Bookman's Price Index

ISSN 0068-0141

Bookman's Price Index

VOLUME 104

A Guide to the Values of
Rare and Other Out of Print Books

Edited by
Anne F. McGrath

GALE
CENGAGE Learning

Farmington Hills, Mich • San Francisco • New York • Waterville, Maine
Meriden, Conn • Mason, Ohio • Chicago

GALE
CENGAGE Learning

Bookman's Price Index, Vol. 104
Anne F. McGrath

Project Editor: Matthew Miskelly

Manufacturing: Rita Wimberley

© 2017 Gale, Cengage Learning
WCN: 01-100-101

ALL RIGHTS RESERVED. No part of this work covered by the copyright herein may be reproduced, transmitted, stored, or used in any form or by any means graphic, electronic, or mechanical, including but not limited to photocopying, recording, scanning, digitizing, taping, Web distribution, information networks, or information storage and retrieval systems, except as permitted under Section 107 or 108 of the 1976 United States Copyright Act, without the prior written permission of the publisher.

This publication is a creative work fully protected by all applicable copyright laws, as well as by misappropriation, trade secret, unfair competition, and other applicable laws. The authors and editors of this work have added value to the underlying factual material herein through one or more of the following: unique and original selection, coordination, expression, arrangement, and classification of the information.

For product information and technology assistance, contact us at
Gale Customer Support, 1-800-877-4253.
For permission to use material from this text or product,
submit all requests online at www.cengage.com/permissions.
Further permissions questions can be emailed to
permissionrequest@cengage.com

While every effort has been made to ensure the reliability of the information presented in this publication, Gale, a part of Cengage Learning, does not guarantee the accuracy of the data contained herein. Gale accepts no payment for listing; and inclusion in the publication of any organization, agency, institution, publication, service, or individual does not imply endorsement of the editors or publisher. Errors brought to the attention of the publisher and verified to the satisfaction of the publisher will be

EDITORIAL DATA PRIVACY POLICY
Does this product contain information about you as an individual? If so, for more information about how to access or correct that information or about our data privacy policies please see our Privacy Statement at www.gale.cengage.com

Gale
27500 Drake Rd.
Farmington Hills, MI 48331-3535

LIBRARY OF CONGRESS CATALOG CARD NUMBER 64-008723

ISBN-13: 978-1-4103-1795-7
ISSN 0068-0141

Printed in the United States of America
1 2 3 4 5 6 7 21 20 19 18 17

Contents

Introduction vii
Dealers Represented in This Volume 1
Bookman's Price Index 11
Association Copies 857
Fine Bindings 1173
Fore-edge Paintings 1227

Introduction

With this 104th edition, Bookman's Price Index marks over 50 years of providing comprehensive information on antiquarian books. Established in 1964, BPI is published twice each year as an index to both the prices and availability of antiquarian books in the United States, Canada, and the British Isles. Each issue of BPI reports the prices and availability of at least 10,000 different antiquarian books. Thus, in the course of an average calendar year, BPI reports the prices and availability of at least 20,000 antiquarian books that are important to readers in the North Atlantic portion of the English-speaking community.

Definition of Antiquarian Books

An antiquarian book is one that is, or has been, traded on the antiquarian book market. It is, or was, traded there because it is important (or in demand) and scarce.

Importance, in the case of antiquarian books, is national. American, Canadian, and British readers buy and sell the artifacts of their own literature and history, science and art as well as a select number of books that document the Continental and Classical origins of certain aspects of their cultures. There are special enthusiasms, too, such as children's books, sporting books, and books that are important principally for their physical beauty; but even the books of these special enthusiasms reflect the national preoccupations of English-speaking readers.

Scarcity means that the number of copies of any book that might come onto the market is measured, at most, in scores, and that only a dozen or a half-dozen, at most, come onto the market during any calendar year.

Lots of important books are not scarce, and lots of scarce books are not important. And, despite the word *antiquarian*, age is no guarantee of either scarcity or importance. Conversely, many books that are less than a generation old bring a handsome price on the market.

The antiquarian books that do appear on the North Atlantic market are a small percentage of the world's entire antiquarian book market, and, necessarily, they are the tiniest fraction of the total number of books published over the centuries.

Despite their thin ranks and scant number, antiquarian books are usually not outrageously expensive. They often range in price from $50 to $500, with most clustering between $100 and $200, and precious few enjoying four-figure prominence.

Prices Reported in *BPI*

The prices reported in *Bookman's Price Index* each year are established by some 100-200 antiquarian booksellers in the United States, Canada, and the British Isles. Usually, about 50 of these booksellers are represented in any one volume of *BPI*. By drawing information from a large number of antiquarian booksellers across English-speaking North America, as well as the British Isles, *BPI* is able to report broad, consistent, and reliable market patterns in the whole North Atlantic English-speaking community.

Within the ranks of the antiquarian booksellers whose prices are reported in *BPI*, the group most interesting is the specialist dealers, whose stock is limited to books in a single subject such as law, or psychiatry, or maritime studies, or horticulture. Such specialists provide readers of *BPI* with information that is not easily available elsewhere.

The prices that all of these antiquarian booksellers report are retail prices that they have established on the basis of their working experience and familiarity with current market conditions, including supply and demand and the effect upon price of the general physical condition of a book, as well as such extraordinary factors as the presence of important autographs.

The willingness of the various antiquarian booksellers to publish their prices in direct comparison with the prices of all other antiquarian booksellers serves as a general indication of the reliability of the prices reported in *BPI* as well as the probity of the antiquarian booksellers. These prices are public market prices, not private deals.

Availability of Books in *BPI*

Every one of the books in *Bookman's Price Index* was recently available in one of the shops of the antiquarian booksellers whose catalogs are included in this volume of *BPI*. It was upon the basis of a hands-on appraisal of each book that an antiquarian bookseller established its price. Thus, the prices reported in *BPI* are actual prices for specific books rather than approximate prices for probable or possible books.

While a particular book may no longer be in the shop of the antiquarian bookseller who established its price, the fact that the book stood on the shelf there recently means that the book is still to be found on the market and that the antiquarian bookseller who established its price may have access to another copy of the same book, or that a different antiquarian bookseller may price another copy of the book in the following issue of *BPI*. Thus, by reporting prices of actual books and their real availability, *Bookman's Price Index* serves as an index to the general market availability of a particular antiquarian book.

Conversely, *BPI* is an index to the absence of certain antiquarian books from the market: books not priced in *BPI* may be presumed to be generally unavailable on the antiquarian book market. *BPI* makes no effort to predict what such unavailable books might be worth if they were perhaps to someday come on the market; *BPI* reports only what is going on in the market, not what might go on.

For example, if a reader were to search the six most recent issues of *BPI* for the price of the first edition of Edgar Allan Poe's *Tamerlane*, he might not find it and could safely conclude that a first edition of *Tamerlane* was not generally available during the past two years or so. If, on the other hand, the same reader were to make a similar search for a first edition of *The Stand* by Poe's spiritual son Stephen King, he might discover that *The Stand* has been found in the shops from time to time and that it is worth about $1600 for a signed first edition, or between $200 and $400 for an unsigned first, depending on condition.

The Importance of Condition

Condition is critical in antiquarian books as in any other antiquarian artifact. The condition of all of the books priced in *Bookman's Price Index* is stated in elaborate detail because it is impossible to understand or justify the price of any antiquarian book without full knowledge of its condition.

Arrangement of *BPI*

The books priced in *Bookman's Price Index* are arranged in a single main alphabet according to the name of the author: in cases of personal authorship, the author's last name; in cases of books produced by corporate bodies such as governments of countries or states, the name of that corporation; in cases of anonymous books, the title; and in cases of anonymous classics such as the *Arabian Nights*, by customary title.

All names of authors, or titles, are standardized according to the usage of American libraries, thus gathering all works by an author.

The works of an author are arranged under his or her name in alphabetical sequence according to the first word of the title, excepting initial articles. However, editions of an author's collected works are listed, out of alphabetical sequence, at the end of the list of his or her individual works.

Different editions of a single work are arranged according to date of publication, with the earlier preceding the later even though this sequence sometimes disrupts alphabetical regularity. In such cases, the editor has sought to consult the reader's convenience rather than any rigid consistency.

The reasons for the occasional disruption of alphabetical regularity are two: the first is that in reporting prices, antiquarian booksellers sometimes refer to a book elliptically, leaving unknown the complete title. The second reason is that certain books change title without changing substance. The most obvious example of this particular editorial problem is the Bible. Title pages of Bibles can begin with such words as Complete, Holy, Sacred, New, Authorized, and so on: it is still the same book. Therefore all English Bibles appear, under the heading BIBLES – ENGLISH, in chronological order. Following the title of each book is its imprint: the place and date of publication and the name of the publisher (or the name of the printer in cases of certain books produced prior to the late eighteenth century).

Description of the Condition of Books

Following the author, title, and imprint of each book is a thorough description of the physical condition of the book, insofar as the bookseller has provided this information. While antiquarian booksellers do not always apply a standard formula in describing the condition of a book, they generally include, as appropriate, most of the following details:

Edition. *BPI* reports which edition of a book is being priced when this information is critical, as in cases when several editions were published in one year. If an edition was published in more than one issue, or state, *BPI* distinguishes among them and identifies them either by the order in which they appeared, or by the physical peculiarities that characterize them. When necessary, *BPI* even describes those obscure details, called "points," that are used to distinguish among issues or states. The points are often minute and consist of such details as one misspelled word buried in the text. Finally, *BPI* identifies limited editions, stating the number of copies in the press run and, if necessary, the types of paper used and the specific number assigned to the book being priced.

Physical Size. *BPI* describes the height and the bulk of each book when this information is available. Height is usually described in the traditional language of the antiquarian book trade: folio, for a tall book; quarto (4to) for a medium-size book; and octavo (8vo) or duodecimo (12mo) for a smaller book. Miniature books are usually described in inches top to bottom and left to right. The bulk of a book is described by stating its pagination, a custom that operates to assure the reader that the book in question is complete.

Illustrations. Since many antiquarian books are more valuable for their illustrations than for their text, *BPI* describes such illustrations carefully, sometimes in considerable detail, as in the case of a book with hand-colored plates.

Binding. All bindings are described fully as to the material used, be it paper, cloth or leather, and even as to the type and color of the material and the time at which it was applied. ("Contemporary tan calf" means that a binding of cattle hide was made for the book contemporaneously with its printing.) Decorations of the binding are also described, and in the cases of twentieth century books, the presence or absence of the dust jacket is always noted.

Authors' Signatures. These are always cited, as they have a significant effect on the price of a book.

General Physical Condition, Specific Flaws, and Relative Scarcity. Usually, *BPI* provides some advice on the general condition of a book by stating that its condition is good, very good, or fine. Additionally, specific flaws are usually listed; some of them are significant, as in the case of a missing leaf or a worn binding, while others are very minor, as in the case of a worm hole in an ancient tome.

Availability. Frequently *BPI* will point out that certain books are of unusual scarcity or rarity. As all antiquarian books are by definition scarce, a special remark that a book is uncommonly scarce should be noted carefully.

Prices. Following the description, *BPI* gives the price of the book along with the name of the antiquarian bookseller who established the price and provided the physical description. Accompanying the antiquarian bookseller's name is the number of the catalog in which he published the price and description of the book, plus the item number of the book in the catalog. The addresses of the antiquarian booksellers whose prices are reported in *BPI* are listed following this Introduction, in the section entitled Dealers Represented in This Volume.

Association Copies, Fine Bindings, and Fore-edge Paintings

Following the main section of *Bookman's Price Index* are three small sections of association copies of books, books in fine bindings, and books decorated with fore-edge paintings. The books in these three sections take on additional interest and value because of features peculiar to them that are not found in other copies of the same books. Their value, or some portion of it, derives from factors not inherent in the text and not identifiable through the name of the author, thereby requiring that they be isolated so that readers can search them out according to the factors that create, or influence, their worth: association, binding or fore-edge painting.

All books priced and described in one of the special sections are also priced and described in the main section of *BPI*, thus permitting the reader to compare an ordinary copy of a book with one that enjoys added attraction because of a unique feature.

Association Copies. Certain antiquarian books acquire added value because of their association with a prominent owner. For instance, an ordinary eighteenth century book would take on enormous extra worth if it had once belonged to George Washington. Association copies of books priced in the special section of *BPI* are arranged according to the name of the person with whom the book was associated rather than according to the name of the author. (The same book is listed in the main body of *BPI* under the name of the author.)

Fine Bindings. Some books are valuable because custom bindings were applied to them alone, and not to other copies of the same book. In the Fine Bindings section of *BPI*, books are gathered under the name of the binder, when known, and then listed according to author. (Each of the books so listed is also listed under the name of the author in the main section of *BPI*.)

Fore-edge Paintings. Fore-edge paintings are original watercolor drawings upon the vertical edges of the leaves of a book. The book is laid flat with the front cover open so that the vertical edges of the leaves slant a little when the painting is applied; when the book is closed, the painting is not visible. These unusual examples of book decoration are gathered in the Fore-edge section under the year of publication of the book, and then arranged according to the name of the author. Generally, fore-edge paintings are not signed and dated, and it is often difficult, if not impossible, to be sure a fore-edge painting was executed in the year of publication of the book. When there is conclusive evidence as to the name of the artist and the date of a fore-edge painting, the book is listed under the year in which the painting was executed. (All books listed in the Fore-edge section are also listed in the main section of *BPI* under the name of the author.)

Errors in *BPI*

The multiple volumes of *BPI* that appear each year combine to include millions of letters and numerals. The editor makes every effort to get them all right, and she asks the reader to be understanding about an occasional typo.

Suggestions Are Welcome

Comments on the *Bookman's Price Index* series and suggestions for corrections and improvements are always welcome. Please contact:

Editor, *Bookman's Price Index*
Gale
27500 Drake Rd.
Farmington Hills, MI 48331-3535
Phone: 248-699-GALE
Toll-free: 800-877-GALE

Antiquarian Book Dealers in Volume 104

Charles Agvent
291 Linden Road
Mertztown PA 19539
USA

Telephone: (610) 682-4750
e-mail: agvent@erols.com
http://www.erols.com/agvent
Contact: Charles Agvent

Aleph-Bet Books, Inc.
85 Old Mill River Road
Pound Ridge NY 10576
USA

Telephone: (914) 764-7410
Fax: (914) 764-1356
e-mail: helen@alephbet.com
http://www.alephbet.com
Contact: Helen & Marc Younger
Specialties: Children's & illustrated books for the collector, first editions, pop-ups, picture books, fairy tales and more.

Andrew Isles, Natural History Books
Rear 115 Greville Street
PO Box 2305
Prahan 3181
Australia

Telephone: 61 03 9510 5750
Fax: 61 03 9529 1256
e-mail: books@AndrewIsles.com
http://www.AndrewIsles.com
Contact: Andrew Isles, Belinda Isles
Specialties: Natural history, wildlife art, birds, mammals, reptiles, amphibians, fish, invertebrates, botany, ecology, paleontology, insects, marine, biology, aviculture, fossils, entomology and conservation. Our natural history stock covers books for Australia, Antarctica, America, Britain, Africa, Europe and Asia.

Any Amount of Books
56 Charing Cross Road
London WC2H 0QA
England

Telephone: 0207 836 3697
Fax: 0207 240 1769
e-mail: charingx@anyamountofbooks.com
http://www.anyamountofbooks.com

Argonaut Book Shop
786-792 Sutter Street
San Francisco CA 94109
USA

Telephone: (415) 474-9067
Fax: (415) 474-2537
e-mail: argonautSF@PacBell.net
http://www.argonautbookshop.com

Athena Rare Books
424 Riverside Drive
Fairfield CT 06824
USA

Telephone: (203) 254-2727
Fax: (203) 254-3518
e-mail: bill@athenararebooks.com
http://www.athenararebooks.com
Contact: William H. Shalberg
Specialties: Fine and rare books on the history of ideas.

B&B Rare Books
30 East 20th Street
Suite 305
New York NY 10003
USA

Telephone: (646) 652-6766
e-mail: info@bbrarebooks.com
http://bbrarebooks.com
Contact: Joshua Mann, Sunday Steinkirchner
Specialties: 19th & 20th century literature; American literature, British literature, children's literature, drama,, espionage, fiction, fine bindings, illustrated books, Irish literature

Gene W. Baade
Books on the West
824 Lynnwood Ave., N.E.
Renton WA 98056-3805
USA

Telephone: (425) 271-6481
e-mail: bookwest@eskimo.com

Beasley Books
1533 W. Oakdale
Chicago IL 60657
USA

Telephone: (773) 472-4528
Fax: (773) 472-7857
e-mail: beasley@beasleybooks.com
http://www.beasleybooks.com
Contact: Paul and Beth Garon; hours by appointment.
Specialties: Modern first editiions, black literature, jazz & blues, radicalism, psychoanalysis.

Bella Luna Books
4697 Stone Canyon Ranch Road
Castle Rock CO   80104
USA

Telephone: 800-497-4717; (303) 663-2202
Fax: (303) 663-2113
e-mail: sales@bellalunabooks.com
http://www.bellalunabooks.com

**Between the Covers
Rare Books, Inc.**
35 W. Maple Ave.
Merchantville NJ   08109
USA

Telephone: (856) 665-2284
Fax: (856) 665-3639
e-mail: mail@betweenthecovers.com
http://www.betweenthecovers.com
Contact: Tom Congalton, Heidi Congalton, Gwen Waring, Jessica Luminoso, Dan Gregory, Jennifer Gregory

Blackwell's Rare Books
48-51 Broad Street
Oxford OX1 3BQ
England

Telephone: 01865 333555
Fax: 01865 794143
e-mail: rarebooks@blackwell.co.uk
http://www.rarebooks.blackwell.co.uk

J & S L Bonham
Flat 14
84 Westbourne Terrace
London W2 6QE
England

Telephone: 20 7402 7064
Fax: 20 7402 0955
e-mail: bonbooks@dial.pipex.com
http://www.bonbooks.dial.pipex.com

David Brass Rare Books, Inc.
PO Box 9029
Calabasas CA   91372
USA

Telephone: (818) 222-4103
e-mail: info@davidbrassrarebooks.com
http://www.davidbrassrarebooks.com
Contact: David Brass

The Brick Row Book Shop
49 Geary Street #230
San Francisco CA
USA

Telephone: (415) 398-0414
Fax: (415) 398-0435
e-mail: books@brickrow.com
http://www.brickrow.com
Contact: John Crighton
Specialties: First editions, rare books & manuscripts from the seventeenth entury through the twientieth centuries, with a strong emphasis on English and American literature.

Buckingham Books
8058 Stone Bridge Road
Greencastle PA   17225-9786
USA

Telephone: (717) 597-5657
Fax: (717) 597-1003
e-mail: buckingham@pa.net
http://www.buckinghambooks.com
Specialties: Western Americana, mystery, detective, and espionage fiction.

By The Book, L. C.
1045 East Camelback Road
Phoenix AZ 85014
USA

Telephone: (602) 222-8806
e-mail: info@bythebooklc.com
http://www.bythebooklc.com
Contact: Sam Hessel
Specialties: First editions, signed works, literature, science, medicine, mathematics, computer science, philoosophy, economics, the Orient, fine art & illustrated works, children's & children's series books, martial arts, and golf.

L. W. Currey, Inc.
P. O. Box 187
Elizabethtown NY 12932
USA

Telephone: (518) 873-6477
http://www.lwcurrey.com
Contact: Lloyd Currey
Specialties: Popular fiction, with emphasis on science fiction and fantasy literature from the earliest times to end of the twentieth century.

Dramatis Personae Bookseller
P.O. Box 1070
Sheffield MA 01257-1070
USA

Telephone: (413) 229-7735
Fax: (413) 229-7735
e-mail: books@dramatispersonae.com
http://www.dramatispersonae.com
Contact: Jonathan and Lisa Reynolds
Specialties: Theatre, drama, conjuring, circus, puppetry, other amusements, all performing arts pre-1930.

John Drury Rare Books
Strandlands, Wrabness
Manningtree
Essex CO11 2TX
England

Telephone: 01255 886260
Fax: 01255 880303
e-mail: mail@johndruryrarebooks.com
http://www.johndruryrarebooks.com
Contact: David Edmunds, Jennifer Edmunds
Specialties: Economics, education. law, philosophy, social history.

Dumont Maps & Books of the West
314 McKenzie Street
P.O. Box 10250
Santa Fe NM 87504
USA

Telephone: (505) 988-1076
Fax: (505) 986-6114
e-mail: info@dumontbooks.com
http://www.dumontbooks.com

I. D. Edrich
17 Selsdon Road
Wanstead
London E11 2QF
England

Telephone: 020 8989 9541
Fax: 020 8989 9541
e-mail: idedrich@idedrich.co.uk
http://www.idedrich.co.uk

Peter Ellis, Bookseller
18 Cecil Court
London WC2N 4HE
England

Telephone: 20 7836 8880
Fax: 20 8318 4748
e-mail: ellisbooks@lineone.net
http://www.peter-ellis.co.uk

Joseph J. Felcone Inc.
P.O. Box 366
Princeton NJ 08542
USA

Telephone: (609) 924-0539
Fax: (609) 924-9078
e-mail: info@felcone.com
http://www.felcone.com

Simon Finch Rare Books Limited
61a Ledbury Road
London W11 2AL
England

Telephone: 20 7792 3303
Fax: 20 7792 2134
e-mail: Rarebooks@simonfinch.com
http://www.simonfinch.com

Gemini Fine Books & Arts Ltd.
917 Oakwood Terrace
Hinsdale IL 60521
USA

Telephone: (630) 986-1478
Fax: (630) 986-8992
e-mail: art@geminibooks.com
http://www.geminibooks.com
Specialties: Art reference and illustrated books, signed first editions, livres d'artistes, surrealism, art deco, art nouveau, and German expressionism

Edwin V. Glaser Rare Books
P.O. Box 755
Napa CA 94559
USA

Telephone: (707) 258-6281
Fax: (707) 258-8625
e-mail: mail@glaserrarebooks.com
http://www.glaserrarebooks.com

James Tait Goodrich
Antiquarian Books and Manuscripts
125 Tweed Boulevard
Grandview-on-Hudson NY 10960
USA

Telephone: (845) 359-0242
Fax: (845) 359-0142
e-mail: jtg@jamestgoodrich.net
Contact: James T. Goodrich
Specialties: Medicine, science, medical instruments, Pre-Columbian artifacts.

Ken Hebenstreit, Bookseller
813 N. Washington Ave.
RoyalOak MI 48067
USA

Telephone: (248) 548-5460
e-mail: ken@khbooks.com
http://www.khbooks.com
Contact: Ken Hebenstreit, Shar Douglas
Specialties: First editioins: mystery, suspense, contemporary fiction.

Heritage Book Shop
9024 Burton Way
Beverly Hills CA 90211
USA

Telephone: (310) 659-3674
Fax: (310) 659-4872
e-mail: heritage@heritagebookshop.com
http://www.heritagebookshop.com
Contact: Ben Weinstein
Specialties: First editions, early printed books, bindings, illustrated books, literature and manuscripts.

Jeff Hirsch Books
39850 N. Dilleys Rd.
Wadsworth IL 60083
USA

Telephone: (847) 662-2665
e-mail: mail@jhbooks.com
http://www.jhbooks.com
Contact: Jeff Hirsch
Specialties: Art, photography, architecture, literary first editions, poetry, drama and signed books

Honey & Wax Booksellers
540 President Street
Third Floor
Brooklyn NY 11215
USA

Telephone: (917) 974-2420
e-mail: info@honeyandwaxbooks.com
http://honeyandwaxbooks.com
Contact: Heather O'Donnell
Specialties: Literature, Graphic Design, the Arts

James S. Jaffe Rare Books
442 Montgomery Avenue
P.O. Box 496
Haverford PA 19041
USA

Telephone: (610) 949-4221
Fax: (610) 649-4542
e-mail: jaffebks@pond.com
http://www.literaryfirsts.com
Contact: James Jaffe, Ingrid Lin, Mark Lowe
Specialties: Rare books, literary first editions, poetry, livres d'artistes, association copies, letters and manuscripts, archives.

Jarndyce Antiquarian Booksellers
46, Great Russell Street
Bloomsbury
London WC1B 3PA
England

Telephone: 020 7631 4220
Fax: 020 7631 1882
e-mail: books@jarndyce.co.uk
http://www.jarndyce.co.uk
Contact: Brian Lake, Janet Nassau
Specialties: Specialty: 18th and particularly 19th century English literature and history; Dickens.

C. R. Johnson Rare Book Collections
4 Keats Grove
London NW3 2RT
England

Telephone: 20 7794-7940
Fax: 20 7433 3303
e-mail: chris@crjohnson.com
http://www.crjohnson.com
Contact: Chris Johnson, Chris Forster

Priscilla Juvelis - Rare Books
11 Goose Fair
Kennebunkport ME 04046
USA

Telephone: (207) 967-0909
e-mail: info@juvelisbooks.com
http://www.juvelisbooks.com
Contact: Priscilla Juvelis
Specialties: Literary first editions, especially women authors, 19th & 20th century book arts, contemporary private press books, artist's books.

Kaaterskill Books
P.O. Box 122
East Jewett, NY 12424

Telehone: (518) 589-0555
e-mail: info@kaaterskillbooks.com
http: www.kaaterskillbooks.com
Contact: Joan and Charles Kutcher
Specialties: the Americas -North, Central, and South, fine, rare, and scholarly books on a wide range of subjects, including Asia, Exploration, Art, Literature, and Books about Books.

The Kelmscott Bookshop
34 W. 25th Street
Baltimore MD 21218
USA

Telephone: (410) 235-6810
Fax: (410) 366-9446
e-mail: info@kelmscottbookshop,com
http://www.kelmscottbookshop.com
Contact: Fran Durako; Susannah Horrom
Specialties: Fine leather bindings, first editions, illustrated books, signed books, books about books and book arts, private press, books about Baltimore,Maryland, art, fashion, film, incunabula, photography, the occult, travel, and literature.

John W. Knott, Jr., Bookseller
8453 Early Bud Way
Laurel MD 20723
USA

Telephone: (301) 512-1300
e-mail: jwk@jwkbooks.com
http://www.jwkbooks.com
Contact: John Knott
Specialties: Fine first editions with an emphasis on science fiction, fantasy, supernatural and horror, mystery & detective fiction, pulp magazines, ephemera, signed books, limited editiions award winners, and popular fiction.

Ken Lopez, Bookseller
51 Huntington Rd.
Hadley MA 01035
USA

Telephone: (413) 584-4827
Fax: (413) 584-2045
e-mail: klopez@well.com
http://www.lopezbooks.com
Specialties: Modern literary first editions, literature of the 1960's, Vietnam War, native American literature, nature writing.

Maggs Bros Ltd.
50 Berkeley Square
London W1J 5BA
England

Telephone: 20 7493 7160
Fax: 20 7499 2007
e-mail: enquiries@maggs.com
http://www.maggs.com

Manhattan Rare Book Company
1050 Second Avenue
Gallery 90
New York NY 10022
USA

Telephone: (212) 326-8907
Fax: (917) 591-8980
e-mail: info@manhattanrarebooks.com
http://manhattanrarebooks.com
Contact: Michael DiRuggiero
Specialties: Literature, History, Culture and Ideas, Science & Technoloby, Art & Photobooks, Illuminated manuscripts

Marlborough Rare Books LTD.
No. 1 St. Clement's Court
London EC4N 7HB England

Telephone: 020 7493 6993
Contact: Jonathan Gestetner
Specialties: Art & architecture, English literature, early books on fine and applied arts, garden design, history of London

Mordida Books
P.O. Box 79322
Houston TX 77279
USA

Telephone: (713) 467-4280
Fax: (713) 467-4182
e-mail: rwilson@mordida.com
http://www.mordida.com

M & S Rare Books, Inc.
P.O. Box 2594
East Side Station
Providence RI 02906
USA

Telephone: (401) 421-1050
FAX: (401) 272-0381
e-mail: dsiegel@msrarebooks.com
http: www.msrarebooks.com
Contact: Daniel G. Siegel

Howard S. Mott, Inc.
PO Box 309
170 South Main Street
Sheffield MA 01257 USA

Telephone: (413) 229-2019 Phone
Fax: (413) 229-8553
Contact: Donald N. Mott
Specialties: Americana, English & American literature, unusual imprints, West Indies, historical manuscripts.

The 19th Century Shop
10400 Stevenson Road, Suite 100
PO Box 410
Stevenson MD 21153
USA

Telephone: (410) 602-3002
Fax: (410) 602-3006
e-mail: info@19thcenturyshop.com
http://www.19thcenturyshop.com
Contact: Stephen Loewentheil, Thomas L. Edsall

Oak Knoll Books
310 Delaware Street
New Castle DE 19720
USA

Telephone: (302) 328-7232
Fax: (302) 328-7274
e-mail: orders@oakknoll.com
http://www.oakknoll.com
Specialties: Bibliography, book collecting, book design, book illustration, book selling, bookbinding, bookplates, fine press books, forgery, libraries, literary criticism, papermaking, printing history, publishing, typography, writing & calligraphy.

Phillip J. Pirages
Fine Books And Manuscripts
P.O. Box 504
2205 Nut Tree Lane
McMinnville OR 97128
USA

Telephone: (503) 472-0476; (800) 962-6666
Fax: (503) 472-5029
e-mail: pirages@onlinemac.com
http://www.pirages.com
Contact: Phil Pirages
Specialties: Early printing, bindings, illuminated manuscripts, illustrated books, private press books.

Bertram Rota Ltd.
31 Long Acre
Covent Garden
London WC2E 9LT
England

Telephone: 020 7836 0723
Fax: 020 7497 9058
e-mail: bertramrota@compuserve.com
http://www.bertramrota.co.uk

Royal Books
32 West 25th Street
Baltimore MD   21218
USA

Telephone: (410) 366-7329
Fax: (443) 524-0942
e-mail: mail@royalbooksonline.com
http://www.royalbooksonline.com
Contact: Kevin Johnson
Specialties: Modern first editions, books on film, jazz and the arts.

Ken Sanders Rare Books
268 South 200 East
Salt Lake City UT   84111
USA

Telephone: (801) 521-3819
Fax: (801) 521-2606
e-mail: books@dreamgarden.com
http://www.kensandersbooks.com
Specialties: Modern first editions, literature of the American west, Edward Abbey, Wallace Stegner, B. Traven, poetry & small presses, western explorations, voyages & travels, Powell, Wheeler, Hayden & King, USGS, Railroad Surveys, Western Americana, Native Americana & Literature, Maps & Atlases, Utah & the Mormons.

Schooner Books Ltd.
5378 Inglis Street
Halifax NS
  B3H 1J5
Canada

Telephone: (902) 423-8419
Fax: (902) 423-8503
e-mail: SchoonerBooks@schoonerbooks.com
http://www.SchoonerBooks.com
Specialties: Second hand and rare books, antique maps & prints.

Second Life Books, Inc.
P.O. Box 242
55 Quarry Road
Lanesborough MA   01237
USA

Telephone: (413) 447-8010
Fax: (413) 499-1540
e-mail: info@secondlifebooks.com
http://www.secondlifebooks.com

Henry Sotheran Limited
Fine and Rare Antiquarian Books & Prints
2 Sackville Street
Piccadilly
London W1S 3DP
England

Telephone: 20 7439 6151
Fax: 20 7434 2019
e-mail: sotherans@sotherans.co.uk
Contact: Andrew McGeachin
Specialties: Fine and rare antiquarian books & prints.

Tavistock Books
1503 Webster Street
Alameda CA   94501
USA

Telephone: (510) 814-0480
Fax: (510) 814-0486
e-mail: vjz@tavbooks.com
http://www.tavbooks.com

Unsworths Booksellers Ltd.
101 Euston Road
London NW1 2RA
England

Telephone: 020 7436-9836
Fax: 020 7383-7557
e-mail: books@unsworths.com
http://www.unsworths.com
Contact: Charlie Unsworth, Leo Cadogan
Specialties: Scholarly and Antiquarian books on the humanities, especially Classics and History.

Jeff Weber Rare Books
PO Box 3368
Glendale CA 91221-0368
(323) 344-9332   Fax: (323) 344-9267

Contacts: Jeff Weber, Linda Weber

Bookman's Price Index

A

A'Beckett, Gilbert Abbott 1811-1856 *The Comic History of Rome.* London: Bradbury & Evans May, 1851-. Jan. 1852. First edition, 10 parts in 9, as initially issued, 10 hand colored plates & 98 intratextual woodcuts by John Leech, 8vo., original blue pictorial wrappers, custom blue morocco pull off slipcase, overall very good to very good+ (bit of chipping to spines as usual and expected).   Tavistock Books   Bibliolatry - 15   2016 $1850

A'Beckett, Gilbert Abbott 1811-1856 *Figaro in London. Volume I for Year 1832.* printed by W. Molineux, published by William Strange Dec. 10, 1831. through Dec. 29 1832, 56 weekly numbers, numerous woodcut illustrations, long tear in 1 leaf, but without loss of text, little foxing at either end, emanating from binding, small folio, contemporary purple moire cloth, spine faded, spine worn at extremities and splits in joints adjoining.   Blackwell's Rare Books   B186 - 13   2016   £200

Abailard, Pierre 1079-1142 *Lettre d'Heloise & Abailard. (with, as issued) Reponse d'Abailard a La Lettre d'Heloise.* Tours: Louis Vauquer, 1695. Extremely rare edition, woodcut ornament on title, little browned in places, 12mo., contemporary mottled calf, spine gilt, upper joint cracked, corners slightly worn, bookplate of Gabriel-Theodore-Francois de Sales d'Olivier, sound.   Blackwell's Rare Books   B186 - 1   2016   £800

Abbey, Edward *The Fool's Progress.* New York: Henry Holt, 1988. First edition, near fine, previous owner's name and gift inscription, dust jacket fine, first state jacket with uncorrected errors on both front and rear flaps 'mist' for 'myth' and 'Mickey' for 'Becky' signed by author.   Bella Luna Books   2016 - 3668   2016 $198

Abbey, Edward *Heaven's Prisoners.* New York: Holt, 1988. First edition, fine, dust jacket near fine, partially price clipped.   Bella Luna Books   2016 - t15831   2016 $198

Abbey, Edward *The Hidden Canyon.* New York: Viking, 1977. First edition, near fine, in fine dust jacket, previous owner's inscription erased from front free endpaper, leaving two small holes and rubbing, dust jacket fine.   Bella Luna Books   2016 - t1760   2016 $165

Abbey, Edward *The Journey Home.* New York: Dutton, 1977. First edition, fine in near fine dust jacket with 1 inch closed tear at heel of spine and light creasing to spine ends.   Bella Luna Books   2016 - t6330   2016 $181

Abbey, Edward *Resist Much, Obey Little - Some Notes on Edward Abbey.* Salt Lake City: Dream Garden Press, 1985. First edition, fine, this copy signed by Greg Mcnamee.   Bella Luna Books   2016 - 3680   2016 $76

Abbey, John Roland *Scenery of Great Britain and Ireland in Aquatint and Lithography 1770-1860. With Life in England. With Travel.* Folkestone: Dawsons of Pall Mall, 1972. Reprint of first editions, 4 volumes, 4to., cloth, dust jackets, plates, many color.   Oak Knoll Books   310 - 223   2016 $750

Abbot, Abiel *Letters Written in the Interior ...* Boston: Bowles and Dearborn, 1829. First edition, quarto, recent brown cloth spine, original drab boards, recent printed paper label, untrimmed, some light browning, small insect damage in upper margin of few signatures, very good.   The Brick Row Book Shop   Miscellany 69 - 78   2016 $500

Abbot, Berenice *Changing New York.* New York: E. P. Dutton, 1939. First edition, near fine in very good plus dust jacket, corners lightly bumped, little soiling to boards, jacket has 3 small internal repairs (not restoration) and few small nicks and closed tears.   Royal Books   48 - 17   2016 $4750

Abbott, John Stevens Cabot *The Mother at Home...* London: John Mason, 1835. Second edition, text foxed, original green cloth, slightly browned paper label, little rubbed & dulled, evidence of label removal from endpapers.   Jarndyce Antiquarian Books   CCXV - 2   2016   £45

Abbott, John Stevens Cabot *The Mother at Home...* London: RTS, circa, 1855. Revised edition, original brown cloth, slightly marked, contemporary signature on leading pastedown, very good.   Jarndyce Antiquarian Books   CCXV - 3   2016   £35

Abbott, John Stevens Cabot *The Mother at Home.* Halifax: Milner & Sowerby, 1858. Frontispiece with small marginal tear, 16mo., original blue cloth, all edges gilt, contemporary inscription, very good.   Jarndyce Antiquarian Books   CCXV - 4   2016   £30

Abdill, David *A New Theory of the Weather and Practical Views of Astronomy.* Wheeling: published by the author, 1842. First edition, 3 folding plates, contemporary calf, very loose and rubbed, early leaves browned.   M & S Rare Books, Inc.   99 - 18   2016 $650

Abecedaire Utile ou Petit Tableau des Arts et Metiers... Leipsic: au Comptaire d'Industrie Chez N. Gluckeberg, n.d. circa, 1825. 4 x 6 inches, blindstamped cloth, some foxing, else near fine in custom cloth box, 24 fine hand colored copperplate engravings on 12 plates, each with 2 illustrations, quite rare.   Aleph-bet Books, Inc.   111 - 1   2016 $2500

Abeking, Hermann *Das Mampampebuch.* Leipzig: Abnel & Muler, n.d. circa, 1921. 4to., cloth backed pictorial boards, some edge rubbing and light soil, very good+, printed on thick board pages one side of page only, illustrations by author.   Aleph-bet Books, Inc.   111 - 44   2016 $1500

Abel, Elie *The Missile Crisis.* Philadelphia and New York: J. B. Lippincott, 1966. First edition, well used, very good, without dust jacket, inscribed by author to Robert Kennedy and wife Ethel, with Kennedy's extensive notes.   Between the Covers Rare Books   204 - 62   2016 $10,000

Abercrombie, John *The Culture and Discipline of the mind.* Edinburgh: William Whyte & Co., 1837. Seventh edition, some foxing and watermarking, original pink cloth, spine faded to brown.   Jarndyce Antiquarian Books   CCXV - 5   2016   £35

Aberdeen, George Hamilton Gordon, Earl of *An Inquiry into the Principles of Beauty in Grecian Architecture...* London: John Murray, 1822. First edition, contemporary or slightly later half tan calf, marbled boards, spine decorated in gilt, dark green morocco label, bookplate of Lord Carlingford, very good.   Jarndyce Antiquarian Booksellers   CCXVII - 1   2016   £85

Abernethy, John *Surgical Observations on the Constitutional Origin and Treatment of Local Diseases...* Philadelphia: Thomas Dobson, 1811. First American edition, 8vo., contemporary calf, red leather spine label, top joint just started, else very good.   Edwin V. Glaser Rare Books   2015 - 10399   2016 $150

Abhedananda, Swami *How to be a Yogi.* New York: Vedanta Society, 1902. First edition, 8vo., original brown cloth with gilt stamped insignia, small closed tear page 171/172, otherwise in very good condition, inscribed with name of previous owner.   Sotheran's   Piccadilly Notes - Summer 2015 - 340   2016   £120

Abraham, James Johnston *Letters His Life, Times, Friends and Descendants.* London: Heinemann, 1933. Numerous text illustrations, 4to., dust jacket, original binding.   James Tait Goodrich   X-78 - 378   2016 $125

Abruzzi, Luigi Amedeo of Savoy, Duke of *On the "Polar Star" in the Arctic Sea.* London: Hutchinson, 1903. First UK edition, octavo, 2 volumes, 212 illustrations in text, 16 tissue guarded photogravure plates, 2 panoramas, 5 maps, original dark green pictorial buckram, top edge gilt, cover faintly scuffed and marked, small snag to head of spine of volume II, very good, handsome.   Peter Ellis   112 - 19   2016   £275

Abse, Dannie *Dannie Abse. The Pocket Poets.* London: Vista, 1963. First edition, fine, inscribed by author for William Meredith.   Charles Agvent   William Meredith - 1   2016 $80

Abse, Dannie *Doctors and Patients.* Oxford: Oxford University Press, 1984. First edition, inscribed for William Meredith, signed twice on titlepage, fine in fine dust jacket.   Charles Agvent   William Meredith - 8   2016 $80

Abse, Dannie *Funland. A Poem in Nine Parts.* Swansea: Portland University Library, 1971. First edition, inscribed and signed by poet for William Meredith, near fine.   Charles Agvent   William Meredith - 2   2016 $80

Abse, Dannie *Modern European Verse. The Pocket Poets.* London: Vista Books, 1964. First edition, inscribed for William Meredith, by Abse, small skim mark on rear, otherwise fine.   Charles Agvent   William Meredith - 9   2016 $80

Abse, Dannie *Poems Golders Green.* London: Hutchinson, 1962. First edition, inscribed for William Meredith, near fine in like dust jacket with some wear to spine.   Charles Agvent   William Meredith - 3   2016 $150

Abse, Dannie *A Strong Dose of Myself.* London: Hutchinson, 1983. First edition, presentation from author for William Meredith, slight dust spotting to top edge, fine in fine dust jacket.   Charles Agvent   William Meredith - 4   2016 $100

Abse, Dannie *Tenants of the House. Poems 1951-1956.* New York: Criterion Books, 1959. First American edition, poet William Meredith's copy with his signature, below inscription from author, laid in is promotional photo of author, fine in near fine dust jacket.   Charles Agvent   William Meredith - 6   2016 $200

Abse, Dannie *Three Question Plays.* Lowestoft: Scorpion Press, 1967. First edition, inscribed by author for William Meredith, pictorial wrappers, some soiling to covers, very good.   Charles Agvent   William Meredith - 7   2016 $60

Absurdities: a Book of Collected Drawings. London: Hutchinson, n.d., 1934. Large 4to., pictorial boards, paper worn on spine ends, slight bit of cover soil, overall clean and very good+ in chipped and soiled dust jacket, nearly 100 illustrations by W. Heath Robinson.   Aleph-bet Books, Inc.   112 - 430   2016 $200

ABT Associates *Counter-Insurgency Game Design Feasibility and Evaluation Study November 1965.* Cambridge: ABT Associates, 1965. First edition, quarto, printed leaves, prong-bound into printed gray wrappers, charts and graphs, some folding, trifle soiled, metal clasp and prong little tarnished, small crease on rear wrapper, slight foxing on bottom edge, else near fine.   Between the Covers Rare Books   204 - 31   2016 $2500

Abu-Hakima, Ahmad Mustafa *Eastern Arabia. Historie Photographs Volume II. Kuwait 1900-1936.* London: Probsthain, 1986. Second printing, 4to., original illustrated wrappers, illustrations.   Sotheran's Travel and Exploration - 295   2016   £125

The Academic. Glasgow: Wardlaw and Cunninghame and Richard Baynes, London, 1826. Excellent set of numbers I to IX, with contemporary inscription to Thomas Campbell, Esq. Lord Rector of University of Glasgow with congratulations of admiring constituent James Blair, very scarce,.   John Drury Rare Books   2015 - 6422   2016 $437

An Account of the Burning of the City of London, as It Was Published by the Special Authority of King and Council to the Year 1666.... (with) The True Protestant Account of the Burning of London....   London: printed and sold by J. Stone, 1720. Printed by R. Baddam and sold by J. Popping, 1720., 8vo., slight browning 40 pages; 40 pages, disbound scarce pair.   Blackwell's Rare Books   B186 - 94   2016   £800

An Accurate Description and History of the Cathedral and Metropolitical Church of St. Peter, York from Its Foundation to the Present Year.   York: printed by G. Peacock, 1790. Third edition, 12mo., 14 folding engraved plates, private library blindstamp at head of titlepage, marginal tear to one leaf without loss, expertly bound in recent quarter sprinkled calf, gilt bands, red morocco label, marbled boards, vellum tips.   Jarndyce Antiquarian Booksellers   CCXVI - 624   2016   £250

Acker, Kathy   *The Adult Life of Toulouse Lautrec.* New York: Kathy Acker/TVRT, 1975-1976. First edition, 6 volumes, octavo, stapled printed wrappers, slightest age toning, else fine, very scarce.   Between the Covers Rare Books   204 - 5   2016 $2850

Acker, Kathy *Algeria: a Series of Invocations Because Nothing Else Works.*   London: Aloes Books, 1984. First edition, octavo, stapled illustrated wrappers, slight sunning on spine, else about fine, signed by Acker, laid in is ANS from Acker to David Reis, uncommon signed.   Between the Covers Rare Books   204 - 6   2016 $1000

Acker, Kathy *The Childlike Life of the Black Tarantula.* New York: TVRT Press, 1975. First one volume edition, photographically illustrated wrappers, some modern stains on front wrapper and bottom back corner little bent, very good.   Between the Covers Rare Books   208 - 3   2016 $150

Acker, Kathy   *Great Expectations.*   San Francisco: Re/Search, 1982. Uncorrected proof, paperback original, "Advance Proof Copy" on titlepage, very near fine in illustrated wrappers, scarce.   Between the Covers Rare Books   208 - 4   2016 $300

Acker, Kathy   *I Dreamt I Became a Nymphomaniac: Imagining.*   San Francisco: Empty Elevator Shaft Poetry Press..., 1974. First edition, complete in 6 volumes, octavo, stapled printed wrappers except for second volume where the wrappers are unprinted as issued, third volume has author's name as 'Peter Gordon' as issued, trifle soiled, else fine.   Between the Covers Rare Books   204 - 3   2016 $2750

Acker, Kathy   *Kathy Goes to Haiti.*   Toronto: Rumour Pub., 1978. First edition, drawings by Robert Kushner, square octavo, 145 pages, illustrated wrappers, slightest of rubbing, else about fine, signed by author.   Between the Covers Rare Books   204 - 4   2016 $850

Acker, Kathy   *Portrait of an Eye.*   New York: Pantheon Books, 1992. Uncorrected proof, printed wrappers, fine, uncommon proof.   Between the Covers Rare Books   208 - 3   2016 $250

Ackermann, Alfred Seabold Eli   *Popular Fallacies.*   London: Cassell & Co., 1907. First edition, half title, frontispiece and plates, original light green decorated cloth, spine slightly dulled, slightly rubbed, very good.   Jarndyce Antiquarian Books   CCXV - 498   2016   £40

Ackermann, Rudolph   1764-1834   *The History of the Abbey Church of St. Peter's Westminster, Its Antiquities and Monuments.* London: for R. Ackermann, 1812. First edition, large 4to., 2 volumes, plan, portrait, 81 hand colored aquatint plates, beautifully found in full straight grain red morocco, spines, covers and turn-ins richly gilt by Bayntun, cloth slipcases, very slight offsetting onto text from some plates as usual, just hint of foxing on two or three plates, else remarkably bright and flawless set, upper hinges just beginning to crack slightly, otherwise binding fine and fresh, fine, very desirable copy.   Joseph J. Felcone, Inc.   Books from Five Centuries: a Miscellany - 1   2016 $3200

Ackermann, Rudolph   1764-1834   *Swiss Views.* London: Ackermann's Repository, 1819. 5 hand colored aquatints.   J. & S. L. Bonham Antiquarian Booksellers   Europe 2016 - 7655   2016   £55

Ackroyd, Peter   *Dickens' London an Imaginative Vision...* London: Guild Publishing, 1987. First edition, half title, illustrations, original white cloth, booklabel, very good in price clipped dust jacket, photos, signed presentation inscription from author for Thelma Grove.   Jarndyce Antiquarian Booksellers   CCXVIII - 1051   2016   £20

Ackroyd, Peter   *Dickens: Public Life and Private Passion.* London: BBC, 2002. First edition, half title, vignette title, illustrations, original grey cloth, mint in dust jacket.   Jarndyce Antiquarian Booksellers   CCXVIII - 1054   2016   £20

Ackroyd, Peter *English Music.* Franklin Center: Franklin Library, 1992. Limited first edition, signed by author, maroon leather, lettered and decoratively stamped in gilt, all edges gilt, very fine, as new.   Argonaut Book Shop   Literature 2015 - 3928   2016 $60

Ackroyd, Peter *Introduction to Dickens.* London: Sinclair Stevenson, 1991. First edition, half title, vignette title, illustrations, original gray cloth, mint in dust jacket.   Jarndyce Antiquarian Booksellers   CCXVIII - 1053   2016   £25

Ackroyd, Peter *The Last Testament of Oscar Wilde.* London: Hamish Hamilton, 1983. First edition, octavo, cheap paper faintly tanned, fine in fine dust jacket.   Peter Ellis   112 - 1   2016   £50

Acta Helvetica, Physico-Mathematico Anatomico-Botanico Medica. Basel: John Rodolph Im-hof, 1751-1777. Volumes, 1, 2, 3, 4, 5, 8, square 8vo., three quarter mottled calf over speckled boards, titles in red and black, engraved head and tailpieces, folding tables, folding plates, light binding wear at extremities, early stamp of Bib. Univ. Heidelbergensis, with their duplicate stamp, very good, crisp, bright.   Edwin V. Glaser Rare Books   2015 - 10412   2016 $2400

Acton, Harold *Four Cautionary Tales.* New York: Wyn, 1948. First American edition, 8vo., little faded yellow cloth, inscribed by author to poet and editor Barbara Howes with her bookplate, included is original photo by Cecil Beaton with his name stamp on verso.   Second Life Books, Inc.   196A - 6   2016 $350

Acton, Harold *An Indian Ass.* London: Duckworth, 1925. First edition, one of 1000 copies, crown 8vo. original red cloth stamped in black to front, blindstamped border to upper board, backstrip slightly faded and lettered in black, edges toned and endpapers browned, photocopy of original dust jacket, good.   Blackwell's Rare Books   B186 - 171   2016   £150

Acton, Harold *Modern Chinese Poetry.* London: Duckworth, 1936. First edition, 8vo., original blue cloth little scuffed overall stamped in gilt to front, backstrip lettered in gilt, little wear at tips, slight lean to spine, top edge gilt, erased ownership inscription, flyleaf and others toned and fore edge untrimmed, good, inscribed by author for (his bibliographer) Neil Ritchie.   Blackwell's Rare Books   B186 - 172   2016   £125

Acton, Harold *Oxford Poetry 1924.* Oxford: Basil Blackwell, 1924. First edition, crown 8vo., original quarter cream boards with blue sides, printed label to upper board and backstrip, latter darkened and little pushed at ends, small amount of rubbing and scuffing to boards, with a pressure mark at head and tail of upper board, edges untrimmed, contemporary Christmas gift inscription.   Blackwell's Rare Books   B186 - 228   2016   £60

Adam, Francis *On Ornithology as a Branch of Liberal Education.* Aberdeen: John Smith, 1859. Few ink corrections, first ad final leaves slightly dusted and marked, vertical fold, sewn as issued, inscribed by author for Sir Thomas Gladstone.   Jarndyce Antiquarian Books   CCXV - 500   2016   £40

Adam, Robert Brothwick *The R. B. Adam Library Relating to Dr. Samuel Johnson and His Era.* Buffalo: printed for the author, London and New York: Oxford University Press, 1929. First edition, one of 500 copies, 3 volumes, quarto, original blue buckram, gilt lettering, top edge gilt, others untrimmed, frontispieces and numerous illustrations, from the library of Walpole bibliographer and scholar Allen Tracy Hazen, with his posthumous booklabel, later ink signature of Johnson scholar Chester Chapin, dated Feb. 27 1986, cloth slightly rubbed and worn, very good.   The Brick Row Book Shop   Miscellany 69 - 50   2016 $500

Adams, Alexander *Geronimo: a Biography.* New York: Putnams, 1971. First edition, 8vo., photos, inscribed by author to poet Paul Metcalf and his wife.   Second Life Books, Inc.   196A - 8   2016 $45

Adams, Ansel *The Four Seasons in Yosemite national Park.* Los Angeles: Yosemite: Yosemite Park and Curry Co. printed by Times Mirror Printing,, 1938. third edition, scarce in this condition, thin quarto, color photo, double page map, printed in brown and blue, profusely illustrated with black and white photos, light green wrappers stamped and lettered in dark green, very fine, bright copy with original glassine jacket, housed in original beige envelope lightly tanned and stained, includes 56 quality half tones after original photos.   Argonaut Book Shop   Natural History 2015 - 8186   2016 $175

Adams, Ansel *Taos Pueblo.* New York: Graphic Society Books, 1977. Facsimile edition of rare original printing, number 822 of 950 copies signed by Adams, photos, bound by Vincent Mullins in half tan Niger leather with orange linen covered boards, title stamped in blind on front cover, marbled ends, very fine, new copy, matching slipcase.   Argonaut Book Shop   Photography 2015 - 7440   2016 $3000

Adams, Ansel *This is the American Earth.* San Francisco: Sierra Club, 1960. First edition, quarto, 84 black and white photos, near fine, pictorial dust jacket.   Argonaut Book Shop   Photography 2015 - 4741   2016 $125

Adams, Ansel *Yosemite and the High Sierra.* Boston: Little Brown, 1994. Second printing, oblong quarto, 75 duotone photos and 6 text illustrations, gray cloth, very fine with pictorial dust jacket.   Argonaut Book Shop   Photography 2015 - 7515   2016 $50

Adams, Frederick Upham *Conquest of the Tropics. The Story of the Creative Enterprises Conducted by the United Fruit Company.* Garden City: Doubleday, 1914. First edition, 8vo., original green cloth, ornamented in blind, lettered in gilt, gilt stamped bunch of bananas on spine and color illustrations laid onto front cover, map endpapers, highly illustrated with plates, photos, minimal bumping to head and tail of spine and one corner, otherwise fine.   Sotheran's Travel and Exploration - 47   2016   £98

Adams, George *An Essay on Electricity.* London: printed and sold by the author at Tycho Brahe's Head no. 60 in Fleet street, 1784. First edition, 8vo., half leather and contemporary marbled boards, skillfully rebacked at some time, red leather spine label, gilt lettering, boards mildly rubbed, mild scattered foxing, soil, tiny worm hole to first few pages, no text or image affected, 6 plates as issued, scarce.   By the Book, L. C.   45 - 8   2016 $3350

Adams, George *Geometrical and Graphical Essays...* London: printed for the author by R. Hindmarsh, 1791. First edition, 8vo., 32 engraved folding plates, edges chipped in places, modern full antique style calf, raised bands, blind and gilt rules, gilt spine title, some brittleness to paper edges, else very good.   Jeff Weber Rare Books   183 - 2   2016 $2000

Adams, George *Mathematical Instrument Maker, the Elder, A Treatise Describing the Construction and Explaining the Use of New Celestial and terrestrial Globes.* London: printed for and sold by the author at Tycho Brahe's Head, 1769. Second edition, 8vo., 14 engraved plates, frontispiece, fore-edge trimmed, left margin frontispiece trimmed, occasional spotting, titlepage defaced bit (eliminating the 'X' from the date, creating at date that didn't exist), offsetting on half title from ads, modern period style calf, gilt stamped, raised bands, elegant red spine label, edges sprinkled red, ownership ink signature of Frank Mergenthaler August 28 1928.   Jeff Weber Rare Books   183 - 1   2016 $1250

Adams, H. M. *Catalogue of Books Printed on the Continent of Europe 1501-1600 in Cambridge Libraries.* Cambridge: University Press, 1967. First edition, thick small 4to., 2 volumes, cloth, dust jackets, loosely inserted 4 page errata and corrigenda pamphlet.   Oak Knoll Books   310 - 224   2016 $600

Adams, Harry *Beyond the Barrier with Byrd. An Authentic Story of the Byrd Antarctic Exploring Expedition.* Chicago and New York: M. A. Donohue & Co., 1932. First edition, first issue binding, 8vo., original green cloth gilt, upper board lettered gilt and blocked to blind with ship, spine lettered in gilt and blocked to blind with penguin, remnant of pictorial dust jacket with picture of Byrd on upper panel, photographic frontispiece and 15 photographic plates, full page facsimile of letter by Byrd, cloth in fine condition, text evenly little browned as usual, signed presentation from Lt. Comdr. Tom Mulroy to Charles L. Kessler.   Sotheran's   Travel and Exploration - 412   2016   £298

Adams, Henry Brooke *Esther. A Novel.* New York: Henry Holt & Co., 1884. First edition, rare, small octavo, original decorated lime green cloth, gilt lettered, edges little rubbed, cloth slightly soiled, paper browning, good copy.   The Brick Row Book Shop   Miscellany 69 - 1   2016 $950

Adams, Jane *Cast the First Stone.* London: Macmillan, 1996. First edition, very fine in dust jacket.   Mordida Books   2015 - 011545   2016 $55

Adams, Joey *The Borscht Belt.* New York: Bobbs Merrill, 1966. First printing, 8vo., illustrations, presentation by Henry Tobias, nice in dust jacket little yellowed and chipped.   Second Life Books, Inc.   196A - 9   2016 $50

Adams, John *Defense des Constitutions Americaines, ou del la Necessite d'une Balance dans les Pouvoirs d'un Gouvernement Libre...* Paris: Chez Buisson, Libraire et Imprimeur, 1792. First edition in French, 2 volumes, octavo, contemporary quarter vellum, blue marbled paper boards, printed paper labels, half title present, bindings little worn, some slight stains and foxing, very good.   The Brick Row Book Shop   Miscellany 69 - 2   2016 $1750

Adams, John *Exposition & Illustration in Teaching.* London: Macmillan, 1910. Half title, original green cloth, very good.   Jarndyce Antiquarian Books   CCXV - 501   2016   £20

Adams, John *Message from the President of the United States, Transmitting a Report of the Secretary of State and Sundry Documents Relative to the Requisition for the Delivery of Jonathan Robins...* Philadelphia: 1800. First edition, 8vo., removed, stab holes at inner margin, still very good+, unopened (uncut).   Kaaterskill Books   21 - 1   2016 $225

Adams, John *The New Teaching.* London: Hodder & Stoughton, 1922. Popular edition, original red cloth, slightly rubbed.   Jarndyce Antiquarian Books   CCXV - 502   2016   £20

Adams, John Quincy   1767-1848 *Oration on the Life and Character of Gilbert Motier De Lafayette...* Washington: 1835. First edition, thick paper copy, inscribed by author on inserted slip in front of titlepage, as usual, signed for Ebenezer Jackson, octavo, contemporary full straight grain navy blue morocco, handsomely rebacked to style, spine stamped and lettered gilt, boards ruled in gilt, blue drab endpapers, original plain wrappers bound in, pages bit toned, inner hinges repaired, previous owners ink signature and address label, some owner's blind embossed notary stamp on signature sheet and page 49, very good.   Heritage Book Shop   Holiday 2015 - 1   2016 $5000

Adams, Leonie *High Falcon & other Poems.* New York: John Day Co., 1929. First edition, tight, near fine copy in near fine dust jacket with some tiny wear at base of front panel, very nice, uncommon.   Jeff Hirsch Books   E-List 80 - 2   2016 $125

Adams, Leonie *Those not Elect.* New York: Robert M. McBride, 1925. First edition, one of just 10 copies on Ingres paper, not for sale, signed by author, 8vo., paper over boards little soiled, near fine.   Second Life Books, Inc.   196A - 12   2016 $700

Adams, Richard *Tales from Watership Down.* London: Hutchinson, 1996. First edition, vignette to titlepage with decoration and full page illustration at head of each section, 8vo., original black boards, backstrip lettered gilt, dust jacket, fine, signed by author.   Blackwell's Rare Books   B186 - 173   2016   £200

Adams, Samuel *The Complete Servant.* London: Knight & Lacey, 1825. First edition, illustrations, later endpapers, contemporary half plain sheep, little rubbed, contemporary signature of Mary Wilson.   Jarndyce Antiquarian Books   CCXV - 6   2016   £125

Adams, W. A. *Grouse and Grouse Moors.* Dumfrieshire: Signet press, 1998. No. 140 of 300 copies, 8vo., original red cloth, gilt decoration to upper board, gilt lettering to spine, fine, illustrations.   Sotheran's   Hunting, Shooting & Fishing - 69   2016   £50

Adcock, A. St. John *The World that Never Was - ...* London: Francis Griffiths, 1908. First edition, octavo, 27 full page black and white drawings by Tom Browne, original floral decorated cloth bit scuffed at edges, front endpapers slightly marked, very good, scarce.   Peter Ellis   112 - 2   2016   £50

Addington, Sarah *Dance Team.* New York: D. Appleton and Co., 1931. First edition, very good in very good plus example of scarce dust jacket, some lean, foxing to page edges, few faint stains to boards, toning and faint staining to jacket, few tiny chips.   Royal Books   49 - 100   2016 $450

Addison, Alexander *Reports of the Cases in the County Courts of the Fifth Circuit and in the High Court of Errors & Appeals...* Washington: John Colerick and May, 1800. First edition, 8vo., new covers, contemporary spine and label.   M & S Rare Books, Inc.   99 - 92   2016 $750

Addison, George Augustus *Original Familiar Correspondence Between Residents in India....* Edinburgh: printed for the editor, sold by William Blackwood & sons, 1846. First edition, half title, largely unopened in original horizontal grained purple cloth, blocked in blind, spine lettered gilt, spine slightly faded, overall very good, well preserved.   Jarndyce Antiquarian Booksellers   CCXVII - 2   2016   £150

Addison, Joseph *Miscellaneous Works, in Verse and Prose.* London: J. and R. Tonson and S. Draper, 1753. 12mo., some gatherings rather browned, contemporary sprinkled calf, spines divided by raised bands between gilt rules, red morocco lettering pieces, compartments below these dyed black and numbered in gilt, little rubbed and chipped, bookplate removed from front pastedown.   Blackwell's Rare Books   B184 - 1   2016   £100

Ade, George *Forty Modern Fables.* New York: R. H. Russell, 1901. First edition, 8vo., original green cloth backed decorated paper covered boards, decorated initials to each fable, very good.   Sotheran's   Piccadilly Notes - Summer 2015 - 13   2016   £78

Adeler, Max *Elbow Room, a Novel without a plot.* London: Ward Lock, 1883. Authorized edition, First UK edition, 8vo., stamped cloth, very good, Bret Harte's copy with bookplate and ex-libris, some external wear, very good.   Second Life Books, Inc.   196A - 730   2016 $150

Adler, Egon *Die Entdeckung Karlsbads Eine Satire.* privately printed, 1922. No. 36 of 50 copies, this with plates hand colored, 4to., pages 63, copiously illustrate in color throughout, name of recipient tipped in at colophon (Walter Quittner) with short handwritten sentiment initialled E.A., original marbled boards over beige cloth lettered gilt at spine, very slight fraying at spine ends, otherwise clean, very good.   Any Amount of Books   2015 - A84565   2016   £550

Adrian, Dennis *See America First.* Chicago: David and Alfred Smart Museum of Art, 2001. Exhibition catalog, fine in French style wrappers.   Jeff Hirsch Books   Holiday List 2015 - 18   2016 $175

The Adventures of Alexander Barclay, Mountain Man. Denver: Old West Pub. Co., 1976. First edition, 5 color plates, numerous illustrations, 3 large folding maps in rear pocket, brown cloth lettered gilt, upper corners slightly jammed, but fine copy (lacking jacket)-.   Argonaut Book Shop   Biography 2015 - 5436   2016 $75

Adventures of Jack Ninepins. New York: Harper Bros., 1944. Stated first edition, 6 1/4 x 8 1/2 inches, cloth, fine in frayed dust jacket, I in color by Averill, this copy from the library of Bertha Mahony Miller with her bookplate, laid in are 6 handwritten letters from Averill to Helen Fay (Juneman) Book Store owner and lecturer on children's books.   Aleph-bet Books, Inc.   111 - 28   2016 $1200

The Adventures of Tommy Teaberry. Pittsburgh: Clark Chrewing Gum Co., 1944. 4t., cloth backed pictorial boards, slightest of tip wear, else fine in dust jacket with corner chip, illustrations in full color by Ben J. Harris, laid in is interesting letter from publisher, great copy. Aleph-bet Books, Inc. 111 - 156 2016 $200

Advice to Certain Lord High Chancellor, Twelve Judges, 600 Barristers 700 English and 800 Irish Students of the law and 30,000 Attornies... London: printed for J. Ridgway, 1791. 8vo., titlepage and final leaf dusted & foxed expertly bound in recent quarter mottled calf, gilt banded spine, red morocco label, marbled boards, vellum tips. Jarndyce Antiquarian Booksellers CCXVI - 356 2016 £750

Advice to Working People. Leith: printed by William Reid, 1823. 16mo., folded as issued, one ink mark. Jarndyce Antiquarian Books CCXV - 7 2016 £125

Aelfric Grammaticus, Abbot of Eynsham *A Testimonie of Antiquitie.* John Day..., 1566? First edition of the first printed Old English text, fore-margin of titlepage sometime torn away (no loss of text, though slight loss to an early inscription at head of title), some mild dampstaining slightly more pronounced at end corners curling, but attractive and large copy, small 8vo., resewn in original binding of limp vellum, being a fragment of a 12th century manuscript, lacking spine, contemporary ownership inscription of Richard Ballett, twice, once in secretary hand and again in italic, early note on upper cover "Broughton Lib". Blackwell's Rare Books B184 - 2 2016 £12,000

Aelianus Tacticus *The Tactiks of Aelian or Art of Embattailing an Army....* Printed at Eliot's Court Press for Laurence Lisle, 1616. First edition in English, engraved titlepage and 50 plates, of which 41 are folding, short tear in 1 plate neatly repaired, minor dust soiling at either end, folio, mid to late 20th century mottled calf, short split at foot of upper joint, good. Blackwell's Rare Books Greek & Latin Classics VII - 1 2016 £3000

Aeschylus *Agamemnon.* Oxford: at the Clarendon Press, 1978. 3 volumes, 8vo., 2 plates, pages 795-822 uniformly toned, otherwise clean and bright inside and out, dark blue cloth, gilt titles to spines, top edges little dusty, light gray dust jackets, spines and edges little faded, some creasing to edges, still very good. Unsworths Antiquarian Booksellers 30 - 1 2016 £300

Aeschylus *The Oresteia.* New York: Heritage Press, 1961. Tall quarto, illustrations by Michael Ayrton, pictorial boards, red cloth spine faded, else fine in slipcase (faded), Sandglass pamphlet laid in. Argonaut Book Shop Heritage Press 2015 - 1860 2016 $40

Aeschylus *Trageodiae Septem cum Versione Latina.* Glasgow: Excudebat Foulis, 1794. Veneunt Londini apud T. Payne, Payne & Mackinlay, Oxoniae apud Jos. Cooke 1806, Large and fine paper copy, half titles discarded, few gatherings rather foxed, some minor spotting elsewhere, few later pencil notes, text numbered as spreads rather than leaves or pages, 8vo., contemporary half dark red skiver, marbled boards, good. Blackwell's Rare Books B184 - 3 2016 £400

Aeschylus *Tragodiai Epta.* Glasgow: in aedibus Academicis, excudebat Andreas Foulis, 1795. One of 52 copies, engraved titlepage and 30 engraved plates by Flaxman, bound in, a numbered golded to fit, several shaved within platemark (one just inside border of image), offsetting from plates, bit of spotting, folio, contemporary russia, boards bordered with decorative roll, spine gilt in compartments, edges gilt, marbled endpapers, bit rubbed and scratched, front joint cracking but strong, slight sunning to top and bottom of boards, good copy. Blackwell's Rare Books Greek & Latin Classics VII - 3 2016 £6000

Aeschylus *Tragodiae VII.* Antwerp: Ex Officina Christophori Plaintini, 1850. First Carter edition, dampmark stretching from upper margin and sometimes fore-edge, some spotting, bound little tightly but unlike many copies not trimmed close at other margins, 16mo., late 19th century vellum boards, spine with three raised bands, red morocco lettering piece, soiled, bookplate and release stamp of Harvard College Library Herbert Weir Smyth gift, good. Blackwell's Rare Books B186 - 3 2016 £950

Aesopus *Fabularum.* Strasbourg: Matthias Schurer, Dec., 1515. Rare Strasbourg edition, small 4to., 19th century marbled boards, title within fine one piece white-on-black woodcut border after Urs Graf incorporating architectural columns, two fools at top and at bottom two putti holding an empty shield, white-on-black initials, light marginal staining and few small wormholes at blank lower margin of last few leaves. Maggs Bros. Ltd. 1474 - 1 2016 £3500

Aesopus *Aesopi Phrygis Fabuale. Elegantissimis Iconibus...* Apud Ioan Tornasium, 1605. Near fine, full cream vellum, handwritten title on spine in brown, exposed stitching, top edge stained black, bottom and fore edges speckled red, near fine with some minor toning to spine, light soiling to binding, some contemporary marginalia to endpapers and titlepage, small wormholes throughout, minor stain to titlepage, few creases to otherwise clean pages, sturdy. B & B Rare Books, Ltd. 2016 - ASP003 2016 $600

Aesopus *Aesopi Phrigis et Aliorum Fabulae Quorum Nomina Sequens Pagella Indicabit.* Venice: Apud Prodoctos, 1686. Rare edition, oval woodcut vignette to titlepage, many more oval woodcuts in text, these showing light coloring in with red crayon or chalk, fables numbered in old hand, one leaf with thin area torn from fore-margin with loss to one letter each in about 10 words, another letter with horizontal closed tear (through two woodcuts with no loss), little other staining and evidence of cheap printing, 12mo. contemporary limp vellum, spine lettered in ink, ruckled, old repair to lower quarter of spine, some wear to edges, label removed, remains of red wax to front flyleaf and rear pastedown, rear flyleaf removed, otherwise inscriptions of Hieronimus Bonanomus (1686) and Canvero Giuseppe (with date 1686, but much later), sound. Blackwell's Rare Books Greek & Latin Classics VII - 4 2016 £1200

Aesopus *Fabulae.* Ex decreto DD Hollandiae Ordinum in Usum Scholarum, 1726. Later edition, small 8vo., 47 woodcuts, text in Greek and Latin, occasional smudges but generally very nice, clean within, lower fore edge corner of leaf G4 lost (possibly due to paper flaw or fold) with resulting loss of few words of text, contemporary limp vellum, edges sprinkled red, little darkened, some smudgy marks, faint cup ring to upper wrapper, very good. Unsworths Antiquarian Booksellers Ltd. E05 - 1 2016 £300

Aesopus *Aesop's Fables.* printed for John Stockdale, 1793. First edition, 8vo., 2 volumes, later full red crushed morocco by F. R. S. Lloyd, boards with gilt panels, spines richly decorated and lettered gilt with green morocco onlay raised bands, 112 engraved plates, including vignette titles, little rubbing to joints, some light offsetting from plates, very good. Sotheran's Piccadilly Notes - Summer 2015 - 14 2016 £1500

Aesopus *Aesop's Fables.* London: A. & C. Black, 1912. Limited to only 250 copies of the deluxe edition, signed by publishees', first edition with these illustrations, illustrations by Charles Folkard with 12 great tipped-in color plates plus numerous illustrations, 4to., white cloth with extensive pictorial decorations, top edge gilt, corner bumped, else fine and bright, rare. Aleph-bet Books, Inc. 112 - 195 2016 $1850

Aesopus *Aesop's Fables.* London: William Heinemann, 1912. Limited to 1450 nmbered copies signed by Rackham, large 4to., white gilt pictorial cloth, small area of cover darkened as is not uncommon with this title, endpapers (plain) foxed, else tight and internally near fine, 13 fabulous tipped-in color plates on brown paper with lettered guards and with 53 fine black and white drawings. Aleph-bet Books, Inc. 112 - 406 2016 $2750

Aesopus *The Fables of Aesop according to Sir Roger L'Estrange.* Paris: Harrison of Paris, 1931. No. 274 of 595 copies on Auvergne from a total edition of 645, 20 of which were not for sale, 257 x 191mm., publisher's cloth backed boards in original pictorial dust jacket, in original (slightly marked) red cardboard chemise and (neatly repaired) slipcase with paper label, 50 drawings by Alexander Calder, original - very frequently missing or damaged - printed paper knife (for opening pages) laid in, pictorial inscription by the artist, Alexander Calder, one leaf with short fore-edge tear, not affecting text, otherwise very fine, pristine internally. Phillip J. Pirages 67 - 84 2016 $5500

Aesopus *Aesop's Fables.* London: George G. Harrap & Co., 1936. No. 5 of 8 copies on vellum, signed by the artist (and 525 on paper), 283 x 213mm., very fine publisher's special russet crushed morocco designed by artist and executed by Sangorski & Sutcliffe (stamp signed on front turn-in), covers gilt with strapwork frame featuring grape clusters in corners and prancing fox in center, raised bands flanked by gilt rules, spine panels with central gilt grape cluster, gilt titling, gilt ruled turn-ins, marbled endpapers, all edges gilt on rough, excellent brown textured cloth box with matching slipcase, 201 charming historiated initials, hand colored in part by a former owner and 12 fine engraved illustrations by Stephen Gooden, including engraved titlepage, couple of these partially hand colored, leather with minor naturally occurring variations in color, one plate with very faint dampstain, handful of tiny marginal smudges of stray coloring, otherwise extremely pleasing copy, vellum particularly smooth and bright and special binding lustrous and unworn. Phillip J. Pirages 67 - 339 2016 $29,000

Aesopus *The Subtyl Historyes and Fables.* San Francisco: Grabhorn Press, 1930. No. 134 of 175 copies (there were also 25 special copies printed for San Francisco bibliophile Herbert Rothchild), 244 x 168mm., original reddish brown morocco, raised bands, spine with titling and date in gilt fore and tail edges untrimmed, decorative with historiated initials as well as 7 illustrations by Valenti Angelo, paragraph marks and illustrations colored by hand in blue, red, yellow or gold, printed in red and black, with original (signed) ink drawing for titlepage laid in, extremities with just hint of rubbing, one opening somewhat foxed in margins (two others trivially so), but excellent copy clean and fresh internally, and in scarcely worn binding. Phillip J. Pirages 67 - 176 2016 $2250

Affecting History of the Dreadful Distresses of Frederic Manheim's Family...with an Account of the Destruction of the Settlements at Wyoming. Philadelphia: by Henry Sweitzer for Mathew Carey, 1800. 48 pages, woodcut frontispiece, modern half crushed brown levant, spine attractively gilt by Morrell, fine, fresh, handsomely bound. Joseph J. Felcone, Inc. Books from Five Centuries: a Miscellany - 80 2016 $4000

Agate, James *Here's Richness.* London: George G. Harrap, 1942. 1/100 copies autographed by author and Osbert Sitwell, provided foreword, three quarter blue morocco, spine gilt, edges of spine slightly scuffed, otherwise nice. Second Life Books, Inc. 196A - 14 2016 $200

Agate, James *Kingdoms for Horses. Boxing. Cricket. Hackneys and Golf.* London: Victor Gollancz, 1936. First edition, square 8vo., original green cloth, drawing on title, 4 plates and 4 headpieces, all by Rex Whistler, inscription on endpaper, very good in slightly soiled and torn dust jacket. Sotheran's Piccadilly Notes - Summer 2015 - 330 2016 £78

Agate, James *A Shorter Ego.* London: Harrap, 1946. Limited edition, of 110 numbered sets, each signed by author, large 8vo., 2 volumes, half morocco, top edge gilt, others uncut, spine sunned, otherwise fine. Second Life Books, Inc. 196A - 15 2016 $125

Agee, James 1909-1955 *Let Us Now Praise Famous Men.* Boston: Houghton Mifflin Co., 1941. First edition, 8vo, photos by Walker Evans, original black cloth, dust jacket price clipped and very slightly rubbed, otherwise exceptionally fine, with absolutely none of the fading that invariably mars the spine of dust jacket on this book, extremely rare in this condition. James S. Jaffe Rare Books Occasional List: Winter 2016 - 1 2016 $12,500

Agee, Jonis *Mercury, a Short Story.* West Branch: The Toothpaste Press, April, 1981. Limited to 900 copies of which this is one of 50 bound thus and signed by Agee and artist, Robert Ferguson, square 8vo., stiff paper wrappers, illustrations. Oak Knoll Books 310 - 160 2016 $150

Agnew, Georgette *Let's Pretend.* London: F. Saville, 1927. Limited to only 156 numbered copies, signed by author and artist (150 for sale), 4to., vellum backed cloth, fine in publisher's slipcase with limitation on spine (few neat mends to case), illustrations by E. H. Shepard. Aleph-bet Books, Inc. 111 - 425 2016 $1275

Agnivtsev, Nikolai *Vinter Chpountik. (The Small Screw).* Leningrad: Radougo, 1925. First edition, 4to., pictorial wrappers, slight cover soil, else very good-fine, color illustrations by V. Tvardovski. Aleph-bet Books, Inc. 111 - 400 2016 $800

Ahlborn, Richard E. *Man Made Mobile. Early Saddles of Western North America.* Washington: Smithsonian Inst. Press, 1980. First edition, green cloth, lettered gilt spine, very fine with pictorial dust jacket, vintage photos. Argonaut Book Shop Native American 2015 - 7664 2016 $50

Aickman, Robert *Sub Rosa: Strange Tales.* London: Victor Gollancz, 1968. First edition, octavo, cloth, fine in fine dust jacket (touch of rubbing to extremities and faint crease to lower left front corner). John W. Knott, Jr./L.W. Currey, Inc. Fall-Winter 2015 - 8662 2016 $500

Aickman, Robert *Tales of Love and Death.* London: Victor Gollancz Ltd., 1977. First edition, signed by author, fine in fine dust jacket, octavo, boards. John W. Knott, Jr./L.W. Currey, Inc. Fall-Winter 2015 - 15911 2016 $750

Aiken, Conrad *The Jug of Forslin.* Boston: Four Seas, 1916. 8vo., bookplate of Thomas Caldecot Chubb, and his name in ink dated Oct. 1919, also signed by Stephen Vincent Benet who signed Christmas 1916, brown stain, top edges darkened, edges of cover and ends of spine little worn, rear cover little spotted, otherwise very good, tight. Second Life Books, Inc. 197 - 2 2016 $125

Aiken, Conrad *Thee: a Poem.* New York: Braziller, 1967. First printing, this one of 200 copies, printed on Arches paper by Meridan Gravure Co., but not numbered, possibly an artist's copy, signed by the artist at colophon and author on half title, drawings by Leonard Baskin, very good, tight copy in printed publisher's box, tall 8vo., bound in paper boards, printed in black. Second Life Books, Inc. 196A - 16 2016 $150

Aikin, John *The Arts of Life.* London: J. Johnson, 1807. Second edition, 12mo., original half green vellum, paper label, marbled boards, very good. Jarndyce Antiquarian Books CCXV - 8 2016 £120

Aikin, John *Letters from a Father to His Son on Various Topics Relative to Literature and the Conduct of Life.* London: printed for J. Johnson, St. Paul's Churchyard, 1794. Second edition, 8vo., titlepage slightly dusted, otherwise nice clean copy, contemporary or slightly later half scarlet calf, armorial gilt stamp of Forbes family at head of spine, little rubbed, corners slightly bumped, armorial bookplate of Castle Forbes Library. Jarndyce Antiquarian Books CCXV - 9 2016 £125

Aikin, John *Letters from a Father to His Son.* London: J. Johnson, 1796. Third edition, 2 volumes, 8vo., uncut in original blue drab boards, cream paper spines, neatly rebacked but with ink volume numbers on spines reversed, contemporary signature of John Allsopp on leading f.e.p. volume 1, very good. Jarndyce Antiquarian Books CCXV - 10 2016 £150

Ainsworth, William Harrison 1807-1896 *Le Gentilhomme Des Grandes-Routes.* Paris: Imprimerie de Dubisson et cie, n.d., First French edition, 4to., original plain wrappers, very good copy, presentation copy from translator, B. H. Revoil to Ainsworth. Second Life Books, Inc. 196A - 18 2016 $750

Aird, Catherine *The Religious Body.* MacDonald, 1965. Uncorrected proof, original wrappers in very good condition, uncommon first book.   I. D. Edrich   Crime - 2016   £45

Airship Panorama Book. London and New York: Nister & Dutton, n.d. circa, 1910. Oblong 4to., cloth backed pictorial boards, slightest bit of cover rubbing, else fine, 4 fabulous pop-up pages, rarely found in such nice intact condition. Alephbet Books, Inc.   112 - 389   2016 $2750

Al'manakh Bibliofila. (The Bibliophile's Almanach). Moscow: n.p., 1975-1993. 8vo., 21 of 28 volumes published to date, cloth, volumes 1, 2, 5, 7, 9, 11-13, 15-20, 22-28.   Oak Knoll Books   310 - 55   2016 $650

Al-Quays, Imru *Weep, ah Weep Love's Losing.* Alton: Clarion Pub., 1996. 57129/199 copies (form an edition of 499 copies), signed by artist Henry Fuller and publisher, 10 illustrations printed in red and gold with 8 of these double spread and 1 full page, calligraphic text printed in red with decorated initial accompanying each stanza, imperial 8vo., original wrappers with Fuller design, illustrated endpapers, original card folder, fine, original prospectus laid in. Blackwell's Rare Books   B184 - 253   2016   £120

Alabama Association of Women's Clubs *Proceedings of the Fifty-ninth Annual Session of the Alabama Association of Women's Clubs Held in Dothan, Alabama June 2, 3, 4, 1957.* Birmingham: Furniss Printing Co., 1958. Octavo, stapled printed pale green wrappers, some foxing, stains on front wrapper, very good.   Between the Covers Rare Books   202 - 122   2016 $450

Albertus Magnus, St. *De Laudibus Beate Virginis Mariae.* Cologne: Ulrich Zel not after, 1473. First edition, folio, 165 leaves (of 166, lacking final blank), Gothic type, 2-4 line initial spaces, alternating spaces filled in red, red paragraph marks, underlining and capital strokes, single pinhole visible in lower margins, early 19th century ochre paper boards, spine label in red lettered in gilt red edges, spine darkened, little soiled and marked, preserved in a box, pinhole visible in lower margin, inner margin of first leaf lightly soiled, otherwise extremely fresh, from Bibliotheae J(ohann Heinrich Joseph) Niesart 1766-1841, pastor in Velen 1816, with his manuscript inscription and his bibliographical notes on loose inserted leaf.   Maggs Bros. Ltd.   1474 - 3   2016   £14,000

Albinus, Petrus *Meifinische Land und Berg-Chronica, in Welcher ein Volinstendige Description des Landes so Zwischen Elbe, Sala...* Dresden: Bergen, 1590. First edition, 2nd issue of part 1, folio, 2 parts in one volume, very good German vellum over wooden boards, spine lettered ink, 2 engravings of several woodcuts in text, both titles within elaborate woodcut borders, first printed in red and black, vellum little spotted, two corners with light wear, ties lacking, about 25 pages in part one supplied in strictly contemporary manuscript by a scribe, as well as small portions of 6 pages, last 3 leaves with old restored corners, affecting half a word supplied in near contemporary manuscript), occasional smudging, varying degrees of browning, as usual, due to paper stock.   Sotheran's   Travel and Exploration - 214   2016   £1450

Albion and Irene: a Political Romance. London: Marcus Ward & Co., 1886. First edition, 8vo., green cloth lettered gilt on spine and cover, tipped in at front is neat publicity sheet of favourable press notices from British and Irish newspapers, very good, clean copy with slight rubbing. Any Amount of Books   2015 - A86039   2016   £150

Albrecht, Lorenz *Euangelisch Prognostic.* Munich: Adam Berg, 1589. Only edition, 4to., modern marbled boards, woodcut lower left hand corner of titlepage of astrologer and his family.   Maggs Bros. Ltd.   1474 - 66   2016   £1250

Alcaforado, Marianna *The Love Letter of a Portuguese Nun...* Oxford: 1901. First English edition, one of 525 copies on Van Gelder, narrow 8vo., uncut, very nice, original, slightly chipped tissue wrapper.   Bertram Rota Ltd. February List 2016 - 1   2016   £65

Alciati, Andrea *Les Emblemes de Nouueau Translatez en Francois.* Lyon: Mace Bonhomme for Guillaume Rouille, 1549. Rare early example, woodcut printer's device on titlepage and 165 woodcut emblematic illustrations, small 8vo., Antique style blind tooled calf, red morocco label, little dampstained in places but generally good copy sympathetically rebound.   Maggs Bros. Ltd.   1474 - 4   2016   £2800

Alciati, Andrea *Emblemata Latinogallica. Les Emblems Latin-Francois... la Version Francoise non Encorveu cy Devant.* Paris: Jean Richet, 1584. First edition thus, woodcut device on titlepage and last leaf, portrait on verso of title and 211 woodcut emblems, 12mo., contemporary vellum, remains of later ties, titlepage with contemporary inscription of Bibliotheque Deprins, bookplate of Samuel Ashton Thompson Yates.   Maggs Bros. Ltd.   1474 - 5   2016   £3000

Alcott, Louisa May   1832-1888 *Jo's Boys and How They Turned Out a Sequel to Little Men.* Boston: Roberts, 1886. First edition, first state with sheets bulking 1 1/16 inch, very good, tight, clean copy, 8vo., brown cloth.   Second Life Books, Inc.   197 - 5   2016 $350

Alcott, Louisa May 1832-1888 *Jo's Boys and How They Turned Out a Sequel to Little Men.* Boston: Roberts, 1886. First edition, 8vo., green cloth, first state with sheets bulking 1 1/16", very good, tight, clean copy.   Second Life Books, Inc.   197 - 4   2016 $350

Alcott, Louisa May 1832-1888 *Little Men.* Boston: Roberts, 1871. First edition, first issue with signature mark 'I' with ad listing "Pink and White Tyranny" as Nearly Ready, green cloth, very little rubbing and some cocked, some spotting to text, very good.   Second Life Books, Inc. 197 - 3   2016 $600

Alcott, Louisa May 1832-1888 *May Flowers.* Boston: Little Brown, 1899. First separate edition, Tan cloth stamped in black and gold, offset on endpaper, else fine, 4 half tone plates, beautiful copy.   Aleph-bet Books, Inc.   111 - 13   2016 $250

Alcott, Louisa May 1832-1888 *"Nelly's Hospital." in Our Young Folks Volume I.* Boston: Ticknor and Fields, 1865. First 12 issues, 8vo., original publisher's green cloth with extensive gilt pictorial spine, occaisonal margin soil, else near fine, profusely illustrated with woodcuts.   Aleph-bet Books, Inc.   111 - 14   2016 $400

Aldam, W. H. *A Quaint Treatise o 'Flees and the Art Artyfichaill Flee Mkaing" by an old man...* London: John B. Day, 1876. First edition, 2nd issue, scarce, 4to., original green cloth decorated in gilt and black to upper board and spine, all edges gilt, two chromolithographs after James Poole on 6 board leaves, extra illustrated with engraved portrait of Aldam to prelim, little spotting, very good, presentation from author to A. W. Cooper.   Sotheran's Hunting, Shooting & Fishing - 106   2016   £2995

Aldan, Daisy *Folder: Volume 1, Number 2 1954.* New York: 1954. Heavy paper folder, holding various single and folded sheets, cover somewhat soiled, some silver fish damage to lower right edge and corner, interior material undamaged, very good.   Second Life Books, Inc.   197 - 6   2016 $45

Aldin, Cecil *Bunnyborough.* London: Humphrey Milford, 1919. Large 4to., cloth backed pictorial boards, rear cover faded, else very good+, 16 rich color plates on heavy stock, pictorial title and pictorial endpapers, extremely scarce.   Aleph-bet Books, Inc.   112 - 16   2016 $1750

Aldin, Cecil *Mac.* New York: Hodder & Stoughton, n.d. circa, 1912. First US edition, 4to., cloth backed pictorial boards, fine, 24 color plates and pictorial titlepage, excellent copy, rare in this condition.   Aleph-bet Books, Inc.   112 - 17   2016 $850

Aldin, Cecil *Pickles.* London: Henry Frowde and Hodder and Stoughton, 1909. First edition, 4to., very good+, mild scattered foxing, cover edge wear, scuffs to covers, spine expertly rebacked in past, 24 fine color plates on heavy stock illustrated recto only, as issued.   By the Book, L. C.   45 - 77   2016 $600

Aldin, Cecil *Puppy Dog Frolics.* London and Glasgow: Collins Clear Type Press, n.d. circa, 1930. Folio, cloth backed pictorial boards, tips rubbed, rear cover soil, very good++, printed on coated paper, 16 full page color illustrations plus 2 black and white illustrations, rare.   Aleph-bet Books, Inc.   112 - 18   2016 $975

Aldin, Cecil *The Twins.* London: Henry Frowde/Hodder & Stoughton, 1910. First edition, 4to., 24 color plates, very good++, original cloth spine and printed illustrated paper boards, owner inscription, small scuff to f.f.ep., minimal soil and edge wear to covers.   By the Book, L. C.   45 - 78   2016 $550

Aldington, Richard *Stepping Heavenword.* Florence: Orioli, 1931. First edition, 40/800 copies of an edition of 808, signed by author, printed on Pescia handmade paper, 8vo., original quarter cream cloth with yellow sides showing few light handling marks, panels of very faint browning to front endpapers, untrimmed and uncut, dust jacket very lightly soiled overall, with some creasing at tips of backstrip and few faint foxspots to rear panel, very good.   Blackwell's Rare Books   B184 - 93   2016   £150

Aldini, Giovanni *Precis des Experiences Galvaniques Faites Recement a Londres et a Calais...* Paris: P. Didot aine, 1803. First edition, slightly browned in places, 8vo., boards, good.   Blackwell's Rare Books   B186 - 6   2016   £700

Aldiss, Brian W. *The Helliconia Trilogy: Helliconia Spring, Helliconia Summer and Helliconia Winter.* New York: Atheneum, 1982-1985. First edition, octavo, cloth backed boards, fine set in fine dust jackets.   John W. Knott, Jr./L.W. Currey, Inc.   Fall-Winter 2015 - 17821   2016 $250

Aldiss, Brian W. *Hothouse.* London: Faber & Faber, 1962. First edition, octavo, cloth, signed by author, fine in fine price clipped dust jacket.   John W. Knott, Jr./L.W. Currey, Inc.   Fall-Winter 2015 - 16872   2016 $1250

Aldiss, Brian W. *Moreau's Other Island.* London: Jonathan Cape, 1980. First edition, octavo, spine slightly bruised at head, otherwise fine in fine dust jacket.   Peter Ellis   112 - 8   2016   £25

Aldridge, Adele *Notpoems.* Riverside: Magic Circle, 1972. Second edition, First printing, 8vo., author's presentation to poet and editor William Claire, 2/17/73, paper wrappers, cover little soiled, otherwise very good, tight.   Second Life Books, Inc.   196A - 22   2016 $50

Aldrin, Buzz *Men from Earth.* New York: Bantam Books, 1989. First edition signed by auhtor, 8vo. original cloth backed paper covered boards with dust jacket, fine. Sotheran's Travel and Exploration - 447 2016 £498

Alembert, Jean Le Rond D' 1717-1783 *Melanges De Litterature D'Histoire, et De Philosophie.* Amsterdam: Zacharie Chatelain & Fils, 1766-1770. Reprint of 1759 edition with few corrections, 5 volumes, 12mo., full calf with raised bands and stained edges, foldout chart, some spines cracked, most of the hinges split, edges and corners of covers rubbed, some foxing through few volumes. Oak Knoll Books 310 - 282 2016 $650

Alexander Aetolus *Alexandri Aetoli Testimonia et Fragmenta.* Florence: Universita degh Studi di Firenze, 1999. First edition, 8vo., paperback, edges slightly dusted, very minor shelfwear, very good, author's inscription. Unsworths Antiquarian Booksellers Ltd. E04 - 25 2016 £30

Alexander, David *Shoot a Sitting Duck.* New York: Random House, 1955. First edition, fine in dust jacket. Mordida Books 2015 - 010150 2016 $65

Alexander, Disney *Prospectus of a Work Intended for Publication and Entitled The Four Gospels....* Halifax: printed by P. K. Holden for the author, 1815. Only edition, 8vo., recent marbled boards lettered on spine, very good. John Drury Rare Books 2015 - 23456 2016 $350

Alexie, Sherman *First Indian on the Moon.* New York: Hanging Loose Press, 1993. First edition, fine copy. Bella Luna Books 2016 - u022a 2016 $165

Alexie, Sherman *The Journal of Ethnic Studies.* Bellingham: JES, 1988. First edition, fine, very scarce, signed by author, paperback original. Bella Luna Books 2016 - 196517 2016 $396

Alexis, Jacques Stephen *In the Flicker of an Eyelid.* Charlottesville: University of Virginia, 2002. First American edition, 8vo., black cloth, review laid in, presentation from Carrol F. Coates, cover very slightly scuffed, otherwise as new. Second Life Books, Inc. 196A - 24 2016 $45

Alger, Horatio *From Canal Boy to President, or the Boyhood and Manhood of James A. Garfield, Illustrated.* New York: John R. Anderson, 1881. First edition, 2nd issue, without errata, 8vo., green cloth stamped in black and green, very good. Second Life Books, Inc. 197 - 7 2016 $150

Alinder, James *Ansel Adams: Classic Images.* Boston: New York Graphic Society Book , Little Brown and Co., 1986. First cloth edition, 75 full duotone illustrations from photos, fine in dust jacket. Argonaut Book Shop Photography 2015 - 953 2016 $40

Alken, Henry *The Art and Practice of Etching; with Directions for Other methods of Light and Entertaining Engraving.* London: S. & J. Fuller, 1849. First edition, square 8vo., original cloth, new spine covering, frontispiece, 8 plates, engraved plates by Alken, bookplate of Gavin Bridson, inside hinges cracked, rebacked with new cloth and with modern paper spine label, ink ownership inscription of titlepage. Oak Knoll Books 310 - 24 2016 $500

Alken, Henry *Illustrations for Landscape Scenery.* London: published by S. & J. Fuller, at the Temple of Fancy, 34 Rathbone Place..., 1821. First edition, scarce edition, oblong small folio, 26 hand colored engraved plates, numbered 1-24 and 2 unnumbered, uncut in original grey boards, upper cover with printed label, rebacked in modern red cloth slipcase, upper cover lettered gilt, bookplate of Joel Spitz. Marlborough Rare Books List 55 - 1 2016 £1500

Alken, Henry *The National sports of Great Britain.* London: Methuen & Co., 1903. New edition, small 8vo., sometime rebound for Sotheran in full red calf, gilt fillets to sides, spine with angle gilt raised band, gilt lettering and horse-shoe tool inside gilt paneling, gilt turn-ins, marbled endpapers, all edges gilt, 50 fine colored plates of sporting subjects, all with tissue guards, spine little sunned, plates in fine state, very clean, very good. Sotheran's Hunting, Shooting & Fishing - 158 2016 £200

Allard, Gerry *Socialist Call.* Chicago: Socialist Party of the US, 1938. Bound copies of the weekly Jan. 8 1938 to Dec. 24, 1938, folio, one year bound in maroon cloth over heavy boards, signed by editor, photos and cartoons, cover somewhat worn and soiled, newspaper leaves creased and little chipped at edges, very good, tight copy. Second Life Books, Inc. 196A - 25 2016 $100

Allbut, Robert *London and Country Rambles with Charles Dickens.* London: Shepherd & St. John, 1888? Frontispiece and plates, original red cloth, spine and front board lettered in gilt, front board with gilt border, spine slightly dulled small mark on front board, armorial bookplate of Edward Andrew Donaldson & his signature on titlepage, all edges gilt, very good plus. Jarndyce Antiquarian Booksellers CCXVIII - 1056 2016 £40

Allbut, Robert *London and Country Rambles with Charles Dickens.* London: Sheppard & St. John, 1894. Reprint of 1886 edition, frontispiece and plates, original green cloth, blocked and lettered gilt, all edges gilt, very good, bright copy. Jarndyce Antiquarian Booksellers CCXVIII - 1057 2016 £35

Allbut, Robert *Rambles in Dickens-Land.* London: Chapman & Hall, 1903. Half title, frontispiece and plates, odd spot, original green cloth, blocked and lettered in blind and gilt, very good, bright.   Jarndyce Antiquarian Booksellers   CCXVIII - 1058   2016   £40

Allchin, William Henry *An Account of the Reconstruction of the University of London.* London: Volume I. H. K. Lewis and volumes II & III HMSO, 1905. 1910? 1912, 3 volumes, larage 8vo., original cloth backed boards, dulled and little worn, presentation inscription from Lady Allchin.   Jarndyce Antiquarian Books   CCXV - 831   2016   £280

Allen, Albert Arthur *The Female Figure.* New York: Arthur Allen Studios, 1915-1925. Photo album portfolio sold to subscribers by Allen, quarto, 40 pages, string bound textured paper wrappers, very good overall, moderate wear to extremities, some waviness to pages and some photo lifting at corners, still firmly secured.   Royal Books   48 - 16   2016 $4500

Allen, Hervey *Sarah Simon.* Garden City: Doubleday Doran, 1929. 1/311 copies, 8vo., unopened, signed by author, paper over boards with cloth spine, illustrated by Frank Peers, cover slightly worn at edges, otherwise very good, tight copy, laid in is original snapshot of author and his wife.   Second Life Books, Inc.   196A - 26   2016 $75

Allen, James Lane *A Kentucky Cardinal.* New York: Harper & Bros., 1895. First edition, 16mo., decorated tan cloth with gilt lettering, 4 black and white illustrations, very fine.   Argonaut Book Shop   Literature 2015 - 1198   2016 $125

Allen, John *European Americana: a Chronological Guide to Works Printed in Europe Relating to the Americas 1493-1650.* New York: Readex Books, 1980. 2 volumes, small 4to., cloth.   Oak Knoll Books   310 - 225   2016 $550

Allen, Michael *Charles Dickens' Childhood.* London: Macmillan, 1988. First edition, half title, plates, maps, original brown cloth, Thelma Grove booklabel, very good in slightly faded dust jacket, signed by author.   Jarndyce Antiquarian Booksellers   CCXVIII - 1059   2016   £25

Allen, Warner *The Devil that Slumbers.* London: John Hamilton, 1925. First edition, rear in or out of jacket, rear board mottled, else very good in like dust jacket (chipped with "T" in "The" on front panel missing), with few short closed tears, light creasing and dampstain to verso of front panel.   Royal Books   51 - 18   2016 $1650

Allfree, P. S. *Hawks of the Hadhramaut.* London: Robert Hale Ltd., 1967. First edition, 8vo., original cloth, dust jacket, sketch map, illustrations from photos, light rubbing to edges of jacket, initially few minor spots, else fine, ownership inscription Noel E. Leat.   Sotheran's   Travel and Exploration - 296   2016   £98

Allingham, Margery *Flowers for the Judge.* New York: Doubleday Doran and Co. Inc., 1936. First US edition, octavo, original tan cloth, spine stamped in red, top edge stained dark red, fore and bottom edges rough trimmed, printed endpapers, nearly fine in very good or somewhat better dust jacket with light shelfwear to spine ends, slight edge rubbing.   John W. Knott, Jr./L.W. Currey, Inc.   Fall-Winter 2015 - 17878   2016 $500

Allingham, Margery *The Mind Readers.* London: Chatto & Windus, 1965. Near fine in dust jacket.   I. D. Edrich   Crime - 2016   £20

Allingham, Margery *Mr. Campion Criminologist....* Garden City: published for the Crime Club Inc. by Doubleday Doran & Co., 1937. First edition, octavo, original black cloth, spine pane stamped in orange, top edge stained red and outer edges rough trimmed, cream endpapers, corners gently bumped, previous owner's bookplate, very good in like dust jacket with rubbing to edges and light shelfwear to spine ends and corner tips and ink to spine panel is sun faded.   John W. Knott, Jr./L.W. Currey, Inc.   Fall-Winter 2015 - 17879   2016 $450

Allingham, Margery *Tether's End.* Garden City: Doubleday, 1958. First American edition, fine in dust jacket.   Mordida Books   2015 - 010115   2016 $65

Allingham, William *Rhymes for the You Folk.* London: Cassell & Co., n.d., 1867. Large 8vo., original illustrated red paper boards over red cloth, lettered black and white on front board, copiously illustrated, signed presentation from one of the artists, Helen Allingham for Claude and Alan Scott, June 1917, some rubbing and slight chipping along edges and corners with faint foxing to prelims, otherwise sound, clean, attractive, very good.   Any Amount of Books   2015 - C8506   2016   £250

Allinson, Francesca *A Childhood.* London: Leonard & Virginia Woolf at Hogarth Press, 1937. First edition, octavo, 6 wood engravings by Enid Marx who also designs dust jacket, slight bruise at head of spine, very good in like dust jacket little nicked, chipped and creased at edges.   Peter Ellis   112 - 172   2016   £200

Allman, George James *Introductory Lecture Delivered to the Students of the Natural History Class in the University of Edinburgh.* Edinburgh: Adam & Charles Black, 1855. Slight damp mark to lower margins, disbound.   Jarndyce Antiquarian Books   CCXV - 633   2016   £20

Allom, Thomas 1804-1872 *Views of Tyrol.* C. Tilt, n.d., 1840. First edition, 8vo. folding map, 45 steel engravings, contemporary black morocco, small wear at head of spine.   J. & S. L. Bonham Antiquarian Booksellers   Europe 2016 - 9947   2016   £180

Allot, Robert *Wit Theater of the Little World.* printed by J(ames) R(oberts) for N(icholas) L(ing), 1599. First edition, few catchwords trimmed, first 2 and last 4 leaves soiled, small hole in blank area of title, repair to lower margin of title, rust hole in X5 with loss of a few leaves, small 8vo., 19th century dark burgundy morocco, double gilt fillets on sides, double gilt rules on either side of 3 raised bands on spine and at head and foot, lettered and dated in gilt direct, signature of John Couchman dated 1699. Blackwell's Rare Books B184 - 4 2016 £5000

L'Alouette: a Magazine of Verse - October 1933 (Volume 4 No. 5). Medford: Charles A. A. Parker, 1933. 12mo., string and black paper wrappers with gilt stamped title on front wrapper, very good or better with non color breaking crease on rear wrapper, and light wear at top of spine and yapped for edges, rare. Between the Covers Rare Books 204 - 150 2016 $350

An Alphabetical List of the Poll for the Election of Two Representatives to Serve in Parliament for the Borough of Newark-upon-Tyne, Taken before the Worshipful Wm. Martin, Esq. Mayor on the 9th day of September 1780.... Newark: printed for James Tomlinson, 1780. Only edition, 12mo., contemporary (original?) elaborately gilt stamped red morocco by James Tomlinson, covers with decorative and ruled borders, "Newark Election 1780" within center gilt ruled rectangular box, spine elaborately tooled in 6 compartments, gilt edges, marbled endpapers, all edges gilt, binding has few trifling imperfections, but lovely copy. Howard S. Mott Inc. 265 - 98 2016 $1250

Althofer, George W. *Cradle of Incense: the Story of Australian Prostanthera.* Melbourne: Society for Growing Australian Plants, 1978. Octavo, illustrations, bookplate, letter from author, slightly worn dust jacket. Andrew Isles Natural History Books 55 - 15543 2016 $30

Altick, Richard D. *The Shows of London.* Cambridge: Belknap Press, 1978. Large 4to., publisher's buckram, color pictorial dust jacket with one small tape repair, previous owner's name to front flyleaf, text in double columns, well illustrated, near fine. Dramatis Personae 119 - 5 2016 $175

Amaral, Anthony *Will James, The Gilt Edged Cowboy.* Los Angeles: Westernlore, 1967. First edition, numerous photographic illustrations, drawings, facsimiles, red cloth, gilt, very fine, pictorial dust jacket. Argonaut Book Shop Biography 2015 - 7176 2016 $150

Ambler, Eric *The Army of the Shadows and Other Stories.* Helsinki: Eurographica, No. 5 of edition limited to 350 numbered copies, signed and dated by author, illustrations, original wrappers, mint. I. D. Edrich Crime - 2016 £75

Ambler, Eric *Dirty Story.* London: Bodley Head, 1967. First edition, fine in price clipped dust jacket with couple of short closed tears. Mordida Books 2015 - 009767 2016 $55

Ambler, Eric *The Light of Day.* New York: Knopf, 1963. First American edition, name on flyleaf otherwise fine in dust jacket with small chip at top corner of back panel. Mordida Books 2015 - 012696 2016 $65

Ambler, Eric *The Night-Comers.* London: Heinemann, 1956. Very good in like dust jacket. I. D. Edrich Crime - 2016 £25

Ambrose, Stephen E. *Crazy Horse and Custer. The Parallel Lives of Two American Warriors.* New York: Doubleday, 1975. First edition, illustrations by Kenneth Francis Dewey, cloth backed boards, fine with dust jacket flap price clipped. Argonaut Book Shop Biography 2015 - 7677 2016 $175

Ambschell, Antonio *Dissertatio de Centro Gravitatis in Subsidium Suorum Discipulorum. (with) Assertiones ex-universa Physica et Mathesi Elememtari....* 1779. First and only edition, 2 works in 1 volume, small 8vo., 2 large folding engraved plates, original full mottled blind ruled calf, spine flat backed but with elaborate gilt tooling, edges red, extremely rare. Jeff Weber Rare Books 183 - 3 2016 $1800

Amend, Ottlile *Jolly Jungle Jingles.* Joliet: Volland, 1929. 4to., cloth backed pictorial boards, fine in original box (color unevenly faded), scarce, illustrations by Eleanor Barte, rare in box. Aleph-bet Books, Inc. 112 - 498 2016 $475

The American book Circular: with Notes and Statistics. New York: Wiley and Putnam, 1843. printed green wrappers, octavo, removed from bound volume, spine perished, slight chipping on front wrapper, modest wear, very good. Between the Covers Rare Books 204 - 97 2016 $450

American Colonization Society *The Twenty-Fourth Annual Report of the American Colonization Society, with Proceedings of the Annual Meeting and of the Board of Directors at Washington City, January 1841.* Washington: Joseph Etter, 1841. First edition, saddle stitched pale pink wrappers, lightly soiled, text little foxed, faint vertical fold, very good. Between the Covers Rare Books 207 - 30 2016 $300

American Domestic Cookery Formed on Principles of Economy or the Use of Private Families. New York: Evert Duyckinck, 1823. Frontispiece, engraved fore title and 7 plates, contemporary marbled leather, very skillfully rebacked with original gilt spine laid down, scattered dampstaining on first and last few leaves, plates foxed but very nice. Joseph J. Felcone, Inc. Books from Five Centuries: a Miscellany - 46 2016 $650

The American Family Receipt Book.... Halifax: Milner & Sowerby reprinted from the American edition, 1856. Second English edition, 16mo., few ink notes, original brown cloth, little marked. Jarndyce Antiquarian Books CCXV - 11 2016 £60

American Institute of Electrical Engineers *Catalogue of the Wheeler Gift of Books, Pamphlets and Periodicals in the Library of....* New York: AIEE, 1909. 3 volumes, thick 8vo., original yellow cloth binding with printed cloth labels, it has been extended to 3 volumes, many blank leaves inserted, covers faded and soiled, inside hinges cracked. Oak Knoll Books 310 - 240 2016 $325

American Printing History Association *The Journal of the American Printing History Association.* V.P.: American Printing History Association, 1979-2008. Volume I no. 1 (whole no. 1), 1979 through volume XXV no. 2 (whole no. 50), illustrations, printed wrappers in very fine, fresh condition. Joseph J. Felcone, Inc. Books from Five Centuries: a Miscellany - 119 2016 $400

American Printing History Association *Printing History, The Journal of the.....* New York: APHA, 1979-1993. 30 issues (in 28), stiff paper wrappers,. Oak Knoll Books 310 - 185 2016 $250

American Readings in Prose and Verse. London: Samuel French, 1884. Part II, original orange printed wrappers, small tear at tail of back wrapper, very good. Jarndyce Antiquarian Booksellers CCXVIII - 393 2016 £30

American Society for Colonizing the Free People of Color of the United States *The Fifth Annual report.... with an appendix.* Washington City: printed by Davis & Force, 1822. First edition, unprinted blue wrappers, errata, page edges untrimmed, foxing, spine partially perished, wrappers bit tattered and worn, near very good. Between the Covers Rare Books 207 - 29 2016 $800

American Type Founders Co. *ATF. Specimen Book and Catalogue.* Jersey City: American Type Founders Co., 1923. Thick 4to., two toned cloth, illustrations, worn at spine ends and tips, slightly shaken. Oak Knoll Books 310 - 189 2016 $350

American Type Founders Co. Kelly Press Division *Style B Kelly Automatic Press Book of Instructions.* Elizabeth: Kelly Press Division, American Type Founders Co., April, 1927. Oblong quarto, original printed red wrappers, 20 illustrations, laid into this copy is typed postcard from printer Lewis Osborne of Ashland, Oregon dated Jan. 9 1973 to printer Adrian Wilson, well used, worn and stained, as one would expect, with scotch tape reinforcement, etc, but complete, and rare. The Brick Row Book Shop Miscellany 69 - 66 2016 $225

Americans in France: a Directory, 1925. Paris: American Chamber of Commerce in France, 1925. First edition, octavo, publisher's maroon leather, color and monochrome illustrations, near fine. Honey & Wax Booksellers 4 - 10 2016 $500

Amir, Eli *Scapegoat: a Novel.* New York: Weidenfeld & Nicolson, 1987. First edition, fine in fine dust jacket. Ken Hebenstreit, Bookseller 2016 - 2016 $95

Amis, Kingsley *The Evans Country.* Oxford: Fantasy Press, 1962. First edition, fine in stapled wrappers as issued, uncommon, as new. Between the Covers Rare Books 204 - 8 2016 $250

Amis, Kingsley *The James Bond Dossier.* New York: NAL, 1965. First American edition, fine in dust jacket. Mordida Books 2015 - 011869 2016 $65

Amis, Kingsley *What Became of Jane Austen? And Other Questions.* London: Cape, 1970. Review copy with review slip loosely inserted, dust jacket with closed tears on tips of spine and edges are chipped, contents in very good condition. I. D. Edrich Crime - 2016 £45

Amis, Martin *Other People: a Mystery Story.* London: Jonathan Cape, 1981. First edition, first state, with top edge blue, fine in fine frontispiece. Peter Ellis 112 - 10 2016 £75

Amis, Martin *Pornoland.* London: Thames and Hudson, 2004. First edition, quarto, 54 color photos by Stefano de Luigi, signed by Amis, fine in near fine dust jacket, just little nicked and creased at top edge. Peter Ellis 112 - 11 2016 £85

Amman, Jost *Bibliorum Utriusque Testamenti Icones, Summor Artificio Expressae Historias Sacras and Vivum Exhibentes & Oculis Summa cum Gratia Repraesentantes....* Frankfurt: Christoph Corvinus & Sigmund Feyerabend, 1571. First edition, 8vo., 19th century blue morocco, triple blind fillet on cover, title lettered in gilt on spine, inner edge richly gilt and signed Bauzonnet-Trautz', marbled edges, gilt edges, silk bookmark, woodcut coats of arms of Johann Fichard and Konrad Weis, 200 fine oval woodcuts within ms. frames by Jose Amman, many signed with his initials, IA, bookplates of Edward Arnold, Dorking, E. Yeminez, Lyon and Allan Heywood Bright, London.   Maggs Bros. Ltd. 1474 - 12   2016   £4500

Amor, Nicholas R.   *Late Medieval Ipswich. Trade and Industry.*   Woodbridge: Boydell Press, 2011. First edition, 8vo., 100 + plates, figures, maps and tables, laminated pictorial boards, as new.   Unsworths Antiquarian Booksellers Ltd.   E05 - 93   2016   £25

Amos 'n Andy with Madam Queen Ruby Taylor in 'Tight Spot'.   Toronto: Goodlesuck Bros. Ltd. (presumed false imprint, circa, 1930. Edition unknown, 16mo., illustrations, stapled wrappers printed in green and black, small tears and creases at edge of front wrapper, few light ink squiggles on unprinted rear wrapper, else very good or better.   Between the Covers Rare Books   207 - 83   2016 $450

Amundsen, Roald   *My Life as an Explorer.*   Garden City: Doubleday, 1927. First edition, 8vo., gift inscription below author's signature, edge wear to covers, owner bookplate, mild scattered foxing, very good.   By the Book, L. C.   45 - 1   2016 $3000

Amusemens Francois, ou Contes a Rire: Trattenimenti Italiani...   Venice: Dominico Pitteri, 1752. 2 volumes bound as 1, 8vo., French and Italian texts, woodcut device to each title, little annotation (page 195), some pencilled notes to front flyleaves, slightly yellowed, few inkspots and smudges, contemporary dark brown calf rebacked in poor quality leather which is now creased and rather rubbed, all edges red, marbled endpapers, upper joint starting at head and tail, edges rubbed, corners worn, flyleaves dusty, still good copy, ownership inscription of Mademoiselle Genevieve Clea(ris?).   Unsworths Antiquarian Booksellers   30 - 3   2016   £160

Anacreon   *Odai, kai to Sapphous kai Erinnas Leipsana.* Edinburgh: Apud Hamilton, Balfour & Neill, 1754. Part of prelims bound after second titlepage, some foxing and soiling around edges, 24mo., contemporary sprinkled calf, rebacked preserving original backstrip, endpapers renewed, scarce, near miniature edition.   Blackwell's Rare Books Greek & Latin Classics VII - 5   2016   £400

Anacreon   *Odai.*   Glasgow: in aedibus academicis, ex Typis Jacobi Mundell, excudebant J. et. J. Scrymgeour, 1801. Some foxing and browning, pages 106, 12mo., contemporary sprinkled calf, boards bordered with gilt roll, neatly rebacked preserving most of original backstrip, new red morocco label, other compartments with central lyre tools, hinges relined, inscription scratched out from front endpaper, good copy.   Blackwell's Rare Books   Greek & Latin Classics VII - 6   2016   £350

Anastasius   *Medicina Salernitana...*   Officina Ioanis Bogaeti, 1611. 12mo., 19th century quarter roan and purple cloth boards, spine worn, title repaired with occasional loss of couple of letters, text foxed.   James Tait Goodrich X-78 - 499   2016 $400

Ancourt, Abbe D'   *The Lady's Preceptor.*   London: printed for J. Watts and sold by B. Dod, 1743. Second edition, 8vo., title in red and black, contemporary full calf, double ruled gilt borders, hinges cracked but remaining firm, little rubbed with slight loss to foot of spine, contemporary ownership signature of Henry Streatfield on title with Streatfield family armorial bookplate.   Jarndyce Antiquarian Books CCXV - 12   2016   £750

Andersen, Hans Christian   1805-1875   *The Emperor's New Clothes.*   Boston: Houghton Mifflin, 1949. Small 4to., cloth, slight bit of cover soil, else fine in dust jacket (very good to fine, very slight wear to spine), illustrations in color, warmly inscribed by artist, Virginia Lee Burton dated 1949, rare thus, beautiful copy.   Aleph-bet Books, Inc.   111 - 68   2016 $850

Andersen, Hans Christian   1805-1875   *Hans Andersen's Fairy Tales.*   London: Frederick Warne, n.d. circa, 1885? Early edition, octavo, illustrations by a number of artists in color and black and white, original brown pictorial cloth, top edge gilt, covers just little blistered at edges, prelims lightly spotted, very good.   Peter Ellis   112 - 12   2016   £95

Andersen, Hans Christian   1805-1875   *Fairy Tales & Stories.*   New York: Century, 1900. First US edition, red pictorial cloth, gilt, fine, illustrations by Hans Tegner with profusion of full and partial page drawings, beautiful. Aleph-bet Books, Inc.   112 - 20   2016 $400

Andersen, Hans Christian   1805-1875   *Hans Andersen's Fairy Tales.*   London: Constable & Co., 1913. Edition Deluxe, 1/100 copies signed by artist, this being #28, quarto, pictorial titlepage, 16 mounted color plates, each with tissue guard, 37 full page and 58 smaller black and white drawings by W. Heath Robinson, publisher's full white vellum over boards, front cover and spine pictorially stamped in gilt, top edge gilt, others uncut, spectacular copy, very rare, housed in leather edged marbled board slipcase.   David Brass Rare Books, Inc.   2015 - 03023   2016 $5500

Andersen, Hans Christian   1805-1875   *Hans Andersen's Fairy Tales.*   London: Boots for Hodder & Stoughton, n.d. circa, 1915. Thick 4to., red cloth stamped in gold, light wear, very good+, illustrations by W. Heath Robinson with 16 wonderful tipped in color plates and full page in text black and whites.   Aleph-bet Books, Inc.   112 - 429   2016 $325

Andersen, Hans Christian   1805-1875   *Fairy Tales.* London: George Harrap, n.d., 1916. Limited to only 125 numbered copies signed by Clarke, tall thick 4to., full vellum, gilt cover, top edge gilt, slight spotting on bottom edge and endpaper, near fine, lavishly illustrated with 16 incredible color plates mounted on heavy stock (with lettered tissue guards), 24 full page black and white plates plus many decorative tailpieces, illustrations illustrations by Harry Clarke are magnificent, beautiful copy of rare book.   Aleph-bet Books, Inc.   111 - 94   2016 $7500

Andersen, Hans Christian   1805-1875   *Fairy Tales.* New York: George H. Doran Co., 1924. First American trade edition, 286 x 222mm., original pictorial cloth, covers in black, silver and orange, flat spine in black and silver with pink labels, pictorial endleaves, hinge neatly reinforced with gray cloth tape, 29 illustrations by Kay Nielsen, comprised of 12 tipped-in color plates, 16 full page black and white drawings, illustrated titlepage, bottom corners little worn, very minor soiling and grazing to covers, 3 inch marginal tear below engraved title repaired (with consequent slight discoloration), other trivial defects, but binding with nothing approaching a serious condition problem, and very clean and fresh internally, all in all, excellent copy.   Phillip J. Pirages   67 - 261   2016 $1000

Andersen, Hans Christian   1805-1875   *Fairy Tales.* London: Hodder and Stoughton, 1924. No. 111 of 500 copies of edition deluxe, signed by artist, 318 x 260mm., publisher's deluxe binding of full vellum, upper cover with gilt embossed vignette (replicating titlepage), flat spine with gilt tree at foot and gilt titling at head, top edge gilt, engraved illustrated titlepage, engraved tailpieces, 16 full page black and white engravings, 12 color plates by kay Nielsen, front free endpaper with remnants of bookplate, hint of splaying to boards, gilt on spine little muted, otherwise only the most trivial imperfections, nearly fine copy, very clean and fresh inside and out.   Phillip J. Pirages   67 - 260   2016 $6000

Andersen, Hans Christian   1805-1875   *Fairy Tales by...* London: Harrap, 1932. One of only 25 copies of a total limited edition of 525 copies (of which 500 were for sale), 4to., publisher's special full green morocco with triple gilt fillet border and pictorial gold design on front cover after Rackham, spine slightly toned, else fine, this copy marked presentation in Arthur Rackham's hand and signed, 12 beautiful color plates, pictorial endpapers, 59 wonderful black and whites, with original drawing by Rackham, signed and dated by him, rare.   Aleph-bet Books, Inc.   111 - 370   2016 $18,500

Andersen, Hans Christian   1805-1875   *Fairy Tales by Hans Andersen.*   Philadelphia: McKay, 1932. First edition, 4to., rose cloth, fine in dust jacket and original publisher's box (small repairs to box flap), illustrations by Arthur Rackham, beautiful copy.   Aleph-bet Books, Inc.   112 - 412   2016 $1500

Andersen, Hans Christian   1805-1875   *Fairy Tales and Legends.*   London: pub. by Cobden Sanderson, 1935. First edition, 8vo., original light green cloth elaborately and highly decoratively stamped in cream, morocco design across both covers and spine, lettered gilt to spine and upper board, pink stained edges, decorative pink endpapers, black and white illustrations after engravings by Rex Whistler, bright and attractive, externally and internally, with fading to pink edges of book block.   Sotheran's Piccadilly Notes - Summer 2015 - 17   2016   £138

Andersen, Hans Christian   1805-1875   *Little Fairy Sleepy Eyes.*   New York: Duffield, 1924. 8vo., fine in lightly chipped dust jacket, every page with vibrant hand colored pochoir illustrations, several pages have cut-out windows to be used to frame pages before and after, rare.   Aleph-bet Books, Inc.   112 - 240   2016 $1500

Andersen, Hans Christian   1805-1875   *Only a Fiddler.* London: H. G. Clarke and Co., 1845. First edition in English, 2 volumes, 12mo., original gift binding, full dark brown morocco elaborately gilt stamped on cover sand spines, half titles in red, blue, green and gold, all edges gilt, previous owner's signatures volume 1, fine set.   Heritage Book Shop   Holiday 2015 - 2   2016 $1500

Andersen, Hans Christian   1805-1875   *A Poet's Day Dreams.*   London: Richard Bentley, 1853. Half title, 4 pages ads, original brown grained cloth by Westleys, gilt spine darkened and slightly rubbed at head, some splits in following hinge.   Jarndyce Antiquarian Booksellers CCXVIII - 884   2016   £85

Andersen, Hans Christian   1805-1875   *Stories from Hans Andersen.*   London & New York: Nister & Dutton, n.d. circa, 1900. 8vo., orange gilt pictorial cloth, all edges gilt, some cover soil and spine faded bit, else very good+, illustrations by E. S. Hardy with 6 amazing chromolithographed plates, lovely full page half tones and profusion of full page and smaller black and whites throughout text.   Aleph-bet Books, Inc.   112 - 21   2016 $225

Andersen, Hans Christian   1805-1875   *Stories from Hans Andersen.*   London: Ernest Nister, 1904. First edition illustrated thus, small 4to., original pictorial pinkish beige cloth over bevelled boards, spine and upper board decorated and lettered in black, white, orange and gilt, all edges gilt, richly printed colored frontispiece and 5 other fine and luxurious chromolithographed plates printed on thicker stock with additional illustrations in monochrome, and line, fine, beautiful copy.   Sotheran's Piccadilly Notes - Summer 2015 - 18   2016   £198

Andersen, Hans Christian 1805-1875 *Stories from Hans Andersen.* London: Hodder & Stoughton, n.d. circa, 1938. Tall 8vo., 28 tipped in color plates, original full light brown cloth, some soiling to fore edges, otherwise near fine. Jeff Weber Rare Books 181 - 56 2016 $300

Andersen, Johannes C. *Bird-song and New Zealand song Birds.* Auckland: Whitcombe and Tombs, 1926. Photographs, publisher's cloth, numbered subscriber's copy signed by author, library stamp and library pocket, very good, scarce. Andrew Isles Natural History Books 55 - 38239 2016 $100

Andersen, Johannes C. *Myths and Legends of the Polynesians.* London: Harrap, 1928. First edition, 16 color plates by Richard Wallwork, 32 plates in half tone and other illustrations, octavo, original dark blue buckram covers elaborately decorated in lighter blue and green, lettered in gilt, pages unopened, free endpapers partially tanned, near fine in scarce dust jacket which is very good, bit tanned at spine and slightly dusty and marked, at tail of spine of dust jacket are three small stickers which served as shelf markers, no other signs of library use. Peter Ellis 112 - 307 2016 £125

Anderson, C. V. J. *A Liturgy for Dragons and 17 other Poems 1953-1961.* New York: Chas P. Young, 1961. First edition, 8vo., paper wrappers, author's (?) presentation, cover soiled, very good. Second Life Books, Inc. 197 - 9 2016 $65

Anderson, F. M. *Upper Cretaceous of the Pacific Coast.* New York: Geological Society of America, 1968. First edition, hundreds of photos on 74 plates, burgundy cloth, gilt, one corner slightly jammed, else very fine. Argonaut Book Shop Natural History 2015 - 5882 2016 $50

Anderson, George William *A New Authentic and Complete Collection of Voyages Round the World...* London: printed for Alex. Hogg at Original king's arms... n.d. circa, 1784-1786. First edition, folio, directions to binder, this copy with title listing dated for first, second and third and final voyages, frontispiece portrait, list of subscriber's bound in at end of volume, undated as per Beddie 18, frontispiece, 156 plates and maps, one of which is folding map, contemporary brown tree calf, spine rebacked to style, contemporary red morocco spine label lettered gilt, board edges tooled gilt, previous owner's old ink signature top margin of leaf 3F, some staining to signatures 4k, pages 493-497, page 515 and facing plate and some minor dampstaining to plate facing page 439, some minor worming to inside of boards and slightly to last few pages, very good, crisp copy, rarely seen with all plates intact. Heritage Book Shop Holiday 2015 - 24 2016 $3750

Anderson, Jon *Counting the Days.* Lisbon: Penumbra, 1974. No. 146 of 200 signed copies, 8vo., author' signature on dedication page, brown cloth, hand printed with Centaur and Arrighi types, fine copy. Second Life Books, Inc. 196A - 30 2016 $95

Anderson, Jon *Cypresses: Poems.* Port Townsend: Graywolf Press, 1981. First edition, one of 325 copies, printed in Bembo type on Frankfurt Creme paper, one of 100 copies, hand bound by Marsha Hollingsworth, this copy # 12 signed by poet. Second Life Books, Inc. 196A - 31 2016 $75

Anderson, Margaret *The Little Review Volume V. No. &.* New York: Margaret Anderson, Nov., 1918. Wrappers, octavo, cheap paper tanned, covers chipping at bottom edges, very good. Peter Ellis 112 - 309 2016 £125

Anderson, Mary *A Few Memories.* New York: Harper, 1896. First edition, 8vo., tipped-in two page autograph letter, 6 photos, moderate wear, front hinge going, top edge gilt, others uncut. Second Life Books, Inc. 196A - 34 2016 $135

Anderson, Mary *Woman at Work.* Minneapolis: University of Minnesota Press, 1951. First edition, 8vo., fine in dust jacket (little worn), signed by author. Second Life Books, Inc. 196A - 33 2016 $85

Anderson, Maxwell *Anne of the Thousand Days.* New York: William Sloan Associates, an Anderson House Book, 1948. First edition, very good, dust jacket little soiled, this copy signed by 5 members of the cast of the play. Second Life Books, Inc. 196A - 35 2016 $125

Anderson, Maxwell *The Wingless Victory.* Washington: Anderson House, 1936. First edition, 8vo., very good in fine dust jacket, inscribed by prodcer of the play to actress Katharine Cornell. Second Life Books, Inc. 196A - 36 2016 $113

Anderson, Poul *The High Crusade.* Garden City: Doubleday and Co., 1960. First edition, octavo, cloth, fine in fine dust jacket. John W. Knott, Jr./L.W. Currey, Inc. Fall-Winter 2015 - 17865 2016 $1500

Anderson, R. C. *Canoeing and Camping Adventures: being an Account of Three Cruises in Northern Waters.* London: C. Gilbert-Wood, 1910. First edition, 8vo., map, diagrams, original blue decorative cloth, spine faded. J. & S. L. Bonham Antiquarian Booksellers Europe 2016 - 6992 2016 £65

Anderson, Reed *American etchers Abroad 1880-1939.* Lawrence: Spencer Museum of Art, University of Kansas, 2004. First edition, 4to., pictorial wrappers, fine, scarce. Gene W. Baade, Books on the West   2015 - 5021045   2016 $65

Anderson, Sherwood   1876-1941   *Alice and the Lost Novel.* London: Elkin Mathews & Marrot, 1929. Number 186 of 500 copies, 8vo., author's signature, paper over boards, uncut, nice in dust jacket.   Second Life Books, Inc.   196A - 37   2016 $165

Anderson, William E.   *Thesis Writing: a Guide for the Preparation of the Master's Thesis.* Montgomery: Paragon Press, 1947. First edition, stapled blue wrappers, tiny name stamp repeated at front and rear wrappers, bit of foxing and soiling, sound, very good.   Between the Covers Rare Books   207 - 7   2016 $275

Ando, Tadao   *Tadao Ando: The Yale Studio & Current Works.* New York: Rizzoli, 1989. Fine in wrappers, very near fine dust jacket signed by Ando and with drawing by him as well.   Jeff Hirsch Books   Holiday List 2015 - 4   2016 $150

Andre, R.   *Colonel Bosey's Sketch Book.* London: Longmans, Green and Co., 1897. First edition, oblong 4to., cloth backed pictorial boards, covers little scratched, hinges neatly strengthened, very good+, rare, illustrations.   Alephbet Books, Inc.   112 - 24   2016 $2000

Andre, Yves Marie   *Essai sur la Beau, ou l'on Examine en Quoi Consiste Precisement le Beau dans la Physique dans le Moral, dans les Ouvrages d'Esprit & dans la Musique.* Paris: Hippolyte-Louis Guerin, 1741. First edition, woodcut device to title, engraved headpiece at start of text, woodcut tail pieces, 12mo., contemporary mottled calf with gilt panelled spines, little craquelure, very good, crisp copy. Blackwell's Rare Books   B186 - 8   2016   £300

Andreae, Johann Valentin   *Seleniana Augustalia....*   Ulm: Balthasar Kuhnen, 1649. First edition, Small 12mo., engraved portrait, engraved title with inset vignettes, 4 full page engraved portraits, full page allegorical woodcut, slight worming to last leaves, slight creasing to portraits, scattered minor stains, early Latin manuscript 2 line note at lower margin page 526, some foxing, contemporary full vellum, very good.   Jeff Weber Rare Books   181 - 10   2016 $1750

Andrews, Alexander   *The Eighteenth Century or Illustrations of the Manners and customs of Our Grandfathers.* London: Chapman & Hall, 1856. First edition, half title, pencil notes on following pastedown, original brown cloth by Burn & Co., spine slightly rubbed at head. Jarndyce Antiquarian Books   CCXV - 13   2016   £50

Andrews, Alexander   *The Eighteenth Century or Illustrations of the Manners and Customs of Our Grandfathers.* London: Chapman & Hall, 1856. First edition, half title, original green cloth, spine decorated in gilt, signature of Lord Carlingford, 1878, very good.   Jarndyce Antiquarian Books   CCXV - 14   2016   £60

Andrews, Edward   *The Shaker Order of Christmas.* New York: Oxford University Press, 1954. First edition, small 8vo., original printed wrappers, wrappers little creased but nice.   Bertram Rota Ltd.   Christmas List 2015 - 1   2016   £20

Andrews, Malcom   *Charles Dickens and His Performing Selves: Dickens and Public Reading.* Oxford University Press, 2007. Half title, illustrations, paperback, mint. Jarndyce Antiquarian Booksellers   CCXVIII - 625   2016   £20

Andrews, Shang   *Chicago After Dark.* Chicago: Chas. J. Heck, 1887. Large 8vo., full page illustrations, original printed wrappers (loose & chipped), 'Copyright 1887' stamped on front wrapper, otherwise undated.   M & S Rare Books, Inc.   99 - 43   2016 $550

Andrews, Shang   *Cranky Ann, the Street Walker: a Story of Chicago in Chunks.* Chicago: Charles J. Heck, 1886. Sixteenth edition, large 8vo., numerous large illustrations, early edges chipped but text complete, original printed wrappers, back wrapper contains a full page ad for the likely publisher, Charles J. Heck, front wrapper contains portrait of Cranky Ann.   M & S Rare Books, Inc.   99 - 44   2016 $350

Andrews, Val   *Sherlock Holmes and the Eminent Thespian.* Romford, Essex: Ian Henry, 1989. First edition, fine in dust jacket.   Mordida Books   2015 - 007868   2016 $60

Andrews, William Loring   *Bibliopegy in the United States and Kindred Subjects.* New York: printed by the Gillis Press for Dodd, Mead and Co., 1902. First edition, deluxe issue, one of 36 copies printed on Imperial Japan vellum, out of an edition of 177, 8vo., frontispiece and color and black and white illustrations, engraved chapter titles and vignettes, original gilt stamped vegetable parchment over boards, silk ribbon marker, dust jacket, neat two inch hairline split in joint near spine of front cover, leather booklabel of Francis Kettaneh on verso of front free endpaper, otherwise fine in dust jacket, sunned at spine panel.   James S. Jaffe Rare Books   Occasional List: Winter 2016 - 32   2016 $875

Andrews, William Loring *An English XIX Century Sportsman Bibliopole and Binder of Angling Books.* New York: Dodd Mead, 1906. One of 125 copies of at taol of 157 copies, engraved titlepage and engraved plates, Japan vellum over boards, fine, fresh in fine dust jacket. Joseph J. Felcone, Inc. Books from Five Centuries: a Miscellany - 4 2016 $500

Aneau, Barthelemy *Imagination Poetique Tradicte en Vers Francois des Latins & Grece....* Lyons: Mace Bonhomme, after 8 September, 1552. Extremely rare first edition, titlepage with Bonhomme's Perseus device and 105 cuts attributed to Pierre Eskrich (from metal plates), small 8vo., limp ivory vellum by Leighton, upper cover with gilt lettered title and date within elaborate frame, flat gilt spine, bookplate of S. A. Thompson Yates 1894. Maggs Bros. Ltd. 1474 - 6 2016 £12,000

Anecdotes of the Chinese Illustrative of their Character and of their Conduct Towards Foreigners. London: T. Allman's, 1847. First edition, 12mo., original red cloth lettered and decorated gilt on spine and cover, all edges gilt, very good+, neat inscription from a teacher to a pupil 1850 and further inscription from father to a daughter 1909. Any Amount of Books 2015 - A76508 2016 £150

Angell, Roger *A Day in the Life of Roger Angell.* N.P.: Viking, 1970. Uncorrected proof copy, near fine in wrappers with small '45' on front cover, presumably the copy number. Ken Lopez Bookseller 166 - 2 2016 $100

Anger, Kenneth *Hollywood Babylone.* Paris: J. J. Pauvert, 1959. First French edition, exceptional copy, fine in plain brown perfect bound wrappers in bright, colorful dust jacket with just touch of fading to pink spine letters and negligible rubbing at corners. Royal Books 52 - 53 2016 $575

Angling: a Poem. London: printed for H. Slater and F. Noble, 1741. Second edition, engraved frontispiece, smal 8vo., 19th century gilt borders with fish in gilt on each cover, spine gilt with rod and net ornaments, very scarce, skilful repair to blank upper margin of plate, but fine. C. R. Johnson Rare Book Collections Foxon: H-P 2015 - 488 2016 $2681

The Anglo-African Magazine August 1859. New York: Thos. Hamilton, 1859. Volume I number 8, octavo original stitched printed self wrappers, large but very faint stain on first few leaves, small creases at page corners, short split at bottom of spine, very good or better, rare. Between the Covers Rare Books 202 - 5 2016 $2500

Anglund, Joan Walsh *Cowboy and His Friend.* New York: Harcourt Brace World, 1961. Stated first edition, 8vo., cloth, fine in dust jacket, illustrations by Anglund, laid in is marvelous drawing of little girl and her cat, inscribed by Anglund and signed by Margaret McElderry. Aleph-bet Books, Inc. 111 - 19 2016 $400

An Animal ABC. New York and Boston: H. M. Caldwell, n.d. circa, 1910. Cloth backed boards, pictorial paste-on, edge stain on cover, some cover soil, edges and tips show wear, overall tight, clean, inside and very good, illustrations by Harry Neilson, with full page color illustrations, super book. Aleph-bet Books, Inc. 112 - 7 2016 $200

Annals of the Rise, Progress and Persecutions of the Famous Reformed Churches in France which are at this Day Groaning Under the Cruel Bondage of Popish Tyranny.... London: by J. Waugh, 1753. Second edition, stitched and untrimmed, as issued, stain at top of titlepage, final leaf bit scruffy around edges, but very good. Joseph J. Felcone, Inc. Books from Five Centuries: a Miscellany - 6 2016 $400

Anouilh, Jean *legend of Lovers.* New York: Coward McCann, 1952. First edition, 8vo., translator's presentation, nice in slightly chipped dust jacket. Second Life Books, Inc. 196A - 42 2016 $45

Anselm, Saint, Bp. of Canterbury 1033-1109 *Operum, quae Quidem Haberi Potuerunt Omnium.* Coloniae: Agrippinae (Cologne): M. Colinus, 1560. 3 volumes bound as 1, folio, woodcut device to titlepage, lightly foxed titlepage creased vertically very occasional spots of foxing elsewhere, some light staining, contemporary blind tooled dark brown calf over wooden boards, metal clasps and corner reinforcements, sturdily rebacked to dark brown morocco, paste downs replaced, upper inner hinge cracked but holding firm, creased and reglued, couple of tiny tears to endcaps, little scuffed but very good overall, small printed label to f.f.e.p. Unsworths Antiquarian Booksellers 30 - 4 2016 £675

Anstis, Marion *Tadpoles of South Eastern Australia; a guide with keys.* Frenchs Forest: New Holland, 2002. Octavo, color photos, text illustrations, maps, dust jacket. Andrew Isles Natural History Books 55 - 15597 2016 $80

An Anthology of Love. Acorn Press and Rampant Lions Press, 1985. First edition, limited to 100 numbered copies, square 8vo., canvas boards with printed paper label, set in Monotype Univers Bold by Stellar Press and hand printed by Sebastian Carter at Rampant Lions Press, Cambridge on Zerkall Ingres Terra, fine, except very slight dust marks on outer boards. Bertram Rota Ltd. February List 2016 - 2 2016 £70

Anthony, Gordon *Studies of Dancers.* London: Home & Van Thal, 1948. First edition, small 4to., 33 mounted plates of which 16 are in color, presentation inscription signed 'Gordon', moderate wear. Second Life Books, Inc. 196A - 44 2016 $75

Anthony, Susan B. *The History of Woman Suffrage.* Rochester: Susan B. Anthony, 1902. First edition, Volume IV only, 8vo., frontispiece, publisher's maroon cloth, front hinge loose, lacks the last 3 leaves of index, good copy housed in cloth clamshell box, inscribed by Anthony for Miss Anna B. Coushaine.   Second Life Books, Inc.   196 B - 685a   2016 $2500

Antoine De Chamerlat, Christian *Falconry and Art.* London: Philip Wilson Publishers Ltd., 1987. 4to., green cloth with gilt lettering and illustrated dust jacket, heavily illustrated, very good.   Sotheran's   Hunting, Shooting & Fishing - 66   2016   £98

Antoninus, Brother   1912-1994 *Poems of Nineteen Forty seven.* Reno: Black Rock Press, 1968. Limited to 180 copies signed by author, 4to., cloth, top edge cut, others uncut.   Oak Knoll Books   310 - 85   2016 $250

Antoninus, Brother   1912-1994 *Single Source. The Early Poems (1934-1940).* Berkeley: Oyez, 1966. First edition, one of 25 numbered copies specially bound and signed by author, 8vo., original leather and boards, dust jacket, as usual text in second corrected state with 'language' on page ix, very fine in dust jacket.   James S. Jaffe Rare Books   Occasional List: Winter 2016 - 58   2016 $1000

Antoninus, Brother   1912-1994 *Tendril in the Mesh.* N.P.: Cayucos Books, 1973. First edition, signed by author, number 20 of 250 copies designed and printed by Clifford Burke, 4to., leather spine, decorated brown and yellow boards, light wear to spine, else fine, printed throughout in gold, brown and black with Goudy Thirty type.   Argonaut Book Shop   Literature 2015 - 6305   2016 $175

Antoninus, Brother   1912-1994 *Tendril in the Mesh.* Aromas: Cayucos Books, 1973. First edition, one of an unspecified number of lettered copies (this copy N) in a total edition of 250 signed by author, printed by Clifford Burke on Wookey Hole Mill paper, 4to., original quarter leather and paste paper over boards, presentation copy inscribed by author to Gary Snyder, spine ends and fore-tips very lightly rubbed, faint offset from binding adhesive along gutters of endsheets, otherwise fine, publisher's prospectus laid in.   James S. Jaffe Rare Books   Occasional List: Winter 2016 - 59   2016 $1250

Apocalypse De Saint Jean. Paris: Joseph Foret, 1961. One of a total of only 8 copies, this unnumbered copy printed for art collector Georges Vic, 2 works in 1 volume, 460 x 385mm., unbound as issued in heavy paper wrappers with gilt titling on upper cover and spine, housed in (somewhat worn) red cloth chemise and white cloth slipcase, with 29 plates depicting scenes from the Apocalypse by Salvador Dali, Jean Cocteau, Foujita, and others; one inch crack to head of front joint of portfolio, otherwise an immaculate copy.   Phillip J. Pirages   67 - 107   2016 $145,000

Apollinaire, Guillaume *Les Mamelles de Tiresias - Drame Surrealiste en Deux Actes et un Prologue.* Paris: Editions Sic, 1918. First edition, 7 drawings by Serge Ferat, wrappers, covers and prelims spotted, spine cracked and defective at tail, cover edges nicked and chipped at lower corners, good serviceable copy of a fragile item.   Peter Ellis   112 - 14   2016   £250

Apollinaire, Guillaume *The Poet Assassinated.* New York: Holt, Rinehart and Winston, 1968. First edition, small 4to., illustrations by Jim Dine, paper over boards, edges soiled, leaves very slightly ripped, otherwise very good, tight in soiled and little chipped dust jacket.   Second Life Books, Inc.   197 - 13   2016 $45

Apollinaire, Guillaume *Zone.* Dublin: Dolmen Press, London: Calder & Boyars, 1972. First edition of this English translation by Beckett, one of 250 numbered copies signed by Beckett, 4to., original black cloth lettered gilt on spine and in blind on boards, fine in slightly creased slipcase.   Sotheran's   Piccadilly Notes - Summer 2015 - 43   2016   £550

Apollonius Pergaeus *The Two Books of Apollonius Pergaeus...* Cambridge: printed by T. Fletcher and F. Hodson, 1764. First edition, 6 folding engraved plates, interleaved with paper watermarked 1827 with notes in a hand of that date, waterstained and foxed, plates with scorch marks in fine margins, latterly entering the plate mark but without loss to figures, 4to., 19th century half vellum over marbled boards, upper cover detached, most of marbled paper missing, spine darkened and defective at head, remains of library labels inside front cover, stamp, accession number and shelf marks of Camberwell Public Library verso of title, Newcastle Lit. & Phil stamp and shelfmark.   Blackwell's Rare Books   Marks of Genius - 1   2016   £950

Apollonius Rhodius *Argonautica; or the Quest of Jason for the Golden Fleece.* New York: Heritage Press, 1960. White boards with red cloth spine, lettered and decorated gilt, very fine in slipcase, with Greek and English text, illustrations by A. Tassos, Sandglass pamphlet laid in.   Argonaut Book Shop   Heritage Press 2015 - 6918   2016 $40

Appel, Karel *Appel & Alechinsky: Two Brush Paintings their Poems by Hugo Claus.* Paris: Yves Riveire, 1980. First edition, 4to., original publisher's printed wrappers, very good, illustrations in black and white and color, inscribed by Hugo Claus to poet William Jay Smith.   Second Life Books, Inc.   196A - 909   2016 $350

Apperly, Charles James *The Chace. The Turf. The Road.* London: John Murray, 1870. New edition, octavo, hand colored frontispiece, extra engraved title in two states, plain and colored, 13 hand colored engraved plates by Alken, some in aquatint, 9 text illustrations black and white by unknown hand, bound c. 1900 by Riviere and Son in full crimson crushed morocco with French fillets, gilt rolled raised bands, decorated and ornamented compartments, gilt rolled board edges, elaborately gilt dentelles, top edge gilt, expertly and rear invisibly rebacked, fine copy.   David Brass Rare Books, Inc.   2015 - 02798   2016 $550

Apple Pie ABC.   New York: McLoughlin Bros., 1899. 4to., stiff pictorial wrappers, fine, full page color illustrations plus 6 full page and one double-page 2 color illustrations, plates mounted on linen, beautiful copy.   Aleph-bet Books, Inc. 111 - 5   2016 $300

Applebroog, Ida   *Ida Applebroog: Are You Bleeding Yet?* New York: La Maison Red, 2002. Numerous color illustrations, fine in fine dust jacket, fresh and clean copy.   Jeff Hirsch Books   Holiday List 2015 - 5   2016 $125

Appleman, Philip   *Kites on a Windy Day.*   Nottingham: The Byron Press, 1967. First edition, inscribed and signed for William Meredith, laid in are two TLS's, along with copies of Appleman's resume and reviews, near fine.   Charles Agvent   William Meredith - 10   2016 $60

Appleton, Elizabeth   *Early Education or the Management of Children Considered with a View to their Future Character.*   London: G. & W. B. Whittaker, 1821. Second edition, 12mo., uncut in original drab boards, paper label, slight rubbing to leading hinge and head and tail of spine, boards little spotted, otherwise very good, Fasque bookseller's ticket, label of E. Willan.   Jarndyce Antiquarian Books CCXV - 506   2016   £280

Apuleius   *The Golden Asse of Lucius Apuleius.*   London: John Lane the Bodley Head, 1923. First edition, limited to 3000 numbered copies, 8vo., gilt pictorial cloth, top edge gilt, fine, 8 color plates, 6 black and whites, 35 half page black and whites and other decorations by Jean De Bosschere, rare in this limited edition.   Aleph-bet Books, Inc.   112 - 136   2016 $325

Apuleius   *The Golden Ass.*   New York: Limited Editions Club, 1932. One of 1500 numbered copies, signed by artist, Percival Goodman, cream calf, rubbed on spine, housed in publisher's box, very good included are 4 original pen and ink drawings nicely framed under glass of illustrations from the book, little browned but in excellent condition.   Second Life Books, Inc.   196A - 46   2016 $750

Arabian Nights   *Ali Baba O'Los Cuarenta Ladrones.*   New York: D. Appleton, 1891. Pictorial wrappers, fine, 4 full page chromolithographs brown line illustrations on every page, and wonderful chromolithographs on front and back covers.   Aleph-bet Books, Inc.   112 - 32   2016 $125

Arabian Nights   *Arabian Nights.*   New York: Dodd Mead, 1925. First American edition, Thick 4to., blue gilt cloth, pictorial paste-on, offsetting from front endpapers and small corner of one tissue guard torn, else near fine, 12 beautifully mounted color plates with tissue guards plus pictorial titlepage and black and whites by Edmund Detmold.   Aleph-bet Books, Inc.   111 - 119   2016 $1100

Arabian Nights   *The Book of the Thousand Nights and a Night.*   H. S. Nichols & Co., 1894. Library edition, royal 8vo., 13 volumes, original black cloth blocked in gilt with elaborate Arabian design to upper covers, top edges gilt, titles printed in red and black, some foxing, mostly to prelims, otherwise very good, clean set.   Sotheran's Piccadilly Notes - Summer 2015 - 62   2016   £1998

Arabian Nights   *The Book of the Thousand Nights and a Night.*   New York: Heritage Press, 1934. 6 volumes in 3, octavo, illustrations by Valenti Angelo, decorated boards with beige cloth spines, lettered gilt, spines darkened with fine set in lightly worn slipcases, Sandglass pamphlet laid in. Argonaut Book Shop   Heritage Press 2015 - 6935   2016 $90

Arabian Nights   *Sinbad the Sailor & Other Stories from the Arabian Nights.*   London: Hodder & Stoughton, 1914. Out-of-Series edition, one of a few copies bound up by Hodder & Stoughton from leftover sheets of signed limited edition, deluxe unrecorded publisher's variant binding with original dust jacket, 23 color plates mounted on cream stock by Edmund Dulac, with decorative border, captioned tissue guards, all text leaves with titlepage border design printed in tan and black, blue-gray papered boards with white parchment spine and corner tips, spine with original blue morocco label lettered in gilt, top edge gilt, others uncut, neat early ink inscription on front free endpaper, very fine in exceptionally scarce white paper dust jacket lettered in black on spine, housed in blue cloth slipcase.   David Brass Rare Books, Inc.   2015 - 03025   2016 $1850

Arabian Nights   *Sinbad Le Marin et D'Autres Contes Des Mille et Une Nuits. (Sinbad the Sailor and Oter Tales from the Thousand and One Nights).*   Paris: H. Piazza, 1919. First edition in French, 305 x 241mm., no. 520 of 1500 copies, espeicaly attractive rich green morocco by Root & son (signed), covers framed in gilt with triple rules, inner rule entwined at corners with ivy leaf terminations, raised bands, spine gilt in compartments formed by double rule and featuring ivy leaf cornerpieces around an inner central panel, wide ruled turn-ins, with foliate cornerpieces, marbled endpapers, top edge gilt, other edges rough trimmed, original wrappers preserved, decorative initials and titlepage, decorative borders throughout and 27 color plates by Edmund Dulac (each laid down within decorative frame, with captioned tissue guard), printed in pale orange and black throughout, pastedown with bookplate of Joseph H. Haines, upper corners slightly bumped, verso of free endpapers, little discolored (from glue?), otherwise very fine.   Phillip J. Pirages   67 - 122   2016 $1950

Arabian Nights *The Thousand and One Nights, Commonly called in England The Arabian Nights' Entertainments.*   London: Charles Knight and Co., 1839-1841. First edition in book form, 3 volumes, 254 x 165mm, pleasing late 19th century crimson half morocco, raised bands, gilt ruled compartments with central ornament of gilt rosette within a star, marbled pastedowns, top edge gilt, more than 300 wood engravings from designs by William Harvey, bookplate of John Watson, volume i with translator's "Advertisement" giving spelling and pronuncication of various bookplate, occasional rust spots, few isolated margin smudges, but really excellent copy with few signs of wear inside or out.   Phillip J. Pirages 67 - 5 2016 $1000

Arabian Nights *The Thousand and One Nights, Commonly Called the Arabian Nights' Entertainments.* London: Chatto & Windus, 1841. 3 volumes, 8vo. handsomely bound set, probably by Bayntun of Bath, late 1940's red half morocco over red cloth boards, spine with raised bands, ornamented and lettered gilt, top edge gilt, marbled endpapers, wood engraved illustrations, light spotting only at beginning and end.   Sotheran's   Travel and Exploration - 335 2016   £1250

Arabian Nights *The Thousand and One Nights, Commonly Called in England, The Arabian Night's Entertainments.* London: Charles Knight, 1841. First edition of volume one, early reprints of 2 volumes, 3 volumes, large 8vo., modern black half morocco over green cloth boards, spine with raised bands, ornamented and lettered gilt, boards with gilt ruled fillets, all edges gilt, patterned endpapers, wood engraved title in pagination, copiously illustrated throughout with superb wood engravings, first engraved title with small repair to lower portion of inner margin, only very light toning here and there, very good set in rather handsome recent binding.   Sotheran's   Travel and Exploration - 334   2016   £998

Arago, Francois *Popular Astronomy.* London: Longmans Brown, Green and Longmans, 1855. 1858, 3 volumes, original green cloth, numerous plates and hundreds of wood engravings, volume 1 rebacked, gilt author, title and volume number to spine, corners bumped but very good, interior pages and plates very good, very handsome set.   The Kelmscott Bookshop   13 - 1   2016 $450

Aragon, Louis *Picasso-Aragon, Shakespeare.* New York: Harry N. Abrams, 1965. First edition, one of 1000 copies, folio of 13 black and white gravure plates, red boards in dust jacket that has couple of small stains, fine.   Second Life Books, Inc. 197 - 14 2016 $350

Arbis, Robert *The Lord's Woods. The Passing of an American Woodland.* New York: Norton, 1971. First edition, inscribed by author for Fanny Parsons, small owner label apparently over another name on front flyleaf, near fine in very good, modestly rubbed and spine faded dust jacket internally tape strengthened at spine base.   Ken Lopez Bookseller   166 - 6 2016 $200

Arblay, Frances Burney D' 1752-1840 *The Diary and Letters of Madame D'Arblay (1778-1840(.*   London: Macmillan and Co. Ltd., 1904. 8vo., 6 volumes i contemporary half polished calf over marbled boards, spines richly gilt with contrasting leather labels, little rubbing to bindings, upper joint of volume 1 rejointed, bookplates, but attractive set.   Sotheran's   Piccadilly Notes - Summer 2015 - 94 2016   £498

Arblay, Frances Burney D' 1752-1840 *Journal.* Philadelphia: Carey Lea and Blanchard, 1835. First US edition, 8vo., untrimmed in original muslin with worn paper label, spine faded and some foxing, front cover of volume one separate, name stamp, good set.   Second Life Books, Inc.   197 - 200 2016 $225

Arbman, Holger *The Vikings.* London: Thames and Hudson, 1962. New edition, 8vo., original cloth and blue wrapper, black and white photos, illustrations and maps, spine of wrapper slightly sunned, very good, signature of R. J. Berry, Emeritus Professor of Genetics of University College London and president of Linnean Society.   Sotheran's   Piccadilly Notes - Summer 2015 - 20   2016   £30

Arbus, Diane *Hubert's Museum Work 1958-1963.* New York: Phillipe de Pury & Co., 2008. First edition, quarto, pictorial glossy stiff wrappers, very good+, back and white and sepia illustrations, minor front cover corner crease and bit of rubbing on spine.   Gene W. Baade, Books on the West   2015 - 1003004 2016 $223

Archer, Michael *Carnivorous Marsupials.*   Sydney: Royal Zoological Survey of New South Wales, 1982. Quarto, 2 volumes, text illustrations, bookplates, very good in dust jackets.   Andrew Isles Natural History Books   55 - 19681 2016 $350

Archer, Michael *Vertebrate Zoogeography and Evolution in Autralasia...* Carlisle: Hesperian Press, 1984. Quarto, text illustrations, signature, very good, in dust jacket, scarce.   Andrew Isles Natural History Books   55 - 9528   2016 $250

Archer, Thomas *Charles Dickens: a Gossip About His Life, Works and Characters.* London: Cassell & Co., 1894? Large folio, titles in red and black, plates, illustrations, original printed boards, maroon cloth spines, very good, clean copy, virtually mint, kept so by early wrapping paper.   Jarndyce Antiquarian Booksellers   CCXVIII - 1069 2016   £150

Archibald, Campbell *Lessons for School Life...* Edinburgh: Thomas Constable & Co., 1853. Second edition, contemporary full calf by Charles Thurman, maroon and green morocco labels, slightly rubbed, inscribed by author for Mrs. Marshall, Apl. 1856, recent ownership label of Dr. Michael Brown.   Jarndyce Antiquarian Books   CCXV - 928 2016   £45

An Architectural Bestiary. New York: High Tide Press, 1993. One of 3 very special copies with color images in an edition of 25 signed copies, 11 structures, collagraph images each on a 30 x 15 inches spread in portfolio, Greek text in red, English text in black, text set in Primer and Greek text set by Cosmos Printing, 4to., signatures and prints loosely inserted in leopard print orange and black faux fur fabric covered clam-shell box.   Oak Knoll Books   27 - 27   2016 $4000

Ardene, Jean Paul De Rome D' *Traite des Renoncules, qui Contient Outre ce Qui Regarde des Fleurs Beaucoup d'Observations, Physiques & de Remarques Utiles Soit Pour l'Agriculture, Soit Pour le Jardinge.* Avignon: Louis Chambeau, 1763. Third edition, small 8vo., contemporary green boards, rebacked in matching morocco with part of original gilt spine preserved, monogram AS in gilt on upper cover, bookplate of NY Horticultural Society, Bequest of Kenneth Mackenzie, inside front cover.   Blackwell's Rare Books   B186 - 9   2016   £600

The Argosy. A Magazine of Tales, Travels, Essays and Poems. London: Strahan & Co., 1866-1873. Volumes I to XVI, frontispiece in volumes I, IV vignette title in volume I, plates, occasional foxing, heavy in places but largely good and clean, uniformly bound in half calf, raised bands, compartments in gilt, black morocco labels, slightly rubbed, overall handsome set. Jarndyce Antiquarian Booksellers   CCXVII - 217   2016   £480

Arguelles, Ivan *New Poetry from California: Dead Requiem.* Berkeley: Pantograph Press, 1998. 4to., Presentation from Jack Foley for William Jay Smith, paper wrappers, as new.   Second Life Books, Inc.   196A - 48   2016 $45

Aristophanes *(Greek) Comoediae Novem with Scholia ed. Marcus Musurus.* Venice: Aldus Manutius 15 July, 1498. Editio princeps, folio, k8 and T6 blank (here lacking), 42 lines Greek type and Roman type, 18th century Dutch? red morocco, spine titled in gilt binding rubbed, spine lightly faded, armorial book stamp on titlepage, small marginal restorations to first and last few leaves stained.   Maggs Bros. Ltd.   1474 - 7   2016   £35,000

Aristophanes *Le Comedie de'l Facetis, Simo Aristofane...* Venice: Appresso Vicenzo Vaugris, 1545. First edition in Italian, some light foxing and few tiny dampmarks to early leaves 18th century vellum boards, spine lettered gilt within yellow dyed compartment, marbled endpapers, little bit soiled, bookplate of Bernardine Murphy, very good.   Blackwell's Rare Books   B186 - 19   2016   £900

Aristotle, Pseud. *Aristotle in three Parts containing I: His Complete Master-Piece: II. His Last Legacy. III. The Family Physician.* N.P.: printed for the booksellers, 1801. Possibly later imprint, 12mo., engraved frontispiece, 4 text woodcuts, circa 1820's sheep, contemporary printed paper spine label, page edges sprinkled red, head of spine worn down, else very good, clean.   Joseph J. Felcone, Inc.   Books from Five Centuries: a Miscellany - 9   2016 $675

Aristotle, Pseud. *The Works of...* Gainsborough: Mozley Printer, for the booksellers, 1811. 4 woodcuts in text, somewhat browned, patchily heavy in places, 12mo., original sheep, gilt ruled compartments on spine, very slightly worn, good, browned.   Blackwell's Rare Books   B186 - 11   2016   £450

Arizona. Live Stock Sanitary Board *Livestock Laws of Arizona. Title XLII Revised Statutes of Arizona 1901.* Phoenix: Live Stock Sanitary Board, 1901. First edition, 8vo., printed wrappers, rare, fine.   Buckingham Books   2015 - 32244   2016 $450

Armati, Mary *E. G. Waterhouse of Eryldene.* Sydney: The Fine Arts Press, 1977. Limited to 550 numbered copies, signed by author, Quarto, photos, publisher's quarter cloth and linen boards, fine.   Andrew Isles Natural History Books   55 - 37165   2016 $100

Armer, Laura Adams *The Trader's Children.* New York: Longmans Green, 1937. Stated first edition, 8vo., cloth, slight bit of cover soil, else fine, photos by Armer and with pictorial initials and endpapers by Armer's husband, Sidney, with handwritten letter from author dated 1963.   Aleph-bet Books, Inc.   111 - 21   2016 $300

Armer, Laura Adams *The Trader's Children.* New York: Longmans, Green, 1937. First edition, full page aquatone reproductions of photos by author, decorations by Sidney Armer, yellow cloth stamped in blue, very fine in very good pictorial dust jacket.   Argonaut Book Shop Native American   2015 - 7035   2016 $90

Armer, Laura Adams *Waterless Mountain.* New York: Longmans Green, 1931. First edition, first printing, 8vo., cloth, fine in dust jacket, some chipping to corners and spine ends but very good, this copy inscribed by author, full page illustrations.   Aleph-bet Books, Inc.   111 - 22   2016 $350

Armer, Laura Adams *Waterless Mountain.* New York: Longmans Green, 1935. 4to., cloth, very good in tattered dust jacket, illustrations by Sidney and Laura Armer, this copy inscribed by Laura and laid in is 2 page handwritten letter from Sidney.   Aleph-bet Books, Inc.   112 - 33   2016 $200

Armitage, George T. *Hawaiian Hospitality.* Honolulu: Hawaiian Service, 1943. First edition?, octavo, photos, vignettes, stapled die-cut wrappers in shape of pineapple, slight creases to wrappers, small ink note on titlepage, else near fine.   Between the Covers Rare Books   204 - 27   2016 $225

Armstrong, Martin *Desert, a Legend.* London: Jonathan Cape, 1926. Crown 8vo., 33 illustrations by Ravilious with full page, one or two light handling marks, crown 8vo., original red cloth with publisher's device blindstamped to lower board, backstrip lettered gilt with slight lean to spine, top edge lightly dust soiled with other edges roughtrimmed, partial browning to free endpapers, dust jacket with Ravilious design, light chipping to corners, contemporary review clipping laid in at front, very good.   Blackwell's Rare Books   B184 - 305   2016   £180

Armstrong, Martin *Desert - a Legend.* London: Jonathan Cape, 1926. One of 100 numbered copies on handmade paper signed by author, first edition, this copy unnumbered but marked 'Presentation', octavo, numerous woodcut illustrations and decorations by Eric Ravilious, full green buckram, top edge gilt, woodcuts greatly enhanced by the fine paper on which they have been printed, small ownership inscription, free endpapers lightly tanned, spine bit faded, very good, internally fine.   Peter Ellis   112 - 322   2016   £275

Armstrong, Terence Ian Fytton *New Tales of Horror by Eminent Authors....* London: Hutchinson & Co. Ltd., 1934. First edition, octavo, original orange cloth, front and spine panels stamped in black, pulp paper text block lightly tanned, fine in fine dust jacket with slight age tanning to spine panel and touch of shelfwear to head of spine panel, superior example of rare jacket.   John W. Knott, Jr./L.W. Currey, Inc.   Fall-Winter 2015 - 16567   2016 $1000

Army, W. F. M. *Indian Agent in New Mexico. The Journal of Special Agent W. F. M. Army 1870.* Santa Fe: Stagecoach Press, 1967. First edition, limited to 750 copies, 12mo., tipped-on frontispiece illustrations, gilt lettered cloth, fine with printed dust jacket, rubber stamp on colophon page.   Argonaut Book Shop   Native American 2015 - 3617   2016 $75

Arndt, Johann *Sechs Bucher vom Wahren Christenhum...* Philadelphia: J. G. Ritter, 1830. 3 parts in one volume, engraved frontispiece, LVI engraved plates in part I and engraved frontispiece and 8 unnumbered plates in part III, some dampstaining and spotting in places, 4to., original plain calf, one of two brass clasps on leather straps, about half of the claspless strap missing, traces of green paper label on lower cover, front hinge strained, good.   Blackwell's Rare Books   B186 - 12   2016   £500

Arne, Thomas A. *The Rose, A Comic Opera.* London: for E. and C. Dilly and W. Griffin, 1773. First edition, disbound, short tear to fore edge of half title.   Dramatis Personae   119 - 10   2016 $80

Arnold, Bion J. *Report on the Pittsburgh Transportation Problem.* Pittsburgh: 1910. First edition, maps, cloth on flexible boards, ex-library with stamps, bookplate, date slip, cover somewhat scuffed and worn, otherwise very good, tight copy, printed presentation by author signed on bookplate.   Second Life Books, Inc.   196A - 50   2016 $40

Arnold, John *Through Hong Kong with Camera.* Middlebrough: Hood & Co., 1910. First edition, 7.5 x 10 inches, original illustrated string wrappers, cover edge wear, rare.   By the Book, L. C.   45 - 38   2016 $1500

Arnold, Matthew 1822-1888 *Culture and Anarchy: an Essay in Political and Social Criticism.* London: Smith, Elder & Co., 1869. First edition, half title, pencil notes, original brown cloth, bevelled boards, little rubbed, armorial booklabel "Presented by Bishop Wordsworth's family", ownership signature of J. Henry Shorthouse.   Jarndyce Antiquarian Booksellers   CCXVII - 15   2016   £420

Arnold, Matthew 1822-1888 *A French Eton or Middle-class Education and the State to Which is Added Schools and Universities in France.* London: Macmillan & Co., 1892. Half title, endpapers and half title browned, partially unopened in original blue cloth, very good.   Jarndyce Antiquarian Books   CCXV - 507   2016   £35

Arnold, Matthew 1822-1888 *Higher Schools and Universities in Germany.* London: Macmillan & Co., 1874. Second edition, half title, 83 page catalog (Oct. 1873), original brown cloth, slightly rubbed and dulled, library label at foot of spine, booklabel of Ian Jack.   Jarndyce Antiquarian Books   CCXV - 508   2016   £35

Arnold, Matthew 1822-1888 *Irish Essays and Others.* London: Smith, Elder and Co., 1882. Blue cloth boards, gilt title to spine, ex-library from St. Felix School Southwold with bookplate, tape remnants to spine and boards, top quarter inch of cloth to head of spine has chipped off, small chip to foot of spine, interior remains very clean, some wear to hinges, very good, presentation inscribed by author's sister, Susy.   The Kelmscott Bookshop   12 - 1   2016 $375

Arnold, Matthew 1822-1888 *Merope: a tragedy.* London: Longman, Brown, Green, Longmans & Roberts, 1858. First edition, presentation copy, inscribed "From the author", with ownership signature of Thomas Arnold, author's brother, dated Dublin 1858, very good in original dark green cloth boards with gilt title to spine and blind stamped decoration to boards, expertly rebacked with original spine laid down, minor rubbing and few spots to boards with minor wear to corners, occasional spots of foxing and light browning to margins of pages, clean overall, type-written description of this book is pasted down to rear free endpaper, very good.   The Kelmscott Bookshop   13 - 2   2016 $450

Arnold, Matthew 1822-1888 *Reports on Elementary schools 1852-1882.* London: Macmillan, 1889. First edition, half title, 2 pages ads, partially unopened, original dark blue cloth, perforated stamp of Homerton New College, Cambridge, very good.   Jarndyce Antiquarian Books   CCXV - 509   2016   £35

Arnold, Matthew 1822-1888 *The Scholar Gypsy.* London: Ivor Nicholson, 1933. gilt cloth, spine toned, else fine, in original slipcase lacking backstrip and chipped, color plate mounted on front, illustrations by Frank Adams with pictorial endpapers, 10 beautiful tipped-in water color plates, 10 full page illustrations in shades of brown plus pictorial borders and initials and detailed pen and inks throughout.   Aleph-bet Books, Inc.   112 - 10   2016 $200

Arnold, Ralph *Fish and Company.* London: Heinemann, 1951. Very good, uncommon, very slightly chipped dust jacket.   I. D. Edrich   Crime - 2016   £25

Arnold, Thomas *Miscellaneous Works.* London: B. Fellowes, 1845. Half title, unopened in original dark green blue cloth, blocked in blind, spine lettered gilt, booklabel with signature of William Wagstaff, attractive copy, near fine. Jarndyce Antiquarian Books   CCXV - 311   2016   £60

Arnold, Thomas Kerchever *A First Verse Book.* London: printed for J. G. F. & J. Rivington, 1841. Final ad leaf, some pencil marks in text, original brown ribbed cloth, paper label, little bumped and marked, ownership inscription of E. J. O'Reilly, 1879.   Jarndyce Antiquarian Books   CCXV - 513   2016   £40

Arnoux, Guy *Tambours et Trompettes.* Paris: Devambez, 1918. No. 287 of 475 copies, from a total issue of 500, loose as issued within original wrappers, housed in publisher's paper board folio, spine repaired with shipping tape, upper cover with hand colored lithograph vignette, original (somewhat worn but intact) tri-color silk ribbon titles, illustrated dust jacket and 10 hand colored plates in pochoir, later board with "can't dupl." in black marking pen, corners and edges somewhat worn, just hint of soiling to boards, very desirable copy, inelegantly repaired portfolio with obvious condition issues, but with richly colored plates, especially clean, fresh and well preserved.   Phillip J. Pirages   67 - 281   2016 $1250

Arnoux, Guy *12 Chansons.* France: no publishing information, n.d. circa, 1910. Large oblong 4to., pictorial boards, slight chipping on spine and light cover soil, else amazingly clean copy, printed on handmade paper, Frenchfold, 12 very fine and vibrant full page pochoir illustrations, this copy inscribed by Arnoux with ink drawing, rare.   Aleph-bet Books, Inc.   111 - 23   2016 $1500

Arrian *De Expedit Alex. magni Historiarum Libri X Ejusdem Indica.* Amstelodami: Joannem Janssonium a Waeserge & Viduam Elizaei Weyerstraet, 1668. 8vo., additional engraved titlepage and portrait , woodcut initials and head and tailpieces, few old annotations, couple of leaves unopened, lower margin of leaf 2L4 abbreviated due to paper flaw, contemporary vellum, title inked to spine, yapp edges, edges sprinkled blue, spine little darkened and marked but vellum otherwise uncommonly clean, pastedown lifted, front little crumpled, revealing manuscript parchment binder's waste used as sewing supports, very good. Unsworths Antiquarian Booksellers Ltd.   E05 - 2   2016   £350

Arrowsmith, Henry William *The House Decorator and Painter's Guide...* London: Thomas Kelly, Paternoster Row, 1840. First edition, 4to. 61 lithograph plates, including 21 hand colored and 6 in bistre, contemporary half calf over marbled paper covered boards with marbled endpapers, spine and four raised bands, gilt foliate decoration and elaborate blind tooling to compartments.   Marlborough Rare Books   List 56 - 3   2016   £650

Ars Antomica: a Medical Fantasia. New York: Medicina Rara, 1972. One of 2800 sets in boxed portfolios, numbered and signed by artist, folio, printed on specially made paper with private watermark, portfolio covered in a Bugra laid paper, box slightly soiled, otherwise very nice.   Second Life Books, Inc.   196A - 51   2016 $200

The Art of Dress; or Guide to the Toilette... London: Charles Gilt, 1839. Half title, hand colored double frontispiece & plates, final ad leaf, occasional light foxing, original dark purple cloth, decorated in gilt, recased, front hinge cracked and roughly repaired, scarce title.   Jarndyce Antiquarian Books   CCXV - 24   2016   £150

Arter, Jared Maurice *Echoes from a Pioneer Life.* Atlanta: A. B. Caldwell Pub. Co., 1922. First edition, small octavo, photos, text wire stitched and bound in publisher's green cloth stamped in black, staples tad oxidized, rear hinge appears to have been repaired (or is perhaps slightly misbound), still sound, very good or better.   Between the Covers Rare Books   207 - 18 2016 $2500

Arthur, Timothy Shay *Anna Lee; or the Maiden, the Wife and the Mother.*   London: W. Nicholson & sons circa, 1890. Half title, 24 page catalog, original red cloth, blocked in blind, lettered in gilt, little dulled and slightly rubbed. Jarndyce Antiquarian Books   CCXV - 25   2016   £20

Arthur, Timothy Shay *The mother: a story for my young countrywomen.*   Halifax: Milner & Sowerby, 1855. 16mo., 2 pages initial ads, half title, frontispiece, original red cloth, blocked in blind and gilt, slightly rubbed, all edges gilt, very good.   Jarndyce Antiquarian Books   CCXV - 26   2016 £35

Artzybasheff, Boris *As I See.*   New York: Dodd Mead, 1954. First edition, 4to., tan cloth, very good+ in chipped dust jacket with some mends on verso, drawings and paintings, include with this is Christmas Greeting poster from artist, 13 1/2 x 12 inches, with intricate and bizarre illustrations, also laid in is greeting card inscribed by artist for Dorothy Lathrop, with illustration on cover.   Aleph-bet Books, Inc. 111 - 26   2016 $800

Artzybasheff, Boris *Seven Simeons.*   New York: Viking, April, 1937. First edition, large 4to., green pictorial cloth, fine in dust jacket rubbed at folds with small piece out of spine, lightly soiled, beautifully printed and illustrated with full and partial page color illustrations.   Aleph-bet Books, Inc.   112 - 35   2016 $200

As the Author of an Article on the Elgin Marbles in No. XXVIII of the Quarterly Review Expresses a Wish to Hear Mr. Payne Knight's Explanation.   N.P.: printed by Schultze and Dean, 13 Poland Street, 1815. 4to., final page blank, folded for insertion in envelope, edges slightly torn. Jarndyce Antiquarian Booksellers   CCXVII - 92   2016   £120

Asbjornsen, Peter Christian *East of the Sun and West of the Moon.*   London: Hodder & Stoughton, 1914. Limited to 500 nyumbered copies signed by artist, large 4to., full vellum stamped in blue and gold, top edge gilt, light cover soil and some rubbing, else very good+, pictorial endpapers, 25 magnificent tipped in color plates with lettered guards as well as numerous detailed black and whites throughout text, rare edition.   Aleph-bet Books, Inc.   111 - 321 2016 $12,750

Asbjornsen, Peter Christian *East of the Sun and West of the Moon: Old Tales from the North.* New York: George H. Doran, n.d. circa, 1925. Considered first US edition, 4to., purple cloth spine, black boards stamped in gold with gold pictorial paste-on, as new publisher's pictorial box (light wear to box), 25 magnificent mounted color plates and many black and whites and pictorial endpapers by Kay Mielsen, extremely rare in this condition in box.   Aleph-bet Books, Inc.   112 - 342   2016 $4500

Asbjornsen, Peter Christian *East of the Sun and West of the Moon.*   New York: George H. Doran, n.d. circa, 1930. Saml 4to., yellow cloth, owner name on endpaper, else nearly as new in dust jacket and publisher's box with color plate on cover, illustrations by Kay Nielsen, magnificent copy, rare in box.   Aleph-bet Books, Inc.   112 - 344   2016 $2000

Asch, Sholem *The Nazarene.* New York: G. P. Putnam's, 1939. First American edition, signed by author, octavo, black cloth, lettered gilt, minor spot to front cover, spine slightly faded, fine.   Argonaut Book Shop   Literature 2015 - 7348   2016 $90

Ash, Bertam S. *Practical Acrobatics.*   London: Link House Publications, 1936. First edition, half title, illustrations, original pictorial paper boards, little rubbed, spine slightly worn at head and tail.   Jarndyce Antiquarian Booksellers CCXVII - 16   2016   £30

Ashbery, John *Three Madrigals.*   New York: Poet's Press, 1968. First edition, one of 150 numbered copies, touch of sunning along spine, else fine in stapled wrappers. Between the Covers Rare Books   204 - 9   2016 $175

Ashbery, John *Who Knows What Constitutes a Life.* Calais: Z Press, 1999. First edition, one of only 26 copies with original 7 color linoleum cut frontispiece signed by artist and colophon signed by poet out of a total edition of 226 printed in Bembo type on Zerkall and Fabriano paper, 8vo., frontispiece, original wrappers with printed label, as new. James S. Jaffe Rare Books   Occasional List: Winter 2016 - 14   2016 $1000

Ashby, Henry *Health in the Nursery.*   London: Longmans, 1902. Third edition, half title, illustrations, occasional ink notes, original dark blue cloth, slightly marked.   Jarndyce Antiquarian Books   CCXV - 27   2016   £35

Ashe, Thomas *Songs of a Year.*   London: Chiswick press, privately printed, 1888. First edition, scrace, original paper wrappers, covers stained, creased on right corner and chipped along edges, hinges tender but text block is tight and clean, very good, presentation copy from author for F. Coylestone Feb. 1888.   The Kelmscott Bookshop   12 - 3 2016 $220

Ashe, Thomas *Songs of a Year.* London: Chiswick Press privately printed, 1888. First edition, paperback edition, scarce, presentation from author to F Coylestone, Feb. 1888, original paper wrappers, covers stained, creased on right corner and chipped along edges, hinges tender but text block in tight and clean, very good.   The Kelmscott Bookshop   13 - 3   2016 $220

Ashmole, Elias   1617-1692 *The Institution, Laws & Ceremonies of the Most Noble Order of the Garter.* London: J. Macock for Nathaniel Brooke, 1672. First edition, folio, 32 leaves of plates, 16 are double page and 5 double sided, occasional ink and wax spots, small number of short closed marginal tears, one closed tear to text pages 67-8, paper flaw to edge of pages 675-6 not affecting text, handful of other more minor examples, plate at page 391 little grubby with some creases suggesting removal and subsequent reinstatement, 20th century blind panelled calf, gilt spine with green morocco label, edges marbled but much faded, endpapers renewed, little rubbed but very good.   Unsworths Antiquarian Booksellers   30 - 9   2016   £2000

Ashton, John *Humour, Wit and Satire of the Seventeenth Century.* London: Chatto & Windus, 1883. First edition, octavo, woodcuts by author, original green gilt pictorial cloth, lettered in gilt, small rubber ex-libris stamp on half title, some spotting, very good, externally bright copy.   Peter Ellis   112 - 21   2016   £85

Ashton, John *Men, Maidens and Manners: a Hundred Years Ago.* London: Field & Tuer, 1888. 12mo., 34 contemporary illustrations, original drab paper wrappers, illustrated labels, leading inner hinge slightly cracking, contemporary inscription, very good.   Jarndyce Antiquarian Books CCXV - 28   2016   £45

Asimov, Isaac *The Dream, Benjamin's Dream and Benjamin's Bicentennial Blast.* New York: privately printed, 1976. Small 8vo., wood engravings by DePol in brown, olive green paper over boards, stamped in gilt, over very slightly faded on spine, little scuffed, otherwise nice.   Second Life Books, Inc.   197 - 16   2016 $30

Asimov, Isaac *Foundation and Earth.* Garden City: Doubleday and Co., 1966. First edition, half red cloth, blue boards, gilt lettered spine, very fine, pictorial dust jacket.   Argonaut Book Shop   Literature 2015 - 4656   2016 $75

Asimov, Isaac *The Foundation Trilogy. Foundation. (with) Foundation and Empire. (with) Second Foundation.* New York: Gnome Press publishers, later Gnome Press, Inc., 1951-1953. First edition, first printings, octavo, first volume in cloth, others in boards, very good in very good dust jackets, previous owner's bookplate.   John W. Knott, Jr./L.W. Currey, Inc.   Fall-Winter 2015 - 17584   2016 $3500

Asimov, Isaac *I. Robot.* New York: Gnome Press, 1950. First edition, octavo, illustrations, cloth, inscribed by author Oct. 14 '82 for Tom Denny, nearly fine in very good dust jacket with moderate rubbing to front panel, light edge wear and light wear to spine ends, closed tear upper front spine fold, spine panel color faded.   John W. Knott, Jr./L.W. Currey, Inc.   Fall-Winter 2015 - 17581   2016 $2500

Aspler, Tony *The Best of Barbaresco.* London: Headline, 1996. First edition, fine in dust jacket.   Mordida Books 2015 - 010650   2016 $65

Aspler, Tony *Death on the Douro.* London: Headline, 1997. First edition, very fine in dust jacket.   Mordida Books   2015 - 1010590   2016 $65

Asprey Miniature Reference Library. Asprey & Co. Ltd., n.d. but circa, 1903-1905. 7 volumes, purple quarter morocco, ruled and lettered in gilt, all edges gilt, some volumes with fading and staining to sides, otherwise very nice set in original inlaid wooden rack.   Bertram Rota Ltd. Christmas List 2015 - 2   2016   £450

Astruc, Jean *A General and Compleat Treatise on all the Diseases Incident to Children, from their Birth to the Age of Fifteen...* London: John Nourse, 1746. First edition in English, 8vo., contemporary calf backed marbled boards, worn, marbled paper sides defective, good, sound copy, entirely uncut and internally fine.   John Drury Rare Books 2015 - 26301   2016 $437

Atherton, Gertrude *A Daughter of the Vine.* London: John Lane, the Bodley Head, 1899. First book edition and first edition with this title, blue-gray cloth lettered and ruled in white, very good, very scarce.   Argonaut Book Shop Literature 2015 - 7257   2016 $300

Atherton, Gertrude *Dido, Queen of Hearts.* New York: Horace Liveright, 1929. First edition, black cloth, gilt, address sticker on inner front cover, fine with dust jacket slightly chipped at spine ends.   Argonaut Book Shop Literature 2015 - 5488   2016 $150

Atherton, Gertrude *The Jealous gods.* New York: Horace Liveright, 1928. First edition, black cloth, gilt, very fine with near fine pictorial dust jacket printed in lavender, orange and black, slight chipping to spine ends of jacket.   Argonaut Book Shop   Literature 2015 - 5492   2016 $75

Atherton, Gertrude *Life in the War Zone.* New York: New York Times, 1916. First book edition, signed by author on titlepage, three quarter quarter white cloth over blue-gray snake skin patterned boards, minor foxing to cloth and very minor rubbing to bottom edge of boards, fine copy.   Argonaut Book Shop   Literature 2015 - 5493   2016 $150

Atherton, Gertrude *Rulers of Kings.* New York & London: Harper & Bros., 1904. First edition with "Published April 1904" on copyright page and with cover lettering in gold, brown decorated cloth, lettered gilt on spine and front cover, cover design in white, pencilled name to front black flyleaf, light soiling to last blank flyleaf, very minor wear to lower corners, overall fine.   Argonaut Book Shop   Literature 2015 - 5494   2016 $75

Atherton, Gertrude *The White Morning: a Novel of the Power of German women in Wartime.* New York: Stokes, 1918. First edition, 8vo., inscribed by author to Clifford Smythe, previous owner's name on endpaper, good, tight copy.   Second Life Books, Inc.   196A - 53   2016 $65

Atkins, F. A. *The Young Man. A Monthly Journal & Review.* 1894-1895. Jan. 1894-Dec. 1895, volume 8/85-volume 9/108, 2 volumes, identically bound.   I. D. Edrich   Crime - 2016   £80

Atkinson, Brooks *Broadway Scrapbook.* New York: Theatre Arts, 1947. First edition, 8vo., cartoons by Al Hirschfeld, author's presentation to Burns Mantle, with Mantle's bookplate, cover little yellowed and worn, else very good, tight copy.   Second Life Books, Inc.   196A - 55   2016 $75

Atkinson, Brooks *The Lively Years 1920-1973.* New York: Association Press, 1973. 8vo., cartoons by Hirschfeld, inscribed by Hirschfeld, top edge of spine damaged, otherwise very good in little worn dust jacket.   Second Life Books, Inc.   196A - 54   2016 $125

Atkinson, Charles *The Life and Adventures of an Eccentric Traveller.* York: printed for the author by M. W. Carroll, 1819. First edition, frontispiece and one other full page woodcut, 6 smaller woodcuts in text, text slightly browned, contemporary full calf, gilt borders and spine, nice.   Jarndyce Antiquarian Booksellers   CCXVII - 17   2016   £480

Atkinson, Ethel Tindal *A Garden of Shadows.* London: Macmillan, 1907. First edition, octavo, 8 full page black and white art nouveau illustrations by Byam Shaw, pages unopened, presentation copy inscribed by author for Edith Lentner, May 1941, free endpapers lightly tanned, edges and prelims spotted, very good in very good slightly rubbed, nicked and creased dust jacket slightly darkened at spine and chipped at tail of spine.   Peter Ellis   112 - 357   2016   £50

Atkinson, George F. *Curry & Rice.* London: and Calcutta: W. Thacker, 1911. Fifth edition, titlepage and 40 tissue guarded color plates, reproductions of watercolors, original pictorial brown cloth, elaborately blocked in gilt, blind and white enamel, all edges gilt, covers slightly marked, very good, bright.   Peter Ellis   112 - 180   2016   £150

Atkinson, J. C. *Forty Years in a Moorland Parish: Reminiscences and Researches on Danby in Cleveland.* London: Macmillan, 1891. Reprint, 8vo., illustrations, maps, original green cloth.   J. & S. L. Bonham Antiquarian Booksellers   Europe 2016 - 5074   2016   £45

Atkinson, Ron *Looking for My Name.* Lenox: Bookstore Press, 1974. First edition, 8vo. paper wrappers, inscribed by author to poet, Paul Metcalf and his wife, two typewritten poems laid in, very good.   Second Life Books, Inc.   196A - 57   2016 $45

Atlas Geographicus Portabilis: XXIX Mappis Orbis Habitabilis Regna Exhibens. Augsburg: Vendit inejus aedib in suburb...n.d. circa, 1750. 16mo., contemporary and probably original blindstamped calf housed in custom cloth box, lacks free endpapers, covers rubbed, generally very good and clean, fine copper plate engravings, double page engraved frontispiece, double page engraved pictorial title.   Aleph-bet Books, Inc.   111 - 265   2016 $2500

Atlas of the Engravings to Illustrate and Practically Explain the Construction of Roofs of Iron... London: John Weale 59 High Holborn1859, 4to., 15 double page and folding engraved plates, clean, original wavy ribbed green cloth with printed paper label on upper cover, bookseller's ticket of T. Fenteman & Sons Theological and General Booksellers, Leeds.   Marlborough Rare Books   List 55 - 72   2016   £225

Attlee, James *Gordon Matta-Clark: the Space Between.* Tucson: Nazraeli Press, 2003. 18 tipped in color and black and white plates, close ot near fine in blue cloth boards, some light fading to spine.   Jeff Hirsch Books   Holiday List 2015 - 83   2016 $85

Attwell, Mabel Lucie *Boo-Boos at Honey Sweet Farm.* London: Dundee; Montreal, Valentine, n.d. circa, 1922. 12mo., boards, pictorial paste -on, some foxing and cover soil else very good, illustrations by Attwell with pictorial endpapers, 14 color plates plus many green line illustrations, very scarce.   Aleph-bet Books, Inc.   111 - 27   2016 $1000

Aubin, Nicolas *Cruels effets de la Vengeance du Cardinal de Richelieu ou Histoire des Diables de Loudun...* Amsterdam: E. Roger, 1716. First edition, 12mo., contemporary calf, edges rubbed, joints tender, marbled endpapers, engraved frontispiece, Grolier Club bookplate and 'sold' stamp.   Edwin V. Glaser Rare Books   2015 - 10408   2016 $450

Aucassin et Nicolete *Aucassin and Nicolete.* London: Adam and Charles Black, 1911. First edition illustrated thus, 4to., white cloth decorated in blue, endpapers toned, else near fine, 6 beautiful color plates with lettered guards by Anne Anderson, text pages have decorative borders in a range of colors, beautiful copy.   Aleph-bet Books, Inc.   112 - 22   2016 $275

Aucassin et Nicolete *Aucassin & Nicolette.* Folio Society, 1947. First edition thus, titlepage illustration and head and tailpieces by Lettice Sandford, crown 8vo., original quarter white cloth patterned paper sides, backstrip lettered in silver, little rubbing to edges, very good.   Blackwell's Rare Books   B184 - 312   2016   £15

Auchincloss, Louis *Love Without Wings.* Boston: Houghton Mifflin, 1991. First printing, 8vo., author's signature on half title, fine in very slightly soiled dust jacket. Second Life Books, Inc.   196A - 58   2016 $45

Auchincloss, Louis *The Winthrop Covenant.* Boston: Houghton Mifflin, 1976. Uncorrected proof, original printed wrappers, slightly soiled, nice, tight copy, signed by author. Second Life Books, Inc.   196A - 59   2016 $75

Auchincloss, Louis *The Winthrop Covenant.* Franklin Center: Franklin Library, 1976. Limited edition, full page drawings by Jerry Pickney, gilt lettered and decorated brown leather, all edges gilt, near fine, as new.   Argonaut Book Shop   Literature 2015 - 2599   2016 $45

Auden, Wystan Hugh   1907-1973   *The Age of Anxiety - a Baroque Eclogue.* London: Faber and Faber, 1948. First UK edition, corners little bruised, very good in very good, slightly chipped dust jacket, bit tanned at spine.   Peter Ellis   112 - 23   2016   £85

Auden, Wystan Hugh   1907-1973   *The Age of Anxiety.* London: Faber & Faber, 1948. First English edition, crown 8vo., original yellow cloth, backstrip lettered in gilt with very slight lean to spine, light dust soiling along top edge and few faint spots to leading edge of upper board, ownership inscription to flyleaf, dust jacket with darkened backstrip panel, good.   Blackwell's Rare Books   B186 - 176   2016   £60

Auden, Wystan Hugh   1907-1973   *The Age of Anxiety.* London: Faber and Faber, 1948. First English edition, crown 8vo., original bright yellow cloth with small strip of bubbling to upper board, small mark to same, very minor bump to top corners, backstrip lettered gilt, top edge slightly dusty, contemporary ownership inscription to flyleaf, dust jacket with little edge darkening and a small amount of chipping to backstrip ends, very good, signed by author. Blackwell's Rare Books   B184 - 94   2016   £400

Auden, Wystan Hugh   1907-1973   *City Without Walls and other Poems.* London: Faber and Faber, 1969. First edition, crown 8vo., original black cloth, backstrip lettered gilt, light dust soiling and few small foxspots to top edge, dust jacket with few small foxspots to top edge, dust jacket with few small nick, very good, inscribed by author.   Blackwell's Rare Books   B184 - 95 2016   £450

Auden, Wystan Hugh   1907-1973   *The Double Man.* New York: Random House, 1941. First edition, 8vo., original brick red cloth stamped in gilt to upper board, backstrip lettered gilt with tiny amount of wear at head, top edge black, faint browning to endpapers, dust jacket price clipped and little frayed, signed by author, with 9 holograph corrections to text.   Blackwell's Rare Books   B184 - 96   2016   £650

Auden, Wystan Hugh   1907-1973   *The Enchafed Flood or the Romantic Iconography of the Sea.* London: Faber and Faber, 1951. First English edition, crown 8vo., original blue cloth, backstrip lettered gilt now dulled, dustiness to boards and textblock, edges of browning to free endpapers, dust jacket browned, frayed and lightly spotted, good, David Gascoyne's copy with his notes, signed by author. Blackwell's Rare Books   B184 - 97   2016   £400

Auden, Wystan Hugh   1907-1973   *Letters from Iceland.* London: Faber and Faber, 1937. First edition, 8vo., signed by author, original green cloth, original illustrated dust jacket, numerous illustrations from photos taken by Auden, diagrams and folding map at rear, dust jacket minimally chipped to extremities, else very good.   Sotheran's Travel and Exploration - 415   2016   £750

Auden, Wystan Hugh   1907-1973   *New Year Letter.* London: Faber and Faber, 1941. First English edition, boards little foxed, small stain on front endpapers, very good in like dust jacket, price clipped with shallow loss at foot and small ink note on rear panel.   Between the Covers Rare Books   208 - 7   2016 $225

Auden, Wystan Hugh   1907-1973   *Poems.* London: Faber & Faber, 1930. First edition, light blue printed wrappers over unprinted card covers, spine bit darkened, light rubbing at extremities, but good copy of fragile book. Joseph J. Felcone, Inc.   Books from Five Centuries: a Miscellany - 11   2016 $750

Auden, Wystan Hugh   1907-1973   *Poesies Choiseies.* Paris: Gallimard, 1976. First edition, printed wrappers, William Meredith's copy signed by poet, near fine.   Charles Agvent   William Meredith - 76   2016 $60

Audsley, George Ashdown *How to Dress: a Manual for Ladies on all Matters Connected with the Proper Selection and Harmonious Combination of Colours Suitable for the Various Complexions.* London: Sampson Low, Marston & Co., 1912. Half title, folding plates, original dark blue cloth, blocked in white with Sanskrit symbol on front board, slightly dulled.   Jarndyce Antiquarian Books   CCXV - 30   2016   £30

Audubon, John James 1785-1851 *Audubon's Birds of America.* New York: Abbeville Press, 1981. First edition, deluxe version, fdolio, original oatmeal cloth backed with black leatherette, gilt spine in oatmeal cloth slipcase with pasted on label, 435 color plates, text fine.   Sotheran's Piccadilly Notes - Summer 2015 - 22   2016   £250

Audubon, John James 1785-1851 *The Quadrupeds of North America.* New York: V. G. Audubon, 1856. Third edition, 3 volumes, publisher's brown morocco, elaborately blindstamped lettering and foliate panels within double fillets to sides, spines tooled in blind, raised bands, gilt lettering, all edges gilt, volumes I and II with marbled endpapers,155 hand colored plates, signature of author tipped in, binding slightly rubbed to edges and joints, very good.   Sotheran's Piccadilly Notes - Summer 2015 - 1   2016   £15,000

Audubon, Maria R. *Audubon and His Journals: with Zoological and other Notes by Elliott Coues.* London: John C. Nimmo, 1898. 2 volumes, photographic plates, publisher's blindstamped cloth, inscription, fine set.   Andrew Isles Natural History Books   55 - 36344   2016 $400

Auel, Jean M. *The Mammoth Hunters.* New York: Crown Pub., 1985. First edition, first issue dust jacket, presentation signed by author, half cloth and boards, very fine, pictorial dust jacket.   Argonaut Book Shop   Literature 2015 - 7036   2016 $200

Auel, Jean M. *The Plains of Passage.* New York: Crown Publisher's, 1990. First edition, red cloth backed tan boards, gilt lettered spine, very fine in pictorial dust jacket.   Argonaut Book Shop   Literature 2015 - 4670   2016 $250

Auel, Jean M. *The Valley of Horses.* New York: Crown Publishers, 1982. First edition, tqan cloth backed blue boards, very minor rubbing to foot of spine, fine in pictorial dust jacket with slight wear to jacket of board of spine.   Argonaut Book Shop   Literature 2015 - 7602   2016 $90

Auel, Jean M. *The Valley of Horses.* New York: Crown Publishers, 1982. First edition, fine in near fine dust jacket (chipped spine ends).   Ken Hebenstreit, Bookseller   2016 - 4   2016 $40

Auel, Jean M. *The Valley of Horses.* New York: Crown, 1982. Eighth printing, one of 2250 copies signed by author, 8vo., nice, in dust jacket with two slight tears.   Second Life Books, Inc.   196A - 60   2016 $100

Augustinus, Arelius, Saint, Bp. of Hippo *De Civitate dei cum Commento.* Venice: Octavianus Scotus, 18th Feb., 1489-1490. Second edition, large woodcut verso of titlepage, woodcut printer's device to final leaf, initials supplied in red or blue and printed capitals, picked out in red, two larger initials on red and blue, 2 cm. tall waterstain with attendant softening to lower margin of first two thirds of volume, first two gatherings with resulting paper repairs, one leaf (A6) stained, small rusthole to final leaf touching one character, little other light browning, intermittent short marginalia in early hand, longer note faded from recto of titlepage, folio, old wooden boards recently recovered in brown calf to period style, tooled to blind, two fore-edge clasps, pastedowns preserving vellum musical manuscript binder's waste from previous binding, good, carefully rubricated throughout, early owner has added a number of annotations out on every page.   Blackwell's Rare Books   B184 - 5   2016   £9500

Aulnoy, Marie Catherine, Comtesse D' *D'Aulnoy's Fairy Tales.* Philadelphia: David McKay Co., 1923. First edition illustrated thus, small quarto, color pictorial titlepage, 8 full page color plates by Gustaf Tenggren, numerous black and white drawings in text, original blue cloth, front cover with paste-on illustration, spine lettered in black, top edge gilt, color pictorial endpapers, fine in original color pictorial dust jacket with few small closed marginal tears.   David Brass Rare Books, Inc.   2015 - 02980   2016 $650

Aulus Gellius *Noctes Atticae, seu Vigiliae Atticae.* Paris: cum privilegio Caesaris et Gallorum Regis, 1585. Paper toned, some spotting, few leaves with light marginal dampmark, one leaf with closed tear vertically through top 9 lines of text (no loss), leaves either side with shorter tears in blank margin, cipher stamp to titlepage with motto 'hoc est signum meu(m)", blank leaf C1 (in second series) discarded (as often), 8vo., early 17th century French brown morocco, boards with central gilt arms (fess between three roses) and border of French fillets, joints, headcap and corners sometime repaired and new leather of front joint now bit worn, but joint itself still strong, spine divided by raised bands, second compartment gilt lettered direct, rest with central gilt monogram "FMTNS" or some combination of those letters, good.   Blackwell's Rare Books   Greek & Latin Classics VII - 8   2016   £1200

Aunt Louisa's Wee Wee Stories. New York: McLoughlin Bros. n.d. circa, 1870. 24 very fine full page chromolithographs, brown cloth decorated in black with round pictorial paste-on, spine ends worn, two minor archival margin mends, else very good.   Aleph-bet Books, Inc.   112 - 308   2016 $325

Aurelius Victor, Sextus *Historia Romana.* Amstelodami: apud Janssonio Waesbergios Trajecti Batav. (Utreccht) apud Joacobum a Poolsum, 1733. 4to., engraved titlepage printed in red and black, woodcut initials and head and tailpieces, numerous illustrations in text, very occasional light foxing, some gatherings toned, contemporary blind tooled vellum, title inked to spine, edges lightly sprinkled red and blue, some smudgy marks to vellum but quite clean and bright overall, top edge darkened, very good bequeathal bookplate to Taylor Institute, overlaid with "Sold by Authority" inkstamp. Unsworths Antiquarian Booksellers   30 - 10   2016   £350

Austen, Ernest Edward *Bombylidae of Palestine.* Long Beach: British Museum (Natural History), 1937. Quarto, colored frontispiece, publisher's cloth, apart from library stamp on titlepage, fine.   Andrew Isles Natural History Books   55 - 35803   2016 $100

Austen, Ernest Edward *A Handbook of the Tsetse-Flies.* London: British Museum, 1911. Octavo, 10 color photographic plates, publisher's cloth, neat library stamp on titlepages, otherwise fine, crisp, clean copy.   Andrew Isles Natural History Books   55 - 35880   2016 $150

Austen, Jane   1775-1817 *Emma: a Novel.* London: printed for John Murray, 1816. First edition, 3 volumes, bound without half titles, some dampstaining to fore-edges, occasional foxing (only becoming unsightly in about a dozen leaves in volume iii), gathering C in volume i little proud, 12mo, contemporary half calf, flat spines gilt, lacking lettering pieces, split at foot of upper joint of volume i and this spine slightly defective at head, corners and board edges slightly worn, good.   Blackwell's Rare Books   Marks of Genius - 4   2016   £10,000

Austen, Jane   1775-1817 *Mansfield Park: a Novel.* London: printed for T. Egerton, 1814. First edition, 12mo., 3 volumes, wanting half titles, with all terminal blanks, contemporary half gray polished calf over marbled boards, gilt stamped spines rebacked to style, boards rubbed as expected, previous owner's contemporary signature on titlepages and armorial bookplates with faint offsetting, overall very good, attractive, clean set.   Heritage Book Shop   Holiday 2015 - 4   2016 $17,500

Austen, Jane   1775-1817 *Northanger Abbey and Persuasion.* London: John Murray, 1818. First edition, 4 volumes, bound without half titles and blanks, sporadic foxing, small hole in C12 in volume i, affecting 2 letters on verso, volume iv, waterstained, 12mo., contemporary half calf, 2 of the spines partially scorched, lacking lettering pieces, 1 spine slightly defective at head, cracks in 4 joints, engraved bookplate in volume I (Rumbold family), pencil ownership inscription on flyleaf (almost loose) of volume iv of C. E. Rumbold, Walton.   Blackwell's Rare Books   Marks of Genius - 6   2016   £6000

Austen, Jane   1775-1817 *Novels.* London: Richard Bentley, 1833. First collected edition, 6 volumes bound in five, octavo, original purple cloth with original labels on spines, gilt stamped spines uniformly sunned, labels bit chipped, minor soiling to covers, very good copy.   Heritage Book Shop   Holiday 2015 - 5   2016 $12,500

Austen, Jane   1775-1817 *Austen's Novels in five volumes with a Memoir.* London: Richard Bentley, 1885-1886. 6 volumes, half title, frontispiece, contemporary half red morocco, spine extra gilt, leading inner hinge of Pride and Prejudice slightly weak but sound, very nice, attractive set, bookplates of John Nairn Marshall.   Jarndyce Antiquarian Booksellers   CCXVII - 18   2016   £1200

Austen, Jane   1775-1817 *The Novels.* London: Dent, 1894-1897. 10 volumes bound in 5, 8vo., mid 20th century half green calf by Bayntun-Riviere, spines gilt, twin red lettering pieces, top edges gilt, bookplate removed, good, attractive set.   Blackwell's Rare Books   B184 - 7   2016   £2000

Austen, Jane   1775-1817 *The Novels.* London: J. M. Dent & Co., 1906-1909. 10 volumes, 8vo., original light blue cloth with pictorial design in dark blue on upper covers which are also lettered gilt, top edge gilt, others uncut, good, attractive set.   Blackwell's Rare Books   B184 - 6 2016   £500

Austen, Jane   1775-1817 *The Novels and Letters.* New York: and Philadelphia: Frank S. Holby, 1914. Hampshire edition, limited to 1250 numbered and registered copies (our copy not numbered), 12 volumes, quite pleasing recent tan crushed half morocco over marbled boards, raised bands, spines with blind wave rule at top and bottom, spine panels with double gilt rules and central gilt fleuron, red and green labels, top edges gilt, other edges untrimmed, letter volumes unopened, colored illustrations by C. E. and H. M. Brock and facsimiles of autograph letters, one leaf with two inch marginal tear (likely from rough opening), otherwise only most trivial imperfections, very fine set, obviously unread in unworn bindings.   Phillip J. Pirages   67 - 19   2016 $2500

Austen, Jane   1775-1817 *Pride and Prejudice: a Novel in Two Volumes.* London: printed for T. Egerton, 1817. Third edition, 2 volumes, bound without half titles or terminal blanks, some foxing, water-staining in lower outer quarter of second half of volume ii, tiny hole in B8 in volume I between lines 7 and 8 (no loss of text), 12mo., contemporary half calf, flat spines, gilt in compartments, lacking lettering pieces, spine of volume I defective at head, rear flyleaf in volume II loose, corners bit worn, early initials at head of titlepages.   Blackwell's Rare Books   Marks of Genius - 5   2016   £5000

Austen, Jane 1775-1817 *Sense and Sensibility.* London: printed for the author by C. Roworth and published by T. Egerton, 1813. Second edition, 3 volumes, bound without half titles and terminal blanks, sporadic foxing as usual, slight defect to inner margin of 1 leaf in volume i, 4 leaves almost loose in volume ii (never caught by edge sewing), minor worming in lower margin volume iii, 12mo., contemporary half calf, flat spines gilt in compartments, lacking lettering pieces, minor wear, engraved armorial bookplate inside front covers volumes i and ii (Rumbold family), good copy. Blackwell's Rare Books Marks of Genius - 3 2016 £8000

Austen, Jane 1775-1817 *Sense and Sensibility.* London: Richard Bentley, 1833. First Bentley edition, frontispiece, engraved title, slight spotting to prelims, contemporary full tan calf, double ruled gilt borders, spine gilt with bands, dark brown morocco label, slightly rubbed, Haverland armorial bookplate, very nice. Jarndyce Antiquarian Booksellers CCXVII - 19 2016 £450

Auster, Paul *Autobiography of the Eye.* Portland: Printed at the Beaverdam Press for Charles Seluzicki, 1993. First edition, one of 35 copies printed (entire edition), 8vo., photographic frontispiece by Karin Welch tipped-in, original string tied French fold unprinted wrappers, printed paper label, publisher's envelope, fine, rare. James S. Jaffe Rare Books Occasional List: Winter 2016 - 28 2016 $850

Auster, Paul *Leviathan.* New York: Viking, 1992. Fine in fine dust jacket, signed by author and additionally signed by dedicatee Don Delillo, very uncommon thus. Jeff Hirsch Books Holiday List 2015 - 19 2016 $175

Austin, Alfred *Lamia's Winter-Quarters.* London: A. & C. black, 1907. First edition, no. 192 of 250 deluxe edition, signed by author, quarto, original ivory decorative cloth, spine faded, cloth cockled. J. & S. L. Bonham Antiquarian Booksellers Europe 2016 - 6259 2016 £50

Austin, Ethel Mildred King Britten *Unending Journey.* London: Thornton Butterworth, 1939. First edition, original brick red cloth, spine lettered gilt, illustrated dust jackets (price clipped), map, spine little sunned, wrappers with few minor chips, very good, from the collection of travel writer Peter Hupkirk, ownership inscription of Wilfred G. Wright dated April 1939. Sotheran's Piccadilly Notes - Summer 2015 - 23 2016 £278

Austin, Mary *The Land of Little Rain.* Boston and New York: Houghton Mifflin, 1903. First edition, fourth impression, octavo, original pictorial olive cloth, gilt lettered, all edges gilt, frontispiece, 3 plates numerous vignettes by E. Boyd Smith, fine, bright copy in original decorated dust jacket, little chipped and torn, but intact, completely unsophisticated and not supplied from another book. The Brick Row Book Shop Miscellany 69 - 9 2016 $900

Austin, Mary *Taos Pueblo.* New York: New York Graphic Society, 1977. Limited signed edition, one of 950 copies signed and numbered by Ansel Adams, 12 gravure reproductions of Adams photos, large folio, original half leather over linen boards, marbled endpapers, original slipcase, fine. Manhattan Rare Book Company 2016 - 1820 2016 $2400

Avannes, Theophile D' *Esquisssses sur Navarre.* Rouen: Imprimerie de Nicetas Periaux, 1839. 8vo., half title, wood engraved titlepage, 7 lithograph plates on india paper by Eugene de Lonlay, numerous decorative initials and wood engraved tailpieces, contemporary quarter dark green morocco, spine gilt in 5 compartments, fore edge of half title repaired, fine. Marlborough Rare Books List 55 - 4 2016 £150

Avedon, Richard *An Autobiography.* New York: Random House, 1993. Signed by Avedon, remarkably fresh and tight, 284 photos, fine in very near fine printed acetate jacket and near fine example of original shipping carton. Jeff Hirsch Books Holiday List 2015 - 66 2016 $400

Avedon, Richard *An Autobiography.* New York: Random House, 1993. First edition, signed limited edition, number 44 of only 250 copies signed by Avedon, special engraver's proof of Marilyn Monroe laid in, lavishly illustrated with 284 photos, folio, original white cloth with gray and black lettering, original slipcase, original publisher's box, just hint of toning to spine, touch of rippling to cloth on front cover, much less than usual, outstanding copy. Manhattan Rare Book Company 2016 - 1799 2016 $4900

Avedon, Richard *An Autobiography. With: Evidence 1944-1994.* New York: Random House, 1994. Limited edition, although limitation states 250 copies, only about 100 actually produced, signed and numbered in box by Avedon, with engraver's proofs of Jasper Johns and Jean Shrimpton, 284 photographs, folio, original matching full linen with colored lettering, matching clamshell box with blindstamped title, engraver's proofs in separate paper folders as issued, with slip "Whitney originals", fine, rare. Manhattan Rare Book Company 2016 - 1640 2016 $6500

Avedon, Richard *In the American West.* New York: Harry N. Abrams, 1985. First edition, signed by Avedon, folio, original pictorial cloth, original acetate, fine. Manhattan Rare Book Company 2016 - 1806 2016 $750

Averani, Benedetto *Benedicti Averanii Florentini in Pisano Lyceo Littearum Humaniorum Professoris Opera Latina Regiae Celsitudini Cosmi III...* Florence: Typis Regiae Celesitudinis Sumptibus Cajetani Tartinii & Sanctis Franchii, 1717. First edition, 3 volumes, tall 4to., volume I engraved frontispiece, volumes II & III engraved titlepage portrait medallion, prominent marginal waterstain especially to lower corners all volumes, not affecting legibility, original full calf, gilt stamped spines and cover edges, 6 raised bands, worn, hinges cracked with leather chipped, spine heads missing pieces, volume 1 free front endpaper loose, small half title tear, Theological Institute of Connecticut blindstamps to first and last few pages, very good (not waterstains), rare.   Jeff Weber Rare Books   181 - 11   2016 $325

Averill, Esther *Eclair.* Paris: Domino Press, 1934. First edition, 4to., cloth backed pictorial boards, fine, color lithos by Rojankovsky, laid in is 1 page handwritten letter from Averill on her personal stationery.   Aleph-bet Books, Inc.   111 - 392   2016 $475

Averill, Esther *Poudre.* Paris: Domino Press, 1933. First edition, 4to., cloth backed pictorial boards, fine, color lithos by Rojankovsky, with 2 page handwritten letter from author.   Aleph-bet Books, Inc.   111 - 394   2016 $475

Averill, Esther *The Voyages of Jacques Cartier retold by....* New York: Domino Press, 1937. Limited to 3000 copies, 4to., cloth, fine in dust jacket (rubbed at folds, piece off top of backstrip, very good), beautifully illustrated with full page and smaller black and white lithographs by Rojankovsky.   Aleph-bet Books, Inc.   111 - 395   2016 $200

Axe, Ruth Frey *The Published Writings of Henry R. Wagner.* New Haven: William Reese, 1988. First edition, one of 500 copies, frontispiece, orange cloth spine, maroon boards, gilt lettering, very fine.   Argonaut Book Shop   Biography 2015 - 7653   2016 $60

Ayliffe, John *The Antient and Present State of the University of Oxford.* London: E. Curll, 1714. First edition, 2 volumes, contemporary brown panelled calf, joints cracked, lacks labels, clean and crisp.   J. & S. L. Bonham Antiquarian Booksellers   Europe 2016 - 8723   2016   £300

Aylmer, Felix *Dickens Incognito.* London: Rupert Hart-Davis, 1959. First edition, half title, frontispiece map, original blue cloth, very good in dust jacket.   Jarndyce Antiquarian Booksellers   CCXVIII - 1070   2016   £25

Aylmer, Felix *The Drood Case.* London: Rupert Hart-Davis, 1964. First edition, half title, frontispiece, plates, original maroon cloth, spine lettered in black, very good in slightly torn dust jacket.   Jarndyce Antiquarian Booksellers   CCXVIII - 666   2016   £20

Ayoux, Jean Jacques *Melville.* New York: Grove Press, London: Evergreen Books, 1960. First edition, small 8vo., illustrations, very nice, inscribed by historian Stefan Lorant to Melville's granddaughter, Eleanor Melville Metcalf.   Second Life Books, Inc.   196 B - 200   2016 $50

Ayrton, Elzabeth *The Doric Temple.* London: Thames & Hudson, 1961. First edition, 4to, 73 plates, gray cloth, gilt slightly discolored edges, very good, dust jacket with some wear to edges with one or two small tears, price clipped, good.   Unsworths Antiquarian Booksellers Ltd.   E05 - 15   2016   £20

B

B. F. Goodrich Co. *Ye Primer. A Rhyme Book on ye letters of ye alphabet.* New York: B. F. Goodrich Co., 1902. First edition (only?), thin 4to., original stiff paper wrappers, printed in black, white and orange, very good. Sotheran's Piccadilly Notes - Summer 2015 - 26 2016 £498

B., F. W. *Woman's Whim; or the Broken Heart.* London: Webb, Millington & Co., 1854. 16mo., color frontispiece and plate, original blue decorated cloth, slightly rubbed, all edges gilt. Jarndyce Antiquarian Books CCXV - 32 2016 £75

B., M. A *Public School Reforms. Few Remarks and Suggestions on the Mental, Moral and Physical Training of Youth.* London: L. Booth, 1872. slight foxing, disbound. Jarndyce Antiquarian Books CCXV - 515 2016 £38

Babbage, Charles 1792-1871 *Observations on the Temple of Serapis at Pozzuoli Near Naples.* privately printed, 1847. First edition, 8vo., 2 lithographed plates, 6 figures, original blind and gilt stamped red cloth with gilt motif of temple on upper cover, gilt spine title, spine ends worn, some soiling, small paper label on upper cover, neat bookplate of Stirling Public Library (The Thomson Collection, Glasgow), very good, inscribed by author for Hon. Charles Villiers, M.P. Jeff Weber Rare Books 183 - 4 2016 $3750

Babington, Thomas *A Practical View of Christian Education in Its Early Stages.* London: J. Hatchard, 1815. Second edition, half title, 2 pages ads, contemporary dark blue morocco, slightly rubbed, bookplate of Christopher Cole, with his signature, very good. Jarndyce Antiquarian Books CCXV - 516 2016 £110

Bacchylides *The Poems of Bacchylides.* London: by order of the trustees of The British museum, 1897. First edition, 8vo, cloth, gilt lettered, spine slightly cocked, spine sunned, toning to upper board, corners and endcaps bumped and starting to fray, edges dusted and uncut, spit to rear endpapers, good, library number cellotaped to spine, ex-libris bookplate of Nan Holley, ownership inscription of N. M. Halley. Unsworths Antiquarian Booksellers Ltd. E05 - 16 2016 £30

Bacheller, Irving *The Scudders a Story of Today.* New York: Macmillan, 1923. First edition, 8vo., fine in chipped and worn dust jacket, signed by author. Second Life Books, Inc. 196A - 64 2016 $45

Bachmair, Johann Jacob *Neue Englische Grammatike...* A. Linde, 1758. Second edition, 8vo., bit damp stained, worming in inner margins occasionally just touching a letter, some old paper repairs, in one case closing a vertical tear through almost the whole leaf without loss), 8vo., contemporary marbled boards, rebacked preserving most of original spine, edges worn. Blackwell's Rare Books B184 - 8 2016 £450

Backker, Metaal *Le Chateau de St. Valerie, Histoire Foundee sur des faits Tites de la Revolution.* London: Dulau et chez l'Auteur, 1817. First edition, tears in inner margins of first few leaves, entering text on 2 leaves without loss, and these repaired, 12mo., contemporary half calf, minor wear, good. Blackwell's Rare Books B184 - 9 2016 £400

Backus, Henry *What are you doing after the orgy?* Englewood Cliffs: Prentice Hall, 1962. First edition, cartoons, presentation by authors Henry and Jim Backus, nice in little scuffed and soiled dust jacket. Second Life Books, Inc. 196A - 65 2016 $45

Bacon, Edgar Mayhew *"A Centennial Souvenir." A Brief History of Tarrytown from 1680 to September 1880.* Tarrytown: Geo. L. Wiley & Bros., 1880. First edition, 24 pages, 1 hand colored folding map, 1 black and white engravings, 8vo., stitched wrappers, about very good, wrappers chipped at edges, front wrapper partially detached, map split at joint, few small tears along folds, otherwise quite bright. Kaaterskill Books 21 - 63 2016 $275

Bacon, Francis 1561-1626 *The Essayes or Counsels Civill and Morall of Francis Lord Verulam Viscount St. Alban.* London: Cresset Press, 1928. No. 32 of 250 copies on paper and 8 on vellum, 390 x 261mm., publisher's vellum over substantial boards, raised bands, gilt titling on upper cover and spine, later suede backed marbled slipcase, titles and initials designed by Joscelyne Gaskin, half dozen abrasions to lower cover, little variation in color of vellum (as almost always), otherwise fine, entirely bright, fresh and clean inside and out. Phillip J. Pirages 67 - 99 2016 $750

Bacon, Francis 1561-1626 *The Essays...* Norwalk: Heritage Press, 1972. Brown leatherette, lettered gilt, very fine in slipcase, Sandglass pamphlet laid in. Argonaut Book Shop Heritage Press 2015 - 6926 2016 $45

Bacon, Francis 1561-1626 *Of Gardens.* London: Eragny Press for Hacon Ricketts, 1902. One of 226 copies, original patterned paper boards, gilt titling on front, wood engraved frontispiece, borders, colophon, printer's device and initials, all by Lucien Pissaro, clipping from promotional material tipped onto front pastedown, front free endpaper with bookplate of Antonio Cippico, front cover with ink inscription "File copy/ not to be/Taken away", paper boards little soiled, usual offsetting to endpapers from binder's glue, half a dozen leaves with faint wrinkling, other minor imperfections but especially interesting copy in very good condition. Phillip J. Pirages 67 - 129 2016 $1500

Bacon, Francis 1561-1626 *The Twoo Bookes of Francis Bacon. Of the Proficience and Advancement of Learning, Divine and Humane.* London: for Henrie Tomes, 1605. First edition, 4to., lacks final blank 3H2 and as always, rare two leaves of errata at end, late 19th century half calf and marbled boards, extremities of boards worn, very skillfully and imperceptibly rebacked, retaining entire original spine, small worm trail at bottom margin of quires 2D-2F, occasional minor marginalia in early hand, else lovely copy, early signature of Row'd Wetherald on title signature of Horatio Carlyon 1861, Sachs bookplate and modern leather book label calf backed clamshell box. Joseph J. Felcone, Inc. Books from Five Centuries: a Miscellany - 10 2016 $7500

Bacon, Francis 1909-1992 *Francis Bacon.* Paris: Galeries Nationales du Grand Palais, 1971. First edition, small quarto, numerous color reproductions, presentation from Bacon for Spanish interior designer Jaime Parlade, one of two of the folding plates creased at fore-edge, very good. Peter Ellis 112 - 26 2016 £1500

Bacon, George Washington *The True Road to Success.* London: G. W. Bacon, circa, 1885? Fourth edition, original orange printed paper wrappers, faded and little worn. Jarndyce Antiquarian Books CCXV - 33 2016 £75

Bacon, Hugh Ford *A Letter to R. M. Beverley, Esq. from an Undergraduate of the University of Cambridge.* London: T. Stevenson, 1833. 28 pages, disbound. Jarndyce Antiquarian Books CCXV - 568 2016 £30

Bacon, Mary Anne *Flowers and Their Kindred Thoughts.* London: Longman & Co., 1848. 8vo., printed in colors and gold, illuminated, printed and designed by Owen Jones, original heavily embossed leather with ivy design repeated in the decorative endpapers. Marlborough Rare Books List 56 - 30 2016 £325

Bacon, Peggy *The Ballad of Tangle Street.* New York: Macmillan, 1929. First edition, cloth backed pictorial boards, edges rubbed, else near fine in very lightly soiled, slightly frayed but very good+ dust jacket, full page pen drawings, scarce, beautiful book. Aleph-bet Books, Inc. 112 - 38 2016 $325

Badminton Library. Hunting. London: Longmans, Green & Co., 1889. 8vo., original brown cloth decorated in black also in gilt to spine, little shaken, nonetheless attractive copy. Sotheran's Hunting, Shooting & Fishing - 30 2016 £55

Baedeker, Karl *Eygpt. First Part. Lower Egypt with the Fayumm and the Peninsula of Sinai.* Leipzig: Karl Baedeker, 1885. Second edition, small 8vo., original publisher's cloth lettered in gold at spine and upper board, 30 plans and 76 vignettes, rear endpaper spotted, front free endpaper reinserted, some tanning to backstrip and little minor chafing to cloth at some extremities, internally bright. Sotheran's Piccadilly Notes - Summer 2015 - 27 2016 £298

Baedeker, Karl *Paris and its Environs with Routes from London to Paris.* Leipzig: Baedeker, 1910. Seventeenth revised edition, small 8vo., original flexible cloth, ornamented in blind, lettered gilt, binding little rubbed, otherwise very good. Sotheran's Travel and Exploration - 217 2016 £78

Baedeker, Karl *Russland nebst Teheran, Port Arthur, Peking....* Leipzig: Baedeker, 1912. Small 8vo., original flexible cloth, ornamented in blind, lettered gilt, marbled edges, 40 maps, 67 plans, 12 architectural diagrams, some of which are folding or double page size, cloth bit darkened and spotted in places, few pages with light crinkling to corners, nonetheless very good with contemporary Aschen bookseller's label inside front cover. Sotheran's Travel and Exploration - 215 2016 £498

Baer, Warren *The Duke of Sacramento.* San Francisco: Grabhorn Press, 1934. One of 550 copies, printed in red and black, illustrations by Arvilla Parker, white cloth backed blue boards, paper spine label, very fine. Argonaut Book Shop Private Press 2015 - 3635 2016 $60

Bagley, Desmond *The Freedom Trap.* London: Collins, 1971. First edition, small light stain on fore-edge, otherwise fine in dust jacket with wear at top of spine and at corners. Mordida Books 2015 - 012568 2016 $65

Bagley, Desmond *The Golden Keel.* London: Collins, 1963. Author's holograph corrected advance proof copy in original wrappers, together with first edition of the book in dust jacket. I. D. Edrich Crime - 2016 £95

Bagnold, Enid *Letters to Frank Harris & Other Friends.* Andoversford: Whittington Press & William Heinemann, 1980. First edition, of a total edition of 400 copies, handset in Caslon and printed on Arches mould made paper, this one of 370 copies bound in cloth, numbered and signed by author, large 8vo., 5 mounted color plates fine, publisher's box. Second Life Books, Inc. 196A - 67 2016 $131

Bahr, Edith-Jane *A Nice Neighbourhood.* Crime Club, 1973. Very good in like dust jacket. I. D. Edrich Crime - 2016 £20

Baikie, William Balfour *Narrative of an Exploring Voyage up the Rivers Kwo'ra and Bi'nue ....* London: Murray, 1856. First edition, 8vo., contemporary full calf, spine with raised bands, richly ornamental to gilt, gilt stamped black morocco lettering piece, marbled endpapers and edges, frontispiece, folding plan of ship, folding map, vignette on title, minor rubbing to binding, very good, clean and fresh copy. Sotheran's Travel and Exploration - 3 2016 £798

Bailer, Adele *Hei von Allerlei.* Leipzig: Hirt & Sohn, 1924. 13 x 10 1/4 inches, cloth backed white pictorial boards, small scrape on cover, else near fine, magnificent silhouettes by Bailer. Aleph-bet Books, Inc. 111 - 194 2016 $650

Bailey, Alfred M. *Subantarctic Campbell Island.* Denver: Denver Musuem of Natural History, 1962. Octavo, photos, publisher's cloth, very good. Andrew Isles Natural History Books 55 - 5186 2016 $80

Bailey, Caroline Sherwin *Miss Hickory.* New York: Viking and Junior Literary Guild, 1946. First edition, 8vo., red cloth, 2 edges dusty, else fine in dust jacket (lightly soiled, slightly frayed but very good+), charming litho illustrations by Ruth Gannett. Aleph-bet Books, Inc. 111 - 29 2016 $150

Bailey, Pearl *Talking to Myself.* New York: Harcourt Brace Jovanovich, 1971. 8vo., author's presentation on title, nice in little curled and yellowed dust jacket. Second Life Books, Inc. 196A - 68 2016 $65

Bailik, H. N. *Sefer Hadvarim. (A Book of Things).* Berlin: Ophir, 1922. First edition, cloth backed pictorial boards, some cover soil, tips rubbed and rubbing at inner hinges, else unusually clean, tight and very good+, 16 striking full page hand colored illustrations by Tom Freud. Aleph-bet Books, Inc. 112 - 207 2016 $4000

Baillie-Grohman, William *Camps in the Rockies: Being a narrative of Life on the Frontier and Sport in the Rocky Mountains...* New York: Charles Scribner's Sons, 1882. First edition, cloth, fair, attractive black line decoration and gilt lettering on upper board and still bright on spine they are slightly faded, although lettering there is still legible, some wear to corners and spine ends of original dark green cloth, interior clean and unmarked, however there is considerable browning to margins of leaves, several chips at front edge, also there are small tears in ads at end of book, folding map remains clean and supple despite several small tears to edges. Simon Finch 2015 - 001110 2016 $205

Baillie, W. W., Mrs. *Days and Nights of Shikar.* John Lane, 1921. First edition, 8vo., original grey cloth, spine titled in gilt, colored frontispiece, little foxing mainly in edges, very good. Sotheran's Hunting, Shooting & Fishing - 1 2016 £50

Bailward, Margaret E. *Mothers and their Responsibilities.* London: Longmans, 1904. First edition, 18 line pencil ms. facing title, ad leaf preceding half title, partially unopened in original blue cloth, spine lettered in gilt, front board spotted by ink, good sound. Jarndyce Antiquarian Books CCXV - 34 2016 £25

Bain, Alexander *Education as a Science.* London: Kegan Paul, Trench & Trubner, 1879. Original red decorated cloth, dulled, library reference on spine, booklabel for the Library of the Faculty of Physicians and Surgeons, Glasgow. Jarndyce Antiquarian Books CCXV - 517 2016 £40

Bain, Alexander *Education as a Science.* London: Kegan Paul, Trench, Trubner & Co., 1892. Eighth edition, half title, 80 page catalog, unopened in original red decorated cloth, spine slightly faded, slight mark to foot of leading and following hinge, nice, bright copy. Jarndyce Antiquarian Books CCXV - 518 2016 £30

Bain, R. Nisbet *Russian Fairy Tales from the Skazki of Polevoi.* London: George Harrap, 1915. 8vo., top edge gilt, cloth with pictorial paste-on, endpapers spotted, else near fine, 4 beautiful color plates, 12 full page black and whites. Aleph-bet Books, Inc. 112 - 442 2016 $150

Baines, Mart Anne *Domestic Servants as They Are and as They Ought to Be.* London: W. Tweedie, 1859. Recent marbled boards, cloth spine, 22 pages. Jarndyce Antiquarian Books CCXV - 35 2016 £120

Baines, Thomas 1806-1881 *Lancashire and Cheshire Past and Present.* London: William Mackenzie, c., 1867. 4 volumes, 4to., 25 plates and engraved titlepages to first part of each volume, some foxing, especially near front and rear, publisher's crimson morocco, heavy gilt spines, boards and dentelles, armorial centre pieces to boards, all edges gilt, spines darkened, joints rubbed, some slight scrapes and dents to boards with very occasional small areas of surface loss, ownership inscription of C. L. Mallinson. Unsworths Antiquarian Booksellers Ltd. E04 - 4 2016 £400

Baird, G. W. *A Report to the Citizens, Concerning Certain late Disturbances on the Western Frontier Involving Sitting Bull, Crazy Horse, Chief Joseph....* Ashland: Lewis Osborne, 1972. first book edition, one of 600 copies, illustrations, gilt lettered and decorated red cloth, very fine. Argonaut Book Shop Native American 2015 - 3638 2016 $50

Baker, E. C. Stuart *The Game-Birds of India, Burma and Ceylon: Volume Two: Bustards and Sand-Grouse.* Bombay: Bombay Natural History Society, 1921. Tall octavo, 19 color plates by H. Gronvold, photos, very good in publisher's brown half morocco.   Andrew Isles Natural History Books   55 - 5209   2016 $450

Baker, Henry *Employment of the Microscope.* London: printed for R. and J. Dodsley, 1764. Second edition, 2 parts in one volume, 8vo., 17 engraved plates, lightly foxed, titlepage creased, plate facing page 422 torn at fold, modern full calf with original calf mounted on sides, gilt stamped motto "Fide et Virtute" belonging to Cha. Brandling, gilt and blindstamped spine, gilt stamped red leather label, new endleaves, bookplates of Cha. Brandling, Charles Adams, Fred C. Luck and Max Erb, very good+.   Jeff Weber Rare Books   183 - 5   2016 $650

Baker, Houston A. *Modernism and the Harlem Renaissance.* Chicago: University of Chicago, 1987. First printing, 8vo., several illustrations, review laid in, author's presentation to Dan Johnson, maroon cloth, edges spotted cover little scuffed at corners and end of spine, otherwise nice in dust jacket.   Second Life Books, Inc.   196A - 70   2016 $75

Baker, Richard M. *The Drood Murder Case. five Studies in Dickens's Edwin Drood.* Berkeley & Los Angeles: University of California, 1951. Half title, original red cloth, spine lettered in black, spine slightly faded, good plus.   Jarndyce Antiquarian Booksellers   CCXVIII - 668   2016   £20

Baker, Richard T. *Woodfibres of Some Australian Timbers: Investigated in Reference to their Prospective Value for Paper-Pulp Production.* Sydney: Government Printer, 1924. Color frontispiece, micro-photographs, publisher's cloth, small stain.   Andrew Isles Natural History Books   55 - 5206   2016 $80

Baker, Samuel White *Cyprus; as I Saw It in 1879.* Macmillan, 1879. First edition, 8vo., frontispiece, contemporary green full polished calf, light fading at top of lower cover, otherwise fine.   J. & S. L. Bonham Antiquarian Booksellers   Europe 2016 - 9736   2016   £550

Baker, Samuel White *Ismailla. A Narrative of the Expedition to Central Africa for the Suppression of the Slave Trade.* London: Macmillan and Co., 1874. First edition, 2 volumes, 2 maps, numerous plates, publisher's green cloth, inner hinges of volume 1 cracked, short tear top of one spine, moderate rubbing of extremities, but very good, rarely found in fine condition, armorial bookplate.   Joseph J. Felcone, Inc.   Books from Five Centuries: a Miscellany - 13   2016 $450

Balaban, John *Walking Down into Cebolla Canyon.* Greensboro: Unicorn, 1980. First edition, wrappers, reproduction of photo by William Clift on cover, broadside poem folded in ours, one of 500 copies, inscribed for William Meredith by Balaban, with original envelope addressed in Balaban's hand, fine.   Charles Agvent   William Meredith - 12   2016 $80

Baldwin, Faith *Sign Posts.* Boston: Small, Maynard & Co., 1924. First edition, small octavo, blue decorated cloth stamped in black and gold, trifle rubbed at spine ends, slight foxing on top edge, else very near fine, lacking dust jacket, inscribed by author to Achmed Abdullah.   Between the Covers Rare Books   204 - 11   2016 $450

Baldwin, James *Giovanni's Room.* New York: Dial Press, 1956. First edition, very slight browning around edges at beginning, small faint stain to top of fore edges, 8vo., original cloth backed boards and dust jacket, small stain to lower cover, bookplate, good.   Blackwell's Rare Books   B184 - 98   2016   £200

Baldwin, James *Going to Meet the Man.* New York: Dial Press, 1965. First edition, advance review copy with author photo laid in, fine in fine dust jacket with virtually none of the usual rubbing, beautiful copy, seldom found thus.   Between the Covers Rare Books   207 - 19   2016 $450

Baldwin, Louisa *The Story of a Marriage.* London: J. M. Dent and Co., 1895. Publisher's dark blue cloth with gilt title and author to spine, bumped, rubbed, light stains and slightly cocked, interior pages very good with typical offsetting to free endpapers, 6 illustrations by J. A. Symington, very good despite binding flaws, very good, inscribed by author to Tris Fleming Nov. 1900.   The Kelmscott Bookshop   13 - 4   2016 $150

Balfour, Clara Lucas *Moral Heroism; or the Trials and Triumphs of the Great and the Good.* London: Houlston & Stoneman, 1853. New edition, frontispiece with small tear to head of titlepage, original purple cloth, spine faded to brown, ownership signature, very good.   Jarndyce Antiquarian Books   CCXV - 36   2016   £35

Balfour, Clara Lucas *Moral Heroism...* London: Houlston & sons, circa, 1878. New edition, half title, frontispiece and plates, original brick red pictorial cloth, blocked in black and gilt, slightly cocked, all edges gilt, stamps of Birkbeck College, very good.   Jarndyce Antiquarian Books   CCXV - 32   2016   £30

Balfour, Graham *The Life of Robert Louis Stevenson.* New York: Charles Scribner's Sons, 1901. First edition, 2 volumes, 2 frontispiece portraits, small folding map, red cloth, top edges gilt, spines slightly faded, bookplate on inner covers with minor offsetting to adjacent endpaper, minor foxing to front endpapers and first few pages in each volume.   Argonaut Book Shop   Biography 2015 - 7648   2016 $60

The Ball-Room Guide. London: Frederick Warne & Co., circa, 1875. 32mo., color frontispiece, additional illustrated title, original green decorated cloth, slightly rubbed, cloth little lifted in places, all edges gilt, good plus. Jarndyce Antiquarian Books   CCXV - 466   2016   £100

Ball, John   *The Cool Cottontail.*   New York: Harper, 1966. First edition, fine in dust jacket.   Mordida Books   2015 - 002740   2016 $55

Ballantine, James   *Poems.*   Edinburgh: Thomas Constable & Co., 1856. First edition, original pink morocco grained cloth by John Gray of Edinburgh, front board with central ornament in gilt, spine lettered gilt, bit rubbed, front boad with 2 small stains and slight crease.   Jarndyce Antiquarian Booksellers   CCXVIII - 885   2016   £50

Ballard, J. G.   *The Four Dimensional Nightmare.*   London: Victor Gollancz ltd., 1963. First edition, octavo, boards, foxing to page edges, nearly fine in nearly fine first printing dust jacket (code X24 at bottom right corner of rear flap and price on front flap), slight age darkening to spine panel, scarce. John W. Knott, Jr./L.W. Currey, Inc.   Fall-Winter 2015 - 15823   2016 $1250

Ballard, J. G.   *The Terminal Beach.*   London: Victor Gollancz Ltd., 1964. First edition, octavo, boards, fine in just about fine dust jacket with small closed tear to upper spine panel, scarce.   John W. Knott, Jr./L.W. Currey, Inc. Fall-Winter 2015 - 15824   2016 $2000

Ballard, J. G.   *The Unlimited Dream Company.*   London: Jonathan Cape, 1979. First edition, hardcover, fine in dust jacket, unclipped.   Jeff Hirsch Books   E-List 80 - 3   2016 $85

Ballard, Philip Boswood   *Group Tests of Intelligence.* London: Hodder & Stoughton, 1928. Fifth impression, half title, original red cloth, very good.   Jarndyce Antiquarian Books   CCXV - 519   2016   £20

Ballard, Philip Boswood   *Mental Tests.*   London: Hodder & Stoughton, circa, 1920. Third impression, half title, occasional pencil notes and underlining, original red cloth, slightly rubbed and marked.   Jarndyce Antiquarian Books CCXV - 520   2016   £20

Ballard, Philip Boswood   *Mental Tests.*   London: University of London Press, 1930. 8th impression, half title, original contemporary brown cloth, slight nick to front board, very good.   Jarndyce Antiquarian Books   CCXV - 521 2016   £20

Ballerini, Luigi   *Italian Visual Poetry 1912-1972.*   New York: Finch College Museum, Inst. Italiano of Cultura, 1973. First edition, Simon Finch   2015 - 2468-05D   2016 $233

Ballin, Ada S.   *The Kindergarten System Explained.*   F. L. Ballin, 1896. First edition, original dark blue cloth, slightly dulled, bookseller's ticket of H. W. Wallis, nice.   Jarndyce Antiquarian Books   CCXV - 522   2016   £40

Balzac, Honore De   *Droll Stories.*   London: Folio Society, 1961. First edition illustrated thus, royal 8vo., recently rebound in half red morocco, spine and top edges gilt, 24 tinted drawings by Mervyn Peake, very good.   Sotheran's Piccadilly Notes - Summer 2015 - 231   2016   £248

Balzac, Honore De   *La Fille aux Yeux d'Or. (The Girl with the Golden Eyes).*   London: Leonard Smithers, 1896. First edition, 6 illustrations engraved on wood by Charles Conder, commonly found in blue cloth, here in original yellow cloth boards with black title to spine and front board, very good plus, minor bumping to spine ends and bottom corners of boards, slight darkening to spine, few spots of foxing to early and late pages, otherwise clean, housed in half morocco slipcase with purple cloth boards, titled in gilt with gilt decoration and raised bands, some discoloration, light soiling and minor rubbing to case.   The Kelmscott Bookshop   12 - 33 2016 $400

Bancroft, Hubert Howe   *History of the life of John G. Downey. A Character Study.*   San Francisco: History Co., 1889. First separate book edition, frontispiece, black cloth, gilt, frontispiece foxed, else fine.   Argonaut Book Shop Biography 2015 - 6580   2016 $50

Bandler, Raymond   *The Hound & Horn: volume III No. 3 April-June 1930.*   Portland: Hound & Horn, 1930. 8vo., paper wrappers, cover fairly heavily spotted, especially in back, corners and edges slightly dog eared, otherwise very good tight.   Second Life Books, Inc.   197 - 17   2016 $45

Bangs, John Kendrick   *Bikey the Skicycle and other Tales of Jimmieboy.*   New York: Riggs, 1902. First edition, 8vo., pictorial cloth, spine crease, one mend, occasional margin soil, very good+, illustrations by Newell.   Aleph-bet Books, Inc.   112 - 337   2016 $200

Bangs, John Kendrick   *The Enchanted Typewriter.*   New York: Harper and Bros., 1899. First edition, fine in dust jacket, illustrated by Peter Newell with 10 monochrome plates, beautiful copy, rare in jacket.   Aleph-bet Books, Inc.   112 - 338   2016 $275

Bangs, John Kendrick   *Pursuit of the House Boat.*   New York: Harper & Bros., 1897. First edition, first state without London on title and listing 7 titles in ads, 24 monotone plates, 12mo., pictorial cloth, 2 small spots on rear cover and spine darkened, else clean and very good-fine.   Aleph-bet Books, Inc.   112 - 340   2016 $200

Banham, Reyner *Theory and Designs in the First Machine Age.* London: Architectural Press, 1960. First edition, octavo, numerous illustrations, near fine in very good dust jacket bit nicked and rubbed at edges, elusive in presentable condition.　　Peter Ellis　　112 - 17　　2016　　£125

Bankes, George Nugent *A Day of My Life.* London: Sampson Low, 1877. First edition, half title, 6 pages ads, original brick red decorated cloth, slight ink mark to front board, little rubbed, bookplate of Oliver Brett & John H. Baker, very good.　　Jarndyce Antiquarian Books　　CCXV - 673　　2016　　£35

Banks, E. T. *Allen Life Guard African Methodist Episcopal Church Manual for Boys.* Norfolk: Allen Life Guard, 1922. First edition, 12mo., photos, stapled brown photographic wrappers, faint wear, very near fine.　　Between the Covers Rare Books　　207 - 85　　2016　　$4500

Banks, Iain M. *The Player of Games.* London: Macmillan, 1988. First edition, octavo, boards, fine in fine dust jacket.　　John W. Knott, Jr./L.W. Currey, Inc.　　Fall-Winter 2015 - 16907　　2016　　$250

Bannerman, David Armitage *Birds of the Atlantic Islands.* Edinburgh: Oliver & Boyd, 1963. Quarto, 4 volumes, color plates and text illustrations, bookplate in each volume, good set in lightly worn dust jackets.　　Andrew Isles Natural History Books　　55 - 15741　　2016　　$850

Bannerman, David Armitage *The Birds of Tropical West Africa...* London: Crown Agents for the Colonies, 1931-1951. Octavo, 8 volumes, plates, text illustrations, folding maps, publisher's cloth, apart from few minor corner bumps, fine set.　　Andrew Isles Natural History Books　　55 - 5239　　2016　　$1250

Bannerman, Helen *Little Black Sambo.* Akron: Saalfield, 1942. Large Format 'cloth like' soft cover, illustrations by Ethel Hays, spine tape repaired, cover retaped on verso, pages intact and in very good shape, fore-edge chipped and worn.　　Second Life Books, Inc.　　197 - 20　　2016　　$75

Bannerman, Helen *Little Black Sambo.* New York: Duenewald, 1943. 8vo., spiral backed pictorial boards, light edge rubbing, else near fine, moveable book, illustrations in color by Julian Wehr and 7 moveable plates plus other color illustrations in text, quite difficult to find complete.　　Aleph-bet Books, Inc.　　112 - 40　　2016　　$600

Bannerman, Helen *Pat and the Spider.* London: James Nisbet, n.d., 1905. First edition, 16mo., pictorial cloth, slight cover soil and spine sunned, else near fine, printed on one side of the paper only, with full page color illustrations facing each page of text.　　Aleph-bet Books, Inc.　　112 - 42　　2016　　$850

Bannerman, Helen *The Story of Little Degchie Head.* London: James Nisbet, 1903. First edition, 16mo., pictorial cloth, spine suned bit and slight soil on rear cover, else near fine.　　Aleph-bet Books, Inc.　　112 - 43　　2016　　$600

Bannet, Ivor *The Amazons.* Golden Cockerel Press, 1948. 45/70 copies (from an edition of 500 copies), signed by author and artist and printed on Arnold mouldmade paper, 12 wood engravings by Clifford Webb, some full page, and reproductions of 3 pen and ink maps by Mina Greenhill, small folio, original dark brown crushed morocco, backstrip lettered gilt, five raised bands, top edge gilt, others untrimmed, brown marbled endpapers with mild offsetting from morocco to outermost borders, gilt chain link design to outer edges and single gilt rule inner borders, brown cloth slipcase, fine.　　Blackwell's Rare Books　　B186 - 309　　2016　　£500

Baraka, Amiri *The Music: Reflections on Jazz and Blues.* New York: Morrow, 1987. first printing, 8vo., illustrations, paper over boards with cloth spine, presentation from author, paper over boards with cloth spine, edges little soiled, otherwise very good, tight, in frontispiece.　　Second Life Books, Inc.　　196A - 73　　2016　　$150

Baraka, Amiri *The Sidney Poet Heroical.* New York: I. Reed Books, 1979. First edition, 8vo., author's signature on gilt, paper wrappers, cover somewhat scuffed, otherwise very good, tight copy.　　Second Life Books, Inc.　　196A - 74　　2016　　$65

Barbara Peek-A-Boos Holiday. London: Humphrey Milford/Oxford University Press, n.d. circa, 1915. Square 4to., pictorial boards, color paste-on, slight wear to paper and slight soil, very good+, 8 fine color plates, numerous black and whites by Chloe Preston.　　Aleph-bet Books, Inc.　　111 - 364　　2016　　$500

Barbaro, Ermolao *Castigationes Plinianae et Pomponii Melae.* Rome: Impressit Eucharius Argenteus... Octavo Kalendas Decembris, 1492. (and) Idibus Feb., 1493. First edition, one leaf with central wax stain causing small area of damage with three letters lost from text on verso, another leaf bit soiled, overall and with short closed split in blank margin, some light spotting to elsewhere but generally clean, fore-edge of first leaf slightly short, small blindstamps to blank margin of first and last leaf, 18th century English red morocco boards gilt in Harleian style, rebacked early 20th century in brick red morocco, lettered gilt direct with narrow paper label above, corners worn, boards bit scratched, hinges reinforced with cloth tape, library bookplate, good copy.　　Blackwell's Rare Books　　Marks of Genius - 36　　2016　　£4500

Barbeau, Marius *Totem Poles.* Canada: National Museum of Canada, 1950. First printing, 2 volumes, profusely illustrated, photographic maps, map endpapers, light green pictorial wrappers stamped in black and red, remnants from removed bookplate, ink numbers on base of spines, general light rubbing, very good set.   Argonaut Book Shop   Native American 2015 - 6031   2016 $125

Barbour, Thomas *A Contribution to the Zoogeography of the West Indies, with Especial Reference to Amphibians and Reptiles.* Cambridge: Museum of Comparative Zoology, 1914. Quarto, one lithographic plate, half green morocco, wrappers retained, handsome copy.   Andrew Isles Natural History Books   55 - 35983   2016 $450

Barbour, Thomas *A List of Antillean Reptiles and Amphibians.* New York: New York Zoological and Amphibians, 1930. Quarto, binder's cloth with title, wrappers retained.   Andrew Isles Natural History Books   55 - 35984   2016 $100

Barcelo, Miquel *Toros.* Zurich: Edition Gallery Bruno Bischolfberger, 1991. First edition, signed, limited edition, #1629 of 2000, color reproductions, black and white photographic images by Lucien Clergue, folio, red cloth, red paper dust jacket with embossed black printing and bull graphic to front panel, light wear, near fine in like dust jacket.   Tavistock Books   Bibliolatry - 30   2016 $300

Barcia Carballido y Zuniga, Andres Gonzales De *Ensayo Cronologico para in Historia General de la Florida....* Madrid: 1723. First edition, folding table, title in red and black, contemporary limp vellum, endpapers discolored and bit wrinkled, very faint dampstain in margin of last several leaves, else near fine.   Joseph J. Felcone, Inc.   Books from Five Centuries: a Miscellany - 62   2016 $2800

Barclay, Robert *Theologiae vere Christianae Apologia.* Amsterdam: Jacob Claus for Benjamin Clark/London: Isaac van Neer; Rotterdam and Heirnich Betke, Frankfurt, 1676. Rare first edition, 4to., contemporary sprinkled calf, blind fillet around covers and run twice along spine, gilt sawtooth roll on board edges, spine with gilt fillet above and below each cord, old paper ms. label, hinges split but held securely by cords, corners bumped and tips worn through, spine with very faint white-ish cast, internally slight dampstain at top margin, some slight sporadic foxing and browning, edges of endpapers discolored from leather turn-ins, very good.   Joseph J. Felcone, Inc.   Books from Five Centuries: a Miscellany - 14   2016 $8000

Bard, Patrick *Transsiberiens.* Paris: Marval, 2003. First edition, 4to., copiously illustrated in color and black and white, fine in fine dust jacket with very slight rubbing, corners very faintly bumped, excellent condition.   Any Amount of Books   2015 - A88409   2016   £170

Barduzzi, Bernardino *A Letter in Praise of Verona (1489).* Verona: Officina Bodoni, 1974. Limited to 150 numbered copies, tall 8vo., quarter vellum with blue Roma paper sides with woodcut pattern in white, top edge gilt, slipcase, printed on Pescia mould made paper by Giovanni Mardersteig at Officina Bodoni in yellow, red and black.   Oak Knoll Books   27 - 47   2016 $500

Baretti, Joseph *A Journey from London to Genoa.* London: T. Davies, 1770. First edition, 4 volumes in 2, volume 1 waterstained in margins, full brown contemporary calf, joints cracked, spines and corners rubbed, some light scuffing, new labels, light browning to prelims.   J. & S. L. Bonham Antiquarian Booksellers   Europe 2016 - 8522   2016   £380

Barham, Richard Harris 1788-1845 *The Ingoldsby legends of Mirth & Marvels.* London: J. M. Dent & Co., 1898. Color and black and white illustrations by Arthur Rackham, original gilt lettered and printed green cloth, rubbing to extremities, chips to spine ends and small chips to front endpaper, very good.   Argonaut Book Shop   Literature 2015 - 1312   2016 $175

Barham, Richard Harris 1788-1845 *Ingoldsby Legends.* London: Dent, 1907. Limited to 560 signed by Rackham, (500 for sale), large thick 4to., full gilt pictorial vellum, inconspicuous mend on 2 text pages, else fine with new ties, 24 beautiful tipped-in color plates mounted on dark paper, 12 full page tinted illustrations and 66 black and white drawings, plus pictorial endpapers, this copy with fine half page watercolor drawing signed by artist, Arthur Rackham.   Aleph-bet Books, Inc.   111 - 372   2016 $13,500

Barham, Richard Harris 1788-1845 *The Ingoldsby Legends: a Gallimaufry.* Mission: Barbarian Press, 2015. 1 of 45 copies from the Standard edition (there are 45 additional copies in the deluxe version), 7 wood engravings by John Lewis Roget, bound with printed red and cream paper boards with deep red silk spine and paper title and press label, printed with Poliphilus & Blado types with Goudy Thirty, on Heine Mouldmade paper, engravings printed on Zerkall Cream smooth, fine, tipped in errata sheet.   The Kelmscott Bookshop   13 - 5   2016 $450

Baring Gould, S. *Amazing Adventures.* London: Skeffington & Son, n.d,, 1903. Cloth backed pictorial boards, corners worn and rear cover soiled, else remarkably clean, tight and very good+, full page chromolithographs by Harry Neilson.   Aleph-bet Books, Inc.   112 - 369 2016 $1250

Barker, Clive *The Books of Blood Volumes.* London: Weidenfeld & Nicolson, 1985-1986. First hardcover editions of volumed 3-6, First separate hardcover editions of volumes one and two, limited to 200 numbered sets, each volume with inserted limitation leaf signed by Barker, this is set number 151, some of the usual age tanning to cheap pulp paper, fine copies in fine dust jackets, enclosed in two cloth slipcases. John W. Knott, Jr./L.W. Currey, Inc. Fall-Winter 2015 - 17556 2016 $750

Barker, George *Poems.* London: Faber and Faber, 1935. First edition, octavo, front free endpaper, bit tanned form news clippings, very good in like dust jacket, bit tanned at spine and edges. Peter Ellis 112 - 27 2016 £45

Barker, George *Collected Poems 1903-1955.* London: Faber and Faber, 1957. First edition, inscribed by author for William Meredith, fine in near fine dust jacket. Charles Agvent William Meredith - 13 2016 $150

Barker, George *Sacred and Secular Elegies.* Norfolk: New Directions, 1943. First edition, inscribed and signed for William Meredith, fine in near fine dust jacket. Charles Agvent William Meredith - 14 2016 $200

Barker, Henry J. *The Comic Side of School Life.* London: Jarrold & sons, 1898. Fourth edition, 17th thousand, original white pictorial paper wrappers, worn but sound, Foyle's bookseller's ticket. Jarndyce Antiquarian Books CCXV - 524 2016 £25

Barker, Mary Anne *Houses and Housekeeping.* London: William Hunt & Co., 1877. Second edition, half title, 12 page catalog, original brown decorated cloth, bevelled boards, slightly dulled, slightly scuffed, bookseller's ticket of W. S. Simons?, very good. Jarndyce Antiquarian Books CCXV - 38 2016 £75

Barker, Nicolas *Two East Anglian Picture Books.* London: Roxburghe Club, 1988. Large folio, 8 leaves of plates + 68 further leaves of colour facsimile plates, titlepage in red and black, sporadic foxing to prelims up to page xi, neat pencil annotations to table of plants and animals depicted to pages 83-5, green cloth, gilt title to spine, boards little dusty, small dent to top edge of upper board, slight spotting to edges. Unsworths Antiquarian Booksellers 30 - 12 2016 £350

Barker, Pat *The Regeneration Trilogy.* Viking, 1996. First single volume edition, 8vo., original black boards, backstrip lettered in red, dust jacket with merest hint of fading to red lettering on backstrip panel, near fine. Blackwell's Rare Books B186 - 177 2016 £50

Barlandus, Hadrianus *Rerum Gestarum a Brabantiae Ducibus Historia - Catalogus Unsignium Oppidorum Germaniae Inferioris.* Antwerp: Johannes Gravius, 1551. Second edition, small 8vo., early 18th century flexible vellum, lettered in ink cursive, printer's woodcut device on title, vellum little spotted, titlepage and final page little dusted, apart from one page with minor spots, very clean, crisp and fresh. Sotheran's Travel and Exploration - 219 2016 £398

Barlow, Jane *The End of Elfin-Town.* London: Macmillan, 1894. First edition, cloth with beautifully elaborate gilt designed covers, all edges gilt, spine darkened, bit of fraying to spine ends, else very good, illustrations by Laurence Housman, 8 full page illustrations and several illustrations in text, increasingly scarce and nice. Aleph-bet Books, Inc. 112 - 247 2016 $750

Barlow, Stephen *The History of Ireland.* London: Sherwood, Neely and Jones, John Cumming and M. Keene, Dublin, 1814. First edition, 2 volumes, half title, frontispiece and engraved title (slightly browned), in both volumes, folding plate and map volume I, slightly later half dark green roan, maroon labels, slight rubbing, good plus. Jarndyce Antiquarian Booksellers CCXVII - 23 2016 £280

Barnabee, Henry Clay *Reminiscences.* Boston: Chapple Pub., 1913. First edition, 8vo., inscribed by author with printed letter laid in, moderate wear illustrations. Second Life Books, Inc. 196A - 76 2016 $45

Barnard, John *Some Rules for the conduct of Life...* London: printed by Witherby & Co., circa, 1949. Rubricated text, original red cloth, very good. Jarndyce Antiquarian Books CCXV - 39 2016 £20

Barnard, M. R. *Sport in Norway and Where to Find It; Together with a Short Account of the Vegetable Productions of the Country...* London: Chapman & Hall, 1864. First edition, 8vo., frontispiece, stains on both covers. J. & S. L. Bonham Antiquarian Booksellers Europe 2016 - 8346 2016 £100

Barnes, Djuna *Nightwood.* London: Faber & Faber, 1936. First edition, 8vo., original purple cloth, dust jacket, few small chips at lower fore-corner of jacket, tiny bit of edgewear elsewhere, otherwise fine, rare, inscribed presentation from author to John Hayward, laid into this copy is brief autographed card signed by Barnes to Hayward, exceptional association. James S. Jaffe Rare Books Occasional List: Winter 2016 - 29 2016 $9500

Barnes, James F. *Authors, Publishers and Politicians for the Quest of an Anglo-American copyright Agreement 1815-1854.* London: Routledge & Kegan Paul, 1974. Half title, original green cloth, mint in dust jacket. Jarndyce Antiquarian Booksellers CCXVIII - 1072 2016 £20

Barnes, Julian *Arthur & George.* London: Review Bookshop Cape, 2005. First edition, xxiii/xxx of an edition of 150 copies, signed by author, 8vo., original quarter orange morocco, backstrip gilt lettered, cream boards with orange pattern overall, cloth and board slipcase, fine. Blackwell's Rare Books   B184 - 99   2016   £350

Barnes, Julian *Cross Channel.* London: Jonathan Cape, 1996. First edition, 44/50 copies signed by author, crown 8vo., original morocco grain dark blue leatherette, backstrip and front cover lettered gilt, all edges gilt, marbled endpapers, fine.   Blackwell's Rare Books   B184 - 100   2016   £400

Barnes, Julian *Fiddle City.* London: Jonathan Cape, 1981. First edition, usual border toning to pages, crown 8vo., original blue boards, backstrip lettered gilt, dust jacket with gentlest of fading to backstrip panel, near fine, signed by Barnes as Dan Kavanagh.   Blackwell's Rare Books   B184 - 104   2016   £120

Barnes, Julian *Flaubert's Parrot.* London: Jonathan Cape, 1984. First edition, 8vo., original green boards, backstrip lettered gilt, dust jacket just little darkened around head to flap-folds, publisher's promotional wraparound band little faded to backstrip, near fine, signed by author. Blackwell's Rare Books   B184 - 101   2016   £300

Barnes, Julian *Going to the Dogs.* London: Jonathan Cape, 1987. First edition, usual border toning to pages, crown 8vo., original blue boards, backstrip lettered gilt, dust jacket with gentlest of fading to backstrip panel, near fine, signed by Barnes as Dan Kavanagh.   Blackwell's Rare Books   B184 - 106   2016   £80

Barnes, Julian *Love etc.* 2000. First edition, fine in slightly creased and rubbed dust jacket, inscribed by author. Bertram Rota Ltd.   February List 2016 - 3   2016   £80

Barnes, Julian *Putting the Boot In.* London: Jonathan Cape, 1985. First edition, usual border toning to pages, crown 8vo., original blue boards, backstrip lettered gilt, dust jacket with laminate little creased and gentle fading to backstrip panel, very good, signed by Barnes as Dan Kavanagh. Blackwell's Rare Books   B184 - 105   2016   £80

Barnes, Linda *Bitter Finish.* New York: St. Martins, 1983. First edition, very fine in dust jacket.   Mordida Books   2015 - 010622   2016 $65

Barnes, Madeline *Fireside Stories.* London: Blackie, 1922. First edition, 4to., cloth backed boards, pictorial paste-on, edges lightly worn, slight cover soil, few spots on title, really nice, very good++, 8 lovely color plates and many lovely black and whires by Anne Anderson.   Aleph-bet Books, Inc.   112 - 23   2016 $300

Barnes, William *A Few Words on the Advantages of a More common Adoption of the mathematics as a Branch of Education...* London: Whittaker & Co., 1834. 12mo., pale green printed paper wrappers, slightly dulled, very good. Jarndyce Antiquarian Books   CCXV - 525   2016   £380

Barnett, Charles Zachary *A Christmas Carol; or the Miser's Warning! (Adapted from Charles Dickens).* London: Thomas Hailes Lacy, circa, 1890. Frontispiece, slightly spotted, disbound.   Jarndyce Antiquarian Booksellers   CCXVIII - 357   2016   £50

Barnett, Louise *Touched by Fire.* New York: Henry Holt, 1996. First edition, numerous historic photos, cloth backed boards, very fine with pictorial dust jacket.   Argonaut Book Shop   Biography 2015 - 7679   2016 $45

Barnett, Vivian Edicott *Kandinsky Watercolours: Catalogue Raisonne Volume One 1900-1921. Volume Two 1922-1944.* Ithaca: Cornell University Press, 1992. 1300 color and black and white illustrations, both books tight and very fine in very near fine dust jackets with some very slight wear, lovely set.   Jeff Hirsch Books   Holiday List 2015 - 13 2016 $375

Barney, Rosset *Evergreen Review: Volume I Number 4 1957.* New York: Grove Press, 1957. First edition, general light rubbing, near fine, inscribed by Allen Ginsberg by his contribution.   Between the Covers Rare Books   208 - 32 2016 $325

Barnum, H. L. *Enoch Crosby or the Spy Unmasked. a Tale of the American Revolution. (with) Book of Heroes....* Cincinnati: U. P. James, n.d., 1855. 24mo., black and white woodcuts, quarter cloth over paper covered boards, very good with wear to bottom corners of lightly soiled boards, contents clean and bright.   Kaaterskill Books   21 - 7 2016 $100

Barnum, Phineas Taylor 1810-1891 *Routledge's Barnum's Show.* London: George Routledge & sons..., 1889. First edition, 4to., 15 chromolithograph plate, including one double page, original glazed chromolithograph covers some small repairs.   Marlborough Rare Books   List 56 - 4   2016   £500

Baron and Feme. A Treatise of the Common Law Concerning Husbands and Wives. London: in the Savoy, printed by Eliz. Nutt and R. Gosling for John Walthoe, 1719. Second edition, 8vo., perforated stamp on titlepage with two holes just touching two letters, old perforated library stamps on two other text leaves, strongly bound in early 20th century in holland cloth with contrasting leather spine labels lettered gilt, Los Angeles Board of Law Library copy, in spite of minor defects noted, acceptable copy.   John Drury Rare Books   2015 - 25950   2016 $437

Baron, Peter *The Round Table Murders.* New York: Macaulay, 1931. First American edition, fine in fine dust jacket with very slight wear at extremities, superb copy. Between the Covers Rare Books   208 - 96   2016 $450

Barrett, Charles *The Bird man: a Sketch of the Life of John Gould.* Melbourne: Whitcombe and Tombs, 1938. Small octavo, illustrations, publisher's paper covered boards, some wear.   Andrew Isles Natural History Books   55 - 5260   2016 $50

Barrett, Charles *Parrots of Australasia.* Melbourne: N. H. Seward, 1949. Octavo, colored frontispiece by Neville Cylely, near fine in dust jacket with owner's signature. Andrew Isles Natural History Books   55 - 15578   2016 $100

Barrett, Geoff *The New Atlas of Australian Birds.* Hawthorn East: Birds Australia, 2003. Quarto, maps, illustrations, laminated boards.   Andrew Isles Natural History Books   55 - 19332   2016 $60

Barrie, James Matthew   1860-1937 *The Admirable Crichton.* London: Hodder & Stoughton, 1914. One of 500 copies, signed by artist, Hugh Thomson, edition deluxe, this copy being no. 94, illustrations by Thomson, with 20 mounted color plates, including frontispiece with descriptive tissue guards, black and white illustrations, original vellum over boards, front cover pictorially stamped and lettered gilt within double gilt rule and triple green rule border, spine decoratively stamped and lettered gilt, top edge gilt, others uncut, silk ties missing, color plate and mount opposite page 36 with vertical marginal crease, vellum slightly dust soiled, otherwise near fine, housed in gray cloth slipcase, laid in is Leicester Galleries exhibition otice for original drawings for the book.   David Brass Rare Books, Inc.   2015 - 02924   2016 $550

Barrie, James Matthew   1860-1937 *Auld Licht Idylls.* London: Hodder and Stoughton, 1888. First edition, 8vo., original bevel edged navy buckram, backstrip lettered gilt with very slight lean to spine, gentlest of rubbing to extremities, top edge gilt, others untrimmed, brown endpapers, very good, inscribed by author for W. C. Fisher.   Blackwell's Rare Books   B186 - 178   2016   £450

Barrie, James Matthew   1860-1937 *Charles Frohman.* London: privately printed by Clement Shorter, 1915. No. 12 of 20 copies, signed by Shorter, 4to., original grey printed wrappers, sewn as issued, very good.   Jarndyce Antiquarian Booksellers   CCXVII - 24   2016   £85

Barrie, James Matthew   1860-1937 *An Edinburgh Eleven.* Office of the British Weekly, 1889. First edition, 4 pages ads, half title, original grey-brow cloth, spine slightly darkened.   Jarndyce Antiquarian Booksellers   CCXVII - 25   2016   £30

Barrie, James Matthew   1860-1937 *Jane Annie or the Good Conduct Prize.* London: Chappell & Co., 1893. Paperback, original printed wrappers, very nice, uncommon, particularly in this condition, variant issue, housed in slipcase, bookplates of Lord Esher and Clark Hunter, very good.   The Kelmscott Bookshop   12 - 5   2016 $700

Barrie, James Matthew   1860-1937 *The Little White Bird.* London: Hodder and Stoughton, 1902. First edition, 8vo., frontispiece map, original navy buckram, backstrip lettered in gilt with gentlest of fading also showing at head of upper board, trifling spots of wear to a couple of corners and faint spotting to fore-edge, top edge gilt, faint partial browning to endpapers, very good.   Blackwell's Rare Books   B186 - 180   2016   £300

Barrie, James Matthew   1860-1937 *Margaret Ogilvy: by Her Son.* New York: Charles Scribner's Sons, 1897. First US edition, 8vo., very good, uncut, stamped tan boards, presentation on endpaper, stamped in gray and gilt.   Second Life Books, Inc.   197 - 21   2016 $45

Barrie, James Matthew   1860-1937 *Peter Pan in Kensington Gardens.* London: Hodder & Stoughton, 1906. True first edition, thick 4to., rust colored cloth stamped in gold, half title foxed, else near fine, 50 mounted color plates with tissue guards and black and white drawings on title and endpaper, by Arthur Rackham.   Aleph-bet Books, Inc.   112 - 409   2016 $2000

Barrie, James Matthew   1860-1937 *Peter Pan in Kensington Gardens.* London: Hodder & Stoughton, n.d., 1912. First edition of Rackham's enlarged edition, first issue with pictorial wrappers, Large 4to., green gilt pictorial cloth, fine in publisher's box and printed glassine wrapper with blindstamped design (dust jacket creased, box dusty with flaps repaired), illustrations by Arthur Rackham, with 50 mounted color plates with tissue guards, 7 full page black and whites, excellent copy, rare in box.   Aleph-bet Books, Inc.   111 - 378   2016 $4500

Barrie, James Matthew   1860-1937 *The Peter Pan Portfolio by Arthur Rackham.* London: Hodder & Stoughton, n.d., 1912. One of 500 numbered copies, signed by Publisher's and engravers/printers, out of a total edition of 600 copies, this being number 498, large quarto, engraved titlepage and limitation statement, 12 large proof size color plates mounted in mats with descriptive tissue guards, original half vellum over light sage green cloth boards, front over lettered gilt, silk ties and all tissue guards present, about fine in original printed publisher's box with restored side panels and missing a couple of small pieces. Heritage Book Shop   Holiday 2015 - 91   2016 $12,500

Barrie, James Matthew 1860-1937 *Peter Pan Portfolio from Peter Pan In Kensington Gardens.* New York: Brentano, 1914. Limited to 300 numbered copies for America, printed on high quality vellum like paper, 12 of the most magnificent large color plates by Arthur Rackham, mounted in mattes with lettered tissue guards, folio, yellow silk moire with tan cloth spine and corners, lacking ribbon ties on cover edges and very slight cover soil, else near fine, rare, great copy of beautiful book. Aleph-bet Books, Inc. 111 - 377 2016 $8000

Barrie, James Matthew 1860-1937 *Peter Pan and Wendy.* London: Hodder & Stoughton, n.d. circa, 1921. Thick 4to., blue cloth, slight fade spots on covers, else very good+, many black and white text illustrations, 12 beautiful tipped-in color plates by Mabel Lucy Attwell, this copy inscribed by artist with lovely full page watercolor, special copy, exceedingly scarce. Aleph-bet Books, Inc. 111 - 31 2016 $2750

Barrie, James Matthew 1860-1937 *Peter Pan and Wendy.* London: Hodder and Stoughton, 1929. Later edition, royal octavo, 12 mounted color plates and numerous black and white drawings by Mabel Lucie Attwell, original blue cloth, front cover bordered in blind, spine lettered gilt, top edge stained blue, pictorial endpapers, some light foxing, neat ink inscription dated 1929 on front pastedown, still very fine in original printed dust jacket with circular illustration pasted onto front panel and price in 10'6d on front flap. David Brass Rare Books, Inc. 2015 - 02944 2016 $375

Barrie, James Matthew 1860-1937 *Quality Street: a Comedy in Four Acts.* London: Hodder & Stoughton, 1903. Edition deluxe, 504/1000 copies, signed and numbered by artist, printed on handmade paper, frontispiece and 21 color printed plates, captioned tissue guards, decorative title border printed in green, several vignettes and 14 line drawings all by Hugh Thomson, prelims lightly foxed (as usual), and occasionally elsewhere, loosely inserted a flyer, printed in red for Leicester Galleries exhibition of original drawings (foxed), original cream vellum lettered and blocked in gilt to design by Thomson, vestiges of green ties, discreet ownership inscription on inside front cover, top edge gilt, others untrimmed, vellum slightly bowed, very good. Blackwell's Rare Books B186 - 345 2016 £300

Barrie, James Matthew 1860-1937 *Quality Street.* London: Hodder & Stoughton, 1913. First trade edition, large quarto, frontispiece and 21 mounted color plates by Hugh Thomson, with descriptive tissue guards, numerous black and white text illustrations, publisher's violet cloth over boards, front cover and spine pictorially stamped and lettered gilt and green, pictorial endpapers, light foxing on half title, ink signature on front free endpaper, fine in original cardboard box with duplicate of color plate facing page 3, pasted on top, box strengthened at corners. David Brass Rare Books, Inc. 2015 - 02984 2016 $450

Barrie, James Matthew 1860-1937 *Quality Street.* London: Hodder & Stoughton, 1913. Limited to 1000 numbered copies, this no. 268, signed by artist, large quarto, frontispiece and 21 mounted color plates by Hugh Thomson with descriptive tissue guards, numerous black and white text illustrations, original vellum over boards, front cover pictorially stamped and lettered in gilt with double gilt rule and triple purple rule border, spine pictorially stamped and lettered gilt, top edge gilt, others uncut, green silk ties renewed, fine. David Brass Rare Books, Inc. 2015 - 02982 2016 $750

Barrie, James Matthew 1860-1937 *Quality Street: a Comedy in Four Acts.* London: Hodder & Stoughton, 1913. First edition, one of 1000 numbered copies, 4to., 22 plates by Hugh Thomson, signed by artist, full vellum boards, stamped gilt, boards little warped, otherwise fine, includes announcement card for exhibition of original drawings by Thomson. Second Life Books, Inc. 196A - 81 2016 $450

Barrie, James Matthew 1860-1937 *Quality Street.* London: Hodder and Stoughton, n.d., 1913. First edition, large thick 4to., purple cloth with elaborate gilt pictorial cover and spine, as new in original box, mounted color plates and plain paper repair (repair to box flaps), 22 beautiful tipped in color plates with pictorial lettered guards plus line illustrations in text and pictorial endpapers, incredible copy in pristine condition. Aleph-bet Books, Inc. 111 - 449 2016 $600

Barrie, James Matthew 1860-1937 *When a Man's Single.* London: Hodder & Stoughton, 1888. First edition, 8vo., original bevel edged navy buckram, backstrip lettered gilt, trifling spot of wear at one corner and odd light graze, top edge gilt, others untrimmed, green endpapers, very good, inscribed by author for W. C. Fisher. Blackwell's Rare Books B186 - 179 2016 £450

Barrington, E. *The Exquisite Perdita.* New York: Dodd, Mead & Co., 1926. Limited to 250 copies, Presetation edition on special paper, extremely scarce presentation edition signed by publisher, Edward H. Dodd, fine, scarce thus, color portrait tipped in. Argonaut Book Shop Literature 2015 - 1203 2016 $100

Barrow, John *Travels into the Interior of Southern Africa.* London: printed for T. Cadell and W. Davies, in the Strand, 1806. Second edition, 4to., 2 volumes, contemporary tree calf, spines ruled in blind, contrasting letter pieces, 8 hand colored plates from original by Samuel Daniell, 9 folding maps and charts (some hand colored in outline), 20th century reback and restoration to corners some heavy embrowning to several maps and ad leaves due to colouring (as usual), two maps neatly repaired to folds, scattered light spotting, else very good. Sotheran's Travel and Exploration - 4 2016 £2750

Barry, Charles *Illustrations of the New Palace of Westminster...* London: Warrington & Son, 27 Strand, Simpkin Marshall & Co., 1849. First edition, 8 steel engraved plates, 8 tinted lithographic plates, several wood engravings in text, contemporary red calf, covers blocked in gilt, double fillet border enclosing four elaborate small cornerpieces, center with decorative cartouche surmounted by royal arms and lettered gilt, spine lettered gilt, spine restored.   Marlborough Rare Books   List 55 - 5   2016   £1850

Barry, Sebastian *A Tale with two Joes In It - a Play for Radio.* London: Bridgewater Press, 2010. First edition, one of 100 copies, this unnumbered, bound in Ratchford Atlantic cloth and printed on five Seasons paper, signed by author, total edition was 138 copies, fine.   Peter Ellis   112 - 28   2016   £75

Barry, Wiliam Whittaker *A Walking Tour in Normandy.* London: Richard Bentley, 1868. First edition, original blue cloth by Edmonds & Remnants, slightly dulled, bookplate of John Etherington Welch Rolls, esq., The Hendre Co. Monmoth, very good.   Jarndyce Antiquarian Booksellers   CCXVII - 26   2016   £75

Bartlett, George Bradford *Mrs. Jarley's Far-famed Collection of Waxworks Volume I.* London: Samuel French, 1889? 4 part, original sky blue pictorial cloth, blocked in red and gilt, bevelled boards, endpapers browned, all edges gilt, very good.   Jarndyce Antiquarian Booksellers   CCXVIII - 1073   2016   £50

Bartlett, William Henry 1809-1854 *Ports, Harbours and Watering Places of Great Britain.* London: Virtue, n.d., 1844. First edition, 2 volumes, quarto, frontispiece (some spotting), 142 plates, contemporary green morocco, gilt raised bands, 2 inch tear to front endpapers, slight rubbing to corners and boards.   J. & S. L. Bonham Antiquarian Booksellers   Europe 2016 - 10296   2016   £300

Bartlett, William Henry 1809-1854 *The Scenery and Antiquities of Ireland, Illustrated from Drawings.* London: Geo. Virtue, n.d., 1841. First edition, 2 volumes quarto, map, 119 steel engravings, some occasional marginal foxing, water staining to margin of few plates, contemporary green half morocco, boards little rubbed, nevertheless an attractive set.   J. & S. L. Bonham Antiquarian Booksellers   Europe 2016 - 10295   2016   £450

Barto, A. *Pesn O Stroike (Song of Construction).* Moscow: Ogiz, Maladai Gvardia (State Publishers), 1932. 8vo., pictorial wrappers, spine and edge mends, very good, printed on orange paper, full color illustrations.   Aleph-bet Books, Inc.   112 - 440   2016 $600

Barzun, Jacques *Romanticism and the Modern Ego.* Boston: Little Brown, 1943. First edition, 8vo., very good, tight, clean copy, inscribed by author to poet/editor Barbara Howes with her bookplate.   Second Life Books, Inc.   196A - 82   2016 $150

Bascombe, M. J. *The Butterflies of Hong Kong.* San Diego: Academic Press, 1999. Quarto, dust jacket, color photos, text illustrations.   Andrew Isles Natural History Books   55 - 12660   2016 $225

Bashford, Herbert *A Man Unafraid. the Story of John Charles Fremont.* San Francisco: Haft Wagner, 1927. First edition, tinted frontispiece, 19 plates, 2 tipped in color illustrations, green cloth, gilt, slight rubbing to edges and covers, light offsetting to front endpaper, very good.   Argonaut Book Shop   Biography 2015 - 6877   2016 $75

Bashford, Herbert *A Man Unafraid. The Story of John Charles Fremont.* San Francisco: Hart Wagner, 1927. First edition, tinted frontispiece, 19 plates, 2 tipped-in color illustrations, green cloth, gilt, minor dampstain at foot of spine, light offsetting to front endpaper, near fine, photos, prints, portraits, two color illustrations after paintings, signature on inner cover of Helen Weber Kennedy, direct descendant of Captain Weber.   Argonaut Book Shop   Biography 2015 - 5429   2016 $90

Basil I *Admonitoria ad Filium Suum Leonem Interprete Ioanne Paradis Beluaco...* Paris: Nicolai Buon, 1637. Rare printing, 12mo., parallel Greek and Latin text, woodcut initials, head and tailpieces, MS. note in old hand opposite titlepage, narrow margins, few occasional spots of foxing, otherwise very nice and bright, contemporary brown mottled calf, gilt spine with burgundy morocco label, edges red, marbled endpapers, joints only slightly cropped, corners worn, slight dent to very edge of upper board.   Unsworths Antiquarian Booksellers   30 - 13   2016   £1250

Baskin, Leonard *An ABC with Best Wishes for 1958: from Esther & Leonard Baskin.* Northampton: Gehenna Press, 1957. First edition, 28 leaves in black and red, 19 wood engravings and stereotypes, line 6 on titlepage omitted entirely, one of 500 copies printed, inscribed by Baskin, fine.   Second Life Books, Inc.   196A - 83   2016 $325

Baskin, Leonard *Ars Anatomica.* New York: Medicina Rara, Number 447 of 2800 copies, signed by artist, printed on specially made paper bearing the private watermarks of Medicina Rara, 13 illustrations, double elephant sized portfolio with title in gilt to spine and "Baskin" in gilt to front cover, minor foxing to some prints, printer's leaflet, fine.   The Kelmscott Bookshop 13 - 6   2016 $175

Bass, Charlotte A. *Forty Years: Memoirs from the Pages of a Newspaper.* Los Angeles: Charlotta A Bass, 1960. First edition, small octavo, maps and photos red cloth gilt, just about fine, issued without dust jacket, inscribed by author, below author's inscription is another inscription by unknown presentee to unknown recipient.   Between the Covers Rare Books   207 - 99   2016 $600

Bassett Hull, A. F. *A List of the Birds of Australia.* Sydney: author, 1909. Octavo, wrappers, recto printed and numbered only, addenda, errata and corrigenda slips bound in, scarce.   Andrew Isles Natural History Books   55 - 5282   2016 $60

Bateman, James *The Orchidaceae of Mexico and Guatemala.* New York: Johnson Reprint, 1973. Facsimile, limited 1000 numbered copies, folio, 40 color plates, publisher's green cloth, fine.   Andrew Isles Natural History Books   55 - 34278   2016 $500

Bateman, Robert *The Art of Robert Bateman.* New York: 1981. First edition, oblong folio, cloth with blindstamped lettering, illustrations by Roger Tory Peterson, fine in dust jacket.   Gene W. Baade, Books on the West   2015 - 9011008   2016 $66

Bates, Herbert Ernest   1905-1974 *Christmas 1930: a Poem.* privately printed, 1930. Issue on japon, with no printed salutation, 4 page leaflet, very slightly creased and dust soiled, otherwise nice, author's signature.   Bertram Rota Ltd.   Christmas List 2015 - 3   2016   £55

Bates, Herbert Ernest   1905-1974 *The Hessian Prisoner.* William Jackson Books ltd., 1930. First edition, limited to 550 copies signed by author, 8vo., original red buckram lettered gilt on spine and upper board, frontispiece by John Austen, spine slightly sunned, otherwise near fine, this copy inscribed by author for film director Bryan Forbes, with bookplate.   Sotheran's   Piccadilly Notes - Summer 2015 - 31   2016   £148

Bates, Herbert Ernest   1905-1974 *The Seekers.* John and Edward Bumpus, 1926. First edition, signed by author on half title, additionally inscribed by author to writer and actor, Bryan Forbes, with Forbes' bookplate, 8vo., original paper covered boards with glassine wrapper, little chipping and loss to glassine, otherwise very good.   Sotheran's Piccadilly Notes - Summer 2015 - 30   2016   £98

Bates, Joseph B. *The Art of the Atlantic Salmon Fly.* Boston: David R. Godine, 1987. First edition, 4to., original cloth and wrapper, 25 color plates, numerous other illustrations, wrapper little sunned to spine, internally fine.   Sotheran's   Hunting, Shooting & Fishing - 108   2016   £100

Bates, Lois *Kindergarten Guide.* London: Longmans Green, 1906. New impression, half title, frontispiece, plates and illustrations, original blue decorated cloth, spine dulled.   Jarndyce Antiquarian Books   CCXV - 526   2016   £25

Bath, William Pulteney, Earl of   1684-1764 *The Negotiators.* London: printed for R. Thompson, 1738. Folio, lacks frontispiece, disbound, dusted edges chipped not affecting text.   Jarndyce Antiquarian Booksellers   CCXVI - 484   2016   £45

Bath, William Pulteney, Earl of   1684-1764 *A State of the National Debt as it stood December the 24th, 1716.* London: R. Francklin, 1727. First edition, 4to., complete with half title, margins of appendix often cut rather clsoe occasioanlly shaving letters but not impairing sense, well bound in old style quarter calf gilt.   John Drury Rare Books   2015 - 8393   2016 $350

Batty, John *The Spirit and Influence of Chivalry.* London: Elliot Stock, 1890. First edition, half title, erratum leaf, slight paper browning, uncut in original olive green cloth, bevelled boards, little rubbed, lower corners slightly worn, 4 page ALS from Batty, 1891 tipped in opposite leading f.e.p., signatures of Richmond Battye 1894 and Ivan(?) Battye 1898.   Jarndyce Antiquarian Books   CCXV - 40   2016   £45

Batty, Robert *German Scenery from Drawings Made in 1820.* London: Rodwell & Martin, 1825. First edition, quarto, 61 steel engravings, vignette on titlepage, original purple decorative straight grained morocco, all edges gilt, joint rubbed, light foxing to prelims, very good.   J. & S. L. Bonham Antiquarian Booksellers   Europe 2016 - 8850   2016   £550

Batty, Robert *Hanoverian and Saxon Scenery from Drawings by Batty.* London: Robert Jennings, 1829. First edition, frontispiece (small tear in margin), vignette on titlepage, 60 steel engraved plates, original brown morocco binding, gilt decorations, raised bands, joints and corners rubbed.   J. & S. L. Bonham Antiquarian Booksellers   Europe 2016 - 8827   2016   £750

Batty, Robert *Scenery of the Rhine, Belgium and Holland.* London: Robert Jennings, 1826. First edition, handsome contemporary dark green half morocco over moss green straight grain buckram, wide raised bands decorated with plain and decorative gilt rules, spine lavishly gilt in compartments with leafy volute cornerpieces and large and intricate central ornament composed of lilies, leaves and small tools radiating from central circlet, marbled endpapers, all edges gilt, joints and morocco corners artfully renewed, with 62 excellent engraved scenic plates printed on china paper and mounted, engravings after drawings by Batty, descriptive text leaves printed in English and in French, spine just slightly sunned, titlepage and four other plates, somewhat foxed, mainly in margins, occasional minor foxing elsewhere, hint of offsetting from plates, otherwise quite fine, handsome binding solid and with bright gilt, text and plates generally very clean and fresh. Phillip J. Pirages 67 - 21 2016 $950

Batty, Robert *Scenery of the Rhine, Belgium and Holland.* London: Robert Jennings, 1826. First edition, quarto, frontispiece, vignette on titlepage, 60 steel engraved plates, some occasional light foxing in margins, original purple morocco, gilt decoration, raised bands, joints and corners rubbed, inner joint cracked. J. & S. L. Bonham Antiquarian Booksellers Europe 2016 - 8828 2016 £380

Baudelaire, Charles *Les Fleurs du Mal. (with) Theophile Gautier.* Paris: Poulet-Malassis, 1857-1859. First edition, first printing with the six suppressed poems, errors in headline on pages 31 and 108, page 45 incorrectly numbered 44, title printed in red and black, with half title; Theophile first edition, one of 500 copies and a few printed on Holland, with title printed in black and red, with half title, frontispiece, both titles bound together in contemporary quarter brown morocco over marbled boards, spine lettered and stamped in gilt, edges speckled brown, marbled endpapers, board edges with some light rubbing, some minor light foxing, mainly to prelims, old inscription in each work, (possibly in author's hand), overall very good. Heritage Book Shop Holiday 2015 - 6 2016 $20,000

Baum, Lyman Frank *Dorothy and the Wizard in Oz.* Chicago: Reilly & Britton, 1908. 4to., blue cloth, pictorial paste-on with gold background, spine stamped in black and silver, with all upper case imprint, ads through John Dough, slight edge and cover rubbing. Aleph-bet Books, Inc. 111 - 34 2016 $2500

Baum, Lyman Frank *Glinda of Oz.* Chicago: Reilly & Lee, 1920. First edition, first state (H-G XIV) with proper ads, 4to., tan cloth, pictorial paste-on, illustrations by J. R. Neill with 12 color plates plus many black and whites. Aleph-bet Books, Inc. 112 - 48 2016 $1250

Baum, Lyman Frank *The Marvelous Land of Oz.* Chicago: Reilly & Britton Co., 1904. First edition, second state with July 1904 copyright page, in the A binding but with second issue text, 16 full color plates inserted throughout, full red cloth, stamped in navy blue, green and silver on front cover, navy blue and green on spine and black on rear cover, front and rear hinges cracked but binding still tight, overall exceptionally clean and fine, housed in custom full black calf clamshell, red morocco label, gilt stamped on spine. Heritage Book Shop Holiday 2015 - 7 2016 $2000

Baum, Lyman Frank *The Marvelous Land of Oz.* Chicago: Reilly & Britton, 1904. First edition, First edition, first state in B binding with red cloth titled in dark blue on spine panel and in blue and silver on front cover, with decorative image of Genera Jinjur standing atop an emerald, first issue sheets, 4to., red pictorial cloth, 6 tiny margin mends, front hinge slightly rubbed but not weak, occasional margin soil and slight cover soil, else near fine, numerous full and partial page black and whites, 16 color plates on glossy stock by J. R. Neill, photo pictorial endpapers, beautiful copy, rare. Aleph-bet Books, Inc. 111 - 33 2016 $12,500

Baum, Lyman Frank *The Master Key. An Electrical Fairy Tale...* Indianapolis: Bowen-Merrill Co., 1901. First edition, third state, illustrations by F. Y. Cory, 12 inserted color plates (including frontispiece), 40 head and tailpieces, 8vo., green cloth with gilt lettering and pictorial pastedown on front board (first state binding), chemised and housed in custom green cloth slipcase with black leather spine labels, near fine, square and tight/bright cloth and gilt, faint discoloration in lower margin of first dozen leaves. Tavistock Books Bibliolatry - 34 2016 $600

Baum, Lyman Frank *Ozma of Oz.* Chicago: Reilly & Britton, 1907. First edition, first state with pictorial endpapers, pictorial rear cover, front ad listing only John Dough and Land of Oz, "O" in Ozma page (11) page 221 in color, many full page and smaller color illustrations, many full page black and whites, lovely copy, rare edition. Aleph-bet Books, Inc. 112 - 46 2016 $2500

Baum, Lyman Frank *Patchwork Girl of Oz.* Chicago: Reilly & Britton, 1913. First edition, first state (H/G VII), 4to., green pictorial cloth, very fine inside and out, illustrations by J. R. Neill, rare in this condition. Aleph-bet Books, Inc. 112 - 45 2016 $2750

Baum, Lyman Frank *The Road to Oz.* Chicago: Reilly & Britton, 1909. First edition, first state, 8vo., green pictorial cloth stamped in black, green, tan and red, fine, bright copy, inscription on ownership page, pictorial endpapers and a profusion of black and whites by J R. Neill. Aleph-bet Books, Inc. 112 - 47 2016 $3000

Baum, Lyman Frank *Wizard of Oz.* Akron: Saalfield, 1944. Wonderful animated edition, small 4to., spiral backed boards, fine in chipped dust jacket, fine moveable plates by Julian Wehr, illustrations throughout the text, scarce. Aleph-bet Books, Inc.   111 - 311   2016 $400

Baum, Lyman Frank *The Wonderful Wizard of Oz.* Chicago: George M. Hill, 1900. First edition, first state of text, large 8vo., pale green cloth stamped in red and green, hinges professionally strengthened, spine ends reinforced, some fading and few faint soil areas on covers, internally with small margin repair to 1 plate, otherwise clean, tight and very good+, wonderful color illustrations by W. W. Denslow.   Aleph-bet Books, Inc.   112 - 44   2016 $22,000

Bauwens, Emile *Livre de Cocktails.* Bruselles: Un coup de Des, 1949. First edition, limited to 2175 copies, 8vo., original printed wrappers, with 10 color plates and 25 caricature line drawings in text by Felix Labisse, front hinge neatly reinforced, otherwise very good, inscribed by author. Sotheran's   Piccadilly Notes - Summer 2015 - 32   2016   £998

Baxter, William *Glossarium Antiquitatum Britannicarum, Sive Syllabus...* London: impensis T. Woodward, C. Davis, J. Hazard, W. Bickerton & R. Chandler, 1773. Second edition, 8vo., frontispiece, woodcut head and last pieces and initials, few old repairs to titlepage, contemporary brown calf, red morocco gilt title label, relaid to spine, double fillet gilt border to boards, edges red, rebacked in slightly lighter shade, chips to label, edges worn, endpapers replaced, but no recently, second bookplate just visible beneath first, armorial bookplate of Frances Mary Richardson Currer. Unsworths Antiquarian Booksellers Ltd.   E01 - Early Printing - 1   2016   £140

Bay, J. Christian *The Pickwick Papers...* Chicago: Caxton Club, 1938. One of 250 copies, half title, plates, original maroon cloth, spine slightly faded and with small hole, without tissue wrapper, very good.   Jarndyce Antiquarian Booksellers   CCXVIII - 137   2016   £25

Bayard, Nicholas *An Account of the Commitment, Arraignment, Tryal and Condemnation of Nicholas Bayard, Esq. for High Treason...* London: printed at New York by order of his Excellency the Lord Cornbury and reprinted at London, 1703. First English and earliest obtainable edition, Modern calf backed marbled boards, very skillfully executed in period style, final leaf H2 supplied from another copy, little lightly browned, else very attractive.   Joseph J. Felcone, Inc.   Books from Five Centuries: a Miscellany - 15   2016 $4800

Bayley, Edric *The Borough Polytechnic Institute: Its Origin and Development.* London: Elliot Stock, 1910. 4to., half title, frontispiece and plates, original green buckram, library label at head of spine slightly dulled, stamps and label of Central Library, Brixton.   Jarndyce Antiquarian Books   CCXV - 527   2016   £110

Bayly, Nathaniel Thomas Haynes *Parliamentary Letters and other Poems.* London: printed for Baldwin, Cradock and Joy and Meyler and Son, Bath, 1818. First edition, scattered foxing, 8vo., original boards, rebacked, fragment of printed label retained, corners worn, still good. Blackwell's Rare Books   B184 - 10   2016   £400

Bazaar and National Exposition of Manufactures *Presented by the Council of the League to the Ladies Who Assisted at the Bazaar and National Exposition of Manufacturers Held in Covent Garden Theatre, London May 1845.* London: designed & printed by Petty & Ernest & Co., 1845. First edition, 4to., ornamental lithograph title, original decorated cloth the upper cover blocked in pattern of gilt and colors, slightly worn at extremities, stamp J. Aked, Bookbinder, Palgrave, London.   Marlborough Rare Books List 56 - 6   2016   £385

The Bazar Book of the Household Marriage Establishment, Children, Servants, Home Life, Housekeeping, Company. New York: Harper & Bros., 1875. Original green cloth, bevelled boards, front board marked and little scuffed, Guille-Alles library stamps, its label removed from front board, sound, booklabel of John Fuller.   Jarndyce Antiquarian Books   CCXV - 41   2016 £30

Beach, Sylvia *Exposition Walt Whitman du 20 Avril au 20 Juin 1926.* Paris: Shakespeare and Co., 1926. Original exhibition catalog, staple bound pamphlet, 12 pages, text in French.   Honey & Wax Booksellers   4 - 11   2016 $500

Beale, Charles Willing *The Secret of the Earth.* London: New York: F. Tennyson Neely, 1899. First edition, octavo, inserted frontispiece, original straw colored cloth, front and spine panels stamped in silver and black, beautiful copy, exceedingly scarce.   John W. Knott, Jr./L.W. Currey, Inc. Fall-Winter 2015 - 17620   2016 $2500

Beale, G. Courtenay *The Complete Husband, a Manual for Men.* London: Wales Pub. Co., 1941. Eleventh edition, half title, final ad leaf, original cream printed paper wrappers, slightly dusted, small indentations to front and back wrappers.   Jarndyce Antiquarian Books   CCXV - 42   2016 £25

Beales, Arthur Charles Frederick *Education Under Penalty: English Catholic Education from the Reformation to the Fall of James II 1547-1689.* London: University of London, The Athlone Press, 1963. First edition, half title, frontispiece, portrait and plates, original dark blue cloth, library stamps on title, signs of labels, removed from leading f.e.p.'s dated 1850.   Jarndyce Antiquarian Books   CCXV - 529   2016   £65

Beard, John Relly *Self Culture: a Practical Answer to the Question "What to learn? How to Learn? When to learn.* Manchester: John Heywood...., 1859. First edition, contemporary half dark blue calf, rubbed, good plus.   Jarndyce Antiquarian Books   CCXV - 530   2016   £38

Beard, Mark *The Utah Reader.* New York: Vincent FitzGerald, 1986. Limited to 40 numbered copies signed by artist, oblong 4to., blue green silk over boards, hand lettered title stamped in orange by Gerard Charriere, inserted in specially constructed black cloth clamshell box with paper spine label, 42 hand colored linocuts, 32 Japanese papers used in collage prints executed by Zahra Partovi, extensively hand colored by artist, offset lithography text printed on Arches paper by John Hutucheson.   Oak Knoll Books   27 - 16   2016 $5000

Beard, Mary R. *On Understanding Women.* New York: Longmans, Green, 1931. First edition, 8vo., very good, laid in is TLS about book from author to Mrs. Margaret Wadsworth Gensmer who is thanked by Beard in prefatory note for having 'volunteered to spend in the Congressional Library at Washington DC such leisure as they could command, helping with researches".   Second Life Books, Inc.   196A - 76   2016 $275

Beard, P. H. *Longing for Darkness - Kamanta's tales from Out of Africa.* New York: Harcourt Brace Jovanovich, 1975. First edition, 108 drawings, 160 photos, unmarked, fine in very good dust jacket, slightly curled dust jacket, some closed tears repaired.   Simon Finch   2015 - 10702   2016 $200

Beard, Peter *The Adventures and Misadventures of Peter Beard in Africa.* Boston: Bullfinch Press/Little Brown and Co., 1993. Numerous images by Beard, tight, near fine with remainder mark to bottom edge which also has couple of ink marks, tight very near fine. signed and inscribed by Beard to a museum curator with additional large embellishment of his inked hand and ink smudge as well. terrific copy, seldom signed.   Jeff Hirsch Books   Holiday List 2015 - 67   2016 $750

Bearden, Romare *Romare Bearden, Paintings and Projections.* Albany: State University of New York at Albany Art Gallery, 1968. First edition, 9 black and white plates and 1 photograph, square 8vo., pictorial paper wrappers, very good with faint soiling on wrappers.   Kaaterskill Books   21 - 30   2016 $400

Bearden, Romare *Romare Bearden: Rituals of the Obeah.* New York: Cordier & Ekstrom, 1984. First edition, oblong octavo, illustrations in color, stapled wrappers, fine exhibition catalog, inscribed by artist to Richard Long, with original mailing envelope hand addressed by Bearden.   Between the Covers Rare Books   207 - 12   2016 $1500

Bearden, Romare *Six Black Masters of American Art.* Garden City: Doubleday & Co./Zenith Books, 1972. Second edition?, hardcover issue, simultaneous issue, octavo, pictorial cloth, fine in near fine dust jacket with short tear and little rubbing, inscribed by Bearden for Richard Romie, very scarce signed.   Between the Covers Rare Books   202 - 7   2016 $1000

Beardsley, Alice *Turn-Around Book.* Indianapolis: Bobbs Merrill, 1914. green cloth, pictorial paste-on, slight spotting on blank endleaves, else fine with white lettering intact, printed on heavy coated paper on one side of page only, full page illustrations.   Aleph-bet Books, Inc.   112 - 341   2016 $450

Beardsley, Aubrey Vincent   1872-1898 *Fifty Drawings by Aubrey Beardsley selected from the collection owned by Mr. H. S. Nichols.* New York: Nichols, 1920. One of 500 copies signed by Nichols, 4to., top edge gilt, very good in chipped dust jacket.   Second Life Books, Inc.   196A - 88   2016 $500

Beardsley, Aubrey Vincent   1872-1898 *Nineteen Early Drawings...from the collection of Mr. Harold Hartley of Brook House, North Soke, S. Oxon.* privately printed, 1919. One of 150 copies, Small 4to., with 4 page brochure and 18 plates (plate 15 is missing), brochure and plates in gray portfolio with worn linen ties, very good.   Second Life Books, Inc.   196A - 89   2016 $450

Beardsley, Aubrey Vincent   1872-1898 *Sous la Colline. (Under the Hill).* Paris: H. Floury, Editeur, 1908. 1 of 1000 copies, First French edition, 13 illustrations and two portraits, all protected by tissue guards, modern black half calf with marbled paper over boards, foxing to frontispiece and last few pages, affecting last illustration, otherwise very good.   The Kelmscott Bookshop   12 - 6   2016 $275

Bearss, Edwin C. *History Basic Data. Redwood National park. Del Norte ad Humboldt Counties, California.* N.P.: Division of History, Office of Archaeology and Historic Preservation, US Dept. of Interior, 1969. First edition, 4to., 41 plates from photos and maps, facsimile illustrations, original pictorial stiff red wrappers, extremities faded, corners slightly bumped, overall fine.   Argonaut Book Shop Natural History   2015 - 7665   2016 $75

Beatitude Anthology. San Francisco: City Lights, 1960. First edition, 8vo., paper wrappers cover little yellowed, otherwise nice.   Second Life Books, Inc.   197 - 48   2016 $45

Beaton, Cecil *Air of glory.* His Majesty's Stationary Office, 1941. First edition, 4to., original cloth, black and white photos, previous owner's signature, little rubbing to wrapper with chips to head and foot of spine, very good.   Sotheran's   Piccadilly Notes - Summer 2015 - 38   2016   £200

Beatson, Alexander *Tracts Relative to the Island of St. Helena....* London: W. Bulmer and Co. for G. and W. Nicol and J. Booth, 1816. First and only edition, 4to. original boards with printed label on spine, aquatint frontispiece, 5 aquatint plates by Daniell after Davis and one engraved plan of the island by Girtin, most plates by tissue guard, some spotting to plates, as usual and occasionally to text, else very good in very good original binding slightly worn, 20th century bookplate of Cornelius Van Heyden De Lancey inside front cover.   Sotheran's   Travel and Exploration - 5   2016   £1795

Beattie, James   1735-1803 *An Essay on the Nature and Immutability of Truth; in Opposition to Sophistry and Scepticism.* Edinburgh: Kincaid & J. Bell, 1770. First edition, octavo, inscribed by author for David Steuart Erskine, 11th Earl of Buchan, beautifully preserved contemporary leather with gilt double lines inscribed on front and back panels, spine has five raised bands and title in gilt lettering on red field, second compartment, with Lord Cardrof's bookplate, ink signature, beautiful copy.   Athena Rare Books   List 15 - 1770   2016 $4500

Beattie, James   1735-1803 *The Minstrel; or the Progress of Genius with Some Other Poems.* London: printed for J. Mawman, 1801. 170 x 102mm., contemporary red straight grain morocco, covers with gilt ruled border, flat spine divided into panels by single gilt rule, gilt titling, turn-ins with decorative bead roll, marbled endpapers, all edges gilt, with pleasing fore-edge painting of the harbor and seaside town of Whitby, in excellent brown morocco pull-off case by Sangorksi & Sutcliffe for J. W. Robinson Co., 4 engravings, front pastedown with engraved bookplate of John Ashley Warre, spine slightly and uniformly sunned to a darker red, occasional spotting or staining, still quite decent copy, binding solid and lustrous, text smooth and fresh, painting very well preserved.   Phillip J. Pirages   67 - 147   2016 $800

Beattie, William *Switzerland: Illustrated in a Series of Views Taken on the spot...* London: Geo. Virtue, 1836. First edition, 2 volumes, quarto, 106 steel engravings, minimal marginal foxing to engravings, contemporary brown half calf, corners little rubbed, excellent set.   J. & S. L. Bonham Antiquarian Booksellers   Europe 2016 - 10297   2016   £350

Beattie, William *The Waldenses: or Protestant Valleys of Piedemont and Dauphiny and the Bar de la Roche...* London: Geo. Virtue, 1838. First edition, quarto, folding map, 70 plates, original dark green, small wear to head of spine, small nick to fore-edge, waterstaining in corner of first few pages.   J. & S. L. Bonham Antiquarian Booksellers   Europe 2016 - 9692   2016   £300

Beaumont, Albanis *Travels through the Rhaetian Alps in the Year MDCCLXXXVI from Italy to Germany, through the Tyrol.* London: C. Clarke, 1792. First edition, folio, 10 uncoloured sepia aquatint plates, contemporary half calf, marbled boards, spine rubbed with small loss to head, internally very good, crisp copy with clean plates.   J. & S. L. Bonham Antiquarian Booksellers   Europe 2016 - 8734   2016   £1650

Beaumont, William *Experiments and Observations on the Gastric Juice and the Physiology of Digestion.* Plattsburgh: printed by F. P. Allen, 1833. First edition, 3 woodcut illustrations, original tan paper covered boards, purple brown linen spine, rebacked retaining 95 per cent of the original spine but largely obscuring the original printed paper spine label, gathering 2L browned as always, usual scattered foxing, else very good, fragile book.   Joseph J. Felcone, Inc.   Books from Five Centuries: a Miscellany - 95   2016 $3000

The Beautes Architecturals De Londres. Paris: H. Mandeville, London: Ackerman & Co. and Read & Co., 1851. Oblong 4to, 35 superbly hand colored engraved plates, including hand colored engraved vignette title, each measuring 27 x 37cm, occasional spotting and one plate trimmed without affecting the images, modern green half green morocco, spines ruled in gilt.   Marlborough Rare Books   List 56 - 34   2016   £5500

Beaver, Herbert *Reports and Letters of 1836-1838.* Portland: Champong Press, 1959. First edition, one of 750 copies, frontispiece, green cloth, slightest of rubbing to head of spine, very fine.   Argonaut Book Shop   Native American 2015 - 7258   2016 $60

Beazley, Charles Raymond *Prince Henry the Navigator.* New York and London: Putnam, 1895. First edition, 8vo., original dark red half morocco over cloth covered boards, spine ornamented and lettered gilt, gilt stamped logo on front cover, only light marking to binding, internally, apart from ownership inscription to front flyleaf and even light toning, very good.   Sotheran's   Travel and Exploration - 448   2016   £98

Beazley, J. D. *The Development of Attic Black Figure.* Berkeley & Los Angeles: University of California Press, 1964. First edition reprinted, large 8vo., grey cloth, gilt lettered to spine, now fading, little shelfwear, very good, no dust jacket, ownership inscription of J. G. Hind.   Unsworths Antiquarian Booksellers Ltd.   E05 - 17   2016   £20

Becher, B. *Industrielandschafen. (Industrial Landscapes).* Munchen: Schirmer Mosel, 2002. Number 93 of only 100 copies, 180 duotone plates, fine, in close to near fine dust jacket with scratch to rear panel and housed in lightly soiled slipcase, chemise with original photo in fine condition, print signed by Bernd and Hilla Becher, also in fine condition.   Jeff Hirsch Books   Holiday List 2015 - 68   2016 $3000

Becke, Louis *Ridan the Devil and Other Stories.* London: T. Fisher Unwin, 1899. First edition, presentation copy inscribed by author for C. A. Wylde, May 10 1899, quite scarce thus, very good in original black cloth boards with gilt title to spine, light rubbing to boards, tips of corners exposed, minor wear to spine ends and hinges, light rubbing to boards, tips of corners exposed, minor wear to spine ends and hinges, slight cock to spine, light foxing to end-pages and few creased corners, else interior clean, very good.   The Kelmscott Bookshop   12 - 9   2016 $250

Becker, Anne *The Transmutation Notebooks: Poems in the Voices of Charles and Emma Darwin.* Washington: Forest Woods Media, 1996. First edition, paper wrappers, author's presentation to poet and editor William Claire, laid in is notecard inviting Claire to a party and flyer announcing poet's readings of her book with note handwritten to invite Claire to same party, fine.   Second Life Books, Inc.   196A - 92   2016 $40

Beckett, Samuel   1906-1989 *All Strange Away.* New York: Gotham Book Mart, 1976. Limited to 200 numbered copies, this copy inscribed by Beckett and signed by artist, 4to., illustrations by Edward Gorey, leather spine, marbled boards, fine in slipcase, laid in is note that explains this one of 5 copies inscribed by author for major Gorey collector.   Aleph-bet Books, Inc.   112 - 220   2016 $3000

Beckett, Samuel   1906-1989 *Come and Go. Dramaticule.* London: Calder & Boyars, 1967. One of 100 numbered copies, signed by author, illustrations, cloth, very fine in original glassine and publisher's slipcase.   Joseph J. Felcone, Inc.   Books from Five Centuries: a Miscellany - 16   2016 $1800

Beckett, Samuel   1906-1989 *Company.* Iowa City: Iowa Center for the Book at the University of Iowa, 1983. First edition thus, one of 52 press-numbered copies (total edition) signed by author and artist, folio, book printed by hand on dampened arches cover paper, folio, 13 full page original etchings by Dellas Henke, original quarter black morocco, black morocco fore-tips and paste paper over boards, speckled endpapers, publisher's slipcase, fine, rare.   James S. Jaffe Rare Books   Occasional List: Winter 2016 - 30   2016 $9500

Beckett, Samuel   1906-1989 *From an Abandoned Work.* London: Faber and Faber, 1958. First edition, fine in stapled wrappers as issued, beautiful copy.   Between the Covers Rare Books   204 - 10   2016 $200

Beckett, Samuel   1906-1989 *The Lost Ones.* London: Calder & Boyars, 1972. First edition in English, signed issue, limited to 100 numbered copies, specially bound, signed by author, 8vo., original quarter vellum and cloth, gilt border and lettering to upper, slipcase, little staining to front endpapers and some staining to slipcase, otherwise near fine.   Sotheran's   Piccadilly Notes - Summer 2015 - 42   2016   £798

Beckett, Samuel   1906-1989 *More Pricks and Kicks.* London: Calder & Boyars, 1970. No. 64 of 100 copies signed by author, 8vo., quarter vellum, orange cloth boards with gilt lettering to upper and spine, matching slipcase, all edges gilt, fine.   Sotheran's   Piccadilly Notes - Summer 2015 - 41   2016   £998

Beckett, Samuel   1906-1989 *More Pricks than Kicks.* London: Calder and Boyars,, 1970. New edition, octavo, slight bruise at head of spine, near fine in very good dust jacket little nicked at edges.   Peter Ellis   112 - 33   2016   £45

Beckett, Samuel   1906-1989 *No's Knife.* London: Calder and Boyars, 1967. First edition, one of 200 numbered copies signed by author, printed 'hors commerce' in advance of first trade edition, 8vo., original cream calf backed buckram boards lettered in gilt on spine and upper board, slipcase, near fine.   Sotheran's   Piccadilly Notes - Summer 2015 - 40   2016   £850

Beckett, Samuel   1906-1989 *Stirrings Still.* New York and London: Blue Moon Books and John Calder, 1988. One of 200 numbered copies of a total edition of 226 copies, signed by Becket and by artist, Louis Le Brocquy, folio, illustrations, including one original duotone lithograph, linen covered boards, vellum spine, as new in publisher's slipcase, beautiful in flawless condition.   Joseph J. Felcone, Inc.   Books from Five Centuries: a Miscellany - 17   2016 $3800

Beckett, Samuel   1906-1989 *The Theatrical Notebooks of Samuel Beckett: Waiting for Godot: Endgame: Krapps' Last Tape.* London: Faber and Faber, 1992-1993. First edition thus, royal 8vo., 3 volumes, (fourth volume of shorter plays was published in 1999), royal octavo, fine set in fine dust jacket, that of first volume being slightly creased at tail of spine, original plain card mailing slipcase.   Peter Ellis   112 - 34   2016   £450

Beckford, William   1760-1844 *Catalogue of the First (to the Fourth) Portion of the Beckford Library Removed from Hamilton Palace, (with) Catalogue of the Hamilton Library.* London: Sotheby, Wilkinson & Hodge, 1882. 1882. 1882, 1883. 1883. 1884, Complete set, 5 volumes bound in 1, thick tall 8vo., half vellum, green pebbled cloth, top edge gilt, first four parts completely priced in pen in margin with buyer's name written in pen in the opposite margin, some soiling to covers with crack along bottom of front hinge, library bookplate is only library marking.   Oak Knoll Books   310 - 56   2016 $800

Beckford, William   1760-1844 *Italy: with Sketches of Spain and Portugal.* London: Richard Bentley, 1834. Second edition, 2 volumes in 1, 8vo., recent brown half calf, good, clean copy.   J. & S. L. Bonham Antiquarian Booksellers   Europe 2016 - 9952   2016   £150

Beckford, William 1760-1844 *Vathek.* Philadelphia: Published by M. Carey, 1816. First American edition, from third London edition, 16mo., original printed paper covered boards, two contemporary or very early owner's names (from the same family), paper lacking from bottom half inch of spine, bound without pages 197-200 (S2), some modest overall rubbing on boards, some foxing to text, overall sound and tight very good.   Between the Covers Rare Books   208 - 112   2016 $2500

Beckford, William 1760-1844 *Vathek.* New York: Limited Editions Club, 1945. Limited to 1500 numbered copies, signed by artist/designer, 16 full page miniature illustrations by Valenti Angelo, heightened in gold by hand, hand set type, full rust morocco stamped in gilt with arabesque pattern, lacking slipcase, fine, clean copy.   Argonaut Book Shop   Literature 2015 - 7379   2016 $125

Beckman, William, Mrs. *Thought-Stitches from Life's Tapestry.* Backman, 1925. Frontispiece, author's presentation on flyleaf, sticker on pastedown, some penciled notes in text, very good.   Second Life Books, Inc.   196A - 94   2016 $75

Becquerel, Antoine Cesar *Des Forces Physico-Chimiques et des Leur Intervention dans la Production des Phenomenes Naturels.* Paris: Didot, 1875. First edition, 8vo., lacks atlas volume, spine sunned, some pages foxed and some pages foxed, very good, quarter calf over marbled boards, gilt spine with four raised bands.   Edwin V. Glaser Rare Books   2015 - 10143   2016 $100

Beddoes, Thomas 1760-1808 *Ueber die Uraschen Fruhen Zeichen und Verhuntung der Lugensucht.* Halberstadt: Im Bureau fur Literatur und Kunst, 1802. 8vo., some browning and spotting (as might be expected), larger stain affecting 3 leaves, 8vo., contemporary marbled boards, little worn at extremities, good.   Blackwell's Rare Books   B186 - 14   2016   £500

Beddow, Mrs. *Use Them; or Gathered Fragments: Missionary Hints and Anecdotes for the Young.* London: Hamilton Adams & Co., 1842. Second edition, 12mo., original brown cloth, contemporary inscription of Elizabeth Peckhove, very good.   Jarndyce Antiquarian Books   CCXV - 531   2016   £50

Bedford, William Riland *The Midland Forester. By a Woodman of Arden.* Birmingham: printed and published by R. Wrightson Athenaeum 8 New Street, 1829. First edition, 12mo., contemporary ownership signature (Mendham) in upper margin of title, bound recently in cloth with printed title label on upper cover, very good, apparently of great rarity.   John Drury Rare Books   2015 - 26076   2016 $437

The Bee, Fire-Side companion with Evening Tales.... (with) The working Bee or Caterer for the Hive. Liverpool: printed at the Caxton Press for Henry Fisher, 1820. 1822. Volumes I and III (of three), frontispiece to both volumes, 24 nos. in 1527 and 1536 columns respectively, contemporary tree calf, slightly rubbed.   Jarndyce Antiquarian Booksellers   CCXVII - 218   2016   £125

Beebe, Lucius *A Bibliography of Edwin Arlington Robinson.* Cambridge: Dunster House Bookshop, 1931. First edition, number 42 of 250 numbered copies, signed by Robinson, octavo, original marbled paper boards and printed paper label, boards little worn, very good.   The Brick Row Book Shop   Miscellany 69 - 70   2016 $150

Beecher, Henry Ward *Norwood: Village Life in New England.* London: Sampson Low, Son and Marston, 1867. First edition, preceding the American edition, 3 volumes, octavo, contemporary maroon quarter calf, marbled sides, leather labels, gilt decorations and lettering, edges little rubbed, some foxing, very good.   The Brick Row Book Shop   Miscellany 69 - 10   2016 $600

Beecher, Henry Ward *Universal Suffrage and Complete Equality in Citizenship, the Safeguards of Democratic Institutions...* Boston: Press of Geo. C. Rand & Avery, 1865. First edition, 8vo., self wrappers, about very good, front wrapper soiled and nearly detached, small dampstain on bottom edge of few leaves.   Kaaterskill Books   21 - 8   2016 $150

Beeching, R. *Electron Diffraction Methuen's Monographs on Chemical Subjects.* London: Methuen & Co. Ltd., 1936. First edition, small 12mo., frontispiece, numerous illustrations in text, publisher's brown cloth covers black lettering and freeze around edges on front and spine, dust jacket, name and address written on f.e.p., bright, attractive copy, fine in very good+ dust jacket.   Simon Finch   2015 - 25368   2016 $280

Beedome, Thomas *Select Poems: Divine and Humane.* Bloomsbury: Nonesuch Press, 1928. Limited edition of 1250 numbered copies, 12mo., original gilt lettered white vellum, very fine, lightly worn slipcase.   Argonaut Book Shop   Literature 2015 - 1224   2016 $150

Beekman, E. M. *Carnal Lent. Poems.* North Hatfield: Pennyroyal Press, 1975. 93/200 copies, printed in black and red on Mohwawk Superfine paper and signed by author and artist, wood engraved portrait of Barry Moser, small 4to., original black cloth, gilt lettered maroon leather backstrip label, fine.   Blackwell's Rare Books   B184 - 298   2016   £150

Beekman, E. M. *Lame Duck a Novel.* Boston: Houghton Mifflin, 1971. First edition, 8vo., fine in slightly worn dust jacket, inscribed by author to poet William Jay Smith, signed again on titlepage.   Second Life Books, Inc.   196A - 95   2016 $45

Beerbohm, Julius *Wanderings in Patagonia; or Life Among the Ostrich-Hunters.* London: Chatto & Windus, 1881. First edition, 8vo., frontispiece, text illustrations, original red decorative cloth, library stamp on titlepage, otherwise very clean. J. & S. L. Bonham Antiquarian Booksellers America 2016 - 9907 2016 £75

Beerbohm, Max 1872-1956 *A Book of Caricatures.* London: Methuen, 1907. Folio, 49 caricature subjects, each protected by tissue guard, bound in original red cloth backed red cloth boards, printed paper label on front cover and gilt title and author to spine, spine has few splits, boards faded and rubbed, bumping to corners, foxing to endpapers, plates clean, very good. The Kelmscott Bookshop 12 - 10 2016 $500

Beerbohm, Max 1872-1956 *Fifty Caricatures.* 1913. First edition, small 4to., spine and top edge of upper cover just little faded, otherwise very nice, previous owner's inscription on front endpaper. Bertram Rota Ltd. Christmas List 2015 - 4 2016 £150

Beerbohm, Max 1872-1956 *Zuleika Dobson.* London: William Heinemann, 1911. First edition, half title and title printed in brown, some spotting, crown 8vo., original mid brown cloth, backstrip gilt lettered and decorated, front cover decorated overall in blind, front hinge just trifle cracked, bookplates (one covering older monogram plate), some light discoloration to boards near fore-edge, good copy. Blackwell's Rare Books Marks of Genius - 8 2016 £150

Beerbohm, Max 1872-1956 *Zuleika Dobson.* London: William Heinemann, 1911. First edition, original reddish brown cloth with light bumping and soiling, some spotting to fore-edges and very occasional light foxing to text pages, but very good in very good dust jacket (front cover is clearly detached, and small chips and tears along top edges, otherwise very good), rare in jacket. The Kelmscott Bookshop 12 - 12 2016 $6000

Beerbohm, Max 1872-1956 *Zuleika Dobson.* Oxford: Shakespeare Head Press, 1975. 185/750 copies, signed by artist, printed in black and cerise, 12 double page spread color plates and reproductions of 5 pencil sketches of Beerbohm, folio, original quarter Oxford blue morocco with vertical gilt rule, blue and white 'Bullingdon' vertical stripe boards, backstrip lettered in gilt with Lancaster illustration the same, top edge gilt, blue page marker, mottled grey endpapers, glassine wrapper browned around backstrip with portions of loss, slipcase, near fine. Blackwell's Rare Books Marks of Genius - 9 2016 £250

Beethoven, Ludwig Van *Ludwig Van Beethoven's Werke.* Leipzig: Breitkopf und Hartel, n.d. circa, 1850's, 4to., contemporary red calf with marbled paper covered boards, all edges gilt, from the reference library of Zaehnsdorf Co. with commemorative booklabel loosely inserted, with their bookplate, wear along hinges. Oak Knoll Books 310 - 276 2016 $300

Beeton, Isabella Mary *How to Manage House and Servants.* London: Ward, Lock & Tyler, circa, 1867. Half title, illustrations, 10 pages ads, ads on endpapers, original yellow printed cloth wrappers, very good. Jarndyce Antiquarian Books CCXV - 43 2016 £240

Beeton, Isabella Mary *Mrs. Beeton's Household Management.* London: Ward, Lock & Co., circa, 1930. New edition, half title, color frontispiece, plates, 16 pages ads, ads on endpapers, original grey brown cloth spine, red cloth boards, slightly rubbed, very good. Jarndyce Antiquarian Booksellers CCXVII - 28 2016 £120

Beeton, Isabella Mary *Mrs. Beeton's Household Management: a complete cookery book.* London: Ward Lock & Co., circa, 1939. New edition, half title, color frontispiece and plates, 8 pages ads, half title slightly creased, original half red embossed cloth, slight rubbing, very good. Jarndyce Antiquarian Books CCXV - 44 2016 £125

Beeton, Samuel Orchart *Family Etiquette.* London: Ward, Lock & Tyler, 1876. 16 page catalog, illustrations, slight paper browning, original brown cloth blocked in black, slightly marked. Jarndyce Antiquarian Books CCXV - 45 2016 £85

Behrman, S. N. *No Time for comedy: a Play in Three Acts.* London: Hamish Hamilton, 1939. First edition, 8vo., original worn printed wrappers, (also issued in cloth), round-robin copy, signed by members of the London production, Diane Wyngard, Rex Harrison, Lilian Palmer, Elizabeth Welch and 3 others. Second Life Books, Inc. 196A - 97 2016 $250

Bein, Albert *Let Freedom Ring.* New York: French, 1936. First edition, 8vo., photos, author's presentation, very good in little worn dust jacket. Second Life Books, Inc. 196A - 98 2016 $45

Beklemishev, W. N. *Principles of Comparative Anatomy of Invertebrates.* Edinburgh: Oliver and Boyd, 1969. Octavo, 2 volumes, 1019 pages, text illustrations, signature, very good. Andrew Isles Natural History Books 55 - 38923 2016 $200

Belardinelli, Dina Bucciarelli *Sillabario E Piccole Letture.* Libreria Della State, 1930. 8vo., cloth backed stiff pictorial wrapper, covers dusty, else very good+, color illustrations by A. Della Torre, illustrations. Aleph-bet Books, Inc. 111 - 366 2016 $900

Belcher's Farmers' Almanack for the year of Our Lord 1867. Halifax: C. H. Belcher, 1867. 8vo., brown pressed cloth with gilt to front cover, small vignette on titlepage and illustrated ads to beginning and ending pages, inner hinge cracks, else very good, blank pages have contemporary black pen notes. Schooner Books Ltd. 115 - 122 2016 $75

Belknap, Jeremy *The Forestry: an American Tale.* Boston: I. Thomas and E. T. Andrews, 1792. First edition, duodecimo, modern calf period style, red leather label, gilt rules and lettering, engraved frontispiece, some slight foxing and stains, few minor tears in margins, very good.   The Brick Row Book Shop   Miscellany 69 - 11   2016 $950

Bell, Arthur G. *Nuremberg: Painted by Arthur G. Bell.* London: A. & C. Black, 1905. First edition, 8vo., top edge gilt, original blue decorative cloth.   J. & S. L. Bonham Antiquarian Booksellers   Europe 2016 - 6261   2016   £45

Bell, Jacob *Historical Sketch of the Progress of Pharmacy in Great Britain.* London: Pharmaceutical Society of Great Britain, 1880. First edition, 8vo., original decorated cloth, binding dull, very good.   Edwin V. Glaser Rare Books   2015 - 10193   2016 $95

Bell, Quentin *An Introductory History of England in the 18th Century...* Charlbury: Senecio Press, 2013. First edition, 36/500 copies, illustrations, imperial 4to.., original quarter brown leather with green patterned boards in facsimile of original binding, introduction by Julian Bell laid in at front on folded sheet with limitation number, slipcase, printed label to front, fine.   Blackwell's Rare Books   B184 - 313   2016   £195

Bell, Thomas *The Thomas Bell Library, The Catalogue of 15,000 Volumes of Scarce & Curious Printed Books and Unique Manuscripts...* Newcastle: J. G. Foster, 1860. Rebound with covers to blue cloth with black and gilt spine label, original wrappers bound in, some bumping and fading, browning wrapper cover and browning to untrimmed edges and to some page margins, not affecting text, very good. The Kelmscott Bookshop   13 - 7   2016 $250

Bell, W. D. M. *The Wanderings of an Elephant Hunter.* Long Beach: Safari Press, 2002. First Select Press edition, 4to., original black cloth with wrapper, 188 black and white plates, fine.   Sotheran's   Hunting, Shooting & Fishing - 3   2016   £130

Bell, William Gardner *Will James. The Life and Works of a Lone Cowboy.* Flagstaff: Northland Press, 1987. First edition, color frontispiece, 13 color plates, 68 reproductions, numerous photos, brown cloth lettered gilt, very fine with pictorial dust jacket.   Argonaut Book Shop   Biography 2015 - 6845   2016 $150

Bellamy, Edward *Looking Backward 2000-1887.* Boston: Houghton Mifflin, 1926. 8vo., very good in publisher's cloth, stain at hinge of rear endpaper, inscribed by author's wife, Emma for Walter James Henry, also inscribed by Bellamy's daughter, Marian Bellamy Ernshaw, liad in 9 x 6 inch handbill advertising talk given by Marian and Emma Bellamy. Second Life Books, Inc.   196A - 103   2016 $300

Bellamy, Edward *Looking Backward.* New York: Limited Editions Club, 1941. First edition, 1/1500 copies, large 8vo., yellow cloth with red design, illustrations by Elise, cover little soiled, otherwise very nice.   Second Life Books, Inc.   196A - 102   2016 $75

La Belle Ali Bois Dormant et Quelques Autres Contes de Jadis. Paris: Piazza & Cie, 1910. First edition in French, 303 x 230mm, no. 258 of 400 copies on Japon signed by Durvand (stamp signed), covers with triple gilt fillet border enclosing an elaborate gilt frame with cupids at corners and fancy gilt title lettering at center, flat spine with gilt decoration and lettering, gilt ruled turn-ins, marbled endleaves, top edge gilt, original wrappers bound in; with head and tailpieces, border designs for text and chapter pages, four decorative initials, two small medallions, 30 color plates by Edmund Dulac, mounted within decorative frames captioned in French, each with tissue guard, thin two inch crack at bottom of front joint, trivial marks and soiling to covers, faint residue from leather dressing, spine evenly sunned, otherwise excellent copy with bright gilt and text plates and tissue guards in pristine condition.   Phillip J. Pirages   67 - 119   2016 $1600

Bellegarde, Jean Baptiste Morvan De *Reflexions Upon Ridicule or What It Is That Makes a Man Ridiculous and the Means to Avoid It. (with) Reflexions Upon the Politeness of Manners, with Maxims of Civil Society...* London: printed for Tho. Newborough, 1707. 8vo., bound in two volumes, contemporary panelled calf, slightly later gilt volume numbers, boards slightly marked with head of spine, volume I slightly rubbed, armorial bookplate of Farquharson of Invercald, very good, first volume with slight paper damage to initial blank.   Jarndyce Antiquarian Books   CCXV - 46   2016   £450

Bellingham, Leo *Oxford: the Novel.* Nold Jonson Books, 1981. First edition, 8vo., original black boards, backstrip lettered gilt, faint foxing to top edge, ownership inscription, dust jacket slightly toned, owner's shelfmark at head of front flap, very good.   Blackwell's Rare Books   B184 - 205   2016   £50

Belloc Lowndes, Marie *Lizzie Border: a Study in Conjecture.* New York: Longmans, Green, 1939. First edition, inscribed by author to actor/writer Ruth Gordon, with bookplate signed by Gordon and husband Garson Kanin, included is TLS by author to Gordon, very good plus in very good dust jacket, jacket spine lightly faded, chipping to edges and light creasing, letter with horizontal fold, near fine overall.   Royal Books   52 - 9   2016 $2500

Bellow, Saul *The Bellarosa Connection.* New York: Penguin Books, 1989. Very near fine copy in wrappers, signed by author, uncommon thus.   Jeff Hirsch Books   Holiday List 2015 - 21   2016 $150

Bellow, Saul *Herzog.* New York: Viking Press, 1964. Near fine in close to near fine dust jacket that has small closed gouge at gutter of front panel and some other minor edgewear and tears, signed by author. Jeff Hirsch Books Holiday List 2015 - 20 2016 $300

Bellow, Saul *Nobel Lecture.* New York: Targ Edition, First edition, limited to 350 copies signed by author, book has been water damaged and covers warped and swelled, pages clean but some wrinkled. Second Life Books, Inc. 196A - 104 2016 $100

Beloved Belindy. Joliet: Volland, 1926. 17th printing, 8vo., pictorial boards, fine in pictorial box, bright color illustrations by Johnny Gruelle, scarce. Aleph-bet Books, Inc. 112 - 63 2016 $750

Belvediere Telephone Company *Belvidere Telephone Company January 1922. Telephone Directory, Belvidere, Illinois.* Belvidere: Belvidere Telephone Co., 1922. First edition, 8vo., lacking stapled paper wrappers, edgeworn, hole punched in top left margin, rust marks at staples, small tear at fore edge throughout, one or two pencil entries. Kaaterskill Books 21 - 33 2016 $200

Bemelmans, Ludwig *The Happy Place.* Boston: Little Brown, 1952. Stated first edition, green cloth, fine in near fine dust jacket, illustrations in full color by author. Aleph-bet Books, Inc. 112 - 52 2016 $225

Bemelmans, Ludwig *Madeline.* London: Derek Verschoyle, n.d., 1952. First edition, first issue, large 4to., pictorial boards, fine in fine dust jacket, not price clipped, wonderful color lithographs on every page. Aleph-bet Books, Inc. 112 - 53 2016 $600

Bemelmans, Ludwig *Madeline: Story and Pictures by....* London: Derek Veraschoyle, 1952. First US edition, first impression with publisher's address matching on copyright page, inscribed by author with drawing to Brianne Rhods, 1952, illustrated paper boards, matching dust jacket with price still intact, tips lightly rubbed, jacket with light wear along extremities, custom beige cloth slipcase, overall very good, very scarce with original signed drawing. Heritage Book Shop Holiday 2015 - 8 2016 $5000

Bemelmans, Ludwig *A Tale of Two Glimps.* New York: Columbia Broadcasting System, 1946. Oblong 4to., pictorial boards, slight toning of covers and slight wear to spine ends, else near fine with original plain paper dust jacket, laid in is CBS card describing the book, scarce with jacket. Aleph-bet Books, Inc. 111 - 43 2016 $800

Ben-Gurion, David *Israel. A Personal History.* New York: Tel Aviv: Funk & Wagnalls/Sabra Books, 1971. First edition, small 4to., fine, original slipcase with mild soil edge wear, slipcase indicates the volume was presented to participants in the United Jewish Appeal 1972 study Conference, presentation for Mr. and Mrs. Donald Hurwitz. By the Book, L. C. 45 - 2 2016 $1600

Benchley, Nathaniel *Catch a Falling Spy.* New York: McGraw Hill, 1963. Third printing, 8vo., very good in wrinkled and worn dust jacket, inscribed by author, probably to poet William Jay Smith. Second Life Books, Inc. 196A - 105 2016 $125

Benedict, Pierce E. *History of Beverly Hills.* Beverly Hills: A. W. Crowston-H.M. Meier, 1934. First edition, one of 125 copies, quarto, 34 plates of views and portraits, publisher's maroon pebble grain cloth, elaborately tooled in blind, front cover and spine lettered gilt, board and spine edges bit rubbed, otherwise near fine. Heritage Book Shop Holiday 2015 - 9 2016 $1000

Benet, Stephen Vincent 1898-1943 *Nightmare at Noon.* New York: Farrar & Rinehart, 1940. First edition, 12mo., bound in gray wrappers, light wear, fine, scarce. Argonaut Book Shop Literature 2015 - 1204 2016 $40

Benjamin, John *Antiquarian Prejudice.* London: Hogarth Press, 1939. First edition, one of 3000 copies, 12mo., original orange sewn wrappers printed in black, near fine. Blackwell's Rare Books B184 - 109 2016 £65

Benjamin, Tritobia Hayes *The Life and Art of Lois Mailou Jones.* San Francisco: Pomegranate ArtBooks, 1994. First edition, hardcover, signed and inscribed by Jones Oct. 7 1995, 130 full color reproductions, very good in purple cloth boards with silver title to spine and front cover, small indent/scuff mark to front cover, small blue marking to fore-edge of text block (not a remainder mark), slight scent of moth balls, in very good black illustrated dust jacket with yellow title to spine and front panels, corresponding indent/scuff mark to front panel of jacket, minor wear to jacket including rubbing to covers, short closed tear along top edge of rear panel, minor wear to edges and small chip to edge of rear flap, large quarto, very good in like dust jacket. The Kelmscott Bookshop 13 - 8 2016 $475

Benn, Robin *Poets in Battledress - a Book of War-time verse.* London: Fortune Press, 1942. First edition, octavo, buckram covers, very good in near fine dust jacket. Peter Ellis 112 - 457 2016 £35

Bennett, Arnold 1867-1931 *Mediterranean Scenes: Rome-Greece-Constantinople.* London: Cassell, 1928. Number 789 of 1000 copies, large 8vo., 40 illustrations, original cloth, covers faded and flecked. J. & S. L. Bonham Antiquarian Booksellers Europe 2016 - 2683 2016 £45

Bennett, Arnold 1867-1931 *The Old Wives' Tale.* London: Chapman & Hall, 1908. First edition, presentation copy, blinstamp to title and following leaf, few spots at beginning, 8vo., original dark rose cloth lettered white on upper cover, spine faded and white lettering gone, Dennis Wheatley's copy with his bookplate, modern bookplate opposite, sound.   Blackwell's Rare Books   B184 - 108   2016   £375

Bennett, Enoch Arnold *A Man from the North.* London: John Lane, Bodley Head, 1898. First edition, half title, 12 page catalog (1897), endpaper neatly replaced, original red cloth, blocked and lettered in white, slight rubbing and marking.   Jarndyce Antiquarian Booksellers   CCXVII - 29   2016   £450

Bennett, George *Gatherings of a Naturalist in Australasia.* London: 1860. Octavo, 8 hand colored lithographs by George French Angas, publisher's blindstamped purple cloth, some fading and blemishes, hinges cracked, front paste down damaged, sound copy.   Andrew Isles Natural History Books   55 - 38810   2016 $850

Bennett, George *Wanderings in New South Wales, Batavia Pedir Coast, Signaproe and China.* London: Richard Bentley, 1834. Octavo, 2 volumes, uncolored frontispieces, attractive early binder's cloth, few spots, otherwise bright pleasant copy.   Andrew Isles Natural History Books   55 - 5337   2016 $400

Bennett, Horace W. *Bright Yellow Gold.* Philadelphia: John C. Winston Co., 1935. First edition, signed by author, 3 color plates, blue cloth, gilt, spine lettering flecked, else near fine.   Argonaut Book Shop   Literature 2015 - 6319   2016 $45

Benson, A. C. *The Book of the Queen's Dolls' House.* London: Methuen & Co., 1924. Limited to 1500 numbered copies, 2 volumes, 4to., quarter cloth, paper covered boards, labels on spine of both volumes, top edge cut, other edges uncut, slipcase, color frontispiece, 92 plates, 24 in color in first volume, 24 plates, six in color in second volume, slipcase worn at edges and corners, boards scuffed at edges, bumped at corners, inside hinges of second volume cracked.   Oak Knoll Books   310 - 205   2016 $550

Benson, A. C. *Fasti Etonenses.* Eton: R. Ingalton Drake, London: Simpkin Marshall, 1899. First edition, half title, frontispiece, plates, partially uncut in original light blue cloth, little rubbed and dulled, top edge gilt.   Jarndyce Antiquarian Books   CCXV - 674   2016   £38

Benson, E. F. *The Angel of Pain.* London: Heinemann, 1906. First edition, owner name, some foxing to fore edge and scattered throughout text, top corners bumped and little soiling to boards, attractive, very good, lacking rare dust jacket.   Between the Covers Rare Books   208 - 114   2016 $450

Benson, Stella *The Man who Missed the Bus.* London: Elkin Mathews & Marrot, 1928. First edition, 1/530 numbered and signed copies, 8vo., tan paper over boards printed in blue, nice in dust jacket.   Second Life Books, Inc.   196A - 108   2016 $65

Bent, Silas *An Address Delivered Before the St. Louis Mercantile Library Association Jan. 8th 1872 Upon the Thermal Paths to the Pole, The Currents of the Ocean and the Influence of the Latter Upon the Climate of the World.* St. Louis: H. P. Shelley Co., 1872. First edition, folding colored plates, original flexible cloth.   M & S Rare Books, Inc.   99 - 256   2016 $250

Bentham, Jeremy 1748-1832 *The Book of Fallacies from Unfinished Papers of Jeremy Bentham.* John and H. L. Hunt, 1824. First edition, contemporary black morocco, gilt foliate borders to sides, gilt lettering and tools to spine, all edges gilt, bookplate of Frank Vanderlip, American banker, another previous owner's signature on titlepage.   Sotheran's   Piccadilly Notes - Summer 2015 - 44   2016   £550

Bentley, E. C. *Trent's Last Case.* Nelson, 1913. Blue cloth, upper case ruled, blocked & lettered in blind, spine lettered gilt, slightly rubbed binding & corners slightly bumped, internally near fine.   I. D. Edrich   Crime - 2016   £85

Bentley, George *Mr. Dickens and Mr. Bentley.* London: 1871. With relevant news clippings loosely inerted, unbound, some minor dusting, scarce.   Jarndyce Antiquarian Booksellers   CCXVIII - 1075   2016   £125

Bentley, John *Mr. Marlow Stops for Brandy.* Boston: Houghton Mifflin, 1940. First American edition, near fine.   Mordida Books   2015 - 010625   2016 $65

Bentley, Nicolas *The Dickens Index.* London: Oxford University Press, 1988. First edition, half title, original dark blue cloth, review copy slip loosely inserted, very good in dust jacket.   Jarndyce Antiquarian Booksellers   CCXVIII - 1076   2016   £20

Bentley's Miscellany. London: Richard Bentley, 1837. First two monthly parts, Jan. 1837 and Feb. 1837, original light brown printed wrappers, spine partially defective, edges and corners little birlle and slightly chipped.   Jarndyce Antiquarian Booksellers   CCXVIII - 766   2016   £85

Bentley's Miscellany. Volumes I-VI. London: Richard Bentley, 1837-1839. Frontsipiece, plates, contemporary half tan calf, marbled boards, lacking spine strips but sound, armorial bookplate of James O'Byrne, decent working copy.   Jarndyce Antiquarian Booksellers   CCXVIII - 765   2016   £350

Bentley's Miscellany Volumes I-IX. London: Richard Bentley, 1837-1841. Frontispieces, plates, contemporary half calf, spines gilt in compartment, black leather labels, marbled boards, hinges and corners little rubbed, signature of Kathleen Tillotson.   Jarndyce Antiquarian Booksellers   CCXVIII - 764   2016   £850

Bentley's Miscellany. Volumes I-IX. London: Richard Bentley, 1837-1841. Volumes I-IX, frontispiece and plates, contemporary half calf, spines gilt in compartments, , black leather labels, marbled boards, hinges and corners little rubbed, signature of Kathleen Tillotson.   Jarndyce Antiquarian Booksellers   CCXVIII - 764   2016   £850

Benyamin, Zvi   *Ha Kepah Hakachla. (Little Blue Riding Hood).* Tel Aviv: B. Barlevi, 1945. Oblong 8vo., pictorial wrappers, some light cover soil, very good+, rare.   Alephbet Books, Inc.   112 - 517   2016 $4250

Bercovitch, Sacvan   *The Puritan Origins of the American Self.* New Haven: Yale, 1975. 8vo., errata slip laid in, author's presentation on flyleaf, very good, tight copy, little chipped and scuffed dust jacket.   Second Life Books, Inc.   196A - 109   2016 $50

Berend, Charlotte   *Anita Berber: acht originallithographieen. (Eight Lithographs of Anita Berber, Weimar's "Priestess of Depravity").* Berlin: Gurlitt Presse, 1919. Elelphant folio, set of eight 20 x 25 inch lithographs housed in portfolio of decorated paper over boards in quarter vellum gilt, each lithograph is laid into thick card matte, some of which shows signs of foxing or light stains, outer portfolio has splits along some folds, with wear some staining and title sheet edgeworn and foxed, overall very good, lithographs near fine or better.   Between the Covers Rare Books   208 - 9   2016 $22,000

Berendt, John   *Midnight in the Garden of Good and Evil.* New York: Random House, 1994. ARC copy, near fine, shows light use, pictorial wrappers.   Bella Luna Books   2016 - t4334   2016 $66

Berg, Elizabeth   *The Art of Mending.* New York: Random House, 2004. First edition, author's presentation on title, paper over boards, top edges slightly spotted, otherwise nice in dust jacket.   Second Life Books, Inc.   196A - 110   2016 $45

Berg, Elizabeth   *Durable Goods.* New York: Random House, 1993. First edition, 8vo., author's signature on title, paper over boards with cloth spine, nice copy in dust jacket.   Second Life Books, Inc.   196A - 111   2016 $45

Berg, Elizabeth   *Say When.* New York: Random House, 2003. first printing, 8vo., author's presentation on title, paper over boards, top edges very slightly spotted, otherwise nice in dust jacket.   Second Life Books, Inc.   196A - 113   2016 $45

Berg, Elizabeth   *We are All Welcome Here.* New York: Random House, 2006. First edition, 8vo., paper over boards, about as new, laid in TLS from author.   Second Life Books, Inc.   196A - 114   2016 $45

Berg, Elizabeth   *The Year of Pleasures.* New York: Random House, 2005. First edition, 8vo., paper over boards, author's presentation on title, top edge faintly spotted, otherwise nice in dust jacket.   Second Life Books, Inc.   196A - 116   2016 $45

Bergen, Jonathan   *Romare Bearden 1911-1988.* New York: ACA Galleries, 1989. One of 2500 copies, 4to., illustrations, photos, blue cloth stamped in gilt, fine in very slightly soiled dust jacket.   Second Life Books, Inc.   197 - 26   2016 $45

Bergengren, Ralph   *David the Dreamer.* Boston: Atlantic Monthly Press, 1922. First American edition, Oblong 4to., green gilt cloth, pictorial paste on, fine in rear dust jacket (chipped and mended on verso), rare in dust jacket.   Aleph-bet Books, Inc.   111 - 189   2016 $2500

Berger, Thomas   *Little Big Man.* New York: Dial Press, 1964. First edition, staining on top edge, very good in moderately rubbed, very good or better dust jacket with shallow chip at foot inscribed by author for his parents.   Between the Covers Rare Books   204 - 13   2016 $7500

Berger,Thomas   *Reinhart in Love.* New York: Charles Scribner's sons, 1962. First edition, stains along edges of boards, thus sound, but good only in good but presentable dust jacket with corresponding stain visible only on rear panel, dedication copy inscribed by author to his parents.   Between the Covers Rare Books   204 - 2   2016 $4500

Berjeau, J. P.   *Book-Worm (First two volumes) the The Bookworm, a Literary and Bibliographical Review.* London: Worm, 1867-1871. volumes 2-5 (of 5 total), tall 8vo., contemporary half blue calf with marbled paper covered boards, top edge gilt, signed bindings by Zaehnsdorf, from the Zaehnsdorf reference library with bookplate, rubbed along hinges,.   Oak Knoll Books   310 - 57   2016 $600

Berkeley, Anthony   *The Poisoned Chocolates Case.* Garden City: published for the Crime Club Inc. by Doubleday Doran & Do., 1929. First US edition, octavo, attractive copy, top page edge little soiled and spotted, nearly fine in nearly fine price clipped dust jacket with mild rubbing and shelf wear to spine ends, little mild soiling, publisher's slip (portion of wrap-around band? laid in).   John W. Knott, Jr./L.W. Currey, Inc.   Fall-Winter 2015 - 17960   2016 $1250

Berkeley, George *Alciphron or the Minute Philosopher in Seven Dialogues.* New Haven: Increase Cooke & Co., 1803. First American edition from fourth London edition, 213 x 130mm, without leaf of ads at end, original American binding of sheepskin, flat spine divided into panels by gilt rules, original red morocco label, front free endpaper and titlepage with ink ownership inscription of "William Tully.... Yale College 1805", front joint cracked with just slight give to board, leather at corner worn through, covers with handful of short scratches and bit of minor soiling, faint offsetting throughout text, excellent example of early America sheep binding, completely unsophisticated, text fresh and clean, generally very much finer state of preservation than is typical.   Phillip J. Pirages   67 - 24   2016 $1500

Berkenhout, John *A Volume of Letters from Dr. Berkenhout to his Son at the University.* Cambridge: printed by J. Archdeacon for T. Cadell, 1790. First edition, 8vo., final errata leaf, contemporary calf with gilt lines and label, little normal wear but very good.   John Drury Rare Books 2015 - 15814   2016 $437

Berlo, Janet Catherine *Plains Indian Drawings 1865-1935: Pages from a Visual History.* New York: 1996. 240 pages, illustrations, near fine in like dust jacket.   Dumont Maps and Books   133 - 44   2016 $100

Berman, Wallace *Radio/Aether Series 1966/1974.* Los Angeles: Gemini G. E. L., 1974. First edition, limited to 50 copies with 10 artist's proofs, signed by Berman on titlepage, portfolio of 13 two color offset lithographs, each photographed from an original verifax collage, and printed on star-white cover mounted on Gemini rag-board, in original screen printed fabric covered box, very fine.   James S. Jaffe Rare Books   Occasional List: Winter 2016 - 5   2016 $10,000

Bernard Da Como *Lucerna Inquisitorum Haereticae Praultatis...* Rome: ex officina Bartholomaei Grassi, (colophon) Excudebat Vincentius Accoltus, 1584. First edition, woodcut printer's device on title, and another at colophon, intermittent foxing and browning, first 4 leaves strengthened in upper margin, last gathering becoming loose, 4to., contemporary limp vellum, lettered ink on spine, soiled, bookplate of Law Society inside front cover, sound.   Blackwell's Rare Books   B184 - 11   2016   £1200

Bernard De Clairvaux, Saint *Opuscula.* Venice: Lucantonio Giunta June, 1503. Rare early collection, 8vo., contemporary German blind tooled pigskin over wooden boards, fine outer roll of half figures on covers (rubbed split at head of upper joint, remains of later spine label one clasp missing), full page woodcut of Annunciation facing the opening text page, title and device, printed in red and opening chapter heading, 8 line white on black initials throughout, printed in double columns, early ownership monastic inscriptions from Memmingen, Bavaria on title dated 1559 and 1560, with ink shields, 19th century printed label of the Redemtionists at Baltimore, later stamp.   Maggs Bros. Ltd. 1474 - 9   2016   £2400

Bernard Shaw & Max Beerbohm at Covent Garden. London: Bodley Head, 1981. First edition, one of 225 copies, press device to titlepage, foolscap 8vo., original sewn card wrappers, dust jacket with Beerbohm caricature, very gentle fading to borders, very good, inscribed by book's designer, John Ryder.   Blackwell's Rare Books   B186 - 282   2016   £30

Bernard, Florence *Through the Cloud Mountain.* Philadelphia: Lippincott, 1922. First edition, 4to., gilt cloth, pictorial paste-on, fine and bright in dust jacket (chipped), illustrations by Kay Gertrude, scarce in dust jacket.   Alephbet Books, Inc.   112 - 275   2016 $300

Bernard, Jacques *Acts and Negotiations Together with the Particular Articles at Large of the General Peace.* London: printed for Robert Clavel at Peacock, and Tim Childe at White Hart, 1698. 8vo., 2 folding plates, first of the work bound upside-down, fore-edges fragile with fly-leaves and final two leaves somewhat worn, occasional light spots and smudges, two identical stubs at front and rear but nothing missing, contemporary speckled calf, Cambridge style boards, two identical stubs at front and rear but nothing missing, contemporary sprinkled calf, Cambridge style boards, neatly rebacked, tan morocco gilt label to spine, edges sprinkled red, few small chips and scrapes, corners little bumped but very good, initial "R" in old hand upper corner f.f..e.p.   Unsworths Antiquarian Booksellers   30 - 15   2016   £400

Berners, Juliana *A Treatyse of Fysshynge wyth an Angle.* Ashendene Press, 1903. One of 150 copies on Batchlor handmade paper, 7 wood engravings reproduced from those used in 1496 edition, initial letter of text printed in red, crown 8vo., original limp cream vellum, backstrip lettered gilt, untrimmed, bookplate, small and faint circular natural variation in colour to vellum at front joint, near fine.   Blackwell's Rare Books   B184 - 250   2016   £1200

Bernhard, Karl *Reise Sr. Hoheit des Herzogs Bernhard zu Sachsen-Weimar- Eisenach Durch Nord-Amerika in de Jahren 125 und 1826.* Weimar: Wilhelm Hoffman, 1828. First edition, 8 black and white maps, 1 folding, 1 folding plan, 4 plates, in text drawings, small 4to., contemporary cloth, paper label, very good, boards and spine sunned, partial paper spine label, some plates moderately toned, light marginal dampstaining.   Kaaterskill Books   21 - 9   2016 $750

Bernhard, Thomas *Correction.* New York: Alfred A. Knopf, 1979. First US edition, extreme edges of covers slightly faded, otherwise fine in near fine, price clipped dust jacket, slightly creased at edges.   Peter Ellis   112 - 37   2016   £45

Bernheim, Hippolyte *De la Suggestion et de ses Applicaions a la Therapeutique.* Paris: Octave Doin, 1886. First edition, small 8vo., several text illustrations, contemporary three quarter morocco, some light foxing, very good. Edwin V. Glaser Rare Books   2015 - 1144   2016 $600

Bernstein, Charles *4 Poem by Charles Bernstein.* Tucson: Chax Press, 1988. 1/125 copies, one sheet, folded twice in paper wrapper, signed by author, very good. Second Life Books, Inc.   196A - 121   2016 $45

Berrigan, Ted *C: a Journal of Poetry Volume 1 No. 4.* New York: Lorenz Gude & Ted Berrigan, 1963. Fourth issue of this mimeographed journal, some edge wear to covers and spine, tear at base of spine, overall very good in stapled wrappers.   Ken Lopez Bookseller   166 - 146   2016 $8500

Berrigan, Ted *"C" a Journal of Poetry.* New York: Lornez Gude et al May, 1963. -May 1966., I: 1-10; II-11 and 13 (of 13), 12 issues, tall legal format, mimeographed and stapled in printed wrappers and in pictorial wrappers with cover design by Joe Brainard, and one issue with silk screen cover design by Andy Warhol, some numbers inscribed by Berrigan and signed by Joe Brainard, presentation inscriptions to Tony Towle from Warhol, Berrigan, Edwin Denby, Gerard Malanga and John Wieners.   James S. Jaffe Rare Books   Occasional List: Winter 2016 - 24   2016 $22,500

Berry, Wendell *Another turn of the Crank.* Washington: Counterpoint, 1995. First edition, 8vo., fine in dust jacket, signed and dated and inscribed by author.   Second Life Books, Inc.   196A - 129   2016 $85

Berry, Wendell *Clearing.* New York: Harcourt, 1977. First edition, 8vo., fine in dust jacket, inscribed by author scarce.   Second Life Books, Inc.   196A - 130   2016 $125

Berry, Wendell *The Cumberlands: Excerpts from Articles on the Region by....* Monterey: Larkspur Press, 2006. First edition thus, 8vo., one of 500 copies, bound in paper covered boards, printed in dust jacket, fine.   Second Life Books, Inc.   197 - 28   2016 $50

Berry, Wendell *Distant Neighbors.* Berkeley: Counterpoint, 2014. First edition, 8vo., fine in dust jacket, signed by author.   Second Life Books, Inc.   196A - 122   2016 $75

Berry, Wendell *Findings.* Iowa City: Prairie Press, 1969. First edition, 8vo., fine in dust jacket, inscribed by author, scarce.   Second Life Books, Inc.   196A - 132   2016 $375

Berry, Wendell *The Gift of Gravity.* Deerfield: Dublin: Deerfield Press/The Gallery Press, 1979. First edition, limited to 300 signed copies, fine in dust jacket with closed tear to rear of dust jacket, brown endpapers, some offsetting from dust jacket, spine title printed in upper and lower case letters, dust jacket state 2 with title on spine in upper and lower case letters.   Second Life Books, Inc.   196A - 133   2016 $225

Berry, Wendell *Given: Poems.* Washington: Shoemaker, Hoard, 2005. First edition, 8vo., fine in fine dust jacket, inscribed by author for Janet 6 3 05.   Second Life Books, Inc.   196A - 123   2016 $95

Berry, Wendell *Harlan Hubbard, Life and Work.* Lexington: University Press of Kentucky, 1990. First edition, 8vo., reproductions by Hubbard, presentation by author, fine in dust jacket.   Second Life Books, Inc.   196A - 134   2016 $95

Berry, Wendell *The Hidden Wound.* Boston: Houghton Mifflin, 1970. First edition, 8vo., fine in dust jacket, signed by author.   Second Life Books, Inc.   196A - 135   2016 $150

Berry, Wendell *The Kentucky River: Two Poems.* Monterey: Larkspur Press, 1976. First edition, limited to 1026 numbered copies, this #226, original wrappers, fine, inscribed by author.   Second Life Books, Inc.   196A - 136   2016 $125

Berry, Wendell *Leavings: Poems.* Berkeley: Counterpoint, 2009. First edition, 8vo., fine in dust jacket.   Second Life Books, Inc.   197 - 27   2016 $65

Berry, Wendell *November Twenty Six Nineteen Hundred Sixty Three.* New York: George Braziller, 1964. First edition, limited to 3013 copes, printed on handmade laid paper by Fabirano, with tipped in colored illustration by Ben Shahn, signed by Berry and artist, Ben Shahn, housed in publisher's slipcase (little faded as usual), very nice.   Second Life Books, Inc.   196A - 137   2016 $300

Berry, Wendell *Remembering a Novel.* San Francisco: North Point Press, 1988. First edition, 8vo., fine in dust jacket, signed by author.   Second Life Books, Inc.   196A - 140   2016 $65

Berry, Wendell *Sabbaths 1987.* Monterey: Larkspur Press, 1991. First edition, 1 of 1000 numbered copies, fine, signed by author, printed brown wrappers.   Bella Luna Books   2016 - s1001   2016 $82

Berry, Wendell *Sabbaths 1987-1990.* London: Golgoonza Press, 1992. First edition, 8vo., little bent original wrappers, very good, signed and dated 1994 by author.   Second Life Books, Inc.   196A - 141   2016 $75

Berry, Wendell *Sayings & Doings (Poems).* Lexington: Gnomon, 1975. First edition, 12mo., second state of binding with cream cloth boards, (1/898 bound thus), stamped in copper/orange, signed by author.   Second Life Books, Inc.   196A - 143   2016 $65

Berry, Wendell *The Selected Poems of.* Washington: Counterpoint, 1998. First edition, fine, dust jacket, signed by author.   Second Life Books, Inc.   196A - 144   2016 $75

Berry, Wendell *The Selected Poems.* Washington: Counterpoint, 1998. First printing, fine in dust jacket, presentation from Berry's bibliographer to his mother-in-law, signed by author.   Second Life Books, Inc.   196A - 124   2016 $125

Berry, Wendell *Traveling at Home.* Lewisburg: Bucknell University Press of Appletree Alley, 1988. First edition, one printing of 150 copies, signed by author, cloth backed boards, fine, issue A of the binding with spine bound in lighter green cloth, fine, printed in Rives Lightweight mould made paper and set in spectrum type.   Second Life Books, Inc.   196A - 147 2016 $600

Berry, Wendell *Watch with me and Six Other Stories...* New York: Pantheon, 1994. First edition, fine in dust jacket, signed by author.   Second Life Books, Inc.   196A - 148   2016 $75

Berry, Wendell *The Way of Ignorance and Other Essays....* Washington: Shoemaker & Hoard, 2005. First edition, 8vo., fine in dust jacket, signed and dated by author.   Second Life Books, Inc.   196A - `16   2016 $75

Berry, Wendell *Window Poems.* Eneryville: Shoemaker and Hoard, 2007. First trade edition, signed by author, 8vo., bound in cloth backed boards, with paper label, fine.   Second Life Books, Inc.   196A - 127   2016 $45

Berryman, John 1914-1972 *Berryman's Sonnets.* New York: Farrar, Straus & Giroux, 1967. Close to near fine with some slight bumping to top corner of first few pages in close to near fine dust jacket with small edge tear to top of spine, signed by author, uncommon thus.   Jeff Hirsch Books Holiday List 2015 - 22   2016 $650

Berssenbrigge. Mei-Mei *Sphericity.* Berkeley: Kelsey St. Press, 1993. First edition, deluxe issue, one of 50 numbered copies, signed by author and artist, in an entire edition of 2000, large square 8vo., illustrations, original illustrated wrappers, original hand colored drawing signed by Richard Tuttle, bound in at back of book, lower fore-corner of wrappers and text block lightly bumped, otherwise fine.   James S. Jaffe Rare Books   Occasional List: Winter 2016 - 23   2016 $1750

Berthelot, Marcelin *Centenaire De Marcelin Berthelot.* Paris: Imprimerie de Vaugirard, 1929. Folio, full leather, spine stamped in gilt with inset profile portrait in relief on cover, all edges speckled, slipcase with protective board, pages with additional leaves of illustrations, few subtle scratches/marks on covers, slipcover shows much wear, rubbing.   Oak Knoll Books   310 - 277   2016 $300

Bertin, Charles *Christopher Columbus.* Roslyn: John Carter Brown Library, 1992. Limited to 200 numbered copies signed by artist, binder and printer, this being one of 20 of the deluxe edition, 8vo., quarter leather, cloth, inserted in clamshell case with separate portfolio containing 6 woodcuts on individaul plates, from the library of Deborah Evetts, binder and contains pen and ink drawing of design used on front cover, stample stamped in green leather of this design.   Oak Knoll Books   310 - 148   2016 $850

Bertolonii, Antonii *Novi Commentarii Academiae Scientiarum Instituti Bononiensis Tomus Tertius.* Bologna: Dall' Olmo et Tio, 1839. Quarto, 14 hand colored engraved plates (five folding), modern binder's cloth, contents fine and crisp.   Andrew Isles Natural History Books   55 - 38818   2016 $1250

Bertozzini, Giancarlo *Yemen del Nord Venti Fotografie Inedite di giancarlo Bertozzini Presentate da Mario Giacomelli.* Pesaro: privately published for the photographer, 1984. first edition, no. 4 of a printing limited to 60, square folio portfolio, original green cloth box, spine lettered gilt, photographer's initials in gilt on front cover, (ff. (7) of creme card, including self wrappers, 20 original color photos mounted on black cards, only minor spotting or scuffing to cloth box, internally near fine.   Sotheran's   Travel and Exploration - 300   2016   £998

Beruldsen, Gordon *A Field Guide to Nests and Eggs of Australian Birds.* Adelaide: Rigby, 1980. First edition, octavo, color photos, signature, fine in dust jacket.   Andrew Isles Natural History Books   55 - 27196   2016 $50

Besant, Walter *Katharine Regina. Arrowsmith's Christmas Annual 1897.* London: J. A. Arrowsmith, 1887. Contemporary half vellum, marbled boards, spine lettered in black, retaining original front wrapper printed in blue, mustard and black.   Jarndyce Antiquarian Booksellers   CCXVII - 30   2016   £125

The Best of Cemetery Dance. Baltimore: Cemetery Dance, 1998. Publisher's copy of the limited edition of 400 copies, fine in fine dust jacket and slipcase, bookplate of horror author, signed by more than 60 authors including Stephen King, Richard Matheson, Campbell, Lansdale, Laymon, Koontz, Ray Garton, Ed Gorman, Jack Ketchum, Graham Masterton, Bill Ponzini, Poppy Brite, Douglas Clegg, and publication founder Richard Chizmar.   Ken Lopez Bookseller   166 - 4   2016 $750

Best, Fritz *Tag und Nacht. (Day and Night).* Berlin: John Gerard, 1992. Limited to 20 numbered copies signed by Gerard and Best, small 4to., gray paper covered boards opening from either end with pages accordion style, 10 leaves printed on both sides, double sided accordion fold book with pulp paper images, on handmade cotton papers, small 4to., gray paper covered boards, opening from either end with pages accordion style, 10 leaves printed on both sides. Oak Knoll Books 27 - 20 2016 $460

Bester, Alfred *The Demolished Man.* Chicago: Shasta Publishers, 1953. First edition, octavo, cloth backed boards, very fine association, signed inscribed by author to his editor Ted Dikty, fine in virtually as new fine dust jacket. John W. Knott, Jr./L.W. Currey, Inc. Fall-Winter 2015 - 18564 2016 $3000

Betham-Edwards, Miss *Holidays in Eastern France.* London: Hurst, Blackett, 1879. First edition, frontispiece, original red cloth, spine faded. J. & S. L. Bonham Antiquarian Booksellers Europe 2016 - 8495 2016 £30

Betjeman, John 1906-1984 *English, Scottish and Welsh landscape 1700-c. 1860.* Frederick Muller, 1944. First edition, crown 8vo., 13 full page illustrations by John Piper, original cloth with Piper lithograph wrapping around, top edge slightly dusty, bookplate of Stephen Bone, flyleaf with little creasing to rear free endpaper, dust jacket repeating cover design little chipped, nicked and rubbed. Blackwell's Rare Books B186 - 183 2016 £100

Betjeman, John 1906-1984 *Ghastly Good Taste; or a Depressing Story of the rise and Fall of English Architecture.* London: 1933. First edition, the copy of Eric Gill. Honey & Wax Booksellers 4 - 15 2016 $500

Betjeman, John 1906-1984 *Ghastly Good Taste.* Blond, 1970. Small 4to., folding plan and drawings in text, little creased in one part where it overhangs textblock when folded, original quarter black cloth, backstrip lettered in silver, printed pink boards with light rubbing to edges and little dust soiling overall, top edge slightly dusty, good, inscribed by author for Toby and Jane. Blackwell's Rare Books B184 - 111 2016 £120

Betjeman, John 1906-1984 *John Piper.* Penguin Books, 1944. First edition, 32 plates, with 16 colorprinted, oblong 8vo., original printed fawn and white stapled card wrappers, covers little dust soiled particularly to rear, staples little rusted, good. Blackwell's Rare Books B184 - 300 2016 £30

Betjeman, John 1906-1984 *John Piper.* Penguin Books, 1944. First edition, 32 plates by John Piper with 16 color printed, short closed tear at foot of page 7, very faint toning to page borders, oblong 8vo., original printed fawn and white stapled card wrappers, covers little dust soiled with some faint foxing carrying around to rear inside covers, good, signed by author. Blackwell's Rare Books B184 - 299 2016 £125

Betjeman, John 1906-1984 *Ode on the Marriage of HRH Prince Charles to Lady Diana Spencer in St. Paul's Cathedral on 29 July 1981.* London: printed by Skelton's Press for Warren Editions, 1981. First edition, one of 125 copies signed by author, decorative 'firework' border of blue and red topped by fleur-de-lys within a crown, whole surrounding text and limitation certificate and printed in blue and red, folio, some very light creasing and small drink spot to outer border, good, with a typescript of same title printed in black on Bejteman's headed paper, original fold, very good, author's signature on tipped-in card. Blackwell's Rare Books B184 - 112 2016 £400

Betjeman, John 1906-1984 *Selected Prose.* London: John Murray, 1955. Fourth printing, 8vo., original cloth with dust jacket little chipped and dusty, otherwise very good. Sotheran's Piccadilly Notes - Summer 2015 - 45 2016 £248

Betjeman, John 1906-1984 *Uncollected Poems.* London: John Murray, 1982. First edition, vignette on titlepage, foolscap 8vo., original green boards, backstrip lettered gilt, top edge trifle dusty, dust jacket, near fine. Blackwell's Rare Books B184 - 114 2016 £30

Beveridge, William H. *Full Employment in a Free Society.* London: George Allen & Unwin, 1944. First edition, 8vo., original black cloth, gilt lettering to spine, diagrams and charts in text, loose news clippings, very good. Sotheran's Piccadilly Notes - Summer 2015 - 46 2016 £120

Beverley, Robert *The History of Virgina in Four Parts...* London: for F. Fayram and J. Clarke and T. Bickerton, 1722. Engraved fore title, 14 engraved plates, slightly later calf, spine rubbed, front hinge beginning to crack but held firmly by cords, some light marginal foxing, but very good, very attractive copy. Joseph J. Felcone, Inc. Books from Five Centuries: a Miscellany - 146 2016 $2800

Bewick, Thomas   1753-1828   *History of British Birds.*   Newcastle: Edward Walker for T. Bewick, 1804, but, 1814-1816.   1804.Fifth edition of volume I (Land Birds), variant B with vignette of ploughman and milkmaid added to page 296; first edition volume II Water Birds, first state of woodcuts, 241 x 149mm., very pleasing contemporary diced calf, covers with triple fillet rules and blindstamped palmette roll border, raised bands, spine compartments with elaborate assemblage of gilt fleurons, gilt titling, gilt rolled turn-ins, marbled endleaves; with 218 fine woodcut figures of birds as well as 227 charming vignettes by Thomas Bewick, large paper copy, verso of front free endpapers with small ink ownership stamp of R. Parker; one joint just slightly rubbed, couple of short black (ink?) marks to one board, one leaf with neat repairs to two short tears at inner margin, one gathering (only) rather foxed, isolated trivial foxing elsewhere, otherwise especially fine, fresh copy internally and in very well preserved original binding.   Phillip J. Pirages   67 - 25   2016 $1600

Bewick, Thomas   1753-1828   *Select Fables with Cuts, Designed and Engraved by Thomas and John Bewick and Others....*   Newcastle: printed by S. Hodgson for Emerson Charnley, 1820.   Demy 8vo. issue, frontispiece, little foxed, titlepage vignette, numerous woodcut illustrations, small corner tear to following f.e.p., uncut in original dull blue boards, fairly recent plain cream paper spine.   Jarndyce Antiquarian Booksellers   CCXVII - 32   2016   £150

Bewick, Thomas   1753-1828   *Vignettes.*   Newcastle-upon-Tyne: printed for Edward Walker, 1827.   4to., vignette title, plus 120 leaves, each with rare woodcuts printed on rectos only, later 19th century half dark green moroccoo, marbled boards, spine gilt, some small hinge repairs, top edge gilt, very nice.   Jarndyce Antiquarian Booksellers   CCXVII - 31   2016   £580

Bewick, Thomas   1753-1828   *Memorial Edition of the Works.*   Newcastle upon Tyne: printed by R. Ward and Sons for Bernard Quaritch... London, 1885-1887.   Limited to 750 numbered copies signed by publisher, 3 volumes, original half brown morocco, spine with raised bands, lettered gilt and with animal and bird tools in top and bottom panels, marbled endpaper, top edges gilt, many wood engravings by Thomas Bewick, very good, TLS dated August 17th 1889 from W J May, VP of Atchison, Topeka and Santa Fe Railroad to Mr. Price urging him to buy this set of books, each volume with bookplate of Margaret Davies Price.   Sotheran's   Piccadilly Notes - Summer 2015 - 47   2016   £1400

Beze, Theodore De   *Propositions and Principles of Divinite, Propounded and Disputed in the Vninersitie of Geneva...*   Edinburgh: printed by Robert Waldengrave, 1591.   First English edition, small quarto, contemporary calf, rebacked, boards ruled in gilt, spine with newer morocco spine label, lettered gilt, spine with newer morocco spine label, lettered in gilt, spine decoratively stamped in gilt, gilt board edges, all edges red inner hinges repaired, small mark where bookplate has been removed to front free endpaper, some repairs to inner margin of titlepage, 2.5 x 1 inch tear to outer margin of leaf Z2, only affecting few letters, final leaf (the table) with some major repairs with loss to few words, some dampstaining and toning throughout, previous owner's old ink marginalia throughout, old ex-library stamps, overall very good.   Heritage Book Shop   Holiday 2015 - 10   2016 $7500

Bhattacharya, Brindavan C.   *Indian Images. Part I. the Brahmanic Iconography.*   Calcutta and Simla: Thacker, Spink & Co., 1921.   Very rare first edition, original blue pebble grained cloth, spine lettered gilt, gilt stamped wheel as centerpiece of front cover, frontispiece with tissue guard, 30 plates after photos, minimal wear to binding, internally, apart from stamps on verso of plates, very good, released from Birmingham University Library.   Sotheran's   Travel and Exploration - 84   2016   £198

Bianchi, Daniel B.   *Some Recollections of the Merrymount Press.*   Berkeley: George I. Harding & Roger Levenson, 1978.   First edition, 12mo., black cloth lettered and decorated in gilt on front cover and spine, bookplate tipped to inner cover, else fine, tipped in bookplates of book collector, Robert Goldman.   Argonaut Book Shop   Private Press 2015 - 6274   2016 $45

Bianco, Pamela   *Beginning with A.*   New York: Oxford University Press, 1947.   First edition, 4to., cloth, fine in dust jacket frayed at spine endds and lightly rubbed, full page illustrations.   Aleph-bet Books, Inc.   112 - 2   2016 $200

Bianco, Pamela   *The Doll in the Window.*   New York: Oxford Press, 1953.   First edition, square 8vo., fine in near fine dust jacket, beautifully illustrated in color.   Aleph-bet Books, Inc. 112 - 57   2016 $125

Biber, Edward   *Christian Education in a Course of Lectures, Delivered in London in Spring 1829.*   London: Effingham Wilson, 1830.   First edition, 32 page catalog, original drab boards, glazed blue cloth spine, slightly dulled, paper label little rubbed, very good.   Jarndyce Antiquarian Books   CCXV - 532   2016   £125

Biber, Edward   *Henry Pestalozzi and His Plan of Education...*   London: John Souter, School Library, 1831.   First edition, frontispiece, browned, original green moire cloth, paper label, spine slightly faded and rubbed at head and tail, book labels of Legge Library.   Jarndyce Antiquarian Books   CCXV - 893   2016   £120

Bibiena, Bernardo Dovizi Da *Calandra. Comedia...* Vinegia: Giolito de' Ferrari, 1562. Early edition, 12mo., later decorative green wrappers, engraved border and printer's device to titlepage, decorative capitals to text, fore-edges trimmed close, very good.   Dramatis Personae   119 - 18   2016 $350

Bible. English - 1703 *The Holy Bible containing the Old Testament and the New. (bound with) The Psalms of David In Meeter.*   London: printed by Charles Bill & the Executrix of Thomas Newcomb...., 1703. Edinburgh: printed by George Mosman, 1693, 8vo., bound in early 19th century full straight grain morocco boards panelled gilt, enclosing elaborate blindstamp border with gilt and blind central panels, richly gilt corner pieces, spine lettered gilt with raised bands gilt and elaborate gaufferig to corners, engraved titlepage, spine little darkened and slightly rubbed on raised bands, pin hole to upper joint, some quires browned, waterstain to inner gutter of last few pages in psalms, otherwise most attractive and decoratively bound.   Sotheran's Piccadilly Notes - Summer 2015 - 48   2016   £1995

Bible. English - 1716 *The Holy Bible Containing the Old Testament and the New... (The Vinegar Bible).*   Oxford: printed by John Baskett, Printer to (the) Kings Most Excellent majesty for Great Britain and for (the) University, 1716. volumes, royal folios, rarer of two known states (the other bearing a 1717 imprint), volume I with illustrated engraved titlepage engraved by John Sturt and dated 1716 and volume 2 issued with engraving of the Annunciation on the letterpress titlepage and dated 1716, rare, magnificent in presentation binding of black levant leather with Royal Cypher of King George III (surmounted by a crown) stamped in gold in five compartments on spines of each volume and the Royal arms with ("G. R. III" above the crown), embossed at center of all four copies, both volumes have marbled endpapers and wove paper flyleaves, royal blue silk ribbons, all edges gilt, according to an early bookseller's description (tipped onto front fly leaf), "this copy possesses even an additional interest beyond being the property of the most likely often read by the Monarch, who expressed a hope "That the time would come when every poor child in his dominions would be able to read the Bible", whether such speculation is true might be subject to some skepticism, but we can only say that this is a presentation binding, exceedingly rare edition.   Between the Covers Rare Books   208 - 23   2016 $45,000

Bible. English - 1791 *The Holy Bible Containing the Old and New Testaments...*   Trenton: Isaac Collins, 1791. First Bible printed in NJ, 4to., contemporary blind paneled sheep by Craig and Lea, with their decorative printed binder's label on front pastedown, binding worn at extremities as usual, front hinge cracking but held strongly by cords, internally the first several leaves have some erosion at extreme edges (about quarter inch) and there is the usual scattered foxing inherent in early American paper, very good, tight copy.   Joseph J. Felcone, Inc.   Books from Five Centuries: a Miscellany - 20   2016 $3000

Bible. English - 1800 *The Holy Bible. The Old Testament.... (with) The New Testament. (and) The Apocrypha.*   London: T. Bensley for T. Macklin (final volume for T. Cadell & W. Davies), 1800. (for the 6 volumes of the Bible. 11816 (for the Apocrypha), First printing of this edition, 7 volumes, once splendid contemporary black straight grain morocco gilt, covers framed by Greek key roll, palmette roll and multiple gilt rules, double raised bands, spine compartments densely gilt with rows of alternating star and circlet tools, gilt titling, turn-ins with gilt chair roll, purple endpaper, all edges gilt (some inexpert but not obvious repairs to joints and backstrips), with more than 100 allegorical headpieces and tailpieces and some 70 splendid large folio size copper plates, extremities rather rubbed, boards bit scuffed, but decorative contemporaneous bindings, solid and not without appeal, plates somewhat foxed (mostly to margins), mild to moderate offsetting from plates, occasional mild offsetting in text bed, still a fresh, wide margined copy.   Phillip J. Pirages   67 - 26   2016 $7500

Bible. English - 1820 *The Holy Bible containing the Old and New Testament translated out of the original tongues...*   Philadelphia: published by Kimber and Sharpless No. 50 North Fourth Street, n.d., 1820? Large 4to., 31 plates, 3 maps, engraved titlepages, without blank, browned and foxed, contemporary green morocco, elaborately gilt, title gilt on spine, all edges gilt, sides and dentelles gilt, marbled pastedowns and endpapers.   Unsworths Antiquarian Booksellers   30 - 16   2016   £150

Bible. English - 1846 *The Illuminated Bible Containing the Old and New Testaments Embellished with Sixteen Hundred Historical Engravings...*   New York: Harper & Bros., 1846. First edition, very thick large 4to., full contemporary gilt tooled black morocco, all edges gilt, edges and spine ends rubbed, very good sound, fine.   M & S Rare Books, Inc.   99 - 25   2016 $1000

Bible. English - 1903 *The English Bible.* Hammersmith: Doves Press, 1903-1905. One of 500 copies, 331 x 235mm., five volumes, original limp vellum by Doves Bindery (stamp signed), gilt titling on spine, housed within two later oatmeal linen dropback clamshell boxes with black morocco spine labels, elegant initial letters in red by Edward Johnston, including an "I" running the length of the page to open Genesis ("In the beginning"), front flyleaf of volume I inscribed in pencil by Madeleine Whyte for Mary Churchill, with Doves Press invoice for Miss Whyte dated June 27 1905, initaled by "B.H." (i.e. Bessie Hooley, a sewer at the bindery and part-time secretary to Cobden-Sanderson) laid in, vellum with just hint of soiling, but very little of the typical variation in grain, two dozen leaves with minor marginal foxing (never approaching any significance), dozen additional leaves with whisper of foxing, otherwise clean, fresh, bright copy inside and out.   Phillip J. Pirages   67 - 115   2016 $19,500

Bible. English - 1909 *The Song of Songs Which is Solomon's.* London: Printed at the Ricardi Press for Philip Lee Warner, Publisher to the Medici Society, 1909. No. 61 of 500 copies, 260 x 194mm., pleasing olive brown crushed morocco by Bumpus (stamp signed), cover framed with three sets of triple fillets, raised bands, spine compartments similarly framed, gilt titling and turn-ins, all edges gilt, vignette on titlepage and colophon, both in blue and 10 color plates by William Russell Flint, mounted on stiff paper, each of the plates accompanied by tissue guard and an additional captioned paper guard, spine faded to soft hazel brown (as usual with green) boards with just hint of same fading, very sight rubbing to small portion of joints, usual offsetting from turn-ins to endleaves, one tissue guard with one inch strip torn at head edge, still very appealing, attractive binding lustrous and with no significant wear and interior clean and fresh.   Phillip J. Pirages   67 - 301   2016 $2250

Bible. English - 1911 *The Holy Bible Containing the Old and New Testaments.* Glasgow: David Bryce and Son, 1911. 42 x 30mm., charmingly original flexible tan roan with ornately blindstamped Renaissance-style covers and gilt titling on spine, lower cover with inside leather pocket containing tiny leather framed magnifying glass, the book attached by six inch chain to wooden lectern approximately 5 1/2 high and containing a small compartment in which the volume is te be stored, with 28 full page illustrations, including frontispiece by C. B. Birch; base of spine with 1 mm. worn away, small hole in front free endpaper, lectern with couple of shallow scratches, other trivial imperfections, still fine specimen that is very well preserved in every important way.   Phillip J. Pirages   67 - 254   2016 $1500

Bible. English - 1925 *The Song of Songs.* Waltham St. Lawrence: Golden Cockerel Press, 1925. One of 720 copies (of a total of 750), 267 x 197mm., original white buckram, spine titled gilt, edges untrimmed, woodcut vignette on title, colophon device, one engraved plate and 17 engravings in text, all by Eric Gill, initials in red, faint sunning to spine, slight discoloration to front free endpaper and tail edge of opening leaves, other trivial defect, occasional marginal smudges or faint foxing, half a dozen leaves with uneven head edge from rough opening, still excellent copy, text fresh and bright and white buckram binding unworn and entirely free of soiling, almost always found on boards of this book.   Phillip J. Pirages   67 - 171   2016 $2500

Bible. English - 1929 *The Apocrypha.* London: Cresset Press, 1929. No. XXX of 30 large paper copies on handmade paper and 450 copies on mould made paper, with additional suite of plates, each signed by artist, 350 x 227mm., publisher's black stiff vellum by Wood (stamp signed), flat spine with gilt titling, yapp edges, top edge gilt, other edges untrimmed, housed with (slightly scuffed) portfolio of plates in later black slipcase, 14 woodcuts, each by different artist, with additional suite of the plates printed on Japanese paper and signed by artist responsible for each, (original?) tissue guards in volume, with two of the original wood blocks for the engravings by Eric Jones and Wladislaw Skoczylas, remains of bookplate, prospectus laid in, spine lightly and uniformly faded, slivers of the binding's black dye faintly worn away along portions of joints and edges (and dye very carefully renewed in few small places, otherwise extremely fine, binding essentially unworn and not splayed, text immaculate, from the collection of John Gribbel (1858-1936) and was lot 217 in the 30 Oct. 1940 sale of his collection at Parke-Bernet.   Phillip J. Pirages   67 - 100   2016 $6500

Bible. English - 1931 *The Four Gospels.* Waltham St. Lawrence: Golden Cockerel press, 1931. No. 392 of 500 copies (first 32 on vellum), 343 x 242mm., publisher's half pigskin and wheat colored buckram sides by Sangorski & Sutcliffe, raised bands, gilt rules and titling on spine, top edge gilt, other edges untrimmed, original (lightly soiled and worn) plain card slipcase, 4 large woodcuts on section titles and scores of striking large and small woodcut illustrations, decorative elements and initials by Eric Gill, printed on Batchelor handmade paper; extraordinarily fine, perhaps unsurpassable copy, pristine internally, binding virtually so.   Phillip J. Pirages   67 - 170   2016 $19,500

Bible. English - 1932 *The Wisdom of Jesus the son of Sirach Commonly called Ecclesiasticus.* Chelsea: Ashendene Press, 1932. One of 250 copies on paper for sale (and 21 vellum copies for sale), 292 x 198mm, original orange vellum, orange silk ties, gilt lettering on spine, edges untrimmed, original marbled slipcase (slightly scratched), initials hand colored in blue and green by Graily Hewitt and his assistants, printed in black and red, single spot of foxing to fore edge of last two leaves, otherwise especially fine, bright, clean, no signs of use.   Phillip J. Pirages   67 - 8   2016 $3250

Bible. English - 1932 *The Revelation of Saint John the Divine.* Montgomeryshire: Gregynog Press, 1932. No. 51 of 250 copies, 347 x 205mm., publisher's deep red Hermitage calf over bevelled boards, top edge sprinkled, housed in (somewhat worn) later quarter leather slipcase; 41 striking wood engraved illustrations by Blair Hughes-Stanton, 13 of them full page, text printed in red and black, first three words on titlepage wood engraved, front pastedown with morocco bookplate of Neva and Guy Littell, spine mildly faded, few minor shallow grazes to leather, otherwise very fine with binding lustrous and showing little use and text and plates especially fresh and clean.   Phillip J. Pirages   67 - 181   2016 $3000

Bible. English - 1932 *The Revelation of Saint John the Divine.* Wales: Gregynog Press, 1932. Limited to 250 numbered copies, 4to., printed in Bembo and Perpetua titling on Japanese vellum, printed in black and red, 41 wood engravings in text by Blair Hughes-Stanton, 4to., full hermitage calf blocked in blind on front cover, some rubbing of covers, spine shows fading, top edge sprinkled, slipcase broken but present and has part of backstrip misising.   Oak Knoll Books   310 - 107   2016 $3500

Bible. English - 1935 *The Holy Bible.* Oxford: University Press, 1935. One of 1000 copies designed by Bruce Rogers for the Oxford University Press, folio, contemporary full red morocco, edges gilt, fine, fresh copy, 1000 copies printed on Wolvercote paper and were marketed largely to churches as a lectern Bible, additional 200 copies were printed damp on slightly larger Batchelor handmade paper, these copies were marketed to the rare book and fine press collecting world, were bound in simple cloth covered boards, this copy fine and fresh and clearly never saw the inside of a church.   Joseph J. Felcone, Inc.   Books from Five Centuries: a Miscellany - 11   2016 $12,500

Bible. English - 1967 *Genesis.* Boston: Pendle Press, 1967. Limited to 20 copies, folio, quarter blue patterned cloth and light blue-gray Fabriano paper covered boards, handprinted on double-fold Japanese Masa paper by McCurdy, very rare, cloth portion of boards stained, paper portion of boards lightly faded at edges.   Oak Knoll Books   310 - 134   2016 $2000

Bible. English - 1970 *The Book of Genesis. King James Bible.* Kentfield: Allen Press, 1970. One of 140 copies printed on Umbria handmade paper in dark brown with running titles and flytitles printed in dark brown, green and orange, titlepage engraving and 23 full page wood engravings by Blair Hughes-Stanton, tissue guards present, folio, original green linen with overall gilt blocked repeated pattern, printed label to lightly faded backstrip, untrimmed, linen slipcase with small waterstain, very good.   Blackwell's Rare Books   B184 - 249   2016   £600

Bible. English - 1999 *The Pennyroyal Caxton Edition of the King James Bible.* North Hatfield: Pennyroyal Caxton Press, 1999. No. 399 of 400 copies (and 30 deluxe copies, 405 x 290mm., 2 volumes, publisher's vellum overboards, covers and pastedowns laced through titling in gilt on front covers and pastedowns laced through, titling gilt on front boards and spines, each volume in original fine cloth bolding box with printed paper label, 232 relief engravings by Barry Moser, initials and three rubrics printed in red, signature of Barry Moser on leaf following colophon, as new.   Phillip J. Pirages   67 - 275   2016 $16,000

Bible. English - 2000 *The Holy Bible.* San Francisco: Arion Press, 2000. One of 400 copies for sale (and 26 copies printed for presentation) and, oft the 400, one of 150 special copies with hand colored and illuminated abstract decoration of the initial letters, original violet crushed morocco boards, black morocco spine, thin strip of red morocco between, flat spine with gilt titling, in sturdy black buckram box with black morocco label, mint.   Phillip J. Pirages   67 - 7   2016 $8000

Bible. Greek - 1524 *Novum Testamentum Graece.* Strasbourg: Wolfgang Cephalaeus, 1524. Title within quadripartie woodcut border, printer's device at centre, large device on verso of last leaf with mottoes in Hebrew, Greek and Latin, uniformly little browned and with some slight dampstaining in upper and fore margins, 8vo., contemporary blindstamped pigskin (or deerskin) over bevelled wooden boards, brass clasps and catches, lacking clasps, very rubbed and darkened, spine partly defective, upper cover held by 1 (of 3) cords, 1529 ownership inscription in 2 places of Johannes Hartmann, purchased, the whole extensively annotated by him in Latin and Greek, sometimes in red ink, 19th century bookplate of Thomas Brooke, of Armitage Bridge (Huddersfield), sound, scarce.   Blackwell's Rare Books   B184 - 13   2016   £5000

Bible. Greek - 1587 *Vetus Testamentum Iuxta Septuaginta ex auctoritate Sixti V. Pont. Max. Editum.* Rome: Francesco Zanetti, 1587. Large engraved vignette on title, initials, headpieces, ruled in red, titlepage little stained and with crease towards inner margin, occasional browning and minor staining, faulty (double) impression, late 18th or early 19th century calf, gilt arms of Abbaye de la Trappe at centre of covers, various inscription and stamps of the Abbaye on titlepage, rebacked preserving.   Blackwell's Rare Books   B184 - 14   2016   £7500

Bible. Greek - 1835 *Vetus Testamentum Graece.* Lipsiae: sumptibus et typis Caroli Tauchnitii, 1835. Editio stereotypa, 8vo., sporadic light foxing, contemporary vellum, gilt spine with two dark green morocco labels, marbled endpapers, all edges red, vellum little darkened, some smudgy marks but still very good, ownership inscriptions, first of J. Thorp, Jan. 1860 and second of William Horbury dated iv, xlii, Thorps's signature again in pencil to titlepage.   Unsworths Antiquarian Booksellers   30 - 17   2016   £60

Bible. Greek - 1838 *New Testament Gospels and Acts in Modern Greek.* Athens: Andreou Koronela, 1838. first edition of this version, one of 2000 copie, 8vo., original calf, rubbed, leather bit dry, but very good, internally fine, co-ownership signature of Baptist missionary Rev. R F. Buel, ex-Colgate University with two early bookplates, small accession number and inconspicuous blindstamp on title.   Howard S. Mott Inc.   265 - 9   2016 $650

Bible. Greek - 1848 *He Palaia Diatheke Kata Tous Ebdomekonta Vetus Testamentum...* Oxonii: e Typographico Academico, 1848. 3 volumes, small 8vo., text in Greek, little toned, endpapers slightly foxed, generally bright and clean within, contemporary dark brown morocco, gilt titles to spines, all edges gilt, marbled endpapers, rubbed, corners bumped and little worn, very good, ownership inscription of A. Staveley, 47th March 1881 to Roger Garth Hooper, 1925 to Peter A. Boyle, September 1952. Unsworths Antiquarian Booksellers   30 - 18   2016   £90

Bible. Italian - 1588 *Figure del Nuovo testamento, Illustrate da Versi Vulgari Italiani.* Lyon: Guillaume Rouille, 1588. Fine illustrated Italian verse adaptation of the New Testament, Rouille's eagle and serpent device on titlepage, and 160 woodcuts, mostly by Pierre Eskrich, fine typographic ornament on verso of otherwise blank final leaf, 8vo., grained brown morocco by Duru dated 1859, title lettered in gilt on spine, inner edges richly gilt, Samuel Ashton Thompson Yates emblematic bookplate dated 1894. Maggs Bros. Ltd.   1474 - 14   2016   £1500

Bible. Latin - 1504 *Biblia Latina cum Postilla Hugonis de Sancto charo.* Basle: Johann Froben for Johann Amerbach & Johann Petri and Anton Koberger in Nuremberg, 1504. Large folio, contemporary South German blind tooled deerskin? over wooden boards, upper panelled in blind and infilled with various large tools, leafy stems thistles and central compartment with acorns and eagle stamps, lower cover with diagonal fillets forming large lozenge, compartments infilled with same large tools plus further ornamental and leafy tool, spine with three raised bands infilled with repeated large leafy tool (some worming and minor areas of wear, lacks clasps and catches), superb example of monastic binding from the turn of the 16th century, ownership inscription in the hand of Bridgettines at Altomunster, Barvaria dated 1537, with title and shelfmark, pencil note recording in duplicate of Royal Library at Munich.   Maggs Bros. Ltd. 1474 - 10   2016   £3500

Bible. Latin - 1512 *Epistola ad Rhomanos. Epistola Prima ad Cori(n)thios etc.* Paris: Henricus Stephanus Dec. 15, 1512. First edition of Lefevre's revision of the Vulgate text of St. Paul's Epistles, woodcut title border, colored red by contemporary hand, 42 fine large crible initials, all but one coloured in red by contemporary hand and numerous smaller initials, rubricated throughout, some passages pasted over or deleted in ink, few manuscript notes, clean tear just into text on K4 with edges marked from sellotape, Blackwell catalog description and illustration pasted to verso of last leaf (small repaired tear) and rear pastedown, folio, contemporary blindstamped calf over wooden boards by the Carthusians at Wedderen, near Dulmen, backstrip with five raised bands and exposed endbands, titled ink on red stained ground, shelfmark on white bound, boards with outer panels with series of blindstamped medallions and inner panels with "IHS", "MA" and "IOHS" circular stamps within diaper pattern, front board more closely filled than the rear, vellum endpapers, two fore-edge clasps sometime renewed, some expert repair to joints, ownership inscription to front flyleaf (one of the Carthusian house at Dulmen, the other dated 1959), bookplate of William Morris and old bookseller's description to front pastedown, very good copy. Blackwell's Rare Books   Marks of Genius - 31   2016   £20,000

Bible. Latin - 1549 *Testamenn Novi Editio Vulgata.* Lyon: Sebastien Gryphe, 1549. One of several illustrated editions produced by Gryphius, 16mo., 19th century half brown morocco, marbled boards, printer's woodcut device on titlepage and 108 woodcuts, three of them signed "IF", few ornamental borders and initials, bookplate of Henri Joseph Francotte, titlepage lightly soiled, otherwise fresh. Maggs Bros. Ltd.   1474 - 11   2016   £1250

Bible. Latin - 1578 *Biblia Sacra Veteris et Novi Testament.* Basle: Thomas Guarinus, 1578. First titlepage within a broad ornamental woodcut border showing Aaron and Moses, incorporating printer's device, larger version of device on titles to other two parts, 190 woodcut illustrations by Tobias Stimmer, 3 double page maps and full page map, 3 parts in one volume, 8vo., contemporary blind tooled pigskin over wooden boards, panelled and outer ornamental roll, inner roll with historiated figure of the virgus Fides, Spes, Fortunado etc. dated 1563, with central panels of the Crucifixion on upper cover with legend below, and of the Resurrection on lower cover with legend below, dated 1583 on upper cover, 7 cornerpieces remain, clasps of catches intact though one replaced, some wear, initials on upper cover erased, superbly illustrated bible, inscribed by Sebastianus Jeniken 1613 with his notes on division of Bible facing the titlepage 18th and 19th century inscriptions on flyleaf, scattering of wormholes towards end, mostly marginal, title lightly soiled, few spots and ink stains, but generally handsome copy in original binding.   Maggs Bros. Ltd. 1474 - 13   2016   £3500

Bible. Latin - 1666 *Novum Testamentum Domini Nostri Iesu Christi.* Cambridge: John Field, 1666. Pretty copy of a pocket New Testament, engraved title within architectural frame with Royal arms at top, few headlines just shaved, minor browning and occasional small stain, small circular indistinct stamp of the Corporation of Southampton thrice on verso of last leaf, 24mo., contemporary Cambridge black morocco richly gilt, gilt edges, trifle rubbed at extremities, early ownership inscription Cath. Eliz. Edridge, very good. Blackwell's Rare Books   B186 - 16   2016   £600

Bible. Latin - 1961 *The Gutenberg Bible.* Paterson and New York: Pageant Books Inc., 1961. One of 1000 numbered sets (996 for sale, this set unnumbered), 2 volumes, 464 x 330mm., very pleasing smooth calf with double fillet border, single fillet panel and cornerpieces in blind, raised bands with gilt rules, spine panels reiterating cornerpieces, dark red and brown morocco spine labels, marbled endpapers, all edges gilt, each text page with rubrication in red and blue, small initials with trailing flourishes in margins, opening leaves of the various books with elaborate initials and marginal embellishment in several colors and gold, chapter initials in red or blue, virtually mint, as new internally.   Phillip J. Pirages   67 - 141   2016 $4500

Bible. Latin - 1977 *The Gutenberg Bible.* Munich: Idion Verlag, 1977-1978. One of a small number of copies in special deluxe binding (of a total of 955 copies printed, 895 of them for sale), 2 volumes, with additional volume of commentary (in German), very ornate blindstamped calf over thick wooden boards by Ernst Ammering, covers panelled with central diapered field, multiple blind rules forming several compartments on covers and spines containing nearly 500 individual stamps (mostly ornamental, but charming stamp of a lute player on either side of central panel on each cover), large brass corner and center bosses, double raised bands, spine panels with decoration in blind similar to the covers, leather thongs with brass clasps and catches, initials, chapter numbers and headlines printed in red and blue, approximately 100 illuminated initials, some with marginal extension, the openings of each of the books of the Bible with large illuminated initials (many of these containing miniatures in several colors and gold and with elaborate fanciful marginal borders, inncorporating flowers, foliage, animals, etc., the whole reproduced in collotype in as many as 10 colors and gold.   Phillip J. Pirages   67 - 142   2016 $11,000

Bible. Polyglot - 1512 *Psalterium Daviticum Materna Lingua Expositum.* Paris: A. Verard, circa, 1512. First edition, in French & Latin, small 8vo., 18th century mottled calf, spine gilt in compartments, red morocco label (one label missing, joints and headcaps restored), titlepage with fine metalcut of David and Bathesheba enclosed within ornate metalcut crible border made up of 8 different strips, printed in red and black throughout, little marginal foxing and toning to places but generally good, 17th century? ownership inscription "Collegii Paris Societ. Jesu", bookseller's label, armorial bookplate of Thomas Brooke, FSA, owner of the Pillone library, inscribed of W. Ingham Brooke of Barford Rectory, Warwick 1908 and pencil acquisition note of Lord Kenyon 20 Dec. 1979.   Maggs Bros. Ltd.   1474 - 67   2016   £1500

Bible. Polyglot - 1665 *Jesu Christi Evangeliorum Versiones Perantique duae Gothica scil. et Anglo-Saxonica Quarum Illam Jesu Christi Evangeliorum Versiones Perantique Duae Gothica....* Dodrecht: typis & sumptibus Juniania excudebant Henricus & Joannes Essaei, 1665. First edition edited by Junius and Marshall, first printing of the Gospels in Gothic with parallel (2nd edition) of the Old English Gospels, 2 volumes in 1, additional engraved titlepage, few spots, occasional mild dampstaining, 4to., 18th century swedish half calf, speckled paper sides, spine richly decorated in compartments, olive leather label, expertly restored, some marginal ink cross referencing in an early hand, handsome copy with a series of 17th century inscription.   Blackwell's Rare Books   B184 - 12   2016   £3000

Bible. Polyglot - 1747 *Biblia Sacra Quadrilinguia Vetris Testamenti Hebraici Cum Versionibus e Regione Positis.* Lipsiae: Sumtibus Haerdum Lanckisianorum, 1747-1751. Text in Latin, German, Hebrew, Greek and Syriac, folio, quarter leather, paper covered boards, boards scuffed and rubbed at edges, soiling on endpapers, some light foxing on titlepages and text, some leaves of text bent at edges. Oak Knoll Books   310 - 278   2016 $6500

Bible. Welsh - 1929 *Psalmali Dafydd Yn Ol William Morgan 1588. (The Psalms of David).* Newtown: Gregynog Press, 1929. No. 199 of 200 copies of a total edition of 225, 298 x 220mm., original Niger backed patterned paper boards (stamped 'Gregynog Press Bindery" on rear pastedown), buckram corners, raised bands, gilt spine titling, top edge gilt, decorative wood engraved openings and initials by Horace Walter Bray, initials in red or blue, wood engraved title (with device) in red and black, part of text printed in blue, head of spine faintly darkened, trivial soiling to front board, mild spots of foxing and one small marginal stain to four leaves, otherwise very fine, binding unworn and text lean, fresh and bright.   Phillip J. Pirages   67 - 182   2016 $1000

Bibliographical Society of the University of Virginia *Studies in Bibliography, Papers of the Bibliographical Society of the University of Virginia.* Charlottesville: Bibliographical Society, 1948-1993. Volumes, I, II III in paper wrappers as issued, then cloth with paper spine labels, complete set from beginning to 1998, a total of 51 volumes.   Oak Knoll Books   310 - 74   2016 $500

Bibliographie Cartographique Internationale.   Paris: Armand Colin, 1946. 28 volumes, 8vo., cloth, with original paper wrappers bound in, complete set, ex-library with markings.   Oak Knoll Books   310 - 255   2016 $1749

Bibliotheque Forney   *Catalogue Matieres: Arts-Decoratifs Beaux-Arts Metiers Techniques.*   Paris: Bibliotheque Forney, 1970-1974. 4 volumes, 4to., cloth, ex-library with markings, front board of first volume torn at top of spine, back top corner of second volume bumped and torn, some soiling to fore-edges.   Oak Knoll Books   310 - 246   2016 $650

Bickerdyke, John   *Practical Letters to Young Sea Fishes.* London: Horace Cox, 1898. First edition, 8vo., original red cloth, gilt lettering to upper board and spine, illustrations, spine dulled, very good.   Sotheran's   Hunting, Shooting & Fishing - 110   2016   £60

Bidart, Frank   *The Book of the Body.*   New York: Farrar, Straus & Giroux, 1977. First edition, this copy inscribed for William Meredith, by author on April 3, 1977, laid in is shipping label from envelope Bidart used to send the book, filled out in Bidart's hand, bit of dust spotting to top edge of bulked text, about fine in close to fine dust jacket.   Charles Agvent   William Meredith - 15   2016 $200

Bidart, Frank   *Golden State.*   New York: George Braziller, 1973. First edition, one of 500 copies, this copy inscribed by author for William Meredith, fine in fine dust jacket. Charles Agvent   William Meredith - 16   2016 $500

Bidder, George Parker   *A Short Account of George Bidder....*   Newcastle: Frederic Crewe, 1850. Fifth edition, slight foxing, contemporary full dark purple grained calf, slightly rubbed, all edges gilt, very good.   Jarndyce Antiquarian Booksellers   CCXVII - 33   2016   £125

Biddle, Nicholas   *The Journals of the Expedition Under the Command of Captains Lewis and Clark.*   New York: Heritage Press, 1962. 2 volumes, watercolors and drawings by Carl Bodmer, printed boards with beige cloth, spines lettered gilt, spine darkened and very minor soiling, else fine in slipcases, Sandglass pamphlet laid in.   Argonaut Book Shop   Literature 2015 - 7029   2016 $75

Bielefeld, Charles Frederick   *On the use of the Improved Papier Mache in Furniture, in the Interior Decoration of Buildings and in Works of Art. (bound with) Ornaments in every Style of Design, Practically Applicable to the Decoration of the Interior of Domestic and Public Buildings...* London: Papier Nache Works No. 15, Wellington Street, Strand, 1850. London: published for the author, 1850. New edition of first work, 2 works bound in one, folio, wood engraved vignette on title engraved frontispiece, 127 engraved or lithograph plates, plate 24 was never issued, original blind stamped green cloth, some minor damp damage to one corner, generally very clean.   Marlborough Rare Books   List 55 - 69   2016   £1100

Bierce, Ambrose   1842-1914   *In the Midst of Life. Tales of Soldiers and Civilians.*   London: Chatto & Windus, 1892. First English edition, scarce, publisher's catalog, blue cloth, very good, clean and bright.   Joseph J. Felcone, Inc. Books from Five Centuries: a Miscellany - 22   2016 $400

Bierce, Ambrose   1842-1914   *The Ocean Wave.*   N.P.: Press of Robert LoMascolo, 2011. Limited to 60 copies signed by LoMascolo, 4to., quarter cloth decorated paper boards, hundreds of handset ornaments printed using gold thermography, and many hand modified and carved ornaments and decorative captials, set in 16 pt. Lucretia Italic, open caps are hand-carved Caslon, modified with a graver. Oak Knoll Books   310 - 142   2016 $500

Bierce, Ambrose   1842-1914   *Tales of Soldiers and Civilians.* San Francisco: E. L. G. Steele, 1891. First edition, octavo, original gray cloth, front and spine panels stamped in gold, presentation copy inscribed by author to fellow journalist Charles Michelson, cloth rubbed at spine ends, bit of darkening to spine panel, minor bubbling to cloth on rear cover, just bit of fading at upper edge of front cover, else fine, very nice, custom cloth slipcase.   John W. Knott, Jr./L.W. Currey, Inc.   Fall-Winter 2015 - 17253   2016 $8500

Bierce, Ambrose   1842-1914   *Tales of Soldiers & Civilians.*   Norwalk: Heritage Press, 1971. Wood engravings by Paul Landacre, dark grey cloth spine, blue mottled boards, very fine with slipcase, Sandglass pamphlet laid in. Argonaut Book Shop   Literature 2015 - 3295   2016 $45

Biggers, Earl Derr   *Seven Keys to Baldpate.*   New York: Grosset & Dunlap, Later reprint edition, small labels removed from front endpapers and pages darkened, otherwise near fine in dust jacket with several short closed tears and minor fraying at top of spine.   Mordida Books   2015 - 011398   2016 $65

Bilderbuch fur Gross Und Klein. (on titlepage). Trau Keinem Fuchs auf Gruener Heid' und Keinem Jud' Bei Seinem Eid. Nurenburg: Sturmer Verlag, 1936. Oblong 4to., cloth backed pictorial boards, slight bit of edge rubbing, else fine, illustrated in bright colors.   Aleph-bet Books, Inc.   111 - 315   2016 $3000

Billington, Elizabeth *The Randolph Caldecott Treasury.* New York & London: Frederick Warne, 1978. First edition, number 4 of only 100 copies, specially bound and signed by Billington, with double page illustration laid-in also with limitation numbered inked in, full leather, all edges gilt, leather darkened on side, else fine.   Aleph-bet Books, Inc.   112 - 90   2016 $350

Bills, Mark *Dickens and the Artists.* New Haven & London: Yale University Press, 2012. Half title, illustrations, across frontispiece and title in color, illustrations in color and black and white.   Jarndyce Antiquarian Booksellers   CCXVIII - 1077   2016   £20

Binet, Etienne *Essay des Merveilles De Nature et des Plus Nobles Artifices.* Rouen: Charles Osmont, 1644. printer's device on title, numerous text engravings, headpieces, occasional marginal dampstaining, contemporary mottled calf, five raised bands, gilt stamped spine, all edges speckled red, covers pockmarked, spine ends showing rear joint split at bottom (to first cord) save for the binding joint, very good.   Jeff Weber Rare Books   181 - 12   2016 $600

Bingham, C. *All Sorts of Comical Cats.* London: Nister, 1902. Small 4to., cloth backed pictorial boards, covers lightly soiled and bottom of inner hinge bumped, else very good+, illustrations by Wain, very scarce.   Aleph-bet Books, Inc.   111 - 471   2016 $700

Bingham, C. *Surprise Pictures from Fairy Land.* London: Nister, n.d. circa, 1907. 4to., cloth backed pictorial boards, near fine, 6 moveable tab-operated plates with double action, when the tab is pulled once, one flap flips over and if it is pulled twice, a second flap flips over the first, illustrations, outstanding copy, rare in this condition.   Aleph-bet Books, Inc.   111 - 310   2016 $1600

Bingham, Edwin *Charles F. Lummis.* San Marino: Huntington Library, 1955. First edition, frontispiece, 4 illustrations, green cloth, very fine, dust jacket with chip and edges bit darkened, as usual.   Argonaut Book Shop Biography 2015 - 5499   2016 $50

Bingham, John *A Case for Libel.* London: Victor Gollancz, 1963. First edition, crown 8vo., original red boards, backstrip lettered gilt with lean to spine, top edge trifle dusty, dust jacket bright but rather frayed, good, inscribed by author to then Director of MIT, Roger Hollis.   Blackwell's Rare Books   B184 - 116   2016   £150

Bingham, John *Murder Plan Six.* London: Victor Gollancz, 1958. First edition, crown 8vo., original red boards, backstrip lettered gilt with lean to spine, top edge trifle dusty, dust jacket bright, backstrip panel shade darkened, light dust soiling to rear panel, some light chipping to corners and backstrip ends and short closed tear at foot of upper joint fold, good, inscribed by author to then Director of MI5, Roger Hollis.   Blackwell's Rare Books   B184 - 117   2016   £200

Bingham, John *Night's Black Agent.* London: Victor Gollancz, 1961. First edition, touch of creasing to bottom corners of two leaves, crown 8vo., original red boards, backstrip lettered in black with lean to spine, top edge trifle dusty, dust jacket bright with light chipping to corners and backstrip ends, small amount of speckling at head of lower joint fold and one or two light marks, good, inscribed by author to then Director of MI5, Roger Hollis.   Blackwell's Rare Books   B184 - 118   2016   £200

Bingham, Kate *Every Girl's Alphabet.* London: 2010. Signed limited edition, one of 56 copies, with original linocut signed by artist, Luke Martineau.   Honey & Wax Booksellers   4 - 43   2016 $250

Binney, Thomas *Is It Possible to Make the Best of Both Worlds?* London: James Nisbet & Co., 1865. Fifteenth edition, pencil signature of Elizabeth Currie on title and preface and pencil note on following f.e.p., fine.   Jarndyce Antiquarian Books   CCXV - 47   2016   £35

Binns, John *Exercises, Instructive and Entertaining in False English.* Leeds: printed by Edward Baines for T. Binns and sold by J. Johnson, D. Goilvy..., 1803. Tenth edition, 12mo., original sheep, little worn, contemporary ownership inscription of Elizabeth Dent 1805, good.   Blackwell's Rare Books   B186 - 18   2016   £90

Binyon, Helen *Eric Ravilious - a Memoir of an Artist.* London: Lutterworth Press, 1983. First edition, quarto, over 100 illustrations lower cover edges slightly rubbed, free endpapers slightly tanned, very good in very good dust jacket little nicked and creased at edges.   Peter Ellis   112 - 323   2016   £55

Binyon, Laurence   1869-1943 *Dream come True.* London: Eragny Press, 1905. One of 175 copies for sale (with 10 copies on vellum), 182 x 110mm., pleasing purple morocco by Stikeman & Co. NY, covers with double fillet border and inner frame with elegant fluoronated cornerpieces, raised bands, spine attractively gilt in compartments, elaborate gilt turn-ins, first two text leaves with woodcut frames and engravings by Binyon in green and red, woodcut initials and publisher's device in colophon, front pastedown with bookplate engraved by Silvain Guillot, joints little worn, otherwise fine, internally with virtually no signs of use.   Phillip J. Pirages   67 - 130   2016 $600

Binyon, Laurence   1869-1943   *The Sirens - an Ode.* Cherlsfield: Stanton Press, 1924. First edition, one of 200 numbered copies on Kelmscott handmade paper, titlepage and firsst page of text have elaborate Celtic-style decorative border, cloth backed patterned paper boards, printed title label on upper cover, corners little rubbed, very good.   Peter Ellis   112 - 40   2016   £45

Binyon, T. J.   *Murder Will Out'.* Oxford: Oxford University, 1989. First edition, fine in price clipped dust jacket.   Mordida Books   2015 - 007591   2016 $65

Bird, J. B.   *The Laws Respecting Parish Matters, Containing the Several Offices and Duties of Churchwardens...* London: J. and W T. Clarke, 1832. Eighth edition, 8vo., occasional spots of foxing, some early leaves little grubby, small tear to titlepage at lower gutter, contemporary half green morocco, gilt spine, marbled paper covered boards, edges sprinkled brown, upper joint splitting at head with some chips to leather, small loss to tail of spine, rubbed with little surface loss to upper board, endpaper bit stained, worn but sound, ownership inscription of R. Chichester dated June 19th 1835, pencilled bookseller's notes.   Unsworths Antiquarian Booksellers   30 - 20   2016   £75

Birds Illustrated. Brentford: Birds Illustrated, 1955-1957. Quarto, photos, color plates, binder's cloth, all wrappers retained, this is the first two volumes of a monthly journal.   Andrew Isles Natural History Books   55 - 37414   2016 $120

Birdwood, James   *Heart's Ease in Heart-Trouble.*   printed for W. Johnston, 1762. Woodcut frontispiece, some spotting and dampstaining, one page creased, 12mo., contemporary canvas over paste boards, split in spine, one cord broken, good.   Blackwell's Rare Books   B186 - 19   2016   £350

Birkbeck, George   *George Birkbeck, the Pioneer of Popular Education.* London and Derby: Bemrose and Sons, 1884. First edition, half title, frontispiece, original brown cloth, bevelled boards, marked, signature of Alfred Sherlock Gooch, April 3, 84, very good.   Jarndyce Antiquarian Books   CCXV - 534   2016   £125

Birmann, Samuel   *Souvenirs de l'Oberland Bernois.* Basle: Birmann et Fils, circa, 1828. Very rare first edition, oblong folio, original tinted lithographic title, stitched as issued, 16 aquatint plates, finely printed with good tonal range and in deep black impressions, wrappers little spotted and with light fraying to margins, apart from light marginal spotting or a few flaws, very good, wide margins.   Sotheran's   Travel and Exploration - 220   2016   £895

Birnarr, Rose De   *Heures du Soir, Livre des Femmes.* Paris: Urbain Canel, Adolphe Guyot, 1833. First edition complete, 6 volumes, octavo contemporary brown quarter calf, marbled paper boards, gilt rules and lettering, rare, spine little faded, some light wear and foxing in fine condition.   The Brick Row Book Shop   Miscellany 69 - 39   2016 $1250

Birrell, Augustine   *Obiter Dicta.* London: Elliott Stock, 1884. First edition, inscribed by author for friend Margaret Muir, interesting hand written sentence on first page of last chapter titled 'Falstaff', very good in original green cloth with gilt title and small rectangle gilt design to front cover, spine faded, some bumping to spine and corners, interior pages clean with slight pulling away of rear hinge, nice, relatively scarce, very good.   The Kelmscott Bookshop   12 - 13   2016 $225

Bishop, Hal   *Romantic Landscape. The Wood Engravings of Raymond Hawthorn.*   Exeter: Bishop Books, printed by Libanus Press, 1999. One of 120 numbered copies of an edition of 140, printed on Zerkall mouldmade paper, this unnumbered and inserted inscribed "presentation copy to Richard at Christmas 1999', 11 wood engravings by Hawthorn, each displayed on separate page, titlepage printed in black and green, royal 8vo., original plain cream sewn card, dust jacket, fine.   Blackwell's Rare Books   B184 - 281   2016   £45

Bishop, Walter W.   *Background to Evolution in Africa.* Chicago: University of Chicago Press, 1967. Octavo, text illustrations, signature, blemished dust jacket.   Andrew Isles Natural History Books   55 - 38814   2016 $60

Bitting, Katherine   *Gastronomic Bibliography.* London: Holland Press, 1981. Reprint of 500 copies, thick 8vo., illustrations, maroon cloth, printed dust jacket, minor abrasion to jacket, very good.   Jeff Weber Rare Books   181 - 50   2016 $100

Bjorndal, Karen   *Biology and Conservation of Sea Turtles.* Washington: Smithsonian, 1981. Quarto, paperback, illustrations.   Andrew Isles Natural History Books   55 - 3253   2016 $60

Black, Dorothy   *The Magic Egg.* London: A. & C. Black, 1922. First edition, 4to., pictorial cloth, except for few spots on fore edge, fine, illustrations by Charles Folkard, with color frontispiece, plus 11 incredibly detailed black and white plates and pictorial endpapers, scarce.   Aleph-bet Books, Inc.   112 - 196   2016 $300

Black, George   *The Young Wife's Advice Book...* London: Ward Lock & Co. circa, 1895? Half title, final ad leaf, original olive green cloth, very good.   Jarndyce Antiquarian Books   CCXV - 71   2016   £40

Black, Robert *Death Wish.* Los Angeles: Holloway House, 1977. First edition, 12mo. paper wrappers, very good, tight. Second Life Books, Inc. 197 - 30 2016 $75

Black, William *The Beautiful Wrench, The Four MacNicols, The Pupil of Aurelius.* London: Macmillan and Co., 1881. First edition, 3 volumes, half titles, 32 page catalog (April 1881) volume I, final ad leaf volume III, untrimmed in original dark blue sand grained cloth, spines lettered gilt, boards blocked with triple ruled borders in black, fine. Jarndyce Antiquarian Booksellers CCXVII - 35 2016 £480

Blackburn, Henry *Artistic Travel in Normandy, Brittany, the Pyrenees, Spain and Algeria.* London: Sampson Low, 1892. First edition, 8vo., ads, numerous illustrations, original blue decorative cloth. J. & S. L. Bonham Antiquarian Booksellers Europe 2016 - 8400 2016 £75

Blackie, John Stuart *Classical Literature in its Relation to the Nineteenth Century and Scottish University Education.* Edinburgh: Sutherland & Knox, 1852. Disbound. Jarndyce Antiquarian Books CCXV - 535 2016 £30

Blackledge, Leonard *Behind the Evidence.* Hutchinson, n.d., Very good copy. I. D. Edrich Crime - 2016 £30

Blackmore, Richard Doddridge 1825-1900 *Lorna Doone a Romance of Exmoor.* George G. Harrap, 1920. First edition thus, original buckram, spine lettered gilt, original buckram, spine lettered gilt, cloth somewhat soiled and extremities lightly rubbed, endpapers browned, still very good, bookplate, inscription and postcard mounted on front endpapers. Bertram Rota Ltd. February List 2016 - 5 2016 £30

Blackstock, Charity *The Foggy, Foggy Dew.* London: Hodder & Stoughton, 1958. First edition, some light spotting on top of page edges, otherwise fine in dust jacket with tiny wear at spine ends. Mordida Books 2015 - 010151 2016 $65

Blackstone, William 1723-1780 *Commentaries on the Laws of England.* Oxford: printed at the Clarendon Press, 1766-1769. Mixed edition, volume 1 second edition, volume II third edition, volumes III and IV first editions, 4 quarto volumes, uniformly bound in contemporary calf, spines with orange and green morocco lettering labels, spine stamped and lettered gilt, board edges tooled in gilt, outer hinges and spines with some professional repairs, inner hinges volume I and II repaired, volume II with some worming to inside of boards and to first and last few leaves, not affecting text, tiny wormhole through a few pages of volume II, not affecting text, otherwise very clean set, previous owner's old ink signature, overall very good and very attractive set. Heritage Book Shop Holiday 2015 - 11 2016 $3500

Blackwell, Elizabeth *The Laws of Life with Special Reference to the Physical Education of Girls.* New York: George P. Putnam, 1852. First edition, slate gray cloth, edges stained red, spine bit faded, few very tiny spots, else remarkably fresh, tight copy as close to fine as one could hope for, contemporary signature of E. H. Cressey, lovely near fine copy, very scarce. Joseph J. Felcone, Inc. Books from Five Centuries: a Miscellany - 24 2016 $12,000

Blackwell, H. F. *The Occupation of Hausaland 1900-1904.* London: printed by the Government Printer, 1927. First edition, 8vo., original blue cloth, gilt lettering to upper board, cloth bit faded, otherwise near fine, from Wigan Public Library with bookplate inside front cover, withdrawal stamp on opposite flyleaf, with their oval blindstamp to title. Sotheran's Travel and Exploration - 2 2016 £198

Blackwood, Caroline *The Fate of Mary Rose.* London: Jonathan, 1981. First edition, octavo, fore-edge very slightly spotted, otherwise fine in very near fine dust jacket, presentation copy from author inscribed for Diana Athill, literary editor. Peter Ellis 112 - 42 2016 £150

Blackwood, Caroline *The Stepdaughter.* London: Duckworth, 1976. First edition, quarto, near fine in like dust jacket slightly creased at bottom edge, presentation copy from author inscribed for fellow writer Francis Wyndham. Peter Ellis 112 - 41 2016 £150

Blacow, Richard *A Letter to William King.* London: printed for R. Griffiths, 1755. Second edition, 8vo., slightly marked, disbound. Jarndyce Antiquarian Booksellers CCXVI - 348 2016 £40

The Blade and the Ear: a Book for Young Men. London: William P. Nimmo, 1875. Half title, frontispiece, plates, 16 page catalog, labels removed from pastedowns, original green cloth, bevelled boards blocked in black and gilt, slightly dulled, with slight marking to back board, labels partly remoed from leading pastedown, all edges gilt. Jarndyce Antiquarian Books CCXV - 72 2016 £25

Blades, William *How to Tell a Caxton with Some Hints Where and How Some Might Be Found.* London: Henry Sotheran & Co., 1870. First edition, 12mo., original printed burnt orange wrappers with black title and decoration on front wrapper, foldout frontispiece and 15 plates, little chipping to wrappers, neat ink name, otherwise very good. Sotheran's Piccadilly Notes - Summer 2015 - 49 2016 £248

Blagdon, Francis William *A New Dictionary of Classical Quotations.* London: printed for Robert Stodart, 1819. First edition, light age toning, 12mo., untrimmed in original boards, paper label to spine, joints rubbed, some slight wear, early ink inscription of Henry Houghton and later monogram stamp of STC, good. Blackwell's Rare Books B186 - 20 2016 £120

Blaikie, Francis *Collection of Works.* printed for John Harding, 1817-1821. 6 works in 1 volume, plate in first work browned, little waterstaining in places, mostly in first work, 12mo., contemporary half calf over drab boards, flat spine with small gilt tool in compartments formed by gilt rules, red lettering piece, slightly worn, boards soiled, ink stamped rest inside front cover with name erased, repeated inside rear cover with name John Jervis Emerson, preserved contemporary bookseller ticket, good.   Blackwell's Rare Books   B186 - 21   2016   £750

Blaine, Delabere P. *Encyclopaedia of Rural Sports or Complete Account...* London: Longman, Brown, Green and Longmans, 1852. New edition, 8vo., sometime bound in serviceable leather, gilt lettering to spine, illustrated in text with wood engravings, splash marks to spine, very good.   Sotheran's   Hunting, Shooting & Fishing - 160   2016   £60

Blair, Hugh *Advice to Youth.* London: B. Crosby & Co., 1808. Third edition, 16mo., 1 woodcut illustration, contemporary half brown calf, maroon morocco label, slightly rubbed.   Jarndyce Antiquarian Books   CCXV - 73   2016   £70

Blake, Nicholas *The Dreadful Hollow.* New York: Harper & Bros., 1953. First American edition, crown 8vo., original quarter black cloth with terra cotta sides, backstrip lettered in white, top edge little dusty, other edges rough trimmed, dust jacket with small amount of fraying and few spots of internal tape repair, good, inscribed by Cecil Day-Lewis for Josie Baird.   Blackwell's Rare Books   B186 - 196   2016   £60

Blake, William   1757-1827 *All Religions are One.* London: Trianon Press, 1970. One of 600 numbered copies out of 662 copies, 10 facsimile leaves plus five page essay by Keynes, morocco backed marbled paper covered boards, green spine sunned to brown, else fine in publisher's slipcase.   Joseph J. Felcone, Inc.   Books from Five Centuries: a Miscellany - 25   2016 $400

Blake, William   1757-1827 *Poems from William Blake's Songs of Innocence.* London: Bodley Head, 1967. Limited to only 275 copies for presentation by publisher,, this copy inscribed by artist to pianist Alvin Novak, with drawing, Dec. '67, pictorial wrappers, fine, illustrations by Maurice Sendak with pictorial cover and 8 color illustrations.   Aleph-bet Books, Inc.   111 - 406   2016 $7500

Blake, William   1757-1827 *Songs of Innocence.* Trianon Press, 1954. Limited to 1600 copies, this copy number 1154 for the American market, 8vo., original full crushed morocco, marbled paper slipcase, 31 color plates printed by collotype and stencil in facsimile of originals by Blake, spine slightly sunned, little wear to slipcase, otherwise very good.   Sotheran's   Piccadilly Notes - Summer 2015 - 50   2016   £350

Blakers, M. *The Atlas of Australian Birds.* Melbourne: Melbourne University Press, 1985. Reprint, octavo, text illustrations, maps, laminated boards.   Andrew Isles Natural History Books   55 - 18075   2016 $50

Blakston, W. A. *The Illustrated Book of Canaries and Cape-Birds British and Foreign.* London: Paris & New York: Cassell, Petter, Galpin & Co., Presumed first edition, 4to., frontispiece and 55 other full color chromolithograph plates, 84 illustrations from wood engravings throughout text, library rebind in red cloth over boards with gilt titles and number on spine, marbled edges, previous owner's name handwritten on titlepage, also couple of samples of blindstamps within, library number on pastedown and reverse of titlepage, bookplate removed from pastedown and there are 2 stamps on endpapers, no other obvious library markings, no foxing, but there is minor marking to some pages.   Simon Finch   2015 - 113   2016 $288

Bland, John *An Essay in Praise of women...* Edinburgh: printed for and sold by W. Darling at his Warehouse Turk's Close, 1767. 12mo., text rather dusted with marginal finger marking, spotting & little creasing and chipping to few corners, old stain at foot of titlepage, small tear to blank corner of I1, old stain to blank lower margin of P3, without final ad leaf, recent quarter tan calf, marbled boards, raised & gilt ruled spine, new endpapers.   Jarndyce Antiquarian Books   CCXV - 74   2016   £320

Bland, Miles *Problems in the Different Branches of Philosophy...* London: Whittaker Treacher & Co., 1830. First edition, half title, errata slip, ad leaf, original green cloth, little marked.   Jarndyce Antiquarian Books   CCXV - 569   2016   £40

Blanton, Catherine *The Three Miracles.* New York: John Day, 1946. First edition, 8vo., fine in fine dust jacket, inscribed by Politi with charming watercolor, scarce.   Aleph-bet Books, Inc.   111 - 350   2016 $700

Blasco Ibanez, Vicente *The Torrent (Entre Naranjos).* New York: E. P. Dutton, 1921. First American edition, contemporary light pencil name, foxing on fore-edge and rubbing on boards, very good in near fine illustrated dust jacket by Dean Cornwell.   Between the Covers Rare Books   208 - 11   2016 $500

Blasingame, Ike *Dakota Cowboy. My Life in the Old Days.* New York: G. P. Putnam's Sons, 1958. First edition, drawings by John Mariani, endpaper maps, brown cloth, gilt, very fine with pictorial dust jacket.   Argonaut Book Shop Biography 2015 - 7684   2016 $175

Blatch, Harriot Stanton *Challenging Years.* New York: Putnams, 1940. First edition, 8vo., very nice in dust jacket, inscribed by author's daughter, Nora Stanton Barney to Winifred A. Tyler.   Second Life Books, Inc.   196A - 157   2016 $150

Blatty, William Peter *The Exorcist.* New York: Harper and Row, 1971. First edition, touch of foxing to top page edges, else lovely, easily near fine in like dust jacket, this the copy of Robert Keeshan (Captain Kangaroo). Royal Books 52 - 14 2016 $1375

Blatz, William Emet *Understanding the Young Child.* London: University of London Press, 1944. First edition, half title, illustrations, original orange cloth, booklabel of National Bureau for the Co-operation in Child Care Library. Jarndyce Antiquarian Books CCXV - 536 2016 £20

Blayney, Major-General Lord *Narrative of a Forced Journey through Spain and France...* London: E. Kerby, 1814. First edition, 2 volumes, 8vo., frontispiece, contemporary brown half calf, inkstain in margin of titlepage, good set. J. & S. L. Bonham Antiquarian Booksellers Europe 2016 - 8433 2016 £400

Blazek, Douglas *Any Typhoons.* Sacramento: Open Skull Press, 1970. First edition, 200 copies, long inscription from Blazek apologizing for contents, signed by author, wrappers, near fine. Simon Finch 2015 - AB116504 2016 $176

Bleecker & Sons, J., New Yor Real Estate Auctioneer *Peremptory Sale of Valuable City Property to be sold at Auction by J. Bleecker & Sons, 13 Broad Street on Thursday the 16th of February 1837 at 12 O'Clock.* New York: Hayward & Co., 1837. 8vo., original plain blue wrappers, wrinkled, 20, i.e. 21, lithographed leaves of maps, stitched, uncut, folded vertically down the middle. Howard S. Mott Inc. 265 - 12 2016 $1750

Bleeker, P. *Over Eenige Visschen van Van Diemensland.* Amsterdam: C. G. Van Der Post, 1855. Quarto, one folding plate, publisher's printed wrappers, rare. Andrew Isles Natural History Books 55 - 38730 2016 $950

Blegvad, Lenore *Kitty and Mr. Kipling: neighbors in Vermont.* New York: McElderry, 2005. First printing, 8vo., illustrations by Erik Blegvad, inscribed by author to poet William Jay Smith, signed by artist as well, paper over boards. Second Life Books, Inc. 196A - 158 2016 $45

Blessington, Marguerite Power Farmer Gardiner, Countess of 1789-1849 *The Keepsake for 1844.* London: Longmans, 1844. Engraved frontispiece and title plates, original maroon cloth, attractively blocked in blind and gilt, rebacked, little darkened and rubbed, signature of Kate Barber 1844, armorial bookplates of Algernon Graves, Renier booklabel. Jarndyce Antiquarian Booksellers CCXVIII - 430 2016 £120

Blewitt, Jonathan *The Matrimonial Ladder.* London: J. Alfred Novello, circa, 1841. Engraved title by George Cruikshank, few marginal tears, disbound, spine and final leaf repaired with cream tape. Jarndyce Antiquarian Books CCXV - 142 2016 £50

Bligh, William 1754-1817 *The Log of the HMS Bounty 1787-1789.* Guildford: Genesis Publications, 1975. 237/500 copies, foldout map at rear printed in black and red, titlepage printed in black and red, full facsimile preceded by frontispiece illustration and newspaper facsimile, imperial 8vo., original half brown leather and blue buckram with ship design stamped in gilt to upper board, backstrip with five raised bands and decorated in gilt with darker leather label lettered in gilt, one or two light surface marks, blue pagemarker, edges sprinkled blue, endpapers with illustrations of ship's design, buckram slipcase with printed label, very good. Blackwell's Rare Books B184 - 15 2016 £450

Bligh, William 1754-1817 *A Narrative of the Mutiny on Board His Majesty's Ship Bounty and the Subsequent Voyage...* London: printed for George Nicol, 1790. First edition, large quarto, folding engraved plan, uncut in original drab blue-green boards, rebacked with quarter paper spine, boards with some soiling and four inch stain to front board, small professional repairs to outer margin of leaves C2, C3, L4 and top margin of B2, overall very good. Heritage Book Shop Holiday 2015 - 13 2016 $19,500

Bligh, William 1754-1817 *The Voyage of the Bounty's Launch as Related in William Bligh's Despatch to the Admiralty and the Journal of John Fryer.* Golden Cockerel Press, 1934. First edition, 190/300 copies printed on Arnold's all rag paper, 12 wood engravings by Robert Gibbings and 2 full page occasional foxspots to borders and gutter, folio, original white and rust red sailcloth canvases, backstrip lettered gilt light overall dust soiling with faint partial ring mark to upper board and small indentation to lower untrimmed, few foxspots to free endpapers, good, signed by Owen Rutter, one of the partners in the Press, with original prospectus. Blackwell's Rare Books B184 - 266 2016 £850

Blish, James *And All the Stars a Stage.* London: Faber and Faber, 1972. First UK edition, octavo, ownership initials, spine little bruised at tail, near fine in like dust jacket just little rubbed at edges. Peter Ellis 112 - 43 2016 £25

Blish, James *A Case of Conscience.* New York: Walker and Co., 1969. First US hardcover edition, octavo, boards, mild age darkening to text block, fine in fine dust jacket with mild age tanning to edges (common to this book). John W. Knott, Jr./L.W. Currey, Inc. Fall-Winter 2015 - 16924 2016 $300

Bloch, Robert *Horror - 7.* New York: Belmont, 1963. First edition, fine, unread copy in wrappers, paperback original. Mordida Books 2015 - 011174 2016 $65

Bloch, Robert *Pleasant Dreams-Nightmares.* Sauk City: Arkham House, 1960. First edition, presentation from author to August Derleth, fine in fine dust jacket, fine association copy, octavo, cloth.   John W. Knott, Jr./L.W. Currey, Inc.   Fall-Winter 2015 - 17254   2016 $2500

Bloch, Robert *Sea Kissed.* London: Utopia Pub. Ltd. n.d., 1945. First edition, small octavo, pictorial wrappers, author's scarce first book, some mild soiling, several small stain spots to rear wrappers, staples rusted, very good to nearly fine.   John W. Knott, Jr./L.W. Currey, Inc.   Fall-Winter 2015 - 17233   2016 $1750

Blochman, Lawrence G. *Clues for Dr. Coffee. A Second Casebook.* Philadelphia: J. B. Lippincott Co., 1964. First edition, signed on titlepage by author, presentation by author for Doc Hasse, exceptional copy.   Buckingham Books 2015 - 29111   2016 $450

Block, Lawrence *The Burglar in the Library.* London: Orion, 1997. First edition, very fine in dust jacket, signed by author.   Mordida Books   2015 - 000014   2016 $55

Block, Lawrence *A Dance at the Slaughterhouse.* New York: Morrow, 1991. First edition, fine in dust jacket, signed by author.   Mordida Books   2015 - 009652   2016 $55

Block, Lawrence *Mona.* Unity: Five-Star, 1999. First hardcover edition, very fine, without dust jacket, as issued. Mordida Books   2015 - 011600   2016 $65

Block, Lawrence *A Week as Andrea Benstock.* New York: Arbour House, 1973. First edition, fine in fine dust jacket, uncommon.   Between the Covers Rare Books   208 - 97   2016 $300

Blonsell, J. R. *The Servant's Book of Reference...* London: Bailey and Co. circa, 1860. Recent marbled boards, crude paper label, tan calf spine, illustrations, little trimmed down.   Jarndyce Antiquarian Books   CCXV - 75   2016   £225

Blossom, Henry M. *Checkers, a Hard Luck Story.* New York: Grosset & Dunlap, 1896. Reprint, inscribed by Blossom and the entire cast, tan linen with photo cover little worn, else nice.   Second Life Books, Inc.   196A - 163   2016 $50

Blount, Thomas Pope *A Natural History Containing Many not Common Observations Extracted Out of the Best Modern Writers.*   London: printed by R. Bentley, 1693. First edition, 16mo., newer three quarter calf, marbled boards, red leather spine label, new endpapers, upper inner corner of title with minor repair, lower corner page 97 torn off affecting one word, expert repair to gutter of text leaf, faint circular enclosed library stamp on title (withdrawn), text sheets lightly browned, handsome copy, fine.   Argonaut Book Shop   Natural History 2015 - 7689   2016 $750

Blumenthal, Joseph *Typographic Years.* New York: printed for members of the Grolier Club, 1982. First edition, one of 300 copies, numbered and signed by author, fine in original slipcase, this copy inscribed on endpaper to Random House founder Donald Klopfer.   Second Life Books, Inc.   196A - 164   2016 $150

Blunden, Edmund *Choice or Chance, New Poems.* London: Cobden Sanderson, 1934. First edition, one of 45 numbered copies, this unnumbered, being one of 10 for presentation, signed by author, 8vo., original pink buckram, gilt lettered backstrip faded, free endpapers, lightly browned, top edge gilt, others untrimmed, with Rex Whistler designed bookplate of Kenneth Rae.   Blackwell's Rare Books   B186 - 184   2016   £160

Blunden, Edmund *Halfway House. A Miscellany of New Poems.* London: Cobden Sanderson, 1932. First edition, one of 70 numbered copies, this unnumbered, being one of 10 for presentation signed by author, 8vo., original orange buckram faintly spotted, gilt lettered backstrip little faded, free endpapers lightly browned, top edge gilt, others untrimmed, good, with Kenneth Rae bookplate designed by Rex Whistler.   Blackwell's Rare Books   B186 - 185   2016   £160

Blunden, Edmund *Retreat.* Cobden-Sanderson, 1928. First edition, one of 112 numbered copies, this unnumbered, being one of 12 for presentation, printed on handmade paper and signed by author title printed in black and red, crown 8vo., original tan buckram, darkened backstrip gilt lettered, free endpapers lightly browned, untrimmed, very good, inscribed by author to Kenneth Rae, with Rae's signature.   Blackwell's Rare Books   B186 - 186   2016   £250

Blunden, Edmund *A Summer's Fancy.* London: Beaumont Press, 1930. Number 123 of 325 copies, 8vo. illustrations by Randolph Schwabe, patterned paper over boards, cloth spine, cover somewhat browned on spine and edges, cover little worn at corners and ends of spine, otherwise very good.   Second Life Books, Inc.   197 - 31   2016 $85

Blunt, Wilfrid Scawen 1840-1922 *The Bride of the Nile: a Political Extravaganza in three acts of rhymed verse.* privately printed, 1907. First edition, slight spotting at beginning and end and little creasing but nice, signed by author on upper wrapper, original purple printed wrappers bound in modern marbled boards, spine with printed label.   Simon Finch   2015 - 4172   2016 $201

Blunt, Wilfrid Scawen 1840-1922 *Esther, Love Lyrics and Natalia's Resurrection.* London: Kegan, Paul, Trench, Trubner & Co. ltd., 1892. First edition, original green cloth lettered and decorated in gilt, cloth little rubbed at edges and endpapers, somewhat browned, otherwise nice, presentation copy inscribed by author for Violet Thurlow.   Bertram Rota Ltd.   February List 2016 - 8   2016   £175

Blunt, Wilfrid Scawen 1840-1922 *The Love Sonnets of Proteus.* London: Kegan Paul, Trench & Co., 1885. Fifth edition, original green cloth lettered and decorated in gilt, cloth just little worn and slight spotting to endpapers, otherwise very nice, presentation inscribed by author for Mrs. Rae.   Bertram Rota Ltd.   February List 2016 - 7   2016   £250

Blunt, Wilfrid Scawen 1840-1922 *My Diaries: Being a Personal Narrative of Events 1888-1914.* London: Martin Secker, 1919-1920. First edition, 2 volumes, original dark blue cloth with gilt title and author to spine and front board, light bumping but in unusually nice condition, offsetting and light spotting to pastedowns and free endpapers, otherwise very good.   The Kelmscott Bookshop   13 - 10   2016 $200

Bly Aleixandre, Vicente *Twenty Poems.* Madison: Seventies Press, 1977. First edition, 8vo., bound in plain paper wrappers with printed dust jacket, inscribed by author to poet Barbara Howes, nice copy.   Second Life Books, Inc.   196A - 166   2016 $65

Bly, Robert *Grass from Two Years and let's Leave.* Denver: Ally Press, 1975. Of a total edition of 200 numbered copies, this one of 50 signed by author, paper wrappers, nice, this copy not numbered.   Second Life Books, Inc.   196A - 171   2016 $75

Blyth, Edmund Kell *Life of William Ellis (founder of the Birkbeck School).* London: Kegan Paul, 1892. Second edition, half title, frontispiece, slight spotting, original dark blue cloth, slight nick to head of following hinge.   Jarndyce Antiquarian Books   CCXV - 641   2016   £75

Boccaccio, Giovanni 1313-1375 *Il Decameron.* Chelsea: Ashendene Press, 1920. One of 80 paper copies for sale (of 105 printed), along with 6 on vellum, 419 x 292 mm., original linen backed blue paper boards, printed paper label on spine, fine printed initials in red and blue designed by Graily Hewitt, text printed in black, red and blue, bookplate of William Henry Smith, 3rd Viscount Hambleden (1903-48), cover with a number of superficial marks and handful of small abrasions (two more prominent), faint fading along two edges of each board, surprisingly solid, only trivial wear to corners and internally pristine.   Phillip J. Pirages   67 - 9   2016 $5000

Boccaccio, Giovanni 1313-1375 *Decameron. the Model of Wit, Mirth, Eloquence and Conversation Framed in Ten Days, of an Hundred Curious Pieces.* Oxford: Shakespeare Head Press, 1934-1935. 15/325 sets (of an edition of 328 sets), printed in double column on Batchelor handmade paper, in black and blue, with large historiated capitals also printed in blue, superb wood engravings, including beautifully executed borders, small folio, original mid-blue hermitage calf trifle edge rubbed, smooth backstrips gilt lettered, blue green and tan marbled endpapers, top edge gilt on rough, others untrimmed.   Blackwell's Rare Books   Marks of Genius - 10   2016   £850

Boccaccio, Giovanni 1313-1375 *Boccaccio's Decameron.* Oxford: Shakespeare Head Press, 1934-1935. No. 88 of 325 copies on paper (and three on vellum), 2 volumes, 289 x 203mm., publisher's blue crushed half morocco over ivory buckram, flat spine lettered in gilt, marbled endpapers, top edge gilt, others untrimmed, housed in later slipcase, with 7 line foliated initials in blue, five elaborate architectural titlepage borders, small woodcut of author appearing on two titlepages, 11 large woodcuts, 100 smaller cuts, printed in blue and black, slight reside from leather preservative, paper covering the upper hinge of first volume split along half its length otherwise quite, fine, easily soiled cream colored sides spotless, bindings with only negligible wear, text quite beautiful.   Phillip J. Pirages   67 - 314   2016 $1500

Boccaccio, Giovanni 1313-1375 *The Nymphs of Fiesole.* Verona: Officina Bodoni, 1952. No. 56 of 225 copies, 288 x 194mm., publisher's quarter vellum over purple patterned boards designed by Hugo Zovetti, vellum tips, flat spine with gilt titling, in a (probably later) green dust jacket and publisher's (just slightly worn) slipcase, latter with label specially printed by previous owner, heliogravure facsimile of titlepage from original 1597 English edition and 23 woodcuts, recut by Fritz Kredel, virtually pristine.   Phillip J. Pirages   67 - 267   2016 $1600

Bock, Carl *The Head-Hunters of Borneo.* London: Sampson Low Marston, Searle & Rivington, 1881. First edition, 4to., original turquoise pictorial cloth lettered gilt on spine and cover, 1 folding map, 20 lithographs, plates and illustrations in text, color plates in excellent condition, some rubbing at hinges and spine ends, slight snag and slight wear at lower hinge, otherwise sound clean, bright, very good.   Any Amount of Books   2015 - C12175   2016   £625

Boddam-Whetham, J. W. *Roraima and British Guiana; with a Glance at Bermuda, the West Indies and the Spanish Main.*   London: Hurst & Blackett, 1879. First edition, 8vo., folding map, frontispiece, original decorative cloth, vignette on titlepage, water on titlepage and frontispiece on corner.   J. & S. L. Bonham Antiquarian Booksellers   America 2016 - 9865   2016   £125

Boddington, Craig *From Mount Kenya to the Cape. Ten Years of African Hunting.*   Long Beach: Safari Press, 1987. Second edition, 8vo., original cloth and wrapper, black and white photos, fine.   Sotheran's   Hunting, Shooting & Fishing - 4   2016   £50

Bodenstedt, Hans *Das Seemanns ABC.* Leipzig: Alfred Hans, 1942. First edition, oblong 4to., cloth backed boards, edges have some wear, front cover scratched, otherwise clean, tight and very good+, illustrations in green line, full page color illustrations, scarce.   Aleph-bet Books, Inc.   111 - 9   2016 $400

Bodmer, Karl *Bodmer's America.* London: Alecto Historical Editions, 1991. No. 23 of 125 copies, 765 x 620mm., loose as issued in five buckram folders inside cloth solander box, paper labels, 81 hand finished color plates, heightened with gum arabic, one corner of (heavy) box expertly repaired, two-inch closed internal tear to title sheet seamlessly mended, other very minor signs of use to box, portfolios and their plates as new, even tissue guards in pristine condition.   Phillip J. Pirages   67 - 80   2016 $45,000

Bodoni, Giovanni Battista   1740-1813 *Manuale Tipografico Del Cavaliere Giambattista Bodoni.* London: Holland Press, 1960. One of 500 copie, exact facsimile of Bodoni specimen book, 2 volumes, 4to., decorated paper covered boards, paper spine labels, lacing slipcase, pristine set.   Oak Knoll Books   310 - 179   2016 $350

Boelter, Homer H. *Portfolio of Hopi Kachinas.* Hollywood: Homer H. Boelter, 1969. First edition, 528 of 1000 numbered copies signed by author, folio, 16 full page chromolithograph plates, numerous text drawings in color and black and white, decorative endpapers, pale green cloth decoratively stamped and lettered in metallic green, plus extra suite of 16 loose folio color plates in light cardboard portfolio, both housed in matching pale green slipcase, very fine.   Argonaut Book Shop   Native American 2015 - 7489   2016 $325

Boer, Charles *Charles Olson in Connecticut.* Chicago: Swallow Press, 1975. First edition, 8vo., nice in little yellowed and chipped dust jacket.   Second Life Books, Inc.   196A - 174   2016 $75

Boer, Charles *Varmint Q.* Chicago: Swallow Press, 1972. 8vo., woodcuts by David Hayes, includes signed letter from author to poet Paul Metcalf laid in, very good in somewhat stained and chipped dust jacket.   Second Life Books, Inc.   196A - 175   2016 $50

Boerio, Giusseppe *Dizionario Del Dialetto Veneziano.* Venice: Andrea Santini E. Figlio, 1829. First edition, 4to., half white vellum and marbled boards with title gilt on light brown leather label, uncommon, sound, clean, very good.   Any Amount of Books   2015 - A74333   2016   £550

Boethius, Anicius Manlius Severinus *De Consolatione Philosophiae, Libri Quinque.* Antwerp: ex officina Plantiniana, 1607. 8vo., printer's device to titlepage and final leaf, woodcut initials, very light toning towards edges, ink blot to page 279-80 not affecting text to recto, obscuring a few letters to verso, contemporary vellum, raised bands, title inked to spine, blind tooled borders, vellum darkened with some marks, corners worn and small areas of loss, narrow strip of vellum lost to top edge of lower board, some bookseller's pencil notes, notes in old hand to rear pastedown, very good, armorial bookplate of William Malsey of St. John's College, Cambridge.   Unsworths Antiquarian Booksellers Ltd.   E05 - 3   2016   £575

Bogan, Louise *Collected Poems 1923-1953.* New York: Noonday, 1954. First edition, 8vo., author's presentation on flyleaf to poet and editor Bill Claire, erratum slip tipped in, yellow cloth, cover little faded and soiled, otherwise very good, tight copy.   Second Life Books, Inc.   196A - 177   2016 $85

Bogira, Steve *$144 a Month.* Chicago: Sherwin Beach Press, 1993. Number 54 of 200 copies, four portraits by photographer Mike Tappin, printed on Johannot paper by Jennifer Hughes and Martha Chiplis, bound in gray soft cover paper wrappers, signed by designer Bob McCamant, fine.   The Kelmscott Bookshop   13 - 53   2016 $450

Bohl, Niels *Atomteori Og Naturbeskrivelse.* Copenhagen: Bianco Lunos Bogtrykkerii, 1929. First edition, 8vo., very good+ in original printed wrappers, spine archivall restored, lettering intact.   By the Book, L. C.   45 - 9   2016 $950

Boileau-Narcejac *Celle Qui n'Etait Plus.* Paris: Denoel, 1952. First edition, near fine in wrappers and lightly rubbed, near fine dust jacket.   Between the Covers Rare Books   204 - 78   2016 $900

Bois, Yve-Alain *Formless: a User's Guide.* New York: Zone Books, 1997. First edition, quarto, copiously illustrated in color and black and white, fine in very good dust jacket little rubbed at top edge.   Peter Ellis   112 - 25   2016   £95

Boisseau, F. G. *Pyretologie Physiologique ou Traite des Fievres Considerees dans l'Esprit de la Nouvelle Doctrine Medicale.* Paris: J. B. Bailliere, 1823. First edition, very good, half calf over marbled boards, gilt spine.   Edwin V. Glaser Rare Books   2015 - 10142   2016 $200

Bokum, Herman *The Stranger's Gift. A Christmas and New Year's Present.* Boston: Light & Horton, 1836. First edition, 12mo., original blindstamped brown cloth, lettered gilt, frontispiece, with half title, very good with some scattered foxing two leaves more heavily, two and a half pages of religious musings in pencil on rear endpapers dated June 1838.   Howard S. Mott Inc.   265 - 32   2016 $850

Bolano, Roberto *Los Detectives Salvajes.* Barcelona: Editorial Anagrams, 1998. First Spanish edition, light rubbing overall, few production wrinkles on spine and nearly imperceptible stain on pge fore edges, else near fine and unread in printed stiff wrappers with French flaps.   Royal Books   48 - 67   2016 $550

Bolano, Roberto *The Savage Detectives.* New York: Farrar Straus & Giroux, 2007. First US edition, octavo, fine in fine dust jacket.   Peter Ellis   112 - 45   2016   £75

Bolognese, Don *Once Upon a Mountain.* Philadelphia: Lippincott, 1967. 8vo., illustrations by author, yellow cloth stamped in pink, cover very slightly scuffed at corners and ends of spine, otherwise nice in chipped and little soiled dust jacket.   Second Life Books, Inc.   197 - 32   2016 $45

Bolsche, Wilhelm *Charles Darwin. Ein Lebensbild.* Leipzig: Voigtlander, 1898. First edition, presentation copy inscribed by author to his brother, Gerhart Hauptmann dated 1898, small 8vo., contemporary red cloth, portrait frontispiece, light wear to binding, few pages with very light spotting, old Polish library stamp on verso of list of contents and release note in pencil on title.   Sotheran's   Piccadilly Notes - Summer 2015 - 51   2016   £248

Boltanski, Christian *Christian Boltanski: lessons of Darkness.* Chicago: Museum of Contemporary Art, 1988. First edition, softcover exhibition catalog, near fine in wrappers, signed by Boltanski, uncommon thus.   Jeff Hirsch Books   E-List 80 - 4   2016 $200

Bolton, Claire *Maziarczyk Paste Papers.* Oxford: Alembic Press, 1991. First edition, limited to 175 numbered copies, 8vo, quarter cloth, paste paper over boards.   Oak Knoll Books   310 - 196   2016 $600

Bolton, Robert *Instructions for a Right Comforting Afflicted Consequences...* imprinted by Felix Kyngston for Thomas Weaver, 1631. First edition, woodut printer's device on title, very slight dampstaining in upper margins, initial blank discarded, small 4to., contemporary mottled calf, blind tooled corner ornaments, author's name in gilt on spine, top compartment of spine defective early initials "PC" opposite signature B, inscription on titlepage "Christo Duce, R.C.", 17th century of T. Browne, 20th century aquisition note by Reginald Chas. Tudor Hutchins, very good.   Blackwell's Rare Books   B186 - 22   2016   £1750

Bonaventura, Saint   1221-1274 *Die Legend des Heyligen Vatters Francisci.* Nuremberg: Hieronymus Holtzel for the heirs of Caspar Rosentalet, April, 1512. First German edition, 4to., titlepage with large woodcut, full page woodcuts, smaller woodcuts, 57 woodcuts in all, all in fine contemporary color, predominantly yellows, greens and browns, 4to., 16th century pigskin over wooden boards, panelled and decorated in blind, remains of clasps (rubbed), rare, from the Virtue and Cahill Library (John Vertue formerly Virtue [1826-1900] and John Baptist Cahill [1841-1910]), overprinted bookplate noting war bomb damage to library in 1941, much used copy with some defects, repaired tear to foot of F3 and V1, no loss, I1, M1 &T4 lower outer corner torn away with loss of some text to lower portion of leaves, N1 woodcut with small hole expertly repaired, some old tears repaired, general staining and soiling throughout.   Maggs Bros. Ltd.   1474 - 16   2016   £12,500

Bonaventura, Saint   1221-1274 *Tractado en la Contempacion de la Vida de Nuestro Senor Iesu Christo Agora Nueuamente Corregdio y Emendado yy con Licentia Impresso.* Valladolid: M. Borras...., 1588. Rare illustrated Spanish edition, small 8vo., blue morocco gilt a la Francaise by Brugalla, title lettered on spine, covers with device of Isidoro Fernandez, gilt turn-ins, all edges gilt, titlepage with woodcut of the Trinity, 21 woodcuts in text, booklabels of Isidoro Fernandez, book collector of Barcelona.   Maggs Bros. Ltd.   1474 - 15   2016   £1800

Bond, Carrie Jacobs *Tales of Little Cats.* Joliet: Volland, 1918. No other printings, 8vo., pictorial boards, fine in original box, box very slightly worn, beautiful color illustrations by Katherine Sturges Dodge, uncommon.   Aleph-bet Books, Inc.   112 - 101   2016 $350

Bond, Earl D. *The Treatment of Behavior Disorders Following Encephalitis.* New York: Commonwealth Fund Division of Publications, 1931. First edition, original cloth, frontispiece, figures, graphs, charts, 8vo., good ex-library.   Edwin V. Glaser Rare Books   2015 - 7746   2016 $45

Bond, Michael *Paddington Abroad.* London: Collins, 1961. First edition, 8vo., newly and handsomely bound in half dark blue calf over dark blue polished cloth sides, spine with 5 raised bands, ruled and lettered gilt with gilt centers, top edge gilt, line drawings by Peggy Fortnum, both externally and internally fine, without inscription.   Sotheran's Piccadilly Notes - Summer 2015 - 52   2016   £168

Bond, Michael *Paddington marches On.* London: Collins, 1964. First edition, 8vo., newly and handsomely bound in half dark blue calf over dark blue polished cloth sides, spine with 5 raised bands ruled and lettered gilt with gilt cebtres, top edges gilt, line drawings by Fortunum, externally and internally fine. Sotheran's Piccadilly Notes - Summer 2015 - 53 2016 £168

Bond, Michael *Paddington Takes the Air.* London: Collins, 1970. First edition, 8vo., newly and handsomely bound in half dark blue calf over dark blue polished cloth sides, spine with 5 raised bands, ruled and lettered gilt with gilt centres, top edges gilt, line drawings by Peggy Fortnum, fine. Sotheran's Piccadilly Notes - Summer 2015 - 54 2016 £168

Bone, Gertrude *Mr. Paul.* London: Jonathan Cape, 1921. One of 750 copies signed by author and artist, illustrations by Stephen Bone, nice, little browned dust jacket. Second Life Books, Inc. 196A - 179 2016 $85

Bonet, Honore *L'Apparition De Jehan de Meun ou Le Songe Du Prieur De Salon.* Paris: Imprime par Crapelet pour la Societe des Bibliophiles Franai, 1845. No. 7 of 17 copies on vellum, plus 100 copies issued on paper, 235 x 181mm., recent fine white pigskin, decorated in blind in medieval style by Courtland Benson, housed in titled custom made morocco backed folding cloth box, 10 engraved plates replicating illustrations from early manuscript copies of the week, pastedown with morocco bookplate of Comte H. De La Bedoyere and engraved bookplate of Marcellus Schlimovich, front free endpaper with embossed library stamp of Dr. Detlef Mauss, half title with ink library stamp of Sociedad Hebraica Argentina, fine, especially clean and bright internally with only most trivial imperfections and in striking new retrospective binding. Phillip J. Pirages 67 - 343 2016 $2750

Bonet, Theophilis *Polyathes sive Thesaurus Medico-Practicus.* Geneva: Leonard Chovet, 1692. First edition, Volume 3 only, folio, contemporary vellum, moderate foxing and dampstains, two inch tear bottom backstrip, wholly legible, good only. Edwin V. Glaser Rare Books 2015 - 10373 2016 $200

Bonington, Chris *Everest the Hard Way.* New York: Random House, 1976. First American edition, numerous color photos, cloth backed boards, thin fade line top edge of boards, else fine with pictorial dust jacket. Argonaut Book Shop Mountaineering 2015 - 4500 2016 $50

Bonington, Chris *Kongur, China's Elusive Summit.* London: Hodder & Stoguhton, 1982. First edition, profusely illustrated, mostly color and black and white photos, maps, cloth, very fine, unclipped pictorial dust jacket. Argonaut Book Shop Mountaineering 2015 - 4471 2016 $75

Bonnardot, A. *Die Kusnt, Kupferstiche zu Restauriren und Flecken aus Papier zu Entfernen.* Quedlinburg: G. Basse, 1859. First German edition, small 8vo., contemporary quarter brown calf, red cloth, top edge gilt, covers rubbed with wear at head of spine, from the reference library of Zaehnsdorf Co. with commemorative booklabel loosely inserted with their bookplate. Oak Knoll Books 310 - 12 2016 $1500

Bonnefoy, Yves *Things Dying things Newborn. Selected Poems.* Menard Press, 1985. First edition thus, K/26 copies signed by translator and artist with signed frontispiece wood engraving by Willow Winston printed in brown, 5 further small wood engravings by same, 8vo., original wrappers with Winston wood engraving to front, glassine jacket little sunned around backstrip panel with some chipping at head of same, very good. Blackwell's Rare Books B184 - 119 2016 £30

Bonner, Mary *Magic Journeys.* New York: Macauley, 1928. First edition, 4to., cloth, fine in slightly frayed dust jacket, color plates frontispiece, pictorial endpapers, plus many full page color illustrations, black and whites throughout. Aleph-bet Books, Inc. 112 - 403 2016 $275

Bonnet, C. *Contemplation de la Nature.* Amsterdam: Marc-Michel Rey, 1764. 8vo., original mottled calf, gilt spine with green and red labels and five raised bands, marbled pastedowns and endpapers very good, volume II only. Edwin V. Glaser Rare Books 2015 - 1070 2016 $125

Bonney, T. G. *Cathedrals, Abbeys and Churches of England and Wales.* London: Cassell & Co., 1891. 2 volumes, 4to., 18 plates as called for, numerous further illustrations in text, some plates little foxed, few neatly pencilled annotations, slightly later cloth, half bound in two shades of green, red morocco gilt title labels to spines, edge sprinkled red, few scratches, joints little rubbed but still very good, recent bookplate of Susan Wade, news clipping pasted to f.f.e.p. and volume I and few other relevant clippings, loosely inserted. Unsworths Antiquarian Booksellers Ltd. E04 - 5 2016 £100

Bonnycastle, John *An Introduction to Mensuration and Practical Geometry.* London: J. Johnson, 1802. Seventh edition, half title, engraved frontispiece, contemporary mottled calf, rubbed and little worn, inscription 'Jonathan Lee's book Dec. 15th 1806", sound. Jarndyce Antiquarian Books CCXV - 542 2016 £60

Bonser, A. E. *Kings of the Forest.* London: Dean & Son ltd., 1905. First edition, 4to., original red cloth with gilt lettering and design on upper board, 2 plates by Stanley Berkeley, very good. Sotheran's Piccadilly Notes - Summer 2015 - 55 2016 £80

The Book & Paper Group Annual. Washington: American Institute for Conservation of Hsitoric and Artistic Works, 1983. 26 volumes, 4to., stiff paper wrappers, very large run. Oak Knoll Books   310 - 206   2016 $500

Book Club of California   *The Hundredth Book, A Bibliography of the Publications of the Book Club of California...* N.P.: Book Club of California, 1958. First edition, limited to 400 copies, folio, half cloth over boards, paper spine label, plain paper dust jacket, many full page plates, 4 pages prospectus loosely inserted, plain paper jacket soiled, book fine.   Oak Knoll Books   27 - 3   2016 $275

The Book of Conversation and Behaviour. London: Printed for R. Griffiths at the Dunciad in St. Paul's Churchyard, 1754. 12mo., contemporary brown calf, sympathetically rebacked, red morocco label.   Jarndyce Antiquarian Books   CCXV - 76   2016   £850

The Book of Courtship or Hymeneal Directory by Amicus Juventutis. London: W. Kidd, circa, 1835. Half title, illustrated title, recent plain blue wrappers.   Jarndyce Antiquarian Books   CCXV - 279   2016   £30

The Book of Elegance or the Ladies' Mirror. London: W. Kidd, circa, 1835. Half title, illustrated title, recent plain blue wrappers.   Jarndyce Antiquarian Books   CCXV - 276   2016   £35

The Book of Fashion: Being a Digest of the Axioms of the Celebrated Joseph Brummell... London: W. Kidd, circa, 1835. Frontispiece, half title, illustrated title and final page, recent plain blue wrappers.   Jarndyce Antiquarian Books   CCXV - 277   2016   £35

The Book of Gems. The Poets and Artists of Great Britain. London and Paris: Fisher Son & Co., 1844. 2 volumes, 222 x 140mm., very pretty crimson morocco handsomely gilt by Doves Bindery (stamp signed and dated 1908 on rear turn-in), covers with line and dot frames, corners adorned with heart shaped leaves, a poppy seed pod, oak leaves, solid heart and gouge work, raised bands, spine compartments with line and dot frames, central poppy seed pod with leaves above and below, turn-ins with gilt rules and oak leaf cluster cornerpieces, all edges gilt, with two rows of gauffered dots (expert repairs to tiny portion of top of spine and three small areas of front joint of second volume), with 106 engraved vignettes and four pages of poets' facsimile signatures at end of each volume, front pastedown with wood engraved bookplate of Charles Walker Andrews, front free endpaper with typed copy of a letter from Andrews to the Doves Bindery, about these bindings (which he commissioned) and Cobden-Sanderson's handwritten and signed reply (first apparently a transcript, with later date of a letter sent 29 Jan. 1909, the second dated 9 Feb. 1909), top corners of volume I bit worn, leaves shade less than bright (no doubt as in all copies because of paper stock, still excellent set that looks very attractive on shelf, binding lustrous and appealing despite its defects and text clean, fresh and unread.   Phillip J. Pirages   67 - 38   2016 $3500

The Book of Gems. The Modern Poets and Artists of Great Britain. London: Henry G. Bohn, 1845. 222 x 140mm., very pretty crimson morocco, handsomely gilt by the Doves Bindery (stamp signed and dated 1908), covers with line and dot frames, corners adorned with heart shaped leaves, a poppy seed pod, oak leaves, solid heart and gouge work, raised bands, spine compartments with line and dot frames, central poppy seed pod with leaves above below, turn-ins with gilt rules and oak leaf cluster cornerpieces, all edges gilt with two rows of gauffered dots (upper cover with small repair at fore edge to fill in a gouge), with 43 engraved vignettes, 40 facsimile signatures of poets on four pages following text, wood engraved bookplate of Charles Walker Andrews, hint of wear at upper corners and along top of spine, gilt frame on front cover slightly affected by repair at fore edge, leaves shade less than bright, still excellent copy, lovely binding especially lustrous and pleasing (even with minor flaws).   Phillip J. Pirages   67 - 39   2016 $1900

The Book of Gentility; or the Why and Because of Polite Society. London: W. Kidd, circa, 1835. Half title, illustrated title, recent plain blue wrappers.   Jarndyce Antiquarian Books   CCXV - 278   2016   £35

The Book of Jade. New York: Doxey's At the Sign of the Lark, 1901. Limited edition, one of 600 numbered copies, this being no. 436, black cloth stamped in orange, 8vo., very good+ with little wear at spine ends.   Beasley Books   2015 - 2016 $1900

Book of Nursery Rhymes.   New York: Doubleday McClure, 1897. Limited to 1030 numbered copies for America, 8vo., boards, light rubbing, near fine, illustrations by F. D. Bedford, 22 rich and beautiful full page color illustrations and with decorations on text pages as well.   Aleph-bet Books, Inc.   111 - 40   2016 $425

The Book of Refinement or Speculurm Mundi.   London: W. Kidd, circa, 1835. Half title, illustrated title, 12mo., recent plain blue wrappers.   Jarndyce Antiquarian Books   CCXV - 279   2016   £35

The Book of Terror.   Toronto: Metropolitan Pub. Co. Dec., 1949. Number 1, large octavo, single issue, pictorial wrappers, stapled, rare, cover restored, very good housed in attractive custom clamshell box.   John W. Knott, Jr./L.W. Currey, Inc.   Fall-Winter 2015 - 17301   2016 $2500

The Book of Tobit and the History of Susanna.   London: Haymarket Press, 1929. Limited to 13 signed copies, this #13, small 4to., rare, near fine, bound in original limp vellum with gilt lettering to front cover, top edge gilt, green ribbon ties, hand set in goudy type and printed by Morton, Burt and Sons Ltd., London, printed in green and black, scattered mild toning page edges, 4 tipped in color plates by Sir William Russell Flint with extra suite of 4 plates in original folding chemise (worn), both book and extra plates in original slipcase as issued, slipcase intact by with soil, wear to edges.   By the Book, L. C.   45 - 60   2016 $1500

The Book of Tobit and the History of Susanna.   London: Haymarket Press, 1929. One of 13 copies signed by artist and printed on vellum along with 100 deluxe copies and 875 regular copies on paper), 254 x 191mm., publisher's limp vellum, gilt titling, cover laced with green silk ribbon, four color plates by W. Russell Flint, printed on paper and mounted on vellum leaves, hint of splaying to covers, minor variation in the grain of the vellum, otherwise very fine, clean, fresh and smooth inside and out.   Phillip J. Pirages   67 - 340   2016 $3500

Boorman, Howard L.   *Biographical Dictionary of Republican China.*   New York & London: Columbia University Press, 1967. First edition, 4 volumes, 4to., ex British Foreign Office library with few library markings, else very good.   Any Amount of Books   2015 - A75346   2016   £150

Boot, Jeremy   *Birds of South Australia.*   Adelaide: Oaklands Publishing, 1985. Quarto, 19 tipped in color plates, publisher's quarter cloth, fine.   Andrew Isles Natural History Books   55 - 32891   2016 $100

Booth, Philip   *The Islanders.*   New York: Viking Press, 1961. First edition, inscribed and signed by author March 26th 1962 for William Meredith, slight dust spotting to top edge, fine in price clipped, near fine dust jacket.   Charles Agvent   William Meredith - 17   2016 $150

Booth, Philip   *Margins. A Sequence of New and Selected Poems.*   New York: Viking Press, 1970. First edition, advance reading copy with letter from editor laid in, inscribed and signed by author April 16th 1971 for William Meredith, mild sunning to top edge, near fine in lightly soiled, near fine dust jacket.   Charles Agvent   William Meredith - 18   2016 $100

Booth, Philip   *Weathers and Edges.*   New York: Viking Press, 1966. First edition, signed with publisher's compliments card laid in, inscribed and signed for William Meredith, slight dust spotting to top edge, fine in lightly soiled, near fine dust jacket.   Charles Agvent   William Meredith - 20   2016 $100

Borden, Mary   *Action for Slander.*   London: Heinemann, 1936. First edition, octavo, presentation from author to C. K. Broadhurst with compliments of author, edges spotted, some offsetting from dust jacket onto spine, very good in scarce dust jacket which is very good, slightly nicked and bit spotted on rear panel, dust jacket design has playing card motif.   Peter Ellis   112 - 306   2016   £150

Borelli, Jules   *Ethiopia Meridionale Journal de Mon Voyage aux Pays Anhara, Oromo et Sidama, Septembre 1885 a November 1888.*   Paris: Ancienne Maison Quantin, 1890. First edition, 4to., contemporary calf backed marbled boards, spine ruled and lettered gilt, 13 plates, 7 double page maps (one colored), numerous wood engravings, extremities little worn, occasional brown spotting, good, contemporary armorial bookplate of Francois Borelli.   Sotheran's   Travel and Exploration - 7   2016   £750

Borges, Jorge Luis   *Labyrinths: Selected Stories & Other Writings.*   New Directions, 1962. First edition, very good in like dust jacket, attractive blue boards backed with black cloth, where silver lettering on spine is as bright as new, black endpapers, top edge colored yellow, interior bright, crisp and clean, price clipped dust jacket chipped at top edge and slightly rubbed and toned.   Simon Finch   2015 - 001519   2016 $175

Borges, Jorge Luis   *A Personal Anthology.*   New York: Grove Press, 1967. Very near fine in like dust jacket.   Jeff Hirsch Books   Holiday List 2015 - 25   2016 $150

Borrow, George   1803-1881   *George Borrow in Vienna.*   London: privately printed by Clement Shorter, 1914. One of 20 copies, 4to., original blue printed wrappers, sewn as issued, very good, 12 pages.   Jarndyce Antiquarian Booksellers   CCXVII - 36   2016   £120

Borrow, George   1803-1881   *Lavengro; The Scholar - the Gypsy -the Priest.*   London: John Murray, 1851. First edition, octavo, 3 volumes, original green ribbed cloth with title labels, title labels dusty, spines slightly faded, heads and tails of spines slightly bumped, very good set.   Peter Ellis   112 - 47   2016   £350

Borrow, George 1803-1881 *Lavengro: The Scholar - the Gypsy - the Priest.* London: John Murray, 1851. First edition, 8vo., publisher's cloth and paper labels (soiled labels), contemporary name on endpapers, some light soiling to titlepage of volume one, first and second volume with ads dated Feb. 1851 and Jan 1851 respectively, volume 3 without any ad, nice, clean set. Second Life Books, Inc. 197 - 33 2016 $600

Bosschere, Jean De 1878-1953 *Beasts and Men.* London: William Heinemann, 1918. First edition, 8vo., green pictorial cloth, few light marks on rear cover, else near fine, 12 fabulous color plates and many black and whites and pictorial endpapers. Aleph-bet Books, Inc. 112 - 134 2016 $275

Bosschere, Jean De 1878-1953 *The City Curious.* New York & London: Dodd Mead & Heinemann, 1920. First edition, 8vo., orange pictorial cloth, owner bookplate, fine, bright copy, 8 color plates and a profusion of odd and intriguing black and whites plus pictorial endpapers. Aleph-bet Books, Inc. 112 - 135 2016 $375

Bossu, Jean Bernard *Nouveaux Voyages aux Indes Occidentales, Contenant une Relation des Differens Peuples qui Habitent les Environs du Grand fleuve Saint Louis...* Paris: Chez le Jay, 1768. First edition, 4 black and white plates, including 2 frontispieces, head and tailpieces, 16mo., later mottled calf, boards ruled in gilt with floral cornerpieces, five raised bands, two compartments with black labels lettered gilt, four compartments decorated in gilt, board edges and turn-ins with gilt dentelle borders, all edges red, marbled endpapers, very good or better, rubbing to head of spine head and front joint, contemporary notations on third blank, else contents clean and bright, very handsome copy. Kaaterskill Books 21 - 10 2016 $1200

Bostwick, F. M. *Oyucha Saun.* Tokyo: T. Hasegawa and Kelly & Walsh, 1892. Second edition, rare, small 4to., original printed self wrappers, within contemporary green morocco backed marbled boards, spine lettered gilt, color printed woodcuts in text, as well as musical notations, extremities of boards with light wear, tail of spine bit more so, internally, apart from minor offsetting here and there, very good, clean. Sotheran's Travel and Exploration - 89 2016 £398

Boswell, David *Fun with Reid Fleming.* Forestville: Eclipse, 1991. One of 300 copies signed by artist, 4to., signed by artist on color illustration tipped on flyleaf, nice, dust jacket some scuffed and soiled. Second Life Books, Inc. 196A - 184 2016 $125

Boswell, James 1740-1795 *An Account of Corsica the Journal of a Tour to that Island, and Memoirs of Pascal Paoli.* Glasgow: Robert and Andrew Foulis for Edward and Charles Dilly, 1768. First edition, with final blank 2A88, leaves E2 and Z3 cancellanda, as usual, large folding map (3 inch tear), contemporary calf, spine richly gilt in compartments, text block lightly dampstained, other than some darkening on endpapers, not the least offensive, attractive copy, modern bookplate. Joseph J. Felcone, Inc. Books from Five Centuries: a Miscellany - 26 2016 $1000

Boswell, James 1740-1795 *Boswell in Holland 1763-1764.* New York: McGraw Hill Book Co., 1952. First edition, blue cloth backed boards, gilt lettering, minor fading to covers, lightly worn with covers bumped and showing, very good in heavily worn dust jacket. Argonaut Book Shop Literature 2015 - 4677 2016 $45

Boswell, James 1740-1795 *Boswell on the Grand Tour: Germany and Switzerland 1764.* New York: McGraw Hill Book Co., 1953. First edition, blue cloth backed boards, gilt lettering, minor fading to covers, fine in lightly worn and chipped dust jacket. Argonaut Book Shop Literature 2015 - 4678 2016 $50

Boswell, James 1740-1795 *The Life of Samuel Johnson, LL.D.* London: printed by Henry Baldwin for Charles Dilly, 1793. First octavo edition, 3 volumes, octavo, original blue paper boards over brown, illustrations by Joshua Reynolds with engraved portrait of Johnson as frontispiece, folding plates, uncut, some rubbing to boards, housed in custom brown cloth open ended slipcase, very good. Heritage Book Shop Holiday 2015 - 12 2016 $3500

Boswell, James 1740-1795 *The Life of Samuel Johnson, LL.D.* New York: Heritage Press, 1963. 3 volumes, frontispiece, brown cloth, marbled slipcases, very slight darkening to fore-edges of slipcases, else very fine, Sandglass pamphlet laid in. Argonaut Book Shop Heritage Press 2015 - 6932 2016 $125

Boswell, Thomas Alexander *The Journal of an Exile.* London: Saunders and Otley, British and Foreign Public Library, 1825. First edition, 2 volumes, some minor foxing, contemporary, probably Scottish binding with thistle motifs on spines, half calf, maroon morocco labels, little rubbed, nice, bookplates of William Money Kyrle. Jarndyce Antiquarian Booksellers CCXVII - 37 2016 £320

Bottome, Phyllis *Stella Benson.* San Francisco: Grabhorn Press, 1934. First edition, 250 copies printed, small 8vo., title printed in red and black, marginal titles, initial and colophon in red, handset Garamond type, Oxford gray cloth boards with yellow spine, paper label printed in red on front cover, spine slightly darkened, but very fine, from the collection of Carl I. Wheat, inscribed by Wheat "From the Library of Albert Bender". Argonaut Book Shop Private Press 2015 - 6276 2016 $60

Bouchot, Henri *L'Epopee Du Costume Militiaire Francais.* Paris: Societe Feancaise D'Editions D'Art/L. Henry May, 1898. First edition, thick 4to., original handsome full embossed leather with gold and red designs, all edges gilt, fine, illustrations by JOB, laid in is 3 page handwritten letter from JOB regarding the publication of one of his books.   Aleph-bet Books, Inc.   112 - 269   2016 $2750

Boudaille, Georges *Picasso's Sketchbook.*   Paris and New York: Harry N. Abrams, 1960. Limited to 1000 copies, facsimile of one of artist's sketchbooks with numerous color and black and white lithographs, with loose text pamphlet, spiral binding in cloth portfolio case, very near fine in like illustrated cloth portfolio, with some very slight wear at base of spine and with about very good printed glassine dust jacket that has several long tears to top of front panel with some wear to printed lettering there as well as some edge chips and other tears due to brittle nature of jacket, very attractive.   Jeff Hirsch Books   Holiday List 2015 - 14   2016 $1500

Boudinot, Elias   1741-1821 *The Second Advent or Coming of the Messiah in Glory.*   Trenton: D. Fenton & S. Hutchinson, 1815. First edition, 8vo., contemporary calf, considerably foxed.   M & S Rare Books, Inc.   99 - 1   2016 $750

Boulenger, George Albert *Catalogue of the Snakes in the British Museum (Natural History).* London: British Museum, 1893-1896. Octavo, 3 volumes, 73 uncolored lithographs, publisher's cloth, some slight wear primarily to top of spine of volume three which has split along upper edge, library accession numbers in copperplate hand on titlepages and endpapers, very good set, scarce.   Andrew Isles Natural History Books   55 - 25316   2016 $2850

Boulnois, H. Percy *The Housing of the Labouring Classes and Back-to-Back Houses.*   London: St. Bride's Press, 1896. First edition, octavo, floorplans, original tan buckram covers, ownership signature, free endpaper tanned, very good, scarce.   Peter Ellis   112 - 175   2016   £65

Bourdaloue, Louis *(Oeures).* Paris: Rigaud, 1707. First collected edition, 16 volumes, first 4 volumes ruled in red throughout, signatures on titles of M. de Chasteaurenault de Port Royal, 8vo., contemporary calf, triple gilt fillets on sides, spines gilt in compartments, contrasting lettering pieces, gilt edges, some wear at extremities, good.   Blackwell's Rare Books   B186 - 24   2016   £300

Bourgoing, Jean Francois *Atlas our servir au Tableau De L'Espagne Moderne.* Leverault: 1803. First edition, quarto, folding map, 3 plans, folding plates, 6 plates, some light waterstaining mainly in margins and prelims, contemporary full speckled calf, atlas complete but lacks the 3 volumes of text.   J. & S. L. Bonham Antiquarian Booksellers   Europe 2016 - 9543   2016   £480

Bourgoing, Jean Francois *Travels in Spain...* London: G. G. J. & J. Robinson, 1789. First English edition, 3 volumes, 8vo., folding map, 11 plates, contemporary brown half calf, spines rubbed with small wear to head and tail of spines.   J. & S. L. Bonham Antiquarian Booksellers   Europe 2016 - 9743   2016   £950

Bourgoing, Jean Francois *Voyage Du Ci-Devat Duc Du chatelet en Portugal...* Paris: F. Buisson, n.d., 1799. First edition, 2 volumes 8vo., folding frontispiece, folding map, contemporary brown full calf, joints rubbed, small loss of leather at base of spines, internally clean.   J. & S. L. Bonham Antiquarian Booksellers   Europe 2016 - 8417   2016   £450

Bourne, Benajmin Franklin *The Giants of Patagonia; Captain Bourne's Account of His Captivity Amongst the Extraordinary Savages of Patagonia.*   Ingram Cooke, 1853. First edition, small 8vo., 5 plates, vignette to titlepage, original green decorative cloth, vignette on upper cover.   J. & S. L. Bonham Antiquarian Booksellers   America 2016 - 9921   2016   £100

Bourne, E. D. *Boy's Games: a Recreation Handbook for Teacher and Scholars.* London: Griffith Farran &c, 1887. Illustrations, binding cracked in places, but still firm, original blue paper wrappers, few small tears, slightly dulled.   Jarndyce Antiquarian Books   CCXV - 544   2016   £35

Boutet De Monvel, Louis Maurice   1850-1913 *La Civilite Puerile et Honnete.* Paris: Plon Nourrit, n.d., 1892. Oblong 10 3/4 x 9 inches, gold pictorial cloth, slight soil, very good, illustrations.   Aleph-bet Books, Inc.   111 - 52   2016 $275

Bova, Ben *The Star Conquerors.* Philadelphia: Toronto: John C. Winston Co., 1959. First edition, touch of shelf-wear to spine ends, fine in very good to nearly fine dust jacket with shelfwear and closed tear to upper right corner tip, small 'v' chip (7 mm deep) at upper front right corner at spine fold, slight edge rubbing.   John W. Knott, Jr./L.W. Currey, Inc.   Fall-Winter 2015 - 17967   2016 $850

Bowen, Clarence Winthrop *The History of Woodstock Connecticut/Genealogies of Woodstock Families.* Norwood: Privately printed by the Plimpton Press, 1926-1943. 4to., 8 volumes, 874 portraits, 145 photo & reproductions and 13 (of 15) maps, dark blue and dark blue green cloth with gilt titles, top edges gilt, rare as complete set, near fine with light rubbing at spine ends and occasional soiling to fore edges.   Kaaterskill Books   21 - 22   2016 $2000

Bowen, W. Wedgwood *Catalogue of Sudan Birds, Based on the Collection in the Sudan Government Museum (Natural History).* Khartounm: Sudan Government Museum (Natural History), 1926-1931. octavo, 2 parts, publisher's wrappers, very good set.   Andrew Isles Natural History Books   55 - 12085   2016 $300

Bowen, William Henry *Charles Dickens and His family: a sympathetic Study.* Cambridge: privately printed by W. Heffer and Sons, 1956. Half title, original green cloth, spine lettered gilt, very good in slightly worn dust jacket. Jarndyce Antiquarian Booksellers   CCXVIII - 1082   2016   £30

Bower, Samuel *The Peopling of Utopia; or the Sufficiency of Socialism for Human Happiness...* Bradford: C. Wilkinson, 1838. First and only edition, small adhesion defect on title causing loss of two letters of word 'social', recently well bound blue boards, upper cover lettered. John Drury Rare Books   2015 - 5717   2016 $437

Bowie, William *The Black Book of Taymouth with other Papers from the Beadalbane Charter Room.* Edinburgh: Bannatyne Club, 1855. First edition, 4to., engraved portrait, 9 colored lithographs by W. H. Lizars and one facsimile original dark brown cloth, spine lettered gilt.   Marlborough Rare Books   List 55 - 7   2016   £350

Bowles, Paul *Paul Bowles Reads a Hundred Camels in the Courtyard.* Santa Barbara: Cadmus Ediions, 1981. Limited edition, copy #29 of only 100 copies signed by author on inserted sheet, 2 LP set, erratum sheet present, fine in near fine cloth sleeve with bit of darkening to upper edge, likely from glue that, by design, adheres the two sides of sleeve, scarce.   Ken Lopez Bookseller   166 - 7   2016 $250

Bowles, Paul *The Thicket of Spring: Poems 1926-1969.* Los Angeles: Black Sparrow Press, 1972. First edition, one of 200 numbered copies signed by Bowles, fine in publisher's acetate.   Second Life Books, Inc.   196A - 185   2016 $225

Bowles, Paul *Things Gone and Things Still Here.* Santa Barbara: Black Sparrow Press, 1977. First edition, paper wrapper issue, publisher's lavender paper wrappers, decorated in purple, blue and green, lettered in red and purple, near fine or better, with only light toning to spine, else fine, very bright and fresh, publisher's review slip laid in.   B & B Rare Books, Ltd.   2016 - PB015   2016 $50

Bowman, A. K. *The Life and Teaching of Sir William MacEwen.* London: 1942. Original binding, frontispiece, nice in original dust jacket, front of jacket with foxing, book near fine.   James Tait Goodrich   X-78 - 387   2016 $135

Boxhorn, Marcus Zuertius *Poetae Satyrici Minores de Corrupto Republicae Statu Marcus Zuerius Boxhornius...* Lugduni Batavorum: ex officina Isaaci Commelini, 1633. First edition, 12mo., titlepage in red and black, splatter marks seemingly ink, to few pages but not interfering with text, paper little browned, marginal paper flaw to very edge of page 101, contemporary vellum title inked to spine, edges sprinkled blue, spine darkened, few grey scuff marks but very good, inscription of Egerton Webbe dated 1837 (1810?-1840).   Unsworths Antiquarian Booksellers Ltd.   E01 - Early Printing - 2   2016   £400

Boyd, John Edward *Reply to Mr. Swinyard's Reports on the prince Edward Island Railway...* Charlottetown: printed by order of the Government of Prince Edward Island, 1875. 8vo., printed wrappers with stitch bound, covers lightly soiled, spine split and pieces missing along spine, very small pieces missing from bottom right corner and small hole through top corner margin through pamphlet but not into text, presentation from G. A. Sharp.   Schooner Books Ltd.   115 - 182   2016 $200

Boyd, William *The History of Western Education.* London: A. & C. Black, 1921. First edition, 1 page ads, half title, original blue cloth, slightly worn dust jacket.   Jarndyce Antiquarian Books   CCXV - 545   2016   £20

Boyd, William *School Ties: Good and Bad....* London: Hamish Hamilton, 1985. First edition, 8vo., fine in very near fine dust jacket very slightly sunned at spine.   Any Amount of Books   2015 - A90762   2016   £170

Boyd, William *Solo.* London: Jonathan Cape, 2013. First edition, signed by author, 8vo., original pictorial boards, dust jacket with cut-out bullet holes, fine.   Blackwell's Rare Books   B186 - 217   2016   £40

Boylan, Grace Duffie *Yama Yama Land.* Chicago: Reilly & Britton, 1909. 8 1/4 x 10 inches, cloth, pictorial paste-on, spine faded, else very good+, illustrated with 12 color plates.   Aleph-bet Books, Inc.   112 - 189   2016 $450

Boyle, Eleanor Vere *Sylvana's Letters to an Unknown Friend.* London: Macmillan and Co., 1900. First edition, 2nd impression, presentation copy inscribed by author for Rose Kerr (1882-1944), with her bookplate, original purple cloth, slightly rubbed, endpapers brown, not in very good condition, black and white illustrations, very good.   The Kelmscott Bookshop   12 - 40   2016 $150

Boyle, Robert *An Essay of the Great Effects of Even Languid and Unheeded Motion.* London: by M. Flesher for Richard Davis, 1685. First edition, 8vo., neat modern calf, antique, retaining original front flyleaf with signature of Mr. Jocelyn, light dust soiling of first few leaves, else fine, clean copy.   Joseph J. Felcone, Inc.   Books from Five Centuries: a Miscellany - 28   2016 $2800

Boyle, T. Coraghessan *The Road to Wellville.* Franklin Center: Franklin Library, 1993. Limited first edition, signed by author, bound in green leather, lettered and decoratively stamped in gilt, all edges gilt, very fine, as new, extremely handsome. Argonaut Book Shop Literature 2015 - 3944 2016 $50

Boyleston, Helen Dore *Sue Barton. Superintendent of Nurses.* Boston: Little Brown and Co., 1940. First edition, 8vo., plates by Forrest Orr, grey cloth with red lettering, black white and grey dust jacket, near fine (slight lean, bookplate), very good (some modest wear and soiling to jacket). Tavistock Books Bibliolatry - 20 2016 $225

Boynton, Susan *Young Choristers 650-1700.* Woodbridge: Boydell Press, 2008. First edition, 8vo., illustrations, blue cloth, gilt lettered, dust jacket, as new. Unsworths Antiquarian Booksellers Ltd. E05 - 68 2016 £25

The Boy's Holiday Book for all Seasons. London: G. H. Davidson, circa, 1845. Second edition, illustrations, original purple cloth, blocked in gilt, rather rubbed, faded and marked, decent copy, scarce. Jarndyce Antiquarian Booksellers CCXVII - 4 2016 £120

Bradbury, Dorothy E. *Nursery School Education.* Washington: National Association for Nursery Education, 1935. Original orange wrappers, ex-Board of Education Reference Library. Jarndyce Antiquarian Books CCXV - 547 2016 £20

Bradbury, Ray *Fahrenheit 451.* New York: Ballantine Books, 1953. True first edition with $.35 price on front cover, 12mo., black and white frontispiece for each story by Joe Mugnaini, mass market paperback, front wrapper deep blue with famous illustration by Mugnaini rear wrapper yellow with black and white photographic image of author, shelfworn with light creasing to spine and joints and minor loss to spine ends, previous owner's ink name to f.f.e.p., short tear to head of half titlepage, leaves age-toned, binding bit tender at hinges, still secure, very good overall. Tavistock Books Bibliolatry - 29 2016 $125

Bradbury, Ray *Fahrenheit 451.* New York: Ballantine, 1953. First edition, binding state D (no established priority), slight rubbing to spine ends and tiny tear to edge of one leaf in text, else fine in lightly soiled, very good plus dust jacket with shallow chip at crown and some of the usual fading to orange '451' on spine, signed by author. Between the Covers Rare Books 208 - 115 2016 $1600

Bradbury, Ray *Fahrenheit 451.* New York: Ballantine Books, 1953. First edition, one of 250 numbered copies signed by author and bound in Johns-Manville Quinterra, an asbestos material, this copy number 77, foxing to endpapers and prelims, fragile asbestos binding is rubbed and foxed, binding tight with no cracks or splits, very good. John W. Knott, Jr./L.W. Currey, Inc. Fall-Winter 2015 - 17587 2016 $8500

Bradbury, Ray *The Martian Chronicles.* Garden City: Doubleday & Co. Inc., 1950. First edition, octavo, cloth, tanning to spine panel, nearly fine in very good dust jacket or somewhat better, with touch of shelfwear to spine ends and light tanning to spine panel and along flap folds, mild dust soiling to rear panel. John W. Knott, Jr./L.W. Currey, Inc. Fall-Winter 2015 - 17580 2016 $3000

Bradbury, Ray *Match to Flame. (issued together with) The Dragon Who Ate His Tail.* Colorado Springs: Gauntlet, 2006. Publisher's copy of the limited edition, 750 copies, signed by author, slight corner tape, else fine in fine dust jacket, slight corner tape, else fine in fine dust jacket, second work with ownrrship stamp of another author inside front cover and slight corner tape, very near fine in wrappers. Ken Lopez Bookseller 166 - 8 2016 $500

Bradbury, Ray *The Wonderful Ice Cream Suit and Other Plays for Today, Tomorrow and Beyond Tomorrow.* London: Hart-Davis, MacGibbon, 1973. First UK edition, octavo, slight bruise at tail of spine, otherwise fine in fine dust jacket. Peter Ellis 112 - 48 2016 £25

Bradford, Ernest *Translations from Heine and Other Verses.* Cambridge: E. Johnson, 1882. First edition, scarce, very good in original grey paper covered boards with printed paper label on spine, title label bit browned and lightly scuffed, printed vertically in brown ink, darkening to spine and minor chipping to head of spine, short closed tear to edge of rear board, offsetting to endpaper, otherwise interior clean. The Kelmscott Bookshop 12 - 87 2016 $150

Bradley-Birt, F. B. *The Romance of an Eastern Capital.* London: Smith, Elder & Co., 1906. First edition, 8vo., original cloth lettered gilt, front cover with gilt stamped vignette of a sailing ship, plates after photos, spine sunned, light offsetting from endpapers very good, presentation copy inscribed by author to Eric Hayward (pictorial bookplate). Sotheran's Travel and Exploration - 91 2016 £198

Bradley, Rose M. *The English Housewife in the Seventeenth & Eighteenth Centuries.* London: Edward Arnold, 1912. Half title, frontispiece, 7 plates, 8 page catalog, slight spotting, original decorated red cloth, spine and back board faded, otherwise very good, bright, presentation copy stamp on titlepage, bookplate of Denis Gray, inserted is ALS recording book as a gift from Frances Lane, Bristol. Jarndyce Antiquarian Books CCXV - 78 2016 £45

Bradley, Will ...His Chap Book: an Account, in the Words of the Dean of American Typographers... New York: Typophiles, 1955. One of 650 copies, small 8vo., patterned paper over boards, about as new in dust jacket.   Second Life Books, Inc.   197 - 36   2016 $45

Bradley, Will Peter Poodle: Toy Maker to the King. New York: Dodd Mead, Oct., 1906. 4to., cloth backed pictorial boards, some edge, corner and cover wear, neat rear hinge repair, very good, 26 full page color illustrations, plus many in text color illustrations.   Aleph-bet Books, Inc.   111 - 54   2016 $1100

Bradshaw, William The Parable of Magpies.   printed for B. Griffitts, 1691. 4to., uncut, unbound, good, slightly frayed and dust soiled at edges.   Blackwell's Rare Books   B186 - 25   2016   £550

Bragdon, Claude Four Dimensional Vistas. New York: Knopf, 1916. First edition, purple cloth stamped in gilt, author's presentation on flyleaf to Florence Kelley, cover somewhat faded and spotted, slightly worn at corners and ends of spine, interior shows light moisture staining bottom of leaves, otherwise very good.   Second Life Books, Inc.   196A - 186   2016 $45

Bragg, George F. Men of Maryland. Baltimore: Church Advocate Press, 1914. First edition, frontispiece, brown cloth gilt, modest chip on rear fly, chip affixed to rear pastedown from binder's glue, trifle worn at thin foot of spine, else near fine, scarce.   Between the Covers Rare Books   202 - 10   2016 $600

Braine, John Room at the Top. London: Eyre & Spottiswoode, 1957. First edition, proof copy, foolscap 8vo., original mid green boards, gilt lettered backstrip with fading to extreme tail edge, usual light browning to endpapers in part, dust jacket with rubbing at head of backstrip panel, bookplate on half title, very good.   Blackwell's Rare Books   B184 - 120   2016   £500

Braithwaite, William Stanley Anthology of Magazine Verse for 1918 and Year Book of American Poetry. Boston: Small, Maynard & Co., 1918. First edition, fine in modestly soiled, very good plus dust jacket with small chips and little discoloration on spine, signed by several poets at each of their contributions, scarce in dust jacket.   Between the Covers Rare Books   207 - 10   2016 $500

Braithwaite, William Stanley Anthology of Magazine Verse for 1920. Boston: Small Maynard, 1920. First edition, corners little bumped, else about fine lacking scarce dust jacket, inscribed by author as well as by dedicatee, Boston bookseller Andrew McCants.   Between the Covers Rare Books   207 - 11   2016 $300

Braithwaite, William Stanley Our Lady's Choir: A Contemporary Anthology of Verse by Catholic Sisters. Boston: Bruce Humphries, 1931. First edition, Japanese vellum and paper covered boards, slight bump at crown else about fine in bit faded, very good, original cardboard slipcase with printed paper label, copy number 280 of 500 numbered copies (of a total numbered issue of 575), signed by Braithwaite.   Between the Covers Rare Books   202 - 12   2016 $250

Bramly, Sophie Walk This Way. Paris: Editions 213/ Steidl, 2015. Deluxe limited edition portfolio, one of five copies (this being copy #1), 47 matte finish photographic prints in both black and white and color, also included is a copy of the limited edition, softcover, published by Galerie 213, one of 500 copies (this being no. 058), containing signed and numbered print by Bramly, limited edition fine in wrappers and a fine printed acetate dust jacket.   Royal Books   51 - 3   2016 $75,000

Bramsen, John Letters of a Prussian Traveller... London: Henry Colburn, 1818. First edition, 2 volumes, 8vo., contemporary brown full polished calf, recently rebacked, internally crisp.   J. & S. L. Bonham Antiquarian Booksellers Europe 2016 - 8715   2016   £850

Brand, Christianna Nurse Matilda. Brockhampton Press, 1964. First edition, 40 illustrations by Ardizzone, 16mo., original mid green boards, backstrip and front cover with overall gilt lettering and designs by Ardizzone, pink cottonmarker, fine.   Blackwell's Rare Books   B186 - 174   2016   £55

Brand, Stewart The Media Lab. New York: Penguin, 1988. First edition thus, softcover, inscribed by author to Gary Snyder in 1990, with Synder's ownership signature, nice association copy.   Ken Lopez Bookseller   166 - 9   2016 $200

Brander, Michael The Roughshooter's Dog. Douglas Saunders, 1957. First edition, 8vo., original cloth and wrapper, black and white photographic plates, little browning to edges of wrapper, otherwise very good, scarce edition.   Sotheran's   Hunting, Shooting & Fishing - 71   2016   £40

Brandi, John Rite for the Beautification of All Beings. West Branch: Toothpaste Press, 1983? 1/555 copies, signed by author, 12mo., pages not numbered, paper wrappers, very good.   Second Life Books, Inc.   196A - 190   2016 $40

Brannan, Robrt Louis Under the Management of Mr. Charles Dickens.... Ithaca: Cornell University Press, 1966. Half title, frontispiece, plates illustrations, original dark green cloth, very good in slightly rubbed dust jacket.   Jarndyce Antiquarian Booksellers   CCXVIII - 552   2016   £35

Branson, Helen Kitchin *Let there Be Life: the Contemporary Account of Edna L. Griffin M.D.* Pasadena: pub. by M. S. Sewn, 1947. First edition, tall octavo, 135 pages, frontispiece, green cloth title stamped on front board in pale yellow, net owner's name Zephyr M. Ramsey, bit of rubbing at spine ends, else very near fine, no dust jacket, almost certainly as issued. Between the Covers Rare Books 202 - 14 2016 $650

Brassey, Annie Allnutt, Baroness 1839-1887 *Aux Indes et en Australie dans le Yacht le 'Sunbeam'.* Tours: Alfred Mame et fils, 1893. Splendid first French edition, small folio, original red pictorial cloth, all edges gilt by A. Souze, numerous wood engraved illustrations (several full page), binding minimally spotted and rubbed, internally, apart from sporadic light spotting, very clean and fresh. Sotheran's Travel and Exploration - 395 2016 £498

Brassey, Annie Allnutt, Baroness 1839-1887 *A Voyage in the Sunbeam: Our Home on the Ocean for Eleven Months.* London: Longmans, Green and Co., 1878. First edition, dark grey cloth with gilt title and author to spine and front cover, gilt illustrations to front and back, cloth chipped and faded but still quite attractive, some soiling to prelim pages and tear to front map, otherwise very good, two foldouts and 118 wood engraved illustrations after drawings by Bingham, ownership signature of George Clayton, very good. The Kelmscott Bookshop 13 - 11 2016 $550

Brassington, W. Salt *A History of the Art of Bookbinding, with Some Account of the Books of the Ancients.* London: Elliot Stock, 1894. First edition, one of 50 large paper copies, 4to., modern full leather, raised designs, red and black leather spine labels, numerous engravings, 10 color and tinted separate plates. Oak Knoll Books 310 - 14 2016 $300

Brauer, George C. *The Age of the Soldier Emperors. Imperial Rome A.D. 244-284.* New Jersey: Noyes Press, 1985. First edition, 8vo., cloth, gilt lettered to spine, endcaps just starting to wear, top edge slightly dusted and spotted, very good, dust jacket, three large tears, one with loss, some smaller closed tears, fraying, faded to spine, good only, ownership inscription J. G. Hind, School of History, Univ. of Leeds with one or two ink annotations. Unsworths Antiquarian Booksellers Ltd. E04 - 35 2016 £30

Bray, F. Sewell *Accounting Research.* London: Cambridge University Press, 1948. First edition, wrappers, 8vo., each issue about 70 pages, 36 issues, from the library of economist Sir Richard Stone. Any Amount of Books 2015 - A72995 2016 £600

Bray, Reginald A. *The Town Child.* London: T. Fisher Unwin, 1912. Second edition, half title, uncut, original maroon cloth, booklabels of Legge Library and another. Jarndyce Antiquarian Books CCXV - 548 2016 £25

Brazil, Angela *A Patriotic Schoolgirl.* Blackie and Son Ltd., 1918. First edition, pictorial cloth little worn and soiled, little foxing, but nice, inscription on front free endpaper. Bertram Rota Ltd. Christmas List 2015 - 5 2016 £50

Breakwall, E. *The Grasses and Fodder Plants of New South Wales.* Sydney: Department of Agriculture, 1923. Octavo, photos, publisher's cloth. Andrew Isles Natural History Books 55 - 14480 2016 $65

Brecht, Bertolt *The Seven Deadly Sins of the Lower Middle Class.* New York: Vincent FitzGerald, 1992. No. 3 in an edition of 50 copies signed by artist and translator and Kurt Weill, etchings and lithographs by Max Beard, printed on rives paper, water colored, folio, bound by Zahra Partovi in association with BookLab in 19th century Hub style binding with black leather and Dacron polyester zebra striped fabric in purple and black, black cloth clamshell box with purple leather cover label, titled gilt. Oak Knoll Books 27 - 15 2016 $7500

Bredsdorff, Elias *Hans Andersen and Charles Dickens a Friendship and its Dissolution.* Cambridge: W. Heffer and Sons, 1956. Printed in Denmark, first edition, half title, frontispiece, plates, illustrations, original orange pictorial cloth, dust jacket, very good. Jarndyce Antiquarian Booksellers CCXVIII - 1060 2016 £25

Breedlove, Dennis E. *The Flowering of Man.* Washington: Smithsonian Institution Press, 1993. First edition, quarto, 2 volumes, 52 figures, 3 maps, 10 appendices, 66 photographic plates, frontispiece in color, peach illustrated wrappers, fine set. Argonaut Book Shop Natural History 2015 - 7569 2016 $125

Breer, Robert *Complete Set of the Galeria Boni Monographs. Floats/More Floats (93 Floats) Constructions and Films.* New York: Galeria Bonino, 1967. Complete set of four matching exhibition catalogs, near fine or better, each in saddle stitched wrappers, with light occasional rubbing. Royal Books 52 - 51 2016 $1500

Breer, Robert *More Floats.* New York: Galeria Bonino, 1967. Exhibition catalog, near fine in saddle stitched wrappers, light rubbing. Royal Books 48 - 46 2016 $325

Breit, Ilse *German, Kindersommer Builder and Verse.* Leipzig: F. Hirt & Sohn, 1924. Large oblong 4to., cloth backed pictorial boards, light cover soil and faint scratch else clean and tight, very good+, 6 magnificent full page color illustrations by Breit. Aleph-bet Books, Inc. 111 - 193 2016 $600

Brereton, Austin *The Life of Henry Irving.* London: Longmans Green, 1908. First edition, 2 volumes, cloth, pictorial gilt, spine ends scuffed, frontisportraits, plates, very good. Dramatis Personae 119 - 19 2016 $45

Breshkovsky, Catherine *The Little Grandmother of the Russian Revolution: Reminiscences and Letters of....* Boston: 1919. Reprint, 8vo., some external wear, very good tight copy, signed by author.   Second Life Books, Inc. 196A - 196   2016 $100

Bressey, Charles *Highway Development Survey 1937.* London: printed and published by HMSO, 1938. First edition, folio, 6 plans and two colored folding maps in pocket at end, original red cloth lettered in blind, ownership label on upper spine.   Marlborough Rare Books   List 55 - 8   2016   £225

Brett, David *Nursery Rhymes and Tales.* London: Dean & son, n.d. circa, 1910. 4to., gilt pictorial cloth, bottom of spine, slightly worn and some fading to cloth, very good+, illustrations by David Brett with striking and fabulous full page color illustrations.   Aleph-bet Books, Inc.   112 - 375   2016 $500

Brett, David *Ten Little Niggers.* London: Dean & Son, n.d. circa, 1910. 4to, flexible pictorial wrappers, slight edge wear, very good-fine, bold and wonderful full page color illustrations by Brett.   Aleph-bet Books, Inc.   112 - 59   2016 $750

Brett, W. H. *The Indian Tribes of Guiana.* London: Bell & Daldy, 1868. First edition, 8vo., folding map, 8 colored plates, illustrations, contemporary brown half calf, handsome copy.   J. & S. L. Bonham Antiquarian Booksellers   America 2016 - 6129   2016   £320

Brewer, Reginald Arthur *Six Hundred American Books Worth Money.* Detroit: Rare Book Information Bureau, 1933. First edition, octavo, original green line spine and decorated cloth boards, little soiled, very good.   The Brick Row Book Shop   Miscellany 69 - 13   2016 $100

Brewer, William Herny *Such a Landscape! A Narrative of the 1864 California Geological Survey Exploration of Yosemite....* Yosemite: Yosemite Association, Sequoia Hist. Assoc., 1987. First edition, number 347 of 500 numbered copies and signed by Alsup, square quarto, frontispiece, 39 plates, half cloth, boards, very fine.   Argonaut Book Shop   Natural History 2015 - 6734   2016 $225

Bridge, Horatio *Journal of an African Cruiser.* New York: George P. Putnam & Co., 1853. 12mo., original blind-stamped cloth, superb copy, inscribed in pencil "Hon. J. Collamer(?)... with respects of the author.   M & S Rare Books, Inc.   99 - 102   2016 $1250

Bridges, Robert 1884-1930 *Eros and Psyce. A Poem in XII Measures.* N.P.: Gregynog Press, 1935. Limited to 300 copies, this being one of 285 copies bound in pigskin, 4to., original cream pigskin blocked gold with circular flower and butterfly device in gold on front cover, top edge gilt, 24 wood engravings from designs of Edward Burne-Jones' drawings, green wood engraved initials by Graily Hewitt, well preserved.   Oak Knoll Books   27 - 24   2016 $1500

Bridges, Robert 1884-1930 *Eros and Pysche: a Poem in XII Measures.* Newtown: Gregynog Press, 1935. One of 285 copies (of 300), counting, 15 copies bound in morocco), 286 x 225mm., publisher's white pigskin blocked in gilt on front cover with medallion of arabesque design incorporating flower and butterflies, straps depicted in gilt on spine where hands would be, gilt top, other edges untrimmed, in (somewhat soiled but apparently original) ivory colored buckram traycase, with initial letters designed by Graily Hewitt and printed in green, and with 24 wood engravings in text, two of them full page, redrawn by Dorothy Hawksley from designs by Edward Burne-Jones and cut by Loyd Haberly and R. John Beedham, printed in red and black on Batchelor handmade paper; just touch of soil to white pigskin, but binding otherwise unworn, especially fine, internally pristine and used so little that the volume opens only reluctantly.   Phillip J. Pirages   67 - 183   2016 $1600

Bridges, Robert 1884-1930 *The Humours of the Court.* London: George Bell & Sons and J. & E. Bumbus, n.d., 1893. First edition, 4to., original grey wrappers, lettered in black, minor dusting to edges of covers, minor spotting to first few leaves, deckled edges.   Dramatis Personae   119 - 20   2016 $55

Bridges, Robert 1884-1930 *John Keats: a Critical Essay.* London: privately printed, 1895. First edition, number 44 of 250 opies, privately printed, inscribed by author, original red buckram, top edge gilt, spine and covers faded and marked, otherwise very good, endpapers browned, interior clean and bright, correction on page 56, scarce, especially inscribed, very good.   The Kelmscott Bookshop   12 - 16   2016 $175

Bridgman, Elijah Coleman *The Chinese Repository. Volume II. From May 1838 to April, 1839.* Canton: printed for the proprietors, 1839, reprinted in Tokyo, Maruzen, 1942. Very rare reprint, 8vo., modern burgundy silk with gilt stamped lettering piece, retaining original light purple endpapers and reproducing the original Japanese binding, which was beyond repair woodcut illustrations, printed on Japanese bamboo (?) paper, few pages yellowed in margins, otherwise very clean and fresh.   Sotheran's Travel and Exploration - 92   2016   £498

Bridgman, L. J. *The Santa Claus Rat and Other Rhymes.* Boston & New York: Caldwell, 1900. 4to., cloth backed pictorial boards, small spot on rear cover, else near fine, illustrations on every page by Bridgman.   Aleph-bet Books, Inc.   112 - 70   2016 $250

Briffault, Robert *Europa in Limbo.* New York: Charles Scribner's sons, 1937. First edition, red cloth with gilt lettering to lightly worn, spine faded dust jacket, fine. Argonaut Book Shop   Literature 2015 - 4672   2016 $45

Briggs, Henry B. *The Musical Notation of the Middle Ages.* London: J. Masters, 1890. First edition, no. 151 of 240 copies, folio, loosely inserted folder with facsimiles, all 20 plates present, printed covers of folded envelope somewhat dust soiled, original red cloth lettered gilt on cover, sound, rebacked with original spine laid down and new endpapers, very good.   Any Amount of Books   2015 - C2305   2016   £170

Briggs, Raymond *Ethel & Ernest.* London: Jonathan Cape, 1998. First edition, color printed illustrations, 8vo., original brown boards, backstrip lettered gilt with very slight lean to spine, dust jacket, near fine, signed by author. Blackwell's Rare Books   B186 - 187   2016   £150

Briggs, Raymond *When the Wind Blows.* New York: Schecken Boks, 1982. Stated first edition, 9 x 12 inches, pictorial boards, very good to fine, color illustrations. Aleph-bet Books, Inc.   112 - 72   2016 $150

Brigham, William T. *Guatemala: the land of the Quetzal, a sketch.* London: T. Fisher Unwin, 1887. First english edition, 8vo., frontispiece, 5 maps, illustrations, original tan decorative cloth, spine faded, corners rubbed, very good, clean copy internally.   J. & S. L. Bonham Antiquarian Booksellers   America 2016 - 7142   2016   £250

Bright, Hemry Arthur *Happy Country This America, the Travel Diary of...* Columbus: Ohio state, 1978. First edition, 8vo., illustrations, inscribed by author, fine in little worn dust jacket.   Second Life Books, Inc.   196A - 750   2016 $45

Bright, Kate C. *Unto the Third and Fourth Generation.* London: Samuel Tinsley & Co., 1881. Half title, 32 page catalog Dec. 1880, original green cloth, pictorially blocked in black, little rubbed and dulled but overall nice, slightly later ownership inscription.   Jarndyce Antiquarian Booksellers   CCXVII - 38   2016   £75

The Brighton Magazine. London: Thomas Hurst, Edward Chance & Co., January-April, 1822. Volume I Nos. I-IV. Frontispiece, index, uncut in original drab boards, drab linen spine, paper label, rubbed and little worn, hinges weakening.   Jarndyce Antiquarian Booksellers   CCXVII - 219   2016   £125

Britaine, William De *Humane Prudence or the Art by Which a Man may Raise Himself and His Fortune to Grandeur.* London: Richard Sare at Gray's Inn Gate in Holborn, 1697. Seventh edition, 12mo., 2 pages ads at end, small paper flaw on F3 slightly touching few letters, contemporary speckled calf expertly & imperceptibly rebacked, various inscriptions & notes, mostly contemporary on endpapers.   Jarndyce Antiquarian Books   CCXV - 79   2016   £250

The British Essayists. London: printed for F. C. and J. Rivington, J. Nichols and Co., 1802. 45 volumes, 12mo., full leather, gilt rules, gilt title and decorations on spine, 3 raised bands, gilt turn-ins, all edges marbled, bookmark ribbon, many of the top or bottom boards loose, boards spotted, leather at edges and spine loose, chipped or flaking, some with boards dented or rubbed, all text block edges soiled, water ring on top board volume 26, top board of volume 23 split, leather beginning to pull away.   Oak Knoll Books   310 - 59   2016 $950

British Museum *List of Serial Publications in the British Museum (Natural History) Library.* London: Trustees of the British Museum (Natural History), 1975. Second edition, 4to., 3 volumes, cloth, dust jacket, ink signature of Gavin Bridson, dust jackets lightly worn with some soiling and spotting.   Oak Knoll Books   310 - 259   2016 $450

Britton, John *Cathedral Antiquities. Historical and Descriptive Accounts (...) of the Following English Cathedrals.* London: M. A. Nattali, 1836. 5 volumes, 4to., each volume contains two or three parts, collates complete, all plates as called for, each volume with a series title, volume title and section title, some woodcuts in text, occasional spot or smudge but overall very clean and bright within, later 19th century half green morocco, gilt spine, marbled boards and endpapers, all edges gilt, boards little rubbed, some scuffed to joints, still very good, handsome set, recent bookplate of Susan Wade to each front pastedown.   Unsworths Antiquarian Booksellers   30 - 25   2016   £750

Britz, Lu *Opera News Alice in Operaland.* New York: Metropolitan Opera Guild Inc. Feb. 6, 1950. Volume XIV number 15, 17.5 x 25.5cm., stapled wrappers, yellow front wrapper with black printing and black and white photo, profusely illustrated with black and white photos, some minimal wear and slight vertical crease, very good.   Ken Sanders Rare Books   E Catalogue # 1 - 29   2016 $40

Brivot, Arsene *Jojo Richissime.* Paris: Editions Prima, 1930. Large 4to., cloth backed pictorial boards, edges worn, some cover soil very good, color illustrations by author.   Aleph-bet Books, Inc.   111 - 184   2016 $150

Broadsides: a Collection of New Irish and English Songs. Dublin: Cuala Press, 1937. broadsides limited to 300 copies, this one of 150 bound sets, signed by W. B. Yeats and Dorothy Wellesley, 25 hand colored woodcut illustrations, errata sheet laid in, leather bookplate on front pastedown, spine and boards slightly soiled, boards bumped at corners, cloth split along front hinge.   Oak Knoll Books   310 - 93   2016 $2250

Brockwell, Charles   *The Natural and Political History of Portugal.*   London: T. Warne, 1726. First edition, 8vo., frontispiece, 2 folding maps, 2 plates, 16 pages browned, contemporary brown full panelled calf, recently rebacked, clean, crisp copy.   J. & S. L. Bonham Antiquarian Booksellers Europe 2016 - 8905   2016   £1250

Brodie, Fawn M.   *No Man Knows My History. The Life of Joseph Smith.*   New York: Alfred A. Knopf, 1971. Second edition, frontispiece, photos, map, black cloth, very fine, printed dust jacket.   Argonaut Book Shop   Biography 2015 - 7147   2016 $60

Brodsky, Joseph   *Collected Poems in English.*   New York: Farrar, Straus and Giroux, 2000. First edition, 8vo., small bump to bottom edge of upper cover, very near fine in fine dust jacket.   Peter Ellis   112 - 49   2016   £35

Brodsky, Joseph   *Selected Poems.*   New York: Penguin Books Inc., 1974. First edition, clean, very near fine copy in wrappers, signed by author, uncommon thus.   Jeff Hirsch Books   E-List 80 - 5   2016 $200

Brodsky, Joseph   *To Urania.*   New York: Farrar Straus & Giroux, 1988. First edition, 8vo., signed by author, black cloth, nice in dust jacket.   Second Life Books, Inc.   196A - 201   2016 $275

Brodsky, Joseph   *Verses on the Winter Campaign.*   London: Anvil Press Poetry, 1981. First edition, one of 250 copies signed by author and translator, Alan Myers, out of a total edition of 500 copies, 12mo., original unprinted wrappers, dust jacket, presentation copy inscribed by author to friend, the poet Mark Strand, with Brodsky's corrections in verse, fine.   James S. Jaffe Rare Books   Occasional List: Winter 2016 - 34   2016 $1250

Brodtmann, Karl Joseph   *Naturgeschichte Und Abbildungen der Saugethiere.*   Zurich: Brodtmann, 1824. First edition, 324 x 235mm., contemporary black quarter roan over green marbled boards, vellum tips, flat dspine with gilt rules, rolls and lettering, 177 hand colored lithographed illustrations, pictorial titlepage and 176 plates, majority with original tissue guards, cover surfaces and extremities somewhat rubbed, corners gently bumped, plate 136 with cracked crease acorss surface, occasional light spots on few plates, some missing and few torn tissue guards, otherwise very attractive, engravings generally quite clean and fresh.   Phillip J. Pirages   67 - 308   2016 $10,000

Broinowski, Gracius J.   *The Cockatoos and Nestors of Australia and New Zealand.*   Melbourne: Lansdowne Editions, 1981. Limited to 500 copies, signed and numbered by author's descendant, facsimile, small folio, 13 plates and accompanying text leaves, black full morocco, fine.   Andrew Isles Natural History Books   55 - 5493   2016 $300

Bromley-Davenport, W.   *Sport.*   London: Chapman & Hall, 1888. New edition, 8vo., original cloth, lettered in black and vignette of stag in red to upper board, gilt lettering to spine, illustrations by Crealock, previous owner's bookplate, very good.   Sotheran's   Hunting, Shooting & Fishing - 161   2016   £70

Bronk, William   *Six Duplicities.*   Brooklyn: Jordan Davies, n.d., Limited to 174 numbered, 24 lettered copies, signed by author, 8vo., quarter cloth, marbled paper covered boards, top edge gilt, other edges uncut, engraved illustration on title.   Oak Knoll Books   310 - 116   2016 $175

Bronk, William   *The Stance.*   Port Townsend: Graywolf Press, 1975. One of 225 copies, signed with author's initials at end of poem, paper wrappers, fine.   Second Life Books, Inc.   196A - 202   2016 $50

Bronk, William   *Two Apostrophes.*   Concord: William B. Ewert, 1985. One of only 86 copies, this copy marked for presentation, printed folded sheet that holds two broadsides that each contain a single poem "Reduction" and "The Incongruities", each printed in two colors, both in fine condition as is the folder, Bronk has signed and inscribed 'Reduction' to noted collector Carter Burden and simply signed the other broadside, very nice.   Jeff Hirsch Books Holiday List 2015 - 23   2016 $125

Bronte, Anne   1820-1849   *The Tenant of Wildfell Hall.*   London: T. C. Newby, 1849. First edition, 3 volumes, volume i bound without half title, not issued in volumes ii and iii, small paper repairs to pages 1/2 volume i affecting 2 words, pages 13/14, 297-8, 360-366 volume ii, handsomely bound in later half dark blue calf, spines with raised bands and devices in gilt, maroon morocco labels, attractive set.   Jarndyce Antiquarian Booksellers   CCXVII - 47   2016   £9800

Bronte, Emily   1818-1855   *The Complete Poems of Emily Jane Bronte.*   New York: Columbia University Press, London: Oxford University Press, 1941. first edition, UK issue, frontispiece, tail of spine bruised, very good in like dust jacket (slightly rubbed and creased and slightly darkened at spine and with few nicks).   Peter Ellis   112 - 50   2016   £75

Bronte, Patrick   1777-1861 *The Cottage in the Wood; or the Art of Becoming Rich and Happy.*   Bradford: T. Inkersley, 1815. Second edition, 18mo., engraved frontispiece after F. James, sculpted by E. Stather, slight offsetting on titlepage, later 19th century full crimson crushed morocco, triple gilt borders, raised bands, gilt compartments and dentelles, green and brown morocco labels, bookplate of George John Armytage, very good.   Jarndyce Antiquarian Booksellers   CCXVII - 48   2016   £2500

Bronte, The Sisters   *The Novels of the Sisters Bronte.* London: Downey and Co. Ltd., 1898. Thornton edition, 12 volumes, contemporary three quarter red morocco leather backed red cloth boards with gilt titles and decoration to spines, binding signed by Bickers and Son, leather on spines browned, though gilt remains bright on all volumes, minor wear/chipping to spine ends of few volumes, minor wear to corners, minor rubbing to hinges and minor scuffing to boards of some volumes, few cracks to spine leather of several volumes, later owner's name neatly handwritten along top of each bookplate, third owner name written in very small neat lettering on top of free front endpaper in few volumes, interiors printed on laid paper and remain very clean, titlepages with tissue guards appear at beginning of most volumes, all volumes tightly bound, very good.   The Kelmscott Bookshop   12 - 17   2016 $1400

Bronte, The Sisters   *Poems by Currer, Ellis and Acton Bell.* Philadelphia: Lea and Blanchard, 1848. First American edition, original brown paper covered boards, printed paper spine label, outer brown paper worn from along hinges and at tips of spine revealing lighter paper underneath, scattered foxing, else very nice, very tight in fragile original boards, 1848 ownership signature of A. G. Trafton.   Joseph J. Felcone, Inc.   Books from Five Centuries: a Miscellany - 29   2016 $2800

Brook, George   *Catalogue of the Madreporian Corals in the British Museum (Natural History).*   London: British Museum (Natural History), 1893. Large quarto, 7 volumes, 240 uncolored photos, publisher's cloth, some wear, upper spine of volume 7 repaired, titlepages with stamp of "Royal Zoological Society of New South Wales", plus a few stamps, sound set, scarce.   Andrew Isles Natural History Books   55 - 20821   2016 $1650

Brook, George Leslie   *The Language of Dickens.* London: Andre Deutsch, 1970. First edition, original blue cloth, half title, very good in slightly torn dust jacket, Robert Gibbing's signed copy.   Jarndyce Antiquarian Booksellers   CCXVIII - 1084   2016   £25

Brooke, Fulke Greville, 1st Baron   *Certaine Learned and Elegant Workes of the Right Honorable Fulke Lord Brooke.* E. P(urslowe) for Henry Seyle, 1633. First edition, tall copy of ordinary paper issue, folio, full morocco gilt by Riviere, all edges gilt, initial and terminal blanks, repaired rust hole in d2 with loss of few letters, slight soiling to first leaves, otherwise very good, large copy, contemporary inscription D. Johannis Mallet, later bookplate of E. M. Cox.   Sotheran's Piccadilly Notes - Summer 2015 - 155   2016   £2750

Brooke, Henry   *Gustavus Vasa the Deliverer of His Country.* London: printed for R. Dodsley, 1739. First edition, 8vo., disbound.   Jarndyce Antiquarian Booksellers   CCXVI - 457   2016   £120

Brooke, Jocelyn   *Conventional Weapons.* London: Faber & Faber, 1961. First edition, foolscap 8vo., original red and black speckled boards, backstrip lettered gilt with slight lean to spine, light foxing to edges and partial browning to front endpapers, dust jacket with backstrip panel faintly sunned, near fine.   Blackwell's Rare Books   B186 - 188   2016   £70

Brooke, Jocelyn   *The Wild Orchids of Britain.* London: Bodley Head, 1950. Limited to 1140 numbered copies, quarto, 40 color plates by Gavin Bone, publisher's cloth.   Andrew Isles Natural History Books   55 - 5497   2016 $100

Brooke, Rupert   1887-1915   *Fragments Now First Collected Being Hitherto Unpublished.*   Hartford: printed at the Press of Finlay Bros., 1925. First edition, one of 99 numbered copies (this one out of series), small quarto, this copy never bound and out of series, first and final blank little smudged, fine.   The Brick Row Book Shop   Miscellany 69 - 15   2016 $175

Brooke, Rupert   1887-1915   *In Remembrance (914) Poems by Rupert Brooke.*   London: J. Curwen & Sons, 1917. First edition, quarto, original printed wrappers, stitched, wrappers little worn and darkened at edges, very good.   The Brick Row Book Shop   Miscellany 69 - 18   2016 $225

Brooke, Rupert   1887-1915   *Lithuania: a Drama in One Act.*   Chicago: Chicago Little Theatre, 1915. First edition, small octavo, original pictorial wrappers, wrappers little worn and soiled, very good.   The Brick Row Book Shop   Miscellany 69 - 17   2016 $375

Brooke, William   *Short Addresses to the children of Sunday Schools....*   London: F. C. & J. Rivington, 1821. 10th, 12mo., some slight browning and marking to text, lacking leading f.e.p., original drab boards, rebacked, slightly worn, contemporary reward label from Fowey Church of England Sunday School, slightly later inscription, sound.   Jarndyce Antiquarian Books   CCXV - 557   2016   £25

Brookes, Richard *An Introduction to Physic and Surgery.* printed for J. Newbery, 1754. 8vo., contemporary speckled calf, double gilt fillets on sides, dark red lettering piece, joints cracked, headcaps defective, corners slightly worn, engraved armorial bookplate of William Turton (overlaying earlier one), sound, small burn hole in Kk2 affecting few words, occasional browning spotting or staining, still good. Blackwell's Rare Books B186 - 27 2016 £500

Brookes, Thomas *Apples of Gold for Young men and women...* London: Book Society for Promoting Christian Knowledge, 1831. New edition, contemporary half purple calf, little rubbed, spine faded, armorial bookplate of Joseph Wilson. Jarndyce Antiquarian Books CCXV - 81 2016 £20

Brooks, Eric St. John *The Irish Cartularies of Llanthony Prima & Secunda.* Dublin: Stationery Office, 1953. 8vo., cloth, gilt lettered, spine sunned and slightly cocked, fabric lifting just slightly at upper top corner, toning to free endpapers, edges lightly dusted, very good, no dust jacket, price stamp on front pastedown. Unsworths Antiquarian Booksellers Ltd. E05 - 96 2016 £35

Brooks, Gwendolyn *To Disembark.* Chicago: Third World Press, 1981. Review copy/complimentary copy with publisher sheets laid in, very near fine with some very slight wear to bottom edge of boards in very fine dust jacket with small tear to base of front panel, signed and inscribed by Gwendolyn Brooks in 1986, much less common in cloth issue. Jeff Hirsch Books Holiday List 2015 - 24 2016 $175

Brooks, Keziah *The Voice and Other Short Stories.* Detroit: Harlo, 1975. First edition, many photos, as new, without dust jacket as issued. Between the Covers Rare Books 202 - 13 2016 $50

Broom, an International Magazine of the Arts Published by Americans in Italy. Rome: Broom, 1921. 4to., paper wrappers, light wear to covers, unopened. Oak Knoll Books 310 - 25 2016 $650

Broonzy, William *Big Bill Blues.* London: Cassell, 1955. First edition, 8vo., dust jacket, photos and drawings, donor's presentation on flyleaf, author's presentation under his frontispiece photo to Mrs. Martha King, top edges slightly soiled, otherwise very good, tight copy, little chipped and somewhat soiled dust jacket, scarce signature. Second Life Books, Inc. 196A - 204 2016 $1500

Brossa, Joan *Oda a Joan Miro.* Barcelona: Edicions Poligrafa, 1973. First edition, one of 350 copies of a total edition of 535 copies, all signed, signed by Miro and Brossa, lithographs by Miro, folio, original pictorial cloth designed by Miro, few tiny spots of soiling to cloth, fine. Manhattan Rare Book Company 2016 - 1731 2016 $2200

Brough, Robert *The Vacant Frame.* Stevenson: The Rocket Press, 1983. Limited to 80 numbered copies, loose leaves inserted in cloth folder, inserted in wooden case in shape of compositor's case with four compartments, one holding book, two holding metal types and a fourth holding a miniature cloth bound book called Walker's Book. Oak Knoll Books 27 - 60 2016 $450

Brougham, Henry Brougham *Practical Observations Upon the Education of the People....* Manchester: printed by Archibald Prentice with the permission of the author), 1825. Recent marbled boards, maroon cloth spine. Jarndyce Antiquarian Books CCXV - 358 2016 £120

Brougham, John *David Copperfield. A Drama in Three Acts.* London: John Dicks circa, Illustrations, odd spot, original wrappers. Jarndyce Antiquarian Booksellers CCXVIII - 486 2016 £250

Brougham, John *Dombey and Son in three acts.* London: John Dicks, 1884. Disbound, illustrations, very good. Jarndyce Antiquarian Booksellers CCXVIII - 460 2016 £25

Broughton, Rhoda *Dear Faustina.* London: Richard Bentley and son, 1897. Scarce first edition, original cloth with blindstamped design to front and rear covers and gilt title and author to spine, very good plus with slight bumping to corners, interior also very good with small brown spots to fore-edge and light offsetting to front free endpaper, very good. The Kelmscott Bookshop 12 - 18 2016 $200

Broughton, T. Alan *The Man on the Moon.* New York: Barlemir House, 1979. First edition, 8vo., paper covered boards, fine, inscribed by author for Ann and Bernard Malamud. Second Life Books, Inc. 196A - 205 2016 $45

Brown Alan K. *Sawpits in the Spanish Red Woods 1787-1849.* San Mateo: San Mateo County Historical Association, 1966. First edition, one of 750 copies, map, 2 plates, gilt lettered green cloth, slight rubbing to spine ends, fine. Argonaut Book Shop Natural History 2015 - 7493 2016 $45

Brown, Alice *Old Crow.* New York: Macmillan, 1922. First edition, 8vo., very good in chipped and nicked dust jacket. Second Life Books, Inc. 197 - 38 2016 $45

Brown, Beatrice Bradshaw *A Doll's Day.* Boston: Little Brown, 1931. First edition, oblong 4to., cloth backed pictorial boards, edges slightly faded, else fine in dust jacket with few chips and fraying, bright full color illustrations plus black and whites by Barbara Hoaven Brown, this copy signed by author and artist, additionally inscribed by author. Alephbet Books, Inc. 112 - 374 2016 $200

Brown, Catherine Hayes *Letters to Mary.* New York: Random House, 1940. First edition, 8vo., one of 350 numbered copies signed by author, inscribed by author, photos, blue moire cloth stamped in gilt, top edge gilt, cover somewhat faded on spine, otherwise nice. Second Life Books, Inc. 196A - 207 2016 $60

Brown, Dee *The Gentle Tamers: Women of the Old Wild West.* New York: Putnam, 1958. First edition, book fine, dust jacket very good with chipping to spine ends, small closed tear and light soiling to rear panel, very nice presentation copy inscribed by author. Bella Luna Books 2016 - u014 2016 $330

Brown, Elder John *Hymns for the use of the United Baptists of Illinois and the West.* Alton: Courier Steam Printing House, 1857. Second edition, 18mo., contemporary gilt stamped calf, last leaf with loss of few letters, stamped "Tobitha Sowell" on inside front cover and ink note indicating that Sowell bought this hymn book with her across the plains in 1863. M & S Rare Books, Inc. 99 - 110 2016 $750

Brown, Francis *A Hebrew and English Lexicon of the Old Testament.* Oxford: Clarendon Press, 1968. First edition, sixth reprint, corrected, 4to., blue boards, gilt lettered to spine, edges spotted, some shelf wear, no dust jacket, still good, ownership inscription of C. D. N. Costa. Unsworths Antiquarian Booksellers Ltd. E05 - 21 2016 £25

Brown, Frank *Frost's Drawings of Ipswich and Sketches in Suffolk.* Ipswich: Published by author, 1895. First edition, no. 3 of 105 copies, folio, 24 collotype plate and 35 views on 28 plates, including hand colored frontispiece, original buckram backed woven silk, somewhat frayed, top edge gilt. Marlborough Rare Books List 55 - 11 2016 £85

Brown, Fredric *Angels and Spaceships.* New York: E. P. Dutton, 1954. First edition, rubbing to board edges, nearly fine in like dust jacket with some tanning to flap edges and rear panel. John W. Knott, Jr./L.W. Currey, Inc. Fall-Winter 2015 - 17588 2016 $250

Brown, Fredric *Angels and Spaceships.* New York: Dutton, 1954. First edition, 8vo., some soiling to rear cover of dust jacket, otherwise fine in fine dust jacket. Second Life Books, Inc. 197 - 281 2016 $300

Brown, Fredric *Handbook for Homicide. in March 1942 Detectives.* Chicago: Popular Publications, 1943. First appearance in pulp magazine, very good. Mordida Books 2015 - 10727 2016 $65

Brown, H. Henry *Co-operation in a University Town...* London: Co-operative Printing Society, 1939. First edition, octavo, 11 drawings by Ronald Searle, photos, edges slightly spotted, very good in very scarce, very good dust jacket, little chipped and nicked on edges and on upper panel. Peter Ellis 112 - 351 2016 £300

Brown, Haydn *The Secret of Good Health and Long Life.* London: James Bowden, 1898. First edition, half ttiel, 10 pages ads, original green cloth, slightly rubbed, inner hinges slightly cracking, contemporary signature. Jarndyce Antiquarian Books CCXV - 82 2016 £30

Brown, J. *Exposition d'un systeme plus Simple de Medecine ou Eclaircissement et Confirmation de la Nouvelle Doctrine....* Paris: Croullebois et al, 1798. 8vo., half calf over speckled boards, some light toning to few leaves, very good. Edwin V. Glaser Rare Books 2015 - 10343 2016 $250

Brown, James S. *California Gold.* Oakland: Pacific Press Pub. Co., 1894. First edition, small 8vo., frontispiece, original printed buff wrappers, minor reinforcement of one corner and spine fold separation, housed in folding chemise and brown morocco slipcase, near fine, rare. Jeff Weber Rare Books 181 - 1 2016 $3500

Brown, John *Barbarossa.* London: J. and R. Tonson and S. Draper, 1755. Disbound, dusting to titlepage and terminal leaf. Dramatis Personae 119 - 21 2016 $40

Brown, John Carter *Bibliotheca Americana, Catalogue of the John Carter Brown Library in Brown University, Providence Rhode Island.* Millwood: Kraus Reprint Co., 1975. Tall 8vo., cloth, 7 volumes. Oak Knoll Books 310 - 231 2016 $700

Brown, Larry *Facing the Music.* Chapel Hill: Algonquin, 1988. First edition, fine in near fine dust jacket, very light sunning and faint damp staining to inside top edge. Bella Luna Books 2016 - 11506 2016 $66

Brown, Leslie *Eagles, Hawks and Falcons of World.* London: Country Life, 1968. Quarto, 2 volumes, text illustrations, color plates, few pale spots, otherwise very good in slipcase. Andrew Isles Natural History Books 55 - 16159 2016 $250

Brown, Louise Fargo *Apostle of Democracy, the Life of Lucy Maynard Salmon.* New York: Harper, 1943. First edition, inscribed by author, frontispiece and 8 plates, nice. Second Life Books, Inc. 196 B - 514 2016 $45

Brown, Marcia *The Blue Jackal.* New York: Scribners, 1977. First edition with first printing with 1-10 code, cloth, as new in dust jacket, 4to., illustrations by author, laid in is 1 page handwritten letter from Brown to a fan. Aleph-bet Books, Inc. 112 - 76 2016 $125

Brown, Marel *Lilly May and Dan: Two Children of the South.* Atlanta: Home Mission Board Southern Baptist Convention, 1946. First edition, illustrations by Lois Maiou Jones, stapled illustrated wrappers, two small chips on front wrapper (larger of which is present but detached), small tear, else very good example of fragile and rare book. Between the Covers Rare Books 202 - 17 2016 $3500

Brown, Margaret Wise *A Child's Good Morning.* New York: William R. Scott, 1952. First edition, 4to., pictorial boards, fine in lightly rubbed dust jacket, illustrations by Jean Charlot with bold bright color lithographs, printed in large font in blue, rarely found in dust jacket in such excellent condition. Aleph-bet Books, Inc. 112 - 78 2016 $1200

Brown, Margaret Wise *A Child's Good Night Book.* New York: William R. Scott, 1943. First edition, 12mo., pictorial boards, spine repaired else very good+ in dust jacket with archival mends on verso, some fading and creasing, magnificent color lithos by Jean Charlot, rare especially in dust jacket wrapper. Aleph-bet Books, Inc. 112 - 79 2016 $1200

Brown, Margaret Wise *The Man in the Manhole and the Fix-It Men.* New York: William R. Scott, 1946. First edition, rare, pictorial boards, corners worn and slight chipping to spine paper, overall very good, rare edition, inscribed by author, color illustrations. Aleph-bet Books, Inc. 111 - 58 2016 $1850

Brown, Margaret Wise *Punch and Judy.* New York: William Scott, 1940. First edition, 4to., pictorial boards, near fine in slightly worn dust jacket, illustrated with bold art deco style illustrations in color by Leonard Weisgard, including stiff color dust jacket that removes to become the stage for cut-out little puppets on back flap of dust jacket, rare in such nice condition. Aleph-bet Books, Inc. 112 - 80 2016 $1200

Brown, Margaret Wise *Pussycat's Christmas.* New York: Thomas Crowell, 1949. first edition, first printing, Square small 4to., cloth, fine in dust jacket (very good condition, few chips), lovely full page and smaller color lithographs by Helen Stone, scarce. Aleph-bet Books, Inc. 111 - 59 2016 $375

Brown, Olympia *Acquaintances, Old and New, Among Reformers.* Milwaukee: by the author, 1911. First edition, grey cloth, photos, fine, inscribed by author to sculptor Adelaide Johnson, Xmas 1913. Second Life Books, Inc. 196A - 216 2016 $950

Brown, Palmer *Cheerful.* New York: Harper Bros., 1957. 12mo., cloth, fine in dust jacket frayed at top of backstrip, else near fine, illustrated with exquisite full color illustrations and equally as lovely black and white drawings. Aleph-bet Books, Inc. 111 - 60 2016 $275

Brown, Pete *Few: Poems.* Birmingham: Migrant Press, 1966. First edition, illustrated wrappers, one of 1000 copies, of which 45 were bound in hardcover, fine. Between the Covers Rare Books 204 - 18 2016 $125

Brown, Robert *A Treatise on Agriculture and Rural Affairs; Being th Substance of the Article Agriculture....* Edinburgh: Oliphant and Balfour and Brown and Crombie and Longman, &c. London, 1811. First separate edition, 2 volumes, 8vo., 6 engraved plates (these little offset), half titles, contemporary uniform mottled calf, spines with gilt lines and labels lettered gilt, very good, sometime in the library of Sir Ernest Ridley Debenham, with his bookplate in each volume. John Drury Rare Books 2015 - 25653 2016 $437

Brown, Robertus *Prodromus Florae Novae Hollandiae et Insulae Van Dieman....* Normibergae: Leonardi Schrag, 1827. Octavo, contemporary half calf, marbled boards, all edges colored, some wear, very scarce. Andrew Isles Natural History Books 55 - 27711 2016 $4500

Brown, Ruth *Miss Rhythm: the Autobiography of Ruth Brown...* New York: Donald Fine, 1996. Second edition, 8vo., fine in dust jacket, inscribed by Miss Brown. Second Life Books, Inc. 196A - 217 2016 $95

Brown, Thomas, the Elder, Pseud. *Bath: a Satirical Novel.* London: printed for the author and sold by Sherwood, Neely and James, 1818. First edition, 3 volumes, 12mo., bound without half titles in contemporary half calf, gilt spines, neat contemporary monogram stamp to endpapers "AJC", very good, attractive copy. Jarndyce Antiquarian Booksellers CCXVII - 50 2016 £1250

Brown, Thomas, the Elder, Pseud. *Brighton or the Steyne.* London: printed for the author, sold by Sherwood, Neely and Jones, 1818. First edition, 3 volumes bound in 1 volume, 12mo., half title volume I with ad on verso, contemporary blue green moire cloth, little rubbed, bookplate of David Milne, Advocate with his trimmed signatures to titles volumes ii and iii, Renier booklabel, nice. Jarndyce Antiquarian Booksellers CCXVII - 51 2016 £750

Brown, Tom, Pseud. *Celebrated Dunces.* London: Sunday School Union, 1883. First edition, frontispiece, illustrations, 6 pages ads, original green decorated cloth, slightly rubbed, presentation stamp completed in ink on recto of frontispiece, all edges gilt, very good. Jarndyce Antiquarian Books CCXV - 51 2016 £30

Browne, Anthony *Gorilla.* New York: Alfred Knopf, 1983. First edition, 2nd printing code 2-10, pictorial boards, fine, illustrations by Browne, this copy signed by Brown with detailed pen drawing of Gorilla's head. Aleph-bet Books, Inc. 112 - 81 2016 $150

Browne, Edgar *Phiz and Dickens as they Appeared to Edgar Browne....* London: James Nisbet & Co., 1913. Limited edition, 4to., half title, frontispiece and plates, uncut in original white cloth, lettered in gilt, bevelled boards, spine little dulled, very good, signed copy, no. 40 of 175. Jarndyce Antiquarian Booksellers CCXVIII - 1087 2016 £40

Browne, Hablot Knight *23 Illustrations to Pickwick Papers.* London: Chapman & Hall, 1881. 23 India proofs after original plates by Phiz, from the deluxe edition of Dickens's Works, some light foxing, occasional chipping to corners, each plate marked on back suggesting removal from album. Jarndyce Antiquarian Booksellers CCXVIII - 120 2016 £40

Browne, Lewis *The Final Stanza.* San Francisco: Book Club of California, 1929. First edition, one of 400 copies, signed by author, large 12mo., initials in blue, vellum backed grey-blue boards, gilt, slight fading to front cover near spine, else fine. Argonaut Book Shop Private Press 2015 - 2380 2016 $40

Browne, Lina Fergusson *J. Ross Browne, His Letters, Journals and Writings.* Albuquerque: University of New Mexico Press, 1969. First edition, presentation signed by author to fellow author, E. Geoffrey Bangs, 15 plates, brown cloth, fine with pictorial dust jacket. Argonaut Book Shop Biography 2015 - 3555 2016 $45

Browne, Moses *Angling Sports in Nine Piscatory Eclogues.* London: printed for Edward and Charles Dilly, 1773. Small 8vo., frontispiece, apparently inscribed by author to Mr. Betteroth?, original calf, rebacked with handsome new spine and red morocco gilt stamped spine label, bookplate of Hastings Nathaniel Middleton, some minor ink annotations to title, very good. Jeff Weber Rare Books 181 - 79 2016 $175

Browne, Phillis, Pseud. *Common-sense Housekeeping.* London: Cassell Petter & Galpin, 1877. Half title 4 pages ads, original decorated blue cloth, slightly rubbed and dulled, all edges gilt, bookseller's ticket of W. & J. Kennedy, Hawick, attractive copy. Jarndyce Antiquarian Books CCXV - 84 2016 £68

Browne, Thomas *Of Garlands and Coronary or Garland Plants .... to John Evelyn.* Northampton: Gehenna Press, 1962. wrappers, uncut, fine signed by Leonard Baskin. Second Life Books, Inc. 196A - 625 2016 $100

Browning, Elizabeth Barrett 1806-1861 *Poems.* London: Edward Moxon, 1844. First edition, 2 volumes, ad leaf at end of volume I, original green vertical fine ribbed cloth, blocked in blind, spines lettered gilt, booklabels of Miss S. Sheppard with her signatures on verso of titlepages and dated may 1848, modern labels of Christopher Clark Geest, slight marking to leading free endpaper from old insertion, otherwise lovely crisp copy, green cloth fold over box. Jarndyce Antiquarian Booksellers CCXVII - 53 2016 £1250

Browning, Elizabeth Barrett 1806-1861 *Sonnets from the Portuguese.* London: Vale Press, 1897. One of 300 copies on paper (and 8 on vellum), 152 x 121mm., pleasing blue-gray crushed morocco by Zaehnsdorf (stamp signed with firm's oval exhibition stamp), covers with delicate gilt frame of swirling tendrils bearing azured leaves, flat spine with gilt tendrils and titling, turn-ins with multiple plain and decorative rules, crimson watered silk endleaves, top edge gilt, 2 large woodcut white vine initials by Charles Ricketts, printed in red, spine evenly sunned, small dark stain, half inch in diameter, at middle of fore-edge of book block (just barely extending onto margin of most pages), otherwise fine, binding unworn and text fresh and clean. Phillip J. Pirages 67 - 79 2016 $750

Browning, Elizabeth Barrett 1806-1861 *Two Poems by Elizabeth Browning an Robert Browning.* London: Chapman & Hall, 1854. First edition, original paper wrappers, sewn as issued. Jarndyce Antiquarian Booksellers CCXVII - 55 2016 £150

Browning, Robert 1812-1889 *Christmas Eve and Easter Day. A Poem.* London: Chapman & Hall, 1850. First edition, half title, 32 page Chapman & Hall cat. Aug. 1849, original dark olive brown vertical fine ribbed cloth, boards blocked in blind, spine lettered in gilt, slight rubbed, nice, crisp copy in primary binding. Jarndyce Antiquarian Booksellers CCXVII - 54 2016 £350

Browning, Robert 1812-1889 *Dramatic Idyls. Second Series.* London: Smith, Elder & Co., 1880. First edition, near fine in original brown cloth with gilt title to spine, light rubbing to edges and corners, browning from paper clip to top edge of first few pages, else interior very clean, near fine. The Kelmscott Bookshop 12 - 19 2016 $3200

Browning, Robert 1812-1889 *Ferishtah's Fancies.* London: Smith, Elder & Co., 1884. First edition, forged presentation "To FG Watts from Robert Browning Dec. 1884" (not in Browning's hand), in very good original dark brown cloth boards with gilt title to spine and black decoration to front board, rubbing to hinges, edges and corners with short open tear to book cloth along front hinge, foxing to first and last few pages with few light pencil bracket marks to text and occasional folded corners, blue endpages, from the collection of Stuart B. Schimmel. The Kelmscott Bookshop 12 - 20 2016 $450

Browning, Robert 1812-1889 *The Pied Piper of Hamelin.* London: George Harrap, 1934. First edition, limited to 400 numbered copies, signed by Arthur Rackham, silhouette endpapers, 4 color plates plus lovely line illustrations in text, beautiful copy, fine in fine original slipcase. Aleph-bet Books, Inc.   111 - 382   2016 $2500

Browning, Robert 1812-1889 *The Ring and The Book.* London: Smith, Elder, 1868-1869. First edition, 4 volumes, 8vo., occasional light scattered foxing to free endleaves, original black stamped green cloth, gilt stamped spines by Harrison, quarter gilt stamped calf over blue cloth slipcase, volume 3 rear hinge cracked with light front pastedown soiling, volumes 1 and 2 hinges cracked, Robert Browning's signature tipped in volume I, opposite titlepage, ownership signatures of W. J. (...?) Settle (Sherborne Dorset, Feb. 21, 1869) and F. Rowlandson, ownership signatures of E. M. Forster in volume 2 to free front endleaf and titlepage, attractive, very good, with cut-out signature tipped in of Robert Browning.   Jeff Weber Rare Books   181 - 42   2016 $4000

Bruccoli, Matthew J. *Fitzgerald Newsletter Number 1, 2, & 3.* Charlottesville: F. Scott Fitzgerald Society, 1958. 3 issues, each consisting of one leaf folded to make four pages, one faint library stamp on no. 3, old staple holes where they were probably stapled, together, else near fine. Between the Covers Rare Books   204 - 47   2016 $300

Bruce, Charles Granville *The Assault on Mount Everest 1922.* New York & London: Longmans, Green and Co. and Edward Arnold,, 1923. First edition, 36 illustrations from photos, 2 folding maps, publisher's blue cloth with titles stamped in gilt, spine sunned but quite legible, light wear to spine ends, dust soil to top edge, binding sound, text quite clean, maps and plates fine.   Simon Finch   2015 - 15363   2016 $275

Bruce, Charles Granville *The Assault on Mount Everest 1922.* London: Edward Arnold & Co., 1923. First edition, frontispiece and 34 of 35 illustrations, 2 folding maps, rebound in maroon cloth covers with gilt lettering and rule on spine, 1 text leaf (page 157-158) and 1 plate (facing p. 156) missing, tissue guard to frontispiece present, some foxing to prelims, some spotting to page edges, internally clean, occasional light foxing, no signatures of stamps, creasing ad 4 inch tear to first folding map, both maps backed with thin card.   Simon Finch   2015 - 00216   2016 $200

Bruce, James *An Interesting Narrative of the Travels of James Bruce Esq. into Abyssinia to Discover the Source of the Nile.* New York: for Berry and Rogers, 1790. First American edition, 12mo, engraved folding map, contemporary sheep, neatly rebacked with original label laid down, 19th century signature of Benj. H. Smith, usual moderate foxing common to American books of this period, else very good.   Joseph J. Felcone, Inc.   Books from Five Centuries: a Miscellany - 30   2016 $550

Bruce, William *Marriage.* London: Jemaes Spiers, 1871. Half title, printed in gold, original white cloth, bevelled boards, elaborately decorated and lettered gilt, little dulled with slight marking to lower board, gift inscription to Mr. & Mrs. Herbert Gill from Mr. and Mrs. Wilkins, March 15 (18)89.   Jarndyce Antiquarian Books   CCXV - 83   2016   £85

Bruff, J. Goldsborough *Gold Rush. The Journals, Drawings and Other Papers of...* New York: Columbia University Press, 1949. California Centennial Edition, thick quarto, color frontispiece plus numerous illustrations and facsimiles, rust cloth, gilt, lower corner slightly jammed, fine with lightly worn dust jacket, lavishly illustrated with Bruff's own drawings and sketches.   Argonaut Book Shop   Biography 2015 - 6592   2016 $90

Brun, Carl *Schweizerisches Kunstler-Lexikon, Herausgegeben Mit Unterstutzung des Bundes Und Kunstrefundlicher Privater vom Schweizerischen Kunstverein.* Frauenfeld: Von Huber & Co., 1905-1917. Thick 8vo., half cloth over pastepaper covered boards loosely inserted commemorative booklabel, which indicates this came from reference library of H. P. Kraus.   Oak Knoll Books   310 - 26   2016 $750

Brunini, John Gilland *Whereon to Stand.* New York: Harper and Bros., 1946. Later printing, light sunning at crown, else fine in spine faded, very good plus with wrinkled on front panel, inscribed by author to author Jean Toomer. Between the Covers Rare Books   207 - 91   2016 $400

Brunner, Hans *The Identification of Mammalian Hair.* Melbourne: Inkata Press, 1974. Quarto, photos, dust jacket, owner's signature, signed by both authors, very good, dust jacket, very scarce.   Andrew Isles Natural History Books   55 - 3693   2016 $300

Bryan, Alfred *A Book of Drawings by A. Bryan, L. Davis, A. T. Elwes, Harry Furniss....* London: privately printed for M. & Mrs. F. T. Davies, 1891. Folio, half title, engraved frontispiece and contents leaf, plates, sewn as issued in original stiff card vellum covered wrappers, lettered on front wrapper in gilt, edges slightly dusted, overall nice. Jarndyce Antiquarian Booksellers   CCXVII - 56   2016   £680

Bryce, William Moir *The Scottish Grey Friars.* Edinburgh & London: 1909. First edition, original brown cloth with gilt letters and blindstamped, Christogram "IHS" as called for, errata, illustrations, including frontispiece with tissue guards, plans, illustrations in text, very good and clean set.   Any Amount of Books   2015 - C507   2016   £170

Brydges, Samuel Egerton 1762-1837 *Censura Literaria.* London: printed for Longman, Hurst, Rees, Orme & Brown, 1813. Second edition, 10 volumes, half titles, initial 4 page catalog volume I, final ad leaf volume III, full index volume X, uncut, original drab boards, paper labels chipped in one or two places, slight wear to heads and tails of spines, corners little knocked, overall very good.   Jarndyce Antiquarian Booksellers   CCXVII - 57   2016   £350

Bryson, Thomas   *A Serious Address to Young and of Both Sexes on the necessity and Advantages of Early Piety.* Printed by J. Skirvens, 1792. 8vo., disbound, title with some foxing.   Jarndyce Antiquarian Books   CCXV - 86   2016   £50

Bysh's Edition of Nursery Rhymes.   London: printed by T. Richardson for J. Bysh, n.d. but owner inscribed, 1828. Pictorial wrappers, bound in later marbled boards, top and bottom margins of front cover trimmed, final leaf lacking a piece from bottom resulting in the last of a few lines of text on each side, housed in custom cloth clamshell box, 6 full page hand colored engravings.   Aleph-bet Books, Inc.   111 - 148   2016 $275

Buaken, Iris B.   *Girl on the Wheel.*   New York: Vantage Press, 1959. First edition, slightly cocked and boards little rubbed, else near fine, good dust jacket with several small chips and tears, some internal tape repairs and slight spot fading to purple, signed by author "Review Copy Iris. B. Buaken".   Between the Covers Rare Books   208 - 45   2016 $500

Buchan, John 1875-1940   *The Complete Richard Hannay.* Blackwood and Hodder & Stoughton, 1916. first editions, 8 volumes, frontispiece map to fourth volume printed in black and red, earlier volumes with some age toning, few with light foxing, more common around prelims and opening pages, one or two light handling marks, crown 8vo., original blue or green cloth, couple of light spotting to edges, most with small amount of foxing or browning to endpapers, endpaper maps to volumes 6 & 7, contemporary ownership inscription of Evelyn Le Marchant (a Naval captain), contemporary gift inscription and bookplate of Philip Waterhouse, bookseller blindstamp to one volume, hinges to first volume touch strained in couple of places, original dust jackets to final three volumes, small amount of rubbing and creasing, odd nick and couple of short closed tears, good.   Blackwell's Rare Books   B186 - 189   2016   £2000

Buchan, John 1875-1940   *The Thirty-Nine Steps.* Edinburgh: William Blackwood, 1915. First edition, usual browning to page edges with one or two foxspots, foolscap 8vo., original blue cloth stamped in navy to front, backstrip lettered navy and little rubbed at tips with short split at foot, small patch of discoloration to upper board, textblock strained between second and third gatherings, very faint browning to free endpapers, very good.   Blackwell's Rare Books   B164 - 121   2016   £1200

Buchanan, George   *Rearum Scoticarum Historia...* Edinburgh: John Paton, 1727. engraved portrait frontispiece, engraved folding map, slightly browned, 12mo., contemporary calf, lettered gilt on spine, minor wear, good. Blackwell's Rare Books   B184 - 17   2016   £300

Buchanan, George   *The Very learned Scotsman, Mr. George Buchanan's Fratres Fraterrimi.*   Edinburgh: printed by the heirs and successors of Andrew Anderson, 1708. First edition, small 8vo., 19th century calf, gilt crest on upper cover by J. Leighton, fine, very scarce, early inscription of Robert Mylne, later bookplate of Robert Crewe-Milnes, Marquess of Crewe.   C. R. Johnson Rare Book Collections Foxon: H-P 2015 - 622   2016 $2298

Buck, Pearl S.   *The Chinese Children next Door.*   New York: John Day, 1942. First edition, drawings by William Arthur Smith, boards slightly soiled else fine in near fine dust jacket with small chip on front panel and few short tears, uncommon.   Between the Covers Rare Books   208 - 17   2016 $500

Buckland, William   *Geology and Mineralogy, considered with Reference to Natural Theology.* London: William Pickering, 1837. Second edition, octavo, 2 volumes, publisher's cloth with printed labels, some foxing, but sound. Andrew Isles Natural History Books   55 - 36575   2016 $450

Buckle, Richard   *John Innocent at Oxford.*   London: Chatto & Windus, 1939. First edition, octavo, illustrations and dust jacket design by author, near fine in very good, slightly nicked, price clipped dust jacket bit tanned at spine. Peter Ellis   112 - 51   2016   £60

Buckler, Ernst   *The Mountain and the Valley.*   New York: Henry Holt and Co., 1952. First edition, light blue cloth, red lettering to spine and top edge pink in dust jacket, 8vo., one corner bumped and some very light shelfwear.   Schooner Books Ltd.   115 - 131   2016 $150

Buckley, Christopher   *Ellis Island Poems.*   N. P.: Duende Press, 1991. Limited to 100 numbered copies, 10 specially bound, signed by author and artist, wood engraving by Paul Ritscher, square 8vo., cloth.   Oak Knoll Books   310 - 96   2016 $125

Bucknill, C. E. R.   *Sea Shells of New Zealand.*   Auckland: Whitcombe and Tombs, 1924. Quarto, 12 uncolored plates, publisher's paper covered boards, tipped on Nautilus plate, fine, scarce in this condition.   Andrew Isles Natural History Books   55 - 38856   2016 $80

Buckrose, J. E., Pseud.   *The Art of Living, Social Problems Solved.*   The Gentlewoman Offices, 1903. Half title, original imitation vellum boards, printed in blue and gilt, yapped edges, top edge gilt, very good.   Jarndyce Antiquarian Books   CCXV - 87   2016   £50

Buday, George *Cries of London. Ancient & Modern.* privately printed, 1954. Advance copy, 20 wood engravings, titlepage printed in red, 24mo., original stapled wrappers printed in red ot front, dust jacket with Buday wood engraving to front and printed Christmas message to front flap, little very light dust soiling, very good.   Blackwell's Rare Books   B186 - 294   2016   £80

Buddignton, Zadel Barnes *The Voice of Christmas Past.* New York: Harper and Bros., 1871. From Harper's Monthly Magazine Volume XLII no. 248 Jan. 1871, slightly marked, recent marbled wrappers, very good.   Jarndyce Antiquarian Booksellers   CCXVIII - 1092   2016   £20

Bude, Guillaume *De Asse et Partibus Etus, Libri Quinque....* Cologne: Johannes Soter, 1528. First American edition, 2 parts in 1 volume, woodcut printer's device on title, title to second part within woodcut border, woodcut initials, more elaborate woodcut device on verso of last leaf, some text in Greek, small hole in titlepage with loss of 1 letter from headline on verso, 2 leaves with small repairs to fore-margin, few gatherings slightly browned, minor dampstaining, small 8vo., contemporary vellum over flexible boards, lettered in ink on spine, minor soiling, some contemporary annotation, the Macclesfield copy with bookplate and blindstamp, very good, scarce.   Blackwell's Rare Books   B186 - 28   2016   £1200

Budge, Ernest Alfred Wallis Thompson 1857-1934 *The Mummy.* Cambridge: University Press, 1925. Royal 8vo., original red cloth, image of Pharaoh in blind to upper cover, lettered in gilt to spine, folding frontispiece, 38 black and white plates from photos, numerous line drawings, lightly sunned on spine, light offsetting from endpapers, spotting to edges, near fine, beautiful copy of the best edition.   Sotheran's   Travel and Exploration - 304   2016   £348

Buff, Mary *Dancing Cloud the Navajo Boy.* New York: Viking, 1957. First edition thus, 8vo., cloth, fine in slightly worn dust jacket, illustrations by Conrad Buff, this copy inscribed and signed by author and artist.   Aleph-bet Books, Inc.   111 - 61   2016 $200

Buff, Mary *Elf Owl.* New York: Viking, 1958. First edition, cloth, fine in lightly frayed, very good dust jacket, this copy warmly inscribed by the Buffs dated 1958.   Aleph-bet Books, Inc.   112 - 82   2016 $150

Buff, Mary *Hah-Nee of the Cliff Dwellers.* Boston: Houghton Mifflin, 1956. 8vo., cloth, fine in very good dust jacket with small piece off backstrip, slight fraying, this copy signed and inscribed by author and artist, full color and black and white lithographs by Conrad Buff.   Aleph-bet Books, Inc.   111 - 63   2016 $150

Buff, Mary *Hurry, Skurry and Flurry.* New York: Viking, 1954. First edition, 8vo., cloth, fine in slightly worn dust jacket, lovely inscribed signed by author and artist, beautiful original cloth by Conrad Buff.   Aleph-bet Books, Inc.   111 - 62   2016 $150

Bugge, Thomas *De Forste Grunde til den Sphaeriske og Theoretiske Astronomie...* Kjobenhavn: S. Poulsens, 1796. Mottled leather spine and tips with tan paste paper covered boards and leather title label to spine, gilt spine label, chipping to top edge of title label which effects few letters in author's name, minor wear to corners and edges of boards, bumping to corners, rubbing to boards and hinges, few chips to paper covering boards, bookplate of Harry Rabinowitz, notes in pen to endpages, soiling to corners of few pages, occasional small spots of foxing, 12 plates, very good.   The Kelmscott Bookshop   13 - 12   2016 $175

Bukha, A. *Chernomorskoe Poberezhe Kaykaza.* Tblisi: Izdanie Gruzinskogo Otdeleniia Muzfonda SSSR, 1960. Oblong 12mo., original pictorial wrappers, illustrations, very well preserved.   Sotheran's   Travel and Exploration - 223   2016   £98

Bukowski, Charles *Flower, Fist and Bestial Waif.* Eureka: Hearse Press, 1960. First edition, one of 200 copies, stapled illustrated wrappers, staples oxidized, else fine, signed by author.   Between the Covers Rare Books   208 - 13   2016 $9500

Bukowski, Charles *Flower, Fist and Bestial Wail.* Eureka: Hearse Press, 1960. First edition, one of no more than five 'author's edition' copies with original illustrations by author bound in, publisher's illustrated saddle stitched wrappers, 28 unnumbered pages, 8 x 5 inches, fine in cloth clamshell box, near fine.   Royal Books   51 - 9   2016 $12,500

Bukowski, Charles *The Last Poem & Tough Company.* Santa Barbara: Black Sparrow Press, 1976. Number 55 from an edition of 176 published as a New Year's Greeting, signed by Bukowski and Wakoski, complimentary slip from publisher laid in, fine copy in paper covered boards with cloth spine, in fine dust jacket.   Jeff Hirsch Books   Holiday List 2015 - 28   2016 $350

Bukowski, Charles *One for the Old Boy.* Santa Barbara: Black Sparrow Press, 1984. Number 193 from an edition of 226 copies, very near fine in paper covered boards with slight lean to spine (from binding process), signed by author. Jeff Hirsch Books   Holiday List 2015 - 27   2016 $150

Bukowski, Charles *2 by Bukowski (2 Poems).* Los Angeles: Black Sparrow Press, 1967. First book of Bukowski's to be published by Black Sparrow, no. 93 of 96 numbered copies of a total edition of 99 copies, signed by author, fine in saddle stitched wrappers, early rarity.   Ken Lopez Bookseller   166 - 11   2016 $1500

Bulgakov, Mikhail *The Master & Margarita.* Collins & Harvill Press, 1967. First English edition, 8vo., original green cloth, backstrip lettered gilt, dust jacket with gentle fading to red of backstrip panel, little rubbing and just hint of creasing to extremities, very good.   Blackwell's Rare Books   B186 - 190   2016   £300

Bulkley, Mary E. *Speaking at Seventy.*   San Francisco: Gelber, Lillienthal, Inc., 1931. First edition, limited to 250 numbered copies printed at the Grabhorn Press, printed in red and black, cloth backed decorated boards, paper spine label, very fine, printed on Van Gelder Paper with Baskerville italic type.   Argonaut Book Shop   Private Press 2015 - 2379   2016 $50

Bullen, Frank T. *The Cruise of the 'Cachalot' Round the World after Sperm Whales.* London: Smith Elder, 1898. First edition, 8vo., folding map, illustrations, original blue decorative cloth, joints slightly rubbed.   J. & S. L. Bonham Antiquarian Booksellers   Voyages 2016 - 6137   2016   £125

Buller, Walter L. *Manual of the Birds of New Zealand.* Wellington: Government Printer, 1882. Octavo, 36 uncolored plates, publisher's red decorated cloth, lower cover stained very good.   Andrew Isles Natural History Books   55 - 30020   2016 $500

Bulls-Eye Bill.   New York: Stoll Edwards, 1921. 4to., stiff pictorial card covers, some cover soil and two small repairs else really very good, each page has large hole cut out in middle, through which can be seen a little black boy, printed on one side of paper, illustrations signed by D. C. Holt.   Aleph-bet Books, Inc.   112 - 61   2016 $450

Bulu, Joel *Joel Bulu: the Autobiography of a Native Minister in the South Seas.* London: T. Woolmer, 1884. Small 8vo., original brick red cloth, lettered gilt, decorated in black, wood engraved frontispiece with tissue guard, this little browned, light offsetting to adjacent leaves, minimal rubbing to extremities, scarce.   Sotheran's   Travel and Exploration - 396   2016   £198

Bunau-Varilla, Philippe *Nicaragua or Panama; the Substance of a Series of Conferences Made Before the Commercial Club of Cincinnati...* New York: Knickerbocker Press, 1901. First edition, 8vo. 4 duotone folding diagrams, stapled wrappers, good+ copy, lacking front wrapper, rear wrapper chipped and nearly detached, spine largely perished and split along signatures, contents clean. Kaaterskill Books   21 - 11   2016 $125

Bunce, Oliver Bell   *Don't: a manual of mistakes and improprieties more or less prevelant in conduct and speech.* London: Ward Lock & Co., circa, 1884. Limp red cloth. Jarndyce Antiquarian Books   CCXV - 88   2016   £35

Bunker, Gerald *The Editor Magazine.*   Cambridge: and Providence: The Editor, 1959. Third issue, octavo, illustrated wrappers, age toning on wrappers, small creases on front wrapper and small tear on final leaf, very good. Between the Covers Rare Books   204 - 19   2016 $250

Bunner, E. *History of Louisiana from Its First Discovery and Settlement to the present Time.* New York: Harper and Bros., 1843. Later printing, 24mo., quarter morocco over cloth boards, gilt titles and decoration on spine, very good ex-library, without usual markings, small split on one side of spine, head and opposite side of spine, tail, few tiny wormholes on backstrip, scuff mark on front board, library label, writing on free front endpaper, scattered foxing.   Kaaterskill Books   21 - 12   2016 $100

Bunny, Edmund *Of Divorce for Adutlerie and Marrying Againe...*   Oxford: Joseph Barnes, 1610. Folindg table, frontispiece, inoffensive staining from **1 to A4 including folding table, foremargin of last 2 leaves trimmed, with minor loss, 20th century full panelled calf, raised bands, spine lettered gilt, some slight rubbing to hinges and extremities, pencil notes on initial inserted blank of the collector Brent Gration-Maxfield.   Jarndyce Antiquarian Booksellers   CCXVII - 58   2016   £3200

Bunting, Eve *Smoky Night.* San Diego: Harcourt Brace, 1994. Stated first edition, pictorial boards, as new in dust jacket, color illustrations by David Diaz, bookplate with large signed drawing by Diaz.   Aleph-bet Books, Inc.   112 - 144   2016 $200

Bunyan, John   1628-1688 *A Book for Boys and Girls or Country Rhymes for Children.* London: Elliot Stock, 1890. Facsimile of first edition, initial ad leaf, half title, uncut, largely unopened, original printed cloth imitating vellum, slightly dulled.   Jarndyce Antiquarian Books CCXV - 561   2016 £58

Bunyan, John   1628-1688 *The Christian Pilgrim.* Worcester: Isaiah Thomas, 1798. First American edition, two tiny octavo volumes in one, each with separate titlepage, frontispiece in volume 1 and numerous small engravings in text, lacks frontispiece to volume two which is a repeat of frontispiece in volume one and oft lacking, modern full brown calf, marbled endpapers, bit of fraying to foreedge of first few pages, some toning and staining throughout, overall very good.   Heritage Book Shop   Holiday 2015 - 14   2016 $5000

Bunyan, John   1628-1688 *The Pilgrims Progress...* Halifax: printed by Nicholsons and Walker, 1800. New edition, 2 parts in 1 volume, 2 engraved frontispieces, some browning, staining and foxing, original sheep, some wear, sound.   Blackwell's Rare Books   B186 - 30   2016   £300

Bunyan, John 1628-1688 *The Pilgrim's Progress...* Cincinnati: printed by J. W. Browne and Co., 1813. 12mo., modern calf backed boards, some browning and staining, little worming at end touching few letters.   Blackwell's Rare Books   B186 - 31   2016   £750

Bunyan, John 1628-1688 *Pilgrim's Progress in Three Parts.* Halifax: printed and published by William Milner, 1841. 12mo., frontispiece and additional engraved titlepage, many illustrations in text, title toned, some sporadic foxing, green publisher's cloth, elaborate gilt spine, blindstamped boards, all edges gilt, rubbed, some tiny holes to upper joint, few marks but still very good.   Unsworths Antiquarian Booksellers Ltd.   E05 - 115   2016   £30

Bunyan, John 1628-1688 *Pilgrim's Progress from this World to that Which is to Come.* London: printed for the Society by J. Haddon, 1847. First edition, 8vo., finely bound by Ramage in full brown morocco boards panelled gilt and black with oak leaf and acorn corner tools and central gilt block, spine panelled and lettered gilt, all edges gilt, uppper joint little rubbed, little spotting to endpapers, leather booklabel of Edith Northbourne, otherwise very good. Sotheran's   Piccadilly Notes - Summer 2015 - 59   2016   £498

Bunyan, John 1628-1688 *The Pilgrim's Progress from this World to that Which is to Come.* London: Essex House Press, 1899. Number 627 of 750 copies, lovely book bound and signed by Bickers and Son in brown crushed pigskin with five bands and blind embossed title on spine, top edges gilt and marbled endpapers, front hinge repaired, printed in black and red type on fine handmade paper, frontispiece illustrations by Reginald Savage protected by tissue guard, very good plus.   The Kelmscott Bookshop   12 - 44   2016 $395

Bunyan, John 1628-1688 *The Pilgrim's Progress.* London: printed by Bernard Newdigate at the Shakespeare Head Press for the Cresset Press, 1928. No. 102 of 195 copies on paper (and 10 on vellum), 2 volumes, 368 x 264mm, publisher's black stained vellum by Sangorski & Sutcliffe (stamp signed), raised bands, gilt titling on upper cover and spine, 2 large vignettes ad 10 engraved plates, by Blair Hughes-Stanton, and Gertrude Hermes, hint of rubbing to extremities, one leaf with closed marginal tear but fine set, quite clean, fresh and bright inside and out. Phillip J. Pirages   67 - 101   2016 $1600

Bunyan, John 1628-1688 *Pilgrim's Progress.* London: printed by Bernard Newdigate at the Shakespeare Head Press for the Cresset Press, 1928. Number 6 of 10 special copies printed on vellum (and 195 on paper), 2 volumes, plus portfolio of plates, fine publisher's russet morocco by Sangorski & Sutcliffe (stamp signed on front turn-in), covers lettered gilt, metal clasps, raised bands, wide turn-ins with multiple ruled border, all edges gilt, volumes housed along with extra suite of engravings, in a (slightly worn but still very good), fleece lined matching cloth box and slipcase, 2 large vignettes and 10 powerful expressionistic engraved plates on vellum, vignettes and 6 of the plates by Blair Hughes-Stanton, the other four by Gertrude Hermes with matted duplicates of all plates (all of the engravings signed), extras done on thin paper and contained in their own portfolio, bookplate of the Garden Collection assembled by Haven O'More, a couple of faint scratches to boards, spines shade darker than covers, small handful of leaves with usual faint discoloration that is inevitable with vellum, otherwise superb set, text clean and fresh, smooth, bright vellum leaves, bindings unworn.   Phillip J. Pirages   67 - 332   2016 $35,000

Bunyan, John, Junior *The Drunkard's Progress...* Edinburgh: Johnstone and Hunter, 1853. 12 full page plates, vignette title and 2 other woodcuts, plate IV, V, VI transposed in binding, contemporary half red calf, cloth boards, front panel lettered with title, ownership inscr. Thos. Carmichael 1854.   Jarndyce Antiquarian Booksellers CCXVII - 59   2016   £65

Buonanni, Filippo 1638-1725 *Observations circa Viventia, quae in Rebus non Viventibus Repriuntur. Cum Micrographia Curiosa....*   Rome: Typs Dominci Antonii Herculis, 1691. First edition, small 4to., 3 parts in one volume, title woodcut vignette, engraved title, 69 engraved copperplate plates, title with mended hole, ownership mark excised on outer margin, with slight affect to 1 letter, frequent browning, lacks famous frontispiece, original full vellum, gilt spine title, added ink manuscript, bookplate of Haskell F. Norman, early ink ownership mark on title 1778. Jeff Weber Rare Books   183 - 7   2016 $3750

Buonarroti, Michel Angelo 1475-1564 *Rime, di Michelangolo Buonarroti Taccolta da Michelangelo suo Nipote.* Florence: Appresson I Giunti, 1623. First edition, small quarto, woodcut device on titlepage, decorative woodcut head and tailpieces and initials, typographic ornaments throughout, uncut and bound in modern full brown speckled calf, decoratively blindstamped on covers, gilt stamped on spine with five raised bands, minimal foxing.   Heritage Book Shop   Holiday 2015 - 79   2016 $5000

Buonarroti, Michel Angelo 1475-1564 *The Sonnets of Michael Angelo Buonarroti and Tommaso Campanella Now for the First time Translated into Rhymed English...* London: Smith Elder & Co., 1878. First complete translation, 8vo., original smooth blue/purple cloth, lettered gilt on spine, borders of lines and stars in black on boards, slightly cocked, spine little darkened, little spotting to prelims, otherwise very good, from the library of Bloomsbury Group publisher and translator, Roger Senhouse.   Sotheran's Piccadilly Notes - Summer 2015 - 203   2016   £198

Bureau of American Ethnology *Bulletin 30: Handbook of American Indians North of Mexico Parts I and II.* Washington: GPO, 1907-1910. First editions, 2 volumes, illustrations, folding map, extremities worn, hinges starting on both volumes, map damaged, internally clean.   Dumont Maps and Books   133 - 59   2016 $65

Burges, Johnson *Pleasant Tragedies of Childhood.* New York: Harper & Bros. Oct., 1905. 4to., blue pictorial cloth, as new in original printed paper wrapper and publishers pictorial box, box soiled some with some wear but very good, printed on heavy coated paper and illustrated by Fanny Cory, outstanding copy.   Aleph-bet Books, Inc.   112 - 117   2016 $275

Burgess, Anthony *A Clockwork Orange.* London: Heinemann, 1962. First edition, first issue black binding, octavo, small contemporary (1964) ownership signature, edges spotted, very good in near fine dust jacket slightly faded at spine.   Peter Ellis   112 - 52   2016   £2750

Burgess, Anthony *The End of the World News.* New York: McGraw Hill, 1983. First edition, fine in little soiled, inscribed by author.   Second Life Books, Inc.   196A - 225   2016 $45

Burgess, Anthony *You've Had your time.* New York: Grove Weidenfeld, 1991. First American edition, first printing, 8vo., paper over boards with cloth spine, edges slightly spotted, otherwise nice in slightly scuffed dust jacket, author's presentation on title.   Second Life Books, Inc.   196A - 226   2016 $75

Burgess, Gelett *Blue Goops and Red Goops.* New York: Frederick A. Stokes, 1909. First edition, 4to., text and illustrations, very good++, mild cover edge wear, owner inscription, each illustrated page has half page overlay, scarce in this condition.   By the Book, L. C.   45 - 79   2016 $450

Burgess, Gelett *Goop Tales Alphabetically Told.* New York: Frederick Stokes, 1904. 4to., blue pictorial cloth, fine, great line illustrations, inscribed by Burgess with drawing.   Aleph-bet Books, Inc.   111 - 64   2016 $1200

Burgess, Gelett *More Goops and How Not to Be Them.* New York: Frederick Stokes, Sept, 1903. First edition, 4to., yellow pictorial cloth, light cover soil rubbing to lettering, occasional finger soil inside, very good+, full page illustrations.   Aleph-bet Books, Inc.   112 - 83   2016 $400

Burgess, Thornton *Animal Pictures.* Akron: Saalfield, 1925. Printed on cloth, lightly frayed and slightly soiled, near fine, rare, full page color illustrations by Harrison Cady. Aleph-bet Books, Inc.   112 - 84   2016 $500

Burgh, James *The Art of Speaking.* London: printed for T. Longman & J. Buckland &c., 1761. 8vo., odd mark and crease, overall nice, clean copy, contemporary full calf, corners repaired, little rubbed, signature of R. Allen, June 21 1799, nice.   Jarndyce Antiquarian Books   CCXV - 89   2016   £380

Burghope, George *Autarachy; or the Art of Self-Government in a Moral Essays.* London: printed for Dorman Newman at the Kings-Arms in the Poulty, 1691. First edition, 8vo., prelim imprimatur leaf and final ad leaf, small paper flaws to margins of D3, F1 & G6, corner fo H3 torn with loss not affecting text, old waterstaining, some browning, contemporary calf, raised bands, original label, neat repairs, boards scratched, 18th century names on front endpaper and inner board and verso of titlepage, two leaves of handwritten 18th century verse at end.   Jarndyce Antiquarian Books   CCXV - 90   2016   £250

Burglon, Nora *Children of the Soil.* New York: Junior Literary Guild and Doubleday Doran, 1933. Stated first edition, rare, 8vo., pictorial cloth, fine in very good dust jacket with some soil and fraying, illustrations by Edgar D'Aulaire. Aleph-bet Books, Inc.   112 - 132   2016 $200

Burgmann, Johann Gustav *An Earnest and Affectionate address to the Jews.* printed by order of the Society for the Promotion of Christian Knowledge, 1774. Small 8vo., woodcut ornaments, disbound, stabbed, very good. Blackwell's Rare Books   B186 - 32   2016   £450

Burke, B. W. *A Compendium of the Anatomy, Physiology and Pathology of the Horse.* Philadelphia: James Humphreys, 1806. First American edition, 2 plates, 12mo., contemporary mottled sheep, plates moderately foxed, upper spine cap partly chipped, small chip from spine label, else very attractive in handsome period binding, ownership signature of Wm. Gunkle, 1818.   Joseph J. Felcone, Inc. Books from Five Centuries: a Miscellany - 31   2016 $1000

Burke, Bernard *A Genealogical and Heraldic History of the Landed Gentry of Great Britain and Ireland.* London: Harrison & sons, 1898. Ninth edition, 2 volumes, rebound in red buckram lettered gilt at spine, illustrations, ex-British Foreign Office library with few library markings, else sound, very good.   Any Amount of Books   2015 - A73018   2016   £170

Burke, Clifford *Heron Light.* Campbell Lake: Margaret's Press, n.d., Numbered edition, 8vo., decorated paper covered boards, presentation from Burke.   Oak Knoll Books   310 - 122   2016 $150

Burke, Edmund   1729-1797 *An Account of the European Settlements in America.* London: John Joseph Stockdale, 1808. New edition, quarto, two engraved maps, contemporary calf, gilt, with two block morocco spine labels, marbled endpapers and matching edges, minor wear to binding, rubbing to joints, some browning and offsetting to first and lost few leaves, overall near fine, armorial bookplate of William Buddell Clarke, small ticket, clipped quotation mounted ot front pastedown.   Heritage Book Shop   Holiday 2015 - 15   2016 $1500

Burke, Edmund   1729-1797 *A Philosophical Enquiry Into the Origin of Our ideas of the Sublime and Beautiful.* London: for R. and J. Dodsley, 1757. First edition, contemporary mottled calf, marbled endpapers, neatly early repair to spine ends, half title with short tear and red stamped name of early owner, occasional minor spotting, withal very good, from the library of Franklin James Didler with his signature, chemise and morocco backed slipcase.   Joseph J. Felcone, Inc.   Books from Five Centuries: a Miscellany - 32   2016 $2000

Burke, Edmund   1729-1797 *The Writings and Speeches.* Boston: Little Brown & Co., 1901. Beaconsfield edition, limited to 1000 numbered sets, 12 volumes, octavo, engraved titlepages and gravure frontispieces and portraits, contemporary three quarter green crushed levant morocco over marbled boards ruled in gilt, spines with two raised bands decorated in black and lettered in gilt, top edge gilt, others uncut, marbled endpapers, spines uniformly faded to olive green, otherwise near fine and very attractive set.   David Brass Rare Books, Inc.   2015 - 03050   2016 $2250

Burke, James Lee *In the Electric Mist with Confederate Dead.* New York: Hyperion, 1993. First edition, still in original shrinkwrap with promotional copy of Lost Get=Back Boogie enclosed, very fine.   Mordida Books   2015 - 001659   2016 $65

Burke, James Lee *The Lost Get Back Boogie.* Baton Rouge: LSU, 1986. First edition, fine in near fine dust jacket, evidence of sticker removal from rear panel.   Bella Luna Books   2016 - 17850   2016 $264

Burke, James Lee *The Lost Get Back Boogie.* Baton Rouge: LSU, 1986. First edition, review copy with slips laid in, fine in very good dust jacket with some rubbing, light soiling and working to front panel, some rubbing and wrinkling to front panel.   Bella Luna Books   2016 - t17851   2016 $198

Burke, James Lee *Texas City, 1947.* Northridge: Lord John Press, 1992. Copy 159 from limited edition of 275 numbered copies, very fine in paper covered boards with cloth spine, signed by author.   Jeff Hirsch Books   Holiday List 2015 - 29   2016 $125

Burke, John *A Hard Day's Night.* Pan Books, 1964. First edition, 8vo., original printed wrappers, 8 pages of photos from the film, little spotting to inside covers, very good.   Sotheran's Piccadilly Notes - Summer 2015 - 33   2016   £50

Burlend, Rebecca *A True Picture of Emigration...* London: G. Berger, 1848. 12mo., original brown printed paper wrappers, sewn as issued, some slight wear to spine and fore-edge, nice.   Jarndyce Antiquarian Booksellers   CCXVII - 60   2016   £250

Burn, Andrew Robert *Persia and the Greeks. The Defence of the West c. 546-478 B.C.* London: Edward Arnold, 1970. 8vo., blue cloth, gilt lettered, slight wear to corners and endcaps, top edge dusted and spotted, very good, blindstamped dust jacket spine faded, few small tears, some with loss, price clipped has price sticker to flap, bit grubby, still good, photocopy of Battle of Salamis loosely inserted, ownership inscription of J. G. F. Hind School of History, University of Leeds.   Unsworths Antiquarian Booksellers Ltd.   E04 - 36   2016   £20

Burnap, George Washington *Lectures to Young Men, on the Cultivation of the Mind, the Formation of Character and the Conduct of Life.* London: Edward T. Whitfield. circa, 1844. Original grey printed paper wrappers, small internal hole to back wrapper, slight creasing, otherwise very good.   Jarndyce Antiquarian Books   CCXV - 91   2016   £75

Burne-Jones, Edward   1833-1898 *The Fairy Family: a Series of Ballads and Metrical Tales Illustrating the Fairy Mythology of Europe.* London: Longman, Brown, Green and Co., 1857. First edition, 8vo., with excellent engraved titlepage, engraved frontispiece, original textured red cloth, simply blind patterned on front and back lettered gilt at spine, slight even surface wear to covers, one small stain, slight rubbing, otherwise close to very good with clean text, reare.   Any Amount of Books   2015 - C15723   2016   £650

Burnet, Gilbert, Bp. of Salisbury   1643-1715 *Bishop Burnet's History of His Own Time.* Oxford: Clarendon Press, 1823. First edition, 8vo., 6 volumes, full brown with gilt decorated spine and five raised bands, top hinge slightly tender on first volume, occasional slight marks to leather, slight rubbing but handsome set with frontispiece portrait, armorial bookplate of Lepel H. Griffin, Glenthorne.   Any Amount of Books   2015 - A82541   2016   £250

Burnett, David *The Heart's Undesign.* Edinburgh: The Tragra Press, 1977. One of 200 copies, titlepage vignette and tailpiece by Joan Hassall, foolscap 8vo., original printed green wrappers, edges rough trimmed, very good, inscribed for Hassall by Burnett.   Blackwell's Rare Books   B184 - 274   2016   £60

Burnett, David *The True Vine.* Hedgehog Press, 1975. One of 100 copies, frontispiece and tailpiece by Joan Hassall, errata slip tipped in at rear, foolscap 8vo., original sewn orange wrappers, little darkened along spine, good, inscribed by author for Joan Hassall.   Blackwell's Rare Books   B184 - 275   2016   £45

Burnett, Frances Hodgson *In the Closed Room.* New York: McClure, Phillips & Co., 1904. First edition, octavo, text printed in green and black, 8 full page color plates by Jessie Willcox Smith, original ribbed green cloth, front cover decoratively stamped in gilt, spine lettered gilt, top edge gilt, others uncut, few leaves roughly opened on fore-edge, otherwise very fine in fine, very scarce original pale green printed dust jacket, top 3/4 inch of jacket spine missing and three are few short tears on extremities, overall very rare dust jacket in very good condition.   David Brass Rare Books, Inc.   2015 - 02973   2016 $650

Burnett, Frances Hodgson *Little Lord Fauntleroy.* New York: Charles Scribner, 1911. First edition with these illustrations, 8vo., blue cloth, pictorial paste-on, top edge gilt, corner of blank endpaper clipped else near fine, this copy inscribed by author to Robert Newell, with lengthy inscription from artist, below is a charming watercolor by artist, super copy, illustrations by Reginald Birch.   Aleph-bet Books, Inc.   111 - 65   2016 $1500

Burnett, Frances Hodgson *Queen Silver Bell.* New York: Century, Nov., 1906. First edition, 12mo., blue cloth, paste-on, fine, wonderfully illustrated by Harrison Cady with 20 fanciful color plates.   Aleph-bet Books, Inc.   112 - 87   2016 $250

Burnett, Frances Hodgson *The Secret Garden.* London: Wm. Heinemann, 1911. 8vo., green cloth decorated in gold, slight edge rubbing, some rear cover soil (not offensive), owner bookplate and inscription, very good, illustrations by Charles Robinson.   Aleph-bet Books, Inc.   112 - 85   2016 $1000

Burnett, Frances Hodgson *The Spring Cleaning.* New York: Century, 1908. First edition, 12mo., blue cloth, pictorial paste-on, fine, illustrations by Harrison Cady.   Aleph-bet Books, Inc.   112 - 86   2016 $250

Burnett, W. R. *Underdog.* New York: Knopf, 1957. First edition, small stamp (a star) on front endpaper, otherwise fine in price clipped dust jacket with couple of tiny tears.   Mordida Books   2015 - 000357   2016 $60

Burningham, John *Granpa.* New York: Crown Pub., 1984. First American edition with 1-10 code, 11 x 9 inches, pictorial boards, fine in dust jacket, lovely color illustrations.   Aleph-bet Books, Inc.   111 - 66   2016 $75

Burns, Robert *The Poems and Songs of Robert Burns.* London: George Newnes Ltd., 1902. 165 x 102mm., very fine crimson morocco lavishly and intricately gilt in a 'Scottish Wheel' design by Morrell (stamp signed on front turn-ins), covers with large central wheel of 20 compartments, each containing elegant gossamer floral tools between two lines of dots radiating from a central rosette, massed tiny circle tools at head and foot of wheel, above and below these circle tools, triangle formed by small scalloped compartments and multiple tiny flowers, corners with large leaf frond tools and covers generally with many accenting small tools, raised bands, spine compartments, with large quatrefoil containing central daisy radiating floral tools surrounded by gilt dots, elegantly and elaborately gilt turn-ins in swag pattern, ivory watered silk endleaves, all edges gilt, rear joint very expertly renewed, frontispiece, rear free endpaper with ink presentation to Ozite Fleming Cox from Benjamin Lloyd Belt dated May 8 1906, front joint beginning to show a thin crack (but mostly masked with dye), paper stock little dingy (as not doubt in all copies), otherwise very fine, covers and spine unworn and lustrous and text without signs of use.   Phillip J. Pirages   67 - 58   2016 $850

Burns, Robert *The Poems of...* Glasgow: Limited Editions Club, 1965. First edition thus, #186 of 1500 copies signed by artist, tall 8vo., calf backed boards, fine in publisher's slipcase, wood engravings by Joan Hassall.   Second Life Books, Inc.   196A - 227   2016 $110

Burns, Walter Noble *Tombstone.* Garden City: Doubleday, 1927. First edition, 8vo., very good+, minimal scuffs to f.f.e.p., foxing to covers and edges in good+ dust jacket with small pieces missing, 2 inch piece missing lower edge rear panel of jacket, soil, short closed tears, signed.   By the Book, L. C.   45 - 63   2016 $1500

Burrand, Gerald *The Modern Shotgun.* London: Herbert Jenkins, 1955-1963. Mixed edition, 8vo., 3 volumes, original blue cloth, gilt lettering to spines, photo plates, very nice.   Sotheran's   Hunting, Shooting & Fishing - 72   2016   £200

Burroughs, Edgar Rice   1875-1950 *'Beware". (in) Burroughs Bulletin 39.* Kansas City: The Burroughs Bulletin, 1974. First edition, tall quarto, illustrated by Richard Cohen, stapled illustrated self wrappers, slight age toning on wrappers, still fine.   Between the Covers Rare Books   208 - 116   2016 $150

Burroughs, Edgar Rice 1875-1950 *A Fighting Man of Mars.* New York: Metropolitan Books, 1931. First edition, octavo, frontispiece, original red mesh weave cloth, front and spine panels stamped in yellow green, top edge stained green, former owner's name and date to front pastedown, fine in fine dust jacket with just touch of edge rubbing, superb copy.   John W. Knott, Jr./L.W. Currey, Inc.   Fall-Winter 2015 - 16002   2016 $4500

Burroughs, William S. *Ghost of Chance.* New York: Library Fellows of Whitney Museum of American Art, 1991. First edition, one of 160 copies printed on Hahnemuhle etching paper by Leslie Miller and signed by author and artist folio, 3 original etchings and several tipped-in color illustrations, pictorial endpapers by George Condo, original black cloth, matching slipcase, as new.   James S. Jaffe Rare Books   Occasional List: Winter 2016 - 35   2016 $1750

Burroughs, William S. *Naked Lunch.* Paris: Olympia Press, 1965. Reprint, printed green wrappers, modest edgewear, slight tear at base of spine, very good or better, without dust jacket, inscribed by author to poet and publisher Charles Plymell, with program for the memorial Service held for Burroughs in Lawrence, Kansas in 1997, fine, with small business card sized poem, signed by Plymell.   Between the Covers Rare Books   208 - 14   2016 $5000

Burt, Cyril *The Backward Child.* London: University of London Press, 1937. Original blue cloth, slightly cocked, library labels of national Bureau of Co-operation in Child Care Library, very good.   Jarndyce Antiquarian Books   CCXV - 563   2016   £45

Burt, Isabella *Historical Notices of Chelsea, Kensington, Fulham and Hammersmith.* Kensington: J. Saunders, 1871. First edition, 8vo., original brick red cloth, spine lettered in gilt, front cover ruled, lettered and decorated in gilt and black, wood engraved frontispiece and four wood engraved plates, all tissue guards preserved, minimal wear to cloth, light spotting only in places, good, uncut, largely unopened.   Sotheran's   Piccadilly Notes - Summer 2015 - 60   2016   £148

Burton, Isabel *The Passion-Play at Ober-Ammergau.* London: Hutchinson, 1900. First edition, 8vo, original cloth lettered gilt on spine and upper board, frontispiece, titlepage printed in red and black, text within red line border, spine slightly sunned, little light spotting to prelims, otherwise very good.   Sotheran's   Piccadilly Notes - Summer 2015 - 61   2016   £128

Burton, John *Lectures on Female Education and Manners.* Dublin: printed for J. Milliken, 1794. Third edition, 12mo., with slight tear with loss to margin not affecting text, tear to following f.e.p., repaired with archvial tape, contemporary calf, stamped "Miss Hodder" on front board, slightly rubbed black morocco label, wear to head and tail of spine, extremities rubbed, good, sound.   Jarndyce Antiquarian Books   CCXV - 92   2016   £180

Burton, Mina E. *Ruling the Planets.* London: Richard Bentley & Son, 1891. First edition, 3 volumes, half titles final ad leaf in all volumes, original royal blue decorated embossed cloth, spines very slightly rubbed at head and tail, stamps of Camberwell Public Libraries on verso of titles, library labels removed from leading pastedowns, bright copy.   Jarndyce Antiquarian Booksellers   CCXVII - 61   2016   £480

Burton, Richard Francis 1821-1890 *The Book of the Thousand Nights and a Night. (and) Supplemental Nights.* Benares: printed by the Kamashastra Society for private subscribers only, 1885-1888. first printing of this edition, 16 volumes, 254 x 159mm., very pleasing rose colored half morocco over buckram boards by Brian Frost & Co. (signed each volume), raised bands, spine panels with gilt floral centerpiece or titling, marbled endpapers, top edge gilt titlepage printed in red and black, first and last few leaves of each volume generally with light foxing to these leaves bit more foxed, text shade less than bright because of paper stock chosen, still very fine, especially lustrous binding without fault with no signs of use internally.   Phillip J. Pirages   67 - 6   2016 $9500

Burton, Richard Francis 1821-1890 *The City of Saints, and Across the Rocky Mountains to California.* London: Longman Green, 1861. First edition, 8vo., folding map, folding plan, frontispiece, 8 plates, original green decorative cloth, gilt vign1612-1680ette, spine slightly faded.   J. & S. L. Bonham Antiquarian Booksellers   America 2016 - 9904   2016   £650

Burton, Richard Francis 1821-1890 *The City of Saints and Across the Rocky Mountains to California.* London: Longman, Green, 1862. Second edition, 8vo., folding map, folding plan, frontispiece, 9 illustrations in text, original green decorative cloth, very good.   J. & S. L. Bonham Antiquarian Booksellers   America 2016 - 7930   2016   £550

Burton, Richard Francis 1821-1890 *First Footsteps in East Africa or an Exploration of Harar.* London: Longman, Brown, Green and Longmans, 1856. First edition, 2nd issue binding, 4 color plates and 2 maps, bound without suppressed fourth appendix, publisher's red cloth, neat early restoration of spine ends and repair of front inner hinge, one lead adhered the next in the gutter, slight darkening of spine and light overall soiling, very good, tight copy.   Joseph J. Felcone, Inc.   Books from Five Centuries: a Miscellany - 33   2016 $3250

Burton, Richard Francis 1821-1890 *The Kasidah of Haji Abdu el-Yezdi.* Philadelphia: David McKay Co., 1931. First US edition, limited to 250 numbered copies, signed by Willy Pogany and Dhan Gopal Murkerji who provided introduction, 4to., contemporary half brown niger morocco over marbled boards, spine with 4 raised bands, ruled and strikingly decorated in gilt to Art Deco design featuring crescent moon and falling stars, top edge gilt, others uncut, frontispiece, black and white lithographed plates by Willy Pogany, very nice, handsomely presented, externally with little rubbing to corners and head and tail of spine, internally fine,. Sotheran's   Piccadilly Notes - Summer 2015 - 238   2016   £450

Burton, Richard Francis 1821-1890 *The Lake Regions of Central America: a Picture of Exploration.* London: Longmans, Green, Longman and Roberts, 1860. First edition, 8vo., 5 volumes, Victorian full red calf by Bickers & Son, spine with raised bands, ornamented in gilt and with contrasting lettering pieces, boards with gilt ruled double fillets, all edges marbled, marbled endpapers, 12 printed plates, combining wood engraving with lithography, 22 wood engraved illustrations, 1 folding colored map, 2 corners with slight bumps, apart from minor spotting initially and at end of volume, very fresh and clean set.   Sotheran's   Travel and Exploration - 9   2016   £3995

Burton, Richard Francis 1821-1890 *Minor Writings of Sir Richard Burton Part One...* Clitheroe: privately published, 1999. First edition, one of 200 copies, 8vo., original illustrated green wrappers, frontispiece, as new. Sotheran's   Travel and Exploration - 453   2016   £28

Burton, Richard Francis 1821-1890 *Paper on Anthropology Travel ad Exploration.* London: A. M. Philpot, 1924. First edition, 8vo., original red cloth, spine faded.   J. & S. L. Bonham Antiquarian Booksellers   Voyages 2016 - 7183   2016   £55

Burton, Richard Francis 1821-1890 *Pilgrimage to El_ Medinah and Meccah.* London: Longman, Brown, Green and Longmans, 1855-1856. First edition, 8vo., 3 volumes, original blue cloth, decorated in black, lettered gilt to spines, uncut, 4 maps and plans, 5 color lithographic plates, 8 tinted lithographic plates, bindings little worn and corners with light bumps, light offsetting from brick-red original endpapers, however, gilt lettering very well preserved, internally notably clean, minimal foxing to plates, one prelim leaf roughly opened, resulting in small marginal flaw, the latter part of third volume largely unopened, each volume with two contemporary engraved armorial bookplates with obliterated names.   Sotheran's   Travel and Exploration - 306   2016   £6750

Burton, Richard Francis 1821-1890 *Wanderings in West Africa from Liverpool to Fernando Po.* London: Tinsley Brothers, 18 Catherine St. Strand, 1863. First edition, 8vo., 2 volumes, original blindstamped maroon cloth lettered gilt to spine, one folding map frontispiece to volume I, wood engraved frontispiece to volume II, very minor rubbing to extremities, nice and clean, engraved armorial bookplates of Edward Joseph Dent and Norman Douglas Simpson.   Sotheran's   Travel and Exploration - 10   2016   £4000

Burton, Virginia Lee *Calico the Wonder Horse.* Boston: Houghton Mifflin, 1950. First edition, 8 1/2 x 6 inches, pictorial cloth, light spotting, else very good+ in fine dust jacket with 2 old tape marks, few very small chips, still attractive and very good, printed on 8 different colors of paper and wonderfully illustrated on every page, this copy inscribed by Burton dated 1950.   Aleph-bet Books, Inc.   111 - 69   2016 $1500

Burton, Virginia Lee *Katy and the Big Snow.* Boston: Houghton Mifflin, 1943. First edition, first printing, oblong 4to., pictorial cloth, slight darkening along edges, else bright and near fine in dust jacket with price intact (dust jacket has some soil, flaking at folds, several closed tears but really very good), illustrations, rare printing.   Aleph-bet Books, Inc.   112 - 88   2016 $3000

Burton, Virginia Lee *Maybelle the Cable Car.* Boston: Houghton Mifflin, 1952. First edition, pictorial cloth, fine in very good+ price clipped dust jacket, this copy signed by author, color illustrations.   Aleph-bet Books, Inc.   111 - 70   2016 $1200

Burton, Virginia Lee *Mike Mulligna and his Steam Shovel.* Boston: Houghton Mifflin, 1939. First edition, Oblong 4to, pictorial cloth, few tiny margin mends and hinge wear, else near fine in amazingly bright price clipped dust jacket with only few tiny closed edge tears and quarter inch chip off top of spine, illustrations in rich colors.   Aleph-bet Books, Inc.   111 - 67   2016 $8000

Burton, William *A Commentary on Antoninus His Itinerary or Journies of the Romanae Empire, so far As It Concernth Britain.* London: printed by Tho. Roycroft for Henry Twyford ad T. Twyford, 1658. Small folio, 2 plates, portrait frontispiece by Hollar, double page map, lacking single leaf 'preface to the reader', titlepage in red and black, woodcut initials, illustrations in text, errata to final leaf verso, small burn hole to pages 33-4 just touching few letters, page 141-2 creased during binding, very occasional spotting and few slight smudges, front and rear blanks darkened at edges, contemporary calf, gilt ruled panels with various mottled effects, all edges gilt, rebacked with dark brown morocco, original spine label retained, spine rubbed, few chips and bookplate of T. H. Ellison, underneath Pemberton plate a piece of paper crossed through in ink, possibly patching a removed third bookplate, Latin annotation in old hand to prelim blank.   Unsworths Antiquarian Booksellers Ltd.   E01 - Early Printing - 3   2016   £750

Bury, J. B. *A History of Greece to the Death of Alexander the Great.* London: Macmillan, 1975. Fourth edition, large 8vo., maps, illustrations, original blue cloth, dust jacket.   J. & S. L. Bonham Antiquarian Booksellers   Europe 2016 - 7346   2016   £20

Bush, Christopher *The Case of the good Employer.* London: Macdonald, 1966. First edition, some tiny light spotting on page edges, otherwise fine in dust jacket. Mordida Books   2015 - 008227   2016 $55

Bush, Vannevar *"As we may think" contained in The Atlantic Monthly Volume CLXXVI no. 1 July 1945.* Boston: Atlantic Monthly Co., 1945. First edition, 4to., 129 pages, original maroon & gold printed wrappers, small hole on spine, minor loss, overall some wear, creasing, six rubber stamped states on page 1, generally very good.   Jeff Weber Rare Books   183 - 8   2016 $800

Bussey, George Moir *History of Napoleon.* London: Joseph Thomas Finch Lane, 1840. First edition, large thick quarto, numerous engravings, some slight foxing, otherwise fine, full page frontispiece, newly bound in half brown calf with matching brown art canvas sides, spine has five raised bands with gilt lines, very good in very good binding. Simon Finch   2015 - 000165   2016 $280

Bustani, Emile *March Arabesque.* London: Robert Hale, 1961. First edition, octavo, presentation from author for friend Paul Ensor, very good in rubbed and creased dust jacket with several short tears.   Peter Ellis   112 - 15   2016   £95

Buster Brown Son Chien Tiger et Leurs Adventures. Paris: Hachette/New York Herald, 1903. 1904., Oblong folio, cloth backed pictorial card covers, corners worn, rear cover lacks a bit of paper and normal soil, very good, 30 folio leaves printed on rectos only.   Aleph-bet Books, Inc. 111 - 329   2016 $500

Butcher, David *Pages from Presses: Kelmscott, Ashendene, Doves, Vale, Eragny & Essex House.*   Risbury: Whittington Press, 2006. No. X of 50 specially bound copies (of 185 total), this copy with Doves Press leaf on vellum and 13 original specimens on paper mounted on stubs, as well as with separate portfolio of fine original leaves, signed by author in colophon, 400 x 298mm., publisher's full scarlet Nigerian goatskin, flat spine with gilt titling, marbled endpapers, quarter buckram portfolio, original red buckram clamshell box with red morocco spine, folding frontispiece, 17 original leaves mounted on 14 protruding stubs (between leaves of commentary text), the 17 comprising the Doves Press vellum leaf protected by tissue guards, 11 single private press leaves, 3 bioflia, one from Kelmscott, one from Doves, one form Vale, portfolio with poster-sized version of frontispiece and five additional original leaves, two from Doves press, one each from Kelmscott, Vale and Eragny, one leaf in portfolio with very neat contemporaneous paragraph marks and marginalia in red and green, four of the leaves in portfolio lightly browned, otherwise mint.   Phillip J. Pirages   67 - 233   2016 $3500

Butcher, John *Instructions in Etiquette, for the Sue of all Five Letters on Important Subjects, Exclusively for Ladies and Conversational Hints to Whom Concerned.*   London: Simpkin Marshall & Co., 1847. Third edition, 12mo., occasional slight spotting, original beige cloth over limp boards printed paper label, slightly marked but nice copy in original green card slipcase, paper labels, rubbed and lacking card at bottom, early 20th century inscription.   Jarndyce Antiquarian Books   CCXV - 93   2016   £150

The Butler: His Duties and How to Perform Them.   London: Houlston & Sons, circa, 1865. 111 page edition, Frontispiece, illustrations, original brown decorated cloth. Jarndyce Antiquarian Books   CCXV - 257   2016   £125

Butler, Arthur Gardiner *Foreign Finches in Captivity.* London: L. Reeve & Co., 1894. Quarto, 59 (of 60) hand colored lithographs by Frohawk, lacks painted Finch plate and Chestnut-breasted Finch/three-coloured Manikin plate is substantially trimmed but no affecting image, publisher's blindstamp burgundy morocco grain cloth with handsome gilt finch design on upper board, top edge gilt, some light wear and few spots.   Andrew Isles Natural History Books 55 - 35346   2016 $2500

Butler, Arthur Gray *The Three Friends: a Story of Rugby in the Forties.*   London: Henry Frowde, 1900. Original maroon cloth, spine little faded, top edge gilt, signed by A. F. Buxton and Kathleen Tillotson, with ALS from Tillotson to Dorothy M. Ward.   Jarndyce Antiquarian Books   CCXV - 927   2016   £35

Butler, Arthur Stanley George *The Lutyens Memorial.* Woodbridge: Antique Collector's Club, 1984. Reprint of 1950 Memorial edition, one of an edition of 1500 numbered sets, this set numbered 228, folio, 3 volumes, publisher's cloth, pictorial jackets, plans and half tone illustrations, expert repair to inner joint of upper board of volume I, otherwise very good set in like dust jacket. Sotheran's Piccadilly Notes - Summer 2015 - 64 2016 £650

Butler, Benjamin Franklin *Ku-Klux Outrages in the South.* Washington: M'Gill & Witherow Printers, 1871. Removed from larger volume, else very good, printed in two columns, 8vo. Kaaterskill Books 21 - 43 2016 $100

Butler, George *Butterfly Babies.* Chicago: Magill Weinsheimer, 1917. 16mo., pictorial boards, light soil and spine rubbing, very good+, quite unusual. Aleph-bet Books, Inc. 111 - 157 2016 $250

Butler, Octavia *Adulthood Rites: Xenogenesis.* New York: Warner, 1988. First printing, author's signature on title, paper over boards with cloth spine, edges very slightly soiled, otherwise fine in dust jacket. Second Life Books, Inc. 196A - 235 2016 $75

Butler, Octavia *Dawn: Xenogenesis.* New York: Warner, 1987. First printing, 8vo., author's signature on titlepage, paper over boards with cloth spine, about as new in dust jacket. Second Life Books, Inc. 196A - 236 2016 $100

Butler, Octavia *Imago.* New York: Warner, 1989. First printing, 8vo., signed by author on title, paper covered boards with cloth spine, small cut at top edge of cover, otherwise nice in dust jacket, remnants of price label on flap. Second Life Books, Inc. 196A - 234 2016 $75

Butler, Octavia *Patern-Master.* New York: Warner, 1995. First Warner Books printing, 12mo., paper wrappers, author's signature on title, nice. Second Life Books, Inc. 196A - 237 2016 $150

Butler, Samuel 1612-1680 *Hudibras. the First Part with The Second Part. The Third and Last Part.* London: by J. G. for Richard Marriot, 1663. London: by T. R. for John Martyn and James Allestry, 1664. London: for Simon Miller, 1678, First authorized editions of volumes 1 and 2, first edition of volume 3, 3 volumes, washed and rebound in uniform simple full brown levant, edges gilt by Zaehnsdorf for A. C. McClurg, some residual soiling, volume 2 with closed tear in title and front hinge cracking slightly and cropped at bit closely cutting into running heads and shoulder notes. Joseph J. Felcone, Inc. Books from Five Centuries: a Miscellany - 34 2016 $2200

Butler, Samuel 1612-1680 *Hudibras.* London: T. Rickaby, 1793. Limited to only 200 copies, this one of those with illustrations in black, large 4to., full leather, gilt turn-ins, gilt design and lettering on spine, gilt rules on boards, marbled endpapers, frontispiece, engraved titlepages, many full page illustrations and head and tailpieces, printed on heavy paper, little offset from few of the illustrations, unfortunately the binding hasn't held up as well as text block, all boards detached, spines holding firmly. Oak Knoll Books 310 - 279 2016 $850

Butler, Samuel 1612-1680 *Hudibras, a poem....* London: printed for Akermann, 1822. 2 volumes, octavo, 12 hand colored engraved plates by J. Clark, full crushed red morocco by Bayntun, covers elaborately tooled and stamped in gilt and black, front boards featuring pictorial inlaid centerpieces made up of several different pieces of dyed morocco, tooled in black, spines tooled, lettered and stamped in gilt in compartments, board edges and turn-ins decoratively gilt, all edges gilt marbled doublures and free endpapers, binding's calligraphic inscription in black and sepia on recto of front free endpapers, occasional light offsetting or spotting, else near fine, clean and bright, fore-edge painting revealed by fanning the outer edge of each text block, after drawing by Hogarth. Heritage Book Shop Holiday 2015 - 40 2016 $6000

Butler, W. F. *The Wild North Land: being the Story of a Winter Journey with Dogs Across Northern North American.* London: Sampson Low, 1874. Second edition, 8vo., folding map, 15 illustrations, contemporary half brown calf, small rubbing to fore-edge. J. & S. L. Bonham Antiquarian Booksellers America 2016 - 5183 2016 £120

Butler, William *Miscellaneous Questions Relating to English History and Biography...* London: Sold by Harris, St. Paul's Churchyard, 1835. 12mo., 12 page catalog, lacking following f.e.p., contemporary tree sheep, little worn, contemporary signature on leading f.e.p. Jarndyce Antiquarian Books CCXV - 564 2016 £30

Butt, John *Dickens at Work.* London: Methuen, 1957. First edition, half title, frontispiece, facsimile plates, original green cloth, gift label, very good in dust jacket. Jarndyce Antiquarian Booksellers CCXVIII - 1099 2016 £35

Butterick Publishing Co. *Home-Making and House-Keeping.* Butterick Pub. Co., 1898. First edition, half title, illustrations, 2 pages ads, original green cloth, slightly rubbed. Jarndyce Antiquarian Books CCXV - 94 2016 £50

Butterworth, Elizabeth *Parrots and Cockatoos.* London: Fischer Fine Art, 1979. Limited to 60 numbered copies, Folio, 20 uncolored aquatints, each signed and numbered by the artist, all plates printed on deckle edge paper and contained in cloth covered folio box, separately printed booklet by Rosemary Low supplied in photocopy, fine. Andrew Isles Natural History Books   55 - 15401   2016 $2650

Butterworth, Elizabeth *Parrots, Macaws and Cockatoos: the Art of Elizabeth Butterworth.* New York: Harry N. Abrams, 1988. Folio, unpaginated, color plates, softcover. Andrew Isles Natural History Books   55 - 2639   2016 $80

By Special Commission. The Trial of Antichrist Otherwise, the Man of Sin, for High Treason Against the Son of God; Tried at the Sessions House of Truth... Dublin: printed for the author and sold by T. Johnstone, London Ogle & Atkman, Edinburgh M. Ogle, Glasgow, 1806. First edition, 12mo. in 6's, some occasional foxing, small piece torn away from margin of pages 189-90 (not touching printed surface), contemporary half sheep over marbled boards, rather worn but sound, rare.   John Drury Rare Books   2015 - 23908   2016 $341

By the Sea Canada Nova Scotia New Brunswick Prince Edward Island. Montreal: Canadian National Railway, 1920's, 9 x 8 inches, color paper cover, two page color map and numerous black and white illustrations, some slight soiling and small tear to outer edge of back cover and some very light wear to edges.   Schooner Books Ltd.   115 - 186   2016 $75

Byars, William Vincent *An American Consumer. the Life and Times of Richard Parks Bland.* Columbia: E. W. Stephens, 1900. First edition, 4to., illustrations, original engraved plates, roan, some binding wear.   M & S Rare Books, Inc.   99 - 35   2016 $225

Bynner, Witter *Light Verse and Satires.* New York: Farrar Straus Giroux, 1978. First edition , from The Works of Witter Bynner, octavo, cover edges slightly bruised, near fine in very good dust jacket, little creased and rubbed at edges.   Peter Ellis   112 - 55   2016   £35

Bynner, Witter *Prose Pieces.* New York: Farrar, Straus, Giroux, 1979. First edition, spine just little bruised at head and tail, near fine in very good dust jacket little creased at edges.   Peter Ellis   112 - 53   2016   £35

Bynner, Witter *Selected Letters.* New York: Farrar Straus, Giroux, 1981. First edition (from the works of Witter Bynner, octavo, fine in very good dust jacket, little nicked and rubbed at edges.   Peter Ellis   112 - 54   2016   £35

Byrd, Richard Evelyn *Discovery. The Story of the Second Byrd Antarctic Expedition.* New York: G. P. Putnam's Sons, 1935. First edition, 8vo., original cloth, gilt, map endpapers, highly illustrated on plates and frontispiece, one stamped on verso.   Sotheran's Travel and Exploration - 416   2016   £695

Byrom, John *The Universal English Short-Hand or the Way of Writing English...* Manchester: printed by Joseph Harrop, 1767. First edition, 13 engraved plates, bound as called for, little marginal dust soiling, line of old paper adhered to verso of last plate, 8vo., wholly untrimmed in plain binding of modern quarter morocco, spine lettered in silver, very good.   Blackwell's Rare Books   B186 - 33   2016   £220

Byron, George Gordon Noel, 6th Baron   1788-1824 *Childe Harold's Pilgrimage.* London: John Murray, 1841. Large 8vo., full red morocco by Riviere, boards with elaborate gilt borders, spine lettered and panelled gilt with gilt centre tools, richly gilt turn ins over patterned endpapers, top edge gilt, frontispiece, engraved title, folding map and 59 engravings in text, handsome volume.   Sotheran's Piccadilly Notes - Summer 2015 - 65   2016   £998

Byron, George Gordon Noel, 6th Baron   1788-1824 *Hebrew Melodies.* London: John Murray, 1815. First edition, 8vo., later three quarter morocco, untrimmed, half title and inserted titles, half titles enabling the pamphlet poems of Byron to date to be bound up in 2 volumes, lacks terminal ads.   Second Life Books, Inc.   197 - 41   2016 $800

Byron, George Gordon Noel, 6th Baron   1788-1824 *Marino Faliero, Doge of Venice...* Vienna and Leipzig: Avalun, 1922. First edition with these illustrations, one of 50 copies numbered in Roman numerals signed by artist who also initials each of the 12 original etchings in text,, small folio, this copy does not have the additional set of etchings called for in colophon, full cream parchment lettered gilt, gilt rules, top edge gilt, covers bit discolored in places as usual, prelims and edges spotted, very good. Peter Ellis   112 - 56   2016   £75

Byron, George Gordon Noel, 6th Baron   1788-1824 *Works.* London: John Murray, 1817. First collected edition, five volumes, 171 x 108mm., very attractive contemporary dark blue straight grain morocco, decorated in gilt and blind, cover with thick and thin gilt rule border, blind tooled palmette frame and large blindstamped arabesque centerpiece, raised bands, spine panels with gilt lyre on top of crossed trumpets, gilt titling and turn-ins, all edges gilt, 11 engraved plates, hint of foxing to engraved material, otherwise only trival imperfections, attractively bound set in especially fine condition, bindings unusually lustrous and text showing almost no signs of use.   Phillip J. Pirages   67 - 82   2016 $2500

Byron, George Gordon Noel, 6th Baron 1788-1824 *The Works.* London: John Murray, 1817. First edition, 6 volumes, full contemporary smooth calf, edges with elaborate floral rolls gilt, sides with trellis pattern within with rectangular frame in black, trellis studded with gilt dots, spines in compartment with raised bands, gilt tooling and leather labels gilt, hinges little weak, some abrasion to front cover of volume IV, still most attractive set. Bertram Rota Ltd. February List 2016 - 10 2016 £285

Byron, George Gordon Noel, 6th Baron 1788-1824 *The Works of Lord Byron in Verse and Prose.* New York: Alexander V. Blake, 1838. Thick 4to., illustrations and facsimiles, fine full contemporary gilt stamped red morocco, some darkening of covers, but very good, browning of text. M & S Rare Books, Inc. 99 - 27 2016 $375

Byron, John *A Voyage Round the World in His Majesty's Ship the 'Dolphin' Commanded by the Honourable Commodore Byron. (with) The Narrative of the Honourable John Byron, Containing an account of the Great Distresses Suffered by himself and His Companions on the Coast of Patagonia...* London: J. Newbury, 1767. London: S. Baker, 1768. First edition, 8vo., frontispiece, 2 plates (slightly frayed in margin not affecting image), contemporary brown full calf, later rebacked, clean and crisp. J. & S. L. Bonham Antiquarian Booksellers Voyages 2016 - 9124 2016 £3000

Byron, May *Cecil Aldin's Merry Party.* London: Henry Frowde Hodder & Stoughton, 1913. First edition, Thick 4to., cloth backed boards, pictorial paste-on top edge gilt, rebacked with original spine laid down, new endpapers, blank prelims foxed, else very good+, 36 tipped in color plates, 6 of which are double page plus 36 full page black and whites. Aleph-bet Books, Inc. 111 - 15 2016 $1850

Byron, May *The Peek-a-Boos Desert Island.* London: Henry Frowde/Hodder & Stoughton, n.d. circa, 1913. Cloth backed pictorial boards, corners worn, covers and edges rubbed, very occasional margin soil or wear, clean, tight and very good, 16 fantastic color plates, may black and whites in text, pictorial endpapers by Chloe Preston, very scarce,. Aleph-bet Books, Inc. 112 - 400 2016 $950

Byron, May *The Peek-A-Boos in War Time.* London: Henry Frowde/Hodder & Stoughton, n.d. circa, 1916. 8 x 9 inches, boards, pictorial paste-on, spine and edge of covers faded, else beautiful, clean very good+ copy, 16 color plates, many black and whites, very scarce. Aleph-bet Books, Inc. 112 - 399 2016 $850

Byron, May *The Poor Dear Dollies.* London & New York: Hodder & Stoughton, n.d. circa, 1910. 8vo., cloth backed pictorial boards, new spine, some edge wear, pencil mark on covers, occasional margin soil, looks much better than it sounds, very good, illustrations by Rosa Petherick with 12 fine and richly colored full page color illustrations and numerous illustrations in line, very scarce. Aleph-bet Books, Inc. 112 - 150 2016 $200

Byron, Robert *First Russia then Tibet.* London: Macmillan and Co. Ltd., 1933. First edition, 8vo., original green cloth lettered gilt, coloured frontispiece and illustrations from photos, cloth minimally rubbed, light offsetting from endpapers, otherwise very good. Sotheran's Piccadilly Notes - Summer 2015 - 66 2016 £298

Byron, Robert *The Road to Oxiana.* London: Macmillan, 1937. First edition, frontispiece, 15 further photo plates, 4 full page maps, very faint foxing to titlepage and to one or two of the plates, crown 8vo., original blue cloth, backstrip lettered in gilt with very slight lean to spine, few pinprick foxspots to endpapers, dust jacket with some tiny faint foxspots at foot of rear panel and one or two further faint marks, tiny amount of deft restoration at tips of corner folds, very good, scarce in dust jacket. Blackwell's Rare Books B184 - 123 2016 £4000

Byron, Robert *The Station. Athos: Treasures and Men.* London: Duckworth, 1928. First edition, original blue cloth lettered gilt at spine, 33 illustrations, slight rubbing at hinge at lower spine end, slight bump to lower edge, otherwise near very good, decent copy. Any Amount of Books 2015 - A96272 2016 £250

Byron, Robert *The Station - Athos: Treasures of men.* London: Duckworth, 1928. First edition, octavo, photos, cover edges little bumped, edges and prelims bit spotted, very good, increasingly difficult to find. Peter Ellis 112 - 58 2016 £275

Bythner, Victorinus *Lyra Prophetica Davidis Regis. Sive Analysis Critico-Practica Psalmorum in quae Omnes & Singulae Voces Hebraeae in Psalterio Contentae...* Londoni: Jacobi Flesher, 1650. First edition, 4to., text in Hebrew and Latin, titlepage in red and black, separate half title to 'Index Libri Psalmorum', final leaf of errata, tidemark to top fore-edge corner from title to page 81 small worm trail to fore-edge margin of page 333 dwindling away to end of textblock, tiny burnhole to page 3-4 touching couple of letters, contemporary brown sprinkled calf, red morocco gilt label to spine, blind tooled borders and additional vertical line to boards, edges sprinkled blue and red, very early rubricated leaves with accompanying manuscript marginalia used as pastedowns, spine rubbed, lower joint split and upper starting but cords holding firm, some scrapes and stains, corners wearing but sound unsophisticated copy, ownership inscription of Stephen Freeman dated 1787 and bookplate of Douglas Cleverdon. Unsworths Antiquarian Booksellers 30 - 28 2016 £175

C

C. W. Stockwell Company *The World is Your Stage When You Dramatize Your Walls with Scenic Wallpapers.* N.P.: C. W. Stockwell Co., n.d., Folio, quarter cloth, illustrated paper covered boards, illustrations in color, boards bumped and scuffed at edges, hinges cracked and final four pages of text detached.   Oak Knoll Books   310 - 307   2016 $1250

Cabell, James Branch   1879-1958 *Sonnets from Antan.* New York: Fountain Press, 1929. First edition, one of 718 numbered copies, signed by author, thin octavo, printed in orange and black, headpiece portrait by William Cotton, handset Lutetia type, gray decorated boards, gray cloth spine, gray spine label printed in black, fine.   Argonaut Book Shop   Literature 2015 - 5846   2016 $100

Cabeo, Niccolo Cabaeus *Philosophia Magnetica in Qua Magnetis Natura Penitus Explicatur, et Omnium quae Hoc Lapide Cernuntur Causae Propriae Afferuntur....* Cologne and Ferrara: Johann Kinckius, Francesco Succi, 1629. First edition, Cologne issue, folio, printer's mark, added fine engraved architectural titlepage with scientific apparatus, wood engravings, including world map, first title and dedication pages, browned as usual, contemporary full vellum, gilt spine title, edges colored.   Jeff Weber Rare Books   183 - 9   2016 $13,000

The Cabinet of Useful Arts and Manufactures.... Dublin: printed by Thomas Courtney, 1821. 10 full page woodcuts, few dogears, modicum of soiling, original tree sheep, gilt lettered library classification on spine, splits in joints and spine defective at foot, inscription inside front cover "Great Ness lending Library. presented by R. A, Slang Esq. 1858", good copy.   Blackwell's Rare Books   B186 - 84   2016   £300

Cable, George Washington   1844-1925 *Bonaventure, a Prose Pastoral of Acadian Louisiana.* New York: Scribner, 1888. First edition, 8vo., ownership signature of Alice Stone Blackwell's copy with her ownership signature, staining to bottom half of covers which bleeds through to endpapers, tight copy otherwise.   Second Life Books, Inc.   196A - 244   2016 $75

Cable, George Washington   1844-1925 *Gideon's Band. A Tale of the Mississippi.* New York: Charles Scribners, 1914. First edition, small octavo, color illustrations, red cloth lettered in gilt, spine slightly faded and there is some very minor rubbing to extremities, fine.   Argonaut Book Shop   Literature 2015 - 1215   2016 $60

Cadman, Samuel Parkes   1864-1936 *The Parables of Jesus.* Philadelphia: McKay, 1931. First edition, 4to., purple cloth, pictorial paste-on, fine in dust jacket (frayed), cover plate, pictorial endpapers, 8 other very beautiful color plates by N. C. Wyeth, especially nice.   Aleph-bet Books, Inc.   112 - 523   2016 $1500

Caesar, Gaius Julius *De Bello Gallo Commnentariorum.* London: Riccardi Press, 1914. No. 5 of 12 copies printed on vellum, 10 of which were for sale and 525 copies on paper, publisher's flexible vellum, gilt titling on upper cover and flat spine, green silk ties, vellum somewhat darkened and with appearance of soiling, though both of these apparently a reflection of the original condition of the skin, in all other ways mint copy.   Phillip J. Pirages   67 - 345   2016 $4500

Caesar, Gaius Julius *Commentaria Caesaris Prius a Locundo Impressioni datae...*   Florence: ex officina Philippi de Giunta, 1514. First Giunti edition of Caesar, 5 full page woodcuts and 2 double page woodcut maps included in pagination, manuscript marginal numbers added to first few pages, some light spotting, one or two small marginal tears, ownership inscription of M. Joh. Jacobus Maierus to titlepage, later ms. Latin quotation recto of final leaf (blank apart from device on verso), 8vo., 17th century walnut brown calf, boards bordered with blind decorative roll inside triple gilt fillet, endpapers renewed early 20th century, recently rebacked in expertly sympathetic fashion, fore-edge lettered in ink (with date '1541'), very good.   Blackwell's Rare Books   Greek & Latin Classics VII - 9   2016   £2500

Caesar, Gaius Julius (Opera). *Commentariourm de Bello Gallico Libri VIII. De Bello Civili Pompeiano Libri IIII. De Bello Alexandrino Liber I. De Bello Hispaniensi Liber I.* Venice: aldo Manuzio and Andrea Torresano, April, 1513. First Aldine edition, double page woodcut map tinted in six colors, stenciled by contemporary hand, 6 full page woodcut illustrations, Aldine anchor device on title and at end, 8vo., mid 16th century German? gilt tooled calf over wooden boards, covers panelled with blind fillets and outer ornamental border with a rosetta at each corner, central panel made up of repeated stamps of curling stems infilled with thistle book, clasps intact, rebacked, new endpapers, corners worn.   Maggs Bros. Ltd.   1474 - 17   2016   £6500

Caesar, Gaius Julius *Quae Extant Omnia.* Venice: Societatis Albritianae, 1737. Engraved frontispiece, folding map, 5 plates (two folding) plus engravings in text area, few leaves with marginal dampmarks, some foxing and finger soiling (heavier in one or two places), one leaf with chip from blank margin, bit of spotting, 4to., contemporary vellum boards, brown morocco lettering piece to spine, soiled and bit scratched vellum covering worn in places (particularly patch at front joint and another at fore-edge of rear board), bookplates of Carrington and David Garrick to front pastedown, good.   Blackwell's Rare Books   B186 - 34   2016   £950

Cage, John *The Wonderful Widow of Eighteen Springs: for Voice and Piano.* New York: Henmar Press, 1960. Folio musical score, 11 x 14 inches, publisher's facsimile proof of Cage's autograph instructions and musical notations, scarce. Honey & Wax Booksellers 4 - 9 2016 $1500

Cahill, Christopher *In Memoriam Darcy O'Brien 1939-1998.* N.P.: Stinehour Press, 1998. 8vo., stiff paper wrappers, photos. Oak Knoll Books 310 - 299 2016 $175

Caille, L'Abbe De La *Lecons Elementaires d'Optique.* Paris: H. L. Guerin & L. F. Delatour, 1756. Second edition, Title vignette, decorative head and tailpieces, 12 folding engraved copperplates, disbound, yet in early marbled wrappers, spine exposed, some signatures loosening, bookplate signed TM of ACS Van Heel, handsome modern blue cloth, drop back box, good, the copy of Abraham Cornelis Sebastian Bram. Jeff Weber Rare Books 183 - 10 2016 $400

Cain, James M. *The Institute.* London: Hale, 1977. First English edition, fine in dust jacket with tiny wear at corners. Mordida Books 2015 - 011677 2016 $65

Cain, James M. *The Postman Always Rings Twice.* New York: Alfred A. Knopf, 1934. First edition, boards slightly soiled and near fine, with supplied proof dust jacket which came directly from estate of artist Arthur Hawkins Jr., jacket folded with crease at spine, Knopf's small Borzoi logo has been cut away , date '1933' on front flap, although book wasn't released until 1934, however this is exceptionally bright and otherwise fine and about 1/4 inch taller than the finished version. Between the Covers Rare Books 208 - 99 2016 $10,000

Calcott, W. *A Candid Disquisition of the Principles and Practices of the Most Antient and Honourable Society of Free and Accepted Masons...* Boston: Brother William M'Alpine, 1772. First American edition, modern quarter calf, marbled paper covered boards, very skillfully executed in period style, top of titlepage including first word "A" neatly replaced at an early date, lower corner of C4 torn off, without loss, text with varying amount of foxing, but very nice in appropriate binding. Joseph J. Felcone, Inc. Books from Five Centuries: a Miscellany - 65 2016 $1800

Caldecott, Randolph *Picture Books.* London: George Routledge, Complete set of 16 picture books, bound in 2 volumes, one 8 1/2 9 the other 9 1/2 x 8, margins trimmed, bindings tight, first volume are all first editions and have both covers bound in, the oblong volume have front cover bound in, presumably first edition but you need the back covers to be definitive, binding is contemporary half leather and marbled boards, gilt spines and raised bands, leather scuffed but not unattractive, edges rubbed, minor foxing on first page, occasional margin mark, no wear to covers or text, very good, internally each book illustrated with 8 wonderful full page color illustrations. Aleph-bet Books, Inc. 112 - 89 2016 $1350

Caldecott, Randolph *R. Caldecott's Picture Books.* London: Frederick Warne & Co., circa, 1900. Later edition, 2 quarto volumes, one in portrait format, one in landscape, contemporary full russet crushed morocco, Art Nouveau botanical designs tooled in blind and gilt, both volumes signed by Guild of Women Binders, color plates and sepia illustrations throughout text, stunning set. Honey & Wax Booksellers 4 - 49 2016 $4500

Calder, Fanny L. *A Teachers' Manual of Elementary Laundry Work.* London: Longmans, Green, 1894. Third edition, half title, original brick red decorated cloth, slight bubbling to lower margin of front board, little dulled. Jarndyce Antiquarian Books CCXV - 565 2016 £35

California Society of Artists *First Exhibition California Society of Artists.* San Francisco: printed by Sanborn Vail for the California Society of Artists, 1902. First edition, square octavo, original pictorial wrappers, 17 plates, slight darkening to edges of wrappers, very good. The Brick Row Book Shop Miscellany 69 - 20 2016 $950

California Sorcery. Abingdon: Cemetery Dance, 1999. Publisher's copy of the limited edition (26 copies), signed by Ray Bradbury, Richard Matheson, Ellison, Nolan, Tomerlin, Sohl, Fritch and others, stamp of another author, fine in fine dust jacket in publisher's printed gray case. Ken Lopez Bookseller 166 - 5 2016 $650

Callahan, Harry *Color 1941-1980.* Providence: Matrix Pub., 1980. First edition, 4to., one of 100 deluxe signed copies, with original color photo, signed by artist laid in, illustrations. full purple morocco, folding cloth clamshell box, fine. James S. Jaffe Rare Books Occasional List: Winter 2016 - 111 2016 $5000

Callahan, Harry *Color 1941-1980.* Providence: Matrix Publications, 1980. First edition, color reproductions, folio, original sage green cloth covered slipcase, title stamped in yellow on front, original shipping box, 96 color plates and one duotone, some rippling to text, otherwise fine. Manhattan Rare Book Company 2016 - 1723 2016 $375

Callieres, Francois De *The Knowledge of the World and the Attainments Useful in the Conduct of Life.* London: printed for the translator and sold by R. Baldwin &c., 1770? half title, 12mo., prelims misbound, corners creased, tear to H4 affecting 4 words, lacking following f.e.p., uncut in contemporary quarter calf, marbled boards, leading hinge little worn, elaborate signature of Maurice Wynne on leading f.e.p., very unsophisticated copy.   Jarndyce Antiquarian Books   CCXV - 95   2016   £520

Callimachus *Hymni, Epigrammata et Fragmenta.* Paris: Excudebat Sebastianus Mabre-Cramoisy, 1675. First Dacier edition, gently washed and pressed at time of rebinding, browned titlepage then also expertly mounted on an old binder's blank, two sets of Macclesfield blindstamps to first three leaves, 4to., 19th century green pebbled morocco by Hatton of Manchester, spine faded, front joint rubbed, Macclesfield arms in gilt to front board, all edges gilt, marbled endpapers, bookplate, good.   Blackwell's Rare Books   B186 - 35   2016   £500

Calonne, Charles Alexandre De *Catalogue of the Superb and Elegant Household Furniture...* London: Skinner and Dyke, 1793. 8vo., mid 20th century red morocco backed marbled boards, spine lettered in gilt.   Marlborough Rare Books   List 56 - 19   2016   £1850

Calverley, Charles Stuart *Fly Leaves.* Cambridge: Deighton Bell and Co., 1872. Second edition, half title, final ad leaf, original green cloth, spine lettered gilt, slight rubbing, very good. Jarndyce Antiquarian Booksellers   CCXVIII - 139   2016   £30

Calvert, Albert F. *The Exploration of Australia from 144 to 1896.* London: George Philip & Son, 1896. First edition, 4to., original eggshell cloth backed blue cloth covered boards, lettered gilt, color printed map, light spotting to spine, internally, apart from one short repaired tear to map, very good, printed on thick laid paper.   Sotheran's Travel and Exploration - 397   2016   £145

Calvino, Italo *Le Cosmicomiche.* Torino: Einaudi, 1965. First edition, 8vo., original pale green cloth, fine in dust jacket with few short tears, presentation copy inscribed by author to William Weaver, the English translator of Cosmicomics, with a number of discreet pencil annotations by Weaver.   James S. Jaffe Rare Books   Occasional List: Winter 2016 - 37   2016 $4500

Cambridge Trifles or Splutterings from an Undergraduate Pen. London: Sampson, Low, Marston, Searle & Rivington, 1881. First edition, dark orange binder's cloth, Bolland collection stamps.   Jarndyce Antiquarian Books   CCXV - 566   2016   £25

Camden, William *Camden's Britannia 1695: a Facsimile of the 1695 Edition.* London: Times Newspapers, 1971. Facsimile reprint of 1695 edition, folio, original publisher's brown cloth over red boards, lettered gilt at spine, color and black and white, neat name plate, very occasional pencil annotation, otherwise clean, very good+.   Any Amount of Books   2015 - C13327   2016   £170

Camden, William *Institutio Graecae Grammatices Compendiaria.* London: Exeuderunt S. Buckley, et T. Longman, 1790. Relatively late edition, 8vo., original linen, covered at an early date with a dust jacket of rough paper, its flaps folded over pastedowns and stitched together rather crudely with green thread, outer surface of paper now worn, inscription 'Jehoshaphat Jones's Book, Bought at Mr. North's Brecon, May 4th 1802", this inscription repeated in various forms on endpapers.   Blackwell's Rare Books Greek & Latin Classics VII - 26   2016   £300

Camden, William *Rerum Anglicarum et Hibernicarum Annales, Regnante Elisabetha.* Lugd. Batavorum: Elzevir, 1639. 8vo, engraved portrait, titlepage in red and black, woodcut printer's device, copious notes in old hand to endpapers and prelim blanks, further marginalia in Latin and English with occasional manicules, few pages with pencil ticks to margins, sporadic light foxing, one or two marginal paper flaws, small hole in centre of page 359, affecting only few letters, contemporary vellum, gilt to spine evidence of lost label replaced with ink title, yapp edges, spine slightly darkened, little soiled with some smudges and stains, small (burn?) hole to spine, some bands broken and inner hinge split but binding sound, small loss ot top corner of f.f.e.p., armorial bookplate of Robert Hinde, bookplate of Frances Massey O'Brien and an anonymous catalogue description affixed to front pastedown, ownership inscriptions of Sunderland Nov. 23rd 1805, Eton, L. M. Robinson 1923, and Frances Massey O'Brien, July 1967, FMO's pencil note.   Unsworths Antiquarian Booksellers Ltd.   E01 - Early Printing - 4   2016   £300

Camerarius, Joachim 1500-1574 *Symbolorum et Emblematum Centuriae Tres....* Heidelberg: Voegelin, 1605. First collected edition, 4 engraved titlepages, 400 circular engraved illustrations, 4to., 4 parts in one volume, contemporary reversed calf, headcap and corners worn, some tears and marks to covers, contemporary ownership inscription "Cambsfort?", titlepage with old repair to tear (no loss), lightly browned throughout, occasional dampstaining.   Maggs Bros. Ltd.   1474 - 18   2016   £4500

Cameron, A. G. *The Wild Red Deer of Scotland.* Edinburgh: William Blackwood and Sons, 1923. First edition, 8vo., original red cloth, gilt to upper board, gilt lettering to spine, 8 photo plates, text illustrations, presentation bookplate to f.f.e.p., spine faded, splash marks to lower board, occasional light spotting, very good.   Sotheran's Hunting, Shooting & Fishing - 53   2016   £40

Cameron, James *Pictonians in Arms a Military History of Pictou County, Nova Scotia.* Fredericton: Nova Scotia University, 1969. 8vo., half title, card covers, numerous black and white photos, previous owner's inscription on half title as well as name written in ink on cover, generally very good.   Schooner Books Ltd.   115 - 134   2016 $45

Cameron, N. C. *The Maritime Retail Merchants Volume I No. I.* St. Johns: Retail Merchants Association of Canada, 1916. Card covers, large 8vo., black and white illustrations, plus illustrated ads, front cover spotted along edges.   Schooner Books Ltd.   115 - 176   2016 $45

Campastri, Tommaso *La Felicita del Matrimonio Opera Morale...* Milano: Nella Stamperia di Antonio Agnelli, 1760. First edition, rare, 8vo., engraved frontispiece, aside from some light foxing in places, clean and fresh throughout, contemporary drab stiff wrappers, later paper spine with handwritten paper label, ink marks on upper cover, good copy.   Marlborough Rare Books   List 56 - 9   2016   £650

Campbell, Archibald James *Golden Wattle: Our National Floral Emblem.* Melbourne: Osboldstone & Co., 1921. Quarto, tipped-in color and black and white photos, publisher's green boards and cloth spine, library stamp on blank front endpaper, very good.   Andrew Isles Natural History Books   55 - 5584   2016 $250

Campbell, Archibald James *Nests and Eggs of Australian Birds Including the Geographical Distribution of the Species and Popular Observations Thereon.* Sheffield: author, 1901. Octavo 28 (of 27 eggs) chromolithographs by Brittlebank, photos, publisher's brown decorated cloth (single volume), bright, crisp copy, scarce in this condition.   Andrew Isles Natural History Books   55 - 36417   2016 $1500

Campbell, Catherine Hayden *Thomas Cantley Remembered.* New Glasgow: Catherine H. Campbell, 2004. Trade paprback, 8vo., photos illustrations, some wear to covers, otherwise very good.   Schooner Books Ltd.   115 - 135   2016 $45

Campbell, Gertrude Elizabeth *Etiquette of Good Society.* London: Cassell & Co., 1898. 78th thousand, 8 page catalog, original light brown cloth, blocked in red, little dulled.   Jarndyce Antiquarian Books   CCXV - 96   2016   £35

Campbell, James Dykes *Poems. MDCCCXXX. MDCCCXXXIII.* Toronto: privately printed, 1862. Pirated edition, uncut in original blue penned paper wrappers, little creased with some very slight wear to head and tail of spine, pencil inscription, given to NIC by Mrs. Dykes Campbell, from JDC's editor, J. Dykes Campbell, library, nice in original wrappers.   Jarndyce Antiquarian Booksellers   CCXVII - 277   2016   £220

Campbell, Janet *The Effect of Adolescence on the Brain of the Girl.* Women's Printing Society, 1908. Original printed paper wrappers, slightly creased.   Jarndyce Antiquarian Books CCXV - 581   2016   £20

Campbell, John Francis *Frost and Fire. Natural Engines, Tool-Marks and Chips.* Edinburgh: Edmonston & Douglas, 1865. First edition, 8vo., 2 volumes, original blue cloth lettered and illustrated in gilt, blindstamped representation of ice marks at St. John, New Brunswick, volume one with wood engraved title, volume two with wood engraving of meteorite on title, numerous wood engravings (some full page), volume 1 with folding lithographic plate printed in black and blue and with red lines added by hand, volume two with lithographic map printed in black and blue as frontispiece, bindings with wear to extremities, rear hinge volume II restored, internally clean and fresh, inscribed by author.   Sotheran's   Travel and Exploration - 417   2016   £298

Campbell, Ramsey *The Inhabitant of the Lake and Less Welcome Tenants.* Sauk City: Arkham House, 1964. First edition, 2009 copies printed, presentation copy with signed inscription by Campbell to August Derleth, fine in fine dust jacket.   John W. Knott, Jr./L.W. Currey, Inc.   Fall-Winter 2015 - 17256   2016 $3500

Campbell, Roy   1901-1957 *The Flaming Terrapin.* New York: Dial Press, 1924. First edition, slim octavo, black cloth backed decorated boards, spine slightly faded and very light rubbing to extremities, else fine.   Argonaut Book Shop   Literature 2015 - 1219   2016 $125

Campbell, Roy   1901-1957 *The Flaming Terrapin.* London: Jonathan Cape, 1924. First edition, frontispiece, crown 8vo. original first state binding of quarter green cloth with patterned boards, backstrip with printed label, light toning to boards, little rubbing to extremities, top edge lightly dust soiled, others untrimmed, free endpapers lightly browned, small bookseller sticker, good, inscribed by Ezra Pound for Bertram Lloyd.   Blackwell's Rare Books   B186 - 273   2016 £300

Campbell, Thomas *The Pleasures of Hope.* Glasgow: At the University Press, printed by J. Mundell, 1800. Fourth edition, 168 x 98mm., very attractive contemporaneous Etruscan style calf featuring blind gilt and acid treated decorations, very possibly by Edwards of Halifax, covers with gilt Greek key border, palmette frame and central panel containing a lyre from which thickening radiations emanate, smooth spine, divided into panels by multiple gilt rules, each panel with blindstamped lyre centerpiece enclosed by gilt flourishes, gilt dots on turn-ins, marbled endpapers, all edges gilt, 4 engraved plates of scenes from the poem, rear joint with thin half inch crack at bottom, extremities slightly rubbed, offsetting from engravings, leaves a shade less than bright, flyleaves faintly spotted, other trivial imperfections, still attractive copy, text with no serious condition issues, very pretty unsophisticated binding, remarkably well preserved.   Phillip J. Pirages   67 - 41   2016 $1100

Camuccini, Vincenzo *Studio del Disegno: Ricavato dall'Estremita delle Figure del Celebre Quadro della Transfiurazione di Raffaelle.* Rome: Studieo di Folo Posto in Piazza di Spragna nume 13, 1806. Folio, engraved title, 31 engraved plates, old stain affecting head of title and first few plates, contemporary marbled boards, sympathetically rebacked. Marlborough Rare Books List 55 - 58 2016 £1250

Camus, Albert *The Stranger.* New York: Heritage press, 1971. Octavo, paintings by Daniel Maffia, yellow cloth stamped in red, lettered gilt, very fine, in slipcase, Sandglass pamphlet laid in. Argonaut Book Shop Heritage Press 2015 - 6937 2016 $40

Canaday, Frank H. *Triumph of Color.* Canaan: Phoenix, 1977. 4to., illustrations in color and black and white, nice in little scuffed and chipped dust jacket, signed by author. Second Life Books, Inc. 196A - 250 2016 $45

Canby, Henry Seidel *The Brandywine Illustrated by Andrew Wyeth.* New York and Toronto: Farrar & Rinehart, 1941. First edition, signed by author, fine in very good illustrated dust jacket, 8vo., original cloth. Howard S. Mott Inc. 265 - 22 2016 $95

Candolle, Augustin Pyramus De *Plantes Rares Du Jardin de Geneve.* Geneva: Barbezat et Delarue, 1825-1827. First edition first issue, 371 x 283mm., 4 separately issued parts bound in one volume, pleasing modern quarter vellum over brown boards, ink titling on flat spine, edges untrimmed, original paper wrappers of parts 3 and 4 bound in at front and rear, with 24 attractive hand finished color plates (as called for), 21 of them by Jean Christophe Heyland, large paper copy, tiny smudge to front board, isolated faint foxing or corner creases, couple of text pages with small brown smudge at tail edge, one plate with short fore-edge tear (not affecting image), other trivial imperfections, but extremely fine, plates especially clean and bright with very pleasing coloring, unworn binding. Phillip J. Pirages 67 - 86 2016 $9500

Canetti, Elias *Kafka's Other Trial.* London: Calder and Boyars, 1974. First English edition, crown 8vo. original black boards, backstrip lettered in silver with very slight lean to spine, ownership inscription, dust jacket, near fine, inscribed by author. Blackwell's Rare Books B186 - 191 2016 £400

Canevaro, Mirka *Three Documents in the Attic Orators Laws and Decrees in the Public Speeches of the Demosthenic Corpus.* Oxford University Press, 2013. First edition, 8vo., 3 tables, dark blue cloth, gilt lettered spine, dust jacket, as new. Unsworths Antiquarian Booksellers Ltd. E04 - 37 2016 £45

Cannon, J. *The Medieval Art, Architecture and History of Bristol Cathedral.* Woodbridge: Boydell Press, 2011. First edition, 8vo., illustrations and plates, black cloth, gilt lettered to spine, dust jacket, as new. Unsworths Antiquarian Booksellers Ltd. E05 - 97 2016 £25

Cantrall, Thomas D. *Ghosts of Ruby Ridge.* Baltimore: 2008. Limited numbered edition, #41 of 100 copies, cover corners curling, but good, sound copy, signed by author. Gene W. Baade, Books on the West 2015 - 5015046 2016 $41

Capaccio, Giulio Cesare *Delle Imprese Trattato in tre Libri Diviso.* Naples: Horatio Salviani for Giovanni Giacomo Carlino and Antonio Pace, 1592. First edition, 3 parts in one volume, 4to., clasped hands printer's device on each titlepage, 303 mostly oval woodcut emblems, cuts on book, 3 have decorative corner pieces filling out the block some groups of shields and circular cuts, woodcut initials, head and tailpieces, contemporary vellum over thin pasteboard, title lettered in ink at head of spine, remains of vellum ties and paper shelflabel at foot of spine, label of Arthur and Charlotte Vershbow. Maggs Bros. Ltd. 1474 - 20 2016 £3500

Capek, Karel *Valka S Mloky. (War with the Newts).* Praha: Nakladatel Fr. Borovy, 1936. First edition, octavo, prelims printed in orange and black, original grey cloth, front panel stamped in brown and back, spine panel stamped in black, 7mm. closed tear to cloth at head of spine, bright nearly fine, scarce. John W. Knott, Jr./L.W. Currey, Inc. Fall-Winter 2015 - 16013 2016 $7500

Capello, Cesare *Ricordo di Napoli.* Milan: Cesare Capello, circa, 1896. 27 concertina-folded views and one panorama extending over five panels in original 8vo., cloth folder with large chromolithographic pictorial paper label on front cover, map endpapers, overall length 350cm., folder with minor wear to extremities, otherwise very well preserved and clean. Sotheran's Piccadilly Notes - Summer 2015 - 67 2016 £98

Capote, Truman 1924-1985 *The Grass Harp: a Play.* New York: Random House, 1952. First edition, fine in fine dust jacket with slight rubbing and tiny 1/8 inch tear in rear panel, beautiful crisp copy. Between the Covers Rare Books 204 - 23 2016 $650

Capote, Truman 1924-1985 *Local Color.* New York: Random house, 1950. First edition, 8vo., very nice, clean copy in little worn dust jacket. Second Life Books, Inc. 197 - 45 2016 $350

Capote, Truman 1924-1985 *Other Voices, Other Rooms.* New York: Random House, 1946. First edition, beige cloth lettered in red, original slate blue dust jacket lettered in white, some faint wear to spine ends, minor toning to spine and board edges, few faint scuffs to otherwise clean binding, hint of offsetting to endpapers and verso of half title, otherwise fresh pages, dust jacket with hint of toning to spine, minor rubbing to extremities, tiny nick to spine head, bright and fresh panels, overall very tight and attractive. B & B Rare Books, Ltd.   2016 - TC059   2016 $250

Capote, Truman 1924-1985 *The Thanksgiving Visitor.* New York: Random House, 1967. First edition, pale pink boards over red cloth spine, lettered in gilt, housed in slate blue slipcase, illustrated with photo of author and his cousin on front panel, book fine, slipcase lightly starting on rear hinge, some light wear and soiling, sunning to front panel and sides, overall about near fine, very pleasing copy.   B & B Rare Books, Ltd.   2016 - TC054   2016 $50

Capote, Truman 1924-1985 *A Tree of Night and Other Stories.* New York: Random House, 1948. First edition, black cloth, spine stamped in silver and yellow, original slate blue dust jacket lettered in white, book about fine, dust jacket with some light toning to spine, minor wear to extremities, few tiny chips to spine ends, hint of soiling to rear panel, otherwise fresh panels, overall very good.   B & B Rare Books, Ltd.   2016 - TC061   2016 $125

Capote, Truman 1924-1985 *A Tree of Night.* London: Heinemann, 1950. First UK edition, octavo, spine slightly darkened, very good in very good, slightly chipped dust jacket with few nicks.   Peter Ellis   112 - 60   2016   £75

Capps, Benjamin *Same Chance.* New York: Duell Sloan and Pearce, 1965. First edition, cloth backed boards, very fine, pictorial dust jacket, scarce in this condition.   Argonaut Book Shop   Literature 2015 - 6402   2016 $45

Capps, Benjamin *The Trail to Ogallala.* New York: Duell, Sloan and Pearce, 1984. First edition, scarce , frontispiece map, cloth backed boards, fine with slightly rubbed pictorial dust jacket.   Argonaut Book Shop   Literature 2015 - 6403   2016 $90

Capstick, Peter Hathaway *Safari. The Last Adventure.* New York: St. Martin's Press, 1984. First edition, 8vo., original cloth and jacket, black and white photos little chipping to edges of jacket, very good.   Sotheran's   Hunting, Shooting & Fishing - 7   2016   £70

Caraboo. A Narrative of a Singular Imposition, Practised Upon the Benevolence of a Lady Residing in the Vicinity of the City of Bristol... Bristol: printed by J. M. Gutch and Pub. by Baldwin Cradock and Joy, Paternoster Row, London, 1817. Half title, frontispiece, large folding full length portrait, plates slightly foxed, uncut in half black sheep, marbled boards, rubbed.   Jarndyce Antiquarian Booksellers   CCXVII - 5   2016   £750

Caraccioli, Louis Antoine *Advice from a Lady of Quality to Her Children in the Last Stage of a Lingering Illness.* Gloucester: printed by R Raikes and sold by J. F. & C. Rivington, 1766. Fourth edition, 8vo., full contemporary green crushed morocco, boards eloabartely blocked in gilt, raised bands, compartments in gilt, spine slightly faded and rubbed, 2 small nicks to front board, presentation inscription "Penelope Phipps given by Revd. James Esqr. August 18th 1805, with additional inscription beneath dated 1851, all edges gilt, very good, handsome copy.   Jarndyce Antiquarian Books   CCXV - 97   2016   £420

Caraccioli, Louis Antoine *The True Mentor or An Essay on the Education of Young People of Fashion.* London: printed for J. Coote, 1760. Contemporary speckled calf, raised bands, red brown morocco label, 12mo., very good.   Jarndyce Antiquarian Books   CCXV - 582   2016   £480

Caradoc, of Llancarvan *The History of Wales.* London: by M. Clark for the author and R. Clavell, 1697. contemporary calf, rebacked in period style, later endpapers, very nice.   Joseph J. Felcone, Inc.   Books from Five Centuries: a Miscellany - 147   2016 $450

Card, Orson Scott *Ender's Game.* New York: Tor, 1985. First edition, octavo, boards, signed label by Card and signed photo of Card laid in, fine in fine dust jacket with touch of rubbing to corner tips and lower rear panel.   John W. Knott, Jr./L.W. Currey, Inc.   Fall-Winter 2015 - 17373   2016 $2500

Card, Orson Scott *Speaker for the Dead.* New York: Tor, 1986. First edition, octavo, boards, signed by author, fine in fine dust jacket with touch of rubbing to head of spine panel.   John W. Knott, Jr./L.W. Currey, Inc.   Fall-Winter 2015 - 17746   2016 $200

Carden, Percy T. *The Murder of Edwin Drood Recounted by John Jasper....* London: Cecil Palmer, 1920. First edition, half title, frontispiece, illustrations, ad on verso of final leaf, original pink cloth, spine faded, Eric Jones-Evans booklabel, very good.   Jarndyce Antiquarian Booksellers   CCXVIII - 664   2016   £25

Cardenas, Jeffrey *Marquesa.* Stone Harbor: Meadow Run Press, 1995. First printing, one of 1500 copies, fine in fine slipcase with promotional postcard laid in, letter from publisher dated Jan 23 1995, transmitting to book to author Peter Matthiesson on behalf of author.   Ken Lopez Bookseller   166 - 16   2016 $350

Cardew, Margaret *A French Alphabet.* London: Circa, 1950. With color lithographs.   Honey & Wax Booksellers   4 - 42   2016 $45

Carey, H. C. *The Slave Trade, Domestic and Foreign.* Philadelphia: A. Hart, later Carey & Hart, 1853. First edition, 8vo., library buckram, foxed.   M & S Rare Books, Inc.   99 - 40   2016 $250

Carey, John *The Violent Effigy: a Study of Dickens' Imagination.* London: Faber, 1973. First edition, half title, original pink cloth, review copy, editor's compliment slip loosely inserted and some pencil association, very good in dust jacket.   Jarndyce Antiquarian Booksellers   CCXVIII - 1100   2016   £20

Carey, John L. *Some Thoughts Concerning Domestic Slavery in a Letter to -- Esq. of Baltimore.* Baltimore: Joseph N. Lewis, 1838. First edition, 16mo., publisher's brown cloth with printed pink label on front board, two early owner's names, front fly affixed to pastedown from excess of binder's glue, small chip at corner of label, some light spotting on boards, modest foxing in text, still handsome very good or better copy.   Between the Covers Rare Books   202 - 15   2016 $650

Carey, Peter *My Life as a Fake.* Sydney: Random House, 2003. First edition, 8vo., original white boards, backstrip lettered in pink, fore edges untrimmed, photographic pastedowns with pink free endpapers, dust jacket with faint ghosting from publisher's sticker, near fine, inscribed by author.   Blackwell's Rare Books   B186 - 192   2016   £80

Carey, Peter *Theft, a Love Story.* Sydney: Knopf, 2006. First Australian edition, true first, fine in like dust jacket, with Victorian Premier's award sticker attached.   Bella Luna Books   2016 - t9227   2016 $82

Carle, Eric *Catch the Ball.* New York: Philopmel Books, 1982. First edition, 8vo. stiff pictorial boards, signed by Carle, just about fine.   Second Life Books, Inc.   197 - 46   2016 $750

Carle, Eric *Where Are You Going? To See My Friend!* Published in Japan by Dashin-Sha Pub. Co., 2001-2002. Pictorial boards, as new in as new dust jacket, illustrations in color, foldout pages, this copy signed by Carle.   Alephbet Books, Inc.   112 - 91   2016 $125

Carleton, William *Traits and Stories of the Irish Peasantry.* Dublin: published by Wm. Curry Junr. & Co., Sackville Street & W. S. Orr & Co., Paternoster Row, London, 1843-1844. Early edition, 2 volumes, 8vo., bound with half titles, each volume also with frontispiece and second illustrated titlepage, 22 further plates to volume i and 14 further plates to volume II, some deterioration, further illustrations in text, foxing, some deterioration to plates, bound in contemporary polished half calf and marbled boards, gilt to spines, labels of black morocco gilt, edges mottled red.   Unsworths Antiquarian Booksellers Ltd.   E04 - 6   2016   £100

Carlile, Henry *Running Lights: Poems by...* Port Townsend: Dragon Gate, 1981. First edition, 1/30 special copies, gray cloth with black spine, hand bound by Marsha Hollingsworth, illustration by Carl Morris applied on front, signed by Carlile and Morris.   Second Life Books, Inc.   196A - 253   2016 $75

Carlisle, Isabella Howard, Countess of *Thoughts in the Form of maxims Addressed to Young Ladies.* London: printed for T. Cornwell, 1790. Second edition, 8vo., half title, contemporary tree calf, neat repairs to extremities expertly rebacked, maroon morocco label, contemporary inscription "E. D. Parr from F. Evans".   Jarndyce Antiquarian Books   CCXV - 98   2016   £30

Carlow, Viscount *On Collecting Books and Printing Them Too.* Quenington: Reading Room Press, 2013. 77/110 copies, tipped in frontispiece by Kennington, titlepage printed in brown, small 4to., original quarter beige cloth with patterned boards, backstrip and upper cloth lettered gilt, foreedge untrimmed, fine.   Blackwell's Rare Books   B184 - 307   2016   £45

Carlton, William John *Charles Dickens Shorthand Writer: the 'Prentice Days of a Master Craftsman.* London: Cecil Palmer, 1926. First edition, half title, frontispiece, plates, 2 pages ads, original pale blue cloth, spine faded, hinges slightly rubbed, presentation from author.   Jarndyce Antiquarian Booksellers   CCXVIII - 1101   2016   £125

Carlyle, Thomas   1795-1881 *Letter to a Young Man.* London: privately printed by Clement Shorter, 1915. 4to., original green printed paper wrappers, sewn as issued, very good.   Jarndyce Antiquarian Booksellers   CCXVII - 63   2016   £120

Carlyle, Thomas   1795-1881 *Oliver Cromwell's Letters and Speeches with Elucidations.* London: Chapman and Hall, 1845. First edition, stout 8vo., 2 volumes bound by Bayntun in half single gilt ruled morocco, spines lettered and panelled in gilt, top edges gilt, frontispiece portrait in volume I extra illustrated with insertion of c. 160 engraved portraits upper joint of volume one little tender with small repaired split in bottom, little occasional light spotting, generally very good set.   Sotheran's   Piccadilly Notes - Summer 2015 - 68   2016   £998

Carlyle, Thomas   1795-1881 *Sartor Resartus.* London: privately printed, James Fraser, 1834. First separate edition, one of only 58 copies, titlepage re-laid, dusted and with few small tears, one affecting final 'v' in imprint date, bound without wrappers in slightly later brown calf by M. Patterson, Glasgow, rubbed, presentation for Edward Irving, from author.   Jarndyce Antiquarian Booksellers   CCXVII - 64   2016   £5800

Carmer, Carl *Genessee River.* New York: Farrar & Rinehart, 1941. First edition, 8vo., good, inscribed by author, Dec. 1941.   Second Life Books, Inc.   196A - 254   2016 $45

Carmer, Carl *Listen to a Lonesome Drum.* New York: Farrar, 1936. First edition, 8vo., cover slightly soiled, very good, presentation by author to art critic and author Thomas Craven.   Second Life Books, Inc.   196A - 255   2016 $65

Carmichael, Harry *Suicide Clause.* London: Collins Crime, 1966. Dust jacket.   I. D. Edrich   Crime - 2016   £30

Carmichael, Waverley Turner *From the Heart of a Folk: a Book of Songs.* Boston: Cornhill Com, 1918. First edition, octavo, quarter cloth gilt and paper covered boards, few spots of foxing, spine gilt faded, overall very good or better, scarce.   Between the Covers Rare Books   202 - 16   2016 $550

Carnarvon, Lord *Portugal and Gallicia with a review of the Social and Political State of the Basques Provinces and a few remarks on recent Events in Spain.* London: John Murray, 1837. First edition, 8vo., 2 volumes, contemporary black half calf, raised bands, very good set.   J. & S. L. Bonham Antiquarian Booksellers   Europe 2016 - 8396   2016   £320

Caron, Francois *A True Description of the Mighty Kingdoms of Japan and Siam.* printed for Robert Boutler, 1671. Second edition in English, large folding engraved map (tears at either end on one fold, no loss and two emanating from inner margin), little discoloration around edges, particularly from turn-ins, some dust soiling among prelims, small 8vo., contemporary speckled calf, fleurons in blind at corners, rebacked, slightly worn at extremities, calf backed folding box, the Macclesfield copy.   Blackwell's Rare Books   B184 - 19   2016   £6500

Carove, F. W. *The Story Without an End.* New York: Scribner Welford, 1868. First American edition printed in England by Leighton Brothers, 4to., green cloth, beveled edges, gilt pictorial cover, all edges gilt, few small insignificant spots on cover, last page of text has margin cut on top and side, lacks one plain paper guard and some other guards slightly frayed, few margin mends in reality, beautiful very good+ copy, 15 magnificent chromolithographed plates plus several engravings in text.   Aleph-bet Books, Inc.   112 - 69   2016 $750

Carpenter, Alejo *The War of Time.* London: Victor Gollancz, 1970. First UK edition, head of spine and one corner slightly bumped, very good in like dust jacket (slightly dusty), presentation copy by translator, Frances Partridge to Bloomsbury artist Eardley Knollys.   Peter Ellis   112 - 63   2016   £200

Carpenter, J. E. *The Study of Theology and the Service of man...* Manchester: H. Rawson & Co., 1887. Original grey printed wrappers, inscription.   Jarndyce Antiquarian Books   CCXV - 584   2016   £20

Carr, Camillus *A Cavalryman in Indian Country.* Ashland: Lewis Osborne, 1974. One of 600 copies, portrait, illustrations, endpaper maps, cloth backed blue boards, printed paper spine label, very fine in plain white dust jacket and publisher's mailing box.   Argonaut Book Shop   Biography 2015 - 7390   2016 $60

Carr, J. L. *The Harpole Report.* London: Secker & Warburg, 1972. First edition, octavo, very good in like dust jacket, nicked, rubbed and creased at edges, presentation from author to Mrs. Waddock and staff of Kenyngton Manor First School.   Peter Ellis   112 - 64   2016   £250

Carr, J. L. *A Month in the Country.* Cornucopia Press, 1990. One of 300 numbered copies signed by author and Ronald Blythe, titlepage printed in black and red, royal 8vo., original mid green cloth, printed backstrip and front cover labels, top edge gilt, glassine jacket, new.   Blackwell's Rare Books   B184 - 124   2016   £200

Carr, John Dickson *The Life of Sir Arthur Conan Doyle.* New York: Harper Bros., 1949. First edition, fine in price clipped dust jacket with light wear to spine ends, corners and extremities.   Buckingham Books   2015 - 39213   2016 $475

Carr, John Dickson *The Men Who Explained Miracles - Six Short Stories and a Novelette.* London: Hamish Hamilton, 1964. First edition, octavo, cover edges bruised and faded, very good in like dust jacket nicked and rubbed at edges.   Peter Ellis   112 - 65   2016   £35

Carr, John Dickson *Nine and Death Makes Ten.* New York: William Morrow & Co., 1940. First edition, octavo, original light blue cloth, spine stamped in yellow, previous owner's stamp, some age darkening to endpapers, very good to nearly fine copy in very good to nearly fine dust jacket with some rubbing to corner tips and spine ends, some tiny chips to spine ends.   John W. Knott, Jr./L.W. Currey, Inc.   Fall-Winter 2015 - 1650   2016 $450

Carr, John Dickson *Scandal at High Chimneys - a Victorian melodrama.* London: Hamish Hamilton, 1959. First edition, octavo, fine in very good, slightly marked, pictorial dust jacket.   Peter Ellis   112 - 66   2016   £55

Carriat-Roland, Gabriel *Moroccan Moods. Twelve Gouache Paintings... Reproduced by Hand.* Casablanca: Laski Bros. for Art Editions Albert Monnet, Dec. 15th, 1958. First edition in English, one of 300 copies printed, large folio, original illustrated wrappers in board wrappers, spine lettered red, within original slipcase, 12 color silkscreen plates, slipcase little worn, few repairs, otherwise fine. Sotheran's Travel and Exploration - 310   2016   £898

Carrigan, Valerie *Messenger.* North Adams: Messenger Press, 2004. Number 26 of 40 copies signed and numbered by book artist Valerie Carrigan, with five loose bird images, each in paper folder with letterpress text on front cover, images began as monotypes and translated to offset lithography, printed on Arches Hot Press, text set in Tiepolo and printed from polymer plates on Mohawk Satin cover, housed in grey silk covered slipcase with bird image inset on top, fine. The Kelmscott Bookshop   13 - 40   2016 $675

Carroll, H. Bailey *Three New Mexico Chronicles.* Albuquerque: Quivira Society, 1942. First edition thus, illustrated with facsimiles, 2 folding maps, small 4to., quarter cloth over paper covered boards, gilt titles, Society medallion, spine bit darkened, else near fine, mostly unopened (uncut).   Kaaterskill Books   21 - 14   2016 $200

Carruth, Hayden *Aura.* West Burke: Janus Press, 1977. First edition, limited to only 50 copies, this copy press lettered especially 'for Michael Boylen' and inscribed by Claire Van Vliet in pencil for Bruce Hubbard, tall folio, printed handmade paper folder, enclosed in publisher's linen folding box with printed paper label on spine, very fine, rare.   James S. Jaffe Rare Books   Occasional List: Winter 2016 - 84   2016 $4500

Carson, Rachel *The Edge of the Sea.* Boston: Houghton Mifflin, 1955. First edition, green cloth, stamped in black, very fine with pictorial dust jacket.   Argonaut Book Shop   Natural History 2015 - 7070   2016 $350

Carson, Rachel *Parker River: a National Wildlife Bridge.* Washington: Fish and Wildlife Service, 1947. Issued as Conservation in Action No. 2, 14 page illustrated booklet written by Carson, uncommon, light creasing and spotting to cover, near fine in stapled wrappers.   Ken Lopez Bookseller   166 - 17   2016 $350

Carson, Rachel *Rivers of Death.* Boston: Houghton Mifflin, 1962. Offprint from Silent Spring printed Chapter 9 pages 192-152 plus footnote, corner crease on one inner page, else fine in stapled wrappers, scarce.   Ken Lopez Bookseller   166 - 18   2016 $375

Carson, Rachel *The Sea Around Us.* New York: Oxford, 1951. First edition, correct first state of the first printing, in correct dust jacket, less than 100 sent out for review.   Beasley Books   2015 - 2016 $2000

Carter, H. J. *Gulliver in the Bush: Wanderings of an Australian Entomologist.* Sydney: Angus and Robertson, 1933. Octavo, photos, bookplate, publisher's cloth, few spots, otherwise good.   Andrew Isles Natural History Books   55 - 5610   2016 $50

Carter, J. C. *Familiar Chinese Faces.* Shanghai: McTavish, circa, 1910. Very rare sole edition, 4to., original cord bound illustrated wrappers, title and 24 photo images mounted on 18 sheets with printed captions and ornamental framework, wrappers bit frayed, rubbed and spotted, internally clean and fresh.   Sotheran's   Travel and Exploration - 97   2016   £1250

Carter, Jimmy *Living Faith.* New York: Times Books, Random House, 1996. First edition, signed by author, blue green boards, gilt, very fine and bright copy with pictorial dust jacket.   Argonaut Book Shop   Biography 2015 - 7071   2016 $250

Carter, Jimmy *Turning Point; A Candidate, A State, and A Nation Come of Age.* New York: Times Books, 1992. Fine copy in about very near fine dust jacket that has some very minor wear, signed by the former President.   Jeff Hirsch Books   Holiday List 2015 - 30   2016 $85

Carter, John *Vindiciae Decimarum. Of Tithes, a Pleas for the Jus Divinum.* London: T. Cotes, 1640. First edition, 4to., title printed in red and black, occasional very minor stains, well bound in old style quarter calf over marbled boards, spine lettered in gilt, very good, crisp copy, scarce. John Drury Rare Books   2015 - 24376   2016 $350

Carter, John   1905-1975 *An Enquiry into the Nature of Certain Nineteenth Century Pamphlets.* London: Constable & Co., 1934. First edition, 8vo., cloth, top edge gilt, dust jacket, this copy inscribed by Carter and Graham Pollard, with bookplate of noted collector Abel Berland, jacket rubbed along spine and hinges along with some fading to spine, rather well preserved.   Oak Knoll Books   310 - 204   2016 $550

Carter, John   1905-1975 *An Enquiry into the Nature of Certain Nineteenth Century Pamphlets.* London: and Berkeley: Scolar Press, 1983. two pamphlets are an original copy of 'Two Poems" by Brownings and "A Note on Two Poems" by Barker, the Note printed in an edition of 80 copies, this number 64, Inquiry is second edition, the other volume is first edition, 3 volumes, volumes I and II bound in full black morocco with gilt titles to spines, third volume is a portfolio that holds two pamphlets and is bound in quarter black moroco with grey paper boards and gilt title to spine, all volumes housed in black cloth slipcase, fine.   The Kelmscott Bookshop   13 - 26   2016 $900

Carter, John   1905-1975 *Printing and the Mind of Man.* Munich: Pressler, 1983. Second edition, folio, original cloth, dust jacket and slip-in case, very good.   Blackwell's Rare Books   B184 - 22   2016   £150

Carter, John 1905-1975 *Working Papers for a Second Edition of an enquiry into the nature of Certain Nineteenth Century Pamphlets.* Oxford: privately printed, 1967. 1969. 1970. First editions of all parts, limited to 140, 200 and 400 copies respectively, volumes, 2, 3 and 4 (of 4), small 8vo., stiff paper wrappers, this set once belonged to Wise bibliographer William Todd, corner of cover loosely inserted photocopy of a review of this title written by Todd and has pencil notes, loosely inserted photocopy of this title, Todd pencil notes throughout.   Oak Knoll Books   310 - 221   2016 $495

Cartier-Bresson, Henry *The Decisive Moment.* 1952. First edition, American issue, publisher's pictorial white boards designed by Herni Matisse, illustrated with abstract cut-out shapes in black, blue and green, lettered in black, publisher's 'Captions' booklet laid in, near fine with light toning and minor wear to spine, few faint spots to otherwise fresh boards, bright and clean interior, very attractive.   B & B Rare Books, Ltd.   2016 - HCAB001   2016 $600

Cartier, Jacques *Voyage de Jaques Cartier au Canada en 1534... with Documents Inedits sur Jaques Cartier et le Canada.* Paris: Librairie Tross, 1865. 2 folding maps, original printed wrappers, light soil and browning to wrappers, internally bright and completely unopened.   Dumont Maps and Books   133 - 45   2016 $75

Cartwright, William *Comedies, Tragi-Comedies with other Poems.* London: for Humphrey Moseley, 1651. First edition, 8vo., engraved portrait, 5 section titles with duplicate leaves U1-3 as usual, blank I4 present, b2 foxed and untrimmed to preserved shoulder notes, modern calf, very skillfully executed in 17th century style, title and dedication leaf and few running heads slightly cropped by binder's knife, and one note to binder cropped, very nice, Arthur Spingarn copy, rebound with his bookplate and collation notes laid in.   Joseph J. Felcone, Inc.   Books from Five Centuries: a Miscellany - 35   2016 $2400

Carvajal, Bernardinus *Sermo in Commemoratione Victoriae Bacensis.* Rome: Stephan Plannk, circa, 1493. Only edition, 4to., lacks final blank, 28 lines, roman letter, 19th century marbled wrappers.   Maggs Bros. Ltd.   1474 - 73   2016   £3500

Carver, Raymond *Fires: Essays Poems Stories.* New York: Vintage, 1984. First Vintage edition, 12mo., author's presentation to publisher, Scott Walker, paper wrappers, cover little soiled, else very good, tight, inscribed by author.   Second Life Books, Inc.   196A - 257   2016 $250

Carver, Raymond *My Father's Life.* Derry: and Ridgewood: Babcock & Koontz, 1986. Limited to 200 numbered copies, signed by author, frontispiece wood engraving by Gaylord Schanilec, sewn into Fabriano Roma wrappers.   Oak Knoll Books   310 - 90   2016 $185

Cary, John *Cary's Survey of the High Roads from London to Hampton Court, Bagshot, Oakingham, Binsfield, Windsor (etc).* London: printed for J. Cary..., 1790. First edition, 4to., engraved throughout, engraved title, engraved 'Explanation... Advertisement', hand colored folding 'General Map' and 'General Plan for explaining the different trusts' and 80 hand colored engraved road maps on 40 leaves, some minor offset foxing, modern half calf over marbled boards, in contemporary style, spine with gilt lettered red label.   Marlborough Rare Books   List 56 - 10   2016   £950

Cary, Joyce *The Moonlight.* London: Michael Joseph, 1946. First edition, 8vo., signed presentation from author for Elsie Carlisle, singer, very good+ in chipped, very good-dust jacket.   Any Amount of Books   2015 - A68594   2016   £150

Cary, M. *The Ancient Explorers.* London: Methuen & Co., 1929. First edition, 8vo., maps, cloth, gilt lettered, spine browned, small mark to lower board, bumping and wear to corners and end caps, edges dusted, light toning to free endpapers, shelfwear, very good, no dust jacket, small white sticker to spine, gilt plate to Bedford College, ownership inscription of Gillian A. Wilkinson.   Unsworths Antiquarian Booksellers Ltd.   E05 - 24   2016   £40

Cary, Thomas G. *Letter to a Lady in France on the Supposed Failure of a National Blank, the Supposed Delinquency of the National Government...* Boston: Benjamin H. Greene, 1844. Second edition, sewn as issued in original pale blue printed wrappers, slight wear to head and tail of spine, bookplate of William Gylde Wilkins, very good.   Jarndyce Antiquarian Booksellers   CCXVIII - 327   2016   £150

Casanova De Seingalt, Girolamo 1725-1798 *The Memoirs.* London: Casanova Society, 1922. One of 1000 copies, 12 volumes bound in 6, 254 x 203mm., attractive later burgundy half morocco over red linen boards by Bayntun (stamp signed), raised bands flanked by gilt rules, spine panels with gilt chandelier-like centerpiece, each spine with two olive brown morocco labels, top edges gilt, 12 frontispieces, large foldout map, foldout facsimile, engraving, two portraits of Casanova, portrait of Manon Baletti, engravings, corners bit worn, joints of early volumes little rubbed (two joints cracked and boards consequently with little wobble), one volume with small loss of leather at bottom of spine, still quite attractive set, bindings entirely sound and withoout any serious wear, wide margined text, virtually unused condition.   Phillip J. Pirages   67 - 87   2016 $750

Casement, Dan Dillon *The Abbreviated Autobiography of a Joyous Pagan.* privately printed, 1944. First edition, original red wrappers, frontispiece, plates, portraits, inscribed by author for family friend, from the library of Clint and Dot Josey with their inked signature and their penciled notation at top of last page, also pencilled notation of collector Larry Myers on last page below Josey notation, laid in is newspaper article dated June 10 1952 advising of Casement's recognition of the Kiwanis Club, a copy of the guest editorial and newspaper clipping advising of Casement's death March 7, 1953, also laid in 1952 Christmas card that pictures Casement, rare, lightly rubbed along spine and covers, else very good, housed in original four-point cloth case with titles stamped in silver on spine. Buckingham Books   2015 - 32934   2016 $4500

Casey, John Albert *Colorless Odorless Tasteless.* Columbia: Sutton Hoo Press, 1993. Limited to 136 copies, 36 signed by author, this copy thus, 4to., cloth, label with title on spine, top edge cut, other edges uncut.   Oak Knoll Books   310 - 153   2016 $125

Caspari, Gertrude *Caspari Fibel: ain Lesenbuch mit Vielen Buntan Bildern fur Die Esrste Schulzeit.* Stuttgart: Volkshurst Rich. Keutel, n.d. circa, 1910. 8vo., pictorical cloth, slight cover soil, otherwise very good+, illustrations in bright colors by Caspari.   Aleph-bet Books, Inc.   111 - 192   2016 $350

Cassay, Neal *O Fatal Practicality!* Louisville: Contre Coup Press, 2014. First edition, limited to 19 copies printed and bound at Campbell-Logan Bindery, Louisville, quarto, tipped-in photo frontispiece and additional tipped in photos of Cassady and Kerouac, quarter gray silk and decorated paper over boards with printed paper spine label, fine. Between the Covers Rare Books   204 - 24   2016 $450

Cassius Dio *E Dione Excerptae Historiae ab Ioanne Xiphilino.* Geneva: Excudebat Henricus Stephanus, 1592. Second Estienne edition of Xiphilnus, folio, Greek and Latin text, printer's device to titlepage, woodcut initials and headpieces, wide margins, occasional light foxing, few wax spots, small closed tear to lower margin pages 263-4, small paper flaw to lower margin pages 301-2, 17th century dark brown calf neatly rebacked with red morocco gilt label, later armorial gilt centrepiece edges, sprinkled red, endcaps and joints weakening, boards bit scuffed with holes for ties (now lost), at fore-edges, corners fraying, endpapers renewed and title finger smudged, very good.   Unsworths Antiquarian Booksellers Ltd.   E04 - 18   2016   £600

Casteel, J. W. *Oklahoma State Penitentiary and Prisons Modern and Medieval.* News Capital Print, n.d. circa, 1915. First edition, 21cm., pictorial wrappers, frontispiece, illustrations, portraits, moderate wear to spine ends, light old waterstains in front and rear covers, slight wear to fore edges of covers, else good, internally clean, rare. Buckingham Books   2015 - 35316   2016 $3750

Castelli, Carlo *L'Arte di Filare la Seta a Freddo ossia senza Fuoco le Bacine delle Fillatrici...* Venice: Domenico Fracasso, 1795. 8vo, 2 folding charts, original stiff paper wrappers, very fine, fresh.   Joseph J. Felcone, Inc.   Books from Five Centuries: a Miscellany - 127   2016 $450

Castello, Alberto De *Sacerdotale Iuxta s Romane Ecclesie & Aliarum Ecclesiarum ex Apostolice Bibliothece...* Venice: heirs of Peiro Ravani and Partners, 1554. 4to., 19th century English blue morocco, gilt panel on covers, printed in red and black throughout with plain chant notation (black on red), numerous woodcuts and woodcut initials, Ravani device on verso of last leaf, Jesuits College at Siena 'di San Vigilio', Law Society bookplate.   Maggs Bros. Ltd. 1474 - 21   2016   £1800

Castle, Irene *My Husband.* London: John Lane, 1919. First UK edition, spine ornamented and lettered gilt, photogravure portrait in sepia, plates after photos, few illustrations in text, only light rubbing to extremities, offsetting from endpapers, one prelim leaf carelessly opened, otherwise good, blindstamped "Review Copy with John Lane's Compliments". Sotheran's   Travel and Exploration - 455   2016   £78

Caswall, Edward *A New Art Teaching How to be Plucked Being a Treatise after the Fashion of Aristotle...* Oxford: J. Vincent, 1835. Second edition, 12mo., contemporary full red calf, limp boards, slightly rubbed and dulled, but nice, ownership Edward W. Bastard 1877.   Jarndyce Antiquarian Books   CCXV - 585   2016   £65

Caswall, Edward *A New Art Teaching How to be Plucked Being a Treatise after the Fashion of Aristotle...* Oxford: Henry Slater, Herald Office, 1836-1837. Third edition, 12mo., original dark green cloth, lettered in gilt, little worn, later signature.   Jarndyce Antiquarian Books   CCXV - 586   2016   £60

Caswall, Edward *Sketches of Young Ladies...* London: Chapman & Hall, 1837. Fourth edition, 6 illustrations by Phiz, with frontispiece and plates, original green printed boards, neatly rebacked, slightly darkened but good plus copy, signature on leading endpaper dated 1854. Jarndyce Antiquarian Booksellers   CCXVIII - 171   2016 £75

Caswall, Edward *Sketches of Young Ladies...* London: Chapman & Hall, 1837. Fifth edition, frontispiece and plates by Phiz, original green printed boards, spine strip missing, little dulled and rubbed, good, sound copy, Kathleen Tillotson's copy.   Jarndyce Antiquarian Booksellers   CCXVIII - 172   2016   £85

Caswall, Edward *Sketches of Young Ladies...* London: Chapman & Hall, 1838. Seventh edition, frontispiece and plates by Phiz, small hole at head of titlepage where name carelessly erased, original purple patterned cloth, spine faded at brown, slightly rubbed, nice.   Jarndyce Antiquarian Booksellers   CCXVIII - 173   2016   £120

Caswall, Edward *The Young Ladies & Gentlemen's Hymeneal Instructor....* Boston: pub. at 66 Cornhill, 1847. 32mo., sewn as issued in original light brown printed paper wrappers, additional blue paper wrappers sewn in, little darkened, but very good.   Jarndyce Antiquarian Books   CCXV - 99   2016   £450

Cather, Willa Sibert   1873-1947 *December Might.* New York: Alfred A. Knopf, 1933. First edition in this format, ink designs by Harold von Schmidt, set by hand and printed on all rag paper by Pynson Printers, thin octavo, original boards, title and rule blind stamped on front cover, previous owner's ink inscription on blank jacket flap, very fine in very elusive decorated dust jacket (chipped on lower spine, less so to upper spine and lower corners).   Argonaut Book Shop   Literature 2015 - 1218   2016 $125

Cather, Willa Sibert   1873-1947 *Lucy Gayheart.* New York: Knopf, 1935. First edition, one of 749 large paper copies, signed by author, 8vo., blue cloth, spine and part of cover faded, uncut, very nice.   Second Life Books, Inc.   196A - 260   2016 $350

Cather, Willa Sibert   1873-1947 *The Novels and Stories.* Boston: Houghton Mifflin, 1937-1941. No. 322 of 970 copies of the autograph edition, volume I signed by author, 232 x 156mm., 13 volumes, publisher's original cream colored linen over gray-blue linen boards, covers with author's ciphers in gilt, black spine label, top edges gilt, other edges untrimmed and unopened in uncommon original oversized dust jackets, 12 frontispieces with tissue guards (volume XIII without frontispiece, as issued), faint browning to spines of few of the dust jackets (this browning extending onto rear panel of one jacket), two jackets with some tears and wrinkling along the bottom foldover flaps, minor rumpling and tears to jacket edges elsewhere, still exceptionally fine, unread volumes, perfectly preserved, jackets with basically minor defects.   Phillip J. Pirages   67 - 88   2016 $600

Cather, Willa Sibert   1873-1947 *The Professor's House.* New York: Knopf, 1925. First edition, limited edition, one of 40 copies on Imperial Japon vellum, signed by author, 8vo., fine, large paper copy, top edge gilt, small owner's bookplate on endpaper, housed in custom clamshell case.   Second Life Books, Inc.   196A - 259   2016 $3000

Catholic Church. Liturgy & Ritual *Canon Missae cum Praefationibus & Aliis non Nullius quae in ea Fere Communiter Dicuntur.* Venice: Ciera, 1630. Large title vignette of Last Supper and full page engraving of the Crucifixion, both signed "Johan, Faber / fecit in Venetia", folio, contemporary Italian brown morocco over paste boards, covers richly gilt in fanfare style incorporating at centre three bees and a sunburst tool repeatedly stamped in inner panel and frame, both familiar emblems of the Barberini family (joints and corners rubbed, small burn hole to upper edge of lower cover), very finely gilt tooled 17th century Italian binding for a member of the Barberini dynasty, decorated with their familiar emblems of 3 bees and sunburst, signs of use throughout but exquisite binding.   Maggs Bros. Ltd.   1474 - 19   2016   £3500

Catholic Church. Liturgy & Ritual *Missale ad Consuetudinem Ecclesie Romanae...* Paris: in alma Parisiorum Academia Impensis Thielmanni Kerver 23 March, 1506. 8vo., Kerver's fine device on titlepage, full page woodcut of Crucifixion, large crible initial of Crucifixion, crible initials, music on four-line staves, printed in red and black, decorative line fillers in red and black, 8vo., 19th century purple brown morocco richly gilt in 16th century style by J. Wright, binder, gauffered edges, headcaps rubbed, bookseller's note stating this was from the library of A. J. Beresford Hope (1820-1887), bookplate and inscription of Herbert Watney (1843-1932).   Maggs Bros. Ltd.   1474 - 53   2016   £4500

Catholic Church. Liturgy & Ritual *Les Tres Riches Heures Du Duc De Berry.* Lucerne: Faksimile Verlag Luzern, 1984. Facsimile, no. 755 of 950 copies, 302 x 216mm., 2 volumes, facsimile plus commentary volume, publisher's replica red morocco binding, covers with gilt ruled border and cresting floral frame, coat of arms with coronet at center, raised bands, spine gilt in compartments with floral spray centerpiece and leafy frond cornerpieces, green silk pastedowns, all edges gilt, commentary volume in red morocco backed green silk, both housed in acrylic case with slideout panel, numerous illuminated initials, many with marginal extensions, 65 small miniatures (measuring approximately 80 x 50mm.), and 66 full page miniatures, nearly mint.   Phillip J. Pirages   67 - 133   2016 $8500

Catleen, Ellen *Peking Studies.* Shanghai: Kelly & Walsh, 1934. First edition, original cloth, photographic illustration mounted to upper cover and title banner to fore-edge of upper cover, numerous illustrations in photogravure, few with additional color printing, color printed city map, thumbnail sketches by Schiff, little spotting to covers, previous owner's inscription, minimal spotting, very good.   Sotheran's   Travel and Exploration - 98   2016   £998

Catlin, George 1796-1872 *O'Kee-Pa: a Religious Ceremony: and Other Customs of the Mandans.* London: Trubner and Co., 1867. First edition, with rare 'Folium Servatum' bound in at rear', presentation copy inscribed by Nicholas Trubner to Thomas Scott, 13 chromolithographed plates, publisher's purple cloth, gilt, all edges gilt, binding lightly soiled and faded, extremities lightly worn, spine ends more so, occasional minor foxing, very good, fragile book difficult to find in fine condition.   Joseph J. Felcone, Inc. Books from Five Centuries: a Miscellany - 36   2016 $20,000

Cats, Jacob *Moral Emblems with Aphorisms, Adages and Proverbs of all Ages and Nations.* London: Longman, Green, Longman and Roberts, 1860. First edition with these illustrations, 276 x 197mm., fine contemporary green straight grain morocco, handsomely gilt, covers framed by mulitple rues and wide, orante dentelle, whole enclosing detailed Greek urn centerpiece, raised bands, spine densely gilt in compartment featuring many small botanical and floral tools, gilt turn-ins, all edges gilt, frontispiece, 60 large tondo emblems and 60 tailpieces, ink presentation 'Wilhemina Colquhoun Jones/1863/ with Charlotte Harriet Jones/ love and best wishes', spine darkened to olive brown (as almost always with green morocco), just faintest hint of wear to joints, occasional minor foxing or stains, extremely attractive, very decorative contemporary binding bright and scarcely worn, text very fresh and showing no signs of use. Phillip J. Pirages   67 - 236   2016 $750

Cats, Jacob *Ouderdom, Buyten-Leven, en hof-gedachten op Sorgh-Vliet.* Amsterdam: Jn Jacobsz Schipper, 1655-1656. First edition, engraved title, added to part 1, two folding plates, signed by Cornelis van Dalen after Adriaen van de Venne, full page plate made up of six vignettes, full page plate and 69 half page engravings, mostly by Van de Venne, one signed Crispijn van der Passe, this copy unfortunately lacks engraved title to part 3, five parts in one volume, 4to., early 18th century Dutch gilt panelled calf over paste boards, spine richly gilt in compartments, headcaps and joints rubbed, unidentified circular monogrammed stamp on titlepage. Maggs Bros. Ltd.   1474 - 22   2016   £7500

Catt, Carrie Chapman *Woman Suffrage and Politics.* New York: Scribner's, 1923. First edition, 8vo., pieces of dust jacket laid in, author's signature on flyleaf, very good, laid in is ribbon from "American Youth Party" Woman Suffrage Day July 7 19(07), torn at extremities but not affecting any text. Second Life Books, Inc.   196A - 261   2016 $750

Catullus, C. Valerius *The Carmina of...* London: printed for the translators, 1894. Limited to 1000 copies, printed on fine hand made paper, half vellum backed boards, corners worn and showing, spine darkened and rubbed, minor foxing to first and last few pages, previous owner bookplate on inner cover, very good. Argonaut Book Shop   Literature 2015 - 4682   2016 $275

Catullus, C. Valerius *The Carmina of Caius Valerius Catullus.* printed for the Translators, 1894. First edition, 145/1000 copies of an edition of 1054, engraved frontispiece, publisher's notice tipped to front endpaper, tissue guard foxed and slightly offset onto titlepage, 8vo., original quarter vellum, spine lettered gilt, corners and fore edges bit worn, endpapers browned, very good. Blackwell's Rare Books   Greek & Latin Classics VII - 11   2016   £150

Catullus, C. Valerius *Catullus, Tibullus, Propertius.* Lutetiae: i.e. Paris: Apud Mamertum Patissonium in Officina Rob. Stephani, 1577. First Scaliger edition, final blank discarded, toned and foxed, 8vo., early 19th century French green roan, boards bordered with gilt roll, spine divided by gilt leaf roll, red morocco lettering piece, somewhat rubbed, very good. Blackwell's Rare Books   Greek & Latin Classics VII - 12   2016   £800

Catullus, C. Valerius *Catullus, Tibullus & Propertius. Opera.* Birmingham: Typis Johannis Baskerville, 1772. Some light spotting, 4to., slightly later straight grained red morocco, boards bordered with double gilt fillet, spine with raised bands between gilt fillets, second compartment gilt lettered direct, marbled endpapers, edges gilt, bookplate removed from front pastedown, spine bit rubbed and darkened, slight wear to corners, good. Blackwell's Rare Books   Greek & Latin Classics VII - 13   2016   £350

Caudle, M. *Everybody's Book of Correct Conduct.* London: W. R. Russell & Co., 1893. Ads on endpapers, original blue printed cloth boards, very good. Jarndyce Antiquarian Books   CCXV - 101   2016   £30

Caudle, M. *Everybody's Book of Correct Conduct.* London: Saxon & Co., 1893. First edition, 16mo., ads on endpapers, original brown pictorial boards, brown cloth spine, rubbed. Jarndyce Antiquarian Books   CCXV - 100 2016   £40

Caudle, M. *Everybody's Book of Correct Conduct.* London: Saxon & Co., circa, 1895. Second edition, 35th thousand, ads on endpapers, original red sheep, worm damage to front board, little rubbed and dulled, hinges slight cracking sound. Jarndyce Antiquarian Books   CCXV - 102 2016   £20

Caulfield, James *Portraits, Memoirs and Characters of Remarkable Persons from the Revolution in 1688 to the End of the Reign of George II.* London: pub. by H. R. Young and T. H. Whitely, 1819-1820. 318 x 254mm., 4 volumes, attractive modern retrospective black half morocco over green marbled boards, flat spines divided into panels with central gilt urns, edges untrimmed, partly unopened, with 155 fine engraved portrait plates, large paper copy, second volume slightly cocked, variable offsetting from virtually all pages, perhaps a third of leaves in volume I faintly browned and somewhat foxed, about half the plates in volume II with small, gray dampstain at lower ouer corner, occasional yellowing and foxing elsewhere, undeniable condition issues, but still satisfactory set, most of the text and plates fresh and clean, bindings with virtually no wear and margins immense.   Phillip J. Pirages   67 - 89   2016 $850

Cave, Nick *King Ink.* London: Black Spring Press, 1988. First edition, octavo, signed and dated 22-06-2015 by author, head and tail of spine bumped, very good in like dust jacket nicked and creased at edges.   Peter Ellis   112 - 68   2016   £225

Cave, Roderick *Private Press Books 1959 to 1933.* Pinner: Private Library Association, 1960-1993. Various limitations ranging from 750 to 1200 copies, 8vo., stiff paper wrappers, 33 volumes.   Oak Knoll Books   310 - 89   2016 $650

Cavendish, George *The Life of Thomas Wolsey, Cardinall Archbishop of York.* London: sold by Reeves & Turner (Hammersmith), 1893. One of 250 paper copies of an edition of 256, octavo, woodcut border to page 1 and numerous initials, full limp vellum with green silk ties, yapp edges, spine lettered gilt, edges uncut, previous owner Crosby Gaige bookplate, vellum slightly warped, and little discoloration, overall very good.   Heritage Book Shop   Holiday 2015 - 63   2016 $2500

Caventou, Joseph Bienaime *Nouvelle Nomenclature Chimique d'Apres la Classification Adoptee par M. Thenard...* Paris: Chez Crochard and Chez Gabon, 1816. First edition, 8vo., half title, vignette, large folding table, index, 1 leaf of errata, quarter calf, paste paper over boards, parchment corners, red leather spine label, ornately gilt spine, rubbed, ownership rubberstamp of Guitet, Pharmacien, very good.   Jeff Weber Rare Books   183 - 11   2016 $750

Cayley, Neville W. *Australian Finches in Bush and Aviary.* Sydney: Angus and Robertson, 1932. Octavo, color plates by author, publisher's cloth, very good.   Andrew Isles Natural History Books   55 - 32256   2016 $150

Cayley, Neville W. *Feathered Friends: a Gould League Annual.* Sydney: Angus and Robertson, 1935. Octavo, color plates by Cayley, library pocket, softcover.   Andrew Isles Natural History Books   55 - 5625   2016 $50

Cayton, Horace *Long Old Road: an Autobiography.* New York: Trident, 1965. First edition, 8vo., author's presentation, brown cloth, edges somewhat spotted and soiled, otherwise very good in chipped and browned dust jacket, very good+.   Second Life Books, Inc.   196A - 265   2016 $125

Cazabon, M. J. *Views of Trinidad from Drawings by J. Cazabon.* Madrid: Julio Soto, 1984. Reprint, oblong 4to., original blue cloth and marbled paper covered boards lettered gilt on spine and cover, 18 plates, neat gift inscription on endpaper, very good.   Any Amount of Books   2015 - A90986   2016   £250

Cebes *Tabula.* Impensis Authoris, 1720. First and last pages slightly dusty, little faint toning, embossmet of Earls of Macclesfield to titlepage, one name in preface corrected in early ink, 8vo., slightly later sprinkled calf, boards bordered with decorative blind roll within double gilt fillet, spine divided by raised bands, red morocco lettering piece, other compartments with gilt acorn tools in quarters within gilt dentelles borders, small paper shelfmark labels at head and foot, Macclesfield bookplate of South Library Shirburn Castle, joints little rubbed, very good.   Blackwell's Rare Books   B186 - 38   2016   £600

Cecil, Henry *The Asking Price.* London: Michael Joseph, 1966. First edition, fine in dust jacket.   Mordida Books 2015 - 00398   2016 $60

Celine, Louis Ferdinand *Journey to the End of the Night.* Boston: Little Brown and Co., 1934. First US edition, octavo, rear blanks tanned, presumably from newspaper cutting, otherwise fine in very good dust jacket with the red bit faded on spine, some shallow chipping to top edge of rear panel.   Peter Ellis   112 - 69   2016   £775

Cellini, Benvenuto *Vita Di Benvenuto Cellini...* Milan: Dalla Societa Tipografica de Classici Italiani, 1811. First edition, 3 volumes, 8vo., rebound in pleasant sky blue buckram lettered gilt on spine, de-accessioned from Birkbeck University library with couple of stamps in each volume, otherwise very good+ with clean text.   Any Amount of Books 2015 - A67973   2016   £150

Cendrars, Blaise *Panama or the Adventures of My seven Uncles.* New York: Harper, 1931. First edition, one of 300 copies printed on Utopian laid paper, numbered and signed by author and translator, John Dos Passos, small 4to., set in Linotype Bodoni and printed from original types, illustrations reproduced by photogelatine proces by four color separation, bound in plain paper wrappers, illustrated paper dust jacket, some toning to cover, lacks top half inch of spine with some wear at bottom, very good.   Second Life Books, Inc.   196A - 267   2016 $450

Cendrars, Blaise *Trans-Siberian Prosody and Little Jeanne from France.* Llandogo: Old Stile Press, 2015. 34/150 copies (from an edition of 160), signed by translator and artist, Natalie D'Arbeloff, text printed in a variety of colours on Canaletto Liscio paper, square 4to., original quarter gold cloth, red and blue boards stamped in silver with lettering by D'Arbeloff, backstrip lettered in black, brown cloth slipcase with portrait of author stamped in black, fine. Blackwell's Rare Books   B186 - 319   2016   £295

Centlivre, Susannah *The Gamester: a Comedy.* London: printed for William Turner and William Davis, 1705. First edition, 4to., without half title, slightly stained, tears from margin from sig. K3 not affecting text, disbound. Jarndyce Antiquarian Booksellers   CCXVI - 458   2016   £180

Centlivre, Susannah *The Works of the Celebrated...* London: printed for J. Knapton, C. Hitch, and L. Hawes, et al, 1761. 1760. First collected edition, 3 volumes, duodecimo, later white three quarter vellum, marbled paper sides, maroon morocco labels, gilt lettering, frontispiece, edges little rubbed, minor waterstaining in lower margin of prelims of volume I, some slight foxing, very good.   The Brick Row Book Shop   Miscellany 69 - 21   2016 $950

Ceravolo, Joseph *Fits of Dawn.* New York: C Press, 1965. First edition, 4to., original illustrated wrappers, stapled as issued, wrappers lightly to moderately soiled, otherwise fine, scarce, presentation from author for Frank Lima and his wife.   James S. Jaffe Rare Books   Occasional List: Winter 2016 - 36   2016 $2250

Cerretti, Luigi *Modonese Notizie Biografiche e Letterrarie Con Prose e Versi Mancanti Nell' Edizioni Dell'autore.* Reggio: Torreggiani, 1833-1837. First edition, 5 volumes, large 8vo., contemporary quarter green gilt leather spine, marbled paper covered boards, all edges speckled blue, slight rubbing on boards, slight damage to top edge of spine on volume five, in all very well preserved set, loosely inserted commemorative book label which indicated this set came from reference library of H. P. Kraus.   Oak Knoll Books   310 - 235   2016 $850

Cerruti, Henry *Rambling in California: the Adventures of Henry Cerruti.* Berkeley: Friends of the Bancroft Library, University of California, 1954. First edition, one of 500 copies, frontispiece, parchment paper spine, light brown boards, fine.   Argonaut Book Shop   Private Press 2015 - 6284   2016 $45

Cervantes Saavedra, Miguel De   1547-1616 *A Collection of Select Novels....* Bristol: printed by S. Farley and sold by F. Wall, bookseller, on the Tolze, James Warriner, in Bath...., 1728. Rare provincial printing, 8vo., modern panelled calf, good, titlepage a little soiled, some browning, especially towards the end.   Blackwell's Rare Books   Marks of Genius - 12   2016   £1800

Cervantes Saavedra, Miguel De   1547-1616 *The Life and Exploits of the Ingenious Gentleman Don Quixote de la Mancha.* London: printed for J. and R. Tonson, 1749. Second edition, 2 volumes, engraved frontispiece, 23 engraved plates, 8vo., some light browning, blank upper corners volume I G5-6 torn away, contemporary calf, gilt ruled borders, expertly rebacked in matching style, raised and gilt banded spines, red morocco labels, armorial bookplate of John Hallifax, Esq., Kenilworth on inner front boards, 19th century bookplate of J. Blackwood Greenshields on front endpapers.   Jarndyce Antiquarian Booksellers   CCXVII - 66   2016   £1500

Cervantes Saavedra, Miguel De   1547-1616 *El Ingenioso Hidalgo Don Quixote de la Mancha.* Madrid: J. Ibarra, 1780. 4 volumes, 4to., additional engraved titles, map, plates and vignettes, contemporary Spanish binding of green marbled calf, covers further 'marbled' with inlaid octagonal panel of brown morocco set in gilt tooled border, spines gilt in compartments, red morocco labels, marbled endpapers, gilt edges, slight worn damage to boot of spine of volume I, head of spine of volume 4 slightly chipped, fine, armorial bookplate of Sarah Sophia Child (Villiers), Countess of Jersey (1785-1867) with old pressmarks of Osterley Park Library, bookplate of Jonathan and Phillida Gili (by Reynolds Stone), it is said about 1500 copies printed, borders of few plates foxed.   Maggs Bros. Ltd.   1474 - 23   2016   £12,500

Cervantes Saavedra, Miguel De   1547-1616 *The History of Don Quixote de la Mancha.* London: Constable and Co. Ltd., 1922. First edition illustrated by De Bosschere, 4to., original purple cloth with gilt vignette on upper cover, wonderful tinted plates, 9 colored plates and numerous illustrations adorning text, spine little rubbed, neat in inscription otherwise very good.   Sotheran's   Piccadilly Notes - Summer 2015 - 71   2016   £148

Cervantes Saavedra, Miguel De   1547-1616 *The First (and Second) Part of The History of the Valorous and Wittie Knight-Errant Don Quixote of the Mancha.* Chelsea: Ashendene Press, 1927-1928. One of 225 copies on paper (and 20 on vellum), 432 x 305mm., 2 volumes, fine original dark green morocco by W. H. Smith & Son (stamp signed inside rear covers), raised bands, gilt titling on spine, lovely woodcut initials and borders designed by Louise Powell, cut on wood by W. M. Quick and George H. Ford, superb copy, entirely fresh, clean and bright internally, and in unworn glittering bindings.   Phillip J. Pirages   67 - 10   2016 $15,000

Cervantes Saavedra, Miguel De   1547-1616 *The Adventures of Don Quixote.* Boston: Houghton Mifflin, 1928. First edition thus, illustrations by Herman Bacharach, medium sized 4to., illustrated endpapers, fine in very slightly chipped, edgeworn dust jacket, scarce.   Gene W. Baade, Books on the West   2015 - SHEL857   2016 $125

Cervantes Saavedra, Miguel De   1547-1616   *Don Quixote De La Mancha.*   London: Nonesuch Press, 1930. First press edition, limited to 1475 copies, 2 volumes, octavo, publisher's full morocco, 21 color plates, presentation from artist, E. McKnight Kauffer to Roger Fry, near fine.   Honey & Wax Booksellers   4 - 2   2016   £2200

Cervantes Saavedra, Miguel De   1547-1616   *Ocho Comedias y Ocho Entemeses Nuevos, Nunca Despresentados (Eight Comedies).*   Madrid: Por la Viudo de Alonso Marin a Costa de Juan de Villarroel, 1615. First edition, very rare edition, period style full vellum, raised bands, text browned, few mended marginal tears, owner ink inscription, evidence of bookplate, minor pencilled annotations on first and final blanks, handsome copy, excellent condition, housed in custom half morocco clamshell box, exceedingly rare first edition.   Heritage Book Shop   Holiday 2015 - 18   2016 $95,000

Cervantes, Enrique A.   *Loza Blanca y Azulejo de Puebla.*   Mexico: privately printed, 1939. Number 751 of a print run of 2000, 4to., 2 volumes, original wrappers, labels printed in blue and black on front covers, highly illustrated with cut out and mounted tinted, black and white and color printed illustrations after photos, minimal rubbing to edges, very good set in original state.   Sotheran's   Travel and Exploration - 49   2016   £298

Chaber, M. E.   *Hangman's Harvest.*   Holt, 1952. First edition, fine in dust jacket with couple of short closed tears.   Mordida Books   2015 - 003339   2016 $55

Chabon, Michael   *The Yiddish Policemen's Union.*   New York: Harper Collins Pub., 2007. First edition, one of 1000 numbered and signed copies, octavo, boards, fine in fine dust jacket in slipcase.   John W. Knott, Jr./L.W. Currey, Inc.   Fall-Winter 2015 - 16962   2016 $150

Chad Gadjo Zeichnungen con Menachem Birnbaum.   Berlin: Welt Verlag, 1920. First edition, folio, original vellum boards with black ties replaced, except for light soil and toning to boards, this is clean very good-fine copy, each page faces striking full page color woodblock illustrations, printed on vellum like parchment, rare.   Aleph-bet Books, Inc.   112 - 268   2016 $3500

Chadwick, Henry   *The Game of Base Ball.*   New York: George Munro & Co., 1868. First edition, 12mo., frontispiece, original quarter brownish red cloth and purple paper covered boards, printed in gold, paper rubbed on boards, particularly at corners, one page little wrinkled from printing flaw, but very nice, particularly fragile construction.   Between the Covers Rare Books   204 - 12   2016 $14,000

Chagall, Marc   *Illustrations for the Bible.*   New York: Harcourt Brace and Co., 1956. First American edition, inscribed by artist with stunning original page color drawing of Moses for Lenette and George Nayor, 1966, and from the collection of Herman Krawitz, former assistant manager of the Metropolitan Opera House, complete with 16 lithographs in color, 12 in black and white plus lithograph cover, also illustrated with reproductions in heliogravuvre of the 106 etchings made by Chagall for the illustrations of the bible, folio, original pictorial boards, original dust jacket, book with tape residue to endpapers, otherwise book and lithographs fine, extremely scarce dust jacket (almost never seen) with chipping, edgewear and damage to spine.   Manhattan Rare Book Company   2016 - 1646   2016 $40,000

Chalfant, W. A.   *The Story of Inyo.*   Chicago: The author, 1922. First edition, very scarce thus, frontispiece map, red cloth, extremities lightly rubbed, spine and top edge of rear cover faded, spotting to rear cover, very good, errata slip tipped-in to inner rear cover.   Argonaut Book Shop   Native American 2015 - 5518   2016 $75

Challinor, William   *The Court of Chancery; its Inherent Defects...*   London: Stevens & Norton, 1849. Second edition, sewn as issued in cream wrappers, very good.   Jarndyce Antiquarian Booksellers   CCXVIII - 519   2016   £450

Chalmers, Floyd   *The Financial Post Survey of Mines Canada and Newfoundland 1929. Description of Camps Company Reviews Tables and Maps.*   Toronto: MacLean Pub. Co., 1929. Fourth Annual edition, quarto, card covers, maps, tables and ads, covers worn and scuffed.   Schooner Books Ltd.   115 - 189   2016 $45

Chalmers, John A.   *Tiyo Soga: A Paper of South African Mission Work.*   Edinburgh, London, Glasgow, Grahamstown, Cape Colony: Andrew Eliot, Hodder & Stoughton, David Bryce & Son, James Kay, 1877. First edition, thick octavo, albumen photographic frontispiece with signature in facsimile, brown cloth decorated in black and stamped in gilt, attractive and small contemporary gift inscription on half title, binding little cocked, modest wear on boards, slight foxing on first few pages, overall nice, very good or better.   Between the Covers Rare Books   207 - 22   2016 $950

Chalmers, Patrick R.   *Deerstalking.*   Philip Allan, 1935. First edition, 8vo., original red cloth, 8 plates, spine sunned, spotting to fore-edge, very good.   Sotheran's   Hunting, Shooting & Fishing - 54   2016   £80

Chalmers, Patrick R.   *A Dozen Dogs or So.*   London: Eyre & Spottiswoode, 1928. First edition, royal octavo, 12 color plates and frontispiece and many fine drawings in text by Cecil Aldin, publisher's tan cloth over beveled boards, front cover and spine lettered brown, neat ink signature dated 1928, fine.   David Brass Rare Books, Inc.   2015 - 02942   2016 $175

Chaloner, Len *What the Vinmers Sell.* London: Heath Cranton Ltd., 1926. Half title, illustrations by Charles Ledger, original purple cloth, spine faded.   Jarndyce Antiquarian Booksellers   CCXVII - 67   2016   £30

Chamberlayne, John *Magnae Britanniae Notitia or the Present State of Great Britain.* printed for Timothy Goodwin...., 1718. 2 parts in 1, second with separate titlepage, engraved frontispiece, one gathering in first part and 5 in second browned, 8vo., contemporary panelled sheep, red lettering piece on spine, date gilt at foot, little worn, cracks in joint headcap defective, agricultural armorial bookplate of Henry Eustachius Strickland, sound.   Blackwell's Rare Books   B186 - 39   2016   £400

Chambers & Knapp's Missouri and Illinois Almanac for the Year... 1847. St. Louis: Missouri Republican Office, 1847. First edition, 12mo., sewn, uncut, some browning at top of spine on front wrapper.   M & S Rare Books, Inc.   99 - 4   2016 $850

Chambers, David *Gogmagog - Morris Cox and the Gogmagog Press.* Pinner: Private Libraries Assoc., 1991. First edition, of 1560 copies this one of 69 numbered 'special copies' signed by Morris Cox on tipped-in colophon lead, followed by 9 tipped in specimen leaves, and original woodcuts signed by artist, 16 color plates, royal octavo, black leather backed cloth, lettered gilt, fine in fine slipcase.   Peter Ellis   112 - 149   2016   £225

Chambers, Robert William *The King in Yellow.* Chicago: F. Tennyson Neely, 1895. First edition, green cloth with lizard on front board, rear board blank, 16mo., on inserted frontispiece, very good+ with mild toning to spine.   Beasley Books   2015 - 2016 $950

Chambers, William *Chambers's Edinburgh Journal: new Series.* Edinburgh: William and Robert Chambers, 1844-1854. 4to., contemporary quarter leather, marbled paper covered boards, title, volume and ornamentation gilt stamped on spine, water damage to edges, back free endpapers and board volume 1 only, previous owner's name H. N. Johnson, inscribed on front free endpaper.   Oak Knoll Books   310 - 60   2016 $450

Chambers, William *The Youth's Companion and Counseller.* London: W. & R. Chambers, circa, 1873? Half title, frontispiece, additional engraved title, original purple cloth, decorated gilt, spine faded and little rubbed at head, prize inscription, all edges gilt.   Jarndyce Antiquarian Books   CCXV - 103   2016   £45

Champney, Julius B. *History of the Champney Family...* Chicago: P. L. Hanscom & Co., 1867. First edition, 8vo., text illustration and 5 plates, original printed wrappers, light wear.   M & S Rare Books, Inc.   99 - 95   2016 $275

Chance, John Newton *A Fall-Out of Thieves.* R. Hale, 1976. Excellent copy in like dust jacket.   I. D. Edrich Crime - 2016   £25

Chance, John Newton *A Place Called Skull.* R. Hale, 1980. Dust jacket, very good.   I. D. Edrich   Crime - 2016   £20

Chance, John Newton *Return to Death Alley.* R. Hale, 1976. Dust jacket.   I. D. Edrich   Crime - 2016   £20

Chancellor, E. Beresford *The London of Charles Dickens...* London: Grant Richards, 1924. First edition, half title, frontispiece, and plates, original maroon cloth, spine lettered in gilt, inner hinges strengthened, labels removed from leading pastedown, good plus.   Jarndyce Antiquarian Booksellers   CCXVIII - 1104   2016   £35

Chancerel, Leon *Piaf Le Cheval Enchante.* Bouasse Jeune et Cie, n.d. circa, 1936. Large 4to. flexible pictorial card wrappers, slight edge wear, near fine, printed on good quality paper with vivid colors, stunning Art Deco illustrations.   Aleph-bet Books, Inc.   111 - 185   2016 $350

Chancerel, Leon *Piphagne.* Bouasse Jeune et Cie, n.d. circa, 1937. Large 4to., flexible pictorial card wrappers, slight edge wear and soil near fine, striking art deco illustrations on every page, printed on good quality paper.   Aleph-bet Books, Inc.   111 - 186   2016 $350

Chancerel, Leon *Sylvestre Le Saltimbanque: Prince Des 4 Chemins.* Bouasse Jeune et Cie, n.d. circa, 1937. Large 4to., flexible pictorial card wrappers, slight edge wear and soil, near fine, illustrations by Turenne Chevaliereau with striking art deco illustrations on every page, printed on good quality paper.   Aleph-bet Books, Inc.   111 - 187   2016 $350

Chandler, L. G. *Bush Charms.* Melbourne: Whitcombe & Tombs, 1922. Small octavo, text illustrations, very good in dust jacket, scarce in this condition.   Andrew Isles Natural History Books   55 - 38496   2016 $40

Chandler, Raymond 1886-1959 *The Big Sleep.* San Francisco: 1989. Reprint edition, photos, fine in dust jacket.   Mordida Books   2015 - 010528   2016 $65

Chandler, Raymond 1886-1959 *Five Sinister Characters.* New York: Avon Book Co., 1945. First edition, digest sized paperback, foxed on inside covers and to few and pages and tiny nick to corner edge of top edge of rear panel and adjacent to spine on top of rear panel, else near fine, tight copy in pictorial wrappers.   Buckingham Books   2015 - 17512   2016 $475

Chandler, Raymond   1886-1959   *The High Window.* New York: Alfred A. Knopf, 1942. First edition, slightly cocked, near fine in nice, near fine dust jacket with tiny nicks and tears at extremities.   Between the Covers Rare Books   208 - 100   2016 $6000

Chandler, Raymond   1886-1959   *Killer in the Rain.* London: Hamish Hamilton, 1964. First edition, very occasional fox, spot towards head of pages in latter half of book, 8vo., original red boards with faint residue line along head of front board from fixing of protective cover, pastedowns show same, backstrip lettered gilt and lightly faded at foot, top edge foxed, dust jacket sunned to backstrip with light soiling on back panel and small tear at head of rear flap, very good. Blackwell's Rare Books   B186 - 193   2016   £150

Chandler, Raymond   1886-1959   *The Lady in the Lake.* New York: Alfred A. Knopf, 1943. First edition, octavo, original green cloth, front and spine panels stamped in black, running Borzoi stamped in black on rear panel, fore and bottom edges rough trimmed, small bookplate of NY University Fales Collection, marked as withdrawn duplicate and collector Scott Cunningham affixed to front pastedown and very faint previous owner's signature, spine lean, very good in very good dust jacket with light wear at spine ends and corner tips, some rubbing along spine folds, just touch of dust soiling to rear panel and printed price clipped from front flap, both book and jacket present well overall.   John W. Knott, Jr./L.W. Currey, Inc.   Fall-Winter 2015 - 16846   2016 $3500

Chandler, Raymond   1886-1959   *The Lady in the Lake.* New York: Alfred A. Knopf, 1943. First edition, slightest bit cocked, else especially bright and fine, lacking dust jacket, scarce.   Between the Covers Rare Books   208 - 101   2016 $2000

Chandler, Raymond   1886-1959   *The Little Sister.* London: Hamish Hamilton, 1949. Cloth covers, little unevenly faded, owtherise very good.   I. D. Edrich   Crime - 2016   £20

Chandler, Raymond   1886-1959   *The Long Good-Bye.* London: Hamish Hamilton, 1953. Precedes American edition, very good.   I. D. Edrich   Crime - 2016   £45

Chandler, Raymond   1886-1959   *Playback.* London: Hamish Hamilton, 1958. Narrow section of fore edge of dust jackets' spine rubbed, otherwise very good copy of trial first with date on verso of titlepage only and silver lettered spine.   I. D. Edrich   Crime - 2016   £65

Chandler, Raymond   1886-1959   *Playback.* Boston: Houghton Mifflin Co., 1958. First American edition, one of 6000 copies original orange cloth, lettered in brown, original pictorial purple dust jacket lettered in white and black, about fine with only hint of wear to spine ends, else fine, jacket with touch of light wear and minor creasing to extremities faint hint of light foxing to spine, bright and clean panels, overall, attractive, near fine copy.   B & B Rare Books, Ltd.   2016 - RC001   2016 $250

Chandler, Raymond   1886-1959   *Spanish Blood - a Collection of short Stories.*   Cleveland and New York: World Pub. Co., 1946. First edition, octavo, cheap paper tanned as ever, head and tail of spine very slightly bumped, very good in very good dust jacket, very slightly nicked, slightly rubbed at edges much better than usual.   Peter Ellis   112 - 72   2016   £125

Channing, William Ellery   *Lectures on the Elevation of the Laboring Portion of the Community.*   Boston: Crosby & Nichols, 1863. Frontispiece, title in red and black, original purple cloth, bevelled boards, largely faded to brown. Jarndyce Antiquarian Books   CCXV - 589   2016   £25

Channing, William Ellery   *Self-Culture and the Elevation of the working Classes.*   London: Groombridge & Sons, circa, 1854. frontispiece, final ad leaf, occasional pencil markings & annotation, original green printed paper boards, slight rubbing, very good.   Jarndyce Antiquarian Books CCXV - 104   2016   £75

Chapin, Frederic   *Toodles of Treasure Town and Her Snow Man.*   Akron: Saalfield, 1908. First edition, 4to., pictorial cloth, small fade stain on corner of cover, some wear to huge paper but not weak, overall very good+ copy, illustrations by Merle Johnson, this copy inscribed by author. Aleph-bet Books, Inc.   112 - 188   2016 $350

Chapin, James P.   *The Birds of the Belgian Congo.*   New York: American Museum of Natural History, 1932-1954. Only 300 copies printed, Octavo, 4 volumes, 3 color plates, photos and other illustrations, binder's red cloth, all edges speckled, bookplate and signatures of Stephen Marchant (previous editor of The Emu), very good, scarce.   Andrew Isles Natural History Books   55 - 12104   2016 $1200

Chapman, Abel   *Memories of Fourscore Years Less Two 1851-1929.*   Gurney and Jackson, 1930. First edition, 8vo., original straight grained green cloth, spine titled in gilt, photo frontispiece, 24 fine colored plates, printed tissue guards, copious illustrations in text by W. H. Riddell, very good.   Sotheran's   Piccadilly Notes - Summer 2015 - 72   2016   £200

Chapman, Abel On Safari Big-Game Hunting in British East Africa. With Studies in Bird-Life. London: Richard Clay & sons, Limited for Edward Arnold, 1908. First edition, 8vo., original blue cloth, gilt lettering and vignette of elephant's head to upper board, gilt lettering to spine, wood engraved illustrations and maps in text after Edmund Caldwell, little rubbed to head and foot of spine, very good, presentation bookplate from author to the captain and officers of HMS Dauntless, Chapman's signature printed but 'Dauntless' written in ink in author's hand, with previous owner's bookplate in f.f.e.p.   Sotheran's   Hunting, Shooting & Fishing - 8   2016   £800

Chapman, Abel Retrospect, Reminiscences and Impressions of a Hunter Naturalist in Three Continents 1851-1928. London and Edinburgh: Oliver and Boyd for Gurney and Jackson, 1928. First edition, 8vo., original dark green cloth, boards with blind-ruled borders, spine lettered and ruled in gilt, top edges gilt, others uncut, color printed frontispiece after William Hatton Riddell retaining printed tissue guard, 19 color printed plates by Riddell retaining printed tissue guards, 34 plates after Riddell, Crawhall, et al, one photogravure plate retaining tissue guard, illustrations and one full page map printed in red and black in text, errata slip tipped onto margin of page xv, extremities slightly rubbed, otherwise very good.   Sotheran's   Hunting, Shooting & Fishing - 164   2016   £250

Chapman, Frederick Open-air Studies in Australia. London: J. M. Dent & sons, 1929. Octavo, photos, dust jacket, scarce in this condition.   Andrew Isles Natural History Books   55 - 5641   2016 $50

Chapman, Roger G. Charles Darwin 1809-1882. A Centennial Commemorative. Wellington: Nova Pacifica, 1982. Limited to 750 copies, this copy unnumbered, out of series copy, presented without the usual slipcase to R. J. Berry, professor, 4to., original half black leather, blue cloth, gilt borders to boards, gilt device to upper gilt spine with contrasting lettering pieces in red and light blue leather, marbled endpapers, 27 tipped in color plates, numerous text illustrations, near fine.   Sotheran's   Piccadilly Notes - Summer 2015 - 73   2016   £400

Chapone, Hester Letters on the Improvement of the Mind, Addressed to a Young Lady. London: printed for J. Walter, Charing Cross and C. Dilly in the Poultry, 1787. New edition, 8vo., , contemporary full speckled calf, rubbed maroon leather label, hinges weakening but sound, slightly chipped at head and tail of spine, armorial bookplate, signature of Martha Campbell & partially removed signature of Harriet Ramsay?, good, sound copy.   Jarndyce Antiquarian Books CCXV - 105   2016   £50

Chapone, Hester Letters on the Improvement of the Mind, Addressed to a Young Lady. London: printed for Scatherd & Letterman, 1810. 12mo., contemporary full tree calf, black morocco label, spine rubbed, ownership inscription of Maria Clarke, 28th Nov. 1810.   Jarndyce Antiquarian Books CCXV - 106   2016   £50

Chapone, Hester The Works of. Edinburgh: James Ballantyne & Co., 1807. Some occasional marking and creasing, contemporary full calf, gilt spine, black morocco label, slightly rubbed, inscribed 'From A. Grant to Jane Grant... May 14th 1809'.   Jarndyce Antiquarian Books CCXV - 107   2016   £60

Chappell, Fred First and Last Words: Poems. Baton Rouge: Louisiana State University, 1989. First printing, 8vo., paper wrappers, author's presentation, cover very slightly soiled, else nice.   Second Life Books, Inc.   196A - 271   2016 $45

Characteristic Sketches of Young Gentlemen. By Quiz Junior. London: published for the author by William Kidd, 1838. Apparently first edition, light waterstain to frontispiece and title, original purple brown patterned cloth, uniformly faded, printed paper label on front board, slight rubbing at head and tail of spine.   Jarndyce Antiquarian Booksellers CCXVIII - 170   2016   £110

The Characters of Freshmen and Other Papers Reprinted from the Cambridge University Magazine. Cambridge: W. P. Grant, 1848. Original printed paper wrappers, little creased, slightly torn with some loss to back wrapper. Jarndyce Antiquarian Books   CCXV - 575   2016   £65

Chargaff, Erwin Heraclitean Fire. New York: Rockefeller University Press, 1980. First edition, near fine, very good dust jacket with edge wear, toning, mild sun to spine, 8vo, with two TLS's by author on his personal stationery laid in, prospectus for the book laid in.   By the Book, L. C.   45 - 23   2016 $500

Charles I, King of Great Britain Historie Entiere & Vertiable du Procez de Charles Stuart, Roy d'Angleterre. I(ohn) G(rismond), 1650. 3 parts in 1, 12mo., contemporary French calf, spine richly gilt, crack at foot of upper joint, very good.   Blackwell's Rare Books   B184 - 24   2016   £750

Charlesworth, Maria Louisa The Broken Looking-Glass or Mrs. Dorothy Cope's Recollections of Service. London: Seeley, Jackson & Halliday, 1880. First edition, frontispiece, plates, 4 pages ads, original light brown decorated cloth, inner leading hinge, slight cracking, contemporary ownership signature, very good.   Jarndyce Antiquarian Books   CCXV - 110   2016   £40

Charlevoix, Pierre Francois Xavier History and General Description of New France. New York: John Gilmary Shea, 1866-1872. First edition, Imperial 8vo., 18 maps, 15 plates and 4 facsimiles, three quarter morocco over marbled boards, five raised bands, gilt rules, titles in two compartments, rosettes in four, marbled endpapers, very good or better, exceptionally clean and wide margined copies, minor rubbing, closed tears to two maps, owner's bookplates. Kaaterskill Books   21 - 15   2016 $3500

Charlevoix, Pierre Francois Xavier *The History of Paraguay.* Lockyer Davis, 1769. First edition, 2 volumes, wormed, contemporary brow full calf, spine rebacked, small loss ot head and tail, some scuffing to leather.   J. & S. L. Bonham Antiquarian Booksellers   America 2016 - 9975   2016   £110

Charlotte Rampling with Compliments.   London: Quartet Books, 1973. First edition, signed by Rampling, near fine in fine dust jacket, photographic plates.   Royal Books   48 - 22   2016 $950

Charteris, Leslie *Thanks to the Saint.* London: Hodder & Stoughton, 1958. First English edition, some staining along fore-edge, otherwise fine in dust jacket with some scattered rubbing on spine.   Mordida Books   2015 - 010923   2016 $65

Charteris, Leslie *Vendetta for the Saint.* London: Hodder & Stoughton, 1965. First English edition, spotting along page edges, otherwise fine in price clipped dust jacket.   Mordida Books   2015 - 010925   2016 $65

Chase-Riboud, Barbara *From Memphis & Peking.* New York: Random House, 1974. First edition, bit of foxing to endpapers, else near fine in dust jacket, inscribed by author to author James Jones and his wife.   Between the Covers Rare Books   207 - 23   2016 $350

Chaskey, Scott *December Songs.* Porthenrys: self published, 1988. Copy #58 of 100, inscribed by author to Peter Matthiessen with TLS laid in, near fine in self wrappers.   Ken Lopez Bookseller   166 - 30   2016 $200

Chatham, Russell *The Theory and Practice of Rivers. (Prints only).* Seattle: Winn Books, 1986. First edition, number 7 of 175 copies (but it appears that they were not all issued), fine, 5 print portfolio by Chatham printed to accompany the book, with original printed envelope, signed by artist.   Bella Luna Books   2016 - 14283N   2016 $660

Chatwin, Bruce *In Patagonia.* London: Jonathan Cape, 1977. First edition, 8vo., illustrations, original boards, dust jacket, fine.   James S. Jaffe Rare Books   Occasional List: Winter 2016 - 39   2016 $750

Chatwin, Bruce *In Patagonia.* London: Jonathan Cape, 1977. First edition, 8vo., frontispiece, illustrations, maps, endpapers with identical maps on them, part of map on lower board missing, original blue cloth with good clean dust jacket.   J. & S. L. Bonham Antiquarian Booksellers   America 2016 - 9823   2016   £85

Chatwin, Bruce *On the Black Hill.* London: Jonathan Cape, 1982. First edition, 8vo., original blue-grey boards, backstrip lettered gilt, dust jacket with touch of very light creasing around head, near fine.   Blackwell's Rare Books   B184 - 125   2016   £90

Chatwin, Bruce *On the Black Hill.* London: Jonathan Cape, 1982. First British edition, true first, fine in fine dust jacket.   Bella Luna Books   2016 - t5467   2016 $72

Chatwin, Bruce *Patagonia Revisited.* Russell, 1985. First edition, textual illustrations, original blue cloth, fine.   J. & S. L. Bonham Antiquarian Booksellers   America 2016 - 9822   2016   £20

Chaucer, Geoffrey   1340-1400 *The Canterbury Tales of Chaucer.* London: 1775-1778. First Tyrwhitt edition, five volumes.   Honey & Wax Booksellers   4 - 26   2016 $3000

Chaucer, Geoffrey   1340-1400 *The Canterbury Tales.* Golden Cockerel Press, 1929-1931. Limited to 500 copies, this number 39 of 485 copies on Batchelor handmade paper, folio, 4 volumes, original quarter niger morocco, spines lettered gilt, decorated board sides, top edges gilt, others uncut, many wood engraved headpieces, tailpieces and leaf spray borders by Eric Gill, initials printed in red and blue, very nice set.   Sotheran's   Piccadilly Notes - Summer 2015 - 2   2016   £8500

Chaucer, Geoffrey   1340-1400 *The Canterbury Tales.* Waltham St. Lawrence: Golden Cockerel Press, 1929-1931. No. 343 of 485 copies on paper (and 15 on vellum), 4 volumes, 318 x 197mm., original morocco backed patterned paper boards by Sangorski & Sutcliffe, raised bands, gilt titling, top edges gilt, others untrimmed, in cloth slipcase, red and blue initials and very pleasing wood engraved borders (frequently inhabited) by Eric Gill on every page except in last part of volume IV, verso of front free endpapers with bookplate of William Risenfield, joints somewhat rubbed and bit darkened (from dye), portions of upper joint volume I cracked (no other cracking), corners rather mashed, leather little marked, but all volumes solid, covers unsoiled, spines uncharacteristically close in color, very fresh, clean and bright internally.   Phillip J. Pirages   67 - 172   2016 $8500

Chaucer, Geoffrey   1340-1400 *The Canterbury Tales of....* New York: Covici Friede, 1930. No. 152 of 924 copies on rag paper, signed by artist, from total edition of 999, 389 x 262mm., 2 volumes, publisher's original page beige linen, top edge gilt, others untrimmed, 50 illustrations by Rockwell Kent, 25 full page in black and brown and 55 black and white head and tailpieces, one spine bit browned, hint of browning to cloth elsewhere, small snag at head of one joint and tail of another, bindings entirely solid and generally very well preserved and especially fine internally, text illustrations quite clean, bright and fresh.   Phillip J. Pirages   67 - 229   2016 $1100

Chaucer, Geoffrey   1340-1400   *The Canterbury Tales: Speical Edition for Young Readers.*   New York: 1961.   First edition, illustrations by Gustaf Tenggren.   Honey & Wax Booksellers   4 - 41   2016 $75

Chaucer, Geoffrey   1340-1400   *The Canterbury Tales.*   New York: Golden Press, 1961.   Deluxe Golden Book (A/A code on pastedown), pictorial boards, some edgewear, very good+, many full and partial page richly colored illustrations.   Aleph-bet Books, Inc.   111 - 443   2016 $125

Chaucer, Geoffrey   1340-1400   *The Romaunt of the Rose.*   London: published for the Florence Press by Chatto and Windus, 1908.   No. 10 of 12 copies on vellum, of 10 were for sale(and 500 copies on paper), 292 x 197mm., original flexible vellum, gilt tilting on upper cover and flat spine, green silk ties, original lightly soiled and faded gray cloth portfolio (for additional suite of plates) both housed in (slightly worn) fleece lined red cloth drop back box, with morocco label, woodcut device on titlepage and 20 color plates by Keith Henderson and Norman Wilkinson, all mounted on gray stock and protected by captioned tissue guards, with additional suite of plates loose in portfolio (as issued), all mounted with tissue guards, especially fine, unusually clean and bright inside and out, without the almost inevitable darkening to vellum leaves with splaying that comes with flexible vellum bindings.   Phillip J. Pirages   67 - 337   2016 $5000

Chaucer, Geoffrey   1340-1400   *Troilus and Criseyde.*   Waltham St. Lawrence: Godlen cockerel Press, 1927.   No. 22 of 225 numbered copies on paper (and six on vellum), 318 x 203mm., original patterned paper sides by Sangorski & Sutcliffe (stamp signed on front pastedown), new replica spine of russet morocco with raised bands and gilt titling by Courtland Benson, top edge gilt, others untrimmed (sides with dots in paper pattern enhanced by previous owner in pleasing, scarcely noticeable manner), in later suede backed marbled paper slipcase, pictorial woodcut borders to fore margins of every text page and five full page wood engravings, all by Eric Gill, setion titlepages with red or blue lettering, occasional text initials in red or blue, light to moderate rubbing along edges, otherwise very fine, expertly renewed binding entirely pleasing, text fresh, bright and immaculate from first leaf to last.   Phillip J. Pirages   67 - 173   2016 $7500

Chaucer, Geoffrey   1340-1400   *The Workes of our Antient and Lernded Engish Poet...*   London: Impensis Geor(ge) Bishop, 1598.   First edition, folio, woodcut title border and 3 divisional titles within repeated woodcut border, woodcut historiated and floral initials, 18th century paneled calf, rebacked with (possible original) spine laid down, bit of rubbing to boards and spine, some worming sporadically throughout, mainly marginal some toning and browning throughout, previous owner's old ink signature on titlepage and old ink notes on dedication page, top margin, overall very good, custom quarter morocco clamshell.   Heritage Book Shop   Holiday 2015 - 19   2016 $12,500

Chaucer, Geoffrey   1340-1400   *The Workes of Our Ancient and Learned English Poet, Geffrey Chaucer.*   London: by Adam Islip, 1602.   Folio, title surrounded by woodcut border, lacking initial blank (a)1, as always and errata leaf 3U8, copperplate portrait , woodcuts, black letter, late 19th century dark brown morocco, blind panel on covers, edges gilt, small worm track in margin of first several gatherings, 2 very minor repaired tears, one blank corner torn away, very clean, attractive copy, gift inscription.   Joseph J. Felcone, Inc.   Books from Five Centuries: a Miscellany - 37   2016 $9000

Chaucer, Geoffrey   1340-1400   *The Works.*   Hammersmith: Kelmscott Press, 1896.   One of 425 copies on paper and 13 on vellum, 457 x 330mm., original holland backed blue paper boards, paper spine label, untrimmed edges, housed in very substantial fleece lined pigskin backed folding box, 87 wonderful large woodcut illustrations after Sir Edward Burne-Jones, redrawn by Robert Catterson Smith and cut by W. H. Hooper, woodcut titlepage, 14 variously repeated woodcut borders, 18 variously repeated woodcut frames around illustrations, 26 19-line woodcut opening words, numerous three-six and 10-line woodcut initial letters and woodcut printer's device, all designed by William Morris and cut by C. E. Keats, Hooper and Spielmeyer, printed in black and red with Chaucer type, titles of longer poems printed in Troy type, tiny tear in spine label (not affecting lettering), hint of soil to covers, one very small shallow dent in back board, one small area where an owner has lightened the paper color by erasure, two conjoint leaves with marginal foxing in one corner, two other conjoint leaves with very slight foxing of same sort but still very fine, all of these imperfections quite minor, the always insubstantial binding with only negligible wear, leaves extraordinarily bright, fresh and clean and text and woodcuts deeply impressed.   Phillip J. Pirages   67 - 218   2016 $95,000

Chaucer, Geoffrey   1340-1400   *Complete Poetical Works of Geoffrey Chaucer.*   New York: Macmillan, Sept., 1912.   First US edition, thick 4to., blue cloth, extensive gilt pictorial cover and spine, top edge gilt, very slight cover rubbing, near fine, illustrations by Warwick Goble, very scarce.   Aleph-bet Books, Inc.   112 - 217   2016 $850

Chaucer, Geoffrey   1340-1400   *Works.*   Oxford: Shakespeare Head Press, 1928-1929.   316/375 sets (of an edition of 386 sets), printed on Kelmscott handmade paper, titles printed in red and the sub-titles and large initial letters printed in blue and red, wood engraved headpieces by Lynton Lamb, paragraph-marks drawn by hand by Joscelyn Gaskin in blue or red and the charming hand colored figures of the Canterbury Pilgrims, engraved from drawings by Hugh Chesterman after those in the Ellesmere Manuscript, leaf acknowledging Chesterman's work with the Chaucerian figures loosely inserted, small folio, original quarter undyed linen, printed labels (with spares loosely inserted), pale blue boards, untrimmed, little minor spotting, very good.   Blackwell's Rare Books   Marks of Genius - 13   2016   £1200

Chaumeton, Francois Pierre *Flore Medicale.* Paris: C. L. F. Panckoucke, 1814-1820. First edition, 236 x 133mm., without separately published 32 page unillustrated section entitled 'Essay d'une Iconographie Elementaire' (sometimes found in or as the final volume), 7 volumes bound in 8, contemporary quarter calf, flat spines divided into panels by plain gilt and decorative blind rules, 3 panels with central quatrefoil blindstamp, each spine with two cream edges and endpapers, 427 engravings, 425 of them quite pleasing botanical plates (one a duplicate), all printed in color and finished by hand, 2 engraved tables, one folding, original tissue guards, evidence of insect activity along 3 joints, sides bit chafed, 3 volumes with small cracks to head or tail of a joint (little rubbing elsewhere to joints) but original bindings entirely sound and without any serious defect, occasional minor foxing and isolated trivial stains or rust spots, two plates with colors slightly smudged, but very pleasing set internally, foxing almost never anything but trivial, leaves quite fresh and clean, plates subtly colored.   Phillip J. Pirages   67 - 90   2016 $8500

Chavasse, Pye Henry *Chavasse's Advice to a Wiffe.* London: J. & A. Churchill, 1898. Fourteenth edition, half title, 30 pages ads, original blue cloth, little rubbed, contemporary signature.   Jarndyce Antiquarian Books   CCXV - 111   2016   £25

Cheadle, Eliza *Manners of Modern Society; being a Book of Etiquette.* London: Cassell Petter & Galpin, circa, 1874. Sixteenth thousand, 4 pages ads, original brown cloth, bevelled boards, blocked in black and gilt, slightly rubbed, lower board little marked.   Jarndyce Antiquarian Books   CCXV - 113   2016   £45

Cheadle, Eliza *Manners of Modern Society.* London: Cassell Petter & Galpin, circa, 1875. 18th thousand, original dark green cloth, slightly rubbed and slightly dulled, all edges gilt, bookseller's ticket of Widdison, Sheffield, nice.   Jarndyce Antiquarian Books   CCXV - 114   2016   £35

Cheetham, Hall *La Vida Breve.* Blewbury: privately printed at the Rocket Press, 1991. One of 75 numbered copies (this unnumbered), signed by artist, 24 wood engravings by John O'Connor, printed in blue, brown, green or orange, tall 8vo., original yellow cloth, printed labels on backstrip and front cover, tail edges rough trimmed, fine.   Blackwell's Rare Books   B184 - 308   2016   £200

Cheever, John   1912-1984 *Atlantic Crossing. Excerpts from the Journal of John Cheever.* Cottondale: Ex Ophidia, 1986. One of only 90 copies, folio, full oasis niger goatskin, as new in equally pristine publisher's cloth clamshell box.   Joseph J. Felcone, Inc.   Books from Five Centuries: a Miscellany - 38   2016 $750

Cheever, John   1912-1984 *Homage to Shakespeare.* Stevenson: Country Squires Books, 1968. First edition, 8vo., fine in dust jacket with couple of light soil marks, one of just 150 numbered copies signed by author.   Second Life Books, Inc.   196A - 274   2016 $150

Chekhov, Anton Pavlovich *The Duel.* St. Petersburg: A S. Surovin, 1897. Sixth edition, some heavy spotting at end, where 2 leaves have tears somewhat crudely repaired (text recoverable), 8vo., recent half calf, original wrappers bound in, upper printed wrapper bit soiled and mounted, sound.   Blackwell's Rare Books   B184 - 25   2016   £1000

Chekhov, Anton Pavlovich *Hmurye lyudi (in Russian) (Gloomy People).* St. Petersburg: A. S. Surovin, 1896. Sixth edition, uniformly slightly browned, half title foxed, 8vo., recent half cloth, good.   Blackwell's Rare Books   B184 - 26   2016   £1200

Chekhov, Anton Pavlovich *Two Plays of.... The Cherry Orchard. Three Sisters.* New York: Limited Editions Club, 1966. First edition, one of 1500 copies signed by artist, Lajos Szalay, quarter black goatskin leather and woven black and cherry-red fabric side, fine in publisher's box.   Second Life Books, Inc.   196A - 277   2016 $45

The Chelsea Historical Pageant June 25th.... July 1st, 1908, Old Ranelagh Gardens, Royal Hospital, Chelsea. London: W. Austin, printer 82 College St. Chelsea, S. W., 1908. First edition, 8vo., 13 leaves of half tone illustrations, original decorated wrapper, upper cover with design by Arthur Blunt, spine slightly torn.   Marlborough Rare Books   List 56 - 12   2016   £85

Chen, Julie *Chrysalis.* Berkeley: Flying Fish Press, 2014. Number 5 of 50 copies, signed and numbered by Chen, letterpress printed on handmade paper using photopolymer plates, terra cotta paper is from Cave Paper and black denim paper is from La Papeterie Saint-Armand, shape of the outer structure is a version of a geometric shape called an olioid, box 6 3/4 x 11 3/4 x 6 5/8 inches, book object size 7 x 11 x 7 when closed and 11 1/2 x 18 inches when opened, fine.   The Kelmscott Bookshop   13 - 17   2016 $1450

Chenery, William *The Fourteenth Regiment Rhode Island Heavy Artillery (Colored) in the War to Preserve the Union 1861-1865.* Providence: Snow and Farnham, 1898. First edition, octavo, 343 pages, frontispiece, one engraving with many portraits, later owner's name on first blank page, couple of small bumps on front board, some very faint spotting, nice, very good plus, uncommon.   Between the Covers Rare Books   202 - 66   2016 $500

Cherryh, C. J. *Downbelow Station.* London: Severn House Publishers, 1985. First British and first trade hardcover edition, crease to upper corner of front free endpaper, some age tanning to text block, fine in fine dust jacket. John W. Knott, Jr./L.W. Currey, Inc. Fall-Winter 2015 - 15905 2016 $250

Cherubin D'Orleans, Francois Lasseri *La Vision Parfaite; ou la Concourt des Dens Asssxis de la Vision et un Seul Poin le O'ject.* Paris: Chez Sebastien Mabre Cramoisy Imprimeur du Roy, 1677. First edition in French, 4 parts in one, folio, large engraved allegorical frontispiece, title vignette, 16 engraved plates, contemporary full calf, gilt spine titles, extremities worn, joints repaired, titlepage with signature of Gilbert Govi, 1854, bookseller's description tipped in , possibly that of Henry Sotheran, rare. Jeff Weber Rare Books 183 - 12 2016 $8000

Chesher, Deborah *Everybody I shot is Dead.* Studio City: Cheshire Cat., 2007. Large format book of photos, inscribed by Chesher, fine in near fine dust jacket with few surface scratches. Ken Lopez Bookseller 166 - 99 2016 $100

Chessman, Caryl *Cell 2455. death Row. A Condemned Man's Own story.* New York: Prentice Hall, 1954. First edition, black cloth, gilt, top of spine crunched with small tear in cloth, pictorial dust jacket (top of jacket spine crunched one inch tear to lower edge). Argonaut Book Shop Biography 2015 - 6562 2016 $75

Chessman, Caryl *Trial by Ordeal.* Englewood Cliffs: Prentice Hal, 1955. First edition, gray cloth stamped in black and red on spine and front cover, fine, pictorial dust jacket, 2 small tears to lower edge of jacket. Argonaut Book Shop Biography 2015 - 6563 2016 $75

Chester, George Randolph *The Wonderful Adventures of Little Prince Toofat.* New York: James McCann, 1922. First edition, 4to., blue grey gilt and pictorial cloth, cover very slightly soiled, else near fine, exceedingly scarce, illustrations by Robert Lawson, rare. Aleph-bet Books, Inc. 112 - 286 2016 $3500

Chesterfield, Philip Dormer Stanhope, 4th Earl of 1694-1773 *Letters Written by the late right Honourable Philip Dormer Stanhope, Earl of Chesterfield to his Son.* London: printed for J. Dodsley, 1774. 2 volumes, half titles, engraved frontispiece, 4to., large uncut, unpressed copy, some slight marginal waterstaining to final few leaves volume I, and to upper margin of some leaves volume II, half titles a little dusty, original boards recovered in blue sugar paper, buff paper spines. Jarndyce Antiquarian Books CCXV - 115 2016 £580

Chesterfield, Philip Dormer Stanhope, Earl of 1694-1773 *Letters by the late Right Honourable Philip Dormer Stanhope, Earl of Chesterfield to his Son Philip Stanhope, Esq....* London: printed for J. Dodsley, 1775. Sixth edition, 2 volumes, 12mo., contemporary tree calf, boards with elaborate gilt borders with cornerpieces, spines richly gilt in compartments with contrasting red and green leather labels, frontispiece in volume I, upper joint of volume I neatly repaired, joints and extremities little rubbed, couple of scrapes to boards of volume i, bookplates to each volume, generally very good in handsome binding. Sotheran's Piccadilly Notes - Summer 2015 - 74 2016 £350

Chesterfield, Philip Dormer Stanhope, Earl of 1694-1773 *Lord Chesterfield's Advice to His Son on Men and Manners or a New System of Education.* Paris: printed for Vergani, the Ninth Year, 1800? 12mo., titlepage little browned, slight tears to blank gutter margin, some age toning, contemporary mottled sheep, gilt spine, dark green morocco label, upper hinge slightly cracked but firm, spine slightly rubbed and chipped at head and tail. Jarndyce Antiquarian Books CCXV - 116 2016 £120

Chesterton, Gilbert Keith 1874-1936 *Appreciations and Criticisms of the Works of Charles Dickens.* London: J. M. Dent & Sons, 1911. First edition, frontispiece and plates, title in red and black, original dark green cloth, spine lettered in gilt, slight rubbing to head and tail of spine, gilt card in envelope tipped into prelims, top edge gilt, very good plus. Jarndyce Antiquarian Booksellers CCXVIII - 1108 2016 £40

Chesterton, Gilbert Keith 1874-1936 *Appreciations and Criticisms of the Works of Charles Dickens.* London: J. M. Dent & Sons, 1933. Half title, original green cloth, spine lettered in gilt, very good. Jarndyce Antiquarian Booksellers CCXVIII - 1110 2016 £30

Chesterton, Gilbert Keith 1874-1936 *Charles Dickens.* London: Methuen & co., 1906. Second edition, half title, frontispiece, plate, prelims little spotted, handsomely bound in full dark green crushed morocco, borders and floral cornerpieces in gilt, spine gilt im compartments, very good. Jarndyce Antiquarian Booksellers CCXVIII - 1111 2016 £50

Chesterton, Gilbert Keith 1874-1936 *Charles Dickens.* London: Methuen & Co., 1907. Fifth edition, half title, frontispiece and plate, 40 page catalog (Nov. 1907) slight spotting, original green cloth, lettered gilt, contemporary gift inscription, very good. Jarndyce Antiquarian Booksellers CCXVIII - 1112 2016 £25

Chesterton, Gilbert Keith 1874-1936 *The Minor Writings of Charles Dickens: a Bibliography and Sketch.* London: Elliot Stock, 1900. First edition, uncut in original olive green cloth, bevelled boards, slight wear to tail of spine, very good,. Jarndyce Antiquarian Booksellers CCXVIII - 1333 2016 £25

Chesterton, Gilbert Keith 1874-1936 *A Short History of England.* London: Chatto and Windus, 1917. Author's original corrected typescript, signed with extensive holograph corrections and additions, 4to., bound in red crushed and polished levant, lettered and bordered in gilt, elaborately gilt dentelles and marbled endpapers by Riviere & son, cloth slipcase, light wear along joint of front cover, light soiling to typescript consistent with use, otherwise fine.   James S. Jaffe Rare Books   Occasional List: Winter 2016 - 41   2016 $25,000

Chesterton, Gilbert Keith 1874-1936 *Simplicity and Tolstoy.* Arthur L. Humphreys, 1912. First separate edition, engraved titlepage, small head and tailpiece plates inserted, title printed in red, 12mo., original printed cream wrappers, covers little darkened from slipcase apertures, untrimmed, board slipcase with printed label and title handwritten in ink to back, very good.   Blackwell's Rare Books   B184 - 126   2016   £55

Chevalier, Maurice *Mome A Cheveux Blancs.* Paris: Presses de la Cite, 1969. First edition, 8vo., author's presentation on half title, photos, nice in slightly chipped dust jacket.   Second Life Books, Inc.   196A - 282   2016 $50

Chevalier, Ulysse *Repertoire des Sources Historiques du Moyen Age, Topo-Bibliographie.* Montbeliard: Societe Anonyme d'Imprimerie Montbeliardaise, 1894-1900. First edition, printed in an edition of 2000 copies, 2 volumes, small 4to., modern cloth, leather spine labels, marginal staining, loosely inserted commemorative booklabel which indicated this set came from reference library of H. P. Kraus.   Oak Knoll Books   310 - 237   2016 $350

Cheyne, John 1671-1743 *An Essay on the Bowel Complaints of Children...* Philadelphia: Anthony Finley, 1813. First American edition, 12mo., engraved illustration in text, early ownership signature, front cover loose, but attached, front free endpaper detached portion of spine perished, corners worn, some moderate staining and browning, good only, original calf with red leather spine labels.   Edwin V. Glaser Rare Books   2015 - 10115   2016 $225

Cheyney, Peter *The Dark Omnibus.* New York: Dodd Mead, 1952. Omnibus edition, fine in dust jacket with tiny wear at spine ends.   Mordida Books   2015 - 011742   2016 $65

Cheyney, Peter *I'll Say She Does!* London: Collins, 1945. Dust jacket grayed, signed by author.   I. D. Edrich Crime - 2016   £40

Cheyney, Peter *No Ordinary Cheyney.* London: Collins, 1948. Very good, frayed dust jacket, signed by author.   I. D. Edrich   Crime - 2016   £45

Cheyney, Peter *Try Anything Twice.* London: Collins, 1948. Dust jacket very slightly frayed, otherwise very good, signed by author.   I. D. Edrich   Crime - 2016   £45

Cheyney, Peter *You Can Call It A Day.* London: Collins, 1949. Very good in frayed dust jacket.   I. D. Edrich   Crime - 2016   £45

Chicago Eye Shield Co. *Spectacles and Goggles.* Chicago: circa, 1916. Small 8vo., half tone text illustrations, original blue printed light green pictorial wrappers.   Marlborough Rare Books   List 56 - 13   2016   £45

Child, Lydia Maria 1802-1880 *The Frugal Housewife.* London: William Tegg, 1860. Twenty-fourth edition, 16mo., original red cloth, spine gilt, slightly rubbed and dulled, signature of Mary Chapman 1868 on leading f.e.p.   Jarndyce Antiquarian Books   CCXV - 117   2016   £48

Children's Singing Games. David Nutt, 1894. First edition, Arts & Craft style illustrations to every page with many borders and some full page, every illustration hand colored by Gloria Cardew, small inkspot at foot of one page, 4to., original mottled brown cloth with illustration stamped in black to upper board, little rubbing to corners and light browning to endpapers, very good, inscribed by Cardew.   Blackwell's Rare Books   B184 - 252   2016   £1000

The Children's Shakespeare. London and New York: Dent & Dutton, 1911. Pictorial cloth, unobtrusive repair to rear hinge and some cover soil, very good+, illustrations by Charles Folkard.   Aleph-bet Books, Inc.   112 - 197   2016 $400

Chile. Constitution *Constitucion de la republic de Chile Jurada y Promulgada el 25 de Mayo 1833.* Santiago de Chile: Imprenta de la Opinion, 1833? Folio, stitched in contemporary blue paper wrappers, as issued, spine scuffed, corners bit worn, else very good, clean copy, rare printing.   Joseph J. Felcone, Inc.   Books from Five Centuries: a Miscellany - 40   2016 $900

Ching, Raymond *Studies and Sketches of a Bird Painter.* Melbourne: Lansdowne Editions, 1981. Folio, color plates by Ching, publisher's cloth, slipcase with pictorial wrappers, owner's expansive signature and address, very good.   Andrew Isles Natural History Books   55 - 1797   2016 $250

Ching, Raymond *Studies and Sketches of a Bird Painter.* Melbourne: Lansdowne Editions, 1981. Limited to 500 copies numbered and signed by artist, Small folio, color plates, text illustrations, publisher's full grey calf and solander box, some marks to box, otherwise fine.   Andrew Isles Natural History Books   55 - 8962   2016 $850

Chisholm, Alec H. *The Story of Elizabeth Gould.* Melbourne: Hawthorn Press, 1944. Limited to 350 copies, octavo, uncolored frontispiece, publisher's green cloth, fine.   Andrew Isles Natural History Books   55 - 30516   2016 $450

Chisholm, Alec H. *Strange Journey: the Adventures of John Gilbert and Ludwig Leichhardt.* Sydney: Angus and Robertson, 1973. Third edition, octavo, endpaper maps, fine.   Andrew Isles Natural History Books   55 - 37707   2016 $60

Chisholm, Alec H. *Observations on the Golden Bower-Bird.* Sydney: Royal Australasian Ornithologiss Union, 1956. Octavo, color frontispiece, publisher's stiff wrappers, fine.   Andrew Isles Natural History Books   55 - 5667   2016 $30

Chisholm, C. R. *Chisholm's All Round Route and Panoramic Guide of the St. Lawrence: the Hudson River; Saratoga; Trenton Falls' Niagara; Toronto...* Montreal: C. R. Chisholm and Bros., 1875. Original burgundy cloth stamped and lettered in gilt on front cover and in blind on back cover, panoramic map in unusually good condition, 6 folded maps, rubbing to spine, nevertheless bright.   Sotheran's   Piccadilly Notes - Summer 2015 - 76   2016   £348

Chisholm, Louey *A Staircase of stories.* London: T. C. and E. C. Jack Ltd. circa, 1919. Early edition, royal 8vo., original brown cloth panelled and lettered in black to spine and upper cover with onlaid pictorial label to upper board, 31 colored plates and other black and white drawings throughout by a variety of artists, externally fine and bright, internally equally fresh with just little speckling to edges of book block and very occasional light browning.   Sotheran's Piccadilly Notes - Summer 2015 - 121   2016   £128

Chittick, Neville *Azania: Journal of the British Institute of History and Archaeology in East Africa.* Nairobi, Addis Ababa, Lusaka: Oxford University Press, 1966-1980. First edition, 15 volumes, 4to., wrappers, consecutive run 1-15, numerous plates, sound, very good in clean covers with only very slight shelfwear and with clean text.   Any Amount of Books   2015 - A89239   2016   £250

Chitty, J. B. *Things Seen in China.* London: Seeley, Service & Co. Ltd., 1909. First edition, 'velvet leather' issue, 8vo., original flexible red reversed calf, prettily blocked in gilt, top edge gilt, marbled endpapers, publisher's illustrated catalog, 248 crisp photographic plates printed in half tones and line illustrations, fine, original publisher's flyer.   Sotheran's   Travel and Exploration - 101   2016   £298

Chiu, Bobby *Pieces of Wonderland.* Toronto: Trinquette Pub.; Imaginism Studios, 2012. First edition, quarto, illustrated paper over boards, fine.   Ken Sanders Rare Books E Catalogue # 1 - 30   2016 $50

Cholmondeley-Pennell, Henry *Modern Babylon and Other Poems.* London: John Camden Hotten, 1872. First edition, half title, original green cloth rubbed but sound.   Jarndyce Antiquarian Booksellers   CCXVII - 68   2016   £350

Cholmondeley-Pennell, Henry *Puck on Pegasus.* London: John Camden Hotten, 1869. Sixth edition, half title, frontispiece, plates and illustrations, slightly later 19th century half scarlet crushed morocco, armorial bookplates of Gelandi & W. A. Locan, all edges gilt, very good.   Jarndyce Antiquarian Booksellers   CCXVII - 69   2016   £125

Choon, Angela *Chris Ofili: Devil's Pie.* New York and Gottingen: Steidl and David Zwimer, 2008. First edition, 4to., original purple cloth lettered silver on spine and cover, signed presentation from Ofili, about fine.   Any Amount of Books   2015 - A75550   2016   £150

Chopin, Kate *The Awakening.* Chicago and New York: Herbert S. Stone & Co., 1899. First edition, 8vo., original decorated light green cloth, top edge gilt, others untrimmed, in extremely rare collector's condition, usually surviving in shabby condition, virtually as new, preserved in half morocco slipcase.   James S. Jaffe Rare Books   Occasional List: Winter 2016 - 42   2016 $17,500

Choukri, Mohamed *Tennessee Williams in Tangier.* Santa Barbara: Cadmus Editions, 1979. First edition, one of 200 copies, signed by author and translator, Paul Bowles, fine in wrappers and fine unprinted acetate dust jacket.   Between the Covers Rare Books   208 - 12   2016 $225

Christie, Agatha   1891-1976 *The Complete Hercule Poirot Short Stories.* London: Folio Society, 2003. 3 volumes, pictorial boards in pictorial slipcase, illustrations by Christopher Brown, near fine.   I. D. Edrich   Crime - 2016   £65

Christie, Agatha   1891-1976 *Curtain. Poirot's last Call.* Collins, 1975. First edition, crown 8vo., original black boards, backstrip lettered gilt with slight lean to spine, thin strip of adhesive residue at centre of each pastedown, news clipping regarding author contemporary with book laid in, dust jacket, good copy, inscribed by author for Mimmie Bush.   Blackwell's Rare Books   B184 - 127   2016   £650

Christie, Agatha   1891-1976 *Endless Night.* Crime Club/Collins, 1967. Dust jacket, very good.   I. D. Edrich   Crime - 2016   £20

Christie, Agatha   1891-1976 *The Hound of Death and Other Stories.* Oldham's Press, 1933. Spine sunned and few small patchy spots on upper case and spine, little fore-edge foxing, very slight, otherwise very good in dull red covers, 'Copyright 1933' on inside of titlepage.   I. D. Edrich   Crime - 2016   £120

Christie, Agatha   1891-1976   *The Murder at the Vicarage.* New York: Dodd Mead and Co., 1930. First US edition, fine, bright, tight copy in spectacular, fine, bright dust jacket, superb copy.   Buckingham Books   2015 - 27194   2016 $3750

Christie, Agatha   1891-1976   *The Murder at the Vicarage.* New York: Dodd, Mead and Co., 1930. First US edition, cloth modestly soiled and sunned on spine, else very good in spectacular fine, bright dust jacket with minor closed tear and some faint creasing to rear flap, exceptional copy. Buckingham Books   2015 - 25491   2016 $3000

Christie, Agatha   1891-1976   *The Mysterious Mr. Quin.* New York: Dodd Mead & Co., 1930. First US edition, in fine, unrestored dust jacket, uncommon, exceptional copy. Buckingham Books   2015 - 265492   2016 $4375

Christie, Agatha   1891-1976   *The Secret Adversary.* New York: Avon, 1946. Paperback original, Avon no. 100, fine, unread copy in wrappers.   Mordida Books   2015 - 011209   2016 $65

Christie, Agatha   1891-1976   *There Is a Tide.*   New York: Dodd, Mead & Co., 1948. First US edition, fine in bright dust jacket with tiny chip to top edge of rear fore corner. Buckingham Books   2015 - 34875   2016 $475

Christie, Manson & Woods   *Catalogue of the Beautiful Collection of Modern Pictures, Water-colour Drawings and Objects of Art of Charles Dickens, with the Whole of the Names of Purchasers and Enormous Prices realised....* London: printed by W. Clowes & Sons, 1870. 12 pages, later marbled protective wrappers, little dusted, stamp of Wigan Public Library, good plus copy, scarce.   Jarndyce Antiquarian Booksellers   CCXVIII - 873   2016   £150

Christie, Thomas   *Letters on the Revolution of France and on the New Constitution Established by the National Assembly...*   London: J. Johnson, 1791. First edition, 2 volumes in one, octavo, part I and only part ever published, 3 large folding charts, half calf over contemporary marbled boards, rebacked and recornered to style, boards and edges bit rubbed, some light foxing, mostly to prelims, some closed tears to first folding chart, but with no loss of text, minor dampstain to bottom of fore-edge, very good.   Heritage Book Shop   Holiday 2015 - 20   2016 $3000

Christopher, A. B.   *The World Accomplished.*   London: World's End Press, 1974. Limited to 75 numbered copies signed by author and artist, Natalie d'Arbeloff, 4to., heavy paper wrapper with (34) very heavy sheets loosely inserted, clamshell box with leather spine and embossed paper covered boards, printed on Barcham Green mould-made paper with etchings printed by artist.   Oak Knoll Books   27 - 8   2016 $650

Christopher, John   *When the Tripods Came.*   New York: E. P. Dutton, 1988. First US edition, octavo, cloth backed boards, fine in fine dust jacket with small closed tear at base of spine panel, sharp copy, scarce.   John W. Knott, Jr./L.W. Currey, Inc.   Fall-Winter 2015 - 17878   2016 $750

Christy, Edwin P.   *Christy's Plantation Melodies No. 2.* Philadelphia: Fisher & Brother, 1853? 18mo, original printed & pictorial wrappers, light staining, some corners lacking. M & S Rare Books, Inc.   99 - 47   2016 $400

Christy, Howard Chandler   *Our Girls.*   New York: Moffat & Yard, Sept., 1907. First edition, 4to., cloth, pictorial paste-on, slight cover rubbing and cover plate, lightly soiled, else near fine, printed on heavy coated paper with decorative border on text pages, beautiful color plates by Christy plus other full page illustrations, beautiful copy.   Aleph-bet Books, Inc.   112 - 109   2016 $200

Chukovsky, Kornei   *The Telephone.*   New York: Delacorte Press, 1977. First edition, 8vo., unpaged, illustrations by Blair Lent, fine in little worn dust jacket signed by translator, William Jay Smith.   Second Life Books, Inc.   196A - 284   2016 $75

Church of England. Book of Common Prayer   *The Book of Common Prayer and Administration of the Sacraments... according to the use of the Church of England. Together with the Psalter or Psalms of David...*   Cambridge: John Baskerville, 1762. Third octavo Baskerville edition, full contemporary red morocco, elaborately tooled in gilt, featuring precise horizontal tooling executed within a framed central lozenge, apparently an English variant on the Scottish 'herring-bone' bindings of the period.   Honey & Wax Booksellers   4 - 4   2016 $2800

Church of England. Book of Common Prayer   *The Book of Common Prayer and Administration of the Sacraments.* London: published for John Reeves...sold and G. and W. Nicol and Satcherd and Letterman, 1807. 2 parts in 1 volume, 12mo., contemporary red straight grained morocco, single gilt fillet on sides and an inner border of 2 blind fillets and a blind roll tool, gilt crown of centre of both covers, spine richly tooled gilt and blind lettered in gilt direct, red morocco label inside front cover, gilt edges, trifle worn at extremities, inner hinge neatly repaired, boards trifle warped, good copy, with a letter of provenance on mourning paper from Isabella Speechly of Peterborough stating "The Prayer Book and Hymn Book (latter not present) which belonging to Queen Caroline, were given to the Lady Egmont by Lady Anne Hamilton the Queen's Lady and she have them to my Great Aunt Miss Martha Speechly then living at Darmouth House...".   Blackwell's Rare Books Marks of Genius - 11   2016   £6000

Church of England. Book of Common Prayer *The Book of Common Prayer...together with the Psalter or Psalms of David...* Oxford: Printed at the Clarendon Press by Samuel Collingwood & Co., 1823. 254 x 152mm., contemporary burgundy straight grain morocco, blindstamped in cathedral style, covers with central panel of an altar with rose window and gothic ownership lettering in gilt ('Eatington Chapel 1826'), panel within a floral frame of gothic motif, wide raised bands, spine panels each blindstamped with two gothic windows, gilt titling, gilt rolled turn-ins, marbled endpapers, all edges gilt; with large fore-edge painting showing Lincoln from the River Witham, spine with hint of sunning, joints and corners slightly worn (front joint perhaps getting ready to crack), final two leaves with faint dampstain at upper right (small, insignificant dampstain at top of some other leaves), very presentable copy, binding solid and not at all unattractive, text unusually bright and quite fresh and painting entirely as it should be.   Phillip J. Pirages   67 - 148   2016 $950

Church, A. H.   *Josiah Wedgewood, Master Potter.* London: Seeley and Co., 1903. Revised edition, small quarto, 4 plates in gravure, 31 further plates in black and white and color, gilt lettered and decorated maroon cloth, top edge gilt, gilt, corner slightly jammed, light extremity rubbing, dent to upper edge of front cover, overall fine.   Argonaut Book Shop   Pottery and Porcelain 2015 - 5012   2016 $150

Church, Roberta   *The Robert R. Churches of Memphis: a Father and Son Who Achieved in Spite of Race.*   Ann Arbor: Edwards Brothers, 1974. First edition, photos, page edges slightly rumpled, still near fine, bit worn but very good dust jacket with some light chipping and faint staining, inscribed by Annette and Roberta Church to Fannie H. Douglas (wife of James H. Douglas).   Between the Covers Rare Books   207 - 27   2016 $250

Churchill, Randolph   *Winston Churchill.*   1966-1967. 4 volumes, illustrations, covers little worn.   I. D. Edrich   Winston Spencer Churchill - 2016   £80

Churchill, Seton   *Forbidden Fruit for Young Men.* London: James Nisbet & Co., circa, 1895. Sixth edition, half title, 6 pages ads, slight spotting, original blue cloth, slightly dulled, signature of F. Raynes 1895.   Jarndyce Antiquarian Books   CCXV - 119   2016   £40

Churchill, Winston Leonard Spencer   1874-1965   *The Aftermath Part 3.*   1909. Errata slip, blue cloth, little bubbly on edge of spine, otherwise very good.   I. D. Edrich   Winston Spencer Churchill - 2016   £125

Churchill, Winston Leonard Spencer   1874-1965   *Great Contemporaries.*   London: Thornton Butterworth, 1937. Advance proof copy of the first edition, rare, octavo, original wrappers, custom silk box, some soiling to wrappers, particularly to spine, small blemish on rear wrapper, excellent copy.   Manhattan Rare Book Company   2016 - 1802   2016 $2700

Churchill, Winston Leonard Spencer   1874-1965   *Here is the Course We Steer.*   London: Conservative Party, 1948. First edition, 8vo., original orange wrappers which are illustrated with black and white photos inside and out, including photo of Churchill on front wrapper, very slight marking to front wrapper and with small tear at top edge, otherwise very good, preserved in custom made cloth covered flapcase with leather label.   Sotheran's   Piccadilly Notes - Summer 2015 - 79   2016   £350

Churchill, Winston Leonard Spencer   1874-1965 *Marlborough: His Life and Times.*   London: George G. Harrap & Co., 1939. First edition thus, 4 volumes, large 8vo., original purple cloth, lettered gilt on spine, illustrations, foldout maps, neat name "J. A Hamilton". otherwise very good+ in like dust jackets (very slight edgewear), slight fading to spines of books and jackets.   Any Amount of Books   2015 - C5426   2016   £650

Churchill, Winston Leonard Spencer   1874-1965   *My African Journey.*   London: Hodder and Stoughton, 1908. First edition, octavo, original pictorial red cloth, publisher's catalog bound in rear (as issued), mild fading to spine (less than usual), slight lean to binding, little foxing to text block edges, exceptionally clean, handsome copy.   Manhattan Rare Book Company   2016 - 1781   2016 $1450

Churchill, Winston Leonard Spencer   1874-1965   *My Early Life.*   London: Thornton Butterworth, 1930. Photo illustrations, library copy in library binding with library bookplate and cancel stamps, folded map frayed at fore-edge but complete, all maps and illustrations present, very good reading and working copy.   I. D. Edrich   Winston Spencer Churchill - 2016   £40

Churchill, Winston Leonard Spencer   1874-1965 *Painting as a Pastime.*   1948. Reproductions in full color, frontispiece, dust jacket slightly rubbed and chipped.   I. D. Edrich   Winston Spencer Churchill - 2016   £25

Churchill, Winston Leonard Spencer   1874-1965   *The Second World War.*   London: Cassell & Co., 1948. First English edition, octavo, modern three quarter red polished calf, decorated spines with gilt lion devices, raised bands, top edge gilt, 6 volumes, fine, very handsomely bound. Manhattan Rare Book Company   2016 - 1628   2016 $2400

Churchill, Winston Leonard Spencer 1874-1965 *The Second World War.* 1948-1954. 6 volumes, all very good in like dust jackets.   I. D. Edrich   Winston Spencer Churchill - 2016   £100

Churchill, Winston Leonard Spencer 1874-1965 *The Second World War.* London: Cassell & Co. Ltd., 1948-1954. First English edition, octavo, original cloth, original dust jackets, 6 volumes, books remarkably fine with spine gilt extremely bright and red top stain rich and unfaded, dust jackets in outstanding condition with volume titles strong on all spines, very rare with this set, extraordinary set.   Manhattan Rare Book Company   2016 - 1662   2016 $1950

Churchill, Winston Leonard Spencer 1874-1965 *Shall the Door be Shut?* Jerusalem: Weiss press, 1939. First edition, 8vo., original wrappers, stapled as issued, some browning with few nicks and creases, otherwise very good, fragile, housed in contemporary green card folder with title typed on front, very rare.   Sotheran's   Piccadilly Notes - Summer 2015 - 78   2016   £2500

Churchill, Winston Leonard Spencer 1874-1965 *The Story of the Malakand Field Force.* London: New York: and Bombay: Aberdeen University Press for Longmans, Green and Co., 1898. First edition, first issue, 8vo., original green cloth, upper board lettered gilt, within panel blocked in blind, spine ruled gilt and lettered gilt, modern black cloth box, gilt green morocco lettering piece on spine, half tone portrait frontispiece with tissue guard, folding tinted lithographic maps, 4 maps, boards lightly rubbed and bumped at extremities, cloth slightly marked, some scattered spotting and occasional light offsetting, otherwise good in original cloth.   Sotheran's   Travel and Exploration - 102   2016   £5500

Churchill, Winston Leonard Spencer 1874-1965 *The War Speeches....* London: Cassel and Co. Ltd., 1941-1946. Complete first edition, 7 volumes, octavo, original blue cloth, original dust jackets, books with mild foxing to edges, much less than usual, dust jackets with slight discoloration and minimal edgewear, otherwise bright and clean copies, one dust jacket with tape inside running along top edge, one dust jacket chipped bottom right corner, one dust jacket with light spotting along right side front panel, one dust jacket with trivial spotting on top left corner of front panel and on left side of back panel as well.   Manhattan Rare Book Company   2016 - 1661   2016 $3900

Churchill, Winston Leonard Spencer 1874-1965 *The Collected Works of Sir Winston Churchill.* London: Library of Imperial History, 1973. Centenary Edition, original vellum, fine, octavo, original full calf skin vellum, 24 carat gold blocking, marbled endpapers, all edges gilt, original slipcases with gilt stamped Churchill coat-of-arms, natural age toning to vellum, slipcases with wear from sticking to each other (very common with this set), beautiful set.   Manhattan Rare Book Company   2016 - 1801   2016 $6000

Churchill, Winston Leonard Spencer 1874-1965 *The World Crisis.* Thornton Butterworth Ltd., 1923-1931. First edition, 6 volumes, numerous maps, plans and illustrations, little spotting to edges, a number stamp to front free endpaper in volume i, remains of subscription library label inside front cover volume ii, with traces of having folded over the front cover for a short way, 8vo., original dark blue cloth, titled in blind within panel on upper covers, and gilt on spine, minimal wear to extremities, very good.   Blackwell's Rare Books   B184 - 129   2016   £1500

Churchill, Winston Leonard Spencer 1874-1965 *The World Crisis. 1916-1918. Part 1.* London: Thornton Butterworth, 1927. First printing, Blue cloth, gilt, maps and charts in excellent condition, name on front pastedown, very good.   I. D. Edrich   Winston Spencer Churchill - 2016   £75

Churchill, Winston Leonard Spencer 1874-1965 *The World Crisis. 1916-1918 Part II.* London: Thornton Butterworth, 1927. First edition, 6 folding maps or charts and 2 facsimiles of letters from Haig as well as further maps within text, occasional pencil markings in margin by Buchan with occasional comment or correction, few very faint foxspots to initial and ultimate leaves and one or two light handling marks, 8vo., original dark blue cloth blindstamped to upper board, backstrip lettered gilt, edges lightly toned and free endpapers little browned, very good, John Buchan's copy with his bookplate and his pencilled notes, superb page letter from author to Buchan 22.2.27.   Blackwell's Rare Books   Marks of Genius - 14   2016   £6000

Churchill, Winston Leonard Spencer 1874-1965 *The World Crisis. 1916-1918. Part 2.* London: Thornton Butterworth, 1927. Second impression, blue cloth, gilt, all maps and charts present in excellent condition, very good copy.   I. D. Edrich   Winston Spencer Churchill - 2016   £25

Churton, Ralph *The Life of Alexander Nowell, Dean of St. Pauls.* Oxford University Press, for the author, 1809. 8vo., 9 plates, some folding, little noted, sporadic foxing, plates offset, tan diced russia, gilt spine and borders, marbled edges and endpapers, binding sound, skillfully rebacked, edges rubbed, corners worn, hinges repaired with marbled paper, armorial bookplate of J. Paul Rylands, , letter to Prof. Patrick Collinson dated 9.ii.80 loosely inserted.   Unsworths Antiquarian Booksellers   30 - 32   2016 $75

Chute, Carolyn *The Beans of Egypt, Maine.* New York: Ticknor and Fields, 1985. Uncorrected proof, with long inscription from author to fellow author Madison Smartt Bell, with Madison Smartt Bell's ownership signature, further inscribed years latter by Chute for book collector Rolland Comstock, faint crease to front cover likely from so much inscribing, near fine in wrappers, laid in is folded five page press release from Ticknor, wonderful association.   Ken Lopez Bookseller   166 - 21   2016 $500

Ciardi, John *Other Skies.* Boston: Little Brown and co., 1947. First edition, inscribed by poet for William Meredith, June 9 1980, fine in close to fine dust jacket with tanned spine.   Charles Agvent   William Meredith - 22   2016 $250

Cibber, Colley 1671-1757 *Perolla and Izadora.* London: for Bernard Lintott, 1706. First edition, small 4to., 19th century morocco backed boards, title gilt to spine, light toning to head of several leaves.   Dramatis Personae 119 - 28   2016 $350

Cicero, Marcus Tullius *Cato Major and His Discourse of Old Age.* Philadelphia: Printed and sold by B. Franklin, 1744. First edition, 4to., printed on imported Genoese 'trois-O' paper, titlepage in red and black, contemporary sprinkled calf, gilt fillet roll around covers, blind sawtooth roll on edges, pages edges sprinkled red, very skillfully and almost imperceptibly rehinged, retaining entire original spine, just the slightest bit of foxing at edges of margins on few pages, else probably the nicest copy we have ever handled, bookplate of 19th century book collector Henry Cunliffe, in neat gold tooled calf backed slipcase.   Joseph J. Felcone, Inc. Books from Five Centuries: a Miscellany - 64   2016 $20,000

Cicero, Marcus Tullius *Three Books Touching the Nature of the Gods.* London: printed for Joseph Hindmarsh, 1683. 12mo., publisher'ds ads to first leaf, edges neatly repaired, little toned, occasional spotting, leaves a7 and 19 grubby at fore edge with few small holes not affecting text, paper flaw to fore-edge margin leaf c2 resulting in small area of loss but not affecting text, contemporary dark brown calf neatly rebacked, raised bands, morocco gilt spine label, blind tooling to boards, edges sprinkled red, rubbed, corners repaired, front endpapers renewed, lower hinge neatly repaired, overall very good, indecipherable ownership inscription and another of Ed. Th. Gosling, Stockwell (?) 1884.   Unsworths Antiquarian Booksellers   30 - 33   2016   £275

Cicero, Marcus Tullius *Opera quae Supersunt Omnia... Voluminibus XX.* Glasgow: Robert and Andrew Foulis, 1749. Pot 8vo. issue, 4 leaves omitted from volume 6 by binder (A3-4 and A7-8), slight browning, 12mo., French black morocco, doublt gilt fillets on spine, flat spines richly gilt, twin red lettering pieces, gilt edges, little wear to extremities, few headcaps chipped, spines faded, top edges dusty, good.   Blackwell's Rare Books   B186 - 42   2016   £900

Cinamon, Gerald *E. R. Weiss: the Typography of an Artist.* Oldham: Incline Press, 2011. First edition, one of 300 numbered copies, 4to., quarter parchment over paper covered boards, slipcase, included are numerous pieces of ephemera and the prospectus.   Oak Knoll Books   310 - 112   2016 $500

Cinderella *Cinderella.* Hamburg: Gustav W. Setiz, circa, 1860. 16mo., pictorial wrappers die-cut in the shape of Cinderella, fine, color lithographs on each page, rare. Aleph-bet Books, Inc.   111 - 420   2016 $800

Cinderella *Cinderella or the Little Glass Slipper.* New York: McLoughlin Bros., n.d. circa, 1865. 12mo., pictorial wrappers highlighted in gold, mounted on linen, fine, illustrations well printed.   Aleph-bet Books, Inc.   111 - 164   2016 $300

Cinderella *Cinderella.* London: & Philadelphia: Wm. Heinemann & Lippinctt, 1919. Limited to only 800 numbered copies for sale signed by Rackham, (525 on handmade paper, 325 on Japanese vellum), this copy on English handmade paper, tipped-in color frontispiece plus beautiful full page silhouette illustrations heightened with color and with other illustrations in black and white, with extra color illustration not found in trade edition, beautiful copy, rarely found with dust jacket.   Aleph-bet Books, Inc.   112 - 414   2016 $2000

Cinderella *Cinderella.* New York: Scribner, 1954. A. First edition, first printing, 4to., cloth, corner slightly worn else fine in very good dust jacket, small chips off spine ends, this copy signed by artist, Marcia Brown.   Aleph-bet Books, Inc.   112 - 77   2016 $1500

The Circulator. A Magazine of Literature, Science and Art. Halifax: R. Leyland & son, 1867. Original dark blue-green cloth, paper spine label, slight rubbing, otherwise very good. Jarndyce Antiquarian Booksellers   CCXVII - 220   2016   £65

Circus Panorama. New York: McLoughlin Bros., 1888. 12 x 8 inches, printed on boards, repair to 3 panels on one side and 1 panel on verse, some edge wear, verso foxed, very good, opens accordion style to produce a continous 8 foot long procession with an 8 foot train on verso, bright, charming chromolithographs on circus side display.   Aleph-bet Books, Inc.   112 - 305   2016 $875

Ciruelo, Pedro *Reprovacion de la Supersticiones y Hechizerias.* Salamanca: Pedro de Castro, 1548. Rare early edition, 8vo., title printed in red and black within woodcut architectural border, woodcut initials, antique style brown blind tooled calf by Arias and Sons, stamped on upper cover, gilt letters on spine, titlepage with neat repairs to edges, small burnhole to folio lxviii affecting one or two letters, lightly spotted and browned in places.   Maggs Bros. Ltd.   1474 - 26   2016   £4500

Ciscar, Francisco *Reflexiones Sabre las Maquinas y Maniobras del Uso de a Bordo.* Madrid: En la Imprenta Real, 1791. First and only edition, folio, 23 folding plates, folding table, contemporary sprinkled calf, red morocco spine label (spine ends chipped, hinges scuffed but very solid), occasional marginal dampstaining but near very good.   Joseph J. Felcone, Inc.   Books from Five Centuries: a Miscellany - 41   2016 $2200

Claire, William *Literature and Medicne: Volume Three. The Physician as Writer.* Albany: SUNY Albany, 1984. First edition, blue printed boards, fine, signed by editor. Second Life Books, Inc.   196A - 289   2016 $450

Claire, William *The Strange Coherence of Our Dreams: Poems by....* Riverside: Magic Circle Press, 1973. First edition, number 2 of 375 copies signed by author and artist, 4to., drawings and by Adele Aldridge, paper wrappers, illustrations in black and white and color, fine.   Second Life Books, Inc.   196A - 287   2016 $65

Clanahan, James F. *The History of Pickens County, Alabama 1540-1920.* Carrollton: Clanahan Publications, 1964. First edition, fine in modestly soiled very good or better dust jacket with couple of stains and small shallow chip at crown, inscribed by Harper Lee.   Between the Covers Rare Books   204 - 66   2016 $3500

Clandel, Paul *The Book of Christopher Columbus.* New Haven: Yale University Press, 1930. First edition, 4to., cloth, fine in worn dust jacket with mends and chips, 100 color drawings and decorated endpapers by Jean Charlot. Aleph-bet Books, Inc.   111 - 87   2016 $300

Clapham, Richard *Rough Shooting for the Man of Moderate Means....* Heath Cranton Ltd., 1923. Early edition, 8vo., original green cloth, gilt lettering to spine, frontispiece and 8 plates, very good.   Sotheran's   Hunting, Shooting & Fishing - 74   2016   £30

Clare, John *The Poems of John Clare.* London: J. M. Dent, 1935. First edition, 2 volumes, frontispiece portrait, frontispiece facsimile, full red cloth lettered in gilt, spines little creased at head, very good set in very good dust jackets torn at edges and chipped at heads of spines.   Peter Ellis 112 - 75   2016   £175

Clare, John *The Village Minstrel and Other Poems.* London: Taylor & Hessey, Fleet Street and E. Drury, Stamford, 1821. First edition, 2 volumes bound in 1, 12mo., modern dark green calf over marbled paper boards, frontispiece in volume 1, ownership signatures of Fenwick Skrimshire, near fine copy.   Honey & Wax Booksellers   4 - 57   2016 $5500

Clare, Martin *The Motion of Fluids, Natural and Artificial.* London: Edward Symon, 1737. Second edition, 8vo., 9 engraved plates, engraved heraldic crest on dedication page, engraved head and tailpieces, red edges, very light foxing on two of the plates, modern half calf, over marbled boards, raised bands, gilt rules on spine, black calf, gilt stamped spine title, fine.   Jeff Weber Rare Books   183 - 13   2016 $575

Clare, Martin *Youth's Introduction to Trade and Business.* London: by Benjamin Webb, G. Keith, J. Fuller & 11 others, 1769. Tenth edition, 8vo., slightly dusted, handsomely rebound in half brown calf, red morocco label, signature of H. Manger, 1853 on leading blank.   Jarndyce Antiquarian Books   CCXV - 120   2016   £280

Clarendon, Henry Hyde *The History of the Rebellion and Civil Wars in Ireland....* London: printed for H. P. for Wilford and T. Jauncy, 1720. First edition, 8vo., engraved frontispiece, extra frontispiece portrait tipped in, final page a bookseller's catalog, decorative initials and head and tailpieces, some light or medium browning, bound in brown quarter calf and rough grained cloth, red morocco gilt label, edges mottled red, tears to leather on spine, overzealous cloth reinforcement of upper hinge causing initial blank to pull away from text block.   Unsworths Antiquarian Booksellers Ltd. E01 - Early Printing - 5   2016   £280

Clark, Ann Nolan *The Little Herded in Summer.* United States Office of Indian Affair, 1942. Oblong 4to., pictorial cloth, slight soil near fine, illustrations, inscribed by artist, Hoke Demetsosie.   Aleph-bet Books, Inc.   111 - 226 2016 $475

Clark, Ann Nolan *Little Navajo Bluebird.* New York: Viking, 1943. Stated first edition, 8vo., cloth, narrow fade spot on spine, else near fine, fine in dust jacket (frayed some at spine ends and corners, very good), illustrations in brown tones by Paul Lantz, very scarce edition.   Aleph-bet Books, Inc.   111 - 93   2016 $150

Clark, Ann Nolan *Magic Money.* New York: Viking, 1950. First edition, 8vo., red cloth, fine in very good dust jacket frayed at head of spine and bit worn at fold, wonderful color illustrations by Leo Politi, laid in is note from Politi and two color photos of him.   Aleph-bet Books, Inc.   112 - 386 2016 $175

Clark, Ann Nolan *The Slim Butte Raccoon.* U.S. Office of Indian Affairs, 1942. Presumable first edition listing this title as "To Be Published in 1942", 10 x 7 inches, edge of cover slightly soiled, else fine, wonderfully illustarted in brown line in native American artist Andrew Standing Soldier, a full blood Sioux, this copy signed by Clark. Aleph-bet Books, Inc.   112 - 259   2016 $175

Clark, Ann Nolan *Who Wants to Be a Prairie Dog?* U.S. Office of Indian Affairs, 1940. Oblong 4to., pictorial cloth, slight cover soil and tiny hole in endpaper, else very good+, inllustrated in brown line by native American artist Tsinnahhjinnie a full blooded Navajo.   Aleph-bet Books, Inc.   112 - 260   2016 $150

Clark, Barrett H. *Intimate Portraits: Being Recollections of Maxim Gorky, John Galsworthy, Edward Sheldon, George Moore, Sidney Howard & others.* New York: Dramatists Play Service, First edition, 8vo., author's presentation, nice in dust jacket (little soiled).   Second Life Books, Inc.   196A - 292   2016 $45

Clark, Edwin *A Visit to South America...* Dean and Son, 1878. First edition, 8vo., folding map, textual illustrations, occasional foxing throughout, original green blindstamped cloth, library stamp on titlepage, sprung.   J. & S. L. Bonham Antiquarian Booksellers   America 2016 - 9911   2016   £120

Clark, Eleanor *Baldur's Gate.* New York: Pantheon, 1970. First edition, 8vo., inscribed by author to noted American poet Barbara Howes, very nice in dust jacket with Howes' notes on rear endpaper.   Second Life Books, Inc.   196A - 293   2016 $75

Clark, Eleanor *Dr. Heart: a Novella & other Stories.* New York: Pantheon, 1976. First edition, 8vo., inscribed by author to poet Barbara Howes.   Second Life Books, Inc.   196A - 294   2016 $65

Clark, Eleanor *Eyes, Etc. a Memoir.* New York: Pantheon, 1977. First edition, 8vo., inscribed by author to poet Barbara.   Second Life Books, Inc.   196A - 295   2016 $65

Clark, Eleanor *Gloria Mundi a Novel.* New York: Pantheon, 1979. First edition, 8vo., inscribed by author for Barbara, fine in dust jacket.   Second Life Books, Inc.   196A - 296   2016 $65

Clark, G. Orr *The Moon Babies.* New York: R. H. Russell, 1900. 12 x 8 3/4 inches, cloth backed pictorial boards, light cover soil and rubbing, very good, illustrations by Helen Hyde, text in calligraphy, very scarce.   Aleph-bet Books, Inc.   112 - 103   2016 $475

Clark, Georgiana C. *Serviettes. Dinner Napkins and How to Fold Them.* London: Dean & Son, 1875. 8 pages ads, illustrations, binding cracking in places but remaining firm, original decorated light brown limp cloth boards, slight rubbing to head and tail of spine, very good, crisp copy.   Jarndyce Antiquarian Books   CCXV - 121   2016   £125

Clark, Helen Mills *Where the Dinner Bell Rings.* Door County, 1944. First edition, pictorial wrappers, drawing by Doris Heise, map, very, very scarce, near fine, no flaws or fading.   Gene W. Baade, Books on the West   2015 - 5004061   2016 $90

Clark, Ira G. *Water in New Mexico: a History of the Management and Use.* Albuquerque: UNM Press, 1987. First edition, illustrations, small stamp to bottom edge, slight fading to dust jacket, internally clean and bright, scarce.   Dumont Maps and Books   133 - 46   2016 $125

Clark, John Heaviside *The Amateur's Assistant; or A Series of Instructions in Sketching from Nature...* London: printed for Samuel Leigh 18 Strand, 1826. First edition, 4to., 10 engraved plates, including 4 in aquatint with hand coloring, original pink boards, upper cover with large engraved title label, rebacked with signs of light waterstaining to foot of first several leaves.   Marlborough Rare Books List 55 - 13   2016   £1250

Clark, John Spencer *Drawing in Public Education, the Features of the Study which Should be Taught in Primary, Grammar and High School.* Boston: L. Prang & Co., 1880. Plates, some color, original printed wrappers, slight wear to back wrapper, small repairs to spine, the copy of journalist politician Henry Norman.   Jarndyce Antiquarian Books CCXV - 594   2016   £48

Clark, Jonathan *On Finding a Possum by the Roadside.* Mountain View: Artichoke Editions, 1977. Limited to 100 numbered copies, 8vo., quarter cloth, marbled paper covered boards, label on front cover, top edge gilt, other edges uncut, relief etching and poem, signed by author, prospectus laid in.   Oak Knoll Books   310 - 78   2016 $125

Clark, Larry *Larry Clark 1992.* New York & Koln: Thea Westreich & Gisela Capitain, 1993. One of 1000 copies, black and white photos, clean, very near fine in photo illustrated wrappers with small crease to bottom corner of front panel, signed by Clark.   Jeff Hirsch Books Holiday List 2015 - 71   2016 $1250

Clark, Larry *Tulsa.* New York: Lustrum, 1971. second edition and first hardcover edition, quarto, fine in fine dust jacket, signed by Clark.   Between the Covers Rare Books 208 - 66   2016 $650

Clark, Leonard *The Mirror and Other Poems.* London: Allan Wingate, 1948. First edition, crown 8vo., original grey-green cloth, backstrip lettered gilt, bottom corners trifle bumped, dust jacket little sunned to borders and backstrip panel with minor chipping to corners and backstrip panel ends, very good, inscribed to fellow poet Louis MacNeice.   Blackwell's Rare Books   B184 - 130   2016   £45

Clark, P. A. G. *Archaeology in the North Report of the Northern Archaeological Survey.* Northern Archaeological Survey, 1976. First edition, folio, figures, plates and maps, recased in green cloth, silver lettered to spine, original paper front cover bound in, minor shelfwear, near fine. Unsworths Antiquarian Booksellers Ltd.   E05 - 98   2016   £20

Clark, Simon *The Puma's Claw.* London: Hutchinson, 1959. First edition, photos and maps, octavo, fine in very good dust jacket little nicked and rubbed at edges.   Peter Ellis   112 - 265   2016   £35

Clark, Walter *Histories of the Several regiments and Battalions from North Carolina in the Great War 1861-1865.* Raleigh: E. M. Uzzell, printer and binder, 1901. First edition, thick 8vo., gray cloth stamped in blue, red, white and lettered gilt, presentation from author to Adjutant Robert M. Freeman, covers rubbed with wear at spine ends, inside hinges cracked with some signatures sprung.   Oak Knoll Books   310 - 280   2016 $650

Clarke, Arthur C. *Childhood's End.* New York: Ballantine Books, 1953. First edition, octavo, cloth, fine in neary fine, bright dust jacket with 10m. closed tear and associated wrinkles at bottom edge of front panel with small internal tape reinforcement to same, light wear to spine ends and upper corner tips and some fading to orange title lettering, publisher's monogram on spine (as usual), very attractive.   John W. Knott, Jr./L.W. Currey, Inc.   Fall-Winter 2015 - 17623   2016 $4500

Clarke, Arthur C. *A Fall of Moondust.* New York: Harcourt Brace and World, 1961. First edition, modest edgewear, very good in near very good dust jacket with some wear and tear, mild stain on rear panel, nicely inscribed by author.   Between the Covers Rare Books   208 - 118   2016 $750

Clarke, Arthur C. *Islands in the Sky.* Philadelphia: John C. Winston, 1952. First edition, small ownership of Ian Macauley, some wear to crown, very good in supplied dust jacket with small chip on front board, couple of tiny tears and some general wear at extremities along with original tattered, poor dust jacket, dedication copy iscribed by author to his protege and friend Ian Macauley.   Between the Covers Rare Books   208 - 117   2016 $25,000

Clarke, Arthur C. *The Sentinel.* New York: Berkley Books, 1983. First edition, one of 465 numbered copies signed by author and artist, Lebbeus Woods, octavo, cloth, fine in nearly fine cloth slipcase with some rubbing.   John W. Knott, Jr./L.W. Currey, Inc.   Fall-Winter 2015 - 17559   2016 $200

Clarke, Arthur C. *2001: a Space Odyssey.* New York: New American Library, 1968. First edition, signed by author, octavo, boards, couple of small abrasions on front free endpaper, page edges just bit tanned, else fine in fine $4.95 first state dust jacket.   John W. Knott, Jr./L.W. Currey, Inc.   Fall-Winter 2015 - 18565   2016 $1000

Clarke, Edward H. *Sex In Education or a Fair Chance for Girls.* Boston & New York: Houghton Mifflin & Co., 1886. 13 page catalog, original green cloth, armorial bookplate of Stephen Ralli, very good.   Jarndyce Antiquarian Books CCXV - 596   2016   £35

Clarke, G. *The Georgian Era memoirs of the Most Eminent Persons Who Have Flourished in Great Britain from the Accession of George the First to the Demise of George the Fourth.* London: Vizetelly, Branston & Co., 1832-1834. First edition of this illustrated collection, 4 volumes, 8vo., frontispieces and plates, contemporary tan calf and buff cloth, spines gilt with red morocco gilt labels, findings slightly chipped and rubbed, spines darkened and loss of part of label to volume I, but very good, top edges gilt.   Unsworths Antiquarian Booksellers Ltd.   E04 - 7   2016   £180

Clarke, Henry *The School Candidates, a Prosaic Burlesque.* Manchester: 18th Jan., 1788. Frontispiece, plates and illustrations, faint signs of label removed from leading pastedown, small Reading's Library stamp, original green cloth, very good.   Jarndyce Antiquarian Books CCXV - 597   2016   £35

Clarke, John Henrik *The Middle Passage: Our Holocaust!* Detroit: Dr. Walter O. Evans, 1991. First edition, one of just 250 copies signed by author and Lawrence, string-bound with surgical silk, rare, 8vo., included is invitation to NY Premeire of film John Henry Clarke a Great Mighty Walk.   Second Life Books, Inc.   196A - 300   2016 $1250

Clarke, Mary Victoria Cowden *The Complete Concordance to Shakespeare.* London: Charles Knight & Co., 1845. First edition in book form, 4to., subscriber's copy, signed by author, clean and bright within, few spots of foxing to prelims, half tan calf, gilt spine with slightly cracked dark brown morocco label, marbled paper boards, endpapers and edges, rubbed spine bit scuffed, lower hinge repaired, very good, faded ownership inscription of 'W. S. Pratten, Compton Lodge".   Unsworths Antiquarian Booksellers Ltd.   30 - 138   2016   £150

Clarke, Susanna *Jonathan Strange & Mr. Norrell.* London: Bloomsbury, 2004. First British edition, illustrations by Portia Rosenberg, fine in fine black dust jacket, signed by author.   Bella Luna Books   2016 - 17160   2016 $82

Clarke, Thurston *Equator: a Journey round the World.* London: Hutchinson, 1988. First edition, 8vo., maps, original black cloth, dust jacket.   J. & S. L. Bonham Antiquarian Booksellers   Voyages 2016 - 9848   2016   £30

Clarke, William *Every night Book or Life after Dark.* London: T. Richardson, Sherwood & Co., 1827. 2 vignette engravings, neatly rebacked in quarter calf, red label, book-label of Shirley Brooks, humorous writer and editor of Punch, with commendatory note which may be in his hand. Jarndyce Antiquarian Booksellers   CCXVII - 71   2016   £225

Clarkson, L. *Heartsease and Happy Days.* New York & London: Dutton & Griffith & Farran, 1883. Folio, blue cloth with elaborate pictorial cover in silver, gold, red and green, all edges gilt, slight wear to spine ends and tips and covers dusty, very good+ clean and tight, 12 exquisite chromolithographed plates with paper guards.   Aleph-bet Books, Inc.   112 - 493   2016 $300

Clarkson, R. D. *Children Who never Grow Up.* Falkirk: John Callander, 1909. Original dark green printed wrappers, art nouveau design, slightly sunned, very good. Jarndyce Antiquarian Booksellers   CCXVIII - 1116   2016   £30

Clarkson, Thomas *Gritos de los Africanos Contra lost Euorpeos sus Opresores o sea Rapida Ojeada sobre el Comercio Homicida llamdo trafico de Negros. (The Cries of Africa to the Inhabitants of Europe....).* Barcelona: Imprenta de Jose Torner, 1825. First Spanish edition, octavo, contemporary calf boards, title and spine decorations gilt, newer marbled endpapers, red morocco spine label, some repair to spine ends, nice, near fine copy, Carey folding plate, neat and professional repairs at folds on verso.   Between the Covers Rare Books   202 - 3   2016 $5500

Clarkson, Thomas *The History of the Rise, Progress and Accomplishment of the Abolition of the African Slave-Trade by the British Parliament.* Wilmington: R. Porter, 1816. Second Wilmington edition?, small octavo, 348 pages, vignette, contemporary full calf with morocco spine label gilt, early gift inscription to Stephen Downing from Charles Collins and signatures, small chip on front fly, light wear on boards, very good or better.   Between the Covers Rare Books   202 - 2   2016 $375

Clason, Clyde B. *Blind Drifts.* New York: Doubleday Doran & Co., 1937. First edition, fine, bright copy in bright, near fine dust jacket with 3 tiny chips to top edge. Buckingham Books   2015 - 38446   2016 $475

Clatyon's Patent Tile, Pipe and Brick Machines *Descriptive Catalogue....* London: George Odell, Printers, 18 Princess Street, Cavendish Square, 1851. 4to., wood engraved illustrations, original decorative printed wrappers, old central fold and remains of three penny reds stamps on back cover.   Marlborough Rare Books   List 55 - 9   2016   £185

Claudianus, Claudius *Opera quae Exstant Omnia ad Membranarum Veterum Fidem Castigata.* Amstelodami: ex officina Schouteniana, 1760. First edition thus 4to., additional presentation certificate bound in, titlepage in red and black, woodcut device, woodcut had and tailpieces and initials, titlepage little dusty, occasional light spots of foxing, slightly toned towards top edge, generally clean within, contemporary Dutch prize vellum, raised bands, blind tooling and black morocco label to spine, gilt panels and centerpieces to both boards with coat of arms of Amsterdam, edges lightly sprinkled blue, two small holes to vellum at spine, label chipped, ties lost, somewhat grubby but very good, sound, overall, printed prize certificate dated 1796 made out by hand to Joanni Petro Pelser and signed by College of Amsterdam rector H. Hana.   Unsworths Antiquarian Booksellers   30 - 36   2016   £350

Clausewitz, Carl Von *On War.* London: N. Trubner & Co., 1871. First edition in English, 3 small quarto volumes in one, mounted photographic frontispiece portrait of author, original full blue cloth, boards ruled in black, spine stamped in gilt, orange paper spine label, lettered in gilt, brown coated endpapers, spine bit darkened, boards bit rubbed, head and tail of spine with some minor shelfwear, front inner hinge starting but firm, previous owner Douglas Dawson's large bookplate, overall very good.   Heritage Book Shop Holiday 2015 - 21   2016 $4000

Clavigero, Francesco Saverio *The History of Mexico Collected from Spanish and Mexican Historians from Manuscripts and Ancient Paintings of the Indians...* Richmond: William Prichard, 1806. First American edition, 3 volumes, black and white plates, 8vo., folding maps, full sheep with red morocco lettering pieces, rare, calf quite dry on all volumes, with good deal of spine on volume I lacking or flaked, half of label gone, front board nearly detached, front joint split but holding on volume 3, few leaves torn, notations on last blank, plates and maps to all volumes foxed, though text leaves quite bright and clean, overall good.   Kaaterskill Books   21 - 18   2016 $300

Claxton, William *Jazzlife: auf den Spuren des Jazz.* Offenburgen (Baden): Burda Druck und Verlag, 1961. First edition, cloth issue includes two rare 45 RPM vinyl records, each in illustrated sleeve that matches jacket design in publisher's pocket mounted at bottom right corner of rear pastedown, book near fine in very good dust jacket, jacket bright and clean with chipping and wear at two of the corners, notably top left corner of rear panel, records and sleeves easily near fine.   Royal Books   49 - 4   2016 $7500

Clay, Felix *Modern School Buildings, Elementary and Secondary....* London: B. T. Batsford, 1902. First edition, half title, folding plans, plates, illustrations, original red cloth, slightly dulled.   Jarndyce Antiquarian Books   CCXV - 598   2016   £60

Clay, John *My Life on the Range.* Chicago: privately printed, 1924. Top edge gilt, little faded, else bright, near fine copy, illustrations.   Dumont Maps and Books   133 - 48   2016 $450

Clay, John Cecil *The Lover's Mother Goose.* Indianapolis: Bobbs Merrill, 1905. 4to., pictorial cloth stamped in gold and green pictorial paste-on, mint in publisher's box (soiled with some wear), 8 beautiful color plates and many full page 3-color illustrations, plus decorations on text pages, beautiful copy.   Aleph-bet Books, Inc.   111 - 302   2016 $450

Clayton, J. W. *The Sunny South, an Autumn in Spain and Majoraca.* London: Hurst and Blackett, 1869. First edition, 8vo., frontispiece, original purple cloth, spine sunned, very clean internally.   J. & S. L. Bonham Antiquarian Booksellers   Europe 2016 - 9735   2016   £220

Cleary, Jon *Fall of an Eagle.* New York: Morrow, 1964. First edition, 8vo., dedication copy, signed by author, with 3 good signed typed letters loosely inserted, with 2 bookplates of recipients, Gordon and Evy Featherstone-Witty, slight tape marks to front endpaper.   Any Amount of Books   2015 - A72358   2016   £150

Cleeves, Ann *Cold Earth.* London: Macmillan, 2016. First edition, very fine, signed by author, jacket fitted with new removable clear cover.   Gemini Books   2016 - 31915   2016 $44

Clegg, Bill *Did You Ever Have a Family.* New York: Scout Press, 2015. Advance reading copy, fine in wrappers, uncommon.   Ken Lopez Bookseller   166 - 22   2016 $125

Cleghorn, Thomas *The Hydro-Aeronaut or Navigators Life Buoy...* London: J. M. Richardson, 1810. First edition, 12mo., half title, frontispiece, engraved title, errata leaf, contemporary sprinkled calf, gilt spine, red morocco lael, some worm damage to head of spine and following hinge, extremities little rubbed, signature of Hugh Hiethold 1946, overall good plus.   Jarndyce Antiquarian Booksellers   CCXVII - 72   2016   £220

Clemens, Samuel Langhorne   1835-1910   *Adventures of Huckleberry Finn.* New York: 1883. First American edition, early issue, with titlepage a cancel, copyright notice dated 1884, page (13), illustration captioned 'Him and another Man' correctly listed last at page 88, page 57 the 11th line from bottom reads 'with the saw', page 283 is a cancel with engraving redone, third state, earliest known to appear in cloth bound copies of book, page 155, the final '5' in the pagination present and larger, frontispiece does not have imprint of Heliotype Printing Co. and tablecloth or scarf on which the bust rests is not clearly visible, octavo, inserted frontispiece, wood engraved text illustrations, octavo, publisher's rare dark green cloth, lettered and pictorially stamped in black and gilt, some wear to spine and corners and on top and bottom of spine, one short tear to front free endpaper, previous owner contemporary inscription, housed in custom quarter morocco clamshell case, gilt stamped, very good.   Heritage Book Shop   Holiday 2015 - 196   2016 $5000

Clemens, Samuel Langhorne   1835-1910   *Adventures of Huckleberry Finn.* New York: Charles Webster, 1885. First edition, first state with naughty picture on page 283, 8vo., three quarter morocco rubbed at extremities of boards, hinges repaired with brown binder's tape, nice, clean copy, names or internal markings.   Second Life Books, Inc.   197 - 328   2016 $13,500

Clemens, Samuel Langhorne   1835-1910   *Adventures of Huckleberry Finn.* Northampton: Pennyroyal Press, 1985. No. 138 of 350 copies, Portfolio, two volumes, including portfolio of prints, publisher's dark green crushed morocco by Gray Parrot, covers bordered by four gilt fillets, upper cover with gilt medallion containing interlinek dates '1885' and '1985', flat spine with gilt titling, housed with beige portfolio in matching linen slipcase, 49 woodcuts by Barry Moser, as called for in volume, with additional suite of plates in portfolio, calligraphy by Rutledge, spine sunned to light green, otherwise near fine.   Phillip J. Pirages   67 - 276   2016 $2400

Clemens, Samuel Langhorne   1835-1910   *Adventures of Tom Sawyer.* Hartford: American Pub. Co., 1876. First American edition, first issue, square 8vo., on wove paper, illustrations, only 200 copies bound in half morocco binding, publisher's original half brown morocco over rust colored cloth, spine lettered in gilt and stamped in blind, boards ruled in blind, boards ruled in blind, all edges gilt, marbled endpapers, boards and edges slightly scuffed, minor stain to outer margin of first few leaves, occasional finger smudging and light spotting, front free endpaper with inner margin minor closed tear, overall exceptional copy, housed in custom full morocco clamshell.   Heritage Book Shop   Holiday 2015 - 108   2016 $25,000

Clemens, Samuel Langhorne 1835-1910 *A Connecticut Yankee in King Arthur's Court.* New York: Webster, 1889. First edition, later state, 8vo., later issue without 'S' like emblem on page 59, illustrations by Daniel Carter Beard, drab green cloth stamped in blue, black and gilt, front hinge tender, good.   Second Life Books, Inc.   197 - 329   2016 $750

Clemens, Samuel Langhorne 1835-1910 *A Connecticut Yankee in King Arthur's Court.* New York: Heritage Press, 1948. Teal boards with tan cloth, very fine in slipcase (faded and rubbed), illustrations by Honore Guilbeau, Sandglass pamphlet laid in.   Argonaut Book Shop   Heritage Press 2015 - 7102   2016 $45

Clemens, Samuel Langhorne 1835-1910 *A Double Barrelled Detective Story.* New York & London: Harper & Bros., 1902. First edition, octavo, on wove paper, 6 of 7 called for plates, including frontispiece with tissue guard, endpapers in mixed A and B state, with no priority, publisher's original red cloth, title stamped in intaglio on gilt background on upper cover, gilt lettered and decorated spine, top edge gilt, few dappled spots to upper cover, bookplate, spine mildly darkened with bit of soiling, otherwise tight, bright, very good copy.   David Brass Rare Books, Inc. 2015 - 01041   2016 $300

Clemens, Samuel Langhorne 1835-1910 *English as She is Taught.* New York: Mutual Book Co., 1900. First edition, second state with correction of word 'five' on page 16, 12mo., green cloth stamped in black and red, little stained on cover and rubbed at extremities of spine, very good, untrimmed.   Second Life Books, Inc.   197 - 330   2016 $125

Clemens, Samuel Langhorne 1835-1910 *Following the Equator.* Hartford: American Publishing Co., 1897. First edition first state, (Single imprint with signature mark on page 161 and terminal flyleaf), 8vo., frontispiece, 192 other illustrations, blue cloth, contemporary name on endpaper, hinges little tender, very good.   Second Life Books, Inc. 197 - 331   2016 $750

Clemens, Samuel Langhorne 1835-1910 *The Innocents Abroad.* Chicago: Sherwin Beach Press, 1998. Number 57 of 200 copie, numbered and illustrated by the bookmakers, 2 volumes, non-adhesive binding with exposed spine sewing consists of 7 black double raised cords attached to hard covers wrapped in red cloth, each volume has cut-out to front cover with small black and white illustrations= along with author, title and volume number, the volumes in turn housed in black and white linen covered hard case wrapper and black leather straps over brass studs and leather suitcase-type label, intended to suggest a portmanteau, printed in Monotype Bell on Johannot paper, designed by Bob McCamant and printed by Martha Chiplis, binding designed and executed by Trisha Hammer, fine.   The Kelmscott Bookshop 13 - 56   2016 $1200

Clemens, Samuel Langhorne 1835-1910 *Life on the Mississippi.* Boston: Osgood, 1883. First edition, intermediate state B (without scene on page 441 and page 443 'St. Louis Hotel'), 8vo., 300 illustrations, original brown cloth stamped in black and gilt, little rubbed at extremities of spine, paper backed on rear hinge, very good.   Second Life Books, Inc.   197 - 332   2016 $900

Clemens, Samuel Langhorne 1835-1910 *The Love Letters of Mark Twain.* New York: Harper Bros., 1949. First edition, no. 6 of 155 special copies with flyleaf signed, 243 x 165, publisher's black cloth with printed spine label, original green dust jacket with printed spine label, housed in publisher's nearly fine slipcase, frontispiece, flawless. Phillip J. Pirages   67 - 92   2016 $11,500

Clemens, Samuel Langhorne 1835-1910 *The Man that Corrupted Hadleyburg and other Stories and Essays.* New York: Harper, 1900. First edition, state 2 , 8vo., gold stamped red cloth, spine little faded, good tight copy, ex-library with bookplates in front and rear, rear hinge starting. Second Life Books, Inc.   197 - 335   2016 $75

Clemens, Samuel Langhorne 1835-1910 *Mark Twain's Letter to William Bowen, Buffalo, Feb. sixth 1870.* San Francisco: Book Club of California, 1938. First edition, one of 400 copies, small quarto, title vignette 4 text illustrations reproduced from first edition of Tom Sawyer, cloth backed blue boards, paper spine label, very light offsetting on ends, small chip to corner of some label, but fine.   Argonaut Book Shop   Literature 2015 - 5689   2016 $125

Clemens, Samuel Langhorne 1835-1910 *Mark Twain's Memoranda from the Galaxy.* Toronto: Wm. Warwich, March, 1871. First edition, octavo, two lithographed illustrations, original black cloth, gilt stamped on front cover, blind-stamped on front and rear covers, small stain to front cover, front outer hinge repaired, otherwise fine.   Heritage Book Shop   Holiday 2015 - 107   2016 $1500

Clemens, Samuel Langhorne 1835-1910 *The Prince and the Pauper, a Tale for Young People of All Ages.* Boston: Osgood, 1882. First edition, first state with Franklin Press imprint on copyright page, original gold stamped green cloth, first state binding with central rosette on spine 1/16 inch above fillet, real binder's endpaper in rear, some very minor external wear, covers little dusty, otherwise very good, usually found in terrible condition, former owner's presentation dated Dec. 24 1881.   Second Life Books, Inc. 197 - 335   2016 $1000

Clemens, Samuel Langhorne 1835-1910 *Pudd'nhead Wilson.* London: Chatto & Windus, 1894. First UK edition, 8vo., catalog dated Sept.1 1894, illustrations by Louis Loeb, red cloth, printed in black, bookplate, very good.   Second Life Books, Inc.   197 - 334   2016 $225

Clemens, Samuel Langhorne 1835-1910 *Roughing It.* Avon: Heritage Press, 1972. Grey cloth lettered in silver, spine faded, else fine in slipcase (darkened), illustrations by Noel Sickles, Sandglass pamphlet laid in. Argonaut Book Shop   Heritage Press 2015 - 7106   2016 $40

Clemens, Samuel Langhorne 1835-1910 *A Tramp Abroad.* London: Chatto & Windus, 1880. Third edition, 2 volumes, half titles, 32 page catalog (April 1880), original olive green cloth, front boards pictorialy blocked and lettered in black, spines blocked in black and lettered in gilt, publisher's monogram at centre of following boards, very slightly rubbed, signed "Kate Restall, May 29th/80", additional inscription "To Mr. E. Galsworthy, 2 Gladstone Terrance, Grosvenor Road".   Jarndyce Antiquarian Booksellers   CCXVII - 287   2016   £120

Clemens, Samuel Langhorne 1835-1910 *Wapping Alice.* Berkeley: Friends of the Bancroft Library, 1981. First edition, frontispiece, 2 plates from early photos, 2 facsimiles, green printed wrappers, very fine.   Argonaut Book Shop   Literature 2015 - 7512   2016 $45

Clement, Lewis *Shooting and Fishing Trips in England, France, Alsace, Belgium, Holland and Bavaria.* London: Chapman and Hall, 1878. Second edition, 8vo., original red cloth, spine lettered gilt, front over designs in black, little shaky, spine sunned, internally clean.   Sotheran's   Hunting, Shooting & Fishing - 166   2016   £50

Clewes, Dorothy *Special Branch Willie.* London: Hamish Hamilton, 1969. First edition, octavo, illustrations, printed in green and black by Edward Ardizzone, pictorial boards, review slip laid in, near fine in very good dust jacket, bit faded at spine and edges, uncommon.   Peter Ellis   112 - 20   2016   £150

Cliff of Worcester *The Cambrian Directory or Cursory Sketches of the Welsh Territories.* Salisbury: printed and sold by J. Easton sold also by others, 1800. First edition, folding table or chart, 8vo., uncut in original boards, boards bit soiled, sometime rebacked, very good, scarce.   Blackwell's Rare Books   B184 - 9   2016   £400

Clifford, Frederick *A History of Private Bill Legislation.* London: Butterworths, 1867-1885. First edition, 2 volumes, 8vo., original green cloth lettered gilt, bindings bit shaken an slight wear to extremities, else good, clean copies.   John Drury Rare Books   2015 - 23924   2016 $341

Clifford, Lucy *Children's Busy, Children Glad, Children Naughty, Children Sad.* Well Gardner, Darton & Co., 1881. First edition, errata slip loose between frontispiece and titlepage with holograph note by author at head suggesting that it was done at Pym's prompting frontispiece and titlepage design by Pym, 20 further illustrations by same with few full page all color printed, interleaved with tisse pages, occasional handling marks with frontispiece re-fixed with cloth tape, original quarter brown cloth with illustrated boards, boards darkened with some soiling and rubbing, some wear to edges and pencil marking to lower board, hinges repaired with cloth tape, spine cocked, sound, inscribed, author's own copy.   Blackwell's Rare Books   B184 - 58   2016   £280

Clifton, Mark *They'd Rather Be Right.* New York: Gnome Press Inc., Publishers, 1957. First edition, octavo, boards, age tanning to text block (common to this book), fine in fine dust jacket, sharp copy.   John W. Knott, Jr./L.W. Currey, Inc.   Fall-Winter 2015 - 16984   2016 $350

Clodd, Edward *Grant Allen. A Memoir.* London: Grant Richards, 1900. First edition, presentation from author to book's publisher, Grant Richards, original dark brown cloth boards, gilt title to spine, minor sunning to spine, small chip to foot of spine and few spots to boards, offsetting to endpapers, else clean, very good.   The Kelmscott Bookshop   13 - 13   2016 $650

Clokey, Richard M. *William H. Ashley.* Norman: University of Oklahoma Press, 1980. First edition, 9 maps, 16 illustrations, brown cloth, very fine with pictorial dust jacket.   Argonaut Book Shop   Biography 2015 - 6973   2016 $75

Clothes and the man: Hints on the Wearing and Caring of Clothes. London: Grant Richards, 1900. First edition, half title, ads on pastedowns, original red pictorial cloth, spine faded, slightly rubbed, bookseller's ticket.   Jarndyce Antiquarian Books   CCXV - 122   2016   £50

Clough, Arthur Hugh *Bothie of Toper-Na-Fuoisich. A Long Vacation Pastoral.* Oxford: Francis Macpherson, 1848. First edition, very good in original blue cloth, flexible boards with gilt title to front cover, minor wear to edges of covers, few small chip to edges of several pages, binding split in few places, however all of the pages remain bound in, bookplate of collector Mark Samuels Lasner, very good.   The Kelmscott Bookshop   12 - 25   2016 $400

Clough, Arthur Hugh *Poems.* Cambridge: Macmillan, 1862. First collected edition, 8vo., original green honeycomb cloth, gilt, minor wear to extremities, good, inscribed by author for Revd. R. P. Graves.   Blackwell's Rare Books   B186 - 43   2016   £375

Clunie, James *First Principles of Working-Class Education.* Glasgow: printed & Pub. by the Socialist Labour Press, 1920. Half title, lacks leading endpaper, following hinge strengthened, numerous folding plates, original blue cloth.   Jarndyce Antiquarian Books   CCXV - 599   2016   £25

Clurman, Harold *Ibsen.* New York: Macmillan, 1977. First edition, inscribed by author to director David Mamet and his then wife, Lindsey Crouse Dec. 31. 1977, near fine in like dust jacket.   Royal Books   48 - 36   2016 $650

Clurman, Harold *Lies Like Truth: Theatre Reviews and Essays.* New York: Macmillan, 1958. First edition, signed by book's dedicatee, actress Stella Adler on dedication page, very good in very good plus dust jacket.   Royal Books   48 - 35   2016 $350

Cluton-Brock, Alan *Murder at Liberty Hall.* New York: Macmillan, 1941. First American edition, fine in very good dust jacket with light fraying at spine ends, chips at corners and couple of closed tears.   Mordida Books   2015 - 010579   2016 $55

Clutton, Henry *Remarks, with Illustrations on the Domestic Architecture of France....* London: published by Day & Son, 1853. Large folio, 16 tinted lithograph plates, some spotting and illustrations in text, original red morocco backed blue cloth, rebacked preserving original lettering to spine, discrete blindstamp on lower corner of title and last plate.   Marlborough Rare Books   List 55 - 14   2016   £650

Clyne, Geraldine *Jolly Jump-Ups Number Book.* Springfield: McLoughlin, 1950. Oblong 4to., pictorial boards, light edge rubbing, very good-fine, 6 great double page color pop-ups.   Aleph-bet Books, Inc.   112 - 387   2016 $200

Coates, Brian *The Birds of Papua new Guniea, including the Bismarck Archipelago and Bougainville Volume One: non Passerines.* Brisbane: Dove, 1985. Quarto, color photos maps, fine in fine dust jacket.   Andrew Isles Natural History Books   55 - 4166   2016 $250

Cobb, James *The Cherokee an Opera as Performed at the Theatre Royal Drury Lane.* London: printed in the year, 1795. Modern wrappers, barely noticeably, early library blindstamps, light soiling and foxing, but very good.   Joseph J. Felcone, Inc.   Books from Five Centuries: a Miscellany - 43   2016 $500

Cobbett, William 1763-1835 *Advice to Young Men and Incidentally to Young Women...* London: published by the author, 1829. First edition, 12mo., 12 page catalog, original drab boards, glazed cloth, spine expertly repaired, very good.   Jarndyce Antiquarian Books   CCXV - 123   2016   £180

Cobbett, William 1763-1835 *Preliminary Part of Paper Against Gold: the Main Object of Which is to Show the Justice and Necessity of reducing the Interest of that Which is called the National Deb...* London: John M. Cobbett, 1821. First edition, 8vo., recently well bound in cloth lettered gilt, good copy, one or two minor stains.   John Drury Rare Books   2015 - 20206   2016 $306

Cobden-Sanderson, Thomas James 1840-1922 *The Ideal book or Book beautiful...* San Francisco: privately printed, 1916. First John Henry Nash edition, number 35 of 165 numbered copies, second American edition overall, quarto, original tan paper boards and printed paper label, fine in original plain and slightly worn dust jacket.   The Brick Row Book Shop   Miscellany 69 - 26   2016 $650

Cobden-Sanderson, Thomas James 1840-1922 *London: a Paper Read at a Meeting of the Art Workers Guild... March 6 1891.* Hammersmith: Doves Press, 1906. One of 5 copies on vellum (and 300 on paper), 235 x 165mm., dark brown crushed morocco by Doves Bindery (stamp signed and dated 1921), gilt ruled covers, raised bands, spine compartments and turn-ins ruled gilt, all edges gilt, neatly rebacked using most of original backstrip, boards with slight humpbacked browning (as nearly always with vellum printed books), hint of rubbing to edges and corners, minor loss of gilt from spine, otherwise near fine.   Phillip J. Pirages   67 - 334   2016 $4500

Cochrane, Charles *Journal of a Residence and Travels in Columbia During the Years 1823 and 1824.* London: Henry Colburn, 1825. First edition, 2 volumes, 8vo., 2 colored frontispieces, folding map, contemporary half green calf, near fine set.   J. & S. L. Bonham Antiquarian Booksellers America 2016 - 8034   2016   £780

Cochrane, Robert *Risen by Perseverance; or Lives of Self-Made Men.* Edinburgh: W. P. Nimmo, 1890. Frontispiece, lacking leading f.e.p., original green decorated cloth, very good.   Jarndyce Antiquarian Books   CCXV - 52   2016   £25

Cochrane, Robert *Risen by Perseverance...* Edinburgh: W. P. Nimmo, circa, 1895? Later reprint, Frontispiece, slightly spotted, original red cloth, slightly rubbed and marked, prize inscription.   Jarndyce Antiquarian Books   CCXV - 53   2016   £20

The Cock, The Mouse and the Little Red Hen. New York: E. P. Dutton, 1946. Oblong 4to., spiral backed pictorial boards, ight wear at spirals, slight edge wear, fine in very good dust jacket with some chipping and small piece off head of spine, fine moveaable plate book, 4 tab operated plates.   Aleph-bet Books, Inc.   112 - 329   2016 $225

Cockburn, James Pattison *Swiss Scenery.* London: Rodwell & Martin, 1820. First edition, quarto, vignette on titlepage, 60 steel engravings, original green decorative morocco, gilt, joints and corners rubbed, light foxing to prelims, good copy.   J. & S. L. Bonham Antiquarian Booksellers   Europe 2016 - 8851   2016   £480

Cockburn, John *A Journey Over Land from the Gulf of Honduras to the Great South-Sea.* London: for C. Rivington, 1735. First edition, folding map, contemporary sprinkled calf, very skillfully rebacked with entire original spine and label retained, lovely copy, text clean and fresh and entirely unfoxed, Wolfgang Herz copy with his small booklabel.   Joseph J. Felcone, Inc.   Books from Five Centuries: a Miscellany - 44   2016 $3500

Cockburn, William *Strictures on Clerical Education in the University of Cambridge.* London: J. Hatchard &c., 1809. Some largely inoffensive dampstaining to upper margins, disbound, ownership signature of James Martineau, 36 pages.   Jarndyce Antiquarian Books   CCXV - 570   2016   £40

Cockerell, S. C. *Some German Woodcuts of the Fifteenth Century.* Hammersmith: Kelmscott Press, 1897. One of 225 copies on paper (and 8 on vellum), 295 x 216mm., original holland backed blue paper boards, untrimmed edges, with 35 reproductions of woodcuts printed on 23 leaves, one six-line woodcut initial, front pastedown with ex-libris and wood engraved bookplate (designed by Lucian Pissaro), printed in red and black, bit of distress to cloth at spine ends, corners mildly bumped and worn, perhaps hint of fading at board edges, but all of these defects minor and otherwise, very fine, fragile, remarkably clean, fresh and bright internally, with deep impressions of type.   Phillip J. Pirages   67 - 219   2016 $6500

Cockin, Joan *Curiosity Killed the Cat.* London: Hodder & Stoughton, 1947. Covers dusty, otherwise very good, scarce.   I. D. Edrich   Crime - 2016   £60

Coddington, Grace *Grace: Thirty Years of Fashion at Vogue.* Paris: Edition 7L, 2002. First edition, photos, fine in very near fine painted acetetate dust jacket and in very good plus slipcase that is lightly soiled and with some minor wear, beautifully printed and designed book.   Jeff Hirsch Books   E-List 80 - 6   2016 $650

Codrescu, Andrei *& Grammar & Money.* Berkeley: Arif Press, 1973. One of 26 copies spined and lettered and signed by author, horizontal 12mo., not numbered, paper wrappers, cover little soiled and faded, else very good.   Second Life Books, Inc.   196A - 308   2016 $95

Codrescu, Andrei *Diapers on the Snow.* Ann Arbor: Crowfoot, 1981. First printing, 8vo., paper wrappers, signed by author, cover slightly faded, else nice.   Second Life Books, Inc.   196A - 307   2016 $45

Codrescu, Andrei *License to Carry a Gun.* Chicago: Big Table, 1970. First printing, 8vo., paper wrappers, author's presentation, cover scuffed and somewhat soiled, otherwise very good, tight copy.   Second Life Books, Inc.   196A - 309   2016 $150

Codrescu, Andrei *The Life and Times of an Involuntary Genius.* New York: Braziller, 1975. First printing, 8vo., paper over boards, note from author laid in, edges soiled, otherwise very good, tight copy in scuffed and somewhat soiled dust jacket.   Second Life Books, Inc.   196A - 310   2016 $75

Codrescu, Andrei *Selected Poems 1970-1980.* New York: Sun, 1983. First edition, author's presentation, paper wrappers, 8vo., edges, cover and half title little spotted, otherwise very good, laid in is 6 line ALS from author and APC to poet Tom Clark.   Second Life Books, Inc.   196A - 314   2016 $150

Codrescu, Andrei *Secret Training.* San Francisco: Grape Press, 1973. One of 350 copies, 8vo., paper wrappers, author's presentation, cover little yellowed and slightly soiled, otherwise very good.   Second Life Books, Inc.   196A - 313   2016 $75

Codrescu, Andrei *Secret Training.* San Francisco: Grape Press, 1973. One of 350 copies, 8vo., paper wrappers, inscribed presentation from author, cover little yellowed and slightly soiled, otherwise very nice.   Second Life Books, Inc.   196A - 312   2016 $45

Codrescu, Andrei *A Serious Morning.* Santa Barbara: Capra, 1973. No. 97 of 100 signed copies, small 8vo., paper over boards, signed and numbered on colophon, fine.   Second Life Books, Inc.   196A - 315   2016 $135

Cody, Sherwin *An Evening with Dickens.* Rochester: Sherwin Cody School of English, 1930. 16mo. slight worming in upper margin of first few leaves, original brown embossed wrappers, little torn at edges.   Jarndyce Antiquarian Booksellers   CCXVIII - 140   2016   £25

Coffield, Glen *The Horned Moon.* Waldport: Untide Press, 1944. Limited to 600 copies, tipped-in photo of author preceded title, 12mo., stiff paper wrappers, chipped and torn, tanning.   Oak Knoll Books   310 - 168   2016 $150

Cogger, Harrold G. *Reptiles and Amphibians of Australia.* Sydney: Reed Books, 1992. Fifth edition, quarto, color photos and text illustrations, signature, very good in dust jacket.   Andrew Isles Natural History Books   55 - 28041   2016 $150

Coggeshall, Edwin W. *The Largest Collection Ever Offered in America of the Autograph Letters of Charles Dickens and Letters and Manuscripts by William M. Thackeray with Original Portraits of Literary Celebrities from the Library of Mr. Edwin Coggeshall of New York. Part II (concluding sale).* New York: Anderson Galleries, 1916. Frontispiece, old pencil annotation, later brown cloth, very good.   Jarndyce Antiquarian Booksellers   CCXVIII - 1491   2016   £35

Cohen-Portheim, Paul *Paris.* Berlin: Klinkhardt & Biermann, 1930. First edition, 8vo., original cloth with scarce illustrated dust jacket, 15 photos of Sacha Stone, front flap of dust jacket removed, couple of creases and repaired closed tears to jacket, remains of pasted slip on front pastedown, otherwise very good.   Sotheran's Piccadilly Notes - Summer 2015 - 284   2016   £850

Cohen, Charles J. *Memoir of Rev. John Wiley Faires, A.M., D. D....* Philadelphia: privately printed, 1926. No. 107 of an edition of 1200, large 8vo., author's signature, photos, foldout classroom plan, paper over boards, three quarter cloth, rear hinge tender, front just beginning at bottom, edges of leaves slightly soiled, edges of cover little scuffed, otherwise very good.   Second Life Books, Inc.   196A - 316   2016 $50

Cohen, Gustavus *The Formation of Character.* Bloomsbury: Gustavus Cohen, 59 Great Russell Street; Liverpool: 40 Bedford Street North, 1884. original blue cloth, bevelled boards decorated in gilt and black, slightly dulled, illustrations by Fritz Braun, inscription from H. G. Cohen 28th July 1886 to R. Cardwell, very good, bright of family presentation copy.   Jarndyce Antiquarian Books   CCXV - 124   2016   £65

Cohen, Henry-Jacques *Sous Le Signe Du Rossignol. (Under the Sight of the Nightingale).* Paris: Sur les Presses de Pierre Frazier, Oct. 15, 1923. First edition, no. 121 of 1500 copies, 306 x 235mm., later coral colored quarter morocco over marbled boards by the Luis Pettingell Bindery of Berkeley, California (ticket), raised bands, gilt ruled compartments with central fleuron, 19 color plates by Kay Nielsen, each mounted within a decorative frame with captioned and decorated tissue guard, spine rather sunned, with gilt bit dulled, light purple stain to edge of front free endpaper, otherwise very fine, no signs of use.   Phillip J. Pirages   67 - 262   2016 $1250

Cohen, Jane R. *Charles Dickens and His Original Illustrations.* Columbus: Ohio University Press, 1980. 4to., half title, frontispiece, illustrations, original dark green cloth, very good in dust jacket.   Jarndyce Antiquarian Booksellers   CCXVIII - 1119   2016   £85

Cohen, Morton M. *Lewis Carroll and Kitchins...* New York: Argosy Bookstore, 1980. Limited edition, copy number 20 in an edition limited to 750 numbered copies, slim quarto, quarter beige cloth with tan and purple floral paper covered boards, near fine, publisher's prospectus laid in.   Ken Sanders Rare Books   E Catalogue # 1 - 24   2016 $75

Coke, Charlotte Talbot *The Gentlewoman at Home.* London: Henry & Co., 1892. Half title, frontispiece, photo portrait, original dark green cloth, corners slightly bumped, very good.   Jarndyce Antiquarian Books   CCXV - 125   2016   £75

Coke, Edward *The Compleate copy-Holder Wherein is Contained a Learned Discourse of the Antiquity and Nature of Manors and Copy-Holds.* London: for Matthew Walbanck and Richard Beel, 1644. Second edition, neat modern full calf in period style, worm trail toward end of text but confined largely to margin, margins close on titlepage but ample, else very good.   Joseph J. Felcone, Inc.   Books from Five Centuries: a Miscellany - 45   2016 $750

Coke, Frederick A. *To the Top of the Continent, Discovery, Exploration and Adventure in Sub-Arctic Alaska.* London: Hodder & Stoughton, 1908. 8vo., original olive green buckram, spine lettered gilt, gilt framed and mounted illustration of the peak on front cover, top edge gilt, color printed frontispiece, 23 leaves of plates with numerous, mainly photographic illustrations, including one double page map, several illustrations, maps and charts in text, spine little sunned, apart from ight offsetting from flyleaves and frontispiece, clean and fresh, some gatherings still unopened, beautiful copy, scarce first UK edition, first issue.   Sotheran's Travel and Exploration - 53   2016   £278

Coke, Richard *Baghdad. the City of Peace.* London: Thornton Butterworth, 1927. First edition, 8vo., original orange cloth lettered gilt, frontispiece and 11 plates after photos, cloth with bit of rubbing and marking, occasional foxing inside, 2 leaves with small marginal flaws.   Sotheran's   Piccadilly Notes - Summer 2015 - 81   2016   £248

Colas, Rene *Bibliographie Generale Du Costume et De La Mode.* Paris: Librairie Rene Colas, 1933. First edition, limited to 1000 numbered copies, tall 8vo., later half red leather with red cloth with original paper wrappers bound in, top edge gilt, plates, rubbed along hinges.   Oak Knoll Books   310 - 239   2016 $325

Colbeck, Alfred *The Fall of the Staincliffes.* London: Sunday School Union, 1891. Frontispiece, illustrations, original pictorial pale green cloth, decorated and lettered in black and gilt, slightly dulled and marked.   Jarndyce Antiquarian Booksellers   CCXVII - 73   2016   £45

Colby Library Quarterly. Edwin Arlington Robinson Centennial Issue #1. Waterville: Colby College, March, 1969. First edition, pictorial wrappers, inscribed and signed by Archibald Macleish for William Meredith, with two ink corrections in his essay and original envelope addressed in MacLeish's hand, fine.   Charles Agvent   William Meredith - 66   2016 $80

Colby, F. T.   *Litton Cheney 1877.*   Warren Editions, 1976. One of 350 copies from an edition of 500, 24mo., original stapled wrappers, covered with patterned papers designed by Reynolds Stone, printed label to front, very good. Blackwell's Rare Books   B184 - 319   2016   £20

Cole, G. D. H.   *Birthday Gifts & Other Stories.*   London: Polybooks, 1946. First edition, Goldstone bookplate, near fine in dust jacket.   Mordida Books   2015 - 011725   2016 $65

Cole, Henri   *The Look of Things.*   New York: Alfred A. Knopf, 1995. First edition, inscribed and signed by poet March 7 1995, for William Meredith, faint dampstain to top of rear panel of both book and dust jacket, not terribly noticeable, near fine in like dust jacket.   Charles Agvent   William Meredith - 23   2016 $150

Cole, John   *Herveiana. Part III.*   Scarborough: printed and published by John Cole, 1826. First edition, woodcut arms on title, 2 woodcuts in text, extra-illustrated, 12mo., contemporary half calf, spine partly defective, author's own copy. Blackwell's Rare Books   B186 - 45   2016   £800

Cole, M. Elizabeth   *Jottings from Overland Trip to Arizona and California.*   Hansman & Pralow, 1908. 7 x 5 inches, printed wrappers, illustrations, covers lightly faded, else very good plus.   Buckingham Books   2015 - 34406   2016 $450

Coleman, Allan D.   *Confirmation.*   Brooklyn: ADCO Enterprises, 1975. Number 86 from an edition of 250, 12 black and white images of Jazz great Charlie Parker grave stone signed by Coleman, also includes signed note from Coleman to curator and author Tom Garver, terrific copy with nice association, fine in wrappers.   Jeff Hirsch Books   Holiday List 2015 - 7   2016 $75

Coleman, Edmund T.   *Scenes from the Snow-Fields: Being Illustrations of the Upper ice-World of Mont Blanc...*   1984. Limited edition, large folio, original purple wrappers, front cover lettered gilt, within drop-back box, front cover lettered gilt, within original cardboard box with label, color plates, as new.   Sotheran's   Travel and Exploration - 226   2016   £298

Coleman, Janet   *Mingus/Mingus: Two Memoirs.*   Berkeley: Creative Arts, 1989. First edition, photos, green cloth, nice in slightly scuffed dust jacket, Al Young's presentation for Andy Davis.   Second Life Books, Inc.   196A - 317   2016 $45

Coleman, Wanda   *Mad Dog Black Lady.*   Santa Barbara: Black Sparrow, 1979. First edition, one of 200 hardcover copies, numbered and signed by author, paper over boards with cloth spine, fine in acrylic dust jacket.   Second Life Books, Inc.   196A - 318   2016 $100

Coleridge, Samuel Taylor   1772-1834   *The Devil's Thoughts and Apologia Pro Vita Sua.*   New York: Kelly Winterton Press, 1989. Limited to 60 numbered copies, 4to., quarter cloth, marbled paper covered boards, top edge gilt, others uncut, hand bound by George and Cathy Wieck. Oak Knoll Books   310 - 120   2016 $225

Coleridge, Samuel Taylor   1772-1834   *Letters, Conversations and Recollections.*   London: Edward Moxon, 1836. First edition, 2 volumes, contemporary black half calf, spines gilt, lacking half titles, binding badly rubbed at extremities and text somewhat browned at margins throughout, very good, each volume with H. M. Tomlinson's ownership signature.   Bertram Rota Ltd.   February List 2016 - 11   2016   £100

Coleridge, Samuel Taylor   1772-1834   *Poems Chosen Out of the Works of Samuel Taylor Coleridge.*   Hammersmith: Kelmscott Press, 1896. One of 300 copies, 210 x 145mm., original limp vellum, gilt titled spine, four silk ties (one with amateur repair, one partly torn away), last third of leaves unopened, gray cloth clamshell box backed with blue calf, very elaborate woodcut title and border around first page of text, handsome woodcut initials throughout, 8 very pleasing engraved plates woodcut borders of vines, leaves and buds, printed in red and black, vellum lightly soiled and tending to splay, but very fine internally, especially clean and fresh, deep impressions of type. Phillip J. Pirages   67 - 220   2016 $2400

Coleridge, Samuel Taylor   1772-1834   *The Rime of the Ancient Mariner.*   London: Oxford University Press, 1930. One of 750 copies printed in Fell types on Barcham Green Charles I handmade paper, marginal notes and colophon printed in brown, typographic border to titlepage and with decorations throughout, crown 8vo., original quarter black cloth with marbled blue and green boards, backstrip lettered in gilt, very light bump to top corners, untrimmed and largely unopened, heavy brown dust jacket, very good. Blackwell's Rare Books   B186 - 333   2016   £175

Coleridge, Samuel Taylor 1772-1834 *The Rime of the Ancient Mariner.* Edinburgh: R. & R. Clark Ltd., 1945. Limited ot 700 copies, frontispiece and color illustrations, five total, by Duncan Grant, marginal notes printed in red, plates made and printed by Raynard Press on Arnold handmade paper, binding executed by Henderson and Bisset, Edinburgh and the medallion and lettering on binding designed by Percy Metcalfe, 8vo., full blue leather, front board stamped with gilt design, top edge gilt, other edges uncut, spine faded, faint stain along bottom of back cover. Oak Knoll Books   310 - 36   2016 $300

Coles, Elisha *The Compleat English Schoolmaster 1674.* Scholar Press, 1969. Facsimile of 1674 edition, original red cloth, very good, Alan Scrivener's copy.   Jarndyce Antiquarian Books CCXV - 601   2016   £25

Coles, Manning *The House at Puck's Gutter.* London: Hodder & Stoughton, 1953. First edition, fine in dust jacket with tiny wear at spine ends.   Mordida Books   2015 - 009761   2016 $65

Coles, Manning *A Knife for the Juggler.* London: Hodder & Stoughton, 1953. First edition, some light spotting and staining on page edges, otherwise fine in dust jacket. Mordida Books   2015 - 008966   2016 $85

Coles, Manning *Pray Silence.* London: Hodder & Stoughton Limited, 1940. First edition, inscribed by author for Julie J. Gladwin, signed by Adelaide Manning, spine slightly browned and light offsetting to front and rear endpapers, else very good in dust jacket with light restoration to spine ends, rare in jacket, rarer still inscribed by author. Buckingham Books   2015 - 2016 $4875

Coles, Manning *A Toast to Tomorrow.* Garden City: Published for the Crime Club by Doubleday Doran and Co. Inc., 1941. First US edition, very good to nearly fine in like dust jacket with light edge rubbing and small tear to upper left front corner, attractive copy.   John W. Knott, Jr./L.W. Currey, Inc.   Fall-Winter 2015 - 17370   2016 $650

Colkett, Victoria Susannah Hine *Ten Etchings of Saint Albans...* 1888. Folio, 10 etchings (29 x 39cm, printed in bisque (two foxed), accompanied by 12 leaf booklet of explanatory text bound with silk ties in original brown cloth backed portfolio, complete set.   Marlborough Rare Books List 55 - 36   2016   £225

Collard, John M. *Arnold Lunn. Ski-Mountaineer Extraordinary.* London: privately printed, 2015. First edition, privately printed, soft cover issue, tall 8vo., original blue cloth covered wrappers, spine and front cover lettered in silver with four plates.   Sotheran's Travel and Exploration - 456   2016   £45

Collard, John M. *The Snow Queen's Magic Gown.* London: privately printed, 2015. Tall 4to., original blue cloth, spine and front cover lettered in silver, very good. Sotheran's Travel and Exploration - 227   2016   £58

Collectanea Graeca Minora, eing Selections from the Greek Authors... Lexington: printed at the office of the Western Monitor, 1823. Foxed and browned, few leaves with blank margins torn, titlepage creased, small dampmark occasionally protruding from gutter, occasional pencil notes, 8vo., original marbled sheep, spine divided by double gilt fillets, red morocco lettering piece, scratched, little wear to spine ends and light rubbing a extremities, flyleaves removed, sound.   Blackwell's Rare Books   B186 - 69   2016   £350

Collier, Jane *An Essay on the Art of Ingeniously Tormenting with Proper Rules for the Exercise of that Pleasant Art.* London: printed for A. Millar in the Strand, 1753. 8vo., engraved frontispiece, very nice, clean copy, contemporary full calf, raised bands, compartments in gilt, brown morocco label, rebacked retaining original spine, leading hinge cracked and little worn, spine rubbed and dulled, repair to following inner hinge, armorial bookplate of Sir George Shuckburgh & later label of E. N. Da C. Andrade, good sound copy.   Jarndyce Antiquarian Books   CCXV - 126 2016   £480

Collier, William Ross *Dave Cook of the Rockies: Frontier General, Fighting Sheriff and leader of Men.* New York: Rufus Rockwell Wilson, 1936. First edition, frontispiece, 13 illustrations from old photographs, maroon cloth lettered in black, fine with slightly chipped and spine darkened pictorial dust jacket (scarce).   Argonaut Book Shop   Biography 2015 - 6289   2016 $90

Collingwood, Charles Stuart *Dr. Cowan and the Grange School, Sunderland with Recollections by Old Scholars.* London: Simpkin, Marshall, Hamilton, Kent & Co., 1897. Half title, original red cloth, slightly dulled.   Jarndyce Antiquarian Books   CCXV - 619   2016   £40

Collins Baker, C. H. *British Painting.* London: Medici Society, 1933. First edition, royal octavo, 140 plates, original red buckram lettered gilt, top edge gilt, spine and top edge of upper cover little faded, very good, no dust jacket, armorial bookplate, beneath which is ownership inscription. Peter Ellis   112 - 191   2016   £45

Collins, Henry Brown *Valentine's Manual of Old New York 1924.* New York: Gracie Mansion, 1923. First edition, 8vo., editior, Henry Brown Collins' presentation on flyleaf, black and white and color illustrations, blue cloth stamped in gilt, top edge gilt, one hinge tender, cover little worn at corners and spine, otherwise very good, inscribed. Second Life Books, Inc.   196A - 211   2016 $65

Collins, Norman *The Bat that Flits.* London: Collins Crime Club, 1952. Dust jacket, very good.   I. D. Edrich Crime - 2016   £30

Collins, Philip *Dickens and Crime.* London: Macmillan, 1962. First edition, half title, original red cloth, very good in slightly torn dust jacket, signed presentation inscription. Jarndyce Antiquarian Booksellers   CCXVIII - 1121   2016   £25

Collins, Philip *Dickens and Education.* London: Macmillan and Co., 1963. First edition, half title, original blue cloth, very good in price clipped dust jacket.   Jarndyce Antiquarian Booksellers   CCXVIII - 1124   2016   £35

Collins, Philip *Dickens: Interviews and Recollections...* London: Macmillan, 1981. First edition, 2 volumes, half titles, plates, original black cloth, very good in dust jackets. Jarndyce Antiquarian Booksellers   CCXVIII - 1127   2016   £60

Collins, Philip *Dickens: the Critical Heritage.*   London: Routledge & Kegan Paul, 1971. Half title, original pale blue cloth, very good in slightly worn dust jacket.   Jarndyce Antiquarian Booksellers   CCXVIII - 1126   2016   £65

Collins, Wilkie   1824-1889 *After Dark.* London: Smith, Elder and Co., 1856. First book edition, 8vo., Riviere & Son full brown calf bindings with elaborate gilt decorated spine, gilt edge tooling, gilt dentelles and marbled paper endpapers, top edge gilt, later maroon leather title labels to spine, original green cloth, covers bound in at rear, minor rubbing to binding extremities, very good+ set.   Tavistock Books   Bibliolatry - 25   2016 $2750

Collins, Wilkie   1824-1889 *Armadale: the Moonstone; No Name and The Woman in White.* London: Folio Society, 1992. 4 volumes frontispiece and plates by Alexy Pendle, fine set.   Bertram Rota Ltd.   February List 2016 - 12   2016   £70

Collins, Wilkie   1824-1889 *Basil: a Study of Modern Life.* London: Richard Bentley, 1852. First edition, 3 volumes bound in two, three quarter tan calf with marbled paper covered boards with red leather labels with gilt titles to spines of both volumes, some rubbing and scuffing to leather, gilt tooling to compartments on spine, some of which have been rubbed, full marbled edges and marbled endpages, book remains quite attractive, though there is minor rubbing to leather along the joints and minor bumping to corners, minor foxing to first and last few pages of both volumes, otherwise interior very bright and clean.   The Kelmscott Bookshop   12 - 27   2016 $3000

Collins, Wilkie   1824-1889 *Memoirs of the Life of William Collins, Esq...with selections from his Journals and Correspondence.*   London: Longman, Brown, Green and Longman, 1848. Uncommon first edition, 8vo., very good in contemporary three quarter brown leather that has some scuffing and rubbing, marbled boards and endpapers, gilt title and rules on spine and gilt to top edges, interior pages clean and solid, engraved portrait, all volumes extra-illustrated by insertion of 57 plates by many artists, very good. The Kelmscott Bookshop   12 - 27   2016 $775

Collins, Wilkie   1824-1889 *The Moonstone.* London: Tinsley Bros., 1868. First edition, first edition, second edition, 3 volumes, half titles, slight marginal staining in first two gatherings volume 1, not affecting text, expertly and sympathetically bound in later half maroon calf marbled boards, spines with devices in gilt, dark green morocco labels, very good.   Jarndyce Antiquarian Booksellers   CCXVII - 74   2016   £3800

Collins, Wilkie   1824-1889 *The Moonstone.*   New York: Limited Editions Club, 1959. No. 1461 of 1500 copies, large 8vo., blue cloth stamped in gilt and red, signed by artist, Dignimont, monthly club letter and flyer about volume laid in, very slight scuffing at lower part of spine, otherwise fine in blue box.   Second Life Books, Inc.   197 - 51   2016 $75

Collins, Wilkie   1824-1889 *The New Magdalen.*   Toronto: Hunter, Rose and Co., 1973. First complete edition, green cloth, gilt titling and decoration on spine, gilt titling and black decoration and border on front, blind stamped border on back, brown endpapers, light wear to corners, more wear to spine ends, some small stains on spine, small pale stain on front, cover has shelfwear, some slightly darkened areas to spine and cover, black leaf between first free endpaper and half title has been removed, presumably to remove the previous center's signature which nevertheless appears as a mirror image transformed to reverse side of first free endpaper, text block edges darkened, interior clean, binding tight. Simon Finch   2015 - 016303   2016 $200

Collins, Wilkie   1824-1889 *Poor Miss Finch as Printed in Cassell's Magazine.*   London: Cassell, Petter and Galpin, 1871. First edition, soft cover, small quarto, contemporary three quarter red leather, raised bands, marbled boards, gilt spine lettering, black and white plates, very good with some very modest shelf wear.   Simon Finch   2015 - 12868   2016 $300

Collins, Wilkie   1824-1889 *The Woman in White.* London: Sampson Low Son & Co., 1861. First one volume edition, half title, oval photographic portrait of author with facsimile signature as frontispiece, engraved title, 1 page ads, excellently rebound in dark green half straight grained morocco, marbled boards, spine bands gilt, morocco label, very good.   Jarndyce Antiquarian Booksellers   CCXVII - 75   2016   £500

Collins, William Lucas *Etoniana Ancient and Modern.* Edinburgh: William Blackwood, 1865. Slightly later half tan calf, brown morocco label, very good.   Jarndyce Antiquarian Books   CCXV - 675   2016   £85

Collis, John Stewart *The Worm Forgives the Plow.* New York: George Braziller, 1975. First American edition, 8vo., illustrations by Oscar Ratti, very good in price clipped dust jacket, inscribed by poet Barbara Howes for her first husband and his wife.   Second Life Books, Inc.   196A - 320   2016 $75

Collison, Beth *Seven Characters.* Colorado Springs: Press at Colorado College, 1980. Limited to 75 numbered copies, bound by James Trissel, oblong 4to., stiff paper wrappers.   Oak Knoll Books   310 - 139   2016 $300

Collyns, Charles Palk *Notes on the chase of the Wild Red Door.* Lawrence and Bullen Ltd., 1902. Royal 8vo., original brown cloth, gilt vignette to lower right corner of upper board, gilt lettering to spine, frontispiece, 7 plates with tissue guards, numerous text illustrations, previous owner's bookplate, black ink mark to upper board, little spotting, very good.   Sotheran's   Hunting, Shooting & Fishing - 55   2016   £100

The Colophon, A Book Collector's Quarterly. New York: Colophon, 1930-1950. Includes the original series, 20 volumes, 4to., boards + index, new series 12 volumes, boards or cloth, The Annual of Bookmaking, thick 8vo., cloth, New Graphic Series, 4 volumes 4to., boards, New Colopon 9 volumes, 4to., boards, except 9th volume which is cloth bound and much thicker than the rest, and Index the Colophon, included is large folder of related ephemeral material including original 4to. prospectus to set.   Oak Knoll Books   310 - 61   2016 $2250

Colquhoun, John *The Moor and the Loch...* William Blackwood and Sons, 1888. New edition, 8vo., original cloth, gilt blocked on upper board, lettered gilt on spine, frontispiece, 14 plates, rubbing to extremities, tipped in frontispiece causing leaf to bow, otherwise very good.   Sotheran's   Hunting, Shooting & Fishing - 169   2016   £90

Colquhoun, John *Sporting Days.* Edinburgh: William Blackwood and Sons, 1866. First edition, 8vo., original green cloth, sometime rebacked with original spine laid down, gilt lettering to upper board and spine, new endpapers, previous owner's inscription, very good.   Sotheran's Hunting, Shooting & Fishing - 170   2016   £90

Colum, Mary *Our Friend James Joyce.* New York: Doubleday, 1958. First edition, little faded spine and couple of minor nicks, inscribed by co-author, Padraic Colum. Second Life Books, Inc.   196A - 322   2016 $150

Colum, Padraic 1881-1972 *Creatures.* New York: Macmillan, 1927. First edition, 8vo., cloth backed decorated boards, near fine in dust jacket with some chips and mends on verso, illustrations by Boris Artzybasheff with striking bold woodcuts, this copy signed by artist.   Aleph-bet Books, Inc.   111 - 25   2016 $225

Colum, Padraic 1881-1972 *The Girl Who Sat by the Ashes.* New York: Macmillan, Dec.., 1919. First edition, 8vo., pictorial cloth, fine in dust jacket (chipped and soiled), color frontispiece and numerous full and partial page pen and inks by Dugald Stewart Walker.   Aleph-bet Books, Inc. 111 - 472   2016 $450

Columbus and His Times. Religious Tract society, 1842. First edition, 12mo., contemporary half morocco over marbled boards, spine, leather on boards and corners richly gilt, all edges gilt, engraved frontispiece, very good.   Sotheran's Piccadilly Notes - Summer 2015 - 82   2016   £250

Colwell, Stephen *The Ways and Means of Payment: a Full Analysis of the Credit System...* Philadelphia: J. B. Lippincott & Co., 1859. First edition, 8vo. very slightly toned but generally clean within, contemporary brown cloth blindstamped gilt title to spine, neatly rebacked, endpapers renewed, little rubbed, some fraying to bottom fore-edge corners, Lane Library Association bookplate, Brandeis University library inkstamp to lower margin of page 15, occasional library codes.   Unsworths Antiquarian Booksellers   30 - 37   2016   £150

Combe, Andrew *The Principles of Physiology Applied to the Preservation of Health...* Edinburgh: Maclachlan, Stewart & Co., 1841. 8 pages ads, illustrations, little spotted, uncut, original drab boards, green cloth spine, paper label, corners slightly bumped, lacking leading f.e.p, nice. Jarndyce Antiquarian Books   CCXV - 603   2016   £45

Combe, Edmund *Voyage en Abyssinie dans la pays des Galla, de Chos et d'ilfat: Precede d'une excursion dans l'Arabie Heureuse... 1833-1857.* Paris: Louis Desessart, 1838. First edition, 4 volumes, 8vo., quarter dark green calf over marbled boards, marbled edges and endpapers, spine with raised bands tooled in gilt and decorated in blind, issued without the map as sometimes the case, little frayed in places, overall sturdy, clean and uniform set.   Sotheran's Travel and Exploration - 11   2016   £498

Combe, George *Education: Its Principles and Practice as Developed by George Combe.* London: Macmillan & Co., 1879. Half title, 4 page ads, original brown cloth, neatly recased, slight mark to back board, prize label from Combe Trust on leading pastedown.   Jarndyce Antiquarian Books CCXV - 605   2016   £58

Combe, George *Lectures on Popular Education Delivered to the Edinburgh Association for Procuring Instruction in Useful and Entertaining Science in April and November 1833.* Edinburgh: John Anderson, Jun., 1833. First edition, disbound, 80 pages. Jarndyce Antiquarian Books CCXV - 606   2016   £30

Combe, George *On the Works of Raphael.* Edinburgh: printed by Neill and Co., 1847. Sewn as issued in plain blue paper wrappers, very good. Jarndyce Antiquarian Books CCXV - 608   2016   £20

Combe, George *On Teaching Physiology and Its Applications in Common Schools.* Edinburgh: Maclachlan & Stewart, 1857. Pamphlet, sewn as issued, old vertical fold, very good. Jarndyce Antiquarian Books CCXV - 607   2016   £20

Combe, George *Reasons for Declining to Subscribe the resolutions in Favorite of National Education in Scotland.* Edinburgh: n.p., 1850. Pamphlet sewn as issued, very good. Jarndyce Antiquarian Books CCXV - 609   2016   £20

Combe, George *Secular Education.* Edinburgh: Maclachlan & Stewart &c, 1851. 2nd thousand, sewn as issued to original pink printed wrappers, very good. Jarndyce Antiquarian Books CCXV - 610   2016   £20

Combe, George *Treasurer Dickson and Secular Schools.* Edinburgh: n.p., 1855. Printed on blue laid paper, sewn as issued. Jarndyce Antiquarian Books CCXV - 611   2016   £20

Combe, William 1742-1823 *The Three Tours of Dr. Syntax. In Search of the Picturesque... In Search of Consoltion... In Search of a Wife.* London: R. Ackermann's Repository of Arts, 1812. 1820. 1821. First editions in book form, 3 volumes, volume III with eight pages of ads and original wrappers and ads from the three monthly parts bound in at rear, very handsome gilt decorated early 20th century dark blue rushed morocco by Riviere & Son (stamp-signed on front turn-in), covers with French fillet border, spines lavishly and elegantly gilt in compartments with flower filled cornucopia centerpiece surrounded by small tools and volute cornerpieces, inner gilt dentelles, top edges gilt, other edges untrimmed, one woodcut illustration, one engraved tailpiece and 80 partfully hand colored aquatint plates by Thomas Rowlandson, engraved armorial bookplate of John Taylor Reynolds, spines uniformly more black than blue, four of the covers with just hint of soiling, most plates with variable offsetting (usually faint but noticeable in half dozen cases), other trivial imperfections, but extremely desirable set, nevertheless with strong impressions and good coloring of first edition plates, with good coloring of first edition plates, very spacious margins, lovely bindings that are lustrous and virtually unworn. Phillip J. Pirages 67 - 306   2016 $3500

Combs, T. *Briefs.* Franklin: Hillside, 1966. No. 259 of 425 copies, 1 5/16 x 2 inches, yellow cloth with drawing on front and lettering on spine in dark blue, drawings by D. Clark, author's presentation for Bill Claire, cover slightly darkened, else nice, little paper folder. Second Life Books, Inc. 196 B - 244   2016 $100

Combs, Trey *The Steelhead Trout: Life History - Early Angling - Contemporary Steelheading.* New York: Salmon Trout Steelheader Co., 1971. First edition, fine in dust jacket. Mordida Books 2015 - 011536   2016 $65

Common Sense or Every Body's Magazine. London: JGF & J. Rivington & Whittaker & Co., 1842. Volume I (of two published), 8 numbers, May-December, original purple brown cloth, slightly faded, early signature of James Dearden, Renier booklabel, very good. Jarndyce Antiquarian Booksellers CCXVII - 221   2016   £45

Compi, Anita De *Mother Goose Parade.* Chicago: Reilly & Britton, 1914. Oblong folio, cloth backed pictorial card covers, some edge and spine wear, otherwise amazingly complete and very good+, 24 full age illustrations and 12 duplicates of the color plates printed only in outline. Alephbet Books, Inc. 112 - 324   2016 $1250

The Compleat Melancholick, Being a Sequence of Found, Composite and Composed Poems... Minneapolis: Bieler Press, 1985. Reprint of handset limited edition, small 8vo., stiff paper wrappers,. Oak Knoll Books 310 - 82   2016 $145

Complete Etiquette for Gentlemen. London: Ward Lock & Co., circa, 1897. Half title, illustrations, index, 6 pages ads, original green cloth, blocked in black, little rubbed and dulled. Jarndyce Antiquarian Books CCXV - 462   2016   £38

Complete Etiquette for Ladies and Gentlemen. London: Ward Lock & Co., circa, 1900. New edition, half title, frontispiece and plate, leaves slightly browned, ads on endpapers, original green cloth, slightly dulled, recent ownership inscription, nice. Jarndyce Antiquarian Books CCXV - 463   2016   £38

A Complete History of the Present War, from Its Commencement in 1756 to the End of the Campaign 1760. London: printed for W. Owen, L. Davis, C. Reymers and J. Scott, 1761. First edition, octavo, contemporary quarter calf, marbled paper boards, gilt lettered, untrimmed, edges little rubbed, some light foxing, very good, untrimmed copy. The Brick Row Book Shop Miscellany 69 - 8   2016 $800

Complete Letter-Writer for Ladies and Gentlemen. London: Ward Lock & co., circa, 1900. New enlarged edition, half title, original blue cloth. Jarndyce Antiquarian Books CCXV - 464 2016   £30

The Complete Young Man's Companion; or Self Instructor.... Manchester: printed by S. Russell, 1805. Frontispiece, slightly offset on title, plates, few small marginal tears to pre-lims & final leaf, rebound in drab brown paper boards, brown cloth spine, paper label.   Jarndyce Antiquarian Books   CCXV - 127   2016   £150

A Concise History of Birmingham....   Birmingham: R. Jabet, 1808. Fourth edition, folding map, 3 plate, original grey boards, spine worn.   J. & S. L. Bonham Antiquarian Booksellers   Europe 2016 - 7280   2016   £60

A Concise View of the Origin, Constitution and Proceedings of the Honourable Society of the Governor and Assistants of London of the New Plantation in Ulster, within the realm of Ireland Commonly Called the Irish Society.   London: printed by order of the Court, by Arthur Taylor, 39, Coleman Street...., 1832. Second edition, 8vo., frontispiece, light browning, foxing, but very good, contemporary green cloth, dark green label stamped in gilt, binding slightly rubbed.   Unsworths Antiquarian Booksellers Ltd.   E04 - 9   2016   £275

A Concise View of the Origin, Constitution and Proceedings of the Honourable Society of the Governor and Assistants of London of the new Plantation in Ulster...   London: printed by order of the court by Arthur Taylor., 1832. Second edition, 8vo., frontispiece, light browning, foxing, very good, contemporary green cloth, dark green label stamped gilt, binding slightly rubbed but very good.   Unsworths Antiquarian Booksellers   30 - 76   2016   £275

Condon, Richard   *Death of a Politician.*   London: Hutchinson, 1979. Very good in like dust jacket.   I. D. Edrich   Crime - 2016   £20

Condon, Richard   *The Venerable Bead.*   Franklin Center: Franklin Library, 1992. Limited first edition, signed by author, red leather lettered and decoratively stamped in gilt, all edges gilt, very fine, extremely handsome.   Argonaut Book Shop   Literature 2015 - 3953   2016 $45

Condorcet, Marie Jean Antoine Nicolas De Caritat, Marquis De   1743-1794   *Outlines of an Historical View of the Progress of the Human Mind.*   London: printed for J. Johnson, 1795. First edition in English, 8vo., light pink staining at upper inner corner, diminishing, uncut, disbound, apparently from wrappers or boards, good.   Blackwell's Rare Books   B184 - 30   2016   £1100

Cone, Claribel   *Alice Derain.*   Woodside: Occasional Works, 1984. First edition, one of a total edition of 250 numbered and signed by author, five tipped-in color reproductions of paintings, hand set type printed on all rag Arches text paper, sewn gray wrappers, paper over and spine labels, very fine, handsome.   Argonaut Book Shop   Literature 2015 - 7448   2016 $90

Cone, Helen   *Tiny Toddlers.*   New York: Stokes, 1890. Folio, loose as issued in pictorial boards with ribbon ties, some margin wear to 2 leaves, else very good+, printed rectos only, 6 magnificent full page chromolithographs of little children, alternating with text in verse, illustrations in line, by Maud Humphrey, rare.   Aleph-bet Books, Inc.   112 - 250   2016 $1500

Congreve, William   1670-1729   *The Way of the World.* London: Haymarket Press, 1928. First edition, number 875 of 875 copies, original signed etching, purple cloth backed velvet with gilt lettering, Japon vellum pages, covers rubbed with top edge faded, very good.   Argonaut Book Shop   Literature 2015 - 1229   2016 $75

Congreve, William   1670-1729   *The Way of the World: Comedy in Five Acts.*   New York: Heritage Press, 1959. blindstamped blue cloth, gilt lettering to spine, spine faded, else fine in slipcase, illustrations by T. M. Cleland, Sandglass pamphlet laid in.   Argonaut Book Shop   Heritage Press 2015 - 6943   2016 $40

Congreve, William   1670-1729   *The Works of Mr. William Congreve.*   Birmingham: printed by John Baskerville for J. and R. Tonson, 1764. First Baskerville edition, 8vo., 3 volumes, handsomely bound by Riviere in full dark green morocco, boards with gilt line and greek key borders, spines richly gilt with contrasting leather labels, all edges gilt, engraved portrait after Kneller, 5 plates engraved by Grignion after Hayman, little occasional light browning, otherwise very nice, much cleaner than usual and in attractive binding.   Sotheran's Piccadilly Notes - Summer 2015 - 83   2016   £1000

Conklin, Groff   *Science Fiction Terror Tales.*   Hicksville: Gnome Press, 1955. First edition, octavo, cloth, mild age toning to text block, fine in fine dust jacket, rare in this condition.   John W. Knott, Jr./L.W. Currey, Inc.   Fall-Winter 2015 - 17366   2016 $750

Connell, Evan B.   *Son of the Morning Star.*   San Francisco: North Point Press, 1984. First edition, frontispiece, map endpapers, cloth backed boards, very fine, pictorial dust jacket.   Argonaut Book Shop   Native American 2015 - 5417   2016 $150

Connell, Mary   *Help is on the Way (Poems).*   Reinhardt, 1896. First edition, line drawings by author, crown 8vo., original light blue card wrappers printed in black, red and white, fine, inscribed by Graham Greene for love of his life Yvonne Cloetta.   Blackwell's Rare Books   B186 - 223   2016   £800

Connelly, Marc *The Green Pastures.* New York: Farrar & Rinehart, 1930. First edition, 4to., #206 of 550 copies signed by author and artist, Robert Edmond Jones, laid in is TLS from author to author Tad Mosel thanking him for his birthday greeting, beautiful pochoir frontispiece, color of boards little retouched, fine in publisher's box.   Second Life Books, Inc.   196A - 325   2016 $350

Connelly, Marc *Voices Offstage: a Book of memoirs.* Chicago: Holt, Rinehart & Winston, 1968. First edition, 8vo., illustrations, fine in fine dust jacket, signed by author.   Second Life Books, Inc.   196A - 327   2016 $56

Connelly, Michael *The Black Echo.* Boston: Little Brown and Co., 1992. Very near fine with some slight bumping to spine in very near fine dust jacket, signed and warmly inscribed by author, terrific copy.   Jeff Hirsch Books Holiday List 2015 - 31   2016 $400

Connelly, Michael *The Black Echo.* Boston: Little Brown, 1992. First edition, near fine, light bumping to spine ends, dust jacket fine, signed by author with no inscription.   Bella Luna Books   2016 - j1423d   2016 $330

Connelly, Michael *The Black Ice.* Boston: Little Brown, 1993. First edition, near fine in like dust jacket, with light creasing at top of spine.   Bella Luna Books   2016 - t6134   2016 $82

Connelly, Michael *Chasing the Dime.* Little Brown, 2002. First edition, very fine in dust jacket, signed by author.   Mordida Books   2015 - 011063   2016 $65

Connelly, Michael *Harry Bosch Three Stories.* New York and Boston: Little Brown and Co., 2011. Advance reading copy, glossy printed wrappers, signed by author, fine, scarce.   Gene W. Baade, Books on the West   2015 - 0521050   2016 $50

Connelly, Michael *Hieronymus Bosch/Mickey Haller.* New York: Mysterious Bookshop, 2008. First edition, very fine in soft covers.   Mordida Books   2015 - 011086   2016 $65

Connelly, Michael *the Overlook.* New York: Little Brown, 2007. First edition, very fine in dust jacket, signed by author.   Mordida Books   2015 - 011064   2016 $55

Connolly, John *Every Dead Thing.* London: Hodder & Stoughton, 1999. First British edition, true first, near fine, very minor bumping to spine ends, fine dust jacket, with promotional sticker intact, signed by author.   Bella Luna Books   2016 - t15520   2016 $66

Connor, Nellie Victoria *Essence of Good Perfume.* Burbank: Ivan Deach Jr., 1940. First edition, one of 100 numbered copies signed by author, frontispiece, cloth soiled, endpapers bit smudged, very good without dust jacket, probably as issued, this copy inscribed twice to Hon. Oscar and Mrs. Du Priest.   Between the Covers Rare Books   207 - 31   2016 $485

Connor, Tony *Kon in Springtime: Poems.* London: Oxford, 1968. 8vo., author's signature on title, nice in price clipped and little chipped dust jacket.   Second Life Books, Inc.   196A - 328   2016 $45

Conover, Anne *Caresse Crosby From Black Sun to Roccasinibalda.* Santa Barbara: Capra Press, 1989. First edition, 8vo., fine in dust jacket, inscribed by author to William Claire.   Second Life Books, Inc.   196A - 152   2016 $750

Conover, Richard Grover *As True as Sea Serpents.* New York: Knickerbocker Press, 1928. First edition, fine in very near fine dust jacket that is trifle faded at spine and has couple of tiny tears, very scarce, especially in dust jacket.   Between the Covers Rare Books   208 - 119   2016 $450

Conrad of Lichtenau, Abbot *Chronicum Abbatis Urspergensis a Nino Rege Assyriorum Magno Usque ad Fridericum II...* Strasbourg: for Crato Mylius, 1537. First illustrated edition, over 100 woodcut medallion portraits of Roman and Austrian emperors, in white on black ground by Heinrich Vogthere the elder, second titlepage with four portraits, small printer's device on titlepage, with almost full page version at end also by Vogthere, folio, contemporary blind tooled calf over pasteboards, covers panelled with broad outer hunting roll and inner floral and ornamental rolls, spine and corners worn.   Maggs Bros. Ltd.   1474 - 28   2016   £2800

Conrad, Joseph 1857-1924 *Alamayer's Folly.* London: Fisher Unwin, 1895. First edition, first state with titlepage printed in black and red with type missing in last 2 lines, very occasional light handling marks, crown 8vo., original green cloth, backstrip lettered in gilt, very light rubbing to extremities, top edge gilt, others untrimmed, bookplate tipped in, very good, exceptional copy.   Blackwell's Rare Books   B184 - 131   2016   £2750

Conrad, Joseph 1857-1924 *The Arrow of Gold.* New York: Doubleday Page, 1919. First edition, octavo, original blue cloth stamped in gilt, from the library of Stanley J. Seeger with his small bookplate, presentation copy from author for Lady (Frances) Colvin, beneath is another presentation inscription to Christopher Wheeler from Sidney Colvin, cover rubbed at spine and edges, cloth bubbled at inside edge of lower cover, good, preserved in green buckram slipcase lettered gilt with inner folding sleeve.   Peter Ellis   112 - 81   2016   £950

Conrad, Joseph 1857-1924 *The Children of the Sea - A Tale of the Forecastle.* New York: Dodd, Mead, n.d. circa, 1908. Early edition, small octavo, original dark blue pictorial cloth, depicting a sailing ship in silhouette against a background of clouds and waves, from the library of Stanley Seeger with his bookplate, contemporary (1908) ownership inscription, covers slightly scuffed, very good.   Peter Ellis   112 - 85   2016   £95

Conrad, Joseph 1857-1924 *The Complete Short Stories of Joseph Conrad.* London: Hutchinson, 1933. First edition, 2nd issue, octavo, original black cloth lettered in yellow, slight crease at outer edge of front free endpaper, near fine in very good pictorial dust jacket little nicked and creased at edges, 3'6 reduced price sticker on spine, from the library of Stanley J. Seeger.   Peter Ellis   112 - 84   2016   £125

Conrad, Joseph 1857-1924 *The First and Last of Conrad - Almayer's Folly, an Outcast of the Islands, the Arrow of Gold & the Rover.* London: Ernest Benn, 1929. First edition, octavo, very good in like dust jacket, slightly marked and little nicked and creased at edges, from the library of Stanley Seeger with his small bookplate.   Peter Ellis   112 - 83   2016   £125

Conrad, Joseph 1857-1924 *Laughing Anne and One Day More - two plays.* London: Castle, 1924. First combined edition, octavo, from the library of Gerard Jean-Aubry, author's close friend and first biographer, from the library of Stanley Seeger with his small bookplate, tipped on blank facing page 19 (a summary description of personages in the play), an original sketch in blue crayon of the stage layout, and positioning of the characters written in black ink by Conrad, at lower corner is note in green ink in Jean-Abury's hand "Plan de la scene - fait par Joseph Conrad", with much rougher sketch for final scene, free endpapers tanned, otherwise fine in very good, nicked and creased dust jacket with enclosed tear at head of upper hinge, preserved in green buckram slipcase lettered gilt and with folding inner sleeve.   Peter Ellis   112 - 82   2016 £1250

Conrad, Joseph 1857-1924 *The Nature of a Crime.* London: Duckworth, 1924. First edition, small octavo, 2 bookplates on front pastedown, on of which is that of travel writer Sean Jennett, typographer at Faber and Faber and that of Conrad collector, Stanley J. Seeger, spine slightly faded at head and just little bumped at tail, very good, preserved in custom made green buckram slipcase, lettered gilt on spine, inner folding sleeve.   Peter Ellis   112 - 78   2016   £95

Conrad, Joseph 1857-1924 *Romance.* London: Smith, Elder & Co., 1903. First edition, original dark blue cloth lettered and decorated in white and gilt, stain to front free endpaper, possibly as result of removal of an inscription, some foxing, little rubbing to extremities and spine bit faded, white lettering and decoration to upper cover, especially bright and fresh.   Bertram Rota Ltd.   February List 2016 - 13   2016   £200

Conrad, Joseph 1857-1924 *The Shadow-Line - a Confession.* London: J. M. Dent, 1917. Second impression, published same month as the first, 2200 copies printed, 8vo., original green decorated cloth, from library of Stanley J. Seeger with his bookplate, presentation from author for The British Farmers' Red Cross Fund No. 1917, cloth little scuffed in two patches on upper board, very good in good only dust jacket, extensively torn at lower hinge and defective at head and tail of spine, preserved in green buckram slipcase lettered gilt with folding inner sleeve.   Peter Ellis   112 - 80   2016   £550

Conrad, Joseph 1857-1924 *The Sisters.* New York: Crosby Gaige, 1928. First edition, one of 926 copies printed on handmade paper by Bruce Rogers, octavo, original marbled paper boards, black leather title bale on spine, 2 bookplates, lower corners little bruised, near fine in original chipped and torn plain dust jacket.   Peter Ellis   112 - 77   2016   £150

Conrad, Joseph 1857-1924 *Tales of Hearsay.* London: T. Fisher Unwin, 1925. First edition, octavo, fomr the library of Conrad collector, Stanley J. Seeger with his small bookplate, prelims and edges little spotted, free endpapers partially and lightly tanned, very good in like pictorial dust jacket with several short clsed tears, one of them at head of spine which is also creased, preserved custom made green buckram slipcase, lettered in gilt on spine, inner folding sleeve.   Peter Ellis   112 - 79   2016   £250

Constable, Henry *National Education. the Case Re-considered a reply to statements of the Bishop of Ossory and of the Author of the Present State of the Controversy.* Dublin: Hodges, Smith & co., 1860. 35 pages, disbound.   Jarndyce Antiquarian Books   CCXV - 616   2016   £20

Constable, John *The Conversation of Gentlemen Considered...* London: printed by J. Hoyles and sold by the booksellers of London and Westminster, 1738. 12mo., engraved frontispiece, late 18th century quarter calf, red morocco label, corners bumped & worn, some slight rubbing, otherwise nice, inscription "John H. Talbot M.P. from his brother D'Arcy Talbot June 28th 1834", armorial bookplate of John H. Talbot.   Jarndyce Antiquarian Books   CCXV - 128   2016   £285

Constant, Alberta Wilson *Paintbox on the Frontier. The Life and Times of George Caleb Bingham.* New York: Thomas Crowell, 1974. First edition, white cloth, color and black and white, very fine, pictorial dust jacket.   Argonaut Book Shop   Biography 2015 - 7683   2016 $75

Constantine, Joseph *Sir Isaac Holden, Bart and His Theory of Healthy Long Life.* London: John Heywood, 1898. First edition, thin 8vo., frontispiece, portrait, engraved illustrations, some ephemera laid in, original brown cloth with gilt title on front cover and spine.   Edwin V. Glaser Rare Books   2015 - 10287   2016 $250

Constantine, Madame, Pseud. *Etiquette for Ladies, containing Hints of Introduction and Acquaintance...* London: J. Dicks, circa, 1867. 32mo., original green limp cloth boards, sewn as issued, very good.   Jarndyce Antiquarian Books CCXV - 129   2016   £125

Contes des Mille et Une Nuits.   Paris: L'Edition d'art H. Piazza, 1912. First French trade edition, quarto, 50 full color plates by Edmund Dulac with captioned tissue guards, mounted on cream colored stock, contemporary three quarter red morocco over cockerel boards, rules in gilt, spine with five raised bands, decoratively tooled and lettered gilt in compartments, top edge gilt, others uncut, Cockerel endpapers, original front wrapper printed in gold and blue bound in at front, marginal rubbing to joints, otherwise near fine. David Brass Rare Books, Inc.   2015 - 02925   2016 $950

Conty, Henry Alexis De   *Suisse Francaise Oberland Bernois. Guide Pratique et Illustre...*   Paris: Faure, circa, 1867. First (?) edition, 12mo., original blue blindstamped flexible cloth, ornamented and lettered gilt, printed on blue paper, wood engravings, folding lithographic map printed in black, red and blue, folding lithographic railway map, 8 page booklet with wood engraved vignette on title inside rear pocket, bold of binding bit faded, only light rubbing, evenly little browned due to paper stock, railway map, little brown spotted, name of Swiss photographer A de Contant-Delessert, inscribed inside front cover.   Sotheran's   Travel and Exploration - 228 2016   £325

Convention of Delegates from the Abolition Societies *Minutes of the Proceedings of the... Convention of Delegates from the Abolition Societies...*   Philadelphia: Printed by Zacharian Poulson Junr., 1794-1801. First, second, third, fourth, fifth and seventh conventions, 6 sewn pamphlets in plain paper wrappers, 3 are untrimmed in original plain paper wrappers, the other three trimmed in early plain paper wrappers, contemporary signature of Samuel Rodman, contemporary signature of Isaac Hicks, front wrapper of fourth pamphlet detached, very good set.   Between the Covers Rare Books   202 - 4   2016 $10,000

Conversations with Mamma on the Peculiarities of Friends. London: Charles Gilpin, 1847. 16mo., frontispiece, lacing leading f.e.p., original green cloth, slightly faded, nice, scarce.   Jarndyce Antiquarian Books   CCXV - 130 2016 £80

Conway, Martin   *Aconcague and Tierra del Fuego: a Book of Climbing, Travel and Exploration.*   London: Cassell, 1902. First edition, 8vo., 27 illustrations, original red cloth, recased using original boards, good, clean copy.   J. & S. L. Bonham Antiquarian Booksellers   America 2016 - 9462 2016   £250

Cook, Jane Elizabeth   *Ye Festival of Ye Sumer Quene. Recollections of Ye Olde English Revels....*   London: Chiswicke Presse, Tookes Courte, Chancerine Lane, 1885. Folio, title printed in red and black, 17 mounted photos on blue card from drawings by Cook, including one in bistre, original portfolio with cloth backed decorated lithograph boards, slightly worn at extremities and cloth spine faded. Marlborough Rare Books   List 55 - 15   2016   £550

Cook, John   *Remarks on the Recommendations and Draft Bill of the Royal Commissioners on Education.*   Edinburgh and London: William Blackwood and Sons, 1858. Sewn as issued, signature Ardgour.   Jarndyce Antiquarian Books CCXV - 617   2016   £30

Cooke, David C.   *c/o American Embassy: a Novel of Suspense.*   New York: Dodd Mead & Co., 1967. First edition, fine in fine dust jacket.   Ken Hebenstreit, Bookseller 2016 - 2016 $40

Cooke, Maude C.   *Social Etiquette or Manners and Customs of Polite Society...*   Cincinnati: W. H. Ferguson Co., 1896. Presentation leaf, frontispiece, plates, illustrations, original blue-gray decorated cloth, little faded. Jarndyce Antiquarian Books   CCXV - 131   2016   £65

Cookery in the Golden State. A Collection of Choice Recipes Tried and Approved by the Ladies of the Unitarian Society. Sacramento: Woodson Bros., 1890. First edition, terra cotta pebbled cloth, binding with gilt stamped title lettering to front board, light shelf wear, age toning to paper, pastedowns with binder's glue discoloration, occasional corner crease, prior owner "Lemon Pie" recipe written in pencil, withal solid very good-very good+ copy.   Tavistock Books Getting Around - 10   2016 $1500

Coolidge, Archibald C.   *Charles Dickens as Serial Novelist.*   Ames: Iowa State University Press, 1967. First edition, half title, original maroon cloth, very good in dust jacket.   Jarndyce Antiquarian Booksellers   CCXVIII - 1130 2016   £25

Coolidge, Calvin   *Have Faith in Massachusetts.*   Boston and New York: Houghton Mifflin, 1919. Second edition, 8vo., inscribed by the President to William F. Prindle, Aug. 1920, very good, tight copy.   Second Life Books, Inc. 196A - 330   2016 $750

Coolidge, Clark   *The So. Poems 1966.*   New York: Adventures in Poetry, 1971. First edition, one of 26 lettered copies signed by author and artist, out of a total edition of 300, 4to., original illustrated wrappers, front cover by Brice Marden, stapled as issued, some light dust soiling to wrappers, otherwise fine.   James S. Jaffe Rare Books Occasional List: Winter 2016 - 12   2016 $1750

Coolridge, Mary Roberts *The Rain-Makers, Indians of Arizona and New Mexico.* Boston: Houghton Mifflin, 1929. First edition, numerous black and white plates, map endpapers, orange lettered blue cloth, spine slightly faded with rubbed ends, else fine.   Argonaut Book Shop   Native American 2015 - 1927   2016 $75

Coomaraswamy, Ananda *Three Poems.* Ditchling: Saint Dominic's Press, 1920. First edition, initial letter in red, full page illustration by Eric Gill with further woodcut by him at rear, 8vo., original sewn self wrappers with Gill woodcut to front printed in red, one or two pinprick foxspots at head, very good, excellent copy, scarce.   Blackwell's Rare Books   B184 - 310   2016   £250

Cooney, Barbara *Chanticleer and the Fox.* New York: Crowell, 1958. First edition (correct issue price), (correct issue price), 4to., cloth, fine in fine dust jacket, brightly illustrated in color by Cooney.   Aleph-bet Books, Inc.   112 - 114   2016 $600

Cooper, Astley *The Lectures of Sir Astley Cooper on the Principles and Practice of Surgery with Additional Notes and Cases.* Philadelphia: Carey & Hart, 1835. Fourth American edition, 6 plates, 2 are hand colored, 3 volumes in one, 8vo., modern quarter morocco and marbled boards.   Edwin V. Glaser Rare Books   2015 - 2260   2016 $135

Cooper, Diana *Autobiography Consisting of the Rainbow comes & Goes, Light of Common Fay. Trumpets from the Steel.* London: Rupert Hart Davis, 1958-1960. First edition, 8vo., 3 volumes, original cloth with dust jackets, photographs, cloth on Rainbow somewhat worn and with repaired and rather tatty dust jacket, dust jackets on other two volumes little chipped, creased and stained, all volumes inscribed by author for friend Nigel Ryan.   Sotheran's Piccadilly Notes - Summer 2015 - 84   2016   £248

Cooper, F. T. *An Argosy of Fables.* New York: Stokes, 1921. Not first edition, thick 4to., blue pictorial cloth, name on verso of frontispiece, else fine in dust jacket (pieces off spine ends and corner of front panel), 12 richly colored and very beautiful color plates plus lovely pictorial endpapers by Paul Bransom.   Aleph-bet Books, Inc.   111 - 55   2016 $250

Cooper, Frederick Fox *Hard Times.* London: John Dicks, circa, 1884. Original pale green printed wrappers, wrappered at edges, spine guarded, illustrations.   Jarndyce Antiquarian Booksellers   CCXVIII - 532   2016   £35

Cooper, Frederick Fox *The Tale of Two Cities.* London: John Dicks, circa, 1885. Disbound, illustrations.   Jarndyce Antiquarian Booksellers   CCXVIII - 568   2016   £20

Cooper, James Fenimore 1789-1851 *The Chronicles of Cooperstown.* Cooperstown: H. & E. Phinney, 1838. First edition, 12m., original plain muslin, some fading, original printed paper label.   M & S Rare Books, Inc.   99 - 67   2016 $650

Cooper, James Fenimore 1789-1851 *The Deerslayer or the First War-Path...* Hartford: Case, Lockwood & Brainard, 1961. First edition thus, 1/1500 numbered copies, signed by artist, illustrations by Edward A. Wilson with pen and brush illustrations, deer skin backed boards, fine, large 8vo.   Second Life Books, Inc.   196A - 333   2016 $50

Cooper, James Fenimore 1789-1851 *Imagination. A Tale for Young Women. (in) Robert's Semi-Monthly Magazine.* Boston: George Roberts Feb. 1 and 15, 1841. 2 volumes, octavo, original printed wrapper, corner torn from one wrapper, very good.   The Brick Row Book Shop   Miscellany 69 - 28   2016 $225

Cooper, James Fenimore 1789-1851 *The Last of the Mohicans a Narrative of 1757.* London: John Miller, 1826. First English edition, 3 volumes, half titles lacking, near contemporary half calf, gilt, name clipped from top margin of titlepage of volume I, stain on 3: 192-3 form laid-in paper, binding lightly rubbed at extremities, but very good.   Joseph J. Felcone, Inc.   Books from Five Centuries: a Miscellany - 50   2016 $1400

Cooper, James Fenimore 1789-1851 *The Last of the Mohicans; a Narrative of 1757.* London: John Miller, 1826. First English edition, 3 volumes, 12mo., slight spotting to prelims, bound without half titles in slightly later 19th century half tan calf, spine with double ruled gilt bands, compartments blocked in blind, volume numbers in gilt, dark green moroco labels, slightly rubbed, Fothergill armorial bookplate, very good.   Jarndyce Antiquarian Booksellers   CCXVII - 77   2016   £2200

Cooper, James Fenimore 1789-1851 *The Monikins.* Philadelphia: Carey Lea & Blanchard, 1835. First edition, 2 volumes, publisher's catalogs, flyleaves at front and back of volme one and at back of volume two, uncut, bound in original linen backed boards, some foxed, boards some soiled, library bookplate, lacks corner of front blank, very good.   Second Life Books, Inc. 197 - 53   2016 $850

Cooper, James Fenimore 1789-1851 *New York.* New York: William Farquhar Payson, 1930. Limited edition, number 38 of 750 numbered copies, slim octavo, black and white frontispiece a contemporary lithograph after a drawing of Aug. Koliner, leaves uncut, brown cloth backed boards, very fine in slightly rubbed slipcase.   Argonaut Book Shop   Literature 2015 - 1223   2016 $125

Cooper, James Fenimore 1789-1851 *The Prairie.* Avon: Heritage Press, 1968. Illustrations by John Steuart Curry, illustrated boards with brown leathette spine, lettered gilt, very fine in slipcase, Sandglass pamphlet laid in.   Argonaut Book Shop   Heritage Press 2015 - 6948   2016 $40

Cooper, Jane *The Weather of Six Mornings. Poems.* New York: London: Macmillan, 1969. First edition, inscribed and signed by author for William Meredith, fine in near fine dust jacket with tanned spine.   Charles Agvent   William Meredith - 24   2016 $100

Cooper, Susan *Silver on the Tree.* New York: Atheneum, 1977. Stated first edition, fine in dust jacket with small closed tear and tiny bit of wear to top of spine, price intact, inscribed by author.   Aleph-bet Books, Inc.   111 - 100   2016 $200

Cooper, William *Love on the Coast.* Macmillan, 1973. First edition, fine in dust jacket.   Bertram Rota Ltd.   February List 2016 - 14   2016   £20

Cooper, William Heaton *The Tarns of Lakeland.* London: Frederick Warne & Co. ltd., 1960. First edition, 4to., original blue cloth, red label to spine, maps to endpapers, 16 color plates and text illustrations by author, spine little rubbed, very good.   Sotheran's   Piccadilly Notes - Summer 2015 - 85   2016   £70

Cope, Edward Drinker *Hitherto Unpublished Plates of Tertiary Mammalia and Permian Vertebrata.* New York: American Museum of Natural History, 1915. Quarto, 64 uncolored lithographs with accompanying text leaves, publisher's blue cloth, few library stamps of Royal Society of Victoria, otherwise very good.   Andrew Isles Natural History Books   55 - 35493   2016 $500

Copeau, Jacques *The House into Which We are Born.* New York: Theatre Arts, 1924. First American edition, 12mo., inscribed by noted US theatre critic John Mason Brown to an American producer, lightly soiled wrappers.   Second Life Books, Inc.   196A - 336   2016 $45

Copeland, Pamela C. *The Five George Masons, Patriots and Planters of Virginia and Maryland.* Lorton: Board of Regents of Gunston Hall, 1989. Second printing, facsimile, map, folding table, genealogical tables, extensive chapter notes, black cloth, very fine with dust jacket.   Argonaut Book Shop   Biography 2015 - 6977   2016 $60

Copelston, Edward *A Reply to the Calumnies of the Edinburgh Review Against Oxford. (with) A Second Reply to the Edinburgh Review.* Oxford: printed for the author..., 1810. Recent blue wrappers.   Jarndyce Antiquarian Books   CCXV - 886   2016   £40

Copley, Esther *Cottage Comforts ...* London: Simpkin Marshall & Co., 1841. Seventeenth edition, original grey-green cloth, boards faded. some rubbing to head pf some, bookplate of W. H. Dalton, bookseller and stationer, good.   Jarndyce Antiquarian Books   CCXV - 132   2016   £50

Copley, Esther *Cottage Comforts ...* London: Simpkin, Marshall & Co., 1858. Twenty-third edition, original grey-green cloth, hand colored armorial bookplate of Hugh Henry Robertson Aikman, embossed library stamp on leading f.e.p., very good.   Jarndyce Antiquarian Books   CCXV - 133   2016   £45

Coppard, A. E. *Adam & Eve and Pinch Me.* London: Golden Cockerel Press, 1921. Limited to 550 copies, 12mo., paper covered boards, label on spine and front cover, spine lightly sunned, covers lightly soiled, endpapers tanned.   Oak Knoll Books   310 - 103   2016 $125

Coras, Jean De *The Qualifications and the Duties of a Good and Complete Judge...* Montreal: 1934. First edition, with his signature dated Autumn 1934, original cloth, spine somewhat rubbed and discolored, else very good, Charles B. Sears's copy.   Simon Finch   2015 - 23032   2016 $250

Corbet, John *Self Employment in Secret.* Hull: printed by J. Ferraby, 1795. New edition, 12mo., contemporary full dark blue calf, gilt bands, compartments gilt, two original brass clasps, slightly rubbed, contemporary signature of Elizabeth Grey, all edges gilt, very good, attractive.   Jarndyce Antiquarian Books   CCXV - 134   2016   £225

Corbett, James J. *The Roar of the Crowd: The True Tale of the Rise and Fall of a Champion.* New York: G. P. Putnam's sons, 1925. First edition, front hinge neatly restored, else fine in very good or better dust jacket with modest chips at spine ends, short split at front flap fold, inscribed by author for boxing champion Dennis Crown.   Between the Covers Rare Books   208 - 133   2016 $2500

Corder, John Shewell *Christchurch, or Witherpole House, a Brief Memorial.* Ipswich: printed and published by S. H. Cowell, Buttermarket, 1893. Small paper edition, folio, tinted printed title, genealogical table and text illustrations, 10 tinted plates, original cloth backed decorated boards, upper cover with illustrations as title and protected by transparent 'waxed' printed paper, loose due to gutta percha binding and some fraying to wrapper and minor top edge damage to leaf of preface.   Marlborough Rare Books   List 55 - 17   2016   £125

Corelli, Marie *The Murder of Delicia.* London: Skeffington and Son, 1896. First edition, very good in original maroon cloth boards with gilt title to spine and front board, slight roll to spine and minor wear to edges and spine ends, endpages browned with small spot of soiling on first two, few spots of foxing to titlepage, inscription from previous owner on half titlepage dated 1896, occasional smudge marks nice despite noted wear, very good.   The Kelmscott Bookshop   12 - 28   2016 $150

Corle, Edwin *Death Valley and the Creek Called Furnace.* Los Angeles: Ward Ritchie Press, 1962. First edition with photos by Ansel Adams, head of spine jammed, very good with pictorial dust jacket (head of jacket spine worn). Argonaut Book Shop   Photography 2015 - 2977   2016 $50

Corman, Cid *Clocked Stone.* Kyoto: Origin Press, 1959. First edition, one of 210 copies signed by author and artist, square folio, collotype plates by Hiedetaka Ohno, original burlap, fine, scarce.   James S. Jaffe Rare Books   Occasional List: Winter 2016 - 44   2016 $1000

Cornelius, Brother *Keith, Old Master of California.* New York: G. P. Putnam's Sons, 1942. Volume 2 St. Mary's College, 1957. First editions, 2 volumes, colored frontispieces and 90 plates, including 16 in color, gray and black cloth, gilt, fine set, perfect dust jacket on volume 2 only. Argonaut Book Shop   Biography 2015 - 5347   2016 $275

Cornelius, Brother *Keith. Old Master of California. Volume II: a supplement.* Moraga: St. Mary's College, 1957. First edition, volume II only, illustrations in color, gray cloth stamped in black and gold, very fine with dust jacket. Argonaut Book Shop   Biography 2015 - 7179   2016 $125

Cornell, Katharine *I Wanted to be an Actress.* New York: Random House, 1939. First printing, 8vo., illustrations, rose moire cloth, one of 550 numbered copies signed by author, this copy also inscribed by author, fine in original glassene (torn).   Second Life Books, Inc.   196A - 338   2016 $125

Cornell, Katharine *I Wanted to be an Actress.* New York: Random House, 1939. First printing, 8vo., illustrations, rose moire cloth, signed by author, worn at corners and some fading on spine, otherwise very good.   Second Life Books, Inc.   196A - 338   2016 $75

Cornwallis, Harris, William *Portraits of the Game and Wild Animals of Southern Africa.* Mazoe: Frank Read Press, 1977. Card portfolio, 66.5 x 49cm., containing 4 prints, each 59 x 43cm., on handmade, painted with Read Press blindstamp, signed by Frank Read and date stamped 9th Dec. 1977, fine.   Sotheran's   Piccadilly Notes - Summer 2015 - 86   2016   £450

Cornwell, Bernard *Sharpe's Eagle.* London: Collins, 1981. First edition, fine in fine, price clipped dust jacket. Buckingham Books   2015 - 27544   2016 $450

Cornwell, Bruce *Life Sketch of Pierre B. Cornwall.* San Francisco: A. M. Robertson, 1906. First edition, very scarce, portraits from early photos, original three quarter brown leather, marbled boards, gilt lettered spine, spine ends slightly rubbed, hint of scattered foxing, free endpapers with offsetting from binders glue, overall fine, by Bruce Cornwall, his son.   Argonaut Book Shop   Biography 2015 - 7392   2016 $325

Cornwell, Patricia D. *Cruel and Unusual.* New York: Scribners, 1993. First edition, very fine in dust jacket. Mordida Books   2015 - 010407   2016 $65

Correlli, Marie *Free Opinions Freely expressed on Certain Phases of Modern Social Life and Conduct.* London: Archibald Constable, 1905. First edition, half title, final ad leaf, 16 page catalog, original dark blue cloth, blocked and lettered in gilt, spine slightly faded, modern bookplate of Ronald George Taylor, inscribed by author on leading f.e.p. "Mr. W. Reede 34 Marstell Place - Leicester".   Jarndyce Antiquarian Books   CCXV - 135   2016   £58

Corso, Gregory *American Express.* Paris: Olympia Press, 1961. First edition, wrappers, owner's name, else fine in lightly rubbed, near fine dust jacket.   Between the Covers Rare Books   204 - 32   2016 $600

Corso, Gregory *Long Live Man.* Norfolk: New Directions, 1962. first printing, 8vo., paper wrappers, cover little scuffed, owner's name inside cover, but very good, tight. Second Life Books, Inc.   197 - 54   2016 $45

Cortazar, Julio *Fantomes Contra Los Vampiros Multinacionales.* Mexico City: Excelsior, 1975. First Mexican edition, preceding all others, inscribed by author, light rubbing overall, owner stamps on front and rear flyleaves, else near fine in saddle stitched illustrated wrappers. Royal Books   48 - 68   2016 $750

Corti, Adolfo *L'Arte del Nuoto Teorico-Pratica Dimostrata Secondo I Principi Della Fisica Con Relative Figure.* Venezia: Tipografia Fracasso, 1819. One of 500 copies, 8vo., 45 figures on 24 plates, contemporary half vellum over grey buckram, spine decorated gilt and with red and gilt title label, deckle edges, top edge gilt, front endpapers stuck together, very slight staining and or foxing to most pages, overall very nice.   Any Amount of Books   2015 - C6274   2016   £600

Cory, Alexander Turner *The Hieroglyphics of Horapollo Nilous.* London: William Pickering, 1840. 193 x 118mm., very attractive contemporary olive green morocco elaborately gilt by Hering (stamp signed), covers with delicate gilt frame of drawer handle, floral sprig and star tools, raised bands, spine gilt in compartments with similar tooling, densely gilt turn-ins, pale yellow endpapers, all edges gilt, frontispiece, numerous representations of hieroglyphics and 3 plates, pencilled presentation from author to the illustrator of the work, Joseph Bonomi, engraved bookplate of Samuel Ashton Thompson-Yates, just slightest hint of rubbing to joints (well marked with dye), faint graze on rear cover, spine probably sunned (though abundance of gilt making this difficult to determine), significant foxing to prelim leaves, frontispiece and titlpage (moderate foxing to plates II and III and adjacent text leaves), but text otherwise clean and fresh, decorative binding lustrous scarcely worn and altogether pleasing. Phillip J. Pirages 67 - 49 2016 $1500

Coryate, Thomas *Coryats Crudities, Hastily gobled up in five Moneths....* London: printed by VV(illiam) S(tansby for the author), 1611. First edition, 4to., full Regency diced tan calf by Charles Hering (engraved label, firm active in London 1794-1844), spine with raised bands, ornamented and lettered gilt, ornamented in blind as well, boards with filigree gilt stamped fleurons in corners, dotted gilt ruling, gothic ornamentation in blind, edges and inner dentelles ornamented in gilt, marbled endpapers, red edges, engraved title, engraved full page portrait and one heraldic engraving, 4 engraved plates, woodcut ornaments in text, rebacked retaining original spine, gathering 2N with tiny traces of worming in upper margins, very light even browning or minimal spotting, folding plate of Strasbourg clock little cropped as usual, title little cropped at upper margin, very good, elaborate binding, bookplate of Henry Yates Thompson (1838-1928). Sotheran's Travel and Exploration - 230 2016 £17,000

Cosnett, Thomas *The Footman's Directory and Butler's Remembrance or The Advice of Onesimus to His Young Friends.* London: Simpkin & Marhsall & Henry Colburn, 1825. New edition, initial, 12 page catalog March 1829, folding plate, uncut in original brown printed paper boards, spine defective with some loss to head and lower hinges. Jarndyce Antiquarian Books CCXV - 136 2016 £250

Cosson, Anthony De *Mareotis, Being a Short Account of the History and Ancient Monuments of the North-Western Desert of Egypt and of Leke Mareotis.* London: Country Life, 1935. First edition, 8vo., original black cloth with illustrated dust jacket, frontispiece in sepia photogravure, photogravure plate, 3 folding plans and folding map (this re-inserted and with repaired tears, see below), cloth lightly rubbed, endpapers with foxing (offsetting to half title), inscribed by R. H. Hase dated Alexandria Dec. 1935. Sotheran's Travel and Exploration - 312 2016 £98

Costello, Louisa Stuart *A Summer Amongst the Bocages and the Vines.* London: Richard Bentley, 1840. First edition, 2 volumes, 8vo., 4 lithographic plates, 8 textual illustrations, some foxing to plates, original green blindstamped cloth, spines faded. J. & S. L. Bonham Antiquarian Booksellers Europe 2016 - 8725 2016 £250

Costello, Ruth *Poems for Evan Connell.* Self published: undated, circa 1980's, Near fine, laid in is printout of 1983 Costello poem "For Lama Anagarika Govinda", unmarked, but from the library of Peter Matthiessen. Ken Lopez Bookseller 166 - 24 2016 $150

Costello, Ruth *Poems for Herb Gold.* undated, circa 1980's, self published, Velobound in gold stamped plastic covers, unmarked, from the library of Peter Matthiessen, highly uncommon. Ken Lopez Bookseller 166 - 23 2016 $150

Coster, Geraldine *Yoga and Western Psychology.* London: Oxford University Press, 1934. First edition, 8vo., original red cloth with gilt lettering on spine, printed green dust jacket, some wear to dust jacket, otherwise fine. Sotheran's Piccadilly Notes - Summer 2015 - 341 2016 £80

Cotes, Roger *Hydrostatical and Pneumatical Lectures.* London: for the editor and sold by S. Austen, 1738. First edition, 5 engraved folding plates, contemporary sprinkled calf, neatly rebacked, name clipped from top corner of front endpaper and repaired with old paper, very good. Joseph J. Felcone, Inc. Books from Five Centuries: a Miscellany - 51 2016 $1200

Cotman, John Sell *Engravings of Sepulchral Brasses in Norfolk and Suffolk, Tending to Illustrate the Ecclesiastical Military and Civil Costume...* London: Henry G. Bohn, 1839. Second edition, 2 volumes, folio, 171 plates as called for, some folding, hand colored frontispiece, very occasional light foxing, slight faint smudging to titlepages, few folded plates just starting to split a little along their folds, generally in good order, half olive green morocco and gold marbled paper covered boards, matching endpapers, gilt spines, top edge gilt and others uncut, spines little faded, rubbed, few small scrapes, edges worn, inner hinges inconspicuously reinforced with green tape, bookplate of Adrian Bullock to front and back pastedown of each volume. Unsworths Antiquarian Booksellers 30 - 38 2016 £650

Cotsell, Michael *The Companion to Our Mutual Friend.* London: Allen & Unwin, 1986. First edition, half title, maps, original green cloth, blocked and lettered gilt, mint in slightly faded dust jacket. Jarndyce Antiquarian Booksellers CCXVIII - 615 2016 £40

Cott, Hugh B. *Adaptive Coloration in Animals.* London: Methuen, 1940. First edition, octavo, colored frontispiece, text illustrations, very good, dust jacket, scarce. Andrew Isles Natural History Books 55 - 37150 2016 $300

The Cottage Fire-Side. Dublin: printed by Napper & White, 1826. Frontispiece, title vignette, illustrations, contemporary full sheep, rubbed and worn, sound copy only. Jarndyce Antiquarian Books CCXV - 137 2016 £38

Cottin, Paul *Memoirs of Sergeant Bourgogne.* London: Heinemann, 1899. First English edition, 8vo., portrait frontispiece, original blue cloth, spine faded, covers speckled. J. & S. L. Bonham Antiquarian Booksellers Europe 2016 - 3477 2016 £20

Cottle, Joseph *Early Recollections: Chiefly Relating to the late Samuel Taylor Coleridge.* London: Longman, Rees & Co., 1837. First edition, 200 x 127mm, 2 volumes, fine polished calf, elegantly gilt by R. W. Smith (stamp signed on front flyleaf), covers bordered with double gilt rules, spines with raised bands and compartments featuring pleasing dense gilt scrollwork, red and deep blue morocco labels, intricately gilt turn-ins, marbled endpapers, top edge gilt, 6 engraved plates, large modern bookplate of Robert Marceau, engravings rather foxed, little darkening and very minor intermittent foxing in text, otherwise excellent internally in beautiful, virtually unworn binding. Phillip J. Pirages 67 - 93 2016 $750

Cotton, Walter *The California Diary.* Oakland: Biobooks, 1948. Reissue, one of 1000 copies, small 4to., 5 plates from drawings, text map, folding facsimile, red cloth, marbled endpapers, fine. Argonaut Book Shop Biography 2015 - 6452 2016 $75

Couchman, Helen *Omani Women. About a Journey.* London: Soloshow Pub., 2015. First edition, 4to., original boards with dust jacket, color illustrations, new, signed by photographer. Sotheran's Travel and Exploration - 313 2016 £29

Coue, Emile *Self Mastery through Conscious Autosuggestion.* New York: American Library Service Pub., 1922. First edition, 8vo., original printed limp wrappers, portrait frontispiece, some rust and paperclip marks to cover and titlepage from previous owner. Sotheran's Piccadilly Notes - Summer 2015 - 87 2016 £40

Coulton, C. G. *The Chronicler of European Chivalry.* Studio Special Winter Number, 1930. First edition, quarto, numerous illustrations, 8 tipped in color plates with captioned tissue guards, red buckram, top edge gilt, fine in very near fine dust jacket, lovely copy. Peter Ellis 112 - 74 2016 £65

Coulton, George Gordon *A Victorian Schoolmaster: Henry Hart of Sedbergh.* London: G. Bell & Sons, 1923. First edition, half title, plates, uncut in original brown buckram, darkened. Jarndyce Antiquarian Books CCXV - 722 2016 £20

Court Etiquette: a Guide to Intercourse with Royal or Titled Persons, to Drawing Rooms, Levees, Courts and Audiences... London: Charles Mitchell, 1849. First edition, 12mo., frontispiece, 1 page ads, original blue grey cloth, dulled and marked by damp, slightly rubbed, all edges gilt, booklabel of Charles Bray, sound. Jarndyce Antiquarian Books CCXV - 138 2016 £85

Courtenay, John *A Poetical review of the Library and Moral Character of the Late Samuel Johnson, LL.D.* London: printed for Charles Dilly, 1786. Second edition, 4to., without half title, last leaves marked by former insert, rebound in pale blue boards. Jarndyce Antiquarian Booksellers CCXVI - 333 2016 £280

Courtivron, Gaspard Le Compasseur Cresquy-Montfort De *Traite d'Optique Ou l'on Done la Theorie de la Lumiere dans le Systeme Newtonien...* Paris: Chez Durand & Pissot, 1752. First edition, small 4to., errors in pagination, collated complete, 7 engraved folding plates, original full mottled calf, raised bands, gilt spine, compartments, brown leather, title label, minor worming to joints and back cover, signature of Barthelemy Lombard, rare. Jeff Weber Rare Books 183 - 14 2016 $3750

Cousin, Victor *Report on the State of Public Instruction in Prussia...* London: Effingham Wilson, 1834. First English edition, half title, 3 folding plans, original brown moire cloth, recased, retaining original spine and paper label. Jarndyce Antiquarian Books CCXV - 618 2016 £85

Coutts, J. *The Complete Book of Gardening.* London: Ward Lock & Co., 1931. Second edition, 8vo., bound by Sangorski & Sutcliffe in half green morocco, spine with gilt raised bands, gilt lettering and gilt foliate centre tools with red morocco inlays, boards and endpapers in matching floral design, top edges gilt, binder's stamp to verso of f.f.e.p., 16 color plates, numerous black and white plates, text illustrations, very good in extremely handsome binding. Sotheran's Piccadilly Notes - Summer 2015 - 88 2016 £150

Couvreur, Jesse Catherine Huybers *In Her Earliest Youth.* London: Kegan Paul, Trench, Trubner & Co., 1891. 8vo., original gilt stamped red cloth, spine slightly faded, author Thomas Hardy's copy signed copy, with his Max Gate bookplate. Howard S. Mott Inc. 265 - 38 2016 $950

Coward, Noel 1899-1973 *Quadrille: a Romantic Comedy in Three Acts.* London: Heinemann, 1952. First edition, signed by 17 members of the English cast and by producer Jack Wilson and by Lynn Fontanne and Alfred Lunt on dedication page (play is dedicated to them), inscribed by Coward to Dorothy Sands (Octavia in the NY production), two more signed cards by Lunt and Fontanne tipped in and 3 notes by Lunt to Sands laid in, with tipped in signed photo of sands, nice in somewhat signed dust jacket. Second Life Books, Inc. 196A - 342 2016 $500

Cowden-Clarke, Mary *Recollections of Writers.* London: Sampson Low, 1878. First edition, half title, facsimile Dickens letter, 32 page catalog (April 1878), preface leaf slightly chipped at fore-edge, original brown cloth, bevelled boards, lettered in gilt, head and tail of spine with small repairs.   Jarndyce Antiquarian Booksellers   CCXVIII - 854   2016   £40

Cowdroy, William *The Vaporish man or Hypocrisy Detected.* Chester: printed for J. Monk, 1782. 8vo., rather browned and foxed, outer pages dusted, blindstamp of Wigan Public Library, ink stamp on verso, final two leaves have paper repairs without loss of text, recent marbled paper wrappers.   Jarndyce Antiquarian Booksellers   CCXVI - 459   2016   £220

Cowles, Frederick *The Night Winds Howls: Complete Supernatural Stories.* Columbia: Ash Tree Press, 1999. Second collected edition, limited to 600 copies, octavo, cloth, some light spotting to page edges, nearly fine in like dust jacket with abrasion to rear panel.   John W. Knott, Jr./ L.W. Currey, Inc.   Fall-Winter 2015 - 18501   2016 $250

Cowley, Abraham   1618-1667 *Poems: viz I. Miscellanies. II. Mistress; or Love Verses. III. Pindarique Odes. and IV. Davides, or a Sacred Poem of the Troubles of David.* London: For Humphrey Moseley, 1656. First collected edition, contemporary paneled calf, edges gilt, very skillfully rebacked to style, later endpapers, occasional minor spots and repaired marginal tears, 3L2 soiled and with paper defect costing several letters, lovely copy, early signature of Edmund Henry Marshal on title "Ex Libris George Bernard Shaw".   Joseph J. Felcone, Inc.   Books from Five Centuries: a Miscellany - 52   2016 $2500

Cowley, Malcolm *Blue Juniata: Collected Poems.* New York: Viking Press, 1968. First edition, 8vo., fine, little worn dust jacket, inscribed by author to poet and editor William Claire.   Second Life Books, Inc.   196A - 344   2016 $85

Cowley, Malcolm *Think Back On us.* Carbondale: Southern Illinois University, 1967. 8vo., author's presentation on half title to Lillian Freedman, green cloth, top edges of leaves little soiled, edges of cover little worn in spots, otherwise very good, tight in chipped dust jacket.   Second Life Books, Inc.   196A - 345   2016 $75

Cowper, William *Memoir of the Early Life of William Cowper, Esq./Cowper Illustrated by a Series of Views...* London: R. Edwards, 1816. First edition, small 8vo., full brown leather decorated gilt, frontispiece, 12 plates, bound together, clean, very good.   Any Amount of Books 2015 - A69176   2016   £150

Cox, Geoffrey *Defence of Madrid.* London: Victor Gollancz, 1937. First edition, scarce hardback issue, book in usual limp orange cloth, octavo, upper corner of front free endpaper creased, otherwise very good in very good, slightly nicked and dusty dust jacket little torn and chipped at tail of spine.   Peter Ellis   112 - 378   2016   £125

Cox, Helen *Mr. and Mrs. Charles Dickens Entertain at Home...* London: Pergamon General Books, 1970. First edition, half title, plate, original white cloth, slightly marked. Jarndyce Antiquarian Booksellers   CCXVIII - 1133   2016   £30

Cox, Irwin Edward Bainbridge *The Country House....* London: Horace Cox, 1883. Third edition, illustrations, slight paper flaw to upper margin of titlepage, original green cloth, front board slightly marked, ex-libris James Gordon, good.   Jarndyce Antiquarian Books   CCXV - 139   2016   £65

Cox, Morris *14 Triads.* London: Gogmagog Press, 1967. Limited to 100 numbered copies, of which 40 were bound in Japanese Hana-asa paper and distributed to the Society of Private printers, 12mo., paper spine label, text printed on dampened Japanese Hoso-shi paper, black on blue print illustrations, printed on blue Mingei paper, publisher's prospectus loosely inserted, beautiful and delicate book, 28 traditional French-fold leaves.   Oak Knoll Books   27 - 23   2016 $350

Cox, Morris *An Impression of Winter: a Landscape Panorama. An Impression of Spring...of Summer...of Autumn....* London: Gogmagog Press, 1966. Limited to 100 copies, 4 volumes, narrow 8vo., each volume illustrated with 3 embossed reverse/direct offset prints joined in continuous strip, very fine set, prospectus laid in.   James S. Jaffe Rare Books   Occasional List: Winter 2016 - 69   2016 $3500

Cox, Morris *Intimidations of Mortality: Poems on Victorian Themes...* London: Gogmagog Private Press, 1977. First edition, no. 58 of 90 copies signed by author, tall 8vo. original red brown Mingei paper boards with black and white title and designs by Cox, publisher's acetate dust jacket, printed on Hodgkinson's and Japanese Mingei handmade papers, fine.   James S. Jaffe Rare Books   Occasional List: Winter 2016 - 70   2016 $375

Cox, Morris *Mummers' Fool.* London: Gogmagog Press, 1965. Copy 53 of 60 copies numbered and signed in ink by author, printed on Barcham Green Roger Powell handmade paper, frontispiece handolored offset print and 6 double page offset prints, quarter natural linen with paper boards, containing actual dried grasses under transparent tissue paper, fine with prospectus laid in.   James S. Jaffe Rare Books   Occasional List: Winter 2016 - 68   2016 $1000

Cox, Palmer *The Brownie Primer Together with Queerie Queers.* Chicago: George M. Hill, 1901. 4to., cloth backed pictorial boards, edges rubbed and few pinholes in spine which is faded, margin soil on epage, very good++, 12 full page color illustrations, rare.   Aleph-bet Books, Inc. 112 - 118   2016 $1200

Cox, Palmer *The Brownies Around the World.*   New York: Century Co., 1894. 4to., glazed pictorial boards, edges and extremities lightly rubbed, first 2 leaves scattered foxing else near fine in original pictorial dust jacket (chip off front panel and soiled), nice, rarely found in jacket.   Aleph-bet Books, Inc.   111 - 101   2016 $975

Cox, Palmer *Queer People Such as Goblins, Giants, Merry-Men and Monarchs and their Kweer Kapers.* Edgewood Pub. Co., 1888. Pictorial boards, some edge wear and nice leather label on spine, very good, profusely illustrated on every page by author, with author's signature on flyleaf.   Aleph-bet Books, Inc.   111 - 102   2016 $475

Cox, Reuben *Corn Close. a Cottage in Dentdale.* Salisbury: Green Shade, 2015. First edition, 4to., illustrations in color, original cloth, dust jacket, limited to 50 copies signed by Cox, Meyer, Midgette, Green and Jaffe, with original photo signed by photographer laid in, as new.   James S. Jaffe Rare Books   Occasional List: Winter 2016 - 148   2016 $250

Coy, Owen C. *A Pictorial History of California.* Berkeley: University of California Press, 1925. First edition, oblong 4to., 281 full page plates, publisher's loose sheets, never bound, fine in broken slipcase.   Argonaut Book Shop Photography 2015 - 7537   2016 $225

Coy, Owen C. *A Pictorial History of California.* Berkeley: University of California, 1925. First edition, oblong 4to., 261 full page plates, publisher's grey-green cloth, gilt, remnants from semi-removed bookplate on inner cover, cloth lightly rubbed at extremities, spine lightly faded, very good. Argonaut Book Shop   Photography 2015 - 5346   2016 $325

Cozzens, Fred S. *The Sayings of Dr. Bushwhacker and Other Learned Men.* New York: Simpson, 1867. First edition, 8vo, little worn purple cloth, leaves browned, very good, inscribed by author to John Elliott, bookplate removed, very good.   Second Life Books, Inc.   196A - 346   2016 $150

Cozzens, James Gould *S. S. San Pedro and Castaway.* New York: Modern Library Paperback by Random House, 1957? 8vo. paperback, spine loose, good, this was poet and editor Barbara Howe's copy and laid in are 10 (6 x 4 inch) sheets of paper on which Howes has commented on Cozzens as a writer and on these short stories.   Second Life Books, Inc.   196A- 75   2016 $350

Crabbe, George *The Life of George Crabbe, by his son.* London: Oxford University Press, Humphrey Milford, 1932. First edition with this introduction, small 8vo., bound by Morrell in full leather, raised bands, gilt decorated spine, gilt rules, marbled endpapers and edges, stamped in gilt with crown and letter K on upper cover, armorial bookplate of Edward Hilton Young, 1st Baron Kennet of the Dene; presentation copy inscribed by author for Kennet, fine.   Peter Ellis   112 - 130   2016   £450

Crace, Jim *The Pesthouse.* New York: Talese/Doubleday, 2007. Advance reading copy, near fine in wrappers.   Ken Lopez Bookseller   166 - 25   2016 $150

Craddock, Harry *The Savoy Cocktail Book.* London: Constable & Co., 1930. First edition, 8vo., original cloth backed boards, attractive Art Deco design to upper cover in green, black and silver and grey,colored decorations throughout by Gilbert Rumbold, little flaking to oxidised silver on boards, as usual little wear to head and tail of spine on which the lettering is dulled, occasional spots of browning to text, generally very good.   Sotheran's Piccadilly Notes - Summer 2015 - 89   2016   £998

The Crafty Princess or the Golden Horse. in four parts. N.P.: i.e. America, n.d. circa 179-?, Rare, 8vo., 8 pages, uncut, nearly fine.   Howard S. Mott Inc.   265 - 3   2016 $600

Craggs, Douglas *A. B. C. of Ventriloquism.* London: Areas, 1944. First edition, folio, sometime rebound in half dark green calf, green cloth sides, spine and upper cover titled gilt, portrait, 30 illustrations in text, fine, author's signed inscription.   Sotheran's Piccadilly Notes - Summer 2015 - 312   2016   £98

Crahan, Marcus *One Hundred Sixteen Uncommon Books on Food and Drink...* Berkeley: Friends of the Bancroft Library, 1975. First edition, 20 photo reproductions, stiff wrappers, spine folded, else fine.   Argonaut Book Shop Private Press 2015 - 7393   2016 $45

Craig, Edward Gordon 1872-1966 *Biographical note.* Florence: n.d. circa, 1919. Sole edition, one or two faint foxspots, 8vo., original self wrappers, paper tabs to spine from having been mounted in album, very good, with annotations by author.   Blackwell's Rare Books   B184 - 132   2016   £550

Craig, Edward Gordon 1872-1966 *Henry Irving.* London: J. M. Dent & Sons, 1930. First edition, this being one of 75 specially bound copies, containing 2 extra illustrations and signed by author, Dame Edith Evans's copy with posthumous bookplate, original quarter leather, spine lettered gilt, top edge gilt, coloured frontispiece, 23 portraits and other illustrations, very good.   Sotheran's Piccadilly Notes - Summer 2015 - 171   2016   £498

Craig, Edward Gordon 1872-1966 *Nothing or the Bookplate.* London: Chatto & Windus, 1924. First edition, limited edition, no. 33 of 280 copies, crown 8vo., original russet buckram lettered gilt on spine and cover, loosely inserted 2 original bookplates by E. G. Craig, this with further bookplate signed by Craig, bookplates hand colored, from the library of James Lee Wilson with his small neat bookplate by Leo Wyatt, loosely inserted compliments slip from London, otherwise very good+.   Any Amount of Books   2015 - C4661   2016   £250

Craig, Maurice J. *Irish Book Bindings 1600-1800.* London: Cassell, 1954. Large 4to., color frontispiece, 58 plates, original full blue gilt stamped cloth, dust jacket with few minor tears to extremities, near fine.   Jeff Weber Rare Books   181 - 52   2016 $175

Craigie, Pearl Mary Theresa Richards 1867-1906 *A Bundle of Life.* London: T. Fisher Unwin, 1893. First edition, near fine in original beige cloth with green title to spine and front board, light sunning to spine and bumping to corners, minor browning to end pages, else interior clean, top edge gilt, near fine.   The Kelmscott Bookshop   12 - 53   2016 $175

Craigie, Pearl Mary Theresa Richards 1867-1906 *A Study in Temptation.* London: T. Fisher Unwin, 1893. First edition, very uncommon, near fine in original beige cloth with green title to spine and front board, minor foxing to endpages, else interior is clean, top edge gilt.   The Kelmscott Bookshop   12 - 54   2016 $225

Craik, Dinah Maria Mulock 1826-1887 *John Halifax Gentleman.* London: Hurst and Blackett, 1856. First edition, 191 x 114mm, 3 volumes with 3 pages of ads at end of first volume and 2 pages at end of third, extremely pleasing medium green straight grain morocco, attractively gilt by Bayntun (stamp-signed on front flyleaf), gilt double fillet border on covers, raised bands, gilt spine compartments with filigree lozenge centerpiece and cornerpiece volutes, blue and red morocco labels, heavily gilt turn-ins, marbled endpapers, all edges gilt, joints of first volume bit flaked, tiny cracks just beginning, two leaves with neatly repaired tear (one in lower fore margin, the other into text, but without loss), text faintly browned at edges because of inexpensive paper, still quite appealing set, decorative bindings bright and almost entirely unworn, text very clean and smooth.   Phillip J. Pirages   67 - 96   2016 $750

Craik, George Lillie *The Pursuit of Knowledge Under Difficulties.* London: M. A. Nattali, 1846. 2 volumes, frontispiece and plates, partially unopened in original green cloth, spines faded with small chip to head of spine, volume i, otherwise very good, contemporary signature of Mrs. D. Lingard.   Jarndyce Antiquarian Books   CCXV - 34   2016   £40

Craik, George Lillie *The Pursuit of Knowledge Under Difficulties.* London: Nattali & Bond, circa, 1857. 2 volumes, frontispiece and plates, original green cloth, spines elaborately gilt blocked, little rubbed and dulled, blindstamps, pressmarks &c. of Bolland Collection LSE Library, good, with signatures of Arthur Bolland Feb. 11th 1857.   Jarndyce Antiquarian Books   CCXV - 55   2016   £40

Craik, George Lillie *The Pursuit of Knowledge Under Difficulties.* London: John Murray, 1858. New edition, 2 volumes in 1, frontispiece, plates and illustrations, original purple cloth, gilt vignette of Craik on frontispiece, faint circular mark on front board, spine faded, all edges gilt, contemporary and recent inscriptions on leading f.e.p, Victor Neuburg's copy.   Jarndyce Antiquarian Books   CCXV - 56   2016   £35

Craik, George Lillie *The Pursuit of Knowledge Under Difficulties.* Edinburgh: William P. Nimmo, 1881. Additional engraved title, frontispiece, plates, original grey decorated cloth, bevelled boards, little rubbed, prize label on leading pastedown.   Jarndyce Antiquarian Books   CCXV - 57   2016   £25

Crain, Jim *California in Depth: a Stereoscopic History.* San Francisco: Chronicle Books, 1994. First edition, small quarto, stereopticon slide reproductions, original folding 3-D stereo viewer in rear pocket, pictorial boards, vey fine, as new in original publisher's shrinkwrap.   Argonaut Book Shop   Photography 2015 - 6896   2016 $45

Crais, Robert *Indigo Slam.* New York: Hyperion, 1997. First edition, very fine in dust jacket, signed by author.   Mordida Books   2015 - 008253   2016 $65

Crais, Robert *The Monkey's Raincoat.* London: Piatkus, 1989. First British edition and first hardcover edition, fine in near fine dust jacket, price clipped, but with publisher's price sticker on front flap.   Bella Luna Books   2016 - t8681   2016 $264

Crais, Robert *The Monkey's Raincoat.* New York: Doubleday, 1993. First US hardcover edition, signed on titlepage by author, fine in dust jacket.   Buckingham Books   2015 - 28958   2016 $450

Crais, Robert *Sunset Express.* New York: Hyperion, 1996. First edition, very fine in dust jacket.   Mordida Books   2015 - 008252   2016 $65

Cramer, J. A. *The Second Book of the Travels of Nicander Nucius of Corcyra.* London: Camden Society, 1841. First edition, small quarto, original dark green blindstamped cloth.   J. & S. L. Bonham Antiquarian Booksellers   Europe 2016 - 9233   2016   £50

Crane, Frances *Horror on the Ruby X.* New York: Random House, 1956. First edition, fine in dust jacket and with tiny wear at top of spine.   Mordida Books   2015 - 010744   2016 $65

Crane, Frances *The Man in Gray.* New York: Random House, 1958. First edition, fine in dust jacket with some tiny wear along edges.   Mordida Books   2015 - 010600   2016 $65

Crane, Hart 1899-1932 *The Bridge.* New York: Horace Liveright, 1930. First American edition, photo by Walker Evans, fine in very good, spine faded dust jacket with couple of internally repaired short tear, in custom cloth chemise and quarter morocco slipcase, inscribed by Crane for Tom Smith.   Between the Covers Rare Books   204 - 30   2016 $50,000

Crane, Hart 1899-1932 *The Bridge. A Poem.* Paris: Black Sun Press, 1930. First edition, one of 200 numbered copies, printed on Holland Paper, 4to., original white printed wrappers, original glassine, publisher's silver gilt paper covered slipcase, touch of discoloration to glassine where the slipcase accommodates finger pulls, original silver foil slipcase edge little cracked at head of spine, otherwise exceptionally fine, preserved in black half moroccco slipcase, 3 photos by Walker Evans.   James S. Jaffe Rare Books Occasional List: Winter 2016 - 45   2016 $15,000

Crane, Hart 1899-1932 *Voyages: Six Poems from White Buildings.* New York: Museum of Modern Art, 1957. First edition, oblong 8vo., this #526 of a limited edition of 975 copies signed and numbered by Leonard Baskin, fine, hand sewn into blue wrappers with paper label in irregularly faded publisher's portfolio that shows some wear at tips, illustrations by Baskin have been printed from six original boxwood engravings and one cherry woodcut on Amalfi Italian handmade paper and on Moriki and mending tissue, both hand made in Japan.   Second Life Books, Inc.   196A - 347   2016 $300

Crane, Lucy *The Baby's Bouquet.* London: George Routledge, n.d., 1878. First edition, 8vo., cloth backed pictorial boards, light cover soil and edge rubbing, very good+, smaller beautiful richly colored illustrations.   Aleph-bet Books, Inc.   112 - 124   2016 $300

Crane, Walter 1845-1915 *The Baby's Opera ....* London: George Routledge, First edition, square octavo, illustrations by Crane, corners scuffed, boards marked, hinges little cracked, very good.   Peter Ellis   112 - 86   2016   £125

Crane, Walter 1845-1915 *Cartoons for the Cause.* Journeyman Press and Marx Memorial Library, 1976. 45/100 copies signed by John Betjeman, titlepage printed in red and black, 12 full page wood engravings by Crane, folio, original brown card wrappers with maroon ribbon tie, printed in brown to front, some light dust soiling to edges and little nicked and creased to borders, where overhanging textblock, edges untrimmed, very good.   Blackwell's Rare Books   B184 - 115   2016   £250

Crane, Walter 1845-1915 *The First of May: a Fairy Masque.* London: Henry Sotheran, 1881. Limited to 300 numbered india proof copies signed by Crane, this number 180, oblong folio, margins trimmed and attractively rebound in cloth with cloth label and decorations from the original folder laid down, marbled endpapers, lovely work, rare.   Aleph-bet Books, Inc.   111 - 103   2016 $900

Crane, Walter 1845-1915 *Flora's Feast.* London: Cassell, 1889. First edition, 4to., cloth backed pictorial boards, tips worn, else very good+, beautiful color illustrations by Crane, lovely book.   Aleph-bet Books, Inc.   111 - 104   2016 $400

Crane, Walter 1845-1915 *Slateandpencilvania.* London: Marcus Ward & Co., 1885. First edition, square quarto, pictorial titlepage, 24 full page color illustrations, monocolor tailpiece, publisher's blue cloth backed pictorial boards, green pictorial endpapers, all edges stained red, corners and board edges little rubbed and worn, otherwise very clean, scarce.   David Brass Rare Books, Inc.   2015 - 02993   2016 $350

Cranmer, Thomas *A Defence of the True and Catholick Doctirne of the Sacrament of the Body and Blood of Our Saviour Jesus Christ....* London: C. and J. Rivington &c., 1825. First edition, uncut in original blue-grey boards, paper label, some slight rubbing with slight cracking to lower corner of front board, from the library of Earl John Eldon with his armorial roundle and signature Eldon, very good in original binding.   Jarndyce Antiquarian Booksellers   CCXVII - 78   2016   £180

Crapsey, Edward *The Nether Side of New York; or the Vice, Crime and Poverty of the Great Metrolpolis.* New York: Sheldon & Co., 1872. First edition, 8vo., original cloth.   M & S Rare Books, Inc.   99 - 206   2016 $175

Crawford, Alexander Robert *Sketches of Missionary Life in Manchuria.* Belfast: R. Carswell & son, 1899. Very rare first edition, 8vo., original blue cloth, spine lettered gilt, frontispiece, illustrations in text, folding map and one sketch plan, minimal wear to extremities, near fine.   Sotheran's Travel and Exploration - 104   2016   £295

Crawford, C. H. *Scenes of Earlier Days in Crossing the Plains to Oregon and Experiences of Western Life.* Petaluma: J. T. Studdert Book and Job printers, 1898. First edition, photographic frontispiece portrait, plates, black cloth over stiff cloth boards, gilt lettered spine, light wear to lower corners, some spotting to front cover, early owner's name in pencil, near fine.   Argonaut Book Shop   Biography 2015 - 6062   2016 $350

Creasey, John *Death of a Stranger.* London: Hodder & Stoughton, 1957. Very good, dust jacket.   I. D. Edrich   Crime - 2016   £20

Creasey, John *The Edge of Terror.* London: Hodder & Stoughton, 1961. Dust jacket, very good.   I. D. Edrich   Crime - 2016   £20

Creasey, John *Murder at End House.* London: Hodder & Stoughton, 1955. Very good in very slightly frayed dust jacket.   I. D. Edrich   Crime - 2016   £25

Creasey, John *The Toff in Town.* London: John Long, n.d., Edge & corners very slightly rubbed, but very good.   I. D. Edrich   Crime - 2016   £30

Creasy, Edward Shepherd *The Fifteen Decisive Battles of the world from Marathon to Waterloo.* London: Richard Bentley, 1851. Second edition, 2 volumes, , inscribed in both volumes to Emma Maria Holmes from ESP April 13th '52 with pencil notes indicating that the volumes were later given to Emma's brother, William George Holmes and suggesting that the original recipient may have been Stanley Poole, very good.   Jarndyce Antiquarian Booksellers   CCXVII - 70   2016   £150

Creasy, Edward Shepherd *The Fifteen Decisive Battles of the World.* New York: Heritage Press, 1969. Red cloth, decorated and lettered in gilt, minor fading to pine, else very fine, slipcase, illustrations by Joseph Domjan, Sandglass pamphlet laid in.   Argonaut Book Shop   Literature 2015 - 6950   2016 $50

Crebillon, Claude Prosper Jolyt De *The Happy Orphans an Authentic History of Persons in High Life.* printed for H. Woodgate and S. Brooks, 1759. First edition of this translation, 2 volumes, occasional minor browning or spotting, few paper repairs (no loss), 12mo., recent half calf by Bayntun, spines gilt, contrasting lettering pieces, good, rare.   Blackwell's Rare Books   B184 - 31   2016   £2500

Creech, William *Letters Addressed to Sir John Sinclair, Bart Respecting the Mode of Living, Arts, Commerce, Literature, Manners &c. of Edinburgh in 1763....* Edinburgh: 1793. First edition, 8vo., half title, final page rather dust soiled with marginal tears, large uncut copy recently bound in old style quarter calf gilt.   John Drury Rare Books   2015 - 12909   2016 $437

Creeley, Robert *The Island a Novel.* New York: Scribners, 1963. First edition, one of 2616 copies, near fine in dust jacket, first state with page 145 a cancel, inscribed by author.   Second Life Books, Inc.   196A - 352   2016 $85

Creeley, Robert *Life and Death.* New York: Grenfell Press, 1993. First edition, limited to 70 copies (entire edition), printed accordion fold on Arches, signed by author and artist, 8vo., 7 original photogravures after paintings by Francesco Clemente, gilt stamped Japanese tea chest paper in black paper chemise, mint.   James S. Jaffe Rare Books   Occasional List: Winter 2016 - 46   2016 $6500

Cressey, Paul G. *The Taxi-Dance Hall.* Chicago: University of Chicago Press, 1932. First edition, 3 folding maps of Chicago bound in, small stains near spine, very good in like or better dust jacket with few small stains, mostly on front panel.   Between the Covers Rare Books   204 - 111   2016 $500

Cresswell, Thomas Estcourt *A Narrative of the Affair Between Mr. Cresswell and Miss Sc—e Address'd to G---V---E SC----E, Esq.* London: Charles Green, n.d., 1747. First edition, uncommon, 8vo., title little dustmarked, small hole in blank margin of final leaf, early 20th century brown cloth, lettered gilt on spine and upper cover, very good.   John Drury Rare Books 2015 - 14690   2016 $350

Crest of Hollywood *Prints by California Artists.* Los Angeles: Crest of Hollywood, 1954. Oblong 4to., 51 unnumbered plates, binder style covers with pink and white decorative paper printed in black with screws holding boards together, mild edge wear, very good, scarce on the market.   Jeff Weber Rare Books   181 - 3   2016 $95

Creuzevault, Colette *Henri Creuzevault 1905-1971.* Paris: Les Editions de Montfort, 1987. First edition, limited to 750 copies, large 4to., stiff paper wrappers, dust jackets, slipcase, color or black and white illustrations, prospectus loosely inserted, slipcase cracked along hinges.   Oak Knoll Books   310 - 15   2016 $950

Crewe, Quentin *Quentin Crewe's Private File of Restaurants.* London: Quentin Crewe, 1972. First edition, large 8vo., small rung bound bolder printed gilt on cover "QC Private File", 11 issues from Jan. 1972 to Nov. 1972, presumably all published, printed on various colours and thicknesses of paper stock, some wear at punch holes at beginning, otherwise decent very good.   Any Amount of Books   2015 - A74694   2016   £150

Crichton, Michael *Disclosure.* New York: Alfred A. Knopf, 1994. First edition, small quarto, very fine, very fine dust jacket.   Argonaut Book Shop   Literature 2015 - 3760   2016 $40

Crichton, Michael *Prey.* New York: Harper Collins, 2002. First edition, very fine, unread copy in very fine dust jacket, signed by author, laid in are two promotional bookmarks. Jeff Hirsch Books E-List 80 - 7 2016 $65

Crichton, Michael *Timeline.* New York: Alfred A. Knopf, 1999. First edition, black cloth backed gray boards, silver lettering to spine, very fine in pictorial dust jacket. Argonaut Book Shop Literature 2015 - 4711 2016 $60

Crispin, Edmund *Fen Country.* London: Gollancz, 1979. First edition, very fine in dust jacket. Mordida Books 2015 - 011769 2016 $65

Crispin, Edmund *Fen Country - Twenty-six stories.* London: Victor Gollancz, 1979. First edition, octavo, fine in fine, price clipped dust jacket. Peter Ellis 112 - 88 2016 £45

Critchley, Mac Donald *James Parkinson 1755-1824.* London: 1955. Occasional marginalia otherwise very good with dust jacket, some light toning, else fine, with facsimile copy of An Essay on the Shaking Palsy, London 1817. James Tait Goodrich X-78 - 451 2016 $95

Croke, Brian *History and Historians in late Antiquity.* Sydney: Pergamon press, 1983. First edition, 4to., boards, black lettered, spine slightly browned, two marks of sticker residue to lower board, lower board bit grubby, light bumping to corners and endcaps, edges dusted, still very good. Unsworths Antiquarian Booksellers Ltd. E05 - 23 2016 £25

Croker, Thomas Crofton *Gooseberry Hall, the Renowned Seat of Sir Hildebrod Gooseberry...* London: T. and W. Bone 29 New Bond Street, 1842. First edition, 4to., 16 wood engraved text illustrations, inlaid on sheets, contemporary half morocco, spine lettered in gilt, uncommon. Marlborough Rare Books List 56 - 53 2016 £1250

Cronin, Edward W. *The Arun: a Natural History of the World's Deepest Valley.* Boston: Houghton Mifflin, 1970. First edition, cloth backed boards, very fine, pictorial dust jacket. Argonaut Book Shop Mountaineering 2015 - 4363 2016 $45

Cronin, Michael *Sweet Water.* Museum Press ltd., 1957. File copy stamp on front endpaper and half title, very slight spotting on edges, not affecting text, dust jacket frayed and torn but largely intact. I. D. Edrich Crime - 2016 £20

Crook, A. H. *The Hong Kong Naturalist; a Quarterly Illustrated Journal...Volume One.* Hong Kong: Newspaper Enterprise, 1930. octavo, 7 color plates, other illustrations. Andrew Isles Natural History Books 55 - 10018 2016 $400

Croom-Johnson, Norman *The Life-Story of Charles Dickens.* London: Stead's Publishing House, circa, 1890. original grey pictorial wrappers, spine slightly rubbed, very good, illustrations. Jarndyce Antiquarian Booksellers CCXVIII - 1134 2016 £20

Crosby, Caresse *Painted Shores.* Paris: Editions Narcisse, 1927. First edition, #121 of 244 copies, small folio, watercolors by Francois Quelvee, original printed wrappers and protective tissue wrappers (slight wear). M & S Rare Books, Inc. 99 - 71 2016 $550

Crosby, Caresse *Poems for Harry Crosby.* Paris: Black Sun Press, 1931. First edition, 8vo., half white morocco (little soiled), 6 1/4 x 1/8 vertical stain on front cover, red diagonal backstrip (faintly faded at bottom), paper label (little soiled, abrasion at bottom taking first two numerals of the date), fore and bottom edges uncut, copy H of 44 lettered copies, on Hollande Van Gelder paper, of an edition of 544, two leaves little roughly opened 15 top, from the collection of Harry Crosby. Howard S. Mott Inc. 265 - 39 2016 $375

Crosby, Elisha Oscar *Memoirs of Elisha Oscar Crosby....* San Marino: Huntington Library, 1945. First edition, frontispiece and 2 plates, black cloth, small oval bookplate, fine chipped dust jacket. Argonaut Book Shop Biography 2015 - 7395 2016 $45

Crosby, Harry *Mad Queen Tirades.* Paris: Black Sun Press, 1929. First edition, number 53 of a limited edition of 100 copies on Holland Van Gelder Zonen, publisher's number 53 still with this copy, frontispiece by Caresse Crosby, 8vo., original printed wrappers, fore and bottom edges uncut, fine in glassine dust jacket and publisher's gold folding portoflio (little rubbed), silk tie,. Howard S. Mott Inc. 265 - 40 2016 $600

Crosby, Harry *Sonnets for Caresse.* Paris: Editions Narcisse, 1927. Edition definitive, i.e. fourth edition, 4to., original printed wrappers, most of front wrapper and all of spine considerably sun darkened, all edges gilt, moderately browned internally. Howard S. Mott Inc. 265 - 41 2016 $350

Croswell, Joseph *Sketches of the Life and Extracts from the Journals and Other Writings of the Late Joseph Croswel...* Boston: Lincoln & Edmonds, 1809. First edition, 12mo., contemporary plain wrappers, some wear to front wrapper. M & S Rare Books, Inc. 99 - 72 2016 $250

Crothers, Samuel McChord *The Children of Dickens.* New York: Charles Scribner's Sons, 1929. 4to., illustrations by Jessie Willcox Smith, half title, color frontispiece and plates, original brown cloth spine lettered gilt, color onlay on front board, following board slightly damp marked, later booklabel. Jarndyce Antiquarian Booksellers CCXVIII - 742 2016 £30

Crow, Gerald H. *William Morris, Designer.* London: The Studio, Special winter edition, 1934. First edition, copiously illustrated, original dark blue cloth lettered in red, near fine in like dust jacket (slightly nicked and creased). Peter Ellis 112 - 263   2016   £95

Crowe, Catherine *The Seeress of Prevost Being Revelations Concerning the Inner Life of Man....* London: J. C. Moore, 1845. First English edition, half title, 2 pages ads, original blue cloth blocked in blind, spine lettered gilt, spine slightly faded, very good, Renier booklabel. Jarndyce Antiquarian Booksellers   CCXVII - 80   2016   £125

Crowe, Catherine *The Story of Arthur Hunter and His First Shilling.* London: James Hogg and Sons, 1861. First edition, 12mo., original blind and gilt stamped purple cloth, gilt lettered, all edges gilt, frontispiece and plates by Dalziel Brothers, scarce, contemporary inscription, later bookplate, spine and edges little worn and faded, very good.   The Brick Row Book Shop   Miscellany 69 - 23   2016 $425

Crowell, Edwin *A History of Barrington Township and Vicinity Shelburne County, Nova Scotia 1604-1870.* Yarmouth: published by author, 1923. First edition, blue cloth with gilt to spine, 8vo., frontispiece, 11 black and white photo illustrations and 1 folding map, covers spotted and faded but binding solid, interior good.   Schooner Books Ltd.   115 - 137   2016 $40

Crucius, Jacobus *Epistolarun Libri IV. Cum Duplici Indice.* Delphis: ex officina Johannes Andreae Koleting, 1633. First edition, 8vo., woodcut initials, f.f.e.p. and following blank both with top fore-edge corner excised, titlepage bit grubby, some light foxing to blanks front and rear, contemporary vellum, title inked to spine, yapp edges, vellum darkened, quite heavily marked especially to spine but entirely sound, inscribed "Antonius (surname obscured) Col. Reg. Oxon ex dondo Guliolmi Preston 1743".   Unsworths Antiquarian Booksellers Ltd.   E01 - Early Printing - 6   2016   £200

Cruikshank, George   1792-1878 *The Comic Almanac... First Series 1835-1843. (offered with) Second Series 1844-1853.* London: Chatto & Windus, circa, 1876? First edition, 12mo., publisher's green cloth, stamped gilt, 2 volumes, foldout frontispiece in second volume, untrimmed, hinges tender, but very good, clean.   Second Life Books, Inc.   197 - 56   2016 $200

Cruikshank, George   1792-1878 *Cruikshank's Water Colours....* London: A. & C. Black, 1903. Half title, color frontispiece and plates, original purple brown cloth, slightly rubbed and marked, top edge gilt.   Jarndyce Antiquarian Booksellers   CCXVIII - 1136   2016   £85

Cruikshank, George   1792-1878 *History of the Irish Rebellion in 1798 with Memoirs of the Union and Emmett's Insurrection in 1803.* Baily Brothers, 1845. 21 engraved plates bound together in later green morocco backed cloth boards lettered on contrasting labels on spine and upper board, captions on couple of plates slightly cropped, little light occasional dusting, otherwise very good, tipped onto front pastedown is typically florid Cruikshank autograph dated March 17th 1846.   Sotheran's   Piccadilly Notes - Summer 2015 - 91   2016   £398

Cruikshank, George   1792-1878 *More Hints on Etiquette...* London: Charles Tilt, 1838. First edition, initial ad leaf, half title, illustrations, final ad leaf, original green brown cloth, limp boards, gilt vignette on front board, spine and leading hinge, slight cracking & some slight rubbing to extremities, all edges gilt.   Jarndyce Antiquarian Books   CCXV - 141   2016   £280

Cruikshank, George   1792-1878 *More Hints on Etiquette for the Use of Society at Large...* London: Charles Tilt, 1838. First edition, ad leaf, half title, illustrations, final ad leaf tipped in 4 page catalog, original dark green cloth, limp boards, gilt vignette on front board, all edges gilt, very good.   Jarndyce Antiquarian Books   CCXV - 140   2016   £350

Cruikshank, Robert James *Charles Dickens and Early Victorian England.* London: Sir Isaac Pitman & Sons, 1949. First edition, half title, illustrations, original buff cloth, lettered with two vignettes on front board in gilt, spine faded.   Jarndyce Antiquarian Booksellers   CCXVIII - 1141   2016   £20

Cruise, William *An Essay on the Nature and Operation of Fines and Recoveries...* London: printed by His Majesty's Law Printers for E. Brooke, 1786. Second edition, 2 volumes, 8vo., contemporary calf, some minor abrasions to bindings and wear to joints, still sound, attractive, original labels, each volume with early 19th century armorial bookplate of John Clarke Stoughton of Wymondham in Norfolk.   John Drury Rare Books   2015 - 22907   2016 $350

Crumley, James *The Muddy Fork: A Work in Progress.* Northridge: Lord John Press, 1984. Number 194 from an edition of 200, fine with paper covered boards, cloth spine, issued without dust jacket, signed by author.   Jeff Hirsch Books   Holiday List 2015 - 33   2016 $85

Crunden, John *Convenient and Ornamental Architecture, Consisting of Original Designs for Plans, Elevations and Sections...* London: printed for author and Henry Webley, 1767. First edition, 4to., 70 numbered illustrations on 56 engraved sheets, engraved by Isaac Taylor, some folding, text on unusually thick paper, occasional light spotting or browning, one folding plate shaved at head, resulting in loss of plate numerals, one folding plate with central 2 inch tear at fold, modern half calf over marbled boards, spine with raised bands and gilt stamped red morocco lettering piece, little rubbed in places. Marlborough Rare Books List 55 - 19 2016 £750

Crusius, Martin *Grammaticae Graecae, cum Latina...* Basle: ex Officina Oporiniana, 1573. Early edition, 2 volumes bound as one, touch of minor spotting, gutter of first titlepage recently reinforced with white tape, 8vo., contemporary pigskin, boards decorated blind including central portraits and latin mottos, two brass clasps pigskin thongs (thongs sometime renewed), soiled, worn at extremities, pigskin cracking ar rear joint. Blackwell's Rare Books B186 - 65 2016 £900

Cruveilhier, Jean *Anatomie Patholgique Du corps Humain.* Paris: J. B. Bailliere, 1829-1842. First edition in book form, 486 x 337mm., 2 volumes, bound from original parts, contemporary marbled boards backed with recent calf, raised bands flanked by gilt fillets, black morocco labels; with 231 lithographed plates (2 folding), of which 167 are in color (many heightened with gum arabic), later tissue guards; corners and edges somewhat rubbed and some loss of paper (as expected), text with variable foxing (persistent, but usually light, never severe and principally confined to margins), handful of black and white plates with moderate spotting, additional small defects internally, otherwise quite commendable copy of a book always found foxed, browned and worse, our volumes solidly restored now, spines unworn, text and remarkable plates with no fatal condition problems. Phillip J. Pirages 67 - 105 2016 $8500

Cudworth, Ralph *A Treatise Concerning Eternal and Immutable Morality.* London: James and John Knapton, 1731. First edition, engraved frontispiece, octavo, contemporary speckled calf, double gilt rule to front and back covers, spine with five gilt bordered raised bands and burgundy morocco lael with gilt lettering, small dark and faded library label at foot of spine, all but impossible to see, front joint cracked but extremely firm, some interior pages browned, overall very pretty, surprisingly uncommon. Athena Rare Books List 15 - 1731 2016 $2000

Culbertson, Charlotte *In My father's House.* Los Angeles: Brookhaven Press, 1939. First edition, author's presentation on title, very good. Second Life Books, Inc. 196A - 357 2016 $75

Cullen, J. M. *Animal Behaviour Monographs.* London: Balliere, Tindal and Cassell, 1968-1976. Quarto, volumes 1-24, all bound in 12 volumes, binder's cloth. Andrew Isles Natural History Books 55 - 36119 2016 $500

Cullen, William *Elemens de Medecine Pratique de M. Cullen, M.D.* Theophile Barrois & Meqignon, 1795. 8vo., 2 volumes, half calf over marbled boards, some foxing, very good. Edwin V. Glaser Rare Books 2015 - 10134 2016 $300

Cullum, Ridgwell *The Vampire of N'Gobi.* Philadelphia: London: J. B. Lippincott Co., 1936. First edition, octavo, original orange cloth, front and spine panels stamped in black, top edge stained black, nearly fine in very good or somewhat better price clipped dust jacket with light shelfwear to spine ends, some tiny chips and creases, light shelfwear along top edge, closed tear and crease and two small closed tears to lower front panel, bright, attractive copy. John W. Knott, Jr./L.W. Currey, Inc. Fall-Winter 2015 - 17384 2016 $450

Cullyer, John *The Gentleman and Farmers' Assistant....* Norwich: printed for the author and sold by Crouse, Stevenson and Matchety...., 1795. First edition, printed on bluish paper, few diagrams in text, signed by author at end of preface, as called for, few manuscript corrections in text, square 12mo., original sheep, joints cracked but firm, corners slightly worn, very good, rare. Blackwell's Rare Books B186 - 47 2016 £600

Culpeper, Nicholas *Culpeper's British Herbal and Complete English Physician.* London: for H. Hogg, undated but early 1800's, 1 volume in 2, frontispiece, 194 botanical plates and 4 anatomical plates, all hand colored, contemporary black calf, very nearly rebacked at early date in black morocco, original spine labels retained, endsheets foxed, few random plates and anatomical plates at end lightly foxed, otherwise all plates and text clean and fresh. Joseph J. Felcone, Inc. Books from Five Centuries: a Miscellany - 54 2016 $1400

Culpeper, Nicholas *Pharmacopia Londiensis or the London Dispensatory Further Adorned by the Studies and Collections of the Fellows...* London: printed by Peter Cole, printer and bookseller...., 1659. (and 1658). One of 3 printing variants of the 6th edition, 8vo., 20th century full calf with raised bands, spine lettered gilt, bound without vertical half title as often, title within two-line typographical border, page 257 with marginal repair, obscuring few words, index with few stains, cut close, never affecting printed surface, little spotted and lightly browned in places, contemporary ink inscription Cordelia Cole, her book, and ink inscription, Benjamin Daves his book. Sotheran's Piccadilly Notes - Summer 2015 - 92 2016 £1250

Cumberland, Henry Frederick, Duke of *Genuine Copies of all the Love Letters and Cards Which Passsed Between an Illustrious Personage and a Noble Lady....* printed for L. Browning, 1770? 8vo., disbound, good. Blackwell's Rare Books B186 - 48 2016 £750

Cumming, Charles *A Divided Spy.* London: Harper Collins, 2016. Waterstones Limited edition, signed by author, good and dust jacket fine, jacket fitted with new removable clear cover.   Gemini Books   2016 - 31891   2016 $44

Cumming, Kate *A Journal of Hospital Life in the Confederate Army of Tennessee from the Battle of Shiloh to the End of the War.* Louisville: John P. Morton & Co., 1866. First edition, 8vo., original cloth, upper corner of back cover worn, slight water staining in upper corners throughout and to back cover.   M & S Rare Books, Inc.   99 - 63   2016 $1500

Cummings, Edward Estlin   1894-1962 *Ciopw.* New York: Covici Friede, 1931. First edition, limited to 391 copies, signed watercolor by author, 4to., brown burlap cloth, little bit of splitting to cloth at extremes of spine, endpapers little toned, very good, tight copy, hinges nice and tight and not split as usual.   Second Life Books, Inc.   197 - 58   2016 $1000

Cummings, Edward Estlin   1894-1962 *Eimi.* New York: William Sloane, 1933. First edition, 8vo., yellow cloth, edges little soiled, one leaf little damaged in printing, text complete, otherwise very good, tight in chipped and soiled. Second Life Books, Inc.   197 - 57   2016 $75

Cummings, Edward Estlin   1894-1962 *50 Poems.* New York: Duell Sloan and Pearce, 1940. First trade edition, one of 1000 copies, 8vo., cloth, very fine in dust jacket (trifle nicked near head of spine), rare in this condition.   James S. Jaffe Rare Books   Occasional List: Winter 2016 - 49   2016 $1250

Cummings, Edward Estlin   1894-1962 *Collected Poems.* New York: Harcourt Brace and co., 1946. Reprint, later printing, William Meredith's copy, signed by poet Princeton 1947, near fine in very good dust jacket.   Charles Agvent   William Meredith - 77   2016 $60

Cummings, Edward Estlin   1894-1962 *Tom.* New York: printed by the Rydal Press for Arrow Editions, 1935. First edition, one of 1500 copies, 8vo., frontispiece by Ben Shahn, original cloth, dust jacket, very fine, uncommon jacket with couple of short closed tears, rare in this condition. James S. Jaffe Rare Books   Occasional List: Winter 2016 - 48   2016 $450

Cummins, Maureen *Aureole to Zingaresca, an Exotic Alphabet Book.* New York: Maureen Cummins, 1994. Limited to 50 numbered copies, 1-25 printed for patrons of the Center of the Book Arts, and 26-50 reserved for purchase, proof copy of the artists book with various pages containing penciled drawings rather than printed text, printed in multi-colors on thick handmade papers with woodblocks with wood type initial caps, designed, printed and illustrated by Cummins, 4to., stiff paper dust jacket printed in colors loosely enclosing text, purple cloth slipcase, 2 folded signatures, one of 12 pages, one of 20 pages, laid into one folded page.   Oak Knoll Books   27 - 7   2016 $750

Cunn, Samuel *A New Treatise of the Construction and Use of the Sector, Containing the Solutions of the Principal Problems...* printed for John Wilcox and Thomas Heath, Mathematical Instrument Maker, 1729. First edition, engraved frontispiece, large folding engraved plates, diagrams in text, bit browned, closed tear in folding plate, not affecting engraved surface, 8vo., contemporary panelled calf, rebacked, ownership inscription inside front cover of E. G. Smith, Caius College Cambridge, 1814, sound. Blackwell's Rare Books   B186 - 49   2016   £950

Cunningham, A B. *Murder at the Schoolhouse.* New York: E. P. Dutton & Co., 1940. First edition, review copy with slip laid-in, plus news clipping of reporter's review of this book, former owner's bookplate, exceptional copy. Buckingham Books   2015 - 35291   2016 $450

Cunningham, Daniel John *Report on Some Points in the Anatomy of the Thylacine (Cuscus and Phascogale) Collected During the Voyage of H. M. S. Challenger in the Years 1873-1876.* London: Challenger Expedition, 1881. Quarto, 13 lithographs, modern half calf nad marbled boards.   Andrew Isles Natural History Books   55 - 38930   2016 $1200

Cunningham, Imogen *After Ninety.* Seattle: pub. by University of Washington Press, 1977. First edition, quarto, 92 black and white photos, mostly full page, gray pictorial cloth lettered in silver, very fine with pictorial dust jacket. Argonaut Book Shop   Photography 2015 - 6119   2016 $90

Cunningham, Peter *The Story of Nell Gwyn and the Sayings of Charles II.* London: Bradbury & Evans, 1852. First edition in book form, 2 volumes, very pretty brown crushed morocco elaborately gilt by Zaehnsdorf, (stamp signed), covers with frame comprising plain and decorative gilt rules, an inlaid maroon morocco strap, ornate gilt corner-pieces of many small floral tools on a stippled background, raised bands, spines densely gilt in compartments with floral branches radiating form a central circle, background stippled and with small circlets, delicate floral frame on turn-ins, leather hinges, olive and gold silk jacquard endleaves, top edges gilt, extra illustrated with 179 engraved plates, (plates listed alphabetically on printed leaves following the Table of Contents obviously prepared either for this copy alone or else for very limited number of copies, engraved armorial bookplate of Thomas McKean, small nick to one board, otherwise just hint of use to attractive lustrous and scarcely worn bindings, majority of inserted plates foxed (two dozen of them noticely so), variable offsetting from engraved material, otherwise excellent internally.   Phillip J. Pirages   67 - 74   2016 $950

Curr, Edward Micklethwaite *Pure Saddle-Horses and How to Breed Them in Australia...* Melbourne: Wilson & Mackinnon, 1863. First edition, large 8vo., original quarter red leather, lettered gilt on spine with brown cloth boards, presentation from "Acclimatisation Society of Victoria", with their neat blindstamp on titlepage and signed presentation from them, sound, near very good, neatly reinforced at spine, loss at top and bottom with slight loss to half of publishing details at foot of spine, "Librairie Parault" bookplate.   Any Amount of Books   2015 - C16482   2016   £170

Curry, Belle, Mrs. *Parsons, Labette County, Kansas, Years from 1869 to 1895. Story of 'The Benders".* Parsons Bell Bookcraft Shop, n.d. circa, 1939. First edition, 8vo., original blue cloth, titles stamped in gold on front cover, rare book, affixed to verso of titlepage is news clipping, some light cosmetic restoration to spine ends and corners, else very good, tight copy, rare.   Buckingham Books   2015 - 32809   2016 $2750

Curtis, George William *Orations and Addresses of....* New York: Harper, 1894. First edition, 3 volumes, 8vo., frontispiece, errata slip in volume II, top edge gilt, rust cloth, partially unopened, hinges tender in volume I, corners of covers little bumped, spine little soiled and rubbed on volume I, otherwise very good set.   Second Life Books, Inc.   196A - 365   2016 $150

Curwen Press *The Curwen Press Miscellany.* London: pub. for the Curwen Press, Plaistow by the Soncino Press, 1931. First edition, limited to 275 numbered copies, 4to., original oatmeal buckram, decorated with red and blue lines, lettered in blue on spine and upper board, type specimens, ornaments, articles and typographical inserts, pages 59-59 with offset browning from now removed news cutting, otherwise very good.   Sotheran's   Piccadilly Notes - Summer 2015 - 93   2016   £998

Curwen, Henry *Plodding on; or the Jog-trot to fame and fortune.* London: Simpkin Marshall & Co., 1879. Plates, frontispiece, original brown cloth, bevelled boards, blocked in black, little rubbed, embossed stamp of J. Woollard bookseller, Liverpool.   Jarndyce Antiquarian Books   CCXV - 58   2016   £35

Curwen, John *Sunday-School Papers reprinted from the 'Independent Magazine Including Proposals for Remodelling a Sunday School, Infants' Classes...* London: Ward Lock, circa, 1875. Original lilac printed wrappers, faded to brown, 32 pages.   Jarndyce Antiquarian Books   CCXV - 622   2016   £20

Cushing, Harvey Williams 1869-1939 *The Life of Sir William Osler.* Oxford University Press, 1926. Fourth impression, nice in bright blue cloth, some discolorations at base of spine and front boards, near fine internally.   James Tait Goodrich   X-78 - 439   2016 $85

Cust, Lionel *A History of Eton College.* London: Duckworth & Co., 1899. Half title, frontispiece and plates, few leaves roughly opened, original dark green cloth, slightly marked, contemporary ownership inscription, very good.   Jarndyce Antiquarian Books   CCXV - 676   2016   £30

Custer, George Armstrong *My Live on the Plains.* Sheldon and Co., 1874. First edition, first issue, original blue decorated cloth with gilt and black stamping on front cover and spine, 8 plates, tiny spot to fore-edges of page 250 to rear pastedown upper corner, else near fine, bright, tight copy, housed in dark blue quarter leather and cloth clamshell case with raised bands and titles, stamped in gold gilt on spine, handsome copy.   Buckingham Books   2015 - 37944   2016 $4875

Cutler, Leland W. *Once Upon a Time.* San Francisco: printed by John Henry Nash, 1934. Number 205 of 600 numbered copies, quarto, decorative chapter heads and initials, cloth backed marbled boards, paper spine label, fine.   Argonaut Book Shop   Private Press 2015 - 6120   2016 $60

Cutler, Thomas W. *Cottage and Country Buildings.* London: published by Horace Cox, Winsor House, Bream's Buildings, E. C., 1896. First edition, oblong 8vo., 44 plates with 36 leaves of descriptive text, original 'art vellum' bevelled boards, upper cover lettered in gilt.   Marlborough Rare Books   List 56 - 15   2016   £350

The Cycle of the Day, a Book of Hours. N.P.: The Press at Colorado College, 1991. Limited to 50 numbered copies, illustrations, designs and diagrams, color plates printed letterpress, few hand done inclusions and hot stamped foil, bird drawings from photos, oblong 4to., 8 loose signatures and colophon section folded in three and loosely inserted in clamshell box, slight bump to top right hand corner of box, else fine.   Oak Knoll Books   27 - 53   2016 $1500

D

D'Abrera, Bernard *Butterflies of Afrotropical Region.* East Melbourne: Lansdowne Editions, 1980. Folio, color photos, inscribed by author, fine in slightly sunned dust jacket.   Andrew Isles Natural History Books   55 - 2692   2016 $400

D'Abrera, Bernard *Butterflies of the Australian Region.* Melbourne: Lansdowne, 1971. First edition, folio, color photos, very good in dust jacket, signed by author Nov. 8 1972.   Andrew Isles Natural History Books   55 - 4851   2016 $350

D'Abrera, Bernard *Butterflies of the Oriental Region, Part Two: Nymphalidae, Satyridae and Amathusidae.* Melbourne: Hill House, 1985. Folio, color photos, inscribed by author, fine in lightly sunned dust jacket.   Andrew Isles Natural History Books   55 - 4138   2016 $300

D'Abrera, Bernard *Butterflies of the Oriental Region, part three: Lycaenidae and Riodinidae.* Melbourne: Hill House, 1986. Folio, color photos, inscribed by author, fine in lightly sunned dust jacket.   Andrew Isles Natural History Books   55 - 26388   2016 $300

D'Ambrosio, Joseph *Daisies Never Tell.* Sherman Oaks: 1982. Limited to 50 numbered copies, signed, titlepage signed and numbered by D'Ambrosio, with 4 original serigraphs, each signed, prelims feature cut out flowers and fan fold action elements, dark green cowhide with two glass windows showing paper folded daises from pages within, housed in green paper clamshell lined in green felt, box broken, fine.   Jeff Weber Rare Books   181 - 53   2016 $850

D'Ambrosio, Joseph *Trapeze.* Chicago: Joseph J. D'Ambrosio, 1976. First edition, no. 2 of 50 copies signed by artist and printer, Elmore Mundell, 257 x 206mm., 48 leaves, creative original tan vinyl cloth over wood by D'Ambrosio, unusual spine hinging vertically in middle with portion to the right becoming a serigraphed shadow box, and with strings running through holes in various locations (spine, wide lip at bottom of front boards and at 11 places on surface of front cover), all contributing to image of circus tent, with taunt ropes holding it up, paper title label on spine portion of shadow box, Japanese mulberry paper endpapers, sturdy card sleeve covered in Japanese mulberry paper, with 20 original color serigraphs signed and numbered by artist, duplicate photocopies of two lettes from artist to original purchaser laid in at front, little creasing to left part of spine, otherwise virtually mint.   Phillip J. Pirages   67 - 108   2016 $950

D'Arbeloff, Natalie *Love.* London: NdA Press, 1992. Limited to 16 numbered copies, plus 2 Artists Proofs, text and illustrations by d'Arbeloff, 34 color etchings with aquatint, printed intaglio and relief on Zerkall, oblong 16mo., concertina binding by Jan Ascoli with cover papers by artist, red slipcase with title in black on spine, 16 leaves.   Oak Knoll Books   27 - 43   2016 $700

D'Arbeloff, Natalie *Pater Noster.* London: NdA Press, 1988. No. 3 in an edition of 5 similar but not identical copies signed by artist, small 4to., printed on Fabriano Satinana paper, blind engraved text on different sized and color papers, titlepage Pater Noster is smallest of successively larger pages, each page has edges of hand color, book glued to back cover which has painted and decorated wood strip on side, title embroidered in red on yellow and blue felt strip edged in same stitching, two press-studs close the book, inside front cover has brightly colored collage of paper, felt and painted decorations against blue cloth background, book laid in hand painted oilcloth with red felt inside on which to place the book, oilcloth trimmed with red and yellow cord, held closed with red and blue cords.   Oak Knoll Books   27 - 44   2016 $2500

D'Arlingcourt, Charles Victor Prevot, Le Vicomte *Ipsiboe.* London: J. Robins & Co., 1823. First English edition, 2 volumes, half titles, later half calf, red and green labels, signature of George Cruikshank at head of titlepage, volume I and dated by him 1823, later c. 1850 bookplates of George S. Davis, very good, attractive copy.   Jarndyce Antiquarian Booksellers   CCXVII - 234   2016   £180

D'Aulaire, Ingri *Abraham Lincoln.* New York: Doubleday Doran and Co., 1939. Stated first edition, first issue with errata slip page 52, large 4to., cloth backed pictorial boards, fine in very good+ dust jacket with just touch of wear on spine, not price clipped, no award sticker, full color lithographs, rare in this condition.   Aleph-bet Books, Inc.   112 - 130   2016 $1750

D'Aulaire, Ingri *Children of the Northlights.* New York: Viking, Sept., 1935. First edition, large 4to., cloth backed pictorial boards, fine in fine dust jacket, signed by D'Aulaire, illustrated with pictorial endpapers plus many fine full page color and black and white lithographs, signed copies quite scarce.   Aleph-bet Books, Inc.   112 - 131   2016 $600

D'Aulaire, Ingri *Columbus.* New York: Doubleday & Co., 1955. Stated First edition, tall 4to., cloth backed pictorial boards, fine in dust jacket (price clipped), beautiful full page color lithographs, this copy inscrybed by D'Aulaire's with pen sketch.   Aleph-bet Books, Inc.   111 - 111   2016 $850

D'Aulaire, Ingri *The Terrible Troll Bird.* New York: Doubleday & Co., 1976. Stated first edition, large 4to., pictorial boards, fine in very slightly worn dust jacket, this copy inscribed by D'Aulaires with full page pen drawing of two Troll Birds.   Aleph-bet Books, Inc.   111 - 113   2016 $650

D'Aulaire, Ingri *Too Big.* New York: Doubleday Doran, 1945. Stated first edition, 8vo., cloth backed pictorial boards, slightest bit of soil and edge rubbing, else very good+ in dust jacket with few archival mends on verso, beautiful color lithos on every page. Aleph-bet Books, Inc. 111 - 112 2016 $400

D'Evelyn, Margaret Muther *Venice and Vitruvius Reading Venice with Daniele Barbaro and Andrea Palladio.* New Haven: Yale University Press, 2012. First edition, 8vo., illustrations, blue cloth, gilt lettered to spine, dust jacket, as new. Unsworths Antiquarian Booksellers Ltd. E05 - 70 2016 £20

D'Ivernois, Francis *Innocence d'Un Magistrat Accuse de Vol Demontree par les Contradictions de Ses Accusateurs et Par les Aveux de Ses Juges Euxmemes.* Londres: imprime part Galabin dans Ingram-Court Penchurch St., 1787. First edition, 8vo., final errata leaf, recent marbled boards lettered on spine, very good, rare. John Drury Rare Books 2015 - 23818 2016 $350

D'Ivray, Jehan *Promenades a Travers le Caire. Ouvrage Illustre par Louis Cabanes.* Paris: Peyronnet, 1928. First edition, number 150 of print run of 350, folio as issued in original wrappers, printed in blue and black, (8) pochoir colored initials in text, color printed, tinted and pochoir coloured plates with captioned tissue guards, wrappers with light wear, good. Sotheran's Travel and Exploration - 315 2016 £698

D'orleans, Henri *From Tonkin to India by the Sources of Irwadi Jan. '95 - Jan. '96.* London: Methuen & Co,, 1898. Large octavo, text illustrations, publisher's green pictorial cloth, slightly shaken, otherwise very good, scarce. Andrew Isles Natural History Books 55 - 17824 2016 $950

Dacey, Philip *Gerard Manley Hopkins Meets Walt Whitman in Heaven and Other Poems.* Great Barrington: Penmaen Press, 1982. First edition, 8vo., wood engravings by Michael McCurdy, printed in an edition of 900 copies, 300 of which were case bound, this one of the 75 case bound copies that were signed by poet and artist, dust jacket, very faintly soiled and bumped at upper corners, otherwise fine. Second Life Books, Inc. 196A - 367 2016 $75

Daelli, Luigi Gino *A Relic of the Italian Revolution of 1849.* New Orleans: At Gibici's Music Stores 39 Camp and 86 Chartres St n.d., i.e., 1854? First edition, oblong 4to., original gilt and blindstamped blue cloth, spine extremities chipped, corners rubbed, little soiled, half title in color, aside from wear to spine tips and rubbing at corners mentioned above, fine. Howard S. Mott Inc. 265 - 43 2016 $1250

Daggett, A. S. *America in the China Relief Expedition.* Kansas City: Hudson Kimberly, 1903. First edition, very good++, mild sun spine, minimal cover edge wear, 8vo., foldout maps, scarce. By the Book, L. C. 45 - 40 2016 $400

Daggett, Thomas F. *The Outlaw Brothers Frank and Jesse James.* Richard K. Fox Proprietor Police Gazette, 1881. Fifth edition, 8vo., pictorial yellow and black wrappers, frontispiece, rare, light wear to spine ends, moderate wear to edges, else very good, housed in quarter leather and cloth clamshell case with raised bands, spine and titles stamped in gilt on spine. Buckingham Books 2015 - 33473 2016 $3750

Dahl, Roald *The BFG.* New York: Farrar Strauss Giroux, 1982. Limited to 500 numbered copies, signed by author and artist, illustrations in black and white by Quentin Blake, 8vo., red cloth stamped in gold, as new in original cloth slipcase. Aleph-bet Books, Inc. 111 - 107 2016 $1500

Dahl, Roald *Boy: Tales of Childhood.* New York: Farrar Straus Giroux, 1984. Number 61 of a limited edition of only 200 numbered copies signed by Dahl, photos, 8vo., cloth, narrow flaw line in cloth on front cover else fine, slipcase. Aleph-bet Books, Inc. 111 - 108 2016 $1000

Dahl, Roald *Charlie and the Chocolate Factory.* New York: Knopf, 1964. First edition (correct printing), 8vo., red cloth, blindstamped on cover, fine in near fine dust jacket only slightly creased at top of spine, illustrations in black and white by Joseph Schindelman, this copy signed by author, outstanding copy. Aleph-bet Books, Inc. 112 - 128 2016 $11,000

Dahl, Roald *Fantastic Mr. Fox.* London: George Allen & Unwin, 1970. First edition, somewhat spotted throughout, still very good in pictorial laminated boards, bookplate, scarce. Bertram Rota Ltd. Christmas List 2015 - 6 2016 £800

Dahl, Roald *The Gremlins.* New York: Random House, 1943. First edition of author's first book, preceding British edition, large quarto, one double page and 12 full page color illustrations, numerous black and white illustrations in text, original red pictorial boards with red cloth backstrip, yellow and red pictorial endpapers, corners and board edges little rubbed, original matching color pictorial dust jacket with $1.00 price, jacket chipped at extremities and some creasing and few short closed tears, otherwise fine. Heritage Book Shop Holiday 2015 - 25 2016 $2500

Dahl, Roald *My Uncle Oswald.* 1979. First edition, fine in slightly browned dust jacket, ownership signature. Bertram Rota Ltd. Christmas List 2015 - 7 2016 £20

Dahl, Roald *Over to You.* London: Hamish Hamilton, 1946. First British edition, fine copy in near fine dust jacket, price clipped but new price stamped on front flap.   Bella Luna Books   2016 - t3611   2016 $165

Dahl, Roald *Someone Like You.* New York: Alfred Knopf, 1953. First edition, gift inscription from author for Nathalie Bell Nov. 9th 1953, tiny bump to top and bottom front corners, former owner's neat stamped name and address on front pastedown sheet (completely covered by front jacket flap), else near fine, bright copy in jacket lightly rubbed at head of spine, excellent copy.   Buckingham Books   2015 - 37651   2016 $3750

Dahl, Roald *The Twits.* London: Jonathan Cape, 1981. Second edition, 8vo., illustrations by Quentin Blake, original red boards, backstrip lettered gilt, dust jacket with minimal rubbing along outer edges, handful of pressure marks overall, very good, inscribed by author.   Blackwell's Rare Books B186 - 194   2016   £300

Dahlbereg, Edward *Can These Bones Live?* New York: New Directions, 1960. First New Directions edition, fine in some soiled dust jacket, first state, 1/1500 copies, inscribed to owners of noted 8th Street bookstore in NYC in a 13 line presentation signed by author.   Second Life Books, Inc. 196A - 368   2016 $150

Daireaux, Godofredo *La Cria Del Ganado en La Pampas....* Felix Lajouane, 1887. First edition, 8vo., 2 folding maps, illustrations, original green decorative cloth, gilt vignette.   J. & S. L. Bonham Antiquarian Booksellers America 2016 - 9922   2016   £80

Dakin, Susanna Bryant *Rose or Rose Thorn? Three Women of Spanish California.* Berkeley: Bancroft Library, 1963. First edition, frontispiece, illustrations, map endpapers, floral decorations on front cover, titlepage and headpieces printed in green and pink, decorated green cloth, gilt lettered spine, very fine.   Argonaut Book Shop   Biography 2015 - 3817   2016 $45

Dakin, Susanna Bryant *The Scent of Violets.* San Francisco: 1968. First edition, fine.   Argonaut Book Shop Biography 2015 - 3547   2016 $60

Dakin, Susanna Bryant *A Scotch Paisano. Hugo Reid's Life in California 1832-1852.* Berkeley: University of California Press, 1939. First edition, illustrations, map, orange cloth, small oval bookplate, fine.   Argonaut Book Shop   Biography 2015 - 3682   2016 $40

Dale, Edward Everett *Lafayette Letters.* Harlow: 1925. First edition, decorated cloth, photos, decorated bookseller's label on Plantation Book Shop, Natchez Miss. on front pastedown, titlepage foxed, paper of rear pastedown has wrinkles, good, very scarce.   Gene W. Baade, Books on the West   2015 - 0711074   2016 $85

Dale, Robert William *Religious Worship and Bible Teaching in Board Schools.* Birmingham: Hudson & Son, 1885. Little dusted, few marginal tears, disbound, 16 pages. Jarndyce Antiquarian Books   CCXV - 623   2016   £20

Dale, Thomas *An Introductory Lecture Delivered to the University of London, Friday Oct. 24 1828.* London: John Taylor, 1828. Original drab brown paper wrappers, paper label, good plus.   Jarndyce Antiquarian Books   CCXV - 832   2016   £35

Dali, Salvador *Salvador Dali: Erotic Sketches/Erotische skizzen.* Munich: Prestel, 2009. Text in English and German, numerous color and black and white illustrations, very near fine in string tied boards, seemingly uncommon. Jeff Hirsch Books   Holiday List 2015 - 8   2016 $150

Dallas, Enaeas Sweetland *Kettner's Book of the Table.* London: Dulau & Co., 1877. First edition, half title, original green cloth by Egleton, blocked in gilt, little rubbed with slight wear to head and tail of spine, contemporary ownership signature & presentation inscription on leading blank. Jarndyce Antiquarian Books   CCXV - 143   2016   £150

Dallas, George *A Vindication of the Justice and Policy of the late Wars Carried on in Hindostan and the Deckan by Marquis Wellesley....* London: for John Stockdale, 1806. First edition, contemporary acid mottled calf, gilt, extremities worn, else very good, Sir Thomas Dallas's copy with his contemporary signature and armorial bookplate.   Joseph J. Felcone, Inc.   Books from Five Centuries: a Miscellany - 79   2016 $400

Dalrymple-Hay, J. C. *Lines from my Log-Books.* Edinburgh: David Douglas, 1898. First edition, 8vo., frontispiece, plates, maps, original blue decorative cloth, corners rubbed, inner hinge cracked.   J. & S. L. Bonham Antiquarian Booksellers   Voyages 2016 - 9396   2016   £60

Dalrymple, Jean *September child.* New York: Dodd Mead, 1963. First edition, author's presentation on half title, photos, nice, in scuffed and chipped dust jacket. Second Life Books, Inc.   196A - 370   2016 $35

Dalrymple, John   1652-1715 *Memoirs of Great Britain and Ireland.* Dublin: printed by Boulter Grierson, 1771. First edition, 3 volumes, 8vo., ex-British Foreign Office library with few library markings, very slight edgewear, spines sunned, else very good.   Any Amount of Books 2015 - A67372   2016   £150

Daly, Elizabeth *Deadly Nightshade.* Hammond, 1948. Edges of cloth faded, dust jacket little chipped & frayed but almost complete, internally very good.   I. D. Edrich   Crime - 2016   £35

Dame Crump and Her Pig. New York: McLoughlin Bros. n.d. circa, 1880. 4t., pictorial wrappers, inconspicuous spine strengthening, 2 tiny closed tears, clean and very good++, 4 fine full page chromolithographs highlighted in gold and with black and whites by J . H. Howard.   Alephbet Books, Inc.   112 - 306   2016 $375

Dampier, William James   *A Memoir of John Carter.* London: John W. Parker, 1850. First edition, frontispiece, plates, original dark blue cloth, spine faded, very good. Jarndyce Antiquarian Booksellers   CCXVII - 65   2016   £150

Dana, Julian   *Sutter of California: a Biography.*   New York: Press of the Pioneers, 1934. First edition, signed by author, illustrations, map, red pictorial cloth, gilt, spine faded, else fine.   Argonaut Book Shop   Biography 2015 - 7272   2016 $75

Dana, Richard Henry   1815-1882   *Two Years Before the Mast.*   New York: Harper & Bros., 1840. First edition, 2nd issue with letter "i" in copyright notice lacking the dot and a broken type in running title of page 9, original tan muslin printed in black, 16mo., few minor nicks to fragile binding and some occasional minor staining to text, otherwise superb, housed in quarter leather and marbled paper over boards clamshell case, raised bands, titles stamped in gold gilt on spine.   Buckingham Books   2015 - 37943   2016 $4875

Dana, Richard Henry   1815-1882   *Two Years Before the Mast.*   London: Edward Moxon, 1841. First English edition, large octavo, modern full blue cloth, gilt stamped on spine, blue endpapers, fine.   Heritage Book Shop   Holiday 2015 - 26   2016 $1000

Dana, Richard Henry   1815-1882   *Two Years Before the Mast.*   New York: Heritage Press, 1947. Small quarto, color engravings by Harri Alexander Mueller, pictorial yellow cloth, fine with faded slipcase.   Argonaut Book Shop   Heritage Press 2015 - 1891   2016 $40

Dana, Richard Henry   1815-1882   *Two years before the Mast.*   New York: Limited Editions club, 1947. 1/1500 copies, 4to., engravings in color by Hans Alexander Mueller, signed by artist, cloth with paper label, cloth covered slipcase, somewhat stained, otherwise nice.   Second Life Books, Inc.   196A - 371   2016 $85

Dane, Clemence   *Come of Age.*   New York: Doubleday, Doran, 1934. First edition, 8vo., very good, inscribed by author and Addinell for Edward Wasserman and signed by actress Judith Anderson who starred in the play.   Second Life Books, Inc.   196A - 372   2016 $150

Dane, Clemence   *Moonlight is Silver.*   London: Heinemann, 1934. First edition, 8vo., author's presentation on flyleaf, very good.   Second Life Books, Inc.   196A - 173   2016 $45

Daniel, Roland   *Again the Remover.*   London: Wright & Brown Ltd., n.d., 1939. First edition, orange boards, spine stamped in black, foxing to edges and pages, very good in very good four color dust jacket with shelfwear to edges and spine ends, some chipping and loss to lower spine panel, price at center of spine has been cut out.   John W. Knott, Jr./L.W. Currey, Inc.   Fall-Winter 2015 - 17870   2016 $225

Daniel, Roland   *The Man from Paris.*   Wright & Brown Ltd., 1958. Dust jacket slightly frayed, very good.   I. D. Edrich   Crime - 2016   £20

Danielewski, Mark Z.   *The House of Leaves.*   New York: Pantheon, 2000. First edition, titlepage states '2nd Edition' but this a deliberately and characteristically misleading, there were several issues in various guises, this is the hardback 2-color issue with ISBN (on rear panel of dust jacket) for the unsigned version, this copy however is signed by author with large 'Z' in blue ink (as called for in signed copies), fine in fine dust jacket.   Peter Ellis   112 - 89   2016   £150

Dante Alighieri   1265-1321   *Dante col Sita, et Forma dell'Inferno (Commedia).*   Vence: Aldus Manutius and Andrea Torresano, 1515. First Illustrated pocket edition of Dante's Commedia, octavo, full 18th century vellum, double page woodcut map and two woodcut charts, text in Italian.   Honey & Wax Booksellers   4 - 51   2016 $15,000

Dante Alighieri   1265-1321   *Divina Commedia.*   Milano: Ulrico Hoepli, 1878. One of 1000 unnumbered copies, 57 x 38mm., pleasing contemporary green moroco, covers gilt with double fillet border enclosing a fame of fleurs-de-lys, large central fleuron, scrolling foliate cornerpieces, raised bands, flanked by double gilt rules, spine panels with small central lozenge, gilt turn-ins, marbled endpapers, frontispiece, spine and upper board uniformly sunned to hazel brown, titlepage with overall light browning, otherwise very fine, binding with virtually no wear and text extremely clean, fresh and smooth.   Phillip J. Pirages   67 - 255   2016 $2250

Dante Alighieri   1265-1321   *La Divina Commedia.* Oxford: M. A. Nella Stameria dell' Universita, 1900. First edition thus, octavo, period binding by W. Matthews of full brown morocco raised bands, gilt rules, all edges gilt, ownership signature of "E(vory) H(amilton) Kennedy - Betchworth 1937, he was Vicar of Betchworth, bound in at front are five pages of his notes, armorial bookplate of Edward Hilton Young, 1st Baron Kennet of Denne, corners slightly bumped, very good.   Peter Ellis   112 - 90   2016   £150

Dante Alighieri 1265-1321 *La Divina Commedia or the Divine Vision of Dante Alighieri in Italian.*   London: Nonesuch Press, 1928. 1199/1475 copies, 42 collotype plates after original drawings by Botticelli, small folio, original bright orange vellum, spine somewhat sunned as almost always, lettering on backstrip and design on front cover blocked in gilt, free endpapers lightly browned, top edge gilt on rough, others untrimmed and uncut, very good.   Blackwell's Rare Books   B184 - 296   2016   £500

Dante Alighieri 1265-1321 *L'Enfer.*   Paris: Chez Jean Porson, 1950. No. 81 of 250 copies, the first 127 printed on velin blanc, all with 18 stunning etchings, 34 hors--texte by Edouard Georg, handsome red and black chemise and matching boxes, one box has slight ding on one top edge and tiny split starting on same edge, beautiful set, folio.   Beasley Books   2015 - 2016 $900

Dante Alighieri 1265-1321 *Dante's Inferno.*   Hopewell: Ecco Press, 1993. First edition, deluxe issue, limited to 125 copies signed by each of the translators, with original etching signed by Francesco Clemente laid in, small folio, quarter black calf and red silk over boards, slipcase by Claudia Cohen, text set in Monotype Dante and printed letterpress by Michael and Winifred Bixler on Rives heavyweight paper, handsome book, as new.   James S. Jaffe Rare Books   Occasional List: Winter 2016 - 78   2016 $3500

Dante Alighieri 1265-1321 *The New Life of Dante Alghieri.*   Cambridge: printed at the Riverside Press, 1892. No. 1 of 250 copies, 202 x 140mm., handsome brown crushed morocco, gilt by Club Bindery (stamp signed), covers with gilt french fillet border, central panel with double gilt rule frame and oblique fleuron cornerpieces, raised bands, spine gilt in compartments with floral cornerpieces and central floral ornament enclosed by a lozenge of small tools, gilt titling, densely gilt turn-ins, top edge gilt, other edges untrimmed, versos of front free endpaper, bookplate of Henry William Poor, "Bound to be the Best: The Club Bindery", just vague hint of rubbing to joints, free endpapers with usual offset shadow from binder's glue, couple of trivial spots internally, but fine, text clean, fresh and bright and in lustrous, scarcely worn binding.   Phillip J. Pirages   67 - 34   2016 $3250

Danticat, Edwidge   *The Coriolis Effect.*   Stockholm: Midnight Paper Sales, 2002. Limited to 170 numbered copies, hand set in monotype Walbaum and signed by him and author, Large 12mo., printed by Gaylord Schanilec on Zerkall paper, cover paper marbled by Carol Scott, bound by Franny Bannen and Lucy Graber, color illustrations.   Oak Knoll Books   310 - 123   2016 $125

Daoust, Edward W.   *The Works of Charles Dickens; First and Subsequent Editions in their Original Bindings...*   New York: American Art Association, 1929. Plates, original cream decorated wrappers, slightly dusted, very good.   Jarndyce Antiquarian Booksellers   CCXVIII - 1493   2016   £20

Darby, Ruth   *Death Boards the Lazy Lady.*   New York: Doubleday, 1939. First edition, 8vo., very good in worn dust jacket.   Second Life Books, Inc.   197 - 60   2016 $250

Dark Forces.   New York: Viking, 1980. Light inkstain throughout first several pages of the introduction, not affecting any text, near fine in near fine dust jacket with light wear to corners, signed or inscribed by 15 writers including, Stephen King, Bloch, Richard Matheson, Joe Haldeman, Gahan Wilson, Campbell, Wolfe, Dennis Etchison, Karl Edward Wagner, Manly Wade Wellman, Edward Bryant, Charles L. Grant and editor, Kirby McCauley, with ownership signature of Stanley Wiater and with his Gahan Wilson bookplate.   Ken Lopez Bookseller   166 - 3   2016 $3000

Darrell, William   *The Gentleman Instructed, in the conduct of a Virtuous and Happy life.*   London: printed by W. B. for E. Smith and sold by Rich. Wilkin, 1720. Seventh edition, 8vo., occasional slight foxing, contemporary panelled calf, brown morocco label, leading hinge with slight cracking, otherwise very good, armorial bookplate of William St. Quintin.   Jarndyce Antiquarian Books   CCXV - 144   2016   £480

Darton, F. J.   *(A Dinner at Popular Walk) Dickens: Positively the First Appearance: a Centenary review with Bibliography of Sketches by Boz.*   Argonaut Press, 1933. First edition, half title, frontispiece, plates, original green cloth backed paper boards, paper label, very good in dust jacket.   Jarndyce Antiquarian Booksellers   CCXVIII - 47   2016   £25

Darwin, Bernard   *The Dickens Advertiser: a Collection of the Advertisements in the Original Parts of the Novels by Charles Dickens.*   London: Elkin Mathews & Marrot, 1930. First edition, half title, plates, facsimiles, original pale blue pictorial cloth, good plus.   Jarndyce Antiquarian Booksellers   CCXVIII - 1494   2016   £35

Darwin, Bernard   *The Golf Courses of the British Isles.*   London: Duckworth & Co., n.d., 1910. First edition, small quarto, 64 illustrations from paintings by artist, Harry Rountree, with descriptive tissue guards, original smooth medium green cloth, front cover ruled and stamped in light green, lettered gilt, spine stamped and lettered gilt, cream endpapers, top edge gilt, extremities very lightly worn, bookplate, 1949 ink inscription, few pages with some very light marginal foxing, still excellent, scarce.   Heritage Book Shop   Holiday 2015 - 27   2016 $750

Darwin, Charles Robert 1809-1882   *The Descent of man and Selection in Relation to Sex.*   New York: Heritage Press, 1972. Drawings by Fritz Kredel, pebbled red cloth, gilt decoration and lettering to spine, spine very lightly faded, else fine in slipcase, Sandglass pamphlet laid in.   Argonaut Book Shop   Heritage Press 2015 - 7127   2016 $60

Darwin, Charles Robert 1809-1882 *The Expression of the Emotions in Man and Animals.* London: John Murray, 1873. Reprint, octavo, 7 heliotype plates, publisher's cloth, contemporary (dated 1883) owner signature, near fine. Andrew Isles Natural History Books 55 - 38625 2016 $600

Darwin, Charles Robert 1809-1882 *Journal of Researches into the Natural History and Geology of Countries Visited During the Voyage HMS 'Beagle' Round the World.* London: John Murray, 1901. New edition, illustrations, and plates, octavo, original green cloth, small ownership signature, cloth little rubbed at head and tail of spine, free endpapers tanned, some sporadic spotting, very good. Peter Ellis 112 - 91 2016 £150

Darwin, Charles Robert 1809-1882 *A Naturalist's Voyage.* London: John Murray, 1889. Early reprint, original green cloth lettered gilt at spine, image in gilt on front cover, illustrations throughout, faint rubbing at edges and hinges, slight foxing to endpapers and prelims, otherwise very good+. Any Amount of Books 2015 - C13675 2016 £170

Darwin, Charles Robert 1809-1882 *On the Origin of Species by means of natural Selection...* London: W. Clowes and Sons for John Murray, 1859. First edition, 8vo. in 12's, original green cloth by Edmonds & Remnants, London retaining their ticket on lower pastedown, boards blocked in blind, rules enclosing foliate designs and central panel, spine gilt, mid brown endpapers, green cloth solander box with printed paper label to spine, 32 publisher's catalog dated June 1859, Freeman variant 3, folding lithographic plate by William West after Darwin, slight rubbing and bumping to extremities with very small ink spot to front board, hinges skillfully restored, little chipped to edges of endpapers and few leaves, nonetheless very bright, fresh copy in original cloth, bookplate of Pownoll William Phipps (b. 1835) using arms and motto of Earls of Mulgrave, whom he was a cousin. Sotheran's Piccadilly Notes - Summer 2015 - 5 2016 £95,000

Darwin, Charles Robert 1809-1882 *On the Origin of The Species by Means of Natural Selection.* New York: D. Appleton and Co., 1860. First American edition, first printing, folding table, original blindstamped boards, expertly respined to style, hinges reinforced, endpapers lightly chipped, previous owner's name on half title, scattered foxing. Dumont Maps and Books 134 - 32 2016 $7500

Darwin, Charles Robert 1809-1882 *The Origin of Species by Means of Natural Selection...* London: John Murray, 1891. Sixth edition, 8vo., original green cloth gilt, one folding chart, binding little rubbed, slight spotting to prelims, partially uncut, very good, presentation from R. J. Wilson to C. E. Byles the antiquarian writer. Sotheran's Piccadilly Notes - Summer 2015 - 95 2016 £450

Darwin, Erasmus 1731-1802 *The Botanic Garden.* London: for J. Johnson, 1791. First edition of part I, third edition of part 2, 2 volume bound as one, 10 plates in each volume, frontispieces, small directions to binder sheet bound between volumes, recent half leather over marbled paper boards with gilt lettering to spine, few short pencilled notes in margin, tidemark and some spotting to few early pages and light offsetting from plates as common with this book, otherwise nice in handsome binding. Any Amount of Books 2015 - A94694 2016 £600

Darwin, Erasmus 1731-1802 *A Plan for the Conduct of Female Education in Boarding Schools.* Derby: printed by J. Drewry for J. Johnson, 1797. First edition, plate slightly spotted and offset, nice, clean copy, handsomely rebound in recent half mottled calf, gilt spine, maroon morocco label. Jarndyce Antiquarian Books CCXV - 624 2016 £850

Dasent, George Webb *Norse Fairy tales Selected and Adapted by...* London: & Philadelphia: George Routledge & Lippincott, n.d. circa, 1912. Thick 8vo., elaborate pictorial boards, some edge and hinge rubbing, very good+, magnificent color pictorial covers and spine, pictorial endpapers, frontispiece and titlepage, 6 color plates plus a profusion of full page and in-text line illustrations by Reginald and Horace Knowles. Aleph-bet Books, Inc. 111 - 239 2016 $600

Dasent, George Webbe *Popular Tales from the Nourse.* Edinburgh: Edmonston and Douglas, 1859. First edition with this collection, 8vo., light browning, bound in brown rough grained publisher's cloth, panelled in blind, title, author and imprint in gilt in spine, binding slightly rubbed, cloth at tail pushed in but good, yellow-brown waxed pastedowns and endpapers, purchase notes of S(pencer) E(rvin) to half title, contents slightly loosening, slight loosening also at hinges. Unsworths Antiquarian Booksellers Ltd. E05 - 72 2016 £150

Daskin, Susanna Bryant *The Lives of William Hartnell.* Stanford: Stanford University Press, 1949. First edition, frontispiece, illustrations, orange cloth lettered and decorated in black, fine, very slightly rubbed pictorial dust jacket. Argonaut Book Shop Biography 2015 - 3597 2016 $50

Datta, Ann *Joun Gould in Australia: letters and Drawings.* Melbourne: Miegunyah Press, 1997. Quarto, color illustrations, fine in dust jacket. Andrew Isles Natural History Books 55 - 10959 2016 $200

Daudet, Alphonse *In the Land of Pain.* London: Jonathan Cape, 2002. First Julian Barnes edition, frontispiece, foolscap 8vo., original black boards, backstrip lettered gilt, dust jacket with 'signed copy' sticker to front, fine, signed by Barnes. Blackwell's Rare Books B184 - 102 2016 £35

Daudet, Alphonse *Lettres De Mon Moulin.* Brussels: Editions du Rond-Point, 1942. One of 6 numbered sets printed on Madagascar paper with color illustrations designed by Andre Collot and containing an extra set of plates, 8vo., stiff paper wrappers with text loosely inserted as issued, unopened, wrappers slightly bent at edges and lightly soiled.   Oak Knoll Books   310 - 28   2016 $550

Daugherty, James *Daniel Boone.* New York: Viking Press, 1939. First edition, first printing, 4to., brown cloth, slightest bit of soil, else fine in very good dust jacket (some edge and corner chips, no award seal), wonderfully illustrated with striking color lithographs.   Aleph-bet Books, Inc.   111 - 110   2016 $400

Daumier, Honore *Daumier et L'Universite: Professerurs et Moutards.* Detroit: Gale Research Co., 1970. 8 black and white lithograph reproductions by Daumier, very slight crease to lower left corners, loosely inserted in an illustrated light brown printed paper folder.   Jarndyce Antiquarian Books   CCXV - 625   2016   £15

Davenant, Francis *What Shall My Son Be?* London: S. W. Partridge & Co., 1870. First edition, half title, 8 pages ads, original light brown decorated cloth, bevelled boards, spine faded, very good.   Jarndyce Antiquarian Books   CCXV - 145   2016   £75

Davenport, Cyril *Mezzotints.* London: Methuen and Co., 1904. First edition, one of 50 bound thus, printed on Japanese paper, small 4to., full vellum with top edge gilt, plates, some cover soiling, bookplate and pencil signature of Gavin Bridson.   Oak Knoll Books   310 - 29   2016 $350

Davenport, Richard Alfred *Lives of Individuals Who Raised Themselves from Poverty to Eminence or Fortune.* London: Thomas Tegg, 1841. First edition, half title, final ad leaf, tipped in label removed from leading pastedown, original printed cloth boards, slightly rubbed and marked, typed booklabel of Granville Garley.   Jarndyce Antiquarian Books   CCXV - 59   2016   £38

Davey, Doris *My Dolly's Home.* London: Simpkin Marshall Hamilton for Arts and General, 1921. Oblong 4to., cloth backed pictorial boards, some cover soil and light stain on bottom of few leaves, else tight and very good complete with two sheets of paper doll figures uncut, 8 pages of text followed by vibrant color lithographed scenes which follow the story, scarce.   Aleph-bet Books, Inc.   111 - 131   2016 $850

Davey, Norman *A History of Building Materials.* London: Phoenix House, 1965. Second impression, royal octavo, frontispiece, 48 plates, 134 illustrations in text, fine in very good dust jacket rubbed at edges.   Peter Ellis   112 - 18   2016   £35

David Copperfield. Strato Publications circa, 1951? Stapled as issued, original color pictorial wrappers, illustrations in comic strip format.   Jarndyce Antiquarian Booksellers   CCXVIII - 483   2016   £20

David Copperfield. New York: Gilberton Co., 1965. Stapled as issued in original color pictorial wrappers, 48 pages, illustrations in comic strip format.   Jarndyce Antiquarian Booksellers   CCXVIII - 484   2016   £20

David Copperfield. New York: Gilberton, 1969. Stapled as issued in original color pictorial wrappers, spine slightly worn, illustrations in comic strip format.   Jarndyce Antiquarian Booksellers   CCXVIII - 485   2016   £20

David, Gary *Eye of the Heart.* Barred Owl Publications, 1981. 8vo., inscribed by author to Paul Metcalf, paper wrappers, very good.   Second Life Books, Inc.   196A - 381   2016 $35

David, Gary *Vineland Distillations.* Rapid City: D'Vine Press, 1980. Paper wrappers, inscribed by author to poet Paul Metcalf and his wife, very good.   Second Life Books, Inc.   196A - 380   2016 $45

Davids, Arthur Lumley *Grammaire Turke: Precedee D'un Discours Preliminaire Sur La Languae et La Litterature Des Nations Orientales.* Londres: W. H. Allen, 1836. First edition of the French translation by Sarah Davids, 4to., publisher's blindstamped cloth, 5 lithographs with errata, wear to head and tail of spine, some small holes to rear hinge, minor discoloration to boards.   Oak Knoll Books   310 - 283   2016 $650

Davidson, Bruce *Time of Change: Civil rights Photographs 1961-1965.* Los Angeles: St. Ann's Press, 2002. Number 90 from a deluxe edition of only 100 copies, signed and numbered by Davidson, with fine original silver gelatin print of the cover image which has also been signed by Davidson on verso, very fine in very fine black cloth slipcase.   Jeff Hirsch Books   Holiday List 2015 - 72   2016 $1200

Davidson, Harold G. *Edward Borein. Cowboy Artist.* New York: Doubleday & Co., 1974. First trade edition, quarto, profusely illustrated with reproductions of drawings, etchings, photos and paintings, including frontispiece and 34 illustrations in color, maroon cloth, gilt, very fine with pictorial dust jacket.   Argonaut Book Shop   Biography 2015 - 7490   2016 $90

Davidson, Homer K. *Black Jack Davidson, a Cavalry Commander...* Glendale: Arthur H. Clark Co., 1974. First edition, although not indicated, one of 1205 copies, 3 color maps, 13 photos, minor rubbing to contents and foot of spine, fine, chipped pictorial dust jacket.   Argonaut Book Shop   Biography 2015 - 5872   2016 $50

Davidson, John *Baptist Lake.* London: Ward and Downey Ltd., 1894. First edition, exceptionally nice, scarce, smooth black cloth with gilt title to front board and spine, near fine, original patterned endpapers, interior pages clean, just showing slightest aging to margins, very slight separation of a middle gathering, caused by book being laid open flat, near fine.   The Kelmscott Bookshop   12 - 29 2016 $175

Davidson, John *The Last Ballad & Other Poems.* London: John Lane, 1899. First edition in rare variant binding, copies usually found in black cloth, this copy bound in red cloth with gilt title, author and Art Novueau influenced flowers and birds to front cover, very good with some light scraping to cloth along bottom of front cover, interior pages are clean and tight, bookplate of artist Pickford Waller, very good.   The Kelmscott Bookshop   12 - 30   2016 $100

Davidson, John *A Queen's Romance: a Version of Victor Hugo's "Ruy Blas".* London: Grant Richards, 1904. First edition, original red cloth with title and author in gilt on spine and front cover, lightly bumped corners but in very good condition, some scattered foxing and offsetting to endpapers but otherwise very nice, very good.   The Kelmscott Bookshop   12 - 31   2016 $300

Davidson, John *Smith: a Tragedy.* Glasgow: Frederick W. Wilson and Brother, 1888. First edition, 300 copies printed, scarce presentation copy inscribed by author to Mrs. John A Cramb, original parchment wrappers, which are browned and lightly soiled, otherwise very good, interior pages clean and bright, very light rippling caused by tight signature, enclosed in red cloth folder, which is inserted into red cloth slipcase with quarter leather spine, gilt title, author, date and 'presentation copy' to spine, very good in wrappers.   The Kelmscott Bookshop   12 - 32   2016 $675

Davidson, Laura *Almost Home.* Boston: 2014. Artist's book, 1 of 8 copies, all on rice paper, each signed and numbered by artist, 9 x 7 1.4 inches, 6 original full page linoleum block prints with hand lettered colophon page, small print incorporating the "A" from the title, that is also an artist's statement, bound loose as issued housed in blue grey cloth over boards clamshell box, small block print on colophon repeated on front panel of box, decorated label on spine, printed housed in tan paper wrapper that is cut with silhouette of bridge suspension cables with small small print from colophon collaged to front wrapper, linoleum block prints printed on antique Kelton Press by artist in two colors. Priscilla Juvelis - Rare Books   66 - 3   2016 $2000

Davidson, Laura *Etui - Portable Necessities.* Boston: 2015. Artist's book one of 10 copies, all on Frankfurt paper, each copy signed and numbered by artist, page size 1 1/2 x 3 3/4 inches, 16 pages, 2 of which are 1 3/8 square fold-overs with fold-over needle case opposite titlepage, bound leporello style, folds going into buff colored Rising Stonehenge paper, painted button closure, which in turn is housed in custom made carrying case of grey Canson paper over boards, solander case, decorated with 4 rows of 3 each mother of pearl shirt buttons sewn on front, title painted on top lid as needlecase, hand painted and hand lettered and hand stitched by Davidson.   Priscilla Juvelis - Rare Books   66 - 4   2016 $1300

Davidson, Rodney *A Book Collector's Notes on Items Relating to the Discovery of Australia the First Settlement and the Early Coastal Exploration of the Continent.*   North Melbourne: Cassell Australia, 1970. Limited to 250 numbered and signed copies, octavo, photos, publisher's cloth and slipcase, bookplate of David McPhee.   Andrew Isles Natural History Books   55 - 37026   2016 $150

Davie, Alan *Drawings.*   Scottish National Gallery of Modern Art, University of Brighton, Paragon Press, 1997. First edition, quarto, 156 reproductions, decorated cloth, signed boldly by artist on half title, fine.   Peter Ellis   112 - 92   2016   £175

Davie, J. C. *Letters from Buenos Ayres and Chili; with an Original History of the Latter Country.*   London: R. Ackermann, 1819. First edition, 8vo., 6 hand colored aquatints, later brown half morocco, light foxing to prelims.   J. & S. L. Bonham Antiquarian Booksellers   America 2016 - 9893   2016   £650

Davies, Henry E. *An Account of the Cavalry Expedition to Richmond Va. by Lt. Col. Henry E. Davies, Commanding the Harris Light Cavalry.*   N.P.: 1963? 4to. bifolium, folded and minor browning.   Howard S. Mott Inc.   265 - 44   2016 $300

Davies, Hunter *The Beatles.*   New York: McGraw Hill Book Co., 1968. First US edition, original cloth, dust jacket, little rubbing to edges of wrapper, but very good.   Sotheran's   Piccadilly Notes - Summer 2015 - 34   2016   £98

Davies, Robertson *Murther & Walking Spirits.*   Franklin Center: Franklin Library, 1991. Limited first edition, signed by author, bound in black leather, lettered and decoratively stamped in gilt, all edges gilt, very fine, as new.   Argonaut Book Shop   Literature 2015 - 3959   2016 $90

Davies, W. E. *Fly Dressing and Some Tackle Making.* Kingswood, Surrey: Elliot's Right Way Books, 1963. First edition, 8vo., original cloth and wrapper, text illustrations, previous owner's bookplate, near fine.   Sotheran's Hunting, Shooting & Fishing - 113   2016   £20

Davies, William Henry 1871-1940 *Shorter Lyrics of the Twentieth Century 1900-1922.* Poetry Bookshop, 1922. First edition, this being one of 200 numbered copies on large paper, inscribed by poet Harold Munro, 8vo., recently finely bound in full dark green morocco, gilt fillet border to sides spine lettered gilt and ruled gilt and with gilt centre tools, marbled endpapers, top edges gilt, fine.   Sotheran's Piccadilly Notes - Summer 2015 - 96   2016   £298

Davies, William Henry 1871-1940 *The Soul's Destroyer and Other Poems.* Alston Rivers, 1970. Second (first trade) edition, foxing throughout, small wormhole at foot of first few leaves, crown 8vo., original grey-green wrappers printed in blue to front, spine little ragged and upper cover detached and held internally by thin strips of brown tape, sound, inscribed by author to E. S. P. Haynes, close friend.   Blackwell's Rare Books   B186 - 195   2016   £700

Davis, Britton *The Truth About Geronimo.* New Haven: Yale University Press, 1929. First edition, very good+ in very good, price clipped dust jacket with few minor chips and tears and old internal repair.   Kaaterskill Books   21 - 25   2016 $175

Davis, Daniel Webster *Weh Down Souf and Other Poems.* Cleveland: Helman-Taylor Co., 1897. First edition, illustrations by William Sheppard, octavo, green pictorial cloth stamped in yellow brown, orange, dark green and black, beautiful fine, scarce.   Between the Covers Rare Books   202 - 27   2016 $650

Davis, John H. *The Guggenheims: an American Epic.* New York: Morrow, 1978. First edition, first printing, 8vo., author's signature on flyleaf, illustrations, paper boards with cloth spine nice in little scuffed and slightly chipped dust jacket, very good+.   Second Life Books, Inc.   196A - 387   2016 $75

Davis, Lavinia *The keys in the City.* New York: Charles Scribner's Sons, 1936. First edition, very good plus in like dust jacket, light toning, spine ends bumped and owner name on front pastedown, jacket spine moderately toned, brief chipping at extremities and light rubbing overall. Royal Books   49 - 98   2016 $350

Davis, Lindsey *A Dying Light in Corduba.* London: Century, 1996. First edition, very fine in dust jacket.   Mordida Books   2015 - 003069   2016 $60

Davis, Lindsey *Three Hands in the Fountain.* London: Century, 1997. First edition, very fine in dust jacket, signed by author.   Mordida Books   2015 - 003070   2016 $55

Davis, Lindsey *Time to Depart.* London: Century, 1995. First edition, very fine in dust jacket.   Mordida Books 2015 - 0030684   2016 $60

Davis, Lindsey *Venus in Copper - a Falcon Novel.* London: Hutchinson, 1991. First edition, octavo, signed by author, cheap paper tanned at edges, fine in fine dust jacket.   Peter Ellis   112 - 93   2016   £75

Davis, Richard Harding *The Deserter.* New York: Scribners, 1917. First edition, 8vo., uncut and partially unopened, fine in very slightly worn original dust jacket, upper corner of first 3 leaves of prelim matter clipped off, inscribed by (introducer) John T. McCutcheon, tipped to endpaper is ALS 12.5/17 from author's brother responding to a request for an autograph, tipped to flyleaf if ALS from author to his brother.   Second Life Books, Inc.   196A - 388   2016 $150

Davis, Richard Harding *In the Fog.* Harper Bros., 1901. Blue boards, gilt, paper illustration tipped on front cover, photo of author extracted from magazine laid in, covers little rubbed, otherwise very good, illustrations by T. M. Pierce & F. D. Steele.   I. D. Edrich   Crime - 2016   £35

Davis, Thulani *Playing the Changes.* Middletown: Wesleyan, 1985. First edition, author's presentation on half title, copies of two photo clippings laid in, paper wrappers, cover scuffed, otherwise very good, tight copt.   Second Life Books, Inc.   196A - 389   2016 $65

Davis, William *A Key to Bonnycastle's Mensuration.* London: printed for the author, 1804. First edition, 12mo., final ad leaf, contemporary mottled calf, worn but sound. Jarndyce Antiquarian Books   CCXV - 543   2016   £30

Davison, Henry *Dove Sono.* London: Kegan Paul Trench, Trubner & Co., 1894. Half title, original olive green cloth, gilt, slightly rubbed, inscribed by Coventry Patmore for Francis Patmore.   Jarndyce Antiquarian Booksellers CCXVII - 82   2016   £125

Davison, Peter *Dark Houses.* Cambridge: Halty Ferguson, 1971. First edition, one of 300 handprinted copies, dark blue decorated wrappers, fine, inscribed by author June 1972 for William Meredith, 3 corrections in text by author.   Charles Agvent   William Meredith - 25   2016 $100

Davison, Peter *Walking the Boundaries. Poems 1957-1974.* New York: Atheneum, 1974. First American edition, inscribed and signed by author June 4 1980, for William Meredith, with author's business card laid in, fine in fine dust jacket.   Charles Agvent   William Meredith - 26   2016 $80

Davys, George *The Saving Bank: Containing the Dialogues of Ralph Ragged and Will Wise...* Liverpool: printed by Michael Heaton and Mitchell, 1836. New edition, 12mo., various pencilled annotations and emphasis marks in early hand with several near contemporary press cuttings inserted or tipped in, original green cloth, fine, apparently of great rarity.   John Drury Rare Books   2015 - 26305   2016 $437

Dawson, Fielding *New Collages.* Syracuse: Light Work, 1978. 1/26 copies signed by author, 8vo. bound in paper wrappers, cover little yellowed, else nice.   Second Life Books, Inc.   196A - 391   2016 $75

Dawson, Fielding *On Duberman's Black Mountain & B. H. Friedman's biography of Jackson Pollock.* Toronto: Coach House Press, 1973. First edition, 12mo., self wrappers, very good, inscribed by author to friend Paul Metcalf.   Second Life Books, Inc.   196A - 392   2016 $75

Dawson, Fielding *On Shortstop as the figure of Kinesis.* Durham: Duke University, 1975. First edition, 1/300 copies, horizontal small 8vo., brown paper wrappers, inscribed by author to Paul Metcalf, very good.   Second Life Books, Inc.   196A - 393   2016 $75

Dawson, Robert *Robert Dawson. Photographs.* Tokyo: Min Gallery & Studio, 1988. First edition, square octavo, over 35 photographic images, bound in pictorial wrappers, upper right corner lightly crease, else fine.   Argonaut Book Shop   Photography 2015 - 2776   2016 $75

Dawson, Samuel *Brest on the Quebec Labrador.* Toronto: Copp-Clark Co., 1905. 8vo. rebound in green cloth, original printed wrappers, pamphlet folded at one time with resulting creases, W. A. Munn's copy with some notations in pencil on outer margins.   Schooner Books Ltd.   115 - 99   2016 $45

Day Lewis, Cecil *Christmas Eve: a Poem.* Ariel Poem, New Series, 1954. First edition, illustrations by Edward Ardizzone, wrappers, fine in publisher's envelope.   Bertram Rota Ltd.   Christmas List 2015 - 8   2016   £20

Day Lewis, Cecil *Country Comets.* Martin Hopkinson, 1928. First edition, foolscap 8vo. original green boards, faded unevenly with paper label to front lettered in black, ight soiling to endpapers around hinge, good, with autograph note form author loosely inserted.   Blackwell's Rare Books   B186 - 197   2016   £60

Day, Charles William *Hints on Etiquette and the Usages of Society...* London: Longmans, Rees, Orme, 1836. Seventh edition, half title, 4 pages ads, original purple brown limp cloth, boards largely faded to brown, hinges slightly cracking, all edges gilt.   Jarndyce Antiquarian Books   CCXV - 146   2016   £75

Day, Charles William *Hints on Etiquette and the Usages of Society...* London: Longmans, Rees, Orme, 1837. Eleventh edition, half title, 4 pages ads, original purple-brown cloth, boards, faded back cover badly faded, ertical owner to front cover, all edges gilt, sound copy only.   Jarndyce Antiquarian Books   CCXV - 147   2016   £45

Day, Charles William *Hints on Etiquette and the Usages of Society...* London: Longmans, 1866. Thirty-first edition, half title, final ad leaf, damp marking to leading endpapers, original purple brown limp cloth boards, slight marking to front board, all edges gilt.   Jarndyce Antiquarian Books   CCXV - 148   2016   £65

Day, Charles William *Hints on Etiquette and the Usages of Society...* London: Turnstile Press, 1946. Reprint of 1836 third edition, half title, color plates, original pictorial boards, contemporary inscription on leading f.e.p., very good.   Jarndyce Antiquarian Books   CCXV - 149   2016   £20

Day, Douglas *Journey of the Wolf.* New York: Atheneum, 1977. First edition, 8vo., paper over boards with cloth spine, review laid in, map on endpapers, nice in little scuffed and slightly chipped dust jacket, author's presentation for Wm. (Jay Smith) & Sonja.   Second Life Books, Inc.   197 - 62   2016 $95

Day, J. Wentworth *King George V as a Sportsman: an Informal Study of the first Country Gentleman.* London: Cassell & Co., 1935. 8vo. in 12's, original green cloth, spine titled gilt, 52 photographic plates and illustrations, spine sunned, otherwise very good, from the library of Kenneth Rose (1924-12014), with his signature.   Sotheran's   Piccadilly Notes - Summer 2015 - 97   2016   £50

Day, Lal Behari *Folk Tales of Bengal.* London: MacMillan, 1912. First edition, red cloth with elaborate gilt pictorial cover, endpapers spotted, very light soil, very good+ tight, 32 magnificent color plates with lettered tissue guards by Warwick Goble.   Aleph-bet Books, Inc.   112 - 215   2016 $475

Day, Lois *The Looker In.* Jonathan Cape, 1961. First edition, crown 8vo., original blue boards, backstrip lettered gilt, top edge blue, ownership inscription to flyleaf, dust jacket designed by Hugh Marshall with merest hint of fading of backstrip panel and at head of upper joint fold, owner's shelfmark to front flap.   Blackwell's Rare Books   B184 - 206   2016   £30

Dazey, Charles T. *In Old Kentucky.* Detroit: Dramatists Play service, 1937. First edition, 1/350 copies in special binding, numbered and signed by author, 8vo., bookplate of Vincent Starrett with his ownership signature, very good in somewhat chipped and soiled dust jacket.   Second Life Books, Inc.   196A - 396   2016 $65

De Angeli, Marguerite *The Door in the Wall.* Garden City: Doubleday & Co., 1949. Stated first edition, 8vo., blue cloth, fine in dust jacket with few small chips, illustrations by author, laid in is wonderful handwritten note about the book written to a fan, special copy.   Aleph-bet Books, Inc.   112 - 133   2016 $600

De Beer, G. R. *Early Travellers in the Alps.* London: Sidgwick & Jackson, 1930. First edition, original cloth in dust jacket, maps and illustrations, one folding map, light soiling to spine of jacket, light spotting to fore edges, else very good.   Sotheran's   Piccadilly Notes - Summer 2015 - 98   2016   £178

De Bernieres, Louis *Birds Without Wings.* London: Secker & Warburg, 2004. First edition, limited to 1000 signed and numbered copies, fine, in fine slipcase.   Bella Luna Books   2016 - 17661   2016 $82

De Bernieres, Louis *Captain Corelli's Mandolin.* London: Secker & Warburg, 1994. First edition, first issue, white boards, octavo, small ownership inscription, slight bruise at head of spine, cheap paper tanned at edges as unusual, near fine in near fine dust jacket, very slightly creased at edges.   Peter Ellis   112 - 95   2016   £250

De Bernieres, Louis *Labels.* London: One Horse Press, 1993. Limited to 2000 copies, pictorial wrappers, fine, wrap-around band, signed and numbered.   Bella Luna Books   2016 - j1000   2016 $82

De Brunhoff, Jean *The Story of Babar.* London: Methuen, 1934. First UK edition, folio, cloth backed pictorial boards, some edge and corner rubbing, very good+, clean copy.   Aleph-bet Books, Inc.   112 - 137   2016 $1250

De Brunhoff, Laurent *Babar's Visit to Bird Island.* New York: Random House, 1952. First edition, folio, cloth backed pictorial boards, fine in dust jacket chipped on edges, color illustrations.   Aleph-bet Books, Inc.   111 - 114   2016 $850

De Brunhoff, Laurent *Babar's Picnic.* New York: Random House, 1949. First edition, folio, cloth backed pictorial boards, near fine, glorious color illustrations.   Aleph-bet Books, Inc.   112 - 138   2016 $425

De Chair, Somerset *The Story of a Lifetime.* Golden Cockerel Press, 1954. 57/100 copies of an edition of 110 copies, signed by author, wood engraved titlepage design, 7 full page wood engravings by Clifford Webb, small folio, original white sheepskin, lettering on backstrip and front cover design gilt blocked, that on backstrip between raised bands, backstrip and immediately adjacent area lightly sunned as usual, head corners trifle bumped, single gilt rule to inner borders, minor stain to rear pastedown, top edge gilt, others untrimmed, good.   Blackwell's Rare Books   B184 - 267   2016   £350

De Fornaro, Carlo *The Arabian Droll Stories.* New York: Lotus Society, 1929. Limited to 550 copies, this one of 100 copies extra illustrated, hand illuminated and signed by author and artist, A. Zaidenberg, 8vo., sometime bound in full cream morocco, boards with elaborate gilt borders enclosing central gilt device with red morocco onlays, spine panelled in gilt with red morocco centre onlays, lettered in blind, upper joint rubbed, boards little dusty, otherwise very good.   Sotheran's   Piccadilly Notes - Summer 2015 - 99   2016   £248

De Fraine, John *The Autobiography of John De Fraine.* London: 1900. Half title, frontispiece, original red cloth, bevelled boards, presentation from author, very good, bright copy.   Jarndyce Antiquarian Books   CCXV - 626   2016   £65

De Garis, Frederic *We Japanese: Being Descriptions of Many of the Customs, Manners, Ceremonies, Festivals....* Miyanoshita: Fujiya Hotel, 1936. Third printing, 8vo., copiously illustrated, paper wrappers, covered with brocade, sewn in Japanese style, with paper label, in cloth covered folding case, fastened with cords and bone pins, cover of book slightly soiled on front, case little worn at corners and slightly unglued at interior spine, otherwise very good, tight copy, presentation from H. S. K. Yamaguchi for Katharine A. Shapes.   Second Life Books, Inc. 196A - 397   2016 $150

De Gasparin, Agenor Etienne, Count *The Family: its Duties, Joys and Sorrows.* London: Jackson, Walford & Hodder, 1867. First English edition, half title, original dark purple cloth bevelled boards, slightly rubbed at head and tail of spine, inner hinges cracking, presentation to the Library of the Ladies Sanitary Association by the translator, library stamps.   Jarndyce Antiquarian Books   CCXV - 150   2016   £48

De Gaya, Louis *Matrimonial Ceremonies Displayed...* London: printed for H. Serjeant & G. Woodfall, 1886. Unopened in original cream boards, cloth spine, slightly dulled.   Jarndyce Antiquarian Books   CCXV - 151   2016   £40

De Gerez, T. *Louhi: Witch of North Farm.* New York: Viking, 1986. First printing (1-5 code), 4to., pictorial boards, as new in dust jacket, magical color illustrations by Barbara Cooney, this copy inscribed by artist.   Aleph-bet Books, Inc.   112 - 115   2016 $100

De Kay, John Wesley *Dictators of Mexico. The Land Where Hope Marches with Despair.* London: Effingham Wilson, 1914. 8vo., original full green morocco, spine and front cover lettered in gilt, inner dentelles gilt, all edges gilt, marbled endpapers, frontispiece, retaining tissue guard, light wear to extremities, spine sunned, little offsetting to initial blank, otherwise very good, inscribed by author for friend.   Sotheran's   Travel and Exploration - 54   2016   £995

De Kooning, Willem *Drawings.* New York: Walker and Co., 1967. First edition, one of only 100 copies signed by artist, beautiful copy in rare original slipcase, 24 charcoal drawings, quarto, original printed boards, original dust jacket, original slipcase, extremely faint evidence of pencil inscription on front free endpaper, small spot of soiling to cloth edge, dust jacket price clipped (as usual) with mild toning to spine, very clean, well preserved in rare slipcase. Manhattan Rare Book Company   2016 - 1635   2016 $2000

De Kooning, Willem *Willem de Kooning.* New York: Museum of Modern Art, 1968. First edition, scarce hardbound issue, square quarto, 115 illustrations, including 16 illustrations in color, near fine in near fine dust jacket faded at spine.   Peter Ellis   112 - 96   2016   £100

De La Bruce, Jean *The Life of that Most Illustrious Prince, Charles V, Late Duke of Lorrain,,,.* London: Randal Taylor, 1691. First edition, 8vo., full leather, covers somewhat scuffed and worn, front board loose, but holding at one hinge, good, clean text.   Any Amount of Books   2015 - A77546   2016   £170

De La Mare, Walter   1873-1956 *Broomsticks & Other Tales.* London: Constable, 1925. First edition, octavo, many wood engravings, gilt pictorial cloth, edges slightly spotted, near fine.   Peter Ellis   112 - 98   2016   £45

De La Mare, Walter   1873-1956 *Crossings.* London: W. Collins, 1923. First edition, 8vo., with music by Cecil Armstrong Gibbs, cloth backed pictorial boards, worn leather label, signed by De La Mare with presentation by Gibbs (?) seemingly signed "Cecil".   Second Life Books, Inc.   197 - 63   2016 $125

De La Mare, Walter   1873-1956 *Memoirs of a Midget.* 1921. First edition, one of 210 numbered copies, this unnumbered, signed by author, drawings by Florence Thompson, 8vo., original oatmeal cloth with grey sides, backstrip with leather label lettered in gilt, bump to top corner of lower board with small amount of wear to all corners, light overall dust soiling, top edge dusty, edges untrimmed and largely uncut, good, this the copy of a Mr. Dewar, with bibliographic notes regarding this book.   Blackwell's Rare Books   B186 - 199   2016   £250

De La Mare, Walter   1873-1956 *Songs of Childhood.* London: Longmans, Green, 1902. First edition, 12mo., blue cloth stamped in gold, parchment spine, top edge gilt, other edges uncut, fine in custom cloth case, gravure frontispiece by Richard Doyle, this copy inscribed by De La Mare and also has 1 page hand written letter from De La Mare laid in, book inscribed by author for friend, J. N. Hart Jan. 1942, and has written 12 lines of verse from his poem 'Gone', plus laid in handwritten letter on 2 sides of an 8vo.. sheet of paper from author to Hart, special copy, rare.   Aleph-bet Books, Inc.   111 - 115   2016 $1850

De La Mare, Walter   1873-1956 *The Veil: and other Poems.* London: Constable, 1921. First edition, #88 of 250 numbered copies, signed, large paper copies, 8vo., untrimmed, bound in cloth backed boards, spine soiled, worn leather label, small bookplate on front endpaper noting that this book was the property of poet laureate John Masefield, also bookplate of Joseph Lilienthal, nice and clean.   Second Life Books, Inc.   197 - 64   2016 $135

De La Pena, D. M. *Manual De Nueva York...* Nueva York: Imprenta de S. W. Benedict, 1851. First edition, 18mo., numerous engravings and small folding map of NY, original cloth.   M & S Rare Books, Inc.   99 - 113   2016 $550

De La Ramee, Marie Louise   1839-1908 *Two Offenders.* London: Chatto & Windus, 1893. First edition, inscribed by author for Sir Philip and Lady Currie, bound in cream cloth with gilt ruling and design to front cover, boards smudged and show other signs of handling, small red spot on front board that may be ink, spine browned and slightly chipped, interior has light foxing to some pages and slight loosening of few signatures, although text block tight, all edges gilt, very good.   The Kelmscott Bookshop   12 - 78   2016 $525

De La Ronciere, Charles *La Decouverte De L'Afrique au Moyen Age Cartographes et Explorateurs.* Le Caire: Societe Royale De Geographie D'Egypte, 1925. 3 volumes in one, folio, half leather, top edge stained green, original paper wrappers bound in, plates, spine rubbed with some loss of leather to head and tail, leather slighty detached at head, wear to edges and corners, boards somewhat worn and slightly faded, wrappers tanned.   Oak Knoll Books   310 - 284   2016 $2500

De Laguna, Frederica *Fog on the Mountain.* New York: Crime Club, 1938. Spine sunned, scarce, very good.   I. D. Edrich   Crime - 2016   £120

De Lyrienne, Richard *The Quest of the Gilt-edged Girl.* London: John Lane, Bodley Head, 1897. First edition, rare, near fine in orange paper wrappers with brown title to spine and front panel, short closed tear to front endpage, otherwise fine, housed in portfolio within grey cloth slipcase with black and gilt leather title label in spine and bookplate of Mark Samuels Lasner on inside board of portfolio, near fine in slipcase.   The Kelmscott Bookshop   12 - 34   2016 $250

De Monvel, M. B. *Jeanne D'Arc.* Paris: Plon Nourrit & Cie, circa, 1900. Early edition, landscape 4to., original mid blue cloth decorated with wreath in green, grey and gilt against decorative background of green wavy lines and seme of fleurs-de-lis and Sacre Coeurs repeated to lower board, blue edges black endpapers, striking colored plates throughout, very good with light rubbing to lower edges and spine, mild cover marking and small abrasions to corners, internally fine bar a 20mm. closed tear to bottom edge of one leaf and small adhesion to another.   Sotheran's Piccadilly Notes - Summer 2015 - 100   2016   £168

De Moraes, Vinicius *O Mergulhador.* Rio De Janeiro: Atelier De Arte, 1968. First edition, 4to., illustrated laminated boards, issued without dust jacket, illustrations in black and white with photos, signed presentation from author and his wife to artist Rosa Fronfins Carless, covers very slightly marked but sound clean, pleasing very good+ copy.   Any Amount of Books   2015 - A90864   2016   £550

De Nascimento, Abdias *Orixas: Os Deuses Vivos da Africa or Orishas: the Living Gods of Africa in Brazil.* Rio de Janeiro: IPEAFRO/Afrodiaspora, 1995. Signed by author, full color, full page reproductions of artist's paintings, very good to tan cloth boards with embossed title to spine and front cover, minor wear to edges of boards including bump to bottom edge of front cover, few splits to interior of binding, all pages remain bound, black illustrated dust jacket with red title to spine and front panels, minor wear to edges of jacket including few small chips and minor rubbing to panels, housed in original black illustrated slipcase with red title to spine and front panels, wear and rubbing to edges and panels of case including an old pricce sticker, very good in like jacket.   The Kelmscott Bookshop   13 - 14   2016 $525

De Quincey, Thomas   1785-1859 *Revolt of the Tatars; or Flight of the Kalmuck Khan and His People from the Russian Territories to the Frontiers of China.* London: Dropmore Press, 1948. first edition thus, quarto, illustrations, including endpapers by Stuart Boyle, printed on handpress on handmade paper, half brown leather with gilt decoration, cloth sides, top edge gilt, presentation copy inscribed "W. Martin from the Dropmore Press Christmas 1948 - Edward Shanks".   Peter Ellis   112 - 106   2016   £85

De Quincey, Thomas   1785-1859 *The Works of...* Edinburgh: Adam and Charles Black, MDCCCLXVIII, reprinted, 1883. Fourth edition, 16 volumes, plates, few illustrations in text, 8vo., contemporary half dark brown morocco, spines gilt in compartments, marbled edges, matching the boards, spines faded, good.   Blackwell's Rare Books B186 - 50   2016   £800

De Salis, Harriet Anne *Tempting Dishes for Small Incomes.* London: Longmans, 1890. First edition, half title, original beige cloth, red cloth spine rather marked, owner inscription of Lucy M. Brett.   Jarndyce Antiquarian Books   CCXV - 152   2016   £45

De St. Croix, G. E. M. *The Class Struggle in the Ancient Greek World from the Archaic Age to the Arab Conquests.* London: Duckworth, 1983. Second corrected impression, 8vo., paperback, creases to cover and spine, edges dusted, some shelfwear, still good.   Unsworths Antiquarian Booksellers Ltd.   E04 - 44   2016   £20

De Tournes, Jean De *Insignium Aliquot Virorum Icones.* Lyons: Jean de Tournes, 1559. First and only edition, 8vo., later vellum with red leather label on spine, some soiling, De Tournes' Viper device on title and 145 woodcut portrait medallions, bookplate of R. E. Cartier, Alfred Cartier's nephew and heir, armorial bookplate of Bibliotheca Trautner-Falkiana, i. e. the Augsburg bibliophile Hans Joachim Trautner (1916-2001), little spotted in places.   Maggs Bros. Ltd.   1474 - 29   2016   £1800

De Valcourt, Robert *The Illustrated Manners Book.* New York: Leland Clay & Co., 1855. original pictorial maroon cloth, decorated in gilt, slightly rubbed, spine little faded, illustrations, tear to lower corner of pages 393/4 with some loss of text, occasional pencil markings.   Jarndyce Antiquarian Books   CCXV - 153   2016   £55

De Valis, Ninette *Come Dance with Me-A Memoir.* London: Hamish Hamilton, 1967. First edition, very good, red cloth, silver titles on spine, some minor wear at edges and covers, book attractive, extensively illustrated including frontispiece, book signed by author and 8 further signatures.   Simon Finch   2015 - 000072   2016 $256

De Visme Shaw, L. H. *Wild Fowl.* London: Longmans, Green and Co., 1912. Reissue, 8vo., original decorative cloth lettered in red with gilt title to spine, illustrations, spine little dulled, very clean internally, very good.   Sotheran's Hunting, Shooting & Fishing - 76   2016   £40

De Waleffe, Maurice *Deuxieme Exposition de l'Arc-en ciel, Groupe Franco-Anglo-Americain du 8 Octobre au 3 Novembre 1183.* Paris: Galerie de Goupil et Cie, 1918. First edition, publisher's white paper wrappers, lettered in blue, near fine, some light soiling to wrappers, light rusting to staple binding, few faint spots ot otherwise clean pages, lovely copy, illustrations.   B & B Rare Books, Ltd.   2016 - AEC001   2016 $350

De Wall, Burt *The International Sherlock Holmes.* Archon Books, 1980. Very good in like dust jacket.   I. D. Edrich Crime - 2016   £40

De Wall, Burt *The World Bibliography of Sherlock Homes and F. Watson.* New York: Bramhall House, 1974. Very good.   I. D. Edrich   Crime - 2016   £40

Deal, Babs H. *Fancy's Knell.* London: Gollancz, 1967. Very nice in dust jacket, uncommon, particularly with jacket. I. D. Edrich   Crime - 2016   £40

Dean, Robert *John Baldessari Catalogue Raisonne: volume On 1956-1974.* New Haven: Yale University Press, 2012. Very fine in very fine slipcase and still in original shrinkwrap, new copy, numerous color illustrations. Jeff Hirsch Books Holiday List 2015 - 6 2016 $100

Dearmer, Mabel *The Book of Penny Toys.* London & New York: Macmillan, 1899. First and only edition, cloth backed pictorial boards, tips worn and foxing, very good, full page color illustrations, rare. Aleph-bet Books, Inc. 112 - 139 2016 $1350

The Death Fetch, or the Student of Gottingen Founded on a Popular Opinion, Prevalent Even at the Present Time.... London: printed for T. Hughes, 35 Ludgate Street, n.d., 1826. First edition, 12mo. inserted folded frontispiece with color frontispiece, original three quarter brown levant morocco, tooled and titled in gold by Morrell of London, armorial bookplate of J. Barton Townsend, later bookplate of William Hartmann Woodin. John W. Knott, Jr./L.W. Currey, Inc. Fall-Winter 2015 - 17501 2016 $2500

Deaver, Jeffery *The Devils Teardrop.* London: Hodder & Stoughton, 1999. First UK edition, octavo, signed by author, fine in very good dust jacket little rubbed at top edge of upper panel. Peter Ellis 112 - 94 2016 £35

Debary, Thomas *Notes of a Residence in the Canary islands, the South of Spain and Algiers.* Francis & John Rivington, 1851. First edition, 8vo., frontispiece lithograph, original blue blindstamped cloth, all edges gilt, small tear to spine, good. J. & S. L. Bonham Antiquarian Booksellers Europe 2016 - 9973 2016 £375

Debreuil, Jean *Practical Perspective or an Easy method of Representing Natural Objects.* London: printed for the proprietors Bowles and Carver at their map and print warehouse, n.d. circ, 1795. Seventh edition, 4to., 150 plates on 81 leaves, 4to., some light toning to plates with offsetting to adjacent pages, titlepage little foxed, contemporary tan sheep boards, recently rebacked in well matched morocco, red gilt label to spine, all edges yellow, endpaper renewed, some scrapes including one repaired to centre of upper board, edges chipped, still good, sound. Unsworths Antiquarian Booksellers 30 - 41 2016 £350

Debs, Joseph *Summa Confutationum Contra Assertiones Sacerdotis Joseph David (also in Arabic).* Beirut: Ex typographia Catholica Sumptibus Rezcalla Micaelis Khadra, 1871. First edition, text in Arabic and latin, 8vo., original calf backed marbled boards, title in gold on spine, ex-Bib. Mt. St Alphonsus, Esopus, NY. Howard S. Mott Inc. 265 - 7 2016 $200

Decker, William *To Be a Man.* Boston: Little Brown, 1967. First edition, inscribed by author to Wallace Stegner's son, the writer Peter Stegner and his wife Marion, nice association, fine in very good dust jacket with few small stains to spine and rear panel which also sports very supportive blurb by Wallace Stegner. Ken Lopez Bookseller 166 - 22 2016 $375

Decremps, Henri *Testament de Jerome Sharp...* Paris: Granger (and others), 1786. Second edition, Disbound, lacking frontispiece, cords loosening to spine, some moderate dampstaining to margins, causing a bit of erosion to upper fore corners of few leaves, woodcut vignette illustrations to text, untrimmed. Dramatis Personae 119 - 41 2016 $125

Dede, John *Der Handel des Russischen Reichs.* Mitau and Leipzig: G. A. Reyher, 1844. First edition, scarce, 8vo., contemporary dark green calf, ornamented in gilt, spine lettered gilt, inner dentelles ornamented in gilt, pink watered endpapers, all edges gilt, tables in text, light wear to extremities, little spotted in places, duplicate from Latvian library crossed out, earlier German stamp of Society for Antiquities of Baltic Provinces of Russia. Sotheran's Travel and Exploration - 234 2016 £895

Defoe, Daniel *The Family Instructor in Three Parts.* London: printed for Eman Matthews, 1715. Second edition, 12mo., some slight worming to lower margin of B1-B12 & F1-F12 with slight loss of text to letter I2 leaves but not affecting sense, contemporary panelled calf, expertly recased, retaining original spine, later gilt title. Jarndyce Antiquarian Books CCXV - 154 2016 £1200

Defoe, Daniel *The Life and Adventures of Robinson Crusoe.* London: printed for John Stockdale, 1804. 8vo., 2 volumes, later speckled calf with double gilt line panels to boards, spines richly gilt with contrasting leather labels, all edges gilt, 17 plates, little rubbing to joints, some offsetting from plates, bookplates, otherwise attractive. Sotheran's Piccadilly Notes - Summer 2015 - 101 2016 £650

Defoe, Daniel *The Life and Adventures of Robinson Crusoe.* London: printed for T. Cadell & W. Davies, 1820. 254 x 159mm., 2 volumes, pleasing late 19th century dark green three quarter morocco, raised bands, spines gilt in compartments with nautical centerpieces, marbled endpapers, top edge gilt; engraved titlepage vignettes and 20 plates (including frontispiece) by Charles Heath after Thomas Stothard, all of the engraved material done on India paper and mounted; large paper copy, spines uniformly faded to olive (vague fading also to parts of leather on sides of volumes), extremities just very slightly rubbed, isolated mild marginal foxing, short closed tear to fore edge of one titlepage, otherwise fine, bindings with no significant wear, leaves clean and fresh, engravings with none of the expected foxing. Phillip J. Pirages 67 - 110 2016 $950

Defoe, Daniel *The Adventures of Robinson Crusoe.* Bickers and Bush, 1862. First edition illustrated thus, 8vo., sometime bound by Bayntun-Riviere in full double gilt line panelled black straight grain morocco, spine lettered and panelled gilt with gilt centre tools, marbled endpapers, all edges gilt, 8 plates and 38 woodcuts, handsome volume. Sotheran's Piccadilly Notes - Summer 2015 - 102 2016 £498

Defoe, Daniel *Robinson Crusoe.* New York: Cosmopolitan, 1920. First edition, 4to., blue gilt cloth, pictorial paste-on, top edge gilt, gilt slightly dulled, else near fine, illustrations by N C. Wyeth. Aleph-bet Books, Inc. 111 - 490 2016 $225

Defoe, Daniel *The Life & Strange Surprising Adventures of Robinson Crusoe of York.* London: Basilisk Press, 1979. No. 6 of 25 specially bound copies with 10 original prints (of a total edition of 515), 328 x 245mm., publisher's original dark blue morocco by Tony Miles of London, upper board with gilt vignette reproducing Craig's woodcut portrait of Crusoe, raised bands, gilt spine titling, gilt dragon ornament to tail panel, decorative blind roll to turn-ins, marbled endpapers, top edge gilt, without publisher's box, with more than 80 small wood engravings in text by Edward Gordon Craig, with 10 original prints, 6 of them signed, with initials and dated, these bound in the rear in windowed French fold leaves, original prospectus laid in, designed by Bernard Roberts and printed at John Roberts Press on Van Gelder mouldmade paper, mint. Phillip J. Pirages 67 - 95 2016 $5000

Defoe, Daniel *The Novels and Miscellaneous Works.* Oxford: Thomas Tegg, 1840. 20 volumes, half titles, contemporary half blue calf by Birdsall, top edge gilt, nice. Jarndyce Antiquarian Booksellers CCXVII - 84 2016 £2850

Defoe, Daniel *The Original Power of the Collective Body of the People of England, Examined and Asserted...* London: printed and sold by R. Baldwin, n.d. circa, 1770. Third edition, 8vo., uncut, evidence of original stab-stitching to gutters, edges little dusty, pencil annotations of page 5 and few pencil marks to titlepage, 19th century half brown calf, textured cloth covered boards, gilt title to spine, spine scuffed with little loss to endcaps, rubbed, corners worn, titlepage separating slightly, some bibliographical pencil notes, binding little shabby but very good internally, label showing book from collection of William Starmer Shaw. Unsworths Antiquarian Booksellers 30 - 42 2016 $95

Defoe, Daniel *A Treatise concerning the Use and Abuse of the Marriage Bed.* London: printed for T. Warner at the Black Boy in Pater-Noster Row, 1727. 8vo., 1 inch tear to upper margin of A2, occasional slight dusting and marking, handsomely rebound in quarter calf, raised bands, compartments ruled in gilt, red morocco label. Jarndyce Antiquarian Books CCXV - 155 2016 £680

Defoe, Daniel *The Voyages and Travels and Surprising Adventures of Captain Robert Singleton.* New York: Everet Duyckinck, 1815. 18mo., frontispiece, contemporary plain boards, spine shot, covers coming loose, text sound and crisp. M & S Rare Books, Inc. 99 - 132 2016 $200

Degrand, Peter Paul Francis *Proceedings of the Friends of a Rail-Road to San Francisco at their Public Meeting Held at the U.S. Hotel in Boston April 19 1849...* Boston: Dutton and Wentworth printers, 1849. Second edition, 24 pages, 8vo., stitched pink paper wrappers, very good, mail fold, tiny deaccession stamp at foot of last leaf. Kaaterskill Books 21 - 28 2016 $325

Dehartington, Michael *Onanism: the Masturbation Panic 1756-1973.* Berkeley: 2006. One of only 100 copies, 8vo., original printed stiff wrappers, fine. Edwin V. Glaser Rare Books 2015 - 19358 2016 $50

Deidier, l'Abbe *La mechanique Generale Contenant La Statique L'Arrometrie, L'Hydrostatique et L'Hydraulique Pour Servir D'Introduction...* Paris: Chez Charles Antoine Jombert, 1741. First edition, 4 books in 1 volume, 4to., elaborate titlepage, 29 engraved plates, 2 allegorical headpieces, engraved and drawn by C. Cochin & Son, original mottled calf, joints cracked, cords holding, extremities quite worn, badly waterstained throughout, as is. Jeff Weber Rare Books 183 - 16 2016 $275

Deighton, Len *The Complete Harry Palmer Novels.* London: Hodder & Stoughton and Jonathan Cape, 1962-1966. First editions, 4 volumes, crown 8vo., original boards, backstrips lettered in gilt with very slight lean to spine of first volume, designs stamped to upper board of all but first volume and illustrated endpapers to same, small bump to bottom corner of upper board of third volume, small patches of offsetting from adhesive tape to free endpapers of second volume, first issue dust jacket with that of final volume little rubbed and crinkled as often found and with two small holes to front flap, dust jacket to second volume price clipped with very minor chipping to corners, very good. Blackwell's Rare Books B184 - 133 2016 £1000

Deighton, Len *An Expensive Place to Die.* London: Jonathan Cape, 1967. First edition, crown 8vo., original black boards, backstrip lettered gilt and slightly softened at head, illustrated endpaper with small amount of adhesive residue to rear free endpaper, dust jacket price clipped with rubbing to extremities and gentle fading to backstrip panel, very good. Blackwell's Rare Books B184 - 134 2016 £100

Deighton, Len *London Dossier.* London: Jonathan Cape, 1967. First edition, crown 8vo., original red boards, backstrip lettered gilt, illustrated endpapers, dust jacket with touch of rubbing at corners and gentlest of fading to backstrip panel, near fine. Blackwell's Rare Books B184 - 135 2016 £100

Deighton, Len *London Match.* London: Hutchinson, 1985. First edition, 8vo., original black boards, backstrip lettered silver with slight lean, red endpapers, dust jacket with gentlest of fading to backstrip panel, very good, signed by author. Blackwell's Rare Books B184 - 136 2016 £70

Delacroix, Henry *Decoration Moderne Dans L'Interieur.* Paris: Editions Art et Architecture, circa, 1925. First edition, oblong quarto, cloth spine portfolio with printed paper over boards with ribbon ties, containing two leaves of text, titlepage, 48 beautifully colored pochoir plates laid in loose as issued, tears along the spine edges, age toning and fading at extremities of portfolio and slight toning in margins (only) of plates, very tiny tears at top margins of plates, overall very good or better, internally near fine. Between the Covers Rare Books 208 - 40 2016 $2600

Deland, Margaret *The Old Garden and Other Verses.* Boston: Houghton Mifflin, 1886. First edition, small 8vo., first issue of author's first book with her signed poem on card laid in, titlepage, bound in original white vellum spine, decoratively printed silk sides, gilt lettering, top edge gilt, cover little browned and worn at edges, slight tear at inside edge of flyleaf, but very good, tight copy. Second Life Books, Inc. 196A - 400 2016 $250

Deland, Margaret *The Old Garden.* Boston: Houghton Mifflin, 1894. first US edition, Owner inscription dated 1893, 8vo., pictorial cloth, colors on covers rubbed, else very good, printed on French-fold paper and illustrated in color on every page by Walter Crane, laid in is 3 page handwritten letter to Sydney Cockerell, from Crane, dated August 1892 with mailing envelope. Aleph-bet Books, Inc. 112 - 123 2016 $750

Delandes, Andre Francois *The Art of Being Easy at all Times and in all Places.* London: printed for C. Rivington at the Bible and Crown, 1724. Second edition, 12mo., leading pastedown not laid down, contemporary half sheep, worn but sound, signature of Ch. Milner & label of Alfred Viscount Milner. Jarndyce Antiquarian Books CCXV - 157 2016 £650

Delany, Patrick *Revelation Examin'd with Candour or a Four Enquiry into the Sense and Use of the Several Revelations....* London: printed for C. Rivington at the Bible and Crown in St. Paul's Church Yard, 1732. First edition, Volume II only of III, 8vo., head and tailpieces, some leaves bit wrinkled or stained, original blindstamped paneled calf with five raised bands and gilt stamped maroon spine label, worn, joints racked but holding, ink ownership signature, bookplate of Hartford Seminary Foundation, good, scarce. Jeff Weber Rare Books 181 - 13 2016 $150

Delany, Samuel R. *Atlantis: Three Tales.* Seattle: Incunabula, 1995. first edition, #297 of 334 copies signed by author, fine in dust jacket. Second Life Books, Inc. 196A - 406 2016 $75

Delany, Samuel R. *Nova.* Garden City: Doubleday, 1968. Book Club?, 8vo., author's presentation on title, paper over boards, edges of cover slightly scuffed, otherwise very good tight copy in price clipped somewhat soiled, nicked and scuffed dust jacket. Second Life Books, Inc. 196A - 407 2016 $65

Delany, Samuel R. *They Fly at Ciron.* Seattle: Incunabula, 1993. First edition, 8vo., fine in dust jacket with 'autographed' sticker on front of dust jacket, signed by author on half title. Second Life Books, Inc. 196A - 408 2016 $65

Delille, Jacques *L'Homme des Champs ou les Georgiques Francoises.... (bound with) Dithyrame sur l'Immoralite de l'Ame, Suivi du Passage du St. Gothard....* Basel: Chez Jacques Decker, 1800. Paris: Chez Giguet et Michaud, 1802. First editions, first work, 4 plates, dampstaining throughout at tail of gutter margin, some browning, second work with frontispiece, bound together, 12mo., contemporary dark blue straight grain morocco, smooth backstrip divided by double gilt rules, second compartment gilt letter direct, single gilt rule on sides, gilt ball roll on board edges and turn-ins, marbled endpapers, touch of rubbing to joints, very good, bookplate of Sir Gore Ouseley, Baronet. Blackwell's Rare Books B186 - 51 2016 £150

Delillo, Don *Americana.* Boston: Houghton Company, 1971. First edition, small very faint sticker shadow on front pastedown, else fine in dust jacket with short tear on front panell that displays old tape repair shadow, visible mostly on inside of jacket, else very good or better. Between the Covers Rare Books 208 - 20 2016 $350

Delisle, Leopold *Histoire Generale De Paris: le Cabinet des Manuscrits De La Bibliotheque Imperiale.* Paris: Imprimerie Imperiale, 1858. Folio, 4 volumes, half cloth, marbled paper covered boards, 51 facsimile plates, covers rubbed and scuffed at edges, bumped at corners. Oak Knoll Books 310 - 180 2016 $750

Dell, Floyd *An Unmarried Father, a Novel.* New York: Doran, 1927. First edition, 8vo., inscribed by author, front hinge loose. Second Life Books, Inc. 196A - 409 2016 $75

Dell, Floyd *Women as World Builders, Studies in Modern Feminism.* Chicago: Forbes, 1913. First edition, 8vo., original olive green cloth stamped in gilt, little wear at top of spine, near fine, scarce. Second Life Books, Inc. 197 - 65 2016 $225

Delord, Taxile *Les Fluers Animees.* Paris: Garnier Freres, 1867. New edition, 2 volumes, 4to., publisher's green leather spine and cloth, all edges gilt, light cover rubbing, faint corner stain on first few leaves of volume one else, tight, clean, very good+ set, 50 magnificent hand colored plates plus 2 hand colored titlepages, by J. J. Grandville, bright and beautiful.   Aleph-bet Books, Inc. 112 - 221   2016 $2000

Demeunier, Jean Nicolas *L'Esprit des Usages et des Coutumes des Differens Peuples, on Observations Tirees des Voyagers & des Historens.*   Londres: Paris: Chez Pissot, 1776. First edition, 3 volumes, 8vo., half titles, title woodcut vignettes, head and tailpieces, original full mottled calf, decorative gilt stamped spine, raised bands, marbled endpapers and edges, joints cracked but holding head and tail worn, head portion missing on volume 3, later shelf sticker on spine foot, ownership signature of C. Francis 1836 and rubber ink and blind embossed stamps on first and last few pages, good, rare.   Jeff Weber Rare Books   181 - 14   2016 $450

Deming, Richard *The Careful Man.*   London: Allen, 1962. First edition, small spot on fore-edge, otherwise fine in dust jacket.   Mordida Books   2015 - 012646   2016 $65

Deming, Therese *Red Folk and Wild Folk with Indian Folk Lore Stories.*   New York: Frederick Stokes, Sept., 1902. 4to., yellow cloth, pictorial paste-on, slight soil, else fine, this copy inscribed and signed by author and artist (Edwin Deming), 12 color plates plus many half tones in text, printed on coated paper, rare inscribed.   Aleph-bet Books, Inc. 111 - 117   2016 $400

Demonferrand, Jean Fermin *Manuel d'Electricite Dynamique ou Traite sur l'Action Mutuelle des Conducteurs Electriques et des Aimans et sur une Nouvelle Theorie du Magnetisme...*   Paris: Bachelier, 1823. First edition, 8vo., five folding engraved plates, light scattered foxing, overall in very good plus condition, handsomely bound in modern calf over marbled boards with gilt stamped spine label, corners rubbed, spine carefully repaired with ends missing small pieces, endpapers renewed, some light foxing to half titlepage and occasional small light brown spot scattered in text, overall interior is in near fine condition, scarce.   Jeff Weber Rare Books   183 - 17   2016 $750

Demosthenes *Selectae Demosthenis Orationes: Quarum Titulos Versa Indicabit Pagina.*   Typis J. Redmayne, 1672. Pocket edition, Large but faint dampmark appearing intermittently, scattering of pinprick wormholes in fore margin of few leaves, occasional underlining or marginal marks in pencil and red crayon, 12mo., original sheep, boards bordered in blind with cornerpieces also in blind, pastedowns from printed work in Italian, somewhat scuffed, small patch of wear to edge of rear board, front flyleaf partly torn away, shelfmark in pink to foot of spine, good.   Blackwell's Rare Books   Greek & Latin Classics VII - 16   2016   £250

Dempsey, G. Drysdale *The Practical Railway Engineeer.* London: John Weale, 1847. First edition, 286 x 291mm., excellent recent retrospective grained calf, raised bands, red morocco label, 50 double page copper engravings showing railway plans, equipment and environmental contexts, as called for, handwritten card with a graph and calculations titled "Stationary Engine Minoris Terminus Blackwall Railway" mounted, plates little browned at edges, about half of them with minor foxing (more conspicuous on the final two plates), occasional minor smudges, thumbing or short marginal tears, otherwise really excellent copy, internally quite fresh and in unworn, attractive binding.   Phillip J. Pirages   67 - 299   2016 $950

Dempsey, Jack *Dempsey.*   New York: Simon and Schuster, 1960. First edition, inscribed by Dempsey to Miss Cordelia, near fine in very good, price clipped dust jacket, toning to extremities, tiny chips and tears at jacket edges, fading to spine and faint stains on front panel. Royal Books   48 - 80   2016 $325

Denby, Edwin H. *Symposium Lincolniana.*   New York: Coq d'or Press, 1942. Limited edition, #140 of special edition of 400 copies, tall quarto or perhaps folio, gilt stamped, handbound, illustrations, affixed slip by publisher with glue shadow verso of slip, moderate wear of extremities of covers, very good.   Gene W. Baade, Books on the West   2015 - 5003049   2016 $61

Dennis, Clarence Michael James Stanislaus *The Singing Garden.*   Australia: Angus & Robertson, 1935. First edition, good to fair copy, illustrations.   Simon Finch 2015 - 012678   2016 $222

Dennis, George *A Summer in Andalucia.*   London: Richard Bentley, 1839. First edition, 2 volumes, 8vo., 2 sepia frontispieces (waterstaining to margin of frontispiece volume II), original black blindstamped cloth, small splits to joints of both volumes.   J. & S. L. Bonham Antiquarian Booksellers   Europe 2016 - 9732   2016   £2000

Denny, Henry *Monographia Pselaphidarum et Scydmaenidarum Britanniae...*   Norwich: S. Wilkin, 1825. 8vo. in 4's, 14 hand colored plates, small paper flaw to p. 3, uncut in original olive green cloth, paper label, signature of Erasmus Wilson, March 1922, very nice.   Jarndyce Antiquarian Booksellers   CCXVII - 85   2016   £450

Denslow, W. W. *Billy Bounce.*   Chicago: Donahue, 1913. 8vo., blue cloth, pictorial paste-on, slight cover soil, near fine, 16 vibrant color plates and black and whites in text by Denslow.   Aleph-bet Books, Inc.   112 - 141   2016 $275

Denslow, W. W. *Denslow's Mother Goose.* New York: McClure Phillips Co., 1901. First edition, 2nd issue, 4to., cloth backed pictorial boards, edges and covers rubbed, else clean, tight and very good+ in original pictorial dust jacket chipped at corner folds, (missing 1 1/2 inch piece off spine with some other chipping, overall very good), this is the Schiller auction copy, this copy with large signature of Denslow plus Seahorse drawing,. Aleph-bet Books, Inc. 112 - 140   2016 $8000

Depew, Chauncey Mitchell *Oration by Hon. Chauncey M. Depew at the Unveiling of the Bartholdi Statue of Liberty Enlightening the World Oct. 28 1886.* New York: n.p., 1886. First edition, small 4to., leaf of plates, three quarter red morocco over marbled boards, very good, splits to joints at head, hinges neatly reinforced, boards rubbed, original wrappers bound in, bookplate, contents crisp. Kaaterskill Books   21 - 29   2016 $450

Derleth, August *Bright Journey.* New York: Charles Scribner's, 1940. First edition, signed by author, map endpapers, black cloth lettered gilt and green, fine with lightly worn pictorial dust jacket. Argonaut Book Shop   Literature 2015 - 472   2016 $75

Derleth, August *No Future for Luana.* Muller, 1948. Very good.   I. D. Edrich   Crime - 2016   £50

Derleth, August *Someone in the Dark.* Sauk City: Arkham House, 1941. First edition, first printing, 1115 copies, octavo cloth, presentation from author to M. P. Shiel, inscribed again by author for Major P. H. Rixey, some tanning to front endpapers, rear endpaper has tape residue to edges and rear paste down has the bookplate of P. H. Rixey affixed to it, top page edges dusty, upper front right corner little bumped, about very good in very good dust jacket which has small tear with wrinkle and small piece missing at upper right front panel affecting the edge of the "E" in title lettering SOMEONE, some light rubs to corner tips and spine ends, some tanning to edges of rear panel.   John W. Knott, Jr./L.W. Currey, Inc.   Fall-Winter 2015 - 16236   2016 $2500

Derleth, August *Travellers by Night.* London: Victor Gollancz, 1968. First UK edition, octavo, on contents page someone has made an ink mark next to one of the titles, head of spine slightly bumped, near fine in very good dust jacket nicked and creased at top edge, bit tanned at spine and with some faint signs of damp, uncommon. Peter Ellis 112 - 99   2016   £35

Derriere le Miroir 133/134. Der Blaue Reiter. Paris: Maeght, 1962. Limited first edition, number 43 of ony 150 copies printed on Velin de Rives, several reproductions, including 2 double page color lithographs after Kandinsky and 1 single page color lithograph after Rousseau, folio, lithographed wrappers, original bound chemise and slipcase. Manhattan Rare Book Company   2016 - 1541   2016 $1100

Derriere Le Miroir: Francis Bacon. Special Issue No. 162. Paris: Maeght, 1966. Limited edition, one of 150 copies on Velin de Rives, folio loose sheets in original pictorial wrappers (as issued), original box and chemise fine, spine fading and touch of wear to box and chemise, beautiful copy, rare. Manhattan Rare Book Company   2016 - 1779   2016 $3000

Desault, P. G. *Lezioni Sopra le Malattie delle vie Orinaris del Signor P. G. Desault Chirugo Primario nel Grande Ospizio d'Umanita di Parigi Estratte dal suo Giornate di Chirurgis...* Napoli: Presso Gaetano Raimondi, 1802. Small 8vo., 2 volumes, covers slightly soiled, lower margins of first two leaves wormed, not affecting text, very good, contemporary vellum, red and green spine labels.   Edwin V. Glaser Rare Books   2015 - 10133   2016 $200

Descartes, Rene *Les Principes de la Philosophie.* Paris: Chez Theodore Girard...., 1668. 4to., engraved title, woodcut illustration, one folding table, contemporary full sprinkled calf, spine gilt in compartments and with raised bands, some minor expertly executed repairs to spine and extremities, very good.   Jarndyce Antiquarian Booksellers   CCXVII - 86   2016   £1250

Deshields, James T. *Tall Men with Long Rifles.* San Antonio: Naylor Co., 1935. First edition, limited to 500 copies signed by author, 8vo., cloth, frontispiece, illustrations, page edges uniformly browned, else very good. Buckingham Books   2015 - 20693   2016 $450

Desinger, Kevin *The Descent of Man.* Unbridled Books, 2011. First edition, cloth and boards, signed by author, fine, like new in dust jacket.   Gene W. Baade, Books on the West   2015 - 5015046   2016 $45

Deslandes, Andre Francois *The Art of Being Easy at all Times and in all Places.* London: printed for C. Rivington at the Bible and Crown, 1724. First edition, 12mo., without half title and final blank but with initial blank leaf, some old waterstaining to edges of first few leaves and neat endpapers and lower margins of main text contemporary unlettered calf, slight wear to head of spine, note on endpaper "Andrew Wilson - Owner 1730".   Jarndyce Antiquarian Books   CCXV - 156   2016   £1100

Desmond, Hugh *Bluebeard's Wife.* Wright & Brown, n.d., Dust jacket chipped and defective at foot of spine, internally very good.   I. D. Edrich   Crime - 2016   £35

Destruction of Life by Snakes, Hydrophobia, etc. in Western India. London: W. H. Allen, 1880. Dudodecimo, publisher's green cloth with titles, few blemishes otherwise very good, rare. Andrew Isles Natural History Books   55 - 36183 2016 $500

Detaille, Edouard *Les Grandes Manoeuvres de l'Armee Russe.* Paris: Boussod, Valadon & cie and Saitn Petersburg, Velten, 1886. First edition, imperial folio, original grey half cloth over printed boards with vignette, 6 full page wood engravings and vignette on title, boards little worn and spotted, offsetting from endpapers to half title and much less to title and to last leaf, inoffensive crease marks to upper outer corners, very rare.   Sotheran's   Travel and Exploration - 235   2016   £995

Deutsche Kunst und Dekoration. Darmstadt: Verlaganstalt Alexander Koch, 1897-1900. Volumes 1, 2, 3, 6, 4to., original binding of decorated cloth, spines faded with wear, front hinge volume 2 broken, plates, some in full color.   Oak Knoll Books   310 - 32   2016 $750

Deutsche Menschen. Eine Folge Von Briefen. Luzern: Vita Nova Verlag, 1936. First edition, one of 2000 copies, 8vo., original cloth, presentation copy inscribed by Walter Benjamin for film maker Hans Richter, rare, inmportant association copy, buff linen lightly soiled, otherwise very good, rare inscribed.   James S. Jaffe Rare Books Occasional List: Winter 2016 - 31   2016 $27,500

Devereux, C., Captain, Pseud. *Venus in India or Love Adventures in Hindustan.* Carnopolis, 1898. Later edition, 2 volumes in 1, contemporary full maroon morocco sides with gilt fillet spine in compartments, raised bands decorated, lettered and dated in gilt, inner dentelles and all edges gilt, silk endpapers, short trivial tear to flyleaf, very nice, scarce edition, sumptuously bound.   Bertram Rota Ltd. February List 2016 - 15   2016   £400

Devine, John *Pentacle.* London: Hale, 1991. First edition, fine in dust jacket.   Mordida Books   2015 - 011826   2016 $65

Devlin, Frank *Reynard Found Out: a Review of the Underworld by a Revolted Wage Slave.* Glasgow/Vienna: L. Whitberg/H. Wagner, 1925. First edition, 12mo., quarter olive cloth and drab printed in black over boards, cheap paper of text little toned, smudging and slight stains on boards, else very good, inscribed by author.   Between the Covers Rare Books   204 - 63   2016 $600

Dewey, Sherman *Account of a Hail Storm which Fell on Part of the Towns of Lebanon, Bozzrah and Franklin on the 15th of July 1799...* Walpole: press of Thomas & Thorne by David Carlisle for the author, 1799. First edition, 12mo., sewn, minor fraying, browned and title stained.   M & S Rare Books, Inc.   99 - 75   2016 $375

Dewhurst, Kenneth *Dr. Thomas Sydenham (1624-1689). His Life and Original writings.* London: Wellcome, 1966. Frontispiece, illustrations, original binding, as new in dust jacket.   James Tait Goodrich   X-78 - 521   2016 $65

Dexter, Colin *Last Bus to Woodstock.* Macmillan, 1975. First edition, few pages browned as usual, crown 8vo., original terra cotta boards, backstrip lettered in black, ownership inscription to flyleaf, dust jacket with owner's shelfmark to front flap, relevant clipping from Oxford Journal laid in, very good, unusually bright.   Blackwell's Rare Books   B184 - 137   2016   £700

Dexter, Colin *Last Seen Wearing.* London: Macmillan, 1976. First edition, pages lightly toned as usual, crown 8vo., original blue boards, backstrip lettered black, very small bump at foot, few faint spots to top edge, ownership inscription, dust jacket with owner's shelfmark, very good. Blackwell's Rare Books   B184 - 138   2016   £500

Dexter, Colin *The Riddle of the Third Mile.* Macmillan, 1983. First edition, foolscap 8vo., unusually faint browning to poor quality paper, original grey boards, backstrip lettered in silver, fine.   Blackwell's Rare Books   B186 - 200   2016 £175

Dexter, Colin *The Silent World of Nicholas Quinn.* London: Macmillan, 1977. First edition, full page diagram, crown 8vo., original black boards, backstrip lettered in white, very light foxing to top edge and one small spot to foreedge, ownership inscription, dust jacket with owner's shelfmark to front flap, very good, splendid copy.   Blackwell's Rare Books   B184 - 139   2016   £700

Dexter, Pete *Brotherly Love.* Franklin Center: Franklin Library, 1991. Limited first edition, signed by author, bound in blue leather, lettered and stamped in gilt, all edges gilt, very fine, as new.   Argonaut Book Shop   Literature 2015 - 3962   2016 $50

Dexter, Walter *The England of Dickens.* London: Cecil Palmer, 1925. First edition, half title, frontispiece, plates, uncut in original dark blue cloth, spine lettered gilt, booklabel, very good.   Jarndyce Antiquarian Booksellers CCXVIII - 1135   2016   £35

Dexter, Walter *The Kent of Dickens.* London: Cecil Palmer, 1924. First edition, half title, frontispiece, plates, uncut in original dark blue cloth, spine lettered gilt, booklabel, very good.   Jarndyce Antiquarian Booksellers CCXVIII - 1156   2016   £20

Dexter, Walter *The London of Dickens.* London: Cecil Palmer, 1924. Second edition, half title. 2 pages ads, uncut in original green vertical grained cloth, front board and spine lettered in black, little faded, good plus.   Jarndyce Antiquarian Booksellers   CCXVIII - 1157   2016   £25

Dexter, Walter *The London of Dickens.* London: Cecil Palmer, 1930. Third & pocket edition, half title, original brown embossed cloth, booklabel on leading pastedown obscuring excised booklabel, very good, signed by author for J. W. Lynne. Jarndyce Antiquarian Booksellers CCXVIII - 1158 2016 £20

Di Lampedusa, Giuseppe *The Leopard.* London: Colins and Harvill Press, 1960. First edition in English, crown 8vo., original mid green cloth, backstrip gilt lettered, dust jacket, bookplate, hint of fading to spine, very good, splendid copy. Blackwell's Rare Books B184 - 140 2016 £300

Di Prima, Diana *Holocene Gazette & County Traveller #1.* Hanover: Center for Paleocybernetic Research, 1970. Presumed first, and only edition, fine copy, uncommon. Jeff Hirsch Books Holiday List 2015 - 34 2016 $200

The Dial: a Magazine of Literature, Philosophy and Religion. Volume 1 no. 1 - July 1840 through volume I no. 4 April 1841. Boston: Weeks, Jordan, London, Wiley and Putnam, 1841. First edition, 8vo., lacks original wrappers, bound in later three quarter maroon morocco by W. Roach of NY, top edge gilt, some foxing and staining, very good, 4 issues, very scarce. Second Life Books, Inc. 197 - 255 2016 $2200

The Dial: a Magazine of Literature, Philosophy and Religion. Volume II no. 1-July 1841 through Volume II no. 4 - april 1842. Boston: Elizabeth Palmer Peabody and London: John Green, 1842. First edition, 8vo., lacks original wrappers, bound in later three quarter maroon morocco by W. Roach of New York with Index, top edge gilt, nice, clean copy, fine, 4 issues, very scarce. Second Life Books, Inc. 197 - 254 2016 $2200

A Dialogue. What! are you in tears again? N.P.: n.p., but ?London, circa, 1750. Outer leaves bit stained, 8vo., loose, disbound. Blackwell's Rare Books B186 - 143 2016 £250

Dialogue. Journal des Livres et des Idees No. 3. Lausanne: September, 1967. Folio, original self wrappers, printed on all sides, light overall toning, quarter folded with horizontal points starting, from the library of actor Douglas Fairbanks Jr. with his loose bookplate in separate envelope, very good, warmly inscribed to Ezra Pound by Piero Sanavio. Blackwell's Rare Books B186 - 274 2016 £650

Diaper, William *The Complete Works of William Diaper.* London: Routledge and Kegan Paul, 1951, i.e., 1952. First edition, small octavo, frontispiece, near fine in near fine dust jacket slightly creased at head of spine. Peter Ellis 112 - 100 2016 £65

Dias, Carlos Malheiro *Historia Da Colonizacao Portugues Do Brasil.* Porto: Litografia Nacional, 1921. First edition, folio, original cloth backed decorated paper covered boards, color plates, tipped-in plates, facsimiles, wear along edges, tear in cloth along front hinge volume two, tear in cloth along back hinge volume three. Oak Knoll Books 310 - 286 2016 $750

Dibdin, Michael *Caval.* London: Faber & Faber, 1992. First edition, specially packaged with promotional copy of author's earlier novel, blue cloth with silver lettering on spine, very fine in pictorial dust jacket. Argonaut Book Shop Literature 2015 - 4718 2016 $65

Dibdin, Michael *Dirty Tricks.* London: Faber, 1991. First edition, fine in dust jacket, signed by author. Mordida Books 2015 - 011076 2016 $65

Dibdin, Thomas Frognall 1776-1847 *A Bibliographical Antiquarian and Picturesque Tour in the Northern Counties of England and Scotland.* London: printed for the author by C. Richards, 1838. First edition, 2 volumes, 251 x 156mm., list of subscribers in volume 1, handsome early 20th century red morocco gilt by Matthews (stamp-signed on front turn-in), covers with gilt French fillet border enclosing a simple lobed panel, raised bands, spines very attractively gilt in compartments with spiral cornerpieces and centerpiece featuring either a fleur-de-lys, a manuscript scroll and quill or Dibdin's cipher, gilt inner dentelles, marbled endpapers, all edges gilt, numerous engravings in text, and 44 engraved plates as called for, tiniest bit of rubbing to joints and corners, minor foxing (mostly marginal) to all but a handful of plates, otherwise, especially pleasing set in fine condition, text clean and bright and decorative bindings very lustrous with almost no signs of use. Phillip J. Pirages 67 - 55 2016 $2250

Dibdin, Thomas Frognall 1776-1847 *Bibliotheca Spenceriana or a Descriptive Catalogue of the Books Printed in the Fifteenth Century...in the Library of George John Earl Spencer (with) Supplement to the Bibliotheca Spenceriana. (with) Aedes Althorpianae; or an Account of the Mansion, Books and Pictures at Althorp (with A Descriptive Catalogue of the Books printed in the Fifteenth Century, Lately forming Part of the Library of the Duke of Dassano Serra and now the Property of George John Earl Spencer.* London: for the author by Shakespeare Press, 1814-1815. 1822-1823, 7 volumes, 4to., profusely illustrated with engraved plates, hundreds of facsimiles of early woodcuts and type, some printed in color, modern full tan morocco, richly gilt, covers with central arms and cornerpieces within two-line fillet, board edges and turn-ins gilt, spines fully gilt in compartments by Edmund Worrall of Birmingham, with his ticket in each volume, engraved plates mostly toned and offset to facing pages, some minor text offsetting, few random gatherings (maybe 12-15 leaves in all), very heavily foxed, else very good set in very fine, fresh bindings. Joseph J. Felcone, Inc. Books from Five Centuries: a Miscellany - 55 2016 $2800

Dibdin, Thomas Frognall 1776-1847 *An Introduction to the Knowledge of Rare and Valuable Editions of the Greek and Latin Classics.* London: printed for Harding & Lepard, 1827. Fourth edition, 2 volumes, 292 x 1977, handsome early 20th century brown straight grain morocco, covers with gilt double fillet border, fleuron cornerpieces, raised bands, spines richly gilt with panels dominated by bold and complex quatrefoil incorporating spade-like tools and with palmette cornerpieces, turn-ins with two gilt fillets, marbled endpapers, all edges gilt, with facsimile of Greek and Latin text from the Complutensian Polyglot and volume I with specimen leaf laid down, as called for, large paper copy, engraved armorial bookplate of John William Pease, rear pastedown with vellum armorial bookplate of Lord Wardington, touch of rubbing to tail edge of boards, one leaf with thin band of soiling along four inches of the fore edge, light glue stain at lower corner of specimen leaf, endpapers with faint fox spots (isolated minor foxing elsewhere), other trivial imperfections but generally, very fine, text clean and fresh with vast margins and decorative bindings with no significant wear.   Phillip J. Pirages   67 - 112   2016 $4500

Dibdin, Thomas Frognall 1776-1847 *The Library Companion or the Young Man's Guide and the Old Man's Comfort in the Choice of a Library.* printed for Harding, Triphook and Legard, 1824. First edition, 8vo., 2 volumes, contemporary full polished calf with gilt and blind panels to boards, both volumes rebacked preserving original spines, little rubbing and scratching to boards, otherwise very good, from the library of Murray A. W. Newman with his bookplate and ownership signature.   Sotheran's   Piccadilly Notes - Summer 2015 - 104   2016   £250

Dick Whittington and His Cat. New York: Scribner, 1950. First edition, 4to., pictorial cloth, fine in nice dust jacket, rubbed at fold with piece missing from spine ends, wonderful linoleum cuts by Marcia Brown, inscribed by Brown.   Aleph-bet Books, Inc.   111 - 56   2016 $750

Dick, Francis *Proof.* London: M. Joseph, 1984. Uncorrected proof copy, in original wrappers, slightly frayed dust jacket.   I. D. Edrich   Crime - 2016   £20

Dick, Philip K. *The Collected Stories of Philip K. Dick.* Los Angeles: Columbia: Underwood Miller, 1987. First edition, one of 500 numbered sets, this one of 400 bound in cloth, octavo, five volumes, laid in is leaflet (single sheet folded to make four pages), fine set in cloth slipcase.   John W. Knott, Jr./L.W. Currey, Inc.   Fall-Winter 2015 - 16485   2016 $750

Dick, Philip K. *Deus Irae.* Garden City: Doubleday & Co., 1976. First edition, octavo, boards, signed by author, fine (no remainder spray) in fine dust jacket with light tanning to spine panel.   John W. Knott, Jr./L.W. Currey, Inc.   Fall-Winter 2015 - 18566   2016 $3000

Dick, Philip K. *Dr. Bloodmoney or How We Got Long After the Bomb.* Boston: Gregg, 1977. First hardcover edition, octavo, cloth, fine.   John W. Knott, Jr./L.W. Currey, Inc.   Fall-Winter 2015 - 16451   2016 $1500

Dick, Philip K. *The Man in the High Castle.* New York: G. P. Putnam's Sons, 1962. First edition, octavo, cloth, publisher's review slip laid in, fine in fine dust jacket with slight stress crease to upper right rear corner with slight soiling to rear spine fold, sharp copy.   John W. Knott, Jr./L.W. Currey, Inc.   Fall-Winter 2015 - 17002   2016 $4500

Dick, Philip K. *The Man in the High Castle.* New York: G. P. Putnam, 1980. Book club edition, 8vo., signed and inscribed by author, fine in fine dust jacket.   By the Book, L. C.   45 - 71   2016 $1750

Dick, Philip K. *Solar Lottery.* Boston: Gregg Press, 1976. First edition, 8vo., fine, green cloth, gilt lettered spine.   By the Book, L. C.   45 - 70   2016 $1250

A Dickens Chronology and Family Tree. London: Dickens House, 1984. Illustrations, stapled as issued, original yellow printed wrappers, very good.   Jarndyce Antiquarian Booksellers   CCXVIII - 1160   2016   £20

Dickens, Al *Uncle Yah Yah.* Detroit: Harlo Press, 1976. First edition, octavo, ordering information rubbert stamped on endpapers, else fine in lightly rubbed, near fine dust jacket, scarce.   Between the Covers Rare Books   202 - 28   2016 $350

Dickens, Charles 1768-1833 *The Life of Charles James Mathews chiefly autobiographical..* London: Macmillan, 1879. First edition, 2 volumes, half titles, frontispiece, 39 page catalog volume I (March 1879) original dark green cloth, slightly dulled, very good.   Jarndyce Antiquarian Booksellers   CCXVIII - 882   2016   £60

Dickens, Charles 1812-1870 *Address Delivered at the Birmingham and Midland Institute on the 27th September 1869.* Birmingham: printed by Josiah Allen, Jun., 1869. First edition, original pale green printed wrappers, slightly spotted.   Jarndyce Antiquarian Booksellers   CCXVIII - 638   2016   £300

Dickens, Charles 1812-1870 *All the Year Round.* London: Wellington Street No. 2, 1859-1868. Complete first series, 20 volumes, contemporary half dark green calf, blue cloth sides, maroon labels, one label missing, several others slightly chipped, spines defective on two volumes, one volume with boards loose, little rubbed but internally clean, good plus working copy.   Jarndyce Antiquarian Booksellers   CCXVIII - 811   2016   £800

Dickens, Charles 1812-1870 *Reisenotizen uber Amerika. (American Notes for General Circulation).* Stuttgart: Verlag von Adoloph Krabbs, 1842. Probable first German edition, Some spotting, slightly later half dark blue morocco, gilt bands, green label, small split at head of leading hinge, good plus. Jarndyce Antiquarian Booksellers CCXVIII - 324 2016 £90

Dickens, Charles 1812-1870 *American Notes for General Circulation.* Leipzig: Bernhard Tauchnitz, 1842. Half title, contemporary half red morocco, red patterned cloth sides, gilt spine, slightly rubbed, very good. Jarndyce Antiquarian Booksellers CCXVIII - 320 2016 £90

Dickens, Charles 1812-1870 *American Notes for General Circulation.* London: Chapman & Hall, 1842. First edition, first issue, 2 volumes, half titles, ad leaf preceding half title volume I, original purple cloth, blocked in blind, spines lettered gilt, expertly recased, spines faded to brown, Kathleen Tillotson's copy. Jarndyce Antiquarian Booksellers CCXVIII - 317 2016 £850

Dickens, Charles 1812-1870 *American Notes for General Circulation.* London: Chapman and Hall, 1842. First edition, first issue, 2 volumes, half titles, ad leaf preceding half title volume I, glazed yellow endpapers, original purple cloth blocked in blind, spines lettered in gilt, some minimal dampstaining to prelims, armorial bookplate of H. C. Embleton volume II, later William Wapler bookplate in both volumes, very good in slipcase. Jarndyce Antiquarian Booksellers CCXVIII - 316 2016 £1600

Dickens, Charles 1812-1870 *American Notes for General Circulation.* London: Chapman and Hall, 1842. First edition, first issue, 2 volumes in 1, half title, volume I only with small tear in outer margin, contemporary half brown calf by Isacke of Edgware Rd., spine gilt in compartments, red and green leather labels, slightly chipped at head of spine , little rubbed, good plus. Jarndyce Antiquarian Booksellers CCXVIII - 318 2016 £250

Dickens, Charles 1812-1870 *American Notes for General Circulation.* London: Chapman & Hall, 1842. Second edition, 8vo., publisher's blindstamped cloth, gilt stamping on spine, cloth worn at extremities of spine, very good, clean copy. Second Life Books, Inc. 197 - 66 2016 $325

Dickens, Charles 1812-1870 *American Notes for General Circulation.* London: Chapman & Hall, 1855. Initial ad leaf, half title, frontispiece by C. Stanfield, 32 page catalog April 1858, original light green cloth, blocked in blind, gilt spine, spine slightly faded, good plus. Jarndyce Antiquarian Booksellers CCXVIII - 321 2016 £35

Dickens, Charles 1812-1870 *American Notes for General Circulation.* London: Chapman & Hall, 1878. Household edition, 4to., frontispiece and plate, illustrations by A. B. Frost and Gordon Thomson, original green cloth, blocked and lettered gilt, very good. Jarndyce Antiquarian Booksellers CCXVIII - 322 2016 £30

Dickens, Charles 1812-1870 *American Notes for General Circulation.* London: Chapman and Hall, circa, 1880. Charles Dickens edition, half title, frontispiece and 7 plates, original red cloth, borders blocked in blind, lettered gilt, very good. Jarndyce Antiquarian Booksellers CCXVIII - 323 2016 £25

Dickens, Charles 1812-1870 *Barnaby Rudge.* London: Chapman & Hall, 1871. Half title, illustrations by Cattermole and Phiz, handsomely bound in contemporary full dark green calf, double ruled borders gilt, spine gilt in compartments, red labels, very good, bright copy. Jarndyce Antiquarian Booksellers CCXVIII - 302 2016 £150

Dickens, Charles 1812-1870 *Barnaby Rudge.* London: Chapman & Hall, 1841. First separate edition, complete in one volume, illustrations by Cattermole and Phiz, original olive green cloth, borders blocked in blind, spine with blind compartments and lettered gilt, spine very slightly faded, booklabel of Leslie C. Staples, very good, bright copy. Jarndyce Antiquarian Booksellers CCXVIII - 297 2016 £1500

Dickens, Charles 1812-1870 *Barnaby Rudge.* London: Chapman & Hall, circa, 1845? Early edition, Complete in one volume, original olive green cloth, borders blocked in blind, spine with blind compartments and lettered gilt, little faded & marked, following hinge splitting, leading inner hinge cracked, good sound copy. Jarndyce Antiquarian Booksellers CCXVIII - 298 2016 £150

Dickens, Charles 1812-1870 *Barnaby Rudge.* London: Chapman & Hall, 1853. Cheap edition, frontispiece, few spots, original light green cloth blocked in bind, gilt spine faded to brown, slightly marked. Jarndyce Antiquarian Booksellers CCXVIII - 299 2016 £30

Dickens, Charles 1812-1870 *Barnaby Rudge.* Paris: Librairie de L'Hachette, 1858. 2 volumes, half title, slightly later half red cloth, black label, good, sound copy. Jarndyce Antiquarian Booksellers CCXVIII - 305 2016 £25

Dickens, Charles 1812-1870 *Barnaby Rudge.* London: Chapman & Hall, 1874. Household edition, 4to., half title, frontispiece, vignette title, illustrations by F. Barnard, original green cloth, lettered gilt, blocked in black, very good. Jarndyce Antiquarian Booksellers CCXVIII - 303 2016 £30

Dickens, Charles 1812-1870 *Barnaby Rudge.* London: Chapman & Hall, circa, 1880. Household edition, 4to., plates and illustrations, original dark green cloth lettered in gilt, blocked in black, slight rubbing.   Jarndyce Antiquarian Booksellers   CCXVIII - 304   2016   £25

Dickens, Charles 1812-1870 *The Battle of Life. A Love Story.* London: Bradbury & Evans, 1846. First edition, 2nd state of engraved title, woodcuts, small 8vo., original red cloth with gilt stamped lettering and cover design, all edges gilt, bright gilt, square and tight, period personal ownership of Susannah Davis dated 21st Dec. 1846, withal pleasing, near fine.   Tavistock Books   Bibliolatry - 6   2016 $1750

Dickens, Charles 1812-1870 *The Battle of Life.* London: Bradbury & Evans, 1846. First edition, fourth issue, half title, frontispiece, engraved title, illustrations, final ad leaf, original red vertical grained cloth, spine slightly rubbed and little faded, good plus.   Jarndyce Antiquarian Booksellers   CCXVIII - 385   2016   £250

Dickens, Charles 1812-1870 *The Battle of Life. A Love Story.* London: Bradbury & Evans, 1846. First edition, fourth issue, very good in original red cloth intricate blind-stamped borders detailed bright gilt vignette to cover and spine, boards lightly soiled with slight bumping to corners, minor wear to head and foot of spine with full gilt edges, interior tight and mostly clean with some light smudging in few areas, pages lightly browned, sporadic faint foxing, wood engraved frontispiece and titlepage and 11 engravings, book has been expertly rebacked with repair hardly noticeable, slight cock to spine, very good.   The Kelmscott Bookshop   12 - 35   2016 $375

Dickens, Charles 1812-1870 *The Battle of Life.* London: Bradbury & Evans, 1846. First edition, 2nd issue, half title, frontispiece, engraved title, illustrations, final ad leaf, original red vertical grained cloth, blocked and lettered gilt, head of spine slightly worn, front board with few tiny ink spots, all edges gilt, good plus in primary binding.   Jarndyce Antiquarian Booksellers   CCXVIII - 374   2016   £650

Dickens, Charles 1812-1870 *The Battle of Life.* London: A. & F. Pears, 1912. Pears Centenary edition, half title, frontispiece and illustrations, original tan cloth, oval red onlay, very good.   Jarndyce Antiquarian Booksellers   CCXVIII - 386   2016   £35

Dickens, Charles 1812-1870 *Bleak House.* London: Bradbury & Evans, 1852-1853. First edition, xx original parts in xix, original pale blue printed wrappers, generally well preserved with some minor repair work in places, two of three backstrips expertly replaced, following wrapper to part in xix/xx repaired in lower inner margin, earlier parts with signature of F. Antrobus and label of Ingalton, the Eton bookseller, nice, clean set in custom made maroon morocco box.   Jarndyce Antiquarian Booksellers   CCXVIII - 500   2016   £3500

Dickens, Charles 1812-1870 *Bleak House.* London: Bradbury & Evans, 1853. First edition, frontispiece and engraved title little browned, plates by Phiz, contemporary half dark green calf, spine with raised gilt bands, maroon leather label, corners little knocked, good plus.   Jarndyce Antiquarian Booksellers   CCXVIII - 505   2016   £380

Dickens, Charles 1812-1870 *Bleak House.* Philadelphia: Getz & Buck, 1853. Appears to be first American edition, Frontispiece, plates, uncut in original pale green printed wrappers, slightly worn in upper and lower margins, contemporary signature of H. P. Hubbell (?) NY.   Jarndyce Antiquarian Booksellers   CCXVIII - 515   2016   £450

Dickens, Charles 1812-1870 *Bleak House.* London: Bradbury & Evans, 1853. First edition, primary binding variant, with date in Roman numerals at tail of spine, half title, frontispiece and engraved title, plates, occasional very slight offsetting, generally very clean and fresh, original olive green fine diaper cloth, blocked in blind, spine lettered gilt, very slightly faded, armorial bookplate of Clement Edward Hoyland with signature in pencil, very good.   Jarndyce Antiquarian Booksellers   CCXVIII - 501   2016   £2500

Dickens, Charles 1812-1870 *Bleak House.* London: Chapman and Hall, 1853. First edition, bound from parts, half title discarded, etched frontispiece with tissue guard, additional titlepage, 39 plates, but much less than usual browning to plates, 8vo., contemporary half dark green morocco spine gilt, marbled edges, slight wear to extremities, good.   Blackwell's Rare Books   B184 - 32   2016   £750

Dickens, Charles 1812-1870 *Bleak House. Oversat fra Engslek ..* Kjovenhavn: Pas F. H. Eibes Forlag, 1858. Danish edition, 2 volumes, final leaf volume II little dusted, later half morocco, brown cloth boards, very good.   Jarndyce Antiquarian Booksellers   CCXVIII - 516   2016   £150

Dickens, Charles 1812-1870 *Bleak House.* London: Bradbury Evans, circa, 1863? First edition, later issue, secondary binding, half title, frontispiece, engraved title, printed title, plates, original green fine diaper cloth blocked in blind, spine lettered gilt, spine very slightly dulled and rubbed, very good.   Jarndyce Antiquarian Booksellers   CCXVIII - 503   2016   £850

Dickens, Charles 1812-1870 *Bleak House.* London: Bradbury & Evans, circa, 1863? First edition, half title, frontispiece, engraved title, plates by Phiz, odd spot, contemporary half black calf by J. Edmond, Aberdeen, spine with raised gilt bands, devices in blind, morocco leather label, slightly rubbed, good plus, attractive.   Jarndyce Antiquarian Booksellers   CCXVIII - 503 2016   £450

Dickens, Charles 1812-1870 *Bleak House.* London: Chapman & Hall, 1865. Cheap edition, half title, frontispiece, slightly spotted, original dark green cloth, blocked in blind, spine blocked and lettered gilt, one or two tiny nicks at head and tail of spine, otherwise very good. Jarndyce Antiquarian Booksellers CCXVIII - 509 2016 £50

Dickens, Charles 1812-1870 *Bleak Hosue.* London: Chapman & Hall, 1873. Household edition, 4to., frontispiece, vignette title, plates and illustrations by F. Barnard, original green cloth, blocked and lettered in black and gilt, very good, later binding variant with address removed from front board. Jarndyce Antiquarian Booksellers CCXVIII - 510 2016 £65

Dickens, Charles 1812-1870 *Bleak House.* London: Chapman and Hall, W. R. Howell & Co., circa, 1875. Half title, frontispiece, engraved plates, slight spotting to prelims, contemporary half black sheep, slight rubbing at extremities. Jarndyce Antiquarian Booksellers CCXVIII - 511 2016 £65

Dickens, Charles 1812-1870 *Bleak House.* London: Chapman & Hall, circa, 1880. Frontispiece and engraved title, plates, contemporary half dark blue morocco, blue cloth, sides, spine lettered and with devices gilt, very good. Jarndyce Antiquarian Booksellers CCXVIII - 512 2016 £120

Dickens, Charles 1812-1870 *Bleak House.* London: Chapman & Hall, circa, 1890? Half title, frontispiece, engraved title and plates by Phiz, partially unopened in original olive green cloth, good plus. Jarndyce Antiquarian Booksellers CCXVIII - 513 2016 £75

Dickens, Charles 1812-1870 *Charles Dickens as editor. Being Letters Written by hi to William Henry Wills.* London: Smith, Elder & Co., 1912. First edition, half title, frontispiece, plates, original red cloth lettered in blind and gilt, spine faded, bookplate of W. Fay, good plus. Jarndyce Antiquarian Booksellers CCXVIII - 866 2016 £35

Dickens, Charles 1812-1870 *Charles Dickens to John Leech: Correspondence Now First Published.* privately printed by Walter Dexter, 1938. One of only 20 copies, illustrations, sewn as issued, original green linen wrappers, very good. Jarndyce Antiquarian Booksellers CCXVIII - 859 2016 £35

Dickens, Charles 1812-1870 *Charles Dickens to John Leech: Correspondence now first published.* London: privately printed by Walter Dexter, 1938. One of only 20 copies, sewn as issued, original green linen wrappers, very good. Jarndyce Antiquarian Booksellers CCXVIII - 758 2016 £35

Dickens, Charles 1812-1870 *A Child's Dream of a Star.* Boston: Fields, Osgood & Co., 1871. First book edition, half title, 11 full page engravings, original brick brown cloth, bevelled boards, pictorially blocked and lettered gilt with additional blocking in black, all edges gilt, very good, handsome. Jarndyce Antiquarian Booksellers CCXVIII - 700 2016 £450

Dickens, Charles 1812-1870 *A Child's History of England.* London: Bradbury & Evans, 1852. 1853. 1854. First edition, 3 volumes, half titles, frontispieces by F. W. Topham, final ad leaves, sumptuously bound in full tan calf by Bayntun Riviere, gilt spines, double ruled borders and dentelles, maroon & tan moroco laels, original maron cloth bound in at end of each volume, all edges gilt, fine. Jarndyce Antiquarian Booksellers CCXVIII - 497 2016 £1500

Dickens, Charles 1812-1870 *A Child's History of England.* London: Bradbury & Evans, 1853-1854. Volume I 1853, volumes II and III first edition, 3 volumes, half titles, frontispiece by F. W. Topham, 1 page ads in all volumes, old tape repairs to inner hinges volume I, original violet pink cloth blocked in blind, front boards decorated n gilt, heads and tails of spine slightly rubbed with some slight loss, boards little dulled and marked, dedication leaf volume i inscribed by author frontispiece Feb. 5th 1854 for Emile de la Rue, signed by De la Rue, later bookplate of H. Lettenorier, fold over box. Jarndyce Antiquarian Booksellers CCXVIII - 495 2016 £16,500

Dickens, Charles 1812-1870 *A Child's History of England.* London: Bradbury & Evans, 1854. 1855. 1855. Early editions, 3 volumes, half titles, frontispieces by Topham, some light damp marking in prelims and outer margins, original pink vertical grained cloth, spines lettered in gilt, boards blocked in gilt and blind, marbled endpapers and edges, carefully rebacked, some expertly executed minor repairs, little dulled. Jarndyce Antiquarian Booksellers CCXVIII - 498 2016 £480

Dickens, Charles 1812-1870 *A Child's History of England.* London: Chapman & Hall, 1879. Household edition, 4to., frontispiece, vignette title, illustrations by Ralston, original green cloth blocked and lettered in black and gilt, very good. Jarndyce Antiquarian Booksellers CCXVIII - 499 2016 £30

Dickens, Charles 1812-1870 *The Chimes.* New York: E. Winchester, New World Press, 1843. woodcut on verso of final leaf, untrimmed, disbound. Jarndyce Antiquarian Booksellers CCXVIII - 373 2016 £80

Dickens, Charles   1812-1870   *The Chimes.*   London: Chapman & Hall, 1844. Proof copy, sent by Dickens to Lady Blessington after 6th December 1844, half title, frontispiece and additional engraved title, illustrations, 19th century full green crushed morocco, hinges skillfully repaired, small mark to front board, bookplates of M. C. Borden and John C. Eckel, all edges gilt. very good, bound after half title is manuscript address leaf in Dickens's hand, cloth slipcase.   Jarndyce Antiquarian Booksellers   CCXVIII - 363   2016   £28,000

Dickens, Charles   1812-1870   *The Chimes.*   New York: E. Winchester, New World Press, 1845. Very early American edition, woodcut on verso of final leaf, uncut in original buff printed wrappers, front wrapper slightly chipped in lower out corner, overall very good.   Jarndyce Antiquarian Booksellers   CCXVIII - 372   2016   £250

Dickens, Charles   1812-1870   *The Chimes.*   Philadelphia: Lea & Blanchard, 1845. frontispiece, engraved title, additional printed title, illustrations, text block slightly browned, some light spotting, original pale blue horizontal grained cloth, front board and spine decorated and lettered in gilt, spine very slightly dulled, very good, almost fine.   Jarndyce Antiquarian Booksellers   CCXVIII - 374   2016   £600

Dickens, Charles   1812-1870   *The Chimes.*   London: Chapman & Hall, 1845. First edition, 2nd issue, frontispiece, engraved title and illustrations, initial ad leaf, original red vertical grained cloth, blocked and lettered gilt, spine slightly faded and very slightly spotted at head, very good.   Jarndyce Antiquarian Booksellers   CCXVIII - 365   2016   £400

Dickens, Charles   1812-1870   *The Chimes.*   London: Chapman & Hall, 1845. Eleventh edition, half title, frontispiece, engraved title and illustrations, initial ad leaf, original red vertical grained cloth, blocked in blind and gilt, slightly dulled, all edges gilt, very good.   Jarndyce Antiquarian Booksellers   CCXVIII - 369   2016   £65

Dickens, Charles   1812-1870   *The Chimes: a Goblin Story of Some Bells...*   London: Chapman & Hall, 1845. First edition, first state, 8vo., original red cloth lettered and decorated with bells, gilt on spine and cover, publisher's name within vignette as called for in first state, very slight lean, covers slightly marked, spine ends rubbed with very slight fraying at lower and slight water staining to engraved titlepage, sound, near very good.   Any Amount of Books   2015 - A89122   2016   £250

Dickens, Charles   1812-1870   *The Chimes.*   London: Chapman & Hall, 1845. First edition, 2nd issue, half title, frontispiece, engraved title and illustrations, initial ad leaf, original red vertical grained cloth, blocked and lettered in gilt, little dulled, spine chipped at head and tail, label carefully removed from leading pastedown, good plus.   Jarndyce Antiquarian Booksellers   CCXVIII - 366   2016   £150

Dickens, Charles   1812-1870   *The Chimes.*   London: Chapman & Hall, 1845. Seventh edition, half title, frontispiece, engraved title and illustrations, initial ad leaf, original red vertical grained cloth blocked in blind and gilt, spine darkened and chipped at head and tail corners little worn, all edges gilt, good, sound copy.   Jarndyce Antiquarian Booksellers   CCXVIII - 367   2016   £45

Dickens, Charles   1812-1870   *The Chimes.*   London: Chapman & Hall, 1845. Ninth edition, frontispiece, engraved title and illustrations, initial ad leaf, original red horizontal grained cloth, blocked in blind and gilt, slightly marked, small split at tail of following hinge, nice, small label of R. Marshall, pharmaceutical chemist, Boston as well as his signature, all edges gilt.   Jarndyce Antiquarian Booksellers   CCXVIII - 368   2016   £65

Dickens, Charles   1812-1870   *The Chimes.*   London: Chapman & Hall, 1845. Twelfth edition, half title, frontispiece, additional engraved title, illustrations, original red cloth gilt, carefully recased, inscribed by author for Thomas Powell, September fourth 1845, later ownership inscription of Ellen Maria Streater, and E. Harrell, all edges gilt, morocco backed box.   Jarndyce Antiquarian Booksellers   CCXVIII - 364   2016   £25,000

Dickens, Charles   1812-1870   *The Chimes.*   London: Chapman and Hall, 1845. Twelfth edition, half title, frontispiece, engraved title and illustrations, initial ad leaf, original red vertical grained cloth blocked in blind and gilt, spine slightly faded and slightly rubbed, all edges gilt, very good.   Jarndyce Antiquarian Booksellers   CCXVIII - 370   2016   £65

Dickens, Charles   1812-1870   *The Chimes.*   London: Hodder & Stoughton, 1913? Half title, color frontispiece and plates tipped in, vignette title printed in red and black, occasional browning and odd spot, original red cloth pictorially blocked and lettered in gilt, spine slightly dulled, gift inscription dated 1919 and later ownership details, very good.   Jarndyce Antiquarian Booksellers   CCXVIII - 371   2016   £60

Dickens, Charles   1812-1870   *The Christmas Books.*   London: Chapman & Hall, 1843-1848. First edition, 5 volumes, full calf with all covers separate, rubbed, complete set needs to be rebound.   Second Life Books, Inc.   197 - 78   2016 $4500

Dickens, Charles   1812-1870   *Les Contes de Noel. (Christmas Books).*   Paris: Librairie des Livres Liturgiques Illustres, 1847-1848. 2 volumes, half titles, frontispiece, illustrations, 6 original French engravings volume I, 8 in volume II, uncut in original printed paper wrappers, small tear without loss in upper margin volume I, slight wear to tails of spines.   Jarndyce Antiquarian Booksellers   CCXVIII - 405   2016   £180

Dickens, Charles   1812-1870   *The Christmas Books.*
London: Chapman & Hall, 1852. First English collectedd edition, frontispiece, final ad leaf, original light green cloth, spine faded, marks on front board, ads printed on endpapers, very good.   Jarndyce Antiquarian Booksellers   CCXVIII - 397   2016   £300

Dickens, Charles   1812-1870   *The Christmas Books.*
London: Chapman & Hall, 1863. Frontispiece, plates, contemporary full green calf, spine gilt in compartments, maroon lather label, slightly marked, contemporary hand written ownership label of Lawson Whittaker, attractive copy.   Jarndyce Antiquarian Booksellers   CCXVIII - 398   2016   £85

Dickens, Charles   1812-1870   *The Christmas Books.*
London: Chapman & Hall, circa, 1868. Half title, frontispiece and 7 plates, plain dark turquoise endpapers, original brown cloth lettered in black and gilt, spine slightly marked, otherwise very good, from the library of Kathleen & Geoffrey Tillotson, numerous notes loosely inserted in unusual variant binding.   Jarndyce Antiquarian Booksellers   CCXVIII - 400   2016   £30

Dickens, Charles   1812-1870   *The Christmas Books.*
London: Chapman & Hall, 1878. Household edition, 4to., frontispiece, vignette title, illustrations by F. Barnard, original green cloth blocked and lettered in black and gilt, very good.   Jarndyce Antiquarian Booksellers   CCXVIII - 401   2016   £65

Dickens, Charles   1812-1870   *The Christmas Books.*
London: Chapman & Hall, circa, 1880. Charles Dickens Edition, 4 page initial ads, frontispiece and 7 plates, original uniform red cloth, little dulled and slightly rubbed, signature of Ada Brampton, 1928.   Jarndyce Antiquarian Booksellers   CCXVIII - 402   2016   £35

Dickens, Charles   1812-1870   *The Christmas Books.*
London: A. & F. Pears,, 1912. Pears Centenary Edition, frontispiece, engraed titles, plates endpapers browned, each volume bound in different colored cloth, uniformly blocked in gilt and black, color onlays on front boards, very slight rubbing in places, spine slightly faded to "Battle for Life", "Haunted Man" worn at head of spine, overall nice bright set.   Jarndyce Antiquarian Booksellers   CCXVIII - 403   2016   £150

Dickens, Charles   1812-1870   *A Christmas Carol.*
Boston: Charles E. Lauriat Co., n.d., Facsimile of original edition, 12mo., cinnamon colored cloth, after original with gilt stamped lettering, all edges gilt, green endpapers, original printed light orange dust jacket, original publisher's white box printed in red and green, book with slight lean, otherwise near fine, dust jacket spine panel bit darkened, some edge chipping, very good, scarce box shows wear, very good.   Tavistock Books   Bibliolatry - 1   2016 $375

Dickens, Charles   1812-1870   *A Christmas Carol.*
London: New York: Toronto: Hodder & Stoughton, n.d., Owner pencilled date of 1912, 4to., 13 full page illustrations by A. C. Michael, plus smaller illustrations in text, owner pencilled date of 1912, red cloth with extensive gilt decoration and pictorial paste-ons, some fraying at spine ends and spine slightly toned, else very good.   Aleph-bet Books, Inc.   111 - 121   2016 $225

Dickens, Charles   1812-1870   *A Christmas Carol. In Prose.* London: Chapman & Hall, 1843. First edition, first issue, "Stave 1" , text entirely uncorrected, cream endpapers, blue half title, red and blue title, small octavo, 4 hand colored steel engraved plates by and after Leech and 4 wood engraved text illustrations by W. J. Linton after Leech, original cinnamon vertically ribbed cloth, covers decoratively stamped in blind, front cover and spine decoratively stamped and lettered gilt, all edges gilt, first issue with unbroken 'D' within wreath and minimum 14mm. gap between blind border and gilt cartouche, previous owner's inscription and bookplate on front pastedown, erased signature on top of front free endpaper, some professional restoration to front outer hinge and at top of spine, overall very good with gold leaf still bright, housed in custom full red morocco clamshell, gilt stamped, attractive copy.   Heritage Book Shop   Holiday 2015 - 32   2016 $10,000

Dickens, Charles   1812-1870   *The Christmas Carol in Prose.* London: Chapman & Hall, 1843. First edition, 2nd issue i.e. 'Stave One', yellow coated endpapers, blue half title, red and blue title, small octavo, four hand colored steel engraved plates by and after Leech, and 4 wood engraved text illustrations by W. J. Linton after Leech, original cinnamon vertically ribbed cloth, covers decoratively in blind, front cover and spine decoratively stamped and lettered gilt, all edges gilt, some mild soiling to binding, hinges professionally and invisibly repaired, very minor wear to spine, extremities, previous owner's contemporary inscription.   Heritage Book Shop   Holiday 2015 - 31   2016 $4500

Dickens, Charles   1812-1870   *A Christmas Carol.*
London: Chapman and Hall, 1843. First edition, first issue, half title, hand colored frontispiece and 3 plates, text woodcuts, 2 page ads, titlepage printed in red and blue, half title and verso of title printed in blue, green endpapers, original salmon pink vertical ribbed cloth, blocked and lettered blind and gilt, spine slightly faded, very tiny nick at tail, very small knock in outer edge of following board, one or two very light almost imperceptible marks on front board, all edges gilt, very good exceptionally well preserved.   Jarndyce Antiquarian Booksellers   CCXVIII - 330   2016   £15,000

Dickens, Charles   1812-1870   *A Christmas Carol.*
London: Chapman & Hall, 1843. Second edition, half title and title in blue, hand colored frontispiece and 3 color plates, text woodcuts, final ad leaf, attractively bound in recent half red morocco, spine with raised gilt bands, and red leather label, maroon cloth boards, all edges gilt, very good.   Jarndyce Antiquarian Booksellers   CCXVIII - 332   2016   £1250

Dickens, Charles 1812-1870 *A Christmas Carol.* London: Chapman & Hall, 1843. Second edition, half title and title in blue, hand colored frontispiece and 3 color plates, text woodcuts, final ad leaf, pale yellow endpapers, original salmon pink vertical fine ribbed cloth, boards blocked with borders in blind, front board and spine decorated and lettered gilt, tiny ink spot on following board, very slight wear to corners and head and tail of spine, signature of Mary Gray 1843, all edges gilt, good plus. Jarndyce Antiquarian Booksellers CCXVIII - 331 2016 £1500

Dickens, Charles 1812-1870 *A Christmas Carol.* New York: Harper & Bros., 1844. First American edition, ad leaf, slightly spotted, nicely bound in later half dark blue morocco. Jarndyce Antiquarian Booksellers CCXVIII - 348 2016 £1500

Dickens, Charles 1812-1870 *A Christmas Carol.* London: Chapman and Hall, 1844. Fourth edition, half title, color frontispiece and 3 other plates by John Leech, text illustrations, original vertical fine ribbed pink cloth, blocked and lettered gilt, spine slightly darkened, expertly rebacked retaining, original spine strip, contemporary owner's signature, all edges gilt, good plus. Jarndyce Antiquarian Booksellers CCXVIII - 334 2016 £850

Dickens, Charles 1812-1870 *A Christmas Carol.* London: Chapman and Hall, 1844. Sixth edition, half title, color frontispiece and 3 other plates by John Leech, text illustrations, final ad leaf, original vertical fine ribbed pink cloth, spine and front board blocked and lettered gilt, spine slightly dulled and very slightly rubbed at head and tail, ownership inscription, struck through, signature of R. Page 1947, all edges gilt, very good. Jarndyce Antiquarian Booksellers CCXVIII - 335 2016 £650

Dickens, Charles 1812-1870 *A Christmas Carol.* London: Chapman & Hall, 1844. Ninth edition, half title, color frontispiece, 3 other plates by John Leech, text illustrations, original vertical grained pink cloth, blocked and lettered gilt, recased retaining upper part of original spine strip (with all gilt blocking), endpapers replaced, all edges gilt, nice, generally well preserved. Jarndyce Antiquarian Booksellers CCXVIII - 336 2016 £650

Dickens, Charles 1812-1870 *A Christmas Carol.* London: Chapman & Hall, 1844. Tenth edition, half title, color frontispiece and 3 other plates by John Leech, text illustrations, final ad leaf, original horizontal grained red cloth, blocked and lettered gilt, bookseller's ticket, all edges gilt, very good. Jarndyce Antiquarian Booksellers CCXVIII - 337 2016 £1500

Dickens, Charles 1812-1870 *A Christmas Carol.* London: Chapman & Hall, 1855. Thirteenth edition, half title, color frontispiece and 3 other plates by John Leech, text illustrations, final ad leaf, original horizontal grained red cloth, blocked and lettered gilt, recased retaining most of original repaired spine strip, corners repaired, all edges gilt. Jarndyce Antiquarian Booksellers CCXVIII - 338 2016 £450

Dickens, Charles 1812-1870 *The Annotated Christmas Carol.* New York: Clarkson N. Potter, circa, 1857? Half title, frontispiece, illustrations, original peal green cloth, spine lettered gilt, very good in edgeworn dust jacket. Jarndyce Antiquarian Booksellers CCXVIII - 350 2016 £30

Dickens, Charles 1812-1870 *A Christmas Carol. in Prose.* Philadelphia: T. B. Peterson, circa, 1857? Disbound, little spotted. Jarndyce Antiquarian Booksellers CCXVIII - 349 2016 £65

Dickens, Charles 1812-1870 *A Christmas Carol.* London: Bradbury & Evans, 1858. Cheap and uniform edition, half title, original green printed wrappers little darkened, spine worn but holding. Jarndyce Antiquarian Booksellers CCXVIII - 339 2016 £75

Dickens, Charles 1812-1870 *A Christmas Carol.* London: Chapman & Hall, 1860. Fourteenth edition, half title, color frontispiece and 3 other plates by John Leech, text illustrations, final ad leaf, original vertical grained red cloth, blocked and lettered gilt, spine very slightly darkened, all edges gilt, very good. Jarndyce Antiquarian Booksellers CCXVIII - 340 2016 £500

Dickens, Charles 1812-1870 *A Christmas Carol.* London: Elliot Stock, 1890. Facsimile reproduction of author's original manuscript, 4to., half title, slightly spotted, uncut in original varnished boards, parchment spine lettered gilt, inner hinges cracking, little dulled & rubbed, leaf of ms. notes loosely inserted. Jarndyce Antiquarian Booksellers CCXVIII - 352 2016 £40

Dickens, Charles 1812-1870 *A Christmas Carol.* 1892. Pears Centenary edition, illustrations, original scarlet cloth lettered gilt, front board with central oval color onlay, spine slightly rubbed, otherwise very good. Jarndyce Antiquarian Booksellers CCXVIII - 341 2016 £40

Dickens, Charles 1812-1870 *A Christmas Carol in Prose.* East Aurora: Roycroft Shop, 1902. First edition thus, printed on Japanese vellum, frontispiece, titlepage decorations, head bands and tailpieces by Samuel Warner, 8vo., three quarter blue morocco binding with marbled paper boards and endpapers, spine gilt decorated, top edge gilt, light wear, handsome, very good+ copy, signed by Elbert Hubbard. Tavistock Books Bibliolatry - 2 2016 $1500

Dickens, Charles 1812-1870 *A Christmas Carol.* London: Henry Frowde, 1904. Miniature edition, 4 x 5.6cm., 7 illustrations, frontispiece and 6 further plates after originals by Leech, original limp wrappers, front wrapper lettered in blind, one or two gatherings slightly proud, all edges gilt. Jarndyce Antiquarian Booksellers CCXVIII - 342 2016 £40

Dickens, Charles 1812-1870 *A Christmas Carol.* London: Simpkin, Marshall, Hamilton, Kent and Co., 1914. 7 color plates by Honor Appleton, original tan cloth lettered and decorated in dark green, color onlay on front board, slightly dulled, contemporary gift inscription. Jarndyce Antiquarian Booksellers CCXVIII - 343 2016 £40

Dickens, Charles 1812-1870 *A Christmas Carol.* London: William Heinemann, 1915. Limited to 525 numbered copies (of 500 were for sale, this number 448), signed by artist, large quarto, 12 color plates mounted on heavy brown paper with descriptive tissue guards and 20 drawings in black and white by Arthur Rackham, original vellum over boards pictorially stamped and lettered gilt on front cover and spine, yellow silk ties renewed, top edge gilt, others uncut, gray and white pictorial endpapers, contemporary ink signature, near fine. Heritage Book Shop Holiday 2015 - 92 2016 $4000

Dickens, Charles 1812-1870 *A Christmas Carol.* London: Heinemann, 1915. Limited ot 525 numbered cpies, large 4to., gilt pictorial vellum, new ribbon ties, small yellow area on rear cover, else fine, signed by artist, Arthur Rackham. Aleph-bet Books, Inc. 112 - 408 2016 $5000

Dickens, Charles 1812-1870 *A Christmas Carol.* London: Odhams Press, circa, 1930. 4to., frontispiece and plates by Gilbert Wilkinson, illustrations on endpapers, original blue cloth imitating leather, blocked and lettered gilt, little dulled, spine slightly worn at head and tail. Jarndyce Antiquarian Booksellers CCXVIII - 344 2016 £20

Dickens, Charles 1812-1870 *A Christmas Carol.* London: Perpetua Books, 1961. Half title, color frontispiece, illustrations in color and black and white by Ronald Searle, original pink cloth lettered gilt, slightly rubbed, good plus in dust jacket. Jarndyce Antiquarian Booksellers CCXVIII - 346 2016 £20

Dickens, Charles 1812-1870 *A Christmas Carol.* London: Dickens House, 1965. Half title, frontispiece, plates, illustrations on endpapers, original imitational vellum lettered gilt, very good in torn mylar wrappers. Jarndyce Antiquarian Booksellers CCXVIII - 347 2016 £30

Dickens, Charles 1812-1870 *A Christmas Carol, the original manuscript.* New York: Dover, 1971. 4to., illustrations, facsimiles, original limp pictorial wrappers, very good, illustrations of John Leech. Jarndyce Antiquarian Booksellers CCXVIII - 353 2016 £20

Dickens, Charles 1812-1870 *A Christmas Carol: the Public Reading Version.* New York: New York Public Library, 1971. First edition, half title, facsimiles, illustrations, original scarlet cloth, lettered in gilt, very good in dust jacket. Jarndyce Antiquarian Booksellers CCXVIII - 356 2016 £50

Dickens, Charles 1812-1870 *A Christmas Carol.* London: Nottingham Court Press, 1987. Facsimile of first edition, frontispiece, printed in color, other three full page illustrations in black and white, title in red and blue, original red cloth, blocked in blind and gilt, int. Jarndyce Antiquarian Booksellers CCXVIII - 355 2016 £20

Dickens, Charles 1812-1870 *A Christmas Carol.* New York: Pierpont Morgan Library, 1993. Facsimile edition of autograph manuscript in the Pierpont Morgan library, color frontispiece and plates, facsimiles, original scarlet cloth, blocked in blind and gilt, all edges gilt, very good in slightly marked dust jacket. Jarndyce Antiquarian Booksellers CCXVIII - 354 2016 £30

Dickens, Charles 1812-1870 *A Christmas Carol.* N.P.: Macawber Fine Editions, 2000. #III of 10 cc hors Commerce, total limitation of 85 cc., signed by R. L. dean and Findeiss, 8vo., illustrated in color by Amy Findeiss, with additional suite of 11 signed/numbered loose plates, full green morocco leather binding with gilt stamped title lettering to spine and full color pictorial onlay to front board, silk moire endpapers, custom clamshell case, fine in near fine case (small bump to upper corner). Tavistock Books Bibliolatry - 3 2016 $950

Dickens, Charles 1812-1870 *A Christmas Carol.* Madrid: Del Prado, 2003. Original maroon leatherette, blocked in black, lettered in yellow, miniature, 5.3 x 6.6cm. Jarndyce Antiquarian Booksellers CCXVIII - 351 2016 £20

Dickens, Charles 1812-1870 *The Christmas Numbers. All the Year Round.* London: 26 Wellington Street, 1868. First collected edition, original fine pebble grained cloth, front and back boards blocked in blind, triple ruled line borders, ornamented at corners with leaves and berries in blind, at centre of front board is Christmas wreath in gilt, all edges gilt, very good, bright. Jarndyce Antiquarian Booksellers CCXVIII - 812 2016 £350

Dickens, Charles 1812-1870 *Christmas Stories from "Household Worlds" and "All the Year Round".* London: Chapman & Hall, 1879. Household edition, 4to., frontispiece, vignette title, plates and illustrations by Dalziel, odd spot, contemporary half calf, spine with raised gilt bands and black leather labels, spine little rubbed, Jas. Robinson with small booklabel, good plus. Jarndyce Antiquarian Booksellers CCXVIII - 774 2016 £35

Dickens, Charles 1812-1870 *Christmas Stories from "Household Worlds" and "All the Year Round".* London: Chapman & Hall, 1879. Household edition, 4to., frontispiece, vignette title, plates and illustrations by E. G. Dalziel, some slight spotting, original green cloth, blocked and lettered in black and gilt, very good.   Jarndyce Antiquarian Booksellers   CCXVIII - 773   2016   £40

Dickens, Charles 1812-1870 *The Cricket on the Hearth.* Boston: Jordan and Wiley, Daily Atlas Building, 1846? Early American edition, outer and lower edges uncut, disbound, retaining original brown illustrated front wrapper.   Jarndyce Antiquarian Booksellers   CCXVIII - 381   2016   £250

Dickens, Charles 1812-1870 *The Cricket on the Hearth.* London: Bradbury & Evans, 1846. First edition, first issue, half title, frontispiece, engraved title and illustrations, original red vertical grained cloth, pictorially blocked and lettered gilt, spine slightly faded, very slightly rubbed at head and tail, very good, all edges gilt.   Jarndyce Antiquarian Booksellers   CCXVIII - 377   2016   £650

Dickens, Charles 1812-1870 *The Cricket on the Hearth.* London: Bradbury & Evans, 1846. First edition, 2nd issue, half title, frontispiece, engraved title, illustrations, final ad leaf in second state, original red horizontal grained cloth, pictorially blocked and lettered gilt, spine slightly faded, all edges gilt, very good.   Jarndyce Antiquarian Booksellers   CCXVIII - 378   2016   £500

Dickens, Charles 1812-1870 *The Cricket on the Hearth.* London: A. F. Pears, 1912. Pears Centenary edition, frontispiece, pictorial title, plates by Charles Green, original olive green decorated cloth, very good.   Jarndyce Antiquarian Booksellers   CCXVIII - 380   2016   £35

Dickens, Charles 1812-1870 *A Curious Dance Round a Curious Tree.* London: St. Luke's Hospital, 1860. First edition, 2nd issue, single vertical fold, original pale pink wrappers, very good in slightly rubbed red silk covered foldover wallet within red crushed morocco slipcase.   Jarndyce Antiquarian Booksellers   CCXVIII - 379   2016   £1500

Dickens, Charles 1812-1870 *A Curious Dance Round a Curious Tree.* London: St. Luke's Hospital, 1860. First edition, 2nd issue, once folded, original pale pink wrappers, slightly dusted, very good in green cloth fold over case.   Jarndyce Antiquarian Booksellers   CCXVIII - 580   2016   £800

Dickens, Charles 1812-1870 *A Curious Dance Round a Curious Tree.* London: St. Luke's Hospital, 1880. Later reprint, Sewn as issued in original pale pink wrapper, edges slightly dusted, very good.   Jarndyce Antiquarian Booksellers   CCXVIII - 581   2016   £180

Dickens, Charles 1812-1870 *Dickens to His Oldest Friend.* London: Putnam, 1932. One of 500 copies, half title, slight foxing to prelims, uncut in original dark green buckram, spine darkened, bookplate of Vera Hodgkinson.   Jarndyce Antiquarian Booksellers   CCXVIII - 848   2016   £30

Dickens, Charles 1812-1870 *The Dent Uniform Edition of Dickens' Journalism Volume IV.* London: J. M. Dent, 2000. Half title, illustrations, original black cloth, very good in dust jacket. Jarndyce Antiquarian Booksellers   CCXVIII - 724   2016   £50

Dickens, Charles 1812-1870 *The Dent Uniform Edition of Dickens's Journalism.* London: J. M. Dent, 1994-2000. 4 volumes, half title, illustrations, original black cloth, very good in slightly faded dust jackets.   Jarndyce Antiquarian Booksellers   CCXVIII - 718   2016   £180

Dickens, Charles 1812-1870 *The Dent Uniform Edition of Dickens' Journalism.* London: J. M. Dent, 1994-2000. 4 volumes, , half titles, illustrations, original black cloth, very good in slightly faded dust jackets.   Jarndyce Antiquarian Booksellers   CCXVIII - 718   2016   £180

Dickens, Charles 1812-1870 *Dickens' Journalism.* Phoenix Giants, 1996. Reprint of volume I of Dent Edition, illustrations, paperback, very good.   Jarndyce Antiquarian Booksellers   CCXVIII - 719   2016   £20

Dickens, Charles 1812-1870 *The Dent Uniform Edition of Dickens' Journalism. Volume II.* London: J. M. Dent, 1996. Half title, illustrations, original black cloth, very good in dust jacket. Jarndyce Antiquarian Booksellers   CCXVIII - 720   2016   £60

Dickens, Charles 1812-1870 *The Dent Uniform Edition of Dickens' Journalism Volume II.* London: J. M. Dent, 1996. Half title, illustrations, original black cloth, very good in dust jacket. Jarndyce Antiquarian Booksellers   CCXVIII - 720   2016   £60

Dickens, Charles 1812-1870 *The Dent Uniform Edition of Dickens' Journalism Volume III.* London: J. M. Dent, 1998. Half title, original black cloth, very good in dust jacket.   Jarndyce Antiquarian Booksellers   CCXVIII - 722   2016   £60

Dickens, Charles 1812-1870 *The Dent Uniform Edition of Dickens Journalism Volume III.* London: J. M. Dent, 1998. half title, original black cloth, dust jacket, very good. Jarndyce Antiquarian Booksellers   CCXVIII - 722   2016   £60

Dickens, Charles 1812-1870 *The Dent Uniform Edition of Dickens' Journalism. volume III.* London: J. M. Dent, 1999. Half title, paperback, very good. Jarndyce Antiquarian Booksellers CCXVIII - 723 2016 £25

Dickens, Charles 1812-1870 *The Dent Uniform Edition of Dickens' Journalism Volume IV.* London: J. M. Dent, 2000. Half title, illustrations, original black cloth, very good in dust jacket. Jarndyce Antiquarian Booksellers CCXVIII - 724 2016 £50

Dickens, Charles 1812-1870 *Dickens to His Oldest Friend. The Letters of a Lifetime from Charles Dickens to Thomas Beard.* London: Putnam, 1932. One of 500 copies, Half title, slight foxing to prelims, uncut, original dark green buckram, spine darkened, bookplates of Vera Hodgkinson. Jarndyce Antiquarian Booksellers CCXVIII - 848 2016 £30

Dickens, Charles 1812-1870 *Doctor Marigold's Prescriptions. Extra Christmas Number of All the Year Round.* Office, 26 Wellington Street, 1965. Sewn as issued original blue printed wrappers, very good, stamp of Wm. Kneale Circulating Library, Douglas, Isle of Man. Jarndyce Antiquarian Booksellers CCXVIII - 822 2016 £30

Dickens, Charles 1812-1870 *Dealings with the Firm of Dombey and Son..* London: Bradbury and Evans, 1846. First edition, all 20 original parts, bound in 19 with last number containing parts xix-xx, original blue printed wrappers, first number frayed around edges, others in excellent condition, couple of covers soiled, some of the plates show wear, very good, housed in well worn, three quarter calf slipcase and chemise. Second Life Books, Inc. 197 - 67 2016 $4000

Dickens, Charles 1812-1870 *Dombey and Son.* London: Bradbury & Evans, 1846-1848. First edition, illustrations by Phiz, xx original parts in xix, original pale blue printed wrappers, some neat professional repair, including substitution of one following wrapper, and replacement of 12 spine strips, internally clean and fresh, well preserved set, retaining most of original ads, custom made dark blue morocco and cloth slipcase. Jarndyce Antiquarian Booksellers CCXVIII - 436 2016 £1500

Dickens, Charles 1812-1870 *Dombey and Son.* Leipzig: Bernh. Tauchnitz Jun., 1847-1848. Copyright edition for continental circulation, 3 volumes, half titles, contemporary half red morocco, red patterned cloth sides, gilt spines, slightly rubbed, very good. Jarndyce Antiquarian Booksellers CCXVIII - 437 2016 £200

Dickens, Charles 1812-1870 *Dombey and Son.* London: Bradbury & Evans, 1848. First edition, half title, frontispiece, engraved title and plates by Phiz, 11 line errata slip, plates spotted, contemporary half tan calf, spines gilt in compartments, olive green leather label, slightly faded, good plus. Jarndyce Antiquarian Booksellers CCXVIII - 443 2016 £240

Dickens, Charles 1812-1870 *Dombey and Son.* London: Bradbury & Evans, 1848. First edition, frontispiece, engraved title and plates by Phiz, 2 errata slips, some foxing to plates, contemporary half dark green calf, spine gilt in compartments, black leather label, little rubbed, contemporary signature of Howard Simcox later details of E. Allen, good, sound copy. Jarndyce Antiquarian Booksellers CCXVIII - 442 2016 £220

Dickens, Charles 1812-1870 *Dombey and Son.* Boston: Bradbury & Guild, 1848. Early American edition, frontispiece and plate by Phiz, title and contents leaf with small repairs in upper margin, name erased from title, nicely rebound in half black cloth, black leather label, some browning and staining to text, otherwise good plus. Jarndyce Antiquarian Booksellers CCXVIII - 456 2016 £200

Dickens, Charles 1812-1870 *Dombey and Son.* London: Bradbury & Evans, 1848. First edition, frontispiece, engraved title and plates by Phiz, 8 line errata, some foxing and browning to plates, contemporary half maroon sheep, spine with raised gilt bands, spine little rubbed and faded to brown, leading hinge carefully repaired, good plus, clean. Jarndyce Antiquarian Booksellers CCXVIII - 441 2016 £260

Dickens, Charles 1812-1870 *Dombey and Sons.* London: Bradbury & Evans, 1848. First edition, bound in 2 volumes, half title, frontispiece and vignette title volume I, plates by Phiz, 8 line errata leaf volume II, later half morocco by Dubois D'Enghlen, spines gilt in compartments, black leather labels, spines uniformly faded, booklabels of Ronald George Taylor, very good, handsome. Jarndyce Antiquarian Booksellers CCXVIII - 440 2016 £380

Dickens, Charles 1812-1870 *Dombey and Son.* London: Bradbury & Evans, 1848. First edition, half title, frontispiece, engraved title and plates by Phiz, slightly spotted, 8 line errata leaf, errata slip, small piece torn from margin of page 129-130, not affecting text, original light green cloth, spine quite heavily embossed with elaborate blind design lettered gilt, boards blocked with line borders, spine faded and slightly rubbed at head and tail, owner's name (1848) erased from pastedown, good plus. Jarndyce Antiquarian Booksellers CCXVIII - 439 2016 £750

Dickens, Charles 1812-1870 *Dombey and Son.* London: Bradbury and Evans, 1848. First edition, engraved title and plates by Phiz, slightly browned, 11 line errata slip, contemporary half dark brown calf, spine with raised gilt bands, maroon leather label, following hinge slightly rubbed, good plus, attractive copy.   Jarndyce Antiquarian Booksellers   CCXVIII - 446   2016   £240

Dickens, Charles 1812-1870 *Dombey and Son.* London: Bradbury & Evans, 1848. First edition, frontispiece, engraved title and plates by Phiz, some browning, contemporary full black calf on heavy boards, rebacked retaining original slightly rubbed spine strip over black cloth.   Jarndyce Antiquarian Booksellers   CCXVIII - 445   2016   £200

Dickens, Charles 1812-1870 *Dombey and Son.* London: Chapman & Hall, 1858. First cheap edition, frontispiece by Phiz, original light green cloth backed in blind, spine blocked and lettered gilt, spine faded and slightly rubbed at head and tail.   Jarndyce Antiquarian Booksellers   CCXVIII - 450   2016   £60

Dickens, Charles 1812-1870 *Dombey and Son.* London: Bradbury & Evans, 1859. First edition, later issue, half title, frontispiece, engraved title, 8 line errata leaf, plates by Phiz, some with waterstain to lower corner, original green cloth, blocked in blind lettered in gilt, spine slightly darkened with slight rubbing and small repairs.   Jarndyce Antiquarian Booksellers   CCXVIII - 447   2016   £250

Dickens, Charles 1812-1870 *Dombey and Son.* Leipzig: Bernhard Tauchnitz circa, 1870. Copyright edition, 3 volumes, half titles, some light foxing, contemporary pink morocco grained cloth gilt spines, spines little faded but good plus.   Jarndyce Antiquarian Booksellers   CCXVIII - 438   2016   £75

Dickens, Charles 1812-1870 *Dombey and Son.* London: Chapman and Hall, circa, 1870. Early edition, half title, frontispiece, engraved title, plates by Phiz slightly spotted, original light green cloth blocked in blind, lettered in gilt, some fading, but very good.   Jarndyce Antiquarian Booksellers   CCXVIII - 448   2016   £85

Dickens, Charles 1812-1870 *Dombey and Son.* London: Chapman and Hall, 1877. Household edition, 4to., half title, frontispiece, vignette title, illustrations by F. Barnard, slight foxing to prelims, original green cloth blocked and lettered in black and gilt, spine slightly rubbed, very good.   Jarndyce Antiquarian Booksellers   CCXVIII - 453   2016   £35

Dickens, Charles 1812-1870 *Dombey and Son.* London: Chapman and Hall, circa, 1877. Charles Dickens edition, 4 page initial ads, series title, frontispiece and 7 plates, original uniform red cloth, little dulled and slightly rubbed.   Jarndyce Antiquarian Booksellers   CCXVIII - 451   2016   £25

Dickens, Charles 1812-1870 *Dombey and Son.* London: Chapman and Hall, circa, 1880. Household edition, reprint, 4to., half title browned, frontispiece, vignette title, illustrations by F. Barnard, original green cloth blocked and lettered in black and gilt, following inner hinge cracking, good, sound copy.   Jarndyce Antiquarian Booksellers   CCXVIII - 454   2016   £25

Dickens, Charles 1812-1870 *The Mystery of Edwin Drood.* London: Chapman and Hall, 1870. First edition, 6 monthly parts, this set is the earliest issue of part 6 with 'eighteenpence' slip pasted over one shilling price on front wrapper, 8vo., blue printed wrappers, lacks a piece of lower left margin of first part, otherwise all are in very good condition with little wear to spine paper, housed in chemise and leather backed slipcase.   Second Life Books, Inc.   197 - 72   2016 $2500

Dickens, Charles 1812-1870 *Edwin Drood and Some Uncollected Pieces.* Boston: Fields, Osgood and Co., 1870. First American edition, 2nd issue, frontispiece and plates by Fildes, original brown pebble grained cloth, front board with borders and publisher's monogram in blind, spine lettered gilt, bookseller's blindstamp on leading f.e.p., Tewksbury & Brother, Manchester, NY, very good, close to fine.   Jarndyce Antiquarian Booksellers   CCXVIII - 646   2016   £420

Dickens, Charles 1812-1870 *Edwin Drood.* London: Chapman and Hall, 1870. First edition, (32 page catalog May 1872, partially unopened and torn), original green cloth blocked in black, lettered gilt, carefully recased, booklabel of Winifred Cerson, good plus, bright copy.   Jarndyce Antiquarian Booksellers   CCXVIII - 642   2016   £250

Dickens, Charles 1812-1870 *Edwin Drood.* London: Chapman & Hall, 1870. First edition, frontispiece, engraved title and plates by S. L. Fidles, dust jacket plain green sand grained binder's cloth, spine lettered gilt, slight rubbing.   Jarndyce Antiquarian Booksellers   CCXVIII - 644   2016   £150

Dickens, Charles 1812-1870 *Edwin Drood.* Boston: Fields, Osgood & Co., 1870. First American edition, 2nd issue, frontispiece and plates by Fildes, original brown pebble grained cloth, front board with borders and publisher's monogram in blind, spine lettered gilt, bookseller's blindstamp on leading f.e.p, Tweksbury & Brother, Manchester NY, very good, close to fine copy.   Jarndyce Antiquarian Booksellers   CCXVIII - 646   2016   £420

Dickens, Charles 1812-1870 *Edwin Drood.* London: Chapman & Hall, 1870. First edition, frontispiece, engraved title and plates by S. L. Fildes, final ad leaf, some light foxing, contemporary half dark green morocco, spine with raised gilt bands, slightly rubbed, good plus.   Jarndyce Antiquarian Booksellers   CCXVIII - 645   2016   £180

Dickens, Charles 1812-1870 *Edwin Drood.* London: Chapman & Hall, 1870. First edition, frontispiece, engraved title and plates by S. L. Fildes, 32 page catalog. (Aug. 31 1870), slight foxing in prelims, remains of text clean and fresh, original green cloth blocked in black, lettered gilt, contemporary signature of Alice Walker, Oakwood, bookseller's blindstamp W. H. Smith & son, very good, bright.   Jarndyce Antiquarian Booksellers   CCXVIII - 641   2016   £500

Dickens, Charles 1812-1870 *Edwin Drood.* London: Chapman & Hall, 1870. First edition, frontispiece, engraved title and plates by S. L. Fildes, 32 page catalog (May 1872, partially unopened and slightly torn), original green cloth, blocked in black, lettered gilt, carefully recased, booklabel of Winifred Cerson, good plus, bright copy.   Jarndyce Antiquarian Booksellers   CCXVIII - 642   2016   £250

Dickens, Charles 1812-1870 *Edwin Drood.* London: Chapman & Hall, 1870. First edition, illustrations by Luke Fildes, 6 original parts, original pale blue printed wrappers, spines splitting and worn, parts V and VI, little dusted and edges slightly chipped in places.   Jarndyce Antiquarian Booksellers   CCXVIII - 640   2016   £650

Dickens, Charles 1812-1870 *Edwin Drood.* London: Chapman & Hall, 1870, 1873? First edition, 2 page ads, slight damp marking, original dull green diaper cloth, small repair to tail of spine, unobtrusive repairs to inner hinges, round booklabel of Henry Stainton.   Jarndyce Antiquarian Booksellers   CCXVIII - 641   2016   £200

Dickens, Charles 1812-1870 *Edwin Drood. Complete (Part Second) by te Spirit-Pen of Charles Dickens, through a Medium).* Brattleboro: T. P. James, 1873. Original brown cloth, bevelled boards, lettered gilt, little rubbed, Suzannet, Starling & Self booklabels, good plus.   Jarndyce Antiquarian Booksellers   CCXVIII - 647   2016   £120

Dickens, Charles 1812-1870 *Edwin Drood.* London: Chapman and Hall, 1873? First edition, slight damp marking, original dull green diaper cloth, small repair to tail of spine, unobtrusive repairs to inner hinges, round booklabel of Henry Stainton, secondary binding.   Jarndyce Antiquarian Booksellers   CCXVIII - 643   2016   £200

Dickens, Charles 1812-1870 *Edwin Drood. Reprinted Pieces and Other Stories.* London: Chapman & Hall, 1879. Household edition, 4to. frontispiece, vignette title, plates, illustrations, original green cloth, blocked in black and gilt, very good.   Jarndyce Antiquarian Booksellers CCXVIII - 648   2016   £35

Dickens, Charles 1812-1870 *Edwin Drood, Completed in 1914 by WEC.* London: J. M. Ouseley & sons, 1914. Half title, illustrations, original red cloth, spine lettered white, front board lettered in blind, spine slightly dulled.   Jarndyce Antiquarian Booksellers   CCXVIII - 651   2016   £35

Dickens, Charles 1812-1870 *Edwin Drood.* London: Queensway Press, 1935. First edition completed by Ruth Alexander, half title, frontispiece and plates, original blue sand-grained cloth, spine lettered black.   Jarndyce Antiquarian Booksellers   CCXVIII - 653   2016   £20

Dickens, Charles 1812-1870 *Edwin Drood: edited by Margaret Cardwell.* Oxford: Clarendon Press, 1972. Definitive edition, Half title, frontispiece, plates, original royal blue cloth, very good in dust jacket.   Jarndyce Antiquarian Booksellers   CCXVIII - 655   2016   £65

Dickens, Charles 1812-1870 *Edwin Drood.* London: Andre Deutsch, 1980. First edition concluded by Leon Garfield, illustrations by Anthony Maitland, frontispiece and illustrations, original brown cloth, very good in dust jacket. Jarndyce Antiquarian Booksellers   CCXVIII - 656   2016   £25

Dickens, Charles 1812-1870 *Gone Astray.* London: Chapman & Hall, 1912. First edition, frontispiece, illustrations, plates, original light green cloth, spine slightly faded, very good.   Jarndyce Antiquarian Booksellers   CCXVIII - 711   2016   £35

Dickens, Charles 1812-1870 *Great Expectations.* London: Chapman & Hall, 1861. First edition, volume I third impression, volume II first impression, volume III first impression, 3 volumes, odd spot in prelims, contemporary full tan calf, gilt dentelles and double ruled borders, spines gilt in compartments, maroon and dark green morocco labels, following board to volume III little marked & scratched, but this remains attractive well preserved copy. Jarndyce Antiquarian Booksellers   CCXVIII - 587   2016   £6500

Dickens, Charles 1812-1870 *Great Expectations.* Philadelphia: T. B. Peterson & Bros., 1861. Half title, frontispiece, engraved and printed title, 34 illustrations, original uniform brown cloth, boards blocked and lettered in blind, spines blocked and lettered gilt, tail of spine little chipped, slight split to head of leading hinge, contemporary signature of A. La Rocher, good plus.   Jarndyce Antiquarian Booksellers   CCXVIII - 590   2016   £450

Dickens, Charles 1812-1870 *Great Expectations.* London: Chapman & Hall, 1861. First edition, send, first and third impression respectively, 3 volumes original triple vertical wavy grained cloth, blocked in blind, spines lettered and decorated gilt, slight signs of library label removal from front boards, careful repairs to tails of spines, corners little rubbed, decent copy as originally issued.   Jarndyce Antiquarian Booksellers   CCXVIII - 586   2016   £2500

Dickens, Charles 1812-1870 *Great Expectations.*
London: Chapman & Hall, 1861. First edition, third impression, third impression and first impression respectively, 3 volumes, half title and color frontispiece volume I, color plates 32 page catalog volume III May 1861, slightly later full scarlet crushed morocco by Riviere & Son, spines gilt in compartments, triple ruled borders and gilt dentelles, original purple cloth bound in at end of each volume, armorial bookplates of Hinton A Stewart, top edge gilt, very good, attractive, handsome copy, extra illustrated by Pailthorpe with 21 full color etchings.   Jarndyce Antiquarian Booksellers   CCXVIII - 588   2016   £6500

Dickens, Charles 1812-1870 *Great Expectations.*
London: Chapman & Hall, 1861. First edition, volume 1 first impression, volume II send impression, volume iii first impression, 3 volumes, occasional interior marking, text block very slightly cut down with no loss of text, contemporary half dark green morcco, spines gilt in compartments, volumes ii and iii spine numbers reversed, spine volume ii (i.e. iii) slightly faded, very good, custom made green slipcase, edges with green morocco.   Jarndyce Antiquarian Booksellers   CCXVIII - 584   2016   £6000

Dickens, Charles 1812-1870 *Great Expectations.*
London: Chapman and Hall, 1861. First edition, first impression of volume one, volume II and III second edition, second impression, 3 volumes, odd spot in prelims, contemporary half dark green calf, spines gilt in compartments, brown morocco spine labels, marbled boards, edges and endpapers, armorial bookplate of Arbuthnot Charles Guthrie Duart, very good, attractive set.   Jarndyce Antiquarian Booksellers   CCXVIII - 585   2016   £6500

Dickens, Charles 1812-1870 *Great Expectations.*
Mobile: S. H. Goetzel & Co. J. Y. Thompson, Printer, 1863. First Confederate edition, Modern blue half morocco leather binding with marbled paper boards, original front wrapper printed on wall paper, bound-in, fine text block, about very good front wrapper with restoration/browning and spotting to text, occasional paper defect, rare imprint.   Tavistock Books   Bibliolatry - 12   2016 $20,000

Dickens, Charles 1812-1870 *Great Expectations.*
London: Chapman & Hall, 1866. Library edition, 8vo., 8 illustrations by Marcus Stone, engraved by Dalziel, finely bound by Bayntun-Riviere in full red crushed morocco with decorated spine, gilt bust of Dickens to front board, gilt facsimile signature to rear board, gilt dentelles, all edges gilt, marbled endpapers, fine, brilliant copy.   Tavistock Books   Bibliolatry - 11   2016 $1250

Dickens, Charles 1812-1870 *Great Expectations.*
Philadelphia: T. B. Peterson & Bros., 1867. 27 original illustrations, original green sand grained cloth, front board lettered and with portrait of Dickens gilt, spine lettered gilt, very slight wear to head and tail of spine, fancy contemporary blindstamp of Jacob Ulp Books, Lock Haven PA, very good, bright copy.   Jarndyce Antiquarian Booksellers   CCXVIII - 591   2016   £300

Dickens, Charles 1812-1870 *Great Expectations.*
London: Chapman & Hall, 1876. Household edition, 4to., half title, frontispiece and illustrations by F. A. Fraser, original green cloth blocked and lettered in black and gilt, slight rubbing, very good.   Jarndyce Antiquarian Booksellers   CCXVIII - 589   2016   £120

Dickens, Charles 1812-1870 *Hard Times for These Times.* London: Bradbury & Evans, 1854. First edition, half title, some light unobtrusive staining pages 11-14, slightly later half red morocco, spine gilt in compartments, marbled boards and edges, booklabel of A. Muriel Ritchie, very good.   Jarndyce Antiquarian Booksellers   CCXVIII - 527   2016   £520

Dickens, Charles 1812-1870 *Hard Times for These Times.* London: Bradbury & Evans, 1854. Half title, original olive green moire cloth, borders blocked in blind, spine lettered gilt, spine little darkened with small neat repairs to head and tail, corners slightly worn.   Jarndyce Antiquarian Booksellers   CCXVIII - 526   2016   £450

Dickens, Charles 1812-1870 *Hard Times for These Times.* London: Bradbury & Evans, 1854. First edition, original olive green horizontal ribbed moire cloth, blocked in blind on boards and spine, spine lettered in gilt, spine little faded and with some expertly executed minor repairs to head and tail of spine, simple bookplate of Alfred Neild, good plus.   Jarndyce Antiquarian Booksellers   CCXVIII - 525   2016   £750

Dickens, Charles 1812-1870 *Hard Times for These Times.* London: Bradbury & Evans, 1854. First edition, half title, original olive green horizontal ribbed moire cloth, blocked in blind on boards and spine, spine lettered gilt, spine only slightly faded, contemporary bookseller's ticket.   Jarndyce Antiquarian Booksellers   CCXVIII - 524   2016   £2200

Dickens, Charles 1812-1870 *Hard Times for These Times.* London: Bradbury & Evans (Chapman & Hall), 1870. First edition, remainder issue using original sheets, remainder binding, original green pebble grained cloth, carefully recased, slight rubbing, good plus, half title obscured by Elsie and Stanley Passmore booklabel, repairs to inner hinges.   Jarndyce Antiquarian Booksellers   CCXVIII - 528   2016   £350

Dickens, Charles 1812-1870 *Hard Times for These Times.* London: Chapman & Hall, 1876. Household edition, first illustrated edition, 4to., frontispiece, vignette title, illustrations by H. French, odd spot, original green cloth, blocked and lettered in black and gilt, slight rubbed.   Jarndyce Antiquarian Booksellers   CCXVIII - 529   2016   £40

Dickens, Charles 1812-1870 *Hard Times for These Times.* London: Chapman and Hall circa, 1877. 8 illustrations, series title, frontispiece and 7 plates, original uniform red cloth, following f.e.p. little creased, slightly dulled. Jarndyce Antiquarian Booksellers CCXVIII - 531 2016 £35

Dickens, Charles 1812-1870 *Hard Times for These Times.* London: Chapman & Hall, circa, 1881. Reprint, 4to., frontispiece, vignette title, illustrations by H. French, odd spot, original green cloth, blocked and lettered in black and gilt, very good, bright copy. Jarndyce Antiquarian Booksellers CCXVIII - 530 2016 £40

Dickens, Charles 1812-1870 *The Haunted Man and the Ghost's Bargain. A Fancy for Christmas-Time.* London: Bradbury & Evans, 1848. First edition, Small 8vo., frontispiece and vignette title leaf, 15 internal illustrations, publisher's original red, vertically ribbed cloth with gilt stamped spine and front board, all edges gilt, gilt bright, modest wear and soiling, slight lean, vew spot of foxing, primarily to prelim and terminal leaves, withal pleasing very good+ copy. Tavistock Books Bibliolatry - 5 2016 $1500

Dickens, Charles 1812-1870 *The Haunted Man and the Ghost's Bargain.* London: Bradbury & Evans, 1848. First edition, frontispiece, engraved title and illustrations, initial ad leaf, original red vertical grained cloth, dulled and rubbed, small chips at head and tail of spine, little loose, all edges gilt, fair good copy only. Jarndyce Antiquarian Booksellers CCXVIII - 390 2016 £85

Dickens, Charles 1812-1870 *The Haunted Man and the Ghost's Bargain.* London: Bradbury & Evans, 1848. First edition, frontispiece, engraved title and illustrations, initial ad leaf, original vertical grained red cloth, blocked and lettered gilt, spine darkened and chipped at head, slightly cocked. Jarndyce Antiquarian Booksellers CCXVIII - 389 2016 £150

Dickens, Charles 1812-1870 *The Haunted Man and the Ghost's Bargain.* London: Bradbury & Evans, 1848. First edition, frontispiece, engraved title and illustrations, contemporary half dark brown morocco, gilt spine, slight rubbing to hinges and head and tail of spine, overall nice, tight copy. Jarndyce Antiquarian Booksellers CCXVIII - 391 2016 £180

Dickens, Charles 1812-1870 *The Haunted Man and the Ghost's Bargain.* London: Bradbury & Evans, 1848. First edition, frontispiece, engraved title and illustrations, initial ad leaf, original horizontal grained red cloth, blocked and lettered gilt, spine very slightly dulled, tiny nick at tail of following hinge, very good, bright copy. Jarndyce Antiquarian Booksellers CCXVIII - 388 2016 £450

Dickens, Charles 1812-1870 *The Haunted Man and the Ghost's Bargain.* New York: Harper & Bros., 1849. First American edition, slightly spotted, sewn as issued in original brown printed wrappers, old stab holes in inner margin, contemporary signature of E. P. Philles, very good. Jarndyce Antiquarian Booksellers CCXVIII - 392 2016 £350

Dickens, Charles 1812-1870 *The Haunted House, Extra Christmas Number of All the Year Round.* London: published at the Office, No. 11 Wellington St., 1859. 48 pages, disbound, very good. Jarndyce Antiquarian Booksellers CCXVIII - 813 2016 £25

Dickens, Charles 1812-1870 *The Heart of Charles Dickens as Revealed in His Letters to Angela Burdett-Coutts...* New York: Duell, Sloan & Pearce, 1952. First edition, half title, frontispiece, original turquoise cloth, very good in slightly rubbed dust jacket. Jarndyce Antiquarian Booksellers CCXVIII - 852 2016 £25

Dickens, Charles 1812-1870 *Holly Berries from Dickens.* Boston: De Wolfe, Fiske & Co., 1898. Small 4to., half title, illustrations in full color, padded faux silk, boards lettered gilt and blocked incolor with holly leaves and berries, spine little worn, gift inscription, Christmas 1904, attractive gilt book. Jarndyce Antiquarian Booksellers CCXVIII - 728 2016 £30

Dickens, Charles 1812-1870 *Household Words.* London: Office, 1850-1859. Complete run, 19 volumes, original green cloth, spine slightly faded and marked on volume XIX only, very good, scarce. Jarndyce Antiquarian Booksellers CCXVIII - 776 2016 £1650

Dickens, Charles 1812-1870 *Household Words. A Weekly Journal.* London: Office, 16 Wellington Street North, 1850-1859. 19 volumes, original green cloth, spine slightly faded and marked on volume XIX only, very good set. Jarndyce Antiquarian Booksellers CCXVIII - 776 2016 £1650

Dickens, Charles 1812-1870 *Extra Christmas Numbers from Household Words and All the Year Round.* London: published at the Office, 1850-1867. complete collection, 19 numbers in total, last 5 numbers sewn as issued in original blue printed wrappers, but with sewing replaced, occaisonal minor rubbing or spotting, 18 extra Christmas Numbers housed in two blue cloth double slipcases, slipcases little damp marked. Jarndyce Antiquarian Booksellers CCXVIII - 772 2016 £550

Dickens, Charles 1812-1870 *Selections from Household Words.* New York: James Miller, 1858-1859. Incomplete run covering majority of May 1858-May-1859, lacking fe.p., 1 volume in original green cloth, spine and front board lettered gilt, very good. Jarndyce Antiquarian Booksellers CCXVIII - 777 2016 £45

Dickens, Charles 1812-1870 *Selections from Household Worlds.* New York: James Miller, 1858-1859. Incomplete run covering the majority of May 1858-May 1859, lacking leading f.e.p., 1 volume in original green cloth, spine and front board lettered gilt, very good.   Jarndyce Antiquarian Booksellers   CCXVIII - 777   2016   £45

Dickens, Charles 1812-1870 *Household Words. Christmas Stories 1851-1858.* London: Ward, Lock & Tyler, 1870. Original blue cloth, bevelled boards, blocked and lettered gilt, black and maroon, minimal rubbing to head and tail of spine, still very good, bright.   Jarndyce Antiquarian Booksellers   CCXVIII - 784   2016   £250

Dickens, Charles 1812-1870 *Household Words. Christmas Stories.* London: Ward, Lock & Tyler, 1870. Original printed wrappers, neatly rebacked, wear to corners, covers little dusted.   Jarndyce Antiquarian Booksellers   CCXVIII - 783   2016   £120

Dickens, Charles 1812-1870 *Hunted Down: a Story.* London: John Camden Hotten, 1871. First UK book edition, half title, vignette title, original pale green printed wrappers, spine chipped at head and tail, good plus.   Jarndyce Antiquarian Booksellers   CCXVIII - 576   2016   £300

Dickens, Charles 1812-1870 *Immorteles from Charles Dickesn.* London: John Moxon, 1856. Half title, few spots, original royal blue cloth by Bone & son, lettered gilt, little worn at corners, bookplate of Samuel J. Mills, good, sound copy.   Jarndyce Antiquarian Booksellers   CCXVIII - 725   2016   £65

Dickens, Charles 1812-1870 *In Memoriam (William Makepeace Thackeray). in The Cornhill Magazine Volume IX no. 50 Feb. 1864.* 1864. Disbound, illustrations, portrait.   Jarndyce Antiquarian Booksellers   CCXVIII - 605   2016   £45

Dickens, Charles 1812-1870 *The Lamplighter.* London: privately printed, 1879. First edition, no. 129 of 250 copies, half title, original blue-gray wrappers bound into contemporary royal blue pebble grained cloth, triple ruled borders in blind, spine and front board lettered gilt, hinges very slightly rubbed, armorial bookplate of Reuben Robert Davis, very good, attractive copy.   Jarndyce Antiquarian Booksellers   CCXVIII - 701   2016   £250

Dickens, Charles 1812-1870 *The Letters of Charles Dickens.* London: Chapman & Hall, 1880-1882. First edition, 3 volumes, half titles, full red morocco, gilt spines, borders and dentelles, hinges rubbed, leading hinge volume i repaired, original cloth bound in, titlepage, very good.   Jarndyce Antiquarian Booksellers   CCXVIII - 836   2016   £150

Dickens, Charles 1812-1870 *The Letters of Charles Dickens.* London: Macmillan and Co., 1893. One volume edition, revised, half title, original green cloth, lettered gilt, slight rubbing at head and tail of spine, otherwise very good.   Jarndyce Antiquarian Booksellers   CCXVIII - 837   2016   £35

Dickens, Charles 1812-1870 *The Letters of Charles Dickens.* London: Macmillan and Co., 1907. Reissue of one volume edition, revised, half title, 32 page catalog (coded 20.4.07), original green cloth, stamps of B. A. Abel, solicitor, Nottingham.   Jarndyce Antiquarian Booksellers   CCXVIII - 838   2016   £30

Dickens, Charles 1812-1870 *Letters to Mark Lemon.* London: printed for Private Circulation, 1927. Printed for Thomas J. Wise, limited to 30 copies, half title, original purple printed wrappers, bound into contemporary half dark blue calf, Clement K. Shorter's booklabel and stamped "C" on initial blank, very good.   Jarndyce Antiquarian Booksellers   CCXVIII - 860   2016   £250

Dickens, Charles 1812-1870 *The Letters of Charles Dickens. Letters Volume IV 1844-1846.* Oxford: Clarendon Press, 1977. original red cloht, very good in worn dust jacket.   Jarndyce Antiquarian Booksellers   CCXVIII - 844   2016   £70

Dickens, Charles 1812-1870 *The Letters of Charles Dickens. Volumes I-VI.* Oxford: Clarendon Press, 1965-1988. Pilgrim edition, volumes I-VI, original pink cloth (volume 1) and red cloth, dulled and marked, volume I with spine strip torn away, volumes III and IV slightly loose, Kathleen Tillotson's copies.   Jarndyce Antiquarian Booksellers   CCXVIII - 840   2016   £380

Dickens, Charles 1812-1870 *The Letters of Charles Dickens.* Oxford: Clarendon Press, 1965-2002. Pilgrim Edition, volume VI is the reprint, 12 volumes, illustrations, original red cloth, dust jackets, generally very good, except for some marking and slight tears to dust jackets.   Jarndyce Antiquarian Booksellers   CCXVIII - 839   2016   £1200

Dickens, Charles 1812-1870 *The Letters of Charles Dickens. Volume I 1820-1839.* Oxford: Clarendon Press, 1982? Later impression, possibly 1982 reprint, Original red cloth, fine in very slightly creased dust jacket,.   Jarndyce Antiquarian Booksellers   CCXVIII - 841   2016   £85

Dickens, Charles 1812-1870 *The Letters of Charles Dickens. Volume II. 1840-1841.* Oxford: Clarendon Press, 1969. Pilgrim Edition, original red cloth, very good in very slightly torn dust jacket.   Jarndyce Antiquarian Booksellers   CCXVIII - 842   2016   £75

Dickens, Charles   1812-1870   *The Letters of Charles Dickens. Volume III 1842-1843.*   Oxford: Clarendon Press, 1974. Original red cloth, very good in dust jacket.   Jarndyce Antiquarian Booksellers   CCXVIII - 843   2016   £50

Dickens, Charles   1812-1870   *The Letters of Charles Dickens. Volume III. 1842-1843.*   Oxford: Clarendon Press, 1974. Pilgrim edition, original red cloth, very good in dust jacket.   Jarndyce Antiquarian Booksellers   CCXVIII - 843   2016   £50

Dickens, Charles   1812-1870   *The Letters of Charles Dickens. volume V. 1847-1849.*   Oxford: Clarendon Press, 1847-1848. Pilgrim edition, original red cloth, fine in dust jacket.   Jarndyce Antiquarian Booksellers   CCXVIII - 845   2016   £90

Dickens, Charles   1812-1870   *The Letters of Charles Dickens. Volume VII 1853-1855.*   Oxford: Clarendon Press, 1993. Pilgrim edition, original red cloth, fine in dust jacket.   Jarndyce Antiquarian Booksellers   CCXVIII - 846   2016   £90

Dickens, Charles   1812-1870   *The Letters of Charles Dickens. Volume VIII. 1856-1858.*   Oxford: Clarendon Press, 2001. Reprint of Pilgrim edition, original black cloth, very good in dust jacket.   Jarndyce Antiquarian Booksellers   CCXVIII - 847   2016   £75

Dickens, Charles   1812-1870   *Letters of Charles Dickens to Wilkie Collins 1851-1876.*   London: James R. Osgood, McIlvaine & Co., 1892. Half title, original dark blue cloth, dulled, inner hinges cracking, inscribed by A. P. Watt for friend George Macdonald.   Jarndyce Antiquarian Booksellers   CCXVIII - 850   2016   £280

Dickens, Charles   1812-1870   *Letters of Charles Dickens to Wilkie Collins 1881-1870.*   London: James R. Osgood, McIlvaine & Co., 1892. First edition, half title, original dark blue cloth lettered gilt, string marks, very good.   Jarndyce Antiquarian Booksellers   CCXVIII - 851   2016   £50

Dickens, Charles   1812-1870   *The Life and Adventures of Martin Chuzzlewit.*   London: Chapman & Hall, 1844. First edition, 2 volumes, contemporary full grained calf, spine gilt in compartments, dark green leather label, hinges & edges slightly rubbed, still good-plus.   Jarndyce Antiquarian Booksellers   CCXVIII - 415   2016   £280

Dickens, Charles   1812-1870   *The Life and Adventures of Martin Chuzzlewit.*   London: Chapman & Hall, 1844. First edition, frontispiece, engraved title rather spotted, plates by Phiz largely clean, contemporary half tan calf, spine gilt in compartments, olive green leather label, spine rubbed and slightly worn at head.   Jarndyce Antiquarian Booksellers   CCXVIII - 414   2016   £250

Dickens, Charles   1812-1870   *The Life and Adventures of Martin Chuzzlewit.*   Leipzig: Bernhard Tacuhnitz Jun., 1844. 2 volumes, half titles, original dark purple brown cloth, spines lettered gilt, spines little faded, slightly rubbed, good, sound copy.   Jarndyce Antiquarian Booksellers   CCXVIII - 417   2016   £85

Dickens, Charles   1812-1870   *The Life and Adventures of Martin Chuzzlewit.*   London: Chapman and Hall, 1844. First edition, later issue, half title, frontispiece and undated engraved title, plates by Phiz, slightly browned in places, contemporary full grained calf, spine gilt in compartments, dark green leather label, hinges and edges slightly rubbed, still good plus copy.   Jarndyce Antiquarian Booksellers   CCXVIII - 415   2016   £280

Dickens, Charles   1812-1870   *The Life and Adventures of Martin Chuzzlewit.*   London: Chapman & Hall, 1844. First edition, half title, frontispiece, engraved title, plates by Phiz, with some slight browning, contemporary half calf, marbled boards and edges, spine with raised gilt bands, spine slightly faded, very good, "£100" on engraved title.   Jarndyce Antiquarian Booksellers   CCXVIII - 413   2016   £380

Dickens, Charles   1812-1870   *The Life and Adventures of Martin Chuzzlewit.*   London: Chapman & Hall, 1844. first edition, first state with '1000' on engraved title, errata pages has 13 lines and thus, according to Hatton and Cleaver is the earlier issue, half title, frontispiece, engraved title, plates by Phiz, plates fairly evenly browned, plate opposite page 415 with small marginal repair, contemporary half black morocco, carefully recased, bookplates of W. H. Wills and Sir W. O. Priestley and handwritten statement inserted in prelims concerning ownership by W. H. Wills, signed J. C. Priestley, cloth slipcase.   Jarndyce Antiquarian Booksellers   CCXVIII - 412   2016   £1800

Dickens, Charles   1812-1870   *The Life and Adventures of Martin Chuzzlewit.*   London: Chapman & Hall, 1852. Cheap edition, half title, frontispiece, original uniform olive green cloth blocked in blind, gilt spine, spine faded little worn at head and tail, good plus.   Jarndyce Antiquarian Booksellers   CCXVIII - 418   2016   £50

Dickens, Charles   1812-1870   *Vie et Aventures du Martin Chuzzlewit. (The Life and Adventures of Martin Chuzzlewit).*   Paris: L. Hachette, 1858. 2 volumes, half titles, uncut, original blue printed wrappers, very good.   Jarndyce Antiquarian Booksellers   CCXVIII - 426   2016   £65

Dickens, Charles   1812-1870   *The Life and Adventures of Martin Chuzzlewit.*   London: Chapman & Hall, circa, 1865. Half title, frontispiece, engraved title and plates by Phiz, contemporary full tan calf, spine gilt in compartmnts, maroon and green leather labels, very good, attractive.   Jarndyce Antiquarian Booksellers   CCXVIII - 419   2016   £110

Dickens, Charles 1812-1870 *The Life and Adventures of Martin Chuzzlewit.* London: Chapman & Hall, c., 1866. People's edition, frontispiece, original uniform green cloth, blocked in blind, spine lettered gilt, ads on endpapers, slightly dulled, good plus, pencil note in prelims notes this edition differed from Cheap edition in that it had no author's preface and a different frontispiece.   Jarndyce Antiquarian Booksellers   CCXVIII - 420   2016   £35

Dickens, Charles 1812-1870 *The Life and Adventures of Martin Chuzzlewit.* London: Chapman & Hall, 1872. Household edition, 4to., frontispiece, vignette title, illustrations by J. Barnard, original green cloth blocked and lettered in black and gilt, very good, presentation from author's daughter, Mamie for Penton Reading Room.   Jarndyce Antiquarian Booksellers   CCXVIII - 421   2016   £120

Dickens, Charles 1812-1870 *The Life and Adventures of Martin Chuzzlewit.* London: Chapman & Hall, 1872. Household edition, 4to., vignette title, illustrations by F. Barnard, original green cloth, blocked in black and gilt, slight rubbing, very good.   Jarndyce Antiquarian Booksellers   CCXVIII - 422   2016   £35

Dickens, Charles 1812-1870 *The Life and Adventures of Martin Chuzzlewit.* London: Chapman and Hall, circa, 1877. Charles Dickens edition, 4 pages initial ads, frontispiece and 7 plates, original uniform red cloth, little dulled and slightly rubbed.   Jarndyce Antiquarian Booksellers   CCXVIII - 423   2016   £25

Dickens, Charles 1812-1870 *The Life and Adventures of Martin Chuzzlewit.* London: Chapman and Hall, 1891. Original format stereotyped from first edition, Half title, frontispiece, engraved title, plates by Phiz, original olive green cloth, spine lettered gilt, blocked in blind, very good.   Jarndyce Antiquarian Booksellers   CCXVIII - 424   2016   £75

Dickens, Charles 1812-1870 *The Life and Adventures of Martin Chuzzlewit.* Oxford: Clarendon Press, 1982. Half title, frontispiece, illustrations, original dark blue cloth, mint, dust jacket.   Jarndyce Antiquarian Booksellers   CCXVIII - 425   2016   £85

Dickens, Charles 1812-1870 *The Life and Adventures of Nicholas Nickleby.* London: Chapman & Hall, 1819. First edition, frontispiece, 39 plates by Phiz, some spotting or browning, small marginal tears to foot of 1 plate, contemporary half black calf, spine with simple raised gilt bands, maroon leather label, some minor repairs to hinges, good plus.   Jarndyce Antiquarian Booksellers   CCXVIII - 224   2016   £350

Dickens, Charles 1812-1870 *The Life and Adventures of Nicholas Nickleby.* London: Chapman & Hall, 1838-1839. First edition, illustrations by Phiz, XX original parts in XIX, some plates little browned, original pale blue printed wrappers, back wrapper missing part XII, some wear to spine, occasional splitting or chipping, good set.   Jarndyce Antiquarian Booksellers   CCXVIII - 222   2016   £2800

Dickens, Charles 1812-1870 *The Life and Adventures of Nicholas Nickleby.* London: Chapman & Hall, 1838-1839. First edition, illustrations by Phiz, original pale blue printed wrappers, one or two expertly executed minor repairs, very good in custom made slipcase and dark blue morocco box, gilt, exceptionally well preserved set, excellent library from the collection of Comte Alain de Suzannet, with his armorial bookplate.   Jarndyce Antiquarian Booksellers   CCXVIII - 221   2016   £5000

Dickens, Charles 1812-1870 *The Life and Adventures of Nicholas Nickleby.* Philadelphia: Lea and Blanchard, 1839. First US edition?, 8vo., scuffed leather backed boards, lacks portrait of Box, with 40 plates, some foxing, good copy, illustrations by Phiz.   Second Life Books, Inc.   197 - 79   2016 $125

Dickens, Charles 1812-1870 *The Life and Adventures of Nicholas Nickleby.* New York: James Turney, 1839. First US edition, 8vo., publisher's plain boards with linen spine and little nicked printed label, bound with portrait of Boz and engraved frontispiece, 2 volumes in one, some light toning, very good, rare book.   Second Life Books, Inc.   197 - 68   2016 $3500

Dickens, Charles 1812-1870 *The Life and Adventures of Nicholas Nickleby.* London: Chapman and Hall, 1839. First edition, half title, steel engraved frontispiece in first state, 39 etched plates, first four in first state with imprint, errors on page 123 and page 160, faint toning and one or two spots, short tears to few plates repaired, generally very clean with plates unusually free from foxing, 8vo., late 19th or early 20th century polished blue calf by Zaehnsdorf, French fillets on sides with floral tools at corners, spine richly gilt in compartments, twin burgundy lettering pieces, top edge gilt, others uncut, very good.   Blackwell's Rare Books   B184 - 33   2016   £1200

Dickens, Charles 1812-1870 *The Life and Adventures of Nicholas Nickleby.* London: Chapman and Hall, 1839. First edition, frontispiece slightly spotted, 39 plates by Piz with slight spotting to edges, contemporary half black calf, spine with raised gilt bands, brown label, good plus.   Jarndyce Antiquarian Booksellers   CCXVIII - 226   2016   £350

Dickens, Charles 1812-1870 *The Life and Adventures of Nicholas Nickleby.* London: Chapman & Hall, 1839. First edition, half title, frontispiece spotted, plates by Phiz, some spotting and browning to edges, primary binding, untrimmed in original dark green cloth, borders blocked in blind, spine lettered gilt, head and tail of spine little worn, small split at tail of following hinge, corners slightly nicked, good, sound copy. Jarndyce Antiquarian Booksellers CCXVIII - 233 2016 £450

Dickens, Charles 1812-1870 *The Life and Adventures of Nicholas Nickleby.* London: Chapman & Hall, 1839. First edition, half title, frontispiece rather spotted, 39 plates by Phiz, slightly marked in places, contemporary half black calf, maroon leather label, slightly rubbed, contemporary signature of Mrs. Pearce, good plus. Jarndyce Antiquarian Booksellers CCXVIII - 225 2016 £300

Dickens, Charles 1812-1870 *The Life and Adventures of Nicholas Nickleby.* Philadelphia: Lea & Blanchard, 1839. First American edition, half title, 39 plates by Phiz, tear in two columns, plates slightly browned, contemporary half dark brown roan, continental style marbled boards, little rubbed, cloth missing from corners. Jarndyce Antiquarian Booksellers CCXVIII - 227 2016 £250

Dickens, Charles 1812-1870 *The Life and Adventures of Nicholas Nickleby.* Leipzig: Bernh. Tauchnitz Jun., 1843. 2 volumes, contemporary half red morocco, red patterned cloth spides, gilt spines, slightly rubbed, very good. Jarndyce Antiquarian Booksellers CCXVIII - 228 2016 £150

Dickens, Charles 1812-1870 *The Life and Adventures of Nicholas Nickleby.* London: Chapman & Hall, 1848. First cheap edition, frontispiece little spotted, original green cloth slightly bubbled, blocked in blind, gilt spine slightly faded and little worn at head and tail, small nick in following hinge, contemporary signature of Josephine Sprowson on leading pastedown, bookseller's blindstamp H. Whitmore, Manchester, good plus. Jarndyce Antiquarian Booksellers CCXVIII - 229 2016 £75

Dickens, Charles 1812-1870 *The Life and Adventures of Nicholas Nickleby.* London: Chapman & Hall, 1857. Early edition, frontispiece, 39 plates by Phiz, contemporary full tan calf by Zaehnsdorf, gilt spine, borders and dentelles, brown morocco labels, all edges gilt, very good. Jarndyce Antiquarian Booksellers CCXVIII - 230 2016 £150

Dickens, Charles 1812-1870 *The Life and Adventures of Nicholas Nickleby.* London: Chapman & Hall, 1857. frontispiece, 39 plates by Phiz, odd spot, contemporary half tan calf by C. Cooper, red morocco label, slightly marked. Jarndyce Antiquarian Booksellers CCXVIII - 231 2016 £120

Dickens, Charles 1812-1870 *The Life and Adventures of Nicholas Nickleby.* London: Chapman & Hall, circa, 1877. Charles Dickens edition, 4 page initial ads, series title, frontispiece & 7 plates, original uniform red cloth, spine slightly dulled, very good. Jarndyce Antiquarian Booksellers CCXVIII - 232 2016 £35

Dickens, Charles 1812-1870 *The Life and Adventures of Nicholas Nickleby.* London: Chapman and Hall, circa, 1885. Household edition, 4to., frontispiece, plates and illustrations by F. Barnard, original dark green cloth, blocked in black and gilt, very good. Jarndyce Antiquarian Booksellers CCXVIII - 234 2016 £50

Dickens, Charles 1812-1870 *The Life and Adventures of Nicholas Nickleby.* London: Chapman & Hall, 1891. Half title, 39 plates by Phiz, contemporary half dark blue morocco, blue cloth sides, spine with raised bands, devices gilt later family inscription "From Joe Dickens". Jarndyce Antiquarian Booksellers CCXVIII - 236 2016 £110

Dickens, Charles 1812-1870 *The Life and Adventures of Nicholas Nickleby.* London: Scolar Press, 1973. Reprinted facsimile of original parts 1838-39, 20 issues in 19 parts, original pale green printed wrappers in facsimile, very good in slipcase. Jarndyce Antiquarian Booksellers CCXVIII - 237 2016 £65

Dickens, Charles 1812-1870 *The Life of Our Lord.* London: Associated Newspapers Ltd., 1934. First edition, half title, frontispiece, illustrations, original maroon cloth, very good in dust jacket, cloth slipcase. Jarndyce Antiquarian Booksellers CCXVIII - 712 2016 £120

Dickens, Charles 1812-1870 *The Life of Our Lord.* London: Associated Newspapers Ltd., 1934. Ordinary first edition, half title, frontispiece, illustrations, original maroon cloth, very good in slightly sunned blue dust jacket. Jarndyce Antiquarian Booksellers CCXVIII - 713 2016 £65

Dickens, Charles 1812-1870 *The Life of Our Lord.* New York: Simon & Schuster, 1934. First American edition, frontispiece, endpapers slightly browned, ordinary copy in green cloth, black spine label, lettered gilt, very good. Jarndyce Antiquarian Booksellers CCXVIII - 716 2016 £20

Dickens, Charles 1812-1870 *Life of Our Lord.* New York: Simon & Schuster, 1934. First American edition, half title, title printed in red and black, deluxe copy in full cream embossed parchment, spine lettered gilt, contemporary gift inscription, booklabel of Margot Couzens Yaw, very good. Jarndyce Antiquarian Booksellers CCXVIII - 715 2016 £70

Dickens, Charles 1812-1870 *Life of Our Lord.* London: Associated Newspapers Ltd., 1934. First edition, ordinary edition, 4to., frontispiece, illustrations, printed on cream paper, original maroon cloth, very good in slightly sunned blue dust jacket.   Jarndyce Antiquarian Booksellers   CCXVIII - 713   2016   £65

Dickens, Charles 1812-1870 *Life of Our Lord.* London: Associated Newspapers, 1934. First edition, half title, frontispiece, illustrations, printed on cream paper, dark blue lambskin, lettered gilt, spine little faded, top edge gilt.   Jarndyce Antiquarian Booksellers   CCXVIII - 714   2016   £35

Dickens, Charles 1812-1870 *The Life of Our Lord.* London: Associated Newspapers, 1934. First edition, 4to., half title, frontispiece, illustrations, printed on cream paper, dark blue lambskin, lettered gilt, spine little faded, very good.   Jarndyce Antiquarian Booksellers   CCXVIII - 714   2016   £35

Dickens, Charles 1812-1870 *Life of Our Lord.* London: Associated Newspapers Ltd., 1934. First edition, half title, frontispiece, illustrations, original maroon cloth, very good in dust jacket, cloth slipcase.   Jarndyce Antiquarian Booksellers   CCXVIII - 712   2016   £120

Dickens, Charles 1812-1870 *The Life of Our Lord.* New York: Simon and Schuster, 1934. First edition, small 8vo., green cloth, stamped in gilt, rear hinge beginning tender, cover slightly scuffed and worn at corners and ends of spine, otherwise very good, tight copy.   Second Life Books, Inc.   197 - 69   2016 $25

Dickens, Charles 1812-1870 *Little Dorrit.* London: Bradbury & Evans, 1855-1857. 20 parts in 19, part 1 lacks 'Norton's Pills', The National Review & Theatre Royal slip at rear, part XIV lacks 'Royal Insurance Co.' at rear, part XVI lacks "Popular Atlases' at rear, 40 steel plates by Phiz, 8vo., blue printed wrappers, housed in custom green morocco quarter leather clamshell case, overall very good-very good+ set, expected moeerate war and chipping, one part split, case near fine.   Tavistock Books   Bibliolatry - 10   2016 $2500

Dickens, Charles 1812-1870 *Little Dorrit.* London: Bradbury & Evans, 1855-1857. First edition, with slip in part 16 alerting the reader to error in printing 'Rigaud' for 'Blandois', illustrations by Phiz, XX original parts in XIX, original pale blue wrappers, occasional slight rubbing, overall very good, unsophisticated set in custom made green cloth fold over box, well preserved.   Jarndyce Antiquarian Booksellers   CCXVIII - 535   2016   £3200

Dickens, Charles 1812-1870 *Little Dorrit.* London: Bradbury and Evans, 1857. First edition, first issue with signature "BB2" signed "B2" without errata slip on page 481, bound from parts, 8vo., bound in little rubbed three quarter leather and boards with labels on spine (lacks one label), 39 plates, some foxed and soiled, good set.   Second Life Books, Inc.   197 - 70   2016 $1250

Dickens, Charles 1812-1870 *Little Dorrit.* London: Bradbury & Evans, 1857. First edition, bound from parts in two volumes, frontispiece, plates by Phiz, little spotted, attractively bound in 2 volumes in later full brown morocco, gilt spines, front boards blocked with floral borders in gilt, further decorated with numerous small hearts and letters "C" and "D" also in gilt, very good, earlier reading of Rigaud for Blandois.   Jarndyce Antiquarian Booksellers   CCXVIII - 537   2016   £480

Dickens, Charles 1812-1870 *Little Dorrit.* London: Bradbury & Evans, 1857. First edition, frontispiece, engraved title and plates by Phiz, contemporary half black calf, spine with raised gilt bands, maroon leather label, slightly rubbed, very good with Blandois reading, plates largely clean.   Jarndyce Antiquarian Booksellers   CCXVIII - 541   2016   £350

Dickens, Charles 1812-1870 *Little Dorrit.* London: Bradbury & Evans, 1857. First edition, first issue with 'Rigaud' for 'Blandois' on pages 469, 470, 472 and 473 in part XV, in 19 parts, 8vo., blue wrappers, 40 inserted plates including frontispiece and added vignette after etchings by Phiz, original blue wrappers printed in black with design by Phiz, original blue wrappers printed in black with design by Phiz on outside front wrappers, excellent set housed in cloth clamshell box.   Second Life Books, Inc.   197 - 71   2016 $3500

Dickens, Charles 1812-1870 *Little Dorrit.* London: Bradbury and Evans, 1857. First edition, with earlier reading of Rigaud for Blandois on page 469 &c, frontispiece, engraved title and plates by Phiz, occasional marginal browning, original olive green cloth, blocked in blind, spine lettered gilt, spine very slightly faded, but overall very good, well preserved.   Jarndyce Antiquarian Booksellers   CCXVIII - 536   2016   £1200

Dickens, Charles 1812-1870 *Little Dorrit.* London: Chapman & Hall, 1865. Cheap edition, half title, frontispiece by Marcus Stone, final ad leaf, original green sand grained cloth, boards blocked in blind, spine blocked and lettered gilt, inner hinges cracking, otherwise very good, bright copy.   Jarndyce Antiquarian Booksellers   CCXVIII - 542   2016   £65

Dickens, Charles 1812-1870 *Little Dorrit.* London: Chapman and Hall, 1866. Cheap edition, half title, frontispiece by Marcus Stone, original green sand grained cloth, boards blocked in blind, spine blocked and lettered gilt, inner hinges cracking and carefully repaired.   Jarndyce Antiquarian Booksellers   CCXVIII - 543   2016   £55

Dickens, Charles 1812-1870 *Little Dorrit.* London: Chapman & Hall, 1873. Household edition, 4to., frontispiece, vignette title illustrations by J. Mahony, original green cloth lettered gilt, blocked in black, very good.   Jarndyce Antiquarian Booksellers CCXVIII - 544   2016   £40

Dickens, Charles 1812-1870 *Little Dorrit.* London: Chapman & Hall, circa, 1880. Frontispiece, engraved title little spotted, plates by Phiz, contemporary half calf, spine with raised gilt bands, green morcoco label, spine slightly rubbed, very good.   Jarndyce Antiquarian Booksellers CCXVIII - 545   2016   £120

Dickens, Charles 1812-1870 *The Loving Ballad of Lord Bateman.* London: Charles Tilt, 1839. First edition, 2nd issue, half title, frontispiece and plates, music, 4 pages of ads, very light spotting, original turquoise green cloth with Cruikshank block, neat repair to inner hinges, very good.   Jarndyce Antiquarian Booksellers   CCXVIII - 256   2016   £380

Dickens, Charles 1812-1870 *The Loving Ballad of Lord Bateman.* London: Tilt & Bogue, 1842? Half title, plates by George Cruikshank, original green cloth blocked gilt, slightly dulled, leading inner hinge slightly cracked and repaired, bookplate of Edward Heron-Allen, good plus.   Jarndyce Antiquarian Booksellers   CCXVIII - 258   2016   £150

Dickens, Charles 1812-1870 *The Loving Ballad of Lord Bateman.* London: Charles Tilt, 1842? Frontispiece and plates by George Cruikshank, spotted, pages vi/vi with small repaired tear, original green cloth, slight lifting from boards with Cruikshank block, little dulled, good plus.   Jarndyce Antiquarian Booksellers   CCXVIII - 257   2016   £150

Dickens, Charles 1812-1870 *The Loving Ballad of Lord Bateman.* London: David Bogue, 1851. Half title, frontispiece and plates by George Cruikshank, original green cloth blocked in gilt, slightly faded, very good.   Jarndyce Antiquarian Booksellers   CCXVIII - 259   2016   £160

Dickens, Charles 1812-1870 *The Loving Ballad of Lord Bateman.* New York: G. W. Carleton & Co., 1871. Disbound, little dusted, Cruikshank illustrations on thick paper with blue printed borders.   Jarndyce Antiquarian Booksellers   CCXVIII - 259   2016   £160

Dickens, Charles 1812-1870 *The Loving Ballad of Lord Bateman.* London: George Bell & sons, 1877. Frontispiece, illustrations, original royal blue cloth, front board lettered gilt, both boards decorated in black, fine.   Jarndyce Antiquarian Booksellers   CCXVIII - 261   2016   £40

Dickens, Charles 1812-1870 *The Loving Ballad of Lord Bateman.* London: George Bell & Sons, 1877. Frontispiece, illustrations, original brick red cloth, front board lettered gilt, front boards decorated black, fine.   Jarndyce Antiquarian Booksellers   CCXVIII - 261   2016   £40

Dickens, Charles 1812-1870 *The Loving Ballad of Lord Bateman.* London: George Bell & Sons, 1883. One of 250 copies, frontispiece and plates, slightly spotted, uncut, contemporary half olive green cloth, turquoise cloth boards, spine lettered in gilt, nice.   Jarndyce Antiquarian Booksellers   CCXVIII - 263   2016   £35

Dickens, Charles 1812-1870 *The Loving Ballad of Lord Bateman.* Glasgow: David Bryce & Son, circa., 1890. Half title, frontispiece and plates, original printed stiff paper wrappers, blue cloth spine, slight damp mark along outer margin of front wrapper, otherwise very good.   Jarndyce Antiquarian Booksellers   CCXVIII - 266   2016   £20

Dickens, Charles 1812-1870 *The Loving Ballad of Lord Bateman.* London: Methuen & Co., 1903. 11 plates by George Cruikshank, frontispiece and plates, some slight internal browning, original turquoise green cloth, Cruikshank block, ownership inscription, very good, bright.   Jarndyce Antiquarian Booksellers   CCXVIII - 267   2016   £20

Dickens, Charles 1812-1870 *Master Humphrey's Clock.* London: Chapman & Hall, 1840. First edition, 3 volumes, little rubbed, three quarter calf with leather label, very good in original binding.   Second Life Books, Inc.   197 - 82   2016 $1500

Dickens, Charles 1812-1870 *Master Humphrey's Clock.* London: Chapman and Hall, 1840. First edition, 3 volumes, publisher's cloth stamped in blind and gilt, some bumped and rubbed, spine worn on volume two, good set in original binding.   Second Life Books, Inc.   197 - 81   2016 $2000

Dickens, Charles 1812-1870 *Master Humphrey's Clock.* London: Chapman & Hall, 1840-1841. in original 88 weekly parts, illustrations by George Cattermole and Phiz, original white decorated wrappers, good plus.   Jarndyce Antiquarian Booksellers   CCXVIII - 270   2016   £1800

Dickens, Charles 1812-1870 *Master Humphrey's Clock.* London: Chapman and Hall, 1840-1841. First edition, 3 volumes, frontispieces, illustrations, original brown cloth, boards blocked in blind with clock centerpieces, gilt spines, slight wear to hinges, otherwise good, signature of Gertrude E. Atkinson 1850 in volume 1, and initials in volumes II and III, bookplates of G. Maitland Gordon, variant marbled endpapers, cloth slipcase.   Jarndyce Antiquarian Booksellers   CCXVIII - 271   2016   £850

Dickens, Charles 1812-1870 *Master Humphrey's Clock.* London: Chapman & Hall, 1840-1841. First edition, 3 volumes, frontispiece and illustrations by George Cattermole and Phiz, prelims rather foxed in all volumes but not affecting text or illustrations, contemporary half red morocco, marbled boards, gilt spines, all edges gilt, very good, bright.   Jarndyce Antiquarian Booksellers   CCXVIII - 275   2016   £380

Dickens, Charles 1812-1870 *Master Humphrey's Clock.* London: Chapman & Hall, 1840-1841. First edition, 3 volumes, frontispieces and illustrations by Cattermole and Phiz, contemporary full scarlet pigskin, spines lettered gilt, little rubbed, top edge gilt.   Jarndyce Antiquarian Booksellers   CCXVIII - 276   2016   £260

Dickens, Charles 1812-1870 *Master Humphrey's Clock.* Calcutta: W. Thacker and Co., 1840-1841. First Indian edition, 3 volumes, vignette title and frontispiece, plates, contemporary half purple calf, brown cloth sides, green leather labels, spines faded to brown, little rubbed, inscriptions torn from leading f,e,p.'s, loosing approximately one third of each leaf, decent set, scarce.   Jarndyce Antiquarian Booksellers   CCXVIII - 278   2016   £500

Dickens, Charles 1812-1870 *Master Humphrey's Clock.* London: Chapman & Hall, 1840-1841. First edition, 3 volumes, frontispieces and illustrations by George Cattermole and Phiz, few spots, contemporary half green morocco, green cloth boards, gilt spines, slight rubbing, bookplates of John Williams, very good, attractive copy.   Jarndyce Antiquarian Booksellers   CCXVIII - 274   2016   £350

Dickens, Charles 1812-1870 *Master Humphrey's Clock.* London: Chapman & Hall, 1840-1841. First edition, 3 volumes, frontispieces, illustrations plates by George Cattermole and Phiz, contemporary full tree calf, gilt spines and borders, maroon and green morocco labels, hinges little rubbed, titlepage, handsome copy, bound with wrappers and extra illustrations.   Jarndyce Antiquarian Booksellers   CCXVIII - 273   2016   £650

Dickens, Charles 1812-1870 *Master Humphrey's Clock.* London: Chapman & Hall, 1840-1841. First edition, frontispiece and illustrations by George Cattermole & Phiz, marbled endpapers, original purple brown vertically ribbed cloth, decorated in blind in gilt, spines slightly chipped at heads and tails, poor copy, booklabels of Ronald George Taylor.   Jarndyce Antiquarian Booksellers   CCXVIII - 272   2016   £200

Dickens, Charles 1812-1870 *Memoirs of Joseph Grimaldi.*   London: Richard Bentley, 1838. First edition, 2nd issue, 2 volumes, half titles, frontispiece and plates by George Cruikshank, some slightly spotted, 36 page catalog volume II, original pink brown cloth, spine blocked gilt, slightly faded, slight wear and repairs to heads and tails, armorial bookplate of Alfred Bleeck, maroon cloth slipcase.   Jarndyce Antiquarian Booksellers   CCXVIII - 214   2016   £500

Dickens, Charles 1812-1870 *Memoirs of Joseph Grimaldi.*   London: Richard Bentley, 1838. First edition, 2nd issue, 2 volumes, half titles, frontispiece, plates, 36 page catalog volume II, some spotting and browning, untrimmed in original black cloth, board blocked in blind, spines pictorially blocked and lettered in black, expertly recased with some minor repairs to head and tail of spines, very good.   Jarndyce Antiquarian Booksellers   CCXVIII - 215   2016   £850

Dickens, Charles 1812-1870 *Memoirs of Joseph Grimaldi.*   London: Richard Bentley, 1838. First edition, 2nd issue, 2 volumes,, half titles, frontispieces and plates, some foxing to plates, little spotted, original purple cloth, spine elaborately decorated in gilt, spines slightly faded, cloth slipcase.   Jarndyce Antiquarian Booksellers   CCXVIII - 213   2016   £2000

Dickens, Charles 1812-1870 *Memoirs of Joseph Grimaldi.*   London: Richard Bentley, 1838. First edition, 2nd issue, 2 volumes, half titles, frontispiece, plates by George Cruikshank, 36 page catalog volume II, later full scarlet morocco for Hatchards. gilt spines and double ruled borders, original pink cloth, spine strips bound in at end of each volume, armorial bookplate of William H. R. Saunders, top edge gilt, very good.   Jarndyce Antiquarian Booksellers   CCXVIII - 216   2016   £420

Dickens, Charles 1812-1870 *Memoirs of Joseph Grimaldi.*   London: Richard Bentley, 1846. New edition, frontispiece, plates, slightly spotted, original buff glazed cloth, printed in red, little dulled and rubbed, bookseller's ticket.   Jarndyce Antiquarian Booksellers   CCXVIII - 217   2016   £65

Dickens, Charles   1812-1870   *Memoirs of Joseph Grimaldi.*   London: G. Routledge, 1853. New edition, 8vo., frontispiece, red pebbled and embossed publisher's cloth, gilt titling on spine, little dusty and some rubbing, hinge tender, good plus.   Second Life Books, Inc.   197 - 80   2016 $75

Dickens, Charles   1812-1870   *Memoirs of Joseph Grimaldi.*   London: George Routledge, 1881? Half title, frontispiece, plates, 6 pages ads, 'yellowback', original pale green printed boards, spine slightly faded, slightly rubbed, very good.   Jarndyce Antiquarian Booksellers   CCXVIII - 218   2016   £65

Dickens, Charles   1812-1870   *A Message from the Sea. Extra Christmas Number of All the Year Round.*   London: published at the Office, No. 26 Wellington Street, 1860. Disbound, very good.   Jarndyce Antiquarian Booksellers   CCXVIII - 814   2016   £25

Dickens, Charles   1812-1870   *Mrs. Lirriper's Legacy. Extra Christmas Number of All the Year Round.*   Published at toeh Office No. 26 Wellington Street, 1864. 4 page additional ads on blue paper tipped in at beginning, as well as advertising slip for Our Mutual Friend, sewn as issued in original blue printed wrappers, stitched slightly weak, spine little worn.   Jarndyce Antiquarian Booksellers   CCXVIII - 819   2016   £45

Dickens, Charles   1812-1870   *Mrs. Lirriper's Lodgings. Extra Christmas Number of All the Year Round.*   London: Published at the Office, No. 26 Wellington Street, 1863. Disbound, very good.   Jarndyce Antiquarian Booksellers   CCXVIII - 817   2016   £50

Dickens, Charles   1812-1870   *The Mudfog Papers.*   London: Richard Bnetley & Son, 1880. First book edition, original red cloth, spine lettered gilt, little faded, inner hinges cracking.   Jarndyce Antiquarian Booksellers   CCXVIII - 703   2016   £75

Dickens, Charles   1812-1870   *The Mudfog Papers.*   London: Richard Bentley & Son, 1880. First edition, original red cloth, spine lettered gilt, little faded, inner hinges cracking.   Jarndyce Antiquarian Booksellers   CCXVIII - 703   2016   £75

Dickens, Charles   1812-1870   *Mugby Junction. Extra Christmas Number of All the Year Round.*   Published at the Office no. 26 Wellington St., 1866. Sewn as issued, original blue printed wrappers, very good, well preserved.   Jarndyce Antiquarian Booksellers   CCXVIII - 826   2016   £40

Dickens, Charles   1812-1870   *No Thoroughfare. Being the Extra Christmas Number of Every Saturday for Chrimas.*   Boston: Ticknor & Fields, 1867. Scarce American issue, 42 pages, original pale blue ad slip for Works of Dickens and Reade inserted between pages 12-13, disbound, retaining original pink front wrapper, edges slightly chipped, overall good.   Jarndyce Antiquarian Booksellers   CCXVIII - 831   2016   £75

Dickens, Charles   1812-1870   *The Old Curiosity Shop.*   London: Chapman and Hall, 1841. First separate edition, contemporary full calf, spine gilt in compartments, maroon and olive green leather labels, little rubbed & marked.   Jarndyce Antiquarian Booksellers   CCXVIII - 282   2016   £250

Dickens, Charles   1812-1870   *The Old Curiosity Shop.*   London: Chapman & Hall, 1841. First separate edition in secondary binding, illustrations by Cattermole and Phiz, complete in one volume, original olive green cloth, borders blocked in blind, spine lettered gilt, spine little faded and slightly rubbed at head and tail.   Jarndyce Antiquarian Booksellers   CCXVIII - 281   2016   £380

Dickens, Charles   1812-1870   *The Old Curiosity Shop.*   London: Chapman & Hall, 1841. First separate edition, frontispiece, illustrations, original maroon cloth blocked in blind, spine lettered gilt, neatly recased, spine and edges faded to brown, corners worn, small booklabel of Elizabeth Brennan, good, sound copy.   Jarndyce Antiquarian Booksellers   CCXVIII - 280   2016   £380

Dickens, Charles   1812-1870   *The Old Curiosity Shop.*   Philadelphia: Lea & Blanchard, 1841. First separate US edition, illustrations, original olive green cloth faded to brown, plain boards, spine blocked and lettered in gilt, carefully rebacked, slightly marked, binding variant II.   Jarndyce Antiquarian Booksellers   CCXVIII - 283   2016   £400

Dickens, Charles   1812-1870   *The Old Curiosity Shop.*   London: Chapman and Hall, 1848. First Cheap edition, frontispiece, spotted, original green cloth, blocked in blind, gilt spine slight faded, very good.   Jarndyce Antiquarian Booksellers   CCXVIII - 284   2016   £65

Dickens, Charles   1812-1870   *The Old Curiosity Shop.*   London: Chapman and Hall, 1858. Cheap edition, spotted, frontispiece, original light green cloth, blocked in blind, gilt spine, very slight rubbing, very good.   Jarndyce Antiquarian Booksellers   CCXVIII - 285   2016   £35

Dickens, Charles   1812-1870   *The Old Curiosity Shop.*   London: Chapman and Hall, 1876. Household edition, 4to., frontispiece, vignette title, illustrations by C. Green, original green cloth lettered in gilt, blocked in black, very good.   Jarndyce Antiquarian Booksellers   CCXVIII - 286 2016   £50

Dickens, Charles 1812-1870 *The Old Curiosity Shope.* Oxford: Clarendon Press, 1997. Half title, illustrations, original dark blue cloth, mint in dust jacket. Jarndyce Antiquarian Booksellers CCXVIII - 287 2016 £65

Dickens, Charles 1812-1870 *Oliver Twist or the Parish Boy's Progress.* Richard Bentley, 1837-1839. Extracted from Bentley's Miscellany, Volumes I-V, Feb. 1837-April 1839, the entire first printing, illustrations by George Cruikshank, plates little browned and spotted, disbound, loose. Jarndyce Antiquarian Booksellers CCXVIII - 174 2016 £350

Dickens, Charles 1812-1870 *Oliver Twist.* London: Richard Bentley, 1838. First edition, first issue with 'Boz' on title and the 'fireside' plate at end of volue III, 8vo., 3 volumes, bound in blind horizontally ribbed stapled cloth, volume I hinges broken, connected to cloth, bookplate, volume II very good, volume III hinges loose; this copy does not have an imprint at bottom of spines, 24 etched plates by George Cruikshank including 'Fireside' plate, 3 volumes housed in full calf slipcase with individual chemises. Second Life Books, Inc. 197 - 74 2016 $5000

Dickens, Charles 1812-1870 *Oliver Twist.* London: Richard Bentley, 1838. First edition, 2nd issue, 3 volumes, half titles volumes I and II, frontispieces and plates by George Cruikshank, original purple-brown cloth, spines lettered gilt, Bentley imprint at tail, spines little faded, armorial bookplates of James Wedderburn, very nice. Jarndyce Antiquarian Booksellers CCXVIII - 176 2016 £2800

Dickens, Charles 1812-1870 *Oliver Twist or the Parish Boy's Progress.* London: Richard Bentley, 1838. First edition, first issue, 3 volumes, half titles in volumes I and II, frontispieces and plates by George Cruikshank, original purple brown cloth, without imprint at tail of spines, spines faded and with expertly executed minor repairs, bookseller's ticket in volume I - G. Simms, Manchester, later signatures of Frank Atkin, good set. Jarndyce Antiquarian Booksellers CCXVIII - 175 2016 £4500

Dickens, Charles 1812-1870 *Oliver Twist.* London: Richard Bentley, 1838. First edition, third issue, 3 volumes, frontispieces and plates by George Cruikshank, occasional spotting or staining, half titles removed, attractively bound in slightly later half dark green morocco, gilt spines, dark green pebble grained cloth sides, withdrawal stamps from Oxford and Cambridge University Club. Jarndyce Antiquarian Booksellers CCXVIII - 177 2016 £950

Dickens, Charles 1812-1870 *Oliver Twist.* Philadelphia: Lea & Blanchard, 1839. First US edition?, illustrated octavo edition, 24 plates by George Cruikshank from parts, bound in original cloth with early rebacking in leather, plate opposite page 200 lacks lower margin below image. Second Life Books, Inc. 197 - 73 2016 $600

Dickens, Charles 1812-1870 *Oliver Twist.* Paris: Baudry's European Library, 1839. Early Paris pirated edition, some spotting and slightly damp stained in lower margin of earlier leaves, contemporary half dark purple calf, gilt spine, lacking label, leading hinge split at head, little rubbed, contemporary signature of E. Smith. Jarndyce Antiquarian Booksellers CCXVIII - 179 2016 £45

Dickens, Charles 1812-1870 *Oliver Twist.* London: Richard Bentley, 1839. Second edition, 3 volumes, frontispieces and plates, volume i unopened, slight spotting to plates, uncut in original purple brown vertical grained cloth, imprints at tails of spines, carefully recased, armorial bookplates and signatures of Henry Maxwell, small bookseller's ticket, good plus. Jarndyce Antiquarian Booksellers CCXVIII - 178 2016 £580

Dickens, Charles 1812-1870 *Oliver Twist.* London: Chapman & Hall, 1841. Third edition, 3 volumes, plates slightly spotted in places, contemporary full tan calf, spines gilt in compartments, maroon morocco labels, single ruled borders in gilt, small monogram booklabels, bookseller's ticket, very good, handsome copy. Jarndyce Antiquarian Booksellers CCXVIII - 180 2016 £750

Dickens, Charles 1812-1870 *Oliver Twist.* London: Bradbury & Evans, 1846. New edition, plates by George Cruikshank, slightly spotted in places, bound without half title, contemporary half dark green calf, spine with raised and gilt bands, maroon leather label, head of leading hinge slightly split, slightly rubbed, good plus. Jarndyce Antiquarian Booksellers CCXVIII - 183 2016 £420

Dickens, Charles 1812-1870 *Oliver Twist.* London: Bradbury & Evans, 1846. New edition, bound without half title, plates by George Cruikshank, contemporary half green calf, spine decorated in blind and with raised gilt bands, maroon leather label, very good, attractive. Jarndyce Antiquarian Booksellers CCXVIII - 182 2016 £500

Dickens, Charles 1812-1870 *Oliver Twist.* London: Chapman & Hall, 1850. First cheap edition, half title, frontispiece by George Cruikshank little spotted, original uniform green cloth, blocked in blind, gilt spine, spine faded, following hinge slightly chipped at head and tail, good plus. Jarndyce Antiquarian Booksellers CCXVIII - 184 2016 £75

Dickens, Charles 1812-1870 *Oliver Twist.* London: Chapman & Hall, 1865. Frontispiece by George Cruikshank, contemporary half maroon sheep, spine slightly rubbed at head and tail, slightly faded, some worming in following hinge, good sound copy. Jarndyce Antiquarian Booksellers CCXVIII - 185 2016 £45

Dickens, Charles 1812-1870 *Oliver Twist.* London: Chapman & Hall, 1871. Household edition, 4to., vignette title, illustrations, original green cloth blocked in black and gilt, slightly rubbed, leading inner hinge slightly cracked, very good.   Jarndyce Antiquarian Booksellers   CCXVIII - 186   2016   £55

Dickens, Charles 1812-1870 *Oliver Twist. (with) Great Expectations.*   London: Chapman and Hall, 1871. 1876. Household edition, 4to., 2 volumes in 1, first work, frontispiece with small tear in outer margin, without loss, illustrations by J. Mahony, second work illustrations by F. A. Fraser, contemporary half dark green morocco, blue patterned cloth sides, spines little faded and slightly rubbed at head and tail, contemporary signature of C. E. Swinnerton.   Jarndyce Antiquarian Booksellers   CCXVIII - 189   2016   £120

Dickens, Charles 1812-1870 *Oliver Twist.* London: Chapman & Hall, 1877. Yellowback, vignette title, final ad leaf, ads on endpapers, original pale green printed boards, spine slightly chipped at head and tail and with some paper missing, hinges rubbed, boards nice and bright.   Jarndyce Antiquarian Booksellers   CCXVIII - 190   2016   £60

Dickens, Charles 1812-1870 *Oliver Twist.* London: Chapman and Hall, circa, 1880. Reprint, 4to., vignette title illustrations by J. Mahoney, original green cloth, blocked in blind and gilt, very good.   Jarndyce Antiquarian Booksellers   CCXVIII - 188   2016   £40

Dickens, Charles 1812-1870 *Oliver Twist.* Manchester & London: John Heywood, 1886. Stapled as issued in buff pink printed wrappers, first wrapper with portrait of Charles Dickens, dusted and marked, tail of spine chipped, good, sound copy, unsigned woodcuts.   Jarndyce Antiquarian Booksellers   CCXVIII - 191   2016   £40

Dickens, Charles 1812-1870 *Oliver Twist.* London: Chapman & Hall, circa, 1890? Large 4to., half title, frontispiece and plates by Cruikshank tipped on to grey paper, some spotting, half red buckram, matching red boards, paper label, little faded and rubbed, bookplate of Frank Staff & Dickens Centenary stamp.   Jarndyce Antiquarian Booksellers   CCXVIII - 192   2016   £75

Dickens, Charles 1812-1870 *Oliver Twist.* London: Chapman & Hall, circa, 1900. Half title, slightly creased, frontispiece, plates, original blue embossed cloth, gilt spine faded, very good.   Jarndyce Antiquarian Booksellers   CCXVIII - 193   2016   £20

Dickens, Charles 1812-1870 *Oliver Twist.* Oxford: Clarendon Press, 1966. Half title, frontispiece, illustrations, map, original dark blue cloth, spine lettered gilt, very good in slightly worn dust jacket.   Jarndyce Antiquarian Booksellers   CCXVIII - 194   2016   £65

Dickens, Charles 1812-1870 *Our Mutual Friend.* London: Chapman & Hall, 1864-1865. First edition, illustrations by Marcus Stone, xx original parts in xix, original green pictorial wrappers, some slightly chipped at fore-edge, spines cracking in places, occasional tear, several spines carefully repaired, spine defective part XVIII, dark blue coth fold over box.   Jarndyce Antiquarian Booksellers   CCXVIII - 607   2016   £1200

Dickens, Charles 1812-1870 *Our Mutual Friend.* London: Chapman & Hall, 1864-1865. First edition, XX original parts of XIX, original green pictorial wrappers, one or two numbers chipped, slight wear to tails of some spines, well preserved and clean set, only minimal expert repair work, in custom made green cloth slipcase, excellent set.   Jarndyce Antiquarian Booksellers   CCXVIII - 606   2016   £1600

Dickens, Charles 1812-1870 *Our Mutual Friend.* New York: Harper & Bros., 1865. First US edition, large 8vo., publisher's brown cloth, covers rubbed, ownership signature on front endpaper dated April 11, 1866, some foxing, good.   Second Life Books, Inc.   197 - 85   2016 $350

Dickens, Charles 1812-1870 *Our Mutual Friend.* New York: Harper & Bros., 1865. First US edition, large 8vo., publisher's brown cloth, hinges tender, name on rear endpaper, ownership signature on front endpaper dated March 31, 1866, some foxing, good.   Second Life Books, Inc.   197 - 84   2016 $350

Dickens, Charles 1812-1870 *Our Mutual Friend.* New York: Harper & Bros., 1865. First American one volume edition, frontispiece, engraved title, illustrations, 2 pages ads, original sand grained purple cloth, double page border in blind spine lettered gilt, slightly dulled, spine excellently repaired at head and tail, good plus.   Jarndyce Antiquarian Booksellers   CCXVIII - 612   2016   £220

Dickens, Charles 1812-1870 *Our Mutual Friend.* London: Chapman & Hall, 1865. First edition, 2 volumes, half titles, frontispieces, plates by Marcus Stone, 36 page catalog (Jan 1865) volume I, final ad leaf, 4 pages ads (Nov. 1865) volume II, occasional light spotting, uncut in original purple sand grained cloth, boards blocked in blind, spines blocked and lettered in gilt, spines very slightly faded, contemporary signature of J. and E.C. Mimms (?), small blindstamps of Bolton & Wilsher, Tenterden, very nice, bright.   Jarndyce Antiquarian Booksellers   CCXVIII - 608   2016   £850

Dickens, Charles 1812-1870 *Our Mutual Friend.* New York: Harper and Brothers, 1865. First American one volume edition, frontispiece, engraved title, illustrations, original sand grained purple cloth, double ruled border in blind, spine lettered gilt, slightly dulled, spine excellently repaired at head and tail, good plus.   Jarndyce Antiquarian Booksellers   CCXVIII - 612   2016   £220

Dickens, Charles 1812-1870 *Our Mutual Friend.* London: Chapman and Hall, 1865. First edition, 2 volumes bound in 1, 8vo., later three quarter calf, some rubbed, very nice clean.   Second Life Books, Inc.   197 - 83   2016 $1200

Dickens, Charles 1812-1870 *Our Mutual Friend.* London: Chapman and Hall, 1865. First edition in book form, octavo, very rare publisher's deluxe morocco, gilt ruled and blindstamped boards, marbled endpapers, all edges gilt, 2 volumes, some scuffing to binding extremities, text and plates exceptionally clean, exquisite set.   Manhattan Rare Book Company   2016 - 1739   2016 $2900

Dickens, Charles 1812-1870 *Our Mutual Friend.* London: Chapman & Hall, 1865. First edition, frontispiece, plates by Marcus Stone, 2 volumes, contemporary half green calf, spines gilt in compartments, red leather labels, slightly rubbed, ownership inscription " N. M. Longhsaw May 1866, Dickens centenary stamps, very good.   Jarndyce Antiquarian Booksellers CCXVIII - 699   2016   £350

Dickens, Charles 1812-1870 *Our Mutual Friend.* London: Chapman & Hall, 1875. Household edition, half title, frontispiece, vignette ttile, illustrations by J. Mahoney, original green cloth, blocked and lettered in black and gilt, slight rubbing to head and tail of spine, else very good.   Jarndyce Antiquarian Booksellers   CCXVIII - 611   2016   £45

Dickens, Charles 1812-1870 *The Personal History of David Copperfield.* London: Bradbury & Evans, 1850. First edition, frontispiece and engraved title, printed title, plates by Phiz, occasional browning or spotting ot plates, contemporary half green calf, spine with raised gilt bands, maroon leather label, boards rubbed, remains of armorial bookplate.   Jarndyce Antiquarian Booksellers   CCXVIII - 474   2016   £280

Dickens, Charles 1812-1870 *The Personal History of David Copperfield.* London: 1849-1850. First edition, illustrations by Phiz, xx original parts in xix, plates slightly browned in places, original blue green pictorial wrappers, two or three parts, very slightly chipped at head of tail of spine, back wrapper carefully reattached part xix/xx part xvii wrappers loose, as issued, never glued to text block, overall very well preserved and clean set, virtually no repair work, custom made blue morocco box, armorial bookplate of Cortlandt F. Bishop.   Jarndyce Antiquarian Booksellers   CCXVIII - 468   2016   £12,500

Dickens, Charles 1812-1870 *The Personal History of David Copperfield.* London: Bradbury & Evans, 1850. First edition, frontispiece and engraved title slightly browned at edges, printed title, plates by Phiz, contemporary half maroon calf, spine gilt to compartments, black leather label, spine faded to tan and slightly rubbed, corner slightly knocked, contemporary signature of M. St. Brague(?) on initial blank, good plus.   Jarndyce Antiquarian Booksellers   CCXVIII - 472   2016   £600

Dickens, Charles 1812-1870 *The Personal History of David Copperfield.* London: Bradbury & Evans, 1850. First edition, frontispiece and engraved title, printed title, plates by Phiz, some browning to plates, lacks leading f.e.p., contemporary full dark blue black morocco, ruled in gilt, little rubbed, repairs to head of leading hinge, contemporary signature of Gerard Johnson, all edges gilt.   Jarndyce Antiquarian Booksellers   CCXVIII - 473   2016   £320

Dickens, Charles 1812-1870 *The Personal History of David Copperfield.* London: Bradbury and Evans, 1850. First edition, half title, frontispiece and engraved title, printed title, plates by Phiz, occasional spotting but plates generally clean and fresh, original olive green fine diaper cloth blocked in blind, spine lettered gilt, front board slightly marked, slight wear to hinges, corners and head and tail of spine, some minor old repairs to following hinge, good, sound copy, difficult title in cloth.   Jarndyce Antiquarian Booksellers   CCXVIII - 470   2016   £500

Dickens, Charles 1812-1870 *The Personal History of David Copperfield.* London: Bradbury & Evans, 1850. First edition, early issue, without half title, engraved frontispiece, title and plates by Phiz, waterstain to lower outer corner of plates, some foxing, original olive green fine diaper cloth, blocked in blind, spine lettered gilt, spine little faded, neat repairs to inner hinges, ownership inscription of A. E. Harwood, superior copy.   Jarndyce Antiquarian Booksellers   CCXVIII - 469   2016   £2500

Dickens, Charles 1812-1870 *The Personal History of David Copperfield.* London: Bradbury & Evans, 1850. First edition, frontispiece and engraved title, printed title, plates by Phiz, contemporary half green calf, spine with raised bands, compartments with embossed wavy design, maroon leather label, very good, attractive.   Jarndyce Antiquarian Booksellers   CCXVIII - 471   2016   £750

Dickens, Charles 1812-1870 *The Personal History of David Copperfield.* London: Bradbury & Evans, 1850. First edition, half title, frontispiece and engraved title, printed title, plates by Phiz, contemporary full ta calf, spine gilt in compartments, black leather label, gilt borders and dentelles, well rebacked retaining original slightly rubbed spine crisp, armorial bookplates, nice, clean.   Jarndyce Antiquarian Booksellers   CCXVIII - 475   2016   £350

Dickens, Charles 1812-1870 *Le Neveu de Ma Tante: Histoire Personnelle de David Copperfield.* Paris: Bureaux de la Revue Britannique, 1851. Third edition, 3 volumes, half titles, uncut, original green printed wrappers bound into half dark green calf, very good.   Jarndyce Antiquarian Booksellers   CCXVIII - 479   2016   £85

Dickens, Charles 1812-1870 *Le Neveu de Ma Tante: Histoire Personnelle de David Copperfield.* Paris: Michel Levy Freres, 1857. 2 volumes, half titles, uncut, original pale green wrappers, spines slightly faded.   Jarndyce Antiquarian Booksellers   CCXVIII - 480   2016   £50

Dickens, Charles 1812-1870 *David Copperfield.* Paris: Librairie de L. Hachette, circa, 1858. Half titles, contemporary brown continental binder's cloth, very good.   Jarndyce Antiquarian Booksellers   CCXVIII - 481   2016   £45

Dickens, Charles 1812-1870 *The Personal History of David Copperfield.* London: Chapman & Hall, 1872. Household edition, 4to., frontispiece, vignette title, plates and illustrations by F. Barnard, original green cloth blocked in black and gilt, leading inner hinge cracking, otherwise very good.   Jarndyce Antiquarian Booksellers   CCXVIII - 476   2016   £45

Dickens, Charles 1812-1870 *The Personal History and Experience of David Copperfield the Younger.* London: Macmillan, 1912. Reprint, octavo, engravings of the first edition, period fine prize binding of full tree calf with raised bands, elaborate decoration to spine and edges, morocco title labels, marbled edges and endpapers, school gilt device on front cover and prize label, near fine.   Peter Ellis   112 - 102   2016   £125

Dickens, Charles 1812-1870 *David Copperfield.* Oxford: Clarendon Press, 1981. Original royal blue cloth, very good in slightly rubbed dust jacket, half title, frontispiece and plates.   Jarndyce Antiquarian Booksellers   CCXVIII - 478   2016   £80

Dickens, Charles 1812-1870 *The Pic Nic Papers.* Paris: A. & W. Galignani & Co., 1841. Titlepage slightly creased, contemporary half calf, later maroon leather label, little rubbed, leading hinge slightly split at head, repaired.   Jarndyce Antiquarian Booksellers   CCXVIII - 312   2016   £85

Dickens, Charles 1812-1870 *The Pic Nic Papers.* London: Henry Colburn, 1841. First edition, 2nd issue with corrected 'young publisher in preface, 8vo., 3 volumes, sometime bound by Riviere & son in full dark green morocco, boards with French fillet panel, spines lettered and decorated in gilt, original boards bound in at rear, frontispiece and plates by George Cruikshank, Phiz, &c., little rubbing to joints, gilt on spines little dulled, otherwise very good set preserved in marbled paper covered slipcase.   Sotheran's Piccadilly Notes - Summer 2015 - 106   2016   £1250

Dickens, Charles 1812-1870 *The Pic Nic Papers.* London: Ward & Lock, circa, 1870. Frontispiece and plates by Cruikshank and Phiz, partially unopened in original green morocco grained cloth, spine blocked in gilt, boards in blind, very good, bright.   Jarndyce Antiquarian Booksellers   CCXVIII - 313   2016   £85

Dickens, Charles 1812-1870 *Pictures from Italy.* London: published for the author by Bradbury & Evans, 1846. first edition, 2nd issue, half title, vignette title, initial and final ad leaves, original blue fine diaper cloth blocked in blind, spine lettered gilt, spine slightly dulled, contemporary signature of H. H. Stanfield, very good in blue cloth slipcase.   Jarndyce Antiquarian Booksellers   CCXVIII - 433   2016   £350

Dickens, Charles 1812-1870 *Pictures from Italy.* London: published for author by Bradbury & Evans, 1846. First edition, vignette title, contemporary full dark green calf, spine gilt in compartments, double ruled borders in gilt, maroon and brown morocco labels, spine slightly rubbed at head and tail contemporary signature of M. E. Martineau, good plus, attractive.   Jarndyce Antiquarian Booksellers   CCXVIII - 434   2016   £250

Dickens, Charles 1812-1870 *Pictures from Italy.* London: published for the author by Bradbury & Evans, 1846. First edition, 2nd issue, half title, vignette title, iniital and final ad leaves, original blue horizontal grained cloth, blocked in blind, spine lettered gilt, some expertly executed minor repairs to head and tail of spine, very good.   Jarndyce Antiquarian Booksellers   CCXVIII - 432   2016   £450

Dickens, Charles 1812-1870 *The Plays and Poems.* London: W. H. Allen, 1885. First edition, 2nd issue, 2 volumes, half titles, original royal blue cloth, spines lettered gilt, spines dulled and rather worn at heads and tails, labels of Constitutional Club library, sound, good copy.   Jarndyce Antiquarian Booksellers   CCXVIII - 705   2016   £180

Dickens, Charles 1812-1870 *The Plays and Poems...* London: W. H. Allen, 1885. First edition, 2nd issue, 2 volumes, half title, original royal blue cloth, spines lettered gilt, spines dulled and rather worn at heads and tails, labels of Constitutioanl Club library, good, sound copy.   Jarndyce Antiquarian Booksellers   CCXVIII - 705   2016   £180

Dickens, Charles 1812-1870 *The Poems and Verses...* London: Chapman & Hall, 1903. First edition, half title, frontispiece, untrimmed in original maroon cloth, beveled boards, lettered gilt, Tillotson signature, top edge gilt, very good.   Jarndyce Antiquarian Booksellers   CCXVIII - 706   2016   £40

Dickens, Charles   1812-1870   *The Poor Traveller; Boots at the Holly-Tree Inn; and Mrs. Gamp.*   London: Bradbury & Evans, 1858. First edition, final ad leaf, original green printed wrappers, small stain on back cover, small chips at head and tail of spine, slightly dusted, good plus.   Jarndyce Antiquarian Booksellers   CCXVIII - 554   2016   £60

Dickens, Charles   1812-1870   *The Poor Traveller; Boots at the Holly-Tree Inn; and Mrs. Gamp.*   London: Bradbury & Evans, 1858. First edition, original green printed wrappers, stitching largely missing, spine defective, lacking back wrappers, signed 'Brandram' on front wrapper, with excisions, annotations and amendments in same hand, Bandram 1824-1892 was a barrister.   Jarndyce Antiquarian Booksellers   CCXVIII - 553   2016   £1500

Dickens, Charles   1812-1870   *The Poor Traveller: Boots at the Holly-Tree Inn; and Mrs. Gamp.*   London: Bradbury & Evans, 1858. First edition, disbound.   Jarndyce Antiquarian Booksellers   CCXVIII - 555   2016   £20

Dickens, Charles   1812-1870   *The Posthumous Papers of the Pickwick Club.*   London: Chapman and Hall, 1837. First edition in book form, 8vo., full brown, straight grained morocco stamped in blind and gilt, all edges gilt, some intermittent foxing and staining especially on plates, very good, tight copy, good looking copy in early binding.   Second Life Books, Inc.   197 - 76   2016 $2500

Dickens, Charles   1812-1870   *The Posthumous Papers of the Pickwick Club.*   London: Chapman & Hall, 1837. First edition, Weller title, frontispiece and engraved title spotted, plates with some marginal spotting and staining, contemporary half calf, black leather label, carefully rebacked, spine and corners rubbed, enw endpapers at some point, contemporary signature of James Lawless, Exeter, good, sound copy.   Jarndyce Antiquarian Booksellers   CCXVIII - 97   2016   £180

Dickens, Charles   1812-1870   *The Posthumous Papers of the Pickwick Club.*   London: Chapman & Hall, 1837. First Edition, Weller title, half title, frontispiece and engraved title and plates, browning to plates, uncut in original purple brown fine diaper cloth, slightly faded with some wear to head and tail of spine, extremities, slightly rubbed, armorial bookplate, cloth slipcase.   Jarndyce Antiquarian Booksellers   CCXVIII - 95   2016   £850

Dickens, Charles   1812-1870   *The Posthumous Papers of the Pickwick Club.*   London: Chapman & Hall, 1837. First edition, Weller title, engraved title and plates, slightly spotted, outer edges of page 393-396 dusted and slightly chipped, one or two gatherings slightly proud, original purple brown fine diaper cloth, boards and spine blocked in blind, spine lettered in gilt with small ink mark, recased with some minor repairs, endpapers replaced, faded, slight creasing to spine, decent of a trifle difficult to cloth grey-green cloth slipcase.   Jarndyce Antiquarian Booksellers   CCXVIII - 91   2016   £500

Dickens, Charles   1812-1870   *The Posthumous Papers of the Pickwick Club.*   London: Chapman & Hall, 1837. First edition, early issue, Weller title, frontispiece and engraved title little spotted, plates with occasional spotting, contemporary half green morocco, green cloth sides, gilt spine, slightly rubbed, good plus.   Jarndyce Antiquarian Booksellers   CCXVIII - 93   2016   £450

Dickens, Charles   1812-1870   *The Posthumous Papers of the Pickwick Club.*   London: Chapman & Hall, 1837. First edition in book form, 43 illustrations, including frontispiece and vignette titlepage, extra illustrated with additional 31 inserted plates by Thomas Onwhyn, 43 engraved plates including frontispiece and engraved titlepage, half title, contemporary half calf over marbled boards, gilt stamped spine, red morocco label, previous owner's contemporary signature, very good, custom green cloth clamshell, gilt stamped.   Heritage Book Shop   Holiday 2015 - 28   2016 $1000

Dickens, Charles   1812-1870   *The Posthumous Papers of the Pickwick Club.*   London: Chapman and Hall, 1837. First edition, Veller title, 2 volumes, additional plates published by E. Grattan in 1817, with original illustrations, in varying states, bound by Root & Son in blue morocco with Dickens's signature in gilt on covers, gilt floral dentelles, edges ruled in gilt spines evenly faded, top edge gilt, in slipcase, extra illustrated with 45 additional plates.   Jarndyce Antiquarian Booksellers   CCXVIII - 92   2016   £2500

Dickens, Charles   1812-1870   *The Posthumous Papers of the Pickwick Club.*   London: Chapman & Hall, 1837. First edition in book form, octavo, extremely rare publisher's deluxe three quarter green morocco, marbled edges and endpapers, toning to engraved title and frontispiece, occasional foxing to plates (generally at edges and less than usual), text exceptionally clean, copies in publisher's morocco are extremely rare.   Manhattan Rare Book Company   2016 - 1734   2016 $4200

Dickens, Charles   1812-1870   *The Posthumous Papers of the Pickwick Club.*   Philadelphia: Carey, Lea & Blanchard, 1838. First American one volume edition, initial 6 page ads (Feb. 1938), frontispiece, engrave dtitle and 19 plates by Crowquill (one missing), slightly dusted and spotted text, well rebound in dark green cloth, quite good.   Jarndyce Antiquarian Booksellers   CCXVIII - 98   2016   £85

Dickens, Charles   1812-1870   *The Posthumous Papers of the Pickwick Club.*   Philadelphia: Lea & Blanchard, 1846. New edition, some internal spotting, pages 111-112 torn and neatly repaired without loss, half black calf, blue cloth boards, spine faded.   Jarndyce Antiquarian Booksellers   CCXVIII - 99   2016   £50

Dickens, Charles   1812-1870   *The Posthumous Papers of the Pickwick Club.*   London: Chapman & Hall, circa, 1865. Cheap edition, half title, frontispiece by C. R. Leslie, original dark green cloth, spine blocked and lettered gilt, spine chipped at tail, following inner hinge slightly cracked, following pastedown little marked.   Jarndyce Antiquarian Booksellers   CCXVIII - 101   2016   £30

Dickens, Charles   1812-1870   *The Posthumous Papers of the Pickwick Club.*   London: Chapman & Hall, 1874. Household edition, 4to., frontispiece and plates, illustrations by Phiz, slight spotting, original green cloth, blocked and lettered im black and gilt very slight rubbing, very good.   Jarndyce Antiquarian Booksellers   CCXVIII - 102   2016   £65

Dickens, Charles   1812-1870   *The Posthumous Papers of the Pickwick Club.*   London: Chapman & Hall, 1877. Vignette title, final ad leaf, ads on titlepage slightly browned, "Yellowback", original pale green printed boards, hinges little rubbed, good plus.   Jarndyce Antiquarian Booksellers   CCXVIII - 103   2016   £120

Dickens, Charles   1812-1870   *The Posthumous Papers of the Pickwick Club.*   London: Hodder & Stoughton, circa, 1910. First edition in book form, 4to., mounted frontispiece plus 24 full page mounted color plates engraved and printed by Henry Stone & Son. Ltd., Banbury, England, light green boards with cloth spine and paper label, some light wear but very good, clean copy with bright illustrations.   Second Life Books, Inc.   197 - 75   2016 $450

Dickens, Charles   1812-1870   *The Posthumous Papers of the Pickwick Club.*   London: Hodder & Stoughton, 1910. 4to., half title, color frontispiece, engraved title, 24 color plates by Frank Reynolds tipped in, original red cloth, lettered gilt, silhouette of Pickwick at centre of front board, slight wear to corners and head and tail of spine.   Jarndyce Antiquarian Booksellers   CCXVIII - 106   2016   £40

Dickens, Charles   1812-1870   *Posthumous Papers of the Pickwick Club.*   New York: E. P. Dutton, n.d., 1910. 2 volumes, large thick 4to., pictorial cloth, light spine rubbing and occasional fox spot, very good+, 24 fabulous color plates plus a profusion of great illustrations all throughout text, lovely set.   Aleph-bet Books, Inc.   112 - 19   2016 $750

Dickens, Charles   1812-1870   *The Posthumous Papers of the Pickwick Club.*   London: Chapman & Hall, Lawrence 7 Jellicoe, 1910. 2 volumes, 4to., half titles, color frontispiece and 22 full color plates, engraved illustrations in text, uncut, original olive brown cloth, pictorially blocked and lettered in dark brown, little dulled and slightly rubbed.   Jarndyce Antiquarian Booksellers   CCXVIII - 105   2016   £150

Dickens, Charles   1812-1870   *The Posthumous Papers of the Pickwick Club.*   London: George G. Harrap & Co., 1930. Half title, color frontispiece and plates, half title and endpapers slightly browned, original brick red cloth, spine lettered in gilt, very good.   Jarndyce Antiquarian Booksellers   CCXVIII - 109   2016   £35

Dickens, Charles   1812-1870   *Los Papeles Posumos del Club Pickwick.*   Barcelona: Ediitorial Tartessos, 1943. No. 145 of 1000 copies, Half title, printed in black, green and red, illustrations, original pale green cloth, lettered in dark green and white, very good.   Jarndyce Antiquarian Booksellers   CCXVIII - 112   2016   £45

Dickens, Charles   1812-1870   *The Posthumous Papers of the Pickwick Club.*   London: Nottingham Court Press, 1979. Facsimile of first edition, color frontispiece, engraved title, additional printed title, plates, original green cloth, blocked and lettered in gilt, mint.   Jarndyce Antiquarian Booksellers   CCXVIII - 110   2016   £35

Dickens, Charles   1812-1870   *The Posthumous Papers of the Pickwick Club.*   Oxford: Clarendon Press, 1986. Half title, frontispiece, I, original dark blue cloth, near mint in slightly faded dust jacket, review slip laid in.   Jarndyce Antiquarian Booksellers   CCXVIII - 111   2016   £110

Dickens, Charles   1812-1870   *The Readings of Mr. Charles Dickens, as Condensed by Himself. A Christmas Carol and the Grial from Pickwick.*   Boston: and New York: Ticknor & Fields, 1868. Illustrated copyright edition, engraved frontispiece and 1 plate by S. Eytinge, original pale blue printed wrappers, spine slightly chipped at head and tail, three small stab holes in inner margin, decent copy.   Jarndyce Antiquarian Booksellers   CCXVIII - 623   2016   £180

Dickens, Charles   1812-1870   *The Short Stories of Charles Dickens.*   New York: Limited Editions Club, 1971. No. 932 of undefined print-run, Illustrated by Edward Ardizzone, half title, frontispiece, vignette title, text illustrations and full page plates, original half black cloth, marbled boards, gilt spine, mint in slightly rubbed, marbled slipcase, signed by artist and J. Blumental, designer and printer.   Jarndyce Antiquarian Booksellers   CCXVIII - 754   2016   £80

Dickens, Charles 1812-1870 *Sketches by Boz. First Series. (with) Second Series.* London: John Macrone, 1836-1837. First edition, frontispiece and plates by George Cruikshank, 2 volumes, uncut in original dark green embossed cloth, heads of spines decorated and lettered in gilt, spines little darkened, carefully recased with some expertly executed minor repairs, second series with half title, frontispiece, engraved title plates, by Cruikshank, 19 page catalog (Dec. 1836), uncut in original pink pebble grained cloth, panelled spine pigmented black at head and tail to give impression of labels, carefully recased with small neat repairs to hinges and head and tail of spine, all volumes with armorial bookplate of Reuben Jay Flick, generally well preserved in custom made dark blue crushed morocco and cloth double slipcase by Heritage Bindery.   Jarndyce Antiquarian Booksellers   CCXVIII - 54   2016   £2800

Dickens, Charles 1812-1870 *Sketches by Boz.* London: John Macrone, 1836-1837. First edition, 2 volumes, 12mo., frontispiece in volume 1 and plates by George Cruikshank, small tear to margin pages 277 and 278 neatly repaired with archival tape, volumes little affected by damp, handsomely rebound in full dark green morocco, gilt dentelles and edges, top edge gilt, cloth slipcase, inscribed "Mrs. George Cruikshank with publisher's best respects" and signed by George Cruikshank.   Jarndyce Antiquarian Booksellers   CCXVIII - 53   2016   £5500

Dickens, Charles 1812-1870 *Sketches by Boz. Second Series. complete in one volume.* London: John Macrone, 1837. (1836). First edition, plates by George Cruikshank, contemporary half dark green calf, spine with raised gilt bands and maroon leather label, monogram bookplate, very good.   Jarndyce Antiquarian Booksellers   CCXVIII - 56   2016   £1200

Dickens, Charles 1812-1870 *Sketches by Boz. (Second Series).* Philadelphia: Carey, Lea & Blanchard, 1837. First American edition, original light brown boards, red cloth spine, paper label, little faded & rubbed, contemporary signature of J. B. Barnum(?), later booklabel of Alfred Knopf, overall good plus, well preserved copy.   Jarndyce Antiquarian Booksellers   CCXVIII - 58   2016   £450

Dickens, Charles 1812-1870 *Sketches by Boz. Second Series.* London: John Macrone, 1837. Second edition, frontispiece, vignette title and plates by George Cruikshank, original pink pebbled grained cloth, blocked in blind, spine lettered in gilt, spine slightly faded, one corner slightly knocked, very good.   Jarndyce Antiquarian Booksellers   CCXVIII - 57   2016   £1200

Dickens, Charles 1812-1870 *Sketches by Boz. First Series.* London: John Macrone, 1837. Third edition, 2 volumes, frontispiece and plates by George Cruikshank, original dark blue green cloth, blocked in blind, spines lettered in gilt, spines slightly faded, overall very good.   Jarndyce Antiquarian Booksellers   CCXVIII - 55   2016   £650

Dickens, Charles 1812-1870 *Sketches by Boz.* Philadelphia: Lea and Blanchard, 1839. First complete American edition, engraved title bound as frontispiece, plates, slight spotting, original purple cloth, faded and slightly rubbed, neatly recased, good.   Jarndyce Antiquarian Booksellers   CCXVIII - 64   2016   £65

Dickens, Charles 1812-1870 *Sketches by Boz.* London: Chapman & Hall, 1839. First collected edition in original cloth, frontispiece, two egnraved titles, one with Chapman and Hall imprint and one without, plates, slight foxing, excellently executed repairs to inner hinges, uncut in original vertical grained cloth, blocked in blind, spine lettered gilt, spine little faded, armorial bookplate of John Wood, green cloth foldover box, slightly spotted, very good, bright.   Jarndyce Antiquarian Booksellers   CCXVIII - 59   2016   £2250

Dickens, Charles 1812-1870 *Sketches by Boz.* London: Chapman and Hall, 1839. Half title, frontispiece, engraved title, plates, uncut in slightly later dark green crushed morocco by Riviere & Son, gilt spine, borders and dentelles, armorial bookplate of John Neville Cross, top edge gilt, very good, handsome copy.   Jarndyce Antiquarian Booksellers   CCXVIII - 60   2016   £850

Dickens, Charles 1812-1870 *Sketches by Boz.* London: Chapman and Hall, 1839. Engraved title, plates, occasional spotting, one plate torn without loss and neatly repaired with archival tape, contemporary full green morocco, green cloth sides, gilt spines slightly faded.   Jarndyce Antiquarian Booksellers   CCXVIII - 61   2016   £420

Dickens, Charles 1812-1870 *Sketches by Boz.* Paris: Baudry's European Library, 1839. Half title, text very lightly spotted, attractively bound in contemporary half green calf, spine gilt in compartments, tan leather label, very slight rubbing to extremities, top edge gilt, very good.   Jarndyce Antiquarian Booksellers   CCXVIII - 62   2016   £85

Dickens, Charles 1812-1870 *Sketches by Boz.* Paris: A. & W. Galignani & Co.,, 1839. Galignani edition, contemporary half dark green calf, spine with raised gilt bands and decorated in blind, slightly rubbed.   Jarndyce Antiquarian Booksellers   CCXVIII - 62   2016   £85

Dickens, Charles 1812-1870 *Sketches by Boz.* Paris: A. & W. Galignani & Co., 1839. Complete in one volume, contemporary half dark green calf, spine with raised gilt bands and decorated in blind, slightly rubbed.   Jarndyce Antiquarian Booksellers   CCXVIII - 63   2016   £85

Dickens, Charles 1812-1870 *Sketches by Boz.* Philadelphia: Lee & Blanchard, 1842. New edition, tall 8vo., engraved frontispiece and 19 plates after George Cruikshank (all present), some browning and staining, few carefully repaired tears, original brown cloth, decorated in blind, gilt spine, expertly recased, neat repairs to corners and head and tail of spine, inscribed Ann (sic) Brown from Catherine Dickens NY June 1842, inscription leaf rather browned and has repaired edges, text clear. Jarndyce Antiquarian Booksellers CCXVIII - 65 2016 £1500

Dickens, Charles 1812-1870 *Sketches by Boz.* London: Chapman & Hall, 1850. First cheap edition, ad leaf preceding half title, frontispiece by George Cruikshank, original light green cloth, blocked in blind, spine blocked and lettered gilt, spine slightly faded, very good. Jarndyce Antiquarian Booksellers CCXVIII - 66 2016 £65

Dickens, Charles 1812-1870 *Sketches by Boz.* London: Chapman and Hall, 1854. Reprint of First cheap edition, frontispiece by George Cruikshank, frontispiece, original light green cloth, blocked in blind, spine blocked and lettered gilt, spine faded and slightly rubbed at head and tail. Jarndyce Antiquarian Booksellers CCXVIII - 67 2016 £40

Dickens, Charles 1812-1870 *Sketches by Boz.* London: Chapman & Hall, 1872. New edition, frontispiece, engraved title, plates by George Cruikshank, handsomely bound in contemporary full dark green calf, double ruled borders gilt, spine gilt in compartments, red labels, very good, bright. Jarndyce Antiquarian Booksellers CCXVIII - 68 2016 £150

Dickens, Charles 1812-1870 *Sketches by Boz.* London: Chapman and Hall, 1876. Household edition, frontispiece, plates and illustrations by Barnard, few spots, original green cloth, blocked in gilt and black, slight rubbing, very good. Jarndyce Antiquarian Booksellers CCXVIII - 69 2016 £40

Dickens, Charles 1812-1870 *Sketches by Boz. (with) Hard Times.* London: Chapman & Hall, 1876-1877. Household edition, vignette titles, illustrations by F. Barnard, 2 volumes in 1, contemporary half dark green morocco, blue patterned cloth sides, spine little faded and slightly rubbed and head and tail, contemporary signature of C. E. Swinnerton, good plus. Jarndyce Antiquarian Booksellers CCXVIII - 70 2016 £50

Dickens, Charles 1812-1870 *Sketches by Boz.* London: Chapman & Hall, 1877. Half title, vignette title, ads on endpapers slightly spotted, 'Yellowback', original pale green printed boards, spine darkened and little worn at head and tail, hinges rubbed, corners slightly knocked, Renier booklabel. Jarndyce Antiquarian Booksellers CCXVIII - 71 2016 £120

Dickens, Charles 1812-1870 *Sketches by Boz.* London: Chapman & Hall, circa, 1880? New edition, half title, frontispiece, engraved title and plates by George Cruikshank, original olive green cloth blocked in blind, spine lettered gilt, spine and edges faded, small ownership label on leading frontispiece, very good. Jarndyce Antiquarian Booksellers CCXVIII - 72 2016 £75

Dickens, Charles 1812-1870 *Sketches of Young Couples.* London: Chapman and Hall, 1840. First edition, half title, frontispiece and plates slightly browned at edges, 4 pages ads, contemporary half black calf, spine with gilt bands and maroon leather label, slightly rubbed, some unobtrusive pencil notes in text. Jarndyce Antiquarian Booksellers CCXVIII - 166 2016 £150

Dickens, Charles 1812-1870 *Sketches of Young Couples.* London: Chapman & Hall, 1840. First edition, half title, frontispiece and plates slightly browned at edges, original green printed boards, slightly dulled and rubbed, spine at some time replaced, hinges weakening, stamps of label of Brooklyn Public Library, poor copy. Jarndyce Antiquarian Booksellers CCXVIII - 167 2016 £120

Dickens, Charles 1812-1870 *Sketches of Young Couples and Young Gentlemen.* London: Chapman & Hall, circa, 1870? Frontispiece and plates by Phiz, original pebble grained maroon cloth, blocked in black, lettered gilt, slightly rubbed, bookplate of Peter & Margery Morris. Jarndyce Antiquarian Booksellers CCXVIII - 165 2016 £85

Dickens, Charles 1812-1870 *Sketches of Young Gentlemen.* London: Chapman & Hall, 1838. Second edition, frontispiece reattached in inner margin, plates, slightly later marbled boards, vellm spine lettered in red and black, little browned. Jarndyce Antiquarian Booksellers CCXVIII - 168 2016 £100

Dickens, Charles 1812-1870 *Sketches of Young Ladies, Young Gentlemen, Young Couples.* London: Chapman & Hall, 1843. First collected edition, 18 illustrations by Phiz, frontispiece and plates, two gatherings slightly proud, original fine grained olive brown cloth, blocked and lettered gilt, all edges gilt, very good, cloth slipcase, scarce edition. Jarndyce Antiquarian Booksellers CCXVIII - 164 2016 £2200

Dickens, Charles 1812-1870 *Some Letters of Charles Dickens.* Pittsburgh: privately printed, 1907. No. 9 of 200 copies, Untrimmed in original green wrappers, spine slightly faded, very good, signed presentation to T. N. Tyrrell. Jarndyce Antiquarian Booksellers CCXVIII - 865 2016 £20

Dickens, Charles 1812-1870 *Speech of Charles Dickens, Esq. as Chairman at the Dinner on Behalf of the Hospital for Sick Children February 9th 1858.* London: printed by R. Folkard & Sons, 1874. Reprint, Original buff wrappers, very good.   Jarndyce Antiquarian Booksellers   CCXVIII - 558   2016   £180

Dickens, Charles 1812-1870 *Speeches, Letters and Sayings of Charles Dickens.* New York: Harper Bros., 1870. First American edition, frontispiece, original buff printed wrappers, little worn and marked, spine chipped but holding.   Jarndyce Antiquarian Booksellers   CCXVIII - 690   2016   £90

Dickens, Charles 1812-1870 *Speeches Literary and Social. Now First Collected.* London: John Camden Hotten, 1870. First edition, original sand grained green cloth, lettering reversed out of black, slightly rubbed.   Jarndyce Antiquarian Booksellers   CCXVIII - 689   2016   £50

Dickens, Charles 1812-1870 *The Speeches of Charles Dickens 1841-1870.* London: Chatto & Windus, 1906. Fine paper edition with portrait, original pale blue cloth lettered in blind, edges slightly spotted, very good in dust jacket.   Jarndyce Antiquarian Booksellers   CCXVIII - 691   2016   £20

Dickens, Charles 1812-1870 *The Speeches of Charles Dickens.* London: Michael Joseph, 1917. Half title, original light blue cloth, very good in dust jacket.   Jarndyce Antiquarian Booksellers   CCXVIII - 692   2016   £20

Dickens, Charles 1812-1870 *The Speeches of Charles Dickens.* Oxford: Clarendon Press, 1960. Definitive edition, half title, original black cloth, mint in slightly tired dust jacket.   Jarndyce Antiquarian Booksellers   CCXVIII - 693   2016   £75

Dickens, Charles 1812-1870 *The Strange Gentleman.* London: Chapman & Hall, 1837. First edition, original pale lavender printed wrappers bound into full tan calf, gilt spine, dentelles and borders, green label, bookplate of Ralph Clutton, very good in cloth slipcase.   Jarndyce Antiquarian Booksellers   CCXVIII - 81   2016   £8500

Dickens, Charles 1812-1870 *The Strange Gentleman.* London: Chapman and Hall, 1871. More common facsimile reprint, largely unopened in original pale pink wrappers.   Jarndyce Antiquarian Booksellers   CCXVIII - 82   2016   £120

Dickens, Charles 1812-1870 *The Strange Gentleman.* London: Chapman and Hall, 1871. Original gray wrappers, later white paper spine.   Jarndyce Antiquarian Booksellers   CCXVIII - 83   2016   £45

Dickens, Charles 1812-1870 *The Strange Gentleman.* London: John Dicks, 1883? Original pink wrappers, split at spine, with loss form top of front cover, illustrations.   Jarndyce Antiquarian Booksellers   CCXVIII - 84   2016   £25

Dickens, Charles 1812-1870 *Sunday Under Three Heads.* London: Chapman & Hall, 1836. First edition, frontispiece, plates by Phiz, original buff pictorial wrappers, at some point neatly respined, good plus in custom made tan calf slipcase by Riviere & Son, imitating a bound volume.   Jarndyce Antiquarian Booksellers   CCXVIII - 78   2016   £1800

Dickens, Charles 1812-1870 *Sunday Under Three Heads.* London: Chapman & Hall, 1836. First edition, half title, engraved frontispiece and two plates after Phiz, marks from adhesion on leading f.e.p., original buff pictorial wrappers, inscribed 'with the publisher's compliments', good copy of fragile item in blue cloth folder, full blue morocco slipcase, scarce.   Jarndyce Antiquarian Booksellers   CCXVIII - 77   2016   £2500

Dickens, Charles 1812-1870 *Sunday Under Three Heads.* London: J. W. Jarvis & son, 1884. Exact facsimile of excessively rare original, illustrations by Phiz, original pale blue printed wrappers, front wrapper fore-edge & corners slightly chipped.   Jarndyce Antiquarian Booksellers   CCXVIII - 79   2016   £45

Dickens, Charles 1812-1870 *Sunday Under Three Heads and other Sketches.* London: George Routledge & sons, circa, 1888. Original pale blue pictorial wrappers printed in black and red, spine neatly replaced with appropriate paper, following wrappers slightly torn withou loss.   Jarndyce Antiquarian Booksellers   CCXVIII - 80   2016   £50

Dickens, Charles 1812-1870 *A Tale of Two Cities.* London: Chapman and Hall, 1859. First edition, 8vo., publisher's catalog, 16 plates by Phiz, 20th three quarter maroon morocco and cloth boards, spine stamped gilt, top edge gilt, some toning to engraved titlepages, otherwise nice, clean copy, first issue with misspelling 'affectionately' on page 134 (line 12 and page 213 mispaginated '113'.   Second Life Books, Inc.   197 - 77   2016 $7000

Dickens, Charles 1812-1870 *A Tale of Two Cities.* London: Chapman and Hall, 1859. First edition, first issue, frontispiece, engraved title and plates by Phiz, 32 page catalog (Nov. 1859), catalog with expertly executed minor repairs, handsomely bound in full scarlet crushed morocco by Bayntun-Riviere, gilt spine, single ruled borders and dentelles, all edges gilt, very good, attractive.   Jarndyce Antiquarian Booksellers   CCXVIII - 559   2016   £3800

Dickens, Charles 1812-1870 *A Tale of Two Cities.* London: Chapman & Hall, 1859. First edition, 2nd issue, frontispiece, engraved title, printed title, plates, small closed tear in inner margin affecting pages 29-68, prelims little browned, some foxing to plates and one or two slightly chipped at edges, contemporary half red morocco, spine gilt in compartments, marbled boards, slightly rubbed, decent in attractive contemporary binding.   Jarndyce Antiquarian Booksellers   CCXVIII - 562   2016   £1250

Dickens, Charles 1812-1870 *A Tale of Two Cities.* London: Chapman & Hall, 1859. First edition, 2nd issue, frontispiece, engraved title, plates by Phiz, uncut, original red cloth, blocked in blind, spine lettered gilt, expertly recased with small repairs to head and tail of spine, odd spot, bookplate of Henry Lea Guillebaud, good plus, scarce in original cloth.   Jarndyce Antiquarian Booksellers   CCXVIII - 561   2016   £1500

Dickens, Charles 1812-1870 *A Tale of Two Cities.* London: chapman & Hall, 1864. First cheap edition, frontispiece, original green sand grained cloth, boards blocked in blind, spine blocked and lettered gilt, very good, bright.   Jarndyce Antiquarian Booksellers   CCXVIII - 563 2016   £280

Dickens, Charles 1812-1870 *A Tale of Two Cities.* London: Chapman & Hall, circa, 1881. Household edition, reprint, 4to., half title, frontispiece, vignette title and plates by F. Barnard, original green cloth, blocked in black and gilt, very good.   Jarndyce Antiquarian Booksellers   CCXVIII - 564   2016   £120

Dickens, Charles 1812-1870 *Tales from Dickens, Engraved in Easy reporting Style of Pitman's Shorthand.* London: Isaac Pitman and Sons, 1902. 20th century edition, illustrations by P. Hudson, original maroon cloth, lettered gilt, Dickens Centenary stamp, very good.   Jarndyce Antiquarian Booksellers   CCXVIII - 729   2016   £25

Dickens, Charles 1812-1870 *Tales from Dickens. Engraved in the Easy Reporting Style of Pitman's Shorthand.* London: Isaac Pitman & Sons, 1902. 20th century edition, illustrations by P. Hudson, 4 pages ads, original mauve cloth lettered gilt, contemporary stamp on leading pastedown, very good.   Jarndyce Antiquarian Booksellers   CCXVIII - 729   2016   £25

Dickens, Charles 1812-1870 *Tom Tiddler's Ground. Extra Christmas Number of All the Year Round.* London: published at the Office No. 26 Wellington Street, 1861. Disbound, very good.   Jarndyce Antiquarian Booksellers   CCXVIII - 815   2016   £25

Dickens, Charles 1812-1870 *The Uncollected Writings of Charles Dickens: Household Words 1850-1859.* London: Allen Lane, Penguin Press, 1969. 2 volumes, original maroon cloth, black labels, very good in slightly rubbed dust jackets, slightly rubbed slipcase.   Jarndyce Antiquarian Booksellers   CCXVIII - 788   2016   £40

Dickens, Charles 1812-1870 *The Uncommercial Traveller.* London: Chapman & Hall, 1861. First edition, half title, 32 page catalog (Dec. 1860), contemporary full dark green crushed morocco by Riviere, gilt spine, borders and dentelles, part of original purple cloth board bound in at end, armorial bookplate of John Neville-Cross, top edge gilt, very good handsome copy.   Jarndyce Antiquarian Booksellers   CCXVIII - 597   2016   £600

Dickens, Charles 1812-1870 *The Uncommercial Traveller.* London: Chapman & Hall, 1861. First edition, 32 page catalog dated Dec. 1860, 8vo., 19th century deep maroon full morocco by Riviere, with elaborate gilt decorated spine, top edge gilt, gilt dentelles, minor extremity wear with lower tips showing slight abrasion, bookplate (Barnton), pencil note to prelim blank, "This copy sold in the McKenzie sale", withal handsome, very good+ copy.   Tavistock Books   Getting Around - 29   2016 $1500

Dickens, Charles 1812-1870 *The Uncommercial Traveller.* London: Chapman & Hall, 1861. Second edition, half title, 32 page catalog (Dec. 1860) original mauve wavy grained cloth, blocked in blind, spine faded, front board slightly unevenly faded, old spot, very good.   Jarndyce Antiquarian Booksellers   CCXVIII - 598   2016   £280

Dickens, Charles 1812-1870 *The Uncommercial Traveller.* London: Chapman & Hall, 1861. Third edition, half title, original mauve wavy grained cloth, blocked in blind, spines faded, very good, signature of dramatist S. Theyre-Smith.   Jarndyce Antiquarian Booksellers   CCXVIII - 599   2016   £250

Dickens, Charles 1812-1870 *The Uncommercial Traveller.* London: Chapman and Hall, 1870. Charles Dickens edition, green cloth, series and half titles, frontispiece slight damp marked in top outer cover, illustrations, original green cloth, bevelled boards, lettered gilt, inner hinges slightly cracked, else very good.   Jarndyce Antiquarian Booksellers   CCXVIII - 600   2016   £85

Dickens, Charles 1812-1870 *The Uncommercial Traveller.* London: Chapman & Hall, 1870. Charles Dickens edition, series and half titles, frontispiece slightly damp marked in top outer corner, illustrations, original green cloth, bevelled boards, lettered gilt, inner hinges slightly cracked, ese very good.   Jarndyce Antiquarian Booksellers   CCXVIII - 600   2016   £85

Dickens, Charles   1812-1870   *The Uncommercial Traveller.*   London: Chapman & Hall, circa, 1872. Charles Dickens edition, half title, frontispiece and 7 plates, original plainer pink cloth, lettered gilt, front cover slightly marked, spine faded.   Jarndyce Antiquarian Booksellers   CCXVIII - 601   2016   £20

Dickens, Charles   1812-1870   *The Uncommercial Traveller.*   London: Chapman and Hall, 1877. Household edition, 4to., frontispiece, plates and illustrations by E. G. Dalziel, original green cloth, blocked and lettered in black and gilt, very good.   Jarndyce Antiquarian Booksellers   CCXVIII - 603   2016   £45

Dickens, Charles   1812-1870   *The Uncommercial Traveller.*   London: Chapman & Hall, 1877. Household edition, 4to., frontispiece and plates and illustrations by E. G. Dalziel, original green cloth blocked and lettered in black and gilt, very good.   Jarndyce Antiquarian Booksellers   CCXVIII - 603   2016   £45

Dickens, Charles   1812-1870   *The Uncommercial Traveller.*   London: Chapman & Hall, circa, 1881. Reprint, 4to., frontispiece, plates, illustrations by E. G. Dalziel, original green cloth, blocked and lettered in black and gilt, leading hinge slightly cracked, otherwise very good.   Jarndyce Antiquarian Booksellers   CCXVIII - 604   2016   £45

Dickens, Charles   1812-1870   *The Uncommercial Traveller.*   London: Chapman and Hall, circa, 1886. Charles Dickens edition, series title, frontispiece, 3 plates, original uniform red cloth, little dulled and rubbed, gift inscription Nov. 1886, bookseller's ticket, Daniel S. Stacy, Islington, good.   Jarndyce Antiquarian Booksellers   CCXVIII - 602   2016   £20

Dickens, Charles   1812-1870   *The Uncommercial Traveller.*   London: Chapman & Hall, circa, 1886. Charles Dickens edition, series title, frontispiece and 3 plates, original uniform red cloth, little dulled and rubbed, gift inscription, bookseller's ticket, good, sound copy.   Jarndyce Antiquarian Booksellers   CCXVIII - 602   2016   £20

Dickens, Charles   1812-1870   *The Unpublished Letters of Charles Dickens to Mark Lemon.*   London: Halton & Truscott Smith, 1927. No. 160 of 525 copies, half title, illustrations, facsimiles, uncut in half vellum, purple cloth boards, top edge gilt, very good.   Jarndyce Antiquarian Booksellers   CCXVIII - 861   2016   £30

Dickens, Charles   1812-1870   *The Village Coquettes.*   London: Richard Bentley (printed by Samuel Bentley), 1836. First edition, title very slightly browned, tiny marginal repair in final leaf, handsome full calf by F. Bedford, gilt spine, borders & dentelles, dark green leather label, armorial bookplate of Ralph Clutton, very good, rare edition. Jarndyce Antiquarian Booksellers   CCXVIII - 86   2016   £1500

Dickens, Charles   1812-1870   *The Village Coquettes.*   London: Richard Bentley, 1836. First edition, slightly later full dark green morocco, single ruled gilt borders, gilt dentelles, hinges slightly rubbed and repaired, top edge gilt, attractive copy.   Jarndyce Antiquarian Booksellers   CCXVIII - 87   2016   £1500

Dickens, Charles   1812-1870   *The Village Coquettes.*   London: Richard Bentley, 1878. Facsimile reprint, later white paper spine strip, final leaf crudely repaired in lower outer corner with white paper.   Jarndyce Antiquarian Booksellers   CCXVIII - 88   2016   £65

Dickens, Charles   1812-1870   *The Works of Charles Dickens.*   New York: Harper and Bros., circa mid 1870's, 16 volumes, original green highly decorative cloth with elaborate gilt lettering and designs, period ownership signature, otherwise bright, fresh, near fine set.   Tavistock Books   Bibliolatry - 4   2016 $750

Dickens, Charles   1812-1870   *Works. The Novels and Tales of Charles Dickens.*   Philadelphia: Lea & Blanchard, 1846. 3 volumes, woodcuts in text, 32 page catalog and 4 pages ads volume III, titlepage and final leaves browned in volume III, original brick red cloth largely faded to brown , blocked in blind, spine lettered gilt, very slight wear to heads and tales of spines, good plus in original cloth.   Jarndyce Antiquarian Booksellers   CCXVIII - 22   2016   £850

Dickens, Charles   1812-1870   *Works.*   London: Chapman and Hall, circa, 1870. Charles Dickens Edition, 18 volumes in 14, contemporary half maroon morocco, marbled boards, gilt spines, slight rubbing, still attractive.   Jarndyce Antiquarian Booksellers   CCXVIII - 24   2016   £680

Dickens, Charles   1812-1870   *Works.*   London: Chapman & Hall, 1871-1879. Household edition, 22 volumes in 8 , frontispiece, plates and illustrations, some hand colored, some spotting in prelims, contemporary half maroon morocco, spines gilt in compartments, maroon leather labels, all edges gilt, handsome set.   Jarndyce Antiquarian Booksellers   CCXVIII - 25   2016   £650

Dickens, Charles   1812-1870   *Works.*   London: Chapman & Hall, 1874. -circa 1880. Illustrated Library edition, 30 volumes, half titles, frontispieces, plates, contemporary half dark green morocco spines with raised gilt bands and gilt devices, dark green cloth sides, occasional slight rubbing, top edge gilt, very good, attractively bound set.   Jarndyce Antiquarian Booksellers   CCXVIII - 26   2016   £2800

Dickens, Charles   1812-1870 *Works.* London: Chapman & Hall, 1880. 16 volumes, frontispiece, 16mo., original green cloth with black and gilt stamping to spine, front board blocked in black and rear board in blind, original green box with gilt stamping to top cover and printed paper label to top cover inside, modest wear to volumes, generally very good+, box shows wear and splitting to cover cloth joints, otherwise very good, quite rare, complete set.   Tavistock Books   Bibliolatry - 13   2016 $1500

Dickens, Charles   1812-1870 *Works.* Boston: Houghton Mifflin, circa, 1880. New Illustrated Library Edition, 30 volumes, half titles, frontispieces and plates, illustrations, contemporary half maroon morocco, spines lettered, with devices in gilt, marbled boards, very slightly darkened in places, very good, attractive set.   Jarndyce Antiquarian Booksellers   CCXVIII - 28   2016   £2500

Dickens, Charles   1812-1870 *Works.* London: Chapman and Hall, circa, 1880. Illustrated Library edition, 30 volumes, frontispiece, plates and illustrations, half titles, original green cloth blocked in black, lettered gilt, very good.   Jarndyce Antiquarian Booksellers   CCXVIII - 27   2016   £1500

Dickens, Charles   1812-1870 *Works.* London: Chapman & Hall, 1880. Pocket Volume edition, 30 volumes, one or two leaves slightly proud in volume 1, uniformly bound in green cloth, blocked in black, lettered gilt, very good, housed in two tiered green cloth presentation box (little tired, with cloth wearing in places, but preserving attractive set).   Jarndyce Antiquarian Booksellers   CCXVIII - 29   2016   £580

Dickens, Charles   1812-1870 *Works.* London: Chapman & Hall, 1881. Edition deluxe, 30 volumes, half titles, frontispieces, illustrations, with India proofs after original plates, some occasional light foxing, contemporary half maroon morocco by Blunson & Co., spines lettered gilt, top edge gilt, very good.   Jarndyce Antiquarian Booksellers   CCXVIII - 30   2016   £3800

Dickens, Charles   1812-1870 *Works.* London: Chapman & Hall, 1890-1892. Crown edition, 17 volumes, half titles, frontispieces and engraved titles, printed titles, illustrations, occasional light spotting, contemporary half tan calf, spines with floral devices in gilt maroon and brown leather labels, slight rubbing to corners and spine ends, overall very good.   Jarndyce Antiquarian Booksellers   CCXVIII - 31   2016   £850

Dickens, Charles   1812-1870 *Works.* London: Chapman & Hall, circa, 1895? Crown edition, 17 volumes, half titles, frontispieces and engraved titles, printed titles illustrations, contemporary half red calf, spines gilt in compartments, maroon and brown morocco labels, occasional rubbing but an attractive set.   Jarndyce Antiquarian Booksellers   CCXVIII - 32   2016   £750

Dickens, Charles   1812-1870 *Works.* London: Chapman & Hall, 1899. Gadshill edition, 34 volumes, frontispieces, engraved titles, plates, titles printed in red and black, contemporary half dark green morocco, gilt spines, handsome set.   Jarndyce Antiquarian Booksellers   CCXVIII - 33   2016   £950

Dickens, Charles   1812-1870 *Works.* London: Chapman & Hall, 1901-1902. Oxford India Paper Dickens, copyright edition with illustrations by Cruikshank, 17 volumes, half titles, illustrations, occasional spotting in prelims, contemporary full dark green crushed and embossed morocco, spine slettered gilt, one or two spines slightly faded, monogram bookplates of Cleland C. Clarke, Southport, top edge gilt, very good.   Jarndyce Antiquarian Booksellers   CCXVIII - 35   2016   £650

Dickens, Charles   1812-1870 *Works.* London: Chapman & Hall, 1901-1905. Authentic Edition, 21 volumes, half titles, color frontispieces and plates with original illustrations, uncut in original olive green cloth, spines and front boards lettered gilt, illustrations on endpapers, spines little dulled and slightly rubbed, top edge gilt.   Jarndyce Antiquarian Booksellers   CCXVIII - 34   2016   £280

Dickens, Charles   1812-1870 *The Complete Works.* New York and London: Harper and Bros. circa, 1902. 213 x 146mm., 20 works in 30 volumes, publisher's appealing deluxe binding of red half morocco over pink marbled boards, raised bands, spine gilt in three small and one large compartment, latter containing elongated Art Nouveau style rose topiary, marbled endpapers, top edge gilt, other edges rough trimmed, all but one of the volumes unopened, illustrated throughout, spines slightly affected by light (each spine evenly so, but with differing resultant shades), little wear to extremities, bottom corner of one leaf torn off with loss of couple of letters, another leaf with smal hole and same degree of loss, other trivial imperfections, excellent set of a readable edition, sturdy bindings show almost no wear to joints and an essentially unread text that obviously shows almost no signs of use.   Phillip J. Pirages   67 - 113   2016 $1750

Dickens, Charles   1812-1870 *Works.* London: Chapman & Hall, 1902-1903. Biographical edition, 19 volumes, frontispiece, plates, illustrations, contemporary half dark green calf, lighter green cloth boards, spine blocked and lettered gilt, spines uniformly browned, very good.   Jarndyce Antiquarian Booksellers   CCXVIII - 36   2016   £1500

Dickens, Charles   1812-1870 *Works.* London: Chapman and Hall, 1903-1906. Biographical edition, 19 volumes, half titles, frontispieces, plates, illustrations, original dark green pebble grained cloth, spines lettered gilt, front boards with CD monograms in gilt, one or two corners slightly bumped, nice, very good, bright set, top edge gilt.   Jarndyce Antiquarian Booksellers   CCXVIII - 37   2016   £750

Dickens, Charles 1812-1870 *Works.* London: Chapman and Hall: and New York: Henry Frowde, 1903-1907. Fireside edition, 22 volumes, half green calf, spines lettered gilt within simple gilt compartments, green cloth sides, bookseller's ticket, top edge gilt, very good, handsome set.   Jarndyce Antiquarian Booksellers   CCXVIII - 39   2016   £850

Dickens, Charles 1812-1870 *Works.* London: Chapman and Hall and New York: Henry Frowde, 1903-1907. Fireside Edition, 23 volumes, half titles frontispieces, original illustrations, 23 volumes, attractively bound in modern half tan morocco, spines gilt in compartments, red and green morocco labels, very good set.   Jarndyce Antiquarian Booksellers CCXVIII - 38   2016   £1200

Dickens, Charles 1812-1870 *Works.* London: Chapman & Hall, 1906-1908. National edition, 40 volumes, half titles, frontispieces and plates, facsimiles, titles printed in red and black, uncut in original green silk, spines blocked and lettered gilt, "CD" monograms on front boards gilt, spines little faded as usual, one or two volumes with light string marking, very good, top edge gilt.   Jarndyce Antiquarian Booksellers CCXVIII - 40   2016   £1500

Dickens, Charles 1812-1870 *Works.* London: Chapman & Hall, 1907-1923. Popular edition, 22 volumes, half titles, frontispieces, illustrations, original olive green cloth, spines lettered in black, very good attractive set.   Jarndyce Antiquarian Booksellers   CCXVIII - 41   2016   £220

Dickens, Charles 1812-1870 *Works.* Waverley Book Co. circa, 1910? Author's Favourite edition, 15 volumes, half titles, frontispieces, illustrations, original scarlet morocco cloth, blocked blind, spines blocked and lettered gilt, very good, bright, custom made wood bookcase.   Jarndyce Antiquarian Booksellers   CCXVIII - 42   2016   £225

Dickens, Charles 1812-1870 *Works.* London: Educational Book Co., 1910. 18 volumes, 1200 illustrations, including 500 special plates, half titles, frontispiece, original vertical grained navy blue cloth, spines lettered gilt, gilt monograms on front boards, very good, bright set in later plain green protective wrappers, top edge gilt.   Jarndyce Antiquarian Booksellers   CCXVIII - 43   2016   £300

Dickens, Charles 1812-1870 *Works.* London: Chapman & Hall, circa, 1930. 20 volumes, frontispieces, plates, illustrations, original blue cloth, gilt spines, top edge gilt, nice set.   Jarndyce Antiquarian Booksellers   CCXVIII - 44   2016   £225

Dickens, Charles 1812-1870 *Works.* London: Nonesuch Press, 1937-1938. 23 volumes, half titles, frontispieces, original illustrations, original cloth, occasional slight mark, top edge gilt with additional woodblock in matching box, very good set.   Jarndyce Antiquarian Booksellers   CCXVIII - 45   2016   £8500

Dickens, Charles 1812-1870 *Works.* London: Orbis, 1986. First edition of the annotated Dickens edited by Edward Guilliano and Philip Collins, 2 volumes, 4to., half titles, frontispiece portraits, illustrations, original maroon imitation leather, lettered and decorated gilt, slight wear to head of spine volume 1, good plus in slipcase.   Jarndyce Antiquarian Booksellers   CCXVIII - 46   2016   £65

Dickens, Henry Fielding *Memories of My Father.* London: Victor Gollancz, 1928. First edition, half title, frontispiece, illustrations, original blue cloth, slightly marked, small split at head of leading hinge.   Jarndyce Antiquarian Booksellers   CCXVIII - 1166   2016   £20

Dickens, Kate *The Comedy of Charles Dickens: a Book of chapters and extracts taken from the writer's novels...* London: Chapman & Hall, 1906. First edition, half title, text and edges little spotted, uncut in original green cloth, lettered in black and gilt.   Jarndyce Antiquarian Booksellers   CCXVIII - 1168   2016   £20

Dickens, Mamie *Charles Dickens.* London: Cassell & Co., 1885. First edition, original mustard cloth, blocked and lettered in red, black and gilt, little dulled owner's inscription dated July 1888, good plus.   Jarndyce Antiquarian Booksellers   CCXVIII - 1169   2016   £40

Dickens, Mamie *My Father as I Recall Him.* Roxburghe Press, 1897. First edition, half title, frontispiece, plates, uncut in original green pictorial cloth, outer edges of boards damp affected, good sound copy.   Jarndyce Antiquarian Booksellers   CCXVIII - 1170   2016   £25

Dickens, Mary Angela *Children's Stories from Dickens retold by....* London: Raphael Tuck & sons, circa, 1911? 4to., illustrations by Harold Copping, half title, color frontispiece and 11 color plates, illustrations, original paper covered pictorial boards, blue cloth spine, spine little dulled, slightly rubbed, gift inscription.   Jarndyce Antiquarian Booksellers   CCXVIII - 732   2016   £50

Dickens, Mary Angela *Dickens' Dream Children.* London: Raphael Tuck & Sons, circa, 1925? Half title, frontispiece, color plates, illustrations, 8 page catalog, small tear to contents leaf without loss, original green cloth, bevelled boards, some slight rubbing, dated Xmas 1936, good sound copy.   Jarndyce Antiquarian Booksellers   CCXVIII - 1171   2016   £30

Dickens, Mary Angela *Little Paul Dombey and Other Stories.* London: Raphael Tuck & Son, circa, 1890. Illustrations, half title, frontispiece and additional color frontispiece, illustrations, original purple paper covered boards, lettered in silver, color onlay on front board, spine little worn at head and tail.   Jarndyce Antiquarian Booksellers   CCXVIII - 461   2016   £30

Dickens, Mary Angela *Stories from Dickens for Boys and Girls.* London: Rapahel Tuck & Sons, 1935. 4to. frontispiece, illustrations, full color pop-up centrefold, 8 pages ads, name cut from leading f.e.p., original pictorial boards, pink cloth spine, spine faded, following hinge split, corners little worn.   Jarndyce Antiquarian Booksellers   CCXVIII - 744   2016   £30

The Dickensian Index for 1905-1934. London: Dickens Fellowship, 1935. Original red cloth, lettered gilt, very good in original glassine wrappers.   Jarndyce Antiquarian Booksellers   CCXVIII - 1202   2016   £55

The Dickensian. London: Chapman & Hall, 1915. Volume 11, original red cloth, spines usually faded, very good in dust jacket.   Jarndyce Antiquarian Booksellers   CCXVIII - 1178   2016   £25

The Dickensian. London: Chapman & Hall, 1916. Volume 12, original red cloth, tonr dust jacket.   Jarndyce Antiquarian Booksellers   CCXVIII - 1179   2016   £25

The Dickensian. London: Chapman & Hall, 1918. Volume 14, original red cloth, slightly faded.   Jarndyce Antiquarian Booksellers   CCXVIII - 1181   2016   £25

The Dickensian. London: Chapman & Hall, 1923. Volume 19, original red cloth.   Jarndyce Antiquarian Booksellers   CCXVIII - 1182   2016   £25

The Dickensian. London: Chapman & Hall, 1923. Volume 23, original red cloth.   Jarndyce Antiquarian Booksellers   CCXVIII - 1183   2016   £25

The Dickensian. London: Chapman & Hall, 1928. Volume 24, original red cloth.   Jarndyce Antiquarian Booksellers   CCXVIII - 1184   2016   £25

The Dickensian. London: Chapman & Hall, 1931. Volume 27, original red cloth.   Jarndyce Antiquarian Booksellers   CCXVIII - 1185   2016   £25

The Dickensian. London: Dickens Fellowship, 1932. Volume 28, original cloth, spine slightly dulled, good plus.   Jarndyce Antiquarian Booksellers   CCXVIII - 1186   2016   £25

The Dickensian. London: Chapman & Hall, 1933. Volume 29, original red cloth.   Jarndyce Antiquarian Booksellers   CCXVIII - 1187   2016   £25

The Dickensian. London: Chapman & Hall, 1934. Volume 30, original red cloth.   Jarndyce Antiquarian Booksellers   CCXVIII - 1188   2016   £25

The Dickensian. London: Chapman & Hall, 1935. Volume 31, original red cloth, very good in torn and repaired dust jacket.   Jarndyce Antiquarian Booksellers   CCXVIII - 1189   2016   £25

The Dickensian. London: Chapman & Hall, 1936. Volume 32, original red cloth.   Jarndyce Antiquarian Booksellers   CCXVIII - 1191   2016   £25

The Dickensian. London: Chapman & Hall, 1937. Volume 33, original red cloth.   Jarndyce Antiquarian Booksellers   CCXVIII - 1192   2016   £25

The Dickensian. London: Chapman & Hall, 1940. Volume 36, original red cloth.   Jarndyce Antiquarian Booksellers   CCXVIII - 1193   2016   £25

The Dickensian. London: Chapman & Hall, 1942. Volume 38, original red cloth.   Jarndyce Antiquarian Booksellers   CCXVIII - 1194   2016   £25

The Dickensian. London: Chapman and Hall, 1945-1946. Original red cloth, volume 42.   Jarndyce Antiquarian Booksellers   CCXVIII - 1195   2016   £25

The Dickensian. London: Chapman & Hall, 1947. Volume 43, original red cloth.   Jarndyce Antiquarian Booksellers   CCXVIII - 1196   2016   £25

The Dickensian. London: Chapman & Hall, 1949. Volume 45, original red cloth, spine lettered vertically.   Jarndyce Antiquarian Booksellers   CCXVIII - 1197   2016   £25

The Dickensian. London: Chapman & Hall, 1950. Volume 46, original red cloth, spine lettered vertically.   Jarndyce Antiquarian Booksellers   CCXVIII - 1198   2016   £25

The Dickensian. London: Chapman & Hall, 1951. Volume 47, original red cloth, spine slightly faded, blindstamped.   Jarndyce Antiquarian Booksellers   CCXVIII - 1199   2016   £20

Dickey, James *Poems 1957-1967.* Middletown: Wesleyan University Press, 1967. First edition, fine in very good dust jacket, inscribed to poet and editor Bill Claire.   Second Life Books, Inc.   196A - 419   2016 $200

Dickey, James *Spinning the Crystal Ball.* Washington: Library of Congress, 1967. 8vo., paper wrappers, fine.   Second Life Books, Inc.   197 - 86   2016 $45

Dickinson, Dorothy *How to Entertain Your Guests.* London: Wells Gardner, Darton & Co., circa, 1920. 8th impression, half title, final ad leaf, original olive green cloth, slightly dulled, slightly later inscription.   Jarndyce Antiquarian Books   CCXV - 158   2016   £25

Dickinson, Emily 1830-1886 *A Thought Went Up in My Mind To-day.* Octon: Verdigris Press, 2014. Artist's book, one of 10 copies from a total issue of 14, all on Hahnemulhe paper, each copy signed and numbered by artist, Judith Rothchild, page size 4 x 3 1/8 inches, 10 pages, bound by printer, Mark Lintott, in Venetian marbled ochre and lime papers over boards, leporello-style title debossed in blind on front cover, also title printed in black on Venetian marbled paper affixed to brown linen spine of book, slipcase housed housed in matching ochre colored paper over boards slipcase.   Priscilla Juvelis - Rare Books   66 - 17   2016 $700

Dickson, Carter *Behind the Crimson Curtain.* London: Heinemann, 1952. First English edition, very good, page edges slightly darkened, otherwise fine in very good dust jacket with nicks at spine ends and along edges and several short closed tears.   Mordida Books   2015 - 007866   2016 $60

Dickson, Moses *Manual of the International Order of Twelve of Knights and Daughters of Tabor...* N.P.: St. Louis: The Moses Dickson Pub. Co., 1907. Fifth edition, octavo, photos, green cloth, gilt, pages toned as usual, modest rubbing on boards, very good or better, usually found well worn, very uncommon, very scarce.   Between the Covers Rare Books   207 - 46   2016 $650

Dickson, Robert *Annals of Scottish Printing from the Introduction of the Art in 1507 to the Beginning of the Seventeenth Century.* Cambridge: Macmillan & Bowes, 1890. Limited to 600 numbered copies signed by John Philip Edmond, this one of the 1000 large paper copies bound thus, illustrations, 4to., original creme colored paper spine with light green paper covers, illustrations, bookplate of Thomas B. Mosher, slight soiling on covers, internally very near fine, unopened.   Oak Knoll Books   310 - 181   2016 $850

Dickson, Sarah Augusta *Tobacco, a Catalogue of the Books, Manuscripts and Engravings Acquire Since 1942 in the Arents Tobacco Collection.... Part IX 1687-1702.* New York: New York Public Library, 1958-1969. 4to., stif paper wrappers, 247 plates, complete 10 volume supplement to original edition.   Oak Knoll Books   310 - 268   2016 $500

Dickson, Violet *The Wild Flowers of Kuwait and Bahrain.* London: George Allen & Unwin, 1955. Very rare first edition, 8vo., original red cloth, spine lettered in gilt, maps, plates and text, spine faded, otherwise very good, contemporary lithographic bookplate.   Sotheran's   Travel and Exploration - 314   2016   £198

The Dictes and Sayings of The Philosophers. Detroit: Cranbrook press, 1901. No. 21 of 244 copies, 282 x 215mm., original half vellum, brown paper sides, calf label on spine, edges untrimmed and unopened, fleece lined slipcase with brown morocco lip, first opening with 3 1/2 x 4 3/4" woodcut vignette on either page, from drawings, vignettes surrounded by elaborate strapwork border, 3 other pages with similar borders, as well as woodcut initials, headpieces and tailpieces, in elaborate style, rear pastedown with library label of Will Ransom, corners slightly bumped, hint of soiling to covers and spine, otherwise very fine, immaculate internally.   Phillip J. Pirages   67 - 98   2016 $1250

Dictionary of American Biography. With Supplements 1-7. New York: Charles Scribner's Sons, 1964-1981. 22 volumes in 11, with 4 volumes containing supplements, small 4to., cloth, ex-library set with markings.   Oak Knoll Books   310 - 287   2016 $300

Dictionary of National Biography, Founded in 1882 by George Smith. London: Oxford University Press, 1973. Complete set up to 1950, 27 volumes, cloth for the first 22 volumes, with dusts jacket on the five supplements, library stamp on front pastedown of all volumes, only library marking.   Oak Knoll Books   310 - 288   2016 $950

Dietrich, Margretta *Doing Fine and Thanks a Million. (with) Hello Many Lucks.* Santa Fe: Santa Fe Press, 1943. 1945. Edition of 500, 2 volumes, illustrations, original printed wrappers, first volume has crease to front wrapper and first 16 pages, wrappers browned, else good, second work has short tear to front wrapper repaired, tiny ink stain to bottom corner of first few pages, else very good.   Dumont Maps and Books   134 - 32   2016 $7500

Digby, Joan *John Depol, from Dark to Light, Wood Engravings for the Stone House Press.* New York: Stone House Press, 1988. Limited to 200 signed and numbered copies, this one of 155 for sale, this copy signed by Digbys, DePol and Gelfand, 60 wood engravings executed by De Pol, 8vo., quarter cloth with patterned paper over boards, this copy inscribed by DePol for Carl Schlesinger.   Oak Knoll Books   310 - 149   2016 $425

Digby, Kenelm Henry *The Broad Stone of Honour; or the True Sense and Practice of Chivalry.* London: Edward Lumley & Bernard Quaritch, 1844-1876. 5 volumes, half titles, frontispiece in volume I, engraved titles, 16 pages ads volume I, final ad leaves in volumes II & III, original red cloth, gilt, very neatly recased, rubbed, dulled and little marked, small library stamp on leading endpapers.   Jarndyce Antiquarian Books   CCXV - 159   2016   £150

Dillard, Annie *Tickets for a Prayer Wheel: Poems.* Columbia: University of Missouri, 1974. First edition, 8vo., author's presentation on half title to poet and editor, William Claire and his wife Helen, orchid cloth over flexible boards, top edges little spotted, otherwise very good tight copy in somewhat toned dust jacket.   Second Life Books, Inc.   196A - 425   2016 $350

Dillard, Richard H. W. *The Day I Stopped Dreaming about Barbara Steele and Other Poems.* Chapel Hill: University of North Carolina, 1966. First edition, 8vo., author's presentation on flyleaf, blue cloth, clipping laid in, top edges little soiled, otherwise very good tight copy in scuffed and chipped dust jacket.   Second Life Books, Inc.   196A - 426   2016 $125

Diller, Phyllis *The Complete Mother.* Garden City: Doubleday, 1969. Second printing, small 8vo., cartoons, author's presentation on flyleaf, very good in dust jacket little soiled and chipped.   Second Life Books, Inc.   196A - 427   2016 $45

Dillon, E. J. *The Eclipse of Russia.* London: J. M. Dent, 1918. First edition, 8vo, original green cloth, slight rubbing to head of spine, clean internally.   J. & S. L. Bonham Antiquarian Booksellers   Europe 2016 - 8847   2016   £45

Dillon, Richard *J. Ross Browne: Confidential Agent in Old California.* Norman: University of Oklahoma Press, 1965. First edition, signed by author, illustrations, photos, very minor soiling to top edges, fine with fine pictorial dust jacket.   Argonaut Book Shop   Biography 2015 - 5122   2016 $45

Dillon, Richard *Maynard Dixon or from Coronado to Canon de Chelly, Artist - Illustrator.* San Francisco: Lester Lloyd, 1976. No. 26 of 200 copies, 8vo., not numbered, signed on colophon by Dillon and printer, Lester Lloyd, paper wrappers, nice.   Second Life Books, Inc.   196A - 428   2016 $50

Diment, Judith *Catalogue of the Natural History Drawings Commissioned by Joseph Banks on the Endeavour Voyage 1768-1771 Held in the British Museum...* London: Bulletin of the British Museum, volume 12, 1987. Octavo, color plate, paperback, fine.   Andrew Isles Natural History Books   55 - 10698   2016 $60

Dinesen, Isak   1885-1962 *Karen Blixens Kunst (Tegninger og Malerier). the Art of Karen Blixen (Drawings & Paintings).* Denmark: Karen Blixen Museet, 2001. First edition, 4to., illustrations in black and white and color, printed boards, near fine, this the copy of William Jay Smith who wrote 16 lines of holograph about his personal memories of his wife, poet Barbara Howes meeting Blixen in Denmark.   Second Life Books, Inc.   196A - 161   2016 $125

Dinesen, Isak   1885-1962 *Last Tales.* London: Putnam, 1957. First UK edition, octavo, near fine in very good dust jacket bit creased at edges.   Peter Ellis   112 - 104   2016   £65

Dinesen, Isak   1885-1962 *Last Tales.* New York: Random House, 1957. First American edition, gray cloth lettered gilt, original pictorial red dust jacket lettered in red and white, near fine with hint of toning to spine and board edges, some offsetting to front endpapers, otherwise bright and clean interior, dust jacket with some light toning to spine, tiny closed tear to front flap fold, some faint rubbing to extremities, minor toning to the otherwise fresh panels, overall tight and very attractive copy.   B & B Rare Books, Ltd.   2016 - ID015   2016 $75

Dinsdale, Alfred *Television.* London: Sir Isaac Pitman & Sons, 1926. First edition, small octavo, frontispiece of John Logic Baird, 5 photographic plates and 6 full page diagrams, first photo printed as it appeared on screen of first television, original printed flexible boards, pictorial dust jacket rubbed along extremities with some light staining, mostly to rear panel, overall very good, very scarce in dust jacket.   Heritage Book Shop   Holiday 2015 - 34   2016 $5000

Dionysius of Halicarnassus *Antiquitates Romanae.* Treviso: per Bernardinum Celerium du Luer, 24th Feb., 1480. Editio princeps, initial blank discarded. first leaf and last leaf little soiled, some light spotting and finger soiling elsewhere, one tiny wormhole in last few leaves, occasional marginal notes and manicules in early hand, sometimes shaved, old inscription, later vellum, early 19th century black lettering piece to spine, slightly soiled, touch of wear to spine ends, small old patch at head of front joint peeling, armorial bookplate of Augusutus Frederick, Duke of Sussex, very good.   Blackwell's Rare Books   B184 - 34   2016   £7500

Dirac, P. A. M. *Quantum Mechanics of Many Electron Systems. in Proceedings of the Royal Society, Series A. Volume 123.* London: Royal Society, 1929. 8vo. entire issue offered, original printed wrappers, finely rebacked to style, library stamps on front cover, front and rear endpapers.   By the Book, L. C.   45 - 10   2016 $750

Discorius, Johannes *Artis Cabalisticae...* Basileae: Sebastianum Henricpetri, 1587. First edition, volume I and only volume published, folio, printer's woodcut device, engraved printer's device and numerous historiated initials, full 18th century calf, rebacked to style, boards ruled gilt, tooled in blind, gilt flroal center device on both boards, red calf spine label, lettered in gilt all edges red, newer endpapers, boards bit scuffed, titlepage with small repair to bottom outer closed tear, no loss of text, bit of light toning, overall very good tall copy with wide margins.   Heritage Book Shop   Holiday 2015 - 89   2016 $12,500

Discours de Son Excellence Monsieur Jean Hancock, President du Congres de Philadelphie. Philadelphia: 1776. First edition, 8vo., contemporary European calf backed boards, spine with label & gilt (worn), all edges red.   M & S Rare Books, Inc.   99 - 101   2016 $2000

Disney, Walt *Adventures of Mickey Mouse Book I.* Philadelphia: McKay, 1931. 8vo., cloth backed stiff pictorial card covers, slight cover soil, near fine and bright, color illustrations on every page of text.   Aleph-bet Books, Inc.   111 - 126   2016 $1000

Disney, Walt *The Adventures of Mickey Mouse Book 2.* Philadelphia: McKay, 1932. 8vo, pictorial boards, fine in dust jacket (neatly repaired), color pictorial endpapers and color illustrations, really nice, very scarce, rare in dust jacket.   Aleph-bet Books, Inc.   111 - 127   2016 $1800

Disney, Walt *Hanky Ventures.* Walt Disney Productions, 1939. First edition, 8vo., very good++, original illustrated string bound wrappers, 6 embroidered hankys folded into pockets, mild cover edge wear, string sunned, mild toning rear cover.   By the Book, L. C.   45 - 81   2016 $475

Disney, Walt *Mickey Hop-Lai Line Partie De Polo.* Paris: Hachette, 1936. 4to., pictorial boards, fine in lightly frayed dust jacket, illustrations, and 3 vibrantly color pop-ups plus color pictorial endpapers, rare in dust jacket.   Aleph-bet Books, Inc.   111 - 353   2016 $1250

Disney, Walt *Mickey Mouse ABC Story Book.* Racine: 1936. 4to., pictorial boards, fine, each page features a fabulous color illustrations done in orange, light orange, black and white by Disney Studios, outstanding copy.   Aleph-bet Books, Inc.   112 - 4   2016 $475

Disney, Walt *Mickey Mouse Bedtime Stories.* London & Glasgow: Sunshine Press, n.d. circa, 1940. Small 4to, flexible pictorial card covers, fine with no wear, 8 full page in color, 6 full page in black and white, and in color black and white on very page.   Aleph-bet Books, Inc.   112 - 146   2016 $325

Disney, Walt *Mickey Mouse Box: Five Books of Adventure Stories with Mickey and His Friends.* Racine: 1939. Box measuring 10 1/2 x 10 inches, 5 books with cloth spines and brightly colored pictorial covers, books as new, box has small repair on flap and is slightly dusty else near fine.   Aleph-bet Books, Inc.   111 - 124   2016 $1250

Disney, Walt *Mickey en Las Carreras. (Mickey Mouse Waddle Book).* Barcelona: Editorial Molina, 1935. Second edition, 4to., pictorial boards, includes 4 waddle figures unpunched and pictorial band that goes around the cover, original printed pictorial instruction envelope, contains the Ramp and the Brass fasteners, stamped 'Archive' on instruction envelope, this the publisher's file copy.   Aleph-bet Books, Inc.   111 - 123   2016 $8750

Disney, Walt *Minnie Mouse.* New York: Blue Ribbon, 1933. 8vo., pictorial boards, slight soil, near fine, illustrations, with 3 marvelous double page color pop-ups plus many black and white in text, especially nice.   Aleph-bet Books, Inc.   112 - 388   2016 $1000

Disney, Walt *Pop-up Silly Symphonies Containing Babes in the Woods and King Neptune.* New York: Blue Ribbon, 1933. 4to., pictorial boards, fine in dust jacket lightly soiled, slightly frayed, full page and in text illustrations plus 4 glorious double page pop-ups.   Aleph-bet Books, Inc.   112 - 390   2016 $1500

Disney, Walt *Walt Disney Annual.* Racine: Whitman, 1937. Large 4to., pictorial boards, paper toned and some rubbing, else fine in dust jacket, slight chipping, creasing, end on verso, really very good+, 8 color plates and large half page black and whites.   Aleph-bet Books, Inc.   112 - 145   2016 $850

Disney, Walt *Walt Disney's Box of Six Pinocchio Books.* Racine: Whitman Pub. Co., 1939-1940. 6 story/paint books, fine, unused condition, beautiful set, rarely found complete in box.   Aleph-bet Books, Inc.   111 - 125   2016 $875

Dissertations and Miscellaneous Pieces Relating to the History and Antiquities, the Arts, Sciences and Literature of Asia. Dublin: printed for Messrs. P. Byrne, Grafton Street and W. Jones, Dame Street, 1793. 8vo., contemporary tree calf, gilt banded spine, red morocco label, joints and head and tail of spine expertly repaired, armorial bookplate of William Perceval, Esq., faint gilt crest and number at foot of spine.   Jarndyce Antiquarian Booksellers   CCXVI - 334   2016   £285

Disturnell, J. *The Great Lakes or Inland Seas of America...* W. B. Zieber, 1871. 18mo., original green cloth, frontispiece, plates, maps, large folding map, very good.   Buckingham Books   2015 - 38098   2016 $475

Ditson, George Leighton *Circassia; or a Tour to the Caucasus.* New York: Stringer, 1850. New edition, small octavo, engraved frontispiece, original green cloth decorated in blind, lettered gilt, ownership signature, cloth just little rubbed at corners, prelims little spotted, one page little chipped and creased at edges, very good, scarce.   Peter Ellis   112 - 67   2016   £375

Dix, Dorothy *Mirandy Exhorts.* Philadelphia: Penn Pub., 1922. First edition, illustrations by E. W. Kemble, owner name on front fly, scattered foxing, light stains to boards and spine, else very good, dust jacket with some chipping and soiling, scarce.   Between the Covers Rare Books   202 - 29   2016 $100

Dixie, Florence *Across Patagonia.* London: Richard Bentley, 1880. First edition, 8vo., frontispiece, illustrations, original green cloth, gilt vignette on upper cover and spine, spine slightly faded. J. & S. L. Bonham Antiquarian Booksellers America 2016 - 9888 2016 £110

Dixon, Franklin W. *The Hardy Boys: The Tower Treasure.* New York: Grosset & Dunlap, 1927. First edition, first issue, with complete 't' in 'talking' to page 31, list 29 Tom Swift titles to second page of publisher's ads, red cloth, lettered in black and olive green gold, about very good with some soiling to boards, spine cracked and holding at pages 204/250 light wear to spine ends, toning to spine, some spotting to page edge and scattered throughout, overall very presentable copy. B & B Rare Books, Ltd. 2016 - FWD002 2016 $400

Dixon, George *A Voyage Round the World, but More Particularly to the North-West Coast of America performed in 1785, 1786, 1787 and 1788...* London: Geo. Goulding, 1789. First edition, 4to., 5 folding maps, 16 engraved plates, leaf of engraved music, modern half calf, very skillfully executed in period style, one of the natural history plates is quite foxed, few others lightly foxed and or offset else very good, clean copy. Joseph J. Felcone, Inc. Books from Five Centuries: a Miscellany - 56 2016 $5500

Dixon, Jeane *My Life and Prophecies: Her Own Story.* New York: William Morrow & Co., 1969. First edition, fine in just about fine dust jacket with slight wrinkling on lamination at the bottom of the front panel, inscribed by Dixon to writer Mr. (and Mrs. Erle Stanley Gardner. Between the Covers Rare Books 208 - 57 2016 $225

Dixon, Richard Watson *Historical Odes and Other Poems.* London: smith, Elder, 1864. First edition, original red cloth with gilt title and author to spine, fading to spine and to part of covers adjacent to spine, otherwise very good, interior clean and tight with light aging to page margins, very nice, uncommon in this condition, very good. The Kelmscott Bookshop 12 - 36 2016 $200

Dixon, Royal *The Human Side of Plants.* New York: Frederick A. Stokes, 1914. Second printing, 8vo., original green cloth, decorative panel pasted on to upper board, lettered in green, black and white plates, very good. Sotheran's Piccadilly Notes - Summer 2015 - 108 2016 £120

Dmitriev, V. N. *Lechenie Morskimi Kupniami v Lalte na Iuzhnom Beregu Kryma.* Saint Petersburg: Shmidt, 1883. First edition, 8vo., modern green half cloth over boards, original printed wrappers bound in, wrappers with marginal repairs, apart from occasional very light spotting internally, very good. Sotheran's Travel and Exploration - 236 2016 £298

Dobie, James Frank 1888-1964 *The Voice of the Coyote.* Boston: Little Brown and Co., 1949. First edition, first issue with extra blank leaf following copyright, signed by author, illustrations, brown cloth gilt, fine in pictorial dust jacket (slightly faded at spine). Argonaut Book Shop Natural History 2015 - 7279 2016 $500

Dobson, Austin 1840-1921 *The Ballad of Beau Brocade and Other Poems of the XVIIIth Century.* London: Kegan Paul, Trench, Trubner & Co., 1892. First edition with these illustrations, one of 450 numbered large paper copies, royal 8vo., original beige cloth, spine lettered gilt, edges uncut and unopened, 50 illustrations by Thomson, including full page plates on Japanese vellum and numerous vignettes and tailpieces, covers trifle marked, blindstamped, armorial bookplate. Sotheran's Piccadilly Notes - Summer 2015 - 301 2016 £148

Dobson, Austin 1840-1921 *Eighteenth Century Vignettes. (and) Eighteenth Century Vignettes. Second Series.* London: Chatto & Windus, 1892. 1894. First editions, 2 separately issued (though obviously companion) volumes, 184 x 127mm, very pleasing black morocco tastefully gilt by C. & C. McLeish (stamp signed on rear turn-ins), covers with gilt rule border and cornerpieces of gilt lilies against a mist of gilt dots, raised bands, each spine compartment with similar design but featuring three inlaid gray morocco lilies at center and trefoil floral ornaments at compartment extremes, all against a stippled ground, turn-ins with gilt fillets and gilt foliate tools at corners, all edges gilt, folding engraved frontispiece to volume 1, large paper copy of each volume, virtually pristine set, nearly as clean and fresh as the day it left the bindery. Phillip J. Pirages 67 - 57 2016 $1250

Dobson, Austin 1840-1921 *Old-World Idyls. (with) At the Sign of the Lyre.* London: Kegan Paul, Trench & Co., 1885. 1886, 159 x 102mm., 2 volumes, very attractive dark green crushed morocco gilt, (stamp-signed "S. E. H. February 23 1907" - binder not identified), covers bordered by double gilt rules with tulip cornerpieces, raised bands, spines gilt in compartments tooled with gilt curls and tulips, gilt titling, turn-ins with plain and decorative gilt rules and volute cornerpieces, brown silk endleaves, top edges gilt, other edges untrimmed in (slightly rubbed) suede lined and morocco lipped marbled paper slipcase, "Lyre" with engraved frontispiece and endpiece, few spots of faint foxing to two plates, faint browning at edges because of paper stock, otherwise very fine set, clean and smooth internally and in lustrous, unworn bindings. Phillip J. Pirages 67 - 37 2016 $750

Dobson, Austin 1840-1921 *Proverbs in Porcelain.* London: Kegan Paul, Trench, Trubner & Co. Ltd., 1893. First edition with this title, large paper edition limited to 250 copies, hand numbered, 25 illustrations by Bernard Partridge, comprised of 11 mounted tissue proof engravings and 14 plates on Japanese vellum paper, rebound in facsimile in dark green cloth with paper spine label, very fine. Argonaut Book Shop Literature 2015 - 1580 2016 $125

Dr. Watts's Plain and Easy Catechisms for children and preservative from the Sins and Follies of Childhood and Youth. Newburyport: Edmund M. Blunt, 1797. First edition, 16mo., leather backed wooden boards covered with paper, lacks free endpapers, paper on boards worn off on corner front cover, spine ends chipped, some foxing, tight and very good.   Aleph-bet Books, Inc.   111 - 141   2016 $1200

Doctorow, E. L.   *Drinks Before Dinner.*   New York: Random House, 1979. First edition, promotional matrial by Random House and glossy portrait of Doctorow laid in, signed by author, fine in slightly scuffed dust jacket. Second Life Books, Inc.   196A - 432   2016 $85

Doctorow, E. L.   *Welcome to Hard Times.*   New York: Simon & Schuster, 1960. First edition, signed by author, 8vo., toned, particularly towards edges, quarter cream buckram with orange paper covered boards, black title to spine and upper board, spine little yellowed, edges very slightly faded, faint mark at lower edge of upper board, still very good, dust jacket little crease and worn at head and tail of spine and joints, bit toned, some shelf wear but good, author's inscription to literary critic Frank Kermode dated 1972.   Unsworths Antiquarian Booksellers   30 - 48   2016   £600

Doderer, Wilhelm, Ritter Von   *Tafeln Fur Eisenbahnhochbau zu den Vorlesungen an der K. K....*   Vienna: Lehmann & Wenzel, 1882. Large folio, title and 23 lithographic plates, evenly little browned due to paper stock, few margins brittle now preserved in modern green cloth portfolio with red morocco label.   Marlborough Rare Books   List 55 - 21   2016   £200

Dodge, Jim   *A Book of Ku.*   N.P.: Tangram, 2013. One of 200 copies, saddle stitched self wrappers, small spot to rear cover, else fine, laid in to this copy is letter from publishers Jerry Reddan to Peter (Matthiessen), uncommon.   Ken Lopez Bookseller   166 - 30   2016 $250

Dodge, Mary Mapes   *Rhymes and Jingles.*   New York: Scribner's, 1898. Reprint, 8vo., illustrations, brown cloth stamped in black and gilt, light rubbing, near fine, inscribed by author, numeral tag on front pastedown.   Second Life Books, Inc.   196A - 435   2016 $65

Dodge, Nehemiah   *A Sermon, Preached in the State Prison in the City of New York the last Lord's Day in Jan. 1825.*   New York: printed at the Office of the Gospel Herald No, 67 Chrystie Street,   First edition, 8vo., removed, foxed. M & S Rare Books, Inc.   99 - 76   2016 $225

Dodgson, Charles Lutwidge   1832-1898   *Alice's Adventures in Wonderland and Through the Looking-Glass.* London: Collins' Clear-Type Press, n.d. but circa 1930's, Red cloth boards, line drawings throughout and 8 color plates by Harry Rountree, front inner hinge starting, else internally very good, all plates intact and bright, significant shelfwear to extremities, spotting and dust to page edges, spine heavily sunned, boards show some rubbing and few small spots fair.   Ken Sanders Rare Books   E Catalogue # 1 - 12   2016 $150

Dodgson, Charles Lutwidge   1832-1898   *Alice's Adventures in Wonderland.*   Chicago: M. A. Donohue & Co.,   Small quarto, light green cloth covered boards, illustrated paper label on front cover, illustrated endsheets good, extremities very lightly soiled, bumped and rubbed, boards just tiny bit concave, cloth at spine ends and corners little frayed, half inch split in front endsheet at base of hinge, hinges are going, browned pages, pages have rare insignificant traces of soiling, illustrations by John Tenniel.   Ken Sanders Rare Books   E Catalogue # 1 - 6   2016 $50

Dodgson, Charles Lutwidge   1832-1898   *Alice's Adventures in Wonderland and Through the Looking Glass.* London: Macmillan, 1866. 1872. First published edition, first issue, 2 volumes, 42 illustrations in volume one and 50 in volume 2 by John Tenniel, original cloth, gilt titles to spine and circular gilt illustrations on both cover, each volume expertly rebacked using original boards, spines and endpapers with repair visible in few places along spine ends and joints, minor fraying and wear to spine ends, corners and edges of boards, spine of Alice darkened and although gilt title remains bright, minor rubbing and few spots of soiling to boards of both volumes, there are two small dampstains on rear board of Through the Looking-Glass, one of which effects the gilt illustration, few bubbles under the cloth of Through the looking Glass, interior of Alice lightly foxed and top margin is lightly browned, verso of front free endpage is Through the Looking Glass has remnants of glue where a bookplate was once adhered, facing half titlepage is lightly browned as a result, both volumes have few light smudge marks and few small spots of soiling, full edges gilt, both volumes housed in red cloth box with gilt titles of both volumes to spine, spine of box faded and panels have minor rubbing and wear, very good.   The Kelmscott Bookshop   12 - 23   2016 $10,000

Dodgson, Charles Lutwidge   1832-1898   *Alice's Adventures in Wonderland.*   New York: Doubleday Page, circa, 1907? 8vo., 13 colored plates, foxed, original red cloth with color pictorial plate on upper cover, spine ends frayed, good.   Jeff Weber Rare Books   181 - 43   2016 $375

Dodgson, Charles Lutwidge   1832-1898   *Alice in Wonderland.*   London: Raphael Tuck, n.d., 1910. First edition, 4to., cloth stamped in gold, all edges gilt, some light foxing and very faint mark on cover, really beautiful near fine copy, 12 fabulous color plates, pictorial endpapers and a profusion of beautiful black and whites throughout text, very scarce.   Aleph-bet Books, Inc.   112 - 91   2016 $1200

Dodgson, Charles Lutwidge 1832-1898 *Alice's Adventures in Wonderland and Through the Looking-Glass.* Chicago: Rand McNally, 1916. First edition thus, illustrated by Milo Winter with pictorial endpapers and 14 fabulous color plates, 4to., green gilt cloth, pictorial paste-on owner inscription, near fine.   Aleph-bet Books, Inc.   112 - 95   2016 $400

Dodgson, Charles Lutwidge 1832-1898 *Alice's Adventures in Wonderland and Through the Looking Glass.* Chicago: Philadelphia and Toronto: The John C. Winston Co., 1925. Early printing, octavo, blue cloth over boards with title stamped in gilt on spine, pictorial paper label on front cover, illustrated endpapers, good, extremities mildly bumped and rubbed, handful of moisture stains on rear cover, rear hinge going, 89 illustrations by John Tenniel, 4 color plates by Edwin John Prittie.   Ken Sanders Rare Books   E Catalogue # 1 - 11   2016 $60

Dodgson, Charles Lutwidge 1832-1898 *Alice's adventures in Wonderland. and Through the Looking-Glass.* London: Macmillan and Co., 1927. 2 volumes, 203 x 130mm, quite appealing dark blue half morocco over blue linen boards by Birdsall (stamp signed on verso of front free endpaper), spines with three raised bands delineating one short and one long compartment, both framed by gilt rules, smaller upper compartment with gilt titling, elongated compartment below featuring ornate gilt hand mirror, marbled endpapers, top edge gilt, other edges untrimmed, with 29 illustrations by John Tenniel as called for, hint of rubbing to extremities, two boards with smattering of tiny faint orange dots, 'Alice' with one inch stain to tail edge of frontispiece titlepage, isolated tears from rough opening, otherwise fine set, very fresh and clean internally, in lustrous virtually unworn bindings.   Phillip J. Pirages   67 - 114   2016 $750

Dodgson, Charles Lutwidge 1832-1898 *Alice's Adventures in Wonderland. (and) Through the Looking-Glass and What Alice Found There.* New York: Limited Editions Club, 1932-1935. Each volume one of 1500 copies, the first #1006, the second #408, 2 separately published (but obviously related) volumes, 225 x 149mm, both signed by Alice Hargreaves, the original Alice, Wonderland also signed by Frederic Warde, publisher's elaborately gilt red morocco for Wonderland and matching blue calf for "Looking-Glass", both bindings designed by Frederic Warde, with publisher's (somewhat darkened and soiled) slipcase that repeats the spine decoration from volume, 94 original illustrations by John Tenniel, the 43 illustrations for Wonderland re-engraved on wood by Bruno Rollitz, the 51 illustrations in 'Looking-Glass' re-engraved by Frederic Warde, just barely perceptible fading to spines, breath of rubbing to extremities, few trivial internal imperfections, still easily and clearing fine copies, fresh, bright, clean inside and out.   Phillip J. Pirages   67 - 238   2016 $5500

Dodgson, Charles Lutwidge 1832-1898 *Alice's Adventures in Wonderland.* New York: Dial, 1935. New edition with these illustrations, 8vo., green cloth, color plate on cover, fine in original pictorial dust jacket and box, both show some minor wear, 12 fine color plates by Gwynned Hudson and with a profusion of wonderful black and whites.   Aleph-bet Books, Inc.   111 - 81   2016 $400

Dodgson, Charles Lutwidge 1832-1898 *Alice's Adventures in Wonderland.* New York: Garden City Pub. Co. Inc, circa, 1936. Later printing, octavo, orange cloth over boards with black ink stamped title on backstrip, pictorial paper label on front board, orange top stain, white and green illustrated endpapers, 8 full color plates, very good, boards bit bowed and spine mildly rolled, endpapers subtly darkened, pages toned, illustrations by A E. Jackson, dust jacket is good plus, with moderate rubbing and discreet tissue repairs backing short closed tears and chips in edges.   Ken Sanders Rare Books   E Catalogue # 1 - 8   2016 $65

Dodgson, Charles Lutwidge 1832-1898 *Alice's Adventures in Wonderland.* London: Hodder & Stoughton, 1938. 12 color plates by Gwynedd Hudson, grey cloth boards with red title and illustration, book has shaky inner front hinge with frontispiece detached, else very good, dust jacket is in poor condition, with large portion missing at head of spine, smaller pieces misising to foot of spine and front panel, large tear to front panel, serious wear at extremities and soiling to rear panel, front flap clipped.   Ken Sanders Rare Books   E Catalogue # 1 - 4   2016 $150

Dodgson, Charles Lutwidge 1832-1898 *Alice's Adventures in Wonderland and Through the Looking Glass.* Stockholm/London: Continental Book Co. Zephyr Books, 1946. First edition in English of the Peake Alice, 12mo., pictorial wrappers, fine in dust jacket (slightly frayed at top of spine), illustrations by Mervyn Peake.   Aleph-bet Books, Inc.   111 - 84   2016 $1500

Dodgson, Charles Lutwidge 1832-1898 *Alisa v Stane Chudes. Skvoz' zerkalo i chto tam uvidela Alisa. (Alice's Adventures in Wonderland. Through the Looking-Glass...* Sofia: Izdatel'stovo Literatury na Inostrannyky Iazykakh, 1967. First Russian edition, quarto, quarter white cloth over blue illustrated boards, very good, illustrations by Peter Chulev.   Ken Sanders Rare Books   E Catalogue # 1 - 13   2016 $1250

Dodgson, Charles Lutwidge 1832-1898 *Alice's Adventures in Wonderland.* Berkeley: University of California Press, 1982. Deluxe issue of the first trade edition, one of 570 copies with an extra wood engraving signed by Moser, 4to., red cloth, top edge red, fine, no slipcase, printed on fine paper, engravings by Barry Moser.   Aleph-bet Books, Inc.   111 - 82   2016 $400

Dodgson, Charles Lutwidge   1832-1898 *Alice's Adventures in Wonderland.*   London: Victor Gollancz, 1984. First edition thus, small quarto, navy blue cloth effect paper over boards, pale blue endpapers, very good, pages ever so slightly ripped, very good dust jacket with several pieces of tape on verso, not visible ad not backing any tears, illustrations by Justin Todd.   Ken Sanders Rare Books   E Catalogue # 1 - 7   2016 $45

Dodgson, Charles Lutwidge   1832-1898 *Alice's Adventrues in Wonderland. Through the Looking-Glass and What Alice Found There.*   London: Folio Society, 1990. Fourth Folio Society Printing, octavo, 1/4 red cloth with light blue and red illustrated paper covered boards, publishers red top stain, blue paper covered slipcase, books near fine, slipcase very good.   Ken Sanders Rare Books   E Catalogue # 1 - 10   2016 $60

Dodgson, Charles Lutwidge   1832-1898 *Alice's Adventures in Wonderland.*   New York: Artisan, 1996. First printing, quarto, bright orange paper over boards with title and decorative borders in red ink on spine, blind stamped title within single ruled borders on front cover, orange and white illustrated endpapers, very good, spine ends and covers rubbed and bumped, top edge of covers bit rubbed, 2 and 1/2 inch closed tear in paper at foot of spine along rear joint, dust jacket near fine, paintings by Angel Dominguez.   Ken Sanders Rare Books   E Catalogue # 1 - 9   2016 $125

Dodgson, Charles Lutwidge   1832-1898 *Alice in (Pop-up) Wonderland.*   New York: Scholastic, 2003. First edition, oblong quarto, pop-up with pictorial boards, art by Otto Seibold and paper engineering by James Diaz, 6 internal pop-up spreads, fine, as new, still in publisher shrinkwrap.   Ken Sanders Rare Books   E Catalogue # 1 - 1   2016 $50

Dodgson, Charles Lutwidge   1832-1898 *Alice in Wonderland.*   Somerville: Templar Books, 2009. First American edition, quarto, 23.5 cm. x 27.5, pictorial slipcase with title in gilt to front and spine and inlaid beads at top and bottom of cover illustration, laminated pictorial boards, deep purple boards, deep purple endsheets, gorgeous full color illustrations, many double page spreads, small smudge to table of contents, slipcase shows some slight wear, near fine, hardcover.   Ken Sanders Rare Books   E Catalogue # 1 - 2   2016 $40

Dodgson, Charles Lutwidge   1832-1898 *Alice's Adventures in Wonderland.*   Mineola: Calla Editions, 2011. Blue paper covered boards with colorful illustrations.   Ken Sanders Rare Books   E Catalogue # 1 - 5   2016 $40

Dodgson, Charles Lutwidge   1832-1898 *The Annotated Alice: 150th Anniversary Deluxe Edition - Alice's Adventures in Wonderland and Through the Looking-Glass.*   New York and London: W. W. Norton and Co., 2015. 150th Annviersary deluxe edition, quarto, decorative red boards with pictorial jacket, fine in fine dust jacket, new, illustrations by John Tenniel.   Ken Sanders Rare Books   E Catalogue # 1 - 14   2016 $40

Dodgson, Charles Lutwidge   1832-1898 *The Collected Verse of Lewis Caroll.*   New York: Macmillan Co., 1933. First edition thus, octavo, light blue cloth, gilt stamped spine title and front board device, no jacket, fading and browning to spine, irregular toning to lightly soiled boards, corners exposed, light chipping and short tears to spine cloth at tips, handful of small dampstains to textblock fore edge, inding sound, ink inscription on front free endpaper, else interior clean and lightly toned, black and white illustrations by Tenniel and others.   Ken Sanders Rare Books   E Catalogue # 1 - 16   2016 $50

Dodgson, Charles Lutwidge   1832-1898 *The Complete Alice and the Hunting of the Snark.*   Topsfield: Salem House Pub., 1987. First edition thus, quarto, tan and white checkerboard patterned endpapers, blue cloth effect paper over boards, very good, bumped at extremities, small stain along bottom edge of front cover, in very good dust jacket with light rubbing and creasing at edges, two pieces of masking tape backing a 1 inch closed tear in paper at foot of jacket's spine.   Ken Sanders Rare Books   E Catalogue # 1 - 17   2016 $175

Dodgson, Charles Lutwidge   1832-1898 *Eight or Nine Wise Words About Letter-Writing.*   Delray Beach: Levenger press, Duodecimo, green leatherette stamped in gilt, fine, still wrapped in publisher's tissue, box very good with several prominent areas of abrasion on front of box, staining to bottom third of rear of box, publisher's prospectus and gray cotton flannel cloth, illustrations by Edward Koren.   Ken Sanders Rare Books   E Catalogue # 1 - 18   2016 $125

Dodgson, Charles Lutwidge   1832-1898 *The Gardener's Song.*   Clun, Shropshire: Redlake Press, 1990. Limited edition of 250 copies, this no. 138, square sextodecimo, quarter red cloth, white and black floral patterned boards, red endpapers, printed on Five Seasons recycled paper, near fine, minor rubbing at spine ends, illustrations by Brian Partridge, set by hand in Perpetua and printed on Arab treadle platen.   Ken Sanders Rare Books   E Catalogue # 1 - 19   2016 $125

Dodgson, Charles Lutwidge   1832-1898   *The Hunting of the Snark. (and) An Easter Greeting to every Child Who Loves Alice.*   London: Macmillan, 1876. First edition, one of 100 copies bound specially for Dodgson (100 in red and gold, 20 in blue and gold, 20 in white and gold), 8vo., bright red cloth with extensive gilt pictorial covers, 6 gilt rules on cover edges, all edges gilt, except for small pinhole in front gutter, near fine and bright, 9 incredibly detailed and fanciful full page illustrations by Henry Holliday, this copy inscribed by author for Beatrix Talhurst.   Aleph-bet Books, Inc.   112 - 97   2016 $9500

Dodgson, Charles Lutwidge   1832-1898   *The Hunting of the Snark and Other Poems.*   New York: Harper & Bros., 1903. First Newell edition, 8vo., white imitation stamped in gold, light cover rubbing, near fine, illustrations by Peter Newell, with tissue guarded color frontispiece plus 39 other plates by Peter Newell, lovely pictorial border, beautiful copy.   Aleph-bet Books, Inc.   111 - 83   2016 $350

Dodgson, Charles Lutwidge   1832-1898   *The Hunting of the Snark and Other Poems.*   New York: Harper & Brothers, 1903. First Newell edition, 6 x 9 inches, white imitation vellum stamped in gold, as new in original cloth backed wrapper and publisher's box (scuffed), illustrations by Peter Newell with tissue guarded color frontispiece plus 39 other fabulous plates done in Newell's uniquely comic style, lovely pictorial border on each text page done by Robert Murray Wright, beautiful copy, rare in box.   Aleph-bet Books, Inc. 112 - 98   2016 $875

Dodgson, Charles Lutwidge   1832-1898   *The Hunting of the Snark.*   New York: Harper and Bros., 1903. First edition, octavo, color frontispiece and 39 monotone plates by Peter Newell, each text leaf with decorated borders by Robert Murray Wright, publisher's red cloth, front cover and spine decorated and lettered gilt, top edges gilt, near fine. David Brass Rare Books, Inc.   2015 - 02954   2016 $275

Dodgson, Charles Lutwidge   1832-1898   *The Hunting with Snark: an Agony in Eight Fits.*   New York: Lewis Carroll Society of North America, 1992. First edition thus, quarto, black cloth over boards, lettering and decorative vignettes in silver on spine and front cover, black endpapers, very good, front cover so slightly concave, several minor dings in bottom edges of covers.   Ken Sanders Rare Books   E Catalogue # 1 - 20   2016 $100l

Dodgson, Charles Lutwidge   1832-1898   *Jabberwocky Re-Versed and Other Guinnes Versions.*   Dublin: Arthur Guinness Son & Co. Ltd., 1935. First edition, slim octavo, stapled pictorial wrappers, good, mildly rubbed wrappers, stained and creased, there are scribbles on rear wrapper and handful of lightly foxed pages have scribbles in pen. Ken Sanders Rare Books   E Catalogue # 1 - 23   2016 $150

Dodgson, Charles Lutwidge   1832-1898   *Jabberwocky and Other Frabjours Nonsense.*   London: Quist Pub., 1967. First British edition, slim quarto, glossy pink and red illustrated paper over boards, very good in dust jacket, light edge wear.   Ken Sanders Rare Books   E Catalogue # 1 - 21 2016 $50

Dodgson, Charles Lutwidge   1832-1898   *Jabberwocky from Through the Looking Glass.*   New York: Harry Abrams, 1989. Slim quarto, glossy pictorial paper over boards, very good, covers very slightly warped, near fine dust jacket with subtle fading to jacket spine.   Ken Sanders Rare Books   E Catalogue # 1 - 22   2016 $60

Dodgson, Charles Lutwidge   1832-1898   *More Annotated Alice: Alice's Adventures in Wonderland and Through the Looking-Glass and What Alice Found There.*   New York: Random House, 1990. First edition, quarto, light brown cloth over boards with title stamped in gilt on spine, gilt stamped design on front cover, brown endpapers, pages printed in black and red, very good, front cover little bit warped, very good dust jacket with moderate wear to surface, publisher's promotional material tucked in.   Ken Sanders Rare Books   E Catalogue # 1 - 28   2016 $60

Dodgson, Charles Lutwidge   1832-1898   *The New Belfry of Christ Church Oxrford. A Monograph.*   Oxford: James Parker and Co., 1872. First edition, first issue, woodcut on titlepage, small tear in upper margin of B7 neatly repaired, 12mo., original printed wrappers, slightly chipped at extremities, very good.   Blackwell's Rare Books   B184 - 21   2016 £800

Dodgson, Charles Lutwidge   1832-1898 *Phantasmagoria and Other Poems.*   London: Macmillan, 1869. 8vo., blue cloth with gilt decorations, all edges gilt, two signatures sprung, light fraying to spine ends, spine and covers darkened a bit, very good in custom cloth clamshell box, this copy inscribed by author to his sister, Mary Dodgson.   Aleph-bet Books, Inc.   111 - 75   2016 $7500

Dodgson, Charles Lutwidge   1832-1898 *Phantasmagoria and other Poems.*   London: Macmillan, 1869. First edition, first issue with page 94 printed correctly, 8vo., beautifully bound by Riviere in full blue calf with extensive gilt toning on spine, gilt rules on covers, gilt turn-ins, all edges gilt and with original covers bound in, fine copy, inscribed by author to Arthur Penrhyn Stanley, beautiful copy.   Aleph-bet Books, Inc.   111 - 77   2016 $6500

Dodgson, Charles Lutwidge   1832-1898 *Phantasmagoria and other Poems.*   London: Macmillan, 1869. 8vo., blue cloth with gilt decorations, all edges gilt, except for light fraying to spine ends, near fine in custom cloth clamshell box, this copy inscribed by author to artist, Thomas Heaphy the Younger.   Aleph-bet Books, Inc.   111 - 76   2016 $5000

Dodgson, Charles Lutwidge   1832-1898   *Rhyme? and Reason?*   London: Macmillan, 1983. First edition, 8vo., white vellum stamped in gold with picture of ghost on cover, all edges gilt, minor insect damage to hinges, else clean, tight and very good+ in custom clamshell box, in rear vellum for presentation, this copy warmly inscribed by author for dear friend Emmie Drury (Wyper), illustrations in color and black and white.   Aleph-bet Books, Inc.   111 - 74   2016 $7500

Dodgson, Charles Lutwidge   1832-1898   *A Sea-Dirge. in College Rhymes.*   London: Griffin, Bohn: Cambridge: Macmillan; Oxford: W. Mansell, 1861. First edition, 8vo., original printed wrappers, upper wrapper providing titlepage, protective marbled card folder, very good.   Blackwell's Rare Books   B184 - 20   2016   £1000

Dodgson, Charles Lutwidge   1832-1898   *Sylvie and Bruno and Sylvie and Bruno Concluded.*   London: Macmillan and Co., 1889. 1893. First editions, each volume contains 46 illustrations by Harry Furniss, both volumes bound in original red cloth with gilt titles to spines, gilt rules to edges of boards, gilt devices to boards, both volumes have full edges gilt and black endpages, spine of first volume browned with chips and minor fraying to spine ends, few light spots of soiling, few scuff marks and small bump to covers of volume as well, both hinges starting, spine lightly rolled, minor foxing to last few pages and previous owner has inscribed the half titlepage in pen dated from late 19th century, second volume noticeably bright and cleaner than the first, probably due to remnants of original jacket which still protect it, it is lightly browned along head of spine and had some rubbing/light wear on spine, covers bright and clean with few bubbles under book cloth, titlepage and frontispiece browned due to tissue guard, otherwise interior very clean with tight binding, this volume does have the front and rear panels of original jacket along with a portion of spine, jacket which was originally blue has browned considerably, spine portion of jacket which had the title is no longer present, however the original price sticker of '8/6 net' is still adhered to bottom edge of spine panel, both volumes housed in red cloth box, box worn along edges and bottom joint beginning to split, very good.   The Kelmscott Bookshop   12 - 22   2016 $250

Dodgson, Charles Lutwidge   1832-1898   *Sylvie and Bruno.*   London: Macmillan, 1889. First edition, 8vo., red cloth stamped in gold, all edges gilt, front gutter and right edge have small holes, rear corner soft, some gilt dulled, prelim pages faded, overall really very good in custom chemise and leather slipcase, this copy inscribed by author for Mrs, Dubourg, wonderfully illustrated by Harry Furniss.   Aleph-bet Books, Inc.   111 - 80   2016 $3250

Dodgson, Charles Lutwidge   1832-1898   *Sylvie and Bruno.*   London: Macmillan, 1889. First edition, 8vo., bound by Riviere in full blue calf with extensive tooling on spine, all edges gilt, gilt turn-ins and with original covers bound in at back, inscribed by author for Lady Harrington, wonderfully illustrated by Harry Furniss with full and partial page drawings.   Aleph-bet Books, Inc.   111 - 78   2016 $3500

Dodgson, Charles Lutwidge   1832-1898   *Sylvie and Bruno Concluded.*   London: Macmillan, 1893. First edition, 8vo., red cloth stamped in gold, all edges gilt, offsetting on half title and tissue guard foxed, else near fine and bright, inscribed by author for Mrs. Dubourg, wonderfully illustrated by Harry Furniss with full and partial page drawings.   Aleph-bet Books, Inc.   111 - 79   2016 $3750

Dodgson, Charles Lutwidge   1832-1898   *Sylvie and Bruno Concluded.*   New York: Macmillan and Co., 1894. Early printing, duodecimo, blue cloth covered boards with gilt and black stamping to front board and backstrip, good only, light soiling to boards, faded at spine, spine slightly rolled and cloth beginning to fray at head and tail of spine, text clean and unmarked, hardcover.   Ken Sanders Rare Books   E Catalogue # 1 - 33   2016 $50

Dodgson, Charles Lutwidge   1832-1898   *A Tangled Tale.*   London: Macmillan, 1885. Third thousand, 12mo., illustrations, rebound in half red calf with cloth sides, gilt decorations and title to spine, all edges gilt, original cloth covers bound in at rear, foxing to tissue guard with some accompanying offsetting to frontispiece, else near fine, 6 black and white illustrations by Arthur Frost.   Ken Sanders Rare Books   E Catalogue # 1 - 35   2016 $250

Dodgson, Charles Lutwidge   1832-1898   *A Tangled Tale.*   London: Macmillan, 1885. First edition, frontispiece with tissue guard and 5 further illustrations with majority full page, musical notation and mathematical formulae, occasional handling mark and even more occasional tiny spot to border, pencilled gift inscription at head of titlepage, crown 8vo., original scarlet cloth with triple fillet border and circular vignette in gilt to each board, backstrip lettered gilt and little faded, touch of wear to bottom corners and minor bumping to top corners, all edges gilt, dark charcoal endpapers with armorial bookplates to each of these at front, good copy.   Blackwell's Rare Books   B186 - 34   2016   £200

Dodgson, Charles Lutwidge   1832-1898   *Through the Looking Glass and What Alice Found There.*   London: Macmillan and Co. 1872, i.e. Dec., 1873. First edition, first issue, with misprint 'wade' for 'wabe' in second line of Jabberwocky on page 21, octavo, wood engraved text illustrations, original red cloth, covers with gilt triple fillet border and central gilt vignette within three circular gilt lines, spine lettered and decoratively stamped in gilt within three gilt fillets, all edges gilt, dark green coated endpapers, cloth lightly frayed at corners and ends of spine, covers slightly rippled and darkened, occasional minor foxing to endpapers and first few leaves, still very good, completely unosphisticated copy.   Heritage Book Shop   Holiday 2015 - 17   2016 $3500

Dodgson, Charles Lutwidge   1832-1898   *Through the Looking-Glass and What Alice Found There.*   New York: Cheshire Hotel, 1931. Limited edition, quarto, white moire cloth over boards with title stamped in silver on spine and silver stamped chess piece designs on covers, top edge gilt, large, but light stain on rear board, measuring roughly 3 x 1 x 1/2 inch wide, corners of covers are bumped, illustrations by Franklin Hughes.   Ken Sanders Rare Books   E Catalogue # 1 - 38   2016 $150

Dodgson, Charles Lutwidge   1832-1898   *Through the Looking-Glass and What Alice Found There.*   Northampton: Pennyroyal Press, 1982. No. 96 of 350 copies (300 for sale), signed by artist, 425 x 279mm., original maroon half morocco over brown paper printed in gray with detail of Moser's portrait of Alice, flat spine with gilt titling interspersed with section of the Queen's scepter, volume, along with extra plates (in folders) contained in original matching folding box of coarsely woven linen with gilt titled (faintly sunned and slightly spotted) morocco spine, volume itself with 92 wood engraved illustrations as usual ('95' mentioned on titlepage is not correct) and with additional suite of plates, each signed by Barry Moser, printed in red and black prospectus laid in, volume virtually mint.   Phillip J. Pirages 67 - 277   2016 $4200

Dodgson, Charles Lutwidge   1832-1898   *Through the Looking-Glass and What Alice Found There.*   New York: Ariel Books/Alfred A. Knopf, 1986. First edition, illustrated by S. Michelle Wiggins, quarto, turquoise cloth over boards titled gilt on spine and front cover and with gilt stamped crown on front cover, illustrated endpapers, very good, gift inscription on ownership page, very good with 1 inch closed tear in top edge of front panel, rear panel has multiple faint indented scratches, over 65 whimsical watercolors.   Ken Sanders Rare Books   E Catalogue # 1 - 37   2016 $30

Dodgson, Charles Lutwidge   1832-1898   *Through the Looking-Glass and What Alice Found There.*   New York: Ariel Books/Alfred A. Knopf, 1986. First edition, illustrations by S. Michelle Wiggins, quarto, turquoise cloth over boards, titled in gilt on spine and front cover and with gilt stamped crown on front cover, illustrated endpapers, very good plus in very good dust jacket with handful of small closed tears and chips in lightly creased edges, longest tear measures 1 inch long, over 65 watercolors.   Ken Sanders Rare Books   E Catalogue # 1 - 36   2016 $45

Dodgson, Charles Lutwidge   1832-1898   *Through the Looking-Glass and What Alice Found There.*   New York: Ariel Books, 1986. First edition thus, small quarto, blue cloth boards with gilt title and decoration to front board, gilt title to spine, pictorial endsheets, illustrated dust jacket, color illustrations by S. Michelle Wiggins, near fine with minor wear in like dust jacket with some slight rubbing.   Ken Sanders Rare Books   E Catalogue # 1 - 35   2016 $50

Dodgson, Charles Lutwidge   1832-1898   *Through the Looking-Glass and What Alice Found There.*   Oxford: Inky Parrot Press, 2015. Limited edition, number 51 of 180 copies, illustrations by Angel Dominguez, signed, quarto, bound for publisher's by Ludlow Bookbinders in red cloth over boards, gilt stamped title on spine, illustrated endpapers, printed on stow book white paper, fine in fine dust jacket.   Ken Sanders Rare Books   E Catalogue # 1 - 39   2016 $250

Dodgson, Charles Lutwidge   1832-1898   *Walt Disney's Alice in wonderland Punch Out Book.*   Racine: Whitman, 1951. Folio, stiff pictorial wrappers, as new, 8 full color die-cut cardboard leaves including covers, each with many characters from Disney's Alice to be used to create 5 scenes.   Aleph-bet Books, Inc.   112 - 93   2016 $750

Dodsley, Robert   1703-1764   *The Oeconomy of Human Life.*   London: printed for R. Dodsley and sold by M. Cooper, 1751. Fourth edition, small tear without loss to leading edge of A4, text foxed, engraved frontispiece, expertly rebound in full mottled calf, raised and gilt banded spine, red morocco label, attractive copy.   Jarndyce Antiquarian Books   CCXV - 160   2016   £250

Dodsley, Robert   1703-1764   *The Oeconomy of Human Life.*   London: printed for W. Gardiner & Vernon Hood & Sharpe, 1806. Handsome contemporary straight grained red morocco, gilt borders & dentelles, slight rubbing, all edges gilt, nice.   Jarndyce Antiquarian Books   CCXV - 161 2016   £75

Dodsley, Robert 1703-1764 *A Select Collection of Old English Plays.* London: Reeves and Turner, 1874. Fourth edition, one of a handful of large paper copies on fine laid paper, one of a handful of large paper copies on fine laid paper, 229 x 152mm., 15 volumes, elegant contemporary polished calf by Mansell (stamp-signed each volume), gilt in compartments, circular brown morocco volume label in garland and wheel pattern, each spine with additional red light brown and black morocco labels, gilt inner dentelles, marbled endpapers, top edges gilt, others untrimmed, 10 woodcut illustrations on one leaf in volume I, front pastedowns with armorial bookplate of Horatio Noble Pym, rear cover of final volume somewhat marked and soiled, spines uniformly just bit darker than boards with occasional minor abrasions, blanks and text leaves lightly foxed at beginning and end of few volumes, otherwise handsome set in fine, clean condition, virtually immaculate internally. Phillip J. Pirages 67 - 52 2016 $2000

Dodson, Owen *Powerful Long Ladder.* New York: Farrar Straus, 1946. Second printing, fine in lightly rubbed, very good plus dust jacket, inscribed for Carl Gardner, by author Dec. 11 1958. Between the Covers Rare Books 207 - 36 2016 $275

Doheny, Estelle *The Estelle Doheny Collection.* New York: Christie's, 1987-1989. 4to., 6 volumes, illustrations in color, cloth. Oak Knoll Books 310 - 239 2016 $300

Dolby, George *Charles Dickens As I Knew Him.* London: T. Fisher Unwin, 1885. First edition, half title, 32 page catalog (1885), occasional browning, contemporary half dark green morocco, spine gilt in compartments, cloth from spine and front board bound into endpapers, top edge gilt, very good. Jarndyce Antiquarian Booksellers CCXVIII - 626 2016 £60

Dolby, George *Charles Dickens as I Knew Him: the Story of the reading Tours in Great Britain and America (1866-1870).* London: T. Fisher Unwin, 1885. First edition, half title, 32 page catalog 1885, occasional browning, contemporary half dark green morocco, spine gilt in compartments, cloth from spine and front board bound into endpapers, top edge gilt, very good. Jarndyce Antiquarian Booksellers CCXVIII - 626 2016 £60

Dolby, George *Charles Dickens as I Knew Him.* London: T. Fisher Unwin, 1887. Popular edition, half title, 32 page catalog, pin holes in title, original red cloth, dulled and marked, inner hinges cracking, full page gift inscription. Jarndyce Antiquarian Booksellers CCXVIII - 627 2016 £40

Dolby, George *Charles Dickens as I Knew Him....* London: T. Fisher Unwin, 1887. Popular edition, half title, pin holes in title, original red cloth, dulled and marked, inner hinges cracking, gift inscription. Jarndyce Antiquarian Booksellers CCXVIII - 627 2016 £40

Dole, Nathan Haskell *Joseph Jefferson at Home.* Boston: Estes and Lauriat, 1898. 8vo., Jefferson's signature pasted on half title, photos, very good. Second Life Books, Inc. 196A - 436 2016 $45

Donahey, William *Alice and the Teenie Weenies.* Chicago: Reilly & Lee, 1927. 4to., pictorial paste-on, soil in front gutter and slight soil, rear cover, very good+, illustrations by author in color on every page, nice, very scarce. Aleph-bet Books, Inc. 112 - 152 2016 $400

Donahey, William *Down with the River the Teenie Weenies.* Chicago: Reilly & Lee, 1921. First edition, 4to., cloth, pictorial paste-on, light finger soil in some margins, else very good+, 8 full color plates by author plus color plate on cover, many full page and smaller black and whites. Aleph-bet Books, Inc. 112 - 153 2016 $650

Donaldson, D. J. *Blood on the Bayou.* New York: St. Martins, 1991. First edition, fine in dust jacket. Mordida Books 2015 - 012725 2016 $65

Donleavy, J. P. *Leila, Further in the Destinies of Darcy Dancer, Gentleman.* Franklin Center: Franklin Library, 1983. First edition, large 8vo., color frontispiece by Stan Hunter, all edges gilt, signed by author, brown leather stamped in gilt, fine. Second Life Books, Inc. 196A - 437 2016 $75

Donnall, Robert Sawle *The Trial of Robert Sawle Donnall, Surgeon and Apothecary, Late of Falmouth in the County of Cornwall, for the Wilful Murder by Poison of Mrs. Elizabeth Downing, Widow, His Mother-in-Law at the Assize at Launceston...* Falmouth: printed by and for James Lake, 1817. First edition, 8vo., one plate, half title, original boards, uncut and unopened, neatly rebacked to match, fine, crisp copy. John Drury Rare Books 2015 - 21527 2016 $350

Donnay, Maurice *Paraitre.* Paris: L'Illustration Theatrale, 1906. First edition, 4to., signed by playwright before his photo, inserted in text are 10 original photos by Paul Boyer, signed by cast members in the scenes, attractive copy in three quarter morocco, fine. Second Life Books, Inc. 196A - 438 2016 $75

Donne, John 1571-1631 *The Love Poems of John Donne.* Boston: Houghton Mifflin & Co., 1905. Printed for 535 numbered copies, 8vo., quarter vellum with paper covered boards, edges uncut, signed by Bruce Rogers on colophon, spine slightly age darkened, lacks slipcase. Oak Knoll Books 310 - 48 2016 $350

Donne, John 1571-1631 *Poems &c.* London: printed by T. N. for Henry Herringman, 1669. Fifth edition according to Keynes, 7th edition according to Wing, contemporary full brown calf, expertly rebacked, covers decoratively ruled in blind, spine decorated in gilt, red morocco label on spine, gilt stamped with five raised bands, previous owner's bookplates, signatures on front free endpapers, corners worn, minor foxing, very good.   Heritage Book Shop   Holiday 2015 - 35   2016 $5500

Donne, John 1571-1631 *The Poems of John Donne.* Cambridge: Limited Editions Club, 1968. Copy #1461 of 1500 copies signed by artist, quarto, quarter burgundy morocco leather and ochre linen boards with front board embossed with oval portrait of Donne, designed by John Dreyfus, 33 wood engravings by Imre Reiner, publisher's fine slipcase.   Second Life Books, Inc.   196A - 439   2016 $85

Donnelly, Ignatius *The Great Cryptogram: Francis Bacon's Cipher in the So-Called Shakespeare Plays.* London: Sampson Low, Marston, Searle & Rivington, 1888. First edition, 2 volumes, large 8vo, illustrated red cloth stamped in black and gilt covers bumped at corners, spines worn, otherwise very good.   Second Life Books, Inc.   197 - 87   2016 $225

Doolittle, Hilda 1886-1961 *Palimpsest.* Paris: Contact Editions, 1926. First edition, crown 8v., original wrappers with very slight dust soiling, one of two marks to front, little chipping to backstrip ends, good, signed by author.   Blackwell's Rare Books   B186 - 201   2016   £425

Doolittle, Hilda 1886-1961 *Collected Poems of H. D.* New York: Boni & Liveright, 1925. First edition, 8vo., covers soiled, but good tight copy, former owner's embossed stamp on titlepage, inscribed by author, scarce thus.   Second Life Books, Inc.   196A - 440   2016 $450

Doolittle, Hilda 1886-1961 *Red Bones for Bronze. Poems.* London: Chatto & Widnus, 1931. First edition, crown 8vo., original red cloth, backstrip lettered in gilt, gentlest of bumps to bottom corner of lower board, top edge red, others rough trimmed, few very faint foxspots, dust jacket with darkened backstrip panel, some very light dust soiling, one or two small nicks, very good, inscribed by author.   Blackwell's Rare Books   B186 - 202   2016   £350

Doolittle, Hilda 1886-1961 *Tribute to the Angels.* London: Oxford University Press, 1945. First edition, crown 8vo., original printed wrappers, small ringstain to front and small trace of surface adhesion at foot of same, otherwise very good, inscribed by author to Gordon Bottomley.   Blackwell's Rare Books   B186 - 203   2016   £500

Doolittle, Hilda 1886-1961 *Trilogy; The Walls Do Not Fall; Tribute to the Angels; and the Flowering of the Rod.* New York: New Directions, 1973. First edition, William Meredith's copy, signed by poet, review copy with slip from publisher laid in, near fine in near fine dust jacket.   Charles Agvent   William Meredith - 78   2016 $50

Doran, John *Knights and Their Days.* London: Richard Bentley, 1856. First edition, half title, frontispiece, lacking following f.e.p., original orange decorated cloth, spine faded, leading inner hinge crudely repaired, bookplate of Robert Washington Oates.   Jarndyce Antiquarian Books   CCXV - 162   2016   £25

Dore, Gustave *The Legend of the Wandering Jew.* Philadelphia: George Gebbie, 1873. Second edition, tall 8vo., 12 plates, some foxing on margins, green cloth (dust stained) stamped in gilt, good.   Second Life Books, Inc.   197 - 89   2016 $150

Dorman, Richard L. *The Chill Line and Santa Fe the City Different.* Santa Fe: R. D. Publications, 2000. Second printing, illustrations, near fine in like dust jacket.   Dumont Maps and Books   133 - 49   2016 $75

Dorris, Michael *A Yellow Raft in Blue Water.* New York: Henry Holt, 1987. First edition, review copy with slip laid in, fine in fine dust jacket, inscribed by atuhor.   Bella Luna Books   2016 - ta175   2016 $99

Dorset, Gerald *Cloud 4 Shadows.* London: Poets and Painters' Press, 1969. First edition, 8vo., publisher's printed wrappers (little bent and soiled), very good, inscribed by author to poet William Jay Smith.   Second Life Books, Inc.   196A - 441   2016 $50

Dos Passos, John 1896-1970 *Most Likely to Succeed.* New York: Prentice Hall, 1954. First edition 1/1000 advance copies, numbered and signed by author, fine in near fine dust jacket.   Second Life Books, Inc.   196A - 442   2016 $150

Dostoevsky, Fyodor Mikhailovich 1821-1881 *Crime & Punishment.* New York: Heritage Press, 1938. Wood engravings by Fritz Eichenbergm red cloth and decorated in gilt, spine slightly faded, else fine in slipcase, Sandglass pamphlet laid in.   Argonaut Book Shop   Heritage Press 2015 - 6981   2016 $45

Dostoevsky, Fyodor Mikhailovich 1821-1881 *New Dostoevsky Letters.* London: Mandrake Press, n.d. circa, 1930. First edition, frontispiece, little ink offsetting to first page, foolscap 8vo., original quarter black cloth with gilt snakeskin patterned sides, backstrip with printed label, top edge little dusty, dust jacket with darkened backstrip panel, one or two small spots and some light handling marks, very good, inscribed by translator, S. S. Koteliansky.   Blackwell's Rare Books   B186 - 249   2016   £150

The Double Perplexity or the Mysterious Marriages. London: printed by J. Roach, at the Britannia Printing Office, 1796. 12mo., some foxing and staining, one section detached in stitching, disbound, from the Renier collection.   Jarndyce Antiquarian Booksellers   CCXVI - 456   2016   £120

Doudney, David Alfred   *Try. A Book for Boys.*   Bonmahon Industrial Printing School, 1857. First edition, 16mo., frontispiece, laid down within printed border, plates, original green cloth, decorated in gilt, recased, dulled, gift inscription on leading f.e.p. for James Bester.   Jarndyce Antiquarian Books   CCXV - 628   2016   £125

Dougall, J.   *Cabinent of the Art: Being a New and Universal Drawing Book Forming a Complete System of Drawing...*   London: R. Ackermann, n.d., 1821. Second edition, text volume only, without the plate volume, 4to., new cloth spine with paper spine label, original paper covered boards, frontispiece, engraved titlepage, bookplate and pencil signature of Gavin Bridson, wear along edges of covers, inner hinges reinforced with archvial paper repair.   Oak Knoll Books   310 - 33   2016 $650

Dougall, James Dalziel   *Shooting: its Appliances; Practice and Purpose.*   London: Sampson Low, Marston Searle & Rivington, 1881. Second edition, 8vo. original burgundy cloth, gilt lettering and firearm design to cover and spine, light surface wear, internally clean, very good.   Sotheran's Hunting, Shooting & Fishing - 78   2016   £175

Doughty, Charles Montagu   1843-1926   *"Documents Epigraphiques Recueillis Dans le Nord de l'Arabie."* in *Notice et Extraits des Manuscrits de la Bibliotheque Nationale et Autres Bibliotheques volume XXIX.*   Paris: Imprimerie Nationale, 1891. First edition, 2nd issue, 4to, original blue wrappers, printed label to spine, 57 plates in various techniques, few folding, wrappers with usual light wear, several plates with traces of humidity, uncut and largely unopened.   Sotheran's   Piccadilly Notes - Summer 2015 - 109   2016   £698

Doughty, Charles Montagu   1843-1926   *Mansoul (Or, The Riddle of the World).*   London: Jonathan Cape & The Medici Society, 1923. Number 122 of first deluxe and revised edition, limited to 500 copies,, signed by author, 8vo., original art vellum, lettered and ornamented in gilt, top edge gilt, original printed wrappers, wrappers bit sunned and with few minor marginal chips little spotted, flyleaves lightly toned, very good, largely unopened.   Sotheran's   Travel and Exploration - 316   2016   £198

Doughty, Charles Montagu   1843-1926   *Under Arms.*   Westminster: Army & Navy Co-operative Society for Constable, 1900. First edition, 4to., original red cloth, front cover lettered gilt, ornamental head and tailpieces in text, printed slip announcing profit of this publication to the Soldier's Widows and Orphans Fund tipped onto titlepage, cloth little sunned, front flyleaf renewed, initially little brown spotted, rare.   Sotheran's   Piccadilly Notes - Summer 2015 - 110   2016   £298

Doughty, Henry Montagu   *Chronicles of Theberton. A Suffolk Village.*   Cambridge: University of Cambridge; London: Macmillan, 1910. First edition, original green cloth, spine ruled and lettered gilt, spine sunned, light bumping to corners, little spotting to endpapers, frontispiece, plates, 3 maps, printed in green and black, occasional light spotting, good, early ownership inscription of Jack Simmons and pictorial bookplate of Claude and Joan Cox, very rare.   Sotheran's   Piccadilly Notes - Summer 2015 - 111   2016   £148

Doughty, Henry Montagu   *Our Wherry in Wendish Lands. From Friesland through the Macklenburg Lakes to Bohemia.*   London: Jarrold and Sons, circa, 1891. First edition, 8vo., dark blue cloth, gilt title and red, black and white colored flag design, publisher's insignia stamped in blind on rear, top edge gilt, patterned endpapers, illustrations in text, two folded lithographic maps in three colors, front edge with spots, repair and light spotting to one map but otherwise in good condition throughout.   Sotheran's   Piccadilly Notes - Summer 2015 - 112   2016   £78

Douglas, James   *Myographiae Comparatae Specimen; or a Comparative Description of all the Muscles in a man and in a Quadruped...*   London: W. B. for G. Strachan, 1707. First edition, 8vo., slight staining to corner of prelims and very slight worming not affecting text to first few pages, otherwise clean, very good in 18th century brown leather calf, little rubbed at spine and edges, no title label at spine and hinges slightly splitting, but holding well.   Any Amount of Books   2015 - A89031   2016   £550

Douglas, Lloyd C.   *White Banners.*   Boston and New York: Houghton Mifflin, 1936. First edition, 8vo., fine, in dust jacket little worn with few small nicks and tears, inscribed by the author for Jewell Allan.   Second Life Books, Inc.   196A - 444   2016 $225

Douglas, Lord Alfred   *Oscar Wilde and Myself.*   London: John Long, 1914. First edition, octavo, photogravure frontispiece, 13 plates and facsimile letters, original blue cloth, top edge gilt, spine just little bumped at head and tail, corners likewise, inner hinges starting, very good.   Peter Ellis   112 - 447   2016   £95

Douglas, Lord Alfred *Tails with a Twist.* London: Edward Arnold, 1898. Oblong 4to., cloth backed pictorial boards, light cover soil, small red area on rear cover, normal edge rubbing and wear, very good+, full page color illustrations by E. T. Reed.   Aleph-bet Books, Inc.   112 - 345   2016 $200

Douglas, Norman   1868-1952 *Birds and Beasts of the Greek Anthology.* Florence: privately printed at the Tipografia Giuntina, 1927. First edition, 444/500 copies, signed by author, frontispiece, 2 smaller plates tipped-in, 8vo., original blue boards, backstrip with printed label, lettered in black, little rubbing to very tip of backstrip, top edge dust soiled, others untrimmed and uncut, dust jacket with few short closed tears, darkened backstrip panel with some liquid staining predominantly to front, adhesive trace at front flap, very good, inscribed by author for Alexander Stuart Frere.   Blackwell's Rare Books   B186 - 204   2016   £360

Douglas, Norman   1868-1952 *How About Europe?* Florence: privately printed, 1929. First edition, 232/550 copies signed by author, one or two very faint foxspots, crown 8vo., original patterned boards, backstrip slightly sunned with printed label lettered in black, tope edge little dust soiled, other edges and endpapers very lightly foxed, dust jacket with short closed tear at head of front panel, faded backstrip panel and light chipping to corners, good.   Blackwell's Rare Books   B186 - 205   2016   £150

Douglas, Norman   1868-1952 *In the Beginning.* Florence: privately printed at the Tipografia Giuntina, 1927. 673/700 copies signed by author, 8vo., original cream patterned boards toned overall with some wear to corners and edges, backstrip darkened with black leather label lettered gilt and small portion of loss ot title, wear at tips of backstrip and some cracking to upper joint, untrimmed, good, inscribed by author.   Blackwell's Rare Books   B186 - 206   2016   £300

Douglas, Norman   1868-1952 *In the Beginning.* Florence: privately printed, 1927. First edition, 8vo., large paper copy, 1/700 signed by author, bound in little bumped paste paper boards with chipped leather label, nice, uncut copy.   Second Life Books, Inc.   196A - 447   2016 $125

Douglas, Norman   1868-1952 *Paneros.* Florence: Orioli, 1930. First edition, 87/250 copies signed by author, foolscap 8vo., original gold vermiculated cloth boards, backstrip with black leather label lettered gilt with little rubbing at head, untrimmed with one or two faint foxspots to fore-edge, dust jacket soiled overall with darkened backstrip, edges frayed with little chipping at corners, external tape repair to rear panel, very good, scarce dust jacket.   Blackwell's Rare Books   B186 - 207   2016   £400

Douglas, Norman   1868-1952 *South Wind.* New York: Dodd Mead and Co., 1928. First American illustrated edition, color illustrated frontispiece, 11 further color plates by Valenti Angelo, royal 8vo., original black buckram stamped in gilt to upper board, backstrip lettered gilt and just little dulled with bruise at head of upper joint, top edge orange, others rough trimmed, illustrated endpapers, slipcase with wear and split along base, otherwise very good, inscribed by the artist for Leon Livingston Sept. 1928.   Blackwell's Rare Books   B186 - 208   2016   £70

Douglas, Norman   1868-1952 *South Wind.* New York: Dodd, Mead, 1928. One of 250 copies signed by author, this copy unnumbered, illustrations in color by Valenti Angelo, large 8vo., red cloth, front flyleaf missing, limitation page and frontispiece loose, extremities of spine show some wear, top edge gilt.   Second Life Books, Inc.   196A - 445   2016 $150

Douglas, Norman   1868-1952 *South Wind.* Norwalk: Heritage Press, 1967. Blue cloth, stamped in blue with gilt lettering to spine, very fine in slipcase (faded), illustrations by Carlotta Petrina, Sandglass pamphlet laid in.   Argonaut Book Shop   Heritage Press 2015 - 6982   2016 $40

Douglas, Norman   1868-1952 *Summer Islands.* New York: Colophon, 1931. One of 500 copies signed by author, blue cloth stamped in orange, nice in somewhat worn box, titlepage design and reproductions of several pen and ink illustrations in text by Howard Willard.   Second Life Books, Inc.   196A - 446   2016 $150

Douglas, Norman   1868-1952 *Together.* London: Chapman & Hall, 1923. First edition, 2 plates, foxing ot half title, occasional spots further in, 8vo., original maroon cloth, backstrip lettered gilt and faded, couple of small marks at foot, rubbing to extremities with mottling to leading edge of both boards, successive bookplates of Lytton Strachey and Miriam Benkovitz, with ownership gift inscription by these respective owners, very good, significant association.   Blackwell's Rare Books   B186 - 209   2016   £150

Douglas, Norman   1868-1952 *Unprofessional Tales.* London: T. Fisher Unwin, 1901. First edition, very light foxing to initial and ultimate pages with isolated outbreaks of same elsewhere, crown 8vo., original white pictorial cloth lettered gilt with small stain at head of lower board, backstrip lettered in gilt and little darkened with light soiling at head and foot and small waterstain above centre, backstrip tips softened and two small faint red marks in upper third, very slight lean to spine, edges browned, very faint and sparse foxing to endpapers, with free endpapers partially browned, bottom corners softened, fore-edge untrimmed, very good.   Blackwell's Rare Books   B186 - 210   2016   £400

Douglas, Stephen A. *Remarks of the Hon. Stephen A. Douglas on Kansas, Utah and Dred Scott Decision Delivered at Springfield, Illinois June 12th 1857.* Chicago: Daily Times, 1857. Uncut as issued, extremities bit chipped and soiled, some foxing and old marks, good copy. Joseph J. Felcone, Inc. Books from Five Centuries: a Miscellany - 57 2016 $400

Douglas, Sylvester *The History of the Cases of Controverted Elections Which were Tried and Determined Ruing the First and Second Session(s) of the Fourteenth Parliament of Great Britain.* London: for G. Robinson, volumes I and II and London for T. Cadell, volumes III & Iv, 1777. (1775). First edition, 4 volumes, 8vo., errata leaves as called for, contemporary uniform calf, neatly and uniformly rebacked, gilt lines and labels, very good. John Drury Rare Books 2015 - 18736 2016 $350

Douglass, Frederick *Life and Times of Frederick Douglass...* Hartford: Park Pub., 1882. Revised edition, 8vo., frontispiece, all edges gilt, brown cloth, some spots where the dye in cloth is missing, printed on poor pulpy paper, small presentation label affixed to front endpaper, very good, scarce. Second Life Books, Inc. 197 - 90 2016 $350

Douglass, Frederick *My Bondage and My Freedom....* New York and Auburn: Miller, Orton & Milligan, 1855. First edition, 8vo., frontispiece, 2 plates, some foxed and stained, bound in publisher's black cloth, (paper on front hinge torn, cloth along front hinge has some small holes in it, endpapers stained), solid good copy, usually found in very worn condition, scarce. Second Life Books, Inc. 197 - 91 2016 $1500

Dousseau, Jean Jacques *Oeuvres Completees.* Paris: Chez A. Belin, imprimeur libraire, 1817. Contemporary full tree calf, spine gilt in compartments, gilt borders and dentelles, maroon and green leather labels, carefully rebacked, slightly rubbed, bookplate of Charles Dickens as well as 'from the Library of Charles Dickens' label, further bookplate of Cordell William Firebrace. Jarndyce Antiquarian Booksellers CCXVIII - 872 2016 £950

Dove, Rita *Mother Love: Poems.* New York: Norton, 1995. First printing, 8vo., author's signature on title, green cloth, nice in near fine dust jacket. Second Life Books, Inc. 196A - 449 2016 $60

Doves Press *Catalogue Raisonne of Books printed & Published at the Doves Press No. 1 The Terrace Hammersmith.* Hammersmith: Doves Press, 1908. One of 300 copies, 234 x 167mm., russet morocco by the Doves Bindery (stamp signed and dated 1908), covers with simple frame of gilt rules accented with circlets where the lines intersect, neatly rejointed, raised bands, gilt titling, all edges gilt, later felt lined green cloth drop-back box; printed in red and black, engraved bookplate of Henry Fairfield Osborn with leather book label of Haven O'More, front free endpaper inscribed to Professor Osborne (sic) by Cobden-Sanderson, signed 'C S' and dated 12 November 1908 accompanied by the booklet "The Closing of the Doves Press: a keepsake from the opening of a 1969 exhibition at Stanford University devoted to Cobden-Sanderson, the Doves Press and the Doves Bindery; spine and significant portion of front cover rather darkened, joints and extremities bit rubbed, half a dozen water spots to boards, restored binding entirely solid and very clean and fresh internally. Phillip J. Pirages 67 - 116 2016 $1250

Dowling, Francis *Fistiana; or the Oracle of the Ring.* London: William Clement, Jun., 1841. First edition, half title, frontispiece and 4 plates, frontispiece slightly foxed, slight adhesive tear to leading endpapers, early 20th century full speckled calf, raised bands, compartments ruled gilt, red morocco label, bound in at front is slightly trimmed down original illustrated cloth binding, armorial bookplate of Sir Charles Alexander Nall-Cain, Baronet, all edges gilt, very good. Jarndyce Antiquarian Booksellers CCXVII - 87 2016 £680

Downes, Olin *A Treasury of American Song.* New York: Howell Soskin, 1940. First edition, 4to., author's presentation on half title, red cloth stamped in gilt, very good, tight copy. Second Life Books, Inc. 196A - 450 2016 $75

Downie, Janet *At the Limits of Art. A Literary Study of Aelius Aristides' Hieroi Logoi.* New York: Oxford University Press, 2013. First edition, 8vo. blue boards, silver lettered to spine, dust jacket, as new. Unsworths Antiquarian Booksellers Ltd. E04 - 45 2016 £25

Dowsett, Charles Finch *Quit You Like Men. A Book for Young Men.* London: James Nisbet & Co., 1887. Fourth edition, 2 pages press opinions preceding title, slight paper browning, original dark maroon cloth, dulled and slightly marked, ownership inscriptions on leading pastedown. Jarndyce Antiquarian Books CCXV - 163 2016 £35

Dowson, Ernest *Adrian Rome.* London: Methuen & Co., 1899. Original blue cloth with gilt authors and title to spine and front cover, spine and cover also have a lovely filigree gilt design, slight bumping and very small strip of cloth missing along top of spine, interior is bright and clean, 39 page publisher's catalog Feb. 1899, very good, quite scarce, rare presentation copy inscribed by Arthur Moore 2nd May 99 for Hugh T. Chilcott. The Kelmscott Bookshop 12 - 37 2016 $850

Doyle, Arthur Conan 1859-1930 *The Adventures of Sherlock Holmes.* London: George Newnes Ltd., 1892. First edition, mixed state, front cover has black and white illustration with banner, "The Strand Library", the street sign is not blank, endpapers variant light orange peacock design, page 317 has uncorrected "Miss Violent' rather than 'Miss Violet", original blue cloth with gilt title and author to spine and front cover, fraying to spine edges and beveled board edges, bumping and rubbing but still nice, hinges expertly restored, interior pages clean and bright except for what appears to be a small cigarette burn affecing bottom margins of pages 282-289, page 285/286 has actual burn hole, illustrations, housed in light blue half morocco slipcase, very good.   The Kelmscott Bookshop   12 - 38   2016 $1850

Doyle, Arthur Conan 1859-1930 *Adventures of Sherlock Holmes.* New York: Harper & Bros., 1892. First US edition, second issue with correction on page 65, line 4, 8vo., some soiled blue cloth stamped in black and gilt, front hinge loose, fly loose as in titlepage, name on endpaper, good, 16 glossy illustrations by Sidney Paget.   Second Life Books, Inc.   197 - 92   2016 $325

Doyle, Arthur Conan 1859-1930 *The Adventures of Sherlock Holmes.* London: G. Newnes, 1902. Souvenir Edition, "Plesant Sunday Afternoon" bookplate, original gilt pictorial cloth, worn on edges, contents still very good.   I. D. Edrich   Crime - 2016   £35

Doyle, Arthur Conan 1859-1930 *The Case for Spirit Photography.* New York: Doran, 1923. First American edition, photos, slight browning to first opening of text, 8vo., original light brown cloth, lettered in black on upper cover, with mounted photographic image, backstrip also lettered in black, endpapers lightly foxed, tail edges rough trimmed, dust jacket defective at head of backstrip panel with loss of 10 letters and partial loss of 3 more, very good.   Blackwell's Rare Books   B186 - 211   2016   £350

Doyle, Arthur Conan 1859-1930 *Danger! And other Stories.* London: John Murray, 1918. (1929). First re-issue, half title, original light brown cloth, ruled and lettered in black.   Jarndyce Antiquarian Booksellers   CCXVII - 88   2016   £65

Doyle, Arthur Conan 1859-1930 *Dangerous Work. Diary of an Arctic Adventure.* London: Great Wall Printing Co. Ltd. for the British Library, 2012. First edition, one of 150 copies, 4to., original cloth backed boards, boards reproducing covers of original notebooks, spine lettered in gilt, printed endpapers, cloth slipcase decorated in gilt on upper panel, frontispiece, imprint and limitation statement on verso, full page color illustrations, maps, fine.   Sotheran's Travel and Exploration - 458   2016   £150

Doyle, Arthur Conan 1859-1930 *Great Stories.* London: John Murray, 1959. First edition thus, near fine in like dust jacket slightly rubbed and crease at top edge.   Peter Ellis   112 - 105 2016   £45

Doyle, Arthur Conan 1859-1930 *His Last Bow.* New York: Union Carbide, 1971. Later edition, fine in dust jacket with some scattered rubbing.   Mordida Books   2015 - 011807   2016 $65

Doyle, Arthur Conan 1859-1930 *The Memoirs of Sherlock Holmes.* London: George Newnes, 1894. First edition, quarto, early blue crushed morocco by Bayntun, gilt dentelles, marbled endpapers, all edges gilt, original cloth front cover and spine bound in superficial split to end of joints (all holding), tied uniform fading to spine, beautiful copy.   Manhattan Rare Book Company   2016 - 1648   2016 $3000

Doyle, Arthur Conan 1859-1930 *The Sign of Four.* London: George Newnes ltd., 1894. New edition, original lilac cloth, front board blocked and lettered in black and orange, spine blocked and lettered in black, orange and gilt, very slight rubbing, very good, crisp copy.   Jarndyce Antiquarian Booksellers   CCXVII - 89   2016   £500

Doyle, Arthur Conan 1859-1930 *The Tragedy of the Korosko.* London: Smith, Elder & Co., 1898. First edition, octavo, 40 monochrome plates by Sidney Paget, 6 page publishers' catalog at rear, red pictorial cloth, gilt, endpapers starting to split at hinges, very good.   Peter Ellis   112 - 104   2016   £175

Doyle, Richard *The Story of Jack and the Giants.* London: Griffith & Farran, 1858. New edition, 8vo., red cloth stamped in blind and gold, all edges gilt, slight cover soil, near fine, printed by the Dalziels, 35 illustrations by Doyle, including 8 incredible full page hand colored plates, very scarce and beautiful.   Aleph-bet Books, Inc.   112 - 155   2016 $1500

Doyle, Roddy *Paddy Clarke Ha Ha Ha.* London: Viking, 1993. First British edition, true first, fine in near fine dust jacket, light creasing to edges and rear flap.   Bella Luna Books   2016 - t3561   2016 $66

Dozy, Reinhart *Spanish Islam: a History of the Moslems in Spain.* London: Chatto & Windus, 1913. First English edition, large 8vo., folding map, photogravure frontispiece, original red cloth, spine slightly faded otherwise very good.   J. & S. L. Bonham Antiquarian Booksellers   Europe 2016 - 8501   2016   £80

Drake, Francis *Drake's Plates of Brass, Evidence of His Visit to California in 1579.* San Francisco: California Historical Society, 1937. First edition, cloth with paper labels on spine and front cover, covers lightly soiled, else fine,.   Argonaut Book Shop   Biography 2015 - 3562   2016 $60

Drake, Nathan *The British Classics. Tatler, Spectator, Guardian, Rambler, Adventurer and Idler. (with) Essays Biographical, Critical and Historical.* London: Sharpe and Suttaby, London: Suttaby Evanc4e and Fox and Sharpe and Hailes, 1803-1815. Second edition, 24 volumes + 3 volumes, small 8vo., occasional toning and light spotting, uniformly bound, half red straight grain morocco with red marbled boards, gilt titles to spines, edges sprinkled, slightly chipped and rubbed, spines darkened, one headpiece loose, good set.   Unsworths Antiquarian Booksellers   30 - 24   2016   £1000

The Drama, Its History, Literature and Influence on Civilization. London: Athenian Society, 1903-1904. Athenian Edition, one of 250 sets, 22 volumes, extremely attractive very deep blue or black half morocco, marbled sides and endpapers, raised bands, top and bottom spine panel with gilt theatrical ornament (lyre or crossed swords), the second and fourth panels with gilt titling and elongated center panel with prominent variable onlays employing one of more flowers in various colors, top edge gilt, other edges rough trimmed, 120 plates, including two frontispieces in each of the first 20 volumes, one in black and white, the other in color) as well as 20 titlepages with illustrated frames (the first in color, the rest in sepia), and 20 borders, one at beginning of each prologue (19 sepia one black and white) and 13 sepia tailpieces, each coming at end of prologue, letterpress tissue guards, one leaf in final volume with paper flaw and two inch closed tear at top, just reaching text, no loss in either case, two other leaves with very minor closed marginal tear, trivial browning at edges of some of the text, otherwise attractively bound set in remarkably fine condition, bindings extremely bright and virtually unworn, text with almost no signs of use.   Phillip J. Pirages   67 - 40   2016 $3900

Drapkin, Frita Roth *A Tanta is Not a Madame!* Flushing: New Voices Pub. Co., 1969. First edition, fine in near fine dust jacket, signed, price clipped dust jacket has minor wear at top of spine and ink marks on rear flap.   Ken Hebenstreit, Bookseller   2016 - 2016 $40

Drayton, Grace *Bettina's Bonnet.* New York: Hearst's Int'l. Library, 1915. First and probably only edition, 12mo., thick pictorial boards with die-cut hole in center through which peeks Bettina's sweet face, neat strengthening to front hinge and verso of one plate, edge scrape on cover, very good, 11 incredible color plates, frontispiece in black and white, rare.   Aleph-bet Books, Inc.   112 - 156   2016 $400

Drayton, Grace *Peek-a-Boo.* New York: Duffield, 1913. 4to., cloth backed pictorial card covers die-cut with shape of little girls head peeking over side of cover, some edge wear, cover soil, some touch-ups, very good+, illustrations on every page, rare.   Aleph-bet Books, Inc.   112 - 157   2016 $600

Drayton, Michael *Poems of Michael Drayton.* London: Routledge and Kegam Paul Ltd., 1953. 2 volumes, 12mo., trifle stained near spines, else near fine in near fine dust jackets, each volume with ownership signature of poet Elizabeth Bishop.   Between the Covers Rare Books   204 - 35   2016 $1200

The Dream Song of Olaf Asteson. Llandogo: Old Stile Press, 1995. 17/140 copies signed by artist, printed on Velin Arches paper, 36 full page woodcuts by Marylcare Foa, oblong 4to., original quarter brown leather with wooden boards made from old reclaimed pitch pine beam, leather strips inserted in top and tail edges of boards, backstrip with blind stamped decorations, untrimmed, fine.   Blackwell's Rare Books   B186 - 320   2016   £180

A Dream of Fair Women. Indianapolis: Bobbs Merrill, Oct., 1907. First edition, 4to., pictorial paste-on, nearly as new with original blue ribbon, glassine wrapper and pictorial box (worn on flaps), printed on heavy coated paper, 20 beautifull full page color illustrations by Harrison Fisher.   Aleph-bet Books, Inc.   111 - 177   2016 $850

Dreamland. New York: Atlantic Books & Art, n.d. circa, 1920. Oblong folio, cloth backed pictorial boards, 14 pages of large full color circus and fair scenes, each page has slot into which the reader can insert a variety of interchangeable paper doll pieces, 50 in all, stunning book, very scarce.   Aleph-bet Books, Inc.   112 - 346   2016 $1200

Drei Karten Von Gerhard Mercator; Europa-Britische Inseln-Weltkarte. Berlin: W. H. Kuhl, 1891. Portfolio with 3 maps in 41 loose plates, illustrates Europe in 15 lves of British Isles in 8 leaves and a world map in 18 leaves, bookplate from Long Island Historical Society, portfolio, half cloth spine, cloth covered boards, portfolio soiled with chipping and cracking to spine, corners worn, map leaves chipped and brittle with loss of paper along edges of plates.   Oak Knoll Books   310 - 289   2016 $2500

Dreier, Katherine S. *Shawn: the Dancer.* New York: Barnes, 1933. First edition, 4to., silver coated cloth, numerous full page photos, inscribed by Shawn to critic Walter Terry, cover slightly soiled, but very good, tight, clean copy.   Second Life Books, Inc.   196A - 452   2016 $200

Dresser, Christopher *The Art of Decorative Design.* London: Day and Son, 1862. First edition, royal 8vo., original red cloth decoratively blocked in gilt to upper board, design repeated in blind to lower board, all edges red, 28 numbered chromolithograph plates, 162 black and white woodcut figures within text, especially bright, fresh copy.   Sotheran's   Piccadilly Notes - Summer 2015 - 113   2016   £1200

Dresser, Christopher *Modern Ornamentation, being a Series of Original designs for the Patterns of Textile Fabrics for the Ornamentation of Manufactures in Wood, Metal, Pottery, &c....* London: B. T. Batsford, 1886. First edition, folio, 50 photo lithographic plates printed in green, brown, black, purple, and blue by Kell, original decorated panelled cloth with bevelled edges, blocked in black and decorative design and gilt lettered, recased with new endpapers. Marlborough Rare Books List 55 - 23 2016 £2500

Dresser, Christopher *Principles of Decorative Design.* London: Cassell, Petter, Galpin and Co., circa, 1887. Fourth edition, half title, color frontispiece and plate, illustrations, 8 page catalog (July 1887), original brown cloth, decorated in black and gilt, some slight wear to head and tail of spine, otherwise very good, signature of G. W. Tucker. Jarndyce Antiquarian Booksellers CCXVII - 90 2016 £280

Dresser, Christopher *The Principles of Decorative Design.* London: Paris and New York: Cassell Petter and Galpin, 1876. Second edition, 4to., 2 chromolithograph plates and numerous wood engraved text illustrations, original purple cloth, upper cover decorated in gilt and black, spine lettered in gilt. Marlborough Rare Books List 56 - 18 2016 £325

Drew, Joseph *The Mystery of Creation: a Lay Sermon.* Wymouth: printed by Sherren and Son, 1879. Half title, text within double rule borders, original black cloth bevelled boards, block in gilt, slightly rubbed and dulled, ownership inscription of J. E. Elliott 1879 and Lawrence Lyall 1903, scarce. Jarndyce Antiquarian Booksellers CCXVII - 91 2016 £45

Drinkwater, John 1882-1937 *The Collected Plays.* London: Sidgwick and Jackson, 1925. First edition, 2 volumes, 8vo., inscribed by playwright in both volumes, top edge gilt, spines little faded and soiled, otherwise nice. Second Life Books, Inc. 196A - 455 2016 $165

Drummond, Harriet *Louisa Moreton; or Children Obey Your Parents in All Things.* Edinburgh: William P. Kennedy, 1850. First edition, frontispiece, vignette title, original red brown vertically grained cloth, decorated in gilt, spine faded, very good. Jarndyce Antiquarian Books CCXV - 164 2016 £75

Drummond, William Blackley *An Introduction to Child Study.* London: Edward Arnold, 1907. First edition, half title, 16 page catalog (Sep. 1907) original blue cloth, booklabels of the Legge library, additional label, very good. Jarndyce Antiquarian Books CCXV - 629 2016 £25

Drury, Clifford *William Anderson Scott "No Ordinary Man".* Glendale: Arthur H. Clark, 1967. First edition, one of 2526 copies, illustrations, fine. Argonaut Book Shop Biography 2015 - 5358 2016 $40

Drury, John *Fire in the Wax Museum.* Colorado Springs: Press at Colorado College, 1980. Limited to 150 numbered copies, signed by author, color illustrations, hand printed and bound, 4to., stiff paper wrappers, top edge gilt, other edges uncut, three metal binding pins. Oak Knoll Books 310 - 140 2016 $225

Druzhinin, N. M. *Ruskie Moreplavateli v Staroi Laponii.* Leningrad: Brokgoaus-Efron, 1924. First edition, 8vo., original illustrated wrappers, frontispiece, with four portraits, vignette on title, one headpiece, sketch map, light wear to wrappers, shelfmark label pasted around spine, internally apart from even light browning, due to paper stock, good copy, Latvian library stamps and cancellation marks to half title and verso of title. Sotheran's Travel and Exploration - 119 2016 £298

Du Bois, W. E. B. *Black Folk Then and Now: an Essay in the History and Sociology of the Negro Race.* New York: Henry Holt, 1939. First edition, older bookplate, light wear at extremities, near fine, in fresh and clean, near fine dust jacket that is lightly rubbed, signed by author. Between the Covers Rare Books 207 - 39 2016 $7500

Du Bois, W. E. B. *The College-Bred Negro: Report of a Social Study....* Atlanta: Atlanta University Press, 1900. First edition, octavo, printed blue wrappers, trifle soiled, slight erosion of paper on unprinted spine, nice, near fine. Between the Covers Rare Books 202 - 21 2016 $1000

Du Bois, W. E. B. *Dark Princess: a Romance.* New York: Harcourt Brace and Co., 1928. First edition, bookplate, tiny bit of wear at extremities, else near fine in very good or better example of the rare dust jacket with modest age toning on spine and few small tears,. Between the Covers Rare Books 202 - 22 2016 $14,000

Du Bois, W. E. B. *Dusk of Dawn.* New York: Harcourt Brace, 1940. First edition, very good+ in very good dust jacket with small chips at folds, 8vo. Beasley Books 2015 - 2016 $850

Du Bois, W. E. B. *Dusk of Dawn: an Essay Towards an Autobiography of a race Concept.* New York: Harcourt Brace and Co., 1940. First edition, bookplate, else near fine in price clipped and moderately worn, very good dust jacket with several small chips and same very neat professional reinforcing at folds, signed by author, very uncommon, especially in jacket and signed. Between the Covers Rare Books 207 - 40 2016 $6000

Du Bois, W. E. B. *Mansart Builds a School.* New York: Mainstream Publishers, 1959. First edition, bookplate, paper over front hinge cracked but hinge still tight, very good, lacking dust jacket, inscribed by author to fellow author Van Wyck Brooks. Between the Covers Rare Books 202 - 25 2016 $4500

Du Bois, W. E. B. *Voices from with the Veil.* New York: Harcourt Brace and Howe, 1920. First edition, bookplate of Wrights, some professional repair to cloth and hinges strengthened, attractive, very good, lacking rare dust jacket, signed by author.   Between the Covers Rare Books   207 - 38   2016 $7500

Du Bois, William Pene *The Great Geppy.* New York: Viking, 1940. First edition, 4to., striped cloth, very good+ in slightly worn dust jacket, 22 color drawings and 48 black and whites by Du Bois, laid in is handwritten letter from Du Bois dated July 10, 1939.   Aleph-bet Books, Inc.   111 - 132   2016 $600

Du Bois, William Pene *Otto in Texas.* New York: Viking, 1959. First edition, 7 x 10 inches, red and tan cloth, fine in very slightly worn dust jacket, color illustrations.   Aleph-bet Books, Inc.   112 - 158   2016 $250

Du Breul, Jacques *Le Theatre des Antiquitez de Paris.* Paris: Claude de La Tour, 1612. First edition, 4to., late 17th century full calf, spine with raised bands, ornamented and lettered in gilt, edges sprinkled in red, woodcut coat of arms on title, 111 engravings in text, few almost full page, wear to corners, head and tail of spines and hinges, lower cover with few small wormholes, even light toning, handful of leaves with inoffensive ink spots, single wormhole from page 1193 to end, good and clean, Portugese bookseller's label and bookplate of Paris collector Goux-Stern.   Sotheran's Travel and Exploration - 237   2016   £1350

Du Cane, Ella *The Canary Islands.* London: Adam and Charles Black, 1911. First edition, 8vo., original cream cloth, lettered and ornamented in gilt and blind, top edge gilt, 20 color plates and captioned tissue guards, one folding map, very good, apart from even light browning to endpapers and minimal spotting to half title, fine.   Sotheran's Travel and Exploration - 238   2016   £198

Du Maurier, George   1834-1896 *Peter Ibbetson.* London: James R. Osgood, McIlvaine & Co., 1892. First English edition, very good in orange beige cloth with brown titles to spines and illustrations to front boards, browning to spines and light soiling to cloth boards, otherwise very bright and clean, half morocco slipcase with red cloth boards, gilt titles to spine, very good.   The Kelmscott Bookshop   12 - 39   2016 $285

Du Perier *A General History of all Voyages and Travels throughout the Old and New World.* London: Edmund Curll, 1708. First UK edition, 8vo., frontispiece, 5 plates, small wormhole in margin of first 76 pages, not affecting text or plates, contemporary brown panelled calf, recently rebacked.   J. & S. L. Bonham Antiquarian Booksellers   Voyages 2016 - 9050   2016   £750

Du Refuge, Eustache *Arcana Aulica; or Walsingham's manual of Prudential Maxims for the States-man and Courtier.* printed for Matthew Gillyflower at the Spread-Eagle in Westminster-Hall, 1694. 12mo., engraved frontispiece, 12mo., little browning, mainly marginal or to original endpapers and pastedowns, recent full antique calf, blind ruled borders, raised bands, retaining original endpapers with bookplate of Randall Hatfeild on leading pastedown.   Jarndyce Antiquarian Books   CCXV - 165   2016   £280

Du Tillet, Jean *Chronicon de regibus Francorum a Faramundo Usque ad Franciscum Primum.* Paris: Apud Fascosanum, 1551. Third edition, little light foxing, 8vo., early 20th century red morocco, boards bordered with triple gilt fillet, spine divided by solid rule between dashed rules, second and third compartments, gilt lettered direct, rest with central urn tools, marbled endpapers, edges gilt, just slightly rubbed at extremities, very good.   Blackwell's Rare Books   B186 - 53   2016   £300

Du Verney, Joseph Guichard *Tractatus de Organo Auditus Continens Structuram usum et Morbos Omnium Auris Partium.* Nuremberg: Johann Zieger, 1684. First edition in Latin, 4to., 16 engraved folding plates, 19th century paper wrappers, plate 16 neatly backed, title very lightly soiled, else very good, Joseph Friedrich Blumenbach's copy with his signature, in fine morocco backed clamshell box.   Joseph J. Felcone, Inc.   Books from Five Centuries: a Miscellany - 96   2016 $4800

Duane, William *Sampson Against the Philistines or the Reformation of Lawsuits and Justice Made Cheap, Speedy and Brought Home to Every Man's Door...* Philadelphia: printed by B. Graves for W. Duane, 1805. Second edition, removed, very good with closed tear to lower edge of title, chips to fore edges and light scattered foxing to last few leaves.   Kaaterskill Books   21 - 45   2016 $175

Dubay, Guy F. *Chez Nous; the St. John Valley.* Brunswick: Maine State Museum, 1983. Glossy card covers, 21.6 x 28cm., photos illustrations, very good.   Schooner Books Ltd.   115 - 19   2016 $45

Duberman, Martin B. *In White America.* Boston: Houghton Mifflin, 1964. First printing, 8vo., author's presentation to his teacher on half title, very good in little worn dust jacket.   Second Life Books, Inc.   196A - 456   2016 $45

Dubie, Norman *The Horsehair Sofa.* Plainfield: Goddard Journal Publications, 1969. Very near fine in stapled wrappers, scarce.   Jeff Hirsch Books   Holiday List 2015 - 35   2016 $350

Dubie, Norman *Popham of the New Song: and Other Poems.... volume one number two of "Twelve Poems"....* Port Townsend: Graywolf Press, 1975. First edition, large 8vo., paper wrappers, author's signature and number on colophon, #12 of 26 signed copies.   Second Life Books, Inc.   196A - 458   2016 $285

Dubie, Norman *Popham of the New Song: and Other Poems.... Volume one Number Two of "Twelve Poems" a poetry quarterly.*   Port Townsend: Graywolf Press, 1975. First edition, large 8vo., paper wrappers, author's presentation and number on colophon, cover very slightly creased at lower corner, otherwise fine, this is number 27 (sic) of 26 numbered copies inscribed from author to publisher Scott Walker.   Second Life Books, Inc.   196A - 457   2016 $400

Dubie, Norman *The Prayers of the North American Martyrs.*   Lisbon: Penumbra Press, 1975. First edition, one of 250 copies signed by author, large 8vo., brown cloth little faded, very good, tight, clean copy.   Second Life Books, Inc.   196A - 460   2016 $75

Dublin, Thomas *Becoming American, Becoming Ethnic: College Students Explore their Roots.*   Philadelphia: Temple University, 1996. First edition, 8vo., photos, blue cloth stamped in copper, cover very slightly wraped, otherwise nice, signed by editor.   Second Life Books, Inc.   196A - 469   2016 $45

Dubroca, Jean Louis *Vida de J. J. Dessaliens, Gefe de Los Negros de Santo Domingto...*   Mexico: en la ofcinia de Mariano de Zuniga y Ontiveros, 1806. First Mexican edition, small quarto, frontispiece and 9 plates, three of which have handsome and vivid contemporary hand coloring, contemporary tree calf with spine gilt, lightly rubbed boards and older private bookplate and stamps, near fine.   Between the Covers Rare Books   207 - 37   2016 $15,000

Duchamp, Marcel *Cheminee Anaglyphe.*   Paris: Fall Edition, 1995. First edition, two original red and blue lithographs of stereoscopic drawings originally made to be issued with deluxe edition, lithographs are held in card frame which allows them to be slid in and out, also present is stereoscopic viewer (3D specs) and 8 page explanatory booklet which contains a French text by Georges Fall, and extract from relevant pages of Duchamp catalogue raisonne, booklet also contains limitation statement which is signed Alexina Duchamp and has estate stamp of Marcel Duchamp's signature, everything is within original black leather solander box, stamped with title in red, fine in original card mailing box which is slightly the worse for wear.   Peter Ellis   112 - 108   2016   £1250

Duckworth, Jeannie *Fagin's Children: Criminal Children in Victorian London.*   Hambledon & London: 2002. First edition, original blue cloth, half title, plates, very good in dust jacket.   Jarndyce Antiquarian Booksellers   CCXVIII - 1208   2016   £20

Dudley, Dud *Dud Dudley's Metallium Martis; or Iron Made with Pit-Coale, Sea Coale &c.*   Wolverhampton?: 1851. New reprint of 1665 edition, 12mo., folding lithograph map, original white glazed paper boards, lettered in black.   Marlborough Rare Books   List 55 - 24   2016   £50

Dudley, Jane *Old Friends and New.*   Fitchburg: Sentinel Printing Co., 1906. First edition, #33 of 290 copies, signed and numbered by author, square oblong 8vo., original cloth backed pictorial boards, becoming loose, but very good.   M & S Rare Books, Inc.   99 - 168   2016 $400

Duellman, William E.   *A Monographic Study of Colubrid Snake Genus Leptodeira.*   New York: American Museum of Natural History, 1958. Large quarto, photos, text illustrations, binder's cloth, publisher's wrappers retained, fine.   Andrew Isles Natural History Books   55 - 35989   2016 $150

Duellman, William E.   *Patterns of Distribution of Amphibians, a Global Perspective.*   Baltimore: Johns Hopkins University Press, 1999. Octavo, illustrations, very good in dust jacket.   Andrew Isles Natural History Books   55 - 38883   2016 $100

Duellman, William E.   *The South American Herpetofauna its Origin, Evolution and Dispersal.* Lawrence: University of Kansas, 1979. Quarto, text illustrations, maps, fine, publisher's cloth.   Andrew Isles Natural History Books   55 - 16520   2016 $200

Duemmler, Ernest *Poetae Latini Aevi Carolini.*   Berlin: Weidmann, 1964. Reprinted from edition of 1881-1896, 4 volumes in 7, including supplement, 8vo., black and white plates to rear of each volume except III, green cloth, gilt, top edge green, slightly faded and dusty, couple of spots to rear endpapers in two volumes, still very good, bookplate of Dr. H. Schmid, Munchen 40.   Unsworths Antiquarian Booksellers   30 - 49   2016   £210

Duerer, Albrecht   1471-1528 *Of the Just Shaping of Letters.*   New York: Grolier Club, 1917. First separate edition in English, one of 215 copies on paper and 3 on vellum, this copy one of 70 bound thus, publisher's quarter vellum over tan boards, 8 full page illustrations of letters, elaborate wood engraved title frame, one wood engraving as headpiece and one or two geometric diagrams for each letter of the alphabet, all by Durer, designed by Bruce Rogers, typical mild soiling to vellum and boards, otherwise fine, especially clean and fresh internally.   Phillip J. Pirages   67 - 123   2016 $1000

Duffy, Patrick Gavin *The Official Mixer's Manual: The Standard Guide for Professional and Amateur Bartenders throughout the World.*   New York: Blue Ribbon Books, 1940. first edition thus, octavo, green pictorial cloth stamped in black and red, endpapers slightly toned, else fine in near fine dust jacket with two small chips at crown.   Between the Covers Rare Books   204 - 28   2016 $225

Dufresne, John *I Will Eat a Piece of the Roof & You Can Eat the Window.* Stockholm: Midnight Paper Sales, 1999. First edition, limited to 220 numbered copies, signed by author and printer/publisher/aritst Gaylord Schanilac, small 12mo., quarter cloth with decorated paper covered boards and paper spine and cover labels, slipcase, five color wood engravings, other engravings decorate beginning of each chapter.   Oak Knoll Books   310 - 124   2016 $100

Dufresne, John *Well Enough Alone: Two Stories and Thirteen Poems.* Candia: LeBow, 1996. First edition, limited to 10 numbered presentation copies, signed by author, fine, illustrations by Dina Knapp, book fine, dust jacket fine, signed by athor and artist.   Bella Luna Books   2016 - 2174   2016 $82

Dugger, Ronnie *Three men in Texas.* Austin: University of Texas Press, 1967. First edition, 3 full page photo portraits, 47 photos, orange cloth, very fine with pictorial dust jacket lightly rubbed at spine ends.   Argonaut Book Shop Literature 2015 - 6239   2016 $75

Dukes, Ashley *Matchmaker's Arms: a comedy in three acts.* Ithaca: Cornell, 1994. First edition, 8vo., author's signature on half title, illustrations, nice in very slightly scuffed and faded dust jacket.   Second Life Books, Inc. 196A - 476   2016 $40

Dulac, Edmund *Edmund Dulac's Fairy Book: Fairy Tales of the Allied Nations.* London: Hodder & Stoughton, n.d., 1916. Limited to only 350 numbered copies signed by Dulac, 4to., white cloth with extensive gilt decorations, light cover soil and light rubbing to gilt else very good+.   Alephbet Books, Inc.   112 - 161   2016 $2500

Dulac, Edmund *Edmund Dulac's Picture Book.* New York: Toronto: Hodder & Stoughton, n.d., Tall 8vo., 18 tipped in color plates, original blue gilt stamped cloth, original printed dust jacket with color plate mounted on upper cover (the Lady Badoura), few minor edge tears, jacket spine back punctured, but near fine.   Jeff Weber Rare Books   181 - 55   2016 $75

Dulac, Edmund *Edmund Dulac's Picture Book.* New York: Toronto: Houghton & Stoughton, n.d., Tall 8vo., 18 tipped in color plates, original blue gilt stamped cloth, original printed dust jacket with color plate mounted on upper cover (nightingale in hand of a lady), few minor edge tears, near fine.   Jeff Weber Rare Books   181 - 54   2016 $75

Dulcken, Augustus *Scenes from "The Pickwick Papers".* London: Bickers & Bush, 1861. Large folio, 4 plates approximately 49 x 38cm., original buff pictorial wrappers, plates slightly creased, bound into later half calf red cloth boards, very good.   Jarndyce Antiquarian Booksellers CCXVIII - 124   2016   £200

Dumas, Alexander *Marguerite De Valois....* New York: Limited Editions Club, 1969. Limited edition of 1500 copies, large 8vo., presentation slip from directors of LEC laid in, drawings by Edy Legrand hand printed and then hand colored, paper specially made by Curtis Paper Co. and binding done by Russell-Rutter Co., this is number "J.W." signed by artist, fine in publisher's slipcase.   Second Life Books, Inc.   196A - 477   2016 $45

Dumas, Alexandre *The Duchess of Berri in La Vendee.* Philadelphia: Carey, Lea & Blanchard, 1833. First American edition, original cloth, printed paper label, piece missing from spine, cloth, very soiled, text considerably foxed, very scarce.   M & S Rare Books, Inc.   99 - 80   2016 $325

Dumouriez, Charles F. *Etat Present Du Royaume De Portugal, en L'Annee MDCCLXVI.* Lausanne: Francois Grasset, 1775. First edition, 12mo., contemporary brown full speckled calf, raised bands, gilt, very good.   J. & S. L. Bonham Antiquarian Booksellers   Europe 2016 - 8450 2016   £380

Dumpty Dumpties. London: Raphael Tuck n.d. circa, 1915. Pictorial boards, small piece of paper off upper corner of last panel, some wear to cloth joints on one side from use, light cover rubbing, else really very good+, double sided 8 section panorama with 16 fabulous color plates, rare.   Alephbet Books, Inc.   112 - 402   2016 $950

Dunbar, George *Key to the Greek Exercises.* Edinburgh: Stirling & Kenney, 1830. Few ink annotations on final page, disbound, contemporary signature of William Forrester, Edinburgh.   Jarndyce Antiquarian Books   CCXV - 630   2016   £28

Dunbar, Paul Laurence *Lyrics of Lowly Life.* London: Chapman & Hall, 1897. First English edition, octavo, publisher's green cloth, frontispiece, ownership signature of Paul Robeson.   Honey & Wax Booksellers   4 - 55   2016 $2500

Duncan, Bob *Buffalo Country.* New York: E. P. Dutton, 1959. First edition, illustrations by author, black cloth, gilt, very fine, pictorial dust jacket.   Argonaut Book Shop Natural History 2015 - 6257   2016 $35

Duncan, George P. *The Gentleman's Book of Manners or Etiquette.* Wakefield: William Nicholson & Cos., circa, 1880? 16mo., half title, color frontispiece, 18 page catalog, original blue glazed cloth, blocked in black, slightly rubbed, booklabel of Allston A. Kisby on leading pastedown. Jarndyce Antiquarian Books   CCXV - 168   2016   £45

Duncan, George P. *The Gentleman's Book of Manners or Etiquette.* London: William Nicholson & Sons, circa, 1890. Half title, frontispiece, final ad leaf, original red cloth, bevelled boards, slight worming to following inner hinge, signature of Bert Wray, Nov. 1904, onc leading f.e.p.   Jarndyce Antiquarian Books   CCXV - 169   2016   £30

Duncan, George P. *How to Talk: a Pocket Manual to Promote Polite and Accurate Conversation...* Wakefield: William Nicholson & sons, 1877. Half title, 3 pages ads, original green cloth blocked in black and gilt, very slight rubbing to spine.   Jarndyce Antiquarian Books   CCXV - 166   2016   £45

Duncan, George P. *How To Talk Correctly.* Wakefield: William Nicholson & Sons, 1888. 128 pages, half title, original brown cloth blocked in gilt, boards very slightly marked.   Jarndyce Antiquarian Books   CCXV - 167   2016   £38

Duncan, Harry *Doors of Perception...* Austin: W. Thomas Taylor, 1983. First edition, 1/325 copies signed by author, 8vo., quarter Niger goatskin with leather corners and handmade paste paper over boards, upper edges very slightly spotted, otherwise fine.   Second Life Books, Inc.   196A - 478   2016 $150

Duncan, John *The Education of the Ordinary Child.* London: Thomas Nelson & Sons, 1942. First edition, Half title, original red cloth, booklabel and stamp of National Bureau for Co-operation in Child Care Library, presented to the library by Dr. W. J. T. Kimber.   Jarndyce Antiquarian Books   CCXV - 631   2016   £20

Duncan, Robert *Caesar's Gate: Poems 1949-1950.* Palma de Majorca: Divers Press, 1955. First edition, one of 10 copies with original collage by Jess and original manuscript poems by Duncan, signed by poet and artist, entire edition consisted of 213 copies, 200 copies for regular circulation and 13 special copies marked A to C and 1 to 10, this copy No. 8, 8vo., illustrations by Jess, original pictorial wrappers, marbled paper slipcase with pictorial label, printed label on spine.   James S. Jaffe Rare Books   Occasional List: Winter 2016 - 52   2016 $12,500

Duncan, Robert *From the Maginogion.* Princeton: Quarterly Review of Literature, 1959. First edition, offprint from Quarterly Review of Lit. Volume XII, 8vo., printed wrappers, one of a small number of special copies used as Christmas greeting by Duncan with original drawing, signed "FD 63" on inside front wrapper, Louis Zukofsky's copy with his ownership signature dated 1963 at top of front wrapper, fine.   James S. Jaffe Rare Books   Occasional List: Winter 2016 - 53   2016 $1250

Duncan, Robert *The Opening Field, (with) The Opening Field (a second copy).* New York: Grove Press, 1960. First edition, 8vo., original printed wrappers, Ted Berrigan's copies with his ownership signature in pencil of first copy, scattered annotations throughout text of first copy with Berrigan's ownership signature, but they appear to be in another hand, titlepage of this copy detached but present with red stain on top edge, covers soiled and lightly rubbed, presentation copy in fine condition.   James S. Jaffe Rare Books   Occasional List: Winter 2016 - 54   2016 $1500

Duncan, Robert *The Year as Catches. First Poems 1939-1946.* Berkeley: Oyez, 1966. First edition, deluxe hardbound issue, one of 30 numbered and signed hors commerce copies with original handmade pan and ink endpaper decorations by Duncan, out of 200 copies comprising the hardbound issue, 8vo., original pictorial boards, dust jacket, very fine.   James S. Jaffe Rare Books   Occasional List: Winter 2016 - 55   2016 $1750

Duncan, Ronald *Judas.* Anthony Blond, 1960. First edition, printed on rose tinted Abbey Mills Glastonbury laid paper, 8 lithographic plates by John Piper, royal 8vo., original blue buckram, upper board blocked in gilt lightest rubbing to extremities, very good, presentation inscribed by author for fellow poet Frank Buchanan.   Blackwell's Rare Books   B184 - 142   2016   £80

Duncombe, John *An Evening Contemplation in a College....* London: printed for R. and J. Dodsley and sold by M. Cooper, 1753. First edition, quarto, disbound, little soiled and browned, very good.   The Brick Row Book Shop   Miscellany 69 - 43   2016 $500

Dundonald, Archibald Cochrane, 9th Earl of *A Treatise Shewing the Intimate Connection that Subsists between Agriculture and Chemistry.* printed for the author and sold by R. Edwards, March, 1795. First edition, printed on blueish paper, inscribed "From the author" and below signature J(ohn) Scott, first Lord Eldon, with his bookplate, 4to., uncut in original drab boards, little soiling and wear, spine defective a little at head and foot, very good.   Blackwell's Rare Books   B186 - 44   2016   £300

Dunham, Curtis *The Casino Girl in London.* New York: R. F. Fenno, 1898. First edition, octavo, original decorated yellow cloth, gilt lettering, frontispiece and 6 photographic plates, 4 pages of publisher's terminal ads, bookseller's stamp on titlepage, cloth little soiled, very good.   The Brick Row Book Shop   Miscellany 69 - 29   2016 $175

Dunlay, Thomas W. *Wovles for the Blue Soldiers. Indian Scouts and Auxiliaries with the United States Army 1860-1890.* Lincoln: University of Nebraska Press, 1982. First edition, numerous black and white photos and maps, gilt lettered blue cloth, very fine with dust jacket.   Argonaut Book Shop   Native American 2015 - 7578   2016 $75

Dunn, Joseph *The Ancient Irish Epic Tale Tain 80 Culange.* London: David Nutt, 1914. First edition, Green cloth, light normal wear, very good+.   Aleph-bet Books, Inc. 111 - 227   2016 $250

Dunne, J. W. *Sunshine and the Dry Fly.* London: Adam and Charles Black, 1950. Second edition, 8vo., original cloth, gold dust jacket, text illustrations, previous owner's bookplate, near fine.   Sotheran's Hunting, Shooting & Fishing - 115   2016   £50

Dunne, Philip *How Green Was My Valley.* Santa Barbara: Santa Teresa Press, 1990. First edition of the screenplay, illustrated with out-takes from the film, author's autograph on flyleaf, fine in dust jacket.   Second Life Books, Inc.   196A - 479   2016 $75

Dunning, John *Booked to Die.* New York: Scribner, 1992. First edition, hardcover, fine in fine dust jacket, signed by author, includes bookmark form Mr. Dunnings bookstore which he has signed Review copy with slips laid in, scarce thus.   Bella Luna Books   2016 - 14013   2016 $1650

Dunning, John *Booked to Die.* New York: Scribner, 1992. Uncorrected proof, near fine, very scarce format, signed by author, printed white wrappers.   Bella Luna Books   2016 - 15994 2016 $924

Dunning, John *Booked to Die.* New York: Scribner, 1992. Second printing, cloth and boards, fine in fine dust jacket, presentation from author.   Gene W. Baade, Books on the West   2015 - 1302041   2016 $95

Dunning, John *Booked to Die.* New York: Scribner, 1992. First edition, later printing, fine in fine dust jacket, signed by author.   Bella Luna Books   2016 - t4208   2016 $66

Dunning, John *The Bookman's Promise.* New York: Scribner, 2004. First edition, fine, soft cover, signed by author.   Bella Luna Books   2016 - t6323   2016 $75

Dunning, John *The Bookman's Wake.* New York: Scribner, 1994. First edition thus, original ARC, near fine, light bumping to base of spine, signed and dated by author.   Bella Luna Books   2016 - t4217   2016 $66

Dunning, John *The Bookman's Wake.* New York: Scribner, 1995. First edition, cloth and boards, signed and dated 3-22-95 by author very soon after publication, fine as new in like dust jacket.   Gene W. Baade, Books on the West   2015 - SHEL136   2016 $98

Dunning, John *Deadline.* Huntington Beach: Cahill, 1995. Limited to 200 numbered copies, fine, signed by author, this copy includes a first edition (second issue) of The Torche Passes also signed by author.   Bella Luna Books   2016 - j1690   2016 $82

Dunning, John *Denver.* New York: Times Books, 1980. First edition, book very good, light dampstaining top corners, dust jacket very good, creasing to spine ends and scratching to front panel, some bleed through folds, signed by author.   Bella Luna Books   2016 - t8221w   2016 $165

Dunning, John *Dreamer.* Huntington Beach: Cahill, 1995. Limited to 26 lettered copies, this being copy O, hardcover, fine, small format.   Bella Luna Books   2016 - ta82   2016 $330

Dunning, John *On the Air.* New York: Oxford University Press, 1998. First edition, fine in fine dust jacket, signed by author.   Bella Luna Books   2016 - t4212   2016 $66

Dunning, John *The Sign of the Book.* New York: Scribner, 2005. First edition, fine in fine dust jacket, signed by author 2-17-06.   Bella Luna Books   2016 - p3059A   2016 $66

Dunning, John *Two O'Clock. Eastern Wartime.* New York: Scribner, 2001. Limited to about 2500 copies, with signed limitation page and pinkie fingerprint by author, double signed by author and signed and dated by author 12-14-00, fine, fine dust jacket.   Bella Luna Books   2016 - p2339P   2016 $330

Dunning, John *Two O'Clock. Eastern Wartime.* New York: Scribner, 2001. Limited edition of about 2500 copies, near fine, front free endpaper creased from top to bottom, dust jacket fine, double signed by author 12-14-00.   Bella Luna Books   2016 - p2383ff   2016 $132

Duplaix, Georges *Gaston and Josephine.* New York: Oxford University Press, 1933. 4to., pictorial boards, top of paper spine has 1 inch chip and base of spine frayed, slight edge rubbing, else very good+ in dust jacket (chips off spine ends and corners and closed tears but overall nice), rare.   Aleph-bet Books, Inc.   112 - 163   2016 $1200

Duplaix, Georges *Gaston and Josephine in America.* New York: Oxford University Press, 1934. First edition, 4to., pictorial boards, small spot on cover size, fine in very good++ dust jacket, full page and partial page color illustrations, unusually fine in scarce dust jacket.   Aleph-bet Books, Inc.   111 - 136   2016 $950

Dupont, Albert *La Societe Paradisiaque ou Le Reve Helateur d'un Hypergraphe Sensible.* Paris: L'Inediteur, 1989. One of 10 numbered copies in total edition of 21 copies, 25 original photos by Dupont, hand colored and worked by Dupont on Arches paper, all signed by Dupont, each volume contains 5 photos illustrating texts and manifestos, volumes also contain small camera, binoculars, compass, hologram and various assorted items, all in their own folders, each portfolio in different colored board folder: red, cerise, yellow, blue and green, each slipcase has a portion of title on spine and is in same colors as portfolio boards, but different that matching portfolio, so effect is even more vibrant, folio, cloth backed portfolios. Oak Knoll Books 27 - 10 2016 $7500

Duppa, Richard *The Classes and Orders of the Linnaean System of Botany, Illustrated by Select Secimens of foreign and indigenous plants.* London: T. Bensley for Longman, Hurst, Rees and others, 1816. 3 volumes, 235 hand colored and three three quarter, tissue guards, early polished olive calf, handsome gilt borders, spines tanned, all edges colored, bookplates. Andrew Isles Natural History Books 55 - 38979 2016 $3500

Durant, Will *A Dual Autobiography.* New York: Simon and Schuster, 1977. First printing, 8vo., photos, signed by Will and Ariel Durant, paper over boards with cloth spine, nice in little chipped dust jacket. Second Life Books, Inc. 197 - 97 2016 $50

Duret, Theodore *Histoire d'Edouard Manet et de Son Oeuvre.* Paris: Floury, 1902. First edition, one of 600 unnumbered copies, two original Manet etchings, 21 full page engravings by Beltrand and Manet, several colored in pochoir, additional in-text illustrations, quarto, contemporary half red morocco, marbled boards, original wrappers bound-in, few scuffs to binding, interior fine, rare. Manhattan Rare Book Company 2016 - 1706 2016 $2900

Durfee, Calvin *Sketch of the late Rev. Ebenezer Fitch D.D., First President of Williams College.* Boston: Mass. Sabbath school Society, 1865. Brown cloth, spine worn at ends, otherwise very good, tight copy, author's presentation. Second Life Books, Inc. 196A - 484 2016 $65

Durham, Jimmie *Columbus Day: Poems, Drawings and Stories about American Indian Life and Death in the Nineteen Seventies.* Minneapolis: West End Press, 1953. First edition, octavo, illustrations, illustrated wrappers little rubbed, very good or better, inscribed by author, relatively uncommon. Between the Covers Rare Books 208 - 56 2016 $200

Durham, John Stephens *Diane, Priestess of Haiti.* (novel in) Lippincott's Monthly Magazine LXIX April 1902. Philadelphia: J. B. Lippincott, 1902. First and apparently only edition, front wrapper detached and chipped at bottom corner as are edges of first two pages, both of ads, last page of novel has short tear and small chip as do a few of the following pages, else sound, readable, good or better copy. Between the Covers Rare Books 202 - 26 2016 $2750

Durham, Mary Edith *Twenty Years of Balkan Tangle.* London: Geo. Allen, 1920. First edition, 8vo. original blue cloth, spine faded, presentation copy Xmas 1933. J. & S. L. Bonham Antiquarian Booksellers Europe 2016 - 8149 2016 £180

Durrell, Gerald *The Stationary Ark.* London: Collins, 1976. First edition, 8vo., photos, endpaper maps, tail of spine slightly bumped, near fine in near fine dust jacket slightly faded at spine. Peter Ellis 112 - 109 2016 £35

Durrell, Lawrence George 1912-1990 *Henri Michaux: the Poet of Supreme Solipism.* Birmingham: Delos Press, 1990. One of 26 lettered deluxe copies out of an edition of 226 copies, signed by Durrell, printed by Jonathan Stephenson at the Rocket Press, Oxford, on Zerkall mould-made paper, tipped in frontispiece illustration by Michaux, small 4to., full light blue goatskin, marbled endpapers, title in gilt on inlaid black leather label on front cover, title in gilt on spine, marbled slipcase with green cloth trimmed, spine slightly faded, else fine. Oak Knoll Books 27 - 61 2016 $300

Durrell, Lawrence George 1912-1990 *Tunc: a novel.* New York: Dutton, 1968. First edition, 8vo. signed by author, little staining on edge and cover, very good. Second Life Books, Inc. 196A - 486 2016 $45

Dussaud, Rene *Les Civilisations Prehelleniques dans le Bassin de la Mer Egee.* Paris: Paul Geuthner, 1914. Second edition, 8vo., contemporary half calf with raised bands, illustrations, binding little rubbed, very light browning, due to paper stock. Sotheran's Travel and Exploration - 239 2016 £85

Dutens, Louis *Journal of Travels made through the Principal Cities of Europe.* London: J. Wallis, 1782. First UK edition, 8vo., contemporary brown half calf, original marbled boards, spine rubbed, joints cracked, internally clean, rare. J. & S. L. Bonham Antiquarian Booksellers Europe 2016 - 8397 2016 £450

The Duties of Servants: a Practical Guide to the routine of Domestic Service. London: Frederick Warne, circa, 1910. Half title, original red decorated cloth, very good. Jarndyce Antiquarian Books CCXV - 15 2016 £45

Duvoisin, Roger *The House of Four Seasons.* New York: Lothrop Lee and Shepard, 1956. 11th printing, 4to., pictorial cloth, durable binding for library use, fine in dust jacket with few small edge chips, artfully illustrated by author, inscribed by author plus laid-in handwritten letter to a fan, very scarce.   Aleph-bet Books, Inc.   111 - 137   2016 $200

Dwight, Timothy *The True Means of Establishing Public Happiness. A Sermon Delivered on the 7th of July 1795 Before the Connecticut Society of Cincinnati and published at their request.* New Haven: printed by T. & S. Green, 1795. First edition, 8vo., stitched paper wrappers, very good with loose stitching, some offsetting and browning at edges of leaves, without half titles.   Kaaterskill Books   21 - 90   2016 $200

Dyer, Thomas Firminger Thiselton *British Parlor Customs, Past and Present.* London: George Bell & Sons, 1876. Later reissue using the first edition sheets with catalog dated 1883, original blue-grey embossed cloth, lettered in blind on front board and gilt on spine with 'Bohn's Antiquarian library', slightly dulled & faded, inner hinges cracking with signs of old cellotape repair.   Jarndyce Antiquarian Books   CCXV - 170   2016   £35

Dyer, Thomas H. *The Ruins of Pompeii; a Series of Eighteen Photographic Views....* London: Bell & Daldy, 1867. First edition, quarto, 18 original photos.   J. & S. L. Bonham Antiquarian Booksellers   Europe 2016 - 3986   2016   £300

Dyott, T. W. *Dr. Robertson's Genuine Patent and Family Medicines.* Philadelphia: printed for the Proprietor by Thomas Town, 1810. First edition, old resewing, uncut, heavily foxed, but very good.   M & S Rare Books, Inc.   99 - 81   2016 $850

Dyson, Walter *Howard University: The Capstone of Negro Education. A History 1867-1940.* Washington: Graduate School Howard University, 1941. First edition, 553 pages, illustrations, fine, lacking dust jacket, inscribed by author for Mr. John M. McDonell, scarce.   Between the Covers Rare Books   202 - 45   2016 $700

E

Eagles, Douglas Eaton *A Genealogical History of Long Island.* Sarnia: Published by the author, 1971. Quarto, black and white photo illustrations, sketches and maps, few spots to white covers,. Schooner Books Ltd. 115 - 138 2016 $55

Earle, Major Cyril *The Earle Collection of Early Staffordshire Pottery.* London: A. Brown and Sons, 1915. First edition, small folio, 270 half tone photographic plates in sepia, 10 color plates, original brick cloth, gilt lettered spine, gilt lettering and pictorial devices to front cover, light wear to spine ends, corners and lower edge of boards, stains from dried flowers to rear endpapers, has leaves with slight crunching to boards near fore-edge, very good. Argonaut Book Shop Pottery and Porcelain 2015 - 5007 2016 $375

Early Marriage and late Parentage the Only Solution of the Social Problem. London: George Standring, 1883. First edition, original black cloth wrappers lettered on front wrapper in gilt, inscribed 'With author's compliments'. Jarndyce Antiquarian Booksellers CCXVII - 209 2016 £350

East Indian Railway Company *Rules and Regulations of the East Indian Railway Company. Together with the act for Regulating Railways in British India.* Calcutta: East Indian Railway Company's Press, 1867. First edition thus, original green cloth backed marbled wrappers, worn with cloth tape spine worn at top and bottom, illustrations from drawings, previous owner's handstamp on inside front cover and rear blank, rare in any condition, owner name Robert Finch with his signature. Simon Finch 2015 - 103632 2016 $220

Eastern Anecdotes of Exemplary Characters with Sketches of the Chinese History. London: printed by Sampson Low, 1799. First edition, 12mo., pages with light dampstain, modern full leather with raised bands, gilt lettering leather spine label, new endpapers, owner name, very good+. By the Book, L. C. 45 - 39 2016 $1250

Eaton, Arthur Wentworth Hamilton *The History of King's County Heart of the Acadian Land.* Milton: Global Heritage Press, 1999. Facsimile of 1910 edition, 8vo., card covers, very good. Schooner Books Ltd. 115 - 139 2016 $55

Eaton, Seymour *The Roosevelt Bears Abroad.* New York: Barse & Hopkins, 1908. First edition, 4to., many drawings an few color plates by R. K. Culver, dark grey paper over boards, cloth spine and color pictorial pasted on front, cover worn at edges, otherwise very good. Second Life Books, Inc. 197 - 98 2016 $300

Eaton, Walter P. *Newark, a Series of Engravings on Wood by Rudolph Ruzicka...* Newark: Carteret Book Club, 1917. Limited to 200 numbered copies, 4to., quarter cloth with marbled paper covered boards, original cardboard slipcase, 5 additional pages of illustrations, each with their own half titlepage, bookplate, light wear to slipcase, book is well preserved, 17 wood engravings. Oak Knoll Books 310 - 49 2016 $1750

Eaton, Walter P. *The Theatre Guild: the First Ten Years...* New York: Brentanos, 1929. First edition, 8vo., pink/purple cloth, one of 350 copies printed on Utopian Deckle edge paper, signed by author and directors, spine faded and stamping moderately chipped off, very good, tight copy, publisher's box that is lacking bottom piece. Second Life Books, Inc. 196A - 488 2016 $125

Eberhard, Frederick G. *Super-Gangster.* New York: Macaulay Co., 1932. First edition, fine, bright square copy in dust jacket with light professional restoration to spine ends,. Buckingham Books 2015 - 33041 2016 $450

Eberhart, Richard *Burr Oaks: (Poems).* London: Chatto & Windus, 1947. First UK edition, 8vo., signed and dated by author, very good. Second Life Books, Inc. 196A - 490 2016 $45

Eberhart, Richard *Free Gunner's Hand Book.* Dam Neck: NAS, Norfolk, 1943? First edition, 12mo, charts, tables, stapled illustrated wrappers, staples little rusted, slight age toning on wrappers, near fine, signed by Eberhart. Between the Covers Rare Books 204 - 36 2016 $2500

Ebersolt, Jean *Constantinople, Byzantine et les Voyageurs du Levant.* Paris: Ernest Leroux, 1918. First edition, small 8vo., original printed wrappers, illustrations in text, wear to spine, covers lightly spotted, internally apart from light marginal toning, good copy. Sotheran's Travel and Exploration - 317 2016 £248

Ebert-Schiefferer, Sybille *Still Life a History.* New York: Harry N. Abrams, 1999. First edition, 4to., bright red cloth, stunningly illustrated, fine in like dust jacket. Gene W. Baade, Books on the West 2015 - 1003038 2016 $482

Ebes, Hank *The John Gould Collection from His Personal Library.* Melbourne: Ebes Douwma Antique Prints and Maps, 1987. Octavo color photos, softcover. Andrew Isles Natural History Books 55 - 15630 2016 $100

Ebutt, Blanche *Dont's for Wives.* London: Gay and Hancock, 1913. 24mo., half title, lacking leading f.e.p., original silver blue glazed cloth, dulled and slightly rubbed. Jarndyce Antiquarian Books CCXV - 173 2016 £40

Eckel, John C. *The First Editions of the Writings of Charles Dickens and their Values: a Bibliography.* London: Chapman & Hall, 1913. First edition, no. 12 of 750 copies, half title, frontispiece, facsimiles, uncut in original brown grained cloth, lettered gilt, slightly dulled, top edge gilt, very good. Jarndyce Antiquarian Booksellers CCXVIII - 1496 2016 £75

Eckel, John C. *The First Editions of the Writings of Charles Dickens.* New York: Maurice Inman Inc., London: Maggs Bros., 1932. Revised edition, illustrations, original cloth, dust jacket in slipcase. Jarndyce Antiquarian Booksellers CCXVIII - 1487 2016 £90

Eckert, Robert P. *Edward Thomas. A Biography and a Bibliography.* London: J. M. Dent, 1937. First edition, frontispiece, 9 further plates, few foxspots to prelims and index, 8vo., original green cloth, backstrip lettered gilt against brown ground with tiny amount of wear to tips of lower joint, little spotting around head of cloth and at foot of upper board, some surface wear to tips of lower joint, little spotting around head of cloth and at foot of upper board, some surface grazing and corners a touch bumped, top edge green, few fos spots to endpapers and two ownership inscriptions, dust jacket frayed with light soiling and some loss at backstrip ends, good, this the copy of Robin Guthrie, artist-son of James Guthrie of Pear Tree press with his ownership inscription dated 1942. Blackwell's Rare Books B186 - 286 2016 £135

Eckley, Sophia May *Minor Chords.* London: Bell and Daldy, 1869. Presentation inscribed by author for Mrs Tipping, original green cloth with black ruling and design to covers and gilt author and title to spine, some bumping and chipping, otherwise very good, spotting to endpaper and occasional spotting in text, very good. The Kelmscott Bookshop 12 - 41 2016 $150

Eco, Umberto *Baudolino.* New York: Harcourt, 2002. 8vo., fine in dust jacket, tipped in bookplate, signed by author. Second Life Books, Inc. 196A - 491 2016 $50

Eco, Umberto *Opera Aperta.* Milano: Bompianai, 1962. First edition, text in Italian, blindstamp on titlepage, fine in very good dust jacket darkened at spine and edges with some staining to spine. Peter Ellis 112 - 110 2016 £125

Ecole Normale *Programme General des Cours Des Ecoles Normales.* Paris: (Forget) I pluviose an III, 1795. First edition, first leaf slightly stained and probably 'soigneusement lavee', last leaf with names and addresses of professors, with repair to lower inner margin, and laid down, short tear in fore-margin of one leaf, 4to., modern calf backed boards, wide margined copy, good, rare. Blackwell's Rare Books B186 - 55 2016 £900

Eddy, Daniel C. *The Young Woman's Friend or the Duties, Trials, Loves and Hopes of Woman.* London: Walter Scott, 1886. New edition, 4 pages ads, original maroon cloth, bevelled boards, gilt spine, slightly rubbed, all edges gilt, very good. Jarndyce Antiquarian Books CCXV - 172 2016 £35

Eddy, Mary Baker Glover *Christ My Refuge: One of Seven Hymns by...* Boston: Pub. by the Trustees under the Will of Mary Baker Eddy, 1939. White cloth, gilt pictorial cover, very good-fine, printed on one side of the page, calligraphic text done in 4 colors with pictorial and illuminated initials, pictorial headpiece and tailipece, title, and cover illustrations plus full page color illustrations by Violet Oakley, beautiful book. Aleph-bet Books, Inc. 111 - 327 2016 $75

Eddy, Mary Baker Glover *Science and Health.* Lynn: Pub by Dr. Asa G. Eddy, 1881. 12mo., frontispiece, blue cloth, volume I-II (all), volume II slightly darker, tiny wear to corners and spinal extremities, internally immaculate, in calf backed new part cloth box, brilliant set. M & S Rare Books, Inc. 99 - 82 2016 $2750

Eddy, William A. *F.D.R. Meets the Saud.* New York: American Friends of the Middle East, 1954. Very rare first edition, 8vo., original blue printed card wrappers, facsimile and two plates, covers faded, interior nonetheless in very good condition. Sotheran's Travel and Exploration - 318 2016 £598

Eden, Anthony *The Memoirs of Sir Anthony Eden 1960-1965.* 1960-1965. 3 volumes, all with dust jackets. I. D. Edrich Winston Spencer Churchill - 2016 £30

Eden, Charles *China. Historical and Descriptive.* London: Marcus Ward & Co., 1877. First edition, scarce, 8vo., recent green crushed morocco over marbled boards, spine with raised bands, ornamented in gilt and with gilt stamped red morocco lettering piece, chromolithographic frontispiece and additional title, folding map in black and blue, numerous text illustrations and plates, light even browning due to paper stock, few minor marginal flaws, map with restortaion on verso, discard stamp of Nahant Public Library in margin of lithographic title. Sotheran's Travel and Exploration - 120 2016 £598

Eden, Frederic Morton *The State of the Poor.* London: J. David for B. & J. White, G. G. & J. Robinson, T. Payne, R. Faulder, T. Gerton, J. Debrett and D. Bremmer, 1797. First edition, 3 volumes, quarto, bound without final leaf of volume III (directions to binder), which was usually omitted when book was bound, superby rebound to style by Trevor Lloyd in full tree calf, covers ruled gilt with a metope-and-septaglyph roll, spines richly gilt with red morocco lettering pieces, volumes numbered on red oval onlays over black morocco labels, inner dentelles ruled in gilt with Greek-key roll, marbled endpapers, an excellent copy,. Heritage Book Shop Holiday 2015 - 36 2016 $10,000

Eden, Ronald *Going to the Moors.* Penrith: David A. Grayling, 1996. No. 207 of a limited edition of 300, signed by author, 8vo., original red cloth with dust jacket, frontispiece, illustrations, fine.   Sotheran's Hunting, Shooting & Fishing - 80   2016   £50

Edgar, James *New Brunswick, as a Home for Emigrants...* Saint John: Barnes and Co., 1860. Paper wrappers, small 8vo., heraldic device on both front cover and titlepage, rear cover detached, slight wear to front cover, previous owner's name inside front cover.   Schooner Books Ltd.   115 - 22   2016 $125

Edgar, John George *The Boyhood of Great men Intended as an Example to Youth.* London: George Routledge & Sons, circa, 1880. New edition, frontispiece and plates, slightly spotted, lacking leading, original green cloth, rubbed and dulled.   Jarndyce Antiquarian Books   CCXV - 60   2016   £20

Edgar, M. G. *A Treasury of Verse for Little Children selected by....* New York: Thomas Crowell, n.d., 1908. 4to., green pictorial cloth, slight cover soil, else near fine, pictorial endpapers and 8 color plates and a profusion of black and whites by Willy Pogany.   Aleph-bet Books, Inc.   111 - 346   2016 $300

Edgeworth, Maria   1768-1849 *Castle Rackrent & The Absentee.* London: Macmillan, 1895. 8vo., uncut, partly unopened, original cloth and pictorial dust jacket, spine of jacket darkened, very good, very scarce in jacket.   Blackwell's Rare Books   B184 - 36   2016   £200

Edgeworth, Maria   1768-1849 *Practical Education.* London: J. Johnson, 1798. 2 volumes, half titles, 2 folded plates with 1 additional plate included in pagination, 4to., occasional light spotting, some pencil underlining and annotation, handsomely rebound in half calf, gilt spines, red morocco labels, marbled boards, very good.   Jarndyce Antiquarian Books   CCXV - 632   2016   £850

Edie, George *The Art of English Shooting.* San Francisco: Arion Press, 1993. Facsimile reprint of 1775, 12mo., original calf backed marbled paper, covered boards, fine in matching slipcase, with prospectus.   Sotheran's Piccadilly Notes - Summer 2015 - 114   2016   £198

Edleston, Richard *Marriage its Uses, Duties and Blessings.* Leeds: J. Heaton, 1849. Occasional ink annotation, original brown cloth, slightly rubbed maroon morocco label, slight damp mark to front board, ownership stamps of G. Mellor.   Jarndyce Antiquarian Books   CCXV - 173   2016   £45

Edmonds, Walter D. *Drums Along the Mohawk.* Boston: Little Brown and Co., 1936. First edition, fine in first issue dust jacket with just touch of toning on spine, signed by author, beautiful copy.   Between the Covers Rare Books   204 - 37   2016 $650

Edwards, Amelia B. *"How the Third Floor Knew the Potteries." in Farmer's Almanac for the Year of Our Lord 1865.* Rahway: D. F. Coles, 1864. Stitched as issued, occasional foxing, first and last leaves bit soiled, corners cut round.   Joseph J. Felcone, Inc.   Books from Five Centuries: a Miscellany - 59   2016 $400

Edwards, Bela Bates *Biography of Self-Taught Men.* London: T. Nelson & sons, 1858. Half title, frontispiece, original pink-brown cloth, spine decorated & lettered in gilt, chip to head of spine, contemporary signature on title.   Jarndyce Antiquarian Books   CCXV - 61   2016   £20

Edwards, Bela Bates *Self-Taught Men...* London: T. Nelson & Sons, 1876. Half title, color frontispiece and additional title plates, final ad leaf, original brown cloth blocked in black and gilt, prize inscription, very good.   Jarndyce Antiquarian Books   CCXV - 62   2016   £25

Edwards, Bela Bates *Self-Taught Men...* London: T. Nelson & sons, 1886. Frontispiece & plates, original brown cloth, slightly dulled, very good.   Jarndyce Antiquarian Books   CCXV - 63   2016   £25

Edwards, Edward *A Sermon Preached in Wrexham Church Nov. 3 1799, being the Sunday after the Interment of Thomas Jones, Esq. Cornet in the Wrexham Yeomanry Cavalry....* Wrexham: printed by John Painter, 1800. Half title discarded, some light dust soiling, 8vo., extracted from bound volume, stab holes also visible, good.   Blackwell's Rare Books   B186 - 56   2016   £200

Edwards, Joseph *Modern Therapeutics of the Diseases of Children with Observations on the Hygiene of Infancy.* Philadelphia: D. G. Brinton, 1885. First edition, 8vo., slight edgewear label on lower spine, very good.   Edwin V. Glaser Rare Books   2015 - 1021   2016 $150

Edwards, Lionel *My Hunting Sketch Book.* London: Eyre and Spottiswoode, 1928. First edition, 4to., original oatmeal cloth, paper label to upper right corner of upper board, 15 plates by Lionel Edwards, colored and mounted, very good, very clean.   Sotheran's Hunting, Shooting & Fishing - 33   2016   £200

Edwards, P. D. *Dickens's "Young Men" George Augustus Sala.* Aldershot: Ashgate, 1997. Half title, illustrations, original black cloth, very good in dust jacket.   Jarndyce Antiquarian Booksellers   CCXVIII - 1213   2016   £30

Egan, Pierce 1772-1849 *Real Life in London or the Rambles and Adventures of Bob Tallyho, Esq. and His Cousin the Hon. Tom Dashall through the Metropolis.* London: printed for Jones and Co., 1821-1822. First edition, first issue with "Oxford Arms Passage" in imprint, complete with two plates not included in list of plates, 8vo., 2 volumes, full red morocco by Riviere and Son, french fillet border to sides, richly gilt panelled spines, gilt turn-ins, all edges gilt, 34 hand colored aquatint plates, including frontispieces and engraved titles, designed and engraved by Alken, Dighton, Brooke and Rowlandson, etc., little spotting to endpapers and edges, some occasional browning, bookplates, otherwise excellent set.   Sotheran's Piccadilly Notes - Summer 2015 - 116   2016   £1000

Egan, Pierce 1772-1849 *Tom & Jerry. Life in London....* London: John Camden Hotten, 1869. Half title, color frontispiece and 35 color plates, text little browned, original blue sand grained cloth, pictorially blocked and lettered gilt, spine little darkened and carefully repaired at head, inner hinge slight splitting, armorial bookplate of Charles Dickens and "From the Library of Charles Dickens" label June 1870.   Jarndyce Antiquarian Booksellers   CCXVIII - 870   2016   £1100

Egerton, Denise *Design for an Accident.* London: Hodder & Stoughton, 1957. Blue boards, gilt titling in lightly marked dust jacket, some edge foxing, not affecting text, contents very good, uncommon.   I. D. Edrich   Crime - 2016   £25

The Eggs-Traordinary Adventures of the Humpty Dumpty Family. London: Anthony Treherne,n.d. circa, 1940. First edition, 3 inch square, pictorial tan cloth, soil on verso of first page of text, light cover rubbing, very good+, printed on board pages on one side of page, each page of text faces charming full page color illustration by author, 24 in all, very scarce.   Aleph-bet Books, Inc.   112 - 252   2016 $750

Eginhartus *De Vita et Gestis Caroli magni.* Traiecti ad Rhenum: Guilielmi Vande Water, 1711. 4to., 2 folding plates, one engraved, the other a table, titlepage in red and black, woodcut printer's device and initials, first plate little creased with 2 cm. closed tear near gutter, adjacent and final leaves, neatly attached, titlepage slightly dusty but generally clean and bright internally, contemporary reversed vellum, ink title to spine, edges sprinkled red and blue, spine slightly darkened bit grubby, front endpapers very slightly toned with some ms. scribbled to f.f.e.p. verso, very good.   Unsworths Antiquarian Booksellers   30 - 50   2016   £200

Egolf, Tristan *Lord of the Barnyard.* London: Picador, 1998. Advance reading excerpt of the First British edition, 19 pages of text, very near fine in stapled wrappers.   Ken Lopez Bookseller   166 - 22   2016 $150

Ehmann, Harold *Encyclopedia of Australian Animals: reptiles.* Sydney: Angus and Robertson, 1992. Quarto, color photos, distribution maps, fine in dust jacket, scarce.   Andrew Isles Natural History Books   55 - 572   2016 $159

Eigner, Larry *On My Eyes.* Highlands: Jonathan Williams, 1960. One of only 500 copies issues in wrappers, no hardcover edition, very good plus in photo illustrated wrappers that have some light soiling and foxing, internally clean copy, somewhat elusive.   Jeff Hirsch Books   Holiday List 2015 - 36   2016 $175

Einstein, Albert 1879-1955 *The Particle Problem in the General Theory of Relativity. in The Physical Review Volume 48, Second Series No. 1 July 1, 1935.* Lancaster: American Institute of Physics, 1935. Entire issue offered, small 4to., near fine, original green printed wrappers finely rebacked to style, tape page 24.   By the Book, L. C.   45 - 11   2016 $750

Einstein, Charles *Willie's Time: a memoir.* New York: Lippincott, 1979. First edition, cloth and boards, pictorial endpapers, signed by Willie Mays, very, very scarce signed, very good+ in dust jacket.   Gene W. Baade, Books on the West   2015 - SHEL689   2016 $135

Eisenberg, John F. *The Mammalian Radiations: an Analysis of trends in Evolution, Adaptation, and Behaviour.* Chicago: University of Chicago Press, 1981. Octavo, text illustrations, publisher's cloth.   Andrew Isles Natural History Books   55 - 38858   2016 $80

Eklekta. In Usum Scholae Regiae Westmonasteriensis. Sumptibus Gulielmi Ginger, ad Insignia Collegii Westmonasteriennsis..., 1781. Sole edition, second leaf of ads, bound following titlepage instead of at end, little minor spotting, 8vo. original linen, bit marked and rubbed, ownership inscription of William Hughes, alumnus of Felsted School to front flyleaf, his name repeated with date 1784 at rear, very good, rare.   Blackwell's Rare Books   Greek & Latin Classics VII - 25   2016   £600

Elder, Annie E. *The History of New Jerusalem.* Fredericton: 1953. Private printing, Card covers, 8vo., small stain on front cover, generally very good.   Schooner Books Ltd.   115 - 23   2016 $55

Elder, William *A Memoir of Henry C. Carey; Read before the Historical Society of Pennsylvania.* Philadelphia: Henry Carey Baird Co., 1880. First edition, 8vo., brown cloth stamped in black, blind and gilt, small scrape on front cover, otherwise very good, presentation "Hon. William D. Kelley/ with the compliments/ Wm. E. Ringwalt/April 2nd/84", from the library of consumer advocate Florence Kelley, this was presented to her father, Judge and Congressman.   Second Life Books, Inc.   196A - 497   2016 $65

Eldridge, Elleanor *Memoirs of Eleanor Eldridge.* Providence: B. T. Albro, 1840. Later edition, 24mo., frontispiece, original quarter cloth and marbled paper covered boards with printed paper spine label toned, possibly lacking rear fly, but no evidence of removal edgewear, very good. Between the Covers Rare Books   202 - 31   2016 $400

An Elegy on the Death and Burial of Cock Robin. Flansham: Pear Tree Press, 1923. One of 100 numbered copies, (this one unnumbered), frontispiece, titlepage decoration and 15 wood engravings by Stuart or Robin Guthrie printed in green to verso, small 4to., original wrappers with titlepage decoration printed in green and press device to rear, wrappers with light overall dust soiling and some crasing to corners, front hinge starting, very good. Blackwell's Rare Books   B186 - 323   2016   £150

Eliot, George, Pseud.   1819-1880 *Adam Bede.* New York: Harper and Bros., 1859. Second American edition, 8vo., original green cloth, covers blocked in blind, spine lettered gilt, spine faded, good.   Blackwell's Rare Books   B184 - 37   2016   £100

Eliot, George, Pseud.   1819-1880 *Adam Bede.* Edinburgh and London: William Blackwood and Son, 1859. Third edition, 3 volumes, 8vo., few spots and minor stains, text block broken in volume ii and couple of gatherings round, original russet pebble grained cloth, blind stamped panels on sides, spine gilt lettered, corners little worn, hinges strained, Maurice Baring's copy with his bookplate in volumes ii and iii, and his signature.   Blackwell's Rare Books   B184 - 38   2016   £100

Eliot, George, Pseud.   1819-1880 *Adam Bede.* Edinburgh and London: William Blackwood and Son, 1859. New and cheaper edition, 2 volumes, little scattered foxing, 8vo., original russet wavy grained cloth, blindstamped panels on sides, spine gilt lettered, upper cover volume ii marked, minor wear, good.   Blackwell's Rare Books   B184 - 39   2016   £80

Eliot, George, Pseud.   1819-1880 *Felix Holt the Radical.* Edinburgh and London: William Blackwood & Sons, 1866. New edition, 2 volumes, original cottage red sand grained cloth, bevelled boards, front boards and spines decorated and lettered in gilt, back boards with borders in blind by Burn, with ticket at end of volume 1, slight marking, half titles,.   Jarndyce Antiquarian Booksellers   CCXVII - 94   2016   £320

Eliot, George, Pseud.   1819-1880 *Middlemarch.* Edinburgh: William Blackwood, 1871-1872. First edition, 4 volumes, half titles, 8 books bound as 4 in slightly later full dark blue morocco by Birdsall, gilt spines, borders and dentelles, top edge gilt, very good, attractive copy, bound in at end are original pale green wrappers to the 8 separately issued books.   Jarndyce Antiquarian Booksellers   CCXVII - 95   2016   £3500

Eliot, George, Pseud.   1819-1880 *The Writings of George Eliot.* Boston: Houghton Mifflin, 1908. Illustrated large paper edition, 25 volumes, contemporary full blue morocco gilt, photogravures in color ALS by author to M. E. Lewes typed into volume I, fine set.   Honey & Wax Booksellers   4 - 6   2016 $7500

Eliot, Thomas Stearns   1888-1965 *After Strange Gods, a Primer of Modern Heresy.* New York: Harcourt Brace, 1934. First edition, issued in an edition of 1500 copies, uncut and partially unopened, some staining to endpapers, very good in torn dust jacket,.   Second Life Books, Inc.   197 - 101   2016 $275

Eliot, Thomas Stearns   1888-1965 *Tam Domov Mas. (East Coker).* East Coker: PEN Clubs, 1941. First Czech edition, one of 750 copies, foolscap 8vo., tipped in frontispiece by John Piper, one or two instances of Pencil annotation to margins, original stapled printed wrappers trifle dust soiled, laid slip laid in, very good, niscribed by translator, Libuse Pankova.   Blackwell's Rare Books   B186 - 212   2016   £300

Eliot, Thomas Stearns   1888-1965 *Ezra Pound: His Metric and Poetry.* New York: Knopf, 1917. first edition of author's second book, one of 1000 copies, 12mo., frontispiece by Henri Gaudier Brzeska, original rose boards, top edge of boards near head of spine bumped, spine faded, otherwise very good, one of Ezra Pound's retained copies, with his contemporary blindstamped address and his holograph annotations to bibliography at back of book, top edge of boards near head of spine bumped, spine faded, otherwise very good.   James S. Jaffe Rare Books   Occasional List: Winter 2016 - 56   2016 $4500

Eliot, Thomas Stearns   1888-1965 *Four Quartets.* London: Faber & Faber, 1940-1942. First editions, 4 volumes, thin 8vo., original printed wrappers, East Coker scarce in first edition, wrappers very slightly soiled, otherwise fine set.   James S. Jaffe Rare Books   Occasional List: Winter 2016 - 57   2016 $1750

Eliot, Thomas Stearns   1888-1965 *Four Quartets - East Coker - Burnt Norton - The Dry Salvages - Little Gidding.* London: Faber & Faber, 1940-1942. First edition, 8vo., 4 volumes in original wrappers, very slightly used, but even so better than most.   Sotheran's   Piccadilly Notes - Summer 2015 - 119   2016   £1500

Eliot, Thomas Stearns   1888-1965 *Murder in the Cathedral.* New York: Harcourt Brace and Co., 1935. First US edition, signed by author, one of 1500 copies, signature little faded, 8vo., original black cloth with dust jacket, wrapper slightly sunned on spine and with fellow shallow chips on top edge, otherwise very good.   Sotheran's   Piccadilly Notes - Summer 2015 - 117   2016   £1250

Eliot, Thomas Stearns 1888-1965 *Murder in the Cathedral.* Canterbury: H. J. Goulden, 1935. First edition, 8vo., original wrappers, small chip to bottom of spine, little sunning to edges of wrappers, discreet gift inscription, otherwise very good.   Sotheran's   Piccadilly Notes - Summer 2015 - 118   2016   £750

Eliot, Thomas Stearns 1888-1965 *The Music of Poetry.* Glasgow: Jackson Son and Co., 1942. First edition, 8vo., original printed wrappers, near fine.   Sotheran's   Piccadilly Notes - Summer 2015 - 120   2016   £125

Eliot, Thomas Stearns 1888-1965 *Collected Poems 1909-1935.* New York: Harcourt Brace and co., 1936. First edition, early printing, William Meredith's copy, signed by poet Princeton 1940, extensively annotated by Meredith in pencil with few pages of notes by Meredith laid in, covers faded and stained, good only, lacking dust jacket.   Charles Agvent   William Meredith - 79   2016 $500

Eliot, Thomas Stearns 1888-1965 *A Presidential Address to the Members of the London Library.* Printed for the London Library by Queen Anne Press, 1952. First edition, one of 500 copies, octavo, sewn wrappers, fine.   Peter Ellis   112 - 113   2016   £65

Eliot, Thomas Stearns 1888-1965 *The Waste Land.* New York: Boni & Liveright, 1922, i.e., 1923. No. 546 of 1000 copies of the second edition/impression, 197 x 130mm., original black buckram, gilt titling on upper cover and spine, unopened, original pale orange dust jacket with black lettering, light uniform fading to spine of jacket, but as close to mint as one could hope to find, surely unsurpassable copy, jacket virtually untouched and with unopened text, obviously never read.   Phillip J. Pirages   67 - 125   2016 $6000

Elison, Hal *The Knife.* New York: Lancer, 1961. First edition, near fine in wrappers.   Mordida Books   2015 - 010705   2016 $65

Elkin, R. H. *The Children's Corner.* London & Philadelphia: Augener & McKay, n.d., 1914. Oblong 4to., gilt cloth, pictorial paste-on, slightest bit of cover soil, near fine, illustrations by H. Willebeek Mair.   Aleph-bet Books, Inc.   112 - 287   2016 $400

Elkus, Richard J. *Alamos: a Philosophy in Living.* San Francisco: Grabhorn Press, 1965. Limited to 487 numbered copies, signed by author/photographer and by Edwin and Robert Grabhorn, folio, 24 mounted photographic plates, half brown suede embossed with title, over hand dyed orange, light brown and yellow striped Mexican cloth, very minor small rubbing to suede at bottom edge of covers, very fine, superb mounted prints.   Argonaut Book Shop   Photography 2015 - 5698   2016 $375

Ellin, Stanley *Kindly Dig Your Grave.* New York: Davis, 1975. First edition, fine in wrappers.   Mordida Books   2015 - 0105781   2016 $65

Elliot, Daniel Giraud *A Classification and Synopsis of the Trochilidae.* Washington: Smithsonian Contributions to Knowledge, 1878. Quarto, text illustrations, contemporary half morocco, all edges colored, two library stamps of the RAOU, otherwise very good.   Andrew Isles Natural History Books   55 - 33278   2016 $250

Elliot, William Hume *The Country and Church of the Cheeryble Brothers.* Selkirk: George Lewis & Son, 1893. First edition, half title, double frontispiece, illustrations, double frontispiece, illustrations, final ad leaf, original blue cloth, slightly rubbed, inscribed to Ruth Browlies "from the author', top edge gilt.   Jarndyce Antiquarian Booksellers   CCXVIII - 249   2016   £30

Ellis, Asa *The Country Dyer's Assistant.* Brookfield: pr. by E. Merriam & Co. for the author, 1798. First edition, 16mo., errata & leaf, contemporary calf, gilt stamping on spine, rubbed but very nice, light foxing, signature of John Brown, Esq.   M & S Rare Books, Inc.   99 - 86   2016 $1250

Ellis, Havelock *The New Spirit.* London: George Bell and Sons, 1890. First edition, very good in original red cloth boards with gilt title to spine, few spots of soiling to boards, minor wear to edges, light browning to spine and few spots of soxing to interior, still nice, signature of previous owner B. Wallis, very good.   The Kelmscott Bookshop   12 - 43   2016 $375

Ellis, James Joseph *Short Lives of me with a Mission.* London: James Nisbet & Co., 1898? Half title, frontispiece, slight paper browning, original blue green cloth, prize inscription on leading pastedown, very good.   Jarndyce Antiquarian Books   CCXV - 64   2016   £25

Ellis, Richard H. *General Pope and U.S. Indian Policy.* Albuquerque: University of New Mexico Press, 1970. First edition, old notes, light brown cloth, very fine with dust jacket.   Argonaut Book Shop   Native American 2015 - 7579   2016 $40

Ellis, Roger *The Oxford History of Literary Translation in English Volume I to 1530.* Oxford University Press, 2008. First edition, 8vo., cloth, gilt lettered, dust jacket, almost as new.   Unsworths Antiquarian Booksellers Ltd.   E05 - 100   2016   £100

Ellis, Sara Stickney *The Daughters of England, Their Position in Society, Character & Responsibilities.* London: Fisher Son & Co., 1842. First edition, frontispiece little spotted, contemporary gilt binding, full dark maroon morocco, decorated in gilt, small repair to leading hinge, boards slightly bowed, all edges gilt, good plus.   Jarndyce Antiquarian Books   CCXV - 174   2016   £65

Ellis, Sara Stickney *The Wives of England, Their Relative Duties, Domestic, Influence & Social Obligations.* London: Fisher Son & Co., 1846. Lacking Leading f.e.p., original scarlet cloth, slightly marked and dulled, frontispiece, nice copy.   Jarndyce Antiquarian Books   CCXV - 175   2016   £50

Ellis, Sara Stickney *The Women of England.* London: Fisher Son & Co., 1841? Half title, original scarlet cloth, dulled, contemporary signature of leading f.e.p., very good.   Jarndyce Antiquarian Books   CCXV - 177   2016   £50

Ellis, Sara Stickney *The Wives of England, Their Relative Duties, Domestic, Influence & Social Obligations.* London: Fisher Son & Co., 1841? Fifteenth edition, Half title, original dark blue cloth with edition statement on spine, slightly rubbed, good.   Jarndyce Antiquarian Books   CCXV - 176   2016   £35

Ellis, William *Philo-Socrates. Part V.* London: Smith, Elder & Co., 1863. Original light brown printed paper wrappers, hinges slightly splitting with some repair to head of leading hinge, inscription Caroline Lindley from her friend William Ellis.   Jarndyce Antiquarian Books CCXV - 640   2016   £85

Ellison, Harlan *Dangerous Visions: 33 Original Stories.* Garden City: Doubleday & Co., 1967. First edition, octavo, cloth, some discoloration to paste-downs with offsetting to free endpapers which is common to this book, fine in fine dust jacket with mild rubbing to corner tips and spine corners, small area of scratches to upper rear panel and two light blue horizontal lines on verso of jacket (offset from previous jacket protector) with slight bleed through to white background of flaps of jacket, attractive copy.   John W. Knott, Jr./L.W. Currey, Inc.   Fall-Winter 2015 - 16589   2016 $350

Ellison, Norman *Out of Doors with Nomad - Further Adventures among the Wild Life of the countryside.* London: University of London Press, 1947. First edition, octavo, wood engravings by C. F. Tunnicliffe, spine faded at head and tail, very good in like dust jacket (chipped).   Peter Ellis   112 - 408   2016   £35

Ellison, Norman *Roving with Nomad.* London: University of London Press, 1949. First edition, octavo, wood engravings by C. F. Tunnicliffe, very good in like dust jacket with chip from top edge of rear panel.   Peter Ellis   112 - 409   2016   £35

Ellison, Norman *Wandering with Nomad...* London: University of London Press, 1946. First edition, octavo, wood engravings by C. F. Tunnicliffe, contemporary (1946) gift inscription, spine bruised, corners slightly bumped, very good in like dust jacket chipped at top edge of upper panel with some loss to lettering of title.   Peter Ellis   112 - 411   2016   £35

Ellison, Ralph *Invisible Man.* New York: The Modern Library, 1952. Modern Library edition, slight wear to boards, near fine in about very good dust jacket with some small chips and repaired along front flap fold with archival tape, inscribed by author to his wife Fanny Mae.   Between the Covers Rare Books   202 - 32   2016 $4500

Ellison, Ralph *Invisible Man.* New York: Random House, 1952. First edition, near fine with spine lettering rubbed as usual, in moderately worn, very good dust jacket with some internal tissue strengthening to joints, jacket designed by E. McKnight Kauffer.   Between the Covers Rare Books   207 - 42   2016 $950

Ellison, Ralph *Invisible Man.* New York: Vintage, 1972. first paperback edition?, small 8vo., author's presentation to Joe Reed and family, paper wrappers, ink markings on front edges, cover creased and scuffed, very good, tight copy.   Second Life Books, Inc.   196A - 499   2016 $700

Ellison, Ralph *Shadow and Act.* New York: Random House, 1964. First edition, small spot on top edge, else fine in fine dust jacket with few tiny spots on rear panel, Advance Review copy with slip and photo of author laid in.   Between the Covers Rare Books   207 - 43   2016 $275

Ellroy, James *The Cold Six Thousand.* New York: Knopf, 2001. First edition, very fine in dust jacket.   Mordida Books   2015 - 012731   2016 $60

Ellroy, James *Hollywood Nocturnes.* New York: Penzler, 1994. First edition, very fine in dust jacket.   Mordida Books   2015 - 011856   2016 $65

Elmslie, Kenward *The Champ.* Los Angeles: Black Sparrow Press, 1968. First edition, illustrations by Joe Brainard, printed wrappers, modest rubbing mostly along spine, else near fine, one of 750 copies, inscribed by Elmslie and Brainard.   Between the Covers Rare Books   208 - 22   2016 $225

Elsler, Robert *The Messiah Jesus and John the Baptist...* London: Methuen, 1931. First edition, original green cloth remains attractive, however spine reinforced with tape where gilt lettering remains clear, several spots on rear board and covers bit bumped, interior shows some foxing with scattered light pencil marks in margins and on rear pastedown, good to very good, 40 plates.   Simon Finch   2015 - 001536   2016 $252

Elsna, Hebe *Unwanted Wife: a Defence of Mrs. Charles Dickens.* London: Jarrolds, 1963. First edition, half title, double leaf title, plates, original maroon cloth, very good in dust jacket.   Jarndyce Antiquarian Booksellers   CCXVIII - 1214   2016   £20

Elson, Louis C. *European Reminicences, Musical and otherwise.* Philadelphia: Theo. Presser, 1896. 8vo., author's presentation, illustrations, green cloth stamped in gilt, cover little spotted and scuffed at corners and spine, otherwise very good.   Second Life Books, Inc.   196A - 50   2016 $45

Ely, David *Seconds.* New York: Pantheon Books, 1963. First edition, octavo, cloth backed boards, fine in fine dust jacket with two light blue horizontal lines on verso of jacket, offset from previous jacket protector with slight bleed through at jacket flap, sharp copy.   John W. Knott, Jr./L.W. Currey, Inc.   Fall-Winter 2015 - 16591   2016 $750

Emancipation of the Negro Slaves in the West India Colonies Considered with Reference to its Impolicy and Injustice, in Answer to Mr. Wilberforce's Appeal. London: Whitmore & Fen, 1824. Half title, slight crease to first 2 leaves, unopened, sewn as isused, backed with later brown paper, slightly worn at head and tail, inscribed "Rt. Hon. Fredk. Robinson MP".   Jarndyce Antiquarian Booksellers CCXVII - 257   2016   £350

Emberley, Ed *Emberley's ABC.* Boston: Little Brown, 1978. Stated first edition, oblong 4to, pictorial cloth, as new in as new dust jacket, every letter has a 2 page spread with fabulous color illustrations, scarce in unusually fine condition.   Aleph-bet Books, Inc.   111 - 3   2016 $100

Emerson, Edwin *Adventures of Theodore Roosevelt.* New York: E. P. Dutton, 1928. Stated first edition, 8vo., gilt cloth, fine in dust jacket with few closd tears, illustrations by Elmer Hader with color dust jacket and endpapers and a profusion of full and partial page black and whites or silhouettes, first editions in dust jackets are rare.   Aleph-bet Books, Inc.   112 - 234   2016 $275

Emerson, Ralph Waldo   1803-1882 *An Address Delivered in the Court House of Concord, Mass. on 1st August 1844 on the Anniversary of the Emancipation of the Negroes in the British West Indies.* Boston: James Munroe, 1844. First edition, 8vo., sewn as issued? browning.   M & S Rare Books, Inc.   99 - 88   2016 $275

Emerson, Ralph Waldo   1803-1882 *Essays (First Series).* Boston: James Munroe and Co., 1841. First edition, octavo, early 20th century black polished calf, gilt ruled and blindstamped spine, boards with gilt ruling surrounding a finely executed blindstamped pattern, gilt dentelles, marbled endpapers, top edge gilt, silk bookmark, spine from original cloth bound in, text remarkably clean.   Manhattan Rare Book Company   2016 - 1772   2016 $2300

Emmons, Earl H. *An Uncensored Anthology: Written by Divers Hands Decorated by Carl Cobbledick....* Mount Vernon: Peter Pauper, 1939. First edition, small 8vo., dark blue cloth with paper labels printed in red, cover little faded, spine label chipped, front label little spotted, otherwise very good, tight in little faded and worn box.   Second Life Books, Inc.   197 - 104   2016 $45

Empson, William *The Gathering Storm.* London: Faber and Faber Ltd., 1940. First edition, James Merrill's copy with his signature dated 1974, signed by William Meredith, faint stain to bottom of front cover, very good in good only dust jacket, split into two pieces.   Charles Agvent   William Meredith - 82   2016 $150

The Emu. Melbourne: Royal Austalasian Ornithologists Union, 1900-1994. Firrst 3 volumes are the Hyett/Cooper facsimile, volumes 1-92, volume six is unbound, volume 8 part one only (lacks three parts), volume nine is in a shabby 'Emu' binding, all other volumes in neat binder's cloth, very good, octavo,.   Andrew Isles Natural History Books   55 - 36419   2016 $5000

The Enchanted Castle: a Book of Fairy Tales for Flowerland. Philadelphia: Altemus, 1906. Pictorial cloth, fine, 40 lovely full and partial page illustrations in red and black, very scarce.   Aleph-bet Books, Inc.   112 - 334   2016 $275

Encyclopaedia Britannica, a Dictionary. Cambridge: At the University Press, 1926. Thirteenth edition, small 4to., original half calf with red cloth covered boards, top edge gilt, minor wear along hinges.   Oak Knoll Books   310 - 241   2016 $350

Enfield, D. E. *Mystery of the Thirties.* London: Hogarth Press, 1928. Illustrated, spine little darkened, name on front endpaper, covers little sunned, pages uncut, outer fore edges little foxed, otherwise very good.   I. D. Edrich Crime - 2016   £25

Enfield, William *The Speaker or Miscellaneous Pieces, Selected or Miscellaneous Pieces...* Paris: sold by F. Louis, 1804. 12mo., final ad leaf, corner creased at beginning and end of volume, uncut in original blue paper wrapper, paper label, corners and edges creased, spine slightly worn, ex-libris Castelli Sanctii Pontii.   Jarndyce Antiquarian Books CCXV - 178   2016   £40

England & Wales *Magna Carta et Cetera Antiqua Statuta Nunc Nouiter per Diuersa Exemplaria Examinata et Summa Diligentia Castigata et Correcta cui Adiecta est Nousa Tabula Valde Necessaria.* London: Thomas Marshe, 1556. Revised edition, 2 parts in 1 volume, woodcut initials, some historiated, lacking blank A1 as often, titlepage browned, brittle and little frayed at edges, clean tear passing through one letter on title, generally little browned around edges, small 8vo., late 19th century half dark green morocco, front inner hinge strained, some early annotations for the most part identifying statutes, sound. Blackwell's Rare Books Marks of Genius - 28 2016 £2500

England, John *Examination of Evidence and Report to the Most Reverend James Whitefield... Upon the Miraculous Restoration of Mrs. Ann Mattingly...* Charleston: James Burges, 1830. First edition, 8vo., contemporary calf backed marbled boards, spine worn, foxed. M & S Rare Books, Inc. 99 - 42 2016 $350

Engle, Lehman *Words with Music.* New York: Macmillan, 1972. First printing, 8vo., author's presentation on flyleaf, edges slightly spotted, otherwise very good, tight copy in soiled and slightly chipped dust jacket. Second Life Books, Inc. 196A - 504 2016 $45

The English Matron. London: Henry Colburn, 1846. First edition, 24 page catalog, new endpapers, uncut in original cream cloth at some time rebacked returning original spine strip, little dulled and marked. Jarndyce Antiquarian Books CCXV - 179 2016 £60

English Forests and Forest Trees, Historical, Legendary and Descriptive. London: Ingram Cooke, 1853. First edition, wood engraved frontispiece, extra engraved title, 42 engraved plates and text illustrations, later three quarter crimson leather, marbled sides, all edges gilt, some rubbing to extremities, armorial bookplate on inner cover, minor foxing to rear blank and leaves with ownership inscription to last leaf, overall fine. Argonaut Book Shop Natural History 2015 - 6752 2016 $325

Enright, D. J. *Selected Poems 1990: Oxford Poets.* New York: Oxford University Press, 1990. First edition, 8vo., printed wrappers, near fine, inscribed by author for William Jay Smith and Sonja. Second Life Books, Inc. 196A - 505 2016 $50

Enslin, Theodore *Ascensions.* Santa Barbara: Black Sparrow, May, 1977. Printed self wrappers, very good inscribed by author to friend, poet Paul Metcalf. Second Life Books, Inc. 196A - 508 2016 $45

Enslin, Theodore *Case Book.* Elmwood: Poets & Poets Press, 1987. First edition, 8vo., printed wrappers, fine, inscribed by author to poet Paul Metcalf. Second Life Books, Inc. 196A - 509 2016 $50

Enslin, Theodore *Circles.* Lewiston: Great Raven Press, 1977. First edition, 8vo., one of 325 copies, printed wrappers, fine, inscribed by author to Paul Metcalf. Second Life Books, Inc. 196A - 519 2016 $50

Enslin, Theodore *Concentrations.* Dennis: Salt Works press, 1977. First edition, 1/400 copies, printed wrappers, fine, inscribed by author to poet Paul Metcalf. Second Life Books, Inc. 196A - 512 2016 $50

Enslin, Theodore *The Country of Our Consciousness.* Berkeley: Sand Dollar Books # 5, 1971. First edition, 8vo., printed wrappers, very good, inscribed by author to poet Paul Metcalf. Second Life Books, Inc. 196A - 513 2016 $65

Enslin, Theodore *Etudes.* New Rochelle: Elizabeth Press, 1972. First edition, 8vo., printed paper wrappers, designed by Martino Mardersteig and printed from Garmond type on rag paper by Stamperia Valdonega, Verona, one of 400 copies, inscribed by author for Paul Metcalf and his wife. Second Life Books, Inc. 196A - 514 2016 $50

Enslin, Theodore *The Fifth Direction.* Markesan: Pentagram Press, 1980. First edition, one of 424 copies in printed wrappers, fine, inscribed by author to poet Paul Metcalf. Second Life Books, Inc. 196A - 515 2016 $50

Enslin, Theodore *The Flare of Beginning is In November.* Brooklyn: Jordan Davis, 1980. First edition, 12mo., printed wrappers, limited to 150 copies, signed, this copy inscribed by author to Paul Metcalf, very nice. Second Life Books, Inc. 196A - 516 2016 $75

Enslin, Theodore *Fragments--- Epigrammata.* Vineyard Haven: Salt-works Press, 1982. First edition, 8vo., of a total edition of 400, handset in Italian oldstyle types on Ticonderoga text paper, this one of 100 bound in cloth, numbered and signed by author, this copy inscribed by author for friend Paul Metcalf, fine. Second Life Books, Inc. 196A - 506 2016 $75

Enslin, Theodore *From Near the Great Pine.* Peoria: Spoon River Poetry Press, 1988. First edition, 8vo., printed wrappers, fine, inscribed by author to poet Paul Metcalf. Second Life Books, Inc. 196A - 517 2016 $50

Enslin, Theodore *The Further Regions.* Milwaukee: Pentagram, 1977. First edition, printed wrappers, fine, of an edition of 376 copies, this one of 300 unsigned, inscribed by author to poet Paul Metcalf. Second Life Books, Inc. 196A - 518 2016 $50

Enslin, Theodore *In the Keeper's House.* Dennis: Saltworks Press, 1973. First edition, printed wrappers, very nice, inscribed by author to poet Paul Metcalf.   Second Life Books, Inc.   196A - 519   2016 $50

Enslin, Theodore *The July Book.* Berkeley: San Dollar, 1976. First edition, 8vo. inscribed by author to poet Paul Metcalf, nice.   Second Life Books, Inc.   196A - 520   2016 $50

Enslin, Theodore *Landler.* New Rochelle: The Elizabeth Press, 1975. First edition, 8vo., printed paper wrappers, one of 250 copies, printed from Baskerville type on Magnani rag paper by Stamperia Valdonega, Verno, nice, inscribed by author to poet Paul Metcalf.   Second Life Books, Inc.   196A - 521   2016 $50

Enslin, Theodore *May Fault.* Fort Kent: Great Raven Press, 1979. First edition, stiff printed wrappers, nice, inscribed by author for poet Paul Metcalf.   Second Life Books, Inc.   196A - 522   2016 $50

Enslin, Theodore *The Mornings.* Berkeley: Shama Drum, 1974. First edition, small 8vo., printed wrappers, fine, one of 500 issued, this copy inscribed by author for poet Paul Metcalf.   Second Life Books, Inc.   196A - 523   2016 $50

Enslin, Theodore *Music for Several Occasions.* Milwaukee: Membrane Press, 1985. First edition, 8vo., printed wrappers, fine, inscribed to poet Paul Metcalf.   Second Life Books, Inc.   196A - 524   2016 $50

Enslin, Theodore *Papers.* New Rochelle: Elizabeth Press, 1976. First edition, 8vo., printed paper wrappers, one of 250 copies, nice, inscribed by author to poet Paul Metcalf, printed from Imprint type on Magnani rag paper by Stamperia Voldonega, Verona.   Second Life Books, Inc.   196A - 525   2016 $50

Enslin, Theodore *Passacaglia (Poems).* Bayonne: Beehive Press, 1982. First edition, spiral bound wrappers, nice, inscribed by author to poet Paul Metcalf.   Second Life Books, Inc.   196A - 526   2016 $50

Enslin, Theodore *Ranger CXXII & CXXVIII.* New York: Station Hill, 1977. First edition, limited to 500 copies, 8vo., paste paper wrappers, fine, inscribed by author to poet Paul Metcalf.   Second Life Books, Inc.   196A - 527   2016 $50

Enslin, Theodore *Sitio January 1969 November 1970.* Hanover: Granite Publications, 1973. First edition, 8vo., printed wrappers, fine, inscribed by author to poet Paul Metcalf.   Second Life Books, Inc.   196A - 528   2016 $50

Enslin, Theodore *Views.* New Rochelle: Elizabeth Press, 1972. First edition, 8vo., printed paper wrappers, designed by Mardersteig and printed from Garamond type on Magnani rag paper, one of 400 copies, nice, inscribed to poet Paul Metcalf.   Second Life Books, Inc.   196A - 529   2016 $50

Enslin, Theodore *With Light Reflected, Poems 1970-1972.* Fremont: Sumac Press, 1973. First edition, 1/1000 copies in printed wrappers, warmly inscribed by author to poet Paul Metcalf and his wife Nancy.   Second Life Books, Inc.   196A - 530   2016 $50

Entick, John *The General History of the late War....* London: Edward and Charles Dilly, 1767. 1766. First volume is third edition, others are second edition, no dust jacket, 5 volumes, 8vo., soundly rebound in 20th century beige buckram with black and red leather spine labels, plans, maps, charts, ex British Foreign Office library with few library markings, else very good.   Any Amount of Books 2015 - A73778   2016   £600

Epictetus *The Discourses in English.* London: Arthur L. Humphreys, 1897. Reprinted from the translation of George Long, first printing of this edition, 229 x 1844m., pleasing contemporary olive green crushed morocco, gilt by Joseph Bretault (stamp signed), covers with triple gilt fillet border, upper cover of both volumes with elaborate heraldic centerpiece bannered beneath a Scottish lion rampant at top and "And Choille" bannered below a crowned lion's head at bottom (centerpiece also featuring a bee to the right, leeks at center, flowered thistle to the left, and at center an opened book with "ET" on left page and "AM" on right, smooth spines with elongated panels formed by concentric fillets, top edges gilt, others untrimmed, large paper copy, titles printed in red and black, woodcut initials, spines uniformly sunned to warm brown, boards with slight fading as well, otherwise fine, leather lustrous and with only trivial signs of use, text immaculate.   Phillip J. Pirages   67 - 128   2016 $1200

Epictetus *The Discourses of Epictetus.* New York: Heritage Press, 1966. Green patterned boards with green cloth spine, lettered gilt, very fine in slipcase, small minor marking to slipcase, illustrations by Hans Erni, Sandglass pamphlet laid in.   Argonaut Book Shop   Heritage Press 2015 - 9686   2016 $40

Epictetus *Epicteti Enchiridion Latinis Versibus Adumbratum.* Oxford: E. Theatro Sheldoniano, 1715. First edition, frontispiece, two leaves with fore-edges dusty, few minor marks elsewhere, 8vo., contemporary sprinkled calf, spine divided by double gilt fillets, black morocco lettering piece, other compartments with gilt wheel tool, edges sprinkled red, slightest bit rubbed at extremities, armorial bookplate of Henry Hobhouse, very good, very pleasant.   Blackwell's Rare Books   B184 - 40   2016   £300

Epictetus *Enchiridion.* Parma: in aedibus Palatinis, typis Bodonianis, 1793. 2 pages with light offsetting from ribbon bookmark, 8vo., contemporary Italian sheep, strikingly marbled in shades of brown and green, boards bordered with triple gilt fillet, gilt flower cornerpieces, spine divided by raised bands, red morocco lettering pieces in second and third compartments, rest with central and corner gilt tools, marbled endpapers, edges gilt, merest touch of rubbing to extremities, modern booklabel, near fine, striking binding. Blackwell's Rare Books   B186 - 58   2016   £1200

Epictetus *Epictetus: a Poem Containing the Maxims of that Celebrated Philosopher...* London: printed and are to be sold by B. Bragge, 1709. First edition, 2nd issue, 8vo., contemporary calf, rebacked, black morocco label, edges and corners rather worn, aside from binding wear, good copy.   C. R. Johnson Rare Book Collections   Foxon: H-P 2015 - 789   2016 $613

Epicurus *Brief an Menoikeus.* N.P.: Fischbachpresse, 2007. Limited to 144 numbered copies signed by binder, Max Krauss, 12 copies, each with different states of binding, bound by Krauss and Wolfgang Kreuzer, woodcut illustrations by Kraus, paper covered boards, sewn, leather spine label, top edge cut, other edges uncut, slipcase, presentation laid in with signatures of Krauss and Kreuzer.   Oak Knoll Books   310 - 100   2016 $350

Epstein, Jacob *Epstein's Rine 'The Hyde Park Atrocity' - Creation and Controversy.* The Henry Moore Centre for the Study of Sculpture, Leeds City Art Galleries, 1988. First edition, illustrations, small folio, wrappers, fine in near fine dust jacket slightly creased at edges.   Peter Ellis   112 - 116   2016   £35

Erasmus, Desiderius 1466-1536 *Adagiorum D. Erasmi Roterodami Epitome.* Amsterdam: Ludovicum Elzevirium, 1650. First Elzevir edition, old calf, titlepage printed in red and black, contemporary limp vellum, endpapers discolored and bit wrinkled, very faint dampstain in margin of last several leaves, else near fine, crisp copy.   Joseph J. Felcone, Inc.   Books from Five Centuries: a Miscellany - 61   2016 $600

Erasmus, Desiderius 1466-1536 *Apophthegmatum, sive Scite Dictorum Libri Sex...* Basle: H. Froben, I. Hervagen & N. Episcopius March, 1531. First edition, superb copy, extremely rare edition, Froben's printer's device on title and somewhat larger version on final leaf verso, 7 large initials (six lines) by Hans Holbein the Younger, with mythological scenes, 4to., contemporary dark brown blind tooled calf over wooden boards, spine with five raised bands, fragments of ties, ms. paper title on head of spine, some wear at head and foot, contemporary mark in ink (M.4 and CH), old ownership crossed on on first endpaper.   Maggs Bros. Ltd. 1474 - 32   2016   £20,000

Erasmus, Desiderius 1466-1536 *L'Eloge de la Folie Nouvellement traduit du Latin d'Esrame par M. De la Veaux.* Basle: imprime avec des characters de G. Haas chez J. J. Thurneysen, le Jeune, 1780. Triple portrait frontispiece, additional engraved titlepage, further portrait engraved by Samuel Granicher, illustrations, few leaves browned or foxed, 8vo., 19th century crushed red morocco by Cape, lettered gilt on spine (giving the place as Berlin), gilt edges, minimal wear to corners, overall morocco book label of Vernon Watney inside front cover and his signature on verso of front free endpaper, very good.   Blackwell's Rare Books   Marks of Genius - 15   2016   £300

Erasmus, Desiderius 1466-1536 *Moriae Encomium Erasmi Roterodami Declamatio....* Paris: Jehan Lalyseau, 1514. 4to., 19th century morocco backed marbled boards, Lalyseau's fine device on titlepage, one large and one small crible initial, extremely rare early Paris edition, 19th century monogramed stamp on flyleaf, Docteur Lucien Graux (1878-1944) with his red label.   Maggs Bros. Ltd.   1474 - 31 2016   £12,500

Erasmus, Desiderius 1466-1536 *Moriae Encomium; or the Praise of Folly.* New York: Limited Editions Club, 1943. Limited to 1500 copies, this #1363, numbered and signed by artist, 4to., 10 mezzotints by Lynd Ward with tissue guards and legends, marginal illustrations & captions, headings and typographical ornaments, printed in red, original black sheep, ivory medallion inset on upper cover, rubbed at corners and spine ends worn and chipped, slight wear to medallion, internally very good, offered without slipcase, laid in is large page of three proofs (2 printed in red one in black) of headings and typographical ornaments that are used in book,.   Second Life Books, Inc.   196A - 531 2016 $200

Erdrich, Louise *Love Medicine.* New York: Holt Rinehart & Winston, 1984. First edition, book near fine with light shelf wear, dust jacket fine, author's scarce first novel, inscribed by author.   Bella Luna Books   2016 - ta83   2016 $132

Erickson, T. C. *Epilepsy and Cerebral Localization. A Study of the Mechanism, Treatment and Prevention of Epileptic Seizures.* Springfield: 1941. 159 illustrations, original cloth, but worn, spine faded, internally good, well illustrated.   James Tait Goodrich   X-78 - 458   2016 $145

Erlenmeyer, Albrecht *Treatment of the Morphine Habit.* Detroit: George S. Davis, 1889. First American edition, spine sunned, boards rubbed, very good.   Ken Lopez Bookseller   166 - 95   2016 $450

Ervine, St. John *Robert's Wife: aa Comedy in Three Acts.* London: Allen & Unwin, 1938. First edition, 8vo., very good, inscribed by author to actor Hugh Beaumont, this a round robin book signed by 15 members of cast and crew. Second Life Books, Inc.   196A - 539   2016 $450

Escritt, L. B. *Rifle and Gun for Practice Competition and Sport.* London: MacDonal and Evans, 1953. First edition, 8vo., illustrations, original red cloth.   J. & S. L. Bonham Antiquarian Booksellers   Europe 2016 - 7713   2016   £18

Eshleman, Clayton *Coils.* Los Angeles: Black Sparrow, 1973. First edition, large 8vo., one of 200 hardcover copies, numbered and signed by author, paper over boards with cloth spine, fine in slightly scuffed acrylic dust jacket.   Second Life Books, Inc.   196A - 540   2016 $45

An Essay Upon the Principles of Political Economy; Designed as a Manual for Practical Men.   New York: Theodore Foster, 1837. First edition, 12mo., large 12mo., original printed wrappers, some light browning and foxing, but very good, scarce.   John Drury Rare Books   2015 - 15790   2016 $437

Esslemont, David *Chili: a Pictorial Recipe.* Decorah: David Esslemont, 2013. Printed in an edition of 30 copies of which this is one of 10 deluxe copies, folio, white alum tawed full pigskin, with design painted in acrylic ink of a bowl of chili on white linen table cloth, blind and gold tooling, sewn on linen tapes with hand sewn headbands and leather jointed paste paper endleaves, felt lined cloth covered drop back box tablecloth, hand printed from original booklocks on Zerkall mould made paper cloth clamshell box, 39 full woodcuts,.   Oak Knoll Books   310 - 98   2016 $4800

Esslemont, David *The Making of Florilegium Solmentes. Nature Prints & Digital Flowers.*   Decorah: Solmentes Press, 2010. 20/30 copies, printed on Zerkall mould made paper, 8 leaf prints by Esslemont, further color printed illustrations, original quarter brown leather and patterned paper sides, new.   Blackwell's Rare Books   B186 - 337   2016   £215

Estienne, Charles   1504-1564 *Dictionarium Historicum, Geographicum, Poeticom....*   Genevae: apud Samuelem de Tournes, 1693. Reissue of the new edition, quarto, titlepage printed in red and black, contemporary binding of full tree calf with gilt decoration, marbled endpapers, from the library of Dutch theologian Johannes Henricus Scholten (1811-1885) tipped in before titlepage is leaf printed with announcement of the Latin School at Delft with Schotlen's name inserted by hand, signed by Rector A. W. Geers and four other teachers, some light foxing here and there.   Peter Ellis   112 - 117   2016   £475

Estienne, Henri   1528-1598 *Schediasmatum Variorum id est Observationum, Emendationum, Expositioum, Didquisitionum Libri Tres....*   Geneva: Excudebat Henricus Stephanus, 1578-1589. First edition, some light browning, few marginal notes in ink, old ownership inscription to titlepage of Johann Geisel?) Zeigler, 8vo, 2 parts bound together in late 18th century mottled calf spine gilt, red morocco lettering piece, "BRUNCK" lettered direct in gilt at foot, marbled endpapers, front joint splitting but strong, some rubbing to joints and edges, good, this the copy of Richard Francois Philippe Brunck (1729-1803).   Blackwell's Rare Books   B184 - 41   2016   £1200

Etiquette. How to Conform to the Rules of Society... London: W. S. Johnson, circa, 1852. 16mo., frontispiece, upper corners slightly creased, original white wrappers printed in green, slight nick to lower margin of front wrapper, few creases, nice.   Jarndyce Antiquarian Books   CCXV - 180   2016   £120

Etiquette. Social Ethics and the Courtesies of Society. London: Wm. S. Orr & Co., 1854. Half title, some slight creasing, original pale brown printed paper wrappers, slightly dusted, creased at corners.   Jarndyce Antiquarian Books   CCXV - 185   2016   £65

Etiquette for Ladies and Gentlemen.   Halifax: Milner & Sowerby, 1851. Small 8vo., half title, hand colored frontispiece, title slightly dusted and marked, original decorated red cloth, expertly recased, contemporary signature, all edges gilt.   Jarndyce Antiquarian Books   CCXV - 181   2016   £110

Etiquette for Ladies and Gentlemen.   Halifax: Milner & Sowerby, 1860. Half title, hand colored frontispiece, original red decorated cloth, little dulled and rubbed, modern ink inscription on leading f.e.p., all edges gilt, nice copy.   Jarndyce Antiquarian Books   CCXV - 182   2016   £65

Etiquette for the Ladies.   London: Tilt & Bogue, 1841. Twenty Fourth edition, 16mo., half title, 16 pages ads, original pink vertical grained cloth, gilt vignette, spine faded, slight mark to back board, bookseller's ticket of Payne's Wallingford, contemporary signature, very good.   Jarndyce Antiquarian Books   CCXV - 183   2016   £75

Etiquette of Good Society.   London: Cassell Petter Galpin & Co., 1893. Thirty-seventh thousand, original cream printed boards, dulled, rubbed and marked, spine with loss to tail, good, sound.   Jarndyce Antiquarian Books   CCXV - 184   2016   £25

Etiquette of the Dinner-Table Including Carving.   London: Frederick Warne & Co., 1866. 32mo., half title, color frontispiece, additional illustrated title, illustrations, original light brown decorated cloth, all edges gilt, very good.   Jarndyce Antiquarian Books   CCXV - 467   2016   £100

Eton College. An Explanation of the Various Local Passages and Allusions in the Appeal &c. of King's College versus Eton College. London: J. Hatchard, 1819. 58 pages, disbound. Jarndyce Antiquarian Books   CCXV - 667   2016   £35

Ets, Marie Hall   *Another Day.*   New York: Viking, 1953. First edition, oblong 4to., cloth, fine in very good+ dust jacket (frayed at spine ends), illustrations.   Aleph-bet Books, Inc.   112 - 170   2016 $200

Ettrick, William   *A Fragment of the History of John Bull, with the Birth, Parentage, Education and Homours of Jack Radical with Incidental Remarks Upon Ancient and Modern Radicalism.*   London: printed for Thomas Wilkie and sold by Akenhead Charnely and Finlay Newcastle Upon Tyne: Renney, Sunderland and Andrews Durham, 1820. First edition, 8vo., half title, well bound fairly recently in cloth backed marbled boards with morocco title label on upper cover, lettered gilt, entirely ucnut, very good, uncommon.   John Drury Rare Books   2015 - 25465   2016 $350

Eubanks, W. Ralph   *Ever is a Long Time.*   New York: Basic, 2003. Advance reading copy, small 8vo., author's signature on flyleaf, paper wrappers, spine slightly yellowed, slightly bumped at bottom, otherwise nice copy.   Second Life Books, Inc.   197 - 105   2016 $45

Euclides   *Elements Book 1-6 Latin and Greek.*   London: Excudebat Gulielmus Iones, 1620. First edition to be printed in England, woodcut ornament on title, woodcut initials and tailpieces, Greek and Latin in parallel columns, 2 sidenotes shaved, little mild dampstaining at beginning, few leaves slightly browned, folio, contemporary calf, blind ruled borders on sides, pair of double rules near spine, hatching in top and bottom compartments, dark blue edges, rather rubbed, corners (especially top front) worn, crack at foot of upper joint and top of lower one, contemporary signature of Will. Whitmore, good.   Blackwell's Rare Books   Marks of Genius - 18   2016   £2750

Euclides   *Geometricorum Elementorum Libri XV.*   Paris: Henri Estienne 7 Jan., 1516-1517. Sixth edition, Roman types, numerous woodcut geometrical diagrams in margins, fine crible initials in a variety of styles and sizes, titlepage soiled and cut down and mounted on old paper, one diagram just cropped at its extreme outer corners, without final blank, folio, 19th century half brown calf by Hatton of Manchester, marbled edges, original order for the binder loosely inserted, the Macclesfield copy with bookplate but no blindstamps and annotated by John Collins, after his death his books were acquired by William Jones and thence to Shirburn Castle, scarce on the market, preserved in cloth folding box, good copy.   Blackwell's Rare Books   Marks of Genius - 16   2016   £12,000

Eugenides, Jeffrey   *The Virgin Suicides.*   New York: FSG, 1993. First edition, fine copy in near fine dust jacket, light creasing to spine ends.   Bella Luna Books   2016 - T6705A   2016 $82

Euler, Leonhard   *Scientia Navalis seu Tractatus de Construendis Ac Dirigendis Navibus Pars Prior Complectens Theoriam Universam de situ A Motu Corporum Aquae Innatantium...*   Petropoli: St. Petersburgh Academaie Scientiarum, 1749. First edition, 65 folding engraved plates of figures, 4to., 2 volumes, contemporary half calf over speckled boards, expertly rebacked, original spines laid down, marginal stain to first and last few leaves, owing to overzealous application of leather dressing, else very good.   Edwin V. Glaser Rare Books   2015 - 10204   2016 $10,000

Euripides   *The Plays of Euripides.*   Newtown: Gregynog Press, 1931. One of 500 numbered copies, folio, 2 volumes in 1, titlepages in red and black, recent very skillful dark brown crushed levant morocco, green title label, covers with blind Greek key roll within gilt rules and cornerpieces, spine gilt in compartments, very fine.   Joseph J. Felcone, Inc.   Books from Five Centuries: a Miscellany - 75   2016 $1200

Euripides   *Tragoedia Phoenissae.*   Lugduni Batavorum: apud samuelem et Joannem Luchtmans, 1802. 4to., stub at front from excised presentation certificate, lightly toned towards top edge, foxing form page 125 of second register onwards corresponding to slightly lower quality paper stock for first gatherings, vellum prize binding, raised bands, gilt spine, borders, frame and central coat-of-arms of Amsterdam, edges sprinkled red and blue, darkened, bit grubby, ties lost, endpapers lifting but revealing interesting binding structure beneath, very good overall.   Unsworths Antiquarian Booksellers   30 - 54   2016   £275

Eusebius   *Evangelica Praeparationis Lib. XV. (with) Evangelicae Demonstrationibus Lib X.*   Paris: Robert Estienne, 1544-1545. Editiones principes, 2 volumes, folio, bound in 1 volume, numerous large foliated and grotesque initials and headpieces, first title slightly soiled, little dampstaining towards the end of the second volume, few dogears, modern calf backed boards, numerous marginal notes in Latin in neat contemporary hand on second work, good.   Blackwell's Rare Books   B184 - 42   2016   £1250

Evans, Arthur *The Palace of Minos of Knossos.* London: Macmillan and Co., 1921-1935. With index 1936. First editions, 4 volumes in 6, with index, making a total of 7 volumes, quarto, profusely illustrated with hundreds of figures in text, plans, tables, colored and supplementary plates, many of which are folding, each volume with frontispiece, many color plates with tissue guards, four volumes with pockets in rear with 11 plans, as issued, publisher's full blue cloth, front boards tooled and stamped in gilt, spines lettered gilt, top edges gilt, 3 volumes with back pockets for folding plans, volume 1 slightly faded with previous owner's signature, some rubbing to top and bottom of spines as usual, scarce index in first edition, overall very good set.   Heritage Book Shop   Holiday 2015 - 37   2016 $6500

Evans, C. S. *Cinderella retold by....* London and Philadelphia: William Heinemann/J. B. Lippincott co., 1919. First edition, deluxe issue, one of 325 numbered copies on Japanese vellum signed by artist, from a total edition of 850, this deluxe issue contains additional color plate, 4to., pictorial endpapers, color frontispiece tipped in, 3 double page color silhouettes, full page color silhouette and 36 silhouette text illustrations in black and white by Arthur Rackham, original vellum backed parchment over boards, lettered gilt on spine and front cover, top edge gilt.   James S. Jaffe Rare Books   Occasional List: Winter 2016 - 122   2016 $2500

Evans, Cerinda W. *Collis Potter Huntington.* Newport News: Manners' Museum, 1954. First edition, 2 volumes, frontispiece, 127 illustrations from photos and prints, gilt lettered green cloth, fine.   Argonaut Book Shop   Biography 2015 - 5552   2016 $175

Evans, Edward *South With Scott...* London: and Glasgow: Collin, 1921. First edition, 2nd impression, 8vo., original dark blue cloth, lettered in red-orange on spine within red orange rules, photogravure frontispiece with tissue guard, 3 folding maps and folding plan, light bubbling to upper quarter of spine, uncut edges with light foxing, as well as offsetting from browned flyleaves to few adjacent pages, otherwise internally clean and fresh, neat contemporary ownership inscription.   Sotheran's   Travel and Exploration - 420   2016   £698

Evans, Henry Herman *Western Bibliographies.* San Francisco: The Peregrine Press, 1951. Second edition, one of 122 copies, octavo, original blue buckram spine, decorated paper boards and printed paper label; titlepage decoration, block print on colophon page and decorated paper boards, fine.   The Brick Row Book Shop   Miscellany 69 - 14   2016 $375

Everard, George *Not Your Own; or Counsels to Young Christians.* London: James Nisbet & Co. circa, 1892. 49th thousand, original olive green cloth, ownership inscription, very good.   Jarndyce Antiquarian Books   CCXV - 186   2016   £20

Everden, William Preston Campbell *Freemasonry and its Etiquette.* London: A. Lewis, 1927. Half title, 7 pages ads, original blue cloth, slightly rubbed, faded booklabel, completed in pencil.   Jarndyce Antiquarian Books   CCXV - 187   2016   £75

Everitt, Alan *Suffolk and the Great Rebellion 1640-1660.* Suffolk Records Society, 1961. First edition, large 8vo., cloth, gilt lettered, few faint marks to lower board, spine slightly browned, very small dark mark to upper board, corners bumped and slightly frayed, edges lightly dusted, still very good, ownership inscription of R. W. Ketton Cremer in pen and bequeathed to him by the Library of the University of East Anglia as noted on the Library's bookplate, various library marks, elsewhere.   Unsworths Antiquarian Booksellers Ltd.   E05 - 102   2016   £45

Every Saturday. Journal of Choice Reading Selected From Foreign Current Literature Volume I-VI. Boston: Ticknor and Fields, Jan- Dec., 1868. 6 of 8 volumes published under this title, small 4to., original cloth, very good, ex-library set.   M & S Rare Books, Inc.   99 - 248   2016 $300

Ewald, Dan *Six. A Salute to Al Kaline.* Detroit: Detroit Tigers and Olympia Entertainment, 2010. First edition, fine, signed by Kaline, oversized paperback original.   Bella Luna Books   2016 - t9510a   2016 $132

Ewald, Herman Frederik *The Story of Waldemar Krone's Youth.* Edinburgh: Edmonston and Douglas, 1867. First edition in English, 2 volumes, 184 x 121mm., attractive Arts and Crafts style dark green morocco elaborately gilt, each cover with 40 gilt lotus flowers (in five vertical rows of eight), flowers all flanked by gilt dot in each of the four corners, raised bands, spine panels with similar floral decoration, gilt titling ad turn-ins, all edges gilt, green spines inevitably sunned to an olive brown, joints and corners little rubbed, very isolated minor foxing, otherwise fine, clean and fresh internally, appealing binding lustrous and without significant wear.   Phillip J. Pirages   67 - 43   2016 $750

Ewald, Johannes *The Death of Balder.* London: Jarrold & sons, 1889. First edition, 8vo., uncut and mostly unopened, publisher's brown cloth, paper label, spine faded, endpapers stained, near fine, one of just 250 copies.   Second Life Books, Inc.   197 - 34   2016 $175

Ewart, Gavin *The Collected Ewart 1933-1980.* London: Hutchinson, 1980. First edition, octavo, spine bruised at tail, very good in near fine dust jacket, slightly creased at edges.   Peter Ellis   112 - 118   2016   £35

Ewing, Juliana Horatia *Jackanapes.* New York: Oxford University Press, 1948. First issue, Slim 8vo., green cloth, fine in dust jacket (very good+ with small closed tear, one corner chipped), pictorial endpapers, full page color illustrations plus black and whites, laid in is 2 page handwritten letter and envelope from Tudor.   Aleph-bet Books, Inc.   111 - 460   2016 $875

Ewing, Juliana Horatia *Leaves from Juliana Horatia Ewing's Canada Home...*   Boston: Roberts Bros., 1896. Pictorial cloth, light cover soil, occasional internal mild mark, very good+, 8 color plates reproducing some of her art and a profusion of half tones and black and whites by Elizabeth Tucker, with chatty handwritten letter from Ewing dated 1881, engraved portrait of Ewing signed by her.   Aleph-bet Books, Inc.   112 - 172   2016 $400

Exley, Frederick *A Fan's Notes - a Fictional Memoir.* New York: Harper & Row, 1968. First edition, octavo, edges and half title faintly spotted, small mark to rear cover, very good in very good slightly nicked dust jacket slightly creased at edges.   Peter Ellis   112 - 119   2016   £125

The Experienced American Housekeeper or Domestic Cookery Formed on Principles of Economy for the Use of Private Families.   New York: Nafis & Cornish, Philadelphia: John B. Perry, 1838. 6 plates, contemporary sheep, very skillfully rebacked in period style with original label preserved, occasional spotting and foxing.   Joseph J. Felcone, Inc.   Books from Five Centuries: a Miscellany - 47   2016 $500

L'Exposition De Paris 1900. Manuel et Catalogues Officiels de la Section de Ceylan.   Colombo: George J. A. Skeen, Imprimerie Nationale, Ceylon, 1900. First edition, 8vo., original tan morocco with onlaid colour printed and varnished panels on both boards, spine with raised bands, spine and boards ruled in gilt, inner dentelles, elaborately ornamented in gilt, watered silk endpapers, all edges gilt, all pages within printed red double fillets, fine photogravure frontispiece, tinted in green after photo by Henry Cave with tissue guard, two color lithographic maps, 24 plates after photos, numerous photographic illustrations in text, extremities minimally rubbed, otherwise fine, with original bronze medal designed by Chaplain, awarded at the Exposition Universelle to the Ceylon Government Printing Office. Sotheran's   Piccadilly Notes - Summer 2015 - 296   2016   £1995

F

F., Mr. *La Retour de Tendresse ou La Feinte Veritable Comedie par Mr. F.* Paris: Chez Briasson, 1728. First edition, old, probably unprinted wrappers, ink blot on inside of front wrapper, foxing to pages, near fine.   Between the Covers Rare Books   208 - 49   2016 $2500

Face to Face. Twelve Contemporary American Artists Interpret Themselves in a Limited Edition of Original Wood Engravings. Great Barrington: Penmaen Busyhaus Pub., 1985. One of 250 numbered sets, 12 engraved self portraits, each numbered and signed by artist and laid into printed folder with page of text about artist, 4to., 14 printed folders with print loosely inserted in all but one, 13 hand printed broadsides, 4 page prospectus with insert describing this production.   Oak Knoll Books   310 - 99   2016 $650

Fainlight, Harry *Sussicran.* London: Turret Books, 1965. First edition, one of 150 copies of a total edition of 200, there were also 50 numbered and signed copies, stapled cream colored self wrappers in silver, modest soiling or age toning, very good or better, signed and inscribed by author.   Between the Covers Rare Books   204 - 39   2016 $950

Fair, A. A. *Fish or Cut Bait.* New York: Mortow, 1967. First edition, fine in dust jacket with some lettering on spine slightly faded.   Mordida Books   2015 - 009006   2016 $55

Fair, Ronald *Many Thousand Gone. An American Fable.* New York: Harcourt Brace & World, 1965. 8vo., author's presentation, green cloth, cover slightly rubbed at corners and ends of spine, otherwise nice in scuffed and chipped dust jacket.   Second Life Books, Inc.   197 - 106   2016 $85

Fairbault, G. B. *Catalogue D'Ouvrages sur L'Historie De L'Amerique et en Particulier Sur Celle du Canada, De La Louisiane.* Quebec: W. Cowan, 1837. 8vo., contemporary leather covered boards, original wrappers bound in, maps, plans, engravings, front cover , front free endpapers plus two blank pages detached, spine heavily worn with loss of leather at head of spine, previous owner's bookplate and binder's label.   Oak Knoll Books   310 - 242   2016 $450

Fairchild, B. H. *Beauty.* Upland: Blackbird Press, 2007. Distributed 2010, Number 40 of 100 copies signed by poet, book artist Jean Gillingwators and illustrator Anna Alquitela, printed with Centaur and Arrighi monotype on Zerkall Book paper, linocuts by Alquitela, housed in gray clamshell box with author in red to spine, fine.   The Kelmscott Bookshop   13 - 9   2016 $750

Fairlie, Gerard *Calling Bulldog Drummond.* London: Hodder & Stoughton, 1951. Red boards, marked and frayed dust jacket, spotting to edges, not affecting text, uncommon.   I. D. Edrich   Crime - 2016   £40

Fairlie, Gerard *Hands off Bulldog Drummond!* London: Hodder & Stoughton, 1949. Blue boards in frayed "H&S" yellow jacket, some foxing to edges, text not affected.   I. D. Edrich   Crime - 2016   £20

Fairmont, Ethel *The Lovely Garden.* Chicago: Volland, 1919. First edition, no additional printings, 8vo., pictorial boards, fine in pictorial box, full page color illustrations by John Rae.   Aleph-bet Books, Inc.   111 - 467   2016 $350

Fairstein, Linda *Final Jeopardy.* New York: Scribners, 1996. First edition, signed by author, very fine in dust jacket.   Mordida Books   2015 - 000744   2016 $65

Fairy ABC. New York: McLoughlin Bros., n.d. circa, 1870. 8vo., pictorial wrappers, inconspicuous small cover and spine, else very good+, large color pictorial illustrations, excellent copy, very scarce.   Aleph-bet Books, Inc.   112 - 5   2016 $450

Falconer, Lanoe *Cecilia de Noel.* London: Macmillan & Co., 1891. First edition, very good, scarce, original dark blue cloth boards, light bumping to corners and chipping to spine, interior pages clean and with some splitting to signatures but text block holding, very good.   The Kelmscott Bookshop   12 - 45   2016 $225

Falconer, William *The Shipwreck, a Poem.* London: printed for William Miller by W. Bulmer, 1811. 197 x 121mm, very pretty mid 19th century green straight grain morocco, intricately decorated in gilt and blind, by W. Barratt (ticket on front flyleaf), covers with broad, densely gilt frame paned central lozenge containing a large and elaborate floral centerpiece, raised bands, spine panels filled with gilt purple watered silk endleaves framed by gilt tolls, all edges gilt, 3 engraved plates and five engraved vignettes, verso of front endleaf with early inscription, "The Bookbinder's Tribute of Gratitude to Benj. Morland" and with bookplate of Cass Canfield, presentation to Canfield from Austen Kark laid in, spine uniformly sunned to olive brown, slight rubbing to corners, bands and joints, muted spotting to silk plates with minor foxing, hint of browning at edges of some leaves, still excellent copy, with none of the condition issues serious and with elaborately decorated covers lustrous and unworn.   Phillip J. Pirages   67 - 27   2016 $750

Falgate, Israel *Interest in Epitome; or Tables in a Shorter method than Hitherto Publish'd...* London: printed for and sold by the author, 1698. First edition, thin 24mo., contemporary marbled paper wrappers, moderate wear to wrappers, very good, signed by author.   Between the Covers Rare Books   208 - 16   2016 $2200

Fall, Anna Christy *The Tragedy of a Widow's Third.* Boston: Fox, 1898. First edition, small 8vo. illustrations by Vesper L. George, author's presentation on flyleaf, dated 1925, brown cloth, top edge gilt, ex-library with stamps and bookplate, cover little scuffed at edges, otherwise very good, tight copy.   Second Life Books, Inc.   196A - 543   2016 $85

Fallows, Noel *Jousting in Medieval and Renaissance Iberia.* Woodbridge: Boydell Press, 2011. First edition, 8vo., maps and illustrations, red cloth, gilt lettered as new, dust jacket little creased and marked, still very good plus.   Unsworths Antiquarian Booksellers Ltd.   E05 - 73   2016   £25

Famous Colorado Men - The Colorado Chronicles. and Famous Colorado Women. Frederick: Jende-Hagen Bookcorp, 1982. Second printings, 4to., 2 volumes, pictorial cloth, illustrations, volume 1 with light wear to extremities, else fine, volume 2 fine, very scarce.   Gene W. Baade, Books on the West   2015 - 1209034   2016 $135

Fante, John *Ask the Dust.* New York: Stackpole, 1939. First edition, inscribed by author to collector and bibliographer of Christopher Morley, Henry Tatnall Brown Jr., dated Nov. 14 1939, Brown's bookplate, slight offsetting from bookplate, else fine in near fine dust jacket, spine sunned with very light edge wear, very nice copy.   Ken Lopez Bookseller   166 - 33   2016 $8500

Farago, Ladislas *The Game of the Foxes: the Untold story of German Espionage in the United States and Great Britain during World War II.* Philadelphia: McKay, 1971. First edition, fine in dust jacket, signed by author.   Mordida Books   2015 - 011012   2016 $65

Farber, Norma *How the Left-Behind Beasts Built Ararat.* New York: Walker and Co., 1978. First printing, (correct number code), 4to., cloth, fine in dust jacket, color woodcuts by Antonio Frasconi, mounted on half title, is decorative typed card with book title, signed by artist.   Aleph-bet Books, Inc.   112 - 199   2016 $125

Farcot, Henri Eugene Adrien *La Navigation Atmospherique.* Paris: A. Bourdilliat et Cie, 1859. 12mo., folding engraved plate, half title, early 20th century dark green quarter morocco and marbled boards, spine gilt and lettered with balloon motif in gilt in compartments, original printed paper wrappers bound in, attractive association copy with red inkstamps of Charles Chavontier, the Paris airship manufacturers.   John Drury Rare Books   2015 - 16246   2016 $437

Faris, John T. *Seeing the Far West.* Philadelphia: J. B. Lippincott, 1920. First edition, colored title vignette, 113 photographic illustrations, 2 maps, pictorial tan cloth stamped in dark green, blue and white, minor rubbing to foot of spine and lower corners, fine, somewhat scarce.   Argonaut Book Shop   Natural History 2015 - 7289   2016 $75

Farjeaon, J. Jefferson *The Crook's Shadow.* New York: Burt, Reprint edition, very good in very fine as new dust jacket.   Mordida Books   2015 - 010749   2016 $65

Farjeon, Eleanor *A Chap-Book of Rounds Parts 1 and 2.* London: J. M. Dent, 1919. First editions, 2 volumes, illustrations around borders, foolscap 4to., original brown wrappers printed in black red and green, little creasing to borders of front on first volume, with darkened strip at head of rear cover on second volume, very good, with original proof for cover illustrations on 14.5 x 1.5 inch white card.   Blackwell's Rare Books   B186 - 213   2016   £250

Farjeon, Eleanor *Come Christmas (Poems).* W. Collins & Sons Co., 1927. First edition, quarter cloth, patterned boards, color printed label on upper cover, binding little soiled, especially at spine, endpapers spotted, otherwise very nice.   Bertram Rota Ltd.   Christmas List 2015 - 9   2016   £60

Farjeon, Eleanor *Miss Granby's Secret.* London: Michael Joseph, 1940. First edition, octavo, cloth faintly spotted at spine, near fine in very good pictorial dust jacket, little nicked and creased at edges and with author's name faded from spine, scarce.   Peter Ellis   112 - 120   2016   £95

Farjeon, Eleanor *Mrs. Malone.* London: Oxford University Press, 1962. First edition, 12mo., pictorial boards, fine in slightly worn dust jacket, illustrations by Edward Ardizzone, this copy inscribed by author to Marc Connelly.   Aleph-bet Books, Inc.   111 - 20   2016 $175

Farley, Harriet *The Lowell Offering. Series 4 no. 8 June 1844.* Lowell: Misses Curtis & Farley, 1844. First edition, little nicked at top of cover, near fine, scarce, former owner's signature "Mary J. Lord".   Second Life Books, Inc.   197 - 107   2016 $150

Farnell, William Keeling *School Steps and Self Instructor's Ladder to Arithmetic, Grammar and Geography.* London: Jarrold, 1857. Disbound, 32 pages, very good.   Jarndyce Antiquarian Books   CCXV - 678   2016   £20

Farnham, Elizabeth W. *The Ideal Attained: Being the Story of Two Steadfast Souls and How they Won their Happiness and Lost it ot.* New York: Plumb & Co., 1865. First edition, 8vo., brown cloth, very fine, bright, rare.   Second Life Books, Inc.   197 - 108   2016 $950

Farningham, Marianne *Girlhood.* James Clarke & Co., 1869. Slight ink marking to leading endpapers, original green cloth, slightly marked, very good.   Jarndyce Antiquarian Books   CCXV - 188   2016   £60

Farquhar, Francis P. *The Books of the Colorado River and Grand Canyon.*   Los Angeles: designed by printed by Ward Ritchie for Glen Dawson, 1953. 8vo., original red cloth, printed label pasted around spine, binding little dusty, light browning to endpapers.   Sotheran's Travel and Exploration - 58   2016   £98

Farquhar, George   *The Works of the late Ingenious Mr. George Farquhar....*   London: printed for John Rivington (and 8 others), 1772. 12mo., full contemporary calf gilt decorated spines, morocco labels, joints slightly cracked but firm.   Jarndyce Antiquarian Booksellers   CCXVI - 460   2016   £125

Farrar, Eliza Ware   *The Young Lady's Friend.*   London: John W. Parker, 1840. Third edition, rebound in olive green boards, green cloth spine, retaining original spine label.   Jarndyce Antiquarian Books   CCXV - 189   2016   £50

Farrar, Eliza Ware   *The Young Lady's Friend.*   London: John W. Parker, 1845. Fifth edition, original olive-green cloth, slightly faded, very nice, contemporary signature.   Jarndyce Antiquarian Books   CCXV - 190   2016   £50

Farrell, J. G.   *The Siege of Krishnapur.*   London: Weidenfeld & Nicolson, 1973. First edition, octavo, spine little bumped at head, near fine in very good dust jacket with couple of closed tears at head of spine repaired on reverse.   Peter Ellis   112 - 121   2016   £150

Farrer, Richard R.   *A Tour in Greece.*   Edinburgh: Blackwood, 1882. First edition, 8vo., 27 plates, original orange decorative cloth, spine lightly rubbed.   J. & S. L. Bonham Antiquarian Booksellers   Europe 2016 - 6254   2016   £110

Farrere, Claude   *Escales d'Asie.*   Paris: Laborey, 1947. First edition, number 122 of 450 copies printed, extremely rare, beautifully produced, 4to., loose sheets in original printed and hand colored wrappers, within original marbled box with printed label, title printed in green and black and with hand colored vignette, one map of Arabia, hand colored vignette, numerous hand colored illustrations, apart from light rubbing to box, very fine.   Sotheran's Piccadilly Notes - Summer 2015 - 123   2016   £2850

Farrow, G. E.   *Pixie Pickles.*   London: Skeffington & Son, n.d, owner dated, 1906. Cloth backed pictorial boards, some cover soil and edge wear very good, wonderful illustrations by Harry Neilson, 20 striking full page chromolithographs with black backgrounds.   Aleph-bet Books, Inc.   112 - 174   2016 $450

Farrow, G. E.   *The Wallypug at Play.*   London: Raphael Tuck, n.d. crica, 1900. Folio, cloth backed pictorial boards, some cover soil and edgewear, very good+, 12 fanciful full page chromolithographs plus numerous 2 color text illustrations by Alan Wright.   Aleph-bet Books, Inc.   112 - 190   2016 $500

Father Tuck's Picture Building Blocks.   London: Raphael Tuck, n.d. circa, 1910. 4to., flexible pictorial card covers, slight bit of spine wear else fine and in unused condition, 8 full page color illustrated pages, divided into a total of 96 squares that illustrate 16 fairy tales, rare in unused condition.   Aleph-bet Books, Inc.   112 - 184   2016 $600

Faulkner, Georgene   *Little Peachling.*   Joliet: Volland, 1928. First edition, no additional printings, 8vo., pictorial boards, fine in original box slightly soiled, illustrations by Frederick Richardson.   Aleph-bet Books, Inc.   111 - 465   2016 $300

Faulkner, Thomas   *An Historical and Topographical Account of Fulham....*   printed for J. Tilling Chelsea for T. Egerton, T. Payne, Becket and Porter..., 1813. First edition, 8vo., sometime finely bound for Tregaskis in half double gilt ruled brown morocco, panelled and lettered in gilt on spine, gilt centre tools, top edge gilt, folding map, 22 plates, little offsetting from couple of plates, very occasional light spotting, bookplate generally very good, handsome binding.   Sotheran's   Piccadilly Notes - Summer 2015 - 124   2016   £498

Faulkner, William Harrison   1896-1962   *Big Woods.*   New York: Random Home, 1955. First edition, 8vo., nice, clean copy in dust jacket.   Second Life Books, Inc.   197 - 109   2016 $400

Faulkner, William Harrison   1896-1962   *Doctor Martino and Other Stories.*   New York: Smith and Haas, 1934. First edition, fine with slightest of seemingly inevitable fading to spine, without dust jacket as issued, copy number 1 of 360 numbered copies, signed by author, with letter from antiquarian bookseller detailing provenance directly from Dean Faulkner Wells who inherited it from her grandmother, Maud.   Between the Covers Rare Books   204 - 40   2016 $12,000

Faulkner, William Harrison   1896-1962   *The Hamlet.*   New York: Random House, 1940. First edition, one of 250 numbered copies, this no. 143, signed by author, scarce signed edition, very good plus lacking the acetate dust jacket, board edges lightly toned, light foxing to page edges and first few leaves.   Royal Books   48 - 73   2016 $4000

Faulkner, William Harrison 1896-1962 *Intruder in the Dust.* New York: Random House, 1948. First edition, 8vo., very good in price clipped dust jacket (couple of words underlined on jacket flap, nick on spine, lacks a triangle (1 l nch) at upper hinge, some rubbed at fore-edge, short inscription on endpaper.   Second Life Books, Inc.   197 - 111   2016 $575

Faulkner, William Harrison 1896-1962 *The Mansion.* New York: Random House, 1959. First edition, one of 500 copies (this being no. 204) signed by author, near fine with some light foxing to page edges, in very good acetate dust jacket.   Royal Books   48 - 75   2016 $1750

Faulkner, William Harrison 1896-1962 *The Town.* New York: Random House, 1957. First edition in second issue dust jacket, without the '5/57' on front flap, signed by author for Miss Adeliade (sic) and Chuck Miller, very near fine with tiny tear at crown in near fine dust jacket with mild foxing to flap folds and on verso very attractive copy, notoriously uncommon signature.   Ken Lopez Bookseller   166 - 34   2016 $12,500

Faulkner, William Harrison 1896-1962 *The Town.* New York: Random House, 1957. First edition, one of 450 numbered copies, this being no. 420, signed by author, near fine, with some light foxing to page edges, in very good acetate dust jacket.   Royal Books   48 - 74   2016 $1250

Faulkner, William Harrison 1896-1962 *The Unvanquished.* New York: Random House, 1938. First edition, fine in fine dust jacket, with short tear on rear panel, lovely copy.   Between the Covers Rare Books   204 - 41   2016 $2000

Fauset, Jessie *The Chinaberry Tree.* London: Elkin Mathew & Marrot, 1932. First English edition, corners slightly bumped, little faded at extremities, about fine in age toned, very good plus dust jacket with 3 unnecessary internal repairs, very attractive copy, extremely uncommon.   Between the Covers Rare Books   202 - 30   2016 $5000

Faust, Bernhard Christoph *Catechism of Health; for the Use of Schools and for Domestic Instruction.* London: printed for C. Dilly in the Poultry, 1794. Woodcut frontispiece, 3 woodcuts in text, 8vo., some foxing and light browning, slight marginal tear to frontispiece and corner of one leaf, both without loss, contemporary half calf, marbled boards, gilt banded spine, red morocco label, boards rubbed and edges slightly worn, contemporary bookplate of 'Montrose Library', scarce.   Jarndyce Antiquarian Books   CCXV - 191   2016   £650

Favorite Fairy Tales. New York: Harper and Brothers c. Oct., 1907. First edition, 8vo., white imitation vellum boards with gilt decoration, top edge gilt, nice, owner bookplate and inscription, near fine in dust jacket (faded on edges, slightly worn), 16 wonderful tinted plates, rare in dust jacket.   Aleph-bet Books, Inc.   112 - 339   2016 $500

Fawcett, John *Advice to Youth or the Advantages of Early Piety...* Halifax: printed and sold by P. K. Holden, 1810. Seventh edition, 12mo., slight spotting, tear to lower margin of G3, contemporary half calf, binding worn, extremities rubbed, bookplate on leading pastedown, contemporary signature, good, sound.   Jarndyce Antiquarian Books   CCXV - 192   2016   £48

Featherstonhaugh, G. W. *A Canoe Voyage Up the Minnay Sotor...* London: Richard Bentley, 1847. First edition, volume one only (of two), 2 folding maps in front pocket, lithographed frontispiece, two folding maps in volume I, original dark green ribbed cloth stamped in blind on covers, gilt lettered spine, slightest of foxing to few prelim leaves, but fine, scarce thus.   Argonaut Book Shop   Native American 2015 - 4529   2016 $300

Feder, Norman *American Indian Art.* New York: Harry N. Abrams, First edition, thick oblong quarto, 302 illustrations, including 60 tipped-in color plates, red cloth decorated and lettered gilt, orange and black, fine copy with pictorial dust jacket.   Argonaut Book Shop   Native American 2015 - 5598   2016 $200

Feist, Raymond E. *Magician.* Garden City: Doubleday & Company, 1982. First edition, octavo, quarter cloth with boards, top corners slightly bumped, nearly fine in nearly fine dust jacket with slight rubbing to corner tips and spine and tiny closed tear to lower left front corner at fold.   John W. Knott, Jr./L.W. Currey, Inc.   Fall-Winter 2015 - 17517   2016 $500

Feldman, Irving *The Pripet Marshes and Other Poems.* New York: Viking, 1965. First edition, signed and inscribed by author in 1971 for William Meredith, laid in is ALS from author to Meredith, some dust spotting to top of bulked text, near fine in very good dust jacket with some darkening to spine and top edges with short tear at rear.   Charles Agvent   William Meredith - 28   2016 $100

Feldman, Irving *Work and Days.* London: Andre Deutsch, 1961. First British edition, inscribed by author in 1971 for William Meredith, some dust spotting to top of bulked text, near fine in like dust jacket with some staining to spine.   Charles Agvent   William Meredith - 29   2016 $80

Feliciano, Felice *Alphabetum Romanum.* Verona: Officiae Bodoni, 1960. Limited to 400 copies, this no. 355, 8vo., prospectus for volume laid in, near fine in original clear plastic dust jacket and fine completely intact original paper covered slipcase with knot design top and bottom of slipcase opening trimmed with brown leather, matching the binding as issued, binding is quarter brown leather and tan paper boards with gilt lettering spine, top edge gilt.   By the Book, L. C.   45 - 58   2016 $750

Fellows, Edward S. *New Brunswick Natural Resources: 105 Years of Stewardship.* Fredericton: 1987. Quarto, card covers, photo illustrations, very good.   Schooner Books Ltd.   115 - 25   2016 $45

Fellows, Muriel *The Land of Little Rain.*   Philadelphia: Toronto: Chicago: John C. Winston, 1936. First edition, 8vo., decorative cloth, fine in dust jacket (frayed, rubbed at fold light soil, very good), illustrations by author with 47 illustrations, many in 5 colors, this copy inscribed by author.   Aleph-bet Books, Inc.   111 - 225   2016 $225

The Female Aegis; or the Duties of Women from childhood to Old Age and in Most Situations of Life Exemplified. London: printed by Sampson Low for J. Gigner, 1798. First edition, frontispiece, 12mo., contemporary mottled calf, black morocco label, hinges cracking, spine worn at head and tail, calligraphic signature of Margaret Watts, 1805, bookseller's ticket, sound copy.   Jarndyce Antiquarian Books   CCXV - 193   2016   £220

Female Excellence or Hints to Daughters.   London: RTS, 1838? Half title, 6 pages ads, contemporary full purple full embossed calf, leading hinges slightly rubbed, all edges gilt, very good.   Jarndyce Antiquarian Books   CCXV - 328   2016   £50

Female Excellence or Hints to Daughters.   London: RTS, circa, 1840. Half title, 6 pages ads, contemporary full maroon grained calf decorated gilt, slightly rubbed, contemporary signature on leading f.e.p.   Jarndyce Antiquarian Books   CCXV - 329   2016   £60

Female Excellence or Hints to Daughters.   London: RTS, circa, 1852. Half title, slight creasing in prelims, uncut in original brown cloth by E. Littler, little dulled with slight rubbing to head and tail of spine, leading f.e.p., signed 'Sophia Spelier, Jan. 31 1852', good plus.   Jarndyce Antiquarian Books   CCXV - 330   2016   £35

The Female Instructor or Young Woman's Companion... Liverpool: Nuttall, Fisher & Dixon, 1812. Stereotype edition, frontispiece and plates, small worm hole to final 3 leaves, contemporary full mottled calf, black morocco label, expert repair to hinges, contemporary signature of Mary Chester, nice.   Jarndyce Antiquarian Books   CCXV - 194   2016   £225

The Female Instructor or Young Woman's Companion... London: Henry Fisher Son & P. Jackson, 1832. (1835), Engraved title, plates, frontispiece, expertly rebound in full brown calf, dark green label.   Jarndyce Antiquarian Books   CCXV - 195   2016   £150

Fenelon, Francois Salignac De La Mothe, Abp.   1651-1715 *The Adventures of Telemachus.* London: printed by W. Wilson for R. Edwards, 1792. 2nd edition, 4to., rubbed full calf, front hinge loose in volume one, contemporary bookplate (Samuel Fothergill Lettsom), later ownership signature of Dr. George Davenport, engraved portrait in volume one, engraved titlepages in both volumes, 24 engraved plates (foxed).   Second Life Books, Inc.   197 - 234   2016 $225

Fenelon, Francois Salignac De La Mothe, Abp.   1651-1715 *Fenelon's Treatise on the Education of Daughters.* Cheltenham: H. Ruff, 1805. Half title, contemporary half calf, maroon morocco label, hinges cracked but remaining firm, little rubbed.   Jarndyce Antiquarian Books   CCXV - 680   2016   £220

Fenelon, Francois Salignac De La Mothe, Abp.   1651-1715 *Instructions for the Education of a Daughter by the Author of Telemachus.*   London: printed for Jonah Bowyer, 1721. Fourth edition, 12mo., lacks plate and leading f.e.p.s, contemporary panelled calf, rubbed, armorial bookplate.   Jarndyce Antiquarian Books   CCXV - 679   2016   £50

Fenelon, Francois Salignac De La Mothe, Abp.   1651-1715 *On the Education of Daughters.* London: W. Darton, 1812. 12mo., frontispiece, slight offsetting, odd spot, handsomely bound in slightly later full light blue grey calf raised bands, gilt compartments, maroon morocco label, little rubbed and marked, attrative copy, gift inscription Juliana St. Aubyn, the gift of Sir. John St. Aubyn.   Jarndyce Antiquarian Books   CCXV - 681   2016   £85

Fenn, George Manville   *Patience Wins or War in the Works.*   Blackie & son, 1886. (1885). First edition, half title, frontispiece, plates, 40 page catalog, original pictorial green cloth, slightly cocked, very good, pencil signature on pastedown.   Jarndyce Antiquarian Booksellers   CCXVII - 97   2016   £45

Fenning, Daniel   *The Young Man's Book of Knowledge.* London: printed for S. Crowder, 1793. Fifth edition, frontispiece and plates, but lacking final music plate, 12mo., contemporary full calf, neat repair to hinges, 19th century inscription on recto of front of Amy Groom.   Jarndyce Antiquarian Books   CCXV - 196   2016   £120

Fenton, Carroll Lane   *Mountains.*   Garden City: Doubleday Doran & Co., 1942. First edition, black and white photos and drawings, blue cloth, white lettering on spine, top corners bumped, else fine, pictorial dust jacket lightly worn and all four inside edges clipped at slight angle, though not affecting text on jacket flaps in any way.   Argonaut Book Shop   Mountaineering 2015 - 723   2016 $40

Fenwick, Eliza *Visits to the Juvenile Library or Knowledge Proved to be the Source of Happiness.* London: printed by Bernard & Sultzer for Tabart & Co...., 1805. First edition, frontispiece, plates, 36 page catalog, 20th century quarter calf with earlier marbled boards, lower board slightly creased, contemporary signature of Susan Wilson. Jarndyce Antiquarian Books   CCXV - 682   2016   £120

Fenwick, Elizabeth *Night Run.* London: Gollancz, 1961. Very good in like dust jacket with slight foxing to prelims and edges.   I. D. Edrich   Crime - 2016   £25

Fenwick, Elizabeth *The Silent Cousin.* London: Gollancz, 1962. Very good in like dust jacket, numbers inked on front endpaper, light foxing of prelims and edges, not affecting text, otherwise very good.   I. D. Edrich   Crime - 2016   £25

Ferber, Edna *Show Boat.* Garden City: Doubleday Page & Co., 1926. One of only 1000 specially bound presentation copies, with rare leaflet "how i happened to write Show Boat', 8vo., original blue cloth backed orange, yellow and blue chequered patterned paper covered boards, top edges red, pictorial endpapers, extremities very slightly rubbed, nonetheless very fresh copy. Sotheran's   Piccadilly Notes - Summer 2015 - 125   2016   £298

Ferguson, Adam *Essay on the History of Civil Society.* Edinburgh: printed for A. Millar & T. Caddel, 1767. First edition, quarto, contemporary full calf, gilt spine with raised bands and red morocco label, edges sprinkled red, joints cracked and tender, edges of boards rubbed, few light pencilled annotations, however very good, crisp copy in red cloth clamshell box.   Heritage Book Shop   Holiday 2015 - 38   2016 $7500

Ferguson, John *Bibliotheca Chemica, A Catalogue of the Alchemical, Chemical.* Glasgow: James Maclehose and Sons, 1906. First edition, 2 volumes, tall 8vo., later library buckram, ex-library with markings and library name perforated on titlepage.   Oak Knoll Books   310 - 244   2016 $300

Ferguson, John Alexander *Bibliography of Australia.* Sydney: Angus and Robertson, 1941-1969. First edition, octavo, 7 volumes, very good set, dust jackets, some wear. Andrew Isles Natural History Books   55 - 36419   2016 $5000

Ferguson, John Alexander *Bibliography of Australia.* Canberra: National Library of Australia, 1975. Volumes 1 and 2 facsimile editions, rest are original, 7 volumes, 4to., cloth, dust jacket, frontispieces, black and white illustrations, all volumes have some minor wear and rubbing at extremities and spine ends bumped, volume 3 missing dust jacket. Oak Knoll Books   310 - 228   2016 $500

Ferguson, Ross *Greening's Popular Reciter and the Art of Elocution and Public Speaking.* Greening & Co., 1904. Half title, original grey-brown pictorial cloth, very good. Jarndyce Antiquarian Books   CCXV - 197   2016   £25

Ferguson, Samuel *The Cromlech on Howth. A Poem...* London: Day & Son, 1861. First edition, very rare, folio, original Celtic green cloth, spine lettered and ornamented gilt, front cover ornamented in gilt, rear cover in blind, all edges gilt, title printed in red and black, additional chromolithographic titlepage, black and white illustrations, 15 chromolithographic plates, ornamental borders, 7 superb mounted chromolithographic landscape plates retaining tissue guards, two minor spots to lower cover, apart from foxing to initial blank, title and to lesser degree to text and plates as usual, very good, Day & Son's contemporary bindery label, slightly later armorial bookplate of Arthur Pendarves Vivian. Sotheran's   Travel and Exploration - 244   2016   £998

Fergusson, C. Bruce *Place Names and Places of Nova Scotia.* Halifax: Public Archives of Nova Scotia, 1967. Red cloth, 8vo., folding maps, very good.   Schooner Books Ltd.   115 - 144   2016 $45

Ferlinghetti, Lawrence *City Lights Journal. Number One.* San Francisco: City Lights, 1963. First edition, photographs, paper wrappers, cover and edges little yellowed, very good, tight.   Second Life Books, Inc.   197 - 114   2016 $75

Ferlinghetti, Lawrence *Endless Life.* San Miniato and Berkeley: Edizioni Canopo, 1999. First of this edition, limited to 35 copies printed on Magnani paper in Atheneum type, signed by poet and artist, text in Italian and English, folio, loose sheets in decorated wrappers, publisher's folding box, very fine, 11 drypoint etchings by Stephanie Peck.   James S. Jaffe Rare Books   Occasional List: Winter 2016 - 61   2016 $1500

Ferlinghetti, Lawrence *The Secret Meaning of Things.* New Directions, 1968. First edition, 1/150 signed copies in publisher's box, fine.   Second Life Books, Inc.   196A - 549   2016 $165

Ferlinghetti, Lawrence *Starting from San Francisco.* Norfolk: New Directions, 1961. First edition, square 8vo., paper over boards, owner's name on pastedown, cover yellowed, somewhat soiled, slightly worn at edges, very good tight copy.   Second Life Books, Inc.   197 - 112   2016 $85

Ferlinghetti, Lawrence *Tentative Description of a dinner given to Promote the Impeachment of President Eisenhower.* San Francisco: Golden Mountain Press, 1958. folded pamphlet, printed in red, cover stained and little chipped, interior slightly stained at edges, otherwise very good.   Second Life Books, Inc.   197 - 113   2016 $45

Fermor, Patrick Leigh *Three Letters from the Andes.* London: John Murray, 1991. First edition, 8vo., map, text illustrations, original blue cloth, dust jacket, fine.   J. & S. L. Bonham Antiquarian Booksellers   America 2016 - 9831   2016   £40

Fermor, Patrick Leigh *A Time of Gifts. On Foot to Constantinople: from the Hook of Holland to the Middle Danube.* London: Murray, 1978. First edition, 2nd issue, 8vo., original blue cloth, upper board with gilt crane design, spine lettered gilt, dust jacket with design after Craxton not price clipped, frontispiece, double page map printed on light brown paper, dust jacket slightly faded on spine (as often), past ownership bookplate attached to front free endpaper, gift inscription dated 1979 by John Murray, probably publisher, dust jacket very slightly rubbed at edges, nonetheless very fresh and bright.   Sotheran's   Travel and Exploration - 247   2016   £75

Fermor, Patrick Leigh *The Traveller's Tree. A Journey through the Caribbean Islands.* London: John Murray, 1950. First edition, 8vo., newly bound in green half calf with green cloth sides, gilt top edge, frontispiece, double page map printed on green paper at front of book, numerous black and white photo plates, captioned on facing page, in a section to rear, fine.   Sotheran's   Travel and Exploration - 245   2016   £498

Fernandiz, Juan *Klaus und Lotte.* Hamburg: Carlsen Verlag, circa 1950's, 4to, pictorial wrappers die-cut in shape of two children in motorcycle, some creasing and few neat mends, still attractive and very good, charming color lithos on every page by author.   Aleph-bet Books, Inc. 111 - 422   2016 $200

Ferrier, Susan Edmonstone 1782-1854 *Destiny; or the Chief's Daughter.* Edinburgh: Printed for Robert Cadell, 1831. First edition, scarce in original light brown paper covered boards, good, spines heavily chipped and worn, signatures visible beneath, though title labels present (though worn on volume 1), boards slightly soiled and worn, corners bumped and worn, rear board volume 2 detached, boards of volume 3 and front board volume 2 loose but still attached, interiors clean, though light spotting is present throughout, text bright and easily readable, bindings strong, no loss pages or signatures, housed in brown cloth covered folding case with brown leather and gilt label to spine, fine, bookplate on inner panel, good.   The Kelmscott Bookshop   12 - 46   2016 $300

Ferrini, Vincent *Hermit of the Clouds, the Autobiography of...* Gloucester: Ten Pound Island Book Co., 1988. First edition, printed wrappers, perfect bound with some loose pages, inscribed by author for Paul Metcalf and his wife Nancy.   Second Life Books, Inc.   196A - 559 2016 $45

Ferrini, Vincent *Know Fish.* Storrs: University of Conn. Library, 1979. First edition, 8vo. printed wrappers, nice, inscribed by author to Paul Metcalf who wrote preface, laid in is 2 page ALS to same from author.   Second Life Books, Inc.   196A - 554   2016 $150

Ferrini, Vincent *Know Fish: Book III, the navigators.* Storrs: University of Conn. Library, 1984. First edition, printed wrappers, nice, inscribed by Paul Metcalf.   Second Life Books, Inc. 196A - 551   2016 $50

Ferrini, Vincent *Know Fish: Book IV & V. The Community of Self.* Storrs: University of Conn. Library, 1986. First edition, 8vo., printed wrappers, nice, inscribed by authr to Paul Metcalf.   Second Life Books, Inc.   196A - 552   2016 $50

Ferrini, Vincent *Know Fish: Book VI & VII This Other Ocean.* Storrs: University of Conn. Library, 1991. First edition, 8vo., printed wrappers, nice, inscribed by author to Paul Metcalf and his wife Nancy.   Second Life Books, Inc. 196A - 553   2016 $50

Ferrini, Vincent *A Tale of Psyche.* Bedford: Igneus Press, 1991. First edition, 8vo., printed wrappers, fine, inscribed by author to Paul Metcalf and wife Nancy.   Second Life Books, Inc.   196A - 555   2016 $50

Ferrini, Vincent *Undersea Bread.* Storrs: University of California Lib., 1989. First edition, 8vo., printed wrappers, very nice, inscribed by author to poet Paul Metcalf and his wife Nancy.   Second Life Books, Inc.   196A - 556   2016 $50

Ferrini, Vincent *War in Heaven.* Storrs: University of CT. Library, 1987. First edition, 8vo., inscribed by author to poet Paul Metcalf, very nice, tight copy.   Second Life Books, Inc.   196A - 557   2016 $50

Ferris, Warren Angus *Life in the Rocky Mountains 1830-1835.* Salt Lake City: Rocky Mountain Book Shop, 1940. First book edition, 4 plates, folding map, publisher's cloth, gilt, light extremity rubbing, spine just bit dulled, two small bookplates on inner cover, overall fine.   Argonaut Book Shop   Biography 2015 - 5437   2016 $350

Ferry, Hypolite *Description de la Nouvelle Californie Geographique, Politique et Moralecontenant l'Histoire de la Decouverte de Cette Contree...* Paris: 1850. Second edition, octavo, large frontispiece folding map, 3 engraved maps, 4 engraved plates, with half title, contemporary quarter red morocco over pebble boards, spine stamped and lettered gilt, edges speckled blue, board edges rubbed, outer hinges cracked but holding, spine with crack across upper top portion, mostly light foxing throughout, two leaves with minor closed tears with no loss of text, large folding map with some minor closed tears and foxing, previous owner Daniel Volkmann Jr. bookplate, other small bookplate as well, overall nice, housed in custom cloth clamshell. Heritage Book Shop   Holiday 2015 - 39   2016 $2500

Feuchtersleben, Ernst Von *The Principles of Medical Psychology.* London: Sydenham Society, 1847. First edition in English, 8vo., original blindstamped dark green cloth, gilt arms on front and back covers, skillfully rebacked with original spine laid down, large armorial bookplate, old faded library stamp, very good.   Edwin V. Glaser Rare Books   2015 - 10404   2016 $125

Feuchtwanger, Lion *Jew Sus: a Historical Romance.* London: Martin Secker, 1926. First edition, 8vo., frontispiece, one of 275 large paper numbered copies signed by author, blue cloth, owner's name on pastedown, cover little bumped at corners and faded on spine, one hinge near tender, but otherwise very good, tight copy.   Second Life Books, Inc.   196A - 558   2016 $150

A Few Words of Advice on Travelling and Its Requirements Addressed to Ladies. London: Thomas Cook & Son, 1876. Second edition, half title, original brown cloth, expertly recased, booksellers stamp and contemporary signature on half title, very good.   Jarndyce Antiquarian Books   CCXV - 198   2016   £150

Fewkes, Jesse Walter *Hopi Katchinas Drawn by native Artists.* Washington: MacRae Publications, 1976. Reprinted from rare first edition of 1903, quarto, color plates, map endpapers, black leatherette stamped in metallic gold, red and blue, fine.   Argonaut Book Shop   Native American 2015 - 5975   2016 $75

Feyrer, Gayle *Demon Letting/Night Blooming.* N.P.: Bieler Press, 1976. Chapbook edition, limited to 100 numbered copies signed by author and artist, large 12mo., stiff paper wrapper, dust jacket, top edge cut, fore and bottom edges deckled, original serigraph by Cathie Ruggie, signed prints, printed in 8 colors.   Oak Knoll Books   310 - 80   2016 $125

Fforde, Jasper *The Eyre Affair.* London: Hodder & Stoughton, 2001. First edition, pictorial wrappers, fine.   Bella Luna Books   2016 - t5399   2016 $181

Fforde, Jasper *The Eyre Affair.* London: Hodder & Stoughton, 2001. First British edition, true first, fine in fine dust jacket, signed by author.   Bella Luna Books   2016 - 515879   2016 $214

Fforde, Jasper *The Eyre Affair.* London: Hodder & Stoughton, 2001. First British edition, true first edition, fine in near fine dust jacket, very slight wear to top edges.   Bella Luna Books   2016 - t4657   2016 $132

Fichte, Johann Gottlieb *Einige Vorlesungen Uber die Bestimmung des Gelehrten.* Jena und Leipzig: Christian Ernst Gabler, 1794. First edition, contemporary grey boards with worn hand written label on spine, small rectangular stamp to front free endpaper, small oval stamp to titlepage, not affecting text, overall, lovely contemporary copy.   Athena Rare Books   List 15 - 1794   2016 $250

Fichte, Johann Gottlieb *Grundlage des Naturrechts nach Principien der Wissenschaftslehre.* Jena und Leipzig: Christian Ernst Gabler, 1796. First edition, contemporary quarter calf with marbled boards, spine with gilt lettering, ornamental devices and four raised bands, from the library of T. De Jonge with his armorial bookplate, minor foxing to text, absolutely beautiful matched set.   Athena Rare Books   List 15 - 1796   2016 $1200

Fiedler, Maggi *Corky's Pet Parade.* New York: Pied Piper books, 1946. 4to., boards, fine in slightly worn dust jacket, color illustrations.   Aleph-bet Books, Inc.   111 - 47   2016 $200

Field, Michael *A Question of Memory: a Play in Four acts....* London: Elkin Mathews and John Lane at the sign of the Bodley Head, 1893. One of 120 copies, uncommon first published edition, original green cloth with red title and author to spine and front cover, offsetting to free front and rear endpapers, pages unopened, very good, 16 page publisher's catalog, very good.   The Kelmscott Bookshop   13 - 15   2016 $625

Field, Rachel *Branches Green.* New York: Macmillan, 1934. First edition, 8vo., cloth, fine in very good dust jacket with few chips and closed tears, lovely full and partial page illustrations by Dorothy Lathrop.   Aleph-bet Books, Inc.   112 - 284   2016 $125

Field, Rachel *Calico Bush.* New York: Macmillan, 1931. First edition, 8vo., multi colored cloth, little worn with labels removed on endpaper, very good, inscribed by author.   Second Life Books, Inc.   196A - 560   2016 $60

Field, Rachel *Eliza and the Elves.* New York: Macmillan, 1926. 8vo., cloth, fine in dust jacket (nickel size piece off upper corner, few other chips), illustrations by Elizabeth Mackinstry, inscribed author author Sept. 19th 1926, quite scarce in dust jacket.   Aleph-bet Books, Inc.   111 - 173   2016 $400

Field, Rachel *Hepatica Hawks.* New York: Macmillan, Oct., 1932. First printing, 8vo., cloth, very good-fine in dust jacket few archival mends on verso, illustrations by Allen Lewis with woodcuts, this copy inscribed by author Oct. 1932.   Aleph-bet Books, Inc.   111 - 174   2016 $275

Field, Rachel *Hepatica Hawks.* New York: Macmillan, 1932. First edition, 2nd printing, 8vo., soiled along hinges and browned on endpapers, otherwise very nice and clean in dust jacket that is torn at extremities of spine, inscribed by author, engravingds on wood by Allen Lewis.   Second Life Books, Inc.   196A - 559   2016 $45

Field, Rachel *Hitty: Her First Hundred Years.* New York: Macmillan, 1930. Early printing, 8vo., patterned cloth, spine and edges faded, else very good+, inscribed by author and dated 1930, laid in is photo of Hitty Inscribed, illustrations by Dorothy Lathrop with 3 color plates and many lovely full page and in-text black and whites.   Aleph-bet Books, Inc.   112 - 191   2016 $500

Field, Rachel *A Little Book of Days.* New York: Doubleday Page, 1927. Stated first edition, green cloth, fine in dust jacket (worn, half inch piece off backstrip, soiled, good condition), each page of text with wonderful full page illustrations by author, this copy inscribed by author in 1927, quite scarce with jacket and inscription.   Aleph-bet Books, Inc.   111 - 175   2016 $225

Field, Rachel *The Pointed People.* New Haven: Yale University Press, 1924. First edition, 8vo., cloth, spine faded, else very good+, 17 full page and many smaller silhouettes, this copy inscribed by author Sept.19 1924 with sketch.   Aleph-bet Books, Inc.   111 - 176   2016 $300

Fielding, Henry   1707-1754 *The History of the Adventures of Joseph Andrews and of his Friend Mr. Abraham Adams.* London: printed for A. Millar, 1742. First edition, bound without ads, K9 in volume i with portion of fore-margin reattached (paperflaw) with glue employed transposing a couple of letters from verso of page opposite the recto, a similar flaw parting the greater part of the inner margin of N8 in same volume, repairs to lower margins of B11 & 12 in volume ii (no loss), 12mo., mid 20th century speckled calf, French fillets on sides, spines gilt in compartments, contrasting lettering pieces, yellow edges, minimal wear, good.   Blackwell's Rare Books   B184 - 43   2016   £1800

Fielding, Henry   1707-1754 *Histoire de Tom Jones Ou L'Enfnat Trouve.* Londre: Jean Nourse, 1750. First edition in French, 4 volumes, period binding of full mottled calf with raised bands, elaborate gilt decorated spines, marbled endpapers, early ownership signature on titlepage of each volume, corners rubbed, otherwise very good, bright and internally fine.   Peter Ellis   112 - 123   2016   £850

Fielding, Henry   1707-1754 *The History of Tom Jones, a Foundling.* New York: Heritage Press, 1952. Marbled boards with beige cloth spine, lettered gilt, very fine in slipcase, illustrations by T. M. Cleland, Sandglass pamphlet laid in.   Argonaut Book Shop   Heritage Press 2015 - 1915   2016 $60

Fielding, John *Sir John Fielding's Jests...* London: printed for the editor and sold by Alex Hogg, 1781. 12mo., engraved frontispiece slightly offset on titlepage and margin slightly torn without loss, disbound.   Jarndyce Antiquarian Booksellers   CCXVI - 323   2016   £350

Fielding, Loraine Hornaday *French Heels to Spurs.* New York: Century Co., 1930. Stated first printing, illustrations, laid in publisher's letter describing the book, bookplate, pencil note on half title, else bright and very good.   Dumont Maps and Books   133 - 51   2016 $50

Fielding, Loraine Hornaday *French Heels to Spurs.* New York: Century Co., 1930. First edition, drawings by Eve Ganson, two-tone blue and orange pictorial cloth stamped in blue and gold, neat contemporary owner's name and date on endpaper (April 1931), very fine, becoming quite scarce.   Argonaut Book Shop   Literature 2015 - 7177   2016 $75

Fielding, Michael *Parenthood: Design or Accident?* London: Williams & Norgate, 1933. 90th thousand, half title, illustrations, original yellow printed wrappers, spine little rubbed, slightly faded.   Jarndyce Antiquarian Books   CCXV - 198   2016   £20

Fielding, Sarah *The Governess or the Little Female Academy....* London: printed for J. Rivington &c, 1789. Seventh edition, 12mo., few gatherings slightly loose, some slight tears to fore edge, close to text, uncut in original hessian cloth, very good.   Jarndyce Antiquarian Books   CCXV - 683   2016   £225

Fielding, Sarah *The Governess...* London: Oxford University Press, 1968. Half title, very good in dust jacket.   Jarndyce Antiquarian Books   CCXV - 684   2016   £15

Fielding, Xan *The Stronghold - an Account of the Four Seasons in the White Mountains of Crete.* London: Secker & Warburg, 1953. First edition, octavo, endpaper maps, folding map, photos by Daphne Bath, endpaper maps and folding map, fore-edge lightly spotted, very good in very good, slightly nicked and chipped dust jacket, bit tanned at spine.   Peter Ellis   112 - 122   2016   £375

Fields, James T., Mrs. *A Shelf of Old Books.* New York: Charles Scribner's Sons, 1895. First edition, 8vo., 54 illustrations and ms. facsimiles, bound in brown gilt stamped cloth, untrimmed, very good, clean, ownership signature on free endpaper "D. J. G. Bromwell/Christmas 1895" with 3 line quote for (S.T.) Coleridge.   Second Life Books, Inc. 196A - 369   2016 $2500

Figuier, Oscar   *Memoire sur la Composition Chimique des Escargots et sur les Preparations Pharmaceutiques dont ils Sont la Base.* Montpellier: F. Gelly, 1840. 8vo., original yellow printed wrappers, very good.   Edwin V. Glaser Rare Books   2015 - 10371   2016 $225

Film Art: Review of the Advance-Guard Cinema.   London: self published, 1933-1934. First edition, first 9 issues, 7.5 x 9.5 inches, saddle stitched, all volumes very good plus with light toning and faint creases and brief notation on front wrapper of Spring 1933 issue.   Royal Books 49 - 23   2016 $875

Finch-Davies, C. G.   *The Bird Paintings of C. G. Finch-Davies.* Johannesburg: Winchester Press, 1984. First edition, profusely illustrated in color and black and white, brown cloth cover with color plates, spine slightly sunned in very good slipcase, else slightly sunned and spotted else fine copy.   Simon Finch   2015 - 606703   2016 $200

Finch-Davies, C. G.   *The Birds of Prey of South Africa.* Johannesburg: Winchester Press, 1980. First edition, limited edition, 859 of 1700 copies, dust jacket, very good, lovely, clean, slightly dusty looking top page block edges and minor bumps to fore edge corners, dust jacket with little edgewear and sun faded with slight loss of spine ends, now protected by removeable jacket sleeve.   Simon Finch 2015 - 006416   2016 $320

Finch-Davies, C. G.   *The Birds of Prey of Southern Africa.* Johannesburg: Winchester Press, 1980. Unauthorized proof of limited edition of 1726, 140 full page color plates, fine in fine dust jacket and slipcase.   Simon Finch   2015 - 14158   2016 $288

Finch-Hatton, Harold   *Advance Australia! An Account of Eight Years Work....* London: W. H. Allen Co., 1885. First edition, 8vo., black and white frontispiece, 13 other black and white plates plus folding black and white map, original blue cloth, gilt spine lettering, gilt vignette to front, rubbed, some marks to boards, frontispiece detached, spotted and with frayed edge, some spots to prelims, plates and text tight and clean, armorial bookplate of Philip Saltmarshe, good++.   Simon Finch   2015 - 8854586565   2016 $320

Finch, Arthur Elley   *On the Inductive Philosophy Including a Parallel Between Lord Bacon and A Comte as Philosophers.... (bound with) The Pursuit of Truth as Exemplified in the Principles of Evidence, Theological, Scientific and Judicial...*   London: Longmans, Green and Co., 1872-1873. First edition, bound together, 8vo., contemporary half calf, bit rubbed, title soiled.   Simon Finch 2015 - 2016 $278

Finch, Christopher   *The Art of Walt Disney from Mickey Mouse to the Magic Kingdoms.*   New York: Harry N. Abrams, 1973. First edition, fine in near fine dust jacket, 763 illustrations, including 351 plates in full color, acetate jacket has three inch tear bottom right corner.   Simon Finch   2015 - 003022   2016 $268

Finch, Christopher   *The Art of Walt Disney.*   New York: Harry N. Abrams Inc., 1973. First edition, fine, acetate dust jacket, acetate cover flawless, front board has raised image of Mickey Mouse holding a paintbrush, with paint bucket nearby, titlepage folds out to four pages wide, profusely illustrated, many color plates.   Simon Finch   2015 - 78242 2016 $250

Finch, Christopher   *The Art of the Lion King.*   Hyperion, 1983. First edition, pictorial wood engraved titlepage, 18 wood engraved plates, oblong folio, original half brown cloth with colored pictorial paper covered upper cover and plain paper covered lower cover, little loose in covers, lower blank margin of paper covered sides of binding worn and dampstained, lower margin of front endpaper dampstained, small light dampstain in lower blank margin of plates.   Simon Finch   2015 - 3547   2016 $240

Finch, Christopher   *Chuck Close Work.*   Prestel, 2010. First edition, very good, dust jacket, folio, signed by author and subject, Chuck Close, dust jacket excellent, text clean and free of marks, binding tight and solid boards clean with no wear.   Simon Finch   2015 - 28253   2016 $300

Finch, Christopher   *Norman Rockwell: 332 Magazine Covers.* New York: Abbeville Press, 1979. First edition, thick folio, green pictorial cloth lettered gilt, pictorial dust jacket, signed by Finch.   Simon Finch   2015 - 2016 $250

Finch, Christopher   *Of Muppets and Men: the making of the Muppets Show.*   New York: Alfred A. Knopf, 1981. First edition, pages in excellent condition, bottom edges scuffed from being shelved, dust jacket has few small edge tears, slight scuffing to jacket, archivally repaired and in mylar. Simon Finch   2015 - S1436627   2016 $250

Finch, Christopher   *Of Muppets & Men: the Making of the Muppets Show.*   New York: Alfred A. Knopf, 1981. First edition, blue cloth, fine, pristine condition, in like dust jacket, in protective plastic cover, no flaws, square quarto.   Simon Finch   2015 - 0178109   2016 $225

Finch, Christopher *Special Effects: Creating Movie Magic - Collectori's edition in Metal Film Case.* Abbeville Press, 1989. First edition, rare, collector's edition, signed on label affixed to front endpage by author, scarce, very limited edition housed in huge metal film case with foam around sides that protect book , some spotting to top edge of case, overall bright and shiny, 4to.   Simon Finch   2015 - 50001116   2016 $225

Finch, Christopher *Twentieth-Century Watercolors.* New York: Abbeville press, 1988. First edition, light blue cloth, fine in fine dust jacket, 303 color illustrations, one tiny bump to front bottom right corner, exceptionally clean, strong, tight and clean, folio.   Simon Finch   2015 - 0178901   2016 $175

Finch, Elley A. *Malthusiana, Illustrations of the Influence of Nature's Law of Increase.* London: G. Standring, 1904. First edition, purple cloth, gilt lettering on front cover and faded spine, ex-academic libris front cover.   Simon Finch   2015 - 1848   2016 $205

Finch, James A. *Federal Anti-Trust Decisions. Cases Decided in the United States Courts Arising Under, Involving or Growing Out of the Enforcement of the Anti-Trust Act of July 2 1890....* Washington: GPO, 1912. First edition, 4 volumes, inscribed by John Qullin Tilson (1866-1958), Conn. Congressman, with stamp of V. N. Roadstrum, attorney for J.P. Morgan Estate, very good or better, edges lightly soiled, otherwise very tight and clean, handsome set, original maroon buckram.   Simon Finch   2015 - 27510   2016 $300

Finch, John *To South Africa and Back.* London: 1880. First edition, inscribed by author, 8 plates, pictorial cloth, bevelled edges, half leather, housed in stunning dark green traycase, absolute mint condition.   Simon Finch   2015 - 2942   2016 $240

Finch, Phillip *Texas Dawn: a Novel.* New York: Seaview Books, 1981. First edition, fine in fine dust jacket, price clipped.   Ken Hebenstreit, Bookseller   2016 - 2016 $45

Finch, R. L. *Story of Minor League Baseball 1901-1952.* Story: Stoneman, 1952. First edition, illustrations, hardcover, good.   Simon Finch   2015 - 16717   2016 $300

Finch, Robert *New Provinces: Poems of Several Authors.* London: Macmillan, 1936. First edition, very good, blue green boards, vibrant dust jacket with moderate edgewear and tanning, corner chipped, light soiling, interior clean, binding solid.   Simon Finch   2015 - 008983   2016 $200

Finch, William Coles *Life in Rural England: Occupations and Pastimes in Field and Villages Farm and Home, Water Mill and Wind Mill.* London: C. W. Daniel, 1928. First edition, engraved photos, very good+.   Simon Finch   2015 - 28819   2016 $215

Finch, William Coles *Watermills and Windmills, a Historical survey of their Rise, Decline and fall as Portrayed by Those of Kent.* London: G. W. Daniel Co., 1933. First edition, red cloth with gilt lettering on spine and front with windmill decoration on front in gilt, photo plates, maps and drawings, inscribed to friend of author, top edge dust soiled, little spotting to fore edge of pages, very good, no dust jacket.   Simon Finch   2015 - 005816   2016 $200

Finley, Mike *Home Trees.* St. Peter Publishing House, 1978. First edition, printed wrappers, very good, laid in is 9 line holograph review by poet Paul Metcalf.   Second Life Books, Inc.   196A - 562   2016 $75

Firbank, Ronald   1886-1926 *Odette d'Antrevernes and A Study in Temperament.* London: Elkin Mathews, 1905. First edition, small 4to., light creasing to top corner of pages 9-42, small 4to., original sea green wrappers stamped in gilt to front, two small internal tape repairs to bottom corner of both panels, small amount of surface removal to bottom corner of rear panel and short closed tear to foot of same, some creasing and rubbing to edges, backstrip darkened with little chipping at tips and two short splits at either end of upper joint, top edge trimmed, protective glassine dust jacket and housed in custom solander box, good, very well preserved.   Blackwell's Rare Books   B186 - 215   2016   £290

Firbank, Ronald   1886-1926 *Valmouth.* London: Grant Richards, 1919. First edition, one of 500 copies, crown 8vo., original black cloth stamped in gilt to upper board, backstrip lettered gilt with touch of softening to tips, top edge green, other edges lightly toned, dust jacket lightly dust soiled overall with chipping to corners and tips of backstrip chip at foot of front panel, good.   Blackwell's Rare Books   B186 - 216   2016   £350

Fischer, Bruno *Crook's Tour.* New York: Dodd Mead, 1953. First edition, fine, inscribed by contributors Lawrence Blochman and Dorothy Gardiner, fine in price clipped dust jacket.   Mordida Books   2015 - 010969   2016 $65

Fischer, Heinrich *Knitische Mikroskopisch-mineralogische Studien.* Freiburg: Carl Troemer, 1869. 1871. 1873. First edition, 3 works in 1, small 8vo., 2 colored plates, some brittleness to paper, quite browned, early half brown morocco, lighter brown pebbled cloth, gilt stamped spine with original yellow printed wrappers, bound in, rubbed, printed wrapper chipped, others fine, ownership signatures of R. Pumpelly, very good, rare.   Jeff Weber Rare Books   183 - 18   2016 $300

Fischer, Henry *Bred in the Bone. an Anthology.* Princeton: Ampersand Press, 1945. First edition, cloth, #300 of 325 printed, inscribed and signed by one of the contributors, Frederick Buechner for William Meredith, Christmas 1974, laid in ALS from Buechner to Meredith, very good, likely issued without dust jacket, with brief ALS by another contributor, Robert Zufall. Charles Agvent William Meredith - 21 2016 $250

Fisher, Aileen *Do Bears Have Mothers, Too?* New York: Thomas Y. Crowell, 1973. First edition, beautifully illustrated by Eric Carle, little wear to plastic covering on rear dust jacket, otherwise fine in dust jacket (not price clipped), inscribed by Carle in ink for Catherine Clark, with added drawing of smiling cat, fine. Second Life Books, Inc. 197 - 47 2016 $1500

Fisher, Anne *The New Pleasing Instructor or Entertaining Moralised.* Halifax: William Milner, 1847. Half title, frontispiece title vignette, plates, lacking leading f.e.p., original blue cloth, gilt spine, slightly later inscription, nice, bright copy. Jarndyce Antiquarian Books CCXV - 200 2016 £35

Fisher, Anne *The New Pleasing Instructor.* Halifax: William Milner, 1847. Half title, 16mo., frontispiece, title vignette, plates, lacking leading f.e.p., original blue cloth, gilt spine, slightly later inscription on half title and recto of following f.e.p., nice, bright copy. Jarndyce Antiquarian Books CCXV - 200 2016 £35

Fisher, Anne *The Pleasing Instructor or Entertaining Moralist....* Newcastle upon Tyne: S. Hodgson, circa, 1800. Title vignette, plates, slightly foxed, contemporary mottled calf, spine rubbed and darkened, hinges cracked, ownership inscription of Mary Marsh 1819, sound. Jarndyce Antiquarian Books CCXV - 686 2016 £48

Fisher, George *The Instructor or Young Man's Best Companion.* London: printed for J. Clarke, 1742. Sixth edition, frontispiece, plates, illustrations, 12mo., pages little browned, handsomely rebound in half calf, vellum tips, red morocco label, inscription "John Webb his book Jan. 24 1837". Jarndyce Antiquarian Books CCXV - 202 2016 £75

Fisher, George *The Instructor.* London: W. Baynes, 1810. Thirty-first edition, 12mo., frontispiece, plate and illustrations, recent functional full brown calf. Jarndyce Antiquarian Books CCXV - 203 2016 £75

Fisher, Harrison *The American Girl.* New York: Scribner, 1909. First edition, large folio, cloth backed boards lettered in gold, pictorial paste-on, light edge rubbing, near fine, 17 color plates, beautiful copy, rarely found in such nice condition. Aleph-bet Books, Inc. 112 - 193 2016 $975

Fisher, Irving 1867-1947 *Stable Money. A History of the Movement.* New York: Adelphi Co., 1934. First edition, limited, no. 634, 8vo., signed and inscribed by Fisher, Frederic Delano and James Rand, original blue cloth with mild wear cover edges, marginal dampstain, very good+. By the Book, L. C. 45 - 28 2016 $3000

Fisher, John *The Magic of Lewis Carroll.* New York: Bramdall House, 1973. Bramdall House Edition, octavo, forest green paper over boards, gilt stamped title on backstrip, very good, moderate bumping to extremities, tanning to pages, very good, mild yellowing at spine, line illustrations by Tenniel, Holiday, Frost, Furniss, etc. Ken Sanders Rare Books E Catalogue # 1 - 47 2016 $50

Fisher, Leona W. *Lemon, Dickens and Mr. Nightingale's Diary; a Victorian Farce.* Victoria: University of Virginia, 1988. Plates, original card wrappers, marked, presentation to Kathleen Tillotson by Reg. Terry in 1989 and heavily annotated. Jarndyce Antiquarian Booksellers CCXVIII - 1225 2016 £35

Fisher, Robert H. *Butterflies of South Australia.* Adelaide: Government Printer, 1978. Octavo, color plates, paperback, very good. Andrew Isles Natural History Books 55 - 6757 2016 $70

Fisher, Vardis *City of Illusion.* New York: Harper & Bros., 1941. First edition, rust cloth, gilt, slightest of rubbing to spine ends, fine, clean copy. Argonaut Book Shop Literature 2015 - 6263 2016 $60

Fisk, Theophilus *Political Reformer volume I no. 1 (all).* Portsmouth: 1840. 8vo., uncut, as issued, some browning. M & S Rare Books, Inc. 99 - 19 2016 $450

Fitz, Henry *The Non-Personality, Origin and End of that Old Serpent Called the Devil and Satan...* New York: printed and for sale at the Office of the Gospel Herald No. 67 Prine Street, 1825. First edition, 8vo., removed, quite foxed. M & S Rare Books, Inc. 99 - 312 2016 $85

Fitzgerald, Errol *A Stranger Intervenes.* Mills & Boon Ltd., 1948. Brown embossed boards in aged, chipped, but complete pictorial dust jacket, light foxing to edges, not affecting text, uncommon. I. D. Edrich Crime - 2016 £30

Fitzgerald, Francis Scott Key 1896-1940 *The Crack-up.* New York: New Directions, 1945. Reprint, 8vo., name on endpaper, very good in some worn dust jacket. Second Life Books, Inc. 197 - 115 2016 $150

Fitzgerald, Francis Scott Key   1896-1940   *The Great Gatsby.*   New York: Scribner, 1925.   First edition, with all first issue points, some wear to extremities of spine and corners, couple of small spots on cover, good copy.   Second Life Books, Inc.   197 - 116   2016 $2750

Fitzgerald, Francis Scott Key   1896-1940   *(Title in Cyrillac) The Great Gatsby.*   Moskva: Khudozhestvennaia Literatura, 1965.   First Russian edition, decorated wrappers, bit cocked and cheap paper bit toned, very good in very good dust jacket with rubbing and few small chips and tears, very uncommon.   Between the Covers Rare Books   208 - 29   2016 $1200

Fitzgerald, Francis Scott Key   1896-1940   *Taps at Reveille.*   New York: Charles Scribner's Sons, 1935.   First edition, first state, Rockwell Kent designed bookplate of Philip Marchant, else superlative, very fine with spine lettering bright, lacking dust jacket.   Between the Covers Rare Books   208 - 28   2016 $2000

Fitzgerald, Francis Scott Key   1896-1940   *Tender is the Night.*   New York: Charles Scribner's Sons, 1934.   First edition, lightly worn cloth, near fine in attractive, first issue dust jacket with unfaded spine and some minor repair and restoration at extremities.   Between the Covers Rare Books   204 - 46   2016 $37,500

Fitzgerald, Kevin   *it's Different in July.*   London: Heinemann, 1955.   Inscribed presentation signed by author, black boards, gilt, frayed and torn dust jacket, slight edge foxing, not affecting text, uncommon, especially with largely intact jacket and signature, very good.   I. D. Edrich   Crime - 2016   £25

Fitzgerald, Kevin   *Kill Him Gently, Nurse.*   London: Heinemann, 1966.   Uncorrected proof copy, original wrappers with name on front wrapper and date on front endpaper.   I. D. Edrich   Crime - 2016   £25

Fitzgerald, Penelope   *The Blue Flower.*   London: Flamingo, 1995.   First edition, octavo, slight bruise at head of spine, near fine in dust jacket.   Peter Ellis   112 - 124   2016   £65

Fitzgerald, Percy   *The Book Fancier or the Romance of Book Collecting.*   London: Sampson, Low, Marston, Searle & Rivington, 1886.   First edition, first and last leaves quite badly spotted, otherwise very nice, cloth lettered in gilt bright, bookplate.   Bertram Rota Ltd.   February List 2016 - 9   2016   £40

Fitzgerald, Percy   *Pickwickian Manners and Customs.*   London: Roxburghe Press, 1897.   First edition, half title, frontispiece, title printed in green, final plate preceding 4 pages ads, uncut in original pale blue cloth, spine in front board blocked and lettered gilt, slightly faded and rubbed, Homeward's Subscription Library label.   Jarndyce Antiquarian Booksellers   CCXVIII - 144   2016   £35

Fitzgibbon, Edward   *A Handbook of Angling Teaching fly-fishing, trolling, bottom-fishing and salmon fishing....*   London: printed for Longman, Brown, Green and Longmans, 1847.   Small 8vo., half title, numerous illustrations, modern blue cloth with silver stamped brown spine label, fine.   Jeff Weber Rare Books   181 - 83   2016 $75

Fitzherbert, Cuthbert   *The Prince and the Pedlar. Stalking Memories.*   Rugby: Anthony Atho Publishers, 1977.   No. 360 of a limited edition of 500, signed by author, 8vo., original green cloth, gilt stag to upper board, gilt lettering to spine, matching slipcase, frontispiece, 5 plates by V. Balfour-Browne, gilt inscription, otherwise fine.   Sotheran's Hunting, Shooting & Fishing - 57   2016   £150

Fitzhugh, Percy   *King Time.*   New York: H. M. Caldwell, 1908.   First edition, cloth with elaborate gilt pictorial cover, front hinge with small repair, else fine, binding bright.   Aleph-bet Books, Inc.   112 - 71   2016 $225

Fitzsimons, Raymond   *The Charles Dickens Show: an account of his public readings 1858-1870.*   London: Geoffrey Bles, 1970.   First edition, half title, plates, cream cloth, very good in slightly rubbed and price clipped dust jacket.   Jarndyce Antiquarian Booksellers   CCXVIII - 628   2016   £20

Flack, Marjorie   *Angus and the Cat.*   New York: Doubleday Doran, 1931.   Stated first edition, oblong 8vo., pictorial boards, near fine in dust jacket with rectangular pieces off blank edge of flap, illustrations on every page, rare.   Aleph-bet Books, Inc.   111 - 178   2016 $850

Flack, Marjorie   *The Story About Ping.*   New York: Viking Press, 1933.   First edition, 8vo., near fine, printing with mild cover edge wear in near fine dust jacket with edge wear, first printing dust jacket with $1.00.   By the Book, L. C.   45 - 82   2016 $675

Flammarion, Camille   *Les Terres du Ciel Voyage Astronomique sur els Autres Mondes et Description des Conditions Actuelles de la Vie sur les Diveres Plantes du System Solaire.*   Paris: C. Marpon et E. Lammrion, 1884.   Eleventh edition, 8 full page plates and numerous in text illustrations, very good in three quarter tan leather over marbled paper covered boards with black and gilt title label to spine, wear to corners, edges of boards, spine ends and hinges, minor rubbing to boards and minor cracks to leather along spine, foxing and browning to interior, very good.   The Kelmscott Bookshop   13 - 16   2016 $150

Flanagan, Hallie *Shifting Scenes of the Modern European Theatre.* New York: Coward McCann, 1928. 8vo., 24 illustrations, owner's name and address in blue pencil opposite title, very good in little worn dust jacket. Second Life Books, Inc. 196A - 566 2016 $45

Flanagan, Thomas Jefferson *The Road to Mount McKeithan and Other Verse.* Atlanta: Indepenedent (sic) Publishers Corporation, 1927. First edition, frontispiece, one printed illustration, paper covered boards, modest erosion to boards, else nice, very good or better, inscribed by author to Professor and Mrs. Edgar H. Webster and dated in year of publication. Between the Covers Rare Books 202 - 33 2016 $750

Flaubert, Gustave 1821-1880 *Herodias.* Paris: Societe des Beaux Arts, 1890's, One of 550 numbered copies of the large paper 'Salon Edition', royal 8vo., original half dark green morocco, spine decorated gilt with curving leafy stems with red floral onlays, small gilt butterflies, marbled paper sides and endpapers, top edges gilt, others untrimmed, color frontispiece, tinted vignette on titlepage, 4 full page tinted engraved plates and numerous timted engraved vignettes, all by Georges Rochegrosse, spine faded to brown, but very nice. Sotheran's Piccadilly Notes - Summer 2015 - 127 2016 £98

Flaubert, Gustave 1821-1880 *Madame Bovary.* Paris: Louis Conard, 1921. Single volume from the Oeuvres Completes, contemporary green half morocco, marbled boards, spine in compartments with raised bands, decorated gilt and with leather labels lettered in gilt, spine sunned to brown, still nice. Bertram Rota Ltd. February List 2016 - 18 2016 £60

Flaubert, Gustave 1821-1880 *Salammbo.* London: Saxon and Co. and New York, 1886. First edition, first edition in Englsih, 8vo., purple cloth stamped in gilt, name stamp on top of titlepage and embossed stamp over imprint, very good. Second Life Books, Inc. 197 - 117 2016 $450

Flaubert, Gustave 1821-1880 *La Tentation De Saint Antoine.* Paris: Henri Reynaud, 1926. No. 196 of 262 copies, on Arches paper, from a total edition of 343, 240 x 190mm., publisher's cream colored printed wrapper, 20 miniatures by Arthur Szyk, colored by Jean Saude, spine of original substantial binding with faint creases and two tears (one short, one three inches long), one gathering becoming loose, binding and contents in extremely clean, fresh and bright. Phillip J. Pirages 67 - 323 2016 $750

Flaubert, Gustave 1821-1880 *Oeuvres Completes.* Paris: Louis Conard, 1910-1954. Mostly late printings, 28 volumes, 8vo, uniformly bound in orange cloth gilt by Morley, spines slightly darkened and edges of some covers little damp marked, associated slight bubbling to pastedown endpapers, otherwise nice. Bertram Rota Ltd. February List 2016 - 17 2016 £500

Flecker, James E. *Letter of... to F. Savery.* Westminster: 1926. Limited to 800 copies, printed on parchment vellum, signed by editor, nice, tight copy. Second Life Books, Inc. 196A - 91 2016 $150

Fleming, Ian Lancaster 1908-1964 *Dr. No.* London: Jonathan Cape, 1958. First edition, brown silhouette on back front cover and fine copy in dust jacket with light professional restoration to head of spine, corners and rear flap foldover, exceptional copy. Buckingham Books 2015 - 37451 2016 $3500

Fleming, Ian Lancaster 1908-1964 *Goldfinger.* London: Jonathan Cape, 1959. First edition, first impression with first published 1959 on copyright page, fine, bright copy in fine, bright dust jacket with earliest state of dust jacket with 19 line publicity blurb about book inside front flap fold, exceptional copy. Buckingham Books 2015 - 37455 2016 $3000

Fleming, Ian Lancaster 1908-1964 *Ian Fleming Introduces Jamaica.* 1965. First edition, color frontispiece and plates, fine in slightly browned dust jacket. Bertram Rota Ltd. Christmas List 2015 - 12 2016 £40

Fleming, Ian Lancaster 1908-1964 *Ian Fleming's Story of Chitty Chitty Bang Bang! The Magical Car.* London: Collins & Harvill, 1969. First edition, near fine in dust jacket. Mordida Books 2015 - 011873 2016 $65

Fleming, Ian Lancaster 1908-1964 *The Man with the Golden Gun.* London: Jonathan, 1965. First edition, fine in price clipped dust jacket (upper panel of which is little damaged), ownership signature and bookseller's small label on front pastedown. Bertram Rota Ltd. Christmas List 2015 - 10 2016 £200

Fleming, Ian Lancaster 1908-1964 *The Man with the Golden Gun.* London: Jonathan Cape, 1965. First edition, first impression, second date as usual, (without gun in gold to front board), binding B (bronze lettering, no priority assigned), black cloth with bronze stamping to spine, green patterned endpapers, original pictorial dust jacket, book fine with just some very minor spotting to top edge, fine dust jacket without any fading or wear, fine and beautiful copy. B & B Rare Books, Ltd. 2016 - IF067 2016 $500

Fleming, Ian Lancaster 1908-1964 *The Man with the Golden Gun.* London: Jonathan Cape, 1965. First edition, crown 8vo., original black boards, backstrip lettered gilt with slight lean to spine, very light central crease to upper board, top edge trifle dusty, single small spot at head of rear pastedown concealed by rear flap, dust jacket with small amount of creasing around head and couple of tiny nicks, very good. Blackwell's Rare Books B184 - 144 2016 £200

Fleming, Ian Lancaster   1908-1964   *The Spy Who Loved Me.*   London: Jonathan Cape, 1962. First edition, fine in very slightly spotted dust jacket spine panel of which is just a little browned.   Bertram Rota Ltd.   Christmas List 2015 - 11   2016   £450

Fleming, Ian Lancaster   1908-1964   *The Spy Who Loved Me.*   London: Jonathan Cape, 1962. First edition, owner bookplate, splendid copy, fine in fine dust jacket.   Ken Hebenstreit, Bookseller   2016 - 2016 $750

Fleming, Ian Lancaster   1908-1964   *Thrilling Cities.*   London: Jonthan Cape, 1963. First edition, 82 illustrations from photos, erratum slip tipped in at page 223, 8vo., original quarter white buckram with grey boards, backstrip lettered gilt, little very faint foxing to cloth, black top edge, contemporary gift inscription to verso of flyleaf, dust jacket price clipped with gentle fading to backstrip panel, very good.   Blackwell's Rare Books   B184 - 145   2016   £150

Fleming, Ian Lancaster   1908-1964   *Thunderball.*   London: Jonathan Cape, 1961. First edition, foolscap 8vo., original black boards with image of skeletal hand blindstamped to upper board, backstrip lettered gilt, gentle bumping to bottom corners, top edge trifle dusty, very short closed tear at head of lower front fold, very good.   Blackwell's Rare Books   B184 - 146   2016   £1200

Fleming, Ian Lancaster   1908-1964   *Thunderball.*   London: Jonathan Cape, 1961. First edition, first issue binding, fine in fine dust jacket.   Buckingham Books   2015 - 37324   2016 $3500

Fleming, Ian Lancaster   1908-1964   *You Only Live Twice.*   London: Cape, 1964. Second edition, erasure on front endpaper, otherwise fine in dust jacket on which someone has drawn picture of a hand on back panel.   Mordida Books   2015 - 006674   2016 $65

Fleming, Ian Lancaster   1908-1964   *You Only Live Twice.*   London: Jonathan Cape, 1964. First edition, first issue, 8vo., original cloth in price clipped dust jacket, spine slightly darkened, otherwise very good.   Sotheran's   Piccadilly Notes - Summer 2015 - 128   2016   £698

Fletcher, Hanslip   *Bombed London - A Collection of Thirty-Eight Drawings ...*   London: Cassell, 1947. First edition, folio, 4 of the plates in color, color pictorial cloth, free endpapers tanned, tail of spine bit darkened, very good in scarce printed tissue dust jacket which is very good, chipped and creased at edges.   Peter Ellis   112 - 125   2016   £95

Fletcher, J. S.   *The Copper Box.*   New York: Grosset & Dunlap, Reprint edition, number on front endpaper, otherwise fine in very fine dust jacket.   Mordida Books   2015 - 011370   2016 $65

Fletcher, J. S.   *Exterior to the Evidence.*   New York: Grosset & Dunlap, Reprint edition, very good, spine darkened and covers worn, otherwise very good in fine dust jacket.   Mordida Books   2015 - 010020   2016 $65

Fletcher, J. S.   *Green Ink.*   New York: Grosset & Dunlap, Reprint edition, fine in very fine, as new dust jacket.   Mordida Books   2015 - 011059   2016 $65

Fletcher, J. S.   *The Green Rope.*   H. Jenkins, 1927. Original pictorial cloth, very good, slight spotting to edges and prelims not affecting text.   I. D. Edrich   Crime - 2016   £20

Fletcher, J. S.   *The Mill of Many Windows.*   New York: Grosset & Dunlap, Reprint edition, number stamped on bottom of page edges and front hinge slightly cracked, otherwise fine in dust jacket.   Mordida Books   2015 - 01022   2016 $65

Fletcher, J. S.   *The Million Dollar Diamond.*   H. Jenkins, 1923. Pictorial cloth little marked, spine creased, crossed out name on front pastedown, endpapers browned, fore edge lightly foxed, not affecting text, otherwise very good.   I. D. Edrich   Crime - 2016   £30

Fletcher, J. S.   *Murder in the Squire's Pew.*   New York: A. Knopf, 1932. First American edition, Red boards little rubbed & age darkened, as are endpapers, still very good.   I. D. Edrich   Crime - 2016   £20

Fletcher, James   *The History of Poland; from the Earliest Period to the Present Time.*   New York: Harper Bros., 1865. Later US edition, small 8vo., frontispiece, original black cloth, small wear to head and tail of spine.   J. & S. L. Bonham Antiquarian Booksellers   Europe 2016 - 8002   2016   £35

Fletcher, John   *The Poems of John Fletcher 1579-1625.*   Stella Press, 2015. 5/150 copies, printed on Fredegoni paper, tipped-in portrait frontispiece, titlepage printed in blue and black, royal 8vo., original quarter blue cloth, mustard boards, printed blue label inset to upper board, printed label to backstrip, fine.   Blackwell's Rare Books   B184 - 317   2016   £50

Fletcher, John   *A Vindication of the Rev. Mr. Wesley's Last Minutes, Occasioned by a circular letter, inviting principal persons, both clergy and laity....*   Bristol: printed by W. Pine in Wine Street, 1771. 12mo., stab-sewn as issued, first and final outer pages dusted and marked.   Jarndyce Antiquarian Booksellers   CCXVI - 605   2016   £150

Flexner, Helen Thomas *A Quaker Childhood.* New Haven: Yale University Press, 1940. First edition, 8vo., photos, tan cloth with paper labels, dust jacket flaps glued on front corners and ends of spine, very good, signed by author.   Second Life Books, Inc.   196A - 567   2016 $45

Flinders, Matthew   1774-1814 *Narrative of His Voyage in the Schooner Francis: 1798.*   Golden Cockerel Press, 1946. First edition, 555/650 copies of a total edition of 750 copies, printed on Arnold pale grey mouldmade paper, frontispiece, 6 large headpieces title vignette and full page map, all wood engraved by John Buckland Wright and printed in dark green, large initial letter to each chapter also printed in green, small folio, original dark green canvas, backstrip lettering and Buckland Wright design on front cover all gilt blocked, top edge gilt, others untrimmed, fine.   Blackwell's Rare Books   B184 - 268   2016   £550

Floire et Jeanne   *The Tale of King Florus and the Fair Jehane.*   Kelmscott Press, 1893. 350 copies printed with an additional 15 copies on vellum, of the 360 copies, 76 copies were purchased in sheets by Tregaskis and sent to book binders, this is probably a trial copy that Rau chose not to send as his exhibition piece but seems more likely that it was a second copy commissioned by a collector who saw the Tretaskis copy in the exhibition or the exhibition catalog, 16mo., choicely bound by E Rau of St. Petersburg in full orange crushed morocco lettered gilt on spine, boards with semi of stylized flowers within a single gilt and dog tooth panel, central initial of 'W" on upper board and "M' on lower, richly gilt inner dentelles over marbled endpapers, double page woodcut border, text printed in black and red in Chaucer type, fine in slipcase, bookplate of Frank Howell and of American collector Charles Walker Andrews, loosely inserted is typed letter from J. and M. L. Tregaskis to Frank Howell.   Sotheran's   Piccadilly Notes - Summer 2015 - 175   2016   £4995

Flora of Australia. Volume 3. Hamamelidales to Casuarinales.   Canberra: Australian Government pub. Service, 1989. Octavo, text illustrations, dust jacket.   Andrew Isles Natural History Books   55 - 1586   2016 $100

Flora of Australia. volume 4. Phytolaccaceae to Cyhenopodiaceae.   Canberra: Australian Government Pub. Service, 1984. Octavo, color photos, text illustrations, fine in dust jacket.   Andrew Isles Natural History Books   55 - 1558   2016 $120

Flora of Australia. Volume 8.   Canberra: Australian Government Pub. Service, 1982. Octavo, text illustrations, slightly blemished dust jacket.   Andrew Isles Natural History Books   55 - 1550   2016 $80

Flora of Australia. Volume 18. Podostemaceae to Combretaceae.   Canberra: Australian Government Pub. Service, 1990. Octavo, text illustrations, fine in dust jacket.   Andrew Isles Natural History Books   55 - 1589   2016 $100

Flora of Australia. Volume 22. Rhizophorales to Celastrales.   Canberra: Australian Government Pub. Service, 1984. Octavo, text illustrations, very good in dust jacket.   Andrew Isles Natural History Books   55 - 1555   2016 $80

Flora of Australia. Volume 29. Solanaceae.   Canberra: Australian Government Pub. Service, 1982. Octavo, color photos, text illustrations, very good, dust jacket.   Andrew Isles Natural History Books   55 - 1485   2016 $80

Flora of Australia. Volume 35. Brunoniaceae, Goodeniaceae.   Canberra: Australian Government Pub. service, 1992. Octavo, text illustrations, fine in dust jacket.   Andrew Isles Natural History Books   55 - 1596   2016 $100

Flora of Australia. Volume 49. Oceanic Islands (part one).   Canberra: Australian Government Pub. Service, 1994. Octavo, dust jacket, text illustrations, fine in dust jacket.   Andrew Isles Natural History Books   55 - 1604   2016 $50

Flora of Australia. Volume 50. Oceanic Islands (part two).   Canberra: Australian Government Pub. Service, 1993. Octavo, text illustrations, fine in dust jacket.   Andrew Isles Natural History Books   55 - 1594   2016 $150

A Floral Fantasy.   London: Harper Bros., 1899. First edition, 4to, pictorial cloth, light cover soil, else fine in original pictorial dust jacket (soiled but generally very good), printed on french-fold paper, each page features fabulous full color illustration portraying a different humanized flower, text in calligraphy, engraved and printed by Edmund Evans.   Aleph-bet Books, Inc.   112 - 121   2016 $1250

Flora's Gala.   London: J. Harris, 1808. 4 x 5 inches, without wrappers, in later full leather binding with gilt design, leather slightly bowed, else fine, fine hand colored copperplate engravings, scarce.   Aleph-bet Books, Inc.   111 - 149   2016 $1200

Florus, Lucius Annaeus *Rerum Romanrum Epitome Interpretatione et Notis Illustravit anna tanaquilli Fabri Filia.* Paris: Apud Fredericum Leonard Typographum Regis, 1674. 4to., additional engraved frontispiece, woodcut printer's device to titlepage, woodcut head and tailpieces and initials through text, lightly toned towards top edge, faint staining to lower margins of first and last two gatherings, binding cracked between frontispiece and titlepage but all still sound, contemporary vellum boards, unusually rebacked in deliberately contrasting late 18th century black morocco, gilt spine and borders, gilt crest to head of spine, all edges gilt, endpapers replaced, spine rubbed, vellum bit darkened, boards little splayed, still very good.   Unsworths Antiquarian Booksellers   30 - 56   2016   £200

Flower, Robin *Love's Bitter-Sweet.* Dublin: Cuala Press, 1925. First edition, one of 500 copies, front and rear free endpapers, little browned, otherwise exceptionally nice. Bertram Rota Ltd.   February List 2016 - 20   2016   £180

Flowers from Shakespear's Garden. London: Cassell, 1906. 4to., cloth backed pictorial boards, one corner bumped, fine in dust jacket, printed on French-fold paper, ach leaf features magnificent full page color illustrations, rare in dust jacket.   Aleph-bet Books, Inc.   112 - 120   2016 $875

Floyd, Silas X. *The New Floyd's Flowers: Short Stories for Colored People Old and Young...* Washington: Austin Jenkins Co., 1922. Revised, frontispiece, heavily illustrated from photos and line drawings, red cloth illustrated in yellow and green, owner's name, hinges tender as always (glossy paper stock is too heavy for binding), thus very good. Between the Covers Rare Books   207 - 24   2016 $375

Fludd, Robert *Utriusque Cosmi Maioris Scilicet et Minoris Metaphysica... (bound with) Tractaus Secundus, De Naturae Simia seu Technica Macrocosmi Historia...* Oppenheim and Frankfurt: Johann Theodore de Bry, Hieronymus Galler (part I) and Kaspar Rotel (part II), 1617-1624. First edition, 2nd impression of part 1, second edition of part 2), 2 parts bound in one, folio, 2 engraved titlepages, approximately 268 text plates by Matthias Merian, five inserted plates in second part, folding plate at page 161 in part II with cellophane tape repairs at folds, some margins folded to protect them from being trimmed short in binding, thus text was preserved, minor marginal wormhole with few page repairs, marginal repair in 5H3, second leaf of index with natural tear, final printed leaf with two cellophane tape repairs at gutter, some leaves browned as usual, very good, early 20th century vellum backed marbled paper covered boards, maroon morocco, gilt stamped spine label, edges red, marbled endpapers, old owner's name, stamps of Bibliothek des Goetheanum.   Jeff Weber Rare Books   183 - 19   2016 $17,500

Foa, Edouard *After Big Game in Central Africa...* New York: St. Martin's Press, 1989. First edition, 8vo., original cloth and wrapper, photo portrait, 29 plates, 1 map, text illustrations, wrapper slightly creased to top edge, very good.   Sotheran's Hunting, Shooting & Fishing - 12 2016 £70

Foerster, Richard *The Hours.* N.P., 1993. Limited to 90 numbered copies, signed by author, , small 4to., stiff paper wrappers, cord tied, wood engraving on title by John DePol. Oak Knoll Books   310 - 30   2016 $100

Fogarty, Mary Beth Schmidt *The Stream of Life.* N.P.: Papierwerkstatt John Gerard, 1995. One of 8 unique variants, with initials of the artist painted in with the work, pulp paper images by Fogarty, folio, textured cream cloth over endboards, gilt title details on front, accordion fold, 8 leaves foled out to 88 inches.   Oak Knoll Books   27 - 18   2016 $1500

Fogelsonger, M. I. *The Secrets of the Liquor Merchant Revealed...* Washington: Mark Green & Bros., 1933. Scarce 1933 edition, 8vo., original blue cloth with slightly chipped dust jacket, scarce in dust jacket.   Sotheran's Piccadilly Notes - Summer 2015 - 132   2016   £298

Foglietta, Uberto *Ex Universa Historia Rerum Europae...* Naples: Giuseppe Cocchi, 1571. First edition, 4to., mid 18th century maroon morocco by Padeloup of Paris (engraved binder's label at lower margin of title), spine ornamented and lettered in gilt, triple fillets around boards in gilt, inner dentelles, gilt, gilt lined edges of boards, all edges gilt, marbled endpapers, woodcut printer's device on title, light wear to hinges and extremities, variable browning (as frequently the case), two prelim leaves remargined in 18th century, f. 94 with small hole, not touching any letter, 16th century inked out Italian ownership inscription.   Sotheran's Travel and Exploration - 253   2016   £1250

Folkard, Henry Coleman *The Wild Fowler: a Treatise on Ancient and Modern Wild-Fowling, Historical and Practical.* Piper, Stephenson and Spence, 1859. First edition, sometime rebound in half green morocco, gilt lettering to spine, marbled boards, marbled endpapers, frontispiece and 12 steel engraved plates, 5 woodcuts in text, spine sunned, very good, bookplate of Thomas Westwood, poet and angling bibliographer.   Sotheran's Hunting, Shooting & Fishing - 81   2016   £300

Follen, Charles *Deutsches Lesebuch fur Anfanger.* Cambridge: Cummings Hilliard, 1826. First edition, 12mo., original cloth backed boards, little stained, corners and spine extremities rubbed, paper label, one letter missing, uncut, very good copy despite binding wear and some very minor browning, in original state.   Howard S. Mott Inc.   265 - 47   2016 $350

Follett, Ken *The Modigliani Scandal.* Collins/Crime Club, 1976. Dust jacket wrapper little chipped and closed tear on top edge of upper panel, otherwise excellent.   I. D. Edrich   Crime - 2016   £85

Follett, Ken *Paper Money.* Collins/Crime Club, 1977. Excellent copy in slightly frayed dust jacket.   I. D. Edrich   Crime - 2016   £80

Follett, Ken *Triple.* New York: Arbor House, 1979. First American edition, fine in price clipped dust jacket.   Mordida Books   2015 - 002437   2016 $60

Folmsbee, Beulah *A Little History of the Horn-book.* Boston: The Horn Book, 1965. Third printing, half title, folding plate, illustrations, original color printed boards, fine.   Jarndyce Antiquarian Books   CCXV - 767   2016   £20

Foner, Philip S. *The Fur and Leather Workers Union.* Newark: Nordan, 1950. 8vo., illustrated with photos and facsimiles, very good in chipped and scuffed dust jacket, author's presentation.   Second Life Books, Inc.   196A - 569   2016 $45

Food for the Young. London: W. Darton Jun., 1818. First edition, small 12mo., frontispiece and 2 further plates, leaves little dusted, 20th century quarter red morocco, presentation inscription on leading blank "H.H. Broughton, a present from Mrs. Nightingale 1819", nice.   Jarndyce Antiquarian Books   CCXV - 687   2016   £95

Foord, James *A Key to the Lock.* London: for Harrison, 1788. First edition, disbound.   Dramatis Personae   119 - 54   2016 $65

Foote, Julia A. J. *A Brand Plucked from the Fire: an Autobiographical Sketch.* Cleveland: Printed for the author by W. F. Schneider, 1879. First edition, red-brown cloth stamped in black and gold, some mottling to boards, else near fine.   Between the Covers Rare Books   207 - 45   2016 $1000

Foote, Mary Hallock *The Valley Road.* Boston: Houghton Mifflin, 1915. First edition, foxing to page edges, offsetting to endpapers and owner name and date 1916 on front endpaper, else near fine in like example of scarce dust jacket.   Royal Books   49 - 97   2016 $500

Foote, Shelby *The Civil War. A Narrative.* New York: Random House, 1958. 1963. 1974. First editions, 3 volumes, complete set, small 4to., very good++ to near fine, in like dust jackets, volume 1 price clipped, volume 1 jacket missing half inch across top spine, no text affected, dampstain, mild sun spine, edge wear, volume 2 jacket price intact and correct for first printing ($12.50), small piece missing across top spine, no text affected, mild sun spine, closed tear rear, mild edge wear, tape verso, volume 3 dust jacket price intact and correct for first printing ($20.00), with mild soil, minimal edge wear, signed, rare thus.   By the Book, L. C.   45 - 3   2016 $2750

The Footman: His Duties and How to Perform Them. London: Houlston & sons, circa, 1870. Original brick brown cloth, blocked in gilt and black, ownership inscription and stamp of John Henry Webber on verso of leading f.e.p., very good.   Jarndyce Antiquarian Books   CCXV - 259   2016   £150

Forbes, David W. *Buniana.* San Francisco: Paul Markham Kahn, 1984. First edition, limited to 300 copies, brown paper wrappers, stitched, printed paper label to front wrapper, fine.   Tavistock Books   Getting Around - 44   2016 $95

Forbes, Henry O. *A Naturalist's Wanderings in the Eastern Archipelago, A Narrative of Travel and Exploration form 1878 to 1883.* London: Sampson Low, Marston, Searle & Rivington, 1885. octavo, chromolithograph frontispiece, text illustrations, publisher's decorated cloth, cracked hinges, otherwise bright, crisp copy.   Andrew Isles Natural History Books   55 - 16657   2016 $1450

Forbes, John *Sight-Seeing in Germany and the Tyrol in the Autumn of 1855.* New York: Smith Elder, 1856. First edition, 8vo., folding map, tinted frontispiece, original purple cloth, skillfully rebacked with new endpapers, spine faded.   J. & S. L. Bonham Antiquarian Booksellers   Europe 2016 - 3944   2016   £110

Ford, Charles Henri *Om Krishna III: Secret Haiku.* New York: Red Ozier Press, 1982. First edition, one of 155 copies signed by author and artist, 8vo., original iridescent gold linen, as new, drawings by Isamu Noguchi.   James S. Jaffe Rare Books   Occasional List: Winter 2016 - 15   2016 $1250

Ford, Charles Henri *Poems for Painters.* New York: View Editions, 1945. First edition, quarto, wrappers illustrated by Pavel Tchelitchew, this is copy number 24 of 500 copies, signed by author (of a total edition of 1500), near fine in stapled wrappers with some light soiling and modest age toning, inscribed by author for Djuna Barnes.   Between the Covers Rare Books   204 - 49   2016 $950

Ford, Charles Henri *View - Series IV No. 1.* New York: March, 1944. First edition, quarto, wrappers, cover design by Alexander Calder, covers rubbed and marked and creased at outer edges, stapled, rusted and covers detached, good.   Peter Ellis   112 - 427   2016   £20

Ford, Charles Henri *View - Series IV No. 3.* New York: View Inc., Oct., 1944. First edition, quarto, wrappers, near fine, magnificent cover design by Leger printed in red, black and yellow. Peter Ellis   112 - 239   2016   £75

Ford, Charles Henri *View - Series IV No. 4.* New York: December, 1944. First edition, quarto, wrappers, cover design by Esteban Frances, covers slightly rubbed and creased at edges, very good.   Peter Ellis   112 - 425   2016   £45

Ford, Charles Henri *View - Series V. No. 3.* New York: October, 1945. First edition, quarto, wrappers, cover edges just little faded and rubbed, very good.   Peter Ellis   112 - 423   2016   £45

Ford, Charles Henri *View - Series V No. 4.* New York: November, 1945. First edition, quarto, wrappers, cover design by Leon Kelly, covers little rubbed at spine, very good.   Peter Ellis   112 - 308   2016   £45

Ford, Charles Henri *View - Series V. No. 5.* New York: December, 1945. First edition, quarto, wrappers upper corner of first page creased, near fine.   Peter Ellis   112 - 424   2016   £65

Ford, Charles Henri *View. Volume VI Nos. 2-3.* New York: March-April, 1946. First edition, quarto, illustrations, wrappers, covers marked and creased, good.   Peter Ellis   112 - 59   2016   £35

Ford, Charles Henri *View - Volume VI. No. 3.* New York: View Inc., May, 1946. First edition, quarto, wrappers, cover design by Jean Helion, some creasing to cover edges, near fine. Peter Ellis   112 - 251   2016   £45

Ford, Charles Henri *View - Series VII No. 1.* New York: October, 1946. First edition, quarto, wrappers, covers lightly dusty and creased at edges, near fine.   Peter Ellis   112 - 426   2016   £45

Ford, George H. *Dickens and His Readers; Aspects of Novel-Criticism Since 1836.* Princeton: Princeton University Press for the University of Cincinnati, 1955. First edition, half title, plates, original pale green cloth, good copy, slightly faded and worn dust jacket.   Jarndyce Antiquarian Booksellers   CCXVIII - 1228   2016   £30

Ford, Hugh *Published in Paris - American and British Writers, Printers and Publishers in Paris 1920-1939.* London: Garnstone, 1975. First UK edition, 77 illustrations, spine just little creased, very good in very good dust jacket slightly creased at head and tail.   Peter Ellis   112 - 128   2016   £50

Ford, James L. *The Story of Du Barry.* New York: Stokes, 1902. Leslie Carter edition, 8vo., illustrations, bound in front is program for the Belasco production, bookplate, signed by Carter, 10 years later Belasco signed and dated page as well, owner's signature on flyleaf, purple cloth stamped in gilt, spine faded, cover little worn, else very good.   Second Life Books, Inc.   196A - 571   2016 $75

Ford, Julia Ellsworth *Imagina.* New York: Duffield, 1914. First edition, 4to., cloth, slight fading on rear cover else, fine, this copy inscribed by Ford to Sarah Latimore, Rackham bibliographer.   Aleph-bet Books, Inc.   111 - 371   2016 $950

Ford, Richard *Independence Day.* New York: Knopf, 1995. First edition, fine, in fine dust jacket, signed by author.   Bella Luna Books   2016 - j1828   2016 $66

Ford, Worthington Chauncey *George Washington.* New York: Goupil & Co. and Charles Scribner's Sons, 1900. One of 200 copies of Edition de Luxe, 267 x 203mm., 2 volumes, attractive green crushed morocco covers with two-line gilt frame, raised bands, gilt framed compartments and gilt titling, red morocco doublures surrounded by inch wide green morocco turn-ins with four gilt fillets, watered silk endleaves, top edges gilt, other edges untrimmed, 88 full page plates, as wll as 32 tailpieces, chapter initials in black and red, bookplate of William P. Olds laid in at front of each volume, large paper copy, hint of wear to joints and extremities, spines mildly faded to olive green (spine of second volume with just slightly irregular fading), still fine copy of this deluxe edition, morocco bindings solid and pleasing, text and plates virtually pristine.   Phillip J. Pirages   67 - 349   2016 $950

Fordyce, James *Sermons to Young Women in Two Volumes.* London: printed for A. Millar & T. Cadell, J. Dodsley & J. Payne, 1767. Fourth edition, 8vo., slight marking to titlepage in volume two, contemporary full lightly speckled calf, raised bands, compartments with double gilt verticle rules, red morocco labels, small chip to front board of volume I with old repair, signature of Renie Fabvi, very good, handsome copy.   Jarndyce Antiquarian Books   CCXV - 204   2016   £380

The Foreigners Guide; or a Necessary and Instructive Companion Both for the Foreigner and Native, in their Tour through the Cities of London and Westminster.   Joseph Pote, 1729. First edition, 8vo., contemporary panel calf.   J. & S. L. Bonham Antiquarian Booksellers   Europe 2016 - 10166   2016   £275

Fores's Sporting Notes and Sketches. London: Simpkin Marshall & Co., 1888. 8vo., 3 parts bound in 1, contemporary full brown calf, contrasting morocco lettering pieces to spine, decorative titlepage, illustrations, previous signature, binding somewhat rubbed, rear hinge starting at foot, very good.   Sotheran's   Hunting, Shooting & Fishing - 202   2016   £100

Forester, Cecil Scott   1899-1966   *The Hornblower Companion.* London: Michael Joseph, 1964. First edition, full page maps and border illustrations, 4to., original red cloth with ship illustration stamped in gilt to upper board against an inset black ground, backstrip lettered in gilt and slightly softened at tips, light foxing to top edge, original Blackwell's invoice laid in, dust jacket with toning to rear panel, very good.   Blackwell's Rare Books   B184 - 148   2016   £90

Forester, Cecil Scott   1899-1966   *The Hornblower Companion.* London: Michael Joseph, 1964. First edition, apparently first issue with blue endpapers, quarto, 30 maps and various black and white drawings by Samuel H. Bryant, laid in is publisher's publicity photo of author, signed by author, dated 1953, spine little bruised at tail, very good in like dust jacket slightly rubbed and creased at edges.   Peter Ellis   112 - 129   2016   £175

Forester, Cecil Scott   1899-1966   *Hornblower During the Crisis and Two Stories: Hornblower's Temptation and The last Encounter.* Boston: Little Brown and Co., 1980. First American edition, fine in fine dust jacket with tiny rubbed tear at foot, tight, fresh, unread copy.   Between the Covers Rare Books   208 - 21   2016 $150

Forester, Cecil Scott   1899-1966   *Poo-Poo and the Dragons.* London: Michael Joseph, 1942. First edition, 8vo., near fine, very good++ price clipped dust jacket with mild soil, scarce in jacket.   By the Book, L. C.   45 - 83   2016 $500

Forester, Cecil Scott   1899-1966   *To the Indies.* Boston: Little Brown, 1940. First edition, 8vo., signed by author, near fine in very good++ dust jacket with mild edge wear and soil.   By the Book, L. C.   45 - 64   2016 $500

Forhan, M. J.   *Salt Lake City. A Sketch of Utah's Wonderful Resources.* Chicago: Rand McNally & Co. for the Chamber of Commerce, Salt Lake City, AD, 1888. Very rare first edition, small 4to., original illustrated wrappers, illustrations in text, frayed corners of wrappers, little loss to spine, internally, apart from very light marginal browning, very good, letter on printed stationery by author presenting this publication, loosening inserted, bookplate and blindstamp of Franklin Institute Library, very good.   Sotheran's   Travel and Exploration - 59   2016   £198

A Form of Prayer and a New Collection of Psalms for the use of a Congregation of Protestant Dissenters in Liverpool. London: printed for the Society and sold by Chr. Henderson under the Royal exchange, London..., 1763. 8vo., ex-Wigan Public Lib., bookplate, first titlepage dusted with clear tape repair to leading edge, old ink splash to leading edge of book block, not intruding on to page surface, cloth backed boards of c. 1920, paper spine labels, knock to edge of back board, attribution in pencil has been alongside many of the psalms in the second part.   Jarndyce Antiquarian Booksellers   CCXVI - 368   2016   £150

Formey, Jean Henri Samuel   *Elementary Principles of the Belles Lettres.*   Glasgow: printed for Robert Urie, 1767. first Glasgow edition, minor soiling, 12mo., contemporary calf, joints cracked, good.   Blackwell's Rare Books   B184 - 44   2016   £600

Forrester, Alfred Henry   1804-1872   *Pictures Picked from the Pickwick Papers.*   London: Ackerman & Co., 1837. Original part, sewn as issued in original cream pictorial wrappers, containing 8 plates, little worn along spine and edges, old small chip, slight browning, fragile but sound copy.   Jarndyce Antiquarian Booksellers   CCXVIII - 123   2016   £35

Forster, Edward Morgan   1879-1970   *The Eternal Moment and Other Stories.*   Sidgwick & Jackson, 1928. First edition, crown 8vo., original maroon cloth, backstrip and front cover lettered and bordered in gilt, few tiny and faint foxspots to top edge, dust jacket with backstrip panel and borders of flaps very gently toned, very good.   Blackwell's Rare Books   B186 - 218   2016   £275

Forster, John   *The Life of Charles Dickens.*   London: Chapman and Hall, 1872-1874. volume I Twelfth edition, volume II 10th thousand, volume III First edition, 3 volumes, half titles, frontispieces and plates, illustrations, some light foxing, original maroon cloth, spines and front boards, lettered gilt and blocked in black, inner hinges strengthened with brown tape volume I, good plus.   Jarndyce Antiquarian Booksellers   CCXVIII - 1233   2016   £125

Forster, John   *The Life of Charles Dickens.*   London: Chapman and Hall, 1872-1874. First edition of volumes II and III, volume I fourth edition, 3 volumes, half titles frontispieces and plates, illustrations, original maroon cloth, spines and front boards lettered gilt and blocked in black, spines little faded, otherwise very good, bright set.   Jarndyce Antiquarian Booksellers   CCXVIII - 1232   2016   £165

Forster, John   *The Life of Charles Dickens.*   London: Chapman & Hall, 1873-1874. Volume I 13th edition, volume II 12th thousand, volume III 10th thousand, frontispiece, plates, illustrations, some occasional light foxing, contemporary half dark green morocco, marbled boards, bit rubbed, good sound.   Jarndyce Antiquarian Booksellers CCXVIII - 1234   2016   £110

Forster, John *Het leven van Ch. Dickens. (The Life of Charles Dickens.* Schiedam: H. A. M. Roelants, 1873-1874. First Dutch edition, 3 volumes half titles, frontispieces volume I and III, contemporary Continental brown cloth spines, brown pebble grained cloth boards, some slight rubbing, good plus.   Jarndyce Antiquarian Booksellers   CCXVIII - 1239   2016   £75

Forster, John *The Life of Charles Dickens.* London: Chapman & Hall, 1876. Illustrated Library edition, 2 volumes, half titles, frontispieces, illustrations, final ad leaf volume II, untrimmed in original green cloth, blocked in black, lettered gilt, very slight rubbing, very good.   Jarndyce Antiquarian Booksellers   CCXVIII - 1235   2016   £45

Forster, John *The Life of Charles Dickens.* London: Chapman & Hall, 1879. Household edition, 4to., frontispiece, vignette title, plates, illustrations, original green cloth, blocked and lettered in black and gilt, very good.   Jarndyce Antiquarian Booksellers   CCXVIII - 1236   2016   £35

Forster, John *The Life of Charles Dickens.* London: Cecil Palmer, 1928. Ley's edition, Half title, frontispiece, illustrations, original blue cloth, lettered gilt, little dulled, good plus.   Jarndyce Antiquarian Booksellers   CCXVIII - 1238   2016   £40

Forsyte, Charles, Pseud. *The Decoding of Edwin Drood.* London: Victor Gollancz, 1980. First edition, half title, original maroon cloth, spine lettered gilt, very good in dust jacket.   Jarndyce Antiquarian Booksellers   CCXVIII - 675   2016   £35

Forsyth, James *The Highlands of Central India...* London: Chapman and Hall, 1871. First edition, 8vo., full green morocco gilt binding identified as "J. S. 1952", page edges trimmed and gilt green marbled endpapers, very light intermittent foxing only, very good, handsome.   Any Amount of Books   2015 - C249   2016   £250

Fort, Paul *Le Livre Des Ballades.* Paris: H. Piazza, 1921. Limited to 1300 copies, this one of 300 with extra color plates, 4to., illustrations by Arthur Rackham, contemporary half leather, marbled paper covered boards with gilt title and decorations on spine, original stiff paper wrappers bound in, marbled endpapers, top edge gilt, other edges uncut, slipcase scuffed at spine edge, boards scuffed at spine edge, pencilled notes on rear free endpaper, original front stiff paper wrapper blue and tan design with Rackham illustration.   Oak Knoll Books   310 - 21 2016 $2500

Fortescue, Hugh, 3rd Earl of *Public Schools for the Middle Classes.* London: Longman Green, 1864. First edition, half title, original brown cloth, bookplate of Thomas Salt, very good.   Jarndyce Antiquarian Books   CCXV - 688   2016   £60

Fortunate Men, How they Made Money and Won Renown.... London: published for the proprietors by James Hogg, 1875. First edition, frontispiece, original purple cloth, bevelled boards, pictorially blocked in gilt, dulled and largely faded to brown, nice, scarce.   Jarndyce Antiquarian Booksellers   CCXVII - 6   2016   £120

Fosbroke, Thomas Dudley *Foreign Topography; or an Encyclopedick Account Alphabetically arranged....* London: J. B. Nichols, 1828. First edition, quarto, 11 plates, illustrations, contemporary full calf, spine little rubbed, there were 22 additional plates issued but not always bound in, bookplate of Duke of Portland.   J. & S. L. Bonham Antiquarian Booksellers   Voyages 2016 - 7712   2016   £120

Foss, Phillip *Somata.* Saint Paul: Bieler Press, 1982. Privately printed and limited to 150 numbered copies, signed by author and artist, Small 4to., stiff paper wrappers, cord-tied in Japanese manner, wraparound paper jacket, accompanied by 7 drawings, printed on dampened Gutenberg laid paper with japanese binding, with soft covers of tan handmade bark paper from Mexico, includes outer wrapper and endsheets, illustrations by Gaylord Schanilec.   Oak Knoll Books   310 - 81   2016 $110

Foster, Arnold, Mrs. *An English and Chinese Pocket Dictionary in the Mandarin Dialect.* Shanghai: Hong Kong: Yokohama: Singapore: Kelly & Walsh, 1903. 12mo., contemporary black half morocco over patterned cloth, front cover lettered gilt, errata, wear to spine and corners, very good and clean.   Sotheran's   Travel and Exploration - 123   2016   £148

Foster, John *An Essay on the Evils of Ignorance.* London: B. J. Holdsworth, 1820. First edition, half title, errata slip, final ad leaf, uncut, original drab boards, neatly rebacked, margins rubbed, slightly worn, front board little marked.   Jarndyce Antiquarian Books   CCXV - 690   2016   £75

Foster, Joseph *Oxford Men & Their Colleges.* Oxford: James Parker & Co., 1893. 2 volumes, folio, half titles, frontispiece, illustrations, plates, original blue cloth, dulled and rubbed, hinges cracking.   Jarndyce Antiquarian Books   CCXV - 887   2016   £50

Fothergill, John *An Innkeeper's Diary, Being the Spread Eagle Section of My Three Inns.* Oxford: Inky Parrot Press, 1987. One of 35 numbered copies printed on mould made paper and hand colored out of a total of 335 copies, 4to., original quarter green morocco and green paper covered boards, title gilt on spine, top edge gilt, illustrated endpapers, all handcolored, matching slipcase, original watercolor by Annie Newnham laid in as called for in this special edition, set on Monoytype Lasercomp at Oxford University Computing Service in 16 pt. Garamond, very scarce.   Oak Knoll Books   27 - 32   2016 $650

Fountain, Richard *Twelfth Century Monasticism in the West.* London: privately printed, 1967. 4to., professionally bound typescript of otherwise unpublished book, 24 maps and ground plans, plain dissertation style buckram with gilt lettering and rules to spine, very good, clean condition. Any Amount of Books   2015 - A83442   2016   £150

Four Toddles Animals. Springfield: McLaughlin, 1929. 4 McLaughlin shape books in original pictorial box, all fine, great color covers and black and whites inside, bound in brightly colored pictorial boards, scarce.   Aleph-bet Books, Inc.   111 - 421   2016 $400

Fourgeres, Gustave *Aux Sanctuaires Grees. Paques 1912.* privately printed by Chelles by A. Foucheaux, 1912. Extremely rare sole edition, number 68 of 130 copies, large folio, original printed wrappers (in color on front cover, both after watercolors by Mme. Brouardel), plates with tissue guards, title printed in red and blue, with initial leaf with text in red and blue and two photos printed in photogravure, map, 446 snapshots printed in photogravure, apart from original spot to title, fine in slightly worn, original patterned box with cloth ties.   Sotheran's   Travel and Exploration - 252   2016   £1995

Fournier, Annie *ABC De La Route.* Paris: Les Editions Sociales Francaises, 1960. 4to., pictorial boards, fine, each page has fantastic gravure photo by Robert Le Pajalec.   Aleph-bet Books, Inc.   111 - 10   2016 $375

Fowler, Gene *Schnozzola: the Story of Jimmy Durante.* New York: Viking, 1951. First edition, 8vo., presentation from Durante, illustrations, very good in somewhat scuffed and chipped dust jacket.   Second Life Books, Inc.   196A - 574   2016 $85

Fowler, Gene *Timber Line. A Story of Bonfils and Tammen.* New York: Covici Friede, 1933. First edition, 2 portraits, tan cloth, spine slightly darkened, spine darkening to endpapers at gutter, owner's signature, overall fine, very scarce.   Argonaut Book Shop   Biography 2015 - 7583   2016 $150

Fowles, John *The Aristos: a Self Portrait in Ideas.* Boston: Little Brown, 1964. Very near fine in close ot near fine dust jacket with couple of faint small spots to spine as well as a tiny bit of wear at spine ends, signed and warmly inscribed by Fowles, uncommon signed.   Jeff Hirsch Books   Holiday List 2015 - 37   2016 $400

Fowles, John *The Collector.* London: Jonathan Cape, 1963. First edition, fine in about fine, first issue dust jacket (without reviews), with couple of minute rub marks.   Between the Covers Rare Books   204 - 50   2016 $950

Fowles, John *Poems.* New York: Ecco Press, 1973. First edition, octavo, fine in fine dust jacket.   Peter Ellis   112 - 134   2016   £75

Fox-Davies, A. C. *The Book of Public Speaking.* Caxton Publishing, 1913. 5 volumes, all published, original cloth, gilt decorations and lettering, all volumes very good.   I. D. Edrich   Winston Spencer Churchill - 2016   £60

Fox, Charles *Education Psychology: Its Problems and Methods.* London: Kegan Paul, 1930. Second edition, 2nd impression, half title, 20 page catalog (1932), original dark blue cloth, Foyles bookseller's label on leading f.e.p., very good.   Jarndyce Antiquarian Books   CCXV - 693   2016   £25

Fox, Jane *The Bowling Ballers.* San Diego: Greenleaf Classics/Heatherpool press, 1977. First edition, paperback original illustrated wrappers, fine, unread copy, rare.   Between the Covers Rare Books   208 - 73   2016 $200

Fox, John *The Little Shepherd of Kingdom Come.* New York: Charles Scribner's, 1931. Limited to 500 numbered copies signed by Wyeth, large 8vo., quarter vellum, blue cloth, top edge gilt, as new in original glassine in publisher's blue box (slight tip rubbing at one corner of box else fine), 16 mounted color illustrations by N. C. Wyeth.   Aleph-bet Books, Inc.   111 - 495   2016 $3850

Foxe, Jeffrey Jay *The Maya Textile Tradition.* New York: Abrams, 1997. First edition, 4to., cloth, lovely illustrations in color and black and white, fine in dust jacket which has couple of indentation scratches on front and back panels which are seen against the light, signed by author, very scarce thus.   Gene W. Baade, Books on the West   2015 - M1004   2016 $150

Francais-Primo, Jean *Frigoulet au Pays des Chiffres.* Paris: Editions Excelsior, 1933. Large 4to., cloth backed pictorial boards slightly toned, tips rubbed, very good.   Aleph-bet Books, Inc.   112 - 359   2016 $500

Francatelli, Charles Elme *A Plain Cookery Book for the Working Classes.* London: George Routledge & Sons, circa, 1869. New edition, slightly later dark blue binders cloth, slightly rubbed, very good.   Jarndyce Antiquarian Books   CCXV - 295   2016   £125

France, Anatole *Filles et Garcons.* Paris: Hachette, n.d. circa, 1910. 12 lovely color plates plus numerous black and whites in text by M. Boutet De Monvel, yellow glazed pictorial boards, cloth spine, some mild cover soil, else very good, clean,.   Aleph-bet Books, Inc.   112 - 66   2016 $125

France, Anatole *Girls and Boys.* New York: Duffield, 1913. First edition in English, 4to., cloth backed boards, corners worn, covers lightly soiled, very good, 12 color plates, illustrations in text, by Boutet De Monvel, quite scarce edition.   Aleph-bet Books, Inc.   111 - 53   2016 $300

France, Anatole *Our Children and Girls and Boys.* New York: Duffield, 1931. 4to., red cloth, fine in slightly worn, very good+ dust jacket, 4 color plates and many black and whites by M. Boutet De Monvel.   Aleph-bet Books, Inc.   112 - 67   2016 $250

Francesco D'Assisi, Saint 1886-1926 *Un Mazzetto Scelto di Certi Fioretti. (Little Flowers).* Chelsea: Ashendene Press, 1904. One of 150 copies on paper and 25 on vellum, 300 x 220mm., original holland backed blue paper boards, titling on upper board and on paper spine label, with 10 one- and two-column woodcut illustrations drawn by Charles Gere and engraved by W. H. Hooper, chapter headings and initials printed in red, initials designed by Graily Hewitt, minor soiling to covers and spine, internally pristine.   Phillip J. Pirages   67 - 12   2016 $2800

Francesco D'Assisi, Saint 1886-1926 *I Fioretti Del glorioso Poverello Di Cristo S. Francesco Di Assisi. (Little flowers).* Chelsea: Ashendene Press, 1922. One of 200 paper copies for sale of 240 printed (and 12 on vellum), 225 x 156mm., original flexible vellum, green silk ties, gilt lettering on spine, edges untrimmed, printer's device and 53 woodcuts in text, printed in black, blue and red, initials in red or blue designed by Graily Hewitt, laid in at front an inked autograph note on personal note card in its original autograph envelope from C. H. St. John Hornby to London bookseller James S Bain, vellum with naturally occurring variations in color, otherwise very fine, binding unworn and text entirely clean, fresh and smooth.   Phillip J. Pirages   67 - 11   2016 $1250

Franchere, G. *Relation d'un voyage a La Cote Du nord-Quest De L'Amerique Septentrionale dans les Annees 1810, 11, 12, 13 et 14.* Pasteur, 1820. First edition, 8vo., contemporary tree sheep, rebacked using original spine, some loss at top and base, small sliver in centre of spine, some waterstaining to prelims, duplicate copy from the famous Edward Everett Ayer Collection, Newberry Library, Chicago.   J. & S. L. Bonham Antiquarian Booksellers   America 2016 - 10232   2016   £5500

Francis, Dick 1920- *Blood Sport.* London: Michael Joseph, 1967. First edition, 8vo., original cloth with price clipped dust jacket little rubbed and chipped, otherwise very good.   Sotheran's   Piccadilly Notes - Summer 2015 - 137   2016   £248

Francis, Dick 1920- *Come to Grief.* London: Michael Joseph, 1995. First edition, very fine in dust jacket.   Mordida Books   2015 - 010402   2016 $65

Francis, Dick 1920- *Knock Down.* London: Michael Joseph, 1974. First British edition, fine, in near fine dust jacket, light edgewear, small stain on verso not visibile on outside of jacket.   Bella Luna Books   2016 - t5498   2016 $66

Francis, Dick 1920- *Odds Against.* London: M. Joseph, 1965. Very small rub mark on upper case and equally small light stain on front endpaper, still very good.   I. D. Edrich   Crime - 2016   £28

Francis, Dick 1920- *Reflex.* London: M. Joseph, 1979. Very good in like dust jacket, personal inscription from author.   I. D. Edrich   Crime - 2016   £40

Francis, Dick 1920- *The Sport of Queens.* London: Michael Joseph, 1957. First edition, color printed frontispiece, numerous monochrome plates, 8vo., original blue cloth, backstrip lettered gilt, very slight lean to spine, faint browning to endpapers and tiny contemporary date stamp to flyleaf, dust jacket with gentle creasing at head, very good, signed by author, scarce thus.   Blackwell's Rare Books   B184 - 150   2016   £400

Francis, Dick 1920- *Under Orders.* London: Michael Joseph, 2006. First edition, very fine in dust jacket.   Mordida Books   2015 - 011894   2016 $65

Francis, Robert *The Face Against Glass.* Amherst: by the author, 1950. First edition, inscribed by author May 2 1960 for William Meredith, near fine, printed wrappers.   Charles Agvent   William Meredith - 30   2016 $60

Frank Russell, or, Living for an Object. London: Knight & Son circa, 1865. Sixth thousand, color frontispiece, additional engraved title and 2 plates, 6 pages ads, original red wavy grained cloth, slightly dulled, binding little weak in places, nice.   Jarndyce Antiquarian Books   CCXV - 206   2016   £40

Frank, Robert *Les Americains.* Paris: Encyclopedie Essentielle, 1958. First edition, oblong 8vo., original laminated boards after design by Saul Steinberg, very fine, none of the usual fading or wear.   James S. Jaffe Rare Books   Occasional List: Winter 2016 - 112   2016 $5000

Frank, Robert *The Americans.* New York: Grove Press, 1959. First American edition, signed by author, photographs, oblong quarto, original black cloth, original dust jacket, book fine, dust jacket price clipped with some edgewear, exceptionally good.   Manhattan Rare Book Company   2016 - 1686   2016 $12,500

Frank, Robert *The Americans.* New York: Grove Press, 1959. First edition, oblong 8vo., very good+ with owner's inscription in very good, price clipped dust jacket with 4 small nicks and short tears on front panel, one small chip and short tears on rear panel, shallow chipping and very light paper loss at spine ends, affecting no type, very presentable copy.   Beasley Books   2015 - 2016 $2500

Franklin, Benjamin 1706-1790 *America's Big Ben.* New York: privately printed, 1963. Small 8vo., woodcuts in dark green and brown by John De Pol, orange paper over boards reverse printed in black, cover little insect nibbled, otherwise very good, tight copy.   Second Life Books, Inc.   197 - 119   2016 $45

Franklin, Benjamin 1706-1790 *The Art of Virtue.* New York: privately printed, 1955. Small 8vo., 2 engravings by John De Pol, rose paper over boards stamped in gilt, cover little scuffed, endpapers little stained, else very good, tight copy.   Second Life Books, Inc.   197 - 120   2016 $45

Franklin, Benjamin 1706-1790 *Experiments and Observations on Electricity Made at Philadelphia in America....to which are added Letters and Papers on Philosophical Subjects.* London: For F. Newbery, 1774. 4to., 7 engraved plates, several woodcut text illustrations, lacks half title, contemporary marbled paper covered boards, calf spine, very skillfully rebacked in period style later endpapers, occasional foxing of both text and plates, some offsetting from few plates, light stains on H3-4 and 2M3-4, withal very good.   Joseph J. Felcone, Inc.   Books from Five Centuries: a Miscellany - 63   2016 $8500

Franklin, Benjamin 1706-1790 *My Dear Girl.* New York: privately printed, 1977. Small 8vo., pink paper over boards, stamped in gilt, wood engravings by John De Pol, cover very slightly faded at upper edge of front, otherwise near fine.   Second Life Books, Inc.   197 - 123   2016 $45

Franklin, Benjamin 1706-1790 *Printing Week Library of Benjamin Franklin Keepsakes.* New York: privately printed, 1953-1982. Large 12mo., 30 volumes, complete set, all paper covered boards with some quarter leather and some patterned boards, variously paginated, this set belonged to Ben Lieberman, inscribed to him by designer, A. Burton Carnes.   Oak Knoll Books   310 - 31   2016 $350

Franklin, Benjamin 1706-1790 *The Silence Dogood Letters.* New York: privately printed, 1968. Small 8vo., wood engravings in tan by John De Pol, tan paper stamped in gilt, cover slightly scuffed, otherwise nice.   Second Life Books, Inc.   197 - 124   2016 $40

Franklin, Benjamin 1706-1790 *The Way to Wealth.* Gillingham: E. Neave, circa, 1810. Original blue paper wrappers, sewn as issued, very good, 12 pages.   Jarndyce Antiquarian Booksellers   CCXVII - 99   2016   £150

Franklin, Benjamin 1706-1790 *What Good is a Newborn Baby?* New York: privately printed, 1964. Small 8vo., woodcuts in rose and green by John De Pol, rose paper over boards stamped in gilt, covr very slightly faded at spine, nice.   Second Life Books, Inc.   197 - 125   2016 $45

Franklin, Colin *Fond of Printing. Gordon Graig (sic) as Typographer & Illustrator.* San Francisco: Book Club of California, 1980. First edition, limited to 450 copies, 12mo., 15 illustrations, some printed on colored paper, cloth backed decorated boards, gilt lettered spine, very fine.   Argonaut Book Shop   Private Press 2015 - 2400   2016 $45

Franklin, Colin *The Mystique of Vellum.* Boston: printed at the Stinehour Press for Anne and David Bromer, 1984. One of 13 copies printed on vellum and 225 on paper, 305 x 229mm., four blank vellum leaves at front and three at back, errata slip in original envelope, laid in, hand bound by Eleanore Ramsey and Janice Schopfer in full burgundy morocco, covers with handsome central panel stamped in blind and titled in gilt, gray silk doublures, gray suede and papers, publisher's fine matching suede endpapers, publisher's fine matching suede lined morocco drop back box, front cover repeating book's design, fine large woodcut on title, delicate woodcut headpiece on contents page, both cuts showing Medieval scribe at work, six highly burnished raised gold initials painted by Thomas Ingmire, printed in russet gray and black, box with small areas of mino discoloration, otherwise mint.   Phillip J. Pirages   67 - 338   2016 $7500

Franquet De Frangueville, Sophia Matilda Palmer, Countess *Mrs. Penicott's Lodger and Other Stories.* London: Macmillan & Co., 1887. Half title, original pale blue cloth, blocked and lettered in red, spine lettered gilt, spine faded, otherwise very good, signed by author "Connaught House" and bookplate of Grosvenor Woods.   Jarndyce Antiquarian Booksellers   CCXVII - 211   2016   £75

Fraser, Antonia *Cool Repentance.* London: Weidenfeld & Nicholson, 1982. very good copy in like dust jacket, loosely inserted invitation card from author presentation from author for Julian (Jebb).   I. D. Edrich   Crime - 2016   £30

Fraser, Antonia *Oxford Blood.* London: Weidenfeld & Nicholson, 1985. First edition, usual toning to pages, 8vo., original terra cotta boards, backstrip lettered gilt, ownership inscription to flyleaf, dust jacket with owner's shelfmark to front flap, very good.   Blackwell's Rare Books   B184 - 207   2016   £30

Fraser, Claud Lovat 1890-1921 *Characters from Dickens.* London: T. C. and E. C. Jack, 1924. Limited edition, no. 60 of 250 copies, 4to., illustrations, original beige wrappers, color illustrations, very good.   Jarndyce Antiquarian Booksellers   CCXVIII - 739   2016   £120

Fraser, George MacDonald *Flash for Freedom.* London: Barrie & Jenkins, 1971. First edition, 8vo., original red boards, backstrip lettered in silver, endpaper maps, dust jacket, slightly bumped at spine, near fine.   Blackwell's Rare Books   B184 - 151   2016   £150

Fraser, George MacDonald *Flashman' Lady.* London: Barrie & Jenkins, 1977. First edition, 8vo. original red boards, backstrip lettered in silver, endpaper maps, dust jacket, near fine.   Blackwell's Rare Books   B184 - 152   2016   £150

Fraser, James A. *Gretna Green a History of Douglastown, New Brunswick, Canada, 17830-1900.* Miramichi Historical Society, 1969. 8vo. card covers, photo illustrations, very good.   Schooner Books Ltd.   115 - 35   2016 $45

Fraser, James A. *A History of Caton's Island.* Chatham: Miramichi Historical Society, Feb. 15, 1968. First printing, limited to 500 copies, this #2, felt covers, small 8vo., 1 map and 11 black and white photo illustrations, very good, author's presentation inscription to Dr Louise Manny.   Schooner Books Ltd.   115 - 32   2016 $55

The Frauds and Abuses of the Coal-Dealers Detected and Exposed: in a Letter to an Alderman of London. London: M. Cooper, 1749. Third edition, 8vo., wanting half title, recently well bound in cloth lettered in gilt, some minor soiling but stil good copy.   John Drury Rare Books   2015 - 20772   2016 $306

Frazer, J. G. *The Belief in Immortality and the Worship of the Dead.* London: Macmillan and Co., 1913. 1922. 1924. First editions (volume 1 second impression), 3 volumes, 8vo., very bright and clean copy, unopened, green publisher's cloth, gilt title to spines, spine little darkened, endcaps creased, top edge dusty, endpapers toned still very good, few neat notes pencilled on f.f.e.p. volume 1.   Unsworths Antiquarian Booksellers   30 - 57   2016   £400

Frazier, Charles *Thirteen Moons.* New York: Random House, 2006. First edition, fine in fine pictorial slipcase, signed and numbered by author.   Bella Luna Books   2016 - t8090   2016 $125

Frederick, Charles *Foxhunting.* London: Seeley Service Co., 1930. First edition, 8vo., original gilt cloth, 4 color plates, 65 other illustrations, previous owner's bookplate and signature, few scratches to front of binding, very good.   Sotheran's Hunting, Shooting & Fishing - 36   2016   £80

Frederick, J. George *Long Island Seafood Cook Book.* New York: Business Course, 1939. First edition, octavo, fine in just about fine dust jacket, inscribed by Frederick for Charles Paoly, Sea Isle Hotel, Miami Beach, beautiful copy.   Between the Covers Rare Books   204 - 33   2016 $800

Fredericton Art Club *25 Years "To Promote Art" by the Fredericton Art Club 1936-1961.* Fredericton: 1963. Card covers stapled at spine, 6 x 9 inches, black and white photo illustrations, fine.   Schooner Books Ltd.   115 - 39   2016 $45

Freedman, Russell G. *Wendell Berry, a Bibliography.* Lexington: University of Kentucky Libraries, Occasional Paper No. 12, 1998. First edition, one of 50 copies bound in cloth and signed by author and Wendell Berry, illustrations.   Second Life Books, Inc.   196A - 150   2016 $150

Freeling, Arthur *A Father's Recollections...* London: Houlston & Stoneman, 1847. First edition, 16mo., half title, frontispiece and additional engraved title, plates damp-stained, occasional pencil markings, ink notes on leading endpapers, original red moire cloth, rubbed at tail of spine.   Jarndyce Antiquarian Books   CCXV - 209   2016   £35

Freeling, Arthur *The Gentleman's Pocket-Book of Etiquette.* Liverpool: Henry Lacey, 1838. Sixth edition, 16mo., half title, engraved title, 8 pages ads, original maroon cloth, slightly rubbed, largely faded to brown, slightly marked by damp, but nice, attractive copy, all edges gilt.   Jarndyce Antiquarian Books   CCXV - 207   2016   £125

Freeling, Arthur *The Gentleman's Pocket-Book of Etiquette.* Liverpool: Henry Lacey, 1838. Eighth edition, 16mo., half title, engraved title, 8 pages ads, original brown cloth, all edges gilt, very good.   Jarndyce Antiquarian Books   CCXV - 208   2016   £110

Freeling, Nicolas *Crime and Metaphysics.* Helsinki: Eurographica, 1990. First edition, 50/350 copies signed and dated by author, printed on Magnani Michelangelo paper, 8vo., original wrappers, edges untrimmed, printed dust jacket with small faint mark at head of backstrip panel, near fine.   Blackwell's Rare Books   B184 - 153   2016   £70

Freeman, Bud *"You Don't Look Like a Musician".* Detroit: Balamp, 1974. First printing, 8vo., author's presentation, paper over boards, titlepage appears to have been miscollated on verso with copyright page as recto, edges of cover very slightly scuffed, otherwise nice in chipped and somewhat soiled dust jacket.   Second Life Books, Inc.   196A - 580   2016 $75

Freeman, Don *Don Freeman's Newsstand. Volume I No. 1 New Series.* April, 1955. 4to., spiral bound, stain on rear cover, very good+, 8 full page and 1 double page woodcuts printed on glossy paper, laid in is inscribed large drawing of Corduroy.   Aleph-bet Books, Inc.   112 - 204 2016 $325

Freeman, Don *Don Freeman's Newsstand. Volume I No. 2 Series III.* n.d., 1945? 4to., spiral bound, fine, laid in is an inscribed large self portrait of Freeman with tiny Mouse sitting on his head, scarce.   Aleph-bet Books, Inc.   112 - 205   2016 $325

Freeman, Don *The Guard Mouse.* New York: Viking Press, 1967. First edition, 4to., pictorial cloth, fine in dust jacket with some archival repair on verso lightly soiled, very good, laid in is charming large 2 color original drawing of guard mouse bone on pictorial greeting card designed by Freeman.   Aleph-bet Books, Inc.   112 - 201   2016 $400

Freeman, Don *Mop Top.* New York: Viking, 1955. First edition, cloth, light cover soil very good+, illustrations in color on every page by Freeman, this copy inscribed by Freeman with large half page drawing.   Aleph-bet Books, Inc.   112 - 203   2016 $225

Freeman, Don *Tilly Witch.* New York: Viking, 1969. 4to., pictorial cloth, slightest bit of cover soil, else fine in dust jacket (price clipped), some fraying, rubbing with very good dust jacket, illustrations in color on every page by Freeman, laid in is large drawing of Corduroy holding a Banner inscribed br Freeman, scarcre.   Aleph-bet Books, Inc.   112 - 202   2016 $475

Freeman, Edward A. *Some Impressions of the United States.* London: Longmans, Green and Co., 1883. 8vo., several gatherings of blanks to rear, clean and bright within, text block parting a little, but sound, half green morocco, gilt spine, marbled paper covered boards, patterned endpapers, cloth hinges, edges sprinkled brown, spine bit darkened, edges little rubbed, very good, catalog entry pasted to f.f.e.p.   Unsworths Antiquarian Booksellers   30 - 58   2016   £30

Freeman, G. J. *Sketches in Wales or a Diary of Three Walking Excursions in that Principality.* London: Longman, Rees Orme, Brown and Green, 1826. First edition, 8vo., full claret leather with attractive gilt tooling, corners and edges lightly bumped and worn, spine has title and lots of gilt tooling, edges lightly bumped internally, marbled endpapers, Duke of Essex bookplate, bookplate of Charles Arthur Wynne Finch, 15 black and white plates.   Simon Finch   2015 - 004316   2016 $296

Freeman, Gage Earle *Five Christmas Poems.* London: Longman and Roberts, 1860. First edition, half title, 24 page catalog, September 1859, original green cloth by Westleys, boards blocked in blind, front board blocked and lettered gilt, inscribed "From the author", very good, crisp copy.   Jarndyce Antiquarian Booksellers   CCXVII - 100   2016   £125

Freeman, James W. *Prose and Poetry of the Live Stock Industry of the United States.* New York: Antiquarian Press, 1959. Facsimile repirnt of the very rare 1905 first edition, limited to 550 copies, numerous illustrations from photos, old prints, etc., thick quarto, half cowhide and gilt stamped buckram, spine lettered gilt, very fine, publisher's slipcase.   Argonaut Book Shop   Literature 2015 - 6135   2016 $350

Freeman, Kathleen *Ancilla to the Pre-Socratic Philosophers.* Oxford: Basil Blackwell, 1956. First edition, 8vo., green cloth, gilt lettered to spine, edges dusted, very good, light green dust jacket, now bit grubby, fraying to top of spine, one 2cm. closed tear to front, price clipped, shelf-wear, good.   Unsworths Antiquarian Booksellers Ltd.   E05 - 27   2016   £20

Freeman, Kathleen *The Work and Life of Solon...* Cardiff: University of Wales, 1926. First edition, 8vo., pages unopened, very good in scarce dust jacket which is very good, slightly darkened at spine and bit creased at edges, presentation from author inscribed for Lilian M. C. Clopet from Kathleen Freeman July 14th 1926.   Peter Ellis   112 - 136   2016   £125

Freeman, Mary E. Wilkins *Jerome a Poor Man.* New York: Harper, 1897. First edition, small 8vo., publisher's cloth, moderate external wear, good copy, signed by author, illustrations, little waterstain at end.   Second Life Books, Inc.   196A - 579   2016 $75

Freeman, R. Austin *Dr. Thorndyke Investigates.* London: London University Press, 1930. Not a first edition, original blue cloth, little worn and marked but contents clean and tight.   I. D. Edrich   Crime - 2016   £20

Freemasons. Grand Lodge of Pennsylvania *Ahiman Rezon Abridged and Digested as a Help to All that Are or Would be Free and Accepted Masons.*   Philadelphia: Hall and Sellers, 1783. First American edition, engraved frontispiece, contemporary sheep, skillfully rebacked in period style, some overall soiling and dampstaining, free endpaper and frontispiece browned at edges and neatly guarded, small early ownership stamp of I. Morrell on first two leaves, good.   Joseph J. Felcone, Inc.   Books from Five Centuries: a Miscellany - 66   2016 $1800

Frees, Harry *The Pot of Gold at Rainbow's End.* Chicago: Manning, 1932. 4to., stiff pictorial card covers slightly dusty, else fine, large photos on every page, nice copy, very scarce.   Aleph-bet Books, Inc.   111 - 338   2016 $250

Freiburg Im Breisgau *Nuewe Stattrechten und Statuten der Statt Fryburg im Pryszgow Gelegen.* Basle: Adam Petri, 1520. Folio, 2 large Holbein woodcuts, modern full calf, light old inkstain in bottom blank margin of two leaves, scattered foxing on few leaves, else clean, very attractive copy with wide margins.   Joseph J. Felcone, Inc.   Books from Five Centuries: a Miscellany - 67   2016 $5500

Freitas, Bernardino Jose De Senna *Uma Viagem a Valle das Furnas na Ilha de S. Miguel em Junho de 1840.* Lisboa: 1845. First edition, folio, 3 lithographed plates, several vignette illustrations in text, later half mottled calf, plates foxed, largely in margins, extremities of binding rubbed, accompanied by fine 1591 engravings, extracted from De Bry's Grand Voyages.   Joseph J. Felcone, Inc.   Books from Five Centuries: a Miscellany - 68   2016 $1200

Freke, William *Select Essays Tending to the Universal Reformation of Learning, Concluded with the Art of War...* printed for Tho. Minors, 1693. First edition, without initial blank, A6 and 7 dust soiled in fore-margin, latter with small hole, neither affecting text, these leaves over-glued in inner margin, 8vo., contemporary panelled calf, rebacked a little crudely, preserving original spine, front joint now cracking again, sound.   Blackwell's Rare Books   B186 - 61   2016   £600

Fremont, Jessie Benton *Letters of Jessie Benton Fremont.* Urbana: University of Illinois Press, 1993. First edition, numerous photos, green cloth, very fine with pictorial dust jacket.   Argonaut Book Shop   Biography 2015 - 7403   2016 $40

Fremont, John Charles *Narrative of the Exploring Expedition to the Rocky Mountains.* London: Wiley and Putnam, 1864. First UK edition, 8vo., folding map, 4 lithographic plates, later 19th century green polished half calf, joints rubbed, fine, crisp copy.   J. & S. L. Bonham Antiquarian Booksellers   America 2016 - 9354   2016   £750

Fremont, John Charles *Report of the Exploring Expedition to the Rocky Mountains in the Year 1842 and to Oregon and North California in the Years 1843-'44.* Washington: Blair and Rives, 1845. House edition, 22 plates, 5 maps, later, probably 19th century binding that has been restored with new hinges, spine quite faded but title still barely legible, large folding map bound into center of book but is now loose, some browning and minor separations, overall better than usually seen, very nice.   Dumont Maps and Books   134 - 34   2016 $2500

French, Frederick *Library of Frederick W. French.* Boston: C. F. Libbie & Co., 1901. 8vo., stiff paper wrappers bound in half cloth, marbled paper covered boards, illustrations, including foldouts, some realized prices, price list and news clippings tipped in, spine slightly faded and with some wear along edges and top of front hinge, bookplate.   Oak Knoll Books   310 - 63   2016 $350

French, Tana *I the Woods.* New York: Viking, 2007. First edition, book has bumped spine ends and lightly bmped corners, fine- in fine dust jacket.   Ken Hebenstreit, Bookseller   2016 - 2016 $45

Frere, Mary *Old Deccan Days; or Hindoo Fairy Legends; Current in Soutehrn India.* London: John Murray, 1868. First edition, 8vo., 4 colored plates, many further illustrations in text, burgundy publisher's cloth, gilt title to spine, gilt stamped illustrations of Ganesh to upper board, endcaps and joints worn, slight loss to head of upper joint little cracked, still very good, 1920's news clipping on subject of folkloric stories for children passed to prelim blank, ownership inscription of Anna M. Orde, 1868 to titlepage, with "Burne-Jones 1880' ms. to titlepage (not the handwriting of the artist, but according to old bookseller's note, from his library).   Unsworths Antiquarian Booksellers   30 - 59   2016   £40

Freud, Sigmund   1856-1939 *An Auto-biographical Study.* London: Hogarth Press, 1950. Fifth impression, 8vo., original green cloth and dust jacket, some sunning to edges of dust jacket, otherwise near fine.   Sotheran's   Piccadilly Notes - Summer 2015 - 139   2016   £25

Freud, Sigmund   1856-1939 *Gesammelte Schriften.* Vienna: Internationaler Psychoanalytischer verlag, 1925. First edition, 11 volumes, also includes the uniform volume XII, volume V has one hinge going, very tender joints.   Beasley Books   2015 - 2016 $1200

Freud, Tom Seidmann *Das Zauberboot.* Berlin: Stuffer, 1930. 4to., cloth backed pictorial boards, light cover soil and few internal spots, else very good-fine and complete, very rare moveable book.   Aleph-bet Books, Inc.   111 - 188   2016 $2000

Freund, Gisele *Gisele Freund, Photographer.* New York: Harry n. Abrams, 1985. First English edition, quarto, numerous photos in black and white and color, gilt lettered tan cloth, very fine in dust jacket.   Argonaut Book Shop   Photography 2015 - 1728   2016 $50

Freundlich, Erwin *The Foundations of Einstein's Theory of Gravitation.* Cambridge: University Press, 1920. First English edition, 8vo., original printed wrappers, disbound.   M & S Rare Books, Inc.   99 - 84   2016 $200

Freygang, F. K. *Letters from the Caucasus and Georgia...* London: John Murray, 1823. First edition, 8vo., folding map, frontispiece, 2 plates, some occasional foxing including to the 2 plates, contemporary brown half calf, gilt spine and raised bands, joint split but repaired.   J. & S. L. Bonham Antiquarian Booksellers   Europe 2016 - 10216   2016   £480

Fridlender, Y. V. *Charles Dickens: Bibliografia...* Moskva: Pub. House of All-Union Palace of Books, 1962. First edition, frontispiece, original paper covered stiff boards, cloth spine, little rubbed, good plus, presentation from co-author I. Katarskii, to Sir John Greaves.   Jarndyce Antiquarian Booksellers   CCXVIII - 1499   2016   £25

Friedlander, Lee *Cherry Blossom Time in Japan.* New York: Haywire, 1986. First edition, large oblong folio, embossed silk cloth in embossed cloth slipcase, engraved titlepage, copy number 28 of 50 copies, there were also lettered artist's copies, 25 exquisitely printed gravure images, each numbered and signed by artist, slightest sunning to delicate pink silk still easily fine.   Royal Books   49 - 2   2016 $40,000

Friedlander, Lee *Factory Valleys: Ohio and Pennsylvania.* New York: Callaway Editions, 1982. First edition, simultaneous paperback issue, 62 duotones, very near fine in wrappers that are bright and clean, signed by author, very fresh copy.   Jeff Hirsch Books   E-List 80 - 2016 $300

Friedman, Kinky *A Case of Lone Star.* New York: Morrow, 1987. First edition, very fine in dust jacket.   Mordida Books   2015 - 010507   2016 $65

Friel, Brian *Molly Sweeney.* Oldcastle Ireland: Gallery Press, 1994. First edition, 8vo., author's signature on title, black paper over boards, near fine in very slightly scuffed dust jacket.   Second Life Books, Inc.   197 - 128   2016 $75

Friendship's Offering and Winter's Wreath: a Christmas and New Year's present for 1837. Edinburgh: W. H. Harrison, Smith, Elder and Co., 1837. Engraved frontispiece and title, plates, contemporary full dark maroon morocco, elaborately gilt spine, borders and dentelles, dark pink moire endpapers with clasp, very good in attractive binding.   Jarndyce Antiquarian Booksellers   CCXVII - 101   2016   £70

Fries, Amos A. *Chemical Warfare.* New York: McGraw Hill, 1921. First edition, 8vo., original cloth olive green boards, frontispiece, numerous illustrations, diagrams and figures, faintest rubbing and creasing at spine ends, otherwise fine, exceptional condition, bright clean copy.   Any Amount of Books   2015 - A83498   2016   £150

Frigge, Karli *Marbled Flowers. Decorated Paper. Volume 5.* Buren, the Netherlands: Fritz Knuf, 1980. Limited to 55 copies, however this one is number '60, signed and numbered by book artist, large folio, bound by artist in black wooden boards with red wooden inlay and leather spine, boards laced on with red parchment straps, text screenprinted, five marbled samples of various sizes, each signed by artist, housed in grey cloth case with calligraphic title to front panel and black ribbon ties, calligraphy by Stan Van Der Weyer, slight discoloration to small spot on edge of case, else fine, book measures 21.5 x 16 inches, 16 pages of text, 5 marbled paper samples, fine.   The Kelmscott Bookshop   13 - 19   2016 $3500

Frink, Maurice *Photographer on an Army Mule.* Norman: University of Oklahoma Press, 1965. First edition, 118 photos, gilt lettered cloth some minor spotting to rear cover, overall fine.   Argonaut Book Shop   Photography 2015 - 3158   2016 $50

Frison-Roche, Roger *Mont Blanc and the Seven Valleys.* New York: Oxford University Press, 1961. First English language, 169 heliogravures, folding map in rear pocket, white cloth stamped in blue and gold, fine, lightly rubbed pictorial dust jacket.   Argonaut Book Shop   Mountaineering 2015 - 727   2016 $75

Friswell, James Hain *About in the World. Essays.* London: Sampson Low, Son & Marston, 1864. Second edition, engraved title, contemporary half brown calf, slightly rubbed.   Jarndyce Antiquarian Books   CCXV - 210   2016   £45

Friswell, James Hain *The Better Self...* London: Henry S. King & Co., 1875. Half title, 48 page catalog, original decorated brown cloth, bevelled boards, ownership stamp of H. T. Harpham.   Jarndyce Antiquarian Books   CCXV - 211   2016   £35

Friswell, James Hain *The Gentle Life.* London: Sampson Low, 1873. 17th edition, original brown cloth, bevelled boards, recased, good, library stamp of Soldier's Home Rawalpindl.   Jarndyce Antiquarian Books   CCXV - 21   2016   £30

Frith, H. J. *The Mallee-Fowl: the Bird that Builds an Incubator.* Sydney: Angus and Robertson, 1962. Octavo, photos, slightly chipped dust jacket.   Andrew Isles Natural History Books   55 - 6212   2016 $80

Frith, William Powell *John Leech His Life and Work.* London: Richard Bentley and son, 1891. First edition, 2 volumes, 222 x 146mm, very handsome scarlet straight grain morocco gilt by Riviere & son (stamp signed on front turn-in), covers with French fillets, raised bands, spine compartments gilt with sporting center ornament and volute cornerpieces, gilt titling, richly gilt turn-ins, all edges gilt, 176 illustrations, comprised of the 97 called for plus 79 extra inserted engraved plates, 49 of these hand colored and 13 double page, except for few inserted plates, light foxing or minor stains, virtually perfect copy, attractive bindings lustrous and unworn, volumes entirely fresh clean inside and out.   Phillip J. Pirages   67 - 234   2016 $1250

Fritsch, F. E. *The Structure and Reproduction of the Algae.* Cambridge: Cambridge University Press, 1935-1945. 2 volumes, octavo, illustrations, 2 folding maps, publisher's cloth, volume one signed by author, very good.   Andrew Isles Natural History Books   55 - 13887   2016 $300

Fritz, Christian G. *Federal Justice, the California Court of Ogden Hoffman 1581-1891.* Lincoln: University of Nebraska Press, 1991. First edition, several photos, tables, maroon cloth lettered in silver, very fine with dust jacket. Argonaut Book Shop   Biography 2015 - 6307   2016 $60

Fritz, Kurt Von *The Theory of the Mixed Constitution in Antiquity: a Critical Analysis of Polybius's Political Ideas.* New York: Columbia University Press, 1958. First edition, second printing, cloth, very good to near fine, attractive maroon cloth in excellent shape but for two bumped corners, gilt titling bright on spines with gently rubbed edges, interior bright, crisp and clean, top edge slate blue, book protected by glassine dust jacket which has served its purpose.   Simon Finch   2015 - 001892   2016 $175

Froebel, Friedrich *Papers on Froebel's Kindergarten...* Hartford: Office of Barnard's American Journal of Education, 1890. Original brown cloth, little rubbed, Russell ownership signature.   Jarndyce Antiquarian Books   CCXV - 694   2016   £50

Frohman, Daniel *Daniel Frohman Presents: an Autobiography.* New York: Claude Kendall, 1935. First edition, 8vo., illustrations, very good, inscribed by author. Second Life Books, Inc. 196A - 582   2016 $45

Frohman, Daniel *Memories of a Manager: Reminiscences of the Old Lyceum and of Some Players of the Last Century.* New York: Doubleday Page, 1911. 8vo., illustrations, author's long presentation, rear hinge tender, cover somewhat worn, else very good.   Second Life Books, Inc.   196A - 584   2016 $75

Froissart, Jean De *Chronicles of England, France, Spain and the Adjoining Counties....* London and New York: George Routledge and Sons, 1868. 2 volumes, many illustrations in text, fore-edge margins somewhat discoloured towards rear of volume 1, contemporary light brown calf, blind tooled with gilt embossed 'Oxford Local Examinations, London' centerpieces, red morocco gilt labels and blind tooling to spines, rebacked well but in different shade, boards scuffed, edges worn, corners neatly repaired, bookplates of M. J. M. Hill from London Committee of Oxford Local Examinations.   Unsworths Antiquarian Booksellers   30 - 60   2016   £140

Froissart, Jean De *Froissarts Cronycles.* Oxford: Basil Blackwell, 1927-1928. One of 350 numbere dcopies, 2 volumes in 8, hand colored heraldic decorations, untrimmed, blue paper covered boards, linen spines with printed paper spine labels, spines bit darkened as usual with some minor soiling of boards and spines and light wear at corners, but very good.   Joseph J. Felcone, Inc.   Books from Five Centuries: a Miscellany - 69   2016 $1500

Frost, John *Portfolio for Youth.* Philadelphia: J. Crissy, 1835. First edition (and probably only edition), 12mo., leather backed boards, ink from owners name bled through to 2 leaves, spine ends worn, edges rubbed, some foxing, tight and very good.   Aleph-bet Books, Inc.   111 - 145   2016 $300

Frost, Joseph *Divine Songs of the Muggletonians in Grateful Praise to the Only True God, the Lord Jesus Christ.* London: printed by R. Brown, 1829. Folding engraved frontispiece, uncut in original drab boards, paper label, spine carefully repaired at head and tail.   Jarndyce Antiquarian Booksellers   CCXVII - 102   2016   £380

Frost, Robert Lee   1874-1963 *Aforesaid.* New York: Henry Holt, 1954. First edition, #271 of 650 numbered copies signed by author, 8vo., fine, publisher's slipcase, little faded and worn.   Second Life Books, Inc.   197 - 129   2016 $600

Frost, Robert Lee   1874-1963 *A Masque of Mercy.* New York: Holt, 1947. First edition, #230 of 751 large paper copies, signed by author, 8vo. fine in torn tissue dust jacket and publisher's box, untrimmed.   Second Life Books, Inc. 197 - 135   2016 $600

Frost, Robert Lee   1874-1963 *A Masque of Reason.* New York: Holt, 1945. First edition, #724 of 800 large paper copies, signed by author, inscribed by author to Florence Parke, 8vo., fine in some worn slip-case, untrimmed.   Second Life Books, Inc.   197 - 136   2016 $650

Frost, Robert Lee   1874-1963 *Mountain Interval.* New York: Holt, 1954. First edition, 8vo., publisher's cloth with original snapshot of Frost tipped to verso of dedication leaf causing some rippling to page, first state with repeated line on page 88, previous owner's bookplate, front hinge little tender, very bright copy.   Second Life Books, Inc.   197 - 130   2016 $500

Frost, Robert Lee   1874-1963 *New Hampshire: a Poem...* New York: Holt, 1923. First edition, limited edition, #136 of 350 copies signed by author, untrimmed, fine.   Second Life Books, Inc.   197 - 137   2016 $4500

Frost, Robert Lee   1874-1963 *New Hampshire: a Poem...* New York: Holt, 1923. First edition, 8vo., untrimmed, name on endpaper, very good.   Second Life Books, Inc.   197 - 138   2016 $350

Frost, Robert Lee   1874-1963 *New Hampshire: a Poem with Notes and Graces Notes.* New York: Holt, 1924. Second printing, 8vo., woodcuts J. J. Lankes who has signed in pencil on blank, dated 1924, paper over boards with cloth spine, edge darkened, cover corners and ends of spine little worn, otherwise very good, tight copy.   Second Life Books, Inc.   197 - 131   2016 $125

Frost, Robert Lee 1874-1963 *The Complete Poems of Robert Frost.* New York: Limited Editions Club, 1950. No. 198 of 1500 copies signed by author, artist and designer, printer, 273 x 189mm., 2 volumes, publisher's blue denim binding, gilt stamped leather, spine labels, original glassine dust jackets in publishers (somewhat worn) slipcase, 10 wood engravings by Thomas Nason, comprised of two title vignettes and 8 section headpieces, with 8 leaf pamphlet 'Thomas W. Nason 1889-1971" and "Monthly Letter of Limited Editions Club" concerning this title laid in, glassine with small chip at spine head of first volume and with other minor imperfections but very fine, entirely fresh and clean inside and out.   Phillip J. Pirages   67 - 239   2016 $2000

Frost, Robert Lee 1874-1963 *Collected Poems.* New York: Henry Holt, 1939. First edition, 8vo., signed by author, very good in rubbed and somewhat worn, price clipped dust jacket.   Second Life Books, Inc.   197 - 134   2016 $900

Frost, Robert Lee 1874-1963 *The Poetry of Robert Frost.* Barre: Imprint Society, 1971. One of 1950 copies, signed by Ruzicka, frontispiece, patterned brown paper over boards, brown cloth spines, nice set in slightly soiled box, 8vo., 2 volumes.   Second Life Books, Inc.   196A - 586   2016 $150

Frost, Robert Lee 1874-1963 *Steeple Bush.* New York: Holt, 1947. First edition, #431 of 751 large papr copies signed by author, 8vo., fine, untrimmed copy in dust jacket and publisher's slipcase.   Second Life Books, Inc.   197 - 139   2016 $750

Frost, Robert Lee 1874-1963 *West Running-Brook.* New York: Henry Holt, 1928. 789/1000 copies, signed by author, woodcut frontispiece, 3 further plates, all with tissue guards and signed by artist, 8vo., original quarter green cloth, leaf patterned boards, backstrip lettered gilt, top edge gilt, others untrimmed, small patch of browning to flyleaf, original tissue jacket with loss to backstrip panel, slipcase with printed label and some wear along edges, very good.   Blackwell's Rare Books   B184 - 154   2016   £500

Frost, Robert Lee 1874-1963 *West-Running Brook.* New York: Holt, 1928. First edition, presumed first issue with 'first printing' on copyright page and with word 'roams' on final line on page 44, paper over boards, cloth spine and gilt paper picture on front, woodcuts by J. J. Lankes, very good.   Second Life Books, Inc.   197 - 132   2016 $150

Frost, Robert Lee 1874-1963 *West-Running Brook.* New York: Holt, 1928. First edition, #618 of 980 large paper copies, signed by author, 8vo., paper over boards with cloth spine and gilt paper picture on front, woodcuts by J. J. Lankes, very good.   Second Life Books, Inc.   197 - 133   2016 $750

Frost, Robert Lee 1874-1963 *A Witness Tree, New Poems.* New York: Holt, 1942. First trade edition, 8vo., pencil signature on endpaper and front paper and front blank, fine in dust jacket.   Second Life Books, Inc.   197 - 140   2016 $145

Froude, James Anthony 1818-1894 *Letters and Memorials of Jane Welsh Carlyle.* London: Longmans, Green and Co., 1883. First edition, octavo, 3 volumes, period binding of half dark green morocco with raised bands, gilt decoration to spine, marbled boards, edges and endpapers, armorial bookplate of Kennet of the Dene in each volume, covers slightly rubbed at edges, very good. Peter Ellis   112 - 62   2016   £225

Fry, Caroline   *The Assistant of Education; Religious and Literary.* London: published for the author by T. Baker, 1823-1824. 2 volumes, 12mo., plates, some light spotting, contemporary half brown calf, little dulled with some slight wear to leading hinge of volume I, inscription on leading blank for Aubrey Lum from sister Mary Greive 2nd July 1869, nice.   Jarndyce Antiquarian Books   CCXV - 695   2016   £75

Fry, Caroline   *The Listener.* London: James Nisbet, 1832. Third edition, 2 volumes, half titles, original pink moire cloth, spines lettered gilt, imprint at tails, price 12s, spine faded, slight damp marking, signature of Anne Webber 1833, nice.   Jarndyce Antiquarian Books   CCXV - 696   2016   £48

Fry, Christopher   *A Sleep of Prisoners, a Play.* London: Oxford University Press, 1951. First edition, presentation from actor Denham Elliott one month after opening in London and signed by author and producer and other members of the cast, fine in dust jacket.   Second Life Books, Inc.   196A - 589   2016 $150

Fry, Christopher   *A Sleep of Prisoners, a Play.* London: Oxford University Press, 1951. Second edition, small 8vo., signed by four members of the Cast, Leonard White, Donald Harron, Hugh Pryse and Stanley Baker, very good. Second Life Books, Inc.   196A - 590   2016 $85

Fry, John   *The Case of Marriages Between Near Kindred Particularly Considered...* London: B. White, 1773. Second edition, half title, 8vo., contemporary sheep, gilt, neatly rebacked and corners restored, very good, sometime in the library of LA board of Law with its bookplate and original ink ownership inscription "W.S. 1773".   John Drury Rare Books   2015 - 25949   2016 $437

Fryer, Jane Eayre   *The Mary Frances Cook Book or Adventures Among the Kitchen People.* Philadelphia: John C. Winston, 1912. 4to., blue cloth, pictorial paste-on, off-setting on endpaper, owner inscription, near fine, illustrations by Jane Eayre Fryer.   Aleph-bet Books, Inc.   112 - 209   2016 $450

Fuchs, Ernest *Text-Book of Ophthalmology.* New York: Appleton, 1896. 788 pages, numerous illustrations, half morocco spine rubbed with front joint starting, internally clean and fine.   James Tait Goodrich   X-78 - 426   2016 $175

Fuentes, Carlos *The Old Gringo.* New York: Farrar Straus and Giroux, 1986. First US edition, fine and tight in fine dust jacket, signed by author and dated in year of publication.   Jeff Hirsch Books   E-List 80 - 9   2016 $85

Fuller, Anna *A Literary Courtship: Under the Auspices of Pike's Peak.* New York: Putnam, 1893. First edition, 8vo., maroon cloth, stamped in gilt, top edge gilt, untrimmed (little worn at hinges), very good.   Second Life Books, Inc.   197 - 141   2016 $45

Fuller, J. F. C. *The Decisive Battles of the Western World and Their Influence Upon History.* London: Eyre & Spottiswoode, 1954-1956. First edition, octavo, 3 volumes, maps and plans, ownership signature on each volume, free endpapers partially and lightly tanned, very good in very good, frayed dust jacket.   Peter Ellis   112 - 432   2016   £225

Fuller, Thomas   1608-1661 *A Pisgah Sight of Palestine and the Confines Thereof...* London: printed by J. E. for John Williams, 1650. First edition, 28 plates + frontispiece and additional titlepage, neat repair to upper corner of pages 279-280, plates mounted on later stubs, exceptionally clean, folio, mid 19th century full dark green crushed morocco, gilt and blind ruled borders, raised bands, ruled in gilt with compartments ruled in blind and gilt, little dulled, bookplate of J. Cresswell on leading pastedown and later bookplate of Helene Jung, inscribed in remembrance of her great kindness to Wm. Howson and his family Dec. 1858, handsome copy. Jarndyce Antiquarian Booksellers   CCXVII - 103   2016   £3500

Funke, Cornelia *Inkheart.* London: Chicken House, 2003. First British edition, fine in fine dust jacket, signed by author.   Bella Luna Books   2016 - t9236   2016 $82

Funny Alphabet. New York: McLoughlin Bros, n.d. circa, 1860. 4.5 x 5.5 inches, pictorial wrappers, spine reinforced and small piece of rear corner off, else very good+, hand colored engravings.   Aleph-bet Books, Inc.   111 - 6   2016 $450

Furbank, P. N. *E. M. Forster: a Life. Volume One. The Growth of the Novelist (1879-1914), Volume two, Polycrates' Ring (1914-1970).* London: Secker & Warburg, 1977-1978. First edition, octavo, illustrations, ownership signature volume 2 scored throughout, near fine set in very near fine dust jackets.   Peter Ellis   112 - 131   2016   £45

Furniss, Harry *The By Ways and Outer Ways of Boxing.* London: Harrison & Sons, 1919. First edition, half title, engraved title, illustrations, date in blue ink on title, endpapers replaced, original green pictorial cloth, bevelled boards, few marks, very good.   Jarndyce Antiquarian Booksellers CCXVII - 104   2016   £160

Furnivall, Frederick James *The Babee's Book: Medieval Managers for the Young...* London: Chatto & Windus, 1923. Engraved title frontispiece and plates, contemporary full brown calf by Bumpus of Oxford, all edges gilt, very good.   Jarndyce Antiquarian Books   CCXV - 213   2016   £38

Furst, Herbert *The Woodcut Annual Numbers I-IV (all published).* Fleuron, 1927-1930. First edition, profusely illustrated with 2 tipped-in samples of Curwen Press patterned paper designed by Enid Marx and Eric Ravilious in the first volume, few foxspots to couple of volumes, imperial 8vo., original quarter black cloth with patterned paper sides designed by Marx, Althea Willoughby and Harry Carter, first volume with plain grey sides, backstrips lettered gilt, occasional rubbing to extremities, few fox spots to endpapers, couple of volumes dust jackets to all but volume 3, very good.   Blackwell's Rare Books   B184 - 263   2016   £650

Fusco, Paul *RFK Funeral Train.* New York: Magnum Photo Books with Umbrage Editions, 2000. First edition thus, signed and warmly inscribed by Fusco on titlepage to curator at High Art Museum in Atlanta, surprisingly uncommon inscribed, fine in very fine dust jacket.   Jeff Hirsch Books   Holiday List 2015 - 73   2016 $375

Fyfe, Thomas Alexander *Who's Who In Dickens: a Complete Dickens Repertory in Dickens' own Words.* London: Hodder & Stoughton, 1912. Original half red buckram, red cloth boards, spine faded, stamps of Standard Library.   Jarndyce Antiquarian Booksellers   CCXVIII - 1247   2016   £20

G

Gabbin, Joanne V. *Furious Flower: a Revolution in Black Poetry.* Charlottesville and Harrisonburg: Virginia Foundation for the Humanities and Public Policy and James Madison University, 1994. First edition, quarto loose leaves laid into printed red portfolio, letterpress printed text and 23 broadside poems, prospectus laid in, one of 300 copies, this copy unnumbered, slightest wear on portfolio, still easily fine. Between the Covers Rare Books 202 - 34 2016 $450

Gadd, W. Laurence *The Great Expectations Country.* London: Cecil Palmer, 1929. First edition, half title, frontispiece, plates, edges slightly spotted, original brown embossed cloth. Jarndyce Antiquarian Booksellers CCXVIII - 594 2016 £30

Gag, Wanda *The Funny Thing.* New York: Coward McCann, 1929. First edition, oblong 8vo., yellow pictorial boards, fine in very slightly soiled dust jacket, illustrations by author. Aleph-bet Books, Inc. 112 - 211 2016 $600

Gag, Wanda *Millions of Cats.* New York: Coward McCann, 1928. First edition, first issue, oblong 4to., yellow pictorial boards, slightest bit of dusting, else fine in very good, lightly soiled dust jacket with slight fraying at spine ends, pictorial endpapers plus beautiful black and white lithos. Aleph-bet Books, Inc. 112 - 210 2016 $2000

Gag, Wanda *Nothing at All.* New York: Coward-McCann, 1941. First edition, orange pictorial boards, fine in very good+ dust jacket with 1 small edge chip, correct price, (no additional printings listed), hand lettered text and beautiful color lithographs on nearly every page, scarce. Aleph-bet Books, Inc. 111 - 190 2016 $750

Gaidzakian, Ohan *Illustrated Armenia and the Armenians.* Boston: 1898. First edition, 8vo., numerous full page illustrations and portraits, original cloth with gilt illustration, some scuffing, but very good. M & S Rare Books, Inc. 99 - 16 2016 $250

Gaiman, Nell *Odd and the Frost Giants.* London: Bloomsbury, 2010. First edition, illustrations by Adam Stower, book and dust jacket fine, signed by author, jacket fitted with new removeable clear cover. Gemini Books 2016 - 31685 2016 $50

Gale, Norman *A June Romance.* Rugby: George E. Over, 1894. Number 28 of 40 copies numbered and signed by publisher, with ALS about the book, letter is 4 x 6 inches and very good except for two inch tear along crease where fold, grey brown paper boards with author and title in black to spine and front cover, some darkening and light staining but very good, offsetting to endpaper, otherwise clean and bright, frontispiece, attractive titlepage with rose vine design, very nice, scarce. The Kelmscott Bookshop 12 - 47 2016 $190

Gale, Zona *The Secret Way.* New York: Macmillan, 1921. First edition, 8vo., bound in cloth backed printed boards, fine, inscribed by author to Dr. William Lyon. Second Life Books, Inc. 196A - 596 2016 $200

Gallagher, Tess *Instructions to the Double.* Port Townsend: Graywolf Press, 1976. First edition, issued and edition of 1500 copies, this one of 1360 in wrappers, 8vo., signed by author. Second Life Books, Inc. 196A - 597 2016 $250

Gallagher, Tess *On Your Own. Poems by...* Graywolf Press, 1978. 12 of 26 copies signed and numbered by author, 8vo., 4 leaves and paper cover, fastened at fold with string, about as new. Second Life Books, Inc. 196A - 598 2016 $200

Gallagher, Tess *On Your own, Poems by...* Graywolf Press, 1978. One of 390 copies, 8vo., 4 leaves and paper cover, fastened at fold with string, signed by author, about as new. Second Life Books, Inc. 196A - 599 2016 $150

Gallagher, Tess *On Your Own.* N.P.: The Graywolf Press, 1978. Limited to 390 copies, this one of 26 numbered copies signed by author, small 4to., self paper wrappers. Oak Knoll Books 310 - 106 2016 $200

Gallagher, Tess *Willingly.* Port Townsend: Graywolf Press, 1984. First printing, no. 3 of 40 copies signed and numbered by author, 8vo., ivory paper over boards with green cloth spine, nice in dust jacket. Second Life Books, Inc. 196A - 600 2016 $250

Gallico, Paul *Confessions of a Story Writer.* New York: Alfred A. Knopf, 1946. First edition, 8vo., original red cloth, spine lettered in gilt, upper board centrally blindstamped, lower board blindstamped with publisher's device in bottom right hand corner in original dust jacket with pink paper wraparound band, top edges orange, extremities very slightly rubbed, very light tearing to head and foot of spine, small triangular tear ad some fading to band, nonetheless very fresh, rare with band, author's inscription to his editor Frances Whiting. Sotheran's Piccadilly Notes - Summer 2015 - 140 2016 £298

Gallo, Philip *Some Roses.* Omaha: University of Nebraska, 1983. One of 192 copies, 12mo., paper wrappers, author's signature on colophon, nice.   Second Life Books, Inc.   196A - 602   2016 $75

Gally, Henry *Some Considerations Upon Clandestine marriages...* London: printed by J. Hughs near Lincoln's-Inn-Fields and sold by J. Roberts &c, 1750. 8vo., slight general paper toning, some very mnor soiling, strongly bound in 20th century in holland cloth, leather spine labels, good copy, sometime in the Los Angeles Board of Law Library, bookplate on pastedown, ink stamps on covers and endpapers, titlepage and text leaves unmarked.   John Drury Rare Books   2015 - 25953   2016 $350

Galsworthy, John   1867-1933   *Carmen. An Opera in Four acts.*   London: Elkin Mathews, 1932. 1/650 copies, 8vo., numbered and signed by John and Ada Galsworthy, cover edge sunned, otherwise nice in little torn and mended dust jacket.   Second Life Books, Inc.   196A - 605   2016 $150

Galsworthy, John   1867-1933   *Flowering Wilderness.*   London: Heinemann, 1932. First edition, one of 400 numbered and signed copies, little warped vellum backed publisher's cloth in most of the original acetate, nice, uncut copy.   Second Life Books, Inc.   196A - 607   2016 $125

Galsworthy, John   1867-1933   *The Forsyte Saga.*   London: Heinemann, 1922. First edition, 84/250 deluxe large paper copies from an edition of 275, signed by author, frontispiece photo of author, captioned tissue guard, folding table, little faint foxing to border of prelims with occasional spot further in, short closed tear at edge of one leaf and little corner creasing, original dark green leather with blind-stamped single fillet border carrying round upper board and backstrip lettered gilt, little rubbing to edges, very minor bumping to corners, top edge gilt, small amount of spotting to endpapers, very good.   Blackwell's Rare Books   B184 - 155   2016 £300

Galsworthy, John   1867-1933   *Glimpses and Reflections.*   London: Heinemann, 1937. First edition, 8vo. inscribed by Ada Galsworthy for Molly Kerr, with Mrs. Galsworthy's compliments card laid in, light foxing on front and back pages and on edges, else very good.   Second Life Books, Inc.   196A - 606   2016 $45

Galsworthy, John   1867-1933   *Loyalties, a Drama in Three Acts.* London: Duckworth, 1930. First edition, one of only 315 copies signed by author, small 4to., 104 pages printed on handmade paper by Camelot Press, fine in little soiled dust jacket that has been strengthened on verso.   Second Life Books, Inc.   196A - 608   2016 $125

Galsworthy, John   1867-1933   *Maid in Waiting.* London: Heinemann, 1931. First edition, one of 525 numbered ccopies, signed by author, uncut, top edge gilt, some warped and faded, publisher's vellum backed cloth, nice, clean copy.   Second Life Books, Inc.   196A - 609   2016 $100

Galsworthy, John   1867-1933   *The Man of Property.*   London: Heinemann, 1906. First edition, some foxing at either end (as often) and on edges, 3 leaves little proud at top edge (for no apaperent reason), 8vo., original cloth, title in gilt on upper cover, spine gilt lettered, little shaken and worn, contemporary signature of Sybil A. Forster dated 1806, modern bookplate.   Blackwell's Rare Books   B184 - 156   2016   £200

Galsworthy, John   1867-1933   *A Rambling Discourse.*   London: Elkin Mathews & Marrot, 1929. First edition, 1/400 numbered copies signed by author, little faded on spine, otherwise fine, uncut copy, 8vo.   Second Life Books, Inc.   196A - 610   2016 $125

Galsworthy, John   1867-1933   *The Silver Spoon.*   London: Heinemann, 1926. First edition, 8vo., fine in publisher's dust jacket, uncut, this one of 265 numbered and signed copies.   Second Life Books, Inc.   196A - 611   2016 $150

Galsworthy, John   1867-1933   *Soames and the Flag.*   London: Heinemann, 1930. First edition, one of 1025 numbered copies, signed by author, 8vo., publisher's vellum somewhat soiled, slipcase.   Second Life Books, Inc.   196A - 613   2016 $85

Galsworthy, John   1867-1933   *Soames and the Flag.*   New York: Scribner, 1930. First edition, 8vo., printed on English handmade paper by William Rudge, in an edition of 600 copies, signed by author, uncut, one small library stamp.   Second Life Books, Inc.   196A - 612   2016 $45

Galt, John   1779-1839   *Les Lairds de Grippy ou le Domaine Substitute Traduit de l'Anglais.*   Paris: Lecomte et Durcy, 1824. First French edition, 4 volumes, uncut in original yellow wrappers, slightly dusted, very good.   Jarndyce Antiquarian Booksellers   CCXVII - 105   2016   £225

Galton, Francis   1822-1911   *The Art of Travel or Shifts and Contrivances Available in Wild Coutnries.*   London: John Murray, 1860. Third edition, woodcut, illustrations, original scarlet cloth by Edmonds and Remnants, spine faded, slightly dulled, leading inner hinge slightly cracked, ex-libris John Woern Hill.   Jarndyce Antiquarian Booksellers   CCXVII - 106   2016   £150

Galton, Francis   1822-1911   *Vacation Tourists and Notes of Travel 1861.*   Cambridge: Macmillan, 1862.   First edition, 8vo., 10 maps, contemporary red calf, rebacked, using original spine, last few sheets waterstained.   J. & S. L. Bonham Antiquarian Booksellers   Voyages 2016 - 9176   2016   £80

Galvan, Manuel Jesus De   *The Cross and the Sword.*   London: Victor Gollancz, 1956.   First UK edition, gilt titles on spine dull, very good in like dust jacket, slightly creased at edges.   Peter Ellis   112 - 154   2016   £45

Gamble, James Alexander   *Roses Unlimited.*   Harrisburg: by the author, 1950.   First edition, frontispiece and 10 full page plates, 6 colored, very good, tight copy, inscribed by author.   Second Life Books, Inc.   196A - 614   2016 $40

Gammon, D. J.   *The Getaway Gang.*   London: Dennis Archer, n.d.,   Price clipped dust jacket slightly fraed, otherwise very good.   I. D. Edrich   Crime - 2016   £20

Gammond, Peter   *A Bibliographical Companion to Betjeman.*   Guilford: Betjeman, 1997.   First edition, one of 250 numbered copies, octavo, fine in plain tissue dust jacket torn and stained with few nicks.   Peter Ellis   112 - 39   2016   £65

Gancel, Joseph   *Gancel's Ready Reference Book of Menu Terms.*   New York: Joseph Joseph Gancel, 1910.   First edition, 8vo., original cloth lettered gilt on upper board, very good, ownership inscription of Emile Durand, head chef for Miami Biltmore Kitchen.   Sotheran's   Piccadilly Notes - Summer 2015 - 141   2016   £298

Ganong, William F.   *The Economic Mollusca of Acadia.*   St. John: Barnes & Co.,, 1889.   Maroon cloth, gilt title to front cover, 8vo., 22 black and white figures, very good.   Schooner Books Ltd.   115 - 47   2016 $45

Ganong, William F.   *The History of Caraquet and Pokemouche.*   St. John: New Brunswick Museum, 1948.   Revised edition, 8vo., maps and illustrations, small waterstain lower spine, generally very good.   Schooner Books Ltd.   115 - 49   2016 $45

Ganong, William F.   *The History of Miscou and Shippegan.*   Saint John: New Brunswick Museum, 1946.   Revised, 9.5 x 6.5 inches, maps and illustrations, previous owner's marginalia and notes in ink and pencil, otherwise very good.   Schooner Books Ltd.   115 - 50   2016 $45

Ganong, William F.   *A Monograph of the Evolution of the Boundaries of the Province of New Brunswick.*   Ottawa: Royal Society of Canada, 1901.   8vo., card covers, 7 folding maps as well as 34 sketch maps, some offsetting to first page, otherwise very good, folding maps very clean.   Schooner Books Ltd.   115 - 43   2016 $125

Gant, Roland   *Mountains in the Mind.*   Andoversford: Whittington Press, 1987.   III/40 copies printed on Zerkall mouldmade paper and signed by author and artist, color printed frontispiece and 5 other wood engravings by Howard Phipps, imperial 8vo., original orange canvas, printed label, one of the engravings inlaid to front cover, untrimmed, with a suite of proofs of the 6 engravings and an extra engraving, all signed by Phipps in pencil, engravings enclosed in protective matching canvas portfolio and book and portfolio further enclosed in board slipcase, fine.   Blackwell's Rare Books   B184 - 320   2016   £2520

Gape, Tim   *The Comical Fellow or Wit and Humour for Town and Country.*   London: printed for W. Lane, 1795?   Third edition, engraved frontispiece, 12mo., good, clean copy, disbound.   Jarndyce Antiquarian Booksellers   CCXVI - 325   2016   £125

Gape, Tim   *Quick's Whim or the Merry Medley.*   London: printed for W. Lane, 1792.   engraved frontispiece, 12mo., titlepage torn with loss of imprint (here supplied in facsimile in old paper), some dusting and light foxing, disbound.   Jarndyce Antiquarian Booksellers   CCXVI - 325   2016   £125

Garcia Lorca, Federico   *Chant Funebre Pour Ignacio Sanchez Mejias.*   Paris: Aux Depens Des Executants De Ce Livre, 1949.   Number 118 of 160 copies on BFK Rives numbered and signed by Krol (from an edition of 225 + 26 HC), folio, 20 engravings + cover, fine although gutter edge of half title is bit rolled, hardcover chemise bears portrait by Roger Tarrov, nice example in near fine matching box.   Beasley Books   2015 - 2016 $2500

Garcia Lorca, Federico   *Romance de la Guardia Civil Espanol.*   Philadelphia: Janus Press, 1962.   First printing of this edition, slim quarto, printed in Monotype Bembo on Okawara paper, one of 45 numbered copies, this being no. 35, signed by artist, Jerome Kaplan, light fading overall and small chip to front wrappers, else near fine, this Denise Levertov's copy.   Royal Books   48 - 69   2016 $650

Garcia Lorca, Federico   *Selected Letters.*   New York: New Directions, 1983.   First edition, photos, blue cloth, cover slightly faded, otherwise nice in little soiled and slightly chipped dust jacket.   Second Life Books, Inc.   197 - 143   2016 $45

Garcia Marquez, Gabriel   *El Otono Del Patricai.*   Barcelona: Plaza & Janes, 1975.   First Spanish edition, near fine, bookstore stamp on titlepage, light shelfwear, very good dust jacket, sunning and light creasing to edges, very good, sunning and light creasing to edges.   Bella Luna Books   2016 - t11716   2016 $66

Garcia Marquez, Gabriel *El Onto del Patricai. (Autumn of the Patriarch).* Barcelona: Plaza & Janes, 1975. First edition, hardbound issue, octavo, head and tail of spine bit bumped, very good in very good dust jacket slightly faded at spine, dust jacket is first issue with photo on rear panel. Peter Ellis 112 - 137 2016 £250

Garcia Marquez, Gabriel *The Autumn of the Patriarch.* New York: Harper and Row, 1976. First American edition, fifth printing, signed by translator Gregory Rabassa, blue cloth lettered gilt, pale blue top stain, original pictorial dust jacket lettered in white and orange, about fine, jacket with hint of rubbing to extremities, faint creasing to spine head, else bright and clean, beautiful copy. B & B Rare Books, Ltd. 2016 - GGM043 2016 $60

Garcia Marquez, Gabriel *La Increible y Triste Historia de la Candida Erendira y de su Abuela Desalmada. (Innocent Erendira).* Mexico: Editorial Hermes, 1972. First Mexican edition, pictorial paper wrappers, illustrations to panels, lettered gilt, presentation inscribed by author to Sylvia Ripstein, his granddaughter, near fine with some light wear to spine ends, faint toning to extremities, minor offsetting from a small piece of removed tape to front free endpaper, otherwise fresh interior, overall bright and attractive copy. B & B Rare Books, Ltd. 2016 - GGM046 2016 $2000

Garcia Marquez, Gabriel *Innocent Erendira and Other Stories.* New York: Harper and Row, 1978. First American edition, signed by translator, Gregory Rabassa, publisher's dark blue cloth, spine lettered gilt, top edge orange, original colorful pictorial dust jacket, about fine with only hint of rubbing to spine ends, else fine, unclipped dust jacket with touch of faint rubbing to extremities, else bright and fresh, very clean and square copy. B & B Rare Books, Ltd. 2016 - GGM042 2016 $150

Garcia Marquez, Gabriel *Leaf Storm and Other Stories.* New York: Harper and Row, 1972. First American edition, teal cloth with bird illustration to front board in green, lettered in green and gilt, pictorial green endpapers, original green pictorial dust jacket, lettered in orange and white, fine. B & B Rare Books, Ltd. 2016 - GGM045 2016 $100

Garcia Marquez, Gabriel *Love in the Time of Cholera.* London: Jonathan Cape, 1988. First UK edition, octavo, slight bruise at head and tail of spine, otherwise very good in like dust jacket little creased at edges. Peter Ellis 112 - 138 2016 £75

Garcia Marquez, Gabriel *Love in the Time of Cholera.* New York: Alfred A. Knopf, 1988. First US edition, octavo, faint bruise at head of spine, otherwise fine in fine dust jacket, little creased at head of spine. Peter Ellis 112 - 139 2016 £75

Garcia Marquez, Gabriel *Love in the time of Cholera.* New York: Alfred A. Knopf, 1988. First American edition, inscribed by translator, Edith Grossman, black cloth lettered gilt, with postcard from publisher's laid in, dust jacket, beautiful copy. B & B Rare Books, Ltd. 2016 - GGM044 2016 $200

Garcia Marquez, Gabriel *Cien Anos de Soledad. (One Hundred Years of Solitude).* Buenos Aires: Editorial Sudamericana, 1967. First Argentine edition, preceding all others, correct first edition, strong, very good plus in illustrated wrappers, slightest lean, minor nicking to crown, light creasing to spine. Royal Books 48 - 63 2016 $6000

The Gardener: A Synopsis of the Principles and Practice of His Art and Calling. London: Houlston & sons, circa, 1870. original brick brown cloth blocked in gilt and black, slightly rubbed few small marks on back board, bookseller's ticket of George H. Shellick, Plymouth on leading pastedown, good plus. Jarndyce Antiquarian Books CCXV - 260 2016 £110

Gardiner, Alan *Egyptian Grammar.* Oxford University Press, 1973. Third edition, large 4to., blue boards, gilt lettered to spine, top edge dated and spotted, little shelfwear, no dust jacket, very good, ownership C. D. N. Costa in pen to front pastedown. Unsworths Antiquarian Booksellers Ltd. E05 - 28 2016 £30

Gardiner, Wrey *The Living Stone.* Billericay: Grey Walls Press, 1941. First edition, 8vo., page edges and endpapers little spotted, very good in very good dust jacket, little creased and darkened at extremities. Peter Ellis 112 - 142 2016 £65

Gardner, Arthur R. L. *Lower Underworld. A Study of Crime in Fictional Form.* Quality Books, 1942. First edition, occasional foxspots to borders, crown 8vo., original red cloth, backstrip lettered in black with lean to spine, little bumping along top edge, light foxing to textblock edges, ownership inscription, scarce, dust jacket frayed with owner's shelfmark, good. Blackwell's Rare Books B184 - 157 2016 £40

Gardner, C. A. *Trees of Western Australia.* Perth: Dept. of Agriculture of Western Australia, 1952-1966. Octavo, text illustrations, 29 pamphlets (numbered 1-to 109, very good set, scarce. Andrew Isles Natural History Books 55 - 23742 2016 $100

Gardner, Erle Stanley *The Case of the Careless Cupid.* New York: Morrow, 1968. First edition, fine in dust jacket. Mordida Books 2015 - 003085 2016 $55

Gardner, John *Grendel.* London: Andre Deutsch, 1972. First UK edition, octavo, illustrations by Emil Antonucci, very near fine in dust jacket. Peter Ellis 112 - 143 2016 £95

Garfield, Brian *Fear in a Handful of Dust.* New York: Dutton, 1978. First edition, fine in dust jacket, inscribed by author.   Mordida Books   2015 - 000853   2016 $60

Garfield, Leon *The Book Lovers; a sequence of love scenes.* London: Ward Lock Limited, 1976. First edition, fine in dust jacket.   Bertram Rota Ltd.   February List 2016 - 21   2016   £25

Garis, Robert *The Dickens Theatre: a Reassessment of the Novels.* Oxford: Clarendon Press, 1965. First edition, half title, original dark blue cloth, spine lettered gilt, library shelf marks and remains of labels, good plus in price clipped dust jacket.   Jarndyce Antiquarian Booksellers   CCXVIII - 1248   2016   £25

Garner, Alan *Red Shift.* London: Collins, 1973. First edition, octavo, free endpapers partially tanned, very good in like dust jacket, price clipped.   Peter Ellis   112 - 144   2016   £35

Garnett, David *Aspects of Love.* London: Chatto & Windus, 1955. First edition, fine in dust jacket.   Bertram Rota Ltd.   February List 2016 - 22   2016   £75

Garnett, David *Lady into Fox.* London: Chatto & Windus, 1922. First edition, frontispiece with tissue guard, titlepage vignette and 9 further illustrations with 1 full page, pare label tipped in at rear, crown 8vo., original black and pink mottled cloth, backstrip with pink printed label, top edge gilt, others rough trimmed, dust jacket with darkened backstrip panel, trifle chipped at head and foot, further very light chipping to corners, very good, signed by author, scarce.   Blackwell's Rare Books   B186 - 219   2016   £450

Garnsey, Peter *Trade in the Ancient Economy.* London: Chatto & Windus, Hogarth Press, 1983. First edition, 8vo., brown cloth, gilt lettered to spine, near fine, orange dust jacket, spine faded, edges slightly worn, few small tears, some with loss, still very good.   Unsworths Antiquarian Booksellers Ltd.   E04 - 51   2016   £25

Garrard, Lewis H. *Wah-to-Yah and the Taos Trail...* H. W. Derby & Co., 1850. First edition, first state, from the library of Clint and Dorothy Josey with their bookplate, original black blindstamped cloth with original spine replaced, original title in gilt on spine, professionally rebacked with title portion of original spine remaining, front and rear endpapers replaced and some pages lightly foxed, else near fine, tight copy, housed in slipcase.   Buckingham Books   2015 - 28736   2016 $3000

Garrick, David *Miss in Her Teens or the Medley of Lovers.* London: printed for J. and R. Tonson and S. Draper, 1747. First edition, octavo, disbound, half title present, first and final leaves bit dust soiled, very good.   The Brick Row Book Shop   Miscellany 69 - 41   2016 $425

Garrison, Fielding H. *The Principles of Anatomic Illustration Before Vesalius.* New York: Paul B. Hoeber, 1926. Limited to 110 signed copies, this no. 48, 8vo., near fine, original canvas spine and blue paper covered boards with printed paper spine label, ribbon bookmark, printed from type on Kelmscott handmade paper, illustrations on Japanese vellum, corners bumped.   By the Book, L. C.   45 - 16   2016 $225

Garstin, Crosbie *Samuel Kelly. An Eighteenth Century Seaman Whose Days Have Been Few and Evil...* New York: Frederick A. Stokes, 1925. Falmouth edition, signed by editor, number 60 of 160 copies, large 8vo., original buckram within green dust jackets lettered in gilt, top edge gilt, title printed in red and black, plates, near fine, uncut and largely unopened.   Sotheran's   Travel and Exploration - 459   2016   £148

Gash, Jonathan *The Judas Pair.* London: Collins, 1977. First edition, 8vo., fine in near fine dust jacket with faint edgewear.   Any Amount of Books   2015 - A48855   2016   £170

Gash, Jonathan *A Rag, a Bone and a Hank of Hair.* London: Macmillan, 1999. First edition, very fine in dust jacket.   Mordida Books   2015 - 000870   2016 $55

Gask, Arthur *The Dark Mill Stream.* n.d., 1947. Good copy, light edgewear in frayed dust jacket.   I. D. Edrich   Crime - 2016   £35

Gaskell, Peter *Artisans and Machinery. The Moral and Physical Condition of the Manfufacturing Population...* London: John W. Parker, 1836. First edition, 8vo., modern black morocco backed cloth, withdrawal stamp of British Library of Political Science.   Marlborough Rare Books   List 55 - 29   2016   £350

Gaskin, G. E. C. *Horn-Book Jingles.* London: Leadenhall Press, 1896-1897. Tall thin 8vo., half title, frontispiece, engravings, secondary binding in plainer grey-green cloth blocked with title in black, slightly dulled.   Jarndyce Antiquarian Books   CCXV - 769   2016   £35

Gaskin, G. E. C. *Horn-Book Jingles.* London: Leadenhall Press, 1896-1897. Tall thin 8vo., half title, frontispiece, engravings, original olive green cloth blocked in black, tiny split at head of spine, very good.   Jarndyce Antiquarian Books   CCXV - 768   2016   £50

Gass, William H. *The First Winter of My married life.* Northridge: Lord John Press, 1979. Limited edition, One of 275 numbered copies signed by author, 8vo., blue paper over boards, cloth spine, cover bumped at corners, otherwise nice.   Second Life Books, Inc.   196A - 622   2016 $125

Gates, Henry Louis *The Signifying Monkey.* New York: Oxford, 1988. Second printing, author's presentation for Dan Johnson, paper over boards, cloth spine, edges of cover slightly rubbed, otherwise nice in dust jacket. Second Life Books, Inc.   196A - 623   2016 $75

Gathorne-Hardy, A. E. *Happy Hunting Grounds.* London: Longmans Green & Co., 1914. First edition, 8vo., original gilt pictorial maroon cloth, photogravure frontispiece, plates, photos, previous owner's bookplate, occasional foxing, otherwise fresh copy.   Sotheran's Hunting, Shooting & Fishing - 174   2016   £60

Gathorne-Hardy, Robert *Coronation Baby.* London: Collins, 1935. First edition, octavo, scarce, endpaper partially tanned, edges very slightly spotted, near fine in like dust jacket little rubbed at edges.   Peter Ellis   112 - 145   2016   £225

Gathorne-Hardy, Robert *Other Seas.* London: Collins, 1933. First edition, octavo, covers little mottled, prelims spotted, very good in like dust jacket with several closed tears at edges and with chip at bottom edge of upper panel. Peter Ellis   112 - 146   2016   £250

Gatty, Margaret 1809-1873 *The Book of Sun Dials.* London: Bell & Daldy, 1872. First edition, 4to., frontispiece and plate, original green pebble grained cloth, bevelled boards, blocked in black and gilt, little rubbed, very good. Jarndyce Antiquarian Booksellers   CCXVII - 107   2016 £250

Gautier, Theophile *Jean and Jeanette.* Paris: Society des Beau Arts, 1890's, One of 550 numbered copies of the large paper 'Salon edition', royal 8vo., original half dark green morocco, spine decorated gilt with curving leafy stems with red floral onlays, small gilt butterflies, marbled paper sides and endpapers, top edges gilt, others untrimmed, engraved frontispiece, tinted vignette on titlepage, numerous tinted plates ad vignettes, all by Lalauze, tissue guards present, spine faded to brown, very nice.   Sotheran's Piccadilly Notes - Summer 2015 - 142   2016   £98

Gautier, Theophile *Jean and Jeanette.* Paris: Societe des Beaux Arts, circa, 1895. One of 20 copies of the edition de Deux Mondes (this copy numbered with a star), 270 x 200mm., sumptuous azure crushed morocco, lavishly gilt and inlaid in Art Nouveau style, covers with large central fleur-de-lys in gilt and lilac morocco within an elaborate frame by lily bouquets and garlands inlaid in lilac, orange and white, raised bands, spine gilt in compartments, smaller ones at head and tail with inlaid maroon fleur-de-lys, large central compartment with spray of lilies in orange and white and two compartments with gilt titling, very wide turn-ins with elaborate gilt floral and foliate decoration enclosing burnt orange morocco doublures, front doublure featuring an oval inset of white kidskin (or perhaps vellum) with hand colored engraving of female nude, ivory watered silk endleaves, blue marbled flyleaves, top edge gilt, other edges untrimmed and unopened with 76 charming engraved vignettes (representing 25 images, one in four states, the others in three states, black and white in text, black and white printed on mounted India paper and hand colored on special textured stock, latter two states with tiny additional accompanying figure in black and white or colored, all by Adolphe Lalauze, tissue guards, large paper copy, small vague scar on front cover (well masked with dye), spine faintly and evenly sunned, otherwise lovely book in fine condition, clean, fresh and bright inside and out.   Phillip J. Pirages   67 - 66   2016 $1250

Gautier, Theophile *King Candaules.* Paris: Societe des Beaux Arts circa, 1895. On of 20 lettered copies of the edition De Dux Mondes (this copy lettered out of sequence and stamped with red star), sumptuous azure crushed morocco, lavishly gilt and inlaid in Art Nouveau style, covers with large central fleur-de-lys in gilt and lilac morocco within an elaborate frame of lily bouquets and garlands inlaid in lilac, orange and white, raised bands, spine gilt in compartments, smaller ones at head and tail with inlaid lilac fleur-de-lys, large central compartment with spray of lilies in orange and white, two compartments with gilt titling, very wide turn-ins with elaborate gilt floral and foliate decoration enclosing burnt orange morocco doublures, front doublure featuring an oval inset of white kidskin with hand colored engraving of female nude, ivory watered silk endleaves, blue marbled flyleaves, top edge gilt, others untrimmed, partially unopened, with 61 illustrations by Paul Avril, comprised of 20 in three states, plain India proof and colored and one in single state, all with tissue guards, spine faintly sunned, otherwise fine as fresh and bright as one could hope for.   Phillip J. Pirages 67 - 67   2016 $2200

Gay, John 1685-1732 *Fables...* London: printed for John Stockdale, 1793. First edition with plates engraved by Blake, 2 volumes, octavo, 71 engraved plates, including titlepage in each volume and engraved dedication plate in volume II, 12 of the plates in volume I, engraved by Blake after designs by Kent, Wooton and Gravelot, list of subscribers in volume II, handsomely bound in half variegated tree calf, ruled gilt, over marbled boards, spines lettered and tooled in gilt in compartments, marbled endpapers, top edge gilt, others trimmed, very minor offsetting from plates to text and some minor edge browning, small tape repair to verso of final leaf in volume 1, not affecting text, near fine. Heritage Book Shop Holiday 2015 - 41 2016 $1000

Gay, John 1685-1732 *Polly: an Opera Being the Second part of the Beggar's Opera.* London: printed for the author, 1729. First edition, quarto, engraved sheet music, title in red and black, original blue paper wrappers, uncut, some professional repairs to wrappers, new stitching to wrappers, 2 previous owner's bookplates tipped in to inside front wrapper, chemised and housed in quarter blue morocco slipcase, very good. Heritage Book Shop Holiday 2015 - 42 2016 $1750

Gay, Theresa *James W. Marshall the Discoverer of California Gold: a Biography.* Georgetown: Tailsman Press, 1967. Limited to 25 copies prined on special paper, specially bound numbered, boxed and signed by author, frontispiece, portrait, both in color, 25 illustrations, 4 facsimile inserts in rear pocket, facsimile map insert missing from this copy, half simulated black morocco over marbled boards, gilt lettered spine, fine, double slipcase (outer slipcase soiled and spotted). Argonaut Book Shop Biography 2015 - 5916 2016 $90

Gaya, Louis De *Marriage Ceremonies; or the Ceremonies Used in Marriages in all Parts of the World.* London: printed for Abel Roper, 1697. Third edition in English, somewhat browned in places, 12mo., original sheep, later paper label on spine lettered in ink, very minor wear, good. Blackwell's Rare Books B186 - 103 2016 £800

Gaze, Harold *The Enchanted Fish.* Melbourne: Auckland: Christchurch: Dunedin and Wellington and London: Whitcome & Tombs Limited, n.d., 1921. 8vo., wrappers, color plate on cover, slight edgewear, near fine, illustrated by Gaze with 3 color plates plus color plate on cover), 3 full page pen and ink plus several smaller text illustrations, rare. Aleph-bet Books, Inc. 112 - 212 2016 $650

Gazzadi, Domenico *Zoologia Morale Exposta in Cento Venti Discrousi in Versi o in Prosa.* Florence: Vincenzo Batelli & Compagni, 1843-1846. First and only edition, folio, 3 volumes, contemporary quarter brown morocco, marbled boards, elaborate gilt tools and lettering to spines, 93 hand colored engraved plates by J. Giarre, binding little rubbed to edges, browning to 3 plates on volume II, closed tear affecting image to bottom margin of plate of St. Bernard's in volume I, occasional marking elsewhere, generally very clean and bright, very good, ownership stamps of Giovanni Borsari, with Borsari's stamp and 2 censor's stamps. Sotheran's Piccadilly Notes - Summer 2015 - 6 2016 £20,000

Gebler, Matthew *Matt. Gebbles' The Clown's Comic Song Book.* Philadelphia: R. f. Simpson, 1864. 12mo., pictorial yellow wrappers, some abrading to rear cover, central vertical crease, narrow dogearing to upper fore-corners, hint of light foxing. Dramatis Personae 119 - 60 2016 $250

Geddes, James *Canal Report Made by the Engineer Employed by the State of Ohio.* Columbus: Office of the Columbus Gazette, 1823. First edition, 8vo., sewn, uncut as issued, few stains. M & S Rare Books, Inc. 99 - 94 2016 $450

Geddes, Vorgo *From the life of George Emery Blum.* Brookfield: Brookfield Payers, 1934. First edition, author's presentation, very good in little worn dust jacket. Second Life Books, Inc. 196A - 624 2016 $65

Geil, William Edgar *The Great Wall of China.* New York: Sturgis & Walton Co., 1909. First edition, illustrations, very good, gilt on binding in excellent condition, some rubbing at head and tail, interior bright, crisp, clean, top edge gilt, hinges reinforced archivally, but there is no wear to binding, copious illustrations. Simon Finch 2015 - 001668 2016 $275

Geil, William Edgar *A Yankee on the Yangtze.* New York: Cincinnati: Eaton and Mains: Jennings and Graham, 1904. First edition, mild soil to covers, cover edge wear, owner name and inkstamp, rear hinge archivally reinforced, 8vo., 100 full page illustrations, very good+ copy. By the Book, L. C. 45 - 41 2016 $200

Geilgud, John *Stage Directions.* New York: Random House, 1963. Second printing, 8vo., frontispiece in color and 11 illustrations, Drama League award to Margaret Jane Fischer and inscription to her from author, fine. Second Life Books, Inc. 196A - 631 2016 $45

Geisel, Theodor Seuss 1904-1994 *And to Think That I Saw It on Mulberry Street.* New York: Vanguard, 1937. Second printing, with dust jacket price $1.25, 4to., pictorial boards, fine in dust jacket, remarkable copy with none of the edgewear usually found and with just touch of toning to white paper spine, dust jacket has minimal soil and few small tears, but this is one of the nicest we've seen, signed by author.   Aleph-bet Books, Inc.   111 - 414   2016 $1950

Geisel, Theodor Seuss 1904-1994 *Because a Little Bus Wen Ka-Choo.* New York: Random House/Beginner Books, 1975. First edition, first printing with 1-0 code, illustrations by Michael Frith, 8vo., pictorial boards small name written on pastedown, near fine,.   Aleph-bet Books, Inc.   112 - 452   2016 $1750

Geisel, Theodor Seuss 1904-1994 *Dr. Seuss from Then to Now.* New York: Random House, 1986. First edition, cloth, fine in fine dust jacket, this copy inscribed by author Christmas 1986.   Aleph-bet Books, Inc.   112 - 458   2016 $600

Geisel, Theodor Seuss 1904-1994 *Green Eggs and Ham.* New York: Random House, 1960. First edition, first issue with '50 Word Vocabulary' statement applied as a sticker on right corner of dust jacket, not printed on paper, 8vo., orange glazed pictorial boards, fine in beautiful dust jacket with 2 small edge mends, great copy.   Aleph-bet Books, Inc.   112 - 451   2016 $4750

Geisel, Theodor Seuss 1904-1994 *Hop of Pop.* New York: Random House, 1963. First edition, 8vo., glazed pictorial boards, slight rubbing, else near fine in slightly soiled, very good+ dust jacket.   Aleph-bet Books, Inc.   112 - 453   2016 $675

Geisel, Theodor Seuss 1904-1994 *I Can Draw It Myself by Me, Myself with a little Help from my Friend Dr. Seuss.* New York: Random House, 1970. Oblong folio, spiral bound flexible card covers, slightest bit of cover soil, else fine and unused, rare.   Aleph-bet Books, Inc.   112 - 454   2016 $1200

Geisel, Theodor Seuss 1904-1994 *I Can Write! A Book by me....* New York: Random House, 1971. First edition, illustrations in color by Roy McKie, rare, 4to., pictorial cloth, covers lightly age toned, else near fine and unused.   Aleph-bet Books, Inc.   112 - 455   2016 $1250

Geisel, Theodor Seuss 1904-1994 *If I Ran the Zoo.* New York: Random House, 1950. First edition, folio, red glazed pictorial boards, fine in near fine dust jacket, amazing copy, exceedingly scarce.   Aleph-bet Books, Inc.   111 - 415   2016 $2500

Geisel, Theodor Seuss 1904-1994 *My Book About Me.* New York: Random House, 1969. First edition, 4to., yellow pictorial cloth, previous owner stamp on endpaper, one corner rubbed, issued without a dust jacket, fine and completely unused, illustrations in color by Roy McKie, rarely found in this condition.   Aleph-bet Books, Inc.   112 - 456   2016 $800

Geisel, Theodor Seuss 1904-1994 *There's a Wocket in My Pocket!* New York: A. Bright and Early Book from Beginner Books/Random House, 1974. First edition (correct code), printed pictorial boards, front tips show wear, light crease on page, very good+.   Aleph-bet Books, Inc.   112 - 457   2016 $700

Geisel, Theodor Seuss 1904-1994 *You're Only Old Once.* New York: Random House, 1986. Limited to 500 copies signed by author, 4to., cloth, fine in slipcase (slightly faded at spine), wonderful illustrations.   Aleph-bet Books, Inc.   111 - 416   2016 $650

Geldart, Hannah Ransome *The Nursery Guide and the Infants first Hymn Book.* London: R. Yorke Clarke & Co., 1850. Third edition, frontispiece, illustrations, slight paper browning, original pink cloth, slightly rubbed at head of tail, spine faded, very good.   Jarndyce Antiquarian Books   CCXV - 214   2016   £75

Gell, Elizabeth Mary Lyttleton *The More Excellent Way,...* London: Henry Frowde, 1898. Half title, original green decorated cloth, very good, bright copy.   Jarndyce Antiquarian Books   CCXV - 215   2016   £25

Gemmell, David A. *The King Beyond the Gate.* London: Century Pub., 1985. First edition, octavo, boards, age darkening to text block, fine in fine dust jacket.   John W. Knott, Jr./L.W. Currey, Inc.   Fall-Winter 2015 - 17423   2016 $1250

Gemmell, David A. *Legend.* London: Melbourne: Auckland: Johannesburg: Century, 1986. First hardcover edition, signed by author, octavo, boards, signed by author, text block age darkened (common to the book), fine in fine dust jacket.   John W. Knott, Jr./L.W. Currey, Inc.   Fall-Winter 2015 - 17422   2016 $1500

Gemmell, David A. *Waylander.* London: Melbourne: Auckland: Johannesburg: Century, 1986. First edition, octavo, boards, age darkening to text block, fine in fine dust jacket.   John W. Knott, Jr./L.W. Currey, Inc.   Fall-Winter 2015 - 17424   2016 $1250

Genard, Francois *The School of Man.* London: printed for Lockyer Davis, 1753. Second edition, 12mo., initial leaf of ads, rebound preserving original lower cover, front cover and spine in matching gilt ruled speckled calf, red morocco label.   Jarndyce Antiquarian Books   CCXV - 216   2016   £150

Gener, S. *Translations of M. Gener, Being a Selection of letters on Life and Manners.* Edinburgh: printed for Peter Hill, 1808. First English edition, half title, contemporary full tree calf, red label, slightly rubbed, booklabel of Maclean of Ardgour, very good. Jarndyce Antiquarian Books CCXV - 217 2016 £65

Genini, Ronald *Romualdo Pacheco, a California in Two Eras.* San Francisco: Book Club of California, 1985. First edition, one of 500 copies, frontispiece, illustrations from photos, brown cloth, embossed portrait on front cover, paper spine label, very fine. Argonaut Book Shop Biography 2015 - 5500 2016 $125

Gent, J. T. *Robert Finch: a Tale of the Old Leicester Stocking Weavers.* London: Leicester: pub. by Simpkin Marshall & Co./De Montford Press, 1893. First edition, 12mo., original cloth, gilt, slightly rubbed at extremities, scarce, very good. Simon Finch 2015 - 028430 2016 $232

The Gentleman's Library, Containing Rules for Conduct in all Parts of Life. London: printed for E. P. for W. Mears, 1715. First edition, 12mo., frontispiece, contemporary panelled calf, later faded and worn paper label, some expert repairs, ownership inscription of Mary Baynes, good plus. Jarndyce Antiquarian Books CCXV - 218 2016 £520

The Gentleman's Library, Containing Rules for Conduct in all Parts of Life. London: published and sold by booksellers, 1813. New edition, 12mo., frontispiece, prelims browned and waterstained, some spotting and slight browning, contemporary full turquoise calf by W. Forester, dulled, spine chipped at head and tail, lacking label, contemporary signature on titlepage. Jarndyce Antiquarian Books CCXV - 219 2016 £45

Geoffroy, Etienne L. *Historie Abregee des Insectes.* Paris: Calixte Volland and Remont an VII i.e., 1799. Later edition, 4to., 2 volumes, folding table, 22 hand colored plates, contemporary half calf, rubbed at extremities, scattered foxing, but very good. Joseph J. Felcone, Inc. Books from Five Centuries: a Miscellany - 70 2016 $120

Geometrical Recreations: affording an Amusing and Familiar Introduction to the Rudiments of Plane Geometry.... London: R. Ackermann, 1815. 15 plates, original black paper boards, little wear, following hinge slightly weak, good plus, original boards, without box mentioned on front board. Jarndyce Antiquarian Books CCXV - 698 2016 £225

George, Emery *A Gift of Nerve.* Ann Arbor: Kylix Press, 1978. 8vo., very good+ in dust jacket, laid in is one page ALS from Herbert Leibowitz, publisher of Parnassus to poet Paul Metcalf requesting a review, also laid in 3 page holograph MS. review of the book by metcalf. Second Life Books, Inc. 196A - 627 2016 $250

George, Jean Craighead *The Big Book for Our Planet.* New York: Dutton, 1993. First edition, boards, fine in fine dust jacket, illustrations, laid in bookplate that is signed by Barbara Cooney and Natalie Babbitt, etc. Aleph-bet Books, Inc. 111 - 464 2016 $200

Georgel, Jean Francois *Voyage a Saint Petersbourg en 1799-1800...* Paris: Eymery and Delaunay, 1818. Scarce first edition, 8vo., contemporary calf backed drab boards, spine with raised bands, ornamented and lettered gilt, hinges at tail of spine repaired, extremities with wear, but stable, internally apart from occasional light browning, good. Sotheran's Travel and Exploration - 253 2016 £498

Georgiadis, Konstantinos *Olympic Revival. The Revival of the Olympic Games in Modern Times.* Athens: Ekdotike Athenson, 2003. First edition, large format, illustrations, blue boards, title and outline of ancient stadium blindstamped, near fine, dust jacket, dust smudge to rear over, else very good. Unsworths Antiquarian Booksellers Ltd. E05 - 116 2016 £45

Gerard De Nerval Labrunie, Known as   1808-1855 *Aurelia.* Monaco: Club International De Bibliophile/Jaspard Polus, 1960. No. 140 of 250 copies from an edition of 300, 34 etchings by Leonor Fini, lovely copy, fine in fine wrappers, publisher's titled clamshell box, 4to. Beasley Books 2015 - 2016 $800

Gerard, John *Trans.* Berlin: John Gerard, 1998. Limited to 20 numbered copies signed by Fritz Best, folio, black linen covers with rectangular cut-out on front board allowing title to show throughout, 7 double page spreads, accordion folded book with images. Oak Knoll Books 27 - 21 2016 $690

Gerard, John   1545-1612 *The Herball or General Histoire of Plantes.* London: by Adam Islip, Joice Norton and Richard Whitakers, 1633. First printing of the second edition, over 2500 woodcuts of plants, early 19th century panelled calf, neatly rebacked retaining original fully gilt spine, title lightly soiled but complete and free of any repair, blank fore and bottom edges of A4-5 neatly extended, few marginal tears neatly closed, intermittent faint dampstain in top margin becoming bit more noticeable toward end of text, marginal repair to 7A1 (index) costing several page numbers, blank lower corner of 7B5 replaced, very good and most attractive copy, without extensive repairing and sophisticated that nearly always comes with early English herbals, ownership inscription and cost dated 1634. Joseph J. Felcone, Inc. Books from Five Centuries: a Miscellany - 72 2016 $8000

Gerhard, Friedrich Wilhelm Eduard *Etruskische und Kampanische Vasenbilder des Koniglichen Museums zu Berlin.* Berlin: Verlag von G. Reimer, 1843. First edition, imperial folio, contemporary calf over marbled blue paper boards, 30 color and five monochrome plates, library label of the Duc de Lynes, text in German, from the library of Honore d'Albert, 8th Duc de Luynes, noted archaeologist and collector of antiquities.   Honey & Wax Booksellers   4 - 5   2016 $9000

Gerning, Johann Isaac Von, Baron *A Picturesque Tour along the Rhine.* London: R. Ackermann, 1820. First edition in English, first issue, one of 50 large paper copies, 422 x 324mm., excellent contemporary red half morocco over marbled boards by Charles Hering (stamp signed), newly rebacked and recornered to style by Courtlad Benson, wide raised bands and panels, attractively gilt in scrolling designs, gilt titling, all edges gilt, 24 hand colored plates of the Rhine (plus one folding map), armorial bookplate "RGV" with evidence of bookplate removal, offsetting onto tissue guards (indicating they have done their job), one tissue guard missing (but not offsetting onto text in this case), isolated trivial thumbing, foxing or rust spots, but fine and especially desirable copy, beautifully restored binding unworn, text and plates with only most minor imperfections and margins of special copy remarkably broad.   Phillip J. Pirages   67 - 167   2016 $10,000

Gerry, Leslie *New York Reflections.* Dowdeswell: Leslie Gerry Editions, 2015. 7/65 copies from an edition of 80 copies, signed by artist, text printed on Somerset mould made paper, frontispiece and 26 color plates largely double spread, 64mo., original quarter yellow leather and black cloth, backstrip lettered in black, cloth slipcase, new.   Blackwell's Rare Books   B186 - 308   2016   £200

Gerry, Leslie *New York Reflections.* Dowdeswell: Leslie Gerry Editions, 2015. 4/55 copies from an edition of 70 copies, signed by artist, text printed in grey, frontispiece and 26 color plates double spread printed on Moulin du Gue mouldmade paper at the Senecio Press using flat bed UV digital printer, large folio, original quarter grey cloth with pictorial sides, backstrip lettered in grey, housed in cloth solander box, inlaid with full color printed metal panels using same technique.   Blackwell's Rare Books   B186 - 307   2016   £2000

Gersaint, Edme Francois *Catalogue Raisonne de Toutes les Pieces qui Forment l'Oeuvre de Rembrandt...* Paris: Chez Hochereau, 1751. First edition, 8vo., errata leaf, half dark brown leather, raised bands on spine, lettered gilt, 2 volumes bound in one, second part is very scarce, sound, very good in scuffed boards, leather little worn and rubbed, neat name on front endpaper, otherwise text clean, portrait in good order.   Any Amount of Books   2015 - C6076   2016   £650

Gershwin, Ira *Lyrics on Several Occasions.* New York: Alfred A. Knopf, 1959. First edition, inscribed by Gershwin to noted pianist and composer, Radie Britain, fine in about near fine dust jacket (spine lightly toned and with few nicks and rubs along top edge), lovely copy.   Royal Books   48 - 23   2016 $1500

Gerstinger, Hans *Die Griechische Buchmalerei. Mit 22 Abbildungen im Textband und 28 Tafeln nach Originalen der Nationalbibliothek in Wien.* Wien: Der Oesterr Staatsdruckerei, 1926. First edition, first printing, folio, 2 volumes, slipcase, paper covered boards, loose plates enclosed in cardboard box with cloth spine, whole enclosed in patterned paper covered slipcase, 5 plates and 28 plates included in the box of leaves, 9 of which are in full color and mounted on white matte board, these plates have minimal wear to edges of matte-boards, bound book has mild wear around edges with moderate rubbing to head and heel of spine, corners lightly bumped, clam shell case with plates moderately worn around edges, spine worn and slightly fragile, slipcase worn and fragile.   Oak Knoll Books   310 - 34   2016 $2500

Die Geschichte der Kinder im Walde Mit Vielen Bunten Bildern Greziert. Harrisburg: G. S. Peters, circa, 1835-1840. First edition?, 18mo., 8 colored illustrations in blue, green, yellow and red, original printed and pictorial orange wrappers.   M & S Rare Books, Inc.   99 - 136   2016 $1000

Gesner, Abraham *New Brunswick: with notes for Emigrants.* London: Simmons and Ward, 1847. First edition, original cloth which has been rebacked with spine repaired and small patch of lower spine cloth replaced, endpapers have been repaired with rear endpaper cleaned, five illustrations and vignette on titlepage, cloth has been repaired with original spine and boards, extreme wear to edges of binding slightly cocked.   Schooner Books Ltd.   115 - 52   2016 $125

Gesner, C. *On the Admiration of Mountains....* San Francisco: Grabhorn Press, 1937. One of 325 copies, unrecorded variant binding with printed paper spine label rather than orange spine lettering, small quarto, 3 illustrated initials by Dorothy Grover, 8 reproductions of early woodcuts by Hans Leonhard Schaufelin, tan decorated boards, tan cloth, spine with printed paper label, light foxing to edges of two pages, small spot to rear cover, else fine.   Argonaut Book Shop   Mountaineering 2015 - 5878   2016 $350

Gesner, Johann Mathias *Scriptores Rei Rusticae Veretes Latini.* Leipzig: sumtibus Caspari Fritsch, 1773. 1774. Second edition, 2 volumes, frontispiece to volume I and 6 further folding plates, engraved vignette to each titlepage, some spotting and browning due to paper quality as usual with fritsch but less than sometimes seen, final plate little oversized and therefore crumpled at edges, contemporary speckled tan calf red and green morocco gilt spine labels, edges sprinkled red, volume I head cap little chipped, few small stains and patchy fading, overall very good, armorial bookplate of Right Hon. Henry Hobhouse (1854-1937) and Stephen Hobhouse (1881-1961) and Arthur Hobhouse (1886-1965).   Unsworths Antiquarian Booksellers Ltd.   E05 - 12   2016   £350

Gessner, Salomon *The Death of Abel.* Newport: printed by Peter Edes, 1787. Rare American printing, browned, text on titlepage underlined with pinpricks, early ownership inscription of Sarah J. Easton, 12mo., contemporary sheep, spine ruled in gilt, rubbed, some wear to front joint and tail of spine, sound.   Blackwell's Rare Books   B186 - 62   2016   £400

Gesta Romanorum cum Applicationibus Moralisatis ac Mysticis. Augsburg: Anton Sorg, 1487. Folio, Gothic letter, 50 or 51-lines per page, initials supplied in red, rubricated throughout, original wooden boards rebacked with half modern calf tooled in blind, spine lettered gilt, brass hardware but lacking clasp closure, wooden boards chipped along edges and with some minor worming, newer endpapers, over partially exposed original endpapers, previous owner's old ink manuscript index, contemporary religious note bottom of leaf b8v and on old owner's inscription on final leaf, some minor worming throughout, mainly marginal, final few leaves have few more wormholes within text, text remains fully legible, marginal closed tear to leaf n5, not affecting text, leaves bit wrinkled and some minor dampstaining to upper margin at end, overall very good, clean.   Heritage Book Shop   Holiday 2015 - 44   2016 $15,000

Ghose, Asutosh *Romance of Plants.* Calcutta: H. C. Gangooly, 1912. First edition, green cloth has some wear and fraying, especially at extremities, very good, apparently uncommon.   Ken Lopez Bookseller   166 - 75   2016 $750

Gibbon, Edward   1737-1794   *The History of the Decline and Fall of the Roman Empire.* London: Strahan and Cadell, 1788-1790. Early octavo edition, 12 volumes, full contemporary polished calf, frontispiece, 3 folding maps, armorial bookplate of James Bruce, Laird of Kinnaird, near fine set with excellent association.   Honey & Wax Booksellers   4 - 56   2016 $5000

Gibbon, Edward   1737-1794   *Gibbon's History of the Decline and Fall of the Roman Empire.* London: printed for G. Kearsley, 1789. 2 volumes, faint foxing in places, text printed on slightly bluer paper than prelims, 8vo., contemporary tree calf, spines divided by gilt fillets, red morocco lettering pieces, circular green numbered pieces (lost from volume I, chipped on volume ii), spines rather rubbed and since conserved, little insect damage to joints, good.   Blackwell's Rare Books   Greek & Latin Classics VII - 78   2016   £900

Gibbon, Edward   1737-1794   *The Decline and Fall of the Roman Empire.* New York: Heritage Press, 1946. 3 volumes, etchings by Gian Battista Piranesi, pictorial boards, brown cloth, spines lettered and decorated in gilt, very fine, slipcases, Sandglass pamphlet laid in.   Argonaut Book Shop   Heritage Press 2015 - 6991   2016 $125

Gibbon, John Murray   *Time and Tide in the Atlantic Provinces.* Sackville: Products Limited, 1952. Quarto, card covers with cover painting by Leonard Lane, other photo illustrations and artwork, folding map, very good.   Schooner Books Ltd.   115 - 191   2016 $45

Gibbons, Stella   *Conference at Cold Comfort Farm.* London: Longmans Green, 1949. First edition, foolscap 8vo., original light blue boards, sunned backstrip lettered in silver, dust jacket chipped, more so to backstrip panel head and tail, good.   Blackwell's Rare Books   B186 - 220   2016   £150

Gibbs, George   *The Vanishing Idol.* New York: D. Appleton Century, 1936. First edition, small owner stamp to front flyleaf, spine lean and trace of rubbing to spine extremities, still near fine in very good, mildly faded and rubbed dust jacket with minor edge wear, especially scarce in jacket.   Ken Lopez Bookseller   166 - 36   2016 $275

Gibbs, May   *Little Ragged Blossom and More About Snugglepot & Cuddlepie.* Sydney: August, 1920. Cloth backed pictorial boards, color paste-on, occasional finger soil, minor wear near fine in dust jacket (with narrow pieces off corners), minor wear, near fine in dust jacket (with narrow pieces off corners), illustrations by Gibbs.   Aleph-bet Books, Inc.   112 - 213   2016 $750

Gibbs, May   *Snugglepot and Cuddlepie their Adventures Wonderful.* Sydney: Angus Robertson, n.d., 1918. First edition, 4to., cloth backed pictorial boards, color paste-on front cover, rear cover blank, light rubbing on cover and margin of one plate very slightly creased, clean, tight very good++ copy, printed in sepia throughout, frontispiece, full page sepia illustrations, several in text illustrations and pictorial endpapers by Gibbs.   Aleph-bet Books, Inc.   112 - 214   2016 $600

Gibson, Ralph *Chiaroscuro.* New York: Hyperion, 1982. First edition, oblong folio, cloth clamshell portfolio containing bifolium limitation leaf and 15 photos, each numbered and signed by artist, one of 100 numbered copies, also five lettered copies, plates, fine, portfolio very good, sensitive portfolio cloth is lightly rubbed and scuffed overall but with no tears or abrasions.   Royal Books   49 - 3   2016 $15,000

Gibson, Wilfrid *Krindlesyke.* London: Macmillan, 1922. First edition, 8vo., original tan boards, printed paper spine label, extreme fore-tips lightly bumped, offset on free endpapers, delimited by jacket flaps, otherwise fine in dust jacket, stained on front panel, presentation copy inscribed by author for Thomas Hardy, with Hardy's Max Gate booklabel. James S. Jaffe Rare Books   Occasional List: Winter 2016 - 75   2016 $750

Gibson, William *Mona Lisa Overdrive.* New York: Bantam Books, 1988. First edition, faint erasure on front fly, else fine in fine dust jacket.   Between the Covers Rare Books   208 - 120   2016 $45

Gibson, William *Neuromancer.* London: Victor Gollancz Ltd., 1984. First British (first hardcover) edition, signed on titlepage by author, octavo, boards, fine in fine dust jacket. John W. Knott, Jr./L.W. Currey, Inc.   Fall-Winter 2015 - 18567   2016 $2500

Giddins, Gary *A Moment's Notice: Portraits of American Jazz Musicians.* New York: Schrimer, 1983. First printing, 4to., presentation by Carol Friedman to Martin Scorsese, paper over boards, nice in slightly browned dust jacket. Second Life Books, Inc.   196A - 629   2016 $95

Gide, Andre   1869-1951 *Theseus.* N.P.: but Covalo: Yolla Bolly Press, 1998. One of 85 copies bound thus by Cardoza-James Binding Co., Folio, quarter suede, paper covered boards, slipcase, paper is mouldmade Somerset Velvet, drawings by Sidney Goodman, signed by Goodman on colophon.   Oak Knoll Books   310 - 178   2016 $900

Gigault De La Salle, Achille Etienne *Voyage Pittoresque en Sicile.*   Paris: P. Didot, l'Aine (second volume: Jules Didot l'Aine), 1822-1826. First editions, 641 x 495mm., 2 volumes, lacking dedication leaf and subscriber list present in Abbey copy, contemporary red straight grain morocco, textured paper boards, gilt titling on spine, edges untrimmed, one map (as called for, though Abbey had two), 92 accomplished and beautifully hand colored aquatint plates of Sicilian Views; moderate rubbing to joints and elsewhere, covers with some scars, other minor problems externally, but original bindings entirely solid and surprisingly so for such an immense book, with so many fabulous picture, prelim leaves and text lightly to substantially foxed, half dozen plates with faint overall browning, one tissue guard missing, margins of perhaps half the engravings with foxing (usually light, though noticeable in three or four cases in the second volumes), still very pleasing copy of beautifully illustrated book, marginal foxing seldom distracting and engraved images themselves clear and clean, affected by neither foxing nor dreaded offsetting from text, extraordinarily rare.   Phillip J. Pirages   67 - 168   2016 $59,000

Gilb, Dagoberto *Winners on the Pass Line, and Other Stories.* El Paso: Cinco Punta Press, 1985. First edition, pictorial wrappers, fine, signed by author.   Bella Luna Books   2016 - t4406   2016 $66

Gilbert, Anthony *The Woman in Red.* London: Collins Crime Club, 1941. First edition, some color fading to top edges of cloth, else near fine in price clipped dust jacket lightly professionally restored at head of spine and lightly sunned on spine, exceptional copy.   Buckingham Books   2015 - 25920   2016 $3750

Gilbert, Cass *Cass Gilbert: Reminiscences and Addresses.* New York: privately printed, 1935. First edition, octavo, navy blue cloth spine and gray cloth boards, some exterior wear to spine ends and corners, gutters bit brown toned, contents otherwise very good, edges untrimmed, frontispiece.   Simon Finch   2015 - 2016 $250

Gilchrist, Alexander *Life of William Blake with Selections from His Poems and Other Writings.* 1880. Second edition, illustrations from Blake's own works, 2 volumes, uncut, blue pictorial cloth, gilt little marked and bumped at corners, lower cover of first volume with some staining and lower joint partly cracked, lower hinge cracked, foxing to endpapers, otherwise nice, with gilt to spines, only little dulled, gilt to upper covers bright of this best edition.   Bertram Rota Ltd.   February List 2016 - 6   2016   £400

Gildersleeve, David H. *Campaign 1888 American Wages for American Workmen, American Markets for American People. Protection.*   New York: David H. Gildersleeve, 1888. First edition, one sheet folded once, near fine, portraits, and 2 color drawings, 16mo., self wrappers. Kaaterskill Books   21 - 32   2016 $100

Gildon, Charles *The New Metamorphosis; or Pleasant Transformation of the Golden Ass.* London: printed for S. Briscoe and sold by J. Morphew, 1708. First edition, 2 volumes, octavo, contemporary panelled calf, rebacked, gilt lettering, 7 engraved plates, foxing and browning, particularly to signatures with poor quality paper, very good.   The Brick Row Book Shop   Miscellany 69 - 30   2016 $1000

Gildzen, Alex *Six Poems/Seven Prints.* Kent: Kent State University, 1971. First edition, one of 50 sets signed by authors and by Smithson, Porter, Quaytman, Sacco, and Piene, out of a total edition of 500 sets, 4to., 14 loose sheets laid into paper portfolio, fine.   James S. Jaffe Rare Books   Occasional List: Winter 2016 - 22   2016 $4500

Giles, Herbert A. *Record of the Buddhistic Kingdoms.* London: Shanghai: Trubner/Kelly & Walsh, 1877. First edition, 8vo., very good+, quarter brown leather and multicolor paper covered boards with raised bands, gilt lettered black leather spine label, tipped-in errata slip as issued, wear to spine label affecting title, minimal scattered foxing, scarce. By the Book, L. C.   45 - 42   2016 $450

Giles, James R. *James Jones.* Boston: Twayne, 1981. One of the dedication copies, inscribed by Giles to Jones's widow, Gloria and their children, boards foxed, very good, without dust jacket, presumably as issued.   Ken Lopez Bookseller   166 - 59   2016 $250

Giles, William *The Guide to Domestic Happiness.* London: William Button, 1811. Ninth edition, 12mo., frontispiece, contemporary mottled calf, borders in gilt, spine decorated in gilt, black morocco label, little rubbed, spine slightly darkened, contemporary gift inscription on leading blank, nice.   Jarndyce Antiquarian Books   CCXV - 220   2016   £75

Gill, Brendan *Many Masks: a Life of Frank Lloyd Wright.* New York: Putnam's, 1987. First printing, photos, author's signature on flyleaf, paper over boards with cloth spine, nice in scuffed and very slightly chipped dust jacket, near fine.   Second Life Books, Inc.   196A - 636   2016 $45

Gill, Eric 1882-1940 *The Engravings of Eric Gill.* Wellingborough: Christopher Skelton, 1983. No. 72 of 85 special copies printed on archival rag paper and 1350 copies of ordinary edition, 2 volumes, plus portfolio, publisher's deluxe biscuit colored morocco over reddish brown linen, flat spines with gilt titling, in original (somewhat worn) slipcase, profusely illustrated with more than 1000 reproductions of Gill's works, special copy accompanied by portfolio of 8 engravings printed directly from original woodblocks, three tiny dark spots to one spine, otherwise in mint condition.   Phillip J. Pirages   67 - 169   2016 $1750

Gill, Eric 1882-1940 *War Memorial.* Ditchling: St. Dominics Press, 1923. First edition, small 8vo., original heavy grey wrappers, with front cover and titlepage illustration from wood engraving by David Jones and single wood engraving by Gill, wrappers slightly browned otherwise, very good, bookplate of Michael Gerveys Sewell.   Sotheran's Piccadilly Notes - Summer 2015 - 145   2016   £495

Gill, Eric 1882-1940 *Wood Engravings: Being a Selection of Deric Gills Engravings on Wood. (with) Engravings by Eric Gill. (with) Engravings 1928-1933.* Sussex: St. Dominics Press, 1924. One of 100 copies in an edition of 150, no limitation statement in this copy, ink notation "No. 5?" added next to bracketed Virgin and Child on titlepage; Bristol: Douglas Cleverdon, 1919. No. 398 in an edition of 400 copies on paper specially manufactured for this edition, total edition of 490, the first authorized edition; London: Faber & Faber, 1934, printed by Hague & Gill at High Wycombe; 4to. and small folio, cloth, frontispiece, plates, very good, handsome set in new matching leather trimmed slipcase.   Oak Knoll Books   27 - 22   2016 $8000

Gill, Thomas *Etiquette for Young Gentlemen or the Principles of True Politeness.* London: Simpkin & Marshall & Thomas Gill, Easingwold, circa, 1847. Small 8vo., 1 page initial ad, original brown cloth blocked in blind and gilt, spine slightly marked by damp, all edges gilt, nice.   Jarndyce Antiquarian Books   CCXV - 221   2016   £180

Gill, Thomas *Report of the Dinner Given to Charles Dickens in Boston February 1 1842.* Boston: William Crosby and Co., 1842. First edition, original pale pink printed wrappers, spine later reinforced with appropriate paper, blind uniersity stamp on title.   Jarndyce Antiquarian Booksellers   CCXVIII - 325   2016   £750

Gillespie, John Birks *To Be or Not to Bop: Memoirs.* Garden City: Doubleday, 1979. First edition, 8vo., notation in ink by musicians, photos, paper over boards with cloth spine, cover very slightly worn at corners and ends of spine, otherwise very good, tight copy, little scuffed and chipped dust jacket.   Second Life Books, Inc.   196A - 637   2016 $350

Gilliam, Albert M. *Travels in Mexico during the Years 1843 and 44.* Aberdeen: George Clark and Son, 1847. New edition, half title, original blue cloth, very slight fading to spine, very good.   Jarndyce Antiquarian Booksellers   CCXVII - 109   2016   £185

Gilliam, Franklin *California Magazines.* San Francisco: Book Club of California, 1975. Facsimile of the first number of "Le Petit Journal des Refusees", fine set, half leather slipcase.   Argonaut Book Shop   Private Press 2015 - 3728   2016 $40

Gillispie, Charles Coulston *Dictionary of Scientific Biography.* New York: Charles Scribner's Sons, 1970-1981. Second edition, 8 volume set (two volumes bound in each volume), green gilt and black stamped, fine.   Jeff Weber Rare Books   183 - 20   2016 $900

Gillman, Richard *Lunch at Carcassonne.* Manchester: The X Press, 1976. First edition, of a total of 500 copies, this one of 450 signed by author, 8vo., printed wrappers, laid in 3 page typed review, with holograph corrections by writer Paul Metcalf.   Second Life Books, Inc.   196A - 639   2016 $125

Gilman, Charlotte Perkins *The Crux, a Novel.* New York: Charlton, 1911. First edition, 8vo., printed wrappers, couple of small chips top of spine, flyleaf soiled, stains on rear cover, very good, quite rare.   Second Life Books, Inc.   197 - 144   2016 $725

Gilman, Charlotte Perkins *The Forerunner.* Volume 4 #1 January, 1913. Printed wrappers, soiled and nicked, nice and clean inside, good copy.   Second Life Books, Inc.   197 - 150   2016 $50

Gilman, Charlotte Perkins *The Forerunner.* Volume 4 #2 February, 1913. Printed wrappers, slightly soiled, nice and clean inside, very good.   Second Life Books, Inc.   197 - 145 2016 $75

Gilman, Charlotte Perkins *The Forerunner.* Volume 5 #1 to Volume 5 #12, 1914. First edition, large 8vo. publisher's cloth, covers show stain effects endpapers, top margin of endpaper and first seven leaves have some of the paper torn (or eaten away, this does not affect text), bindings show varying degrees of wear,.   Second Life Books, Inc.   197 - 153   2016 $700

Gilman, Charlotte Perkins *The Forerunner.* Volume 5 #2, Feb., 1914. Printed wrappers, soiled, nice and clean inside, very good.   Second Life Books, Inc.   197 - 151   2016 $60

Gilman, Charlotte Perkins *The Forerunner.* Volume 5, #4, April, 1914. printed wrappers, some soiled, nice and clean inside, very good.   Second Life Books, Inc.   197 - 152   2016 $60

Gilman, Charlotte Perkins *The Forerunner.* Volume 5 #8, August, 1914. Unbound and untrimmed, unopened sheets, very good, untrimmed, these sheets probably never bound.   Second Life Books, Inc.   197 - 149   2016 $65

Gilman, Charlotte Perkins *The Forerunner.* Volume 5 # 9, Sept., 1914. Printed wrappers, some soil, nice and clean inside, very good.   Second Life Books, Inc.   197 - 148   2016 $60

Gilman, Charlotte Perkins *The Forerunner.* Volume 5 #12, Dec., 1914. Unbound and untrimmed, unopened, very good.   Second Life Books, Inc.   197 - 147   2016 $60

Gilman, Charlotte Perkins *The Home, Its Work and Influence.* New York: McClure Phillips, 1903. First edition, 8vo., cloth stamped in gilt fine in dust jacket, some chipping at top of spine above title, very rare in dust jacket, uncommon book, this copy probably inscribed for architect Mary J. Coltor "For Mary J. Coutler (sic)".   Second Life Books, Inc.   197 - 155   2016 $3750

Gilman, Charlotte Perkins *The Home, Its Work and Influence.* New York: McClure Phillips, 1903. First edition, 8vo., rear hinge repaired, private bookplate on endpaper, some rubbing along hinges, better than good, scarce.   Second Life Books, Inc.   197 - 154   2016 $600

Gilmour, James *Among the Mongols.* London: Religious Tract Society, 1883. Early or first edition, 8vo., publisher's original blue cloth, illustrated, decorated and lettered in gilt and black, patterned endpapers, numerous wood engravings, some full page, minor rubbing to head and tail of spine, light offsetting from endpapers and light even browning, due to paper stock, good copy.   Sotheran's   Travel and Exploration - 125   2016   £198

Gilpin, John, Mrs. *Pakwan-Ki-Kitab Memsahib's Guide to Cookery in India.* Bombay: A. J. Combridge & Co., 1914. Original printed cream boards, brown cloth spine, covers little rubbed.   Jarndyce Antiquarian Books   CCXV - 222   2016   £125

Gilpin, Joshua *Twenty-One Discourses Delivered in the Parish Church of Wrockwardine in the County of Salop.* London: John Hatchard and Son, 1827. Apparently first edition, 219 x 133mm., appealing contemporary red straight grain morocco, covers with gilt rule border and small sunburst cornerpieces, raised bands flanked by plain and decorative gilt rules, turn-ins with decorative gilt roll, marbled endpapers, all edges gilt, front joint very expertly renewed, with very accomplished fore-edge painting of West Gate, Canterbury; flyleaf facing titlepage with faint but readable offset of the (backward) text of a previously tipped in presentation letter from author; corners bit bruised, spine little dried, leather slightly marked and soiled, expertly repaired binding sound and attractive with lustrous covers, two inch horizontal tear to front endpaper, titlepage bit soiled, text remarkably clean, bright and fresh.   Phillip J. Pirages   67 - 155   2016 $1250

Gilpin, Laura *The Enduring Navaho.* Austin: University of Texas, 1968. First edition, quarto, profusely illustrated with black and white color photos, map, green cloth stamped and lettered in silver and black, fine with pictorial dust jacket with some damage to head and foot of spine.   Argonaut Book Shop   Photography 2015 - 4801   2016 $175

Gilroy, Frank *About Those Roses or How not to Do a Play and Succeed.* New York: Random House, 1965. First edition, 8vo., signed by Irene Dailey who played Nettie Cleary in the 1964 production, very good in little worn dust jacket. Second Life Books, Inc. 196A - 642 2016 $65

Gingerbread Boy. New York: Dutton, 1943. 8vo., spiral backed boards, light edge wear, very good+, 6 fine moveable plates and other color illustrations by Julian Wehr. Aleph-bet Books, Inc. 111 - 313 2016 $200

Gingold, Hermoine *Sirens Should be Seen and Not Heard.* Philadelphia: Lippincott, 1963. First edition, 8vo., author's presentation on flyleaf, nice, slightly chipped and soiled dust jacket. Second Life Books, Inc. 196A - 643 2016 $45

Ginsberg, Allen *Empty Mirror.* New York: Totem Press/Corinth, 1961. First edition, paper wrappers, paper yellowed, owner' name inside cover, cover slightly spotted, otherwise very good. Second Life Books, Inc. 197 - 156 2016 $50

Ginsberg, Allen *First Blues: Rags, Ballads and Harmonium Songs 1971-1974.* New York: Full Court Press, 1975. First edition, signed by author, publisher's olive grey cloth, lettered in silver, original pink dust jacket lettered in white and blue-gray, near fine, very slight lean to spine, three tiny spots to edge, spine head with lightly bumped, unclipped dust jacket, some light toning to front panel, minor sunning to spine, some faint rubbing to extremities, very clean and fresh. B & B Rare Books, Ltd. 2016 - AG008 2016 $150

Ginsberg, Allen *Howl and Other Poems.* San Francisco: City Lights Pocket Bookshop, 1956. First edition, one of 1000 copies printed letterpress, 12mo., original printed wrappers, printed cover label lightly soiled, otherwise fine, presentation from author to poet Jack Gilbert. James S. Jaffe Rare Books Occasional List: Winter 2016 - 64 2016 $15,000

Ginsberg, Allen *Howl.* New York: Harper & Row, 1986. First edition thus, limited edition, quarto, slightly bowed boards with some spotting, else about near fine in about fine dust jacket, signed by author, with elaborate illustration to writer Colleen Watt. Between the Covers Rare Books 208 - 33 2016 $500

Ginsberg, Allen *Journals: Mid Fifties 1954-58.* New York: Harper Collins, 1995. First edition, 1/150 signed copies, publisher's slipcase, fine. Second Life Books, Inc. 196A - 644 2016 $135

Ginsberg, Allen *Kaddish.* San Francisco: City Lights, 1961. First edition, printed wrappers, inscribed and signed by the poet for William Meredith, with several drawings by Ginsberg, light wear, near fine. Charles Agvent William Meredith - 32 2016 $1000

Ginsberg, Allen *Kaddish: and other Poems 1958-1960.* San Francisco: City Lights, 1961. First edition, 12mo., paper wrappers, cover slightly soiled and chipped, owner's name inside cover, otherwise very good, tight copy. Second Life Books, Inc. 197 - 157 2016 $200

Ginsberg, Allen *Photographs.* Altadena: Twelvetrees Press, 1990. Fine in very near fine dust jacket with uncommon original wraparound in close to near fine condition with small tear, signed and with extensive and much better than usual two page drawing by Ginsberg. Jeff Hirsch Books Holiday List 2015 - 74 2016 $1000

Ginsberg, Allen *Reality Sandwiches 1953-1960.* San Francisco: City Lights, 1963. First edition, one of 3000 copies, 12mo., paper wrappers, cover little soiled and slightly rubbed at corners, owner's name inside cover, otherwise very good, tight. Second Life Books, Inc. 197 - 158 2016 $235

Giovanni, Nikki *Cotton Candy on a Rainy Day.* New York: Morrow, 1978. First printing, author's presentation, paper over boards with cloth spine, cover slightly faded at edges, otherwise nice in dust jacket. Second Life Books, Inc. 196A - 645 2016 $75

Giradoux, Jean *The Madwoman of Chaillot.* New York: Random, 1947. First printing, 2 photos, presentation on flyleaf by Alfred de Liagre, Jr., director of the 1948 production of Belasco Theatre on Dec. 27 1948. Second Life Books, Inc. 196A - 646 2016 $50

Giraldus Cambrensis *Itinerary through Wales.* Newtown, Powys: Gregynog Press, 1989. 128/280 copies from an edition of 300 copies, signed by artist, Colin Paynton, printed on Zerkall mouldmade paper, 33 wood engraved vignettes with two-colour borders, title panel designed by Michael Harvey, title and chapter numbers printed in red, folio, original quarter scarlet goatskin with vertical gilt, rule, grey boards, backstrip lettered gilt, top edge gilt, others untrimmed, cloth slipcase, fine. Blackwell's Rare Books B184 - 270 2016 £1000

Giraud, S. Louis *Bookano Stories No. 4.* London: Strand, n.d. circa, 1937. 8vo., pictorial boards, slight rubbing, near fine, 5 action packed double page color pop-ups, illustrations in color and black and white, beautiful copy. Aleph-bet Books, Inc. 111 - 352 2016 $350

Giraud, S. Louis *Bookano Stories No. 5.* London: Strand, n.d. circa, 1938. 8vo., pictorial board, light spine wear, near fine and bright, 5 particularly wonderful double page color pop-ups, illustrations in color and black and white, beautiful copy. Aleph-bet Books, Inc. 112 - 392 2016 $400

Giraud, S. Louis *Bookano Stories No. 9.* London: Strand, n.d. circa, 1940. 4to., pictorial boards, fine, 5 particularly wonderful double page color pop-ups, illustrations in color and black and white. Aleph-bet Books, Inc. 112 - 393 2016 $450

Giraud, S. Louis *Old Rhymes and New Stories (Bookano Living Model Edition No. 3 on Spine).* London: Strand, n.d. circa, 1940. Pictorial boards, slightest bit of rubbing, else near fine, 3 very fine double page color pop-ups, charming black and whites throughout text. Aleph-bet Books, Inc. 112 - 394 2016 $250

The Girl in the Apple. Ashford: Worlds End Press, 1984. 79/120 copies, signed by translator, Helen Attlee and artist, Ann Brunskill, titlepage and colophon vignette printed in terracotta with 15 further woodcut illustrations, all hand colored by artist, tissue guards, 4to., original quarter red cloth, little very faint dust soiling to edge of lower board, slipcase, very good. Blackwell's Rare Books B186 - 350 2016 £80

Gisborne, Thomas *An Enquiry into the Duties of Men in the Higher and Middle Classes of Society, in Great Britain, Resulting from their Respective Stations, Professions and Employments.* London: J. Davis, 1795. Third edition, 2 volumes, 8vo., small stain to upper corner of final leaves volume II endpapers lightly foxed, otherwise good, clean copy, contemporary half calf, marbled boards, gilt banded spine, black labels, joints cracked but firm, slight wear to head and tail of spine volume. Jarndyce Antiquarian Books CCXV - 223 2016 £110

Gisborne, Thomas *An Enquiry into the Duties of Men in the Higher and Middle Classes of Society, in Great Britain, Resulting from their Respective Stations, Professions and Employments.* London: printed for B. and J. White, Fleet Street, 1797. Fourth edition, 8vo., full contemporary calf, raised and gilt banded spines, red morocco labels, slight wear to upper rear hinge volume I, spines rubbed, 19th century note on inner front board, Ebbetston Library No. 84 in later hand, gift from Mrs. Baker. Jarndyce Antiquarian Books CCXV - 224 2016 £200

Gissing, George 1857-1903 *Charles Dickens: a Critical Study.* London: Gresham Pub. Co., 1902. Imperial edition, half title, some spotting, original red cloth lettered gilt, unevenly faded, top edge gilt. Jarndyce Antiquarian Booksellers CCXVIII - 1253 2016 £20

Gissing, George 1857-1903 *The Collected Works of George Gissing on Charles Dickens.* London: Grayswood Press, 2004-2005. 3 volumes, half titles, frontispiece, volumes uniformly bound in different color cloth, red, blue and green, mint in dust jackets. Jarndyce Antiquarian Booksellers CCXVIII - 1251 2016 £85

Gissing, George 1857-1903 *Collected Works of George Gissing on Charles Dickens.* London: Grayswood Press, 2004-2005. Paperback edition, 3 volumes, half titles, frontispieces, mint. Jarndyce Antiquarian Booksellers CCXVIII - 1252 2016 £55

Gissing, George 1857-1903 *Critical Studies of the Works of Charles Dickens.* New York: Greenberg, 1924. First edition, half title, frontispiece, original brown cloth with paper label, very good in dust jacket. Jarndyce Antiquarian Booksellers CCXVIII - 1255 2016 £35

Gissing, George 1857-1903 *Forster's Life of Dickens Abridged and revised by George Gissing.* London: Chapman & Hall, 1903. Portraits, illustrations, facsimiles, half title, original blue cloth, blocked and lettered in black, very good. Jarndyce Antiquarian Booksellers CCXVIII - 1254 2016 £45

Gissing, George 1857-1903 *The Immortal Dickens.* London: Cecil Palmer, 1925. First English edition, half titles, frontispiece, some browning, original mauve cloth, paper label browned, spine faded and slightly rubbed, good, sound copy. Jarndyce Antiquarian Booksellers CCXVIII - 1256 2016 £25

Gissing, George 1857-1903 *The Private Papers of Henry Ryecroft.* London: Methuen, 1960. First edition, 8vo., original cloth lettered gilt on upper board and backstrip, merest hint of fading to backstrip, excellent. Blackwell's Rare Books B184 - 158 2016 £200

Glasby, C. J. *Fauna of Australia Volume 2A: Amphibia and Reptilia.* Canberra: Australian Government Pub. Service, 1933. Quarto, text illustrations, signature, sunned dust jacket. Andrew Isles Natural History Books 55 - 1605 2016 $80

Glascock, William Nugent *Land Sharks and Sea Gulls.* London: Richard Bentley, 1838. First edition, 3 volumes, frontispiece and plates, small marginal tear to plate facing page 58 volume III, handsomely rebound by J. Larkins in half red morocco, raised bands, decorated and lettered gilt, top edge gilt, very good. Jarndyce Antiquarian Booksellers CCXVII - 110 2016 £450

Glasgow, Ellen 1874-1945 *Barren Ground.* Garden City: Doubleday Page & Co., 1925. Later printing, presentation inscription signed and dated in pencil by author, decorated blue cloth, lettered in silver, spine in lightly faded and has some rubbing, ex-library with stamping at head of titlepage and no fore-edge, pocket and call slip removed from inner front over with remnants, library stamp to inner front cover, very good.   Argonaut Book Shop   Literature 2015 - 4765   2016 $125

Glasgow, Ellen 1874-1945 *The Deliverance.* New York: Doubleday Page, 1904. First edition, 8vo., 3 illustrations by Frank Schoonover, author's signature tipped in, red cloth stamped in gilt, cover slightly worn at ends of spine, small spot on front, otherwise nice.   Second Life Books, Inc. 196A - 650   2016 $75

Glasgow, Ellen 1874-1945 *Deliverance.* New York: Doubleday, Page & Co., 1904. first edition, first issue, red cloth, lettered gilt, some rubbing to cover extremities and light soiling to covers and spine, upper front corner jammed, lower rear corner less so, , lower front corner just showing, near fine.   Argonaut Book Shop   Literature 2015 - 4766   2016 $90

Glasgow, Ellen 1874-1945 *Letters of Ellen Glasgow.* New York: Harcourt Brace and Co., 1958. First edition, red cloth with silver lettering to spine, dust jacket faded along extremities and lightly worn, otherwise fine.   Argonaut Book Shop   Literature 2015 - 4791   2016 $40

Glasgow, Ellen 1874-1945 *The Miller of Old Church.* Garden City: Doubleday Page & Co., 1911. First edition, green cloth with gilt lettering, covers have minor scuffing and light wear, slight bump to open and lower edge, small scratch to spine, near fine.   Argonaut Book Shop Literature 2015 - 4769   2016 $40

Glasgow, Ellen 1874-1945 *The Romance of a Plain Man.* New York: Macmillan Co., 1909. First edition, maroon cloth decorated and lettered in gilt, top corner of leaves slightly jammed, inner front hinge cracked, minor soiling to cover with wear to extremities of covers and spine, ver6y good.   Argonaut Book Shop   Literature 2015 - 4771 2016 $40

Glasgow, Ellen 1874-1945 *The Romantic Comedians.* Garden City: Doubleday Page & Co., 1926. First edition, printed endpapers, purple blind stamped cloth cover, paper label on spine, some fading to spine and outer edges of covers, spine slightly cocked, near fine.   Argonaut Book Shop   Literature 2015 - 4778   2016 $75

Glasgow, Ellen 1874-1945 *The Romantic Comedians.* Garden City: Doubleday Page, 1926. First edition, trade issue, spine tanned, owner's name neatly erased on half title, thus very good in like dust jacket with small chips at spine ends, inscribed by author, attractive copy.   Between the Covers Rare Books   208 - 34   2016 $500

Glasgow, Ellen 1874-1945 *The Shadowy Third and other Stories.* Garden City: Doubleday Page and Co., 1923. First edition, frontispiece by Elenore Abbott, news editoral pasted onto inner rear cover with offsetting to adjoining free endpaper, rear free endpaper also stamped with library markings, some light rubbing to front cover and spotting to lower corner, very good.   Argonaut Book Shop   Literature 2015 - 4779   2016 $125

Glasgow, Ellen 1874-1945 *The Sheltered Life.* Garden City: Doubleday, Doran & Co., 1932. First edition, gilt decorated red cloth, faded at spine and upper edge of covers, badly worn original pictorial dust jacket, very good. Argonaut Book Shop   Literature 2015 - 4782   2016 $40

Glasgow, Ellen 1874-1945 *They Stopped to Folly.* Garden City: Doubleday Doran & Co., 1929. Second impression, black cloth with paper spine label, corners of covers lightly bumped, near fine in heavily worn pictorial dust jacket.   Argonaut Book Shop   Literature 2015 - 4783   2016 $40

Glasgow, Ellen 1874-1945 *Vein of Iron.* New York: Harcourt Brace & Co., 1935. First edition, blue cloth, dust jacket worn along upper and lower edges, fine.   Argonaut Book Shop   Literature 2015 - 4786   2016 $60

Glasgow, Ellen 1874-1945 *The Voice of the People.* New York: Doubleday Page & Co., 1900. First edition, tan cloth stamped in green, spine slightly darkened and light soiling to covers, previous owner's bookplate to inner cover, fine.   Argonaut Book Shop   Literature 2015 - 4788   2016 $75

The Glass of Fashion: a Universal Handbook... London: John Hogg, 1881. Half title, frontispiece, final ad leaf, original brown decorated cloth, little rubbed, inner hinges cracked with some crude repairs, bookseller's embossed stamp on leading f.e.p.   Jarndyce Antiquarian Books CCXV - 225   2016   £35

Glavin, John *Dickens on Screen.* Cambridge: University Press, 2003. First edition, very good, illustrated with film stills, paperback, very good.   Jarndyce Antiquarian Booksellers   CCXVIII - 1258   2016   £25

Glaze, Andrew *The Trash Dragon of Shensi.* Providence: Copper Beech Press, 1978. First edition, printed wrappers, very good, laid in is 1 page typed ms. review of this book by poet Paul Metcalf.   Second Life Books, Inc.   196A - 651 2016 $100

Gluck, Louise *The House on Marshland.* New York: Ecco Press, 1975. First edition, review copy with material from publisher laid in, although there is no indication of such, this book came from the library of William Meredith, fine in close to fine dust jacket.   Charles Agvent   William Meredith - 33   2016 $200

Go Ahead. Davy Crockett's Almanack of Wild Sports in the West and Life in the Backwoods, Volume I No. 2. Nashville: published for the author, 1835. First edition, 12mo., vignette and text illustrations, whip stitched, title substantially intact, but torn and crudely reinforced on verso with contemporary stiff paper, last leaf pasted down to stiff paper with loss to full page illustration on last page, tear to another page repaired with thread, &c.   M & S Rare Books, Inc. 99 - 70   2016 $950

Goddard, Robert H.   *The Autobiography of Robert Hutchings Goddard Father of the Space Age.*   Worcester: 1966. Number 67 of 1920 printed in Holland to commemorate 40th anniversary of the liquid propelled rocket, frontispiece, illustrations, miniature book, 3 x 2 1/4 inches, full leather, all edges gilt, near fine.   Dumont Maps and Books 133 - 52   2016 $65

Godfrey, J. H.   *Jugoslavia.*   London: Naval Intelligence, 1944. First edition, 8vo., numerous maps (2 in slipcase), illustrations, plans, original tan cloth.   J. & S. L. Bonham Antiquarian Booksellers   Europe 2016 - 7176   2016   £40

Godin, Charline Jenkins   *Memories of the Escuminac Diaster June 159.*   Moneton: Published by author, 1998. Quarto, card covers with plastic comb binding, photocopies of news photos throughout, very good.   Schooner Books Ltd.   115 - 56   2016 $45

Godine, David R.   *Lyric Verse: a Printer's Choice.* Lunenburg: Stinehour Press, 1966. One of 280 copies, out of a total of 500, large 8vo., presentation in pencil on colophon page, marbled paper over boards, paper spine, spine little worn at both ends, otherwise nice.   Second Life Books, Inc.   196A - 654   2016 $200

Godley's Lady's Book and Magazine Volume LXXIV (Volume LXXV).   Philadelphia: 1867. Issues for January to December 1867, hand tinted foldout fashion plate frontispieces, some medium browning but good, bound in half black morocco gilt rubbed, marbled boards, marbled edges, binding rubbed at joints at sides.   Unsworths Antiquarian Booksellers   30 - 61   2016   £150

Godman, Frederick Du Cane   *Natural History of the Azores or Western Islands.*   London: John Van Voorst, 1870. First edition, 8vo., original red cloth, blindstamped borders to sides, gilt lettering to spine, two maps at rear, foxing to titlepage, little bumping to extremities, very good. Sotheran's   Travel and Exploration - 254   2016   £80

Godwin, Gail   *Father Melancholy's Daughter.*   Franklin Center: Franklin Library, 1991. Limited first edition, signed by author, lavender leather, lettered and decoratively stamped in gilt, all edges gilt, book mistakenly bound with cover upside down, otherwise very fine, as new.   Argonaut Book Shop   Literature 2015 - 3970   2016 $40

Godwin, William   1756-1836   *Enquiry Concerning Political Justice and Its Influence on Morals and Happiness.* Philadelphia: Bioren and Madan, 1796. First American edition, 2 volumes, 12mo., contemporary mottled sheep, spines with title labels and dark green volume number labels with gilt ovals, quarter size piece torn from one front endpaper, one gathering slightly pulled, occasional very light scattered foxing but fine, clean copy in lovely period binding, quite unusual in this condition.   Joseph J. Felcone, Inc.   Books from Five Centuries: a Miscellany - 73   2016 $2600

Godwin, William   1756-1836   *Things as They Are, or the Adventures of Caleb Williams.*   London: printed for B. Crosby, 1794. First edition, 12mo., some spotting, early signature (largely illegible, but from the Gell family), and watercolour coat of arms on half titles, critical quotation from Monthly Review to verso volume i titlepage (partly cropped), early quarter blue roan, marbled boards, spines divided by gilt fillets and lettered direct to gilt, marbled endpapers, little bit rubbed, modern bookplate, very good.   Blackwell's Rare Books   Marks of Genius - 19   2016   £5000

Goethe, Johann Wolfgang Von   1749-1832   *Eventyret: Das Marchen. (Fairy Tales).*   Kobenhavn: Farlaget Kronos, 1949. Limited to 350 numbered copies, 4to., loose as issued in decorative boards and slipcase, illustrations by Kay Nielsen, with 2 full page and one almost full page black and white, rare.   Aleph-bet Books, Inc.   111 - 323   2016 $2500

Goethe, Johann Wolfgang Von   1749-1832   *Faust.* London: Hutchinson, 1908. First edition, 4to., red pictorial cloth, top edge gilt, light cover soil, very good-fine, 30 beautiful and richly colored plates with lettered tissue guards plus pictorial titlepage, elaborate pictorial initials by Willy Pogany. Aleph-bet Books, Inc.   112 - 377   2016 $400

Goethe, Johann Wolfgang Von   1749-1832   *Wilhelm Meister's Apprenticeship.*   New York: Heritage Press, 1959. Light blue cloth lettered gilt, fading to spine with tiny bit of rubbing, else fine in slipcase (some fading), illustrations by William Sharp, Sandglass pamphlet laid in.   Argonaut Book Shop   Heritage Press 2015 - 6993   2016 $40

Goetzmann, William H.   *The West of the Imagination.* Norman: University of Oklahoma, 2009. Second and best edition, quarto, color and black and white illustrations, dark brown cloth, fine with pictorial dust jacket.   Argonaut Book Shop   Photography 2015 - 6406   2016 $75

Going, Jo   *Wild Cranes.*   Washington: National Museum of Women in the Arts, 1997. Limited to 125 numbered copies signed by Going, 4to., green cloth painted with blue, gold and silver with cut-out in both front and back which show a feather, plus a string of beads in front board, double sided accordion fold, brightly colored prints of paintings, drawings and poems by Going, each fore-edge is jointed by a colored cloth which contains a colored pick-up-stick.   Oak Knoll Books   27 - 41   2016 $450

Gold, Joseph *Charles Dickens: Radical Moralist.* Toronto: Copp Clark Pub. Co., 1972. First edition, half title, original black cloth, very good in slightly faded dust jacket. Jarndyce Antiquarian Booksellers   CCXVIII - 1260   2016   £20

Goldberg, Michael *Carlyle and Dickens.* Athens: University of Athens Press, 1972. First edition, half title, frontispiece, original sage green cloth, mint in dust jacket. Jarndyce Antiquarian Booksellers   CCXVIII - 1262   2016   £25

Goldberg, Rube *Rube Goldbereg's Guide to Europe.* New York: Vanguard, 1954. First edition, 8vo., author's presentation on half title, cover slightly worn, otherwise nice. Second Life Books, Inc.   196A - 655   2016 $75

Golden Looks and Pretty Frocks. London: Raphael Tuck, n.d. circa, 1915. 4to. red cloth, pictorial paste-on, all edges gilt, light cover soil, very good-fine, illustrations by Agnes Richardson with 12 beautiful color plates, pictorial endpapers and many black and whites, beautiful book.   Aleph-bet Books, Inc.   112 - 183   2016 $450

Golden, Arthur *Memoirs of a Geisha.* New York: Knopf, 1997. First edition, fine in fine dust jacket, signed by author. Bella Luna Books   2016 - T7748   2016 $264

Golden, John *Stage-Struck John Golden.* New York: Samuel French, 1930. First edition, 8vo., photos and drawings, author's presentation on flyleaf, presentation letter from Golden to Robert Coleman at The Mirror in NY laid in, very good in worn dust jacket.   Second Life Books, Inc.   196A - 656   2016 $75

Golding, Godfrey *How to Get On; Being the Book of Good Devices.* London: Cassell, Petter & Galpin, circa, 1878. Fifth edition, half title, original brown cloth, spine rubbed at head and tail, all edges gilt.   Jarndyce Antiquarian Books   CCXV - 226   2016   £25

Golding, Louis *Pale Blue Nightgown.* Corvinus Press, 1936. first edition, one of 60 copies printed on Potal Whitechurch paper, numbered and signed by author, this copy 17, 8vo., limited to 100 signed by author, quarter blue leather and gray cloth with all four corners bound in blue leather and titles stamped in gold gilt on spine, affixed to front flyleaf is statement of provenance advising that this copy came from the library of Ellery Queen, former owner's armorial bookplate, front pastedown sheet, blue spine panel lightly sunned, else near fine.   Buckingham Books   2015 - 38201   2016 $3500

Goldsmith, Oliver   1730-1774 *Dr. Goldsmith's History of Greece....* Gainsborough: H. Mozley, 1814. New edition, 12mo., frontispiece, contemporary full speckled sheep, spine slightly rubbed at head and tail back board slightly marked, inscription "James Lawson Feb. 24 1818", good plus. Jarndyce Antiquarian Books   CCXV - 701   2016   £35

Goldsmith, Oliver   1730-1774 *The Good Natur'd Man.* London: for W. Griffin, 1780. New edition, disbound. Dramatis Personae   119 - 62   2016 $45

Goldsmith, Oliver   1730-1774 *She Stoops to Conquer.* London: Hodder & Stoughton, n.d., 1912. Limited to 350 numbered copies signed by Hugh Thomson, this copy not numbered for presentation with original drawing signed by Thomson, large thick 4to., full vellum elaborately stamped in gold, top edge gilt, ties renewed, fine, 26 beautiful tipped in color plates plus many more illustrations.   Aleph-bet Books, Inc.   111 - 448   2016 $3750

Goldsmith, Oliver   1730-1774 *She Stoops to Conqueror the Mistakes of a Night.* New York: Limited Editions Club, 1964. First edition thus, one of 1500 copies signed by artist, T. M. Cleland, yellow buckram, fine in publisher's box (little rubbed).   Second Life Books, Inc.   196A - 658   2016 $150

Goldsmith, Oliver   1730-1774 *Le Ministre de Wakefield.* Londres: et se trouve a Paris: Chez Pissot & Chez Desaint, 1767. First edition in French, 2 volumes in 1, duodecimo, recent calf spine and marbled boards, period style gilt decorartions and lettering, upper corners of two leaves signed, not touching text, early ink signature scratched out and replaced on titlepage, some scattered light foxing and staining, very good.   The Brick Row Book Shop   Miscellany 69 - 44   2016 $675

Goldsmith, Oliver   1730-1774 *The Vicar of Wakefield.* Halle: printed and sold by J. Friedrich Daniel Francke, 1787. Engraved frontispiece and engraved vignette on title, 8vo., original paper boards, gilt lettered spine label, few chips, very good.   Blackwell's Rare Books   B186 - 63   2016   £600

Goldsmith, Oliver   1730-1774 *The Vicar of Wakefield.* New York: printed by James Oram for Christian Brown, 1803. First illustrated edition published in America and the first NY edition in any form, 2 volumes in one, 12mo., contemporary tree calf, rebacked old back laid down, corners rubbed, leather label, 4 wood engraved plates by Alexander Anderson, including frontispiece, oval handmade early bookplate, lettered and decorated by one 'Elen Thompson' and bookseller's label on free half of front free endpaper advertising 'Lottery Tickets Sold at the Book Store of Thomas & Whipple, Market Square, Newburyport", pencil note that this copy was purchased from Goodspeed in 1955.   Howard S. Mott Inc.   265 - 54   2016 $450

Goldsmith, Oliver   1730-1774   *The Vicar of Wakefield, a Tale.*   London: R. Ackermann, 1823. Secnd edition, reissue of the plates form first edition of 1817, hand colored aquatint plates by Thomas Rowlandson, full tan polished calf, richly gilt, spine gilt in compartments with red and green labels by Morrell, occasional very minor spots of foxing or offsetting, else fine and fresh, in chemise and red polished calf slipcase.   Joseph J. Felcone, Inc.   Books from Five Centuries: a Miscellany - 74   2016 $750

Goldsmith, Oliver   1730-1774   *The Vicar of Wakefield.*   Philadelphia: David McKay Co., 1929. No. 95 of 200 copies for American and 575 for England, signed by artist, 10 1/2 x 8 1/8 inches, very attractive red three quarter morocco gilt, stamp signed 'Putnams' along front turn-in), raised bands, spine handsomely gilt in compartment formed by plain and decorative rules, quatrefoil centerpiece surround by densely scrolling cornerpieces, sides and endleaves of rose colored linen, top edge gilt, other edges untrimmed and mostly unopened, 12 color plates by Rackham, including frontispiece, as well as five full page and several smaller illustrations in text by Arthur Rackham, front board with insignificant small round spot to cloth, but fine, unusually bright and clean inside and out with almost no signs of use.   Phillip J. Pirages   67 - 292   2016 $2500

Goldsmith, Oliver   1730-1774   *Vicar of Wakefield.*   London: Harrap, 1929. First edition, 4to., gilt cloth, top edge gilt, endpaper foxed, light wear, very good+, illustrated by Arthur Rackham, this copy has large half page pen drawing signed and dated Nov. 1929 by artist.   Aleph-bet Books, Inc.   112 - 407   2016 $2200

Goldsmith, Oliver   1730-1774   *The Vicar of Wakefield.*   London: Bombay. Sydney: George G. Harrap & Co., 1929. First trade edition, appealing publisher's special gray persian morocco upper cover with multi color pictorial inlays reproducing illustration "an Epitaph for my Wife", flat spine with gilt titling, pictorial endpapers, top edge gilt, other edges untrimmed, 35 illustrations by Arthur Rackham, front free endpaper with neatly inked contemporary gift inscription, slight uniform sunning to spine, boards with hint of splaying, title with very faint mottled foxing, other trivial imperfections, still very pleasing copy, binding unworn and lustrous, volume clean and fresh inside and out.   Phillip J. Pirages   67 - 59   2016 $1000

Goldsmith, Oliver   1730-1774   *The Works of Oliver Goldsmith.*   London: John Murray, 1854. 4 volumes, additional engraved titlepage in each volume, frontispiece volume 1, contemporary red pebble grain moroco prize binding from Trinity College, Cambridge, boards with college arms blocked in gilt, spines lettered gilt direct with arms at head and foot, prize label to front pastedown with ownership labels to endpapers, edges gilt, merest touch of rubbing, few minor marks, very good, award as prize at Trinity College Cambridge, to Henry Thornton Forster, label of L. M. Forster (Laura Mary Forster), Edward Morgan Llewellyn Forster's label, then to Novelist E. M. Forster.   Blackwell's Rare Books   B184 - 45   2016   £600

Goll, Claire   *Love Poems.*   New York: printed by Profile Press for Hemispheres, 1947. First edition, deluxe issue, one of 40 copies numbered in roman on Velin d'Arches signed by authors and by artist, Marc Chagall, large 8vo., tipped in frontispiece and full page illustrations by Chagall, original printed gold-foil wrappers, extremities of wrappers somewhat rubbed, light offset to titlepage from facing frontispiece, ink ownership inscription, otherwise fine, unopened copy.   James S. Jaffe Rare Books   Occasional List: Winter 2016 - 8   2016 $2500

Goll, Ivan   *La Chanson De Jean Sans Terre. Poeme en 9 Chants. Dessin de Marach Chagall.*   Paris: Editions Poesie & Cie, 1936. First edition, one of only 6 copies printed on Japon Imperial paper out of a total edition of 500 copies, 8vo., original pictorial wrappers, with design by Marc Chagall, fine.   James S. Jaffe Rare Books   Occasional List: Winter 2016 - 7   2016 $750

Golovnin, Vasily Mikhailavich   *Narrative of my Captivity in Japan During the Years 1811, 1812 and 1813.*   London: for Henry Colburn, 1818. First edition in English, 2 volumes, contemporary or slightly later half calf with binder's ticket 'Bound at Ford's late Barratt's Library... Bath", turn-in at top of each spine chipped off, early stamp of private school library on front pastedowns and an early paper pocket on rear pastedowns, otherwise unmarked and very clean, bookseller's ticket of J. L. Thompson and Co. Ltd. Kobe, Japan.   Joseph J. Felcone, Inc.   Books from Five Centuries: a Miscellany - 83   2016 $1600

Gombrich, Ernst Hans   *Art and Scholarship.*   London: University College London, 1957. Original grey printed paper wrappers, sewn as issued, slightly creased.   Jarndyce Antiquarian Books   CCXV - 702   2016   £20

Gomme, A. W.   *A Historical Commentary on Thucydides.*   Oxford: Clarendon Press, 1945. 1979. 1978. 1981, 8 books in 5 volumes, 8vo., cloth, gilt lettered bump to top edge of lower wrapper volume III, light toning to upper board volume I, spine of volume IV lightly sunned, edges dusted, all very good, no dust jackets, made up set but with ownership inscription of C. D. N. Costa.   Unsworths Antiquarian Booksellers   30 - 62   2016   £300

Goncourt, Edmond *L'Amour Au Dix-Huiteme Siecle.* Paris: E. Dentu, 1875. First separate edition, 194 x 143mm., elegant fin-de-Siecle brown crushed morocco by A. Taffin of Paris (stamp-signed), covers with ornate gilt frame of flowers, leaves and small tools enclosing two inlaid salmon pink morocco bands separated by a gilt chain roll, raised bands, spine gilt in compartments with floral frame, gilt titling, turn-ins lavishly gilt, green silk endleaves, top edge gilt, other edges untrimmed, original wrappers bound in, text within full woodcut inhabited frames, engraved frontispiece, headpiece and tailpiece and extra illustrated with 19 engravings in black and white or bistre, spine mildly but uniformly sunned towards a chocolate brown, other trivial imperfections, very fine, extremely pretty decorative binding lustrous and virtually unworn and text clean and fresh.   Phillip J. Pirages   67 - 68   2016 $1000

Gonzalez, Julio *Julio Gonzalez.* London: The Gallery, 1970. First edition, scarcer hardbound issue, square octavo, fine in near fine dust jacket slightly faded at spine. Peter Ellis   112 - 150   2016   £25

Good Advice to Apprentices or the Covenants of the City Indenture Familiarly explained and Enforced in Scripture. London: n.p., circa, 1863? 16mo., half title, rubricated text, original brick brown cloth, slight marking to front board, all edges gilt, very good.   Jarndyce Antiquarian Books   CCXV - 227   2016   £35

Goodall's *Good Things made Said and Done for Every Home and Household.* London: Goodall Backhouse & Co., 1896. Thirty fourth edition, illustrations, staples slightly rusted, ads on endpapers, original red decorated cloth, very good.   Jarndyce Antiquarian Books   CCXV - 228   2016   £40

Goodchild, George *McLean Prevails.* London & Melbourne: Ward, Lock & Co., 1935. First edition, 8vo., original olive green cloth, lettered black on spine and front cover, from the Donald Rudd collection, very slight browning to endpapers with small Father Christmas sticker, otherwise near fine in price clipped, very good+ dust jacket, very slight shelfwear, excellent condition.   Any Amount of Books   2015 - C11014   2016   £170

Goodchild, George *Stout Cortez.* London: Ward Lock & Co., 1949. Very good in like dust jacket.   I. D. Edrich Crime - 2016   £25

Goode, John *Freshwater Tortoises of Australia and New Guinea (in the family Chelidae).* Melbourne: Lansdowne, 1967. Octavo, color photos, very good in dust jacket, scarce.   Andrew Isles Natural History Books   55 - 6316   2016 $350

Goodis, David *Black Pudding. in Dec. 1953 issue of Manhunt.* New York: Flying Eagle, 1953. Fine in wrappers.   Mordida Books   2015 - 011965   2016 $65

Goodis, David *Nightfall.* New York: Julian Messner Inc., 1947. First edition, octavo, cloth, mild bruises to upper spine end and lower corner tips, nearly fine in bright, nearly fine dust jacket with mild rubs at upper spine nd and lower front corner tips, very nice.   John W. Knott, Jr./L.W. Currey, Inc.   Fall-Winter 2015 - 17180   2016 $1250

Goodis, David *Of Missing Persons.* New York: William Morrow & Co., 1950. First edition, mild bruises to upper spine an lower corner tips, nearly fine in bright, nearly fine dust jacket with mild rubs at upper spine ends and lower front corner tips, very nice.   John W. Knott, Jr./L.W. Currey, Inc.   Fall-Winter 2015 - 17818   2016 $1500

Goodman, Paul *Making Do.* New York: Random House, 1980. 8vo., author's presentation, endpapers and dust jacket slightly soiled, small tear in dust jacket, else very good. Second Life Books, Inc.   196A - 660   2016 $65

Goodman, Paul *Tragedy & Comedy, Four Cubist Plays.* Los Angeles: Black Sparrow Press, 1970. First edition, large 8vo., of a total of 750 copies, this one of 200 bound in cloth backed boards and signed by author, fine.   Second Life Books, Inc.   196A - 659   2016 $100

Goodrich, E. S. *No. 2 Mormonism Unveiled. The Other Side from an American Standpoint.* Salt Lake City?: 1884. First edition, 8vo., original printed wrappers, old binding holes.   M & S Rare Books, Inc.   99 - 190   2016 $175

Goodrich, Samuel Griswold 1793-1860 *What to Do and How to Do It...* London: Darton & Clark, 1844. 12mo., frontispiece and additional engraved title, illustrations, 4 pages ads, frontispiece and engraved title slightly browned, binding split in places but still firm, original green pictorial cloth, spine slightly faded, very good.   Jarndyce Antiquarian Books   CCXV - 350   2016   £120

Goodwin, Derek *Estrildid Finches of the World.* Natural History Mus., 1982. First edition, shows some signs of wear and may have some markings on inside.   Simon Finch   2015 - 2016 $185

Goodwin, Grenville *The Social Organization of the Western Apache.* Chicago: 1942. First edition, illustrations, dust jacket soiled with couple of minor chips, owner's name on flap, else clean and very good.   Dumont Maps and Books   133 - 53   2016 $100

Goodwin, Hezekiah *A Vision Shewing the Sudden and Surprising Appearance, the Celestial mein!...* New York: printed for the Purchase, 1800? 16mo., sewn as issued. M & S Rare Books, Inc.   99 - 98   2016 $225

Gordimer, Nadine *Jump and Other Stories.* Franklin Center: Franklin Library, 1991. Limited first edition, signed by author, red leather, lettered and decoratively stamped in gilt, all edges gilt, very fine.   Argonaut Book Shop   Literature 2015 - 3972   2016 $75

Gordon, A. M. *The New Domestic Cookery.* London: W. Tweedie, 1853. Initial 4 page catalog, frontispiece and illustrations, few internal marks, handsomely rebound in half calf, gilt bands, green label.   Jarndyce Antiquarian Booksellers   CCXVII - 111   2016   £180

Gordon, Alison *Night Game.* Toronto: McClelland & Stewart, 1992. First edition, very fine in dust jacket, signed by author.   Mordida Books   2015 - 006492   2016 $55

Gordon, Elizabeth *The Butterfly Babies Book.* Chicago: Rand McNally, 1914. First edition, 8vo., cloth backed pictorial boards, covers lightly soiled and rubbed, else very good, each page with wonderful color illustrations by Penny Ross, quite scarce.   Aleph-bet Books, Inc.   112 - 218   2016 $275

Gordon, Elizabeth *Mother Earth's Children: the Frolics of the Fruits and Vegetables.* Chicago: Volland, 1914. 29th printing, 8vo., pictorial boards, slightest bit of soil, else fine in pictorial box, small repair to box (small repair to box flaps, else very good+), printed on coated paper, illustrations by M. T. Penny Ross.   Aleph-bet Books, Inc.   112 - 500   2016 $300

Gordon, Elizabeth *The Turned Into's.* Chicago: Volland, 1920. First edition, no additional printings, 8vo., pictorial boards, fine in original box (with light soil and some repair on flaps), illustrations by Janet Laura Scott, scarce.   Aleph-bet Books, Inc.   111 - 468   2016 $350

Gordon, J. P. *The Master - New Type of Microwave Amplifier, Frequency Standard and Spectrometer. in The Physical Review Volume 99, Second Series.* Lancaster: American Institute of Physics, 1955. Small 4to., entire issue offered, finely rebacked original wrappers.   By the Book, L. C.   45 - 12   2016 $650

Gordon, Mary *Men and Angels.* New York: Random House, 1985. First edition, 8vo., author's presentation on flyleaf, news clipping about author laid in, maroon cloth, edges slightly spotted, cover little warped, otherwise very good, tight copy in price clipped and scuffed dust jacket.   Second Life Books, Inc.   196A - 662   2016 $45

Gordon, Mary *Temporary Shelter: Short Stories.* New York: Random House, 1987. First edition, maroon cloth, 8vo., author's presentation on flyleaf, remainder mark on top and bottom edges, very good, tight copy, slightly chipped and soiled dust jacket.   Second Life Books, Inc.   196A - 663   2016 $45

Gordon, W. *Every Young Man's Companion.* London: J. Hodges, 1757. Second edition, 12mo., occasional ink marks, lacking f.e.p.'s, contemporary full brown sheep, rubbed and edges worn but sound.   Jarndyce Antiquarian Books   CCXV - 229   2016   £125

Gordon, William *The Separation of the Jewish Tribes after the Death of Solomon....* Boston: J. Gill, 1777. First edition, 8vo., sewn as issued, but without half title, little weary, some ink stains.   M & S Rare Books, Inc.   99 - 130   2016 $4750

Gore, Al *Earth in the Balance.* Boston: Houghton Mifflin, 1992. Proof copy, very good, light rubbing, scarce format, signed by author.   Bella Luna Books   2016 - t566   2016 $132

Gore, Al *Earth in Balance.* Boston: Houghton Mifflin, 1992. First edition, fine in fine dust jacket, inscribed by author for Tony Delcavo.   Bella Luna Books   2016 - ta87   2016 $396

Gorey, Edward *Amphigorey Too.* New York: G. P. Putnams, 1983. First edition, tiny spot on fore edge, boards little bumped, very nar fine in very near fine dust jacket.   Between the Covers Rare Books   208 - 35   2016 $100

Gorey, Edward *The Chinese Obelisks. The Osbick Bird. Donald Has a Difficulty.* New York: Fantod Press, 1970. First edition, 3 books, stapled wrappers in publisher's printed envelope as issued, books as new, envelope fine but for touch of discoloration.   Between the Covers Rare Books   204 - 52   2016 $1000

Gorey, Edward *The Deranged Cousins. The Eleventh Episode. (The Untitled Book).* Fantos Press, 1971. Limited to 500 sets, signed by Gorey, 3 books, pictorial wrappers, faint crease on one cover, else fine in publisher's very good+ tan printed envelope, fine.   Aleph-bet Books, Inc. 111 - 203   2016 $1200

Gorey, Edward *The Dwindling Party.* New York: Random House, 1982. 4to., 6 pop-up scenes, paper over boards, slight soil on cover, otherwise nice, excellent, unread copy with original $8.95 peelable sticker to front.   Second Life Books, Inc.   197 - 159   2016 $300

Gorey, Edward *A Gorey Festival.* New York: Ivan Obolensky, 1968. All four books tight, seemingly unread but with some miniscule wear, all housed in very near fine slipcase, lovely set.   Jeff Hirsch Books   Holiday List 2015 - 39   2016 $150

Gorey, Edward *The Green Beads.* New York: Albondaconi Press, 1978. Limited to 400 numbered copies signed by Gorey, printed on fine paper on one side of the page and handsewn, each page has full page illustration with no text, 12mo., pictorial wrappers, fine.   Aleph-bet Books, Inc.   111 - 200   2016 $500

Gorey, Edward *Loathsome Couple.* New York: Dodd, Mead, 1977. Limited to 250 numbered copies, signed by Gorey, very scarce, pictorial boards, fine in dust jacket and slipcase.   Aleph-bet Books, Inc.   111 - 201   2016 $1200

Gorey, Edward *The Prune People II.* New York: Albondocani Press, 1985. First edition, stapled wrappers, fine, as new, prospectus for the edition laid in, one of 400 numbered copies, signed by Gorey.   Between the Covers Rare Books   204 - 53   2016 $425

Gorey, Edward *The Raging Tide or the Black Doll's Imbroglio.* New York: Beaufort Books, 1987. Limited to 200 numbered copies and 26 lettered copies reserved for the author and distributor, this one of the lettered copies signed by Gorey, boards, fine in fine dust jacket, full page illustrations, rare.   Aleph-bet Books, Inc.   111 - 202   2016 $2000

Gorey, Edward *The Remembered Visit - a Story Taken from Life.* New York: Simon and Schuster, 1965. First edition, oblong octavo, pictorial boards, front endpapers tanned, otherwise fine in near fine dust jacket.   Peter Ellis   112 - 151   2016   £50

Gorey, Edward *Story for Sara.* New York: Albondocani Press, 1971. Limited to 26 lettered copies for use of author, published and signed by Gorey, pictorial wrappers, fine, laid in is publisher's order card illustrated by Gorey, also signed by Gorey, with prospectus.   Aleph-bet Books, Inc.   112 - 219   2016 $1300

Gorham, Beryl *Gorham Homestead a Family Farm 1784-1984.* 1984. Card covers, quarto, very good.   Schooner Books Ltd.   115 - 57   2016 $45

Gorham, Charles *The Gold of Their Bodies: a Novel about Gaugin.* New York: Dial Press, 1955. First edition, owner bookplate, fine copy, near fine- dust jacket with chipping at spine and flap fold ends and slightly sunned spine.   Ken Hebenstreit, Bookseller   2016 - 2016 $40

Gorton, J. *The Mariner's Chronicle of Shipwrecks, Fires, Famines and Other Disasters at Sea...* Philadelphia: Jesper Harding, 1848. Later printing, 12mo., cloth with gilt title and decoration stamped in blind, 6 black and white engravings, about very good, split ends, light soiling on boards, scattered foxing.   Kaaterskill Books   21 - 33   2016 $100

Gosse, P. H. *The Aquarium: an Unveiling of the Wonders of the Deep Sea.* London: John Van Voorst, 1854. Second edition, octavo, 6 chromolithographs, frontispiece, all by Gosse, text illustrations, publisher's cloth, some wear, front endpaper loose, sound.   Andrew Isles Natural History Books   55 - 38941   2016 $250

Gosse, Philip *The Pirates 'Who's Who' giving Particulars of the Lives and Deaths of the Pirates and Buccaneers.* London: Dulau, 1924. First edition, 8vo., map on endpapers, 6 plates, original red cloth, from the library of J. C. Beaglehole.   J. & S. L. Bonham Antiquarian Booksellers America 2016 - 9924   2016   £70

Gottschalk, Paul *The Earliest Diplomatic Documents on America, the Papal Bulls of 1493 and the Treaty of Tordesillas Reproduced and Translated.* Berlin: Paul Gottschalk, 1927. 172 copies printed, of which 150 are for sale, folio, quarter vellum, cloth, 130 plates, soiling to vellum, cloth curled away from vellum slightly on front cover, corners bumped with minor wear to extremities.   Oak Knoll Books   310 - 290   2016 $1750

Goubert, Jean Pierre *Description et Usage des Barometres, Thermometre et autres Instrumens Meteorologiques.* Paris: chez l'Auteur et chez Jombert, 1781. First edition, 8vo., disbound, sound, woodcut device of sphere and compass on title, one folding table, first few leaves browned, last few also to a lesser extent.   Blackwell's Rare Books   B186 - 64   2016   £500

Goude, Jean Paul *Jungle Fever.* New York: Xavier Moreau, 1982. Fine in very near fine dust jacket with small, nearly invisible edge tear to top of front panel, very fresh and bright.   Jeff Hirsch Books   Holiday List 2015 - 76   2016 $300

Goudy's Illinois Farmer's Almanac and Repository of Useful Knowledge... 1844. Springfield: Robert Goudy, Alton, sold by Wm. A. Holton, 1843. 12mo., sewn and uncut, last leaf with small tear and without loss.   M & S Rare Books, Inc.   99 - 3   2016 $550

Gough, Henry *The Register of the Fraternity or Guild of the Holy and Undivided Trinity and Blessed Virgin Mary in the Parish Church of Luton in the county of Bedford from AD MCCCLXXV to MDCXLVI.* London: Chiswick Press, 1906. First edition, 6 illustrations, 10 plates, folio, original navy blue cloth with black leather spine lettered gilt, printed on handmade paper bearing watermark of the Chiswick Press, some rubbing at hinges, otherwise sound, very good.   Any Amount of Books   2015 - 2016   £250

Gould, John   1804-1881 *Australian Marsupials and Monotremes with Modern Commentaries by Joan Dixon.* South Melbourne: Macmillan, 1974. Folio, color plates, publisher's cloth, cardboard slipcase.   Andrew Isles Natural History Books   55 - 21594   2016 $60

Gould, John 1804-1881 *The Birds of Australia and the Adjacent Islands.* East Melbourne: Lansdowne, 1979. Facsimile, limited to 500 copies numbered and signed by Alan McEvey, 20 color plates, folio, publisher's decorated cloth, fine.   Andrew Isles Natural History Books   55 - 8968   2016 $400

Gould, John 1804-1881 *The Birds of Australia. Volume Five.* Melbourne: Hill House, 1989. Folio, 92 color plates, publisher's green cloth, fine.   Andrew Isles Natural History Books 55 - 3952   2016 $2250

Gould, John 1804-1881 *The Birds of Great Britain.* published by the author, 1862-1873. First edition, imperial folio, 25 parts in 5 volumes, bound by George Gregory of Bath in half green morocco, spines with gilt raised bands, lettering and elaborate tooling in custom made (c. 1990) walnut display case 38 x 36 x 25 inches, with lockable drawers, one for each volume, together with lockable hinged glass compartment that can be positioned like a lectern; with 367 hand colored lithographs, one text gathering bound in upside down in volume IV, slightly rubbed at extremities, occasional spots, otherwise extremely clean, very good, subscriber's copy with bookplate of Sir John William Cradock-Hartopp, 4th Baronet (1829-1888).   Sotheran's Piccadilly Notes - Summer 2015 - 7   2016   £90,000

Gould, John 1804-1881 *Handbook to the Birds of Australia.* London: author, 1865. Octavo, 2 volumes, publisher's handsome decorated cloth, bookplate, few minor splits in cloth, otherwise fine.   Andrew Isles Natural History Books   55 - 26957   2016 $2500

Gould, John 1804-1881 *Handbook to the Birds of Australia.* London: published by the author, 1865. First edition thus, 2 volumes, 8vo., original green cloth lettered and decorated gilt, gilt lyre bird on cover of both, only faults are short nicks at head of both spines, head of volume one has very slight loss, front inner hinges of both volumes slightly tender and volume one has one page tipped in with ads of books by Gould, neat name label to each volume, handsome, very good+.   Any Amount of Books   2015 - A83227   2016   £550

Gould, John 1804-1881 *Kangaroos: with Modern Commentaries by Joan Dixon.* Melbourne: Macmillan, 1973. Folio, color plates, publisher's cloth, slipcase.   Andrew Isles Natural History Books   55 - 878   2016 $60

Gould, John 1804-1881 *A Monograph of the Macropodidae or Family of Kangaroos.* Melbourne: Lansdowne Editions, 1981. Facsimile, limited edition of 750 copies, numbered and signed by Joan Dixon, folio, color plates, publisher's cloth with locket portrait, very good.   Andrew Isles Natural History Books   55 - 13996   2016 $250

Gould, John 1804-1881 *Monograph of the Pittidae.* Melbourne: Hill House, 1989. Folio, 9 color plates and accompanying text leaves, publisher's blue cloth, fine.   Andrew Isles Natural History Books   55 - 3953   2016 $350

Gould, John 1804-1881 *A Synopsis of the Birds of Australia and the Adjacent Islands.* Melbourne: Queensberry Hill Press, 1979. Facsimile, quarto, 73 colored plates by Elizabeth Gould, each plate accompanied by single text leaf, publisher's half morocco slipcase.   Andrew Isles Natural History Books   55 - 3675   2016 $650

Gould, Nat *The Magic of Sport; Mainly Autobiographical.* London: John Long, 1909. First edition, bookplate and owner's inked name of William Benezet Rogert, spine ends bit chipped, else near fine in modestly chipped and internally repaired, about very good, very scarce.   Between the Covers Rare Books   208 - 134   2016 $225

Gould, Nat *The Stolen Racer.* J. Long, 1909. Original pictorial cloth, very good.   I. D. Edrich   Crime - 2016   £45

Gould, R. T. *The Case for the Sea-Serpent.* London: Philip Allan and Co., 1930. Octavo, photos, publisher's cloth, slightly grubby, hinges lightly cracked.   Andrew Isles Natural History Books   55 - 30847   2016 $60

Goyen, William *Selected Letters from a Writer's Life.* Austin: University of Texas Press, 1995. First edition, 8vo., fine in dust jacket, inscribed by editor to poet William Jay Smith.   Second Life Books, Inc.   196A - 670   2016 $65

Goyen, William *Wonderful Plant.* Winston-Salem: Palaemon Press ltd., 1980. Limited numbered edition of 160, 100 numbered 1-100 for public sale, 60 numbered i-lx for distribution, marbled boards made by Daniel Guyot of Seattle, this copy No. 1 signed by author, presentation from author to publisher Stuart Wright, note from author to publisher laid in along with copy of news clipping.   Oak Knoll Books   310 - 130   2016 $300

Grace, Dick *Squadron of Death: the True Adventures of a Movie-Plane Crasher.* Garden City: Doubleday Doran, 1929. First edition, signed by author, uncommon in scarce dust jacket, very good plus in very good plus, price clipped jacket, toning and bumps at extremities, faint bruise on front endpaper, jacket spine and folds toned, with tiny chips on tears at edges.   Royal Books   49 - 22   2016 $650

Grace, James *Green Willow and Other Japanese Fairy Tales.* London: Macmillan & Co., 1910. Limited to 500 copies, large thick 4to., publisher's full vellum, silk ties, top edge gilt, some soil and rubbing to vellum, internally clean and fine and overall very good+, 40 magnificent tipped-in color plates with printed guards by Warwick Goble, rare.   Aleph-bet Books, Inc.   111 - 197   2016 $2000

Gracian Dantisco, Lucas *Narcissus; or the Young Man's Entertaining Mirror...* printed for J. Bew, 1778. First edition of this translation, minor spotting and staining, small hole in F3 just touching a couple of letters on recto, 12mo., contemporary sheep, sometime rebacked, later but not very recent endpapers, corners worn, some contemporary annotations in ink.   Blackwell's Rare Books   B184 - 46   2016   £750

Graham, Arthur Harrington *Master and Servant.* London: W. Foulsham & Co., 1899. Half title, original mustard cloth, slightly rubbed and dulled, but nice, W. Foulssham & Co's label laid down over original imprint.   Jarndyce Antiquarian Books   CCXV - 230   2016   £85

Graham, Ernest G. C. *A History of the Anglican Church in the Parish of Springfield.* Sussex: 1983. Quarto, card covers with functional library type binding, some photo illustrations very good.   Schooner Books Ltd.   115 - 58   2016 $50

Graham, Frank *The Audubon Ark. A History of the National Audubon Society.* New York: Alfred A. Knopf, 1990. First edition, illustrated from photos, maroon cloth backed boards, very fine with pictorial dust jacket.   Argonaut Book Shop   Natural History 2015 - 7156   2016 $45

Graham, James Robert George *Corn and Currency in an Address to the land Owners.* London: James Ridgway, Piccadilly, 1826. Second edition with additions, 8vo., original grey boards, printed label to spine, upper cover loose, bookplate of Royal Agricultural Society.   Marlborough Rare Books   List 56 - 22   2016   £100

Graham, Neill *Murder Made Easy.* John Long, 1964. Review copy, review slip loosely inserted, dust jacket, very good.   I. D. Edrich   Crime - 2016   £30

Graham, W. A. *The Custer Myth.* Harrisburg: Stackpole, 1953. First edition, numerous black and white plates, printed brown cloth with slightly rubbed ends, else fine.   Argonaut Book Shop   Native American 2015 - 1933   2016 $75

Grahame, Kenneth 1859-1932   *Dream Days.* London & New York: John Lane/Bodley, 1898. 1902. First Parrish edition, 8vo., green cloth with elaborate gilt pictorial cover, top edge gilt, others uncut, fine, illustrations by Maxfield Parrish.   Aleph-bet Books, Inc.   112 - 363   2016 $475

Grahame, Kenneth 1859-1932   *The Wind in the Willows.* London: Methuen & Co., 1908. First English edition, 8vo., original dark green cloth, little rubbed, front cover and spine stamped in gilt, frontispiece, top edge gilt, uncut, jacket with some illustrations on front panel and spine as does books covers, very good with scattered foxing of text, foxing of endpapers, dust jacket has no tears or repairs, excellent example, little dusty and showing some rubbing at folds, morocco backed cloth folding case.   Howard S. Mott Inc.   265 - 59   2016 $9500

Grahame, Kenneth 1859-1932   *The Wind in the Willows.* London: Methuen and Co., 1908. First edition, gilt lettering and designs fresh and bright, little wear at edges and covers, few very light stains, some professional color restoration, prelims and endleaves somewhat darkened and foxed as usual and edges of some leaves also foxed, nice, increasingly scarce, ownership inscription erased from flyleaf, but from the library of Dame Freya Stark and husband Stewart Perowne, bearing their Asolo bookplate.   Bertram Rota Ltd.   Christmas List 2015 - 13   2016   £4000

Grahame, Kenneth 1859-1932   *The Wind in the Willows.* London: Methuen, 1931. First edition with Shepard illustrations, 8vo., green gilt cloth, book has an ever so slight lean, light foxing, else fine in lovely pictorial dust jacket (slightly frayed at spine ends, spine slightly toned), illustrations by E. H. Shepard, pictorial endpapers, illustrations.   Aleph-bet Books, Inc.   111 - 204   2016 $2000

Grahame, Kenneth 1859-1932   *The Wind in the Willows.* London: Methuen & Co. Ltd., 1959. First edition thus, 8vo., original turquoise cloth lettered and decorated in gilt to spine, pictorial map endpapers, preserved in pictorial dust jacket, with 8 exquisite full bleed coloured plates printed in rich matt tones and line drawings, externally and internally very good and attractive copy with perhaps a touch of discoloration to spine and mild toning to edges of book block, protected by a very attractive, unclipped dust jacket with dusting and slight marking to lower panel and little light rubbing.   Sotheran's   Piccadilly Notes - Summer 2015 - 149   2016   £298

Grahame, Kenneth 1859-1932   *The Wind in the Willows.* London: Methuen Childrens Books, 1971. First edition thus, 8vo., original chocolate brown cloth lettered gilt to spine with vignette in blind to upper board, pictorial map endpapers, preserved in pictorial dust jacket, colored illustrations by E. H. Shepard, externally fine, internally very good with very minor dusting to edges of book block, protected by an uncommonly good, unclipped dust jacket with little of the usual light toning, slight spotting to lower flap and single vertical crease to same.   Sotheran's   Piccadilly Notes - Summer 2015 - 148   2016   £288

Gramatry, Hardie *Bolivar.* New York: G. P. Putnam, 1961. First edition, 8vo., cloth, fine in near fine dust jacket, this copy inscribed by Gramatky with sketch of Bolivar, great copy.   Aleph-bet Books, Inc.   111 - 205   2016 $325

Graner, Cyrus *Bland Tomtar och Troll. (Among Gnomes and Trolls).* Stockholm: Ahlen & Akerlunds, 1921. First edition, small quarto, 10 full page color plates and 4 black and white illustrations by Gustaf Tenggren, original color pictorial wrappers with additional color illustration on front wrapper and another illustration printed in brown on back wrapper, near fine, very scarce. David Brass Rare Books, Inc. 2015 - 02987   2016 $750

Granger, Bill Schism *Schism.* New York: Crown, 1981. First edition, fine in dust jacket. Mordida Books   2015 - 011923   2016 $65

Grant, Anne MacVicar   1755-18838 *Essays on the Superstitions on the Highlanders of Scotland.* London: and Edinburgh: Longman, Hurst, Rees, Orme, etc., 1811. First edition, octavo, 2 volumes, period binding fo full calf with gilt decorated spines, gilt rules, black leather title labels, lettered gilt, bookplate of English schoolmistress Richmal Mangnall (1769-1820) ad armorial bookplate of each volume, covers little rubbed and bruised at corners and just little defective at extreme head of volume 1, prelims spotted, very good. Peter Ellis   112 - 350   2016   £195

Grant, Gordon *Ship Ahoy: a Construction Book for Fireside Sailors.* Garden City: Doubleday Doran, 1934. Stated first edition, oblong large folio, spiral backed thick cardboard cover, some edge rubbing and slight soil, else very good+ and completely unused, large full color illustrations, rare. Aleph-bet Books, Inc.   112 - 347   2016 $850

Grant, Jerry V. *Shaker Furniture Makers.* Hanover: University Press of New England, 1989. First printing, inscribed by authors, copiously illustrated with photos, brown cloth, nice in lightly scuffed and slightly faded dust jacket. Second Life Books, Inc.   196A - 671   2016 $40

Grant, Joseph D. *Redwoods and Reminiscences.* San Francisco: Ave the Redwoods League, 1973. First edition, color frontispiece, illustrations from photos, brick pictorial cloth, gilt, fine. Argonaut Book Shop   Natural History 2015 - 7304   2016 $60

Grant, Maxwell *The Eyes of the Shadow.* New York: Street & Smith, 1931. First edition, inscribed by author for Walter B. Gibson, front hinge cracking, else very good, attractive copy, fragile cheaply made book in pictorial papers over boards, issued without. Buckingham Books   2015 - 6358   2016 $450

Grant, Ruth Winona *Bel Viso Hillman History in New Brunswick from Hillman Papers and other Records.* Woodstock: Laren Offset Printing, 1978. Card covers, 8vo., folding map at rear, other photo illustrations, square piece cut from upper top of titlepage, otherwise very good. Schooner Books Ltd.   115 - 64   2016 $40

Grant, Ruth Winona *Now and Then. A History of the Southampton Area Along the Saint John river.* Woodstock: Published by author, 1967. Card covers, 19.6 x 28cm, photo illustrations, covers worn and tears to spine, good, some ink notations correcting photo captions, possibly by author. Schooner Books Ltd.   115 - 65   2016 $45

Grant, Ulysses S. *Message from the President of the United States, Transmitting in Answer to a Senate Revolution of July 20 1876...* Washington: GPO, 1876. First edition, octavo, removed, small nicks and stab holes along spine, else near fine. Between the Covers Rare Books   207 - 47   2016 $500

Granville, A. B. *The Spas of Germany.* London: Henry Colburn, 1839. Second edition, 8vo., 5 maps, 13 plates, illustrations, original red blindstamped cloth, head of spine has small tear, corners bumped, internally clean, good. J. & S. L. Bonham Antiquarian Booksellers   Europe 2016 - 9609   2016   £150

Graphical Representation of the Coronation Regalia of the Kings of England; with the Degrees and Costume of Different Ranks. Philadelphia: Morgan and Year, n.d. circa, 1825. 4 1/4 x 7 inches, some offsetting and slight foxing, very good+, printed on one side of paper, 12 very fine hand colored copperplate engravings, very scarce. Aleph-bet Books, Inc.   111 - 140   2016 $1500

Graphis, Graphic and Applied Art. Zurich: Graphis Press, 1946-1951. 23 issue run, starts with issue 14 (lacks covers) and goes through issue 37 (lacking only issue 18), 4to., stiff paper wrappers, some covers detached and spine coverings worn, filled with graphic art illustrations in color. Oak Knoll Books   310 - 37   2016 $450

Grasberg, Eugene *The New Brunswick Economy and Proposed Passaquoddy Tidal Power Project 1936-1980.* Fredericton: University of new Brunswick, 1958. Large 8vo., tables and graphs, very good, card covers with pastic comb binding. Schooner Books Ltd.   115 - 66   2016 $45

Grass, Gunter *The Tin Drum.* London: Secker & Warburg, 1962. Proof copy, 8vo, half title and final page little toned, small diminishing stain to fore-edge, margin beginning to half title and vanishing around page 50, green paper covers, spine sunned and creased, lightly toned towards edges, few tiny marks to edges, inner hinge separating, very slightly at gutter still very good, inkstamp to upper cover, "Date and price subject to alteration August 30sOd". Unsworths Antiquarian Booksellers   30 - 64   2016   £35

Grattan, William *Arden. the Unfortunate Stranger Who was Tried for Murder of Miss Harriet Finch....* Philadelphia: published and sold wholesale only by Freeman Scott, 1827. First edition thus, 24mo., printed self wrappers, sewn, titlepage moderately soiled and rubbed, partially obscuring publication date beneath publisher's imprint, few leaves creased at tips of corners, else good to very good. Simon Finch 2015 - 63234   2016 $285

Graves, Alfred Perceval *Songs of Killarney.* London: Bradbury Agnew & Co., 1873. First edition, half title, vignette signed AC, slightly dusted, original green cloth, front board and spine decorated in black, lettered gilt, back board in blind, half title inscribed "With the author's Respects", Grenville Matheson MacDonald's bookplate, later ownership inscription of R. G. F. Sandbach, nice.   Jarndyce Antiquarian Booksellers   CCXVII - 112   2016   £150

Graves, Charles B. *Lore and Legends of the Klamath River Indians.* Yreka: Press of the Times, 1929. First edition, 24 photographic plates and portraits, red cloth, gilt, spine slightly faded, very fine, scarce.   Argonaut Book Shop   Native American 2015 - 1935   2016 $175

Graves, Ida *Epithalamion.* Colchester: Gemini Press, 1934. 76/280 copies from an edition of 330 copies printed on Basingwerk paper and signed by artist, Blair Hughes Stanton, 23 full page wood engravings, small folio, original pale green boards, printed label, edges untrimmed, remnants of tissue jacket laid in, board slipcase.   Blackwell's Rare Books   B184 - 264   2016   £1000

Graves, Ida *Epithalamion.* Higham, Colchester: Gemini Press, 1934 but released by Basilisk Press in, 1980. No. 252 of 280 copies on paper (of a total of 330), our copy signed by artist, 349 x 207mm., 23 dramatic full page wood engravings by Blair Hughes-Stanton, publisher's light brown morocco designed by Hughes-Stanton and executed by Paul Collet and David Sellars, flat spine with vertical gilt titling, mint condition.   Phillip J. Pirages   67 - 197   2016 $1000

Graves, Robert   1895-1985 *Antigua, Penny, Puce.* Deya, Majorica: Seizin Press, Constable, 1936. First edition, with misprints as called for on pages 100, 103 and 293, crown 8vo., original maroon cloth, backstrip lettered white, bookplate, dust jacket with front flap of panel and price 7/6, trifle frayed at head of backstrip panel, very good.   Blackwell's Rare Books   B186 - 221   2016   £275

Graves, Robert   1895-1985 *The Big Green Book.* New York: Crowell-Collier, 1962. Stated first printing in new format, 8vo., pictorial cloth, fine in dust jacket, illustrations on every page by Maurice Sendak, this copy with marvelous pen drawing signed by artist.   Aleph-bet Books, Inc.   111 - 412   2016 $1200

Graves, Robert   1895-1985 *Collected Short Stories.* London: Cassell, 1965. First British edition, blue cloth with gilt lettering to spine, fine in browned dust jacket.   Argonaut Book Shop   Literature 2015 - 4819   2016 $75

Graves, Robert   1895-1985 *Colophon to Love Respelt: Poems.* privately printed, 1967. First edition, one of 386 copies signed by author, this copy unnumbered and marked "Out of Series - for Presentation".   Bertram Rota Ltd. February List 2016 - 23   2016   £75

Graves, Robert   1895-1985 *The Infant with the Globe.* New York: Thomas Youseloff, 1959. First American edition, orange cloth, slight bump to lower edge of front cover, else fine in worn and torn dust jacket.   Argonaut Book Shop Literature 2015 - 4811   2016 $60

Graves, Robert   1895-1985 *The Islands of Unwisdom.* Garden City: Doubleday & Co., 1949. First edition, red cloth with gilt lettering to spine, corners to front cover jammed, dust jacket worn at edges, near fine.   Argonaut Book Shop   Literature 2015 - 4812   2016 $50

Graves, Robert   1895-1985 *The Isles of Unwisdom.* London: Cassell, 1950. First English edition, double page map, foolscap 8vo., original black cloth, backstrip gilt lettered, light edge spotting, dust jacket with backstrip panel trifle sunned and with internal sellotape repair at head, very good, inscribed by author for Charles (Morgenstern). Blackwell's Rare Books   B186 - 222   2016   £450

Graves, Robert   1895-1985 *John Kemp's Wager: a Ballad Opera.* Oxford: Basil Blackwell, 1925. First edition, one of 100 numbered copies printed on Kelmscott handmade paper and signed by author, 8vo., quarter parchment and patterned boards, plain dust jacket, superb copy, virtually as new.   James S. Jaffe Rare Books   Occasional List: Winter 2016 - 71   2016 $850

Graves, Robert   1895-1985 *King Jesus.* New York: Farrar, Straus and Cudahy, Inc., 1955. Reprint, gray cloth some minor markings along edges of covers, else fine in dust jacket.   Argonaut Book Shop   Literature 2015 - 4813 2016 $40

Graves, Robert   1895-1985 *Proceed, Sergeant Lamb.* New York: Random House, 1941. First edition, red cloth, paper labels to cover and spine, spine faded, very good. Argonaut Book Shop   Literature 2015 - 4814   2016 $75

Graves, Robert   1895-1985 *The Real David Copperfield.* London: Arthur Barker, 1933. First edition, half title, original blue cloth, pencil inscription of John Butt 1938, stamps of B. A. Abel, solicitor, Nottingham, good plus in slightly worn dust jacket.   Jarndyce Antiquarian Booksellers   CCXVIII - 491 2016   £65

Graves, Robert   1895-1985   *Sergeant Lamb's America.*   New York: Random House, 1940. First edition, red cloth with paper labels to cover and spine, upper corners lightly bumped, faded at spine and along upper edge of covers, very good.   Argonaut Book Shop   Literature 2015 - 4815   2016 $50

Graves, Robert   1895-1985   *Seven Days in New Crete.*   London: Cassell & Co., 1949. First edition, black cloth with gilt lettering to spine, pictorial dust jacket with some inner wear to edges, some foxing to extreme outer edge of pages, fine.   Argonaut Book Shop   Literature 2015 - 4816   2016 $60

Gray, Annie P.   *Bird Hybrids: a check-list with bibliography.*   Farnham Royal: Farnham Royal Commonwealth Agricultural Bureau, 1958. Quarto, fine in dust jacket, bookplate of Roy Cooper.   Andrew Isles Natural History Books   55 - 6349   2016 $250

Gray, Blaine   *The Siren Trophies.*   Chicago: Celebrity Print, 1905. First edition, 12mo., photographic portrait frontispiece, wood blocks by author, printed in different colors throughout, full decorative stamped leather, wear to crown of thin spine and couple of rings at bottom of front board, some light rubbing, sound and very good, internally fine, nicely inscribed by author, author's letter press calling card laid in.   Between the Covers Rare Books   202 - 35   2016 $2500

Gray, Harold   *Little Orphan Annie and Jumbo the Circus Elephant.*   Chicago: Pleasure Books, 1935. Square 4to., pictorial boards, covers slightly soiled, else near fine, 3 marvelous double page color pop-ups and many black and whites.   Aleph-bet Books, Inc.   111 - 356   2016 $525

Gray, John Edward   *Catalogue of Reptiles... in the Collection of the British Museum.*   London: British Museum, 1844-1845. 2 volumes, duodecimo, publisher's blue wrappers with title labels on upper covers, handwritten title labels on upper covers and handwritten paper label on spine, fine set contained in handsome modern half calf solander box.   Andrew Isles Natural History Books   55 - 36424   2016 $850

Gray, Thomas   1716-1771   *An Elegy wrote in a Country Churchyard.*   London: printed for R. Dodsley and sold by M. Cooper, 1751. Second edition, slight stain on upper margin of titlepage, some light foxing, very good, bookplate of Charles Walker Andrews.   The Brick Row Book Shop   Miscellany 69 - 52   2016 $1000

Gray, Thomas   1716-1771   *Elegy Written in a Country Church-Yard.*   Norwalk: Heritage Press, 1951. Navy blue cloth, lettered and decorated in silver, bookplate, else fine in faded slipcase, illustrations by Agnes Miller Parker.   Argonaut Book Shop   Heritage Press 2015 - 6996   2016 $45

Gray, Thomas   1716-1771   *The Poems of Gray.*   London: printed by T. Bensley, 1800. 6 engraved plates, light foxing throughout, 8vo., contemporary diced russia, a Trinity College Dublin prize binding with their oval stamp in gilt to boards, boards bordered with gilt rope tool, spine divided by decorative gilt rolls, second compartment gilt lettered direct, rest with central tools of urn beneath overhanging branches, marbled endpapers, joints bit rubbed, very good.   Blackwell's Rare Books   B184 - 47   2016   £400

Gray, Thomas   1716-1771   *The Poems of Thomas Gray.*   London: printed for White, Cochrane & Co., 1814. Octavo, portrait frontispiece and one engraved plate, full contemporary red straight grain morocco, covers elaborately decorated in gilt, spine with raised bands decoratively lettered and tooled in gilt, gilt board edges, gilt turn-ins, all edges gilt, marbled endpapers, 2 neat ink inscriptions on blank leaves, fine, with a 'two-way-double' fore-edge painting by Martin Frost (signed with initials on right-hand side of oval of the Tomb scene) of a bucolic rural scene and a view of Gray's tomb at Stoke Poges, tipped in at back of book is Martin Frost's printed certificate "hidden under the gilt edge of the book you can find a FORE-EDGE PAINTING by Martin Frost", fine example by Frost.   David Brass Rare Books, Inc.   2015 - 02892   2016 $1850

Gray, Thomas   1716-1771   *The Poetical Works of Thomas Gray....*   York: printed by A. Ward and sold by J. Dodsley and J. Todd, York, 1775. First edition, 4to., contemporary full calf, spine with contrasting red leather label, frontispiece, joints cracking at top head of spine with little chipping, some scrapes to boards and rubbing to spine, little browning to endpapers, otherwise very good, ink note on front free endpaper by Richard Hooper of Upton Vicarage, Berks dated Jul 12 1872, bookplate of Baron Carlingford.   Sotheran's Piccadilly Notes - Summer 2015 - 150   2016   £275

Gray, Thomas   1716-1771   *The Works of Thomas Gray.*   London: Harding, Triphook and Lepard, 1825. 2 volumes, extremely appealing contemporary red straight grain morocco, attractively gilt by Ingalton of Eton (with their ticket), 197 x 114mm., covers with double fillet border enclosing a triple fillet frame with gilt tooled leafy cornerpieces, central panel enclosed by single fillet with roundel corners, raised bands, spine compartments gilt with leafy frames, turn-ins with dense gilt roll, all edges gilt, engraved frontispiece portrait of gray, first prelim leaf to volume I with inked inscription 'George Chester Cooper/Given to him by his friend George Pickering/Eton. March 1830", just vaguest rubbing and abrasions to covers, minor foxing to frontispiece and prelim leaves, pretty set in very fine condition, clean and fresh internally, gleaming bindings with virtually no wear.   Phillip J. Pirages   67 - 45   2016 $950

Grazzini, Antonis Francesco, called II Lasca   1503-1584
The Story of Doctor Manente.   Florence: Orioli, 1929. First edition, 49.200 copies signed by author, printed on Binda handmade paper (of an edition of 1200), frontispiece, 2 further plates, original vellum, oval ornament stamped in red to upper board, little browning and few small foxspots to lower board, backstrip lettered in red and darkened Lawrence phoenix bookplate and Stephen Gooden, bookplate for John Raymond Danson, untrimmed, protective glassine jacket, good.   Blackwell's Rare Books   B184 - 176   2016   £350

The Great American Circus.   New York: McLoughlin Bros., 1889. Large 8vo., stiff card covers with chromolithographed illustration, stapled, moderate wear and dusting to covers, wear to backstrip, chromolithographed illustrations to each page, very minor foxing and thumb soiling to margins.   Dramatis Personae   119 - 33   2016 $150

Great Britain.   Naval Intelligence Division - 1944   *The Belgian Congo.*   London: OUP for H. M. Stationery Office, April, 1944. First edition, 8vo., original grey cloth, spine and front cover lettered in gilt, highly illustrated with plates, maps and plans, two large color map in rear pocket, as new, with "This book is for offficial use of persons in HM Service only....".   Sotheran's   Travel and Exploration - 24   2016   £128

Great Britain.   Parliament - 1754   *An Act to Continue the Duties for Encouragement of the Coinage of Money and from Removing Doubts Concerning the Continuance of the Duty of Twenty Shillings for Every Ton of Brandy Wines and strong Waters, Imported.*   London: printed by Thomas Baskett, printer to the King's most excelent Majesty, 1754. Folio, self wrappers.   Jeff Weber Rare Books   181 - 80   2016 $100

Great Britain.   Parliament - 1777   *The Parliamnetary Register; or History of the Proceedings and Debates of the House of Commons... volume 6.*   London: printed for J. Almon, 1777. First edition, 8vo., contemporary calf, five raised bands, red morocco spine label gilt, armorial gilt device at foot, marbled endpapers, very good, wear and sunning to boards, spine rubbed, headband lacking, some minor browning to leaves, small loss of paper at lower fore edge of titlepage.   Kaaterskill Books   21 - 5   2016 $1200

Great Britain.   Parliament - 1778   *An Act to Enable His Majestly to Appoint Commissioners with Sufficient Powers to Treat consult and Agree Upon the means of Quieting the Disorders ow Subsisting in Certain of the Colonies, Plantations and Provinces of North America.*   London: printed by Charles Eyre and William Stahan..., 1778. First edition, 30.5 x 19.5cm., marbled paper covered boards, originally removed from large volume, title within double line border, headpiece, initial, small stab holes at inner margin, else fine in mildy rubbed boards.   Kaaterskill Books   21 - 4   2016 $450

Great Britain.   Parliament.   House of Lords - 1776   *The Humble Address of the Right Honourable The Lords Spirial and Temporal in Parliament Assembled. Presented to His Majesty...*   London: Charles Eyre and William Strahan, 1776. First edition, printed on handmade laid paper with 'Bankers Linen' watermark,.   M & S Rare Books, Inc.   99 - 263   2016 $4500

Great Britain.   Parliament.   House of Lords - 1862   *Papers Relating to the Rebellion in China and the Trade in the Yang-Tze-Kiang River... with (further Papers relating to the Rebellion in China. (with) Further Papers Relating to the Rebellion in China.*   London: Harrison and Sons, 1862. First edition of all parts, foolscap folio, 3 volumes in one, modern boards with printed label on spine, 5 lithographic maps and plans, one with additional color, 3 folding, apart from light even browning, fine, very rare.   Sotheran's Travel and Exploration - 93   2016   £1995

Great Britain.   Treaties, etc. - 1840   *Correspondence Relating to the Boundary Between the British Possessions in North America and the United States of America under the Treaty of 1783.*   London: Government of Great Britain, 1840. 2 volumes, quarto, 2 large folding map, 5 small diagrams, original blue paper wrapper, part I with covers detached and soiled, part of front cover missing, with titles on both front and back covers, top margins is soiled to first 20 pages and last 50 pages have a tear to top margin and few pages have some loss, not into text, interior very good with one map in very good condition and largest has tears to folds that have been repaired and some light browning along folds.   Schooner Books Ltd.   115 - 198   2016 $450

Great Britain.   War Office - 1940   *Notes on Map Reading 1929.*   London: His Majesty's Stationary Office, 1940. Second edition, 8vo., publisher's printed wrappers, 20 monthly folding plates, maps, illustrations in text, wrappers little foxed, otherwise good, HM Stationery Office stamp.   Sotheran's   Travel and Exploration - 480   2016   £85

Greco, Gioachino   *Le Jeu des Eschets.*   Paris: N. Pepingue, 1669. First edition in French, 12mo., contemporary French calf, marbled endpapers, page edges colored and sprinkled, light rubbing at extremities, but very good and very attractive.   Joseph J. Felcone, Inc.   Books from Five Centuries: a Miscellany - 39   2016 $2500

Greely, Adolphous W.   *Report on the Climate of New Mexico with Particular Reference to Questions of Irrigation and Water Storage in the Arid Regions.*   Washington: GPO, 1891. Tables, 8 folding maps, offprint, original printed wrappers soiled, small corner chip with library notation on front wrapper, pages browned, else good.   Dumont Maps and Books   133 - 54   2016 $100

Greely, Adolphus W. *Three Years of Arctic Service. An Account of the Lady Franklin Bay Expedition of 1881-84 and the Attainment of the Farthest North.* London: Bentley, 1886. First UK edition, 8vo., 2 volumes, original blue cloth, spine ornamented and lettered gilt, front covers with Arctic landscapes blocked in white within gilt oval frame, 44 steel engraved portait, folding facsimiles, 41 wood engraved plates, many after photos, 8 maps, one large lithographic folding map printed in two colours bound in, numerous text illustrations, recased at early stage restorations to worn extremities, portrait with repaired tears as well as large map at folds, some spotting to few pages, including portrait, one plate and prelims.   Sotheran's   Travel and Exploration - 423   2016   £228

Green, Ellen *Propertius.* Oxford University Press, 2012. First edition, as new, paperback.   Unsworths Antiquarian Booksellers Ltd.   E04 - 56   2016   £20

Green, George Smith *The Life of Mr. John Van a Clergyman's Son of Woods in New Hampshire.* London: printed for Francis Noble and John Noble, 1757? Rare, 2 volumes, 8vo., near fine, contemporary calf, gilt ruled borders, raised and gilt banded spines, original red gilt labels, small expert repairs to heads of spine.   Jarndyce Antiquarian Booksellers   CCXVII - 113   2016   £3000

Green, H. Gordon *The Silver Dart: the Authentic Story of the Hon. J. A. D. McCurdy, Canada's First Pilot.* Fredericton: Brunswick Press, 1959. First printing, blue cloth, dust jacket, half title, 43 black and white photos, very good in worn dust jacket.   Schooner Books Ltd.   115 - 147   2016 $45

Green, J. W. *Kingia (volume one).* Perth: Western Australian Herbarium, 1988-1990. 4 parts, wrappers.   Andrew Isles Natural History Books   55 - 37623   2016 $80

Green. Frederick Lawrence *Odd Man Out.* New York: Reynal & Hitchcock, 1947. First US edition, fine in fine dust jacket, octavo, cloth, sharp copy.   John W. Knott, Jr./L.W. Currey, Inc.   Fall-Winter 2015 - 18499   2016 $375

Greenaway, Kate   1846-1901 *Almanack for 1925.* London: Frederick Warne & Co., 1925. First edition, yellow cloth and pictorial cream boards, lettered in black, pale teal endpapers, very good or better, some light soiling to boards, minor wear to extremities, touch of light sunning and soiling to endpapers, otherwise bright and clean pages, overall attractive copy.   B & B Rare Books, Ltd.   2016 - KG002b   2016 $60

Greenaway, Kate   1846-1901 *Kate Greenaways Birthday Book for Children.*   London: George Routledge, n.d. circa, 1881. New edition, 24mo., red cloth with bevelled edges, stamped in black and gold, round glazed pictorial paste-on, near fine and unused, 12 beautiful color plates and hundreds of illustrations, this copy signed by Greenaway and has stamp with her address on verso presentation page.   Aleph-bet   Books, Inc.   112 - 223   2016 $1250

Greenaway, Kate   1846-1901 *Under the Window.* London: George Routledge & Sons, New York: 416 Broome St., n.d., 1878. First edition, green glazed pictorial boards, blue spine, blue endpapers, yellow edges, light edgewear an hinge rubbing, half title quite foxed, else very good+, this copy signed by Sarah Orne Jewett, her copy.   Aleph-bet Books, Inc.   112 - 224   2016 $600

Greenaway, Kate   1846-1901 *Under the Window.* London: George Routledge & sons, 1879. First edition, first issue, small quarto, numerous color printed wood engraved illustrations in text, original green glazed boards with dark green cloth backstrip, covers illustrated, all edges stained yellow, dark green coated endpapers, some minor rubbing to corners, few short marginal tears, some light foxing to prelim leaves, overall an excellent copy, first book written and illustrated by Greenaway.   David Brass Rare Books, Inc.   2015 - 02992   2016 $450

Greenberg, Martin *Journey to Infinity.* New York: Gnome Press Inc., 1951. First edition, octavo, cloth backed boards, some mild discoloration of cloth at spine ends, nearly fine in about fine dust jacket with light crease along upper front edge and some mild stress crease to upper left front corner.   John W. Knott, Jr./L.W. Currey, Inc.   Fall-Winter 2015 - 17037   2016 $75

Greenberg, Martin *Men Against the Stars.* New York: Gnome Press, 1950. First edition, octavo, cloth backed boards, fine in fine dust jacket, sharp copy.   John W. Knott, Jr./L.W. Currey, Inc.   Fall-Winter 2015 - 17036   2016 $250

Greenberg, Martin *The Robot and the Man.* New York: Gnome Press Inc., 1953. First edition, octavo, cloth, thin ink mark along upper edge of front free endpaper, fine in fine dust jacket.   John W. Knott, Jr./L.W. Currey, Inc.   Fall-Winter 2015 - 17039   2016 $250

Greenberg, Martin *Travelers of Space.* New York: Gnome Press Inc., 1951. First edition, octavo, cloth backed boards, fine in fine, first state dust jacket with tiny closed tear at head of spine panel.   John W. Knott, Jr./L.W. Currey, Inc.   Fall-Winter 2015 - 17038   2016 $150

Greene, Graham 1904-1991 *The Basement Room and Other Stories.* London: Cresset, 1935. First edition, first issue, 8vo., original green cloth little soiled overall with rubbing at corners, backstrip lettered in gilt with rubbing to tips, top edge lightly dust soiled with faint hit of foxing to foreedge and endpapers, ownership inscription, very good. Blackwell's Rare Books   B186 - 224   2016   £450

Greene, Graham 1904-1991 *Collected Essays.* London: Bodley Head, 1969. First edition, original cloth with dust jacket, spine of jacket little browned with couple of closed tears, otherwise very good.   Sotheran's   Piccadilly Notes - Summer 2015 - 151   2016   £148

Greene, Graham 1904-1991 *The Complaisant Lover.* New York: 1961. First American edition, very nice in slightly rubbed dust jacket, commercially produced bookplate which carries author's autograph signature, it would appear Greene signed this bookplate at the request of a previous owner.   Bertram Rota Ltd.   February List 2016 - 25   2016   £450

Greene, Graham 1904-1991 *The Confidential Agent.* Viking Press, 1939. First US edition, fine, bright, clean copy in wonderful dust jacket, fine and fresh except for trace of rubbing to front flap fold, exceptional copy.   Buckingham Books   2015 - 36923   2016 $3500

Greene, Graham 1904-1991 *The End of the Affair.* London: William Heinemann, 1951. First edition, slight fading at head and foot of spine, otherwise very nice in slightly chipped and soiled dust jacket, booklabel and bookseller's label on front pastedown.   Bertram Rota Ltd.   February List 2016 - 24   2016   £220

Greene, Graham 1904-1991 *England Made Me.* London: Heinemann, 1935. First edition, pages lightly toned, 8vo., original red cloth with publisher's device blindstamped at foot of lower panel, backstrip lettered in gilt and faded, slightly softened ead, edges toned, very good. Blackwell's Rare Books   B186 - 226   2016   £500

Greene, Graham 1904-1991 *Collected Essays.* London: Bodley Head, 1969. First edition, octavo, upper cover little spotted, very good in very good slightly nicked dust jacket with closed tear of approximately 3 inches at fold of lower flap.   Peter Ellis   112 - 155   2016   £75

Greene, Graham 1904-1991 *Getting to Know the General.* London: Bodley Head, 1984. First edition, 8vo., original cloth, near fine, inscribed by author for Lady Diana Cooper.   Sotheran's   Piccadilly Notes - Summer 2015 - 152   2016   £1250

Greene, Graham 1904-1991 *In Search of a Character. Two African Journals.* London: Bodley Head, 1961. First British edition, true first, fine, near fine dust jacket with very light wear.   Bella Luna Books   2016 - t5400   2016 $165

Greene, Graham 1904-1991 *The Ministry of Fear.* London: William Heinemann, 1943. First edition, original yellow cloth, cloth moderately soiled, former owner's inked name on front flyear, else very good in professionally restored dust jacket, news clipping taken from Sunday Supplement May 29 1943, pasted to newspaper. Buckingham Books   2015 - 29296   2016 $3750

Greene, Graham 1904-1991 *The Name of Action.* London: Heinemann, 1930. First edition, light foxing to prelims and very occasionally to text, original blue cloth with publisher's device and border, blindstamped to lower and upper board respectively, backstrip lettered gilt and trifle rubbed at tips, edges and endpapers foxed, very good. Blackwell's Rare Books   B186 - 227   2016   £300

Greene, Graham 1904-1991 *The Old School. Essays by Divers Hands.* London: Jonathan Cape, 1934. First edition, faint foxing to prelims and final text pages, occasional faint spot further in, 8vo., original black cloth lettered in blue to upper board with publisher's device in same to lower backstrip lettered in blue, few faint foxspots to gently toned edges, tail edge rough trimmed, few faint spots to endpapers, good, bright copy, scarce edition, with 1 page ALS from H. E. Bates to Greene.   Blackwell's Rare Books B186 - 225   2016   £800

Greene, Graham 1904-1991 *Why the Epigraph?* London: Nonesuch Press, 1989. First edition, limited to 950 numbered copies signed by Greene, 8vo., gilt stamped cloth, fine in original clear wrappers.   Aleph-bet Books, Inc.   112 - 225   2016 $300

Greene, W. C. *Parrots in Captivity.* London: George Bell and Sons, 1884-1887. First edition, 3 large octavo volumes, with 2 additional pages numbered 50' and 50", 81 wood engraved plates, printed in colors and beautifully finished by hand, publisher's second issue binding of original dark teal cloth dated 1892, at foot of spines, front covers stamped with central gilt parrot vignette, teal coated endpapers, spines lettered gilt, spines with very light rubbing at extremities, corners little rubbed, overall fine, all plates extremely clean and bright.   Heritage Book Shop   Holiday 2015 - 49   2016 $4500

Greenewalt, Crawford H. *Hummingbirds.* Garden City: American Museum of Natural History, 1960. Quarto, 68 tipped-in color photos by author, text illustrations, fine, slightly chipped dust jacket, bookplate of Norman Wettenhall.   Andrew Isles Natural History Books   55 - 13280   2016 $400

Greenhow, Robert *Memoir, Historical and Political on the Northwest Coast of North America and the Adjacent Territories.* Washington: Blair and Rives, 1840. Folding map laid in, disbound from larger volume, text block clean and bright.   Dumont Maps and Books   134 - 35   2016 $450

Greenleaf, Stephen *Fatal Obsession.* New York: Dial, 1983. First edition, signed by author, fine in dust jacket. Mordida Books   2015 - 007924   2016 $55

Greenleaf, Stephen *State's Evidence.* New York: Dial, 1982. First edition, fine in dust jacket.   Mordida Books 2015 - 011975   2016 $60

Greenough, Horatio *Form and Function.* Berkeley: University of California Press, 1944. One of 75 copies, 12mo., printed in red and black, half gilt lettered vellum, marbled boards, slight wear to corners, but fine.   Argonaut Book Shop   Private Press 2015 - 6311   2016 $50

Greenough, Sarah *On the Art of Fixing a Shadow.* Boston: Little Brown and Co. in association with national Gallery of Art and Art Institute of Chicago, 1989. First edition, oblong quarto, hundreds of reproductions, beige cloth, very fine with cover fading to pictorial dust jacket. Argonaut Book Shop   Photography 2015 - 7305   2016 $90

Greenwald, Maurine Weiner *Women, War and Work: the Impact of World War I on Women Workers in the United States.* Westport: Greenwood, 1980. First edition, 8vo., illustrations, author's TLS laid in, black cloth, few pencil marks, top edge spotted, otherwise very good, tight copy in scuffed and chipped dust jacket.   Second Life Books, Inc. 196A - 676   2016 $45

Greenwood, Jeremy *Ravilious Engravings.* Woodbridge: Wood Lea Press, 2008. Limited to 8000 copies bound thus, over 400 engravings, drawings, illustrations, folio, cloth, slipcase.   Oak Knoll Books   310 - 176   2016 $620

Greenwood, Robert *The California Outlaw, Tiburcio Vasquez.* Los Gatos: Talisman Press, 1960. First edition, limited to 975 copies, illustrations, portrait, facsimiles, cloth backed boards, very fine, dust jacket.   Argonaut Book Shop   Biography 2015 - 5545   2016 $125

Gregg, Ellen E. *Kirk-McColl 1785 to 1980 - 195 Years of Christian Witness.* St. Stephen: Print'N Press, 1980. 8vo., card covers, photo illustrations, very good.   Schooner Books Ltd.   115 - 67   2016 $45

Gregg, Jarvis *Elisama or the Captivity and Restoration of the Jews.* Philadelphia: American Sunday School Union, 1835. First edition, 16mo., frontispiece map, contemporary calf backed marbled boards, hinges cracked, front hinge weak, text stained toward back.   M & S Rare Books, Inc. 99 - 131   2016 $125

Gregg, Linda *Eight Poems.* Port Townsend: Graywolf Press, 1982. Copy M of 26 lettered copies out of 312, small 8vo., signed and lettered on colophon by author, paper wrappers, as new.   Second Life Books, Inc.   196A - 677   2016 $125

Gregory, Brian *In Winter Vineyards, Poems by Brian Gregory.* Auckland: Pear Tree Press, 1999. Limited to 50 numbered copies, signed by Gregory, Richard McWhannell and Tara McLeod, woodcuts by McWhannell, on Lana Royal mouldmade paper with 6 tipped in woodcut images printed from wood blocks, 4to., black cloth spine, red cloth covered boards, paper cover label.   Oak Knoll Books   27 - 50 2016 $575

Gregory, John *A Father's Legacy to his Daughters.* London: for W. Strahan and T. Cadell, 1784. New edition, 8vo., half title, frontispiece, small paper flaw to B2 causing loss of page number, contemporary full tree calf, elaborate gilt spine, dark green morocco label, corners little bumped, some slight rubbing, Conyngham armorial bookplate, signature of 'Denison', handsome copy.   Jarndyce Antiquarian Books   CCXV - 231   2016   £75

Gregory, John *A Father's Legacy to His Daughters.* London: printed at the Minerva Press for lane Newman & Co., 1808. New edition, 32mo., frontispiece, original sheep, slightly worm damaged.   Jarndyce Antiquarian Books CCXV - 232   2016   £65

Gregory, John *A Father's Legacy to His Daughters.* London: John Sharpe, 1822. Half title, frontispiece and plates, full tan calf, blocked in blind and gilt, raised bands, compartments in gilt, maroon morocco label, little rubbed, contemporary calligraphic ownership signature of Miss Barbara Barla, bookseller's ticket, Maurice Ogle, Glasgow, nice copy.   Jarndyce Antiquarian Books   CCXV - 233 2016   £50

Gregory, Saint, the Great *Opera.* Paris: Francois Regnault, 1521. Early reissue of 1518 editio princeps, titlepage printed in red and black, scattering of small wormholes in title and first section (index), reducing to 3 by the start of text and wholly extinguished by f. 50, 3 further small holes in last 30ff., sometimes touching a character but rarely affecting legibility, frequent short marginal early ink notes, bit of dust soiling and marginal damp marking at end, folio, early 19th century English sprinkled calf, backstrip with four raised bands, remains of old label in second compartment, boards bordered in blind, front joint and backstrip ends expertly renewed, bit rubbed and scratched, ownership inscription with Latin motto dated 1578 at head of title with initials T. G. (further initial lost), 17th century inscription by Roger Kay, early 19th century bookplate of Fulwar William Fowle, good.   Blackwell's Rare Books   Marks of Genius - 20   2016   £950

Gregory, William King *The Anatomy of the Gorilla; the Studies of Henry Cushir Raven.* New York: Columbia University Press, 1950. Quarto, 4 folding plates, publisher's cloth, chipped dust jacket, some grubby marks and library stamp of Royal Society of Victoria, very good. Andrew Isles Natural History Books 55 - 35882 2016 $400

Gregson, J. M. *Murder at the Nineteenth.* London: Collins Crime Club, 1989. First edition, pages slightly darkened and some scattered light spotting on page edges, otherwise fine in dust jacket. Mordida Books 2015 - 011347 2016 $65

Gressitt, J. L. *Biogeography and Ecology of Mew Guinea.* The Hague: Junk, 1982. Octavo, photos, publisher's cloth, ex-library with stamps, library pocket, nonetheless sound set, scarce. Andrew Isles Natural History Books 55 - 10413 2016 $250

Grey, Edward William *The History of and Antiquities of Newbury and Its Environs, Including Twenty-Eight Parishes, Situate in the County of berks...* Speenhamland: Hall and Marsh, 1839. 8vo., 19 plates, folding frontispiece map laid down on tissue and with repaired tear stretching 12mm. from mount, some foxing and spotting elsewhere, half title discarded, later polished green calf, boards with gilt border, spine gilt, green morocco lettering piece, somewhat rubbed, spine sunned, bookplate of Piscatorial Society recording book's gift to Society by Robert Blundell in 1911, good. Blackwell's Rare Books B184 - 48 2016 £120

Grey, William, Mrs. *Journal of a Visit to Egypt, Constantinople, The Crimea, Greece, etc. in the Suite of the Prince and Princess of Wales.* London: Smith Elder, 1870. Second edition, 8ov., original purple cloth, spine lightly faded. J. & S. L. Bonham Antiquarian Booksellers Voyages 2016 - 8407 2016 $65

Grey, Zane 1872-1939 *An American Angler in Australia.* New York and London: Harper & Bros., 1937. First edition (so stated and with correct 'B-M' code, 35 photographic halftone plates, titlepage printed in ochre and black, publisher's gilt stamped green cloth, fine with very good pictorial dust jacket (chipped at foot of spine and lower corners, less so to rear lower edge), scarce. Argonaut Book Shop Literature 2015 - 7587 2016 $900

Grey, Zane 1872-1939 *Betty Zane by Znae Grey.* New York: Charles Francis Press, 1901. First edition, presentation copy inscribed by him, octavo, 6 inserted plates including frontispiece, publisher's light grey cloth, spine lettered gilt, front cover decoratively stamped in yellow, brown and burgundy, this title was not issued with dust jacket, spine rubbed and lightly soiled, some rubbing to front cover, slightly skewed, still near fine, rare. Heritage Book Shop Holiday 2015 - 50 2016 $5000

Grey, Zane 1872-1939 *Tales of Fishes.* New York: Grosset & Dunlap, 1937. First reprint by this publisher, color frontispiece and over 60 photo half tone illustrations by the author, yellow cloth stamped in dark green, spine slightly darkened, fine copy with pictorial dust jacket worn and torn. Argonaut Book Shop Literature 2015 - 7589 2016 $150

Grey, Zane 1872-1939 *Tales of Southern Rivers.* New York: Harper and Bros., 1924. First edition, ownership stamp of a Boy Scout troops, gilt lettering little tarnished, near fine in price clipped very good photographically illustrated white dust jacket with some rubbing and small nicks on spine, and some overall smudges, some modest flaws still nice copy. Between the Covers Rare Books 208 - 135 2016 $1200

Grey, Zane 1872-1939 *Tales of Swordfish and Tuna.* New York: Harper & Bros., 1927. First edition (so sated and with correct "H-B" code, quarto, 90 photographic halftone plates, drawings, publisher's gilt stamped dark blue cloth, tiny bump to lower edge of front cover, very fine with pictorial dust jacket (slight wear to jacket spine ends), lovely copy with jacket, quite scarce in this condition. Argonaut Book Shop Literature 2015 - 7590 2016 $1500

Grey, Zane 1872-1939 *Tales of the Angler's Eldorado, New Zealand.* New York: Grosset & Dunlap, 1937. First reprint by this publisher, quarto, 100 photographic half tone illustrations by author and drawings by Frank Phares, publisher's dark blue cloth lettered in light blue, upper fore-edge of two leaves slightly shaved, fine copy with pictorial dust jacket lightly worn and chipped. Argonaut Book Shop Literature 2015 - 7588 2016 $300

Grey, Zane 1872-1939 *The Vanishing American.* New York and London: Harper & Bros., 1925. Octavo, rust colored cloth with blue printing and decoration on cover and spine, publisher's printing code 'L-Z' on copyright page indicates this is later printing, printed Nov. 1925, minor wear to head and foot of spine, else fine. Argonaut Book Shop Native American 2015 - 7738 2016 $40

Gribble, Harry Wagstaff *March Hares. (The Tempermentalists).* Cincinnati: Stewart Kidd, 1923. First edition, 8vo., author's presentation on flyleaf, very good in little worn, price clipped dust jacket. Second Life Books, Inc. 196A - 679 2016 $65

Grierson, James *Delineations of St. Andrews...* Edinburgh: printed for Peter Hill et al, 1807. First edition, 198 x 114mm., publisher's original blue boards, paper label on spine, edges untrimmed, felt lined morocco backed folding box, 4 engraved plates, inscribed "Edin. 27th April 1807/ Agnes Cockburn/in memory/ of the author", boards little soiled, front joint cracked (rear joint starting at tail), extremities with the expected considerable wear, spine label chipped (with a fourth of the letters gone), but with boards still attached and extremely insubstantial publisher's binding still appealing because of its original materials, titlepage with bit of offsetting from frontispiece, isolated minor foxing in text, other trivial imperfections, but excellent internally, untrimmed leaves bright fresh and clean, with all of their ample margins intact.   Phillip J. Pirages   67 - 175   2016 $6500

Griffin, Jasper *Homer on Life and death.* Oxford: Clarendon Press, 1983. First paperback edition, 8vo., spine slightly faded, very minor shelfwear, very good, ownership inscription of C. D. N. Costa and one or two pencil annotations.   Unsworths Antiquarian Booksellers Ltd.   E05 - 30   2016   £30

Griffin, W. E. B. *The Aviators.* New York: Putnam, 1987. First edition, fine in dust jacket.   Mordida Books   2015 - 011927   2016 $65

Griffin, W. E. B. *The New Breed.* New York: Putnam, 1987. First edition, fine in dust jacket.   Mordida Books   2015 - 011926   2016 $65

Griffith, Aline *The Earth Rests Lightly Earth.* Holt: Rinehart & Winston, 1964. First edition, fine in fine dust jacket (minor edge wear).   Ken Hebenstreit, Bookseller   2016 - 2016 $125

Griffith, George *The Endowed Schools of England and Ireland.* London: Whittaker & Co., 1864. Original blue pictorial paper boards, neatly rebacked with brown cloth, slight waterstain to front board.   Jarndyce Antiquarian Books   CCXV - 706   2016   £85

Griffith, George *Going to Markets and Grammar Schools...* London: William Freeman, 1870. First edition, 2 volumes, half titles, frontispiece, illustrations, original maroon cloth, spines slightly faded, good plus.   Jarndyce Antiquarian Books   CCXV - 707   2016   £85

Griffith, George *The White Witch of Mayfair.* London: F. V. White & Co. Ltd., 1902. First edition, presumed later or variant binding, 8vo., illustrated red cloth, publisher's monogram stamped in black on rear panel, lettered black at spine, neat short gift inscription on half title, very faint mottling to spine, bright, clean, very good copy.   Any Amount of Books   2015 - A71382   2016   £150

Griffiths, David N. *The Bibliography of the Book of Common Prayer 1549-1999.* New Castle: Oak Knoll Press, 2002. First edition, large 8vo., cloth, dust jacket, 15 full color illustrations.   Oak Knoll Books   310 - 248   2016 $350

Griffiths, Julia *Autographs for Freedom.* Auburn/ Rochester: Alden, Beardsley & Co./Wanzer Beardsley & Co., 1854. Second edition, publisher's brown figured cloth, gilt (no priority), slight contemporary name stamp of George H. Dickerson, slight spotting on boards and light wear at extremities, else near fine.   Between the Covers Rare Books   207 - 3   2016 $600

Griffon, Jules *It's Orgy Time.* Los Angeles: Ultima Books, 1971. First edition, trade paperback small octavo, explicit photos, mostly in color, illustrated wrappers, modest edgewear, about near fine,.   Between the Covers Rare Books   208 - 76   2016 $250

Griggs, Sutton E. *According to Law.* Memphis: National Public Welfare League, 1916. First edition, 12mo., printed gray wrappers, small tears at edges of yapped wrapper, modest rubbing, very good or better.   Between the Covers Rare Books   202 - 36   2016 $700

Grigsby, Joan S. *Lanterns by the Lake.* London and Kobe: Kegan, Paul, Trench, Trubner & J. L. Thompson, 1929. First edition, frontispiece and 5 further woodblock illustrations tipped to thick brown paper with printed captions below, few faint foxspots to prelims and gentle knock to top corner of textblock, 8vo., original black cloth with sewn Japanese style binding, lantern shaped title label pasted to upper board, slight knock to top corners, pages uncut, red gold speckled endpapers, straining to hinges particularly at front, very good.   Blackwell's Rare Books   B186 - 230   2016   £275

Grimaldi, Stacey *A suit of Armour for Youth.* published by the proprietor, 1824. First edition, engraved frontispiece, 11 engraved plates each with flap, 1 of the flaps re-attached, some offsetting, 12mo., contemporary calf, gilt roll tooled borders on sides, spine gilt, rebacked (little crudely), corners worn, contemporary ownership inscription of Jane Janvrin and inscription by her presenting volume to her brother, Francis, sound.   Blackwell's Rare Books   B186 - 70   2016   £450

Grimble, Augustus *Highland Sport.* London: Chapman & Hall, 1894. First edition, 4to., original vellum backed paper covered board, gilt lettering to spine, frontispiece and 10 black and white plates by Archibald Thorburn, binding little sunned, occasional sporting mainly to endpapers, very good.   Sotheran's   Hunting, Shooting & Fishing - 175   2016   £300

Grimble, Augustus *More Leaves from My Game Book.* London: printed for R. Clay and Sons Ltd., 1917. First edition, limited to 250 copies, 8vo., original half vellum over marbled boards with red leather label on spine, 45 illustrations, vellum bit rubbed and discolored but good, inscribed by author to Maurice Hill Aug. 1917.   Sotheran's Hunting, Shooting & Fishing - 176   2016   £300

Grimble, Augustus *Salmon Rivers of England and Wales.* London: Kegan Paul, Trench, Trubner & Co. Ltd., 1913. Second edition, 8vo., original green cloth, gilt, folding map, 89 illustrations, previous owner's signature, extremities slightly bumped, otherwise very good.   Sotheran's Hunting, Shooting & Fishing - 119   2016   £300

Grimes, Martha *Rainbow's End.* New York: Knopf, 1995. First edition, very fine in dust jacket, signed by author.   Mordida Books   2015 - 010818   2016 $65

Grimke, Angelina W. *Rachel: A Play in Three Acts.* Boston: Cornhill Co., 1920. First edition, cloth and paper covered boards, gilt , very slight foxing on prelim leaves, spine gilt little faded, otherwise nice and square, near fine.   Between the Covers Rare Books   202 - 38   2016 $2500

Grimm, The Brothers *The Bear and the Kingbird.* New York: Farrar, Strauss, Giroux, 1979. 8vo., cloth, soil along inner edge of rear cover, very good in dust jacket (soil on rear cover), color illustrations by Chris Conover, laid in is charming letter from Conover discussing her book 'Simple Simon' thanking recipient for hr kind words and with a little ink drawing.   Aleph-bet Books, Inc.   111 - 98   2016 $125

Grimm, The Brothers *The Fairy Tales of the Brothers Grimm.* London: Constable & Co. Ltd, 1909. No. 732 of 750 copies signed by artist, 292 x 235mm., very attractive red three quarter morocco gilt stamp signed 'Putnams' along front turn-in, raised bands, spine handsomely gilt in compartments formed by plain and decorative rules, quatrefoil centerpiece surrounded by densely scrolling cornerpieces, sides and endleaves of rose colored linen, top edge gilt (front joint and headcap very expertly repaired by Courtland Benson), titlepage with pictorial frame, numerous black and white illustrations in text, 10 full page black and white illustrations and 40 color plates by Arthur Rackham, as called for mounted on cream stock and protected by lettered tissue guards, front cover with faint minor soiling, just hint of wear to corners, small corner tear to one plate, two tissue guards with minor creasing or chipped edges, otherwise fine, handsome binding, text and plates clean, fresh and bright.   Phillip J. Pirages   67 - 293   2016 $3750

Grimm, The Brothers *Grimm's Fairy Tales.* New York: Charles Scribner's Sons, 1920. 8vo., plates, original black cloth with mounted color plate on upper cover, very good+.   Jeff Weber Rare Books   181 - 65   2016 $250

Grimm, The Brothers *Grimm's Fairy Tales.* Philadelphia: Penn, 1922. First edition, thick 4to., gilt cloth, pictorial paste-on, fine, 23 beautiful color plates plus many black and white text illustrations.   Aleph-bet Books, Inc.   112 - 119   2016 $300

Grimm, The Brothers *The Fisherman and His Wife.* New York: Farrar, Straus Giroux, 1908. Stated first edition, cloth, fine in dust jacket creased on corner, else very good+, full and partial page color illustrations by Margot Zemach, laid in are 2 handwritten letters from artist.   Aleph-bet Books, Inc.   112 - 530   2016 $150

Grimm, The Brothers *Grimm Tales for Young and Old.* Penguin, 2012. First edition of this new version by Philip Pullman, 8vo. original red boards, backstrip lettered in white, red page marker, dust jacket, fine.   Blackwell's Rare Books   B184 - 223   2016   £150

Grimm, The Brothers *Grimms Marchenschatz.* Berlin: Hermann Klemm, 1923. First edition, quarto, 32 fine tipped-in color plates, by Gustaf Tenggren, original quarter black calf over batik boards, front cover and spine pictorially stamped in gilt, four plates with very slight corner creases, inner hinge little shaken, corners of binding little rubbed, overall excellent, scarce.   David Brass Rare Books, Inc.   2015 - 02979   2016 $750

Grimm, The Brothers *Hansel and Gretel.* New York: Macmillan, Aug., 1827. First edition, many full and partial page color lithograph by the Haders, 8vo., pictorial boards, minor shelf wear, very good-fine.   Aleph-bet Books, Inc.   111 - 211   2016 $200

Grimm, The Brothers *Hansel and Gretel and Other Stories by the Brothers Grimm.* London: Hodder & Stoughton, n.d., 1925. Limited to 600 numbered copies signed by artist, large 4to., quarter cloth and batiked paper over boards, fine in original plain paper slipcase, lacks a flap, 12 magnificent tipped in color plates plus decorative endpapers, beautiful copy, scarce.   Aleph-bet Books, Inc.   112 - 343   2016 $6000

Grimm, The Brothers *Juniper Tree and Other Tales from the Brothers Grimm.* New York: Farrar, Straus & Giroux, 1973. Limited to 500 numbered copies, signed by artist, Maurice Sendak and by translator Lore Segal, 2 volumes, top edge gilt, dust jackets, fine in slipcase (slightly shelfworn and faded), illustrations by Sendak with extra suite of illustrations printed on Beckett paper, beautiful set, increasingly scarce.   Aleph-bet Books, Inc.   111 - 409   2016 $1100

Grimm, The Brothers *The Juniper Tree and Other Tales from Grimm.* 1974. First English edition, 2 volumes, illustrations by Maurice Sendak, 2 volumes, spines slightly faded, otherwise very nice in dust jackets and publisher's slipcase that is little marked and worn.   Bertram Rota Ltd. Christmas List 2015 - 38   2016   £100

Grimm, The Brothers *Little Brother & Little Sister.* London: Constable, 1917. Limited to 525 numbered copies signed by Arthur Rackham, folio, grey cloth, pictorial label stamped in gold, top edge gilt, slight bit of rubbing and light rubbing of spine ends, else fine, illustrations by Rackham, with additional signed color plate in envelope.   Aleph-bet Books, Inc.   112 - 410   2016 $7500

Grimm, The Brothers *Little Brother & Little Sister.* New York: Dodd, Mead, 1917. First edition, thick 4to., red gilt cloth, tiny margin creases on some plates, else fine in original publisher's box with mounted color plate on cover (box with flap repaired), 12 beautiful tipped in color plates, 43 black and white drawings plus pictorial endpapers by Arthur Rackham, rare in box.   Aleph-bet Books, Inc.   111 - 375   2016 $1850

Grimm, The Brothers *Rapunzel.* New York: Dutton, 1997. Stated first edition, first printing with 1-10 code, pictorial boards, as new in as new dust jacket, illustrations by artist, Paul Zelinsky, this copy inscribed by artist.   Aleph-bet Books, Inc.   112 - 529   2016 $225

Groff, Lauren *Fates and Furies.* London: Heinemann, 2015. Advance reading copy of first British edition, fine in wrappers, apparently uncommon.   Ken Lopez Bookseller   166 - 38   2016 $125

Grolier Club *Catalogue of an Exhibition of the Works of Charles Dickens...* New York: Grolier Club, 1913. One of 300 copies on handmade paper, frontispiece, uncut, original gray boards, maroon leather label, spine chipped at head and worn at hinges, good, sound copy.   Jarndyce Antiquarian Booksellers   CCXVIII - 1501   2016   £20

Groner, Augusta *Mene Tekel: a Tale of Strange Happenings.* New York: Duffield, 1912. First American edition and first edition in English, small contemporary owner's initials on front pastedown, white painted spine lettering rubbed but readable, some modest foxing in text, sound, very good or better.   Between the Covers Rare Books   204 - 109   2016 $150

Grose, Francis   1731-1791 *A Treatise on Ancient Armour and Weapons.* London: for S. Hooper, 1786. First edition, 4to., profusely illustrated, 1 text engraving, 48 engraved plates by John Hamilton, contemporary sprinkled calf, spines gilt, hinges cracked but held by cords, extremities worn, light scattered foxing, but very good.   Joseph J. Felcone, Inc.   Books from Five Centuries: a Miscellany - 10   2016 $600

Grosse, E. M. *Series of Seventeen Colour Lithographed Plates from the 1913 Expedition to the Coral Reefs of the Torres Straits of Department of Marine Biology of the Carnegie Inst. of Washington.*   Sydney: Government Printer, 1914. Quarto, 17 plates (numbered to 19), typescript insert inscribed to J. Lane Mullins by F. Walsh.   Andrew Isles Natural History Books   55 - 38216   2016 $650

Grosvenor, Frederika *A Very Small Tale of Two Very Small Bears.* New York: McLoughlin Bros., 1905. Folio, cloth backed boards, slight cover and corners worn else very good+ fine chromolithographs, quite scarce.   Aleph-bet Books, Inc.   111 - 277   2016 $350

Groth, John *Studio Europe.* New York: Vanguard, 1945. First edition, presentation copy from author, cover slightly soiled, very good, tight, illustrations.   Second Life Books, Inc.   196A - 681   2016 $45

Grotius, Hugo   1583-1645 *De Iure Belli ac Pacis Libri Tres.* Frankfurt: typis & Sumptibus Wechelianorum D & D. Aubriorum & c Schleichii, 1626. Pirated edition, 8vo., last 2 leaves blank, contemporary English calf over pasteboard, repairs to spine,.   Maggs Bros. Ltd.   1474 - 38   2016   £2500

Grover, Sherwood *Common Place Book six.*   Aptos & Woodside: Grace Hoper Press, 1983. One of 200 copies signed by printer and author, 32cmo., illustrations, quarter beige cloth, decorative printed boards, gilt stamped spine title, plain wrapper, fine, prospectus laid in.   Jeff Weber Rare Books   181 - 64   2016 $55

Groves, Jay *Fireball at the Lake: a Story of Encounter with Another World.*   New York: Exposition Press, 1967. First edition, little spotting on front board, else near fine in good dust jacket with long tear and sticker remnant, both on front panel, very scarce.   Between the Covers Rare Books   208 - 121   2016 $225

Gruelle, Johnny *Friendly Fairies.* Chicago: Volland, 1919. First edition, No additional printings, 8vo., pictorial boards, light wear to spine ends, half title spotted, very good+ in publisher's box (flaps repaired), illustrated with bright colors.   Aleph-bet Books, Inc.   111 - 297   2016 $675

Gruelle, Johnny *Orphan Annie Story Book.* Indianapolis: Bobbs Merrill, 1921. 8vo., cloth, pictorial paste-on, fine, many full and partial page color illustrations, pictorial endpapers as well.   Aleph-bet Books, Inc.   112 - 228   2016 $450

Gruelle, Johnny *Raggedy Ann's Lucky Pennies.* Joliet: Volland, 1932. First edition, 4to., cloth backed pictorial boards, owner inscription dated 1932 with postage stamp size Christmas stamp, fine in fine box, full page and partial page color illustrations, amazing copy. Aleph-bet Books, Inc. 112 - 226 2016 $450

Gruelle, Johnny *Wooden Willie.* Chicago: Volland, 1927. First edition, 8vo., pictorial boards, few tiny pinholes in gutter, else very good to fine, wonderful color illustrations. Aleph-bet Books, Inc. 112 - 227 2016 $500

Grundberg, Andy *Brodovitch.* New York: Harry N. Abrams, 1989. 340 illustrations, 70 in color, fine in very near fine dust jacket. Jeff Hirsch Books Holiday List 2015 - 69 2016 $150

Gruner, Ludwig *The Decorations of the Garden Pavilion in the Grounds of Buckingham Palace.* London: Published by John Murray, 1846. First edition, large folio, 15 engraved plates, some light spotting, original red cloth, upper board lettered and tooled in gilt, rebacked, armorial bookplate of Samuel Rogers. Marlborough Rare Books List 55 - 31 2016 £950

Grunsky, Carl Ewald *Stockton Boyhood, Being the Reminiscences of Which cover the Years from 1855 to 1877.* Berkeley: Friends of the Bancroft Library, 1959. First edition, limited to 800 copies, frontispiece, illustrations, green cloth, gilt lettered spine, illustration on front cover, slight offsetting to endpaper, but very fine. Argonaut Book Shop Biography 2015 - 3600 2016 $75

Gudde, Edwin Gustav *Edward Vischer's First Visit to California.* San Francisco: California Historical Society, 1940. First separate edition, tipped on frontispiece, title printed in red and black, stiff tan wrappers printed in red, some offsetting from portrait, very fine. Argonaut Book Shop Biography 2015 - 3807 2016 $60

Gudger, Eugene Willis *The Bashford Dean Memorial Volume, Archaic Fish Part One.* New York: American Museum of Natural History, 1930-1933. Quarto, text illustrations, plates, binder's cloth, some stamps, very good. Andrew Isles Natural History Books 55 - 35890 2016 $250

Guedalla, Philip *Bonnet and Shawl.* New York: Crosby Gaige, 1928. First edition, 1/571 copies, author's signature on blank opposite title, patterned paper over boards, gray spine stamped in gilt, part of owner's bookplate, slightly scuffed at corners and ends of spine, otherwise nice. Second Life Books, Inc. 196A - 686 2016 $45

Guelloz, Ezzedine *Pelerinage a la mecque.* Lausanne and Paris: La Bibliotheque des Arts, copyright Sud Editions in Tunis, 1977. First edition, folio, original white leatherette, lettered gilt, photographic dust jackets, illustrated paste downs, illustrations, near fine, presentation inscription, very rare. Sotheran's Travel and Exploration - 322 2016 £248

Guerassimov, A. *Excursion are Caucase Littoral de la mer Noire.* Leningrad and Moscow: Imprimerie au nom d'Eugenie Sokolova, 1937. Rare first edition, original grey cloth, front cover lettered blue, 3 plates after photos, one large folding table, folding map, sketch maps and diagrams in text, wear and spotting to binding, internally apart from one gathering toned due to paper stock, very good and clean copy, Polish library in Leningrad with stamp on blank page and stamp. Sotheran's Travel and Exploration - 256 2016 £198

Guerin, Maurice De *From Centaur to Cross the Unpublished Correspondence & the Centaur.* New York: Covici Friede, 1929. First edition, 8vo., corners slightly bumped, some wear along spine, fine. Argonaut Book Shop Literature 2015 - 1250 2016 $45

Guest, Author Unknown, 17th Century Christ Church Manuscript with Wood Cuts By Helen Siegl. West Burke: Janus Press, Christmas, 1976. Limited to 300 numbered copies signed by Siegl, this one of 50 copies bound thus and accompanied by extra suite of plates, contained in paper portfolio, 8vo., cloth backed decorated paper covered boards, paper spine label, stiff paper wrappers, both enclosed in slipcase, printed on French-folded Hosho Speical with woodcut illustrations printed in blue with decorations in gold, spine of paper portfolio faded. Oak Knoll Books 310 - 111 2016 $300

Guest, Barbara *Poems: the Location of Things, Archaics, the Open Skies.* Garden City: Doubleday, 1962. First edition, 8vo., original boards, dust jacket, fine, jacket slightly dust soiled, presentation copy inscribed by poet to Ted Berrigan, with his ownership signature in pencil. James S. Jaffe Rare Books Occasional List: Winter 2016 - 73 2016 $1250

Guevara, Antonio De *The Praise and Happinesse of the Countrie-Life.* Newtown: Powys, Gregnog Press, 1938. 66/380 copies of an edition of 400 copies, printed on Arnold handmade paper, 6 head and tailpieces and title vignette by Reynolds Stone, usual foxing to blank leaves at beginning and end, 16mo., original quarter red morocco trifle chipped at beginning and end, 16mo., original quarter red morocco trifle chipped at backstrip head, backstrip gilt lettered, mid green boards, printed front cover label, red morocco tipped corners, untrimmed, dust jacket soiled and price clipped, good. Blackwell's Rare Books B184 - 269 2016 £200

Guibelet, Jourdain *Examen de l'Examen des Esprits.* Paris: M. Soly, 1631. First edition, 8vo., contemporary vellum, engraved printer's device on title, very scarce, bit of soiling to binding, else very good, large armorial bookplate of Duke of Portland.   Edwin V. Glaser Rare Books   2015 - 10407   2016 $1200

Guigo *On the Solitary Life.* Pawlet: Banyan Press, 1977. Limited to 240 numbered copies, 4to., stiff paper wrappers, top edge cut, others uncut, publisher's printed manila envelope.   Oak Knoll Books   310 - 79   2016 $150

Guilbert, Rita *Seven Voices: Seven Latin American writers Talk to...* New York: Knopf, 1973. First edition, 8vo., photos, donor's presentation taped on front flyleaf, author's presentation on half title, nice, in little chipped and soiled, price clipped dust jacket.   Second Life Books, Inc.   196A - 690   2016 $45

Guileville, Guillaume De *The Ancient Poem of Guillaume de Guileville Entitled La Pelerinage de l'Homme.* London: Basil Montagu Pickering, 1858. First edition, quarto, plates, some colored, photo frontispiece, decorated cloth gilt, covers little rubbed at corners, very good.   Peter Ellis   112 - 156   2016   £75

Guillemard, N. *La Peche a La Ligne et a Filet.* Paris: Librarie de L. Hachette et Cie, 1857. First edition, 8vo., original paper wrappers, custom made green fall-down back box, frontispiece, text illustrations, previous owner's signature, little staining to first few leaves, generally very good.   Sotheran's   Hunting, Shooting & Fishing - 121   2016   £100

Guillemeau, Jacques *Child-Birth or the Happy Delivery of Women Wherein is Set Down the Government of Woman in the Time of their Breeding Childe...* London: Anne Griffin for Joyce Norton and Richard Whitaker, 1635. Small 4to., new English style panel calf with raised bands, text foxed and some marginal dampstaining, title soiled and institutional stamp, lower portion of X4 torn with text loss, original French edition, bookplate, noting this was a gift of William Osler.   James Tait Goodrich   X-78 - 398   2016 $2500

Guiterman, Arthur *The School for Husbands.* New York: Samuel French, 1933. 8vo., illustrations, signed by Guiterman and Lawrence Langner, very good in little worn dust jacket.   Second Life Books, Inc.   196A - 691   2016 $50

Gunn, John C. *Gunn's Domestic Medicine or Poor Man's Friend, the Diseases of Men, Women and Children...* Philadelphia: G. V. Raymond, 1840. Revised edition, 8vo., frontispiece, text block sound, but covers becoming detached, text foxed throughout.   M & S Rare Books, Inc.   99 - 100   2016 $300

Gunn, Thom *Fighting Terms.* Swinford, Eynsham: Fantasy Press, 1954. First edition, first issue lacking final t of word 'thought' in line one of poem, Tamer and Hawk on page 38, faint signs of damp to bottom corner of rear cover, otherwise fine.   Peter Ellis   112 - 158   2016   £275

Gunning, Henry *The King v. the Vice-Chancellor of Cambridge.* Cambridge: Deighton & Sons, 1824. Disbound, 95 pages.   Jarndyce Antiquarian Books   CCXV - 572   2016   £35

Gunther, Albert C. L. G. *The Reptiles of British India.* London: Ray Society, 1864. Folio, 26 uncolored lithographic plates, contemporary half morocco and marbled boards, top edge gilt, upper corner very slightly bumped and few spots, otherwise handsome.   Andrew Isles Natural History Books   55 - 35992   2016 $2250

Gurney, J. H. *The Gannet: a Bird with a History.* London: Witherby & Co., 1913. Octavo, frontispiece amp, plates, two colored, and illustrations, publisher's gilt decorated cloth, back hinge weakened, gilt edges, prospectus enclosd, near fine.   Andrew Isles Natural History Books 55 - 26962   2016 $300

Guterson, David *The Country Ahead of Us, the Country Behind: Stories.* New York: Harper & Row, 1989. First edition, signed by author, fine in dust jacket.   Gene W. Baade, Books on the West   2015 - SHEL764   2016 $136

Guterson, David *Moneyball.* Stamford: Champion International Caorproation, 1995. First separate edition, comics and artwork by Michael Kress-Russick, with two fold out illustrations, quart, stapled wrappers printed on Kromekote paper, near fine, with light wear, including couple of creases to spine.   Between the Covers Rare Books 208 - 136   2016 $350

Guterson, David *Snow Falling on Cedars.* New York: Harcourt Brace & Co., 1994. First edition, cloth and boards, signed by author, fine in dust jacket.   Gene W. Baade, Books on the West   2015 - 1402058   2016 $58

Guthrie, A. B. *The Big Sky.* New York: Sloane, 1947. First edition, signed by author and inscribed in Lexington Kentucky for Elizabeth and Virgil (Steed), moderate dampstaining to cloth with loss to spine lettering, very good in very good spine sunned dust jacket with small, internally tape reinforced edge chips.   Ken Lopez Bookseller   166 - 40   2016 $575

Guthrie, A. B. *Wild Pitch.* Boston: Houghton Mifflin, 1973. First edition, fine in dust jacket with crease tear on front panel.   Mordida Books   2015 - 002914   2016 $60

Guthrie, James *The Elf.* Pear Tree Press, printed at the Old Bourne Press, 1903. One of 250 numbered copies, this unnumbered, Autumn number, titlepage with elaborate woodcut border printed in terra cotta, frontispiece and 6 further full page wood engravings, with one printed in terra cotta and one with tissue guard, 3 pages with decorative borders in terracotta small 4to., original quarter beige cloth, blue board with floral design printed in terra cotta, printed label to upper board, small amount of wear to corners and some light dust soiling, edges untrimmed, endpapers with repeated wood engraved illustrations, good, inscribed by James Guthrie for Stuart Guthrie.   Blackwell's Rare Books   B186 - 325   2016   £450

Guthrie, James *The Elf, a Magazine of Drawings and Writings by James Guthrie.* Harting: Pear Tree Press, 1905, but actually, 1912. No limitation, but prospectus states 80 copies only printed, 4to., original cloth backed boards, 21 separate plates of illustrations, very minor wear at head of spine and rubbing to covers, ink ownership inscription.   Oak Knoll Books   27 - 49   2016 $650

Guthrie, James *Root and Branch. Volume Two Nos. 1-4.* Morland Press, n.d. circa, 1918. First edition, decorations and illustrations, many full page, full page illustrations, predominantly wood engraved, one or two small spots with small hole in margin of page 61 and indentation on surrounding leaves, 8vo., original quarter brown cloth with grey sides, light overall rubbing and soiling, edges rough trimmed and lightly toned, partial browning to free endpapers, good, signed by Stuart Guthrie.   Blackwell's Rare Books   B186 - 327   2016   £275

Guthrie, James *A Second Book of Drawings.* Edinburgh: T. N. Foulis, 1908. First edition, frontispiece, titlepage and each drawing by Guthrie tipped-in, small 4to., gray paper covered boards with paper cover label with illustration on front, uncommon, minor shelfwear at edges, else very good.   Oak Knoll Books   27 - 25   2016 $395

Guthrie, Stuart *A Little Anthology of Hitherto Uncollected Poems.* Bognar: Pear Tree Press, n.d. but, 1922. Limited to 80 numbered copies, 8vo., quarter cloth, paper covered boards, label on front cover, frontispiece, hand printed on Antique laid paper, foxing of endpapers.   Oak Knoll Books   27 - 51   2016 $265

Guthrie, Thomas *Seed-time a Harvest of Ragged Schools...* Edinburgh: Adam and Charles Black, 1860. Half title, frontispiece, 9 pages ads, some slight dusting, original maroon cloth by Westleys & Co., slightly rubbed, publisher's ad slip tipped in, bookseller's ticket, very good.   Jarndyce Antiquarian Books   CCXV - 710   2016   £150

Guthrie, Thomas Anstey *Baboo Jabberjee B. A.* London: J. M. Dent & Co., 1897. Half title, frontispiece, illustrations, partially uncut, original blue cloth, slightly rubbed, little cocked, top edges gilt.   Jarndyce Antiquarian Booksellers   CCXVII - 13   2016   £75

Guthrie, W. K. C. *A History of Greek Philosophy.* Cambridge: Cambridge University Press, 1978. 1977. 1979. 1986. 1990, Set of 6 volumes in 7, 8vo., paperbacks, creases along length of spines of volumes I and II, spines sunned, minor shelfwear, price sticker to lower wrapper of volumes III and VI, all very good, ownership inscription of C. D. N. Costa in pen to verso of upper jacket of all volumes.   Unsworths Antiquarian Booksellers Ltd.   E05 - 31   2016   £175

Guyer, William *The Merry Mixer or Cocktails and their Ilk.* London: Jos. S Finch & Co., 1933. First edition, original orange printed wrappers, very good, small piece of tape to top of spine, tear at base of spine, light wear to page corners, light occasional edge wear, rare.   Simon Finch   2015 - 141229002   2016 $250

Guzman, Francisco De *Triumphos Morales...* Seville: Alonso Escribano, 1575. 8vo., red morocco gilt a la Francaise by Brugalla dated 1937, with gilt emblematic stamp on covers, printer's device on t itle, 14 full page woodcuts, title with marginal repairs, repaired tear to K3 and N3 with some smaller repairs to other leaves, whole lightly washed, washed out inscriptions on titlepage of the library of Compania de Jesus, Barcelona, green morocco booklabel of Isidoro Fernandez (1876-1963).   Maggs Bros. Ltd.   1474 - 39   2016   £4000

H

H., M. B. *Home Truths for Home Peace, or "Muddle" Defeated, a Practical Inquiry....* London: Longmans, 1854. Sixth edition, original green cloth by Westley & Co., slightly rubbed, nice, contemporary signature of Joseph R. Aston. Jarndyce Antiquarian Books   CCXV - 234   2016   £65

Habberton, John *Bructon's Bayou.* London: Chatto & Windus, 1886. First edition, half title, 32 page catalog (Sept. 1886) ads on endpapers, yellowback, original printed pale yellow boards, bit rubbed, but above average copy. Jarndyce Antiquarian Booksellers   CCXVII - 114   2016   £40

Haberly, Lord *Mediaevel English Pavingtiles.* Oxford: Shakespeare Head Press, 1937. One of 425 copies printed in black and red, over 270 wood engraved examples, almost all printed in red, errata sip tipped in, large 4to., original half rust hermitage calf lettered and patterned in gilt on backstrip, cream buckram sides lightly foxed, backstrip head and tail lightly rubbed, buckram sides bordered by gilt dot blocked border, endpapers foxed, top edge gilt, others untrimmed, very good.   Blackwell's Rare Books   B184 - 314   2016   £465

The Habits of Good Society: a Handbook of Etiquette for Ladies and Gentleman. London: James Hogg & Sons, 1859. First edition, half title, frontispiece, 6 pages ads, original red cloth, blocked and lettered gilt, slightly dulled, nice. Jarndyce Antiquarian Books   CCXV - 235   2016   £120

The Habits of Good Society: a Handbook of Etiquette for Ladies and Gentleman. London: James Hogg & sons, 1859. First edition, original brown cloth, recased, rubbed and dulled, signature of Robert White, sound copy only. Jarndyce Antiquarian Books   CCXV - 236   2016 £50

The Habits of Good Society: a Handbook of Etiquette for Ladies and Gentleman. London: Virtue & co., 1890. New edition, half title, frontispiece, paper repair to upper margin of title, contemporary half dark purple calf, hinges cracked, little rubbed, cocked, sound copy only.   Jarndyce Antiquarian Books   CCXV - 237   2016   £25

Hackenbroch, Yvonne *Chelsea and other English Porcelain, Pottery and Enamel in the Irwin Untermyer Collection.* London: Thames and Hudson, 1957. First edition, quarto, 47 pages of color plates and 100 pages of black and white reproductions, cloth backed boards, gilt, very fine. Argonaut Book Shop   Pottery and Porcelain 2015 - 5014   2016 $100

Hackett, Maria *A Brief Account of Cathedral and Collegiate Schools.* London: J. Nichols & Son, 1824. 8 pages plates in facsimile dated 1860, original drab printed paper wrappers, slightly rubbed and marked, very good. Jarndyce Antiquarian Books   CCXV - 711   2016   £125

Hackett, R. G. *South African War Books. an Illustrated Bibliography of English Language Publications Relating to the Boer War of 1899-1902.* London: privately printed for Lotz, 1994. first edition, one of 1200 copies, 4to., original boards within illustrated dust jacket, highly illustrated, very well preserved.   Sotheran's   Travel and Exploration - 13   2016   £68

Hader, Berta *The Big Snow.* New York: Macmillan, 1948. First edition, first printing, 4to., cloth, slight rubbing, else near fine, dust jacket with slight wear to spine ends and folds, otherwise rally nice, color and black and white illustrations by Haders.   Aleph-bet Books, Inc.   112 - 233   2016 $1650

Hader, Berta *The Friendly Phoebe.* New York: Macmillan, 1953. 8vo., cloth, fine in dust jacket with some fraying, illustrated by the Haders in color and black and white, with lovely nearly full page watercolor of a bird on a branch overlooking a River, with mountains and boats in background, inscribed to Berta's sister, Leota.   Aleph-bet Books, Inc.   111 - 208   2016 $850

Hader, Berta *Jamaica Johnny.* New York: Macmillan, Oct., 1935. First edition, 8 3/4 inch square, green pictorial cloth, fine in very good+ dust jacket with few chips and small closed tears, wonderful full page color lithographs and smaller black and white lithos, this copy has fabulous full page watercolor signed by Berta and Elmer Hader.   Aleph-bet Books, Inc.   111 - 210   2016 $1500

Hader, Berta *The Little Stone House.* New York: Macmillan, 1944. Third printing, 4to., cloth, fine in dust jacket with chip out of spine and old tape mends on verso, full color illustrations, this copy has beautiful full page watercolor by the Haders on half title, illustrations is inscribed and signed by each of the Haders.   Aleph-bet Books, Inc.   112 - 229   2016 $1200

Hader, Berta *Little Appaloosa.* New York: Macmillan, 1949. Stated first edition, 4to., cloth, slight fading, else very good+, charming watercolor self portraits by Haders inscribed by them.   Aleph-bet Books, Inc.   112 - 232   2016 $600

Hader, Berta *Little Chip of Willow Hill.* New York: Macmillan, 1958. Stated first edition, 8vo., cloth, fine in dust jacket, inscribed by Haders with lovely double page watercolor drawing.   Aleph-bet Books, Inc.   112 - 230   2016 $875

Hadfield, P. Heywood *With an Ocean Liner (Orient Line) as 'Otranto' through the Fiords of Norway...* Stereoscopic & Photographic Co. Ltd. n.d., 1907. Ninth edition, quarto, black and white photos, folding map, original dark green cloth, corners rubbed, inner hinge cracked.   J. & S. L. Bonham Antiquarian Booksellers   Europe 2016 - 9869   2016   £75

Hadrian VI, Pope *Questiones Quotlibetice.* Louvain: Thierry Martens, March, 1515. First edition, folio, 2 columns, errata on folio CXXXII verso, followed by Tabula, early 20th century old style blindstamped calf, large device on titlepage with side border of small metal cuts, 12 line and 7 line woodcut initials, last leaf with arms etc. on verso, uncommon edition.   Maggs Bros. Ltd.   1474 - 40   2016   £3500

Hagelin, Ove *Rare and Important Medical Books in the Library of the Swedish Society of Medicine.* Stockholm: Svesko Lakarsdilskpet, 1989. 125 illustrations, corrigends slip tipped in, tall 8vo. fine, original binding.   James Tait Goodrich   X-78 - 417   2016 $125

Haggard, Henry Rider   1856-1925 *King Solomon's Mines.* Barre: Imprint Society, 1970. No. 903 of 1950 copies, large 8vo., illustrations, nubered and signed by David Gentleman, tan linen, stamped in dark red, green leather spine stamped gilt, green box with gilt decoration, book slightly rubbed at edges of spine, otherwise near fine, box slightly scuffed.   Second Life Books, Inc.   197 - 163   2016 $75

Haggard, Henry Rider   1856-1925 *Pearl-Maiden - a Tale of the Fall of Jerusalem.* London: Longmans, Green, 1903. First edition, octavo, black and white illustrations by Byam Shaw, original dark blue cloth lettered in gilt, cover edges little bumped, spotting here and there, very good.   Peter Ellis   112 - 161   2016   £100

Haggard, Henry Rider   1856-1925 *Stella Fregelius - a Tale of Three Destinies.* London: Longman Green, 1904. First edition, octavo, original blue cloth lettered gilt, two page list of publishers' list at rear, edges and prelims spotted, head and tail of spine and corners slightly bumped, rear cover slightly marked, very good.   Peter Ellis   112 - 160   2016   £75

Haggard, Henry Rider   1856-1925 *The Wizard.* Bristol: J. W. Arrowsmith, 1896. first edition in cloth, publisher's brown cloth blocked in black on front cover, blind on rear cover and gilt on spine, charcoal endpapers, spine ends lightly worn, corners rubbed, front inner hinge very slightly cracked, but very good, from the library of H. Buxton Forman, with his bookplate and initialled note in pencil on front endpaper.   Joseph J. Felcone, Inc.   Books from Five Centuries: a Miscellany - 76   2016 $650

Haile, Berard, Father *Prayer Stick Cutting in a Five Night Navaho Cermonial of the male branch of Shootingway.* Chicago: University of Chicago Press, 1947. 9 folding plates, illustrations, original printed wrappers, dampstain to some pages of fore edge and waviness to those surrounding, previous owner name stamp to front cover and f.f.e.p. of Edward Hall.   Dumont Maps and Books   134 - 36   2016 $125

Hailey, Arthur *Strong Medicine.* Garden City: Doubleday, 1984. First edition, author's signature, owner's embossed stamp, paper over boards with cloth spine, nice in little torn and yellowed dust jacket.   Second Life Books, Inc.   197 - 164   2016 $50

Hain, Ludovici *Repertorium Bibliographicum in Quo Libri Omnes Ab Arte Typographica Inventa Usque Ad Annum Md.* Stuggart & Paris: Cottae et Renouard, 1826-1838. Thick 8vo., half cloth, marbled paper covered boards, split along hinges, appears to be a reprint.   Oak Knoll Books   310 - 250   2016 $450

Haines, John *In a Dusty Light.* Port Townsend: Graywolf Press, 1977. One of a total edition of 1000 copies, this #12 of 20 numbered copies, 8vo., several drawings by Gue Walker, author's signature on title, paper wrappers, about as new.   Second Life Books, Inc.   196A - 697   2016 $150

Haines, John *In a Dusty Light.* Port Townsend: Graywolf Press, 1977. One of 62 copies, 8vo, several drawings by Gue Walker, author's signature on title, brown cloth, about as new in dust jacket.   Second Life Books, Inc.   196A - 695   2016 $125

Haines, John *New Poems: 1980-88.* Brownsville: Story Line Press, 1990. First edition, 8vo., author's presentation to publisher of Graywolf Press, Scott (Walker), paper wrappers, cover scuffed, but very tight.   Second Life Books, Inc.   196A - 699   2016 $150

Haines, John *Rain Country.* Richmond: Mad River Press, 1990. First edition, no. 24 of 250 numbered copies signed by author, paper wrappers, fine.   Second Life Books, Inc.   196A - 700   2016 $45

Haines, John *Where the Twilight Never Ends. Poems.* Boise: Limberlost Press, 1994. One of 400 copies, 12mo., author's presentation to Scott Walker, publisher of Graywolf Press, paper wrappers, nice.   Second Life Books, Inc.   196A - 701   2016 $125

Haining, Peter *Movable Books: an Illustrated History.* New English Library, 1979. First and only edition, cloth, fine in dust jacket, fabulous color photos and other illustrations.   Aleph-bet Books, Inc.   112 - 332   2016 $150

Haldane, Richard Burdon, Viscount *Universities and national Life. Three Addresses to Students.* London: John Murray, 1910. First edition, half title, 2 pages ads, original light green cloth, slightly faded.   Jarndyce Antiquarian Books   CCXV - 712   2016   £20

Hale, Edward Everett *How They Lived in Hampton...* Boston: Stilman Smith, 1888. First edition, 8vo., very good, tight, signed by author.   Second Life Books, Inc.   196A - 703   2016 $125

Hale, Edward Everett *Seven Spanish Cities and the Way to Them.* Boston: Roberts, 1883. First edition, 8vo., blue cloth stamped in gilt (worn at top of spine), front flyleaf separate, ownership signature of Caroline H(ealey) Dall, contemporary book review tipped to front pastedown, very good.   Second Life Books, Inc.   196A - 702   2016 $150

Hale, Herbert M.   *The Crustaceans of South Australia.* Adelaide: Government Printer, 1927-1929. Octavo, uncolored plates, text illustrations, publisher's wrappers, signatures, minor blemishes, otherwise sound set.   Andrew Isles Natural History Books   55 - 21341   2016 $60

Hale, Kathleen *Orlando and the Three Graces.* London: John Murray, 1965. First edition, numerous lithographic illustrations in color and black and white by author, few faint spots to first and last text pages, oblong 8vo., original pictorial boards with few faint spots to edges, dust jacket clipped but still showing price (as issued) with few faint spots, signed by author, bookplate of Camilla Bryden Brown, artist.   Blackwell's Rare Books   B186 - 231   2016   £175

Hale, Sarah J.   *Aunt Mary's New Stories for Young People.* Boston and Cambridge: James Munroe & Co., 1849. First edition, remarkably fresh copy, 12mo., original elaborately blind and gilt stamped green cloth, frontispiece, remarkably fresh copy.   Howard S. Mott Inc.   265 - 61   2016 $250

Hale, Virginia Sidney   *A Book of Etiquette, good form on all occasions.* New York: Dell Pub. Co., 1923. Original illustrated cream wrappers, stapled as issued, illustrations, bookplate of Christopher Clark Geest.   Jarndyce Antiquarian Books   CCXV - 238   2016   £45

Haley, Alex   *Roots: the Saga of an American Family.* Garden City: Doubleday, 1976. Near fine in close to near fine dust jacket with few edge tears to rear panel and some very slight wear, signed and nicely inscribed by author.   Jeff Hirsch Books   Holiday List 2015 - 40   2016 $150

Haley, Alex   *Roots.* Garden City: Doubleday, 1976. Uncorrected proof, inscribed by author for Jim Butler, about very good in plain beige printed wrappers as issued, wrappers creased at corners and first few dozen leaves creased at bottom right corner from reading, some occasional spotting on pages as well, presentable example, scarce.   Royal Books   52 - 30   2016 $2850

Haley, James Evetts   *The XIT Ranch of Texas.*   Chicago: Lakeside Press, 1929. First edition, folding map, near fine, signed and inscribed by author.   Dumont Maps and Books 134 - 37   2016 $1750

Half Hours with Foreign Novelists. London: Chatto & Windus, 1882. Second edition, 2 volumes, half titles, 32 page catalog Nov. 1881 volume i, original grey decorated cloth, very good, bright copy.   Jarndyce Antiquarian Booksellers   CCXVII - 14   2016   £120

Halfer, Josef   *Die Fortschritte der Marmorierkunst. ein Praktisches Handbuch fur Buchbinder und Buntpapierfabrikanten.*   Stuttgart: Wilhelm Leo, 1891. Second edition, 8vo., later half red calf, marbled paper covered boards, five raised bands, top edge gilt, signed binding by Zaehnsdorf, with 5 leaves of single mounted marbled paper specimens + 5 leaves each with 6 mounted marbled paper specimens, from the reference library of Zaehnsdorf and Company with commemorative booklabel loosely inserted, with bookplate of Zaehnsdorf Co., tipped in is two page ALS by Richard Leo to Mr. Zaehnsdorf, rubbed along hinges and soiled along edges.   Oak Knoll Books   310 - 9   2016 $3500

Halfer, Josef   *Die Fortschritte der Marmorierkunst.* Stuttgart: Wilhelm Leo, 1891. Second edition, 8vo., contemporary quarter leather with marbled paper covered boards, all edges stained red, red leather spine label, rubbed along hinges and edges.   Oak Knoll Books   310 - 197   2016 $2250

Halford, Frederic M.   *Dry Fly Entomology.*   London: Vinton & Co. Ltd., 1902. Second edition, 8vo., original blue cloth, titled in gilt to upper cover and spine, little worn, with some creasing and past ownership inscription.   Sotheran's Hunting, Shooting & Fishing - 122   2016   £50

Halford, Frederic M.   *Modern Development of the dry Fly. The New Dry Fly Patterns, the Manipulation of Dressing Them and Practical Experiences of their Use.*   London: George Routledge and Sons, 1910. First edition, 8vo., original black cloth, spine lettered, frontispiece, 9 colored plates of flies, color chart on 18 plates, 16 photogravure plates, text illustrations, presentation inscription, head of spine worn, boards little scuffed, otherwise very good. Sotheran's   Hunting, Shooting & Fishing - 123   2016 £450

The Halfpenny Magazine. London: R. Seton at the Tatler Office, Covent Garden, 1832. Nos. 1-13, 16-17, May-August 1832, contemporary marbled boards, later paper spine, hand lettered, booklabels of R. G. Scotland and Reniers.   Jarndyce Antiquarian Booksellers   CCXVII - 222 2016   £65

Halifax, Charles Montagu, Earl of *The Works and Life of the Right Honourable Charles, Late Earl of Halifax.* London: printed for E. Currll, J. Pemberton and J. Hooke, 1715. First edition, octavo, contemporary blindstamped sprinkled calf, leather label, gilt decorated and lettered spine, engraved frontispiece, fine.   The Brick Row Book Shop   Miscellany 69 - 59   2016 $475

Halkett, Samuel *Dictionary of Anonymous and Pseudonymous English Literature New and Revised Edition by Dr. James Kennedy, W. A. Smith and A. F. Johnson.* Edinburgh: Oliver and Boyd, 1926-1934. 1956. Revised edition, 7 volumes with Volume VIII, 1900-1950, 4to., cloth, top edge gilt, ex-library with markings and stamps, binding still tight.   Oak Knoll Books   310 - 291   2016 $350

Hall, Adam *The Quiller Memorandum.* New York: Simon & Schuster, 1964. First edition, tall galley style uncorrected proofs, about good copy in string tied wrappers with some chipping and tears, some pencil notations on front cover and some other wear as well, very scarce in this format.   Jeff Hirsch Books   E-List 80 - 10   2016 $150

Hall, Brian *Stealing from a Deep Place.* London: Heinemann, 1988. First edition, 8vo., map, original green decorative cloth, dust jacket torn at top of spine.   J. & S. L. Bonham Antiquarian Booksellers   Europe 2016 - 98121   2016   £25

Hall, Caroline Arabella *Songs of the Grange set to the Music and Dedicated to the Order of Patrons of Husbandry in the United States.* Philadelphia: Wagenseller, 1873. First edition, 12mo., light blue wrappers (little worn, lacks half of paper on spine), very good, previous owner's name on over and titlepage.   Second Life Books, Inc.   197 - 165   2016 $125

Hall, Charles A. *The Manly Life and How to Live It.* Paisley: Alexander Gardner, 1908. Half title, frontispiece, 1 page ads, original light brown cloth, damp marked, Fasque Old Maine Library label on front board and spine, presentation label.   Jarndyce Antiquarian Books   CCXV - 239   2016   £25

Hall, Donald *Kicking the Leaves. A Poem in Severn Parts with Colophonic Boxwood Engraving by Reynolds Stone.* Mt. Horeb: Perishable Press, 1976. First edition, thin oblong 12mo., original wrappers, one of 125 copies (entire edition), signed by author, mint.   James S. Jaffe Rare Books   Occasional List: Winter 2016 - 74   2016 $450

Hall, H. Fielding *Margaret's Books.* London: Hutchinson, n.d., 1913. First edition, Thick small 4to., red gilt cloth, all edges gilt, near fine and bright, illustrations by Charles Robinson, 12 tipped in color plates with lettered tissue guards, plus a profusion of black and whites in text, beautiful copy, uncommon and particularly lovely.   Aleph-bet Books, Inc.   111 - 387   2016 $650

Hall, Samuel Carter 1800-1889 *The Book of the Thames. From Its Rise to Its Fall.* London: Alfred W. Bennett, 5 Bishopgate Without, Virtue & Co. Ivy Lane, 1867. First edition, first issue, small 4to., 15 albumen plates by Francis Frith, including frontispiece, engraved illustrations, contemporary black panelled morocco, gilt edges.   Marlborough Rare Books   List 56 - 24   2016   £650

Hall, Samuel R. *Lectures on School-Keeping.* Boston: Richardson, Lord and Holbrook, 1829. First edition, 12mo., contemporary quarter morocco over marbled boards, red morocco spine label and rules, nice, very good, one inch split to front joint free front endpaper torn with loss, owner's signature, some foxing, mostly to endpaper, nice, scarce, usually not found in such good condition.   Kaaterskill Books   21 - 34   2016 $925

Hall, Wade *The Smiling Phoenix.* Gainesville: University of Florida Press, 1968. Second printing, large 8vo., very good in torn in dust jacket, inscribed by author to pot William Jay Smith.   Second Life Books, Inc.   196A - 709   2016 $45

Hall, William Clarke *Children's Courts.* London: George Allen & Unwin, 1926. First edition, half title, original green cloth, spine faded, bookplate of Legge Library, additional label on leading f.e.p., presentation inscription.   Jarndyce Antiquarian Books   CCXV - 713   2016   £40

Hallam, Isaac *The Cocker, a Poem.* Stanford: Francis Howgrave, 1742. First edition, 4to., frontispiece, full brown morocco gilt, all edges gilt, by Riviere & Son, fine, very rare.   C. R. Johnson Rare Book Collections   Foxon: H-P 2015 - 4397h-p   2016 $5363

Hallam, Margaret *Dear Daughter of Eve: a Complete Book of Health and Beauty.* London: W. Collins and Co., 1924. Second impression, half title, frontispiece and photographic plates, original maroon cloth, rubbed.   Jarndyce Antiquarian Books   CCXV - 240   2016   £30

Hallas, Richard *You Play the Black and the Red Comes Up.* New York: McBride, 1958. First edition, minute bumps to crown and foot else fine in lovely, about fine example of scarce dust jacket with few rubbed spots, slight loss at spinal extremities (affecting a couple of letters), some very professional reinforcing at folds, uncommon, genuinely rare in jacket.   Between the Covers Rare Books   208 - 105   2016 $17,500

Hallberrg, Garth Risk *City on Fire.* New York: Knopf, 2015. Advance reading copy, with letter from publisher bound in dated March 2015, book was published in Oct. 2015, scarce, fine in self wrappers.   Ken Lopez Bookseller   166 - 41   2016 $125

Haller, Ablrecht Von, Baron *Letters from Baron Haller to His Daughter...*   London: printed by J. Murray, 1780. Half title, contemporary speckled calf, raised bands, maroon morocco label, neat repairs to hinges, spines slightly rubbed, presentation inscriptions on leading pastedown and initial blank, gift of Queen Charlotte to Mary Hamilton, Queen's House, London Jan. 19th 1781.   Jarndyce Antiquarian Books   CCXV - 241   2016   £1500

Halley, Anne *Between the Wars and Other Poems.* Northampton: Gehenna Press, 1965. First edition, green cloth stamped in gilt, little faded and worn dust jacket, #11 of 500 copies, this copy inscribed by author for writer/critic Alfred Kazin, fine.   Second Life Books, Inc.   196A - 710   2016 $125

Halsman, Phillipe *Halsman: Portraits.* New York: Harry N. Abrams, 1983. First edition, black and white photos, clean, very near fine in close to near fine dust jacket with some very slight wear, nicer than usual copy.   Jeff Hirsch Books   E-List 80 - 11   2016 $100

Hamady, Walter *Closing Flowers.* Mt. Horeb: Perishable Press, 1966. First edition, one of only 30 copies printed on variegated handmade paper, some copies bound in cloth, present copy is one of the majority of copies issued as unbound signatures, fine, rare.   James S. Jaffe Rare Books   Occasional List: Winter 2016 - 107   2016 $3500

Hamady, Walter *The Disillusioned Solipist and Nien Related Poems.* N.P.: Perishable Press, 1964. First edition, small 4to., 2 original signed etchings, original photo and 2 drawings by author, original brown paper wrappers, limited to 60 copies, this no. 36 and signed by Walter Hamady, staining from glue used to tip-in the illustrations, otherwise fine, extremly rare.   James S. Jaffe Rare Books Occasional List: Winter 2016 - 106   2016 $5000

Hamady, Watler *Wowa's First Book.* Mt. Horeb: perishable Press, 1977. First edition, 2 x 1 1/34 inches, original Swedish marbled paper wrappers handmade by author, one of only 60 copies salvaged from an intended edton of 365, very rine, rare.   James S. Jaffe Rare Books   Occasional List: Winter 2016 - 109   2016 $1500

Hamilton, Anthony   1646-1720   *Memoirs of Count Grammont.* London and Edinburgh: printed by Ballantyne, Hanson and Co., 1889. Number 101 of 780 copies, 292 x 191mm., extended to 2 volumes and extra illustrated with portraits, views etc. by John Runkle, very fine contemporary scarlet morocco elaborately gilt by Marius Michel (stamp signed on front doublures), covers featuring concentric French fillet panels with intricate cornerpieces between them, raised bands, gilt ruled spine of compartments with elegant foliate curls and complex central lozenge composed of several fleurons, forest green morocco doublures with large central panel formed by lobed French fillets, gilt tooled inner and outer cornerpieces and sidepieces, gilt decorated turn-ins, marbled endpapers, 33 etchings, along with 167 engraved extra illustrations for a total of 200 images, large paper copy, color of spines just shade different from cover, isolated vague spotting of no consequence in the text, inserted plates occasionally with minor foxing, especially attractive set in fine condition, text clean and fresh, margins vast and bindings lustrous and unworn.   Phillip J. Pirages   67 - 53   2016 $1250

Hamilton, Anthony   1646-1720   *Memoirs of the Count De Grammont.* London: John Lane The Bodley Head, 1928. Numbered, limited edition of 1000 copies, 8vo., bound for Bumpus in contemporary half brown moroco over marbled boards, lettered gilt on spine, top edges gilt, wood engravings by Wilfred Jones, little light spotting to few leaves, otherwise very good.   Sotheran's   Piccadilly Notes - Summer 2015 - 156   2016   £98

Hamilton, Clive *Dymer.* London: J. M. Dent, 1926. First edition, titlepage printed in grey and black, very faint offset to half title verso, faint browning to half title and some light foxing to ads at rear, few faint spots to borders of prelims, odd spot recurring further in, crown 8vo., original pale blue and grey sprinkled cloth, Knowles figure design blocked in black to upper board with blindstamped single fillet border to same, backstrip lettered gilt (publisher in black) and sunned with light rubbing to corners and small spot of rubbing at head of upper board, top edge now faded with couple of small spots to other edges, bookseller sticker, crease to flyleaf, couple of handling marks at head of rear free endpaper, good.   Blackwell's Rare Books   B186 - 256   2016   £1500

Hamilton, Elizabeth *Letters on the Elementary Principles of Education.* London: G. & J. Robinson, 1801. Volume I second edition, volume II first edition, half title in volume II, 1 page ads in both volumes, uncut in contemporary light blue paper boards, red morocco labels, some slight rubbing, overall, nice, bookplate of John Lawson.   Jarndyce Antiquarian Books   CCXV - 714   2016   £240

Hamilton, Elizabeth *A Series of Popular Essays, Illustrative of Principles Essentially Connected with the Improvement of the Understanding, the Imagination and the Heart.* Edinburgh: printed for Manners and Miller and Longman &c. London, 1813. 2 volumes, 8vo, half titles, contemporary calf, flat spines gilt and labelled, but numbering pieces wanting, very good contemporary armorial bookplate in each of Maclean of Ardgour. John Drury Rare Books 2015 - 25845 2016 $437

Hamilton, Elizabeth *A Series of Popular Essays Illustrative of Principles Essentially Conncted with the Improvement of the Understanding, the Imagination and the Heart.* Edinburgh: printed for Manners and Miller, 1813. First edition, 2 volumes, 5 pages ads volume II, contemporary full tan calf, gilt spines, , red morocco labels, some slight rubbing, bookplates of William Jacomb and Joseph Stancliffe Hurst, handsome. Jarndyce Antiquarian Books CCXV - 715 2016 £320

Hamilton, Elizabeth *A Series of Popular Essays.* Edinburgh: printed for Manners and Miller, 1815. Second edition, 2 volumes, 5 pages ads volume II, handsomely rebound in half calf, gilt spines, green morocco labels. Jarndyce Antiquarian Books CCXV - 716 2016 £280

Hamilton, Ian *In Search of J. D. Salinger.* New York: Random House, 1988. First edition, purple cloth, very fine in original dust jacket. Argonaut Book Shop Literature 2015 - 5505 2016 $45

Hamilton, Ian Standish Monteith *The Danlanelles. An Epic told in Pictures.* London: Alferi Picture Service, circa, 1917. Second edition, oblong small 4to., original cloth backed wrappers, raised brown lettering and mounted photogravure in sepia on front cover, lower cover and embossed Anzac log and flags, full page illustrations after photos, sketch map, minor rubbing to binding, very light spotting initially, good copy, duplicate from Imperial War Museum of Duxford with note pencille onto initial blank. Sotheran's Travel and Exploration - 319 2016 £498

Hamilton, James *Arthur Rackham: A Biography.* New York: Arcade/Little Brown, 1990. Stated first edition, first printing with 1-10 code, illustrated with a profusion of color and black and whites, cloth, fine in dust jacket. Aleph-bet Books, Inc. 111 - 384 2016 $150

Hamilton, Jane *The Book of Ruth.* New York: Ticknor & Fields, 1988. First edition, book near fine, very light use, dust jacket fine. Bella Luna Books 2016 - t3409 2016 $198

Hamilton, John R. *Our Royal Guests a Souvenir of the Visits of the Duke and Duchess of Cornwall and York and Other Members of the Royal Family to St. John and the Province of New Brunswick, Canada.* St. John and Boston: John R. Hamilton, 1902. 19 x 30cm., maroon cloth with gilt titles and crest on front board, photo illustrations, double page panorama view, previous owner's inscription, binding shaky with inner hinge starting to separate, interior generally good. Schooner Books Ltd. 115 - 71 2016 $95

Hamilton, Owen *Tyrolean Summer.* London: Williams & Norgate, 1934. First edition, 8vo., illustrations, original brown cloth. J. & S. L. Bonham Antiquarian Booksellers Europe 2016 - 5320 2016 £30

Hamilton, Richard Winter *The Institutions of Popular Education.* London: Hamilton, Adams & Co., 1845. Second thousand, half title, 16 page catalog on thin paper, original purple maroon cloth, spine faded to brown, booklabel of United College, Bradford on leading pastedown, inscription on leading f.e.p., very good. Jarndyce Antiquarian Books CCXV - 717 2016 £140

Hamilton, Thomas *Men and Manners in America.* Edinburgh: William Blackwood and T. Cadell, London, 1833. First edition, 2 volumes, 8vo., original green patterned cloth, paper labels (little browned), uncut, old repair to front inner hinge of volume 1, rare in original condition, without foxing, rarer still inscribed, presentation copy inscribed by author for Charles Mont(gomer)y Campbell. Howard S. Mott Inc. 265 - 62 2016 $650

Hamilton, W. D. *The Julian Tribe.* Fredericton: Micmac-Maliseet Institute University of New Brunswick, 1984. 8vo., card covers, illustrations, very good. Schooner Books Ltd. 115 - 73 2016 $45

Hamilton, W. D. *Old North Esk on the Miramichi.* Fredericton: Published by the author, 1979. Green cloth, gilt title to spine, dust jacket, 8vo., 12 maps and illustrations, 4 tables, very good. Schooner Books Ltd. 115 - 72 2016 $60

Hammer-Purgstall, Joseph Von *Histoire de l'Ordre des Assassins...* Paris: Paulin, March, 1833. First edition in French, 8vo., original printed wrappers, rebacked, margins of wrappers frayed, occasional spotting to browning, still good. Sotheran's Travel and Exploration - 323 2016 £248

Hammer, Meredith *The Auncient Ecclesiastical Histories of the First Six Hundred Yeares After Christ.* London: Richard Field, 1129. Third edition, folio, gap in pagination as called for but lacking first and final blank, separate half title to each section with woodcut device, woodcut decorations, very lightly toned towards edges, few underlinings, occasional specks of wax, green morocco with green cloth boards, previous spine label retained, endpapers and endbands renewed, very good, armorial bookplate of John (Russell), Duke of Bedford.   Unsworths Antiquarian Booksellers   30 - 55   2016   £650

Hammerton, J. A. *Harmsworth's Household Encyclopedia.* Harmsworth Encyclopedias, n.d. circa, 1920. 8vo., 6 volumes, leather backed green cloth boards, occasional discoloration to covers, otherwise in very good condition.   Sotheran's   Piccadilly Notes - Summer 2015 - 157   2016   £298

Hammerton, John Alexander *The Dickens Companion.* London: Educational Book Co., 1912. 72 illustrations, frontispiece, original blue cloth, gilt, little dulled.   Jarndyce Antiquarian Booksellers   CCXVIII - 1276   2016   £25

Hammett, Dashiell *The Big Knock-Over.* New York: Spivak, Later edition, very good in wrappers.   Mordida Books   2015 - 012019   2016 $65

Hammett, Dashiell *The Dain Curse.* New York: London: Alfred A. Knopf, 1929. First edition, octavo, titlepage printed in brown and black, original decorated tan cloth, front and spine panels stamped in red and brown, running Borzoi stamped in brown on rear panel, top edge stained brown, fore and bottom edges rough trimmed, small inked number at the upper left corner of the front free endpaper, just hint of soiling to cloth, square, tight, clean, very good.   John W. Knott, Jr./L.W. Currey, Inc.   Fall-Winter 2015 - 164847   2016 $1500

Hammett, Dashiell *The Glass Key.* New York: Alfred A. Knopf, 1931. First American edition, very slight sunning on boards, little rubbing at extremities, but much nicer than usual, very near fine copy, lacking dust jacket, attractive.   Between the Covers Rare Books   208 - 103 2016 $1200

Hammett, Dashiell *The Maltese Falcon.* New York: Alfred A. Knopf, 1930. First edition, owner's name on front fly, bit of soiling on boards, nice, near fine, lacking dust jacket, nice, clean copy.   Between the Covers Rare Books   208 - 102   2016 $2100

Hammett, Dashiell *Selected Letters of Dashiell Hammett 1921-1960.* New York: Counterpoint, 2001. First edition, fine, in printed wrappers, uncorrected proof copy.   Mordida Books   2015 - 008327   2016 $55

Hammett, Dashiell *Ten Digest Size Dashiell Hammett Collection.* Lawrence E. Spivak, 1944-1962. First editions, 10 original digest size booklets of Hammett's short stories in near fine to fine condition.   Buckingham Books   2015 - 35905   2016 $2750

Hammond, George P. *G. P. H. an Informal Record of George P. Hammond and His Era in the Bancroft Library.* Berkeley: University of California Press and Friends of the Bancroft Library, 1965. First edition, signed by Hammond, frontispiece, 10 plates, brick cloth, gilt, very fine, frontispiece, 10 plates, brick cloth, gilt, very fine.   Argonaut Book Shop   Biography 2015 - 3598   2016 $60

Hammond, George P. *New Spain and the Anglo-American West.* Los Angeles: privately printed at Lancaster Press, 1932. First edition, signed by Hammond and Bolton, scarce such, frontispiece, small 4to., red cloth, very good+, partially uncut, unopened set, gilt slightly faded.   Kaaterskill Books   21 - 35   2016 $300

Hammond, George P. *The Weber Era in Stockton History.* Berkeley: University of California Press, 1982. First edition, 4to., frontispiece, illustrations, 4 maps, light brown stiff wrappers and pictorial endpapers, very minor scar to head of spine, very fine.   Argonaut Book Shop   Biography 2015 - 7592   2016 $40

Hammond, James *An Elegy to a Young Lady.* London: printed for J. Roberts, 1733. First edition, folio, recent marbled boards, printed paper side label, very good.   C. R. Johnson Rare Book Collections   Foxon: H-P 2015 - 440   2016 $689

Hammond, James *Love Elegies. Written in the year 1732.* London: printed for G. Hawkins and sold by T. Cooper, 1743. First edition, folio, sewn as issued, cloth folding case, stitching tifle loose, fine, fresh copy, entirely uncut.   C. R. Johnson Rare Book Collections   Foxon: H-P 2015 - 441   2016 $689

Hammond, Mrs. *The Horse Opera; and other poems.* Columbus: Ohio State University, 1966. First edition, author's presentation to poet William Claire, blue cloth, top edges slightly spotted, otherwise nice in very slightly chipped and faded dust jacket.   Second Life Books, Inc.   196A - 712   2016 $45

Hamod, Sam *Dying with the Wrong Name.* Princeton: Contemporary Poetry Press, 2013. New edition, inscribed by author for poet Bei Dao, near fine in near fine dust jacket, laid in typescript copy of Hamod's poem "Sabra/Shatilla: In Sorrow".   Ken Lopez Bookseller   166 - 42   2016 $150

Hampl, Patricia *Resort: a Poem by...* St. Paul: Bookslinger Editions, 1982. One of 50 copies numbered and signed by author, 8vo., frontispiece and ornamental rose by Gaylord Shanilec, author's presentation and signature on half title, also signed by artist, paper wrappers, cover very slightly scuffed at top of spine, faintly dog eared, otherwise nice, inscribed by author for Scott Walker, signed by artist in pencil "Hi Scott Gaylord". Second Life Books, Inc. 196A - 715   2016 $250

Hampl, Patricia *Resort.* St. Paul: Bookslinger Editions, 1982. One of 300 copies, this one of 50 numbered copies, signed by artist, presentation by author, frontispiece and ornamental rose by Gaylord Schanilec, 8vo., stiff paper wrappers, label on front cover, top edge gilt, other edges uncut.   Oak Knoll Books   310 - 161   2016 $125

The Hampstead Congress; or the Happy Pair. London: printed and sold by M. Cooper, A. Dodd and G. Woodfall (sic), 1745. First edition, 4to., recent half calf and marbled boards, very good, from the Macclesfield library.   C. R. Johnson Rare Book Collections   Foxon: H-P 2015 - 442   2016 $2681

Hanaford, Phebe A. *The Life and Writings of Charles Dickens.* Boston: B. B. Russell, 1871. First edition, frontispiece, foxed tissue guard, plate, original purple cloth lettered gilt, bevelled boards, few slight marks, spine faded. Jarndyce Antiquarian Booksellers   CCXVIII - 1277   2016   £50

Hand-Book of Etiquette: Being a Complete Guide to the Usages of Polite Society. London: Cassell, Petter & Galpin, Half title, 24 page catalog, original red brown limp cloth boards, little faded, slight lifting of cloth on front board, pencil inscription of Alfred Diggle, nice copy.   Jarndyce Antiquarian Books   CCXV - 242   2016   £75

Handel, George Frederic *Israel in Egypt.* London: printed for William Randall Successor to the late Mr. I. Walsh, circa, 1770. First edition of the score, engraved frontispiece portrait by Houbraken, all pages apart from 2 leaves of subscribers also engraved, folio, original quarter sheep, marbled boards, green morocco lettering piece (lettered vertically), spine rather rubbed with loss of surface, extremities worn, good, scarce first printing.   Blackwell's Rare Books   Marks of Genius - 21   2016   £3000

Handforth, Thomas *Faraway Meadow.* New York: Doubleday, 1939. Stated first edition, Oblong large 4to., cloth, narrow band of darkening on bottom edge of cover and small chip, spine end frayed in dust jacket with old repairs on verso and some chipping, overall very good. Aleph-bet Books, Inc.   112 - 236   2016 $200

Handforth, Thomas *Mei Li.* New York: Doubleday Doran, 1938. Stated first edition, Large 4to., orange cloth, fine in near fine dust jacket, without medal and not price clipped, magnificently illustrated by author with black and white lithos on every page, rare in this condition.   Aleph-bet Books, Inc. 111 - 213   2016 $1250

Handy, W. C. *Saint Louis Blues.* New York: Handy Brothers Music Co. Inc., 1940. Quarto, bi-folium with loose leaf laid in as issued, some rubbing with faint creases, very good, small affixed typed label "When Mary Mac's review of W. C. Handy's autobiography appeared in the Memphis Commerical Appeal in June 1941, Handy in appreciation sent her this autographed presentation copy, insbcribed to same by author for Mary Mac Franklin, note laid in by recipient reiterating information on typed label.   Between the Covers Rare Books   202 - 62   2016 $550

Handy, W. C. *Unsung Americans Sung.* New York: Handy Brothers, 1946. Second edition, fine in little rubbed and worn dust jacket.   Second Life Books, Inc.   197 - 168 2016 $125

Handyside, P. D. *Observations on the Arrested Twin Development of Jean Battista Dos Santos, Born at Faro in Portugal in 1846.* Edinburgh (and) London: Maclachlan and Stewart (and) Robert Hardwicke, 1866. First edition, octavo, later decorated wrappers, 2 rather graphic woodcuts, laid in is TNS by book dealer James Tait Goodrich sending the pamphlet to Lee Ash.   Between the Covers Rare Books 204 - 71   2016 $450

Hanff, Peter E. *Cyclone on the Prairies.* San Francisco: Book Club of California, 2011. First edition, one of 300 copies, quarto, over 77 color illustrations, original leaf tipped-in, errata slip, half silk cloth, pictorial boards, with accompanying work by Riley in stiff wrappers, housed in publisher's dark brown silk and cloth slipcase, very fine set. Argonaut Book Shop   Literature 2015 - 7432   2016 $450

Hanken, James *The Skull.* Chicago: University of Chicago Press, 1993. Octavo, 3 volumes, text illustrations, softcover.   Andrew Isles Natural History Books   55 - 9538 2016 $120

Hanley, James *At Bay and Other Stories.* New York: Faber and Faber, 1944. First trade edition, small octavo, gray cloth, edges of covers lightly faded, gray dust jacket with small quarter inch chip missing from bottom edge, fine. Argonaut Book Shop   Literature 2015 - 484 2016 $50

Hanley, James *The Last Voyage.* London: Joiner & Steele, 1931. Limited to 550 copies (500 of which ere for sale), hand numbered and signed by author, frontispiece, green cloth lettered gilt, faded at spine and edges of covers, minor soiling to rear cover, otherwise fine.   Argonaut Book Shop   Literature 2015 - 4842   2016 $100

Hanley, James *Sailor's Song.* London: Nicholson & Watson, 1943. First edition, yellow cloth, cover spotted and lightly worn, sunned dust jacket with half inch chip missing at base of spine, very good.   Argonaut Book Shop   Literature 2015 - 4847   2016 $50

Hanley, James *The Secret Journey.* London: Chatto & Windus, 1936. First edition, octavo, very slight bumping and fading to head and tail of spine, near fine in very good, slightly nicked and rubbed dust jacket, designed by Harold Jones, with short tear on rear panel and tape marks on reverse.   Peter Ellis   112 - 162   2016   £150

Hanley, James *The Welsh Sonata. Variations on a Theme.* London: Derek Verschoyle, 1954. First edition, green cloth with gilt lettering to spine, minor offsetting to endpapers, very minor bump to upper edge of front cover, pictorial dust jacket with small tear to upper front corner, fine.   Argonaut Book Shop   Literature 2015 - 4848   2016 $75

Hanley, William *Slow Dance on the Killing Ground.* New York: Random House, 1964. First printing, 8vo., author's presentation on flyleaf, very good in dust jacket.   Second Life Books, Inc.   196A - 716   2016 $65

Hanmer, Karen *Star Poems.* Glenview: Karen Hammer, 2008. Number 17 of 30 copies, text paired with 17th century mythological images of constellation forms and images, on background of photo of the Milky Way, book can be held in hand and read page by page like a traditional book, can be removed from its jacket and unfolded flat to reference historical astronomical charts or contemporary NASA photos, or can be folded into an infinite variety of sculptural shapes, 6.75 x 5.75. x .75 closed, 17.5 x 23 inches open, housed in blue cardstock box with velcro closure, fine.   The Kelmscott Bookshop   13 - 20   2016 $725

Hannay, James *History of the War of 1812.* Toronto: Morang & Co. Ltd., 1905. 8vo., brown cloth with gilt titles to spine and front cover, map frontispiece and numerous black and white illustrations and maps, very good.   Schooner Books Ltd.   115 - 215   2016 $85

Hannay, James *The Life and Times of Sir Leonard Tilley.* St. John: no printer no publisher, 1897. 8vo., cloth, gilt titles to spine and gilt signature of Tilley on front board, frontispiece, cloth slightly worn at edges, generally very good.   Schooner Books Ltd.   115 - 75   2016 $75

Hanni, Romano *Worte Machen das Unendliche Endlich VI. Words Make the Infinite Finite VI.* Basel: Romano Hanni, 2015. Number 57 of 187 copies, hand printed in black, red, yellow and blue ink, it is an accordion structure with stiff paper illustrated book which, when removed, allows the 12 pages of content to be unfolded into one continuous strip, paper band closure for folded book, small book measuring 3.25 inches wide by 5 inches tall, fine.   The Kelmscott Bookshop   13 - 21   2016 $130

Hannigan, Paul *The Carnation.* Boston: Barn Dream Press, 1972. First edition, of an edition of 1100 copies, this one of 100 in printed wrappers, 8vo., inscribed by author to poet Paul Metcalf, in addition there is one page TLS from author to Metcalf laid in.   Second Life Books, Inc.   196A - 718   2016 $45

Hansberry, Lorraine *A Raisin in the Sun.* London: Methuen, 1960. First English edition, little creasing at bottom corner of final quarter textblock, foolscap 8vo., original blue boards, backstrip lettered gilt one or two faint spots to endpapers, dust jacket rubbed at extremities, with little waterstaining around head of backstrip panel, good.   Blackwell's Rare Books   B184 - 159 2016   £150

Hanscome, Alberta V. *History of the Saint John General Hospital and School of Nursing.* St. John: Lingley Printing Co. Ltd., 1955. 8vo. blue cloth, photo illustrated endpapers, black and white photos throughout, very good, slight wear to cloth.   Schooner Books Ltd.   115 - 78   2016 $55

Hansen, Joseph *Brandstetter and others.* Woodstock: Foul Play, 1984. First edition, very fine in dust jacket, included is promotional pamphlet containing short story Election day, signed by Hansen.   Mordida Books   2015 - 011999   2016 $65

Hansen, Sikker *Danish Summer.* Copenhagen: Politikens Ferlag, 1950. First English edition, original buff boards decorated with gentle washed patterned in green and blue, with onlaid lettering label to upper cover, illustrated on every page with a total of 27 colored plates which form 13 double page spreads and one single image, all printed in sunny lithographic colours in impressionist style, fine, clean copy, both externally and internally with only trace of light dusting to cover.   Sotheran's   Piccadilly Notes - Summer 2015 - 103   2016   £98

Hanshew, Mary E. *The Riddle of Spinning Wheel.* New York: A. L. Burt, Reprint edition, very good in fine dust jacket.   Mordida Books   2015 - 008831   2016 $65

Hanway, Jonas *Domestic Happiness Promoted: in a Series of Discourses....* London: J. G. & F. Rivington, 1832. New edition, 12mo., lacking leading f.e.p., contemporary full brown sheep for Society for Promotion of Christian Knowledge with its stamp on front board, slight loss to tail of spine.   Jarndyce Antiquarian Books   CCXV - 243   2016   £35

Happy Hours with Mamma. Edinburgh: William Oliphant & sons, 1835. Second edition, 24mo., frontispiece, plates, 4 pages ads, rather crude repairs to tears to pages 202-205, contemporary full dark blue morocco, gilt bands.   Jarndyce Antiquarian Books   CCXV - 719   2016   £45

Harbage, Alfred B. *A Kind of Power, the Shakespeare Dickens Analogy.* Philadelphia: American Philosophical Society, 1975. First edition, Half title, original blue cloth, lettered gilt, very good in dust, presentation to Kathleen Tillotson.   Jarndyce Antiquarian Booksellers   CCXVIII - 1278   2016   £20

The Harbinger. London: William Freeman, 1862. 12 issues, Jan.-Dec., lacking leading f.e.p., original wavy grained green cloth, gilt, Renier booklabel.   Jarndyce Antiquarian Booksellers   CCXVII - 223   2016   £35

Harcourt, Edward Vernon   *A Sketch of Madeira.* London: John Murray, 1851. First edition, 8vo., 2 folding maps, 5 illustrations, some occasional light foxing, original brown decorative cloth, spine and corners rubbed.   J. & S. L. Bonham Antiquarian Booksellers   Europe 2016 - 8965   2016   £125

Hardie, Andrew   *Ballet Exercises for Athletes.* London: Amateur Athletic Association/Royal Academy of Dancing, 1960. First edition, octavo, color pictorial wrappers, Fougasse illustrates the various exercise routines, covers slightly creased, very good, scarce.   Peter Ellis   112 - 133   2016   £25

Hardie, D. W. F.   *The Case of the Praying Evangelist.* London: Nicholson & Watson, 1950. First, fine in dust jacket.   Mordida Books   2015 - 008655   2016 $55

Hardie, Martin   *The Etched Work of W Lee--Hankey, R. E. from 1904 to 1920.* L. H. Lefevre & Son, 1920. Limited edition, 122/350 copies, copiously illustrated, 4to., original cream cloth, lettered gilt on upper cover and on spine, good.   Blackwell's Rare Books   B186 - 312   2016   £200

Harding, George   *Henry Raup Wagner 1862-1957.* San Francisco: Lawton Kennedy, 1957. First book edition, one of 200 copies printed for members of the Roxburge Club and Zamorano Club thin quarto, 2 tipped-on portraits, light gray stiff wrappers printed in blue and black, lower corner slightly bent, fine.   Argonaut Book Shop   Biography 2015 - 7654   2016 $50

Hardinge, Francis   *The Lie Tree.* London: Macmillan Children's Books, 2016. Special edition, double signed by author and artist, Chris Riddell, beautifully illustrated, book and jacket fine, jacket fitted with new removable clear cover.   Gemini Books   2016 - 31899   2016 $40

Hardwick, Michael   *The Charles Dickens Companion.* London: John Murray, 1965. First edition, half title, frontispiece, illustrations, original green cloth, very good in slightly rubbed, price clipped dust jacket.   Jarndyce Antiquarian Booksellers   CCXVIII - 1279   2016   £15

Hardy, Arthur Sherburne   *Diane and Her friends.* Boston: Houghton Mifflin Co., 1914. First edition, 8vo., original yellow cloth lightly soiled and spine panel bit darkened, else near fine, internally clean, illustrations by Elizabeth Shippen Green.   Buckingham Books   2015 - 34216   2016 $450

Hardy, Florence   *The Early Life of Thomas Hady 1840-1891. (and) The Later Years of Thomas Hardy 1892-1928.* London: Macmillan, 1928-1933. First editions, 2 volumes, frontispiece portraits, plates, 8vo., original mid green cloth, lettering on backstrips and hardy medallion on front covers, all gilt blocked, faint endpaper foxing, small newspaper clipping pasted to rear free endpaper, top edge gilt, dust jackets chipped with short tears, very good, Doctor Vandermin's copy, with presentation to same from Florence Hardy.   Blackwell's Rare Books   B186 - 233   2016   £550

Hardy, Thomas   1748-1798   *The Patriot. Addressed to the People on the Present State of Affairs in Britain and in France.* Edinburgh: printed for and sold by J. Dickson, London, sold by G. Niccol, 1793. First edition, 8vo., half title and final ad leaf, recently well bound in cloth, spine gilt lettered, very good.   John Drury Rare Books   2015 - 25901   2016 $350

Hardy, Thomas   1840-1928   *The Hand of Ethelberta.* London: Smith, Elder & Co., 1876. First edition in book form, 2 volumes, B4 and F1 both cancels (as usual), some foxing, especially in volume ii which is affected (though not stained) by damp, 1 leaf with large portion torn off and somewhat crudely reattached, 1 plate with small piece of the surface lifted off and now adhering to the page opposite, 8vo., original red brown cloth blocked in black and gilt, ex-circulating library with traces of labels on upper covers, recased with new endpapers, wear to extremities, spine of volume ii less bright than that of volume 1.   Blackwell's Rare Books   B186 - 234   2016   £1800

Hardy, Thomas   1840-1928   *Human Shows, Far Phantasies.* London: Macmillan, 1925. First edition, 8vo., green cloth stamped in gilt, uncut, spine little faded, some light soiling, inscription on endpaper very good.   Second Life Books, Inc.   197 - 170   2016 $85

Hardy, Thomas   1840-1928   *An Indiscretion of the Life of an Heiress.* London: privately printed for the author's Widow, 1934. First edition, 94/100 copies, crown 8vo., original limp cream vellum, yapped fore edges, backstrip gilt lettered, gilt edges, fine with Hardy's Max Gate booklabel.   Blackwell's Rare Books   B186 - 235   2016   £400

Hardy, Thomas   1840-1928   *Jude the Obscure.*   New York: Limited Editions club, 1969. No. 1461 of 1500 copies, 8vo., gray granite paper over boards with black leather spine, all edges gilt speckled in grey, spine slightly faded, otherwise fine in granite paper covered box, 21 black and white wood engraved illustrations and 6 two-color illustrations, two color wood engravings on Japanese paper, signed by artist.   Second Life Books, Inc.   197 - 171   2016 $125

Hardy, Thomas   1840-1928   *Tess of the D'Urbervilles.*   London: 1892. First edition, 2nd impression, 3 volumes, octavo, original smooth tan cloth, front covers stamped gilt after a design by Charles Ricketts, spines decoratively stamped and lettered gilt, plain endpapers, previous owner's bookplates in all 3 volumes, edges and spine bumped, extremities lightly worn, spines darkened, very good, housed in full morocco clamshell, first printed serially.   Heritage Book Shop   Holiday 2015 - 51   2016 $2500

Hardy, Thomas   1840-1928   *Under the Greenwood Tree.*   London: Tinsley Bros., 1872. First edition, 2 volumes, 192 x 130mm., one of presumably 500 copies (according to Purdy), fine maroon crushed morocco by Zaehnsdorf (stamp signed), covers with triple gilt fillet border, raised bands, spines gilt in compartments with vase and garland centerpiece, gilt titling, turn-ins with gilt floral vine roll, marbled endpapers, top edges gilt, beautiful copy, bindings entirely unworn and unusually bright, text with no signs of use, handsomely bound.   Phillip J. Pirages   67 - 190   2016 $5000

Hardy, Thomas   1840-1928   *Under the Greenwood Tree - a Rural Painting of the Dutch School.*   London: Chatto & Windus, 1913. First edition, octavo, 10 color plates by Keith Henderson, original green gilt decorated cloth, prelims quite heavily spotted, edges spotted, very good in good, scarce dust jacket little defective at head and tail of spine.   Peter Ellis   112 - 165 2016   £65

Hardy, Thomas   1840-1928   *The Well Beloved.*   Osgood McIlvaine & Co., 1897. First edition, with etching, map, tissue guard of frontispiece foxed and this affecting small extent the adjacent pages, 8vo., original dark green ribbed cloth, gilt monogram within wreath on front cover, spine gilt, spine slightly darkened, corners little bumped , bookplate, very good.   Blackwell's Rare Books   B184 - 160   2016   £175

Hardy, Thomas   1840-1928   *Wessex Poems and Other Verses.*   Harper, 1898. First edition, 31 illustrations, tissue guard to frontispiece foxed, pastedowns and endleaves foxed, 8vo., good in original presentation binding white bevel edged cloth, backstrip and front cover blocked in gilt and conforming to that of ordinary green cloth issue, covers and endpapers foxed and backstrip sunned, gilt edges, slightly marked, rare, presentation gift binding.   Blackwell's Rare Books   B184 - 161   2016   £1500

Hare, Augustus J. C.   *Walks in Rome.*   London: George Allen, 1903. Sixteenth edition, small octavo, 2 volumes, each volume with 40 albumen plates, double page maps, publisher's deluxe binding of full vellum with elaborate decoration in gilt with morocco onlaid strips also gilt decorated, morocco onlays chipped, very good.   Peter Ellis   112 - 336   2016   £175

Hare, Kenneth   *Three Poems.*   printed for C. L. F, and A. F. by A. T. Stevens, 1916. First edition, 24mo., 2 full page and 1 near full page illustrations by Claud Lovat Fraser, couple of very faint handling marks, original cream wrappers, very good.   Blackwell's Rare Books   B186 - 261   2016   £50

Haresfoot & Rogue, Pseud.   *How to "Make-up". A Practical Guide to the Art of "Making-up for Amatuers 7c....*   London: Samuel French, 1877. 6 color plates, 6 page ads, original grey printed wrappers, spine dulled and slightly worn, faint library stamp on front wrapper.   Jarndyce Antiquarian Booksellers   CCXVII - 118   2016   £50

Harlan, Robert   *Chapter Nine: the Vulgate Bible & Other Unfinished Projects of John Henry Nash.*   San Francisco: Book Club of California, 1982. First edition, one of 1000 copies printed and designed by Abe Lemar. 12mo., gilt lettered tan boards, upper corners just showing, else very fine.   Argonaut Book Shop   Private Press 2015 - 2377   2016 $40

Harlan, Robert   *William Doxey's San Francisco Publishing Venture at the Sign of the Lark with an Annotated Bibliography.*   San Francisco: Book Club of California, 1983. First edition, one of 550 copies, octavo, purple cloth, gilt lettered, frontispiece and 7 illustrations, Harlan's copy with his pencil signature and notation, various typos annotated in margins by Harlan, fine copy with all faults.   The Brick Row Book Shop   Miscellany 69 - 45   2016 $150

Harman, S. W.   *Hell on the Border: He Hanged Eighty-Eight Men.*   Fort Smith: Phoenix Publishing Co., 1898. First edition, illustrations, rebound in green three quarter leather and green marbled paper with green leather corner tips and raised bands with titles stamped in gold on black leather without retaining wrappers or frontispiece.   Buckingham Books   2015 - 25238 2016 $2750

Harman, S. W.   *Hell on the Border: He Hanged Eighty-Eight Men.*   Fort Smith: Phoenix Pub. Co., 1898. First edition, original light green printed wrappers, frontispiece, numerous illustrations, portraits, lightly chipped along front fore-edge, spine ends reinforced with archival tape, else very good, clean copy housed in cloth slipcase, rare.   Buckingham Books   2015 - 33474   2016 $3250

The Harmsworth Monthly Pictorial Magazine. London: Harmsworth Bros., 1898-1902. Volumes I-VII, volumes 1-5 bound with frontispieces, half titles, general titles and indexes, attractively bound in uniform light green cloth, decorated in gilt, lettered in black, some slight rubbing, overall very good, bright set.   Jarndyce Antiquarian Booksellers   CCXVII - 224   2016   £380

Harmsworth, R. Leicester   *The Harmsworth Trust Library. Part 1-35 (lacking no. 14). (with) Catalogue of Books Omitted or Returned from Previous Sales (1954)...*   London: Sotheby & Co., 1939-1954. 8vo., stiff paper wrappers.   Oak Knoll Books   310 - 249   2016 $500

Harney, Gilbert Lane   *Philoland...*   New York and London: F. Tennyson Neely Co., 1900. First edition, octavo, original tan cloth, front and spine panels stamped in dark brown, charming gift inscription in rhyme about the book written in pencil on front free endpaper, very good, rare.   John W. Knott, Jr./L.W. Currey, Inc.   Fall-Winter 2015 - 1726   2016 $3750

Harper & Brothers   *Harper's Illustrated Catalogue of Valuable Standard Works, in the Several Departments of General Literature.*   New York: Harper & Bros., 1847. Printed wrappers, illustrations, bound in contemporary half morocco, spine gilt in compartments, binding worn at extremities, else very good.   Joseph J. Felcone, Inc.   Books from Five Centuries: a Miscellany - 58   2016 $200

Harper, Frances E. W.   *Iola Leroy, or Shadows Uplifted.*   Philadelphia: Garrigues Brothers, 1892. First edition, brown cloth, gilt, frontispiece, fine with just slightest of bumping at corners and hinges repaired, gilt bright and unrubbed, small stamp of Anti-Slavery and Aborigines Protection Society, inscribed by author for Catherine Impey.   Between the Covers Rare Books   207 - 50   2016 $35,000

Harper, Frances E. W.   *Minnie's Sacrifice Showing and Reaping Trial and Triumph.*   Boston: Beacon, 1994. First printing, 8vo., paper over boards with cloth spine, near fine in little soiled dust jacket.   Second Life Books, Inc.   197 - 172   2016 $35

Harper, John   *The History of New Brunswick and Other Maritimes Provinces.*   St. John: J. & A.. McMillan, 1876. Small 8vo., cloth, blindstamped on front and back cover, inscribed by previous owners top titlepage, cloth damaged to right front cover, spine worn.   Schooner Books Ltd.   115 - 79   2016 $45

Harper, L.   *Preliminary Report on the Geology and Agriculture of the State of Mississippi.*   Jackson: 1857. Folding map, plus 4 single page hand colored county maps, plates and illustrations, original stamped boards, some foxing to map and some of the plates browned, minor loss along one edge of map, overall tight and very good.   Dumont Maps and Books   133 - 55   2016 $175

Harper, Michael   *Photographs: Negatives: History at Apple Tree.*   San Francisco: Scarab Press, 1972. First edition, one of 500 numbered copies, signed by author, near fine in slightly foxed and soiled, near fine dust jacket, this copy inscribed to fellow poet Gwendolyn Brooks 26 July 72.   Between the Covers Rare Books   207 - 49   2016 $500

Harrington, Oliver W.   *Where is the Justice.*   Detroit: Typocraft Printing, 1991. First edition, one of 250 copies signed by author, sewn wrappers, fine, scarce.   Second Life Books, Inc.   196A - 724   2016 $100

Harris, Frank   *My Life and Loves...*   New York: Grove Press, 1963. First Grove edition, 2nd printing, 5 volumes in 1, thick volume, green cloth in orange and white, pictorial dust jacket,.   Simon Finch   2015 - 005624   2016 $175

Harris, Joanne   *Chocolat.*   New York: Viking, 1999. First edition, fine in fine dust jacket, signed by author.   Bella Luna Books   2016 - t6014   2016 $66

Harris, Joel Chandler   1848-1908   *Uncle Remus.*   London: Raithby, Lawrence, n.d., circa, 1915. Folio, cloth, one inconspicous mend, else very good+ in dust jacket with mounted color plate, illustrations by Harry Rowntree.   Aleph-bet Books, Inc.   111 - 215   2016 $900

Harris, Joel Chandler   1848-1908   *Uncle Remus: His Songs and Sayings.*   New York: D. Appleton, 1935. Deluxe gift edition, Thick 4to. green gilt cloth ever so slightly darkened on top edge of covers, else bright and very good+, illustrations.   Aleph-bet Books, Inc.   111 - 214   2016 $400

Harris, Joel Chandler   1848-1908   *Wally Wanderoon and His Story Telling Machine.*   New York: McClure Phillips, 1903. First edition, first state, 8vo., minimal foxing to edges and endpapers, in original rare color printed dust jacket with 3 inch piece missing lower spine tip of jacket, chips, short closed tears, 8vo.   By the Book, L. C.   45 - 84   2016 $350

Harris, John   *Right of Reply: a Novel of International Crisis.*   New York: Coward McCann, 1968. First edition, fine-, lettering on spine faded and sunned bottom board edges, near fine+ dust jacket with wear at spine and flap fold ends.   Ken Hebenstreit, Bookseller   2016 - 41   2016 $40

Harris, Thomas   *Black Sunday.*   New York: G. P. Putnam's, 1975. First edition, fine in dust jacket with one half inch closed tear to bottom edge of front panel.   Buckingham Books   2015 - 26212   2016 $450

Harris, Tony *Shrikes of Southern African: True Shrikes.* Cape Town: Struik Winchester, 1988. Quarto, olor plates by Graeme Arnott, publisher's half morocco and marbled boards, slipcase, collector's issue limited to 100 numbered and signed copies.   Andrew Isles Natural History Books   55 - 34284   2016 $350

Harris, William *An Historical and Critical Account of Hugh Peters, After the Manner of Mr.. Bayle.* London: printed for J. Noon and A. Millar, 1751. 8vo., woodcut printer's device of an angel to titlepage, slight foxing, lightly toned throughout but with some pages more affected, later half tan sheep with marbled paper boards, black morocco label and gilt title to spine, marbled endpapers, little surface peeling to spine and corners, boards rubbed and edges wear, upper inner hinge cracked but holding firm, clipped out catalog descriptions of other books on Petters tipped to front pastedown, news article dated 20/3/12 tipped to f.f.e.p., illegible ownership inscription.   Unsworths Antiquarian Booksellers Ltd.   E01 - Early Printing - 8   2016   £200

Harrison, A. R. W. *The Law of Athens Procedure.* Oxford: Clarendon Press, 1971. First edition, 8vo., cloth, gilt lettered, spine slightly cocked, edges dusted, very good, no dust jacket, crossed out ownership inscription of Birthe Elkrog and gift inscription of Chris (Carey).   Unsworths Antiquarian Booksellers Ltd.   E04 - 57   2016   £30

Harrison, Florence *The Man in the Moon and Other Verses.* London: Blackie, 1918. First edition, small 4to., very good+, original cloth spine and paper covered boards with color pastedown illustration to front cover, pictorial endpapers, mild soil and edge wear covers, owner inscription, 12 color plates.   By the Book, L. C.   45 - 85   2016 $400

Harrison, Jim *The Beast God Forgot to Invent.* Atlantic Monthly Press, 2000. First edition, fine in like dust jacket, signed by author.   Bella Luna Books   2016 - p2326   2016 $200

Harrison, Jim *The Big Seven.* New York: Crown, 2015. Advance reading copy, marked "Uncorrected Proof", fine in wrappers, uncommon.   Ken Lopez Bookseller   166 - 47   2016 $125

Harrison, Jim *The Great Leader.* New York: Crown, 2011. Advance reading copy, fine in pictorial wrappers marked "Uncorrected Proof" by publisher, uncommon issue.   Ken Lopez Bookseller   166 - 46   2016 $125

Harrison, Jim *Legends of the Fall.* New York: Delacorte, n.d., 1979. Uncorrected proof copy, near fine in spine sunned wrappers, scarce.   Ken Lopez Bookseller   166 - 44   2016 $450

Harrison, Jim *The Raw and the Cooked.* New York: Dim Gray Bar Press, 1992. First edition, number 46 of only 100 numbered copies, fine copy.   Jeff Hirsch Books   E-List 80 - 12   2016 $350

Harrison, John *Oure Tounis Colledge. sketches of the History of the Old College of Edinburgh.* Wm. Blackwood, 1884. First edition, half title, 24 pages ads, original maroon cloth, spine faded.   Jarndyce Antiquarian Books   CCXV - 634   2016   £25

Harrison, Michael *Charles Dickens: a Sentimental Journey in Search of an Unvarnished Portrait.* London: Cassell & Co., 1953. First edition, half title, frontispiece and plates, slight foxing in prelims and edges, original dark blue cloth, very good in price clipped dust jacket.   Jarndyce Antiquarian Booksellers   CCXVIII - 1291   2016   £20

Harrison, Peter *Seabirds; an Identification Guide.* Beckenham: Croom Helm, 1983. First edition, octavo, color plates by author, maps, very good in dust jacket.   Andrew Isles Natural History Books   55 - 21264   2016 $60

Harrison, Rex *Rex, an Autobiography.* New York: Morrow, 1975. First printing, 8vo., illustrations, author's signature on flyleaf, nice in slightly scratched and chipped dust jacket.   Second Life Books, Inc.   196A - 726   2016 $45

Harrison, Sarah *The House-Keeper's Pocket-Book and Compleat Family Cook...* London: for J. Rivington and Sons, 1777. Ninth edition, modern paneled calf antique, few tiny unobtrusive worn trails in bottom margin, very minor foxing, else very good, clean copy, several leaves of contemporary interest tables bound in after contents leaf.   Joseph J. Felcone, Inc.   Books from Five Centuries: a Miscellany - 48   2016 $1200

Hart-Davis, Rupert *The Lyttelton Hart-Davis Letters. Correspondence of George Lyttelton and Rupert Hart-Davis.* London: John Murray, 1978-1984. First edition, 8vo., 6 volumes in original cloth with dust jackets, near fine set, this set from the library of historian Kenneth Rose, without ownership markings, occasional marginal lines in his hand.   Sotheran's   Piccadilly Notes - Summer 2015 - 159   2016   £198

Hart, Gordon *Woman and the Race.* Westwood: Ariel Press, 1911. Second edition, title slightly stuck to leading pastedown at inner margin, lacking leading f.e.p., original grey green heavy paper boards, white paper spine and label on front board little rubbed.   Jarndyce Antiquarian Books   CCXV - 244   2016   £48

Hart, James D. *A Tribute to Edwin Grabhorn & the Grabhorn Press.* San Francisco: Friends of the SF Library, 1969. First edition, one of 1000 copies, 12mo., printed in red and black, 4 photos, light blue paper covered boards, paper label, very fine.   Argonaut Book Shop   Private Press 2015 - 2390   2016 $50

Hart, Jerome   *Two Argonauts in Spain.*   London: Longmans Green, 1905. New edition, 8vo., illustrations, origial blue decorative cloth.   J. & S. L. Bonham Antiquarian Booksellers   Europe 2016 - 8429   2016   £25

Hart, John   *Herodotus and Greek history.*   New York: St. Martin's Press, 1982. First edition, 8vo., maps, cloth, gilt lettered top edge, slightly dusted, otherwise near fine, yellow dust jacket, spine bit faded, little shelfwear, very good, ownership inscription of C. D. N. Costa and Croom Helm LTD publisher card with compliments from author.   Unsworths Antiquarian Booksellers Ltd.   E05 - 35   2016   £20

Hart, Joseph C.   *Miriam Coffin; on the Whale Fisherman: a Tale.*   New York: G. & C. & H. Carvill et al, 1834. First edition, 2 volumes in 1, duodecimo, 19th century brown half calf, marbled paper boards, gilt rules and lettering, half titles present, 19th century signature of D. R. Coleman, 517 Ellis St., SF, who apparently had this bound for him, his name gilt stamped at foot of spine, edges bit rubbed, date trimmed by binder on titlepage of volume two, some light foxing, very good.   The Brick Row Book Shop   Miscellany 69 - 46   2016 $500

Harte, Bret   1836-1902   *Colonel Starbottle's Client and Some Other People.*   Boston: Houghton Mifflin, 1892. First American edition, variant brown cloth stamped in black and gilt, recipient's name blacked out by author, fine.   Second Life Books, Inc.   196A - 729   2016 $150

Harte, Bret   1836-1902   *Dickens in Camp.*   San Francisco: John Howell, 1922. First edition, one of an edition of 350 (#72) copies, large 8vo., titlepage and decorations by Joseph Sinel, cloth backed boards little soiled, very good, untrimmed copy, titlepage printed in blue and black.   Second Life Books, Inc.   197 - 173   2016 $125

Harte, Bret   1836-1902   *Dickens in Camp.*   San Francisco: Book Club of California, 1923. Although not indicated, one of 250 copies printed by John Henry Nash as a gift to the Book Club of California, thin quarto, 3 facsimiles pages tipped, red boards decorated with tan, black, green and white leaf pattern, printed paper label on front cover, fine.   Argonaut Book Shop   Literature 2015 - 7309   2016 $175

Harte, Bret   1836-1902   *"Lanty Foster's Mistake." in Overland Monthly an Illustrated Magazine of the West, December 1901.*   San Francisco: Frederick Marriot, 1901. First edition, printed wrappers, numerous black and white illustrations, internally clean, light chipping to spine ends, fine.   Argonaut Book Shop   Literature 2015 - 1255   2016 $75

Harte, Bret   1836-1902   *The Luck of the Roaring Camp.*   San Francisco: Ranssohoffs, 1948. One of 300 copies, quarto, four full page color plates and initial designed and illustrated by Mallette Dean, printed in red and black, maroon boards, decorated and lettered gilt, maroon cloth spine, paper spine label printed in gold, very fine.   Argonaut Book Shop   Literature 2015 - 5850   2016 $175

Harte, Bret   1836-1902   *A Millionaire of Rough and Ready.*   Kentfield: The L-D Allen Press, 1955. One of 220 copies, printed on all rag paper, printed throughout in 3 colors, handset Bulmer type printed on all rag rives paper from France, bound in two contrasting brown Oriental papers, lettered and decorated in gold, very fine.   Argonaut Book Shop   Literature 2015 - 5851   2016 $275

Harte, Bret   1836-1902   *Mliss.*   San Francisco: Grabhorn Press, 1948. One of 300 copies, printed with handset Goudy modern style, small folio, initials and 4 full page illustrations in color, engraved by Mallette Dean, half red linen and decorated boards, printed paper spine label, spine ever so slightly faded, but very fine.   Argonaut Book Shop Literature 2015 - 5852   2016 $175

Harte, Bret   1836-1902   *The Right Eye of the Commander. A New Year's Legend of Spanish California.*   Berkeley: Wilder and Ellen Bentley, 1937. One of 350 copies, designed, hand printed on handpress, illustrations by Hans, pictorial cloth, slight offsetting to endpapers as usual, otherwise fine, signed by artist and the Bentley's.   Argonaut Book Shop   Private Press 2015 - 2885   2016 $60

Harte, Bret   1836-1902   *Tales of the Gold Rush.*   New York: Heritage Press, 1944. printed boards with beige cloth spine, spine slightly darkened, else fine in slipcase, illustrations by Fletcher Martin, Sandglass pamphlet laid in.   Argonaut Book Shop   Heritage Press 2015 - 6665   2016 $40

Harte, Bret   1836-1902   *The Writings of Bret Harte.*   Boston and New York: Houghton Mifflin,, 1896. Standard Library edition, 2 volumes, engraved frontispiece, extra engraved titles, photogravures throughout, three quarter dark blue crushed morocco, light blue cloth sides, spines with raised bands and gilt elements between panels, top edge gilt, spines very slightly faded, but very fine, uncut, very handsome collection.   Argonaut Book Shop Literature 2015 - 6770   2016 $2750

Harte, Walter *Essays on Husbandry.* London: printed for W. Frederick in Bath, and sold by J. Hinton, 1764. 8vo., small tear repaired at head of titlepage not affecting text, full contemporary calf, raised and double gilt banded spine, red morocco label, very good, 5 engraved plates, numerous woodcuts.   Jarndyce Antiquarian Booksellers   CCXVII - 119   2016 £620

Harte, Walter *Poems on Several Occasions.* London: printed for Bernard Lintot, 1727. First edition, frontispiece, 8vo., contemporary speckled calf, gilt, spine gilt, green morocco label, slight cracks in lower joint.   C. R. Johnson Rare Book Collections   Foxon: H-P 2015 - 448   2016 $689

Hartley, Gilfrid W. *Wild Sport and Some Stories.* Edinburgh: William Blackwood and Sons, 1912. First edition, 8vo., original blue decorative cloth, gilt lettering to upper board and spine, 3 color plates, numerous black and white plates and text illustrations, previous owner's inkstamp to front pastedown and signature ot f.f.e.p., little spotting to edges, very good.   Sotheran's   Hunting, Shooting & Fishing - 177   2016   £80

Hartley, L. P. *The Brickfield.* London: Hamish Hamilton, 1964. First edition, signed by author, 8vo., little light foxing to half title and titlepage, green cloth, gilt tile to spine, faint whitish mark to upper board, some very light foxing to edges, very good, Val Biro dust jacket little creased at top edge with some closed tears, very good overall, author inscription to Billy Jan. 1965.   Unsworths Antiquarian Booksellers   30 - 66   2016   £175

Hartley, L. P. *A Perfect Woman.* 1955. First edition, slight spotting at upper margin, otherwise very nice in slightly soiled dust jacket which has few short tears and small stain to lower panel, inscription and date stamp on front free endpaper.   Bertram Rota Ltd.   February List 2016 - 26   2016   £30

Hartley, Marie *The Yorkshire Dales. (with) The Yorkshire Dales - a Further Selection.* Wakefield: for Smith Settle, 1989. 1991. Limited, 234/250 copies and 203/250 copies signed by author and printed on mould made paper, numerous wood engravings, small folio, first work original quarter brown cloth, slipcase fine, second work original quarter green cloth, fine in slipcase.   Blackwell's Rare Books   B184 - 258   2016   £400

Hartshorne, Anna C. *Japan and Her People.* London: Kegan Paul, Trench, Trubner, 1904. First UK edition from American sheets, 2 volumes, octavo, 50 photogravure plates with captioned guards, folding colored map, original blue cloth with spectacular gilt design of flying cranes, top edge gilt, upper corners slightly bumped, faint tapemarks on free endpapers, very good.   Peter Ellis   112 - 192   2016   £250

Hartwell, James *The Cat and the Mouse: A Book of Persian Fairy Tales.* Philadelphia: Henry Altemus, 1906. fine, scarce, illustrations by John R. Neill with 40 2-color illustrations and in line.   Aleph-bet Books, Inc.   112 - 333   2016 $275

Harvard, Andrew *Mountain of Storms: the American Expeditions to Dhaulagiri 1969 & 1973.* New York: Chelsea House, 1974. First edition, small quarto, color and black and white photos, maps, cloth, fine in pictorial dust jacket (slight rubbing to upper edge and corners, one very small rubbed spot on front, small half inch tear to rear of jacket and light soiling).   Argonaut Book Shop   Mountaineering 2015 - 4496   2016 $55

Harvey, George *Women, etc. Some Leaves from an Editor's Diary.* New York: Harper, 1908. First edition, 8vo., brown cloth stamped in gilt, very good, inscribed by author and play on words 'women's rights'.   Second Life Books, Inc.   196A - 733   2016 $85

Harvey, Marion *The Mystery of the Hidden Room.* New York: Edward J. Clode, 1922. First edition, near fine, bright copy in dust jacket with light professional restoration to spine ends and extremities.   Buckingham Books   2015 - 33040   2016 $450

Harvey, William 1578-1657 *De Motu Cordis et Sanguinis in Animalibus Anatomica Exercitatio....* Padua: Cadorinum, 1689. 12mo., old vellum, base of spine with old nicely done repair, author's name in ink on spine, few old ink ownership marks on blindstamped, leather slipcase with mild edge wear, bookplate of Malan de Merindol, very good+.   By the Book, L. C.   45 - 17   2016 $3000

Harvey, William Henry *Phycologia Britannica.* London: Reeve and Benham, 1846-1852. Octavo, 172 (of 360) hand colored plates with accompanying text leaves, each plate accompanied by a single text leaf, handsome contemporary full green blindstamped polished morocco, gilt spines with colored label, all edges speckled.   Andrew Isles Natural History Books   55 - 38817   2016 $1200

Harvie-Brown, J. A. *Travels of a Naturalist in Northern Europe.* London: T. Fisher Unwin, 1905. First edition, scarce, 8vo., 2 volumes, original brown ribbed cloth, gilt lettering to spines, 2 color plates, 4 maps, black and white plates, fine, scarce.   Sotheran's   Piccadilly Notes - Summer 2015 - 160   2016   £400

Haskins, Sam *November Girl.* New York: Madison Square Press, 1967. First US edition, photographs, close to near fine copy with light crease to front free endpaper, minor darkening to edge of boards and some of usual waviness to cloth, in close to near fine dust jacket with few small edge tears, crease to front flap and some other minor wear, still much nicer than usual.   Jeff Hirsch Books   E-List 80 - 13   2016 $250

Haslam, John *Sound Mind; or Contributions to the Natural History and Physiology of the Human Intellect.* London: Longman Hurst Rees Orme and Brown, 1819. First edition, few early reader's marks and annotations, light foxing of few early leaves, later 19th century half calf with label, little rubbed but very good, old bookplate of M. A. Broadwood. John Drury Rare Books   2015 - 13669   2016 $437

Haslem, John *The Old Derby China Factory: the Workmen and Their Productions.* London: George Bell and Sons, 1876. First edition, 1 plain and 11 chromolithograph plates, maroon cloth, gilt, corners show light expertly recased, endpapers renewed, very good, tight, internally clean. Argonaut Book Shop   Pottery and Porcelain 2015 - 5002   2016 $250

Hassall, Christopher *Eddie Narsh.* 1959. Proof copy, in original drab wrappers, dust jacket. I. D. Edrich   Winston Spencer Churchill - 2016   £25

Hassall, Joan *Dearest Joana. a Selection of Joan Hassall's Lifetime Letters and Art.* Denby Dale: Fleece Press, 2000. One of 40 sets with an additional section of engravings (from an edition of 300 sets), printed on Zerkall mouldmade paper, titles printed in black and red, both titlepages with typographic border design, numerous engravings, royal 8vo. original quarter vellum with marbled boards, backstrips lettered gilt, rough trimmed, cloth edge board slipcase, fine. Blackwell's Rare Books   B186 - 298   2016   £525

Hassell, John *Picturesque Rides and Walks with Excursions by Water Thirty Miles round the British Metropolis.* London: printed for J. Hassell, 1817-1818. First edition, 162 x 102mm, quite attractive late 19th century jade green crushed morocco in Arts and Crafts designs by Wood of London, stamp signed, covers with gilt rule border and stippled cornerpieces incorporating drawer handles and three graceful tulips, raised bands, spines gilt im compartments with wide frame formed by drawer handles, heart ornaments and much stippling, turn-ins decorated with charming gilt tulips, marbled endpapers, top edges gilt, other edges rough trimmed, 120 hand colored aquatint engravings, front joint of one volume with just hint of rubbing at head, faint minor spotting to covers, spines just slightly sunned to richer green, trivial imperfections internally, but particularly fine and pretty set, text and plates very clean and fresh, ornate bindings lustrous and no significant wear. Phillip J. Pirages   67 - 191   2016 $2400

Hastings, Michael *Cork on Water.* London: Joseph, 1951. First edition, fine in dust jacket with couple of short closed tears and wear at corners. Mordida Books   2015 - 012627   2016 $65

Haston, Dougal *In High Places.* New York: Macmillan, 1973. First edition, black and white photos, cloth, very fine, pictorial dust jacket. Argonaut Book Shop   Mountaineering 2015 - 4491   2016 $60

Haswell, William A. *A Catalouge of the Australian Stalk and Sessile Eyed Crustacea.* Sydney: The Australian Museum, 1882. Octavo, 4 uncolored chromolithographs, substantially foxed, early binder's cloth, bookplate and library pocket. Andrew Isles Natural History Books   55 - 6504   2016 $80

Hatton, Henry Charles *An Occasional Satyr.* London: printed for J. Jackson and sold by J. Peele, 1725. First edition, folio, disbound, good. C. R. Johnson Rare Book Collections   Foxon: H-P 2015 - 452   2016 $2681

Hatton, Joseph *Cigarette Papers: for After-Dinner Smoking.* Philadelphia: Lippincott, 1892. 8vo., drawings, letter from author to dramatist William Winter laid in, gray cloth stamped in black, red, gilt and white, cover somewhat worn, hinge tender, otherwise very good. Second Life Books, Inc.   196A - 736   2016 $65

Hatton, Thomas *A Bibliography of the Periodical Works of Charles Dickens...* London: Chapman & Hall, 1933. First edition, 4to., half title, frontispiece, plates, facsimiles, uncut in original green cloth, bevelled boards, lettered gilt, very good. Jarndyce Antiquarian Booksellers   CCXVIII - 1503   2016   £180

Hauck, Louise Platt *Joyce a Novel.* New York: Grosset & Dunlap, 1927. Reprint, blue cloth, moderate wear to extremities, very scarce. Gene W. Baade, Books on the West   2015 - 5019043   2016 $121

Haury, Emil W. *Recently Dated Pueblo Ruins in Arizona.* Washington: Smithsonian Institution, 1931. Illustrations, 27 plates, original printed wrappers, discrete owner's name on front wrapper, else very good. Dumont Maps and Books   133 - 57   2016 $50

Hausman, Gerald *Circle Meadow.* Lenox: Bookstore Press, 1972. Paper wrappers, inscribed by author to poet, Paul Metcalf, very good. Second Life Books, Inc.   196A - 739   2016 $355

Hausman, Gerald *New Marlboro Stage.* Lenox: Bookstore Press, 1971. 8vo., paper wrappers, inscribed by author to poet Paul Metcalf, very good. Second Life Books, Inc.   196A - 741   2016 $45

Haverschmidt, F. *Birds of Surinam.* Edinburgh: Oliver and Boyd, 1968. First edition, quarto, color plates by Paul Barruel, folding map, very good in dust jacket. Andrew Isles Natural History Books   55 - 1112   2016 $150

The Hawaiian Spectator. volume I Number 1 1838. Honolulu: printed for the Proprietors, 1838. Rare separate issue, chart, original tan printed wrappers, printed in black on front and back wrapper, front wrapper with lower corner chipped and chips along spine, backstrip with large chips missing, still held together tightly, some foxing and toning, overall very good.   Heritage Book Shop   Holiday 2015 - 52   2016 $5000

Haweis, Hugh Reginald *Ideals for Girls.*   London: James Clarke & co., circa, 1900. New edition, half title, 32 page catalog, prelims and catalog browned, lacking following f.e.p. original red cloth, dulled, inner leading hinge slightly cracked, later ink inscription, sound.   Jarndyce Antiquarian Books   CCXV - 245   2016   £25

Hawes, Charles Boardman *Dark Frigate.*   Boston: Atlantic Monthly Press, 1923. First edition, 8vo., orange pictorial cloth, fine in pictorial dust jacket (very good with chip off top of spine and wear at rear fold), illustrations by A. L Ripley with half tone frontispiece, 8 full page pen and ink drawings, rare in jacket.   Aleph-bet Books, Inc.   112 - 237   2016 $850

Hawes, Donald *Who's Who in Dickens.*   London: Routledge, 1998. First edition, large format paperback, very good.   Jarndyce Antiquarian Booksellers   CCXVIII - 1294   2016   £20

Hawes, Robert *The History of Framingham in the County of Suffolk, Including Brief Notices of the Masters and Fellows of Pembroke-Hall in Cambridge, from the Foundation of the College to the Present Time.* Woodbridge: printed by and for R. Loder, 1798. 4to., frontispiece, 10 further engraved plates, final ad leaf list of subscribers, inside cockled towards the front, plates somewhat foxed, contemporary half tan calf, gilt spine, marbled boards, edges sprinkled red, very much rubbed with some surface, loss to spine, label lost, upper just beginning to split at head, edges worn, ownership inscription of H. S. Merritt (?).   Unsworths Antiquarian Booksellers Ltd.   E01 - Early Printing - 9   2016   £250

Hawke, Edward *A Poem Upon the Law, Occasioned by a Late Act of Parliament, Entituled, an Act for the Amendment of the Law and the Better Advancement of Justice.* London: printed in the year, 1707. First edition, 4to, blue cloth boards, dark blue morocco spine (bit scuffed), fine, very rare.   C. R. Johnson Rare Book Collections   Foxon: H-P 2015 - 453   2016 $3064

Hawker, Peter *The Diary of Colonel Peter Hawker.* London: Longmans Green and Co., 1893. First edition, 2 volumes, 8vo., original brown cloth, little surface wear, light foxing with past ownership bookplate.   Sotheran's Hunting, Shooting & Fishing - 84   2016   £150

Hawker, Peter *Instructions to Young Sportsmen in all that relates to Game and Shooting...*   London: Longman, Rees, Orme, Brown and Longman, 1833. Seventh edition, 8vo., recent half morocco, spine with gilt raised bands, green morocco label with gilt lettering, marbled endpapers, engraved frontispiece, stipple engraved portrait, 8 engraved plates and several wood engraved illustrations in text, binding sunned to spine and top edge, little foxing to frontispiece and occasionally very good.   Sotheran's   Hunting, Shooting & Fishing - 83   2016   £300

Hawkes, John *The Lime Twig.*   New Directions, 1961. First edition, 2nd printing, printed wrappers, 8vo., John Clellon Holmes's copy with his ownership signature on half title and his underlining in text.   Second Life Books, Inc. 196A - 744   2016 $150

Hawkins, Bisset *Germany; the Spirit of Her History, Literature, Social Condition and National Economy.* London: John W. Parker, 1838. First edition, 8vo., contemporary green straight grained morocco, spine faded with small wear to head and tail.   J. & S. L. Bonham Antiquarian Booksellers   Europe 2016 - 5502   2016   £115

Hawkins, John *The Life of Samuel Johnson, LL.D.* London: printed for J. Buckland, J. Rivington and Sons, T. Payne and Sons, 1787. First separate edition, octavo, quarter brown paper over original drab boards, two manuscript paper spine labels, uncut, boards rubbed and bumped, spine chipping and flaking, occasional signature coming loose, chemised and housed on cloth slipcase with red leather label, overall very good.   Heritage Book Shop   Holiday 2015 - 58   2016 $1500

Hawks, F. L. *Japan Opened.*   London: Religious Tract Society, 1858. First edition, 16mo., original cloth wigh gilt lettered spine and front cover, spine sunned, minimal spine edge wear, soil to rear endpaper, 11 woodcut illustrations, very good+.   By the Book, L. C.   45 - 48   2016 $600

Hawksley, Enid Dickens *Charles Dickens Birthday Book.* London: Faber, 1948. Drawings by Edward Ardizzone, half title, original pictorial cloth boards, printed in pink, black and green, very good in sightly creased dust jacket.   Jarndyce Antiquarian Booksellers   CCXVIII - 763   2016   £35

Hawley, Donald *The Trucial States.*   Allen & Unwin, 1971. First edition, 2nd printing, 8vo., original cloth, ornamented dust jacket, top edge red, rear map endpapers, sketch map, 4 pages of plates, apart from minor marginal fraying to wrappers, fine.   Sotheran's   Travel and Exploration - 325   2016   £128

Haworth-Booth, Mark *E. McKnight Kauffer: a Designer and His Public.*   Gordon Fraser, 1979. 4to., original boards, dust jacket, illustrations in color and black and white, very good, inscribed to art design critic, Bevis Hillier from author.   Sotheran's   Piccadilly Notes - Summer 2015 - 197   2016   £198

Hawthorne, Hildegarde *Arabian Nights.* Philadelphia: Penn Pub. Co., 1928. First Sterrett edition, Large thick 4to., dark blue gilt cloth, pictorial paste-on, as new in original glassine and original box with color plate on cover, some wear at box flaps, illustrations by Virginia Sterrett. Aleph-bet Books, Inc.   111 - 440   2016 $1250

Hawthorne, Hildegarde *Poems.* Boston: Badger, 1905. First edition, 8vo., picture of author pasted in black, but presentation on front flyleaf, green cloth stamped in gilt, cover somewhat soiled, slight foxing on few pages, else very good.   Second Life Books, Inc.   196A - 746   2016 $45

Hawthorne, Nathaniel   1804-1864 *The House of the Seven Gables, a Romance.* Avon: Heritage Press, 1963. printed boards with black leatherette spine, lettered in silver, very fine, in slipcase, illustrations in color by Valenti Angelo, Sandglass pamphlet laid in.   Argonaut Book Shop Heritage Press 2015 - 7002   2016 $40

Hawthorne, Nathaniel   1804-1864 *The Marble Faun.* Boston: Ticknor & Fields, 1860. First US edition, first printing, 12mo, March 1860 catalog, cloth, worn at extremities of spines, rear hinge of volume 1 loose, very good set. Second Life Books, Inc.   197 - 185   2016 $300

Hawthorne, Nathaniel   1804-1864 *The Marble Faun or the Romance of Monte Beni.* Boston and New York: printed at the Riverside Press for Houghton Mifflin and Co., 1890. 2 volumes, quite pretty contemporary sky blue crushed morocco lavishly gilt, covers with multiple plain and decorative rules enclosing a central panel seme with gilt daisies, raised bands, spine compartments densely gilt with central daisy enclosed by small tools and filigree cornerpieces, marbled endpapers, all edges gilt, 51 photogravure plates, including portrait of Hawthorne, front pastedowns and verso of front free endpapers, bookplate of Edward Karfiol, spines just slightly different shade of blue, especially fine set, bindings lustrous and unworn, immaculate internally.   Phillip J. Pirages   67 - 48   2016 $950

Hawthorne, Nathaniel   1804-1864 *The Marble Faun or the Romance of Monte Beni.* Zurich: Fretz Bros. for the Limited Editions Club, 1931. First edition thus, 12mo., 20 colored plates, one of 1500 copies signed by artist, Carl Strauss, 2 volumes, full flexible tan tweed cloth with gold stamped orange cloth labels, slightly worn, very good. Second Life Books, Inc.   196A - 748   2016 $100

Hawthorne, Nathaniel   1804-1864 *Our Old Home: a Series of English Sketches.* Boston: Ticknor and Fields, 1863. First edition, 2nd state with page (399) blank, brown cloth decorated in blind, lettered gilt, brown coated endpapers, about near fine with some light wear to extremities, tiny holes to hinges at spine tail, boards lightly rubbed, otherwise bright and sturdy binding, Christopher Geest's bookplate, former owner's pencil inscription, faint tide marks to bottom corners of last few leaves, otherwise very bright and fresh, overall very clean and sturdy copy.   B & B Rare Books, Ltd.   2016 - NH024   2016 $100

Hawthorne, Nathaniel   1804-1864 *Passages from the American Notebooks.* London: 1868. First English edition, Honey & Wax Booksellers   4 - 33   2016 $550

Hawthorne, Nathaniel   1804-1864 *The Scarlet Letter.* Boston: Ticknor, Reed and Fields, 1850. First edition, first issue with ads dated march 1 1850 with misprint on page 21 line 20 'redupliciate' for 'repudiate', 181 x 111mm., fine modern dark brown crushed morocco by Bayntun (stamp-signed on front turn-in), covers with single gilt fillet border, raised bands, spine gilt in single ruled compartments containing antique style letter 'A', gilt titling and turn-ins, marbled endpapers, all edges gilt, original blindstamped brown cloth covers bound in at rear, bookplate of Robert Le Gresley, leaves shade less than bright (as in the typical copy), occasional corner creases, isolated spots of mild foxing, otherwise fine, text clean and fresh, pristine binding.   Phillip J. Pirages   67 - 192   2016 $3900

Hawthorne, Nathaniel   1804-1864 *The Scarlet Letter.* Boston: Ticknor, Reed and Fields, 1850. First edition, 12mo., later full crimson morocco (original cloth and endpapers bound in), inscribed ads dated March 1, 1850, pasted opposite title, which is printed in black and red-orange, is fine example of Hawthorne's holograph signature, signed as surveyor of the port of Salem, Mass., 19h century ownership signature 'Emily G. Freeman, nearly fine with bookplate of Carolyn Wells, author.   Howard S. Mott Inc.   265 - 65 2016 $2000

Hawthorne, Nathaniel   1804-1864 *Twice-Told Tales.* New York: Heritage Press, 1966. printed yellow boards and yellow cloth spine, lettered gilt, spine faded and slightly soiled, else fine in slipcase, illustrations by Valenti Angelo, Sandglass pamphlet laid in.   Argonaut Book Shop Heritage Press 2015 - 1999   2016 $40

Hawthorne, Nathaniel   1804-1864 *A Wonder Book and Tanglewood Tales for Girls and Boys.* New York: Duffield, 1910. First Parrish edition, 4to., 10 full page illustrations in full color, bookplate, illustrated blue cloth, untrimmed, previous owner's inscription, clean.   Second Life Books, Inc. 197 - 174   2016 $300

Hawthorne, Nathaniel 1804-1864 *The Complete Works.* Cambridge: Printed at the Riverside Press, 1883. No. 68 of 250 copies of the Riverside edition, 248 x 159mm. restrained but attractive early 20th century brown crushed morocco by Ernst Hertzberg & Sons (stamp-signed), covers with frame formed by pairs of plain gilt rules and single gilt dot at each corner, raised bands, spine compartments gilt in same design as covers, gilt titling, turn-ins densely gilt in palmette pattern, marbled endpaper, top edges gilt, other edges rough trimmed, all volumes with frontispieces and titlepages with etched vignette, large paper copy on laid paper, titlepages in red and black, spines faintly and evenly sunned, just hint of wear to tops of three spines, beautiful set, lustrous bindings almost entirely unworn and text unusually clean, fresh and bright.   Phillip J. Pirages   67 - 193   2016 $2000

Hawtrey, Louisa *Castle Cornet or the Island's Trouble in the Troublous Times.* London: SPCK, 1872. Half title, frontispiece and plates, original grey green pictorial cloth, slightly marked, nice.   Jarndyce Antiquarian Booksellers   CCXVII - 121   2016   £45

Hawtrey, Stephen Thomas *Reminiscences of a French Eton.* London: printed by Mary S. Rickerby, 1847. Original green cloth wrappers, red edges, presentation inscription "R. Howard Esq. from the writer".   Jarndyce Antiquarian Books   CCXV - 723   2016   £35

Hawtrey, Stephen Thomas *The Story of a Week Spent by St. Mark's School on Board of a Man-of-War...* London: printed by W. Whittington, 1859. Plates, original pale blue printed paper wrappers, slightly marked, very good.   Jarndyce Antiquarian Books   CCXV - 724   2016 £85

Hay, George *The Architecture of Scottish Post-Reformation Churches 1560-1843.* Oxford: Clarendon Press, 1957. First edition, royal 8vo., photos, 60 figures in text, blue buckram covers, laid in is ALS by author 2 Nv. 1959 to a Mr. Edwards, letter folded twice, very good, book with ownership inscription, near fine in very good, slightly rubbed and nicked dust jacket.   Peter Ellis   112 - 16   2016   £95

Hay, Helen *Little Boy Book.* New York: R. H. Russell, 1900. First and probably only edition, large 4to., cloth backed pictorial boards, tips rubbed and light rubbing to rear cover, else very good+, illustrations by Frank Ver Beck, rare in such nice condition.   Aleph-bet Books, Inc.   112 - 492   2016 $650

Hayden, Arthur *Old English Porcelain. The Lady Ludlow Collection.* London: John Murray, 1932. First edition, limited to 100 numbered copies signed by author, 91 hand printed photogravures, 41 tipped-on color plates, printed throughout in light blue and black, handset type, beautifully bound by Sangorski & Sutcliffe in three quarter turquoise blue levant morocco, light blue cloth boards gilt emblem on front cover and spine, gilt lettered spine, raised bands, top edges gilt, very fine, very rare.   Argonaut Book Shop Pottery and Porcelain 2015 - 4994   2016 $2750

Hayden, Robert *Kaleidoscope: Poems by American Negro Poets.* New York: Harcourt, Brace & World, 1967. First edition, blue cloth, corners and ends of spine slightly rubbed, otherwise nice in dust jacket little soiled and chipped.   Second Life Books, Inc.   197 - 176   2016 $45

Hayder, Mo *The Treatment.* London: Bantam, 2001. First edition, very fine in dust jacket, signed by author. Mordida Books   2015 - 012649   2016 $65

Haye, Louise Marie De La, Vicomte de Cormenin *L'Education et L'Enseignement en Maitre d'Instruction Secondaire...* Paris: Pagnere, Editeur, 1847. Half title, contemporary quarter tan calf, black morocco label, little rubbed, library label of Bib. de Mpl. Laurent Pichat. Jarndyce Antiquarian Books   CCXV - 725   2016   £40

Hayek, Friedrich August Von *The Constitution of a Liberal State.* Il Politico, University of Pavia, 1967. Offprint, first separate edition, 8vo., very good++, toning and mild spotting covers, text in English, rare.   By the Book, L. C.   45 - 30   2016 $500

Hayek, Friedrich August Von *Freiburger Studien.* Tubingen: J. C. B. Mohr (Paul Siebeck), 1969. First edition, 8vo., very good++ dust jacket with mild soil and edge wear, near fine copy.   By the Book, L. C.   45 - 29   2016 $300

Hayes, Dorsha B. *Chicago; Crossroads of an American Enterprise.* New York: Messner, 1944. First edition, very good, tight copy, 8vo., little nicked and chipped dust jacket lacking lower portion of spine, inscribed by author for cousin, Margaret Cook, with her pencil ownership signature. Second Life Books, Inc.   196A - 752   2016 $65

Hayman, Peter *Shorebirds: an Identification Guide to the Waders of the World.* London: Croom Helm, 1995. Reprint, octavo, color plates, bookplate, fine in dust jacket. Andrew Isles Natural History Books   55 - 18711   2016 $100

Haynes, Samuel *A Sermon Lately Delivered on Universal Salvation...* Boston: printed for Nathaniel Coverly, 1818. Later printing, printed self wrappers, 12 pages, untrimmed and partially unopened, light edgewear and little soiling, very good or better, fragile pamphlet, uncommon.   Between the Covers Rare Books   202 - 37   2016 $700

Hayward, Henry *How the Pox May Be taught without Compromise of Principles or Opinions.* London: F. W. Calder, 1855. Disbound.   Jarndyce Antiquarian Books   CCXV - 625   2016   £65

Haywood, William D. *Bill Haywood's Book.* New York: International Pub., 1929. First edition, owner's signature, Patience W. Norman, else fine in attractive, very good or better dust jacket with couple of modest chips and tears, nice, clean copy.   Between the Covers Rare Books   204 - 64   2016 $350

Hazard, Caroline *Threads from the Distaff of History and Contemplation.* Providence: Roger Williams Press, 1934. First edition, 8vo., frontispiece, paper over boards, cloth back, paper labels, author's presentation to William Mellinger, president of Wellesley College on flyleaf, another owner's name on flyleaf, cover little scuffed and worn at edges, else very good, tight copy.   Second Life Books, Inc.   196A - 756   2016 $45

Hazard, Joseph *Poems on Various Subjects.* Brooklyn: publ. by author, 1814. First edition, Duodecimo, original brown sheep, ink signature on front free endpaper stated Sept. 29 1815, with price 6/0 paid and on rear free endpaper in same hand is written that the book was received from the hand of the author, binding little worn, text somewhat foxed very good.   The Brick Row Book Shop   Miscellany 69 - 5   2016 $950

Hazlitt, William   1778-1830 *Lectures on the English Poets.* Philadelphia: Thomas Dobson and son, 1818. First American edition, Tall 8vo., original two-toned paper covered boards, printed paper label, uncut, spine little worn ad stained, early printed bookplate with terms of Library of Immanuel Parish of Bellows Falls VT.   M & S Rare Books, Inc.   99 - 104   2016 $225

Hazlitt, William   1778-1830 *Liber Armoris: or the New Pygmalion.* London: printed for John Hunt, 1823. First edition, engraved titlepage, ink with greenish tinted with vignette portrait of Sarah Walker after Hazlitt's drawing, some foxing, 8vo., uncut in original pink boards, spine of drab paper, printed label partly defective, rubbed and corners worn, sound.   Blackwell's Rare Books   B184 - 49   2016   £800

Hazlitt, William   1778-1830 *Political Essays, with Sketches of Public Characters.* London: William Hone, 1819. First edition, 8vo., well bound in modern half calf over marbled boards, spine gilt with contrasting labels and raised bands, entirely uncut, large copy.   John Drury Rare Books   2015 - 25445   2016 $350

Hazlitt, William   1778-1830 *A Reply to Z.* London: First Edition Club, 1923. One of 300 hand numbered copies, slim octavo, red and black cloth, spine faded, else fine.   Argonaut Book Shop   Literature 2015 - 1302   2016 $75

Hazo, Samuel *Once for the last Bandit.* Pittsburgh: University of Pittsburgh, 1972. 8vo., author's presentation to poet William Claire, orchid cloth, top edges slightly spotted, otherwise nice, in somewhat soiled and chipped dust jacket.   Second Life Books, Inc.   196A - 759   2016 $45

Hazo, Samuel *Sexes: the Marriage Dialogues.* Byblos Press, 1965. First edition, 8vo., author's presentation to William Claire, very good.   Second Life Books, Inc.   196A - 760   2016 $45

Hazzard, Margaret *Australia's Brilliant Daughter Ellis Rowan - artist, naturalist, explorer 1848-1922.* Melbourne: Greenhouse Publications, 1984. Octavo, color plates, very good in dust jacket.   Andrew Isles Natural History Books   55 - 3671   2016 $40

Head, Francis *A Faggot of French Sticks.* London: John Murray, 1952. First edition, octavo, 2 volumes, publisher's catalog dated Jan. 1952 at rear, original blue marbled cloth, decorated gilt, contemporary 1857 ownership signature, some foxing, some pages creased, hinges cracking, cloth slightly rubbed at edges, good.   Peter Ellis   112 - 286   2016   £65

Headley, Justina Chen *The Patch.* Watertown: Charlesbridge, 2006. First edition, as new, 4to., pictorial hardbound, illustrations by Mich Vane, fine, like new in dust jacket.   Gene W. Baade, Books on the West   2015 - JUV001   2016 $45

Heal, Ambrose *Old London Ridge Tradesmen's Cards and Tokens.* London: John Lane, 1931. 8vo., original printed wrappers, inscribed by author "With A. H. Compliments".   Marlborough Rare Books   List 55 - 33   2016   £15

Health & Strength Magazine. Tricks and Tests of Muscle. London: Athletic Pub., 1908. Revised edition, original printed paper boards, slightly rubbed, slight marginal tear to front board.   Jarndyce Antiquarian Books   CCXV - 246   2016   £45

Heaney, Seamus   1939- *Commencement Address. the University of North Carolina at Chapel Hill May 12 1996.* Chapel Hill: University of North Carolina, 1996. First edition, one of 100 numbered copies signed by author, out of a total edition of 500 copies, 12mo., original unprinted wrappers, dust jacket, stitched as issued, fine.   James S. Jaffe Rare Books   Occasional List: Winter 2016 - 77   2016 $1000

Heaney, Seamus   1939- *Door into the Dark.* London: Faber and Faber, 1968. First edition, 8vo., original black cloth, backstrip lettered gilt, few tiny foxspots to top edge, dust jacket with one or two faint spots to rear panel, near fine.   Blackwell's Rare Books   B184 - 162   2016   £525

Heaney, Seamus   1939-   *Door into the Dark.*   London: Faber & Faber, 1969. Tight very near fine in near fine dust jacket.   Jeff Hirsch Books   Holiday List 2015 - 42   2016 $450

Heaney, Seamus   1939-   *The Government of the Tongue.*   London: Faber & Faber, 1988. First edition, crown 8vo., original red boards, backstrip lettered in white, dust jacket, fine.   Blackwell's Rare Books   B186 - 237   2016   £75

Heaney, Seamus   1939-   *North.*   London: Faber and Faber, 1975. First edition, 8vo., original light blue cloth, backstrip lettered in gilt, faint foxing to top edge and few small spots to fore-edge, front endpapers browned, dust jacket with areas of very gentle fading to front and backstrip panel (but much less than usually found), tiny nick at foot of front panel, very good, superb copy.   Blackwell's Rare Books   B186 - 236   2016   £500

Heaney, Seamus   1939-   *Opened Ground: Selected Poems 1966-1996.*   New York: Farrar, Straus & Giroux, 1998. First American edition, signed by author, publisher's black cloth and red orange boards, lettered in black and gilt, original pictorial dust jacket designed by Cynthia Krupat, lettered in black and yellow-orange, fine in fine dust jacket, lovely copy.   B & B Rare Books, Ltd.   2016 - SH015   2016 $300

Heaney, Seamus   1939-   *Poems & a Memoir.*   New York: Limited Editions Club, 1982. First edition, tall 8vo., one of 200 copies signed by author, Henry Pearson and Thomas Flanagan, embossed brown morocco by Robert Bulen & son, in brown cardboard slipcase, this copy inscribed by author for Bill Claire, fine.   Second Life Books, Inc.   196A - 761   2016 $1200

Heap, Gwinn Harris   *Central Route to the Pacific from the Valley of the Mississippi to California.*   Philadelphia: 1854. 13 plates, facsimile map, original cloth covered boards are worn with some damage including loss of some cloth to rear cover, front hinge and joint starting but holding, slight interior foxing, withal complete with sound binding.   Dumont Maps and Books   134 - 38   2016 $450

Heard, H. F.   *The Great Fog and Other Weird Tales.*   New York: Vanguard Press, 1944. First edition, beige cloth with minor spotting to spine, else fine in slightly chipped dust jacket.   Argonaut Book Shop   Literature 2015 - 4856   2016 $75

Hearn, Chester   *Admiral David Glasgow Farragut. The Civil War Years.*   Annapolis: Naval Institute Press, 1998. First edition, photos and early prints, purple cloth, gilt, over beige boards, very fine, pictorial dust jacket.   Argonaut Book Shop   Biography 2015 - 5923   2016 $45

Hearn, Gordon   *A Handbook for Traveller's in India and Pakistan, Burma and Ceylon, Including the Portuguese and French Possessions and the Indian States...*   London: Murray, 1952. 8vo., original orange cloth, lettered in gilt, rarely seen dust jacket, printed in red, large folding map in rear pocket, numerous folding maps and plans, small repaired tear to wrappers, bought from Calcutta booksellers by C. R. Hottelet of NY.   Sotheran's   Travel and Exploration - 130   2016   £128

Hearn, Lafcadio   1850-1904   *Japanese Fairy Tale Series Rendered into English.*   Philadelphia: Macrae Smith Co., n.d. circa, 1915. 5 volumes, silk ties and printed on crepe paper, housed in publisher's folding cloth case with pictorial lining and ivory clasps, spine of case faded and two joints on other side of backstrip neatly reinforced, case wound and complete with ivory clasps, each book fine in right condition, all have original rice paper sleeves.   Aleph-bet Books, Inc.   112 - 238   2016 $2500

Hearst, James   *My Shadow Below me.*   Ames: Iowa State, 1981. First edition, signed by author, cloth, signed presentation (non-authorial), fine in dust jacket.   Gene W. Baade, Books on the West   2015 - FTR185   2016 $49

Heath, Henry   *Domestic Bliss. (with) Domestic Miseries.*   London: D. Bogue, 1848. Oblong folio, 6 numbered plates, all with numerous caricature sketches, all slightly dusted, small tear to upper margin of no. 3., marginal tears to number 6, repaired with archival tape, Miseries with plates number 7, 8 and 9, creased, dusted and with numerous marginal tears repaired, archival tape, recent black cloth, fold over case, booklabel of Anthony David Estill.   Jarndyce Antiquarian Books   CCXV - 247   2016   £350

Heath, William   *Pickwickian Illustrations, Twenty Plates by Heath.*   London: T. McLean, 1837. 20 leaves, rather browned and spotted, original green wrappers, green cloth spine, corners folded and chipped, decent copy, scarce collection.   Jarndyce Antiquarian Booksellers   CCXVIII - 125   2016   £250

Heath, William   *Pickwickian Illustrations.*   London: T. McLean, 1837. First edition with publisher's imprint on first four plates, 8vo., sometime bound in patterned paper covered boards, retaining original gilt lettered black paper label, 20 plates, little loss to spine of wrappers, otherwise very good, clean set, scarce.   Sotheran's   Piccadilly Notes - Summer 2015 - 105   2016   £850

Heavisides, Edward Marsh   *The Poetical and Prose Remains.*   London: Longmans, Stockton Jennett & Co, 1850. First edition, original purple cloth by Remnant & Edmonds, decorative borders in blind, spine blocked and lettered gilt, spine slightly faded, very good.   Jarndyce Antiquarian Booksellers   CCXVIII - 1296   2016   £60

Hebblethwaite, Abraham Rhodes *Hints on Child-Training.* Leeds: John Parrott, 1875. Original limp green cloth, contemporary signature, f.e.p., very good. Jarndyce Antiquarian Books CCXV - 248 2016 £58

Hecht, Anthony *Aesopic-Couplets to Accompany the Thomas Bewick wood engravings.* Northampton: Gehenna Press, 1967. First edition, 1/500 copies, oblong boards, wood engravings from blocks by Thomas Bewick. Second Life Books, Inc. 196A - 763 2016 $325

Hecht, Anthony *The Hard Hours. Poems.* New York: Atheneum, 1967. First edition, issue in wrappers, inscribed and signed for William Meredith, near fine. Charles Agvent William Meredith - 35 2016 $100

Hecht, Anthony *Jiggery-Pokery: a Compendium of Double Dactyls.* New York: Atheneum, 1967. First edition, inscribed and signed by author for William Meredith, illustrations by Milton Glaser, fine in near fine dust jacket. Charles Agvent William Meredith - 34 2016 $150

Hecht, Anthony *A Love for Four Voices: Homage to Franz Joseph Hayden.* Great Barrington: Penmaen Press, 1983. First edition, 8vo., illustrations by Michael McCurdy, one of 50 numbered copies signed by author and artist, one small scrape on edge of front cover, otherwise nice. Second Life Books, Inc. 196A - 762 2016 $150

Hecht, Ben *The Kingdom of Evil.* Chicago: Pascal Covici, 1924. Limited to 2000 numbered copies, 1900 of which were for sale, 8vo., top edge gilt, others untrimmed, some minor abrasion on corner of endpaper, else fine in dust jacket that is faded on spine and top 2 inches of cover, 12 absolutely stunning full page black and white illustrations and pictorial endpapers. Aleph-bet Books, Inc. 112 - 186 2016 $275

Hecht, Roger *Burnt Offerings. Poems by.* Santa Fe: The Lightning Tree, 1979. First printing, small 8vo., author's presentation to poet William Claire, paper wrappers, cover ad edges little foxed, otherwise nice. Second Life Books, Inc. 196A - 767 2016 $45

Hecht, Roger *27 Poems.* Denver: Alan Swallow, 1966. First edition, 8vo., paper over boards, cover slightly bumped at ends of spine, otherwise nice in slightly scuffed and chipped dust jacket, presentation from author to William Claire. Second Life Books, Inc. 196A - 766 2016 $50

Heck, Christian *Le Bestiaire Medieval: L'Animal dans les Manuscrits Enlumines.* Paris: Citadelles & Mazenod, 2011. First edition, limited to 2000 copies, folio, cloth, dust jacket, slipcase, top edge gilt, frontispiece full color illustrations, ex-library with markings. Oak Knoll Books 310 - 38 2016 $450

Hecox, Margaret M. *California Caravan: the Overland Trail memoir of.* San Jose: Harla Young Press, 1966. First edition, signed by editor, 6 illustrations from photos, tan cloth lettered in brown, very fine, pictorial dust jacket. Argonaut Book Shop Biography 2015 - 7311 2016 $50

Hedderwick, James, & Son *Reference Book of James Hedderwick & Son, Printers, Mellville, Place, Glasgow, Exhibiting the Various Sizes of Printing Types with Which their Office is Furnished.* Glasgow: Britannia Press, 1823. Half title, drop head at beginning of text on page 10, contemporary or slightly later, dark green grained calf, marbled boards. Jarndyce Antiquarian Booksellers CCXVII - 124 2016 £280

Hedderwick, Robert Grosvenor *The Story of Self-Made Men or Industry, Perserverance, Application and Enterprise Exemplified in Real Life.* London: Simpkin, Marshall, Hamilton, Kent & Co. circa, 1885. Second edition, illustrations, half title, frontispiece and plates, original green cloth, slightly rubbed and dulled, prize label on leading f.e.p. Jarndyce Antiquarian Books CCXV - 65 2016 £25

Hedericus, Benjamin *Lexicon Manuale Graecum, Omnibus sui Generis Lexicis quae quidem Exstant...* London: Excudit S. Palmer, Impensis J. & J. Knapton et al, 1727. 4to., titlepage in red and black, final leaf with publisher's catalog, occasional light spots and smudges, generally clean, closed tear to leaf M4, trimmed little close but never touching text, contemporary tan calf boards, neatly rebacked, raised bands, gilt to spine, older label retained, edges patterned, endpapers renewed, some scratches and stains, area of lower board neatly patched with calf, corners fraying, still very good and sound, armorial bookplates of Rev. Samuel Kettilby, and Edward Oates, and Robert Washington Oates, commentary of Oates to first flyleaf verso, pencilled inscription "From Henry (Cooper?) to Mrs. Edward Oates 17 Nov. 1849". Unsworths Antiquarian Booksellers 30 - 68 2016 £175

Hedin, Sven *The Flight of the 'Big Horse'.* New York: Darton and Co., 1936. First US edition, publisher's blue cloth, pictorial dust jacket, red lettering to spine and upper cloth cover, map endpapers (browned as usual, over 10 full page illustrations from photos, rubbing and creasing to extremities of dust jacket with closed tear to back, very good, bookplate of Neville Howell Ehmann. Sotheran's Piccadilly Notes - Summer 2015 - 162 2016 £298

Hedin, Sven *The Flight of the "Big Horse" the Trail of War in Central Asia.* New York: Dutton, 1936. First US edition, 8vo., publisher's blue cloth, pictorial dust jacket, red lettering to spine and upper cloth cover, map endpapers (browned as usual) over 100 full page photo illustrations, rubbing and creasing to extremities of dust jacket ad closed tear to back, very good, bookplate Neville Howell Ehmann. Sotheran's Travel and Exploration - 132 2016 £298

Hedin, Sven *Trans-Himalaya. Discoveries and adventures in Tibet.* London: R. & R. Clark, Limited for Macmillan and Co. Limited, 1910-1913. First English edition, 8vo., 3 volumes, original red cloth, upper boards blocked with gilt vignette, spines lettered gilt, top edges gilt, frontispieces, retaining tissue guards, hundreds of plates, extremities little worn and bumped, light offsetting onto free endpapers, some occasional light spotting, short, skillfully repaired tears on 2 folding maps, nonetheless very good, clean set in original cloth, all volumes with neat ownership inscription of L. V. Halward dated Cambridge Feb. 1921.   Sotheran's Piccadilly Notes - Summer 2015 - 161   2016   £498

Heebner, Mary *Western Trilogy. the Desert. The Prairie. The Ocean.* Santa Barbara: Simplemente Maria Press, 2000. Limited to only numbered 20 sets, 15 for sale, 3 volumes, small 8vo., cloth with paper covered boards, slipcase, original watercolor paintings and text by Heebner on Zekishu Nautral paper, accordion fold, typeset digitally in Bembo & Trajan and printed letterpress from polymer plates by John Balkwill of Lumino Press, textured blue/tan cloth slipcase.   Oak Knoll Books 27 - 62   2016 $2750

Hegetschweiler, Johann *Sammlling Von Schweizer-Pflanzen. (Collection of Swiss Plants).* Zurich: Essligner, 1825-1834. 191 x 12mm., 43 fascicles (of 80) in four portfolios (lacking the text leaf for "chrysanthemum leucanthemum" and with text leaves for "luxus sempervirens' and 'mespilus germanica' in contemporaneous manuscript, loose as issued in printed stiff board portfolios, flat spines with black leather labels, ribbon ties at fore edge of two volumes (missing on others), original cardboard slipcases, with 257 hand colored lithographs by Jonas Labram David (of 258, missing 'urtica urens'), bound portfolios, little soiled, couple of trivial stains (only), otherwise fine, both attractively colored plates and text leaves consistently quite clean and fresh.   Phillip J. Pirages 67 - 81   2016 $2400

Heinecken, Robert *Heinecken.* Carmel: Friends of Photography in Conjunction with Light Gallery, 1980. First edition, one of 2000 copies, as new in cloth binding, still in original publisher shrinkwrap and in original shipping carton, signed by Heinecken, beautiful copy.   Jeff Hirsch Books E-List 80 - 16   2016 $300

Heinecken, Robert *Heinecken: Selected Works 1966-1986.* Tokyo: Gallery Min, 1986. First edition, text in English and Japanese, numerous color and black and white photos, near fine in wrappers, uncommon.   Jeff Hirsch Books   E-List 80 - 15   2016 $100

Heineman, Ben Walter *Some Personal Views.* Chicago: Falcon Press, 1974. First edition, tan cloth binding with brown spine and front cover lettering, one small tear to lower part of rear hinge, color photo inset on front cover, slipcase with minimal shelfwear, 17 color photos.   Simon Finch 2015 - 006064   2016 $200

Heinemann, William *The First Step: a Dramatic Moment.* London: John Lane, 1895. 1 of 500 copies, first edition, original grey-green boards with paper title label, label chipped and corners of boards slightly bumped, interior clean and with most of the pages unopened, near fine.   The Kelmscott Bookshop   12 - 49   2016 $200

Heinlein, David *Micro Mono.* Piscataway: self published, 1995. One of 15 self-published copies of the second edition, fine in stapled wrappers, with ANS by author laid in.   Ken Lopez Bookseller 166 - 142   2016 $75

Heinlein, Robert Anson 1907-1988 *To Sail Beyond the Sunset.* New York: G. P. Putnam's Sons, 1987. First edition, blue cloth backed boards, lettered in silver, very fine in pristine dust jacket.   Argonaut Book Shop   Literature 2015 - 4858   2016 $100

Heinlein, Robert Anson 1907-1988 *Tunnel in the Sky.* New York: Scribners, 1955. First edition, near fine, very good+ first state dust jacket with chips, front flap clipped with price intact, minimal scuffs, 8vo.   By the Book, L. C. 45 - 72   2016 $650

Helle, Andre *Alphabet De La Grande Guerre 1914-1916.* Paris: Berger Leverault, 1915. 4to, cloth backed pictorial boards, covers dusty and slightly soiled, else clean, tight and very good+, full color illustrations, very scarce.   Alephbet Books, Inc. 111 - 216   2016 $1500

Helle, Andre *Images Drolatiques.* Paris: 1923. First edition, color lithographs, text in French.   Honey & Wax Booksellers   4 - 44   2016 $800

Helle, Andre *Le Tour Du Monde en 80 Pages.* Paris: J. Ferenczi et Fils, 1927. 4to., cloth backed pictorial boards, slight bit of edge rubbing, else near fine, every page has color illustrations.   Aleph-bet Books, Inc. 112 - 242   2016 $500

Heller, Joseph *Now and Then from Coney Island to Here.* New York: Simon & Schuster, 1998. First edition, faint toning to borders of cheap paper, original black boards, backstrip lettered in gilt, small amount of transfer from dust jacket to interior, ownership inscription, contemporary review clipping and publisher letter laid in, near fine, signed and dated by author.   Blackwell's Rare Books B184 - 153   2016   £50

Heller, Thomas Edmund *The New Code (1884-1885) of Minutes of the education Department...* London: Bemrose & Sons, 1884. Ninth edition, 5 initial ads, 10 pages ads, original printed paper wrappers, rebacked.   Jarndyce Antiquarian Books CCXV - 727   2016   £40

Hellman, Lillian *The Autumn Garden.* Boston: Little Brown, 1951. First edition, 8vo., very good in dust jacket mended on verso, presentation from author to Paul (Metcalf) and wife. Second Life Books, Inc. 196A - 771 2016 $450

Helm, Clementine *Cecily (Elf Goldenhair).* Philadelphia: Lippincott, 1924. First edition, 4to., red cloth stamped in gold, pictorial paste-on, spine bit dull and few marks on rear covers, clean and very good+, illustrations by Gertrude Kay. Aleph-bet Books, Inc. 112 - 276 2016 $200

Helmuth, J. Henry C. *A Short Account of the Yellow Fever in Philadelphia for the Reflecting Christian.* Philadelphia: Jones, Hoff & Derrick, 1794. First edition in English, old plain wrappers, text foxed and brown, rare. James Tait Goodrich X-78 - 569 2016 $250

Heming, W. T. *The Needle Region and Its Resources.* Redditch: printed and published at Indicator Office, 1877. First edition, 8vo., folding lithograph panorama, numerous wood engraved text illustrations, original blind stamped red cloth, upper cover lettered gilt, slightly worn and loose. Marlborough Rare Books List 55 - 34 2016 £45

Hemingway, Ernest Millar 1899-1961 *A Farewell to Arms.* New York: Charles Scribner's Sons, 1929. First edition, copy number 280 of 510 numbered copies, signed by author on Japanese vellum and paper covered boards, spine little tinted and slight glue stain to top of leather spine label, in a worn original matching numbered publisher's cardboard slipcase with top panel supplied in facsimile, some neat internal repair. Between the Covers Rare Books 204 - 56 2016 $10,000

Hemingway, Ernest Millar 1899-1961 *A Farewell to Arms.* New York: Scribner, 1929. First edition, first state withou disclaimer on page x, 8vo., very good. Second Life Books, Inc. 197 - 179 2016 $450

Hemingway, Ernest Millar 1899-1961 *For Whom the Bell Tolls.* New York: Charles Scribner's Sons, 1940. First edition, first printing,, beige cloth stamped in black and red, original pictorial first issue dust jacket without photographer's credit to rear panel with an illustration of mountain scene to front panel, white, black and blue lettered in red and white, book about fine, with only some faint offsetting to endpapers, else fine, dust jacket with some loss and closed tears to spine head, wear and chipping to extremities, light toning to spine, fiant rubbing to clean panels, overall very good, presentable copy. Manhattan Rare Book Company 2016 - EH182 2016 $400

Hemingway, Ernest Millar 1899-1961 *For Whom the Bell Tolls.* New York: Charles Scribner's Sons, 1940. First edition, first issue with Scribner's 'A' on copyright page, in first issue dust jacket (no photographer's credit on rear of jacket), original nubby oatmeal cloth, front board stamped in black with Hemingway's signature, spine stamped in red and black boards and spine, cloth extremely bright and completely unfaded, usual binder's glue stains at hinges, jacket bright with no fading, minimal flaking to corners but mostly at top and bottom of spine, superb copy. Heritage Book Shop Holiday 2015 - 53 2016 $3500

Hemingway, Ernest Millar 1899-1961 *God Rest You Merry Gentlemen.* New York: House of Books, 1933. Limited to 300 copies, this #154, 12mo., red cloth with gilt lettering spine and front cover, very good++, mild sun spine and covers. By the Book, L. C. 45 - 65 2016 $750

Hemingway, Ernest Millar 1899-1961 *God Rest You Merry Gentlemen.* New York: House of Books, 1933. First limited edition, one of 300 copies, publisher's red cloth, front board lettered in black, spine lettered gilt, near fine with some faint toning to spine and board edges, hint of bowing to front board, bright and fresh interior, glassine with some wear and close to extremities, some loss to spine and panel edges, overall very clean and pleasing copy in scarce original glassine dust jacket. B & B Rare Books, Ltd. 2016 - EH039 2016 $1500

Hemingway, Ernest Millar 1899-1961 *In Our Time.* Paris: Three Mountains Press, 1924. First edition, of 170 copies printed on rives hand-made paper, this is number 42, glue stain on endpaper, as usual, tiny chips at spinal extremities and slight browning of covers, excellent, very fine copy, in custom quarter morocco clamshell case. Between the Covers Rare Books 204 - 55 2016 $55,000

Hemingway, Ernest Millar 1899-1961 *Islands in the Stream.* New York: Charles Scribner's Sons, 1970. First edition, bright green cloth, lettered gilt, pictorial yellow endpapers illustrated with maps, original green pictorial dust jacket, lettered in yellow and white, about near fine with hint of wear to spine ends, light spotting to page edges, few faint spots to otherwise fresh interior, dust jacket with hint of toning to extremities, bright spine, few faint spots to verso, bright spine, else bright and fresh, overall very tight and square copy. B & B Rare Books, Ltd. 2016 - EH012 2016 $200

Hemingway, Ernest Millar 1899-1961 *A Moveable Feast.* New York: Charles Scribner's Sons, 1964. Unbound folded and gathered signatures, 8 signatures, the first and last signature with endpapers attached, page edges untrimmed and consequently the signatures have minor height variations, fine. Between the Covers Rare Books 208 - 1 2016 $3500

Hemingway, Ernest Millar 1899-1961 *Der alter un Der Yam. (Old Man and the Sea).* New York: Der Kval, 1958. 8vo., yellow cloth boards with drawing of Hemingway by Leonard Baskin on front panel, glassine tissue dust jacket, signed by Baskin, fine.   Second Life Books, Inc.   196A - 772   2016 $225

Hemingway, Ernest Millar 1899-1961 *The Sun Also Rises.* New York: Charles Scribner's Sons, 1926. First edition, 2nd issue, 8vo., bound in black publisher's cloth with paper label (chipped on spine, affecting couple of letters), good clean, Florence Eldridge's copy with her bookplate.   Second Life Books, Inc.   197 - 178   2016 $350

Hemingway, Ernest Millar 1899-1961 *The Torrents of Spring.* New York: Charles Scribner's Sons, 1926. First edition, first printing, publisher's dark green black cloth, lettered in red in original light tan first issue dust jacket, with nine titles to rear panel, book about fine, with one or two very faint scuffs to first and last leaves of the text block, hint of rubbing to extremities, bookseller's plate to rear pastedown, else bright and clean, unclipped dust jacket with some closed splitting to front hinge, some minor loss to spine ends, light toning to spine, fine minor chips to corners, few faint scuffs to the otherwise very bright and clean panels, near fine, handsome copy in fragile dust jacket, much nicer and brighter than usually found.   B & B Rare Books, Ltd.   2016 - EH183   2016 $5000

Hemphill, Samuel *The Diatessaron of Tatian a Harmony of the four Holy Gospels...* London: Furst and Hodder & Stoughton, 1888. First edition, near fine, original brown stitched pattern cloth, gilt, dark brown endpapers, foxing to verso of f.f.e.p. and title and verso of last leaf recto of rear f.e.p., otherwise near fine, tight copy, signed, scarce.   Simon Finch   2015 - 5404   2016 $192

Henbeck, Alfred *A Commentary on Homer's Odyssey.* Oxford: Clarendon Press, 1990-1992. 3 volumes, 8vo., figures, paperbacks, spines faded, one light crease along length of spine to volume II and III, little shelfwear, very good set, ownership inscription of C. D. N. Costa with few small and neat annotations to volume II.   Unsworths Antiquarian Booksellers Ltd.   E05 - 36   2016   £90

Henderson, Bernard *Wonder Tales of Ancient Wales.* Boston: Small Maynard, 1921. 4to., blue pictorial cloth, top edge gilt, slightest cover soil, very good+, illustrations by Doris Williamson.   Aleph-bet Books, Inc.   111 - 170   2016 $250

Henderson, G. E. *Princess Patricia's Canadian Light Infantry Allied with the Rifle Brigade 34d Green Jackets, Rifle Brigade volume XVII.* May, 1964. Jubilee edition, gold card covers, 8vo., photos, very good.   Schooner Books Ltd.   115 - 217   2016 $45

Henderson, George Wylie *Ollie Miss.* New York: Stokes, 1935. First edition, woodblock illustrations by L. Balcom, slight soiling to binding, else about fine in nice, very good dust jacket with some light scuffing on spine and some light nicking at crown, very nice.   Between the Covers Rare Books   207 - 48   2016 $350

Henderson, Mrs. *Etiquette of the Ballroom, and Guide to all the New and Fashionable Dances...* London: Routledge, circa, 1857. Eighth edition, ads on endpapers, original decorated purple cloth, very slight marking to front board, all edges gilt, nice, bright copy, 32m.   Jarndyce Antiquarian Books   CCXV - 250   2016   £110

Henderson, Mrs. *The Young Wife's Own Book.* Glasgow: W. R. M'Phun, 1856. 16 pages ads, originl green printed paper wrappers, slightly rubbed, all edges gilt.   Jarndyce Antiquarian Books   CCXV - 249   2016   £120

Henderson, Scott *Silent Swift Superb: the Story of the Vickers VCF10.* Newcastle-upon-Tyne: Scoval, 1998. First edition, large 4to., original illustrated boards, lettered black on spine and white and blue on covers, copiously illustrated in color and black and white, about fine, lower spine slightly bumped.   Any Amount of Books   2015 - C6989   2016   £170

Henderson, Thulia Susannah *The Good Steward: a Manual for Sunday School Teachers.* London: Sunday School Union, circa, 1860. Final ad leaf, original purple cloth, slightly rubbed.   Jarndyce Antiquarian Books   CCXV - 729   2016   £25

Hendrickson, Janis *My Lichtenstein.* Koln: Benedikt Taschen, 1988. First edition, 4to., copiously illustrated, nice in slightly scuffed dust jacket.   Second Life Books, Inc.   196A - 774   2016 $75

Hendy, Philip *Matthew Smith. Penguin Modern Painters.* Penguin Books, 1944. First edition, 32 plates, 16 color printed, oblong 8vo., original printed fawn and white stamped card wrappers, covers lightly dust soiled with faint spot to inside front cover, staples little rusted, good.   Blackwell's Rare Books   B184 - 315   2016   £25

Henham, Ernest G. *Tenebrae. A Novel.* London: Skeffington & Son, 1898. First edition, 8vo., titlepage printed in red and black, original pictorial green cloth, front and spine panels stamped in brown and black, publisher's monogram stamped in blind on rear panel, fore and bottom edges untrimmed, white endpapers with floral pattern printed in green, fine, lovely rare.   John W. Knott, Jr./L.W. Currey, Inc.   Fall-Winter 2015 - 17627   2016 $3500

Henley, William Ernest   1849-1903   *A Book of Verses.* London: Published by David Nutt, 1897. 171 x 18mm., fine scarlet crushed morocco elaborately gilt by Zaehnsdorf (blindstamped exhibition mark to lower pastedown), covers with gilt ruled border enclosing panel of double fillets capturing a field with rows of repeated gilt flowers (28 on each cover), flowers on stems with azured leaves and delicate gilt dotted element below each, gilt ruled raised bands and gilt spine compartments repeating these floral and foliate tools, red silk endleaves, all edges gilt, engraved vignette to title, spine uniformly sunned to darker red, very slight rubbing to joints, well masked with dye, otherwise fine, lovely binding especially bright and text showing no signs of use.   Phillip J. Pirages   67 - 75   2016 $850

Henley, William Ernest   1849-1903   *For England's Sake: Verses and Songs in Time of War.*   London: David Nutt, 1900. First edition, signed presentation from author for Mrs. Henry Head, wife of Sir Henry Head, brownish purple wrappers with faded gold lettering on stiff archival boards, sunning to spine and edges of boards, interior yellowed but text clear and crisp, housed in brown cloth covered box, scarce in presentation from, very good-.   The Kelmscott Bookshop   12 - 50   2016 $175

Henry, Barbara   *Walt Whitman's Faces. A Typographic Reading.*   Jersey City: Harsimus Press, 2012. 19/30 copies, from an edition of 80 copies signed by Barbara Henry, these copies with additional two color pints of 4 lino-cut Whitman portraits signed by Henry, large frontispiece linocut portrait of Whitman by Henry with further small portraits by the same to contents page and section title, each printed in black against a yellow or red ground, printed in various colors and types with two photographic plates of street scenes both contemporary to Whitman and modern, royal 8vo., original quarter green morocco with grey boards, illustration printed in black to each board, backstrip with printed label, edges untrimmed, prospectus and press ephemera loosely inserted, new.   Blackwell's Rare Books   B184 - 273   2016   £500

Henry, James   *Sketches of Moravian Life and Character.* Philadelphia: J. B. Lippincott, 1859. First edition, 8vo., frontispiece, original purple cloth, faded, lacks free endpaper.   J. & S. L. Bonham Antiquarian Booksellers   Europe 2016 - 7384   2016   £40

Henry, John M.   *Nine Above the Law: Our Supreme Court.* Pittsburgh: R. T. Lewis Co., 1936. First edition, small quarto, red brown cloth gilt, some rubbing to extremities, very good or better, inscribed by author, to Sinclair Lewis, also with bookplate of Lewis's wife, activist/author Dorothy Thompson.   Between the Covers Rare Books   208 - 37   2016 $300

Henry, Marguerite   *Misty of Chincoteague.*   Chicago: Rand McNally, 1959. Reprint, illustrations by Wesley Dennis, author's signature on bookplate, notes in ink are characters in book, light blue paper over boards, edges little soiled, otherwise very good, tight copy in somewhat chipped and soiled dust jacket.   Second Life Books, Inc.   196A - 776   2016 $65

Henshaw, Samuel   *Some Chinese Vertebrates.* Cambridge: Museum of Comparative Zoology, 1912. Quarto, six colored plates, publisher's printed upper wrapper, lower wrapper missing, badly chipped.   Andrew Isles Natural History Books   55 - 6533   2016 $100

Henty, George Alfred   1832-1902   *In the Hands of the Cave Dwellers.*   Blackie, 1902. First English bookform edition, 2 plates, 8vo., original olive green cloth, not blue as called for by Newbolt, pictorial front cover and darkened backstrip blocked in grey, orange and black, lettered gilt and orange, short split at head of backstrip, contemporary prize bookplate, ownership signature, good.   Blackwell's Rare Books   B184 - 164   2016   £150

Hepworth, Barbara   *A Pictorial Autobiography.*   London: Adam & Dart, 1970. First edition, quarto, black and white reproductions, photos, review slip laid in, very near fine in dust jacket, slightly creased at top edges.   Peter Ellis   112 - 166   2016   £150

Herbach, Chad   *The Art of Fielding.*   New York: Little Brown, 2011. Advance reading copy, near fine, light wear to extremities.   Bella Luna Books   2016 - t9976   2016 $82

Herbert, Auberon   *The Sacrifice of education to Examination.*   London: Williams & Norgate, 1889. Errata leaf, original printed paper boards, blue cloth spine, little rubbed and marked, library numbers on spine, from the library of Faculty of Physicians and Surgeons, Glasgow. Jarndyce Antiquarian Books   CCXV - 731   2016   £35

Herbert, Frank   *Children of Dune.*   New York: Berkeley/ G. P. Putnam, 1976. True first edition, signed and inscribed by author, 8vo., near fine with minimal cover edge wear, very good++ dust jacket with edgewear, 8vo.   By the Book, L. C.   45 - 73   2016 $325

Herbert, Frank   *The Dragon in the Sea.*   Garden City: Doubleday, 1956. First edition, 8vo., near fine, minimal cover edge wear, near fine dust jacket, signed by author. By the Book, L. C. 45 - 74   2016 $500

Herbert, Frank   *Dune.*   Philadelphia and New York: Coward McCann, Inc., 1954. First edition, octavo, cloth, fine in fine dust jacket, sharp copy.   John W. Knott, Jr./L.W. Currey, Inc. Fall-Winter 2015 - 17097   2016 $15,000

Hercules, Frank *Where the Hummingbird Flies.* New York: Harcourt Brace, 1961. First edition, author's presentation on flyleaf for Bill Goodman, Feb. 10 1970, rust cloth, cover little soiled, but very good tight copy in scuffed and slightly chpped dust jacket, scarce first book.   Second Life Books, Inc.   196A - 777   2016 $150

Hergesheimer, Joseph *The Party Dress.* New York: 1930. First edition, limited to 225 large paper copies signed by author, vellum backed boards, little worn at spine in worn original box.   Second Life Books, Inc.   196A - 779   2016 $50

Hermes, Gertrude *Wood Engravings for "The Lovers" Song Book.* Newtown, Powys: Gregynog Press, 1993. 18/50 copies, 10 engravings printed on Japanese vellum and mounted, book with titles printed in red, tall 8vo., original grey printed wrappers, tail edge untrimmed, book with prints and descriptive pamphlet, housed in gray cloth drop down box lettered gilt to front and backstrip, fine. Blackwell's Rare Books   B184 - 271   2016   £1200

Hernandez, Miguel *Viento del Pueblo - Poesia en la Guerra.* Valencia: Ediciones 'Socorro Rojo, 1937. First edition, octavo, photos, recent French binding of vellum backed patterned boards with leather spine label, titlepage cropped at margin, otherwise fine, rare.   Peter Ellis   112 - 372   2016   £3750

Hernton, Calvin C. *Coming Together: Black Power, White Hatred and Sexual Hang-Ups.* New York: Random House, 1971. First edition, bottom corner of few pages creased, tiny burn mark on fore-edge else near fine in lightly soiled about fine dust jacket, effusively inscribed by author for Roy Hill, poet/author.   Between the Covers Rare Books   207 - 52   2016 $125

Herodian *Historiarum Libri Octo Graece.* Halle: in libraria Orphanotrophei, 1792. First Wolf edition, poor quality paper browned and bit spotted, 8vo., untrimmed in contemporary quarter red straight grained morocco by Thouvenin, signed at foot of spine, red paste paper boards, spine divided by five raised bands, second and fourth compartments gilt lettered, rest with central gilt stamps of harp-shapes formed with scallop and beasts' heads tools, marbled endpapers, 2 additional binder's blanks (one paper, one vellum), board edges little worn, leather slightly darkened and rubbed, very good.   Blackwell's Rare Books   Greek & Latin Classics VII - 29   2016   £200

Herodotus *Herodoti Libri Novem. Quibus Musarum Sunt Nomina.* Venice: Aldus Manutius, 1502. First edition, folio, printed in Green type with Aldine anchor on title and last page, full 18th century French crimson levant morocco stamped in gilt, triple gilt fillets on sides and gilt inside borders, marbled endpapers, all edges gilt, previous cataloger noted the binding was probably done by Derome, part of lower right of titlepage restored, barely affecting few letters of dedication letter, contemporary manuscript marginalia on some leaves, fine, large copy, wide margins, bookplate of Edith Rockefeller McCormick.   Second Life Books, Inc.   197 - 180   2016 $47,500

Herodotus *Historiarum Libri IX...* Lugduni Batavorum: apud Samuelem Luchtmann, 1715. Engraved frontispiece titlepage dated 1716, first edition, folio, without separate titlepage to appendix (after page 554), found in some copies, half title, additional engraved title, titlepage in red and black, foldout engraved illustration after page 135, two small illustrations in text (pages 912 and 997), woodcut initials, engraved tailpieces, Greek and Latin parallel text, occasional small annotations, some light ink spotting to half title, little toned in gutters and towards end of text, small ink blot to top edge sporadically visible at upper margins but never approaching text, contemporary vellum, raised bands, gilt morocco spine label, blind tooled boards, edges sprinkled red and blue, bit grubby, prelim blanks tattered with some loss, old discolored repair to top corner but very good, ownership inscriptions of Henry Gahagan, student at Christ Church Oxford and Rev. Reginald (Lake?) Nov. 30 1880. Unsworths Antiquarian Booksellers Ltd.   E04 - 21   2016 £650

Herodotus *Historiarum Libri IX....* Lugduni Batavorum: apud Samuelem Luchtmans, 1715. First edition, engraved frontispiece titlepage dated 1716, folio, without separate titlepage to appendix, found in some copies, half title, additional engraved title, titlepage in red and black, foldout engraved illustration after page 138, 2 small illustrations to text, without initials, engraved tailpieces, Greek and Latin parallel text, occasional small annotations, some light ink spotting to half title, little toned in gutters and towards end of text, small ink blot to top edge sporadically visible upper margin but nver approaching text, contemporary vellum, raised bands, gilt morocco spine label, blind tooled boards, edges sprinkled red and blue, bit grubby, prelim blanks tattered with some loss, old discolored repair to top corner, but very good overall, ownership inscription of Henry Gahagan, student of Christ Church, Oxford and Rev. Reginald (Lake?) Nov. 30 1880.   Unsworths Antiquarian Booksellers   30 - 69   2016   £650

Herodotus *The History of...* printed for A. Bell (and others), 1720. Second edition of the first full translation into English, 2 volumes, 3 folding engraved maps, some spotting and browning, 8vo., contemporary calf, rebacked, sound. Blackwell's Rare Books   B186 - 72   2016   £950

Herodotus *Historia.* Glasgow: In aedibus Academicis, excuderbant Robertus et Andreas Foulis, 1761. First Foulis edition, first issue on less fine paper but with all blanks present and correct, 8vo., contemporary calf, spines gilt, red and green morocco lettering pieces (about half of them renewed with consummate skill), joints and extremities worn, some leather cracking but all boards firm held, front endpapers volume I renewed, bookplate of G. Devisme in all volumes except first, good copy.   Blackwell's Rare Books   Greek & Latin Classics VII - 30   2016   £1500

Herodotus *Historia.* Glasgow: in aedibus Academicis excudebant Robertus et Andreas Foulis, 1761. First Foulis edition, issue on less fine paper but with all blanks present and correct, 8vo., contemporary calf, spines gilt, red and green morocco lettering pieces (about half of them renewed with consummate skill), joints and extremities worn, some leather cracking but all boards firmly held, front endpapers volume 1 renewed, bookplate of G. de Visme in all volumes, except the first, good.   Blackwell's Rare Books   B186 - 71   2016   £1500

Herodotus *Historiarum Libri IX.* Amsterdam: sumptibus Petri Schovtenii, 1763. Folio, additional engraved title and 1 folding plate, parallel Latin and Greek text, prelims in Latin, titlepages in red and black, engraved vignette, woodcut initials and head and tailpieces, small illustrations in text with half title, some leaves lightly toned near text but uncommonly bright and clean overall, contemporary blind tooled vellum, ink title to spine, edges gilt over marbling, spine and head of boards slightly darkened, little grubby, still very good.   Unsworths Antiquarian Booksellers Ltd.   E04 - 22   2016   £1000

Herodotus *Historiarum Libri IX.* Amstelodami: sumptibus Petri Schovtenii, 1763. Folio, engraved additional titlepage and 1 folding plate, Greek and Latin text, titlepage in red and black with engraved vignette, half title, engraved initials and head and tailpieces, internally bright and clean, contemporary brown calf boards, neatly rebacked in slightly lighter shade, spine heavily gilt, older red morocco spine label, edges sprinkled red, marbled endpapers little rubbed, few light scratches, rear flyleaf repaired with tape, very good, ownership inscription of W. Cokayne Frith, bookbinders label E. A. Weeks & Son, London.   Unsworths Antiquarian Booksellers   30 - 71   2016   £1000

Herodotus *Historiarum Libri IX.* Amstelodami: Sumptibus Petri Schovtenii, 1763. Folio, engraved title, 1 folding plate, parallel Latin and Greek text, titlepage in red and black with engraved vignette, woodcut initials and head and tailpieces, small illustrations in text, half title, some leaves lightly toned near text but uncommonly bright and clean overall, contemporary blind tooled vellum, ink title to spine, edges gilt over marbling, spine and nead of boards slightly darkened, little grubby, still very good.   Unsworths Antiquarian Booksellers   30 - 70   2016   £1000

Herrick, Robert 1591-1674 *The Hesperides & Noble Numbers.* London: Lawrence & Bullen, 1898. Revised edition, small octavo, 2 volumes, superb period bindings by Riviere of full dark pink morocco with raised bands, ornate gilt spine with inner dentelles, gilt rules, top edge gilt, bookplate of poet H. W. Harding, spines little darkened and joints just faintly rubbed, very good.   Peter Ellis   112 - 167   2016   £650

Herriot, James *All Creatures Great and Small.* New York: St. Martin's Press, 1972. Presumed later printing in black boards, slight slant and lightly bumped top corners, fine- in near fine-, price clipped dust jacket jacket has chipping at spine ends.   Ken Hebenstreit, Bookseller   2016 - 2016 $55

Herrligkoffer, Karl M. *Nanga Parbat: Incorporating the Official Report of the Expedition of 1953.* London: Elek Books, 1954. First English translation, color frontispiece, photographics, maps, turquoise cloth, gilt lettered spine, fine.   Argonaut Book Shop   Mountaineering 2015 - 4461   2016 $90

Herron, Don *Willeford.* Tucson: Dennis McMillan, 1997. First edition, very fine in dust jacket, signed by author.   Mordida Books   2015 - 010414   2016 $65

Hersey, John *Blues.* Franklin Center: Franklin Library, 1987. Limited first edition, signed by author, blue leather lettered and decoratively stamped in gilt, color pastedown illustration to front cover, all edges gilt, very fine, as new.   Argonaut Book Shop   Literature 2015 - 3973   2016 $45

Hersey, John *Too Far to Walk.* New York: Alfred A. Knopf, 1966. First edition, blue cloth lettered in gilt and black, fine in price clipped dust jacket.   Argonaut Book Shop   Literature 2015 - 4861   2016 $50

Hersholt, Jean *Evergreen Tales or Tales for the Ageless...* New York: Limited Editions Club, 1949-1952. First edition thus, small folio, 15 volumes, original variously coloured linen and silk bindings, decorated in gilt and color, pictorial endpapers, contained within 5 separate red slipcases with printed paper labels at spines, each volume circa 45 pages, lithographed color illustrations, most volumes signed by Hersholt with additional signatures.   Sotheran's Piccadilly Notes - Summer 2015 - 122   2016   £898

Herskovits, Melville J. *The Anthropometry of the American Negro.* New York: Columbia University Press, 1930. First edition, boards little bowed, else fine, without dust jacket, possibly as issued, inscribed by author for Prof. H. Labourer with compliments and kind regards of the author, scarce.   Between the Covers Rare Books   202 - 39   2016 $650

Herst, Beth Francine *The Dickens Hero: Selfhood and Alienation in the Dickens World.* London: Weidenfeld & Nicholson, 1990. First edition, half title, original dark blue cloth, spine lettered in silver, very good in dust jacket. Jarndyce Antiquarian Booksellers   CCXVIII - 1298 2016 £20

Hertel, Niels Theodor Axel *Overpressure in High Schools in Denmark.* London: Macmillan, 1885. First English edition, half title, charts, original blue cloth, dulled and bit worn, booklabel of Library of Faculty of Physicians and Surgeons, Glasgow.   Jarndyce Antiquarian Books   CCXV - 732 2016   £20

Hertz, Louis H. *The Handbook of Old American Toys.* Wethersfield: Mark Haber, 1947. First edition, 2nd printing, 8vo., author's presentation on flyleaf, red cloth, cover slightly worn bumped at corners and edges, otherwise very good tight copy.   Second Life Books, Inc.   196A - 780   2016 $45

Hervey, Elizabeth *The History of Ned Evans.* Dublin: P. Wogan, 1805. Scarce edition, later issue, contemporary full brown leather with red title label and brown volume number label to spine, binding is mottled with bumping and boards of volume 2 starting to split from spine, binding still solid, however text blocks are tight, browning and some foxing to interior pages, otherwise very good, bookplate affixed to front pastedown to volume I and ink ownership signature, very good.   The Kelmscott Bookshop   12 - 51   2016 $500

Hesiod *Epga Kai Hmepai di Esiodo Traduzione Presentata a S. E. ser Giovanni Donado Veneto Senatore...* Padua: per li Conzantti, 1765. First edition entirely in Italian, woodcut textural diagrams and tables, touch of light foxing to places, corner of few leaves lightly damp marked, few small tidy repairs to surface abrasions from stamp removal, 4to., contemporary vellum, boards decorated in blind with large central lozenge and fillet border, spine divided by blind fillets, second compartment stained orange and lettered and bordered gilt, remainder with central blind flower tools, red star-design bunt papier pastedowns, slightly soiled, touch of inset damage to joints, armorial bookplates, good. Blackwell's Rare Books   Greek & Latin Classics VII - 32 2016   £500

Hesiod *Opera et Dies. Theogonia. Scutum Herculis.* Venice: in aedibus Batholomaei Zanetti, 1537. First edition with Scholia, first text leaf printed in red and black, several woodcuts within text, including one full page, margins of early leaves dusty and with one or two small tidy repairs, occasional dampstaining to lower margin, particularly at end, gathering (omicron) bound out of order and inside gathering, occasional old underlining and notes in red crayon, 4to., 17th century English calf, boards ruled in gilt and blind with central decorative gilt lozenge, rebacked preserving old backstrip, little marked and chipped, gift bookplate of James Yorke, bishop of Ely, good.   Blackwell's Rare Books   Greek & Latin Classics VII - 31   2016   £300

Hesiod *Opera et Dies.* Venice: in aedibis Bartholomaei Zanetti, 1537. First edition with Scholia, first text leaf printed in red and black, several woodcuts within text, margins of early leaves dusty and with one or two small tidy repairs, occasional dampstaining to lower margin (particularly at end), gathering (omicron) bound out of order and inside gathering (xi), occasional old underlining and notes in red crayon, 4to., 17th century English calf, boards ruled in gilt and blind with central decorative gilt lozenge, rebacked preserving old backstrip, little marked and chipped, gift bookplate of James Yorke, Bishop of Ely, good.   Blackwell's Rare Books   B186 - 73   2016   £3000

Hesychius of Alexandria *Lexicon cum Variis Doctorum Virorum Notis vel Editis Antehac vel Ineditis....* Leiden & Rotterdam: Ex Officina Hackiana, 1668. First Variorum edition, ownership inscription struck through at foot of titlepage, very faint edge browning, 4to., contemporary vellum boards, spine lettered in ink, just slightly dusty, turn-ins lifting, front hinge cracking bit at titlepage, very good.   Blackwell's Rare Books   B186 - 74   2016   £500

Hesychius of Alexandria *Lexicon Ailiou Diogeneianou Periergopentes Editionem Minorem....* Jenae: sumptibus Hermanni Dufftii (Libraria Maukiana), 1867. Large 8vo., sporadic foxing heavier at front and rear, some neat pencil annotations, later half brown morocco with green cloth covered boards, green gilt spine label, top edge red, rubbed, few scuffs, corners wearing but very good, sound copy, penciled ownership inscription of E. Ken Borthwick to f.f.e.p. Unsworths Antiquarian Booksellers   30 - 72   2016   £90

Hewett, Edward *Convivial Dickens: the Drinks of Dickens and His Times.* Athens: Ohio University Press, 1983. First edition, 4to., half title, illustrations, original red-brown cloth, very good in dust jacket.   Jarndyce Antiquarian Booksellers CCXVIII - 1299   2016   £25

Hewitt, Edward Ringwood *Secrets of the Salmon.* New York: Charles Scribner's, 1922. No. 639 of limited edition of 780, 8vo., original green cloth backed green paper covered boards, 53 illustrations, occasional light spotting, previous owner's signature to f.f.e.p., very good.   Sotheran's Hunting, Shooting & Fishing - 124   2016   £250

Hewitt, Graily *Lettering for Students and Craftsmen.* London: Seeley, Service & Co. Ltd., 1930. No. 324 of 370 copies for sale (from a total edition of 380), signed by author, 200 x 264mm, publisher's original white buckram, flat spine with gilt titling, top edge gilt, other edges untrimmed, first third of leaves unopened, 183 figures, including tipped in plates and two plates with alphabets of Roman capitals by author, final two leaves of appendix, and first two of index with two inch closed tear at bottom, not affecting text, otherwise very fine, white cloth remarkably clean and bright, text immaculate.   Phillip J. Pirages   67 - 194   2016 $1000

Hey, Richard *Observations on the Nature of Civil Liberty and the Principles of Government.* London: for T. Cadell and T. and J. Merrill, 1776. First edition, neat modern boards, morocco backed folding box, near fine.   Joseph J. Felcone, Inc.   Books from Five Centuries: a Miscellany - 77   2016 $850

Heyeck, Robin *Marbling at the Heyeck Press.* Woodside: Heyeck, 1986. Limited to 150 numbered copies, signed by author, 4to., quarter morocco with marbled paper covered sides, slipcase, printed on dampened handmade paper and having a total of 28 samples, loosely inserted is a bill for this copy made out to collector, Pat England with note by Robin Heyeck written on it, also present is Christmas card from Heyeck to England.   Oak Knoll Books   27 - 37   2016 $850

Heyen, William *The Ash.* Potsdam: Tamarack Editions, 1978. First edition, of a total edition of 326, this #48 of 126 to contain a special drawing, hand colored by Kristen Heyen, 12 year old daughter of author, and signed by author and artist, inscribed and signed by same for William Meredith, original envelope addressed in Heyen's hand to Meredith, fine.   Charles Agvent   William Meredith - 36   2016 $100

Heyen, William *The Chestnut Eain.* New York: Ballantine, 1986. First edition, author's presentation on half title to poet and editor, William Claire, paper wrappers, cover slightly soiled and creased, otherwise very good, right copy.   Second Life Books, Inc.   196A - 781   2016 $85

Heyen, William *Depth of Field. Poems.* Baton Rouge: Louisiana State University Press, 1970. First edition, inscribed and signed by author for William Meredith, slight wrinkling to top of text and dampstaining to top of dust jacket, still near fine in very good dust jacket.   Charles Agvent   William Meredith - 37   2016 $80

Heyen, William *Erika. Poems of the Holacaust.* St. Louis: Time Being Books, 1991. New edition, lengthily inscribed and signed by author for William Meredith, slight dust spotting to top edge, fine in fine dust jacket.   Charles Agvent   William Meredith - 38   2016 $100

Heyen, William *Fires.* Athens: Croissant & Co., 1977. First edition, printed red wrappers, #87 of 300 copies, this copy inscribed and signed by author for William Meredith in 1977, fine, original envelope addressed in Heyen's hand to Meredith.   Charles Agvent   William Meredith - 39   2016 $100

Heyen, William *Long Island Light. Poems and a Memoir.* New York: Vanguard Press, 1979. First edition, inscribed and signed in 1979 by author for William Meredith, slight dust spotting to top edge of text, fine in near fine dust jacket.   Charles Agvent   William Meredith - 40   2016 $100

Heyen, William *My Holocaust Songs.* Concord: William B. Ewert, 1980. First edition, #146 of 180 signed by author and artist, Michael McCurdy, signed and inscribed by author for William Meredith, slight dust spotting to top edge of text, mild sunning to spine, near fine, issued without dust jacket.   Charles Agvent   William Meredith - 41   2016 $100

Heyen, William *Noise in the Trees: poems and memoir.* New York: Vanguard, 1974. First edition, author's presentation to poet William Claire, Oct. 20 1989, pale blue cloth stamped in white, edges little spotted, cover slightly faded, otherwise very good, tight copy in price clipped and little scuffed dust jacket.   Second Life Books, Inc.   196A - 782   2016 $95

Heyen, William *Noise in the Trees. Poems and a Memoir.* New York: Vanguard Press, 1974. First edition, copy 28 of 50 signed copies from a total edition of 2500, additionally inscribed and signed by author for William Meredith, slight dust spotting to top edge of text, fine in fine dust jacket.   Charles Agvent   William Meredith - 42   2016 $150

Heyen, William *XVII Machines.* Pittsburg: and Derry: Sisyphus Editions, 1976. First edition, printed wrappers, #20 of 503, inscribed and signed in 1977 by author for William Meredith, laid in is 4 page ALS from author to Meredith, in original envelope addressed in Heyen's hand, fine.   Charles Agvent   William Meredith - 44   2016 $150

Heyen, William *The Swastika Poems 1957-1974.* New York: Vanguard Press, 1977. First edition, signed and inscribed by author for William Meredith, fine in close to fine dust jacket with short tear at rear.   Charles Agvent   William Meredith - 43   2016 $100

Heynen, James *The Funeral Parlor.* Port Townsend: Graywolf Press, 1976. No. 12 of 60 copies, 8vo., one of an edition of 225 limited copies, printed from handset Palatino types on Curtis rag paper, wrapper is Strathmore Rhododendron, this is one of the copies signed by author, paper wrappers, about as new.   Second Life Books, Inc.   196A - 783   2016 $65

Heynen, James *The Man Who Kept Cigars in His Cap.* Port Townsend: Graywolf Press, 1979. One of 26 signed copies, illustrations by Tom Pohrt, signed by author and artist, tan cloth, nice in dust jacket, little scuffed and torn.   Second Life Books, Inc.   196A - 786   2016 $200

Heyrick, Thomas *Miscellany Poems.* Cambridge: by John Hayes for the author, 1691. First edition, very scarce, woodcut alma mater device on title, late 19th century half morocco (hinges lightly scuffed), some foxing and light browning, chiefly on first and last few pages and largely confined to margins, small piece torn from upper corner of titlepage, short marginal tear on K1, signature of Rd. Habgood 1774.   Joseph J. Felcone, Inc.   Books from Five Centuries: a Miscellany - 78   2016 $3000

Heywood, B. A. *Addresses Delivered at the Meetings of the Proprietors of the Liverpool Royal Institution on the 27th February 1822 and 13 February 1824.* Liverpool: printed by Harris and Co., 1824. First edition, 4to., frontispiece woodcut on India paper laid down on blank, vignette of the seal and one plate, on India paper of the Minerva Ergane, excellently rebound in half calf, marbled boards, maroon morocco label, from the library of John Gladstone, Fasque House, very good.   Jarndyce Antiquarian Booksellers   CCXVII - 125   2016   £280

Heywood, James *The Ancient Laws of the Century, for King's College, Cambridge and for the Public School of Eton College.* London: Longman, 1850. First edition, frontispiece and plate, original dull green cloth by Westleys, small labels and stamps of the British Library of Political Science, otherwise very good.   Jarndyce Antiquarian Books   CCXV - 573   2016   £45

Hiaasen, Carl *A Death in China.* New York: Atheneum, 1984. First edition, near fine, shows light use, in like dust jacket with very light edge wear, small crease on front flap, signed by author.   Bella Luna Books   2016 - t1537   2016 $231

Hiaasen, Carl *Native Tongue.* New York: Knopf, 1991. First edition, fine in pictorial wrappers, signed by author, advance reading copy.   Mordida Books   2015 - 010444   2016 $55

Hibberd, Shirley *The Book of the Quarium; or Practical Instructions on the Formation, Stocks and Management in All Seasons...* London: Groombridge and Sons, 1869. Small octavo, text illustrations, publisher's decorated cloth, grubby but sound.   Andrew Isles Natural History Books   55 - 6554   2016 $100

Hickey, Emily *Poems.* London: Elki Mathews, 1896. Scarce first edition, original light green cloth boards with gilt title to spine and front board, browning to spine and edges of boards, few markings to rear board, includes frontispiece by Mary Swan with browned tissue guard, ex-library from St. Mary's Clapham Library, no library markings aside from their modest bookplate, interior clean and bright, very good.   The Kelmscott Bookshop   12 - 52   2016 $150

Hiebert, Helen *Interluceo.* Red Cliff: Helen Hiebert Studio, 2015. Artist's book, one of 25 copies, each signed by Hiebert and dated on titlepage, all on her own handmade papers, 75% cotton, 25% abaca blend paper to showcase watermarks, pigmented abaca pulp to create rainbow spectrum of translucent papers, 9 3/16 x 9 3/16 inches, bound by Claudia Cohen, handsewn exposed spine, grey paper wrapper printed with title and geometric shapes in darker grey on front panel, housed in custom made plum silk over boards box with title printed blind on grey paper laid onto spine, 7 handcut paper illustrations,.   Priscilla Juvelis - Rare Books   66 - 5   2016 $1750

Higgins, Colin *Harold and Maude.* Philadelphia and New York: J. B. Lippincott Co., 1971. First edition, fine in near fine dust jacket with modest creased tear on rear panel and couple of other tiny tears.   Between the Covers Rare Books   208 - 25   2016 $200

Higgs, P. W. *Broken Symmetries Massless Particles and Gauge Fields. in Physics Letters Volume 12 1964.* Amsterdam: North Holland Pub., 1964. 8vo., modern cloth, gilt lettered spine with ink note verso titlepage, mild spotting top edge.   By the Book, L. C.   45 - 13   2016 $1000

Highsmith, Patricia *The Blunderer.* New York: Coward McCann Inc., 1954. First edition, octavo, cloth, fine in nearly fine dust jacket with some light creases to heel of spine panel and some mild rub spots to rear panel, uncommon in nice condition.   John W. Knott, Jr./L.W. Currey, Inc.   Fall-Winter 2015 - 17964   2016 $850

Highsmith, Patricia *Deep Water.* New York: Harper Bros., 1957. First edition, octavo, boards, fine in fine dust jacket with some mild rubbing, mainly to folds and slight shelfwear to spine ends.   John W. Knott, Jr./L.W. Currey, Inc.   Fall-Winter 2015 - 17963   2016 $1500

Highsmith, Patricia *A Dog's Ransom.* London: Heinemann, 1972. Proof copy, original wrappers, glassine protected dust jacket.   I. D. Edrich   Crime - 2016   £30

Highsmith, Patricia *The Glass Cell.* Garden City: Doubleday & Co. for the Crime Club, 1964. Tight, very near fine copy in close to near fine dust jacket that has tiny bit of wear to corners, lovely copy.   Jeff Hirsch Books   Holiday List 2015 - 43   2016 $450

Highsmith, Patricia *Nothing that Meets the Eye.* London: Bloomsbury, 2005. First edition, very fine in dust jacket.   Mordida Books   2015 - 010718   2016 $55

Highsmith, Patricia *The Price of Salt.* New York: Coward McCann, 1953. First edition, fine, bright copy in dust jacket with light professional restoration to spine ends, corners and extremities, lovely copy.   Buckingham Books   2015 - 27091   2016 $4750

Highsmith, Patricia *Ripley Under Water.* Bloomsbury: London Limited Editions, 1991. Limited to 150 copies, numbered, signed by author, specially bound, mint in tissue dust jacket.   I. D. Edrich   Crime - 2016   £60

Highsmith, Patricia *Ripley's Game.* New York: Knopf, 1974. First American edition, some light staining on spine, otherwise fine in dust jacket.   Mordida Books   2015 - 012050   2016 $65

Highsmith, Patricia *Strangers on a Train.* London: Cresset Press, 1950. First UK edition, publisher's file copy with slip affixed to front flyleaf, near fine in dust jacket with some light professional restoration to spine ends and corners, exceptional copy.   Buckingham Books   2015 - 26687   2016 $3750

Highsmith, Patricia *Strangers on a Train.* London: The Cresset Press, 1950. Uncorrected proof of first English edition, fine in unprinted wrappers with applied label of Paul Popper & Co. Literary Services, page edges trifle soiled, else about fine.   Between the Covers Rare Books 208 - 106   2016 $2000

Highsmith, Patricia *The Talented Mr. Ripley.* New York: Coward McCann, 1955. First edition, some light offsetting to front and rear endpapers, else near fine, tight copy in dust jacket lightly sunned on spine and with light professional restoration to spine ends and corners.   Buckingham Books   2015 - 28615   2016 $3750

Highsmith, Patricia *The Talented Mr. Ripley.* New York: Coward McCann Inc., 1955. First edition, original black cloth stamped in green, fine in very good dust jacket with touch of fading to green background on spine panel and along narrow vertical strip of front panel near spine fold and light wear to spine ends and corners, two short closed tears at top edge with mild associated creases and a 25 x 11 mm. abrasion to spine panel restored by professional paper conservator.   John W. Knott, Jr./L.W. Currey, Inc.   Fall-Winter 2015 - 17500   2016 $2500

Hijuelos, Oscar *Mr. Ives' Christmas.* New York: Harper Collins, 1995. First edition, fine in fine dust jacket, inscribed by author for Reynolds Price.   Between the Covers Rare Books   208 - 38   2016 $275

Hildrop, John *Free Thoughts Upon the Brute Creation; or an Examination of Father Bougerant's Philosophical Amusement &c.* London: printed for R. Minors, 1742-1743. First edition, 2 parts in 1 volum, engraved frontispiece, piece torn from fore-margin of H2 in first part with loss of 8 letters on recto and 2 on verso (sense recoverable), some spots and stains outside pages browned, 8vo., calf backed boards, circa 1950, red lettering piece, sound.   Blackwell's Rare Books   B186 - 75   2016   £750

Hill, Aaron *Alzira. A Tragedy.* London: printed for John Osborn, 1736. First edition, 8vo., title in red and black, disbound.   Jarndyce Antiquarian Booksellers   CCXVI - 461   2016   £50

Hill, Aaron *The Works of the Late Aaron Hill, Esq.* London: printed for the benefit of the family, 1753. First edition, 8vo., 4 volumes, contemporary mottled calf, gilt, spines gilt, red morocco labels, just trifle rubbed, very slight wear to tips of spines, handsome set on fine paper, watermarked with Strasburg bend, copies on ordinary paper have no watermark, fine condition.   C. R. Johnson Rare Book Collections   Foxon: H-P 2015 - 461   2016 $3064

Hill, David Octavius *Sketches of Scenery in Perthshire.* Perth: Published by Thos. Hill and sold by W. Blackwood, Edinburgh & Matin & Ackermann, London and printed by J. Roberston, Edinburgh, 1821-1823. First edition, 6 parts, oblong folio, 30 lithographed plates, parts 1-3 printed by J. Robertson, Edinburgh, parts 4-6 printed by Hulmandel, stitched as issued in original buff wrappers, preserved in modern green cloth, folder, upper with gilt morocco label, the copy of James Drummond, later 8th Viscount Strathallan, fine.   Marlborough Rare Books   List 55 - 35   2016   £5500

Hill, Elisabeth *The Poetical Monitor...* London: printed by J. Skirven, sold by Longman & Co., 1812. Sixth edition, final ad leaf, contemporary full speckled sheep, red morocco label, very good handsome copy.   Jarndyce Antiquarian Books   CCXV - 733   2016   £180

Hill, Grace Livingston *The White Flower.* New York: Grosset & Dunlap, Reprint edition, fine in dust jacket with faint crease on spine.   Mordida Books   2015 - 010759   2016 $65

Hill, John *The Conduct of a Married Life.* London: printed for R. Baldwin, 1753. 12mo., tear to lower corner of H*5 with no loss of text, contemporary full brown calf, double ruled gilt borders, raised bands, compartments, double ruled in gilt, some expert repairs to hinges, slightly rubbed, later pencil signature of A. H. Foot, nice.   Jarndyce Antiquarian Books   CCXV - 251   2016   £950

Hill, Joseph *Lexicon Manuale Graeco-Latinum a Josepho Hillio Aliquot Vocum Millibus Locupletatum.* Amstelodami: ex officina Heinrici & Viduae Theodori Boom, 1709. 8vo., frontispiece, additional engraved titlepage, engraved vignette to titlepage, little yellowed, some occasional light spotting and staining, slightly later vellum, tan sheep label to spine, edges sprinkled red and blue, spine darkened, label worn, small stains and smudgy marks, tiny chip to bottom edge of lower board, small tear to front pastedown, pencilled inscripiton 'A gift from JPB/ 9 April 1991'.   Unsworths Antiquarian Booksellers Ltd.   30 - 133   2016   £125

Hill, Leslie Pinckney *Toussaint L'Ouverture: a Dramatic History.* Boston: Christopher Pub. House, 1928. First edition, owner's stamp of Harrison A. Ridley Jr., repeated on prelim leaves, numbers on bottom page (as was Ridley's custom), else near fine, handsome, very near fine dust jacket (scarce).   Between the Covers Rare Books   207 - 53   2016 $750

Hill, Reginald *An Advancement of Learning.* London: Collins, 1971. First edition, fine in dust jacket. Buckingham Books   2015 - 31374   2016 $450

Hill, Reginald *Brother's Keeper and Other Stories.* Helsinki: Eurographica, 1992. First edition thus, 60/350 copies signed and dated by author, printed on magnani Michelangelo paper, original wrappers, edges untrimmed, printed dust jacket with gentle fading to backstrip panel, near fine.   Blackwell's Rare Books   B184 - 155   2016   £100

Hill, Richard *An Address to Persons of Fashion. Relating to Balls...* Shrewsbury: printed by J. Eddowes, 1771. Sixth edition, half title, 12mo., good clean copy, manuscript footnote on page 34, blue marginal line marking a paragraph on pages 154-155, recent full tan calf, raised bands, red morocco label, fresh contemporary endpapers and pastedowns, early signature of Peter Dean on titlepage. Jarndyce Antiquarian Books   CCXV - 252   2016   £200

Hill, Richard *The Blessings of Polygamy Displayed in an Affectionate Address to the Rev. Martin Madan Occaisoned by His late Work Entitled Thelypthora or a Treatise on Female Ruin.* London: sold by J. Mathews, C. Dilly and J. Eddowes in Shrewsbury, 1781. First edition, errata slip tipped in before dedication leaf, original boards, little worn, else fine, uncut.   John Drury Rare Books   2015 - 19118   2016 $350

Hill, Robin *Australian Birds.* Melbourne: Nelson, 1976. Second edition, folio, color illustrations by the author, publisher's full brown leather and slipcase, limited to 200 numbered copies, signed by author, deluxe edition.   Andrew Isles Natural History Books   55 - 16570   2016 $300

Hillary, Edmund *From the Ocean to the Sky.* New York: Viking Press, 1979. First American edition, numerous color and black and white plates, cloth backed boards, owner's neat inscription, else fine, pictorial dust jacket.   Argonaut Book Shop   Mountaineering 2015 - 4487   2016 $75

Hillary, Edmund *High in the Thin Cold Air.* Garden City: Doubleday, 1962. First edition, photos in color and black and white, drawings, gray cloth, one corner slightly jammed, else fine with pictorial dust jacket slightly torn and scarred at upper left corner of front cover.   Argonaut Book Shop   Mountaineering 2015 - 7159   2016 $50

Hillenbrand, Laura *Seabiscuit.* New York: Random House, 2001. First edition, near fine, light bumping to spine ends, near fine dust jacket with light wear to top corners, first state dust jacket, inside back flap does not promote the Random House Audio Book, back panel lists 'advance praise' reviews in correct order.   Bella Luna Books   2016 - t6328   2016 $66

Hillengrand, Laura *Unbroken.* New York: Random House, 2010. Advance reading copy, couple of tiny creases to covers, very near fine in wrappers.   Ken Lopez Bookseller   166 - 50   2016 $125

Hillerman, Tony *Skeleton Man.* New York: Harper Collins, 2004. First edition, 8vo., fine in dust jacket, signed by author.   Second Life Books, Inc.   196A - 792   2016 $65

Hillerman, Tony *Talking God.* New York: Harper, 1989. First edition, very fine in dust jacket.   Mordida Books   2015 - 011080   2016 $60

Hillhouse, James A. *Dramas, Discourses and Other Pieces.* Boston: Charles C. Little & Brown, James, 1839. First edition, 2 volumes, 12mo., presentation copy with tipped-in autograph card signed by author, as well as presentation by author, binding K, both volumes have bottom 2 inches cut away from spine, otherwise clean tight copies. Second Life Books, Inc.   196A - 793   2016 $85

Hilliard, Timothy *A Sermon Delivered December 10 1788 at the Ordination of the Rev. John Andrews to the Care of the First Church and Society in Newburyport.* Newburyport: John Mycall, 1789. First edition, 8vo., self paper wrappers, side sewn binding, 44 pages, half title lightly soiled, ink notations including author's, side sewn binding holds together, loosely, on first three sections, fore-edges and bottoms of leaves with small creases, chips and closed tears.   Oak Knoll Books   310 - 3   2016 $1850

Hillman, Brenda *Coffee. 3 A.M.* Lisbon: Penumbra Press, 1981. Limited to 250 numbered copies, 125 in cloth signed by author and artist, illustrations on title with relief blocks and pochoir by Bonnie P. O'Connell, cloth, illustration to front cover, fore-edge uncut, paper spine label.   Oak Knoll Books   310 - 136   2016 $125

Hillyer, Robert *The Death of Captain nemo.* New York: Knopf, 1949. First edition, 8vo., laid in ALS from author to bookseller Maurice Firusky, May 1949 on Poetry Socetiy of America Stationary, nice in little faded dust jacket.   Second Life Books, Inc.   196A - 794   2016 $45

Hime, Maurice Charles *Efficiency of Irish Schools and their Superiority to English Schools...* London: Simpkin Marshall & Co., 1889. First edition, half title, final ad leaf, original blue cloth slightly dulled, library numbers on spine, booklabel of Library of faculty of Physicians and Surgeons, bookseller's ticket James Maclehose, Glasgow.   Jarndyce Antiquarian Books   CCXV - 734   2016   £45

Himes, Chester *A Case of rape.* New York: Targ, 1980. One of 350 copies, first edition in English, author's signature on colophon, paper over boards with cloth spine, nice in chipped original tissue dust jacket.   Second Life Books, Inc.   196A - 795   2016 $200

Himes, Chester *If He Hollers Let Him Go.* Garden City: Doubleday Doran, 1945. First edition, fine in attractive, very good dust jacket with couple of small internal repairs and bit of soiling and rubbed, better than usual copy, increasingly scarce. Between the Covers Rare Books 207 - 54   2016 $825

Himes, Chester *Lonely Crusade.* New York: Alfred A. Knopf, 1947. First edition, slight stain on rear board, else near fine in attractive, very good dust jacket, long tear on front panel, small chips on rear panel and some modest stains on rear panel, mostly externally invisible. Between the Covers Rare Books   207 - 55   2016 $600

Himes, Chester *La Croisade de Lee Lordon. (Lonely Crusade).* Paris: Correa, 1952. First French edition, pages with little browning, else fine in lightly worn, near fine dust jacket, inscribed by Himes to Michael Fabre, a Sorbonne professor. Between the Covers Rare Books 202 - 41   2016 $2000

Himes, Chester *The Quality of Hurt: the Autobiography of... Volume I.* Garden City: Doubleday, 1972. First edition, 8vo., author' signature on blank, cover bumped at corners, otherwise very good in some worn dust jacket, review copy with slip laid in. Second Life Books, Inc.   196A - 796   2016 $475

Himes, Chester *Rififi No Harlem.* Rio de Janeiro/ Sao Paulo: Distribuidora record, 1965. First Brazilian edition and first edition in Portuguese, illustrated self wrappers, bit of spine sunned and small stain on edge of first few leaves, else near fine, signed by author, very uncommon thus. Between the Covers Rare Books   208 - 104   2016 $500

Himma 3 December 1977. Indianapolis: Ron Bernard, 1977. Oblong octavo, stapled gray decorated wrappers, little rust on staples, else fine, signed by Gerard Malanga, contributor. Between the Covers Rare Books   204 - 70   2016 $150

Hinckley, Mary *Sequel to the Seymour Family or Domestic Scenes.* Boston: Leonard C. Bowles, 1830. First edition, 18mo., engraved frontispiece, contemporary calf backed marbled boards, light foxed, lacking back endpapers. M & S Rare Books, Inc.   99 - 165   2016 $125

Hincliff, Thomas Woodbine *Over the Sea and Far Away.* London: Longman, Green, 1876. First edition, 8vo., 14 illustrations, recent brown half calf, rare, Charles Wheatley's copy. J. & S. L. Bonham Antiquarian Booksellers Voyages 2016 - 9874   2016   £220

Hinde, George Jennings *Catalogue of the Fossil Sponges in the Geological Department of the British Museum (Natural History).* London: British Museum (Natural History), 1883. Quarto, 38 uncolored lithographic plates, publisher's cloth, very good. Andrew Isles Natural History Books   55 - 35490   2016 $250

Hines, J. W. *Touching Incidents in the Life and Labors of a Pioneer on the Pacific Coast Since 1853.* San Jose: Eaton & Co., 1811. First edition, small octavo, 198 pages, frontispiece, brown cloth stamped in dark brown on spine and front cover, some light spotting to lower front cover, else very fine. Argonaut Book Shop   Biography 2015 - 6667   2016 $90

Hingston, R. W. G. *The Meaning of Animal Colour and Adornment.* London: Edward Arnold, 1933. Octavo, text illustrations, bookplate of Roy Cooper, dust jacket. Andrew Isles Natural History Books   55 - 6584   2016 $150

Hinkhouse, F. M. *Levier.* Paris: Editions d'Art des Champs-Elysees, 1961. One of 1500 numbered copies, 4to., author's presentation on title, 3 pieces of promotional material for an exhibition at the Galaxy Gallery in Phoenix AZ laid in, 27 color plates tipped in, cover slightly soiled and scuffed on edges, otherwise very good, tight copy in torn dust jacket. Second Life Books, Inc.   196A - 798   2016 $150

Hippocrates *Aphorismi, Hippocratis et Celsi Locis Parallelis Illustrati....* Paris: Theophilus Barrois, 1784. Scarce edition, woodcut head and tailpieces, Greek and Latin texts, few leaves trifle browned, lacking half title, contemporary French red morocco, wide gilt fillet border on sides with dot at each corner, spine gilt in compartments, dark green lettering piece, gilt inner dentelles, gilt edges, very slight rubbing to corners, choice copy, scarce edition. Blackwell's Rare Books   B186 - 76   2016   £1200

Hippocrates *Coacae Praenotiones.* Paris: Sumptibus Gaspari Maturas, 1658. Folio, title in red and black, light to moderate browning, very good in original calf spine richly gilt with six raised bands. Edwin V. Glaser Rare Books   2015 - 9370   2016 $650

Hird, Lewis A. *The Distinguished Collection of First Editions, Autographs, Manuscripts.* New York: Parke Bernet Galleries, 1953. Vellum spine, marbled boards, brown leather label, very good, excellent collection. Jarndyce Antiquarian Booksellers   CCXVIII - 1504   2016   £20

Hirschfeld, Al *Harlem as Seen by Hirschfeld.* New York: Hyperion Press, 1941. First edition, limited to 1000 numbered copies, this being no. 511, large folio, 6 pages of text by William Saroyan, 24 original lithographic captioned plates, printed on handmade Canson paper, original cream cloth lettered on front cover and spine, with illustration from book reproduced and colored by hand on front cover, spine bit bumped and rubbed, some minor spotting and soiling to cloth, as often seen, else very good, handsome copy, plates, clean and bright.   Heritage Book Shop   Holiday 2015 - 99   2016 $3000

Hirschfeld, Al *Hirschfeld: Art and Recollections from Eight Decades.* New York: Charles Scribner's, 1991. Signed and inscribed by Hirschfeld in year of publication, tight, close to near fine copy in vert good, price clipped dust jacket.   Jeff Hirsch Books   Holiday List 2015 - 10   2016 $150

Hirschhorn, Clive *The Films of James Mason.* London: LSP Books, 1975. 4to., heavily illustrated, signatures of Mason and his second wife Clarissa and Joan Bennet, appearing on their pictures, very good in chipped and soiled dust jacket.   Second Life Books, Inc.   196A - 799   2016 $225

Hirth, Friedrich *China and the Roman Orient Researches into their Ancient and Mediaeval Relations as Presented in old Chinese Records.* Leipsic & Munich: Shanghai & Hong Kong: Georg Hirth/Kelly & Walsh, 1885. First edition, 8vo., original printed wrappers, rebacked, f.f.e.p. and half titlepages present, 2 folding facsimiles of Chinese text and folding map, as issued, original invoice (1894) laid-in, mild soil and edge wear covers, mild scattered foxing.   By the Book, L. C.   45 - 43   2016 $500

Histoire de l'Academie Royale des Sciences avec les Memoires de Mathematique & de Physique. Amsterdam: Pierre de Coup Pierre Morlier, 1715-1735. 12mo. and thick 12mo., 30 volumes, full calf, spines gilt, red morocco spine labels, allegorical frontispiece in each volume, hundreds of full page engravings, many folding, earlier owner's name on title neatly crossed, occasional marginal staining on front pastedowns and flyleaf resulting from overzealous leather treatments, near fine.   Edwin V. Glaser Rare Books   2015 - 10396   2016 $5750

Histoire Veritable et Merveilleuse d'une Jeune Angloise.... Imprime a Physicopolis & se Trouve a Paris chez Lottin, 1772. First edition, A4 with old repair to tear in fore-margin, entering printed area but not affecting text, outer leaves trifle soiled, one or two spots or dust stains, 12mo., modern vellum backed boards, very good.   Blackwell's Rare Books   B186 - 127   2016   £1100

The Historie of Frier Rush: How He Came to a House of Religion to Seeke Service... London: Harding and Wright for Robert Triphook, 1810. One of 4 copies on vellum, contemporary red velvet by H. Faulkner (ticket on verso front flyleaf), covers with wide Greek key border rolled in blind, flat spine with small remnant of leather backstrip (that has been laid on to hide a binder's titling error), red moire silk endleaves, turn-ins and pastedowns with rolls in blind, all edges gilt, housed in very good later leather edged slipcase, woodcut vignette on title, verso to front flyleaf with bookplate of Edward Vernon Utterson and morocco bookplate of Hans Furstenberg, bookplate of John Kershaw, contemporary inked note listing original owner of each of the four vellum copies of the present book, later pencilled note on same "Ths copy was after-wards in the possession of Mr. George Smith and it was (sold in his (s)ale for £9.15.0", spine mostly covered with (glue?) residue left by now basically missing leather backstrip, corners rubbed to board, portions of the joints torn, velvet nap somewhat diminished, a bit of natural rumpling to the vellum, very few inoffensive spots to margins, entirely solid (apart from spine remnants) an agreeable copy of this curious book.   Phillip J. Pirages   67 - 341   2016 $4500

The History of Printing from Its Beginnings to 1930: the Subject Catalouge of the American type Founders company Library in the Columbia University Libraries. Millwood: Kraus reprint, 1980. First edition, 4 volumes, 4to, cloth.   Oak Knoll Books   310 - 186   2016 $399

The History of the House That Jack Built. London: Houlston & Son, n.d. circa, 1820. 24mo., pictorial wrappers, fine, woodcuts.   Aleph-bet Books, Inc.   111 - 147   2016 $350

Hitchcock, Alfred *Rope - the Book of the Film (and) Under Capricorn - Photo Preview.* London: Word Film Pub., 1948. First edition, octavo, pictorial wrappers, covers bit dusty, very good.   Peter Ellis   112 - 170   2016   £25

Hitchens, Robert *The Near East: Dalmatia, Greece and Constantinople.* New York: Century Co., 1913. First edition, 8vo., illustrations, original blue decorative cloth.   J. & S. L. Bonham Antiquarian Booksellers   Europe 2016 - 8706   2016   £45

Hively, William *Nine Classic California Photographers.* Berkeley: Friends of the Bancroft Library, 1980. First edition, photos, 10 plates, stiff printed black wrappers, fine.   Argonaut Book Shop   Photography 2015 - 2477   2016 $45

Hoadly, Benjamin *The Suspicious Husband.* London: printed for and sold by W. Oxlade, 1777. 12mo., disbound, a piracy.   Jarndyce Antiquarian Booksellers   CCXVI - 462   2016   £50

Hoagland, Richard C. *The Breakthroughs of Cydonia.* N.P.: privately printed, 1991. First edition, very good, printed on cheap paper with melon colored covers which are slightly faded, 8 1/4 x 10 3/4 inch booklet, photos, diagrams, drawings, minor creasing but no abrasions, 2 very short edge tears to front cover, no chips, very good used condition.   Gene W. Baade, Books on the West   2015 - SHEL663   2016 $359

Hoare, Louisa *Hints for the Improvement of Early education and Nursery Discipline.*   London: J. Hatchard & Son, 1841. Fourteenth edition, original blue grey cloth, spine faded and slightly rubbed, 2 small ink marks, inscription Diana Smyth 23 Wilton Place, May 1844, nice.   Jarndyce Antiquarian Books   CCXV - 235   2016   £45

Hoare, Louisa *Hints for the Improvement of Early Education and Nursery Discipline.*   London: Thomas Hatchard, 1853. 16th edition, 32 page catalog, June 1858, original purple cloth, faded, spine slightly bubbled.   Jarndyce Antiquarian Books   CCXV - 736   2016   £35

Hoban, Russell *Mouse and His Child.*   New York: Harper & Row, 1967. First edition, (correct price, which must be present to determine edition), pictorial cloth, fine in dust jacket with price intact, dust jacket rubbed on corners, light soil to rear panel, very good, illustrations by Lillian Hoban.   Aleph-bet Books, Inc.   111 - 219   2016 $600

Hobson, Charles *Dancing with Amelia: Amelia Earhart's Six Years of Marriage...*   San Francisco: Pacific Editions, 2000. Limited to 38 numbered copies signed by Hobson, small 8vo., laser cut 8-ply cover over blue cloth, gray cloth covered chemise, gray ribbon ties, accordion fold.   Oak Knoll Books   27 - 48   2016 $1750

Hobson, Fred *Mencken: a Life.*   New York: Random House, 1994. First edition, gilt lettered black cloth backed boards, very fine in pictorial dust jacket.   Argonaut Book Shop   Literature 2015 - 5027   2016 $50

Hobson, Geoffrey Dudley *English Binding Before 1500. the Sandars Lectures 1927.*   Cambridge: Cambridge University Press, 1929. Limited to 500 copies, folio, title vignette, illustrations, 55 plates, original blue cloth, printed dust jacket, top edge gilt, jacket extremities torn with loss (to edges), preserved with original 4 page prospectus plus added copy of plate 39.   Jeff Weber Rare Books   181 - 61   2016 $325

Hobson, Geoffrey Dudley *English Binding Before 1500.*   Cambridge: Cambridge University Press, 1929. Limited to 500 copies, folio, cloth, top edge gilt, 55 full page plates, minor rubbing, scarce.   Oak Knoll Books   310 - 16   2016 $325

Hoch, Edward D. *Best Detective Stories of the Year 1978.*   New York: Dutton, 1978. First edition, fine, inscription, otherwise fine in dust jacket.   Mordida Books   2015 - 012507   2016 $65

Hocking, Anne *A Reason for Murder.*   London: W. H. Allen, 1955. Red cloth, gilt, slightly aged & frayed dust jacket, endpapers slightly age marked, edges lightly spotted, not affecting text, uncommon title.   I. D. Edrich   Crime - 2016   £25

Hoddinott, R. F. *The Thracians.*   London: Thames and Hudson, 1981. First edition, 8vo., 168 illustrations, red cloth, gilt, near fine, dust jacket with few tears, some with loss ot corners and edges, couple of creases, price sticker adhered to rear, good copy.   Unsworths Antiquarian Booksellers Ltd.   E04 - 58   2016   £20

Hodgdon, Moses *The Complete Justice of the Peace, Containing Extracts from Burn's Justice and Other Justiciary Productions....*   Dover: Charles Peirce, Nov., 1806. First edition, 8vo., recent calf backed cloth, label.   M & S Rare Books, Inc.   99 - 145   2016 $225

Hodges, C. E. *Little Plays from Dickens.*   London: Evans Bros., 1916. Original grey printed wrappers, spine gilt at head and tail, stitching slightly loose, ownership details on initial blank.   Jarndyce Antiquarian Booksellers   CCXVIII - 736   2016   £20

Hodges, Margaret *The Kitchen Knight: a Tale of King Arthur.*   New York: Holiday House, 1990. Stated first edition, cloth backed boards, fine in fine dust jacket, beautiful color illustrations by Hyman, this copy signed by artist.   Aleph-bet Books, Inc.   111 - 223   2016 $275

Hodges, Margaret *Saint George and the Dragon, retold by...*   Boston: Little Brown, 1984. Stated first edition, first printing designated on jacket flap but no "1" in the number line, cloth, fine in dust jacket with no award medal, illustrations by Trina Hyman.   Aleph-bet Books, Inc.   112 - 256   2016 $250

Hodgkin, John *Calligraphia Graeca et Poecilographia Graeca.*   n.p., 1794-1807. Engraved titlepage, dedication and 17 other engraved plates, plates toned and somewhat spotted, letterpress more heavily spotted, ownership inscription of Thomas Jessop to titlepage, folio, contemporary quarter red roan, marbled boards, spine lettered vertically in gilt, front binder's blank with hand lettered 'half title' reading 'Poikilographia Ellenika' in Greek alphabet, followed by reference to discussion of the work in the Classical Journal, rubbed, some light wear to extremities, ownership stamp of Grace Richardson to endpaper, good.   Blackwell's Rare Books   Greek & Latin Classics VII - 27   2016   £800

Hodgman, Carolyn *How Santa Filled the Christmas Stockings.* Rochester: Stecher Litho. Co., 1916. Folio, flexible pictorial card covers, very good-fine, beautiful color lithos by W. F. Stecher.   Aleph-bet Books, Inc.   111 - 92   2016 $200

Hodgson, Isaac *A Practical English Grammar for the Use of Schools and Private Gentlemen and Ladies...* London: printed for B. Law & J. Linden & J. Wise, Southampton, 1777. New edition, 12mo., few smallink marks, slight tear to lower corner of final leaf, lacking f.e.p.s, original hessian-cloth, little marked and worn.   Jarndyce Antiquarian Books   CCXV - 737   2016   £120

Hodgson, W. B. *Exaggerated Estimates of reading and writing...* London: W. W. Head, 1868. One ink correction, stabbed as issued.   Jarndyce Antiquarian Books   CCXV - 738   2016   £20

Hodson, W. *Hodson's Self Instructing Copy Book.* London: W. Hodson, circa, 1860. Engraved head lines partially completed in ink and pencil, 7 leaves without ms., original orange illustrated printed paper wrappers, wrappers sewn as issued, inscription "Charles Rayner, Schoolmistress, Miss A. B. Rayner, Wallinton, Herts".   Jarndyce Antiquarian Books   CCXV - 739   2016   £30

Hoefer, M. Le *Nouvelle Viographie Generale Depuis Les Temps Les Plus Recules Jusqu'a Nos Joures Avec Les Renneignements Bibliographiques Et L'Indication des Sources a Consulter.* Copenhague: Rosenkilde et Bagger, 1963. Reprint of original, 46 volumes bound in 23, 8vo., cloth.   Oak Knoll Books   310 - 292   2016 $775

Hoffer, Johann *Icones Catecheseos, et Virtutum ac Uitiorum Illusrtatae Numeris...* Wittenberg: Johannes Crato, 1558. Small 8vo., fine device on titlepage and larger version on recto of final leaf, 77 half page woodcuts by Jakob Lucius?, late 19th century brown morocco by Riviere & Son, covers panelled in blind, spine lettered gilt, gilt edges, bookplate of Samuel Ashton Thompson-Yates, 1894.   Maggs Bros. Ltd.   1474 - 41   2016   £2500

Hoffman, Alice *Turtle Moon.* Franklin Center: Franklin Library, 1992. Limited first edition, signed by author, bound in tan leather lettered and decoratively stamped in gilt, all edges gilt, very fine, as new.   Argonaut Book Shop   Literature 2015 - 3976   2016 $50

Hoffman, Daniel *An Armada of Thirty Whales.* New Haven: Yale, 1954. First edition, 8vo., author's presentation opposite title to poet William Claire, paper over boards, first book scarce, edges little spotted, otherwise very good tight in somewhat soiled and little chipped dust jacket with corner of front flap torn off.   Second Life Books, Inc.   196A - 803   2016 $75

Hoffman, Daniel *An Armada of thirty Whales.* New Haven: Yale University Press, 1954. First edition, inscribed by author for William Meredith, with small original color photo of Meredith with little girl annotated on rear by Hoffman, with ALS from Hoffman to Meredith on postcard, fine in lightly soiled, near fine dust jacket with tanned spine.   Charles Agvent   William Meredith - 47   2016 $350

Hoffman, Daniel *Brotherly Love.* New York: Vintage/Random House, 1981. 8vo., several illustrations, paper wrappers, author's signature on title, cover little scuffed and creased, otherwise very good, tight copy.   Second Life Books, Inc.   196A - 805   2016 $75

Hoffman, Daniel *The Center of Attention.* New York: Random House, 1974. First edition, 8vo., author's presentation verso of half title, black cloth, top edges slightly spotted, otherwise nice in price clipped, very slightly chipped and yellowed dust jacket.   Second Life Books, Inc.   196A - 806   2016 $50

Hoffman, Daniel *The City of Satisfaction.* New York: Oxford University Press, 1963. First edition, fine in near fine dust jacket with sunned spine, inscribed by author for William Meredith.   Charles Agvent   William Meredith - 48   2016 $50

Hoffman, Daniel *A Little Geste and Other Poems.* New York: Oxford University Press, 1958. First edition, inscribed and signed by author April 75 for William Meredith, fine in near fine dust jacket with tanned spine.   Charles Agvent   William Meredith - 49   2016 $50

Hoffman, Daniel *A Little Geste; and other poems.* New York: Oxford, 1960. 8vo., author's presentation to poet William Claire, signed under crossed-out author's name, green cloth, edges slightly soiled, corners of cover little rubbed, otherwise very good, tight copy in little chipped and soiled dust jacket.   Second Life Books, Inc.   196A - 804   2016 $75

Hoffman, Daniel *Striking the Stones: Poems.* New York: Oxford, 1968. 8vo., author's name crossed out and 'Dan' written below and presentation to William Claire, from author, light yellow cloth, top edges of leaves and edges of cover slightly soiled, very good, tight in little chipped and soiled dust jacket.   Second Life Books, Inc.   196A - 807   2016 $45

Hoffman, J. W. *Cyclopaedia of Foods condiments and beverages.* London: Simpkin Marshall & Co., 1890. First edition, half title, original brick brown cloth, blocked in black and gilt, little rubbed.   Jarndyce Antiquarian Books   CCXV - 255   2016   £85

Hoffman, Malvina *Heads and Tales.* New York: Scribners, 1936. First edition, 8vo., 416 pages, illustrations, signed by author on half title, no dust jacket, bookplate, nice. Second Life Books, Inc. 196A - 808 2016 $45

Hoffmann-Donner, Heinrich 1809-1894 *English Struwwelpeter...* Leipsic: Friedruch Volckmar, 1848. First edition in English, 4to., original decorative boards with vignette on rear cover, recased with new spine, old endpapers, tear on titlepage repaired, some soiling throughout, paper on cover is worn off on corners and edges, overall very good. Aleph-bet Books, Inc. 112 - 243 2016 $25,000

Hofner, Carl *Seinen Gonern Und Theatrefreunden in... Dresden Empfiehlt Sich Mit Den Worten des Abschieds Beim....* Dresden: for the author, circa, 1830. 4to., decorative border to titlepage, early reinforcement to backstrip, mild foxing, soft horizontal crease. Dramatis Personae 119 - 70 2016 $425

Hogarth, George *Memoirs of the Musical Drama.* London: Richard Bentley, 1838. First edition, half title, frontispiece, portraits, final ad leaf volume I, more recent half green cloth, black leather labels, very good. Jarndyce Antiquarian Booksellers CCXVIII - 883 2016 £150

Hogarth, William 1697-1764 *The Complete Works.* London and New York: London Printing and Pub. Co. Ltd., 1861. New and revised edition, 324 x 241mm., extremely attractive contemporary crimson pebble grain morocco, elaborately blindstamped and gilt, covers with gilt oval framed vignette of Hogarth at center, raised bands flanked by decorative gilt rolls, spine panels with central gilt lozenge or gilt titling, gilt turn-ins, all edges gilt, 150 attractive steel engravings on 146 plates, all with guards, trivial pale blotchy fox spots here and there, otherwise a beautiful copy, hefty decorative binding, virtually unworn and text and plates showing no perceptible signs of use. Phillip J. Pirages 67 - 196 2016 $1000

Hogg, James *The Business Man's Note Book for the Year 1856.* Edinburgh: James Hogg; London: R. Groombridge and Son, end of Dec., 1855. 12mo., 5 folding outline maps, original maroon roan, upper cover with neat guide to locating dates in year and ruler blocked in gilt, inside cover with gilt metal circular volvelle perpetual calendar, rear joint repaired, rare. Marlborough Rare Books List 55 - 37 2016 £225

Hoggson, Thomas *The Squire's Home-Made Wines...* London: printed by Prynson, 1924. Small 4to., uncut, original paper boards, hinges worn, flyer tipped on to leading pastedown. Jarndyce Antiquarian Books CCXV - 378 2016 £20

Holbach, Paul Von, Baron *Histoire Critique de Jesus-Christ, ou, Analyse Raisonnee des Evangiles.* N.P. (Amsterdam): n.p. (Marc-Michel Rey), 1770. First edition, wrapped in old, multi-colored paper cover with floral design, paper has the pattern and impression showing through on back side and it looks very much like piece of wallpaper, titlepage browned along right edge, suggesting the book at one time had another cover, small part of titlepage missing along upper, inside gutter (no loss of text), someone has written '1872' at bottom titlepage, completely uncut, despite rather garish wrappers, this copy very nice. Athena Rare Books List 15 - 1770 2016 $750

Holbein, Hans *Icones Historiarum Veteris Testaementi.* Lyon: Jean Frellan, 1547. Fifth edition, small quarto, modern full dark brown morocco gilt, printer's device on titlepage, two woodcut initials, 94 woodcut after designs by Holbein, four later woodcuts by unknown hand, text in Latin and French, near fine. Honey & Wax Booksellers 4 - 46 2016 $10,000

Holbein, Hans *Les Images de la Mort, aux Quelles Saint Adioustees Douze Figures.* Lyon: Jean Freelon, 1547. Third edition in French, seventh edition overall, small octavo, modern full black morocco, printer's device on titlepage, woodcut initials throughout text, 53 woodcuts after designs by Holbein, bookplate and owner signatures of 19th century collector Elias Harry Frost, text in French, near fine. Honey & Wax Booksellers 4 - 47 2016 $17,500

Holbein, Hans *Le Triomphe De La Mort.* Paris: Simon Racon et Comp. 1780 (but mid 19th century), 146 x 114mm., very pleasing 19th century maroon crushed morocco, Jansenist, by Cape Masson-Debonnelle (stamp signed), covers with central gilt skull with crossbone cornerpieces, raised bands, spine panels alternating gilt skull and crossbones, gilt titling densely gilt turn-ins, marbled endpapers, al edges gilt, fine black quarter morocco folding box, with 47 copper engravings by Christian Von Mechel, 46 of these after original designs of Holbein, one (double page plate) added by Mechel, quarter inch at top of front joint, bit rubbed, occasional faint offsetting from plates, otherwise very fine, especially clean, fresh and bright internally with rich impressions of the plates in lustrous, essentially unworn. Phillip J. Pirages 67 - 109 2016 $4500

Holberg, Ludvig, Baron *Voyage de Nicolas Limius dans le Monde Souterrain Contenant une Nouvelle Teorie de la Terre et l'"histoire d'une Clinquieme Monarchie Inconnue Jusqu'a present.* Copenhagen: Jacob Preuss, 1741. 8vo., title printed in red and black, engraved frontispiece, folding map, 2 plates, uniformly slightly browned, 8vo., contemporary Scandinavian calf, spine decorated in blind, tan lettering piece, little rubbed, headcap defective, contemporary ownership inscription on title, good. Blackwell's Rare Books B184 - 50 2016 £3000

Holden, William Curry *The Spur Ranch. A Study of the Inclosed Ranch Phase of the Cattle Industry in Texas.* Boston: Christopher Pub. Co., 1934. First edition, 8vo., inscribed by author, cloth, fine, bright, tight copy, lacking original glassine dust jacket, very scarce.   Buckingham Books   2015 - 32584   2016 $450

Holdsworth, William *A History of English Law.* London: Methuen, 1924-1972. Mixed editions, 17 volume set, some first editions, mostly later printings, original blue cloth lettered gilt at spin, all books very good, 3 volumes have slight fading to cloth, occasional slight tape marks at endpapers in few volumes, later volumes near fine.   Any Amount of Books   2015 - A99410   2016   £600

The Holkham Bible. London: Folio Society, 2007. Limited, numbered edition of 1750 copies, with 25 lettered copies not for sale also printed, 4to., facsimile volume, half leather, decorated cloth, gilt decoration with raised bands on spine, companion volume quarter cloth, paper covered boards, label on front board, decorated clamshell box.   Oak Knoll Books   310 - 102   2016 $460

Holland, Henry *Travels in the Ionian Isles, Albania, Thessaly, Macedonia, et. During the Years 1812 and 1813.* London: Longman, Hurst, 1815. First edition, quarto, 12 plates, occasional foxing, contemporary half calf, corners and spine rubbed, split at head of spine.   J. & S. L. Bonham Antiquarian Booksellers   Europe 2016 - 8823   2016   £650

Holland, J. G. *Lessons in Life: a Series of Familiar Essays.* New York: Charles Scribner, 1861. 8vo., author's presentation, cover little worn, otherwise nice and tight.   Second Life Books, Inc.   196A - 809   2016 $45

Holland, James R. *Tanglewood.* Barre: Barre Pub., 1973. First edition, small 4to., printed wrappers, photos, signed by composer Aaron Copeland, very good+.   Second Life Books, Inc.   196A - 810   2016 $250

Holland, Rupert Sargent *Pirates of the Delaware.* Philadelphia: Lippincott, 1925. First edition, author's presentation to poet Barbara Howes, cream cloth, pictorial stamping in dark blue, edges slightly spotted, cover somewhat scuffed and soiled, spine little worn at ends, else very good, tight copy.   Second Life Books, Inc.   196A - 811   2016 $65

Hollander, Bernard *Abnormal Children.* London: Kegan Paul, Trench & Trubner, 1916. First edition, half title, plates, original blue cloth, slightly rubbed.   Jarndyce Antiquarian Books   CCXV - 740   2016   £25

Hollander, Bernard *Abnormal Children.* London: Kegan Paul, Treach & Trubner & Co., 1916. Second edition, original blue cloth, boards marked by damp, booklabels of Leage Library. Jarndyce Antiquarian Books   CCXV - 741   2016   £20

Hollander, John *A Book of Various Owls.* New York: W. W. Norton, 1963. Stated first edition, pictorial boards, near fine in very good+ dust jacket with light rubbing, illustrations by Tomi Ungerer, very scarce in jacket.   Aleph-bet Books, Inc.   112 - 488   2016 $200

Hollander, John *A Crackling of Thorns.* New Haven: Yale University Press, 1958. First edition, inscribed and signed by poet for William Meredith, May 1958, near fine in very good dust jacket.   Charles Agvent   William Meredith - 50   2016 $200

Hollander, John *Movie-going and Other Poems.* New York: Atheneum, 1962. First edition, wrapper issue, inscribed and signed by author for William Meredith, near fine.   Charles Agvent William Meredith - 51   2016 $80

Hollander, John *Reflections on Espionage. The Question of Cupcake.* New York: Atheneum, 1976. First edition, inscribed and signed by author for William Meredith, fine in near fine dust jacket.   Charles Agvent   William Meredith - 53   2016 $80

Hollander, John *Tales Told of the Fathers. Poems.* New York: Atheneum, 1975. First edition, inscribed by author for William Meredith, fine in near fine dust jacket.   Charles Agvent William Meredith - 54   2016 $100

Holldobler, Bert *The Ants.* Cambridge: Belknap Press, 1990. Quarto, illustrations, inscription, fine, dust jacket.   Andrew Isles Natural History Books   55 - 24545   2016 $250

Holling, Holling C. *Claws of the Thunderbird.* Joliet: Volland, 1928. First edition, 8vo., cloth, cover faded, slight wear to spine ends, bold full page and in text color illustrations plus black and whites.   Aleph-bet Books, Inc.   111 - 220   2016 $150

Hollinghurst, Alan *The Line of Beauty.* London: Picador, 2004. First edition, fine in near fine dust jacket, light creasing to top edge.   Bella Luna Books   2016 - t7634   2016 $66

Hollinshead, John *Hints to Country Gentlemen and Farmers on the Importance of Using Salt as a General Manure.* Blackburn: printed by Hemingway and Crook, 1800. Second edition, titlepage little soiled and with library blindstamp in lower margin, efficiently bound fairly recently in marbled boards with printed paper spine label, rare.   John Drury Rare Books   2015 - 20996   2016 $306

Holloway, William *The Baron of Lauderbrooke.* printed by T. Maiden for Ann Lemoine and sold by T. Hunt, 1800. First edition, rare, additional engraved title, engraved frontispiece, uniformly slightly browned, few spots, contemporary tree calf, spine gilt, black lettering piece, joints cracked, corners worn, sound.   Blackwell's Rare Books   B184 - 51   2016   £2000

Holman, John P. *Sheep and Bear Trails: a Hunter's Wanderings in Alaska and British Columbia.* New York: Frank Walters, 1933. 8vo., original dark blue cloth, titled gilt on spine and upper cover, upper cover with centrally placed gilt vignette, original dust jacket, photo frontispiece, 42 other photographic plates on 23 leaves, dust jacket little creased to bottom of front panel, near fine.   Sotheran's Piccadilly Notes - Summer 2015 - 165   2016   £450

Holman, Shireen *Time.* Montgomery Village: Shireen Holman, 2013. Number 15 of 20 copies, signed and numbered by artist, complex artist's book, finished book consists of woodcuts printed onto pulp-painted handmade paper, text was letterpress printed on gampi paper and then pasted onto handmade sheets, pages folded in such a way that one can see little of each of the subsequent pages from the current page, thus from beginning to end of the book one can see a little of the future from the present, each page has semicircular areas cut out so that the calendar at bottom right of the colophon page is visible at all times, housed in cream paper clamshell box witt title "Time" in raised letters affixed vertically to cover, linen spine, fine, accompanied by softcover book titled "The making of the Artist Book 'Time' ", fine.   The Kelmscott Bookshop   13 - 23   2016 $2000

Holmes, Oliver Wendell   1809-1894 *Boylston Prize Dissertations for the Years 1836 and 1837.* Boston: Charles C. Little and James Brown, 1838. First edition, octavo, folding map frontispiece with state borders outlined by hand in colors, brown ribbon embossed cloth (oak-leaf and acorn pattern), gilt spine title, couple of short closed tears at spinal extremities and few scattered spots of light foxing in text, lovely near fine, this copy inscribed by author to William Hussey Page, Boston physician.   Between the Covers Rare Books   208 - 39   2016 $4950

Holmes, Oliver Wendell   1809-1894 *Dorothy Q. Together with A Ballad of the Boston Tea Party & Grandmother's Story of Bunker Hill Battle.* Cambridge: printed at the Riverside Press, 1893. Edition deluxe, one of 250 copies, first edition, first issue with 'flashed' instead of 'dashed' on page 50 line 8, this being #119, small octavo, frontispiece and 61 illustrations by Howard Pyle, text leaves with decorations in red, publisher's yapp edged vellum, covers decorated gilt, top edge gilt, original silk ties, minimal soiling to vellum otherwise fine.   David Brass Rare Books, Inc.   2015 - 02962   2016 $350

Holmes, Oliver Wendell   1809-1894 *John Lothrop Motley: a Memoir.* Boston: Houghton, Osgood and Co., 1879. First US edition, large 8vo., original orange cloth lettered gilt on spine and on front cover, signed presentation from author to Countess of Minto, slight mottled and very slight rubbing, else clean, very good+.   Any Amount of Books   2015 - C12763   2016   £170

Holt, Francis Ludlow *The Law of Libel; in Which is Contained a General History of this Law in the Ancient Codes and of Its Introduction and Successive Alterations in Law of England.* London: J. Butterworth and Son and J. Cooke, Dublin, 1816. First American edition, large 8vo., old library inkstamp on blank verso of title, repeated at lower margin of final leaf, reboundf recently in workmanlike but unsympathetic half cloth over marbled boards, spine lettered gilt, nonetheless, good fresh copy.   John Drury Rare Books   2015 - 24105   2016 $350

Holt, Gavin *Send No Flowers.* New York: Howell Soskin, 1947. First American edition, pages darkened, otherwise fine in dust jacket.   Mordida Books   2015 - 012065   2016 $65

Holt, Gavin *Tonight if for Death.* London: Hodder & Stoughton, 1952. Red boards little marked and aged in slightly grubby, frayed and torn dust jacket, edge foxing not affecting text, contents very good, uncommon title.   I. D. Edrich   Crime - 2016   £30

Holyoake, George Jacob *The Jubilee History of the Leeds Industrial Co-Operative Society from 1847 to 1897.* Leeds: Central Cooperative Offices, 1897. First edition, 8vo., publisher's cloth somewhat worn, spine lacking cloth at extremities, corporate library bookplate, inscribed for friend Dr. Hollrik (sp?), good copy, large foldout map of the ity of Leeds with stores run by Industrial Society noted, photos.   Second Life Books, Inc.   196A - 812   2016 $65

Holyroyd, Michael *Bernard Shaw.* New York: Random House, 1988. First American edition, cloth backed boards, minor fading and a bit of rubbing, fine set in pictorial dust jackets. Argonaut Book Shop   Literature 2015 - 5522   2016 $120

Holzenberg, Eric *Three Gold Bezants, Three Silver Stars; the Arms of the Grolier Club 1884-1984.* New York: Grolier Club, 1999. Limited to 240 copies, 22 illustrations, many printed from original blocks, three tipped in bookplates, hardcover.   Oak Knoll Books   310 - 209   2016 $100

Holzworth, John M. *The Wild Grizzlies of Alaska.* New York: G. P. Putnam's Sons, 1930. First edition, frontispiece, 94 photogravure plates, endpaper map, rust pictorial cloth stamped in black, spine ever so slightly faded but fine, clean and tight.   Argonaut Book Shop   Natural History 2015 - 6482   2016 $150

Homans, J. Smith *The Banker's Common Place Book....* New York: Office of the Banker's Magazine, 1870. 8vo., original cloth, discoloration from old offset on title and flyleaf. M & S Rare Books, Inc.   99 - 20   2016 $500

A Home for Hominstructs. New York: High Tide Press, 1996. Limited to 15 numbered copies signed by John Ross, folio, tan cloth portfolio box with magnetized covers that opening the middle, two front boards each have two recesses with matching wood veneer and two flat knobs, giving effect of a cupboard with opening front doors, boxing made by James DeMarcantonio, text printed from Linotype Helvetica on Vandercook proofing press, with display letters from wood type printed on Coventry paper, book cut paper accordion that folds into a 3-D house.   Oak Knoll Books   27 - 26   2016 $2000

The Homeric Hymn to Aphrodite. London: Golden Cockerel Press, 1948. Limited to 750 numbered copies, this one of 100 specially bound numbered copies, signed by translator, 10 engravings, including frontispiece by Mark Severin, full red leather, covers and spine gilt stamped, top edge gilt, other edges uncut, two raised bands on spine, slipcase scuffed at corners.   Oak Knoll Books   310 - 104   2016 $1200

Homerus *Ilias (and) Odyssea. Batrachomyomachia. Hymni XXXII. Eorundem Multiplex Lectio.*   Venice: in officina Lucaeantonii Iuntae, 1537. 8vo., woodcut device with initials "LA on titlepages, some light spotting, titlepage and last page dusty in each volume, second gathering in third section either misbound or misnumbered (but all there), late 18th century red morocco boards, bordered with gilt fillet, spine divided by dotted gilt rules, second and third compartments, gilt lettered direct, rest with small central flower tools, marbled endpapers, edges red, just little rubbed, spines slightly sunned, very good, the Chatsworth copy. Blackwell's Rare Books   Greek & Latin Classics VII - 33   2016   £5000

Homerus *The Iliad of Homer.* London: printed by W. Bowyer for Bernard Lintott, 1715-1720. First edition translated by Alexander Pope, folio, plates and maps, period full paneled calf, bindings with spine labels to volumes 1, 5 and 6 only, personal owner gilt stamped name ("I. Phelipps Y", label to volume 6 chipped, some wear to spines and joints tender though bindings overall sound and quite appealing, minor worming to margins of volumes 1, 3, 5 and 6, some gatherings little browned as often found, short tear to volume II f.f.e.p., period personal ownership signature to front free endpapers, withal very good set.   Tavistock Books   Bibliolatry - 16   2016 $7500

Homerus *The Iliad. (with) The Odyssey.* London: printed by W. Bowyer for Bernard Lintott, 1715-1726. First editions translated by Alexander Pope, 11 volumes bound as 6, large paper copies, titlepages of Odyssey printed in red and black, with all plates except Troy plate (often missing), double page map hand colored in outline, some spotting in volume iii of the Iliad, less in v, worming in lower margins of iv of Odyssey extending slightly into v, no loss of text, one or two other minor faults, sporadic minor dust staining in upper margins, staining to 2 leaves in postscript to Odyssey, folio, uniform contemporary mottled calf, spines richly gilt in compartments, tan lettering pieces, some joints cracked, some wear, engraved bookplate of Thomas Edwards Freeman in most volumes (removed from others), good.   Blackwell's Rare Books   Marks of Genius - 38   2016   £6000

Homerus *The Iliad of Homer. (with) The Odyssey of Homer.* London: printed for J. Whiston &c., 1771. 1771, Iliad in 4 volumes, Odyssey in 5 volumes, together 9 volumes, engraved portraits, 2 plates, 2 folding maps, folding plate uniformly bound in slightly later full sprinkled calf, spines gilt in compartments, maroon and green morocco labels, armorial bookplate in all volumes of Elizabeth Bell, very good, attractive set, fine in 18th century binding. Jarndyce Antiquarian Booksellers   CCXVII - 232   2016   £4250

Homerus *Ilias. Graece et Latine.* London: Impensis J. F. & C. Rivington et al, 1790. 8vo., 2 folding engraved maps, little minor spotting, ownership inscriptions, contemporary biscuit calf, boards bordered with gilt fillet, spines divided by raised bands between gilt fillets, green morocco lettering pieces, extremities rubbed, slight wear to foot of volume i spine, good.   Blackwell's Rare Books   Greek & Latin Classics VII - 36   2016   £100

Homerus *Ilias kai Odysseia.* Oxonia: ex Ergasteriou Typographikou Akademias, 1800. One of the rare and spectacular copies of the Grenville Homer, only 25 copies printed and used as presentation copies, inscribed by editors, William Wyndham, Lord Grenville and his brother Thomas Grenville, 4to., 5 engraved plates, plates spotted, some light offsetting to text, contemporary red morocco, boards with central gilt stamp, arms of the Earl of Cawdor, spines lettered gilt, red morocco doublures with border of fourteen gilt fillets, edges gilt on rough, spines unned, touch of rubbing to extremities, doublures offset onto endpapers and outermost leaves of each volume, very good. Blackwell's Rare Books   Greek & Latin Classics VII - 37   2016   £12,000

Homerus *Ilias cum brevi annotatione curante C. G. Heyne. (with) Odyssea cum scholiis veteribus Accedunt Batrachomyomachia, Hymni, Fragmenta. (and) C. G. Henii Excursus in Homerum ....* Oxford: e typographeo Clarendoniano, 1821-1827. Large paper copies, 252mm. tall, some spotting and foxing, large 8vo., uniformly bound in later vellum over wooden boards, spines lettered in black and red, marbled endpapers, top edge gilt, others untrimmed, vellum soiled, front boards with gift inscription in initial blank in volume i, very good.   Blackwell's Rare Books   Greek & Latin Classics VII - 38   2016   £250

Homerus *Iliad.* London: printed for F. C. and J. Rivington, 1822. 12mo., frontispiece and additional engraved titlepage plates little stained, few spots of foxing, but internally bright and clean overall, dark green sheep, burgundy gilt label to spine, raised bands, marbled edges, rubbed, color little faded in places, but good, sound copy.   Unsworths Antiquarian Booksellers Ltd.   E05 - 37   2016   £40

Homerus *Ilias. (and) Odysseia.* London: Gulielmus Pickering, 1831. engraved in volume i (dampmarked as often), bit of minor spotting elsewhere, 32mo., contemporary stiff vellum, boards bordered with gilt fillet, red morocco lettering pieces, marbled endpapers, labels bit chipped, some cracking to hinges and boards splayed outward slightly good.   Blackwell's Rare Books   Greek & Latin Classics VII - 40   2016   £100

Homerus *Illias.* Leipzig: sumptibus Ottonis Holtze, 1876. 12mo., slightly toned towards edges, occasional light foxing, half brown sheep, textured cloth boards, gilt spines, marbled edges and endpapers, rubbed, joints and corners worn, but handsome little set.   Unsworths Antiquarian Booksellers Ltd.   E05 - 38   2016   £30

Homerus *The Odyssey of Homer.* London: printed for Bernard Lintot, 1725. First Pope edition, folio, 5 volumes in 3, each volume with separate titlepage printed in red and black, volume i with engraved vignette on titlepage, each of the volumes with half title which is printed on recto and dedication printed on verso, bound with the frontispiece portrait which is found inserted into some copies, numerous historiated initials an elaborate head and tailpieces, uniformly bound in contemporary marbled boards, handsomely rebacked and recornered in half modern calf, spines each with red and black spine label, spines stamped and lettered gilt, boards rubbed and somewhat worn, inner hinges of all volumes professionally repaired, some toning and staining to endpapers, internally quite clean, overall very good set.   Heritage Book Shop   Holiday 2015 - 54   2016 $5000

Homerus *The Odyssey of Homer.* London: printed for John Bell, 1774. 2 volumes, some light spotting, later ownership inscription of Thomas Hutchinson of St. John's College to titlepages (possibly the vicar of Kimbolton and nephew of William Wordsworth), 8vo., contemporary sprinkled sheep, rubbed and worn, red and green morocco lettering pieces to volume i (lost from volume ii), joints cracking, sound, rare.   Blackwell's Rare Books   Greek & Latin Classics VII - 35   2016   £400

Homerus *The Odyssey of Homer.* London: printed for C. and J. Rivington (and 16 other firms), 1823. 12mo., additional engraved titlepage and frontispiece, untrimmed in original printed boards, front board replicating the titlepage and rear board, rubbed, some wear to extremities, ownership inscription of H. Murray dated 1844 on front pastedown, good, scarce in original boards.   Blackwell's Rare Books   Greek & Latin Classics VII - 39   2016   £150

Homerus *The Odyssey of Homer.* Boston: Houghton Mifflin, 1929. Limited to 550 numbered copies signed by author and artist, 4to., blue gilt pictorial cloth backed with pigskin and leather label, spine with some soil, else near fine (no extra plates), illustrations by N. C. Wyeth.   Alephbet Books, Inc.   111 - 494   2016 $2000

Homerus *The Odyssey.* Garden City: Anchor Press/ Doubleday, 1961. Reprint, illustrations by Hans Erni, inscribed and signed by translator Robert Fitzgerald for William Meredith in 1979, also inscribed in Greek and signed by folk singer Richard Dyer-Bennet, laid in is ticket and program to a Library of Congress event presenting Dyer-Bennet premier, fine in close ot fine dust jacket.   Charles Agvent   William Meredith - 55   2016 $100

Homerus *The Odyssey of Homer.* New York: Limited Editions Club, 1981. 740/2000 copies, signed by Barry Moser, the artist, and Jeremy Wilson, who provided preface, frontispiece and 24 further full page wood engravings, royal 8vo., original olive cloth, stamped in red, slipcase, fine.   Blackwell's Rare Books   B184 - 283   2016   £100

Homerus *The Iliads of Homer Prince of Poets (with) Homer's Odysses. (with) The Crowne of all Homers Worckes Batrachomyonmachia or the Battaile of Frogs and Mise...* London: printed (by Richard Field) for Nathaniel Butter, 1611-1615. Worckes - London: printed by Iohn Bill, 1624. First Complete edition in English of first two works, first edition in English of third, titlepage engraved (some expert repair work around outer edges), inner edge just disappearing into gutter, initial blank discarded, final blank present, additional leaves of sonnets bound in prelims, some dust soiling and marks; titlepage engraved (some expert repair work around edges), initial and final blanks discarded, Y2 slightly shorter and probably supplied, little marginal worming in second half expertly repaired, occasionally touching letter, no significant loss; top edge gilt (earliest state with "Worckes" instead of "Workes"), initial blank discarded, folio, 3 volumes, washed and pressed in 19th century red morocco by Riviere, boards with central lozenge shape made of wreaths and flowers and containing a circular frame, blocked in gilt, spines elaborately gilt, bookplate of Thomas Gaisford, leather booklabel of 'Terry' and small booklabel of J. O. Edwards, modern bookplate, very good. Blackwell's Rare Books Marks of Genius - 22 2016 £40,000

Homerus *Opera Omnia ex recensione et cum notis Samuelis Clarkii...* Glasgow: Excudebat Andreas Duncan, 1814. Large paper copy, 5 volumes, 2 folding engraved maps (offset onto facing pages), touch of light spotting, 8vo., contemporary Italian black sheep, spines divided by a triple gilt fillet between blind rolls, second compartment gilt lettered direct, rest with central blind tools, name 'Caissotti' blocked in gilt to front boards, rubbed and scratched, gold and green mottled endpapers, edges untrimmed, good. Blackwell's Rare Books B186 - 77 2016 £800

Homerus *The Works.* Oxford: Shakespeare Head Press, 1930-1931. No. 302 of 450 copies on paper (and 10 on vellum), five volumes, 292 x 203mm., original burnt-orange half morocco over cream colored buckram, edges untrimmed, later paper covered slipcase, 52 wood engravings by John Farleigh, comprised of two frontispieces, woodcut framed titlepages to volumes I and V, and 48 full page cuts, ink ownership inscription of Daisy Patterson Hall, overall fading and significant chafing to spines, minor dressing residue to leather, faint dampstain covering about a third of back cover of volume V (few tiny stray stains on spine and of same volume), bindings showing little wear, other sides of other volumes, often found foxed, virtually spotless and very pleasing, internally beautiful copy, as fresh and clean as one could hope for. Phillip J. Pirages 67 - 315 2016 $1250

Hone, William *The Every-Day Book and Table Book or Everlasting Calendar of Popular Amusements, Sports, Pastimes....* London: William Tegg and Co., 1847. 1848., Volumes I-III + Year Book, 8vo., frontispiece to each volume, publisher's catalog rear of first volume, volume III final leaf loosening, small paper repair to Year Book not affecting text, little toned, occasional marginal smudges, recent red cloth, black morocco gilt spine labels, endcaps creased little rubbed, some light scratches, edges uncut and dusted, bookplate of Wyatt-Paine. Unsworths Antiquarian Booksellers 30 - 75 2016 £140

Hood, Thomas *The Headlong Career and Woeful Ending of Precocious Piggy.* London: Griffith and Farran, 1859. 4to., dsalmon colored pictorial boards, respined with matching paper, some cover soil, else remarkably tight and clean, hand colored illustration, sold with 1969 facsimile of original manuscript. Aleph-bet Books, Inc. 112 - 246 2016 $1500

Hood, Thomas *Poems by Thomas Hood.* London: E. Moxon, 1871. First edition thus, 22 exquisite engravings by Birket Foster, quarto, fine period binding by H. Sotheran of full straight grain morocco with raised bands, gilt decoration and rules, all edges gilt, bit of foxing here and there, otherwise fine. Peter Ellis 112 - 132 2016 £500

Hoods Ltd. *International Exhcange, Birmingham. Enamelled Goods of General Hardware, List 112 September 1908.* Birmingham: 1908. 8vo., profusely illustrated, original decorated red paper covers. Marlborough Rare Books List 55 - 32 2016 £95

Hoogstraten, Franz Van *Het Voorhof der Ziele, Behangen met Leerzaeme Prenten en Zinnebeelden.* Rotterdam: Francois van Hoogstraeten, Boeckverkooper, 1668. First edition, rare, 4to., contemporary mottled calf, gilt spine, red speckled edges, etched engraved title, 60 half page etchings by Romeyn de Hooghe, Allan Heywood Bright bookplate. Maggs Bros. Ltd. 1474 - 42 2016 £4500

Hooker, J. D. *Handbook of the New Zealand Flora...* London: Lovell Reeve, 1864-1867. Octavo, 2 volumes, publisher's cloth on stiff boards, contents slightly loose, bookplates, sound. Andrew Isles Natural History Books 55 - 17966 2016 $400

Hoole, John *Cyrus: a Tragedy.* London: for T. Davies, 1768. Later crude cloth backed boards, lacking half title, dust soiling to titlepage, else very good. Dramatis Personae 119 - 71 2016 $150

Hoole, John *Cyrus; a Tragedy.* London: printed for T. Davies, 1772. Third edition, half title, 8vo., disbound. Jarndyce Antiquarian Booksellers CCXVI - 463 2016 £50

Hoole, Samuel *Modern Manners or the country Cousins in a Series of Poetical Epistles.* London: printed for J. Dodsley in Pall Mall, 1782. Second edition, engraved frontispiece, bound without half title, 8vo., text slightly browned and foxed, quite heavy in places, contemporary half calf, marbled boards, raised and gilt banded spine, red morocco label, joints slightly cracking, but firm, slight wear to head of spine, nice.   Jarndyce Antiquarian Books   CCXV - 256   2016   £320

Hooper, Franklin William *Plan of an Institution Devoted to Liberal Education.* New York: S. W. Green's Sons, 1881. Folding plate, later grey paper wrappers, rebacked, inscribed "Henry Norman with compliments of Edward T. Fisher".   Jarndyce Antiquarian Books   CCXV - 743   2016   £85

Hooper, George *The Parsons Case Under the Present Land Tax Recommended in a letter to a member of the House of Commons.* London: printed in the year, 1689. First edition, 4to., title soiled, modern boards, spine lettered.   John Drury Rare Books   2015 - 8139   2016 $350

Hoover, Herbert *The Problems of Lasting Peace.* Garden City: Doubleday Doran and Co., 1942. 2nd printing (as per jacket),, about fine in very good, internally tape repaired dust jacket with several small nicks and tears, inscribed by author for Norman Vincent Peale.   Between the Covers Rare Books   204 - 57   2016 $950

Hope, Anthony *The Dolly dialogues.* London: Westminster Gazette, 1894. First edition, scarce first issue, small octavo, four black and white illustrated plates in half tone by Arthur Rackham, yellow pictorial wrappers, blue lettering and illustrations, mild wear and soiling to wrappers, especially on spine, titlepage signed in black ink by author, excellent copy.   David Brass Rare Books, Inc.   2015 - 02921   2016 $950

Hope, Anthony *The Prisoner of Zenda.* New York: Limited Editions Club, 1966. First edition thus, one of 1500 copies, this is copy "JW" signed by Donald Spencer, large 8vo, leather backed cloth, fine in publisher's slipcase.   Second Life Books, Inc.   197 - 182   2016 $75

Hopkins, G. H. *Mosquitoes of the Ethiopian Region.* London: British Museum (Natural History), 1936-1941. Octavo, 3 volumes, color photo plates, publisher's cloth, neat library stamp on titlepages, otherwise fine, crisp copy.   Andrew Isles Natural History Books   55 - 35904   2016 $450

Hopkins, Pauline E. *Contending Forces: A Romance.* Boston: Colonel Co-Operative Pub., 1900. First edition, illustrations and cover designed by R. Emmett Owen, red cloth decorated in pink and yellow, front hinge professionally and invisibly strengthened, else love, just about fine, very scarce.   Between the Covers Rare Books   207 - 56   2016 $8500

Hopkins, William John *The Clammer.* Boston: Houghton Mifflin and Co., 1906. First edition, later printing, publisher's decorative green cloth designed and signed by Amy Sacker, with illustration of sunset over water within decorative torch, clam, trident, vine and banner border to front board in pale green, pale blue and gilt, near fine with slight lean to spine, minor rubbing to extremities, otherwise fresh binding, bright and clean interior, attractive copy.   B & B Rare Books, Ltd.   2016 - WJH001   2016 $50

Hopper, Nora *Under Quickens Boughs.* London: John Lane, Bodley Head, 1896. First edition, highly decorated green cloth with red and black floral designs on front and back boards, title and author in gilt to spine, very good with light bumping to corners, interior very good, untrimmed foreedges, inscription and poem in th hand of Jessica Duncan Jamieson, as well as tipped in rebuttal poet title to JDJ with slip of paper reading "William Parker" securing it, another poem written in pencil.   The Kelmscott Bookshop   12 - 55   2016 $175

Hopwood, John *The Toyland Convention.* Springfield: McLoughlin, 1928. Cloth backed pictorial boards, some edge and tip wear, else very good+, clean and tight, full and partial page color illustrations.   Aleph-bet Books, Inc.   112 - 477   2016 $375

Horatius Flaccus, Quimtus *Cum Commentariis & Enarrationibus Commentatoris Veteris, et Iacobi Cruquii Messenii...* Antwerp: Ex officina Plantiana Raphelengii, 1611. Final Plantin edition, 4to., paper toned, some spotting, gift inscription dated 1643 (to Ludovicus Chimaer from G. van Alphen) and ownership inscription dated 1669, contemporary vellum, board fore-edges overlapping, spine lettered in ink, soiled and bit nicked, hinges cracking but sound, rear flyleaf removed, armorial bookplate of Rich. Palmer, Esq.   Blackwell's Rare Books   Greek & Latin Classics VII - 41   2016   £500

Horatius Flaccus, Quintus *Ad Nuperam Richardi Bentleii Editionem Accurate Expressus. Notas Addidit Thomas Bentleius, A. B. Collegii S. Trinitatis apud Cantabrigienses Alumnus.* Cambridge: Typis Academicis Impensis Cornelii Crownfield`, 1713. 8vo., bit of light browning, some marginal annotations, contemporary calf, black morocco, boards panelled in gilt and blind, spine divided by raised bands, flower head tool in gilt to each compartment, marbled endpapers, bound with half a dozen additional binder's blanks at front and rear, the last at front excised, these filled closely with manuscript notes, joints and edges rubbed, small crack to foot of rear joint, bookplate of William Michael Collett, ownership inscription of Woodthorpe Scholefield Collet, struck through, another C. S. Collett, Grammar School, Ipswich to binder's blank, very good.   Blackwell's Rare Books   Greek & Latin Classics VII - 42   2016   £900

Horatius Flaccus, Quintus *Ex Antiquissimus Undecim Lib. M. S. et Schedis Aliquot Emendatus.* Antwerp: Christophori Plantini, 1578. Small 4to., printer's device to titlepage, some small illustrations in text, woodcut initials, occasional tiny annotations and underlinings in old hand, few small paper flaws, two marginal and one affecting couple of words to page 441-2, little light toning towards edges, odd spots of ink, modern green morocco, red label to spine, edges red, marbled endpapers, spine faded to yellowish tan, little shelfwear, very good, signature of Ludovicus Martellus Rotomagoeus, illegible library ink stamp, few ms. codes to prelim blanks.   Unsworths Antiquarian Booksellers Ltd.   E01 - Early Printing - 11   2016   £475

Horatius Flaccus, Quintus *Carmina.* Strasbourg: Typis et Sumtu Rollandi et Jacobi Nunc Postant apud Georgium Treutell, 1788. Splendid copy of the 'correct edition by Oberlin, 4to., few leaves somewhat mottled and lightly browned, occasional spotting elsewhere, half title, bit soiled, 4to., contemporary red straight grained morocco, boards bordered with decorative gilt roll, spine divided by doule gilt fillets, circular gilt tools to compartments, marbled endpapers, front joint repaired, hinges relined with morocco, old scratches and marks to boards, good.   Blackwell's Rare Books   Greek & Latin Classics VII - 46   2016   £450

Horatius Flaccus, Quintus *Carmina Sapphica. (and) Carmina Alcaica.* Chelsea: Ashendene Press, 1903. One of 150 copies on Japanese paper (25 on vellum), 185 x 128mm., 2 volumes, original flexible vellum, gilt titling on spine, housed in custom cloth folding box with separate compartments for each book, initials hand painted by Graily Hewiett, printed in red and black, "Carmina Alcaica" inscribed to Philip Webb by printer and dated 1903 with further ink notation that was given by Webb's executor to Walter Knight Shirley, Earl Ferrers on 22 Feb. 1916 and by him to Charles Winmile Jan 1937, verso of 'Carmina Sapphica" with morocco bookplate of Cortlandt Bishop, pastedowns little waffled, otherwise mint.   Phillip J. Pirages   67 - 13   2016 $4000

Horatius Flaccus, Quintus *Epistolae ad Pisones et Augustum With an English Commentary and Notes.* London: printed for W. Thurlbourne, 1753. One of 750 copies of the second edition, 2 volumes, 8vo., few pencil corrections in text, stamps of Jesuit Library at Milltown Park, contemporary mid-brown calf, labels lost from spines, little rubbing to extremities, short cracks and spot of insect damage to heads of joints, good.   Blackwell's Rare Books   Greek & Latin Classics VII - 44   2016   £150

Horatius Flaccus, Quintus *Poemata: ex antiquis Codd. & Certis Observationibus...* Londoni: apud Fratres Vaillant et N. Prevost, 1721. First edition, personal copy of Henry Nelson Coleridge, with his ownership signature dated 'Hampstead 1832' to titlepage, full vellum, spine ruled and decorated in blind, handwritten title to spine, all edges stained red, pink marbled endpapers, very good or better, some bowing to boards, minor spotting at spine heads, otherwise sturdy binding, small loss to bottom corner of pages 213;214, few minor and scattered pieces of pencil marginalia, light soiling to pages and page edges, else bright and clean, very good overall, tight copy in early binding.   B & B Rare Books, Ltd.   2016 - STC005   2016 $350

Horatius Flaccus, Quintus *Satires and Epistles of Horace done into English, with Notes.* London: printed by M. Jenour for D. Browne...., 1712. Second edition, 8vo., frontispiece, woodcut initials and interleaves with gathering 'B' of Art of Poetry misbound, interleaved with gathering "C" which is then duplicated afterwards, some ink spots and smudges, contemporary light brown calf with blind tooled borders, rebacked in lighter shade with raised bands and black morocco and gilt spine label, edges sprinkled red, scuffed, corners bumped but good, sound copy.   Unsworths Antiquarian Booksellers   30 - 79   2016   £125

Horatius Flaccus, Quintus *Opera ad Optimorum Exemplarum Fidem Recensita.* Cambridge: Typis Academicis, impensis Jocobi Tonson, 1699. 4to., engraved frontispiece, engraved head and tailpieces, browned, particularly towards front, sporadic foxing, some neat pencil annotations, pen line to title also visible to verso, small dark patch to lower margins pages 224-5, contemporary brown calf, gilt borders and frame, rebacked in lighter calf with raised bands, gilt and red morocco label, corners repaired, all edges gilt, marbled endpapers, part of spine label lost, some scrapes and blackening to boards, edges chipped, solid working copy, tiny bookseller's label of B. Diver & Son, Cambridge.   Unsworths Antiquarian Booksellers   30 - 77   2016   £275

Horatius Flaccus, Quintus *(Opera) ex recensione & cum Notis Atque Emendationibus.* Cantabrigiae: 1711. First edition, 4to., engraved additional titlepage, half title, engraved printer's device to title, 'Notae & Emendationes' has separate half title, title, pagination and register, some library stamps, occasional slight dustiness to head margins, additional engraved title somewhat foxed, paper flaw to pages 165-6 affecting few letters, faint stain to bottom fore-edge corner pages 329-32, contemporary brown calf boards with gilt frame and border, sturdily rebacked, edges sprinkled red endpapers replaced, few scrapes, corners worn, very good, sound, Library inkstamps of Royal College of Physicians of London, and of Metropolitan Special Collection Southwark to title, library codes to title verso, ownership inscription f J. S. Davies in old hand.   Unsworths Antiquarian Booksellers   30 - 78   2016   £650

Horatius Flaccus, Quintus *(Opera) ex recensione & cum notis atque Emendationiibus Richardi Bentleii.* Amsterdam: Apud Rod. & Gerh. Wetstenios, 1713. Second Bentley edition, large paper copy, engraved frontispiece, lightly toned, some dampmarking to outer edge, occasional spotting, two small holes to blank area of final leaf, half title to section two discarded (as usual when bound in one volume), 4to., contemporary Cambridge style panelled calf, somewhat crudely rebacked, preserving most of original red morocco lettering piece, new endpapers, scratched and marked, extremities worn, sound.   Blackwell's Rare Books   B186 - 79   2016   £500

Horatius Flaccus, Quintus *Opera.* Londini: Iohannes Pine, 1733. 1737. First issue with "Post Est" rather than correct "Potest" engraved around Caesar medal volume 2 page 108), 2 volumes, 8vo., multiple lists of subscribers to each volume, but without letterpress printed list of antiquities sometimes found, entirely engraved by John Pine, with frontispieces, title vignettes, 8 full page illustrations, culs-de-lampe and 4 line opening initial to each poem, volume I has small intermittent stain to lower margin near gutter, handful of upper corners creased, occasional light foxing, contemporary dark brown calf, gilt spines with red and green title labels, green possibly replaced or sympathetically retooled, all edges red, spines rubbed with tail of volume II quite worn, joints neatly repaired, few scuffs, endpapers little toned, very good, armorial bookplate of Francis Eyre (c. 1732-104) of Warkworth, serviceable copy.   Unsworths Antiquarian Booksellers   30 - 80   2016   £850

Horatius Flaccus, Quintus *Quinti Horatii Flacci Opera.* London: Aeneis tabulis Incidit Johannes Pine, 1733-1737. Second impression with mistake page 108 corrected, each page entirely engraved, some light spotting and toning, 8vo., 19th century blue dark blue roan, boards bordered gilt and blind, spines with raised bands, compartments panelled in gilt and lettered direct, yellow chalked endpapers, edges gilt, spines sunned and rubbed, touch of wear to extremities, good.   Blackwell's Rare Books   Greek & Latin Classics VII - 43   2016   £400

Horatius Flaccus, Quintus *Opera.* Londini: prostant apud Gul. Sandby typis Jacobi Bettnham 25 Julli, 1749. 2 volumes, 8vo., 35 engraved plates, including frontispiece, titlepage to each volume in red and black with engraved portraits, list of plates on single leaf, without final leaf of binder's instructions, some occaisonal light foxing, very small number of pencilled marginal notes, tiny paper repair to page 193, contemporary light brown calf, neatly (if not invisibly) rebacked with original gilt spines retained, all edges red, spines worn and crackled, few scuffs and faded patches, but very good set, inscribed for Thomae Coombe, pencilled bookseller's comment, early 20th century bookplate of Arthur Coombe.   Unsworths Antiquarian Booksellers   30 - 81   2016   £250

Horatius Flaccus, Quintus *The Works of Horace.* Edinburgh: printed for J. Dickson, Exchange, and James Duncan, Glasgow, 1777. 18mo., somewhat spotted and soiled, contemporary sheep, rubbed and worn, lettering pieces lost, joints cracking, spine of volume cracking and one compartment partly defective, front flyleaves excised, remaining endpapers with various scribbles and inscriptions in ink and pencil (including, Andrew Brown of Egypt Park in Paisley dated 1842).   Blackwell's Rare Books   Greek & Latin Classics VII - 45   2016   £200

Horatius Flaccus, Quintus *Opera cum Scholiis Veteribus Castigavit....* Glasgow: in Aedibus Academicis Excudebat Jacobus Mundell, 1796. 8vo., some light foxing, Jesuit library stamp of Milltown Park to titlepage, ownership inscription of C. J. Tindal, Trinity College, 1838 to initial blank, 8vo., contemporary straight grained red morocco, boards bordered with single gilt fillet, spine divided by single gilt fillet, gilt crest in top compartment, title lettered direct in second and pale and date at foot, spine bit darkened, few tiny marks here and there, marbled endpapers, all edges gilt, with thin roll of gauffering near front and back hinge, cracking little at titlepage and headband partly loose, label removed from front pastedown, good.   Blackwell's Rare Books   Greek & Latin Classics VII - 47   2016   £500

Horatius Flaccus, Quintus *Opera, cum Scholiis Veteribus Castigavit et Notis Illustravit Gulielmus Baxteruus...* Edinburgh: Ex Prelo Academico... apud Mundell Doig et Stevenson, 1806. 4to., contemporary red straight grained morocco, boards bordered in gilt and blind enclosing a further frame combining a rectangle and lozenge shape, spine lettered gilt and also decorated in gilt and blind, marbled endpapers, edges gilt and minimally guaffered, bit rubbed at joints and extremities, few small marks, bookplates and ownership inscription of Chandos Leigh, very good.   Blackwell's Rare Books   Greek & Latin Classics VII - 48   2016   £550

Horatius Flaccus, Quintus *(Opera).* Londini: Gulielmus Pickering, 1824. Large paper copy, 32mo., portrait frontispiece, 1 engraved plate, very light occasional foxing but still nice and bright inside, contemporary red morocco by Joubert, gilt title to spine, gilt dentelles, bright blue morocco doublures, top edge gilt, joints and corners little worn, small split starting at head of lower board, slight discoloration to free endpapers from leather joints, illegible inscription ot f.f.e.p, verso bookseller's pencilled notes to rear.   Unsworths Antiquarian Booksellers   30 - 44   2016   £250

Horatius Flaccus, Quintus *(Opera).* Gulielmus Pickering, 1826. Large paper copy, engraved titlepage (slightly browned), bound without engraved frontispiece dated 1828 and the letterpress titlepage dated 1824, 8vo., original rose cloth, printed paper label to spine, sunned and little bit marked, spine ends chipped, cloth cracked at front joint, pencilled purchase note of Thomas Thorp, dated 13th oct. 1928, earlier bookplate of William Ellis Wall, good.   Blackwell's Rare Books   B186 - 78   2016   £120

Horatius Flaccus, Quintus *(Opera).* Londini: Gulielmus Pickering, 1828. second titlepage dated 1824 and frontispiece dated 1828. Second edition from Pickering's Diamond Classics series, 48mo., 2 plates, engraved frontispiece and titlepage, plates very slightly toned but generally bright and clean within, contemporary tan calf, gilt title to spine, all edges gilt, little rubbed, few light scuffs to spine, very good gift inscription, plus name Nigel Temple pencilled in. Unsworths Antiquarian Booksellers   30 - 45   2016   £100

Horgan, Paul *A Certain Climate: Essays in History, Arts and Letters.* Middletown: Wesleyan University, 1988. First edition, with short note from author to Tad Mosel laid in, as well as clipping of Horgan's obit, fine in dust jacket. Second Life Books, Inc.   196A - 819   2016 $45

Horgan, Paul *Everything to Live For.* New York: Farrar, Straus and Giroux, 1968. First edition, black cloth, gilt lettered spine, dust jacket shows light wear and minor soiling and is price clipped, fine.   Argonaut Book Shop   Literature 2015 - 4865   2016 $50

Horgan, Paul *Humble Powers.* London: Macmillan, 1954. First British edition thus, cloth, laid into corner photo mounts on f.f.e.p is black and white photo of Horgan with his aunt, and godchild, gilt inscription written by his aunt, Marie Rhor to Isabelle Hinsdale, fine in slightly edge worn dust jacket with two small chips and couple of short tears, very scarce.   Gene W. Baade, Books on the West   2015 - FTR091   2016 $131

Horgan, Paul *Lamy of Santa Fe: His Life and Times.* New York: Farrar, Straus & Giroux, 1973. First edition, large paper limited edition of 490 copies signed by author, this number 12, tall 8vo., 20 black and whites plates, and 12 beautifully colored plates, cloth backed paper boards, top edge gilt, couple of light age spots on titlepage, else fine in publisher's box, presentation copy from author for Leon Edel, with his ownership signature.   Second Life Books, Inc.   196A - 821   2016 $275

Horgan, Paul *Memories of the Future.* New York: Farrar Straus and Giroux, 1966. First edition, black cloth with gilt lettering to spine, dust jacket shows some light rubbing and is chipped at head of spine, else fine.   Argonaut Book Shop   Literature 2015 - 4866   2016 $50

Horgan, Paul *Mexico Bay.* New York: Farrar, Straus and Giroux, 1982. First edition, black cloth with lettering to spine, very fine in original dust jacket.   Argonaut Book Shop   Literature 2015 - 4867   2016 $50

Horgan, Paul *Peter Hurd: a Portrait Sketch from Life.* Austin: University of Texas, 1965. First edition, 4to., 16 black and white illustrations and 6 color plates, author's presentation on flyleaf, dated 1989, paper over boards with cloth spine, cover bumped at corners, slightly scuffed at ends of spine, otherwise very good, tight.   Second Life Books, Inc.   196A - 822   2016 $125

Horgan, Paul *Whitewater.* New York: Farrar, Straus and Giroux, 1970. First edition, blue cloth with gilt lettering to spine, fine in slightly rubbed dust jacket.   Argonaut Book Shop   Literature 2015 - 4869   2016 $75

The Horn Book Crier. Boston: The Horn Book, 1964-1975. Jan. - Sept. 1971; Jan, March, July, Sept. 1972; May, Nov. 1974. May July, Sept. 1975, newsletter, folding for posting. Jarndyce Antiquarian Books   CCXV - 770   2016   £20

Hornby, C. H. St. John *A Descriptive Bibliography of Books printed at the Ashendene Press MDCCCXCV-MCMXXXIV.* Chelsea: Ashendene Press, 1935. No. 41 of 390 copies of the original edition, signed by Hornby, 343 x 235mm., publisher's polished cordovan calf, gilt titling on front cover ad spine, edges untrimmed, modern morocco edged slipcase, with 33 plates, several initials hand painted by Graily Hewitt, very good autograph letters from Hornby to London bookseller James Bain, in marbled paper folders laid in, errata and additional errata slips laid in at rear, spine somewhat rubbed and marked with two small dark spots, faint fading to spine and top edge of covers, otherwise binding lustrous and pleasing with virtually no wear to joints, very faint offset to front free endpaper, handful of light and neglibile rust spots, otherwise very fine internally.   Phillip J. Pirages   67 - 14   2016 $2500

Hornby, Nick *Songbook.* New York: McSweeney's, 2002. True first edition, fine, pictorial boards, includes 11 song CD, signed by author.   Bella Luna Books   2016 - t5556   2016 $82

Horne, Herbert Percy *Diversi Colores.* London: published by author at the Chiswick Press, 1891. First edition, probably one of 250 copies, duodecimo, original gray-green boards and printed paper label, decorated titlepage and colophon designed by author, form the library of school teacher Thomas Hutchinson with his initials and shelf number on front pastedown and note on front free endpaper, scarce little book, label little darkened, edges slightly rubbed, fine copy.   The Brick Row Book Shop   Miscellany 69 - 47   2016 $225

Horowitz, Anthony *The Magpie Murders.* London: Orion, 2016. First edition, book and dust jacket mint, signed and dated 6/10/6 by author, publisher's erratum slip loosely inserted, jacket fitted with new removable clear cover. Gemini Books   2016 - 31900   2016 $50

Horowitz, Anthony *Moriarty.* London: Orion, 2014. First edition, book and dust jacket fine unread condition, very slight tinge to upper closed page edges, signed by author, jacket fitted with new removable clear cover.   Gemini Books   2016 - 31892   2016 $39

Horowitz, Anthony *Trigger Mortis.* London: Orion, 2015. First edition, black dust jacket, fine copy in like jacket, signed by author.   Gemini Books   2016 - 31905   2016 $57

Horton, Robert Wilmot *First Letter to the Freeholders of the County of York, on Negro Slavery, Being an Inquiry into the Claims of the West Indians for Equitable Compensation.* London: Edmund Lloyd, 1830. First edition, recent cloth backed marbled boards, morocco label on upper cover lettered gilt, very good.   John Drury Rare Books   2015 - 25629   2016 $350

Hotten, John Camden *Charles Dickens the story of his life by the author.* London: John Camden Hotten, 1870. First edition, vignette title, plates, 20 page catalog, original green cloth by W. Bone & Son, slight rubbing.   Jarndyce Antiquarian Booksellers   CCXVIII - 1306   2016   £35

Houbart, Jacques *Haute Societe - Revue Bimestrielle nos 1-3 (all published).* Paris: Juin-Novembre, 1960. Quarto, wrappers, cover for each issue is lithograph by Andre Francois Roland Topor and Bassiak, respectively, very good.   Peter Ellis   112 - 289   2016   £575

Houghton, Claude *Birthmark.* London: Collins, 1950. Author's own copy with his pencilled signature, Savage Club address and note, covers little marked and sunned, front hinge tender.   I. D. Edrich   Crime - 2016   £45

Houghton, Claude *Christina.* London: Collins, 1950. red clop, dust jacket little torn and frayed, contents very good, signed by author.   I. D. Edrich   Crime - 2016   £35

Houghton, Claude *The Quarrel.* London: Collins, 1948. Red cloth, little faded in slightly marked and chipped dust jacket, inscribed by author for Gilda.   I. D. Edrich   Crime - 2016   £50

Houghton, Norris *But Not Forgotten.* New York: William Sloane Associates, 1951. First edition, near fine in near very good dust jacket with couple of chips and long closed tear, signed by three members of the troupe, Henry Fonda, Joshua Logan and Mildred Narwick.   Between the Covers Rare Books   204 - 58   2016 $500

Houghton, Thomas Shaw *The Printers' Practical Every-Day Book Calculated to assist the Young Printer to Work with Ease and Expedition.* London: Simpkin, Marshall & Co., 1841. First edition, original drab boards, original purple cloth, spine faded to brown, paper label darkened, price 3s, scarce.   Jarndyce Antiquarian Booksellers   CCXVII - 128   2016   £185

Houghton, William *British Fresh Water Fishes.* Hull and York: A Brown and Sons Ltd., 1895. Second edition, large 8vo., original green cloth, gilt lettering to spine, 24 plates of views, numerous text illustrations, very good.   Sotheran's Hunting, Shooting & Fishing - 126   2016   £500

Houplain, Jacques *La Genese.* Paris: Chez Jean Porson, 1949. Copy #32 of 75 copies from an edition of 250, with an extra set of illustrations, 2 volumes, wrappers, unbound gatherings in chemise and slipcase, 13 planches inutilisees, copper plate and original drawing corresponding to copper plate, 4to.   Beasley Books   2015 - 2016 $1200

The House in the Wood and Other Old Fairy Stories. London: Frederick Warne, 1909. First edition, pictorial cloth, slight bit of cover soil, else near fine, illustrations by Leslie Brooke.   Aleph-bet Books, Inc.   112 - 75   2016 $275

Household Conveniences. Being the Experience of Many Practical Writers. New York: Orange Judd Co., 1884. First edition, original blue decorative cloth, gilt lettering to upper board and spine, illustrations throughout, very good, bookplate of Gunn Memorial Lib. Washington, Conn. with circular label.   Sotheran's Piccadilly Notes - Summer 2015 - 19   2016   £50

Household Tales and Fairy Stories. New York and Manchester: George Routledge, 1893. Thick 8vo. brown cloth with beautiful gilt cover and spine, very good-fine, nearly 50 fairy tales, over 1000 very fine engravings.   Aleph-bet Books, Inc.   111 - 162   2016 $300

Household, Geoffrey *A Rough Shoot.* M. Joseph, 1951. Dust jacket chipped, with tears at head and foot of spine.   I. D. Edrich   Crime - 2016   £20

Household, Geoffrey *The Salvation of Pisco Gabar and other Stories.* London: Chatto & Windus, 1938. First edition, fine in fine dust jacket, slightly creased at edges, exceptionally bright, octavo.   Peter Ellis   112 - 174   2016   £250

Household, Geoffrey *The Three Sentinels.* London: Michael Joseph, 1972. First edition, fine in dust jacket.   Mordida Books   2015 - 001128   2016 $55

The Housemaid. London: Houlston & Stoneman, circa, 1860. Leaves little dusted, original limp green cloth boards, dulled and slightly affected by damp, signature "Staryley' on title.   Jarndyce Antiquarian Books   CCXV - 261   2016   £125

The Housemaid. London: Houslton & sons, circa, 1870. Original brown cloth boards cut flush, slightly rubbed, very good.   Jarndyce Antiquarian Books   CCXV - 262   2016   £150

The Housemaid. London: Houslton & sons, circa, 1879. Little spotted, original brick brown cloth, blocked in gilt and black, very good.   Jarndyce Antiquarian Books   CCXV - 263   2016   £125

Houseman, John *Entertainers and the Entertained.* New York: Simon & Schuster, 1986. First printing, 8vo., signed on flyleaf by author, nice in slightly soiled dust jacket. Second Life Books, Inc.   196A - 818   2016 $45

Housman, Laurence   1865-1959 *All-Fellows, Seven Legends Of Lower Redemption with Insets in Verse.* London: Kegan-Paul, Trench, Trubner & Co., 1896. First edition, presentation copy inscribed by author Feb. 18th 1897 to W. B. Blaikie, master printer at T. and A. Constable, lovely engravings, cover design, titlepage and initial letters by Housman, original green cloth with bumping, fading and sunning to spine, interior pages very nice light browning to margins and deckled edges, very good.   The Kelmscott Bookshop   13 - 24   2016 $450

Housman, Laurence   1865-1959 *Prunella or Love in a Dutch Garden.* London: Sigwick & Jackson, 1911. Third edition, new impression, square 8vo., untrimmed frontispiece by Housman, printed boards, bookplate removed from front pastedown, closed tear to front blank, very good, signed and dated by actor George Odell who played the Tenor, in addition this copy signed by about 25 members of the NY cast,.   Second Life Books, Inc.   196A - 830   2016 $225

Housman, Laurence   1865-1959 *Stories front the Arabian Nights.* Garden City: n.d., Drawings and color illustrations by Edmund Dulac, black cloth, large pictorial label, edges darkened, covers scuffed at edges and at ends of spine, rear hinge tender, otherwise very good.   Second Life Books, Inc.   197 - 183   2016 $50

Housman, Laurence   1865-1959 *Stories from the Arabian Nights Retold by....* London: Hodder & Stoughton, 1907. first Dulac illustrated edition, Tall 8vo., 50 tipped in plates by Edmund Dulac, original red black and gilt stamped cloth, color printed dust jacket, jacket torn, piece missing at head, some nicks at dust jacket spine back, jacket rare, very good. Jeff Weber Rare Books   181 - 58   2016 $675

Housman, Laurence   1865-1959 *Stories from the Arabian Nights, retold by.* London: Hodder & Stoughton, 1907. Limited to only 350 numbered copies signed by Dulac, thick 4to., gilt pictorial vellum, top edge gilt, few very small areas of soil, else near fine with new ties and one of the warping that is usually found in this title, 50 tipped in color plates by Edmund Dulac.   Aleph-bet Books, Inc.   112 - 160   2016 $4250

Housman, Laurence   1865-1959 *Stories from the Arabian Nights Retold by...* London: Hodder & Stoughton, n.d., 1907. First edition in this preferred format, 50 beautiful tipped in color plates with guards, thick large 4to., gilt decorated cloth, fine in lovely pictorial dust jacket with mounted color plate (soiled areas on dust jacket), beautiful copy, increasingly scarce, rarely found in dust jacket.   Aleph-bet Books, Inc.   111 - 134   2016 $2200

Houston, Pam *Cowboys are my Weakness.* New York: W. W. Norton, 1992. First edition, very good, light shelf wear, 'not for resale' stamped on top edge, small ink mark to front pastedown, dust jacket fine.   Bella Luna Books   2016 - t3356   2016 $66

Houston, T. F. *Dragon Lizards and Gonnas of South Australia.* Adelaide: South Australian Museum, 1978. First edition, octavo, attractive color plates by author, maps, softcover.   Andrew Isles Natural History Books   55 - 2207   2016 $50

Houx-Marc, Eugene *French Tribulations De La Mere Goody.* Paris: Bedelet, n.d. circa, 1840. 12mo., pictorial boards, spine paper chipped and some edge rubbing, tight clean and very good+, 14 lovely hand colored plates. Aleph-bet Books, Inc.   112 - 169   2016 $600

Hoving, Thomas *Tutankhamun: the Untold Story.* New York: Simon and Schuster, 1978. First printing, 8vo., photos, map on endpapers, author's signature on blank, tank cloth, nice in slightly scuffed and chipped dust jacket, near fine.   Second Life Books, Inc.   196A - 832   2016 $50

How to be Happy or Fairy Gifts...   London: John Harris, 1828. Frontispiece, plates, 1 page ads, contemporary marbled boards, maroon morocco, spine slightly rubbed, contemporary signature N. R. Brown on leading f.e.p., very good.   Jarndyce Antiquarian Books   CCXV - 264 2016   £125

How to Behave: a Pocket Manual of Etiquette and Guide to Correct Personal Habits.   Glasgow: John S. Marr & Sons, 1883. Half title, 2 pages ads, original yellow printed paper wrappers, rubbed and slightly dulled, loss to spine strip. Jarndyce Antiquarian Books   CCXV - 265   2016   £45

Howard, Elizabeth Jane *We Are for the Dark: Six Ghost Stories.* London: Jonathan Cape, 1951. First edition, 8vo., original maroon cloth lettered silver on spine, about fine in very good clean price clipped dust jacket, very slight wear at spine and with no loss, very slight edgewear with no loss and slight rubbing at corners, decent copy.   Any Amount of Books   2015 - A99788   2016   £250

Howard, H. Eliot *An Introduction to the Study of Bird Behaviour.* Cambridge: Cambridge University Press, 1929. Quarto, 10 uncolored plates, contemporary red half calf by Walbys of Oxford, apart from few minor spots, handsome copy.   Andrew Isles Natural History Books   55 - 28239   2016 $300

Howard, John Galen *Brunelleschi, a Poem.* San Francisco: John Howell Books, 1913. First edition, one of 480 numbered copies, tall 8vo., original paper covered boards, paper spine label, bit of minor soiling to covers, very tiny nick to foot of spine, else fine.   Argonaut Book Shop Private Press 2015 - 5322   2016 $50

Howard, Richard *Fellow Feelings. Poems.* New York: Atheneum, 1976. First edition, issue in wrappers, inscribed and signed by author for for William Meredith, foxing to top and side edges, very good.   Charles Agvent   William Meredith - 56   2016 $80

Howard, Richard *Quantities. Poems.* Middletown: Wesleyan University Press, 1962. First edition, issue in wrappers, signed and inscribed by author for William Meredith, additionally signed by Bernard Malamud , to Meredith, with TLS from Malamud apologizing for signing the book, some dust spotting to top edge, near fine.   Charles Agvent   William Meredith - 57   2016 $500

Howard, Richard *Two-Part Inventions. Poems.* New York: Atheneum, 1974. First edition, issue in wrappers, inscribed and signed by author for William Meredith, some dust spotting to top edge, near fine.   Charles Agvent   William Meredith - 58   2016 $150

Howard, Richard *Untitled Subjects. Poems.* New York: Atheneum, 1969. First edition, paperback original, inscribed and signed by author for William Meredith, some dust spotting to top edge, near fine.   Charles Agvent   William Meredith - 59   2016 $200

Howard, Robert *The Committee, a Comedy.* London: i.e. The Hague: printed for the Company i.e. T. Johnson, 1728? 8vo., disbound.   Jarndyce Antiquarian Booksellers   CCXVI - 464   2016   £85

Howard, Robert E. *Conan the Barbarian. (in) Weird Tales 1932-1936.* Indianapolis: 1932-1936. Octavo, 26 issues, pictorial wrappers, darkening to pages to a number of copies, little color fade to few issues and some edge rubs, overall condition of issues nearly fine, very attractive set.   John W. Knott, Jr./L.W. Currey, Inc.   Fall-Winter 2015 - 15172   2016 $12,500

Howard, Robert E. *Conan the Barbarian.* New York: Gnome Press, 1954. First edition, upper right front corner little bumped, some rubbing to bottom edges, nearly fine in virtually as new fine dust jacket with light vertical crease to rear panel near spine.   John W. Knott, Jr./L.W. Currey, Inc.   Fall-Winter 2015 - 17867   2016 $750

Howard, Robert E. *Night Images: a Book of Fantasy Verse.* Leawood/New York:: Morning Star Press, 1976. First edition, limited to 1000 numbered copies of which this is one of approximately 750 unsigned trade copies, this one of publisher's overrun, large octavo, illustrations, fine in fine dust jacket with touch or rubbing.   John W. Knott, Jr./L.W. Currey, Inc.   Fall-Winter 2015 - 18008   2016 $125

Howard, Sidney *Yellow Jack, a History...* New York: Harcourt Brace, 1933. First edition, 8vo., full brown morocco by Brentanos, spine gilt in compartments, this copy presented by author to play's director Guthrie McClintic, with initials 'G McC' on front board.   Second Life Books, Inc.   196A - 833   2016 $375

Howchin, Walter *The Building of Australia and the Succession of Life with Special Reference to South Australia.* Adelaide: Govenment Printer, 1925-1930. Octavo, 3 volumes, text illustrations, publisher's wrappers, very good.   Andrew Isles Natural History Books   55 - 6647   2016 $100

Howell, James *Dendrologia (Greek letters) Dodona's Grove or the Vocall Forest.* London: printed by Thomas Warren for Humphrye Moseley, n.d., 1649. 3 works in one, 12mo., lacks one folding plate and one leaf of text, with penultimate leaft of England's Tears, with alterations to pagination and catchword to disguise the loss, lightly toned, edges little browned and fragile with some occasional chipping, closed tear to plate with paper tape repair to verso, recently rebound in tan calf with red morocco gilt label and blind tooling to spine, upper board onlaid with panel of original darker brown calf with gilt centerpiece showing three trees within wreath and lettered with title, endpapers renewed, few very faint scuffs.   Unsworths Antiquarian Booksellers   30 - 83   2016   £250

Howell, James *Epistolae Ho-Eliana. Familiar Letters Domestic and Forren...* London: printed for Humphrey Moseley, 1645. First edition, small 4to., lacking additional engraved titlepage, woodcut initials and head and tailpieces, few pencil marks and underlinings, some MS. notes in old hand including dates and sometimes locations, occasional wax marks not affecting text, 19th century plum colored faux morocco, gilt label to spine, blindstamped spine and boards, edges sprinkled red, marbled endpapers, rubbed, edges bit worn and some fraying to covers, spine label lifting, armorial bookplate of Frederick William Cosens, MS gift inscription to Allan H. Bright, dated 30th May 1891, from HYS, armorial bookplate of Douglas Kinnaird, tipped to f.f.e.p. a page of handwritten notes on the content of the book with brief chronology of Howell's life in pencil, with note book was purchased from Cosens through Quaritch.   Unsworths Antiquarian Booksellers   30 - 82   2016   £300

Howes, Barbara *The Blue Garden.* Middletown: Wesleyan University Press, 1972. First edition, stiff wrappers, very good, inscribed by authr.   Second Life Books, Inc.   196A - 838   2016 $45

Howes, Barbara *The Blue Garden.* Middletown: Wesleyan Univ. Press, 1972. First edition, very good in little stained and worn price clipped dust jacket, inscribed by author to first husband William Jay Smith and his wife.   Second Life Books, Inc.   196A - 839   2016 $200

Howes, Barbara *From the Green Antilles...* New York: Macmillan, 1966. First edition, 8vo., very good, tight copy, dust jacket little wrinkled and soiled, inscribed by author to her first husband William Jay Smith.   Second Life Books, Inc.   196A - 835   2016 $150

Howes, Barbara *Light and Dark: Poems.* Middletown: Wesleyan, 1959. First edition, 8vo., very good in dust jacket, little soiled, inscribed by author to husband William Jay Smith.   Second Life Books, Inc.   196A - 836   2016 $200

Howes, Barbara *A Private Signal, Poems New and Selected.* Middletown: Wesleyan Univ., 1977. First edition, 8vo., fine in little soiled and stained dust jacket, inscribed by author for her ex-husband William Jay Smith and his wife.   Second Life Books, Inc.   196A - 842   2016 $200

Hoyt, Ray *We Can Take It: a Short Story of the C. C. C.* New York: Cincinnati: American Book Co., 1935. First edition, octavo, illustrations by Marshall Davis, quarter canvas and illustrated green wrappers, bot of foxing on wrappers and fore edge, very good.   Between the Covers Rare Books   204 - 25   2016 $150

Hozier, H. M. *The Franco Prussian War: its Causes, Incidents and Consequences.* London: William Mackenzie, circa, 1870. First edition, crown 4to., 7 divisions, original maroon cloth blocked in gilt black and blind, all edges gilt, engraved title 24 maps and plans, 56 engraved plates and portraits, stain on lower cover of first volume, occasional internal foxing, otherwise very good set.   Sotheran's Piccadilly Notes - Summer 2015 - 166   2016   £498

Huarte De San Juan, Juan *Essame de gl'Ingegni de gl'Huomini....* Cremona: C. Draconi, 1588. Early Italian edition, small 8vo., 18th century half morocco over patterned boards, red morocco spine label, morocco rubbed at extremities, fore-edges trimmed with occasional loss of letter or two in marginal side notes, very good,.   Edwin V. Glaser Rare Books   2015 - 10211   2016 $950

Hubback, Theodore R. *To Far Western Alaska for Big Game....* London: Rowland Ward, 1939. First edition, 8vo., map in pocket, illustrations, original green decorative cloth, zebra endpapers, fine.   J. & S. L. Bonham Antiquarian Booksellers   America 2016 - 10030   2016   £750

Hubbard, Elbert   1856-1915 *Little Journeys to the Homes of Good Men and Great.* New York & London: G. P. Putnam's Son, 1895. Portrait, 4 pages ads, slightly spotted, stapled as issued in original wrappers, untrimmed, printed in black and red, slightly dusted.   Jarndyce Antiquarian Booksellers   CCXVIII - 1309   2016   £35

Hubbard, Elbert   1856-1915 *Complete Writings of Elbert Hubbard.* East Aurora: Roycrofters, 1908. Author's edition, #432 of 1000 sets, 20 volumes, large quarto, each hand numbered and signed by author, beautifully printed in letterpress in reddish brown and black on handmade Roycroft watermarked paper, titlepage design and inked letters designed by Dard Hunter, decorated initials printed in black, reddish brown and light green, etched portraits and duo-tones, 2 pages of original ms. bound into volume I, publisher's three quarter crushed brown morocco, tooled in dark brown with an art nouveau design, light brown paper sides, raised bands, gilt spine lettering and decoration, top edges gilt, very slight damage to head of spine of volume I, just few minor scuff marks, overall fine, very attractive set.   Argonaut Book Shop   Literature 2015 - 5073   2016 $3250

Hubner, Alexander, Graf von *Promenade Autour du Monde 1871.* Paris: Hachette & Cie, 1877. Folio, 316 woodcuts, original paper wrappers and spine reinforced with paper tape, rear wrapper torn, wrappers soiled, dampstain in last fifth, mainly to margins but affecting some text and few illustrations, still complete usable wide margined and untrimmed copy with terrific plates and illustrations, call it fair to good.   Kaaterskill Books   21 - 36   2016 $100

Huddesford, George *A Proper reply to a Pamphlet entitled, A Defence of the Rector ad Fellows of Exeter College &c.* Oxford: printed at the Theatre for Richard Clements & sold by J. and J. Rivington, London, 1755. 4to. disbound.   Jarndyce Antiquarian Booksellers   CCXVI - 349   2016   £30

Hudson-Fulton Celebration Commission *Official Program. Hudson-Fulton Celebration September 25 to October 9 1909, Brooklyn Edition.* New York: Redfield Brothers, 1909. First edition, 32 pages, black and white photos and reproductions, 4to. stapled paper wrappers, scarce edition, very good, top half of wrappers detached, small chips to sunned front wrapper, 3 inch long chip to upper corner of rear wrapper, two leaves with tears to fore edge.   Kaaterskill Books   21 - 37   2016 $50

Hudson, Derek *Arthur Rackham: His Life and Work.* New York: Charles Scribner, 1960. 1975, 4to., fine in dust jacket slightly worn on corners and spine ends, excellent copy, many mounted color plates plus line illustrations by Arthur Rackham.   Aleph-bet Books, Inc.   111 - 385   2016 $150

Hudson, G. V. *New Zealand Neuroptera: a Popular Introduction to the life Histories and Habits of My Flies, Dragon Flies, Caddis Flies...* London: West, Newman & Co., 1904. Octavo, 11 colored plates, publisher's green cloth, fine.   Andrew Isles Natural History Books   55 - 33668   2016 $500

Hudson, Mike *Private Impressions, a Second Collection of Four Monographs About Printing and Other Arts.* Katoomba: The Wayzgoose Press, 2001. One in an edition of 15 signed and numbered copies, 4to., full bottle green cloth, two recessed labels on cover, slipcase, original two-color wood engraving printed from block tipped in.   Oak Knoll Books   27 - 68   2016 $700

Hudson, William Henry 1841-1922 *Birds of La Plata.* London: J. M. Dent & sons, 1920. Limited to 3000 copies, 22 color plates, large octavo, 2 volumes, publisher's decorated cloth, fragments of dust jacket for both volumes, very good.   Andrew Isles Natural History Books   55 - 6652   2016 $450

Hudson, William Henry 1841-1922 *Idle Days in Patagonia.* London: Chapman & Hall, 1893. First edition, one of 1750 copies, 8vo., 27 illustrations, original red cloth, gilt vignette, spine little faded.   J. & S. L. Bonham Antiquarian Booksellers   America 2016 - 9928   2016   £125

Hudson, William Henry 1841-1922 *The Naturalist in La Plata.* London: J. M. Dent, 1929. Second edition, octavo, text illustrations, bookplate, fine in chipped dust jacket. Andrew Isles Natural History Books   55 - 37617   2016 $60

Huet, Pierre Daniel *De Imbecillitate Mentis Humanae Libri Tres.* Amsterdam: Apud H. Du. Sauzet, 1738. 12mo., title in red and black, engraved frontispiece, portrait, spine strengthened with clear tape, good copy in contemporary grey blue boards, presentation slip "With the compliments of Dr. Richard A. Hunter" laid in, with Stonor armorial bookplate.   Edwin V. Glaser Rare Books   2015 - 19212   2016 $300

Hueter, Diane *Kansas: Just Before Sleep...* Lawrence: Cottonwood Review, 1978. First edition, printed wrappers, very good, this copy belonged to Paul Metcalf and several of the poems have pencil marks next to them in his holograph, in addition, laid in is 2 page typed review of the book with line in his holography.   Second Life Books, Inc.   196A - 844   2016 $85

Huffard, Grace Thompson *My Poetry Book.* Chicago: John C. Winston Co., 1934. First edition, octavo, 8 full page color plates and 24 full page line drawings by Willy Pogany, publisher's blue cloth, front cover and spine decoratively tooled and lettered gilt, top edge stained blue, pictorial endpapers, very fine in original pictorial dust jacket. David Brass Rare Books, Inc.   2015 - 02956   2016 $250

Hughes-Stanton, Blair *Wood-Engravings.* Pinner: Private Libraries Association, 1991. First edition, 19/112 deluxe copies (of an edition of 1862 copies)m reproductions of 138 wood engravings, 16 reproductions of photos of artist and his family and friends, extra Deluxe issue plates, small folio, original quarter black morocco, backstrip gilt lettered, black cloth sides, cloth slipcase, fine.   Blackwell's Rare Books   B184 - 277   2016   £200

Hughes, Glenn *Mrs. Carlyle, an Historical Play.* Seattle: University of Washington, 1950. First edition, 8vo., illustrations, author's presentation on flyleaf, very good in slightly worn, price clipped dust jacket.   Second Life Books, Inc. 196A - 845   2016 $50

Hughes, J. Trevor *Thomas Willis 1621-1675.* London: Royal Society of medicine, 151 pages, illustrations, portraits, tall 8vo., stiff printed wrappers, color frontispiece. James Tait Goodrich   X-78 - 561   2016 $85

Hughes, Jabez *The Rape of Prosperine, from Claudian.* London: printed for J. Watts and sold by W. Meares, 1723. Second edition, 12mo., disbound, very good, very scarce. C. R. Johnson Rare Book Collections   Foxon: H-P 2015 - 477   2016 $613

Hughes, James L. *Dickens as an Educator.* New York: D. Appleton & Co., 1914. Original dark green cloth, blocked in red and black, spine lettered gilt, very good. Jarndyce Antiquarian Booksellers   CCXVIII - 1310   2016   £30

Hughes, Langston *I Wonder as I Wander.* New York: Rinehart & Co., 1956. First edition, some edgewear to boards, thus very good in fine dust jacket, nice.   Between the Covers Rare Books   202 - 43   2016 $350

Hughes, Langston *Laughing to Keep from Crying.* New York: Henry Holt, 1952. First edition, fine in slightly soiled, near fine dust jacket with modest tanning to spine, nicely inscribed by author in year of publication.   Between the Covers Rare Books   202 - 44   2016 $1750

Hughes, Langston *One-Way ticket.* New York: Alfred A. Knopf, 1949. First edition, inscribed by author for Moses Asch, Aug. 15 1955, near fine in very good dust jacket, jacket bright with some rubbing at folds and small chip at crown, no titling affected.   Royal Books   48 - 28   2016 $1500

Hughes, Langston *Simple Stakes a Claim.* New York: Rinehart, 1957. First edition, poor quality paper yellowed as always, else fine in near fine dust jacket with some slight wear at crown in scarce, collector's conditionw.   Between the Covers Rare Books   202 - 46   2016 $200

Hughes, Langston *Troubled Island: an Opera in Three Acts by William Grant Still, Libretto by Langston Hughes.* New York: Leeds Music Corp., 1949. First edition, 8vo. little soiled light blue printed wrappers, near fine, inscribed by Hughes for Richard M. Lourie.   Second Life Books, Inc.   196A - 849   2016 $600

Hughes, Langston *Troubled Island. An Opera in three acts.* New York: Leeds Music. Corporation, 1951. First edition of the libretto, 8vo., original printed wrappers, fine.   Sotheran's   Piccadilly Notes - Summer 2015 - 167   2016   £398

Hughes, Langston *The Weary Blues.* New York: Alfred A. Knopf, 1926. First edition, one of 1500 copies, small 8vo., original blue cloth backed decorated boards, inscribed by author to Ira Gershwin, covers lightly rubbed, lacking rare dust jacket, otherwise very good.   James S. Jaffe Rare Books   Occasional List: Winter 2016 - 81   2016 $35,000

Hughes, Langston *The Weary Blues.* New York: Knopf, 1944. Ninth printing, 8vo, yellow cloth, dust jacket lacks some paper at extremities of spine and small hole which affects two letters of author's name, very good, inscribed by author for Mrs. Lester Holt Nov. 14 1945.   Second Life Books, Inc.   196A - 851   2016 $450

Hughes, Richard *A High Wind in Jamaica.* London: Chatto & Windus, 1929. First edition, little foxing at beginning and little less at end, 8vo., original bright green cloth, dust jacket, slightly skewed, spine little spotted, very minor fraying to jacket, bookplate, good.   Blackwell's Rare Books   B184 - 166   2016   £250

Hughes, Richard *In the Lap of Atlas. Stories of Morocco.* London: Chatto & Windus, 1979. First edition, red cloth with gilt lettering to spine, fine in dust jacket.   Argonaut Book Shop   Literature 2015 - 4874   2016 $45

Hughes, Richard *The Spider's Palace - and Other Stories.* London: Chatto and Windus, 1931. First edition, one of 110 numbered copies signed by author, octavo, drawings by George Charlton, frontispiece in color, buckram backed decorated boards, top edge gilt, spine slightly faded, very good.   Peter Ellis   112 - 176   2016   £85

Hughes, Richard *The Wooden Shepherdess.* London: Chatto & Windus, 1972. First edition, octavo, fine in fine dust jacket, publisher's wraparound band.   Peter Ellis   112 - 177   2016   £45

Hughes, Richard *The Wooden Shepherdess. The Human Predicament volume II.* London: Chatto & Windus, 1973. First edition, fine in dust jacket designed by John Ward, inscribed by author to Joe Brewer, laid in is autograph card from Hughes.   Second Life Books, Inc.   196A - 853   2016 $225

Hughes, Richard B. *Pioneer Years in the Black Hills...* Glendale: Arthur H. Clark Co., 1957. First edition, 1000 copies, illustrations, maps, portraits, red cloth, gilt, library stamp to top edge of text block, almost unnoticeable smudge to foot of spine, else fine, bright and uncut.   Argonaut Book Shop   Biography 2015 - 5788   2016 $250

Hughes, Robert Edward *The Making of Citizens: a Study in Comparative Education.* London: Walter Scott Pub. co., 1902. First edition, Half title, 24 page catalog, original maroon cloth, slightly dulled, library numbers on spine, booklabel for the library of the faculty of Physicans and Surgeons, Glasgow.   Jarndyce Antiquarian Books   CCXV - 791   2016   £35

Hughes, Ted 1930-1998 *Chiasmadon.* Baltimore: Charles Seluzicki, 1977. First edition, #75 of 120 copies for sale, printed by Susan Johanknecht and Claire Van Vliet at the Janus Press, West Burket VT, signed by author and Van Vliet, bound in printed wrappers, fine.   Second Life Books, Inc.   196A - 854   2016 $425

Hughes, Ted 1930-1998 *Chiasmadon.* Baltimore: Charles Seluzicki, 1977. First edition, one of 5 or 6 copies specially bound for participants of the edition, out of a total of 175 copies, square 8vo., original quarter black leather and decorated paper boards by Susan Johanknecht, this ad personam copy, designated for "Victoria Fraser" in Van Vliet's hand, very fine copy.   James S. Jaffe Rare Books   Occasional List: Winter 2016 - 82   2016 $4500

Hughes, Ted 1930-1998 *Moon-Bells and Other Poems.* London: Bodley Head, 1986. First illustrated edition, with 3 additional poems, illustrations by Bowers, fine in fine dust jacket, as new.   Between the Covers Rare Books   204 - 60   2016 $40

Hughes, Ted 1930-1998 *Scapegoats and Rabies.* London: Poet & Printer, 1967. First edition, self wrappers, fine, as new one of little more than 400 copies printed.   Between the Covers Rare Books   204 - 59   2016 $50

Hughes, Ted 1930-1998 *Sean, the Fool, the Devil and the Cats - a Play in One Act.* Chicago: Dramatic Pub. Co., 1974. First separate edition, small octavo stapled wrappers, chart of stage positions, seven blank pages for director's notes, fine, scarce.   Peter Ellis   112 - 178   2016   £110

Hughes, Ted 1930-1998 *Winter Pollen.* New York: Picador, 1995. First American edition, 8vo., original quarter black cloth with blue boards, backstrip lettered in silver, dust jacket with just small amount of creasing to extremities, various clippings about author laid in, inscribed by author for mentor, Doris Wheatley.   Blackwell's Rare Books   B186 - 240   2016   £1500

Hughes, William Richard *A Week's Tramp in Dickens Land.* London: Chapman & Hall, 1893. Second edition, half title, frontispiece, illustrations, original red cloth, pictorially blocked and lettered gilt, spine slightly faded, tiny nick at head of leading hinge, owner's inscription, good, sound copy.   Jarndyce Antiquarian Booksellers   CCXVIII - 1311   2016   £45

Hugo, Richard *Rain Five Days and I Love It.* Port Townsend: Graywolf Press, 1975. One of 512 copies, this is one of 25 signed in wrappers, 8vo., paper wrappers, cover slightly faded, otherwise nice, prospectus for this title indicated that of the 512 total copies, 20 were hand colored and remainder were in wrappers, 25 of those wrappered copies, signed by author on colophon.   Second Life Books, Inc.   196A - 855   2016 $75

Hulbert, Archer Butler *The Niagara River.* New York: Putnam, 1908. First edition, large 8vo., original ribbed blue cloth, lettered gilt with mounted photographic illustration on front cover, top edge gilt, photogravure frontispiece in sepia, numerous plates after photos, fine, presentation inscription to initial blank.   Sotheran's   Travel and Exploration - 60   2016   £125

Hulbert, Homer *Omjee the Wizard.* Springfield: Milton Bradley, 1925. First edition, 4to., black pictorial cloth, fine in frayed dust jacket, illustrations by Hildegard Lupprian with full color illustrations, pictorial boards, pages printed in a range of colors, rare in dust jacket.   Aleph-bet Books, Inc.   111 - 241   2016 $275

Hulme, F. Edward *Bards and Blossoms or the Poetry, History and Associations of Flowers.* London: Marcus Ward & Co., 1877. First edition, half title, colour frontispiece and 7 further color plates, original green cloth beveled boards, elaborately decorated in gilt, black and pink, all edges gilt, attractive gift inscription "L. A. Richardson from her loving friend M. Randall, June 15 1878", fine, attractive copy.   Jarndyce Antiquarian Booksellers   CCXVII - 130   2016   £180

Hulme, F. Edward *Faimilar Wild Flowers.* London: Cassell, Petter, Galpin and Co., 1877-1885. First edition, octavo, five volumes, 200 colored plates, publisher's handsome decorated green cloth, all edges gilt, fine, crisp set.   Andrew Isles Natural History Books   55 - 38884   2016 $400

Humair, Daniel *Pulsations. Interventions by Daniel Humair. Eaux-fortes by Bertrand Dorny.* Paris: n.p., 1979. Limited to 54 numbered copies, of which 50 copies were for sale, signed by Humair and Dorny, 3 black and white etchings by Dorny, 5 pages of drawings of musical symbols on architectural vellum, square 8vo., white card wrappers with pages loosely inserted, laid loose in charcoal card cover with title in white spine, yellow cloth slipcase.   Oak Knoll Books   27 - 30   2016 $450

Humbert, L. M. *Memorials of the Hospital of St. Cross and Alms House of Noble Poverty.* Winchester and London: William Savage and Messrs. Parker & Co., 1868. 4to., cloth, gilt decorated, all edges gilt, 13 photos and 16 woodcut illustrations, scuffed at edges along spine, slight tear in cloth at bottom rear fore-edge, inscription, foxing on endpapers and on paper guards.   Oak Knoll Books   310 - 50   2016 $350

Humbly Inscribed to Parliament. Two Letters on the Flour Trade and Dearness of Corn... London: W. Flexney, 1766. First edition, 8vo., titlepage just little dusty and marked, bound in mid 20th century marbled boards with printed spine label, very good, very scarce.   John Drury Rare Books   2015 - 26319   2016 $437

Hume, Abraham *The Learned Societies and printing Clubs of the United Kingdom...* London: G. Willis, 1853. Half title, original brown cloth, little rubbed, inner hinges cracking, monogram bookplate of Allan Freer, Fordel, good plus.   Jarndyce Antiquarian Booksellers   CCXVII - 131   2016   £85

Hume, Allan C. *Stray Feathers: a Journal of Ornithology for India and Its Dependencies.* 1872-1878. Octavo, 8 volumes (lacking last 3 volumes), hand colored plates, contemporary green half calf with red labels, some rubbing, the set of the Royal Australasian Ornithologist' Union with library stamps.   Andrew Isles Natural History Books   55 - 30873   2016 $1500

Hume, David *An Enquiry Concerning the Principles of Morals.* London: printed for A. Millar, 1751. First edition, 2nd state, first four leaves, including on errata leaf and with leaf L3 a cancel, 12mo., half title and ads, contemporary speckled calf, rebacked to style, boards double ruled in gilt, spine ruled in gilt in compartments with gilt center tool and red morocco gilt lettering label, bottom margin of titlepage trimmed short about one inch no loss of text, occasional old ink notes making errata corrections, leaf M4 with a two inch closed tear with no loss of text, overall very good.   Heritage Book Shop   Holiday 2015 - 55   2016 $3000

Hume, David *Essays and treatises on Several Subjects.* London: printed for A. Millar and A. Kincaid and A. Donaldson, 1764. London: Printed for A. Millar in the Strand, and A. Kincaid, and A. Donaldson at Edinburgh, 1764. New edition, 2 volumes, 8vo., clean, crisp copy throughout, contemporary sprinkled calf, spines with contrasting red and black morocco labels, lettered and numbered in gilt, some light chipping to head and feet of spines, still fine inscribed by Thomas Bowles and dated 13 1767.   Marlborough Rare Books   List 56 - 25   2016   £950

Hume, David *Letters of David Hume to William Strahan.* Oxford: Clarendon Press, 1888. First edition, original olive green cloth bit rubbed at extremities and spine darkened but gilt lettering still clearly legible, binding firm despite touch of white on black endpapers, inside bright and clean with about half of the leaves still unopened, top edge of text block little dusty, facsimile letter in excellent condition.   Simon Finch   2015 - 000894   2016 $252

Hume, Ian D. *Digestive Physiology and Nutrition of Marsupials.* Cambridge: Cambridge University PRess, 1982. Octavo, photos, signature, very good in dust jacket.   Andrew Isles Natural History Books   55 - 1175   2016 $80

Hume, Ian D. *Marsupial Nutrition.* Melbourne: Cambridge University Press, 1999. Octavo, text illustrations, signature, paperback.   Andrew Isles Natural History Books   55 - 21397   2016 $80

Humphrey, James *An Homage the End of some More Land.* Woods Hole: the Job Shop, 1972. First edition, 1/500 copies, 8vo. paper wrappers, inscribed by author to poet Paul Metcalf, very good.   Second Life Books, Inc.   196A - 858   2016 $40

Humphrey, Mabel *Little Soldiers and Sailors.* New York: Frederick Stokes, 1899. 4to., cloth backed pictorial boards light cover soil and edge wear, else very good++, illustrations by Maud Humphrey.   Aleph-bet Books, Inc.   112 - 249   2016 $700

Humphreys, Henry Noel *Maxims and Precepts of the Saviour.* London: Longmans, Green & Co., 1848. 8vo., 16 chromolithograph leaves that constitute title and plates numbered 1-31, descriptive index, original heavily gilt and colored pressed paper mache binding, spine lettered but slight loss.   Marlborough Rare Books   List 55 - 38   2016   £450

Humphries, Sydney *A Calendar of Verse.* London: privately printed, 1912. One of 20 copies, 225 x 155mm., printed recto only, excellent full vellum over boards by Riviere & Son (stamp-signed), compiler's gilt coat of arms on each cover and foot of spine, flat spine with gilt titling, densely gilt turn-ins, ivory moire silk endleaves, top edge gilt, other edges untrimmed, fleece lined blue cloth slipcase, frontispiece with monographs of Humphires and his wife, surrounded by putti and other symbols of love, engraved coat of arms on title, ink inscription from author to William Maxwell, master printer at R. & R Clark, where the volume was printed, extremely pleasing, binding unworn, entirely clean, fresh and bright, inside and out.   Phillip J. Pirages   67 - 244   2016 $1250

Humphry, Charlotte Eliza *Manners for Men.* London: Ward Lock and Co., 1897. First edition, tall 8vo., original grey decorated cloth, very good, nice.   Jarndyce Antiquarian Books   CCXV - 266   2016   £65

Humphry, Charlotte Eliza *Manners for Men.* London: James Bowden, 1898. Sixth edition, tall 8vo., original grey decorated cloth, very good, nice.   Jarndyce Antiquarian Books   CCXV - 267   2016   £50

Hundert Meister Der Gegenwart: proben Zeitgenössischer Deutscher Malerei in Farbiger Wiedergabe.   Leipzig: Verlag von E. A. Seemann, 1902-1904. Folio, half leather, marbled paper covered boards, marbled endpapers, original paper wrappers bound in at end, tipped in color illustrations, covers rubbed and scuffed at edges, marbling on covers worn, previous owner's bookplate and inkstamp of a library stating 'withdrawn', some leaves of text chipped at edges.   Oak Knoll Books   310 - 39   2016 $500

Huneker, James *Painted Veils.* New York: Boni & Liveright, 1920. One of 1200 copies numbered and signed by author, large 8vo., paper over boards, spine browned, edges little scuffed, cover shows little insect damage, otherwise very good, tight copy.   Second Life Books, Inc.   196A - 862   2016 $45

Hungry Bibliophiles. An Experiment in Utilitarian Bookmaking.   New York: Russell Maret, 2015. 13/75 copies, printed on handmade paper using typefaces of Maret's own design, folio, original printed wrappers, prospectus loosely inserted, new.   Blackwell's Rare Books   B184 - 286   2016   £500

Hunt, Aurora *Kirby Benedict. Frontier Federal Judge. An Account of Legal and Judicial Development in the Southwest 1853-1874.*   Glendale: Arthur H. Clark Co., 1961. First edition, frontispiece, illustrations, maps, red cloth, gilt, very fine, uncut.   Argonaut Book Shop Biography 2015 - 5769   2016 $60

Hunt, John *The Ascent of Everest.* London: Hodder & Stoughton, 1953. First edition, signed by Sir Edmund Hillary, 48 black and white photos, 8 color photos, numerous maps, drawings, etc., blue cloth, fine, lightly chipped and faded pictorial dust jacket.   Argonaut Book Shop Mountaineering 2015 - 7162   2016 $500

Hunt, Leigh *A Jar of Honey from Mount Hybla.* London: Smith Elder, 1848. First edition, 8vo., text illustrations, orange blindstamped cloth.   J. & S. L. Bonham Antiquarian Booksellers Europe 2016 - 7058   2016   £40

Hunt, Leigh *Lord Byron and Some of His Contemporaries.* London: Henry Colburn, 1828. Second edition, 2 volumes, engravings, rebound in green cloth, endpapers renewed, cloth from original spines preserved, sporadic spotting, very good set.   Peter Ellis   112 - 57   2016   £185

Hunt, M. Stuart *Nova Scotia's Part in the Great War.* Halifax: Nova Scotia Veteran Pub. Co., 1920. Red cloth with N.S. coat of arms decoration to front, half title, 8vo., frontispiece, half tones, cloth quite worn and darkened, interior good.   Schooner Books Ltd.   115 - 219   2016 $50

Hunt, P. Francis *Orchidaceae.* Bourton: Bourton Press, 1973. Limited to 600 numbered copies, signed, Folio, 40 colored plates by Mary Grierson, publisher's full vellum by Zaehnsdorf, all edges gilt, cloth slipcase, fine.   Andrew Isles Natural History Books   55 - 3535   2016 $750

Hunt, Rockwell *Mr. California. Autobiography of Rockwell D. Hunt.* San Francisco: Fearon Pub., 1956. First edition, fine with dust jacket, presentation inscription signed by fellow author, Julie Altrocchi, also signed by author.   Argonaut Book Shop   Biography 2015 - 2016 $40

Hunter, Agnes Sophia *Miscellany.* London: printed by Robert Armstrong, 1811. Second edition, 12mo., original pale green paper boards, dark green cloth spine, red morocco label, little rubbed but nice in original binding, "Daughter of Dr. Henry Hunter..." written in pencil on title.   Jarndyce Antiquarian Books   CCXV - 268   2016   £150

Hunter, Dard *Dard Hunter and Son.* Newtown: Bird & Bull Press, 1998. No. 174 of 225 copies, 324 x 235 mm., publisher's black quarter morocco over red Japanese cloth, flat spine with red morocco label, in original tan silk covered folding box with red morocco label, with 30 pages of black and white illustrations, 30 tip-ins (many in full color), seven original folio or quarto leaves from Mountain House Press books, and four original samples of papers made by all three generations of Hunters, prospectus laid in at front, mint.   Phillip J. Pirages   67 - 200   2016 $1600

Hunter, Dard *The Life Work of Dard Hunter.* Chillicothe: Mountain House Press, 1981-1983. Nos. 11 (volume I) and 96 (volume II) of 100 copies of the regular edition, signed by Dard Hunter, there were an additional 50 'special copies in red morocco binding), original quite attractive chestnut brown half morocco over paper boards printed with Roycroft pattern of pink roses and green leaves, flat spines with gilt titles, leather hinges, edges untrimmed, in original sturdy linen clamshell boxes with tan morocco labels on spine volume I with 194 specimens and 65 black and white illustrations, many of those painstakingly hand printed to resemble paper and color from Hunter's original drawings, volume II with 25 color and 75 black and white illustrations, 34 paper specimens and 23 titlepage reproductions, prospectus laid in at front, mint.   Phillip J. Pirages   67 - 199   2016 $7200

Hunter, Dard *Papermaking by Hand in India.* New York: Pynson Printers, 1939. No. 87 of 370 copies signed by author and publisher, Elmer Adler, 292 x 229mm., original black quarter calf over Indian cloth in floral design, flat spine with gilt titling, publisher's (slightly worn) lettered brown cardboard slipcase, with 85 photogravure illustrations of papermaking in India and 27 specimens of Indian paper, short indentation to spine light thumbing to couple of leaves, otherwise fine, clean and bright in unworn binding.   Phillip J. Pirages   67 - 198   2016 $3200

Hunter, Dard *Papermaking by Hand in India.* New York: Pynson Printers, 1939. Limited to 370 numbered copies, signed by Hunter and by Elmer Adler, small folio, hand blocked India print cloth covered boards, black calf back by Gerhard Gerlach, deckled fore and bottom edges, slipcase, 42 leaves of illustrations, 27 actual specimens of handmade paper, slipcase rubbed on spine, few tiny scuff marks on leather spine, much better preserved binding than usually found.   Oak Knoll Books   310 - 194   2016 $1000

Hunter, Dard *A Papermaking Pilgrimage to Japan, Korea and China.* New York: Pynson Printers, 1936. First edition, limited to 370 numbered copies, signed by Hunter and designer, Elmer Adler, 4to., half leather, paper covered boards, slipcase, slight wear to leather spine, slipcase rubbed, light foxing to some of the specimen pages, prospectus loosely inserted.   Oak Knoll Books   310 - 195   2016 $2750

Hunter, George *Reminiscneces of an Old Timer.* Battle Creek: Review and Herald, 1889. Fourth edition, 8vo., illustrations, warmly inscribed "Compliments of the author..... to J. T. Hunter, as in other words Hunter to Hunter.... July 8th 90", also signed with his Indian name, red cloth stamped in gilt, little worn, hinge tender, very good.   Second Life Books, Inc.   196A - 864   2016 $350

Hunter, George W. *Mohammedan "Narrative of the Prophets" covering from Zacharias to Paul.* Tihwafu: Sinking, the editor, 1916. First and only edition, one of 100 copies, 4to., original stab-sewn Chinese style wrappers, text mimeographed on rectos only of concertina folded sheets of wrappers, slightly rubbed and chipped at edges, very light even browning, but very good, rare and fragile.   Sotheran's Travel and Exploration - 137   2016   £1795

Hunter, John   1728-1793 *A Treatise on the Blood, Inflammation and Gun-Shot Wounds by the late John Hunter.* London: printed by John Richardson for George Nicol, 1794. First edition, 4to., near fine, modern quarter leather and marbled paper boards with raised bands spine, gilt lettered spine, marbled endpapers, scattered foxing to text and plates, frontispiece, 9 additional plates.   By the Book, L. C.   45 - 18   2016 $4500

Hunter, John Marvin *The Trail Drivers of Texas.* Nashville: Cokesbury Press, 1925. Second edition, illustrations, wear to extremities, noticeable at top and bottom of spine, endpapers foxed, internally clean, very good. Dumont Maps and Books   133 - 60   2016 $175

Hunter, Joseph *Hallamshire. The History and Topography of the Parish of Sheffield in the County of York...* London: printed for the author by Richard and Arthur Taylor, published by Lackington Huges, Harding, Mavor and Jones, 1819. Large paper copy, folio, engraved portrait frontispiece and 8 further plates, further engravings in text, list of subscribers, occasional marginalia, plates slightly foxed, small tears to frontispiece, title and leaf 2Q all repaired, recent half brown calf with marbled paper boards, gilt and blind tooling to spine, top edge gilt, other edges uncut, some light scuffs to spine, edges dusty, very good, embossed ex-libris stamp, letter to Mrs. Dearden of Amercliffe Commons, Sheffield loosely inserted. Unsworths Antiquarian Booksellers   30 - 84   2016   £300

Hunter, Kenneth *Convention Song: Jobs, Security, Democracy and Peace.* New York: Workers Bookshop, 1938. 4to., illustrated cover, inscribed by author, very good. Second Life Books, Inc.   196A - 865   2016 $75

Hunter, Kristin *The Lakestown Rebellion.* New York: Scribner's, 1978. First printing, 8vo., author's signature on title, paper over boards, edges very slightly soiled, otherwise nice in somewhat soiled and chipped dust jacket. Second Life Books, Inc.   196A - 866   2016 $75

Hunter, Thomas *Moral Discourses on Providence and Other Important Subjects.* Warrington: printed by William Eyres, 1774. 2 volumes, 8vo., handsomely bound in dust jacket full calf, raised bands, compartments ruled in gilt, red morocco labels, superb copy. Jarndyce Antiquarian Booksellers   CCXVII - 132   2016   £680

Hurd, Edith Thacher *It's Snowing.* New York: Sterling Pub. Co., 1937. First edition, silver cloth, near fine in lightly frayed but very good+ dust jacket, wonderful lithographs in shades of black and grey one very page by Clement Hurd, rare first edition. Aleph-bet Books, Inc.   112 - 253   2016 $300

Hurlbutt, Frank *Bow Porcelain.* London: G. Bell and Sons, 1926. First edition, quarto, 56 halftone photographic plates and 8 color plates, original maroon cloth, gilt, spine and edges of front cover faded, else fine and clean copy. Argonaut Book Shop   Pottery and Porcelain 2015 - 4995   2016 $225

Hurry, William *Proceedings of the Assizes at Thetford on the 18th of March 1786 and the 24th of March 1787 in the Trial of William Hurry, Merchant of the Borough of Great Yarmouth on an indictment Preferred against him by John Watson...* Norwich: printed and sold by Chae and Cco. in Cockey-Lane, 1787. 4to., side stabbed sheets as issued, stitching now missing, gatherings loose, old central fold mark, some marginal dustiness. Jarndyce Antiquarian Booksellers   CCXVI - 572   2016   £50

Hurst, Fannie *Appassionata.* New York: Knopf, 1926. First edition, 8vo., limited edition, 1/220 signed by author, printed paper over boards, cloth back with paper label, unopened, cover little worn at edges, otherwise very good, tight. Second Life Books, Inc.   196A - 868   2016 $65

Hurst, Fannie *Imitation of Life.* New York: Harper & Bros., 1933. First edition, fine in red cloth, boards with fresh paper labels on spine and front board in very good dust jacket with few scattered spots on front panel, some sunning to spine and light wear to edges, with few nicks, remarkably scarce, particularly in jacket. Between the Covers Rare Books   202 - 48   2016 $5000

Hurston, Zora Neale *Jonah's Gourd Vine.* Philadelphia: Lippincott, 1934. Scarce first edition, octavo, original dust jacket, presentation inscription from author to Kate Thompson. Honey & Wax Booksellers   4 - 54   2016 $5200

Hustin, Willis *Around the World on 30 Cents or; Hop-Scotching the Globe for Fun.* Chicago: Regan Press, 1905. First printing, illustrations, pictorial paper wrappers printed in red and blue on white paper, some wear and soiling to wrappers, with closed tear to rear wrapper, bookseller ticket of Charles S. Pratt, NY, age toning to paper, withal very good, scarce. Tavistock Books   Getting Around - 53   2016 $75

Hutcheson, Francis *A Short Introduction to Moral Philosophy....* Glasgow: Robert Foulis, 1747. First English edition, 12mo. in sixes, contemporary calf with gilt ruled covers and spine, binding extremities lightly rubbed, spine with vertical cracks showing, overall clean, tight and bright. Athena Rare Books   List 15 - 1747   2016 $2500

Hutchins, John Nathan *Almanack and Ephemeris of the Motions of the Sun and the Moon The True Places and Aspects of the Planets....* Alexander Ming, 1810. First edition, small 8vo., text illustrations, pages lightly browned, original light brown pamphlet, crudely rebacked, 2 corners chipped, no loss of text, pages lightly browned, some contemporary annotations. J. & S. L. Bonham Antiquarian Booksellers   America 2016 - 9737   2016   £60

Hutchinson, Horace G. *Fishing.* Pub. at the Office of "Country Life" by George Newnes Ltd., 1907. Second edition, 2 volumes original red cloth, red lettering to spines, color and black and white plates and illustrations, previous owners' bookplates, very good. Sotheran's Hunting, Shooting & Fishing - 127   2016   £100

Hutchinson, Thomas *The Hutchinson Papers.* Albany: Prince Society, 1865. Limited to 160 numbered copies, this one of 10 large paper copies, 2 volumes, wrappers soiled, chipping to edges of both volumes, first and last several sheets on both volumes detached, text block volume two cracked at center, paper on spines worn with some loss of paper to tail of spine volume one, spine labels on both volumes chipped, mostly uncut.   Oak Knoll Books   310 - 293   2016 $450

Hutchinson, Veronica *Chimney Corner Fairy Tales.* New York: Minton Balch, 1926. First edition, 4to., orange cloth, fine in very good+ dust jacket lightly worn at spine ends and corners, 6 color plates plus numerous black and whites, beautiful copy, quite scarce.   Aleph-bet Books, Inc.   111 - 259   2016 $450

Hutchinson, W. H. *Oil, Land and Politics. The California Career of Thomas Robert Bard.* Norman: University of Oklahoma Press, 1965. First edition, 2 volumes, presentation inscription signed by author, numerous illustrations from photos, maps, grey cloth printed in black and gold, very fine set, slipcase.   Argonaut Book Shop   Biography 2015 - 7421   2016 $175

Hutton, Laurence *Plays and Players.* New York: Hurd and Houghton, 1875. 8vo., owner's bookplate, author's presentation and picture pasted on blank, cover worn, otherwise very good.   Second Life Books, Inc.   196A - 870   2016 $75

Hutton, Samuel King *A Shepherd in the Snow. The Life Story of Walter Perrett of Labrador.* London: Hodder & Stoughton, 1936. 8vo., cloth worn and darkened, some offsetting and foxing to endpapers and paper edges. Schooner Books Ltd.   115 - 104   2016 $175

Huttton, Paul Andres *Soldiers West. Biographies from the Military frontier.* Lincoln: University of Nebraska Press, 1987. First edition, numerous portraits, beige cloth, very fine, pictorial dust jacket.   Argonaut Book Shop   Biography 2015 - 7423   2016 $45

Huxley, Elspeth *White Man's Country. Lord Delamere and The Making of Kenya.* London: MacMillan, 1935. First edition, 8vo., 2 volumes, original orange cloth, spine lettered in gilt, plate sand four folding maps, light marking to cloth, internally, apart from very few faint discolorations, very good, inscribed by athor on both half titles to Joy and George Adamson, dated Dec. 1956, contemporary name boldly on both front covers.   Sotheran's Travel and Exploration - 14   2016   £498

Huxley, Julian *A Scientist Among the Soviets.* New York: Harper and Bros., 1932. First US edition, original cloth and jacket, spine little sunned, ner fine.   Sotheran's Piccadilly Notes - Summer 2015 - 169   2016   £110

Hyde, J. A. Lloyd *Oriental Lowestoft Chinese Export Porcelain. Porcelaine de la Cie des Indes.* Newport: The Ceramic Book Co., 1964. Third edition, limited to 1000 copies, quarto, numerous black and white plates and color frontispiece, gilt lettered orange cloth, spine faded, else fine. Argonaut Book Shop   Pottery and Porcelain 2015 - 1618   2016 $90

Hyde, Philip *The Last Redwoods.* San Francisco: Sierra Club, 1963. First edition, presentation inscription, signed by Francois Leylet, 78 black and white photos and 8 color photos, large folding map, grayish brown cloth, very fine with pictorial dust jacket.   Argonaut Book Shop Photography 2015 - 7165   2016 $150

Hyett, Jack *A Bushman's Year.* Melbourne: F. W. Cheshire, 1959. Octavo, photos, signed by author, fine in dust jacket.   Andrew Isles Natural History Books   55 - 21414   2016 $30

A Hymn to the Chair; or Lucubrations, Serious and Comical on te Use of Chairs, Benches, Forms, Joint-Stools, Three Legged Stools... London: printed for B. Dickinson, Tho. Corbet and R. Montague and sold by E. Nutt..., 1732. First edition, 8vo., disbound, very good, rare.   C. R. Johnson Rare Book Collections   Foxon: H-P 2015 - 484   2016 $3448

Hymns for Children. printed by A. Pari, and sold by Henry Haslop and at the Chapels of the United Brethren in Great Britain and Ireland, 1797. 12mo., some foxing and staining, latter particularly at end, original sheep, spine defective at either end, corners worn, piece cut from top of front flyleaf, ownership inscription, with just surname Crawford. Blackwell's Rare Books   B184 - 55   2016   £750

I

Ibarruri, Dolores *Speeches & Articles 1936-1938.* London: Lawrence & Wishart, 1938. First UK edition, from Russian sheets of the first English language edition, octavo, photos, wrappers, cover edges nicked and rubbed, text block bit bumped at corners, very good.   Peter Ellis   112 - 371   2016   £35

Ibsen, Henrik *A Doll's House.* New York: D. Appleton, 1890. First American edition, 8vo., cream vellum boards and green cloth, little soiled, untrimmed.   Second Life Books, Inc.   197 - 188   2016 $135

Ibsen, Henrik *Peer Gynt.* London: George G. Harrap & Co. Ltd., 1936. First (British) printing of this edition, 260 x 197mm., original linen boards, original pictorial dust jacket, 12 color plates , including frontispiece, by Arthur Rackham, all protected by tissue guards with descriptive letterpress, dust jacket with tiny chip out of bottom edge of back panel and two very minor closed tears at bottom of front panel, little chafing at folds, still very fine in fine dust jacket.   Phillip J. Pirages   67 - 294   2016 $1950

Ibsen, Henrik *Peer Gynt.* London: George Harrap, 1936. Limited to 460 copies signed by Rackham, 4to., full vellum decorated in gold, top edge gilt, some discoloration of vellum, else near fine, pictorial endpapers, 12 color plates, plus numerous fanciful black and whites by Arthur Rackham, beautiful copy.   Aleph-bet Books, Inc.   111 - 383   2016 $1850

Ibsen, Henrik *Haermaende Pa Helgeland... (The Vikings of Helgeland).* Kobenhavn: Gylendalske, 1873. Second edition, small 8vo., half roan, worn, contents good.   Dramatis Personae   119 - 72   2016 $50

The Idler, a Treasury of Essay, Criticism and General Literature. London: Houlston and Stoneman, 1856. 6 numbers, all published, contemporary half roan, bit rubbed and worn.   Jarndyce Antiquarian Booksellers   CCXVII - 225   2016   £125

Ignatius, David *Agents of Innocence.* New York: Norton, 1987. First edition, very fine in printed wrappers, with copy of promotional pamphlet containing excerpts from the novel, uncorrected proof.   Mordida Books   2015 - 012073   2016 $65

Ihimaera, Witi *The Whale Rider.* Auckland: Heinemann, 1987. First edition, 8vo., original cloth boards, dust jacket, illustrations by John Howell, spine ends and extreme foretips very slightly rubbed, otherwise fine in trifle edgeworn dust jacket, original edition scarce, presentation inscribed by author.   James S. Jaffe Rare Books   Occasional List: Winter 2016 - 83   2016 $850

Illinois Central Railroad Company *Sectional Maps showing 2,500,000 Acres (of) Farms and Wood Lands... in all parts of the State of Illinois...* Chicago: Office in Central Rail Road, 1856. First edition, 8vo., 34 full page black and white maps, 2 folding, original printed wrappers, lightly dust soiled, spine worn, wrappers starting, rare.   M & S Rare Books, Inc.   99 - 118   2016 $1650

The Illiterati Proposes: Creation, Experiment and Revolution to Build a Waterless Free Society....No. 4 Summer 1945. Waldport: Illiterati, 1945. octavo, stapled illustrated wrappers, tiny crease on edge of couple of pages, else fine.   Between the Covers Rare Books   204 - 38   2016 $225

The Illustrated London Almanack. London: published at the Office of the Illustrated London News, 1845-1849. 1850-1854. 1865-1874, 20 volumes bound in 3, large 8vo., each 74 pages, those 1865-1874 with coloured illustrations and original coloured wrappers bound in, contemporary half calf, spines with black labels lettered gilt, marbled edges.   Marlborough Rare Books   List 55 - 3   2016   £750

Illustrated London News. 1954. Color and black and white illustrations, very small color bleeding from margin of front red cover on front blank free endpaper, otherwise very good.   I. D. Edrich   Winston Spencer Churchill - 2016   £20

Imprimerie Royale *Notice Sur les Types Etrangers du Specimen de L'Imprimerie Royale.* Paris: Imprimerie Royale, 1847. First edition, 4to., original printed paper covered boards, spine rubbed, corners of boards rubbed and scuffed at edges, boards soiled and stained, stamp in modern Turkish on front board, titlepage stamped with stamp of director's office.   Oak Knoll Books   310 - 190   2016 $650

Incbold, Stanley *Lisbon and Cintra.* London: Chatto & Windus, 1907. First edition, 8vo., illustrations (1 torn), original red decorative cloth.   J. & S. L. Bonham Antiquarian Booksellers   Europe 2016 - 9862   2016   £45

Inchbald, Elizabeth *A Simple Story.* London: printed for G. G. J. and J. Robinson, 1791. Second edition, half titles discarded, ownership inscription of Jan Panton, touch of light soiling and browning, one leaf in volume I with small paper flaw to blank margin, one gathering in volume iii rough at bottom edge (missed by binder's knife), 8vo., late 19th century half calf, sometime rebacked to style, dark brown morocco lettering pieces, marbled boards, edges and endpapers, slightly rubbed, corners bit worn, hinges neatly relined, good.   Blackwell's Rare Books   B186 - 80   2016   £500

Infidelity Punished. report of a Remarkable Trial The King vs. The Rev. Robert Taylor, a Minister of the Established Church of England for a Blasphemous Discourse Against Our Lord Jesus Christ....   New York: printed and published by Robert Wauchope No. 11 spring Street, First American edition, 8vo., removed, quite browned and foxed.   M & S Rare Books, Inc.   99 - 73   2016 $175

Ingegneri, Giovanni *Fisionomia Naturale nella Quale con Ragioni Tolte dalla Filosofia della Medicina & dall' Anatomia.* Milan: Gio. Pietro Giovanini, 1607. 12mo., woodcut printer's device on title, large woodcut initials throughout, some marginal worming to first few leaves, some soiling and staining to first few leaves, very good in contemporary vellum.   Edwin V. Glaser Rare Books   2015 - 19419   2016 $650

Ingelow, Jean *Mopsa the Fairy.* New York: Harper & Bros., 1927. First edition, 8vo., maroon cloth, pictorial paste on, fine in dust jacket (frayed, light soil), rare in dust jacket, color frontispiece, 12 full page black and whites plus numerous half page black and whites and pictorial endpapers.   Aleph-bet Books, Inc.   111 - 249   2016 $750

Inglis, Henry David *Spain in 1830.* London: Whittaker Treacher, 1831. First edition, 2 volumes, 8vo., contemporary black half morocco, raised bands and gilt, minimal rubbing to spine, handsome set.   J. & S. L. Bonham Antiquarian Booksellers   Europe 2016 - 9746   2016   £1250

Inglow, Jean *Mopsa the Fairy.* New York: Macmillan, Sept., 1927. First Walker edition, 8vo., blue pictorial cloth, very good- fine in dust jacket with color plate but lacking spine panel, pictorial endpapers, color frontispiece, many full page and partial black and whites by Dugald Stewart Walker.   Aleph-bet Books, Inc.   112 - 508   2016 $250

Ingraham, J. H. *Scarlet Father or the Young Chief of the Abeanaquies a Romance of the Wilderness of Maine.* Boston: F. Gleason, 1845. First edition, 12mo., illustrations, engraved vignette on title and at conclusion of text, sewn, spine worn, front wrapper loose, uncut, heavily foxed.   M & S Rare Books, Inc.   99 - 125   2016 $225

Ingraham, Prentiss *Merle, The Boy Cruiser; or Brandt, the Buccanner.* New York: Beadle & Adams, volume XVIII no. 227 May 16, 1888. First printing thus, large wood engravings to front wrapper, 8vo., printed self wrappers, staple, minor soiling, very good, fragile.   Tavistock Books   Getting Around - 3   2016 $175

Ingram, James *Memorials of Oxford.* Oxford: John Henry Parker; H. Slatter and W. Graham, 1837. First edition, Volume I-(III), 3 general views as frontispieces, folding plan in volume iii, and 94 plates, all steel engraved, some foxing as usual, wood engraved titlepage vignettes and numerous text illustrations, 8vo., contemporary green morocco by W. Hayes of Oxford, extremities very slightly rubbed, spine with raised bands, gilt lettered direct in second and third compartments, remainder panelled with wheel decoration, sides gilt panelled with wide gilt borders, single fillet on board edges, gilt roll on turn-ins, gilt edges, very good.   Blackwell's Rare Books   B186 - 109   2016   £70

Ingram, James *Memorials of Oxford.* Malvern: Cappella Archive, 2007. 17/100 copies,, frontispiece engravings, 300 further illustrations by James Ingram, 8vo., original cream cloth stamped in blue to front and backstrip, blue pages markers, endpaper maps of contemporary Oxford, matching slipcase, fine.   Blackwell's Rare Books   B184 - 278   2016   £150

Innes, Doreen *Ethics and Rhetoric.* Oxford: Clarendon Press, 1995. First edition, 8vo., blue boards, gilt lettered to spine, 93cm. scratch to spine, spot of wear to top board, blue dust jacket, spine slightly faded, very good, ownership inscription of C D. N. Costa, complimentary copy note loosely inserted.   Unsworths Antiquarian Booksellers Ltd.   E05 - 41   2016   £65

Innes, Emily *Chersonese with the gilding Off.* London: Richard Bentley, 1885. First edition, 2 volumes, frontispiece illustrations, original green pictorial cloth lettered gilt, from the library of John William Darwood with his bookplate in each volume, founder of the tram system in Burma as well as the Strand Hotel in Rangoon, with errata slip, covers little marked and little bruised at edges, edges of free endpaper to volume I, just little chipped, very good, scarce.   Peter Ellis   112 - 246   2016   £550

Innes, Hammond *Dead and Alive.* London: Collins, 1946. First edition, very good in good dust jacket with few nicks and chips.   Peter Ellis   112 - 183   2016   £85

Innes, Michael *Appleby Talks Again.* London: Gollancz, 1956. First edition, fine in blindstamped dust jacket with darkened spine and chipping at top of spine.   Mordida Books   2015 - 012083   2016 $60

Innes, Michael *Lord Mullion's Secret.* London: Victor Gollancz, 1981. First edition, octavo, bookplate with owner's signature on top edge and with author's signature at bottom, near fine in like dust jacket slightly creased at head and tail of spine.   Peter Ellis   112 - 184   2016   £35

L'Innocence de la Tresillustre. Tres-chaste, et Debonnaire Princesse, Madame Marie Royne d'Escosse. n.p. Iprime an, 1572. 8vo., signature O omitted in make up, text complete, all pages faintly rubricated, very nice, bound by Bedford in dark blue morocco gilt, dentelles, marbled endpapers, all edges gilt, ownership signature of A. Elphinston(e) on titlepage with dated in lower margin 1600, later armorial bookplate of James Wyllie Guild and Thomas Brooke, FSA, Armitage Bridge, ownership inscription Alexander W. Ruthven Stuart 1923.   Jarndyce Antiquarian Booksellers   CCXVII - 182   2016   £1500

The Innocent Epicure; or the Art of Angling. London: printed by H. Meere for R. Gosling, 1713. Second edition, small 8vo., contemporary calf, gilt, neatly rebacked, spine gilt, red morocco label, presentation copy, inscribed 'Ex dono authoris', fine, bookplates of Edwin Snow and Henry Sherwin. C. R. Johnson Rare Book Collections   Foxon: H-P 2015 - 487   2016 $3831

Ionesco, Eugene *Double Act.* Canberra: Raft Press, 1992. Limited to 6 numbered copies, small 4to., gray handmade thick paper folded case with paper cover label, exposed cord binding, green cloth slipcase with paper spine label, heavy leaves, some printed text, some blank and 4 with illustrations.   Oak Knoll Books   27 - 56   2016 $500

Iraq Petroleum Company *An Account of the Construction in the Years 1932 to 1934 of the Pipe-Line of the Iraq Petroleum Company Limited ...* London: St. Clements Press, Oct., 1934. First edition, very rare, folio, original petrol blue quarter leather over boards, spine lettered gilt and with two panels blocked in gilt on front cover, folding plan, folding map, numerous superb illustrations in text, wear to extremities of binding, internally fine, contemporary bookplate of A. Denys Cadman, later in the Library of the University of Wyoming with stamp (cancelled), shelfmark label removed.   Sotheran's   Travel and Exploration - 329   2016   £798

Ireland, Alexander *The Book-Lover's Enchiridion.* London: Simpkin Marshall and Co., 1883. Third edition, octavo, finely bound by Sangorski & Sutcliffe circa 1930 in full red calf covers with double gilt rules, front cover lettered gilt, spine with five raised bands, decoratively tooled in gilt in compartments, two blue morocco labels lettered gilt, gilt board edges and decorative turn-ins, top edge gilt, marbled endpapers, fine binding example.   David Brass Rare Books, Inc.   2015 - 03007   2016 $225

Ireland, Alleyne *The Far Eastern Tropics, Studies in the administration of tropical Dependencies.* Boston and New York: Houghton Mifflin and Co., 1905. First edition, 8vo., original green ribbed cloth lettered in gilt, very light toning, near fine, signed presentation inscribed by author to John C. Phillips.   Sotheran's   Travel and Exploration - 138   2016   £398

Ireland, John *Hogarth Illustrated. (with) Graphic Illustrations of Hogarth from Pictures, Drawings and Scarce Prints.* J. J. Boydell and R. Faulder, 1791-1794. First edition, 8vo., 3 volumes, uniformly bound in contemporary full diced Russia calf, spines ruled in gilt contrasting black leather labels, 154 engraved plates, spines slightly sunned, some browning and offsetting, otherwise very good, from the library of Sir James Colquhoun of Luss with bookplate. Sotheran's   Piccadilly Notes - Summer 2015 - 170   2016   £1000

Ireland, Samuel *Picturesque Views on the Thames from Its Source in Gloucestershire to the Nore with Observations on the Public Buildings and Other Works of Art.* London: Egerton, 1792. First edition, 2 volumes, 8vo., 2 maps, sepia aquatint titlepages, 52 sepia aquatints, some light occasional spotting mainly in margins, contemporary speckled calf, volume i neatly rebacked using original spine with some small loss at head.   J. & S. L. Bonham Antiquarian Booksellers   Europe 2016 - 9236   2016   £500

Ireland, William Henry 1777-1835 *Memoirs of Jeanne D'Arc Surnamed La Pucelle D'Orleans with the History of Her Times.* London: Robert Triphook, 1824. 2 volumes bound in 4, 241 x 152mm., pleasing 19th century dark blue three quarter morocco flat spines decorated in gilt and inlaid with four tan fleurs-de-lys, marbled sides and endpapers, top edge gilt, with 27 plates, including five called for (one a double page, another folding color scene) and extra-illustrated with 22 plates, four of them in color, large paper copy, front flyleaf with signature of Charles G. Dill dated 31 May 1909; joints and extremities with hint of rubbing (but well masked with dye), small chip out of spine top, backstrips lightly and uniformly sunned, but the pretty bindings solid and with no serious condition issues, flyleaves and final leaf in each volume somewhat browned, (one opening with small portion of pages similarly browned from a laid-in acidic object), variable offsetting from the plates (perhaps a dozen rather noticeably offset), intermittent spotted foxing (isolated leaves more heavily foxed), not without problems internally, but with text still fresh, without many signs of use and printed within vast margins.   Phillip J. Pirages   67 - 204   2016 $850

Ireland, William Henry 1777-1835 *Memoirs of Jeanne D'Arc surnamed La Pucelle D'Orleans with the History of Her Times.* London: printed for Robert Triphood, 1824. 2 volumes, 8vo., 2 plates, sporadic foxing, some toning to plates and offsetting to facing pages, half green morocco marbled paper covered boards, raised bands, gilt title to spine, top edge gilt, other edges uncut, marbled endpapers, spines faded and little scratched, joints and endcaps rubbed, little scuffed, still very good, armorial bookplate of Sir Robert Peel, later bookplate of John Porter, small ink-stamp "Mentmore".   Unsworths Antiquarian Booksellers   30 - 87   2016   £180

The Iris. London: printed for E. Livermore, published by J. Gifford, 1825. Volume I, nos. I-XXVI, contemporary boards, rather worn, roughly rebacked, 4to., Renier booklabel.   Jarndyce Antiquarian Booksellers   CCXVII - 226   2016   £85

Irving, Henry   *The Drama. Addresses...* London: Heinemann, 1893. Small 8vo., white boards, mild staining to extremities of covers, spine darkened, frontispiece, tissue guarded, "Presentation Copy" in blind stamp to front flyleaf.   Dramatis Personae   119 - 74   2016 $50

Irving, John 1942- *The 158-Pound Marriage.* New York: Random House, 1974. First edition, inscribed and signed by author for William Meredith, fine in near fine dust jacket.   Charles Agvent   William Meredith - 60   2016 $300

Irving, John 1942- *The Pension Grillparzer.* Logan: Perfection Form Co., 1980. First separate appearance, clean, near fine copy with some of the usual light fading to spine, uncommon.   Jeff Hirsch Books   Holiday List 2015 - 46   2016 $175

Irving, John 1942- *The World According to Garp.* New York: Dutton, 1978. First edition, author's signature on half title, owner's name on flyleaf, very good in little scuffed and chipped dust jacket.   Second Life Books, Inc.   196A - 877   2016 $450

Irving, Washington 1783-1859 *The Adventures of Captain Bonneville or Scenes Beyond the Rocky Mountains of the Far West.* London: Richard Bentley, 1837. First English edition, 3 volumes, contemporary half calf, spines gilt in compartments, brown and maroon leather labels.   Jarndyce Antiquarian Booksellers   CCXVII - 135   2016   £650

Irving, Washington 1783-1859 *The Adventures of Captain Bonneville.* New York: and London: printed by Knickerbocker Press for G. P. Putnam's, 1895. No. 3 of 100 copies of the Colorado edition, 253 x 180mm., 2 volumes, handsome scarlet crushed morocco by Zaehnsdorf (stamp signed), covers with gilt triple fillet border, raised bands, spines gilt in double-ruled compartments with anthemion centerpiece in gilt and inlaid black morocco, gilt titling, richly gilt turn-ins, marbled endpapers, all edges centerpiece in gilt and inlaid black morocco, gilt titling, richly gilt turn-ins, marbled endpapers, all edges gilt, folding map, 28 plates printed on Japan as called for, all with captioned tissue guards, text framed in gold, small faintly darkened area at top of front cover of volume II, otherwise especially beautiful set in extraordinarily fine, bindings remarkably lustrous and entirely unworn, text and plates pristine.   Phillip J. Pirages   67 - 201   2016 $1250

Irving, Washington 1783-1859 *Bracebridge Hall.* London: John Murray, 1822. First British edition, 2 volumes, second issue of volume II with text finishing on page 404, contemporary three quarter dark green calf, marbled boards, covers bit rubbed, some edge wer, especially at corners, overall attractive, clean set.   Argonaut Book Shop   Literature 2015 - 4879   2016 $300

Irving, Washington 1783-1859 *Chronicle of the Conquest of Granada. (and) The Alhambra.* New York and London: Printed at the Knickerbocker Press for G. P. Putnam's Sons, 1893-1894. 229 x 165mm., 4 volumes, representing two separately published works, each in two volumes, publisher's ivory buckram, ornately embellished with Moorish inspired design by Alice Cordelia Morse, covers with elaborate decoration in colors and gilt, flat spines with gilt titling, decoration and patterned endpapers, top edge gilt, in original blue cloth dust jacket, gilt titling on spine, 61 photogravures of the Alhambra and Granada, each with lettered tissue guard, engraved bookplate of Ella C. Smith (Alhambra) and Harold Randolph (Granada), mild browning to leaves opposite illustrations from acidic tissue guards, otherwise extraordinarily fine set, clean and fresh in very pretty publisher's bindings beautifully protected by original fine dust jackets.   Phillip J. Pirages   67 - 202   2016 $950

Irving, Washington 1783-1859 *The Legend of Sleepy Hollow.* London: George Harrap, 1928. First edition with these illustrations, 4to., publisher's full brown leather, top edge gilt in original publisher's box with label (box repaired with wear), color plates and black and white drawings by Arthur Rackham, special binding is rare, especially in box.   Aleph-bet Books, Inc.   111 - 374   2016 $1250

Irving, Washington 1783-1859 *The Life and Voyages of Christopher Columbus.* New York: N. and J. White, 1834. Plates, contemporary straight grain morocco, title with gilt box on front cover, marbled endpapers and edges, foxing, hinges cracking very slightly but quite secure, presentation inscribed by author for Mary Rhinelander, uncommon.   Joseph J. Felcone, Inc.   Books from Five Centuries: a Miscellany - 81   2016 $2600

Irving, Washington 1783-1859 *Rip Van Winkle.* London & New York: Heinemann & Doubleday Page, 1905. First edition, first impression, 4to., green gilt cloth, small snag at head of spine, text pages foxed, else tight and very good+, 51 magnificent color plates plus several black and whites by Arthur Rackham. Aleph-bet Books, Inc. 111 - 379 2016 $1350

Irving, Washington 1783-1859 *Rip Van Winkle.* Philadelphia: McKay, 1921. First edition, first issue, 4to., brown cloth, pictorial paste-on, very slight edge rubbing, neat owner inscription, fine in worn and chipped dust jacket, illustrations by N. C. Wyeth, this copy signed by Wyeth and dated 1822. Aleph-bet Books, Inc. 112 - 524 2016 $3500

Irving, Washington 1783-1859 *Tales of a Traveller.* London: John Murray, 1824. First edition with five items not included in later First American edition, 232 x 143mm., publisher's blue paper boards, paper labels on spine, edges untrimmed, recently resewn and rebacked, using original backstrips), in blue cloth chemise and inside a matching (slightly rubbed and soiled), slipcase, black morocco backed spine designed to appear on shelf as two volumes with raised bands and gilt titling, engraved booklabel from which the name has been removed, corners worn, boards slightly soiled, original temporary bindings expertly restored now and extremely pleasing, very faint offsetting here and there, just most trivial isolated soiling, otherwise a fine copy internally, leaves especially fresh and clean and margins inordinately ample. Phillip J. Pirages 67 - 203 2016 $2250

Is She His Wife? Or, Something Singular. Boston: James R. Osgood & Co., 1877. Original brick brown cloth, spine lettered in black, front board lettered gilt and blocked in black, ads on endpapers, little rubbed at head and tail of spine, front board slightly marked, Poughkeepsie bookseller's ticket partially removed, good plus. Jarndyce Antiquarian Booksellers CCXVIII - 163 2016 £450

Isaacs, Susan *Shining Through.* New York: Harper & Row, 1988. First printing, 8vo., author's signature on title, white cloth, almost as new in very slightly yellowed dust jacket, fine. Second Life Books, Inc. 196A - 878 2016 $65

Isherwood, Christopher *The Condor and the Cows.* London: Methuen, 1949. First edition, 8vo. map, illustrations, original red cloth, some splash marks on upper cover, dust jacket worn with small loss, internally clean. J. & S. L. Bonham Antiquarian Booksellers America 2016 - 9839 2016 £50

Isherwood, Christopher *Lions and Shadows an Education the Twenties.* London: Hogarth Press, 1938. First edition, photographic frontispiece, foolscap 8vo, original blue cloth, first issue with backstrip blocked in black, partial browning to free endpapers, dust jacket with design by Robert Medley reproduced on front panel, backstrip panl darkened and trifle frayed at head and tail, few small ink spots to rear panel, good, bookplate of Paul Tabori. Blackwell's Rare Books B186 - 241 2016 £200

Isherwood, Christopher *The Memorial - Portrait of a family.* London: Hogarth Press, 1932. First edition, pink linen lettered in blue, octavo, 1222 copies printed, free endpapers very lightly spotted, otherwise fine in near fine dust jacket, designed by John Banting, hint of fading to spine, bright copy. Peter Ellis 112 - 186 2016 £575

Isherwood, Christopher *The Mortmere Stories.* London: Enitharmon Press, 1994. First edition, one of 50 copies signed by Edward Upward, Graham Crowley and Katherine Bucknell, specially bound, octavo, images by Graham Crowley, one mounted in panel on upper cover, fine in near fine plain acetate dust jacket with short tear on rear panel. Peter Ellis 112 - 187 2016 £275

Ishiguro, Kazuo *An Artist of the Floating World.* London: Faber & Faber, 1986. First edition, fine in fine dust jacket. Bella Luna Books 2016 - t9432 2016 $99

Ishiguro, Kazuo *The Remains of the Day.* London: Faber and Faber, 1989. First edition, crown 8vo., original black boards, backstrip lettered in silver, dust jacket with mereest hint of fading to backstrip panel, touch of light creasing at head of same, near fine, very bright, first state dust jacket. Blackwell's Rare Books B184 - 167 2016 £100

Ives, Gordon Langley *Conversations of Bigfoot.* Cedarville: Floating Island Press, 1998. First edition, pictorial wrappers, vignette illustrations, bottom corner of front cover faded, else fine. Gene W. Baade, Books on the West 2015 - 5016070 2016 $42

Ives, Joseph C. *Report Upon the Colorado River of the West... (with) Hydrographic Report. (with) Geological Report. (with) Botany. (with) Zoology. (with) Appendices.* Washington: GPO, 1861. 1860, 5 parts in 1, 4to., fine illustrations, 2 large folding lithographed maps, 8 fine folding panoramic views, 8 chromolithographic plates, numerous steel engravings, minor tears to maps repaired, some browning, spotting and engraving offsetting, page 108 glue spot on plate has pulled some facing text, titlepage with small perforated LC and dated 1908, rubber stamp on verso, otherwise clean pages, original pictorial gilt and blind stamped dark brown cloth covers, recent new spine of similarly toned cloth, LC bookplate, very good, clean and well maintained. Jeff Weber Rare Books 181 - 6 2016 $1400

Ives, Joseph C. *Report Upon the Colorado River of the West.* Washington: GPO, 1861. First edition, quarto, 2 large folding maps (1 repaired, tape used in margin of one of the profiles), 14 plates, 8 folding panoramas, original black blind stamped cloth, gilt vignette on upper cover, little wear to head of spine, corner bumped, good, clean.   J. & S. L. Bonham Antiquarian Booksellers   America 2016 - 9188   2016   £590

Ivey, Eowyn *The Snow Child.* New York: Little Brown & Co., 2012. First edition, cloth and boards, signature of author, fine in dust jacket.   Gene W. Baade, Books on the West   2015 - 5002055   2016 $50

J

Jack and the Beanstalk. New York: George Sully, 1920. 8vo. pictorial boards, slight spine wear, else fine, publisher's pictorial box, illustrations by W. Stecher.   Aleph-bet Books, Inc.   111 - 166   2016 $125

Jack Dandy's Delight or the History of Birds and Beasts: in Prose and Verse. York: Kendrew, n.d. circa, 1820. 16mo. yellow wrappers, fine, 13 woodcuts.   Aleph-bet Books, Inc.   111 - 151   2016 $175

Jack the Giant Killer and Other Tales. New York: Blue Ribbon, 1932. Thick 4to., pictorial boards, usual hinge strains, else unusually fine in fine dust jacket, illustrations by Harold Lentz, nicest copy you're likely to find.   Aleph-bet Books, Inc.   111 - 357   2016 $900

Jack, Marian   *Christmas Brownie in Christmas Land.* London: Frederick Warne, n.d. circa, 1915. Cloth backed boards, pictorial paste-on, near fine, publisher's file, so stamped, 8 great color plates, full page brown illustrations and brown line in-text.   Aleph-bet Books, Inc.   112 - 108   2016 $300

Jackman, S. W.   *Tasmania.* Newton Abbot: David & Charles, 1974. First edition, 8vo., original cloth and dust jacket, black and white illustrations, dust jacket price clipped, near fine.   Sotheran's   Piccadilly Notes - Summer 2015 - 172   2016   £30

The Jacks Put to their Trumps; a Tale of a King James's Irish Shilling. London: printed and sold by R Burleigh, 1714. First edition, 8vo., disbound blank outer margin of half title trimmed bit close, but very good, very rare.   C. R. Johnson Rare Book Collections   Foxon: H-P 2015 - 491   2016 $3064

Jackson, Alfred   *Time from an Amateur's Palette or a Few Stray Lines of Thorugh.* London: Effingham Wilson, 1849. 12 page catalog (Aug. 1849), pages slightly dusted throughout, original red cloth, borders, spine lettered in gilt, little rubbed and dulled.   Jarndyce Antiquarian Booksellers   CCXVIII - 886   2016   £40

Jackson, Charles   *The Lost Weekend.* New York: Farrar & Rinehart, 1944. First edition, Fine bright copy in dust jacket with some minor professional restoration to spine ends, sharp copy, author's warm contemporary presentation inscription to Dick May Jan. 27 '44.   Buckingham Books   2015 - 26213   2016 $3750

Jackson, Helen Hunt   *Ramona.* Los Angeles: Limited Editions Club, 1959. One of 1500 numbered copies, signed by artist, handsomely printed, color illustrations from drawings, multicolored buckram, printed paper spine label, very fine in slipcase.   Argonaut Book Shop   Literature 2015 - 7597   2016 $175

Jackson, Jack   *Shooting the Sun: Cartographic Results of Military Activities in Texas 1689-1829.* Austin: Book Club of Texas, 1998. Limited edition 299 of 325, 2 volumes, illustrations, slipcase slightly rubbed, volumes near fine.   Dumont Maps and Books   134 - 40   2016 $750

Jackson, John J.   *Bermuda.* Newton Abbot: David & Charles, 1988. First edition, 8vo., original cloth and dust jacket, black and white illustrations, near fine.   Sotheran's Piccadilly Notes - Summer 2015 - 173   2016   £30

Jackson, Mary Catherine   *Word-Sketches in the Sweet South.* London: Richard Bentley, 1873. First edition, 8vo., frontispiece, late 19th century full red calf, gilt spine, raised bands, school crest on upper cover, fine.   J. & S. L. Bonham Antiquarian Booksellers   Europe 2016 - 8978   2016   £350

Jackson, S. W.   *Egg Collecting and Bird Life of Australia, Catalogue and Date of the "Jacksonain Oological Collection".* Sydney: Author, 1907. Quarto, photos, publisher's printed wrappers, fine.   Andrew Isles Natural History Books   55 - 8802   2016 $4500

Jackson, Shirley   *Hangsaman.* New York: Farrar Straus and Young, 1951. First edition, extremities of boards little worn, else fine in price clipped, very good dust jacket with some foxing on rear panel, inscribed by author for Joseph Mitchell and his wife, very nice copy.   Between the Covers Rare Books   208 - 41   2016 $4800

Jackson, Thomas Graham   *Six Ghost Stories...* London: John Murray, 1919. First edition, octavo, original decorated grey cloth, front and spine panels stamped in black, right, near fine, excellent copy, uncommon, rarely found in superior condition.   John W. Knott, Jr./L.W. Currey, Inc.   Fall-Winter 2015 - 17628   2016 $750

Jackson, William   *A Lecture on Rail Roads Delivered Jan. 12 1829.* Boston: Henry Bowen, 1829. Second edition, 18mo., sewn and uncut as issued.   M & S Rare Books, Inc.   99 - 258   2016 $450

Jacob, Giles   *New Law Dictionary.* London: In the Savoy; printed by E. and R. Nutt and R. Gosling..., 1729. First edition, large quarto, contemporary full calf, rebacked, boards tooled in blind, spine with newer red morocco spine label, boards rubbed, previous owner's old ink signature on front free endpaper, front and rear endpapers, laid down, some light toning, overall very good, internally very clean.   Heritage Book Shop   Holiday 2015 - 56   2016 $2850

Jacob, Hildebrand *Chiron to Achilles: a Poem.* London: i.e. Edinburgh: printed for J. R. i.e. Allan Ramsey, 1732. Scottish reprint, 8vo., disbound, fine.   C. R. Johnson Rare Book Collections   Foxon: H-P 2015 - 497   2016 $689

Jacobsen, Josephine *The Animal Inside.* Athens: Ohio University, 1966. First edition, yellow cloth, errata slip in between pages, 2 articles about author laid in, edges of cover little soiled, otherwise very good, tight copy in scuffed and chipped dust jacket, author's presentation to poet William Claire.   Second Life Books, Inc.   196A - 884   2016 $45

Jacobsen, Josephine *For the Unlost. Volume four of the Distinguished Poets Series of Contemporary Poetry.* Baltimore: Contemporary Poetry, 1946. First edition, 8vo., frontispiece, author's presentation to poet William Claire, signed again on title, gray cloth, cover slightly yellowed and little scuffed at corners and ends of spine, else nie.   Second Life Books, Inc.   196A - 887   2016 $50

Jacobsen, Josephine *On the Island.* Princeton: Ontario Review Press, 1989. First printing, 8vo., signed on titlepage by author, presentation from author to editor Barbara Howes, gray-green cloth, nice in slightly chipped dust jacket.   Second Life Books, Inc.   196A - 885   2016 $65

Jacobsen, Josephine *The Shade-Seller New and Selected Poems.* Garden City: Doubleday and Co., 1974. First edition, hardbound issue, inscribed and signed by author for William Meredith, offsetting from clippings slightly affecting inscription, near fine in soiled, very good dust jacket.   Charles Agvent   William Meredith - 61   2016 $60

Jacobsen, Josephine *The Sisters.* Columbia: The Bench Press, 1987. First printing, author's presentation on half title to poet William Claire, paper wrappers, about as new.   Second Life Books, Inc.   196A - 886   2016 $45

Jacobson, C. M. *Intrauterine Diagnosis and Management of Genetic Defects.* American Journal OB-Gyn 99: 796-807, 1969. Entire issue offered in nice condition.   James Tait Goodrich   X-78 - 417   2016 $125

Jacobson, Wendy S. *The Companion to the Mystery of Edwin Drood.* London: Allen & Unwin, 1986. Half title, illustrations, map, original green cloth, very good in dust jacket.   Jarndyce Antiquarian Booksellers   CCXVIII - 678   2016   £30

Jacobus De Varagine   1230-1298 *The Golden Legend of Master William Caxton done anew.* Hammersmith: Kelmscott, 1892. One of 500 copies, 3 volumes, 2 illustrations by Edward Burne-Jones, blue paper covered boards, linen spines with printed paper labels, spines rather worn at extremities and splitting along some hinges, one inch tide line along bottom edge of several boards, not affecting pages, internally lovely and in need of conservation of spines, as often the case with this book.   Joseph J. Felcone, Inc.   Books from Five Centuries: a Miscellany - 87   2016 $5500

Jacques, Brian *Outcast of Redwall.* New York: Philamel, 1996. Stated first American edition, first printing (1-10 code), 8vo., cloth backed boards, as new in like dust jacket, chapter headings by Allan Curtiss, this copy signed by Jacques.   Aleph-bet Books, Inc.   111 - 228   2016 $100

Jadeja, Princesse V. *Adventures de Pirouli le Petit Negre.* Paris: Editions de L'Ecureuil, 1946. Cloth backed pictorial boards, fine, every page has wonderful color lithographs by author.   Aleph-bet Books, Inc.   112 - 64   2016 $200

Jaeger, C. K. *The Man in the Top Hat.* London: Grey Walls Press, 1949. First edition, octavo, contemporary gift inscription, dust jacket designed off-set onto spine, edges spotted, very good in very good nicked and chipped dust jacket, little defective at head of spine.   Peter Ellis   112 - 189   2016   £125

Jaeger, Oscar *The Great Grand Canyon Adventure.* Dubuque: Pub. by the author, 1932. printed cloth, binding staples exposed at front hinge, else clean and bright.   Dumont Maps and Books   134 - 41   2016 $250

Jaffin, David *The Half of a Circle.* New Rochelle: Elizabeth Press, 1977. First edition, limited to 400 copies printed from Centaur type by Stamperia Valdonega Verona, very lightly soiled printed wrappers, nice.   Second Life Books, Inc.   196A - 889   2016 $75

James, George Payne Rainsford   1799-1860 *The Gipsy, a Tale.* London: George Routledge & Co., 1858. Frontispiece, 96 page catalog, crease to titlepage, original red pebble grained cloth, "Routledge's Standard Novels" enbossed on front board, slightly dulled.   Jarndyce Antiquarian Booksellers   CCXVII - 137   2016   £30

James, George Payne Rainsford   1799-1860 *The History of Chivalry.* London: Henry Colburn & Richard Bentley, 1830. Second edition, frontispiece, engraved title, original green glazed cloth, dark blue paper label lettered gilt, spine very slightly faded, contemporary signature of J. Clark on engraved title, very good, crisp copy.   Jarndyce Antiquarian Books   CCXV - 269   2016   £75

James, George Payne Rainsford 1799-1860 *The Huguenot: a Tale of the French Protestants.* London: George Routledge & Co., 1858. New edition, 96 page catalog, frontispiece, some leaves roughly opened, few tiny tears not affecting text, original red pebble grained cloth, slightly dulled. Jarndyce Antiquarian Booksellers CCXVII - 138 2016 £30

James, George Payne Rainsford 1799-1860 *The Last of the Fairies.* London: Parry & Co., 1848. Frontispiece, additional engraved title, illustrations, text within colored floral borders, plates slightly dusted, original red decorated cloth, spine darkened, little dulled, leading inner hinge slightly cracking, all edges gilt, overall good. Jarndyce Antiquarian Booksellers CCXVII - 139 2016 £85

James, George Payne Rainsford 1799-1860 *The Last of the Fairies.* London: Parry & Co., 1848. First edition, illustrations by John Gilbert, frontispiece and engraved title, printed title with red loral border, illustrations, original red cloth, spine darkened, blocked in blind, lettered and decorated gilt, spine little dulled and slightly rubbed at head and tail, contemporary gift inscription, all edges gilt. Jarndyce Antiquarian Booksellers CCXVIII - 406 2016 £200

James, Henry 1843-1916 *The Complete Tales of Henry James.* London: Rupert Hart-Davis, 1962-1964. First edition of the UK issue, 8vo., 12 volumes, original cloth with harlequin colored dust jackets, little sunning to few wrappers which have old nick, otherwise very good set. Sotheran's Piccadilly Notes - Summer 2015 - 174 2016 £498

James, Henry 1843-1916 *Daisy Miller.* Cambridge: Printed for members of the Limited Editions Club at the University Printing House, 1969. First edition thus, limited to 1500 numbered copies signed by artist, Gustave Nebel, 8vo., full red morocco, fine in publisher's box. Second Life Books, Inc. 196A - 890 2016 $75

James, J. T. *Journal of a tour in Germany, Sweden, Russia, Poland During the Years 1813 and 1814.* London: John Murray, 1816. First edition, quarto, 6 etched plates, 12 sepia aquatint plates (some light browning opposite), vignette on titlepage, plate, 50mm. split at head of spine, good. J. & S. L. Bonham Antiquarian Booksellers Europe 2016 - 9755 2016 £550

James, John Angell *The Young Man from Home.* London: RTS, circa, 1830. Second edition, frontispiece, engraved title, original green glazed cloth, dark blue paper label lettered gilt, spine very slightly faded, contemporary signature of J. Clark on engraved title, very good, crisp copy. Jarndyce Antiquarian Books CCXV - 270 2016 £40

James, John T. *The Benders in Kansas.* Kan Okl Pub. Co., 1913. First edition, 12mo., rebound in quarter leather and marked paper over boards, brown endpapers, rare, handsomely bound. Buckingham Books 2015 - 26242 2016 $3750

James, Montague Rhodes *Ghost Stories of an Antiquary.* London: Edward Arnold, 1904. First edition, octavo, pub catalog dated Nov. 1904, original tan buckram, front and spine panels stamped in orange and black, rear panel stamped in orange, fore and bottom edges untrimmed, attractive private owner's printed book label affixed to front pastedown, minute spot on front cover, hint of tanning to half title leaf and frontispiece tissue guard, fine, quite scarce in this condition. John W. Knott, Jr./L.W. Currey, Inc. Fall-Winter 2015 - 17267 2016 $4000

James, Montague Rhodes *A Thin Ghost and Others.* London: Edward Arnold, 1919. First edition, 8vo., original black cloth with pale blue lettering and spider's web, slight rubbing at spine ends, lower corners slightly rubbed and slightly bumped, endpapers slightly browned, otherwise clean, very good+. Any Amount of Books 2015 - A83874 2016 £150

James, Montague Rhodes *The Western Manuscripts in the Library of Trinity College, Cambridge, a Descriptive Catalogue.* Cambridge: University Press, 1900. 4to., cloth, title, author's name, volume and Cambridge arms gilt-stamped on spine, plates, boards faded, front board volume 2 bumped, text very lightly tanned. Oak Knoll Books 310 - 251 2016 $950

James, Nicholas *Poems on Several Occasions.* Truro: printed by Andrew Brice, 1742. First edition, small 8vo., contemporary calf, gilt, spine gilt and small piece chipped from top of spine, fine, very scarce. C. R. Johnson Rare Book Collections Foxon: H-P 2015 - 499 2016 $3831

James, P. D. *Cover Her Face.* London: Faber & Faber, 1962. First edition, top corner page 237/238 torn away touching one letter, 8vo., original green cloth, backstrip lettered gilt, front hinge strained, backstrip ends lightly bumped and rubbed, dust jacket little soiled overall, some fraying to backstrip panel ends and chip from foot of rear panel (with cloth sunned beneath), crease to rear flap, ownership stamp to front flyleaf also offset to front flap, sound, scarce in any condition. Blackwell's Rare Books B186 - 242 2016 £1500

James, P. D. *A Taste for Death.* London: Faber, 1986. Uncorrected advance proof copy, original wrappers, in slightly frayed first edition dust jacket. I. D. Edrich Crime - 2016 £40

James, P. D. *A Taste for Death.* London: Faber, 1986. First edition, fine in dust jacket. Mordida Books 2015 - 011082 2016 $65

James, Will 1892-1942 *All in the Day's Riding.* New York: Charles Scribner's Sons, 1933. First edition, first issue with date at bottom of titlepage and Scribner's 'A' on the copyright page, small quarto, 104 black and white drawings, plus 2 more on jacket, red cloth stamped in black and gold, very slight rubbing at foot of spine, neat contemporary owner's name and date (1932) on endpaper, very fine with lightly worn pictorial dust jacket. Argonaut Book Shop Literature 2015 - 7168 2016 $900

James, Will 1892-1942 *Flint Spears, Cowboy Rodeo Contestant.* New York: Charles Scribner's Sons, 1938. First edition, without the Scribner's 'A' on copyright page and with "New York" at bottom of titlepage, photographs, full color frontispiece, 30 black and white drawings, orange red cloth stamped in black, neat contemporary owner's name and date fine copy, pictorial dust jacket with short half inch tear near lower spine, head of spine very slightly chipped. Argonaut Book Shop Literature 2015 - 7169 2016 $400

James, Will 1892-1942 *Home Ranch.* New York: Charles Scribner's Sons, 1935. First edition, 54 black and white drawings by author plus full color painting, drawing and screened photo on dust jacket, light brown cloth stamped in black, one lower corner slightly jammed, neat contemporary owner's three line inscription at top of endpaper, dated Christmas 1935, fine with pictorial dust jacket bit rough at edge and with corner of jacket flap slightly creased. Argonaut Book Shop Literature 2015 - 7170 2016 $400

James, Will 1892-1942 *Lone Cowboy. My Life Story.* New York: Charles Scribner's, 1930. First edition, frontispiece, 71 drawings by author, forest green pictorial cloth stamped in black, title stamped in gilt, light rubbing to spine ends, less so to lower corners, spine darkened, owner's neat signature on endpaper, near fine. Argonaut Book Shop Biography 2015 - 7172 2016 $175

James, Will 1892-1942 *Sand.* New York: Charles Scribner's Sons, 1929. First edition, date at bottom of titlepage and three line copyright notice, 47 black and white drawings by author, green cloth, stamped in black and red rule, slight rubbing to foot of spine, previous owner's short inscription to endpaper, fine,. Argonaut Book Shop Literature 2015 - 7173 2016 $175

James, Will 1892-1942 *Young Cowboy.* New York: Charles Scribner's Sons, 1935. First edition, oblong 4to., cloth, pictorial paste-on, fine in dust jacket with some soil and fraying but overall very good, illustrations by James, great copy, rare in jacket. Aleph-bet Books, Inc. 111 - 229 2016 $1200

James, William *The Letters of...* Boston: Atlantic Monthly, 1920. Limited edition, #1 of 600 sets, 2 volumes, 8vo., photos and facsimiles, gray paper over boards, embossed medallion on front and blue cloth spine, paper label, top edge gilt, little foxing here and there, covers little worn at edges and corners, otherwise very good, tight set, Alice James' copy of the set with her name on blank, perhaps written by publisher. Second Life Books, Inc. 196A - 891 2016 $350

James, William F. *Saint Patrick of England.* San Francisco: printed for the author, 1955. One of 200 copies, numbered and signed by author, our copy being number 85, signed on last page, quarto, title in red and black, woodcut by Mallette Dean, printed on English handmade paper, green cloth, natural linen back, title in red on spine, very fine. Argonaut Book Shop Biography 2015 - 5789 2016 $150

Jameson, Anna Brownell 1794-1860 *Characteristics of Women, Moral, Poetical and Historical.* London: Saunders & Otley, 1832. First edition, 2 volumes, half titles volume I, illustrated with tiny vignette etchings bound in later olive green binder's cloth, maroon leather labels, spines slightly foxed, contemporary signature of Frances Bass on half title, later signature E. V. Arnold, good plus. Jarndyce Antiquarian Books CCXV - 272 2016 £150

Jameson, Anna Brownell 1794-1860 *Memoirs of Early Italian Painters.* London: John Murray, 1891. New edition, octavo, 58 engraved portraits, bound by Bayntun (stamp-signed on front turn-in) circa 1925, full purple morocco over beveled boards, covers ruled gilt, spine with fine raised bands, paneled and lettered gilt, decorative gilt board edges, decorative gilt turn-ins, all edges gilt, marbled endpapers, spine slightly faded, otherwise near fine. David Brass Rare Books, Inc. 2015 - 03011 2016 $175

Jameson, Anna Brownell 1794-1860 *Shakespeare's Heroines - Characteristics of Women Moral, Poetical and Historical.* London: Ernest Nister, 1904. First edition with these illustrations, octavo, 6 color plates and numerous black and white illustrations by W(alter) Pater, original striking art nouveau pictorial cloth, all edges gilt, contemporary (1909) gift inscription, fine in exceedingly scarce, very good, nicked and chipped dust jacket with gilt embossed lettering and floral design on upper panel. Peter Ellis 112 - 355 2016 £250

Jameson, Storm *A Cup of Tea for Mr. Thorgill.* London: Macmillan, 1957. First edition, crown 8vo., original green cloth, backstrip lettered gilt, light dust soiling to top edge, ownership inscription to flyleaf, dust jacket with owner's shelfmark to front flap, backstrip panel and head of rear panel lightly sunned, very good. Blackwell's Rare Books B184 - 208 2016 £30

Jamieson, John *Catalogue of the Extensive Library, Bronzes, Roman Antiquities, Prints &c &c.* Edinburgh: Colston, Printer, East Rose Street Lane, 1839. 8vo., modern red cloth, spine lettered gilt, book label of J. L.. Weir, inserted on title by the famous Glasgow bookseller, John Smith, rare. Marlborough Rare Books List 56 - 27 2016 £325

Jane, Fred T. *The Lordship The Passen and We.* London: A. D. Innes, 1897. First edition, 8vo., original blue cloth lettered gilt on spine and cover, pages uncut, signed presentation from author to Commander Robinson. Any Amount of Books 2015 - A99784 2016 £250

Janscha, Laurens *Collection de Cinquante Vues du Rhin les Plus Interessantes et les Plus Pittoresques...* Edinburgh: Harris, 1980. First facsimile edition, large folio, original half morocco over cloth covered boards, spine ornamented and lettered gilt in half morocco drop-down box with large oval lettering piece on lide, black lining, 50 color facsimile plates, with prospectus and original styrofoam lined shipping box. Sotheran's Travel and Exploration - 258 2016 £598

Jansson, Tove *The Book about Moomin, Mymble and Little My.* London: Ernest Benn, 1953. First English language edition, 4to., cloth backed pictorial boards, slight cover soil else fine, bold color illustrations, quitae scarce edition. Aleph-bet Books, Inc. 112 - 261 2016 $700

Jansson, Tove *The Dangerous Journey.* London: Ernest Benn, 1978. First English edition, cloth backed pictorial boards, no dust jacket as issued, fine, every page with wonderful color lithographs. Aleph-bet Books, Inc. 112 - 264 2016 $150

Jansson, Tove *Mumintrollet.* Gebers, n.d. circa, 1955. 9 x 7 inches, cloth backed pictorial boards, very good+, each page illustrated with black and white panels, rare. Aleph-bet Books, Inc. 112 - 263 2016 $225

Jansson, Tove *Who Will Comfort Topple?* London: Ernest Benn, 1960. First English langauge edition, Boards, very faint stain on edge of first few leaves, else very good+ in very good dust jacket with some soil and fraying, bold full color illustrations on every page. Aleph-bet Books, Inc. 112 - 262 2016 $200

Jantz, Harold S. *German Baroque Literature, a Descriptive Catalogue of the Collection of Harold Jantz and a Guide to the Collection on Microfilm.* New Haven: Research Publications, 1974. First edition, small 4to., cloth, some underlining in red, wrinkling of fabric along hinges, scarce book. Oak Knoll Books 310 - 252 2016 $400

Japanese Pictures of Japanese Life. Tokyo: T. Hasegawa, 1929. Third edition, 8vo., crepe paper, silk ties, as new, illustrations, scarce. Aleph-bet Books, Inc. 111 - 230 2016 $850

Jardine, William *British Salmonidae.* London: Decimus Pub., 1979. Limited to 500 numbered copies, folio, 12 color plates, text illustrations, quarter morocco over green cloth, slipcase, very good. Andrew Isles Natural History Books 55 - 38749 2016 $350

Jardine, William *Erythura Cheef. The Closet Finch Plate XXXIV.* Edinburgh: Published by W. H. Lizars, 1839. First edition, original hand colored plate by Edward Lear, some very faint discoloration to paper, illustration clean and bright, small chip at fore-edge of last leaf in very good condition. Simon Finch 2015 - 53512 2016 $240

Jardine, William *The Naturalist's Library Ornithology. Volume X. Birds of Great Britain and Ireland. Part II Incessores.* Edinburgh: W. H. Lizars, 1839. First edition, 12mo., very good, original cloth with hand colored vignette titlepage and 30 hand colored plates. Simon Finch 2015 - 031870 2016 $192

Jarmuth, Sylvia L. *Dickens' Use of women in His Novels.* New York: Excelsior Publishing Co., 1967. Original wrappers. Jarndyce Antiquarian Booksellers CCXVIII - 1317 2016 £25

Jasper, Herbert *Epilepsy and the Functional Anatomy of the Human brain.* Boston: Little Brown & Co., 1954. Colored frontispiece, 8 colored plates and three quarter black and white illustrations, original blue cloth, bit worn and rubbed, internally fine. James Tait Goodrich X-78 - 459 2016 $135

Jaubert, Amedee *Voyage en Armenie et en Perse, fait Dans les Annees 1805 et 1806....* Paris: Pelicier et Nepveu, 1821. First edition, 8vo., contemporary French black polished calf backed marbled boards, spine lettered and ruled gilt, sprinkled edges, frontispiece and 9 plates in charcoal lithography, all tissue guards preserved, large folding engraved map, part from light wear to extremities and occasional negligible spotting, clean and fresh, unopened since binding prior to collating. Sotheran's Travel and Exploration - 331 2016 £1698

Jean, Fritz *Man Who Loved Books.* New York: G. P. Putnam, 1981. Stated first impression, fine in near fine dust jacket with tiny closed tear, illustrations in full color by Rina Hyman. Aleph-bet Books, Inc. 111 - 224 2016 $100

Jefferies, Richard   1848-1887 *The Amateur Poacher.* London: Smith, Elder & Co., 1903. New edition, 8vo., original dark khaki cloth, gilt central design to upper board, gilt lettering to spine, previous owner's inscription to titlepage, very good.   Sotheran's   Hunting, Shooting & Fishing - 180   2016   £50

Jefferies, Richard   1848-1887 *Sun, Sea and Earth.* Manor Farm, Andoversford: Whittington Press, 1989. One of 100 copies (of 125 total), and 12 double leaves, 8 leaves on toned laid handmade paper and 4 leaves on cream laid paper, folded at fore-edge, 8 copper engravings by Brian Hanscomb, limited supply of handmade papers for the engravings, very scarce.   Oak Knoll Books   310 - 170   2016 $450

Jeffers, Robinson   1887-1962 *Californians.* New York: Macmillan Co., 1916. First edition, 1200 copies printed, small octavo, blue cloth lettered in gilt on spine and front cover, pictorial element on front cover in light blue, gold and black, very minor rubbing to spine ends and corners, light foxing to 6 prelim leaves, overall fine.   Argonaut Book Shop   Literature 2015 - 7424   2016 $275

Jeffers, Robinson   1887-1962 *Cawdor and Other Poems.* New York: Horace Liveright, 1928. First edition, number 346 of 375 numbered and signed copies, title printed in red and black, two-tone salmon and tan cloth, spine and edges of covers bit darkened, near fine.   Argonaut Book Shop   Literature 2015 - 4803   2016 $350

Jeffers, Robinson   1887-1962 *Granite & Cypress: Rubbins from the Rock.* University of California at Santa Cruz: Lime Kiln Press, 1975. Limited to 100 numbered copies, exceptionally rare, Oblong folio, printed on English Hayle handmade paper, titlepage woodcut by William Prochnow, bound by Schuberth Bookbindery in German linen, open laced deerskin over Monterey Cypress spine, Japanese Uwa endpapers, custom slipcase made of Monterey Cypress inlaid with square 'window' of granite from Jeffers; stoneyard (drawn by the poet from the sea), built to stand erect on felt lined cypress stand case, with hairline crack, else fine, signed by printer, William Everson, presentation signed by Everson and three proof sheets laid in.   Jeff Weber Rare Books   181 - 67   2016 $15,000

Jeffers, Robinson   1887-1962 *Medea.* New York: Random House, 1946. Second printing, autographed to Doris Rich by Dedicatee Judith Anderson on dedication page, with short TLS from Anderson to Rich dated Feb. 6 1948, laid in, some notes in pencil that appear to show changes made in production, owner's bookplate, nice in worn dust jacket.   Second Life Books, Inc.   196A - 892   2016 $125

Jefferys, Nathaniel *An Englishman's Descriptive account of Dublin and the Road from Bangor Ferry to Holy Head....* London: Cadell & Davies, 1810. First edition, octavo, engraved folding map, original boards, covers worn and defective at spine, boards dampstained, internally very good, rare.   Peter Ellis   112 - 185   2016   £1150

Jekyll, Gertrude *Wall and Water Gardens.* London: Country Life, n.d., 1901. First edition, plates, buckram covers with gilt decorations on spine, contemporary ownership inscription, spine slightly faded and bumped at head and tail some faint spotting to prelims, one plate partially loose and bit creased at fore-edge, very good.   Peter Ellis   112 - 140   2016   £125

Jellinek, Frank *Civil War in Spain.* London: Victor Gollancz, 1938. First edition, octavo, spine superficially affected by damp at head and tail, cheap quality paper tanned at edges, endpapers lightly spotted, very good in very good, nicked and rubbed dust jacket darkened a little stained at spine.   Peter Ellis   112 - 374   2016   £125

Jellinek, Joanna *A Tale of Two Cities.* London: Studio Vista Books, 1973. 4to., folding frontispiece, plates, illustrations, original black cloth, lettered red, very good in blue dust jacket. Jarndyce Antiquarian Booksellers   CCXVIII - 569   2016   £20

Jennens, William *The Great Jennens Case...* Sheffield: printed by Pawson & Brailsford, 1879. Frontispiece and plates, fold out table, original red cloth blocked and lettered gilt, spine dulled and little rubbed at some point carefully recased, good plus.   Jarndyce Antiquarian Booksellers   CCXVIII - 520   2016   £60

Jenner, Bruce *Decathlon Challenge. Bruce Jenner's Story.* Englewood Cliffs: Prentice Hall, 1977. First edition, inscribed to author, fine in very good, price clipped dust jacket.   Ken Lopez Bookseller   166 - 121   2016 $375

Jennings, Elizabeth *Poems.* Eynsham: Fantasy Press, 1953. First edition, octavo, wrappers, covers bit dusty and spotted, very good.   Peter Ellis   112 - 194   2016   £35

Jensen, Laura *Tapwater: Poems by....* Port Townsend: Graywolf Press, 1978. First edition, one of 26 lettered copies signed by author of a total edition of 450 printed using Palatino typefaces on Rives light paper, grey boards with paper label, fine, drawings by author.   Second Life Books, Inc.   196A - 893   2016 $125

Jenyns, Soane *The Modern Fine Lady.* London: printed for R. Dodsley in Pall Mall, 1751. First edition, 4to., slightly trimmed copy only affecting extreme edge of one page number and brackets, old fold mark on titlepage, recent sugar paper wrappers, woodcut ornament to titlepage, decorative woodcut headpiece.   Jarndyce Antiquarian Booksellers CCXVI - 316   2016   £285

Jenyns, Soane *A Scheme for the Coalition of Parties, Humbly Submitted to the Publick.* London: printed for J. Wilkie in St. Paul's Church Yard, 1772. 34 pages, 8vo., without half title, disbound, unstitched, very good. Jarndyce Antiquarian Booksellers CCXVI - 317 2016 £45

Jenyns, Soane *The Squire and the Parson, an Eclogue.* London: Printed for R. Dodsley, 1749. 4to., light browning, some foxing and old fold mark to titlepage, recent sugar paper wrappers, armorial bookplate of H. & M. Berens, signed by H. (Ber(ens). Jarndyce Antiquarian Booksellers CCXVI - 318 2016 £285

Jenyns, Soane *Thoughts on the Causes and Consequences of the Present High Price of Provisions.* London: printed for J. Dodsley, 1767. Second edition, 8vo., half title, final blank signature, entirely untrimed, stitched as issue, signature of Robt. Digby, very good. Jarndyce Antiquarian Booksellers CCXVI - 319 2016 £85

Jepson, Edgar *Sibyl Falcon: a Study in romantic Morals.* London: Tower Pub., 1895. First edition, very good, original red cloth boards with gilt title to spine and front board, front cover illustrated with ship and spine with man hailing a ship from the shore, minor wear to edges of boards and there are few dark markings to boards spine, aside from few light smudge marks, interior clean and bright with 8 illustrations and cover design by Harold Piffard, bookplate,. The Kelmscott Bookshop 12 - 57 2016 $275

Jepson, Selwyn *The Assassin.* London: Collins, 1956. Signed presentation copy from author, recipient's name removed, some spotting of top edge not affecting text, but none the less, very good copy. I. D. Edrich Crime - 2016 £20

Jernegan, Marcus Wilson *Progress of Nations. The Story of the World And Its Peoples from the Dawn of History to the Present Day.* Chicago: Dept. of Rehabilitation, Disabled American Veterans of the World War, 1930-1931. Unknown Soldier edition, 10 volumes, 229 x 156mm., this copy #604 especially prepared for Mrs. Eli K. Robinson, remarkably fine publisher's deluxe black pebble grain morocco, ornately gilt, front covers with decorative gilt rule border enclosing elaborate floral rococo-style frame, frame around a central medallion featuring a knight's plumed helmet, raised bands, gilt titling, gilt turn-ins with compartments elegantly decorated with volutes and small floral tools, gilt titling, gilt turn-ins with curling floral rolls, sky blue pictorial endpapers, all edges gilt, with more than 2000 illustrations, including more than 200 maps and charts, 53 images in color, perhaps trivial imperfection somewhere, but essentially in as new condition, amazingly well preserved set, virtually as it was delivered to its original owner. Phillip J. Pirages 67 - 195 2016 $1800

Jerome, J. K. *The Idler.* 1893. Volumes 1-3, Feb.-July 1893, volumes 1 and 2 publisher's original gilt pictorial green cloth, volume 3 half calf spine cracked. I. D. Edrich Crime - 2016 £65

Jerome, J. K. *The Idler.* 1894. Volume 5 Feb-July 1894, half calf. I. D. Edrich Crime - 2016 £30

Jerrold, Blanchard 1826-1884 *The Life of George Cruikshank.* London: Chatto & Windus, 1882. First edition, 2 volumes, half titles, frontispieces, vignette titles, plates and illustrations, 32 page catalog (Feb. 1882) volume II, original brown pictorial cloth, spines slightly bubbled, otherwise very good. Jarndyce Antiquarian Booksellers CCXVIII - 1138 2016 £110

Jerrold, Walter *The Big Book of Fables.* London: Blackie, n.d., 1912. Thick 4to., red cloth with elaborate gilt spine and cover blindstamped in red, top edge gilt, plain endpapers, spine lightly sunned, else near fine, 28 color plates, 100 full page black and whites, plus numerous smaller black and whites in text. Aleph-bet Books, Inc. 112 - 425 2016 $450

Jess *Jess: Grand Collage 1951-1993.* Buffalo: Albright Knox Gallery, 1993. First edition, softcover, set of folded and gathered sheets laid into a trial dust jacket, illustrations in color and black and white, about near fine set of sheets in very good plus dust jacket with crease to front panel, scarce in this format. Jeff Hirsch Books E-List 80 - 16 2016 $150

Jessel, George *Halo Over Hollywood.* Van Nuys: Toastmaster, 1963. First edition, author's presentation on flyleaf, very good. Second Life Books, Inc. 196A - 895 2016 $45

Jevons, W. Stanley *The Principles of Economics: a Fragment of a Treatise on the Industrial Mechanisms of Society and Other papers.* London: Macmillan and Co. Ltd., 1905. First edition, octavo, publisher's full brick cloth, boards ruled in blind, spine lettered and ruled in gilt, partially unopened, previous owner's name twice on front free endpaper, once on titlepage, not affecting text, another previous signature has been extracted from front free endpaper, leaving 2 1/2 inch hole, corners bit bumped, spine slightly darkened with gilt bit rubbed, some light foxing to endpapers, overall very good. Heritage Book Shop Holiday 2015 - 57 2016 $750

Jewett, Norman *Monkey Shines of Marseleen and Some of His Adventures.* New York: McLoughlin Bros., 1906. 10 x 12 3/8 inches, cloth backed pictorial boards, some edge wear, corners worn, clean tight and very good, cartoons, printed on coated paper, rare. Aleph-bet Books, Inc. 112 - 100 2016 $400

Jewett, Sarah Orne   1849-1909   *The White Heron.*   New York: Crowell, 1963. 1-10 code. First edition, first printing, cloth, fine in very good+ dust jacket darkened on edge of rear panel with price intact, beautifully illustrated in color by Barbara Cooney, laid in is signed card written by Cooney responding to collector's request to sign exhibition catalogue.   Aleph-bet Books, Inc.   111 - 99   2016 $150

Jewry, Mary   *Warne's Model Cookery and Housekeeping Book...*   London: Frederick Warne & Co., 1892? Color frontispiece and 3 further colour plates, illustrations, few minor paper flaws, original brown cloth, blocked in black, very good.   Jarndyce Antiquarian Books   CCXV - 273   2016   £75

Jhabvala, Ruth Prawer   *Heat and Dust.*   London: 1975. First edition, very fine in dust jacket, bookplate.   Bertram Rota Ltd.   Christmas List 2015 - 15   2016   £100

Jhabvala, Ruth Prawer   *In Search of Love and Duty.*   1983. First edition, fine in dust jacket, bookplate.   Bertram Rota Ltd.   February List 2016 - 29   2016   £30

Joans, Ted   *Honey Spoon.*   Vilnius: Handshake Press, 1993. Reprint of 1991 Paris edition, square 12mo., autographed by author on title, 2 illustrations, paper wrappers, cover little yellowed and slight soiled, autographed sticker on front, otherwise very good, tight copy.   Second Life Books, Inc.   197 - 191   2016 $75

Jocelyn, H.   *Mostly Alkali.*   Caldwell: The Caxton Printers, 1953. First edition, numerous black and white plates, maps, map endpapers, fine copy with dust jacket.   Argonaut Book Shop Native American 2015 - 1943   2016 $150

Jocosus, Gaudentius, Pseud.   *Doctoae Nugae Gandentii Jonsi, Consistentes in Diversis Narrationibus et Eventibus Buyus Temporis...*   Solisbaci: Impens J. L. Bugelii, 1713. Second edition, copperplate frontispiece, contemporary paste paper covered boards, lacks spine, generally good.   Jeff Weber Rare Books   181 - 17   2016 $225

Johanknecht, Susan   *Waste Incant. Words and Images by Susan Johanknencht.*   Newark: Janus Press, 2007. Limited to 150 numbered copies, oblong small 8vo., bound with woven strips of silver colored paper and encased in same vinyl, loose vinyl protective cover, clear acrylic slipcase, 12 leaves, printed on Barcham Green Cambers and Cairo from Hayle Mill in England, each leaf interspersed with textured sheets of flexible vinyl and illusion polycaronate.   Oak Knoll Books   27 - 33   2016 $300

Johannes De Aquila   *Sermones Quadragesimales (with the Collaboration of Daniel Vincentius).*   Venice: Petrus de Quarengiis, Bergomensis for Alexander Calcedonius, 21 October, 1499. Second edition, fine woodcut, opening historiated initial, rubricated in red and black headings and large initials rubricated in red throughout, 8vo., double columns, 19th century French marbled calf, flat spine richly gilt with red morocco label, marbled edges, neat repair to headcap, contemporary inscription, ex libris P H Chavoix typographi.   Maggs Bros. Ltd.   1474 - 43   2016   £3000

John, Juliet   *Dickens's Villains: melodrama, Character, Popular Culture.*   London: Oxford University Press, 2001. Half title, original black cloth, mint, dust jacket.   Jarndyce Antiquarian Booksellers   CCXVIII - 1319   2016   £35

John, W. D.   *Nantgarw Porcelain.*   Newport, Monmouthshire: R. H. Johns Ltd., 1948. First edition, tall quarto, 42 color and 143 black and white plates, lacking 2 supplements, original leather worn, externally good, internally fine.   Argonaut Book Shop   Pottery and Porcelain 2015 - 100   2016 $200

Johnck & Seeger   *Type Faces Available From the Typographic Shop of Johnck & Seeger.*   San Francisco: Johnck & Seeger, n.d. but circa, 1950. Octavo, original printed red wrappers, stapled, wrappers little faded and soiled, fine.   The Brick Row Book Shop   Miscellany 69 - 80   2016 $175

Johns, W. E.   *Biggles Takes it Rough.*   Leicester: Brockhampton Press, 1963. First edition, octavo, illustrations by Leslie Stead, tail of spine slightly bumped, very good in very dust jacket, slightly nicked and rubbed, price clipped dust jacket.   Peter Ellis   112 - 196   2016   £50

Johnson, Charles   1679-1748   *The Complete Art of Writing Letters.*   London: printed for T. Lowndes, 1779. Sixth edition, engraved frontispiece, typographic head piece decorations, 12mo., some occasional minor browning and very slight foxing, small ink splash to titlepage, rather faded, expertly bound in recent quarter sprinkled calf, raised and gilt banded spine, red morocco label, marbled boards, vellum tips, fresh contemporary endpapers and pastedowns. Jarndyce Antiquarian Booksellers   CCXVI - 326   2016   £280

Johnson, Charles Plumptre   *Hints to Collectors of Original Editions of the Works of Charles Dickens.*   London: George Redway, 1885. First edition, half title, 4 page catalog, uncut, full parchment by Westleys, lettered gilt, bevelled boards, spotted and marked, large format.   Jarndyce Antiquarian Booksellers   CCXVIII - 1506   2016   £30

Johnson, Crockett *The Frowning Prince.* New York: Harper & Bros., 1959. 8vo., cloth backed pictorial boards, fine in very good dust jacket with small piece off base of spine, small rub area on cover, wonderful illustrations on nearly every page by Johnson.   Aleph-bet Books, Inc.   112 - 271   2016 $350

Johnson, Crockett *Harold's Trip to the Sky.* New York: Harper Bros., 1957. First edition, 16mo., tan cloth, spine and pictorial boards, fine in near fine, price clipped dust jacket, rare in such beautiful condition.   Aleph-bet Books, Inc.   112 - 272   2016 $1275

Johnson, Crockett *Who's Upside Down?* New York: William R. Scott, 1952. First (probably only) edition, 4to., pictorial boards, slightest of edge rubbing, else fine in dust jacket with some old repairs on verso, marvelous full page illustrations.   Aleph-bet Books, Inc.   112 - 273   2016 $1250

Johnson, Edgar *Charles Dickens: His Tragedy and Triumph.* New York: Simon & Schuster, 1952. First edition, 2 volumes, half titles, frontispiece, plates, illustrations, original pale blue-gray cloth, lettered in gilt, very good in slightly worn dust jacket.   Jarndyce Antiquarian Booksellers   CCXVIII - 1321   2016   £60

Johnson, Edgar *Charles Dickens: His Tragedy and Triumph.* London: Victor Gollancz, 1953. First English edition, 2 volumes, half titles, frontispiece, plates, illustrations, original dark blue cloth, lettered gilt, very good in dust jackets.   Jarndyce Antiquarian Booksellers   CCXVIII - 1322   2016   £50

Johnson, Edgar *The Dickens Theatrical Reader.* Boston and Toronto: Little Brown and Co., 1964. First edition, half title, illustrations, original blue cloth, very good in slightly worn dust jacket.   Jarndyce Antiquarian Booksellers   CCXVIII - 751   2016   £20

Johnson, Emma Dora *Poems.* Huntington: Emma Mae Dora Johnson, 1914. First edition, small quarto, frontispiece, stapled printed brown wrappers, very faint waterstain on upper corner of pages (but not wrapper), very good or better.   Between the Covers Rare Books   207 - 57   2016 $900

Johnson, Foster M. *Thomas Short and the First Book Printed in Connecticut.* Meriden: Bayberry Hill Press, 1958. Limited to 50 numbered copies, being a keeepsake for the Columbiad Club, 12mo., full leather, dust jacket, extremely scarce.   Oak Knoll Books   310 - 203   2016 $950

Johnson, George W. *The Cottage Gardeners' Dictionary.* London: William S. Orr & Co., 1852. First edition, excellently rebound in half dark green calf, gilt, maroon label, very good.   Jarndyce Antiquarian Booksellers   CCXVII - 140   2016   £280

Johnson, Georgia Douglas *Bronze.* Boston: B. J. Brimmer Co., 1922. First edition, printed paper over boards, boards slightly splayed and corners little worn, else near fine, fragile volume, without dust jacket, rear panel and rear flap are laid in, warmly inscribed by author to Roscoe Conkling Simmons.   Between the Covers Rare Books   202 - 50   2016 $4500

Johnson, Georgia Douglas *Bronze.* Boston: B. J. Brimmer Co., 1922. First edition, boards slightly splayed, slight offsetting to endpapers from jacket flaps, very near fine in lightly foxed, very good dust jacket with few very small chips at extremities, housed in custom cloth clamshell case with morocco spine label.   Between the Covers Rare Books   207 - 58   2016 $9500

Johnson, Georgia Douglas *My Regal Rose.* Chicago and Tuskegee: N. Clark Smith Music Pub. and Tuskegee Inst., Folio, illustrated wrappers printed in red, few tears, two small chips on front wrapper, about very good.   Between the Covers Rare Books   202 - 51   2016 $2500

Johnson, James Weldon *The Book of American Negro Poetry.* New York: Harcourt Brace and Co., 1922. First edition, fore edge somewhat foxed, else fine in very attractive near fine example of very scarce dust jacket with small chip on front panel, negligible wear at spine ends and some small loss at crown, rare in dust jacket, unusually nice copy.   Between the Covers Rare Books   202 - 6   2016 $2000

Johnson, John *The Clergyman's Vade-Mecum or an Account of the Ancient and Present Church of England... (with) Part II.* London: printed for Robert Knaplock and Ballard, 1731. 1723. Sixth edition and third edition of part II, 12mo., contemporary gilt ruled calf, lettered only with volume number, just little wear to extremities, but very good with 18th century signature of W. Harbin; part II with few leaves creased, but very good, crisp copy also with Harbin's signature and in matching binding.   John Drury Rare Books   2015 - 228827   2016 $350

Johnson, John *Original Letters Written by the Late Mr. John Johnson of Liverpool.* Norwich: printed and sold by Crouse, Stevenson and Matchett, sold also by W. Robinson, Liverpool, 1798-1800. First edition, 2 volumes, some foxing to both volumes, some worming in volume I, confined to upper and lower margins, 8vo., contemporary brown straight grained morocco by S. Curtis with his ticket, triple blind ruled borders on sides, black lettering pieces in 2nd and 4th of 5 compartments on spine, raised bands, gilt tooled, hinges rubbed, small knock at foot of spine of volume I, some contemporary annotations to first letter, sound.   Blackwell's Rare Books   B186 - 82   2016   £300

Johnson, Joseph *Clever Boys of Your Time and How They Became Famous Men.* London: Gall & Inglis, 1878. Frontispiece and plates, original blue decorated cloth, bevelled boards, spine slightly rubbed at head and tail, inner hinge slightly cracking, all edges gilt, prize inscription. Jarndyce Antiquarian Books CCXV - 66 2016 £28

Johnson, Kenneth M. *The Life and Times of Edward Robeson Taylor....* San Francisco: Book Club of California, 1968. First edition, limited to 400 copies, folded broadside tipped-in, plates from photos, gold cloth lettered and decorated in gilt, very fine, original prospectus laid in. Argonaut Book Shop Biography 2015 - 3769 2016 $45

Johnson, Lionel *The Art of Thomas Hardy.* London: John Lane, 1895. Second edition, frontispiece by Herbert Strang, 16 page publisher's catalog dated 1894 at rear, green buckram covers, attractive art nouveau pictorial bookplate, rear hinge cracking but tight, spine faded, very good. Peter Ellis 112 - 195 2016 £45

Johnson, Lyndon Baines *State of the Union Message...* 8vo., inscribed by a secreaty, not Johnson, for friend Myron Black, fine copy. Second Life Books, Inc. 196A - 898 2016 $50

Johnson, Merle *American First Editions, bibliographic Checklists of the Works of 105 American authors.* New York: Bowker, 1929. First edition, one of 1000 copies, 8vo., rubbed blue cloth with paper label, untrimmed, some annotations by previous owner, good copy. Second Life Books, Inc. 197 - 195 2016 $95

Johnson, Merle *A Bibliography of the Works of Mark Twain.* New York: Harper, 1910. First edition, 8vo., untrimmed and partially unopened, some pages little roughly opened, bound in cloth (little soiled), paper label, very good, tight copy, one of 500 numbered copies signed by author and publisher. Second Life Books, Inc. 196A - 302 2016 $250

Johnson, Merle *Howard Pyle's Book of the American Spirit.* New York: Harper & Bros., 1923. First edition, first issue with B-X on copyright page, folio, 22 full page color plates and 180 black and white illustrations, original black cloth over tan boards, front cover with color illustration laid-on and lettered in dark brown, spine lettered gilt, top edge stained orange, one small marginal tear (7/8 inch) on pages 223/224, otherwise very fine in original tan paper dust jacket. David Brass Rare Books, Inc. 2015 - 02966 2016 $950

Johnson, Michael *Masters of Crime. Lionel Davidson & Dick Francis.* Herefordshire: Scorpion Press, 2006. First edition, one of 52 lettered deluxe copies signed by Davidson, Francis and all contributors, very fine leather bound copies with raised bands, gold stamping on spine and in transparent dust jacket, numerous pen and ink illustrations. Buckingham Books 2015 - 24248 2016 $450

Johnson, Richard *The History of a Little Boy Found Under the Haycock.* York: Kendrew, n.d. circa, 1820. 16mo., yellow wrappers, fine, 14 woodcuts. Aleph-bet Books, Inc. 111 - 150 2016 $175

Johnson, Richard *The History of North America Containing a Review of the Customs and Manners of the Original Inhabitants the Final Settlement of the British Colonies and their Rise and Progress.* Lansingburgh: printed for Samuel Shaw, bookbinder, by Charles R. and George Webster, Albany, 1805. 12mo., contemporary sheep, spine with gilt fillets, otherwise undecorated, corner torn from #2 with loss of text, both endpapers torn, some soiling and foxing, but very tight. Joseph J. Felcone, Inc. Books from Five Centuries: a Miscellany - 84 2016 $1000

Johnson, Richard *A New Roman History.* London: printed for F. Newbery, 1770. 18mo., plates, original quarter green vellum, dark blue boards, rubbed printed paper spine label, good plus. Jarndyce Antiquarian Booksellers CCXVI - 327 2016 £75

Johnson, Richard *Rural Felicity or the History of Tommy and Sally Embellished with Cuts.* printed for E. Newbery, 1788? First edition, frontispiece and 7 woodcuts in text, one or two spots, 32mo., original green floral wrappers, good, rare. Blackwell's Rare Books B184 - 54 2016 £1500

Johnson, Samuel 1709-1784 *A Dictionary of the English Language.* London: printed by W. Strahan for J. and P. Knapton...., 1755. First edition, 2 volumes, titlepages printed in red and black, smallish (?wax) stain in last leaf of prelims, few leaves little browned, crease in 29F2 (no loss), small circular ink spot 2952v, couple of contemporary notes on sources added in margins, folio, contemporary calf, double gilt fillets on sides, stoutly and skillfully rebacked, repairs to corners, contemporary ownership inscription of Champion Branfill, engraved armorial bookplate of Joseph Cator, very good. Blackwell's Rare Books B184 - 52 2016 £17,500

Johnson, Samuel 1709-1784 *The Idler.* London: J. Newbery, 1761. First collected edition, small octavo, contemporary full calf, housed in custom case, 2 volumes, rubbing to spines and boards, particularly near edges, rubbing to spines of box as well, browning to pages from binding, otherwise text fine with wide margins, rare set in urnestored contemporary bindings. Manhattan Rare Book Company 2016 - 189 2016 $1100

Johnson, Samuel 1709-1784 *The Idler.* London: printed for J. Hodges and 6 others, 1790. Sixth edition, 8vo., some browning, waterstain to upper corner of first three leaves of volume II, full contemporary tree calf, gilt borders, smooth spines, gilt decoration, black morocco labels, some rubbing to hinges and spines, early ownership name of Thos. Kennard. Jarndyce Antiquarian Booksellers CCXVI - 329 2016 £125

Johnson, Samuel 1709-1784 *A Journey to the Western Islands of Scotland.*   London: printed for A. Strahan and T. Cadell, 1791. New edition, 8vo., some browning to lower margins of final hundred pages, occasionally rather intrusive, full contemporary sheep, gilt decorated spine, original morocco label, spine slightly chipped at head and tail, joints cracked but firm, armorial bookplate of Revd. James Burnell, with his name on titlepage.   Jarndyce Antiquarian Booksellers   CCXVI - 330   2016   £150

Johnson, Samuel 1709-1784 *The Lives of the Most Eminent English Poets...*   London: printed for J. Buckland, C. Bathurst and T. Davies, 1793. New edition, frontispiece, 12mo., some browning to endpapers and pastedowns, some marginal browning to next few leaves, each volume, one leaf torn right across in volume III, without loss, full contemporary sprinkled calf, gilt banded spines, rather dry & rubbed, red morocco labels intact, two joints cracked but firm, wear to one headcap and to foot of one spine, contemporary bookplate of John Headlam, and his signature dated 1796.   Jarndyce Antiquarian Booksellers   CCXVI - 331   2016   £200

Johnson, Samuel 1709-1784 *Lives of the Most Eminent English Poets with Critical Observations on their Works.*   London: John Murray, 1854. Good library edition, 8vo., 3 volumes, contemporary half dark green morocco, panelled spines very elegantly tooled in gilt with flowers in vase and various other small tools, marbled endpapers, top edges gilt, handsome set.   Sotheran's Piccadilly Notes - Summer 2015 - 175   2016   £398

Johnson, Samuel 1709-1784 *New Annals of the Club.*   the Club, 2014. First edition, limited to 250 copies, 8vo., original cloth, 41 color illustrations.   Sotheran's Piccadilly Notes - Summer 2015 - 257   2016   £100

Johnson, Samuel 1709-1784 *Political Tracts Containing the False Alarm, Falkland's Islands, The Patriot and Taxation no Tyranny.*   London: printed for W. Strahan and T. Cadell, 1776. First edition, octavo, original drab boards, uncut, front cover off, boards rubbed and stained, spine chipped and splitting, previous owner's old ink note on titlepage, overall good, chemised and housed in cloth slipcase, morocco spine label.   Heritage Book Shop   Holiday 2015 - 59   2016 $1500

Johnson, Samuel 1709-1784 *The Rambler.*   London: Payne and Bouquet, 1750. First editions, first printings of all 208 original issues, original 208 parts bound in two volumes, small folio, contemporary full calf elaborately gilt decorated spines with leather labels, gilt ruled boards, light rubbing to joints, corners bumped, chips to volume 1 spine ends, text clean with very wide margins, exceedingly rare complete and in beautiful full (unrestored) contemporary bindings, extraordinary set.   Manhattan Rare Book Company   2016 - 1629   2016 $9500

Johnson, Samuel 1709-1784 *The Rambler.*   London: printed for J. Hodges and 6 others, 1791. 4 volumes, 8vo., some foxing, faint waterstaining, one opening with old ink splash, top corner volume I B6 torn with slight loss to page number, full contemporary tree calf, gilt borders, smooth spines, gilt decoration, black morocco labels, some rubbing to hinges and spines, early ownership name of Thos. Kennard.   Jarndyce Antiquarian Booksellers   CCXVI - 332   2016   £200

Johnson, Theodora *The Swedish System of Physical Education.*   Bristol: John Wright & Co.,, 1897. First edition, half title, frontispiece, plates and illustrations, uncut in original blue cloth, bevelled boards, very good.   Jarndyce Antiquarian Books   CCXV - 794   2016   £45

Johnson, Virginia *Catskill Fairies.*   New York: Harper Bros., 1875. 4to., brown cloth, beveled edges, extensive gilt decorated cover, all edges gilt, spine ends worn, still attractive, tips slightly rubbed, very good+, 7 engraved plates, numerous partial page engravings.   Aleph-bet Books, Inc.   112 - 177   2016 $300

Johnston, Charles *Incidents Attending the Capture, Detention and Ransom of Charles Johnston of Virginia.*   Cleveland: Burrows Brothers Co., 1905. Number 201 of 267copies, map, facsimile titlepage, maroon cloth, gilt, some rubbing to spine ends and spine extremities, very good. Argonaut Book Shop   Native American 2015 - 5950   2016 $90

Johnston, Charles *A Narrative of the Incidents Attending the Capture, Detention and Ransom of Who Was made prisoner by the Indians on the River Ohio, in the Year 1790.*   New York: J. & J. Harper, 1827. First edition, 12mo., contemporary three quarter calf, marbled boards, extremities and boards rubbed, spine shows some horizontal cracking, short crack to lower front hinge, text lightly foxed, spotted or lightly browned, rear free endpaper exposed, binding soiled, polished and well preserved, very good.   Argonaut Book Shop   Native American 2015 - 5949   2016 $900

Johnston, Jennifer *The Christmas Tree.*   1981. First edition, fine in slightly rubbed and soiled dust jacket, bookplate. Bertram Rota Ltd.   Christmas List 2015 - 16   2016   £35

Johnston, Ollie *The Disney Villain.*   New York: Hyperion, 1993. First edition, first printing with 1-10 code, 4to., cloth backed boards, as new in as new dust jacket, profusely illustrated in color including holographic image, signed by Ollie Johnston and Frank Thomas.   Aleph-bet Books, Inc.   112 - 147   2016 $300

Johnstone, George *The Speech of Mr. Johnstone, on the Third reading of the Bill for Preventing the Gold Coin of the Realm From Being Paid or Accepted for a Greater Value than the Current Value of Such Coin, Commonly Called Lord Stanhope's Bill Friday the 19th of July 1811.* London: J. Booker, 1811. First edition, 8vo., wanting half title, recently well bound in linen backed marbled boards lettered, very good.   John Drury Rare Books   2015 - 19821   2016 $350

The Jolly Jig-Saw Book: Dogs Allowed. London: John Leng, n.d. circa, 1935. 4to., cloth backed pictorial boards, some edge and corner wear, faint tinting on small guide pictures, very good+, full page brightly colored jig saw puzzle, five in all, great book in nice condition.   Aleph-bet Books, Inc.   112 - 405   2016 $275

The Jolly Old Man Who sings Down Derry Down. London: Dean & song 65, Ludgate Hill, 1865. Small 4to., 8 leaves, very good, hand colored pictorial engraving on front board, including cover there are 8 hand colored engravings, rear board has notices of other Dean publications, paper loss lower rear board, cloth spine nicely repaired in the past, fore-edge trimmed, no loss to text or images, mild soil to few pages, rare.   By the Book, L. C.   45 - 80   2016 $1000

Jolly Old Sports. London: Blackie, n.d. circa, 1915. Folio, cloth backed boards, pictorial paste-on, corners rubbed and light cover soil, very good+, 37 fabulous color plates by Frank Adams.   Aleph-bet Books, Inc.   112 - 9   2016 $400

Jones, A. H. M. *The Later Roman Empire 284-602. A Social, Economic and Administrative Survey.* Oxford: Basil Blackwell, 1986. Reprint in 2 volumes, 8vo., cloth, gilt lettered, faint mark to upper boards, edges lightly dusted, very good, dust jackets, spine sunned, minor shelfwear, very good, ownership inscription of C. D. N. Costa.   Unsworths Antiquarian Booksellers Ltd.   E05 - 43   2016   £180

Jones, Charlotte Rosalys *The Hypnotic Experiment of Dr. Reeves and other Stories.* London and New York: Bliss, Sands and Foster, Brentano's, 1894. First edition, brown cloth with delicate cream and green design in gilt, edges worn and chipped, interior pages have some browning along margins, some splitting of signatures but text block remains solid, very good, presentation copy from author to Star Barker, further inscribed to Karl Martin.   The Kelmscott Bookshop   12 - 58   2016 $300

Jones, D. L. *Orchids of Australia, the Complete Edition Drawn in Natural Colour by W. H. Nicholls.* Melbourne: Nelson, 1969. Large quarto, 476 color plates by W. H. Nichols, fine in very good dust jacket.   Andrew Isles Natural History Books   55 - 30582   2016 $200

Jones, David *The Anathemata - Fragments of an Attempted Writing.* London: Faber and Faber, 1952. First edition, octavo, black and white plates and one red, black and white plate by author, near fine in very good, slightly nicked dust jacket faintly tanned at spine.   Peter Ellis   112 - 199   2016   £175

Jones, David *The Chester Play of the Deluge.* London: printed by Will Carter at the Rampant Lions Press for Clover Hill Editions, 1977. No. XXXII of 80 copies on handmade paper from a total edition of 337 copies, including 7 on vellum, publisher's russet morocco backed marbled boards, morocco title label on upper cover, housed in lightly soiled cloth slipcase along with matching cloth chemise containing additional suite of plates, with 10 wood engravings by David Jones, and with additional suite of plates on Japon, engravings printed from original wood blocks on an Albion hand press by Ian Mortimer at I. M. Imprimit, except for bit of wear to bottom corners, mint.   Phillip J. Pirages   67 - 206   2016 $1900

Jones, David *The Chester Play of the Deluge.* London: printed by Will Carter at the Rampant Lions Press for Clover Hill Editions, 1977. Copy "E" of 7 copies printed on vellu, 343 x 264mm., 2 volumes, including portfolio, original special russet crushed morocco by Sangorski & Sutcliffe (stamp-signed), raised bands, gilt titling, turn-ins ruled in gilt and black, marbled endpapers, portfolio in marbled paper clamshell box backed with matching morocco, both in lightly rubbed felt lined slipcase, 10 wood engravings by David Jones and three additional suites of plates, one on vellum, another on handmade paper and third on Japon, engravings printed from original wood blocks on an Albion handpress by Ian Mortimer at I. M. Imprimit, errata slip laid in at colophon, pristine.   Phillip J. Pirages   67 - 342   2016 $15,000

Jones, David *In Parenthesis.* London: Faber and Faber, 1961. Second edition, deluxe issue, limited ot 70 numbered copies (50 for sale), specially bound and signed by Jones and T. S. Eliot, this copy no. 1, 8vo., original blue buckram, spine lettered on grey background within gilt panel, frontispiece and full page plate at rear both by David Jones and map in text, fine.   Sotheran's Piccadilly Notes - Summer 2015 - 176   2016   £4995

Jones, David *An Introduction to the Rime of the Ancient Mariner.* London: Clover Hill Editions, 1972. One of 115 numbered special copies signed and dated by David Jones in an edition of 330, 4to., quarter vellum and green cloth covered boards title in gilt on spine, top edge gilt, slipcase of green and blue marbled paper, set in Monotype Ehrhardt, printed on paper handmade by W. S. Hodgkinson, slipcase, edges slightly worn, else fine.   Oak Knoll Books   27 - 58   2016 $350

Jones, David *The Paintings of David Jones.* London: John Taylor/Lund Humphries in association with the Tate Gallery, 1989. First edition, quarto, 62 color plates, 6 black and white illustrations, fine in near fine dust jacket little creased at edges.   Peter Ellis   112 - 198   2016   £75

Jones, David Martin *Conscience and Allegiance in Seventeenth Century England: the Political Significance of Oaths and Engagements.* Rochester: University of Rochester Press, 1999. First edition, 8vo., fine in very good+ dust jacket.   Any Amount of Books   2015 - A96294   2016   £170

Jones, Henry *Poems on Several Occasions.* London: printed for R. Dodsley and W. Owen, 1740. First edition, 8vo., contemporary half calf and marbled boards, spine gilt, rubbed, spine worn, lower joint cracked but firm, good, wanting flyleaf at end, blank strip torn from foot of last leaf, otherwise good.   C. R. Johnson Rare Book Collections   Foxon: H-P 2015 - 507   2016 $613

Jones, Henry Arthur *The Crusaders: an Original Comedy of Modern London Life.* London: Macmillan & Co., 1893. First edition, presentation copy inscribed by author "To the Green Room Club, from Henry Arthur Jones Sept. 16 1893", vellum with gilt title to spine, yapp edges and original green ties, vellum spotted and darkened with age and front cover has curled, interior bright and tight with some spotting and darkening along untrimmed edges, large octavo, very good.   The Kelmscott Bookshop   12 - 59   2016 $150

Jones, Henry Arthur *Patriotism and Popular Education...* London: Chapman & Hall, 1919. Presentation inscription, from author for Gilbert Parker.   Jarndyce Antiquarian Books   CCXV - 795   2016   £65

Jones, I. McHenry *Harts of Gold.* Wheeling: Daily Intelligence Steam Job Press, 1896. First edition, octavo, errata, green cloth decorated in gilt, contemporary owner's name on front pastedown, some spotting and light bowing on boards, cheap paper little toned, couple of pages little loose, still nice about very good copy of this uncommon novel.   Between the Covers Rare Books   202 - 54   2016 $2000

Jones, J. Elizabeth *The Young Abolitionists or Conversations of Slavery.* Boston: The Anti-Slavery Office, 1848. First edition, 16mo., green embossed publisher's cloth, worn, pencil doodling to pastedowns and flyleaves, titlepage with small chip to upper corner and staining, staining/soiling to some lower margins, last leaf blank, with loss, some minor issues or other minor flaws, five different Jones names written in ink in back.   M & S Rare Books, Inc.   99 - 291   2016 $1250

Jones, Jack *Birds of the Footscray District.* Melbourne: author, 1939. Octavo, printed wrappers, fine, scarce.   Andrew Isles Natural History Books   55 - 6846   2016 $80

Jones, James *From Here to Eternity.* New York: Scribner, 1951. Advance copy, couple of slight textual differences from published book, together with (secretarially) typed letter signed by author in Paris in 1963, conveying a signed book not included here to a fan in Dublin, sheets are fragile at edges and have professional restoration to first several pages, but are near fine and preserved in several faded numbers marked on it in pencil, letter fine, folded in fourths and laid in, including for comparison is early printing of the book in dust jacket.   Ken Lopez Bookseller   166 - 58   2016 $2500

Jones, Jefferson *The Fall of Tsingtau.* Boston: Houghton Mifflin, 1915. First edition, 8vo., original yellow cloth, soil to covers, cover edge wear, owner inscription, scarce.   By the Book, L. C.   45 - 44   2016 $200

Jones, John *The Theory and Practice of Notes of Lessons.* London: Simpkin Marshall, 1856. Second edition, 2 pages ads, half title, original blue cloth, very good.   Jarndyce Antiquarian Books   CCXV - 796   2016   £30

Jones, Joseph *Historical Sketch of the Art and Literary Institutions of Wolverhampton...* London: Alexander & Shepherd, 1897. Half title, frontispiece, plates, original blue cloth, slightly rubbed and dulled, signature of W. Trimmington, nice.   Jarndyce Antiquarian Books   CCXV - 799   2016   £40

Jones, M. D. *A Murder in West Covina: Chronicles of the Finch-Tregoff Case.* West Covina: Chappard, 1992. First edition, fine in fine dust jacket, black boards, blood red metallic titling on cover and spine (jacket in Brodart), signed by author, scarce thus.   Simon Finch   2015 - 011202   2016 $220

Jones, Mary Gladys *The Charity School Movement.* London: Frank Cass & Co., 1964. New impression, half title, plates, original turqoise cloth, very good in slightly torn dust jacket with repair to tail of spine, Victor Neuburg's copy.   Jarndyce Antiquarian Books   CCXV - 798   2016   £20

Jones, Owen   1809-1874 *One Thousand and One Initial Letters Designed and Illuminated by Owen Jones.* London: Day & Son, 1864. Folio, chromolithograph title and 27 plates, printed in gold and colors, 5 cm. edge tear to plate for letter A without loss, original bevelled maroon cloth, upper cover and spine blocked with title in gilt, edges gilt recased.   Marlborough Rare Books   List 55 - 40   2016   £1500

Jones, Owen   1809-1874 *The Sermon on the Mount.* London: Longman & Co., 1844. 36 pages, text illuminated by Owen Jones & chromolithographed in color, some spotting and (mainly) marginal marking, original dark purple by Hayday, blocked in blind with onlaid paper labels to both boards, all edges gilt, contemporary gift inscription, very rare.   Jarndyce Antiquarian Booksellers   CCXVII - 142   2016   £280

Jones, Paul *Flora Magnifica: Selected and Painted by the Artist.* London: Tryon Gallery, 1976. Limited to 506 numbered and signed copies, Folio, 15 plates with tissue guards, publisher's half vellum, and maroon cloth boards by Zaehnsdorf, slipcase.   Andrew Isles Natural History Books   55 - 31426   2016 $650

Jones, Robert *Artificial Fireworks, Improved to the Modern Practice, from the Minutest to the Highest Branches.* Chelmsford: printed and sold by Meggy and Chalk, 1801. 210 x 137mm., very pleasing recent retrospective smooth calf, raised bands, red morocco label, edges entirely untrimmed, with 20 copper engraved plates (printed on both sides of leaves) showing various pyrotechnical apparatuses, inscription in 19th century hand for Mrs. S. Pearson, Steeton; minor foxing and soiling there, but generally text in excellent condition, unexpectedly clean and fresh, unworn sympathetic binding.   Phillip J. Pirages   67 - 290   2016 $950

Jones, Terry *Lady Cottington's Pressed Fairy Book.* Atlanta: Turner Pub. Inc., 1994. First US edition, beautiful illustrations, padded boards simulated to look like old worn leather, pressed fairy bookmark laid in and in perfect condition, band for 'protection of the innocent' included and still intact, small inked owner's signature on upper corner of front free endpaper, else fine, beautiful copy.   Argonaut Book Shop   Literature 2015 - 4717   2016 $275

Jones, Terry *Lady Cottington's Pressed Fairy Book.* Atlanta: Turner Pub. Co., 1994. First edition, first printing with 1-10 code, instead of pressed flowers in a book, this features pressed fairies, full page color illustrations by Brian Froud, fairy bookmark, imitation leather, pictorial boards, fine.   Aleph-bet Books, Inc.   112 - 208   2016 $200

Jones, Tessie *Bagatelles.* Paris: M. Darantiere, 1926. One of 100 copies, 225 x 162mm., publisher's blue green paper wrappers, color illustration on upper cover, 11 vignette headpieces and 8 tailpiece ornament by Robert Bonfils, all coloured using pochoir technique, spine faded, some fading to covers with areas recolored by a previous owner, slight fraying at spine ends and edges of fragile binding, otherwise fine.   Phillip J. Pirages   67 - 282   2016 $750

Jones, Thomas *Classical Education.* Bristol: printed by J. Rudhall, circa, 1790. Prospectus, formerly folded twice, central section on verso of second leaf slightly soiled, few tin holes at folds, 4to., good.   Blackwell's Rare Books   B184 - 53   2016   £600

Jones, William M. *Planning for Limited Nuclear Operation: Procedures and Problems.* Santa Monica: The RAND Corporation, 1969. Quarto, printed rectos only, stapled self wrappers, just about fine.   Between the Covers Rare Books   208 - 42   2016 $700

Jong, Erica *Fruits and Vegetables: Poems.* New York: Holt Rinehart & Winston, 1971. First edition, 8vo., paper wrappers, signed by author, some underlining in colored ink, cover little scuffed, otherwise very good.   Second Life Books, Inc.   196A - 900   2016 $50

Jonson, Ben 1572-1637 *The Key Keeper.* Tunbridge Wells: Foundling Press, 2002. First modernised edition, 97/300 copies printed on Zerkall mouldmade paper, 11 line drawings by David Gentleman, title printed in red, original dark blue cloth, backstrip gilt lettered, tail edges rough trimmed, dust jacket, fine.   Blackwell's Rare Books   B186 - 305   2016   £70

Jonson, Ben 1572-1637 *Volpone; or the Foxe.* New York: John Lane, 1898. No, 43 of 100 copies on Japanese Imperial vellum, each containing an extra suite of plates (of a total edition of 1100 for England and America), 295 x 225mm., publisher's original vellum over bevelled boards, upper cover elaborately gilt in design by Beardsley, smooth spine lettered gilt, top edge gilt, others untrimmed, housed in later cloth slipcase, 13 illustrations by Aubrey Beardsley, woodcut bookplate of John Quinn, splaying to boards, otherwise especially fine, very clean and smooth and fresh inside and out.   Phillip J. Pirages   67 - 22   2016 $2900

Jonson, Ben 1572-1637 *The Workes.* London: Will Stansby, 1616. London: Richard Meighen, 1640, 3 volumes in 2, engraved title by W. Hole in volume I, 2 divisional titles within woodcut border, engraved portrait by Vaughan inserted from second edition, engraved title neatly repaired at inner margin of A4 of "The Magnetic Lady" restored at margins, very small hole in penultimate leaf of the second volume, occasional light browning, folio, red crushed morocco by Riviere, French fillets on sides, spines richly gilt, gilt edges, upper hinges slightly rubbed, very good.   Blackwell's Rare Books   Marks of Genius - 23   2016   £15,000

Joppien, Rudiger *The Art of Captain Cook's Voyages.* Melbourne: Oxford University Press, 1985. Reprint, 2 volumes, 4to., copiously illustrated in color and black and white, neat collector's blindstamp, otherwise very good+ in like dust jacket with slight fading and very slight creasing, otherwise excellent.   Any Amount of Books   2015 - A76751   2016   £150

Joris, Pierre *Turbulence.* Rhinebeck: St. Lazaire, 1991. First edition, 8vo., paper wrappers, inscribed by author for poet Paul Metcalf.   Second Life Books, Inc.   196A - 902   2016 $45

Josephson, Kenneth *Selected Photographs.* Berlin: Only Photography, 2013. Number 401 from an edition of 500, very fine in illustrated boards, signed by Josephson, beautifully printed book, numerous black and white images.   Jeff Hirsch Books   Holiday List 2015 - 79   2016 $175

Josephy, Alvin M. *The Nez Perce Indians and the Opening of the Northwest.* New Haven and London: Yale University Press, 1965. First edition, scarce thus, presentation inscription signed by author, frontispiece, eleven maps, 24 contemporary photographs and sketches, original tan cloth, very fine with pictorial dust jacket. Argonaut Book Shop   Native American 2015 - 7598   2016 $225

Joslyn, Sesyle *What Do You Do Dear?* New York: Young Scott, 1961. First edition, Pictorial cloth, near fine in dust jacket, illustrations in color by Maurice Sendak, this copy signed by artist with particularly charming drawing by Sendak.   Aleph-bet Books, Inc.   111 - 411   2016 $1500

The Journal of Nervous and Mental Diseases. Special Number Dedicated to Howard C. Nafziger, M.D. 1944. Volume 99 issue #5, 1944, original full morocco binding with some wear, particularly at joints, Nafziger's copy with his name embossed in gold on front board.   James Tait Goodrich   X-78 - 407   2016 $1295

Jourtel, Henri *A Journal of the Last Voyage Perform'd by Monsr. de la Sale to the Gulph of Mexico to find out the Mouth of the Mississippi River...*   London: for A. Bell, B. Lintot and J. Baker, 1714. First edition in English, engraved folding map, short closed tear, contemporary calf, extremities rubbed, top of spine bit worn, else lovely untouched copy, text clean and fresh and entirely unfoxed, Peter A Porter bookplate and Wolfgang Herz label.   Joseph J. Felcone, Inc.   Books from Five Centuries: a Miscellany - 85   2016 $15,000

Joyce, James 1882-1941 *The Dead.* Dublin: Stoney Road Press, 2014. 59/150 copies (from an edition of 175 copies), signed by artist, Robert Berry and by David Norris, printed on Arches Blanc paper, 14 full page drawings by Robert Berry, titlepage printed in lilac, 4to., original grey boards, illustrations in black, white and blue with publisher's device blindstamped at head of upper board, backstrip of black cloth, lettered in black, edges black, illustrated endpapers, cloth slipcase stamped in white, fine.   Blackwell's Rare Books   B186 - 342   2016   £1250

Joyce, James 1882-1941 *Finnegans Wake.* London: Faber & Faber, New York: Viking Press, 1939. First edition, no. 206 of 425 copies, signed by Joyce, 260 x 171mm., original brick red buckram, gilt titling on spine, edges untrimmed and mostly unopened, in original (very slightly soiled) yellow cloth slipcase and housed in extremely attractive modern dark red morocco backed folding box, remnants of bookplate glue on front pastedown, especially fine, binding unworn, virtually pristine internally and even slipcase very well preserved.   Phillip J. Pirages   67 - 208   2016 $16,000

Joyce, James 1882-1941 *Haveth Childers Everywhere.* Paris: Henry Babou and Jack Kahane; New York: Fountain Press, 1930. No. 24 of 100 copies on iridescent handmade Japan, signed by author (plus an additional 500 on paper and 75 writer's copies), 283 x 191mm., original white paper covers with printed titling on front and spine, leaves untrimmed and unopened in original glassine protected wrapper, the whole in original (slightly rubbed) three panel stiff card folder covered with gilt paper, without original slipcase, title printed in green and black, initials and headlines printed in green, inside front cover of folder and bookplate of John Kobler, corners just slightly bumped, one small faint brown spot to tissue cover, outstanding copy, very fragile and always torn glassine entirely intact, text with no signs of use, most of it never having seen the light of day.   Phillip J. Pirages   67 - 209   2016 $15,000

Joyce, James 1882-1941 *The Mime of Mick, Nick and the Maggies.* The Hague: The Servire Press, New York: Gotham Book Mart, 1934. First edition, no. 631 of 1000 copies on Old Antique Dutch (and 29 special signed copies on Japon), 241 x 162mm., plain paper wrappers in white dust jacket, front cover with design by Lucia Joyce printed in blue and silver, blue titling on front cover and spine, entirely unopened, with very rare original glassine and housed in slightly worn brown cardboard slipcase, with opening initial and tailpiece designed by Lucia Joyce, glassine little wrinkled, one corner just lightly bumped, otherwise pristine.   Phillip J. Pirages   67 - 210   2016 $2000

Joyce, James 1882-1941 *Collected Poems.* New York: Black Sun Press, 1936. First edition, no. 166 of 800 copies, publisher's cream colored paper boards, covers printed in blue with a floral frame enclosing a central panel of alternating rows of fleurons, blue titling on flat spine, frontispiece of author by Augustus Johns, printed in dark blue, spine slightly sunned to creamier color, light soiling along bottom inch of back cover, one small faint spot to margin of one page, otherwise very fine, clean and bright inside and out.   Phillip J. Pirages   67 - 107   2016 $1000

Joyce, James 1882-1941 *Collected Poems of....* New York: Black Sun Press, 1936. First edition, limited to 50 copies on Japanese vellum, signed by Joyce on frontispiece, this copy number 18, also signed below colophon for publisher Caresse Crosby, small octavo, printed in blue ink, all in italic, lithographed portrait frontispiece in crayon by Augustus John, publisher's cream white parchment over boards, stamped in gilt with arabesque border around a central panel patterned with all all over design of 23 floral ornament, gilt title on spine, blue ribbon marker bound in, top edge gilt, publisher's original glassine, protective wrapper (chipped with some loss principally to lower panel), original gilt slipcase with extremities worn and some tears to joints, overall pristine, housed in custom blue morocco clamshell.   Heritage Book Shop   Holiday 2015 - 60   2016 $12,500

Joyce, James 1882-1941 *A Portrait of the Artist as a Young Man.* New York: B. W. Huebsch, 1916. First edition, 194 x 127mm., publisher's blue cloth, blindstamped title on front cover, flat spine with gilt tilting, bookplates of John Kobler and of "Porcaro", very slight chafing to joints and extremities, spine ends just little curled, otherwise fine, binding especially clean, spine gilt very bright, text virtually pristine. Phillip J. Pirages 67 - 211 2016 $7000

Joyce, James 1882-1941 *Stephen Hero.* New Directions, 1944. First American edition, the copy of Lionel Trilling. Honey & Wax Booksellers 4 - 39 2016 $600

Joyce, James 1882-1941 *Stephen Hero.* London: Jonathan Cape, 1944. First edition, one of 2000 copies, crown 8vo., original black cloth, backstrip lettered gilt with very slight lean to spine, tail edges rough trimmed with top edge a trifle dusty, ownership inscription to front pastedown concealed by dust jacket flap, dust jacket lightly soiled overall with darkened backstrip panel, little fraying at tips of backstrip panel and chipping to corners, good. Blackwell's Rare Books B186 - 244 2016 £200

Joyce, James 1882-1941 *Tales Told of Shem and Shaun. Three Fragments from Work in Progress.* Paris: Black Sun Press, 1929. First edition, no. 249 of 500 copies on Van Gelder Zoenen paper (plus 50 copies hors commerce and 100 copies on Japanese vellum) 210 x 168mm., original white paper wrappers, title printed in black and red on front cover and spine, printer's device on back cover, in original glassine dust jacket, in (slightly worn and expertly repaired) cardboard slipcase of orange cloth covered with gilt paper and with orange ribbon pull (apparently a variant of publisher's slipcase described in Slocum & Cahoon), frontispiece by Constantin Brancusi, original tissue guard, printed in red and black, minuscule chip to glassine at head and tail of spine, otherwise in pristine condition. Phillip J. Pirages 67 - 212 2016 $2500

Joyce, James 1882-1941 *Tales Told of Shem and Shaun.* Paris: Black Sun Press, 1929. First edition, 124/500 copies (from an edition of 650 copies) printed in black and red on Holland Van Gelder Zonen paper, frontispiece by Brancusi with tissue guard, 4to., original white wrappers, backstrip and front cover printed in black and red, some light dust soiling with little chipping at foot of backstrip and front cover printed in black and red, some light dust soiling, little chipping at foot of backstrip, two gold slipcase boards and salmon pink ribbon pull remaining only, very good. Blackwell's Rare Books B186 - 243 2016 £850

Joyce, James 1882-1941 *Ulysses.* Paris: Shakespeare and Co., 1922. First edition, one of 750 numbered copies on handmade paper from a total edition of 1000, this no. 878, 4to., original blue paper printed wrappers, some restoration of paper to spine, light soiling to wrappers but very good, notoriously fragile book in solander cloth case. Sotheran's Piccadilly Notes - Summer 2015 - 8 2016 £39,950

Joyce, James 1882-1941 *Ulysses.* New York: Limited Editions Club, 1935. No. 1367 of 1500 copies signed by Matisse, 305 x 235mm., publisher's original brown buckram, embossed in gilt and titled on front cover and on flat spine, decorations from design by LeRoy H. Appleton, housed in original slightly worn but generally well preserved board slipcase with brown titling on spine, with 26 illustrations by Henri Matisse, with book review from 24 Nov. 1935 NY Times laid in, slipcase with minor soiling and with discreet minor and very neat head and tail of spine, otherwise solid and excellent, volume itself virtually mint. Phillip J. Pirages 67 - 240 2016 $5500

Joyce, James 1882-1941 *Ulysses.* London: John Lane, the Bodley Head, 1936. One of 100 copies signed by author, there were also 100 unsigned copies, first edition printed in England, original vellum, gilt titling on spine, large stylized gilt bow on each cover, top edge gilt, other edges untrimmed and mostly unopened, original (slightly worn but very solid) black and white patterned paper slipcase with paper label housed in fine silk lined grey morocco clamshell box by Sangorski & Sutcliffe, title printed in blue and black, prospectus laid in at front, perhaps hint of smudging to vellum (or perhaps just natural variation in color), but in any case, virtually mint, binding entirely unworn and especially bright and mostly unopened text pristine. Phillip J. Pirages 67 - 213 2016 $36,000

Joyce, Patrick Weston *A Hand-Book of School Management and Methods of teaching.* Dublin: M. H. Gill & Son, 1879. Sixth edition, illustrations, original purple cloth, unevenly faded, presentation from author for Alfred P. Grams. Jarndyce Antiquarian Books CCXV - 799 2016 £48

Joyce, William *The Leaf Men and the Brave Good Bugs.* New York: Harper Collins, 1996. Stated first edition, pictorial boards, as new in as new contemporary, marvelous full page color illustrations, this copy signed by Joyce with small sketch. Aleph-bet Books, Inc. 112 - 274 2016 $125

Joyce, William *Santa Calls.* New York: Harper Collins, 1993. Limited to 250 numbered copies signed by Joyce, with small drawing, 11 1/4 inch square, cloth pictorial boards, as new in slipcase (slightly faded at edge), small pen drawing, rich color illustrations. Aleph-bet Books, Inc. 111 - 237 2016 $400

Jubilee of Acadia College and Memorial Exercises. Halifax: Holloway Bros., 1889. 8vo., brown pressed cloth boards, gilt to front and spine, frontispiece, black and white illustrations, portraits, plan, top and bottom of spine frayed and small portion of cloth on spine missing, corners bumped and worn, interior very good. Schooner Books Ltd. 115 - 126 2016 $75

Judah, Samuel Benjamin Helbert *Gotham and the Gothamites. a Medley.* New York: Pub. for the author by S. King, 1823. First edition, small 12mo, original printed paper covered boards, untrimmed and largely unopened, endpapers slightly foxed, boards bit scuffed and worn at extremities, else remarkably well preserved, with entire spine and letterpress title intact.   Joseph J. Felcone, Inc.   Books from Five Centuries: a Miscellany - 2   2016 $2200

Judd, Donald *Donald Judd Furniture Retrospective.* Rotterdam: Museum Boymans-van Beuingen, 1993. Color illustrations, clean and tight, very near fine in close to near fine dust jacket with some very slight wear, lovely copy, much less common cloth issue.   Jeff Hirsch Books   Holiday List 2015 - 12   2016 $1500

Jung, Carl G. *Eranos 1941.* Zurich: 1941. Mimeographed, 182 pages bound in stiff boards, signed by poet Barbara Howes, very good.   Second Life Books, Inc.   196A - 904   2016 $50

Junius, Franciscus *Etymologicum Anglicanum.* Oxonii: e Theatro Sheldoniano, 1743. Folio, frontispiece, corrigenda and list of subscribers, bound out of order at front, occasional light foxing towards edges, leaf 352 folded and therefore partially uncut, recent blind tooled brown morocco with green morocco spine label by Bernard Middleton, few slight scuffs, endpapers little toned, very good.   Unsworths Antiquarian Booksellers   30 - 89   2016   £500

Junius, Pseud. *The Letters of Junius.* London: printed in the year, 1789. 12mo., scattered light foxing, margins slightly discolored, neatly and attractively rebound in quarter speckled calf, marbled paper boards, vellum tips, spine ruled in gilt, red morocco label, very good.   Jarndyce Antiquarian Booksellers   CCXVI - 335   2016   £110

Junius, Pseud. *The Letters of Junius.* London: n.p., 1791. New edition, 12mo., scattered light foxing, edges dusted, uncut as issued in blue boards, blue paper spine chipped with ink title added, some wear.   Jarndyce Antiquarian Booksellers   CCXVI - 336   2016   £55

Junius, Pseud. *Stat Nominis Umbra.* London: printed by T. Bensley for Vernor & Hood, 1801. 8vo., 2 volumes, in full Spanish calf, boards with gilt border, spines gilt with contrasting leather labels, 21 engraved portraits and 69 vignettes, volume I with small hole to upper joint and pin hole on upper board, spines and joints little rubbed, some occasional browning, otherwise very good.   Sotheran's Piccadilly Notes - Summer 2015 - 177   2016   £250

Jury, David *Book Art Object 2: Second Catalogue of the Codex Foundation Biennial International Book Exhibition and Symposium, Berkeley 2011.* Berkeley: Codex Foundation, 2013. 1133 color images, new in white cloth boards with red title to front cover and spine, new white dust jacket with red title to spine and front cover, fine in fine jacket.   The Kelmscott Bookshop   13 - 27   2016 $150

Jusserand, J. J. *La Vie Nomade et Les Routes D'Angleterre au XIVe Siecle.* Paris: Hachette, 1884. 8vo., quarter black roan with marbled boards, spine in seven compartments with raised bands, gilt, rubbed, corners bit bumped and worn, marble endpapers, prelims darkened a little but text block clean, edges uncut, general dustiness but still good, author's inscription to Gaston Paris, philanthropist, stamp of St. Ignatius College Amsterdam.   Unsworths Antiquarian Booksellers   30 - 90   2016   £60

A Just, Genuine and Impartial History of the Memorable Sea-Fight in the Mediterranean Between the Combined Fleets of France and Spain... printed of the author and sold by R. Walker, 1745. First edition, folding engraved plate as frontispiece and folding engraved plate with 2 maps, uniformly slightly browned, minor soiling, frontispiece foxed and with short tear (no loss), old flyleaf at front, defective in lower outer corner, bearing ownership inscription of Philip Moore, dated 2nd 1745, 8vo., modern leatherette, sound.   Blackwell's Rare Books   B184 - 71   2016   £850

Justice, James *The British Gardener's Director...* Edinburgh: printed for A. Kincaid and J. Bell and R. Fleming, 1764. 8vo., some very slight marginal worming, well clear of text, only affecting few leaves, contemporary sheep neatly rebacked, with plain raised bands, original red morocco label, contemporary signature of J. P. Wm. Ellis.   Jarndyce Antiquarian Booksellers   CCXVI - 338   2016   £320

Juvenalis, Decimus Junius *Satyrae with commentary of Domitius Calderinus.* Venice: Bartholomaeus de Zanis 3 Oct., 1487. Folio, spaces left for capitals illuminated with four large white vine initials of 4 to 8 lines in size, initials in gold with swirling white stems surrounding them against backgrounds of red, green and blue, two small 3 line initials and gold against a red and green background, some rubrication in blue and red, two smaller initials in gold against red and green background, some rubrication in blue and red, lacking final blank, Roman letter, 61 lines of commentary surrounding text, 19th century half brown morocco, rubbed and scuffed, tear to upper margins of ff. b1 and b2, neatly repaired, one or two wormholes at beginning and end, little browned or stained in places, Kenneth Rapoport copy.   Maggs Bros. Ltd.   1474 - 44   2016   £7500

Juvenalis, Decimus Junius *Satyrae.* Utrech: Rudolphi a Zyll, 1658. 4to. engraved title, contemporary calf, neatly rebacked in period style, some light stains on first and last few leaves, covers bit scuffed and corners worn through, else very good.   Joseph J. Felcone, Inc.   Books from Five Centuries: a Miscellany - 86   2016 $425

Juvenalis, Decimus Junius *Satyrae.* Dublin: ex officina Georgii Grierson, 1728. 12mo., engraved frontispiece, titlepage in red and black, touch of faint spotting, 12mo., contemporary calf, spine with four raised bands, red morocco lettering piece, bit marked, tiny chips to tail of spine, very good.   Blackwell's Rare Books   Greek & Latin Classics VII - 52   2016   £120

Juvenalis, Decimus Junius *Satyrae.* Birmingham: Typis Johannis Baskerville, 1761. Cancel leaves #2, K4, V4, Z3 and gatherings Ee-Ggprinted on poorer quality paper and dampmarked in upper margin and lower fore corner, just little minor spotting elsewhere, 4to., 19th century half black calf, marbled boards and endpapers, spine with raised bands, lettered direct in gilt, extremities rubbed, little wear, good.   Blackwell's Rare Books   Greek & Latin Classics VII - 53   2016   £250

Juvenalis, Decimus Junius *Satyrae.* Cambridge: Prostant Venales Londini apud Gul. Sandby, 1763. 8vo., 15 engraved plates (including frontispiece), light spotting, contemporary mid-brown calf, boards bordered with gilt roll, gilt in compartments, lettering piece in second compartment (rather chipped), boards with later Chancellor's Prize stamp in blind (i.e. arms of Baron Grenville, as chancellor of Oxford), marbled endpapers, extremities rubbed, head of spine chipped, front joint cracking but strong, armorial bookplate of Revd Charles Lyttelton, good.   Blackwell's Rare Books   Greek & Latin Classics VII - 54   2016   £250

Juvenalis, Decimus Junius *The Satires of Juvenal.* Cambridge: printed for J. Nicholson, 1777. Some light soiling and toning, frequent underlining and marginal notes in early hand, 8vo., later mottled calf, rebacked preserving original endpapers, spine gilt somewhat crudely, armorial bookplate of Thomas Hesketh and shelfmark and label of Easton Neston library, good.   Blackwell's Rare Books   Greek & Latin Classics VII - 51   2016   £400

The Juvenile Biographer, Containing the Lives of Little Masters and Misses....   Worcester: Isaiah Thomas..., 1767. First Worcester edition, 32mo., two faint blindstamps on title, occasional spot else very good in (later?) floral patterned paper wrappers, housed in custom cloth box, 20 woodcuts, tailpieces & ornaments, quite scarce.   Aleph-bet Books, Inc.   111 - 139   2016 $1950

Juvenile Philosophy....   London: Vernor & Hood, 1801. Free endpapers removed, 16mo., original quarter dark green roan, marbled paper boards, small repair to leading hinge, rubbed.   Jarndyce Antiquarian Books   CCXV - 801   2016   £65

K

Kaberry, Charles *The Book of Baby Dogs.* London: Henry Frowde, n.d., 1915. 4to., cloth backed boards, round pictorial paste-on, corners rubbed, else clean, tight and very good+, 19 incredible and unusual mounted color plates in his unique style, quite scarce. Aleph-bet Books, Inc. 112 - 143 2016 $425

Kadryskoya, Natalya *The Little Man in the Globe.* Paris: Ourlet Freres, 1954. 4to., boards, pictorial paste-on, fine, illustrations by Rojankovsky. Aleph-bet Books, Inc. 111 - 393 2016 $300

Kafka, Franz 1883-1924 *America.* London: George Routledge & sons, 1938. First UK edition, 8vo., burgundy cloth, some spotting to fore edge and endpapers, very good in little nicked and worn, price clipped dust jacket. Second Life Books, Inc. 197 - 197 2016 $850

Kafka, Franz 1883-1924 *The Diaries of Franz Kafka 1910-1923.* London: Secker and Warburg, 1948-1949. First UK edition, 8vo., 2 volumes, 3 sketches by author reproduced, spines and cover edges slightly faded as usual, top edges little spotted, very good set in very good, slightly nicked and rubbed dust jackets, bit tanned at spine and edges. Peter Ellis 112 - 200 2016 £185

Kahn, Edgar M. *Bret Harte in California, A Character Study.* San Francisco: privately printed and designed for the author by Haywood H. Hunt, 1951. First edition, one of 200 copies, this being number 2, signed 'Author's copy', frontispiece, tan cloth backed marbled boards, paper cover label, slight offsetting to front and leaves, tape residue to upper edge of inner cover, else fine. Argonaut Book Shop Private Press 2015 - 7599 2016 $60

Kajiyama, Y. *Studies in Buddhist Philosophy.* Kyoto: Rinsen Book Co., 1989. First edition, small 4to., housed in original printed paper covered slipcase with soil, mild wear, scarce. By the Book, L. C. 45 - 49 2016 $250

Kallman, Chester *Storm at Castelfanco.* New York: Grove Press, 1956. First edition, one of only 15 copies signed by Kallman and containing an original drawing signed by Larry Rivers tipped in as frontispiece, offsetting to titlepage from original drawing, otherwise very good, small 8vo., original cloth backed boards, glassine dust jacket. James S. Jaffe Rare Books Occasional List: Winter 2016 - 19 2016 $7500

Kamante *Longing for Darkness: Kamanate's Tales from Out of Africa.* Harcourt Brace Jovanovich, 1975. First edition, very good in like dust jacket, photos. Simon Finch 2015 - 0026212 2016 $250

Kaminsky, Stuart M. *Exercise in Terror.* New York: St. Martin's, 1985. First edition, some tiny spotting on edges, otherwise fine in dust jacket with slightly faded spine. Mordida Books 2015 - 006824 2016 $60

Kanin, Garson *Blow Up a Storm a Novel.* New York: Random House, 1959. First edition, 8vo., very good in somewhat soiled dust jacket inscribed by author. Second Life Books, Inc. 196A - 908 2016 $35

Kanin, Garson *Hollywood.* New York: Viking Press, 1974. First edition, 8vo., inscribed by author to wife Ruth Gordon, with notations by Gordon, a working copy. Second Life Books, Inc. 196A - 906 2016 $75

Kann, Eduard *The Currencies of China.* Shanghai: Kelly & Walsh, 1926. First edition, 8vo., minimal sun spine, small dent to front cover, foxing, gift inscription, dust jacket missing front flap, lower edge of front and rear panels, dust jacket laid down on matching tan colored paper to fill the missing sections, scarce, especially with dust jacket. By the Book, L. C. 45 - 45 2016 $400

Kanter, Larry *On Firm Ground.* Urbana: University of Illinois, 2001. First edition, oblong 4to., cloth, signed by Kanter, splendid book, fine in scarce dust jacket, photos. Gene W. Baade, Books on the West 2015 - 0903082 2016 $61

Kantor, MacKinlay *Arouse and Beware.* London: Victor Gollancz, 1937. First English edition, foxing on page edges and first few leaves, else near fine in near fine dust jacket with couple of very short tear, publisher's file copy, so stamped. Between the Covers Rare Books 208 - 43 2016 $250

Kapham, Mortimer *Dickens Children Stories.* Chicago and New York: Donohue, 1929. Half title, frontispiece, plates, illustrations by Ella Dollbear Lee, 4to., original olive green cloth, lettered gilt, front board with rubbed color onlay, booklabel of Donald S. Gray, this copy inscribed by author. Jarndyce Antiquarian Booksellers CCXVIII - 743 2016 £40

Kapham, Mortimer *Dickens Children Stories.* Chicago & New York: Donohue, 1929. 4to., illustrations by Ella Dolbear, color frontispiece and plates, original olive green cloth, lettered gilt, front board with rubbed color onlay, bookplate of Donald S. Gray, this copy inscribed by author. Jarndyce Antiquarian Booksellers CCXVIII - 744 2016 £30

Kaplan, Fred *Dickens: a Biography.* London: Hodder & Stoughton, 1988. First edition, half title, plates, original black cloth, very good in dust jacket. Jarndyce Antiquarian Booksellers   CCXVIII - 1326   2016   £20

Kaplan, Fred *Dickens and Mesmerism: the Hidden Springs of Fiction.* Princeton: Princeton University Press, First edition, half title, plates, original brown cloth, very good in dust jacket, Kathleen Tillotson's copy with notes relating to this work. Jarndyce Antiquarian Booksellers   CCXVIII - 1325   2016   £45

Kapp, Friedrich *Leben des Americanischen Generals Johann Kalb, Mit Kalb's Portrait.* Stuttgart: Cotta, 1862. First edition, very scarce in original wrappers and very scarce in this country, scattered foxing. Howard S. Mott Inc.   265 - 76   2016 $300

Karamisheff, W. *Mongolia and Western China.* Tientsin: La Librairie Francaise, 1925. First edition, 8vo., voxing, very good++, very good + dust jacket with chips and mild sun spine, scuffs and minimal foxing, 3 foldout maps, rare. By the Book, L. C.   45 - 46   2016 $1200

Karberry, C. J. *Our Little Neighbours Animals of the Farmland and Woodland.* London: Humphrey Milford/ Oxford University Press, n.d, 1921. 4to., cream colored boards, pictorial paste-on, slight cover soil, else fine in dust jacket (repaired with some pieces off), 11 magnificent mounted color plates by Edmund Detmold, rare in dust jacket. Aleph-bet Books, Inc.   112 - 142   2016 $650

Karlsen, Carol F.. *The Devil in the Shape of a Woman.* New York: Norton, 1987. First printing, 8vo., paper over boards, cloth spine, owner's name on flyleaf, author's presentation on title, top edge spotted, otherwise very good in little faded dust jacket. Second Life Books, Inc.   196A - 910   2016 $45

Karnilov, Boris *Kak Ot Meda U Medvedi a Zuby Nachali Bolet. (The Honey Bear with Toothache).* Moscow: State Oybkusger, 1935. Large 4to., pictorial wrappers, several edge repairs, very good, illustrations by K Rotov. Aleph-bet Books, Inc.   112 - 441   2016 $500

Karr, Mary *Abacus.* Middletown: Wesleyan University Press, 1987. First edition, inscribed by author for another writer, fine in very near fine with faint edge creasing to rear panel, uncommon in hardcover, especially signed. Ken Lopez Bookseller   166 - 60   2016 $500

Kassil, Lev *Tisiachu Platev V Den. (A Thousand Dresses a Day).* Moscow: Ogiz, 1931. 4to., pictorial wrappers, fine, 4 page panoramic view. Aleph-bet Books, Inc.   111 - 398   2016 $1200

Katzenbach and Warren, New York *Mural-Scrolls (Mural Scrolls).* New York: Katzenbach and Warren, 1949. First edition, rare portfolio with original silkscreens by Matisse, Calder, Miro and Matta, sample book, folio, original spiral bound color boards, few spiral loops broken, some wear and soiling to boards, patch of old tape to cloth inside covers offsetting on last page of text, silkscreens show small spots from burlap pushing through, few spots of paste-action at extreme top margin of the Miro, stunning set, remarkably bright. Manhattan Rare Book Company   2016 - 1616   2016 $2700

Katzenbach, F. *Genl. Tom Thumb's Polka.* Memphis: F. Katzenbach, 1863. First edition, folio, removed, light soiling, spine resewn, colored lithograph center on title leaf of Tom Thumb bride, best man and bridesmaid. M & S Rare Books, Inc.   99 - 23   2016 $1250

Kaufman, George *Beggar on Horseback.* New York: Boni & Liveright, 1924. First edition, 8vo., nice in little chipped dust jacket, section of joike newspaper pasted in on page 167, inscribed by Anne Carpenter (Gladys in the play). Second Life Books, Inc.   196A - 912   2016 $125

Kaufman, George *Beggar on Horseback.* New York: Boni & Liveright, 1924. First edition, 8vo., 2 pages in the middle of text quite darkened from old news clipping that had been laid in, top edges of boards sunned, otherwise very good tight copy in very good, bright dust jacket, inscribed by producer Winthrop Ames to George Barbier who played Mr. Cady, also inscribed by both playwrights, George Kaufman and Marc Connelly, splendid association. Second Life Books, Inc.   196A - 913   2016 $1500

Kaufman, Margaret *Aunt Sallie's Lament.* Burke: Janus Press, 1988. Limited to 150 copies, first edition, 8vo., original multi color paperwork, in floral print cloth folding box with printed label on spine, printed on richly colored cut out pages that create layered patchwork effect similar to actual quilt, box faded, book/paperwork fine. James S. Jaffe Rare Books   Occasional List: Winter 2016 - 85   2016 $1000

Kaufman, Margaret *Praise Basted In.* Vermont: Janus Press, 1995. Limited to 100 copies, signed by all participants, waverley upholstery cotton covered box, 9 squares creating friendship quilt, each with its own greeting card. Oak Knoll Books   310 - 113   2016 $750

Kauufman, S. Jay *Highlowbrow and Other Sketches.* New York: Samuel French, 1942. 8vo., author's presentation on flyleaf, nice in little worn dust jacket. Second Life Books, Inc.   196A - 914   2016 $45

Kavanagh, James William *Mixed Education. the Catholic Case Stated.* Dublin: John Mullany, 1859. Original green cloth, recased, slightly marked, spine faded. Jarndyce Antiquarian Books   CCXV - 802   2016   £40

Kavanagh, Patrick *Lapped Furrows - Correspondence 1933-1967 Between Patrick and Peter Kavanagh with other Documents.* New York: Peter Kavanagh Hand Press, 1969. First edition, octavo, presentation copy inscribed by editor for Brendan Lynch, octavo, covers slightly marked, near fine.   Peter Ellis   112 - 201   2016   £85

Kay-Shuttleworth, James *Four Periods of Public education as reviewed in 1832-1839-1846-1862.* London: Longman, 1862. First edition, half title, library stamps, crossed out in ink, slight signs of label removed from leading pastedown, original brown cloth by Westley & Co., slightly rubbed.   Jarndyce Antiquarian Books   CCXV - 803   2016   £110

Kay-Shuttleworth, James *Public Education as Affected by the Minutes of the Committee of Privy council from 1846 to 1852.* London: Longman, Brown, Green & Longmans, 1853. Folding tables, original brown cloth, plainly rebacked, Bookseller's ticket of R. Slocombe, Leeds.   Jarndyce Antiquarian Books   CCXV - 804   2016   £65

Kay, Gertrude *The Friends of Jimmy.* Joliet: Volland, 1926. Stated first edition, 8vo., pictorial boards, spine lightly rubbed and toned, else very good+, in fine box, illustrations by Kay.   Aleph-bet Books, Inc.   112 - 277   2016 $350

Kaye-Smith, Sheila *The History of Susan Spray, The Female Preacher.* London: Cassell, 1931. 1/150 copies, 8vo., signed by author, very good.   Second Life Books, Inc.   196A - 915   2016 $45

Keach, Benjamin *War with the Devil; or the Young Man's Conflict with the Powers of Darkness.* London: printed for H. P. and sold by Han(nah) Tracy, n.d. circa, 1720. 18th impression, Small 8vo., 19th century divinity calf, red edges, double page woodcut frontispiece (neatly trimmed and mounted), 15 further woodcuts in text, excellent, armorial bookplate of Joseph Beard of Alderley, later book label of L. G. E. Bell.   C. R. Johnson Rare Book Collections   Foxon: H-P 2015 - 509   2016 $689

Keane, A. H. *Asia with Ethnological Appendix.* London: Stanford, 1882. First edition, 8vo., original green pictorial cloth, blocked in black and gilt, 11 folding color printed maps apart from few repaired marginal tears to maps, near fine.   Sotheran's Travel and Exploration - 139   2016   £225

Keane, A. H. *Central & South America.* London: Edward Stanford, 1909. Second edition, octavo, 2 volumes, 32 page publisher's catalog dated 1911 at rear of second volume, illustrations, numerous folding color maps, green buckram decorated in gilt, Army and Navy Club bookplates, no other signs of library usage, chipping to overlapping edge of one of the maps (not affecting image), very good, bright set.   Peter Ellis   112 - 211   2016   £175

Keast, Allen *Ecological Biogeography of Australia.* The Hague: Dr. W. Junk, 1981. Octavo, 3 volumes, text illustrations, map, publisher's cloth and slipcase, fine.   Andrew Isles Natural History Books   55 - 26357   2016 $600

Keating, H. R. F. *Agatha Christie: First Lady of Crime.* London: Weidenfeld & Nicolson, 1977. First edition, very fine in dust jacket.   Mordida Books   2015 - 012096   2016 $65

Keating, William H. *Narrative of an Expedition to the Source of St. Peter's River, Lake Winnepeek, Lake of the Woods...* Philadelphia: Carey & Lea, 1824. First edition, folding map, 15 plates, with both half titles, original cloth backed boards, original paper labels to spines, spines faded, one label rubbed, light foxing.   M & S Rare Books, Inc.   99 - 137   2016 $1850

Keats, John   1795-1821 *Life, Letters and Literary Remains. (and) The Poetical Works.* London: Edward Moxon & Co., 1848. First edition of the first work, all volumes with half title, 3 volumes, 171 x 108mm., very pretty early 20th century slate blue crushed morocco by Zaehnsdorf (stamp signed, oval exhibition stamp), covers with delicate gilt rule frame, inlaid red morocco tulips at corners, raised bands, spines gilt in compartments with inlaid red tulip, gilt titling, turn-ins with leafy gilt border, marbled endpapers, top edges gilt, frontispiece in each volume with tissue guard; spines lightly and uniformly sunned, free endpapers with offset shadow from binder's glue, frontispiece from 'Remains' detached and little soiled, still pretty set in excellent condition, text clean and fresh, decorative bindings unworn.   Phillip J. Pirages   67 - 76   2016 $1000

Keats, John   1795-1821 *The Poems.* Cambridge: Limited Editions Club, 1966. First edition thus, copy 1461 of 1500, large 8vo., illustrations by David Gentleman, bound in bright red cowhide leather and black line with gold embossed portrait of poet in center of front cover, nearly 80 line drawings, including 16 full page drawings colored with panel tints by David Gentleman and signed by artist on colophon page, fine.   Second Life Books, Inc.   196A - 917   2016 $125

Keats, John   1795-1821 *Poetical Works.* London: Macmillan & co., 1927. 146 x 92mm., lovely turquoise crushed morocco intricately gilt by Ramage of London (stamp signed on front turn-in), covers with multiple gilt rolls bordering a rich an densely gilt plaitwork frame enclosing an open panel with petite, gilt tooled cornerpieces, raised bands, spine compartments reiterating the frame's design, turn-ins decorated with decorative rolls and small tools, ivory moire silk endleaves, all edges gilt, titlepage with engraved vignette, first prelim blank with neat inked inscription, faintest hint of scratch on one cover, spine probably darker than boards (though hard to tell, with so much gilt in the way), but very fine, text clean and fresh, elaborately decorated binding, lustrous and virtually unworn.   Phillip J. Pirages   67 - 60   2016 $850

Keeler, Henry Stephen *The Spectacles of Mr. Cagliostro.* New York: Dutton, 1929. First American edition, near fine, without dust jacket.   Mordida Books   2015 - 006867   2016 $55

Keene, Day *Take a Step to Murder.* Greenwich: Fawcett, 1959. First edition, fine, unread copy in wrappers.   Mordida Books   2015 - 010696   2016 $60

Keene, Henry George *A Hand-Book for Visitors to Lucknow.* Calcutta: Thacker, Spink & Co., 1875. First edition, 6 3/4 x 4 5/8 inches, 6 panel foldout plan, original terra cotta cloth with printed paper title onlay to front cover, slight lean, modest binding wear, prior owner signature on title label, very good+ rare.   Tavistock Books   Getting Around - 42   2016 $325

Keenleyside, Miles H. A. *Cichlid Fishes: Behaviour, Ecology and Evolution.* London: Chapman & Hall, 1991. Octavo, text illustrations, signature, laminated boards.   Andrew Isles Natural History Books   55 - 967   2016 $80

Keith, Arthur *The Antiquity of Man.* London: Williams and Norgate, 1915. First edition, octavo, text illustrations, publisher's decorated cloth, signature, very good.   Andrew Isles Natural History Books   55 - 38873   2016 $100

Keith, E. C. *A Countryman's Creed.* London: Country Life Ltd., 1938. First edition, 4to., original cloth and wrapper, colored frontispiece and 12 pencil illustrations by Archibald Thorburn, chipping and loss to corners of dust jacket, previous owner's signature, internally very clean and fresh.   Sotheran's   Hunting, Shooting & Fishing - 181   2016   £100

Keith, Thomas *The Complete Practical Arithmetician.* London: printed for J. Scatcherd etc., 1798. Second edition, 12mo., page of ads for books, occasional ink blot or other sign of use, lower corners bit creased, contemporary sheep spine gilt ruled, unlettered, bit worn, corners bumped, signature of B. Eamonson 1832.   Jarndyce Antiquarian Books   CCXV - 806   2016   £120

Keller, Helen *The Story of my Life with Her Letters (1887-1901) and a Supplementary Accounr of Her Education...* New York: Doubleday, 1935. Reprint of 1904 edition, 8vo., photos, cover some faded, little soiled, endpapers stained, very good, inscribed by author, laid in paper and stamps from mail wrapper addressed in another hand.   Second Life Books, Inc.   196A - 921   2016 $750

Kellerman, Jonathan *The Butcher's Theater.* New York: Bantam, 1988. First edition, fine in dust jacket.   Mordida Books   2015 - 012588   2016 $65

Kelley, A. R. *The Great Chinese Awakening. Glimpses at China and Its People.* London: Robert Culley, 1909. First edition, rare on the market, small 8vo., original red cloth, spine lettered and ornamented in gilt, front cover lettered and ornamented in blind, color printed folding map, light marking to binding, map with repaired tears along folds, light offsetting from endpapers, good copy.   Sotheran's   Travel and Exploration - 140   2016   £198

Kelley, William D. *Speeches, Addresses and Letters on Industrial and Financial Question...* Philadelphia: Henry Carey Baird, 1872. First edition, 8vo., bound in green cloth, some external wear, cloth torn along lower hinge, hinges starting, good copy, presentation from author's daughter, Florence Kelley to her son Nicholas.   Second Life Books, Inc.   196A - 923   2016 $300

Kelley, William D. *Why Colored People in Philadelphia are Excluded from the Street Cards.* Philadelphia: Benjamin Bacon, 1866. Printed wrappers, handsomely bound in modern marbled paper covered boards, leather spine label, very light toning of first gathering, unobtrusive archival repair to gutter of front wrapper, very good.   Joseph J. Felcone, Inc.   Books from Five Centuries: a Miscellany - 42   2016 $1500

Kelley, William Melvin *A Different Drummer.* Garden City: Doubleday, 1962. First edition, 8vo.,author's presentation for William Raney, paper over boards, cloth spine, very good, tight copy in little scuffed and soiled dust jacket.   Second Life Books, Inc.   196A - 924   2016 $225

Kellor, Frances *Out of Work.* New York: Putnam's, 1915. Revised edition, 8vo. author's presentation on blank, red cloth, stamped in gilt, hinges tender, cover scuffed at edges, otherwise very good.   Second Life Books, Inc.   196A - 926   2016 $45

Kellsall, Charles *Classical Excursion from Rome to Arpino.* London: Richard Phillips, 1821. First edition, 8vo., 2 maps, 3 plates, recent brown quarter calf.   J. & S. L. Bonham Antiquarian Booksellers   Europe 2016 - 6404   2016   £55

Kelly, Edward F. *Steady-On! The Combat History of Co C 25th Tank BN.* Munich: Buch un Kunstdruckerei Hanns Lindner, 1945. First edition, quarto, photos, maps, stapled wrappers, small tears at spine ends, slightly age toned, very good or better, signed by the commanding officer Lt. Col. Andrew Winiarczyk, very uncommon.   Between the Covers Rare Books   204 - 145   2016 $250

Kelly, Ellsworth *Plant Drawings.* New York: Published by Matthew Marks Gallery, 1992. First edition, number 31 of 1000 (of planned but unrealized edition of 150) hardbound copies, signed by Kelly and Ashbery, octavo, original white cloth, original dust jacket, fine, rare.   Manhattan Rare Book Company   2016 - 1736   2016 $2000

Kelly, George *Behold the Bridegroom.* Boston: Little Brown, 1928. First edition, 8vo., frontispiece, blue cloth with paper label, else near fine in little nicked and soiled dust jacket, rare in dust jacket, inscribed by author for Mr. Barrett Clark, May 1929.   Second Life Books, Inc.   196A - 927   2016 $350

Kelly, George *Craig's Wife, a Drama.* Boston: Little Brown, 1926. First edition, 8vo., very nice tight copy, inscribed by author for Josephine Williams (played part of Mrs. Harold in NY production), also signed by rest of the cast and inscribed by producer Rosalie Stewart.   Second Life Books, Inc.   196A - 929   2016 $1500

Kelly, George *Daisy Mayme.* Boston: Little Brown, 1927. First edition, blue cloth with little nicked paper label, inscribed by author for Barrett Clarke, laid in is clipped signature of Jessie Busley who played the title role and to whom the plays was dedicated.   Second Life Books, Inc.   196A - 930   2016 $225

Kelly, George *The Deep Mrs. Sykes.* New York: Samuel French, 1946. First edition, 8vo., photos of two sets, fine in little nicked dust jacket, inscribed by author for Mr. Rubin.   Second Life Books, Inc.   196A - 932   2016 $225

Kelly, George *The Deep Mrs. Sykes.* New York: Samuel French, 1946. First edition, photos of two sets, fine, inscribed by author for Jean Dixon, she starred in this play.   Second Life Books, Inc.   196A - 933   2016 $350

Kelly, George *Philip Goes Forth.* New York: Samuel French, 1931. First edition, 8vo., fine in dust jacket missing some pieces at edges and corners, inscribed by author to Dorothy Stickney with her name stamp, also signed by the complete cast.   Second Life Books, Inc.   196A - 936   2016 $650

Kelly, George *Philip goes Forth.* New York: Samuel French, 1931. First edition, 8vo., fine, inscribed by author to Barrett Clarke from George Kelly.   Second Life Books, Inc.   196A - 935   2016 $188

Kelly, George *Reflected Glory.* New York: Samuel French, 1937. First edition, 8vo., fine in dust jacket faded on spine and internally mended, illustrated with stills from the film.   Second Life Books, Inc.   196A - 937   2016 $150

Kelly, George *The Show-Off.* Boston: Little Brown, 1924. First edition, 8vo., frontispiece, inscribed by author for Barrett H. Clarke, very good.   Second Life Books, Inc.   196A - 938   2016 $350

Kelly, George *The Torch Bearers.* New York: Samuel French, 1924. First Acting edition, 8vo., publisher's wrappers, uncut and unopened, inscribed by author for Barrett Clarke, recipient's bookplate, very good.   Second Life Books, Inc.   196A - 939   2016 $94

Kelly, Michael *Cinderella or the Little Glass Slipper.... altered by Michael Kelley.* New York: pub. by D. Longworth at the Dramatic Repository, Shakespeare Gallery, 1807. First American edition, 12mo., disbound, small spot on title, otherwise fine.   Howard S. Mott Inc.   265 - 153   2016 $500

Kelly, Mike *"Play Ball" Stories of the Diamond Field by Mike Kelly of the Boston Base Ball Club.* Boston and New York: Kean & Kelly, 1889. Second edition, octavo, publisher's printed brown wrappers, front cover with engraved portrait of Kelly, spine and covers lightly worn, small chip from bottom end of spine, previous owner's name in pencil at head of titlepage, custom brown cloth clamshell box.   Between the Covers Rare Books   208 - 137   2016 $15,000

Kelly, Sean *Irish Folk and Fairy Tales.* New York: Galley Press, 1982. First printing, 8vo. editor's presentation, 8vo., paper over boards, edges of cover slightly scuffed, otherwise nice in little chipped and scuffed dust jacket.   Second Life Books, Inc.   197 - 199   2016 $45

Kemble, E. W. *A Coon Alphabet.* New York: London: Russell & John Lane, 1898. First edition, cloth backed pictorial boards, covers lightly soiled and rubbed on edges, else tight, clean, very good+, black and white illustrations.   Aleph-bet Books, Inc.   112 - 58   2016 $2200

Kemp, Alan *The Birds of Southern Africa.* Johannesburg: Winchester Press, 1982. quarto, 176 color plates by Claude Gibney Finch-Davies, fine in dust jacket with bookplate and prospectus tipped in, limited to 2750 copies.   Andrew Isles Natural History Books   55 - 23857   2016 $300

Kemp, Alan *The Birds of Southern Africa.* Winchester Press, 1982. First edition, 176 paintings, magnificent presentation, boxed, fine in fine dust jacket.   Simon Finch   2015 - 000190   2016 $176

Kendall, Edward Augustus *The Crested Wren.* London: printed for E. Newbery at the Cornr of St. Paul's Church Yard, 1799. 12mo., half title and final ad leaf, engraved frontispiece, titlepage vignette, lacking ads pages 155-156, B3 torn with slight loss to blank top corner, original dark green vellum spine, marbled boards, chipped paper spine label, corners little worn, A Swinburne family copy with signature.   Jarndyce Antiquarian Booksellers   CCXVI - 340   2016   £85

Kendall, Henry A. *Trinity River Diversion?* Eureka: The author, 1942. First edition, green wrappers printed in black, 12mo., quite scarce.   Argonaut Book Shop   Natural History 2015 - 7180   2016 $75

Keneally, Thomas *Schindler's List.* New York: Simon & Schuster, 1982. First edition, digitized illustrations from photos, half tan cloth over gray boards, spine lettered in black, very fine with spine faded dust jacket.   Argonaut Book Shop   Literature 2015 - 4887   2016 $175

Kennedy, E. D. *The Automobile Industry. The Coming of Age of Capitalism's Favourite Child.* Reynal & Hitchcock, 1941. First edition, original cloth, dust jacket, very good bright copy.   Sotheran's   Piccadilly Notes - Summer 2015 - 179   2016   £248

Kennedy, Ellen Conroy *The Negritude of Poets.* New York: Viking, 1975. 8vo., presentation form editor for William Claire, paper over boards with cloth spine, edges little spotted, otherwise very good, tight copy, little chipped and scuffed dust jacket.   Second Life Books, Inc.   196A - 942   2016 $45

Kennedy, James *The Bankrupt Act. Together with the Chancellor's Orders...* New York: Edward B. Gould, 1826. First American edition?, 8vo., contemporary calf backed printed boards, uncut, 1832 ink signature on title and signature on front cover, some pencilling.   M & S Rare Books, Inc.   99 - 22   2016 $450

Kennedy, John Fitzgerald   1917-1963 *We Remember Joe.* Cambridge: University Press, privately printed, 1945. First edition, 2nd issue, octavo, 33 black and white photos, including frontispiece, publisher's original full burgundy cloth, front cover stamped in black and gilt, spine lettered gilt, fore edge with some minor foxing, back cover with some light soiling, near fine.   Heritage Book Shop   Holiday 2015 - 64   2016 $2500

Kennedy, Richard *A Parcel of Time.* Andoversford: Whittington Press, 1977. First edition, frontispiece and 20 further drawings by author with majority full page and some double spread, 4to., original brown boards, backstrip lettered gilt, scuff to tail edge of lower board, yellow endpapers, dust jacket with backstrip panel very gently faded, very good, with uncorrected proof copy of the same in printed pink wrappers with some light dust soiling to covers and small pen mark to front.   Blackwell's Rare Books   B184 - 321   2016   £150

Kennedy, William   1928- *Ironweed.* New York: Viking, 1983. Uncorrected proof, signed by author, near fine in wrappers, with two page letter from publisher to a reviewer at the Chicago Tribune laid in.   Ken Lopez Bookseller   166 - 65   2016 $450

Kennedy, William   1928- *Legs.* New York: Coward McCann, 1975. Uncorrected proof copy, signed by author, fine in wrappers but for mild spine fading, title written on spine, publisher's slip written for advance readers and reviewers laid in, very uncommon, especially signed.   Ken Lopez Bookseller   166 - 64   2016 $750

Kennedy, X. J. *French Leave.* Florence: Robert L. Barth, 1983. Number F of 200 signed and numbered copies, 8vo, presentation for Willia Jay Smith, paper wrappers, nice, near fine.   Second Life Books, Inc.   196A - 945   2016 $45

Kenney-Herbert, Arthur Russell *Culinary Jottings. A Treatise in Thirty Chapters on Reformed Cookery for Anglo-Indian Exiles...* Madras: Higginbotham & Co., 1891. Half title, some offset browning from f.e.p.'s, original brown cloth, slightly rubbed, signature of Elsie Stockley Secunderabad, Oct. 1898, nice.   Jarndyce Antiquarian Books   CCXV - 274   2016   £120

Kennion, Edward *An Essay on Trees in Landscape.* London: printed by T. Bensely for C. J. Kennion, 1815. First edition, 362 x 292mm., pleasing recent sympathetic sprinkled half calf, marbled sides, raised bands, morocco label, spine with multiple decorative gilt rules, new endpapers, aquatint title vignette of the three principal types of English trees and 54 engravings showing trees and leaves, with four double page plates, one single page plate and engraved title vignette colored by later hand; titlepage neatly remargined, almost invisible repair at extreme inner margin of one plate, two plates with small faint dampstain at fore edge outside plate mark, small area at bottom of one plate with tiny speckles of paint, very slight darkening or foxing at extreme outer margins of most leaves, slight offsetting from plates (especially double page images), single page plates somewhat more noticeably affected by foxing (one or two plates rather foxed), but foxing almost entirely marginal, never offensive and entirely absent from more than 20 of the plates, pleasing copy despite imperfections, excellent new binding.   Phillip J. Pirages   67 - 228   2016 $2500

Kennon, J. L. *The Planet Mars and Its Inhabitants.* N.P.: 1922. First printing, frontispiece, map, 8vo., white paper wrappers, printed in red and green, age toning & dusting to wrappers, very good.   Tavistock Books   Getting Around - 50   2016 $175

Kenrick, Thomas *The British Stage and Literary Cabinet, August 1820.* London: J. Chappell, 1820. Disbound, engraved frontisportrait, bit foxed, offsetting to first page of text.   Dramatis Personae   119 - 92   2016 $50

Kenrick, Tony *The Only Good Body's a Dead One.* New York: Simon and Schuster, 1971. First American edition, fine in price clipped dust jacket.   Mordida Books   2015 - 004528   2016 $55

Kenrick, William *Falstaff's Wedding.* London: J. Wilkes (and others),, 1766. Second edition, 12mo., modern wrappers, foxed, closed tear form gutter to terminal leaf, reinforcements of verso of titlepage.   Dramatis Personae   119 - 93   2016 $40

Kent, Charles *Charles Dickens as a Reader.* London: Chapman & Hall, 1872. First edition, plates, facsimiles, original green cloth, blocked in blind, spine lettered gilt, slightly rubbed, nice.   Jarndyce Antiquarian Booksellers   CCXVIII - 631   2016   £45

Kent, Charles *The Humour and Pathos of Charles Dickens.* London: Chapman and Hall, 1884. First edition, half title, frontispiece, 4 pages ads dusted, careless opening in places, original green cloth, blocked and lettered gilt in black, slight rubbing, very good.   Jarndyce Antiquarian Booksellers   CCXVIII - 726   2016   £45

Kent, Rockwell *Rockwell Kent's Greenland Journal.* New York: Ivan Obolensky Inc., 1962. First edition, inscribed by Kent for friend Maxwell Geismar, drawings by Kent, 8vo., green cloth, silver stamped lettering to spine, map endpapers, dust jacket, very good+ in similar jacket which has slightly sun tanned spine panel.   Tavistock Books   Getting Around - 31   2016 $750

Kent, William Saville *The Great Barrier Reef of Australia: Its Products and Potentialities.* Melbourne: John Currey, 1972. Facsimile, quarto, color plates, text illustrations, lengthy biro inscription, grubby dust jacket.   Andrew Isles Natural History Books   55 - 11210   2016 $100

Kenyon, Frederic G. *Ancient Books and Modern Discoveries.* Chicago: Caxton Club, 1927. First edition, limited to 350 copies, 4to., vellum backed marbled boards, top edge gilt, others uncut, plain paper dust jacket, slipcase shows wear along edges with some cracking, book very fine, collotype plates made by Emery Walker.   Oak Knoll Books   310 - 210   2016 $300

Kenyon, Michael *The Shooting of Dan McGrew.* London: Collins Crime Club, 1972. First edition, some scattered very light spotting on fore edge, otherwise fine in price clipped dust jacket with publisher's price sticker, tiny wear at base of spine and at lower front corner of front panel and short closed tear.   Mordida Books   2015 - 011349   2016 $65

Kepler, Johann *Prodromus Dissertationum Cosmographicarum Continens Mysterium Cosmographicum de Admirabili Proportione Orbium Coelestium...* Frankfurt: Erasmus Kempfer for G. Tampach, 1621-1622. Second edition, 2 parts in one, folio, contemporary speckled calf, spine gilt in compartments, binding slightly rubbed, 4 folding woodcut plates, woodcut figures in text, lacking engraved plate at page 26, some browning.   Maggs Bros. Ltd.   1474 - 45   2016   £10,000

Kerouac, Jack   1922-1969 *The Dharma Bums.* New York: Viking, 1958. First edition, octavo, original cloth, original dust jacket, book near fine, very good dust jacket with some of the rubbing almost ubiquitous with this jacket, tape reinforcements and small amount of light dampstaining to verso (not visible from front of jacket).   Manhattan Rare Book Company   2016 - 1791   2016 $650

Kerouac, Jack   1922-1969 *Two Early Stories.* New York: Aloe editions, 1973. Limited to 175 copies, 8vo., stiff paper wrappers, fore edge uncut.   Oak Knoll Books   310 - 126   2016 $175

Kerouac, Jack   1922-1969 *Visions of Cody.* New York: McGraw Hill, 1972. First edition, fine in fine dust jacket, beautiful copy, seldom found thus.   Between the Covers Rare Books   208 - 44   2016 $500

Kerr, J. M. M. *Historical Review of British Obstetrics and Gynaecology 1800-1950.* Edinburgh: Livingstone, 1954. Royal 8vo., very good, original binding, dust jacket.   James Tait Goodrich   X-78 - 419   2016 $195

Kerr, John *Memories Grave and Gay....* Edinburgh: William Blackwood & Sons, 1902. Half title, frontispiece, plates, 32 page catalog, few leaves roughly opened causing tear to pages 287/288, original green cloth, slightly rubbed and dulled, gift inscription from James Christie, Carlisle 25th March 1902.   Jarndyce Antiquarian Books   CCXV - 809   2016   £20

Kerr, Orpheus C. *The Cloven Foot...* New York: Carleton, 1870. First edition, original green cloth, spine lettered gilt, lilac endpapers, slightly rubbed, very good.   Jarndyce Antiquarian Booksellers   CCXVIII - 658   2016   £150

Kersh, Gerald *Faces in a Dusty Picture.* London: Heinemann, 1944. First edition, octavo, near fine in good, chipped and rubbed dust jacket.   Peter Ellis   112 - 202   2016   £45

Kertesz, Andre *Day of Paris.* New York: J. J. Augustin, 1945. First edition, 103 black and white photos, quarto, original cloth, original dust jacket, custom box, neat owner signature on front free endpaper, cloth near fine with few spots of foxing to rear board, little browning on free endpapers (offset from dust jacket flaps as usual), dust jacket with minor edgewear and creasing, light soiling to rear panel, excellent copy.   Manhattan Rare Book Company   2016 - 1729   2016 $1900

Kesey, Ken *Demon Box.* N.P.: Viking, 1987. Uncorrected proof copy, signed by author, fine in wrappers.   Ken Lopez Bookseller   166 - 66   2016 $350

Kesey, Ken *Kesey's Garage Sale.* New York: Viking, 1973. First edition, quarto, very good in dust jacket, scarce cloth edition, illustrations, inscribed by author.   Second Life Books, Inc.   196A - 950   2016 $325

Kesey, Ken *Kesey's Jail Journal.* New York: Viking, 2003. First edition, large 8vo., fine in dust jacket, signed by Ed McClanahan (introducer).   Second Life Books, Inc.   196A - 949   2016 $45

Kesey, Ken *Spit in the Ocean Number 6.* Pleasant Hill: Intrepid Trips, 1981. First edition, Cassady Issue, original printed wrappers, scarce, very good.   Second Life Books, Inc.   197 - 201   2016 $45

Kett, Henry *Elements of General Knowledge.* London: Rivington, 1803. Third edition, 2 volumes, contemporary half calf, spines with surface rubbing, otherwise nice and clean, sound copy, bookplates of Charles Constable. Jarndyce Antiquarian Books   CCXV - 810   2016   £120

Kettilby, Mary *A Collection of Above Three Hundred Receipts in Cookery, Physick and Surgery; for the Use of all Good Wives, Tender Mothers and Careful Nurses.* London: for Richard Wilkin, 1714. First edition, contemporary paneled calf, neatly rebacked, light overall toning, minor marginal foxing and dampstaining, upper margin of A3 clipped and neatly restored, just grazing running head on verso, 3 leaves of early owners' recipes bound in at end, early ownership signature of Tho. tipping, dated at several locations in Herfordshire 1714-1739, later signature of Elizabeth Randall 1771, modern cookery bookplate, very nice in portfolio and leather backed slipcase.   Joseph J. Felcone, Inc.   Books from Five Centuries: a Miscellany - 49 2016 $2800

Keynes, John Maynard, 1st Baron 1883-1946 *How to Pay for the War.* Macmillan, 1940. First edition, crown 8vo., original blue green boards printed in black to front and backstrip, very good.   Blackwell's Rare Books   B184 - 168   2016   £100

Keys, John *The Practical Bee Master....* Printed for the author and sold by him at his house..., 1780. First edition, folding engraved plate, uncut in original wrappers, spine hand lettered in ink, spine partly defective, preserved in cloth folding box, very good.   Blackwell's Rare Books   B186 - 88   2016   £950

Khaled, Hossesini *The Kite Runner.* Doubleday, 2003. First edition, fine in fine dust jacket. Bella Luna Books   2016 - t336   2016 $150

Kherdian, David *David Meltzer.* Berkeley: Oyez, 1965. Frontispiece, paper wrappers, signed by author, nice. Second Life Books, Inc.   196A - 953   2016 $75

Kherdian, David *On the Death of my father and Other Poems.* Fresno: Giligia Press, 1870. First edition, printed wrappers, very nice, full page inscription by author on endpaper, very nice.   Second Life Books, Inc.   196A - 954   2016 $65

Khuhn, Carolva Gottlob *Medicorvm Graecorvan Opera Qvae Exstant.* Lipsiae: 1821-1833. 20 volumes, 19th century buckram, ex-library with stamp on title, bindings worn in parts, couple of volumes have front joint split, overall clean, tight.   James Tait Goodrich   X-78 - 360   2016 $4500

Kidder, A. V. *The Artifacts of Pecos.* New York: Yale University Press, 1932. Bright, near fine copy, illustrations. Dumont Maps and Books   133 - 62   2016 $150

Kidson, Joseph R. *Historical Notices of the Leeds Old Pottery with a Description of Its Wages.* Leeds: J. R. Kidson, 1892. First edition, one of 250 copies on Dutch handmade paper, 21 photographic plates, maroon cloth, gilt, wear to spine ends, extremities rubbed or worn, very good, complete copy.   Argonaut Book Shop   Pottery and Porcelain 2015 - 5008   2016 $450

Kilmer, Joyce *The Circus and Other Essays.* New York: Laurence J. Gomme, 1916. First edition, first state without Mitchell Kennerly slip on front pastedown, very good++, minimal cover edge wear, very good dust jacket with mild chips, scuffs, soil, 12mo, signed and inscribed by author and by his mother.   By the Book, L. C.   45 - 66   2016 $750

Kilner, Ann *A Course of Lectures for Sunday Evenings Containing Religious Advice to Young Persons.* London: printed and sold by John Marshall 124, 1737-1787. 12mo., ink splash to first titlepage, slight tear to gutter margin first half title, two volumes bound in one, contemporary quarter calf, marbled boards, vellum tips, board edges worn, some slight rubbing to joints, inscribed on front endpaper "Wm. Jones bought miss Baldock's sale 1845", signatures of Martha Baldock 1844 and Eleanor Jones.   Jarndyce Antiquarian Booksellers   CCXVI - 341   2016   £225

Kilvert, Francis *A View of Kilvert. Passages from the Diary of Reverend Francis Kilvert.* Glasgow: Foulis Archive Press, 1979. Limited to 50 numbered copies signed by artist, 4to., printed in Monotype Baskerville on Strathmore Grandee paper, 4to., 10 full page colored illustrations in line and color wash and reproduced by lithography, brown cloth stamped in gilt, dust jacket torn with small piece missing along edge.   Oak Knoll Books   27 - 46   2016 $350

Kimber, Edward *The London Magazine; or Gentleman's Monthly Intelligencer for Nov. 1774.* London: printed for R. Baldwin, 1774. First edition, engraved plate, musical score, small mathematical drawing, small 4to., stitched paper wrappers, very good, untrimmed, original stitching, mostly loose, occasional soiled spot, few creased corners, one leaf with pin hole in lower margin, offsetting from plate.   Kaaterskill Books   21 - 42   2016 $225

Kimber, John *The Trial of Captain John Kimber for the Murder of Two Female Negro Slaves on Board the Recovery, African Slave Ship.*   London: printed and sold by C. Stalker, No. 4 Stationer's-Court, circa, 1792. 8vo., half title, final two leaves have marginal repairs, last page and half title dusted, late 19th century gilt lettered black cloth, backstrip neatly relaid.   Jarndyce Antiquarian Booksellers CCXVI - 342   2016   £850

Kincaid, James Russell *Dickens and the Rhetoric of Laughter.*   Oxford: Clarendon Press, 1971. First edition, half title, original blue cloth, very good in slightly faded dust jacket.   Jarndyce Antiquarian Booksellers   CCXVIII - 1328   2016   £20

Kindersley, David *Mr. Eric Gill: Recollections of...*   Typophiles, 1967. One of 400 copies, small 8vo., illustrations, yellow cloth stamped in red, cover slightly soiled, otherwise nice.   Second Life Books, Inc.   197 - 202   2016 $45

King, A. W. *An Aubrey Beardsley Lecture.*   London: R. A. Walker, 1924. One of 500 copies signed by author, small 4to., blue cloth with worn leather label, corners and ends of spine little worn, otherwise very good.   Second Life Books, Inc.   196A - 955   2016 $225

King, A. W. *An Aubrey Beadsley Lecture...*   London: R. Walker, 1924. First edition, 1/450 copies signed by Walker, 4to., cloth with leather label, good, tight copy, drawings. Second Life Books, Inc.   196A - 90   2016 $100

King, Charles *A Daughter of the Sioux. A Tale of the Indian Frontier.*   New York: Hobart Co., 1903. True First edition with 'Published March 15, 1903' on copyright page, 8 black and white plates, red pictorial cloth, gilt lettering, color photographic pastedown of Indian maiden on front cover, top edge gilt, original owner' neat inscription Dec. 25 1903, very fine, very bright.   Argonaut Book Shop   Literature 2015 - 7428   2016 $250

King, Coretta Scott *My Life with Martin Luther King Jr.* New York: Holt Rinehart Winston, 1969. First edition, some staining to fore edge and little soiling to cover, very good, tight copy, inscribed by author.   Second Life Books, Inc. 196A - 957   2016 $150

King, Frank *The Ghoul.*   London: Geoffrey Bles, 1928. First edition, very good in about very good example of rare dust jacket, jacket chipped with loss to title and author name at crown, spine toned, vertical creasing to front panel, but illustration still crisp and bright.   Royal Books   51 - 19   2016 $3500

King, Louis Magrath *China as it Really is.*   London: Eveleigh Nash, 1912. First edition, 8vo., original yellow orange cloth, spine and front covered lettered in black, Chinese ornament as centerpiece on front cover, binding little marked, initially little foxed, otherwise good, very rare. Sotheran's   Travel and Exploration - 141   2016   £398

King, Martin Luther *The Montgomery Story Address by Rev. Dr. Martin Luther King, Pastor of the Dexter Avenue Baptist Church and President of the Montgomery Improvement Association....*   San Francisco: NAACP Annual Convention, 1956. First edition, five folio leaves mimeographed in blue ink on rectos only, stapled in upper left hand corner, slight age toning at extremities, else very near fine, very rare.   Between the Covers Rare Books 207 - 59   2016 $17,500

King, Martin Luther *Where Do We Go From Here: Chaos or Community?*   New York: Harper & Row, 1967. First edition, fine in fine dust jacket, inscribed by author to Mrs. Thomas Taylor.   Between the Covers Rare Books   207 - 61   2016 $12,500

King, Peter *The History of the Apostles Creed with Critical Observations on the Several Articles.*   London: printed by W. B. for R. Robinson, 1737. Fifth edition, 8vo., contemporary blind ruled calf, upper hinge cracking, label missing, scattered pencil underlining, very good.   Jarndyce Antiquarian Booksellers   CCXVI - 343   2016   £50

King, Ronald *The Song of the Solomon from the Old Testament.*   Guilford: Circle press, 1968. Limited to 150 copies, this marked "AP" (artist's proof) of an edition of 150 with 15 artist's proofs and 5 H.C. copies, this one of the proofs in original printed wrappers, folio, 2 color silk screen illustrations on covers and 47 additional color illustrations throughout text, some abrasion or rubbing to covers, cellophane tape applied to inner dentelles folds, slipcase not present, rare.   Jeff Weber Rare Books   181 - 49   2016 $750

King, Samuel William *Notes on a Roman Kiln and Urns Found at Hedenham Near Bungay.*   Norwich: Cuddle, Miller & Leavens, 1864. 8vo., chromolithograph frontispiece, original green cloth, upper over blocked in blind and lettered gilt, presentation inscription from author for J. W. ? Marlborough Rare Books   List 55 - 41   2016   £85

King, Stephen 1947- *Blockade Billy.*   Baltimore: Cemetery Dance Pub., 2010. First edition, illustrations by Alex McVey, blue cloth, original pictorial mustard yellow dust jacket housed in publisher's brown slipcases, lettered in gilt, as new in original publisher's shrinkwrap.   B & B Rare Books, Ltd.   2016 - SK024   2016 $100

King, Stephen 1947- *Cujo.*   New York: Viking Press, 1981. First edition, fine in fine dust jacket.   Between the Covers Rare Books   208 - 122   2016 $100

King, Stephen 1947- *11/22/63.* New York: Scribner, 2011. First edition, special collector's issue, signed by King, with publisher's DVD, red and black boards, lettered in white, publisher's pictorial tan dust jacket, housed in red slipcase, lettered in black, as new in publisher's shrinkwrap, fine slipcase.   B & B Rare Books, Ltd.   2016 - SK025   2016 $1000

King, Stephen 1947- *The Green Mile...* Burton: Subterranean Press, 2006. First separate hardcover edition, one of 148 numbered and signed copies by King, octavo, 6 volumes, leather backed cloth, fine set, cloth slipcase.   John W. Knott, Jr./L.W. Currey, Inc.   Fall-Winter 2015 - 17118   2016 $2500

King, Stephen 1947- *Salem's Lot.* New English Library, 1976. First English edition, 8vo., original black boards with minor dent ot front fore-edge, backstrip lettered in gilt, edges toned, dust jacket, very good.   Blackwell's Rare Books   B186 - 247   2016   £400

King, Stephen 1947- *Under the Dome.* New York: Simon & Schuster, 2009. First edition, deluxe limited issue of 1500 copies, signed by author, black cloth, lettered in white, pictorial endpapers, black ribbon bookmark, original pictorial dust jacket with wraparound illustration, with the publisher issued set of 27 cards illustrated by Matthew Diffee, as new in publisher's shrinkwrap with original affixed price sticker.   B & B Rare Books, Ltd.   2016 - SK023   2016 $500

King, William *The Art of Cookery.* London: printed by Bernard Lintott, 1708. First authorized edition third edition overall, octavo, contemporary sprinkled panelled calf, neatly rebacked, gilt lettering, half title present, lacking final blank, very good.   The Brick Row Book Shop   Miscellany 69 - 31   2016 $650

King, William *Chelsea Porcelain.* London: Benn Bros., 1922. First edition, thick quarto, 171 photographs, 7 in color, gray-brown beveled cloth, gilt spine lettering, gilt pictorial element on front cover, light rubbing to extremities, head of spine slightly jammed, owner's name on inner cover, fine.   Argonaut Book Shop   Pottery and Porcelain 2015 - 4996   2016 $175

King, William *Doctor King's Apology or Vindication of Himself from the Several Matters charged on him by the Society of Informers.* Oxford: printed at the Theatre for S. Parker & sold by W. Owen, London, 1755. 4to., disbound.   Jarndyce Antiquarian Booksellers   CCXVI - 346   2016   £30

King, William *Eulogium Famae Inserviens Jacci Etonensis sive Gigantis or the Praises of Jack of Eton...* Oxford: printed for S. Parker and sold by W. Owen, London, 1750. First edition, 8vo., half blue morocco, top edge gilt, very good.   C. R. Johnson Rare Book Collections   Foxon: H-P 2015 - 520   2016 $689

King, William *The Fairy Feast.* London: printed in the year, 1704. folio, some browning and light foxing, repair to verso of small gutter tears to first two leaves, woodcut ornament to titlepage, disbound.   Jarndyce Antiquarian Booksellers   CCXVI - 344   2016   £450

King, William *The Toast, an Epic Poem in Four Books.* Dublin: i.e. London?: printed in the year, 1732. First edition, 8vo., disbound, fine.   C. R. Johnson Rare Book Collections   Foxon: H-P 2015 - 522h-p   2016 $5363

King, William *The Original Works of William King, LL.D.* London: printed for the Editor and sold by N. Conant, successor to Mr. Whiston in Fleet street, 1776. 8vo., 3 volumes, half titles, engraved vignette portrait to each titlepage, one full page woodcut, one very slight marginal tear to T1 volume II, some offset browning on endpapers, fine, clean set bound in full contemporary sprinkled calf, smooth spines, gilt bands, red morocco title labels, dark green oval volume labels set within gilt wreaths, from the library of Invercauld Castle, Braemar.   Jarndyce Antiquarian Booksellers   CCXVI - 345   2016   £680

Kingdom, William *The Secretary Assistant...* London: Whittaker & Co., 1838. Seventh edition, original purple cloth, largely faded to brown, booklabel of A. Scott over earlier removed label, very good.   Jarndyce Antiquarian Books   CCXV - 280   2016   £60

Kings of Jazz. New York: A. S. Barnes for Perpetua Books, 1963. Eleven octavo volumes, glossy color pictorial wrappers, black and white photographs, housed in original publisher's slipcase, striking boxed set, fine and bright.   Honey & Wax Booksellers   4 - 12   2016 $300

Kingsford, Anna Bonus *Health, Beauty and the Toilet.* London: Frederick Warne & Co., 1886. First edition, endpapers with marginal tear to leading f.e.p., original light brown cloth, bookseller's ticket of W. Whiteley, very good.   Jarndyce Antiquarian Books   CCXV - 281   2016   £150

Kingsley, Amis *Colonel Sun.* London: Jonathan Cape, 1968. First edition, crown 8vo., original black boards, backstrip lettered gilt with very slight lean to spine, endpaper maps, direction pointer points vertically, few tiny foxpots to top edge, Tom Adams designed the dust jacket with just touch of rubbing at extremities very good.   Blackwell's Rare Books   B184 - 146   2016   £120

Kingsley, Charles 1819-1875 *The Water-Babies; a Fairy Tale for a Land-Baby.* London: Macmillan and Co., 1889. New edition, King Edward VI School, Berkhamsted, Prize Binding with prize label, maroon full calf, sides ruled in gilt with armorial crest gilt on upper cover, spine in compartments with raised bands, elaborately gilt and green leather label, lettered gilt by Bickers & Son, extremities with very slight wear, very nice.   Bertram Rota Ltd.   Christmas List 2015 - 17   2016   £150

Kingsley, Charles 1819-1875 *Water Babies.* London: Macmillan, 1909. Deluxe edition, limited to 260 copies printed on handmade paper and illustrated by Warwick Goble with 32 mounted color plates with lettered tissue guards, very scarce, full vellum with gilt pictorial cover, top edge gilt, silk ties, slight spotting on cover edge and endpaper and cover very slightly bowed, very good+, clean and fresh.   Aleph-bet Books, Inc.   111 - 198   2016 $2500

Kingsley, Charles 1819-1875 *The Water Babies.* London: Macmillan, 1909. First Goble edition, thick 4to., green gilt pictorial cloth, all edges gilt, spine faded and offsetting on endpapers, else fine, illustrations by Warwick Goble with 32 magnificent tipped-in color plates mounted on heavy stock with lettered tissue guards, nice, clean copy.   Aleph-bet Books, Inc.   111 - 199   2016 $1200

Kingsley, Charles 1819-1875 *Water Babies.* London: Paris: Raphael Tuck & New York: David McKay, n.d. circa, 1920. First US edition, 4to., blue cloth, light cover soiled, very good+, 12 beautiful color plates plus many charming illustrations.   Aleph-bet Books, Inc.   112 - 37   2016 $675

Kingsley, Charles 1819-1875 *The Water-Babies.* London: Ward Lock & Co. Ltd. circa, 1950. Early edition, small 4to., original mid green cloth lettered in yellow, double page pictorial endpapers, top edge green, preserved in pictorial dust jacket with beautiful wrap around design, plates in color and sepia by Harry Theaker, very good with some marking to green top edge, internally clean with minor speckling in edges of book block, protected by a highly attractive, partially clipped, dust jacket with nicking to spine ends and corners with neat paper strengthening and some spotting to reverse.   Sotheran's   Piccadilly Notes - Summer 2015 - 181 2016   £78

Kingsley, Charles 1819-1875 *Westward Ho!* New York: Limited Editions Club, 1947. 2 volumes, 4to., signed by artist, Edward A. Wilson, nice in little faded slipcase.   Second Life Books, Inc.   196A - 958   2016 $75

Kingsley, Charles 1819-1875 *Westward Ho!* Norwalk: Heritage Press, 1975. Maroon cloth, decorated and lettered gilt, very fine in slipcase, illustrations by Edward Wilson, Sandglass pamphlet laid in.   Argonaut Book Shop   Heritage Press 2015 - 7020   2016 $50

Kingsley, Sidney *Detective Story.* New York: Random House, 1949. First edition, 8vo., illustrations, author's presentation to one of the cast members, very good in some worn dust jacket.   Second Life Books, Inc.   196A - 959   2016 $75

Kingsley, Sidney *Men in White.* New York: Covici Friede, 1933. First edition, First edition, 8vo., printed cloth in crinkled and worn dust jacket, advance review with slip tipped to front endpaper, inscribed by author to columnist Louis Sobol.   Second Life Books, Inc.   196A - 961   2016 $500

Kingsolver, Barbara *Animal Dreams.* New York: Harper Collins, 1990. First edition, 8vo., fine in price clipped dust jacket, name blacked out on endpaper, inscribed by author.   Second Life Books, Inc.   196A - 964   2016 $50

Kingsolver, Barbara *The Bean Trees.* New York: Harper & Row, 1988. First edition, fine in near fine dust jacket with minor creasing at top of spine.   Bella Luna Books   2016 - t11410   2016 $165

Kingsolver, Barbara *Homeland.* New York: Harper & Row, 1989. First edition, fine in near fine dust jacket, with very minor creasing to top of spine.   Bella Luna Books   2016 - t3281   2016 $66

Kingsolver, Barbara *Pigs in Heaven.* New York: Harper Collins, 1993. First edition, 8vo., name covered with magic marker on endpaper, else fine in dust jacket, signed by author.   Second Life Books, Inc.   196A - 965   2016 $75

Kinkead, Eugene *Spider, Egg and Microcosm.* New York: Knopf, First edition, mild offsetting to rear endpapers, else fine in near fine dust jacket with trace fading to red on spine, not uncommon, but difficult to find in nice condition.   Ken Lopez Bookseller   166 - 150   2016 $100

Kinman, Diane *Franca's Story Survival in World War II Italy.* Mercer Island: Wimer Pub. Co., 2005. First edition, signed by author and Franca Mercati Martin, illustrations by Martin, endpaper maps, as new.   Gene W. Baade, Books on the West   2015 - 5021022   2016 $121

Kinnell, Galway *Two Poems.* Newark: Janus Press, 1979. Limited to 185 numbered copies, signed by author and artist on colophon, 8vo., quarter cloth, illustrated paper covered boards, illustrated endpapers, offset lithographs by Claire Van Vliet.   Oak Knoll Books   310 - 114   2016 $150

Kinsella, W. P. *The First and Last Annual. Six Towns Area Old Timer's Baseball Game.* Minneapolis: Coffee House Press, 1991. Limited to 150 numbered copies signed by author and artist, color wood engravings by Gaylord Schanilec, set of five loose engravings also in text laid in, 4to., quarter leather, paper covered boards, top edge gilt, others uncut.   Oak Knoll Books   310 - 91   2016 $250

Kinsella, W. P. *Shoeless Joe.* Boston: Houghton Mifflin Co., 1982. First edition, fine in fine dust jacket.   Between the Covers Rare Books   208 - 138   2016 $250

Kinsey, W. M. *Portugal Illustrated.* Valpy, 1828. First edition, large 8vo., folding frontispiece, double page map, 16 plates, 10 plates of music, 9 colored plates, 19th century half green morocco, spine gilt with raised bands, handsome binding.   J. & S. L. Bonham Antiquarian Booksellers Europe 2016 - 9513   2016   £750

Kipling, Rudyard   1865-1936   *A Book of Words.*   London: Macmillan and Co., 1928. First edition, half title, 4 pages ads, original maroon cloth, original dust jacket, top edge gilt, very good, crisp copy.   Jarndyce Antiquarian Booksellers   CCXVII - 143   2016   £200

Kipling, Rudyard   1865-1936   *The Five Nations.*   London: Methuen and Co., 1903. one of only 30 large paper copies on Japanese paper, half title, uncut and unopened, original white limp vellum, very small knock to tail of spine, top edge gilt, very nice, crisp copy.   Jarndyce Antiquarian Booksellers   CCXVII - 146   2016   £480

Kipling, Rudyard   1865-1936   *Home Before Action.*   London: Methuen & Co., 1915. Illuminated Edition, 8 page pamphlet printed in colors, sewn as issued in original grey printed envelope, little dusted.   Jarndyce Antiquarian Booksellers   CCXVII - 147   2016   £35

Kipling, Rudyard   1865-1936   *In Black and White.*   Allahabad: A. H. Wheeler & Co., 1890. Third Indian edition, original grey-green illustrated printed paper wrappers, front wrapper faded to brown with small ink mark, little worn and fragile.   Jarndyce Antiquarian Booksellers   CCXVII - 148   2016   £45

Kipling, Rudyard   1865-1936   *The Jungle Book & The Second Jungle Book.*   London: Macmillan, 1894. 1895. First editions, 2 volumes, half titles, frontispiece in volume I, illustrations, slight spotting to prelims in volume II, some off-setting from dentelles on f.e.p.'s, finely bound in full dark blue crushed morocco by J. Larkins, double ruled gilt borders with floral corner pieces, raised gilt ruled bands, compartments in gilt, elaborate gilt dentelles, very light rubbing to extremities, fine and handsome set.   Jarndyce Antiquarian Booksellers   CCXVII - 149   2016   £1500

Kipling, Rudyard   1865-1936   *The Jungle Book. (with) The Second Jungle Book.*   London: Macmillan and Co., 1894-1895. First editions, small octavo, frontispiece, text illustrations, second work small octavo with text illustrations, original bright blue cloth pictorially gilt stamped on front covers and spines, all edges gilt, tips rubbed, mostly at top and bottom of spines, corner of tissue guard torn in volume 1, beautifully housed together in custom quarter snakeskin slipcase by Sangorski & Sutcliffe, gilt stamped morocco label on spine, very handsome set.   Heritage Book Shop Holiday 2015 - 66   2016 $4250

Kipling, Rudyard   1865-1936   *The Jungle Book; the Second Jungle Book.*   New York: 1894-1899. First American edition, later American edition of "Second Jungle Book", original green pictorial cloth lettered and decorated in gilt and gilt black, just little spotting, but bright handsome copies, neat ownership inscriptions.   Bertram Rota Ltd. Christmas List 2015 - 19   2016   £450

Kipling, Rudyard   1865-1936   *Just so Stories.*   London: Macmillan, 1902. Reprint, October 1902, slim 4to., red cloth stamped in black and white, little rubbed at extremities, very good, issued one month after first edition, name stamp on endpaper, ad brochure laid in.   Second Life Books, Inc. 197 - 203   2016 $700

Kipling, Rudyard   1865-1936   *Just So Stories for Little children.*   New York: Doubleday Page and Co., 1909. Pocket edition, 12th impression, half title, original limp maroon cloth, front board and spine gilt, spine slightly darkened with some repairs, signed presentation by author for Mary Rankin Xmas 09.   Jarndyce Antiquarian Booksellers   CCXVII - 150   2016   £380

Kipling, Rudyard   1865-1936   *Just So Stories.*   London: Macmillan, 1913. First edition, 4to., 12 color plates by Joseph Gleeson, illustrations in black and white very good+.   Aleph-bet Books, Inc.   111 - 238   2016 $250

Kipling, Rudyard   1865-1936   *Limits and Renewals.*   London: Macmillan ad Co., 1932. First edition, half title, original maroon cloth, gilt, top edge gilt, very good in slightly marked original dust jacket.   Jarndyce Antiquarian Booksellers   CCXVII - 151   2016   £150

Kipling, Rudyard   1865-1936   *Plain Tales from the Hills.*   London: Macmillan and Co., 1928. Pocket edition on India paper, half title, frontispiece, slight worming at end, original flexible maroon cloth, front board and spine gilt, spine slightly darkened with minimal repairs, signed presentation from author to J. G. Kiefer.   Jarndyce Antiquarian Booksellers   CCXVII - 152   2016   £225

Kipling, Rudyard   1865-1936   *A Song of the English.*   London: Hodder & Stoughton, n.d., 1909. Limited to only 500 copies signed by Robinson, large 4to., full vellum stamped in red, gold and green, new ties, light cover soil, very good+, printed on handmade paper, illustrations by W. Heath Robinson with 30 magnificent tipped in color plates with illustrated/lettered guards and with 59 line illustrations.   Aleph-bet Books, Inc.   111 - 391   2016 $2200

Kipling, Rudyard   1865-1936   *A Song of the English.*   London: Hodder & Stoughton, 1909. First American edition, large quarto, 30 color plates, including frontispiece, mounted on leaves with color border decorations, descriptive tissue guards, each with miniature line illustration, pictorial title and 59 black and white line illustrations by W. Heath Robinson.   David Brass Rare Books, Inc.   2015 - 02968   2016 $550

Kipling, Rudyard   1865-1936   *Songs from Books.*   London: Macmillan and Co., 1913. First edition, half title, original maroon cloth, original dust jacket, spine slightly darkened.   Jarndyce Antiquarian Booksellers   CCXVII - 153   2016   £150

Kipling, Rudyard   1865-1936   *The Story of the Gadsbys; a Tale Without a Plot.*   Allahabad: A. B. Wheeler & Co., 1890. Third Indian edition, Original grey green illustrated printed paper wrappers, small tear with loss to back wrapper, 2 small marks to leading edge of front wrapper, overall very good.   Jarndyce Antiquarian Booksellers   CCXVII - 154   2016   £220

Kipling, Rudyard   1865-1936   *Verse. Inclusive Edition 1885-1918.*   Garden City: Doubleday Page and Co., 1926. US Inclusive edition, 8vo., handsomely bound in full tan morocco, boards panelled in gilt with leaf and flower corner pieces, spine lettered and decorated gilt, rich gilt turn-ins over marbled paper, all edges gilt, printed on India paper, attractive copy.   Sotheran's   Piccadilly Notes - Summer 2015 - 182   2016   £498

Kipling, Rudyard   1865-1936   *Wee Willie Winkle and Other Stories.*   Allahabad: A. H. Wheeler & Co., 1890. Third Indian edition, initial ad leaf, original grey green illustrated printed paper wrappers, front wrapper faded to brown, little worn and fragile, small elaborate circular label to upper margin of front cover.   Jarndyce Antiquarian Booksellers CCXVII - 155   2016   £45

Kipling, Rudyard   1865-1936   *The Years Between.* London: Methuen, 1919. First edition, half title, 32 page Methuen catalog at end coded IK/2/19, uncut in original maroon cloth, spine lettered gilt, top edge gilt, original dust jacket, tear to back wrapper repaired without loss, bookplate of John H. Mills, Derby, small ownership stamp of F. Alan Underwood.   Jarndyce Antiquarian Booksellers   CCXVII - 156   2016   £150

Kippis, Andrew   1725-1795   *The New Annual Register or General Repository of History, Politics and Literature for the Year 1791.*   London: G. G. J. and J. Robinson, 1792. 8vo., modern half dark broon morocco and red cloth, 6 raised bands, original gilt stamped red calf spine label, Hartford Theological Seminary blindstamp, titlepage and last page, very good.   Jeff Weber Rare Books   181 - 18   2016 $65

Kirchmann, Johannes   *De Annulis Liber Singularis. Accedunt Georgii Longi Abraham Gorlaei et Henr. Kornmanni De Iisdem.*   Lugd. Batv:: apud Hackios, 1672. 4 works issued as one volume, 12mo., additional engraved titlepage, three divisional titles bearing same date and printer's device to titlepage, one engraved illustration within text, some woodcut initials, Latin text with some Greek excerpts, few faint marginal stains, otherwise internally bright, contemporary vellum, faded ink title to spine, edges lightly sprinkled brown, little yellowed, some smudgy marks, small spot of wax (?) to upper board, pastedowns lifted and quite tattered at gutters, very good, tiny ms. note in old hand to front pastedown.   Unsworths Antiquarian Booksellers   30 - 92 2016   £200

Kirchner, Athanasius   1602-1680   *Ars Magna Lucis et Umbrae: in decem Libros Digesta.*   Rome: Sumptibus Hermanni Scheus, 1645. 2 volumes bound in one, engraved frontispiece and 38 plates, 2 double sided tables, engraved frontispiece has been expertly backed, fore edge of pages 513/4 slightly shaved affecting headline, lower margin of pages 563/4 also slightly shaved just affecting catchword, full modern brown morocco, covers panelled in blind, spine with four raised bands ruled in blind and lettered in gilt, all edges sprinkled red, excellent and very fresh copy, rebound about 20 years ago, little tightly but this only affects ease of opening large double page folding plate, ownership inscription of Thomas Tyrwhitt at top of frontispiece.   David Brass Rare Books, Inc.   2015 - 02989   2016 $14,500

Kirk, Robert   *The Secret Commonwealth of Elves, Fauns and Fairies.*   London: David Nutt, 1893. Limited to 550 copies, 8vo., frontispiece, publisher's list to rear, limp cream paper wrappers, black title and vignette, edges uncut, little darkened, spine creased, some small smudges, still very good.   Unsworths Antiquarian Booksellers   30 - 93   2016 £300

Kirk, Robert   *Secret Commonwealth or a Treatise Displaying the Chiefe Curiosities a they are in Use Among Diverse of the People of the Scotland to this Day...* Llandogo: Old Stile Press, 2005. 29/150 copies from an edition of 160 signed by artist, printed on Hahnemuhle Old Antique laid paper, woodcut illustrations, 4to, original brown leather, section of woodcut illustrated green paper at foot, backstrip lettered in blind, top edge purple, others untrimmed, fine.   Blackwell's Rare Books   B184 - 297 2016   £200

Kirk, T.   *The Forest Flora of New Zealand.*   Wellington: Government Printer, 1889. Small folio, 159 uncolored plates, publisher's elaborately blindstamped cloth, some slight rubbing, otherwise very good.   Andrew Isles Natural History Books   55 - 15066   2016 $400

Kirke, Edmund   *Among the Pines.*   New York: Carleton, 1862. Thirty fourth thousand, 8vo., very good, tight, clean copy.   Second Life Books, Inc.   197 - 20   2016 $85

Kirkpatrick, Karey   *James & The Giant Peach.*   New York: Walt Disney Co., 1996. First edition of this retelling, special limited edition of 1000 numbered copies signed by Lane Smith, the artist and Kirkpatrick, with wonderful color lithograph that does not appear in the trade edition and this copy also has a pen sketch signed by Smith on half title, full page color illustrations, brown cloth with elaborate gilt pictorial design, as new in publisher's cloth slipcase.   Aleph-bet Books, Inc.   111 - 109   2016 $200

Kirkwood, Edith   *Animal Children.*   Chicago: Volland, 1913. 26th edition, 8vo., pictorial boards, slightest bit of cover soil, else fine in original pictorial box, color illustrations on every page by Penny Ross, scarce.   Aleph-bet Books, Inc.   112 - 495   2016 $350

Kirwan, Andrew Valentine *Host and Guest.* London: Bell & Daldy, 1864. First edition, half title, uncut in original blue cloth by Bone & Son, little rubbed and dulled, recent booklabel of Alan Davidson, good plus. Jarndyce Antiquarian Books   CCXV - 282   2016   £120

Kish, Matt *Moby-Dick in Pictures.* Portland: Tin House, 2011. Limited edition, oblong 4to., pictorial slipcase, illustrations in color with some black and white images, with rare 8 x 10 staple bound publishers' promo booklet, pictorial wrappers, 12 pages, including covers. Gene W. Baade, Books on the West   2015 - SHEL737   2016 $500

Kitchiner, William   1775-1827 *The Art of Invigorating and Prolonging Life...* London: Hurst & Robinson & Co., 1822. third edition, 12mo., half title, final ad leaf, uncut in original blue drab boards, neatly rebacked with grey paper spine retaining original label, slight damp mark to back board, signature and booklabel of J. C. Bruce. Jarndyce Antiquarian Books   CCXV - 283   2016   £120

Kitchiner, William   1775-1827 *The House Keeper's Oracle.* London: Whittaker, Treacher & Co., 1829. Frontispiece, illustrations, title trimmed close at foot with loss of date, slightly later full maroon calf, raised gilt bands, green morocco label, spine faded to brown, little rubbed at hinges and head and tail of spine, armorial bookplate of Thomas Dawson, nice. Jarndyce Antiquarian Books   CCXV - 284   2016   £180

Kitton, Frederic George *Charles Dickens: His Life, Writings and Personality.* London: T. C. & E. C., 1902. First edition, half title, frontispiece, plates, slight spotting, original red cloth, lettered gilt, spine slightly faded, otherwise very good. Jarndyce Antiquarian Booksellers   CCXVIII - 1335   2016   £30

Kitton, Frederic George *Dickens and His Illustrators...* London: George Redway, 1899. Second edition, half title, plates and illustrations, small repair to outer margin of front, not affecting image, little spotted, uncut in original green buckram, spine and front board lettered in gilt, bevelled boards, slightly dulled, top edge gilt, good plus. Jarndyce Antiquarian Booksellers   CCXVIII - 952   2016   £125

Kitton, Frederic George *Dickens and His Illustrators...* New York: AMS Press, 1975. Reduced size facsimile reprint of 1899 second edition, 22 portraits and facsimiles of 70 original drawings, original brown cloth, booklabel, very good. Jarndyce Antiquarian Booksellers   CCXVIII - 953   2016   £30

Kitton, Frederic George *The Dickens Country.* London: Albert & Charles Black, 1905. First edition, Half title, frontispiece, 50 plates, mostly from photos, initial and 2 final ad leaves, original dark green cloth, blocked and lettered gilt, owner's inscription dated April 1906, top edge gilt, very good, bright. Jarndyce Antiquarian Booksellers   CCXVIII - 1336   2016   £35

Kitton, Frederic George *The Dickens Country.* London: Adam & Charles Black, 1911. Second edition, 4 pages ads, frontispiece, plates, original blue cloth, portrait onlay, slightly rubbed and dulled, illustrations from photos. Jarndyce Antiquarian Booksellers   CCXVIII - 1337   2016   £20

Kitton, Frederic George *Dickens Illustrations, Facsimiles of Original Drawings, Sketches and Studies for Illustrations in the Works of Charles Dickens...* London: George Redway, 1900. Folio, half title, list of plates (unopened), 28 plates, loosely inserted into original green cloth foldover case, bookplate of W. Miller, the Dickensian, very good. Jarndyce Antiquarian Booksellers   CCXVIII - 955   2016   £100

Kitton, Frederic George *Dickensiana: a Bibliography of the Literature Relating to Charles Dickens and His Writings.* London: George Redway, 1886. First edition, only 500 copies printed, half title, title, frontispiece, 24 page catalog (1886), untrimmed in original fine grained green cloth by Westleys, spine lettered gilt, leading inner hinge cracking, booklabel of William Grist, good plus. Jarndyce Antiquarian Booksellers   CCXVIII - 1329   2016   £75

Kitton, Frederic George *John Leech: Artist and Humourist....* London: George Redway, 1883. New edition, half title, frontispiece, illustrations, ad on verso of final leaf, original brown printed wrappers, old repair to spine, chipped along spine and edges. Jarndyce Antiquarian Booksellers   CCXVIII - 1356   2016   £25

Kitton, Frederic George *The Novels of Charles Dickens; a bibliography and Sketch. (with) The Minor writings of Charles Dickens; a bibliography and sketch.* London: Elliot Stock, 1897. 1900. first edition, 2 volumes, titles printed in red and black, uniformly bound and uncut in original dark blue cloth, dark blue buckram spines, lettered gilt, very good. Jarndyce Antiquarian Booksellers   CCXVIII - 1331   2016   £75

Kitton, Frederic George *The Novels of Charles Dickens: a Bibliography and Sketch.* London: Elliot Stock, 1897. First edition, frontispiece, uncut in original olive green cloth, bevelled boards, lettered gilt, prelims rather browned, otherwise very good. Jarndyce Antiquarian Booksellers   CCXVIII - 1332   2016   £25

Kitton, Frederic George *"Phiz".* London: George Redway, 1882. First edition, half title, frontispiece, plates, 2 page 'note', original brown wrappers, slightly chipped with minor loss to edges and spine, bookplate of Anne & Fernand Renier. Jarndyce Antiquarian Booksellers   CCXVIII - 1089   2016   £35

Klane, Robert *Where's Poppa?* New York: Random House, 1970. First edition, fine in fine- dust jacket with couple of nicks on front panel. Ken Hebenstreit, Bookseller   2016 - 2016 $175

Klein, C. C. *Bemerkungen uber die bisher angenonumene Folgen des Sturzes der Kunder auf den Boden bey Schnelien Geburten Wichtlige Beytrage zu der Gerichtlichen...* Stuttgart: Metzler, 1817. First edition, stiff contemporary paper boards, some wear, early ownership signature on title, some light foxing, very uncommon. James Tait Goodrich   X-78 - 356   2016 $795

Klein, Gilbert *Fat Chance. Misfits, Rejects and Ne'er-Do-Wells Running a Radio Station.* Chula Vista: Main Frame Press, 2012. Review copy, ANS by Klein laid in, addressed "Editor" and serving as review slip, fine in fine dust jacket. Ken Lopez Bookseller   166 - 67   2016 $150

Kleist, Heirnich Von *On Puppet Shows.* Hamburg: Otto Rohse Press, 1991. Limited to 75 numbered copies signed by Rohse, folio, leather, cloth slipcase, engravings by Rohse, binding by Christian Zweig.   Oak Knoll Books   310 - 127   2016 $1500

Kleivan, Helge *The Eskimos of Northeast Labrador a History of Eskimo-White Relations 1771-1955.* Oslo: Norsk Polarinstitutt, 1966. Quarto, card covers, 1 map, edges sunned and slightly browned.   Schooner Books Ltd.   115 - 105   2016 $45

Klempner, John *Letter to Five Wives.* London: Sampson Low Marston & Co., 1946. First UK edition, extremely scarce, about very good in very good dust jacket, some odd indentations to soft spine as result of overstamping in production, right at application of gilt titles, otherwise book lightly rubbed at extremities and quite clean, jacket rubbed and bit nicked at extremities, light soil to rear panel, very presentable copy overall.   Royal Books   49 - 70   2016 $450

Kloot, Tess *Birds of Australian Gardens.* Adelaide: Rigby, 1980. Folio, color plates by Peter Trusler, dust jacket. Andrew Isles Natural History Books   55 - 16462   2016 $50

Kloss, C. Boden *Bulletin of the Raffles Museum: Singapore, Straits Settlements.* Singapore: Raffles Museum, 1928-1952. 24 volumes bound in 10, contemporary binder's red cloth (some size variation), all edges speckled, typed titlepage for volume one, fine set, very scarce.   Andrew Isles Natural History Books   55 - 26987   2016 $2850

Klykov, Andrei *U Beregov Turkmenii.* Moscow: Molodaia Gvardiia, 1929. First edition, very rare, 8vo., original illustrated wrappers, photos, sketch map, lightly toned due to paper stock, very rare.   Sotheran's Travel and Exploration - 142   2016   £198

Kneale, Nigel *The Year of the Sex Olympics and Other TV Plays.* London: Ferret Fantasy, 1976. First edition, original ochre cloth lettered gilt on spine, ownership signature of S(tephen) Wyatt, author of Doctor Who books, about fine in very good, slightly tanned dust jacket, complete with no nicks or tears, excellent condition.   Any Amount of Books 2015 - A6882   2016   £150

Kneeland, Abner *Ancient Universalism as Taught by Christ and His Apostles...* New York: Office of the Gospel Herald no. 67, 1823. First edition, 8vo., removed, foxed. M & S Rare Books, Inc.   99 - 139   2016 $175

Kneeland, Abner *Three Sermons Delivered in the First Universalist Church in... New York on Easter Sunday March 26, 1826.* New York: J. Finch, 1826. 8vo., removed, lightly toned.   M & S Rare Books, Inc.   99 - 142   2016 $150

Knerr *The Katzenjammer kids.* Kenasha: John Martin, 1945. 8 inch square, spiral backed pictorial boards, some rubbing on rear cover, else near fine, color illustrations on every page, uncommon book.   Aleph-bet Books, Inc.   112 - 395   2016 $300

Knie, J. G. *A Guide to the Proper Management and Education of Blind Children During their Earlier Years.* London: Sampson Low, Marston & Co., 1894. New edition, contemporary half calf, black cloth boards, slightly rubbed. Jarndyce Antiquarian Books   CCXV - 813   2016   £45

Knight, C. *Mind Amongst the Spindles.* Boston: Jordan, Swift & Wiley, 1845. First edition, 12mo., black cloth (slit along hinge), very good, clean, scarce.   Second Life Books, Inc.   197 - 205   2016 $350

Knight, Ellis Cornelia   1757-1837 *A Description of Latium; or La Campagna Di Roma.* London: Longman Hurst, 1805. First edition, quarto, map, 20 tinted sepia etchings, map lightly foxed, contemporary brown speckled calf, joints split, covers rubbed, corners worn.   J. & S. L. Bonham Antiquarian Booksellers   Europe 2016 - 9598 2016   £600

Knight, Gwen *The Art of Gwen Knight...* Seattle: University of Washington Press, 2003. First edition, oblong 8vo., color illustrations, fine in dust jacket, inscribed by Knight as Gwendolyn Lawrence.   Second Life Books, Inc. 196A - 971   2016 $150

Knight, Richard Payne *An Analytical Inquiry into the Principles of Taste.* London: printed by Luke Hansard... for T. Payne, 1806. Third edition, 8vo. slight foxing, old closed tear towards foot of titlepage, contemporary half calf, marbled boards, gilt spine, boards slightly rubbed, with Fasque library bookplate of the Gladstone family, inscription "the gift of Cha. Blundell Esq. ... to John Gladstone.. 17 Nov. 1827. Jarndyce Antiquarian Booksellers   CCXVI - 350   2016 £90

Knopf, Alfred A. *Portrait of a Publisher.* New York: Tye typophiles, 1965. One of 2000 copies, 2 volmes, small 8vo., photos, volume i dark grey cloth, red spine, volume ii green cloth, nice copies in dust jackets, little yellowed at spine, little soiled yellow box. Second Life Books, Inc. 197 - 206 2016 $75

Knoth, Louis *Aufgeklarte Mosaische Archi-Geschichte (with) Offener brief an den Deutschen Reichskanzler Bismark (sic).* New York: Wolff & Co., 1881-1887. First edition, folio, contemporary pebbled brown cloth with morocco spine label, lettered gilt, very good, boards rubbed, spine ends renewed, manuscript titlepage soiled, few edge tears and institutional library stamps. Kaaterskill Books 21 - 41 2016 $750

Knott, Robert R. *The new Aid to memory.* London: Whittaker & Co., 1839. First edition, frontispiece and plates, plates slightly browned, original blue green cloth, small repair to tail of spine, all edges gilt, contemporary inscription. Jarndyce Antiquarian Books CCXV - 814 2016 £38

Knott, Robert R. *The new Aid to memory...* London: printed for the author, circa, 1840. New edition, half title, color plates, original red cloth, slightly dulled and marked, all edges gilt, very good, Leslie Shepard's copy. Jarndyce Antiquarian Books CCXV - 815 2016 £75

Knott, Robert R. *The New Aid to Memory.* London: Whittaker & Co., 1841. Second edition, plates, some marking, binding cracked in places but largely firm, lacking f.e.p., original green blue cloth, slightly rubbed and damp marked, all edges gilt. Jarndyce Antiquarian Books CCXV - 816 2016 £25

Knowles, Horace *Peeps into Fairyland.* London: Thornton Butterworth, 1924. First (probably only edition), large 4to., gold cloth, slight fading of cloth in corner and some margin foxing, else fine with original pictorial dust jacket (well worn lacking spine and with pieces of both panels), illustrations by author, unusually clean, rare. Alephbet Books, Inc. 112 - 279 2016 $2500

Knowles, Richard *Two Superiors. the Motor-Cycling Friendship of George Brough and T. E. Lawrence.* Upper Denby: Fleece Press, 2005. One of 300 copies printed on Monadnock Dulcet paper, titles printed in blue, 30 illustrations with majority photos, 4to., original green cloth with Shaw monogram blindstamped to upper board, backstrip with printed label, fine. Blackwell's Rare Books B186 - 299 2016 £250

Knowlton, William *The Boastful.* New York: Alfred Knopf, 1970. Cloth, light soil on inner edges, else very good in dust jacket (price clipped, faded on edge, slight fraying very good), wonderful color linoleum block illustrations. Alephbet Books, Inc. 111 - 73 2016 $150

Knox, A. E. *Game Birds and Wild Fowl; their Friends and their Foes.* London: John Van Voorst, 1850. First edition, 8vo., original cloth, lettered gilt on spine, gilt block of game bird attacking a duck with feathers flying on upper board, 4 tinted lithographs by J. Wolf, previous owner's inscriptions, spine sunned with chipping to head, little foxing, especially to first plate, top of titlepage clipped, otherwise very good. Sotheran's Hunting, Shooting & Fishing - 85 2016 £120

Knox, Ronald A. *The Viaduct Murder.* London: Methuen & Co., 1925. First edition, author's first book, lightly foxed, former owner ownership stamp, front panel of dust jacket affixed to front pastedown sheet, story map affixed to rear pastedown sheet, else very good, very scarce. Buckingham Books 2015 - 28286 2016 $450

Knox, Vicesimus 1752-1821 *Essays Moral and Literary.* Basle: printed and sold by James Decker, 1800. First Basle edition, little minor spotting, generally crisp and clean, one leaf in volume 1 with original paper flaw affecting a few words, 8vo., contemporary vellum backed boards, blue morocco lettering pieces to spines, boards just slightly soiled, very good. Blackwell's Rare Books B186 - 89 2016 £220

Kobrin, Bill *The Kobrin Collection 'Sixty Years Behind the Camera'.* Indigo: Bighorn Enterprises, 2007. First edition, elegant silver stamped cloth with blindstamped decorative motifs, folio, black and white photos, very minor small indentation about size of half grain of rice in cloth near bottom back cover, else fine, inscribed. Gene W. Baade, Books on the West 2015 - SHEL411 2016 $563

Koch, Rudolf *The Typefoundry in Silhouette: How Printing Type is Developed at Klingspor Bros. in Offenbach on the River Main.* San Francisco: Arion Press, 1982. Limited edition of 500 copies, oblong 4to., portfolio, title printed in red and black, preserved in publisher's red cloth chemise, fine. Jeff Weber Rare Books 181 - 40 2016 $80

Koehler, Wilhelm *Die Karolingischen Miniaturen.* Berlin: Deutschen Vereins fur Kunstwissenschaft, 1963. Reprint of 1390 edition, text in German, 5 volumes in 6, with 5 plate volumes, folio, cloth, editor and title stamped on spine, decorative stamping on front boards, bookplate each volume , some of plate volumes damaged at bottom of spine. Oak Knoll Books 310 - 211 2016 $2500

Koeman, I. C. *Links with the Past. the History of Cartography of Surinam 1500-1971.* Amsterdam: Theatrum Orbis Terrarum, 1973. First edition, large folio, original blue cloth, ornamented and lettered gilt, housed in original box made from Surinam wood', text highly illustrated, 39 maps and charts, loosely in box, with separate list of maps, within stiff card folder, box lacking claps, with little repair, list of plate with two small folds to corner, otherwise fine. Sotheran's Travel and Exploration - 62 2016 £298

Kohl, J. G. *Die Beiden Altesten General - Karten Von America.* Weimar: Geographisches Institut, 1860. Folio, paper covered boards, this copy from American Geographical Society, bookplate and stamps, covers detached from block, and are rubbed and worn, spine missing, pages tanned and chipped along edges, sheets loose, very scarce.   Oak Knoll Books   310 - 294   2016 $3000

Kohut, Rebekah *My Portion.* New York: Boni, 1927. Third printing, small 8vo., author's presentation to her grand daugter, latter glued to cover, black cloth, cover scuffed and little worn at corners and ends of spine, else very good. Second Life Books, Inc.   196A - 974   2016 $75

Kolesnikov, A. I *Arkhitectura Parkov Kavkaza I Kryma.* Moscow: Government Architectural Publisher, 1949. First edition, 4to., original illustrated cloth backed boards, one color plate and 14 plates and plans, numerous text illustrations, extremities with wear, internally, apart from occasional very light spotting, clean and fresh.   Sotheran's Travel and Exploration - 259   2016   £128

Kolkin, Jon *Inner Harmony: Learning from the Buddhist Spirit.* Raleigh: Jon Kolkin, 2014. Number 37 of 50 copies, inscribed by Kolkin, beautiful book with 30 black and white images, bound in black Japanese cloth and bound using a traditional Chinese binding technique, fine, 12 x 13 inches.   The Kelmscott Bookshop   13 - 29   2016 $485

Kolliker, Albert *Handbuch der Gewebelebre des Menschen fur Arzie und Studirende.* Leipzig: Wilhelm Engelmann, 1852. First edition, 8vo., 313 figures, early half maroon sheep, marbled boards, black leather gilt stamped label, extremities worn, spine faded, ownership signature of G. G. Bichlmaier, ink inscription on half title.   Jeff Weber Rare Books   183 - 21   2016 $875

Kolliker, Theodore *Die Verletzungen und Chirurgischen Erkrankungen der Peripherischen Nerven.* Stuttgart: Ferdinand Enke, 1890. Original half morocco and marbled boards, issued here as a separate volume.   James Tait Goodrich   X-78 - 358   2016 $250

Kondoleon, Harry *The Cote D'Azur Triangle.* New York: Vincent FitzGerald & Co., 1985. Signed limited edition, one of 125 copies only on rives BFK, all signed by author and artist, hand set in Janson, lithographs and etchings, bound by Gerard Charriere, 12 x 14 cloth of vibrant yelow, title stamped in blue within red triangle on front cover, housed in black clamshell box by Charriere.   Oak Knoll Books   310 - 101   2016 $4000

Kondrashev, S. K. *Izyskanilia v Bassein r. Amu-Dari. Oroshaemoe Khoziaistvo i Vodopolozovanie Khivinskago Oazisa.* Moscow: Sazonov for Ministerstvo Zemledeliia Otdel Zemelnyck..., 1916. Extremely rare, large 8vo., original purple printed wrappers, sketch map, diagrams, tables, numerous plates after photographs, wrappers little marked, internally rather clean and fresh, from an Estonian library with stamps.   Sotheran's Travel and Exploration - 143   2016   £1250

Konigsburg, E. L. *From the Mixed Up Files of Mrs. Basil E. Frankweiler.* New York: Atheneum, 1967. First edition, 8vo., cloth, half title toned, else fine in fine dust jacket (price clipped), illustrations by author, with warm inscription dated 1967 by author.   Aleph-bet Books, Inc.   111 - 240   2016 $1200

Koontz, Dean R. *Chase.* London: Arthur Barker, 1974. First UK edition, fine, dust jacket near fine with light wear to spine ends.   Bella Luna Books   2016 - t6843   2016 $66

Koontz, Dean R. *Cold Fire.* New York: Putnam, 1991. First edition, very fine, inscribed by author, dust jacket. Mordida Books   2015 - 012122   2016 $65

Koppe, Johannes *Halpert & Co.* Leipzig: 1927. Oblong folio, 17 mounted photos, each mount stamped in purple ink 'Archikekj Johannes Koppe, Leipzig", original padded black morocco album held with cords.   Marlborough Rare Books List 56 - 31   2016   £2850

Kops, Bernard *Four Plays. The Hamlet of Stepney Green. Enter Solly Gold. Home Sweet Honeycomb. The Lemmings.* London: Macgibbon & Kee, 1964. First edition, author's presentation, much pencil marking, otherwise very good in chipped and yellowed dust jacket.   Second Life Books, Inc. 196A - 978   2016 $45

Kordosi, Michael S. *Contribution to the History of Topography of the Cornith region in the Middle Ages.* Athens: Dionesinos Notis Karavas bookshop, 1981. First edition, 8vo., paperback, edges uncut, minor signs of shelf-wear, very good, author's card with his signature added in ink, loosely inserted.   Unsworths Antiquarian Booksellers Ltd.   E05 - 77   2016   £45

Kosinski, Jerzy 1933-1991 *The Painted Bird.* Boston: Houghton Mifflin, 1976. Uncorrected proof copy of the revised second edition, signed by author on titlepage and additionally inscribed by him, light bump to spine base, else fine in wrappers, uncommon, especially signed.   Ken Lopez Bookseller   166 - 68   2016 $375

Kovner, Michael *Portscapes: Childhood Landscapes: the Mountain and the Valley.* Ein Harod: Museum of Art, 2007. First edition thus, 4to., pictorial stiff wrappers, 3 volumes, original custom slipcase (bit of scuffing to latter), color and black and white illustrations, fine, very scarce. Gene W. Baade, Books on the West 2015 - M1006 2016 $200

Koyama, Fujio *Ten Thousand Years of Oriental Ceramics.* New York: Harry N. Abrams Inc., 1960. First edition, large quarto, 175 photographic illustrations, including 54 tipped-in color plates, gold cloth, gilt, fine with lightly worn pictorial dust jacket. Argonaut Book Shop Pottery and Porcelain 2015 - 6502 2016 $150

Kozisek, Joseph *A Forest Story.* New York: Macmillan, 1929. First English edition, cloth backed decorative boards, 2 tips rubbed, else fine in original pictorial slipcase, magnificent book illustrated by Rudolf Mates with vibrant full page color illustrations. Aleph-bet Books, Inc. 112 - 126 2016 $300

Kraft, Irma *Plays Players Playhouses.* New York: George Dobsevage, 1928. First edition, photos and drawings, author's presentation, very good in worn dust jacket. Second Life Books, Inc. 196A - 981 2016 $45

Krag, Martha Ann *Martha Jane.* Indianapolis: Bowen Merrill, 1896. Oblong 4to., red cloth stamped in gold, all edges gilt, very slight finger soil on covers, else fine, printed on heavy cards, each page individually hinged into book. Aleph-bet Books, Inc. 112 - 420 2016 $650

Krakauer, Jon *Into the Wild.* New York: Viking, 1996. First edition, fine in fine dust jacket, review copy with slip laid in. Bella Luna Books 2016 - t9630r 2016 $165

Kramm, Joseph *The Shrike.* New York: Random House, 1952. First edition, 8vo., illustrations, author's presentation, nice in little browned dust jacket. Second Life Books, Inc. 196A - 982 2016 $45

Krantz, Albert *Saxonia.* Cologne: Johannes Soter, 1520. First edition, folio, fine woodcut titlepage, some old marginalia, some pinhole worming (more prominent at rear), modern half morocco, five raised bands, title label, minor dampstains in rear inner margin, paper clean, crisp condition. Jeff Weber Rare Books 181 - 16 2016 $1500

Krapf, Norbert *Heartwood.* Roslyn Harbor: Stone House Press, 1983. Limited to 150 numbered copies signed by author, presentation from artist, John DePol, wood engravings by DePol, 8vo., cloth backed decorated paper boards. Oak Knoll Books 310 - 150 2016 $135

Krasna, Norman *Who Was that lady I Saw You With?* New York: Random House, 1958. First edition, 8vo., very good in little soiled and worn dust jacket, cast member Roland Winters' copy, signed by 30 members of the cast. Second Life Books, Inc. 196A - 984 2016 $325

Krause, Fedor *Surgery of the Brain and Spinal Cord Based on Personal Experiences.* New York: Rebman, 1909-1912. 62 plates all in color except 2, 119 text illustrations, some in color, 3 volumes, original cloth, worn and shaken, backstrips loose and detached, old spine labels removed from volumes. James Tait Goodrich X-78 - 359 2016 $595

Krauss, Ruth *Charlotte and the White Horse.* New York: Harper, 1955. First edition, 12mo., cloth backed pictorial boards, fine in near fine dust jacket with price intact, this copy inscribed by author, especially nice, scarce. Aleph-bet Books, Inc. 111 - 408 2016 $850

Krauss, Ruth *A Hole is to Dig.* New York: Harper and Row, 1952. Later printing, 12mo., pictorial cloth, fine in dust jacket, illustrations by Maurice Sendak, this copy inscribed by artist for Herbert Hosmer. Aleph-bet Books, Inc. 111 - 413 2016 $850

Krefft, Gerard *The Mammals of Australia.* Melbourne: Lansdowne, 1979. Limited to 350 copies signed by Basil Marlow, folio, monochrome plates, publisher's quarter brown calf, illustrations by Harriet Scott and Helena Forde. Andrew Isles Natural History Books 55 - 15180 2016 $100

Krefft, Gerard *The Snakes of Australia.* Sydney: Thomas Richards, 1869. Quarto, 12 uncolored plates, modern binder's cloth with gilt title, stiff card wrappers, retained, plates with some minor repairs and upper wrapper stained, sound pleasant copy. Andrew Isles Natural History Books 55 - 14159 2016 $1250

Krefft, Gerard *The Snakes of Australia.* Brisbane: Lookout Publications, 1984. Facsimile, quarto, color plates. Andrew Isles Natural History Books 55 - 4109 2016 $80

Kretschmer, Konrad *Die Entdeckung Amerika's in Ihrer Bedeutung Fur Die Gesccchchichte Des Weltbildes.* Berlin: W. H. Kuhl, 1892. Folio, 2 volumes contemporary quarter leather, marbled paper covered boards, atlas volume has 40 color lithograph maps, volume one has scratching on spine with loss of leather to head and tail of spine, boards rubbed and faded with wear to corners, cracking to hinge at half title, volume two has scratching and wear to spine with loss of leather at head and tail, wear to boards and at corners, atlas very slightly cocked. Oak Knoll Books 310 - 295 2016 $1500

Kriegel, Volker *The Truth About Dogs.* Bloomsbury: 1988. First Julian Barnes edition, Kriegel cartoons, 12mo., original yellow boards, backstrip lettered gilt, dust jacket near fine, signed by Julian Barnes, beneath his crossed through printed name.   Blackwell's Rare Books   B184 - 107   2016   £35

Kristeller, Paul *Early Florentine Woodcuts.* London: Kegan Paul, Trench, Trubner and Co., 1897. Limited to 300 numbered copies, 4to., original quarter leather, cloth, top edge gilt, other edges uncut, 193 black and white illustrations, corners bumped, corners rubbed and scuffed, front free endpaper chipped at fore-edge, inside hinges cracked, light tanning near edges of text. Oak Knoll Books   310 - 41   2016 $300

Kroeber, Theodore *Ishi Last of his Tribe.* Berkeley: Parnassas Press, 1964. First edition, cloth, offsetting on endpapers, else fine condition in slightly soiled, price clipped dust jacket.   Aleph-bet Books, Inc.   112 - 257   2016 $125

Kroll, Ernest *Marianne Moore at the Dial Commissions - an article on the Movies.* Colorado Springs: Press at Colorado College, n.d., Limited to 100 numbered copies, 8vo., quarter faux leather, marbled paper covered boards, paper spine label, printed accordian style, with two page ALS from the printer, Jim Trissel, to editor, Kroll.   Oak Knoll Books   310 - 141   2016 $400

Krumgold, Joseph *And Now Miguel.* New York: Crowell, 1953. Stated first printing, 8vo., cloth, fine in price clipped dust jacket with small rubbed area on spine, color endpapers and wrapper plus full and partial page black and whites by Jean Charlot.   Aleph-bet Books, Inc.   112 - 102   2016 $250

Kubasta, V. *An American Indian Camp.* Bancroft & Co., 1962. First edition, near fine with pop-up in perfect working order, 3 dimensional pop-up, with 3 tab activated pieces along outer perimeter, illustrations, scarce, uncommon.   Buckingham Books   2015 - 38298   2016 $475

Kubasta, V. *Red Riding Hood.* London: Bancroft & Co., 1956. Most likely First English edition, illustrated stiff paper boards, cloth spine, full color pop-up illustrations, quite minor wear, very good, all tabs present and working, two narrow folds archivally repaired.   Gene W. Baade, Books on the West   2015 - 5012051   2016 $142

Kuczynski, Jurgen *Labour Conditions in Western Europe 1820 to 1935.* London: Lawrence and Wishart, 1937. First edition, black cloth, author's presentation, very good, tight in worn dust jacket.   Second Life Books, Inc.   196A - 989   2016 $75

Kuczynski, Jurgen *A Short History of Labour Conditions Under Industrial Captialism.* London: Muller, 1973. 1943. First edition of volume 2, third edition of volume 2, small 8vo., author's presentation, blue cloth, top edge somewhat soiled, edges of cover slightly scuffed and bumped, otherwise very good, tight copy in chipped and scuffed dust jacket.   Second Life Books, Inc.   196A - 990   2016 $45

Kumin, Maxine *The Long Approach. Poems.* New York: Viking, 1985. First edition, inscribed and signed by author for William Meredith, near fine in fine dust jacket.   Charles Agvent   William Meredith - 62   2016 $50

Kumin, Maxine *Looking for Luck. Poems.* New York: W. W. Norton & co., 1992. First edition, inscribed and signed on titlepage by author for William Meredith, laid in is 1994 flyer announcing Kumin reading and addressed to Meredith, fine in fine dust jacket.   Charles Agvent William Meredith - 63   2016 $80

Kumin, Maxine *Nurture. Poems.* New York: Viking, 1989. First edition, signed on titlepage for William Meredith, fine in fine dust jacket.   Charles Agvent   William Meredith - 64   2016 $60

Kumin, Maxine *Women, Animals and Vegetables. Essays and Stories.* New York: W. W. Norton and Co., 1994. First edition, inscribed and signed for William Meredith, laid in is photographic Christmas card signed by Kumin, fine in fine dust jacket.   Charles Agvent   William Meredith - 65   2016 $100

Kunitz, Stanley *A Kind of Order, a Kind of Folly.* Boston: Atlantic Monthly, Little Brown, 1975. First edition, 8vo., author's presentation for William Claire, paper over boards with cloth spine, edges little marked and soiled, edges of cover little scuffed, otherwise very good tight in chipped and lightly soiled dust jacket.   Second Life Books, Inc.   196A - 992   2016 $75

Kunitz, Stanley *Passport to the War.* New York: Holt, 1944. First edition, 8vo. fine in nicked and some worn dust jacket, inscribed by author for William Claire.   Second Life Books, Inc.   196A - 994   2016 $300

Kunitz, Stanley *The Poems of 1928-1978.* Boston: Little Brown, 1979. First edition, 8vo., author's affectionate presentation to Bill Claire, tan cloth, nice, little soiled and stained dust jacket.   Second Life Books, Inc.   196A - 993   2016 $75

Kunitz, Stanley *The Testing-Tree.* Boston: Atlantic Monthly, 1971. First edition, 8vo., fine in little nicked dust jacket, inscribed by author for William Claire.   Second Life Books, Inc.   196A - 995   2016 $225

Kuo Mo-Jo *Culture and Education in New China.* Beijing: Foreign Language Press, 1950. First edition, 8vo., original wrappers printed in red and black, 8 leaves of plates, light marginal spotting to wrappers, internally very good. Sotheran's   Travel and Exploration - 144   2016   £48

Kurt, Weill *An American Opera.* New York: Chappell & Co., 1948. First edition, large quarto, printed wrappers, top corner very slightly bumped, trifle age toned on wrappers, publisher's price sticker on titlepage, near fine, ownership signature of Daniel Rule, director of NYC Opera.   Between the Covers Rare Books   204 - 77   2016 $900

Kurutz, Gary F. *Benjamin C. Truman: California Booster & Bon Vivant.* San Francisco: Book Club of California, 1984. First edition, limited to 600 copies, frontispiece, gilt lettered green cloth, very fine.   Argonaut Book Shop   Biography 2015 - 3772   2016 $50

Kurzweil, Arthur *The Encyclopedia of Jewish Genealogy volume I.* Northvale: Jason Aronson, 1991. First edition, 8vo., presentation to William Claire, black cloth, top edges slightly soiled, otherwise very good, tight copy in browned and little soiled, slightly chipped, dust jacket.   Second Life Books, Inc.   196A - 996   2016 $50

Kussmaul, Adolf *Die Storungen der Sprache.* Leipzig: von F. C. W. Vogel, 1877. First edition, 8vo., very good, clean copy, original brown cloth.   James Tait Goodrich X-78 - 351   2016 $1495

Kwik and Kwak. New York: Crown, 1942. First edition, 4to., cloth backed pictorial boards, fine in frayed but very good dust jacket, illustrations in color by Forbes.   Aleph-bet Books, Inc. 112 - 518   2016   £400

Kyd *The Characters of Charles Dickens, Portrayed in a Series of Original Water Colour Sketches by Kyd.* London: Raphael Tuck & sons, 1889. Engraved title, 24 chromo-lithographs, original green cloth, front board pictorially blocked and lettered gilt, slight rubbing to head of spine, ownership inscription, Dec. 1892, very good.   Jarndyce Antiquarian Booksellers   CCXVIII - 956   2016   £120

Kyd *The Characters of Charles Dickens.* London: Raphael Tuck & Sons, 1889. Engraved title, 24 chromo-lithographs, original turquoise cloth, front board pictorially blocked and lettered gilt, inner hinges, strengthened with linen, leading f.e.p. loose, slightly rubbed.   Jarndyce Antiquarian Booksellers   CCXVIII - 957   2016   £85

Kyd *Some Well-Known Characters from the Works of Charles Dickens.* London: Hildesheimer & Faulkner, 1892. First edition, half title, 16 color plates, original brown cloth, bevelled boards, pictorially blocked & lettered gilt, spine slightly darkened and slightly rubbed at head and tail, all edges gilt, good plus.   Jarndyce Antiquarian Booksellers CCXVIII - 958   2016   £75

L

L'Engle, Madeleine *A Wrinkle in Time.* New York: Ariel Books Farrar, Strauss & Cudahy, 1962. Stated first edition, first printing, faint fading on edge of boards as usual, else fine in dust jacket, dust jacket in beautiful condition with no fraying or tears, price clipped but price is not a factor, exceptionally nice.   Aleph-bet Books, Inc.   111 - 257   2016 $9000

L'Heureux, John *Rubrics for a Revolution.* New York: Macmillan, 1967. First printing, author's presentation to William Claire, black cloth, top edges slightly soiled, otherwise very good, tight in browned and little soiled, slightly chipped dust jacket.   Second Life Books, Inc.   196B - 997   2016 $75

L., A. E. *"Prof. Charley": A Sketch of Charles Thompson.* Boston: D. C. Heath, 1902. First edition, frontispiece, paper over stiff card wrappers, some splitting along edges of paper spine, yapped edges, bit bumped, very good.   Between the Covers Rare Books   202 - 61   2016 $400

La Belle Manufacturing Company *The La Belle Manufacturing Company: Sole Proprietors of the La Belle Letter-Copying Book and Ink.* Chicago: 1878. First edition, 4to., self wrappers, quite scarce as printed, on tissue paper, some browning on last page with small tear, else near fine.   Kaaterskill Books   21 - 44   2016 $250

La Branche, George M. L. *The Salmon and Dry Fly.* Boston: Houghton Mifflin, 1924. first edition, limited to 775 numbered copies, signed by author, 8vo., original calf backed marbled paper boards in remains of dust jacket, color frontispiece depicting 4 flies, little rubbing to spine ends, otherwise much nicer than usual, scarce with dust jacket in any state, preserved in custom made morocco backed fall down back box.   Sotheran's   Piccadilly Notes - Summer 2015 - 183   2016   £698

La Fontaine, Augustine Heinrich Julius *Henriette Bellman ou Dernier Tableau.* Paris: chez J. Garnier, 1803. Second edition, engraved frontispiece, 2 engraved plates, titlepage roundel to first volume, 12mo., full contemporary tree calf, gilt spines, small floral motifs, black gilt labels, head of spines slightly worn, some light rubbing to gilt.   Jarndyce Antiquarian Booksellers   CCXVI - 351   2016   £85

La Fontaine, Jean De   1621-1695 *Fables and Tales from La Fontaine.* London: printed for A. Bettesworth and C. Hitch and C. Davis, 1734. 8vo., titlepage dusted, slight edge wear, lower corner a2 torn without loss of text, some occasional marking and light browning, few slight edge chips, faint contemporary note to page 21, expertly bound in recent full mottled calf, raised and gilt banded spine, small gilt devices, red morocco label.   Jarndyce Antiquarian Booksellers   CCXVI - 352   2016   £1250

La Fontaine, Jean De   1621-1695 *Fables Choisies ...* Paris: chez Desaint & Saillant et Durond..., 1755. First edition, large paper copy, 4 volumes, handsomely bound in contemporary French mottled calf, red and green morocco spine labels with rich gilt detailing, marbled endpapers and all edges marbled, discrete repairs to spine ends without rebacking, internal contents are generally in excellent condition although with occasional spot of foxing and with few warm pinholes running through the blank margins, front inner hinge of volume IV cracked but holding and slight age toning to text leaves in volume, engraved frontispiece, extra engraved portrait (found only in some copies) and 275 other engraved plates, bookplate of John Drummond in all volumes volume and second bookplate with name illegible.   Heritage Book Shop   Holiday 2015 - 69   2016 $35,000

La Fontaine, Jean De   1621-1695 *Fables Choisies Mises en Vers...* Paris: Le Breton, 1769. Nouvelle edition, 2 parts in 1, half titles, titlepages printed in red and black, engraved frontispiece, 12mo., fine, clean copy, full contemporary calf, raised and gilt banded spine, red morocco label, paper flaw to blank lower corner L1, from the library of Invercauld Castle, Braemar.   Jarndyce Antiquarian Booksellers   CCXVI - 353   2016   £250

La Fontaine, Jean De   1621-1695 *Fables.* Paris: H. Fournier Aine, 1838. First edition, illustrations by Grandville, more than 100 full page engravings and many vignettes, contemporary three quarter brown leather with blue marbled paper boards, spines with five raised bands with gilt title, volume number and ornaments in each compartment, corners bumped, some nicks to leather, still very good, interior pages have some foxing, gutter visible in volume I from opening book flat, text blocks still tight, very good.   The Kelmscott Bookshop   13 - 30   2016 $600

La Fontaine, Jean De   1621-1695 *Fables De La Fontaine.* Nancy: Berger, circa, 1925. Large 4to., cloth backed pictorial boards, slightest bit of cover soil, else fine, illustrations by Andre Helle with vibrant pochoir color illustrations, beautiful copy.   Aleph-bet Books, Inc.   112 - 241   2016 $750

La Fontaine, Jean De   1621-1695 *The Fables of La Fontaine.* New York: Viking, 1954. First edition, one of 400 large copies, large 8vo., fine copy, not signed by inscribed by translator, Marianne Moore for Dr. Harold Baldwin, red cloth, bookplate, neatly removed, fine.   Second Life Books, Inc.   196 B - 259   2016 $325

La Fontaine, Jean De   1621-1695   *Fables of De La Fontaine.*   Paris: Hachette, n.d. circa, 1982. Cloth backed pictorial paste-on, edges and spine worn, same else tight and very good, illustrations by Felix Lorioux.   Aleph-bet Books, Inc.   112 - 299   2016 $450

La Fontaine, Jean De   1621-1695   *Tales and Novels in Verse.*   London: Society for English Bibliophilists, 1896? First edition thus?, only a limited number will be printed, quarto, 2 volumes, 123 plates from original copper, original silk moire covers, top edges gilt, some sporadic foxing, covers slightly marked, spines slightly marked, spines bit dull, very good.   Peter Ellis   112 - 204   2016   £125

La Martiniere, Bruzen   *Introduction a l'Histoire de L'Asie de l'Afrique, et de L'Amerique.*   Amsterdam: Zacharie Chatelain, 1735. First edition, 2 volumes, small 8vo., 4 folding maps, contemporary full calf, joints cracked, wear and rubbing to head and tail of spine.   J. & S. L. Bonham Antiquarian Booksellers   Voyages 2016 - 6015   2016   £240

La Mettrie, Julien Offray De   *Aphorismes de Monsieur Herman Boerhaave sur la Connaissance et la Cure des Maladies.*   Rennes: Place du Palais, 1738. First edition, 12mo., contemporary full leather with five raised bands on spine with gilt title and decorations, there is 1 inch gouge to lower front cover, two-line inscription in fading contemporary ink, bridging ornamental device center of page, otherwise tight, clean, remarkably well preserved.   Athena Rare Books   List 15 - 1738   2016 $1000

La Mettrie, Julien Offray De   *Observations de Medicine Pratique.*   Paris: Chez Huart, Briasson & Durand, 1743. First edition, contemporary full leather with five raised bands on spine with gilt decorations and gilt title in red field, spine edges lightly worn and just bit chipped at top, covers have few light gouges front and back but nothing unsightly, overall very acceptable tight and clean copy.   Athena Rare Books   List 15 - 1743   2016 $1250

La Mettrie, Julien Offray De   *Systeme de Monsieur Herman Boerhaave sur les Maladies Veneriennes.*   Paris: Chez Prault fils, 1735. First edition, contemporary full leather, 12mo., five raised bands on spine with gilt decorations and title in red field, spine just bit worn, otherwise tight, clean and remarkably well preserved.   Athena Rare Books   List 15 - 1735   2016 $1750

La Mettrie, Julien Offray De   *Traite de la Matiere Medicale, Pour Servir a la Composition des Remedes Inndique's dans les Aphorismes.*   Paris: Chez Huart & Briasson, 1739. First edition, 12mo., contemporary full leather with five raised bands on spine, gilt title and decorations, heavily overstruck two-line inscription in contemporary ink on titlepage to right of ornmental device in center of page, otherwise tight, clean, very well preserved.   Athena Rare Books   List 15 - 1739   2016 $850

La Mettrie, Julien Offray De   *Traite de la Petite Verole, avec la Maniere de Guerir Cette Maladie Suivant les Principes de Mr. Herman Boerhaave.*   Paris: Chez Huart & Briasson, 1740. First edition, contemporary full leather with five raised bands on spine and gilt decorations and gilt title, few light gouges to covers both front and back, but nothing unsightly, lovely contemporary bookplate of J. F. Brossard 1752, otherwise tight, clean, remarkably well preserved.   Athena Rare Books   List 15 - 1740   2016 $1500

La Motte, Guillame Mauquet De   *Traite Complet des Accouchemens Naturels non Naturels et Conetre Nature.*   Paris: Chez Laurent d'Houry, 1721. Tall 4to., contemporary full mottled calf, gilt panelled spine, joints cracked, corners and edges rubbed, contemporary signature on title dated 1753.   James Tait Goodrich   X-78 - 366   2016 $995

La Plante, Lynda   *Cold Blood.*   London: Macmillan, 1996. Very good, signed by author, Selfridges stamp pasted on to front, otherwise very good.   I. D. Edrich   Crime - 2016   £30

La Rochefoucauld, Francois Duc De   1613-1680   *Maxims.*   Haworth Press, 1931. One of 1075 copies, Text in French and English.   Honey & Wax Booksellers   4 - 20   2016 $150

Labillardiere, J. J.   *Novae Hollandiae Plantarum Specimen...*   Lehre: J. Cramer, 1966. Facsimile, uncolored plates, small quarto, publisher's cloth, fine.   Andrew Isles Natural History Books   55 - 10751   2016 $400

Labillardiere, J. J.   *Sertum Austro-Caledonicum.*   Lehre: Verlag von J. Cramer, 1968. Facsimile, Small folio, 80 plates publisher's cloth, fine, scarce.   Andrew Isles Natural History Books   55 - 18407   2016 $400

Laborde, J. V.   *Le Ramollissement et La Congestion Du Cerveau Principalement Cnsideres Chez Le Vielliard. Etude Clinique et Pathogenique.*   Paris: Adrien Delahaye, 1866. Original quarter morocco and marbled boards, clean, tight copy.   James Tait Goodrich   X-78 - 362   2016 $495

Labrosse, F.   *The Navigation of the Pacific Ocean, China Seas, etc.*   Washington: GPO, 1875. First edition in English, 8vo., original green cloth lettered gilt, very light wear to edges, internally apart from very light browning or spotting, very good.   Sotheran's   Travel and Exploration - 403   2016   £598

Lack, David   *Darwin's Finches.*   Cambridge: University Press, 1947. First edition, near fine in dust jacket also near fine, original cloth, 27 figures, 8 plates.   Simon Finch 2015 - 20336   2016 $250

Laconics or New Maxims of State and Conversation. printed for Thomas Hodges..., 1701. 8vo., nice, clean copy, contemporary panelled calf, red morocco label, rebacked retaining original spine, armorial bookplate of William Lord North of Carthage and Baron Grey of Rolleston 1703. Jarndyce Antiquarian Books   CCXV - 205   2016   £250

Lacy, Ed   *Sin in their Blodd.*   New York: Eton, 1952. First edition, short corner crease on front cover and some tiny wear along edges, otherwise fine in wrappers.   Mordida Books   2015 - 010706   2016 $65

Lada, Joseph   *Halekacky nasi Kacky.*   Praze: Melantricha, 1932. Stiff pictorial wrappers, minimal wear, near fine, absolutely stunning picture book, this illustrated by Joseph Lada and 24 fabulous bold full page color illustrations. Aleph-bet Books, Inc.   112 - 125   2016 $1500

Laden, Nina   *Roberto the Insect Archtiect.*   San Francisco: Chronicle Books, 2000. First edition, as new, signed and dated by author in year of publication, illustrations.   Gene W. Baade, Books on the West   2015 - JUV011   2016 $50

The Ladies Charity School House Roll of Highgate or a Subscription of Many Noble, Well Disposed Ladies for the Ease of Carrying it On.   London: 1670. First edition, octavo, contemporary red morocco with elaborate gilt decorated patterns of floral ornaments, handles, knobs and shells on covers and five compartments on spine, with repeating pattern of smaller handles and knobs around spider like figures, 4 engraved plates, edges rubbed, two silk ties lacking (two present), lacking front free endpaper, very good, ink signature of Thomas Stedman, Oct. 1763.   The Brick Row Book Shop   Miscellany 69 - 12   2016 $2750

The Lady's Book of Manners or Etiquette Showing How to Become a Perfect Lady.   Wakefield: William Nicholson & sons, circa, 1870. Half title, color frontispiece, original mauve cloth faded and worn.   Jarndyce Antiquarian Books   CCXV - 286   2016   £30

Laennec, Rene Theophile Hyacinthe   1751-1826   *De l'Ausculation Mediate ou Traite du Diagnostic des Maladies des Poumons 35 de Couer.*   Paris: 1831. First edition to include notes by author's cousin, Mertadec, 2 hand colored lithograph plates, 4 double page aquatint plates, 8vo., 3 volumes in recent quarter calf with gilt spines and marbled boards, light text foxing at beginning and end, all edges marbled, plates clean, very nice, clean, tight set.   James Tait Goodrich   X-78 - 365   2016 $495

Laennec, Rene Theophile Hyacinthe   1751-1826   *A Treatise on the Diseases of the Chest and the Mediate Auscultation...*   London: T. and G. Underwood, 1827. Second edition in English, 8vo., modern quarter tan calf and marbled boards, black morocco spine label, opening leaves foxed, otherwise clean tight copy, 8 engraved plates. James Tait Goodrich   X-78 - 363   2016 $500

Laennec, Rene Theophile Hyacinthe   1751-1826   *A Treatise on the Diseases of the Chest in which they are Described according to the Anatomical Characters...* London: 1834. Final edition of the Forbes translation, half title, 2 engraved plates, large 8vo., modern cloth, internally very clean, tight, uncut.   James Tait Goodrich   X-78 - 364   2016 $450

Laforgue, Jules   *Moral Tales.*   New Directions, 1985. First edition, 8vo., fine in dust jacket, signed by William Jay Smith.   Second Life Books, Inc.   196 B - 1   2016 $145

Lafragua, Jose Maria   *Reglamento de la Direccion De Colonizacion.*   Mexico: Reglamento de la Direccion, 1846. First edition, 16mo., contemporary calf, bookplate of A. Salazar, very good, boards lightly scuffed, some faded ink spots on titlepage, small bookplate on front pastedown. Kaaterskill Books   21 - 13   2016 $1000

Lagerbring, Sven   *Dissertatio Historica de Distinctione Fidelium in Clericos et Laicos Quam Adspirante Summon Numine et Calculo...*   Lund: Typis Reg. Aul. Gamer & Direct Reg. Acad. Carolinae, Typog. Caroli Gustavi Berling, 1766. Small 4to., 18 pages, engraved headpiece and initial, small hole on title, disbound withdrawn from Pitts Theology Library rubber stamp, rare, very good.   Jeff Weber Rare Books   181 - 19   2016 $125

Laishley, Richard   *Education and Educators.*   London: Waterlow & Sons, March, 1884. inscribed by author for Prof. S. Stephens, original red cloth, spine faded. Jarndyce Antiquarian Books   CCXV - 817   2016   £20

Lalanne, Leon   *Manuel de Service De La 2e Section de la navigation de la Marne.*   Paris: Thumot, 1867. First edition, 8vo., original green cloth, spine lettered ink, ornamented in blind, folding table, 65 cm. long folding map, long folding section, folding plate, plates in black and blue, corners little worn, covers with light spots, internally, apart from even toning due to paper stock, good copy.   Sotheran's   Travel and Exploration - 260   2016   £225

Lamb, Caroline   1785-1828   *Ada Reis, a tale.*   London: John Murray, 1823. First edition, 3 volumes, small octavo, early 19th century purple half morocco, drab paper boards, gilt decorations and lettering, half titles present, edges little rubbed, uncommon.   The Brick Row Book Shop Miscellany 69 - 52   2016 $1750

Lamb, Charles   1775-1834   *The Works of Charles and Mary Lamb and the Life of Charles Lamb.*   London: Methuen & Co., 1903-1905. 9 volumes, 222 x 146mm., especially attractive contemporary red morocco, elaborately gilt (stamp signed 'Charles E. Lauriat'), covers framed by two plain gilt rules, raised bands, spines lavishly gilt in compartments with large central fleuron surrounded by a lozenge of small tools and intricate scrolling cornerpieces, densely gilt turn-ins, top edges gilt, extravagantly extra illustrated with 653 plates, five of these folding, two double page, and two colored, engraved bookplate of Joel Cheney Wells, just vaguest hint of rubbing to extremities, isolated small marginal stains, still handsomely bound in fine condition, fresh and clean internally and in lustrous bindings with few signs of wear.   Phillip J. Pirages   67 - 132   2016 $4500

Lamb, Dana   *Enchanted Vagabonds: the Story of a 16,000 mile Cruise from San Diego to Panama.*   London: Hamish Hamilton, 1938. First edition, 8vo., maps, illustrations, original green cloth, dust jacket (small tear).   J. & S. L. Bonham Antiquarian Booksellers   America 2016 - 9955   2016   £95

Lamb, Ruth   *Servants and Service.*   London: RTS, 1888. Half title, 16 page catalog, original olive green cloth, fine.   Jarndyce Antiquarian Books   CCXV - 287   2016   £85

Lambarde, William   *Archaionomia sive de Prisis Anglorum Legibus Libri....*   John Day, 1568. First edition, first of 3 issues with Lambarde's MS. corrections at 264 found in some copies, full page woodcut map in text (trimmed at foot), dampstaining at head, small 4to., contemporary calf ruled in blind, blindstamped arabesque to both boards, back ties, rebacked.   Blackwell's Rare Books   B184 - 57   2016   £10,000

Lambe, Robert   *An Exact and Circumstantial History of the Battle of Floddon.*   Berwick upon Tweed: printed and sold by R. Taylor and E. and C. Dilly in the Poultry and G. Freer, Bell Yard, London, 1774. 8vo., frontispiece, erratum leaf + ads at end, 19th century half calf, marbled boards, grey sprinkled edges, leading hinge weakening, booklabel of John Murray Aynsley.   Jarndyce Antiquarian Booksellers   CCXVI - 354   2016   £75

Lambert, John   *Trial of the Information ex Officio the King Versus John Lambert and Another on a Charge of Libel on His Majesty's Person Inserted in the Morning Chronicle.*   London: edited by James Perry and printed by John Lamber for James Ridgway, 1810. First edition, 8vo., upper margin of one leaf damaged but not touching printed text, titlepage just little soiled and creased, recently well bound in linen backed marbled boards lettered, good, uncommon.   John Drury Rare Books   2015 - 22898   2016 $350

Lambert, Mark   *Dickens and the Suspended Quotation.*   New Haven: Yale University Press, 1981. First edition, half title, original white cloth, very good in dust jacket.   Jarndyce Antiquarian Booksellers   CCXVIII - 1341   2016   £20

Lambert, Samuel W.   *When Mr. Pickwick Went Fishing.*   New York: Edmond Byrne Hackett, Brick Row Book Shop, 1924. Half title, vignette title, 11 plates by Seymour, uncut in original blue drab boards, white cloth spine, paper label, very good in slightly dulled dust jacket.   Jarndyce Antiquarian Booksellers   CCXVIII - 150   2016   £30

Lambert, W. G.   *Babylonian Wisdom Literature.*   Oxford: Clarendon Press, 1975. First edition, second reprint with corrections, 4to., 38 leaves of plates, blue boards, gilt lettered to spine, edges slightly spotted, light blue dust jacket, little faded to spine and top extremities, very good, ownership inscription of C. D. N. Costa in pen and sheet of typed note to text loosely inserted.   Unsworths Antiquarian Booksellers Ltd.   E05 - 45   2016   £35

Lana, Francesco   *Prodromo Ouero Saggio di Alcune Inuentoni Premesso all'Arte Maestra....*   Brescia: per li Rizzardi, 1670. First edition, 20 engraved plates with figures numbered I-LXX, folio, contemporary mottled calf over pasteboard, spine wrongly titled, expert repair at edges, possibly belonged to mathematician John Collins (1625-1683), fellow of the Royal Society, first three leaves neatly restored at fore-edges, flyleaves defective at fore-edges, otherwise very clean, crisp copy.   Maggs Bros. Ltd.   1474 - 46   2016   £4500

Lancaster, G. B.   *Jim of the Ranges.*   London: Constable and Co., 1913. 4 initial ads, 6 pages ads, slight paper browning, original pictorial wrappers, printed in black and white with color illustrations, back cover ad, very good.   Jarndyce Antiquarian Booksellers   CCXVII - 159   2016   £25

Lancaster, Joseph   *Improvements in Education.*   London: printed & sold by J. Lancaster, Free School, Borough Rd., 1806. Fourth edition, full contemporary tree calf, gilt spine, black morocco label, little rubbed and worn at corners, inscribed by author for P. Debary in the Egham Coach Apt. 25 1807.   Jarndyce Antiquarian Books   CCXV - 819   2016   £380

Lancelyn-Green, R.   *A Bibliography of A. Conan Doyle.*   Clarendon Press, 1983. Mint copy.   I. D. Edrich   Crime - 2016   £60

Landacre, Paul *California Hills and Other Wood Engraivngs by Paul Landacre from Original Blocks.* Los Angeles: Bruce McCallister, 1931. Limited edition, signed by Landacre, issued in numbered print run of 500 copies (this no. 35), 14 large woodblock prints, 1 small print on colophon, original orange and grey patterned paper boards, printed and engraved cover title label, spine expertly restored retaining all the original patterned paper, rear hinge reinforced, near fine.   Jeff Weber Rare Books   181 - 7   2016 $4000

Landels, William *Woman's Sphere and Work...*   London: James Nisbet, 1884. Thirteenth edition, half title, original brown cloth, blocked in black, spine lettered in gilt, very slightly rubbed, very good.   Jarndyce Antiquarian Books   CCXV - 288   2016   £35

Lander, George *Bleake House; or Poor "Jo" a drama in four acts.*   London: John Dicks, circa, 1883. Illustrated, disbound.   Jarndyce Antiquarian Booksellers   CCXVIII - 517   2016   £30

Landon, Joseph *School Management Including Organisation, Discipline and Moral Training.* London: Kegan Paul, Trench & Co., 1889. Seventh edition, half title, 8vo. pages catalog June 1892, uncut in original blue green cloth, blocked in red and black, slightly rubbed.   Jarndyce Antiquarian Books   CCXV - 820   2016   £20

Landor, Arnold Henry Savage   1865-1924 *Across Unknown South America.* London: Hodder & Stoughton, 1913. First edition, 2 volumes, large 8vo., numerous illustrations, original decorative cloth, slight rubbing at base of spines and fore edge, good and clean.   J. & S. L. Bonham Antiquarian Booksellers   America 2016 - 10206   2016   £180

Landor, Arnold Henry Savage   1865-1924 *In the Forbidden Land.* London: William Heinemann, 1899. First one volume edition, 8vo., original green pictorial cloth, vignette of prayer wheel and manades blocked in colors to upper board, lettered in red to upper cover and in gilt and black to spine, frontispiece, numerous black and white illustrations, 1 large folding map, edges untrimmed, presentation inscription, light rubbing to extremities, neat repair to front inner hinge, handsome copy.   Sotheran's Travel and Exploration - 146   2016   £158

Landor, Walter Savage   1775-1864 *Satire on Satirists and Admonition to Detractors.* London: Saunders and Otley, 1836. First edition, duodecimo, later polished calf, gilt decorations and lettering, very good.   The Brick Row Book Shop   Miscellany 69 - 53   2016 $350

Landowska, Wanda *Landowska on Music.* New York: Stein & Day, 1964. First edition, 8vo., frontispiece, photos, nice in scuffed slipcase, this copy neatly signed in ink by editors, Denise Restout and Robert Hawkins.   Second Life Books, Inc.   196 B - 8   2016 $100

Lang, Andrew *The Blue Fairy Book.* London: Longmans, 1889. First edition, 8vo., blue cloth, gilt pictorial cover, all edges gilt, binding leaning, spine faded bit, slightly soiled, blindstamped, illustrations by H. J.Ford and G. P. J. Hood, nice copy, very elusive edition.   Aleph-bet Books, Inc.   111 - 243   2016 $3500

Lang, Andrew *The Blue Fairy Book.* London: Longmans, Green and Co., 1905. Early edition (11th impression), 8vo., original dark blue cloth elaborately blocked in gilt with striking design to upper board, spine lettered and decorated gilt, all edges gilt, profusely illustrated by H. J. Ford, fine, exceptional copy.   Sotheran's Piccadilly Notes - Summer 2015 - 185   2016   £198

Lang, Andrew *Blue Poetry Book.* London: Longmans Green, 1891. First edition, first printing, 8vo., blue gilt pictorial cloth, all edges gilt, slight bit of cover soil and rubbing, neat previous owner name, near fine with gilt cover, still sparkling.   Aleph-bet Books, Inc.   112 - 281   2016 $300

Lang, Andrew *The Green Fairy Book.* London: Longmans, Green and Co., 1906. Early edition, 7th impression, 8v8vo., original dark green cloth elaborately and pictorially gilt to spine and upper cover, all edges gilt, engravings by Ford, fine in exceptionally fresh and clean condition, both internally and externally.   Sotheran's Piccadilly Notes - Summer 2015 - 187   2016   £168

Lang, Andrew *Letters to Dead authors.*   London: and New York: Longmans, Green, 1892. New edition, original blue cloth lettered gilt, small 8vo., spine little rubbed at head and tail, endpapers spotted, very good.   Peter Ellis   112 - 208   2016   £25

Lang, Andrew *Old Friends Among the Fairies...* London, et al: Longmans, Green, 1926. First edition, 8vo., green pictorial cloth, very good+, 4 beautiful tipped in color plates lovely cover design and pictorial endpapers by H. J. Ford, also with a profusion of black and whites by Ford and others.   Aleph-bet Books, Inc.   111 - 168   2016 $175

Lang, Andrew *The Pink Fairy Book.* London: Longmans Green and Co., 1906. New impression, 8vo., original pink cloth elaborately and decoratively blocked in gilt to spine and upper cover, all edges gilt, illustrations after engravings by H. J. Ford, particularly nice, scarce, only minor fading to spine and dulling to spine gilt, touch of light soiling and rubbing, internally fine.   Sotheran's Piccadilly Notes - Summer 2015 - 186   2016   £178

Lang, Andrew *Prince Ricardo of Pantouflia: Being the Further Adventures of Prince Prigio's Son.* Bristol: Arrowsmith, n.d., 1893. First edition, 4to., three quarter vellum and brown cloth, vellum slightly age toned, else fine, large paper presentation copy (so stamped), rare in this edition, 12 plates plus 12 illustrations in text by Gordon Browne.   Aleph-bet Books, Inc.   111 - 244   2016 $500

Lang, Andrew *Rainbow Fairy Book.* New York: Wiliam Morrow, 1993. Limited to only 50 numbered copies signed by Hague and with 4 inch drawing of wizard, 4to. cloth pictorial paste-on, spine faded, else fine in cloth slipcase which is faded on edges, rare edition, illustrations by Michael Hague. Aleph-bet Books, Inc.   111 - 212   2016 $350

Lang, Andrew *The Red Book of Heroes.* London: Longmans, Green, 1909. First edition, first printing, 8vo., red gilt cloth, all edges gilt, spine very slightly dull else fine, beautiful and elaborate gilt cover design, 8 lovely color plates, 17 black and white plates, and 23 black and whites in text and pictorial endpapers.   Aleph-bet Books, Inc.   111 - 245   2016 $300

Lang, Andrew *The Red Fairy Book.* London: Longmans Green, 1890. First edition, first printing, 8vo., red gilt pictorial cloth, all edges gilt, spine slightly dulled, scattered foxing, slight lean, overall tight and very good, illustrations by H. J. Ford, laid in is humourous note from Lang, rare. Aleph-bet Books, Inc.   112 - 280   2016 $1500

Lang, Andrew *The Violet Fairy Book.* London: Longmans, Green and Co., 1902. 8vo., original deep violet cloth elaborately blocked in gilt to spine and upper cover, all edges gilt, black endpaper, full color frontispiece and 7 other fine and glorious coloured plates alongside engravings by H. J. Ford, remarkably bright and attractive copy with only very minor rubbing and suggestion of dulling, to cover gilt, internally fresh with mild toning to endleaves.   Sotheran's Piccadilly Notes - Summer 2015 - 184   2016   £225

Lang, Andrew *The Yellow fairy Book.* London: Longmans, Green and Co., 1906. Early edition, 8vo., original yellow cloth, pictorially blocked in gilt to spine and upper cover, all edges gilt, black endpapers, engravings by H. J. Ford, attractive copy, some light soiling to spine, cover bright, internally fine and immaculate.   Sotheran's Piccadilly Notes - Summer 2015 - 188   2016   £168

Lang, Anton *Reminiscneces.* Munich: Seyfried, 1934. 12mo., signed and dated by author, many illustrations, very good in worn dust jacket.   Second Life Books, Inc.   196 B - 8   2016 $45

Lang, Harry *The Corpse in the Hearth.* Philadelphia: Macrae Smith, 1946. First edition, fine in dust jacket with tiny wear at base of spine and couple of short closed tears. Mordida Books   2015 - 010762   2016 $65

Langdale, Charles *Memoirs of Mrs. Fitzherbert; with an Account of Her Marriage with H. E. H. the Prince of Wales, Afterwards King George IV.* London: R. Bentley, 1856. First edition, 225 x 140mm., pleasing early 20th century turquoise crushed morocco by Bayntun of Bath for C. E. Lauriat of Boston (stamp-signed on front turn-in), covers with two interlaced rectangular frames of gilt and black, foliate cornerpieces, raised bands, spine compartments with concentric black and gilt frames, gilt titling, turn-ins with gilt French fillet frame and arabesque cornerpieces, marbled endpapers, all edges gilt, housed in felt lined blue buckram slipcase, 38 engraved plates, 10 in color comprised of hand colored frontispiece portrait (as issued) and 37 extra illustrations, all with tissue guards, spine sunned to olive brown, otherwise fine, leather lustrous and virtually by unworn, text with almost no signs of use, tissue guards preventing offsetting the frequently affects extra illustrated copies.   Phillip J. Pirages   67 - 28   2016 $1000

Langdon-Davies, John *Russia Puts the Clock Back.* London: Victor Gollancz, 1949. First edition, single faint foxspot to prelims, foolscap 8vo., original green cloth, backstrip lettered red, faint foxing to top edge and inner margin of endpapers, ownership inscription, dust jacket with few short closed tears, few foxspots, some light dust soiling, owner's shelfmark at head of front flap, good.   Blackwell's Rare Books   B184 - 169   2016   £30

Langhorne, John *The Correspondence of Theodosius and Constantia.* printed and embellished under the Direction of C. cook, 1796. 2 volumes, first with an engraved frontispiece and letterpress title, second with engraved frontispiece and title, uncut, original pink printed wrappers, some fraying, good, rare survival in wrappers. Blackwell's Rare Books   B186 - 46   2016   £300

Langhorne, John *The Effusions of Friendship and Fancy.* London: printed for T. Becket and P. A De Hondt, 1766. Second edition, 12mo., 2 volumes, fine, clean copy, full contemporary calf, raised and gilt banded spine, red and black morocco labels, from the Library of Invercauld Castle, Braemar.   Jarndyce Antiquarian Booksellers   CCXVI - 355   2016   £350

Langley, Batty *The City and Country Builders and Workman's Treasury of Designs of the Art of Drawing and Working the Ornamental Parts of Architecture Illustrated.* London: printed for J. Ilive for Thomas Langley, 1740. First edition, bookplate, signature and stamp of Robert Lancaster, one of the listed subscribers, 4to., contemporary full calf rebacked with original red leather spine label laid down, spine in 6 compartments, 187 engraved plates, mild wear to cover edges, mild scattered foxing, soiling, bit of worming lower margin of first third of volume, no text or plates affected later owner name f.f.e.p., scarce.   By the Book, L. C. 45 - 4   2016 $2750

Langrand, Olivier *Guide to the Birds of Madagascar.* New Haven: Yale University Press, 1990. Octavo, color plates, very good in dust jacket.   Andrew Isles Natural History Books   55 - 25897   2016 $100

Langstaff, John *David Copperfield's Library...* London: George Allen & Unwin, 1924. First edition, half title, frontispiece, plate, illustrations, original dark blue cloth, blocked in red, Langstaff's visiting card attached to title, 'with author's compliments'.   Jarndyce Antiquarian Booksellers   CCXVIII - 1345   2016   £25

Langstaff, John *Frog Went A-Courtin'.* New York: Harcourt Brace, 1955. Stated first edition, boards, fine in very good+ dust jacket with tiny hole in spine and slightest bit of rubbing, illustrated by Rajan with lithographs.   Aleph-bet Books, Inc.   112 - 433   2016 $1350

Langton, Robert *The Childhood and Youth of Charles Dickens.* London: published by the author, 1883. Half title, frontispiece, numerous illustrations, final ad leaf, original green cloth, lettered gilt, bookplate, very good.   Jarndyce Antiquarian Booksellers   CCXVIII - 1346   2016   £25

Langton, Robert *The Childhood and Youth of Charles Dickens.* London: Hutchinson & Co., 1891. First Published edition, half title, frontispiece, illustrations, original pale green cloth, lettered gilt, little dulled, front board slightly creased, signature of Thelma Weatherall April 1891, top edge gilt.   Jarndyce Antiquarian Booksellers   CCXVIII - 1347   2016   £20

Langton, Robert *The Childhood and Youth of Charles Dickens.* London: Hutchinson & Co., 1912. Reprint, half title, frontispiece, illustrations, final ad leaf, original green cloth, lettered gilt, very good, bright.   Jarndyce Antiquarian Booksellers   CCXVIII - 1348   2016   £35

Lankester, Edwin *Half Hours with the Microscope.* London: Robert Hardwicke, 1860. New edition, illustrated by Tuffen West, half title, frontispiece, plates, 2 pages ads, original pink brown cloth by W. Bone & Son, spine slightly faded, very good.   Jarndyce Antiquarian Booksellers   CCXVII - 160   2016   £50

Lansdowe, George Granville *Dramatic Works.* Glasgow: printed by Robert Urie, 1752. 12mo., publisher's catalog to rear, titlepage little grubby, few occasional smudges and spots of foxing, generally clean, later half green calf, marbled paper covered boards, spine gilt with red morocco label, spine faded and little worn, edges rubbed, portion of flyleaf excised seemingly to remove the name of a previous owner.   Unsworths Antiquarian Booksellers   30 - 63   2016   £125

Lapidario Del Rey D. Alfonso X. Codice Original. Madrid: Imprenta de la Iberia a Cargo de J. Blasco, 1881. Facsimile edition, 4to., modern half calf with brown cloth covered boards, five raised bands, 638 full color miniuates and initial letters, well preserved.   Oak Knoll Books   310 - 42   2016 $1500

Lardner, Dionysius *Popular Lectures on Science and Art, Delivered in the Principal Cities and Towns of the United States.* New York: Greeley & McLerath, 1846. First edition, 8vo, 2 volumes, illustrations, some dampstaining to spine and upper corners of 16 pages in volume I, not affecting legibility, covers of both volumes rubbed and slightly chipped, very good set, original half calf over marbled boards.   Edwin V. Glaser Rare Books   2015 - 10280   2016 $150

Larkin, David *Fairies.* New York: Harry N. Abrams, 1978. Large 4to., gilt pictorial cloth, fine in near fine dust jacket, touch of soil 185 illustrations, including 147 in full color by Froud and Alan Lee.   Aleph-bet Books, Inc.   112 - 176   2016 $200

Larkin, George *The Visions of John Bunyan....* London: printed for A. Millar, W. Law and R. Carter and for Wilson, Spence and Mawman, York, 1793. 12mo., some browning, contemporary half calf over marbled boards, large vellum corner pieces, themselves marbled, rebacked, a series of 3 early 19th century inscriptions inside front cover and on flyleaves passing the book on, sound.   Blackwell's Rare Books   B186 - 90   2016   £180

Larkin, Philip 1922-1985 *All What Jazz - a Record Diary 1961-1968.* London: Faber and Faber, 1985. Second edition, octavo, spine slightly bumped at head and tail, near fine in fine dust jacket.   Peter Ellis   112 - 209   2016   £65

Larkin, Philip 1922-1985 *Jill.* Fortune Press, 1946. First edition, odd faint foxspot to handful of pages, crown 8vo., original pale green cloth, backstrip lettered gilt that is slightly dulled, top edge sprinkled red, few faint foxspots to endpapers, faint partial browning from dust jacket flaps, dust jacket, bright but split along upper joint fold, light chipping to corners and heavier at backstrip panel ends, publisher's repricing to front flap, good, inscribed by author.   Blackwell's Rare Books   B184 - 170   2016   £7000

Larkin, Philip 1922-1985 *The Less Deceived: Poems.* Hessle: Marvell Press, 1955. First edition, This is an early copy (one of 120) of the first impression with flat spine and the misprint on page 38 (which is here corrected in pencil), little foxing, very nice in dust jacket which has touch of wear at head and foot of spine panel, signed by author in pencil on front free endpaper with few pencil markings and annotations by Anthony Thwaite, loosely inserted are 3 carbon typescript poems by Larkin.   Bertram Rota Ltd.   Christmas List 2015 - 20   2016   £2000

Larkin, Philip 1922-1985 *Miscellaneous Pieces 1955-1982.* London: Faber and Faber, 1983. First edition, first impression, paperback original, 8vo., original photographic wrappers, soft crease in top corner of front wrapper, otherwise very fine, presentation by author for Michael Wright of Faber and Faber.   James S. Jaffe Rare Books   Occasional List: Winter 2016 - 90   2016 $3500

Larned, W. T. *Fairy Tales from France.* Chicago: Volland, 1920. 14th edition, 8vo, pictorial boards, fine in box (one flap repaired, else box very good+), illustrations by John Rae.   Aleph-bet Books, Inc.   112 - 497   2016 $300

Larrieu, Odette *Roman De Renard.* Paris: Hachette, 1925. 4to.,, 4to., decorative cloth, pictorial paste-on, top edge gilt, light wear and soil, near fine, illustrations by Felix Lorioux, quite uncommon.   Aleph-bet Books, Inc.   112 - 300   2016 $600

Larronde, Olivier *Rien Voila l'Ordre.* Decines: L'Arbalete, 1959. First edition, limited to 1325 copies of which this is one of 150 with "H.C." on limitation page, 4to., paper covered boards with illustration on front board, pencil drawings by Alberto Giacometti, spine and boards slightly soiled, small scuff on back board.   Oak Knoll Books   310 - 35   2016 $350

Larsen, Ellouise Baker *American Historical Views on Staffordshrie China.* New York: Doubleday Doran & Co., 1939. First edition, small 4to., frontispiece in color, photographs, dark blue cloth, gilt, pictorial pastedown on front cover, spine bit faded, minor spotting to front cover, owner's name on front flyleaf, fine.   Argonaut Book Shop   Pottery and Porcelain 2015 - 5003   2016 $125

Larsson, Carl *Larssons.* Stockholm: Albert Bonniers, 1902. First edition, large folio, pictorial cloth dulled bit, else very good++, pen and ink illustrations, followed by 32 fabulous color plates,.   Aleph-bet Books, Inc.   112 - 282   2016 $550

Larsson, Stieg *The Millenium Trilogy: The Girl with the Dragon Tattoo: The Girl Who Played with Fire: The Girl who Kicked the Hornet's Nest.* London: Maclehose, 2008. First edition, 8vo., 3 volumes, fine in fine dust jackets.   Any Amount of Books   2015 - A96808   2016   £650

Lary, Nikita Michael *Dostoevsky and Dickens: a Study of Literary Influence.* London: Routledge & Kegan Paul, 1973. First edition, half title, original blue cloth, publisher's compliments slip loosely inserted, very good in dust jacket.   Jarndyce Antiquarian Booksellers   CCXVIII - 1350   2016   £25

The Last Blow or an Unanswerable Vindication of the Society of Exeter College. London: printed for S. Crowder, H. Woodgate &c., 1755. Second edition, 4to., slightly dusted, title leaf laid down, without half title, disbound.   Jarndyce Antiquarian Booksellers   CCXVI - 347   2016   £30

Last, P. R. *Sharks and Rays of Australia.* Melbourne: CSIRO, 1994. First edition, quarto, color plates, maps, very minor blemishes, laminated boards.   Andrew Isles Natural History Books   55 - 1533   2016 $100

Lastanosa, Vincencio Juan De *Tratado de la Moneda Iaquesa y de Otras de Oro y Plata del Reyno de Aragon.* Zaragoza: 1681. First and only edition, 4to., late 19th century Spanish red morocco with title boldly lettered on upper cover in gilt, unidentified ownership initials TXE stamped at foot, cruciform ornaments in gilt on lower cover.   Maggs Bros. Ltd.   1474 - 48   2016   £3000

Lastman, Cornelius Jansz *Konst der Stuuruiden.* Amsterdam: by Hendrik Donkker in Compagnie met Jacob en Casporus Loots-Man, 1675. 3 parts in one volume, 4to., contemporary Dutch mottled calf, spine decorated gilt (tulip motifs), raised bands, red morocco lettering piece, marbled edges, 2 woodcut title vignettes, numerous woodcut diagrams and tables in text, slightly rubbed with small splits to upper joint at head and foot of spine and little loss to lettering piece, page 133 with flawed corner, marginal paper flaw to page 201, affecting one word, table on page 209 shaved at lower margin, due to extension, occasionally lightly spotted or browned, very good and clean.   Sotheran's Travel and Exploration - 463   2016   £4950

The Late Gallant Exploits of a Famous Balancing Captain: a New Song. London: printed for J. Huggonson, 1741. First edition, folio, disbound, fore edge of titlepage bit trimmed, some marginal tears and few minor pen trials, but sound, very scarce.   C. R. Johnson Rare Book Collections   Foxon: H-P 2015 - 526   2016   £613

Latham, Hiram *Trans-Missouri Stock Raising.* Denver: Old West Pub. Co., 1962. 1 of 999 copies, map endpapers, near fine in dust jacket.   Dumont Maps and Books   133 - 64   2016 $50

Latham, Wilfrid *The States of the River Plate; their Industries and Commerce.* London: Longman, Green, 1868. Second edition, 8vo., folding map, original green blindstamped cloth, neatly rebacked.   J. & S. L. Bonham Antiquarian Booksellers   America 2016 - 9913   2016   £100

Lathrop, Dorothy *Animals of the Bible.* New York: Frederick F. Stokes, 1937. First edition, first state with Lathrop's name misspelled 'Lathop' on spine of book and spine of jacket), 4to., mild toning and foxing to endpapers and pastedown, pictorial endpapers, binding tight in very good+ dust jacket with chips, stain to rear panel of dust jacket, mild scuff.   By the Book, L. C.   45 - 86   2016 $1000

Lathrop, Dorothy *The Fairy Circus.* New York: MacMillan, Nov., 1931. First edition, first printing, oblong 4to., orange pictorial cloth, covers faded with some soil, rear cover crease, mend on endpaper and blank leaf, tight and good-very good in very good dust jacket (frayed at fold and head of spine), 8 magnificent and enchanting color plates, as well as 12 beautiful full page black and white plates, inscribed by Lathrop, scarce.   Aleph-bet Books, Inc.   112 - 283   2016 $1650

Lathrop, Dorothy *The Lost Merry-go-Round.* New York: Macmillan, Oct., 1934. First edition, 8vo., red pictorial cloth, cover faded along bottom and side edges, else very good+ in dust jacket (some soil, worn on corners and small pieces off backstrip), illustrations by author, rare.   Aleph-bet Books, Inc.   111 - 246   2016 $750

Lathrop, Dorothy *The Skittle-Skattle Monkey.* New York: Macmillan, Oct., 1945. First edition, 8vo., red boards, very good+ in dust jacket (soiled, few closed tears, better than good), beautiful full page illustrations.   Aleph-bet Books, Inc.   111 - 247   2016 $200

Latimer, John *The Annals of Bristol in the Sixteenth and Seventeenth Centuries in the Eighteenth Century, in the Nineteenth Century.* Bath: Kingsmead Reprints, 1970. 3 volumes, 8vo., lightly dusted to top board edges and browned to page edges, dust jackets little worn in extremities, still very good, ownership signature.   Unsworths Antiquarian Booksellers Ltd.   E04 - 11   2016   £75

Latimer, Jonathan *Black is the Fashion for Dying.* New York: Random House, 1959. First edition, spine foxed and rubbed, very good in like dust jacket, signed by author, uncommon thus.   Between the Covers Rare Books   208 - 107   2016 $225

Lattier De Laraoche, T. M. A. A. *Memoire sur la Cataracte et Guerison de Cette Maladie sans Operation Chirurgicale.* Delaunay, Bechet, Paris: Carpentier Mericourt for the author, 1833. Second enlarged edition, original printed paper wrappers, 8vo., covers very lightly soiled, near fine, untrimmed.   Edwin V. Glaser Rare Books   2015 - 10291   2016 $450

Laughlin, James *New Directions in Poetry and Prose.* Norfolk: New Directions, 1936. First edition, 8vo., printed boards, somewhat soiled, signed by author to Aquinto Jack, one of 513 copies.   Second Life Books, Inc.   196 B - 14   2016 $300

Laughlin, James *New Directions in Poetry and Prose. Number 11.* Norfolk: New Directions, 1949. First edition, 8vo., tan cloth and nicked and somewhat worn dust jacket, inscribed by poet Stanley Moss for Ella, with ink drawing, he has also made ink corrections in text of his poems.   Second Life Books, Inc.   196 B - 15   2016 $85

Laughlin, James *Selected Poems.* Norfolk: New Directions, 1959. First edition, 8vo., author's presentation on flyleaf to poet William Claire, paper over boards, little foxing on endpapers, otherwise very good, tight copy in little chipped and somewhat soiled dust jacket.   Second Life Books, Inc.   196 B - 20   2016 $75

Laughlin, James *Quello Che La Maitta Scrive...* Parma: Guanda Editore, 1970. First edition, 12mo., printed wrapper over stiff wrapper, inscribed to poet William Claire, slight tanning to text block, near fine.   Second Life Books, Inc.   196 B - 16   2016 $75

Laughlin, James *The Wild Anemone & Other Poems.* New York: New Directions, 1957. First edition, 12mo., printed wrapper over stiff wrapper, inscribed by author for William Claire, slight tanning to text block, nar fine.   Second Life Books, Inc.   196 B - 19   2016 $75

Laurence, Dan *Shaw on Dickens.* Lorrimer Pub., 1986. Half title, original beige cloth, very good in dust jacket.   Jarndyce Antiquarian Booksellers   CCXVIII - 1439   2016   £20

Laurence, William L. *The Hell Bomb.* Hollis & Carter, 1951. First English edition, full page map, crown 8vo., original red cloth, backstrip lettered in gilt and gentle faded, ownership inscription and some faint foxing to inner margin of endpapers, dust jacket with touch of fading to backstrip panel and light rubbing to extremities, very good.   Blackwell's Rare Books   B184 - 171   2016   £30

Laurie, James Stuart *Rhymes, Jingles and Songs with Music for Voice and Piano...* London: Longman, Brown, Longman & Roberts, circa, 1862. Oblong 8vo., original blue cloth, slightly dulled, very good.   Jarndyce Antiquarian Books   CCXV - 821   2016   £65

Lauterbach, Ann *Later that Evening.* Brooklyn: Jordan Davies, 1981. Limited to 210 copies, signed by author, 8vo., quarter cloth, paper covered boards, top edge cut, other edges uncut.   Oak Knoll Books   310 - 117   2016 $225

Laval, Jerome D. *As "Pop" Saw It. The Great Central Valley of California...* Fresno: Pub. by Graphic Technology, 1975-1976. First edition, Volumes I and II, quarto, profusely illustrated with hundreds of photos, pictorial cloth, owner's inscription in each volume, light rubbing to spine ends, else fine.   Argonaut Book Shop   Photography 2015 - 7604   2016 $100

Lavelli, Jacapo *De Pulsibus ad Tyrones...* Venice: apud in Baptisam Clotium Senensem, 1602. 4to., contemporary limp vellum, recased with renewal of endpapers, engraved printer's device on title, woodcut block initials, title in red and black, old ownership signature on title, light foxing, else nice, clean copy, rare. James Tait Goodrich X-78 - 368 2016 $495

Lavender, David *Nothing Seemed Impossible.* Palo Alto: American West Pub., 1975. First edition, frontispiece, illustrations, fine with lightly chipped pictorial dust jacket. Argonaut Book Shop Biography 2015 - 7453 2016 $45

Lavery, Emmet *The Magnificent Yankee. A Play in Three Acts.* New York: Samuel French, 1946. 8vo., illustrations, author's presentation, nice in chipped dust jacket. Second Life Books, Inc. 196 B - 23 2016 $40

Lavoisier, Antoine Laurent 1743-1794 *Methode de Nomenclature Chimique Proposee...* Paris: Chez Cuchet, 1787. First edition, 2nd issue, 2nd printing with flowered vase on titlepage, 8vo., half title, woodcut titlepage vignette, headpiece, tailpieces, 6 folding tables, 1 folding plate, page 1 of text trimmed at top margin and mounted on stub, foxed, contemporary full mottled calf, red leather spine label, gilt spine, foot of spine chipped, corners of rear cover chewed ownership signature on title, good. Jeff Weber Rare Books 183 - 22 2016 $1750

Law, Edmund *An Enquiry into the Ideas of Space, Time, Immensity and Eternity....* Cambridge: printed by W. Fenner and R. Beresford for W. Thurlborn, 1734. First edition, octavo, contemporary full paneled calf with lovely design work on both front and back covers, leather (but not the board) on front panel wormed in irregular pattern (1 1/4 inch) on lower edge front cover, spine with five raised bands and burgundy morocco spine label with gilt lettering, contemporary ink notation on front endpaper including dates 1736-7, really beautiful, crisp, clean, bright, rare. Athena Rare Books List 15 - 1734 2016 $1500

Lawhead, Terry *Nothing Lives Long.* Port Townsend: Graywolf Press, No. 1 of 50 copies, numbered and signed by author, 8vo., paper wrappers, sewn at spine, inscribed to publisher and dedicatee, Scott (Walker), cover slightly faded, otherwise nice. Second Life Books, Inc. 196 B - 25 2016 $50

Lawrence, A. W. *T. E. Lawrence by His Friends.* 1937. signature of James Hanley, illustrations, dust jacket slightly discolored. I. D. Edrich Winston Spencer Churchill - 2016 £125

Lawrence, Alfred Henry *Reminiscences of Cambridge Life.* London: for private circulation only, 1889. Half title, original light blue cloth, bevelled boards, all edges gilt, later presentation inscription from author's wife to Mr. Dyer, very good. Jarndyce Antiquarian Books CCXV - 574 2016 £65

Lawrence, David *Death Has two Hands.* London: Ward Lock, 1958. First edition, fine in dust jacket with tiny wear at corners, base of spine and along edges, signed by author. Mordida Books 2015 - 004603 2016 $55

Lawrence, David Herbert 1885-1930 *Kangaroo.* London: Martin Secker, 1923. First edition, 8vo., brown cloth, gilt stamped lettering to spine, rule stamped in blind to boards, cream dust jacket with printed red lettering, ex-university library with only small one line name stamp to head of contents page, no other library markings, faint sunning to edges of rear board, light toning to page block and endpapers, pages clean and bright, binding sound, dust jacket lightly worn at extremities, and sunned to spine, sticker shadow and small abrasion to spine panel, neat tape repair to folds at interior, including strip of archival paper reinforcing spine panel, very good+ in very good- dust jacket. Tavistock Books Getting Around - 43 2016 $300

Lawrence, David Herbert 1885-1930 *Lady Chatterly's Lover.* Florence: privately printed, 1928. Limited to 100 numbered copies, signed by author, small 4to., original brown printed boards, black phoenix insignia on upper cover printed paper spine label, plain cream jacket, top edge rough trimmed, faint trace of foxing to fore-edges, jacket extremely fine, and as well preserved copy as one might hope to find, near fine. Jeff Weber Rare Books 181 - 68 2016 $;18,000

Lawrence, David Herbert 1885-1930 *Lady Chatterly's Lover.* Harmondsworth: 1960. First authorised unexpurgated English edition, wrapper, fine, as new. Bertram Rota Ltd. February List 2016 - 32 2016 £120

Lawrence, David Herbert 1885-1930 *The Lost Girl.* London: Secker, 1920. First edition, first state with unaltered text on pages 256 and 268, some browning to half title, crown 8vo., original brown cloth, blindstamped double border, backstrip lettered gilt, top edge trimmed, little dust soiling, edges toned, browning to free endpapers, very good. Blackwell's Rare Books B184 - 172 2016 £200

Lawrence, David Herbert 1885-1930 *Love Among the Haystacks and Other Pieces.* London: Nonesuch Press, 1930. First edition, one of 1600 numbered copies, uncut and unopened, endpapers just little browned, otherwise very nice in dust jacket. Bertram Rota Ltd. February List 2016 - 31 2016 £225

Lawrence, David Herbert 1885-1930 *The Man Who Died.* London: Martin Secker, 1931. First English edition, 8vo., original green buckram with Lawrence phoenix stamped in gilt to upper board, backstrip lettered in gilt and lightly faded, small amount of very gentle fading through jacket at head of upper board, free endpapers browned, original 1931 Bumpus sales invoice laid in, dust jacket slightly frayed, some light toning and dust soiling and small amount of foxing at flap-folds, very good. Blackwell's Rare Books B186 - 250 2016 £175

Lawrence, David Herbert 1885-1930 *Mornings in Mexico.* London: Secker, 1927. First edition, small amount of foxing at head of prelims, 8vo., original tan cloth little soiled overall, backstrip lettered gilt and slightly sunned, top edge green, others untrimmed and foxed, faint browning to endpapers, dust jacket with few foxspots and some browning to lfaps, good, contemporary review clipping loosely inserted.   Blackwell's Rare Books   B184 - 173   2016   £350

Lawrence, David Herbert 1885-1930 *The Paintings of D. H. Lawrence.* Mandrake Press, 1929. 131/500 copies printed on Arches mouldmade paper (of an edition to 510), 26 color reproductions of paintings of which 13 are oil and 13 watercolors, each with caption leaf and printed on recto, imperial 4to., original half brown morocco with green cloth boards, Lawrence Phoenix stamped in gilt to both, backstrip lettered in gilt, top corners bumped and all corners little rubbed, black ink mark along foot of lower board, top edge gilt, others untrimmed, browning to free endpapers, good.   Blackwell's Rare Books   B184 - 174   2016   £240

Lawrence, David Herbert 1885-1930 *A Propos of Lady Chatterley.* Mandrake Press, 1930. First edition thus, advance copy, foolscap 8vo., original blue cloth with lettering and single fillet border in red ot upper board, backstrip lettered in red and gentley faded, dust jacket, very good.   Blackwell's Rare Books   B186 - 251   2016   £125

Lawrence, David Herbert 1885-1930 *Rawdon's Roof.* London: Elkin Mathews & Marrot, 1928. First edition, one of 500 signed copies out of a total edition of 530, 8vo., near fine in slightly nicked dust jacket.   Second Life Books, Inc.   196 B - 27   2016 $650

Lawrence, David Herbert 1885-1930 *Snake.* Octon: Verdigris Press, 2014. Artist's book, one of 4 deluxe copies, from a total edition of 50, deluxe with original copperplate drawing, page size 5 1/4 x 12 inches, bound by Mark Lintott, leporello style in brown boards with title printed in blind on front panel, drawing housed in same brown paper over boards, housed in gold faux snakeskin portfolio laid into clamshell box, copperplate inset into front panel of clamshell box, slipcase and clamshell box of same gold faux snakeskin, man made material, painted and sanded by artist to resemble belly of a snake, title printed in brown on front panel, title, author, artist and press printed in brown on spine, four mezzotints by Judith Rothchild.   Priscilla Juvelis - Rare Books   66 - 18   2016 $2200

Lawrence, David Herbert 1885-1930 *Sons and Lovers.* London: Duckworth, 1913. First edition, cancel titlepage with date, very occasional light foxspots, small nick to edge of few leaves, 8vo., original blue cloth stamped in gilt, blind-stamped double rule border to upper board and publisher's device to lower, few light marks, backstrips lettered gilt with slender waterstain to centre, slight lean to spine, free endpapers faintly browned, two ownership inscriptions, good.   Blackwell's Rare Books   B184 - 175   2016   £700

Lawrence, David Herbert 1885-1930 *Tortoises.* New York: Seltzer, 1921. First edition, titlepage printed in black and red, patches of very faint browning to prelims, 8vo., original green boards with illustration to front backstrip slightly chipped, printed label lettered in black, some fading overall and rubbed at extremities with small hole at head of upper joint, free endpapers browned unevenly, untrimmed, good.   Blackwell's Rare Books   B184 - 177   2016   £240

Lawrence, David Herbert 1885-1930 *The Trespasser.* London: Duckworth, 1912. First edition, light creasing to top corner of few leaves, 8vo., original blue cloth and lightly soiled overall with bump to corners of upper board, stamped in gilt to front with publisher's device blindstamped to lower board, backstrip lettered gilt and rubbed, spine shaken, cocked and worn along joints, edges and endpapers browned, bookplate.   Blackwell's Rare Books   B184 - 178   2016   £200

Lawrence, Jacob *Harriet and the Promised Land.* New York: Simon & Schuster, 1968. Second edition, thin folio, bit of mustiness and slight foxing on boards, thus very good in like dust jacket with scrape on rear panel, some foxing and clipped price, publisher's supplied price sticker present, inscribed by artist Jacob Lawrence 1/9/87.   Between the Covers Rare Books   202 - 18   2016 $750

Lawrence, Jacob *The Migration Series.* Washington: Rappahannock Press, 1993. First edition, large quarto, slight foxing on endpapers, about fine in dust jacket with foxing, visible only on inside of jacket, signed by author.   Between the Covers Rare Books   202 - 56   2016 $650

Lawrence, James *On the Nobility of the British Gentry.* London: James Fraser, 1840. Fourth edition, 12mo., half title, final ad leaf, faint signs of label removed from leading pastedown, original dark brown cloth, damp marked, good.   Jarndyce Antiquarian Books   CCXV - 289   2016   £75

Lawrence, Jerome *The Gang's All Here.* Cleveland: World Pub., 1960. First edition, small 8vo., inscribed by both authors, very nice in dust jacket.   Second Life Books, Inc.   196 B - 28   2016 $45

Lawrence, John *The Clergy-Man's Recreation...* London: printed for Bernard Lintott, 1714. Second edition, engraved frontispiece, 8vo. contemporary manuscript index has been written on both sides of a final blank leaf, there are a number of annotations in margins, one noting other gardening works, slight browning, faint waterstaining to few leaves, modern full dark brown crushed morocco, gilt spine bands, black gilt label.   Jarndyce Antiquarian Booksellers   CCXVI - 357   2016   £520

Lawrence, Thomas Edward 1888-1935 *Correspondence with E. M. Forster and F. L. Lucas.* Fordingbridge: Castle Hill Press, 2011. First edition, 114/225 copies, from an edition of 377, tipped in color printed frontispiece, royal 8vo., original grey cloth, backstrip lettered gilt, top edge gilt, original invoice laid in, dust jacket fine. Blackwell's Rare Books B184 - 179 2016 £180

Lawrence, Thomas Edward 1888-1935 *Correspondence with Henry Williamson.* Fordingbridge: Castle Hill Press, 2000. First edition, 168/600 copies (from a edition of 702 copies), frontispiece, royal 8vo., original brown cloth, backstrip gilt lettered, front cover blocked in blind, top edge gilt, bookplate, dust jacket with short closed tear at foot of front joint fold, near fine. Blackwell's Rare Books B184 - 180 2016 £90

Lawrence, Thomas Edward 1888-1935 *Crusader Castles.* Golden Cockerel Press, 1936. 638/1000 copies, printed on mould-made paper, 166 reproductions of drawings, photographs and diagrams, 2 maps printed in black and red laid down within original envelope which is lightly foxed, crown 4to., original half red morocco with cream cloth, backstrips lettered in gilt with five raised bands, little overall spotting and some light soiling, hint of rubbing to extremities, top edge gilt, others untrimmed with one or two foxspots, bookplate to front pastedowns, faint foxing to rear pastedown of first volume, good. Blackwell's Rare Books B186 - 310 2016 £1200

Lawrence, Thomas Edward 1888-1935 *An Invitation to British Columbia. A Letter from T. E. Lawrence to Martin A. Grainger.* Vancouver: Heavenly Monkey, 2005. First edition, limited to 50 numbered copies signed by Jeremy Wilson and Don Stewart, an extra 20 copies printed for private distribution, 8vo., original speckled faux parchment stamped in black, printed on handmade paper, frontispiece, plus facsimile of original letter, fine. Sotheran's Piccadilly Notes - Summer 2015 - 190 2016 £598

Lawrence, Thomas Edward 1888-1935 *Letters to E. T. Leeds.* Andoversford: Whittington Press, 1988. First edition, 179/650 copies from an edition of 750 copies printed on Zerkall mouldmade paper, 13 plates reproducing 25 photos, line drawings by Richard Kennedy printed in brown, 4to., original quarter brown cloth with cinnamon boards, upper board with line drawing by Kennedy printed in brown, backstrip lettered gilt with slight bump at head, untrimmed, bookplate, cloth and board slipcase, very good. Blackwell's Rare Books B184 - 322 2016 £80

Lawrence, Thomas Edward 1888-1935 *"The Mint" and Later Writings about Service Life.* Castle Hill Press, 2009. 29/50 copies from an edition of 277, tipped-in sepia frontispiece from drawing by Augustus John, parts 1 and 2 of the diary printed on grey paper, all prelims and remainder of text on white paper, royal 8vo., original full goatskin, backstrip lettered gilt with five raised bands, all edges gilt, grey endpapers, pale grey cotton marker, blue cloth slipcase, fine. Blackwell's Rare Books B186 - 254 2016 £700

Lawrence, Thomas Edward 1888-1935 *Revolt in the Desert.* New York: George H. Doran Co., 1927. First US edition, first impression, 8vo., original brick red cloth lettered in black on spine and upper board, pictorial endpapers after watercolor, 16 portraits and color printed folding map, light discoloration to foot of spine and small portion of lower cover, apart from light browning to plates, good copy, gift inscription dated March 30 1927. Sotheran's Travel and Exploration - 336 2016 £248

Lawrence, Thomas Edward 1888-1935 *Seven Pillars of Wisdom & Triumph.* London: Jonathan Cape, 1935. Limited to 750 copies in special binding with color plates and facsimile manuscript leaves not found in standard trade edition, this being 477, quarto, numbered limitation leaf, frontispiece, 3 pages of facsimile manuscript, 43 illustrations and four maps inserted, facsimile pages have tissue guards, quarter brown levant morocco over brown cloth boards, gilt stamped front board and spine, bottom and fore-edge uncut, top edge gilt, several pages unopened, marbled endpapers, fine. Heritage Book Shop Holiday 2015 - 70 2016 $2250

Lawrence, Thomas Edward 1888-1935 *Seven Pillars of Wisdom.* London: Jonathan Cape, 1935. First trade edition, 3 facsimiles, 48 plates and 4 folding maps, some very occasional clusters of light foxing to leading edge, 4to. original brown buckram stamped in gilt to front, backstrip lettered gilt and lightly sunned through dust jacket, untrimmed, top edge brown with fore-edges lightly foxed, dust jacket with few tears and attendant creasing, some pressure marks to rear panel, good. Blackwell's Rare Books B186 - 253 2016 £350

Lawrence, Thomas Edward 1888-1935 *Translating the Bruce Rogers 'Odyssey'.* Salisbury: Castle Hill Press, 2014. 22/45 copies from an edition of 377, frontispiece tipped in photo, tipped in photo of Isham, 4 further photographic plates, royal 8vo., original tan goatskin, backstrip with maroon leather label lettered gilt between 7 raised bands, all edges gilt, cloth slipcase, new. Blackwell's Rare Books B184 - 186 2016 £600

Lawrence, Thomas Edward 1888-1935 *Translating the Bruce Rogers 'Odyssey'.* Salisbury: Castle Hill Press, 2014. 232/250 copies from an edition of 377, frontispiece tipped-in photo, tipped in photo of Ralph Isham and 4 further photos plates, royal 8vo., original red cloth, backstrip lettered gilt, top edge orange, dust jacket, new. Blackwell's Rare Books B184 - 185 2016 £150

Laws Concerning Masters and Servants... London: printed by his Majesty's Law-Printers for W. Owen, 1768. Second edition, 12mo., contemporary sheep, rebacked and with repairs to inner hinges. Jarndyce Antiquarian Books CCXV - 290 2016 £380

The Laws of Etiquette; or Short Rules and Reflections for Conduct in Society. Philadelphia: Carey, Lea & Blanchard, 1836. Second edition, slight spotting, original brown cloth, expertly recased.   Jarndyce Antiquarian Books   CCXV - 291   2016   £60

Lawson-Hall, Claire   *Oxford Doors.*   Marcham: Alembic Press, 1997. 38/40 copies signed by author and artist, line drawings, etching and linocuts printed in various colours with predominance of brown dictated by subject, text printed in brown, small faint spot at border of frontispiece, folio, original Coptic gatefold binding of a wood grain textured Maziarczyk pastepaper boards, with asymmetric pages of varying width, edges untrimmed, terra cotta cloth solander box, near fine.   Blackwell's Rare Books   B186 - 292   2016   £850

Lawson, John   *The Upper Gallery. A Poem.*   Dublin: printed by George Faulkner, 1733. First edition, small 8vo., disbound, very slight paper loss among blank inner margins, otherwise very good, rare.   C. R. Johnson Rare Book Collections   Foxon: H-P 2015 - 527   2016 $2681

Lawson, Robert   *Ben and Me.*   Boston: Little Brown, 1939. First edition, 8vo., brown cloth, fine in dust jacket slightly faded on edge with one small closed tear otherwise beautiful and much nicer than usually found, printed in brown and featuring many wonderful full and partial page endpapers, this copy inscribed by Lawson.   Aleph-bet Books, Inc.   111 - 251   2016 $1500

Lawton, W. J. Henri   *Champion Club Swinging Series Containing Upwards of 1000 Exercises.*   Leamington: Churches & Womersley, Daily Circular Office, 1898. First edition, initial ad leaf, half title, illustrations, original royal blue moire cloth boards, front blocked in black, slight rubbing, very good.   Jarndyce Antiquarian Books   CCXV - 292   2016   £75

Layard, G. S.   *Kate Greenaway.*   London: Adam and Charles Black, 1995. Edition deluxe, one of 500 signed copies of which this is number 342, original pencil sketch by Greenaway, quarto, 53 color illustrations and numerous black and white illustrations, publisher's white beveled cloth, geometric blindstamping to front and spine, gilt cover and spine lettering, decorative color endpapers, top edge gilt, some light wear to spine extremities, front and rear hinge starting, very attractive.   Heritage Book Shop   Holiday 2015 - 46   2016 $2000

Layman, Pseud.   *The Independence of the Universities of Oxford and Cambridge.*   Oxford: Parker, 1838. Partly unopened, sewn as issued, bit dusted, 43 pages.   Jarndyce Antiquarian Books   CCXV - 822   2016   £35

Layman, Pseud.   *Remarks on the Rev. Dr. Vincent's Defence of Public Education with an Attempt to State Fairly the Question....*   London: J. Hatchard, 1802. Second edition, disbound, signature of M. Bagot.   Jarndyce Antiquarian Books   CCXV - 996   2016   £40

Le Blanc, Charles   *Manuel De l'Amateur D'Estampes Contenant Le Dictionnaire des Graveurs de Toutes Les Nations.*   Paris: Emile Bouillon, 1854-1890. 8vo., contemporary quarter leather, marbled paper covered boards, original paper wrappers bound in, 4 volumes, illustrations, laid in letter from Mr. James Hillhouse of New Haven to Mr. Dougall Hawkes of NY describes research done on this copy, ex-library, bookplate and markings, spines of first 3 volumes loose, front hinges of first two volumes cracked, scuffing and rubbing at edges of all volumes.   Oak Knoll Books   310 - 43   2016 $450

Le Boe, Sylvius Franciscus De   *Opera Medic Tam Hactenus Inedita...*   Paris: Apud Frederick Leonard, 1679. First edition, title printed in red and black, inserted large folding engraved portrait, 4to, modern brown calf, gilt spine with raised bands, black leather gilt label, some early ink inscriptions, title with marginal loss and two repairs to verso final index leaf with hole and loss of test, very pale mostly marginal dampstaining at beginning and end, very good, Paris bookseller's label pasted over imprint, portrait appears to be a later insertion.   James Tait Goodrich   X-78 - 370   2016 $650

Le Brocquy, Louis   *Louis Le Brocquy.*   Dublin: Ward River Press, 1981. First edition, octavo, numerous illustrations in color and black and white, fine in very near fine dust jacket.   Peter Ellis   112 - 212   2016   £85

Le Carre, John 1931-   *Call for the Dead.*   Walker and Co., 1962. First American edition, 8vo., paper over boards with cloth spine, near fine in slightly scuffed dust jacket with very small tear at bottom front, scarce.   Second Life Books, Inc.   197 - 207   2016 $75

Le Carre, John 1931-   *The Honoruable Schoolboy.*   New York: Alfred A. Knopf, 1977. First American edition, fine in dust jacket.   Bertram Rota Ltd.   Christmas List 2015 - 21   2016   £25

Le Carre, John 1931-   *The Naive and Sentimental Lover.*   London: Hodder and Stoughton, 1971. First edition, 3 corners bumped, otherwise nice in price clipped dust jacket, with publisher's small price label on inner panel.   Bertram Rota Ltd.   February List 2016 - 33   2016   £20

Le Carre, John 1931- *A Perfect Spy.* London: London Limited Editions, 1986. First edition, 91/250 copies, signed by author, 8vo., original quarter grey cloth with vertical gilt rule and marbled boards, backstrip lettered in gilt, tissue dust jacket with backstrip panel, little browned and small portion of loss at foot of rear panel, carrying around to backstrip, very good.   Blackwell's Rare Books   B184 - 190   2016   £100

Le Carre, John 1931- *The Spy Who Came in from the Cold.* London: Victor Gollancz, 1963. First edition, original blue cloth, somewhat darkened throughout and spine slightly faded, otherwise very nice in similarly faded dust jacket, small ink note on front free endpaper, cutting of quotation from Graham Greene ("Best spy story I've ever read), possibly clipped from later dust jacket, has at some time been taped onto front free endpaper, tape has long since oxidised and fallen away, leaving some staining that has bled throughout onto half title.   Bertram Rota Ltd.   Christmas List 2015 - 22   2016   £500

Le Clerc, Daniel *Bibliotheca Anatomica; sive Recens in Anatomia Inventorum Thesaurus Locupielissimus....* Geneva: Jean Antoine Chouet, 1685. First edition, 2 volumes, large folio, lacks portrait, 87 plates, engraved vignette on titles, contemporary vellum, boards worn, some warping, text foxed and browned in parts, some of the folding plates have been repaired at fold.   James Tait Goodrich   X-78 - 371   2016 $2450

Le Clert, Louis *Papier, Recherches et Notes Pour Servir a L'Histoire Du Papier, Principalement a Troyes et Aux Environs Depuis le Quatorzieme Siecle.* Paris: a L'Enseigne du Pegase, 1926. First edition, limited to 711 numbered copies, 2 volumes, with 75 (of 78) fold-out plates reproducing watermarks and over 300 figures in text, some of the plates in color, folio, quarter vellum, blue cloth boards, top edges gilt, covers rubbed and soiled.   Oak Knoll Books   310 - 200   2016 $550

Le Corbeau, Adrien *The Forest Giant.* London: Jonathan Cape, 1924. First English edition, frontispiece and decorative border to titlepage with decorations at head of each text page, little very faint foxing to prelims and pencil note identifying Lawrence to titlepage, foolscap 8vo., original quarter yellow cloth with green boards, backstrip with printed label, a touch of wear to one corner, edges rough trimmed, dust jacket with darkened backstrip panel frayed at either end with some loss at foot, little chipping to corners, darkened overall, good, presentation copy inscribed by Charlotte F. Shaw to J. G. Wilson of Bumpus.   Blackwell's Rare Books   B186 - 252   2016   £400

Le Corbeau, Adrien *The Forest Giant.* London: Jonathan Cape, 1935. First illustrated edition, 8vo., original cloth with illustrated dust jackets, not price clipped, full page woodcuts in text, wrappers little dusted, otherwise near fine.   Sotheran's   Piccadilly Notes - Summer 2015 - 189   2016   £198

Le Corbeau, Adrien *La Gigantesque.* Fordingbridge: Castle Hill Press, 2004. 25/40 copies (from an edition of 352 copies), tipped in frontispiece facsimile, 8 further plates, 8vo., original maroon goatskin with design and double fillet border blind stamped to upper board, backstrip lettered in gilt, all edges gilt, marbled endpapers, cloth slipcase, fine.   Blackwell's Rare Books   B184 - 188   2016   £435

Le Fanu, Joseph Sheridan 1814-1873 *Green Tea and other Ghost Stories.* Sauk City: Arkham House, 1945. First edition, octavo, illustrations by Ronald Clyne, cloth, some darkening to pastedowns, previous owner's bookplate to front pastedown, fine in nearly fine dust jacket with some rubbing along upper edges and small closed tears at upper front panel.   John W. Knott, Jr./L.W. Currey, Inc.   Fall-Winter 2015 - 17866   2016 $450

Le Gallienne, Eva *Eva Le Gallienne's Civic Repertory Plays.* New York: Norton, 1928. First edition, one of 500 signed by author, 8vo., slipcase, owner's name on flyleaf, photos and stage plans, cover slightly soiled, case little worn, otherwise nice.   Second Life Books, Inc.   196 B - 33   2016 $65

Le Guin, Ursula K. *The Compass Rose Short Stories.* London: Victor Gollancz, 1983. First UK edition, fine in fine dust jacket, very slightly creased at top edge.   Peter Ellis   112 - 216   2016   £45

Le Guin, Ursula K. *The Dispossessed; a Ambiguous Utopia.* New York: Evanston: San Francisco: London: Harper Row, 1974. First edition, signed by author, octavo, cloth backed boards, fine in nearly fine dust jacket with tiny closed tears at upper spine end professionally mended.   John W. Knott, Jr./L.W. Currey, Inc.   Fall-Winter 2015 - 18569   2016 $750

Le Guin, Ursula K. *The Eye of the Heron.* London: Victor Gollancz, 1982. First UK edition, fine in fine dust jacket slightly creased at top edge.   Peter Ellis   112 - 217   2016   £45

Le Guin, Ursula K. *The Farthest Shore.* New York: Atheneum, 1972. First edition, octavo, cloth, fine in fine dust jacket.   John W. Knott, Jr./L.W. Currey, Inc.   Fall-Winter 2015 - 16673   2016 $650

Le Guin, Ursula K. *The Lathe of Heaven.* New York: Charles Scribner's Sons, 1971. First edition, octavo, quarter cloth with boards, fine in fine dust jacket.   John W. Knott, Jr./L.W. Currey, Inc.   Fall-Winter 2015 - 179130   2016 $850

Le Guin, Ursula K. *The Tombs of Atuan.* New York: Atheneum, 1971. First edition, octavo, cloth, fine in just about fine first state dust jacket, tiny closed tear to upper front panel and some mild edge rubs.   John W. Knott, Jr./L.W. Currey, Inc.   Fall-Winter 2015 - 16672   2016 $850

Le Guin, Ursula K. *A Wizard of Earthsea.* Berkeley: Parnassus Press, 1968. First edition, first printing, publisher's library cloth binding, octavo, fine in fine dust jacket with some light scratch marks to upper front panel in area of 'art' of Earthsea title lettering, lower front flap corner clipped, $3.95 price present at upper corner, excellent copy.   John W. Knott, Jr./L.W. Currey, Inc.   Fall-Winter 2015 - 16671   2016 $4500

Le Queux, William *Mysteries.* London: Ward Lock & Co., 1913. Black boards, slightly rubbed on edges, tissue protected frontispiece/illustration, price certificate on front pastedown, slight edge foxing, otherwise very good, scarce.   I. D. Edrich   Crime - 2016   £35

Le Quoy, R. *An Account of the Model in Relievo of the Great and Magnificent City and Suburbs of Paris.* London: printed by H. Reynell, 1779. 8vo. in 4's, some very slight marginal waterstaining to final leaves, very good, disbound.   Jarndyce Antiquarian Booksellers   CCXVI - 359   2016   £480

Le Roy Achille *La Liberte de l'Amour.* Paris: Librairie Socialiste Internationale, 1887. First edition, 12mo., original printed and pictorial pink wrappers, fading at top.   M & S Rare Books, Inc.   99 - 146   2016 $125

Le Sage, Alain Rene   1668-1747 *The Adventures of Gil Blas of Santillane.* London: printed for Richard Phillips, 1807. 203 x 121mm., 4 volumes, extremely pleasing contemporary deep blue straight grain morocco, handsomely gilt by Samuel Welcher (with his ticket on verso of front endpaper), covers bordered gilt with triple rules and framed with palmette roll, inside is a rule with small ring and floral tools at corners, raised bands, spines ornately gilt in lobed compartments, featuring stippled ground, quatrefoil centerpiece with delicate foliate, sprays at sides and fleurons at ends, turn-ins gilt with single rule and fleuron and ring tools at corners, all edges gilt, with 160 engravings comprised of 100 copperplates by Warner, Tomlinson and others, and extra illustrated with 60 plates by Conrad Martin Metz, armorial bookplate of H. Holland Edwards, Pennant Erithlyn, North Wales; front joints just little flaked, backstrips slightly sunned, covers with minor variation in color, several plates little foxed, generally only in margins and more frequently on added plates), one leaf with light ink stain in lower margin, light dampstain in margin at head of one plate, isolated very minor marginal soiling, very pleasing set, decorative bindings very well preserved and internally clean, fresh and bright.   Phillip J. Pirages   67 - 72   2016 $1750

Le Sage, Alain Rene   1668-1747 *The Adventures of Gil Blas of Santillane.* London: J. C. Nimmo and Bain, 1881. 191 x 121mm., 3 volumes, reddish brown crushed morocco gilt by Bayntun (stamp signed on front turn-in), covers with gilt French fillet border and cricket cornerpieces, raised bands, spine compartments similarly decorated, gilt ruled turn-ins, marbled endpapers, all edges gilt, 12 original etchings as called for and extra illustrated with 95 hand colored plates, one board detached, other joints rather worn, couple with older cracks repaired by glue, spines bit scuffed, other general wear couple of tiny fore-edge tears to one plate, otherwise text and inserted plates especially fine.   Phillip J. Pirages   67 - 237   2016 $850

Le Vaillant, Francois *A New and Improved Edition of Histoire Naturelle des Perroquets by...* Sydney: Imprime, 1989. Elephant folio, 2 volumes, 144 loose plates, publisher's handsome green cloth, solander boxes with colored label, fine set.   Andrew Isles Natural History Books   55 - 13390   2016 $3500

Lea, Tom *The King Ranch.* Kingsville: King Ranch, 1957. First edition, special limited 'Saddle Blanket issue', one of 3000 copies, none intended for sale, octavo, original tan and brown heavy crash linen in the design of saddle blankets woven and used on King Ranch, 2 volumes, original slipcase, handsome presentation inscription 1967, volume I hinge with paper split but holding, wear to edges on leather label on box (as usual due to softness of leather), exquisite production.   Manhattan Rare Book Company   2016 - 1642   2016 $1450

Leach, J. A. *Nature-Study: a Descriptive List of the Birds Native to Victoria, Australia.* Melbourne: Government Printer, 1909. Octavo, binder's red cloth, publisher's wrappers retained, handsome copy, scarce.   Andrew Isles Natural History Books   55 - 36370   2016 $60

Leach, MacEdward *The Book of Ballads.* New York: Limited Editions Club, 1967. This lettered copy "JW", large 8vo., red paper over boards with cloth spine, woodcuts by Fritz Kredel, fine in publisher's slipcase, illustrations cut in wood and hand colored, near fine.   Second Life Books, Inc.   196 B - 35   2016 $75

Leacock, Stephen *The Dry Pickwick and Other Congruities.* London: John Lane, Bodley Head, 1932. First edition, half title, 8 pages ads, original purple cloth lettered in white, spine faded, contemporary pencil signature of Fred Barrett.   Jarndyce Antiquarian Booksellers   CCXVIII - 152   2016   £25

Leaf, Munro *The Story of Ferdinand.* New York: Viking, 1936. First printing, 8vo., cloth backed pictorial boards, corners worn, covers and spine lightly soiled, very good in dust jacket from a later printing, spine faded, some closed tears and soil, good condition and $1.00 price intact, illustrations by Robert Lawson, this copy has 3 Christmas Cards from the leaf Family laid in, each card has an illustration, rare. Aleph-bet Books, Inc. 111 - 253 2016 $2500

Leake, Chauncey D. *Some Founders of Physiology.* Washington: 1956. Photos, original binding. James Tait Goodrich X-78 - 369 2016 $75

Leake, William Martin *Travels in Morea.* London: John Murray, 1830. First edition, 3 volumes, 8vo., 17 maps, 13 plates, contemporary half calf, raised bands and gilt on spine. J. & S. L. Bonham Antiquarian Booksellers Europe 2016 - 10265 2016 £1750

Leapor, Mary *Poems Upon Several Occasions.* London: printed and sold by J. Roberts, 1748. First edition, 2 volumes, near fine, 8vo., contemporary half calf, spine gilt, red morocco labels, just trifle rubbed, very slightly chipped at tops of spines, fine set, the second volume has always been difficult to find. C. R. Johnson Rare Book Collections Foxon: H-P 2015 - 530 2016 $3831

Lear, Edward 1812-1888 *A Book of Lear.* Harmondsworth: Penguin Books, 1939. First edition, drawings by Lear, wrappers, text just little browned, otherwise very nice, slightly darkened and torn dust jacket. Bertram Rota Ltd. Christmas List 2015 - 23 2016 £25

Lear, Edward 1812-1888 *The Book of Nonsense to which is Added More Nonsense.* London: Frederick Warne & Co. Ltd., 1900. Copyright edition, oblong quarto, 109 illustrated limericks in first part and 103 in second, publisher's brown cloth over beveled boards, front cover decorated and lettered in black, spine lettered gilt, minimal wear to extremities, excellent copy. David Brass Rare Books, Inc. 2015 - 02951 2016 $350

Lear, Edward 1812-1888 *Illustrations of the Family of Psittacidae or Parrots the Greater Part of Them Species...* London/New York: Pion/Johnson Reprint, 1978. Folio, 42 colored plates and accompanying text, publisher's red half morocco, very good. Andrew Isles Natural History Books 55 - 12934 2016 $1250

Lear, Edward 1812-1888 *Nonsense Botany and Nonsense Alphabets.* London: Frederick Warne & Co., 1888. Half title, vignette title, illustrations, final ad leaf, original blue bevelled boards, pictorially blocked in red, yellow, black and gilt, very bright and attractive copy. Jarndyce Antiquarian Booksellers CCXVII - 163 2016 £85

Lear, Edward 1812-1888 *Nonsense Songs and Stories.* London: Frederick Warne & co., 1888. Seventh edition, half title, vignette title, illustrations, final ad leaf, original light brown pictorial cloth, bevelled boards, lettered in black and gilt, very slightly dulled, attractive copy. Jarndyce Antiquarian Booksellers CCXVII - 164 2016 £125

Least Heat Moon, William *Blue Highways.* Boston: Little Brown, 1982. First edition, 18th printing, 8vo., nice in little chipped and worn, price clipped dust jacket, signed by author for friend Bill Smith. Second Life Books, Inc. 196 B - 36 2016 $75

Leatham, A. E. *Sport in Five Continents.* William Blackwood, 1912. First edition, 8vo., frontispiece, illustrations, original green decorative cloth, foxing to endpapers. J. & S. L. Bonham Antiquarian Booksellers Voyages 2016 - 10283 2016 £120

Leatherman, Leroy *Martha Graham.* New York: Knopf, 1966. First edition, 4to., photos by Martha Swope, signed by Leatherman and Swope, inscribed by Swope to Helen Hayes, nice copy. Second Life Books, Inc. 196 B - 37 2016 $250

Leavis, Frank Raymond *Dickens the Novelist.* London: Chatto & Windus, 1970. First edition, half title, original purple brown boards, very good in dust jacket. Jarndyce Antiquarian Booksellers CCXVIII - 1354 2016 £30

Leavitt, Joshua *Emancipator and Free American. (with) National Anti-Slavery Standard, The Liberator, Herald of Freedom and Christian Investigator.* Boston: Dexter S. King, 1842-1843. 1838, Elephant folio, contemporary quarter calf, marbled boards, with clear tape on spine and corners, very good with scattered spotting and small owner's signature. Between the Covers Rare Books 202 - 57 2016 $6500

Lecky, William Edward Hartpole *The Map of Life...* London: Longmans, 1902. New impression, half title, 40 page catalogue, page 165 onwards creased by damp, original maroon cloth, back board slightly damp marked, sound. Jarndyce Antiquarian Books CCXV - 293 2016 £20

Leclercq, Jules *Un Sejour Dans l'Ile de Java. Le Pays, Les Habitants, Le Systeme Colonial.* Paris: Librarie Plon, 1898. 8vo., plates, slightly toned, green cloth, gilt title to spine, edges sprinkled brown, spine little darkened, very good, pencilled ownership inscription of Spencer Ervin. Unsworths Antiquarian Booksellers 30 - 94 2016 £30

Lederer, Charles *Queertown: the Home of the Funniest of Funny Talk.* Chicago: Monarch, 1906. First and probably only edition, cloth backed pictorial boards, tips worn, some cover soil and crease on 2 pages, really clean, tight and very good, 13 full page color illustrations, this copy not colored in, with original drawing of a wizard inscribed by Lederer, special copy of rare book.   Aleph-bet Books, Inc.   112 - 371   2016 $800

Lee, Hannah F. *Elinor Fulton.* Boston: Whipple & Damrell, 1837. First edition, 12mo., original printed and pictorial pink wrappers (fading at spine).   M & S Rare Books, Inc.   99 - 147   2016 $250

Lee, Harper *To Kill a Mockingbird.* London: Heinemann, 1960. First edition, very good with new facsimile dust jacket, burgundy boards, spine stamped in silver, octavo, spine ends gently bumped, tidy gift inscription and vintage bookseller's label affixed to front pastedown, text block slightly and uniformly yellowed with light touches of soiling, binding square and sound, tips sharp, nice collector's copy.   Simon Finch   2015 - 1115418   2016 $250

Lee, Harper *(title in Cyrillic and English) Ubit Peresmeshnika/To Kill a Mockingbird.* Moskva: Moldodaia Gvardiia, 1964. First Russian book edition, octavo, text in Russian, octavo, quarter black cloth printed in white and illustrated paper over boards, attractive bookplate in Cyrillic of A. P. Chubova, owner's name in Cyrillic on both sides of first leaf, binding little cocked and spine lettering little rubbed, modest edgewear on edges of paper, overall very good.   Between the Covers Rare Books   204 - 67   2016 $2200

Lee, Laurie *Cider with Rosie.* London: Hogarth Press, 1959. First edition, first issue, very nice in like dust jacket and Book Society Choice wraparound band.   Bertram Rota Ltd.   Christmas List 2015 - 24   2016   £450

Lee, Laurie *We Made a Film in Cyprus.* London: Longmans, Green, 1947. First edition, 8vo., illustrations, original buff cloth, small stain to base, dust jacket (small tear).   J. & S. L. Bonham Antiquarian Booksellers   Europe 2016 - 9770   2016   £45

Lee, Sarah Bowdich *Familiar natural History.* London: 1860. Wood engravings.   Honey & Wax Booksellers   4 - 32   2016 $200

Lees-Milne, James *Heretics in Love.* London: Chatto & Windus, 1973. First edition, spine little bruised at head and tail, very good in near fine dust jacket, little creased at edges.   Peter Ellis   112 - 214   2016   £45

Lees-Milne, James *Round the Clock.* London: Chatto and Windus, 1978. First edition, octavo, spine just trifle bumped at head and tail, near fine in very good dust jacket creased at edges.   Peter Ellis   112 - 215   2016   £75

Lefeuvre, Marie Anne *Bazareries.* Paris: Lefeuuvre, 1991. Limited to 47 numbered copies, written and illustrated by Lefeuvre, small square 4to., four signatures loose in cover, folded white card covers decorated with relief title and illustrations on front cover and turn-ins.   Oak Knoll Books   27 - 35   2016 $450

Lefevre D'Etaples, Jacques *Musica Libris Quatuor Demonstrata.* Paris: Guillaume Cavellat, 1551. First separate edition and first illustrated edition, 4to., large woodcut printer's device on title, text diagrams, tables, woodcut initials, early 19th century calf, gilt, neatly rebacked retaining original spine, title very slightly soiled, faint marginal foxing, modern booklabel.   Joseph J. Felcone, Inc.   Books from Five Centuries: a Miscellany - 88   2016 $4800

Lehane, Dennis *A Drink Before the War.* New York: HBJ, 1994. First edition, book near fine, bottom corners bumped, dust jacket fine, signed by author.   Bella Luna Books   2016 - t668   2016 $99

Lehane, Dennis *Mystic River.* New York: Morrow, 2001. First edition, very fine in dust jacket.   Mordida Books   2015 - 009675   2016 $65

Lehane, Dennis *Prayers for rain.* New York: Morrow, 1999. First edition, fine in dust jacket.   Mordida Books   2015 - 009674   2016 $65

Lehane, Dennis *Shutter Island.* New York: Mottow, 2003. First edition, very fine in dust jacket, signed by author.   Mordida Books   2015 - 008846   2016 $55

Lehman, Frederic *The Sacred Landscape.* Berkeley: Celestial Arts, 1988. Special slipcased edition, original pictorial and gilt stamped cloth, 4to., custom slipcase with silk ribbon, illustrated with landscape photos, long and warm inscription by Lehman, fine in slipcase.   Gene W. Baade, Books on the West   2015 - SHEL715   2016 $150

Lehmann, Frederick W. *A Charles Dickens Collection of Superlative Merit and Equally fine First Editions of American and English Authors: The Library of the Hon. Frederick W. Lehmann.* New York: American Art Association Anderson Galleries, 1930. Illustrations, original cream printed wrappers, slightly dusted, very good.   Jarndyce Antiquarian Booksellers   CCXVIII - 1508   2016   £20

Lehmann, John *Poems for Spain.* London: Hogarth Press, 1939. First edition, cloth little faded at spine and edges, free endpapers spotted and browned, very good in good soiled, rubbed and heavily spotted dust jacket.   Peter Ellis   112 - 379   2016   £45

Lehmann, John *Virginia Woolf and Her World.* London: Thames and Hudson, 1975. First edition, royal octavo, copiously illustrated, fine in near fine dust jacket very slightly creased at edges.   Peter Ellis   112 - 452   2016   £25

Leibovitz, Annie *Photographs.* New York: Rolling Stone Press, 1983. First edition, quarto, gray cloth, minor indentation to small spot of front cover, else fine in worn and lightly soiled dust jacket, photos.   Argonaut Book Shop   Photography 2015 - 4083   2016 $45

Leibovitz, Annie *Photographs 1970-1990.* New York: Harper Collins, 1991. First edition, one of 300 specially bound and slipcased copies, signed by Leibovitz, 4to., illustrations, original cloth, cloth slipcase, as new.   James S. Jaffe Rare Books   Occasional List: Winter 2016 - 113   2016 $1500

Leibovitz, Annie *Pilgrimage.* New York: Random House, 2011. Color photographs, very fine in like dust jacket with fine wraparound band, signed by Leibovitz in year of publication.   Jeff Hirsch Books   Holiday List 2015 - 81   2016 $1100

Leigh, Charles *The Natural History of Lancashire, Cheshire and the Peak in Derbyshire with an Account of the British, Phoencian, Armenian...* Oxford: printed for the author, 1700. First edition, folio, 24 plates, including portrait frontispiece, 2 further plates of subscribers; coats of arms plus folding, hand colored map, old spots of foxing, edges little toned, occasional dirt to top margins, portrait repaired at gutter, closed tear to first page of Book II affecting text but with no loss, recent half tan calf, spine blind tooled with gilt title and raised bands, brown cloth boards, endpapers renewed, spine little sunned, few white specks, very good, sound.   Unsworths Antiquarian Booksellers Ltd.   E05 - 6   2016   £650

Leighton, Edward *Joseph, a Model for the Young...* Hamilton, Adams & Co., 1838. Second edition, 12mo., original blue cloth, spine lettered gilt, back board slightly damp marked, presentation label of Sheffield Lancasterian School, fine.   Jarndyce Antiquarian Books   CCXV - 294   2016   £48

Leighton, John *Select Views of Glasgow and Its Environs.* Glasgow: published by Joseph Swan, 1828. First edition, 276 x 216mm., handsome 19th century polished calf, covers with elaborate floral roll fame in gilt and blind, raised bands decorated with four gilt rules terminating in an arabesque at either end, gilt compartment formed by thick, thin and dotted rules, tan morocco title label, turn-ins tooled in blind, all edges gilt, 33 engraved scenic plates printed on india paper and mounted, original tissue guards (one missing), very thin crack along top three inches of front joint, joints otherwise not seriously worn, one large and two small abrasions to lower cover, original decorative binding solid, especially lustrous and altogether pleasing, hint of foxing (only) to some plates (two plates bit more foxed), endpapers and first few leaves at front and back with faint discoloration at corners (apparently from glue), otherwise fine internally - fresh, bright and clean throughout, first-rate impressions of engravings.   Phillip J. Pirages   67 - 235   2016 $950

Leiris, Michel *Verve - The French Review of Art Volume VIII No. 29/30.* Paris: Teriade, 1954. First English edition distributed in Great Britain by A. Swemmer, folio, double number devoted to Picasso, 180 drawings, 16 color lithographs, 164 heliogravures, color pictorial boards by Picasso, ownership signature of Ronald Searle, covers bit rubbed at edges, tail of spine slightly chipped, very good.   Peter Ellis   112 - 296   2016   £1500

Lemaistre, John Gustavus *Frederick Latimer or the History of a Young Man of Fashion.* London: printed by Luke Hansard No. 6 Great Turnstile..., 1799. 12mo., contemporary mottled calf, gilt borders, very skillfully rebacked with triple gilt bands, small gilt device in each compartment, red and gilt morocco labels, original silk markers in each volume, some very slight rubbing to board edges.   Jarndyce Antiquarian Booksellers   CCXVI - 360   2016   £650

Lemant, Albert *Bebetes.* N.P.: Albert Lemant, 1991. Limited to 50 numbered copies signed by Lemant, titlepage and colophon page hand lettered, portfolio containing 6 engravings, each number 24/50 signed by Lemant, 4to., stiff paper portfolio with sheets loosely inserted, wooden slipcase with color image mounted on front.   Oak Knoll Books   27 - 36   2016 $450

Lemarchand, Elizabeth *Alibi for a Corpse.* London: Harte Davis, 1969. First edition, fine in dust jacket, signed by author.   Mordida Books   2015 - 012161   2016 $65

Lemarchand, Georges *Conseil Municipal de Paris 1911.* Paris: Imprimerie Municipole, 1911. First edition, 4to., contemporary blue half cloth over marbled boards, spine lettered gilt, marbled endpapers, 37 plates, maps and plans, title little browned and with small old repair to corner, signed presentation inscription to poet Jules Condere, with his etched bookplate and signature and address, author's business card tipped in.   Sotheran's Travel and Exploration - 262   2016   £248

Lemon, Mark *The Chimes... a drama in four quarters...* London: Webster and Co., 1845. Original buff printed wrappers, spines slightly split at head, very good, frontispiece.   Jarndyce Antiquarian Booksellers   CCXVIII - 375   2016   £250

Lendenfeld, R. Von *Descriptive Catalogue of the Medusae of the Australian Seas.* Sydney: Australian Museum, 1887. Octavo, 2 parts, early binder's cloth, titlepage lightly spotted, very good, scarce.   Andrew Isles Natural History Books   55 - 36436   2016 $450

Lennox, Charlotte   1720-1804 *The Female Quioxte, or the Adventures of Arabella.* London: printed for A. Millar...., 1752. First edition, 12mo., small marginal tear without loss to C2 volume I, long vertical tear to left hand edge N2 in same volume, possibly original paper flaw, several gatherings little proud in binding, full contemporary sprinkled calf, raised & gilt banded spines, red morocco labels, gilt volume numbers, small gilt device for each compartment, from the library of Invercauld Castle, Braemar.   Jarndyce Antiquarian Booksellers   CCXVI - 361   2016   £850

Lenrow, Elbert *The Letters of Richard Wagner to Anton Pusinelli.* New York: Knopf, 1932. first edition, 1/200 copies, numbered and signed by author, 8vo., spine sunned, else nice in box, little faded and worn.   Second Life Books, Inc.   196 B - 43   2016 $75

Lenski, Lois *Coal Camp girl.* Philadelphia: Lippincott, 1959. Stated first edition, 8vo., cloth, fine in dust jacket (small chip, slight fraying and slight soil, very good+), illustrations by author.   Aleph-bet Books, Inc.   111 - 260   2016 $200

Lenski, Lois *Little Farm.* New York: Oxford University Press, 1942. First edition, 8vo., pictorial cloth, fine in dust jacket (slightly faded else near fine), full page color and grey tone illustrations.   Aleph-bet Books, Inc.   112 - 288   2016 $425

Lenski, Lois *Two Brothers and their Animal Friends.* New York: Stokes Co., 1929. First edition, landscape small 8vo., original mid green sand grained cloth with single line pastel in blind to upper board, lettered in black to spine, onlaid pictorial label to upper cover, pictorial green endpapers, 12 whimsical colored plates and others in line, attractive copy, some light external dusting, small rubbing to spine ends and small and difuse, white mark to lower cover, internally clean, neat contemporary gift inscription, scarce in commerce.   Sotheran's   Piccadilly Notes - Summer 2015 - 191   2016   £248

Lenski, Lois *The Wonder City.* New York: Coward McCann, 1929. First edition, 4to., pictorial boards, fine in dust jacket (very good with some chips, wear at folds, one mend), illustrations by author, rare.   Aleph-bet Books, Inc.   112 - 289   2016 $1200

Leonard, Elmore *Bandits.* New York: Arbor House, 1987. First edition, very fine in dust jacket.   Mordida Books   2015 - 006846   2016 $65

Leonard, Elmore *Freaky Deaky.* New York: Arbor House, 1988. First edition, fine in dust jacket, signed by author.   Mordida Books   2015 - 012164   2016 $65

Leonard, Elmore *Get Shorty.* New York: Delacorte, 1990. First printing, 8vo, paper over boards with cloth spine, author's presentation to Bill Claire, cover slightly darkened at ends of spine, otherwise near fine in sightly yellowed dust jacket.   Second Life Books, Inc.   197 - 208   2016 $200

Leonard, Elmore *Gold Coast.* Allen, 1982. First hardback edition, usual marginal browning to text leaves, foolscap 8vo., original light blue boards, backstrip gilt lettered, dust jacket trifle creased at head of rear panel with light foxing to flaps, very good.   Blackwell's Rare Books   B186 - 255   2016   £400

Leonard, Elmore *The Law at Randado.* Boston: Houghton Mifflin Co., 1955. First edition, octavo, boards, signed by author, some rubbing at board corners, very good in good dust jacket with chips at upper corners and upper left spine fold, 1 x 3cm. piece missing from lower left spine panel, spine panel background color faded from orginal light green to pale blue and some mild rubbing, front panel largely complete and presents well.   John W. Knott, Jr./L.W. Currey, Inc.   Fall-Winter 2015 - 16850   2016 $1750

Leonard, Elmore *Mr. Majestyk.* New York: Dell, 1974. First edition, fine, some tiny nicks along front cover edge and nick at base of spine, otherwise fine, unread copy in wrappers.   Mordida Books   2015 - 012137   2016 $65

Leonard, Herman *Jazz Memories.* Levallois-Perret: Editions Filipcachi, 1995. Text in French with English translation inserted, black and white photos, fine in fine dust jacket, signed by Leonard, fresh copy.   Jeff Hirsch Books   Holiday List 2015 - 82   2016 $200

Leonardo, Richard *History of Gynecology.* New York: Froben Press, 1944. Frotnsipiece, 25 illustrated plates, very good in original blue cloth, clean and tight.   James Tait Goodrich   X-78 - 421   2016 $125

Leonardo, Richard *History of Surgery.* New York: Froben Press, 1943. 100 plates, original green pbulisher's cloth, some light wear, overall very nice.   James Tait Goodrich   X-78 - 374   2016 $175

Lerner, Nathan *Modernist Eye: the Art and Design of Nathan Lerner.* Raleigh: Gallery of Art & Design, 2000. First edition, softcover exhibition catalog, numerous color and black and white images, very fine in stapled wrappers, fairly uncommon.   Jeff Hirsch Books   E-List 80 - 19 2016 $75

Leroux, Gaston *The Phantom of the Opera.* New York: Dell, 1943. Paperback edition, some binding wrinkling on spine, otherwise fine unread copy.   Mordida Books   2015 - 1161   2016 $65

Leslie, Charles *A Short and Easy method with the Deists...* London: printed for F. & C. Rivington, 1799. 12mo., uncut in later purple brown sugar paper wrappers. Jarndyce Antiquarian Booksellers   CCXVI - 362 2016 £45

Leslie, George Dunlop *Letters to Marco.* London: Macmillan, 1893. Presentation to John Ruskin from G. D. Leslie, Dec. 20, 1993, very good in original dark green cloth boards, gilt title to spine and gilt floral decoration to front cover, minor wear to edges of boards and corners, interior clean overall, occasional spots of foxing, short closed tear to bottom edge of titlepage, minor repairs to both interior hinges, very good.   The Kelmscott Bookshop   13 - 31   2016 $450

Lesseps, Ferdinand De *Compagnie Universelle de Canal Maritime de Suez.* Paris: typogrpahie de Henri Plon, 1869. First edition, 8vo., original printed wrappers, 3 prelim leaves, 4 maps and 2 folding tables, uncut, excellent copy. Howard S. Mott Inc.   265 - 121   2016 $250

Lester, Julius *The Last Tales of Uncle Remus.* New York: Dial, 1994. First edition, 8vo., illustrations by Jerry Pinkey signed by artist on title, paper over boards with cloth spine, about as new in dust jacket.   Second Life Books, Inc.   196 B - 46   2016 $50

Lester, Julius *Look Out Whitey! Black Power's gon' get your mama.* New York: Dial, 1968. Third printing, 8vo., author's presentation on flyleaf, black cloth, edges slightly soiled, otherwise very good, tight in scuffed dust jacket. Second Life Books, Inc.   196 B - 47   2016 $45

Lestock, Richard *Vice Adm-l L-st-k's Account of the Late Engagement Near Toulon, Between His Majesty's Fleet and the Fleets of France and Spain...* London: printed for M. Cooper, 1745. 8vo., ad on titlepage verso, some light damp marking to upper margins, disbound.   Jarndyce Antiquarian Booksellers   CCXVI - 363   2016   £110

A Letter from a Mother to her Daughter at a Boarding School. London: RTS, 1802. Disbound.   Jarndyce Antiquarian Books   CCXV - 295   2016   £25

The Letter Sent from Don Blass de Lezo the Spanish Admiral at Carthegena to Don Thomas Geraldino, Versify'd. N.P.: London: published from the copy printed at Jamica and now reprinted for T. Gardner, 1740. First London edition, folio, disbound, fine.   C. R. Johnson Rare Book Collections Foxon: H-P 2015 - 535   2016 $3064

A Letter to the Author of An Enquiry into the Revenue, Credit and Commerce of France. London: J. Roberts, 1742. First edition, 8vo., without half title, but with two folding tables, large crisp copy bound in early 20th century half roan, joints worn, uncut.   John Drury Rare Books   2015 - 14634   2016 $350

Letters Concerning the Labors of Mr. John Augustus, the Well Known Philanthropist from one Who Knows Him. Boston: published for private circulation, Dec., 1858. First edition, 8vo., sewn as issued.   M & S Rare Books, Inc.   99 - 28   2016 $350

Letters, Poems and Tales: Amorous, Satyrical and Gallant. London: printed for E. Curll, 1718. First edition, 8vo, disbound, fine.   C. R. Johnson Rare Book Collections Foxon: H-P 2015 - 536   2016 $2661

Lettsom, John Coakley *An Address to Parents and Guardians of Children and Others on Variolous and Vaccine Inoculations.* London: J. Nichols, 1803. Rare, , early 20th century paste boards with leather spine label, text uncut, well margined, some light foxing and toning.   James Tait Goodrich   X-78 - 377   2016 $495

Lettsom, John Coakley *History of the Origin of Medicine: an Oration Delivered at the Anniversary Meeing of the Medical Society of London Jan. 19 1778.* London: printed by J. Phillips, 1778. Portrait as frontispiece with hand colored engraved folding plate, second uncolored plate is not present in this copy, this plate identical to colored, 4to., contemporary full sheep, some rubbing, text with light foxing and browning, otherwise very good, tall uncut copy.   James Tait Goodrich   X-78 - 375   2016 $1250

Lettsom, John Coakley *The Naturalist's and Traveller's Companion.* London: printed for the author, 1772. First edition, Hand colored frontispiece, contemporary marbled wrappers, worn, rare, with plate hand colored and beautifully preserved.   James Tait Goodrich   X-78 - 376   2016 $695

Lever, Charles *The Martins of Cro' Martin.* London: Chapman and Hall, 1856. First edition, numerous full page plates, illustrations by Phiz, contemporary three quarter polished calf binding, light rubbing to extremities, half inch split at top of front hinge, small bump to top edge of front cover, first few leaves foxed, very good.   Argonaut Book Shop Literature 2015 - 4894   2016 $150

Lever, Christopher *The Cane Toad; the History and Ecology of a Successful Colonist.* Otley: Westbury Academic and Scientific Pub., 2001. Octavo, color photos, fine in dust jacket. Andrew Isles Natural History Books 55 - 18339   2016 $150

Levertov, Denise *Embroideries.* Los Angeles: Black Sparrow, 1969. First edition, of a total edition of 700, this is one of 250 copies sewn in wrappers, 8vo., wrappers little soiled, this copy signed by author Oct. 6th 1984, very good. Second Life Books, Inc.   196 B - 49   2016 $50

Levertov, Denise *The Jacob's Ladder.* New Directions, 1961. First edition, original wrappers, some rubbed, good copy, signed by author.   Second Life Books, Inc.   196 B - 52   2016 $125

Levertov, Denise *Wanderer's Daysong.* Copper Canyon Press, 1981. One of approximately 240 copies, small 4to., paper over boards with cloth spine, author's signature on colophon, cover little faded at spine, otherwise nice. Second Life Books, Inc.   196 B - 51   2016 $100

Levesque, Pierre Charles *Collection des Moralistes Anciens Dediés au Roi.* Paris: Didot and Burre, 1782-1783. First French edition, 12mo., 2 volumes in one, calf backed pebble grained cloth of about 1835, spine ruled and lettered gilt, marbled endpapers, head and tail of spine little worn, internally clean and fresh, ink name of Joseph Mazzini Wheeler, translator and editor.   Sotheran's   Travel and Exploration - 149   2016   £348

Levi, Primo *Se Questo e un Uomo. (If This a man).* Torino: Einaudi, 1963. Fourth edition, 8vo., original cloth, dust jacket, signed by author, cocked, ink owner's name, otherwise very good in somewhat worn jacket, reinforced with cellotape in few places, from the library of Dr. Cesare Lombroso, of Harvard med. School, rare signed.   James S. Jaffe Rare Books   Occasional List: Winter 2016 - 92   2016 $2500

Levret, Andre *Essay Sur l'Abus des Regles Generales et Contre Les Prejuges qui s'upposent aus Progres de L'Art Des Accouchemens Avec Figures.* Paris: Prault, 1766. First edition, 8vo., one folding plate, contemporary full calf, newly rebacked in calf, internally very nice.   James Tait Goodrich   X-78 - 379   2016 $595

Levy, D. A. *Prose: on Poetry in the Wholesale Education and Cultural System.* Milwaukee: Gunrunner Press, 1968. Uncommon first edition, one of 300 copies printed, mild edge sunning, else fine in stapled wrappers.   Ken Lopez Bookseller   166 - 69   2016 $500

Levy, Jacques *Cesar Chavez: Autobiography of La Causa.* New York: W. W. Norton, 1975. First edition, inscribed by Chavez for Ben Barken, fine in bright, near fine dust jacket.   Royal Books   48 - 79   2016 $350

Levy, Jo Ann *Unsettling the West Eliza Farnham and Georgiana Bruce Kirby in Frontier California.* Santa Clara and Berkeley: Santa Clara University and Heyday Books, 2004. First edition, presentation inscription, signed by author, illustrations, cloth backed boards, very fine with dust jacket.   Argonaut Book Shop   Biography 2015 - 6786   2016 $50

Lewandowski, Ranier *Die Filme von Volker Schlondorff.* Hildesham: Olma Presse, 1981. First edition, trade softcover original, inscribed by Volker Schlondorff for Pierre Goulliard, near fine, profusely illustrated with photos, stiff perfect bound wrappers, fine, 8.5 x 9.5 inches.   Royal Books   49 - 24   2016 $1250

Lewin, John William *A Natural History of the Birds of New South Wales...* Melbourne: Queensberry Hill Press, 1978. Limited to 500 numbered copies, folio, text erratically paginated, color plates, publisher's handsome brown full calf, solander box.   Andrew Isles Natural History Books   55 - 15097   2016 $500

Lewis, Caroline *Lost in Blunderland: the Further Adventures of Clara.* London: William Heinemann, 1903. Tenth edition, duodecimo, olive green cloth over boards lettered and pictorially stamped in red and black, very good, extremities bumped and mildly rubbed, spine subtly darkened, rolled, endpapers, prelims and terminal pages foxed, cloth on lower third of rear board rippled, text block is cracked at center, book still very sturdy.   Ken Sanders Rare Books   E Catalogue # 1 - 26   2016 $50

Lewis, Clive Staples   1898-1963 *The Four Loves.* London: Geoffrey Bles, 1960. First edition, Christian themed bookplate, extreme head of spine faded, very good in very good price clipped and slightly spotted dust jacket with closed tear at hinge of upper flap.   Peter Ellis   112 - 218   2016   £75

Lewis, Clive Staples   1898-1963 *The Lion, The Witch and the Wardrobe.* New York: Macmillan, 1905. Stated first printing, 8vo., cloth, except for bit of inevitable fading and always occurs with this title, fine in near fine dust jacket (with touch of fading on rear panel and ever so slightly rubbed), illustrations in black and white by Pauline Baynes, amazingly nice, rare in this condition.   Aleph-bet Books, Inc.   112 - 293   2016 $3000

Lewis, Clive Staples   1898-1963 *Out of the Silent Planet.* London: Bodley Head, 1938. First edition, occasional light foxing to borders with couple of pages more heavily spotted, crown 8vo., original burgundy cloth, backstrip lettered gilt with slight lean to spine, very slight bowing to boards, edges little rubbed, top edge dust soiled with color faded, few spots to other edges, pencilled numerals (some dates) to rear pastedown, bookseller label at foot, ownership inscription of Geoffrey Faber.   Blackwell's Rare Books   B186 - 257   2016   £1750

Lewis, Clive Staples 1898-1963 *Surprised by Joy - the Shape of My Early Life.* London: Geoffrey Bles, 1955. First edition, octavo, spine bumped at head, prelims spotted, very good in very good dust jacket creased and nicked at edges.   Peter Ellis   112 - 219   2016   £75

Lewis, E., Mrs. *Domestic Service in the Present Day.* London: Elliot Stock, 1889. Fifth thousand, small tear to upper corner of page 77/76, original blue grey cloth, slightly dulled, recent bookseller's ticket on following pastedown. Jarndyce Antiquarian Books   CCXV - 296   2016   £75

Lewis, F. G. *Characters from Dickens.* London: Chapman & Hall, 1912. 4to., portfolio of 20 Vandyck gravures from drawings by Lewin, 4to. the 20 leaves with sepia printed plates laid in, loosely inserted (as issued) into drab pictorial boards, red cloth spine, slightly rubbed, one silk tie broken. Jarndyce Antiquarian Booksellers   CCXVIII - 959   2016   £75

Lewis, Griselda *A Picture History of English Pottery.* London: Hutton Press, 1956. First edition, 4to., numerous color and black and white plates, black cloth, spine ends rubbed, dust jacket worn, else fine.   Argonaut Book Shop Pottery and Porcelain 2015 - 1495   2016 $35

Lewis, Isaac *The Political Advantages of Godliness. A Sermon, Preached before his Excellency the Governor.* Hartford: printed in Hudson & Goodwin, 1797. First edition, 8vo., stitched paper wrappers, half title, bottom quarter of last leaf torn away without loss of text, else very good, untrimmed, contemporary owner's signatures on half title. Kaaterskill Books   21 - 46   2016 $200

Lewis, Janet *The Wheel in Midsummer.* Lynn: Lone Gull, 1927. First edition, octavo, original decorated stiff paper wrappers and printed paper label, rare, fine.   The Brick Row Book Shop   Miscellany 69 - 54   2016 $375

Lewis, Jenny *(Poetry in the making). Catalogue of an Exhibition of Poetry Manuscripts in the British Museum April-June 1967.* London: Turret Books, 1967. First edition, limited to 126 copies signed by Philip Larkin, Day Lewis, Skeat and Jenny Lewis, fine in dust jacket, 8vo., illustrations, original cloth.   James S. Jaffe Rare Books   Occasional List: Winter 2016 - 91   2016 $400

Lewis, John *A Complete History of the Several Translations of the Holy Bible.* London: printed by H. Woodfall for Joseph Pote, 1739. Full contemporary sprinkled calf, gilt ruled borders, neatly rebacked retaining gilt decorated spine, red morocco label, 8vo., engraved folding plate, some slight browning and occasional minor foxing, front edge of titlepage.   Jarndyce Antiquarian Booksellers CCXVI - 364   2016   £3800

Lewis, Leon *The Landscape of Contemporary Cinema.* Buffalo: Buffalo Spectrum Press, 1967. First edition, octavo, illustrated perfect bound wrapper, very slight soiling on wrappers, still fine, inscribed by William David Sherman to author John Barth with Barth's ownership signature and ownership stamp, laid in ALS from Sherman to Barth sending the book.   Between the Covers Rare Books   204 - 43   2016 $225

Lewis, Matthew Gregory 1775-1818 *Tales of Wonder.* London: Printed by W. Bulmer & Co, for the author, 1801. First edition, royal octavo, 2 volumes, period binding of full marbled calf with intricate gilt decoration, leather title labels, marbled edges and endpapers, in the middle of each cover is gilt monogram initial "D" surmounted by winged crown, few stains in margins of first volume, upper joint of second volume cracking, very good set, armorial bookplate (Frederick Leigh Colvile) with inscription "from my Uncle Chandos Leigh".   Peter Ellis   112 - 220   2016   £675

Lewis, Matthew Gregory 1775-1818 *Tales of Wonder.* London: printed by W. Bulmer and Co. for the author, 1801. First edition, 2 volumes, 260 x 159mm., contemporary calf in Etruscan style, possibly by Edwards of Halifax, each cover with gilt floral spray border (unusual for this style of binding) surrounding a terra cotta and deep burnt orange frame with palmettes stamped in black and blind, this frame enclosing panel diced and dotted in blind and with gilt cornerpieces and central medallion featuring an incised monochrome mythological painting, double raised bands flanking gilt pentaglyph and metope roll, gilt ruled spine compartments with open gilt dots and classical ornaments in blind, turn-ins with greek key gilt roll, marbled edges, neatly rebacked using most of original spines, hinges reinforced with matching paper in first volume and matching cloth in second, bookplate of E.L.", bookplate of Harry H. Blum, central images on covers of volume II somewhat indistinct, few leaves with faint spots, otherwise excellent, carefully restored binding, still retaining much of its original impressiveness and text very crisp and clean.   Phillip J. Pirages   67 - 42   2016 $1500

Lewis, Meriwether 1774-1809 *Original Journals of the Lewis and Clark Expedition 1804-1806.* New York: Dodd, Mead & Co., 1904. One of 200 numbered copies on Van Gelder handmade paper, large quarto, 7 volumes, extended to 14, plus atlas volume, with a profusion of plates, facsimiles, folding maps &c., green cloth, bindings moderately worn at extremities, cloth lightly discolored as usual, but very good with largely unopened text.   Joseph J. Felcone, Inc. Books from Five Centuries: a Miscellany - 89   2016 $8000

Lewis, Meriwether 1774-1809 *Original Journals of the Lewis and Clark Expedition 1804-1806.* New York: Dodd, Mead & Co., 1904. First edition, first printing, edition deluxe limited to 50 copies, this number 34 printed on Imperial Japan paper with all volumes marked on colophons, large quarto, 33 plates in two states, black and white and hand tinted in color, 15 folio volumes, including atlas, original tan buckram, decoratively stamped in gilt, front covers inset with color portraits of Lewis and Clark, frontispieces in all volumes with tissue guards, with all 54 maps. Heritage Book Shop   Holiday 2015 - 73   2016 $22,500

Lewis, Meriwether 1774-1809 *Travels to the Source of the Missouri River and Across the American Continent to the Pacific Ocean...* London: Longman, Hurst, Rees, Orme and Brown, 1814. First English edition, quarto, contemporary marbled boards, superbly rebacked in style in modern three quarter calf, fine, text very clean, map with slight offsetting, otherwise with no tears, rare in such good condition. Manhattan Rare Book Company   2016 - 1793   2016 $38,000

Lewis, Michael *Liar's Poker.* New York: Norton, 1989. First edition, different paper stocks used in production resulting in three quarter of the pages being mildly age toned, otherwise fine in fine dust jacket with slight push at crown, uncommon.   Ken Lopez Bookseller   166 - 70   2016 $350

Lewis, Norman *Darkness Visible - a Novel.* London: Jonathan Cape, 1960. First edition, octavo, little bumped and faded at edges, very good, in very good dust jacket, marked, nicked and rubbed at edges, presentation copy inscribed by author for S. J. Perelman and his wife.   Peter Ellis   112 - 224   2016   £650

Lewis, Norman *Samara.* London: Jonathan Cape, 1949. First edition, octavo, very scarce, presentation copy inscribed by author to American humourist S. J. Perelman, very good in very good price clipped dust jacket, tanned and little defective at head and tail of spine and little torn, nicked and creased at edges.   Peter Ellis   112 - 221   2016   £1250

Lewis, Norman *A Single Pilgrim - a Novel.* London: Jonathan Cape, 1953. First edition, octavo, presentation copy inscribed by author for S. J. Perelman, covers bruised at head of spine and at top edge of upper board, very good in very good nicked, rubbed and creased dust jacket with closed tear at fold of upper flap.   Peter Ellis   112 - 222   2016   £650

Lewis, Norman *The Tenth Year of the Ship.* London: Collins, 1962. First edition, octavo, head of spine and upper corners little bruised, very good in very good dust jacket, nicked and rubbed, little defective at tail of spine, presentation copy inscribed by author for S. J. Perelman and his wife.   Peter Ellis   112 - 225   2016   £650

Lewis, Oscar *A Family of Builders.* San Francisco: privately printed, 1961. First edition, one of 1000 copies, 12 leaves of photos, handset type in red and black, brown and white decorated boards, reddish brown cloth spine, printed paper spine label, very fine.   Argonaut Book Shop   Private Press 2015 - 6333   2016 $60

Lewis, Oscar *Hearn and His Biographers.* San Francisco: Westgate Press, 1930. First edition, variant binding, one of 350 copies printed, facsimile photo tipped in, 3 facsimile letters, 2 facsimile leaflets, printed tissue guards, dark grey cloth, patterned floral cloth boards, printed paper spine label, titlepage slightly soiled, fine.   Argonaut Book Shop   Literature 2015 - 5687   2016 $175

Lewis, Oscar *The Lost Years. A biographical fantasy.* New York: Alfred A. Knopf, 1951. First edition, presentation inscription signed by author to bookbinder and designer, Herbert Fahey, illustrations by Mallette Dean, brown and white decorated boards, fine with pictorial dust jacket (slight chip), laid in is photos of author.   Argonaut Book Shop   Literature 2015 - 7190   2016 $60

Lewis, Sinclair 1885-1951 *Ann Vickers.* London: Cape, 1933. Second impression, 8vo., publisher's cloth some soiled, very good, inscribed by author for Elizabeth Farmer Feb. 23 1933, bookplate of author Barbara Howes.   Second Life Books, Inc.   196 B - 65   2016 $600

Lewis, Sinclair 1885-1951 *Dodsworth.* New York: Harcourt Brace and Co., 1929. First edition, Near fine, dark blue cloth stamped in orange, hint of sunning to spine, very lightly starting at page 376/377, otherwise sturdy binding, few faint spots to top edge, otherwise fresh pages, overal very clean and attractive.   B & B Rare Books, Ltd.   2016 - SL016   2016 $50

Lewis, Sinclair 1885-1951 *Elmer Gantry.* New York: Brace and Co., 1927. First edition, first issue with 'Gantry' spelled 'Cantry' on spine, endpapers slightly toned, fine in about very good dust jacket with several internal tape repairs, very small shallow chips at spine ends, light erasure on front panel, despite several flaws, presentable copy.   Between the Covers Rare Books   204 - 65   2016 $800

Lewis, Sinclair 1885-1951 *Kingsblood Royal.* New York: Random House, 1947. First edition, limited to 1050 copies signed by author, large paper copy, nice, tight copy.   Second Life Books, Inc.   196 B - 66   2016 $225

Lewis, Sinclair 1885-1951 *Main Street.* New York: Harcourt Brace and Co., 1920. Later printing, presentation signed by author, small octavo, blue cloth, minor wear to spine ends, spine and cover slightly faded, else fine.   Argonaut Book Shop   Literature 2015 - 7349   2016 $500

Lewis, Wilmarth Sheldon *One Man's Education.* New York: Knopf, 1967. First edition, 8vo., 32 pages of illustrations, author's presentation on flyleaf, obits and other clippings laid in, blue cloth, slightly scuffed at edges of cover, otherwise nice in price clipped and little chipped and faded dust jacket.   Second Life Books, Inc.   196 B - 67   2016 $56

Lewis, Wyndham   1882-1957 *Apes of Gold.* London: Arthur Press, 1930. First edition, limited numbered, signed edition, no. 92 of 750 copies, original cream colored cloth in discolored as shown in images of actual book, but turquoise lettering still bright on spine, extremities bumped, interior remains bright, crisp, clean, despite some pale spotting to titlepage, endpapers and text block edges, small tear to fore-edge of pages 307-313 perhaps from original publication, no text affected.   Simon Finch   2015 - 001707   2016 $195

Lewis, Wyndham   1882-1957 *The Apes of God.* Arthur Press, 1930. First edition, 341/750 copies signed by author, recurrent light foxing to borders, royal 8vo., original tan cloth with little spotting overall, backstrip lettered in green spotting to edges, armorial bookplate of Wyndham Edward Buckley Lloyd, foxing to free endpapers, dust jacket darkened and lightly dust soiled overall, rubbed at folds with edges little frayed, light chipping to corners and tips of backstrip panel with small hole at foot of Latter, good.   Blackwell's Rare Books   B186 - 259   2016   £425

Lewis, Wyndham   1882-1957 *The Diabolical Principle and the Duhyramble Spectator.* London: Chatto & Windus, 1931. First edition, first issue, octavo in red buckram with gilt lettering on spine, fine in very good dust jacket, slightly creased with no fading at all to end parts, lovely bright copy.   Peter Ellis   112 - 227   2016   £450

Lewis, Wyndham   1882-1957 *Francois Villon.* New York: Literary Guild of America, 1928. Signed by author 8vo., little soiled cloth, very good.   Second Life Books, Inc.   196 B - 55   2016 $45

Lewis, Wyndham   1882-1957 *The Jews - Are they Human?* London: George Allen & Unwin, 1939. First edition, octavo, small patch of fading at tail of spine and another at bottom edge of rear cover, very good in very good dust jacket, slightly nicked with some fading to spine.   Peter Ellis   112 - 229   2016   £575

Lewis, Wyndham   1882-1957 *Left Wings Over Europe: or How to Make a War About Nothing.* London: Jonathan Cape, 1936. First edition, octavo, TLS Sept. 26 1936 by author mounted on front endpaper, recipient unknown, fine in scarce, very good dust jacket little nicked and rubbed at edges and repaired on reverse in three places.   Peter Ellis   112 - 232   2016   £750

Lewis, Wyndham   1882-1957 *The Mysterious Mr. Bull.* London: Robert Hale, 1938. First edition, octavo, tapemarks at outer corners of free endpapers, very good in very good dust jacket nicked and rubbed at edges, closed tear of approximately a inch at tail of spine.   Peter Ellis   112 - 231   2016   £250

Lewis, Wyndham   1882-1957 *One-Way Song.* London: Metheun, 1960. Second edition but first to contain foreword by T. S. Eliot, octavo, fine in near fine dust jacket, slightly darkened at spine.   Peter Ellis   112 - 226   2016   £35

Lewis, Wyndham   1882-1957 *Snooty Baronet.* London: Cassell, 1932. First edition, first issue in brown cloth lettered in gilt, octavo, fine in scarce very good dust jacket little faded at spine and edges and with minuscule chip at bottom edge of lower panel.   Peter Ellis   112 - 230 2016   £600

Lewis, Wyndham   1882-1957 *The Vulgar Streak.* London: Robert Hale, 1941. First edition, octavo, head of spine bit bumped, small scuff to tail of spine, very good in very good, slightly nicked dust jacket slgthly faded at spine, scarce.   Peter Ellis   112 - 227   2016   £575

Ley, Madeleine *La Nuit De La St. Sylvain.* Paris: Calmann-Levy, 1935. First edition, large 4to., pictorial boards, slight edge wear and rear cover soil, really very good+ to fine in dust jacket (frayed, some chips but very good+), printed on colored paper.   Aleph-bet Books, Inc.   111 - 256   2016 $250

Liberty Belles: Eight Epochs in the Making of the American Girl. New York: The Bobbs Merrill Co., 1912. First edition, folio, cloth, title and illustrator gilt stamped on front cover dust jacket, fore-edge uncut, drawings by Howard Chandler Christy, dust jacket chipped at edges, previous owner's name on front endpaper.   Oak Knoll Books   310 - 27   2016 $1000

The Library of Fiction, or Family Story-Teller... London: Chapman and Hall, 1836-1837. First edition, first issue, 2 volumes, half titles, plates by Robert Seymour, Buss &c., uncut in later 19th century full crushed red morocco by Grieve of Edinburgh, gilt spines, borders & dentelles, elaborate gilt cornerpieces, original spine strips laid in, slight rubbing, overall very good, handsome, top edge gilt.   Jarndyce Antiquarian Booksellers   CCXVIII - 52   2016   £1250

The Library of Fiction, or Family Story-Teller... London: Chapman & Hall, 1836-1837. First edition, first issue, 2 volumes, half title volume 1 only, plates by Robert Seymour, Buss, etc, original dark blue diaper cloth, boards blocked in blind, spines lettered gilt within triple border frame, small repairs to spines & hinges, bookplates of Walter Thomas Wallace.   Jarndyce Antiquarian Booksellers   CCXVIII - 51 2016   £1600

Lichfield, Frederick *The Collection of Old Worcester Porcelain Formed by the late Mr. Robert Drane Exhibited by Albert Amor.* London: Albert Amor, 1922. First edition, very scarce, large thin quarto, 48 photographic plates, contemporary red cloth, gilt, bookplate, fine. Argonaut Book Shop Pottery and Porcelain 2015 - 4997 2016 $375

Lichten, Frances *Decortive Art of Victoria's Era.* New York: Scribner's, 1950. First edition, 4to., 96 pages of illustrations, 14 two-color pages, illustrated presentation from author on flyleaf, blue cloth stamped in black and gilt, edges little soiled, otherwise very good, tight copy in somewhat chipped, scuffed and soiled dust jacket. Second Life Books, Inc. 196 B - 70 2016 $150

Liddell, Mary *Little Machinery.* New York: Doubleday Page, 1926. First edition, 4to., cloth backed pictorial boards, owner inscription, fine in near fine dust jacket, rare, illustrations by author. Aleph-bet Books, Inc. 112 - 294 2016 $900

Liechtenstein, Princess Marie *Holland House.* London: Macmillan and Co., 1874. First edition, 2 volumes, handsome early 20th century blue gray crushed morocco by Bayntun, signed on front turn-ins, covers with double gilt fillet border, large central frame of gilt and black, elegant interlacing quatrefoil centerpiece (also in gilt and black), raised bands decorated with gilt dots, spines gilt in compartments repeating cover design elements, turn-ins with gilt French fillet, marbled endpapers, all edges gilt, original cloth binding at back of each volume, titlepage portrait miniatures, numerous woodcut illustrations in text, three portraits and 8 autograph facsimiles as called for, extra illustrated with 140 plates, 20 of these colored, mostly portraits, but with 24 views, three of these double page, isolated faint offsetting and other trivial imperfections, especially fine and pretty set, clean, fresh and bright internally, in lustrous virtually unworn binding. Phillip J. Pirages 67 - 30 2016 $1750

Life and Adventures of Robert, the Hermit of Massachusettes who has Lived 14 Years in a Cave Secluded from Human Society... Taken from his own mouth... Providence: H. Trumbull, 1829. One of two slightly varying editions, frontispiece, stitched in contemporary plain wrappers, some browning and soiling, else very nice. Joseph J. Felcone, Inc. Books from Five Centuries: a Miscellany - 90 2016 $450

The Life of Sir Robt. Cochran, prime-Minister to King James III of Scotland. London: printed and sold by A. Dodd &c, 1734. 8vo., disbound, slightly dusted. Jarndyce Antiquarian Booksellers CCXVI - 588 2016 £25

Lightwood, James Thomas *Charles Dickens and Music.* London: Charles H. Kelly, 1912. First edition, half title, frontispiece by George Cruikshank, original pale brown cloth, decorated and lettered in gilt, endpapers little browned, very good, bright copy. Jarndyce Antiquarian Booksellers CCXVIII - 1358 2016 £25

Liltved, William Rune *Cowries and Their Relatives of Southern Africa.* Cape Town: Seacomber Publications, 1989. Quarto, color photos, publisher's half morocco and marbled boards, collector's issue, this copy number 5 and signed by author. Andrew Isles Natural History Books 55 - 30871 2016 $300

Lily, William *Lily's Rules Construed Where Unto are Added Tho. Robinson's (sic) Heteroclites the Latin Syntaxis also there are added the rules for the Genders of Nouns and Preterperfect Tenses and Supines of Verbs in English alone.* London: printed by S. Buckley and T. Longman, 1736. Small 8vo., contemporary American speckled calf, minor browning, excellent copy. Howard S. Mott Inc. 265 - 79 2016 $350

Lily, William *A Short Introduction of Grammar, Generally to be Used.* printed by Bonham Norton, 1630. 4to., titlepage dusty, dampmark to fore-corners, some other spots and stains, repairs to blank, corners of titlepage and also to just some corners tips of next two and last six leaves, contemporary ownership inscription of William Houghton to titlepage and third leaf, 4to., sometime stitched into limp wrappers reusing a parchment manuscript of the sixteenth century, parchment somewhat unevenly trimmed around edges and externally dust soiled, sound. Blackwell's Rare Books Greek & Latin Classics VII - 55 2016 £1500

Lincoln, C. Eric *The Avenue, Clayton City.* New York: Morrow, 1988. First edition, paper over boards with cloth spine, author's signature on flyleaf, very slightly soiled at edges, else nice in yellowed dust jacket. Second Life Books, Inc. 196 B - 73 2016 $65

Lincoln, Leo L. *Postal History of Berkshire County Massachusetts 1790-1981.* Williamstown: Drickamer, 1982. 4to., signed by author, copiously illustrated, paper wrappers, nice. Second Life Books, Inc. 196 B - 72 2016 $45

Lind, L. R. *Studies in Pre-Vesalian Anatomy, Biography, Translations, Documents.* Philadelphia: 1975. Large 4to., original binding, illustrations, nic ein dust jacket. James Tait Goodrich X-78 - 380 2016 $125

Lindanus, Wilhelmus *Panoplia Evangelica, Sive De Verbo Dei Evangelico Libri Quinque. (bound with) Loci Communes Theologici Pro Ecclesia Catholica.* Coloniae: Agrippiane; Coloniae: Maternus Cholinus; Arnodi Birchmanni, 1560. 1559, Small folio, contemporary full leather over boards, rolled designs in blind, it had clasps at one time evidenced by nail marks, staining and small loss of leather on bottom board, edges soiled, as are first and last few pages, there are also quite worn at corners with some small paper loss, some small stains and very minor smudges throughout, attractive volume with hard-to-find texts. Oak Knoll Books 310 - 183 2016 $2750

Lindbergh, Anne Morrow *Gift from the Sea.* New York: Pantheon, 1955. First edition, review copy with publisher's slip laid in, light foxing to top page edges, light foxing to extremities and jacket and short closed tear to jacket heel, else near fine in near fine dust jacket, brief pencil notation on review slip.   Royal Books   48 - 78   2016 $475

Lindley, John   1799-1865 *The Elements of Botany, Structural, Physiological and Medical.*   London: Bradbury & Evans, 1849. Text illustrations, owner's inscription, some foxing throughout, grubby publisher's cloth.   Andrew Isles Natural History Books   55 - 11819   2016 $60

Lindley, John   1799-1865 *Pomologia Britannica; or Figures and Descriptions of the Most Important Varieties of Fruit Cultivated in Great Britain.*   London: Henry G. Bohn, 1841. First edition, 3 volumes, 245 x 150mm, contemporary green half morocco with marbled boards, spine gilt with fruit motifs, raised bands, red and brown morocco labels, gilt edges, 152 beautiful hand colored plates, bookplate of Joseph Greene and that of Sir Thomas Neame, edges and joints, bit rubbed, covers little scuffed, couple of minor marginal stains and occasional foxing, mostly on paper guards and very rarely affecting leaves with text, otherwise all plates fine, with particularly bright colors.   Phillip J. Pirages   67 - 242   2016 $15,000

Lindley, John   1799-1865 *Sertum Orchidaceum: a Wreath of the Most Beautiful Orchidaceous Flowers.*   New York: Johnson Reprint, 1973. Facsimile, limited to 1000 numbered copies, folio, 49 color plates, publisher's green cloth, fine.   Andrew Isles Natural History Books   55 - 15398   2016 $300

Lindsay, David *A Voyage to Arcturus.*   London: Methuen & Co., 1920. First edition, first issue, first binding, 1250 copies printed of which one of 500 to 600 in first issue binding, octavo, original red cloth, spine panel stamped in gold, front cover stamped in blind, endpapers replaced, some spotting and dustiness to edges, staining to front cover, spine dull with several small stains, gold spine lettering dull but complete, solid good copy.   John W. Knott, Jr./L.W. Currey, Inc.   Fall-Winter 2015 - 16568   2016 $950

Lindsay, Jack *William Blake.* Creative Will and the Poetic Image, 1927. First trade edition, one of 500 copies, printed on Japon vellum, decoration by Norman Lindsay, crown 8vo., original red cloth with green sides, backstrip lettered gilt, top corners lightly bumped, dust jacket with very light soiling, small penmark to front panel, very good, original prospectus also printed on Japon and order form laid in.   Blackwell's Rare Books   B184 - 256   2016   £80

Linduska, Joseph P. *Waterfowl Tomorrow.* Washington: United States Dept. of Interior, 1964. First edition, gilt pictorial cloth, illustrations, fine.   Gene W. Baade, Books on the West   2015 - 5001116   2016 $61

Lines, Samuel *A Few Incidents in the Life of Samuel Lines, Sen.* Birmingham: printed by Josiah Allen, Jun., 1862. First edition, 8vo., inscribed " To my granddaughter, Kate Lines May 31st 1862, original embossed cloth, printed paper label, clean copy.   Marlborough Rare Books   List 55 - 43   2016   £185

Ling, Nicholas *Politeuphuia, Wits Common-wealth...* London: printed by J. H. for W. Freeman at the Bible against the Middle Temple Gate.., 12mo., small ink splash to blank outer margin of N8-N12, engraved title mounted and neatly repaired along outer edge, printed titlepage little dusty, corners of first few leaves just slightly chipped, excellently rebound in quarter sprinkled calf, raised and gilt banded spine, red morocco label, marbled boards, vellum cornerpieces, fresh contemporary endpapers.   Jarndyce Antiquarian Booksellers   CCXVI - 365   2016   £3800

Lingwood, James *Franz Xaver Messerschmidt: Character Heads 1770-1783....*   London: Institute of Contemporary Arts, 1986. First edition, 4to., wrappers, loosely inserted 6 page ICA leaflet on the show, copiously illustrated in black and white, clean, bright, very good+.   Any Amount of Books   2015 - A90076   2016   £250

Linklater, Eric *Crises in Heaven: an Elysian comedy.* London: Macmillan, 1944. First edition, little worn dust jacket, signed by 17 members of the cast of the first London production. Second Life Books, Inc.   196 B - 76   2016 $225

Linstrum, Derek *Sir Jeffry Wyatville: Architect to the King.* Oxford: Clarendon Press, 1972. First edition, 4to., copiously illustrated in black and white, about fine in very good+ dust jacket slightly rubbed at edges, very slight fading at spine, neat name and date on verso of titlepage.   Any Amount of Books   2015 - A77851   2016   £170

Linton, William *Colossal Vestiages of the Older nations.* London: Longman, Green, Longman & Roberts, 1862. First edition, frontispiece, foldout diagram, untrimmed in original red wavy grained cloth, blocked in blind, front board lettered gilt, some minor repairs to head and tail of spine, bookplates of Charles Dickens, Sara R. Dunn and J. R. Ainslie, with "from the Library of Charles Dickens" label, very good in brown cloth foldover box, inscribed by Marion Bell to Dickens.   Jarndyce Antiquarian Booksellers   CCXVIII - 871   2016   £1650

Lionnet, Guy *The Seychelles.* Newton Abbot: David & Charles, 1972. First edition, 8vo., original cloth and wrapper, black and white illustrations, slight dampstain to top edges, very good, signature of R. J. Berry, professor.   Sotheran's Piccadilly Notes - Summer 2015 - 192   2016   £30

Lionni, Leo *Fredericks's Fables.* New York: Pantheon, 1985. Limited to 500 numbered copies signed by author, very scarce edition, 4to., cloth, touch of soil on corner, else fine in cloth slipcase (darkened on part of rear cover and edge else very good), illustrations in color, very scarce. Aleph-bet Books, Inc.   111 - 261   2016 $300

Lionni, Leo *Tico and the Golden Wings.* New York: Pantheon, 1964. Cloth backed pictorial boards, near fine in lightly soiled dust jacket, illustrations in color by author. Aleph-bet Books, Inc.   111 - 262   2016 $150

Lipton, Lew *Ideas.* New York: Chatham, 1937. First edition, 8vo., author's presentation on flyleaf, very good in dust jacket.   Second Life Books, Inc.   196 B - 77   2016 $45

A List of the Minority in the House of Commons who Voted Against the Bill to Repeal the American Stamp Act. Paris: chez J. W. (i.e. London: Almon?), 1766. First edition, neat modern half cloth, edges quite brittle with some chipping, fore edge of title repaired.   Joseph J. Felcone, Inc.   Books from Five Centuries: a Miscellany - 134   2016 $400

A List of the Union soldiers Buried at Andersonville. New York: Tribune Association, 1866. First edition, small 4to., original printed wrappers.   M & S Rare Books, Inc.   99 - 48   2016 $275

List, Freidrich *Das Nationale System der Politischen Oekonomie....* Stuttgart: J. G. Gotto'scher Verlag, 1841. First edition, volume I only (all published), contemporary half patterned brown cloth over marbled boards, spine lettered gilt, cloth and tips rubbed, especially at top and bottom of spine, occasional browning to some pages, as usual, professional triangle shaped repair to page 503 on right hand blank, bottom corner not affecting text, overall very good. Heritage Book Shop   Holiday 2015 - 75   2016 $7500

Lister, Martin *Conchyliorum Bivalvium Utriusque Aquae Exercitatio Anatomica Tertia...* London: Sumptibus authoris impressa, 1696. 4to., 10 engraved plates, complete with terminal blank Z4 in first work, contemporary sprinkled calf, very skillfully rebacked in period style, small early shelfmark in red ink on endpaper and on title, minor paper flaw in S2 just grazing catchword, very faint foxing in fore-edge, very lovely copy with text and plates clean and fresh, armorial bookplate of A. Gifford, DD of the Museum, presentation copy inscribed by author for Mr. Dalone.   Joseph J. Felcone, Inc.   Books from Five Centuries: a Miscellany - 91   2016 $10,000

Lister, R. P. *Allotments.* Manor Farm: Whittington Press, 1985. First edition, limited to 335 numbered copies signed by author and artist, oblong 8vo., quarter cloth, printed paper covered boards, paper spine label, slipcase, 41 wood engravings by Miriam Macgregor.   Oak Knoll Books   310 - 171   2016 $300

Lister, Valerie Browne *Phiz, the man who Drew Dickens.* London: Chatto & Windus, 2004. First edition, half title, vignette title, plates and illustrations, original mauve cloth, mint in price clipped.   Jarndyce Antiquarian Booksellers   CCXVIII - 1090   2016   £20

The Literary Museum or Monthly Magazine for April 1797. West Chester: printed by Derrick & Sharples, 1797. First edition, 8vo., removed, very good, front leaf detached and creased, few chips, rear two leaves creased, otherwise clean.   Kaaterskill Books   21 - 3   2016 $400

Lithgow, William *The Totall Discourse of the Rare Adventures & Painefull Peregrinations.* James MacLehose, 1906. First edition thus, 8vo., illustrations, original red decorative cloth, spine little faded.   J. & S. L. Bonham Antiquarian Booksellers   Voyages 2016 - 10016   2016   £45

Little Bo Peep. New York: McLoughlin Bros. n.d. circa, 1865. 4to., pictorial wrappers, small chip off upper corner, else fine, 7 fine hand colored illustrations, scarce.   Aleph-bet Books, Inc. 111 - 273   2016 $600

Little Boys and Girls ABC. New York: McLoughlin Bros., 1884. 8vo., pictorial wrappers, old neat strengthening inside cover, else very good+, 8 pages of chromolithographs. Aleph-bet Books, Inc.   111 - 7   2016 $225

Little Heroes. New York: Philadelphia: Chicago: et al: International Art Pub. Co., n.d. circa`, 1900. Book is shaped like an ax with real wood dowel, some edgewear and fraying at binding, overall very good+, illustrations in green line by F. Holms and with 4 chromolithographs, very scarce.   Aleph-bet Books, Inc.   111 - 418   2016 $400

Little Marian. Philadelphia: American Sunday School Union n.d. circa, 1860. 8vo., pictorial wrappers, neat spine mends, tight, very good+, diecut in shape of little girl and delicately illustrated with color lithos by F. Maras, quite rare. Aleph-bet Books, Inc.   111 - 423   2016 $1200

Little Old Woman. New York: McLoughlin Bros., n.d. circa, 1865. 12mo., pictorial wrappers highlighted in gold, mounted on linen, fine, full page color pictorial title plus 8 brightly colored three quarter page illustrations, beautiful copy. Aleph-bet Books, Inc.   111 - 274   2016 $300

Little Pig's Ramble from Home. London: Dean & Son, 1857. 12mo., pictorial wrappers, archival repair to spine and corner worn, else very good+.   Aleph-bet Books, Inc. 112 - 168   2016 $750

Little Prattle Over a Book of Prints with Easy Tales for Children. Philadelphia: J. Johnson, 1808. First American edition, marbled wrappers, some chipping and a few tiny mends, light soil, very good+, fine woodcuts throughout text, quite scarce.   Aleph-bet Books, Inc.   111 - 142   2016 $1200

Little Red Riding Hood. New York: Blue Ribbon, 1934. 4to., pictorial boards, black and white illustrations, 3 double page color pop-ups by Harold Lentz, very good+.   Aleph-bet Books, Inc.   111 - 358   2016 $300

Littlejohns, R. T. *Birds of Our Bush, or Photography for Nature-Lovers.* Melbourne: Whitcombe and Tombs, 1927. Octavo, illustrations from photos by author, publisher's decorated cloth, fine, crisp copy, very scarce in this condition.   Andrew Isles Natural History Books   55 - 7078   2016 $60

Littleton, Adam *Latin Dictionary.* London: printed for J. Walthoe, J. J. and P. Knapton, et al, 1735. Sixth edition, 4to., frontispiece and 2 maps, lacking front and rear free endpapers, little yellowed, some light ink spots and smudges, contemporary brown calf boards rebacked in vellum, slotted to accommodate raised bands, ownership inscriptions to frontispiece and titlepage of Edward Oliver Osborn, also to titlepage, inscription of William Osborn dated 1739.   Unsworths Antiquarian Booksellers   30 - 96   2016   £150

Liu, Cch'eng-chao *Amphibians of Western China.* Chicago: Chicago Natural History Museum, 1950. Quarto, 10 plates, publisher's printed wrappers, fine, magnificently housed in quarter morocco solander box.   Andrew Isles Natural History Books   55 - 35995   2016 $400

Livesey, Joseph *The Staunch Teetotaler.* London: Tweedie, 337 Strand, Manchester: Tubbs & Brook..., 1869. 8vo., frontispiece, photo on card with lithographic signature below, original green cloth, spine lettered gilt.   Marlborough Rare Books   List 55 - 44   2016   £75

Livingston, Luther *Frank and His Press at Passy, an Account of the Books, Pamphlets and Leaflets Printed...* New York: Grolier Club, 1914. First edition, limited to 303 copies, designed by Bruce Rogers and well printed on Van Gelder paper, 8vo., cloth backed marbled paper covered boards, paper spine label, illustrations, foldout plates, well preserved, lacks slipcase.   Oak Knoll Books   310 - 182   2016 $375

Livingstone, David 1813-1873 *Missionary Travels and Researches in South Africa...* London: Ward Lock & Co. n.d., 1899. New edition, octavo, plates, red cloth gilt, contemporary (1905) gift inscription, very good.   Peter Ellis   112 - 233   2016   £35

Le Livre, Revue Mensuelle Bibliographie Ancienne. Paris: A. Quantin, 1880-1886. Large run, small 4to., variously bound in original paper wrappers, later cloth and contemporary half cloth with leather spine labels and marbled paper covered boards, present are volumes 1-3 and 5 and 6, part one of the first volume bound in later cloth, part two unbound, others bound in period half cloth with leather spine labels and marbled boards.   Oak Knoll Books   310 - 65   2016 $700

Livy *Historiarum ab urbe Condita Libri qui Extant.* Venice: Apud Paulum Manutium, 1566. Second edition, tidy repairs to blank verso of titlepage and one or two other leaves, some staining to titlepage and occasionally elsewhere, few gatherings browned, occasional marginal notes in early hand, few leaves with ink splashes (not obscuring text), old inscription rubbed out from margin of titlepage, folio, 18th century Italian vellum, brown morocco lettering to spine, slightly soiled, good.   Blackwell's Rare Books   B186 - 92   2016   £1500

Livy *Historiarum Libri, Qui Supersunt Omnes et Deperditorum Fragmenta.* Oxonii: Talboys, 1840. 1840. 1841. 1841, 8vo., 4 volumes, little light foxing to front and rear generally clean and bright, v4ellum, gilt red morocco spine labels, marbled endpapers, all edges red, endcaps little creased, sme smudges and shelfwear to vellum, generally very good, armorial bookplate of James Frank Bright, stamped "Bound by Wheeler".   Unsworths Antiquarian Booksellers   30 - 97   2016   £240

Livy *Morceaux Choisis de Tite-Live.* Marseille: Chez Jean Mossy, 1781. 2 volumes, small wormhole to lower blank margin throughout volume i and in second half of volume ii, never touching text, contemporary marbled sheep, spines divided by decorative gilt rolls, yellow and green lettering pieces, labels bit rubbed, slight wear to headcaps, little unobtrusive surface damage to spine volume i, very good.   Blackwell's Rare Books   Greek & Latin Classics VII - 56   2016   £400

The Lizard's Question. N.P.: The Press at Coilorado College, 1996. Limited to 51 numbered copies signed by Prince Philip, Duke of Edinburgh, 4to., green cloth, green paper slipcase, original cardboard mailing envelope that was used to mail the book after it had been signed.   Oak Knoll Books   27 - 54   2016 $1500

Llanos Gutierrez, Valentin *Don Esteban or Memoirs of a Spaniard.* London: Henry Colburn, New Burlington Street, 1825. First edition, 3 volumes, 8vo., minor ink stain in volume III, contemporary light green calf, spines decorated in gilt with black lettering pieces, spines slightly sunned.   Marlborough Rare Books   List 56 - 33   2016   £450

Llewellyn, Richard *How Green wa My valley.* London: Michael Joseph, 1939. First edition, 8vo., signed by author, very good+, with soil and foxing to edges, in good dust jacket with pieces missing top and bottom spine affecting lettering, chips, tape verso, rare.   By the Book, L. C.   45 - 67   2016 $1000

Lloyd-Jones, H. *Sophocles Second Thought.* Gottingen: Vandenhoeck und Ruprecht, 1997. First edition, 8vo., near fine, paperback, author's gift inscription to Chris Carey.   Unsworths Antiquarian Booksellers Ltd.   E04 - 70   2016   £20

Lloyd, Charles *The Anatomy of a late Negociation.* London: printed for J. Wilkie, 1763. Second edition, 4to., half title, small stain to lower outer blank corner of signature (C2), disbound, very good.   Jarndyce Antiquarian Booksellers   CCXVI - 369   2016   £60

Lloyd, Charles *Principles for the Conduct of Life.* London: printed by J. Masters, 1848. Second impression, contemporary full brown calf, gilt spines, black morocco labels, boards rubbed, gift inscription "Miss Anderson with Mrs. Sherry's love", booklabel of Hairlie Lloyd-Jones, nice.   Jarndyce Antiquarian Books   CCXV - 297   2016   £125

Lloyd, Charles *A True History of a late Short Administration.* London: printed for J. Almon, 1766. 8vo. some foxing, disbound.   Jarndyce Antiquarian Booksellers   CCXVI - 370   2016   £75

Lloyd, H. E. *The German Tourist.* London: D. Nutt, 1837. First edition, 8vo., 17 steel engravings, contemporary purple blindstamped morocco bound boards, all edges gilt, joints little rubbed, plates foxed of browned, original blind stamped morocco, all edges gilt, spine rubbed.   J. & S. L. Bonham Antiquarian Booksellers   Europe 2016 - 3960   2016   £160

Lloyd, Lester *XXX Plus One.* Lafayette: A. R. Tommasini, 1978. First edition, limited to 200 copies, 32mo., brown cloth, text printed in red and black, very fine.   Argonaut Book Shop   Private Press 2015 - 2376   2016 $45

Lobel, Arnold *Frog and Toad All Year.* New York: Harper & Row, 1976. early but not first edition, 8vo., pictorial boards, fine in dust jacket, this copy inscribed by author with sketch, illustrations by author.   Aleph-bet Books, Inc.   112 - 295   2016 $100

Lobel, Arnold *A Treeful of Pigs.* London: Julia MacRae/ Franklin Watts, 1980. First British edition, oblong 4to., pictorial boards, tiny edge ding else fine, this copy signed by author and artist, with Arnold drawing of a pig, illustrations by Anita Lobel.   Aleph-bet Books, Inc.   112 - 296   2016 $175

Lobel, Edgar *Poetarum Lesbiorum Fragmenta.* Oxford: Clarendon Press, 1997. Reprint of first edition, 8vo. dark blue boards, gilt lettered, one crease along spine, else near fine, lacks dust jacket, ownership inscription of C. D. N. Costa to front pastedown.   Unsworths Antiquarian Booksellers Ltd.   E05 - 48   2016   £28

Lock, Graham *Forces in Motion: Anthony Braxton and the Meta-Reality of Creative Music.* London: Quarter, 1988. First edition, 8vo., presentation on flyleaf from Braxton, photos, paper over boards, nice in dust jacket.   Second Life Books, Inc.   196 B - 80   2016 $85

Lockdridge, Richard *Murder Can't Wait.* Philadelphia: Lippincott, 1964. First edition, fine in dust jacket.   Mordida Books   2015 - 010538   2016 $65

Locke, John 1632-1704 *An Essay Concerning Humane Understanding in Four Books.* London: for Awnsham and John Churchil (sic), 1700. Fourth edition, engraved portrait, some browning and spotting, purchase inscription 'Fromanteel pr. 13s' to titlepage, gift inscription 'The gift of Abraham Fromanteel of London, to Daniel Fromanteel Sen. of Norwich after his decease to be & remaine in hs family, London November 27 1709', folio, contemporary Cambridge style panelled calf, rebacked, hinges relined, boards pitted, edges worn, sound.   Blackwell's Rare Books   Marks of Genius - 25   2016   £950

Locke, John 1632-1704 *Du Gouvernement Civil ou l'on Traite de l'Origine, des Fondemens, de la Nature, du Pouvoir & Des Fins des Societes Politiques.* Amsterdam: Abraham Wolfgang, 1691. First edition in French, 12mo., woodcut printer's device on title, bound without final blank 1 or 2 leaves little spotted or browned, contemporary speckled calf, spine gilt, red lettering piece, headcaps defective, corners little worn, 2 early ownership inscriptions on title, good.   Blackwell's Rare Books   B184 - 59   2016   £2500

Locke, John 1632-1704 *The Literary Diary or Improved Common-Place-Book...* Taylor & Hessy, 1811. First edition?, contemporary calf, sides diced, gilt roll tooled border, rounded spine lettered in gilt direct and with gilt compartments, spine very slightly faded, first couple of gatherings proud, good.   Blackwell's Rare Books   B184 - 29   2016   £450

Locke, Richard Adams *Great Astronomical Discoveries Lately Made by Sir John Herschel, LL.D.* N.P.: n.d. New York: New York Sun Office, 1835. First edition, octavo, uncut, sewn, first leaf bit tanned, but basically fine.   John W. Knott, Jr./L.W. Currey, Inc.   Fall-Winter 2015 - 17461   2016 $8500

Lockhart, John Gibson 1794-1854 *Memoirs of the Life of Sir Walter Scott.* Boston and New York: Houghton Mifflin and Co., 1902. Cambridge edition, 5 volumes, 213 x 149mm., lovely contemporary red half morocco, beautifully gilt in style of Doves Bindery, raised bands, spines in fine gilt compartments featuring sprays of tulips, marbled boards and endpapers, top edges gilt, other edges untrimmed and (except for prefatory material in first volume) entirely unopened, frontispiece portraits, small portions of two spine bands, corners and just few joints and insignificant wear (rubbing carefully refurbished), one leaf with jagged fore-edge from rough opening, lovely set, nearly fine condition, bindings unusualy lustrous and text virtually pristine because obviously unread.   Phillip J. Pirages 67 - 313 2016 $2250

Lockman, John *The History of Greece.* London: printed for R. Dodsley in Pall Mall, 1743. First edition, ad leaf discarded, little minor spotting, 12mo., later marbled calf, spine gilt, joints and corners expertly renewed, new green morocco lettering piece, good, rare.   Blackwell's Rare Books Greek & Latin Classics VII - 20 2016   £700

Lockman, John *The History of Greece.* printed for C. Hitch and L. Hawes, 1761. Third surviving edition, lightly browned and spotted, 8vo., contemporary mottled calf, quite rubbed, bit of wear to head of spine, red morocco lettering piece partly defective, sound.   Blackwell's Rare Books Greek & Latin Classics VII - 21 2016   £150

Lockman, John *A New Roman History, by Question and Answer.* London: T. Astley, 1737. First edition, titlepage fore-edge little creased, last two leaves containing publisher's ads, 12mo., contemporary sheep, joints cracked and strengthened with glue internally, extremities worn, label lost, early inscriptions of Caleb Lomax to flyleaves, sound. Blackwell's Rare Books   Greek & Latin Classics VII - 77   2016   £150

Lockman, John *Verses to His Royal Highness the Duke of Cumberland...*   London: printed for H. Chapelle and sold by J. Robinson, 1743. First edition, folio, recent stiff wrappers, narrow slip cut from middle of titlepage and made good (presumably to remove ownership inscription), outer edges bit dusty and ragged, but acceptable copy.   C. R. Johnson Rare Book Collections Foxon: H-P 2015 - 541 2016 $689

Lockridge, Ross *Raintree County.* Boston: Houghton Mifflin, 1948. First edition, fine, good dust jacket, price clipped, moderate chipping and creasing.   Bella Luna Books 2016 - t17982 2016 $198

Lockroy, Edouard *La Marine de Guerre.* Paris and Nancy: Berger Leverault, 1897. First edition, scarce, 8vo., contemporary dark green cloth, spine lettered and ruled gilt, very light rubbing, internally apart from even browning, as usual due to paper stock, very good, from the Inst. of Naval Architects with bookplate.   Sotheran's Travel and Exploration - 464   2016   £198

Lockwood, Frank *The Law and Lawyers of Pickwick. A Lecture.* London: Roxburghe Press, 1894. Frontispiece, title and 12 page publisher's catalog printed in green, uncut in original blue cloth, bevelled boards, lettered and pictorial blocked in gilt, spine slightly dulled and rubbed, very good.   Jarndyce Antiquarian Booksellers   CCXVIII - 153   2016   £35

Loewenstein, Louis J. *History of the St. Louis Cathedral of New Orleans.* New Orleans: Times Democrat, 1882. First edition, 8vo., later half calf, marbled boards, original printed wrappers bound in, small withdrawn stamp.   Howard S. Mott Inc.   265 - 81   2016 $125

Loft, Milton *Dance Back the Buffalo.* Boston: Houghton Mifflin, 1959. First edition, map endpapers, rust cloth lettered in black fine with lightly rubbed and chipped pictorial dust jacket.   Argonaut Book Shop   Literature 2015 - 1949 2016 $50

Lofting, Hugh *Doctor Dolittle and the Green Canary.* London: Jonathan Cape, 1951. First edition, 8vo., original green cloth stamped in darker green, pictorial endpapers, preserved by pictorial dust jacket, colored frontispiece and line drawings by Lofting, very fresh with just little dusting to edges of book block, protected by near fine dust jacket with only very minor nicks to head and tail of spine.   Sotheran's Piccadilly Notes - Summer 2015 - 193   2016   £128

Lofting, Hugh *Doctor Doolittle's Zoo.* New York: Frederick Stokes, 1928. 8vo, grey pictorial cloth, pictorial paste-on, fine in very good dust jacket (some closed tears, chips, light soil), illustrations by author.   Aleph-bet Books, Inc.   112 - 297   2016 $400

Lofting, Hugh *Noisy Nora.* New York: Frederick Stokes, 1929. First edition, pink cloth, pictorial paste-on, spine faded, else fine, full page and partial page of full color illustrations and black and whites as well, rare, great copy. Aleph-bet Books, Inc.   112 - 298   2016 $675

Logan, John *The Anonymous Lover: new Poems by...* New York: Liveright, 1973. First edition, 8vo., author's presentation on half title to poet and editor William Claire, also signed on title, 3 photos by Aaron Sisking, paper over boards with cloth spine, very slight foxing on first and last two leaves, otherwise nice in dust jacket.   Second Life Books, Inc.   196 B - 85   2016 $75

Logan, John *The Bridge of Change.* Brockport: BOA editions, 1978. One of 200 copies, 8vo., author's presentation on flyleaf to poet and editor William Claire, signed on title, paper wrappers, slight spot on back cover, otherwise nice. Second Life Books, Inc.   196 B - 87   2016 $45

Logan, John *Cycle for Mother Cabrini.* Cloud Marauder Press, 1971. Second printing, 8vo., author's presentation to poet William Claire, woodcuts by James Brunot, paper wrappers, cover slightly faded and very small bump at upper corner, otherwise nice.   Second Life Books, Inc.   196 B - 88   2016 $45

Logan, John *Ghosts of the Heart: New Poems...* Chicago: University of Chicago, 1960. First edition, 8vo., signed by author, presentation from author for poet William Claire, red cloth, nice, scuffed and little chipped, dust jacket. Second Life Books, Inc.   196 B - 89   2016 $75

Logan, John *The House that Jack Built.* Omaha: University of Nebraska, Abattoir Editions, 1974. No. 61 of 300 copies, large 8vo., drawings by James Brunot, author's signature with his presentation, ivory cloth with paper label, fine.   Second Life Books, Inc.   196 B - 90   2016 $125

Logan, John *Spring of the Thief: Poems 1960-1962.* New York: Knopf, 1963. First edition, 8vo., author's signature and presentation to William Claire, blue cloth stamped in red and gilt, cover very slightly scuffed at corners and ends of spine, otherwise very good, tight copy in scuffed and chipped dust jacket.   Second Life Books, Inc.   196 B - 91   2016 $95

Logan, Joshua *Josh. My Up and Down, In and Out Life.* New York: Delacorte, 1976. First printing, 8vo., photos, five line presentation by author, nice in little scuffed dust jacket. Second Life Books, Inc.   196 B - 92   2016 $45

Logan, William Hugh *Little Bo-Peep; or Harlequin and The Little Girl that Lost Her Sheep.* (bound with) *St. George & ye Dragon or Harlequin and Ye Seven Champions of Christendom.* Edinburgh: printed by Schenck & McFarlane, 1857. Edinburgh: Schenck & McFarlane, 1857. First editions, small 4to., later cloth, original yellow pictorial wrappers printed in gold bound in, extra illustrated title printed in red, 4 plates printed in gold, drawn and lithographed by Haswelle, 5 plates printed in gold, drawn and lithographed by Haswelle, minor foxing.   Howard S. Mott Inc.   265 - 82   2016 $950

Loggan, David *Cantabrigia Illustrata...* Cambridge: Macmillan & Bowes, 1905. Facsimile of 1690 edition, folio, original cloth spine, blue papered boards, lettered black on spine and front cover, neat inscription, slight abrasion at top edge of front board, some rubbing and browning at spine and slight scuffing, otherwise sound, about very good, with clean plates.   Any Amount of Books   2015 - C8312   2016 £250

Loggan, David *Oxonia Illustrata, sive Omnium Celebrrimae Istius Universitatis Collegiorum, Aularum, Bibliothecae Bodleianae, Scholarum Publicaruum...* Oxford: Senecio Press, 1970. One of 1000 numbered copies (this unnumbered), 40 plates of copper engraved illustrations with 11 topographical, 1 costume and 28 of colleges and halls, all of which are double sheet except Christ Church, folio, original half brown leather with blue cloth sides, backstrip lettered and decorated in gilt with 5 imitation raised bands, little surface grazing and one or two faint marks, good. Blackwell's Rare Books   Marks of Genius - 26   2016 £500

Lohrli, Anne *Household Words: a Weekly Journal 1850-1859.* Toronto: University of Toronto Press, 1973. Half title, original maroon cloth, slightly marked, Kathleen Tillotson's copy, with occasional pencil annotations in text. Jarndyce Antiquarian Booksellers   CCXVIII - 780   2016 £50

London County Council *Re-Planting London Schools, a Short Account of the Development Plan for Primary and Secondary Education Prepared by the London County Council...* London: London County Council, 1947. Original light green illustrated wrappers, stapled as issued, slightly dulled, staples rusted, very good.   Jarndyce Antiquarian Books   CCXV - 829   2016   £20

London, Jack   1876-1916 *The Call of the Wild.* London: William Heinemann, 1903. Reprint, half title, color frontispiece, engraved title, 10 colored plates, illustrations, illustrated endpapers, untrimmed, original dark blue vertical grained cloth, front board and spine pictorially blocked in maroon, black and white, lettered black and gilt, bookseller's ticket Flor and Findel, Florence, very good.   Jarndyce Antiquarian Booksellers   CCXVII - 165   2016   £125

London, Jack   1876-1916 *John Barleycorn.* New York: Century, 1913. First edition, first printing, with single blank leaf in rear, 8vo., illustrations by H. T. Dunn, dark blue cloth, little rippling to cloth, very good.   Second Life Books, Inc. 197 - 214   2016 $150

London, Jack   1876-1916 *The Sea Wolf.* New York: Heritage Press, 1961. printed gray cloth, lettered gilt, spine faded with few spots from foxing, very good in slipcase (fading to extremities), illustrations by Fletcher Martin, Sandglass pamphlet laid in.   Argonaut Book Shop Heritage Press 2015 - 7029   2016 $40

London, Jack   1876-1916 *The Sea-Wolf.* Hartford: Connecticut Printers, 1961. First edition thus, quarto, full imported flexible Irish linen with silkscreen design by artist on cover, 12 full page, full color paintings plus 2 double spreads in full color and 16 line drawings by Fletcher Martin, one of 1500 copies signed by artist.   Second Life Books, Inc.   196 B - 93   2016 $75

London, Jack 1876-1916 *Smoke Bellew.* New York: Century Co., 1912. First edition, 8vo., couple of nicks, very nice in original cloth.   Second Life Books, Inc.   197 - 215   2016 $150

London, Jack 1876-1916 *The Turtles of Tasman.* New York: Macmillan, 1916. First edition, 8vo. mauve cloth stamped in yellow, orange and blue, little light soiling on cover and nick at extremities of spine, otherwise near fine.   Second Life Books, Inc.   197 - 216   2016 $300

Long, A. A.   *The Hellenistic Philosophers.* Cambridge: Cambridge University Press, 1990. 1989, 8vo., 2 volumes, paperback .5cm closed tear to spine of volume II, .3cm. closed tear to spine of volume I, bump to top corner of volume II, edges slightly dusted, price stickers to lower wrappers, very good, ownership inscription of C. D. N. Costa.   Unsworths Antiquarian Booksellers Ltd.   E05 - 49   2016   £40

Long, George   *An Introductory Lecture Delivered in the University of London, Tuesday Nov. 4 1828.* London: John Taylor, 1829. Second edition, damp marks to title, original drab wrappers, little torn, paper label.   Jarndyce Antiquarian Books   CCXV - 833   2016   £30

Long, Max   *Murder Between Dark and Dark.* Philadelphia: J. B. Lippincott, 1939. First edition, small inked numbers to top edge of front flyleaf, else fine, tight, bright green and orange dust jacket with light restoration to head of spine, attractive copy.   Buckingham Books   2015 - 37552   2016 $475

Longfellow, Henry Wadsworth 1807-1882 *The Courtship of Miles Standish and Other Poems.* Boston: Ticknor and Fields, 1858. First edition, first issue, 12mo., original brown embossed cloth, gilt lettered spine, general wear to extremities, spine ends chipped, good copy.   Argonaut Book Shop   Literature 2015 - 1325   2016 $250

Longfellow, Henry Wadsworth 1807-1882 *The Courtship of Miles Standish and Other Poems.* Boston: Ticknor & Fields, 1859. first edition, third/fourth printing, 8vo., blindstamped brown cloth, very good.   Second Life Books, Inc.   197 - 217   2016 $125

Longfellow, Henry Wadsworth 1807-1882 *Evangeline.* Chicago: Reilly & Britton, 1909. 8vo., cloth, pictotial paste-on, top edge gilt, slight cover soil else very good+, illustrations by John R. Neill, beautiful copy.   Aleph-bet Books, Inc.   111 - 316   2016 $150

Longfellow, Henry Wadsworth 1807-1882 *The Golden Legend.* Boston: Ticknor Reed and Fields, 1851. First edition, first issue, 12mo., original brown embossed cloth with gilt lettered spine, general wear to extremities, spine ends chipped, previous owner's bookplate, good copy.   Argonaut Book Shop   Literature 2015 - 1326   2016 $300

Longfellow, Henry Wadsworth 1807-1882 *The Song of Hiawatha.* Boston: Ticknor & Fields, 1855. first edition, 2nd printing (1/3000 copies printed Nov. 22nd), 8vo., ad dated Nov. 1855, brown cloth, some external wear, good tight copy.   Second Life Books, Inc.   197 - 218   2016 $300

Longfellow, Henry Wadsworth 1807-1882 *Voices of the Night.* Cambridge: published by John Owen, 1840. Third edition, large paper issue, uarto, original black morocco by Peter Low, gilt rules, decorations and lettering, all edges gilt, edges little rubbed, some light foxing, rear free endpaper, chipped at corner, very good.   The Brick Row Book Shop   Miscellany 69 - 55   2016 $900

Longley, Michael   *Sea Asters.* Rochdale: Andrew J. Moorhosue, 2015. 10/75 copies (from an edition of 125 signed by author and artist, printed on Zerkall paper, titlepage printed in purple and black titlepage vignette and 12 full page pen and ink drawings by Longley, additional vignette at close of text, royal 8vo., original quarter mustard yellow leather with maroon cloth, printed label inset to upper board, tail edges untrimmed, fine.   Blackwell's Rare Books   B186 - 260   2016   £95

Longshore-Potts, Anna M.   *Discourses to Women on Medical Subjects.* London: published by the author, 1895. English edition, 40th thousand, half title, frontispiece, illustrations, original brown cloth, little rubbed, ownership inscription dated 26/3/59.   Jarndyce Antiquarian Books   CCXV - 298   2016   £35

Longshore-Potts, Anna M.   *Love, Courtship and Marriage.* London: published by the authoress, circa, 1894. Half title, frontispiece, original blue pictorial cloth bevelled boards, little rubbed and dulled, ownership inscription on initial blank and half title dated 1906.   Jarndyce Antiquarian Books   CCXV - 299   2016   £35

Longstreet, Abby Buchana   *Cards: Their Significance and Proper Uses as Governed by Their Usages of New York Society.* New York: Frederick A. Stokes and Brother, 1889. Few leaves roughly opened, original green cloth, very good.   Jarndyce Antiquarian Books   CCXV - 300   2016   £50

Longus   *Les Amours Pastorales De Daphnis et Chloe.* Chelsea: Ashendene Press, 1933. One of 250 paper copies for sale (of a total of 290) and 20 on vellum, 261 x 185mm., in original peacock green paper boards with vellum spine and tips, circular gold stamping on front cover by Gwendolen Raverat, in original patterned paper slipcase (slightly soiled and rubbed), 29 charming woodcuts by Raverat, four full page; morocco bookplate of C. R. and J. E. Ashbee, marginal notes printed in red, initials and paragraph marks in blue added by hand by Graily Hewitt, half dozen tiny chips missing where paper covering boards meets vellum, spine, otherwise fine, entirely clean, fresh and bright inside and out.   Phillip J. Pirages   67 - 15   2016 $3800

Longus *The Pastoral Loves of Daphnis and Chloe done into English by George Moore.* London: Heinemann, 1924. First edition, one of 1280 large paper copies signed by author, cloth backed boards, uncut.   Second Life Books, Inc.   196 B - 258   2016 $45

Lons, Hermann *Luttjemann und Ruttjerinchen.* Hanover: Sponholtz, 1924. Small 4to., cloth backed pictorial boards, near fine, illustrations by Fritz Hans Eggers.   Aleph-bet Books, Inc.   111 - 195   2016 $225

Lonsdale Library *Hounds & Dogs.* London: Seeley Service & Co., 1932. First edition, 8vo., publisher's quarter green leather, top edges gilt, green silk marker, illustrations in black and white, spine faded as usual, otherwise very nice.   Sotheran's   Hunting, Shooting & Fishing - 182   2016   £198

Lonsdale, Henry *A Sketch of the Life and Writings of Robert Knox the Anatomist.* London: Macmillan, 1870. Engraved frontispiece, ex-library, original binding, good copy.   James Tait Goodrich   X-78 - 357   2016 $95

Lopez, Barry *River Notes, The Dance of Herons.* Kansas City: Andrews and McMeel, 1979. First edition, near fine, previous owner's embossing stamp on front free endpapers, dust jacket near fine, small rubbed spots and soiling, small printing, elusive title, signed by author.   Bella Luna Books   2016 - ta120   2016 $99

Lorac, E. C. R. *Shroud of Darkness.* Garden City: Doubleday, 1954. First American edition, fine in dust jacket.   Mordida Books   2015 - 003120   2016 $60

Loraine, Philip *White Lie the Dead.* London: Hodder & Stoughton, 1950. Very good, frayed dust jacket.   I. D. Edrich   Crime - 2016   £20

Lorant, Stefan *The New World.* New York: Duell, Sloan and Pearce, 1966. First revised edition, numerous black and white plates and maps, fine with lightly worn dust jacket.   Argonaut Book Shop   Native American 2015 - 1948   2016 $50

Lord John Signatures. Northridge: Lord John Press, 1961. First edition, limited to 150 deluxe copies, signed by Stephen King (provided introduction), very fine in decorated cloth, slipcase, signed by over 40 contributors.   Buckingham Books   2015 - 21530   2016 $450

Lord, Albert *Russian Folk Tales.* Avon: Heritage Press, 1970. Patterned red boards with red cloth spine, lettered gilt, very fine in slipcase (fading to extremities), illustrations by Teje Etchemendy, Sandglass pamphlet laid in.   Argonaut Book Shop   Heritage Press 2015 - 7031   2016 $45

Lord, Clive E. *A Synopsis of the Vertebrate Animals of Tasmania.* Hobart: Oldham, Beddome and Meredith, 1924. Octavo, text illustrations, very good, publisher's cloth.   Andrew Isles Natural History Books   55 - 7095   2016 $80

Lorenzini, Carlo   1829-1890 *Story of a Puppet or the Adventures of Pinocchio.* London: T. Fisher Unwin, 1892. First edition in English, 12mo., decorative cloth with design repeated on edges, cloth lightly faded and spine age toned, else very good+, charmingly illustrated by C. Mazzanti.   Aleph-bet Books, Inc.   112 - 111   2016 $8000

Lorenzini, Carlo   1829-1890 *The Story of the Puppet or the Adventures of Pinocchio.* London: C. Fisher Unwin, 1892. First edition in English, small octavo, half title and title printed in red and black, 41 black and white vignette drawings by Mazzanti, rare publisher's variant binding of patterned sand grain medium blue cloth over bevelled boards, title stamped in blue at head of spine, matching blue patterned endpapers, all edges in matching blue pattern, spine lightly sunned and skewed, very good, housed in full blue morocco clamshell case, gilt stamped on spine.   Heritage Book Shop   Holiday 2015 - 23   2016 $6500

Lorrain, Jean *La Maison Philibert.* Paris: G. Cres et Cie, 1925. No. 159 of 300 copies on Rives paper from a total edition of 365 copies, 15 of which were not for sale`, 197 x 248mm., attractive contemporary olive brown morocco, gilt, covers with French fillet border and frame composed of swirling vine enclosed by fillets, raised bands, spine compartments with gilt fillet frames, gilt titling, broad turn-ins densely gilt, marbled endpapers, top edge gilt, other edges untrimmed, original wrappers bound in, 88 illustrations by Andre Dignimont, 16 of these full page printed in rich colors using pochoir technique, two inch crack at head of front joint, spine evenly sunned (as expected, otherwise fine), binding escpecially lustrous, text fresh and clean, illustrations very richly colored.   Phillip J. Pirages   67 - 283   2016 $750

Lossing, Benson John *The Illustrated New World.* New York: H. Phelps & Co., 1848. First edition, black and white plate, 50 engravings, 8vo., illustrated paper wrappers, very good, wrappers browned at edges, inch tears at spine head and tail, some offsetting of engravings, curl at one corner,.   Kaaterskill Books   21 - 48   2016 $100

Loti, Pierre *An Iceland Fisherman.* Stockholm: printed for the LEC by Norstedt & Soner, 1931. First edition thus, 4to., fine in box, signed by artist, printed on handmade linen rag paper by Van Gelder Zonen, lithographs by Yngve Berg.   Second Life Books, Inc.   196 B - 38   2016 $50

Loti, Pierre *La Maison des Aieules.* Paris: Henri Floury, 1927. Limited to 302 numbered copies, printed on velin d'Arches, 4to., pictorial wrappers, 77 fabulous pochoir illustrations, scarce.   Aleph-bet Books, Inc.   111 - 217   2016 $1200

Loti, Pierre *La Maison des Aieules suivie de Mademoiselle Anna, Tres Humble Pupee...* Paris: Henry Floury, 1927. No. 270 of 274 copies on velin d'Arches (of a total edition of 302), 245 x 192mm., publisher's color illustrated wrappers, original glassine, 76 illustrations including wrapper image by Andre Helle, hand colored in gouache via pochoir stenciling by J. Saude, half inch joint split at spine head and tail, mild edgewear, glassine with many small chips to spine and edges, extremely appealing copy, fragile book quite solid, internally quite clean, fresh and bright with very rich colouring. Phillip J. Pirages 67 - 284 2016 $1000

Loti, Pierre *La Mort De Notre Chere France en Orient.* Paris: Calmann-Levy, 1920. Third edition, chipped wrappers, cover separate, this was the copy of consumer advocate, Florence Kelley with her signature and 12 lines of her hologoraph, fragile pulpy paper. Second Life Books, Inc. 196 B - 94 2016 $50

Lott, Milton *Dance Back the Buffalo.* Boston: Houghton Mifflin, 1959. First edition, map endpapers, red cloth lettered in black, fine with lightly rubbed and chipped pictorial dust jacket. Argonaut Book Shop Native American 2015 - 1949 2016 $50

Lougy, Robert E. *Martin Chuzzlewitt: an annotated Bibliography.* New York: Garland Pub., 1990. Half title, original green cloth, very good. Jarndyce Antiquarian Booksellers CCXVIII - 428 2016 £20

Louichheim, Katie *With or Without Roses.* Garden City: Doubleday, 1966. First edition, 8vo., author's presentation n title to poet William Claire, tan cloth, top edges slightly spotted, few ink marks in contents pages, otherwise very good, tight, scuffed and lightly soiled dust jacket. Second Life Books, Inc. 196 B - 97 2016 $40

Louisa, Aunt *A Book of Drolleries.* London/New York: Frederick Warne/Scribner, Welford and Armstrong, circa, 1874. First edition, 4to., very good+, rebacked with original spine laid down, original green cloth covered boards with gilt lettered spine, gilt lettering and design to front cover, color illustrations, with large horizontal full color illustration, faint owner inscription, scattered soil and foxing, scarce. By the Book, L. C. 45 - 87 2016 $300

Loutherbourg, Philipp Jakob De *The Romantic and Picturesque Scenery of England and Wales.* London: printed for Rober Bowyer for T. Bensley, 1805. First edition, first issue, wit signature and imprint underneath each plate and watermarks no later than 1805, folio, 2 titlepages and two leaves of descriptive text for each plate, 18 hand colored aquatint plates, text and plates watermarked J. Whatman 1801 and 1805, few light marginal stains to some text leaves, overall near fine, recently rebound in contemporary style in full dark green straight grain morocco, covers with gilt rubbed borders enclosing decorative gilt border, spine richly gilt decorated and lettered in compartments, decorative gilt turn-ins, marbled endpapers. David Brass Rare Books, Inc. 2015 - 02690 2016 $4500

Louvet De Couvray, Jean Baptiste *An Account of the Dangers to Which I Have Been Exposed Since the 31st of May 1793.* Perth: printed by R. Morison Junior for R. Morison & Son, 1795. 12mo., very clean, tear without loss to C3, pencil puzzle on rear endpaper, contemporary quarter calf, gilt banded spine, red morocco label, marbled board, vellum cornerpieces. Jarndyce Antiquarian Booksellers CCXVI - 372 2016 £150

Louys, Pierre *The Adventures of King Pausole.* Paris: Fortune Press, 1929. first edition of this translation by Charles Hope Lumley, royal 8vo., one of 1125 copies on handmade paper, this being unnumbered, color illustrations by Beresford Egan, black buckram backed paper boards, laid in is a Fuller d'Arch Smith catalogue of Fortune Press titles gilt titles on spine, bit dull, near fine in near fine dust jacket, bookplate designed by Egan Beresford. Peter Ellis 112 - 111 2016 £225

Love is Strange: Stories of Postmodern Romance. New York: W. W. Norton & Co., 1993. First edition, illustrated self wrappers, slight waviness on pages, rear bottom corner bumped, else near fine, 'Autographed Copy' sticker, nicely inscribed by contributor, Kathy Acker with drawing, inscription below in unknown hand. Between the Covers Rare Books 204 - 7 2016 $275

Love, Nat *The Life and Adventures of Nat Love Better Known in the Cattle Country as Deadwood Dick by Himself.* Los Angeles: Nat Love, author, 1907. First edition, tall octavo, photographic frontispiece, illustrations, pictorial brown cloth, couple of tape shadows on front and rear free endpapers, else near fine, nice, very uncommon. Between the Covers Rare Books 202 - 60 2016 $1200

Lovecraft, Howard Phillips *Dreams and Fancies.* Sauk City: Arkham House, 1962. First edition, one of 2000 copies, fine in very good dust jacket little creased at tail of spine. Peter Ellis 112 - 235 2016 £250

Lovecraft, Howard Phillips *The Shadow Over Innsmouth.* Everett: Visionary Pub. Co., 1936. First edition, octavo, illustrations by Frank Utpatel, original black cloth, front and spine panels stamped in silver, of the two known bindings, this copy has title on front panel stamped in upper and lower case letters, fine in fine printed dust jacket, lettering in silver matching the book, printed ertrata leaf laid in, excellent copy.   John W. Knott, Jr./L.W. Currey, Inc.   Fall-Winter 2015 - 16569   2016 $3500

Lovelace, Maud Hart *Betsy's Wedding.* New York: Crowell, 1955. Stated first printing, 8vo., cloth, owner name on endpaper, fine in very good dust jacket with few closed tears, illustrations by Vera Neville, laid in is handwritten letter from author to friend in envelope, very scarce with letter. Aleph-bet Books, Inc.   111 - 264   2016 $575

Lovesey, Peter *Wobble to Death.*   London: Macmillan, 1970. First edition, signed by author, page edges uniformly tanned, else fine in price clipped dust jacket with light professional restoration to front corners.   Buckingham Books 2015 - 30619   2016 $450

Lowe, Joseph *The Present State of England in Regard to Agriculture, Trade, and Finance with a Comparison of the Prospects of England and France.* London: Longman, Hurst Rees, Orme and Brown and J. Richardson, 1822. First edition, 8vo., bound without half title, contemporary half calf, spine gilt in compartments with label, very good.   John Drury Rare Books   2015 - 14259   2016 $350

Lowe, P. R. *British Antarctic ("Terra Nova") Expedition, 1910. Zoology. Birds.* London: Trustees of the British Museum, 1930. Quarto, 16 plates, publisher's printed wrappers, some slight chipping.   Andrew Isles Natural History Books   55 - 7112   2016 $300

Lowe, P. R. *A Naturalist on Desert Islands.* London: Witherby & Co., 1911. First edition, 8vo., original pale blue cloth, spine titled gilt, incorporating vignette of rocky shore with palm trees, in rear original pale blue dust jacket, 32 photographic plates and double page colored map, single page colored map, some spotting to endpapers and edges, previous owner's inscription, very good.   Sotheran's Piccadilly Notes - Summer 2015 - 194   2016   £198

Lowe, Peter *A Discorvse of the Whole Art of Chyrvrgerie.* London: printed by Thomas Pvrfoot, 1636. Third edition, woodcut on verso of title and number of text woodcuts, some full page, 4to., recent full English paneled calf, raised bands, gilt spine, burgundy spine label, endpapers renewed, title with toning, text with toning and browning and areas of foxing, page 147 lacking part of lower blank margin, page 203 lacking part of lower blank margin just catching one letter of text, overall most pleasing copy, contemporary inked line outs and corrections.   James Tait Goodrich   X-78 - 372   2016 $3950

Lowell, Amy *Six French Poets.* New York: Macmillan, 1916. First edition, 2nd printing, 8vo., blue cloth stamped in gilt, very good, tight copy, inscribed by author for Helen Lehmann.   Second Life Books, Inc.   196 B - 99   2016 $200

Lowell, Amy *Some Imagist Poets 1916.* Boston & New York: Houghton Mifflin, 1916. First edition, 8vo., printed wrappers, front hinge torn, spine paper worn, inscribed by Lowell for Helen Lehmann.   Second Life Books, Inc.   196 B - 98   2016 $250

Lowell, James Russell 1819-1891 *The Biglow Papers. Second Series.* Boston: Ticknor and Fields, 1867. First edition, 12mo., original brown embossed cloth with gilt lettered spine, general wear to extremities, edges and endpapers foxed, front cover has several minor scuffs, good copy. Argonaut Book Shop   Literature 2015 - 1323   2016 $50

Lowell, James Russell 1819-1891 *The Complete Writings.* Cambridge: Riverside Press, 1904. Edition de luxe, one of 1000 copies, 222 x 146mm., 16 volumes, last 3 volumes containing 'Letters' edited by Charles Eliot Norton, very handsome dark green morocco extravagantly gilt, covers with wavy gilt border and charming floral ornaments at corners, central panel with square notched corners formed by 6 parallel gilt lines, raised bands, spine compartments attractively gilt with scrolling flowers and foliage enclosing floral fleuron centerpiece, wide turn-ins with elaborate gilt decoration featuring many large and small roses and leaves on stylized lattice work, turn-ins enclosing scarlet colored polished morocco doublures, crimson watered silk free endleaves, top edge gilt, other edges rough trimmed, mostly unopened (6 of the volumes entirely unopened and all but one of the others largely so), 80 mounted photogravure illustrations on India paper (including frontispieces, one double plate and one plate with four portraits), original tissue guards, joints of volume I with hint of wear (half dozen other joints with very slight rubbing), spines evenly sunned to attractive olive brown (though a handful of spines bit lighter than others), one small cover scuff, two leaves roughly opened (with no serious consequences), other isolated trivial imperfections, near fine set in quite attractive binding, leather lustrous and mostly unopened, text essentially undisturbed.   Phillip J. Pirages   67 - 51   2016 $2500

Lowell, Percival *Noto an Unexplored corner of Japan.* Boston: Houghton Mifflin/Riverside Press, 1891. First edition, small 8vo., presentation slip from author tipped-in, very good++, black cloth covered boards with gilt lettered spine, red ink stamped design front cover, titlepage, minimal scuffs spine, soil to reaf endpaper, bookplate of Frederic J. Stimson.   By the Book, L. C.   45 - 50   2016 $650

Lowell, Robert 1917-1977 *For the Union Dead.* London: Faber and Faber, 1965. First UK edition, octavo, free endpapers faintly tanned, fine in very good dust jacket little nicked and creased at top edge, but with none of the usual fading to the red.   Peter Ellis   112 - 236   2016   £45

Lowell, Robert 1917-1977 *Notebook 1967-1968.* New York: Farrar Straus Giroux, 1969. First edition, fine in about fine dust jacket with small crease on rear flap, from the library of author Peter Taylor and his wife, Eleanor Ross Taylor, inscribed by Lowell to same.   Between the Covers Rare Books   208 - 2   2016 $2750

Lowenfels, Walter *Song of Peace.* New York: Roving Eye Prress, 1959. One of 125 copies in hardcover, Blockprints by Anton Refregier, folio, cloth and illustrated paper over boards, cloth quite foxed, thus about very good, laid in broadside on card with block print by Refregier and with blurb by Linus Pauling (foxed and with crease), volume signed by Lowenfels and Refregier, also inscribed for James Roman by Lowenfels', laid in letter dated 9/4/65 on Lowenfels' stationary.   Between the Covers Rare Books   204 - 68   2016 $150

Lowry, Lois *Number the Stars.* Boston: Houghton Mifflin, 1969. Reprint, 8vo., fine in slightly worn dust jacket, signed with 2 hearts by author on titlepage.   Second Life Books, Inc.   196 B - 100   2016 $45

Lowry, Malcolm 1909-1957 *Ultramarine.* London: Jonathan Cape, 1933. First edition, 8vo., original blue cloth lettered gilt on spine, prelims very slightly foxed, very slight fading, spine lettering very slightly flecked, otherwise sound, clean, very good.   Any Amount of Books 2015 - A93279   2016   £600

Lowry, Malcolm 1909-1957 *Under the Volcano.* London: Jonathan Cape, 1947. First edition, octavo, small ownership signature at top corner of front free endpaper, slight pinhole damage to spine, head of spine bit faded, very good in like dust jacket, nicked, slightly rubbed with few short tears.   Peter Ellis   112 - 238   2016   £650

Lowry, Malcolm 1909-1957 *Under the Volcano.* London: Jonathan Cape, 1947. First edition, octavo, just hint of fading at head of spine, very good in like, chipped dust jacket with some small loss to bottom edges and with two closed tears and multiple creasing at bottom edge of lower panel, quite bright.   Peter Ellis   112 - 237   2016   £850

Lubbock, John *British Wild Flowers Considered in Relation to Insects.* London: Macmillan, 1909. Octavo, text illustrations, bookplate, publisher's cloth, corner of front free endpaper removed, otherwise fine, crisp copy.   Andrew Isles Natural History Books   55 - 38045   2016 $80

Lubieniecki, Stanislaw *Historia Cometarum a Diluvio Usque ad Praesentem Annum Vulgaris Epochae a Christio Nao 1665... (with) Theatri Cometici Exitus de Significatione Cometarum.* Amsterdam: apud Danielem Baccamude..., 1668. Amsterdam: 1668. First edition, Volume two parts II and III only, folio, 26 hand colored plates, 2 hand colored titlepages, 2 hand colored double page plates, 21 full page hand colored plates, pages 3/4 with considerable loss to lower corner, pages 57/58, 175/176, 203/204 torn (no loss), original full dark calf (circa 1668), with gilt fillets and wreath-like device on both upper and lower covers, all edges gilt and guaffered, crudely rebacked with blackish corded cloth (no attempt to match leather), with very old spine mounted and weirdly stained white, spine gilt decoration obscured by white and yet with enough manuscript title for this volume to indicate it belongs together, imitation 19th century style marbled leaves and later endleaves, 7 leaves with faint waterstaining to outer margin at front, some minor foxing, inscription of Collegii Neoburgensis... Jesu 1667, 2 plates with manuscript notations to margins, one line manuscript with internal references at rear, very good.   Jeff Weber Rare Books   183 - 23   2016 $20,000

Lubin, R. P. A. *Mercure Geographique ou Le Guide du Curieux des Cartes Goegraphiques.* Paris: Chez Christophie Remy, 1678. First edition, 12mo., frontispiece, woodcut on titlepage, page of 'table' torn without loss, contemporary brown full calf, gilt, covers rubbed, neatly rebacked using original spine, good tight copy.   J. & S. L. Bonham Antiquarian Booksellers   Voyages 2016 - 8924   2016 $950

Lucanus, Marcus Annaeus *Pharaslia, cum Commentario Petri Burmanni.* Leidae: apud Conradum Wishoff, Danielem Goetval et Georg. Jacob Wishoff fil, Conrad, 1740. 4to., presentation certificate bound in, titlepage in red and black with large engraved vignette, some woodcut initials, 3 page errata to rear, occasional light foxing, some leaves little grubby towards top and fore-edges, contemporary prize vellum, gilt spine and boards with Utrecht coat-of-arms centerpiece to both boards, edges sprinkled red and blue, spine darkened, quite soiled, joint beginning to crack but holding firm, endpapers bit dusty, very good, presentation certificate dated 1776 bound in before titlepage, inscribed to Henrico Petro van Hurck and signed by various academics, small leaf of calculations in old hand loosely inserted.   Unsworths Antiquarian Booksellers   30 - 98   2016   £300

Lucanus, Marcus Annaeus *Pharsalia.* Twicknham: Strawberry Hill, 1760. 4to., engraved vignette on titlepage and dedication, prelims in first state, some light spotting, contemporary calf, rebacked and recornered in slightly different shade, preserving original lettering piece, spine gilt in compartments, marbled endpapers preserved, old leather scratched, bookplate of Earl of Guildford to front pastedown, good.   Blackwell's Rare Books   Greek & Latin Classics VII - 57   2016   £500

Lucas, John *The Melancholy Man: a Study of Dickens's Novels.* London: Methuen & Co., 1970. First edition, half title, original green cloth very good in slightly torn dust jacket.   Jarndyce Antiquarian Booksellers   CCXVIII - 1361   2016   £20

Lucas, John *The Poetry of Theodore Roethke.* Oxford Review, 1968. Offprint, 8vo., stapled wrappers, inscribed by author for William Claire, laid in TLS to Claire.   Second Life Books, Inc.   196 B - 101   2016 $85

Lucas, Richard *An Enquiry into the Happiness.* London: printed by J. Buckland (and 8 others), 1764. Tenth edition, 8vo, near fine in full contemporary sprinkled calf, raised and gilt banded spines, red morocco labels, from the library of Invercauld Casatle, Braemar.   Jarndyce Antiquarian Booksellers   CCXVI - 373   2016   £450

Lucas, Robert *Below the Belt.* New York: Universal, 1953. First edition, digest size paperback original, especially fine, crisp and unread copy, rare.   Between the Covers Rare Books   202 - 69   2016 $450

Lucas, W. F. *Bottom Fishing: a Novella and Other Stories.* Knoxville: Carpetbag Press, 1974. First edition, 8vo., 8vo., author's presentation on inside of cover for David Henderson, some very light spots at bottom of some leaves, cover soiled, otherwise very good, tight copy.   Second Life Books, Inc.   196 B - 102   2016 $150

Lucianus Samosatensis *Dialogorum Selectorum Libri Duo Graecolatini.* Ingolstadt: Ex officinia typogrpahica Adami Sartorii, 1598. 8vo., final blank discarded, errata leaf present, top margin of last few leaves worn (with loss to running title), titlepage dust soiled and bit frayed at fore-margin, small paper flaw in leaf y4 affecting few characters, occasional marginal annotations in Latin and Greek in early hand, gathering v bound out of order, 8vo, contemporary dark sheep, paper label to spine, rubbed and scratched, some wrear to joints, leather since treated to conserve it, various inscriptions in English, Latin and Greek - Andrew Baxter and his son Alexander of Duns Castle, also of Thomas Mein.   Blackwell's Rare Books   Greek & Latin Classics VII - 58   2016   £750

Lucianus Samosatensis *Gli Dilettevoli Dialogi la vere Narrationi.* Venice: Bernardin Bindoni, 1543. Small 8vo., late 19th century vellum backed cloth boards, original gilt guaffered edges remain, title within one piece historiated border and 30 large woodcut illustrations, fine woodcut printer's device of a full on verso of otherwise blank final leaf, blank margin at foot of titlepage cut away and repaired, few light stains but otherwise fresh copy.   Maggs Bros. Ltd.   1474 - 49   2016   £1250

Lucianus Samosatensis *Part of Lucian Made English from the original in the Year 1638. (bound with) Certain Select Dialogues of Lucian...* Oxford: printed by H. Hull for R. Davis, 1664. Oxford: printed for Richard Davis, 1663. First English editions, second issue of volume 1, folio, 2 volumes in one, engraved frontispiece, full contemporary calf rebacked to style, brown morocco spine label lettered in gilt, edges dyed green, newer endpapers, edges and corners of boards chipped and boards rubbed, corner marginal paper flaw to leaves F, L. not affect text, small nole on page number of leaf M3, 3 3/4 inch closed tear to leaf P, occasional old ink markings from previous owner, some foxing, overall very good, rare.   Heritage Book Shop   Holiday 2015 - 64   2016 $2000

Lucianus Samosatensis *Opera (with) Index Verboru ac Phrasutti Luciani sive Lexicon Lucianeum...* Amsterdam: sumptibus Jacobi Wetstenii, 1743. Utrecht: ex typographia Hermanni Besseling, 1746, Engraved frontispiece in first volume, light toning and spotting, browned in places, 4to., uniformly bound in contemporary Spanish marbled sheep, spine with five raised bands, red and green morocco lettering pieces, other compartments infilled with gilt volute, flower and circle tools, marbled endpapers, edges red, rubbed, some surface damage to leather, good.   Blackwell's Rare Books   B186 - 96   2016   £800

Luckombe, Philip *The History and Art of Printing.* printed by W. Adlard and J. Browne for J. Johnson, 1771. 8vo., woodcut frontispiece, woodcut illustrations in text, type specimens, text within decorative border, waterstaining at either end, chiefly confined to flyleaves, contemporary calf, spine with gilt fleuron in each compartment, red lettering pieces, cracking to joints, some wear, sound.   Blackwell's Rare Books   B184 - 60   2016   £600

Lucretius Carus, Titus *De Rerum Natura libri Sex.* Paris: in Guilielmi Rouillij et Philippi G. Roullij, Nep., 1563. First edition edited by Lambin, 4to., several library stamps to titlepage, one leaf with substantial manuscript note in early hand, 4to., 18th century vellum boards, spine divided by raised bands, second compartment gilt lettered direct, scattering of wormholes to backstrip, vellum partly defective in lower compartment, worn area partly covered by library shelfmark label, front hinge splitting at titlepage, library label with 'withdrawn' stamp, endpapers treated (successfully to stop worming coming through covers), sound.   Blackwell's Rare Books   Greek & Latin Classics VII - 59   2016   £900

Lucretius Carus, Titus *De Rerum Natura Libri Sex.* Paris: in aedibus Rouilli, 1565. 16mo., titlepage with woodcut border, this just shaved at head and with slim strip of blank area excised at foot, two blank leaves VI and +8 discarded, light browning in places, little dampmarking at end, 17th century sprinkled calf spine gilt in compartments, red morocco lettering piece little chipped, some wear to foot of spine and front joint printed label partially removed from front pastedown, old ownership inscription, some other pencil marks, good.   Blackwell's Rare Books B184 - 61   2016   £800

Lucretius Carus, Titus *De Rerum Natura Libri VI.* Frankfurt: heirs of Andreas Wechel, 1583. Fourth Lambin edition, woodcut printer's device on title, slightly browned, last few leaves with stain in lower margin, 12mo., modern vellum in old style, good.   Blackwell's Rare Books   B186 - 97   2016   £600

Lucretius Carus, Titus *Der Rerum Natura Libri Sex.* Birmingham: Typis Johannis Baskerville, 1772. 12mo. light age toning, few marginal pencil marks, contemporary calf, spine divided by gilt fillets, red morocco lettering piece, other compartments with centural gilt fillets, rubbed, front joint cracking but strong, bookplate of Charles Wordsworth (1806-1902) covering earlier bookplate, good.   Blackwell's Rare Books   Greek & Latin Classics VII - 60   2016   £150

Lucretius Carus, Titus *De Rerum Nature Libros Sex, ad Exemplarium Mss. Fidem Recensitos...* Impensis editoris typis A Hamilton, 1796-1797. First Wakefield edition, large paper copy, engraved frontispiece, little spotting and dust soiling here and there, tall 4to., contemporary vellum, boards bordered with gilt roll with central gilt stamp of arms of Duke of Devonshire, spines titled gilt, deep blue endpapers, edges gilt and marbled underneath vellum on each spine split horizontally, just above middle, volume ii in two places (with slight loss of vellum on volumes ii and iii), otherwise just little bit age yellowed and with touch of wear to spine ends, bookplates of Chatsworth Library, red morocco gilt booklabels of Baron Holland, plus modern paper booklabel in volume i, very good.   Blackwell's Rare Books   B186 - 98   2016   £3000

Lucretius Carus, Titus *De Rerum Nature Libri Sex.* in aedibus Richardi Taylor, 1832. 4to., contemporary polished russia, boards bordered with double gilt fillet, spine divided by raised bands with gilt fillets, second and fourth compartments gilt lettered direct, rest with gilt borders and arabesques in blind, boards bit marked, joints and extremities rubbed.   Blackwell's Rare Books   Greek & Latin Classics VII - 62   2016   £150

Lucretius Carus, Titus *De Rerum Natura Libri Sex.* Berlin: Impensis Georgii, 1850. 8vo., 2 volumes bound as one, little foxing at beginning and end, contemporary vellum, boards ruled in blue, spine gilt, red and green morocco lettering pieces, green morocco date piece at foot (albeit with wrong date, 1840), marbled edges and endpapers, boards just slightly bowed, touch of rubbing to extremities, bookplate and ownership inscription of William Dickinson (Trinity college 1851), very good.   Blackwell's Rare Books   Greek & Latin Classics VII - 63   2016   £1000

Ludecke, Kurt G. W. *I Knew Hitler - the Story of a Nazi Who Escaped the Blood of Purge.* London: Jarrolds, 1938. First UK edition, octavo, photos, very good in very good, nicked and creased dust jacket with closed tears at head of upper hinge and hinge of upper flap, uncommon.   Peter Ellis   112 - 458   2016   £125

Ludlum, Robert *The Materese Circle.* New York: Marek, 1979. First edition, fine in dust jacket.   Mordida Books   2015 - 012143   2016 $55

Ludlum, Robert *The Osterman Weekend.* Cleveland: World Publ Co., 1972. First edition, fine in very good+ dust jacket with pieces missing at bottom of spine and top of spine and flap folds.   Ken Hebenstreit, Bookseller   2016 - 2016 $65

Ludlum, Robert *The Road to Omaha.* New York: Random House, 1992. First edition, very fine in dust jacket.   Mordida Books   2015 - 004726   2016 $55

Ludolf, Hiob *A New History of Ethiopia.* London: for Samuel Smith, 1682. First edition in English, folio, 8 engraved plates, engraved plate of Ethiopic alphabet and folding genealogical table, contemporary or early 18th century calf, front hinge cracked but held by cords, corners worn, some light browning, but very good with signatures of Edmund and Rufus Marsden, latter dated 1762, Herz booklabel.   Joseph J. Felcone, Inc.   Books from Five Centuries: a Miscellany - 92   2016 $2200

Lugar, Robert *Villa Architecture: a Collection of Views with Plans, of Buildings Executed in England, Scotland &c.* London: J. Taylor, 1828. First edition, folio, 42 plates, of 2hich 26 are handcolored aquatints, 16 floral plans, modern hal red morocco, margins of first two leaves bit soiled, few tiny chips, two leaves of preface moderately foxed, occasional spot of foxing, but plates clean and bright and fine, signature of H. LeRoy Newbold, NY 1836.   Joseph J. Felcone, Inc.   Books from Five Centuries: a Miscellany - 7   2016 $4500

Luhan, Mabel Dodge *Taos and Artists.* New York: 1947. First edition, 56 full page plates, dust jacket spine faded, edgewear with slight soil and loss, internally clean and very good.   Dumont Maps and Books   133 - 65   2016 $100

Luhan, Mabel Dodge *Una and Robin.* Berkeley: Bancroft library, 1976. First edition, photo frontispiece, 4 black and white plates, original printed gray wrappers, fine.   Argonaut Book Shop   Private Press 2015 - 2482   2016 $45

Luhan, Mabel Dodge *Winter in Taos.* New York: Harcourt Brace and Co., 1935. First edition, 16 black and white photographic reproductions, 8 1/4 x 5 3/4 inches, tan cloth with maroon topstain, brown stamped lettering, orange and white dust jacket with black borders and black and white illustrations, light age toning to leaves, small booksellers label to front pastedown, gutter at half title slightly strained, one dog eared page, text clean, binding square, dust jacket somewhat edgeworn, small chips/loss to spine ends and tips, flaps machine clipped only with $.275 intact on flap, very good in about very good dust jacket.   Tavistock Books   Getting Around - 15   2016 $125

Luhrs, Victor *The Longbow Murder.* W. W. Norton & Co., 1941. First edition, cloth, spine lightly faded, page edges uniformly tanned, else fine in dust jacket with minor, tiny professional restoration to spine ends, attractive copy. Buckingham Books   2015 - 35815   2016 $475

Lunch, Lydia *Adulterers Anonymous.* New York: Grove press, 1982. Signed by Lunch and co author Exene Cervenka at publication party, fine in wrappers.   Ken Lopez Bookseller   166 - 71   2016 $175

Lupton, Thomas *A Thousand Notable Things on Various Subjects....* London: printed for Walker, Edwards & Reynolds, 1815. 12mo., some spotting throughout, 19th century half black calf, nice.   Jarndyce Antiquarian Books   CCXV - 301   2016   £120

Lushington, A. M. *Stories from French History.* London: Saunders, Otley and Co., 1868. Half title, frontispiece and 7 further plates by William Wheelwright, original green moire cloth, bevelled boards, pictorially blocked on front board with two jousting knights, all edges gilt, near fine.   Jarndyce Antiquarian Booksellers   CCXVII - 167   2016   £250

Luther, Martin *Dris Martini Luthri Colloquia Mensalia or the Dr. Martin Luther's divine Discourses at His Table, etc.* London: printed by William Du Gard, 1652. First English edition, large quarto, recent full calf period style, red morocco label, gilt lettering, some spotting and foxing to text, fine. The Brick Row Book Shop   Miscellany 69 - 56   2016 $2500

Lutoslawaki, Wincenty *The Origin and Growth of Plato's Logic.* London: Longmans, Green & co., 1897. First edition, good, original maroon cloth, rubbed at extremities, some spotting and fox bumps, gilt lettering on spine clearly legible, split at front joint has been almost imperceptibly repaired.   Simon Finch   2015 - 001053   2016 $194

Luzi, Mario *In the Dark Body of Metamorphosis & Other Peoms.* New York: Norton, 1972. First edition, blue cloth, nice in little scuffed and soiled dust jacket, presentation by translator to I. L. Salomon.   Second Life Books, Inc.   197 - 219   2016 $45

Lydekker, Richard *The Deer of All Lands: a History of the Family Cervidae Living and Extinct.* Rowland Ward Ltd., 1898. First and only edition, large 4to., original pale green cloth, upper cover and spine titled gilt, all edges gilt, 24 fine hand colored lithographed plates by J. Smit, many photos and wood engraved illustrations, previous owner's blindstamp, signature verso of f.f.e.p., binding little rubbed, occasional faint foxing, very good.   Sotheran's Hunting, Shooting & Fishing - 60   2016   £4000

Lydekker, Richard *The Royal Natural History.* London: Frederick Warne and Co., 1893-1896. Quarto, 6 volumes, chromolithographs and text illustrations, handsome publisher's decorated cloth, some spotting, otherwise very good. Andrew Isles Natural History Books   55 - 7131   2016 $500

Lydekker, Richard *The Royal Natural History.* London: Frederick Warne & Co., 1893-1896. First edition, 6 volumes, original tan cloth, bevelled boards, each volume richly blocked in gold, silver and black with gilt title surmounting a rectangular panel containing a vignette of an exotic catalog, 72 chromolithographed plates, wood engraved illustrations, light rubbing to extremities, little scattered foxing, binding very bright, very good.   Sotheran's Piccadilly Notes - Summer 2015 - 195   2016   £300

Lydius, Jacobus *Syntagma Sacrum De Re Militairi: Nec Non De Jure Jurando Dissertation Philologica.* Dordaci: apud Cornelium Willegardum Bibliopolam, 1698. First edition, 4to., 12 plates, 4 of which are folding, additional engraved titlepage, woodcut device to titlepage and further woodcut head and tailpieces and initials, generous margins, couple of small closed marginal tears, paper flaw to bottom edge of pages 89-90, not affecting text, very occasional spots, few small stains to engraved title, some light marginal smudges but generally clean and bright within, 19th century marbled paper covered boards with tan calf corners, recently rebacked in tan speckled calf with raised bands, red morocco gilt label, edges very lightly sprinkled red, boards bit rubbed, corners worn, very good. sound, Oxford University bookplate with "Rejected 1925" overwritten in pencil.   Unsworths Antiquarian Booksellers   30 - 99   2016   £450

Lyell, Charles *The Geological Evidences of the Antiquity of Man...* London: John Murray, 1873. fourth edition, octavo, uncolored frontispiece, contemporary full calf prize binding, all edges marbled, both boards detached, ex-library. Andrew Isles Natural History Books   55 - 38606   2016 $100

Lyman, George D. *John Marsh, Pioneer. The Life Story of a Trail-Blazer on Six Frontiers.* New York: Charles Scribner's Sons, 1930. First edition, presentation inscription signed and dated by author, 24 illustrations, map endpapers, gilt lettered dark blue cloth, very fine copy. Argonaut Book Shop   Biography 2015 - 7608   2016 $60

Lyman, George D. *John Marsh Pioneer, The Life Story of a Trail Blazer on Six Frontiers.* New York: Charles Scribner's Sons, 1930. First limited, signed edition, number 5 of 150 numbered copies signed by author, four facsimile folding letters tipped in, 24 illustrations, map endpapers, publisher's two-tone red cloth, black leather spine label, very fine, slipcase, very scarce.   Argonaut Book Shop Biography 2015 - 7433   2016 $425

Lyman, Theodore *The Diplomacy of the United States...* Boston: Wells and Lilly, 1828. Second edition, 2 volumes, 8vo., full leather, lettered gilt at spine, ex-Foreign and Commonwealth Office library with their label and stamps and few library marks, covers worn and scuffed, front board loose on volume one with clean text.   Any Amount of Books   2015 - A49587   2016   £165

Lynam, C. C. *To Norway and the North Cape in 'Blue Dragon II' 1911-1912.* London: Sidgwick & Jackson, 1913. First edition, scarce, in later variant binding, 8vo., original blue cloth, ornamented and lettered in black, circular illustration from a photo mounted on front cover, map endpapers, highly illustrated with maps and plates after photos and drawings, color frontispiece, binding restored and with light marking, apart from very light browning, internally very good, early ownership inscription, scarce.   Sotheran's Travel and Exploration - 266   2016   £125

Lynam, Edward *Richard Hakluyt and His Successors.* London: Hakluyt Society, 1946. First edition, 8vo., illustrations, original blue cloth.   J. & S. L. Bonham Antiquarian Booksellers   Voyages 2016 - 7364   2016   £40

Lyndon, Barre *The Amazing Dr. Clitterhouse.* London: Hamish Hamilton, 1936. First edition, 8vo. fine in little soiled and worn dust jacket, photos, signed by 12 members of the first NY production, including Alexander Field, Edward Fulang, Muriel Hutchinson, Stephen Fox and others.   Second Life Books, Inc.   196 B - 108   2016 $225

Lyne, A. G. *Biology of the Skin and Hair Growth Proceedings of a symposium Held at Canberra, Australia, August 1964.* Sydney: Angus and Robertson, 1965. Octavo, text illustrations, very good in dust jacket, signed by Lyne.   Andrew Isles Natural History Books   55 - 35908   2016 $100

Lynes, H. *Review of the Genus Cisticola.* London: the Ibis, 1930. Octavo, two volumes, 20 color plates, handsome publisher's 'ibis' red cloth, very good.   Andrew Isles Natural History Books   55 - 35616   2016 $850

Lyons, Albert S. *Medicine an Illustrated History.* New York: Abrams, 1978. 615 pages, many illustrations, color and black and white, large tall 4to., dust jacket, light wear, else near new.   James Tait Goodrich   X-78 - 383   2016 $148

Lyons, Anthony *Observations on My First visit to Ireland.* Norton, Malton: T. Baker & Son, Printers, circa, 1924. Photo illustrations, original grey printed boards, slightly marked.   Jarndyce Antiquarian Booksellers   CCXVII - 168   2016   £60

Lyons, Arthur *At the Hands of Another.* New York: Holt Rinehart & Winston, 1983. First edition, very fine in dust jacket, inscribed by author.   Mordida Books   2015 - 009093   2016 $55

Lyons, Daniel *Magna Britannia; Being a Concise Topographical Account of the Several Counties of Great Britain.* London: printed for T. Cadell and W. Davies, 1806-1822. Large paper copy, 346 x 260mm., 6 volumes bound in 10, pleasing contemporary red hard-grain half morocco over marbled boards by J. Mackenzie & son (stamp signed), raised bands, spines attractively gilt in compartments with very large and complex central fleuron surrounded by small tools and volute cornerpieces, gilt titling, marbled endpapers, all edges gilt, with 398 plates of maps, plans, views and architecture, 264 as called for and extra illustrated with 134, the total including 72 double page, 7 folding and 13 in color, engraved armorial bookplate of Arthur Soames, signed and dated in the plate by C. Hebard, paper boards somewhat chafed, extremities (especially bottom edge of boards), rather rubbed, spines slightly (but uniformly) darkened, few of the leather corners abraded, small portions of morocco dulled from perservatives, but bindings completely solid with no cracking to joints and still impressive on shelf, handsomely decorated spines unmarked, majority of plates with variable foxing (usually minimal, but perhaps two dozen noticeably foxed), a number of engravings with small, faint dampstains at very edge of top margin, text itself very fine, looking remarkably clean, fresh, smooth within its vast margins.   Phillip J. Pirages   67 - 245   2016 $5900

Lyotard, Jean Francois *Pacific Wall.* Venice: Lapis Press, 1990. first edition in English, small 4to., folding photographic plate, original photo illustrated paper over boards, publisher's sepia colored acetate dust jacket and printed acetate wrap-around band, publisher's cloth traycase, very fine.   James S. Jaffe Rare Books   Occasional List: Winter 2016 - 89   2016 $1250

Lyric Love. London: and New York: Macmillan and Co., 1892. 159 x 105mm., lovely contemporary blue-gray crushed morocco elegantly and elaborately gilt by Bumpus (stamp signed), covers with delicate filigree frame and large densely intricate central medallion composed of hundreds of small tools, fan shaped cornerpieces of similar design, raised bands, spine gilt in compartments with central medallion and scrolling cornerpieces, pastedowns framed by turquoise morocco with gilt filigree borders, fleuron cornerpieces and alternating dot and crescent tools along the four sides, ivory silk endleaves, all edges gilt, titlepage vignette, front pastedown with engraved bookplate of Victoria Sackville-West, spine sunned to pleasant slightly darker blue green, joints with just a hint of water, light offsetting to free endleaves from turn-ins as usual, isolated corner creases, other trivial imperfections, but most attractive little book, especially smooth and clean internally and in flamboyant binding showing almost no wear.   Phillip J. Pirages   67 - 33   2016 $1500

Lysons, Daniel *Magna Britannia Being a Concise Topographical Account of the Several Counties of Great Britain. (Cambridgeshire).* London: printed for T. Cadell and W. Davies, 1808. Volume II Part I Cambridgeshire, large 4to., large paper copy, extra illustrated, 23 engraved plates as called for, plus 9 extra, some foxing to frontispiece with occasional light spotting elsewhere, some smudge marks early and late in text, pasted to page 268, next to entry on Trumpington is news clipping on Trumpington Cross causing little offset browning to adjacent pages, later quarter crimson roan with green cloth boards, brown morocco gilt label to spine, raised bands, top edge cut with others deckled, spine rubbed and faded but holding firm, few marks, edges dusty, very good, loosely inserted, previous owner's hasty list of extra plates, tiny news clipping from the Times dated Sept 5th 1898 reporting death of Rev. George Charter of Cambridgeshire. Unsworths Antiquarian Booksellers Ltd. E04 - 12 2016 £275

Lysons, Daniel *Magna Britannia....* London: printed for T. Cadell and W. Davies, 1810. Volume II Part II, large 4to., large paper copy, extra illustrated, all 35 plates called for plus 29 additional plates, occasional foxing, particularly to some plates, few plates repaired at edges and one bound upside down, contemporary vellum boards, brown, calf corners recently rebacked in brown morocco with gilt spine label, all edges gilt, endpapers renewed, some staining and smudgy marks to boards, corners worn, still very good, ownership inscription. Unsworths Antiquarian Booksellers 30 - 101 2016 £275

Lyttelton, Edward *Mothers and Sons or Problems in the Home Training of Boys.* London: Macmillan and Co., 1893. Half title, 4 pages ads, original blue cloth, contemporary signature of Danny Wilson, very good. Jarndyce Antiquarian Books CCXV - 302 2016 £25

Lyttelton, Edward *Thirteen Essays on Education.* London: Percival & Co., 1891. First edition, original dark green cloth. Jarndyce Antiquarian Books CCXV - 1891 2016 £20

Lyttelton, Thomas, Baron *Letters of the late Lord Lyttelton.* London: printed for J. Bew, 1780. 1792. First edition of volume I, fourth edition of volume II, 2 volumes, 8vo., contemporary half calf, marbled paper boards, lacking labels. Jarndyce Antiquarian Booksellers CCXVI - 374 2016 £45

Lytton, Edward George Earle Lyton, Bulwer-Lytton, 1st Baron 1803-1873 *The Pilgrims of the Rhine.* London: Saunders & Otley, 1834. First edition, 8o., plates, vignettes, contemporary brown calf, spine rubbed and worn, corners rubbed. J. & S. L. Bonham Antiquarian Booksellers Europe 2016 - 6258 2016 £65

Lytton, Edward George Earle Lyton, Bulwer-Lytton, 1st Baron 1803-1873 *The Works of Edward Lytton Bulwer...* Philadelphia: E. L. Carey and A. Hart, 1836. Small 4to., 2 volumes, fine contemporary gilt stamped red morocco, some wear but very good, rare set. M & S Rare Books, Inc. 99 - 26 2016 $450

Lytton, Edward George Earle Lyton, Bulwer-Lytton, 1st Baron 1803-1873 *Works.* London: G. Routledge and Co., Chapman and Hall, 1851-1860. New edition, 19 titles in 20 volumes, frontispieces, occasional spotting and dusting, one or two gatherings slightly proud, uniformly bound in contemporary half maroon calf blocked in blind, spines decorated in gilt, dark green leather labels, armorial bookplates of Charles Dickens, with "From the Library of Charles Dickens" label in all volumes. Jarndyce Antiquarian Booksellers CCXVIII - 869 2016 £4500

Lytton, Edward George Earle Lyton, Bulwer-Lytton, 1st Baron 1803-1873 *Works.* London: George Routledge and Sons, circa, 1870. Large 8vo., late 19th century green half hard grained morocco, spine with gilt ornaments in compartments, lettered direct, marbled edges, spines faded, bookplate of John Camm Buckley, good. Blackwell's Rare Books B186 - 29 2016 £300

Lytton, Edward Robert Bulwer-Lytton, 1st Earl of 1831-1891 *After Paradise or Legends of Exile with Other Poems.* London: David Stott, 1887. First edition, original blue cloth with gilt title to spine, minor wear to edges, interior is very clean with some light foxing to last few pages, tight binding, nice copy apart from presence of a circulating library label, bookplate stating the book was presented to the Norfolk and Norwich Library by the Rev. Elwin in 1907, scarce, very good, presentation copy inscribed W. E. by author (Rev. Warwick Elwin, close friend). The Kelmscott Bookshop 12 - 61 2016 $175

M

M'Crie, James *Autopaedia or Instructions on Personal Education.* Aberdeen: John Smith, 1866. First edition, photo frontispiece, few leaves roughly opened, original maroon cloth, spine dulled, slightly later gift inscription. Jarndyce Antiquarian Books   CCXV - 839   2016   £48

M'Dougall, John *High Court of Admiralty Edinburgh 9th May 1821. Trial of John M'Dougall & James Menzies, before Sir John Connell, Knt. Judge Admiral of Scotland, for casting away a vessel the Friends of Glasgow and of John M'Dougall and Archibald M'Lachlan for Abstracting Goods from a Vessel called the Mary and afterwards Scuttling her.* Glasgow: printed by Young and Gallie for Maurice Ogle, 1821. First edition, 8vo., disbound.   Howard S. Mott Inc.   265 - 137   2016 $300

M'Harry, Samuel *The Practical Distiller; or an Introduction of making Whiskey, Gin, Brandy, Spirits &c.* Harrisburg: John Wyeth, 1809. Contemporary sheep, corner extremities uniformly clipped, front free endpaper wanting, some marginal staining, but very good in very tight and attractive original binding, rare.   Joseph J. Felcone, Inc.   Books from Five Centuries: a Miscellany - 101   2016 $4000

M'Intosh, Charles *The Greenhouse, Hot House and Stove..* London: Wm. S. Orr and Co., Amen Corner, Paternoster Row, 1838. 8vo., 18 hand colored engraved plates, including frontispiece and additional titlepage, numerous wood engraved text illustrations, original green cloth blocked in blind and gilt.   Marlborough Rare Books   List 56 - 36   2016   £500

M., C. A. *Notes on the Horn Book.* Northampton: printed by H. Butterfield, Herald and Daily Chronicle, Offices for Taylor & Son, Dryden Press,, 1901. Half title, illustrations, folded as issued, splitting at fold.   Jarndyce Antiquarian Books   CCXV - 774   2016   £25

Maaskamp, E. *Afbeeidingen van de Kleeding, Zeden en Gewoonten in Holland...* Amsterdam: E. Maaskamp Aupres du Palais, 1811. 4to., finely and handsomely bound in half tan Regency calf over marbled boards, spine with 5 raised bands exquisitely and extravagantly decorated in gilt in compartments with repeating scroll tool design, lettered direct in gilt, marbled endpapers and edges, housed within custom made beige cloth covered fall down back box with green cloth label lettered gilt, with fine stipple engraved and hand colored allegorical frontispiece, 20 other fine and exquisite engraved plates with detailed and expert hand coloring, wonderfully pleasing copy, externally fine, recently expertly and invisibly rejointed at upper board by Charles Gledhill, internally also preserved in exceptionally crisp state with occasional very light and inoffensive, browning and spotting almost exclusively confined to text pages, neat contemporary inscription.   Sotheran's   Travel and Exploration - 240   2016   £1400

Mably, Gabriel Bonnot, Abbe De *Observations sur les Grecs.* Geneve: par la Compagnie des Libraires, 1749. First edition, 12mo., half title, leaf of errata, contemporary calf, spine gilt with raised bands and label, very good, crisp copy.   John Drury Rare Books   2015 - 23281   2016 $350

MacArthur, Bessie J. B. *The Clan of Loghlann and Silis: Two celtic Plays.* Edinburgh: Urquhart, 1928. First edition, 8vo., als from author laid in, paper wrappers, very good. Second Life Books, Inc.   196 B - 111   2016 $45

Macaulay, Rose *The Towers of Trebizond.* London: Collins, 1956. First edition, few spots and thumb-marks, 8vo., original black cloth, spine lettered green, dust jacket backstrip trifle faded, good.   Blackwell's Rare Books   B184 - 192   2016   £75

MacCann *Ride through the Argentine Provinces; being an Account of the Natural Products of the Country and Habits of the People...* London: Smith Elder, 1853. First edition, 8vo., 2 volumes, colored frontispieces, folding map, illustrations, original decorative cloth, gilt vignettes, spines faded with small wear to heads, very good.   J. & S. L. Bonham Antiquarian Booksellers   America 2016 - 9885   2016   £420

MacCarthy, Fiona *Stanley Spencer - an English Vision.* New Haven: Yale University Press, 1997. First edition, quarto, copiously illustrated in color, fine in near fine dust jacket just little nicked and rubbed at head of spine.   Peter Ellis   112 - 380   2016   £50

Macclesfield, George Parker, Earl of *Remarks Upon the Solar and Lunar Years The Cycle of 19 Years, Commonly Called the Golden Number....* printed for Charles Davis, 1750. First separate edition, 4to., folding table at end, later (not recent) marbled boards, very good.   Blackwell's Rare Books   B186 - 112   2016   £350

MacDiarmid, John *An Inquiry into the System of National Defence in Great Britain.* London: C. and R. Baldwin, 1805. First edition, 2 volumes, 8vo., without half titles, recently rebound in good matching cloth backed boards, spine labels lettered gilt, marbled edges, very good, surprisingly rare.   John Drury Rare Books   2015 - 25371   2016 $350

MacDonald, A. C. *Euphrates Exile.* London: Bell, 1936. First and only edition, original orange-red cloth, spine lettered in black, map endpapers, plates from photos, extremities little worn and marked, light offsetting from endpapers, otherwise internally good, inscribed by author July 1937, map endpapers with additional Iraqi place names in manuscript.   Sotheran's   Travel and Exploration - 340   2016   £148

MacDonald, Christine Lewis *The story of an Island.* Edinburgh: Macdonald Pub., 1982. First edition, 8vo., original glossy paper covered boards, black and white photos upper board, little sunned to top, internally fine.   Sotheran's Piccadilly Notes - Summer 2015 - 196   2016   £30

MacDonald, Clyde F. *Sunny Brae a Village Since 1802.* New Glasgow: Clyde F. MacDonald, 2002. Trade paperback, 8vo., illustrations, signed by author, very good.   Schooner Books Ltd.   115 - 155   2016 $40

MacDonald, George 1824-1905 *At the Back of the North Wind.* London: Strahan & Co., 1871. (1870). First edition, half title, 76 illustrations after Arthur Hughes, 13 page catalog, original green cloth blocked in black, gilt and blind by Burn and Co. with their ticket, slight marking to endpapers, some mottling and rubbing of cloth, all edges gilt, still very good, scarce edition.   Jarndyce Antiquarian Booksellers CCXVII - 171   2016   £2500

MacDonald, George 1824-1905 *The Golden Key.* New York: Farrar Straus and Giroux, 1967. First printing, 8vo., illustrations by Maurice Sendak, blue cloth with decorative stamping in silver, William Jay Smith's copy with his signature, little scuffed at top edge of spine, otherwise nice in slightly soiled dust jacket.   Second Life Books, Inc.   197 - 220   2016 $135

MacDonald, George 1824-1905 *Phantastes: a Faerie Romance for men and women.* London: Smith, Elder and Co., 1858. First edition, half title, original green cloth, recased, retaining original spine, endpapers replaced with contemporary cream paper, nice.   Jarndyce Antiquarian Booksellers CCXVII - 172   2016   £580

MacDonald, George 1824-1905 *The Princess and the Goblin.* Philadelphia: David McKay Co., 1920. First edition illustrated thus, binding, B, quarto, color pictorial titlepage and 8 full page color plates by Jessie Willcox Smith, publisher's beige line cloth, front cover bordered and lettered in blue with additional color illustration pasted on, spine decoratively lettered in blue, to edge gilt, color pictorial endpapers, neat ink inscription, fine in original color pictorial dust jacket.   David Brass Rare Books, Inc.   2015 - 2016 $550

MacDonald, George 1824-1905 *The Princess and the Goblin.* Philadelphia: David McKay, 1920. 4to., gilt cloth, pictorial paste-on, top edge gilt, light corner stain on corner of rear cover, rubbing very good, cover plate, pictorial endpapers, top edge gilt and 8 color plates by Jessie Willcox Smith.   Aleph-bet Books, Inc.   111 - 433   2016 $200

MacDonald, George 1824-1905 *Warlock O'Glenwarlock. A Homely romance.* Boston: D. Lothrop and Co., copyright, 1881. First edition, 4to., original tartan boards, spine paper considerably rubbed off, tips worn, rubbed at edges and corners, printed paper label on front cover, slightly chipped at one corner, just touching one letter, despite rubbing of boards, very good.   Howard S. Mott Inc.   265 - 83   2016 $950

MacDonald, George 1824-1905 *Works of Fancy and Imagination.* London: Strahan and Co., 1871. First edition, 16mo., 10 volumes, half titles, original green cloth, beveled boards, elaborately blocked in gilt by Burn, all edges gilt, very good apart from rubbing to gilt on spine volume VI, scarce first edition.   Jarndyce Antiquarian Booksellers CCXVII - 173   2016   £1200

MacDonald, John D. *The Deep Blue Good-by.* Greenwich: Fawcett, 1964. First edition, naer fine in wrappers.   Mordida Books   2015 - 009102   2016 $65

MacDonald, John D. *The Empty Trap.* New York: Popular Library, 1957. First edition, very good in wrappers.   Mordida Books   2015 - 010703   2016 $65

MacDonald, John D. *One Fearful Yellow Eye.* Philadelphia: Lippincott, 1977. First US hardcover edition, fine, bright copy in bright, fine dust jacket.   Buckingham Books   2015 - 31317   2016 $475

MacDonald, John D. *The Only Girl in the Game.* London: Robert Hale Limited, 1962. First hardcover edition, octavo, boards, nearly fine in very good or somewhat better dust jacket with light edge rubbing and light shelf wear to spine ends, moderate soiling to spine panel and several tiny closed tears to lower front panel with crease, uncommon.   John W. Knott, Jr./L.W. Currey, Inc.   Fall-Winter 2015 - 17244   2016 $1250

MacDonald, John D. *Slam the Big Door.* London: Robert Hale Limited, 1961. First hardcover edition, octavo, boards very good in like or somewhat better dust jacket with mild creasing and edge wear, rub mark to lower right front corner. John W. Knott, Jr./L.W. Currey, Inc. Fall-Winter 2015 - 17242 2016 $1000

MacDonald, Philip *Patrol.* New York: Harper & Bros., 1928. First US edition, fine in professionally restored dust jacket, presentation inscription by author, exceptional copy of scarce book, rare in dust jacket. Buckingham Books 2015 - 25705 2016 $3500

MacDonald, Ross *Black Money.* New York: Knopf, 1966. First edition, inscribed by author to poet Donald Davie and wife, Doreen, fine in dust jacket with one tiny rub at head of spine. Buckingham Books 2015 - 20957 2016 $2750

MacDonald, Ross *The Doomsters.* London: Cassell & Co., 1958. First English edition, fine in near fine dust jacket with some rubbing and tiny, internally tape repaired nick at crown. Between the Covers Rare Books 204 - 79 2016 $50

MacDonald, Ross *The Far Side of the Dollar.* New York: Alfred A. Knopf, 1965. First edition, 8vo., fine in fine dust jacket, inscribed Jan. 15 1965 for Bill Gault, by author, exceptional copy, housed in cloth slipcase with red leather labels on spine, titles and date stamped in gold. Buckingham Books 2015 - 25474 2016 $2750

MacDonald, Ross *Find a Victim.* New York: Alfred A Knopf, 1954. First edition, signed by author, small octavo, patterned paper over boards, original dust jacket some rubbing to jacket, very tiny chip on rear of jacket at top, with two small creases nearby, some rubbing to book, still near fine. Heritage Book Shop Holiday 2015 - 76 2016 $3000

MacDonald, Ross *The Galton Case.* New York: Knopf, 1959. First edition, 8vo., signed by author, fine in price clipped dust jacket with light wear to spine ends and with tiny closed tears to top edge of rear panel, beautiful copy housed in black cloth slipcase with three red leather labels on spine with ties stamped in gilt. Buckingham Books 2015 - 25780 2016 $3000

MacDonald, Ross *The Goodbye Look.* London: Collins Crime Club, 1969. First English edition, fine in dust jacket with tiny wear at corners and tiny tear. Mordida Books 2015 - 011383 2016 $65

MacDonald, Ross *The Instant Enemy.* New York: Alfred A. Knopf, 1968. First edition, octavo, blue cloth backstrip over yellow paper boards, dust jacket with mild toning to jacket, recipient's name in inscription, presentation inscribed by author for Paul Nelson. Heritage Book Shop Holiday 2015 - 76 2016 $1250

MacDonald, Ross *The Underground Man.* New York: Knopf, 1971. First edition, fine in dust jacket with short crease on inner front flap. Mordida Books 2015 - 012713 2016 $65

MacDonald, Ross *The Wycherly Woman.* New York: Knopf, 1961. First edition, presentation inscription dated 1961, month of publication to the Marshall McLuhans, fine in dust jacket lightly soiled on rear panel and with some very minor restoration to spine ends and corners. Buckingham Books 2015 - 31440 2016 $3750

MacDonell, Arthur Anthony *A Practical Sanskrit Dictionary.* London: Oxford University Press, 1976. First edition, 7th photographic reprint, 4to., cloth, gilt lettered, light toning to upper board, 12 small brown marks to endpapers, edges lightly dusted, very good, no dust jacket, ownership inscription of C. D. N. Costa. Unsworths Antiquarian Booksellers Ltd. E05 - 51 2016 £25

MacDonough, Glen *Babes in Toyland.* New York: Fox Duffield, Sept., 1904. First edition, illustrations by Ethel Betts with cover design, color pictorial endpapers, 7 beautiful color plates plus many black and white line illustrations, 4to., tan pictorial cloth, slightest bit of finger soil, near fine. Aleph-bet Books, Inc. 112 - 54 2016 $450

MacEwen, William *Atlas of Head Sections. Fifty-Three Engraved Copperplates of Frozen Sections of the Head and Fifty-Three Key Plates with Descriptive Texts.* New York: Macmillan, 1893. First edition with NY cancel title, 4to., later plain buckram, internally quite clean. James Tait Goodrich X-78 - 386 2016 $995

MacEwen, William *The Growth and Shedding of the Antler of the Deer the Histological Pheneomna and their Relation to the Growth of Bone.* Glasgow: Maclehose, Jackson and Co., 1920. Octavo, photos, publisher's cloth, fine. Andrew Isles Natural History Books 55 - 34930 2016 $400

MacEwen, William *Pyogenic Infective Diseases of the Brain and Spinal Cord.* Glasgow: Maclehose, 1893. 60 illustrations, original green cloth, light wear, internally fresh, clean and uncut, penned "With Mess. Maclehose Compliments, and "William Thorburn Reviewer for Medical Chronicle", this appears to have been sent by publisher for review. James Tait Goodrich X-78 - 384 2016 $1295

MacEwen, William *Pyogenic Infective Diseases of the Brain and Spinal Cord.* Glasgow: Maclehose, 1893. Original cloth, illustrations, rebacked with original spine laid down, faded spine call number, otherwise internally fresh, clean and uncut. James Tait Goodrich X-78 - 385 2016 $695

MacFall, Haldane *Aubrey Beardsley...* New York: Simon & Schuster, 1927. First edition, 4to., black cloth, one of 300 signed by author. Second Life Books, Inc. 196 B - 113 2016 $250

MacFarlan, Allan *American Indian Legends.* New York: Heritage Press, 1968. Printed green boards with yellow cloth spine, fine in slightly soiled slipcase, illustrations by Everett Gee Jackson, Sandglass pamphlet laid in. Argonaut Book Shop Heritage Press 2015 - 7033 2016 $45

MacFarlan, Allan *American Indian Legends...* New York: printed for Members of the Limited Editions Club by the Ward Ritchie Press, Los Angeles, 1968. First edition, one of 1500 copies signed by artist, this number J.W., 4to., half tan calf and boards, slipcase, fine, illustrations by Everett Gee Jackson. Second Life Books, Inc. 196 B - 114 2016 $85

MacGill-Eain, Somhairle *Hallaig.* Isle of Skye: Urras Shomhairle/the Sorley MacLean Trust, 2002. One of 10 (actually 50 copies) signed by Seamus Heaney (translator), first edition, 9/50 copies, from an edition of 200 copies, crown 8vo., original stapled green wrappers, printed in black to front, fine, scarce. Blackwell's Rare Books B186 - 238 2016 £500

MacGillivray, E. J. *The Copyright Act 1911, Annotated.* London: Stevens and Sons, 1912. Original light blue cloth, lettered in black, little marked and dulled. Jarndyce Antiquarian Booksellers CCXVII - 239 2016 £65

MacGillivray, William *Rob Lindsay and His School...* London: T. N. Foulis, circa, 1910. Half title, frontispiece, illustrations, plates, 15 page catalog, original brown pictorial boards, cream paper spine, very good in slightly faded dust jacket. Jarndyce Antiquarian Books CCXV - 827 2016 £35

MacGowan, John *Death, a Vision or the Solemn departure of Saints and Sinners...* London: printed for G. G. J. & J. Robinson, 1789. Fifth edition, half title, 12mo., some slight foxing, full contemporary calf, gilt banded spine, red morocco label, joints slightly cracked but very firm, some insect damage to lower corner of upper board, early name of Thos. Smith on front endpaper, later inscription to half title "Hephzibah Smith the gift of her affectionate mother Feb. 3rd 1828". Jarndyce Antiquarian Booksellers CCXVI - 375 2016 £125

MacGregor, James G. *Edmonton Trader: the Story of John A. McDougall.* Toronto: McClelland & Stewart, 1963. First edition, map endpapers numerous photos, brown and cream cloth, fine, pictorial dust jacket. Argonaut Book Shop Biography 2015 - 5923 2016 $45

MacGregor, John *On Training Boys for Soldiers.* London: W. Mitchell & Co., 1875. First edition, original mauve wrappers, slightly creased and faded with small tear without loss at back, in ink "Gordon' Boys Camp 20 Cockspur Street S.W.". Jarndyce Antiquarian Books CCXV - 835 2016 £38

Machado, Antonio *I Never Wanted Fame.* St. Paul: Ally Press, 1979. First edition, limited to 1629 numbered copies, 26 lettered handcased in boards and signed by translator and binding craftsman, this one of the 26 lettered copies bound thus, oblong 32mo., pebbled cloth, illustrated label on front cover, decorated endpapers. Oak Knoll Books 310 - 162 2016 $100

Machen, Arthur 1863-1947 *The Carleon Edition of the Works of Arthur Machen.* London: Martin Secker, 1923. Limited to 1000 numbered sets signed by author, this number 392, octavo, 9 volumes, inserted frontispiece in volume one, original sage green cloth, front panels stamped in gold and ruled in blind, spine panels stamped in gold, rear panels ruled in blind, top edge gilt, other edges untrimmed, spines slightly age darkened, volume 5 has dampstain to front cover, nearly fine set with 6 volumes having good dust jackets 2 volumes having partial dust jackets and one volume with no dust jacket. John W. Knott, Jr./L.W. Currey, Inc. Fall-Winter 2015 - 15916 2016 $1250

Machiavelli, Niccolo 1469-1527 *Tutte le Opere.... Divise in V parti.* Geneva: 1550, circa, 1610. 1619. First Testina edition, although dated 1550 on titlepage, was in fact published in early 17th century, 5 parts in one volume, 4to., contemporary vellum, over paste boards, woodcut head and shoulders portrait on each title, little light dampstaining in places, few small wormholes, mostly marginal to Istorie Florentine. Maggs Bros. Ltd. 1474 - 50 2016 £2500

MacIntosh, Charles *Biographical Memoir of the late Charles Macintosh...* Glasgow: printed by W. G. Blackie and Co., Villafield, 1847. Frontispiece, half title, 8 plates, some folding at end with facsimiles of 57 signatures and handwriting of Macintosh's correspondents, original dark green cloth, little dulled, inscribed "with the author's best regards". Jarndyce Antiquarian Booksellers CCXVII - 174 2016 £125

Mack, Ebenezer *The Cat-Fight: a Mock Heroic Poem...* New York: sold at 350 Water Street, 1824. First edition, 12mo., five full page engravings, original plain boards, lacking front cover, uncut, some stains, especially last leaf, foxing. M & S Rare Books, Inc. 99 - 109 2016 $525

Mack, Robert *The Golden Treasury of Art and Song.* London & New York: Nister & Dutton, n.d. circa, 1890. Folio, brown cloth with elaborate gilt and silver pictorial cover, beveled edges, all edges gilt, endpapers mounted on cloth, tips and spine ends show some wear else very good+, 18 beautiful chromolithographs by Robert Bell. Aleph-bet Books, Inc. 112 - 50 2016 $250

Mackail, John William *Biblia Innocentium...* London: sold by Reeves & Turner, 1892. Limited to 20 paper copies, octavo, printed in Golden type, decorative woodcut border and initials, printed by William Morris at Kelmscott Press, original stiff vellum with yapp edges, spine lettered gilt, gold silk ties, pages uncut, two previous owner's bookplates, few leaves very lightly browned, excellent copy.   Heritage Book Shop   Holiday 2015 - 62   2016 $3000

MacKail, John William *William Morris, an Address Delivered the XIth November MDCCCC at Kelmscott House, Hammersmith, before Hammersmith Socialist Society.* London: Doves Press, 1901. One of 300 copies (of an edition of 315), printed in black and red on handmade paper, 8vo., original limp cream vellum by Doves Bindery, backstrip gilt lettered, untrimmed, slight wear to head of boards, bookplate of Charles Walker Andrews, very good, Andrews pencil note records that the book came from Salem Hyde's Library (Hyde being his father in law).   Blackwell's Rare Books Marks of Genius - 30   2016   £500

Mackail, John William *William Morris: an Address Delivered the XIth November MDCCCC at Kelmscott House Hammersmith Before the Hammersmith Socialist.* Hammersmith: Doves Press, 1901. Limited to 300 copies, 8vo., limp vellum, limited toning to vellum.   Oak Knoll Books   310 - 95   2016 $750

Mackarness, Matilda Anne *Old Jolliffe; not a Goblin Story.* London: W. N. Wright, 1850. Sixth edition, half title, original purple grey cloth, lettered in gilt, slightly faded, very good, all edges gilt.   Jarndyce Antiquarian Booksellers   CCXVIII - 376   2016   £45

MacKay, Henry Fowler *Orders and Regulations framed by Capt. Henry Fowler Mackay, Chief Constable for the Eastern Division of the County of Sussex for the Government of the Police....* Lewes: printed by Geo. P. Bacon Sussex Advertiser Office, 1858. First and only edition, 8vo., original but soiled printed boards, corners worn with loss of two letters from text on upper board, neatly rebacked, spine lettered, good copy,.   John Drury Rare Books   2015 - 26140   2016 $437

MacKay, Wallis *Wallis MacKay His Horn Book.* London: John MacQueen, 1898. Original yellow printed wrappers, dulled, illustrations, publisher's presentation copy.   Jarndyce Antiquarian Books   CCXV - 775   2016   £35

MacKaye, Percy Wallace *Johnny Crimson: a Legend of Hollis Hall.* Boston: Kiley, Printer, 1895. First edition one of 50 copies printed, small quarto, original pictorial wrappers, 22 pages, frontispiece, few slight stains, fine.   The Brick Row Book Shop   Miscellany 69 - 6   2016 $475

Macke, August *Tunisian Watercolours and Drawings.* New York: Harry N. Abrams, 1959. First US edition, quarto, 16 color plates loosely inserted inside mounts, black and white drawings, most unusually there are two empty mounts in pocket at rear for many illustrations in the book one might care to frame, very good.   Peter Ellis   112 - 241   2016   £75

MacKenzie, Compton *Gallipoli Memories.* London: Cassell and Co., 1929. First edition, top corners very slightly bumped, very near fine in handsome, very good or better dust with shallow chips at crown, little toning and faint 'x' on front panel.   Between the Covers Rare Books   204 - 141   2016 $200

MacKenzie, Compton *Our Street.* Garden City: Doubleday Doran & co., 1934. first American edition, fine in price clipped, fine dust jacket, woth original mailing carton for "Doubleday Dollar Book Club", beautiful, almost new.   Between the Covers Rare Books   208 - 46   2016 $225

MacKenzie, Compton *Thin Ice.* London: Chatto & Windus, 1956. First edition, inscribed by author, bright and clean internally, blue cloth, gilt title to spine, edges faintly foxed, strip of light toning to each endpaper near gutter, very good, dust jacket spine little sunned causing lettering to blend in, as is usual here, some light shelfwear, verso little toned but not outwardly visible, very good, inscription Sept. 2 1956.   Unsworths Antiquarian Booksellers   30 - 102   2016   £275

MacKenzie, Henry *Julia De Roubigne a Tale.* London: printed for W. Strahan, 1777. One of two imprints of the first edition of 17777, this one without addition of W. Creech, Edinburgh, half titles and final ad leaf volume II, 12mo., slight browning and offsetting from turn-ins of first few and final leaves, 2 volumes in one, contemporary mottled calf, boards slightly pitted, corners worn, expertly rebacked with raised and gilt banded spine, red morocco label, near contemporary ownership signature of Harriet West.   Jarndyce Antiquarian Booksellers   CCXVI - 376   2016   £280

MacKenzie, Henry *The Lounger: a Periodical Paper.* Edinburgh: published by William Creech, 1785-1787. First edition, with a duplicate of number II in second edition bound in and of No. XCVII loosely inserted (the latter frayed in inner and oute3r margins, pagination at head cropped); Second edition of No. ((, usual fold marks, some of which little discolored, complete set of 101 numbers, folio, contemporary calf backed marbled boards, vellum tips to corners, red lettering piece on spine, sides slightly rubbed, repairs to lower joint and foot of spine, good.   Blackwell's Rare Books   B186 - 100   2016   £1200

MacKenzie, Minnie Anna Baskerville *Verses Part I, Part II.* London: privately printed, n.p.,, 1900. Frontipsiece portraits to both parts, contemporary plain purple cloth, slightly faded.   Jarndyce Antiquarian Booksellers   CCXVII - 175   2016   £50

MacKenzie, Robert Shelton *Life of Charles Dickens.* Philadelphia: T. B. Peterson & Bros., 1870. First edition, frontispiece, original royal blue cloth, little worn at head and tail of spine, but good copy. Jarndyce Antiquarian Booksellers   CCXVIII - 1369   2016   £40

MacKenzie, William *Traite Pratique des Maladies de l'Oeil.* Victor Masson, 1856-1865. Quatrieme edition, 8vo., 3 volumes, numerous illustrations in text, uniformly bound with scarce supplement volume, trace of paper labels on spine, else fine, half cloth over marbled boards.   Edwin V. Glaser Rare Books   2015 - 10340   2016 $275

MacKenzie, William Leslie *The Medical Inspection of School Children...* Edinburgh & Glasgow: William Hodge & Co., 1904. First edition, Half title, folding plate, original maroon cloth, slightly rubbed, ownership inscription "Peter L. Sutherland Feb. 1908".   Jarndyce Antiquarian Books   CCXV - 836   2016   £38

Mackey, Nathaniel *Four for Trane. Poems.* Los Angeles: Golemics, 1978. First edition, one of 250 copies, narrow small 4to., illustrations, original printed wrappers, stapled as issued, very fine, scarcer than limitation would suggest. James S. Jaffe Rare Books   Occasional List: Winter 2016 - 94   2016 $750

Mackie, Peter Jeffrey *The Keeper's Book.* London: G. T. Foulis and Co. Ltd., 1929. Reprint, 8vo., recently rebound in quarter tan calf, marbled boards, spine with raised bands, gilt rules and contrasting morocco lettering pieces, marbled endpapers, frontispiece and 11 plates mounted at large, text illustrations, closed tear to bottom pages, otherwise very good.   Sotheran's   Hunting, Shooting & Fishing - 234 2016   £100

Mackinstry, Elizabeth *The Fairy Alphabet as Used by Merlin.* New York: Viking, 1933. First edition, 4to., cloth pictorial paste-on, fine in very good fine in very good dust jacket with small piece off top edge, intricate black and white drawings.   Aleph-bet Books, Inc.   112 - 1   2016 $375

Macky, A. *A Journey through the Australian Netherlands.* Pemberton, 1732. Second edition, 8vo., contemporary brown panelled calf, lacks morocco label, otherwise very good and clean.   J. & S. L. Bonham Antiquarian Booksellers   Europe 2016 - 10018   2016   £250

MacLane, Mary *My Friend Annabel Lee.* Chicago: Herbert S. Stone and Co., 1903. First edition, olive cloth lettered in black, frontispiece, covers with spine lightly worn and rubbed, minor soiling, previous owner's inscription, very good.   Argonaut Book Shop   Literature 2015 - 4897   2016 $45

MacLean, Alistair *Force 10 from Navarone.* London: Collins, 1968. First edition, fine in dust jacket with slightly faded spine.   Mordida Books   2015 - 010325   2016 $65

MacLean, Alistair *Force 10 from Navarone.* London: Collins, 1968. First edition, octavo, near fine in very good dust jacket, bit faded at spine.   Peter Ellis   112 - 242 2016   £25

MacLean, Fitzroy *Back to Bokhara.* London: Jonathan Cape, 1959. First edition, 8vo., original blue cloth by A. W. Bain & Co., spine lettered gilt, top edge blue, photographic endpapers, dust jacket retaining price, double page map printed in ochre and black, 8 monochrome plates, bearing photographic illustrations recto and verso dust jacket minimally rubbed, price clipped, otherwise very good, author's presentation 1959.   Sotheran's   Travel and Exploration - 150   2016   £178

MacLean, Norman *A River Runs through it.* Minneapolis: Tunhein Santrizos Co., 1992. Limited to 325 copies produced as a holiday gift for clients of Twin Citites based ad firm, printed on mould-made Frankfurt text paper with three wood engravings by Kent Aldrich, fine in marbled paper covered boards, cloth spine, very attractive despite misspelling author's name.   Jeff Hirsch Books   Holiday List 2015 - 48 2016 $175

MacLean, R. A. *The Casket 1852-1992 from Gutenberg to Internet.* Antigonish: Casket Printing & Pub. Ltd., 1992. Quarto, imitation red leather with gilt titles to spine and front cover, 81 black and white illustrations, very good to fine. Schooner Books Ltd.   115 - 159   2016 $40

MacLeish, Archibald *An Evening's Journey to Conway Massachusetts.* Northampton: Gehenna Press, 1967. Trade edition, small 4to., inscribed by Archibald and Ada Macleish, original wrappers, very good.   Second Life Books, Inc.   196 B - 115   2016 $65

MacLeish, Archibald *The Fall of the City.* London: Boriswood, 1937. First English edition, 8vo., author's presentation, nice in slightly worn dust jacket.   Second Life Books, Inc.   196 B - 116   2016 $75

MacLeish, Archibald *Herakles.* Boston: Houghton Mifflin, 1967. First edition, fine in dust jacket, laid in 1 page TLS from author.   Second Life Books, Inc.   196 B - 120   2016 $45

MacLeish, Archibald *New and Collected Poems 1917-1976.* Boston: Houghton Mifflin, 1976. First printing, fine in near fine dust jacket, inscribed for William Claire. Second Life Books, Inc.   196 B - 117   2016 $75

MacLeish, Archibald *Panic.* Boston: Houghton Mifflin, 1935. First edition, signed by author, about fine in slightly chipped dust jacket.   Second Life Books, Inc.   196 B - 118 2016 $45

MacLeish, Archibald *Public Speech, Poems by...* New York: Farrar & Rinehart, 1936. Limited to 276 copies signed and hand numbered by author, blue cloth, gilt lettered red leather labels to spine and front cover, spine faded and slightly rubbed at ends, otherwise fine, original slipcase lightly worn and beginning to crack on lower edge. Argonaut Book Shop Literature 2015 - 1327 2016 $125

MacLeish, Archibald *Songs for Eve.* Boston: Houghton Mifflin, 1954. First edition, fine in nice and some worn dust jacket, inscribed by author for William Claire. Second Life Books, Inc. 196 B - 119 2016 $45

MacLeod, George Husband Baird *Notes on the Surgery of the War in the Crimea with Remarks on the Treatment of Gunshot Wounds.* Philadelphia: 1862. First American edition, 12mo., original cloth, spine varnished, spine chipped. James Tait Goodrich X-78 - 388 2016 $595

MacLiammoir, Michael *Each Actor on His Ass.* London: Routledge and Kegan Paul, 1961. First edition, drawings, author's presentation n title, nice copy in slightly worn dust jacket. Second Life Books, Inc. 196 B - 110 2016 $45

MacLochlin, J. *Education.* London: Elliot Stock, 1881. Half title, original brown cloth, slightly rubbed. Jarndyce Antiquarian Books CCXV - 837 2016 £60

MacLow, Jackson *Barnesbook: Four Poems Derived from Sentences by Djuna Barnes.* Los Angeles: Sun & Moon Press, 1996. First edition, small octavo, illustrated wrappers, fine inscribed by author to Judith Malina. Between the Covers Rare Books 204 - 69 2016 $450

MacLow, Jackson *36th Light Poem in Memoriam Buster Keaton.* London and New York: Permanet Press, 1975. printed in an edition of 275 on the occasion of JML's first English Tour, near fine in stapled wrappers, signed and warmly inscribed by author. Jeff Hirsch Books Holiday List 2015 - 49 2016 $100

MacMullen, Ramsey *Soldier and Civilian in the later Roman Empire.* Cambridge: Harvard University Press, 1967. First reprinting, small 8vo. 4 plates, cloth, gilt lettered spine slightly cocked, edges dusted, very good, dust jacket with 1.7 cm. closed tear to lower jacket, few small tears to headcap with bit of loss, .8cm. closed tear to top edge of upper jacket, spine lightly sunned, two small pencil marks to upper jacket, minor shelfwear, top corner of front flyleaf clipped, very good, ownership inscription J. G. Hind. Unsworths Antiquarian Booksellers Ltd. E05 - 52 2016 £30

MacNally, Lea *Highland Deer Forest.* London: J. M. Dent & sons Ltd., 1970. First edition, 8vo., original green cloth, stag motif stamped in black to upper cover, illustrated dust jacket (spine sunned, price clipped), good copy, internally clean and sound. Sotheran's Hunting, Shooting & Fishing - 61 2016 £30

MacNally, Lea *Highland Year.* London: J. M. Dent & Sons Ltd., 1968. 8vo., original brown cloth, gilt title, without dust jacket, very good, small past ownership inscription. Sotheran's Hunting, Shooting & Fishing - 183 2016 £20

MacNally, Lea *Torridon - Life and Wildlife in the Scottish Highlands.* Shrewsbury: Airlife Pub. Ltd., 1993. First edition, 8vo., original green cloth with illustrated dust jacket, near fine, price clipped. Sotheran's Hunting, Shooting & Fishing - 186 2016 £30

MacNally, Lea *The Ways of an Eagle.* London: Collins & Harville Press, 1977. First edition, 8vo., original green cloth, illustrated dust jacket, spine sunned, price clipped, otherwise very good internally clean. Sotheran's Hunting, Shooting & Fishing - 184 2016 £30

MacNally, Lea *Wild Highlands.* London: J. M. Dent and sons Ltd., 1972. First edition, 8vo., original terracotta cloth, illustrated dust jacket, spine of jacket sunned, price clipped, internally clean throughout, ownership inscription. Sotheran's Hunting, Shooting & Fishing - 184 2016 £30

MacNally, Lea *The Year of the Red Deer.* London: J. M. Dent Ltd., 1975. First edition, large 8vo., original green cloth, illustrated dust jacket used, otherwise very good. Sotheran's Hunting, Shooting & Fishing - 62 2016 £30

MacNeice, Louis *Autumn Sequel - a Rhetorical Poem in XXVI Cantos.* London: Faber and Faber, 1954. First edition, free endpapers faintly tanned, near fine in very good dust jacket slightly darkened at spine and creased at top edge. Peter Ellis 112 - 245 2016 £45

MacNeice, Louis *Collected Poems 1925-1948.* London: Faber and Faber, 1949. First edition, quarto, fore-edge very slightly spotted, otherwise fine in very good dust jacket a bit tanned at spine and edges. Peter Ellis 112 - 244 2016 £75

MacPherson, James *The Poems of Ossian.* London: printed for Cadell and Davies, 1807. New edition, 2 volumes, 8vo., half title, some light browning, full contemporary tree calf, gilt decorated spines, dark green morocco label, spines and joints little rubbed, armorial bookplate of Sir Jas. Montgomery Bart. of Stanhope. Jarndyce Antiquarian Booksellers CCXVI - 377 2016 £150

MacQueen, Daniel *Letters on Mr. Hume's History of Great Britain.* Edinburgh: A. Kincaid and A. Donaldson, 1756. First edition, half title, occasional light spotting, contemporary calf gilt with raised bands and label, joints worn and beginning to split but cords still strong and even so a very good copy.   John Drury Rare Books   2015 - 14894   2016 $438

Macrobius, Ambrosius Aurelius Theodosius *Quae Exstant Omnia Diligentissime Emendata et cum Optimis Editionibus Collata....* Padua: excudebat Josephus Comimus, 1736. 8vo., engraved vignette to titlepage, occasional diagrams in text, woodcut initials and head and tailpieces, very light sporadic foxing but generally bright within, contemporary half vellum, cream colored boards, orange morocco gilt label to spine, edges uncut and some unopened, label bit chipped with small loss, some smudge marks and light stains, small dent to lower board at fore-edge, top edge dusty.   Unsworths Antiquarian Booksellers Ltd.   E01 - Early Printing - 13   2016   £200

Madden, Samuel *Boutler's Monument.* Dublin: printed by George Faulkner, 1745. First Dublin edition, 8vo., disbound, old perforated stamp of mercantile Library of Philadelphia, some light browning and scattered soiling, sound.   C. R. Johnson Rare Book Collections   Foxon: H-P 2015 - 558   2016 $3064

Madison, James *Message from the President of the United States to both Houses of Congress at the Commencement of the Second Session of the Twelfth Congress Nov. 4 1812...* Washington: A. & G. Way, 1812. First edition, black and white folding chart, 8vo., removed, very good.   Kaaterskill Books   21 - 111   2016 $400

Maeterlinck, Maurice *The Blue Bird.* New York: Dodd Mead, Oct., 1911. First US deluxe edition, 4to., blue cloth extensively stamped in gold, pink and blue, top edge gilt, faint crease on 3 corners, else very fine in original glassine and original box, illustrations by F. Cayley Robinson with 25 very beautiful tipped in color plates, beautiful copy.   Alephbet Books, Inc.   112 - 427   2016 $450

Maeterlinck, Maurice *The Blue Bird.* New York: Dodd Mead, 1911. First illustrated American edition, untrimmed, bound in blue cloth stamped in gilt, very good, tight, clean copy.   Second Life Books, Inc.   197 - 221   2016 $150

Maeterlinck, Maurice *The Inner Beauty.* London: Humphreys, 1912. Reprint, small octavo, top edge gilt, full red morocco stamped in gilt by Sangorski & Sutcliffe, inner dentelles, little rubbed along hinge, nice, clean copy.   Second Life Books, Inc.   197 - 222   2016 $75

Maeterlinck, Maurice *The Treasure of the Humble.* London: George Allen, 1897. octavo, Pickford Waller's copy with his bookplate, designed by him, book specially bound by him in full cream parchment on which he has painted red tulips, together with leaves, three on upper cover and one on lower, book's title and author's name written in his hand on both upper cover and spine, laid in is what appears to be part of a dust jacket, prelims spotted, covers in excellent state , bright and clean.   Peter Ellis   112 - 431   2016   £150

Magee, David *A Course in Correct Cataloguing or Notes in the Neophyte.* San Francisco: NCC/ABAA, 1977. First collected edition, printed in red and black, original printed wrappers, mint.   Argonaut Book Shop   Private Press 2015 - 6339   2016 $50

Magnus, Philip *Educational Aims and Efforts 1880-1910.* Aberdeen: John Smith, 1866. First edition, frontispiece, few leaves roughly opened, original maroon cloth, spine dulled later gift inscription.   Jarndyce Antiquarian Books   CCXV - 840   2016   £25

Magny, M. Le Vicomte De *La Science Du Blason: Accompagnee d'un Armorial General des Familles Nobles de L'Europe.* Paris: L'Institut Heraldique, n.d., 1858. First edition, 4to., dark red half leather over marbled boards, gilt decoration to spine with gilt lettering, five raised bands and marbled endpapers, illustrations, text in French, some rubbing to boards, slight foxing to endpapers, else sound, very good with clean plates.   Any Amount of Books   2015 - C11870   2016   £170

Magowan, Ronald *Barracuda.* R. Hale, 1972. Proof copy, original wrappers, very good.   I. D. Edrich   Crime - 2016   £24

Mahabharata *Harivansa ou Histoire de la Famille de Hari Ouvrage Formant un Appendice du Mahabharata...* Paris and London: for the Oriental Translation Fund, 1834-1835. 4to., contemporary green cloth, leather spine labels, partially unopened, bindings slightly worn, spine labels scuffed, endpapers browned, foxing in text, good, tight copy in contemporary binding.   Joseph J. Felcone, Inc.   Books from Five Centuries: a Miscellany - 93   2016 $400

Mahfouz, Naguib *Atlas of Mahoufz's Obstetric and Gynaecological Museum.* Altrincham: Sherratt, 1949. 7313 text figures and plates, about half in color, 3 volumes, 4to., original binding, presentation with compliments of Egyptian Majesty's Ambassador in London.   James Tait Goodrich   X-78 - 422   2016 $350

Mahfouz, Naguib *Palace Walk, Palace of desire and Sugar Street.* New York: Doubleday, 1990. all 3 books in near fine condition or better and in very near fine or better dust jackets.   Jeff Hirsch Books   Holiday List 2015 - 59   2016 $150

Mahony, Francis Sylvester *Facts & Figures from Italy.* London: Richard Bentley, 1847. First edition, 4 pages ad, original pale yellow vertical fine ribbed cloth blocked with gilt lettering and blind decoration, papal marks in black on front and in blind on back board, spine slightly sunned, marks on front board, small tear in leading f.e.p., Ecclesiastical bookplate of Gerald J. Hardman.   Jarndyce Antiquarian Booksellers   CCXVIII - 435   2016   £300

Mahurin, Matt *Matt Mahurin: Photographs.* Pasadena: Twelvetrees Press, 1989. First edition, one of 3000 copies, quarto, 47 photo plates, titlepage printed in red and black, original red cloth, printed in black, very fine with brick dust jacket printed in black, very scarce, especially in this condition.   Argonaut Book Shop   Photography 2015 - 2717   2016 $300

Maiden, J. H. *The Weeds of New South Wales Part One.* Sydney: Government Printer, 1920. Octavo, color plates, text illustrations, publisher's cloth, very good.   Andrew Isles Natural History Books   55 - 7187   2016 $120

Maidment, James *A Book of Scotish Pasquils 1568-1715.* Edinburgh: William Paterson, 1868. One of 3 copies on vellum (and limited but unspecified number of copies printed on paper), 210 x 130mm., handsome contemporary crimson morocco, attractively gilt by Andrew Grieve (stamp signed on front turn-in), covers gilt with multiple plain and decorative rules enclosing a delicate frame, large and intricate fleuron at center of each cover, spine gilt in double ruled compartments with complex fleuron centerpiece and scrolling floral cornerpieces, turn-ins decorated with plain and decorative gilt rules, patterned burgundy and gold silk endleaves, top edge gilt, slightly worn matching morocco lipped slipcase, woodcut titlepage illustrations, numerous decorative tailpieces and occasional woodcut vignettes in text, front pastedown with armorial bookplate of H. D. Colvill-Scott, armorial bookplate of Clarence S. Bemens, tiny dark spot on spine corners and just hint of rubbing, couple of leaves with slightly rumpled fore edge, still fine, text clean, smooth and bright and binding unusually lustrous, virtually no wear.   Phillip J. Pirages   67 - 346   2016 $4500

Mailer, Norman 1923-2007 *Ancient Evenings.* Boston: Little Brown, 1983. Third printing, very good in little worn dust jacket, signed by author.   Second Life Books, Inc.   196 B - 124   2016 $45

Mailer, Norman 1923-2007 *The Homosexual Villain (in) One. The Homosexual Magazine, Volumes III number 1, January 1955.* Los Angeles: One, Inc., 1955. First edition, softcover, Second anniversary issue, clean, near fine in stapled wrappers with some very slight wear.   Jeff Hirsch Books   E-List 80 - 20   2016 $85

Mailer, Norman 1923-2007 *The Time of Our Time.* New York: Random House, 1998. First edition, 8vo., author's signature on blank nice in slightly scuffed dust jacket.   Second Life Books, Inc.   196 B - 123   2016 $75

Maillart, Ella K. *Turkestan Solo. Ome Woman's Expedition from the Tien Shan to the Kizil Kum.* New York: Putnam, 1935. First English language edition, US issue, 8vo., original grey cloth, lettered and decorated in black, map endpapers, highly illustrated with black and white photographic plates, light marking to cloth, little spotted at beginning and end, otherwise clean and fresh, name on front pastedown, signed by author.   Sotheran's   Travel and Exploration - 151   2016   £298

Main, Ernest *In and Around Baghdad.* Baghdad: The Times Press Ltd., circa, 1930. First edition, 8vo., original blue watered cloth, front cover lettered gilt, spine faded, lower cover little marked, good copy, very rare.   Sotheran's   Travel and Exploration - 341   2016   £298

Maintenon, Francoise D'Aubigne, Marquise De *The Life and Letters of Madame de Maintenon.* London: printed for Lockyer Davis, 1772. 12mo., trifle browned in places, one or two minor stains, paper flaw in volume i touching two letters and a numeral, original speckled calf, spines darkened and chafed, lacking 2 headcaps, corners worn, good.   Blackwell's Rare Books   B186 - 101   2016   £350

Mair, John *An Introduction to Latin Syntax...* Philadelphia: printed for Campbell Conrad & Co. by J. Bioren, 1799. First American edition, lightly toned and spotted, ownership inscription of Daniel Turny to titlepage and Jacob Mechlin to second leaf, contemporary marbled sheep, rubbed, worn at extremities, red morocco lettering piece partly worn away, sound.   Blackwell's Rare Books   B186 - 102   2016   £200

Mais, S. P. B. *Who Dies?* Hutchinson, 1949. First edition, crown 8vo., original blue cloth, publisher stamped in gilt at foot of upper board, backstrip lettered gilt with touch of fading at foot and slight lean to spine, top edges slightly dusty, ownership inscription, engraved plates frayed with small section missing at foot of backstrip panel and owner's shelfmark at head of front flap, good.   Blackwell's Rare Books   B184 - 210   2016   £30

Maison Murat *Petite Orfevrerie. Bourses (cover title).* Paris: 62 Rue des Archives, circa, 1907. Folio, trade catalogue, plates, 2 section titles printed in brown paper, final plate printed in red and black, 2 plates with silverfish holes, one plate cropped on upper margin, few little foxed, original green cloth, lettered and ruled in blind, lightly worn in places, loosely inserted is 29 page price list dated March 1 1908 and one ms. letter on printed stationery by Maison Murat to a customer dated Dec. 12.   Marlborough Rare Books   List 55 - 62   2016   £425

Maitland, James A. *Reminiscences of a Retired Physician.* London: G. Routledge and Co., 1854. First edition, little cut down in contemporary half purple calf, spine gilt, slightly faded, from the Headfort Library, signed Bective 1854.   Jarndyce Antiquarian Booksellers   CCXVII - 176   2016   £65

Maitre-Jan *Traite des Maladies de l'Oeil.* Paris: Ve D'Houry, 1740. Enlarged edition, 12mo., very good copy, contemporary calf, spine richly gilt.   Edwin V. Glaser Rare Books   2015 - 10094   2016 $1500

Majnep, Ian Saem *Birds of My Kalam Country.* Auckland: Auckland University Press, 1977. Quarto, photos and text illustrations, slightly blemished dust jacket.   Andrew Isles Natural History Books   55 - 12236   2016 $60

A Make-Belief of Funny Beasts. New York: New York Book Co., n.d., circa, 1890. Cloth backed pictorial boards, near fine, 4 chromolithographed tab operated moveable plates, moveable pages have color pictorial border and there are half page brown illustrations on every page of text.   Alephbet Books, Inc.   111 - 309   2016 $800

Malamud, Bernard   1914-1986 *The Fixer.* New York: FSG, 1966. First edition, inscribed by author for Katharine Shattuck and Michael Seide, fine in near fine dust jacket with mild foxing to spine lettering and bit of wear to crown, excellent association copy.   Ken Lopez Bookseller   166 - 72   2016 $750

Malamud, Bernard   1914-1986 *Pictures of Fidelman.* New York: FSG, 1969. First edition, inscribed by author for Michael Seide and wife Katharine Shattuck, fine in near fine dust jacket.   Ken Lopez Bookseller   166 - 73   2016 $350

Malamud, Bernard   1914-1986 *The Tenants.* New York: FSG, 1971. First edition, inscribed by author for Catharine and Mike, (Katharine Shattuck and Michael Seide), fine in near fine dust jacket, fading to spine lettering and wear to crown.   Ken Lopez Bookseller   166 - 74   2016 $250

Malaurie, Jean *The Last Kings of Thule.* London: Allen & Unwin, 1956. First edition in English, small 4to., original cloth, dust jacket, errata slip tipped in, black and white photo plates, numerous figures to text, wrappers with damage, else very good, 7 line authorial presentation inscription.   Sotheran's   Travel and Exploration - 427   2016   £128

Malcolm X   1925-1965 *The Autobiography of Malcolm X.* New York: Grove Press, 1965. First edition, front hinge professionally repaired, else near fine in price clipped, near fine dust jacket with small tears and rubbing to spine ends, none of the usual fading to the light sensitive orange spine lettering.   Between the Covers Rare Books   207 - 61   2016 $1250

Malcolm X   1925-1965 *Two Speeches by....* New York: Merit, First edition, 8vo, cover portrait, paper wrappers cover yellowed and very slightly chipped, otherwise very good, scarce.   Second Life Books, Inc.   197 - 224   2016 $100

Maldon. Dublin: Salvage Press, 2014. 10/40 copies from an edition of 65 copies, signed by artist and printer, printed on Zerkal mouldmade paper, 2 full page wood engravings, calligraphic titles after designs by Frances Breen, title and initial letter in red, original half cloth, patterned paper sides, printed label inset to upper board, untrimmed, cloth slipcase with title blindstamped, fine.   Blackwell's Rare Books   B186 - 334   2016   £225

Malle, Louis *Malle on Malle.* London: Faber and Faber, 1993. First edition, slight smudge on fore edge, else fine in fine dust jacket.   Between the Covers Rare Books   208 - 26   2016 $375

Malles De Beaulieu, Mme. *The Modern Crusoe. A Narrative of the Life and Adventures of a French Cabin boy, who was Shipwrecked on an Uninhabitated Island.* Boston: James Loring, 1827. First American edition, 12mo., frontispiece, contemporary sheep backed printed boards, front cover detached.   Joseph J. Felcone, Inc.   Books from Five Centuries: a Miscellany - 94   2016 $450

Mallory, Jay *Sweet aloes: a Play in Three Acts.* London: Cassell, 1935. First edition, orange cloth, very good, tight copy, inscribed by author for producer Hugh Beaumont, also inscribed by actress, Joyce Carey, and signed by 12 members of the cast.   Second Life Books, Inc.   196 B - 126   2016 $225

Malone, Michael *Psychetypes: a New Way of Exploring Personality.* New York: E. P. Dutton & Co., 1977. First edition, fine in fine dust jacket.   Between the Covers Rare Books   208 - 50 2016 $250

Malory, Thomas *Le Morte D'Arthur. The History of King Arthur of His Noble Knights of the Round Table.* Boston: Medici Society circa, 1920. First trade edition, 2 volumes, illustrations by W. Russell Flint, cloth, fine in very good dust jackets with just slightest spine discoloration, as fresh a copy as one could hope.   Joseph J. Felcone, Inc.   Books from Five Centuries: a Miscellany - 127   2016 $450

Malory, Thomas *The Noble & Joyous Boke Entytled Le Morte D'arthur.* Oxford: Shakespeare Head Press, 1933. No. 171 of 350 copies for sale (of a total edition of 370), 2 volumes, 264 x 191mm., publisher's terra cotta half morocco over ivory buckram, flat spines with gilt titling, marbled endpapers, top edges and other edges untrimmed, 22 woodcuts and other edges untrimmed, 22 woodcuts, all hand colored, printed in red and black in Caslon type, unusually fine copy inside and out entirely fresh, bright and clean.   Phillip J. Pirages   67 - 316   2016 $1800

Malory, Thomas *Le Morte D'Arthur.* Norwalk: Heritage Press, 1955. Navy blue cloth decorated and lettered gilt, very fine in slipcase (bit faded), illustrations by Robert Gibbings, Sandglass pamphlet laid in.   Argonaut Book Shop   Heritage Press 2015 - 7039   2016 $45

Malory, Thomas *Sir Thomas Malory's Chronicles of King Arthur.* London: Folio Society, 1982. 3 volumes, 8vo., full red leather with decorative gilt stamping to spines and covers, signed on half title by artist, Edward Bawden, faint rubbing and slight fading at spines, otherwise fine in very good+ slipcase.   Any Amount of Books   2015 - A91761   2016   £170

Malpighi, Marcello *Tetras Anatomicarum Epistolarum de Lingua et Cerebro Quibus Anonymi Accessii Exercitatio de Ormento.... (bound with) De Extrno Tactus Organ Anatomica Observatio.* Bologna: Vittorio Benacci, 1665. Naples: Vittorio Benacci, 1665. First edition, second complete issue, 12mo, two works bound in one volume, 3 folding engraved plates, 18th century full calf, spine gilt panelled, vellum label applied to upper spine, one plate has a tear repaired, light wear, else very good, tight copy.   James Tait Goodrich   X-78 - 390   2016 $12,500

Malpighi, Marcello *Opera Medica et Anatomica Varia...* Venice: Andrea Poletti, 1743. Half title, engraved frontispiece, 20 engraved plates, folio, bound in contemporary vellum boards, boards slightly wraped, short crack at top of front joint and bottom of rear joint, some minor foxing on few plates, bookplate of Carlo Chiaveroti on title verso, adhesive discoloration showing through on recto.   James Tait Goodrich   X-78 - 391   2016 $1250

Malthus, Thomas Robert   1766-1834 *Additions to the Fourth and Former Editions of an Essay on the Principle of Population.* London: John Murray, 1817. First edition, original blue paper boards, neatly rebacked in buff paper, original printed paper spine label, 229 x 152mm., untrimmed edges, 19th century bookplate, spine label chipped and rubbed, significant loss of legibility, little soil and wear to original sides (as expected), but boards surprisingly well preserved and the well restored binding, absolutely tight, first few leaves and last three gatherings freckled with foxing, minor foxing elsewhere, few trivial spots, excellent internally, still rather fresh and not at all darkened or browned.   Phillip J. Pirages   67 - 247   2016 $950

Malthus, Thomas Robert   1766-1834 *An Essay on the Principle of Population...* London: printed for J. Johnson, by C. Bensley, 1803. Second edition, quarto, contemporary calf, skillfully rebacked to style with corners renewed, spine decoratively tooled in compartments with burgundy morocco gilt lettering label, endpapers renewe, occasional light foxing, titlepage with publisher's diagonal paper flaw crease, overall very good.   Heritage Book Shop   Holiday 2015 - 78   2016 $6500

Malton, Thomas *Views of Oxford.* London: White & Co.; Oxford: R. Smith, 1810. First complete edition, appealing 19th century (circa 1860's?), dark green half morocco over lighter green textured cloth by T. Aitken (stamp signed), upper cover with gilt titling, raised bands, spine gilt in compartments with elongated fleuron centerpiece and scrolling cornerpieces, gilt titling, marbled endpapers, all edges gilt (small, very expert repairs to upper outer corners and perhaps at top of joints), mezzotint frontispiece, engraved title, 30 fine plates of interior and exterior views, armorial bookplates of Sir Mayson M. Beeton and Sir Richard Farrant, verso of front free endpaper, ink presentation inscription from author for Sir Charles Locock, Nov. 1860, subscription proposal for work printed by T. Bensley and dated "London, May 30, 1301 (i.e. 1801)", laid in at front, couple of small smudges to boards, portrait faintly foxed and browned, isolated small stains, not affecting images, but fine, plates especially clean and fresh, smooth and pleasing binding with virtually no wear.   Phillip J. Pirages   67 - 248   2016 $8500

Mamet, David *American Buffalo.* New York: Grove Press, 1976. First edition, fine in fine dust jacket, except for touch of age toning to flaps, spectacular, as new copy.   Between the Covers Rare Books   208 - 47   2016 $2500

Mamet, David *Poet and the Rent.* Flossmoor: David Mamet, 1973. Quarto, 41 pages, mimeographed playscript printed in purple, printed rectos only, prong-bound into manila folder, hand titled by Mamet on front wrapper "Poet and the Rent by David Mamet. This Copy Belongs to David Mamet" and the number "19" in upper right hand corner, very good, heavily annotated throughout in his hand.   Between the Covers Rare Books   204 - 72   2016 $25,000

Mamma's Absence; or the Written Rules. London: Seeley's, 1854. Small 4to., frontispiece foxed, original brown limp cloth boards, hinges slightly cracking.   Jarndyce Antiquarian Books CCXV - 305   2016   £38

The Man Trap. Boston: Riverton Press, 1910. First edition, fine in soft covers, with special notice of explanation, with the cancellation stamps and added notice.   Mordida Books   2015 - 011569   2016 $65

Manarin, Louis H. *North Carolina Troops 1861-1865. A Roster.* Raleigh: State Division of Archives and History, 1988-2003. Second printing with addenda of first two volumes, 15 volumes, thick 8vo., cloth, dust jackets, well preserved set.   Oak Knoll Books   310 - 296   2016 $675

Manassas Review. William Heyen Issue. Manassas: Northern Virginia Community College, 1978. First edition, printed wrappers, this copy signed and inscribed by William Heyen for William Meredith, laid in is full ALS from Heyen to Meredith in original envelope addressed in Heyen's hand to Meredith, fine.   Charles Agvent   William Meredith - 46   2016 $100

Mandela, Nelson *The Illustrated Long Walk to Freedom.* Little Brown, 1996. First Illustrated edition, 144/425 copies with photographic portrait signed by author, richly illustrated with photos, royal 8vo., original quarter South African Wassa goastskin with jagged gilt rule and terracotta cloth sides, all edges gilt, lined dropdown box with pictorial onlay and original publisher's cardboard packaging, fine.   Blackwell's Rare Books   B186 - 262   2016   £3000

Mandelbrot, Benoit *The Variation of Certain Speculative Prices. In the Journal of Business Volume XXXVI October 1963 (with) The Variation of Some Other Speculative Prices. in The Journal of Business Vol. 40 October 1967 . (with) Correction of an Error in The Variation of Certain Speculative Prices. in The Journal of Business Volume 45 October 1972.*   Chicago: University of Chicago Press, 1963-1972. 3 entire issues, very good+ to near fine in original printed wrappers, 1963 issue with mild soil and stains to wrappers, 1967 issue with library ink stamps on front and back wrappers and each page, all 3 issues housed in custom made quarter leather clamshell box with gilt lettering to spine and front cover.   By the Book, L. C.   45 - 31   2016 $1650

Mandragora; or the Quacks.   London: printed and sold by John Morphew, 1718. Second edition, 8vo., disbound, fine. C. R. Johnson Rare Book Collections   Foxon: H-P 2015 - 589   2016 $2681

Manfred, Frederick *Dinkytown.*   Minneapolis: Dinkytown Antiquarian Bookstore, 1984. Limited to 526, this one of 26 lettered copies signed by author, printed on Frankfurt White and bound thus, set in Italian Olde Style on Adorra text and sewn into Grande wrappers,.   Oak Knoll Books   310 - 163   2016 $200

Mangoian, L. *The Island of Cyprus.*   Nicosia: Mangoian Bros., 1947. First edition, 8vo., original cloth, lettered gilt, folding map at rear, highly illustrated, minor wear to extremities, few spots to endpapers, good.   Sotheran's   Travel and Exploration - 270   2016   £75

Manilius, Marcus *Astronomicon Interpretatione et Notis ac Figuris Illustravit Michael fayus...*   Parisiis: Apud Fredericum Leonard, 1679. 4to., engraved additional titlepage, woodcut head and tailpieces, initials and device to titlepage, several illustrations and tables in text, toning to some gatherings occasional very light smudges, contemporary brown speckled calf, rebacked neatly but in slightly lighter ton, raised bands, recent black and gilt spine label, edges sprinkled red and brown, rubbed, few scrapes, corners fraying but very good, bookplate of Charles William Hamilton Sotheby (a1820-1887).   Unsworths Antiquarian Booksellers   30 - 104   2016   £450

Manilius, Marcus *(Astronomicon). The Five Books - Containing a System of the Ancient Astronomy and Astrology, together with the Philosophy of the Stocks.*   London: printed for Jacob Tonson, 1697. First English edition, 8vo., contemporary paneled calf, rebacked, corners rubbed, new endpapers, recent leather label, 6 leaves of plates, including frontispiece, leaves age toned, some foxing towards rear.   Howard S. Mott Inc.   265 - 86   2016 $250

Manilius, Marcus *Astronomicon ex Recensione et cum Notis Richardi Bentletii.*   Henry Woodfall for Paul and Isaac Vaillant, 1739. First Bentley edition, engraved frontispiece by vertue and folding plate of marble globe in Palazzo Fanese in Rome, engraved arms at head of dedication, some spotting and dust soiling, faint dampmark at head, 4to., modern dark brown diced calf, boards bordered with gilt fillet, spine with raised bands, between double gilt fillets, red morocco lettering piece, other compartments with central blind tool, marbled endpapers, edges gilt, good. Blackwell's Rare Books   Greek & Latin Classics VII - 64 2016   £600

Manilius, Marcus *Astronomicon ex Recensione et cum Notis Richardi Bentleii.*   London: Typus Henrici Woodfall Sumptibus Pauli et Isaac Vaillant, 1739. 4to., 2 engraved plates, frontispiece folding celestial map, woodcut device to titlepage, engraved headpiece to dedication, occasional neatly pencilled marginal notes, closed tear (85mm. approx) to page 145-6, sporadic light worming to top fore-edge, corner not affecting text, small closed tear to map attachment, some edges little toned, 19th century half vellum, black morocco gilt spine label, marbled paper covered boards, fore and tail edges deckled, vellum darkened, rubbed, edges worn, corners frayed, inkstamp and signature of writer and book collector Walter Ashburner (1864-1936), signature of W. Oates dated 1746.   Unsworths Antiquarian Booksellers Ltd.   E01 - Early Printing - 14   2016   £850

Manilius, Marcus *Astronomicon. Liber Quintus.*   London: Richards Press, 1930. One of 400 copies, 8vo. original tape backed printed boards, printed paper spine label, with ALS by A. E. Housman to G. N. Wiggins, tipped to front free endpaper, spine panel lightly sunned, dust soiling to top edge of textblock, few fox marks and fold from mailing letter is fine.   James S. Jaffe Rare Books   Occasional List: Winter 2016 - 80   2016 $1000

Mankowitz, Wolf *Wedgwood.*   New York: E. P. Dutton, 1953. , limited to 1500 copies, 8 color plates, 118 monochrome illustrations, original blue cloth lettered gilt, light rubbing to extremities, spine slightly faded, fine.   Argonaut Book Shop   Pottery and Porcelain 2015 - 5010   2016 $90

Manley, Marie De La Riviere *Secret Memoirs and Manners of Several Persons of Quality of Both sexes. (with) Secret Memoirs...the Second Volume.* London: printed for John Morphew and J. Woodward, 1709. Second edition of first part, first edition of second part, 2 volumes, octavo, contemporary panelled calf, small hand lettered paper spine labels, bindings similar in style but not identical, engraved frontispiece in volume 2 (none called for in 1), on rear blanks and free endpaper of volume 1 are contemporary ink notations, identifying over 80 characters in the text by name and page number, waterstain to front board and spine of volume I, edges little rubbed, very good.   The Brick Row Book Shop   Miscellany 69 - 57   2016 $1250

Manlius; or the Brave Adventurer. A Poetical Novel. Edinburgh: printed by Donald Muchieson for Fergus Philabeg, 1749. First edition, fine, 4to., quarter red morocco, very rare, fine, outer edges uncut, few small ms. corrections, no doubt authorial.   C. R. Johnson Rare Book Collections   Foxon: H-P 2015 - 570   2016 $2681

Mann, Horace   *Report of an Educational tour in Germany and Parts of Great Britain and Ireland...*   London: Simpkin, Marshall & Co., 1846. Half title, some pencil markings and annotations, original purple cloth, largeley faded to brown, spine rubbed and head and tail following inner hinge cracking, inscribed "Robert Con Esq. with kindest regards from W. B. Hodgson, Liverpool Feb. 1846".   Jarndyce Antiquarian Books   CCXV - 842   2016   £85

Mann, J. H.   *A History of Gibraltar and Its Sieges.* London: Provost, 1873. Second edition, 8vo., map, 16 photos, some foxing throughout, mainly in margins, plate frayed on fore-edge not affecting image, all photos clean, original red decorative cloth, rebacked using original spine.   J. & S. L. Bonham Antiquarian Booksellers   Europe 2016 - 9420   2016   £550

Mann, Thomas   *Death in Venice.*   New York: 1965. New edition, endpapers somewhat browned, otherwise very nice in slightly chipped dust jacket, slightly worn and soiled slipcase.   Bertram Rota Ltd.   February List 2016 - 33   2016   £20

Mann, Thomas   *Joseph the Provider.*   New York: Alfred A. Knopf, 1944. First American edition, black cloth with gilt lettered spine, gilt wearing from spine and spine ends very lightly rubbed, else fine.   Argonaut Book Shop   Literature 2015 - 1325   2016 $45

Mann, Tom   *From Single Tax to Syndicalism.*   London: Guy Bowman, 1913. 8vo., few slight smudges to title, otherwise very bright outside, half black morocco, dark grey cloth boards, gilt title to spine, edges sprinkled red, spine rubbed and worn but holding firm, corners rubbed, owner hinges reinforced with cloth tape, very good, ownership inscription of Rufus Godson.   Unsworths Antiquarian Booksellers   30 - 105   2016   £50

Manners and Rules of Good Society...   London: Frederick Warne & Co., 1896. 21st edition, original red cloth, lettered in black and gilt, small mark to front board, otherwise very good.   Jarndyce Antiquarian Books   CCXV - 16   2016   £60

Manners and Rules of Good Society...   London: Frederick Warne, 1898. Fifth edition, half title, 12 page catalog, original mustard cloth, lettered gilt.   Jarndyce Antiquarian Books   CCXV - 18   2016   £45

Manners and Rules of Good Society...   London: Frederick Warne, 1898. Twenty third edition, half title, original red cloth lettered in black and gilt, small mark to front board, otherwise very good.   Jarndyce Antiquarian Books   CCXV - 17   2016   £40

Manners for All.   London: Ward Lock & Co., 1898. Final ad leaf, illustrations, leaves browned, original illustrated wrappers, stapled as issued, chipped, staples rusted.   Jarndyce Antiquarian Books   CCXV - 306   2016   £30

Mannes, Marya   *Subverse: Thymes for Our Times.*   New York: Braziller, 1959. First edition, small 4to., drawings by Robert Osborn, signed by author, cover little yellowed and bumped at corners, very good tight.   Second Life Books, Inc.   196 B - 129   2016 $45

Manning, John   *Dickens on Education.*   Toronto: University of Toronto Press, 1959. First edition, half title, very good in slightly torn dust jacket.   Jarndyce Antiquarian Booksellers   CCXVIII - 1374   2016   £20

Mannix, Daniel   *A Sporting Chance Usual methods of Hunting.*   London: Longmans, 1968. First UK edition, 8vo., original cloth and wrapper, black and white photos, previous owner's bookplate, very good.   Sotheran's   Hunting, Shooting & Fishing - 187   2016   £40

Mansfield, Brian   *Ring of Fire: a Tribute to Johnny Cash.* Nashville: Rutledge Hill Press, 2003. First edition, Photo illustrations by Lee Leverett, fine in fine dust jacket, includes CD, signed by Cash on bookplate laid in.   Bella Luna Books   2016 - t8236   2016 $99

Mantel, Hilary   *Eight Months on Ghazzah Street.*   London: Viking, 1988. First edition, signed by author, 8vo., margins toned, black cloth, red title to spine, few tiny dents, light stain to top edge, still very good, dust jacket lightly shelf worn, very good, autographed by author.   Unsworths Antiquarian Booksellers   30 - 106   2016   £125

Mantel, Hilary   *An Experiment in Love.*   1955. First edition, fine in dust jacket, bookplate.   Bertram Rota Ltd.   Christmas List 2015 - 26   2016   £25

Mantle, Mickey *The Mickey Mantle Story.* New York: Henry Holt, 1957. First edition, illustrated from photographs, corners little bumped, near fine in near very good dust jacket with some chipping near spine ends, inscribed by Mantle.   Between the Covers Rare Books   208 - 140   2016 $900

A Manual of Etiquette for Gentlemen or, True Principles of Politeness.   London: Allman & Son, 1859. 16mo., frontispiece, sewing little loose, original purple cloth, limp boards, blocked gilt, little rubbed and dulled, all edges gilt, contemporary signature on leading f.e.p., good, sound copy.   Jarndyce Antiquarian Books   CCXV - 307   2016   £75

A Manual of the Etiquette of Love, Courtship and Marriage. London: Allman & Son, 1859. 16mo., frontispiece, original red decorated cloth, rubbed, dulled and slightly marked, all edges gilt, contemporary signature of Sarah Welfare.   Jarndyce Antiquarian Books   CCXV - 308   2016   £45

Manzel, Josef   *Bruin Furryball in the Circus.* Prague: Artia, 1954. Cloth backed pictorial boards, light tip wear, very good+, fantastic full page and smaller color lithographs by Jiri Trnka, very scarce.   Aleph-bet Books, Inc.   111 - 453   2016 $250

Manzel, Josef   *Bruin Furryball in the Zoo.* Prague: Artia, 1954. Cloth backed pictorial boards light tip wear, very good+, fantastic full page and smaller color lithographs by Jiri Trnka, very scarce.   Aleph-bet Books, Inc.   111 - 454   2016 $250

Maraini, Fosco   *Where Four World Meet, Hindu Kush 1959.* New York: Harcourt World, 1964. First American edition, boards, very fine with slightly chipped pictorial dust jacket.   Argonaut Book Shop   Mountaineering 2015 - 4464   2016 $60

March, Joseph Moncure   *The Wild Party.* New York: Pascal Covici, 1928. First edition, preceding all others, one of 750 copies (this being no. 141) published for subscribers, tan and gold paper over boards, quarterbound in dark gray cloth with titles stamped in gilt on spine and in black on front board, deep yellow topstain, attractive example of the extremely uncommon original slipcase, matching paper spine label as issued, easily near fine in very good slipcase.   Royal Books   48 - 71   2016 $1500

March, Sandra   *I Hear(t) you.* Barcelona: Printed at the Folio Club for Sandra March, 2014. Number 83 of 100 copies signed and numbered by March, contents comprise the book, two posters and CD, bound in white cardboard CD case, posters attached to the back cover by pink elastic band and CD held on middle fold of case, fine.   The Kelmscott Bookshop   13 - 34   2016 $200

March, Sandra   *Projecte Anatomica - Soft & Economy.* Barcelona: printed at the Private Space for Sandra March, 2012. One of 100 copies, 8 x 11 inches, 10 booklets housed in brown paper envelope that in turn is in tulle bag, each piece 8 x 11 inches, fine.   The Kelmscott Bookshop   13 - 35   2016 $250

Marchand, Prosper   *Dictionnaire Historiques ou Memoires Critiques et Litterires, Concernant La Vie et les Ouvrages de Divers Personnage Distingues, Particulierement Dans La Republique des Lettres.* La Haye: Pierre de Hondt, 1758-1759. 2 volumes bound as one, three quarter brown leather with decorated brown paper boards, six raised bands to spine with brown leather title label in second compartment, chipping and small tears to leather as well as to paper covers, interior pages show light aging, otherwise lean and bright, offsetting on free endpapers from leather borders, previous owner bookplate and small stamp "Holstein-Hoisteinborg", very good.   The Kelmscott Bookshop   13 - 36   2016 $750

Marchionni, Domenico   *Discorsi Morali Intorno alla Venuta del Messia Alla Verginita di Maria anche dopo il Parto....* Ferrara: per Alonso, e Gio. Battista Maresti, 1664. Small emblematic device on titlepage, title in red and black, woodcut device on page 219, woodcut initials, small 4to., contemporary Italian red morocco gilt over paste board, cover's elaborately decorated with four outer narrow decorative rolls enclosing central panel of large circular fan ornament with four corner fan sections, flat spine richly decorated, gilt edges, some rubbing to extremities, lacks silk ties, Towneley Library near Burnley, Lancashire copy, 19th century pencil note inside cover, sold in Towneley Hall library auction.   Maggs Bros. Ltd.   1474 - 51   2016   £2800

Marciano, Georges   *Guess.* London: Guess, 1991. First edition, folio, original cream boards lettered gilt on spine and front cover, copiously illustrated in color and black and white, fine in fine dust jacket.   Any Amount of Books   2015 - C11474   2016   £170

Marciano, John Bemelmans   *Madeline and the Cats of Rome.* New York: Viking, 2008. First edition, as new, fine in dust jacket, 4to., pictorial hardbound.   Gene W. Baade, Books on the West   2015 - JUV022   2016 $45

Marcoy, Paul   *A Journey Across South America from the Pacific Ocean to the Atlantic Ocean.* Blackie, 1873. First edition, 2 volumes, large quarto, numerous maps and illustrations, brown half calf, corners rubbed, otherwise very clean.   J. & S. L. Bonham Antiquarian Booksellers   America 2016 - 10303   2016   £350

Marcus, Subcomandante   *The Story of Colors.* El Paso: Cinco Puntos Press, 1999. First edition, fine, in fine dust jacket.   Bella Luna Books   2016 - 4362   2016 $66

Mardersteig, Giovanni 1892-1977 *The Officina Bodoni an Account of the Work of a Hand Press 1923-1977.* Verona: Officina Bodoni, 1980. No. 21 of 125 copies (99 of these for sale), 305 x 203mm., 2 volumes, with second volume containing original plates, from a total edition of 1500, publisher's brown quarter morocco over beige vellum, housed in publisher's (slightly worn) moroco lipped buckram slipcase, frontispiece, many illustrations, second volume with 10 biofolio within brown lettered guards, woodcut illustrations, mint.   Phillip J. Pirages   67 - 268   2016 $1000

Mardrus, J. C. *Histoire Charmante De L'Adolescente Sucre D'Amour.* Paris: F. L. Schmied, 1927. First edition, no. 50 of 170 copies signed by artist, 318 x 241mm., unbound as issued in original printed paper wrappers, 14 full page color wood engravings, including frontispiece, signed in pencil by artist, Francois Louis Schmied, and 635 color panel borders, line fillers and tailpieces in Art Deco style, all by Schmied, recto of limitations page with facsimile inscription by author to Schmied, short ink mark to margin of titlepage, just faintest isolated smudge or freckled foxing, otherwise very fine, clean, fresh, fragile wrapper unsoiled and remarkably well preserved.   Phillip J. Pirages   67 - 309   2016 $6500

Mare, A. C. De La *Bartolomeo Sanvito: the Life and Work of a Renaissance Scribee.* London: Internationale de Bibliophile, 2009. Large 4to., cloth, dust jacket, 196 images,.   Oak Knoll Books   310 - 146   2016 $350

Maret, Russell *Interstices & Intersections or an Autodidact Comprehends a cube, Thirteen Euclidean Propositiones.* New York: 2014. 42/75 copies (of an edition of 92), printed in full color on Zerkall mould-made paper, illustrations, all printed from photopolymer plates, accordion folded, original quarter real goatskin with dark grey boards, leather cut to form peak from which extends a single white rule stretching horizontally across board, fine.   Blackwell's Rare Books   Marks of Genius - 17   2016   £4000

Maret, Russell *Linear A to Linear Z: Twenty-Six Linoleum Cuts by Russell Maret.* New York: Russell Maret, 2015. Limited to 90 copies, this one of 70 copies bound in paper wrappers by Nancy Loeber.   Oak Knoll Books   310 - 121   2016 $675

Margam Abbey an Historical romance of the Fourteenth Century. London: John Green, 1837. Marginal tear to pages 117-119 without loss to text, full dark green grained calf, attractively blocked in gilt, rubbed, chip to head and tail of spine, inscription to Miss Steel, March 18th 1849, all edges gilt.   Jarndyce Antiquarian Booksellers   CCXVII - 7   2016   £250

Margrie, William *The Pickwicks of Peckham: being the Book of the London Explorer's Club.* London: Watts and Co., 1938. Half title, frontispiece, plates, original pale blue cloth, lettered gilt, very good in reinforced dust jacket.   Jarndyce Antiquarian Booksellers   CCXVIII - 154   2016   £20

Marguerite D'Angouleme, Queen of Navarre 1492-1549 *The Heptameron of the Tales of Margaret, Queen of Navarre.* London: privately printed for the Navarre Society, 1922. 232 x 152mm., five volumes, original white buckram, gilt, covers with double fillet border and central medallion containing a fleur-de-lys, flat spines outlined by double fillet and featuring a tall tree with a grape vine twining around its trunk, gilt titling, top edges gilt, other edges untrimmed and mostly unopened in original gray dust jackets, 150 head and tailpieces by Dunker and 73 engraved plates designed by S. Freudenberg, as called for, all plates with tissue guards, spines of dust jackets little sunned and with very slight traces of use, one fore edge uneven (paper flaw), one tissue panel creased, remarkably fine set, in close to original condition as one could hope to find.   Phillip J. Pirages   67 - 258   2016 $750

Mariana *P'Sich.* F. A. R. Gallery, n.d. circa, 1945. Limited to 500 numbered copies signed by author, most copies neither signed nor numbered, 8vo., cloth backed boards, tiny bit of toning on bottom edge, else very fine in slipcase with mounted color plate (slipcase soiled), beautiful copy.   Aleph-bet Books, Inc.   111 - 266   2016 $375

Marie, Pierre *Contribution a l'Etude et au diagnostic Des Formes Fruste de la Maladie De Basedow.* Paris: A. Delahaye et E. Lecrosnier, 1883. Half title, recent marbled boards, author's presentation.   James Tait Goodrich   X-78 - 392   2016 $695

Marie, Pierre *Lectures on Diseases of the Spinal Cord.* London: New Sydenham Society, 1895. 244 woodcuts and photos, original Sydneham cloth, bit worn, base of spine chipped, internally very good.   James Tait Goodrich   X-78 - 393   2016 $150

Marie, Queen of Romania *The Dreamer of Dreams.* London: Hodder & Stoughton, n.d., 1915. 4to., grey gilt cloth stamped in blue, circular fade spot on rear cover, not visible with dust jacket, else fine with mounted color plate, dust jacket frayed with some soil but very good, illustrations by Edmund Dulac, 6 beautiful tipped in color plates with tissue guards, quite scarce in dust jacket.   Aleph-bet Books, Inc.   111 - 133   2016 $750

Marie, Queen of Romania *The Story of Naughty Kildeen.* London: et al: Oxford University Press, 1922. First edition, folio gilt pictorial cloth, near fine, minor tip and edge wear, magnificent hand colored illustrations plus detailed black and whites by Job.   Aleph-bet Books, Inc.   111 - 236   2016 $1850

The Mariner's Concert, Being a New Collection of the Most Favorite Sea Songs... printed by J. Evans, 1797. Large woodcut vignette on title, poorly printed on cheap paper with bit of consequent browning, 4to., early 20th century navy blue buckram, lettered on upper cover, slight worn, pencil note inside front cover, form the library of Lovat Fraser, good, rare. Blackwell's Rare Books B186 - 141 2016 £250

Marivaux, Pierre Carlet de Chamblain *The Fortunate Villager; or Memoirs of Sir Andrew Thompson.* Dublin: printed for Sarah Cotter and James Williams, 1765. 2 volumes, 12mo., contemporary calf, slight wear. Jarndyce Antiquarian Booksellers CCXVI - 399 2016 £150

Mark, Joan *Silver Gringo, William Spratling and Taxco.* Albuquerque: University of New Mexico Press, 2000. First edition, small quarto, drawings, numerous photos, ochre cloth, very fine, pictorial dust jacket. Argonaut Book Shop Biography 2015 - 7611 2016 $75

Markey, Gene *Literary Lights. A book of Caricatures.* New York: Alfred A. Knopf, 1922. First edition, 50 full page illustrations, cloth backed decorated boards, spine darkened, rubbing to corners, very good, signed by author with full page original drawing in ink, very nice. Argonaut Book Shop Literature 2015 - 4931 2016 $65

Markfield, Wallace *Multiple Orgasms.* Bloomfield: Bruccolli Clark, 1977. No. 255 of 300 copies, 12mo., signed and numbered by author, paper over boards with cloth spine, cover very slightly faded at top edge, otherwise nice. Second Life Books, Inc. 196 B - 135 2016 $45

Markham, Clements Robert 1830-1916 *Book of the Knowledge of all the Kingdoms, Lands and Lordships or the Kings and Lords Who Possess Them.* London: Hakluyt, 1912. First edition, 8vo., 20 color plates, original blue decorative cloth, near fine. J. & S. L. Bonham Antiquarian Booksellers Voyages 2016 - 8796 2016 £75

Markland, George *Pteryplegia; or the Art of Shooting-Flying.* London: printed and sold by J. Roberts, 1717. First edition, 8vo., disbound, variant with errata on verso of titlepage, fine. C. R. Johnson Rare Book Collections Foxon: H-P 2015 - 573h-p 2016 $4597

Markland, George *Pteryplegia; or the Art of Shooting-Flying.* London: printed for Stephen Austen, 1727. Second edition, 8v., disbound, titlepage slightly spotted, very good, contemporary signature of George Weller. C. R. Johnson Rare Book Collections Foxon: H-P 2015 - 574 2016 $613

Marklew, William *Our Home.* Birmingham?: 1934. 12mo., original red cloth, upper cover lettered gilt, spine slightly sunned. Marlborough Rare Books List 55 - 45 2016 £75

Marlowe, Christopher 1564-1593 *Hero and Leander.* London: printed at the Ballantyne Press, 1894. One of 220 copies, 200 for sale, publisher's full vellum by Henry Leighton (stamp signed with his cipher at lower right corner of covers), tooled in gilt, abstract geometric design by Charles Ricketts, covers with compartmentalized central panel, large gilt leaves at corners interlocking "Cs" and date in Roman numerals, spine with gilt title at head and "VI" device at tail, fine modern navy folding cloth box; with elaborate woodcut initials, full white vine border on opening page and 7 wood engravings by Ricketts and Shannon, bookplate of "Beach", significant splaying to covers, one leaf with old repair to corner (torn by rough opening?), three openings and rear flyleaves rather foxed, text a shade less than bright, other minor problems internally, still pleasant copy because of clean, unworn binding. Phillip J. Pirages 67 - 329 2016 $2200

Marmodoro, Anna *The Author's Voice in Classical and Late Antiquity.* Oxford University Press, 2013. First edition, 8vo., figures and illustrations, dark blue cloth, gilt lettered to spine, dust jacket, as new. Unsworths Antiquarian Booksellers Ltd. E04 - 72 2016 £45

Marmontel, Jean Francois 1723-1799 *The Incas or the Destruction of the Empire of Peru.* London: printed for J. Nourse (and 3 others), 1777. First English edition, 12mo., half titles, fine, clean copy, full contemporary sprinkled calf, raised and gilt banded spines, red morocco labels, gilt volume numbers, from the library of Invercauld Castle, Braemar. Jarndyce Antiquarian Booksellers CCXVI - 402 2016 £580

Marmontel, Jean Francois 1723-1799 *Les Incas; ou la Destruction d l'Empire de Peru.* Paris: chez Lacombe, 1777. First edition in French, 2 volumes, half titles, engraved frontispiece, 10 engraved plates, 12mo., very clean, slight waterstain to blank upper margin of one plate, small tear without loss to leading edge of first titlepage, full contemporary English sprinkled calf, raised and gilt banded spines, red morocco labels, gilt volume numbers, from the Library of Invercauld Castle, Braemar, very good. Jarndyce Antiquarian Booksellers CCXVI - 401 2016 £480

Marquis, T. G. *Canada's Sons on Kopje and Veldt.* Toronto: Canada's Sons Pub. Co., 1900. Blue pebbled cloth with gilt and black design and titles to front board, 8vo., richly illustrated with black and white photos, cloth worn along edges, some offsetting to endpapers, interior very good. Schooner Books Ltd. 115 - 220 2016 $45

Marr, Melissa *Untamed City: Carnival of (Secrets).* New York: Harper, 2012. First edition, signed by author, limited edition stated on titlepage, very hard to come by, fine in fine dust jacket. Gene W. Baade, Books on the West 2015 - 5011076 2016 $49

Marriott, Joseph *Prosaic Effusions or Essays on Various Subjects and Miscellaneous observations.* Whitchurch: printed and sold by R. B. Jones, circa, 1829? Index, errata leaf, uncut in original blue boards, drab paper spine & label, hinges weakening, early ownership stamp of John Gregory with his signature. Jarndyce Antiquarian Booksellers CCXVII - 181   2016   £120

Marrtinson, Harry *Wild Bouquet.* Kansas City: BKMK Press, 1985. First edition, 8vo., fine in dust jacket, signed by Smith with his bookplate on endpaper, dust jacket little toned, otherwise fine.   Second Life Books, Inc.   196 B - 147   2016 $45

Marryat, Francis S. *Mountains and Molehills.* London: Longmans, 1855. First edition, 8vo., 8 colored lithographs, contemporary brown half calf, spine gilt, raised bands, joints and corners rubbed, good, clean copy.   J. & S. L. Bonham Antiquarian Booksellers   America 2016 - 8991   2016 £600

Marryat, Frederick   1792-1848   *Japhet in Search of a Father.* Macmillan, 1895. 8vo., uncut and unopened, original cloth, pictorial dust jacket, spine of jacket darkened and spotted, bookplate, very good, very scarce with jacket. Blackwell's Rare Books   B184 - 62   2016   £200

Marryat, Frederick   1792-1848   *Mr. Midshipman Easy.* Boston: Lothrop, 1899. Square 8vo., 4 color lithographic plates, black and white illustrations, quarter red cloth and pictorial boards with very attractive lithographic mounted plate for upper cover, showing one boy rescuing another from a sinking ship, very good.   Jeff Weber Rare Books 181 - 46   2016 $40

Marryat, Frederick   1792-1848   *Peter Simple.* Macmillan, 1895. 8vo., uncut, unopened in original cloth and pictorial dust jacket, bookkplate, very good.   Blackwell's Rare Books   B184 - 63   2016   £200

Marsh, A. E. W. *Sketches and Adventures in Madeira, Portugal and the Andalusias of Spain.* New York: Harper Bros., 1856. First edition, 8vo., frontispiece, illustrations, original blue decorative cloth, small wear to head and tail of spine, very good.   J. & S. L. Bonham Antiquarian Booksellers   Europe 2016 - 8937   2016   £200

Marsh, Dorothy *I Want to Be.* London: B. Walker & Sons, 1942. First edition, royal 8vo., original pictorial wrappers stapled to spine, die-cut window to upper panel, illustrations in orange and blue, scarce,.   Sotheran's Piccadilly Notes - Summer 2015 - 218   2016   £128

Marsh, Ngaio *Black Beech and Honeydew.* Boston: Little Brown, 1965. First American edition, fine in dust jacket. Mordida Books   2015 - 009362   2016 $55

Marsh, Richard Ogelsby *White Indians of Darien.* New York: Putnam's Sons, 1934. First edition, 8vo., original red buckram, lettered in black, map endpapers, frontispiece and plates after photos, very good and fresh, library card pocket removed from rear flyleaf, provenance of Monsigneur Joseph M. Gleason's pictorial engraved bookplate. Sotheran's   Travel and Exploration - 64   2016   £198

Marshak, S. *Charushin Detke V Kletke. (Animal Babies in a Cage - Zoo Babies).* Leningrad: Ogiz, 1935. First edition, 4to., cloth backed pictorial boards, edges rubbed and cover toned, else very good, with Charushin's illustrations. Aleph-bet Books, Inc.   112 - 438   2016 $800

Marshak, S. *Vchera I Segodnia I Segodnia. (Yesterday and today).* Leningrad: Guiz, 1928. Third printing, 4to., pictorial wrappers, light cover soil, almost invisible spine repair very good+, illustrations by Lebedev.   Aleph-bet Books, Inc.   111 - 255   2016 $1200

Marshall, A. J. *Bower-Birds: their Displays and Breeding Cycles.* Oxford: Clarendon Press, 1954. Octavo, text illustrations, good copy in worn and chipped dust jacket. Andrew Isles Natural History Books   55 - 20594   2016 $80

Marshall, Edison *The Doctor of Lonesome River.* New York: Cosmopolitan Book Corp., 1931. First edition, contemporary ownership signature, very good in very good, slightly nicked and dusty dust jacket.   Peter Ellis   112 - 5 2016   £35

Marshall, Edison *The Isle of Retribution.* Boston: Little Brown and Co., 1923. First edition, frontispiece, pictorial green cloth stamped in yellow and black, near fine in very good nicked and slightly chipped dust jacket.   Peter Ellis 112 - 4   2016   £35

Marshall, Edison *The Land of Forgotten Men.* Boston: Little Brown and Co., 1923. First edition, frontispiece by W. Herbert Dunton, pictorial green cloth blocked in orange and lighter green, contemporary ownership signature, fine in very good, slightly torn and rubbed dust jacket, chipped at head of spine.   Peter Ellis   112 - 7   2016   £35

Marshall, Edward *Four on the shore.* New York: Dial Books, 1985. First printing (code 1-10), 8vo., pictorial boards, as new in as new dust jacket, wonderful color illustrations by James Marshall to his life partner and dedicatee of the book, Joe Bryan, with charming ink drawing.   Aleph-bet Books, Inc.   111 - 270   2016 $1000

Marshall, Francis James Charles *Physical Education in Boys' Schools.* London: University of London Press, 1933. First edition, half title, frontispiece, plates and illustrations, original light blue cloth, spine faded, slightly dulled, booklabel of W. Meenger, St. Luke's College, Exeter.   Jarndyce Antiquarian Books   CCXV - 856   2016   £20

Marshall, James *The Cut-Ups.* New York: Viking Kestrel, 1984. First printing (code 1-3), 4to., pictorial boards, as new in as new dust jacket. Aleph-bet Books, Inc. 111 - 267 2016 $100

Marshall, James *Speedboat.* Boston: Houghton Mifflin, 1976. First edition, first printing (1-10 code), 8vo., fine in very slightly soiled dust jacket, inscribed to Marshall's life partner with 3/4 page drawing of Jasper. Aleph-bet Books, Inc. 111 - 268 2016 $1200

Marshall, John 1755-1835 *The Life of George Washington.* London: printed for Richard Phillips by T. Gillet, 1804-1807. First English edition, five volumes, 279 x 216mm., large paper quarto edition, publisher's quarter red roan over green paper boards, raised bands, spines attractively rebacked to style in modern times in panels with blind tooling and foliate gilt centerpiece, apparently original endpapers (hinges expertly reinforced with matching paper), 16 engravings as called for, including 12 folding maps, portrait of Washington and 3 views, paper boards bit soiled and chafed, extremities little rubbed, sympathetically rebacked bindings sturdy and attractive on shelf, one leaf with three inch tear into text (minimal loss) another with light brown stain touching but not obscuring text, one gathering somewhat foxed, occasional mild offsetting, otherwise clean and fresh internally with wide margins and few signs of use. Phillip J. Pirages 67 - 350 2016 $3500

Marshall, Paule *Brown Girl, Brownstone.* New York: Random House, 1959. First edition, octavo, original dust jacket. Honey & Wax Booksellers 4 - 59 2016 $450

Marshall, Paule *The Chosen Place, the Timeless People.* New York: Vintage, 1984. First Vintage Books edition, 8vo., author's signature on title, paper wrappers, edges and covers little soiled, cover creased front and back at lower corners, otherwise very good, tight copy, very good. Second Life Books, Inc. 196 B - 140 2016 $75

Marshall, Paule *Praisesong for the Widow.* New York: Putnam, 1983. First edition, 8vo., fine, dust jacket little nicked and worn, inscribed by author to poet William claire. Second Life Books, Inc. 196 B - 142 2016 $85

Marshall, Thomas *Aristotle's Theory of Conduct.* London: T. Fisher Unwin, 1906. First edition, half title, original dark green cloth, very good. Jarndyce Antiquarian Books CCXV - 23 2016 £30

Marston, Edward *Dovedale Revisited with other Holiday Sketches.* London: Sampson Low, Marston and Co., 1902. First edition, 1 of 250 numbered copies on Van Gelder paper signed by author, 8vo. original vellum backed green cloth boards, lettered in gilt on spine, illustrated with woodcuts and photogravures, spine slightly darkened otherwise, very good. Sotheran's Piccadilly Notes - Summer 2015 - 199 2016 £198

Marston, Edward *On a Sunshine Holyday by the Amateur Angler.* London: Sampson Low and Co., 1897. First edition, 1 of 250 numbered copies on Van Gelder paper initialled by author, 8vo., original vellum backed green cloth boards lettered gilt on spine, frontispiece and 15 India paper proof plates, spine slightly darkened, otherwise very good, bookplate of angling author Joe Brooks. Sotheran's Piccadilly Notes - Summer 2015 - 198 2016 £198

Marston, John Westland *The Patrician's Daughter.* London: C. Mitchell, 1843. Fifth edition, Half title slightly stained in outer margin, disbound. Jarndyce Antiquarian Booksellers CCXVIII - 315 2016 £120

Marston, Philip Bourke *Song-Tide and Other Poems.* London: Ellis and Green, 1871. First edition, inscribed presentation from author for aunt E. A. Singleton, exceptionally uncommon inscription, very good in original green cloth with gilt title to spine and front board, bump to head of spine ad to lower front cover, slight wear to boards, browning to endpages and few small spots of foxing to interior, very good. The Kelmscott Bookshop 12 - 64 2016 $300

Marston, William Moulton *F. F. Proctor.* New York: Richard Smith, 1943. First edition, photos and program reproductions, inscribed by Mrs Proctor to Governor Dewey of NY, nice, little scuffed and chipped dust jacket. Second Life Books, Inc. 196 B - 143 2016 $75

Martell, C. H., Mrs. *Historical Sketch of the United Baptist Woman's Missionary Union of the Maritime Provinces.* Wolfville?: United Baptist Woman's Missionary Union, 1920. Green cloth, gilt title to front cover, small 8vo., frontispiece, cloth slightly worn, previous owner's name on front endpaper. Schooner Books Ltd. 115 - 194 2016 $45

Martial Reviv'd or Epigrams, Satyrical, Panegyrical, Political, Moral, Elegiacal, Whimsical and Comical. London: printed for Tho. Atkins, n.d., 1722. First edition, 8vo., disbound, fine, complete with half title, very rare. C. R. Johnson Rare Book Collections Foxon: H-P 2015 - 575 2016 $3831

Martial De Salviac, P. *Un People Antique Au Pays De Menelik Les Galla.* Paris: H. Oudin, 1991. Second edition, 4to., slightly later crushed orange red morocco with raised bands, top edge gilt, dust jacket in half orange-red morocco over marbled paper boards, inside lined with black calf, spine lettered gilt, marbled paper covered slipcase with morocco edges, original printed wrappers bound in (these little spotted and with wear to spine), black and white illustrations after drawings and photos, near fine, incredibly luxurious binding, very rare. Sotheran's Travel and Exploration - 20 2016 £298

Martialis, Marcus Valerius *Epigrammaton Libri XIII.* Lyon: Apud Seb. Gryphium, 1546. Pocket edition, few minor spots, ownership inscription erased from titlepage, 16mo., 19th century mottled calf, spine gilt in compartment, boards bordered with triple gilt fillet, marbled endpapers, label lost from spine, extremities worn, label removed from front pastedown, ownership inscription of F. G. Kenyon, good.   Blackwell's Rare Books   Greek & Latin Classics VII - 65   2016   £250

Martialis, Marcus Valerius *Epigrammaton Libri XV....* Argentinae: Lazari Zetzneri, 1595. 16mo., slight worming to approximately first 50 pages at top of gutter plus single wormhole to lower margin throughout textblock, neither affecting text, paper flaw to bottom corner page 195-6 causing small tear, but no loss, occasional small spots and stains, trimmed little close at head but not touching, 17th century speckled calf, raised bands, double line blind tooling to boards, edges sprinkled red, little light creasing to spine, joints and endcaps worn, lower paste down lifted, very good, illegible ownership inscriptions.   Unsworths Antiquarian Booksellers   30 - 107   2016   £300

Martialis, Marcus Valerius *Epigrammaton Libri.* Londini: Excudebat Felix Kingstonius impensis Gulielmi Welby, 1615. Small 8vo., woodcut headpieces and motif to titlepage, light toning, small piece missing from bottom corner of editor's dedication and small stain to margin of following page but neither affecting text, very good overall, recent light brown morocco, blind tooled raised bands to spine with black morocco gilt label, gilt date to tail of spine, all edges red, endpapers replaced, tan buckram slipcase, binding and case fine, ownership inscription of Edward Wilson in old hand to initial blank and titlepage, second similar ownership inscription also to title with first name William but illegible surname, some numbers in old hand to rear blank tiny binder's stamp 'Delrue'.   Unsworths Antiquarian Booksellers 30 - 108   2016   £500

Martialis, Marcus Valerius *Epigrammata Demptis Obscenis.* Paris: Apud Viduam Simonis Benard, 1693. 12mo., contemporary brown morocco, covers with gilt fleur-de-ls and interlaced crescents at alternate corners, large central gilt arms of town of Bordeau, edges gilt, very pretty copy, bookplates (two) of Camille Aboussouan.   Joseph J. Felcone, Inc.   Books from Five Centuries: a Miscellany - 23   2016 $600

Martin, A. E. *The Outsiders.* New York: Simon & Schuster, 1945. First American edition, fine in dust jacket with tiny wear at corners.   Mordida Books   2015 - 004922   2016 $55

Martin, Edward Sandford *The Unrest of Women.* New York: Appleton, 1913. First edition, 8vo., ex-library with bookplate, cloth, very good, author Martha Deland's copy with her ownership signature and note that it was presented from publisher, note from the Library of Lorin Deland and library bookplate.   Second Life Books, Inc.   196 B - 144   2016 $75

Martin, Francois Xavier *The History of Louisiana from the Earliest Period.* New Orleans: printed by Lyman and Beardslee and A. T. Penniman & Co., 1827. First edition, 2 volumes, 248 x 165mm., pleasing later 19th century dark green crushed morocco by Stikeman (signed on front turn-in), covers with triple gilt fillet border and floral sprig corner-pieces, raised bands, spines densely gilt in compartments with center floral sprig in oval medallion, surrounded by swirling gilt tooling accented with small tools, gilt titling, gilt turn-ins, marbled endpapers, top edges gilt, other edges entirely untrimmed, front pastedown with leather bookplate of Marshall Clifford Lefferts and bookplate of Mrs. L. Bartlett, spines sunned to pleasing honey brown (covers bit sunned at edges, with front cover volume II inconspicuously sunned, and showing the darker silhouette of a bookend), few small stains to edges of same board, bindings virtually unworn and otherwise quite pleasing, minor foxing or browning throughout (no doubt affecting all copies because of inferior paper stock), five quires in volume I with one inch dampstain at head, one gathering in volume II noticeably browned, not without condition issues, but with much to please internally, including vast margins, consistent freshness and absence of soiling.   Phillip J. Pirages   67 - 250   2016 $1800

Martin, Frank *The Wood Engravings.* Church, Hanborough: Previous Parrot Press, 1998. XIV/36 copies, from an edition of 360 copies, signed by artist and compiler, printed on Mohawk paper, illustrations, some with color printing, this special edition with 8 Martin wood engravings signed and title by artist, printed from blocks by David Esslement and housed in separate card folder, this one of a number of copies issued with only 4 extra engravings, but with missing 4 supplied by publisher, folio, original quarter morocco with grey boards, Martin illustration to upper board, backstrip lettered in gilt, Martin design to endpapers, slipcase with patterned paper repeating a Martin design, fine. Blackwell's Rare Books   B186 - 329   2016   £500

Martin, Gabriel *Catalogus Librorum Bibliothecae Illustrissimi Viri Caroli Henrici Comitis de Hoym...* Parisiis: Gabriele & Claudium Martin, 1738. Small 8vo., 18th century quarter calf, blue paper covered boards, red leather spine label, all edges stained red, individual lots priced in ink in margins, dampstaining to titlepage and few pages that immediately follow, wear to extremities with small chips to head and tail of spine and to one panel between raised bands, small corner of page 99 lacking, bookplate of Paul Lacombe and A. Aubry, loosely inserted is commemorative booklabel which indicates the book came from reference library of H. P. Kraus.   Oak Knoll Books   310 - 64   2016 $1750

Martin, George R. R. *A Game of Thrones Book One of a Song of Fire and Ice.* New York: Toronto: London: Bantam Books, 1996. First edition, octavo, boards, signed by author, corners and base of spine slightly bumped, nearly fine in nearly fine dust jacket with corner tips slightly bumped, tiny nick to mid front panel spine fold and little lamination separation to few spots on front panel.   John W. Knott, Jr./L.W. Currey, Inc.   Fall-Winter 2015 - 17386   2016 $850

Martin, George R. R. *A Game of Thrones Preview Edition.* London: Harper Collins/Voyager, 1996. First edition, trade paperback, small octavo, fine in illustrated wrappers, signed by author on label affixed on dedication page.   Between the Covers Rare Books   204 - 110   2016 $950

Martin, H. Bradley *The Library of H. Bradley Martin.* New York: Sotheby's, 1989-1990. Complete set, 9 volumes, small 4to., cloth, paper cover labels, illustrations.   Oak Knoll Books   310 - 256   2016 $375

Martin, Mary *My Heart Belongs.* New York: Morrow, 1976. First printing, 8vo., author's presentation on half title, nice, dust jacket little torn.   Second Life Books, Inc.   196 B - 146   2016 $45

Martin, Paul S. *The SU Site Excavations at a Mogolian Village Western New Mexico 1939/1941/1946.* Chicago: Field Museum of Natural History, 1940. 1943. 1947, 3 volumes, numerous plates, maps, illustrations and charts, original printed wrappers, some browning to wrappers especially on volume 1, scuff marks on covers of two volumes, internally bright.   Dumont Maps and Books   133 - 66   2016 $125

Martin, William *Noble Boys: Thei Deeds of Love and Duty.* London: Strahan and Co., 1870. First edition, half title, frontispiece, plates and illustrations, 32 page catalog (Nov. 1870), original brick red cloth by Burn & Co., little dulled, some slight repair to following hinge, prize label and school report laid on to leading free endpapers, good plus.   Jarndyce Antiquarian Books   CCXV - 67   2016   £38

Martindale, C. C. *Charles IXth Duke of Marlborough, K. G.* 1934. Original wrappers.   I. D. Edrich   Winston Spencer Churchill - 2016   £80

Martineau, Harriet 1802-1876 *The Crofton Boys; a Tale.* New York: Appleton, 1857. first American edition, small 8vo., engraved frontispiece, original blindstamped brown cloth little faded, very good, tight copy.   Second Life Books, Inc.   197 - 227   2016 $65

Martineau, Harriet 1802-1876 *How to Observe. Morals and Manners.* London: Charles Knight & Co., 1838. First edition, 2 pages ads, original dark green cloth, slightly rubbed and tail of spine otherwise nice, crispy copy, bookseller's ticket of C. Ambery, Manchester.   Jarndyce Antiquarian Books   CCXV - 309   2016   £125

Martson, John Westland *Gerald: a Dramatic Poem and Other Poems.* London: C. Mitchell, 1842. First edition, leading f.e.p. removed, original dark blue cloth, blocked in blind, spine lettered gilt, boards rather severely affected by damp but text block largely undamaged.   Jarndyce Antiquarian Booksellers   CCXVIII - 887   2016   £80

Maruki, Tashi *Hiroshima No Pika.* New York: Lathrop Lee & Shepard, 1980. Stated first edition, first printing with 1-10 code, pictorial boards, fine in dust jacket, color illustrations.   Aleph-bet Books, Inc.   111 - 487   2016 $125

Marvin, Charles *The Region of the Eternal Fire.* London: Allen, 1891. Revised edition, 8vo., original red pictorial cloth, mounted woodbury type photographic portrait frontispiece with tissue guard, maps and wood engraved plates, light marking to binding, spine little faded, internally apart from light spotting to few illustrations, very clean and fresh.   Sotheran's   Travel and Exploration - 269   2016   £598

Marvin, Charles *The Russians at the Gates of Herat.* London: New York: Scribner, 1885. First US edition, 8vo., original sand colored cloth, lettered in black, map frontispiece, 6 portraits, one further map, light even toning to paper, near fine.   Sotheran's   Travel and Exploration - 152   2016   £298

Mascall, Leonard *A Book of Fishing with Hooke and Line...* London: S. Watchell, 1884. One of 200 copies, 222 x 178mm., original brown quarter morocco over cloth boards, flat spine with titling in gilt, marbled endpapers, top edge gilt, 12 illustrations, from woodcuts, front pastedown with bookplate of R. A. G. Festing, extremities slightly rubbed, spine with minor marks, endpapers bit foxed, otherwise excellent copy, binding completely sound and without any major flaw and text clean and pleasing.   Phillip J. Pirages   67 - 3   2016 $750

Masefield, John 1878-1967 *August 1914 & Reynard the Fox or the Ghost Heath Run 1918.* Market Drayton: Tern Press, 2005. Limited to 40 numbered copies, signed by Nicholas and Mary Parry, first titlepage portrait of Masefield plus 55 full page black and white illustrations, set in Caslon type on Magnani paper with pencil illustrations reproduced by North Shropshire Print, brown cloth covers with paper title label on spine and front, tan endpapers, with over 50 original graphite drawings by Nicholas Parry used in the book, as well as others not used in the book, drawings on card stock, all in tan cloth drop-back box with toning leather title label on spine, rare.   Oak Knoll Books   27 - 64   2016 $6500

Masefield, John 1878-1967 *Poetry.* London: William Heinemann Ltd., Limited to 275 copies`, signed and numbered by author, tan cloth boards lettered gilt, top edge gilt, covers darkened and offsetting to endpapers, otherwise fine.   Argonaut Book Shop   Literature 2015 - 4932   2016 $50

Masefield, John 1878-1967 *Rosas.* New York: Macmillan Co., 1918. First edition, number 313 of 750 numbered copies out of a total edition of 950, signed by author, 16mo., vellum backed light blue boards, lettered gilt, corners rubbed and soiled, darkened spine, lower corners showing, bookplate, very good.   Argonaut Book Shop   Literature 2015 - 7347   2016 $50

Maskell, W. M. *An Account of the Insects Noxious to Agriculture and Plants in New Zealand.* Wellington: Government Printer, 1887. Octavo, 23 chromolithograph plates, publisher's cloth, very good. Andrew Isles Natural History Books 55 - 7234 2016 $60

Mason, Alfred Edward Woodley 1865-1948 *Miranda of the Balcony.* London: Macmillan and Co. Limited, 1899. First edition, inscribed on titlepage by Anne Crawford Flexner who secured the dramatic rights for Mason's Novel, original blue cloth with bright gilt title stamped to cover and spine, along with lovely embossed floral design, top edge gilt, light wear to edges and spine ends, foxing to endpapers but rest of interior is extremely clean and bright, tightly bound, very good. The Kelmscott Bookshop 12 - 65 2016 $150

Mason, Bobbie Ann *In Country, a Novel.* New York: Harper Row, 1985. First edition, 8vo., signed by author, fine in dust jacket. Second Life Books, Inc. 196 B - 149 2016 $65

Mason, Clifford *Jamaica Run.* New York: St. Martin's, 1987. First edition, very fine in dust jacket. Mordida Books 2015 - 001535 2016 $55

Mason, James *Cornelia and Alcestis: Two Operas.* London: printed for T. Payne, 1810. First edition, 194 x 124mm., harmless contemporary purple straight grain morocco, covers with gilt fillet border, raised bands flanked by plain gilt rules, gilt titling, all edges gilt, excellent later fore-edge painting of the Acropolis, joints somewhat rubbed and flaked, boards little stained and rather faded, rear board with two small abraded patches, otherwise excellent copy, clean, fresh internally, solid, inoffensive binding with vividly colored painting in fine condition. Phillip J. Pirages 67 - 156 2016 $1100

Mason, Mason Jordan *The Twenty-Third of Love.* Eureka: Hearse Press, n.d., Number 94 of 125 copies, close to near fine in stapled wrappers illustrated by Ben Tibbs and with some rusting at staples, uncommon. Jeff Hirsch Books Holiday List 2015 - 32 2016 $75

Mason, Ronald *The Spirit above the Dust: a Study of Herman Melville.* New York: Paul Appel, 1972. Second edition, 8vo., inscribed by author and Howard Vincent (provided introduction), fine, without dust jacket. Second Life Books, Inc. 196 B - 201 2016 $45

Mason, Stuart *Bibliography of Oscar Wilde.* London: T. Werner Laurie, 1914. First edition, edition deluxe, number 29 of 100 copies numbered and signed, frontispieces, bookplate of Willis Vickery, near fine in beige cloth boards with gilt titles to spines and front boards, few spots of foxing to top edges of boards, good - but rare - brown dust jackets with black titles to spines and front panels, heavy chipping rubbing, browning and wear to jackets, they are protected from further wear with archival plastic cover,. The Kelmscott Bookshop 13 - 37 2016 $975

Mason, William 1725-1797 *Elegies.* London: printed for Robert Horsfield, 1763. First edition, half title, 4to., little dusted, some modern pencil notes in margins, disbound. Jarndyce Antiquarian Booksellers CCXVI - 403 2016 £220

Mason, William 1725-1797 *Elfrida, a Dramatic Poem.* London: printed for J. & P. Knapton, 1752. Third edition, 8vo., title printed in black and red, without half title, disbound. Jarndyce Antiquarian Booksellers CCXVI - 404 2016 £20

Mason, William 1725-1797 *Poems.* London: printed for Robert Horsfield and sold by J. Dodsley and C. Marsh, also by W. Thurlbourn and J. Woodyer in Cambridge..., 1764. First edition, 8vo., titlepage vignette by S. Wale, contents leaf at end, excellently rebound half calf, red label. Jarndyce Antiquarian Booksellers CCXVI - 405 2016 £110

Mason, William Shaw *Bibliotheca Hibernicana or a Descriptive Catalogue of a Select Irish Library.* Dublin: printed by W. Fold and Son, 1823. Limited to 50 copies, 8vo., original boards soiled and worn, backstrip chipped and worn away, missing portion at heel, bookplate, small institutional release stamp, occasional finger soiling, marginal damp stain toward end, second front blank has short tear with no loss. Oak Knoll Books 310 - 257 2016 $2200

Massachusetts *Resolves of the General Court of the Commonwealth of Massachusetts Passed at their Session, which Commenced on Wednesday, the Second of January and Ended on Thursday, the Twenty-Eighth of March, One Thousand Eight Hundred and Thirty Three.* Boston: Dutton and Wentworth, 1833. First edition, small 4to., original blue gray wrappers, stitched, lacking rear wrappers, scattered foxing, else very good, untrimmed. Kaaterskill Books 21 - 66 2016 $150

Massachusetts Historical Society *Collections of the Massachusetts Historical Society Volume II of the Second Series.* Boston: printed by John Eliot, 1814. First edition, signed with gift inscription to the American Antiquarian Society by Isaiah Thomas, 8vo., original blue gray paper covered boards with paper label on spine, spine and label well worn, ends and joints chipped, institutional stamp on title, gift inscription on free front endpaper, leaves untrimmed, about good.   Kaaterskill Books   21 - 50   2016 $500

Massett, Stephen C. *Stephen C. Massett. The First California Troubadour.* Oakland: Biobooks, 1954. First edition, one of 500 copies, frontispiece, 3 facsimile programs, 1954 menu tipped in, dark green cloth, copper boards, foot of spine jammed, fine.   Argonaut Book Shop   Biography 2015 - 7612   2016 $45

Massie, Robert K. *Peter the Great: His Life and World.* New York: Knopf, 1980. First edition, 8vo. illustrations, maps on endpapers, author's signature on blank, black cloth, very good, somewhat scuffed and chipped dust jacket.   Second Life Books, Inc.   197 - 228   2016 $60

Massime Cristiane. Proposte a Meditarsi in Ciascun Giorno Del Mese. Milano: Per Federico Agnelli, 1774. 10th printing, page text with double rule border, head - tailpieces, decorative initial capital letters, 12mo., white cloth with green, black, yellow, pink and blue flower embroidery, all edges gilt, average wear and soiling to binding, period personal owner signature to front pastedown, respecable copy, rare.   Tavistock Books   Bibliolatry - 24   2016 $950

Masson, Elsie *Folk Tales of Brittany.* Philadelphia: Macrae Smith, 1929. First edition, 4to., cloth backed pictorial boards, corner rubbed, else fine in dust jacket (very good, with few mends on verso and half inch piece off top of backstrip), pictorial endpapers, 15 full page illustrations plus many partial page illustrations and striking color wrapper by Thornton Oakley, with Oakley inscription and sketch.   Aleph-bet Books, Inc.   111 - 326   2016 $450

Masters, Edgar Lee *Spoon River Anthology.* New York: Limited Editions Club, 1942. Number 815 from an edition of 2000 copies, illustrations by Boardman Robinson, clean, very near fine in very good plus slipcase that has some minor wear, signed by Masters and Boardman Robinson.   Jeff Hirsch Books   Holiday List 2015 - 51   2016 $150

Mastin, John *Through the Sun in an Airship.* London: Charles Giffin, 1909. First edition, 2nd issue, slight spotting to front board, modest scattered foxing, very good plus in near fine dust jacket with couple of small nicks at crown, very scarce in jacket.   Between the Covers Rare Books   208 - 125   2016 $650

Mather, Cotton **1662-1727** *Ratio Disciplinae Fratrum Nov-Anglorum. A Faithful Acount of the Discipline Professed and Practiced in the Churches of New England.* Boston: printed for S. Gerrish in Cornhill, 1726. First edition, 12mo., modern calf with new endpaper, original blanks, "by Cotton Mather" inscribed on titlepage and manuscript number inscribed verso of titlepage, foxing throughout, intermittent marginal wear, leaf Ee2 slightly defective with minute loss of text, inscriptions by early owners and titlepage, still about very good.   Kaaterskill Books   21 - 52   2016 $3750

Mather, George *Lectures on the Beautiful and Sublime in Nature and in Morals.* London: pub. for the author at the Wesleyan Conference Office, 1874. Second edition, 4th thousand, half title, 16 page catalog, original dark green cloth, bevelled boards, blocked in black and gilt, contemporary presentation inscription on half title.   Jarndyce Antiquarian Books   CCXV - 310   2016   £35

Mathers, Edward Powys *Eastern Love: Prose and Verse Translations.* privately for subscribers by John Rodker, 1927-1930. First edition of these translations, one of 1000 numbered sets, 12 volumes, copper plate engravings by Hester Sainsbury, 12 volumes, quarter pink calf, black cloth sides with gilt devices on upper covers, spines faded and little rubbed, some foxing (particularly of prelims and endleaves), some corners bruised, otherwise very good, ownership signature volumes I 50 VIII, bookplates ot each volume.   Bertram Rota Ltd.   February List 2016 - 35   2016   £500

Matheson, Richard *The Shrinking Man.* London: David Bruce & Watson, 1973. First hardcover edition, signed by author, 8vo., fine in very good++ dust jacket with soil and scuffs, 8vo.   By the Book, L. C.   45 - 75   2016 $900

Matheson, Robert *Born of Man and Woman: Tales of Science Fiction and Fantasy.* Philadelphia: Chamberlain Press Inc., 1954. First edition, octavo, cloth, signed by author, fine copy in fine dust jacket, brilliant copy.   John W. Knott, Jr./L.W. Currey, Inc.   Fall-Winter 2015 - 17147   2016 $1500

Mathews, G. M. *Birds and Books the Story of the Mathews Ornithological Library.* Canberra: Verity Hewitt Bookshop, 1942. Limited to 200 copies, numbered and signed by author, octavo, photos, publisher's titled wrappers.   Andrew Isles Natural History Books   55 - 16347   2016 $200

Mathews, G. M. *The Call of China and the Islands. Report of the Foreign Deputation 1911-1912...* Dayton: Foreign Missionary Society, 1912. First edition, 8vo., very rare, original yellow cloth, frontispiece and illustrations in text, light toning and ms. note to titlepage, previous owner's ink-stamp.   Sotheran's   Travel and Exploration - 153   2016   £178

Mathews, G. M. *A Manual of the Birds of Australia. Volume One. Orders Casuarii to Columbae.* London: H. F. & G. Witherby, 1921. Large octavo, 36 plates, by Lilan Medland, fine in dust jacket.   Andrew Isles Natural History Books   55 - 18492   2016 $150

Mathews, Nancy Mowell *Paul Gauguin - an Exotic Life.* New Haven and London: Yale University Life, 2001. First edition, quarto, well illustrated, fine in fine dust jacket.   Peter Ellis   112 - 147   2016   £25

Mathews, William *Getting on in the World or Hints on Success in Life.* Chicago: S. C. Griggs & Co., 1874. Original brick red cloth, very good, bright.   Jarndyce Antiquarian Books   CCXV - 311   2016   £35

Mathias, Thomas James *The Pursuits of Literature... (bound with) A Translation of the Passages from Greek, Latin, Italian and French Writers.* London: printed for T. Becket, 1798. Dublin: printed for J. Milliken... 1799. Fifth edition of first work, 8vo., very light marginal damp marking, slightly more intrusive at end, contemporary half vellum, marbled paper boards, little rubbed, little wear to lower joint, green morocco label, blue sprinkled edges, bookplate of William Bisset, Lessondrum, his signature dated 1798 and of Francis White Popham, sound, attractive copy.   Jarndyce Antiquarian Booksellers   CCXVI - 406   2016   £785

Matrix 1-26 (with index to volumes 1-21). Whittington Press, 1980-2006. Together 27 volumes, 4to, original harlequin wrappers, profusely illustrated, near fine run, with ALS from John Randle to Howard Gerwing.   Sotheran's Piccadilly Notes - Summer 2015 - 307   2016   £3750

Matrix 1. Number One Autumn 1981. Manor Farm: Whittington Press, 1981. First edition, limited to 30 numbered copies, 4to., stiff paper wrappers, very scarce, fading to spine and spine edges of back cover/top of front cover, inserted is ALS form John Randle, slight shelfwear, some sunning to spine.   Oak Knoll Books   310 - 172   2016 $1000

Matrix 2. Andoversford: Whittington Press, 1993. Reprint of 2nd issue, 4to., original rust colored paper covered boards and dust jacket, fine.   Sotheran's Piccadilly Notes - Summer 2015 - 309   2016   £148

Matrix 4. Andoversford: Whittington Press, 1984. Limited to 590 numbered copies, this one of 65 copies, specially bound, folio, original morocco backed patterned paper covered boards, fine, without slipcase.   Sotheran's Piccadilly Notes - Summer 2015 - 308   2016   £998

Matrix 05. Cheltenham: Whittington Press, 1985. Limited to 715 copies, plates, tipped-in samples, small 4to., stiff paper wrappers, very slight sun fading to spine.   Oak Knoll Books   310 - 173   2016 $325

Matrix 33. Risbury: Whittington Press, 2015. One of 655 copies, from an edition of 715 copies printed on Matrix Laid Zerkall mould made and naturalis papers, decorative borders and initial letters, numerous illustrations with many tipped in, some of these foldouts, loosely inserted erratum slip, 4to., original mint green boards with Tom Mayo decorated initial to upper board, dust jacket with Joe MacLaren illustrations on front, edges roughtrimmed.   Blackwell's Rare Books   B186 - 347   2016   £135

Matrix 33. Risbury: Whittington Press, 2015. Limited to 715 copies, this being one of 60 of the deluxe edition bound thus with extra material, 8 pages of color plates, typ specimens, linocut and line and color illustrations.   Oak Knoll Books   310 - 174   2016 $580

Matson, Donald D. *Neurosurgery of Infancy and Childhood.* Springfield: Charles C. Thomas, 1968. Second edition, numerous text illustrations, original cloth and dust jacket, near fine.   James Tait Goodrich   X-78 - 394   2016 $195

Matthews, William *Sticks and Stones.* Milwaukee: Pentagram Press, 1975. First edition, one of 600 copies, pictorial wrappers, inscribed by author for William Meredith, quarter size light stain on front cover, near fine.   Charles Agvent   William Meredith - 69   2016 $100

Matveld, H. J. T. *Prentenboer.* Leyden: circa, 1840. 16mo., printed wrappers, fine, hand colored illustrations.   Aleph-bet Books, Inc.   111 - 146   2016 $300

Matz, Bertam Waldron *Character Sketches from Dickens.* London: Rapahel Tuck & Sons, 1924. 4to., half title, facsimile, frontispiece, plates, color plates, original red embossed lettered in gilt, booklabel, very good.   Jarndyce Antiquarian Booksellers   CCXVIII - 740   2016   £50

Matz, Bertam Waldron *Dickensian Inns & Taverns.* London: Cecil Palmer, 1922. First edition, half title, frontispiece, plates, original blue cloth, lettered in blind and gilt, spine slightly faded, very good.   Jarndyce Antiquarian Booksellers   CCXVIII - 1377   2016   £45

Matz, Bertam Waldron *The Inns & Taverns of 'Pickwick' with Observations on their Other Associates.* London: Cecil Palmer, 1921. First edition, half title, frontispiece and plates, original maroon cloth, lettered in blind and gilt, spine slightly faded, endpapers browned, good plus.   Jarndyce Antiquarian Booksellers   CCXVIII - 156   2016   £25

Mauduit, Israel *Considerations on the Present German War.* London: printed for John Wilkie at the Bible in St. Paul's Churchyard, 1760. 8vo. in 4's, titlepage little dusty, otherwise good, clean copy, disbound.   Jarndyce Antiquarian Booksellers   CCXVI - 407   2016   £85

Maugham, William Somerset 1874-1965 *Liza of Lambeth.* London: Heinemann, 1947. Jubilee edition, 8vo., one of 1000 numbered copies signed by author, cloth backed patterned boards, original acetate little torn, very good, clean, tight copy.   Second Life Books, Inc.   196 B - 154   2016 $225

Maugham, William Somerset 1874-1965 *The Making of a Saint.* London: T. Fisher Unwin, 1898. First English edition, uncommon second book, original green cloth with gilt title to spine, minor rubbing to boards and minor wear to spine ends, text and endpages slightly browned as is usual with this book, bookplates of three previous owners, A. S. Alexander, Eleanor Jacott and Mark Samuels Lasner, very good.   The Kelmscott Bookshop   12 - 66   2016 $300

Maugham, William Somerset 1874-1965 *Of Human Bondage.* London: William Heinemann, 1915. First edition, small stain in upper margin affecting about 50 leaves, browned, original cloth, spine little faded, inner hinges strained.   Blackwell's Rare Books   B184 - 193   2016   £150

Maugham, William Somerset 1874-1965 *The Summing Up.* Garden City: Doubleday Doran, 1938. First edition, 8vo., black and white frontispiece, large paper limited edition of a total edition of 291 copies, this one of 375 copies, signed by author, gold cloth stamped in red and gold, title gilt on red background on spine, printed on watermarked rag paper by James Leach at Country Life Press, deckle edge, top edge gilt, fine.   Second Life Books, Inc.   196 B - 155   2016 $250

Maundeville, John *The Voiage and Travaile of Sir John Maundevile, Kt.* New York: printed by the Grabhorn Press, San Francisco for Random House, 1928. No. 104 of 150 copies, 368 x 242mm., publisher's Philppine mahogany boards backed with brown Niger morocco by William Wheeler, raised bands, spine with tilting in blind "TKD" embossed in blank on portion of spine leather extending onto front board, paragraph marks in red or blue, 32 woodcut in text, 34 large hand illuminated initials in red, blue and gold by Valenti Angelo, one page with faint paint residue in margin, but very fine, binding extremely bright and virtually unworn, text showing no signs of use.   Phillip J. Pirages   67 - 178   2016 $2500

Maupassant, Guy De 1850-1893 *The Tales of...* London: Limited Editions Club, 1963. No. 1461 of 1500 copies, 8vo., illustrations by Gunter Bohmer, signed on colophon by artist, light blue cloth, tan cloth labels applied front and spine, stamped in gilt, monthly letter of the club laid in, about as new in box, covered with marbled paper.   Second Life Books, Inc.   197 - 229   2016 $50

Maurice, C. Edmund *Life of Octavia Hill as told in her Letters.* London: Macmillan, 1913. First edition, 8vo., portraits, untrimmed and partially unopened, very good, clean tight copy, this the copy of author and feminist, Jane Addams (Hull House), from the library of consumer advocate Florence Kelley.   Second Life Books, Inc.   196 B - 157   2016 $250

Maurois, Andre *Serge Mendjinsky...* Paris: 1963. 4to., Medjinsky's presentation with large ink drawing of sunflower, color and black and white reproductions, cover slightly scuffed and soiled, otherwise very good, tight copy.   Second Life Books, Inc.   196 B - 158   2016 $450

Maurois, Andre *Women of Paris.* London: Andre Deutsch, 1958. First UK edition, small octavo, 125 plates, original wrappers, near fine, only slight rubbing to cover edges.   Peter Ellis   112 - 248   2016   £50

Mawer, John *The Progress of Language, an Essay, Wherein is Prov'd the First Language.* London: printed for John Clarke, 1726. First edition, folio, disbound, very good, rare.   C. R. Johnson Rare Book Collections   Foxon: H-P 2015 - 581   2016 $3064

Mawson, Thomas H. *The Art and Craft of Garden Making.* London: B. T. Batsford, 1901. Second edition, folio, photos, plans, drawings, green cloth decorated gilt, top edge gilt, cover shakey and bruise at one corner, cloth rubbed at head and tail of spine, tail of spine waterstained, good.   Peter Ellis   112 - 141   2016   £200

Master Roberts' Bridget Kehoe Songster. New York: A. J. Fisher, 1880. 12mo., printed wrappers, pictorial front cover, colored by hand, minor wear to spine, hint of foxing to edges of few leaves, publisher's ads at end, overall very good.   Dramatis Personae   119 - 142   2016 $175

Maxims, Morals and Golden Rules. London: J. Madden & Co., 1839. Original limp green cloth, creased and rubbed, all edges gilt, contemporary gift inscription on leading pastedown from Frances Anne Dodgson for father, additional later presentation leaf tipped in.   Jarndyce Antiquarian Books   CCXV - 313   2016   £60

Maxwell, James *Divine Miscellanies; or Sacred Poems.* Birmingham: printed for the author by T. Warren, 1756. First edition, engraved frontispiece, 12mo., contemporary sheep, rebacked in paler calf, black morocco label, wanting flyleaf at front, some early pencil trails and scribbled but sound, uncommon.   C. R. Johnson Rare Book Collections   Foxon: H-P 2015 - 582   2016 $689

Maxwell, Marius *Stalking Big Game with a Camera in Equatorial Africa.* London: William Heinemann, 1925. First 'royal 4to." (an imperial 4to. edition limited to 550 copies was published in 1924, but without the monograph on elephant, present here), royal 4to., original blue cloth, gilt lettering to spine, top edge gilt, large folding sepia photographic plate of a herd of elephants, 2 plates of photographic equipment itself, 110 black and white plates, several folding on multiple image, folding lithographed map of Kenya Colony, colored in outline, previous owner's inscription to front pastedown, slight rubbing to extremities, otherwise good.   Sotheran's   Hunting, Shooting & Fishing - 15   2016   £300

Maxwell, William *The Chateau.* New York: Knopf, 1961. First edition, inscribed by author to author Oliver La Farge and wife Consuelo, fine in very near fine dust jacket with slight loss of crimson to spine extremities.   Ken Lopez Bookseller   166 - 78   2016 $575

Maxwell, William Hamilton *Rambling Recollections of a Soldier of Fortune.* Dublin: William Curry, Jun. & Co., 1842. Frontispiece and plates by Phiz, frontispiece, slightly foxed, contemporary half brown calf, maroon morocco label, slightly rubbed with slight sign of library label removal from spine, from the Headfort library, 'Bective 1856', nice copy.   Jarndyce Antiquarian Booksellers   CCXVII - 183   2016   £150

Mayer, Edwin Justus *The Firebrand.* New York: Boni & Liveright, 1924. First edition, 8vo., black cloth, water mark in lower inner margin, very good, 2 illustrations from the play tipped in, signed by 6 members of the cast.   Second Life Books, Inc.   196 B - 160   2016 $250

Mayer, Johann Tobias *Lehrbuch uber die Physische Astronomie, Theorie der Erde und Meteorolgoie.* Gottingen: Heinich Dieterich, 1805. Black paper covered boards with red and gilt title label on spine, wear to hinges, edges of boards and corners, heavy rubbing to paper covering boards, stamp from Meteorological Society to titlepage and remnant of stamp to endpage, previous owner signature dated 1825 to front endpaper, occasional spots of foxing to interior and minor toning to pages in German, 2 plates, very good, scarce.   The Kelmscott Bookshop   13 - 38   2016 $175

Mayer, John *The Sportsman's Directory; or Park and Gamekeeper's Companion.* London: Baldwin, Cradock and Joy, Paternoster Row and Swinborne and Walter Colchester, 1819. Third edition, bound in three quarter red leather with red cloth covered boards and black title label to spine, five raised bands to spine with gilt decoration to each compartment, slight fading to spine, rubbing to spine ends and minor wear to corners of boards, occasional spots of foxing throughout text and offsetting to titlepage, frontispiece, marbled endpages and top edges gilt, attractive book, very good.   The Kelmscott Bookshop   13 - 39   2016 $175

Mayer, John *The Sportsman's Directory or Park and Gamekeeper's Companion.* London: printed for Baldwin and Cradock et al, 1828. Fifth edition, 191 x 121mm., appealing mid 19th century black straight grain half morocco over marbled paper boards, raised bands, gilt spine titling, marbled endpapers, top edge gilt, woodcut tailpiece, sewn illustrations in text and one engraved plate, titlepage with ink ownership signature of John Sadlier Moody, upper corners slightly bumped, top edge gilt obviously browned from facing frontispiece, light offsetting and isolated trivial foxing in text, excellent copy, binding without significant wear and leaves almost entirely quite fresh and clean.   Phillip J. Pirages   67 - 4   2016 $750

Mayhew, Augustus *Acting Charades; or Deeds not Words.* London: D. Bogue, 86 Fleet Street, n.d. c., 1850. First edition, square 16mo., hand colored engraved title and frontispiece, tailpiece by George Cruikshank, original red cloth, upper cover and spine blocked in gilt, lightly dust soiled and rubbed to extremities, inscribed "W. J. Clarke & Julia Maria Clarke from Papa".   Marlborough Rare Books   List 55 - 47   2016   £125

Mayhew, Henry *The Criminal Prisons of London and Scenes of Criminal Life.* London: Charles Griffin & Co., 1862. First edition, 8vo., 111 wood engravings, including 47 wood engraved plates, 2 folding, original red cloth, decorated spine, gilt somewhat worn, uncommon.   Marlborough Rare Books   List 56 - 37   2016   £300

Mayo, Herbert *Anatomical and Physiological Commentaries No. 1 August 1822 with Number II July 1823.* London: Thomas and George Underwood, 1822. 1823., 8vo., 2 parts in 1 volume, recent quarter calf and marbled boards with vellum corner tips, 8 folding lithographed plates, seven plates, some soiling and foxing to text, fore edges of two plates soiled and chipped, presentation from author, signed.   James Tait Goodrich   X-78 - 395   2016 $575

Mc Spadden, J. Walker *Stories from Dickens.* London: George G. Harrap, 1914. Color frontispiece, black and white plates, original purple pictorial cloth, lettered in black, ownership inscription Xmas 1919, very good, bright copy in slightly worn dust jacket.   Jarndyce Antiquarian Booksellers   CCXVIII - 734   2016   £35

McAlmon, Robert *Being Geniuses Together.* London: Secker & Warburg, 1938. First edition, 8vo., original blue cloth, dust jacket, rare, extremely so in such fine condition in dust jacket, preserved in half calf folding box.   James S. Jaffe Rare Books   Occasional List: Winter 2016 - 94   2016 $7500

McArthur, Molly *Tribute.* Pelican Press, 1924. 195/250 copies signed by author, woodcut head and tailpieces, faint foxing to limitation page, imperial 8vo., original quarter black cloth, little waterstaining at foot of upper board and light overall soiling, rubbing to extremities with light wear to top corners, patterned endpapers, good.   Blackwell's Rare Books   B186 - 328   2016   £50

McBain, Ed *The Pusher: a Novel of the 87th Precinct.* London: New York: T. V. Boardman & Co. Ltd., 1959. First hardcover edition, signed by author, octavo, cloth, some mild discoloration to cloth at base of spine, light residue from label removal to front pastedown, very good to nearly fine in nearly fine dust jacket with some black ink touch up to head and heel of spine panel with tape re-enforcement to verso of head of spine panel, uncommon signed.   John W. Knott, Jr./L.W. Currey, Inc.   Fall-Winter 2015 - 17240   2016 $1250

McBeth, Brian S. *British Oil Policy 1919-1939.* London: Frank Cass, 1985. First edition, 8vo., original red boards, spine lettered gilt, pictorial dust jacket, plates from historic photographs, apart from small spot to fore edges, near fine, inscribed by author.   Sotheran's   Travel and Exploration - 343   2016   £128

McBride, James J *Interned: Internment of the SS Columbus Crew at Fort Stanton, New Mexico 1941-1945.* Santa Fe: self published, 2003. Second edition, illustrations, wrappers, light wear, else very good.   Dumont Maps and Books   133 - 67   2016 $75

McCabe, Olivia *The Rose Fairies.* Chicago: Rand McNally, 1911. First edition, small 4to., cloth, pictorial paste-on, slight cover soil, near fine, 12 color plates and black and whites in text, with pictorial endpapers by Hope Dunlop.   Aleph-bet Books, Inc.   111 - 163   2016 $275

McCall Smith, Alexander *Bertie's Guide to Life and Mothers.* London: Polygon, 2013. First edition, book and dust jacket fine, slight tinge to closed page edges, signed by author, jacket filled with new removable clear cover.   Gemini Books   2016 - 31876   2016 $44

McCall Smith, Alexander *The Importance of Being Seven.* London: Polygon, 2010. First edition, book and dust jacket fine, signed by author, jacket supplied in new removable clear cover.   Gemini Books   2016 - 31868   2016 $44

McCall Smith, Alexander *The Novel Habits of Happiness.* London: Little Brown, 2015. First edition, book and dust jacket fine, signed by author, jacket fitted with removable clear cover.   Gemini Books   2016 - 31881   2016 $50

McCall Smith, Alexander *Precious and Grace.* London: Little Brown, 2016. First edition, signed by author, fine, in jacket fitted with new removable clear cover.   Gemini Books   2016 - 31879   2016 $50

McCall Smith, Alexander *The Uncommon Appeal of Clouds.* London: Little Brown, 2012. First edition, book and dust jacket fine, as new, signed by author, jacket fitted with new removable cover.   Gemini Books   2016 - 31879   2016 $50

McCall Smith, Alexander *The Woman Who Walked in Sunshine.* London: Little Brown, 2015. First edition, book and dust jacket in new-fine condition, jacket fitted with new removable clear cover.   Gemini Books   2016 - 31680   2016 $44

McCardell, Roy L. *Conversations of a Chorus girl.* New York: Street & Smith, 1903. First edition, 12mo., cartoons, orange cloth stamped in black, yellow and white, author's presentation on flyleaf, owner's bookplate, nice.   Second Life Books, Inc.   196 B - 164   2016 $75

McCarthy, Charlotte *Justice and Reason, faithful Guides to Truth.* London: printed for the author, 1767. First edition, octavo, later tree calf rebacked, green morocco label, gilt lettering, fine.   The Brick Row Book Shop   Miscellany 69 - 48   2016 $3000

McCarthy, Cormac *Blood Meridian or the Evening Redness in the West.* Random House, 1985. First edition, 8vo., review copy with slip laid-in, two tone red cloth with red paper over boards, fine, bright, unread copy in fine dust jacket, full imitation leather slipcase with books dust jackets front panel duplicated on front panel, spine panel and rear panel matching dust jacket, exceptional copy.   Buckingham Books   2015 - 26129   2016 $3750

McCarthy, Cormac *The Counselor.* New York: Vintage Books, 2013. Uncorrected proof, paperback original, very near fine in wrappers, very uncommon format.   Jeff Hirsch Books   Holiday List 2015 - 52   2016 $450

McCarthy, Cormac *No Country for Old Men.* New York: Alfred A. Knopf, 2005. First edition, signed by author on titlepage (not as more commonly found - on tipped in sheet, fine, original cloth, original dust jacket.   Manhattan Rare Book Company   2016 - 1814   2016 $950

McCarthy, Cormac *The Road.* New York: Alfred A. Knopf, 2006. First edition, octavo, boards, slight lean, nearly fine in like dust jacket with touch of shelfwear to corner tips.   John W. Knott, Jr./L.W. Currey, Inc.   Fall-Winter 2015 - 17864   2016 $125

McCarthy, Eugene *Other Things and the Aardvark.* Garden City: Doubleday and Co., 1970. Limited to 250 copies, first trade edition, tall 8vo., publisher's boards, inscribed by author for Bill Claire, very good, tight copy. Second Life Books, Inc.   196 B - 165   2016 $75

McCarthy, Jack *New Guinea Journeys.* Adelaide: Rigby, 1970. First edition, octavo, photos, endpaper maps, fine in very good dust jacket little rubbed at head of spine.   Peter Ellis   112 - 278   2016   £30

McCarthy, Justin *The "Daily News" Jubilee: a Political and Social Retrospect of Fifty Years of the Queen's Reign.* London: Sampson Low, 1896. Half title, frontispiece, plates, original green pictorial cloth, lettered in blue and gilt, spine slightly dulled, good plus.   Jarndyce Antiquarian Booksellers   CCXVIII - 1364   2016   £45

McCarthy, Justin *A History of Our Own Times.* London: Chatto & Windus, 1880-1905. First editions, 7 volumes, large 8vo., contemporary half blue morocco, spine gilt ruled in compartments and lettered direct by Bicker and Son, last 3 volumes signed, small piece missing form foot of spine, some shelfwear, armorial bookplate inside front cover of R. D. Jackson, sound.   Blackwell's Rare Books   B186 - 99   2016   £250

McCarthy, Lillah *Myself and My Friends.* London: Butterworth, 1933. First edition, 8vo., illustrations, frontispiece by Edward Dulac, presentation copy, signed by actress, very good.   Second Life Books, Inc.   196 B - 169   2016 $75

McCarthy, Muriel *All Graduates & Gentlemen.* Dublin: O'Brien Press, 1980. First edition, 8vo., illustrations, author's presentation on half title, purple cloth, stamped in gilt, cover very slightly scuffed and faded, otherwise nice copy.   Second Life Books, Inc.   196 B - 170   2016 $50

McClintock, F. R. *Holiday in Spain: Being some Account of Two Tours in the Country in the Autumns of 1880 and 1881.* London: Ed Stanford, 1882. First edition, 8vo., frontispiece, 3 plates, original gred decorative cloth, waterstain on spine, small area excised from front endpaper, good copy.   J. & S. L. Bonham Antiquarian Booksellers   Europe 2016 - 8427   2016   £150

McCloskey, Robert *Lentil.* New York: Junior Literary Guild and Viking, 1940. First edition, large 4to., cloth, fine in very good+ dust jacket slightly frayed at edges.   Aleph-bet Books, Inc.   111 - 272   2016 $1250

McCloskey, Robert *One Morning in Maine.* New York: Viking, 1952. First edition, 4to., pictorial cloth, fine in very good dust jacket with few mends on verso, chips on spine ends, every page illustrated by author.   Aleph-bet Books, Inc.   112 - 303   2016 $850

McCloy, Helen *The Deadly Truth.*   New York: William Morris and Co., 1941. First edition, near fine in fine dust jacket.   Buckingham Books   2015 - 30534   2016 $450

McClung, J. W. *McClung's St. Paul Directory and Statistical Record for 1866.* St. Paul: J. W. McClung, 1866. First edition, 8vo., original cloth, printed sheets on covers. M & S Rare Books, Inc.   99 - 183   2016 $425

McClure, James *The Sunday Hangman.* New York: Harper & Row, 1977. First US edition, TLS by author to European literary critic dated May 28 1978 additionally book inscribed to same, with recipient's neat bookplate, else fine in dust jacket, lightly sunned on spine and with light restoration to spine ends.   Buckingham Books   2015 - 33710   2016 $450

McClure, Michael *Rare Angel.* Los Angeles: Black Sparrow, 1974. One of 200 hardcover copies, numbered and signed by poet, 8vo., nice in slightly chipped acrylic dust jacket.   Second Life Books, Inc.   196 B - 171   2016 $95

McClure, Pamela *Holding the Air.* Winona: Sutton Hoo Press, 1996. Small 4to., decorated paper covered boards, handmade kozo and abaca paper flecked with cattail, two linoleum cuts on endpapers, publisher's statement laid in. Oak Knoll Books   310 - 154   2016 $125

McConaughy, J. E. *Capital for Working Boys.* London: Hodder & Stoughton, 1884. First edition, half title, original blue decorated cloth, very good.   Jarndyce Antiquarian Books   CCXV - 303   2016   £40

McConchie, Rob *Northern Territory Naturalist.* Darwin: Northern Territory Naturalists Club, 1978-1985. Quarto, first 8 parts, photos, text illustrations, soft covers.   Andrew Isles Natural History Books   55 - 38859   2016 $60

McConnell, Francis John *Borden Parker Bowne, His Life and Philosophy.* New York: Abingdon Press, 1929. First edition, 8vo., very good, Alice Stone Blackwell's copy with her ownership signature.   Second Life Books, Inc.   196A - 155   2016 $75

McCord, David *Twelve Verses from XII Night.* Boston: St. Botolph Club, 1938. First edition, 8vo., one of 120 opies, this numbered 129! printed paper over boards, paper label, author's presentation to John Mason Brown and his wife, spine little browned and faded, two small spots on front, otherwise nice.   Second Life Books, Inc.   196 B - 172   2016 $50

McCormick, Elsie *Audacious Angles of China.* Shanghai: Chinese American Pub. Co., 1922. First book edition, printed marbled card stock covers, printed cloth tape spine (added later?), average wear, tightly bound, pulling on beginning & terminal leaves, very good, signature of former owner Addie Viola Smith (1893-1975).   Tavistock Books   Getting Around - 41   2016 $250

McCourt, Frank *Angela's Ashes.* London: Harper Collins, 1996. First British edition, fine in fine dust jacket.   Bella Luna Books   2016 - t8012   2016 $66

McCourt, Frank *Angela's Ashes.* New York: Scribner, 1998. First edition, true first, fine in fine dust jacket.   Bella Luna Books   2016 - 52921u   2016 $350

McCourt, Frank *Teacher Man.* London: Fourth Estate, 2005. First British edition, fine in fine dust jacket, signed and dated 1/30/06 by author.   Bella Luna Books   2016 - k184   2016 $66

McCoy, Horace *They Shoot Horses, Don't They?* New York: Simon and Schuster, 1935. First edition, signed by author, very good in very good dust jacket, boards very lightly soiled, tiny tear at one hinge, jacket complete but rubbed at hinges and spine panel and minutely chipped at extremities, very presentable example.   Royal Books   49 - 69   2016 $2500

McCready, T. L. *Increase Rabbit.* New York: Ariel/Farrar Straus, Cudahy, First edition, first printing, 8vo., yellow pictorial cloth, fine in frontispiece, slight wear at head of spine, illustrations in color and black and white by Tasha Tudor, unusually bright, very scarce.   Aleph-bet Books, Inc.   112 - 486   2016 $700

McCutcheon, George Barr *Graustark. The Story of a Love Behind a Throne.* Chicago: Herbert S. Stone and Co., 1901. First edition, 2nd issue, blue cloth lettered and decorated in white, light rubbing to extremities, fine.   Argonaut Book Shop   Literature 2015 - 1332   2016 $45

McDougall, William *Character and the Conduct of Life.* London: Methuen, 1928. Third edition, Half title, 8 pages ads, original blue cloth, signature of L. R. Adams 1930.   Jarndyce Antiquarian Books   CCXV - 304   2016   £25

McEvey, Allan *John Cotton's Birds of the Port Phillip District of New South Wales 1843-1849.* Sydney: Collins, 1974. Limited to 850 numbered copies, oblong format, color plates, slipcase, fine.   Andrew Isles Natural History Books   55 - 11   2016 $200

McEwan, Ian *The Cement Garden.* London: Jonathan Cape, 1978. First edition, octavo, fine in fine dust jacket.   Peter Ellis   112 - 249   2016   £225

McEwan, Ian *First Love Last Rites.* London: Jonathan Cape, 1975. First edition, endpapers little spotted, very nice in dust jacket with has just little trivial wear at head of spine panel, Anthony Thwaite's ownership signature and inscription from author Nov. 1990.   Bertram Rota Ltd.   February List 2016 - 37   2016   £1000

McFarland, J. Horace *Modern Roses II.* New York: Macmillan, 1940. Second edition, 8vo., color and black and white photos, red cloth, author's signature on back of frontispiece photo, fine, from the library of Alta Rockefeller Prentice.   Second Life Books, Inc.   196 B - 176   2016 $45

McGahern, John *The Dark.* London: Faber, 1965. First British edition, near fine, light bump to top front corner, dust jacket very good, light 1 inch diameter dampstain to rear panel, light chipping and small closed tears to spine, very good, light 1 inch diameter dampstain to rear panel, light chipping and small closed tears to spine.   Bella Luna Books   2016 - t18484   2016 $330

McGillivray, Nora Lee *Moon.* Shoreview: Nora Lee McGillivray, 1992. 2000. Limited to 10 numbered and initialled copies, small 4to., unsupported, exposed spine, wire-edge binding, wove with silver thread, cotton/linen cloth covered conservation board, original text in XPSchooner, hand traced and screen printed in grey on black Arches cover, semi-circular pages with endpages of a painted night sky scene, all images of moon are hand painted, circle in relief on front and back covers, silver painted paper crescent inset on front board, front doublure shows phases of the moon in gray, doubling as contents page, title in silver paint.   Oak Knoll Books   27 - 38   2016 $650

McGivern, William P. *Odds Against Tomorrow.* New York: Dodd, Mead and Co., 1957. First edition, presentation from author, cloth lightly sunned on spine, hinge of old tiny waterstain to fore-edges of first two pages, page 7 has a repaired tear, else very good in dust jacket with light professional restoration to spine ends, corners and extremities.   Buckingham Books   2015 - 31993   2016 $450

McGrew, Charles H. *Reminiscences of Our Mother.* 1888. 8vo., portrait, photo and drawing, author's presentation on blank, mustard colored cloth over boards, stamped in gilt, first few leaves bumped at top, small tears on four, cover slightly worn at edges, otherwise very good, tight copy.   Second Life Books, Inc.   196 B - 180   2016 $75

McGuane, Thomas *Keep the Change.* Boston: Houghton Mifflin, 1989. First edition, publisher's pale beige cloth and olive green paper boards, lettered in gilt and metallic green, about fine with hint of sunning to extremities, dust jacket with touch of wear to spine ends, hint of faint toning to top edge of panels, overall very bright and pleasing copy.   B & B Rare Books, Ltd.   2016 - TMG005   2016 $45

McGuane, Thomas *Panama.* New York: Straus & Giroux, 1978. First edition, signed and inscribed by author for Sherman Kaplan, green cloth and green paper boards, lettered in blind and silver, top edge green, orgiinal white dust jacket lettered in red and black, near fine with some light offsetting to boards, else bright and clean, dust jacket with some faint toning to extremities, few faint spots of light soiling, very tight copy.   B & B Rare Books, Ltd.   2016 - TMG002   2016 $50

McGuane, Thomas *Some Horses.* New York: Lyons Press, 1999. Limited to 250 copies, illustrations by Buckeye Blake, fine slipcase, signed by author and publisher.   Bella Luna Books   2016 - t4052   2016 $66

McGuane, Thomas *Something to be Desired.* New York: Random House, 1984. First edition, signed by author, blue cloth and ivory boards, lettered in blind and silver, original pictorial dust jacket with very short closed tear to rear panel at spine head, few faint scuffs, else bright and clean, beautiful copy, signed by author.   B & B Rare Books, Ltd.   2016 - TM0003   2016 $40

McGuane, Thomas *The Sporting Club: a Novel.* New York: Simon & Schuster, 1968. First edition, red cloth lettered gilt, yellow top stain, original white pictorial dust jacket, lettered in black, about fine, jacket with only some faint toning to spine, hint of light soiling to verso of rear wrapper, else bright and clean, overall a beautiful copy.   B & B Rare Books, Ltd.   2016 - TMG001   2016 $200

McGuane, Thomas *To Skin a Cat.* New York: E. P. Dutton, 1986. First edition, signed and dated by author in year of publication, ivory cloth and black paper boards, lettered in copper, original brown dust jacket lettered in black, white, orange and pale green, fine, unclipped dust jacket with hint of faint sunning to spine, else bright and clean, beautiful copy, inscribed by author.   B & B Rare Books, Ltd.   2016 - TMG004   2016 $75

McGuire, James Patrick *Iwonski in Texas, Painter and Citizen.* San Antonio: San Antonio Museum Assoc., 1976. First edition, color and black and white plates and photos, square 8vo., cloth with gilt titles, inscribed by author, fine in fine dust jacket.   Kaaterskill Books   21 - 53   2016 $200

McHugh, Heather *Dangers: Poems by.* Boston: Houghton Mifflin, 1977. First printing, 8vo., half title, author's presentation to poet William Claire, red cloth stamped in silver, nice, little chipped and soiled dust jacket.   Second Life Books, Inc.   196 B - 182   2016 $125

McKee, George Wilson *The McKees of Virginia and Kentucky.* Pittsburgh: from the Press of J. B. Richards, 1891. First edition, frontispiece, small 8vo., full leather, all edges gilt, gilt title and decoration, good backstrip worn, chipped at ends, front joint split, front board very tender, with first signature detached, inscribed by author with tipped in news photo, few entries corrected in ink.   Kaaterskill Books   21 - 54   2016 $350

McKenney, Thomas Lorraine   1785-1859 *History of the Indian Tribes of North America with Biographical Sketches and Anecdotes of the Principal Chiefs.* Philadelphia: J. T. Bowen, 1848. 1849-1850. First octavo edition, Royal 8vo., 3 volumes, contemporary ornate gilt stamped dark morocco, new spines, text and tissues with light foxing and occasional penciling, but plates in excellent condition, binding with only slight wear, spines most appealingly done to match by Green Dragon Bindery.   M & S Rare Books, Inc.   99 - 177   2016 $35,000

McKenney, Thomas Lorraine   1785-1859 *Memoirs, Official and Personal...* New York: Paine and Burgess, 1846. Second edition, 2 volumes bound as one, lithographed frontispiece, ne facsimile, 11 lithographed plates by F. O. C. Darley, 1 hand colored lithograph, new full dark green morocco, raised bands, gilt lettered maroon leather labels, occasional minor spotting or darkening, but fine.   Argonaut Book Shop   Native American 2015 - 7438   2016 $450

McKenzie, Charles *The Religious Sentiment of Charles Dickens Collected from His Writings by Charles H. McKenzie.* London: Walter Scott, 1884. First edition, 16 page catalog (Sept. 1884), original maroon cloth, bevelled boards, endpapers little browned, good plus, scarce.   Jarndyce Antiquarian Booksellers   CCXVIII - 1367   2016   £60

McKeon, Hugh *An Inquiry into the Rights of the Poor, of the Parish of Lavenham, in Suffolk with Historical Notes and Observations.* London: Baldwin and Cradock and sold by Loder Woodbridge &c., 1829. First edition, 8vo., later 19th century half morocco over marbled boards, spine lettered gilt with raised bands, top edge gilt, others uncut by W. J. Scopes of Ipswich, with his ticket, very good.   John Drury Rare Books   2015 - 19691   2016 $323

McKillip, Patricia *The Riddle Master Trilogy. The Riddle Master of Hed. Heir of Sea and Fire. Harpist in the Wind.* New York: Atheneum, 1976-1979. First editions, 3 volumes, octavo, fine in fine dust jackets with close tear to upper front panel of Heir and touch of shelfwear to spine ends of Harpist, which is the correct first state dust jacket.   John W. Knott, Jr./L.W. Currey, Inc.   Fall-Winter 2015 - 17527   2016 $450

McKinney, John A. *The Lincoln Secret.* Dixon: Martin Pearl Pub., 2008. First edition, pictorial trade wrappers, signed by author, scarac4e thus.   Gene W. Baade, Books on the West   2015 - SHEL532   2016 $40

McKuen, Rod *The Seas Around Me... The Hills Above.* London: Elm Tree Boks, 1976. Copy 24 from an edition of 1000 specially bound and numbered copies, fine in very good acetate jacket with small chip to top of spine and another to top front corner in near fine slipcase, signed by author on limitation page and then additionally signed and inscribed with drawing by author, lovely copy.   Jeff Hirsch Books   Holiday 2015 - 53   2016 $150

McLaurin, Charles *To Overcome Fear.* Cambridge: Massachusetts Boston Friends of SNCC, circa, 1965. First edition, one leaf folded to make four pages, illustrations, vertical crease, else near fine.   Between the Covers Rare Books   202 - 19   2016 $275

McLaverty, Michael *In This Day Thy Day.* London: Jonathan Cape, 1945. First edition, 200 pages, very good in very good, slightly chipped and nicked dust jacket.   Peter Ellis   112 - 250   2016   £150

McLean, Alick M. *Prato Architecture Piety and Political Identity in a Tuscan City-State.* New Haven: Yale University Press, 2008. First edition, 4to., illustrations, brown boards, gilt lettered to spine, dust jacket, mint, still in publisher's shrink wrap, as new.   Unsworths Antiquarian Booksellers Ltd.   E05 - 79   2016   £20

McLean, Donald B. *The Plumber's Kitchen.* Arizona: Normount Technical Publications, 1975. First edition, 4to., original paper wrappers, black and white photos, little fading to rear wrapper, insect damage to edges of f.f.e.p., very good.   Sotheran's   Piccadilly Notes - Summer 2015 - 200   2016   £80

McLean, Ruari *Benjamin Fawcett Engraver and Colour Printer, with List of His Books and Plates.* Hampshire: Scolar Press, 1988. First edition, limited to 750 numbered copies, of which this is one of 25 special copies with 3 actual plates, loosely inserted in pocket at back, special binding with limitation page bound in and with McLean's signature, many black and white illustrations, plus 9 color plates, spine of jacket faded.   Oak Knoll Books   310 - 243   2016 $315

McMahon, Valerie *Bumps the Golfball Kid and Little Caddie.* East Aurora: Roycrofters, 1929. First edition, 4to., red cloth, fine in pictorial dust jacket worn on spine, 12 full page and 5 half page color illustrations plus 9 full page black and whites as well as smaller black & whites in text, full color endpapers mounted on linen, very scarce.   Alephbet Books, Inc.   112 - 436   2016 $1250

McMahon, Valerie *Travel Stories of Fan. Fan-ie, Ginger and Little Stitches. The Baseball Kids...* Alexandria: Children's Library, 1933. First edition, Volumes one, two and three, each die-cut in shape of humanized baseball child, one back cover slightly out of register size, nearly as new, rare as a group, each book with 6 fine full page color illustrations including covers plus black and whites.   Alephbet Books, Inc.   111 - 32   2016 $1200

McMaster, Juliet *Dickens the Designer.* London: Macmillan, 1987. First edition, half title, illustrations, original purple cloth, very good in dust jacket.   Jarndyce Antiquarian Booksellers   CCXVIII - 1370   2016   £20

McMillan, Margaret *The Camp School.* London: George Allen & Unwin, 1919. Half title, frontispiece, 8 pages ads, original olive green cloth, very good.   Jarndyce Antiquarian Books   CCXV - 838   2016   £25

McMillan, Terry *Breaking Ice: an Anthology of Contemporary African American Fiction.* New York: Viking, 1990. First printing, 8vo., presentation form editor, edges slightly soiled, otherwise fine, little scuffed dust jacket.   Second Life Books, Inc.   196 B - 185   2016 $125

McMillan, Terry *A Day Late and a Dollar short.* New York: Viking, 2001. first printing, 8vo., author's signature on title nice, little wrinkled and soiled dust jacket.   Second Life Books, Inc.   196 B - 186   2016 $45

McMurtrie, Douglas C. *A Project for Printing in Bermuda 1772.* Chicago: privately printed, 1928. One of 250 copies, thin octavo, decorative border around titlepage, True-Cut Caslon type, light green wrapper printed in black on front over, very fine.   Argonaut Book Shop   Private Press 2015 - 6828   2016 $50

McMurtry, Larry 1936- *Anything for Billy.* New York: Simon & Schuster, 1988. First edition, blue cloth backed light blue boards, spine lettered gilt, very fine with pictorial dust jacket.   Argonaut Book Shop   Literature 2015 - 7717   2016 $75

McMurtry, Larry 1936- *Boone's Lick.* New York: Simon & Schuster, 2000. First edition, two-toned boards, very fine with pictorial dust jacket.   Argonaut Book Shop   Literature 2015 - 7732   2016 $90

McMurtry, Larry 1936- *Buffalo Girls.* New York: Simon & Schuster, 1990. First edition, red cloth backed grey boards, gilt lettered spine, very fine with pictorial dust jacket.   Argonaut Book Shop   Literature 2015 - 7727   2016 $90

McMurtry, Larry 1936- *By Sorrow's River.* New York: Simon & Schuster, 2003. First edition, green cloth and beige boards, very fine, pictorial dust jacket.   Argonaut Book Shop   Literature 2015 - 7713   2016 $50

McMurtry, Larry 1936- *Comanche Moon.* New York: Simon & Schuster, 1997. First edition, dark blue and tan boards, very fine with pictorial dust jacket.   Argonaut Book Shop   Literature 2015 - 7728   2016 $75

McMurtry, Larry 1936- *Dead man's Walk.* New York: Simon & Schuster, 1995. First edition, blue cloth backed boards, very fine with pictorial dust jacket.   Argonaut Book Shop   Literature 2015 - 7722   2016 $50

McMurtry, Larry 1936- *Desert Rose.* New York: Simon & Schuster, 1983. First edition, violet cloth backed grey boards, very fine with pictorial dust jacket.   Argonaut Book Shop   Literature 2015 - 7723   2016 $75

McMurtry, Larry 1936- *Duane's Depressed.* New York: Simon & Schuster, 1999. First edition, red and blue boards, very fine with dust jacket.   Argonaut Book Shop   Literature 2015 - 7730   2016 $75

McMurtry, Larry 1936- *The Evening Star.* New York: Simon & Schuster, 1992. First edition, red cloth backed boards, slight dent to head of spine, else very fine with dust jacket.   Argonaut Book Shop   Literature 2015 - 7726   2016 $50

McMurtry, Larry 1936- *Folly and Glory.* New York: Simon & Schuster, 2004. First edition, tan cloth backed beige boards, spine lettered in metallic silver, very fine with pictorial dust jacket.   Argonaut Book Shop   Literature 2015 - 7714   2016 $60

McMurtry, Larry 1936- *Lonesome Dove.* New York: Simon & Schuster, 1985. First edition, first issue with error 'he had none nothing' on page 621, and with the $18.95 price on jacket flap unclipped, black cloth backed boards, small library bookplate on front free end, minor wear to upper edge of rear endpaper, else fine with perfect pictorial dust jacket.   Argonaut Book Shop   Literature 2015 - 7724   2016 $425

McMurtry, Larry 1936- *Loop Group.* New York: Simon & Schuster, 2004. First edition, grey cloth backed light gray boards, very fine with pictorial dust jacket, publisher's review copy with review slip and announcement laid in.   Argonaut Book Shop   Literature 2015 - 7731   2016 $60

McMurtry, Larry 1936- *Pretty Boy Floyd.* New York: Simon & Schuster, 1994. First edition, red cloth backed black boards, slight buping to foot of spine, very fine with pictorial dust jacket.   Argonaut Book Shop   Literature 2015 - 7716   2016 $50

McMurtry, Larry 1936- *Roads. Driving America's Great Highways.* New York: Simon & Schuster, 2000. First edition, two-tone dark brown and beige boards, spine lettered in gold, very fine with pictorial dust jacket.   Argonaut Book Shop   Literature 2015 - 7715   2016 $50

McMurtry, Larry 1936- *Sin Killer.* New York: Simon & Schuster, 2002. First edition, brown and beige boards, very fine with pictorial dust jacket.   Argonaut Book Shop   Literature 2015 - 7711   2016 $50

McMurtry, Larry 1936- *Somebody's Darling.* New York: Simon & Schuster, 1978. First edition, blue cloth, gilt lettering to spine, fine in dust jacket.   Argonaut Book Shop   Literature 2015 - 4902   2016 $90

McMurtry, Larry 1936- *Streets of Laredo.* New York: Simon & Schuster, 1993. First edition, dark blue cloth backed beige boards, gilt lettered spine, very fine with pictorial dust jacket.   Argonaut Book Shop   Literature 2015 - 7725   2016 $225

McMurtry, Larry 1936- *Terms of Endearment.* New York: Simon & Schuster, 1975. First edition, very good, moderate browning to pages, brief noted ined on pastedown under front flap, remainder strip on bottom edge, dust jacket near fine with fading to edges of front panel, light general wear,.   Bella Luna Books   2016 - t7958b   2016 $165

McMurtry, Larry 1936- *Texasville.* New York: Simon & Schuster, 1987. First edition, dark blue cloth backed boards, spine lettered in white, very fine with pictorial dust jacket (price intact).   Argonaut Book Shop   Literature 2015 - 7729   2016 $75

McMurtry, Larry 1936- *Walter Benjamin at the Dairy Queen.* New York: Simon & Schuster, 1999. First edition, photos, photographic endpapers, two-tone dark blue and tan boards, spine lettered gold, remainder mark to bottom edge of text block, else very fine with pictorial dust jacket.   Argonaut Book Shop   Literature 2015 - 7733   2016 $60

McMurtry, Larry 1936- *The Wandering Hill.* New York: Simon & Schuster, 2003. First edition, two-tone beige and tan boards, spine lettered in metallic blue, very fine with pictorial dust jacket.   Argonaut Book Shop   Literature 2015 - 7712   2016 $60

McNeer, May *The Golden Flash.* New York: Viking, 1947. First edition, signed by author and artist, presented to owner by Harry Ward (Lynd Ward's father), cloth, slight soil, near fine in dust jacket with edge chipping and archival mends on verso, color lithos by Lynd Ward.   Aleph-bet Books, Inc.   112 - 510   2016 $200

McNeer, May *The Wolf of Lamb's Lane.* Boston: Houghton Mifflin, 1967. First edition, stated first printing, 8vo., cloth, near fine in dust jacket (some soil), full page and smaller color illustrations by Lynd Ward, this copy inscribed by author and artist.   Aleph-bet Books, Inc.   111 - 473   2016 $200

McPhee, John *Annals of the Former World.* New York: FSG, 1998. First edition, signed by author, with signature of 1987 Nobel Prize winning chemist, Donald J. Cram, bit of shelfwear to lower edges of cloth, slight spine lean, very near fine in fine dust jacket.   Ken Lopez Bookseller   166 - 83   2016 $1000

McPhee, John *The Fair of San Gennaro.* Portland: Press-22, 1981. First signed limited edition, of a total edition of 250 copies, this copy no. 26 of 200 numbered copies in cloth and marbled paper boards, issued without slipcase, signed by author, fine, scarce.   Ken Lopez Bookseller   166 - 81   2016 $1750

McPhee, John *Rising from the Plains.* New York: FSG, 1986. First edition, signed by author on half titlepage, mild foxing, near fine in very near fine dust jacket with trace shelfwear.   Ken Lopez Bookseller   166 - 82   2016 $150

McPherson, Sandra *Sensing.* San Francisco: Meadow Press, 1980. No. 67 of 100 copies, signed by author and Leigh McLellan, woodcut and printing by McLellan, patterned paper over boards with cloth spine, nice in little yellowed and chipped plain paper dust jacket.   Second Life Books, Inc.   196 B - 190   2016 $65

McSpadden, J. Walker *Stories from Dickens.* London: George G. Harrap, 1914. Color frontispiece, black and white plates, original purple pictorial cloth, lettered black, ownership inscription Xmas 1919, very good, bright, slightly worn dust jacket.   Jarndyce Antiquarian Booksellers   CCXVIII - 734   2016   £35

McSpadden, J. Walker *Stories from Dickens.* London: George G. Harrap & Co., 1927. Reprint, half title, frontispiece, 7 black and white plates, original brown grained cloth, blocked and lettered gilt, tail of following hinge slightly tender, Church prize label on leading pastedown July 1929, very good.   Jarndyce Antiquarian Booksellers   CCXVIII - 735   2016   £25

McTaggart, M. F. *From Colonel to Subaltern; Some Keys for Horse Owners.* London & New York: Country Life & Charles Scribner's, 1928. First edition, royal 4to., original grey cloth backed red cloth covered boards, lettered in black to upper board and spine, numerous illustrations, previous owner's bookplate, very good.   Sotheran's Hunting, Shooting & Fishing - 188   2016   £100

McWaters, George S. *Knots Untied; or Ways and by-Ways in the Hidden Life of American Detectives.* Hartford: J. B. Burr and Hyde, 1871. First edition, cloth, frontispiece, illustrations, former owner's name, else good.   Buckingham Books   2015 - 7135   2016 $450

Mead, Richard *A Mechanical Account of Poisons in Several Essays.* London: printed by J. M. for Ralph Smith, 1708. Second edition, half title, cancel titlepage, folding plate, 8vo., very good, clean copy, plate detached from binding, full contemporary mottled calf, raised bands, morocco label, expert repairs to joints, very slight wear to corners.   Jarndyce Antiquarian Booksellers   CCXVI - 408   2016   £450

Meade, Elizabeth Thomasina *Miss Nonentity.* London: W. & R. Chambers, 1900. Half title, frontispiece, plates, original brown cloth pictorially blocked and lettered in pink, white, black and gilt, slight rubbing, but nice, city of Manchester prize label 1905.   Jarndyce Antiquarian Booksellers   CCXVII - 184   2016   £35

Meakin, Budgett *The Land of the Moors.* London: Swan, Sonnenschein & Co. and New York: Macmillan, 1931. First edition, American issue, 8vo., original pictorial cloth, very attractively decorated with gilt image of the Gate of the Citadel in Tangier, lettering and image of nature scene in gilt to spine, numerous illustrations, mostly from photos, one folding map, rear inner hinge strengthened, Nashua, NH Public Library bookplate and discard stamp, Boston bookseller's label, light marginal browning, still very good.   Sotheran's Travel and Exploration - 344   2016   £298

Meath, Reginald Brabazon, Earl of *Some National and Board School Reforms.* London: Longmans, 1887. Half title, presentation from the author, 24 page catalog (Jan. 1887), original pictorial printed boards, spine chipped at tail, hinges cracking, worn but sound, contemporary signature.   Jarndyce Antiquarian Books   CCXV - 546   2016   £35

Mech, L. David *Wolves: Behaviour, Ecology and Conservation.* Chicago: University of Chicago Press, 2003. Quarto, photos, text illustrations, fine, in dust jacket.   Andrew Isles Natural History Books   55 - 19288   2016 $80

Mechoulam, Raphael *Marijuana: Chemistry, Pharmacology, Metabolism and Clinical Effects.* New York: Academic Press, 1971. First edition, mottling to cloth, very good in like dust jacket.   Ken Lopez Bookseller   166 - 76   2016 $125

Medicina Flagellata; or the Doctor Scarified. London: printed for J. Bateman and J. Nicks, 1721. First edition, with additional letterpress title with engraved vignette, 8vo., contemporary tree calf, flat spine gilt in compartments, red lettering piece, minor wear, top of upper joint snagged, foot of spine chipped, contemporary signature of W. Beeson, MD, engraved bookplate of Sir Thomas Hesketh and Easton Neston Library shelf label, very good.   Blackwell's Rare Books   B186 - 126   2016   £550

Mee, Margaret Ursula *Flowers of the Brazilian Forests Collected and Painted by Margaret Mee.* London: L. van Leer & Co. for the Tryon Gallery in association with George Rainbird, 1968. First and only edition, limited to 500 copies, this no. 27 of 100 deluxe copies signed by Mee and with original gouache by Mee, folio, original full natural vellum by Zaehnsdorf gilt facsimile of author's signature blocked on upper board, vignette of a teja-assu lizard after Mee blocked in gilt on lower board, spine lettered in gilt, endpapers with printed vignettes of teja assu after Mee, top edges gilt, original green cloth slipcase with gilt lettering piece on upper panel, original shipping carton address to Richard Mitchell, Aldham, Essex with limitation numbers, printed in green and black, loose original prospectus, fine.   Sotheran's Piccadilly Notes - Summer 2015 - 9   2016   £7000

Meggendorfer, Lothar *Curious Creatures.* London: H. Grevel, n.d. circa, 1892. First English edition, folio, cloth backed pictorial boards, some soil, cover corners bit worn, metal pieces rusty, really very good+ and fully operational, 8 fine hand colored tab operated hinged plates.   Aleph-bet Books, Inc.   111 - 279   2016 $3250

Meggendorfer, Lothar *Gute Bekannte.* Stuttgart: W. Nitzschke, n.d., 1880. Folio, cloth backed pictorial boards, except for a very few tiny margin mends and margin finger soil this is bright near fine, 25 fantastic full page color lithographed plates that appear to be heightened with hand coloring, rare.   Aleph-bet Books, Inc.   112 - 310   2016 $2750

Meggendorfer, Lothar *Prinzessin Rosenhold.* Eldington & Munchen: Schreiber, circa, 1900. Oblong folio, cloth backed pictorial boards, small chip on top edge of cover spine has some wear, near fine in custom cloth box, 6 vibrant color tab operated moveable plates by Meggendorfer, lovely black and whites on all text pages, each moveable has several parts, very uncommon.   Aleph-bet Books, Inc.   112 - 309   2016 $3250

Meggendorfer, Lothar *Zum Zeitvertreib.* Munchen: Braun & Schneider, n.d. circa, 1890. Cloth backed pictorial boards, new spine nearly identical to original, some finger soil from usage, otherwise in very good+ condition and bright copy, fully operational.   Aleph-bet Books, Inc.   112 - 311   2016 $3000

Meiggs, Russell *The Athenian Empire.* Oxford: Clarendon Press, 1979. First paperback edition, 8vo., figures and maps, edges faded and worn, creased, bit grubby, still good, correspondence from author to J. G. Hind loosely inserted.   Unsworths Antiquarian Booksellers Ltd.   E04 - 75   2016   £20

Meiklejohn, J. M. D. *The Golden Primer Parts I and II.* London: Meiklejohn and Holden, n.d. circa, 1910. 8vo, white cloth, pictorial paste-on, light cover soil, very good+, 2 volumes in 1, pictorial endpapers, color pictorial titlepage plus beautiful full page color illustrations on every other page by Walter Crane, engraved and printed by Edmund Evans, nice, clean copy.   Aleph-bet Books, Inc.   112 - 122   2016 $275

Meinertzhagen, R. *Birds of Arabia.* Edinburgh: Oliver and Boyd, 1954. Quarto, 19 color plates, other illustrations, folded map in back cover pocket, fine in near fine dust jacket, desirable in this condition.   Andrew Isles Natural History Books   55 - 30578   2016 $850

Melanchthon, Philipp   1497-1560 *Epigrammata Selectiota Formulis Precum, Historiis Paraphrasi Dictorum Divinorum...* Frankfurt: Johanne & Sigismund Feyerabend, 1583. First edition edited by Peter Jensen, 4to., printer's device on titlepage and larger version on recto of penultimate leaf, woodcut dedicatory arms, map, 95 oval woodcuts within fine mannerist borders, many signed I.A. (Jost Amman), late 18th century calf, sides with gilt ruled and blind roll tooled border, gilt edges, spine with later gilt lettering, marbled endpapers, neat repairs to head and foot of spine, joints rubbed, blank corner of titlepage cut away and neatly replaced, few spots and stains but generally fresh, inscription dated 1818 of Rev. Henry White of Lichfield, dated 1818, armorial bookplate of Henry Latham.   Maggs Bros. Ltd.   1474 - 52   2016   £2800

Melanga, Gerard *Poetry on film.* New York: Telegraph Books, 1972. First edition, 8vo. stiff wrappers, very good, inscribed by author.   Second Life Books, Inc.   196 B - 19194   2016 $50

Melfi, Leonard *Encounters: Six One-Act Plays.* New York: Random House, 1967. First printing, 8vo., author's 10 line presentation to playwright Langford Wilson, with recipient's name stamp, nice, scarce.   Second Life Books, Inc.   196 B - 196   2016 $100

Meline, Frank *Las Vegas Cocktail Girl.* Hollywood: France Book, 1963. First American edition, pages little toned, faint stain on rear wrapper and bit rubbed, but very good or better, very scarce.   Between the Covers Rare Books   204 - 29   2016 $175

Mell, Max *Paradeisspiel in der Steiermark.* Grundlsee: Stamperia del Santuccio, 1936. No. VI of 25 numbered copies (of 36 total), 23- x 175mm, publisher's(?) later(?) oxblood paper boards, spine with letterpress label, text in black and red, virtually pristine.   Phillip J. Pirages   67 - 186   2016 $1500

Mellers, H. F. *Hints for the Improvement of the Manners and Appearance of Both Sexes.* London: Dean and Munday, 1838. Half title, frontispiece with slight waterstain, few gatherings slightly proud, original light purple embossed glazed cloth, spine faded, all edges gilt, gift inscription on verso, very good.   Jarndyce Antiquarian Books   CCXV - 314   2016   £120

Melling, Antoine Ignace *Voyage Pittoresque de Constatinople des Rives du Bosophore.* Bern: Ertug & Kocabiyuk, 2002. No. 46 of 50 specially bound copies, (of a total edition of 350), 670 x 508mm., publisher's scarlet morocco by Buchbinderei Burkhardt AG, covers with gilt rolled border, cornerpieces tooled in gilt, upper cover with gilt calligraphic Arabic centerpiece, lower cover with gilt central heraldic device, marbled endleaves, all edges gilt, frontispiece, 48 double page plates and 3 double page maps, virtually as new.   Phillip J. Pirages   67 - 143   2016 $12,500

Melmoth, William *The Letters of Sir Thomas Fitzosborne on Several Subjects.* London: printed for J. Dodsley in Pall-Mall, 1784. Ninth edition, 8vo. full contemporary tree calf, attractive gilt decorated spine, red morocco label, slight wear to head and tail of spine and small section of leather on upper board with insect damage.   Jarndyce Antiquarian Booksellers   CCXVI - 409   2016   £40

Meltzer, David *Hero/Lil.* Los Angeles: Black Sparrow, 1973. First edition, large 8vo., one of 175 hardcover copies numbered and sigend by poet, paper over boards with cloth spine, fine in slightly scuffed acrylic dust jacket.   Second Life Books, Inc.   196 B - 197   2016 $85

Meltzer, David *Ragas.* San Francisco: Discovery, 1959. First edition, 8vo., former owner's name on inside front cover, paper wrappers, cover slightly soiled, otherwise very good.   Second Life Books, Inc.   197 - 232   2016 $45

Melville, Herman   1819-1891 *Cock-a-Doodle-Doo! or The Crowing of the Noble Cock.* N.P.: Otto Rohse Press, 1986. Limited to 150 numbered copies, signed by Otto Rohse, wood engravings by Rohse, 4to., paper covered boards, illustrated front cover, top edge cut, other edges uncut, slipcase, binding by Christian Zweig.   Oak Knoll Books   310 - 128   2016 $300

Melville, Herman   1819-1891 *Melville's Agatha Letter to Hawthorne.* Portland: Southworth Press, 1929. First separate printing, green paper wrapper, spine little discolored, very good, signed by Melville's granddaughter Elenaor M(elville) Metcalf, rare.   Second Life Books, Inc.   196 B - 199   2016 $750

Melville, Herman   1819-1891 *Moby-Dick or the Whale.* Chicago: Lakeside Press, 1930. One of 1000 copies, 3 volumes, original publisher's black cloth decorated and titled in silver, one quarter of the leaves unopened, housed in fine later dark blue folding cloth box, more than 250 large and small woodcut illustrations by Rockwell Kent, backstrips slightly and evenly sunned, tiny signs of wear at top of spines of first two volumes, negligible to light illustration offset, otherwise very fine, cloth internally clean and with no signs of internal use.   Phillip J. Pirages   67 - 230   2016 $5000

Melville, Herman   1819-1891 *Omoo.* New York: Heritage Press, 1967. Engravings by Reynolds Stone, pictorial cloth, lettered silver, slight wear to extremities, more so to foot of spine, fine in slipcase (slightly faded), Sandglass pamphlet laid in.   Argonaut Book Shop   Heritage Press 2015 - 7045   2016 $45

Memoire pour la Demoiselle Le Guay d'Oliva...   Paris: chez P. G. Simon & N. H. Nyon, 1786. 4to., half title, final blank, signature F4 preserved, outer margins of half title and title folded in, titlepage trimmed at foot with loss of date from imprint?, text trimmed a bit close at top and outer margins, recent grey paper boards, red sprinkled edges.   Jarndyce Antiquarian Booksellers   CCXVI - 571   2016   £45

Memoirs of the Public and Private Life, Adventures and Wonderful Exploits of Madame Vestris, the Female Giovanni.... London: printed and published by William Chubb, circa, 1830. First edition, octavo, modern gray boards, printed paper label, fine.   The Brick Row Book Shop   Miscellany 69 - 33   2016 $375

Memorials of Early Genius and Achievements in the Pursuit of Knowledge. London: Thomas Nelson, 1851. frontispiece and additional engraved title, contemporary full tan calf, maroon morocco label, little rubbed, leading hinge with slight cracking, prize label on leading pastedown.   Jarndyce Antiquarian Books   CCXV - 48   2016   £30

Mencken, Alice Davis *On the Side of mercy: Problems in Social Readjustment.* New York: Covici Friede, 1933. First edition, 8vo., fine in little worn dust jacket, inscribed by author.   Second Life Books, Inc.   196 B - 204   2016 $65

Mencken, H. L. *The Diary of H. L. Mencken.* New York: Alfred A. Knopf, 1989. First edition, 8 pages of black and white photos, tan cloth stamped in gilt, very minor rubbing, very fine in pictorial dust jacket.   Argonaut Book Shop   Literature 2015 - 5030   2016 $50

Mencken, H. L. *A Mencken Chrestomathy.* New York: Alfred A. Knopf, 1949. First edition, blue cloth with gilt lettering to spine, spine very slightly faded, fine in worn pictorial dust jacket. Argonaut Book Shop   Literature 2015 - 5043   2016 $75

Mencken, H. L. *Newspaper Days 1899-1906.* New York: Alfred Knopf, 1941. First edition, tan buckram, minor darkening to edges, slight remainder from a removed sticker on front free endpaper, fine copy in worn dust jacket. Argonaut Book Shop   Literature 2015 - 5044   2016 $125

Menken, Adah Isaacs *Infelicia.* London: Paris: New York: Privately printed, 1868. First edition, first issue, half title, frontispiece, illustrations, original green cloth, bevelled boards by W. Bone and Co., all edges gilt, nice, inscribed by author.   Jarndyce Antiquarian Booksellers   CCXVIII - 862   2016   £125

Menken, Adah Isaacs *Infelicia.* London: Paris: New York: privately printed, 1868. Half title, frontispiece, portrait, illustrations, original green cloth, bevelled boards by W. Bone, bit rubbed, all edges gilt.   Jarndyce Antiquarian Booksellers   CCXVIII - 863   2016   £100

Mennie, Donald *The Grandeur of the Gorges.* Shanghai: A. S. Watson & Co. (The Shanghai Pharmacy Ltd.), Kelly & Walsh Limited, 1926. First edition, no. 889 of 1000 copies, 4to, original silk, image of Yangtze Gorge in colours to upper cover, 50 mounted plates from photos, including 12 colored, nice, bright copy, inscribed by Margaret Lo for Mrs. W. J. Souchow?   Sotheran's   Travel and Exploration - 155   2016   £1950

Menninger, Karl *The Crime of Punishment.* New York: Viking, 1973. Eleventh printing, 8vo., author's presentation, black cloth, nice, little scuffed dust jacket.   Second Life Books, Inc. 196 B - 205   2016 $45

Menno, Simons *Ein Fundament und Klare Anweisung. (A Judgment and Clear Instruction to the Blessed teachings of our Lord Jesus Christ).* Lancaster: Johann Baer, 1835. 8vo, contemporary calf over boards, original clasps.   M & S Rare Books, Inc.   99 - 231   2016 $350

Menzies, W. J. M. *Salmon Fishing.* London: Adam and Charles Black, 1950. Reprint, 8vo., original cloth and wrapper, frontispiece, 10 plates, text illustrations, closed tear to head of spine of wrapper, internally very fresh, very good. Sotheran's   Hunting, Shooting & Fishing - 136   2016   £30

Mercurius Publicus. Comprising the Sum of all Affairs Now in Agitation in England, Scotland and Ireland. London: printed for Peter Lillicap, 1662. Number 18, Thursday May to Thursday May 8 1662, disbound, trimmed close. Jarndyce Antiquarian Booksellers   CCXVII - 200   2016   £75

Mercurius Publicus. Comprising the Sum of all Affairs Now in Agitation in England, Scotland and Ireland. London: printed by Richard Hodgkinson, 1662. Number 39 from Thursday Sept 25 to Thursday Oct. 2 1662, 4to., untrimmed, small repair to page 650, not affecting text, especially clean, disbound.   Jarndyce Antiquarian Booksellers   CCXVII - 201   2016   £120

Mercurius Publicus. Comprising the Sum of all Affairs Now in Agitation in England, Scotland and Ireland. London: printed for James Cottrel, 1663. Number 14 from Thursday April 2 to Thursday April 9, 1663, Untrimmed, tear to final leaf not affecting text, leaves slightly loose, disbound. Jarndyce Antiquarian Booksellers   CCXVII - 202   2016   £100

Meredith, George   1828-1909 *Diana of the Crossways.* New York: Scribner's, 1910. one hinge slightly tender, otherwise very good, 8vo., frontispiece, presentation by author's daughter, Marie Sturgis.   Second Life Books, Inc. 196 B - 206   2016 $75

Meredith, George   1828-1909 *Farina: a Legend of Cologne.* London: Smith, Elder and Co., 1857. First edition, rare, inscribed by author for friend, F. Maxse, original apple green cloth, professionally recased, binding rubbed and easily soiled, interior pages clean and bright, July 1857 publisher's catalog, bookplate of noted collector, H. Bradley Martin, green cloth clamshell box with paper title and author label to spine, exceptional association copy in extremely scarce original cloth, very good.   The Kelmscott Bookshop 12 - 68   2016 $4900

Meredith, George   1828-1909 *One of Our Conquerors.* London: Chapman and Hall, 1891. 3 volumes, original royal blue coarse morocco grained cloth, front board blocked in black back board with publisher's monogram in blind, spine gilt lettered and ruled, fine, pale yellow endpapers, signature of Fritz Kamp.   Jarndyce Antiquarian Booksellers   CCXVII - 175   2016   £220

Meredith, George   1828-1909 *A Reading of Earth.* Macmillan and Co., 1888. First edition, apparently a presentation copy with inserted sheet printed "From the author" and with bookplate of recipient G. W. Foote, original dark blue cloth with light bumping to corners, interior page very good with light aging to margins and occasional pencil mark next to passage, inserted sheet has a browned crease along top edge, very good.   The Kelmscott Bookshop   12 - 69   2016 $175

Meredith, Louisa A. *Bush Friends in Tasmania, Native Flowers, Fruits and Insects Drawn from Nature...* London: Macmillan, 1891. One of 700 numbered copies signed by author, folio, 15 chromolithographs, publisher's decorated cloth, some wear, contents loose and shaken, sound internally, lengthy contemporary inscription.   Andrew Isles Natural History Books   55 - 7346   2016 $300

Meredith, William *The Cheer.* New York: Alfred A. Knopf, 1980. First edition, limited edition, this #5 of 100 signed by poet, from poet's own library, several pages have post-its, possibly to mark poems for readings, fine in fine dust jacket. Charles Agvent   William Meredith - 72   2016 $125

Meredith, William *The Cheer.* New York: Alfred A. Knopf, 1980. First edition, Limited edition, #11 of 100 signed by poet, from poet's own library, laid in on 13 1/2 x 8 1/2 inch sheet of paper folded in fours is manuscript of last poem from the book, written and signed by Meredith and dated Jan. 1976, also with color snapshot of his home briefly annotated by him on rear, fine in fine dust jacket.   Charles Agvent   William Meredith - 71   2016 $250

Meredith, William *The Cheer.* New York: Alfred A. Knopf, 1980. First edition, uncorrected proof in printed wrappers with 7 x 5 inch card with manuscript poem from the book, 'Country Stars" by William Meredith dated Jan. 1975. Charles Agvent   William Meredith - 70 2016 $200

Meredith, William *Earth Walk: new and selected poems.* New York: Alfred A. Knopf, 1970. First edition, signed on titlepage, from poet's own library, several pages have yellow post-its, likely to mark poems for readings, fine in near fine dust jacket.   Charles Agvent   William Meredith - 73   2016 $80

Meredith, William *Hazard the Painter.* N.P.: Ironwood Press, 1972. First edition, 8vo. scarce, inscribed by author for William Claire.   Second Life Books, Inc.   196 B - 209   2016 $150

Meredith, William *Hazard, the Painter.* New York: Alfred A. Knopf, 1975. First edition, author's own copy of the uncorrected proof, tall wrappers, signed on titlepage, near fine.   Charles Agvent   William Meredith - 74   2016 $150

Meredith, William *Ships and Other Figures.* Princeton: Princeton University Press, 1948. First edition, signed on titlepage, this copy from poet's own library, he has corrected text in three places, initialling two of them, several pages have yellow post-its, fine in fine dust jacket.   Charles Agvent   William Meredith - 75   2016 $200

Merian, Matthaeus *Topographia Germainiae.* Kassel and Basel: Brenreiter Verlag, 1959-1965. 16 volumes, 305 x 203mm., publisher's vellum like paper in shades of ivory, upper covers blindstamped with Habsburg double headed eagle crest, flat spines with brown morocco labels, hundreds of folding plates, inscribed "John A. A. des V. G./Haywood", occasional small marks to boards or smudges to edges, essentially unused and virtually mint.   Phillip J. Pirages   67 - 144   2016 $1250

Merimee, Prosper *Carmen and Letters from Spain.* Paris and New York: Harrison of Paris, 1931. One of 50 numbered copies of Japan vellum, designed and signed by Monroe Wheeler, signed by Barbara Harrison and Glenway Wescott, illustrations by Maurice Barraud, illustrated boards, morocco spine, spine cords scuffed, trifle darkened, else very good, bookplate in publisher's box (soiled).   Joseph J. Felcone, Inc.   Books from Five Centuries: a Miscellany - 100   2016 $600

Merimee, Prosper *Carmen.* New York: Limited Editions Club, 1941. Limited to 1500 copies, 4to., buckram spine and stunning marbelized silk cloth, near fine in slipcase, some soil and short splitting, 37 stunning color lithographs drawn on plates by Jean Charlot, laid in is Charlot's peronsal Christmas card with by Charlot, signed by Jean Chalot and wife.   Aleph-bet Books, Inc.   111 - 86   2016 $450

Merrick, Pliny *Renunciation of Free Masonry.* Worcester: C. A. Blanchard, 1871. 12mo., original printed wrappers, little worn.   M & S Rare Books, Inc.   99 - 159   2016 $85

Merrifield, Mary Philadelphia *The Art of Fresco painting as Practised by the Old Italian and Spanish Masters with a Preliminary Inquiry into the nature of the Colours Used in Fresco Painting...* for the author by Charles Gilpin and Arthur Wallace, Brighton, 1846. First edition, half title, index, largely unopened, fine, bright in original green cloth blocked in blind, lettered gilt, Reynolds Stone booklabel of Pamela and Raymond Lister.   Jarndyce Antiquarian Booksellers   CCXVII - 186   2016   £125

Merrill, James *The Changing Light at Sandover.* New York: Atheneum, 1982. First edition, 8vo, photographs inside covers, paper wrappers, author's presentation to Barbara Howes, errata slip laid in, first five leaves loose, else very good.   Second Life Books, Inc.   196 B - 212   2016 $300

Merrill, James *First Poems.* New York: Knopf, 1951. First edition, one of 999 copies, this #564, 8vo., near fine in dust jacket, inscribed by author for William Claire.   Second Life Books, Inc.   196 B - 213   2016 $975

Merrill, James *Marbled Paper.* Riverside: Rara Avis Press for Charles Seluzicki Fine Books, 1982. Limited to 200 copies signed by author, 8vo, stiff paper wrappers, illustrations.   Oak Knoll Books   310 - 143   2016 $125

Merrill, James *Mirabell: Books of Number.* New York: Atheneum, 1978. Review copy with slip and publisher material laid in, close to near fine with some bumping to bottom of spine, near fine dust jacket with bump to bottom of spine, signed by author.   Jeff Hirsch Books   Holiday 2015 - 54   2016 $125

Merrill, James *Peter.* Dublin: Old Deerfield: The Deerfield Press/The Gallery Press, 1982. First edition, one of 300 numbered copies by poet on colophon page, this copy inscribed by author and Peter Hooten for William Meredith, fine in fine dust jacket.   Charles Agvent   William Meredith - 81   2016 $350

Merrill, James *The Seraglio.* New York: Knopf, 1957. First edition, 8vo., very good tight in scuffed and chipped dust jacket, inscribed by author to Bill Claire.   Second Life Books, Inc.   196 B - 214   2016 $175

Merrill, Marion *Three Little Pigs.* New York: Citadel Press, 1946. 4to., spiral backed pictorial boards, slight joint and edge rubbing, name on title else very good+ in dust jacket (with few closed tears), 4 moveable plates in the style of Weir, plus color lithographed in text.   Aleph-bet Books, Inc.   111 - 308   2016 $225

Merrill, William L. *Anthropology, History and American Indians: Essays in Honor of William Curtis Sturtevant.* Washington: Smithsonian Inst. press, 2002. First edition, quarto, frontispiece, 86 photographic figures, 13 tables, maps, peach wrappers, fine, printed on coated paper.   Argonaut Book Shop   Native American 2015 - 7613   2016 $50

Mershon, William B. *Recollections of My Fifty Years Hunting and Fishing.* Boston: Stratford & Co., 1923. First edition, gilt stamped cloth, illustrations, inscribed in 1944 by author's son, near fine, untrimmed fore edge and couple of pages with small tears, slight fading at spine.   Gene W. Baade, Books on the West   2015 - SHEL816   2016 $125

Mertens, Robert *Die Familie der Warane (Varanidae).* Frankfurt: Senchenbergischen Naturforschenden Gesellschaft, 1942. Quarto, 3 parts, photos plates, publisher's printed wrappers, fine set.   Andrew Isles Natural History Books   55 - 35836   2016 $600

Merton, Thomas 1915-1968 *Thirty Poems.* Norfolk: New Directions/Poets of the Year, 1944. First edition, 8vo., original printed boards, dust jacket, scarce hardbound issue, few faint creases in jacket, having been preserved folded and placed in the book, virtually as new.   James S. Jaffe Rare Books   Occasional List: Winter 2016 - 96   2016 $1250

Merwin, W. S. *Asian Figures.* New York: Atheneum, 1975. First edition, pictorial wrappers, inscribed by poet for Richard Harteis via Bill Meredith and Bill Merwin, laid in is brief ANS from Meredith to Harteis, his partner of many years, fine.   Charles Agvent   William Meredith - 83   2016 $150

Merwin, W. S. *Mary.* Brooklyn: Jordan Davies, 1976. First edition, one of 175 copies signed by author, fine, printed boards.   Second Life Books, Inc.   196 B - 215   2016 $135

Meserve, Frederick Hill *Lincoln's Ellsworth Letter.* New York: n.p., 1916. Limited to 250 copies, 8vo., paper covered boards, chipping with minor paper loss to head and tail of spine, some rubbing to covers at corners, slight cracking of inside hinges, offsetting to titlepage from one of the photos.   Oak Knoll Books   310 - 212   2016 $525

Meston, William *Mob contra Mob or the Rabblers Rabbled.* Edinburgh: printed and sold at Mr. Freebalm's shop in the Parliament-Close, 1714. 8vo., disbound, light creasing and outer pages dusted.   Jarndyce Antiquarian Booksellers   CCXVI - 410   2016   £225

Meston, William *The Poetical Works of the Ingenious and Learned William Meston, A.M....* Edinburgh: printed by Wal. Ruddiman, Junior, for Francis Robertson, 1767. Sixth edition, 12mo., recent blue boards, drab paper spine, very good.   C. R. Johnson Rare Book Collections   Foxon: H-P 2015 - 584   2016 $613

Metcalf, Colin *Gum Debut Issue.* Berkeley: Ginko Press, 2003. First edition, unopened pictorial plastic package of the Debut issue which houses a book (180) pages, comic (20 pages), trading cards (6), sticker sheet (1) and chewing gumm (1), very scare, fine.   Gene W. Baade, Books on the West   2015 - SHEL681   2016 $85

Metcalf, Paul *Both.* N.P.: Jargon Society, 4to., signed by author, nice in little chipped and soiled dust jacket.   Second Life Books, Inc.   196 B - 218   2016 $65

Metcalfe, Frederick *The Oxonian in Iceland; or Notes of Travel in that Island in the Summer of 1860.* London: Longman, Green, Longman, and Roberts, 1864. First edition, 8vo., contemporary half calf, marbled boards, spine panelled and lettered gilt, in 6 compartments with piscatorial gilt centre tools, top edge gilt, 3 wood engraved plates and illustration and folding engraved map, coloured in outline, little rubbing to joints, otherwise very good.   Sotheran's Piccadilly Notes - Summer 2015 - 202   2016   £350

Metcalfe, John *The Feasting Dead.* Sauk City: Arkham House, 1954. First edition, octavo, cloth, presentation from author to his publisher August Derleth, fine in fine dust jacket, rare signed or inscribed.   John W. Knott, Jr./L.W. Currey, Inc.   Fall-Winter 2015 - 17275   2016 $3000

Meteyard, Eliza *The Life of Josiah Wedgwood from His Private Correspondence and Family Papers with an Introductory Sketch of the Art of Pottery in England.* London: Hurst and Blackett, 1865. First edition, 2 volumes, two steel engraved frontispieces, 2 chromolithographs, three quarter brown morocco, marbled boards, top edge gilt, some light general scuffing to extremities, owner's name to endpapers, but fine set.   Argonaut Book Shop   Pottery and Porcelain 2015 - 5009   2016 $350

Methodist Church, Newfoundland *Minutes of the Proceedings of the Twelfth Session of Newfoundland Conference of the Methodist Church, Held in the Wesley Methodist Church, Harbor Grace, June 25th 1895 to the Twentieth Sesson June 24th 1903.* St. Johns: The Methodist Church, 1895-1903. 8vo., green cloth with gilt title to spine, 5 black and white illustrations in 1899 session and numerous tables, binding worn with spine sunned, interior very good with exception of 1900 session which has hole to inner margin of titlepage not into text.   Schooner Books Ltd.   115 - 109   2016 $225

Metropolitan Grievances; or a Serio-Comic Glance at Minor Mischiefs in London and on Vicinity.... London: printed by Charles Squire, for Sherwood, Neely & Jones, 1812. 12mo., color folding frontispiece by George Cruikshank, quarter dark brown morocco, marbled boards, slightly rubbed.   Jarndyce Antiquarian Booksellers   CCXVII - 8   2016   £280

Metropolitan Improvements; or London in the Nineteenth Century... London: Jones, 1827. First edition, octavo, 157 tissue guarded plates, finely engraved by William Wallis after drawings by Thomas Shepherd, folding map of Regent's Park, 20th century binding of quarter calf with marbled boards, gilt decorated spine, endpapers renewed, some light spotting to margins of plates, very good.   Peter Ellis   112 - 234   2016   £500

Mettler, Cecilia C.   *History and Medicine.*   Philadelphia: Blakiston, 1947. 16 plates, nice in original cloth.   James Tait Goodrich   X-78 - 396   2016 $175

Metz, Leon   *Robert E. McKee: Master Builder of Structures Beyond the Ordinary.*   El Paso: Robert E. & Evelyn McKee Foundation, 1997. First edition, 4to., attractive pictorial silver stamped cloth, illustrations, signed by Metz and Louis McKee, fine in fine slipcase, very scarce. Gene W. Baade, Books on the West   2015 - 1111113   2016 $356

Metz, Nancy Ayrcock   *The Companion to Martin Chuzzlewit.*   London: Helm Information, 2001. First edition, half title, illustrations, maps, original dark green cloth, booklabel of Thomas Grove, mint in dust jacket.   Jarndyce Antiquarian Booksellers   CCXVIII - 429   2016   £35

Meyer Bros. Drug Co.   *Annual Prices Current of Meyer Bros. & Co.....*   St. Louis: Meyer Bros. Drug Co., 1884. Small 4to., copious illustrations, flexible cloth, gilt on front cover, covers rubbed and soiled, hinges started, ownership signature of Thomas Kimbley Druggists - Hartford KY, good copy only.   Edwin V. Glaser Rare Books   2015 - 19299   2016 $450

Meyerstein, E. H. W.   *Joshua Slade - A Novel.*   London: Richards, 1938. First edition, octavo, near fine in very good dust jacket, slightly nicked, marked and chipped.   Peter Ellis   112 - 252   2016   £85

Meynell, Alice   *Children of the Old Masters.*   London: Duckworth, 1903. First edition, quarto, numerous fine photogravure plates, some foxing to edges and endpaper, fine in original tissue dust jacket which is bit chipped.   Peter Ellis   112 - 253   2016   £85

Meynell, Katherine   *Mare Fecundditatis: Seas of the Moon.*   London: Gefn Press, 1988. One of 40 numbered copies printed by Susan Johanknecht at Gefn Press and Camberwell Press, signed by Meynell and Johandknecht, 8 deeply textured collagraphs by Johanknecht, printed on thick paper and thinner, tissue guard type leaves with printed lunar surface details, small square 4to., flexible paper wrappers covered with bubbled type of iridescent plastic, stitching along cover fore-edges, inserted in dark blue denim cloth sleeve.   Oak Knoll Books   27 - 19   2016 $300

Meynell, Laurence   *The Frightened Man.*   London: Collins, 1952. Maroon cloth, silver titling in slightly aged and chipped but complete dust jacket, uncommon.   I. D. Edrich   Crime - 2016   £40

Meynell, Laurence   *Strange landing.*   London: Collins, 1946. First edition, fine in price clipped dust jacket.   Mordida Books   2015 - 012243   2016 $65

Meyrick, Samuel Rush   *Specimens of Ancient Furniture.*   London: William Pickering, 1836. First edition, 4to., original half brown morocco, marbled paper covered boards, spine gilt stamped, illustrations by Henry Shaw, rubbing at edges and along spine, foxing in text and on illustrations.   Oak Knoll Books   310 - 51   2016 $350

Meyrink, Gustav   *The Golem.*   London: Gollancz, 1928. First English edition, half title, original black cloth in pictorial dust jacket by Edward McKnight Kauffer, spine of dust jacket slightly dulled, Gollanz family copy.   Jarndyce Antiquarian Booksellers   CCXVII - 187   2016   £580

Michaels, Barbara   *The Master of Blacktower.*   New York: Appleton Century, 1966. First edition, owner name and date on front f.e.p., fine in fine dust jacket, price clipped with light rubbing at spine ends.   Ken Hebenstreit, Bookseller   2016 - 2016 $110

Michaels, Barbara *Someone in the House.* New York: Dodde Mead, 1981. First edition, fine in dust jacket. Mordida Books   2015 - 010411   2016 $55

Michalopoulos, Takis *Engravings. Piraeus & Ports of the Mediterranean Sea.* Athens: Eurodimention LTD for Hellenic Republic Ministry of Mercantile Marine, 2000. Large 8vo., original brown color hot stamped folder, 84 color printed or tinted views and maps on 55 loose plates, folder with few repaired tears, otherwise fine, preserved in custom made cloth drop back box with morocco lettering piece on spine, extremities rare.   Sotheran's   Travel and Exploration - 270   2016   £748

Micheaux, Oscar *The Forged Note.* Lincoln: Western Book Supply Co., 1915. First edition, gilt stamped cloth, 13 drawing by Heller, supremely rare, good+, hinges carefully and professionally repaired, spine speckled with small light spots and slightly faded, front and back covers acceptably bright, rear joint has very narrow broken band of light stain or bleach running along limited distance, occasional light prior crease to few leaves.   Gene W. Baade, Books on the West   2015 - 5005011   2016 $688

Michell, Thomas *History of the Scottish Expedition to Norway in 1612.* London: T. Nelson & Sons, 1886. First edition, 8vo., map, illustrations, original brown decorative cloth, spine faded, small wear to upper fore edge (4mm).   J. & S. L. Bonham Antiquarian Booksellers   Europe 2016 - 8980   2016   £65

Michener, James A. *Kent State What Happened and Why.* New York: Random House, 1971. Uncorrected proof, tall sheets, comb-bound, pencil date and annotation to front cover and ink publication date and proposal price on first leaf, overall near fine and scarce.   Ken Lopez Bookseller   166 - 85   2016 $350

Michener, James A. *A Michener Miscellany 1950-1970.* New York: Random House, 1973. First edition, black cloth, lettered in silver, fine in dust jacket.   Argonaut Book Shop Literature 2015 - 504   2016 $90

Michener, James A. *The Modern Japanese Print.* Rutland & Tokyo: Charles E. Tuttle, 1962. First edition, one of 510 numbered copies, this being number 214, signed by author and 10 contribution artists, large folio, original full page prints, each signed by artist, text handset in Perpetua type, printed on handmade kyokushi or Japanese vellum, bound in Okamoto Bindery in original tri-tone linen, stamped in gilt on front boards and spine, uncut, housed in original slipcase of unvarnished spruce or Japanese cedar, Japanese title burned onto wood on front panel of slipcase, spine sunned, slipcase and book with some scuffs, altogether very good copy of exquisite book with 10 original signed prints.   Heritage Book Shop   Holiday 2015 - 80   2016 $3500

Michener, James A. *My Lost Mexico.* Austin: State House Press, 1992. Limited edition of 350 copies, this being #198, fine, drawings and photos by author, cloth slipcase with iny bump on bottom edge, signed by author. Bella Luna Books   2016 - j11027   2016 $132

Michener, James A. *Recessional.* New York: Random House, 1994. First trade edition, purple cloth backed boards, lettered gilt, only tiny blemish to lower edge of cover, else very fine in dust jacket.   Argonaut Book Shop Literature 2015 - 5049   2016 $40

Michener, James A. *Return to Paradise.* New York: Random House, 1951. First edition, tan cloth with green decoration, lettered in gilt, very minor soiling to covers, just bit of foxing to fore edge.   Argonaut Book Shop   Literature 2015 - 5048   2016 $50

Michener, James A. *The World is My Home: a Memoir.* New York: Random House, 1992. First edition, 16 pages of black and white photos, blue cloth backed white paper boards, lettered gilt, minor bits of foxing along top edge, otherwise very fine in pictorial dust jacket.   Argonaut Book Shop   Literature 2015 - 5046   2016 $50

Middle East Pipelines Limited *Report on Trans-Desert Survey in Iraq. General Report on Alignment.* Westminster: Rendel, Palmer & Tritton..., 1949. Foolscap folio, original green printed boards, linen backed, typescript, sectional titles printed on green cards with 24 printed photographs on 12 plates, one folding color lithographic map with key pasted down and six roneographed folding maps with sections, several with hand coloring, name on front cover, extremities little rubbed, very well preserved.   Sotheran's   Piccadilly Notes - Summer 2015 - 204   2016   £1795

Middleton, Christopher *Nonsequences.* London: Longmans, 1965. First edition, quarto, numerous fine photogravure plates, some foxing to edges and endpaper, fine in original tissue dust jacket which is bit chipped.   Peter Ellis   112 - 254   2016   £45

Middleton, Conyers *De Medicorum apud Veteres Romanos Degentium Conditione Dissertatio...* Cambridge: apud Edmundum Jeffery, 1726. 4to., disbound, number label to upper left corner of title, text lightly foxed.   James Tait Goodrich   X-78 - 397   2016 $450

Middleton, George *Hiss! Boom!! Blah!!!* New York: Samuel French, 1933. 8vo., author's presentation to Eva Le Gallienne with her bookplate, lacks dust jacket.   Second Life Books, Inc.   196 B - 224   2016 $45

Middleton, John Izard *Grecian Remains in Italy.* London: printed for Edward Orme by W. Bulmer and Co., J. F. Dove 1812, but, 1811-. circa 1823. First edition, 480 x 335mm, modern retrospective red half morocco over older marbled boards, front cover with original red morocco title label, flat spine with densely gilt panels at head and tail gilt titling with original red morocco title label, flat spine with densely tooled gilt panels at head and tail, gilt titling expertly reinforced hinges, all edges gilt, with 2 beautifully engraved plates, 23 of them hand colored aquatints (3 double page), two of them plain line engravings, inconspicuous abrasions to paper boards, minor stain to fore edge of front flyleaf, handful of leaves with inconsequential small, faint spots at margins, vaguest hint of offsetting onto small portions of two plate, quite fine, binding expertly restored and certainly pleasing, engravings richly colored as well as entirely clean and fresh. Phillip J. Pirages   67 - 252   2016 $19,500

Midgley, Samuel *Halifax and Its Gibbet Law Placed in a True Light.* Halifax: printed by P. Darby for John Bentley, 1761. First edition thus, small 8vo., frontispiece and 1 additional folding plate, little toned, occasional underlining, light foxing, frontispiece edges delicate with few small repairs, later tan marbled calf, apparently by Riviere, spine gilt, raised bands, all edges gilt, endpapers renewed, joints creased, upper just starting, free endpapers toned at edges, very good, handsome copy, elaborate ownership inscription of William Jackson, Halifax 1679.   Unsworths Antiquarian Booksellers Ltd.   E05 - 8   2016   £175

Miers, John *Travels in Chile and La Plata.* London: Baldwin, Cradock & Joy, 1826. First edition, 2 volumes, 8vo., 3 maps, 19 plates, contemporary brown half calf, joints and corners slightly rubbed, crease on lweor cover, very good set.   J. & S. L. Bonham Antiquarian Booksellers America 2016 - 9902   2016   £900

Mignan, Robert *Travels in Chaldaea, Including a Journey from Bussourah to Bagdad, Hillah and Babylon, performed on foot in 1827...* London: Henry Colburn, 1829. First edition, 8vo., contemporary original blue cloth, yellow endpapers, aquatint frontispiece and five aquatint plates printed in sepia, retaining tissue guards, two engraved folding maps, wood engraved illustrations in text, light rubbing to cloth, here and there little spotted, very good in rarely seen publisher's binding, contemporary ownership inscription of R. E. Plunkett.   Sotheran's   Travel and Exploration - 346   2016   £798

Miles, Bernard *Curtain Calls.* Guilford, Surrey: Lutterworth, 1981. First edition, inscribed by author, nice in little scuffed dust jacket.   Second Life Books, Inc.   196 B - 229   2016 $45

Miles, Eustace *Better Food for Boys.* London: George Bell & Sons, 1909. Second edition, half title, 1 page ads, leading f.e.p. removed, original light grey decorated boards, spine uplettered in brown, very good.   Jarndyce Antiquarian Books   CCXV - 315   2016   £45

Milhouse, Katherine *Through These Arches: the Story of Independence Hall.* Philadelphia: Lippincott, 1964. First edition, 10 x 8 inches, cloth, fine in dust jacket with one spot of soil and tiny bit of edgewear, illustrations by author, this copy signed by Milhouse on titlepage and additionally inscribed.   Aleph-bet Books, Inc.   112 - 312   2016 $175

Milhouse, Katherine *With Bells On.* New York: Charles Scribner, 1955. A. First edition, 4to., aqua pictorial cloth, fine in dust jacket with piece out of corner, many full page color illustrations by author, this copy inscribed by Milhous to author Ruth Hutchinson with color pencil drawing, also signed by her, laid in are two handwritten letters from Milhouse to Hutchinson.   Aleph-bet Books, Inc.   111 - 281   2016 $450

Mill, John Stuart   1806-1873 *Principles of Political Economy with some of Their Applications to Social Philosophy.* John W. Parker, 1849. Second edition, 8vo., 2 volumes, contemporary half calf over marbled boards, spines with new morocco labels with gilt lettering, neat repairs to joints and extremities, spines little darkened, very clean internally, very good, bookplate of Frederick Henry Norman.   Sotheran's   Piccadilly Notes - Summer 2015 - 205   2016   £700

Mill, John Stuart   1806-1873 *A System of Logic, Ratiocinative and Inductive, Being a Connected View of the Principles of Evidence and the Methods of Scientific Investigation.* London: John W. Parker, 1851. Third edition, 8vo., 2 volumes, contemporary calf gilt with raised bands and labels, all edges gilt, very good.   John Drury Rare Books   2015 - 26011   2016 $350

Millais, John Guille   1865-1931 *British Deer and Their Horns....* Henry Sotheran & Co., 37 Piccadilly, W. and 140 Strand W.C., 1897. First edition, folio, original cream pictorial cloth, frontispiece printed in colors by Wilhelm Grieve of Berlin, 10 full page etched plates, 10 full page black and white plates, 173 illustrations, binding unusually bright, previous owner's signature, very good.   Sotheran's   Hunting, Shooting & Fishing - 63   2016   £850

Millais, John Guille   1865-1931 *Game Birds and Shooting Sketches.* London: Henry Sotheran and Co., 1894. Second edition, 8vo., original pale brown cloth, ink designs of birds to front cover and spine, spine darkened from exposure, attractively so, small ownership inscription, good copy.   Sotheran's   Hunting, Shooting & Fishing - 88   2016   £100

Millais, John Guille 1865-1931 *The Wildfowler in Scotland.* London: Longmans, Green and Co., 1901. First edition, 4to., original half vellum, spine titled in gilt, blue paper boards, top edge gilt, etched frontispiece, 20 other full page plates, some colored by Millais and others, wood engraved illustrations, previous owner's signature to half title, spine scuffed and slightly darkened, boards rubbed, but internally very clean, very good. Sotheran's Hunting, Shooting & Fishing - 89 2016 £300

Millar, H. R. *The Dreamland Express.* New York: Dodd Mead/London: Humphrey Milford, Oxford University Press, 1927. Oblong 4to., cloth backed pictorial boards, edges rubbed, some light cover soil, clean, tight and very good, illustrations by Millar. Aleph-bet Books, Inc. 111 - 291 2016 $1250

Millay, Edna St. Vincent 1892-1950 *The King's Henchmen.* New York: Harper, 1927. First edition, limited to 150 large paper copies signed by author on Tuscany handmade paper, very good in worn publisher's box. Second Life Books, Inc. 196 B - 231 2016 $300

Millay, Edna St. Vincent 1892-1950 *The Lamp and Bell.* New York: Frank Shay, 1921. First edition, bookplate of previous owner, wrappers heavily worn, internally fine, good reading copy. Argonaut Book Shop Literature 2015 - 1369 2016 $75

Miller, Andrew M. *From Delos to Delphi. A Literary Study of the Homeric Hymn to Apollo.* Leicen: E. J. Brill, 1986. First edition, 8vo, very light shelfwear, near fine. Unsworths Antiquarian Booksellers Ltd. E04 - 77 2016 £45

Miller, Arthur *After the Fall.* New York: Viking, 1964. First edition, one of 500 large paper copies, signed by author, fine in original tissue and publisher's box. Second Life Books, Inc. 196 B - 234 2016 $300

Miller, Arthur *All My Sons.* New York: Reynal & Hitchcock, 1947. First edition, celery cloth boards, also issued in gray cloth, no priority, fine with some expert restoration to extremities of dust jacket, which is fine, scarce. Between the Covers Rare Books 204 - 74 2016 $250

Miller, Arthur *Arthur Miller's Collected Plays.* New York: Viking Press, 1957. First edition, top edge little toned, rubbing on spine and some foxing on endpapers, very good in price clipped, near fine dust jacket with single short tear, inscribed by author. Between the Covers Rare Books 204 - 75 2016 $600

Miller, Arthur *Death of a Salesman...* New York: Limited Editions Club, 1984. First edition, 1/500 copies, signed by author and artist, five etchings by Leonard Baskin, bound in full brown morocco by Gray Parrot, fine in little worn original slipcase, 4to. Second Life Books, Inc. 196 B - 235 2016 $750

Miller, Arthur *You're Next.* New York: Stage for Action/American Youth for Democracy, circa, 1946. Playscript, quarto, printed pink paper self wrappers mimeographed rectos only and stapled at upper left corner, minor handling and wear, first and last sheets nearly detached from staple, else near fine, rare. Between the Covers Rare Books 204 - 73 2016 $12,000

Miller, C. William *Benjamin Franklin's Philadelphia Printing 1728-1766. A Descriptive Bibliography.* Philadelphia: American Philosophical Society, 1974. First edition, 8vo., illustrations, original tan cloth, fine in fine dust jacket. Howard S. Mott Inc. 265 - 49 2016 $30

Miller, George *A Lessening.* Oswestry: Hedge Sparrow Press, 2007. 29/45 copies, full page wood engraving by Alan May, crown 8vo., original grey paper wrappers printed in silver and blue, backstrip unevenly applied to textblock and front flyleaves creased, edges untrimmed, near fine. Blackwell's Rare Books B184 - 276 2016 £25

Miller, Gerrit S. *Catalogue of the Mammals of Western Europe (Europe Exclusive of Russia) in the Collection of the British Museum.* London: Trustees of the British Museum, 1912. Octavo, text illustrations, publisher's cloth, neat library stamp on titlepage, otherwise fine. Andrew Isles Natural History Books 55 - 7358 2016 $80

Miller, Helen Sullivan *The History of Chi Eta Phi Sorority Inc. 1932-1967.* Washington: Association for the Study of Negro Life and History, 1968. First edition, small quarto, yellow cloth lettered green, photos, fine in very near fine dust jacket, with very light wear. Between the Covers Rare Books 202 - 121 2016 $300

Miller, Henry 1891-1980 *Henry Miller's Book of Friends.* Santa Barbara: Capra Press, 1976. First printing, 8vo., photos, small drawings by author, erra slip laid in, red cloth, cover slightly faded, otherwise very good, tight copy in scuffed and chipped dust jacket. Second Life Books, Inc. 197 - 236 2016 $50

Miller, Henry 1891-1980 *Maurizius Forever.* San Francisco: Colt Press, 1946. One of 500 copies, title in brown and black with illustration in color, 8 illustrations in color drawings and water colors by Miller, green boards lettered in white, very fine. Argonaut Book Shop Literature 2015 - 6355 2016 $200

Miller, Henry   1891-1980   *The Mezzotints.*   Ann Arbor: Roger Jackson, 1993. One of 100 copies signed and numbered by Roger Jackson, portfolio, covered with blue marbled paper and containing a booklet (paper wrappers), 17 pages plus facsimiles of mezzotints, signed on title by publisher, 5 x 7 inch color photo, near fine.   Second Life Books, Inc.   196 B - 238   2016 $150

Miller, Hugh   *My Schools and Schoolmasters or the Story of My Education.*   Edinburgh: Thomas Constable and Co., 1858. contemporary speckled calf, gilt spine, lacking label, little rubbed, contemporary gift inscription on leading pastedown "Jeffery Edwards from his friend & school fellow, Henry Lee Warner....".   Jarndyce Antiquarian Books   CCXV - 838   2016   £38

Miller, James Russell   *Home Making or the Ideal Family Life.*   London: Sunday School Union, 1896. Half title, original dark blue cloth, little rubbed, prize label on leading pastedown.   Jarndyce Antiquarian Books   CCXV - 316   2016   £38

Miller, Joaquin   1841-1913   *The Building of the City Beautiful.*   Trenton: Albert Brandt, 1905. First edition, 12mo., frontispiece, red cloth decoratively stamped in gilt, slight fading to lower spine, contemporary dated inscription on inner cover, fine.   Argonaut Book Shop   Literature 2015 - 7614   2016 $150

Miller, Kelly   *The Disgrace of Democracy: Open Letter to President Woodrow Wilson.*   Washington: Kelly Miller, 1917. Stated 'Over 100,000 copies distributed' (?), stapled printed gray wrappers, small stain on edges of pages, near fine.   Between the Covers Rare Books   207 - 69   2016 $475

Miller, Philip   *The Gardeners Kalendar...*   London: printed for the author and sold by John Rivington in St. Paul's Church Yard, C. Hitch (and 14 others), 1760. Engraved frontispiece, 5 folding plates, 8vo., lacking leading endpaper, contemporary calf, neatly rebacked with new red gilt label, covers worn, contemporary armorial bookplate of Antipas Church with signature at head of titlepage, notes on Sea kale written on frontispiece recto, several marginal pen strokes & underlinings.   Jarndyce Antiquarian Booksellers   CCXVI - 412   2016   £240

Miller, R. S.   *The Lowan, Parts One and Two (all published).*   Melbourne: Bird Observers' Club, 1935-1936. Octavo, 2 colored plates by Neville W. Cayley, publisher's printed wrappers, fine, scarce.   Andrew Isles Natural History Books   55 - 23884   2016 $300

Miller, Walter   *A Canticle for Leibowitz.*   Philadelphia & New York: J. B. Lippincott Co., 1960. First edition, octavo, cloth backed boards, light offsetting to front and rear pastedowns and endpapers with exception of lower left front pastedown and lower right front free endpaper edge which shows 7.4mm. long darker strip-perhaps from previous jacket protector, nearly fine to fine copy in fine dust jacket with 1.2 mm. stress crease at upper right front corner and tiny soil spot to upper right corner edge, rare orange wraparound advertising band present, superior copy, seldom found in this condition.   John W. Knott, Jr./L.W. Currey, Inc.   Fall-Winter 2015 - 17165   2016 $4500

Millet, Gabriel   *Recherches sur l'Iconogaphie de l'Evangile aux XIVe, XVe et SVIe Siecles D'Apres Les Monuments De Mistra, De La Macedoine et Du Mt. Athos.*   Paris: Editions E. de Boccard, 1960. Second edition, reprint of 1916 edition, text in French, 8vo., cloth, dust jacket torn at edges and lightly soiled, edges lightly soiled, 670 black and white illustrations.   Oak Knoll Books   310 - 44   2016 $650

Milligan, Spike   *Goodbye Solider - War Biography Vol. 6.*   London: Michael Joseph/Jack Hobbs, 1986. First edition, octavo, photos, signed by author, tail of spine bit bumped, otherwise fine in near fine dust jacket with red on spine, bit faded.   Peter Ellis   112 - 255   2016   £125

Millikan, Robert A.   *The Isolation of an Ion, a Precision Measurement of Its Charge...*   New York: Physcial Review, 1911. First edition offprint, extremely rare, octavo, early (no original) wrappers, (original wrappers lacking), touch of nearly invisible dampstaining evident at bottom margin of some leaves, rare.   Manhattan Rare Book Company   2016 - 1821   2016 $1900

Mills, Alfred   *Pictures of Roman History, in Miniature.*   Philadelphia: Johnson & Warner, 1811. First edition, 2.5 x 2 inches, original printed boards, spine shot.   M & S Rare Books, Inc. 99 - 134   2016 $300

Mills, James W.   *The Labyrinth and Other Poems.*   London: Williams & Norgate, 1930. First edition, titlepage vignette and 6 full page wood engravings, occasional foxspots throughout, crown 8vo., original quarter black cloth with blue boards, backstrip lettered gilt, lightly rubbed and spotted overall, some wear to corners, edges toned, light foxing to endpapers, good, inscribed by author for Lilian & Dick.   Blackwell's Rare Books   B184 - 194   2016   £30

Mills, John   *Christmas in the Olden Time.*   London: H. Hurst, 1846. First edition, red and green titlepage, two early Peabody Library 'Rules' sheets pasted in, 12mo., original gilt and blind decorated red cloth, 6 leaves of plates, including frontispiece, all edges gilt, excellent copy.   Howard S. Mott Inc.   265 - 33   2016 $75

Milne, Alan Alexander 1882-1956 *House at Pooh Corner.* London: Methuen, 1928. First edition, deluxe edition, 8vo., publisher's full blue calf with double gilt rules, floral decorations in corners and picture in center, gilt, pictorial spine, all edges gilt spine slightly sunned, else fine.   Aleph-bet Books, Inc.   112 - 316   2016 $2000

Milne, Alan Alexander 1882-1956 *The House at Pooh Corner.* London: Metheun & Co., 1928. First edition, deluxe leather bound edition with bright gilt decorations and lettering, small 8vo., all edges gilt, bright and unmarked in original box with original printed paste on labels on box top and one edge, as issued, box top, label soiled.   By the Book, L. C.   45 - 88   2016 $1750

Milne, Alan Alexander 1882-1956 *The House at Pooh Corner.* London: Methuen & Co., 1928. First edition, one of 350 numbered copies printed on handmade paper, signed by author and artist, presentation copy inscribed by author to Louis Grobosky on titlepage, with his small bookplate, small quarto, text illustrations, original quarter blue cloth over cream colored boards, printed paper label on front cover, rare bottom right corner bumped with professional repair, some foxing to covers, dust jacket with repairs to verso folds, very good, housed in custom blue cloth chemise and quarter blue morocco slipcase, gilt stamped.   Heritage Book Shop   Holiday 2015 - 81   2016 $6500

Milne, Alan Alexander 1882-1956 *Now We Are Six.* London: Methuen, 1927. 8vo., gilt cloth, top edge gilt, fine in dust jacket (slightly chipped at spine extremes and slightly darkened), illustrations by E. H. Shepard.   Aleph-bet Books, Inc.   112 - 315   2016 $900

Milne, Alan Alexander 1882-1956 *Now We Are Six.* London: Methuen, 1927. Deluxe edition, 8vo., full publisher's morocco, gilt pictorial cover with extensive gilt pictorial spine, all edges gilt, fine in original publisher's box with printed labels on cover and flap (box with some soil and flap mends), illustrations by E. H. Shepard.   Aleph-bet Books, Inc.   111 - 293   2016 $2850

Milne, Alan Alexander 1882-1956 *Now We Are Six.* London: Methuen, 1927. First edition, original red pictorial cloth, gilt, top edge gilt, slight browning to half title and final page with imprint but very nice, bright copy in slightly chipped and frayed and somewhat dust soiled dust jacket, which is browned at spine panel.   Bertram Rota Ltd.   Christmas List 2015 - 27   2016   £600

Milne, Alan Alexander 1882-1956 *The Secret and Other Stories.* New York: Fountain Press, 1929. Limited to 700 copies for sale, signed by Milne (400 for US 300 for England), slim 8vo., red cloth, paper spine label, fine, beautiful copy.   Aleph-bet Books, Inc.   111 - 295   2016 $750

Milne, Alan Alexander 1882-1956 *When We Were Very Young.* London: Methuen, 1924. Limited to only 100 numbered copies signed by author and artist, 4to., cloth backed boards, offsetting on rear endpaper and 3 oxidation marks on cover label and tip very slightly worn, else near fine in slightly soiled very good dust jacket with old tape marks on verso lightly visible on front, housed in custom leather backed case.   Aleph-bet Books, Inc.   112 - 314   2016 $16,000

Milne, Alan Alexander 1882-1956 *When We Were Very Young.* London: Methuen, 1924. First edition, decorations by E. H. Shepard, few hinges little strained, crown 8vo., original bright clean mid blue cloth, backstrip lettering and Shepard designs on covers all gilt blocked, free endpapers browned, owner's short gift inscription on front free endpaper, top edge gilt, others untrimmed, very good.   Blackwell's Rare Books   B186 - 264   2016   £1200

Milne, Alan Alexander 1882-1956 *When We Were Very Young.* London: Methuen & Co. Ltd., 1932. Twenty-third edition, 8vo., original royal blue cloth panelled and prettily decorated gilt with vignettes to both boards, others untrimmed, pictorial endpapers, protected by the pictorial dust jacket, line drawing throughout by E. H. Shepard, fine and exceptional copy protected by a particularly nice dust jacket, price 7/6 to spine with slight rubbing and dusting to spine.   Sotheran's   Piccadilly Notes - Summer 2015 - 207   2016   £148

Milne, Alan Alexander 1882-1956 *When We Were Very Young.* London: Methuen Children's Books, 1974. No. 157 of 300 copies signed by Christopher Milne, 194 x 121mm., publisher's sky blue crushed morocco, upper cover with gilt figure of Little Bo Peep holding a shepherd's crook at center, flat spine adorned with twining floral vine around which cherubic children frolic, all edges gilt, illustrations by E. H. Shepard, five of these full page, spine and edges of covers slightly sunned, otherwise pristine.   Phillip J. Pirages   67 - 253   2016 $950

Milne, Alan Alexander 1882-1956 *When We Were Very Young. Winnie-the-Pooh. Now We Are Six. The House at Pooh Corner.* New York: Dutton Children's Books, 1992. Color edition, one of 1000 copies signed by one of trustees of the Pooh Properties, five volumes, fine set in very slightly rubbed slipcase, including separate reproduction of the Winnie-the-Pooh Christmas print, secured with silk ribbon in maroon cloth binding, Pooh trustees party invitation and two Winnie-the-Pooh postage stamps loosely inserted.   Bertram Rota Ltd.   Christmas List 2015 - 29   2016   £250

Milne, Alan Alexander 1882-1956 *Winnie the Pooh.* London: Methuen, 1926. One of only 20 copies printed on vellum and signed by author and artist, 4to., full vellum, very light soil else fine, rare.   Aleph-bet Books, Inc.   111 - 292   2016 $57,500

Milne, Alan Alexander 1882-1956 *Winnie the Pooh.* London: Methuen, 1926. First edition, large paper copy limited to 350 numbered copies on handmade paper, signed by Milne and Shepard, 4to., cloth backed boards, fine in dust jacket (very good with some toning with small repair to chips at folds), housed in custom chemise and quarter leather case, illustrations by E. H. Shepard.   Aleph-bet Books, Inc.   111 - 294   2016 $16,500

Milne, Alan Alexander 1882-1956 *Winnie-the-Pooh.* London: 1926. First trade edition, illustrations by E. H. Shepherd.   Honey & Wax Booksellers   4 - 23   2016 $4500

Milne, Alan Alexander 1882-1956 *Winnie the Pooh.* London: Methuen, 1926. First edition, first printing, illustrations in line by E. H. Shepard, 8vo., green gilt cloth, fine in very good+ dust jacket (light soil and slight wear to spine ends).   Aleph-bet Books, Inc.   112 - 313   2016 $6500

Milne, Alan Alexander 1882-1956 *Winnie-the-Pooh.* London: Macmillan and Co. ltd., 1933. Twelfth edition, 8vo., original dark green polished cloth panelled and lettered gilt, with vignette in upper board, top edge gilt, others untrimmed, pictorial map endpapers, line drawings by E. H. Shepard, externally and internally fine, bright, protected by an unusually fresh dust jacket with spine panel mildly dusted, faint vertical crease and neat tape strengthening to reverse at spine ends.   Sotheran's   Piccadilly Notes - Summer 2015 - 208   2016   £148

Milne, Alan Alexander 1882-1956 *Winnie-the-Pooh and Eeyore's Tail: a Pop-up Picture Book.*   London: Methuen & Co., 1953. First edition, 4 color pop-up pictures and color plates, spiral bound pictorial boards, boards just little rubbed, but very nice.   Bertram Rota Ltd.   Christmas List 2015 - 29   2016   £150

Milnor, William   *An Authentic Historical Memoir of the Schuylkill Fishing Company of the State in Schuylkill from Its Establishment on the Romantic Stream near Philadelphia...*   Philadelphia: Judah Dobson, 1830. First edition, errata leaf, 5 plates, original reddish pink linen covered boards, printed paper label on front cover, some foxing as always.   Joseph J. Felcone, Inc.   Books from Five Centuries: a Miscellany - 103   2016 $1200

Milosz, Czeslaw   *Bells In Winter.*   New York: Ecco Press, 1978. First edition, review copy with photo of author and broadside with poem 'Encounters' laid in, inscribed by author for William Meredith, fine in fine dust jacket.   Charles Agvent   William Meredith - 84   2016 $500

Milosz, Czeslaw   *Unattainable Earth.*   New York: Ecco, 1986. First edition, 8vo., author's presentation on flyleaf, paper over boards with cloth spine, fine in price clipped dust jacket.   Second Life Books, Inc.   196 B - 243   2016 $125

Milton, John 1608-1674 *L'Allegro and Il Penseroso.* New Rochelle: Elston Press, 1903. Limited to 160 copies printed in red and black on English handmade paper watermarked with the 'cat', decorative titlepage and some initial letters and 17 illustrations cut on wood from designs by H. M. O'Kane, bookplate, small ink ownership stamp, lacks spine label.   Oak Knoll Books   310 - 97   2016 $450

Milton, John 1608-1674 *Comus, a Mask.*   London: Essex House Press, 1901. No. 14 of 150 copies on vellum, 195 x 125 mm., original stiff vellum over thin boards, front cover with embossed rose design, rubricted by Florence Kingsford throughout, one two-line and one very large 10 line gilt initial, illustated colophon, woodcut frontispiece by Reginald Savage, both hand colored, vellum pastedowns lifting at edges, otherwise in especially fine condition, binding extraordinarily clean and text essentially faultless.   Phillip J. Pirages   67 - 335   2016 $1250

Milton, John 1608-1674 *Comus.*   New York and London: Doubleday and Heinemann, n.d., 1921. First US edition, 4to., green cloth, top edge gilt, spine slightly dull else near fine, 24 very beautiful tipped-in color plates with lettered guards, 37 line illustrations and pictorial endpapers by Arthur Rackham.   Aleph-bet Books, Inc.   112 - 415   2016 $500

Milton, John 1608-1674 *Comus.*   New York: Doubleday Page, London: William Heinemann, n.d., 1922? Limited to 550 copies, numbered and signed by author, 4to., original quarter vellum, cream gilt stamped boards, top edge gilt, some darkening to boards, lower edge dented slightly very good.   Jeff Weber Rare Books   181 - 63   2016 $700

Milton, John 1608-1674 *Four Poems by John Milton L'Allegro, Il Penseroso, Arcades, Lycidas.*   Newtown: Gregynog Press, 1933. No. 172 of 235 copies (of a total of 250, including 15 bound in morocco), 264 x 171mm., publisher's reddish brown Hermitage calf, upper cover blocked in blind with titling, press device and figure of Euphrosyne, one of the Three Graces, designed by Blair Hughes-Stanton, four of them full page, printed on Japanese vellum, hint of rubbing to leather, one tiny spot on spine, otherwise very fine, immaculate internally.   Phillip J. Pirages   67 - 184   2016 $1000

Milton, John 1608-1674 *The Masque of Comus.* Cambridge: Heritage Press, Watercolors by Edmund Dulac, printed boards with black cloth spine, lettered in gilt, very fine in slipcase (faded at extremities), Sandglass pamphlet laid in.   Argonaut Book Shop   Literature 2015 - 7046   2016 $60

Milton, John   1608-1674   *On the Morning of Christ's Nativity.*   Flansham: Pear Tree Press, 1930. 48/100 copies printed in black and gold, frontispiece and further wood engraved decorations, patches of colour bleeding from gold ink throughout as well as a couple of other small stains, 12mo., original silver boards decorated in black with woodcut frontispiece, paper label printed in gold and black to front, backstrip lettered in gold and slightly rubbed, decorated endpapers, pastedowns little foxed along head, original tissue wrappers, good.   Blackwell's Rare Books   B186 - 326   2016   £200

Milton, John   1608-1674   *Paradise Lost. A Poem in Twelve Books. (and) Paradise Regain'd. A Poem in Four Books. to which is added Samson Agonistes and Poems upon Several Occasions.*   London: Jacob Tonson, 1705. Seventh and fourth edition, issued in two volume set with general half title in first volume, octavo, in first volume is portrait frontispiece engraving and 12 engraved plates, as well as engraved coat of arms of Lord Sommers at head of first verse, 19th century bindings of half dark burgundy morocco with raised bands, gilt rules, pebbled cloth sides, marbled endpapers, all edges stained red, couple of stains in margins, otherwise internally fine, covers faintly rubbed at edges, very good.   Peter Ellis   112 - 257   2016   £950

Milton, John   1608-1674   *Paradise Lost... (with) Paradise Regained.*   London: Printed for J. Tonson, 1711. 1713. Ninth edition and fifth edition, 2 volumes, engraved frontispiece and 12 engraved plates, 11 engraved plates, 12mo., some foxing in second volume 19th century dark green pebble grained morocco, raised bands, gilt lettered spines, marbled endpapers, all edges gilt.   Jarndyce Antiquarian Booksellers   CCXVI - 413   2016   £380

Milton, John   1608-1674   *Paradise Lost.*   London: printed for Jacob Tonson, 1730. Fourteenth edition, titlepage printed in red and black, 12 engraved plates, 12mo., some browning, old signature on versos of titlepage, slight showing through to recto, several pages with pencil marks, full contemporary calf, spine very slightly rubbed and chipped at head and tail, joints cracked but firm, lacking label, inscription dated 1903.   Jarndyce Antiquarian Booksellers   CCXVI - 414   2016   £75

Milton, John   1608-1674   *Paradise Lost and Paradise Regained to Which is Added Samson Agonistes and Poems Upon Several Occasions.*   Birmingham: John Baskerville, 1760. 8vo. 2 volumes, contemporary full red calf, boards with rich gilt borders, corner pieces and central gilt decoration, spines with contrasting leather labels richly gilt in compartments, repair to head of spine volume I, joints little rubbed, some staining to lower board of volume I, neat ink poem in contemporary hand, ink name on titlepage, generally very good.   Sotheran's   Piccadilly Notes - Summer 2015 - 209   2016   £1500

Milton, John   1608-1674   *Paradise Lost. (and) Paradise Regain'd.*   London: printed at the Shakespeare Head Press for Cresset Press, 1931. No. 80 of 195 copies on handmade paper and 10 on vellum, 2 volumes 375 x 260mm., original white buckram boards, gilt titling on spine, edges untrimmed, headpiece, two tailpieces and 16 wood engravings by D. Galanis, titlepage and initial letters designed by Anna Simons, extremities lightly bumped, upper cover of one volume with short faint pencil mark, unusually fine, easily soiled binding unusually clean and interior entirely fresh and bright.   Phillip J. Pirages   67 - 102   2016 $4800

Milton, John   1608-1674   *The Complete Poetical Works of John Milton.*   London: Henry Frowde/Oxford University Press, 1908. First Oxford edition, octavo, full green pebbled leather, raised bands, gilt inner floral dentelles, lettered in gilt, all edges gilt, marbled endpapers, spine little faded, covers slightly rubbed at joints, very good.   Peter Ellis   112 - 258   2016   £125

Milton, John   1608-1674   *Samson Agonistes; a Dramatic Poem.*   New Rochelle: Elston Press, 1904. One of 125 copies, 229 x 152mm., publisher's quarter linen over blue gray paper boards, printed spine label, woodcut headpieces, initials and inhabited border from designs by H. M. O'Kane, mild toning to two board edges, minor spotting to back cove, trivial wear to corners, still very near fine and pristine internally.   Phillip J. Pirages   67 - 126   2016 $1000

Milton, John   1608-1674   *Samson Agonistes.*   Florence: Stamperia del Santuccio, 1931. No. 51 of 95 copies, 340 x 229mm., in peculiar amateur binding of blue crushed morocco, upper cover with short black and orange lines onlaid at upper left and lower right corners, centerpiece of onlaid black coffin like ornament entwined by orange snake flat spine with onlaid orange sword with gilt titling, ivory moire silk endleaves, matching velvet lined orange linen, folding box with orange morocco back and lip, onlaid sword on back, printed in black and bistre, bookplate of Norman J. Sondheim, leather little spotted, soiled and with slight variation of color, isolated very trivial flecks of foxing, otherwise fine, text brilliantly white and clean, binding unworn.   Phillip J. Pirages   67 - 187   2016 $5500

Minchin, H. Cotton   *The Legion Book.*   Curwen Press, 1929. Limited to 600 copies, red/brown buckram, covers slightly worn, uncommon first impression.   I. D. Edrich   Winston Spencer Churchill - 2016   £65

Mingus, Charles   *Beneath the Underdog.*   New York: Alfred A. Knopf, 1971. First edition, faint "H" stamp on printed front endpaper, else about near fine in like dust jacket, signed by Mingus.   Royal Books   52 - 29   2016 $4500

The Mining Catalog for the Year 1921. Pittsburgh: Keystone Consolidated Pub. Co. Ltd.1, 1921. 8vo., fully illustrated with black and white photo illustrations, blue cloth, extreme wear to edges, inner hinge cracks, some light soiling to outer margins, good only.   Schooner Books Ltd.   115 - 195   2016 $125

Minney, R. J.   *The War Incorporating War Pictorial.*   1939-1941. No. 1-85. Oct. 1939 - Aug. 5 1941, original wrappers, very fragile, photos, diagrams and maps.   I. D. Edrich Winston Spencer Churchill - 2016   £95

Minshull, Mr.   *The Miser, a Poem.*   London: printed and sold by A. Dodd, Mr. Penn, E Nutt and by booksellers of London and Westminster, 1735. First edition, folio, sewn as issued, very uncommon, last leaf torn and rather fragile, no loss of text, otherwise good in original condition, entirely uncut.   C. R. Johnson Rare Book Collections   Foxon: H-P 2015 - 596   2016 $689

Mirabeau, Honore Gabrielle Riquetti, Comte De   1749-1791   *Considerations on the Order of Cincinnatus. To Which are Added Several Original Papers...*   Philadelphia: printed by T. Seddon, 1786. New edition, first American edition, 8vo. 19th century three quarter morocco over marbled boards. very good copy, untrimmed, chips to spine ends, scuffed tips, owner's bookplate son front free endpapers and first blank, tight binding, the copy of Frank Maier and William S. S. Horton, M. De. with armorial bookplate.   Kaaterskill Books   21 - 55   2016 $750

Miro, Joan   *Maitres-Gravures-Contemporains 1970.* Paris: Benggruen & Cie, 1970. First edition, pictorial wrappers, wraparound original five color lithograph by Miro, publisher's price slip laid in, about fine, one or two very tiny underlines to one of the last leaves of text, bookseller's plate inside rear wrapper, else bright and fresh, beautiful copy.   B & B Rare Books, Ltd.   2016 - JMO001   2016 $100

Miron, Charles   *Murder on the 18th Hole.*   New York: Manor, 1978. First edition, paperback original, fine in wrappers.   Mordida Books   2015 - 011359   2016 $65

Mirth in Ridicule; or a Satyr Against Immoderate Laughing. London: printed and sold by J. Morphew, 1708. First edition, small 4to., stitched as issued, fine, rare.   C. R. Johnson Rare Book Collections   Foxon: H-P 2015 - 599   2016 $3831

A Miscellaneous Collection of Poems, Songs and Epigrams. Dublin: printed by A. Rhames, 1721. First edition, 2 volumes in one, 12mo., contemporary panelled calf spine gilt bit worn, remains of morocco label, very good, early armorial bookplate.   C. R. Johnson Rare Book Collections Foxon: H-P 2015 - 600   2016 $3831

Miscellaneous Poems by Several Hands.   London: printed by J. Watts, 1726. First edition, 2 volumes, 8vo., contemporary panelled calf, spines rubbed, joints slightly cracked, one label missing, slight foxing, but very good, traces of bookplate removed from verso of titlepage volume II, bindings vary slightly as often.   C. R. Johnson Rare Book Collections   Foxon: H-P 2015 - 602   2016 $689

Mises, Ludwig Von   *A Critique of Interventionism.*   New Rochelle: Arlington House, 1977. First edition in English, 8vo., near fine, age darkening endpapers, very good+ dust jacket with minimal chips and short closed tears, scarce. By the Book, L. C.   45 - 33   2016 $250

Mises, Ludwig Von   *Epistemological Problems of Economics.*   Princeton: D. Van Nostrand, 1960. First edition in English, 8vo., near fine, in very good++ dust jacket with sun spine, as usual for this book, minimal edge wear, scarce in original dust jacket.   By the Book, L. C.   45 - 34   2016 $325

Mises, Ludwig Von   *Nation, State and Economy.*   New York: New York University Press, 1983. First edition, owner name, 8vo., near fine in like dust jacket with minimal edgewear, owner name front pastedown.   By the Book, L. C.   45 - 35   2016 $175

Mises, Ludwig Von   *The Ultimate Foundation of Economic Science.*   Princeton: D. Van Nostrand, 1962. First edition, 8vo., fine in very good++ dust jacket with sun spine per usual for this jacket and edge wear.   By the Book, L. C.   45 - 32   2016 $375

Mitchell, George   *Kernel Cob and Little Miss Sweetclover.* Chicago: Volland, 1918. No additional printings, 8vo., quarter pictorial boards, small mend to paper on spine, slight wear to spine ends, very good++, full color illustrations by Tony Sarg, rare.   Aleph-bet Books, Inc.   112 - 444   2016 $625

Mitchell, George   *Little Bass.*   Chicago: Volland, 1919. No additional printings, 8vo., pictorial boards, fine in pictorial box (box with some light wear), scarce, illustrations by Arthur Henderson with charming full page and smaller color illustrations.   Aleph-bet Books, Inc.   112 - 499   2016 $350

Mitchell, James   *Smear Job.*   New York: G. P. Putnam's Sons, 1977. First edition, fine in near fine dust jacket (chip at top of rear flap fold and minor wear at bottom of spine). Ken Hebenstreit, Bookseller   2016 - 2016 $60

Mitchell, Joseph *The Shoe-Heel: a Rhapsody.* London: printed for Tho. Astley, 1727. First edition, 8vo., recent boards, original pale blue wrappers preserved, fine, fresh copy in original wrappers, entirely uncut as issued, printed on thick unwatermarked paper and very possibly a fine paper copy.   C. R. Johnson Rare Book Collections   Foxon: H-P 2015 - 609   2016 $3831

Mitchell, Margaret   1900-1949 *Gone with the Wind.* New York: Macmillan Co., 1936. First edition, first issue with published May 1936 on copyright page and no note of further printing, 222 x 152mm., signed by author, very pleasing gray crushed morocco by Sangorski & Sutcliffe (stamp-signed), covers with single gilt rule border, raised bands decorated with stippled rule and flanked by gilt rules, panels with intricate gilt fleuron centerpiece and gilt titling, gilt ruled turn-ins, marbled endpapers, top edge gilt, upper right corner of back cover slightly soiled (with a series of short, thin, faint parallel lines about two to three inches in length descending from top edge), spine slightly and evenly sunned to pleasant light brownish gray, trivial internal imperfections, otherwise very fine.   Phillip J. Pirages 67 - 256   2016 $5000

Mitchell, Margaret   1900-1949 *Gone with the Wind.* New York: Heritage Press, 1968. 2 volumes, illustrations by John Groth, blue and grey cloth lettered in gilt, very fine in slipcase, fading to fore edge of one slipcase, Sandglass pamphlet laid in.   Argonaut Book Shop   Heritage Press 2015 - 7048   2016 $40

Mitchell, Margaret   1900-1949 *Gone with the Wind.* Franklin Center: Franklin Library, 1976. First edition, book has slight scuff on gilt leaf on top paper edges, heavy full red leather with bright gilt lettering and design, 3 raised bands on spine, all edges gilt, red moire endpapers, red silk bookmark sewn in, illustrations in color by Robert Reid, set in Fairfield typeface, printed on 50 pound Finch Special Book paper, Bicentennial edition limited (but no number indicated), beautiful copy.   Simon Finch 2015 - 17469   2016 $250

Mitchell, Silas Weir   1829-1914 *Hugh Wynne, Free Quaker.* New York: Century Co., 1897. First edition, first issue, 2 volume set, 12mo., black and white frontispiece plate, grey cloth with red printing and decoration, spines of both volumes slightly cocked and soiled, light wear to spine ends, else near fine set.   Argonaut Book Shop   Literature 2015 - 1342   2016 $225

Mitchell, Silas Weir   1829-1914 *Lectures on Diseases of the Nervous System.* Philadelphia: Henry C. Lea, 1881. Small 8vo., five text plates, original green cloth from publisher, near fine in both binding and internally.   James Tait Goodrich X-78 - 400   2016 $695

Mitchell, Silas Weir   1829-1914 *Researches Upon the Venom of the Rattlesnake with an Investigation of the Anatomy and Physiology of the Organs Concerned.* Washington: Smithsonian, 1850. Tall 4to., new cloth.   James Tait Goodrich   X-78 - 401   2016 $175

Mitchell, Silas Weir   1829-1914 *The Wonderful Adventures of Fuz-Buz the Fly and Mother Grabem.* Philadelphia: Lippincott, 1867. (1866). First edition, 12mo., green cloth, gilt cover, beveled edges, some foxing very good++, this copy inscribed Dec. 25th 1866, this state of the book is quite rare, illustrated with 9 plates plus 1 black and white by Henry Bispham.   Aleph-bet Books, Inc. 111 - 296   2016 $1200

Mitchell, William *General Greely: The Storty of a great American.* New York: G. P. Putnam's Sons, 1936. First edition, 10 photographic plates, blue cloth, very fine.   Argonaut Book Shop   Biography 2015 - 6788   2016 $50

Mitford, Mary Russell   1787-1855 *Our Village, Illustrated.* London: Sampson Low, 1879. First edition thus, full straight grained dark green morocco by F. Bedford, gilt rules and spine decoration, all edges gilt, very good, attractive copy, 4to.   Jarndyce Antiquarian Booksellers   CCXVII - 188   2016   £280

Mitford, Mary Russell   1787-1855 *Our Village.* London: Macmillan and co., 1893. First edition with Hugh Thomson illustrations, this one of 470 copies of the large paper edition, royal 8vo., recently rebound in half red morocco, spine lettered gilt and with gilt rules and centre tools, top edges gilt, 100 illustrations by Hugh Thomson, very nice.   Sotheran's   Piccadilly Notes - Summer 2015 - 302   2016   £298

Mitford, Nancy   1904-1973 *Noblesse Oblige - an Enquiry into the Identifiable Characteristics of the English Aristocracy.* London: Hamish Hamilton, 1956. First edition, octavo, several full page black and white cartoons by Osbert Lancaster, free endpapers partially tanned, head and tail of spine very slightly bumped, near fine in very good, slightly nicked dust jacket.   Peter Ellis 112 - 260   2016   £85

Mittelholzer, Edgar *Shadows Move Among Them.* Philadelphia: Lippincott, 1951. First edition, 8vo., paper over boards, cover slightly faded in spots, otherwise very good, bright copy in worn dust jacket.   Second Life Books, Inc. 197 - 237   2016 $95

Mittelholzer, Edgar *The Weather in Middenshot.* New York: John Day, 1953. First American edition, 8vo., paper over boards, cover little scuffed and bumped at edges, few small stains, otherwise very good, tight copy.   Second Life Books, Inc. 197 - 239   2016 $45

Mixter, William J. *Rupture of the Invertebral Disc with Involvement of the Spinal Canal.* Reprinted from New England Journal of Medicine, Folding table, illustrations, original offprint. James Tait Goodrich   X-78 - 402   2016 $150

Mizauldo, Antonio *Centuriae IX Memorabilium Utilium Ac Juncdorum in Aphorismos...* Frankfurt: Nicolas Hoffman, 1613. Small folio, 3 parts in 1 volume, some misnumbering of pages, printer's device on each of the three titles, light paper toning, occaisonal stains, contemporary limp vellum, manuscript spine title, lacks ties, rear joint partly torn, bookplate signed by Fritz Laber of Dr. Carl Wurth, early ownership signatures of Ernnet Casparus Maismis, very good. Jeff Weber Rare Books   181 - 21   2016 $600

Mo, Timothy *Sour Sweet.* London: Deutsch, 1982. First British edition, near fine, browning to edges, near fine second state dust jacket (with Book nomination mention). Bella Luna Books   2016 - t17671   2016 $66

Modern Etiquette in Public and Private. London: Frederick Warne & Co., circa, 1880. Revised edition, half title, original red decorated cloth, some slight marking, very good. Jarndyce Antiquarian Books   CCXV - 318   2016   £45

The Modern Letter Writer or Art of Polite Correspondence for Ladies and Gentlemen... Glasgow: Cameron & Ferguson, 1871. Prelims browned, original pale blue cloth little dulled, ownership stamp on title. Jarndyce Antiquarian Books   CCXV - 319   2016   £28

Modern Quality. London: printed for J. Huggonson, 1742. First edition, 12 pages, folio, disbound, short tear in inner margins, not touch text, otherwise good. C. R. Johnson Rare Book Collections   Foxon: H-P 2015 - 613   2016 $613

A Modest Defence of Publick Stews; or an Essay Upon Whoring... London: printed by A. Monroe near St. Paul's, 1724. Half title, slight worming in lower margin, not affecting text, contemporary full panelled calf, at some point neatly rebacked, very good.   Jarndyce Antiquarian Booksellers CCXVII - 9   2016   £2800

Modius, Franciscus *Cleri Totius Romanae Ecclesiae Subiecti, seu Pontificirum ordinum Omnium Omnino Utriusqve Sexus Habitus, Artificiosissimis Figuris...* Frankfurt: Sigismund Feyerabend, 1585. First edition, 4to., near contemporary limp vellum with yapp edges, later vertical letter in ink on spine, woodcut printer's device on main title and later repeated twice, 103 costume woodcuts by Jost Amman (one repeated), vellum little spotted and lightly rubbed, only very light spotting here and there internally, lower outer corner of F2 expertly repaired, E4 with small hole in lower outer corner filled, very clean and good, near immaculate copy.   Sotheran's   Travel and Exploration - 271   2016   £2995

Moe, Louis *The Forest Part.* New York: Coward McCann, 1930. First edition, Large oblong 4to., cloth backed pictorial boards, fine in original glassine dust jacket (chipped, missing piece on back), each page of text surrounded by black and white scenes and each faces a full page, rich color illustration, 10 full pages in color plus color pictorial dust jacket, rare jacket.   Aleph-bet Books, Inc.   112 - 319   2016 $400

Moffat, W. D. *The Mentor. May 1924.* Springfield: Crowell, 1924. Small 4to., illustrations, cover little soiled, slightly chipped (small tape mend a top of spine, small bit missing at bottom), otherwise very good, tight copy. Second Life Books, Inc.   197 - 336   2016 $75

Mogensen, Allan H. *Common Sense Applied to Motion and Time Study.* Factory and Industrial management, 1932. First edition, 8vo., very good++, minimal soil edges and scuffs to covers, foldout chart, scarce.   By the Book, L. C.   45 - 36   2016 $225

Mogridge, George *Learning to Act.* London: RTS, 1848. Additional engraved title, illustrations, original black cloth, spine slightly faded, prize presentation to J. R. Chatterton by Sabbath school teacher.   Jarndyce Antiquarian Books CCXV - 320   2016   £40

Mogridge, George *Sergeant Bell and His Raree-show.* London: Thomas Tegg, First edition, frontispiece illustrations, contemporary half red sheep, marbled boards, little rubbed and worn, bookplate of novelist John Fowles, news clipping relating to Seregeat Bell publishing history tipped in, good plus, internally clean, scarce.   Jarndyce Antiquarian Booksellers   CCXVIII - 268   2016   £200

Moholy-Nagy, Laszlo *Bauhaus Buchet 14: Von matrial zu Architektur.* Munchen: Albert Langen Verlag, 1929. First edition, small quarto, extensively illustrated with photos, yellow cloth decorated in red, some rubbing on spine lettering and age toning on boards, very good in very good original card slipcase rubber stamped with title and publisher, inscribed by author to his wife Lucia.   Between the Covers Rare Books   208 - 65   2016 $8000

Moholy-Nagy, Laszlo *Moholy-Nagy: a New Vision for Chicago.* Springfield & Chicago: University of Illinois Press and The Illinois State Museum, 1990. Numerous color and black and white illustrations, close to near fine in wrappers with vertical crease to front cover near spine and some slight wear, seemingly fairly uncommon.   Jeff Hirsch Books Holiday List 2015 - 85   2016 $100

Moir, John *Female Tuition or an Address to Mothers on the Education of Daughters.* London: printed for J. Murray, 1786. Second edition, 8vo., expertly bound in recent quarter sprinkled calf, gilt banded spine, red morocco label, marbled boards, vellum tips.   Jarndyce Antiquarian Books CCXV - 860   2016   £680

Moivre, Abraham De 1667-1754 *The Doctrine of Chances on a Method of Calculating Probabilities of Events in Play.* London: A. Millar, 1756. Third edition, quarto, portrait medallion vignette on title, original full calf, joints repaired, fine.   Jeff Weber Rare Books   183 - 15   2016 $2500

Molesworth, Mary Louisa Stewart 1839-1921 *The Girls and I.* London: Macmillan, 1892. First edition, red pictorial cloth, binding tight and light cover soil, else very good+, this copy inscribed and dated 1892 by author, illustrations by Leslie Brooke.   Aleph-bet Books, Inc.   112 - 74   2016 $275

Molier, Ernest *Cirque Molier 1880-1904.* Paris: Paul Depont, n.d., 1905. First edition, large 4to., original decorative printed wrappers, mounted photo on front cover, frontispiece, titlepage in red and black, profusely illustrated with photos, drawings and reproductions of programs.   Dramatis Personae   119 - 115   2016 $350

Moliere, Jean Baptiste Poquelin De 1622-1673 *The Misanthrope.* New York: Harcourt Brace, 1955. First edition translated by Richard Wilburn, 8vo., 1/1500 copies signed by Wilbur, drawings by Enrico Arno, very good in faded cloth.   Second Life Books, Inc.   196 B - 885   2016 $65

Moliere, Jean Baptiste Pouquelin De 1622-1673 *Le Tartuffe. (and) Don Juan.* Nice and Paris: l'Imprimerie Nationale de Monaco, 1954. No. IX of XXV copies reserved for the collaborators and friends of the artist (in addition to 700 regular copies), 241 x 191mm., contemporary green crushed morocco by Jean Santin (stamp-signed), smooth spine with gilt titling, gilt ruled turn-ins, pale green watered silk endleaves, all edges gilt, titlepage vignettes, frontispiece at beginning of each work and numerous illustrations in text by Jean Gradassi, all hand colored by atelier of Edmond Vairel using pochoir technique, with extra suite of 45 illustrations, bound in after text and with original version of an illustration from Don Juan inscribed by the artist to Madame Hicks and identified by him on verso, bound in at front, pages ruled in red, two half titles printed in red, joints little rubbed, spine uniformly sunned, just hint of soiling to covers, otherwise very fine, binding lustrous and text immaculate.   Phillip J. Pirages   67 - 285   2016 $850

Moll, Elick *Seidman and Son.* New York: Samuel French, 1963. First edition, 8vo., author's full page presentation on flyleaf, nice in little soiled dust jacket.   Second Life Books, Inc.   196 B - 250   2016 $50

Moll, Herman *The British Empire in America, Containing the History of the Discovery, Settlement, Progress and Present State of all the British Colonies...*   London: printed for John Nicholson at the King's Arms in Little Britain, Benjamin Took at Middle Temple Gate, Fleetstreet and Richard Parker and Ralph Smith...., 1708. First edition, 8 engraved folding maps, small 8vo. contemporary paneled calf, rebacked in morocco, raised bands, red morocco lettering piece, gilt, very good set, boards rubbed with one small split small stickers on each front cover and front pastedown, browning to corners, volume I has damp marking to upper part of title and first few leaves of introduction, volume II has worming to corners of free front endpapers and first blank, faint damp marking along top edge, tear to one map through blank area, few minor nicks to edges of two other maps, stickers from Dr. Winslow Lewis (1799-1875) of Boston.   Kaaterskill Books   21 - 67   2016 $5000

Moll, Herman *Thirty Two new and Accurate maps of the Geography of the Ancients....* London: printed for and sold by H. Moll, 1732. 4to., double page engraved cartouche titlepage, 32 double page copper engraved maps, 4to., very good, clean copy, arly 19th century half calf, marbled boards, expert repairs to joints and corners.   Jarndyce Antiquarian Booksellers   CCXVI - 415   2016   £650

Mollien, Gaspard *Travels in the Republic of Colombia in the Years 1822 and 1823.* London: C. Knight, 1824. First edition, 8vo., frontispiece (marginal waterstain), folding map, brown half calf (split at base of spine).   J. & S. L. Bonham Antiquarian Booksellers   America 2016 - 6645   2016   £250

Mollien, Gaspard *Voyage Dans L'Interieur De L'Afrique Aus Sources Du Senegal et de La Gamble, Fait en 1818.* Paris: Mme. Ve. Courcier, 1820. First edition, 8vo., 2 volumes, contemporary calf backed marbled boards, spine lettered and ornamented in gilt, sprinkled edges, folding engraved map with routes in red and blue, 4 engraved plates by Ambroise Tardieu, first title signed on verso by author to guarantee authenticity of the edition, spines little faded, half titles with minimal offsetting from pastedown, one leaf with marginal spots, few negligible spots elsewhere, otherwise near immaculate set in stylish binding.   Sotheran's   Travel and Exploration - 23   2016   £798

Monaldini, Giuseppe Antonio *Instituzione Antiquaria Numismatica o sia Introduzione allo Studio delle Antiche Medaglie in due Libri Proposa.* Rome: A Spese di Venanzio Monaldini nella Stamperia Giovanni Zempel, 1772. First edition, title printed in red and black with engraved vignette, 3 folding engraved plates, half title, apparently lacking initial blank, 8vo., contemporary sheep backed russet boards, all but 1 of the sheep tips lacking, stamp (19th century) on half title of English numismatics dealer, F. J. Jefferey, good, scarce.   Blackwell's Rare Books   B184 - 66   2016   £350

Monck, Mary *Marinda. Poems and Translations Upon Several Occasions.* London: printed by J. Tonson, 1716. First edition, very good, 8vo., contemporary calf, gilt, rebacked, very good, early signatures of John Brace (crossed out) and Elizabeth Lovell, later bookplates of G. W. F. Gregor and Oliver Brett, Viscount Esher.   C. R. Johnson Rare Book Collections   Foxon: H-P 2015 - 617   2016 $2298

Money, John *Historie de la Campagne Faite en 1792...* E. Harlow, 1794. 8vo., some browning and foxing, uncut in original boards, spine lettered, good.   Blackwell's Rare Books   B184 - 67   2016   £400

Mongez, Antoine *Tableaux, Statues, Bas Reliefs E5 Camera De La Galerie De Florence et du PalaisPitti...* Paris: Lacombe, 1789-1814. 4 volumes bound in 2, frontispiece, 187 engraved illustrations on 200 sheets of India paper laid down on thick paper, with accompanying leaves of descriptive text, foxing as usual, some offsetting, tear to inner margin of dedication leaf, folio, contemporary green hard grained morocco by Fairbairn, multiple gilt and blind fillets on sides, outermost being wide and gilt, spines similarly decorated gilt, gilt edges, corners bumped and joints little rubbed.   Blackwell's Rare Books   B184 - 68   2016   £2000

Mongorgueil, G. *Murat.* Paris: Hachette, 1903. gilt pictorial cloth, endpaper slightly frayed, slight cover rubbing, else fine, 40 magnificent full page color illustrations by JOB, this copy inscribed by him.   Aleph-bet Books, Inc.   112 - 270   2016 $2250

Mongtomery, Florence *Behind the Scenes in the Schoolroom...* Leipzig: Bernhard Tauchnitz, 1913. Copyright edition, half title, publisher's pink boards, cloth spine, very good, bright copy.   Jarndyce Antiquarian Books   CCXV - 862   2016   £20

Monod, Louis *De L'Encephalopathie Albuminurique Algue et Desc Caracters Qu'Elle Persente en Particular Chez Les Enfants.* Paris: Adrien Delahaye, 1858. New boards, front blank leaf has top 2 inches cut away, outer lower third of pages with dampstaining, text lightly foxed.   James Tait Goodrich   X-78 - 403   2016 $175

Monotype Corporation of London *Pastonchi a Specimen of a New Letter for the Use on the 'Monotype'.* London: Lanston Monotype Corporation, 1928. Limited to 200 copies on special Fabriano paper, small 4to., half vellum with marbled paper covered boards, remnants of slipcase, light foxing, trade edition also issued.   Oak Knoll Books   310 - 125   2016 $350

Monro, Alexander *Dissertatio Medica De Testibus et de Semine in Variis Animalibus Quam Annuente Summo Numine...* Edinburgh: Apud G. Hamilton & J. Balfour, 1755. Folding engraved plates with mutiple engravings, recent light blue sugar board style with printed paper label, endpapers renewed, light foxing of text otherwise clean, near fine, rare.   James Tait Goodrich   X-78 - 404   2016 $1250

Monro, Alexander *New Brunswick with a Brief Outline of Nova Scotia and Prince Edward Island...* Belleville: Mika Studio, 1972. Facsimile of 1855 edition, 8vo., 2 folding maps to front and tables, cloth faded, very good.   Schooner Books Ltd.   115 - 197   2016 $45

Monro, Alexander *Three Treatises on the Brain, the Eye and the Ear.* Edinburgh: Bell & Bradfute, G. G. & J. Robinson and J. Johnson, Edinburgh, 1797. First edition, 24 engraved plates, some folding, one partially hand colored, first two leaves moderately browned with occasional light toning throughout, margins of title expertly mended, some offsetting from a number of plates, signature of William Ryland, Edinburgh dated 1819, very attractive, untrimmed copy.   Edwin V. Glaser Rare Books   2015 - 10131   2016 $2500

Monro, Donald *Praelectiones Medicae Ex Cronii Institutio Annis 1774 et 1775 et Oratio Anniversaria ex Harveii Instituto die Octobris 18 anni 1775.* London: Gul. Hay, 1776. First edition, errata, ad leaf, newly rebound in full English style morocco, uncut, fine, scarce.   James Tait Goodrich   X-78 - 406   2016 $795

Monro, George *Extracts. Doctrinal, Practical and Devotional.* London: William Darton and Son, 1836. 19th century blind stamped binding, inscribed by editor, Joseph Fry for Raymond & Louisa Polly, , octavo, full contemporary decoratively blindstamped blue morocco, spine lettered gilt, all edges gilt, near fine.   David Brass Rare Books, Inc.   2015 - 03012   2016 $150

Monroe, Anne Shannon *Feelin' Fine!* Garden City: Doubleday Doran, 1930. First edition, 8vo., photos frontispiece, signed by author, green cloth with paper labels, map on endpapers, cover slightly faded and worn, otherwise very good, tight copy.   Second Life Books, Inc.   196 B - 254   2016 $85

Monsarrat, Nicholas *The Cruel Sea.* N.P.: Book Club Associates, 1971. First edition thus, 8vo., full red faux leather lettered gilt on spine and cover, limitation label on front endpaper, this no. 89 inscribed by author for Lord Butler of Saffron Walden, covers very slightly bumped, otherwise very good, sound.   Any Amount of Books   2015 - A84859   2016   £250

Monsivais, Hector *Principados y Potestades.* Mexico City: Liberia Madero, 1969. First Mexican edition, preceding all others, slim quarter, perfectbound softcover, yellow wrappers (also noted in green wrappers, with no known priority), near fine.　Royal Books　48 - 64　2016　$4250

Montagu, Lord Robert *Topicorum Liber: a Roberto de Monte Acuto.* London: printed by Harrison and sons, St. Martin's Lane, 1868. First edition, folio, printed in galley form, with wide gutter margins, title foxed, contemporary black straight grain morocco cloth.　Marlborough Rare Books　List 55 - 49　2016　£1850

Montagu, Mary Pierrepone Wortley　1689-1762 *The Poetical Works of the Right Honourable Lady...* London: printed for J. Williams, 1768. First edition, small 8vo., contemporary calf, spine gilt, ends of spine defective, joints cracked, aside from binding wear, very good.　C. R. Johnson Rare Book Collections　Foxon: H-P 2015 - 621　2016　$613

Montaigne, Michel De　1533-1592 *Les Essais.* Leyden: par Jean Doreau, Geneva printed), 1602. Second of two Geneva editions published in 1602 under the false imprint of Leyden, 8vo., contemporary vellum, title inked on spine, vellum ties missing, paper flaw in D1 with slight loss, lightly browned throughout.　Maggs Bros. Ltd.　1474 - 54　2016　£2750

Montaigne, Michel De　1533-1592 *Essays of Michael Seigneur de Montaigne in Three Books.* London: printed for T. Basset, 1693. Early edition, 3 volumes, small 8vo., engraved frontispiece portrait of author, some early ink underlining, lacks rear free endpaper (volume I), original full mottled calf (mismatched set), raised bands, gilt spines, red leather title labels, inner joints reinforced with Kozo, worn, ownership signatures of J. Merton (?), Arthur Rogers - June 1933, Reverend James Jenkyn (d. 1825 of Herfordshire?) and Myles Standish Slocum, Pasadena.　Jeff Weber Rare Books　181 - 22　2016　$275

Montaigne, Michel De　1533-1592 *The Essays of Michel de Montaigne.* New York: Heritage Press, 1946. 3 volumes, thick 12mo., marbled boards with brown cloth spines, lettered gilt, very fine, slipcases with minor fading, Sandglass pamphlet laid in.　Argonaut Book Shop　Heritage Press 2015 - 2022　2016　$90

Montaut, Henri De *Vertus & Qualities.* Paris: chez Arnuald de Vresse, n.d. circa 1860's, Colored issue, oblong folio, 12 hand colored lithographed plates with interleaves, each plate imprinted 'chez Aubert', original cloth with blind-stamped arabesque panel enclosing an elaborately gilt centerpiece with title within, few very light marginal fingermarks, inner hinges expertly strengthened, excessively scarce.　David Brass Rare Books, Inc.　2015 - 02896　2016　$4800

Monteiro, Jose Leite *Estampas Antigas de Paisagem e Costumes de Madeira.* Funchal: Club Roatrio, 1951. First edition, quarto, 76 illustrations, original buff decorative wrappers.　J. & S. L. Bonham Antiquarian Booksellers　Europe 2016 - 8963　2016　£75

Montesquieu, Charles Louis De Secondat, Baron De La Brede　1689-1755 *Persian Letters.* London: privately printed, 1892. first edition, number 123 of a total of 320 of this new translation, 8vo., 2 volumes, original blue cloth, printed labels on spines, two gold and color printed half title surrounds, etched portrait and 8 etchings on India paper, all retaining tissue guards, label little chipped, few corners lightly bumped, internally very good, contemporary bookplates of Paisley Free Library and Museum, discard stamp.　Sotheran's　Travel and Exploration - 348　2016　£298

Montgomery, James *Poems on the Abolition of the Slave Trade...* London: printed for R. Bowyer, the Proprietor, 1809. First edition, large quarto, sympathetically rebound in later period style quarter morocco and marbled paper covered boards, dark red spine label, engraved title and 12 plates, some staining and foxing to title and plates, smudging to front fly, else handsome, very good.　Between the Covers Rare Books　207 - 1　2016　$2250

Montgomery, L. M. *Anne's House of Dreams.* New York: Stokes, 1917. First edition, 8vo., lavender cloth, pictorial paste-on, fine in dust jacket (some chips and creases), illustrations by Maria Kirk with tissue guarded frontispiece repeated on cover, nice, rare in dust jacket.　Aleph-bet Books, Inc.　111 - 297　2016　$2000

Montgomery, L. M. *Emily of New Moon.* New York: Stokes, 1923. First edition, 8vo., blue cloth, pictorial paste-on, fine in dust jacket heavily worn with old tape repair, illustrations by Maria Kirk with color frontispiece.　Aleph-bet Books, Inc.　112 - 320　2016　$850

Montgomery, L. M. *Jane of Lantern Hill.* Toronto: McClelland and Stewart, 1937. First Canadian edition, 8vo., green cloth gilt titles to front and spine with top edge green, color frontispiece, cloth sunned and slightly worn along spine, slight staining to paper edges, signed by author.　Schooner Books Ltd.　115 - 181　2016　$475

Montgomery, L. M. *Magic for Marigold.* New York: Frederick Stokes, 1929. First edition, 8vo. green cloth, pictorial paste-on, fine in near fine dust jacket, illustrations by Edna Cooke Shoemaker, very scarce, magnificent copy.　Aleph-bet Books, Inc.　112 - 321　2016　$1200

Montgomery, L. M. *Rainbow Valley.* New York: Frederick Stokes, 1919. First edition, 8vo., green cloth, pictorial paste-on, near fine in dust jacket (chipped with some soil), illustrations by Maria Kirk with tissue guarded frontispiece repeated on cover, scarce in dust jacket.　Aleph-bet Books, Inc.　111 - 298　2016　$1000

Montgomery, Robert *The Sacred Annual; Being the Messiah, a Poems.* London: John Turrill, 1834. Fourth edition, 191 x 121mm, appealing 19th century black straight grain morocco, covers with gilt filigree and blind rolled frame, raised bands, spine compartments gilt with curling cornerpieces and lancet tools radiating from a central circle, black morocco label, blind rolled turn-ins, marbled endpapers, all edges gilt, extra chromolithographed 'missal' titlepage woodcut tailpiece by John Franklin and 10 color lithographs mounted on heavy stock, 3 of these by John Martin, all lithographs with captioned tissue guards, front pastedown with armorial bookplate, engraved bookplate of George Oliver Clark, with inscription, joints little rubbed (part of front joint with thin crack), spine gilt little muted, corners very slightly worn, binding without any serious condition issues and pleasing, isolated faint spots internally, text and plates generally very clean and fresh.   Phillip J. Pirages   67 - 251   2016 $1500

The Monthly Photographic Illustration.   Japan: Taisho, n.d., 1916. First edition, oblong folio, folding maps, numerous photos, original brown decorative cloth.   J. & S. L. Bonham Antiquarian Booksellers   Voyages 2016 - 2016   £100

Montmort, Pierre Remond De   *Essay d'Analyse sur les Jeux de Hazard.*   Paris: Chez Jacque Quillau, 1708. First edition, 4to, engraved title vignette, 3 vignettes depicting gambling scenes, decorative initials and tailpieces, 3 folding tables, occasional browning, pages 127-8 with closed tear, small marginal burn hole pages 101-102, original full vellum with maroon calf spine label, ink inscription of author, armorial bookplate of Sir Francis Hopkins, 1st Baronet 1756-1814, very good.   Jeff Weber Rare Books   183 - 24   2016 $7000

Moorcock, Michael   *Elric at the End of Time.*   New England Library, 1964. First edition, as new in like dust jacket, signed by author.   Simon Finch   2015 - 9990   2016 $200

Moore, Alan   *From Hell: Book One, The Compleat Scrips.*   Baltimore: Borderlands Press, Wilmington: Spiderbaby Grafix, 1994. Limited to 1026 copies, this one of 1000 numbered copies signed by author, artist and editor, Stephen R. Bissette, illustrations by Eddie Campbell, octavo, cloth, fine in fine dust jacket.   John W. Knott, Jr./L.W. Currey, Inc.   Fall-Winter 2015 - 17302   2016 $500

Moore, Catherine L.   *Shambleau and Others.*   New York: Gnome Press, 1953. First edition, 8vo., fine in dust jacket (rear panel little soiled, cover illustrations by Binkley.   Second Life Books, Inc.   197 - 282   2016 $250

Moore, Christopher   *Coyote Blue.*   New York: Simon & Schuster, 1994. First edition, near fine, minor bumping to base of spine, dust jacket fine, signed by author.   Bella Luna Books   2016 - t4883   2016 $66

Moore, Christopher   *Lamb: The Gospel According to Biff, Christ's Childhood Pal.*   New York: William Morrow, 2002. First edition, fine, fine dust jacket.   Bella Luna Books   2016 - t9610   2016 $195

Moore, Christopher   *Lamb: The Gospel According to Biff, Christ's Childhood Pal.*   New York: William Morrow, 2002. First edition, near fine, light bumping to spine ends, fine dust jacket.   Bella Luna Books   2016 - t8537   2016 $181

Moore, Christopher   *The Stupidest Angel.*   New York: Morrow, 2004. First edition, fine, fine dust jacket, signed by author.   Bella Luna Books   2016 - t6959a   2016 $66

Moore, Clement Clarke   1779-1863   *The Night Before Christmas. in The New York Book of Poetry.*   New York: George Dearborn, 1837. First edition state A, tall 8vo., pinkish brown cloth blindstamped and stamped in gold with gilt vase on covers, cloth on spine ends chipped off, foxing, front outer joint rubbed, altogether tight and very good.   Aleph-bet Books, Inc.   112 - 106   2016 $2000

Moore, Clement Clarke   1779-1863   *Night Before Christmas.*   Akron: Saalfield, n.d. circa, 1910. 4to., cloth, slight bit of fraying, very good+, color illustrations on every page.   Aleph-bet Books, Inc.   111 - 91   2016 $600

Moore, Clement Clarke   1779-1863   *Santa Claus. (The Night Before Christmas).*   London: Dean's Rag Book, n.d. circa, 1920. 8vo., brightly illustrated in full color by Harry Rountree, printed cloth rag book, light cover soil, near fine, rare in such clean condition.   Aleph-bet Books, Inc.   112 - 107   2016 $875

Moore, Clement Clarke   1779-1863   *The Night Before Christmas.*   Philadelphia: J. Lippincott & Co., 1931. No. 249 of 275 copies for American and 275 for England, signed by artist, 231 x 150 mm., publisher's limp vellum gilt titling on upper cover, pictorial endpapers designed by Rackham, original (slightly worn) slipcase, 17 black and white illustrations in text and four color plates, all by Arthur Rackham, titlepage and page 33 with faint ink stamp of Glen Rdge Free Public Library, verso of title and page 33 with small neatly inked accession number, vellum and content very faintly rumpled, otherwise fine, very fresh inside and out.   Phillip J. Pirages   67 - 295   2016 $1250

Moore, Clement Clarke   1779-1863   *The Night Before Christmas.*   Akron: Saalfield, 1932. Folio, flexible pictorial card covers, very slight wear, near fine, 12 beautiful color illustrations by Fern Bisel Peat.   Aleph-bet Books, Inc.   112 - 1o5   2016 $175

Moore, Clement Clarke 1779-1863 *Poems.* New York: Barlett & Welford, 1844. First edition, 12mo., finely bound in recent half red morocco over marbled boards, half title, uncut, inscribed by author July 1848 for Mrs. Murray, excellent copy with minor scattered foxing.   Howard S. Mott Inc.   265 - 34   2016 $8500

Moore, Edward *Poems, Fables and Plays.* London: printed by J. Hughes for R. and J. Dodsley, 1756. First edition, contemporary calf, spine scuffed, joints cracked but firm, remains of brown morocco label, handsome collected edition, aside from wear to spine, fresh copy.   C. R. Johnson Rare Book Collections   Foxon: H-P 2015 - 623   2016 $613

Moore, George 1852-1933 *Aphrodite in Aulis.* London: Heinemann; New York: Fountain Press, 1930. First edition, one of 1825 large paper copies, large 8vo., uncut and signed by author, page or two at end somewhat chipped in cutting, cover little scuffed and spotted, otherwise nice, no slipcase.   Second Life Books, Inc.   196 B - 256   2016 $75

Moore, George 1852-1933 *The Apostle.* London: Heinemann, 1923. First edition, 8vo., one of 1000 copies, numbered and signed by author, paper boards, dust jacket of the same paper, cover little worn at ends of spine, else very good in chipped dust jacket.   Second Life Books, Inc.   196 B - 255   2016 $85

Moore, George 1852-1933 *Confessions of a Young Man.* London: Swan Sonnenschein, Lowrey & Co., 1888. First edition, author's presentation copy to his brother Maurice Moore, tipped in at back is autograph letter from Moore to editor C. Lewis Hind, dated June 18 1900, original cloth with pictorial illustration of a young woman on cover, spine somewhat darkened as usual, corners of book and spine bumped, still nice, hinges tender, otherwise very good, tipped in is an ad for Moore's Parnell and His Island, housed in grey cloth chemise and quarter leather slipcase, very good.   The Kelmscott Bookshop   13 - 42   2016 $3000

Moore, George 1852-1933 *Letters from.... to Ed. DuJardin 1886-1922.* New York: Crosby Gaige, 1929. First edition, one of 668 copies, signed by author, 8vo., nice.   Second Life Books, Inc.   196 B - 257   2016 $45

Moore, George 1852-1933 *Martin Luther. A Tragedy in Five Acts.* London: Remington & Co., 1879. First edition, original blindstamped black cloth with gilt title and authors to front cover and title to spine, corners lightly bumped and small piece missing from top on spine, interior pages very nice, ownership signature of Henry Knight, bookplate of Rosita de Texada, very good, housed in green silk folding case.   The Kelmscott Bookshop   13 - 41   2016 $2550

Moore, George 1852-1933 *Mike Fletcher: a Novel.* London: Ward and Downey, 1889. First edition, probable second state with leaf of press notices for Moore's novels, with tipped in two-page letter from Moore to his secretary, Miss Gough on administrative matters, blue cloth boards with gilt title to spine, orange patterned decoration to spine and front board, minor wear to edges and corners, bookplate of John Stuart Groves, clean interior and tight binding, housed in turquoise half morocco slipcase, very good plus.   The Kelmscott Bookshop   12 - 71   2016 $225

Moore, George 1852-1933 *Ulick and Soracha.* New York: Boni & Liveright, 1826. First edition, limited to 1250 copies signed by author, spine end lightly rubbed, rubbing to the extremities, spine has some discoloration, dust jacket lightly worn, very good.   Argonaut Book Shop   Literature 2015 - 1343   2016 $125

Moore, John *Edward. Various Views of Human Nature...* London: printed for A. Strahan and T. Cadell Jun. and W. Davies, 1796. 2 volumes, 8vo., very good, clean, contemporary marbled boards, vellum tips, ex-expertly rebacked, calf spines, double gilt bands, red morocco title labels, small circular green morocco volume numbers, armorial crest & booklabel of Thomas Hammond Foxcroft and his signature at head of each titlepage.   Jarndyce Antiquarian Booksellers   CCXVI - 415   2016   £160

Moore, John *A Sermon Preached Before the House of Lords in the Abbey Church of Westminster on Thursday Jan. 30 1777....* London: printed for J. Robson, 1777. 4to., most attractive copy, bound in near contemporary Dutch gilt floral wrappers, slight central crease, several small disposal stamps fro Lambeth Palace Library, all edges gilt.   Jarndyce Antiquarian Booksellers   CCXVI - 417   2016   £125

Moore, John *A View of the Society and Manners in Italy.* London: printed for W. Strahan and T. Cadell, 1783. Third edition, 2 volumes, 8vo., some old mottling from damp to margins of titlepages, preface leaves and a number of other pages, expertly rebound in quarter calf, raised and gilt banded spines, red morocco labels, marbled boards.   Jarndyce Antiquarian Booksellers   CCXVI - 418   2016   £250

Moore, John *A View of Society and Manners in France, Switzerland and Germany.* London: A. Strahan & T. Cadell, 1786. Sixth edition, 2 volumes, contemporary brown full calf, upper cover of volume 1 detached, joints and corners rubbed, labels chipped, internally clean.   J. & S. L. Bonham Antiquarian Booksellers   Europe 2016 - 9180   2016   £130

Moore, John A. *The Frogs of Eastern New South Wales.* New York: American Museum of Natural History, 1961. Text illustrations, wrappers.   Andrew Isles Natural History Books   55 - 7398   2016 $60

Moore, Joshua J. *The Traveller's Directory or a Pocket Companion...* Philadelphia: Mathew Carey, 1802. First edition, 8vo. 38 engraved strip maps on 22 plates, later cloth backed boards, half title and title darkened and slightly soiled, text lightly foxed and with minor offsetting of maps, as always with this book, good plus. Joseph J. Felcone, Inc. Books from Five Centuries: a Miscellany - 104 2016 $8500

Moore, Marianne 1887-1972 *The Arctic Ox.* London: Faber and Faber, 1964. First edition, one of 1500 copies, presentation copy inscribed by author for Elizabeth Mayer, 8vo., original cloth, dust jacket, light offsetting from binding adhesive on rear free endpaper, else very fine in jacket. James S. Jaffe Rare Books Occasional List: Winter 2016 - 99 2016 $850

Moore, Marianne 1887-1972 *Eight Poems.* New York: Museum of Modern Art, 1962. Limited to 195 numbered copies, 4to., original cloth, backed boards, publisher's slipcase, very fine, publisher's prospectus laid in, lacking erratum slip. James S. Jaffe Rare Books Occasional List: Winter 2016 - 98 2016 $500

Moore, Marianne 1887-1972 *Le Mariage.* New York: Ibex Press, 1965. First edition, one of 26 lettered copies from a total edition of 50 copies, 12mo., original unprinted wrappers, illustrated dust jacket by Laurence Scott, publisher's printed envelope, presentation inscribed by author for Glenway Wescott, binding adhesive lightly offset to spine portion of jacket, otherwise fine in lightly toned and dust soiled publisher's envelope, scarce. James S. Jaffe Rare Books Occasional List: Winter 2016 - 100 2016 $1250

Moore, Marianne 1887-1972 *Collected Poems.* New York: Macmillan Co., 1951. First edition, American issue, 8vo., original reddish orange cloth, dust jacket, errata sheet tipped to page 9, one of 1500 copies printed (out of total printing of 5000 copies), presentation inscribed by author for Katherine Anne Porter, Dec. 3 1951, covers bit splayed, small photo of Moore affixed to front pastedown, otherwise very good in jacket (spine tanned with few small chips and split along spine gold). James S. Jaffe Rare Books Occasional List: Winter 2016 - 97 2016 $2250

Moore, Raymond C. *Treatise on Invertebrate Paleontology part R: Arthropoda volume four (Crustacea).* Lawrence: University of Kansas, 1969. Octavo, 2 volumes, text illustrations, very good in cloth binding, signed by author for Edgar Riek. Andrew Isles Natural History Books 55 - 20337 2016 $250

Moore, Samuel *An Accurate System of Surveying... the Whole Being Performed without the Use of Scale and Compasses or a Table of Logarithums.* Litchfield: T. Collins, 1796. First edition, 8vo., illustrations, contemporary unlettered sheep, spine rubbed, browned. M & S Rare Books, Inc. 99 - 188 2016 $725

Moore, Samuel *Melodies, Songs, Sacred Songs and National Arts.* New York: George Long, 1821. First American edition, old calf, rubbed, 16mo. M & S Rare Books, Inc. 99 - 189 2016 $125

Moore, Suzanne *A Musings.* Vashon Island: 2015. Artist's Book, one of 26 copies, all on Rives BFK paper and Revere papers, lettered A to Z, signed and dated by artist, page size 9 x 15 inches, bound by artist, painted maized colored Magnani paper with letter "A" tooled in silver and gold gilt on front panel, rather abstract as if assemblage of bamboo, paper portfolio to house book, titlepage extends across two pages and features a large script A followed by smaller printed MUSINGS, separated by gold gilt dot, designed, hand lettered and painted and collaged, printed monotype debossed and handcut by artist with handset type composition and letterpress printing by Jessica Spring at Springtide Press, each page an original composition capable of standing on its own. Priscilla Juvelis - Rare Books 66 - 9 2016 $1100

Moore, Thomas *Letters and Journals of Lord Byron with Notices of His Life.* London: John Murray, 1830. First edition, 273 x 216mm., 2 volumes, especially pleasing contemporary deep blue half roan over marbled boards, spines attractively gilt in compartments with fleuron centerpieces and entwined vines filling corners, gilt titling, marbled endpapers and edges, frontispiece in volume 1, front pastedown with armorial bookplate of Robert Dillon, 3rd Baron Clonbrook (1807-93), hint of rubbing to leather, paper boards, very faintly chafed, one small marginal wax spot, exceptionally fine, clean, smooth and bright internally and in virtually unworn decorated period binding. Phillip J. Pirages 67 - 83 2016 $950

Moore, Thomas *Tom Crib's Memorial to Congress.* New York: For Kirk and Mercein, etc, William A. Mercein,, 1819. First American edition, later half morocco, nice, tight copy with half title, scarce edition. Joseph J. Felcone, Inc. Books from Five Centuries: a Miscellany - 27 2016 $400

Moore, Thomas Sturge 1870-1944 *Corregio.* London: Duckworth, 1906. First edition, octavo, plates, endpapers little spotted, small nick at outer edge of front free endpaper, very good. Peter Ellis 112 - 262 2016 £35

Moore, Thomas Sturge 1870-1944 *The Little School a Posy of Rhymes.* Eragny Press, 1905. First edition, one of 175 copies of an edition of 185, printed on handmade paper, 4 wood engravings by author, decorative wood engraved capitals throughout by Lucien Pissaro, press device printed in green, 16mo., original quarter pale grey boards, cracking to front joint, front cover lettered gilt (oxidised), green patterned boards, browning to free endpapers, good. Blackwell's Rare Books B184 - 255 2016 £450

Moorehead, Alan *The White Nile.* London: Hamish Hamilton, 1900. First edition, octavo, plates and endpaper maps, edges very slightly spotted, very good in dust jacket slightly rubbed at top edge.   Peter Ellis   112 - 261   2016   £25

Moorehead, Warren K. *The Bird-Stone Ceremonial.* Saranac Lake: 1899. One of 600 copies privately printed, large 4to., illustrations, plate, wrappers, very fine, fresh, from the library of antiquarian Hiram E. Deats.   Joseph J. Felcone, Inc.   Books from Five Centuries: a Miscellany - 105   2016 $450

Moral Precepts. Dampur: published under the patronage of His Majesty the King of Oude, 1834. 24mo., lithographed throughout, original red morocco, singl gilt fillet on sides, slip-in case of same material, edges gilt, upper cover and one side of slip-in case faded, good, of exceptional rarity.   Blackwell's Rare Books   B184 - 65   2016   £900

More, Hannah   1745-1833 *Essays on Various Subjects...* Edinburgh: Oliver & Boyd, circa, 1810. New edition, 24mo., half title, frontispiece, additional engraved title, contemporary green calf, rubbed, lacking title label, contemporary inscription.   Jarndyce Antiquarian Books   CCXV - 322   2016   £25

More, Hannah   1745-1833 *Essays on Various Subjects, Principally Designed for Young Ladies.* London: Sharpe and Hailes, 1810. Contemporary panelled calf, gilt spine, borders and dentelles, black leather label, small chip at head of spine, small wormhole at lower leading hinge, some rubbing, good plus copy.   Jarndyce Antiquarian Books   CCXV - 321   2016   £45

More, Hannah   1745-1833 *An Estimate of the Religion of the Fashionable World.* London: T. Cadell, 1793. Fifth edition, 8vo., very slight worm damage in lower margins of prelims bound without half title but with ad leaf, contemporary tree calf, spine gilt in compartments, red label, slight rubbing, armorial bookplate of William Anthony Glynn, nice copy.   Jarndyce Antiquarian Booksellers   CCXVI - 419   2016   £65

More, Hannah   1745-1833 *Moral Sketches of Prevailing Opinions and Manners.* London: T. Cadell & W. Davies, 1819. Second edition, some slight foxing, marbled boards, excellently rebacked in half brown calf, spine tooled gilt and blind, very good.   Jarndyce Antiquarian Books   CCXV - 323   2016   £120

More, Hannah   1745-1833 *Strictures on the Modern System of Female Education.* London: printed for T. Cadell Jun. and W. Davies, 1799. Second edition, 2 volumes, handsomely bound in full tree calf, spines ruled and decorated gilt, red and black morocco labels, some slight rubbing, but very good, attractive copy, inscription.   Jarndyce Antiquarian Books   CCXV - 864 2016   £280

More, Hannah   1745-1833 *Thoughts on the Importance of the Manners of the Great to General Society.* London: printed for T. Cadell, 1788. First edition, 8vo., slight foxing to final page, half red morocco with gilt ruled spine.   Jarndyce Antiquarian Books   CCXV - 324   2016 £180

More, Hannah   1745-1833 *Thoughts on the Importance of the Manners of the Great to General Society.* London: printed for T. Cadell, 1788. Fifth edition, half title, 8vo., expertly rebound in half calf, gilt ruled spine, red morocco label, very good.   Jarndyce Antiquarian Books   CCXV - 325   2016   £125

More, Henry *Enchiridion Ethicum, Praecipua Moralis Rhilosophiae Rudimenta Complectens Illustrata Utplurimum Veterum Monumentis...* London: J. Downing, 1711. Fourth edition, 8vo. engraved portrait, frontispiece trimmed, contemporary blind tooled calf, rebacked, 4 raised bands, gilt title, new endleaves, signature of Edmund Quincey 1718, donor's note (to Jeremiah Dummer, (Silversmith) dated 1718, signatures of 'William B. Calhoun', foxing, some leaves toned, marginal pen lines, title + first leaf perforated and embossed, very good.   Jeff Weber Rare Books   181 - 23   2016 $295

More, Thomas   1478-1535 *De Optimo Republicae Statu, Deque Nova Insula Utopia...* Hanover: printed by Hans Jacob Henne for Peter Kopf, 1613. Relatively early edition, woodcut printer's device on top edge gilt, slightly soiled, occasional minor browning, 12mo., contemporary? English calf, double blind ruled borders on sides, blind ruled compartments on spine, spine slightly rubbed, lacking pastedown, good.   Blackwell's Rare Books   Marks of Genius - 29   2016   £1200

Moreas, Jean *Ausgewalte Gedichte.* Frankfurt am Main: Trajanus Presse n.d. but circa, 1979. Limited to 100 numbered copies, small folio, paper covered boards, top edge cut, other edges uncut, cover illustration and five signed original etchings in text by Willy Meyer-Osburg, covers lightly soiled.   Oak Knoll Books   310 - 167   2016 $650

Morehouse, Ward *Miss Quis.* New York: Random House, 1937. Special edition, 1/150 copies, signed by Morehouse, very good in chipped and little soiled dust jacket, 8vo.   Second Life Books, Inc.   196 B - 260   2016 $50

Moreland, Arthur *Dickens Landmarks in London.* London: Cassell & Co., 1931. 4to., half title, illustrations, original orange printed boards, very good.   Jarndyce Antiquarian Booksellers CCXVIII - 1385   2016   £40

Morell, Thomas *Thesaurus Graecae Poeseros; sive Lexicon Graeco-Prosodiacum Versus et Synonyma....* Etonae: Ex Typographia et Impensis Josephi Pote, Bibliopolae, 1762. First edition, large 4to., frontispiece, but lacking half title (with bookseller's catalog to verso), titlepage in red and black with engraved vignette, light sporadic foxing, some leaves little yellowed, slightly later half dark brown calf with marbled paper covered boards, neatly rebacked with spine retained, raised band, gilt title to spine, corners reinforced, edges sprinkled reddish brown, rubbed, some loss of surface pattern to marbled pages, edges worn, endpapers little dusty with short closed tear to f.f.e.p., but sound and very good overall, bookplate of Stanley family, Earls of Derby.   Unsworths Antiquarian Booksellers   30 - 110   2016   £225

Morford, Henry *John Jasper's Secret.*   London: Pub. Offices No. 342 Strand, 1872, i.e. Oct., 1871-. May 1872. First edition, original 8 monthly parts, as issued, 20 inserted plates, collates complete per Sadleir, except with the two leaf 'sewing machine' in beginning of Part VI instead of Part V, original blue green printed wrappers, text and plates exceptionally clean and bright, wrappers slightly chipped, page 252 mispaginated 521, professioanal restoration to cover with upper right corner replaced from another part to first few leaves of part V, sharp, fresh set of very rare parts issue of this, housed in custom quarter morocco clamshell gilt stamped.   Heritage Book Shop   Holiday 2015 - 29   2016 $4000

Morford, Henry *John Jasper's Secret....*   London: publishing Offices no. 142 Strand, 1872. First UK edition, frontispiece and plates, contemporary half purple morocco by Root & Son, spine with floral devices in gilt, leading hinge little worn with small split at head, marbled boards, slightly rubbed, original blue part wrapper bound in at end, along with original ads, front wrapper to part IV dampstained, otherwise very good.   Jarndyce Antiquarian Booksellers CCXVIII - 660   2016   £280

Morford, Henry *John Jasper's Secret....*   London: Publishing Offices No. 342, Strand, 1872. First edition, frontispiece and plates, little foxed, contemporary half dark green calf, spine with gilt bands and maroon leather label, near repairs to hinges.   Jarndyce Antiquarian Booksellers CCXVIII - 662   2016   £250

Morgagni, Giovanni Battista   1682-1771 *The Seats and Causes of Diseases Investigated by anatomy in Five Books.* London: printed for A. Millar & T. Cadell and Johnson and Payne, 1769. First edition in English, 3 volumes, 4to., very good++ in contemporary marbled boards, modern half leather rebacking and corners, leather spine label, gilt lettering, cover edges mild wear, scattered mild foxing, owner bookplate, handsome set.   By the Book, L. C.   45 - 19   2016 $4500

Morgagni, Giovanni Battista   1682-1771 *The Seats and Causes of Disease Investigated by Anatomy in the Books Containing a Great Variety of Dissections with Remarks.* London: for A. Millar and others, 1769. First edition in English, thick 4to., 3 volumes, recent quarter morocco and linen boards, raised bands, gilt spine lettering, lacking half title in volume one, neat repairs on verso of titlepages, light text browning, early ownership markings on title, signature of John Redman Coxe.   James Tait Goodrich   X-78 - 405   2016 $3750

Morgan, Gwenda *Wood Engravings.*   Andoversford: Whittington Press, 1985. 71/300 copies (from an edition of 335 copies), signed by artist and printed on Zerkall mould-made paper, 52 wood engravings by Gwenda Morgan, all but one printed from original wood blocks, many full page, titlepage printed in black and red, imperial 8vo., original grey cloth with wood engraving on inset label to upper board, backstrip with printed label, top edge brown, untrimmed, fine.   Blackwell's Rare Books   B186 - 348   2016   £300

Morgan, H. *Cynegetica or the Force and Pleasure of Hunting...*   London: printed for William Chetwood, 1718. First edition, frontispiece, 12mo., half vellum and marbled boards, gilt, spine gilt, black morocco label (label bit worn), fine.   C. R. Johnson Rare Book Collections   Foxon: H-P 2015 - 626h-p   2016 $6895

Morgan, Henry J. *Sketches of Celebrated Canadians and Persons Connected with Canada....*   Quebec: Hunter, Rose & Co., 1862. First edition, thick octavo, black embossed cloth, gilt lettered spine, gilt pictorial element on front cover, library stamping to top and bottom edges, minor spotting to front cover, bookplate, overall very good.   Argonaut Book Shop   Biography 2015 - 2932   2016 $125

Morgan, Kenneth *Australia Circumnavigated. The Voyage of Matthew Flinders in HMS Investigator 1801-1803.* London: Hakluyt Society, 2014. 4to., 2 volumes, new. Sotheran's   Travel and Exploration - 404   2016   £120

Morgan, Nigel *Early Gothic Manuscripts 1190-1250. With 1250-1285.*   New York: Harvey Miller Publications, 1982. 1988. First US editions, 2 volumes, tall 4to., cloth, dust jackets, 330 and 462 illustrations respectively, some in color, jacket spines faded, chipped around edges.   Oak Knoll Books   310 - 40   2016 $500

Morgan, Sydney Owenson *France.* London: Henry Colburn, 1817. First edition, 4to., 2 volumes in 1, map, contemporary diced calf, spine fully gilt in panels, edges marbled, corners worn, hinges cracked but held by cords and endpapers, light scattered foxing on few gatherings, else fine internally in very nice period binding, R. H. A. Bennet armorial bookplate.   Joseph J. Felcone, Inc.   Books from Five Centuries: a Miscellany - 107   2016 $800

Morgan, W. G. Curtis *An Oxford Romance.* Carmathen: The Druid Press, 1948. First edition, small spot at leading edge of first few leaves with smattering of very faint foxing at head of final page, foolscap 8vo., original white wrappers printed in blue, faint overall spotting, light rubbing to extremities with spine slightly cocked, good. Blackwell's Rare Books B184 - 211 2016 £50

Morgenstaler, Goldie *Dickens and Heredity...* London: Macmillan Press, 2000. Inscribed by author to Thelma Grove and with some loosely inserted correspondence, half title, original black cloth, very good in dust jacket. Jarndyce Antiquarian Booksellers CCXVIII - 1386 2016 £30

Morhof, Daniel Georg *Polyhistor, in Tres Tomos, Literarium....* Lubeck: Peter Boeckmann, 1708. First Moller edition, thick 4to., contemporary vellum, red spine label. Edwin V. Glaser Rare Books 2015 - 10138 2016 $600

Morice, Anne *Nursery, Tea and Poison.* London: Macmillan, 1975. Uncorrected proof, original wrappers in excellent condition. I. D. Edrich Crime - 2016 £20

Morier, James *The Adventures of Hajji Baba or Ispahan.* London: Richard Bentley, 1851. Half title, frontispiece, original brown cloth, small mark on front board, armorial bookplate, very good. Jarndyce Antiquarian Booksellers CCXVII - 189 2016 £45

Morison, Stanley *A Tally of Types Cut for Machine Composition and Introduced at the University Press, Cambridge 1922-1932.* Cambridge: privately printed by the University Printer, 1953. First edition, one of 4to., copies printed in black with 6 wood engraved panels by Reynolds Stone, each printed in orange a separate example of an engraving used by press heads several of chapters, each of the chapters being printed in different typeface, 8vo., original orange linen, backstrip lettered and decorated in gilt, fine. Blackwell's Rare Books B186 - 295 2016 £75

Morley, Christopher 1890-1957 *I Know a Secret.* Garden City: Doubleday Page, 1927. First edition, 8vo., author's presentation in blank, hinges tender, cover somewhat warped, otherwise very good. Second Life Books, Inc. 196 B - 264 2016 $40

Morley, Christopher 1890-1957 *Where the Blue Begins.* New York: Doubleday Page, 1922. Small 8vo., paper over boards tamed in blue, cloth spine, author's presentation, ex-library, bookplate, cover little soiled, spine little torn at top, otherwise very good. Second Life Books, Inc. 196 B - 265 2016 $45

Morley, Christopher 1890-1957 *The Worst Christmas Story.* New York: Random House, 1928. One of 365 copies signed by author and artist, large 8vo., illustrations by Marguerite Jones, red patterned paper over thin boards, paper somewhat chipped and torn, interior very good. Second Life Books, Inc. 196 B - 266 2016 $100

Morley, Henry *A Defence of Ignorance.* London: Chapman and Hall, 1851. Original royal blue cloth, slight rubbing. Jarndyce Antiquarian Books CCXV - 865 2016 £50

Morley, Robert *A Musing Morley.* London: Robson Books, 1974. First edition, 8vo., inscribed on half title by author, illustrations, fine in somewhat scuffed and soiled dust jacket. Second Life Books, Inc. 196 B - 267 2016 $45

Morrice, Bezaleel *An Essay on the Poets.* London: printed for Daniel Brown and sold by A. Baldwin, 1712. First edition, 8vo., disbound, fine, rare. C. R. Johnson Rare Book Collections Foxon: H-P 2015 - 633 2016 $3831

Morrice, Bezaleel *An Essay on the Poets.* London: printed for T. Bickerton, 1721. Third edition, 8vo., disibound, some worming in blank lower margins, otherwise very good, very rare. C. R. Johnson Rare Book Collections Foxon: H-P 2015 - 634 2016 $2298

Morrice, Bezaleel *Love and Resentment: a Pastoral.* London: printed for R. Burleigh and Arrabella Morric3e, 1717. First edition, very good, disbound, outer margin trimmed a trifle close, but very good, rare. C. R. Johnson Rare Book Collections Foxon: H-P 2015 - 635 2016 $2298

Morrice, Bezaleel *The Present State of Poetry a Satire...* London: printed and sold by J. Roberts and booksellers of London and Westminster, 1726. Second edition, 8vo., recent grey wrappers, some browning, otherwise good with small Folger duplicate stamp, rare. C. R. Johnson Rare Book Collections Foxon: H-P 2015 - 636 2016 $2298

Morrice, Bezaleel *A Voyage from the East-Indies.* London: printed and sold by Roberts, 1716. First edition, 8vo., disbound, fine, engraved frontispiece. C. R. Johnson Rare Book Collections Foxon: H-P 2015 - 637 2016 $3831

Morris, Brian *The Epiphytic Orchids of Malawi.* Malawi: The Society of Malawi, 1970. Octavo, five color plates, text illustrations, ex-library, very good in dust jacket. Andrew Isles Natural History Books 55 - 38602 2016 $60

Morris, Charles V. *B. Franklin: Innovator.* New York: privately printed, 1961. Small 8vo., illustrations by John DePol in dark green and rose, cover printed in rose with white illustration, cover bit faded at spine, slightly scuffed at corners and on interior edges, otherwise very good, tight copy. Second Life Books, Inc. 197 - 241 2016 $40

Morris, Charles V. *A Quart of Oysters and Other Bon Mots of Bon Homme Richard.* New York: privately printed, 1972. small 8vo., small illustrations and fancy capitals in maroon by John De Pol, deep yellow paper over boards stamped in gilt, top edges very slightly spotted, otherwise near fine. Second Life Books, Inc. 197 - 240 2016 $65

Morris, Corbyn *A Letter from a By-stander to a Member of Parliament...* London: printed for J. Roberts, 1742. Second edition, half title, 8vo., half title, spotted at end, disbound. Jarndyce Antiquarian Booksellers CCXVI - 420 2016 £35

Morris, Earl J. *The Cop.* New York: Exposition Press, 1951. First edition, some sunning on bottom of front board and front panel of jacket, else near fine in very good or better dust jacket with additional modest sunning on spine, warmly inscribed by author to co-worker. Between the Covers Rare Books 202 - 62 2016 $350

Morris, Francis Orpen 1810-1893 *A History of British Birds.* London: Bell and Aldy, 1870. Second edition, octavo, 6 volumes, 365 hand colored plates, publisher's handsome gilt original cloth, very good. Andrew Isles Natural History Books 55 - 20517 2016 $950

Morris, Francis Orpen 1810-1893 *History of British Butterflies.* London: John C. Nimmo, 1864. Second edition, 8vo., sometime rebound in half red morocco, marbled boards, spine with elaborate panels in blind and gilt lettering, marbled endpapers, 71 hand colored plates, 2 black and white plates, little sunning to top of upper board, very fresh internally, very good. Sotheran's Piccadilly Notes - Summer 2015 - 210 2016 £400

Morris, Francis Orpen 1810-1893 *A Series of Picturesque Views of Seats of the Noblemen and Gentlemen of Great Britain and Ireland.* London: William Mackenzie, n.d. circa, 1880. 6 volumes, 4to., color plates, few leaves loose to volumes I & VI, sporadic foxing, some text pages affected by offset browning from plates, handsome red, black and heavily gilt pictorial cloth, all edges gilt, endcaps and corners fraying, joints little rubbed, edges faded in places, endpapers bit foxed and beginning to split at upper of joints volume I, but still sound. Unsworths Antiquarian Booksellers Ltd. 30 - 111 2016 £300

Morris, Frank T. *Birds of the Australian Swamps.* Melbourne: Lansdowne Editions, 1978-1981. Folio, publisher's quarter brown calf, limited to 500 copies, numbered and signed by author, fine. Andrew Isles Natural History Books 55 - 26755 2016 $650

Morris, Hugh *How to Make Love the Secret of Wooing and Winning the One You Love.* New York: Padell Book Co., 1936. First edition, illustrations, leaves little browned, original illustrated yellow wrappers, stapled as issued, slightly dulled but nice. Jarndyce Antiquarian Books CCXV - 326 2016 £65

Morris, Jan *Hav.* Viking, 2006. First edition, 8vo., map, original black clorh, dust jacket, fine. J. & S. L. Bonham Antiquarian Booksellers Europe 2016 - 9764 2016 £25

Morris, Jan *Spain.* Barrie & Jenkins, 1988. First edition, large 8vo., illustrations, original black cloth, dust jacket. J. & S. L. Bonham Antiquarian Booksellers Europe 2016 - 9820 2016 £25

Morris, John *Traveller from Tokyo.* London: Cresset Press, 1943. First edition, octavo, very good in slightly chipped dust jacket tanned at spine, presentation from author inscribed for Clifford & Sibyl Lawton Reece, 2 Oct. 1943. Peter Ellis 112 - 193 2016 £35

Morris, Laura *What time Is It On the Sun?* Mass Moca/ Getty Foundation, 2008. First edition, quarto, yellow cloth boards with blindstamped lettering to front board and red lettering to spine, illustrated endpapers, foldout poster to reverse of f.e.p., illustrations, very good, slight soiling to board edges in slipcase, very good+. Simon Finch 2015 - 2f38a/17 2016 $262

Morris, Mart *The Norman Conquest.* London: Hutchinson, 2012. First edition, 8vo., 8 plates, boards, silver lettered, small mark to upper board, edges lightly dusted, dust jacket with minor shelfwear, very good. Unsworths Antiquarian Booksellers Ltd. E05 - 107 2016 £20

Morris, Peter M. *A Survey of Dickens' Employments.* London: Peter Morris Books, 1996. Illustrations, paperback, very good. Jarndyce Antiquarian Booksellers CCXVIII - 1387 2016 £20

Morris, R. R. *Juvenile Catechism: First Lesson for Children and Instructions in the History, Doctrines and Usages of the A. M. E. Zion Church...* Charlotte: A. M. E. Zion Publications House, circa, 1890. Revised edition, 16mo., stapled printed green wrappers, vertical crease, couple of tiny tears at edge of front wrapper, very good, very cheaply produced pamphlet, rare. Between the Covers Rare Books 207 - 25 2016 $1200

Morris, Robert *The Confidential Correspondence of Robert Morris, the Great Financier of the Revolution and Signer of the Declaration of Independence...* Philadelphia: Stan V. Henkels, 1917. First edition, small 4to., paper wrappers, Henkel's Notice tipped onto front wrapper, very good, spine ends chipped, darkened wrappers, small price stamp on front wrapper, clean contents. Kaaterskill Books 21 - 56 2016 $225

Morris, William 1834-1896 *An Address Delivered by William Morris at the Distribution of Prizes of Students of the Birmingham Municipal School of Art on February 21, 1894.* London: Longmans & Co., 1898. Exceptionally nice bound in blue paper boards with grey linen spine and title printed on cover, light wear and slight darkening to edges of boards, interior bright and clean save for offsetting to rear endpapers and few brown spots to fore edge, pages unopened. The Kelmscott Bookshop 12 - 72 2016 $150

Morris, William 1834-1896 *The Earthly Paradise.* London: Ellis and Green, 1872. Popular edition in 10 parts, 10 volumes, frontispiece volume I, original flexible blue green cloth, slight lifting in places, otherwise good plus, ownership inscribed in all volumes of Elizabeth Izou. Jarndyce Antiquarian Booksellers CCXVII - 190 2016 £125

Morris, William 1834-1896 *The Earthly Paradise.* London: Reeves and Turner, 1890. Unusual presentation copy inscribed by author for Miss Edith Lamb July 15 1891, she was the family's nurse, bound in three quarter vellum with black leather title, author and date spine labels and gilt decorated compartments, boards marbled blue, gilt and cream paper, as are the end pages bumping and some chipping to top of boards and spine and along edge of rear board, vellum has light smudging, paper boards have faded, interior very good, housed in modern white cloth clamshell box, very good. The Kelmscott Bookshop 12 - 73 2016 $2200

Morris, William 1834-1896 *Gothic Architecture: a Lecture for the Arts and Crafts Exhibition Society.* Hammersmith: Kelmscott Press 1893, One of 1500 copies on paper (and 45 on vellum), 146 x 108mm., original holland backed blue paper boards, woodcut initials and small woodcut decorations in text, headlines and sidenotes printed in red; tiny tears to spine ends, otherwise very fine, binding remarkably clean and text showing signs of use. Phillip J. Pirages 67 - 222 2016 $1100

Morris, William 1834-1896 *News from Nowhere; or an Epoch of Reset, Being Some chapters from a Utopian Romance.* London: Reeves & Turner, 1891. No. 1 of 250 large paper copies, first British edition, 8vo. original blue-gray paper boards with Japanese paper spine, spine quite browned and bumped and label has half inch tear on its upper left corner, joints somewhat rubbed, free endpages have light outlines of what looks like scotch tape, and their may have been a bookplate removed from front pastedown, light browning to rear endpapers, save for browning along uncut edges of fore-edge, interior pages bright and clean, printed on high quality French paper, binding tight except for an old gap at bottom of gathering between pages 96 and 97, gatherings firmly attached, small section of binding material visible, despite these flaws, very good. The Kelmscott Bookshop 12 - 74 2016 $595

Morris, William 1834-1896 *A Note by William Morris on his Aims in Founding the Kelmscott Press Together with a Short Description of the Press by S. C. Cockerell...* Hammersmith: Kelmscott Press, 1898. One of 525 copies on paper (and 12 on vellum), 210 x 150mm., original holland backed gray boards, very nice folding box covered with navy blue cloth, spine with morocco label reading "C. H. St.. J. H./ S. C. C./ W.M.", elaborate borders around frontispiece and first page of text, frontispiece drawn by Edward Burne-Jones and cut by William Morris, large decorative woodcut initials, device on last page of text and one full page woodcut of ornaments used in Kelmscott edition of "Love is Enough", printed in red and red black, bookplate of Charles Harry St. John Hornby, presentation from Cockerell to Hornby and his wife as well as tipped-on letter to Hornby, describing, this work, rear pastedown with clipped signature of William Morris pasted down, pristine. Phillip J. Pirages 67 - 221 2016 $19,500

Morris, William 1834-1896 *Socialism, Its Growth and Outcome.* London and New York: Swan Sonnenschein & Co./Charles Scribner's, 1893. First edition, large paper edition, limited to 275 copies, 8vo., original buckram with printed label on spine, top of spine rubbed, spine lightly faded, else very good. James S. Jaffe Rare Books Occasional List: Winter 2016 - 101 2016 $350

Morris, William 1834-1896 *The Sundering Flood.* Hammersmith: Kelmscott Press, 1897. 1 of 300 copies, 10 other copies printed on vellum, pages printed in Chaucer type on Flower paper, text printed in black with red chapter titles and shoulder notes, beautiful borders and initials designed by Morris, quarter holland blue paper with modern white linen spine and modern paper title label, light rubbing to boards and slight browning to edges as is common, light scuff mark to front cover and small dampstain along top edge of rear cover, corners worn and lightly bumped, very lightly foxing to rear endpages and few small spots of foxing to few interior pages but overall, interior remains very clean, original pastedown with map illustration, very good. The Kelmscott Bookshop 12 - 60 2016 $1800

Morris, William 1834-1896 *The Tale of the Emperor Coustans and of Over the Sea.* Hammersmith: Kelmscott Press, 1894. One of 525 copies on paper (and 20 on vellum), 150 x 110mm., original holland backed blue gray paper boards, untrimmed edges, boarders of twining leaves and grape clusters around each of the two full page woodcuts as well as on first page of text of both stories, woodcut foliated three-line initials, rubrics to every page; armorial bookplate bearing Pepperell coat of arms, two tiny white spots to upper board, just hint of soil to covers, otherwise very fine, binding unworn and especially clean, fresh and bright internally.   Phillip J. Pirages   67 - 223   2016 $1750

Morris, William 1834-1896 *The Tale of the Emperor Coustans and of Over Sea.* Hammersmith: Kelmscott Press, 1894. Limited to 545 copies, this being one of 525 paper copies, 32mo., quarter cloth, paper covered boards, edges uncut, 3 and 6 line initials, shoulder notes and some lines, in red, covers lightly soiled, slightly scuffed at lower fore-edge corners, previous owner's bookplate, foxing on endpapers.   Oak Knoll Books   310 - 1   2016 $2250

Morris, Willie *A Prayer for the Opening of the Little League Season.* New York: Harcourt Brace, 1996. Limited to 300 copies, this E4, illustrations by Barry Moser, fine, signed by author and artist.   Bella Luna Books   2016 - t13105   2016 $132

Morris, Wright *Cause for Wonder.* New York: Atheneum, 1963. First edition, brown cloth, lettered gilt on spine, minor foxing to spine and upper edge of covers, fore-edge lightly foxed, else fine in dust jacket.   Argonaut Book Shop   Literature 2015 - 6861   2016 $75

Morris, Wright *Collected Stories 1948-1986.* New York: Harper & Row, 1986. First edition, blue cloth, silver lettering to spine, offsetting to front endpaper, very small puncture to dust jacket, fine in fine dust jacket.   Argonaut Book Shop   Literature 2015 - 6869   2016 $50

Morrison, Alex *The Breed of Manly Men: The History of the Cape Breton Highlanders.* Sydney: published by authors, 1994. red cloth boards, gilt to front and spine in dust jacket, photos illustrations, previous owner's name written on endpaper, generally very good.   Schooner Books Ltd.   115 - 223   2016 $40

Morrison, Arthur *Martin Hewitt Investigator.* London: Ward Lock & Bowden, 1895. Second edition, illustrations by Sidney Paget, little light rubbing, very good in original pictorial boards, gilt, very uncommon in early editions.   I. D. Edrich   Crime - 2016   £150

Morrison, C. T. *The Flame of the Icebox: an Episode of the Vietnam War.* New York: Exposition Press, 1968. First edition, owner's stamp, else fine in fine dust jacket with just touch of rubbing, very uncommon.   Between the Covers Rare Books   207 - 68   2016 $275

Morrison, Thomas *Manual of School Management for the Use of Teachers, Students and Pupil Teachers.* Glasgow: Wm. Hamilton, 1868. Third edition, Original purple cloth, very good.   Jarndyce Antiquarian Books   CCXV - 866   2016   £38

Morrison, Toni *The Bluest Eye.* London: Chatto & Windus, 1979. First British edition, 8vo., signed by author, near fine in in fine dust jacket.   By the Book, L. C.   45 - 68   2016 $850

Morrison, Toni *Jazz.* Franklin Center: Franklin Library, 1992. Limited first edition signed by author, purple leather, lettered and decoratively stamped in gilt, all edges gilt, very fine, as new, extremely handsome edition.   Argonaut Book Shop   Literature 2015 - 3996   2016 $175

Morrison, Toni *Love.* New York: Knopf, 2003. First edition, 8vo., author's signature on title, maroon cloth, nice in very slightly soiled dust jacket.   Second Life Books, Inc.   196 B - 272   2016 $75

Morrison, Toni *Paradise.* New York: Alfred A. Knopf, 1998. Stated 'Second Printing Before Publication", black cloth with gilt lettering and front cover, fine with fine pictorial dust jacket with Oprah's Book Club sticker on front cover, publisher's bookplate signed by author laid in.   Argonaut Book Shop   Literature 2015 - 5591   2016 $40

Morrison, Toni *Paradise.* New York: Knopf, 1998. First edition, 8vo., black cloth, author's signature on bookplate, fine in dust jacket.   Second Life Books, Inc.   196 B - 269   2016 $75

Morrison, Toni *Sula.* New York: Knopf, 1976. Fifth printing, 8vo., author's presentation on flyleaf, small stain on flyleaf, black cloth, very good, tight in somewhat chipped and faded dust jacket.   Second Life Books, Inc.   196 B - 271   2016 $75

Morshead, O. F. *Everybody's Pepys. the Diary of Samuel Pepys.* London: G. Bell and Sons, 1926. First edition illustrated thus, thick 8vo., newly and handsomely bound in half dark blue calf over dark blue polished cloth boards, spine with 5 raised bands, ruled and lettered gilt with gilt centres, top edges gilt, original pictorial cloth cover, 2 double page map endpapers, expertly rebacked, fine, line illustrations by E. H. Shepard.   Sotheran's   Piccadilly Notes - Summer 2015 - 234   2016   £188

Mortensen, Greg *Three Cups of Tea.* New York: Viking, 2006. First edition and a copy of the advance reading copy, 2 volumes, signed by Mortenson (advance reading copy signed by Mortenson and Relin), the first edition fine in fine dust jacket with tick and program for Mortenson reading of the sequel laid in, each book in custom clamshell case.   Ken Lopez Bookseller   166 - 86   2016 $1000

Mortensen, Greg *Three Cups of Tea.* New York: Viking, 2006. 10th printing, illustrations, signed by Mortenson and David Oliver, scarce thus, fine in dust jacket.   Gene W. Baade, Books on the West   2015 - SHEL787   2016 $75

Mortimer-Granville, Joseph *Youth: Its Care and Culture.* London: David Bogue, 1880. Half title, 1 page initial ads, 22 page catalog, original decorated brown cloth, leading hinge slightly cracking.   Jarndyce Antiquarian Books CCXV - 327   2016   £35

Mortimer, J. *The Whole Art of Husbandry...* London: printed by J. H. for J. Mortlock and J. Robinson, 1708. Second edition, 8vo., some woodcut illustrations in text, little toned towards edges, occasional spots and stains, one or two small annotations, recently rebound in half brown cloth with marbled paper covered boards, red cloth and gilt label to spine, endpapers renewed, very good, sound copy, recent bookplate of Brian Fortune.   Unsworths Antiquarian Booksellers Ltd.   30 - 112   2016   £250

Mortimer, Raymond *Channel Packet.* London: Hogarth Press, 1942. First edition, octavo, fine in very good dust jacket, slightly nicked and creased at edges, presentation copy inscribed by author for John (Lehmann), managing director of Hogarth Press.   Peter Ellis   112 - 264   2016   £150

Mortimer, Ruth *Catalogue of Books and Manuscripts Part I: French 16th Century Books.* Cambridge: Belknap Press of Harvard University Press, 1964. 2 volumes, 4to., cloth, slipcase cracked along hinge.   Oak Knoll Books   310 - 258   2016 $375

Moscicki, Henryk *Wilno. Fotografje J. Bulhaka.* Warsaw: P. Hoesicki and J. Zawadzki in Vilnius, 1922. First edition, very rare, 8vo., contemporary linen backed cloth covered boards, illustrated front wrapper bound in, photogravure plates on 16 leaves, printed on both sides, photographic frontispiece, illustrations after photo pasted in at end as tailpiece, shelfmark stamped in black on spine and in ink at foot of half title, otherwise very good.   Sotheran's Travel and Exploration - 222   2016   £498

Mosel, Ariene *The Funny Little Woman.* New York: Dutton, 1972. Stated first edition, fine in dust jacket with seal and some soil, color illustrations by Blair Lent, laid in are 2 letters by Lent.   Aleph-bet Books, Inc.   112 - 291   2016 $475

Mosely, Alfred *Reports of the Mosely Education Commission to the United States of America, October - December 1903.* London: published for the proprietor by the Co-operative Printing Society, 1904. Plates, slight paper browning, original dark green cloth, library marks on spine, from the Library of Faculty of Physicians and Surgeons, Glasgow.   Jarndyce Antiquarian Books   CCXV - 867   2016   £25

Moser, Barry *Fifty Wood Engravings.* Northampton: Pennyroyal Press, 1978. No. 24 of 100 copies signed by artist, 575 x 445mm., unbound as issued in linen chemise and portfolio backed with mahogany morocco by E. Gray Parrot, 50 wood engravings on 38 plates, mint.   Phillip J. Pirages   67 - 278   2016 $2400

Mosley, Walter *Always Outnumbered, Always Outgunned.* New York: Norton, 1998. First printing, 8vo., author's signature on title, paper over boards, fine, dust jacket with booksellers sticker on front, fine.   Second Life Books, Inc.   196 B - 276   2016 $75

Mosley, Walter *Blue Light.* Boston: Little Brown, 1998. First edition, 8vo., author's presentation, paper over boards, about as new in dust jacket.   Second Life Books, Inc.   196 B - 277   2016 $75

Mosley, Walter *Devil in a Blue Dress.* New York: Norton, 1990. First printing, 8vo., author's signature on half title, paper over boards with cloth spine, nice, as new, except for bookseller's label on front of dust jacket, fine.   Second Life Books, Inc.   196 B - 278   2016 $300

Mosley, Walter *Fearless Jones.* Boston: Little Brown, 2001. First printing, 8vo., author's signature on title, paper over boards, dust jacket, fine.   Second Life Books, Inc.   196 B - 279   2016 $75

Mosley, Walter *Gone Fishin'.* Baltimore: Black Classic Press, 1997. Limited edition, 1/1000 copies, although publisher says less were distributed, 8vo., black cloth with paper label on front, author's signature, issued without dust jacket, fine, as new.   Second Life Books, Inc.   196 B - 280   2016 $700

Mosley, Walter *Life Out of Context.* New York: Nation Books, 2006. First Printing, 8vo., author's presentation to Katherine Tarr, paper wrappers, near fine.   Second Life Books, Inc.   196 B - 281   2016 $75

Mosley, Walter *RL's Dream.* New York: Norton, 1995. First printing, 8vo., author's signature on half title, paper boards with cloth spine, dust jacket, near fine.   Second Life Books, Inc.   196 B - 282   2016 $125

Moss, Arthur B. *The Workman's Foe.* London: Watts & Co., 1898? Presentation copy inscribed by author for Joseph Fay 25 June 98, brown cloth with titles and author in gilt to cover and original wrappers bound in, waterstaining on pastedowns and free endpapers, partially affecting inscription, some pages loose and paper has browned, cloth binding slightly rubbed and worn, very good given fragility of the items.   The Kelmscott Bookshop   12 - 75   2016 $750

Moss, Graham *Bookplates of Enid Marx.* Oldham: Incline Press, 1997. 70/150 copies signed by author, printed on handmade paper, 10 tipped in plates with 8 wood engraved and the remainder drawn, foolscap 8vo., original sewn plain wrappers, edge sun trimmed, dust jacket, printed label to front, press prospectus loosely inserted, fine. Blackwell's Rare Books   B186 - 314   2016   £80

Moss, Howard *Buried City.* New York: Atheneum, 1975. First edition, inscribed and signed by poet for William Meredith, near fine in fine dust jacket.   Charles Agvent   William Meredith - 85   2016 $130

Moss, Howard *A Swimmer in the Air: Poems.* New York: Charles Scribner's Sons, 1957. First edition, inscribed by the poet for William Meredith, fine in near fine dust jacket.   Charles Agvent   William Meredith - 87   2016 $150

Moss, Howard *A Swim off the Rocks. Light Verse.* New York: Atheneum, 1978. First edition, pictorial wrappers, inscribed by poet on front endpaper for William Meredith, fine.   Charles Agvent   William Meredith - 86   2016 $50

Moss, Sidney P. *American Episodes Invovling Charles Dickens.* London: Whitston Pub. Co., 1999. First edition, half title illustrations, original dark blue cloth, inscribed and signed by authors, mint in dust jacket.   Jarndyce Antiquarian Booksellers   CCXVIII - 1390   2016   £20

Moss, Sidney P. *The Charles Dickens - Thomas Powell Vendetta the story of Documents.* Troy: Whiston Pub. Co., 1996. First edition, half title, illustrations, original red cloth, inscribed by authors to unidentified recipient, very good in dust jacket.   Jarndyce Antiquarian Booksellers   CCXVIII - 1389   2016   £25

Mostel, Zero *Zero by Mostel.* New York: Horizon, 1965. First edition, 4to., presentation by Max Waldman, many photos of Mostel in pantomine and section on his role as Tevye in Fiddler, drawings by Mosel and interview, very good in chipped and soiled dust jacket.   Second Life Books, Inc.   196 B - 284   2016 $60

Mostyn, John *History and Antiquities of the County of Norfolk.* Norwich: printed for J. Crouse for M. Booth, Bookseller, 1781. 10 volumes, 8vo., plates, sporadic foxing occasionally becoming heavy, some offsetting from plates, closd tear to page 27 volume VIII repaired with tape, some library stamps, contemporary lightly speckled brown calf, neatly rebacked, spines gilt with burgundy straight grain morocco labels and darker brown calf onlays to alternate compartments, lower board of volumes III and IX covered with tan cloth, gilt single line borders, some corners reinforced, edges sprinkled grey and red, replacement marbled endpapers, edges rubbed, few chips and scratches, very good overall, bookseller's annotations to front of volume IV notes lack of appendix to North Greenhoe section, inkstamps of Richmond Free Public Library, Surrey to titlepages, front and rear of each section and plates, bookseller's collation notes.   Unsworths Antiquarian Booksellers   30 - 7   2016   £600

Mother Goose *Bo-Peep Rhymes.* London: Dean, circa, 1938. Pictorial cloth, as new, Dean's Rag book 336, charming color illustrations by Margaret Ethel Banks, well printed, great copy.   Aleph-bet Books, Inc.   111 - 299   2016 $150

Mother Goose *The Golden Mother Goose ABC.* Cincinnati: Peter G. Thomson, 1885. 4to., flexible card wrappers, neat spine, strengthening near fine, 8 superb color lithographs highlighted in gold by Walter Stranders plus great color covers, quite scarce.   Aleph-bet Books, Inc.   112 - 6   2016 $475

Mother Goose *The History of Old Mother Goose and Golden Egg.* Baltimore: William Raine, n.d. circa, 1840. 12mo., green pictorial wrappers, neat obtrusive spine strengthening else very good+, excellent copy.   Aleph-bet Books, Inc.   112 - 164   2016 $600

Mother Goose *Jolly Rhymes of Mother Goose.* Platt & Munk, 1941. Housed in publisher's pictorial box, 5 Mother Goose books bound in pictorial wrappers, illustrations.   Aleph-bet Books, Inc.   112 - 290   2016 $275

Mother Goose *Little Mother Goose.* New York: McBride Nast, 1915. 4to., boards, pictorial paste-on, fine in rare pictorial dust jacket (chipped, missing large piece off front panel), 16 color plates by Willy Pogany and in brown line on every page, incredibly rare in dust jacket.   Aleph-bet Books, Inc.   111 - 345   2016 $900

Mother Goose *Mother Goose.* New York: McLoughlin Bros, 1895. Folio, pictorial card covers, die-cut in shape of Mother Goose, sight spine rubbing, else very good+, fabulous color cover, 4 pages have great chromolithographs and 10 remaining pages have charming line illustrations.   Aleph-bet Books, Inc.   111 - 303   2016 $325

Mother Goose *Mother Goose.* Akron: Saalfield, 1910. Narrow 4to., cloth, cover margin crease, else very good-fine, bright color illustrations on every page and printed on cloth. Aleph-bet Books, Inc.   111 - 301   2016 $275

Mother Goose *Mother Goose.* Chicago: Volland, 1915. First edition arranged by Eulalie Grover, Folio, blue gilt cloth, pictorial paste-on, fine in original box (flaps repaired, else very good), magnificently illustrated by Frederick Richardson, with colored full page illustrations on every page, wonderful copy.   Aleph-bet Books, Inc.   111 - 304   2016 $1200

Mother Goose *Mother Goose.* New York: Oxford University Press, 1944. Limited to only 500 copies for private distribution, signed by artist, Tasha Tudor, cloth, fine in dust jacket (chips of spine ends, else very good), illustrations on every page by Tudor, most in full color, with letter from publisher presenting the book.   Aleph-bet Books, Inc.   111 - 461   2016 $1500

Mother Goose *Mother Goose Book.* London: Frederick Warne, n.d. circa, 1905. Red and salmon colored cloth stamped in brown, pictorial paste-on, pages mounted on cloth, fine+ condition, publisher's file copy so stamped, printed on one side of page, 8 full page chromolithographs and many color illustrations in text pages as well.   Aleph-bet Books, Inc.   112 - 323   2016 $600

Mother Goose *Mother Goose in Hieroglyphics.* New York: Sherman & Co., 1855. Nice early edition, Oblong 8vo., gilt and blindstamped flexible cloth covers, occasional spot, very good+, 12 nice cuts replacing words, nearly 400 cuts in total.   Aleph-bet Books, Inc.   112 - 322   2016 $200

Mother Goose *Mother Goose Nursery Rhymes.* London: Raphael Tuck, n.d. circa, 1915. 4to., cloth backed pictorial boards, tips and edges rubbed, else very good+, pages on thin boards, featuring 16 fine full page color illustrations by Lucie Mabel Attwell.   Aleph-bet Books, Inc.   112 - 36   2016 $750

Mother Goose *Mother Goose Rhymes.* London: Dent, circa, 1915. Pictorial cloth, as new, Dean's Rag book 118 with color illustrations by Dorothy Goddard, great copy. Aleph-bet Books, Inc.   111 - 300   2016 $150

Mother Goose *Mother Goose: the Old Nursery Rhymes.* London: Heinemann, 1913. First edition, limited to 1130 numbered copies signed by Rackham, original white gilt pictorial cloth, top edge gilt, few light marks on cover and spine toned as is common, else very good, fine, tight and clean with no foxing, 13 fabulous tipped-in color plates, mounted on heavy paper plus a profusion of beautiful black and whites, nice.   Aleph-bet Books, Inc.   112 - 416   2016 $2850

Mother Goose *Mother Goose's Rag Book.* London: Dean, n.d. circa, 1918. 4to., cloth, small tan spot on edge of some pages, near fine, brightly colored illustrations by Hilda Cowham.   Aleph-bet Books, Inc.   112 - 325   2016 $300

Motley. An Ephemeral Magazine. Number II, July 10th, 1933. First edition, 17 plates, original grey wrappers printed in red, backstrip little rubbed, some loss and splitting at tips, creasing to corners, good.   Blackwell's Rare Books   B184 - 122   2016   £400

Mott, Abigail *Observations on the Importance of Female Education and Maternal Instruction with Their Beneficial Influence on Society.* New York: printed and sold by Mahlon Day, 1825. First edition, 12mo., old boards, detached, title loose, printed copyright slip pasted to verso of title leaf, printed early bookplate of Susan Bell.   M & S Rare Books, Inc.   99 - 338   2016 $1250

Mottistone, John Edward Bernard Seely, 1st Baron *My Horse Warrior.* London: Hodder & Stoughton, 1934. First edition, small 4to., original light blue cloth pictorially decorated and lettered in black, double page pictorial endpapers, preserved in original pictorial dust jacket, full and double page plates in monochrome by Alfred Munning, externally near fine with very weak vertical crease to spine, internally near fine with only faint foxing to endpapers, protected by the scarce, unclipped dust jacket in remarkably clean and complete state, with some light dust soiling, especially to spine panel, rubbing to folds, small triangular loss to heel of spine and small chipping at head and edges with near old tape repairs to reverse.   Sotheran's   Piccadilly Notes - Summer 2015 - 321   2016   £650

Moule, Arthur E. *The Glorious Land Short Chapters on China and Missionary Work There.* London: Church Missionary Society, 1891. First edition, 8vo., original cloth, gilt, folding map as frontispiece, illustrations in text, partial browning to map, else very good.   Sotheran's Travel and Exploration - 157   2016   £198

Moule, Arthur E. *The Story of the Cheh-Kiang Mission of the Church Missionary Society.* London: Church Missionary Society, 1891. 8vo., original pictorial cloth, one folding map, wood engraved illustrations, presentation for Millie Ashe, from author Christmas 1895, very good.   Sotheran's Travel and Exploration - 158   2016   £348

Moule, Thomas *Great Britain Illustrated.* London: Charles Tilt, 1830. First edition in book form, striking, contemporary embossed 'Relievo' burgundy morocco by Remnant & Edmonds (their stamp), covers densely patterned with three very complex foliate frames around a central medallion featuring the muses Erato, Calliope and Euterpe, flat spine with gilt titling at head and an elaborate embossed pattern below, turn-ins with floral gilt roll all edges gilt, extra engraved titlepage with vignette and 118 engraved views on 59 plates by William Westall, as called for, original tissue guards, front pastedown with armorial bookplate of William Perceval, majority of plates with minor foxing and offsetting (two or three engravings foxed, bit more, engraved title and facing page rather noticeably affected), spine slightly and uniformly sunned, joints with vaguest hint of rubbing but text especially fresh clean and bright and strikng binding virtually unworn, very lustrous covers that retain all of the original sharpness of their intricate blind decoration. Phillip J. Pirages 67 - 62 2016 $1000

Mounsey, George Gill *Authentic Account of the Occupation of Carlisle in 1745 by Prince Charles Edward Stuart.* London: Longman and Co., Carlisle: James Steel, 1846. First edition, 8vo., original cloth with elaborate blind-stamped borders on boards, gilt block on upper board, lettered gilt on spine, vignette titlepage, folding map and 5 engraved plates, spine faded, otherwise very good, bright, clean. Sotheran's Piccadilly Notes - Summer 2015 - 28 2016 £98

Mountfort, Guy *The Hawfinch.* Collins, 1957. First edition, small octavo, green buckram boards with gilt lettering to spine, illustrations, very good+, light speckling to fore-edges, in very good dust+ dust jacket, light soiling, small closed tears at extremities, scarce. Simon Finch 2015 - 211/83 2016 $250

Mozart, Wolfgang Amadeus *Messa in C a Quattro Voci in Piena Partitura...* Florence: Ferdinando Lorenzi between, 1836-1856. Folio, entirely engraved, some foxing, Continental armorial ownership stamp to titlepage, folo, contemporary quarter green sheep, marbled boards, spine lettered in gilt, little rubbed and worn, gutter cracking in places but binding strong, good, rare. Blackwell's Rare Books B184 - 70 2016 £750

Mozeen, Thomas *Young Scarron.* London: Printed & sold by T. Trye & W. Reeve, 1752. 8vo. half title, contemporary calf, rather rubbed, rebacked, red label, 2 armorial bookplates of Earl of Clanricarde. Jarndyce Antiquarian Booksellers CCXVI - 421 2016 £520

Mrabet, Mohamnmed *Love with a few Hairs.* New York: George Braziller, 1968. Very near fine in near fine , signed and inscribed by Paul Bowles the translator for Mary Allen, 21/5/69, very nice, uncommon. Jeff Hirsch Books Holiday List 2015 - 55 2016 $300

Muddock, James Edward Preston *Stories Weird and Wonderful.* London: Chatto & Windus, 1889. First edition, octavo, chromo-lithograph plate with portrait, 32 page publisher's catalog dated May 1903, octavo, original white pictorial boards printed in red and black, pulp paper endpapers painted with ads, light wear at upper spine end and corner tips, lower spine and rubbed, overall stunning, rare. John W. Knott, Jr./L.W. Currey, Inc. Fall-Winter 2015 - 17466 2016 $7500

Mudie, Robert *The Feathered Tribes of the British Islands.* London: Whittaker, 1834. First edition thus, no edition stated, 2 volume set, bound into attractive green leather spine and corners over green cloth, gilt titles, five raised bands to spine, top edge gilt, marbled endpapers, both volumes in like condition, covers lightly rubbed, some offsetting to endpapers from leather, tissue guards tinted, frontispiece has light spotting, light to moderate foxing to prelims, text complete, binding tight, remarkably bright illustrations, gorgeous illustrations, attractive binding. Simon Finch 2015 - 346 2016 $200

Mueller, Ferdinand Von *The Plants Indigenous to the Colony of Citoria.* Melbourne: Government Printer, 1860-1865. (-1910), Quarto, 3 volumes, 120 lithographic plates, first volume in binder's cloth, second volume in publisher's cloth, final Ewart supplement (limited to 484 copies), original printed wrappers, some foxing, scarce, complete. Andrew Isles Natural History Books 55 - 18410 2016 $1200

Mueller, Ferdinand Von *Western Australia.* Perth: Government Printer, 1882. Quarto, two (folding) colored maps, one tinted and 20 uncolored lithographic plates, publisher's cloth with label, hinges cracked, crudely repaired, bookplate of R. Schomburgk, director of Adelaide Botanic Gardens. Andrew Isles Natural History Books 55 - 37716 2016 $450

Mueller, Lisel *The Private Life.* Baton Rouge: Louisiana State University Press, 1976. Fine in fine dust jacket with laid in Lamont card, signed and inscribed by author, lovely copy, uncommon signed. Jeff Hirsch Books Holiday List 2015 - 56 2016 $150

Muenster, Sebastian 1489-1552 *Rudimenta Mathematica.* Basel: H. Petrus, 1551. First edition, folio, large woodcut on title, woodcuts throughout text, large double page woodcut attributed to Hans Holbein the Younger (as are several in text woodcuts), is laid in loose and appears to be from another copy, early vellum, ties, dampstain in gutter, occasionally entering text, otherwise clean copy, early institutional bookplate, otherwise unmarked. Joseph J. Felcone, Inc. Books from Five Centuries: a Miscellany - 108 2016 $2000

Muesebeck, C. E. W. *Hymenoptera of America North of Mexico.* Washington: United States Dept. of Agriculture, 1951-1967. Octavo, 3 volumes, publisher's cloth, folding map.   Andrew Isles Natural History Books   55 - 20330   2016 $300

Muggleton, Lodowick   *The Acts of the Witnesses of the Spirit in Five Parts.* London: 1764. Small 4to., very lightly yellowed, occasional light smudges, tiny chip to head of titlepage, contemporary marbled calf, green morocco gilt, spine label, edges sprinkled blue, joints and edges bit rubbed, corners starting to wear a little, endpapers heavily foxed, very good, handsome.   Unsworths Antiquarian Booksellers Ltd.   30 - 113   2016   £300

Muir, Edwin   *Prometheus.* London: Faber and Faber, 1954. First edition, 2 full page illustrations by John Piper, crown 8vo., original sewn printed wrappers, original envelope which is lightly dust soiled with few tiny foxspots, book itself fine.   Blackwell's Rare Books   B184 - 303   2016   £30

Muir, John   1838-1914   *Rambles in King's River Country.* Ashland: Lewis Osborne, 1977. First book edition, limited to 600 copies, frontispiece, single page map, 13 illustrations, beige cloth spine, brown pictorial boards, gilt very fine.   Argonaut Book Shop   Natural History 2015 - 7618   2016 $75

Muir, John   1838-1914   *Travels in Alaska.* Boston and New York: Houghton Mifflin Co., 1916. Second impression, octavo, plates from photos, grey buckram covers with color plate mounted on front, top edge gilt, rear cover lightly marked, very good.   Peter Ellis   112 - 266   2016   £65

Muir, John   1838-1914   *Writings of John Muir. Together with The Life and Letters of John Muir...* Boston: Houghton Mifflin and Co., 1916-1924. Manuscript edition, ultra deluxe special copies, numbered 126 of 750 of the standard edition), 10 volumes + 2 added volumes, octavo, extra illustrated, with more than 260 added plates, with 114 edition plates the set is now 374 (mostly photographic), full set, 10 volumes, original full crushed green morocco, four ruled borders on covers with corner florets, six spine compartments, each ornately tooled in gilt naming the series title and titles contained within each volume at foot of spine, full in laid morocco doublures with massed ornate gilt stamped panel at center, silk free endleaves, top edge gilt, bound at Riverside Press, spine gilt stamped, some fading to covers (to brownish color) as usual with green bindings exposed to sunlight, near fine, the Life and Letters in 2 volumes, uniformly bound in later full red crushed morocco, ruled and tooled in gilt, all edges gilt, fine.   Jeff Weber Rare Books   181 - 70   2016 $45,000

Muir, John   1838-1914   *The Yosemite.* San Francisco: Sierra Club, 1989. First edition, signed by photographer, Galen Rowell, 4to., 101 full color plates, many full page, black cloth, gilt, very fine in original pictorial dust jacket.   Argonaut Book Shop   Natural History 2015 - 7460   2016 $175

Muirhead, Findlay   *Switzerland wit Chamonix and the Italian Lakes.* London: Macmillan, 1930. Second edition, small 8vo., numerous maps , original blue cloth.   J. & S. L. Bonham Antiquarian Booksellers   Europe 2016 - 7834   2016   £16

Muldoon, Paul   *I Might Make Out with You.* New York: Lofi Bookstein Fine Art, 2006. First edition, small square 8vo., original unprinted white wrappers, stamped in relief, one of 10 numbered copies in a total edition of 1000, signed by author and artist, original monotype by Wendy Mark, as new.   James S. Jaffe Rare Books   Occasional List: Winter 2016 - 102   2016 $4000

Muldoon, Paul   *Selected Poems 1968-1986.* New York: Ecco., 1987. First edition, 8vo., author's presentation, paper over boards with cloth spine, nice in lightly scuffed dust jacket.   Second Life Books, Inc.   196 B - 286   2016 $65

Mulford, Prentice   *Prentice Mulford's Story. Life by Land and Sea.* New York: F. J. Needham, 1889. First edition, small octavo, maroon cloth, stamped in red and gold, very fine and bright.   Argonaut Book Shop   Biography 2015 - 7619   2016 $175

Muller, Eugene   *La Mionette.* Paris: Librairie L. Conquet, 1885. No. 12 of 150 large paper copies (and 850 regular copies), 197 x 133mm., lovely dark green crushed morocco, gilt and inlaid by Marius Michel (stamp signed on front turn-in), covers with double gilt rule frame enclosing central floral wreath bearing red and white morocco roses, leafy rose branch at corners with red or white blossom, tiny gilt bees whimsically buzzing around flowers (one on upper cover, three on lower), raised bands, spine gilt in compartments with central rose sprig bearing a red or white bloom, foliate cornerpieces, densely gilt turn-ins, marbled endpapers, all edges gilt, original pink wrappers bound in (front cover with small portrait), housed in marbled paper slipcase, with a total of 84 illustrations by Oreste Cortazzo (two large and 26 smaller vignettes, each in three states, eau fort pure, before letters and complete, the third state of the smaller vignettes always printed in the text, rest on pages that are otherwise blank), with an additional state of the wrapper portrait printed on China paper, quite minor offsetting from engravings (though always onto blank page, never onto text), otherwise virtually perfect, lovely binding and unworn, text and cuts in very fine condition.   Phillip J. Pirages   67 - 54   2016 $850

Muller, Johann Ernst Friedrich Wilhelm *Versuch eienr Asthetik der Toilette oder Winke fur Damen, sich nach den Grundregeln der Malerei Heschmackvoll zu Kleiden...* Leipzig: im Industrie Comptoir, circa, 1805. First edition, 18 leaves of plates of which 8 are colored, one bound as frontispiece, 8vo., contemporary green boards imitating morocco, edged and tooled in gilt, spine ruled and lettered gilt, some loss to paper on spine, boards and spine generally worn, stamp at foot of title of initials PvH surmounted by a crown, sound, very rare.   Blackwell's Rare Books   B186 - 104   2016   £2000

Muller, Victor *En Syrie avec les Bedouins. Les Tribus du Desert.* Paris: Ernest Leroux, 1931. First edition, 8vo., original printed wrappers, 9 maps, apart from light even browning, near fine, uncut and unopened.   Sotheran's Travel and Exploration - 349   2016   £455

Mullins, Helen *Earthbound & Other Poems.* New York: Harper, 1929. First edition, 8vo., one of 250 copies, numbered and signed by author, rear hinge beginning tender, cover little scuffed at edges, otherwise very good.   Second Life Books, Inc.   196 B - 287   2016 $75

Mullins, Jane E. *Some Liverpool Chronicles.* C. D. Hemeon, 1980. Reprint, limited edition, card covers, 8vo. black and white photo illustrations, very good.   Schooner Books Ltd.   115 - 166   2016 $55

Mulvaney, D. J. *"So Much that is new" Baldwin Spencer 1860-1929; a biography.* Melbourne: Melbourne University Press, 1985. Octavo, text illustrations, very good in dust jacket.   Andrew Isles Natural History Books   55 - 1259   2016 $100

Mumford, Erasmus *A Letter to the Club at White's. In Which are Set forth the Great Expediency of repeating the laws Now in Force Against Excessive Gaming and the Many Advantages that Would Arise to this Nation from It.* London: for W. Owen, 1750. First edition, 8vo., recent marbled boards lettered on spine, very good.   John Drury Rare Books   2015 - 25390   2016 $350

Munari, Bruno *Who's There? Open the Door!* Cleveland: World, 1957. Folio, cloth backed pictorial boards, slight cover soil, margin mend on one leaf, very good+, bright full color illustrations.   Aleph-bet Books, Inc.   111 - 314   2016 $500

Munby, A. N. L. *Philipps Studies.* Cambridge: Cambridge University Press, 1951-1960. 8vo., cloth, dust jackets, dust jacket of volume 2 age darkened, owner's booklabel to corner of back pastedown.   Oak Knoll Books   310 - 67   2016 $450

Mundell, E. H. *Madison Presses and Imprints.* Portage: Compulsive Printer, 1980. 8vo., paper covered boards, note by collector Michael Peich on front free endpaper states only five copies printed, but no limitation statement.   Oak Knoll Books   310 - 92   2016 $125

Mundy, Francis Noel Clarke *Needwood Forest. (bound with) The Fall of Needwood.* Lichfield: printed by John Jackson; Derby: printed at the Office of J. Drewry, 1766. or c. 1790, & 1808. First editions, 4to., frontispiece, some foxing to 3 leaves of second work, contemporary ink note to one passage, pencil quotation from the Letters of Anna Seward in first work, 2 volumes in one, bound in early 19th century half red morocco, marbled boards, some rubbing to boards, corners worn, ownership name of Henry Smedley 1812 and Millicent Crompton, tipped in as a slip of blue sugar paper for Miss Mary French's friend.   Jarndyce Antiquarian Booksellers   CCXVI - 422   2016   £180

Mungo, Raymond *Return to Sender.* Boston: Houghton Mifflin, 1975. First edition, 8vo., very good in little chipped dust jacket, signed by author.   Second Life Books, Inc.   196 B - 288   2016 $75

Munoz, Rie *Rie Munoz: Artist in Alaska.* Juneau: R. Munoz, 1987. First edition, silver stamped cloth, illustrations, signed by author, fine in dust jacket.   Gene W. Baade, Books on the West   2015 - 1408103   2016 $50

Munro, H. H. *The Novels and Plays of Saki.* New York: Viking Press, 1933. Stated "Second Omnibus" volume, rebound in blue half morocco gilt, paper covered boards, probably soon after publication, spine expertly preserved, otherwise nice, near fine, with two identical examples of the armorial bookplate of Thomas Ruggles Pynchon, presumably that of author Thomas Pynchon's father.   Between the Covers Rare Books   204 - 99   2016 $950

Munro, Thomas *The Life of Major General Sir Thomas Munro, Bart....* London: Henry Colburn and Richard Bentley, 1830. First edition, 3 volumes, frontispiece, folding map volume I, contemporary half red morocco, marbled boards, ownership inscription in all volumes of Robert Macfie, Ardis. 1865, very good, attractive copy.   Jarndyce Antiquarian Booksellers   CCXVII - 194   2016   £380

Murakami, Haruki *Colorless Tsukuru Tazaki and His Years of Pilgrimage.* Harvill Secker, 2014. First edition, signed by author, 8vo., original illustrated boards, sticker sheet laid in, dust jacket, fine.   Blackwell's Rare Books   B186 - 266   2016   £275

Murakami, Haruki *Dance Dance Dance.* New York: Kodansha International, 1994. First edition, fine in fine dust jacket.   Between the Covers Rare Books   208 - 52   2016 $225

Murakami, Haruki *Kafka on the Shore.* London: Harvill, 2005. First edition, 93/100 copies signed and stamped by author on tipped in bookplate, 8vo., original white leather with inlaid black cat to front, backstrip lettered black, tiny speck to lower board, black page marker, wave patterned endpapers, slipcase, near fine.   Blackwell's Rare Books   B186 - 265   2016   £950

Murakami, Haruki *A Wild Sheep Chase.* Tokyo and New York: Kodansha International, 1989. First American edition, fine in fine dust jacket, publisher's postcard for the book and publisher's catalog laid in.   Between the Covers Rare Books   208 - 51   2016 $175

Murakami, Haruki *A Wild Sheep Chase.* London: 1990. First edition, first impression, 8vo., fine in fine dust jacket, inevitable slight tanning to edges of cheap paper.   Any Amount of Books   2015 - A85920   2016   £165

The Murdered Bride or the Victim of Treachery: a Tale of Horror. London: William Emans, 1837. First edition?, small quarto, engraved frontispiece, additional engraved titlepage and 6 other engraved plates, contemporary half calf over marbled boards, original parts bound together with stabmarks, bound by G. J. Sutton (?) with small binder label on front endpaper, spine heavily tooled gilt in compartments, green morocco spine label, lettered gilt, spine with name M. N. Bourne in gilt at foot, all edges marbled, green endpapers, some toning to plates, bit of foxing throughout, boards bit rubbed, previous owner Bruce Ismery's armorial bookplate, overall very good, extremely rare.   Heritage Book Shop   Holiday 2015 - 3   2016 $3000

Murdoch, Iris *The Book and the Brotherhood.* London: Chatto & Windus, 1987. First edition, octavo, cheap paper faintly tanned as usual, fine in fine dust jacket.   Peter Ellis   112 - 267   2016   £25

Murdoch, Iris *The Philosopher's Pupil.* London: Chatto & Windus, Hogarth Press, 1983. First edition, crown 8vo., original blue boards, backstrip lettered gilt, light foxing to edges, dust jacket, good, inscribed by author.   Blackwell's Rare Books   B184 - 186   2016   £120

Murdoch, Iris *The Philosopher's Pupil.* London: Chatto & Windus/The Hogarth Press, 1983. First edition, octavo, very good in like dust jacket, little creased at top edge.   Peter Ellis   112 - 268   2016   £30

Murdoch, Iris *The Sea.* London: Chatto & Windus, 1978. First edition, crown 8vo., original turquoise boards, backstrip lettered gilt, sprinkling of tiny foxspots to top edge, dust jacket price clipped, very good.   Blackwell's Rare Books   B184 - 197   2016   £70

Murdoch, W. G. Burn *From Edinburgh to the Antarctic: an Artist's Notes and Sketches....* London: Longmans, Green and Co., 1894. First edition, 8vo., original dark green cloth with cover design in silver and brown, spine in silver, monochrome illustrations, one folding map, some occasional spotting (chiefly to edges), otherwise good, bright copy.   Sotheran's   Travel and Exploration - 428   2016   £1150

Murdock, Charles A. *Horatio Stebbins. His Ministry and His Personality.* Boston: Houghton Mifflin Co., 1921. First edition, signed by author, frontispiece, original blue cloth stamped in gilt on spine and front cover, slight rubbing to spine ends, but fine.   Argonaut Book Shop   Biography 2015 - 6748   2016 $60

Murphy, Arthur *Ranger's Progress; Consisting of a Variety of Poetical Essays....* London: printed for the author and sold by T. Kinnersly in St. Paul's Church Yard and to be had of all other Booksellers in Town and Country, 1760. 8vo., full contemporary calf, gilt ruled border, spine gilt in six compartments with repeat floral device, upper inch of joints little cracked, head and tail chipped, signature of C. R. Rintoul 1888 on f.e.p., very good, clean copy.   Jarndyce Antiquarian Booksellers   CCXVI - 423   2016   £280

Murphy, Claire Rudolf *The Prince and the Salmon People.* New York: Rizzoli, 1993. First edition, 4to., fine, illustrations by Duane Pasco, signed by author, fine in dust jacket, scarce.   Gene W. Baade, Books on the West   2015 - 1104108   2016 $41

Murphy, Henry C. *Anthology of New Netherland or Translations from the Early Dutch Poets of New York with Memoirs of their Lives.* New York: Bradford Club, 1865. Number 86 of an edition of 125 copies, 4to., later flexible leatherette, frontispiece, accompanied by two manuscript letters, first from John B. Moreau making the presentation to Benson Lossing on behalf of Bradford Club and second from Lossing to Moreau, very good copy.   Edwin V. Glaser Rare Books   2015 - 10275   2016 $450

Murphy, Robert Cushman *Oceanic Birds of South America...* New York: Macmillan, 1936. Quarto, 2 volumes, color plates, photos, very slight wear to publisher's cloth.   Andrew Isles Natural History Books   55 - 13002   2016 $80

Murray, David *Some Early Grammars and Other School Books in Use in Scotland More Particularly those Printed at or Relating to Glasgow.* Royal Philosophical Society of Glasgow, 1905. Contemporary half tan calf, brown morocco label, spine lettered gilt, slightly rubbed, signature and bookplate of author.   Jarndyce Antiquarian Books   CCXV - 869   2016   £58

Murray, Edward *Enoch Restituts or an Attempt to Separate from the Books of Enoch...* London: J. G. & F. Rivington, 1836. First edition, 8vo., all edges gilt, neat inscription, bookplate, otherwise very good in fine red full leather. Any Amount of Books 2015 - 2016 £150

Murray, George *Phycological memoir, Being Researches Made in the Botanical Department of the British Museum.* London: Dulau and Co., 1892-1895. Quarto, 20 lithographed plates (some colored), publisher's morocco grained cloth, near fine. Andrew Isles Natural History Books 55 - 32440 2016 $350

Murray, James A. H. *A New English Dictionary on Historical Principles.* Oxford: Clarendon Press, 1888-1928. First edition, 10 volumes, large quarto, bound in twenty volumes, original deluxe half burgundy morocco, gilt ruled cover heavy grain maroon cloth, spines gilt, top edge gilt, original coated stock endpapers, one volume with professional repair to top of spine, minor wear to some tips, overall fine. Heritage Book Shop Holiday 2015 - 82 2016 $8500

Murray, Joan *Poems.* New Haven: Yale University Press, 1947. First edition, although there is not indication, this book came from William Meredith's library, slight dust spotting to top edge of text, near fine in near fine dust jacket. Charles Agvent William Meredith - 88 2016 $100

Murray, John *Jerubbaal or Tyranny's Grove Destroyed and the Altar of Liberty Finished.* Newbury-port: John Mycalf, 1784. First edition, 12mo., three quarter morocco over marbled boards, few spots and stains but very good, from the Gordon Lester Ford Collection of NY Public Library with their duplicate sold stamp, lacks final four leaves. Edwin V. Glaser Rare Books 2015 - 10379 2016 $240

Murray, John *John Murray 50 Albermarle St. 1768-1930.* London: Artist Illustrators, n.d., 1930. First edition, 8vo., illustrations, original brown wrappers. J. & S. L. Bonham Antiquarian Booksellers Europe 2016 - 9232 2016 £50

Murray, L. *The Young Man's Best Companion and Book of General Knowledge...* London: Thomas Kelly, 1822. Additional engraved title, plates, some occasional pencil markings, heavy in places, lacing following f.e.p., contemporary black calf, borders in gilt and blind, gilt bands and compartments, red morocco label, boards little marked, signature of Ernest Phillips 1892, good plus. Jarndyce Antiquarian Books CCXV - 331 2016 £110

Murray, L. *The Young Man's Best Companion and Book of General Knowledge...* London: printed for Thos. Kelly, 1824. Frontispiece, additional engraved title, plates, damp marking to prelims and final 3 leaves and endpapers, folding plate facing page 53 with marginal tears and backed with brown paper, handsomely bound in recent half brown calf, vellum tips, gilt bands, red morocco label. Jarndyce Antiquarian Books CCXV - 332 2016 £110

Murray, L. *The Young Man's Best Companion and Book of General Knowledge...* London: printed for Thomas Kelly, 1834. Frontispiece, additional engraved title, plates, contemporary full tree calf, gilt borders & spine, maroon morocco label, slight wear to head and tail of spine, nice. Jarndyce Antiquarian Books CCXV - 333 2016 £120

Murray, Lindley *Memoir of the Life and Writings of Lindley Murray....* York: Wilson & Sons, 1827. Second edition, plate, uncut, recent quarter calf, gilt library reference at foot of spine, booklabel & stamps of Camden & Hampstead libraries. Jarndyce Antiquarian Books CCXV - 870 2016 £48

Murray, Louise Welles *The Story of Some French Refugees and their 'Azilum' 1793-1800.* Athens: 1903. First edition, number 20 of 250 copies signed by author, this copy additionally inscribed by author for friends, tall 8vo., original cloth backed boards, minor edge wear, paper label on front cover, plates, folding map, uncut. Howard S. Mott Inc. 265 - 95 2016 $225

Murray, Thomas Boyles *The Home of the Mutineers.* Philadelphia: American Sunday School Union, 1854. First edition thus, publisher's brown purple cloth, spine lettered and decorated in gilt, boards decorated in blind, very good or better, with some rubbing to extremities, toning to spine and board edges, slight lean to spine, former owner's pencil inscription to front free endpaper, few light and scattered spots to otherwise fresh interior, overall attractive and unsophisticated copy, free of any repairs or restoration. B & B Rare Books, Ltd. 2016 - TBYM001 2016 $200

Murray, Thomas Boyles *Pictairn: the Island, the People and the Pastor...* London: Society for Promoting Christian Knowledge, 1854. Fourth edition, 8vo., original brown grained cloth, spine lettered gilt, vignette blocked in gilt onto upper cover ornamented in blind, 13 engraved plates, very light marking to binding, very good, contemporary bookplate of George William Mercer Henderson. Sotheran's Travel and Exploration - 405 2016 £225

Musapaedia or Miscellany Poems Never Before Printed. London: printed for R. Francklin, 1719. First edition, 8vo., disbound, fine, very scarce. C. R. Johnson Rare Book Collections Foxon: H-P 2015 - 643 2016 $2298

Musgrave, Anthony *Bibliography of Australian Entomolgy 1775-1930 with Biographical notes on Authros and Collectors.* Sydney: Royal Zoological Society of New South Wales, 1932. Octavo, wrappers, chipped and some creasing, owner's sticker. Andrew Isles Natural History Books 55 - 35166 2016 $50

Musil, Robert *The Man Without Qualities. Volume III. Into the Millennium.*   London: Secker & Warburg, 1959, but, 1960. Uncorrected proof copy, correction to publication date on titlepage and extensive notes in pencil and red ink by Roger Senhouse, crown 8vo., original printed wrappers, little fading to backstrip and borders and slight lean to spine, pencilled note of date going to press to front, short split at head of upper joint, good.   Blackwell's Rare Books   B186 - 267   2016   £1000

Muybridge, Eadweard *Animals in Motion.*   London: Chapman and Hall, 1918. Fourth impression, oblogn 4to, original maroon cloth, titled in gilt on spine and in blind on upper cover, frontispiece, photos, lightly bumped at top of spine, otherwise very nice, bright copy, scarce in this condition.   Sotheran's   Piccadilly Notes - Summer 2015 - 212   2016   £198

Muybridge, Eadweard *Animals in Motion.*   New York: Dover Pub., 1967. First edition, quarto, original cloth, fine with pictorial dust jacket.   Argonaut Book Shop   Photography 2015 - 2564   2016 $60

My Picture Story-Book, in Prose and Poetry for Little Ones.   Philadelphia: 1878. First edition, wood engravings.   Honey & Wax Booksellers   4 - 30   2016 $250

Myers, Alfred Moritz *The History of a Young Jew or of Alfred Moritz Myers....*   Chester: printed by T. Thomas Eastgate Street, 1840. First edition, 12mo., frontispiece, original blue cloth covered boards, slightly rubbed label on front cover, 'price one shilling', little rubbed.   Jarndyce Antiquarian Booksellers   CCXVII - 195   2016   £75

Myers, Walter *Harlem.*   New York: Scholastic Press, 1997. First edition, folio, pictorial boards, new in dust jacket, illustrations by Christopher Myers with color collages, this copy signed by author and artist, with signed poster laid in.   Aleph-bet Books, Inc.   111 - 48   2016 $125

Myles, Eileen *The Irony of the Leash.*   New York: Jim Brodey Books, 1978. First edition, one of 200 copies, 4to., original illustrated wrappers, stapled as issued, light use, short soft crease in first few leaves, otherwise fine in dust jacket.   James S. Jaffe Rare Books   Occasional List: Winter 2016 - 103   2016 $750

Myths of the Ancient World.   Norwalk: Easton Press, 1997. 10 volumes, color frontispiece in each volume, bound in full green leather with gilt and black stamped cover designs, orange silk moire endpapers, all edges gilt, silk ribbon permanent markers, near fine set.   Tavistock Books   Bibliolatry - 18   2016 $875

N

N., J. *Select Lessons in Prose and Verse, from Various Authors...* Bristol: printed by S. Farley, 1774. 8vo., 4 lines crossed out in contemporary ink, 19th century marbled boards, handsomely rebacked in brown calf, red morocco label, signature of J. Raymond 1778.   Jarndyce Antiquarian Books   CCXV - 334   2016   £220

Nabokov, Vladimir   1899-1977 *Ada; or Ardor a family Chronicle.* London: Weidenfeld and Nicolson, 1969. First UK edition, octavo, very near fine in near fine dust jacket, slightly faded at spine and bit rubbed at tail of spine.   Peter Ellis   112 - 269   2016   £75

Nabokov, Vladimir   1899-1977 *The Gift.* London: Weidenfeld and Nicolson, 1963. First UK edition, octavo, spine creased, very good in very good dust jacket, slightly faded at spine and little nicked at head of spine.   Peter Ellis   112 - 270   2016   £55

Nabokov, Vladimir   1899-1977 *Lolita.* Jerusalem: printed in Israel for the Olympia Press by Steimatzky's Agency, 1955. First Israeli edition, first hardcover edition, 2 volumes in one, original blue leather textured paper covered boards in dust jacket, offsetting to front and rear endpapers as usual, small and light stain on rear flyleaf, else near fine in modestly rubbed, very good dust jacket with some tanning to white portion of spine and few modest chips, first hardcover edition.   Between the Covers Rare Books   208 - 55   2016 $2000

Nabokov, Vladimir   1899-1977 *Lolita.* Paris: Olympia Press, 1955. First edition, first issue with 900 Francs on rear wrappres and no evidence of later price sticker, this copy from the Bureau Litteraire Clairouin Nabokov's literary agency who was instrumental in its publication, octavo, original green paper wrappers, custom box, 2 volumes, little edgewear and few spots of soiling, usual spine creases, excellent copy, rare first issue.   Manhattan Rare Book Company   2016 - 1738   2016 $8500

Nabokov, Vladimir   1899-1977 *Look at the Harlequins!* New York: McGraw Hill, 1974. First edition, fine in fine dust jacket, inscribed by author for Gordon Lish, with author's corrections, housed in cloth chemise and quarter morocco and cloth slipcase.   Between the Covers Rare Books   204 - 84   2016 $9500

Nabokov, Vladimir   1899-1977 *Nikolai Gogol.* New Directions, 1944. First edition, Honey & Wax Booksellers   4 - 45   2016 $275

Nabokov, Vladimir   1899-1977 *Poems and Problems.* London: Weidenfeld and Nicolson, 1972. First UK edition, fine in fine dust jacket with tiny nick at top edge, uncommon, especially in this kind of condition.   Peter Ellis   112 - 272   2016   £125

Nabokov, Vladimir   1899-1977 *Strong Opinions.* London: Weidenfeld and Nicolson, 1974. First UK edition, octavo, fine in very good dust jacket with small chip at head of spine.   Peter Ellis   112 - 271   2016   £45

Nagel, Paul C. *Descent from Glory: Four Generations of the John Adams Family.* New York: Oxford, 1983. First printing, 8vo., illustrations, author's signature, paper over boards with cloth spine, nice in scuffed dust jacket, near fine.   Second Life Books, Inc.   196 B - 294   2016 $45

Nagy, Gregory *Pindar's Homer. A Lyric Possession of an Epic Past.* Baltimore: Johns Hopkins University Press, 1990. First edition, 8vo., beige cloth, endcaps just starting to wear, tiny bump to top edge of upper board, edges slightly dusted, otherwise very good, black dust jacket, corners worn, one or two tiny closed tears, still very good, Inter-Library Loan card loosely inserted, some pencil annotations and underlining.   Unsworths Antiquarian Booksellers Ltd.   E04 - 79   2016   £25

Nahm, Milton C. *Selections from Early Greek Philosophy.* New York: F. S. Crofts, 1945. Second edition, fifth edition, small 8vo., original cream cloth lettered brown on spine and cover, Allen Ginsberg's copy with his name written 3 times on front endpaper.   Any Amount of Books 2015 - A71815   2016   £550

Naipaul, V. S. *Between Father and Son, Family Letters.* New York: Alfred A. Knopf, 2000. First edition, tight very near fine in copy in very near fine dust jacket, signed by author on tipped in page by publisher, uncommon thus.   Jeff Hirsch Books   E-List 80 - 21   2016 $150

Naipaul, V. S. *Guerrillas.* London: Deutsch, 1975. Uncorrected proof of the first edition, spine slanted and title and author written on spine in red ink, near fine, extremely uncommon proof.   Ken Lopez Bookseller   166 - 87   2016 $550

Naipaul, V. S. *A Turn in the South.* Franklin Center: Franklin Library, 1989. Limited first edition signed by author, brown leather, lettered and decoratively stamped in gilt, all edges gilt, very fine, as new copy, extremely handsome edition.   Argonaut Book Shop   Literature 2015 - 3999   2016 $100

Naipaul, V. S. *A Turn in the South.* Viking, 1989. First edition, 8vo., original red cloth, some light staining to fore-edge, dust jacket, signed.   J. & S. L. Bonham Antiquarian Booksellers   America 2016 - 9771   2016   £85

Naissance Poems - Prose No. 5 and 6 (Double issue). Winchester: Naissance, n.d., First edition, 4to., decorated stapled wrappers, very good.   Simon Finch   2015 - 14604   2016 $250

Nansen, Fridtjof   1861-1930   *"Farthest North" being the Record of a Voyage of Exploration of the Ship Fram 1893-96 and of a Fifteen Months' Sleigh Journey....*   London: George Mewnes, 1898. Second English edition, 8vo., 2 volumes, original blue cloth over bevelled boards, upper boards blocked in gilt, silver and red with vignettes, spines blocked in gilt and silver with titles and vignettes, black endpapers, all edges gilt, frontispiece, 64 monochrome plates, one color printed plate, monochrome illustrations and diagrams, 46 full page one full page map and letterpress tables to text, little shaky with some minor bumping, more attractive than most.   Sotheran's   Travel and Exploration - 431   2016   £598

Napier, William Francis Patrick   *History of the War in the Peninsula and in the South of France from the Year 1807 to the Year 1814.*   London: John Murray/Thomas and William Boone, 1828. Mixed edition, 6 volumes, 8vo., full leather, almost all with loose boards, 6th volume lacking boards, otherwise internally clean and bright set, good working copies.   Any Amount of Books   2015 - A42359   2016   £165

Napoleon, Bonaparte   *Maxims of Napoleon.*   London: Arthur I. Humphreys, 1906. 8vo., half gilt ruled red morocco, spine panelled and lettered gilt, top edge gilt, very good.   Sotheran's   Piccadilly Notes - Summer 2015 - 213   2016   £298

Nash, Graham   *The Graham Nash Collection.*   Los Angeles: Nash Press, 1978. First edition, one of 100 numbered copies specially bound and signed by Nash, oblong 4to., illustrations, leather backed cloth over boards, marbled front pastedown, original illustrated front wrapper, bound in publisher's matching slipcase, very fine, scarce, presentation from author to Lydia Modi Vitale, laid is is carbon copy signed of single page TL from Nash to an administrator at the University, also laid in is 1 page TLS to Vitale from visitor to the exhibition.   James S. Jaffe Rare Books Occasional List: Winter 2016 - 115   2016 $1000

Nash, John   *Real Algebraic Manifolds.*   Baltimore: Princeton University Press, 1952. First edition, octavo, original printed wrappers, toning to spine and some light toning to rear wrappers, hint of edgewear, extremely well preserved, rare in original wrappers, without any institution markings.   Manhattan Rare Book Company   2016 - 1659   2016 $1900

Nash, Paul   *Dear Mercia - Paul Nash Letters to Mercia Oakley 1909-18.*   Wakefield: Fleece Press, 1991. First edition, 4to., illustrations include facsimiles of drawings in the letters, as well as color plate in rear pocket, quarter cloth with interesting patterned paste paper boards by Clare Maziarcyk in NY, one of 300 printed on Zerkall paper, fine in fine slipcase.   Peter Ellis   112 - 273   2016   £85

Nash, Paul   *The Wood Engravings of Paul Nash.*   Woodbridge: Wood Lea Press, 1997. One of 490 copies, frontispiece wood engraved self portrait and several tipped in color printed plates and numerous reproductions of engravings by Nash, addendum sheet laid in at rear, folio, original quarter grey cloth with patterned paper sides after a Curwen design, backstrip lettered in gilt, slipcase, near fine.   Blackwell's Rare Books   B186 - 349   2016   £150

Nasti, Mauro   *Schmied.*   Vicenza: Guido Tamoni, 1991. No. LVI of LVI Delux copies (and 1000 regular copies), publisher's deluxe vellum binding by I. Zanardi, volume housed in dark brown gilt titled folding cloth box, profusely illustrated with examples of Schmied's work, this copy with biofolium on Lamb's vellum (from 1930-33 edition of L'Odyssee), featuring an illustration after Schmied colored au pochoir by Jean Saude, biofolium laid in inside vellum folder, box with few small marks, otherwise mint.   Phillip J. Pirages   67 - 311   2016 $1500

Nathan, George Jean   *Art of the Night.*   New York: Knopf, 1928. First edition, 8vo., laid in autograph note and postcard by nathan to critic John Mason Brown, moderate wear.   Second Life Books, Inc.   196 B - 301   2016 $50

Nathan, George Jean   *Land of the Pilgrims' Pride.*   New York: Knopf, 1927. First edition, 1/140 copies printed on all rag paper and signed by author, large 8vo., library bookplate, cover little faded and worn at edges, otherwise very good, tight.   Second Life Books, Inc.   196 B - 302   2016 $65

Nathan, George Jean   *The Theatre of the Moment.*   New York: Knopf, 1938. First edition, nice, moderately worn dust jacket, inscribed by author to critic John Mason Brown.   Second Life Books, Inc.   196 B - 303   2016 $65

Nathan, Robert   *There is Another Heaven.*   Indianapolis: Bobbs Merrill, 1929. First edition, 8vo., author's presentation on half title, owner's bookplate, spine faded, else very good, tight copy.   Second Life Books, Inc.   196 B - 304   2016 $56

Nathanason, E. M.   *The Dirty Dozen.*   Arthur Barker, 1966. First UK edition, 8vo, original cloth, dust jacket little rubbed with some internal residual tape marks, small stain to top edge of front endpaper, otherwise very good, signed by actor Donald Sutherland who played Vernon Pinkley in the Aldrich film.   Sotheran's   Piccadilly Notes - Summer 2015 - 214   2016   £98

National American Woman Suffrage Association
Victory: How Women Won It.   New York: Wilson, 1940. First edition, 8vo., pages 174, illustrations, blue cloth, spine little faded, otherwise fine, one of 300 Honor Copies inscribed by Carrie Chapman Catt.   Second Life Books, Inc.   196 B - 305   2016 $450

National Association of Teachers of the Deaf
Proceedings of the International conference on the Education of the Deaf...   Edinburgh: Darien Press1907, Original maroon cloth, frontispiece, illustrations, very good.   Jarndyce Antiquarian Books   CCXV - 872   2016   £35

National Gallery   *Report from the Select Committee of the National Gallery....*   London: Henry Hansard Ordered by the Printer 16th August, 1853. Folio, lithograph plate, 1 double page lithograph plate, 1 hand colored lithograph plan, 1 folding double page lithograph plan, contemporary full red morocco, marbled edges.   Marlborough Rare Books   List 56 - 39   2016   £950

National Photographic Index   *Cuckoos, Nightbirds and Kingfishers of Australia.*   Pymble: Angus and Robertson, 1994. Quarto, color photos, maps, fine in dust jacket.   Andrew Isles Natural History Books   55 - 576   2016 $150

National Photographic Index   *Finches, Bowerbirds and Other Passerines of Australia.*   Sydney: Angus and Robertson, 1996. Quarto, color photos, fine in dust jacket.   Andrew Isles Natural History Books   55 - 9159   2016 $200

National Photographic Index   *Parrots and Pigeons of Australia.*   Sydney: Angus and Robertson, 1992. Quarto, color photos, very good in dust jacket.   Andrew Isles Natural History Books   55 - 20736   2016 $400

National Photographic Index   *The Seabirds of Australia.*   North Ryde: Angus and Robertson, 1986. Quarto, color photos, fine in dust jacket.   Andrew Isles Natural History Books   55 - 542   2016 $200

National Photographic Index   *The Shorebirds of Australia.*   North Ryde: Angus and Robertson, 1987. Quarto, color photos, dust jacket rubbed and grubby, otherwise very good.   Andrew Isles Natural History Books   55 - 20565   2016 $300

National Photographic Index   *The Waterbirds of Australia.*   North Ryde: Angus and Robertson, 1985. Quarto, color photos, fine in dust jacket.   Andrew Isles Natural History Books   55 - 25362   2016 $150

National Photographic Index   *The Wrens and Warblers of Australia.*   London: Angus and Robertson, 1982. Quarto, color photos, bookplate, fine in dust jacket.   Andrew Isles Natural History Books   55 - 530   2016 $50

National Training School for Cookery   *High Class Cookery Recipes as Taught in School.*   London: W. H. Allen & Co., 1885. 10 pages ads, 44 page catalog (July 1883), 4 pages ads, ink recipe for Xmas cake on verso of title, endpapers brittle, leading f.e.p. loose, original contemporary signature of Susan Roger.   Jarndyce Antiquarian Books   CCXV - 335   2016   £45

Naumann, I. D.   *The Insects of Australia: a Textbook for Students and Research Workers (with supplement).*   Melbourne: Melbourne University Press, 1979. -1974 Reprint, quarto, 2 volumes, color plates, very good in dust jackets.   Andrew Isles Natural History Books   55 - 13599   2016 $100

Navari, Leonora   *Greece and the Levant, the Catalogue of the Henry Myron Blackmer Collection of Books and Manuscripts.*   London: Maggs Bros. Ltd., 1989. Limited to 300 copies, folio, cloth, 16 color plates, bumping to bottom of corners and spine ends, slight fading to spine and covers at top, spine label removed.   Oak Knoll Books   310 - 215   2016 $2249

Nawrath, Ernest Alfred   *The Glories of Hindustan.*   London: Methuen, 1935. First edition, square 8vo., 240 full page gravure plates, man on front endpapers, superb photos and descriptions facing each of them, endpapers and fore edge little spotted, very good in scarce, very good, rubbed, nicked and creased price clipped dust jacket with small chip at tail of spine, larger one at top edge of rear panel.   Peter Ellis   112 - 182   2016   £350

Naylor, Gloria   *Mama Day.*   New York: Ticknor & Fields, 1988. First printing, 8vo., author's presentation on title, map on endpapers, paper over boards with cloth spine, nice in somewhat scuffed dust jacket.   Second Life Books, Inc.   196 B - 307   2016 $75

Naylor, Gloria   *The Women of Brewster Place.*   New York: Viking, 1982. First edition, 8vo., author's signature on title, paper over boards with cloth spine, fine in dust jacket.   Second Life Books, Inc.   196 B - 308   2016 $500

Neale, Charles Montague   *An Index to Pickwick.*   London: printed for the author by J. Hitchcock, 1897. 4to., addenda slip tipped in uncut in grey printed boards, green cloth spine, little rubbed, leading inner hinge starting, contemporary signature of James H. Baylis.   Jarndyce Antiquarian Booksellers   CCXVIII - 159   2016   £30

Neale, Cornelius   *Emblems for the Young, From Scripture, Nature and Art.*   London: RTS, 1835. Third edition, illustrations, leaves slightly dusted, original dark green cloth, slight damp mark to back board and tail of spine, otherwise very nice.   Jarndyce Antiquarian Books   CCXV - 336   2016   £40

Neale, Richard *A Pocket Companion for Gentleman and Ladies...* London: Clue's Printing Office in Bow Church-Yard, 1724. First edition, octavo, contemporary crimson morocco gilt, engraved frontispiece, prelims and musical scores with lyrics for dozens of songs, two early ownership inscriptions, beautiful copy, scarce. Honey & Wax Booksellers 4 - 8 2016 $1850

Neil, Alexander Sutherland *A Dominie's Five or Free School.* London: Herbert Jenkins, circa, 1910. Second printing, Half title, original orange cloth, very good in slightly torn dust jacket. Jarndyce Antiquarian Books CCXV - 876 2016 £20

Neil, Charles Lang *After Dinner Sleights and Pocket Tricks.* London: Hamley Bros., 1904. First edition, half title, illustrations, original yellow pictorial paper boards, printed in red and black, back cover ad, very good. Jarndyce Antiquarian Booksellers CCXVII - 197 2016 £50

Neil, Samuel *The Home Teacher....* London: Wm. MacKenzie, 1886-1888. 2 volumes, 4to., engraved titles, numerous plates and woodcut vignettes, half red calf, black and red labels, handsome. Jarndyce Antiquarian Books CCXV - 875 2016 £75

Neiman, Catrina *View: parade of the Avant Garde - an Anthology of View Magazine (1940-1947).* New York: Thunder's Mouth press, 1991. First edition, square quarto, illustrations, fine in near fine dust jacket just little creased at edges. Peter Ellis 112 - 422 2016 £30

Neinhauser, William H. *The Indiana Companion to Traditional.* Bloomington: Indiana University Press, 1986. First edition, large fat 8vo., uncommon, very good+ in like dust jacket, excellent condition. Any Amount of Books 2015 - A71204 2016 £150

Neira, Francisco *Larvae of Temperate Australian Fishes: Laboratory Guide for Larval Fish Identification.* Nedlands: UWA Press, 1998. Quarto, text illustrations, maps, laminated boards. Andrew Isles Natural History Books 55 - 14034 2016 $100

Nella, Nella *Prince Babillon.* New York: Mitchell Kennerley, 1910. First American edition, 6 full page drawings by Charles Robinson, including frontispiece, and numerous text illustrations, all printed in red and black, publisher's cream boards, front cover and spine decoratively stamped in black, red and gilt, pictorial endpapers printed in green, boards little dust soiled and rubbed at edges, otherwise very good. David Brass Rare Books, Inc. 2015 - 02998 2016 $175

Nelson, Charles A. *Waltham, Past and Present and Its Industries.* Cambridge: Thomas Lewis, Landscape Photographer, 1879. First edition, one of 900 copies, 55 albumen photos on 31 pages of photographic paper, small 8vo., brown cloth with beveled edges, gilt title, head and foot of spine expertly repaired, else near fine, faintly sunned spine. Kaaterskill Books 21 - 51 2016 $675

Nelson, Robert *A Companion for the Festivals and Fasts of the Church of England with Collects and Prayers for Each Solemnity.* London: Rivington, Johnson, Richardson, 1807. 30th edition, 8vo., period binding of full leather with gilt decoration to spine, spine little defective at head, upper joint cracking but tight, contemporary ownership signature on first blank, couple of small stains to fore-edge, very good. Peter Ellis 112 - 274 2016 £125

Nelson, William *The Office and Authority of a Justice of Peace....* In the Savoy: printed by E. & R. Nutt & R. Gosling, 1726. Ninth edition, 8vo. very nicely rebound in half sprinkled calf, raised and gilt banded spine, red gilt label, marbled boards, slight marginal worming not affecting text, pages 335-361, old waterstaining to lower margin, only noticeable towards end. Jarndyce Antiquarian Booksellers CCXVI - 424 2016 £450

Nemerov, Howard *Gnomes & Occasions. Poems.* Chicago and London: The University of Chicago Press, 1973. First edition, inscribed and signed by author for William Meredith, near fine. Charles Agvent William Meredith - 90 2016 $100

Nemerov, Howard *The Oak in the Acorn; on Remembrance of Things and on Teaching Proust...* Baton Rouge & London: Louisiana State University Press, 1987. First edition, inscribed and signed by author for William Meredith, near fine in like dust jacket. Charles Agvent William Meredith - 91 2016 $100

Nemerov, Howard *The Collected Poems of....* Chicago and London: University of Chicago Press, 1977. First edition, inscribed and signed by author for William Meredith, fine in near fine dust jacket. Charles Agvent William Meredith - 89 2016 $250

Nemerov, Howard *War Stories. Poems About Long Ago and Now.* Chicago & London: University of Chicago Press, 1987. First edition, inscribed and signed by author for William Meredith, near fine in like dust jacket with glass ring on front cover. Charles Agvent William Meredith - 92 2016 $100

Nemerov, Howard *The Western Approaches. Poems 1973-75.* Chicago: and London: University of Chicago Press, 1975. First edition, inscribed and signed on half title by author for William Meredith, slight dust spotting to top edge, fine in fine dust jacket. Charles Agvent William Meredith - 93 2016 $150

Nepos, Cornelius *Quae extant ex Editione Io. And. Bosil.* Amsterdam: Typis Petri Mortier, 1704. Pleasant copy of this pocket edition, ownership inscription of William Gibson dated 1746, 16mo., contemporary sprinkled calf, spine with four raised bands, red morocco lettering piece, other compartments decorated in gilt, little rubbed and much worn at extremities, slightly scratched, good.   Blackwell's Rare Books   B186 - 105   2016   £125

Neruda, Pablo *Alturas de Macchu PicchuAlturas.* Chile: Nascimento, 1954. First printing of this edition, one of 1000 numbered copies, this No. 680, signed by author, photos by Martin Chambi, moderate toning and light rubbing overall with light bumps at extremities, else near fine.   Royal Books   48 - 66   2016 $4500

Neruda, Pablo *Bestiary.* New York: Harcourt Brace, World, 1965. Limited to 300 copies, signed by artist and printer, part of a special unstated limitation with original 3 color woodcut signed by artist, printed on Rives mouldmade paper, striking woodcuts in black and orange by Antonio Frasconi, cloth backed pictorial boards, fine in glassine and slipcase, printed label.   Aleph-bet Books, Inc.   111 - 181   2016 $850

Neruda, Pablo *Cien Sonetos de Amor. (100 Love Sonnets).* Chile: Editorial Universitaria, 1959. First Chilean edition, preceding all others, folio, stiff wrappers, signed by author and artist, Nemesio Antunez, slight spine lean and moderate toning, else near fine, lacking scarce original glassine.   Royal Books   48 - 65   2016 $5000

Neruda, Pablo *Skystones.* Easthampton: Emanon Press, 1981. Limited to 60 numbered copies signed by Ben Belitt, Debra Weier and Bill Bridges, bound by Gray Parrot in Fabriano over boards printed to a design by Debra Weier and brown leather trim, beige cloth clamshell box with author's name in gilt on spine, box lined with paper to match binding, handset in Virgin Bodoni Book by artists and Bill Bridgers, printed on Arches buff and Rives BFK tan, with one page of Japanese paper, five two-plate color etchings printed on Rives BFK and Arches.   Oak Knoll Books   27 - 14   2016 $1500

Neruda, Pablo *Cancion de Gesta (Song of Protest).* N.P.: Imprenta Nacional de Cuba, 1960. True first edition, inscribed by author to Manuel Rivero de la Calle, 1960, mild foxing to pages, multiple dampstains to boards, tiny pencil annotations on cover, good copy.   Ken Lopez Bookseller   166 - 91   2016 $2500

Neruda, Pablo *'u de Noviembre Oda a un Dia de Victorias'.* N.P.: Ediciones 'Espana Popular', 1941. First edition, 8vo., original stapled self wrappers, photographic portrait of Neruda on front wrapper, presentation copy from author with 3 line inscription, signed by him, old vertical fold, few soft corner creases, few nicks and closed edge tears on front wrapper, acidic paper, somewhat brittle from age, but good copy of this fragile 7 page leaflet.   James S. Jaffe Rare Books   Occasional List: Winter 2016 - 104   2016 $2500

Nesbit, Edith *The Magic World.* London: Macmillan, 1912. First edition, octavo, 24 black and white plates, original red gilt pictorial cloth, top edge gilt, ownership inscription in red ink on front endpaper, covers little marked, endpapers tanned and spotted, very good.   Peter Ellis   112 - 273   2016   £250

Nesbit, Edith *The Pilot.* London: von Partheim & Co., n.d. circa, 1892. 8vo., flexible pictorial card covers, string binding, fine in original dust jacket (chipped) gorgeous chromolithographs, remarkable copy, rare in dust jacket.   Aleph-bet Books, Inc.   111 - 317   2016 $275

Nesbit, Edith *A Pomander of Verse.* London: John Lane at the Bodley Head, 1895. First edition, 1 of 750 copies, inscribed by author's cousin, Paris Nesbit, tan boards with gilt cover design by Laurence Housman, who also did the charming illustration for titlepage, very good with bumping to board corners and chipping to spine edges, interior clean with slight aging to margins of untrimmed pages, very good-.   The Kelmscott Bookshop   12 - 76   2016 $250

Nesfield, William Eden *Specimens of Mediaeval Architecture, Chiefly Selected from Examples of the 12th and 13th Centuries in France and Italy.* London: Day and Son at gate Street Near Lincoln Inn Fields, Jan. A.D., 1862. First edition, folio, wood engraved title by Dalziel after author, including figures by Albert Moore, 100 lithographic plates, including one in chromolithography by A. Newman, original purple roan backed brick colored cloth blocked in black, upper cover reproducing title leaf with inlaid panel of red calf blocked in gold spine decorated and lettered gilt and black, all edges gilt, binder ticket of Leighton Son and Hodge, contemporary bookplate of Frederick Stacey.   Marlborough Rare Books   List 55 - 50   2016   £250

Ness, Patrick *The Ask and the Answer.* London: Walker Books, 2009. First edition, book and glassine dust jacket fine, signed by author, glassine jacket fitted with new removable clear cover.   Gemini Books   2016 - 31795   2016 $63

Neuburger, Max *The Historical Development of Experimental Brain and Spinal Cord Physiology Before Flourens.* Baltimore: Hopkins, 1981. Original binding.   James Tait Goodrich   X-78 - 409   2016 $85

Neueste Kleinigreiten fur Liebe Jugend Ein Bilderbuch Zum Nuzen Und Bergnugen. Vienna: Johann Neidl, n.d. circa, 1810. 20 fine hand colored engravings, original marbled wrappers with printed label, near fine, rare. Aleph-bet Books, Inc. 111 - 152 2016 $2000

Neueste *Neueste Lander-Fiebel.* n.p.: n.d., but circa, 1830. 114 x 140mm., double sided concertina fold-out with 12 panels, original yellow printed paper wrappers, with 24 maps, little light soiling to wrapper, tiny chip lost at one corner, one or two panels, bit faintly printed, exceptionally fine, clean, fresh and remarkably well preserved in general. Phillip J. Pirages 67 - 249 2016 $2900

Neuhaus, Eugen *The Art of the Exposition.* San Francisco: Paul Elder, 1915. First edition, 8vo., illustrations, untrimmed, dust jacket with pieces missing to fore-edge, part of lower corner of front board nicked and about 1 inch of paper missing, good copy, this the copy of consumer advocate Florence Kelley, presentation to Kelley from Katherine Philips Edson May 29th 1915, nice association. Second Life Books, Inc. 196 B - 310 2016 $95

Neuhaus, Eugen *William Keith the Man and the Artist.* Berkeley: University of California Press, 1938. First edition, thin 4to., color frontispiece, 11 black and white reproductions, original cloth, very fine. Argonaut Book Shop Biography 2015 - 7316 2016 $150

Neukrantz, Amandus Ferdinand *Ausfuhrlicher Bericht uber die Grobe Allgemeine Deutshe gwerbe-Ausstellung in Berlin im Jahre 1844.* Berlin: M. Simion, 1844. First edition, 8vo., contemporary quarter cloth over marbled boards, spine lettered gilt, large lithographic folding plan, light wear to extremities, little browned, due to paper stock, oval stamp of Lower Austrian Trade Association on title and page 3. Sotheran's Travel and Exploration - 273 2016 £198

Nevins, Allan *Fremont, the West's Greatest Adventurer.* New York: Harper and Bros., 1928. First edition, 2 volumes, frontispiece in each volume, 62 plates, errata slip tipped in, , gilt lettered navy blue cloth, fine set. Argonaut Book Shop Biography 2015 - 5431 2016 $200

A New Ballad, Inscrib'd to the Polly Peachum. London: printed for A. Moore, n.d., 1728. First edition, 8 pages, folio, later wrappers, in half blue morocco slipcase, very good, outer edges untrimmed. C. R. Johnson Rare Book Collections Foxon: H-P 2015 - 854-h-p 2016 $6129

A New Bloody Ballad on the Bloody Battle at Dettingen... London: printed for W. Webb, 1743. First edition, folio, folded sheets as issued, fine. C. R. Johnson Rare Book Collections Foxon: H-P 2015 - 657h-p 2016 $4597

The New Family Cook or Housekeeper's Guide.... London: printed for the Booksellers, 1838. Some slight spotting, original brown cloth, slightly rubbed and marked, good, sound copy. Jarndyce Antiquarian Books CCXV - 337 2016 £125

The New Female Instructor; or Young Woman's Guide... London: Thomas Kelly, 1822. Frontispiece, additional engraved title, plates, frontispiece strengthened using original endpaper, plates slightly browned and with some damp marking, paper repair to contents leaf, handsomely rebound in half tan calf, black morocco label, signature of Sarah Jane Hemsworth, April 1829. Jarndyce Antiquarian Books CCXV - 338 2016 £180

New Granada Mineral Land Company *The Charter and by-laws of the New Granada Mineral Land Company...* Philadelphia: printed by C. Sherman & Son, 1856. First edition, 8vo., 1 (of 2) plates, folding map, original beige wrappers, stitched, overall good, map detached, otherwise fine. Kaaterskill Books 21 - 57 2016 $250

The New History of the Trojan Wars and Troy's Destruction. Paisley: printed and sold by Alex Weir, 1774. Very rare provincial printing, 12mo., somewhat toned, contemporary decorated boards backed with sheep, spine very rubbed, extremities worn, front flyleaf lost, sound. Blackwell's Rare Books Greek & Latin Classics VII - 22 2016 £750

New Miscellaneous Poems, with Five Love-Letters from a Nun to a Cavalier. London: printed for A. Bettesworth and C. Hitch, 1731. Seventh edition, very good, engraved frontispiece, 12mo., contemporary calf, spine gilt (spine trifle rubbed front cover loose), small patched repair to foot of titlepage, touching ruled border, but very good, complete with engraved frontispiece. C. R. Johnson Rare Book Collections Foxon: H-P 2015 - 661 2016 $3064

A New Primary Dictionary of the English Language. Philadelphia: 1902. Early owner's embroidered binding. Honey & Wax Booksellers 4 - 38 2016 $400

The New Primer. Groton: Alpheus Richardson, circa, 1830. printed wrappers, illustrations, some edgewear and soiling, but very good, rare complete copy. Joseph J. Felcone, Inc. Books from Five Centuries: a Miscellany - 110 2016 $650

New Provinces. Poems of Several Authors. Toronto: Macmillan Company, 1936. First edition, very good, clean condition, previous owner's name on f.f.ep., green hardcovers with black titles, very light wear on corners and edges, green dust jacket with black titles, spine yellowed, small closed tear on front jacket of spine, rare book, very good+ in very good dust jacket. Simon Finch 2015 - 212823 2016 $230

A New Translation of Aesop in a Hundred Select Fables Burlesq'd.   London: printed and sold by S. Malthus and William Lucas, 1705. First edition, 8vo., panelled calf antique, red morocco label, some foxing, very slight marginal restoration to first and last leaves, otherwise very good, very rare.   C. R. Johnson Rare Book Collections   Foxon: H-P 2015 - 667   2016 $3064

New York Academy of Medicine, Author Catalog.   Boston: G. K. Hall, 1969. First edition, folio, cloth.   Oak Knoll Books   310 - 298   2016 $749

New York Public Library   *Guide to Festschriften the Retrospective Festschriften Collection of the New York Public Library. With a Dictionary Catalogue of Festschriften in the New York Public Library (1972-1976) and the Library of Congress.*   Boston: G. K. Hall & Co., 1977. 4to., cloth, 2 volumes, library markings on front covers and spines and stamps on front free endpapers and titlepages.   Oak Knoll Books   310 - 245   2016 $350

New York Public Library   *The Hornbook.*   New York: New York Public Library, 1927. Plates, original grey printed wrappers.   Jarndyce Antiquarian Books   CCXV - 776   2016   £20

Newbery, E.   *The Royal Genealogical Pastime of the Sovereigns of England.*   London: pub. by E. Newbery, the corner of St. Paul's Church Yard & John Wallis, No. 16, Ludgate Street, Nov. 30th, 1791. 12 sections mounted on linen, with hand colored playing area, printed rules down each side, some minor edge wear without loss, light browning, corners of few sections lifting from linen backing, stitching to linen on verso, original marbled card slipcase, little worn at edges but engraved oval label intact.   Jarndyce Antiquarian Booksellers   CCXVI - 425   2016   £280

Newbigin, Alice M. S.   *A Wayfarer in Spain.*   London: Methuen, 1926. First edition, 8vo., map on endpaper, illustrations, original brown cloth, small stain where label removed, small nick at head of spine.   J. & S. L. Bonham Antiquarian Booksellers   Europe 2016 - 6377   2016   £30

Newbolt, Henry   *Drake's Drum and the Songs of the Sea.*   London: Hodder and Stoughton, 1914. First edition, quarto, 12 tissue guarded tipped in color plates, pictorial endpapers, original lavish gilt decorated cloth, titlepage (1914) gift inscription on verso of front free endpaper and bookplate on blank opposite, covers slightly marked and just little rubbed at head an tail of spine, free endpapers tanned, prelims spotted, very good.   Peter Ellis   112 - 277   2016   £150

Newby, Eric   *Love and War in the Apennines.*   London: Hodder and Stoughton, 1971. First edition, 8vo., original cloth in dust jacket, frontispiece, one sketch map, near fine, ownership inscription.   Sotheran's   Piccadilly Notes - Summer 2015 - 215   2016   £68

Newby, P. H.   *Something to Answer For.*   London: Faber and Faber, 1968. First edition, crown 8vo., original orange cloth, backstrip lettered in dark blue, dust jacket with lamination wrapped around to rear panel as usual, mildest of toning to leading edge of same, near fine.   Blackwell's Rare Books   B186 - 268   2016   £350

Newby, P. H.   *The Young May Moon.*   London: Cape, 1950. First edition, foolscap 8vo., original fawn cloth, backstrip and front cover blocked in red, tail edges untrimmed, dust jacket lightly soiled, backstrip panel faded and chipped, good, inscribed by author.   Blackwell's Rare Books   B186 - 269   2016   £60

Newcomb, Thomas   *Bibliotheca; a Poem.*   London: printed and are to be sold by J. Morphew, 1714. Second edition, 8vo., disbound, fine.   C. R. Johnson Rare Book Collections   Foxon: H-P 2015 - 869   2016 $2298

Newcome, Peter   *The History of the Ancient and Royal Foundation, Called the Abbey of St. Alban in the County of Hertford, from the Founding Thereof in 793 to the dissolution in 1339.*   London: printed for the author by J. Nichols, 1795. Reissue, 4to., some slight foxing, generally very clean, bound red labels, some wear to head and tail of spine, gilt little rubbed, minor abrasions to boards, early signature of Mary Bagot.   Jarndyce Antiquarian Booksellers   CCXVI - 426   2016   £225

Newell, Peter   *The Hole Book.*   New York: Harper & Bros. Oct., 1908. First edition, 8vo., blue cloth, pictorial paste-on, fine in dust jacket (very good- with pieces off spine ends and rear cover, few closed tears), marvelous full page illustrations by Newell, rare in dust jacket.   Aleph-bet Books, Inc.   111 - 318   2016 $2750

Newell, Peter   *The Slant Book.*   New York: Harper, Nov., 1910. First edition, 8vo., cloth backed pictorial boards, tips and edges slightly rubbed, else fine in pictorial dust jacket (very good+ lightly soiled and chipped), housed in custom cloth box, full page color illustrations, real rarity in fragile dust jacket.   Aleph-bet Books, Inc.   111 - 319   2016 $3000

The Newes, published for Satisfaction and Information of the People with Privilege Number 86 Thursday Nov. 10 1664.   London: printed for Richard Hodgkinson, 1664. 4to., slightly dusted, bound with numerous blanks into modern quarter calf.   Jarndyce Antiquarian Booksellers   CCXVII - 203   2016   £280

Newhall, Nancy   *Ansel Adams. Volume I. The Eloquent Light.*   San Francisco: Sierra Club, 1963. First edition, 87 black and white photos, fine, dust jacket (bit of minor staining to edges and bottom of last few leaves), scarce.   Argonaut Book Shop   Photography 2015 - 4742   2016 $90

Newhall, Nancy *Cedric Wright: Words of the Earth.* San Francisco: Sierra Club, 1960. First edition, folio, 50 black and white photos by Wright plus a portrait by Ansel Adams, brown cloth lettered in silver, fine with pictorial dust jacket. Argonaut Book Shop   Photography 2015 - 7203   2016 $75

Newland, Henry *South Church Union Lectures.* London: Joseph Masters, 1853. Third edition, half title, 1 page ads, original purple brown cloth covered wrappers, cut flush, original paper label on front board, inscribed "With Bp. of Moray's regards".   Jarndyce Antiquarian Booksellers   CCXVII - 198   2016   £30

Newman, Isidora *Fairy Flowers: Nature Legends of Fact and Fantasy.* New York: Henry Holt, 1928. 4to., cloth backed boards with floral design, fine in original dust jacket, 15 beautiful tippe-in color plates and 15 lovely full page black and whites by Willy Pogany.   Aleph-bet Books, Inc.   111 - 344   2016 $475

Newman, John Henry, Cardinal   1801-1890 *The idea of a University Defined and Illustrated.* London: Longmans, 1907. New impression, half title, original dark blue cloth, slight mark to front board, later ownership inscription. Jarndyce Antiquarian Books   CCXV - 877   2016   £20

Newman, John Henry, Cardinal   1801-1890 *Sermons Bearing on Subjects of the Day.* London: J. G. F. and J. Rivington, 1843. First edition, half title, original blue green cloth, slightly browned and chipped paper label, small nick to lower margin of spine with slight loss, spine rubbed at head and tail, inner hinges little weak, presentation inscription "Ambrose St. John with affectionate regards of JHN DEC. 8 1843".   Jarndyce Antiquarian Booksellers   CCXVII - 199   2016   £1250

Newman, John Henry, Cardinal   1801-1890 *Tracts for the Times.* London: printed for J. G. and F. Rivington & J. H. Parker, Oxford, 1834-1841. First editions, complete set, Volume I 1834-4 - Volume V for 1838-40 and Volume VI for 1841, complete set of 90 tracts bound in 6 volumes with titlepages and prelim matter for the first 5 volumes, no volume title to last volume, due no doubt to sudden cessation of the series, contemporary divinity calf, spine little bit scuffed, 1885 inscription A. Murray Browne, later inscription by William Bevil Browne, some pencil underlinings and marginal notes, good.   Blackwell's Rare Books   B186 - 106   2016   £600

Newton, A. Edward *Derby Day: and Other Adventures.* Boston: Little Brown, 1934. One of a limited edition of 1129 numbered copies signed by author, large 8vo., photos, partially unopened, leaf from unopened volume, with facsimile of its manuscript in pocket at rear of book, light green paper over boards, tan cloth spine stamped in green, cover little faded and worn at corners, otherwise very good, tight copy. Second Life Books, Inc.   196 B - 311   2016 $120

Newton, A. Edward *The Format of the English Novel.* Cleveland: Rowfant Club, 1928. One of 289 numbered copies, with separate colored plate as frontispiece, marbled cloth, maroon base color, box with wrap around label.   Oak Knoll Books   310 - 66   2016 $300

Newton, A. Edward *The Trollope Society.* Philadelphia: privately printed by author, 1934. First edition, small 8vo., paper wrappers, sewn at back, frontispiece, original mailing envelope, fine.   Second Life Books, Inc.   197 - 247   2016 $45

Newton, Chambers & Co. *Patterns of Palisading & Gates, Balconies, Staircases, Staircase Banisters, Verandahs...* Birmingham: Cund Bros. Printers, 1882. Oblong folio, title printed in red and black, 112 chromolithograph plates, 4 folding, printed index on front pastedown, original blue cloth, upper cover blocked with gilt title, fine.   Marlborough Rare Books   List 56 - 11   2016   £1250

Newton, Charles Thomas *A History of Discoveries at Hallcarnassus, Cnidus and Branchidae.* London: Day & Son, 1862. Volume 2 part 1 only, 8vo., folding frontispieces, map, 2 plates, 14 woodcuts, light foxing to map, else very good. Edwin V. Glaser Rare Books   2015 - 8332   2016 $300

Newton, Isaac   1642-1727 *Correspondence Respecting the Prince Edward Island Raily and Report of....* Charlottetown: 1873. 8vo., printed wrappers stitch bound, browned along edges and with some foxing, very small pieces misising from spine and small hole through top corner margin through pamphlet but not into text, presentation from G. A. Sharp.   Schooner Books Ltd.   115 - 183   2016 $175

Newton, Isaac   1642-1727 *Philosophiae Naturalis Principia Mathematica.* London: William and John Innys, 1726. Third edition, title printed in red and black, engraved frontispiece, 1 engraving and numerous diagrams in text, complete with half title and final ad leaf, some foxing at beginning and end, few scattered minor stains, repairs to margins of front flyleaves, late 19th century half red hard grained morocco, spine gilt in compartments and lettered direct, red edges, rebacked preserving previous spine, early inscription at head of title, little cropped at top and faded, seems to say 'gifted to Mr. William Scott of Babecan advocate by me ( ) Foulis', 19th century signature stamp of Dugald Macdonald at centre of titlepage, bookplate of Quebecois George G. Leroux, very good.   Blackwell's Rare Books   Marks of Genius - 32   2016   £11,000

Newton, Isaac 1642-1727 *The Mathematical Principles of Natural Philosophy.* London: for Benjamin Motte, 1729. First edition in English, 2 octavo volumes, engraved frontispiece after and by A. Motte in each volume, 47 folding engraved plates, 2 folding letterpress tables, 3 engraved headpieces by Motte, numerous woodcut head and tailpieces and historiated and ornamental woodcut initials, section title ot Machin's "Laws of the Moon's Motion", contemporary brown calf, rebacked to style, decoratively gilt stamped on spine with five raised bands, each volume with red morocco spine label, lettered in gilt, titlepage of volume one supplied from another copy and professionally repaired along outer margin and 1 small hole, also professionally repaired, small wormhole to lower inner margin to beginning pages of volume, one previous owner's contemporary small signature on titlepage of volume 2, otherwise very clean and tight, handsome set.   Heritage Book Shop   Holiday 2015 - 84   2016 $45,000

Newton, Isaac 1642-1727 *Principes Mathematiques de la Philosophie Naturelle.* Paris: Desaint & Saillant, Lambert, 1759. First and only French translation, 2 volumes, 4to., 14 folding engraved plates, woodcut head and tailpieces, occasional minor foxing, modern half calf stamp of the London Institution and U. of L. withdrawn stamp on titles and final page.   Blackwell's Rare Books   Marks of Genius - 34   2016   £3500

Newton, Isaac 1642-1727 *Mathematical Principles of Natural Philosophy Book the First (all published).* London: printed by A. Strahan for T. Cadell, Jun. and W. Davies, 1802. 22 folding engraved plates, some dampstaining mainly throughout, usually pale but little more pronounced in places, the last leaf a cancel, 4to., 19th century half calf and marbled boards, flat spine gilt tooled on either side of raised bands, skillfully rebacked and recornered, new labels, stamp of Melchet Court, Romsey with initial A circled by a crown in centre, few mathematical notes in margins, good.
Blackwell's Rare Books   Marks of Genius - 33   2016   £2500

Newton, Isaac 1642-1727 *Opticks or a Treatise of the Reflections, Refractions, Inflections and Colours of Light.* London: printed by William Bowyer for William and John Innys, 1721. Third edition, 8vo., folding engraved plates, contemporary panelled calf, skillfully rebacked in period style, light dampstain on front and rear endpapers, else very good, clean.   Joseph J. Felcone, Inc.   Books from Five Centuries: a Miscellany - 112   2016 $4500

Neyt, Francois *La Grande Statuaire Hemba Du Zaire.* Louvain- La Neuve: Institute Superieur d'Archeologie & D'Histoire De L'Art, First edition, 4to., original bright blue cloth, lettered gilt on spine and cover, copiously illustrated in black and white, very good+ in dust jacket, excellent condition.   Any Amount of Books   2015 - C396   2016   £600

Nicholls, W. H. *Orchids of Australia, Drawn in Natural Colour.* Melbourne: Georgian House, 1951. Limited to 1050 numbered copies, Small folio, 96 colored plates with accompanying text leaves, full red morocco with gilt spine and contrasting black label, wrappers retained, very fine in scarce presentation binding.   Andrew Isles Natural History Books   55 - 25244   2016 $1850

Nichols, Francis *The Irish Compendium; or Rudiments of Honour....* London: printed for J. Knapton, 1756. Fifth edition, frontispiece, 85 engraved plates, 12mo., full contemporary calf, neatly rebacked with recent black gilt label. Jarndyce Antiquarian Booksellers   CCXVI - 427   2016   £280

Nichols, John *Genuine Works of William Hogarth...* London: Longman, Hurst, Rees, & Orme, 1808. 1810, 2 volumes, 4to., frontispiece portraits, plates, some light foxing overall, nice, clean copy, contemporary full calf, elaborate blind and gilt borders, raised gilt bands, spines in blind and gilt, some rubbing to hinges, armorial bookplate of Joseph Ffeilden, Esq., Lancaster, bookseller's ticket of Row & Waller, London, fine and handsome.   Jarndyce Antiquarian Booksellers   CCXVII - 127   2016   £450

Nichols, John *The Sterile Cuckoo.* New York: David McKay, 1965. First edition, trifle toned on top edge soil easily fine in fine dust jacket, superior copy.   Between the Covers Rare Books   204 - 85   2016 $250

Nichols, John Treadwell *The Fresh-Water Fishes of China.* New York: American Museum of Natural History, 1943. Quarto, text illustrations, publisher's yellow printed cloth, fine.   Andrew Isles Natural History Books   55 - 36002   2016 $200

Nichols, Thomas Low *Behaviour, a manual of manners and Morals.* London: Longmans, 1874. Half title, 1 page ads, original light brown decorated cloth, bevelled boards, slightly dulled and rubbed, small ink mark to front board, all edges gilt, good plus.   Jarndyce Antiquarian Books   CCXV - 339   2016   £45

Nicholson, Ben *Ben Nicholson.* Zurich: Galeri Andre Emmerich, 1975. First Edition, quarto, color plates and photo of the artist, fine.   Peter Ellis   112 - 279   2016   £25

Nicholson, Edward *Indian Snakes. An Elementary Treastise on Ophiology with a descriptive Catalogue of the Snakes Found in India and the Adjoining Countries.* Madras: Higginbotham and Co., 1893. Second edition, octavo, 20 lithographic plates, many figures hand colored, publisher's brown cloth with gilt cobra, titlepage and early leaves laid down, otherwise very good.   Andrew Isles Natural History Books   55 - 35837   2016 $850

Nicholson, William *An Introduction to Natural History Illustrated with Copperplates.* Philadelphia: T. Dobson, 1795. 8vo., half title, 25 folding illustrated plates, recent quarter calf and marbled boards, some light marginal worming, text brown and foxed in parts, plates, clean ter to plate XXII, overall nice. James Tait Goodrich X-78 - 413 2016 $750

Nicholson, William *The Pirate Twins.* London: Faber and Faber, 1929. Special edition limited to 60 numbered copies signed by author, oblong 8vo., pictorial boards, covers very slightly dusty, else fine, color lithographs, very rare edition. Aleph-bet Books, Inc. 111 - 320 2016 $6500

Nicholson, William *The Wind Singer.* London: Mammouth, 2000. First British edition, true first, fine in fine dust jacket, signed by author. Bella Luna Books 2016 - t8063 2016 $82

Nicklin, John Arnold *Dickens-Land Described by....* London: Blackie & Son, 1939. Color frontispiece, plates, original drab boards, lettered in green, very good. Jarndyce Antiquarian Booksellers CCXVIII - 1393 2016 £30

Nicklin, Susan *Address to a Young Lady on Her Entrance into the World.* London: printed for Houlston and Carpenter, 1796. 8vo., 2 volumes, slight tears to inner margin of titlepage volume I, small hole at foot of A1 affecting signature letter (probably printing fault), slight damp marks to fore-edge final three leaves, faint waterstaining towards end volume II, full contemporary tree calf, gilt spines with sunburst & floral devices, black morocco labels spines, rubbed, slight abrasions to boards, corners bumped. Jarndyce Antiquarian Books CCXV - 340 2016 £520

Nicolas, Pierre Francois *Memoires sur les Maladies Epidemiques qui ont Regne dans la Province de Deuphine depuis l'annee 1780....* Grenoble: l'Imprimerie Royale, 1786. First edition, light stain to upper margin of final few leaves, very good, contemporary quarter calf over speckled boards. Edwin V. Glaser Rare Books 2015 - 10315 2016 $250

Nicoll, M. J. *Three Voyages of a Naturalist....* London: Witherby, 1908. First edition, 8vo., maps, illustrations, original blue cloth. J. & S. L. Bonham Antiquarian Booksellers Voyages 2016 - 8791 2016 £80

Nicoll, William Robertson *Literary Anecdotes of the Nineteenth Century Contributions Towards a Ltierary History of the Period.* London: Hodder & Stoughton, 1895-1896. First edition, 2 volumes, 8vo., original cloth, scarce, inner hinge of first volume cracked but solid, better condition than most sets seen. Oak Knoll Books 310 - 222 2016 $300

Nicoll, William Robertson *The Problem of 'Edwin Drood' a study in the methods of Dickens.* London: Hodder & Stoughton, 1912. First edition, half title, frontispiece, original full vellum, spine and front board lettered gilt, slightly spotted, very good, signed presentation from author to Captain Douglas Stuart William Milne on his marriage in 1916. Jarndyce Antiquarian Booksellers CCXVIII - 682 2016 £45

Nicols, Arthur *Chapters from the Physical History of the Earth.* London: C. Kegan Paul & Co., 1880. First edition, half title, 32 page catalog 10/79, tipped in 'Opinions of the Press' leaf, original dark brown cloth, little marked, author's own copy with his notes, corrections amendments together with insertions, 4 page ALS from F. W. Ridler of Museum of Practical Geology, brief note from Kegan Paul, brief ALS from H. G. Seeley, ALS postcard from Sir Stanley Lathes. Jarndyce Antiquarian Booksellers CCXVII - 205 2016 £380

Nicolson, Harold *Small Talk.* London: Constable & Co., 1937. Second edition, half title, original red cloth, slightly marked, spine faded. Jarndyce Antiquarian Books CCXV - 341 2016 £15

Niemeyer, A. H. *Travels on the Continent and in England.* London: Richard Phillips, 1823. First English edition, 8vo., original grey boards. J. & S. L. Bonham Antiquarian Booksellers Europe 2016 - 6584 2016 £25

Nietzsche, Friedrich Wilhelm *Also Sprach Zarathustra.* Leipzig: Verlag von C. W. Fritzsch, 1886. Leipzig: Druck and Verlag von C. G. Numann, 1891. First collected edition, parts 1-3 are first edition, second issue as these first three parts are put together from sheets of first edition, first issue which were all issued separately, for this issue the titlepages for each part were cancelled and a new volume title was created and half titles for each part added, part 4 is the first trade edition, 4 octavo volumes in one, contemporary half pebble brown cloth over marbled boards, spine lettered gilt, tiny one quarter inch split to top rear joint, boards slightly rubbed at edges and joints, previous owner's bookplate on front pastedown, previous owner's small old ink note and date stamp on front pastedown, some very slight discoloration to main titlepage, overall very nice and clean copy. Heritage Book Shop Holiday 2015 - 83 2016 $4000

Nihell, Jacobo *Novae Raraeque Observationes Circa Variarum Crislum Praedictionme....* Venetiis: Thoman Bettineli, 1748. Original stiff paper boards, very clean, crisp copy. James Tait Goodrich X-78 - 414 2016 $225

Nin, Anais *Children of the Albatross.* New York: Dutton, 1947. First edition, 8vo., fine in near fine dust jacket, inscribed by author for Bill Claire. Second Life Books, Inc. 196 B - 315 2016 $400

Nin, Anais *The Diary of Anais Nin. Volume Two 1934-1939.* New York: Swallow Press/Harcourt Brace and world, 1967. First edition, 8vo., photos, very good, tight copy, dust jacket little scuffed and chipped, inscribed by author for Bill Claire.   Second Life Books, Inc.   196 B - 317   2016 $400

Nin, Anais *The Diary of.... Volume 3 1939-1944.* New York: Harcourt Brace and World, 1969. First edition, 8vo., very nice in dust jacket, complimentary slip from author laid in.   Second Life Books, Inc.   197 - 250   2016 $45

Nin, Anais *The Diary of.... 1944-1947.* New York: Harcourt Brace Jovanovich, 1971. First edition, 8vo. illustrations, with photos, cover lightly stained, otherwise very good, tight copy in little scuffed and nicked price clipped dust jacket, laid in is advance copy complimentary slip with author's card, also inscribed by author to poet William Claire.   Second Life Books, Inc.   196 B - 318   2016 $600

Nin, Anais *The Four Chambered Heart.* New York: Duell, Sloan and Pearce, 1950. First edition, 8vo., grey cloth, pages little toned, very good, inscribed by author for William Claire.   Second Life Books, Inc.   196 B - 319   2016 $300

Nin, Anais *House of Incest.* Paris: Siana Editions, 1936. First edition, 4to., stain to endpapers and blanks opposite frontispiece and in rear, printed wrappers, some shelf wear and browning, front hinge strengthened, nice, untrimmed copy in cloth slipcase, one of only 249 copies, numbered and signed by author.   Second Life Books, Inc.   196 B - 320   2016 $1250

Nin, Anais *Ladders to Fire.* New York: Dutton, 1946. First edition, 8vo., very good in little chipped and worn dust jacket (lacks some of jacket at extremities of spine and on corners), inscribed by author for Bill Claire.   Second Life Books, Inc.   196 B - 321   2016 $450

Nisbet, Ada *Dickens Centennial Essays.* Berkeley: University of California Press, 1971. First edition, half title, illustrations, orginal pale blue cloth, editor's compliments slip loosely inserted, very good in dust jacket.   Jarndyce Antiquarian Booksellers   CCXVIII - 1395   2016   £20

Nisbet, Alexander *An Essay on the Ancient and Modern Use of Armories; Shewing their Origin, Definition and Division of them into their Several Species.* Edinburgh: printed by William Adam Junior, for Mr. James Mackeuen, 1718. First edition, fine in beautiful binding, 4to., mid 19th century full red morocco 18th century style, bound by John Whiteford MacKenzie, elaborately gilt, gilt spine (slightly faded) in 7 compartments, raised bands, black leather label, gilt edges, inner gilt dentelles, marbled endpaper, engraved plates, all edges gilt.   Howard S. Mott Inc.   265 - 101   2016 $600

Nisbet, Hume *Her Loving Slave.* London: Digby, Long & Co., 1894. First edition, half title, frontispiece, illustrations, title, original pictorial light blue cloth, very good.   Jarndyce Antiquarian Booksellers   CCXVII - 206   2016   £180

Nissen, Claus *Die Illustrierten Vogelbucher: ihre Geschichte und Bibliographie.* Stuttgart: Hiersemann Verlag, 1953. Quarto, photos, very good in dust jacket.   Andrew Isles Natural History Books   55 - 10803   2016 $200

Nissenwurzel, Paul Arthur Amadeus *Doomsday Books.* San Francisco: printed for Herbert Rothchild for members of the Roxburghe Club, 1928. One of 150 copies printed by Grabhorn Press, tall quarto, titlepage printed in black and red, handset Janson type, black cloth backed gray boards, small bookplate on inner cover, very minor wear to foot of spine, fine.   Argonaut Book Shop   Literature 2015 - 5854   2016 $150

Nix, Nelleke *Zones of Time, Sand and Rain.* Washington: Library Fellows of the National Museum of Women in the Arts, 2000. Limited to 125 numbered copies signed by Nix, small 4to., boards made of specialty plywood with open sewn spine, sepia photo on front board, 3-D viewer included inside back cover, red cloth dropback box, with cut-out rectangle allowing viewer to see the image on front board, titlepage, blockprints and linocuts done at Sideral Press.   Oak Knoll Books   27 - 45   2016 $300

Nixon, Ed *The Nixons. A Family Portrait.* Bothell: Book Pub. Network, 2009. First edition, gilt stamped hardbound, signed by Nixon and Karen Olson, fine, like new in dust jacket.   Gene W. Baade, Books on the West   2015 - P2036b   2016 $50

Nixon, Richard Milhous *Six Crises.* New York: Doubleday, 1962. First edition, large 8vo., very good, tight in little worn but unclipped dust jacket, inscribed by author for Patti Vickery.   Second Life Books, Inc.   196 B - 322   2016 $600

Noakes, David L. G. *The Ecology and Ethology of Fishes.* The Hague: Dr. W. Junk, 1981. Small quarto, photos, very good.   Andrew Isles Natural History Books   55 - 38866   2016 $220

Nobbes, Robert *The Compleat Troller or the Art of Trolling with a Description of all the Utensils, Instruments, Tackling and Materials Requisite Thereto...* London: by T. James for Tho. Helder 1682, i.e. circa, 1790. 18th century facsimile reprint, 2 woodcuts in text, contemporary blue paper wrappers (front dampstained), neatly rebacked, dampstain to first few leaves, title bit soiled, else very good in neat portfolio and morocco backed slipcase.   Joseph J. Felcone, Inc.   Books from Five Centuries: a Miscellany - 5   2016 $750

Noble, Richard *Mr. Noble's Speech to My Lord Chief-Justice Parker at his Tryal at Kingston Assizes on Friday March 13 1712.* London: printed for Bernard Lintott, 1713. Folio, uncut, light fold marks.   Jarndyce Antiquarian Booksellers   CCXVI - 429   2016   £520

Noffenegger, Audrey *The Time Traveler's Wife.* London: Jonathan Cape, 2005. First limited edition, fine, in fine dust jacket, still original plastic wrapper, signed on a publisher's bookplate attached to half titlepage.   Bella Luna Books 2016 - k170   2016 $198

Nogales, Rafael De *Vier Jahre unter dem Halbmond. Erinnenrungen aus dem Weltkriege.* Berlin: Reimar Hobbing, 1925. First German edition, 8vo., original red cloth, lettered in black with illustrated dust jackets, highly illustrated with plates after photos, folding map, printed in red and black, fine.   Sotheran's   Travel and Exploration - 353   2016   £198

Nomachi, Kazuyushi *Sahara.* Newton Abbot: Westbridge Books, 1978. First English edition, large 4to., original sand colored cloth, dust jacket price clipped, full page illustrations and color and black and white, very good, contemporary bookplate inside front cover.   Sotheran's   Travel and Exploration - 354   2016   £48

"Nomad." Occasional Shots. A Collection of Anglo-Indian Incidents. London: printed at the Victoria Press, Quetta 9278, 1906. Original red cloth wrappers cut flush, printed in black with price "One Rupee".   Jarndyce Antiquarian Booksellers   CCXVII - 207   2016   £85

Nonesuch Press *Retrospectus and Prospectus. The Nonesuch Dickens.* London: Nonesuch Press, 1937. Half title, illustrations, uncut, original blue cloth, very good in glassine wrapper, original slightly worn orange box.   Jarndyce Antiquarian Booksellers   CCXVIII - 1510   2016   £30

Norie, John William *A Complete Epitome of Practical Navigation...* London: printed for the author and sold by Charles Wilson, 1856. Sixteenth (Stereotyped) edition, 222 x 137mm., very plain contemporary sprinkled sheep, flat spine divided into panels by single gilt rules, dun-colored endpapers, 9 engraved plates, 19th century ink signature of Charles Watson, tiny cracks just beginning at top and bottom of joints, minor smudge upper cover, lower board with small trailing wormhole, minor offsetting from plates, still especially fine, entirely bright, fresh and clean inside and out.   Phillip J. Pirages   67 - 266   2016 $750

Norrcena Society *The Flatey Book and Recently Discovered Vatican Manuscripts Concerning America as Early as the Tenth Century.* Flatey: London, 1906. Facsimiles, endpaper maps, binding slightly shaken, generally very good.   Dumont Maps and Books   133 - 69   2016 $50

Norre, Erhardt *Chirurgischer Webweiser samt Einem Reise-und Fel-Kasten fur die Chirurgos...* Nuremberg: Johann Stein, 1736. 12mo., quite scarce, titlepage loose, one clasp broken, lightly browned throughout, lacks frontispiece and leaves E4-6, contemporary blindstamped calf with leather and brass clasps.   Edwin V. Glaser Rare Books   2015 - 9403   2016 $300

Norris, Frank *A Novelist in the Making.* Cambridge: Harvard University Press, 1970. First edition, presentation signed by editor, frontispiece facsimile, grey cloth, very good, lightly chipped and soiled pictorial dust jacket.   Argonaut Book Shop   Literature 2015 - 74444   2016 $60

Norris, Joan *Banquet.* Lincoln: Penmaen Press, 1978. First edition, one of 225 copies, signed by authors and artist, printed paper over boards, 3/4 tan cloth, without slipcase, very nice.   Second Life Books, Inc.   196 B - 325   2016 $150

Norris, Kathleen *Dedications.* Berkeley: Charles G. Norris, 1936. First edition, one of 100 copies printed, cloth backed blue boards, printed paper cover label, spine darkening to extremities of covers and spine, overall fine, scarce, previous owner has very discreetly noted that one dedication is to the authors younger brother, and another address to CGN was her husband, Charles Norris.   Argonaut Book Shop   Literature 2015 - 7445   2016 $125

North Lee, Brian *Bookplates by Richard Shirley Smith.* Upper Denby: Fleece Press, 2005, i.e., 2006. One of 235 copies from an edition of 275, printed on Saunders paper, 65 illustrations by Richard Shirley Smith, including 9 engravings, and 12 from line block, 6 of the illustrations tipped in, photographic reproductions of Shirley Smith also tipped in, title printed in brown, crown 8vo., original quarter lime green linen, printed label, matching stained wood veneer boards, untrimmed, green linen slipcase with printed label, fine.   Blackwell's Rare Books   B184 - 259   2016   £140

North, Alfred J. *Nests and Eggs of Birds found Breeding in Australia and Tasmania.* Sydney: Australian Museum, 1901-1914. Quarto, 4 volumes, 25 egg plates, uncolored vignettes by Neville Cayley senior, photos by author and H. Barnes, handsome modern green morocco and cloth boards, all edges speckled, fine, clean set.   Andrew Isles Natural History Books   55 - 13882   2016 $1800

North, Charles *Elizabethan & Nova Scotian Music.* New York: Adventures in Poetry, 1974. First edition, limited issue, one of 26 lettered copies signed by author and artist, 4to., original illustrated wrappers, stapled as issued, drawings by Jane Freilicher, fine.   James S. Jaffe Rare Books   Occasional List: Winter 2016 - 9   2016 $1500

North, Gil *A Corpse for Kofi Katt.* R. Hale, 1978. Very good in like dust jacket.   I. D. Edrich   Crime - 2016   £20

North, John *Sherlock Holmes and the Arabian Princess.* Romford, Essex: Ian Henry, 1990. First edition, fine in dust jacket.   Mordida Books   2015 - 007876   2016 $60

North, William *The City of the Jugglers or Free Trade in Souls.* H. J. Gibbs, 1850. First edition, plates as per titlepage, uniformly slightly browned, plates offset, frontispiece slightly foxed, bound without ads, inscription at top of titlepage cropped, contemporary half black calf, worn at extremities, spine chipped, lacking label, small hole in upper board at fore-edge penetrating into first 20 pages (no more than a nick by the time it reaches paper), sound, rare.   Blackwell's Rare Books   B186 - 107   2016   £3000

Northcote, William *The Anatomy of the Human Body.* 8vo., full modern brown calf with raised bands, gilt leather spine label in red, endpapers renewed, titlepage repaired with top and bottom margins repaired which has resulted in eliminating the first line, text has some soiling and foxing of paper, nice copy.   James Tait Goodrich   X-78 - 416   2016 $850

Northleigh, John *Topographical Descriptions; with Historico-Political Observations; made in Two Several Voyages through most parts of Europe.* London: Tooke, 1702. First edition, 2 parts in one volume, 8vo., 2 leaves of catalog creased and lightly soiled, contemporary brown panelled calf, scuff mark on upper cover, good copy.   J. & S. L. Bonham Antiquarian Booksellers   Europe 2016 - 8398   2016   £350

Norton, Andre *Operation Time Search.* New York: Harcourt Brace and World, 1967. First edition, octavo, fine in fine dust jacket with touch of rubbing and shelfwear.   John W. Knott, Jr./L.W. Currey, Inc.   Fall-Winter 2015 - 16694   2016 $350

Norton, Andre *Star Man's Son 2250 A.D.* New York: Harcourt Brace and Co., 1952. First edition, octavo, red boards, front and spine panels stamped in black, fine in fine dust jacket with mild fade to upper eighth of spine panel, sharp copy, scarce, rarely found in superior condition.   John W. Knott, Jr./L.W. Currey, Inc.   Fall-Winter 2015 - 17174   2016 $1250

Norton, Mary *The Borrowers.* New York: Harcourt Brace, 1953. Stated first UK edition, first printing, 8vo., blue pictorial cloth, slight cover fading and mark on endpaper, else near fine in like dust jacket, illustrations in black and white by Beth and Joe Krush.   Aleph-bet Books, Inc.   111 - 325   2016 $500

Norton, Mary *The Borrowers.* New York: Harcourt Brace and Co., 1953. First US edition, original light blue cloth lettered in darker blue to spine with small vignette in blue to upper cover, preserved in pictorial dust jacket with photographic portrait of author to lower panel, drawings, attractive copy with touch of fading to spine and flecking to joints, internally fresh with small contemporary ownership inscription upside down to rear free endpapers, dust jacket with light overall dusting and faint toning, 2 short closed tears to spine ends (maximum 20mm), tiny nicking to spine ends and corners, one small (15mm) circular and unobtrusive, mark to lower panel.   Sotheran's   Piccadilly Notes - Summer 2015 - 217   2016   £168

Norwich, John Julius *A Christmas Cracker: being a Commonplace Selection.* N.P.: 1993. wrappers, slight damp marks throughout, otherwise very nice, inscribed by compiler for Victor and Dorothy, from the library of V. S. Pritchett.   Bertram Rota Ltd.   Christmas List 2015 - 30   2016   £20

Notley, Alice *How Spring comes.* West Branch: Toothpaste Press, 1981. Limited to 100 numbered copies, signed by author, errata.   Oak Knoll Books   310 - 164   2016 $175

Nottingham, Daniel Finch, Earl of *Vindication of the Earl of Nottingham.* London: printed for J. Roberts, 1714. First edition, 8vo., disbound, half title present, fine.   Simon Finch   2015 - 84156   2016 $240

Novik, Naomi *Temeraire 2: Throne of Jade....* Burton, Subterranean Press, 2009. First edition in English, signed and lettered, one of 52 copies, illustrations by Dominic Harman and Anka Eissmann.   Simon Finch   2015 - 12602   2016 $230

Nowlan, James *Shall Irish Americans Countenance England's Demand for free Trade with America.* Chicago: J. C. Drake, printer, circa, 1884. First edition, 8vo., self wrappers, very good with mail fold.   Kaaterskill Books   21 - 65   2016 $175

Noyes, Alfred *A Pickwick Portrait Gallery from the Pens of Divers Admirers of the Illustrations Members of the Pickwick Club...* London: Chapman & Hall, 1936. Half title, frontispiece, plates, original pale red cloth, lettered and with small vignette of Mr. Pickwick in black, very good in slightly worn dust jacket.   Jarndyce Antiquarian Booksellers   CCXVIII - 160   2016   £35

Noyes, Charles *Redwood and Lumbering in California Forests.* San Francisco: E. Cherry, 1884. First edition, 4to., 24 mounted original albumen photos, with 15 captioned in purple ink, original brown cloth, green patterned paper endpapers, housed in custom chemise and quarter leather slipcase, binding show wear with some cloth loss (two horizontal strips 1 inch wide) to rear board, with board showing, first gathering coming loose, last quarter of text block has tide-line in upper and right margins (not affecting text), prior owner inscriptions to first blank page, including presentation inscription to contributor, Robert Dollar 1844-1932 (unknown inscriber), occasional marginal note, some photos with age fading to edges though not adversely affecting overall image, good+ to very good.   Tavistock Books   Bibliolatry - 38   2016 $7500

Noyes, John H. *The Berean: A Manual for the Help of Those Who Seek the Faith of the Primitive Church.* Putney: Office of the Spiritual Magazine, 1847. First edition, 8vo., original cloth, spine chipped, sound.   M & S Rare Books, Inc.   99 - 216   2016 $650

Nugent, Robert, Earl of *An Essay on Happiness.* London: printed for J. Walthoe, 1737. First edition, folio, later drab wrappers, very good, uncut.   C. R. Johnson Rare Book Collections   Foxon: H-P 2015 - 677   2016 $613

Nugent, Robert, Earl of *An Inquiry into the Origin and Consequences of the Influence of the Crow over Parliament etc.* London: printed for J. Dodsley, 1780. 8vo., without half title, disbound.   Jarndyce Antiquarian Booksellers CCXVI - 432   2016   £45

Nunis, Doyce B. *Josiah Belden. 1841. California Overland Pioneer: His memoir and early letters.* Georgetown: Talisman Press, 1962. First edition, one of 750 copies, illustrations, map endpapers, gray cloth with printed pink paper spine label, very fine with dust jacket.   Argonaut Book Shop   Biography 2015 - 3543   2016 $60

Nursery ABC. London: Dean, 1905. Slight cover soil and slight fraying, very good+, illustrations by Jessie Aitcheson Walker.   Aleph-bet Books, Inc.   112 - 3   2016 $275

Nutt, Alfred *Popular Studies in Mythology, Romance and Folklore.* London: David Nutt, 1899-1902. Volumes 1-12 bound as 1, 8vo., original green wrappers bound in, little toned, some occasional foxing, some wrappers faded, bound together in red buckram, gilt title to spine, edges little rubbed, top edge dusty but robustly bound and very good, nos. 11 and 12 signed " John F. Kelly".   Unsworths Antiquarian Booksellers Ltd.   30 - 114   2016   £300

Nye, Naomi Shihab *On the Edge of the Sky.* Madison: Iguana Press, 1981. Limited to 190 numbered copies, 12mo., stiff paper wrappers, dust jacket, top edge cut, others uncut, printed on handmade paper.   Oak Knoll Books 310 - 110   2016 $125

Nyholm, Janet *From a Housewife's Diary...* West Burke: Janus Press, 1978. First edition, no. 213 of 250 copies with Claire Van Vilet's presentation on colophon, large 8vo., illustrations hand colored with pencils, two flyers for Janus Press laid in, almost as new, bound in full cloth (red and white disthtowel) with paper spine label, printed on Mohawk Superfine by Van Vliet, illustrated with eraser stamps by Jerome Kaplan which were "colored 31 times eventually 37, by Victoria Fraser & anyone else she could con".   Second Life Books, Inc.   196 B - 330   2016 $175

Nyquist, Harry *Certain Topics in Telegraph Transmission Theory.* New York: American Institute of Electrical Engineers, 1928. First edition, extremely rare first printing, quarto, original wrappers, custom box, corners bumped, upper outer corner of first few leaves, bit wrinkled but nowhere near text, spine ends bit worn, exceedingly rare.   Manhattan Rare Book Company   2016 - 1792   2016 $7500

O

O'Brian, Patrick *The Commodore.* New York: W. W. Norton & Co., 1995. First American edition, frontispiece, blue cloth backed boards, gilt lettering to spine, very fine in pictorial dust jacket.   Argonaut Book Shop   Literature 2015 - 5301   2016 $90

O'Brian, Patrick *The Reverse of the Medal.* London: Collins, 1986. First edition, usual browning to poor quality, crown 8vo., original dark green boards backstrip lettered gilt, few small spots to top edge, dust jacket with gentle fading to backstrip panel, very good.   Blackwell's Rare Books   B184 - 200   2016   £350

O'Brien, Conor Cruise *Maria Cross Imaginative Patterns in a Group of Modern Catholic Writers.* New York: Oxford University Press, 1952. First edition, fine in attractive, near fine dust jacket with tiny tears, inscribed by Daniel and Philip Berrigan, uncommon title.   Between the Covers Rare Books   208 - 58   2016 $500

O'Brien, Robert *Mrs. Frisby and the Rats of Nimh.* New York: Atheneum, 1971. Stated first edition, 8vo., fine in fine dust jacket, illustrations by Zena Bernstein, rare, great copy.   Aleph-bet Books, Inc.   112 - 349   2016 $2500

O'Brien, Tim *The Things They Carried.* Boston: Houghton Mifflin, 1990. First edition, fine in fine dust jacket.   Bella Luna Books   2016 - 2833   2016 $200

O'Bryen, Denis *Utrum Horum? The government or the Country?* London: printed for J. Debrett, 1796. 8vo., half title, final blank Q2, disbound, slightly dusted, signature of Anne Renier.   Jarndyce Antiquarian Booksellers   CCXVI - 435   2016   £40

O'Connor, Edwin *The Oracle.* New York: Harper and Bros., 1951. First edition, 8vo., paper over boards, top edge slightly darkened, corners of cover and ends of spine little scuffed, otherwise nice, little chipped and soiled dust jacket.   Second Life Books, Inc.   197 - 251   2016 $45

O'Connor, Flannery 1925-1964 *Wise Blood.* New York: Harcourt Brace & Co., 1952. First edition, modest stain on top edge that is just touching top of boards and split at bottom front joint, spine worn down to text block, sound, good copy in presentable supplied, about very good dust jacket, ownership name of Miller Williams stamp on top of page edges, inscribed to same by author.   Between the Covers Rare Books   204 - 1   2016 $12,000

O'Connor, Frank *Guests of the Nation.* London: Macmillan and Co., 1930. First edition, 8vo., original cloth, dust jacket little chipped at head of spine, otherwise very good.   Sotheran's Piccadilly Notes - Summer 2015 - 219   2016   £498

O'Connor, John *Knipton, a Leicestershire Village.* Risbury: Whittington Press, 1996. Limited to 200 numbered copies, this one of 45 lettered copies to be bound thus and to contain separate portfolio of engravings, signed by O'Connor, woodcuts printed in different colors, 35 wood engravings by artist, small folio, quarter Oasis, paper covered boards, accompanied by a separate portfolio of 8 of the engravings inserted in cloth backed paper covered board portfolio, all inserted in slipcase.   Oak Knoll Books   310 - 175   2016 $600

O'Dell, Scott *Island of the Blue Dolphins.* Boston: Houghton Mifflin, 1960. First edition, first printing, 8vo., cloth, fine in dust jacket (not price clipped, no award seal, irregular piece off top of spine, ink name on flap, few closed tears), still very good-, this copy inscribed by O'Dell and laid in is TLS by artist, Eveline Ness in 1976 on her personal letterhead, Ness illustrated the color dust jacket, also laid in 4 page playbill for the movie made in 1964, signed by Celia Kay who starred in the movie.   Aleph-bet Books, Inc.   112 - 350   2016 $875

O'Dogherty, William *An Epitome of the History of Europe, from the Reign of Charlemagne, to the Reign of George III.* printed for T. Hookham, 1788. First edition of this title, one leaf with portion torn out of fore-margin (not affecting text), occasional spots or stains, 8vo., contemporary calf backed marbled boards, vellum tips to corners, flat spine with gilt tooled compartments, slightly worn, childish and somewhat messy scribblings in pencil to endpapers and flyleaves, good.   Blackwell's Rare Books   B186 - 108   2016   £450

O'Donnell, Donat *Maria Cross Imaginative Patterns in a Group of Modern Catholic Writers.* New York: Oxford University Press, 1952. First edition, preceding the British edition by 2 years, owner's name front fly, some passages underlined and notes in text in ink, else about very good in internally repaired near very good dust jacket with modest chips and tears.   Between the Covers Rare Books   204 - 86   2016 $150

O'Donoghue, Heather *English Poetry and Old Norse Myth: a History.* Oxford University Press, 2014. First edition, 8vo. black boards, gilt lettered spine, dust jacket, near fine.   Unsworths Antiquarian Booksellers Ltd.   E05 - 108   2016   £35

O'Faolain, Sean *A Summer In Italy.* New York: Devin-Adair, 1950. First edition, 8vo., signed by author, bookplate of Barbara Howes.   Second Life Books, Inc.   196 B - 332   2016 $40

O'Hamaguchi San *Fortune Telling by Japanese Swords from Old Japanese Mss.* London: John Lane, Bodley Head, 1905. First edition, 8vo., very good+, red cloth with gilt lettering and Japanese sword illustration spine, gilt Japanese sun design front cover, top edge gilt, mild spotting to covers, scattered foxing, few pages unopened, rare, signed and inscribed by Talbot Clifton.   By the Book, L. C. 45 - 51   2016 $650

O'Hara, Mary *Green Grass of Wyoming.* Philadelphia: J. B. Lippincott, 1946. First edition, gray cloth stamped in dark green and gold, fine with pictorial dust jacket (very slight wear to head of jacket spine).   Argonaut Book Shop   Literature 2015 - 7205   2016 $175

O'Hara, Mary *Thunderhead.* Philadelphia: J. B. Lippincott, 1943. First edition, blue cloth, some light spine fading, nice in lightly worn and tape repaired pictorial dust jacket.   Argonaut Book Shop   Literature 2015 - 7208   2016 $375

O'Keefe, Georgia *Georgia O'Keefe Drawings.* New York: Atlantis Editions, 1968. First edition, signed, limited edition, one of only 290 copies out of a total edition of 250, 10 very large lithographs, fine.   Manhattan Rare Book Company   2016 - 1817   2016 $16,500

O'Keefe, Georgia *Some Memories of Drawings.* New York: Atlantis Edition, 1974. First edition, limited, one of 20 presentation copies, out of a total edition of 120, signed by artist, and book's designer, Leonard Baskin, extraordinary copy, given by O'Keeffe's long time agent Doris Bry to her friend and noted psychiatrist Dr. Lucie Jessner, with letters from Bry to Jessner, 21 charcoal and pencil drawings reproduced on Arches Silkscreen in 300-line offset lithography, each laid into lettered folded leaf of Arches paper.   Manhattan Rare Book Company   2016 - 1626   2016 $10,000

O'Malley, C. D. *Andreas Vesalius of Brussels 1514-1564.* UC Press, 1964. 64 pages, original binding, very good.   James Tait Goodrich   X-78 - 535   2016 $85

O'Malley, C. D. *Leondaro da Vinci on the Human Body....* New York: Schumann, 1952. Large 4to., dust jacket worn and torn, original binding, text and book fine, illustrations.   James Tait Goodrich   X-78 - 425   2016 $250

O'Malley, C. D. *Leondaro da Vinci on the Human Body....* New York: Schuman, 1952. Large 4to., pictorial boards, original binding, nice, tight copy, illustrations.   James Tait Goodrich   X-78 - 373   2016 $125

O'Nan, Stewart *Snow Angels.* New York: Doubleday, 1994. First edition, near fine, spine ends wrinkled, dust jacket near fine with light creasing, signed by author.   Bella Luna Books   2016 - t4255   2016 $66

O'Neil, George *The Cobbler in Willow Street, and Other Poems.* New York: Boni & Liveright, 1919. First edition, small octavo, beige cloth backed olive green boards, extremities rubbed and corners showing, spine darkened, previous owner's bookplate, untrimmed edges, some pages uncut, very good.   Argonaut Book Shop   Literature 2015 - 7345   2016 $75

O'Neill, Eugene Gladstone   1888-1953 *Ah, Wilderness!* Avon: Heritage Press, 1972. Light blue boards with dark blue cloth spine, very fine in slipcase, illustrations by Shannon Stirweis, Sandglass pamphlet laid in.   Argonaut Book Shop   Heritage Press 2015 - 2024   2016 $45

O'Neill, Eugene Gladstone   1888-1953 *The Hairy Ape.* New York: Horace Liveright, 1929. First edition, limited large paper copy, 591/775 copies signed by author, 8vo., paste paper backed by cloth and dust jacket somewhat soiled, and worn at extremities, split along rear hinge, very good in original very worn box.   Second Life Books, Inc.   196 B - 336   2016 $450

O'Neill, Eugene Gladstone   1888-1953 *The Iceman Cometh.* New York: Limited Editions Club, 1982. First edition, small 4to., one of 2000 copies for the LEC, all copies signed by artist, in this copy the lithograph is signed, as new in original slipcase.   Second Life Books, Inc.   196 B - 337   2016 $400

O'Neill, Rose *The Kewpies their Book.* New York: Frederick Stokes, Nov., 1913. 4to., boards with pictorial paste-on, slightest bit of rubbing, else near fine, illustrations by author, with the book is boxed set of Kewpie handkerchiefs, 10 3/4" square and are silk screened with color images, box has flaps strengthened and with great pictorial cover, rare.   Aleph-bet Books, Inc.   111 - 328   2016 $2200

O'Reilly, J. A. *The Last Sentinel of Castle Hill A Story of Newfoundland.* London: Eliot Stock, 1916. 8vo. red cloth with gilt to spine & black lettering to front cover, spine sunned, small light stain to front over and boards, lightly soiled, half title missing.   Schooner Books Ltd.   115 - 114   2016 $45

Oakley, Violet *Cathedral of Compassion.* Philadelphia: Women's International League, 1955. Limited edition, 8vo., uncut, ivory cloth, stamped in red, signed by author, owner's name and address on verso of flyleaf, ex-library with stamps, cover somewhat soiled and little worn at corners and ends of spine, otherwise very good.   Second Life Books, Inc.   196 B - 341   2016 $65

Oates, Eugene W. *The Fauna of British India, Including Ceylon and Burma.* London: Taylor & Francis, 1889-1898. Octavo, 4 volumes, text illustrations, contemporary half morocco, slight wear and previous owner's notes, otherwise sound set.   Andrew Isles Natural History Books   55 - 21235   2016 $600

Oates, Joyce Carol 1938- *All the Good People I've Left Behind.* Santa Barbara: Black Sparrow Press, 1979. First edition, some sunning at edge of boards, very good or better in fine, original unprinted glassine dust jacket, one of 1000 hardbound copies, dedication copy inscribed by author Herb Yellin.   Between the Covers Rare Books   204 - 90   2016 $1500

Oates, Joyce Carol 1938- *All the Good People I've Left Behind.* Santa Barbara: Black Sparrow, 1979. First edition, of a total edition of 1000, this one of 300 copies that have been numbered and signed by author, 8vo., fine in original acetate.   Second Life Books, Inc.   196 B - 342   2016 $100

Oates, Joyce Carol 1938- *Do With Me what You Will.* New York: Vanguard Press, 1973. Uncorrected proof, pink wrappers, applied printed label, very good with bottom corner bumped, signed by author and uncommon thus.   Between the Covers Rare Books   204 - 88   2016 $300

Oates, Joyce Carol 1938- *Fertilizing the Continent.* Northridge: Santa Susana Press/California State University, 1976. First edition, copy number 10 of 12 signed copies, signed by Oates, quarter red calf and marbled paper covered boards, spine irregularly sunned, else near fine in slipcase,.   Between the Covers Rare Books   208 - 61   2016 $800

Oates, Joyce Carol 1938- *New Heaven, New Earth: The Visionary Experience in Literature.* New York: Vanguard Press, 1974. First edition, fine in fine dust jacket, inscribed by author to Herb Yellin, fairly uncommon.   Between the Covers Rare Books   208 - 60   2016 $250

Oates, Joyce Carol 1938- *On Boxing.* Garden City: Dolphin/Doubleday, 1987. First edition, fine in fine dust jacket, signed by author.   Between the Covers Rare Books   208 - 141   2016 $100

Oates, Joyce Carol 1938- *Queen of the Night.* Northridge: Lord John Press, 1979. First edition, copy 1 of 350 numbered and signed by author, quarter cloth and decorated paper covered boards.   Between the Covers Rare Books   208 - 62   2016 $250

Oates, Joyce Carol 1938- *Season of Peril.* Santa Barbara: Black Sparrow Press, 1977. First edition, small quarto, fine in modestly rubbed, near fine acetate dust jacket, number 1 of 3 copies for presentation, signed and with original drawing by author tipped-in.   Between the Covers Rare Books   204 - 89   2016 $750

Oates, Joyce Carol 1938- *The Time Traveler.* Northridge: Lord John Press, 1987. First edition, quarter morocco and marbled paper covered boards, fine, letter A of 26 lettered copies specially bound and signed by author.   Between the Covers Rare Books   204 - 87   2016 $500

Oates, Joyce Carol 1938- *With Shuddering Fall.* New York: Vanguard Press, 1964. First edition, near fine in spine sunned, very good dust jacket with ink spot on front panel, warmly inscribed by Oates to Herb Yellin.   Between the Covers Rare Books   208 - 59   2016 $400

Obama, Barack   *The Audacity of Hope.* New York: Crown, 2006. First edition, near fine, shows very light use, fine dust jacket.   Bella Luna Books   2016 - t9068   2016 $115

Obedience to Parents. N.P.: 1839. 16mo., original dark green cloth, lettered gilt on front board, slightly rubbed, all edges gilt, very good.   Jarndyce Antiquarian Books   CCXV - 342   2016   £125

Obloler, Arch   *Night of the Auk.* New York: Horizon, 1958. First edition, 8vo., nice, little chipped dust jacket, author's presentation.   Second Life Books, Inc.   196 B - 344   2016 $45

Obrecht, Ulrich   *Historiae Augustae Scriptores sex, Aelnus Spartianus, Indius Capitolinus, Aelius Lampridius Vulcatius Gallicarnus, Trebellius Pollio, Flavius Vepiscus.* Argentorati: In Frid. Spoor & Reinh. Waechtler, 1677. 8vo., titlepage in red and black, generous margins, few marginal paper flaws, neatly repaired tear to page 53, neither of which affect text, contemporary vellum, title inked to spine, yapp edges, edges sprinkled blue, some smudgy marks particularly to spine, top dusty, faint library inkstamp to titlepage verso.   Unsworths Antiquarian Booksellers Ltd.   E01 - Early Printing - 10   2016   £200

Odes on Various Subjects, Humbly Address'd to the Right Honourable the Lord Walpole... London: printed and sold by J. Roberts, 1741. First edition, very rare, disbound, 4to., fine.   C. R. Johnson Rare Book Collections   Foxon: H-P 2015 - 687   2016 $2298

Odier, Louis   *Manuel de Medecine Pratique ou Sommaire d'un Cours Gratuit...* Geneva: J. J. Paschod, 1803. First edition, 8vo., original half calf over boards, paper spine label, gilt title, five bands on spine.   Edwin V. Glaser Rare Books   2015 - 19141   2016 $250

Odum, Howard W.   *The Negro and His Songs: a Study of Typical Negro Songs of the South.* Chapel Hill: University of North Carolina, 1925. First edition, thin horizontal strip of cloth, neatly removed from rear board some splash marks on spine, hinges show evidence of old repair, still pleasant, near very good, lacking dust jacket.   Between the Covers Rare Books   207 - 71   2016 $9500

Ogawa, Kazumasa *Japanese Costumes Before the Restoration.* Tokyo: K. Ogawa, 1893. First edition, folio, 17 full page plates printed recto only, plates beautiful, very good+, original printed wrappers, replaced ribbon tie, top 1 inch corner front cover replaced, mild soil covers.   By the Book, L. C.   45 - 53   2016 $800

Ogawa, Kazumasa *Military Costumes in Old Japan.* Tokyo: K. Ogawa, 1893. First edition, folio, 15 photographic plates, original printed wrappers, replaced ribbon tie, soil to covers, original printed wrappers.   By the Book, L. C.   45 - 54   2016 $800

Ogawa, Kazumasa *Scenes in the Eastern Capital of Japan.* Tokyo: Ogawa, 1912. Third edition, 4to., grey cloth with color illustration, cover edge wear, corners bumped, mild soil and scuffs to covers, 107 pages of photos, 105 in black and white, 2 in color, scarce, very good+.   By the Book, L. C.   45 - 52   2016 $450

Ogden, Peter Skene *Traits of American Indian Life and Character.* London: Smith Elder and Co., 1853. First edition, original cloth, ex-library with 1.5 inch library stamp verso of titlepage and in lower fore-corner of 3 other pages, previous owners name and date on top edge of front free endpaper, some modest sunning to spine and some very slight edgewear, else near fine, rare, slipcase.   Buckingham Books   2015 - 26900   2016 $3000

Ogilvie-Grant, W. R. *Report on the Birds Collected by the British Ornithologist's Union Expedition in Dutch New Guinea.* London: The Ibis, 1915. Quarto, 8 chromolithographs by Gronvold, two folding maps, contemporary binder's blue cloth, fine.   Andrew Isles Natural History Books   55 - 38393   2016 $650

Ogle, George *The Fifth Epistle of the First Book of Horace Imitated.* London: printed for R. Dodsley, 1738. First edition, 4to., disbound, some foxing, otherwise very good.   C. R. Johnson Rare Book Collections   Foxon: H-P 2015 - 689   2016 $2298

Ohaejesi, Chidi M. *How to Write Love Letters and Win Girls' Love 95 Love Letters and How to Compose Them.* Onitsha-Nigeria: Minaco "Nig" Bookshops/Do-well Printing Press, circa, 1969. First edition?, octavo, stapled photographically illustrated wrappers, very faint stain in bottom margin, barely visible, near fine.   Between the Covers Rare Books   207 - 3   2016 $225

Olafsen, O. *Through Hardanger. A Handbook for Travellers.* Bergen, Nilssen & Son for the author and cartographer in Oddo, 1914. First edition, small 8vo., original red printed wrappers, folding lithographic map, printed in three colors, occasional very light spotting, otherwise very good.   Sotheran's   Travel and Exploration - 274   2016   £148

The Old Ballad of Dick Whittington. London: Warne, n.d. circa, 1870. 4to., wrappers, slight offsetting on text pages, else near fine, each page mounted on linen, very fine full page chromolithographs.   Aleph-bet Books, Inc.   111 - 165   2016 $300

Old French Nursery Songs. London: George Harrap, n.d. circa, 1915. 4to., cloth backed pictorial boards, fine in slightly worn dust jacket, 8 beautiful color plates and many lovely black and whites by Anne Anderson.   Aleph-bet Books, Inc.   111 - 17   2016 $400

Old Nick's Pocket-Book.... London: printed by J. Moyes for Sherwood Neeley and Jones, 1808. Onlye edition, apparently very scarce, folding frontispiece, 8vo., original boards rebacked in cloth, entirely uncut, very good.   John Drury Rare Books   2015 - 26116   2016 $437

Old Old Tales Retold: the Best Loved Folk Stories for children. Chicago: Volland, 1923. 13th edition, oblong 4to., blue gilt cloth, pictorial paste-on, fine in original box, flaps strengthened, wonderfully illustrated by Frederick Richardson, 51 full page colored illustrations and black and whites in text, printed on coated paper, beautiful copy, rare in box.   Aleph-bet Books, Inc.   112 - 421   2016 $650

The Old Wives Tales: a Poem. Part I. London: printed and sold by John Morphew, 1712. First edition, 8vo., disbound, fine, rare.   C. R. Johnson Rare Book Collections   Foxon: H-P 2015 - 695   2016 $2298

Olfers, Sibylle *Prinzeschen im Walde.* Esslingen und Munchen: J. F. Schreiber, n.d. circa, 1915. First edition, 4to., cloth backed pictorial boards, light cover rubbing, very good+, illustrations by Olfers.   Aleph-bet Books, Inc.   112 - 351   2016 $600

Oliphant, Laurence 1829-1888 *Altiora Peto.* Leipzig: Bernhard Tauchnitz, 1883. First Tauchnitz edition, small octavo, 2 volumes, bound by Giulio Giannini of Florence, in full parchment with elaborate gilt stencilling and handpainting tempura in green and red, in manner that has been dubbed 'Florentine style", book's title on spine in black mediaeval script with red uncials, gilt floral endpapers, all edges gilt, binding is roughly contemporaneous with book's publication date, early gift inscription, very good.   Peter Ellis   112 - 281   2016   £125

Oliphant, Laurence 1829-1888 *Minnesota and the Far West.* Edinburgh: 1855. Folding map, illustrations, rebound in utilitarian brown cloth, bottom corner of text block bumped, clean and very good, presentation copy inscribed by author.   Dumont Maps and Books   133 - 70   2016 $175

Oliphant, Laurence   1829-1888 *The Russian Shores of the Black Sea in the Autumn of 1852 with a Voyage down the Volga and a Tour through the Country of the Don Cossacks.*   Edinburgh: and London: William Blackwood and Sons, 1854. Fourth edition, 8vo., original brown ribbed cloth, all over decorated in blind, spine lettered gilt, front cover with gilt stamped vignette of a camel-drawn wagon, tinted lithographic frontispiece (tissue guard), wood engraved head and tailpieces and illustrations, lithographic maps, rare folding and with route added in red by hand, minimal rubbing to cloth, internally few pages little dusty, contemporary ownership inscription of Miss Pringle.   Sotheran's   Travel and Exploration - 275   2016   £198

Oliver, Anthony *The Elberg Collection.*   London: Heinemann, 1985. First edition, erasure on front pastedown, otherwise fine in dust jacket.   Mordida Books   2015 - 008425   2016 $60

Oliver, James Edward *A Treatise on Trigonometry.*   Ithaca: Finch & Apgar, 1881. First edition, signed by one of the authors, Lucian Wait, covers marked at edges of spine.   Simon Finch   2015 - 006069   2016 $300

Olivier, J. *Fencing Familiarized; or a New Treatise on the Art of Sword Play.*   London: John Bell, 1771-1772. First edition, 8vo., contemporary polished calf, sometime rebacked with contrasting leather spine label, engraved folding frontispiece and 8 plates, some rubbing and wear to boards, small wormhole to top corner of first 15 pages, offsetting from plates, little occasional browning, bookplate of Wilfrid Evill, otherwise very good.   Sotheran's   Piccadilly Notes - Summer 2015 - 220   2016   £398

Olmsted, Duncan H. *Seventy Years. A Checklist of Book club Publications 1914-1983.*   San Francisco: Book Club of California, 1984. First edition, one of 1500 copies, quarto, light grey printed wrappers, spine faded to white, else fine.   Argonaut Book Shop   Private Press 2015 - 3732   2016 $60

Olney, Peter J. S. *The Wildfowl Paintings of Henry Jones.*   London: Threshold/Harrap, 1987. Folio, oblong format, 60 color plates, publisher's quarter blue calf and blue cloth, blue cloth case, limited edition of 350 copies signed and numbered by author fine.   Andrew Isles Natural History Books   55 - 3516   2016 $600

Olsen, Penny *Feather and Brush: Three Centuries of Australian Bird Art.*   Melbourne: CSIRO Pub., 2001. Quarto, color illustrations, signature of Janet Flinn (an artist represented in the book), very good in dust jacket.   Andrew Isles Natural History Books   55 - 14253   2016 $120

Olson, Charles *The Maximus Poems/ 1-10.*   Stuttgart: Jonathan Williams, 1953. First edition, Deluxe issue of 50 copies, signed by Olson, Introduction by Robert Creeley laid in, calligraphic covers by Jonathan Williams, spine little sunned, else near fine in stiff wrappers, in original age toned, very good slipcase.   Between the Covers Rare Books   204 - 91   2016 $3500

Olson, Charles *Maximus Poems IV, V, VI.*   London: Cape Goliard, 1968. First UK edition, 4to., wrappers, hardbound issued was limited to 126 copies, small inkmark on upper cover, very good.   Peter Ellis   112 - 283   2016   £45

Olson, James C. *Red Cloud and the Sioux Problem.*   Lincoln: University of Nebraska Press, 1965. First edition, 32 historic photographs, 2 maps, rust cloth gilt, owner's name, fine with pictorial dust jacket.   Argonaut Book Shop   Native American 2015 - 5879   2016 $75

Olson, Keith *The Art of Terry Redlin, Opening Windows to the Wild.*   Plymouth: Hadley House, 1987. First edition, one of the limited, numbered and signed versions, large 4to., full leather, gilt lettering, leather slipcase, with light wear to corners and edges, and few minor scratches, 117 reproductions, most in color.   Oak Knoll Books   310 - 47   2016 $375

Olson, Sigurd F. *Listening Point.*   New York: Alfred A. Knopf, 1958. First edition, 28 drawings by Francis Lee Jacques, green cloth stamped in silver and gold, superior copy, very fine with pictorial dust jacket.   Argonaut Book Shop   Natural History 2015 - 7207   2016 $90

Olson, Toby *Fishing.* Driftless: Perishable Press, 1973. First edition, one of only 50 copies printed on Shadwell, signed by artist, William Weege Da Barba, cover is six vertical scraps of variegated Shadwell randomly zig-zagged together with the text block sewed to one end of the blank side, cover folded under and around the text block with real fishing fly affixed to cover, very fine.   James S. Jaffe Rare Books   Occasional List: Winter 2016 - 108   2016 $4500

Olson, Toby *Two Standards.*   Madison: Salient Seedling Press, 1982. Limited to 175 copies, graph paper illustrations, including pop-up on title, foldout page, 12mo., stiff paper wrapper, dust jacket, title stamped on front cover, top edge cut, other edges uncut, printed on handmade paper.   Oak Knoll Books   310 - 145   2016 $100

Omand, Donald *The New Caithness Book.*   Caithness: North of Scotland Newspapers, 1992. 8vo., figures and plates, green cloth, gilt lettered spine, endcaps just starting to wear, dust jacket, price sticker to rear, minor shelfwear, very good.   Unsworths Antiquarian Booksellers Ltd.   E05 - 109   2016   £20

Omar Khayyam *The Rubaiyat of Omar Khayyam.* London: Bernard Quaritch, 1859. First edition of Edward Fitzgerald's translation, one of 250 copies printed, very scarce in any state, rare in wrappers, large square 8vo., original printed wrappers, slight staining to fore-edge of wrappers and fly-leaves (possibly from some former protective wrapper), traces of old bookseller's catalogue description inside front cover, preserved in chemise and cloth folding box, excellent.   Blackwell's Rare Books   Marks of Genius - 39   2016   £40,000

Omar Khayyam *Rubaiyat of Omar Khayyam and the Salaman and Absal of Jami Rendered into English.* London: Bernard Quaritch, 1879. Fourth edition, 8vo., original half Roxburgh binding with cloth sides lettered in gold, very good.   Sotheran's   Piccadilly Notes - Summer 2015 - 221   2016   £498

Omar Khayyam *Rubaiyat.* Boston: L. C. Page and London: Macmillan, 1898. First edition thus, octavo, 2 volumes, tissue guarded photogravures from paintings by Edmund H. Garrett and engravings by Gilbert James, handsome period binding of three quarter vellum with batik paper boards, floral gilt spines, brown leather title labels lettered gilt, top edge gilt, pink silk ties, very good set, early gift inscription, prelims spotted.   Peter Ellis   112 - 343   2016   £275

Omar Khayyam *Rubaiyat.* London: Macmillan and Co., 1905. Small octavo, magnificently bound by Ramage, elaborate contemporary binding of dark green morocco inlaid in Padeloup-style mosaic pattern, covers bordered with decorative and plain gilt rules, rest of boards entirely covered with inlaid diapering featuring rows of pale yellow lozenges tooled gilt with gilt fleurons, these flanked on all four sides with inlaid navy circles, green morocco tooled with curving gilt lines attracted to the dots, spine compartments with similar inlaid pale yellow lozenges tooled gilt and title in gilt, pastedowns framed by dark green morocco inlaid with pale yellow circles at corners and with gilt floral tooling, cream colored watered silk endleaves, faint evidence of owner stamp on verso of front free endpaper tiny chip to top of spine, outstanding binding, extremely well preserved.   Manhattan Rare Book Company   2016 - 1707   2016 $2400

Omar Khayyam *Rubaiyat of Omar Khayyam.* New York: George H. Doran, 1909. 8vo., 16 plates by Dulac, quarter red cloth, orange boards, original printed dust jacket with small tears to extremities, spine faded, very good and rare in dust jacket.   Jeff Weber Rare Books   181 - 87   2016 $75

Omar Khayyam *Rubaiyat of Omar Khayyam.* New York: Thomas Y. Crowell & Co., 1910. First American trade edition, quarto, 14 tipped-in color plates, including frontispiece by Willy Pogany, all mounted onto heavy stock card, publisher's tan buckram over pictorial paper boards, spine decoratively tooled and lettered gilt, top edge gilt, others uncut, pictorial endpapers, few of the tipped-in color plates have light crease on lower corner and couple of heavy card mounts have been neatly repaired with archival tape, otherwise this is very fine in original brown paper dust jacket decoratively printed in dark brown, housed in cloth slipcase.   David Brass Rare Books, Inc.   2015 - 02957   2016 $550

Omar Khayyam *Rubaiyat of Omar Khayyam.* New York: E. P. Dutton, 1922. First US edition, 4to., newer cloth, original patterned covers, original dust wrapper bound in, fine, illustrations by Anne Harriet Fish.   Aleph-bet Books, Inc.   112 - 437   2016 $850

Omar Khayyam *Rubaiyat.* New York: Thomas Y. Crowell Co., 1930. First revised American trade edition, 12 tipped-in color plates, including frontispiece, by Willy Pogany, text leaves additionally decorated with 40 mounted black and gold illustrations and head and tailpieces in black and white, original orange silk cloth, front cover lettered in gilt with black and gold illustration, spine decoratively tooled and lettered gilt, top edge gilt, others uncut, original decorative tan paper dust jacket printed on orange, original tan cardboard box decoratively printed in dark brown, ink signature, very fine, woth original Crowell 8 page leaflet described the work of Pogany loosely inserted.   David Brass Rare Books, Inc.   2015 - 02958   2016 $1100

Omar Khayyam *The Golden Cockerel Rubaiyat of Omar Khayyam.* Golden Cockerel Press, 1938. One of 200 numbered copies, folio, original white quarter morocco, spine lettered gilt, cloth sides with gilt design on upper cover, top edges gilt, others untrimmed, 8 full page copper engravings by John Buckland Wright, nice.   Sotheran's   Piccadilly Notes - Summer 2015 - 222 2016   £1250

Omar Khayyam *The Original Rubaiyat of Omar Khayyam.* Garden City: Doubleday & Co., 1968. First edition, limited to 500 numbered copies signed by Graves, 8vo., original cloth backed paper covered boards with slipcase, previous owner's inkstamp of bee on front free endpaper, otherwise fine.   Sotheran's   Piccadilly Notes - Summer 2015 - 223   2016   £275

On the Edge: Images from 100 Years of Vogue. New York: pub. by Random House, 1992. First edition, small folio, photos, navy blue cloth, very fine with pictorial dust jacket.   Argonaut Book Shop   Photography 2015 - 7663   2016 $50

On the Folly and Wickedness of War. Minneapolis: Solentes Press, 2004. 57/100 copies, printed on Zerkall mouldmade paper, titlepage and illustrations printed in red and black, 5 lino-cut based on 18th century woodcuts with 2 full page and one double spread, 8vo., original paste paper boards in red and black, printed label to backstrip, edges untrimmed, fine.   Blackwell's Rare Books   B186 - 338   2016   £70

On the Origin of Sam Weller and the Real Cause of the Success of the Posthumous Papers of the Pickwick Club by a Lover of Charles Dickens's Works. Together with a Facsimile Reprint of the Beauties of Pickwick.   London: J. W. Jarvis, 1883. Frontispiece, title in red and black, original blue printed wrappers, small tear in outer margin of front cover not affecting text, ownership signature of E. Kendall Pearson.   Jarndyce Antiquarian Booksellers   CCXVIII - 134   2016   £20

Ondaatje, Michael   *The English Patient.*   London: Bloomsbury, 1992. First British edition, true first, near fine, bumping to spine ends, dust jacket very good, creasing and closed tears to spine ends, price clipped but part of price still present.   Bella Luna Books   2016 - t58863   2016 $82

Ono, Yoko   *Penny Views.*   Santa Barbara: Turkey Press, 1995. First edition, one of 125 numbered copies (entire edition) and signed by Ono, hand printed artist's book consisting of 24 letter press drawings by Ono on black Mingei and kakishibu (a handmade persimmon washed kozo) Japanese paper, and bound by hand, as new, small 8vo., illustrations by Ono, original boards with polished copper spine lettering in original printed paper envelope.   James S. Jaffe Rare Books   Occasional List: Winter 2016 - 16   2016 $1500

Onwhyn, Thomas   *Sketches in the Mining Districts, Cornwall.*   Rock & Co. May 7th, 1861. Oblong 8vo., 6 wood engraved plates dated Nov. 6th, 9th, 1858 (one inadvertently dated 1850), stitched as issued in original yellow wrappers, upper wrappers with title and view of the workings at the face of the mine, rare.   Marlborough Rare Books List 55 - 51   2016   £750

Onwhyn, Thomas   *Thirty-Two Plates to Illustrate the Cheap Edition of Nicholas Nickelby.*   London: J. Newman, 1848. 8 parts, plates slightly browned but not foxed, original green printed wrappers to each part, 1 split along spine and slight chipped, 4 with some splitting, good set, scarce.   Jarndyce Antiquarian Booksellers   CCXVIII - 246   2016   £280

Onwhyn, Thomas   *Twelve Illusrations to The Pickwick Club.*   London: Albert Jackson, 1894. Uncoloured plates loose in original green wrappers, wrappers with small repairs, very good.   Jarndyce Antiquarian Booksellers   CCXVIII - 130   2016   £110

An "Open Sesame" for the Black Consumer Market.   New York: L H. Stanton Publications Inc., 1972. Quarto, 19 pages, photocopied rectos only, plastic three hole binder, wrappers rubbed and modest age toning, very good or better, publisher's rare card laid in loosely.   Between the Covers Rare Books   207 - 21   2016 $350

Opie, Amelia   *Illustrations of Lying in all Its Branches.*   London: Longman, 1825. First edition, 2 volumes, 12mo., contemporary half calf, black labels, hinges slightly splitting, contemporary signature of Dr. Brand(?).   Jarndyce Antiquarian Books   CCXV - 343   2016   £120

Oppenheim, E. Phillips   *The Cinema Murder.*   New York: Burt, Reprint edition, fine in dust jacket.   Mordida Books   2015 - 010030   2016 $65

Oppenheim, E. Phillips   *Harvey Garrad's Crime.*   New York: Burt, Reprint edition, inscription, otherwise fine in dust jacket with faint crease on spine.   Mordida Books   2015 - 012276   2016 $65

Oppenheim, E. Phillips   *Mr. Grex of Monte Carlo.*   New York: Burt, Reprint edition, fine in very fine, as new dust jacket.   Mordida Books   2015 - 010029   2016 $65

Oppenheim, E. Phillips   *Nobody's Man.*   New York: A. L. Burt, Reprint edition, fine in very fine, as new dust jacket.   Mordida Books   2015 - 011060   2016 $65

Oppenheim, E. Phillips   *The Profiteers.*   New York: A. L. Butt, Reprint edition, spine slightly darkened, otherwise very good in fine dust jacket.   Mordida Books   2015 - 011053   2016 $65

Oppenheim, E. Phillips   *Stolen Idols.*   Boston: Little Brown, 1925. First American edition, previous owner's stamp and date on front endpaper, else near fine in very fine Burt reprint jacket.   Mordida Books   2015 - 010800   2016 $65

Oppenlander, Ella Ann   *Dickens' All the Year Round Descriptive Index and Contributor List.*   Troy: Whitman Pub. Co., 1984. Half title, original olive green cloth, slightly rubbed.   Jarndyce Antiquarian Booksellers   CCXVIII - 835   2016   £65

Orczy, Emmuska   *The Emperor's Candlesticks.*   London: C. Arthur Pearson Limited, 1899. First edition, original tan cloth boards with brown title to spine and front board, minor wear to edges and spine ends, light rubbing to boards, few spots of foxing to interior, else very clean, bookplate of collector Mark Samuels Lasner, tipped in, very good.   The Kelmscott Bookshop   12 - 77   2016 $550

Orczy, Emmuska *The Man in the Corner.* New York: Dodd, Mead & Co., 1909. First US edition, very good in pictorial cloth, illustrated by H. M. Brock.   Buckingham Books   2015 - 31330   2016 $450

The Order of Chivalry. Kelmscott Press, 1892-1893. One of 225 copies of an edition of 235 copies, printed in black and red in Chaucer type on Flower paper of two sizes, woodcut frontispiece designed by Burne-Jones, first woodcut initial, recently hand colored with green and red, small 4to. and 8vo., original limp vellum, backstrip lettered gilt, green silk ties, just lightly soiled, bookplate of Harry Alfred Fowler, very good.   Blackwell's Rare Books   B184 - 279   2016   £3000

Orlen, Steven *Sleeping on Doors.* Lisbon: Peumbra Press, 1975. No. 51 of 200 copies signed by author, 8vo., hand printed on Nideggen paper, ivory cloth with paper label on spine, nice.   Second Life Books, Inc.   196 B - 351   2016 $75

Orosius, Paulus *Adversus Paganos Historiarum Libri Septem ut et Apologeticus Contras Pelagium de Arbitrii Libertate.* Lugduni Batavorum: apud Gerardum Potuleit, 1738. First edition, 4to., title in red and black with engraving of both sides of an ancient coin, numerous further engravings of coins in text, occasionl light spots and smudges, generally clean, 3 library inkstamps to titlepage verso with one slightly offset to first page of text, contemporary vellum, title inked to spine, all edges red, darkened, bit grubby, small stain to upper board, endpapers smudgy with library code to front pastedown, still very good.   Unsworths Antiquarian Booksellers Ltd.   30 - 115   2016   £375

Orr, William *The History of the Classical High School...* Springfield: Classical High School Alumni Assn., 1936. Large 8vo., author's presentation on blank, clippings, graduation program from 1898 and order form laid in, illustrations, blue cloth stamped in gilt, cover slightly scuffed, very good, tight.   Second Life Books, Inc.   196 B - 352   2016 $75

Ortmann, Otto *The Physiological Mechanics of Piano Technique.* London: Kegan Paul, Trench, Trubner & Co. Ltd. and Curwen & Sons, 1929. First edition, diagrams in text, photographic plates, original cloth, blindstamped borders on sides, spine gilt lettered, spine and portion of boards faded, lower outer corner of upper board completely faded or perhaps affected by Damp, Tobias Matthay's copy annotated in pencil, extensively dog-eared, good.   Blackwell's Rare Books   B184 - 72   2016   £750

Orton, Joe *Entertaining Mr. Sloane.* Hamish Hamilton, 1964. First edition, slight browning to endpapers, otherwise very nice in slightly frayed and soiled dust jacket, bookplate.   Bertram Rota Ltd.   Christmas List 2015 - 31   2016   £180

Orton, Joe *Entertaining Mr. Sloane.* London: Hamish Hamilton, 1964. First edition, foolscap 8vo., original green boards, backstrip lettered silver, dust jacket with price lightly crossed through in pencil, very small chip at one corner, short tear at head of front and rear panel, very good.   Blackwell's Rare Books   B184 - 201   2016   £180

Orwell, George   1903-1950 *Animal Farm: a Fairy Story.* London: Secker & Warburg, 1945. First edition, original green cloth, spine panel stamped in white, fine in very good or better dust jacket (printed in green and gray on paper stock with discarded 'Searchlight Books' design in red on verso), light wear at spine ends and corner tips, rubbing along spine folds, two tiny closed tears at bottom edge of front panel, light dust soiling to rear panel, nice, fragile wartime book.   John W. Knott, Jr./L.W. Currey, Inc.   Fall-Winter 2015 - 17469   2016 $8500

Orwell, George   1903-1950 *Down and Out in Paris and London.* New York: Harper and Bros., 1933. First American edition, scarce, 8vo., trifle browned, few dog ears, original lilac cloth, spine lettered and banded in black, pictorial endpapers, spine slightly faded, slight wear to extremities, bookplate verso of flyleaf where pencil inscription has been erased, sound.   Blackwell's Rare Books   B184 - 202   2016   £450

Orwell, George   1903-1950 *Keep the Aspidistra Flying.* London: Gollancz, 1936. First edition, trifle browned, 8vo., original pale blue cloth, spine lettered in dark blue, bit skewed, slightly soiled, labels removed from paste downs and front free endpapers, bookplate, sound.   Blackwell's Rare Books   B184 - 203   2016   £300

Orwell, George   1903-1950 *The Road to Wigan Pier.* London: Victor Gollancz, 1937. First trade edition, 32 plates, 8vo., original mid blue cloth, dust jacket, spine slightly darkened, jacket foxed and defective about 3cm. at foot of backstrip panel, small circular label to backstrip panel, illegible signature dated 1945 and later bookplate.   Blackwell's Rare Books   B184 - 204   2016   £6000

Orwell, George   1903-1950 *The Road to Wigan Pier.* London: Victor Gollancz, 1937. First edition, octavo, cloth wrappers, photos, laid in is publisher's membership prospectus, ownership signature on front free endpaper, edges faintly spotted, near fine.   Peter Ellis   112 - 284   2016   £175

Orwell, George   1903-1950 *The Complete Works of George Orwell.* London: Secker & Warburg, 1998. First complete edition, from the library of publisher, Tom Rosenthal with his bookplate, 8vo., 20 volumes in original cloth with dust jackets, little light sunning to spines of few wrappers, otherwise near fine set.   Sotheran's Piccadilly Notes - Summer 2015 - 224   2016   £2750

Osborn, Paul *On Borrowed Time.* New York: Knopf, 1938. First edition, very good, tight copy in little worn dust jacket, laid in is program from Chicago production of the play from 1938 that includes some of the NY cast, signed by director, Joshua Logan as well as all of the cast.   Second Life Books, Inc.   196 B - 353   2016 $350

Osborn, Stellanova *A Tale of Possum Poke in Possum Lane.* Poulsan: Osborn, 1946. Tall 8vo., photos and drawings, author's presentation on flyleaf, orange cloth with silver lettering on spine, nice.   Second Life Books, Inc.   196 B - 354   2016 $45

Osborne, Dorothy *Letters from Dorothy Osborne to Sir William Temple 1652-54.* London and Manchester: Sherratt and Hughes, 1903. 184 x 127mm, quite pretty russet crushed morocco by Roger De Coverly & Sons (signed on rear turn-in), covers with double gilt rule border, raised bands, spines richly gilt in compartments with quatrefoil centerpiece surrounded by daisies, shamrocks and rose leaves, gilt titling, turn-ins ruled in gilt with trefoil cornerpieces, all edges gilt, portraits of Osborne and Temple and a plate depicting Osborne's family home, Chicksands Priory, front free endpaper with engraved bookplate of Katherine Nora Sturdy, usual offsetting to free endpapers from turn-in glue, mild foxing to blanks at beginning and end, as well as to leaves opposite two of the plates, but fine, clean, fresh internally and in a bright, unworn binding.   Phillip J. Pirages   67 - 36   2016 $950

Osgood, Harriet *Presents from Pam Pam.* London: Oxford University Press, 1945. first printing, square 8vo., very nice in dust jacket, inscribed by author.   Second Life Books, Inc.   196 B - 355   2016 $45

Osler, William   1849-1919 *Bibliotheca Osleriana.* Montreal: 1969. Thick 4to., original red cloth, light wear, from the collection of Saul Jarcho, M.D. with his signature, photocopied addenda and corrigenda laid in.   James Tait Goodrich   X-78 - 439   2016 $125

Osler, William   1849-1919 *The Growth of Truth as Illustrated in the Discovery of the Circulation of the Bood being the Harveian Oration Delivered at the Royal College of Physicians London Oct. 18 1906.* London: Henry Frowde, 1906. Original blue cloth, some light rubbing, else good.   James Tait Goodrich   X-78 - 532   2016 $350

Osler, William   1849-1919 *Incunabula Medica.* printed for the Bibliographical Society at Oxford Univesity Press, 1923. Photogravure as frontispiece, title in red and black, text uncut, original quarter linen backed boards, mild wear to binding, very good, internally clean and bright.   James Tait Goodrich   X-78 - 433   2016 $595

Osler, William   1849-1919 *The Master Word in Medicine. An Address to the Medical Students on the Occasion of the Opening of the New Building of the Medical Faculty of the University of Toronto Oct. 1 1903.* Baltimore: 1903. Original printed wrappers.   James Tait Goodrich   X-78 - 446   2016 $125

Osler, William   1849-1919 *Michael Servetus.* Baltimore: 1909. Plates, rebound in new cloth, 4to., uncut, separate printing originally published in Johns Hopkins Hospital Bull. 21 1910.   James Tait Goodrich   X-78 - 448   2016 $150

Osler, William   1849-1919 *The Old Humanities and the New Science. An Address Before the Classical Association Oxford May 16th 1919.* London: John Murray, 1919. Red printed wrappers.   James Tait Goodrich   X-78 - 434   2016 $125

Osler, William   1849-1919 *On Chorea and Choreiform Affections.* Philadelphia: B. Blakiston, 1894. Tables, original cloth, library stamp on title, removed marking on spine, some rubbing to binding, otherwise quite nice.   James Tait Goodrich   X-78 - 431   2016 $1495

Osler, William   1849-1919 *The Principles and Practice of Medicine.* New York: Appleton, 1892. First edition, 2nd issue, original half sheep, newly rebacked in matching black calf, raised bands, corner torn off rear blank fly, internally very good.   James Tait Goodrich   X-78 - 436   2016 $695

Osler, William   1849-1919 *The Principles and Practice of Medicine.* New York: Appleton, 1900. Third edition, original green cloth, some binding wear, internally very good very nice and clean, unsophisticated copy in original binding.   James Tait Goodrich   X-78 - 437   2016 $125

Osler, William   1849-1919 *The Principles and Practice of Medicine.* Edinburgh: Young J. Pentland, 1901. Fourth edition, original blue cloth, lightly rubbed else very good, tight copy.   James Tait Goodrich   X-78 - 438   2016 $165

Osler, William   1849-1919 *Sir Kenelm Digby's Powder of Sympathy an unfinished Essay by....* Los Angeles: Plantin Press, 1972. Limited to 275 copies, 3 plates, near fine, original binding.   James Tait Goodrich   X-78 - 440   2016 $75

Osler, William   1849-1919 *Unity, Peace and Concord a Farewell Address to the medical profession of the United States.* Oxford: Horace Hart, 1905. Original printed wrappers (soiled), uncut, on heavy rag stock.   James Tait Goodrich   X-78 - 445   2016 $75

Osler, William 1849-1919 *A Way of Life. An Address Delivered to Yale Students on the Evening of Sunday April 20th 1913.* New York: Harper, 1937. Small 8vo., marbled boards, nice. James Tait Goodrich X-78 - 435 2016 $45

Ossoli, Sarah Margaret Fuller, Marchesa D' 1810-1850 *At Home and Abroad; or Things and Thoughts in America and Europe.* Boston and London: Crosby, Nichols and Samson Low, 1856. Fifth printing, 8vo., some wear at extremities of spine (cloth worn away from crown, rubbed along extremities and tips), bound in black, good clean copy internally. Second Life Books, Inc. 197 - 256 2016 $75

Ossoli, Sarah Margaret Fuller, Marchesa D' 1810-1850 *Papers on Literature and Art.* New York: Wiley and Putnam, 1846. First edition, 2 volumes in 1, duodecimo, original blindstamped brown cloth, gilt lettering, four page publisher's catalog in volume one, text little foxed, cloth repaired at edges, very good. The Brick Row Book Shop Miscellany 69 - 40 2016 $300

Ossoli, Sarah Margaret Fuller, Marchesa D' 1810-1850 *Summer on the Lakes in 1843.* Boston: Charles Little and James Brown; New York: Francis, 1844. First edition, 8vo., frontispiece and 6 plates by Sarah Clark, publisher's black cloth, gilt stamped spine title, sides blocked in blind, faded pink endpapers (small nick at head of spine and rubbing at bottom), truly fresh and crisp, just couple of spots of foxing, publisher's black cloth, gilt stamped spine title, sides blocked in blind, faded pink endpapers. Second Life Books, Inc. 197 - 257 2016 $7500

Osterhuber, Magda *The Onus of Existence.* Iowa City: Finial Press, 1960. First edition in book form, narrow 4to., illustrations, original Japanese paper over boards, printed paper label on front cover by Elizabeth Kner, one of 50 numbered copies in Arrighi type on Asahi paper signed by author, illustrations by Al Doyle Moore, some light rubbing at extremities of spine and covers, otherwise fine, rare. James S. Jaffe Rare Books Occasional List: Winter 2016 - 62 2016 $750

Ostriker, Alicia *Once More Out of Darkness and Other Poems.* Berkeley: Berkeley Poet's Workshop & Press, 1974. First edition, pictorial wrappers, inscribed by poet for William Meredith, fine. Charles Agvent William Meredith - 94 2016 $50

Ostriker, Alicia *Songs.* New York: Rinehart and Winston, 1969. First edition, 8vo., inscribed by author for Paul Metcalf, and his wife, very good in dust jacket little yellowed. Second Life Books, Inc. 196 B - 357 2016 $50

Otis, James *Toby Tyler or Ten Weeks with a Circus.* New York: Harper & Bros., 1881. First edition, 12mo., brown cloth stamped in gilt, red and black, patterned endpapers, spine printing in the middle of the spine, except for light rubbing this is in near fine condition in custom cloth chemise and slipcase, rare. Aleph-bet Books, Inc. 112 - 352 2016 $600

Otter, R. H. *Winters Abroad, Some Information Respecting Places Visited by the Author on Account of His Health.* London: John Murray, 1882. First edition, 8vo., original red cloth, faded in parts, sprung but joints intact. J. & S. L. Bonham Antiquarian Booksellers Voyages 2016 - 8480 2016 £45

Ottley, Allan R. *John A. Sutter's Last Days. The Bidwell Letters.* Sacramento: Sacramento Book Collector's Club, 1986. First edition, one of 410 copies, frontispiece, 5 portraits, cloth backed printed gray boards, small oval bookplate, fine, original prospectus laid in. Argonaut Book Shop Biography 2015 - 7507 2016 $75

Our Exagmination Round His Factification for Incamination of Work in Progress. Paris: Shakespeare and Co., 1929. First printing, one of 96 special copies in the limited edition (and 200 copies in the trade edition), 191 x 140mm., original printed paper wrappers designed by Sylvia Beach, front flyleaf with ink ownership inscription of "Arthur W. Poulin/ November 1944/San Francisco", one inch tears top of front and bottom of rear joint, spine little scuffed, covers with faint soiling, two small chips to fore edge of front cover, otherwise fragile wrappers in excellent condition, except for slight browning at edges because of paper stock, fine internally. Phillip J. Pirages 67 - 217 2016 $4000

Our Paper. Jan. to Dec., 1856. (1855).with No. 10 being for Oct. -Dec., editor's own copy, with his monogram stamp on leading free endpaper and titlepage and signed by him on leading blank, A. C. Lyster Grennan Lodge, Lessners, Heath, Kent St., contemporary red binder's cloth, little worn, recased, all edges gilt. Jarndyce Antiquarian Booksellers CCXVII - 227 2016 £1250

Oury, Marcelle *Lettre a Mon Peintre Raoul Dufy.* Paris: Librairie Academique Perrin, 1965. First edition, no. 468 of 975 copies (from an edition of 6000), unbound signatures laid into wrappers, 4to., with an extra suite of lithographs, 27 full color lithographs, 8 of which are double page spreads, fine in very close to fine wrappers with merest trace of wear at spine end corners, in board chemise with white leather spine stamped in gold, in decorated box, lovely copy. Beasley Books 2015 - 2016 $825

Out of the West. Northridge: Lord John Press, 1979. First edition, 4to., limited to 150 copies signed by all the poets, cloth backed boards, fine. Second Life Books, Inc. 196 B - 639 2016 $150

Outcault, R. F. *Buster Brown His Dog Tige and their Jolly Times.* New York: Cupples and Leon, 1906. Oblong folio, cloth backed flexible card covers rear cover crease, some minor mends on blank versos, really clean and near fine in printed pictorial dust jacket, rare in jacket, beautiful copy. Aleph-bet Books, Inc.   112 - 354   2016 $650

Outcault, R. F. *Buster Brown's Autobiography.* New York: Frederick Stokes, 1907. First edition, 4to. pictorial cloth, some slight cover soil, very small margin mend on one plate, very occasional soil, clean, tight and very good+, 16 color plates and numerous illustrations in text.   Aleph-bet Books, Inc.   112 - 355   2016 $225

Outram, George *Legal & Other Lyrics.* London: T. N. Foulis, 1916. First edition thus, tipped-in frontispiece and plates by Edmund J. Sullivan, top edge gilt, others uncut, very attractive copy in dust jacket.   Bertram Rota Ltd. Christmas List 2015 - 32   2016   £90

The Outsider 3. New Orleans: Loujon Press, 1963. Third issue, near fine in printed wrappers.   Ken Lopez Bookseller 166 - 12   2016 $300

Overton, Thomas Collins *Original Designs of Temples and Other Ornamental Buildings for Parks and Gardens, in the Greek, Roman and Gothic Taste.* London: printed for the author and sold by Henry Webley, 1766. First edition, royal 8vo., contemporary full speckled calf, gilt spine, red morocco and gilt label, little worn at head and foot of spine, 50 engraved plates printed on thick paper, early bookplate of John Ward, recent bookplate of John Harris, particularly fine copy.   Sotheran's   Piccadilly Notes - Summer 2015 - 227   2016   £2400

Ovidius Naso, Publius *Ovid's Art of Love....* London: printed by William Smith, Nelson St., circa, 1845. 32mo., frontispiece, original green cloth, decorated in gilt, very good.   Jarndyce Antiquarian Books   CCXV - 344   2016   £40

Ovidius Naso, Publius *Liber Heroidum Epistolarum. Liber Sapphus Libellus in Ibin...* Lyon: JeanThomas & Stephane Gueynard, Nov., 1513. 4to., 19th century blind tooled calf, title lettered gilt on spine, title within fine four piece white-on-black border made up of putti and classical ornaments, woodcut, title in red and black, large opening woodcut and 21 woodcuts in text, some pages with ornamental borders, numerous initials verso of final leaf with circular diagram of winds and regions of the globe, beautifully produced, early 20th century signature and bookplate of Erwin Mosch. Maggs Bros. Ltd.   1474 - 56   2016   £2800

Ovidius Naso, Publius *Herodium Epistoale. Amorum Libri III De arte Amandi Libri III De Remedio Amoris Libri II.* Antwerp: Christopher Plantin, 1575. 16mo., contemporary blind tooled pigskin over paste boards dated 1577 on upper cover, covers with fine outer ornamental roll incorporating the medallion heads of reformers, superb central panel stamp of seated Justice with her sword and scales against an arched architectural background with banner, legend beneath the panel, finely preserved binding, copious contemporary underlinings throughout in red ink and some marginalia, ownership inscription inside front cover dated 1624, inscription in same hand at foot of titlepage ruled out in ink, later inscriptions dated 1664.   Maggs Bros. Ltd. 1474 - 57 2016   £2000

Ovidius Naso, Publius *Metamorphoses in Fifteen Books.* Dublin: printed by S. Powell for G. Risk, G. Ewing and W. Smith, 1727. 12mo., engraved frontispiece, 16 plates, few plates little frayed at edges, one with part of fore-and lower-edge lost outside of platemark, some soiling and staining, early ownership inscription of Owen and Mary Wynne to titlepage, contemporary dark calf label lost from spine, rear flyleaf excised, two corners and head of spine, some old scratches and little rubbing, sound.   Blackwell's Rare Books   Greek & Latin Classics VII - 66   2016   £200

Ovidius Naso, Publius *Stories from the Metamorphoses.* Shanty Bay Press, 2013. 16/60 copies (from an edition of 70 copies), signed by artist and printer, printed on Arches Cover mouldmade paper author's name to titlepage, initial letters and additional decorations printed in red against grey ground, 16 charcoal drawings by Jon Goodman printed using photograuvre, original quarter tan calf with Japanese Gampi paper boards, backstrip lettered in blind, edges untrimmed, slipcase, fine.   Blackwell's Rare Books   B186 - 336   2016   £2000

Ovidius Naso, Publius *Opera.* Leiden: ex officina Elzeviriana, 1629. First edition thus, 3 volumes, 16mo., engraved titlepage to volume I, 'Kalendarium' in red and black, occasional foxing mostly to endpapers, 35mm. closed tear to page 393, volume III, volume I has top fore-edge corner of r.f.e.p. excised, contemporary vellum, titles inked to spines, yapp edges, edges speckled blue, little yellowed, some smudgy marks, top edges darkened, still very good, armorial bookplate of Cecil Thompson to each front pastedown.   Unsworths Antiquarian Booksellers Ltd.   E01 - Early Printing - 15   2016   £500

Owen, John *The Fashionable World Displayed by Theophilus Christian (Pseud.).* London: printed for J. Hatchard, 1804. First edition, octavo, original blue boards, half title, 3 pages of publisher's ads, edges little rubbed and chipped at head and foot of spine, very good in original state.   The Brick Row Book Shop   Miscellany 69 - 60   2016 $225

Owen, Mary Alicia *Old Rabbit The Voodoo and Other Sorcerers.* London: T. Fisher Unwin, 1893. First edition, octavo, frontispiece and 57 line drawings in text, 10 of the drawings signed by Louis Wain, publisher's light blue cloth, front cover pictorially stamped in colors, spine lettered gilt and black partially uncut, spine slightly faded, few leaves poorly opened at top edge, otherwise near fine. David Brass Rare Books, Inc. 2015 - 02959 2016 $550

Owen, Robert *Debate on the Evidences of Christianity Containing an Examination of The Social System and of All Systems of Scepticism....* Cincinnati: Robinson & Fairbank, 1829. 8vo., contemporary gilt stamped calf, top of spine worn, text heavily browned in places, lacking front blank, early Cincinnati ownership. M & S Rare Books, Inc. 99 - 225 2016 $300

Owen, Wilfred *The End.* N.P.: but Leonia, NJ: Lois Morrison, 1999. The only one for sale of 2 copies, signed by Morrison, various colored stitching and collage against a pale green see through fabric, text printed on thin strips of cloth and stitched on by hand, binding technique of 4 strips of cloth tied to a brown wood spine with rounded ends, these strips contain the text and to continue to the edge of the pages, illustrations and designs by Morrison, small square 4to., stitched collage fabric book, plum cloth clamshell box, further protected by brown cloth bag, 10 leaves. Oak Knoll Books 27 - 40 2016 $2000

Owens, Harry J. *Doctor Faust: a Play Based Upon German Puppet Versions.* Chicago: Caxton Club, 1953. Apparently No. 2 of 3 hand colored copies (of 350 total), 264 x 171mm., publisher's gray cloth backed paper boards, later sturdy marbled paper slipcase, with 20 hand colored 15th century style woodcuts by Fritz Kredel, signed by Kredel, Victor Hammer and Elizabeth Kner in colohpon, with yellow folded card in announcing this copy as one of three hand colored copies; tiny area of soiling top of spine, otherwise very fine inside and out. Phillip J. Pirages 67 - 231 2016 $950

Oxfam *Ox Travels. Meetings of Remarkable Travel Writers.* London: MPG Biddles for Profile Books, 2011. First edition, limited to 250 numbered copies, this one of 100 special copies signed by contributing authors, 8vo., original dark blue cloth, upper board with impressed panel lettered in white, spine lettered in white, pictorial endpapers, red cloth slipcase, yellow fabric marker, frontispiece, full page portraits, fine. Sotheran's Travel and Exploration - 467 2016 £250

Oxford Bibliographical Society *Occasional Publications.* Oxford: Oxford Bibliographical Society, 1967-1992. Run of issues from inception through volume 24 (volume 9 missing), large 8vo., stiff paper wrappers, last 4 volumes with blue covers, others red, few spines sunned, volume 20 comprised almost entirely of foldout plates. Oak Knoll Books 310 - 261 2016 $450

The Oxford Packet. London: printed J. Roberts, 1714. First edition, 8vo. disbound, scarce, fine. C. R. Johnson Rare Book Collections Foxon: H-P 2015 - 705 2016 $2298

Oxford Poetry 1915. Oxford: B. H. Blackwell, 1915. First edition, tiny amount of waterstaining to top corner of final few leaves, crown 8vo., original blue wrappers with printed label to front and backstrip, backstrip sunned and chipped at ends, very gentle fading to borders, little creasing to yapped edges, textblock edges untrimmed, top edge lightly dust soiled, good. Blackwell's Rare Books B184 - 241 2016 £400

Ozell, John *The Cid; or The Heroick Daughter.* London: for J. W., 1714. First edition, 12mo., disbound, engraved frontispiece. Dramatis Personae 119 - 123 2016 $85

P

Pack, Richardson *Religion and Philosophy: a tale.* London: printed for E. Curll, 1720. First edition, 8vo., recent marbled wrappers, titlepage rather dust soiled, small piece torn from blank lower corner.   C. R. Johnson Rare Book Collections   Foxon: H-P 2015 - 716   2016 $613

Packard, Francis R. *History of Medicine in the United States.* New York: 1931. Second edition, 2 volumes, light cloth wear, else very good, from the library of Saul Jarcho, MD with his signature on each of front flyleaves.   James Tait Goodrich   X-78 - 449   2016 $250

Packard, Frank L. *Pawned.* New York: Burt, Reprint edition, fine in dust jacket.   Mordida Books   2015 - 010035   2016 $65

Packard, Frank L. *The Sin That Was His.* New York: Burt, Reprint edition, white paint streak on spine, otherwise fine in very fine dust jacket.   Mordida Books   2015 - 011369   2016 $65

Packer, Z. Z. *Drinking Coffee Elsewhere.* New York: Riverhead Books, 2003. Second printing, signed by author on titlepage, 8vo.   Second Life Books, Inc.   196 B - 362   2016 $45

Page, Augustine *Memoranda Concerning the Boys' Hospital at Hampton, in Suffolk, Founded by James Calthorpe, Esq. A.D. 1702.* Ipswich: printed by J. Page St. Clement's Fore Street, for private circulation, 1838. First edition, 4to., several early ms. annotations in ink, original boards with printed short title on upper cover, boards generally bit grubby, neatly rebacked with cloth, armorial bookplate of William Edward Layton, very rare.   John Drury Rare Books   2015 - 21915   2016 $350

Page, D. I. *Poetae Melici Graeci Alcamanais steischori Ibyci Anacreontis Simonidis Corinnae Poetarum Minorum Reliquias Carmina Popularia Et Convivialia.* Oxford: Clarendon Press, 1967. First reprint, 8vo., red boards, gilt lettered, spine faded, endcaps slightly worn, little shelfwear, very good, ownership inscription of C. D. N. Costa to front pastedown and with few pencil annotations.   Unsworths Antiquarian Booksellers Ltd.   E05 - 54   2016   £50

Page, H. A. *Noble Workers: a Book of Examples for Young Men.* London: Daldy Isbister & Co., 1875. First edition, half title, frontispiece, original blue cloth, prize label on leading pastedown, very good.   Jarndyce Antiquarian Books   CCXV - 68   2016   £35

Page, John *Receipts for Preparing and Compounding This Principal Medicines Made Use of by the Late Mr. Ward....* London: Henry Whitbridge, 1763. First edition, first issue, disbound, bit toned and spotted, some light foxing, last two blank leaves stained at edges, good copy.   Edwin V. Glaser Rare Books   2015 - 10220   2016 $300

Page, Norman *A Dickens Chronology.* London: Macmillan Press, 1988. First edition, half title, table, original black cloth, very good.   Jarndyce Antiquarian Booksellers   CCXVIII - 1399   2016   £25

Page, Thomas Nelson *Red Rock. A Chronicle of Reconstruction.* New York: Charles Scribner's Sons, 1898. Decorated green cloth, lettered gilt, previous owner's inscription, small spot worn on spine, near fine.   Argonaut Book Shop   Literature 2015 - 1361   2016 $75

Paget, Thomas Catesby, Baron *An Essay on Human Life.* London: printed and are to be sold by Fletcher Gyles, 1736. Second edition, 4to., disbound, very good, titlepage slightly soiled, very uncommon.   C. R. Johnson Rare Book Collections   Foxon: H-P 2015 - 719   2016 $613

Paher, Stanley W. *Nevada: an Annotated Bibliography.* Las Vegas: 1980. Illustrations, fine.   Dumont Maps and Books   133 - 71   2016 $50

Paine, Albert Bigelow *The Hollow Tree Stories.* New York: R. H. Russell, 1898. 8vo., cloth backed pictorial boards, some mild cover soil and one margin mend, very good+, illustrations by J. M. Conde, quite scarce.   Alephbet Books, Inc.   112 - 357   2016 $2500

Paine, Martyn *Letters on the Cholera Asphyxia as It Has Appeared in the City of New York.* New York: Collins & Harvey, 1832. First edition, thin 8vo., spine label and covers chipped and slightly soiled, library label on front pastedown, some marginal staining on few pages, some scattered foxing, inscription to Rev. Lucius Smith, very good, untrimmed, cloth backed paper boards with paper spine label.   Edwin V. Glaser Rare Books   2015 - 10282   2016 $150

Paine, Mary M. *In the Land of Make Believe.* London: Elliot Stock, 1901. First edition, 8vo., two page poem on rear blanks in rear in author's hand, signed, partially unopened, very good.   Second Life Books, Inc.   196 B - 363   2016 $50

Paine, Thomas 1737-1809 *Letter Addressed to the Addressers of the late Proclamation.* London: printed for H. D. Symonds, 1792. 8vo., disbound.   Jarndyce Antiquarian Booksellers   CCXVI - 437   2016   £200

Paine, Thomas   1737-1809   *Miscellaneous Articles by Thomas Paine.*   London: printed for J. Ridgway...., 1792. First edition, 8vo., disbound.   Jarndyce Antiquarian Booksellers   CCXVI - 438   2016   £250

Paine, Thomas   1737-1809   *The Rights of Man; Being an Answer to Mr. Burke's Attack on the French revolution...*   Boston: printed by I. Thomas and E. T. Andrews, 1791. First Boston edition, self wrappers, stitched as issued, untrimmed, some light foxing, wear and scattered stains, overall very good in original state, contemporary ink notation "Essex Hist. Soc./fr. G. A. Ward".   The Brick Row Book Shop   Miscellany 69 - 61   2016 $1250

Paine, Thomas   1737-1809   *Rights of Man.*   London: part I printed for J. S. Jordan, Part II printed for H. D. Symonds, 1792. 12mo., cheap coarse paper, old but not intrusive waterstaining, occasional dusting, bound in contemporary calf backed marbled boards, vellum fore-edges, boards rubbed and neatly rebacked, Michael Foot's copy with his signature and note on front endpaper.   Jarndyce Antiquarian Booksellers   CCXVI - 439   2016   £2500

Paine, Thomas   1737-1809   *Die Rechte des menschen. (The Rights of Man).*   Copenhagen: Christ. Gotti. Proft, 1793. Second improved edition, engraved portrait, 8vo., 3 volumes in 1, contemporary paper covered boards, very good, clean.   Joseph J. Felcone, Inc.   Books from Five Centuries: a Miscellany - 113   2016 $750

Paine, Thomas   1737-1809   *Two Letters to Lord Onslow, Lord Lieutenant of the County of Surrey and one to Mr Henry Dundas, Secretary of State on the Subject of the late Excellent Proclamation.*   London: printed for James Ridgway, 1792. Fourth edition, 36 pages, 8vo., some foxing and old waterstain to head of pages, not too intrusive, disbound, without two final ad leaves.   Jarndyce Antiquarian Booksellers   CCXVI - 440   2016   £125

Paine, Thomas   1737-1809   *The Whole Proceedings on the Trial of an Information Exhibited ex officio by the king's Attorney Against Thomas Paine for a Libel Upon the Revolution and the Bill of Rights....*   London: sold by Martha Gurney No. 128, Holborn Hill, 1793. 8vo., contemporary half calf, expertly rebacked, gilt banded spine, red morocco label, marbled boards, corners neatly repaired, bookplate of Michael Foot with pencil notes to front endpaper, pencil underlinings with the ownership signature of Thomas Holcroft 1745-1809.   Jarndyce Antiquarian Booksellers   CCXVI - 441   2016   £1800

Palahniuk, Chuck   *Invisible Monsters.*   New York: Norton, 1999. Advance reading copy, issued as a trade paperback original, this copy signed by author, two nicks to lower edge of front over, near fine in wrappers, scarce, especially signed.   Ken Lopez Bookseller   166 - 96   2016 $200

Palanco, Francisco   *Cursus Philosophicus Juxta Miram Angelici Praeceptoris Doctrinam Digestus et Pro Communi Studentium Utilitate Tribes Tomis Absolutus.*   Madrid: Lucan Antonium Bermar & Narbez, 1703. Third edition, Volume I only, 8vo., engraved titlepage vignette and headpiece, all edges marbled, offsetting to free endpapers and pastedowns, contemporary mottled calf, 5 raised bands, gilt stamped spine, rubbed, especially at spine ends, Theological Institute of Connecticut blindstamps to first and last few pages, rare, very good.   Jeff Weber Rare Books   181 - 24   2016 $150

Palermo, Francesco   *I Manoscritti Palatini Di Firenze.*   Firenze: Biblioteca Palatina, 1853-1869. First edition, 4to. modern cloth, leather spine labels, uncut, 4 pages of plates and facsimiles, light foxing throughout, bookplate indicates this book came from the reference library of H. P. Kraus.   Oak Knoll Books   310 - 216   2016 $450

Paley, Grace   *Just as I Thought.*   New York: Farrar Straus, Giroux, 1998. First edition, 8vo., fine in little soiled dust jacket, inscribed by author for poet William Jay Smith.   Second Life Books, Inc.   196 B - 365   2016 $75

Palgrave, Frances Turner   1824-1897   *The Golden Treasury of the Best Songs and Lyrical Poems in the English Language.*   Cambridge and London: Macmillan and Co., 1861. First edition first binding, 500 copies only, half title, original glazed green cloth, gilt, very nice.   Jarndyce Antiquarian Booksellers   CCXVII - 210   2016   £350

Palingenio Stellato, Marcello, Pseud.   *Zodiacus Vitae, hoc est. De Hominis Vita Studio ac Moribus Optime Instintuendis Libri XII.*   Paris: Hierome de Manref and Guillaume Cavellat...., 1580. 16mo., woodcut printer's device on title, tear through last leaf and this also with few small holes on blank area, 2 small neat rectangles excised from titlepage, near contemporary red morocco, panelled gilt, spine gilt in compartments, minor wear.   Blackwell's Rare Books   B186 - 110   2016   £650

Palladio, Andrea   *Le Termi Dei Romani...*   Vicenza: Giovanni Rossi, 1797. Smudged inscription inside front cover apparently recording the purchase of the book in Rome by a British traveller, ink title on spine in English, frontispiece, 24 engraved plates, minor foxing to text, original carta rustica, splits in joints and spine little defective, good.   Blackwell's Rare Books   B184 - 73   2016   £900

Pallenberg, Rospo   *Stephen King's The Stand. (Screenplay).*   Burbank: Warner Bros., 1989. Quarto, first draft, computer generated sheets in bradbound studio wrappers, light wear at edges of wrappers, very near fine.   Between the Covers Rare Books   208 - 124   2016 $200

Pallis, Marco *Peaks and Lamas.* London: Cassell and Co. Ltd., 1939. First edition, 8vo., original black cloth, dust jacket, photographic illustrations, 3 sketch maps, minimal rubbing, light spotting to fore edge, else very good. Sotheran's Travel and Exploration - 160   2016   £198

Pallot, Bill *The Art of the Chair in Eighteenth Century France.* Dourbevoie: A.C.R. Gismondi Editeurs, 1989. Third edition, 4to., original black cloth, lettered gilt on spine and on front cover, copiously illustrated in color and black and white, slightly bumped, otherwise very good+, slightly chipped and nicked, very good.   Any Amount of Books 2015 - Cc1459   2016   £250

Palmer, Charles John *The Perlustration of Great Yarmouth with Gorleston and Southtown.* Yarmouth: George Nall, 1872. First edition, fair copy, cloth spine, marbled boards, volume I only, lacks all of the plates, some foxing mainly to prelims and occasionally thereafter, printer's proof copy complete with author's corrections in ink to text and margins, when bound the margins have been trimmed and some of Palmer's comments have been truncated, inscription records this was William Finch Crisp's copy, original 19th century photo of St. Nicholas Church pasted on back of front endpaper, on back of final leaf has been pasted engraving of Burgh Castle.   Simon Finch   2015 - 91344 2016 $320

Palmer, H. R. *Sudanese Memoirs: Being Mainly Translations of a Number of Arabic manuscripts Relating to the Central and Western Sudan.*   Logos: Government Printer, 1998. First edition, 8vo., 3 volumes, original purple cloth, gilt, 4 plates from photos, 3 maps, some fading to cloth, else very good.   Sotheran's Travel and Exploration - 26   2016   £598

Palmer, Helen *Do You Know What I'm Going to Do Next Saturday?* New York: Beginner Books, 1963. First edition, 8vo., glazed pictorial boards, slight bit of edge rubbing, very good-fine in very good+ dust jacket with few small closed tears, illustrations by Lynn Fayman.   Aleph-bet Books, Inc. 111 - 41   2016 $125

Palmer, Herbert *A Sword in the Desert: a Book of Poems and Verses for the Present Times.* London: George G. Harrap and Co. Ltd., 1946. First edition, 8vo., original blue cloth lettered silver on spine, signed presentation, spine and edges little rubbed, slight fading, else sound, near very good, slight rubbed, else very good.   Any Amount of Books 2015 - C11581   2016   £650

Palmer, Stuart *The Adventure of the Marked Man and One Other.* Boulder: Aspen, 1973. First edition, fine in stapled wrappers.   Mordida Books   2015 - 012462   2016 $65

Palmer, Stuart *The Green Ace.* New York: Mill Morrow, 1950. First edition, name stamp on front endpapers, otherwise very good in dust jacket.   Mordida Books   2015 - 012660   2016 $65

Palmer, T. S. *Biographies of Members of the American Ornithologists' Union.* Washington: Auk, 1954. First edition, octavo, bookplate, fine.   Andrew Isles Natural History Books   55 - 37578   2016 $200

Palmquist, Peter E. *Fine California Views. The Photographs of A. W. Ericson.* Eureka: Inerface California Corporation, 1975. First edition, square quarto, 92 photo reproductions, 20 smaller reproductions, two tone brown and tan cloth, two wine labels pasted to front fixed endpaper, fine, slightly soiled pictorial dust jacket, two short edge tears.   Argonaut Book Shop   Photography 2015 - 6799 2016 $60

Palmquist, Peter E. *Redwood and Lumbering in California Forests: a Reconstruction of the Original Edgar Cherry Edition.*   San Francisco: Book Club of California, 1983. First edition in this format, limited to 600 copies printed at Yolly Bolly Press, frontispiece, numerous photographic plates, full linen stamped in brown to spine, pictorial pastedown to front cover, very fine.   Argonaut Book Shop Natural History 2015 - 2880   2016 $150

Palsits, Victor Hugo *A Narrative of the Captivity of Nehemiah How in 1745-1747.* Cleveland: Burrows Bros. Co., 1904. Number 180 of 250 copies, facsimile titlepage, maroon cloth, gilt top edges gilt, light rubbing to spine ends, front and rear inner hinges just starting, two leaves bit roughly opened, very good.   Argonaut Book Shop   Native American 2015 - 5951   2016 $90

Pamuk, Orhan *Istanbul.* London: Faber and Faber, 2005. First UK edition, octavo, numerous rather murky photos, signed by author on titlepage, spine slightly bumped at head and tail, near fine in very good, slightly marked dust jacket little creased at edges.   Peter Ellis 112 - 285   2016 £85

A Panegyrick in Answer to a Lible (sic) on the Late Famous D---- of T. C. Deceas'd. N.P.: Dublin: printed in the year, 1730. First edition, small 8vo., disbound, very rare, wanting blank at beginning and end, but very good.   C. R. Johnson Rare Book Collections   Foxon: H-P 2015 - 723   2016 $2298

Panius Diaconus *Pauli Warnefridi Langobardi Filii Duiaconi Foroiuliensis De Gestis Lagobardorum Libri VI...* Leiden: ex officina Plantianiana Paud Franciscum Raphelengium, 1595 circa, 1586. 12mo., woodcut device to titlepage of first work, slightly toned with some occaisonal foxing, small scorch mark to text page 16 (no loss of sense), prelim blanks and one leaf loosening, some underlining to one page in second section, later vellum possibly retaining old boards, ink title to spine, yapp edges, edges sprinkled red, endcaps creased a little darkened at fore-edges, otherwise bright, pastedowns lifting to reveal manuscript binder's waste, some booksellers notes and a pasted catalog entry to front pastedown, 2 works bound together.   Unsworths Antiquarian Booksellers Ltd.   E01 - Early Printing - 16   2016   £675

Panton, Edward *Speculum Juventutis; or a True Mirror...* London: printed for Charles Smith & Thomas Burrell, 1671. Licence leaf preceding title and final ad leaves, 8vo., attractively rebound in 20th century full calf, spine ruled in gilt, red morocco label, embossed stamps of Free Public Library, Wigan, faint 20th century library stamp.   Jarndyce Antiquarian Books   CCXV - 345   2016   £750

Paola, Tomie *Merry Christmas. Strega Nona.* New York: Harcourt Brace Jovanovich, 1986. Second printing, 4to., cloth, fine in dust jacket, illustrations by author in bright colors, this copy inscribed by author.   Aleph-bet Books, Inc.   111 - 116   2016 $100

Paolini, Christopher *Eragon.* New York: Knopf, 2003. Advance galley copy, near fine, 1/16" tear on front cover spine.   Bella Luna Books   2016 - p3731   2016 $99

Papers Relative to the Discussion with Spain in 1802, 1803 and 1804. London: A. Strahan, 1805. First edition, contemporary mottled calf, spine gilt ruled and with black label, spine rubbed, upper joints cracked but holding, bookplate of Aurberon Finch with his stamp, scarce.   Simon Finch   2015 - 22284   2016 $102

Paquier, Jean Baptiste *Le Pamir. Etude Geographie Physique Historique.* Paris: Maisonneuve et Cie, 1876. First edition, scarce, 8vo., original printed wrappers, five lithographic maps, minor marginal chipping to wrappers, maps evenly browned as usual, due to paper stock, errata leaf with faint marginal trace of humidity, entirely uncut, and unopened, scarce.   Sotheran's   Travel and Exploration - 161   2016   £448

Paracelsus 1493-1541 *Operum Medico-Chimicorum Sive Paradoxorvm.* Frankfurt: Collegia Museum Pathentianarum, 1603-1605. First complete Latin edition, 13 volumes bound in 6, portrait, with duplicates of volumes, 5, 6, 9, 10, mixed set with four bindings bound in full contemporary calf with raised bands and gilt spines, one volume in 18th century half calf, one volume in matching full calf in matching style, all volumes have heavy browning in text, along with extensive early if not contemporary annotations and marginalia in brown in, copy obviously used by early scholar.   James Tait Goodrich   X-78 - 450   2016 $7500

Pardon, George Frederick *The Faces in the Fire; a Story for the Season.* London: Willoughby & Co., 1849? First edition, half title, color frontispiece, original title and 2 plates, woodcut vignettes, original vertical grained red cloth, blocked and lettered gilt, slight rubbing to tail of spine, one small ink mark to lower margin of front board, good plus. Jarndyce Antiquarian Booksellers   CCXVIII - 407   2016   £180

Pardon, George Frederick *The Faces in the Fire; a Story for the Seasons.* London: Willoughby & Co., 1849? First edition, frontispiece, engraved title and 2 plates, woodcut vignettes, slight staining to pages 128/9, handsome crimson straight grained morocco, gilt spine, borders and dentelles, bookplate of Edward Thomson, all edges gilt, very good. Jarndyce Antiquarian Booksellers   CCXVIII - 408   2016   £150

Parenthesis: the Newsletter of the Fine Press Book Association No. 3. Vancouver: Sheffield: FPBA, 1999. Deluxe issue, liited to 75 copies and bound thus, small 4to., paper covered boards, slipcase, this issue with separate portfolio containing three signed and numbered wood engravings by Miriam MacGregor, Frank Martin and Gaylord Schanilec, as well as separate material from Bird and Bull Press.   Oak Knoll Books   310 - 133   2016 $225

The Parent's High Commission. London: J. Hatchard & Son, 1843. First edition, half title, final ad leaf, original blue grey cloth, front board unevenly faded, slight damp mark to lower corner of front board.   Jarndyce Antiquarian Books CCXV - 346   2016   £50

Parfit, Joseph T. *Among the Druzes of Lebanon and Bashan.* London: Hunter & Longhurst, 1917. First edition, octavo, photos, original green cloth, scarce, presentation copy inscribed by author for Mr. and Mrs. Warmington Reed, covers little marked and rubbed at edges, free endpapers tanned, very good.   Peter Ellis   112 - 107   2016   £250

Paris Review No. 43 Summer 1968. New York: Paris Review, 1968. First edition, publisher's paper wrappers, with illustrations of Eiffel Tower in purple and black to front wrapper, lettered in black, near fine with some minor wear to extremities, light soiling to bottom edge of front panel and fore edge, else bright and clean.   B & B Rare Books, Ltd. 2016 - JK044   2016 $65

Paris, Louis Philippe Albert D'Orleans, Comte De   1838-1894   *Damas et le Liban. Extraits du Journal d'un Voyage en Syrie au Printemps de 1860.*   London: W. Jeffs... Foreign Bookseller to the Royal Family, 1861. First edition, 8vo., original maroon cloth by Westleys in London, spine (rebacked) lettered and dated gilt, covers ornamented in blind, covers with few minor spots, half title, little dusted, name of anonymous author supplied in pencil and with underlining in crayon.   Sotheran's   Travel and Exploration - 358   2016   £448

Paris, Matthew   1200-1259   *Flores Historiarum per Matthaeum Westmonasteriensem Collecti, Praecipue de rebus Britannicis ab Exordio Mundi Usque ad Annum Domini 1307.*   ex officina Thomae Marshii, 1570. Folio, titlepage trimmed close to woodcut border, final blank leaf discarded, index bound at front of text, one leaf with original paper flaw affecting few characters, first leaf of index with bottom margin folded over to preserve early manuscript note, verso of title also filled with text in early manuscript (trimmed at bottom), few short notes or marks later on, last dozen leaves showing a faint but substantial dampmark, some soiling/minor staining elsewhere, touch of worming to blank fore-edge margin, two leaves remargined, gathering Ttt in earlier (?) state without (and not calling for) additional unsigned singleton leaf, folio, 18th century mottled calf, spine with five raised bands, red morocco lettering pieces in second and third compartment, rubbed, front joint cracking (but strong) with little peeling to leather, light wear to endcaps, marbled endpapers, bookplates of Robert Surtees and his Mainsforth Library, sound.   Blackwell's Rare Books   B186 - 111   2016   £1100

Parish, Morris L.   *Charles Kingsley and Thomas Hughes. First editions (with a Few Exceptions) the library of Dormy House, Pine Valley, New Jersey.*   London: 1936. One of 150 numbered copies, 4to., plate, facsimiles, addenda/errata, cloth, pristine, lovely dust jacket with just few tiny chips at spine ends, the personal copy of Alexander Wainwright (curator of Parrish collection of Victorian novelists at Princeton), lovely copy.   Joseph J. Felcone, Inc.   Books from Five Centuries: a Miscellany - 114   2016 $600

Parkeharrison, Robert   *Counterpoint.*   Santa Fe: Twin Palms, 2008. First printing of only 3000 copies, 33 color plates, very fine in very fine dust jacket, signed by Parkeharrison, scarce thus.   Jeff Hirsch Books   Holiday List 2015 - 86   2016 $175

Parker, B.   *Arctic Orphans.*   London and Edinburgh: W. & R. Chambers, n.d circa, 1920. Oblong folio, pictorial boards, slight tip rubbing, else fine in dust jacket (chipped with few mends), 13 incredible full page full color illustrations plus illustrations in text by N. Parker, rare, beautiful.   Aleph-bet Books, Inc.   111 - 331   2016 $2000

Parker, B.   *Cinderella at the Zoo.*   London: & Edinburgh: W. & R. Chambers, n.d. circa, 1917. First edition, large 4to., pictorial boards, neat spine repair and edges rubbed, else very good-fine, 16 full page chromolithographs, rare.   Aleph-bet Books, Inc.   112 - 360   2016 $1250

Parker, B.   *Frolic Farm.*   London: Chambers Pub. n.d. circa, 1910. Oblong 4to., pictorial boards, slightest of spine and tip wear, else very good-fine, full page color lithographs and brown illustrations by N. Parker.   Aleph-bet Books, Inc.   112 - 362   2016 $1200

Parker, B.   *Funny Bunnies.*   London: W. & R. Chambers, n.d. circa, 1905. Oblong folio, pictorial boards, light rubbing on edges and corners, near fine, illustrations by N. Parker.   Aleph-bet Books, Inc.   112 - 361   2016 $1200

Parker, B.   *The Hole and Corner book.*   London & Edinburgh: W. & R. Chambers, n.d. circa, 1910. Oblong folio, pictorial boards, fine in original dust jacket (minor wear else very good-fine), full page color lithographed plates plus illustrations in brown line on text pages by Nancy Parker, very scarce, rarely found in dust jacket.   Aleph-bet Books, Inc.   111 - 332   2016 $1850

Parker, Chan   *To Bird with Love.*   Poitiers: Editions Witzlov, 1981. First edition, folio, fine in very good box with rubbed edges and one internal joint mend, this copy signed and inscribed by Chan Parker unusual thus.   Beasley Books   2015 - 2016 $1200

Parker, Emma   *Important Trifles Chiefly Appropriate to Females on Their Entrance into Society.*   London: printed for T. Egerton, 1817. First edition, 12mo., half title, uncut in original drab boards, pink paper label, really nice in original binding.   Jarndyce Antiquarian Books   CCXV - 348   2016   £750

Parker, Eric   *Shooting by Moor, Field & shore.*   London: Seeley Service & Co. circa, 1940. Early edition, 8vo., original quarter yellow buckram over brown cloth, dust jacket used, though still bright and retaining attached photographic illustrations as issued, internally sound.   Sotheran's Hunting, Shooting & Fishing - 86   2016   £90

Parker, Fred B. *The Crowded Vacancy: Three Los Angeles Photographers.* Davis: Memorial Union Art Gallery, University of California, Davis, 1971. Exhibition catalog, printed in an edition of 700 copies, black and white photos by Lewis Baltz, Anthony Hernandez and Terry Wild, close to near fine in stapled wrappers with small sticker shadow on verso of front cover and miniscule spot to bottom edges, very nice.   Jeff Hirsch Books   Holiday List 2015 - 87   2016 $175

Parker, Harry *Mail & Passenger: Steamships of the Nineteenth Century, the MacPherson Collection...* London: Sampson Low, 1928. First edition, quarto, 16 color plates, numerous black and white illustrations, original beige cloth, near fine.   J. & S. L. Bonham Antiquarian Booksellers   Voyages 2016 - 5600   2016   £300

Parker, John Henry *The Architectural Antiquities of the City of Wells.* London: James Parker and Co., 1866. First edition, vignette title, 29 numbered plates, plate XVII foxed, sewing of plates slightly weak, original purple cloth, slightly faded and marked, inscribed "From the author" verso of leading f.e.p., armorial bookplate of Robert Daubeney.   Jarndyce Antiquarian Booksellers   CCXVII - 212   2016   £40

Parker, M. *The Arcana of Arts and Sciences or Farmer's and Mechanics' Manual...* Washington: Grayson, 1824. First edition, 16mo., contemporary calf, leather label, browned, lacking front endleaves and evidently two plates.   M & S Rare Books, Inc.   99 - 226   2016 $650

Parker, Robert B. *Chance.* New York: Putnam, 1996. First edition, signed by author, very fine.   Mordida Books   2015 - 010774   2016 $55

Parker, Robert B. *The Godwulf Manuscript.* Toyko: Hayaskawa, 1976. First Japanese edition, very fine, unread copy in wrapper, signed by author.   Mordida Books   2015 - 011304   2016 $65

Parker, Robert B. *Leichte Beute Fur Profis (Promised Land).* Frankfurt: Ulstein Buch, 1977. First German edition, very fine, unread copy in wrappers, signed by author.   Mordida Books   2015 - 011290   2016 $65

Parker, Robert B. *Poodle Springs.* New York: Putnam, 1989. First edition, very fine in printed wrappers, advance reading copy.   Mordida Books   2015 - 010875   2016 $65

Parker, Robert B. *Ramdam-Dame (Looking for Rachel Wallace).* Paris: Gallimard, 1981. First French edition, very fine unread copy in wrappers, signed by author.   Mordida Books   2015 - 011289   2016 $65

Parker, Robert B. *Small Vices.* New York: Putnam, 1997. First edition, very fine in dust jacket, signed by author.   Mordida Books   2015 - 010773   2016 $55

Parker, Robert B. *Stardust.* New York: Putnam, 1990. First edition, very fine in dust jacket, inscribed by author.   Mordida Books   2015 - 010101   2016 $65

Parker, Robert B. *Walking Shadow.* New York: Putnam, 1994. First edition, very fine in dust jacket, signed by author.   Mordida Books   2015 - 010775   2016 $55

Parker, Theodore *Lessons from the World of Matter and The World of Man.* Boston: Published by Charles W. Slack, 1865. First edition, green cloth, gilt, few tears at bottom of spine, short crack to paper over front hinge, modest wear to boards, very good, inscribed by editor to author and Thomas biographer, Frank B. Sanborn.   Between the Covers Rare Books   202 - 71   2016 $600

Parkes, Harry *The Man who Would Like to marry.* London: Frederick Warne & Co., circa, 1887. Oblong folio, 12 lithographic plates, title plate spotted, otherwise plates good and clean, original pale green wrappers, sewn as issued, spine slightly worn, spotted.   Jarndyce Antiquarian Books   CCXV - 349   2016   £50

Parkinson, James *An Essay on the Shaking Palsy.* Birmingham: Classics of medicine library, 1817. Facsimile reprint, 8vo., full dark brown calf with gilt boards, all edges gilt, marbled endpapers, fine.   James Tait Goodrich   X-78 - 452   2016 $65

Parkman, Francis   1823-1893 *The Discovery of the Great West; an Historical Narrative.* London: John Murray, 1869. First edition, 8vo., frontispiece map, original purple cloth, spine faded.   J. & S. L. Bonham Antiquarian Booksellers   America 2016 - 9614   2016   £150

Parkman, Francis   1823-1893 *The Oregon Trail.* Boston: Little Brown, 1925. Limited to 950 numbered copies,, cloth backed boards, cloth tips, top edge gilt, fine in dust jacket with slipcase and limitation number on printed label of case, dust jacket with repair piece off back panel, case is very good, strengthened along joints, 10 tipped in plates by N. C. Wyeth and 5 in monotone by Frederick Remington, great copy, scarce, rare with dust jacket and slipcase.   Aleph-bet Books, Inc.   112 - 525   2016 $1250

Parks, Annette White *Qh awala-li 'water coming down place.' A History of Gualala Mendocino County California.* Uklah: Fresh Cut Press, 1980. First edition, quarto, well illustrated with 56 historical images, maps, maroon cloth, gilt, very fine with pictorial dust jacket, scarce thus.   Argonaut Book Shop   Native American 2015 - 7214   2016 $60

Parnell & Sons, Limited *Architectural Ironfounders, W. & T. Avery Ltd. Supplementary List No. 226...*   Bristol: 1916. 4to., profusely illustrated with half tone illustrations, original decorated buff wrappers.   Marlborough Rare Books   List 56 - 2   2016   £250

Paroissien: Elzevir, Rite Romain.   Paris: Gruel et Englemann, 1889. 165 x 83mm., striking contemporary burgundy morocco, elaborately gilt by Gruel (stamp signed at tail of spine), upper cover with large and richly detailed oval bas-relief plaquette of the last supper framed above and below by a large panel of interlacing open strapwork comprised of abstracted gilt floral and foliate curls and other decorative elements, lower cover similarly decorated, with its central medallion containing a gilt cipher in intertwined majuscules, raised bands, spine gilt in double ruled compartments with central arabesque, gilt filigree turn-ins, claret moire silk endleaves, all edges gilt, original brass clasps with strapwork decoration, with 26 illustrations, composed of 22 large black and white woodcut headpieces and four chromolithographed plates with gold highlights, along with numerous uncolored woodcut initials, front free endleaf gilt stamp '24 Mai 1891', first Communion card of Andre Gallien dated 9 May 1895, laid in, very fine, morocco lustrous and leaves entirely crisp and clean.   Phillip J. Pirages   67 - 47   2016 $1100

Paroissien, David   *A Companion to Charles Dickens.*   London: Blackwell, 2008. First edition, 4to., half title, original black cloth, mint in dust jacket.   Jarndyce Antiquarian Booksellers   CCXVIII - 1400   2016   £50

Paroissien, David   *The Companion to Great Expectations.*   London: Helm Information, 2000. First edition, half title, illustrations, maps, original green cloth, mint in dust jacket.   Jarndyce Antiquarian Booksellers   CCXVIII - 596   2016   £45

Parone, Edward   *Collision Course.*   New York: Random House, 1968. First printing, 8vo., illustrations, author's presentation on flyleaf, very good in somewhat chipped and scuffed dust jacket.   Second Life Books, Inc.   196 B - 371   2016 $65

Parr, Martin   *7 Cups of Tea.*   Portland: Nazraeli Press, 2012. Number 261 of 500 copies, 6 color images along with original tipped in color photo by Parr, very fine in publisher's bag.   Jeff Hirsch Books   Holiday List 2015 - 88   2016 $75

Parr, Samuel   *A Letter from Irenoplis (sic) to the Inhabitants of Eleutheropolis or a Serious Address to the Dissenters of Birmingham.*   Birmingham: printed by John Thompson for C. Dilly, London, 1792. Second edition, 8vo., with half title and final leaf, mid 20th century roan backed marbled boards, spine lettered gilt, very good, scarce.   John Drury Rare Books   2015 - 21127   2016 $306

Parrish, Anne   *The Story of Appleby Capple.*   New York: Harper & Bros., 1950. First edition, 4to., yellow cloth, very good+ in dust jacket with some soil and chipping, color endpapers and more than 50 black and whites, each letter in humanized form.   Aleph-bet Books, Inc.   112 - 8   2016 $250

Parrott, J. Edward   *A Christmas Carol...arranged for dramatic representation by...*   London: J. Curwen & Sons, 1896. 4to., illustrations, text with printed music, sewn as issued, original pink pictorial wrappers, printed in red, very good.   Jarndyce Antiquarian Booksellers   CCXVIII - 358   2016   £65

Parry, Judge   *The Scarlet Herring.*   London: Smith, Elder, 1899. Limited to 50 numbered copies printed on Japan vellum, signed by author, tall 8vo., white boards, covers toned and has some soil, else very good, illustrations by Athelstan Rusden with red half title, 8 plates and 21 illustrations in text.   Aleph-bet Books, Inc.   112 - 181   2016 $300

Parsons, Anthony   *Bush Gypsies.*   London: Grayson & Grayson, 1932. First edition, 8vo., original publisher's blue cloth, lettered black on spine, very slight lean at spine, otherwise lean, bright and very good+ in near very good dust jacket, slightly chipped and nicked (dime sized chip at head of spine not affecting lettering), and mild surface wear, front panel of jacket in good order.   Any Amount of Books   2015 - C7190   2016   £170

Parsons, Elsie Clews   *Isleta Paintings.*   Washington: Smithsonian Institution, 1962. First edition, 140 reproductions, including frontispiece in color, light brown cloth, gilt, fine with pictorial dust jacket.   Argonaut Book Shop   Native American 2015 - 5713   2016 $125

Parsons, Flora   *Calisthentic Songs Illustrated for the Use of Both Public and Private Schools.*   New York: Ivison Blakeman Taylor, 1869. 7 x 5 inches, gilt lettered cloth, light shelf wear, very good+, nearly every page of musical notation faces an illustrated page of calisthenics and detailed directions.   Aleph-bet Books, Inc.   111 - 143   2016 $200

Parsons, John   *Probably Without Equal Frank Mercer and the Newfoundland Rangers.*   Shearstown and St. Johns: Grassy Pond Pub. & DRC, 2003. Second edition, trade paperback, very good, signed by author.   Schooner Books Ltd.   115 - 115   2016 $40

Parsons, Julie   *Mary, Mary.*   London: Macmillan, 1998. First edition, very fine in dust jacket with publisher's wraparound intact.   Mordida Books   2015 - 001777   2016 $55

Parsons, Louella *The Gay Illiterate.* Garden City: Doubleday Doran, 1944. First edition, fine in price clipped, very good dust jacket with slight loss at crown, inscribed by Parson for Betty Grable and husband Harry James. Between the Covers Rare Books   204 - 51   2016 $650

Parsons, Lucy E. *Life of Albert R. Parsons with Brief History of the labor Movement in America.* Chicago: 1889. First edition, slight shelfwear and couple of internal smudges, overall remarkably nice.   Dumont Maps and Books   134 - 43   2016 $500

Partlow, Robert R. *Dickens the Craftsman: Strategies of Presentation...* Carbondale: Southern Illinois University Press, 1970. First edition, original black cloth, spine, grey patterned paper boards, very good in slightly rubbed, dust jacket.   Jarndyce Antiquarian Booksellers   CCXVIII - 1401   2016   £20

Partridge, Ralph *Broadmoor. A History of Criminal Lunacy and Its Provisions.* London: Chatto & Windus, 1953. First edition, 8vo., original cloth and dust jacket, 12 illustrations, small chip to top edge of jacket, very good, scarce. Sotheran's   Piccadilly Notes - Summer 2015 - 228   2016   £50

Partridge, Samuel William *Upward and Onward: a Thought Book for the Threshold of active Life.* London: S. W. Partridge & Co., circa, 1858? 12th thousand, half title, 4 pages ads, original brown cloth, bevelled boards, slight nick to spine, otherwise very good, crisp copy, all edges gilt, presentation inscription on half title.   Jarndyce Antiquarian Books   CCXV - 351   2016   £30

Party-Giving on Every Scale or the Cost of Entertainments with the Fashionable Modes of Arrangement. London: Frederick Warne & Co., 1882. Second edition, half title, original mustard decorated cloth, slightly rubbed and marked, signature of J. M. Wilson.   Jarndyce Antiquarian Books   CCXV - 19   2016   £75

Parvan, Vasile *Dacia. An Outline of the early Civilizations of the Carpatho-Danubian Countries.* Cambridge University Press, 1928. First edition, 8vo., plates and maps, green cloth, gilt lettered spine, some separation at gutter between pages 64/65, little wear to endcaps and corners, but binding sound, still good copy, ownership inscription of G. N. G. Smith.   Unsworths Antiquarian Booksellers Ltd.   E05 - 55   2016   £20

Pascal, Blaise *Les Provinciales; or The Mysterie of Jersuitisme.* London: printed by J.. G. for R. Royston, 1657. First edition in English, 12mo., prelim blank, postscript leaf, two final leaves of errata and ads, added engraved titlepage by Robert Vaughan, 18th century panelled calf, neatly rebacked, retaining old morocco lettering label, spine lettered gilt with decorative gilt board edges, 18th century armorial bookplate of John Hustler of Acklam mounted on verso of engraved titlepage, early ink notations at bottom of engraved titlepage, leaves Q thru Q12 have been affected by printer's ink, mostly just little snugging, verso of Q10 is the only page where two lines of text have been affected, apart from few flaws, fine copy, very rare. Heritage Book Shop   Holiday 2015 - 86   2016 $2000

Pascal, Blaise *Les Provinciales ou Lettres Ecrites par Louis de Montalte...* Paris: Charpentier, 1875. New edition, octavo, period binding of full blue straight grain calf, raised bands, gilt decorated spine, gilt rules and inner and outer dentelles, marbled endpapers, all edges gilt, armorial bookplate of Edward Hilton Young, 1st Baron Kennet of the Dene, gift inscription "Arthur William Young with best wishes from Margaret Lucia Young 27th June 1882", slight scuffing to hinges, very good.   Peter Ellis   112 - 287   2016   £150

Pascal, Blaise *Thoughts on Religion and Other Subjects.* Edinburgh: printed by R. Fleming for W. Gray, 1751. 12mo., old ink splash to leading edge of book block, intruding on to page but disappearing by page 28, ownership name of James Ford 1828, some underlining to text, marginal pen strokes, expertly bound in recent quarter sprinkled calf, marbled boards, vellum tips, raised and gilt banded spine, red morocco label.   Jarndyce Antiquarian Booksellers   CCXVI - 442   2016   £280

Pastan, Linda *Aspects of Eve. Poems.* New York: Liveright, 1975. First edition, hardcover issue, inscribed and signed for William Meredith, faint spotting to cloth, very good in like dust jacket.   Charles Agvent   William Meredith - 96   2016 $100

Pastan, Linda *Aspects of Eve: Poems.* New York: Liveright, 1975. First edition, 8vo., author's presentation on title to poet Bill Claire, brown cloth, nice in slightly scuffed and soiled dust jacket.   Second Life Books, Inc.   196 B - 374   2016 $45

Pastan, Linda *Aspects of Eve. Poems.* New York: Liveright, 1975. First edition, wrapper issue, inscribed and signed for William Meredith, near fine.   Charles Agvent   William Meredith - 95   2016 $50

Pastan, Linda *The Five Stages of Grief. Poems.* New York: W. W. Norton & co., 1978. First edition, inscribed and signed on titlepage for William Meredith, also signed in full by Pastan, near fine in near fine dust jacket.   Charles Agvent   William Meredith - 97   2016 $80

Pastan, Linda *On the Way to the Zoo.* Washington: Dryad, 1975. No. 81 of 600 copies, small 8vo., not numbered, author's presentation on title, covers slightly soiled, nice.   Second Life Books, Inc.   197 - 258   2016 $45

Pastan, Linda *A Perfect Circle of Sun.* Chicago: Swallow, 1971. First edition, brown cloth, cover very slightly scuffed at corners and ends of spine, but nice in scuffed and little soiled dust jacket, author's presentation to poet William Claire.   Second Life Books, Inc.   196 B - 376   2016 $45

Pastan, Linda *Waiting for My Life. Poems.* New York: W. W. Norton & Co., 1981. First edition, inscribed and signed by author for William Meredith, near fine in like dust jacket.   Charles Agvent   William Meredith - 98   2016 $80

Pasternak, Boris 1890-1960 *Doktor Zywago.* Milan: Feltrinelli Editore, n.d. circa, 1958. First official edition in Russian, 8vo., finely bound in full dark green leather lettered gilt and decorated at spine, edges of pages slightly browned, otherwise fine.   Any Amount of Books   2015 - A44995   2016   £600

Pastimes of James Joyce. New York: Joyce Memorial Fund, 1941. First edition, no. 37 of 300 copies signed by editors and artist and 700 unsigned copies, 305 x 229mm., original blue-gray paper boards, facsimile of Joyce's signature on upper cover, flat spine, frontispiece by Jo Davidson, 3 pages of facsimile manuscript, laid in at rear an article from the 28 September 1961 edition of "The Listener" entitled 'James Joyce: a First Impression" by James Stern, Slocum and Cahoon A-50, half the length of each joint with thin crack, faint offsetting (from news article?) to titlepage and frontispiece, otherwise especially clean and fresh inside and out.   Phillip J. Pirages   67 - 216   2016 $800

Paston, George *At John Murray's - Records of a Literary Circle 1843-1892.* London: John Murray, 1932. First edition, plates, head and tail of spine slightly bumped, near fine in very good, slightly torn and repaired price clipped dust jacket faded at spine and edges, presentation copy inscribed for Henry Schollick, by John G. Murray, below that his Son John R. Murray has added his signature.   Peter Ellis   112 - 318   2016   £75

Paston, George *At John Murray's Records of a Literary Circle 1843-1892.* London: John Murray, 1932. First edition, 8vo., frontispiece, plates, original black cloth, presentation from John Murray to Mr. Williams.   J. & S. L. Bonham Antiquarian Booksellers   Voyages 2016 - 8794   2016   £65

Pate, Janet *The Book of Bleuths.* London: New English Library, 1977. First edition, fine in dust jacket.   Mordida Books   2015 - 010780   2016 $65

Pater, Walter *Appreciations with an Essay on Style.* London: Macmillan, 1890. Third impression, bound for George Allison Armour by Doves Bindery in 1894, very good in full green morocco with gilt title, gilt clover decoration and five raised bands to spine, browning to spine and edges of boards, minor rubbing to hinges, corners and bands, decorative dentelles and full edges gilt, offsetting to endpapers and slight toning to margins of pages, else clean and bright, very good.   The Kelmscott Bookshop   13 - 41   2016 $850

Pater, Walter *Essays from the Guardian.* London: Macmillan and Co., 1901. Second printing, extremely pleasing crimson crushed morocco attractively gilt by Zaehnsdorf (stamp signed), covers with multiple gilt rule frame, central panel with azured cornerpieces and central oval medallion, flat spine in three unequal panels, two with oval medallion tools, one with gilt titling, gilt ruled turn-ins, marbled endpapers, top edge gilt, bookplate of Charles Walker Andrews, spine uniformly sunned to a dark red, light offsetting on free endpapers from turn-in glue, otherwise very fine, binding unworn and especially lustrous, text showing virtually no signs of use.   Phillip J. Pirages   67 - 77   2016 $800

Paterson, James Graham *Sowing Beside All Waters: a narrative of a Journey of 66,000 miles over land and seas through Australia, New Zealand, Tasmania, Fiji, Friendly Islands, Cape Colony, Transvaal natal, Orange Free State, Madagascar &c.* Glasgow: David Bryce & Son, 1891. Folding map, plates, illustrations, printed paper boards, blue cloth spine, little rubbed.   Jarndyce Antiquarian Booksellers   CCXVII - 213   2016   £68

Paterson, Katherine *Bridge to Terabithia.* New York: Crowell, 1977. First edition, first printing (correct code), cloth, fine in fine dust jacket, not price clipped, no seal, extremely scarce in such nice condition.   Aleph-bet Books, Inc.   112 - 364   2016 $750

Paterson, Michael *Voices from Dickens' London.* London: David Charles, 2006. Half title, plates, illustrations, original pale blue cloth, mint in dust jacket, Jarndyce Antiquarian Booksellers   CCXVIII - 1402   2016   £25

Patmore, Brigit *The Impassioned Onlooker.* London: Robert Holden, 1926. First edition, one or two faint foxspots to prelims with occasional spot further, few faint handling marks, crown 8vo., original red and black patterned cloth, backstrip gently faded with printed label, small amount of creasing to cloth of upper board, little bleed from red of cloth to top edge and dust jacket interior (single spot showing to front panel), dust jacket with light overall dust soiling and small amount of chipping at corners, good, inscribed by author for Kathleen Byass.   Blackwell's Rare Books   B186 - 271   2016   £600

Patmore, Coventry *The Angel of the House and Espousals.* London: John Parker & Son, 1854. 1856. First edition, inscribed 'with the author's compliments' in first volume, bound in original rippled brown cloth with paper spine labels, rubbed and bumped and tears to the Espousals label, interior pages generally very good, pastedown to first volume stained and has remains of bookplate, second volume has light ink inscription and signature, very good.   The Kelmscott Bookshop   12 - 80   2016 $450

Patmore, Coventry *Poems. I. Amelia. II. Angel in the House. III. Victories of Love. IV. The Unknown Eros.* London: George Bell & sons, 1879. Half titles, 4 volumes, contemporary quarter green morocco, green sand grained cloth sides, spines lettered gilt, slight rubbing, very good, discreet presentation inscription from author for H. R. (likely Harriet Robson who became Patmore's third wife).   Jarndyce Antiquarian Booksellers   CCXVII - 214   2016   £320

Patrick, John *The Teahouse of the August Moon.* New York: Putnam, 1952. Second impression, 8vo., Harry Jackson's copy (Sgt. Gregovich in the play), signed by David Wayne and 15 members of the cast, presentation from Jackson, light edge bumps, tear on blank, otherwise very good in little chipped and stained dust jacket.   Second Life Books, Inc.   196 B - 380   2016 $200

Patrick, Robert *Untold Decades.* New York: St. Martins, 1988. First edition, 8vo., illustrations, author's presentation on fly, nice in dust jacket.   Second Life Books, Inc.   196 B - 381   2016 $45

Patriotic Competition Against Self-Interested Combination, Recommended by a Union Between the Nobility, the Landed and Independent... London: James Ridgway, 1800. First edition, 8vo., recently bound in calf backed marbled boards, gilt, very good, presentation copy inscribed "From the Author", very scarce.   John Drury Rare Books   2015 - 5292   2016 $437

Patten, Robert L. *Charles Dickens and His Publishers.* Oxford: Clarendon Press, 1978. First edition, half title, nd plates, folding, original dark blue cloth, very good in slightly faded dust jacket, publisher's compliments slip loosely inserted.   Jarndyce Antiquarian Booksellers   CCXVIII - 1403   2016   £65

Patterson, Charles F. *The Petrified Heart.* Livermore: Rockbridge Baths: Signal Time Publications, 2002. First edition, bump to crown, else fine in like dust jacket, uncommon.   Ken Lopez Bookseller   166 - 143   2016 $75

Patterson, Frederick B. *African Adventures.* New York: Putnam's, 1928. First edition, 4to., 50 full page illustrations in black and white, rebound in full leather with leather title label on spine along with gilt line decorations and raised ribs, slight edgewear to cover, contents tight, clean and without marks or inscriptions, very good.   Simon Finch   2015 - W27179   2016 $225

Pauker, John *Yoked by Violence: Poems by...* Denver: Alan Swallow, 1949. Small 8vo., author's presentation to The Cosmos Club and poet William Claire, paper on boards, edges and cover slightly soiled and cover little peeled at lower front edge, otherwise very good, tight copy.   Second Life Books, Inc.   196 B - 384   2016 $75

Paul VI, Pope *Allocutio Pro Pace. (with) Facsimile - Bodoni Imprint) Oratorio Dominica in CLV Linguas.* Parma: Franco Maria Ricci, 1967. One of 700 copies, 2 volumes, publisher's excellent red straight grain morocco, covers with gilt frame and central coat of arms, raised bands flanked by decorative gilt rules, panels with gilt lettering or central fleuron, original morocco lipped marbled paper slipcase.   Phillip J. Pirages   67 - 273   2016 $750

Paul, Elliott *The Life and Death of a Spanish Town.* London: Peter Davies, 1937. First UK edition, octavo, edges very slightly spotted, very good in like dust jacket (chipped, nicked, faded at spine).   Peter Ellis   112 - 370   2016   £175

Pauly, Bettina *A Sun that rises.* San Francisco: Bettina Pauly, 2013. Number 7 of 10 copies, signed and numbered by book artist, book is an accordion structure letterpress printed on BFK paper, text and red stitching printed atop an abstract etching that darkens with each page, hand died red ribbons attached, housed in clamshell box with title label and cut-out windows, fine, 6 x 5.5 inches (44 inches fully extended).   The Kelmscott Bookshop   13 - 44   2016 $750

Paxson, Frederic L. *Pre-War Years 1913-1917.* Boston: Houghton Mifflin, 1936. First edition, 8vo., photos, orange cloth, signed by author, very good.   Second Life Books, Inc.   196 B - 387   2016 $40

Paxton, Joseph *A Pocket Botanical Dictionary, Comprising the names, History and Culture of all Plants Known in Britain.* London: Bradbury & Evans, 1849. New edition, half title, original green cloth blocked in blind and gilt, attractive copy.   Jarndyce Antiquarian Booksellers   CCXVII - 215   2016   £85

Payne Gallwey, Ralph *The Fowler Ireland.* London: John Van Voorst, Paternoster Row, 1882. First edition, inscribed by author for H. Rouse, large 8vo., recently rebound in half blue morocco over blue cloth, spine decorated in gilt and stamped with hunting motifs, marbled endpapers, top edge gilt, very good, internally clean.   Sotheran's   Hunting, Shooting & Fishing - 91   2016   £200

Payne, Alfred C. *Little People's Book of Fun.* London: Nister, n.d, circa, 1910. Cloth backed pictorial boards, some edge rubbing and minor soil, else very good-fine, fabulous full page and large partial page chromolithographs, many by G. H. Thompson, also many brown illustrations including 7 large illustrations by Louis Wain, rare, especially in such nice condition. Aleph-bet Books, Inc. 112 - 370 2016 $800

Payne, Ed. *Billy the Boy Artist's Book of Funny Pictures.* Boston: C. M. Clark, 1910. Oblong large 4to., pictorial boards, except for very slight wear to paper spine and corners, near fine condition, every page illustrated with cartoons, really scarce. Aleph-bet Books, Inc. 112 - 99 2016 $400

Payne, Edward F. *The Charity of Charles Dickens, His Interest in the Home for Fallen Women...* Boston: printed privately for Charles E. Goodspeed, 1929. One of 100 ordinary copies, original cream paper boards, printed paper label in slightly dulled slipcase, very good. Jarndyce Antiquarian Booksellers CCXVIII - 1405 2016 £20

Payne, Edward F. *The Charity of Charles Dickens....* Boston: printed for members of the Bibliophile Society, 1929. First edition, one of 425 copies, half title, plate, frontispiece letter, uncut in full tan calf, gilt borders, little marked, good plus, double slipcase, top edge gilt. Jarndyce Antiquarian Booksellers CCXVIII - 1095 2016 £35

Payne, Edward F. *Dickens Days in Boston: a Record of Daily Events.* Boston & New York: Houghton Mifflin Co., Riverside Press, Cambridge, 1927. First edition, plates, original maroon cloth, front board blocked with central vignette in gilt within blind floral border, spine lettered gilt, spine slightly rubbed at head and tail, three small nicks in leading hinge, good plus. Jarndyce Antiquarian Booksellers CCXVIII - 1404 2016 £45

Paz, Octavio *Premier de L'an.* Paris: Marchant Ducel, 1989. First printing of this edition, octavo, one of 24 numbered copies, this being no. 23, out of a total limitation of 49, signed by Paz and artist, Dominique Gutherz, about fine, small circular sticker on jacket spine, scarce. Royal Books 48 - 70 2016 $850

Paz, Octavio *Three Poems. Tres Poems.* New York: Limited Editions Club, 1987. Limited to 750 signed copies, this #543, elephant folio, original lithographs by Robert Motherwell with tissue guards, bound in linen with red paper label front cover, black lettering spine, types used are Bauer Bodoni Bold and Bauer Bodoni Bold Italic, cast by Fundicion Tipografica Neufville, text handset at Stamperia Valdonega, with label rear paste-down staining the book was hand-sewn and bound by Carol Joyce, text printed on mould made paper from Cartiere Enrico Magnani, lithographs printed at Trestle Editions on various handmade Japanese papers, in fine original clamshell box with black lettering on spine. By the Book, L. C. 45 - 62 2016 $2700

Peacock, Lucy *The Visit for a Week...* London: printed for Hookham and Carpenter, 1794. 12mo., paper flaw to G9 affecting a few letters, leading blank edge of K10 torn with loss, tear without loss to edge of O4, some occasional slight browning, one gathering a little proud in binding, near contemporary ownership name at head of titlepage, full contemporary sheep, simple gilt banded spine, expert repairs to joints and corners. Jarndyce Antiquarian Booksellers CCXVI - 443 2016 £250

Peacock, Thomas Love *Prose Works.* London: J. M. Dent & Co., 1891-1893. Small 8vo., 10 volumes, original fawn cloth, blocked in black and red with attractive design on upper covers of a street sign bearing title of each volume surrounded by elaborate ironwork, 2 portraits and other frontispieces, slight variance in color of cloth, little bubbling to couple of volumes, ink name, otherwise very good, preserved in cloth covered slipcase. Sotheran's Piccadilly Notes - Summer 2015 - 229 2016 £298

Peacock, Thomas Love *Sir Hornbook or Childe Lancelot's Expedition...* London: printed for John Sharpe, 1815. Third edition, frontispiece and 7 hand colored plates, slight dampstaining in inner margin, original dark printed wrappers, spine slightly chipped, nice. Jarndyce Antiquarian Books CCXV - 777 2016 £350

Peacock, Thomas Love *Sir Hornbook or Childe Lancelot's Expedition...* London: printed for N. Hailes, Juvenile Library, 1817. Fourth edition, frontispiece and 7 plates, dated 1813, original grey printed wrappers, edges slightly chipped. Jarndyce Antiquarian Books CCXV - 778 2016 £200

Peacock, Thomas Love *Sir Hornbook or Childe Lancelot's Expedition...* London: printed for N. Hailes,, 1818. Fifth edition, frontispiece and 7 plates dated June 1813, final ad leaf, original pink printed wrappers,l little rubbed and repaired in places, contemporary signatures of G. Davies & P. Cain. Jarndyce Antiquarian Books CCXV - 779 2016 £150

Peake, Mervyn *Captain Slaughterhouse Drops Anchor.* London: Eyre & Spottiswoode, 1945. Second edition, royal 8vo., original fine cream cloth lettered in green, original pictorial dust jacket, line drawings on variously colored grounds, near fine with one small adhesion to inner gutter of titlepage and slight crinkling to free endpapers, irregularly price clipped dust jacket with some light general dusting, one short and unobtrusive closed tear to bottom edge of upper panel, another equally short split to front flap at top of edge (10mm). Sotheran's Piccadilly Notes - Summer 2015 - 230 2016 £298

Peake, Mervyn *The Gormenghast Trilogy: Titus Groan; Gormenghast; Titus Alone.* London: Eyre & Spottiswoode, 1968-1970. First edition thus, drawings by author, 3 volumes, octavo, first volume little creased at spine, small stain on upper cover, bruised at upper corners, small ownership signature, very good in very good dust jacket, nicked and internally repaired at edges, some show through from sellotape, second volume very good in like dust jacket, price clipped, small ownership signature, third volume fine in near fine dust jacket slightly creased at edges.   Peter Ellis   112 - 288   2016   £200

Peake, Mervyn *Mr. Pye.* London: Heinemann, 1953. First edition, 31 line drawings by author as chapter headpieces, crown 8vo., original blue cloth, publisher's device blindstamped to lower board, backstrip lettered gilt with touch of rubbing at tips, little faint spotting to top edge, price penned to top corner of flyleaf, dust jacket with Peake design, repriced in pen to front flap, some fraying and light soiling with backstrip panel gently faded, good.   Blackwell's Rare Books   B184 - 215   2016   £80

Peake, Mervyn *Sketches from Bleak House.* London: Methuen, 1983. First edition, illustrations, original sky blue cloth, very good in dust jacket.   Jarndyce Antiquarian Booksellers   CCXVIII - 518   2016   £20

Peake, Mervyn *Titus Groan.* London: Eyre & Spottiswoode, 1946. First edition, title vignette by author, single faint foxspot at head of prelims, 8vo., original red cloth, backstrip lettered in gilt now little dulled, minor bumping to corners of lower board, small amount of light foxing to edges with few very faint foxspots to endpapers, contemporary ownership inscription, small bookseller sticker at foot of rear pastedown, dust jacket with light overall toning, little chipping at head of backstrip panel and small amount of soiling to rear panel, very good.   Blackwell's Rare Books   B184 - 216   2016   £325

Pearce, Barry *Australian Artists, Australian Birds.* Drummoyne: Angus and Robertson, 1989. Quarto, color illustrations, very good in dust jacket.   Andrew Isles Natural History Books   55 - 564   2016 $100

Pearce, James Alfred *Old Line Whigs for Buchanan & Breckinridge. Letters from Hon. James Alfred Pearce and Hon. Thoms G. Pratt to the Whigs of Maryland...* Washington: J. W. Crisfield and James B. Clay, 1856. 8vo., 16 pages, self wrappers, closely trimmed on fore edge, loss of few letters not affecting legibility, else very good.   Kaaterskill Books   21 - 69   2016 $75

Pearce, Michael *The Mingrelian Conspiracy.* London: Harper Collins, 1995. First edition, very fine in dust jacket.   Mordida Books   2015 - 008130   2016 $55

Pearse, Ruth *The Underground Press.* New York: Composing Room, n.d., First edition, octavo, illustrations, illustrated orange wrappers, trifle soiled, very near fine.   Between the Covers Rare Books   204 - 144   2016 $250

Pearson, Edward *The Angler's Garland and Fisher's Delight.* London: Bickers & Son, 1871. First edition, limited to 350 copies, 4to., contemporary half green double gilt ruled morocco over marbled paper boards, spine richly gilt, woodcuts by Bewick and extra illustrated with six other plates, 3 are hand colored, little offsetting from inserted plates, otherwise very good.   Sotheran's Piccadilly Notes - Summer 2015 - 232   2016   £1250

Peck, Bradford *The World a Department Store.* Lewiston: Bradford Peck, 1900. First edition, 8vo., lacks half of folding frontispiece, inscribed with compliments of author for E. W. Tyler.   Second Life Books, Inc.   196 B - 782   2016 $175

Peck, Francis *Academia Tertia Anglicana; or the Antiquarian Annals of Stanford (sic) in Lincoln, Rutland and Northampton Shires....* London: printed for the author by James Bettenham, 1727. First edition, 14 books in one, bound in early 19th century panelled russia, attractively tooled in blind, rebacked period style by Bernard Middleton, all edges gilt, 33 engraved plates, including large folding engraved frontispiece, 4 small engraved plates within text, numerous attractive wood engraved tailpieces, bright, clean, early 19th century engraved armorial booklabel of Earls of Abingdon, bookplate of John Lea Nevinson (1905-1985).   Sotheran's Piccadilly Notes - Summer 2015 - 233   2016   £695

Peck, G. W. *Aurifodina or Adventures in the Gold Region. A Fantastical '49er Novel.* San Francisco: Book Club of California, 1974. Limited to 400 copies, printed by Andrew Hoyem, illustrations, gilt stamped and decorated black cloth, fine.   Argonaut Book Shop   Private Press 2015 - 3705   2016 $45

Peck, John Mason *A New Guide for Emigrants to the West....* Boston: Gould, Kendall & Lincoln, 1836. First edition thus, 16mo., blind embossed green cloth, gilt titles, very good or better, minor wear at extremities, faint browning on spine, else fresh, bright copy.   Kaaterskill Books   21 - 70   2016 $450

Peck, Samuel *Fair Women of To-Day.* New York: Stokes, 1895. 4to. , three quarter blue cloth, fine, beautiful full page chromolithographs by Caroline Lovell, great copy of beautiful book.   Aleph-bet Books, Inc.   112 - 194   2016 $600

Pedant, Gilles *Recueil de Diverses Sentences, Prouerbes & Dictions Remarquables.* Paris: Pierre Ramier, 1628. 8vo., marbled wrappers, upper cover nearly detached, little browned and minor staining, bookplate of Colonel Victor De Guinzbourg, sound.   Blackwell's Rare Books   B186 - 114   2016   £850

Peddle, Mrs. *Rudiments of Taste.* London: printed for C. Dilly in Poultry, 1789. 12mo., rebound in quarter brown calf, gilt spine, red morocco label, very good. Jarndyce Antiquarian Books   CCXV - 352   2016   £480

Pedley, Mrs. *Practical Housekeeping or the Duties of a Home-Wife.* London: George Routledge & Sons, 1867. First edition, half title, 10 page catalog, original illustrated printed orange cloth, spine dulled, nice. Jarndyce Antiquarian Books   CCXV - 353   2016   £120

Peel, Dorothy Constance *Waiting at Table; a Practical Guide Including Parlourmaid's Work in General.* London: Frederick Warne & Co., 1929. First edition, half title, original brick red cloth, very good in slightly torn and dusted dust jacket. Jarndyce Antiquarian Books   CCXV - 354   2016   £40

Peile, Solomon Charles Frederick *Lawn Tennis as a Game of Skill...* London: William Blackwood and Sons, 1887. Fourth edition, half title, slight creasing to upper corners, original orange pictorial cloth, slightly rubbed, nice, attractive copy. Jarndyce Antiquarian Booksellers   CCXVII - 162   2016   £150

Peixotto, Ernest *Through Spain and Portugal.* New York: Scribners, 1922. First edition, 8vo., illustrations, original decorative cloth. J. & S. L. Bonham Antiquarian Booksellers Europe 2016 - 8959   2016   £20

Pelecanos, George *Down by the River Where the Dead Men Go.* New York: St. Martin's Press, 1995. First edition, fine in like dust jacket, signed by author. Bella Luna Books 2016 - p3290   2016 $82

Pemberton, Henry *A View of Newton's Philosophy.* S. Palmer, 1728. First edition, 4to., recent half mottled brown calf, marbled boards, spine with raised bands and red morocco label with gilt lettering, 12 unnumbered folding plates, engraved titlepage vignette, initials, headpieces and tailpieces by John Pine after J. Grison, very bright and clean, very good, engraved bookplate and library labels of Duke of Leinster.   Sotheran's   Piccadilly Notes - Summer 2015 - 216   2016   £1500

Pemberton, J. Edgar *Charles Dickens and the Stage.* London: George Redway, 1888. First edition, half title, frontispiece and 2 plates, uncut in original green cloth, spine lettered gilt, very good, bright. Jarndyce Antiquarian Booksellers   CCXVIII - 1407   2016   £35

Pemble, William *A Briefe Introduction to Geography Containing a Description of the Grounds, and Generall part Thereof...* Oxford: Iohn Lichfield for Edward Forest, 1630. First edition, small 4to., 1 folding table, printer's device on titlepage, 2 woodcut headpieces, very faint waterstain on a few pages, modern full vellum, gilt stamped spine title, booklabel of John Lawson, fine, rare. Jeff Weber Rare Books 181 - 25   2016 $2500

Penfield, Wilder *The Cerebral Cortex of Man.* New York: MacMillan, 1950. 121 text illustrations, signed by Theodore Rasmussen on title in pen, nice in original red cloth. James Tait Goodrich   X-78 - 480   2016 $125

Penfield, Wilder *The Excitable Cortex in Conscious Man.* Liverpool: 1958. Original binding, with tipped in reprint of review of this book by Stanley Cobb, note on front fly "James C. White set by W. P. 5-15-58" in White's hand. James Tait Goodrich   X-78 - 461   2016 $125

Penman, Sharon Kay *The Sunne in Splendour.* New York: Holt Rinehart & Winston, 1982. First edition, fine in near fine dust jacket with chipping at spine and flap fold ends. Ken Hebenstreit, Bookseller   2016 - 2016 $55

Penn, Granville *Remarks Preparatory to the Issue of the Reserved Negotiation for Peace.* London: printed by James Bateson for T. Beckett, Pall Mall, 1797. 8vo., presentation inscription to Earl of Haddington from his father the author, very good, clean copy, disbound. Jarndyce Antiquarian Booksellers   CCXVI - 444   2016   £75

Penn, Richard *Maxims and Hints for an Angler...* Philadelphia: F. Bell, 1855. First American edition, 12mo, numerous full page plates, original gilt stamped cloth, lightly soiled, foxed, collector's ownership label. M & S Rare Books, Inc.   99 - 298   2016 $475

Penn, William *Some Fruits of Solitude.... (with, as issued) More Fruits....* Newport: printed by James Franklin, 1749. First American edition, 12mo., 2 parts in 1 volume, occasional browning and spotting, few leaves little defective in fore margin, original sheep, cracks in joints, upper one repaired, corners worn, slip-in case ownership inscription of Mary Monry 1876, later bookplate of Paul Jordan-Smith. Blackwell's Rare Books   B186 - 115   2016   £2250

Pennant, Thomas   1726-1798 *A Tour from Downing to Alston Moor.* London: Oriental Press, 1801. First edition, quarto, 27 plates, light occasional foxing, recent brown half calf. J. & S. L. Bonham Antiquarian Booksellers Europe 2016 - 9113   2016   £250

Pennington, Sarah *An Unfortunate Mother's advice to her Absent Daughters in a Letter to Miss Pennington.* London: printed by S. Chandler & sold by W. Bristow, 1761. half title, 8vo., signed in Ms. S. Pennington, contemporary half sheep, marbled boards, rubbed, hinges slightly worn, armorial bookplate of La Grange on leading pastedown, nice, unsophisticated copy. Jarndyce Antiquarian Books CCXV - 355 2016 £680

Pennington, Sarah *An Unfortunate Mother's advice to her Absent Daughters in a Letter to Miss Pennington.* London: J. Hatchard, 1802. 12mo., half title, frontispiece, contemporary tree calf, red morocco label, extremities slightly worn, rubbed, contemporary signatures, good, sound. Jarndyce Antiquarian Books CCXV - 356 2016 £65

Penrose, Thomas *Poems.* London: printed for J. Walter, 1781. First edition, 8vo., titlepage and final page little dusted, tiny expert repair to head of final leaf, some light browning, expertly bound in recent quarter sprinkled calf, gilt ands, red morocco label, marbled boards, vellum tips, fresh contemporary endpapers and pastedowns. Jarndyce Antiquarian Booksellers CCXVI - 445 2016 £280

Penzer, Norman *The Most Noble and Famous Travels of Marco Polo, Together with the Travels of Nicolo de Conti.* London: Argonaut Press, 1937. First edition thus, quarto, one of 1050 numbered copies, color frontispiece, titlepage vignette by William Monk, several maps, one of which is folding, original binding of quarter vellum backed with yellow buckram sides, armorial shield on upper cover, printed on Japon vellum, presentation copy from editor Norman Penzer May 28th 1934 for Nancy and Wilfred Greene, armorial bookplate of recipient, bookplate, edges bit spotted, very good. Peter Ellis 112 - 247 2016 £175

Pepler, Hillary Douglas Clark *The Devil's Devices..* S. Dominic's Press, 1915. First edition, 11 wood engravings by Eric Gill, foolscap 8vo., original quarter black cloth, scarlet boards, Gill engraving and lettering on front cover, all printed in black, cover rubbed, more so to rear cover, untrimmed, good, Eric Gill's bookplate. Blackwell's Rare Books B184 - 311 2016 £300

Pepper & Salt or Seasoning for Young Folk. New York: Harper and Bros., 1886. First edition, large quarto, pictorial titlepage printed in red and black and 75 black and white illustrations by Howard Pyle, original tan cloth pictorially decorated in red and black, very fine. David Brass Rare Books, Inc. 2015 - 02963 2016 $950

Pepper, William *An American Text-Book of the Theory and Practice of Medicine.* Philadelphia: 1893. Royal 8vo., 2 volumes, original full sheep, red burgundy spine label, raised bands, other than some light wear to leather, very good. James Tait Goodrich X-78 - 462 2016 $495

Peppin, Brigid *Dictionary of British Book Illustrators: The Twentieth Century.* London: John Murray, 1983. First edition, quarto, copiously illustrated, fine in near fine dust jacket, very slightly rubbed at head of spine. Peter Ellis 112 - 46 2016 £45

Pepys, Samuel 1633-1703 *Bibliotheca Pepysiana, a Descriptive Catalogue of the Library of Samuel Pepys.* London: Sidgwick & Jackson Ltd., 1914. 1914. 1923. 1940, Volumes I-III quarter cloth with paper covered boards, paper spine label, dust jacket, volume IV cloth with paper spine label, dust jacket, large 8vo., all but fourth volume signed and dated by previous owners, extra spine label laid-in and bookseller's ticket on front pastedown in third volume, volume IV stamped on front free endpaper, volumes I and II have glassine wrapper under dust jacket, all volumes with corners bumped, jacket soiled in places and tanned at edges and spine, worn at edges, volume I and II boards tanned at head, some loss at head and tail of spine of wrapper, paper loss at spine of jacket, jacket loose at upper joint, volume III boards lightly tanned, cloth at spine foxed, two small yellow stains on upper board, volume IV minor wear to boards. Oak Knoll Books 310 - 262 2016 $300

Pepys, Samuel 1633-1703 *Memoirs of Samuel Pepys: Comprising his Diary from 1659 to 1669 and a Selection from His Private Correspondence.* London: Henry Colburn, 1825. First decoded edition, 295 x 229mm., 2 volumes, fine honey brown morocco by Bayntun (stamp signed), covers with intricate strapwork frame in gilt and black, raised bands, spines with similar strapwork compartments, gilt turn-ins with complex fleuron cornerpieces, marbled endpapers, leather hinges, all edges gilt, 21 called-for illustrations, including folding map, 7 portraits and an interior view (13 illustrations hand colored) and extra illustrated with 158 plates, 31 of these in color, 20 of them folding, three or four trivial (neatly refurbished) nicks in leather, paper used for mounting extra illustrated material acidic and consequently browned (and with facing pages slightly darkened as well), index in first volume faintly spotted, couple of short marginal tears to folding plates, other insignificant imperfections, but extremely attractive set, text clean and fresh, animated decorative bindings lustrous and scarcely worn. Phillip J. Pirages 67 - 31 2016 $3900

Percival, James G. *Poem Delivered Before the Connecticut Alpha of the Phi Beat Kappa Society September 13 1925.* Boston: Richardson & Lord, 1825. First edition, 8vo., removed, but preserving original printed wrappers. M & S Rare Books, Inc. 99 - 247 2016 $150

Percy, Stephen *Robin Hood and His Merry Foresters.* London: Bradbury & Evans, 1849. New edition, half title, original green cloth, blocked in blind and gilt, attractive copy. Jarndyce Antiquarian Booksellers CCXVII - 216 2016 £40

Percy, Walker *The Thanatos Syndrome.* Franklin Center: Franklin Library, 1987. Limited first edition, signed by author, bound in green leather, lettered and decoratively stamped in gilt, all edges gilt, very fine, as new.   Argonaut Book Shop   Literature 2015 - 4770   2016 $100

Perelman, S. J. *Chicken Inspector No. 23.* New York: Simon and Schuster, 1966. First edition, yellow cloth backed red boards, some minor spoiling to cover, pictorial contemporary in excellent condition other than a quarter inch tear to upper edge, fine.   Argonaut Book Shop   Literature 2015 - 5308   2016 $50

Perelman, S. J. *The Rising Gorge.* New York: Simon and Schuster, 1961. First edition, original cloth backed red boards, spine slightly bumped, minor rubbing to extremities and small bit of fading to upper edge of covers, near fine in chipped, rubbed and lightly soiled pictorial dust jacket.   Argonaut Book Shop   Literature 2015 - 5310   2016 $60

The Perfect Gentleman; or Etiquette and Eloquence.   New York: Dick & Fitzgerald, 1860. 12 page catalog, small tear to leading blank, some occasional slight spotting, lacking leading f.e.p., original green cloth, very good.   Jarndyce Antiquarian Books   CCXV - 357   2016   £65

Perfect, Thomas, Pseud.   *The Practice of Gardening.* London: printed for M. Cooper, 1759. One of 3 editions published in 1759, this issue is the same as the second edition except for new titlepage with statement "By. T. Perfect, a pupil of Dr. Hill', 8vo., disbound, ad leaf separated, but present, first and last leaf dusty.   Howard S. Mott Inc.   265 - 67   2016 $600

Perkin, J. R. C.   *Morning in His Heart The Life and Writings of Watson Kirkconnell.*   Hantsport: Pub. for Acadia University Library by Lancelot Press, 1986. 8vo., half title, red buckram with gilt titles to front cover and spine, black and white frontispiece ad black and white illustrations, very good.   Schooner Books Ltd.   115 - 170   2016 $75

Perkins, Edith Forbes   *Letters and Journal 1908-1925.* privately printed at the Riverside Press, 1931. 4 volumes, 8vo., photos, editor's presentation on flyleaf of volume I, spines little faded, otherwise nice.   Second Life Books, Inc.   196 B - 394   2016 $125

Perkins, Jacob   *Description of the Patent Improved Fire Engines and Other Hydrolic Machines Invented by Jacob Perkins and Manufactured by S. V. Merrick & Co.* Philadelphia: 1821. Only edition, 8vo., original plain gray wrappers (little worn), hand lettered, 2 full page engraved plates, stitched, plates mildly foxed.   Howard S. Mott Inc.   265 - 106   2016 $3500

Perkins, Jacob   *On the Explosion of Steam Borders.* N.P.: n.d. i.e. London, 1827. First edition, rare, 8vo., disbound, folding plate, rare.   Howard S. Mott Inc.   265 - 105   2016 $3500

Perkins, Lucy Fitch   *A Book of Joys" The Story of a New England Summer.*   Chicago: McClurg, Oct. 19, 1907. First edition, 8vo., green cloth, pictorial paste-on, slight bit of fading, else near fine, 5 lovely color plates, quite scarce in this condition.   Aleph-bet Books, Inc.   112 - 366   2016 $100

Perkins, William   *The Workes of the Famous and Worthy Minister of Christ...(The First Volume) The Foundation of Christian Religion, Gathered into Six Princples. (with) A Golden Chaine or the Description of Theologie...*   London: Iohn Legatt, printer to the Universitie of Cambridge, 1616. Second collected edition, Volume 1 (of 3), folio, 6 tables, lacking first four leaves (general title, address to the reader and table of contents) and folding table, margins dust soiled and dampstained, few leaves frayed to blank margin, modern half dark brown calf with marbled boards, spine in 7 compartments with raised bands, red morocco compartment, little cocked when upright, but binding sound, 19th century ownership inscription of John Morgan of Warrington to title.   Unsworths Antiquarian Booksellers Ltd.   30 - 118   2016   £600

Perlutsky, Jack   *Scranimals.*   New York: Greenwillow, 2002. First edition, 4to., pictorial hardbound, illustrations by Peter Sis, signed and dated, fine, like new in dust jacket.   Gene W. Baade, Books on the West   2015 - JUV010   2016 $50

Pernkoff, Eduard   *Atlas of Topographical and Applied Human Anatomy.*   Philadelphia: Saunders, 1963. 4to., original quarter calf and linen cloth, light wear, else fine, 332 illustrations, most in color.   James Tait Goodrich   X-78 - 463   2016 $275

Perowne, J. T. Woolrych   *Russian Hosts and English Guests in Central Asia.*   London: Scientific Press, 1898. First edition, 8vo., original cloth, spine lettered gilt, gilt stamped publisher's logo on upper cover, frontispiece, 10 plates, illustrations in text, one folding map, route in red, spine darkened, initial blank little spotted, else very good.   Sotheran's   Travel and Exploration - 162   2016   £298

Perrault, Charles 1628-1703 *Cendrillon et Les Fees. La Barbe Bleue et La Belle au Bois Dormant.* Paris: Boussod Valadon, 1886-1887. 2 volumes folio, top edges gilt, printed on heavy wove velin on one side of paper only with each page individually hinged into the binding, beautiful contemporary full morocco with extensive gilt tooling, spines in compartments with raised bands, gilt dentelles, silk doublures and end leaves (instead of paste-down and free endpapers), housed in custom marbled slipcase, joint of Barbe Bleu lightly worn and slipcases strengthened on edges, else fine, 73 magnificent aquarelles, color photogravure illustrations printed integrally with text, by Edouard De Braumont, exquisite set. Aleph-bet Books, Inc. 112 - 150 2016 $5500

Perrault, Charles 1628-1703 *Contes des Fees, Contenant Le Chaperon Rouge.* Paris: a la Librairie Economique, 1810. 1809., 12mo., 2 volumes in one, half titles, engraved titlepages, 12 engraved plates, some age toning and light foxing, contemporary sprinkled calf, gilt floral borders, gilt spine, black morocco labels, joints cracked but firm, spine rubbed, one corner worn. Jarndyce Antiquarian Booksellers CCXVI - 446 2016 £180

Perrault, Charles 1628-1703 *Les Contes De. Ch. Perrault.* Paris: Librairie des Bibliophiles, 1876. No. 54 of 200 copies, 216 x 197mm., 2 volumes, half titles, lovely contemporary dark green crushed morocco, attractively gilt by Thibaron-Joly (stamp signed), covers with French fillets, raised bands, spine gilt in compartments with central rose sprig and floral cornerpieces, marbled endpapers, all edges gilt, frontispiece and 11 engraved plates, one illustrating each tale, large paper copy, bookplate in each volume of W. Vincens Bouguereau, faint offsetting from engravings, text shade less than bright, couple of vaguest scratches on covers, otherwise very fine, text and plates smooth, fresh and clean, margins far beyond ample and beautifully executed bindings virtually perfect. Phillip J. Pirages 67 - 69 2016 $1500

Perrault, Charles 1628-1703 *Old-Time Stories.* New York: Dodd Mead & Co., 1921. First American edition, quarto, 6 tipped-in color plates mounted on gray card, 28 full page black and white illustrations and 24 line drawings in text by W. Heath Robinson, publisher's blue cloth, front cover lettered gilt and with duplicate of color frontispiece pasted on, spine lettered gilt, one color plate (facing page 99) with light crease to front right corner, one leaf with marginal tear neatly repaired, 2 leaves poorly opened, two bookplates, bright and near fine. David Brass Rare Books, Inc. 2015 - 02969 2016 $450

Perreau, Jean Andre *Le Roi Voyageur ou Examen des abus de l'Administration de la Lydie.* Londres: chez T. P. Cadel dans le Strand, 1784. First edition, 8vo., minor stain just visible at head of title and foxing to contents leaves, otherwise clean crisp copy, in recent marbled boards, scarce. Marlborough Rare Books List 56 - 42 2016 £750

Perreaux, Louis Guillaume *Lois De L'Univers: Principe de la Creation.* Paris: Edouard Baltenweck Editeur 7 rue Horore Chevalier, 1877. First edition, 2 volumes, 8vo., titles printed in red and black, colored frontispiece in first volume, paper discolored in places, original printed wrappers, joints to wrappers to volume on repaired, some minor chipping to edge of upper wrapper in volume two, inscribed by author to Leon Duru, rare. Marlborough Rare Books List 56 - 43 2016 £550

Perrot, Paul *Tableaux sacrez.* Frankfurt: de l'Impression de lean Feyrabendt aux depends de Theodore de Bry, 1594. Only edition of extremely rare French Protestant emblem book, 8vo., contemporary limp vellum, rubbed and wrinkled, printer's device on titlepage, 13 woodcut tableaux by Jost Amman. Maggs Bros. Ltd. 1474 - 58 2016 £8500

Perry, John *The State of Russia Under the Present Czar.* London: Benjamin Tooke, 1716. 8vo., fine folding map by Moll, contemporary full panelled calf, rebacked sensitively using original spine, new black morocco label. J. & S. L. Bonham Antiquarian Booksellers Europe 2016 - 8661 2016 £750

The Persecuted or the Days of Lorenzo de Medici. Florence: n.p., 1842. Sole edition, Half title, slight marking to text, Continental half calf, marbled boards, slightly rubbed, good plus copy, scarce. Jarndyce Antiquarian Booksellers CCXVII - 10 2016 £350

Persius *Satyrae sex.* Paris: Apud Sebastianum Cramoisy, Architypographum Regium & Gabrielem Cramoisy, 1644. Scarce small format printing, some spotting and light browning, contemporary vellum, slightly soiled letterpress booklabel of Etienne-Francois Dutour (1711-1784), very good. Blackwell's Rare Books Greek & Latin Classics VII - 67 2016 £500

Persoz, Jean Francois *Traite Theorique et Practique de l'Impression Des Tissues....* Paris: Victor Masson, 1846. First edition, 4 text volumes, 8vo., 429 fabric samples mounted throughout, Atlas volume, 4to., 20 plates of which are chromolithographs, lightly foxed in places due to paper stock, text volumes, bound in contemporary red morocco backed marbled boards, spines decoratively tooled and lettered in gilt, small chip to head of volume IV, and light rubbing to boards and extremities, atlas volume in calf backed marbled boards, spine decorated and lettered in gilt, light surface wear and rubbing to extremities, otherwise appealing copy. Marlborough Rare Books List 56 - 44 2016 £2750

Pertwee, Guy *Scenes from Dickens for Drawing Room and Platform Acting.* London: George Routledge, 1912. Second edition, half title, plates, little spotted, original green cloth, lettered in blind and gilt. Jarndyce Antiquarian Booksellers CCXVIII - 733 2016 £20

Pescott, Edward Edgar *The Native Flowers of Victoria.* Melbourne: George Robertson & Co., 1914. Octavo, 4 tipped in color plates, photos, fine in fine dust jacket, scarce in this condition.   Andrew Isles Natural History Books   55 - 13982   2016 $80

Pesotta, Rose *Bread Upon the Waters.* New York: Dodd, Mead, 1944. First edition, 8vo., red cloth, stamped in black, author's presentation, cover little faded and scuffed at edges, interior slightly rippled on first few leaves, otherwise very good.   Second Life Books, Inc.   196 B - 396 2016 $75

Pessoa, Fernando *35 Sonnets.* Lisbon: Montiero and Co., 1918. First edition, one of Pessoa's first books, 8vo., original printed wrappers, eith exception of Mensagem, all extremely rare, fine copy.   James S. Jaffe Rare Books Occasional List: Winter 2016 - 110   2016 $15,000

Petau, Denis *...Opus de Theologicis Dogmatibus Nunc primum Septem Voluminibus Comprehensum, in Mediorem Ordinem Redactum...* Venice: Remondiana, 1757. Best edition, 6 books in 7 and bound in 2 volumes, folio, title in red and black, half title, each book with its separate title, titlepage portrait engraving of Denis and additional woodcut initials and head and tailpieces all volumes, first volume free endpapers slightly torn, contemporary full vellum, gilt stamped spines, first volume stained, second volume lower corners gently bumped, bookplates of Ex Oblatororum S. Caroli Bibliotheca Bayswater (Henry Edward Manning 1808-1892), Pitts Theology Library bookplates, C. J. Stewart bookseller label, titlepage ownership signatures and inscriptions of Engelbert Klupfel, 1769 and Steph. Wirelo(?), rare, fine.   Jeff Weber Rare Books   181 - 26   2016 $750

Peter Cunningham's New Jest Book; or Modern High Life Below Stairs. London: printed for Funny Joe (Alex Hogg). No. 16 Pater-noster Row, 1780? 12mo., disbound, several fore edges slightly browned, frontispiece.   Jarndyce Antiquarian Booksellers   CCXVI - 320   2016   £320

Peters, Ellis *An Excellent Mystery.* New York: Morrow, 1985. First American edition, fine in dust jacket.   Mordida Books   2015 - 010816   2016 $60

Peters, Ellis *The Lily Hand: and Other Stories.* London: Heinemann, 1965. First edition, octavo, boards, signed inscriptions, first from author to brother Edmund Ellis Pargeter, second to Sue (could be Sue Feder), fine in nearly fine dust jacket with touch of dustiness and very mild stress wrinkle to lower front panel.   John W. Knott, Jr./L.W. Currey, Inc.   Fall-Winter 2015 - 16212   2016 $325

Peters, Ellis *The Summer of the Danes.* New York: Mysterious Press, 1991. First American edition, very fine in dust jacket, signed by author.   Mordida Books   2015 - 010849   2016 $65

Peters, Jason *Wendell Berry/Life and Work.*   Lexington: The University of Kentucky, 2007. First edition, first issue with paper flaw at bottom of titlepage, 8vo., fine, issued in an edition of approximately 3000 copies, this copy signed by Berry and 6 contributors Guy Mendes, Ed McClanahn, Morris Grubbs, Norman Wirzba, Katharine Dalton & Jack Shoemaker.   Second Life Books, Inc.   196 B - 397   2016 $150

Peters, Jason *Wendell Berry/Life and Work.*   Lexington: The University Press of Kentucky, 2007. Second printing with titlepage without paper flaw, 8vo., fine in dust jacket, this is the third (?) issue with titlepage replaced and bound in, this copy signed by Berry.   Second Life Books, Inc.   196 B - 398   2016 $50

Petersham, Maud *Get-a-way and Harry Janos.* New York: Viking, 1933. First edition, 9 x 11 inches, cloth backed pictorial boards, slightest bit of edge wear, else fine in very good+ dust jacket chipped at spine ends, illustrations by Petershams, beautiful, increasingly scarce.   Aleph-bet Books, Inc.   112 - 367   2016 $425

Peterson, Allan *Stars on a Wire.* N.P.: Parallel Editions, 1989. Limited to numbered copies, signed by author, 8vo., stiff paper wrappers, top edge cut, other edges uncut, titlepage calligraphy by Frances Dunham, titlepage shapes derived from lithograph by Sharon Long, erratum laid in.   Oak Knoll Books   310 - 132   2016 $110

Peterson, Allan *Stars on a Wire.* N.P.: Parallel Editions, 1989. Limited to 80 numbered copies, 20 bound in quarter French chagrain leather, signed by author, this copy is thus, titlepage calligraphy by Frances Dunham, titlepage shapes derived from lithograph by Sharon Long, erratum sheet laid in.   Oak Knoll Books   310 - 131   2016 $225

Petillon, Corentin *Allusions Litteraires...* Shanghai: Imprimerie de la Mission Catholique a l'Orphelinat de..., 1909. 8vo., contemporary dark brown cloth, spine lettered and ruled gilt, little worn around edges, internally very clean, apart from ocasional light browning, printed label of French Bookstore in Peiping (Beijing) inside rear cover.   Sotheran's   Travel and Exploration - 162   2016   £198

Petit, Francois Pourfour Du *Lettre dans Laquelle Il Demontre Que la Cristallin est Fort Gras pres de l'uvee et Rapporte de Nouvelles Preuves qui Concernentl... (bound with) Lettre de m. Petit Contenant des Reflexions sur ce que M. Hecquet...* Paris: Chaubert, 1729. Full modern calf, light staining to final leaf of second letter, very few neat corrections in contemporary hand, very good, 4to.   Edwin V. Glaser Rare Books   2015 - 10095   2016 $750

Petit, Jean Louis *Traite des Maladies Chirurgicales et des Operations qui Leur Conviennent Ouvrage Posthume...* Paris: Chez P. Fr. Didot, 1774. First edition, 3 volumes, engraved frontispiece in volume 1, half titles, 90 engraved plates, contemporary full mottled polished calf, gilt panelled spine with small armorial stamps, edges in red, some wear to boards, else near fine set in contemporary binding, plates fine.   James Tait Goodrich   X-78 - 464   2016 $3750

Petrie, Henry *Monumenta Historica Britannica,, or Materials for the History of Britain, from the Earliest Period.* London: printed by George E. Eyre and William Spottiswoode...., 1848. First edition, folio, 27 plates, foldout map, half title and titlepages in red and black, plates rather foxed as usual, occasional slight staining, some toning from plates to adjacent pages, small closed tear to map, sturdy 20th century quarter morocco, orange buckram boards, gilt title to spine, edges uncut, replacement endpapers with cloth hinges, spine lttle scuffed, corners worn, few marks here and there but sound, bookplate of Jesuit Community Library at 114 Mount St., London to front pastedown.   Unsworths Antiquarian Booksellers Ltd.   30 - 119   2016   £375

Petronius *The Satyricon of T. Petronius Arbiter.* London: Simpkin Marshall, Hamilton, Kent and Co., circa, 1926. 8vo., original blue cloth, lettered gilt on spine, gilt very dulled, ornaments of Martin Travers, slight rubbing to extremities, otherwise very good, without dust jacket, Christopher Isherwood's copy with ownership signature dated Oxford Dec. 1926.   Sotheran's   Piccadilly Notes - Summer 2015 - 235   2016   £750

Pettibon, Raymond *Thinking of You.* Chicago: The Renaissance Society at the University of Chicago, 1998. First edition, tight, very near fine copy, hardcover.   Jeff Hirsch Books   E-List 80 - 22   2016 $75

Pettit, Eber M. *Sketches in the History of the Underground Railroad Comprising Many Thrilling Incidents of the Escape of the Fugitives from Slavery....* Fredonia: W. McKinstry & Son, 1879. First edition, tall octavo, original decorated cloth stamped in black and titled gilt, contemporary owner's signature and Chicago address, small tear on front fly, little rubbing on boards, else especially bright and near fine, usually found well worn.   Between the Covers Rare Books   202 - 72   2016 $1800

Pevtsov, M. V. *Puteshestviia po Kitaiu i Mongolii.* Moscow: Government Publisher of Geographical Literature, 1951. First edition, tall 8vo., original cloth backed illustrated boards, spine ornamented in black, lettered in gilt, front cover lettered gilt, double page sketch map, vignettes in text, color printed map loosely inserted, edges of covers with wear, apart from offsetting from front flyleaf to title, internally very good, withdrawn from Warsaw public library with stamps.   Sotheran's   Travel and Exploration - 164   2016   £398

Phaedrus *Phaedri Fabulae et P. Syrimimi Sententiae.* Hagae Contitum: apud Petrum Gosse, 1723. 8vo., titlepage printed in red and black, engraved vignette frontispiece, full contemporary sheep, raised bands, gilt decorated spine red morocco label, joints cracked but firm, head of spine chipped, engraved bookplate and label of Lord Lilford's Library at Lilford Hall, Northamptonshire.   Jarndyce Antiquarian Booksellers   CCXVI - 447   2016   £125

Phalaris, Pseudo *Epistolae.* Rome: Ulrich Han Udalricus Gallus, 1470. Second Latin edition, 4to., few contemporary marginal marks in ink, carta rustica of an indeterminate date (not very recent, not very old), red sprinkled edges, old headbands, good, rare.   Blackwell's Rare Books   Greek & Latin Classics VII - 68   2016   £18,500

Phelps, H. P. *Players of a Century.* Albany: McDonough, 1880. First edition, 8vo., one of 250 copies for subscribers, initialled by author, red cloth stamped in black, moderate wear, very good.   Second Life Books, Inc.   196 B - 404   2016 $85

Philately. The Stamp Collector's Magazine. London: E. Marlborough & Co., 1863-1865. Volumes I-III, 4to., illustrations, original green cloth, bevelled boards, decorated in gilt and blind with stamp laid down in circular centerpiece, volume I slightly dulled, little rubbed, sale descriptions laid onto leading pastedown, volume I, very good.   Jarndyce Antiquarian Booksellers   CCXVII - 230   2016   £150

Philby, Harry St. John Bridger *Iraq in War time.* Basrah: printed and Engraved by Government Press, 1919. Folio, original brown cloth, front cover illustrated and lettered in gilt (in English), rear cover lettered in Arabic, hundreds of photographic illustrations, text in English and Arabic, only minor rubbing to binding in places, only, internally clean and fresh.   Sotheran's   Travel and Exploration - 361   2016   £2850

Philby, Harry St. John Bridger *Sheba's Daughters being a Record of travel in Southern Arabia.* London: Methuen & Co., 1939. First edition, crown 8vo., publisher's original green cloth, lettered gilt, numerous illustrations form photos, large folding map at rear, binding non-uniformly faded (as often), internally a remarkably clean and fresh.   Sotheran's   Travel and Exploration - 360   2016   £398

Philip, Alex J. *A Dickens Dictionary.* London: the Librarian, 1928. Second edition, half title, frontispiece, illustrations, original blue cloth.   Jarndyce Antiquarian Booksellers   CCXVIII - 1410   2016   £25

Philip, Alex J. *Dickens Dictionary.* London: Bracken Books, 1989. Reprint of 1928 edition, original green cloth, very good in dust jacket.   Jarndyce Antiquarian Booksellers   CCXVIII - 1411   2016   £20

Philip, Alex J. *Dickens's Honeymoon and Where He Spent It.* London: Chapman & Hall; Gravesend: Bryant and Rackstraw, 1912. First edition, half title, frontispiece and 3 plates, uncut in original grey-green printed wrappers, slightly creased ad slightly damp marked in inner margin, good plus, signed by author.   Jarndyce Antiquarian Booksellers   CCXVIII - 1409   2016   £35

Philip, Neil *Charles Dickens: a December Vision.* London: Collins, 1986. First edition, 8vo., half title, vignette title, illustrations in black and white, original green cloth, booklabel of Thelma Grove, very good in price clipped dust jacket.   Jarndyce Antiquarian Booksellers   CCXVIII - 1412   2016   £20

Philip, Robert *The Hannahs or Maternal Influence on Sons.* London: William S. Orr & Co., 1851. Original green cloth, slight marking to back board, all edges gilt, contemporary ownership inscription on titlepage, attractive copy.   Jarndyce Antiquarian Books   CCXV - 358   2016   £60

Philips, Ambrose *An Epistle to the Right Honourable Charles Lord Halifax, one of the Lords Justices Appointed by His Majesty.* London: printed for J. Tonson, 1714. First edition, folio, disbound, fine, half title present, scarce.   C. R. Johnson Rare Book Collections   Foxon: H-P 2015 - 736   2016 $613

Philips, John *Blenheim, a Poem.* London: printed for Tho. Bennet, 1705. First edition, variant with "Army, Death..." p. 8 line 12, Folio, foxed and browned, disbound.   Jarndyce Antiquarian Booksellers   CCXVI - 449   2016   £225

Philips, John *Bleinheim, a Poem.* London: printed for Tho. Bennet, 1705. First edition, folio, recent boards, foxed, otherwise very good from the library of John Brett-Smith.   C. R. Johnson Rare Book Collections   Foxon: H-P 2015 - 744   2016 $2298

Philips, John *The Splendid Shilling.* London: printed for Tho. Bennet, 1705. Folio, half title, some foxing and light browning, disbound.   Jarndyce Antiquarian Booksellers   CCXVI - 448   2016   £225

Philips, John *The Works of Mr. John Philips.* London: printed and sold by E. Curll, 1712. First edition, frontispiece, 8vo., contemporary panelled calf, neatly rebacked, margins of half title brown stained, otherwise very good.   C. R. Johnson Rare Book Collections   Foxon: H-P 2015 - 739   2016 $613

Phillipps, Henry *History of Cultivated Vegetables, Comprising their Botanical, Medicinal, Edible and Chemical Qualities, Natural History, and Relation to Art, Science and Commerce.* London: Henry Colburn, 1822. Octavo, 2 volumes, early full calf, Signet Library stamp on boards, shelf label, expertly rebacked.   Andrew Isles Natural History Books   55 - 38999   2016 $400

Phillips, Anghalen Arrington *Gingerbread Houses: Haiti's Endangered Species.* Port Au Prince: Henri Deschamps, 1984. Limited edition, 4to., copiously illustrated in black and white, bound in full grey leather, signed presentation from Phillips.   Any Amount of Books   2015 - A70520   2016   £150

Phillips, Charles Henry *The History of the Colored Methodist Episcopal Church in America....* Jackson: Pub. House C. M. E. Church, 1925. Third edition of Book one, first edition of book two, publisher's cloth gilt, frontispiece, photos, couple of small tears on spine, else nice, near fine, inscribed by author to another Bishop in the Church, Collins Drury Feb. 15 1926.   Between the Covers Rare Books   207 - 81   2016 $950

Phillips, Edward *Theatrum Poetarum Anglicanorum,...* London: Canterbury, 1800. First printing of this enlarged, updated edition, 203 x 121mm., appealing recent brown quarter morocco over linen boards, raised bands, red morocco label, front flyleaf with ownership inscription of 'G.D./Canonbury' (George Daniel of Canonbury Square, Islington, titlepage with small discreet embossed stamp of 'Mark Pattison, Lincoln College, Oxon", in exceptionally fine condition inside and out.   Phillip J. Pirages   67 - 243   2016 $750

Phillips, Jayne Anne *How Mickey Made It.* St. Paul: Bookslinger Editions, 1981. Limited to 26 lettered copies, signed by author and artist, small 4to., quarter cloth, Murehitome paper covered boards, label on front cover, 8 illustrations by Gaylord Schanilec.   Oak Knoll Books   310 - 88   2016 $250

Phillips, Jayne Anne *How Mickey Made It.* St. Paul: Bookslinger Editions, 1981. Limited to 100 numbered copies, signed by author, 8 illustrations by Gaylord Schanilec, small 4to., cloth label on front cover.   Oak Knoll Books   310 - 87   2016 $110

Phillips, Louis *Haunted House Jokes.* New York: Viking Kestrel, 1987. First printing, (code -15), 8vo., as new, pictorial boards, illustrations by James Marshall, this copy inscribed to Marshall's life partner, Joe Bryan.   Aleph-bet Books, Inc.   112 - 302   2016 $450

Phillips, Richard *A Letter to the Schoolmasters and Governesses of England and Wales on the New Theories of Education...* London: Sherwood, Gilbert & Piper, 1835. First edition, 16 page catalog, disbound, crease in first 3 leaves, slight marking.   Jarndyce Antiquarian Books   CCXV - 895   2016   £65

Phillips, Richard *A Million of Facts of Correct Data and Elementary Constants in the Entire Circle of the Sciences....* London: Darton & Clark, 1840. Stereotyped edition, full contemporary diced brown calf, black morocco label, slightly rubbed, faint damp mark to front board, contemporary signature on title and later ownership signature on leading blank, good plus.   Jarndyce Antiquarian Books   CCXV - 896   2016   £38

Phillips, Richard *A Million of Facts of Correct Data and Elementary Constants in the Entire Circle of the Sciences....* London: Darton & Co., 1855. Original grey cloth, dulled.   Jarndyce Antiquarian Books   CCXV - 897   2016   £20

Phillips, Richard *A Million of Facts.* London: Ward Lock & Co., circa, 1890. Stereotyped edition, half title, frontispiece, 16 page catalog, original green cloth, slightly rubbed, prize label.   Jarndyce Antiquarian Books   CCXV - 898   2016   £28

Phillips, Richard *The Vocal Library: being the Largest Collection of English, Scottish and Irish Songs..* London: printed for Sir Richard Phillips and Co. Bride Court, Bridge Street, Blackfriars by J. and C. Adland, 28 Bartholomew Close, 1826. Square 12mo., wood engraved frontispiece and 4 scenes, original green calf, spine decorated and lettered.   Marlborough Rare Books   List 55 - 53   2016   £225

Phillips, Robert Randal *The Servantless House.* London: published at the offices of Country Life, 1923. Second edition, half title, photo illustrations, original cloth backed grey boards, very good.   Jarndyce Antiquarian Books   CCXV - 359   2016   £45

Phillips, Samuel *Guide to the Crystal Palace and Park.* London: Bradbury & Evans, 1856. First edition, 8vo., 1 folding map, 2 folding plates, contemporary black half morocco, joints and corner scrubbed.   J. & S. L. Bonham Antiquarian Booksellers   Europe 2016 - 8366   2016   £195

Phillips, Teresia Constantia *A Letter Humbly Address'd to the right Honourable the Earl of Chesterfield.* London: for the author, 1750. First edition, removed, modern wrappers, lacks half title, signed in ink by author at conclusion, but cropped by binder's knife.   Joseph J. Felcone, Inc.   Books from Five Centuries: a Miscellany - 115   2016 $400

Phillips, Walter C. *Dickens, Reade and Collins.* New York: Columbia University Press, 1919. Half title, original dark green cloth, lettered gilt, very good.   Jarndyce Antiquarian Booksellers   CCXVIII - 1414   2016   £30

Phillpotts, Eden   1862-1960 *The End of a Life.* Bristol and London: J. W. Arrowsmith and Simpkin, Marshall, Hamilton, Kent & Co. Ltd., 1891. Presentation copy inscribed to G. B. Burgin, presentation copies from Phillpotts are scarce, very good in original brown cloth with gilt title to spine and black title to front board, front board slightly bowed and spine is somewhat cocked, hinges rubbed, minor soiling to boards, corners bumped, bookplate of Alastair Forbes, text remains bright although there is browning to margins of interior, ?evidence of a repair to front and rear interior hinges, very good.   The Kelmscott Bookshop   12 - 81   2016 $225

Phillpotts, Eden   1862-1960 *Folly and Fresh Air.* London: Trischler and Comany, 1891. First edition, inscribed by author to Daniel Frohman 18 June 1892, very good in green cloth boards with dark red title and author to spine and dark red author, title and design to front cover, some chipping and bumping and bit of light soilig to boards, floral decorated endpages, endpages and text pages lightly browned from age.   The Kelmscott Bookshop   12 - 82   2016 $150

Phillpotts, Eden   1862-1960 *In Sugar-Cane Land.* McClure, 1892. First edition, 8vo., original blue cloth.   J. & S. L. Bonham Antiquarian Booksellers   America 2016 - 9594   2016   £20

Phillpotts, Eden   1862-1960 *Portrait of a Scoundrel.* London: John Murray, 1938. First edition, fine in dust jacket with light professional restoration to spine ends and corners, old original label at base of spine , evidently done by publisher.   Buckingham Books   2015 - 28265   2016 $475

Philo, Judaeus *In Libros Mosis: De Mundi Opificio, Historicos, de Legibus Eiusdem Libri Singulares.* Paris: e officina Adriani Turnebi typographi Regii, 1552. Editio princeps, lightly toned, titlepage little dusty, 3 small wormholes, briefly stretching to a short trail in blank margin at beginning, blindstamp of Earls of Macclesfield to initial leaves, folio, 18th century panelled calf, rubbed and scuffed, some wear to joints, bookplate of Shirburn Castle, good.   Blackwell's Rare Books   Greek & Latin Classics VII - 69   2016   £2750

Philobiblon, Eine Vierteljahrsschrift fur Buch-Und Graphik-Sammler. Hamburg: Dr. Ernst Hauswedell & Co., 1957-1974. Second series, complete run, volume one number 1 (1957) - volume eighteen number 4 (1974), 8vo., stiff paper wrappers, 18 volumes, very fine set, each volume of 4 quarterlies in is protected by cardboard case.   Oak Knoll Books   310 - 68   2016 $400

Philp, Robert Kemp *Best of Everything.* London: Frederick Warne and Co., 1873? Sixty thousand, color frontispiece, original brown cloth, slightly torn paper price label on spine, slightly dulled, very good. Jarndyce Antiquarian Books   CCXV - 360   2016   £65

Philp, Robert Kemp *Enquire within Upon Everything.* London: Houlston & Stoneman, 1856. First edition, 2 lines ms. notes on page 352, original blue green cloth, blocked in blind and gilt, spine faded and slightly rubbed at head and tail, contemporary inscription of G. F. Truscott, booksellers embossed stamp, nice.   Jarndyce Antiquarian Books   CCXV - 361   2016 £250

Philp, Robert Kemp *Enquire within Upon Everything.* London: Houlston & Wright, 1867. 325th thousand, lacking leading f.e.p., original dark blue publisher's cloth. Jarndyce Antiquarian Books   CCXV - 362   2016   £50

Philp, Robert Kemp *Enquire within Upon Everything.* London: Houlston & sons, 1899. 96th edition, title browned, ads on endpapers, original maroon decorated cloth, very good.   Jarndyce Antiquarian Books   CCXV - 363   2016   £45

Philp, Robert Kemp *Enquire within Upon Everything.* London: Houlston & sons, 1902. 99th edition, title browned, original maroon decorated cloth, very good.   Jarndyce Antiquarian Books   CCXV - 364   2016   £40

Philp, Robert Kemp *Lady's Every-Day Book...* London: Bemrose & Sons, 1880. Original brick red decorated cloth, slightly rubbed.   Jarndyce Antiquarian Books   CCXV - 365   2016   £45

Philp, Robert Kemp *The Practical Housewife, a Complete Encyclopaedia of Domestic Economy and Family Medical guide.* London: Houlston & Wright, 1860. New edition, half title, frontispiece, illustrations, original dark green cloth, blocked in blind and gilt, expertly recased, ownership signature of Hadie Pilgate, inscription, nice.   Jarndyce Antiquarian Books   CCXV - 366   2016   £85

Philpotts, Trey *The Companion to Little Dorrit.* London: Helm Information, 2003. Half title, illustrations, maps original green cloth, blocked and lettered in gilt, mint in dust jacket.   Jarndyce Antiquarian Booksellers   CCXVIII - 550   2016   £45

Phipps, Constantine John *The Journal of a Voyage undertaken by Order of His Present Majesty.* London: printed for F. Newbery at the Corner of St. Paul's Church Yard, 1774. One of two variants, this with ruled lines on titlepage both thin, 8vo., folding map, one engraved plate, but lacking frontispiece map, titlepage dusted, final leaf creased and dusted, disbound.   Jarndyce Antiquarian Booksellers   CCXVI - 450   2016   £150

Picart, J. M. *Album De La Revolucion Cubana.* Habana: Editorial Echevarria circa, 1960-1961. Oblong 4to., pictorial wrappers, covers worn and several neat margin mends, good-very good and complete,.   Aleph-bet Books, Inc.   112 - 404   2016 $4500

Picasso, Pablo   1881-1973 *Picasso 1901-1925.* Tokyo: circa, 1930. First edition, 2 titlepages one with photo of Picasso, followed by color plate and 60 monochrome plates, 16 pages Japanese text at end, spiral bound into covers, covers bit tanned at edges, very good, scarce.   Peter Ellis   112 - 295   2016   £250

Picasso, Pablo   1881-1973 *Picasso: Torreos.* New York: George Braziller, 1961. 4 original lithographs, one in color, very good plus in red cloth boards with some fading top top and bottom edges, small crease to top corner of two pages in close to near fine dust jacket with some very minor wear, lithographs are all fine.   Jeff Hirsch Books   Holiday List 2015 - 15   2016 $1750

Picasso, Pablo   1881-1973 *Picasso's Vollard Suite.* London: Thames & Hudson, 1956. First edition thus, some mustiness, else fine in fair or better dust jacket with snag/ wrinkled upper corner of front panel.   Gene W. Baade, Books on the West   2015 - SHEL890   2016 $160

Pickens, William *Bursting Bonds...* Boston: Jordan & More Press, 1923. Second edition, 8vo., boards with paper label, lacking some of the paper on spine, some staining to cover, nice and clean inside, inscribed by author to consumer advocate Florence Kelley from her library.   Second Life Books, Inc.   196 B - 406   2016 $325

Pickering, Harold G. *Dog-Days on Trout Waters.* New York: Derrydale Press, 1933. One of 199 numbered copies signed by author, this additionally inscribed by Pickering to good friend Irene Holden, illustrations by Donald Gardner, paper covered boards, cloth spine, printed paper labels, bookplate, very light soiling and fading of boards, two facing leaves darkened from laid-in news cutting, else very good, not quite fine.   Joseph J. Felcone, Inc.   Books from Five Centuries: a Miscellany - 116   2016 $800

Pictet, Benedict *An Antidote Against a Careless Indifferency in Matters of Religion...* North Allerton: printed by J. Langdale, 1802. Third edition, 8vo., partially unopened, full contemporary tan sheep, simple blind-stamped border, spine rubbed, slight insect damage to upper board.   Jarndyce Antiquarian Booksellers   CCXVI - 452   2016   £65

Pictorius, Georg *Apotheseos tam Exterarum Gentium Quam Romanorum Deorum Libri Tres.* Basle: Nicolaus Brylinger, 1558. First illustrated edition, printer's device on titlepage, 25 woodcuts, woodcut initials, small 8vo., late 19th century half brown morocco by Roger De Coverly, spine lettered gilt, gilt edges, bookplate of Samuel Ashton Thompson Yates dated 1894.   Maggs Bros. Ltd.   1474 - 59   2016   £2500

Picture of New York. New York: Mahlon Day n.d., circa, 1830. 2 1/8 x 3 1/2 inches, pictorial wrappers, small chip off rear cover and first leaf, else very good+, 10 woodcuts including one of Mahlon Day's Juvenile Bookstore, charming and scarce.   Aleph-bet Books, Inc.   112 - 165   2016 $600

Pictures for the little Ones to Brighten Dull Days. London: Ernest Nister, 1902. First edition, 4to., original beige cloth backed chromolithographed boards, 18 fine chromolithographed plates and other illustrations and text in sepia, very attractive clean copy with only tiny wear to corner tips and an area of light browning in bottom fore corner of lower cover, internally bright with neat inscription, dated 1906. Sotheran's   Piccadilly Notes - Summer 2015 - 77   2016   £148

Picturesques Freeport.   Freeport: W. H. Wagner & Sons, 1900. First edition, oblong string tied dark gray wrappers, half tone illustrations, truly rare, fair copy.   Gene W. Baade, Books on the West   2015 - SHEL565   2016 $270

Pierce, Charles *The Household Manager...* London: Geo. Routledge & Co., 1857. First edition, half title, original red decorated cloth, blocked in gilt and blind, very good, attractive.   Jarndyce Antiquarian Books   CCXV - 367   2016   £120

Pierce, Gene *Black Experience Metamorphosis: the Black Poet.* Philadelphia: Pierce Publications, 1970. First edition, softcover, fine in stapled wrappers, signed and warmly inscribed, scarce.   Jeff Hirsch Books   E-List 80 - 23   2016 $100

Pierce, Gilbert A. *The Dickens Dictionary.* London: Chapman & Hall, 1878. First English edition, half title, original green cloth, recased retaining most of original spine strip, endpapers replaced.   Jarndyce Antiquarian Booksellers   CCXVIII - 1415   2016   £20

Pierce, Ray Vaughn *The People's Common Sense Medical Adviser in Plain English or Medicine Simplified.* Buffalo: World's Dispensary Printing Office & Bindery, circa, 1900. frontispiece, color plates, illustrations, original black cloth, llittle rubbed.   Jarndyce Antiquarian Books   CCXV - 368   2016   £48

Pierre Legrain, Relieur. Repertoire Descriptif et Bibliographique de Mille Deux Trente-Six reliures. Paris: Libraire Auguste Blaizot, 1965. Limited to 600 numbered copies, 4to., signatures loosely inserted in white stiff paper wrapper, brown cloth slipcase, 205 pages in full color, 243 reproductions in collotype, leather bookplate of Julia Parker Wightman, only minor fading of spine.   Oak Knoll Books   310 - 17   2016 $800

Piers, Harry *Master Goldsmiths and Silversmiths of Nova Scotia and Their marks.* Halifax: Antiquarian Club, 1948. 8vo., blue cloth boards, gilt decoration and title to front cover, half title, frontispiece and 60 plates, some wear to edges and front hinge crack, otherwise very good. Schooner Books Ltd.   115 - 173   2016 $125

Pietas Academiae Oxoniensis in Obitum Augustissimae et Desideratissimae Reginae Carolinae. Oxford: e typographeo Clarendoniano, 1738. First edition, folio, contemporary panelled calf, red morocco label, very good, large paper copy.   C. R. Johnson Rare Book Collections   Foxon: H-P 2015 - 752   2016 $613

Piggott, Tom *Iraq Petroleum .... The Magazine of the Iraq Petroleum Company Limited and Its Associated Companies.* London: Iraq Petroleum Co., 1954-1960. 21 issues in one volume, 4to., modern private blue half cloth over boards, original illustrated wrappers bound in, highly illustrated and printed on heavy glossy paper, few wrappers lightly rubbed or little frayed, cut close by binders.   Sotheran's   Travel and Exploration - 362   2016   £895

Pike, John Gregory *Parental Care for the Salvation of Children Explained and Enforced with Advice on their Religious Education.* London: RTS, 1839. Original brown cloth, signature of J. H. Ross Farquharson, very good. Jarndyce Antiquarian Books   CCXV - 901   2016   £35

Pike, Robert L. *Mute Witness.* New York: Doubleday & Co., 1963. First edition, former owner's small inked name and date on front free flyleaf, else fine in dust jacket with orange and red inks lightly faded on spine and hint of rubbing to bottom fore corners, scarce unaccountably, exceptional copy.   Buckingham Books   2015 - 31937   2016 $2750

Pike, Zebulon Montgomery 1779-1813 *Exploratory Travels through the Western Territories of North America....* London: printed for Longman, Hurst, Rees, Orme and Brown, 1811. First English edition, quarto, contemporary sprinkled calf, marbled paper endpapers, red morocco label, gilt decorations and lettering, 2 maps, one folding, half title, lower margins of maps trimmed to border, edges and spine little rubbed, fine.   The Brick Row Book Shop   Miscellany 69 - 63   2016 $7500

Pilkington, Mary *Asiatic Princess.* London: printed for Vernor and Hood in the Poultry, 1800. 12mo., engraved frontispiece, slight marginal waterstain to leading edge towards end of second volume, little light browning, otherwise clean, 2 volumes in 1, contemporary drab paper boards, dark green roan spine, spine worn at head with traces of original paper label, leading edge worn.   Jarndyce Antiquarian Booksellers   CCXVI - 453   2016   £280

Pilkington, Mrs. *Marmontel's Tales, selected and abridged for the instruction and amusement of Youth by....* London: Vernor and Hood, 1799. First edition, engraved frontispiece and 26 woodcuts, little spotted, 12mo., original sheep, joints cracked but cords firm, corners worn, contemporary signature of Louisa Morton, 2 brief lines of inscription scored out, good.   Blackwell's Rare Books   B186 - 85   2016   £350

Pilley, Dorothy *Climbing Days.* London: Secker & Warburg, 1965. Second edition, photos, boards, tear to head of spine repaired, light stain to rear board, else fine.   Argonaut Book Shop   Mountaineering 2015 - 4489   2016 $45

Pilley, John J. *Chemistry of Common Objects...* London: George Gill & Sons, 1898. Half title, illustrations, original brown cloth, very good.   Jarndyce Antiquarian Books   CCXV - 902   2016   £30

Pilon, Frederick *The Drama, a Poem.* London: for J. Williams, 1775. First edition, disbound, half title present.   Dramatis Personae   119 - 127   2016 $200

Pim, Bedford *The Gate of the Pacific.* London: Lovell Reeve, 1863. First edition, half title, 7 engraved maps, 9 lithographs, light foxing in few places, original blue decorative cloth, string mark on lower cover, occasional mark but very bright, clean copy.   J. & S. L. Bonham Antiquarian Booksellers   America 2016 - 7042   2016   £320

Pinchard, Elizabeth Sibthorpe *The Blind Child or Anecdotes of the Wyndham Family.* London: printed for E. Newbery, 1795. 12mo., frontispiece with contemporary coloring, slightly creased with few chips repaired along foreedge, young reader has neatly amended final paragraph, contemporary sheep, gilt banded spine, small neat repairs, nice.   Jarndyce Antiquarian Books   CCXV - 369   2016   £125

Pinchard, Elizabeth Sibthorpe *The Blind Child.* London: printed for E. Newbery, 1798. Fifth edition, 12mo., some foxing to frontispiece, titlepage dusted and little browned, full contemporary tree calf, double gilt banded spine, red morocco label, joints cracked but firm, some slight wear, inscription "given to the Miss Fludyers by Lady Charlotte Duncombe, June 1801".   Jarndyce Antiquarian Books   CCXV - 370   2016   £75

Pinchard, Elizabeth Sibthorpe *The Two Cousins a Moral Story...* London: printed for E. Newbery, 1798. 12mo., half title, fine copper engraved frontispiece, full contemporary tree sheep, double gilt banded spine, hinges cracked but firm.   Jarndyce Antiquarian Books   CCXV - 371   2016   £150

Pindarus *Odes of Pindar.* London: printed for R. Dodsley, 1749. First edition of Gilbert West's translation, quarto, contemporary full speckled calf, rebacked to style, original and morocco spine label, lettered gilt, spine stamped gilt, title printed in red and black, edges speckled in red, outer front hinge cracked and loose, but holding, outer back hinge cracked but firm, head and tale of spine chipped, very good.   Heritage Book Shop   Holiday 2015 - 87   2016 $1250

Pindarus *The Isthmian Odes of Pindar.* London: Macmillan and Co., 1892. First edition, 8vo., dark green cloth, gilt lettered to spine, edges uncut, separating between gatherings of gutters, almost split at page 80-1, but very worn binding sill holding, reading copy only, no dust jacket, editor's corrections slip loosely inserted, pencil underlining and annotations throughout.   Unsworths Antiquarian Booksellers Ltd.   E04 - 82   2016   £30

Pindarus *Olympia. Pythia. Nemea. Isthmia. Meta Exegeseous Palais Pany...* Rome: per Zachariam Calergi Cretensem, 1515. Second edition of text but editio princeps of scholia, first leaf of text printed in red and black, that leaf with two small abrasions and one vertical hole, hole also reaching, though less so, next leaf, with one or two letters lost about 2 dozen words in total, intermittent dampmark in lower margin, some soiling and spotting, foliated in later hand, early annotations and manicules to last three leaves, 4to., 18th century calf, spine and corners skillfully repaired, new labels, leather little darkened and marked in places, sound.   Blackwell's Rare Books   B184 - 74   2016   £6500

Pindarus *Olympia, Pythia, Nemea, Isthmia.* Lyon: Apud Ioan Pillehotte, 1598. Probably pirated edition, 16mo., browned and spotted, some old annotations in ink and pencil, contemporary limp vellum, spine lettered in ink, darkened and rubbed, no flyleaves, hinges cracking and little wear to joints.   Blackwell's Rare Books   Greek & Latin Classics VII - 70   2016   £600

Pindarus *Olympia, Nemea, Pythia, Isthmia.* Oxford: E. Theatro Sheldoniano, 1697. First English edition of the Greek text, edited by Richard West and Robert Welsted, engraved frontispiece and large titlepage vignette by M. Burghers, final section printed on poorer paper and rather browned, some spotting and toning elsewhere, folio, 18th century speckled calf, spine gilt in compartments, marbled endpapers, rather rubbed, joints cracking at ends, bookplate of Skene Library and early 20th century Blackwell's bookseller label to front pastedown, good.   Blackwell's Rare Books   Greek & Latin Classics VII - 71   2016   £700

Pinel, Philippe *Nosographie Philosophique, ou le Methode de l'Analyse Appliquee a la Medecine Tome Premier (-Second).* Paris: Crapelet An VI, 1798. First edition, 2 volumes, 8vo., contemporary calf backed boards, spines slightly faded, corners slightly worn, very good. Blackwell's Rare Books   B186 - 117   2016   £750

Pinel, Philippe *Tratado Medico-Filosofico de la Enangenacion Del Alma 6 Mania, Escrito en Frences por Felipe Pinel.* Madrid: en la Imprenta Real, 1804. First edition in Spanish, 2 engraved plates and folding table, little browned or foxed in places, small 8vo., original tree sheep, spine gilt ruled in compartments, red lettering piece, red edges, very minor wear, very good. Blackwell's Rare Books   B186 - 118   2016   £950

Pinero, Arthur W. *The Times.* London: Heinemann, 1891. 12mo., rebound in full morocco, rubbed along hinge, original wrappers bound in at back, top edge gilt, author's presentation on blank, 5 leaves loose to front, otherwise nice. Second Life Books, Inc.   196 B - 408   2016 $75

Pinkerton, J. *Petralogy: a Treatise on Rocks.* London: White, Cochrane and Co., 1811. Octavo, two volumes, two (of three?) engraved plates, early binder's cloth, skillfully rebacked, some paper browning and spotting, otherwise sound set. Andrew Isles Natural History Books   55 - 36644   2016 $400

Pinkerton, J. *Recollections of Paris in the Years 1802, 3-4-5.* London: Longman, Hurst, Rees & Orme, 1806. First edition, 2 volumes, 8vo., full tree calf lettered gilt on spine on black label, spine label rubbed and only part legible, hinges slightly rubbed, endpapers slightly foxed and browned, label removed from pastedown, otherwise sound, very good. Any Amount of Books   2015 - C1133   2016   £170

Pinney, Peter *Anywhere but Here.* London: Angus and Robertson, 1957. First edition, octavo, photos endpaper map, fine in very good dust jacket (slightly rubbed at top edge). Peter Ellis   112 - 3   2016   £45

Pinnock, William *Pinnock's Juvenile reader...* London: G. & W. B. Whittaker, 1822. Eleventh edition, 12mo., frontispiece, illustrations, contemporary mottled tree sheep, red morocco label, slight wear to foot of spine, corners slightly bumped, armorial bookplate of Thomas Fitzgerald & bookseller's ticket of King & Co., Cork. Jarndyce Antiquarian Books   CCXV - 903   2016   £40

Pinnock, William *Roman History made easy...* London: W. Sell, 1831. Color map frontispiece, plate and illustrations, slight spotting, slight paper damage to inner margin of front and title, original printed paper boards, paper label slightly rubbed, contemporary ownership signatures of Charles Little, bookplate of Anthony David Estill, nice. Jarndyce Antiquarian Books   CCXV - 904   2016   £68

Pinsky, Robert *An Explanation of America.* Princeton: Princeton University Press, 1979. First edition, inscribed and signed by author for William Meredith, fine in near fine dust jacket with sunned spine. Charles Agvent   William Meredith - 100   2016 $250

Pinsky, Robert *Sadness and Happiness. Poems.* Princeton: Princeton University Press, 1975. First edition, inscribed and signed by author for William Meredith, fine in fine dust jacket. Charles Agvent   William Meredith - 101   2016 $150

Pinter, Harold *Accident.* London: Joseph Losey/The Grade Organization May 4th, 1966. Screenplay, photomechanically duplicated sheets bradbound into unprinted blue wrappers, die cut to reveal title, 100 leaves printed rectos only, fine. Between the Covers Rare Books   208 - 67   2016 $3500

Pinter, Harold *Betrayal.* London: Eyre Methuen, 1978. First edition, 8vo., signed by author on titlepage, rear cover bit bumped at corners, otherwise fine in very near fine dust jacket. Peter Ellis   112 - 299   2016   £475

Pinter, Harold *The Birthday Party.* London: Encore Pub., 1959. First edition, trifle rubbed, still fine in wrappers, uncommon true first edition of author's first play, inscribed by him to his first wife, Vivien Merchant Dec. 59, very uncommon, housed in custom full cloth clamshell box. Between the Covers Rare Books   204 - 83   2016 $40,000

Pinter, Harold *The Birthday Party and other Plays.* London: Methuen & Co., 1960. First hardcover edition, uncommon acting edition in wrappers, fine in rubbed, very good or better dust jacket, signed by Pinter. Between the Covers Rare Books   204 - 94   2016 $1000

Pinter, Harold *The Homecoming.* London: Methuen, 1965. First edition, foolscap 8vo., original black boards, backstrip lettered in silver with very slight lean to spine, top edge trifle dusty, dust jacket with some light rubbing, very good. Blackwell's Rare Books   B184 - 218   2016   £60

Pinter, Harold *Landscape.* London: Emanuel Wax, 1968. First edition, 8vo., limited to 1/2000 copies, signed by author, fine. Second Life Books, Inc.   196 B - 409   2016 $65

Pinter, Harold *Mountain Language (and) Ashes to Ashes.* London: Faber and Faber for the Royal Court, 2001. New edition, octavo, glossy wrappers, signed by author on titlepage, fine. Peter Ellis   112 - 300   2016   £45

Pinter, Harold *No Man's Land.* London: Eyre Methuen, 1975. First edition, fine in fine dust jacket, beautiful copy. Between the Covers Rare Books   208 - 68   2016 $200

Pinter, Harold *Press Conference.* London: Faber and Faber, 2002. First edition, octavo, signed by author, fine in near fine dust jacket, slightly marked on rear panel.   Peter Ellis   112 - 298   2016   £125

Pinter, Harold *Various Voices - Prose, Poetry, Politics 1948-1998.* New York: Grove Press, 1999. First Grove press paperback edition, octavo, glossy color wrappers, signed by author, fine.   Peter Ellis   112 - 297   2016   £65

Piorry, Pierre Adolphe *De la Percussion Mediate et des Signes Obienus a l'Aide de ce Nouveau Moyen d'Exploration dans les Maladies des Organes Thoraciques et Abdominaux.* Paris: J. S. Chaude, 1828. First edition, half title, 2 engraved plates, contemporary half green roan and marbled boards, some wear, text browning, rather scarce.   James Tait Goodrich   X-78 - 467   2016 $1500

Piranesi: the Magnificence of Rome. New York: A. Helen & Kurt Wolff Book, Harcourt. Brace and World, 1962. Limited to 200 numbered copies, 28 plates, folio, paper covered boards, edges uncut, slipcase, bottom and top of slipcase missing, illustrations on front of slipcase torn at bottom.   Oak Knoll Books   310 - 45   2016 $500

Pirsig, Robert M. *Zen and the Art of Motorcycle Maintenance: an Inquiry into Values.* New York: William Morrow & Co., 1974. First edition, very good to near fine dust jacket, book fine to as new, black paper covered boards in excellent shape, black cloth covering spine with bright silver lettering, shows merest touch of wear at head, interior with white endpapers looks as though it has not been read through, price clipped jacket has one mark and hint of sunning.   Simon Finch   2015 - 001600   2016 $175

Pitati, Pietro *Compendivm.... Super Annua Solaris Atque Lunaris anni Quantitate...* Verona: Paolo Ravagnano, 1560. First edition, woodcut printer's device on title, woodcut initials, Register and colophon on recto and heraldic woodcut on verso of last leaf, lacking final (blank) leaf, few headlines shaved, little waterstaining at beginning towards top, 4to., 18th century ?Italian mottled calf, spine gilt in compartments, unlettered green lettering piece, yellow marbled edges, Macclesfield copy with bookplate and blindstamps.   Blackwell's Rare Books   B186 - 119   2016   £1500

Pitcher, Oliver *Dust of Silence.* New York and San Francisco: Troubador Poets, 1958. First edition, clean, near fine in black boards, about very good dust jacket with number of small chips and edge tears, much less common than softcover edition.   Jeff Hirsch Books   E-List 80 - 24   2016 $125

Pitman, Charles R. S. *A Guide to the Snakes of Uganda.* Kampala: Uganda Society, 1938. Quarto, 23 colored plates, publisher's quarter cloth and marbled boards with title label, some wear, but good copy, scarce and sought after book.   Andrew Isles Natural History Books   55 - 21227   2016 $1500

Pitman, Isaac *The Reporter; or Phonography.* Bath & London: Isaac Pitman at the Phonographic Institution, 1846. Original maroon cloth, blocked in blind, lettered gilt, spines slightly faded, otherwise very good, bright.   Jarndyce Antiquarian Booksellers   CCXVIII - 1416   2016   £125

Pitt, Christopher *An Essay on Virgil's Aeneid.* London: printed for a Bettesworth and W. Hinchliffe, 1722. First edition, 8vo., fine, uncommon.   C. R. Johnson Rare Book Collections   Foxon: H-P 2015 - 756   2016 $613

Pitt, Christopher *Poems and Translations.* London: printed for Bernard Lintot and Arthur Bettesworth, 1727. First edition, folio, contemporary panelled calf, red morocco label, very good on large paper, early signature of James Smyth.   C. R. Johnson Rare Book Collections   Foxon: H-P 2015 - 752   2016 $613

Pitt, Robert *The Antidote; or the preservative of Health and Life and the Restorative of Physick to its Sincerity and Perfection.* London: printed for John Nutt near Stationers Hall, 1704. One of two issues of the first edition, this issiue with second line of imprint beginning "Stationers", 8vo. half title, very good, clean copy, full contemporary panelled calf, raised bands, slight wear to head of spine, very slight crack to upper section of front joint, small faint ink splash to leading edge of book block, bookplate of William Wollascott.   Jarndyce Antiquarian Booksellers   CCXVI - 454   2016   £350

Pitter, Ruth *The Art of Reading in Ignorance.* London: Constable, n.d. circa, 1971. First edition, wrappers, presentation from author, inscribed to Norah Cruikshank from Ruth Pitter 19 Mar 71, staples rusted, covers slightly marked and creased, small smudge on upper cover slightly affecting presentation inscription, very good.   Peter Ellis   112 - 302   2016   £75

Pitter, Ruth *Persephone in Hades.* Auch, Gers, France: privately printed by A. Sauriac, 1931. First edition, one of 100 numbered copies, this being no. 1, octavo, wrappers, printed on Pur Fil Lafuma, covers marked and darkened at edges, short closed tear at top edge of lower cover, very good, rare, presentation from author for Lorna Kenyon-Lees, Jan. 1933.   Peter Ellis   112 - 303   2016   £275

Pius XI, Pope *Climbs on Alpine Peaks.* Boston: Houghton Mifflin, 1923. First American edition, frontispiece, black and white photo plates, gray cloth lettered in white, very minor rubbing to spine ends, but fine, fresh.   Argonaut Book Shop   Mountaineering 2015 - 4484   2016 $125

Pizzey, Graham *A Garden of Birds: Australian Birds in Australian Gardens.* Ringwood: Viking O'Neil, 1988. First edition, quarto, photos, text illustrations by Richard Weatherly, inscription, very good in dust jacket. Andrew Isles Natural History Books 55 - 36390 2016 $30

Plain Truth, or Downright Dunstable. A Poem.... London: printed for J. Roberts, 1740. First edition, 4to., sewn as issued, very rare, titlepage dusty, upper margins trimmed and slightly stained, not affecting printed portion, otherwise very good. C. R. Johnson Rare Book Collections Foxon: H-P 2015 - 763 2016 $2298

Plan for Expediting the Mail From London to Edinburgh: So That It Shall Arrive at One O'Clock on the Second day... Edinburgh: Balour and Clarke for William Blackwood, 1822. First edition, final leaf with seal tear with loss of part of three or four words on recto and one word on verso, recent marbled boards lettered on spine, scarce. John Drury Rare Books 2015 - 26004 2016 $323

Planche, J. R. *Descent of the Danube from Ratisbon to Vienna During the Autumn of 1827.* London: James Dunkan, 1828. First edition, 8vo., map, frontispiece, vignette on titlepage, light foxing to map and margins of frontispiece, contemporary black polished calf with gilt spine and raised bands, handsome. J. & S. L. Bonham Antiquarian Booksellers Europe 2016 - 9110 2016 £200

Plannck, Stephen *The Letter of Columbus on His Discovery of the new World.* Los Angeles: USC Fine Arts Press, 1989. Limited to 326 n7umbered copies, this being one of the trade editions tound thus, 8vo., quarter leather, elephant hide paper over boards. Oak Knoll Books 310 - 169 2016 $320

Plath, Sylvia 1932-1963 *Ariel.* New York: Harper & Row, 1966. First edition, William Meredith's copy signed by poet with several annotations in pencil, near fine in very good dust jacket. Charles Agvent William Meredith - 80 2016 $300

Plath, Sylvia 1932-1963 *The Bell Jar.* London: Heinemann, 1963. First edition, crow 8vo., original black boards with publisher device blindstamped to lower board, backstrip lettered gilt, little foxing to top edge, dust jacket with just little rubbing to extremities and light dust soiling to rear panel, custom drop-down box, very good, excellent. Blackwell's Rare Books B184 - 219 2016 £6000

Plath, Sylvia 1932-1963 *The Bell Jar.* London: Heinemann Contemporary Fiction, 1964. First Book Club Edition, crown 8vo., original green boards, backstrip lettered in silver and little softened at head, top edge purple and foxing to fore-edge, light bump to bottom corners, dust jacket with backstrip panel gently faded, small amount of surface soiling and light rubbing to extremities, little foxing along rear flap fold, very good. Blackwell's Rare Books B184 - 220 2016 £385

Plath, Sylvia 1932-1963 *Crystal Gazer and Other Poems.* London: Rainbow Press, 1971. First edition, one of 400 numbred copies, quarto, blue quarter linen, decorative paper boards, gilt lettering, vignette titlepage, one plate after drawings by Ted Hughes, fine in publisher's slipcase. The Brick Row Book Shop Miscellany 69 - 64 2016 $275

Plath, Sylvia 1932-1963 *Winter Trees.* London: Faber and Faber, 1971. First edition, fine in fine dust jacket, Poetry Book Society promotional material laid in, immaculate copy. Between the Covers Rare Books 204 - 96 2016 $350

Plato *Septem Selecti Dialogi.* Dublin: E Typographia Academiae, 1738. 8vo., titlepage printed in red and black, prelim blank present, 8vo., original mottled calf, Trinity College gilt medallion to boards, spine with five raised bands, replacement red morocco lettering piece, rubbed, gilt faded from backstrip, some scrapes and old repairs to boards, joints cracking but strong, algebraic notation in ink to front pastedown, sound. Blackwell's Rare Books Greek & Latin Classics VII - 74 2016 £350

Plato *Platonis Dialogui V.* Oxonii: E Typogrpaheo Clarendoniano, 1752. 8vo., titlepage vignette, few pencil underlinings, full contemporary sprinkled caf raised & gilt banded spine, small gilt device in compartment, red morocco label, armorial bookplate of Marquess of Headfort. Jarndyce Antiquarian Booksellers CCXVI - 455 2016 £85

Plato *Plato's Phaedo.* London: Routledge & Kegan Paul, 1955. First edition, 8vo., cloth, gilt lettered, spine slightly cocked, edges dusted, top edges slightly foxed, light toning to free endpapers, very good, white dust jacket bit grubby, minor shelfwear, very good, ex-libris of Barbara McBride. Unsworths Antiquarian Booksellers Ltd. E04 - 85 2016 £25

Plato *The Republic of Plato.* Glasgow: Robert & Andrew Foulis, 1763. First edition in English, full contemporary calf, rebacked to style, spine stamped in gilt, red morocco spine label, lettered gilt, newer rear endpapers and front pastedown, original front flyleaf with old ink notes, previous owner's old ink signature on titlepage, repairs to top margin of titlepage and front free flyleaf, some dampstaining and toning throughout, leaf S4 with a small closed tear, professionally repaired leaf DDD2, corner torn, not affecting text, overall very nice. Heritage Book Shop Holiday 2015 - 90 2016 $10,000

Plato *Omnia Opera cum Commentariis Procli in Timaeum & Politica...* Basel: Apud Ioan Valderum, 1534. Editio princeps of the Scholia, 2 volumes bound as 3, some minor spotting and staining, old (probably 17th century) manuscript annotations in ink (in Latin, some shaved) and underlining in red, plus later marginal numbered in pencil, one or two later ink notes in French, marginal dampstaining in volume III, 17th century inscription of 'Ant. Carpetnarius, Doct. med. Paris', folio, late 17th century brown goatskin, spines gilt in compartments with second and third lettered and central tool of a crowned goat's head in others, marbled pastedowns, colouring different in each volume, some wear and old repairs to head and foot of spines, volume i with front flyleaf filled with 8 paragraphs of bibliographic detail in French in later (late 18th century) hand, good.   Blackwell's Rare Books   Greek & Latin Classics VII - 72   2016   £5000

Plato *The Works of Plato Abridg'd.* London: printed for A. Bell, 1701. First English edition, few leaves browned or spotted, one or two corrections in manuscript, faint dampmark to upper forecorner of first 50 leaves, 8vo., contemporary Cambridge stype panelled calf, red morocco label to spine, slightly rubbed and marked bookplate of Seton of Ekoslund and ownership inscription of Duncan Campbell, more recent chess bookplate of Bruno Bassi, name 'Greeg' in blank area of first page of text, blindstamped.
Blackwell's Rare Books   Greek & Latin Classics VII - 73   2016   £2500

Platt, S. H. *The Martyrs and the Fugitive: or a Narrative of the Captivity, Sufferings and Death of an African Family and the Slavery and Escape of their Son.* New York: Daniel Fanshaw, 1859. First edition, 12mo., brown cloth gilt, dampstain at top of pages, which becomes progressively lighter after first few leaves and some minor, not very obvious loss at spine extremities, still handsome, very good with gilt lettering on front board bright and unrubbed.   Between the Covers Rare Books   202 - 97   2016 $450

Platt, William *Love Triumphant.* London: Charles Hirsch, 1896. First edition, uncommon, original green cloth, somewhat rubbed and bumped, interior pages have browning to margins, offsetting to free endpapers and chip to rear free endpaper, still very good.   The Kelmscott Bookshop   12 - 83   2016 $200

Platt, William *Men, Women and Chance.* London: T. Fisher Unwin, 1898. First edition, rare, very nice in original grey cloth with gilt cover design, bookplate of Mark Samuels Lasner.   The Kelmscott Bookshop   12 - 84   2016 $200

Plautus, Titus Maccius *Commoediae XX.* Venice: Lazarus Soardus, 14 August, 1511. first illustrated edition, folio, lacks final blank, 18th century calf covers panelled with blind fillets and large ornamental roll spine gilt in compartments, light wear to extremities, one or two small wormholes to spine, occasional faint dampstaining to lower outer corners, some marginal brown staining to first and last leaves, light browning to few leaves, minor worming to lower margins of last leaves, small corner restoration on HH8.   Maggs Bros. Ltd.   1474 - 62   2016   £9000

Plautus, Titus Maccius *Comoediae Viginti.* Lyons: Apud Seb. Gryphium, 1549. Pocket Gryphius edition, ruled in red, touch of worming to gutter of first few leaves (affecting one word of dedication), paper evenly toned brown, few minor spots, two leaves near end with small tears from blank margins, 16mo., early calf boards, boarded with gilt roll and with small floral cornerpieces, spine with four raised bands between double gilt fillets and dentelle tools, second compartment gilt lettered direct, mottled endpapers, all edges gilt, touch rubbed, few tiny wormholes to spine, old scrape to lower board, good.   Blackwell's Rare Books   Greek & Latin Classics VII - 75   2016   £450

Plautus, Titus Maccius *Comoediae Superstites Virginti cum Fragmentis Deperdiatrum ex Optimis Quibuesque Editionibus.* Patavii: excudebat Josephus Cominus, 1725. 1 volume bound as 2, 8vo., vignette to titlepages, woodcut colophon to final leaf (verso of volume II), contemporary vellum red morocco gilt labels to spine, edges sprinkled blue, bit yellowed, some greyish marks, lower board of volume II worn at head edge, but very good.   Unsworths Antiquarian Booksellers Ltd.   E01 - Early Printing - 17   2016   £200

Plautus, Titus Maccius *Plautus Integer cum Interpretatione Joannisba Pristae.* Milan: Ulrich Scinzenzelet, 18 Jan., 1500. Folio, 60 lines of commentary plush headline, Roman and Greek letter, some printing in red (on Aa2), last leaf with register, 17th century Parisian binding of citron morocco, gilt panel on covers, spine elaborately gilt, marbled edges, few marginal wormholes in first 3 leaves, covers of binding with some abrasions (no loss of leather), some annotations slightly cropped by binder, finely bound copy, the copy of Jean Francois Theuart of Paris, 1674, to whom awarded as a prize, inscription "ex libris JF Theuart".   Maggs Bros. Ltd.   1474 - 61   2016   £9000

Plautus, Titus Maccius *(Opera) ex fide Atque Auctoriatate Complurium Librorum...* Lyon: apud Ioannem Macaeum, 1577. First Lambind edition, top edge of first few leaves slightly affected by damp with little resulting fraying, occasional spotting and signs of use elsewhere, scattered contemporary ink annotations, folio, early dark brown morocco, much darkened and surface mottled from acid, spine in compartments with impression of gilt center pieces visible, second compartment plainly gilt lettered sometime later, extremities rubbed and little bit worn but binding overall quite sturdy, sound.   Blackwell's Rare Books   B186 - 121   2016   £650

The Players: a Satire. London: printed for W. Mears, 1733. First edition, second issue with cancel titlepage, 8vo., fine, disbound.   C. R. Johnson Rare Book Collections   Foxon: H-P 2015 - 766   2016 $3064

Playfair, Lyon *An Address Delivered by Dr. Lyon Playfair...* Sheffield: printed by Leader Independent Office, 1853. Disbound, 12 pages.   Jarndyce Antiquarian Books   CCXV - 904   2016   £48

The Pleasures of Cotton; or the Nightly Sports of Venus: A Poem. London: printed for E. Curll, 1721. First edition, engraved frontispiece, 8vo., contemporary polished calf, gilt, spine gilt, green morocco label, very good.   C. R. Johnson Rare Book Collections   Foxon: H-P 2015 - 767   2016 $2298

Plicka, Karel   *Slovakia/La Slovaquie.*   Prague: Artia, 1955. Early reprint, quarto 224 full page photos, small address label on front pastedown, fine in very good dust jacket torn, rubbed and tanned at spine and in good only card slipcase.   Peter Ellis   112 - 294   2016   £95

Plimpton, George   *The Curious Case of Sidd Finch.* Franklin Center: Franklin Library, Jan., 1987. First edition, fine in like dust jacket, signed by author, personal ownership blindstamp.   Simon Finch   2015 - 2016 $190

Plimpton, George   *The Curious Case of Sidd Finch.* Franklin Center: Franklin Library, 1987. First edition, limited edition, fine, accented in 22kt. gold, printed on archival paper with gilded edges, smyth sewing and concealed muslin joints, bound in full leather with rubbed spines, pristine. Simon Finch   2015 - 61482   2016 $275

Plinius Caecilius Secundus, Gaius   *The Letters of Pliny the Counsul; with Occasional Remarks.*   London: printed for J. Dodsley, 1748. Third edition, 2 volumes, 8vo., titlepages printed in red and black with small numismatic engravings, half title in each volume, occasional light foxing, particularly to front and rear, few smudgy marks, contemporary dark brown speckled calf, neatly rebacked, gilt borders, edges sprinkled red, spines darkened and bit creased, few small chips and scrapes, very good, ownership inscription of F. Mashiter to each front pastedown, together with several library codes, pictorial bookplate, ownership inscription of Thomas Short to each titlepage122.   Unsworths Antiquarian Booksellers Ltd.   30 - 122   2016   £160

Plinius Secundus, C. *Historiae Mundi Libri Triginta Septem.*   Lyons: Ex officina Godefridi et Marcelli Beringorum, 1548. Reprint of Gelen's edition, short wormtrack to final 15 leaves affecting few characters in index, few early ink splashed in text, variably browned and lightly foxed in places, several leaves with small old paper repairs in blank margin, early ownership inscription cancelled from head of titlepage, small splashmark to fore-edge, Erasmus's name censored at head of dedication, 18th century catspaw calf, spine gilt with floral tools and corner sprays, 2 original patches to leather of rear board, few tidy recent repairs including spine ends, some old scrapes to fore-edges, front flyleaf sometime reglued, overall still good.   Blackwell's Rare Books   Marks of Genius - 35   2016   £950

Plomer, William   *A Choice of Ballads.*   London: printed for private distribution by Jonathan Cape, Christmas, 1960. First edition of this selection, octavo, red buckram backed decorated paper boards, one of 350 numbered copies signed by author, prelims very faintly foxed, otherwise fine. Peter Ellis   112 - 305   2016   £35

Plomer, William   *Paper Houses.* London: Hogarth Press, 1929. First edition, free endpapers partially tanned, head of spine faded, very good in like dust jacket, nicked and slightly chipped with couple of short closed tears, scarce.   Peter Ellis   112 - 304   2016   £550

Plot, Robert   *The Natural History of Oxfordshire.* Oxford: printed at the Theater in Oxford, 1677. First edition, folio, contemporary full panelled calf, skillfully rebacked period style by Bernard Middleton, spine divided into six compartments, red morocco and gilt lettering piece to second compartment, all edges red, engraved titlepage vignette, engraved folding map, 16 numbered engraved plates, light browning to margins, few dust marks, otherwise very good, with map usually lacking.   Sotheran's Piccadilly Notes - Summer 2015 - 237   2016   £1800

Plot, Robert   *The Natural History of Oxford-shire.* Oxford: printed by Leon Litchfield for Charles Brome... and John Nicholson, 1705. Second edition, folio, 17 plates including folded map, occasional spotting but generally bright and clean, map very slightly toned with small tear near attachment, contemporary tan calf boards, neatly rebacked in marginally lighter shade, raised bands, green morocco gilt title label, all edges red upper hinge reinforced, little ms. to f.f.e.p., rear endpapers renewed, few small scrapes and marks but very good, armorial bookplates of Powell Snell and Robert Biddulh Phillipps, bookseller's ticket of Myers and Co.   Unsworths Antiquarian Booksellers Ltd.   E05 - 9   2016   £1500

Plowhead, Ruth Gipson   *Holiday's with Betty Sue and Sally Lou.*   Caldwell: Caxton, 1939. First edition, 8vo., color and black and white by Agnes Randall Moore, author's presentation, top edges slightly soiled, otherwise nice in dust jacket.   Second Life Books, Inc.   196 B - 412   2016 $45

La Plus Vielle Histoire Du Monde. Paris: Jardin des Modes, n.d., 1931. Oblong 4to., printed on cloth, slightest of cover soil, near fine, one of the first Batik printed books (using vegetable dyes), with charming illustrations by Francoise, nice copy. Aleph-bet Books, Inc. 111 - 180 2016 $1200

Plutarchus *Vitae Illustrium Virorum.* Rome: Ulrich Han, 1470. First edition, volume I, large folio, mid to late 19th century dark brown morocco over bevelled boards by William Townsend and Son, Sheffield with other blindstamp inside front covers panelled with simple blind fillets and ornamental rolls, spine decorated in same way, red morocco label, illuminated opening page with white vine stem border, on three sides extending into fore-margin, border incorporates 9 line initial "I" in gold and wreath on each border, one in lower margin left blank for a coat-of-arms, remaining two with rosettes, also four birds found in lower border, all in burnished gold, blue, green, purple, 54 further initials in gold, mostly 9 to 11 lines, against intricate white vine backgrounds infilled with blue green and purple, which extend into margins, 4 line initial in gold infilled with green and purple against blue background, some rubrication, early ms. headings and foliaton, heavy inkstain affecting ff. vIv and v2r and initial, some dampstaining, mostly marginal but heavier towards end affecting c. 9 initials, foxed and spotted in places, near contemporary marginal annotations plentiful for first 35ff and intermittent thereafter, acquisition note of Dom Munor de Suessa, Dean of Labelda-Logrono 1632, 18th century inscription of D. Gregorio Lopez Malo, 2 pages of 19th century bibliographical notes cut down and mounted at end. Maggs Bros. Ltd. 1474 - 64 2016 £45,000

Plutarchus *Select Lives.* London: i.e. Edinburgh: sold by A. Manson, R. Williams, J. Hammond, B. White, H. Newton, W. Middleton, P. Thomson and S. Bland, circa, 1775. 2 volumes, engraved frontispiece in volume i, 8vo., contemporary sheep, spines with five raised bands, labels lost from second compartments. green numbering pieces, rest with central gilt stamps, joints cracked but boards firmly held, spines darkened, extremities little worn, recently polished, rare. Blackwell's Rare Books Greek & Latin Classics VII - 78 2016 £450

Plutarchus *The Lives of the Noble Grecians and Romanes Compared Together by that Grave Learned Philosopher....* Stratford-on-Avon: Shakespeare Head Pres, 1928. No. 6 of 100 sets, on handmade paper and in deluxe binding, signed by artist (along with 500 regular copies), 241 x 159 mm., publisher's black half morocco over burnt orange linen by Morley of Oxford (stamp signed), raised bands decorated with thick and thin gilt rules, top edges gilt, tondo portrait of author on titlepage, portrait of Elizabeth I a head of dedication page and portrait of appropriate subject at beginning of each biography, laid-in carbon copy of description from Philip C. Duschnes ((perhaps 1960-70s) describing this set as in perfect condition, one cover with tiny blemish and vague dent to tail edge, but beautifully well preserved, entirely clean, fresh and bright internally, virtually unworn binding. Phillip J. Pirages 67 - 317 2016 $4500

Plutarchus *(Moralia) Opuscula LXXXXII.* Venice: Aldus Manutius & Andreas Asulanus, March, 1509. Editio princeps, 4to., Greek and Roman type, 16th century vellum, Aldus' device on titlepage, light staining, heavier waterstaining to front and last quire to title leaf restored, small wormholes to first quire. Maggs Bros. Ltd. 1474 - 63 2016 £17,500

Poage, Michael *Handbook of Ornament.* San Francisco: Black Stone Press, 1979. Limited to 500 copies, this one of 26 numbered copies, signed by author, hand bound by Shelley Hoyt-Koch, 8vo., quarter cloth, paper covered boards, label on spine. Oak Knoll Books 310 - 86 2016 $125

Pocock, Arthur *Red Flannel and Green Ice.* London: Herbert Jenkins, 1950. 22.2 x 15.2cm, green cloth with map endpapers, dust jacket, black and white frontispiece, 14 black and white photo illustrations, very good in dust jacket with wear to spine and small tears and nicks to edges. Schooner Books Ltd. 115 - 115 2016 $40

Podeschi, John B. *Dickes and Dickensiana. A Catalogue of the Richard Gimbal Collection in the Yale Unviersity Library.* New Haven: Yale University Press, 1980. Half title, frontispiece, original olive green cloth, paper label, very good. Jarndyce Antiquarian Booksellers CCXVIII - 1513 2016 £45

Poe, Edgar Allan 1809-1849 *Aventures D'Arthur Gordon Pym.* Paris: Michel Levy Freres, 1858. First edition, original green printed wrappers, few spots of soiling to wrappers, outstanding copy, very rare in such good condition. Manhattan Rare Book Company 2016 - 1646 2016 $1800

Poe, Edgar Allan 1809-1849 *The Bells and Other Poems.* London: Hodder and Stoughton, 1912. First trade edition, large quarto, 28 mounted color plates by Edmund Dulac, with descriptive tissue guards, 10 black headpieces on tan backgrounds and portrait of Poe on titlepage, also in black ink on tan background, original gray-green cloth, gilt stamped on front cover with all over Dulac design of clusters of bells lettered gilt, spine lettered gilt and with similar design, early ink presentation, minimal rubbing to extremities, otherwise very fine, loosely inserted is Leicester Galleries notice of the exhibition of the watercolors for the book. David Brass Rare Books, Inc. 2015 - 02937 2016 $850

Poe, Edgar Allan 1809-1849 *The Bells & Other Poems.* London & New York: Hodder & Stoughton, n.d., 1912. Limited to only 650 copies signed by Dulac, large 4to., full vellum binding extensively decorated in gold, top edge gilt, new silk ties, most minor cover soil, bump at head of spine, else fine, none of the bowing of covers usually affecting this book, 28 magnificent color plates with guards and many large pictorial headpieces by Edmund Dulac. Aleph-bet Books, Inc. 112 - 159 2016 $2500

Poe, Edgar Allan 1809-1849 *The Bells & Other Poems.* New York & London: Hodder and Stoughton, n.d., 1912. First American trade edition, 4to., blue cloth with elaborate black cover design, fine in original publisher's pictorial box (scuffed), 28 magnificent color plates framed in green borders, plus many large pictorial headpieces and pictorial endpapers, great copy, rare in this box. Aleph-bet Books, Inc. 112 - 162 2016 $1500

Poe, Edgar Allan 1809-1849 *Les Cloches et Quelques Autres Poemes.* Paris: L'Edition D'Art H Piazza, 1913. French Limited edition, one of 400 copies, printed on Papier Du Japon, large quarto, 28 color plates with captioned tissue guards, 39 decorated initials, 9 headpieces and 34 tailpiece designs by Edmund Dulac, original tan wrappers printed in gilt and rust, bound circa 1913 in three quarter brown morocco over batik boards ruled gilt, spine decoratively tooled and lettered in compartments, top edge gilt, handmade gold, green and tan endpapers, housed in original brown leather edged slipcase, neat ink inscription, fine copy. David Brass Rare Books, Inc. 2015 - 02938 2016 $950

Poe, Edgar Allan 1809-1849 *The Journal of Julius Rodman.* San Francisco: Colt Press, 1947. First book apperance, limited to 500 copies printed by Grabhorn Press, small quarto, seven color wood engravings by Mallette Dean, handset Oxford type, cloth backed decorated boards, paper spine label printed in blue and brown, fine. Argonaut Book Shop Literature 2015 - 5343 2016 $150

Poe, Edgar Allan 1809-1849 *"Murders in the Rue Morgue." "A Descent into the Maelstrom." "To Helen." (and other tales, poems, essays by Poe) in Graham's Lady's and Gentleman's magazine Volumes 1-19, 1841.* Philadelphia: George G. Graham, 1841. Bound magazine, 2 volumes in one, octavo, contemporary half morocco and marbled paper boards, binding worn with some paper on front board torn away and cracked near front hinge with few leaves, creased at gutter, sound, near very good copy with scattered foxing. Between the Covers Rare Books 208 - 110 2016 $4500

Poe, Edgar Allan 1809-1849 *The Purloined Letter.* Ulysses Bookshop, 1931. Reprinted here for the first time in edition of 325 copies, original green wrappers, edges stained, internally very good, uncommon. I. D. Edrich Crime - 2016 £60

Poe, Edgar Allan 1809-1849 *Tales of Mystery and Imagination.* New York: Brentanos, n.d. circa, 1923. Large thick 4to., black cloth, pictorial paste-on, top edge tinted black, others trimmed, no decorations on spine, 412 numbered pages, black endpapers, slightest bit of fading, near fine in dust jacket (frayed), 8 tipped-in color plates, 24 detailed black and white plates and 26 vignettes by Harry Clarke. Aleph-bet Books, Inc. 111 - 95 2016 $950

Poe, Edgar Allan 1809-1849 *Tales of Mystery and Imagination.* Philadelphia: Lippincott, 1935. First American Rackham illustrated edition, 4to., red pictorial cloth, old paper clip mark on edge of endpaper, else fine in dust jacket (with 'v' shaped piece off top of spine, frayed at base of spine), pictorial endpapers, 12 fine color plates with tissue guards plus many black and whites by Arthur Rackham. Aleph-bet Books, Inc. 111 - 381 2016 $875

Poe, Edgar Allan 1809-1849 *Tales of Mystery and Imagination.* Franklin Center: Franklin Library, 1987. 8vo., illustrations by Harry Clarke, all edges gilt, leatherette over boards, stamped in gilt, fine. Second Life Books, Inc. 197 - 261 2016 $45

Poems, Amicis Candisqe Legenda. N.P. London: n.d., 1745. First edition, 8vo., disbound, very good, very rare. C. R. Johnson Rare Book Collections Foxon: H-P 2015 - 772 2016 $3064

Poems (Eight Northwest Poets). Portland: Portland Art Museum, 1959. Portfolio, 8 gatefold pamphlet, each made from folio sheets folded twice to form 8 pages, all housed in envelope hand labelled "Eight Northwest Poets" along with each poet's name, near fine with very light toning and chip to corner of one pamphlet (that of William Stafford) in very good envelope toned and chipped at corners. Between the Covers Rare Books 208 - 82 2016 $3500

Poems on Several Occasions. Manchester: printed for the author by R. Whitworth, 1733. First edition, 8vo., original pale blue wrappers, some wear to spine, rare, excellent copy. C. R. Johnson Rare Book Collections Foxon: H-P 2015 - 776-h-p 2016 $6895

Pomes on Several Occasions. London: printed for W. Mears, 1733. First edition, very good, engraved frontispiece, 8vo., disbound, slight marginal worming in last few leaves, but very good, very rare. C. R. Johnson Rare Book Collections Foxon: H-P 2015 - 775 2016 $3064

Poems, Riddles &c. London: printed and sold by John Marshall No. 4, Aldermary-Church Yard in Bow Lane, Cheapside, circa, 1802. 12mo., hand colored frontispiece, prelim and final blanks, titlepage marked at foot, some offsetting from frontispiece, final page of text torn with loss to blank lower corner, some light browning and occasional fingermarking to text, stitched in recent marbled paper wrappers. Jarndyce Antiquarian Booksellers CCXVI - 339 2016 £225

Poetae Graeci Veteres Carminis Heroici Scriptores, Qui Extant, Omnes. Geneva: Sumptibus Caldorianae Societatis, 1606. Titlepage in red and black, first three leaves creased vertically, dampmark in lower corner, some light browning and spotting elsewhere, title slightly dusty and paper softened, showing two ownership stamps, small inscription and page numbers added to listing of contents, folio, contemporary acid speckled calf, spine with six raised bands second compartment gilt lettered direct, remainder with gilt decoration and cornerpieces, boards bordered with double gilt fillet, central gilt stamp of French bishop's arms, leather flaked, worn at extremities, joints cracking bit but strong, sound.   Blackwell's Rare Books   Greek & Latin Classics VII - 19   2016   £500

Poetical Reflexions Moral, Comical, Satyrical &c. on the Vices and Follies of the Age... London: printed by J. Read, 1708. First edition, 8vo., 19th century half roan and marbled boards (scuffed), inner margins strengthened at beginning and end, otherwise good.   C. R. Johnson Rare Book Collections   Foxon: H-P 2015 - 782   2016 $613

Poetry: The Fiftieth Anniversary: October-November 1962 Volume 11, Numbers 1 and 2 (double issue). Chicago: Modern Poetry Association, 1962. First edition, printed wrappers bit rubbed, else near fine, signed by a number of the contributors.   Between the Covers Rare Books 208 - 8   2016 $500

Poets & Writers, Inc.   *...Tenth Birthday Party: Roseland October 22 1980.* New York: Poets & Writers Inc., 1980. Small 4to., paper wrappers, laid in note to poet and editor William Claire, on blue paper with heading Saturday Review, edges very slightly spotted, front corners of cover slightly worn, otherwise very good, tight copy.   Second Life Books, Inc.   196 B - 414   2016 $50

Pogany, Elaine   *Peterkin.* Philadelphia: McKay, 1940. First edition, cloth backed pictorial boards, slightest bit of edge rubbing, else fine in very good+ dust jacket (lightly frayed at spine ends, slightly rubbed at folds), 15 full page and smaller color illustrations by Willy Pogany, inscribed by Pogany, nice.   Aleph-bet Books, Inc.   111 - 343   2016 $350

Pogany, Willy   *Willy Pogany's Mother Goose.* New York: Nelson, 1928. Limited to 500 copies, numbered and signed by artist, 4to., quarter cloth, blue boards, fine, full page color illustrations, many half page and marvelous black and whites, exceptionally rare.   Aleph-bet Books, Inc.   112 - 376   2016 $2750

Pogany, Willy   *Willy Pogany's Mother Goose.* New York: Thomas Nelson, 1928. First trade edition, 8vo., blue cloth stamped in gilt in pictorial dust jacket (worn original tissue over that), small bookseller's price label on dust jacket flap and top edge of front flyleaf, little browning to fore edge and bottom of leaves, near fine, beautifully illustrated in back and white and color throughout, pictorial endsheets, top edge gilt.   Second Life Books, Inc.   197 - 263   2016 $400

Poggendorff, J. C.   *Biographisch-Literarisches Handworterbuch zur Geschichte der Exacten Wissenschaften...* Ann Arbor: J. W. Edwards, 1945. 7 volumes in 10, accompanied by 19 parts bound in 2 volumes, for a total of 12 volumes, thick 8vo., cloth, ex-library set with markings, accompanied by various supplements extending the set up through 1960.   Oak Knoll Books   310 - 263   2016 $1250

Pogzeba, Wolfgang   *New Vision. Photographs of the Americn West.* Flagstaff and Cody: Northwest Press and Buffalo Bill Historical Center, 1977. First edition, oblong quarto, profusely illustrated with black and white reproductions, half black leather stamped in silver, granite boards, very fine with black slipcase, no. 29 of 100 copies especially bound, slipcased and numbered and containing original full page watercolor, signed by artist.   Argonaut Book Shop   Photography 2015 - 6848   2016 $350

Pohl, Frederik   *Gateway.* New York: St. Martin's Press, 1977. First edition, octavo, boards, fine in nearly fine dust jacket with some rubbing to edges.   John W. Knott, Jr./L.W. Currey, Inc.   Fall-Winter 2015 - 18570   2016 $1000

Pohl, Frederik   *Slave Ship.* New York: Ballantine Books, 1957. First edition, 8vo., fine in very good++ dust jacket with minimal edgewear, signed and inscribed by author.   By the Book, L. C.   45 - 76   2016 $600

Point, Nicolas   *Wilderness Kingdom. Indian Life in the Rocky Mountains.* New York: Holt Rinehart and Winston, 1967. First edition, scarce thus, 283 reproductions, navy blue cloth, very fine with pictorial dust jacket.   Argonaut Book Shop   Native American 2015 - 6366   2016 $125

Point, Nicolas   *Wilderness Kingdom. Indian Life in the Rocky Mountains 1840-1847.* New York: Holt, Rinehart and Winston, 1967. Second printing, 4to., 288 reproductions paintings, rubbed spine ends, lightly worn dust jacket, else fine copy.   Argonaut Book Shop   Native American 2015 - 1959   2016 $50

Poiret, Pierre *The Divine Oeconomy; or an Universal System of the Works and Purposes of God Towards Men, Demonstrated.* printed for R. Bonwicke, M. Wotton, S. Manship and R. Parker, 1713. 6 volumes bound in 4, each volume with its own titlepage, slight browning, 8vo. contemporary panelled calf, rubbed, 1 headcap defective, sound armorial bookplate, engraved by A. Johnston in each volume of Hon. George Baillie (of Jerviswood). Blackwell's Rare Books B186 - 124 2016 £1500

Poisson, Simeon Denis *Recherches sur la Probabilite des Jugements en Matiere Criminelle et en Matiere Civile Precedes des Regeles Generales de Calcul des Probabilites.* Paris: Bachelier, 1837. First edition, half title, light foxing within, original quarter dark green gilt stamped calf, marbled boards, extremities worn, very good, signature of Karl Pearson (1857-1936). Jeff Weber Rare Books 183 - 25 2016 $4000

Pole, Thomas *A History of the Origin and Progress of Adult Schools...* Bristol: printed: New Yor: reprinted and sold by Samuel Wood, 1815. Folding table at end, generally little foxed, recently rebound in half black calf, marbled boards. Jarndyce Antiquarian Books CCXV - 906 2016 £85

Poleni, Giovanni *Memorie Istoriche Della gran Cupola Del Tempio Vaticano...* Padova: Nella Stamperia dei Seminario, 1748. Folio, five books in one volume, contemporary quarter calf over patterned paper covered boards, brown morocco and gilt lettering piece to spine, all edges speckled red, folding etched plates, binding rather rubbed at extremities, corners bumped some loss of paper covering boards, internally bright, crisp copy, ink signature of John Lewis Wolfe, engraved armorial bookplate of Joseph Gwilt (1784-1863), engraved bookplate of Sir Albert Richardson (1880-1964). Sotheran's Piccadilly Notes - Summer 2015 - 239 2016 £3955

Polezhaev, Petr Vasilevich *Za Shest let (1906-1912 g.g.).* Saint Petersburg: A. S. Surovin, 1912. First edition, 8vo., contemporary black quarter morocco over marbled boards, spine lettered vertically in gilt art nouveau type, very light wear to edges only, apart from light even browning due to paper stock, very good, 1930's Estonian stamp and release stamp dated 2002, beautiful copy. Sotheran's Travel and Exploration - 277 2016 £598

Polidori, John William *The Vampyre a Tale.* London: printed for Herwood, Neely and Jones, 1819. First edition, first printing, octavo, 16 page publisher's catalog Nov. 2d 1818, original unprinted drab paper wrappers, all edges untrimmed, contemporary owner's attribution to 'Mary Shelley' spine panel professionally rebacked to style, very light foxing early and late, very good or better copy overall, enclosed in custom cloth slipcase. John W. Knott, Jr./L.W. Currey, Inc. Fall-Winter 2015 - 17170 2016 $12,500

Poliroux, Jacques Barthelemy *Traite de Medecine Legale Criminelle.* Paris: Levrault, 1834. First edition, last leaf slightly stained, small circular library stamp on verso of title, 8vo., uncut, original yellow paper wrappers, paper label on spine lettered in ink, small label inside front cover partly excised, minor defects to spine, very good. Blackwell's Rare Books B186 - 123 2016 £600

Politi, Leo *Angeleno Heights.* Los Angeles: pub. by Leo Politi, 1989. Limited to 40 linen bound books signed by Politi, large 4to., gilt pictorial cloth, fine, fabulous full and partial page color illustrations and line illustrations, scarce. Aleph-bet Books, Inc. 112 - 380 2016 $500

Politi, Leo *A Boat for Pepe.* New York: Charles Scribner, 1950. First edition, 4to., cloth, fine in dust jacket with wear at folds and frayed, brightly colored illustrations, full page watercolor filling front free endpaper, rare thus. Aleph-bet Books, Inc. 111 - 347 2016 $1500

Politi, Leo *Juanita.* New York: Charles Scribner's Son, 1948. A. First edition, cloth, fine dust jacket, inscribed and dated 1948 to Sarah Latimore, with very fine finished watercolor. Aleph-bet Books, Inc. 112 - 381 2016 $850

Politi, Leo *Little Leo.* New York: Charles Scribner's Sons, 1951. First edition, "A" on titlepage, 4to., cloth durable binding, fine in slightly worn dust jacket, illustrations in color. Aleph-bet Books, Inc. 112 - 382 2016 $400

Politi, Leo *Little Pancho.* New York: Viking, 1938. First edition, Pictorial boards, fine in lightly worn but very good+ dust jacket, this copy inscribed by author, he has hand water colored 5 of the illustrations. Aleph-bet Books, Inc. 112 - 383 2016 $1200

Politi, Leo *My Fong's Toy Shop.* New York: Charles Scribner's Sons, 1978. First edition, first printing with number beginning with 1, 4to., pictorial sturdy cloth, fine in dust jacket, this copy inscribed by Politi, scarce in excellent condition. Aleph-bet Books, Inc. 111 - 348 2016 $500

Politi, Leo *The Poinsettia.* Best West Pub., 1967. First edition, Folio, pictorial cloth, fine in dust jacket, this copy has a large finished watercolor on blank prelim page signed by Politi, rare thus. Aleph-bet Books, Inc. 111 - 349 2016 $1500

Politi, Leo *Saint Francis and the Animals.* New York: Charles Scribner's Sons, 1959. First edition, 4to., cloth, durable binding, fine in near fine dust jacket, warmly inscribed to friends with watercolor embellishments dated 1959, illustrations in full color by Politi. Aleph-bet Books, Inc. 112 - 384 2016 $350

Politi, Leo *Song of the Swallows.* New York: Charles Scribner, 1949. 4to., cloth, fine in really nice, very good dust jacket frayed at spine ends and corners and 2 small closed tears, full color illustrations by author. Aleph-bet Books, Inc. 112 - 385 2016 $750

Pollan, Michael *The Idea of a Garden.* New York: Atlantic Monthly Press, 1991. Uncorrected proof copy, mild wrinkling to couple of pages, apparently in production, fading to spine, near fine in wrappers, scarce. Ken Lopez Bookseller 166 - 100 2016 $250

Pollitt, Katha *Antarctic Traveller: Poems.* New York: Alfred A. Knopf, 1982. First edition, inscribed and signed by author for William Meredith, Dec. 7 1984, fine in fine dust jacket. Charles Agvent William Meredith - 102 2016 $150

Pollitt, Katha *Antarctic Traveller. Poems.* New York: Alfred A. Knopf, 1982. First edition, uncorrected proof, printed white wrappers, with TLS for William Meredith, forwarding the galleys 'with warm regards from your old student', near fine. Charles Agvent William Meredith - 103 2016 $150

Pollux, Julius *Onomasticon Graece & Latine.* Amsterdam: Ex Officina Wetsteniana, 1706. 2 volumes, folio, 1 folding plate, half title to each volume, volume I an engraved title and engraved frontispiece, volume I titlepage in red and black, woodcut initials, parallel Greek and Latin texts, foldout plate of coins in volume II, first page of text in each volume has portion of fore-edge margin excised, seemingly to remove ms., occasional faint staining to fore edge margins, few wax spots, upper half of r.f.e.p. excised, contemporary blind tooled vellum, titles inked ot spines, edges sprinkled red, spines little darkened, slightly rubbed, contemporary blind tooled vellum, titles inked to spines, edge sprinkled red, spines little darkened, slightly grubby with few small ink stains, but very good, partially erased ownership inscription dated 1837. Unsworths Antiquarian Booksellers Ltd. E04 - 23 2016 £750

Polovtsoff, Pierre *Monte Carlo Casino.* London: Stanley Paul, 1937. First edition, 8vo., half blue leathear lettered and decorated gilt on spine, marbled boards, 5 raised bands, about fine. Any Amount of Books 2015 - A99417 2016 £250

Pona, Francesco *Cardiomorphoseos sive ex Corde Desumpta Emblemata Sacra.* Verona: Superiorum Permissu, 1645. First and only edition, 4to., century marbled paper over pasteboards (spine faded), allegorical title, engraved by "GG" 101 numbered oval etchings of emblems. Maggs Bros. Ltd. 1474 - 65 2016 £4000

Pool, J. Lawrence *Acoustic Nerve Tumors. Early Diagnosis and Treatment.* Springfield: Thomas, 1970. Original binding, near fine in dust jacket, presentation from author to Ed Houseplan. James Tait Goodrich X-78 - 471 2016 $175

Pool, J. Lawrence *Adventures and Ventures of a New York Neurosurgeon.* published by the author, 1988. Blue printed wrappers, illustrations, nice, presentation note to Edgar Houseplan from author. James Tait Goodrich X-78 - 473 2016 $95

Pool, J. Lawrence *Aneurysma and Arteriovenous Snomnalies of the Brain Diagnois and Treatment.* New York: Hoeber, 1965. 271 illustrations, 4 in full color, near fine, original binding, dust jacket, presentation form author March 16 1965 to Ed Houseplan. James Tait Goodrich X-78 - 469 2016 $150

Pool, J. Lawrence *The Early Diagnosis and Treatment of Acoustic Nerve Tumors.* Springfield: Thomas, 1957. Original binding, near fine in dust jacket, presentation copy to Ed Houseplan from author Oct. 29 1957. James Tait Goodrich X-78 - 470 2016 $125

Pool, J. Lawrence *Fighting Ships of the Revolution on Long Island Sound 1775-1783.* privately published, 1990. Original printed wrappers, signed by author. James Tait Goodrich X-78 - 474 2016 $45

Pool, J. Lawrence *Nature's Masterpiece. The Brain and How It Works.* New York: Walker, 1987. Hardcover, laid in at from "With compliments of Larry Pool". James Tait Goodrich X-78 - 476 2016 $75

Pool, J. Lawrence *The Neurological Institute of New York 1909-1974.* Pocket Knife Press, 1975. Original printed wrapers, spine soiled, illustrations, presentation by author for Edgar Houseplan. James Tait Goodrich X-78 - 475 2016 $125

Pool, J. Lawrence *The Neurosurgical Treatment of Traumatic Paraplegia.* Springfield: Thomas, 1981. Original binding, 24 figures, nice copy. James Tait Goodrich X-78 - 472 2016 $75

Poole, George Ayliffe *An Historical and Descriptive Guide to York Cathedral and its Antiquities with a History and Description of the Munster Organ.* York: published by R. Sunter, 1850. 4to., 41 lithographic plates of which 3 are double page and 3 are colored, bit toned, particularly to titlepage, sporadic foxing, later quarter tan calf, brown morocco label with gilt title to spine, marbled paper covered boards, edges uncut, spine faded, little shelf wear, endpapers slightly grubby but overall very good, sound, ownership inscription of S. M. Wade. Unsworths Antiquarian Booksellers Ltd. E04 - 14 2016 £175

Poole, Matthew *Synopsis Criticorum Aliorumque Sarae Scripturae Interpretum et Commentatorum Summo Studio et Fide Adornata....* Frankfurt am Main: Balthasar Christopher Wurst, 1678. Early edition, volumes I, II & IV of V, only, folio, engraved titlepage vignettes, initials and head and tailpieces, woodcut, titlepages in red and black, contemporary blind stamped vellum, 6 raised bands, holograph spine titles, lightly soiled, rubbed, Hartford Theological Foundation/Case Memorial Library bookplates, very good.   Jeff Weber Rare Books 181 - 29   2016 $650

Poole, Monica *The Wood Engravings of John Farleigh.* Henley-on-Thames: Gresham Books, 1985. 24/100 copies from an edition of 110 signed by author with hand printed proof from original Farleigh engraved block within bound-in envelope, illustrations, some in black and red, folio, original quarter brown leather with yellow cloth stamped in gilt to upper board, backstrip lettered gilt, terracotta endpapers, brown cloth, slipcase with printed paper label, near fine.   Blackwell's Rare Books   B184 - 257   2016   £150

Pooley, Charles *Notes on the Old Crosses of Gloucestershire.* London: Longmans, Green and Co., 1868. First and only edition, 8vo., maroon cloth stamped with cross design and title in gilt and ruled in black, color frontispiece, tinted lithographs and engravings, some wear to head of cover, interior occasionally discolored mainly on page four and back of plate facing page 5.   Sotheran's Piccadilly Notes - Summer 2015 - 240   2016   £68

Poor Cock Robin. London: Darton & Co., Holborn Hill, n.d. circa, 1859. 4to., cloth backed pictorial boards, some soil, spotting on blank pages and normal wear, excellent copy, fine hand colored moveable plates operated with tabs, plus pictorial titlepage and frontispiece signed 'Calvert', when the tab is pulled, several pieces move simultaneously, extremely rare.   Aleph-bet Books, Inc.   111 - 306   2016 $3500

Pope, Alexander   1688-1744 *The Poetical Works of Alexander Pope.* London: printed for private circulation by Bradbury & Evans,, 1848. Contemporary full dark green morocco, spine with blindstamped compartments, blind and gilt borders, gilt dentelles, slightly rubbed, small mark on front board, all edges gilt, attractive, well preserved, presentation from editor, William Macready to Mrs. Charles Dickens, then in turn, given by her to writer Edward Dutton Cook.   Jarndyce Antiquarian Booksellers   CCXVIII - 878   2016   £350

Pope, Alexander   1688-1744 *The Poetical Works of.* Edinburgh: James Nichol (and others in London and Dublin), 1856. 2 volumes, few scattered spots slightly more pronounced in volume ii, 8vo., contemporary polished calf, double gilt fillets on sides, spines gilt in compartments, contrasting lettering pieces, spine slightly dulled, good.   Blackwell's Rare Books   B186 - 125   2016   £150

Pope, Alexander   1688-1744 *Selecta Poemata Italorum qui Latine Scripserunt.* London: impensis J. & P. Knapton, 1740. 2 volumes, 8vo., touch of foxing to titlepages, contemporary sprinkled calf, spines in six compartments with raised bands, numbered in gilt, rest with gilt decoration, much rubbed, joints and corners neatly repaired, spines bit darkened with endcaps worn down and labels lost, but sound, ownership inscriptions of Geoffrey Woledge, Birmingham 1937 and A. Montague Summers (1899).   Unsworths Antiquarian Booksellers Ltd.   E01 - Early Printing - 18   2016   £300

Pope, Alexander   1688-1744 *The Works of....* Edinburgh: printed for J. Balfour, 1764. Volumes I-VI, engraved portrait frontispiece in volume one, one titlepage bit browned, 12mo., contemporary speckled calf, single gilt fillets on sides, spines with double gilt rules either side of raised bands, tan lettering pieces, minor wear to extremities, very good.   Blackwell's Rare Books   Marks of Genius - 37   2016   £900

Pope, Alexander   1688-1744 *The Works of Alexander Pope, Esq.* Warrington: printed for the authors by W. Eyres and old by Payne...., 1794. 8vo., large uncut, some occasional foxing, original boards covered with printers' waste sheets, expertly rebacked in sprinkled calf, raised and gilt banded spine, red morocco label.   Jarndyce Antiquarian Booksellers   CCXVI - 477   2016   £285

Pope, Jessie *The Story of Flip & Fuzzy.* New York: Dodge, n.d. circa, 1910. 4to., pictorial boards, spine repaired maintaining original ribbon tie, very good+, tight and clean.   Aleph-bet Books, Inc.   112 - 62   2016 $400

Pope, Joseph John *Number One and How to Take Care of Him.* London: Allman & Son, 1883. Half title, original red cloth, little rubbed and dulled, ownership inscription.   Jarndyce Antiquarian Books   CCXV - 372   2016   £40

Pope, Norris *Dickens and Charity.* London: Macmillan, 1978. First edition, half title, plates, original light brown cloth, booklabel, very good, in slightly faded dust jacket.   Jarndyce Antiquarian Booksellers   CCXVIII - 1418   2016   £20

Popeye and the Pirates. New York: Duenewald, 1945. 8vo., pictorial boards, light cover soil, else near fine, full color illustrations featuring 4 color moveable plates by Julian Wehr, scarce.   Aleph-bet Books, Inc.   112 - 331   2016 $300

Popeye Funny Face Maker. New York: Jaymar, 1962. Square pictorial boards, come edge wear, very good+, designed so by rotating any or all 5 discs a complete face appears, thousands of combinations are possible.   Aleph-bet Books, Inc.   112 - 326   2016 $350

Popham, A. E. *Catalogue of Drawings in the Collection Formed by Sir Thomas Phillipps, Bart, F.R.S. Now in the Possession of his Grandson T. Fitzroy Phillipps Fenwick of Thirlestaine House, Cheltenham.* N.P.: privately printed for T. Fitzroy Fenwick, 1935. Limited to 150 numbered copies, 2 collotype portraits and 100 separate plates, small 4to., polished brown buckram stamped in gilt, signed and dated in lower corner of front free endpaper by Agnes Mongan, covers show light rubbing, book cocked.   Oak Knoll Books   310 - 46   2016 $650

Popham, William Home   *The Nursery Guide or Practical Hints on the Diseases and Management of Children.* London: Simpkin Marshall & Co., 1847. First edition, half title, original black grey cloth, spine faded, little rubbed and marked, but nice.   Jarndyce Antiquarian Books   CCXV - 373   2016   £90

Poppe, Guido T.   *European Seashells.*   Wiesbaden: Christa Hemmen, 1991-1993. Octavo, laminated boards, 2 volumes, color photos, fine set with few very lightly bumped corners.   Andrew Isles Natural History Books   55 - 4676   2016 $300

Porta, Giovanni Battista Della   1535-1615
Physiognomiae Coelestis Libri Sex. Leiden: H. de Vogel, 1645. 12mo., contemporary vellum, engraved title, tears without loss to leaves K3 and K4, else very good.   Edwin V. Glaser Rare Books   2015 - 10413   2016 $750

Portal, Antoine   *Cours d'Anatomie Medicale or Elamens de l'Anatomie de l'Homme.*   Paris: Baoudouin, 1804. 5 volumes, 4to., tall handsome set in contemporary full calf gilt, light text browning, some early wear to joints and corners, otherwise clean, crisp set, large, uncut margins in contemporary binding.   James Tait Goodrich   X-78 - 477   2016 $695

Porter, Anne   *The Birds of Passage.*   New York: Groundwater Press, 1989. First edition, large 8vo., glossy illustrated wrappers after design by Fairfield Porter, one of 26 copies, signed by author, out of a total of 100 copies, about fine.   James S. Jaffe Rare Books   Occasional List: Winter 2016 - 18   2016 $350

Porter, Bern   *From: Bern Porter: To: The World!*   1999. 1/100 copies, 4to., paper wrappers, spiral bound, pages not numbered, drawings, collage, photos, short bits of text, cover little soiled, otherwise nice, this copy inscribed by author with 2 quatrains.   Second Life Books, Inc. 196 B - 422   2016 $100

Porter, Bern   *A Sex Oriented, Woman connected Guy Doing His Own Thing...*   Ann Arbor: Roger Jackson, 1996. One of 75 copies signed and numbered by publisher, nice in little worn matching envelope, paper wrappers, 4to., drawings and photos, pocket at back with color photos of Porter, facsimile of a questionnaire page.   Second Life Books, Inc. 196 B - 421   2016 $175

Porter, Jane   *Thaddeus of Warsaw.*   London: Richard Bentley, 1849. half title, frontispiece, original brown cloth.   Jarndyce Antiquarian Booksellers   CCXVII - 233   2016   £50

Porter, Joyce   *It's Murder with Dover.*   London: Weidenfeld & Nicolson, 1973. Uncorrected proof, slightly rubbed and creased original wrappers.   I. D. Edrich   Crime - 2016   £30

Porter, Katherine Anne   1890-1980   *A Christmas Story.* New York: Delacorte, 1967. First edition, 12mo., very good, tight, clean copy in little toned dust jacket, inscribed by author for friend, poet Barbara Howes, 12mo., very good, clean, tight copy in little toned dust jacket.   Second Life Books, Inc.   196 B - 425   2016 $700

Porter, William Sydney   1862-1910   *The Best of O. Henry.*   London: Hodder and Stoughton, 1956. Reprint of the first collected edition, 8vo., recently rebound in half red morocco by Bayntun, spine lettered gilt, gilt centre tools, marbled endpapers, top edge gilt, near fine.   Sotheran's Piccadilly Notes - Summer 2015 - 163   2016   £148

Porter, William Sydney   1862-1910   *The Stories of O'Henry.*   New York: Limited Editions Club, 1965. First edition, one of 1500 numbered copies, signed by artist, large 8vo., bound in cloth with leather label in publisher's slipcase. Second Life Books, Inc.   196 B - 333   2016 $65

Porteus, Beilby   *Death. A Poetical Essays.*   Cambridge: printed by J. Bentham printer to the University, 1760. Third edition, 4to., slightly dusted, some light browning disbound.   Jarndyce Antiquarian Booksellers   CCXVI - 478   2016   £75

Portis, Charles   *True Grit.*   New York: Simon and Schuster, 1968. First edition, inscribed by author for Aunt Cecil and Aunt Katherine, June 17 1968, some staining to bottom edges and page fore edges, else near fine in attractive, near fine dust jacket.   Royal Books   49 - 74   2016 $3500

Portrait and Biographical Record of Denver and Vicinity. Chicago: Chapman Pub. Co., 1898. Photos, full decorated leather, all edges gilt, leather rubbed with scuffed extremities, spine faded, gilt title still quite legible, binding sound, internally clean with no stains, writing, tears or water damage.   Dumont Maps and Books   134 - 31   2016 $450

Poston, Charles D.   *Apache-Land.*   San Francisco: A. L. Bancroft & Co., 1878. Frontispiece, 12 litho views, remains of label on spine, front hinge starting, previous owner's bookplate of David Laird, bookseller and bibliographer, else good.   Dumont Maps and Books   133 - 74   2016 $125

Pote, Joseph *The Foreigner's Guide; or a Necessary and Instructive Companion, both for the Foreigner and Native, in their Tour through the Cities of London and Westminster.* Pote, 1729. First edition, small 8vo., contemporary brown panelled calf, small wear to spine, recent black morocco label, rare. J. & S. L. Bonham Antiquarian Booksellers Europe 2016 - 10085   2016   £1250

Political Merriment; or Truths Told to Some Tune. London: printed for A. Boutler and sold by S. Keiemr, 1714. First edition, 12mo., contemporary sheep, rebacked, old spine laid down, spine gilt, red morocco label, very good. C. R. Johnson Rare Book Collections   Foxon: H-P 2015 - 783   2016 $613

Potter, Beatrix   1866-1943 *Appley Dapply's Nursery Rhymes.* London: Frederick Warne and New York: n.d., 1917. 16mo., green boards stamped in red, some light cover soil and spine wear, else tight and internally clean and very good, color illustrations. Aleph-bet Books, Inc.   112 - 397   2016 $600

Potter, Beatrix   1866-1943 *The Fairy Caravan.* Philadelphia: David McKay Co. Washington Square, 1929. First trade edition, large 8vo., original dark green grained cloth with pictorial plate to upper cover, spine decorated gilt, preserved in pictorial dust jacket, 6 colored plates and 42 line illustrations, fine and immaculate copy, protected by uncommonly fresh example of scarce dust jacket with little light dusting, 3 short and barely open tears to top edge (maximum 5mm), tiny nicks to spine ends and very small loss to lower joint fold (10 x 3mm). Sotheran's Piccadilly Notes - Summer 2015 - 242   2016   £1350

Potter, Beatrix   1866-1943 *The Fairy Caravan.* London: Frederick Warne and Co., 1952. First UK trade edition, square 8vo., recently attractively bound in half dark green calf over green cloth sides, spine ruled and lettered gilt with gilt centres, top edge gilt, original green cloth cover bound in at rear, numerous line drawings and 6 full page colored plates by Potter, near fine, just touch of fading to spine. Sotheran's Piccadilly Notes - Summer 2015 - 245   2016   £225

Potter, Beatrix   1866-1943 *The Roly-Poly Pudding.* London: Frederick Warne and Co., 1908. First edition, first issue, large 8vo., original red grained cloth lettered green and gilt with onlaid pictorial label to upper cover, pictorial endpapers, illustrations in color and with line vignettes by Potter, unusually attractive copy of elusive title with some fading to spine and lower board and some light general rubbing, internally fresh and clean and perhaps touch shaken. Sotheran's Piccadilly Notes - Summer 2015 - 241   2016   £798

Potter, Beatrix   1866-1943 *Sister Anne.* Philadelphia: David McKay, 1932. First edition, 2nd issue with frontispiece correctly positioned, 8vo, original royal blue grained cloth decorated and lettered gilt to spine and upper cover, top edge orange, 13 full page black and white plates by Katherine Sturges, generally very good, minor marking to lower board and spine gilt dulled, board and spine gilt dulled, internally fresh with contemporary gift inscription dated Jan. 16th 1938. Sotheran's Piccadilly Notes - Summer 2015 - 243   2016   £268

Potter, Beatrix   1866-1943 *The Tale of Jemima Puddle-Duck.* London: Frederick Warne and Co. Ltd., 1943. Early edition, 12mo., original green paper covered boards with onlaid pictorial label to upper cover, pictorial endpapers, color illustrations after watercolours by author, very good and clean, externally lightly rubbed with couple of tiny closed nicks to joints at head of spine, now neatly repaired and almost unnoticeable, internally a touch shaken and sometime expertly tightened, some sporadic light thumbing, pale marking and occasional minor cracking, scarce signed, presentation copy inscribed "For Isabel/from Mrs. Heelis/Beatrix Potter/Feb. 16th 1943". Sotheran's Piccadilly Notes - Summer 2015 - 244   2016   £1400

Potter, Beatrix   1866-1943 *The Tale of Little Pig Robinson.* London: Frederick Warne, 1930. First edition, 8vo., blue gilt pictorial cloth, slight wear, fine in fine dust jacket with mounted color plate, fine color plates and numerous line illustrations in text and pictorial endpapers, beautiful copy. Aleph-bet Books, Inc.   111 - 361   2016 $1200

Potter, Beatrix   1866-1943 *The Tale of Peter Rabbit.* London: Frederick Warne, n.d., 1902. First trade edition, 12mo., brown boards, most minor of cover rubbing, else near fine in custom box, text and illustrations engraved and printed by Edmund Evans, rare in such fresh condition. Aleph-bet Books, Inc.   112 - 396   2016 $13,500

Potter, Beatrix   1866-1943 *The Tale of Peter Rabbit.* New York: Blue Ribbon, 1934. 16mo., pictorial boards, rubbing on edges and spine ends, else very good+, double page color pop-up, full page black and whites, very scarce. Aleph-bet Books, Inc.   111 - 362   2016 $650

Potter, Beatrix   1866-1943 *Tale of Pigling Bland.* London: Warne, 1913. First edition, 12mo. green boards, pictorial paste-on, some light wear to spine ends, else near fine, color plates by author. Aleph-bet Books, Inc.   111 - 360   2016 $750

Potter, Beatrix   1866-1943 *The Tale of the Flopsy Bunnies.* London: Warne, 1909. First edition, 12mo., brown boards, previous owner inscription dated 1912, otherwise fine in original printed glassine dust jacket, color frontispiece plus 26 color illustrations printed on glossy paper, rare in wrapper. Aleph-bet Books, Inc.   112 - 398   2016 $2850

Potter, Beatrix 1866-1943 *Tale of Timmy Tiptoes.* London: Warne, 1911. 12mo., dark green boards, pictorial paste-on, small owner inscription, else fine, original printed glassine wrapper (with half inch chip top of spine, base of spine has "1-net' price, few smaller chips elsewhere), overall very good, color frontispiece and 26 color plaes and pictorial endpapers, exceptional copy, rare in wrapper. Aleph-bet Books, Inc. 111 - 359 2016 $3250

Potter, Beatrix 1866-1943 *The Tale of Timmy Tiptoes.* London: Warne, 1911. First edition, first and second impressions are identical, 27 full page color printed illustrations, frontispiece and title vignette, all by author, 16mo., original dark green boards, backstrip and front cover lettered in white, onlaid illustration, tiny scuff mark to front cover just affecting 'W' in Wanre, covers overall very nice, short gift inscription, very good. Blackwell's Rare Books B186 - 272 2016 £500

Pottle, Frederick A. *James Boswell: the Earlier Years 1740-1769.* New York: McGraw Hill Book Co., 1966. First edition, cloth, gilt lettering, illustrations, some extremely minor fading to edges of covers, fine, dust jacket has creases on inner flaps. Argonaut Book Shop Literature 2015 - 4675 2016 $45

Potts, Stacy G. *Village Tales or Collections of By-Past Times.* Trenton: Joseph Justice, 1827. First and only edition in book form, Mid 19th century half sheep, rubbed, worn at extremities, but tight, foxing and some browning. Joseph J. Felcone, Inc. Books from Five Centuries: a Miscellany - 118 2016 $450

Pouchet, Felix Archimede *Theorie Postive l'Ovulation Spontanee de la Fecondation des Mammiferes et de l'Espece Humaine...* Paris: J. B. Bailliere, 1847. First edition, original printed paper wrappers, foldout table, 8vo., covers lightly soiled, small tear on text spine, text volume partially unopened, atlas volume neatly rebacked, small, light rubbed library stamp on title, very good. Edwin V. Glaser Rare Books 2015 - 10173 2016 $850

Poulin, A. *Catawba: Omens, Prayers & Songs: Poems by...* Port Townsend: Graywolf Press, 1977. One of 640 copies, small 8vo., illustration by Roy Nydorf, author's signature on title, with presentation to poet William Claire, flyer for book laid in, signed by author, cover slightly spotted, otherwise nice. Second Life Books, Inc. 196 B - 428 2016 $75

Poulin, A. *Catawba: Omens, Prayers & Songs: Poems by...* Port Townsend: Graywolf Press, 1977. No. 69 of 100 copies, small 8vo., illustration by Roy Nydorf, author's signature on title, brown cloth, about as new. Second Life Books, Inc. 196 B - 427 2016 $50

Poulin, A. *A Momentary Order: Poems by...* St. Paul: Graywolf, 1987. First printing, authors's presentation to poet William Claire, signed, paper wrappers, cover slightly scuffed, otherwise nice. Second Life Books, Inc. 196 B - 430 2016 $50

Poulin, A. *The Widow's Taboo: Poems after the Catawba.* Tokyo: Mushinsha, 1977. First edition, small 4to., tipped in illustrations by Nydorf, author's signature and presentation to poet William Claire, brown cloth, nice in chipped, scuffed and little worn dust jacket. Second Life Books, Inc. 196 B - 431 2016 $225

Pound, Ezra Loomis 1885-1972 *ABC of Reading.* London: Faber and Faber, 1951. New edition, octavo, spine creased and faded at head and tail, very good in good, chipped and marked dust jacket defective at head of spine and torn at tail. Peter Ellis 112 - 310 2016 £30

Pound, Ezra Loomis 1885-1972 *Antheil and The Treatise on Harmony.* Chicago: Pascal Covici, 1927. First American edition, fine in slightly age toned very near fine dust jacket, although this post dates the Paris edition, it is much less common in this condition. Between the Covers Rare Books 204 - 100 2016 $1750

Pound, Ezra Loomis 1885-1972 *Cavalcanti Poems.* New York: New Directions, 1966. First edition, limited issue, one of 190 numbered copies signed by author and printed on Pescia paper, this one of 115 for sale in the US, 4to., original quarter vellum and paper over boards, top edge gilt, acetate dust jacket, publisher's card slipcase, very fine. James S. Jaffe Rare Books Occasional List: Winter 2016 - 119 2016 $2250

Pound, Ezra Loomis 1885-1972 *Diptych Rome-London. Homage to Sextus Propertius ....* New York: New Directions, 1957. Limited to 200 numbered copies, signed by author, this one of 125 for distribution in the US, 4to., original boards, top edge gilt, publisher's matching cloth and boards slipcase with printed label, very fine in slipcase. James S. Jaffe Rare Books Occasional List: Winter 2016 - 118 2016 $2250

Pound, Ezra Loomis 1885-1972 *Drafts & Fragments of Cantos CX-CXVII.* London and Iowa City: Faber & Faber/ Stone Wall Press, 1968. First edition, no. 273 of 310 copies, English issue, numbered and signed by Pound, fine in fine slipcase, but for little mild sunning, errata slip laid in, 4to., printed on handpress by K K Merker on Umbria paper. Beasley Books 2015 - 2016 $900

Povey, Charles *The Visions of Sir Hesiter Ryley with Other Entertainments.* London: 1710-1711. Volume I nos. 1-80, August 21 1710-Feb. 21 1710 (i.e. 1711), 4to., occasional repairs to worming in fore-edge margins, rebound in half calf, marbled boards, very good. Jarndyce Antiquarian Booksellers CCXVI - 479 2016 £650

Powell, A. N. W. *Call of the Tiger.* Robert Hale Ltd., 1957. First edition, 8vo, original cloth and wrapper, occasional light spotting, very good, scarce. Sotheran's Hunting, Shooting & Fishing - 17 2016 £150

Powell, Allan *The Metropolitan Asylums Board and Its Work 1867-1930.* London: Metropolitan Asylums Board, 1930. First edition, 8vo., original two-toned cloth, numerous photograph illustrations, many full page, fine. Edwin V. Glaser Rare Books 2015 - 19405 2016 $60

Powell, Anthony *Agents and Patients.* London: Duckworth, 1936. First edition, faint foxing to prelims and final few leaves, little to edges, foolscap 8vo., original pink cloth cocked, faded backstrip gilt lettered with chafing to its head and tail, good, with friendly 2 page ALS from Powell loosely tucked into book, addressed to Gerald Reitlinger. Blackwell's Rare Books B186 - 275 2016 £800

Powell, Anthony *The Soldier's Art.* London: Heinemann, 1946. First edition, crown 8vo., original red cloth, backstrip lettered gilt against black ground, few faint foxspots to edges, rear free endpaper faintly browned, dust jacket with gentle sunning to backstrip panel, very good. Blackwell's Rare Books B184 - 221 2016 £90

Powell, Anthony *Talk about Byzantium: Anthony Powell & the BBC.* Charingworth: Evergreen, 2006. First edition, stitched paper wrappers, one of 200 numbered copies, hand set and printed by John Grice in Centaur type on Zekall mouldmade paper, laid in original letter from Powll to William Claire, with ink corrections and additions. Second Life Books, Inc. 196 B - 432 2016 $1200

Powell, E. Alexander *In Barbary Tunisia, Algeria, Morocco and the Sahara.* New York: Century Co., 1926. First edition, 8vo., original pictorial cloth, colored printed folding map, tinted folding map, sepia tinted plates after photos on eggshell glossy paper, apart from hinges strengthened, fine, gift inscription. Sotheran's Travel and Exploration - 363 2016 £98

Powell, J. W. *Eleventh Annual Report of the United States Geological Survey Part II - Irrigation.* Washington: GPO, 1891. Maps and illustrations, original cloth, gilt spine title bright, internally clean and very good. Dumont Maps and Books 134 - 45 2016 $135

Powell, J. W. *Report on the lands of the Arid Region of the United States with a More Detailed Account of the lands of Utah.* Washington: 1879. Second edition, 3 folding maps in rear pocket, original cloth, extremities worn, binding tight, internally clean and very good. Dumont Maps and Books 134 - 44 2016 £350

Powell, Lawrence Clark *A Passion for Books.* Cleveland: World, 1958. One of 975 copies, 8vo., marbled paper over boards, red cloth spine stamped in gilt, spine slightly faded, two very tiny nicks where paper joins cloth, otherwise fine in gray box. Second Life Books, Inc. 197 - 264 2016 $45

Powell, Lawrence Clark *Robinson Jeffers, the Man and His Work.* Los Angeles: Primavera Press, 1934. First edition, one of 750 copies, presentation inscription, signed by author, frontispiece, 2 plates from photos, 2 reproductions of titlepages, map, brown cloth, printed paper spine label, spine and edges of covers lightly faded, spine label soiled, two small repairs to inner front hinge, slight offsetting to front endpapers, very good. Argonaut Book Shop Literature 2015 - 4806 2016 $250

Powell, Michael *A Life in the Movies - an Autobiography.* London: Heinemann, 1986. First edition, octavo, several pages just little thumbed at outer edges, very good in very good, slightly nicked dust jacket. Peter Ellis 112 - 312 2016 £350

Powell, Michael *200,000 Feet on Foula.* London: Faber and Faber, 1938. First edition, octavo, frontispiece map, photos, covers grubby and rubbed at edges and hinges, free endpapers renewed, good reading copy, scarce. Peter Ellis 112 - 313 2016 £75

Powell, W. J. *The Zulu Rebellion of 1906.* Johannesburg: Transvaal Leader, 1906. First edition, oblong 4to., original green illustrated cloth, illustrated mainly with photographs, binding minimally spotted and rubbed, good, clean copy, neat contemporary ownership inscription Thomas Goodman from Tom, very rare. Sotheran's Piccadilly Notes - Summer 2015 - 246 2016 £995

Power, J. W *Elements de la Construction Picturale.* Paris: Editions Antoine Roche, 1932. first edition, French language issue, of a total of 550 copies, this one of 500 numbered, quarto, diagrams and black and white reproductions, in six pockets at rear are envelopes which contain 'analyses' of paintings by various artists, comprising black and white reproductions of the paintings, together with printed tracing paper overlays and 'formats mouvants' on celluloid, all intended to reveal the diagrammatic bases of the pictures, linen backed boards, covers rubbed at edges, corners bumped, head of spine scuffed and snagged, very good, scarce. Peter Ellis 112 - 314 2016 £110

Powers, Kevin *The Yellow Birds.* London: Sceptre, 2012. The First and second issue uncorrected proof copies, 2 volumes, faint handling apparent to crown, very near fine in wrappers, the second issue proof bound in medium yellow wrappers with photo of author on inside front cover, fine in wrappers with publicity sheet laid in. Ken Lopez Bookseller 166 - 101 2016 $350

Powers, Stephen *California Indian Characteristics & Centennial Mission to the Indians of Western Nevada and California.* Berkeley: Friends of the Bancroft Library of California, 1975. First book edition, color frontispiece, five photographic plates, portrait, self red wrappers, fine. Argonaut Book Shop   Native American 2015 - 1960   2016 $45

Powlett, Edmund *The General Contents of the British Museum; with Remarks Serving as a Directory...*   London: printed for R. and J. Dodsley, 1762. Second edition, half title, 12mo., some light browning, but very good, clean copy, full contemporary sprinkled calf, gilt ruled borders, raised and gilt banded spine, red morocco label, expert repairs to joints and corners, armorial bookplate of Strahallan contemporary signature on front endpaper of S. M. Savage dated 1762 with a number of ms. corrections and observations. Jarndyce Antiquarian Booksellers   CCXVI - 480   2016   £1250

Powys, John Cowper 1872-1964 *Poems.* London: William Ryder and Son Ltd., 1899. First edition, uncommon, very good in original white parchment covered boards with gilt title to spine and front board, elaborate gilt cover with floral and geometric design by Gleeson White, browning to spine and rubbing to spine and boards, minor wear to joints, signed by previous owner, otherwise interior clean, attractive copy, scarce.   The Kelmscott Bookshop   12 - 85   2016 $225

Powys, Theodore Francis 1875-1953 *Fables.* London: Chatto & Windus, 1929. One of 750 copies, 8vo., author's signature on colophon, green cloth with somewhat worn, leather label on spine, top edge gilt, cover little worn at corners and ends of spine, otherwise very good, tight copy. Second Life Books, Inc.   196 B - 435   2016 $175

Powys, Theodore Francis 1875-1953 *Mr. Tasker's Gods.* London: Chatto & Windus, 1925. First edition, 8vo., near fine in dust jacket, signed by author on endpaper. Second Life Books, Inc.   196 B - 437   2016 $150

Powys, Theodore Francis 1875-1953 *Mockery Gap.* London: Chatto & Windus, 1925. First edition, 8vo., fine in little soiled dust jacket (spine browned), signed by author. Second Life Books, Inc.   196 B - 436   2016 $175

Poynder, Frederick *A Few Words of Advice to a Public School Boy.* London: SPCK, circa, 1870. Original limp blue cloth boards, slightly rubbed.   Jarndyce Antiquarian Books   CCXV - 907   2016   £20

Poynter, F. N. L. *The History and Philosophy of Knowledge of the Brain and Its Functions.* Springfield: 1958. Original binding, nice in lightly worn dust jacket. James Tait Goodrich   X-78 - 478   2016 $145

Practical Economy or the Application of Modern Discoveries to the Purposes of Domestic Life. London: Henry Colburn and Co., 1822. Second edition, half title, 4 pages ads, endpapers replaced, uncut in original blue paper boards, modern blue speckled paper spine, paper label, boards slightly worn.   Jarndyce Antiquarian Books   CCXV - 374   2016   £220

The Practical Joke; or the Christmas Story of Uncle Ned. Third Series No. 3. New York: Kiggins & Kellog, 88 John Street, n.d., 32mo., illustrated with 7 cuts, titlepage cut replicated on front wrapper, printed pale yellow paper wrappers, sewn, modest wear and soiling, period personal owner inscription to front wrapper, very good-very good+. Tavistock Books   Bibliolatry - 32   2016 $75

Praslow, J. *The State of California: a Medico-Geographical Account.* San Francisco: John J. Newbegin, 1939. First English translation, one of 250 copies, presentation inscription signed by translator, one plate, brick cloth, pictorial pastedown on front cover, paper spine label, covers lightly spotted, spine label darkened, very good.   Argonaut Book Shop   Biography 2015 - 3680 2016 $50

Pratt, Samuel *The Regulating Silver coin Made Practicable and Easie to the Government and Subject.* printed for Henry Bonwick, 1696. First edition, 8vo., original speckled calf, double blind fillets on sides with fleurons at corners, plain spine, lettering piece lost, minor wear to spine, very good.   Blackwell's Rare Books   B184 - 75   2016   £550

Prendergast, Thomas F. *Forgotten Pioneers Irish Leaders in Early California.* San Francisco: Trade Pressroom, 1942. First edition, limited to 1500 copies, 6 portraits, green cloth, gilt lettering to spine, very fine in elusive printed dust jacket (chipped with repaired tears, mylar protected). Argonaut Book Shop   Biography 2015 - 3818   2016 $90

Prentice, Archibald *Historical Sketches and Personal Recollections of Manchester.* London and Manchester: Charles Gilpin and J. T. Parkes, 1851. Second edition, 8vo., somewhat toned, publisher's faded purple cloth, gilt title to spine, blindstamped boards, edges worn, edges uncut, spine sunned, endcaps and corners tattered, endpaper split at front hinge but holding firm, still good working copy, illegible ownership inscription pencilled to f.f.e.p. Unsworths Antiquarian Booksellers Ltd.   30 - 127   2016   £40

A Present for Good Little Boys and Girls. New York: Holiday House, 1937. Set of 4 stocking stuffer books in original slipcase, cloth backed pictorial boards, except for edge toning on one book, all in fine condition, publisher's pictorial slipcase (with small stain), rare, illustrations. Aleph-bet Books, Inc.   111 - 169   2016 $375

Preston, Chloe *Chunky Cottage.* London: Humphrey Milford, 1925. First edition, very good+, large black and white illustrations, original colored pictorial boards with scattered foxing, mild cover, spine wear binding intact. By the Book, L. C. 45 - 89 2016 $350

Preston, Chloe *Cuddly Kiddies.* London: Tuck, n.d. circa, 1915. 4to., pictorial boards, some cover rubbing. else very good+, 8 section panorama with 16 fabulous color plates, scarce. Aleph-bet Books, Inc. 111 - 363 2016 $1200

Preston, Chloe *The Good-Ship Chunky.* Springfield: McLoughlin Bros., 1929. First American edition, each page with decorated borders and different large color illustrations, original colored pictorial boards with mild cover, spine wear, binding intact, rare. By the Book, L. C. 45 - 90 2016 $350

Preston, Margaret J. *Old Song and New.* Philadelphia: Lippincott, 1870. First edition, small 8vo., author's presentation on title, top edge gilt, green cloth, stamped in gilt, cover somewhat worn at corners and ends of spine, otherwise very good. Second Life Books, Inc. 196 B - 439 2016 $75

Prevert, Jacques *Le Cirque D'Izis.* Monte Carlo: Andre Sauete Editeur, 1965. Numerous black and white photos along with 4 color illustrations by Marc Chagall, tight near fine in red cloth boards, in very good dust jacket that has some minor edgewear and some small edge tears as well, printed acetate jacket has a number of edge chips and tears, some creases to flap, overall nice, attractively printed book. Jeff Hirsch Books Holiday List 2015 - 16 2016 $150

Prevert, Jacques *Fetes.* Paris: Maeght, 1971. One of 25 de tete copies on Auvergne from a total issue of 225, 200 ordinary copies, 25 copies on Richard de Bas paper, these signed by author and artist, Alexander Calder, with an extra suite of the aquatints with pochoir in colors, each aquatint in extra suite signed in pencil by artist (this copy) and 25 copies hors commerce, 7 full page aquatints with pochoir color with text, page size 18 x 14 1/4 inches, printed by Fequet et Baudier, this homage to Calder is brilliant, loose in original wrappers with title printed in orange on blue balloons across front panel, housed in publisher's bright red orange clamshell box, with title, author and artist stamped in black on spine, extra suite of aquatints in bright red orange portfolio into box behind book, box bit rubbed and faded on back, text pages of book bit toned but aquatint pages bright and fresh, first etching of extra suite with bit of rumpling to top left and right edge (where lifted out of portfolio). Priscilla Juvelis - Rare Books 66 - 1 2016 $32,000

Prevost, Antoine Francois, Called Prevost D'Exiles 1697-1763 *Histoire Du Chevalier Des Grieux et De Manon Lescaut.* Stamford: Overbrook Press, 1958. One of 200 copies, 302 x 222mm., publisher's old calf, spine ruled in blind, red morocco lipped slipcase, 43 full color silk screened illustrations, comprised of frontispiece, title frame, 37 vibrant text water colors, two headpieces and no initials, original prospectus laid in, shallow chip across half an inch at spine head, leather (including label) with few marks and scratched, spine and two small areas discolored, paper covering upper hinge with two inch split at head, binding entirely firm and not at all unpleasant, extremely fine with no signs of use. Phillip J. Pirages 67 - 270 2016 $1000

Prevost, Antoine Francois, Called Prevost D'Exiles 1697-1763 *Manon Lescaut.* New York: Dodd Mead and Co., 1928. First American edition, folio, partially uncut, titlepage printed in black and red, 11 full page black, red and white plates by Alastair with captioned tissue guards, original gray cloth, front cover stamped and spine lettered red, pictorial endpapers printed in black and red, top edge trimmed, others uncut, spine slightly faded with small quarter inch tear at top, original pictorial dust jacket printed in black and red (torn at folds), excellent copy. David Brass Rare Books, Inc. 2015 - 02941 2016 $350

Price-Jones, Humphrey *Australian Birds of Prey.* Lane Cove: Doubleday, 1983. Limited to 250 signed and numbered copies and containing a loose illustration signed by artist, folio, full brown calf, illustration of white morph Grey Goshawk pasted onto front cover, all edges gilt, slipcase, color plates, fine. Andrew Isles Natural History Books 55 - 8965 2016 $300

Price-Mars, Jean *Ainsi Parla L'Oncle: Essais D'Ethnographie.* Haiti: Imprimerie De Compiegne, 1928. First edition, large octavo, printed wrappers, little soiling and light wear, very good, errata slip laid in, inscribed by author. Between the Covers Rare Books 202 - 80 2016 $3500

Price, Edward *Norway; Views of Wild Scenery and Journal.* Hamilton Adams, 1834. First edition, quarto, 21 aquatint plates, contemporary plum half morocco, joints and corners rubbed, very good and clean. J. & S. L. Bonham Antiquarian Booksellers Europe 2016 - 9731 2016 £550

Price, Leontyne *Aida.* San Diego: Harcourt Brace Jovanovich, 1990. Limited to only 250 copies specially bound and signed by Price and the Dillons, magnificently illustrated in color by Leo and Diane Dillons, 4to., purple gilt cloth, fine in slipcase. Aleph-bet Books, Inc. 111 - 122 2016 $200

Price, Lucien *Another Athens Shall Arise.* Kent: Kent State University, 1956. First edition, 8vo., author's presentation, nice copy in slightly faded dust jacket. Second Life Books, Inc. 196 B - 440 2016 $45

Price, Robin *An Annotated Catalogue of Medical Americana in the Library of the Wellcome Institute for the History of Medicine.* London: Wellcome Institute, 1983. Original cloth, fine. Edwin V. Glaser Rare Books 2015 - 3444 2016 $75

Price, Thomas W. *Brief Notes Taken on a Trip to the City of Mexico in 1878.* privately printed, 1878. First edition, 8 x 5 inches, original cloth with title stamped in black, presentation copy inscribed by author, spine ends and corners worn, good copy. Buckingham Books 2015 - 37029 2016 $475

Prichard, H. Hesketh *Through the Heart of Patagonia.* London: Heinemann, 1902. First edition, large 8vo., colored frontispiece, 3 maps, numerous illustrations, original red decorative cloth, spine slightly faded, very good. J. & S. L. Bonham Antiquarian Booksellers America 2016 - 9887 2016 £280

Priest-Craft and Lust; or Lancelot to His Ladies. An Epistle from the Shades. London: printed for W. Webb, 1743. First edition, folio, recent marbled wrappers, very good, some light browning, but very good, very scarce. C. R. Johnson Rare Book Collections Foxon: H-P 2015 - 795 2016 $2681

Priestley, Joseph 1733-1804 *A Description of a System of Biography; with a Catalogue of all the names inserted in it...* Philadelphia: printed by Ackerman & Hancock for Mathew Carey, 1803. New edition, folded leaf, black and white foldout chart, 8vo., quarter cloth over paper covered boards, very good, boards scuffed and soiled, spine ends worn, with half title and chart and inch tear to top margin. Kaaterskill Books 21 - 77 2016 $250

Priestley, Joseph 1733-1804 *A Familiar Introduction to the Study of Electricity.* London: Dodsley, 1768. First edition, Four full page engraved plates, modern half calf and marbled boards, front joint just starting, slight foxing and browning, otherwise very good. James Tait Goodrich X-78 - 479 2016 $1395

Priestley, Joseph 1733-1804 *The History and Present State of Discoveries Relating to Vision, Light and Colours.* London: printed for J. Johnson, 1772. First edition, 4to., folding frontispiece, errata, 24 folding plates, the copy of John Knott, MD Nov. 21 1904, red inked signature on title and frequent marginal notes, bookplate of Trinity College, Dublin, lending Library, duplicate sold. Jeff Weber Rare Books 183 - 27 2016 $1600

Priestley, Joseph 1733-1804 *Lectures on History and General Policy...* London: Thomas Tegg, 1826. 2 folding plates, later functional purple cloth, spine faded, later signature of Alfred H. Robinson. Jarndyce Antiquarian Books CCXV - 908 2016 £60

Priestley, Joseph 1733-1804 *Miscellaneous Observations relating to Education.* Bath: printed for R. Cruttwell for J. Johnson, 1778. 8vo., occasional slight damp marking, some long and shorthand contemporary annotations, attractively rebound in quarter calf, raised bands, red morocco label, vellum tips, ownership signature of Rich'd Watson, later inscription "Presented to me by Dr. Williams' Library London...". Jarndyce Antiquarian Books CCXV - 909 2016 £580

Prince, F. T. *Drypoints of the Hassidim.* London: Menard Press, 1975. First edition, slim book, near fine in stapled wrappers with some faint creasing to top corner of pages, in about very good dust jacket with some slight wear to top, spine and top of rear panel, signed and inscribed by author to Ted and Alice Berrigan, nice association, laid in is article about this book. Jeff Hirsch Books E-List 80 - 25 2016 $100

Prince, F. T. *Collected Poems.* London: Anvil Press Poetry/The Menard Press, 1979. First edition, octavo, presentation from author for Patrick Garland, actor and artistic director, fine in very good dust jacket faded at spine and edges. Peter Ellis 112 - 315 2016 £150

Prince, Richard *HMS Sulphur at California 1837 and 1839.* San Francisco: Book Club of California, 1969. First edition, limited to 450 copies, frontispiece map in color, 2 facsimiles, portrait, 3 plates, cloth backed decorated boards, gilt lettered spine, very fine, original prospectus laid in. Argonaut Book Shop Private Press 2015 - 2875 2016 $60

Prince, Richard *Inside World.* New York: Thea Westreich, 1989. Signed limited edition, number 68 of 250 copies, signed by Prince with accompanying handwritten joke, also signed, octavo, original red cloth, original slipcase, fine exhibition catalog. Manhattan Rare Book Company 2016 - 1733 2016 $5500

Prior, Matthew 1664-1721 *Colin's Mistakes.* London: printed for Jacob Tonson, 1721. First edition, folio, sewn as issued, signs of prior folding, last leaf fragile with portions missing from blank inner margin, not affecting printed portion, otherwise good, stitched and uncut. C. R. Johnson Rare Book Collections Foxon: H-P 2015 - 602 2016 $613

Prior, Matthew 1664-1721 *A New Collection of Poems on Several Occasions.* London: printed for Tho. Osborne, 1725. 12mo., some browning, mainly affecting endpapers, and pastedowns, engraved frontispiece, 3 engraved plates, full contemporary panelled calf, raised bands, joints cracked but firm, spine and corners rather rubbed, 19th century bookplate of Arthur Headlam. Jarndyce Antiquarian Booksellers CCXVI - 482 2016 £65

Prior, Matthew 1664-1721 *An Ode Humbly Inscrib'd to the Queen.* London: printed for Jacob Tonson, 1706. Folio, stained at tail, slight wears to A1 and A2 without loss, lacks half title, disbound.   Jarndyce Antiquarian Booksellers CCXVI - 481   2016   £90

Prior, Matthew 1664-1721 *Poems on Several Occasions.* London: printed for Jacob Tonson and John Barber, 1718. Large folio, fine, engraved frontispiece, contemporary black morocco, covers panelled gilt, spine and inner dentelles gilt, dark red morocco label, all edges gilt, joints and corners bit rubbed, sumptuous edition, this one of a relatively small number of copies printed on superfine copy, with watermark of a fleur-de-lys surmounting a shield as opposed to ordinary copies for subscribers with a Strasburg band watermark and copies of the trade issue with London arms watermark, numerous engraved headpieces and tailpieces, some dampmarks in blank upper margins, otherwise fine in handsome morocco binding of the period, bold armorial bookplate of Philip Southcote and booklabel of bibliography A. N. L. Munby.   C. R. Johnson Rare Book Collections   Foxon: H-P 2015 - 798   2016 $2298

Prior, Matthew 1664-1721 *Poems on Several Occasionas.* London: for Jacob Tonson and John Barber, 1718. First collected edition, large paper copy, gift from Edward Harley for Mary Popham, royal folio, engraved frontispiece, titlepage vignette, headpieces and initial letters, engraved portrait of Prior dated 1719 neatly mounted to front flyleaf, contemporary calf, boards with two-line gold fillet enclosing blind decorative roll, board edges with gold decorative roll, spine very skillfully rebacked retaining original label, recornered, marbled endpapers, just lightest occasional foxing, else very good, lovely copy.   Joseph J. Felcone, Inc.   Books from Five Centuries: a Miscellany - 120   2016 $1400

Prior, Matthew 1664-1721 *To a Young Gentleman in Love. A Tale.* London: printed for J. Tonson, 1702. First edition, folio, recent marbled wrappers, very good.   C. R. Johnson Rare Book Collections   Foxon: H-P 2015 - 804h-p   2016 $5363

Pritchard, Andrew   *History of Infusoria Living and Fossil...* London: Whittaker, 1841. First edition, subscriber's copy with ownership signature on title, of J. Jones Tucker, R. N., Dublin, tipped in notice of author, errata, 1 figure, 12 plates, heavy staining between pages 126-178, original brown embossed cloth, rebacked preserving original spine, very good but for internal staining.   Jeff Weber Rare Books 183 - 26   2016 $175

Pritchard, Andrew   *The Microscopic Cabinet of Select animated Objects....* London: Whittaker, Treacher and Arnot, 1832. First edition, 8vo., numerous figures, 13 plates, modern quarter calf, original marbled boards, black spine label, original calf corners, new endleaves, bookplate of Fred C. Luck, early pencil ownership signature of Thomas B. Hart(?) 1834, very good.   Jeff Weber Rare Books   183 - 28   2016 $875

Pritchard, James   *How to Make a Good Girl and a Useful Woman.* London: William Lister, 1868. 12mo., frontispiece, illustrations, 1 page ads, original purple cloth, blocked in gilt, largely faded to brown.   Jarndyce Antiquarian Books   CCXV - 375   2016   £85

Pritchard, N. H.   *The Matrix. Poems 1960-1979.* Garden City: Doubleday, 1970. Complimentary copy with Doubleday 'compliments of' card laid in, signed by author, modest glue bleed to hinges, light corner tap, else near fine, dust jacket near fine.   Ken Lopez Bookseller   166 - 102   2016 $150

Pritchard, Ronald Edward   *Dicken's England: Life in Victorian Times.* Sutton Pub., 2002. First edition, illustrations, original black cloth, mint in dust jacket.   Jarndyce Antiquarian Booksellers   CCXVIII - 1422   2016   £25

Pritchett, V. S.   *Christmas with the Cratchits: a Sketch.* Berkeley: Hart Press, 1964. First edition, wrappers somewhat faded and soiled, internally nice, author's own copy with VSP booklabel.   Bertram Rota Ltd.   Christmas List 2015 - 36   2016   £50

Pritchett, V. S.   *Marching Spain.* London: Ernest Benn, 1928. First edition, octavo, 8 photos, ownership signature of one of the Cholmondeleys, edges bit spotted, cloth bubbled in places, corner bruised, very good in very good, chipped and slightly marked dust jacket bit tanned at spine.   Peter Ellis   112 - 317   2016   £125

Prize Stories of 1951: The O. Henry Awards. Garden City: Doubleday, 1951. First edition, fine in very good dust jacket with some spine fading and tiny nick and tears, handsome copy.   Between the Covers Rare Books   204 - 17   2016 $350

Procter, Adelaide Anne   *Legends and Lyrics. A Book of Verses.* London: George Bell & sons, 1827. 29th and 19th thousand, 2 volumes, half titles, frontispiece volume i, original royal blue cloth, spines lettered gilt, contemporary owner's inscription on half title volume i, small stain on front board volume ii, otherwise very good.   Jarndyce Antiquarian Booksellers   CCXVIII - 619   2016   £25

Procter, Adelaide Anne   *Legends and Lyrics: a Book of Verses...* London: George Bell & Sons, 1877. 29th thousand and 19th thosuand, 2 volumes, half titles, frontispiece, original royal blue cloth, spines lettered gilt, contemporary owner's inscription, small stain o front board volume II, otherwise very good.   Jarndyce Antiquarian Booksellers   CCXVIII - 619   2016   £25

Proctor, Henry Hugh   *Between Black and White: Autobiographical Sketches.* Boston: Pilgrim Press, 1925. First edition, fine in modestly age toned dust jacket with some shallow chipping at crown, affecting no lettering.   Between the Covers Rare Books   207 - 77   2016 $500

Proctor, Richard A. *Watched by the Dead...* London: W. H. Allen & Co., 1887. First edition, engraved title, 48 page catalog (Nov. 1887), original brown cloth, lettered gilt, spine very slightly rubbed at head and tail.   Jarndyce Antiquarian Booksellers   CCXVIII - 685   2016   £90

Proctor, Richard A. *Watched by the Dead: a Loving Study of Dicken's Half-told tale.* London: W. H. Allen & Co., 1887. First edition, engraved title, 48 page catalog (Nov. 1887), original printed pictorial boards, spine little rubbed and slightly chipped at head and tail.   Jarndyce Antiquarian Booksellers   CCXVIII - 684   2016   £75

Prokofieff, Serge *Peter and the Wolf.* New York: Alfred Knopf, 1940. Stated first edition, Oblong 4to., cloth, pictorial paste-on, fine in faded dust jacket with few mends, inscribed by artist with lovely drawing of Peter laid in note signed by artist on his personal stationery with mailing envelope, super copy, illustrations by Warren Chappell.   Aleph-bet Books, Inc.   111 - 85   2016 $400

Proudfit, Isabel *The Bottle Family.* Philadelphia: McKay, 1938. 8vo., pictorial boards, fine in fine dust jacket, charming full page color lithos by Caroline Whitehead.   Aleph-bet Books, Inc.   112 - 28   2016 $150

Proudfit, Isabel *The Broom Closet Family.* Philadelphia: McKay, 1938. 8vo., pictorial boards, light rubbing on edges, else near fine, in slightly frayed dust jacket, full page color lithos by Caroline Whitehead.   Aleph-bet Books, Inc.   112 - 29   2016 $150

Proudfit, Isabel *The Ice Box Family.* Philadelphia: McKay, 1945. 8vo., pictorial boards, fine in slightly worn dust jacket, charming full page color lithos by Caroline Matson.   Aleph-bet Books, Inc.   112 - 30   2016 $150

Proudfit, Isabel *The Pencil Box Family.* Philadelphia: McKay, 1945. 8vo., pictorial boards, fine in very slightly worn fine dust jacket, full page color lithos by Caroline Matson.   Aleph-bet Books, Inc.   112 - 31   2016 $150

Proulx, E. Annie *Heart Songs.* New York: Scribner, 1988. First edition, fine in fine dust jacket, signed by author. Bella Luna Books   2016 - 6409   2016 $264

Proulx, E. Annie *Postcards.* London: Fourth esstate, 1993. Proof of First British edition, fine copy, uncommon state, signed by author on laid in book plate, printed matrix wrappers.   Bella Luna Books   2016 - t202   2016 $165

Provensen, Alice *Who's in the Egg?* Western Pub. Co., 1970. presumable first edition, 4to., pictorial boards, near fine in very good-fine price clipped dust jacket, charming color lithographers on nearly every page.   Aleph-bet Books, Inc.   111 - 367   2016 $200

Prudentius Clemens, Aurelius *Opera.* Amsterdam: Apud Danielem Elzevirium, 1667. 12mo., title in red and black with printer's device and hand ruled lines, separate half title to Heinsius notes, occasional engraved initials and head and tailpieces, little toned but generally clean, contemporary vellum, title inked to spine in old hand, yapp edges, edges sprinkled blue, some smudgy marks, endcaps creased, turn-ins lifting slightly causing cracks to edges of endpapers, but all holding firm, Pardonneau of Tours to front pastedown, armorial bookplate of Samuel Alfred Steinthal. Unsworths Antiquarian Booksellers Ltd.   E01 - Early Printing - 19   2016   £175

Prudhomme, Louis Marie *Les Crimes des Reines de France....* Paris: Bureau des Revolutions de Paris et a Lyon, Prudhomme, 1791. First edition, 8vo., half title in contemporary boards, leather spine (rubbed along edges), 1 inch of leather chipped off at extremities of spine, untrimmed, very nice, 5 engraved plates, signed by author. Second Life Books, Inc.   196 B - 442   2016 $450

Ptolemaeus, Claudius *Geography of...* New York: New York Public Library, 1932. Limited edition translated and edited by Edward Luther Stevenson, one of 250 numbered copies, printed on Charing handmade paper, collotypes by Max Jafee, 27 maps, folio, half leather, cloth, five raised bands, cardboard box with paper cover label, box soiled, worn and split at joints and corners, very minor wear at spine ends.   Oak Knoll Books   310 - 306   2016 $3500

Puckle, James *The Club; or a Grey-Cap for a Green-Head in a Dialogue Between Father and Son.* Glasgow: printed at the University Press, circa, 1890? Half title, frontispiece, rubricated text, uncut. original suede blocked in blind, retaining ties, contemporary signature.   Jarndyce Antiquarian Books   CCXV - 376   2016   £35

Pudney, John *It Breathed Down My Neck.* London: John Lane, 1946. First UK edition, 8vo., author's presentation on flyleaf, cover little worn and faded, otherwise very good. Second Life Books, Inc.   196 B - 443   2016 $45

Puffendorf, Samuel, Freiherr Von 1632-1694 *The Compleat History of Sweden....* London: printed for J. Brudenell, 1701. 8vo., some browning to several gatherings, otherwise very good, clean, full contemporary calf, lighter mottled board panels, blindstamped tulip cornerpieces, ornate gilt panelled spine, red morocco label, armorial bookplate with Medlicott family motto.   Jarndyce Antiquarian Booksellers   CCXVI - 483   2016   £350

Pugh, Edwin *The Charles Dickens Originals.* London: T. N. Foulis, 1912. First edition, half title, frontispiece and plates, endpapers replaced at some point, uncut in original red cloth, spine little faded, owner's inscription, top edge gilt, good plus.   Jarndyce Antiquarian Booksellers   CCXVIII - 1423   2016   £20

Pugh, S. S. *Life's Battle Lost and Worn...* London: RTS, circa, 1880. Original light brown decorated cloth, spine slightly dulled and rubbed at head and tail, contemporary signature, frontispiece, illustrations, 16 page catalog. Jarndyce Antiquarian Books   CCXV - 377   2016   £20

Puig, Manuel *The Buenos Aires Affair.* New York: E. P. Dutton and Co., 1976. About near fine with some slight fading to top edge of boards in near fine dust jacket, signed by author.   Jeff Hirsch Books   Holiday List 2015 - 59   2016 $85

Pullman, Philip *The Amber Spyglass. His Dark Materials III.* New York: Knopf, 2000. First edition, fine in fine dust jacket.   Bella Luna Books   2016 - t9609   2016 $165

Pullman, Philip *The Amber Spyglass. His Dark Materials III.* London: Scholastic Press, 2000. First British edition, hardcover, book fine, fine dust jacket, scarce, laid in is 'How to Read the Alethiometer'.   Bella Luna Books   2016 - t9226   2016 $264

Pullman, Philip *Lyra's Oxford.* Oxford: David Fickling books, 2003. First UK edition, signed by author, fine. Bella Luna Books   2016 - t6855   2016 $82

Pullman, Philip *Once Upon a Time in the North.* Oxford: David Fickling Books, 2008. First edition, signed by author and artist, John Lawrence, wood engravings by John Lawrence, folded sheet 'Perils of the North' tucked into pocket on rear pastedown, 16mo., original dark blue cloth, backstrip and rear cover printed in pale blue, front cover with two printed labels, fine.   Blackwell's Rare Books   B184 - 222   2016   £50

Pumpelly, Raphael *Across America and Asia: Notes of Five Years' Journey Around the World and of Residence in Arizona, Japan and China.* London: Sampson Low, 1870. First edition, 8vo., 4 colored woodcuts, 8 plates, illustrations, original red decorative cloth, inner joints cracked, very good, clean.   J. & S. L. Bonham Antiquarian Booksellers   Voyages 2016 - 6813   2016   £170

Punctuation: a Printer's Study. Stroud: Evergreen Press, 2001. 200/200 copies, printed in red and black, original grey linen with irregular shaped grey label to upper,. Blackwell's Rare Books   B186 - 297   2016   £130

Punshon, E. R. *Everybody Always Tells.* London: Gollancz, 1950. Dust jacket little frayed & torn at foot of spine, slight foxing to edges and prelims, otherwise very good, uncommon.   I. D. Edrich   Crime - 2016   £25

Punshon, E. R. *The Secret Search.* London: Gollancz, 1951. Dust jacket little spotted, frayed, closed tear to base of spine, contents very good, uncommon.   I. D. Edrich Crime - 2016   £25

Purdy, James *A day After the Fair...* New York: Note of Hand, 1977. First printing, 8vo., one of 1000 copies, fine in dust jacket, this copy not numbered but signed by author and inscribed.   Second Life Books, Inc.   196 B - 446   2016 $150

Purdy, James *Two Plays.* Dallas: New London Press, 1979. First printing, 8vo., limited edition, 1/150 copies, signed by author, near fine.   Second Life Books, Inc.   196 B - 447   2016 $45

Purmannus, Mattheus Gothofredus *Chirurgia Curiosa; or the Newest and Most Curious Observations and Operations in the Whole Art of Chirurgery.* London: printed for D. Browned, 1706. 5 folding engraved plates, errata leaf, small folio, contemporary 18th century paneled calf with spine repaired with early spine laid down, original endleaves and pastedowns saved as part of the binding.   James Tait Goodrich   X-78 - 480   2016 $3500

Purnell, Thomas *Dust and Diamonds.* London: Ward & Downey, 1888. First edition, half title, unopened, 16 page Ward & Downey catalog Nov. 1888, original turquoise cloth, gilt, very good, armorial bookplate of Sir Alfred Sherlock Gooch.   Jarndyce Antiquarian Booksellers   CCXVII - 242   2016   £45

Purney, Thomas *The Chevalier de St. George: an Hero-Comick Poem in Six Canto's.* London: printed or W. Chetwood, 1718. First edition, engraved frontispiece, 12mo., disbound, very rare.   C. R. Johnson Rare Book Collections   Foxon: H-P 2015 - 813   2016 $3064

Purney, Thomas *Pastorals. Viz. The Bashful Swain: and Beauty and Simplicity.* London: printed by H. P. for Jonas Brown, 1717. First edition, fine, 8vo., disbound, very scarce.   C. R. Johnson Rare Book Collections   Foxon: H-P 2015 - 816   2016 $2298

Purton, Peter *A History of the Early Medieval Siege. A History of the Late Medieval Siege c. 450-1200 1200-1500.* Woodbridge: Boydell Press, 2009-2010. First edition, large 8vo., cloth, gilt lettered, slight dustiness to edges, otherwise as new, dust jacket little bit of shelfwear, otherwise as new. Unsworths Antiquarian Booksellers Ltd.   E05 - 86   2016 £60

Pushkin, Alexander Sergeevich   1799-1837 *Boris Goudounov.* Paris: Editions de la Pleiade, J. Schiffrin et Cie, 1925. Number 73 of 390 copies on verge paper, signed by publisher, from a total edition of 445 copies, 430 for sale, 311 x 241mm., original dun colored printed wrappers, decorative head and tailpieces and 18 color pochoir plates by Vassili Choukhaeff (Shukhayev), spine with vertical crack and some looseness (though the insubstantial volume still intact), expected minor wear at extremities, clean inside and out, with richly colored plates.   Phillip J. Pirages   67 - 286   2016 $1250

Pushkin, Alexander Sergeevich 1799-1837 *Boris Godunov.* Leamington Spa: Sixth Chamber Press, 1985. First edition of this translation, octavo, morocco backed patterned paper boards, one of 30 copies this unnumbered, on Hahnemuhle mould-made paper, signed by translator, there were also 200 copies of the ordinary edition, small mark on spine which is just trifle rubbed at head, near fine in fine, matching slipcase.   Peter Ellis   112 - 321   2016   £100

Puss in Boots. London: Raphael Tuck, n.d,, Inscribed 1905, narrow folio, pictorial wrappers, mid spine wear and owner inscription in corner of cover, very good+ 4 full page chromolithographs plus 10 illustrations in brown.   Aleph-bet Books, Inc.   112 - 182   2016 $250

Puss in Boots. London: Frederick Warne, n.d. circa, 1910. Large 4to., green decorative cloth, large pictorial paste-on, light rubbing to spine ends, slight fox spot, really very good-fine, illustrations by H. M. Brock with 8 mounted color plates with captioned guards, rarely found in this format in such nice condition.   Aleph-bet Books, Inc.   112 - 73   2016 $350

Putnam-Jacobi, Mary *Stories and Sketches.* New York: Putnam, 1907. First edition, 8vo., fine, scarce.   Second Life Books, Inc.   197 - 265   2016 $750

Putnam, Wallace *Moby Dick Seen Again.* New York: Blue Moon Press, 1975. First edition, issued in an edition of 365 copies+, 4to., some toning to top of some leaves, 35 loose folders, 11.25 x 9.25 inches, each enclosed in wrap-around folder with author an title on cover, printed on Crane Artificial parchment rag paper by Yorktown Printing Corp., 15 of these also included original drawing, imperfect copy issued without box, signed and inscribed by the artist to David Metcalf, also signed on colophon noting this is a "HC" copy, this was actually given to Paul Metcalf, Melville's great grandson.   Second Life Books, Inc.   196 B - 202   2016 $2000

Puzo, Mario *The Fourth K.* New York: Random House, 1990. First edition, some moderate dampstaining on boards, good copy in stained but presentable dust jacket, inscribed by author to close friend.   Between the Covers Rare Books   208 - 70   2016 $350

Puzo, Mario *The Last Don.* New York: Random House, 1996. First edition, near fine in near fine dust jacket with faint stain on base of spine, inscribed by author to close friend and neighbour.   Between the Covers Rare Books   204 - 80   2016 $250

Puzo, Mario *The Sicilian.* New York: Random House, 1984. First edition, modest wear, very good or better in near fine dust jacket with crease on rear flap, inscribed by author to close friend and neighbour.   Between the Covers Rare Books   208 - 69   2016 $400

Pye, John *Patronage of British Art, an Historical Sketch...* London: Longman, Brown, Green and Longmans, 1845. First edition, presentation from author, royal 8vo., engraved portrait, one folding table, several facsimile signatures and 17 illustrations in text, original dark green vertically ribbed cloth, spine lettered gilt, inscribed "To C. R. Cockerell Esq. R. A., Professor of Architecture in the Royal Academy &c &c. with John Pye's Compls.", some pencil marginalia in recipient's hand.   Marlborough Rare Books   List 55 - 57   2016   £100

The Pyed Pyper. Llandogo: Old Stile Press, 2002. 84/175 copies signed by artist, woodcuts and linocuts printed in a variety of colours on Fabriano Ingres paper, 4to., original full tan calf with blindstamped design to front, tiny adhesive mark to front and band of slight fading around head of same, prospectus laid in at front, very good.   Blackwell's Rare Books   B186 - 321   2016   £150

Pyle, Howard *Otto of the Silver Hand.* London: Sampson Low, Marston & Co., 1893. Ad leaf preceding half title, frontispiece, plates, original turquoise cloth by Leighton Son & Hodge, pictorially blocked and lettered in black, silver and gilt, slightly dulled, contemporary ownership inscription, top edge gilt, good plus.   Jarndyce Antiquarian Booksellers   CCXVII - 243   2016   £85

Pyle, Katharine *Fairy Tales from India.* Philadelphia: Lippincott, 1926. First edition, 8vo., red gilt decorated cloth, near fine dust jacket with color plate on cover (dust jacket reinforcement on verso), 12 color plates, 2 pictorial head-pieces and pictorial titlepage, scarce in dust jacket.   Aleph-bet Books, Inc.   111 - 368   2016 $225

Pyle, Katharine *In the Green Forest.* Boston: Little Brown, Oct., 1902. First edition, 8vo., green pictorial cloth, rear cover has some inoffensive but visible stains, faint corner stain actually looks much better than it sounds, very good, illustrations by Pyle with 5 full page half-tone plates plus many black and whites in text.   Aleph-bet Books, Inc.   111 - 369   2016 $200

Pym, Horace N. *Chats in the Book-room.* London: 1896. Number 73 of 150 copies, signed and inscribed to Douglas Carnegie, vellum backed green cloth with gilt title and author to front board and spine, vellum discolored and corners bumped, printed on Arnold's unbleached handmade paper, interior very good except for foxing to frontispiece verso, which are printed on different paper, very good.   The Kelmscott Bookshop   12 - 86   2016   £160

Pynchon, Thomas *Inherent Vice.* New York: Penguin Press, 2009. Advance reading copy issued in very limited quantities to sales reps and reviewers, book review editor's name and affiliation on titlepage, light wear and crease to fore edge of covers, near fine in wrappers, extremely scarce.   Ken Lopez Bookseller   166 - 103   2016 $2500

Q

Qoyawayma, Polingaysi *No Turning Back.* Albuquerque: University of New Mexico, 1964. First edition, pictorial cloth, inscription by Carlson, very scarce thus. Gene W. Baade, Books on the West 2015 - 1402122 2016 $125

Quadri, Antonio *Il Canal Grande Di Venezia Descritto Da Antonio Quadri...* Venezia: Dalla Tipografia Armena Di S. Lazzaro, 1838. Second edition, oblong folio, 48 hand colored engravings, original quarter red morocco and printed boards, 48 panoramic views, aside from some slight rubbing to covers, fine condition. James S. Jaffe Rare Books Occasional List: Winter 2016 - 43 2016 $15,000

Quammen, David *The Soul of Victor Tronko.* New York: Doubleday, 1987. First edition, fine in like dust jacket, signed and dated by author 4/96. Bella Luna Books 2016 - ta272 2016 $132

Quammen, David *To Walk the Line.* New York: Knopf, 1970. First edition, fine, dust jacket fine with letter to Dr. Highfield, handwritten, signed and dated by author 1/31/71, inscribed by author. Bella Luna Books 2016 - ta276 2016 $132

Quarles, Benjamin *Allies for Freedom: Blacks and John Brown.* New York: Oxford University Press, 1974. First edition, fine in attractive, near fine dust jacket with very slight fading to spine lettering and very small nick on rear panel, inscribed by author for Clarence Holte, ad exec. Between the Covers Rare Books 202 - 82 2016 $350

Quarles, Benjamin *Black History's Diversified Clientele: a Lecture at Howard University.* Washington: Dept. of History, Howard University, 1971. First edition, blue cloth boards, gilt, fine, issued without dust jacket. inscribed by historian Rayford Logan to Cynthia Gray in year of publication, very scarce. Between the Covers Rare Books 202 - 81 2016 $650

Quarles, Francis *Divine Fancies Digested into Epigrams, Meditations and Observations.* London: T(homas) D(awks) for John Williams, 1675. Seventh edition, 8vo., small dampstain to upper margin and very light foxing to titlepage, large rust spot to centre of B2 and C1, dampstain in corner of D2-N2, early 19th century half russia and marbled boards, reback, boards soiled and corners worn, from the library of James Stevens Cox (1910-1997). Maggs Bros. Ltd. 1447 - 344 2016 £120

Quarles, Francis *Divine Poems.* London: by Edward Okes for Benjamin Tooke and Thomas Sawbridge...., 1669. 8vo., engraved frontispiece/title, engraved title and final leaf repaired and strengthened at fore edge, later 20th century calf, from the library of James Stevens Cox (1910-1997), various pen trials, inscription "John Barnard/of Fallm(outh); in/Cornwall" and "To James Edgecom/John Symmons", presumably of Edgcumbe or Edgcombe. Maggs Bros. Ltd. 1447 - 345 2016 £180

Quarles, John *Divine Meditations Upon Several Subjects.* London: by Thomas Johnson for Peter Parker, 1671. Third edition, 8vo., engraved portrait, title roughly torn along inner margin and mounted on stub (with slight loss to imprint), browned and foxed throughout (more so in margins), corners of B8 and C1 bumped and with some light worming, scorchmark (45 x 25mm.) to centre of L2 (and with loss to upper margin) also affecting L3, contemporary sheep rebacked, corners repaired, new endleaves, from the library of James Stevens Cox (1910-1997). Maggs Bros. Ltd. 1447 - 346 2016 £180

Quasha, George *Giving the Lily back her Hands.* Barrytown: Station Hill Press, 1979. First edition, tall 8vo., paper wrappers, inscribed by author for Paul Metcalf, very good. Second Life Books, Inc. 196 B - 448 2016 $45

Quayle, Eric *The Collector's Book of Children's Books.* New York: Potter, 1971. First American edition, fine in dust jacket. Mordida Books 2015 - 010985 2016 $65

Quayle, Eric *The Collector's Book of Detective Fiction.* London: Studio Vista, 1972. Photos by Gabriel Monro, terracotta cloth, gilt, slightly rubbed dust jacket, spine of which is sunned, contents very good. I. D. Edrich Crime - 2016 £20

Queen Summer or the Journey of the Lily and the Rose. London: Paris: Melbourne: Cassell, 1891. First edition, 4to., cloth backed pictorial boards, some mild edge rubbing, slight toning on edges, very good+, printed on one side of the paper, calligraphic text, color illustrations by Walter Crane. Aleph-bet Books, Inc. 111 - 105 2016 $475

Queen, Ellery, Pseud. *The American Gun Mystery.* New York: Dell, 1943. Paperback edition, Dell no. 4, fine in wrappers. Mordida Books 2015 - 011109 2016 $65

Queen, Ellery, Pseud. *A Study in Terror.* New York: Lancer, 1966. First edition, fine, creases at lower corner of front cover, otherwise fine, unread copy in wrappers. Mordida Books 2015 - 008284 2016 $60

The Queen's Beasts. London: Newman Neame, 1953. One of 200 numbered copies, quarto, 6 color plates by Edward Bawden, 5 by Cecil Keeling, black and white photos of James Woodford's original statues, genealogical charts on endpapers, cover slightly bumped at one corner, near fine in very good dust jacket with couple of nicks. Peter Ellis   112 - 30   2016   £75

Quested, John   *The Art of Land Surveying Explained by Short and Easy Rules...*   London: Relfe Bros., circa, 1850. Eighth edition, plates and illustrations, original pale blue cloth, slight nick to leading hinge, otherwise good. Jarndyce Antiquarian Books   CCXV - 912   2016   £30

Quetelet, Lambert Adolphe Jacques   *Letters Addressed to H. R. H the Grand Duke of Saxe Coburg and Gotha on the Theory of Probabilities as Applied to the Moral and Political Sciences.*   London: Charles & Edwin Layton, 1849. First edition in English, 8vo., tables, original blind-stamped brown cloth by Lewis (binder's ticket at rear), rebacked, new spine label, fine, inscribed by translator Olinthus Gregory Downes to J. J. Sylvester, Esq., bookplate of Percy Alexander MacMahon, bookplate of Francis Galton Laboratory, initials of Florence Nightingale David, 1845. Jeff Weber Rare Books   183 - 29   2016 $1000

Quevedo, Francisco De   *Fortune in Her Wits; or the Hour of all Men.*   London: for R. Sare, F. Saunders and Tho. Bennet, 1697. First edition in English, 8vo., minor worming to inner margin of A1-A3 touching printed border of top edge gilt and two letters of text on A3, small stain to lower inner margin of D5-D6, small ink stain to blank lower margin of f1, early ownership inscription cropped from head of titlepage, 19th century calf, corners bumped and chipped, joints rubbed, from the library of James Stevens Cox (1910-1997), inscribed "W(illiam) M. Marrow, his booke 1720", inscription of Alicia Anne Shring 1835. Maggs Bros. Ltd.   1447 - 347   2016   £350

Quiller-Couch, Arthur Thomas   1863-1944   *In Powder and Crinoline.*   London: Hodder and Stoughton, 1913. 318 x 229mm., fine green morocco by Sangorski & Sutcliffe (stamp-signed), covers with single gilt fillet border upper cover with gilt titling, raised bands, gilt ruled compartments, turn-ins with single gilt fillet, marbled endleaves, top edges gilt, 26 color plates by Kay Nielsen, tipped-in on gray stock with decorative frames, each with captioned and decorated tissue guards, two leaves with short closed tear to fore margin, slight browning to edges of leaves additional trivial defects, but quite fine, clean internally in unworn binding. Phillip J. Pirages   67 - 263   2016 $2900

Quiller-Couch, Arthur Thomas   1863-1944   *The Twelve Dancing Princesses and Other Fairy Tales Retold by Sir Arthur Quiller-Couch.*   New York: George H. Doran, n.d. circa, 1915. 8vo., blue gilt pictorial cloth, fine in dust jacket, dust jacket very good to fine with some minor wear, this copy inscribed by artist, Kay Nielsen to Sarah Briggs Latimore, 16 magnificent tipped-in color plates, black and whites in text, pictorial endpapers, cover and dust jacket design, beautiful copy.   Aleph-bet Books, Inc.   111 - 324   2016 $2000

Quillet, Aristide   *Histoire du Livre et d'Une Librairie Moderene.*   Paris: Quillet, 1937. Large 8vo., pages not numbered, illustrated and printed in colors, author's presentation on half title, paper wrappers, little stain on flyleaf and cover, otherwise very good.   Second Life Books, Inc.   196 B - 449   2016 $75

Quinn, Tom   *BB. A Celebration.*   Barnsley: Wharncliffe Publishing Ltd., 1993. First edition, 8vo., original cloth and dust jacket, photographic plates, illustrations by author, presentation inscription, price clipped, otherwise fine. Sotheran's   Hunting, Shooting & Fishing - 243   2016   £150

Quinnell, A. J.   *The Mahdi.*   London: Macmillan, 1981. First edition, fine in dust jacket.   Mordida Books   2015 - 011502   2016 $65

Quintilianus, Marcus Fabius   *De Institutione Oratoria Libri Duodecim ad Codicum Veterum Fidem...*   Lipsiae: Sumtibus Siegfried Lebrecht Crusi (Volumes I_IV) Sumptiubs Frid. Christ. Guil. Vogelii (Volumes V-VI), 1798-1834. 6 volumes, 8vo., occasional spots of foxing, generally bright, small closed tear to vol. IV titlepage, mid 20th century half light tan calf, red morocco spine labels, red marbled paper boards, edges lightly sprinkled brown, contrasting marbled endpapers, some patchy color variation to spines, possibly from leather dressing, little rubbed but very good set, with "David M. Gaunt (rebound Jan. 1968)".   Unsworths Antiquarian Booksellers Ltd.   E05 - 10   2016   £675

Quisumbing, Eduardo A.   *The Complete Writings of....on Philippine Orchids.*   Manila: Eugenio Lopez Foundation, 1981. Octavo, 2 volumes, color plates, publisher's vinyl binding, very good.   Andrew Isles Natural History Books 55 - 38083   2016 $100

R

R. & A. Main, Ltd., Gothic Iron Works *London and Falkirk Contractors to the Admiralty and War Office.* London?: 1923. 4to., half tone illustrations, original red boards, upper cover with title gilt on black.   Marlborough Rare Books   List 55 - 16   2016   £125

Raban, Jonathan *Hunting Mister Heartbreak.* London: Collins Harvill, 1990. First edition, 8vo., original ivory cloth, dust jacket.   J. & S. L. Bonham Antiquarian Booksellers America 2016 - 9798   2016   £25

Rabelais, Francois *Pantagruel.* Paris: Albert Skira, 1943. No. 85 of 275 copies on velin d'arches, signed by artist, 350 x 285mm., magnificent contemporary chocolate brown crushed morocco, elaborately inlaid and gilt by Leon Gruel (stamp signed on front turn-in), covers with exuberant Groliersque design of intricate dark red morocco strapwork accented with swirling azured gilt foliage and small tools, raised bands, spine in compartments framed by red morocco inlays, gilt fleuron centerpieces, gilt titling, chocolate brown morocco doublures framed with multiple gilt rules and azured foliate cornerpieces, rose colored watered silk endleaves, all edges gilt, original printed wrappers bound in, housed in original suede-lined chestnut morocco backed chemise and matching morocco trimmed slipcase, with 180 hand colored wood engravings by Andre Derain, 22 of them full page, 94 in text, 34 initials, 27 tailpieces, title engraving to front wrapper, frontispiece and title vignette, printed in Garamond typeface by Georges Gerard, wood engravings printed by Roger Lacouriere, flawless copy.   Phillip J. Pirages   67 - 46   2016 $33,000

Rabelais, Francois *The Works of the Famous Mr. Francis Rabelais, Doctor in Physick...* London: for Richard Bentley and are to be sold by John Starkey, 1664. First edition in English, 2nd issue, small rust spot on E8 and G1, small piece torn away from fore-edge of M8 (not touching text), dark stain near inner margin of D1, minor tear to lower edge of (2) N& (just touching last line of text), lower edge of)2 uncut, contemporary sheep ruled in blind, rebacked, corners repaired, new endleaves, from the library of James Stevens Cox (1910-1997), contemporary ink signature of James Chamberlayne.   Maggs Bros. Ltd.   1447 - 348   2016   £950

Rabier, Benjamin *Le Buffon de Benjamin Rabier.* Paris: Librairie Garnier Freres, n.d., 1913. First edition, 4to., contemporary quarter red morocco, gilt lettering and decoration to spine, marbled boards, marbled endpapers, top edges gilt, 33 full color plates, color text illustrations, little rubbing to edges of binding, little chipping to fore-edge of first couple of leaves, otherwise very good, prize bookplate and ex-libris bookplate of Frazier McCann.   Sotheran's   Piccadilly Notes - Summer 2015 - 248   2016   £800

Raby, Peter *The Stratford Scene.* Toronto: Clarke Irwin, 1968. First edition, oblong quarto signed by numerous actors and actresses at their inclusions - Kate Reid, Douglas Campbell, Helen Burns, Richard Monette, Alan Bates, Christopher Walken, very good plus, lacking dust jacket, slight spine lean and light soil.   Royal Books   48 - 37   2016 $475

Racine, Jean *Andromache: a Tragedy, Freely Translated into English in 1674.* Lexington: Anvil Press, 1986. Limited to 100 numbered copies, Small 4to., cloth backed boards, paper spine label, dust jacket, very fine.   Oak Knoll Books   310 - 77   2016 $850

Rackham, Arthur *Arthur Rackham's Book of Pictures.* London: William Heinemann, 1913. No. 511 of 1030 copies signed by artist, 294 x 230mm., appealing burgundy morocco by Zaehnsdorf for E. Joseph (stamp-signed), upper cover with gilt titling and pelican insignia, raised bands, densely gilt turn-ins, marbled endpapers, top edge gilt, other edges untrimmed, few vignettes in text, 44 color plates mounted on brown paper, all with lettered tissue guards, faint crease to frontispiece plate, tiny notch at bottom edge of frontispiece mount, otherwise extremely fine, binding unusually lustrous and virtually unworn, plates clean and fresh, bright copy. Phillip J. Pirages   67 - 291   2016 $1900

Rackham, Bernard *Catalogue of English Porcelain, Earthenware, Enamels and Glass Collected by Charles Schreiber and the Lady Charlotte Elizabeth Schreiber.* London: Victoria and Albert Museum, 1924. New edition, 3 volumes, small quarto, 230 black and white photographs, blue cloth, gilt, light rubbing to extremities, very light wear to spine only, near fine set.   Argonaut Book Shop   Pottery and Porcelain 2015 - 4999   2016 $275

Rackham, Bernard *Catalogue of the Glaisher Collection of Pottery & Porcelain in the Fitzwilliam Museum, Cambridge.* Cambridge: Cambridge University Press, 1935. First edition, scarce thus, thick folio, 37 color plates and 286 black and white multi-image plates, blue cloth gilt bevelled edges, two upper corners and foot of spine of volume I bit jammed, overall fine, with slightly chipped and spine darkened dust jacket printed in red and black, magnificent catalogue.   Argonaut Book Shop   Pottery and Porcelain 2015 - 4998   2016 $900

Radbill, Samuel X. *Bibliography of Medical Ex Libris Literature.* Los Angeles: Hilprand Press, 1951. 15 plates plus tipped in frontispiece, with autograph letter from author tipped in plus two articles.   James Tait Goodrich   X-78 - 452   2016 $125

Radcliffe, Alexander   *Ovidius Exulans ur Ovid Travestie.* London: by Peter Lillicrap for Samuel Speed, 1673. First edition, small 8vo., engraved portrait bust, washed and pressed, late 19th century polished calf by F. Bedford, covers with triple gilt fillet, gilt spine, marbled endleaves, gilt edges, joints rubbed. from the library of James Stevens Cox (1910-1997). the copy of W. E. Bonds, of Enderby House, Clapham, London, the copy of George Thorn Drury.   Maggs Bros. Ltd.   1447 - 350   2016   £1100

Radcliffe, Ann Ward   1764-1823   *The Romance of the Forest.* London: printed for T. Hookham and J. Carpenter, 1792. Third edition, 3 volumes, 12mo., old stain to gutter margin pages 200-206 volume I, otherwise very clean, early ownership name of Fanny (?) Hunt, Christian names erased causing hole to volume 1 titlepage, key pattern bands, gilt stars, red and black morocco labels, hinges and spines little rubbed, very good.   Jarndyce Antiquarian Booksellers   CCXVI - 485   2016   £280

Radcliffe, Ann Ward   1764-1823   *A Sicilian Romance.* London: printed for Hookham and Carpenter, 1796. Volume I second edition, volume II third edition, 12mo., some faint waterstaining to upper margins, horizontal crease to volume II D3 (original flaw in binding), contemporary quarter calf, marbled boards, vellum tips, gilt banded spines, black morocco labels, some rubbing to boards, joints slightly cracked, volume II bound without half title, final digit of imprint date in volume I has been amended to 6 probably by publisher.   Jarndyce Antiquarian Booksellers   CCXVI - 486   2016   £380

Rae, John   *Why: Reflections for Children.*   New York: Dodd, Mead, Oct., 1910. Thick blue cloth, pictorial paste-on, slight cover rubbing, else complete and very good-fine, illustrations by author on every page.   Aleph-bet Books, Inc.   112 - 418   2016 $400

Rae, Simon   *Allotment.*   Alton: Prospero Press, 1996. 57/60 copies from an edition of 499 copies, signed by poet and by artist, frontispiece, titlepage vignette and 4 further small wood engravings by Miriam Macgregor, crown 8vo., original boards with MacGregor wood engraving printed in green to front, fine.   Blackwell's Rare Books   B184 - 254   2016   £55

Raffray, Achille   *Coleoptera: Family Pselaphidae.* Brussels: L. Desmet-Verteneuil, 1908. Quarto, 9 lithographed plates, contemporary half green morocco, rubbed, the copy of Erasmus Wilson.   Andrew Isles Natural History Books   55 - 38319   2016 $350

Ragland, J. Farley   *Rhymes of the Times.*   New York: Wendell Malliet and Co., 1946. First edition, owner's name front pastedown, else fine in very good dust jacket with slight chipping and short tears to upper extremities, signed by author, uncommon.   Between the Covers Rare Books   202 - 86   2016 $250

Raine, Kathleen   *Autobiography - Farewell Happy fields - Memories of Childhood: the Land Unknown; The Lion's Mouth - Concluding Chapters of Autobiography.*   London: Hamish Hamilton, 1973-1977. First edition, 3 volumes, octavo, photos, ownership signature, spines little creased, very good in like dust jacket (slightly creased).   Peter Ellis   112 - 319   2016   £75

Raine, Kathleen   *Cecil Collins. Painter of Paradise.* Piswich: Golgonooza Press, 1979. First edition, 38/100 copies signed by author, original sewn blue card wrappers printed in blue and copper, backstrip very slightly faded, fine.   Blackwell's Rare Books   B186 - 276   2016   £40

Raine, Kathleen   *The Collected Poems of Kathleen Raine.* London: Hamish Hamilton, 1956. First edition, fine in fine dust jacket, from the library of Stephen Spender with his bookplate.   Peter Ellis   112 - 320   2016   £65

Raine, William MacLeod   *The Vision Splendid.*   New York: Grosset & Dunlap, Reprint edition, near fine in fine dust jacket with closed tear.   Mordida Books   2015 - 010036   2016 $65

Rainforth, S. I.   *The Stereoscopic Skin Clinic.*   New York: Medical Art Pub. Co. n.d. circa, 1910. First edition, Series of 132 colored stereoscopic cards, complete with viewer, in original box, box lightly soiled, paper label rubbed, viewer and cards very good, completely functioning.   Edwin V. Glaser Rare Books   2015 - 10100   2016 $1800

Rait, Robert Sangster   *The Universities of Aberdeen. A History.*   Aberdeen: James Gordon Bisset, 1895. First edition, half title, frontispiece and plates, unopened in original black buckram, bevelled boards, very good.   Jarndyce Antiquarian Books   CCXV - 916   2016   £30

Rajic, Jovan   *Istoriia Raznykh Slavenskikh Narodov, Naipache Bolgar, Khorvatov, I Serbov.*   V Budinom Grade, tipografie Kvolevskago Universa? teta Ungarskago, 1823. Third edition of volume II (of 4), 8vo., contemporary marbled boards, faded ms. lettering piece on spine, engraved frontispiece, engraved portraits of rulers in text, folding engraved map, 4 folding typographical genealogical tables at end, binding with minor wear to extremities, title with old repair (loss of one letter), occasionally little spotted, one text leaf with marginal paper flaw, otherwise titlepage, contemporary typographical bookplate of Greek-Catholic Monastery i Przemyal, South Eastern Poland.   Sotheran's   Travel and Exploration - 278   2016   £2998

Raleigh, Walter *The Council Cabinet....* printed by Tho. Newcomb for Tho. Johnson, 1658. First edition, frontispiece (sometimes wanting), frontispiece soiled, and cut down and mounted (complete as to text and image), repair to foot of titlepage, bit browned and with minor staining towards edges, 1 headline cropped and few others just trimmed, 12mo., early 19th century calf panelled in blind, twin maroon longitudinal lettering pieces on spine, sound.   Blackwell's Rare Books   B184 - 76   2016   £2000

Raleigh, Walter *The Historie of the World in Five Books.* London: printed for B. White I. Place & G. Dawes, 1666. Early edition, small folio, 8 double page engraved maps, modern full brown calf, decoratively blindstamped on spine with five raised bands, few contemporary notations throughout, Cecil B. De Mille's copy with his bookplate.   Heritage Book Shop   Holiday 2015 - 96   2016 $2000

Raleigh, Walter *Judicious and Select Essayes and Observations.* London: by T. Warren for Humphrey Moseley, 1650. First edition, small 8vo., engraved portrait, but without 4 leaves of Moseley's ads, blank verso of engraved portrait and blank verso of last leaf stained by turn-ins and with edges slightly chipped, small repair to foot of titlepage, just touching decorated border, minor closed tear in lower inner margin of A1-2, dampstaining to inner margins of G4-(2)C8 (touching text in places), small hole through (3)A-3 (touching two lines of text), some occasional rust spotting, mid 20th century calf, from the library of James Stevens Cox (1910-1997), early inscription of John Spelman, signature Robertus (?) Culsett, armorial bookplate of William Miller Ord (1834-1902).   Maggs Bros. Ltd.   1447 - 351   2016   £350

Ralph James *The Touch-Stone or Historical, Critical, Political, Philosophical and Theological Essays....* printed and sold by the booksellers of London and Westminster, 1728. First edition, woodcut initials, head and tailpieces bit browned and spotted in places, apparently lacking half title, 19th century half calf, flat spine gilt in compartments, red lettering piece, skillfully rebacked, book label inside front cover of Mr. B. Warren, sound.   Blackwell's Rare Books   B186 - 128   2016   £950

Ramazzini, Bernardini *Opera Omnia Medica et Physiologica in Duos Tomos Distributia.* Venetiis: Apud Andream Poletti, 1750. 4to., 5 engraved plates, early limp boards, text foxed, uncut.   James Tait Goodrich   X-78 - 483   2016 $1250

Ramey, John *A Letter to R. F. Esq.* Yarmouth?: printed in the year, 1759. First (only) edition, old (original?) marbled wrappers, very good, very rare.   John Drury Rare Books   2015 - 20547   2016 $306

Ramon T Cajal, Santiago *Degeneration and Regeneration of the Nervous System.* London: Oxford University Press, 1928. First English edition, Engraved frontispiece, near fine set, original binding, original dust jackets, second jacket has tear to front, rare in this condition.   James Tait Goodrich   X-78 - 484   2016 $1595

Ramsay, Allan   1686-1758 *The Gentle Shepherd, a Scotch Pastoral.* London: printed for the author by T. Bensley, 1790. Octavo, recent half morocco and marbled boards, period style, dark green morocco label, gilt rules and lettering, boards little rubbed, fine.   The Brick Row Book Shop   Miscellany 69 - 67   2016 $300

Ramsay, Allan   1686-1758 *Thoughts on the origin and Nature of Government. Occasioned by the Late Disputes between Great Britain and Her American Colonies.* London: for T. Becket and P. A. de Hondt 1769, i.e., 1768. Neat modern paper covered boards, fine in morocco backed cloth folding box.   Joseph J. Felcone, Inc.   Books from Five Centuries: a Miscellany - 121   2016 $1500

Ramsay, E. Pierson *Catalogue of the Australian Accipitres or Diurnal Birds of Prey Inhabiting Australia in the Collection of the Australian Museum at Sydney.* Sydney: The Minister of Justice and Public Instruction, 1876. Octavo, early binder's cloth, gilt title, rebacked with new endpapers.   Andrew Isles Natural History Books   55 - 7727   2016 $60

The Rand-McNally Atlas of China. Chicago: Rand McNally & Co., 1900. First printing thus (presumed), 6 full color maps, 4 double page, text illustrated with 16 photographic images, folio, green paper wrappers, printed in blue, light toning and edge chipping to wrappers, with 2 1/2 x 2 1/2 inch triangle of loss to lower corner of front wrapper, faint dampstain to foot of front wrapper and gutter foot throughout, small closed tear to fore-edge of rear wrapper and last few leaves, pages otherwise clean and bright, about frontispiece.   Tavistock Books   Getting Around - 40   2016 $395

Rand, Ayn *Atlas Shrugged.* New York: Random House, 1957. Tenth Anniversary edition, limited to 2000 signed copies, this no. 526, 8vo., original clear plastic dust jacket, near fine original paper covered slipcase with mild sunning.   By the Book, L. C.   45 - 5   2016 $2350

Rand, Ayn *Atlas Shrugged.* New York: Random House, 1957. First edition, first issue, fine, thick octavo, original green cloth, original dust jacket, beautiful, outstanding copy.   Manhattan Rare Book Company   2016 - 1807   2016 $3900

Rand, Ayn *Atlas Shrugged.* New York: Random House, 1957. First edition, fine and unread in about fine dust jacket, jacket unrestored with uniformly deep colors and brilliant unblemished and unfaded topstain, only touch of rubbing at crown to note and none of the usual toning to spine, wonderful association copy, inscribed by author for William W. Brainard, Jr.   Royal Books   52 - 1   2016 $25,000

Rand, Gloria *Sailing Home: a Story of a Childhood at Sea.* New York: North South Books, 2001. First edition, signed by Gloria and Red Rand, fine, like new in dust jacket, illustrations.   Gene W. Baade, Books on the West   2015 - 5009072   2016 $41

Rand, Harry *The Clouds.* Washington: Dove Press, 1996. Limited to 35 numbered copies, this one of 25 regular signed copies, 4to., gray cloth with darker gray morocco, spine printed in palladium, publisher's slipcase, 10 original lithographs by Elaine Kurtz, 8 full page lithographs hand pulled by Judith Slodkin in collaboration with the artist at Solo Impressions, NY, with two double-page images of approximately 14 x 20 inches, many images required multiple plates and the artist's hand applique of color and mica, design and typography of book by Jerry Kelly, text printed letterpress by Stinehour Press, Lunenberg, VT, type face is Robert Slimbach's Minion Paper for both text and images is Heavyweight Rives BFK 250 gsm., each print has Japanese paper overlay imprinted with short segment from the text, sewn and hand bound by Judi Conant, 4to., gray cloth with darker gray morocco spine printed in palladium, publisher's slipcase.   Oak Knoll Books   27 - 9   2016 $1250

Randolph, Peter *From Slave Cabin to Pulpit, the Autobiography of the Rev. Peter Randolph: The Southern Question Illustrated and Sketches of Slavery.* Boston: James H. Earle, 1893. First expanded edition, octavo, frontispiece, illustrated cloth boards, small label with 1894 copyright date and author's name on titlepage, contemporary owner's name, cheap paper browned as always, front hinge tender, modest rubbing to pictorial binding, very good.   Between the Covers Rare Books   202 - 76   2016 $500

Randolph, Thomas *Poems.* London: for F. Bowman, and are to be sold by William Roybould, 1652. Fourth edition, small 8vo., engraved titlepage, small stain at head of engraved titlepage, paper flaw in lower corner of (2)(N), upper corners of (2)C1-7 dampstained, rust spot to head of I1, type ornament border of title closely shaved and border of subtitle to 'Aristippus' slightly shaved, early 19th century calf, covers ruled in blind, front joint cracked, lower joint and headcaps rubbed, small hole in spine, from the library of James Stevens Cox (1910-1997), contemporary signature of Dorothy Howland with crude ink drawing.   Maggs Bros. Ltd.   1447 - 353   2016   £150

Randolph, Thomas *The Poems with Muses Looking Glass and Amyntas.* Oxford: Printed for F. Bowman, 1668. Fifth edition (though titlepage reads sixth edition), engraved frontispiece, 8vo., full gilt in 19th century paneled calf, elaborate gilt spine and panels, all edges gilt.   James Tait Goodrich   X-78 - 485   2016 $750

Randolph, Thomas *Poems with the Muses Looking-Glasse, and the Amyntas.* London: in the year, 1643. Third edition, titlepage lightly soiled, some light soiling and staining, full modern calf, from the library of James Stevens Cox (1910-1997), with his pencil annotations to front pastedown, signature of Thomas Stringer, 1678, (K?) Stringer signature dated 1693,.   Maggs Bros. Ltd.   1447 - 352   2016   £250

Randolph, Thomas *Poems with the Muses Looking-Glass and Amyntas.* Oxford: for F. Bowman and are to be sold by John Crosley, 1668. Fifth (i.e. sixth) edition, small 8vo., with half title, leaves A1-P8 lightly browned, small piece torn away from blank corner of C4 and with small closed tear to lower margin of L4, some small spots, minor hole through P7 (touching text) and with sheet S closely trimmed, but with no loss of text, early 20th century calf, gilt spine by Birdsall & Son of Northampton, joints rubbed and slightly cracked at head and tail, some insect damage at foot of spine, from the library of James Stevens Cox (1910-1997), armorial bookplate, Ambrose Isted (1717-81) of Ecton Hall, Northamptonshire.   Maggs Bros. Ltd.   1447 - 354   2016   £180

Ranjitsinhji, K. S. *The Jubilee Book of Cricket.* Edinburgh and London: 1898. First edition, frontispiece, plates, covers little marked, titlepage shaved and some spotting, especially to endpapers, very good.   Bertram Rota Ltd.   Christmas List 2015 - 37   2016   £60

Rankin, Ian *Set in Darkness.* London: Orion, 2000. First edition, fine in dust jacket.   Mordida Books   2015 - 012732   2016 $65

Ransom, Will *Selective Check Lists of Press Books, a Compilation of all Important & Significant Private Presses, or Press Books Which are Collected.* New York: Philip C. Duschnes, 1945-1950. Complete set of the supplements, 12 parts in 9 volumes, 8vo., paper wrappers, some fading along edges of covers.   Oak Knoll Books   310 - 265   2016 $125

Ransome, Arthur *Aladdin and His Wonderful Lamp.* London: Nister, n.d., 1919. Limited to only 250 numbered copies signed by MacKenzie, large 4to., white cloth with elaborate gilt pictorial cover, top edge gilt, other edges uncut, slightest of fading to spine, else fine, 12 magnificent tipped in color plates with tissue guards, decorative initials and text borders, profusion of stunning black and whites on every page by Thomas Mackenize.   Aleph-bet Books, Inc.   112 - 301   2016 $6250

Ransome, Arthur *The Picts and the Martyrs or Not Welcome at All.* London: Jonathan Cape, 1941. First edition, 8vo., recently attractively bound in half dark green calf over dark green cloth boards, spine with 5 raised bands, ruled and lettered gilt with gilt centres, top edge gilt, original pictorial map endpapers laid down and bound in at rear, black and white illustrations, fine.   Sotheran's Piccadilly Notes - Summer 2015 - 251   2016   £225

Raoul-Duval, Robert *Au Transvaal et dans le Sud-Africain avec les Attachees Militaires.* Paris: Charles Delagrave, 1902. First edition, 8vo., privately bound for publisher in tan goatskin, ornamented in blind, lettered in gilt, including Delagrave's name on front cover, original purple wrappers printed in white bound in (vignette of a machine gunner at end), top edge gilt, marbled endpapers, title with vignette printed in red and black, frontispiece with tissue guard, facsimile of author's dedication note, tinted portrait of South African president and numerous facsimiles, photographic illustrations, many full page, most of them tinted in various colours, binding minimally rubbed, two illustrations little smudged during printing, fine.   Sotheran's Travel and Exploration - 29   2016   £348

Raphael, John Nathan *Pictures of Paris & Some Parisians.* London: Adam & Charles Black, 1908. Proof copy, 8vo., 12 half tone plates and numerous text illustrations, contemporary blue half morocco, spine decorated and lettered gilt, top edge gilt, inscribed "The Proofs of a small book for the sweetest of small darlings, John N. Raphael Paris July 1908".   Marlborough Rare Books   List 55 - 59   2016   £185

Raphaelson, Samson *Jason.* New York: Random House, 1942. First printing, 8vo., author's presentation on flyleaf, very good in chipped and torn dust jacket.   Second Life Books, Inc.   196 B - 453   2016 $40

Rapilly, Georges *Catalogue de Livres D'Art Architecture et Decoration Peinture, Sculpture, Gravure, Arts Industriels et D'Estampes, Anciennes, et Modernes en Vente Chez Georges Rapilly Marchand D'Estampes De La Bibliotheque Nationale Libraire De L'Ecole Nationale Des Beaux Arts.* Paris: Georges Rapilly, 1888-1908. 4 volumes, each contains about 20 sales catalogues (each of which is 40 pages long), small 8vo., volume 1 half leather with marbled paper covered boards, volume 2 full cloth, volume 3 and 4 quarter cloth with marbled paper covered boards, original paper wrappers bound in, rear board detached on volume one, some early pages have also detached, minor rubbing and chipping to covers.   Oak Knoll Books   310 - 302   2016 $350

Rappoport, Lisa *A Flame in the Heart.* Oakland: Littoral Press, 2002. Number 6 of 125 copies, this one of 10 from the deluxe edition and signed on colophon by 16 of the 17 contributors, beautiful accordion book bound in red and black Thai Unryl reversible paper with black title label to front over, printed with handset Garamond type on Joahhnot paper with black and blood-red ink, each volume has unique pastepaper endpapers, book 11 x 7 inches folded and 18 feet long unfolded, fine.   The Kelmscott Bookshop   13 - 32   2016 $500

Rarey, J. S. *The Modern Art of Taming Wild Horses.* Columbus: printed by the Ohio State Journal Co., 1857. 16mo., original printed wrappers, spine worn, corner chipped, light stain and short tear on front wrapper, very good, very rare.   M & S Rare Books, Inc.   99 - 259   2016 $425

Raspe, Rudolf Erich   1737-1794 *Surprisng Adventures of the Renowned Baron Munchausen...* London: Thomas Tegg, 1809. Half title, folding frontispiece and 8 plates after Rowlandson, hand colored, small closed tear in out margin of frontispiece, late 19th century half red morocco, spine gilt, very slight rubbing, top edge gilt, very good, with 2 rare original drawings by Rowlandson.   Jarndyce Antiquarian Booksellers   CCXVII - 244   2016   £1850

Raspe, Rudolf Erich   1737-1794 *The Travels of Baron Munchausen...* Duncombe: 19 Little Queen Street, Holborn, 1829. 12mo., frontispiece and 3 other illustrations, final page torn without loss, original half red roan, marbled boards, little rubbed, ownership inscription recto of frontispiece of Samuel Elliot Jan. 125 1830.   Jarndyce Antiquarian Booksellers   CCXVII - 245 2016   £125

Raswan, Carl R. *Black Tents of Arabia.* London: Hutchinson, 1935. Scarce first edition, 8vo., original black cloth, lettered in white (remainder binding), numerous illustrations from photos, one folding table of named horses, cloth little browned with lettering of spine partially lost, else very good.   Sotheran's Travel and Exploration - 364   2016   £798

Rathbone, Frederick *Old Wedgwood. The Decorative or Artistic Ceramic Work in Colour and Relief Invented and Produced by Josiah Wedgwood 1760-1794.* Merion: Bulen Museum of Wedgwood, 1968. Reprint, 67 full page illustrations, smaller text illustrations, green cloth, gilt, very fine. Argonaut Book Shop   Pottery and Porcelain 2015 - 5006   2016 $75

Rather, Lois *R. W. Emerson. Tourist. the Story of Ralph Waldo Emerson's Visit to California in 1871.* Oakland: Rather Press, 1979. First edition, number 22 of 150 copies, bound by Clif and Lois Rather at the Rather Press, 8 illustrations, decorative boards, green cloth spine, upper corners slightly bumped, else fine.   Argonaut Book Shop   Biography 2015 - 3559   2016 $60

Ratisbon, Rosa Mullholland *The First Christmas for Our Dear Little Ones.* New York: Cincinnati: Frederick Pustet, 1875. 4to., cloth backed pictorial boards, edges rubbed, else very good+, printed on rectos only, 15 fine and beautifull full page color illustrations by Diefenbach, beautiful book. Aleph-bet Books, Inc. 111 - 89 2016 $400

Rattigan, Nancy *The Confessions of a Siamese Cat Prince.* Lahore: printed at the Civil and Military Press, 1914. 4to., original illustrated cream printed paper boards, light blue cloth spine, inscription "To Lady Kensington with love from Nancy 12 March 1914". Jarndyce Antiquarian Booksellers CCXVII - 246 2016 £180

Rattigan, Terence *The Deep Blue Sea: a New Play.* London: Hamish Hamilton, 1952. First edition, 8vo., nice in dust jacket, signed by members of the NY production, including director Frith Banbury, Betty Sinclair, Margaret Sullavan, Stella Andrew and 4 others. Second Life Books, Inc. 196 B - 454 2016 $250

Rattigan, Terence *The Winslow Boy.* London: Hamish Hamilton, 1946. First edition, 8vo., very good, signed by 10 of the 11 cast members,. Second Life Books, Inc. 196 B - 455 2016 $350

Rauch, Earl Mac *New York, New York.* New York: Simon and Schuster, 1977. First edition, fine in very near fine dust jacket with slight toning on spine and tiny tear on front panel, uncommon. Between the Covers Rare Books 204 - 101 2016 $300

Rauch, S. A. *Catalogue De Beaux Livres; Ventes Rausch.* Geneve: N. Rauch, 1948-1964. Sales catalogues, 8vo., auction catalogues large 8vo., cloth with paper or leather spine labels, stiff paper wrappers, 3 additional catalogues from the early 1960's in stiff paper wrappers, and three slim bulletins. Oak Knoll Books 310 - 69 2016 $750

Raulston, Marion Churchill *Memories of Owen Humphrey Churchill and His Family.* Los Angeles: by the author, 1950. First edition, printed in small edition, presentation inscription, signed by author, numerous photos and portraits, one color plate, half cloth and boards, small remnants to inner cover from removed news article, but fine copy. Argonaut Book Shop Biography 2015 - 7631 2016 $125

Raven, Simon *Alms for Oblivion. The Rich Pay late. friends in Low Places....* Anthony Blond or Blond & Briggs, 1964-1976. First editions, small stain at head of one page in 6th volume, occasional top corner creasing to same, corrective pencil note to margin of 9th volume, original boards, backstrips lettered silver, gilt or white, very occasional spotting or toning to edges, bookplate of M. Bernard Thorold to fourth volume, ownership inscription to flyleaf of 9th volume, few handling marks to rear free endpaper of final volume, dust jackets in good shape with that to last volume price clipped, very good overall. Blackwell's Rare Books B184 - 224 2016 £900

Raven, Simon *The Feathers of Death.* A. Blond, 1959. Very good, slightly marked, rubbed and frayed dust jacket. I. D. Edrich Crime - 2016 £30

Ravenscroft, Edward *The London Cuckolds.* London: for Jos. Hindmarsh, 1688. Second edition, small 4to., small dampstain to blank fore-margin throughout, closely cropped along lower edge with occasional cropping of signatures, 20th century half morocco and marbled boards, from the library of James Stevens Cox (1910-1997) with note of Maggs Bros. sale to him and his notes on front pastedown. Maggs Bros. Ltd. 1447 - 355 2016 £150

Raverat, Gwen *The Wood Engravings.* Cambridge: Silent Books, 1989. Second edition, numerous examples of artist's work, 4to., original blue boards, backstrip lettered gilt, small bump to bottom corner of lower board, few faint foxspots to top edge, illustrated endpapers, dust jacket with backstrip panel very gently faded, very good. Blackwell's Rare Books B186 - 331 2016 £60

Ravilious, Eric *Wood Engravings.* Lion and Unicorn Press, 1972. 108/120 copies from an edition of 500 copies printed, printed on Basingwerk Parchment paper, 421 wood engravings reproduced as line drawings on 113 plates, including some folding plans, double page titlepage, frontispiece portrait, folio, original fawn canvas, backstrip little darkened and blocked in black, front cover with title and author at head of cover, large Ravilious engraving beneath, all in black, patterned endpapers, cloth slipcase, near fine. Blackwell's Rare Books B184 - 285 2016 £600

Rawlet, John *Poetick Miscellanies of Mr. John Rawlet, B.D.....* London: for Samuel Tidmarsh, 1687. First edition, 8vo., portrait trimmed down and mounted at later date, without first blank leaf, long crease with very small closed tear (5mm) to titlepage, two ink spots recto of K4 (one just touching text), small rust spot, modern half red morocco and cloth boards, from the library of James Stevens Cox (1910-1997). Maggs Bros. Ltd. 1447 - 356 2016 £320

Rawlings, Marjorie Kinnan *Cross Creek.* New York: Scribner's, 1945. Reprint, 8vo., decorations by Edward Shenton, author's signature on blank, green cloth stamped in silver, ex-library with stamps, spine label and pocket, cover scuffed and somewhat worn at edges and spine ends, otherwise very good.   Second Life Books, Inc.   196 B - 457   2016 $45

Rawlinson, Richard *The English topographer or an Historical Account (as far as can be collected from Printed books and manuscripts).* London: printed for T. Jauncy at the Angel without Temple-Bar, 1720. First and sole 18th century edition, engraved text illustrations, one pasted in, 8vo., some foxing and light browning, full contemporary calf, gilt ruled border, gilt decorated spine, morocco label, spine rather rubbed, label chipped, upper joint cracked but firm, slight insect damage to boards, good plus.   Jarndyce Antiquarian Booksellers   CCXVI - 487   2016   £220

Rawson, Elizabeth *The Spartan tradition in European Thought.* Oxford: Clarendon Press, 1969. First edition, 8vo., 6 plates, blue boards, gilt lettered to spine, little shelf-wear, very good, dust jacket, spine faded and fraying, corners worn, few small tears, some with loss, shelfworn, but still good.   Unsworths Antiquarian Booksellers Ltd.   E04 - 92   2016   £30

Ray, David *Gathering Firewood. New Poems and Selected.* Middletown: Wesleyan University Press, 1974. First edition, decorated wrappers, inscribed and signed in 1974 for William Meredith, ALS with postcard by Ray to Meredith as well as large promotional card for the book from David Ingatow, near fine.   Charles Agvent   William Meredith - 104   2016 $60

Ray, John *Catalogus Plantarum Circa Cantabrigiam Nascentium....* Cambridge: Excudebat Joann. Field., Impensis Gulielmi Nealand, 1660. First edition, 8vo., Keynes' corrected titlepage 'B', lightly browned throughout and with some spotting to D1-4 and L4, contemporary limp vellum, painted green (paint rubbing away) particularly on spine, from the library of James Stevens Cox (1910-1997). Maggs Bros. Ltd.   1447 - 157   2016   £575

Ray, John *A Collection of English Proverbs Digested into a Convenient Method for the Speedy Finding Any One Upon Occasion; with Short Annotations.* Cambridge: by John Hayes for W. Morden, 1678. Second edition, 8vo., light intermittent soiling and dampstaining throughout, blank margin of B5 soiled, 19th century calf, ruled in blind, rebacked, new endpapers, from the library of James Stevens Cox (1910-1997), 18th century ownership inscription James Nicol, Traquair Manse.   Maggs Bros. Ltd.   1447 - 358   2016   £300

Ray, John *Synopsis Methodica Animalium Quadruperdum et Serpentini Generis.* London: Impensis S. Smith & B. Walford, 1693. First edition, 8vo., engraved portrait, sheets B-M browned due to poor paper quality, all others clean, printer's crease across lower corner of page 67 but no loss of text, contemporary sprinkled calf, front cover detached, label missing, from the library of James Stevens Cox (1910-1997), contemporary inscription 'AAA 50', inscription 'E Libris Eduardi Nelthorpe Admi/1720', and "E Libris G. D. Kent CCC Oxon".   Maggs Bros. Ltd.   1447 - 359   2016   £220

Ray, John *The Wisdom of God Manifested in the Works of the Creation, in Two Parts.* London: for Samuel Smith, 1692. Second edition, 8vo., contemporary calf, covers panelled gilt with vase and flower tool in each corner, gilt spine with red morocco label (corners worn, top corner of lower cover chewed, area of surface insect damage at foot of the lower cover), from the library of James Stevens Cox (1910-1997), inscribed "The Gift of Mrs. Ray to John Morley July 31 1707", and signatures 'Jane Dorothy Harvey 1849' and 'C. H. Rikerman(?) 1885'.   Maggs Bros. Ltd.   1447 - 360   2016   £500

Ray, Milton S. *The Poet and the Messenger.* San Francisco: Grabhorn Press, 1945. First edition, one of 250 copies, very scarce, printed in Franciscan handset type on French handmade paper, quarto, initials by Mallette Dean on title and throughout text in red, decoration on title, opening lines of dedication, numbering of poems, all in turquoise, opening initials of foreword in gold, colophon printed in red, printer's device in turquoise, orange decorated boards, white vellum back lettered in gold, bookplate, minor offsetting to endpapers, very fine.   Argonaut Book Shop   Literature 2015 - 5856   2016 $175

Rayment, Tarlton *Bees of the Portland District.* Portland: Portland Field Naturalist Club, 1953. Octavo, wrappers, text illustrations fine, scarce.   Andrew Isles Natural History Books   55 - 19708   2016 $40

Rayment, Tarlton *A Cluster of Bees: Sixty Essays on the Life Histories of Australian Bees.* Sydney: Endeavour press, 1935. Octavo, colored frontispiece and numerous illustrations, publisher's gilt decorated rexine, very good, scarce.   Andrew Isles Natural History Books   55 - 7757   2016 $1800

Raymond, Joseph Howard *History of the Long Island College Hospital and Its Graduates Together with Hoagland Laboratory...* Brooklyn: 1899. Frontispiece, text illustrations, original red gilt cloth, spine faded.   James Tait Goodrich   X-78 - 381   2016 $150

Rayner, Barnabas *The Dumb Man of Manchester.* London: E. Lloyd, n.d. circa, 1837. Small 4to., unbound, engraved illustration to first page, uncut and unopened, some dusting and fraying to edges.   Dramatis Personae 119 - 133   2016 $85

Rayner, Menzies *Universalism a Doctrine of Works of all Acceptance. A Sermon Delivered at Monroe, Conn....* 1827. First edition, 8vo., removed, foxed.   M & S Rare Books, Inc.   99 - 313   2016 $125

Razmara, Haj Ali *The Military Geography of the Caspian Sea.* Tehran: Government Printing House, 1941. First edition, original red cloth, lettered gilt, ornamented in blind, wire stitched, few photographic illustrations in text, 4 folding lithographic maps in rear pocket, cloth little rubbed, one map with repaired tears at folds, presentation inscription, extremely rare.   Sotheran's   Piccadilly Notes - Summer 2015 - 254   2016   £1895

Razvozzhaev, S. M. *Gde Shumit Padun.* Iirkutsk: Irkutskoe Izdatelstvo, 1957. Oblong large folio, original cloth backed illustrated boards, cord bound, 20 tinted lithographic pages in different colors, light wear to extremities, internally very good, released from Latvian library in early 1990s, with stamps on title verso and in margin of last plate, one plate with ms. shelfmark, extremely rare.   Sotheran's Travel and Exploration - 172   2016   £1950

Rea, John *Flora: seu de Florum Cultura.* London: by T. N. for George Marriott, 1676. Second edition, folio, engraved title, 8 plates, lightly browned, upper margins dusty, worming close to inner margin towards top edge, extends throughout getting worse in middle and then fanning out into a trial in text, hole in Y1 (affecting two lines), closed tear on two of the plate leaves about 3cm. long, contemporary calf, covers panelled in blind, rebacked, lower corners repaired, upper corners worn, new endleaves, old flyleaves preserved, from the library of James Stevens Cox (1910-1997), engraved label inserted between pages 52 and 53 'Laura A(nne) Calmady' of Langdon Court, ms. note on label dated 23 Oct. 1889 and states the book was bought from Wm. Wade at sale of Langdon books by Vincent Pollexfen Calmady.   Maggs Bros. Ltd.   1447 - 361   2016   £500

Read, Daniel *The Columbian Harmonist No. 1. Containing First A Plain and Concise Introduction in Psalmody fitly Calculated for the use of Singing Schools....* New Haven: printed for & sold by the editor, sold also by the Principal Booksellers in the United States, 1793-1794. first edition, 2nd issue, with variant imprint, oblong 8vo., original flexible marbled boards (goodly portion of marbled paper is no longer), last blank leaf pasted down, stitched, some browning and staining throughout, still very good.   Howard S. Mott Inc.   265 - 108   2016 $2250

Read, George *The Confectioner's and Pastry-Cook's Guide or Confectionery Made Easy...* London: Dean & Son, circa, 1855. Fifth edition, 12mo., final ad leaf, original limp green cloth, spine and back cover neatly replaced.   Jarndyce Antiquarian Books   CCXV - 360   2016   £65

Reade, Charles   1814-1884 *Christie Johnstone.* London: Richard Bentley, 1853. First edition, octavo, later brown full calf, red morocco label, gilt decorations and lettering, edges slightly rubbed, smidgen of foxing, very good.   The Brick Row Book Shop   Miscellany 69 - 68   2016 $250

Reade, Charles   1814-1884 *The Cloister and the Hearth.* London: Trubner and Co., 1861. First edition, 4 volumes, octavo, black half morocco by Tout, marbled paper sides, matching endpapers, gilt rules and lettering, top edge gilt, some foxing to blanks on volume one (apparently caused by manuscript leaf), fine, enclosed in blue cloth slipcase.   The Brick Row Book Shop   Miscellany 69 - 69   2016 $2500

Reade, Charles   1814-1884 *Peg Woffington.* London: George Allen, 1899. First Thomson illustrated edition, 8vo., rebound in full dark blue morocco by Sangorski & Sutcliffe, spine lettered and ruled in gilt with emblematic gilt centre tools, single gilt fillet border to sides, gilt border to turn-ins, marbled endpapers, all edges gilt, illustrations by Hugh Thomson, very nice.   Sotheran's   Piccadilly Notes - Summer 2015 - 303   2016   £198

Reader's Digest Complete Book of Australian Birds. Sydney: Reader's Digest, 1983. Second edition, quarto, color photos, maps, handsome modern grey morocco (Newbold and Collins, Sydney), with raised bands and two colored title inlays, decorative gilt rule, marbled endpapers, fine.   Andrew Isles Natural History Books   55 - 26559   2016 $400

Reagh, William *A Long Walk Downtown. Photographs of Los Angeles and Southern California 1936-1991.* San Francisco: Book Club of California, 2012. First edition, one of 350 copies, 130 photos by Reagh, printed letterpress by Reagh, half orange linen printed in black, gray linen boards, very fine, housed in matching slipcase.   Argonaut Book Shop   Photography 2015 - 7632   2016 $350

Rebman, Sybil *Animal Alphabet.* Chicago: Volland, 1917. 4to., cloth backed pictorial boards, some tip and edge wear, very good+, full page color illustrations by author.   Aleph-bet Books, Inc.   111 - 12   2016 $900

Rebuffat, Gaston *Mont Blanc to Everest.* London: Thomas and Hudson, 1956. First English edition, 69 photogravure plates, 8 in color, blue cloth decorated gilt, fine, pictorial dust jacket rubbed along upper edge ad has 1 1/2 inch tear to lower rear edge, half inch section missing.   Argonaut Book Shop   Mountaineering 2015 - 4482   2016 $75

Reciusione Militare *Album per l'Esposizione di Belle Arti e Mestieri in Savona.* Savona: Tip Della reciusione Militare, 1864. Text in Italian, each page framed by beautifully color printed ornaments and borders, folio, contemporary green morocco with covers with gilt fillet and corner ornaments, gilt center ornament, 32 unnumbered leaves printed on rectos only.   Oak Knoll Books   310 - 5   2016 $5000

Record, Robert *Records Arithmetick or the Ground of Arts.* London: by J. Flesher for John Harrison..., 1652. 8vo., numerous engraved tables and mathematical illustrations, large dampstains to corners in places, very small hole through 2N4 (just touching text), text-block starting to split in places, contemporary sheep spine rubbed and creased, corners slightly rubbed, from the library of James Stevens Cox (1910-1997).   Maggs Bros. Ltd.   1447 - 362   2016   £650

Record, Robert *Records Arithmetick; or the Ground of Arts...* London: by James Flesher and are to be sold by Joseph Cranford, 1662. 8vo., rust holes through E8, F8, 2A2, 2A5 and 2H4, ink blots on F2v and F34, S1-T1 lightly browned and with occasional light damp staining along the fore-margins, contemporary calf, surface cracking on spine, area of surface insect damage on lower corner, joints, corners and edges rubbed, from the library of James Stevens Cox (1910-1997).   Maggs Bros. Ltd.   1447 - 363   2016   £600

Red Riding Hood and Nursery Friends.   London: Raphael Tuck, n.d. circa, 1910. Narrow folio, pictorial boards with wrap-around color covers that are die-cut in shape of Red Riding Hood's hood, light edge wear and rubbing, very good+, full page color illustrations and large well printed brown illustrations in text by Beatrice Mallet in the style of Attwell.   Aleph-bet Books, Inc.   111 - 4   2016 $450

Redding, Cyrus *Every man His Own Butler.* London: Whitaker & Co., 1839. First edition, engraved title, original ribbed purple cloth, gilt illustrated, largely faded to brown, spine slightly rubbed at head and tail, signs of label removal, later signature of W. S. Hill, good plus copy.   Jarndyce Antiquarian Books   CCXV - 381   2016   £480

Redgrove, Peter *The God-Trap.* London: Turret Books, 1966. First edition, octavo, wrappers with flaps, number 1 of 5 copies signed by author out of a total edition of 150.   Peter Ellis   112 - 324   2016   £35

Redmond De Sainte Albine, Pierre *Le Comedine.* Paris: Vincent, 1749. Nouvelle edition, contemporary calf, worn, joints cracked but firm, top of lower joint repaired, dust soiling to edges of titlepage, engraved vignette to titlepage, 3 engraved vignettes in text.   Dramatis Personae   119 - 134   2016 $100

Redoute, Pierre Joseph *A Catalogue of Redouteana Exhibited at the Hunt Botanical Library 21 April to 1 August 1963.* Pittsburgh: Hunt Botanical Library, 1963. Octavo, illustrations, very good in slightly chipped publisher's wrappers.   Andrew Isles Natural History Books   55 - 9445   2016 $70

Reece, Erik *Field Work: Modern Poems from Eastern Forests.* Lexington: The University Press of Kentucky, 2008. First edition, 8vo., fine in dust jacket, signed by contributors Eric Reece, James Baker Hall, Wendell Berry and Richard Taylor.   Second Life Books, Inc.   196 B - 461   2016 $45

Reed, Eliot *The Maras Affair.* Garden City: Doubleday Crime Club, 1953. First edition, advance review copy with review slip laid in, signed by Dorothy Hughes, very good in dust jacket with chipped spine ends, slightly faded spine and wear at corners.   Mordida Books   2015 - 012572   2016 $65

Reed, Isaac *The Christian Traveller in Five Parts.* New York: J. & H. Harper, 1828. First edition, 18mo., errata leaf, contemporary calf backed plate boards, front cover detached, some foxing and few moderate stains.   M & S Rare Books, Inc.   99 - 261   2016 $2500

Reed, Jeremy *For David Gascoyne's Eightieth Birthday.* Edinburgh: privately printed for Alan Clodd and the author at the Tragara Press, 1996. First edition, octavo, wrappers with flaps, one of 80 unnumbered copies, signed by author, fine.   Peter Ellis   112 - 325   2016   £25

Reed, Rex *Travolta to Keaton.* New York: Morrow, 1979. First edition, 8vo., portraits, signed by Jimmy Stewart, very good in dust jacket.   Second Life Books, Inc.   196 B - 463   2016 $65

Reed, St. Clair Griffin *A History of the Texas Railroads and of Transportation Conditions Under Spain and Mexico and the Republic and the State.* Houston: St. Clair Pub., 1941. First edition, 8vo., blue cloth, gilt titles, presentation copy warmly inscribed by author to Sam Chiles, longtime railroad associate of author, no. 1733 of numbered limited edition signed by author, very good+, faint darkening of spine.   Kaaterskill Books   21 - 79   2016 $400

Reeringh, P. C. *Buchenwald: Mijn Dagboek. (Buchenwald: My Diary).* e-Gravenhage: P. C. Reeringh, 1945. First edition, quarto, 58 mimeographed leaves printed rectos only, with 10 unnumbered inserted pages with printed plates, printed stapled wrappers, rear wrapper detached, text in Dutch, very cheap paper browned with modest chip at top corner of first couple of leaves affecting no text, good copy, rare.   Between the Covers Rare Books   204 - 143   2016 $2500

Rees, Ennis *More of Brer Rabbit's Tricks.* New York: Young Scott Books, 1968. Horizontal 8vo., illustrated and signed by Edward Gorey, green cloth with pictorial stamping in red, black and white, slight nick and scuff on front cover, nice, lacks dust jacket, very good+.   Second Life Books, Inc.   196 B - 465   2016 $150

Rees, James *The Life of Edwin Forrest.* Philadelphia: Peterson, 1874. First edition, 8vo., frontispiece, gold lettering on morocco, edge rubbed, some foxing, otherwise very good.   Second Life Books, Inc.   196 B - 466   2016 $45

Reese, David M. *A Plea for the Intemperate.* New York: John S. Taylor & Co., 1841. First edition, original cloth, outer edges chewed (text margin slightly), some browning staining on lower edges.   M & S Rare Books, Inc.   99 - 305   2016 $125

Reicher, Otto *Das Faschingrennen: ein Volksbralich in der Oberen.* Grundlsee: Stamperia del Santuccio, 1937. No. 1 of 24 copies, No. 236 x 171mm., publisher's(?) later(?) oxblood paper boards, spine with letterpress label, unopened, virtually mint.   Phillip J. Pirages   67 - 188 2016 $1500

Reicher, Otto *Die Taliernreise.* Florence: Stamperia del Santuccio, 1931-1932. One of 69 copies, this being one of 14 unnumbered (reserved?) copies, 260 x 175mm., publisher's(?) later(?) oxblood paper boards, spine with letterpres slabel, in extraordinarily fine condition inside and out.   Phillip J. Pirages   67 - 189   2016 $1500

Reichlin Von Meldegg, Anton Philipp Franz Frober, Baron *A Treatise on Patroling, from the German of...* London: Calkin and Budd Booksellers to His Majesty Pall Mall, 1830. First edition, 8vo., original pink boards with some edge wear, rebacked in cloth, spine lettered, sometime in the Library of the Royal United Services Institutions, with his old blindstamp on title (and also marked for disposal on front free endpaper), very good, crisp copy, entirely uncut.   John Drury Rare Books   2015 - 22914   2016 $350

Reid, Alastair *To Lighten My House.* New York: Morgan & Morgan, 1953. One of 850 copies, 8vo., author's presentation on half title to author and editor, Barbara Howes, with her bookplate, gray cloth, stamped in red, edges little soiled, cover slightly faded, otherwise nice in very slightly chipped and soiled dust jacket.   Second Life Books, Inc.   196 B - 469   2016 $100

Reid, Forest *Pender Among the Residents.* London: W. Collins, 1922. First edition, octavo, original dark blue cloth lettered in red, spine superficially rubbed at joints, bookplate remoed, very good.   Peter Ellis   112 - 326   2016   £95

Reid, Thomas 1710-1796 *Essays on the Active Powers of Man.* Edinburgh: printed for John Bell and G. G. J. and J. Robinson, 1788. First edition, quarto, contemporary half calf with marbled boards with calf, edges gilt ruled, spines decorated in blindstamp and gilt lettering and lightly cracked, but extremely firm, little discolored with joints lightly rubbed, bookplate removed from inside front cover, but with another small bookplate remaining there, light, small early manuscript initials to titlepage, bright and clean, wide margined copy.   Athena Rare Books   List 15 - 1788   2016 $2750

Reider, William D. *The New Tablet of memory...* London: John Clements, 1841. Slightly browned, contemporary half calf, lacking label, little rubbed, later ownership signature of R. Nicholls.   Jarndyce Antiquarian Books   CCXV - 917   2016   £48

Reik, Theodor *The Unknown Murderer.* London: Hogarth Press and Institute of Psycho-Analysis, 1936. First UK edition, octavo, fine in very good dust jacket faded at spine and edges, creased at head of spine and with small chip, bright copy.   Peter Ellis   112 - 173   2016   £125

Reinhart, Matthew *Star Wards: a Pop-up Guide to the Galaxy.* New York: Orchard Books, 2007. First edition, 4to., pictorial hardbound, fine, new condition, with publisher's advance promotional signed by Reinhart, rare.   Gene W. Baade, Books on the West   2015 - SHEL593   2016 $180

A Relation of Several Hundreds of Children and others that Prophesie and Preach in Their Sleep &c. London: for Richard Baldwin, 1689. First edition, small 4to., some light soiling to first few leaves, mid 20th century half blue morocco and marbled boards by William Matthews for Maggs, from the library of James Stevens Cox (1910-1997).   Maggs Bros. Ltd.   1447 - 364   2016   £180

Remington, Frederic 1806-1919 *Crooked Trails.* New York and London: Harper and Bros., 1898. First edition, 49 plates after illustrations by author, original pictorial yellow orange cloth stamped on spine and front cover in gold, turquoise, white and lavender, binding slightly soiled, slight rubbing to spine ends, lower corners just a tad bent, very good, tight, internally fresh and clean.   Argonaut Book Shop   Literature 2015 - 6807   2016 $275

Rendell, Ruth *Heartstones.* London: Hutchinson, 1987. First edition, very fine in dust jacket.   Mordida Books   2015 - 007133   2016 $60

Rendell, Ruth *The Veiled One.* London: Hutchinson, 1988. First edition, very fine in dust jacket.   Mordida Books   2015 - 001913   2016 $60

Rentoul, Annie *Fairyland.* New York: Frederick A. Stokes, 1929. First American edition, folio, red gilt cloth, pictorial paste-on, light fading on spine, else fine in dust jacket (large piece off top edge of front cover, 2 pieces off spine, archival mends on verso), pictorial endpapers, 19 magnificent large color plates, 32 large and incredibly detailed black and white plates, plus drawings in text.   Aleph-bet Books, Inc.   111 - 330   2016 $3250

Rentoul, Annie *Little Green Road to Fairyland.* London: A. & C. Black, 1922. First edition, 4to., floral patterned boards, pictorial label, slight foxing, else near fine, 8 black and 6 white plates, 8 color plates by Ida Rentoul Outhwaite, very scarce.   Aleph-bet Books, Inc.   112 - 356   2016 $1875

Renwick, George *Romantic Corsica: Wanderings in Napoleon's Isle with a Chapter on Climbing by T. G. Ouston.* London: Fisher Unwin, 1909. First edition, folding color map, frontispiece, illustrations, original blue cloth, gilt vignette.   J. & S. L. Bonham Antiquarian Booksellers   Europe 2016 - 6409   2016   £30

Renwick, Thomas *Narrative of the Case of Miss Margaret McAvoy....* London: Baldwin Cradock and Joy (&c), 1817. First edition, 4to., frontispiece, 6 line errata slip, excellently rebound in half calf, dark green label, very good.   Jarndyce Antiquarian Booksellers   CCXVII - 247   2016   £580

Repton, Humphry   1752-1818 *An Enquiry into the Changes of Taste in Landscape Gardening to Which are Added Some Observations on Its Theory and Practice....* London: J. Taylor, 1806. First edition, 8vo., original blue paper covered boards, original titled paper label to spine, half title, some wear to spine, internally very good, Dr. Nigel Temple copy with his booklabel.   Sotheran's Piccadilly Notes - Summer 2015 - 255   2016   £2500

Reresby, John *The Memoirs of the Hon. Sir John Reresby, Bart....* London: printed for Samuel Harding, 1734. First edition in 8vo, 2 titlepages with slightly different content, first in red and black, each with woodcut device, lightly toned, sporadic foxing, few smudgy marks particularly to first titlepage, pages 225-6 torn with loss to upper corner affecting about a quarter of the text, infilled with plain paper, contemporary light brown calf, gilt label to spine, edges lightly sprinkled blue, scuffed, joints neatly repaired, some speckled marks to upper board, bookplate little offset to f.f.e.p., very good, armorial bookplate of Henry Merrik Hoare.   Unsworths Antiquarian Booksellers Ltd.   30 - 129   2016   £125

Reuter, F. Turner *Animal & Sporting Artists in America.* Middleburg: National Sporting Library, 2008. No. 139 of limited edition of 175 copies, 4to., original cloth and decorative wrapper, slipcase, color plates, black and white text illustrations, fine.   Sotheran's Hunting, Shooting & Fishing - 191   2016   £550

A Review of the Principles and Conduct of the Judges of His Majesty's Supreme Court of Judicature in Bengal... London: printed in the year, 1782. First edition, wanting half title, well bound recently in cloth, spine lettered gilt, very good, rare.   John Drury Rare Books   2015 - 19374   2016 $437

Revised Laws of Lawn-Tennis as Adopted by the Marylebone Cricket Club and the All England Croquet and Lawn Tennis Club. London: Horace Cox, The Field Office, 1881. Fourth edition, original yellow printed wrappers with ads, markef and little worn, spine repaired.   Jarndyce Antiquarian Booksellers   CCXVII - 161   2016   £580

Rewald, Sabine *The Romantic Vision of Caspar David Friedrich.* New York: Metropolitan Museum, 1990. First edition, author's presentation, small 8vo., very good.   Second Life Books, Inc.   196 B - 472   2016 $50

Rey, H. A. *Look for the Letters: a Hide and Seek Alphabet.* New York: Harper Bros., 1945. First edition, Oblong 4to., cloth backed pictorial boards, slight edge rubbing else very good+ in dust jacket (frayed on edges and 2 closed tears), full color illustrations, rare.   Aleph-bet Books, Inc.   112 - 421   2016 $750

Rey, H. A. *The Stars: a New Way to See Them.* Boston: Houghton Mifflin, 1952. First edition, 4to., pictorial cloth, small bit of edge fading, else fine in dust jacket (some soil, fraying and few closed tears), inscribed by author for Adlai Stevenson.   Aleph-bet Books, Inc.   112 - 422   2016 $1750

Rey, H. A. *Zebraology.* London: Chatto & Windus, 1953. First edition, fourth impression, landscape large 8vo., original glazed cream pictorial boards with red tie to spine, complete with original mailing envelope, pictorial printed in red and priced 2/0 net., 8 color printed plates, immaculate copy, externally and internally complete with extremely scarce original mailing envelope with just little shadowed dust soiling.   Sotheran's Piccadilly Notes - Summer 2015 - 256   2016   £188

Reynolds, Baille, Mrs. *The Lost Discovery.* New York: Doran, 1923. First edition, very good, fine in Burt reprint dust jacket.   Mordida Books   2015 - 010787   2016 $65

Reynolds, Joshua *The Works Containing His Discourses, Idlers, A Journey to Flanders and Holland....* London: printed for T. Cadell Jun. and W. Davies, 1797. 2 volumes in one, 4to., frontispiece causing light offset to title, some lower and outer margins untrimmed, volume 1 title and one or two gatherings in volume 2 lightly foxed, closed tears in lower blank portion of last leaf, contemporary gilt ruled diced calf, spine ruled and decorated in gilt, brown morocco label, marbled endpapers and edges, silk marker, trifle rubbed, engraved bookplate of Revd. Willm. G. Phillips, Elling. Hants, very handsome, clean copy with wide margins.   Jarndyce Antiquarian Booksellers   CCXVI - 490   2016   £380

Rhijne, Willem Ten *Meditationes.* Leiden: Johannes van Schuylenburgh, 1672. First edition, engraved frontispiece and folding engraved plate both designed by Ten Rhijne, little damp staining in upper margins, 12mo., original vellum over boards, lettered ink on spine, minor staining, contemporary ownership inscription of Venetian Jesuit, very good. Blackwell's Rare Books   B186 - 130   2016   £1500

Rhoads, Dorothy *Bright Feather and Other Maya Tales.* New York: Doubleday Doran and Co., 1932. Stated first edition, 8vo., fine in dust jacket chipped, few closed tears), illustrations by Lowell Houser with color frontispiece and 8 full page black and whites plus color dust jacket and endpapers, scarce.   Aleph-bet Books, Inc.   111 - 271   2016 $150

Rhodes, Eugene Manlove *The Best Novels and Stories of Eugene Manlove Rhodes.* Boston: Houghton Mifflin Co., 1949. First collected edition, map endpapers, tan cloth lettered red, fine.   Argonaut Book Shop   Literature 2015 - 7634   2016 $75

Rhodiginus, Caelius *Lectionum Antiquarum Libri Triginta.* Frankfurt: Apud Heredes Andreae Andreae Wecheli, Claudium Marnium & Ioannem Aubrium, 1599. Folio, some light foxing, ownership inscription 'Fletcher', two more inscriptions, early Dutch vellum, boards with central decorative frame blocked in blind, spine lettered in ink, little soiled, two small gouges to rear board, good.   Blackwell's Rare Books   B186 - 131   2016   £900

Rhymers' Club *The Second Book of the Rhymers' Club.* London: Elkin Mathews & John Lane, 1894. One of 650 copies, presentation from publisher John Lane, inscribed in pencil to Irish poet and novelist Katharine Tynan Hinkson, extremely uncommon thus, original brown cloth with gilt title to spine, light browning to margins of interior pages, bookplates of writer J. G. E. Hopkins, culinary writer Helmut Lothar Ripperger and collector Mark Samuels Lasner, very good.   The Kelmscott Bookshop   13 - 59   2016 $950

Rhymes of Old Times. Boston & London: Medici Society, 1925. First American edition, octavo, 16 mounted color plates and 136 silhouette and black and white drawings by Margaret Tarrant, publisher's blue cloth, front cover pictorially stamped in yellow. spine lettered in yellow, pictorial endpapers, near fine in original color pictorial dust jacket.   David Brass Rare Books, Inc.   2015 - 02977   2016 $350

Rhys, Ernest *Fairy Gold: a Book of Old English Fairy Tales.* London and New York: Dent & Dutton, 1906. First edition, thick 8vo., gilt lettered cloth, top edge gilt, light cover rubbing, else very good+, 12 color plates and 70 beautiful drawings by Herbert Cole.   Aleph-bet Books, Inc.   111 - 161   2016 $450

Ribalaigna, Constantino *Florida Bar Cocktails.* Havana: La Florida Bar Restaurant, 1935. First edition, 12mo., stapled illustrated wrappers, staples little oxidized and pressed-out crease on rear wrapper, else barely worn, near fine copy.   Between the Covers Rare Books   208 - 18   2016 $600

Ricci, James V. *One Hundred Years of Gynecology 1800-1900.* Philadelphia: Blakiston, 1945. Very faint dampstaining to top edges of pages, overall nice, author's presentation.   James Tait Goodrich   X-78 - 423   2016 $195

Riccoboni, Marie Jeanne *Letters from Juliet Lady Catesby to her friend Lady Henrietta Campley.* London: printed for R. and J. Dodsley in Pall Mall, 1764. Fourth edition, 12mo., offset browning to titlepage margins, small brown stain to upper corner of first seven leaves, small tears with slight loss to outer lower corner of few leaves not affecting text, very nicely rebound in quarter sprinkled calf, raised and gilt banded spine, red gilt morocco label, marbled boards, vellum tips.   Jarndyce Antiquarian Booksellers   CCXVI - 491   2016   £185

Rice, Anne *Interview with the Vampire.* New York: Alfred A. Knopf, 1976. First edition, fine in fine dust jacket with just touch of rubbing, housed in custom cloth clamshell case with leather spine label, lovely copy.   Between the Covers Rare Books   208 - 127   2016 $650

Rice, Anne *Interview with the Vampire.* New York: Alfred A. Knopf, 1976. Tight near fine copy with bright red top stain but with faint and tiny red dot to bottom edge of the last two pages, close to near fine dust jacket with some minor scratches, slight wear and small crease to rear flap, still lovely.   Jeff Hirsch Books   Holiday List 2015 - 60   2016 $400

Rice, Elmer *The Left Bank.* New York: Samuel French, 1931. First edition, very good, tight copy, with card list from original play program tipped to front free endpaper and printed photo of leading lady tippped to front pastedown, this copy signed by Katharine Alexander, Horace Braham and Donald Macdonald.   Second Life Books, Inc.   196 B - 475   2016 $125

Rich, Adrienne *Diving into the Wreck.* New York: W. W. Norton, 1973. First edition, as usual, price at bottom corner of front flap clipped, with price present at top, review copy with material from publisher laid in, although no indication of such, this book from William Meredith's library, fine in near fine dust jacket with small tear at rear.   Charles Agvent   William Meredith - 105   2016 $150

Rich, Adrienne *Letters Censored, Shredded, Returned to Sender or Judged Unfit to Send.*   Hopewell: Pied Oxoen Press, 2009. First edition, one of 85 numbered copies hand set and printed in ATF Garamond types, intaglio prints by Nancy Grossman, printed by Marjorie Van Dyke at Van Deb Editions in NY, signed by poet and artist and printer, David Sellers, entire edition consisted of 100 copies of which 15 wsere hors commerce and 85 for sale, folio, illustrations, original Belgian linen covered boards, recessed printed paste paper labels, as new.   James S. Jaffe Rare Books   Occasional List: Winter 2016 - 121   2016 $3500

Richard, Timothy *Forty-Five Years in China. Reminiscences.* London: T. Fisher Unwin, 1916. First edition, 8vo., very good++, orange cloth with gilt lettering to spine, minimal soil to covers, mild foxing edges, scarce, 18 photographic illustrations on coated stock printed one side only.   By the Book, L. C.   45 - 47   2016 $600

Richards, J. M. *The Castles on the Ground.* Architectural Press, 1946. First edition, frontispiece and 7 other lithographic plates in brown from drawings by John Piper, crown 8vo., original dark brown cloth, backstrip lettered gilt, faint endpaper foxing, very good, inscribed by Hubert De Cronin Hastings, for Dick & Bride.   Blackwell's Rare Books   B184 - 304   2016   £60

Richards, John William *Municipalisation of Secondary Education.* London: Simpkin, Marshall, Hamilton, Kent & Co., 1903. stapled as issued, original green wrappers, lightly dulled, library stamp on front wrapper.   Jarndyce Antiquarian Books   CCXV - 918   2016   £20

Richards, L. A. *Coleridge's Minor Poems.* N.P.: n.p., n.d., circa, 1970. First edition, octavo, wrappers, printed label on upper cover, presentation copy inscribed by author to Cleanth Brooks, wrappers faintly faded at edges, very good.   Peter Ellis   112 - 330   2016   £45

Richards, Laura E. *Captain January.* Boston: Estes & Lauriat, 1898. Edition deluxe limited to only 100 numbered copies, signed by Richards and the publisher Estes Lauriat, 12mo., printed on handmade Japanese paper and illustrated with frontispiece.   Aleph-bet Books, Inc.   111 - 386   2016 $300

Richards, Laura E. *The Silver Crown: another Book of Fables.* Boston: Little Brown, 1906. First edition, fine in pictorial boards and near fine dust jacket with very small chip at crown and other light wear, lovely copy, scarce jacket.   Between the Covers Rare Books   204 - 21   2016 $200

Richards, Laura E. *Stepping Westward.* New York: D. Appleton, 1931. First edition, 8vo., cloth backed cloth, signed by author, very good, photos.   Second Life Books, Inc.   196 B - 477   2016 $45

Richardson, Benjamin Ward *The Guild of Good Life.* London: 1884. First edition, original light brown cloth, very good, bright.   Jarndyce Antiquarian Books   CCXV - 382   2016   £65

Richardson, Ethel M. *The Lion and the Rose.* New York: E. P. Dutton & Co., 1923. First edition, fine, 1920's Grolieresque binding by Stikeman & Co., 18 full page illustrations on art paper, 2 volumes, octavo, 16 photogravure plates, handsomely bound by Stikeman (stamp signed on rear turn-ins), in full contemporary red crushed levant morocco, covers elaborately stamped in gilt marked endpapers, fine set.   David Brass Rare Books, Inc.   2015 - 03049   2016 $1950

Richardson, James Nicholson *Concerning Servants.* Gloucester: printed by John Bellow, circa, 1900. 24mo., contemporary half maroon calf, all edges gilt, inscription, initials written on titlepage.   Jarndyce Antiquarian Books   CCXV - 383   2016   £60

Richardson, John *Arctic Ordeal. The Journal of John Richardson, Surgeon-Naturalist with Franklin 1820-1822.* Kingston and Montreal: McGill - Queen's University Press and Gloucester Alan Sutton, 1984. First edition, 4to., original blue cloth, spine lettered silver, illustrated dust jacket, wrappers little sunned.   Sotheran's Travel and Exploration - 435   2016   £98

Richardson, John *A Dictionary, Persian, Arabic and English...* London: printed by J. L. Cox, 1829. large 4to., mid 20th century half calf over cloth covered boards, spine with gilt raised bands and red morocco lettering piece, signed by binder on rear turn-ins, half title discarded a long time ago, offsetting from title to old initial blank, spine little sunned, internally, apart from occasional very light spotting and toning, very good and clean copy, weight just under 7 kilos.   Sotheran's Travel and Exploration - 365   2016   £1950

Richardson, John Maunsell *Gentlemen Riders Past and Present.* Vinton, 1909. First edition, half black leather over vellum covers, very clean, tight text but endpapers spotted, inscription of owner , hinges cracking at top, extremities of covers bit worn and vellum little marked, truly presentable copy.   Simon Finch   2015 - 2016 $190

Richardson, Samuel 1689-1761 *A Collection of the Moral and Instructive Sentiments, Maxims, Cautions and Reflexions...* London: printed for S. Richardson and sold by C. Hitch & L. Hawes &c., 1755. 12mo., contemporary calf, gilt borders, red sprinkled edges, recently well rebacked with gilt bands, red label.   Jarndyce Antiquarian Booksellers   CCXVI - 492   2016   £380

Richardson, Samuel 1689-1761 *The History of Sir William Harrington.* London: printed for John Bell and C. Etherington at York, 1772. Second edition, 4 volumes, 12mo., half title to each volume, leaf of ads at end of volumes 2 and 4, all volumes affected by damp, more seriously in volume 3, completely uncut in original drab sugar paper wrappers, dampstained at top of each volume, spines little worn, remains of old ms. labels.   Jarndyce Antiquarian Booksellers   CCXVI - 493   2016   £500

Richardson, Samuel 1689-1761 *Nouvelles Lettres Angloises ou Histoire du Chevalier Grandisson.* Amsterdam: 1770. 8 volumes in 4, half titles, 12mo., 6 titlepage outer margin torn with loss, not affecting text, full contemporary mottled calf, attractive gilt decorated spines, red and black gilt labels, mottled page edges, slight wear to corners, very nice set.   Jarndyce Antiquarian Booksellers   CCXVI - 494   2016   £250

Richardson, Samuel 1689-1761 *Pamela, ou La Vertu Recompensee.* Paris: De l'Imprimerie de Plassan, 1821-1822. 2 volumes, 212, 133mm., very attractive quarter calf blindstamped in 'cathedral' style over marbled boards by by Thouvenin (stamp signed in gilt at foot of spine), corners tipped with green vellum, green blindstamped with design of Gothic arched windows, gilt titling, marbled endpapers and edges, half title with ink inscription in French stating that this book was purchased at the sale of the library of Duc de Coigny at Chateau de Franquetot on 24 April (19)12, occasional insignificant smudges or spots of foxing, paper little on inexpensive side, otherwise appealing copy with virtually no signs of use.   Phillip J. Pirages   67 - 302   2016 $900

Richmond, Florence *Golden Lark, a Symphony of Reincarnation in Seven Tableaux.* New York: Roger, 1911. First edition, 8vo., uncut in publisher's cloth, lacks front flyleaf, very good, inscribed by author to her sister.   Second Life Books, Inc.   196 B - 478   2016 $45

Richmond, Legh *Domestic Portraiture or the Successful Application of Religious Principled in the Education of a Family...* London: R. B. Seeley & W. Burnside, 1833. First edition, half title, contemporary full calf, gilt monograms, spine decorated in gilt, maroon leather label, front board scuffed, slightly rubbed, Trinity College Dublin prize label on leading pastedown.   Jarndyce Antiquarian Books   CCXV - 919   2016   £48

Richmond, William *A Series of Maritime and Mercantile Tables Illustrative of the Shipping as Connected with the Trade and Commerce of Great Britain..* Newcastle upon Tyne: printed by Hernaman and Perring, 1833. First and only edition, Large folio, handsome presentation binding of black morocco, embossed in blind, sides gilt panelled and gilt lettered on upper cover, all edges gilt, spines and extremities rather worn and covers just little warped, contents in fine state of preservation, notable presentation copy inscribed and signed in ink by author to Duke of Northumberland with Duke's armorial bookplate, scarce.   John Drury Rare Books   2015 - 26048   2016 $437

Richter, Paul *L'Art et La Medecine.* Paris: Gaultier Magnier, n.d., Tall 4to., 345 figures and illustrations, original half red roan leather and marbled boards, ex-library with stamp on title, call number on spine, spine internally very good, spine rubbed at head and tail, overall good tight copy.   James Tait Goodrich   X-78 - 488   2016 $595

Rickards, Colin *Mysterious Dave Mather.* Santa Fe: The Press of Terriorian, 1968. Limited to 1500 copies, frontispiece, illustrations, dust jacket with some light spotting, book near fine.   Dumont Maps and Books   133 - 75   2016 $50

Rickwood, Edgell *Invocations to Angels and The Happy New Year.* Wishart, 1928. First edition, foolscap 8vo., original quarter black cloth with patterned paper boards, just little rubbed to edges, edges rough trimmed, dust jacket, very good, inscribed by author to C. J. Greenwood.   Blackwell's Rare Books   B186 - 277   2016   £275

Rideal, Charles F. *Wellerisms from "Pickwick" and "Master Humphrey's Clock".* London: Roxburghe Press, 1894. Third edition, title in green, 34 page catalog (1895), uncut in original olive green cloth, bevelled boards, spine and front board lettered gilt, slightly rubbed, frontispiece by George Cruikshank.   Jarndyce Antiquarian Booksellers   CCXVIII - 162   2016   £40

Rideing, William H. *A Saddle in the Wild West.* New York: D. Appleton and Co., 1879. First edition, 12mo., orange cloth, black ink and gold lettering on front cover and spine, tan endpapers, small abrasion to lower portion of front pastedown sheet, light wear to spine ends and corners, else very good, solid copy.   Buckingham Books   2015 - 37939   2016 $475

Ridge, John Rollin *A Trumpet of Our Own.* San Francisco: Book Club of California, 1981. Limited to 650 copies, photos, cloth backed boards, gilt lettered spine, very fine with plain brown dust jacket.   Argonaut Book Shop   Native American 2015 - 5714   2016 $75

Ridgely, Robert S. *The Birds of South America.* Austin: University of Texas Press, 1989. 1964. First editions, Volumes I and II, profusely illustrated in color and black and white, very good.   Simon Finch   2015 - 162825   2016 $200

Riding, Laura *It Has Taken Long...* Chelsea: 1976. One of 200 special copies signed by author, original wrappers, fine.   Second Life Books, Inc.   196 B - 479   2016 $75

Riding, Laura *Some Communications of Broad Reference.* Northridge: Lord John Press, 1983. First edition, 8vo., 1/125 numbered copies, signed by author, nice.   Second Life Books, Inc.   196 B - 480   2016 $100

Ridley, Gloster *Melampus: a Poem in Four Books with notes.* London: J. Dodsley, 1781. First edition, 4to., titlepage author's portrait medallion engraved by John Hall after painting by Scouler, occasional light foxing, scattered throughout, marginal tears pages 169-172, disbound, leaves untrimmed, ink holograph '5' on titlepage, as is, rare. Jeff Weber Rare Books 181 - 32 2016 $75

Ridley, Henrici *Anatomia Cerebri Complectens ejus Mechanismum & Physiologiam Simulque Nova Quaedam Inventa...* Lugduni Batavorum: Apud Joh. Arn. Langerak, 1725. First edition in Latin, 5 folding engraved plates, 8vo., recent half calf and marbled boards, endpapers renewed, nice large uncut copy. James Tait Goodrich X-78 - 489 2016 $2500

Ridpath, George *The Stage Condem'd and the Encouragement Given to the Immoralities and Profaneness of the Theatre....* London: for John Salusbury, 1698. First edition, foxed and browned throughout, heavily in places and dampstained at end, contemporary panelled calf, rebacked, leather crackled by damp, corners repaired, new endleaves, from the library of James Stevens Cox (1910-1997), 'E- libris Ge(o)r(ge) Luke pr. 0£ 2s-6d". Maggs Bros. Ltd. 1447 - 365 2016 £220

Riesner, Charles *Little Inch High People.* New York: Junior Progress, 1937. 4to., cloth backed pictorial boards, slightes bit of edge rubbing, else fine, 13 color plates, 6 half page color illustrations, 38 3-color illustrations and pictorial endpapers by George Wolfe. Aleph-bet Books, Inc. 112 - 187 2016 $225

The Rights of the Clergy of Ireland Candidly Considered. Dublin: printed by G. Faulkner, 1767. First edition, rare outside Ireland, final leaf blank, dampstain at head of leaves throughout, recent plain wrappers. John Drury Rare Books 2015 - 19046 2016 $350

Rike, Rainer, Maria 1875-1926 *The Astonishment of Origins.* Port Townsend: Graywolf Press, 1982. First printing, 12mo., blue cloth, stamped in gilt, signed by translator, A. Poulin, nice in dust jacket. Second Life Books, Inc. 196 B - 481 2016 $95

Rikhoff, Jim *Hunting the African Leopard.* Clinton: Anwell Press, 1995. First edition thus, limited to 1000 copies signed Rikhoff, this copy #458, textured black leather, gold stamping on spine, linen endpapers, frontispiece, illustrations, as new, unread, housed in original cloth slipcase. Buckingham Books 2015 - 22702 2016 $450

Riley, Athelston *Aths; or the Mountain of the Monks.* London: Longmans, Green, 1887. First edition, 8vo., ads, map, 8 plates, textual illustrations, original red cloth, very clean, scarce. J. & S. L. Bonham Antiquarian Booksellers Europe 2016 - 9617 2016 £650

Riley, Henry Alsop *An Atlas of the Basal Ganglia, Brain Stem and Spinal Cord.* New York: Hafner Pub., 1960. Oblong 4to., original binding, very nice, excellent illustrations, signature of E. H. Houseplan. James Tait Goodrich X-78 - 491 2016 $395

Riley, James Whitcomb 1849-1916 *A Host of Children.* Indianapolis: Bobbs Merrill, 1920. Gilt cloth, pictorial paste-on, light cover rubbing, else fine, illustrations by Ethel Betts with 16 beautiful color plates plus many black and whites in text, beautiful book, excellent condition. Aleph-bet Books, Inc. 112 - 55 2016 $200

Riley, James Whitcomb 1849-1916 *Out to Old Aunt Mary's.* Indianapolis: Bobbs Merrill, 1904. First edition, drawings by Howard Chandler Christy, decorations by Margaret Armstrong, pictorial green cloth stamped in white and gilt on cover and spine, first issue binding with printed endpapers, second printing with 4 dots at end of line 2 on (page 40), fine. Second Life Books, Inc. 197 - 269 2016 $150

Rilke, Rainer Maria 1875-1926 *Duineser Elegien.* London: Hogarth Press, 1931. First edition, one of 230 numbered copies printed at the Cranach Press on handmade Maillol Kessler paper with watermark of Cranach Press and signed by translators, 8vo., initials designed by Eric Gill, original vellum backed boards, top edge gilt plain unprinted dust jacket, publisher's slipcase, dust jacket lightly sunned along spine, slipcase lightly tanned, some very slight foxing to text, otherwise fine, one of very few we have seen in original dust jacket. James S. Jaffe Rare Books Occasional List: Winter 2016 - 79 2016 $7500

Rilke, Rainer Maria 1875-1926 *From the Remains of Count C. W.* London: Hogarth Press, 1952. First UK edition, octavo, free endpapers partially and faintly tanned, near fine in very good dust jacket, little nicked and creased at edges. Peter Ellis 112 - 331 2016 £45

Rilke, Rainer Maria 1875-1926 *The Roses and the Windows.* Port Townsend: Graywolf Press, 1979. One of 48 copies numbered and inscribed by translator, A. Poulin and W, D. Snodgrass, 12mo., green cloth stamped gilt, about as new in dust jacket. Second Life Books, Inc. 196 B - 482 2016 $250

Rilke, Rainer Maria 1875-1926 *The Roses & the Windows.* Port Townsend: Greywold press, 1979. First edition, presentation from translator, A. Poulin for William Claire, green cloth stamped in gilt, nice in very slightly yellowed and soiled dust jacket. Second Life Books, Inc. 196 B - 483 2016 $75

Rimbaud, Arthur *Une Saison en Enfer.*   M. J. Poot et Compagnie, 1873. First edition, 12mo., original wrappers printed red and black, contemporary inscription from Rimbaud enthusiast, minor foxing to front cover, else fine, housed in custom full morocco clamshell.   Heritage Book Shop   Holiday 2015 - 95   2016 $19,500

Rimbaud, Arthur *A Season in Hell.*   New York: Limited Editions Club, 1986. No. 787 of 1000 copies, signed by translator and artist, 292 x 191mm., publisher's crimson Nigerian Oasis goatskin stamped in black, in original black linen slipcase, 8 hand rubbed photogravures by Robert Mapplethorpe, printed in English and French, small (naturally occurring?) dimple on front board, otherwise mint.   Phillip J. Pirages   67 - 241   2016 $950

Rimmer, Alfred *A History of Shrewsbury School from the Blakeway Mss....*   Shrewsbury: Adritt & Naunton, London: Simpkin, Marshall &c., 1889. Original brown cloth, slightly marked, very good, illustrations.   Jarndyce Antiquarian Books   CCXV - 946   2016   £35

Rindl, Deb *Requiem for My Sister.*   London: Deb rindl, 1997. Limited to 40 numbered and initialled copies, small 4to., black stiff paper wrappers with four metal screws and nuts, cameo cut-out exposing part of the title on front cover, housed in box, 33 leaves.   Oak Knoll Books   27 - 59   2016 $350

Ringwaldt, Bartholomaus *Buchlein des Hans Frummann Welcher Von Himmel und Holle Zeuget und Die gotteslasterer Vor der Heissen Holle Treulich Warnet.*   Harrisburg: Gedrudt fur den Verleger, 1826. First edition, 16mo., stitched paper wrappers, rare, good copy, lacking front wrapper, rubbed rear wrapper, soiling to titlepage, paper loss at lower corner, untrimmed, light foxing, leaves browned.   Kaaterskill Books   21 - 80   2016 $250

Rinkefeil, Rudolf *Schlierilei Ein Tiermarchen.*   Baden: Volksunst und Volksildung, richard Keutel, 1925. First edition, early issie (8-12 Thousand), folio, original emerald green cloth pictorially blocked and lettered gilt to upper cover, double page forest endpapers preserved in buff dust jacket in buff dust jacket panelled and illustrated in brown, black and green, printed throughout on coated stock and with some line drawings and 12 fine coloured plates, both externally and internally fine an exceptional copy with only very minor and sporadic internal browning, protected by the elusive dust jacket which has archivally repaired to reverse with tissue, small chipping to spine ends, few other tiny nicks and chips, remarkably scarce in jacket.   Sotheran's Piccadilly Notes - Summer 2015 - 143   2016   £298

Ripley, C. Peter *The Black Abolitionist Papers. Volume II.*   Chapel Hill: University of NC, 1986. First edition, 8vo., portraits and maps, inscribed by author, brown cloth, top edge spotted, upper corners of cover and leaves bumped, otherwise very good, tight copy.   Second Life Books, Inc.   196 B - 484   2016 $45

Ripley, S. Dillon *Rails of the World: a Monograph of the Family Rallidae.*   Boston: David R. Godine, 1977. Small folio, color plates by J. Fenwick Lansdowne, fine in dust jacket.   Andrew Isles Natural History Books   55 - 23732   2016 $200

Ripley, S. Dillon *Trail of the Money Bird: 30000 Miles of Adventure with a Naturalist.*   London: Longman, Green and Co., 1947. Octavo, photos, fine in fine dust jacket, scarce in this condition.   Andrew Isles Natural History Books   55 - 4219   2016 $100

Risk, Robert K. *Songs of the Links.*   London: Duckworth, 1919. First edition with these illustrations, small quarto, black and white illustrations by H. M. Bateman, original green cloth, prelims and edges spotted, free endpapers little tanned, very good, no dust jacket.   Peter Ellis   112 - 29   2016   £75

Ritchie, Leitch *Picturesque Annual for 1835.*   Longmans, 1835. First edition, 8vo., 20 engravings, original red decorative cloth, vignette on titlepage, slight rubbing to head and tail of spine, foxing to frontispiece and titlepage.   J. & S. L. Bonham Antiquarian Booksellers   Europe 2016 - 9985   2016   £50

Ritchie, Ward *The Year's at the spring.*   Los Angeles: Ward Ritchie Press, 1938. First edition, 12mo. one of 150 copies, 9 decorations by Paul Landacre, unprinted wrappers with title label on upper cover, printed on handmade paper, laid in is printed sheet with heading By Way of Explanation, with statement about pamphlet and a Christmas greeting from Ritchie family, covers little nicked and creased at edges, tear at head of spine, very good, scarce.   Peter Ellis   112 - 332   2016   £225

Ritson, Joseph *Gammer Garton's Garland; or the Nursery Parnassus.*   London: printed for R. Tiphood, 1810. First complete edition, octavo, modern dark purple morocco by Philip Dusel, gilt decorations and lettering, paper with scattered light browning, fine with wide margins.   The Brick Row Book Shop   Miscellany 69 - 24   2016 $2750

Ritter, H. *Historia Philosophiae.*   Gothae: sumtibus Frider Andr. Perthes, 1878. Sixth edition, 8vo., pencil underlinings and annotations, little toned, light foxing to prelims, half tan morocco, darker brown cloth, gilt and blind tooling to spine, marbled endpapers, edges sprinkled red, rubbed, joints slightly worn, very good, ownership inscription of L. F. Richardson.   Unsworths Antiquarian Booksellers Ltd.   30 - 131   2016   £30

Ritz, Charles *A Fly Fisher's Life.*   London: Max Reinhardt, 1965. Revised and updated edition, 4to., original yellow cloth, illustrated dust jacket, dust jacket slightly used on whole, very good.   Sotheran's   Hunting, Shooting & Fishing - 138   2016   £80

Riviere, P. *Poh-Dena Scenes De La Vie Siamoise.* Paris: L'Edition D'Art, 1913. #183 of 288 copies, originl wrappers, near fine with deep crease in spine, 8vo., beautiful book with many of the 50 color illustrations by Neziere enriched with gold. Beasley Books 2015 - 2016 $1700

RKO Radio Pictures 1940-1941 Annual. Los Angeles: RKO-Radio Pictures, 1940. First edition, large quarto, brown alligator leather with beveled edges and brown comb binding, very good plus with fragile comb binding undamaged, moderate wear at corners, quite attractive overall. Royal Books 52 - 54 2016 $1850

RKO Radio Pictures 1941-1942 Annual. Los Angeles: RKO Radio Pictures, 1941. First edition, large quarto, brown morocco leather with beveled edges and brown comb binding, very good plus, fragile binding undamaged, moderate wear at corners, quite attractive overall. Royal Books 52 - 55 2016 $1250

Robbins, Tom *Villa Incognito.* New York: Bantam, 2003. First edition, fine in fine dust jacket. Bella Luna Books 2016 - t5630 2016 $66

Robert Frank: Fotografias/Films. 1948/1984. Vallenia: Sara Parpallo/Instiucio Alfons et Magnanim, 1985. Stiff perfect bound wrappers, 8.5 x 9.5 inches, fine, superbly illustrated with photos. Royal Books 49 - 25 2016 $725

Roberti, Antonius *Clavis Homerica. Sive Lexicon Vocabulorum Omnium Quae Continentur in Homeri Iliade et Potissima Parte Odysseaeae.* London: Impensis J. Walthoe, J. Knapton, R. Knaplock, J. & B. Sprint (etc), 1727. Ad leaf discarded, ownership inscriptions of Charles and Edward Hendrick to titlepage, along with ink blot causing small hole in blank area, short wormtrack in blank gutter of last 5 leaves, just some minor soiling otherwise, 8vo., contemporary Cambridge style panelled calf, bit rubbed, touch of wear to extremities, some old scratches, good, pleasant copy, scarce printing. Blackwell's Rare Books Greek & Latin Classics VII - 23 2016 £200

Roberts, Elizabeth Madox *A Buried Treasure.* New York: Viking, 1931. First edition, 8v., uncut, #6 of 200 large paper copies, signed by author, spine lightly faded, otherwise fine in broken publisher's box, inscribed and dated Feb. 21 1933 by author. Second Life Books, Inc. 196 B - 488 2016 $85

Roberts, George *The Four Years Voyages of Capt. George Roberts....* London: printed for A. Bettesworth, 1726. 8vo., folding frontispiece map, 4 engraved plates, paper rather browned but in good sound condition, full contemporary panelled calf, raised bands, expert repairs to joints and head and tail of spine, from the library of Perceval-Maxwell with shelf number at head of titlepage, faint gilt crest and number at foot of spine. Jarndyce Antiquarian Booksellers CCXVI - 495 2016 £480

Roberts, George *The History of Lyme Regis, Dorset...* Sherborne: Printed for the author by Langdon and Harker, and for Baldwin, Cradock and Joy and S. Bagster, London, 1823. First edition, 8vo., 2 hand colored folding lithograph plates by C. Hullmandel after Thomas Mann Baynes, later black morocco backed boards, armorial bookplate of Cornelius Walford. Marlborough Rare Books List 55 - 60 2016 £375

Roberts, Georgia *The Toy Village.* London & New York: Nister & Dutton, n.d. circa, 1906. Oblong 4to., cloth backed pictorial boards, edges rubbed, else very good+, illustrations by Katharine Greenland with 20 full page chromolithographs. Aleph-bet Books, Inc. 111 - 341 2016 $500

Roberts, Jack *La Croisiere Blanche ou l'Expedition Moko-Moka Kokola.* Paris: Talmar, 1928. Oblong small 8vo., cloth backed picotiral boards, slightest bit of dustiness on cover, else fine, color illustrations on each page in Art Deco style, 8 hand colored figures in slits, some of which stand, there is also an alligator hinged into rear cover that can swivel. Aleph-bet Books, Inc. 111 - 339 2016 $2599

Roberts, Kenneth *Sun Hunting.* Indianapolis: Bobbs Merrill, 1922. First edition, first state, very good+ in dark green cloth covered boards, faded gilt text on spine and bold gilt text stamped on front board, 12mo., without dust jacket, signed warmly inscribed by author to Helen Bess Finch, black and white photos. Simon Finch 2015 - TB01648 2016 $200

Roberts, Kenneth *Trending Into Maine.* Boston: Little Brown, June, 1938. First edition, 8vo., tan stamped cloth, fine in dust jacket and publisher's pictorial box, illustrations by N. C. Wyeth, signed by author. Aleph-bet Books, Inc. 111 - 491 2016 $1200

Roberts, Kenneth *Trending into Maine.* Boston: Little Brown, May, 1938. Limited to 1075 numbered copies signed by author and artist, 4to., white cloth spine, blue cloth, spine slightly toned, else fine in publisher's slipcase (few small neat repairs on edge), great copy. Aleph-bet Books, Inc. 112 - 522 2016 $2500

Roberts, Luke *Harlem Doctor.* New York: Universal, 1955. First edition, digest size paperback original, very slight offsetting on rear panel, else especially fine, crisp and unread. Between the Covers Rare Books 202 - 70 2016 $450

Roberts, Robert *The House Servant's Directory or a Monitor for Private Families Comprising Hints to the Arrangement and performance of Servants' Work.* Boston: Monroe & Francis, 1827. First edition, 12mo., contemporary American tree calf with black morocco spine label gilt, joints starting a little, some slight loss at crown, usual light spotting in text, small dampstain on last three leaves, sound and pleasing, very good, handsome in nice contemporary American binding. Between the Covers Rare Books 202 - 20 2016 $20,000

Roberts, S. C. *Doctor Watson.* Faber, 1931. Original wrapper marked and little frayed, humorous poem by E. V. Lucas pasted on blank endpaper. I. D. Edrich Crime - 2016 £20

Roberts, Thomas P. *Report of a Reconnaissance of the Missouri River in 1872.* Washington: GPO, 1875. First edition, limited to 250 copies, original brown cloth, spine stamped in gilt, 1 plate, 3 tables, 2 folding charts, 2 folding diagrams, 2 folding maps, 3 very large folding maps, rare, near fine, slightest edgewear to original binding, preserved in attractive cloth clamshell box with leather label on spine. Buckingham Books 2015 - 35989 2016 $3500

Robertson-Miller, Ellen *Butterfly and Moth Book: personal Studies and Observations of the More Familiar Species.* New York: Charles Scribner's Sons, 1912. First edition, publisher's decorative gray cloth with art Nouveau stylized illustration of a butterfly, caterpillars and leaves in pale chartreuse and blue, lettered in blue and black, fine, few faint scuffs to otherwise fresh binding, former owner's inscription, otherwise bright and clean pages, beautiful copy. B & B Rare Books, Ltd. 2016 - ERM001 2016 $50

Robertson, Fred W. *Two Lectures on the Influence of Poetry on the Working Classes....* Brighton: Henry S. King, 1853. Second edition, half title, new preface, original green cloth wrappers. Jarndyce Antiquarian Books CCXV - 922 2016 £48

Robertson, John W. *Edgar A. Poe: a Study.* San Francisco: Bruce Brough, 1921. First edition, 8vo., illustrations, fine, untrimmed copy in slightly worn dust jacket. Second Life Books, Inc. 197 - 262 2016 $75

Robertson, Robin *Love Poet, Carpenter. Michael Longley at Seventy.* Enitharmon Press, 2009. First edition, 160/195 copies signed by contributors, frontispiece by Jeffrey Morgan and full page charcoal drawing by Sarah Longley, 8vo., original blue cloth with small inset portrait by Morgan to upper board, backstrip lettered gilt, matching slipcase, fine. Blackwell's Rare Books B184 - 191 2016 £500

Robeson, Paul *Here I Stand.* London: Dennis Dobson, 1958. first UK edition, octavo, spine just little faded, free endpapers partially tanned, front free endpaper little creased, very good in like dust jacket, little nicked and rubbed at edges, presentation inscribed by author to Joseph Griffiths. Peter Ellis 112 - 333 2016 £350

Robimson, Will H. *Under Turquoise Skies.* New York: Macmillan Co., 1928. First edition, numerous black and white plates, gilt lettered red cloth, corners and spine ends rubbed, else fine. Argonaut Book Shop Native American 2015 - 1966 2016 $50

Robin Hood *Robin Ballestero.* New York: D. Appleton, 1891. Pictorial wrappers, fine, 4 full page chromolithographs, brown line illustrations on every page, wrap around chromolithographs. Aleph-bet Books, Inc. 112 - 424 2016 $125

Robinson, Doane *South Dakota, Stressing the Unique and Dramatic in South Dakota History.* American Historical Society, 1930. First edition, 3 volumes, marbled endpapers and edge of text block of all 3 volumes, numerous illustrations, charts, tables, very slight sunning to spines and very light spotting to back panel of first volume, else near fine, attractive set. Buckingham Books 2015 - 25759 2016 $450

Robinson, Edward Arlington 1869-1935 *Sonnets 1889-1927.* New York: Crosby Gaige, 1928. First edition, limited to 561 large paper copies signed by author, near fine, uncut. Second Life Books, Inc. 196 B - 489 2016 $100

Robinson, Gertrude *Floral Fairies: The Little Miss Hollies.* New York: Floral Fairy Pub. Co., 1912. Oblong 4to., cloth backed pictorial boards, slight cover soil, else near fine, illustrations by F. A. Carter. Aleph-bet Books, Inc. 112 - 178 2016 $300

Robinson, Gertrude *Floral Fairies: the Mistletoe's Pranks.* New York: Floral Fairy Pub. Co., 1913. 9 color plates by F. A. Carter 12 9 inches, cloth backed pictorial boards, rare in beautiful copy. Aleph-bet Books, Inc. 112 - 173 2016 $450

Robinson, Herbert C. *The Birds of the Malay Peninsula: a General Account of the Birds Inhabiting the Region from the Isthmus of Kra to Singapore with the Adjacent Islands.* London: H. F. & G. Witherby, 1927-1976. Small quarto, five volumes, 125 color plates by Gronvold, publisher's red cloth (volume 5 in dust jacket), fine set. Andrew Isles Natural History Books 55 - 25785 2016 $1850

Robinson, Jacob *North Country Sports and Pastimes. Wrestling and Wrestlers...* London: Bemrose & Sons, Carlisle: The Wordsworth Press, 1893. First edition, scarce, 8vo., contemporary half red morocco by Fazakerley, lettered to gilt on spine, original printed wrappers bound in, little occasional browning, otherwise very good. Sotheran's Hunting, Shooting & Fishing - 192 2016 £498

Robinson, John *An Account of Sweden; Together with an Extract of the History of the Kingdom.* London: Tim Goodwin, 1694. First edition, 8vo., initial leaf with half title on recto and ad on verso, A1-4 browned, E8-8 and O1-2 browned and spotted, small semi-circular chip from fore-edge of front flyleaf, contemporary sprinkled calf, spine with gilt thistle crest in fourth panel and gilt shelf mark in final one (covers detached, edges and corners worn, headcaps torn away and with small white splash of paint on upper board), from the library of James Stevens Cox (1910-1997) the copy of Rev. Kene Percival (1709?-74?) with his gilt thistle crest, S. or J. Foley signature. Maggs Bros. Ltd. 1447 - 366 2016 £100

Robinson, John *An Account of Sueden; together with an Extract of the History of that Kingdom.* London: Tim Goodwin, 1717. Third edition, 12mo., ads, contemporary brown speckled calf, spine rubbed. J. & S. L. Bonham Antiquarian Booksellers Europe 2016 - 8421 2016 £200

Robinson, John *A Description of and Critical Remarks on the Picture of Christ Healing the Sick in the Temple...* Philadelphia: published by S. W. Conrad for the Pennsylvania Hospital, William brown, 1818. First edition, 8vo., 2 leaves of plates, stitched uncut, somewhat rough copy, rarely encountered, foxed and uncut edges, somewhat ragged, issued in printed wrappers, not here, somehow missing. Howard S. Mott Inc. 265 - 111 2016 $450

Robinson, Nicholas *A New System of the Spleen, Vapours and Hypochrondriack Melancholy.* London: printed for A. Bettesworth, W. Innys and C. Rivington, 1729. Full contemporary English paneled and polished calf, front joint cracked and starting to split, part of spine label lacking, spine gilt. James Tait Goodrich X-78 - 492 2016 $1500

Robinson, Philomena *Completing the Circle.* Washington: Library Fellows of the National Museum of Women in the Arts, 1996. Limited to 125 numbered copies signed by artist, on Lanaquarelle 90lb hotpress, quotes typeset in Helvetica, handmade paper of cotton abaca created by Marilyn Sward, photos, hand painted watercolor symbols, embossed copper and paper-cut designs by Robinson, oblong small 8vo., handmade paper binding with titled wrappers, loosely inserted in green cloth covered folding portfolio. Oak Knoll Books 27 - 42 2016 $395

Robinson, Thomas *An Essays Towards a National History of Westmorland and Cumberland.* London: printed by J. L. for W. Freeman, 1709. 8vo., lower edge of final ad leaf worn and repaired with no loss of text, some light browning and occaisonal minor foxing, 19th century ownership name, Anthony Barker at head of titlepage, expertly bound in recent quarter mottled calf, raised and gilt banded spine, red morocco label, marbled boards, vellum tips. Jarndyce Antiquarian Booksellers CCXVI - 496 2016 £380

Robinson, William Heath *Bill the Minder.* New York: Henry Holt, 1912. First US edition, 4to., olive cloth, pictorial paste-on, gilt cover and spine slightest of cover soil, else near fine. Aleph-bet Books, Inc. 111 - 390 2016 $750

Robinson, William Heath *How to be a Motorist.* Hutchinson & Co., 1939. First edition, crown 8vo., recently rebound in half red morocco, spine lettered and ruled in gilt, gilt centres, top edges gilt, one set of original pictorial endpapers, bound in at end, drawings, very nice. Sotheran's Piccadilly Notes - Summer 2015 - 258 2016 £198

Robinson, William Heath *Railway Ribaldry.* London: Great Western Railway, 1935. First edition, 4to., stiff pictorial card covers, fine. Aleph-bet Books, Inc. 112 - 428 2016 $400

Robson, Peter *Mountains in Kenya...* Nairobi: East African Pub. House, 1969. First edition, hardback issue, 8vo., original black cloth with illustrated dust jackets, frontispiece, text illustrations, color plates, one sketch map, cloth little marked, light warping to paper, else very good. Sotheran's Travel and Exploration - 30 2016 £78

Roche, Paul *The Rat and the Convent Dove and Other Tales and Fables.* Aldington, Kent: Hand & Flower Press, 1952. First edition, 8vo., signed by author, very good, clean copy in dust jacket. Second Life Books, Inc. 196 B - 490 2016 $50

Rochester, John Wilmot, 2nd Earl of 1647-1680 *Perfect and Imperfect Enjoyments. Poems.* Folio Society, 1992. 46/50 copies (from an edition of 500), signed by artist with separate folder of illustrations each numbered and signed in pencil, frontispiece and 7 further full page illustrations color printed using photo lithographs at Senecio Press, imperial 8vo., original full vellum, backstrip lettered gilt, upper board bowing slightly, top edge gilt, others untrimmed, cloth drop-down box with printed label inset to front, near fine. Blackwell's Rare Books B184 - 262 2016 £800

Rochester, John Wilmot, 2nd Earl of 1647-1680 *Poems (&c) on Several Occasions.* London: for Jacob Tonson, 1696. Reprint of 1691 edition, 8vo., slightly dusty in places, very small worm trail in lower inner margin of final few leaves, contemporary plain mottled calf, covers ruled in blind, joints rubbed, stain on rear endleaves, from the library of James Stevens Cox (1910-1997). Maggs Bros. Ltd. 1447 - 367 2016 £750

Rock, William Frederick *The Anniversary: a Christmas Story.* London: David Bogue, 1856. First edition, half title, frontispiece, engraved title and 6 further plates by Thomas Onwhyn, original red wavy-grained cloth by Bone & Son, blocked in blind, lettered and decorated gilt, small split in following inner hinge, all edges gilt, very good, bright. Jarndyce Antiquarian Booksellers   CCXVIII - 409   2016   £120

Rodd, Rennell *Raleigh. Recited in the Theatre June 9 1880.* Oxford: T. Shrimpton and Son, 1880. First edition, very good in blue paper wrappers with black title to front panel, browning to edges of wrappers and few chips to rear panel, pencilled initials in front cover, interior remains clean and bright, housed in fine, light brown cloth box with gilt and black leather title label to spine, very nice, fragile, uncommon.   The Kelmscott Bookshop   12 - 88   2016 $525

Roden, Barbara *Lady Stanhope's Manuscript and Other Supernatural Tales.* Pennyffordd, Chester: Ash-Tree Press, 1994. First edition, 150 copies printed, octavo, stiff printed wrappers, fine.   John W. Knott, Jr./L.W. Currey, Inc.   Fall-Winter 2015 - 18477   2016 $650

Rodker, John *Poems.* London: privately printed for the author, n.d., 1914. First edition, octavo, wrappers, some faint spotting, small nick to fore-edge of titlepage, covers slightly nicked and creased at overlapping edges and slightly dusty, spine rubbed, very good.   Peter Ellis   112 - 334   2016   £175

Rodney, Bryan *The Owl Flies Home.* Wright & Brown, n.d., Red boards, little spotted in slightly worn and frayed dust jacket, contents very good, scarce.   I. D. Edrich   Crime - 2016   £50

Roederer, Joannis Georgii *Elementa Artis Obstetriciae in Usum Auditorum Denuo Edidit.* Gottingen: apvd Vidvan Abrami Vandenhoeckii, 1766. Third Latin edition, Engraved title, 8vo., early calf and patterned boards, rubbed, corners bumped, some light foxing and staining.   James Tait Goodrich   X-78 - 424   2016 $595

Roentgen, Wilhelm *Ueber Eine Neue Art Von Strahlen Erste Mittheilung. (with) Ueber Fine Neue Neue Art Von Strahlen. Zweite Mittheilung. (with) Weitere Beobachtungen Uber dei Eigenschaften der X-Strahlen. Dritte Mittheilung. In the Annalen der Physik und Chemie, Neue Folge, Band 64 (1898).* Leipzig: Johann Ambmrosius Barth., 1898. 8vo., entire volume offered, very good+, half cloth and marbled boards with gilt lettering to spine, mild cover edgewear, owner bookplate, mild scattered foxing.   By the Book, L. C.   45 - 20   2016 $1500

Roethke, Theodore *Open House.* New York: Alfred A. Knopf, 1941. First edition, one of 1000 numbered copies, just about fine in about very good dust jacket with slight chipping at crown and chipping and internal repair to flap folds.   Between the Covers Rare Books   204 - 102   2016 $200

Roethke, Theodore *Sequence Sometimes Metaphysical. Poems.* Iowa City: Stone Wall Press, 1963. First edition, small 4to., original quarter leather and pictorial boards, publisher's slipcase, one of only 60 specially bound copies signed by author and artist, wood engravings by John Roy, fine.   James S. Jaffe Rare Books   Occasional List: Winter 2016 - 123   2016 $3500

Roger Eliot Stoddard at Sixty-Five, a Celebration. New York: Thornwillow Press, 2000. First edition, one of 300 numbered copies with addenda laid in, 8vo., tipped in plates, plain wrappers, dust jacket, fine.   James S. Jaffe Rare Books   Occasional List: Winter 2016 - 33   2016 $75

Roger, Noelle *He Who Sees.* London: George G. Harrap & Co., 1935. First English edition, boards slightly bowed and some very light scattered foxing, else about fine in very attractive, near fine dust jacket with rubbed tear at crown, rare in jacket.   Between the Covers Rare Books   208 - 126   2016 $1000

Rogers, Fred Blackburn *William Brown Ide, Bear Flagger.* San Francisco: John Howell Books, 1962. First edition, limited to 750 copies, frontispiece, 6 plates, map, pictorial tan cloth stamped in white and red, gilt lettered spine, very fine.   Argonaut Book Shop   Biography 2015 - 3611   2016 $90

Rogers, Samuel *Italy, a Poem (and) Poems.* London: printed for T. Cadell, 1830. First illustrated editions, 202 x 135mm., 2 separately published works, bound in two volumes, (but often found as companion volumes), very pretty sky blue morocco gilt, by Root & son (stamp-signed on front turn-ins), covers with gilt frame bedecked with a profusion of flowers, raised bands, spines gilt in compartments with large floral spray centerpiece, gilt titling, turn-ins decorated with gilt rules and floral garland, marbled endpapers, all edges gilt, 2 volumes with a total of four plates, 20 illustrations in text, more than 100 fine steel engraved headpieces and tailpieces after deisgns, mostly by J. M. W. Turner and Thomas Sothard, spines slightly and uniformly sunned, trivial defects internally, extremely pretty set in very fine condition, immaculate text with virtually no signs of use and glittering rulings, unworn.   Phillip J. Pirages   67 - 65   2016 $950

Rogers, Thomas *A Posie for Lovers; or the Terrestrial Venus Unmaskt.* London: for Thomas Speed, 1694. First edition, small 4to., titlepage and verso of final leaf lightly soiled and with a number of uncut edges, early 20th century half calf and marbled boards, from the library of James Stevens Cox (1910-1997) with his cipher pencilled on front pastedown and notes attributing the work to Rogers. Maggs Bros. Ltd. 1447 - 368 2016 £1250

Rogers, W. G. *Wise Men Fish Here...* New York: Harcourt Brace & World, 1965. First edition, yellow cloth, cover lightly stained, otherwise nice in some soiled and chipped dust jacket, inscribed by author for William Claire, with TLS from author to Claire. Second Life Books, Inc. 196 B - 493 2016 $85

Rogers, William *Reminiscences of William Rogers.* London: Kegan Paul, Trench & Co., 1888. First edition, half title, frontispiece, 43 page catalog (11.87), 4 pages ads, original maroon cloth, bevelled boards, little rubbed, presentation inscription on title for Frank Lawson. Jarndyce Antiquarian Books CCXV - 923 2016 £40

Rogerson, Ian *Moods and Tenses. the Portraits and Characters of Peter Reddick.* Denby Dale: Fleece Press, 1999. First edition, one of 220 copies printed on mouldmade paper, titles printed in orange, two folding leaves displaying a number of 30 wood engravings by Peter Reddick, 4to., original quarter orange cloth, printed label, orange pastepaper boards, grey board and cloth slipcase, fine. Blackwell's Rare Books B186 - 300 2016 £110

Rohelm, Geza *Australian Totemism: a Psycho-Analytic Study in Anthropology.* London: George Allen & Unwin, 1925. First edition, good to very good, dust jacket poor, drawings, original cloth shows spotting with tear at lower front joint, gilt titling remains bright on spine and front board, interior remains bright, despite pale toning to maps and dust spotting on top edge, endpapers show offsetting, all 11 folding maps present and in excellent condition, unclipped dust jacket is in two pieces but has done a good job in protectig the book. Simon Finch 2015 - 001525 2016 $195

Rohmer, Eric *Hitchcock.* Paris: Editions Universitaires, 1957. First French edition, inscribed by Rohmer and co-author, Claude Chabrol, also laid in is small publisher's prospectus for this title, very good in wrappers. Royal Books 51 - 37 2016 $3500

Rohmer, Sax *The Book of Fu-Manchu.* London: Hurst & Blackett, n.d., Black boards with paper title labels pasted on front and spine, both inner and outer front hinge cracked, otherwise good, uncommon. I. D. Edrich Crime - 2016 £25

Rohr, Karl *Teddy Eine Lustige Barengeschichte.* Easslingen und Munchen: J. F. Schreiber, n.d. circa, 1910. 4to., pictorial boards, some margin soil and rubbing, very good, die cut in shape of toy bear with blue ribbon around its neck, front cover embossed giving it a three dimensional effect, illustrations by Rohr with 8 full page color illustrations and 8 full pages in various shades of brown depicting Teddy getting into all kinds of mischief. Aleph-bet Books, Inc. 112 - 459 2016 $600

Rolland, Francisco Hueso *Exposicion de Encuadernaciones Espanolas Siglos XII Al XIX.* Madrid: Sociedad Espanola de Amigos del Arte, 1934. First edition, one of 100 numbered copies, samll folio, cloth, dust jacket, 61 full page plates, scarce, jacket chipped with small tears. Oak Knoll Books 310 - 18 2016 $1500

Rolleston, Thomas William Hazen 1856-1920 *The Tale of Lohengrin: Knight of the Swan ....* London: Harrap, n.d., 1913. First edition, 4to., brown gilt pictorial cloth, inconspicuous rub spot on endpaper, else fine in original pictorial slipcase (scuffed, neatly strengthened), illustrations by Willy Pogany, beautiful copy, scarce. Aleph-bet Books, Inc. 112 - 379 2016 $1000

Rollins, Carl Purlington *Theodore Low De Vinne (Volume I).* New York: Typohpiles, 1968. One of 500 copies, 2 volumes, small 8vo., illustrated Aqua cloth in paper covered box, box little faded, 3 very small holes at bottom corner, otherwise near fine. Second Life Books, Inc. 197 - 270 2016 $85

Rollo, John *Remarks on the Disease Lately Described by Dr. (James) Hendy.* Printed for C. Dilly, 1785. First edition, little dust soiling to some upper margins, outer pages slightly foxed from flyleaves, small 8vo., partly unopened, original blue paper boards, rebacked, little soiled, contemporary engraved armorial bookplate inside front cover, name erased, good, rare. Blackwell's Rare Books B186 - 132 2016 £800

Rolls, Eric *A Million Wild Acres.* Melbourne: Nelson, 1981. Ocatvo, photos, bookplate, shelfwear, very good in dust jacket. Andrew Isles Natural History Books 55 - 365 2016 $50

Roman, C. V. *American Civilization and the Negro: the Afro-American in Relation to National Progress.* Philadelphia: E. A. Davis, 1916. First edition, photos slight rubbing on spine, else neart fine. Between the Covers Rare Books 202 - 88 2016 $475

Rombauer, Irma *The Joy of Cooking.* St. Louis: A. C. Clayton Printing Co., 1931. First edition, privately published by author in an edition of 3000 copies, 8vo., illustrations by Marion Rombauer, original cloth, pictorial dust jacket, miraculous survival, virtually as new in dust jacket, showing only faintest of toning to spine of book and dust jacket, enclosed in cloth folding box. James S. Jaffe Rare Books Occasional List: Winter 2016 - 47 2016 $40,000

Romer, Isabella Frances *Filia Dolorosa. Memoirs of Marie Therese Charlotte, Duchess of Angouleme, The Last Dauphnies.* London: Richard Bentley, 1852. First edition, 225 x 140mm., 2 volumes, attractive later sky blue crushed morocco by Bayntun of Bath for his bookseller Charles E. Lauriat co. of Boston (stamp signed on front turn-in), covers with frame of black and gilt rules cinched to the center of each side by a decorative quatrefoil, raised bands, spine compartments framed by black and gilt rules, gilt titling, turn-ins ruled in gilt and black with decorative cornerpieces, marbled endpapers, all edges gilt, hand colored frontispiece portrait, extra illustrated with portraits and views, 20 of the portraits hand colored, bookplate of Joel Cheney Wells, designed by Elisha Brown Bird, spines uniformly faded further toward gray than blue, isolated trivial defects internally, otherwise very pleasing copy, entirely clean and fresh as in bindings with spine lustrous covers and virtually no signs of use. Phillip J. Pirages 67 - 39 2016 $750

The Romish Mass-Book Faithfully Translated into English with Notes and Observations Thereupon... London: printed by George Larkin for Thomas Malthus, 1683. 12mo., engraved frontispiece, publisher's catalog, frontispiece almost detached, little yellowed, with few small spots, worming to lower margin page 12 onwards, final leaf slightly adhered to r.f.e.p. causing some tearing near gutter, contemporary brown sheep, edges sprinkled reddish brown, spine worn and narrow 4cm. piece missing at tail and adjacent stain to lower board, some other small stains and speckling, pastedowns lifting with lower part of front pastedown excised, number 17 inked in old hand in inner front board where exposed to lifted pastedown and to fore edge, ownership inscription of Isabella Raymond dated 1756. Unsworths Antiquarian Booksellers 30 - 5 2016 £450

Ronalds, Alfred *The Fly-Fisher's Entomology with Coloured Representations of the Natural and Artificial Insect and a Few Observations ad Instructions on Trout and Grayling Fishing.* London: Longman, Green and Co., 1883. Ninth edition, 8vo., original dark green cloth lettered gilt and blocked in blind, 20 hand colored engraved plates of flies, frontispiece, slight spotting to prelims, ownership inscription on half title, very good. Sotheran's Hunting, Shooting & Fishing - 139 2016 £650

Ronsard, Pierre De *Choix De Sonnets.* London: Eragny Press for Hacon Ricketts, 1902. One of 226 copies, 219 x 149mm, original patterned paper boards, gilt titling on front cover, woodcut frontispiece with elaborate woodcut border, same border around titlepage, large decorative initial on each page, printer's device at end, all by Pissarros, first opening printed in red and black; spine rather darkened, paper boards with minor stains, tiny tears and other signs of use to joints and extremities, offsetting to endpapers from binder's glue but binding not at all weakened, clean fresh copy internally. Phillip J. Pirages 67 - 131 2016 $1200

Rooke, Octavius *The Channel Islands; Pictorial, Legendary and descriptive.* London: L. Booth, 1856. First edition, 8vo., text illustrations, contemporary green morocco, gilt, handsome copy. J. & S. L. Bonham Antiquarian Booksellers Europe 2016 - 8349 2016 £280

Roos, William *January Thaw.* Chicago: Dramatic Pub., 1946. 8vo., 2 photo, one stage diagram, author's presentation on half title to producer Mike Todd, cover slightly worn at corners and spine, else very good. Second Life Books, Inc. 196 B - 495 2016 $45

Roosevelt, Eleanor 1884-1962 *Christmas.* New York: Alfred Knopf, 1940. First edition, 16mo., pictorial boards, corner of rear cover discolored, else very good+ in dust jacket with corner chip, this copy inscribed by Roosevelt on half title, full page and smaller in-text pen and ink illustrations and color dust jacket and endpapers by Fritz Kredel. Aleph-bet Books, Inc. 111 - 396 2016 $2850

Roosevelt, Eleanor 1884-1962 *It's Up to Women.* New York: Stokes, 1933. First edition, 8vo., chipped and worn dust jacket, fine, scarce. Second Life Books, Inc. 197 - 271 2016 $650

Roosevelt, Kermit *The Long Trail.* New York: Metropolitan Magazine, 1921. Autographed edition, small 8vo., several illustrations, author's autograph, tan paper over boards, cloth spine, printed in black and gilt, slightly worn at corners and ends of spine, but very good, tight copy. Second Life Books, Inc. 196 B - 498 2016 $75

Roosevelt, Theodore 1858-1919 *The Rough Riders.* New York: Charles Scribners, 1899. First edition, signed by Roosevelt, octavo, original gilt stamped cloth, custom box, spine slightly faded, cloth with only trivial wear, outstanding copy, extremely rare signed. Manhattan Rare Book Company 2016 - 1776 2016 $5000

Root, Riley *Musical Philosophy...* Galesburg: Wm. J. Mourer, Book and Job Printer, 1866. First edition, 12mo., text printed within ornamental border throughout, original printed wrappers, touch of spotty foxing, nice. M & S Rare Books, Inc. 99 - 117 2016 $375

Roper, Abel *Cursory but Curious Observations of Mr. Ab-l R--er upon a late Famous Pamphlet entituled, Remarks on the Preliminary Articles offer'd by the F. K. in Hopes to Procure a General Peace.* London: printed for John Morphew..., 1711. 8vo., traces of old paste at inner margin of titlepage, small ink splah at edge of final page, disbound. Jarndyce Antiquarian Booksellers   CCXVI - 497   2016   £50

Roper, Walter F. *Experiments of a Handgunner.* New York: Stackpoole & Heck Inc., 1949. First edition, 8vo., original cloth with dust jacket, 60 illustrations, very good. Sotheran's Hunting, Shooting & Fishing - 194 2016   £175

Ros, Amanda M. *Fumes of Formation.* Belfast: R. Carswell & Son, 1933. First edition, 8vo., 2000 copies, one of only 160 bound up, remaining sets of sheets were estroyed, head and tail of spine slightly bumped, very good in good chipped, nicked, dusty and slightly creased dust jacket darkened at spine.   Peter Ellis   112 - 337   2016   £200

Roscoe, William *Considerations on the Causes, Objects and Consequences of the Present War and on the Expediency or the Danger of Peace with France.* London: printed by J. McCreery for Cadell & Davies, 1808. First edition, title little browned, uncut sewn as issued, small library duplicate stamp on final page, contemporary signature of William Strickland on titlepage, very good.   Jarndyce Antiquarian Booksellers   CCXVII - 250   2016   £95

Roscoe, William *Strictures on Mr. Burke's Two Letters Addressed to a Member of the Present Parliament.* printed for G. G. J. and J. Robinson, 1796. First edition, outer leaves trifle soiled, 8vo., disbound, good.   Blackwell's Rare Books B186 - 133   2016   £375

Rose Fyleman Fairy Book. London: Methuen, 1923. First edition, 4to., blue cloth, very good, illustrations by Hilda Miller. Aleph-bet Books, Inc.   111 - 159   2016 $475

Rose, Thomas *Vues Pittoresques des Comtes De Westmorland, Cumberland, Durham et Northumberland.* London: A. Fisher, B. Fisher, et P. Jackson, 1834-1836. First edition in French, 3 volumes, 286 x 222cm., very pleasing contemporary dark green half morocco over lighter green moire cloth, covers with gilt fillet and blind rolled lattice border, spines with gilt tooled raised bands at head and tail, with two elongated raised panels elegantly gilt in gothic pattern, 3 brown morocco labels, marbled endleaves and edges, engraved titlepage with vignette in volume 1, frontispiece in volumes 2 and 3, 213 steel engravings on 108 plates, original tissue guards, tips of corners bruised, just small number of plates with easily tolerable foxing or browning, otherwise especially fine, text and plates unusually clean and entirely fresh, very pleasing bindings bright, lustrous and altogether attractive on the shelf.   Phillip J. Pirages   67 - 232   2016 $2800

Rose, Walter *Snakes: Mainly South African.* Cape Town: Maskew Miller, 1955. Octavo, photos, signature, tape marks, dust jacket.   Andrew Isles Natural History Books 55 - 38976   2016 $80

Rosenbach, Abraham Simon Wolf 1876-1952 *Early American Children's Books.* Portland: Southworth Press, 1933. First edition, one of 585 numbered copies signed by Rosenbach, 4to., levant backed pictorial boards, top edge gilt, slipcase slightly soiled.   Oak Knoll Books   310 - 70   2016 $350

Rosenberg, Hogler *Det Nya Sibirien. En Skildring af Det Genom Den Sibirska Jarnvagen Oppanade....* Stockholm: Fahlcrantz, 1904. First Swedith edition, 8vo., 9 parts, original printed wrappers, one color printed map and numerous illustrations after photos in text, wrappers of last part little spotted, otherwise fine, each issue with neat ownership inscription to upper margin of front wrapper.   Sotheran's Travel and Exploration - 173   2016   £498

Rosenberg, Samuel *Naked is the Best Disguise.* Indianapolis: Bobbs Merrill, 1974. First edition, octavo, brown cloth backed tan boards with gilt lettering on spine, fine in fine pictorial dust jacket.   Argonaut Book Shop Literature 2015 - 5124   2016 $50

Rosenthal, Ed *Marijuana Beer.* Berkeley: Quick American Publishing & And/Or Press, 1984. First edition, fine in wrappers, with labels and stickers intact.   Ken Lopez Bookseller   166 - 77   2016 $150

Rosenthal, Irving *Big Table. Number 1 Spring 1959.* Chicago: Big Table, 1959. First edition, small 8vo., paper wrappers, cover little soiled and somewhat scuffed, otherwise very good.   Second Life Books, Inc.   197 - 272   2016 $100

Rosenthal, Leonard *The Kingdom of the Pearl.* New York: Brentano's, circa, 1920. First American edition, no. 12 of 675 copies printed for sale in the US (with an additional 10 copies signed in quarter vellum, a total of 775 American copies), 297 x 236mm., publisher's ivory colored cloth over gray patterned boards, top edge gilt, others untrimmed, rare original dust jacket, housed in sturdy (slightly soiled) slipcase, 20 color plates by Edmund Dulac, with original descriptive tissue guards, tissue guards uniformly toned as usual, jacket with extensive neat repairs to underside, small looses along top edge, sunning to spine and other minor defects, volume itself in very fine condition. Phillip J. Pirages   67 - 121   2016 $1000

Rosenthal, Leonard *Au Royaume De La Perle. (The Kingdom of the Pearl).* Paris: H. Piazza, 1920. First printing with these illustrations, no. 430 of 1500 copies, 289 x 230mm., fine later black crushed morocco gilt by Bayntun-Riviere (stamp signed), covers with dotted roll border incorporating gilt cornerpieces, upper cover with lobed centerpiece panel enclosing gilt crown set with 26 tiny seed pearls, raised bands, gilt ruled and decorated compartments, wide turn-ins with gilt rolls and cornerpieces, marbled endpapers, top edge gilt, housed in somewhat worn and faded but still sturdy felt-lined drop-back clamshell cloth box; decorated title, initials, head and tailpieces, borders, 10 color plates by Edmund Dulac, mounted within decorative frames, captioned tissue guards, four initials carefully hand colored by previous owner, imitation page with convincing signature of Dulac, which appears to be a forgery, beautifully bound in pristine condition.   Phillip J. Pirages   67 - 120   2016 $1900

Rosenus, Alan *General M. G. Vallejo and the Advent of the Americans. A Biography.* Albuquerque: University of New Mexico Press, 1996. First edition, signed by author, 29 illustrations, green cloth, mint copy in pictorial dust jacket.   Argonaut Book Shop   Biography 2015 - 1767   2016 $60

Rosevear, D. R. *The Carnivores of West Africa.* London: British Museum (Natural History), 1974. Octavo, color plates, text illustrations, fine in dust jacket.   Andrew Isles Natural History Books   55 - 1291   2016 $250

Rosevear, D. R. *The Rodents of West Africa.* London: British Museum (Natural History), 1969. Octavo, 11 color plates, text illustrations, fine in fine dust jacket.   Andrew Isles Natural History Books   55 - 6757   2016 $250

Rosler, Christian Friedrich *De Variis Disputandi Methods Veteris Eccesiae Rectore Universitatis Eberhardinae Carolinae Magnificentissimo Seremissimo or Potentessimo Duce et Domino....* Tubingen: Schrammianis, 1784. 4to., disbound, library number rubber stamp to titlepage with verso "Withdrawn from Pitts Theology Library" rubber stamp, clean text, very scarce, good.   Jeff Weber Rare Books   181 - 33   2016 $45

Ross, D. K. *The Pioneers and Churches The Pioneers and Families of Big Brook and West Branch E.R. and Surrounding Sections Including Lorne, Glengarry, Elgin, Centerdale....* Halifax: Saint Mark's Church, 8vo., card covers stapled and taped spine, photo illustrations, covers scuffed and stained, paper edges, some dampstaining.   Schooner Books Ltd.   115 - 175   2016 $45

Ross, Frank Alexander *A Bibliography of the Negro Migration.* New York: Columbia University Press, 1934. First edition, bottom corner little bumped, else near fine in near fine green dust jacket with small nicks and tears, very nice in scarce jacket.   Between the Covers Rare Books   202 - 89   2016 $350

Ross, Isie Younger *Feeding the Child - All Ages Foods that Promote Growth, Health, Mental and Physical Development....* London: Frederick Warne, 1929. First edition, frontispiece, illustrations, endpapers replaced, original orange cloth, very good in slightly dulled and rubbed dust jacket.   Jarndyce Antiquarian Books   CCXV - 384   2016   £20

Ross, Margaret *Tiger Island.* London: Gawthorn, n.d. circa, 1940. First edition, oblong 4to., cloth, very good in dust jacket (dust jacket worn), full page color illustrations by author.   Aleph-bet Books, Inc.   111 - 46   2016 $200

Ross, Patricia *The Hungry Moon: Mexican Nursery Tales.* New York: Alfred Knopf, 1946. Stated first edition, 4to, cloth, small stain bottom edge of front cover, else very good in dust jacket with small pieces of spine ends, illustrations in full colors.   Aleph-bet Books, Inc.   111 - 280   2016 $150

Rossetti, Charles *Maude: a Story for Girls.* London: James Bowden, 1897. Limited edition, 1 of 500 copies, blue cloth boards with gilt title to spine and gilt facsimile of author's signature, browning to spine, interior very clean with minor browning to top edge of pages, text bright, tight binding, frontispiece with tissue guard, previous owner's bookplate, very good.   The Kelmscott Bookshop   12 - 89   2016 $125

Rossetti, Christina 1830-1894 *Goblin Market.* London: Macmillan, 1893. First edition with these illustrations, narrow octavo, tissue guarded titlepage, 12 full page other illustrations and other vignettes by Laurence Housman, original green elaborate gilt cloth, all edges gilt, bookplate, cloth superficially rubbed at head and tail of spine, endpapers spotted as usual, very good.   Peter Ellis   112 - 340   2016   £375

Rossetti, Christina 1830-1894 *Goblin Market.* London: George G. Harrap & Co., 1933. No. 347 of 410 copies (400 for sale) signed by artist, 241 x 165mm., original limp vellum, original (?) tissue dust jacket, original slipcase with printed paper label, illustrated endpapers, half title and titlepage, text illustrations, four color plates by Arthur Rackham, titlepage partly printed in green, slight fraying and tiny chips missing along top of front panel of dust jacket, otherwise almost amazing copy, even slipcase being unusually clean and volume itself virtualy pristine.   Phillip J. Pirages   67 - 296   2016 $1900

Rossetti, Christina 1830-1894 *Goblin Market.* Philadelphia: Lippincott, 1933. First US edition, 8vo., red cloth, pictorial paste-on, two tiny edge mends on endpaper else, fine in dust jacket (very good lightly soiled with few small chips), illustrations by Rackham, nice.   Aleph-bet Books, Inc.   112 - 413   2016 $325

Rossetti, Dante Gabriel 1828-1882 *Ballads and Sonnets.* London: Ellis and White, 1881. First edition, exceptional association copy, inscribed by author for Frederick Leyland (1832-1892), original green cloth with gilt flower and lattice design by Rossetti on covers and spine, spotting to prelim leaves and at emd of book, including inscription page, but this does not obscure inscription, closed half inch margin to page 327, very good plus, housed in modern green cloth clamshell box. The Kelmscott Bookshop 12 - 91 2016 $4500

Rossetti, Dante Gabriel 1828-1882 *The Early Italian Poets from Ciullo d'Alcamo t Dante Alighieri....* London: Smith, Elder & Co., 1861. First edition, one of 600 copies, presentation copy inscribed by author to Thomas Keightley, original brown cloth, gilt title to spine and cover design by author, professionally recased, common repair for this title due to text block being too heavy for binding, light rubbing to edges and boards, short, expertly repaired closed tear to book cloth along rear board and spine, interior clean and bright, housed in handsome green half morocco slipcase with few scuff marks to spine, very good. The Kelmscott Bookshop 12 - 92 2016 $3200

Rossetti, Dante Gabriel 1828-1882 *Letters of Dante Gabriel Rossetti.* Oxford: at the Clarendon Press, 1965-1967. First edition, 4 volumes, bound in original dark blue cloth with title and editors to spines, interior pages bright and clean, near fine, in publisher's very dust jackets in light red and cream with Rossetti portrait on front cover, price clipped, otherwise very good. The Kelmscott Bookshop 13 - 46 2016 $250

Rossetti, Dante Gabriel 1828-1882 *Poems.* London: F. S. Ellis, 1870. 8vo., presentation inscription from author for friend, Arthur Hughes; dark green cloth boards with gilt title to spine, attractive gilt decoration to spine and boards, minor wear to edges and slight discoloration to boards, clean, bright interior with decorative endpieces, housed in black cloth covered clamshell box, gilt label to spine, very good. The Kelmscott Bookshop 12 - 93 2016 $6400

Rossetti, Dante Gabriel 1828-1882 *The Poems of Dante Gabriel Rossetti.* London: Ellis & Elvey, 1904. No. 7 of 30 numbered copies, with plates on Japanese vellum, 25 copies for subscribers and 5 for presentation, lovely set, bound in full vellum, top edge gilt, slight soiling in gilt on fore-edge of volume II, beautifully printed with 18 full page illustrations and frontispieces from Rossetti's paintings and drawings, each protected by tissue guard giving the name of the work, vellum binding in very good condition with just lightest signs of handling, gilt title and author to spine, interior pristine, bookplate of Frederick William Brown affixed to each front pastedown, original blue ribbon placemarks present, housed in modern green cloth slipcase, fine. The Kelmscott Bookshop 13 - 47 2016 $1300

Rossetti, Dante Gabriel 1828-1882 *So This Then is the House of Life: Being a Collection of Sonnets by....* Aurora: Roycroft Shop, 1899. Copy# 15 out of 25 copies specially illuminated by hand and bound in suede, signed by Elbert Hubbard and illuminator Frances Kelly, this book is number 15, bound in three quarter red suede with soft leather edges, gilt title stamped to leather title label, red ribbon placemarker attached to spine, suede and leather edges show some wear as is their wont. Tavistock Books Bibliolatry - 23 2016 $600

Rossetti, Dante Gabriel 1828-1882 *The Collected Works of Dante Gabriel Rossetti.* Ellis and Elvey, 1897. New edition, 2 volumes, original dark blue cloth with elaborate gilt design to spine and covers, pale blue decorated endpapers, cloth just very little marked and rubbed in places, gilt design in particulary clean and bright state, bookplate volume i. Bertram Rota Ltd.   February List 2016 - 46 2016   £150

Rossetti, Dante Gabriel 1828-1882 *The Collected Works of...* London: Ellis, 1905-1906. Reprint, 8vo., 2 volumes, attractive period binding of half parchment with green cloth, art noveau gilt design on spines, dark green leather title labels lettered gilt, marbled endpapers, top edge gilt, silk ties, near fine set. Peter Ellis 112 - 341 2016 £275

Rossetti, Maria Francesca *Aneddoti Italian. Italian Anecdotes.* London and Edinburgh: William and Norgate, 1867. First edition, octavo, original blindstamped green cloth, gilt lettering, cloth slightly worn, small early library pocket on rear pastedown, stamped discard notice, very good. The Brick Row Book Shop   Miscellany 69 - 71 2016 $400

Rossetti, William Michael 1829-1919 *Notes on the Royal Academy Exhibition 1868.* London: John Camden Hotten Piccadilly, 1868. First edition, original cream paper wrappers with black title to front panel, covers darkened along edges with minor soiling and few spots of foxing, few chips to spine panel and to rear corner, interior clean overall with few splits to binding and few small spots of foxing on first and last few pages, housed in modern green cloth covered slipcase with black leather title label to spine and pull out chemise, very good. The Kelmscott Bookshop 12 - 96 2016 $750

Rossi-Wilcox, Susan M. *Dinner for Dickens the Culinary History of Mrs. Charles Dickens's Menu Book.* London: Prospect Books, 2005. Loosely inserted newspaper articles relating to publication, half title, plates, original blue cloth, very good in dust jacket. Jarndyce Antiquarian Booksellers CCXVIII - 1427 2016 £22

Rostand, Edmond *Cyrano De Bergerac.* Orleans: Maurice Rouam, 1947. No. 1049 of 1500 copies for slae (and 26 copies ot for sale),, 330 x 257mm., unbound as issued in illustrated paper wrappers with (presumably) original glassine, in a (somewhat marked and soiled but very sturdy) cloth clamshell box, numerous illustrations in text, 19 plates, one double page, all by Albert Dubout, with pochoir coloring by Bellande, presentation copy signed by artist for Louis Lek, 3 inch tear lower inside corner of rear wrapper, glassine slight damaged, otherwise in very fine condition.   Phillip J. Pirages   67 - 287   2016 $750

Rostand, Edmond *Cyrano de Bergerac.* New York: Heritage Press, 1964. printed red boards, lettered gilt, spine faded and slightly rubbed, fine in slipcase, illustrations by Pierre Brissaud, Sandglass pamphlet laid in.   Argonaut Book Shop   Heritage Press 2015 - 2032   2016 $45

Rostenberg, Leona *Old & Rare.* New York: Schram, 1974. First edition, 8vo. photos, author's presentation, edges little spotted, otherwise very good, tight copy in somewhat soiled dust jacket.   Second Life Books, Inc.   196 B - 504   2016 $45

Rostinio, Pietro *Compendio Di Tvita La Cirvgia per Peitro & Leoducio Rostini Medici...* Venice: Spineda, 1630. 8 plates, small 8vo., early vellum, text foxed in parts.   James Tait Goodrich   X-78 - 493   2016 $495

Rotary Club of Signapore *A Handbook of Information Presented by the Rotary Club and Municipal Commission of the Town of Singapore.* Singapore: Publicity Committe of the Rotary Club of Singaproe, 1933. Large 4to., original decorated wrappers, illustrations, front cover little marked, internally very good, very rare.   Sotheran's   Travel and Exploration - 174   2016   £498

Roth, Philip *The Human Stain.* Franklin Library, 2000. First edition, one of 1300 copies, signed by author, frontispiece by Dante Da Vinci, 8vo., original grey leather stamped gilt to both boards, backstrip lettered gilt with four imitation raised bands, all edges gilt, page marks, marbled endpapers, fine.   Blackwell's Rare Books   B184 - 226   2016   £200

Roth, Philip *Operation Skylock.* New York: Simon & Schuster, 1993. Uncorrected proof, Harold Bloom's copy, with TNS by Roth from two years prior laid in, note folded, else fine, proof has Bloom's notations on front cover and summary page, handling apparent to covers, very good in wrappers, good association.   Ken Lopez Bookseller   166 - 108   2016 $1500

Roth, Philip *Operation Shylock: a confession.* New York: Simon & Schuster, 1993. First edition, signed by author, grey cloth backed boards, gilt lettering to spine, fine, in dust jacket.   Argonaut Book Shop   Literature 2015 - 5316   2016 $300

Roth, Philip *The Plot Against America.* Boston: New York: Houghton Mifflin, 2004. Advance reading copy, Literary critic Harold Bloom's copy, with his signature, age toning to pages, near fine in wrappers.   Ken Lopez Bookseller   166 - 109   2016 $350

Roth, Philip *Portnoy's Complaint.* New York: Random House, 1969. First edition, inscribed by author in month of publication to photographer Naomi Savage and her husband the artist, David Savage, bit of offsetting to endpapers and between pages 200-201, small spot to topstain near fine in very near fine, corner clipped but not price clipped dust jacket with slightest wear to spine extremities.   Ken Lopez Bookseller   166 - 107   2016 $2500

Rothfield, Otto *With Pen and Rifle in Kishtwar.* Bombay: D. P. Taraporevala Sons & Co., 1918. First edition, small 8vo., original green cloth, gilt, 6 photo plates, slightly rubbed, else very good.   Sotheran's   Hunting, Shooting & Fishing - 19   2016   £950

Rothschild, James De, Le Baron *Catalogue Des Livres Composant La Bibliotheque De Feli M. Le Baron James De Rothschild.* Paris: Damascene Morgand, 1884-1920. First edition, no. 400 of 400 copies, 260 x 171mm., 5 volumes, pleasing red three quarter morocco, raised bands, gilt titling, top edges gilt, other edges untrimmed, frontispiece, numerous illustrations in text and 52 plates, 14 of these folding, 8 plates in color highlighted with gold, front free endpaper with tiny 'EK' ink stamp of Ernst Kyriss, extremities just slightly rubbed, isoalted, mild offsetting from in-text illustrations, but fine, clean, fresh and bright inside and out.   Phillip J. Pirages   67 - 305   2016 $2250

Rothschild, Walter *The Genus Dendrolagus (Three Kangaroos).* London: Transactions of the Zoological Society of London, Volume 21, 1935. Quarto, 16 chromolithographic plates by Frohawk, 7 photos, quarter red morocco and papered boards, fine.   Andrew Isles Natural History Books   55 - 7867   2016 $2500

Rottenberg, D. A. *Neurological Classics in Modern Translation.* New York: Hafner, 1977. Nice copy, original binding.   James Tait Goodrich   X-78 - 494   2016 $75

Roucher-Deratte, Claude *Lecon Physiologico-Meteorologique sur les Constitutions des Saisons Relativvement a l'Economie Animale et Vegetale....* Montpellier: Auguste Ricard le 11 1804. First edition, some light dampstaining in gutters to few gatherings, last two leaves repaired in inner margin, 8vo., largely unopened in contemporary pink wrappers with handwritten paper label on spine, spine bit frayed, very good.   Blackwell's Rare Books   B186 - 134   2016   £500

Roughley, T. C *Fishes of Australia and their Technology.* Sydney: Government printer, 1916. Color plates, publisher's green decorated cloth, inscribed by author to A. G. Butler, very good.   Andrew Isles Natural History Books   55 - 38723   2016 $300

Roulin, M. *Memoire Pour Servir a l'Histoire du Tapir, et Description d'une Espece Nouvelle Appartant aux hautes Regions de la Cordillere des Andes.*   Paris: Annales des Science Naturele Zoologie, 1829. Quarto, 3 folding uncolored lithographed plates, binder's half cloth and marbled boards, partly unopened, fine.   Andrew Isles Natural History Books   55 - 12548   2016 $300

The Roumaunt of the Rose.   Florence Press, 1908. 7/12 copies, printed on vellum, text in double columns, 20 color printed plates by Norman Wilkinson and Keith Henderson (10 each) tipped to grey paper and bound after text, captioned tissue guards present, lighter than usual offsetting to guards, fly-title and initial leaves printed in blue, imperial 8vo., original limp vellum, green silk ties (two at rear sometime split and skillfully glued back in), front cover and spine lettered gilt, little crease to head of spine, very good.   Blackwell's Rare Books   Marks of Genius - 40   2016   £5500

Rourke, J. P.   *The Proteas of Southern Africa.*   Cape Town: Purnell, 1980. Folio, color plates by Fay Anderson and others, rebound in full blue morocco, fine.   Andrew Isles Natural History Books   55 - 9693   2016 $600

Rouse, William Henry Denham   *Greek Votive Offerings.* Cambridge: at the University Press, 1902. 8vo., unopened, brown publisher's cloth, gilt titling to spine, gilt illustration to front cover, top edge gilt, some small spots of rubbing and wear, good binding.   Unsworths Antiquarian Booksellers Ltd.   E04 - 91   2016   £60

Rousseau, Jean Jacques   1712-1778   *The Confessions.* New York: Brentano's, 1928. 8vo., 2 volumes, contemporary half purple morocco, gilt panelled spines, floral centre tools, marbled endpapers, top edge gilt, others uncut, 13 plates, little chip to top edge of front free endpaper, otherwise very nice.   Sotheran's   Piccadilly Notes - Summer 2015 - 259   2016   £350

Rousseau, Jean Jacques   1712-1778   *Eloisa; or a Series of Original Letters.*   Philadelphia: Samuel Longscope, 1796. First American edition, Volume i-(iii), uniformly slightly browned, occasional light foxing, few leaves frayed at edges, 12mo. in 6's, contemporary tree sheep, flat spines with gilt ruled compartments, red lettering pieces, numbered gilt direct, cracks in joints (volume ii the worst), some wear to extremities, labels of Tremont (Subscription) Library, Boston, inside front covers, slipcase.   Blackwell's Rare Books   B186 - 135   2016   £1200

Rousseau, Jean Jacques   1712-1778   *Emilius and Sophia or a New System of Education.*   London: printed by H. Baldwin, 1783. 4 volumes, frontispiece, 3 further frontispieces, 2 engraved plates, 12mo., 4 volumes, bound without half titles, paper flaw to foot of volume III, B2 with loss to a catchword, contemporary tree calf, gilt banded spines, red morocco labels, hinge cracked, spines rubbed and slightly chipped at head and tail.   Jarndyce Antiquarian Books   CCXV - 925   2016   £280

Routh, C. H. F.   *Infant Feeding and Its Influence on Life or the Causes and Prevention of Infant Mortality.*   New York: Wood, 1879. Third edition, original binding.   James Tait Goodrich   X-78 - 453   2016 $95

Routledge's Etiquette for Gentlemen.   London: George Routledge & sons, 1864. Half title, color frontispiec eand additional title, original blue decorated cloth, leading inner hinge slightly cracking, all edges gilt, very good.   Jarndyce Antiquarian Books   CCXV - 385   2016   £75

Routledge's Etiquette for Ladies.   London: George Routledge & Sons, 1864. Half title, color frontispiece and additional title, original brick-red decorated cloth, all edges gilt, very good.   Jarndyce Antiquarian Books   CCXV - 386   2016   £85

Routledge's Etiquette of Courtship and Matrimony.   London: Routledge Warne and Routledge, 1865. 32mo., color frontispiece and additional title, original green decorated cloth, all edges gilt, very good, crisp.   Jarndyce Antiquarian Books   CCXV - 389   2016   £85

Routledge's Etiquette of Courtship and Matrimony.   London: George Routledge & sons, 1865. 32mo., color frontispiece and additional title, original red-brown decorated cloth, little dulled, all edges gilt.   Jarndyce Antiquarian Books   CCXV - 388   2016   £75

Routledge's Everlasting Alphabet and Little Words. London: George Routledge, n.d. circa, 1880. 12mo., flexible card wrappers, slight bit of some wear and soil, 6 different alphabets in varying fonts and arrangements, 3 letter words, with 2 lovely full page chromolithographs, printed on cloth by Kronheim.   Aleph-bet Books, Inc.   111 - 11   2016 $200

Routledge's Japanese Almanac.   Boston: W. B. Clark & Curruth, 1886. Printed in New York, 24mo., cloth backed pictorial boards, 8 beautiful full page chromolithographs. Aleph-bet Books, Inc.   111 - 233   2016 $325

Rowe, Elizabeth Singer *Friendship in Death in Letters from the Dead to the Living.* London: C. Cooke, 1797. 12mo., 4 engraved plates, tailpieces, small engraving on title, stained, foxed throughout, original dark calf, heavily worn, cover off, ink signatures on titlepage and title verso (Madam Codman, Josh Brooksby and George Wilson), rubber ink stamped numbers on title verso, blind emboss stamps on first and last few leaves, including title, bookplate of Charles T. Congdon (1821-1891).   Jeff Weber Rare Books   181 - 34   2016 $35

Rowe, James *Five Years to Freedom.* Boston: Little Brown, 1971. First edition, signed by author, additionally this copy inscribed and annotated by Elizabeth Starkey, a nurse at the 24th Evac. Hospital in Long Binh where Rowe was taken, inscribed by Starkey with long paragraph telling her story, near fine in very good dust jacket with internal tape mending.   Ken Lopez Bookseller   166 - 138   2016 $450

Rowe, Nicholas *Tamerlane, a Tragedy.* London: printed for and sold by W. Oxlade, 1776. 12mo., disbound, a piracy.   Jarndyce Antiquarian Booksellers   CCXVI - 463   2016   £25

Rowland, Mabel *Bert Williams: Son of Laughter: a Symposium of Tribute to the Man and to His Work...* New York: English Crafters, 1923. First edition, neat contemporary gift inscription, fine in attractive, very good dust jacket that is chipped at crown, affecting bout onee half of thet title.   Between the Covers Rare Books   202 - 99   2016 $1500

Rowlands, Henry *Mona Antiqua Restaurata.* Dublin: printed by Aaron Rhames for Robert Owen, 1723. First edition, 4to., 10 plates, titlepage in red and black, woodcut initials, some lineages illustrated in text, lightly toned, occasional light foxing, small blind embossed coat of arms to titlepage and following three pages, contemporary brown mottled calf, gilt spine with brown label, raised bands, all edges red, marbled endpapers, rubbed, endcaps worn with some loss, joints split but cards holding, very good, armorial bookplate of Earls of Macclesfield.   Unsworths Antiquarian Booksellers Ltd.   E05 - 11   2016   £360

Rowley, Hugh *Advice to Parties About to Marry.* London: John Camden Hotten, 1872. Half title, illustrations, lacking following endpaper, original green cloth, bevelled boards, blocked gilt, little rubbed and dulled, all edges gilt.   Jarndyce Antiquarian Books   CCXV - 390   2016   £45

Rowley, Ian *Behavioural Ecology of the Galah, Eolophus Roseicapillus in the Wheatbelt of Western Australia.* Chipping Norton: Surrey Beatty, 1990. Octavo, color photos, laminated boards.   Andrew Isles Natural History Books   55 - 4000   2016 $40

Rowling, J. K. *Harry Potter and the Chamber of Secrets.* New York: Scholastic Press, 1999. First American edition, later printing, with 'ancestor' instead of 'descendant' to page 332, in second state binding and dust jacket, with 'Year 2' badge on spine, and priced $17.95, inscribed by author, royal blue boards and green cloth, checker pattern to boards in blind, spine lettered in silver, original pictorial dust jacket designed by the artist, illustrations by Mary GrandPre, near fine with corners very lightly bumped and tiny scuff to bottom of front board, else fine, dust jacket with touch of light creasing to extremities, else bright and clean, overall very tight and fresh.   B & B Rare Books, Ltd.   2016 - JKR006   2016 $600

Rowling, J. K. *Harry Potter and the Chamber of Secrets.* New York: Scholastic Press, 2002. Collector's edition, publisher's Taratan bonded leather, with two raised bands to spine, onlay illustration to front panel, lettered in gilt, all edges gilt, blue and green diamond patterned endpapers, full color illustration after original dust jacket art laid in at rear, original acetate dust jacket, lettered in white, with publisher's gold sticket to front panel, near fine or better with just hint of rubbing to spine ends, else fine, dust jacket with few very minor scuffs, else fine, lovely deluxe copy, illustrations by Mary GrandPre.   B & B Rare Books, Ltd.   2016 - JKR007   2016 $150

Rowling, J. K. *Harry Potter and the Goblet of Fire.* London: Bloomsbury, 2000. First edition, first printing "First published in Great Britain in 2000/.../First edition" on copyright page, signed by author, octavo, cloth backed boards,.   John W. Knott, Jr./L.W. Currey, Inc.   Fall-Winter 2015 - 18571   2016 $3000

Rowling, J. K. *Harry Potter and the Goblet of Fire.* London: Bloomsbury, 2000. First edition, fine in near fine dust jacket, light creasing on bottom edge, this copy contains errors of the first printing that were corrected in later copies.   Bella Luna Books   2016 - t9459   2016 $82

Rowling, J. K. *Harry Potter and the Half-Blood Prince.* New York: Scholastic Inc., 2005. First American deluxe edition, illustrations by Mary GrandPre, publisher's black cloth lettered in metaliic purple, original pictorial dust jacket, housed in publisher's pictorial green slipcase, with illustrations to panels, lettered in gilt, in publisher's shrinkwrap, original ad and price stickers, as new with small opening to shrinkwrap.   B & B Rare Books, Ltd.   2016 - JKR010   2016 $100

Rowling, J. K. *Harry Potter and the Order of the Phoenix.* New York: Scholastic Press, 2003. First American edition, illustrations by Mary GranPre, bright blue boards and gray cloth, with checker pattern to boards in blind, spine lettered in metallic blue, original pictorial dust jacket, dust jacket with some very slight creasing to spine head, else fine, handsome copy, fine.   B & B Rare Books, Ltd.   2016 - JKR008   2016 $50

Rowling, J. K. *Harry Potter and the Sorcerer's Stone.* New York: Scholastic Press, 2000. Collector's edition, green-black Taratan bonded leather, two raised bands to spine, onlay illustration from front panel, lettered gilt, all edges gilt, red and blue diamond patterned endpapers, publisher's acetate dust jacket, lettered in white, near fine, tiny split to front hinge at spine tail, minor rubbing to spine head, else fine, dust jacket with some light wear to spine and few minor scuffs, else fine, overall attractive deluxe copy.   B & B Rare Books, Ltd.   2016 - JKR009   2016 $150

Rowson, Susanna *Reuben and Rachel or Tales of Old Times.*   sold by him and by author (and others),   1798. First edition, 2 volumes in 1, browning and foxing (as usual), staining from turn-ins, textblock strained and few gatherings proud, contemporary ownership inscription of Miss Lucy H. Boice, Worcester, 8vo., original sheep, red lettering piece, worn, spine slightly defective at head and foot, sound.   Blackwell's Rare Books   B186 - 136   2016   £1500

Roy, Arundhati *Address to the Lannan Foundation.*   n.p.: Klean Karma Press, 2002. Chapbook printing, signed by author, uncommon.   Ken Lopez Bookseller   166 - 111   2016 $450

Roy, Arundhati *The God of Small Things.*   London: Flamingo, 1997. First edition, near fine, light shelfwear, fine dust jacket.   Bella Luna Books   2016 - t2405   2016 $82

Royal Asiatic Society *Catalogue of Printed Books Published Before 1932 in the Library of the Royal Asiatic Society.*   London: Royal Asiatic Society, 1940. Cloth, 4to., bumped at head and tail of spine and corners.   Oak Knoll Books   310 - 266   2016 $300

Royal Dublin Society *Essays and Observations on the Following Subjects Viz. O Trade - Husbandry of flax - raising Banks Against Tides and Floods - Hops....*   Dublin: pritned: London: Reprinted and sold by Charles Corbett, 1740. 4 engraved folding plates, 8vo., fine, clean copy, full contemporary calf, raised and gilt banded spine, repeat gilt flower head device, red morocco label, from the Library Of Invercauld Castle, Braemar.   Jarndyce Antiquarian Booksellers   CCXVI - 498   2016   £1500

Royal Society of Canada *Proceedings and Transactions of the Royal Society of Canada Second Series Volume II Meeting of May 1896.*   Toronto and London: John Durie & Son, The Copp-Clark Co. & Bernard Quaritch,   1896. Quarto, dark blue cloth, gilt tiles to spines, half title 4 maps and black and white illustrations, inner hinge cracks due to size and wear to edges.   Schooner Books Ltd.   115 - 200   2016 $45

Royal Society of Canada *Proceedings and Transactions of the Royal Society of Canada Third Series Volume VI Meeting of May 1912.*   Toronto & London: James Hope & son, The Copp Clark Co. & Bernard Quaritch, 1913. Dark blue cloth with gilt titles to spines, half title, quarto, diagrams, figures, maps and black and white illustrations, some wear to covers, otherwise very good.   Schooner Books Ltd.   115 - 201   2016 $45

Royde-Smith, Naomi *The Lover.*   London: Constable, 1928. First edition, 8vo., author's presentation, light blue patterned cloth over flexible boards, paper spine label, cover somewhat faded, very good, tight copy.   Second Life Books, Inc.   196 B - 510   2016 $65

Ruby, Robert H. *Dreamer Prophets of the Columbia Plateau.*   Norman: University of Oklahoma Press/,   1988. First edition, 4to., color and black and white reproductions, green cloth, very fine with pictorial dust jacket.   Argonaut Book Shop   Native American 2015 - 7247   2016 $45

Ruby, Robert H. *Myron Eells and the Puget Sound Indians.*   Seattle: Superior Pub. Co., 1976. First edition, 4to.m frontispiece, profusely illustrated with text illustrations, early photos, red cloth, fine with slightly rubbed pictorial dust jacket.   Argonaut Book Shop   Native American 2015 - 3370   2016 $50

Rudland, E. M. *Selection from Ballads of Old Birmingham.* Birmingham: printed for Private Distribution, Leonard Jay, 1945. First edition, one of 85 copies, printed in black and red, typographic border to titlepage and armorial bearings by A. Michael Fletcher also printed in red, small folio, original quarter tan cloth, backstrip gilt lettered, grey-green boards, foxed endpapers, very good.   Blackwell's Rare Books   B186 - 293   2016   £60

Ruines d'Angkor.   Saigon: Edition Photo Nadal, circa, 1925. Oblong large 4to., original grey wrappers, lettered gilt, illustrated in brown, 48 full page photographic illustrations in sepia photogravure on 24 leaves, backstrip renwed, very light wear to edges of wrappers, otherwise good.   Sotheran's   Travel and Exploration - 156   2016   £198

Rukeyser, Muriel *The Green Wave.*   New York: Doubleday, 1948. First edition, 8vo., very good in little soiled dust jacket, inscribed by author for Bill Claire.   Second Life Books, Inc.   196 B - 511   2016 $100

Rules and Orders of the Public Infirmary at Liverpool. Liverpool: printed by John Sadler, 1749. Some browning and dustiness, disbound, stamp of Wigan Public Libraries on titlepage verso.   Jarndyce Antiquarian Booksellers   CCXVI - 367   2016   £225

Runsell, Frank *The Pima Indians. in Twenty Sixth Annual Report of Bureau of American Ethnology.* Washington: GPO, 1908. 47 plates, illustrations, original cloth, extremities rubbed, internally clean.   Dumont Maps and Books 133 - 76   2016 $75

Runyon, Alfred Damon *The Army of God Knows Where.* Chicago: American Asphalatum& Rubber Co., 1911. First edition, one sheet folded and ribbon tied to make four pages, very light pencil name, light edgewear, still just about fine, attractively printed pamphlet, rare, possibly unique.   Between the Covers Rare Books   208 - 71   2016 $16,000

Ruppert, Karl *The Caracol; at Chichen Itz Yucatan, Mexico.* Washington: Carnegie Inst., 1935. First edition, frontispiece, illustrations, all maps and plates present, original blue cloth with some rubbing at extremities, patches of discoloration and affecting sturdy binding or the gilt titling on spine and upper board which remains bright, interior leaves bright and crsip despite considerable age discoloration to front and rear endpaper, no markings in text.   Simon Finch 2015 - 001723   2016 $250

Ruscha, Edward *Every Building on the Sunset Strip.* Los Angeles: Edward Ruscha, 1966. Limited to 1000 copies, though not explicity stated, first edition, first issue with small folded flap at end of book, unfolded it is 24 feet long, original white wrappers prited in silver on front an spine, accordion folded book with numerous black and white photos take by Ruscha, spine slightly creased, otherwise near fine, housed in publisher's original silver slipcase.   Heritage Book Shop Holiday 2015 - 97   2016 $6500

Ruscha, Edward *Thirtyfour Parking Lots in Los Angeles.* Los Angeles: Edward Ruscha, 1967. First edition, signed by Ruscha, 31 black and white photos, quarto, original printed paper wrappers, without scarce glassine, wrappers with little toning around edges, near fine, rare signed. Manhattan Rare Book Company   2016 - 1624   2016 $2300

Rusden, Moses *A Further Discoverry of Bees.* London: for the author and by Henry Million, 1679. First edition, engraved frontispiece and 3 folding plates (out inch of first plate is missing where it would have been folded-in, with loss to image), some heavy browning and spotting, stronger in margins, short (25mm) closed tear to fore margin of C5 (just touching text), frontispiece and first plate heavily browned, contemporary sheep, rebacked, large areas of insect damage to covers, corners worn, old reback wearing again with an area of insect damage at foot, from the library of James Stevens Cox (1910-1997).   Maggs Bros. Ltd. 1447 - 369   2016   £300

Rush, Benjamin   1745-1813 *Medical Inquiries and Observations Upon the Diseases of the Mind.* Philadelphia: Kimber & Richardson, 1812. First edition, 2nd state, 8vo., contemporary tree calf, front cover detached, blank piece tor from top of title leaf, text foxed.   M & S Rare Books, Inc. 99 - 284   2016 $950

Rush, Norman *Mating a Novel.* New York: Knopf, 1991. First edition, cloth and boards, endpaper maps, inscribved by author, fine in dust jacket.   Gene W. Baade, Books on the West   2015 - SHEL750   2016 $50

Rushdie, Salman *Midnight's Children.* London: Jonathan Cape, 1981. First English edition, one of only 2500 copies, fine in about fine dust jacket with with typical slight sunning on spine and tiny stain on inside front wrapper.   Between the Covers Rare Books   204 - 101   2016 $1500

Rushdie, Salman *Two Stories.* London: privately printed, 1989. First edition, one of 12 specially bound copies signed by Rushdie, with separate suite of the 8 prints, each signed by artist, large 4to., original full leather with gilt leather onlays by Sally Saumarez Smith, publisher's full cloth folding box, five woodcuts and 3 linocuts by Bhupen Khakhar, as new.   James S. Jaffe Rare Books   Occasional List: Winter 2016 - 124   2016 $10,000

Rushton, Charles *Furnace for a Foe.* H. Jenkins, 1951. First English edition, very good, uncommon, red boards in slightly aged but complete dust jacket, contents very good. I. D. Edrich   Crime - 2016   £20

Ruskin, John   1819-1900 *Dame Wiggins of Lee and Her Seven Wonderful Cats.* Sunnyside, Orpington, Kent: George Allen, 1885. Large paper copy from a later edition, inscribed by the artist, Kate Greenaway for F. Locker-Lampson, 1886, illustrations by Greenaway, original brown cloth with gilt title and illustration on front cover, binding rubbed and bumped, with few light stains, interior pages are generally clean, this copy has a plate of Bert M. Barwis Fund of Trenton Public Library stating the book was a personal gift to the library from Miss Barwis, she was the Supervisor of Kindergartens and Primary Schools for the City of Trenton NJ, call number written in white ink on spine and library ownership indicated by stamp to titlepage, despite flaws, still very nice, desirable copy.   The Kelmscott Bookshop   12 - 48   2016 $400

Ruskin, John   1819-1900 *The Harbours of England.* London: E. Gambart & Co. n.d., 1856. First edition, small folio, 12 beautiful seteel engravings in book, nicely rebacked with original reddish brown cloth, bumping and chipping and fading, still solid, bottom edges of first few pages chipped, otherwise interior very good, previous owner taped an early bookseller auction listing to front free endpaper, very good. The Kelmscott Bookshop   13 - 49   2016 $1500

Ruskin, John 1819-1900 *An Ill-Assorted Marriage.* London: privately printed by Clement Shorter..., 1915. 4to., original red printed wrappers, sewn as issued, very good. Jarndyce Antiquarian Booksellers   CCXVII - 251   2016   £120

Ruskin, John 1819-1900 *Letter to Young Girls.* n.p., 1876. 8 page pamphlet, sewn as issued.   Jarndyce Antiquarian Books   CCXV - 391   2016   £40

Russ, L. B.   *Poems.*   N. P.:: the author, 1940. First edition, 24mo., stapled blue wrappers, photographic portrait of author on front panel, faint crease on rear wrapper, else fine.   Between the Covers Rare Books   207 - 82   2016 $650

Russel, John   *Letters from a Young Painter Abroad to His Friends in England.*   London: printed for W. Russel, 1748. First edition, 8vo., some light foxing, offset browning to titlepage border, alter ownership stamp "Isherwood" at head, contemporary calf, gilt ruled borders, expertly rebacked in matching style, raised & gilt bands, red morocco label. Jarndyce Antiquarian Booksellers   CCXVI - 500   2016   £480

Russell, Alan   *The Forest Prime Evil.*   New York: Walker, 1992. First edition, signed by author, very fine in dust jacket.   Mordida Books   2015 - 001961   2016 $60

Russell, Bertrand   1872-1970   *History of Western Philosophy and Its Connection with Political and Social Circumstances from the Earliest Times to the Present Day.* London: George Allen and Unwin, 1946. First edition, 8vo., newly bound in half black morocco, spine lettered and ruled gilt, top edges gilt, very nice.   Sotheran's Piccadilly Notes - Summer 2015 - 262   2016   £598

Russell, Bertrand   1872-1970   *On Education, Especially in Early Childhood.*   London: George Allen & Uwin, 1927. Third edition, half title, final ad leaf, original blue cloth, blocked in red, slightly rubbed, signature of G. Beeson. Jarndyce Antiquarian Books   CCXV - 929   2016   £20

Russell, Bertrand   1872-1970   *Our Knowledge of the External World.*   New York: W. W. Norton and Co., 1929. Second US edition, original cloth and dust jacket, little browning to endpapers, partially uncut, near fine.   Sotheran's   Piccadilly Notes - Summer 2015 - 264   2016   £220

Russell, Charles Edward Bellyse   *Lads Clubs: Their History, Organisation and Management.*   London: A. & C. Black, 1932. Half title, frontispiece, original red brown cloth, very good in browned, and slightly torn dust jacket. Jarndyce Antiquarian Books   CCXV - 930   2016   £24

Russell, D. A.   *Antonine Literature.*   Oxford: Clarendon Press, 1990. First edition, 8vo., blue boards, gilt lettered to spine, green dust jacket, near fine, ownership inscription of C. D. N. Costa, Oxford University Press complimentary advice note loosely inserted.   Unsworths Antiquarian Booksellers Ltd.   E05 - 59   2016   £35

Russell, Franklin   *The Mountains of America: from Alaska to Great Smokies.*   New York: Harry N. Abrams, 1975. Folio, profusely illustrated with color photos, gray cloth lettered in silver, some minor rubbing to rear pocket, very slight bump to upper front corner, else fine.   Argonaut Book Shop Mountaineering 2015 - 706   2016 $45

Russell, George   *Sunday School and Other Anecdotes.* London: printed by Pewtress, Low & Pewtress, 1819. Errata slip, contemporary tree calf, gilt spine and borders, leading hinge slightly splitting, Renier booklabel, nice. Jarndyce Antiquarian Books   CCXV - 931   2016   £25

Russell, Jerry   *On the Loose.*   San Francisco: Sierra Club, 1967. First edition, 63 color and black and white photos, half blue cloth, blue decorated boards, very fine with slipcase.   Argonaut Book Shop   Natural History 2015 - 710   2016 $75

Russell, John   *Seurat.*   London: Thames & Hudson, 1965. First edition, octavo, lavishly illustrated, presentation copy inscribed by author, small bump at top edge, otherwise near fine in near fine, slightly marked dust jacket with one nick.   Peter Ellis   112 - 352   2016   £35

Russell, John Fuller   *The Ancient Knight or Chapters on Chivalry.*   London: W. J. Cleaver, 1849. Frontispiece, 14 page catalog, original scarlet cloth by Bone & Son, largely faded to brown, little rubbed, spine chipped at head, contemporary signature of Leo. G. Watlyn Thomas.   Jarndyce Antiquarian Books   CCXV - 392   2016   £40

Russell, John Scott   *Systematic Technical Education for the English People.*   London: Bradbury & Evans & Co., 1869. First edition, half title, 1 page ads, odd spot, original brown cloth, bevelled boards, maroon labels, darkened and rubbed, booklabel of Library of Faculty of Physicians and Surgeons, Glasgow.   Jarndyce Antiquarian Books   CCXV - 932   2016   £35

Russell, Phillips   *Bud 2nd: a Collection of Literary Stories...*   Chapel Hill: Phillips Russell's Class, 1934. Quarto, quarter canvas and blue card wrappers with title either hand inked or dittoed on front wrapper, 40 mimeographed leaves printed rectos only, trifle age toned, else very near fine, frontispiece.   Between the Covers Rare Books   204 - 104   2016 $500

Russia and America A. D. 1830. London: n.p., 1831. 16 pages, sewn as issued in original drab wrappers, slight dampstain in lower inner margin, all edges gilt. Jarndyce Antiquarian Booksellers CCXVII - 11 2016 £150

Rust, Art *The Art Rust Jr. Baseball Quiz Book.* New York: Facts On File Publications, 1985. First edition, fine in fine dust jacket, inscribed to Joe DiMaggio 7/13/85, with letter of provenance signed by DiMaggio's two granddaughters. Between the Covers Rare Books 202 - 11 2016 $600

Rutari, A. *Charles Dickens.* Bielsfeld and Leipzig: Velhagen & Klasing, 1912. Original stiff grey card wrappers, portrait onlay, very good, illustrations. Jarndyce Antiquarian Booksellers CCXVIII - 1428 2016 £20

Rutherford, Samuel *Joshua Redivivus or Mr. Rutherford's Letters, Divided in two parts.* Rotterdam: in the Year, 1664. First edition, 8vo., some occasional light dampstaining, larger ink blots, very small hole through V1 (touching text on verso), late 19th century 'Presbyterian blue' morocco by Riviere & Son, panelled and lettered gilt, gilt gauffered edges, contemporary flyleaves and 'Dutch-gilt' pastedowns preserved from original binding, from the library of James Stevens Cox (1910-1997), 17th century calligraphic inscription 'Mrs. Anna Montgomerie Her Booke", long list of numbers and letters written in ink on front flyleaf, mid 19th century bookplate of John Whitefoord Mackenize. Maggs Bros. Ltd. 1447 - 370 2016 £500

Rutherford, William *A View of Antient History...* London: printed for the author and sold by J. Mururay, 1788. 1791, 2 volumes, large folding engraved map, mounted on linen, 8vo., some light pencil notes and crosses in margins, otherwise clean, fresh copy, full contemporary calf, gilt ruled spine, red gilt morocco labels. Jarndyce Antiquarian Booksellers CCXVI - 501 2016 £185

Rutkow, I. M. *The History of Surgery in the United States 1775-1900.* San Francisco: Norman, 1988. Original binding, as new in dust jacket. James Tait Goodrich X-78 - 495 2016 $175

Rutkow, I. M. *The History of Surgery in the United States Volume 2.* San Francisco: Norman, 1992. Original binding, as new in dust jacket. James Tait Goodrich X-78 - 496 2016 $175

Ruyl, Beatrie Baxter *Little Indian Maidens at Work and Play.* London & New York: Nister & Dutton, n.d. circa, 1909. Small 4to., pictorial paste-on, slight rubbing, near fine, each page features bold color illustrations depicting the daily lives of Indian girls, text calligraphic with large red decorative initials at start of each page. Aleph-bet Books, Inc. 112 - 258 2016 $250

Ryan, J. S. *Charles Dickens and New Zealand: a Colonial Image.* Wellington: A. H. & A. W. Reed, 1965. no. 301 of 750 copies, illustrations, facsimiles, original red cloth, very good in dust jacket. Jarndyce Antiquarian Booksellers CCXVIII - 1429 2016 £25

Ryder, John *The Case for Legibility.* London: Bodley Head, 1979. First edition, foolscap 8vo., original blue cloth, backstrip lettered in gilt with very slight lean to spine, dust jacket with very gentle fading to backstrip panel, very good, inscribed by author for Susan La Roux.   Blackwell's Rare Books B186 - 278 2016 £50

Ryff, Walter Hermann *Der Erste Theyl der Kleynen Teutschen Apoteck.* Strasburg: S. Emmel, 1559-1566. 3 parts in 1 volume, 4to., contemporary full blindstamped vellum over wood boards, clasps present but defective, extremely rare. James Tait Goodrich X-78 - 497 2016 $4750

Ryley, Elizabeth *Homicide with Charm.* Gerald G. Swan, 1946. Blue cloth, gilt, largely complete but frayed dust jacket with tear to base of front panel, top corner of front endpaper has been excised and there is name on half titlepage, otherwise very good, nonetheless uncommon with jacket. I. D. Edrich Crime - 2016 £45

Rymer, Thomas *The Tragedies of the Last Age Consider'd and examin'd by the Practice of the Ancients and by the Common sense of All the Ages.* London: for Richard Tonson, 1678. First edition, 8vo., A1-4 lightly foxed, short tear at foot of title, small stains to corner of C5-6, rust spot to E8, F4, leaves K4-8 heavily foxed, 45 x 25mm. piece cut from flyleaf, probably to removed earlier signature, early 19th century half calf and marbled boards, rubbed, corners bumped, from the library of James Stevens Cox (1910-1997). Maggs Bros. Ltd. 1447 - 371 2016 £180

S

Sabin, Ethridge H. *Prince Trixie or Baby Brownie's Birthday.* Chicago: Rand McNally, 1914. First edition, 8vo., cloth pictorial paste-on, mint condition in dust jacket with several edge chips, 8 lovely color plates by Frances Beem and 30 delicate and detailed half page line illustrations. Aleph-bet Books, Inc. 112 - 179 2016 $225

Sacheverell, Henry *Collection of Passages referr'd to by Dr. Henry Sacheverell in His Answer to the Articles of Him Impeachment.* London: printed for Henry Clements, 1710. folio, disbound, half title. Jarndyce Antiquarian Booksellers CCXVI - 502 2016 £85

Sacheverell, Henry *The Speech of Henry Sacheverell, D.D. Upon His Impeachment at the Bar of the House of Lords in Westminster Hall March 7 1709/10.* London: printed in the year, 1710. Folio, some foxing, small marginal ink stain to extreme upper edge of a few leaves, disbound. Jarndyce Antiquarian Booksellers CCXVI - 504 2016 £85

Sacheverell, Henry *The Speech... upon His Impeachment at the Bar of the House of Lords, in Westminster Hall March 7 1709/10.* London: printed in the year, 1710. 8vo., browned, one corner creased, disbound. Jarndyce Antiquarian Booksellers CCXVI - 503 2016 £20

Sachs, Nelly *Selected Poems Including the Verse Play, Eli.* London: Jonathan Cape, 1968. First UK edition, head and tail of spine slightly bruised, very good in very good dust jacket, slightly rubbed at edges, octavo, cloth backed boards. Peter Ellis 112 - 344 2016 £45

Sackheim, Eric *The Blues Line: a Collection of Blues Lyrics.* New York: Grossman Pub., 1969. First edition, quarto, fine in age toned, very good dust jacket, author Ralph Ellison's copy with his ownership signature. Between the Covers Rare Books 207 - 41 2016 $800

Sackman, Douglas Cazaux *Wild Men. Ishi and Krober in the Wilderness of Modern America.* New York: Oxford University Press, 2010. First edition, numerous period photos, maps, two-tone boards, very fine with pictorial dust jacket. Argonaut Book Shop Native American 2015 - 7483 2016 $40

Sackville West, Victoria Mary 1892-1962 *The Garden.* London: Michael Joseph, 1946. First edition number 386 of 750 numbered copies, printed on handmade paper and signed by author, 8vo., original brown buckram, lettered gilt on spine and upper cover, top edges gilt, slight sunning to top of upper board and to spine, internally very clean, very good. Sotheran's Piccadilly Notes - Summer 2015 - 263 2016 £378

Sackville West, Victoria Mary 1892-1962 *Solitude a Poem.* London: Hogarth Press, 1938. First edition, 88/100 copies numbered and signed by author, printed on vellum paper, original quarter parchment with terra cotta cloth, backstrip lettered gilt, edges untrimmed, dust jacket with few tiny foxspots at foot of front panel, backstrip panel shade darkened and small amount of very light soiling, very good. Blackwell's Rare Books B186 - 279 2016 £750

Sadler, Marie *Mamma's Angel Child in Toyland.* Chicago: Rand McNally, 1915. First edition, boards, pictorial paste-on, near fine in dust jacket, black and whites in text and 24 full color illustrations plus numerous smaller color illustrations by M. T. Ross. Aleph-bet Books, Inc. 112 - 434 2016 $425

Sage, Betty *Rhymes of Real Children.* New York: Fox Duffield, Oct., 1903. First edition, large square 4to., cloth backed pictorial boards, slight edge and corner wear, else near fine, 6 large color plates, orange and black pictorial border on every page of text, plus small color illustration on dedication page, by Jessie, Willcox Smith, scarce. Aleph-bet Books, Inc. 111 - 434 2016 $600

St. Nerses The Graceful Patriarch of Armenia. Venetiis: in Insula S. Lazari, 1823. Polyglot edition, Small 8vo., frontispiece, engraved titlepage, occasional minor browning, contemporary speckled calf, gilt roll tooled borders on sides flat spine gilt in compartments, red lettering piece, very minor wear, very good. Blackwell's Rare Books B184 - 79 2016 £250

Saint-Cricq, Laurent *Voyage a travers l'Amerique du Sud de L'Ocean Pacifique a L'Ocean Atlantique.* Paris: Librairie de L. Hachette, 1869. First edition, 2 volumes, large quarto, original red quarter morocco, blindstamped red cloth boards, gilt decorations and lettering, all edges gilt, frontispiece, 20 maps, 626 illustrations, by Edouard Riou, edges little rubbed and some light foxing, nearly fine. The Brick Row Book Shop Miscellany 69 - 79 2016 $1750

Saint-Joseph, Pierre De *Idea Philosophiae Naturalis seu Physica.* Paris: G. Josse, 1659. Second edition, 12mo., contemporary calf, engraved frontispiece, front cover detached but present, frontispiece loose, mearly marginal notations first 30 pages, else rather good. Edwin V. Glaser Rare Books 2015 - 10385 2016 $200

St. James's Repartee; or the Witticisms of Fashion, Taste and the Bon Ton.   London: printed for W. Lane, 1791. Engraved frontispiece, 12mo., slight waterstain to foot of frontispiece, old ink splash to page 7, otherwise clean copy, very slightly browned, disbound.   Jarndyce Antiquarian Booksellers   CCXVI - 321   2016   £320

Saint Phalle, Niki De   *Aids - You Can't Catch it Holding Hands.*   Munich and Lucerne: Verlag C. J. Bucher, 1986. First edition, color pictorial laminated boards, quarto, facsimile reproduction of author/artist's original illustrated manuscript, presentation copy inscribed by author for Erica Brausen and Toto Koopman, corners bumped at corners, very good.   Peter Ellis   112 - 345   2016   £225

Saint Pierre, Jacques Henri Bernardin De   1737-1814   *Beauties of the Studies of nature Selected form the Works of.*   New York: Davis for Caritat, 1799. First American edition, 8vo., contemporary calf, front cover nearly detached, signature of RI reformer T(homas) W(ilson) Dorr.   M & S Rare Books, Inc.   99 - 78   2016 $750

Saint Pierre, Jacques Henri Bernardin De   1737-1814   *Paul and Mary an Indian Story.*   London: printed for J. Dodsley, Pall Mall, 1789. 2 volumes, bound without half titles, 12mo., tears with slight loss to blank lower margin of few leaves, final blank removal from end of volume II, early 19th century half calf, gilt banded spines, black labels, marbled boards, some rubbing and slight wear to middle of spine volume II, one section little loose, armorial bookplate of Charles Barclay and W. Douro Hoare.   Jarndyce Antiquarian Booksellers   CCXVI - 505   2016   £150

Saint Pierre, Jacques Henri Bernardin De   1737-1814   *Paul and Virginia.*   London: printed for Vernor & Hood, 1799. Fourth edition, frontispiece, engraved title and printed title, 6 plates and numerous woodcuts, 8vo., frontispiece and engraved title browned, some staining to text, contemporary full dark green morocco, gilt spine, borders and dentelles, slight rubbing to spine, good plus, Renier bookplate.   Jarndyce Antiquarian Booksellers   CCXVI - 506   2016   £85

Saint Pierre, Jacques Henri Bernardin De   1737-1814   *Studies of Nature.*   London: printed by J. W. Myers for W. West, 1798. 8vo., without half title, contemporary half mottled calf, gilt spine, green label, very good, signature of E. Ann Oakes.   Jarndyce Antiquarian Booksellers   CCXVI - 507   2016   £180

Saint Yves, Charles De   *A New Treatise of the Diseases of the Eyes.*   London: Society of Booksellers, 1741. 8vo., modern calf, some light browning and foxing, 18th century ownership signature, very good.   Edwin V. Glaser Rare Books   2015 - 10097   2016 $950

Sainte-Maure, Charles De   *A New Journey through Greece, Aegypt, Palestine, Italy, Swisserland, Alsatia and the Netherlands.*   London: J. Battey, 1735. Second edition, 8vo., contemporary full specked calf, joints cracked, covers worn, clean and crisp.   J. & S. L. Bonham Antiquarian Booksellers   Europe 2016 - 8974   2016   £280

Saito, Shozo   *Bookplates in Japan.*   Tokyo: Meiji-Shobo, 1941. Limited edition of 350 copies, this no. 195, 50 original Japanese bookplates, many in color, each tipped on separate numbered 8.5 x 7 inch tan sheet of handmade rice paper, many bookplates are woodblock prints, each a small jewel in itself, additional printed rice paper sheet of a teapot which serves as endpaper to these bookplates, 10 leaf booklet on rice paper accompanies the bookplates, all bookplates and text fine, bookplates and booklet in original orange chemise which has been archivally strengthened, new label on cover of chemise, chipped label on spine, chemise has done its job well protected text and bookplates the chemise is modern cloth covered clamshell box with paper label on spine.   By the Book, L. C.   45 - 55   2016 $1250

Sala, George Augustus   *Charles Dickens.*   London: George Routledge and Son, 1870. First edition, lacking leading f.e.p., original maroon cloth, front board lettered and blocked gilt with blind borders, little rubbed, good sound copy, quite scarce in cloth.   Jarndyce Antiquarian Booksellers   CCXVIII - 1431   2016   £40

Salinger, Jerome David   *Franny and Zooey.*   Boston: Little Brown and Co., 1961. Uncorrected galleys, string-tied in unprinted gray wrappers with applied paper title label, printed rectos only, slight crease on front wrapper, modest age-toning, else near fine with title handwritten on spine, laid in are press release a publicity statement to booksellers, and seasonal pamphlet reviewing the book press release on Little Brown stationery is interesting as it details an August publication date (eventually published in September) and also announces that the book contain an introduction by Salinger (little additional text that he reluctantly provided was used on jacket flaps and there is no introduction within book itself), additionally these galleys lack dedication page added to published book, rare.   Between the Covers Rare Books   208 - 74 2016 $15,000

Salinger, Jerome David   *Franny and Zooey.*   Boston: Little Brown and Co., 1961. First edition, gray cloth with gilt lettered spine, original green and white dust jacket, near fine with hint of sunning to extremities, else fine, unclipped dust jacket with some light rubbing to spine ends, very tiny nick to front hinge, bright and clean panels, very handsome, fresh copy.   B & B Rare Books, Ltd.   2016 - JDS058   2016 $450

Salinger, Jerome David *Raise High the Roof Beams, Carpenters and Seymour - an Introduction.* Boston: Little Brown and Co., 1959. First edition, usual Third issue with dedication leaf, publisher's blue gray cloth, lettered gilt, original mustard yellow and white dust jacket lettered in black, fine boo, dust jacket with hint of sunning to spine, touch of wear to spine ends else bright and clean, overall near fine and very attractive copy.   B & B Rare Books, Ltd.   2016 - JDS059   2016 $200

Salinger, Jerome David *Raise High the Roof Beam, Carpenters and Seymour an Introduction.* Boston: Little Brown, 1959. First and only edition, later state with dedication page bound in, 8vo., very good plus in dust jacket (some light spotting on endpaper, very good.   Second Life Books, Inc.   197 - 275   2016 $325

Salis, Harriet De *Wrinkles and Notions for Every Household.* London: Longmans, 1890. First edition, half title, 12 page catalog, Aug. 1889, original decorated olive green cloth, leading inner hinge slightly cracking, slightly rubbed.   Jarndyce Antiquarian Books   CCXV - 393   2016   £40

Sallustius Crispus, C. *Bellum Catilinarium et Juugurthinum cum Versione Libnera...* Gloucester: printed by R. Raikes, 1789. Scarce provincial printing, some browning, foxing and minor staining, few wax marks and slight abrasions to blank area of titlepage, 8vo., contemporary sheep, joints and edges repaired, front flyleaf excised, gift inscription dated 1841 to front pastedown, ownership inscription of same era to rear flyleaf, good.   Blackwell's Rare Books   Greek & Latin Classics VII - 80   2016   £250

Sallustius Crispus, C. *La Conjuracion e Catilina y la Guerra de Jugurta.* Madrid: J. Ibarra, 1772. Folio, contemporary Spanish binding of red morocco, covers decorated with gilt Greek key border having gilt suns at corners, enclosing an inner roll border of foliate design, flat spine gilt at either end with central neo-classical motif built of various tools, green morocco label, green silk doublures and marker, edges gilt, slight chip at headband, small worm holes at head and foot of spine, excellent copy, engraved titlepage by Montfort, portrait, 3 engraved plates (including a map) and numerous engravings by Montfort and Carmona after Maella, 3 engraved plates by Fabregat and Ballester and two plates of scripts, one of Phoenician coins, without half title found in most copies, bookplate of Jonathan and Phillida Gili, by Reynolds Stone.   Maggs Bros. Ltd.   1474 - 71   2016 $8500

Sallustius Crispus, C. *Opera.* Birmingham: Typis Johannis Baskerville, 1773. Paper lightly age toned, 4to., contemporary tree calf, boards bordered with gilt roll, marbled endpapers, rebacked preserving lettering piece, corners repaired, old leather scratched, good.   Blackwell's Rare Books   Greek & Latin Classics VII - 79   2016   £200

Sallustius Crispus, C. *Opera quae Supersunt, Omnia.* Andreapoli (St. Andrews): in aedibus academicis excudebat Jacobus Morison, 1796. half title discarded, 12mo., contemporary sprinkled calf, spine divided by double gilt fillet, black morocco lettering piece, arms of City of Edinburgh blocked in gilt to boards, somewhat rubbed, very good.   Blackwell's Rare Books   Greek & Latin Classics VII - 81   2016   £400

Sallustius Crispus, C. *Opera Quae Suerpsunt Omnia.* Andreapoli: in aedibus academicis excudebat Jacobus Morison, 1796. 12mo., half title, lightly dust soiled in places, largely untrimmed in early 20th century green pebbled cloth, spine lettered gilt, backstrip sunned, headcap lightly worn, ownership inscription of G. H. Robinson, good.   Blackwell's Rare Books   B186 - 138   2016   £200

Sallustius Crispus, C. *Opera Quae Supersunt, Omnia.* Andreapoli: in aedibus academicis excudebat Jacobus Morison, 1796. 12mo., contemporary sprinkled calf, spine divided by double gilt fillet, black morocco lettering piece, arms of the city of Edinburgh blocked in gilt to boards, somewhat rubbed, very good.   Blackwell's Rare Books   B186 - 137   2016   £400

Salmon, William *Seplasium. The Compleat English Physician or the Druggist's Shop Opened.* London: for Matthew Gilliflower and George Sawbridge, 1693. First edition, half title and errata/ad leaf and a4 with table on verso that is meant as a slip cancel for the table on X8v bound after X8, small hole through centre of Z8 (damaging two lines), 19th century paper slip tipped in between E32-3 (obscuring small portion of text on first 13 lines), rust spots on Gg1-3, fore corner of Ooo4 folded-in, small rust spot on Ffff4, contemporary calf, front joint and spine repaired, 19th century endleaves, from the library of James Stevens Cox (1910-1997), old signature "R. L. Carr ex donis C. C. Cocks".   Maggs Bros. Ltd.   1447 - 373   2016   £650

Salomon, Charlotte *Charlotte: Life or Theater? An Autobiographical Play.* New York: Viking Press in association with Gary Schwartz, 1981. 769 paintings, very near fine in like dust jacket, tight and lovely copy.   Jeff Hirsch Books   Holiday List 2015 - 17   2016 $100

The Salt Water Gazette for MDCCCXXXV. Glasgow: James Hedderwick & son, 1835. Issues 1 to 14 (all published), later maroon morocco grained cloth, probably 1857 from pencil date, spine lettered gilt, publisher's own copy.   Jarndyce Antiquarian Booksellers   CCXVII - 228   2016   £180

Salt, Henry *A Voyage to Abyssinia and Travels into the Interior of that Country...* London: W. Bulmer & Co. for F. C. and J. Rivington, 1814. First edition, large paper copy in good Regency binding, large 4to., contemporary full tan calf, spine gilt in compartments and lettered in one, highly decorated in gilt, all edges gilt, 28 engraved plates, 2 engraved head and tailpieces, 6 engraved maps, 5 folding and one hand coloured in outline, illustrations in text, roman, greek and arabic types, retaining half title, only minor rubbing to extremities, expertly rebacked, some variable light spotting and browning, armorial bookplate of Frederick Ducane Godman inside front cover.   Sotheran's   Travel and Exploration - 31   2016   £2995

Salten, Felix *A Forest World.* Indianapolis: Bobbs Merrill, 1942. First edition, illustrations by Bob Kuhn, green cloth, short tear to bottom edge of jacket, but fine with pictorial dust jacket. Argonaut Book Shop   Literature 2015 - 7221   2016 $90

Salter, James *Light Years.* New York: Random House, 1975. First edition, fine in fine dust jacket with tiny crease on front flap.   Between the Covers Rare Books   208 - 77   2016 $400

Salter, Robert B. *Textbook of Disorders and Injuries of the Musculoskeletal System.* Baltimore: 1970. Light wear, else good, from the library of Frank H. Netter, with note to that effect on front fly, original binding.   James Tait Goodrich   X-78 - 498   2016 $75

Salter, T. F. *The Angler's Guide...* London: 1825. Sixth edition, small octavo, frontispiece, numerous wood engravings, period binding in full red morocco, raised bands, gilt decorated spine, gilt rules, inner and outer dentelles, top edge gilt, marbled endpapers, 1939 gift inscription on first blank, spine little rubbed at hinges and at head and tail, frontispiece spotted, very good.   Peter Ellis   112 - 13   2016   £195

Saltmarsh, John *Perfume Against the Sulpherous Stinke of the Snuffe of the Light for Smoak, called Novello-Mastix.* London: by Elizabeth Purslow, April 19, 1646. First edition, small 4to., small defect from paper fault in lower fore-corner of title (touching type-ornament border), disbound, uncut, from the library of James Stevens Cox (1910-1997).   Maggs Bros. Ltd.   1447 - 373   2016   £200

Salvin, Osbert *Catalogue of the Picariae in the Collection of the British Museum.* London: British Museum (Natural History), 1892. Octavo, 14 chromolithograph plates, publisher's cloth, 2 small library stamps of Royal Society of Victoria, ownership signataure of J. A. Kershaw (ornithologist of Horn Expedition), fine.   Andrew Isles Natural History Books   55 - 15576   2016 $750

Salzman, L. F. *The History of the County of Warwick.* London: Archibald Constable Oxford University Press, 1904. First edition, 4to., original red cloth lettered gilt on spine with gilt coat of arms on covers, photos, 6 volumes, good very good+ with some fading to covers and spine of volume 1 and 4, slight foxing on prelims, some ghost tape marks in some volumes, some neat scholarly inked notes in volume I of Natural History section.   Any Amount of Books 2015 - A90096   2016   £250

Salzmann, Christian Gotthilf *Gymnastics for Youth.* London: J. Johnson, 1800. First UK edition, octavo, 10 copper engravings, including folding frontispiece, contemporary quarter calf with marbled boards, burgundy leather title label on spine lettered gilt, spine scuffed and little cracked at head and cover edges rubbed, frontispiece little spotted, very good, rare.   Peter Ellis   112 - 159   2016   £850

Salzmann, Christian Gotthilf *Gymnastic's for Youth...* Philadelphia: printed by William Duane, 1802. First American edition, small quarto, 10 engraved plates, contemporary tree calf, rebacked to style at early date, smooth spine with gilt rules and red morocco gilt spine label, some pencil notations on front and rear endpapers, contemporary signature and date, folding map with few short closed tears, staining to inner margin of first quarter of book, not affecting text, except for titlepage, offsetting from plates to text and foxing throughout, as usual, very good.   Heritage Book Shop   Holiday 2015 - 98   2016 $1750

Sampson, Anthony *Mandela. the Authorised Biography.* London: Harper Collins, 1999. First edition, signed and inscribed by Jo. Mandell, who co-directed the 1996 official film biography of Nelson Mandela, for Gritta Weil (1924-2009).   Sotheran's   Travel and Exploration - 33   2016   £78

Samuel Smith & Son Ltd. *Beehive Foundry, Smethwick Section 1. Range List.* Birmingham: Hudson & Son, 1915. 4to., 26 pages, profusely illustrated, stapled as issued in original red wrappers printed in black.   Marlborough Rare Books   List 55 - 42   2016   £100

San Francisco Art Association *Catalogue of the San Francisco Art Association, Mark Hopkins Institute of Art.* San Francisco: Art Association, 1903. First edition, octavo, original pictorial gray wrappers, frontispiece and 11 photographic illustrations, little fading on rear wrapper, fine.   The Brick Row Book Shop   Miscellany 69 - 19   2016 $400

San Francisco Art Association *Catalogue of the Second San Francisco Photographic Salon at the the Mark Hopkins Institute of Art.* San Francisco: San Francisco Art Association & the California Camera Club, 1902. First edition, square octavo, original printed wrappers, 31 illustrations, edges slightly creased, fine.   The Brick Row Book Shop   Miscellany 69 - 62   2016 $900

Sanchez, Thomas *Mile Zero.* New York: Knopf, 1989. First edition, 8vo., paper wrappers signed and dated by author, cover slightly scuffed, otherwise as new in publisher's box, this seems to be some kind of advance copy in black wrappers in paper slipcase with author and publisher's name on cover.   Second Life Books, Inc.   196 B - 515   2016 $150

Sand, George, Pseud. of Mme. Dudevant   1804-1876
Andre. Paris: Felix Bonnaire Editeur, 1837. Second edition, octavo, 19th century dark red straight grained half morocco, marbled boards, gilt rules and lettering, 2 armorial Selden bookplates, some spotting to front endpapers, edges slightly rubbed, minor foxing, very good in handsome binding.   The Brick Row Book Shop   Miscellany 69 - 36   2016 $300

Sand, George, Pseud. of Mme. Dudevant   1804-1876
Lelia. Paris: Henri Dupuy, Imprimeur Editeur, L. Tenre, Libraire, 1833. First edition, 2 volumes, octavo, 19th century dark red straight grained half morocco, marbled paper boards, gilt rules and lettering, two armorial Selden bookplates, spotting to front endpapers, moderate foxing, very good in handsome binding.   The Brick Row Book Shop   Miscellany 69 - 37   2016 $600

Sand, George, Pseud. of Mme. Dudevant   1804-1876
Mauprat. Paris: Felix Bonnaire, Editer, 1837. First Paris edition in book form and first authorized edition, 2 volumes, octavo, 19th century dark red straight grained half morocco, marbled paper boards, gilt rules and lettering, frontispiece, light spotting to front endpapers, some light foxing, very good in handsome binding, two armorial Selden bookplates.   The Brick Row Book Shop   Miscellany 69 - 38   2016   £750

Sandburg, Carl   1878-1967 *Abraham Lincoln: the Prairie Years.* New York: Harcourt Brace, 1926. Sixth Printing, 2 volumes, large 8vo., three quarter leather, autographed on half title of volume I by author, front cover and half title of volume I separate, worn set.   Second Life Books, Inc.   196 B - 516   2016 $75

Sander, Bruno *Einfuhrung in die Gefugekunde der Geologischen Korper.* Insbruck: Springer Verlag, 1948-1950. First editions, 2 volumes, illustrations, black gilt stamped cloth, heavily worn with kozo repairs, ex-library with usual stamping, good, but rare complete.   Jeff Weber Rare Books   183 - 30   2016 $95

Sanders, Andrew *The Companion of a Tale of Two Cities.* London: Unwin Hyman, 1988. First edition, half title, illustrations, original green cloth, very good in slightly dusted dust jacket, Kathleen Tillotson's copy with some of her notes loosely inserted.   Jarndyce Antiquarian Booksellers   CCXVIII - 571   2016   £30

Sanders, Dennis *The Agatha Christie Companion.* New York: Delacorte, 1984. First edition, fine in dust jacket.   Mordida Books   2015 - 009459   2016 $55

Sanders, Ed *Fuck You: number 2: a Magazine of the Arts.* New York: April, 1962. First edition, 4to., 22 mimeographed leaves on pink paper, covers little soiled, very good, very scarce.   Second Life Books, Inc.   197 - 279   2016 $950

Sanders, Prince *Haytian Papers.* Boston: Caleb Bingham and Co., 1818. First American edition, small octavo, original printed orange paper over boards, sympathetically rebacked, lovely untrimmed, seldom found thus.   Between the Covers Rare Books   207 - 84   2016 $2500

Sanderson, James *The Affair of the Blood Stained Egg Cosy.* London: Constable, 1975. Very good in slightly aged but complete dust jacket.   I. D. Edrich   Crime - 2016   £25

Sandford, Elizabeth Poole *Woman in her Social and Domestic Character.* London: Longman, Rees, Orme, Brown, Green & Longman, 1834. Fourth edition, 19th century plain purple cloth.   Jarndyce Antiquarian Booksellers   CCXVII - 252   2016   £75

Sandford, John *The Empress File.* New York: Holt, 1991. First edition, very fine in dust jacket.   Mordida Books   2015 - 012331   2016 $65

Sandifort, Eduard *Exercitationes Academicae.* Leiden: S. and J. Luchtmans, P. Van der Eyk and D. Vygh, 1783-1785. First edition, 2 parts in one, 4to., half title and 15 engraved folding anatomical plates, bound out of sequence at end, early 19th century calf backed patterned boards, showing wear, some dampstaining throughout.   James Tait Goodrich   X-78 - 500   2016 $1250

Sandlin, Lee *Saving His Life.* Chicago: Sherwin Peach Press, 2008. Number 18 of 50 copies, signed by author and bookmakers, numerous family photos by Nina Sandlin, designed by Martha Chiplis, set in Monoytype Ehrhardt by Winifred and Michael Bixler, printed by Chiplis on hanmdade Twinrocker Taupe paper, photo etchings from family photos printed on Hosho, inset into book in debossed panels, map, Trisha Hammer has designed and executed a hidden crossed-structure binding in Nigerian goatskin with endpapers of Japanese silk housed in silk drawstring bag, fine.   The Kelmscott Bookshop   13 - 54   2016 $1915

Sandomirskogo, M. *Zyheleznaya Doroga. (Railroad).* Moscow: G. F. Mirimanova, 1927. Large oblong 4to., pictorial wrappers, some cover and internal soil, corner worn, very good, illustrations by Vasily Vatagin with 12 full page stunning, richly colored lithographs.   Aleph-bet Books, Inc.   111 - 492   2016 $850

Sandow, Eugen *Strength and How to Obtain It...* London: Gale & Polden, 1897. First edition, illustrations, 11 pages ads, original red cloth, bevelled boards, slightly marked, bookseller's ticket on leading pastedown, contemporary signature on leading f.e.p., very good.   Jarndyce Antiquarian Books   CCXV - 394   2016   £48

Sands, J. Cooper *Dramatised Version of 'Pickwick Papers' 'the Pickwickians'.* Nottingham: Jno. Sands & Son, 1936. Stapled as issued, original green printed wrappers, spine slightly faded and slightly chipped at head and tail. Jarndyce Antiquarian Booksellers   CCXVIII - 118   2016   £35

Sandys, William *Christmastide: In History, Festivities and Carols.* London: John Russell Smith, 1852. First edition, 8vo., original blindstamped blue cloth, minor corner wear, spine elaborately gilt, 8 lithographed plates, inlcuding frontispiece, 17 in text vignettes, with 1856 ownership signature of G(ulian) C(rommelin) Verplanck (1786-1870), excellent copy. Howard S. Mott Inc.   265 - 34a   2016 $350

Sanger, Margaret *Woman and the New Race.* New York: Brentano's, 1923. Sixth printing, 8vo., red cloth, stamped in black, author's presentation on half title under scotch tape, ex-library with bookplate and stamps, rear hinge near tender, otherwise very good.   Second Life Books, Inc.   196 B - 520   2016 $50

Sansom, William *The Equilibriad.* London: Hogarth Press, 1948. Limited to 750 numbered copies signed by author, this copy numbered 172, 8vo., original quarter brown buckram over marbled paper covered boards with very rare glassine dust jacket printed with title and price on front flap, with five full page plates after drawings by Lucien Freud, two closed tears to glassine dust jacket, small marks to top edge of same, but rare survival.   Sotheran's   Piccadilly Notes - Summer 2015 - 138   2016   £1400

Sansom, William *Fire Over London 1940-1941.* London: County Council, 1941. First edition, royal octavo, photos, wrappers, corners little bumped, very good.   Peter Ellis   112 - 456   2016   £35

Santa Croce, Antonio *Secretaria di Apollo or Letters from Apollo....* London: printed for R. Smith at the Angel and Bible...., 1704. 8vo., engraved frontispiece, very crisp, clean, fine full contemporary panelled calf, simple raised spine bands, from the library of Invercauld Castle Braemar, armorial bookplate.   Jarndyce Antiquarian Booksellers   CCXVI - 508   2016   £480

Santayana, George   1863-1952 *The Last Puritan: a memoir in the Form of a Novel.* New York: Charles Scribner's Sons, 1936. First edition, small octavo, green cloth lettered in gilt, lightly rubbed with minor wear to corners and ends of spine, very good in chipped dust jacket. Argonaut Book Shop   Literature 2015 - 5501   2016 $100

Sappho *Sappho. The Text Arranged with Translations, Introduction and Notes by E. M. Cox.* Manaton: Boar's Head Press, 1932. XX/XXV copies printed on Japanese vellum (from an edition of 250 copies), 6 full page wood engravings by Lettice Sandford with tissue guards, crown 8vo., original full tan morocco, backstrip lettered in gilt, some rubbing, soiling and marking overall with two notable scrapes at foot of lower board, top edge gilt, others untrimmed, leather and gilt bookplate to pastedown, compliments slip from Sandfords with wood engraved press device laid in at front, good.   Blackwell's Rare Books   Marks of Genius - 41   2016   £800

Sappington, John *The Theory and Treatment of Fevers.* Arrow Rock: 1844. First edition, contemporary full polished sheep, only light wear else binding quite tight, text foxed and browned in parts, typical for this period.   James Tait Goodrich   X-78 - 501   2016 $495

Sarbiewski, Maciej Kazimierz   1595-1640 *Mathiae Casimiri Sarbievii Lycircorum Libri IV.* Cambridge: Richard Green, 1684. 12mo., fore-margin of A1-4 (and second flyleaf) dampstained and slightly ragged, contemporary calf, ruled in blind with small tool in each corner, front joint rubbed, from the library of James Stevens Cox (1910-1997), the copy of John Loveday (1711-1689) with signature. Maggs Bros. Ltd.   1447 - 374   2016   £120

Sargeant, Charlotte Eliza *Self-reliance: a Book for Young Men...* London: Partridge & Oakey, 1853. Half title, original dark blue green embossed cloth, slightly rubbed & marked, front board slightly cracked, contemporary gift inscription.   Jarndyce Antiquarian Books   CCXV - 69   2016   £20

Sargent, Shirley *Solomons of the Sierra. The Pioneer of the John Muir Trail.* Yosemite: Flying Spur Press, 1989. First edition, 4to., photos, glossy pictorial boards, lower front corner slightly jammed, very fine.   Argonaut Book Shop Biography 2015 - 7638   2016 $150

Saroyan, William *An Act or Two of Foolish Kindness...* Lincoln: Penmaen press, 1977. First edition, 8vo., 178 of 300 copies signed by author and artist, engravings by Helen Siegl, printed on Curtis Rag paper, paste paper bindings by Carol Blinn, fine.   Second Life Books, Inc.   196 B - 522   2016 $75

Saroyan, William *Don't Go Away Mad.* New York: Harcourt Brace, 1949. First edition, 8vo., full page inscription, nice in dust jacket.   Second Life Books, Inc.   196 B - 523   2016 $375

Sarton, George *Introduction to the History of Science.* Baltimore: Williams & Wilkins, 1927. 3 volumes in five, original blue cloth, volumes 1 and 2/2 recased, some wear overall.   James Tait Goodrich   X-78 - 503   2016 $495

Sarton, May *Anger, a Novel.* New York: Norton, 1982. First edition, 8vo., fine, inscribed by author, dust jacket. Second Life Books, Inc.   196 B - 525   2016 $65

Sarton, May *The Fur Person.* Rinehart, 1957. First edition, near fine, very light crease on front of boards, bookplate under flap, dust jacket near fine with light soiling to lighter areas, light wear to extremities.   Bella Luna Books 2016 - 6340   2016 $75

Sarton, May *Mrs. Stevens Hears the Mermaids Singing.* New York: Norton, 1965. First edition, 8vo., very good in price clipped dust jacket that show some marginal wear, former owner's bookplate tipped in is Sarton's 1963 Christmas poem "The House in Winter" signed by Sarton.   Second Life Books, Inc.   196 B - 524   2016 $400

Sassoon, Siegfried Lorraine   1886-1967 *Memoirs of a Fox Hunting Man.* London: Faber and Gwyer Ltd., 1928. First edition, edition deluxe, limited to 260 numbered copies, signed by author, original blue buckram, lettered gilt on spine, top edges gilt, others uncut, spine and small section of upper board faded, light foxing to endpapers, previous owner's signature, fresh.   Sotheran's   Piccadilly Notes - Summer 2015 - 265   2016   £998

Sassoon, Siegfried Lorraine   1886-1967 *The Old Century and Seven More Years.* London: Faber and Faber, 1938. First edition, titlepage vignette by Reynolds Stone, octavo, covers little bumped at corners, very good in very good dust jacket rubbed at edges and creased and spotted at spine.   Peter Ellis   112 - 346   2016   £75

Sassoon, Siegfried Lorraine   1886-1967 *Poems.* London: Duckworth, 1931. First edition, crown 8vo., couple of occasional faint foxspots at head of pages and light handling marks, original black boards, stamped in green to upper board, faint foxing to free endpapers, very good, this copy inscribed by Christabel McLaren May 14th 1931 to Clive Bell.   Blackwell's Rare Books   B186 - 280   2016 £100

Sassoon, Siegfried Lorraine   1886-1967 *Something about Myself.* Worcester: Stanbrook Abbey Press, 1966. First edition, one of about 400 copies, printed on Millbourn Lexpar paper, calligraphic script and marginal decorations by Margaret Adams, reproduced from line blocks in black, blue and brown, illustrations in blue and brown, faintest of spotting dimly visible to borders of first few pages, royal 8vo., original stiff white wrappers, design of cat reproduced in gilt at centre front cover, tail edges untrimmed, near fine. Blackwell's Rare Books   B186 - 340 2016   £70

Satchell, William *The Angler's Notebook and Naturalist's Record.* London: William Satchell, Elliot Stock, 1880. 1888, Square 8vo., 12 illustrations, occasional marginalia, original dark green blind and gilt stamped cloth, extremities worn, spine ends chipped especially on second series volume, bookplate of John H. Crossley, good.   Jeff Weber Rare Books   181 - 84   2016 $100

Saude, Jean *Traite D'Enluminure D'Art Ali Pochoir.* Paris: Aux Editions de l"ibis, 1925. No. 431 of 500 copies signed by Saude, 328 x 256mm., loose as issued in publisher's blue-gray paper portfolio backed with matching cloth, upper cover with printed gilt titling and onlaid brightly colored pochoir color print, lower cover with onlaid pochoir roundel, pochoir endpapers, without publisher's slipcase, titlepage vignette, headpieces and tailpieces, numerous illustrations in text (all colored using pochoir plates), comprised of full page sample of Chapuis-designed endpaper and 29 other plates, depicting 20 subjects, four of these in multiple states, as called for, many with tissue guards, fragile paper boards somewhat soiled, rubbed and marked with bit of wear along joints but entirely solid, one plate with minor crease to fore margin and couple of small closed tears to same, otherwise fine internally clean and fresh, with vibrant colors.   Phillip J. Pirages   67 - 280   2016 $3000

Saunders, Eileen *Wagtails book of Fuchsias.* Henfield: Author, 1971. Quarto, four volumes, color plates, very good set, lacks volume 5, publisher's printed boards and plastic sleeves.   Andrew Isles Natural History Books   55 - 38263 2016 $100

Saunders, George *Civil War Land in Bad Decline: Stories and a Novella.* New York: Random House, 1996. First edition, fine in fine dust jacket, signed by author and dated in 2006.   Between the Covers Rare Books   204 - 106 2016 $375

Saunders, George *Civil War Land in Bad Decline - Stories and a Novella.* New York: Random House, 1996. First edition, octavo, laid in is publisher's publicity photo of author, fine in fine dust jacket.   Peter Ellis   112 - 347 2016   £75

Saunders, Howard *Catalogue of the Gaviae and Tubinares in the Collection of the British Museum. (Catalogue of Birds in the British Museum volume 25).* London: British Musuem (Natural History), 1896. octavo, 8 chromolithograph plates by Smith, publisher's cloth, fine. Andrew Isles Natural History Books   55 - 15575   2016 $400

Saunders, J. B. *Andreas Vesalius Bruxellensis: The Bloodletting Letter of 1539. An Anatomical translation and Study of the Evolution of Vesalius's Scientific Development.* New York: Schuman, 1948. Original binding.   James Tait Goodrich   X-78 - 531   2016 $125

Saunders, J. B. *Vesalius. The Illustrations from his works.* New York: 1950. original binding, very good in dust jacket, showing some wear, signed presentation by Doris Appel. James Tait Goodrich   X-78 - 537   2016 $500

Saunders, Louise *Knave of Hearts.* New York: Scribner, 1925. First edition, Folio, black cloth, pictorial paste-on, fine in original box (restored as usual), incredibly beautiful copy, glorious pictorial endpapers, really magnificent full page color illustrations (printed rectos only), numerous rich color illustrations in text by Maxfield Parrish, all printed on heavy thick coated paper.   Aleph-bet Books, Inc.   111 - 333   2016 $4000

Saunders, Louise *The Knave of Hearts.* New York: Charles Scribner's Sons, 1925. First edition, publisher's brightly colored pictorial cloth, pictorial endleaves, original glassine dust jacket, housed in publisher's matching pictorial box, 26 very pleasing partial and full page illustrations by Maxfied Parrish, nearly mint, perhaps unsurpassable copy. Phillip J. Pirages   67 - 272   2016 $5500

Saunders, Montagu *The Mystery in the Drood Family.* Cambridge: University Press, 1914. Half title, original light green cloth, paper label, spine little faded, Starling booklabel, very good.   Jarndyce Antiquarian Booksellers   CCXVIII - 686   2016   £25

Sauvages De La Croix, Francois Boissier De *Pathologia Methodica....* Leiden: Fratrum de Toumes, 1759. Third edition, 12mo., original mottled calf, gilt spine, red spine label.   Edwin V. Glaser Rare Books   2015 - 10135   2016 $225

Sauvan, Jean Baptiste Balthazar *Picturesque Tour of the Seine From Paris to the Sea: With Particulars Historical and Descriptive.* London: R. Ackermann, 1821. First edition, 346 x 273mm., publisher's red buckram, covers with blind-stamped frame upper cover with gilt titling, flat spine stamped with gilt strapwork panels and with gilt titling, all edges gilt, with engraved color vignette on titlepage, unsigned aquatint vignette at foot of last page, engraved color map, 24 fine hand colored aquatint plates, by Augustus Pugin and John Gendall, presentation bookplate "Master E. Cockayne, as the reward of merit by Mr. Bowling Milk Street Academy Sheffield June 23rd 1848, binding little soiled, joints and extremities bit worn, just the slightest off-setting from some plates onto text, one plate with offsetting from text and half a dozen others with just hint of same, other trivial imperfections, still very desirable, binding sturdy and without any major defects, beautiful scenic plates with particularly attractive coloring.   Phillip J. Pirages   67 - 307   2016 $5500

Sava, A. B. *Twenty-Five Caricatures.* London: Elkin Mathews, 1926. First edition, quarto, linen backed boards, caricatures, each with captioned tissue guard, signed by author on half title, someone has written '250 copies' on same page, covers bit rubbed and tanned, inner front hinge cracked, very good.   Peter Ellis   112 - 61   2016   £200

Savage, Colleen King *Echoing Women.* self published, 2001. Signed "Artist's Proof 2001, CH5", ring-bound with rubbed acetate covers, else fine, text and illustrations by Savage.   Ken Lopez Bookseller   166 - 116   2016 $200

Savage, Richard *Sir Thomas Overbury.* London: printed by William Woodfall for Francis Newbery, 1777. First edition, 8vo., later beige buckram, spine dulled.   Jarndyce Antiquarian Booksellers   CCXVI - 466   2016   £40l

Savage, Thomas *Lona Hanson: a bold woman with a Lust for Power.* New York: Signet Books July, 1949. Abridged paperback edition, pictorial wrappers, very good, offered with full page TLS from author to poet and editor Bill Claire. Second Life Books, Inc.   196 B - 528   2016 $125

Savidge, Eugene Coleman *The American In Paris.* Philadelphia: Lippincott, 1896. Second edition, 12mo., brown cloth stamped in silver, inscribed by author to Professor Phelps with author's compliments, very good, tight copy.   Second Life Books, Inc.   196 B - 530   2016 $85

Savile, George *Miscellanies Historical and Philological.* London: printed for J. T. and sold by the Booksellers of London and Westminster, 1703. 8vo., half title, one text woodcut on page 3, but frontispiece noted in preface was never published, very good, clean, late 19th century bibliographical notes to endpaper & prelim blank, late 19th century gilt panelled calf, ornate gilt spine, upper joint slightly cracked but very firm, all edges gilt.   Jarndyce Antiquarian Booksellers   CCXVI - 509   2016   £225

Sawyer, Charles J. *Dickens v. Barabbas: Forster Intervening, a Study Based Upon Some Hietherto Unpublished Letters.* London: 1930. Number 16 of 90 copies on handmade paper, half title, facsimiles, uncut in original olive green buckram, spine and front board lettered in gilt, bevelled boards, top edge gilt, very good in original glassine wrappers.   Jarndyce Antiquarian Booksellers CCXVIII - 857   2016   £35

Sawyer, James *Notes on Medical Education.* Birmingham: Cornish Brothers, 1889. Half title, final ad leaf, original red cloth, little dulled, slight mark to front board, stamp of Society of Knights Bachelor.   Jarndyce Antiquarian Books   CCXV - 935   2016   £38

Sawyer, Ruth *Journey Cake Ho!* New York: Viking, 1953. First edition, 4to., patterned cloth, fine in very good dust jacket with fraying at spine ends and 2 small closed tears, color illustrations by Robert McCloskey. Aleph-bet Books, Inc. 112 - 304 2016 $1400

Say, Allen *El Chino.* Boston: Houghton Mifflin, 1990. First printing (1-10 code), 4to., cloth backed boards, fine in dust jacket (soiled along edge and slightly frayed at top of spine but still presents well), illustrations in color by Say, this copy inscribed by Say with 5 inch drawing. Aleph-bet Books, Inc. 111 - 405 2016 $125

Sayansky, L. *Trans Siberian Express.* Moscow: Intourist, circa, 1929. First edition, 12mo., original illustrated wrappers printed in orange, black and sepia, very light wear to margins of wrappers, few crinkles internally due to matching binding, very good, extremely rare. Sotheran's Travel and Exploration - 175 2016 £298

Sayers, Dorothy *The Unpleasantness at the Bellona Club.* New York: Payson & Clarke Ltd., 1928. First US edition, 8vo., lavender colored cloth moderately faded at margins of front and rear covers and spine panel, else very good in strikingly beautiful, fine, used jacket. Buckingham Books 2015 - 32216 2016 $3750

Sayler, Oliver M. *Playwright, Actress, Creator: a Study of the many-sided art of Cornelia Otis Skinner.* New York: Horizontal, 8vo., not numbered, paper wrappers, stapled with decorative yellow card tie, portraits and photos, signed on cover by Skinner, in linen covered folder with ribbon ties, and Skinner's name in gilt on front, booklet slightly soiled and faintly dog eared in glassine dust jacket, folder with one tiny spot, otherwise near fine. Second Life Books, Inc. 196 B - 534 2016 $85

Scarborough, Dorothy *On the Trail of Negro Folk-Songs.* Cambridge: Harvard University Press, 1925. First edition, trifle rubbed, still fine, lacking uncommon dust jacket, nice. Between the Covers Rare Books 202 - 92 2016 $350

Scarlett, P. Campbell *South American and the Pacific Comprising a Journey across the Pampas and the Andes.* London: Henry Colburn, 1838. First edition, 2 volumes, 8vo., frontispiece, 4 folding maps, 3 plates, original blue decorative cloth, very good. J. & S. L. Bonham Antiquarian Booksellers America 2016 - 9944 2016 £650

Scarpa, Antonio *Atlante Delle Opere Complete.* Florence: V. Batelli, 1839. Folio, 54 double page plates plus 10 outline plates, overall very good, extra title soiled and there is very occasional light foxing to soiling and few sheets, uncommon, unbound, untrimmed, cloth clamshell box. Edwin V. Glaser Rare Books 2015 - 10072 2016 $4500

Scenes from the War. London: Dean & Son, n.d., 1859. 4to., 8 leaves with first mounted inside front over, pictorial wrappers, spine has some wear, very good+, printed on one side of paper, with fine large hand colored illustrations, quite scarce. Aleph-bet Books, Inc. 111 - 282 2016 $750

Schacht, A. *My Own Particular Screwball....* Garden City: Doubleday, 1955. First edition, 8vo., author's presentation on flyleaf, very good in little soiled dust jacket. Second Life Books, Inc. 196 B - 535 2016 $50

Schaeffer, Jacob C. *... Elementa Entomologica...* Regensburg: Gedruckt mit Weissischen Schriften, 1766. First edition, rare, 140 beautifully engraved and hand colored plates on 72 leaves, margins of first few leaves stained from turn-in of original binding, very minor occasional foxing, light old mildew stain on upper corners of binding, else very good, with beautiful, clean plates. Joseph J. Felcone, Inc. Books from Five Centuries: a Miscellany - 124 2016 $6000

Schaf, Philip *Anglo-Germanism or the Significance of the German Nationality in the United States, an Address Delivered March 10 1846 before the Schilder Society of Marshall College.* Chambersburg: printed at the publication Office of the Ger. Reformed Cruch (sic), 1846. First English edition, 8vo., paper wrappers, very good, lightly soiled wrappers, contents clean. Kaaterskill Books 21 - 84 2016 $250

Scharder, Paul *Mishima - a Life in four Chapters.* London: Warner Bros., 1985. A4 sheets printed on recto only and ring-bound in card wrappers, distributor's compliments slip clipped to first leaf, some creasing to covers, very good. Peter Ellis 112 - 259 2016 £50

Scharlieb, Mary *The Welfare of the Expectant Mother.* London: Cassell & Co., 1919. First edition, half title, frontispiece, original blue grey cloth, slight marking to back board, library labels on leading pastedown and f.e.p., very good. Jarndyce Antiquarian Books CCXV - 395 2016 £20

Schawlow, Arthur *Infrared and Optical Lasers. In The Physical Review volume 112 Second Series No. 6 Dec. 15 1958.* Lancaster: American Institute of Physics, 1958. 4to., entire issue offered, fine, original printed wrappers finely rebacked to style. By the Book, L. C. 45 - 14 2016 $1000

Scheiner, Christof *Oculus hoc est: Fundamentum Opticum.* London: J. Flesher, 1652. Second edition, numerous illustrations in text, 8vo., light foxing at leaf edges, fine, crisp copy in early vellum, old library stamps on title. Edwin V. Glaser Rare Books 2015 - 10098 2016 $3500

Scherzer, Carl *Travels in the Free States of Central America....* London: Longman, Brown, Green, 1857. First English edition, 2 volumes in 1, 8vo., half titles, folding colored map, folding plan colored in outline, contemporary polished calf, spine richly gilt, gilt fillets and rules on covers, green label, very slightly rubbed, ink inscription on upper free endpaper, attractive copy. J. & S. L. Bonham Antiquarian Booksellers America 2016 - 2131 2016 £450

Schevill, James *The Black President: and other Plays.* Denver: Alan Swallow, 1965. First edition, 8vo., illustrations, signed on half title by author, paper wrappers, owner's stamp on half title, cover slightly soiled, otherwise nice. Second Life Books, Inc. 196 B - 536 2016 $40

Schiele, Egon *Egon Schiele, Aquarelle und Zeichnungen.* Salzburg: Verlag Galerie Welz, 1968. Large folio, red cloth portfolio containing the loose sheets, 15 pages of text followed by 64 reproductions. Oak Knoll Books 27 - 13 2016 $1350

Schildkraut, Joseph *My Father and I: as told to Leo Lania.* New York: Viking, 1959. First edition, 8vo., author's presentation on flyleaf, photos, very good in little chipped dust jacket. Second Life Books, Inc. 196 B - 537 2016 $45

Schiller, Johann Christoph Friederich Von   1759-1805 *The Fight with the Dragon a Romance.* London: (S. and R. Bentley) for Septimus Powett 23 Old Bond Street, 1825. First illustrated and separate English edition, 4to., 16 plates engraved by Henry Moses, text almost spotless, plates with minor foxing only here and there, 3 plates with minor marginal waterstains, all tissue guards present, original publisher's illustrated boards, spotted, traces of humidity, surface scuffing to front cover, extremities and spine worn. Marlborough Rare Books List 55 - 61 2016 £100

Schiller, Johann Christoph Friederich Von   1759-1805 *The Robbers.* London: for G. G. and J. Robinson, 1795. Disboune, some dusting to half title, small light stain to head of few leaves, embrowning to terminal leaf. Dramatis Personae 119 - 153 2016 $40

Schiller, Johann Christoph Friederich Von   1759-1805 *Wallenstein.* New York: David Longworth, 1805. First American edition, minor dampstaining, 19th century marbled boards, original wrappers bound in, wrappers slightly soiled and mounted at inner margin, good. Blackwell's Rare Books B184 - 28 2016 £400

Schillibeer, John *A Narrative of the Briton's voyage to Pitcairn's Island.* Tanto: for the author by J. W. Marriott, published by Law and Whittaker, 1817. First edition, 16 etchings on 12 plates (some folding), contemporary calf, central blindstamped design on covers, gilt decoration (outer hinges cracked), plates and facing pages foxed, just hint of mustiness, contemporary bookplate. Joseph J. Felcone, Inc. Books from Five Centuries: a Miscellany - 126 2016 $1500

Schlegel, Gustave *Unranographie Chinoise ou Preuves Directes que l'Astronomie Primitive est Originaire de la Chine...* La Haye: Librairie de Martinus Nijhoff, Lyede: Imprimerie de E. J. Brill Relie, 1875. First edition, 2 volumes, with separate atlas volume, large 8vo., atlas with 7 large plates, modern quarter navy blue cloth, marbled paper over boards, gilt spine, atlas wrapper is a remnant, but printed cover present, preserved in modern navy blue quarter cloth folder with inner pocker, overall very good, very rare. Jeff Weber Rare Books 183 - 31 2016 $985

Schlegel, Johann Christian Traugott *Collectio Opusculorum Selectorum ad Medicinam Forensem Spectantium.* Leipzig: C. F. Schneider, 1784-1791. Small 8vo., 5 volumes of 6 (lacking volume 2), occasional foxing and browning, good set, early marbled boards paper spine labels. Edwin V. Glaser Rare Books 2015 - 10223 2016 $200

Schlegel, Johann Elias *Le Triomphe des Bonnes Femmes Comedie, en Cinq Actes Traduite de Pallemand...* Londres: imprimee dans l'annee, 1763. 8vo., titlepage little stained, minor foxing at either end, disbound, good. Blackwell's Rare Books B186 - 139 2016 £500

Schlegel, Jorgen U. *The Luger.* Independence: International University Press, 1989. First edition, printed wrappers, slight vertical crease to back cover, else fine, very scarce. Gene W. Baade, Books on the West 2015 - 5004042 2016 $81

Schlesinger, Max *Saunterings in and About London.* London: Nathaniel Cooke, 1853. First English edition, half title, frontispiece, added engraved title, plates, original deep brown cloth, spine faded, very good, crisp copy. Jarndyce Antiquarian Booksellers CCXVII - 253 2016 £120

Schlicke, Paul *Dickens and Popular Entertainment.* London: Allen & Unwin, 1985. First edition, half title, illustrations, original scarlet cloth, very good in dust jacket. Jarndyce Antiquarian Booksellers CCXVIII - 1434 2016 £20

Schlicke, Paul *Oxford Reader's Companion to Dickens.* Oxford: Oxford University Press, 1999. First edition, half title, illustrations, original dark blue cloth, very good in dust jacket. Jarndyce Antiquarian Booksellers CCXVIII - 1433 2016 £35

Schmauk, Theodore E. *Good Conversation its Charms & Secrets.* London: W. R. Russell & Co., circa, 1890. Original olive green cloth, very good. Jarndyce Antiquarian Books   CCXV - 396   2016   £35

Schmid, Christoph Von *Cuentecitos para Ninos y Ninas Compuestos en Aleman paar D. Cristobal de Schmid.* Barcelona: Oficina de Piferrer, 1856. First edition in Spanish, small octavo, contemporary red quarter calf, green cloth boards, gilt decorations and lettering, two plates, half title present, fine.   The Brick Row Book Shop   Miscellany 69 - 25   2016 $250

Schmidt, Adolf *Bucheinbande Aus Dem XIV-XIX Jahrhundert in Der Landesbibliothek zu Darmstadt.* Leipzig: Karl W. Hiersemann, 1921. Thick folio, cloth, leather spine label, 41 pages followed by 100 full page plates, magnificent folio, some spotting of covers, with Randeria bookplate.   Oak Knoll Books   310 - 19   2016 $550

Schmidt, Johann Jacob *Biblischer Medicus oder Betrachtung des Menschen nach der Physiologie Pathologie...* 1743. Thick 8vo., full contemporary vellum, some soiling, text has browning and staining, some water spots, early ownership inscription on title.   James Tait Goodrich   X-78 - 504   2016 $895

Schmidt, Martin *Imprint: Oregon. VI/1-V2/2.* 1974-1975, 4 issues, all in original pictorial wrappers, illustrations, excellent condition, though 3 have faint rubber library stamps in their upper panels.   I. D. Edrich   Winston Spencer Churchill - 2016   £100

Schmoller, Tanya *Remondini and Rizzi, a Chapter in Italian Decorated Paper History.* New Castle: Oak Knoll Books, 1990. Limited to 215 numbered copies, set in Perpetua and printed letterpress on Johannot mould-made paper by Henry Morris, 8vo., cloth backed, patterned paper (in facsimile of an original Remondini pattern specially executed by Morris), leather spine label, illustrations include a three-color facsimile of Remondini woodblock, and a foldout reproduction of a decree authorizing the sale of gilt paper, there are also four pages of genuine Rizzi paper samples, prospectus loosely inserted.   Oak Knoll Books   27 - 2   2016 $400

Schnabel, Julian *Works on Paper 1975-1988.* Munich: Prestel, 1990. First edition, with English text, one of 100 numbered copies with an original painting by Schnabel (signed) on front cover, inscribed to reader and signed by the artist, 4to., illustrated cloth, fine, publisher's note laid in. James S. Jaffe Rare Books   Occasional List: Winter 2016 - 21   2016 $2000

Schodde, Richard *Nocturnal Birds of Australia.* Melbourne: Lansdowne, 1980. Limited to 750 copies numbered and signed by authors and artist, this copy has attractive signed lithograph (limited to copies) of a black-shouldered kite, folio, 22 color plates by Jeremy Boot, text illustrations, publisher's brown full morocco.   Andrew Isles Natural History Books   55 - 1796   2016 $550

Scholarly Publishing, a Journal for Authors & Publishers. Toronto: University of Toronto Press, 1969-1999. 8vo., 3 volumes, composing 118 (of 120) issues, lacks only 25, 4 and 30, 2, stiff paper wrappers.   Oak Knoll Books   310 - 72   2016 $450

Schonbrunner, J. *Handzeichnungen Alter Meister aus Der Albertina Und Anderen Sammlungen.* Wien: Gerlach & Schenk, 1896-1908. First edition, folio, 12 volumes, half calf portfolio, cloth backed boards, gilt stamping and illustration on upper boards with tipped in illustration, hundreds of plates, commemorative booklabel which indicates this set came from the H. P. Kraus reference library.   Oak Knoll Books   310 - 303   2016 $2000

School Exercises. 1761. The Hat. The Peruke. The Breeches. Ramsgate: Burgess printer, circa, 1800. 16 pages, disbound.   Jarndyce Antiquarian Booksellers CCXVII - 12   2016   £250

Schoolcraft, Henry Rowe   1793-1864 *Historical and Statistical Information, Respecting the History, condition and Prospects of the Indian Tries of the United States...* Philadelphia: Lippincott, Grambo and Co., 1851-1857. 6 volumes, thick folio, 330 lithographed and steel engraved plates, many tinted, some hand colored or chromolithographed, largely after artist Seth Eastman, original half dark green morocco, marbled paper sides, reddish brown endpapers, in remarkably fine condition, bright and fresh, fore titles moderately foxed, black and white plates and tissue guards range from entirely unfoxed to moderately foxed with most lightly foxed in margins, color plates largely unfoxed, few lightly foxed in margins.   Joseph J. Felcone, Inc. Books from Five Centuries: a Miscellany - 125   2016 $20,000

Schoolcraft, Henry Rowe   1793-1864 *Journal of a Tour into the Interior of Missouri and Arkansas.* London: Richard Phillips, 1821. First UK edition, 8vo., folding map, recent brown calf.   J. & S. L. Bonham Antiquarian Booksellers America 2016 - 7314   2016   £380

Schott, Gaspar *Magia Optica Das ist Geheime doch Naturmassige Gesicht und Augen-Lehr...* Bamberg: Johann Martin Schonwerters, 1677. First German edition, small 4to., allegorical frontispiece, 25 engraved copper plates, variously browned, foxed or stained, contemporary quarter calf, decorative boards, extremities very worn, ownership signature L. Orssinger and inscription Ex Libris P. Lemigii Antles, Ludovii Kappourr?   Jeff Weber Rare Books   183 - 32   2016 $3000

Schott, Gaspar *Schola Steganographica in Classes Octo Distributa...* Nuremberg: Jobus Hertz for Johann Andrea..., 1665. First edition, small 4to., extra engraved titlepage, half title, titlepage printed in red and black, engraved arms of Ferdinand Maximilan, 1625-1669, 3 tables, text engravings, woodcut initials, head and tailpieces, contemporary vellum, title in old hand on spine, edges speckled red, monor toning and foxing, vellum browned as usual, one tie remains, bookplate of Hedwig & Eberhard Frey dated 1920, one plate with repaired tears at blank table, otherwise fine.   Jeff Weber Rare Books   183 - 33   2016 $3250

Schrader, Franz *Mitosis.* New York: Columbia University Press, 1949. Third printing, 8vo., signed by Erwin Chargaff, fine, hardback.   By the Book, L. C.   45 - 24   2016 $250

Schrank, Joseph *Seldom and the Golden Cheese.* New York: Dodd, Mead and Co., 1933. First edition, octavo, color frontispiece, 6 full page black and white illustrations and numerous black and white drawings by Gustaf Tenggren, publisher's tan cloth, front cover and spine stamped in black, tan pictorial endpapers printed in blue, early ink inscription, near fine in original color pictorial dust jacket with lower corner of front panel torn away and few other small chips.   David Brass Rare Books, Inc.   2015 - 02996   2016 $350

Schreiber, Charlotte *Lady Charlotte Screiber's Journals.* London: John Lane, The Bodley Head, 1911. First edition, 2 volumes, thick royal octavo, upwards of 100 plates, , 8 in color, dark blue cloth lettered gilt on spines and front covers, pictorial elements in white, top edge gilt, light extremity rubbing, two corners jammed short half inch tear to upper front hinge of volume II, very good set.   Argonaut Book Shop   Pottery and Porcelain 2015 - 5005   2016 $400

Schreiber, Hazel Snell *Coastland Curfew and Other Poems.* San Francisco: Privately published, 1957. One of 250 copies, Memorial edition, presentation from Beryl Schreiber Jespersen to Ina Coolibrth Circle SF, titlepage printed in red and black, tan cloth backed blue/gray boards, gilt, fine.   Argonaut Book Shop   Private Press 2015 - 6377   2016 $60

Schreiner, Olive 1855-1920 *The Story of an African Farm.* Westerham: Limited Editions Club, 1961. first edition thus, one of 1500 numbered copies, signed by artist, large 8vo., bound by Russell-Rutter Co. in full bark cloth from Uganda, title stamped in gold, illustrations are drawings and original color lithographs by Paul Horgan.   Second Life Books, Inc.   196 B - 539 2016 $75

Schulman, Max *The Tender Trap, a Comedy.* New York: Random House, 1955. First edition, 8vo., illustrations, very good in little worn dust jacket, signed by 5 cast members.   Second Life Books, Inc.   196 B - 542   2016 $75

Schulz, Herbert Clarence *Monograph on the Italian Choir Book.* San Francisco: David Magee, 1941. One of 75 copies, 387 x 279mm., publisher's original oatmeal colored and red cloth upper cover with red lettering, 13 modern three line initials and one seven line initial with tissue guard, in colors and gold by Valenti Angelo, bound in substantial portion of early 16th century(?) illuminated manuscript Gradual leaf on vellum, colophon printed in red, some rubbing to extremities, cloth bit soiled, internally fine with striking manuscript leaf well preserved.   Phillip J. Pirages   67 - 177   2016 $1250

Schumann, Peter *Tatata, 24 Cordells. Twenty-Four Chapbooks Drawn and Written by Peter Shumann.* Newark: Janus Press, 2011. Limited to 120 numbered copies signed by Schumann, charcoal and ink drawings on Mohawk Superfine eggshell white 100 lb. text, crayon cover drawings on Mohawk Via cream linen 65 lb cover by Andrew Miller-Brown, small 4to., 8 booklets laid in colored paper pockets agains each of the three colored sides of strong navy book cloth folder with title on top side and colophon details on inside, light tan bristol slipcase with printed spine label, stiff illustrated paper wrappers, 8 pages each for the 24 booklets.   Oak Knoll Books   27 - 34   2016 $350

Schwartz, Jerome *Oxcar the Ostrich.* New York: Random House, 1940. First edition, 8vo., pictorial boards, owner inscription, fine in very good+ price clipped dust jacket, full page black and white lithographs by Mark David.   Aleph-bet Books, Inc.   112 - 519   2016 $450

Schwartz, Lynne Sharon *The Accounting.* Great Barrington: Penmaen Press, 1983. First edition, title illustration by Michael McCurdy, with original print of same wood engraving, signed by artist, laid in, one of 50 copies numbered and signed by author and artist and casebound by Deborah Wender, fine in little chipped and soiled tissue dust jacket.   Second Life Books, Inc.   196 B - 546   2016 $150

Schwarzbach, Fredric *Dickens and the City.* London: University of London, Athlone Press, 1979. First edition, half title, plates, original blue cloth, very good in dust jacket.   Jarndyce Antiquarian Booksellers   CCXVIII - 1437   2016   £20

Schwechten, Eduard *Das Lied vom Levfi. (The Song of Levi).* Koln: Verlag der Antisemitischen Buchhandlung (Eduard Hentel), 1895. First edition, 8vo., pictorial wrappers, some cover soil, corners chipped and one edge mend on rear cover, spine reinforced stamp on titlepage, really sound and very good, rare edition, 50 full page disgusting anti Semitic half tone illustrations by Siegfried Horn, rare.   Aleph-bet Books, Inc.   111 - 235   2016 $2000

Schwechten, Eduard *Das Lied Vom Levi. (The Song of Levi).* Dusseldorf: J. Knippenberg, 1933. First edition, 8vo., wrappers, very good+, full and partial page illustrations.   Aleph-bet Books, Inc.   112 - 267   2016 $850

Schweinfurth, Charles *Orchids of Peru.* Chicago: Chicago Natural History Museum, 1958-1970. Octavo, 5 volumes (first supplement), text illustrations, publisher's printed wrappers with separately issued titlepage. Andrew Isles Natural History Books 55 - 7965 2016 $200

Sciascia, Leonardo *The Council of Egypt.* London: Jonathan Cape, 1966. First UK edition, near fine in near fine dust jacket, octavo, uncommon. Peter Ellis 112 - 349 2016 £85

Sciascia, Leonardo *Equal Danger.* London: Jonathan Cape, 1974. First UK edition, octavo, near fine in near fine dust jacket, uncommon. Peter Ellis 112 - 348 2016 £45

Sclater, Philip Lutley *The Book of Antelopes.* R. H. Porter, 1894-1900. First edition, scarce, 4to., 4 volumes, original green cloth, gilt vignette of antelope to uppers, gilt rules to boards, spines with gilt rules and lettering, 100 hand colored lithographs, 121 text illustrations, spines little darkened, repair to one text page in volume 1, otherwise very good, plates clean. Sotheran's Hunting, Shooting & Fishing - 20 2016 £8500

Sclater, Philip Lutley *Catalogue of the Passeriformes or Perching Birds, in the Collection of the British Museum.* London: British Museum Natural History, 1888. Octavo, 18 chromolithograph plates by Smit, publisher's cloth, two small library stamps of Royal Society of Victoria, ownership signature of J. A. Kershaw (ornithologist of Horn Expedition), fine. Andrew Isles Natural History Books 55 - 37794 2016 $500

Sclater, Philip Lutley *The Ibis.* London: British Ornithologists' Union, 1909. Octavo, photos, binder's cloth, wrappers retained. Andrew Isles Natural History Books 55 - 36653 2016 $300

Scoles, Ignatius *Sketches of African and Indian Life in British Guiana.* Demerea: The 'Argosy Press' Georgetown, 1885. Original light green printed boards, green cloth spine, boards little rubbed, doodle on leading endpaper. Jarndyce Antiquarian Booksellers CCXVII - 254 2016 £65

The Scots Angler. A Monthly Magazine of River and Loch. D. Douglas, R. R. Clark, 1896-1897. Complete run, 4to., 12 issued, without original wrappers, bound together in recent red cloth with leather spine label from an earlier binding, marbled edges, drawings, cartoons and photos, very good. Sotheran's Piccadilly Notes - Summer 2015 - 126 2016 £498

Scott, A. W. *Mammalia, Recent and Exticnt: an Elemnetary Treatise for the Use of the Public Schools of New South Wales.* Sydney: Government printer, 1873. Octavo, quarter calf on marbled boards, some foxing, bookplate of John Lane Mullins, inscription from author, scarce. Andrew Isles Natural History Books 55 - 7985 2016 $300

Scott, Anna M. *The Flower Babies.* Chicago: Rand, McNally, 1914. First edition, 8vo., cloth backed pictorial boards, some cover rubbing else very good+, wonderful illustrations. Aleph-bet Books, Inc. 112 - 175 2016 $275

Scott, C. Rochfort *Excursions in the Mountains of Ronda and Granada.* London: Henry Colburn, 1838. First edition, 2 volumes, 8vo., frontispieces (light foxing in margins), original purple blindstamped cloth, very small ownership stamp at base of titlepages, very good set. J. & S. L. Bonham Antiquarian Booksellers Europe 2016 - 9734 2016 £1750

Scott, David *The History of Scotland.* Westminster: J. Cluer and A. Campbell, 1727. First edition, folio, engraved frontispiece and foldout map, very lightly toned towards edges, generally bright, contemporary tan calf Cambridge boards, gilt title and blind tooling to spine, edges sprinkled red, lighter tan used to reback and repair in sturdy but somewhat inelegant style boards, scuffed, lacks f.f.e.p., inner hinges reinforced with cloth tape, alternative impression of the royal paper edition of 1727, this time with prelims reset, first word of last line on page (iii) being 'And'. Unsworths Antiquarian Booksellers Ltd. E01 - Early Printing - 20 2016 £700

Scott, Edward *How to Dance and Guide to the Ball-Room.* London: Ward, Lock and Co., circa, 1898. Original pictorial green cloth, very good, half title, frontispiece. Jarndyce Antiquarian Books CCXV - 397 2016 £85

Scott, George Ryley *The History of Cockfighting.* London: Charles Skilton, 1957. Limited to 1095 numbered copies, quarto, colored frontispiece, contemporary half red morocco and marbled boards, top edge gilt and other edges uncut, limited to 1095 numbered copies, fine. Andrew Isles Natural History Books 55 - 38617 2016 $400

Scott, H. *A Monograph of Nototherium Tasmanicum.* Hobart: John Vail, 1915. Quarto, 22 plates, publisher's green boards. Andrew Isles Natural History Books 55 - 21528 2016 $70

Scott, Herbert *In the Realm of Space.* Winona: Sutton Hoo Press, 2001. Limited to 126 copies, 12mo., quarter cloth, marbled paper covered boards. Oak Knoll Books 310 - 155 2016 $125

Scott, Jack Denton *Forests of the Night.* Robert Hale, 1960. First UK edition, 8vo., original cloth and wrapper, 13 photos by author's wife, occasional spots, very good. Sotheran's Hunting, Shooting & Fishing - 21 2016 £30

Scott, Jock *Salmon and Trout Fishing Up To Date.* London: Seeley Service & Co., 1960. 8vo., original green cloth, bronze lettering to spine, illustrated dust jacket, slight wear to dust jacket, otherwise near fine, not price clipped, past ownership bookplate attached to front pastedown. Sotheran's Hunting, Shooting & Fishing - 142 2016 £38

Scott, John Anthony *The Defense of Gracchus Babeuf before the High Court of Vendome.* Northampton: Gehenna Press, 1964. First edition, 4to., full leather chemise laid in cloth covered clamshell box with leather spine, 21 etched portraits printed on special paper and loosely inserted, paper is Nideggen made in Germany, suite of etchings printed by Emiliano Sorini in NY and designed by Leonard Baskin, printed in an edition of 300 numbered copies, this 'printer's copy' signed by Baskin which contains portraits, signed by Thomas Cornell, on blue fabriano, enclosed in unbound, uncut signatures. Second Life Books, Inc. 196 B - 549 2016 $1450

Scott, Jonathan *The Arabian Nights Entertainments, Carefully Revised and Occasionally Corrected from the Arabic.* London: printed for Longman, 1811. 12mo., some dusting and occasional staining to text, one gathering little proud, contemporary half calf, marbled boards, gilt spines, rather rubbed, several joints cracked but firm, slight chipping to headcaps, ink splashes to leading edge of one book block. Jarndyce Antiquarian Booksellers CCXVI - 510 2016 £125

Scott, Peter *My Favourite stories of wild life.* Lutterworth press, 1965. First edition, 8vo., original cloth and dust jacket, illustrations by Keith Shackleton, some chipping to top edge of jacket, very good. Sotheran's Piccadilly Notes - Summer 2015 - 268 2016 £30

Scott, Thomas *An Impartial Statement of the Scripture Doctrine in Respect of Civil Government and the Duties of Subjects.* London: printed and sold by C. Watts, Queen Street, Grosvenor Square by J. Johnson...., 1792. Large 12mo. in 6's, titlepage and final leaf rather dusted with some light creases, original paper flaw to A6, stitched as issued. Jarndyce Antiquarian Booksellers CCXVI - 511 2016 £50

Scott, Walter 1771-1832 *The Abbot.* Edinburgh: Longman, Hurst, Rees, Orme and Brown, 1820. First edition, first issue, 3 volumes, finely bound in tan calf and green marbled boards, four raised bands to spines, contrasting dark red title labels to spines, lettered gilt, spine bands decorated gilt, spine compartments decorated blind, boards ruled gilt, all edges marbled, green marbled endpapers, near fine, some light rubbing to boards and extremities, faint toning to spines, booksellers plates to front free endpapers, lacking half titles, few faint spots to otherwise fresh interiors, overall very clean and pleasing. Manhattan Rare Book Company 2016 - SWS074 2016 $225

Scott, Walter 1771-1832 *Border Antiquities of England and Scotland...* London: printed for Longman, Hurst, Rees, Orme and Brown, J. Murray...., 1814. 1817. First edition, large paper copy, 2 volumes, folio, 94 engraved plates, including 2 engraved titlepages, Morpeth Castle plate loose, volume I engraved title almost loose, pages civ-cv little discolored apparently by insertion of a leaf between them, occasional light foxing with volume I engraved titlepage bit more affected, contemporary half deep red straight grain morocco, green marbled paper covered boards, edges uncut, endcaps, joints and board edges worn, boards much rubbed, edges little toned but still good copy overall, front pastedown of each volume is ownership inscription of H. C. Rigg, Crossrigg Hall and recent bookplate of Susan Wade. Unsworths Antiquarian Booksellers Ltd. 30 - 135 2016 £200

Scott, Walter 1771-1832 *The Doom of the Devorgoil, A Melo-Drama. (and) Alichindrane or the Ayrshire Tragedy.* Edinburgh: printed by Ballantyne for Cadell and Co., Edinburgh and Simpkin and Marshall, London, 1830. First separate and complete edition, 229 x 1522m., attractive late 19th century dark green armorial morocco by Maclehose of Glasgow (stamp signed), covers gilt with heraldic pelican crest of Thomas Glen Arthur of Garrick House, Ayr, flat spine with title at head and author at tail and five gilt ornaments in between (comprised of three thistles and two heraldic devices), gold endleaves, top edge gilt, other edges untrimmed (front hinge and joint with careful repairs, front free endpaper and first flyleaf cut near gutter and reattached with cellophane), large paper presentation copy, inscribed by Harry A. Sickles, Christmas 1917 for friend Frank P. Leffingwell, short crack beginning at bottom of front joint, hint of fading and leather dressing residue to covers, otherwise in excellent, binding solid and lustrous, text clean and fresh, margins very commodious. Phillip J. Pirages 67 - 312 2016 $1000

Scott, Walter 1771-1832 *Ivanhoe.* Edinburgh: Archibald Constable and Co., 1820. First edition, first issue, complete with half titles and publisher's ads, 3 volumes, octavo, original boards rebacked, some wear to boards, text extremely clean, faint signature and date (1820) of Sophia Tathwell, tiny faint library stamp on ad leaf of volume 1 and second half titles of volumes 2 and 3. Manhattan Rare Book Company 2016 - 1756 2016 $5500

Scott, Walter 1771-1832 *The Lay of the Last Minstrel, a Poem.* London and Edinburgh: printed for Longman, Hurst Rees and Orme and for A. Constable by James Ballantyne, 1805. Second edition, 213 x 133mm., contemporary red straight grain morocco, covers bordered by gilt rule and cresting blind roll, flat spine divided into panels by single gilt rules, gilt titling, turn-ins with gilt bead roll, marbled endpapers, all edges gilt, with fore-edge painting of Dumbarton Castle and the River Clyde, in paper slipcase, joints significantly rubbed (but this well masked with dye), small notch out at top of front joint, slight wear with bit of loss at corners and spine ends, minor spotting and darkening to boards, other trivial defects externally but binding, still firm and entirely satisfactory, scattered foxing at edges, leaves less than bright because of paper stock, but text still fresh and dramatic fore-edge painting well preserved.   Phillip J. Pirages   67 - 160   2016 $1400

Scott, Walter 1771-1832 *Peveril of the Peak.* Edinburgh: printed for the Archibald Constable and Co., 1822. First edition, first issue, lacking half titles, 4 volumes, finely bound in brown calf and tan marbled boards, three raised bands to spines, contrasting dark red title labels to spines, lettered gilt, spines decorated and ruled gilt, boards ruled in blind and gilt, all edges marbled, very good or better, some light wear to boards and extremities, faint toning to spines, bookeller's plates to front pastedown, volume III with minor split to front outer hinge and lacking errata slip, spines very lightly starting at endpapers, otherwise sturdy bindings, few minor ceases to otherwise fresh pages, overall very bright, attractive set.   Manhattan Rare Book Company   2016 - SWS075   2016 $300

Scott, Walter 1771-1832 *Redgauntlet. A Tale of the Eighteenth Century.* Edinburgh: printed for Archibald Constable and Co., and Hurst, Robinson and Co., London, 1824. First edition, 2nd issue, first gathering in volume ii loosening, few other nearly loose leaves, 8vo., uncut in original cloth backed blue boards, recovered in paper, drab spines, blue covers, various poetical handbills used as pastedowns, printed labels on spine, worn at extremities, covers unevenly faded, inner hinges weak, sound.   Blackwell's Rare Books   B186 - 140   2016   £200

Scott, Walter 1771-1832 *Rob Roy.* Edinburgh: printed by James Ballantyne and Co. for Archibald Constable and Co., 1818. First edition, 3 volumes, with half titles, finely bound in tan polished calf and brown marbled boards by Carss and Coy of Glasgow, five raised bands to spine, contrasting maroon title labels to spine, lettered and ruled in gilt, spine compartments decorated in blind, all edges speckled, green ribbon bookmarks, near fine, volume with some discreet repairs to leaves 33-41 and first two leaves washed, some minor wear to boards and extremities, light toning to spines, few faint spots to calf, volume III with minor spot to top edge, few scattered spots to otherwise fresh pages, overall very clean and handsome.   B & B Rare Books, Ltd.   2016 - SWS078   2016 $750

Scott, Walter 1771-1832 *The Talisman.* New York: Heritage Press, 1972. Red cloth, lettered gilt, slight fading to spine, else fine in slipcase (slight fading), illustrations by Federico Castellon, Sandglass pamphlet laid in.   Argonaut Book Shop   Heritage Press 2015 - 2036   2016 $40

Scott, Walter 1771-1832 *Waverley; or the Sixty Years Since.* New York: Heritage Press, 1961. Printed orange boards with orange cloth spine, lettered gilt, slight fading to spine, else fine in slipcase, illustrations by Robert Ball, Sandglass pamphlet laid in.   Argonaut Book Shop   Heritage Press 2015 - 2037   2016 $40

Scott, Walter 1771-1832 *Woodstock; or the Cavelier: a Tale of the Year Sixteen Hundred and Fifty-One.* Edinburgh: printed for Archibald Constable and Co., 1826. First edition, 3 volumes, finely bound in tan polished calf and blue marbled boards, 3 raised bands to spines, contrasting maroon title labels, lettered and decorated gilt, all edges marbled, blue marbled endpapers, green ribbon bookmarks, about very good, outer hinges lightly cracked, volume III with spine slightly lifting at head, some wear to the extremities, light rubbing to boards and hinges, minor fading to edges of endpapers, bound without half titles, otherwise fresh interior, overall very presentable set.   B & B Rare Books, Ltd.   2016 - SWS077   2016 $250

Scott, William *The Complete Works... with a biography...* New York: Conner & Cooke, 1833-1835. Tall 8vo., 7 volumes, slightly later full morocco, gilt stamping, majority of covers detached, but present.   M & S Rare Books, Inc.   99 - 287   2016 $275

Scribner, Tom *Lumberjack with Appendix on Musical Saw.* Santa Cruz: privately printed, 1967. Revised 4th printing, 4to., printed pink wrappers, stapled, good copy, minor cover edge tears and light soiling.   Gene W. Baade, Books on the West   2015 - 1402140   2016 $95

Scriptores Rei Rusticae Veretes Latini. Lipsiae: sumptibus Caspari Fritsch, 1773-1774. Second edition, 2 volumes, 4to., frontispiece to volume 1, 6 further folding plates, engraved vignette to each titlepage, some spotting and browning due to paper quality as usual with Fritsch (but less than sometimes seen), final plate little oversized and therefore crumpled at edges, contemporary speckled tan calf, red and green morocco gilt spine labels, edges sprinkled red, volume 1 head-cap little chipped, few small stains and patchy fading but overall very good set, armorial bookplate of Right Hon, Henry Hobhouse (1854-1937).   Unsworths Antiquarian Booksellers Ltd.   30 - 136   2016   £350

Scrope, George Poulett *Principles of Political Economy Deduced from the National Laws of Social Welfare and Applied to the Present State of Britain.* London: Longman, Rees, Orme, Brown, Green & Longman, 1833. First edition, 8vo., engraved frontispiece, map, contemporary polished calf, spine decorated in gilt with red skiver label, ex-library from Queen's College, Oxford with discreet ink stamps.   Marlborough Rare Books   List 56 - 50   2016   £750

Scrope, William *The Art of Deer-Stalking.* London: Edward Arnold, 1897. New edition, 8vo., original half vellum, marbled board sides, gilt lettered spine, leather label, top edges gilt, 10 plates, previous owner's inkstamp, binding little discolored as usual, boards rubbed, very good.   Sotheran's   Hunting, Shooting & Fishing - 64   2016   £400

Scrope, William *Days and Nights of Salmon Fishing in the Tweed with a Short Account of the Natural History of the Habits of the Salmon...* Edward Arnold, 1898. New edition, 8vo. original publisher's half vellum, gilt lettering to spine, marbed boards, 13 lithographed plates, including two color printed plates, wood engravings in text, previous owner's bookplate, spine little dulled, very nice.   Sotheran's   Hunting, Shooting & Fishing - 143   2016   £400

Scruton, James *The Practical Counting House...* Glasgow: printed for James Duncan, 1777. 8vo., titlepage dusted and foxed, some worming ot upper margin at start of book, disappearing to single hole by page 26 ending at page 103, some pen marks against entries, other ink splashes to few pages and edge of book block, pen calculations on inner front board, without free endpapers, Fasque library bookplate of Gladstone family, full contemporary calf, raised and gilt banded spine, red morocco label, covers rubbed, some old ink marks to boards.   Jarndyce Antiquarian Booksellers   CCXVI - 512   2016   £420

Scurfield, Harold *Infant and Young Child Welfare.* London: Cassell & Co., 1919. First edition, half title, frontispiece, original blue grey cloth, damp mark to back board, library labels on leading pastedown and f.e.p., good plus.   Jarndyce Antiquarian Books   CCXV - 398   2016   £20

Seager, Robin *Amnianus Marcellinus. Seven Studies in His Language and Thought.* Columbia University of Missouri Press, 1986. First edition, 8vo., cloth, blue lettered, some very small marks to spine, edges dusted, jacket has closed tears to top edge of upper jacket, minor shelfwear, very good, from the library of Prof. J. G. Hind, with his ms translation of sections of annotations loosely inserted.   Unsworths Antiquarian Booksellers Ltd.   E05 - 61   2016   £35

Sealey, J. Robert *A Revision of the Genus Camelia.* London: Royal Horticultural Society, 1958. Quarto, colored frontispiece, text illustrations, few tape marks on endpapers, otherwise very good, scarce.   Andrew Isles Natural History Books   55 - 32200   2016 $400

Sealsfield, Charles *Life in the New World; or Sketches of American Society.* New York: J. Winchester, New World Press, 1844. First edition in English, octavo, original 7 parts bound in one volume 19th century black quarter calf and cloth boards, gilt lettered, text somewhat foxed and little stained in spots, very good.   The Brick Row Book Shop   Miscellany 69 - 74   2016 $300

Sealts, Merton M. *Melville as Lecturer.* Cambridge: Harvard, 1957. First edition, several facsimiles, author's presentation on flyleaf, red cloth, corner of flyleaf clipped, otherwise very good, tight copy in scuffed and chipped dust jacket.   Second Life Books, Inc.   196 B - 551   2016 $45

Searle, Ronald *More Scraps in no Particular Order.* (with) *Watteau Revisited.* Church Hanborough: Inky Parrot Press, 2008. 48/204 sets (from an edition of 246 sets), 2 volumes, first signed by artist, printed on mouldmade paper with Searle drawings throughout, titlepage to first volume printed in red and black, royal 8vo., original wrappers with Searle illustrations, backstrips lettered in black, untrimmed, Searle designs on endpapers, together in cloth, slipcase, fine.   Blackwell's Rare Books   B186 - 315   2016   £250

Sears, W. W. *This is Sackville.* Sackville: 1966. Quarto, decorative card covers with ring binding, black and white illustrations, 2 folding maps, very good.   Schooner Books Ltd.   115 - 88   2016 $45

Seaton, J. *The Ball-Room Manual and Etiquette of Dancing...* Halifax: Milner & Sowerby, 1867? 32mo., half title, hand colored frontispiece, slight browning, original red cloth, pictorially blocked in gilt, slightly dulled.   Jarndyce Antiquarian Books   CCXV - 399   2016   £120

Seaver, George *Edward Wilson of the Antarctic.* London: John Murray, 1933. First edition, 2nd printing, 8vo., original blue cloth with gilt stamped cream cloth label to spine and direct lettering in gilt, color and black and white plates, 3 maps, light markings to binding, internally amost spotless, gift inscription to WSD.   Sotheran's   Travel and Exploration - 438   2016   £78

Sebald, W. G. *Austerlitz.* Hamilton, 2001. Uncorrected proof, 89/100 copies signed by author with illustrations, crown 8vo., original cream boards, printed in black, white and yellow and illustrated overall on front cover, fine.   Blackwell's Rare Books   B186 - 281   2016   £600

Sebon, Raymond *La Theologie Naturelle...* Rouen: Jean de la Marc, 1641. 8vo., title printed in red and black, woodcut Jesuit device to title, paper flaw at foot of 4L2 separating several letters on recto but without any loss, contemporary limp vellum, later tan label, remains of ties, engraved armorial bookplate of Edward Joshua Cooper of Markree, with label above it marking re-arrangement of castle library by Bryan Cooper, in 1913, good copy.   Blackwell's Rare Books   B184 - 69   2016   £1750

Seccombe, Captain *Army and Navy Drolleries.* London: Frederick Warne, n.d. circa, 1870. First edition, 4to., gilt pictorial cloth, light normal wear, very good++, printed on one side of the paper, fine full page chromolithographs, rare edition, nice copy. Aleph-bet Books, Inc. 111 - 8 2016 $850

Secker, William *The Wedding Ring.* Wakefield: William Nicholson & sons, circa, 1870. Original yellow wrappers, decorated title onlay with embossed gilt floral border, illustrated and lettered in blue, exceptional copy, custom made foldover case, label of Anthony David Estill. Jarndyce Antiquarian Books CCXV - 400 2016 £120

The Secret of the Bay City Rollers. circa, 1976. Octavo, photographically illustrated, stapled photographically illustrated wrappers, owner's neat name on front wrap, spine reinforced with tape and corners bit worn, about very good. Between the Covers Rare Books 208 - 51 2016 $125

Sedgwick, Adam *A Discourse on the Studies of the University.* Cambridge: printed at the Pitt Press for J. & J. J. Deighton, 1834. 16 page catalog, occasional pencil marks and annotations, original dark green glazed cloth, slightly rubbed at head and tail of spine, little cocked. Jarndyce Antiquarian Books CCXV - 577 2016 £75

Sedgwick, William Ellery *Herman Melville: the Tragedy of Mind.* Cambridge: Harvard, 1944. First edition, green cloth, cover very slightly scuffed at corners and ends of spine, ownership signature of Alfred Kazin, 1944, some pencil marking throughout, otherwise very good, tight, price clipped, chipped and browned dust jacket. Second Life Books, Inc. 196 B - 203 2016 $100

See-Paynton, Colin *The Incisive Eye.* Aldershot: Scolar Press & Glynn Vivian Art Gallery, 1996. First edition, 15/100 copies signed by artist, illustrations throughout many full page, 4to., original black cloth, backstrip lettered gilt, signed note by author laid in, dust jacket, numbered card slipcase, fine. Blackwell's Rare Books B186 - 135 2016 £250

Seebohm, Henry *The Birds of Siberia: a Record of a naturalist's Visits to the Valleys of the Petchora and Yenesi.* London: John Murray, 1901. Octavo, 512 pages, text illustrations, publisher's decorated cloth, some minor blemishes, otherwise very good. Andrew Isles Natural History Books 55 - 7995 2016 $250

Seeley, Mabel *The Chuckling Fingers.* Garden City: Doubleday Doran & Co., 1941. First edition, very good in price clipped dust jacket with light professional restoration to spine ends and corners. Buckingham Books 2015 - 27208 2016 $475

Segal, Lore *All the Way Home.* New York: Farrar Straus Giroux, 1973. Stated first edition, 8vo., cloth, fine in fine dust jacket, great color illustrations by James Marshall. Aleph-bet Books, Inc. 111 - 269 2016 $150

Segaloff, Jean *Literary Women of the Left Bank, Paris 1900-1940.* Cambridge: 2014. Artist's book, one of 3 copies, all on Arches hot pressed watercolor paper and transparent polyester film with matte finish (Grafix) signed by artist/author, page size 11 3.4 x 7 inches, 12 original drypoint etchings made on polyester plates that have been hand watercolored and 12 pages of computer generated text preceding each image, bound pages hinged with metal screws on boards covered with gold cloth, front panel with typed label of author/artist and title , green and gold and gold-gilt endpapers, custom made purple cloth over boards clamshell box with purple leather label stamped in gold. Priscilla Juvelis - Rare Books 66 - 13 2016 $1500

Segar, Simon *Honores Anglicani or Titles of Honour the Temporal Nobility of the English Nation.* London: printed for John Baker at the Black Boy in Pater Noster Row, 1712. 8vo., some foxing and browning, contemporary panelled calf, raised bands, red morocco label, faint gilt crest at foot, expert repairs to joints and head and tail of spine, armorial bookplate of William Perceval, signature on titlepage and shelf number at head and early name Alex. McNaghton. Jarndyce Antiquarian Booksellers CCXVI - 513 2016 £380

Seguin, Lisbeth Gooch *Walks in Algiers and Its Surroundings.* London: Daldy Isbister & Co., 1878. First edition, scarce, 8vo., original decorated blue cloth gilt, frontispiece, wood engraved illustrations in text, folding plans, light wear to extremities, front inner hinge reinforced, few pages with minor spotting, else very good. Sotheran's Travel and Exploration - 369 2016 £148

Seguy, E. A. *Floreal Dessins et Coloris Nouveaux.* Paris: A. Calavas, circa, 1925. First edition, 514 x 394 mm., 22 folio leaves, (20 plates, half title and title), loose as issued, publisher's portfolio of ivory quarter linen over terra cotta boards, upper cover with printed title label, original ribbon ties, 76 full color designs in pochoir on 20 plates, a number of small tears, noticeable spotting, and slight soiling and abrasions to covers, edges and corners bit rubbed, portfolio stull sturdy and much more than functional with its original ribbons still intact, light freckling to half title, small minor dampstain in upper gutter margin of three or four plates (trace of this dampstain on few other plates), but internally (where it counts), very pleasing copy, clean margins and especially vibrant colors. Phillip J. Pirages 67 - 288 2016 $1900

Seitz, Don C. *The Buccaneers rough Verse.* New York: Harper & Bros., 1912. First edition, decorations by Howard Pyle, octavo, with frontispiece and two text illustrations, publisher's black cloth, front cover with additional Pyle color plate pasted on, lettered gilt, inscribed by author to American impressionist George Wharton Edwards, near fine.   David Brass Rare Books, Inc.   2015 - 02981   2016 $350

Selbourne, Joanna   *Gwen Raverat, Wood Engraver.* Denby Dale: Fleece Press, 1996. One of 260 copies (from an edition of 300), printed on Zerkall mouldmade paper, printed in black title and chapter headings printed in brown, numerous reproductions of wood engravings by Raverat, small number tipped-in, with tipped-in color printed self portrait of artist, original quarter mustard yellow cloth, backstrip with printed label, marbled brown and yellow boards, rough trimmed, cloth and board slipcase couple of strips of surface removal to paper, fine.   Blackwell's Rare Books   B186 - 302   2016   £350

Selden, George   *The Cricket in Times Square.*   New York: Farrar Straus and Cudahy, 1960. Stated first printing, 8vo., pink cloth, fine in very good+ dust jacket (price clipped, no award seal), illustrations by Garth Williams, signed by Selden with TLS by Williams laid in.   Aleph-bet Books, Inc.   111 - 482   2016 $750

Selden, John   1584-1654   *The Priviledges of the Baronage of England, when they Sit in Parliament.* London: by T. Badger for Matthew Wallbanck, 1642. First edition, small 8vo., without first blank leaf, dampstained and browned throughout, shaved at head, with some loss to page numbers, late 19th century vellum (label missing), from the library of James Stevens Cox (1910-1997), bookplate of Charles Edward Doble (d. 1914).   Maggs Bros. Ltd.   1447 - 375   2016   £170

Selden, John   1584-1654   *Table-Talk: Being the Discourses of John Selden Esq. or His Sence of Various Matters of Weight and High Consequence Relating Especially to Religion and State.*   London: for E. Smith, 1689. First edition, small 4to., browned throughout, dampstain to fore-margin, of (A)4 and D1, very small hole through inner margin of C3, foxing to edges of H3-4, lower corner of last leaf torn-away (just touching two letters), some lower edges uncut, mid 20th century half calf and marbled boards, from the library of James Stevens Cox (1910-1997).   Maggs Bros. Ltd.   1447 - 376   2016   £400

Selden, John   1584-1654   *Table Talk.*   London: J. M. Dent, 1906. 16mo., full blue calf by Riviere & Son circa 1920, covers double ruled gilt, spine decoratively tooled in compartments, two tan morocco labels lettered gilt, gilt board edges and turn-ins, marbled endpapers, all edges gilt, fine.   David Brass Rare Books, Inc.   2015 - 03010   2016 $150

Selden, John   1584-1654   *Theanthropos; or God Made Man.*   London: by J. G. for Nathaniel Brooks, 1661. First edition, 8vo., engraved portrait, contemporary calf, covers ruled in blind, gilt spine with red morocco label, inside joints broken, spine defective at head and tail, covers rubbed, pastedowns unstuck, flyleaves include waste from 12mo. edition of Cicero, from the library of James Stevens Cox (1910-1997), bookplate and signature of John, first and last Baron Rolle of Stevenstone (1750-1842), Exeter.   Maggs Bros. Ltd.   1447 - 377   2016   £160

The Self-Instructor or Young man's Companion...   London: Henry Fisher, c., 1823. Additional engraved title and 8 plates, plates slightly browned and with small damp marking, contemporary half calf, red morocco label, rubbed, overall nice, signature of Henry S. Peacock, Maddlockstones.   Jarndyce Antiquarian Books   CCXV - 401   2016   £220

Self, William E.   *Auction Catalogue. The William E. Self Family Collection.*   London and: New York: Christie's, 2008. First edition, half title, color facsimiles and photos, original scarlet cloth, front board with portrait onlay of Dickens lettered in gilt, mint.   Jarndyce Antiquarian Booksellers   CCXVIII - 1515   2016   £35

Seller, Abednego   *The Antiquities of Palmyra.*   London: printed for S. Smith and B. Watford, 1696. First edition, scarce, 8vo., modern panelled and sprinkled calf, raised bands, red lettering piece, blindstamped fleurons in corners, large folding panoramas, one plate of coins, some light waterstaining to fore edges, neat repairs to coin plate, otherwise good, ownership inscription.   Sotheran's Piccadilly Notes - Summer 2015 - 269   2016   £895

Selz, Peter   *New Images of Man.*   New York: Museum of Modern Art/Doubleday, 1959. First edition, small square quarto, illustrations, laminated boards, errata slip laid in, slight bruise at tail of spine, otherwise fine in very good, slightly nicked dust jacket with short tear.   Peter Ellis   112 - 280   2016   £35

Semenov, Petr Petrovich   *Travels in the Tian'-Shan' 156-1857.*   London: Hakluyt Society, 1998. First edition, plates, fine in very near fine dust jacket.   Peter Ellis   112 - 70   2016   £35

Semon, Richard   *In the Australian Bush and on the Coast of the Coral Sea...*   London: Macmillan, 1899. Large octavo, 552 pages, 4 folding colored maps and text illustrations, publisher's green cloth, few spots but sound.   Andrew Isles Natural History Books   55 - 7999   2016 $350

Sencourt, Robert   *Spain's Ordeal - a Documented Survey of Recent Events.*   London: Longmans, Green and Co., 1938. First edition, octavo, 9 sketch maps, one folding, contemporary (1938) ownership signature, head of spine, bit bumped, near fine in very good, slightly creased dust jacket, bit tanned at spine.   Peter Ellis   112 - 373   2016   £125

Sendak, Jack *Circus Girl.* New York: Harper & Bros., 1957. First edition, 4to., pictorial cloth, covers slightly faded, else near fine in dust jacket with price intact, some soil to dust jacket with chip off top of spine, illustrations by Maurice Sendak.   Aleph-bet Books, Inc.   112 - 447   2016 $1250

Sendak, Maurice *Some Swell Pup.* New York: Farrar Straus Giroux, 1976. Stated first edition, first printing, illustrated in bright color on every page, cloth, fine in slightly worn, near fine dust jacket, this copy inscribed and dated by Sendak with charming small pen drawing.   Aleph-bet Books, Inc.   112 - 449   2016 $600

Sendak, Maurice *Max en De Maximonsters. (Where the Wild things Are).* Rotterdam: Leminscoat, 1981. Dutch edition, glazed pictorial boards, near fine, this edition signed by Sendak with pen drawing.   Aleph-bet Books, Inc.   111 - 407   2016 $400

Sendak, Maurice *Where the Wild Things Are.* New York: Harper & Row, 1988. Limited to 220 numbered copies signed by Sendak, including original pen an dink drawing of wild thing signed by Sendak, this copy additionally inscribed by Sendak to fellow artist James Marshall, fine association copy, oblong, publisher's full blue leather stamped in gold, all edges gilt, fine in original cloth box with large color plate on cover.   Aleph-bet Books, Inc.   112 - 446   2016 $10,500

Sender, Ramon J. *Seven Red Sundays.* London: Faber and Faber, 1936. First UK edition, octavo, covers marked and bruised at one corner, endpapers and edges spotted, very good in good striking dust jacket designed by Eric Fraser, little nicked and rubbed at edges and marked on lower panel, scarce.   Peter Ellis   112 - 376   2016   £125

Seneca, Lucius Annaeus *Seneca's Morals by Way of Abstract.* London: printed for J. and R. Tonson, 1764. 12mo., several ink splashes, early names and pen strokes to endpapers and inner boards, full contemporary calf, raised and gilt bands, red morocco label, covers rather rubbed, head of spine chipped, corners bumped, pen initials on upper board.   Jarndyce Antiquarian Booksellers   CCXVI - 514   2016   £65

Seneca, Lucius Annaeus *Singulares Sententiae Centum Aliquot Versibus ex Codd Pall & Frising Auctae & Correctae, Studio & Opera Jani Gruteri...* Lugduni Batavorum: apud Johannem du Vivie, 1708. 8vo., additional engraved titlepage, titlepage in red and plate with engraved vignette, woodcut head and tailpieces, sporadic light foxing, evidence in gutter preceding engraved title of presentation certificate removal, contemporary vellum prize binding, gilt spine with red morocco label, gilt crest of The Hague to each board, edges sprinkled red, spine label little chipped, some greyish marks, boards slightly bowed, top edge dusty, bookplate of Maurice B. Worms, modern ink inscription "A.S.B. from A.J.C. Easter mcmlx".   Unsworths Antiquarian Booksellers Ltd.   30 - 137   2016   £200

Seneca, Lucius Annaeus *Tragoediae: Post Omnes Omnium Editiones Recensione Editae Denuo & Notis....* Excudebat Rogerus Daniel, 1659. 12mo., first leaf blank, one leaf with paper flaw to fore-edge affecting few characters of side note, small wormhole in gutter of a few gatherings sometimes touching a line number, few minor marks, bookplate of Robert Maxwell of Finnebrogue to titlepage verso, 12mo., original blind ruled sheep, worn paper label to spine, rear joint damaged near head revealing structure of binding, but binding still entirely sound, slightly marked and rubbed, good.   Blackwell's Rare Books   Greek & Latin Classics VII - 82   2016   £200

Senior, Nassau William   1790-1864 *A Journal Kept in Turkey and Greece, in the Autumn of 1857 and the Beginning of 1858.* London: Longman, Brown, Green, 1859. First edition, 8vo., half title, 2 double page maps colored in outline, 2 colored lithographs, original green blind-stamped cloth, corners rubbed, small evidence of rubbing on upper cover, very good.   J. & S. L. Bonham Antiquarian Booksellers   Europe 2016 - 9174   2016   £680

Senn, Charles Herman *The Art of the Table...* London: Ward, Lock & Co., 1923. Third edition, half title, photo frontispiece and illustrations, original grey decorated cloth, ex-libris Barbara Jones, very good.   Jarndyce Antiquarian Books   CCXV - 402   2016   £40

The Series of Dramatic Entertainments Performed by Royal Command Before Her Majesty the Queen, His Royal Highness Prince Albert, the Royal Family and the Court at Windsor Castle 1848-1849. London: Mr. Mitchell, Royal Library, 1849. One of 200 copies, 254 x 20mm., publisher's very decorative deluxe binding of crimson pebble grain morocco, covers colored by plain rules and dogtooth roll, central panel with elaborate gilt frame enclosing imperial crown, flat spine with filigree, gilt decoration, gilt turn-ins, ivory watered silk endleaves, all edges gilt, 10 chromolithographs heightened with gilt, including frontispiece depicting a royal performance, a decorative titlepage and 8 decorative play titles, with five delicate printed cut-paper dollies serving as playbills for plays performed by royal command, quarter inch abrasion at spine tail (with small loss of gilt), one inch closed tear to bottom margin of one plate, quite fine, binding lustrous and otherwise unworn, text basically undisturbed.   Phillip J. Pirages   67 - 326   2016 $1500

Sermon, William *A Friend to the Sick or the Honest English Mans Preservations.* London: printed by W. Downing for Edward Thomas, 1673. First edition, lacks frontispiece, stamp on title, some dampstaining, small 8vo., contemporary full calf, some wear and corners bumped, rare.   James Tait Goodrich   X-78 - 506   2016 $795

Serres De La Tour, Alphonse De *Londres et ses Environs ou Guide des Voyageurs, Curieux et Amateurs dans Cette Partie de l'Angleterre qui fait Connoitre tout ce qui Peut Interesser & Exciter la Curiosite des Voyageurs des Curieux & des Amateurs de tous les Etat...* Paris: chez Buisson, 1788. First edition, 2 volumes, thick 12mo., contemporary quarter calf, gilt, over paste paper boards, morocco labels, 9 large folding engraved plates, large folding map, all edges red, excellent copy.   Howard S. Mott Inc.   265 - 115   2016 $800

Serventy, D. L. *The Emulet: an ornithological souffle (and) an ornithological omulet.* Melbourne: privately published, 1949-1952. Limited to 150 copies, Octavo, 52 pages, text illustrations, publisher's printed wrappers, very good set.   Andrew Isles Natural History Books   55 - 6020   2016 $250

Serventy, D. L. *The Western Australian Naturalist. (volumes 1-23).* Perth: Western Australian Naturalist's Club, 1947-2001. Octavo, 23 volumes, publisher's wrappers (except the first two volumes which are bound together in binder's cloth, very good set.   Andrew Isles Natural History Books   55 - 18909   2016 $350

Servos, Launcelot Cressy *Practical Instruction in Golf.* Emmaus: Rodale Press, 1938. Second edition, ink price marked on front pastedown, some bleed thought from binder's glue, else near fine in very good dust jacket with tear on front panel and few small spots, scarce in dust jacket.   Between the Covers Rare Books   208 - 143   2016 $225

The Session of the Poets, Holden at the Foot of Parnassus-Hill July the 9th 1696. London: for Elizabeth Whitlock, 1696. First edition, 8vo., uncut, engraved frontispiece, little dusty, some creasing to edges, small piece torn away from lower corner of D1, unsophisticated copy, sewn as issued in original pale blue paper wrappers, wrappers creased, short tear at head and tille stained, (original stitching partly loose), from the library of James Stevens Cox (1910-1997).   Maggs Bros. Ltd.   1447 - 378   2016   £1500

Setoun, Gabriel *The Child World.* London: John Lane, The Bodley Head, 1896. First American edition illustrated by Charles Robinson, small octavo, profusely illustrated, small octavo, publisher's ribbed dark red cloth, front cover and spine pictorially stamped gilt, top edge gilt, others uncut, small marginal tear on pages 131/132, otherwise very fine.   David Brass Rare Books, Inc.   2015 - 02967   2016 $450

Settle, Elkanah *The New Athenian Comedy...* London: for Campanella Restio, 1693. First edition, small 4to., browned throughout, author's name written in pencil on titlepage, late 19th century half morocco and marbled boards by Kerr and Richardson (head and foot of spine chipped, front joint lightly chipped), from the library of James Stevens Cox (1910-1997), 20th century signature of James Bell.   Maggs Bros. Ltd.   1447 - 379   2016   £250

Settle, Mary Lee *Charley Bland.* Franklin Center: Franklin Library, 1989. Limited first edition, signed by author, bound in green leather, lettered and decoratively stamped in gilt, all edges gilt, very fine, as new, extremely handsome edition.   Argonaut Book Shop   Literature 2015 - 4016   2016 $45

The Seven Wonderful Brothers. London: Dean and Son, 1855. 4to., pictorial wrappers, top margin slightly trimmed and spine unobtrusively strengthened, very good+, printed on one side of paper, hand colored illustrations.   Aleph-bet Books, Inc.   112 - 167   2016 $725

Severance, Frank H. *The Captivity and Sufferings of Benjamin Gilbert and His Family.* Cleveland: Burrows Brothers Co., 1904. One of 267 numbered copies reprinted from original 1784 edition, 2 facsimiles, folding map in rear, maroon cloth, gilt, all edges gilt, very minor rubbing to spine ends, inner rear cover with pencilled note, fine.   Argonaut Book Shop   Native American 2015 - 5952   2016 $125

Sevigne, Marie De Rabutin Chantal, Marquise De   1626-1696 *Letters of Madame de Rabutin Chantal, Marchioness de Sevigne in the Comtess (sic) de Grignan, her Daughter.* London: printed for N. Blandford at the London Gazette, Charing Cross, 1727. Tear across volume I, E9, with old repairs in margins, lacking free endpapers, old notes on inner rear board volume I, volume II has half title only, contemporary panelled calf, red labels, attractive copy.   Jarndyce Antiquarian Booksellers   CCXVI - 515   2016   £125

Sewall, Joseph *A Sermon Preached at the Thursday-Lecture in Boston, September 16, 1761 Before the Great and General Court... on the Joyful news of the Reduction ...* Boston: by John Draper and by Edes and Gil, 1762. Stitched and untrimmed, stitching breaking, else very good, contemporary signature of Jos. Green, chemise and cloth slipcase.   Joseph J. Felcone, Inc.   Books from Five Centuries: a Miscellany - 53   2016 $550

Seward County, Hand-Book. From the "Modern Argo" Kansas City, Mo. Kansas City: Modern Argo Print, n.d. circa, 1883? 8vo., original pale blue pictorial wrappers printed in purple, spine worn, diagonal repaired tear in front wrapper repaired on verso, with no loss, edges slightly ragged.   Howard S. Mott Inc.   265 - 96   2016 $350

Sewell, Anna *Black Beauty: His Grooms and Companions.* London: Jarrold & sons, 1877. First edition, octavo, black and white wood engraved frontispiece by C. Hewitt, original cloth, Carter's variant 'C' binding, terracotta cloth blocked in black and gilt, brown coated endpapers, spine lightly sunned and some minor rubbing at extremities, recased with some professional restoration to top and bottom of spine, few thumb marks to first few pages, good copy.   Heritage Book Shop   Holiday 2015 - 100   2016 $4500

Sewrin, Charles Augustin *Brick Bolding, ou Qu-est-ce Quae la Vie?* Paris: chez Roux (et) Marchand, 1800. Nouvelle edition, 12mo., burn hole to blank leading edge of one leaf, oldstain to outer lower corner of M2 and M3 volume I, uncut in original sugar paper wrappers, chipped spine labels, outer cover stop short of leading edges of volumes causing creasing and dustiness to corners & edges of some leaves, wear to backstrips but in generally good condition.   Jarndyce Antiquarian Booksellers   CCXVI - 516   2016   £200

Seyd, Ernest *California and Its Resources. A Work for the merchant, The Captialist and the Emigrant.* London: Trubner and Co., 1858. Plates, 2 folding maps, original pebbled boards, front free endpaper removed, some foxing, extremities rubbed, front hinge cracked but holding, withal good copy.   Dumont Maps and Books   134 - 46   2016 $1500

Seymour, Richard Arthur *Pioneering in the Pampas; or the First Four Years of a Settler's Eperience in the La Plata Camps.* London: Longmans Green, 1869. First edition, folding map, original green cloth, spine faded with small wear to head and tail.   J. & S. L. Bonham Antiquarian Booksellers   America 2016 - 9916   2016   £150

Sforzosi, Luigi *Tesoretto dello Studente della Lingua Italiana.* Boston: William D. Ticknor, 1835. First American edition, original pebble grain cloth, extremities rubbed, spine ends chipped, some foxing, annotated in pencil in margins of first 16 pages.   Joseph J. Felcone, Inc.   Books from Five Centuries: a Miscellany - 82   2016 $275

Shaberman, R. B. *Lewis Carroll and Mrs. Liddell, a Study of Their Relationship Based on New Material Together with a Review of the Unpublished Diaries of Lewis Carroll.* London: M. Tickner and Co. Ltd., 1982. Limited edition, number 132 of 300 copies, signed by Shaberman, slim octavo, stapled green and black printed wrappers, near fine.   Ken Sanders Rare Books   E Catalogue # 1 - 25   2016 $75

Shadwell, Thomas *Epsom-Wells.* London: printed for R. Wellington, 1704. 4to., early strengthening to title leaf which is dusted and bears a small paper label, small repair to corner of last leaf, disbound.   Jarndyce Antiquarian Booksellers   CCXVI - 467   2016   £75

Shadwell, Thomas *The History of Timon of Athens, the man-hater.* The Hague: printed by T. Johnson, 1712. 8vo., some light foxing, recent full polished tree calf, gilt label.   Jarndyce Antiquarian Booksellers   CCXVI - 469   2016   £450

Shaftesbury, Anthony Ashley Cooper, 3rd Earl of   1671-1713 *Characteristicks of Men, Manners, Opinions, Times.* N.P.: n.p., 1708-1711. 3 volumes, , lovely contemporary boards with spines beautifully and unobtrusively rebacked to style, top front spine edge of volume three just beginning to crack (about 2") but very firm, small bookplate to inside front cover of volume I (Walter T. Shirley II), contemporary ink signature, overall very pretty, rare first issue.   Athena Rare Books   List 15 - 1711   2016 $4500

Shaftesbury, Anthony Ashley Cooper, 3rd Earl of   1671-1713 *Characteristicks of Men, Manners, Opinions, Times &c.* London: printed in the year, 1733. 3 volumes, 12mo., collective titlepage in volume I, separate titles with imprint for each volume, some light browning to paper, several leaves of index, untrimmed in top corner and folded back into binding, contemporary mottled calf, spines rubbed, only faint traces of black morocco labels, armorial bookplate of Marquess of Headfort, nice, unsophisticated copy.   Jarndyce Antiquarian Books   CCXV - 400   2016   £225

Shaftesbury, Anthony Ashley Cooper, 3rd Earl of   1671-1713 *Characteristicks of Men, Manners, Opinions, times.* printed for James Purser, 1737. Sixth edition, 8vo., 3 volumes, handsome contemporary London bindings, black morocco, richly gilt tooled to cottage roof pattern, gilt edges, frontispiece, title vignettes, headpieces, little rubbing to joints, spines slightly sunned, heads and tails of spines worn, otherwise very good.   Sotheran's   Piccadilly Notes - Summer 2015 - 270   2016   £2995

Shakespeare, William   1564-1616 *As You Like It.* London: Hodder & Stoughton, n.d., 1909. Limited to 500 numbered copies signed by Thomson, this copy 0000 for presentation, presentation inscription from artist to J. E. Hodder Williams, director at Hodder & Stoughton, this is accompanied by lovely watercolor on half title, printed on fine paper, illustrated with 40 beautiful tipped in color plates by Hugh Thomson, with lettered tissue guards, large thick 4to., full vellum, gilt pictorial cover, original silk ties, few minor marks on cover and endpaper, boxed as usual, else fine.   Aleph-bet Books, Inc.   112 - 475   2016 $5000

Shakespeare, William 1564-1616 *Comedies, Histories and Tragedies.* London: printed for H. Herringman, E. Brewster and R. Bentley, 1685. Magnificent engraved portrait by Martin Doreshout above the verses To the Reader on verso of first leaf, title with fleur-de-lis-device, double column text within typographical rules, woodcut initials, frontispiece skillfully repaired at inner margin, tear (repaired) in top inner corner just passing through engraved surface for about 1 cm. (hatched area), titlepage with tears repaired, 2 small lacunae filled in, some of the repaired tears passing through letters but without loss, paperflaw in *BBB1 with loss of 7 letters on recto and several more on verso (failure to print), waterstaining in inner margins at beginning, diminishing until absent in gathering E, intermittent waterstaining to lower margins, last leaf mounted and defective at head and foot without loss of text, minor worming strictly in fore-margin in third pagination, few ink splashes here and there and odd small rust hole, tears in lower margin of 'Bbb6 with loss to blank margin not affecting text, another Kkk4 entering the text but without losse, modern panelled calf over boards by James Brockman, spine richly gilt contrasting lettering pieces, black velvet lined maroon buckram folding box with black lettering piece, good.   Blackwell's Rare Books   Marks of Genius - 42   2016   £85,000

Shakespeare, William 1564-1616 *The Comedies: the Histories: the Tragedies.* New York: Heritage Press, 1958. 3 volumes, illustrations, printed boards, beige cloth spines, lettered gilt, spines darkened, Tragedies volume has very slight rubbing to head of spine and soiled and faded slipcase, else fine set in slipcases, Sandglass pamphlets laid in.   Argonaut Book Shop   Heritage Press 2015 - 7063   2016 $90

Shakespeare, William 1564-1616 *The Dramatic Works.* London: 1876. 6 volumes.   Honey & Wax Booksellers   4 - 24   2016 $850

Shakespeare, William 1564-1616 *Hamlet.* New York: Composing Room & Graphic Arts Typographers Inc., 1972. Square 8vo., illustrations by Jack Wolfgang Beck, gray cloth with imitation black morocco spine, stamped in gilt, fine in cloth covered box.   Second Life Books, Inc.   197 - 284   2016 $45

Shakespeare, William 1564-1616 *The Histories.* Norwalk: Heritage Press, 1986. illustrations by John Farleigh, 2 volumes, printed beige cloth, gilt lettering to spines, very fine, slipcase with minor soiling, Sandglass pamphlet laid in.   Argonaut Book Shop   Heritage Press 2015 - 7075   2016 $90

Shakespeare, William 1564-1616 *King Lear.* London: Gamymed Original Editions, 1963. Limited to 279 oies, signed by artist, this number 87, folio, beautifully illustrated with 16 lithographs by Oskar Kokoschka, original full vellum, gilt stamped on spine, marbled endpapers, gray cloth slipcase, slightly frayed, vellum little soiled, otherwise fine.   Heritage Book Shop   Holiday 2015 - 67   2016 $3000

Shakespeare, William 1564-1616 *The Tragedie of King Lear.* Bangor: Theodore Press, 1986. Limited to 160 signed and numbered copies, small folio, printed with hand-set type at Theodore Press on light gray paper handmade especially for this book by Kate MacGregor and Bernie Vinzani, Claire Van Vliet woodcuts, superb edition, quarter leather with birch boards in non-adhesive binding with exposed sewing, chemise and slipcase.   Oak Knoll Books   310 - 115   2016 $2000

Shakespeare, William 1564-1616 *The Tragical History of King Richard III.* London: printed for J. Tonson & J. Watts and sold by W. Feales, 1736. Frontispiece with corner torn from margin, title in red and black, slight damp marking to inner margin, 12mo., disbound.   Jarndyce Antiquarian Booksellers   CCXVI - 468   2016   £75

Shakespeare, William 1564-1616 *The Tragedy of MacBeth.* London: Hacon & Ricketts, 1901. Uncut in light green cloth, blocked in blind, spine decorated and lettered gilt at head, very good.   Jarndyce Antiquarian Booksellers   CCXVII - 255   2016   £180

Shakespeare, William 1564-1616 *The Merry Wives of Windsor.* New York: Frederick A. Stokes Co., 1910. Edition deluxe, limited to 350 numbered copies, this one of 100 reserved for sale in the US, signed by artist, this no. 290, quarto, frontispiece and 39 color plates by Hugh Thomson on heavy brown stock, descriptive tissue guards, black and white text illustrations, original vellum over boards, pictorially stamped and lettered gilt on front cover and lettered gilt on spine, top edge gilt, others uncut, covers very slightly dust soiled, lacking silk ties, frontispiece with very small crease in right hand lower corner, small close marginal tear on fore-edge of pages 83/84, still excellent copy.   David Brass Rare Books, Inc.   2015 - 02981   2016 $650

Shakespeare, William 1564-1616 *Merry Wives of Windsor.* New York: Frederick Stokes, 1910. First US edition, thick 4to., green gilt pictorial cloth, owner inscription, else as new in publisher's box with printed label (box rubbed, flaps repaired), 40 beautiful tipped in color plates by Hugh Thomson, with guards, uncommon, rare in box.   Aleph-bet Books, Inc.   112 - 476   2016 $600

Shakespeare, William 1564-1616 *The Merry Wives of Windsor.* London: William Heinemann, 1910. first edition thus, large quarto, vellum over boards, pictorially tooled in gilt, 40 colored plates, including frontispiece, mounted on heavy brown paper and protected by lettered tissue guards, untrimmed, top edge gilt, number 183 of 350 numbered copies, signed by artist, silk ties laid in, front hinge paper starting, still tight, some minor rubbing to covers, very good.   Second Life Books, Inc.   196 B - 557   2016 $50

Shakespeare, William   1564-1616   *A Midsummer Night's Dream.*   London: J. M. Dent & Aldine House, 1895. First edition with these illustrations, 8vo., gold cloth with ornate gilt design, top edge gilt, others uncut, very light cover soil and one margin of a text page irregular from being opened roughly, very good-fine, 10 full page, 3 double page and many smaller beautiful Art Nouveau illustrations by Robert Bell.   Aleph-bet Books, Inc.   112 - 51   2016 $375

Shakespeare, William   1564-1616   *A Midsummer Nights Dream.*   New York & London: Doubleday Page & William Heinemann, 1908. 4to., cloth backed leaf patterned boards with gilt picture, fine in original dust jacket printed with spider web design and in publisher's pictorial box (dust jacket chipped with few mends, box with some wear), box has charming line illustration, illustrations by Arthur Rackham, with 40 magnificent color plates on heavy paper with lettered guards, plus many lovely black and whites in text, great copy, rare with wrapper and box.   Aleph-bet Books, Inc.   111 - 376   2016 $3000

Shakespeare, William   1564-1616   *Shakespeare's Comedy of a Midsummer-Night's Dream.*   London: Constable & Co., 1914. Edition Deluxe, 1/250 copies signed by artist, this being #68, quarto, 12 mounted color plates, each with titled tissue guard, 46 full page and 17 smaller black and white drawings by W. Heath Robinson, publisher's primary binding of full white vellum over boards, front cover and spine pictorially stamped in gilt, top edge gilt, others uncut, vellum very slightly dust soiled, light offsetting onto pastedowns, otherwise spectacular copy, housed in blue cloth slipcase.   David Brass Rare Books, Inc.   2015 - 03022   2016 $5000

Shakespeare, William   1564-1616   *A Mid-Summer Night's Dream.*   New York: Henry Holt, 1914. First US edition, 4to., blue cloth pictorially stamped in green and gold, top edge gilt, covers very slightly dulled, else near fine, illustrations by W. Heath Robinson.   Aleph-bet Books, Inc.   112 - 431   2016 $850

Shakespeare, William   1564-1616   *Othello, the Moor of Venice.*   Covent Garden: printed for the Proprietors and sold by all the Booksellers of London and Westminster, 1770. Rare acting edition, engraved frontispiece, some browning and few spots, first 2 leaves dog eared, 8vo., uncut, stitched in original wrappers, bit soiled and frayed, sound.   Blackwell's Rare Books   B184 - 77   2016   £450

Shakespeare, William   1564-1616   *Othello.*   New York: Composing Room, 1974. Square 8vo., illustrations by Isadore Seltzer, black cloth with black morocco grained plastic spine, stamped in gilt, fine in very slightly faded black cloth covered box.   Second Life Books, Inc.   197 - 285   2016 $45

Shakespeare, William   1564-1616   *The Plays of William Shakespare.*   London: Longman, Rivington, Richardson, Hatchard et al, 1847. First edition, octavo, 8 volumes, portrait frontispiece and various other engravings, fine period binding of full tan panelled calf with raised bands, elaborate gilt decoration and inner dentelles, red and green morocco title labels, marbled endpapers, all edges gilt, armorial bookplate, some foxing here and there, some mild wear to edges of covers, near fine set, handsomely bound.   Peter Ellis   112 - 354   2016   £1200

Shakespeare, William   1564-1616   *Plays and Poems.*   New York: Limited Editions Club, 1939-1941. Limited to 195 numbered sets, 39 volumes, original cloth backed patterned boards top edges gilt, other untrimmed, each play illustrated by a different artist, spines slightly darkened, couple with little spotting, generally very nice.   Sotheran's Piccadilly Notes - Summer 2015 - 272   2016   £1995

Shakespeare, William   1564-1616   *Shakespear's Sonnets.*   London: Daivd Nutt, 1890. First edition, octavo, 8 page publisher's catalog at rear, 3 plates, very good, scarce.   Peter Ellis   112 - 353   2016   £85

Shakespeare, William   1564-1616   *The Sonnets.*   Birmingham: Birmingham Guild of Handicraft Press, 1895. One of 500 copies, and 50 large paper copies, 222 x 178mm, pleasing rich brown morocco in the Arts and Crafts style by Winifred Turner (signed and dated by her in 1930), covers divided into geometric compartments by blind and gilt rules, at center a lozenge filled with entwined gilt roses, raised bands, spine compartments ruled in gilt and blind, linen pastedowns framed by gilt beading, top edge gilt, with woodcut white vine initials, some with extensions, 12 half borders and two three quarter borders, all by Ernest G. Treglown, engraved on wood by Charles Carr Tomkinson, spine lightly sunned, little soiling to lower cover, neither trivial nor serious, titlepage bit foxed, other insignificant imperfections internally, but excellent copy, text clean and lustrous binding essentially unworn.   Phillip J. Pirages   67 - 73   2016 $900

Shakespeare, William   1564-1616   *The Sonnets.*   London: published by George Bell and Sons, 1899. 164 x 130mm, very pretty burgundy crushed morocco gilt, by Zaehnsdorf (stamp signed and with firm's oval stamp in blind, covers with thin fillet borders enclosing a central panel featuring rose medallions in each corner and at center a lobed and leafy lozenge contain Shakespeare's initials within flames, raised bands, spine compartments with either lozenge, rose or "W S" monogram at center, gilt titling , turn-ins with foliate tooling, red linen endleaves, top edge gilt, other edges untrimmed and unopened, woodcut initials and elaborate Kelmscott-style white-vine woodcut borders around first opening, hint of rubbing to upper joint, spine just shade darker than covers, pages faintly browned at edges, otherwise fine, binding lustrous, text obviously never read.   Phillip J. Pirages   67 - 78   2016 $950

Shakespeare, William 1564-1616 *Complete Sonnets.* Sylvan Press, 1955. Limited to 1050 copies, this one of 500 for Balding & Mansell Ltd., 4to, recently finely bound in half russet morocco with gilt rules, lettered gilt on spine, top edge gilt, fine.   Sotheran's   Piccadilly Notes - Summer 2015 - 271   2016   £248

Shakespeare, William 1564-1616 *The Sonnets of William Shakespeare.* Los Angeles: Zeitlin & Ver Brugge April, 1974. Limited to 120 numbered copies, this number 74, small 8vo., 2 illustrations, original binding by Max Adjarian in quarter levant morocco, decorative paper, raised bands, gilt spine, fine.   Jeff Weber Rare Books   181 - 72   2016 $5500

Shakespeare, William 1564-1616 *The Sonnets & a Lover's Complaint.* Folio Society, 1989. Wood engravings, quarter cloth, patterned boards, fine in slipcase.   Bertram Rota Ltd.   February List 2016 - 48   2016   £25

Shakespeare, William 1564-1616 *The Taming of the Shrew.* New York: Composing Room, 1973. Square 8vo., illustrations by Isadore Seltzer, orchid cloth with black imitation morocco spine, stamped in gilt, near fine in slightly faded box.   Second Life Books, Inc.   197 - 286   2016 $45

Shakespeare, William 1564-1616 *Shakespeare's Comedy of The Tempest.* London: Hodder & Stoughton, n.d., 1908? Tall 8vo., 40 color tipped in plates by Edmund Dulac, original blue gilt stamped cloth, printed dust jacket with couple of small chips to edges with small hole, bit rubbed, jacket rare.   Jeff Weber Rare Books   181 - 60   2016 $400

Shakespeare, William 1564-1616 *The Tempest.* London: Hodder & Stoughton, 1908. Limited to only 500 numbered copies signed by artist, 40 beautiful tipped-in color plates on heavy stock by Edmund Dulac, large 4to., full gilt vellum, silk ties renewed, top edge gilt, near fine. Aleph-bet Books, Inc.   111 - 138   2016 $2500

Shakespeare, William 1564-1616 *The Tempest.* London & New York: Heinemann & Doubleday, 1926. Limited to 520 copies, 4to., quarter vellum, white gilt pictorial boards, top edge gilt, fine in original dust jacket, illustrations by Arthur Rackham with 21 magnificent tipped-in color plates plus pictorial titlepage and several black and white devices, printed on handmade paper, magnificent copy. Aleph-bet Books, Inc.   111 - 380   2016 $3000

Shakespeare, William 1564-1616 *The Tempest.* New York: Composing Room & Graphic Arts Typographers, 1971. Square 8vo., illustrations by Jack Wolfgang Beck, bookmark laid in tan cloth with black imitation morocco spine, stamped in gilt, fine in tan box, very slightly worn at one corner.   Second Life Books, Inc.   197 - 283   2016 $45

Shakespeare, William 1564-1616 *Troilus and Creside.* New York: Limited Editions Club, 1939. 153/950 copies, frontispiece and 5 further full page wood engravings printed in black and brown, folio, original tan bucckram with patterned boards, backstrip little darkened and lettered gilt, touch of wear to corners, top edge gilt, others untrimmed and lightly toned, bookplate and ownership inscription of Roy. C. Barker, 4 page descriptive leaflet laid in, very good. Blackwell's Rare Books   B186 - 316   2016   £60

Shakespeare, William 1564-1616 *Shakespeare's Comedy of the Twelfth Night.* London: Hodder & Stoughton, 1908. Limited to 350 numbered copies, signed by artist, thick 4to., full vellum stamped in gold, new ties, light cover soil, else near fine, illustrations by Charles Robinson with 40 beautiful tipped in color plates, this copy has fantastic detailed full page drawing signed by Robinson on verso of limitation page.   Aleph-bet Books, Inc.   111 - 389   2016 $5250

Shakespeare, William 1564-1616 *The Works of William Shakespeare.* London: Macmillan & Co., 1899. Eversley edition, 10 volumes, half titles, some slight foxing, occasional pencil marking, armorial bookplate of Arthur & Dorothy Hazlerigg, contemporary half olive green morocco, spines with gilt floral motif, some very slight rubbing to extremities, attractive set.   Jarndyce Antiquarian Booksellers   CCXVII - 256   2016   £1850

Shakespeare, William 1564-1616 *The Works.* London: Macmillan and Co., 1902-1905. Cambridge edition, 9 volumes, 235 x 159mm, very appealing in brown half morocco over green linen by Zaehnsdorf (stamp signed on verso of front free endpaper), raised bands, spines gilt in double ruled compartments with dotted inner frame and floral cornerpieces as well as large central ornament formed by two crossed swords, crown and garland, marbled endpapers, top edge gilt, other edges rough trimmed, spines uniformly sunned ot very pleasing honey brown, first volume with shallow chipping at top of spine with one band little abraded, otherwise only trivial defects, bindings in other ways showing only very minor signs of use, text quite clean and fresh. Phillip J. Pirages   67 - 319   2016 $1900

Shakespeare, William 1564-1616 *The Works of William Shakespeare.* New York: Random House, 1929-1933. Limited to 1600 sets, 7 volumes, 8vo., original full gilt stamped Niger morocco, top edge gilt, clean and unfaded, near fine, originally issued in individual slipcases, not present here, this is the Milton S. Slocum San Marino, CA copy with original invoice from 1955.   Jeff Weber Rare Books 181 - 71   2016 $2000

Shakespeare, William 1564-1616 *The Works.* New York: Nonesuch Press, 1929-1933. One of 1600 copies, 242 x 155mm., 7 volumes, original russet niger morocco by A. W. Bain, covers with gilt double fillet frame, raised bands, gilt titling on spines, a total of five (oil?) spots (one the size of a quarter, the others smaller), spines sunned as always (but atypically uniform in color), free endpapers with offset shadow from binder's glue, otherwise very fine, bindings with virtually no wear and interiors essentially undisturbed. Phillip J. Pirages 67 - 264 2016 $3600

Shakespeare, William 1564-1616 *The Works of Shakespeare.* London: Nonesuch Press, New York: Random Huse, 1929-1933. Limited to 1600 sets, this number 359 (of 1050 sets for Great Britain and Ireland and 550 sets for America), 7 volumes, octavo, on Pannekoek mould made paper, publisher's full nger morocco, corners with gilt double fillet border blind and lettered in gilt in compartments, gilt turn-ins, top edge colored pale pink and gilt on rough, others uncut, some very slight variations in colors of spines as usual, some minor offsetting to endpapers, bookplate of previous owner, Harry Lawrence Bradfer-Lawrence, covers and spines with occasional minor discoloration, overall near fine. Heritage Book Shop Holiday 2015 - 85 2016 $3000

Shakespeare, William 1564-1616 *Complete Works.* London: Oxford University Press, 1969. 8vo., publisher's cloth, very good, tight copy, bookseller, author, Larry McMurtry's copy, with his 1969 ownership signature, card with 7 lines of holograph and slip with 6 lines of holograph laid in. Second Life Books, Inc. 196 B - 555 2016 $50

Shakespeare, William 1564-1616 *The Complete Works.* Norwalk and London: Easton Press, 1992. 286 x 197mm., 39 volumes, publisher's original burgundy morocco, elaborate gilt, moire silk endleaves, all edges gilt, all but one of the volumes in original shrinkwrap, colored wood engravings, lithographs, line drawings in color and pencil and collotypes throughout by Gill, Rackham, Gibbings, Dwiggins, Sauvage, Charlot, Angelo and others, extraordinary copy essentially fresh from publisher's bindery, couple of decades later. Phillip J. Pirages 67 - 124 2016 $3600

Shange, Ntozake *For Colored Girls Who Have Considered Suicide When the Rainbow is Enuf.* New York: Macmillan, 1977. First printing, 8vo., paper over boards with cloth spine, slightly scuffed at ends of spine, otherwise nice in dust jacket (little scuffed). Second Life Books, Inc. 197 - 287 2016 $50

Shange, Ntozake *Melissa & Smith.* St. Paul: Bookslinger Editions, 1976. No. 276 of 300 copies, 12mo., author's signature on colophon, printed on handmade Japanese paper, endpapers made in India, paper cover from France, nice. Second Life Books, Inc. 196 B - 558 2016 $100

Shange, Ntozake *Melissa & Smith.* St. Paul: Bookslinger Editions, 1976. Limited to 300 numbered copies, signed by author, printed on Kochi handmade in Japan, 12mo., stiff paper wrappers, fore edge uncut, cord tied. Oak Knoll Books 310 - 166 2016 $110

Shanks & Co. *Illustrated Catalogue of Sanitary Appliances Manufactured by Shanks & Co. Ltd. Tubal Works, Barrhead, Scotland.* Glasgow: A. D. Goldie, 1899. Folio, 31 chromolithograph plates, some with gold, several tinted leaves and plates and remaining leaves, half tone illustrations, original hesian backed green cloth, upper cover gilt, cover somewhat worn. Marlborough Rare Books List 56 - 56 2016 £950

Shannon, Francis, Viscount *Discourses Useful for the Vain Modish Ladies and their Gallants.... (bound after) Essays and Discourses, Moral and Divine, Upon Several Subjects.* London: for J. Taylor, 1696. Second edition, the two parts usually bound in reverse, lacking combined general titlepage, old ink stain along lower edge of D5 and centre of B1, contemporary mottled calf, corners bumped and spine split, from the library of James Stevens Cox (1910-1997). Maggs Bros. Ltd. 1447 - 380 2016 £750

Shannon, Monica *Dobry.* New York: Viking Press, 1934. First edition, 8vo., cloth, tiny bit of edge soil, fine in dust jacket (very good, no award medal, tanned on edges with some edge chipping on rear panel), striking color and black and white lithographs by A. Katchamakoff, this copy inscribed by author Nov. 1934. Aleph-bet Books, Inc. 111 - 417 2016 $400

Shapcote, Emily Mary *Swan Rhymes in Honour of Our Blessed Lady.* N.P.: privately published, 1894. First edition, 8vo., original printed blue cloth, lettered gilt on front cover and illustrated in blind, minor dampstain at lower corner not affecting text, inked stamp of Hawkesyard Priory Library with slight rubbing and slight wear at spine ends and corners, otherwise sound, close to very good. Any Amount of Books 2015 - C15916 2016 £175

Shapiro, Harvey *Lauds.* New York: Sun, 1975. First edition, 8vo., author's presentation for Bill Smith, paper wrappers, cover slightly soiled, otherwise nice. Second Life Books, Inc. 197 - 288 2016 $45

Sharman, Miriam *Death Pays All Debts.* London: Gollancz, 1965. good copy, in good yellow dust jacket. I. D. Edrich Crime - 2016 £20

Sharp, Granville 1734-1813 *A Circular Letter to the Several Petitioning Counties, Addressed to their General Meeetings Against the Late Proposition for a Triennial Election of Representatives.* N.p.: 1780. Fourth edition, folded and unopened as issued, slightly creased at foreedge, extremities slightly dusted. Jarndyce Antiquarian Booksellers CCXVI - 518 2016 £150

Sharp, Granville   1734-1813   *The Claims of the People of England.*   London: printed for J. Stockdale, 1782.   Fifth edition, uncut, unsewn as issued, very slight dusting, very good.   Jarndyce Antiquarian Booksellers   CCXVI - 520   2016   £110

Sharp, Granville   1734-1813   *A Dissertation on the Supreme Divine Dignity of the messiah...*   London: printed by R. Edwards, 1806.   Original pink paper wrappers, slightly defective at tail of spine, generally slightly dusted, original printed paper label on front wrappers, nice.   Jarndyce Antiquarian Booksellers   CCXVI - 521   2016   £90

Sharp, Granville   1734-1813   *The Legal Means of Political Reformation Proposed in Two Small Tracts.*   London: 1780?   Fourth edition, general half title only, as issued, with edition statement, uncut and unopened, stained as issued, very good.   Jarndyce Antiquarian Booksellers   CCXVI - 522   2016   £180

Sharp, Granville   1734-1813   *A Short Tract Concerning the Doctrine of "Nullum Tempus Occurit Regi" Shewing the Particular Cases to Which it is Applicable...*   London: printed in the year, 1779.   8vo., stabbed as issued, in contemporary orange brown paper wrapper lettered "Nullm Tempus 1779", small paper label at tail of spine.   Jarndyce Antiquarian Booksellers   CCXVI - 523   2016   £180

Sharpe, R. Bowdler   *Catalogue of the Passeriformes, or Perching Birds, in the Collection of the British Museum. Fringilliformes: part three.*   London: British Museum, 1888.   Octavo, 16 chromolithograph plates by Hart and Keulemans, publisher's cloth, double page manuscript letter from Salvadori to Sharpe tipped-in.   Andrew Isles Natural History Books   55 - 9260   2016 $500

Sharpe, R. Bowdler   *Catalogue of the Passeriformes, or Perching birds, in the Collection of the British Musueum. Sturniformes containing the Familes Artamidae, Sturnidae, Ploceidae, Alaudidae. Also the familes Atrichiidae and Menuridae.*   London: British Museum, 1890.   Octavo, 15 color plates by Smith, publisher's cloth, fine.   Andrew Isles Natural History Books   55 - 9261   2016 $400

Sharrock, Robert   *The History of the Propagation & Improvement of Vegetables by the Concurrence of Art and Nature...*   Oxford: A. Lichfield for Tho. Robinson, 1660.   First edition, small 8vo., with two additional illustrated leaves and ad at end, very inky thumb prints on titlepage, very occasional minor rust spotting, endleaves stained by turn-ins, early 20th century calf, from the library of James Stevens Cox (1910-1997), with bookplate.   Maggs Bros. Ltd.   1447 - 381   2016   £700

Shatto, Susan   *The Companion to Bleak House.*   London: Unwin Hyman, 1988.   First edition, half title, illustrations, maps, original green cloth, very good in dust jacket.   Jarndyce Antiquarian Booksellers   CCXVIII - 521   2016   £30

Shaw, Alexander P.   *What Must the Negro Do to Be Saved.*   Baltimore: Bishop Alexander P. Shaw/Clarke Press, circa, 1935.   First edition, 24mo., stapled printed wrappers, 31 pages, very good, with 1 inch split at top of spine, toned wrappers and tidemark on upper part of wrappers (not affecting interior pages).   Between the Covers Rare Books   202 - 93   2016 $475

Shaw, George Bernard   1856-1950   *The Adventures of the Black Girl in Her Search for God.*   London: Constable, 1932.   First edition, pictorial titlepage, 19 other wood engraved illustrations, some faint foxing to prelims and odd spot further on, crown 8vo., original boards with Farleigh design, light rubbing, endpapers with Farleigh design, very good.   Blackwell's Rare Books   B184 - 227   2016   £60

Shaw, George Bernard   1856-1950   *Androcles and the Lion, Overruled, Pygamlion.*   London: Constable, 1916.   First English edition, 8vo., original green cloth, lettered gilt on spine, very good.   Blackwell's Rare Books   B184 - 228   2016   £200

Shaw, George Bernard   1856-1950   *Back to Methuselah.*   New York: Limited Editions Club, 1939.   1335/1500 copies, signed by artist, 8vo., original pale green cloth, green leather label to front board lettered gilt featuring Farleigh design, backstrip label faded to brown and cloth also just slightly sunned, top edge green, slipcase with label, very good.   Blackwell's Rare Books   B184 - 284   2016   £60

Shaw, George Bernard   1856-1950   *Cashel Byron's Profession.*   London: Modern Press, 1886.   First edition, tall 8vo., pebbled binder's cloth (lacking original wrappers.   Second Life Books, Inc.   197 - 289   2016 $900

Shaw, George Bernard   1856-1950   *The Intelligent Woman's Guide to Socialism and Capitalism.*   London: Constable, 1928.   First edition, royal octavo, decorated cloth in gilt and green, designed by Douglas Cockerell, top edge gilt, fore-edge slightly spotted, near fine in very good, price clipped dust jacket designed by Eric Kennington, little wrinkled and stained at spine and with several nicks and short tears and little defective at top right corner of upper panel.   Peter Ellis   112 - 356   2016   £150

Shaw, George Bernard   1856-1950   *Love Among the Artists.*   Chicago: 1900.   First edition, decorated cloth, prelim blank and rear endpapers tape stained, otherwise nice, name on prelim blank.   Bertram Rota Ltd.   February List 2016 - 49   2016   £100

Shaw, George Bernard   1856-1950   *Man and Superman.*   London: Constable and Co. ltd., First edition, 8vo., original green cloth, spine gilt lettered, spine faded, inscribed by author for F. Collinson.   Blackwell's Rare Books   B184 - 229   2016   £1500

Shaw, George Bernard 1856-1950 *Man and Superman.* New York: Dodd, Mead, 1947. First edition, 8vo., very good in little worn dust jacket, some of the photos show little watermark at edge, written on endpaper is note this book is the property of "Maurice Evans Prod. Inc." and is to be returned, this copy signed by Malcolm Keen, Chester Stratton, Victor Sutherland, Carmen Mathews, Jack Manning, Phoebe Mackay and Tony Bickley.   Second Life Books, Inc.   196 B - 562   2016 $450

Shaw, George Bernard 1856-1950 *Man and Superman.* New York: Heritage Press, 1962. Marbled boards with maroon cloth spine, lettered gilt, spines faded with free minor scuff marks, fine in slipcase with special pocket which houses The Revolutionist's Handbook & Pocket Companion, slipcase faded with bit of wear and small crack near the special pocket, Sandglass pamphlet laid in.   Argonaut Book Shop   Heritage Press 2015 - 7076   2016 $45

Shaw, George Bernard 1856-1950 *Passion Play, a Dramatic Fragment 1878.*   Iowa: Windhover Press, 1971. First edition, one of 350 numbered copies printed by hand, small folio, printed in red, brown, blue an black, Roman type on Italian Umbria paper, line backed decorated boards, paper label, very fine with slightly soiled cloth slipcase. Argonaut Book Shop   Literature 2015 - 1365   2016 $250

Shaw, George Bernard 1856-1950 *Saint Joan.* London: Constable, 1924. First edition, inscribed by author for Lilian Throckmorton, with original silverprint of Shaw and recipient posing in a garden, with Throckmorton's bookplate, fine. Second Life Books, Inc.   196 B - 561   2016 $750

Shaw, George Bernard 1856-1950 *Sixteen Self Sketches.* London: Constable and co., 1949. First edition, presentation copy inscribed by author for Judy Gillmore Cahworth, frontispiece, 23 plates, 8vo., original red cloth, dust jacket, backstrip chipped at head and foot with closed tear, very good.   Blackwell's Rare Books   B184 - 230   2016   £650

Shaw, George Bernard 1856-1950 *Two Plays for Puritans.* New York: Heritage Press, 1966. Drawings by George Him, blind stamped green cloth, gilt lettering to spine, minor fading to spine and very slightly bumped at head of spine, fine, slipcase lightly worn and soiled, Sandglass pamphlet laid in.   Argonaut Book Shop Heritage Press 2015 - 2040   2016 $45

Shaw, George T. *History of the Athenaeum.* Liverpool: printed for the Committee of the Athenaeum by Rockcliff Bros. Ltd. 44 Castle Street, 1898. Small folio, contemporary full chocolate brown crushed morocco by Fazakerley of Liverpool, gilt stamped monogram to centre of the upper board, spine divided into six compartments with raised bands, lettered and dated in second and third compartments, gilt ruled edges, gilt dentelles, top edge gilt, marbled endpapers, gilt lettered brown morocco, presentation label to front pastedown, black and white photo frontispiece and 6 plates, 3 plans, bright, crisp, copy, presentation to Mandell Creighton, Bp. of London, bookplate of Sir Albert Richardson (1880-1964).   Sotheran's   Piccadilly Notes - Summer 2015 - 273   2016   £295

Shaw, Joseph T. *The Hard-Boiled Omnibus: Early Stories from Black Mask.* New York: Simon & Schuster, 1946. First edition, octavo, cloth, slight bump to upper right front corners, spine ends little bumped, nearly fine in fine dust jacket with touch or rubbing to corner tips and small crease at upper right front corner, perhaps just hint of fade to orange background of spine panel, ever so slight, superior example of jacket, attractive copy.   John W. Knott, Jr./L.W. Currey, Inc.   Fall-Winter 2015 - 15917   2016 $500

Shawn, Ted *One Thousand and One Night Stands.*   New York: Doubleday, 1960. First edition, signed by Shawn and inscribed by his collaborator Gray Poole, very good. Second Life Books, Inc.   196 B - 563   2016 $75

Shefrin, Jill *One Hundred Books Famous in Children's Literature.* New York: Grolier Club, 2014. First edition, deluxe issue limited to 50 copies, this copy unnumbered, with signed note from Chris Loker loosely inserted, 4to., original blue morocco backed boards, lettered gilt on spine in slipcase, illustrations.   Sotheran's   Piccadilly Notes - Summer 2015 - 75   2016   £1500

Sheldon, Charles M. *The Crucifixion of Phillip Strong.* Chicago: Advance Printing Co., 1898. Later edition, 12mo., original cloth.   M & S Rare Books, Inc.   99 - 288   2016 $150

Shelley, Mary Wollestonecraft Godwin 1797-1851 *Frankenstein or the Modern Prometheus.* Northampton: Pennyroyal Press, 1983. No 175 of 305 copies, 2 volumes (including portfolio of prints), original tan quarter morocco over maroon with boards by Sam Ellenport at the Harcourt Bindery, raised bands, maroon leather label with calligraphic titling, matching publishers' folding cloth box just slightly marked, with the extra suite of plates by Barry Moser signed by him, very faint foxing to fore and tail edges of book block, half dozen pages with hardly perceptible very small spots of foxing, otherwise spotless and unworn.   Phillip J. Pirages 67 - 279   2016 $3000

Shelley, Mary Wollestonecraft Godwin   1797-1851
History of a Six Weeks' Tour Through a Part of France, Switzerland, Germany and Holland.   London: published by T. Hookham Jun., 1817. First edition, little light soiling, 8vo., early 20th century olive morocco by Tout, boards with gilt frame and spine, elaborately gilt top edge gilt, others untrimmed, joints rather rubbed, little wear to headcap, bookplates of H. Bradley Martin and of Robertson Trowbridge (this inscribed to Mark Trowbridge's gift of the volume to Thomas Pym Cope) and of Thomas Jefferson McKee, very good.   Blackwell's Rare Books   Marks of Genius - 43   2016   £3500

Shelley, Mary Wollestonecraft Godwin   1797-1851
Rambles in Germany and Italy in 1840, 1842, 1843. London: Edward Moxon, 1844. First edition, 2 volumes, 8vo., early 20th century red half morocco, top edge gilt, others uncut, joints and corners rubbed, good.   Blackwell's Rare Books   Marks of Genius - 44   2016   £500

Shelley, Percy Bysshe   1792-1822   *The Cenci. A Tragedy, in Five Acts.*   Italy (Livorgno): printed for C. and J. Ollier, 1819. First edition, only 250 copies printed, without initial blank, 8vo., brown crushed morocco gilt by Zaehnsdorf with their exhibition stamp, wide multiple roll tooled borders on sides, gilt in gilt on cover (within a frame) and spine, gilt edges and iner dentelles, Estelle Doheny's copy with her morocco gilt book label inside front cover, fine. Blackwell's Rare Books   Marks of Genius - 45   2016 £4000

Shelley, Percy Bysshe   1792-1822   *Letters... to Leigh Hunt.*   London: privately printed, 1894. First edition, one of 6 copies on vellum, with first and last blank leaves, 30 copies were printed on Whatman paper, 8vo., crushed black morocco by Ramage, Herbert S. Leon and Alington bookplates, fine.   Blackwell's Rare Books   Marks of Genius - 48   2016   £6000

Shelley, Percy Bysshe   1792-1822   *The Poetical Works of Percy Bysshe Shelley...*   Henry Frowde, 1908. Oxford edition, contemporary full tree calf, sides with gilt roll, spine in compartments, raised bands elaborately gilt and with red leather label lettered gilt, all edges and inner dentelles gilt, fine copy in Oxford binding.   Bertram Rota Ltd.   February List 2016 - 50   Th   £250

Shelley, Percy Bysshe   1792-1822   *Prometheus Unbound. A Lyrical Drama in Four Acts with Other Poems.* London: C. and J. Ollier, 1820. First edition, 2nd issue, with half title, ads at end discarded, 8vo., early 20th century red crushed morocco for William Brown (booksellers), Edinburgh, French fillets on sides, crowned initial B on the upper cover, spine panelled in gilt in compartments, gilt edges, surface of joints partly lifted, F. E. Smith's copy (crowned initial on upper cover), with his bookplate inside front cover as Viscount Birkenhead, bookplate of Fernand Spaak opposite, good.   Blackwell's Rare Books   Marks of Genius - 49   2016   £2500

Shelley, Percy Bysshe   1792-1822   *Queen Mab.* London: W. Clark, 1821. First published edition, final ad leaf present, this copy (as issued) without dedication leaf found in some copies, little light spotting, edges untrimmed, 8vo., original drab paper boards, printed paper backstrip label (stained), joints bit worn but strong, small losses from backstrip ends, some light scratches and marks, bound in brown cloth felt-lined solander box, very good.   Blackwell's Rare Books   Marks of Genius - 46   2016   £1250

Shelley, Percy Bysshe   1792-1822   *Rosalind and Helen, a Modern Eclogue, with Other Poems.*   London: printed for C. and J. Ollier, 1819. First edition, with final ad leaves, first few leaves slightly spotted, 8vo., polished calf by F. Bedford, spine gilt red lettering piece, gilt edges, minimal wear to extremities, the Hibbert-Esher copy with bookplates and acquisition notes by Oliver Brett, good.   Blackwell's Rare Books   Marks of Genius - 47   2016   £2500

Shelley, Percy Bysshe   1792-1822   *The Sensitive Plant.* London: William Heinemann, 1911. First edition thus, 4to., original publisher's green cloth, illustrated and lettered black leaves faintly browned, one or two leaves, little loose, extremities very lightly rubbed and light wear elsewhere, but nice.   Bertram Rota Ltd.   February List 2016 - 51   2016 £300

Shelton, Thomas   *Tachygraphy.*   London: by Thomas Milbourn for Dorman Newman, 1693. Small 8vo., additional engraved architectural title, 9 pages of engraved examples, engraved title frayed at head and repaired (touching frame) and shaved at foot affecting second line of imprint, small pin-hole through centre of first 15 leaves, letterpress title dampstained in upper inner margin, little soiled throughout and with margins closely trimmed in places, mid 20th century half calf and marbled boards, Edmund Herbert's early signature, from the library of James Stevens Cox (1910-1997). Maggs Bros. Ltd.   1447 - 382   2016   £350

Shen, Juliet   *Searching for Morris Fuller Benton: Discovering the Designer through his Typefaces.*   Chicago: Sherwin Beach Press, 2011. No. 65 of 75 copies, signed by author, designed by Robert McCamant, set in Cloister Oldstyle cast by Dale Guild Type Foundry from ATF matrices and typeset by Art Larson and Rose Wisotzky at Horton Tank Graphics, printed on Mohawk Superfine, letterpress by Micahl Russeum of Kat Ran Press, offset illustrations and captions by Capitol Offset, Trisha Hammer designed and executed the black cloth binding with red stiching to open spine, fine.   The Kelmscott Bookshop   13 - 55   2016 $450

Shepard, Leslie   *The History of the Horn Book.*   London: 1977. Original printed wrappers, bound into marbled boards, brown cloth spine, handmade paper endpapers, compliments slip bearing note from John Foreman to Leslie Shepard.   Jarndyce Antiquarian Books   CCXV - 781 2016   £20

Shepard, Odell *Connecticut Past and Present.* New York: Knopf, 1939. First edition, 8vo., bound in blue cloth with colored map on endpapers, little chipped dust jacket, inscribed by author for William Jay Smith. Second Life Books, Inc. 196 B - 565 2016 $75

Shepard, Sam *Hawk Moon.* Los Angeles: Black Sparrow, 1973. First edition, one of 200 hardcover copies, numbered and signed by author, paper over boards, cloth spine, very nice in little chipped arcylic dust jacket. Second Life Books, Inc. 196 B - 566 2016 $225

Shephard, Mark *The Great Victoria Desert: North of the Nullarbor, South of the Centre.* Sydney: Reed, 1995. Quarto, color photos, very good in slightly sunned dust jacket, scarce. Andrew Isles Natural History Books 55 - 9093 2016 $80

Shepherd, Rob *Lost on the Titanic.* London: Shepherds Sangorski & Sutcliffe and Zaehnsdorf, 2001. Limited to 750 numbered copies, 4to., cloth, tipped in color frontispiece and tipped-in color illustrations in text, black and white illustrations, lacks poster which accompanied this book, 4to., cloth. Oak Knoll Books 310 - 20 2016 $350

Shepherd, Thomas H. *Modern Athens! Displayed in a Series of Views.* James & co., 1832. 4to., publisher's half brown morocco over marbled boards, all edges marbled, spine in six compartments with lettering to second and third, marbled endpapers, engraved title, title, interleaves with 48 engraved plates, spine and edges rubbed, some offsetting, otherwise very good. Sotheran's Piccadilly Notes - Summer 2015 - 275 2016 £155

Shepperd, Ted *Pack & Paddock.* New York: Derrydale Press, 1938. First edition, number 74 of 950 copies, 12mo., illustrations by Paul Brown, publisher's three quarter red leatherette, gilt label on front cover, very fine. Argonaut Book Shop Literature 2015 - 5808 2016 $175

Sherburne, John Henry *The Life of Paul Jones from Original Documents in the Possession of....* London: John Murray, 1825. First edition, half title, uncut in original drab boards, paper spine label, price 7s 6d, slight rubbing, especially to hinges, very good or originally published. Jarndyce Antiquarian Booksellers CCXVII - 141 2016 £750

Sheridan, Richard Brinsley Butler 1751-1816 *The Speech of...delivered in the House of Commons Monday the Second of April 1787...* London: printed for W. Lowndes No. 77 Fleet Street, 1787. 8vo., half title, small hole to top margin of B4, well clear of text, disbound. Jarndyce Antiquarian Booksellers CCXVI - 526 2016 £110

Sheridan, Richard Brinsley Butler 1751-1816 *The Speech of R. B. Sheridan, Esq. member for Stafford on Wednesday the 7th of Feb. 1787.* London: printed for J. French Bookseller no. 164 Fenchurch Street, 1787. Second edition, 8vo., some pencil lines in margins, disbound. Jarndyce Antiquarian Booksellers CCXVI - 525 2016 £110

Sheridan, Richard Brinsley Butler 1751-1816 *Verses to the Memory of Garrick. Spoken as a Monody at the Theatre Royal in Drury Lane.* London: published by T. Evans, J. Wilkie, E. and C. Dilly, A. Portal & J. Almon, 1779. First edition, first issue, 4to., half title, front plate bound before half title, slightly later half green morocco, spine faded to brown. Jarndyce Antiquarian Booksellers CCXVI - 527 2016 £480

Sheridan, Richard Brinsley Butler 1751-1816 *The Works of the late Right Honourable Richard Brinsley Sheridan.* London: J. Murray, James Ridgway and Thomas Wilkie, 1821. First collected edition, 2 volumes, 236 x 154mm., contemporary dun colored publisher's boards, flat spines with paper labels, edges untrimmed, modern blue buckram, chemises inside matching morocco backed slipcases with gilt titling on spines, engraved armorial bookplate of R. B. AE Macleod of Cadboll, Invergordon Castle, 1877, paper boards little soiled, extremities with vague wear, occasional was drippings (noticeable, without being disfiguring, at bottom of perhaps 20 openings), otherwise excellent, leaves fresh and bright with generous signs and unsubstantial boards entirely solid and showing, very few signs of use. Phillip J. Pirages 67 - 320 2016 $1000

Sheridan, Thomas *British Education or the Source of the Disorders of Great Britain.* London: printed for R. and J. Dodsley, 1756. Half title, 8vo., early 19th century calf, expertly rebacked, raised bands, gilt motifs, original red morocco, armorial bookplate of Marquess of Headfort. Jarndyce Antiquarian Books CCXV - 845 2016 £480

Sherman, Frederick Barreda *From the Guadalquivir in the Golden Gate by Way of Lima, Baltimore, New York, Newport, Washington, London, Paris....* Mill Valley: Hall and Smith Co., 1977. First edition, one of 125 copies printed for prviate distribution, presentation inscription, signed by author to the California Genealogical Society, frontispiece, facsimiles, portraits, rust cloth, gilt, fine. Argonaut Book Shop Biography 2015 - 7841 2016 $175

Sherry, Norman *The Life of Graham Greene.* London: Jonathan Cape, 1989-2004. First edition, 8vo., 3 volumes, original cloth with dust jackets, small snag on jacket volume I, otherwise near fine. Sotheran's Piccadilly Notes - Summer 2015 - 153 2016 £498

Sherwood, Bob *Hold Yer Hosses!* New York: Macmillan, 1932. First edition, 16 illustrations, long inscription by author, photo of Sherwood pasted in, hinges tender, else very good.   Second Life Books, Inc.   196 B - 569   2016 $75

Sherwood, Mary Martha Butt 1775-1851 *The History of Susan Gray as Related by a Clergyman...* London: Houlston & Co., 1840. New edition, frontispiece, engraved title additional printed title later green endpapers, original quarter black calf, slight rubbing, ownership inscriptions on verso of engraved title and on blank immediately preceding text, good plus copy.   Jarndyce Antiquarian Books   CCXV - 404   2016   £65

Sherwood, Robert Emmet *The Road to Rome.* New York: Scribner's, 1927. First edition, 8vo., author's presentation on flyleaf, very good in little worn dust jacket.   Second Life Books, Inc.   196 B - 570   2016 $85

Shields, Carol *The Stone Diaries.* Toronto: Random House, 1993. First Canadian edition, near fine, small spot of sticker residue on front free endpapers, near fine dust jacket, light wear to extremities.   Bella Luna Books   2016 - t685   2016 $198

Shiers, William *A Familiar Discourse or Dialogue Concerning the Mine-Adventure.* London: in the year, 1700. First edition, 8vo., light dampstaining to fore-margins, tables spotted, first one torn affecting five lines of text, book block split, pastedowns detached, contemporary sheep, panelled in blind, spine split with dust jacket paper label, shelfmark, spine worn and torn at foot, sewing broken, coming loose in case, endleaves unstuck, from the library of James Stevens Cox (1910-1997).   Maggs Bros. Ltd.   1447 - 383   2016   £700

Shinoyama, Kishin *Harata Hi - a Fine Day.* Tokyo: Heibonsha, 1975. First edition, hardcover, color photos, clean, close to near fine in about near fine printed acetate dust jacket with some wear and minor chips to spinal ends and corners, signed by Shinoyama, quite uncommon thus.   Jeff Hirsch Books   E-List 80 - 26   2016 $1250

Shipway, Verna Cook *The Mexican House: Old & New.* New York: Architectural Book Pub., 1960. First edition, 4to., photos and drawings, author's presentation on flyleaf, cover somewhat soiled, but very good, tight copy.   Second Life Books, Inc.   196 B - 571   2016 $65

Shirley Smith, Richard *Wood Engravings. A Selection 1960 to 1977.* Pinner: Cuckoo, 1983. 82/180 copies from an edition of 187 copies, printed on Basingwerk parchment paper and signed by artist, frontispiece and 48 other wood engravings by Shirley Smith, 8vo., original quarter black morocco with vertical gilt rule, grey cloth sides, backstrip lettered in gilt between raised bands, marbled endpapers, slipcase, fine.   Blackwell's Rare Books   B186 - 296   2016   £120

Shirley, James 1596-1666 *Via ad Latinam Linguam Companta.* London: by R. W. for John Stephenson, 1649. First edition, 8vo., lacking engraved title by Thomas Cross, some light soiling to titlepage and A2, two small inkstains to A24 and A3v, edges slightly bumped throughout and with some gatherings beginning to come loose, contemporary blind ruled sheep (corner of upper board chewed, bumped and rubbed), from the library of James Stevens Cox (1910-1997), 18th century name of Joseph Spry.   Maggs Bros. Ltd.   1447 - 384   2016   £200

Shirley, Walter Augustus *Letters to Young People.* London: Thomas Hatchard, 1850. First edition, 36 page catalog Nov. 1856, original brown cloth, slightly rubbed, spine little darkened.   Jarndyce Antiquarian Books   CCXV - 403   2016   £45

Shoebotham, H. Minar *Anaconda. Life of Marcus Daly, the Copper King.* Harrisburg: Stackpole Co., 1956. First edition, 10 illustrations from photos, copper boards lettered in dark green, spine ends and lower edges of boards bit rubbed, near fine with slightly chipped and price clipped pictorial dust jacket.   Argonaut Book Shop   Biography 2015 - 5179   2016 $75

Shokunbi, Mae Gleaton *Songs of the Soul.* Philadelphia: Dorrance & Co., 1945. First edition, little toning in gutters, else fine in very good with quote from G. W. Carver on front flap, modest chipping to spine ends, some soiling and splitting along edge of spine fold, warmly inscribed by author with Christmas card inscribed by her laid in.   Between the Covers Rare Books   202 - 94   2016 $450

Shore, Stephen *Pet Pictures.* Portland: Nazareli Press, 2012. Number 259 from an edition of 500 copies, 17 color images along with original tipped in color photo by Shore, very fine in publisher's bag, signed by Shore.   Jeff Hirsch Books   Holiday List 2015 - 90   2016 $125

Shore, Stephen *Signs of Life: Symbols in the American City.* New York: Aperture, 1976. First edition, exhibition catalog, very good plus in stapled wrappers with some slight wear and small spot to rear panel.   Jeff Hirsch Books   E-List 80 - 27   2016 $65

Shortridge, G. C. *The Mammals of South West Africa.* London: William Heinemann, 1934. Octavo, 2 volumes, photos, folding map, publisher's cloth, few blemishes, signature.   Andrew Isles Natural History Books   55 - 8039   2016 $150

Shoson Ohara *Process of Wood-cut Printing.* Kyoto: Unso-do, circa 1930's, 9.5 x 15 inches, near fine, accordion fold plates bound in silk covered boards with printed paper title label, 14 progressive plates mild cover edge wear, owner inscription, , scattered foxing, in very good++ original chitsu with archival cloth restoration to sides, faux bone clasps, printed paper title on front chemise, scarce.   By the Book, L. C.   45 - 56   2016 $1000

Shotterel, Robert *Archerie Reviv'd or the Bow-Man's Excellence.* London: by Thomas Roycroft, 1676. First edition, 8vo., first blank leaf, light marginal browning, a number of margins have also been closely trimmed, contemporary sheep, covers ruled blind (slightly rubbed, front cover with 90mm scuff and with some minor staining on rare board, from the library of James Stevens Cox (1910-1997). Maggs Bros. Ltd.   1447 - 385   2016   £750

Shove, Fredegond *Fredegond and Gerald Shove.* Cambridge: Privately printed at the University Press, 1952. First edition, one of 250 copies, frontispiece, 4 further photo plates, few faint foxspots, 8vo., original quarter blue cloth with patterned paper sides, backstrip lettered gilt and little creased, with slight lean, some wear to corners and edge of upper board, endpapers foxed, contemporary gift inscription, good.   Blackwell's Rare Books   B184 - 231   2016   £175

Shreffler, P. A. *The Baker Street Reader.* New York: Greenwood Press, 1984. Very good in like dust jacket.   I. D. Edrich   Crime - 2016   £40

Shui Hu Zhuan *All Men are Brothers.* London: Methuen, 1933. First UK edition, 8vo., original black cloth, spine lettered in gilt, top edge gilt, frontispiece and few illustrations in text, restored short split at lower hinge, light rubbing to binding, little offsetting from endpapers.   Sotheran's   Travel and Exploration - 178   2016   £98

Shumate, Albert *The Stormy Life of major Wm. Gouverneur Morris in California and Alaska.* San Francisco: California Historical Society, 1993. First edition, presentation inscription signed by author, one of 500 copies, frontispiece, 11 illustrations, red cloth, very fine in pictorial dust jacket.   Argonaut Book Shop   Biography 2015 - 7642   2016 $45

Shuster, W. Morgan *The Strangling of Persia.* New York: Century, 1912. First edition, 8vo., photos and map, presentation on flyleaf, top edge gilt, covers little scuffed on edges, otherwise nice.   Second Life Books, Inc.   196 B - 572   2016 $150

Shute, E. L. *What the Toys Did!* London: Frederick Warne, n.d., 1904. Oblong folio, cloth backed pictorial boards, some edge wear, small barely visible crack on cover, very good+, full page color illustrations.   Aleph-bet Books, Inc.   112 - 26   2016 $475

Shvarc, E. *Lager (Camp).* Leningrad: Giz, 1925. 4to., pictorial wrappers, fine, great color lithographs by Alexi Pakhomov.   Aleph-bet Books, Inc.   111 - 399   2016 $950

Siddons, George A. *The Cabinet-Maker's Guide; or Rules and Instructions in the Art of varnishing, Dying, Staining, Japanning, Polishing, Lackering, and Beautifying Wood Ivory....* Greenfield: Re-printed by Ansel Phelps and for sale by him at the Bookstore also by West & Richardson, Cummings, Hilliard & Co. Boston and Wilder & Campbell, New York, 1825. First American edition, 12mo., original cloth backed printed boards, covers present but separated, corners slightly rubbed, uncut, in folding case, cover separated, lovely copy, completely unsophisticated, as issued, with no foxing.   Howard S. Mott Inc.   265 - 116   2016 $4500

Sidney, Margaret *Old Concord Her Highways and Byways.* Boston: Lothrop Pub. Co., 1892. Revised and enlarged edition, 8vo., green gilt pictorial cloth, all edges gilt, spine slightly darkened, else near fine, this copy inscribed by author, special copy of beautiful book.   Aleph-bet Books, Inc.   111 - 426   2016 $750

Sidney, Philip 1554-1586 *Astrophel & Stella.* London: Nonesuch Press, 1931. One of 1210 copies, inscribed by Cyril Conolly to a colleague at the London Sunday times, with Connoly's funeral program laid-in.   Honey & Wax Booksellers   4 - 21   2016 $350

Siebner, Herbert *Herbert Siebner Travel Sketches 1962-1963.* Victoria: Classic Engraving, 1997. Limited edition, number 242 of an edition of 350, signed by Siebner & publisher, oblong stiff boards with plastic spiral type binding, 72 glossy prints, fine scarce.   Gene W. Baade, Books on the West   2015 - 5014049   2016 $162

Siegel, Jeff *The American Detective.* Dallas: Taylor, 1993. First edition, very fine in dust jacket.   Mordida Books   2015 - 010782   2016 $65

Sieveking, Lance *The Woman She Was.* London: Cassell, 1934. First edition, 2 plates, presentation from author, inscribed for Sir Philip Sassoon, edges spotted, spine dull, good in good, chipped and torn dust jacket defective at head and tail of spine.   Peter Ellis   112 - 358   2016   £95

Sigaud De La Fond, Joseph Aignan *Precis Historique et Experimental Des Phenomenes Electriques, Depuix L'Origine De Cette Decouverte Jusqu'a Ce Jour.* Paris: 1781. First edition, printed glosses, illustrated with 9 folding copperplate engravings, head and tailpieces 8vo., period full leather of speckled calf with elaborate gilt decorated spine, edges stained red, marbled endpapers, bit of splay to boards, tips show some wear, joints starting at ends, withal very good.   Tavistock Books   Bibliolatry - 35   2016 $1250

Sigonius, Carolus *De Rep. Atheniensum Libri III.* Venice: apud Vinventium Valgrisium, 1565. Second edition, lightly toned, little minor spotting, 8vo., 18th century mid-brown sheep (probably German), boards elaborately panelled in blind in imitation of 16th century Italian style, spine also decorated in blind, green shelfmark label at foot, touch rubbed, one scrape to forecorner of rear board, German bookseller's label to front pastedown, very good. Blackwell's Rare Books   B186 - 66   2016   £600

Sigourney, Lydia Huntley *Letters to Mothers.* New York: Harper & Bros., 1839. Second edition, 8vo., original cloth. M & S Rare Books, Inc.   99 - 289   2016 $175

Sigourney, Lydia Huntley *Letters to Young Ladies.* London: Thomas Ward & Co., 1834. First English edition, 16mo., frontispiece, original brown patterned cloth, contemporary signature of Maria Denbigh on leading free endpaper, very good.   Jarndyce Antiquarian Books   CCXV - 408   2016   £75

The Siliad or the Siege of the Seats. Beeton's Humorous Books. No. 28. London: Ward Lock & Tyler, n.d. circa, 1874. First edition thus, 12mo., intratextual cuts, printed paper wrappers, very good+ minor wear and light foxing to edges.   Tavistock Books   Bibliolatry - 17   2016 $125

Silius, Italicus *De Secundo Bello Punico.* Amsterdam: G. Jansson, 1620. Engraved titlepage, ruled in red, 16mo., exquisite binding by Mace Ruette, contemporary gilt tooled red morocco, covers framed by outer double fillet, central panel of strait and curved double fillets with small vase of flowers tool at each outer corner in centre of covers a quadrilobe inlay with monogram of H. L. Habert de Montmort and four "S" forms with elaborate pointille sprays of spirals, circles and dots on all four sides, spine with five raised bands, decorated in compartments, inner edges gilt, marbled endpapers, gilt edges, headcaps and joints lightly rubbed, the copy of Habert de Montmort (1600-1679), Colonel Thomas Stanley (1749-1818), William Beckford with his bookseller George Clarke's pencil collation mark, Hamilton Palace Library sale, Thore Virgin inscription dated 1916 with his book label (1886-1957).   Maggs Bros. Ltd.   1474 - 72   2016   £2500

Sillitoe, Alan *The Loneliness of the Long-Distance Runner.* London: W. H. Allen, 1959. First edition, 8vo., original grey green cloth, backstrip gilt lettered, free endpapers partly lightly browned as usual, dust jacket little foxed and with faint stain to upper side, good.   Blackwell's Rare Books   B184 - 232   2016   £550

Sillitoe, Alan *Saturday Night and Sunday Morning.* London: W. H. Allen, 1958. First edition, author's signature, 8vo., very slightly toned but clean within, red cloth, gilt title to spine, endcaps little creased, few very faint smudges to endpapers, tiny pencilled code to rear pastedown, top edge little dusty, very good dust jacket spine faded with very small losses at head and tail, rubbed, tiny chips to fore-edge corners, little shelfworn but whole and still good.   Unsworths Antiquarian Booksellers Ltd.   30 - 139   2016   £650

Silsby, Wilson *Etching Methods and Materials.* New York: Dodd Mead & Co., 1943. First edition, 8vo., cloth, presentation copy to artist Lee Le Blanc, signed by author and by Le Blanc, small spot on fore edge of front cover, else near fine.   Gene W. Baade, Books on the West   2015 - 5001115   2016 $109

Silveira, Humberto Da *Najd.* Paris: Ideatis Creation, 1992. First edition, very rare, large 4to., original cloth, illustrated dust jacket, cloth slipcase, highly illustrated from black and white photos, near fine.   Sotheran's   Piccadilly Notes - Summer 2015 - 276   2016   £398

Silveira, Humberto Da *Najd.* Paris: Ideatis Creation, 1992. First edition and very rare, large 4to., original cloth, illustrated dust jackets, cloth slipcase, highly illustrated from black and white photos, near fine, together with a set of 14 promotional cards from photos.   Sotheran's   Travel and Exploration - 370   2016   £895

Silverstein, Shel *The Missing Piece Meets the Big O.* New York: Harper & Row, 1981. First edition, royal octavo, pictorial cloth, fine in near fine dust jacket with small nick. Peter Ellis   112 - 359   2016   £25

Silvestre, Armand *Roses D'Octobre.* Paris: G. Charpentier et Cie, 1890. No. 9 of 10 copies on Holland paper, 187 x 12mm., charming contemporary dark green morocco gilt and inlaid by Salvador David (stamp-signed on front turn-in), covers framed by gilt branches, entwined with inlaid pink morocco roses, raised bands, spine compartments with central inlaid pink now surrounded by gilt foliage, densely gilt turn-ins, all edges gilt, original wrappers bound in, bookplate of Daniel Henry Holmes Jr., tiny fox spot every 40 pages, text with overall faint darkening (perhaps as in all copies because of paper stock), spine probably just a shade darker than the covers, still obviously fine, completely clean and smooth internally, and in unworn, lustrous binding. Phillip J. Pirages   67 - 35   2016 $750

Sime, James *The Kingdom of All-Israel: Its History, Literature and Worship.* London: Nisbet, 1883. First edition, uncommon, 8vo., original brown cloth, spine lettered gilt, professionally restored binding, endpapers renewed, even light browning due to paper stock, final 5 leaves and browning to lower margins, otherwise clean and sound, from NY Mercantile Library with stamp, uncommon.   Sotheran's Travel and Exploration - 179   2016   £198

Simenon, Georges *Betty.* London: Hamish Hamilton, 1975. Uncorrected proof copy of the First English edition, nice copy in slightly dusty original wrappers.   I. D. Edrich   Crime - 2016   £20

Simenon, Georges *Five times Maigret.* New York: Harcourt, 1964. Omnibus edition, fine in price clipped dust jacket.   Mordida Books   2015 - 005793   2016 $55

Simenon, Georges *Maigret and the Calame Report.* New York: Harcourt Brace & World, 1969. First American edition, 8vo., bookplate with signature of author, slightly scuffed at corners and ends of spine, otherwise nice in little chipped dust jacket.   Second Life Books, Inc.   196 B - 5y3   2016 $169

Simenon, Georges *Maigret and the Hotel Majestic.* London: Hamilton, 1977. First English edition, fine in dust jacket with price on inner flap partially marked out.   Mordida Books   2015 - 002034   2016 $55

Simenon, Georges *Maigret and the Wine Merchant.* London: Hamilton, 1971. First English edition, fine in dust jacket010658.   Mordida Books   2015 - 010658   2016 $85

Simenon, Georges *Maigret's memoirs.* London: Hamilton, 1963. First English edition, fine in dust jacket with lightly soiled back panel and some spine fading.   Mordida Books   2015 - 008454   2016 $55

Simenon, Georges *Maigret's Pipe.* London: Hamish Hamilton, 1977. Very good in maroon boards, gilt, price clipped dust jacket.   I. D. Edrich   Crime - 2016   £20

Simenon, Georges *The Rich Man.* London: Hamish Hamilton, 1970. Advance proof copy, slightly dusty original wrappers.   I. D. Edrich   Crime - 2016   £20

Simic, Charles *Dismantling the Silence Poems.* New York: George Braziller, 1971. First edition, printed wrappers, inscribed and signed by author for William Meredith, 4-2-75, with personal letter from publisher and handwritten description of book in uknown hand, near fine.   Charles Agvent   William Meredith - 106   2016 $200

Simic, Charles *On the Music of the Spheres.* New York: Library Fellows of the Whitney Museum of American Art, 1996. First edition, deluxe issue, one of 100 numbered copies signed by Simic and photographer, Linda Connor, square 4to., 15 tipped in photographic plates, original navy cloth, black morocco labels lettered gilt, publisher's slipcase, specially bound, with original signed platinum palladium print by artist, as new in dust jacket.   James S. Jaffe Rare Books   Occasional List: Winter 2016 - 127   2016 $1500

Simic, Charles *Return to a Place Lit by a Glass of Milk. Poems.* New York: George Braziller, 1974. First edition, printed wrappers, inscribed and signed for William Meredith, by author, 4-19-77, near fine.   Charles Agvent   William Meredith - 107   2016 $150

Simmons, Henry Bradford *The Jingle Jangle Rhyme Book.* London: H. Grevel, Stokes, 1898. Oblong 4to., cloth backed pictorial boards, edges worn, some cover soil, interior clean, very good-, full color lithographs, rare.   Aleph-bet Books, Inc.   112 - 368   2016 $300

Simms, Rupert *Bibliotheca Staffordiensis.* Lichfield: A. C. Lomax, 1894. Limited to 200 numbered copies, large 4to., original cloth, uncut pages with top edge gilt, bookplate of Donald and Mary Hyde, ink inscription by Henry Elwell, also signed by Elwell, hinges, head and tail of spine worn, corners rubbed, both covers scuffed.   Oak Knoll Books   310 - 267   2016 $350

Simon, Andre *Bibliotheca Bacchica. Bibliographie Raisonne des Ouvrages Imprimies avant 1600...* London: Holland Press, 1972. Reprint edition, limited to 250 copies, 2 volumes in 1, thick 4to., illustrations, red cloth, printed dust jacket cloth edges with some discoloring, very good.   Jeff Weber Rare Books   181 - 51   2016 $100

Simon, Andre *A Catechism concerning Cheeses with a Glossary of Cheeses and Cheese Dishes. (cover title).* Wine and Food Society, printed at Chiswick Press, 1936. First edition, wrappers little dust soiled, otherwise very nice.   Bertram Rota Ltd.   Christmas List 2015 - 39   2016   £45

Simonde De Sismondi, Jean Charles Leonard *Tableau De l'Agriculture Toscane.* Geneve: J. J. Paschoud, 1801. First edition, 210 x 140mm., very pleasing recent retrospective smooth half calf over convincing marbled paper boards, raised bands, maroon morocco label, new well matching endpapers, folding frontispiece, folding plate, first 3 leaves and 3 other leaves with marginal patches up to two inches square (not affecting text), probably due to removal of library stamp, aisde from patches mentioned above, very fine inside and out in convincing, binding, unworn and text unusually clean, fresh and bright.   Phillip J. Pirages   67 - 1   2016 $950

Simons, Mathew *A Direction for the English Traveller.* London: are to be sold by Thomas Jenner at the South Entrance of the Exchange, 1643. Fourth edition, small 4to., engraved leaves, paginated in manuscript by near contemporary hand, few pen trials to titlepage, occasional spotting and soiling, contemporary blind ruled sheep (front cover with early repair, covers with scrapes, piece torn from rear cover, edges chipped, joints cracked), with 8 page manuscript of Dance Steps by choreographer, Kenelm Tomlinson, with Tomlinson signature, from the library of James Stevens Cox (1910-1997).   Maggs Bros. Ltd.   1447 - 387   2016   £6000

Simple Simon. New York: McLoughlin Bros., 1804. 4to., pictorial stiff wrappers, illustrations in black and white and 6 full color chromolithographs, very good plus.   Second Life Books, Inc.   197 - 292   2016 $75

Simpson, C. L.   *The Memoirs of C. L. Simpson: the Symbol of Liberia.*   London: Diplomatic Press and Pub. Co., 1961. First edition, octavo, blue cloth gilt, trifle rubbed, paper edges slightly toned, still about fine, inscribed by Simpson to Adlai Stevenson.   Between the Covers Rare Books   202 - 95   2016 $450

Simpson, Dorothy   *No Laughing Matter.*   London: Michael Joseph, 1993. First edition, very fine, signed by author.   Mordida Books   2015 - 010633   2016 $55

Simpson, George   *A Journey Round the World During the Years 1841 and 1842.*   London: Henry Colburn, 1847. First edition, 2 volumes, 8vo., portrait, folding map, contemporary green half calf, slight rubbing to joints, very good, crisp copy.   J. & S. L. Bonham Antiquarian Booksellers America 2016 - 7882   2016   £550

Simpson, J. Y.   *Anesthesia or the Employment of Chloroform and Ether in Surgery, Midwifer, etc.*   Philadelphia: Lindsay & Blakiston, 1849. First American edition, 8vo., original cloth, very worn, becoming loose, heavily foxed with tide mark in text.   M & S Rare Books, Inc.   99 - 8   2016 $475

Simpson, James   *The Philosophy of Education...*   Edinburgh: Adam & Charles Black, 1836. Second edition, largely unopened in original grey green moiree cloth, paper label, slightly marked by damp but nice.   Jarndyce Antiquarian Books   CCXV - 947   2016   £68

Simpson, James Y.   *Anaesthesia, Hospitalism, Hermaphroitisim. Proposal to Stamp Out Small-Pox and other Contagious Diseases.*   New York: D. Appleton, 1872. First American edition, 8vo., original pebbled cloth, good reading copy only, ex-library with markings on spine and elsewhere.   Edwin V. Glaser Rare Books   2015 - 10367   2016 $50

Simpson, James Y.   *Clinical Lectures on the Diseases of Women.*   New York: D. Appleton, 1977. First American edition, 8vo., original pebbled cloth, 142 illustrations in text, publisher's catalog bound in, good reading copy only.   Edwin V. Glaser Rare Books   2015 - 10366   2016 $50

Simpson, James Y.   *History of Modern Anaesthetics.*   Edinburgh: Edmonston and Douglas, 1870. 8vo., orginal purple paper wrappers, some wear, else good.   James Tait Goodrich   X-78 - 507   2016 $595

Simpson, Louis   *North of Jamaica.*   New York: Harper & Row, 1972. First American edition, 8vo., author's signature on presentation card laid in, paper over boards with cloth spine, edges little spotted, otherwise very good, tight copy in little scuffed and chipped dust jacket.   Second Life Books, Inc.   196 B - 577   2016 $75

Simpson, Louis   *Selected Poems.*   New York: Harcourt Brace & World, 1965. First edition, 8vo., author's presentation for William Claire, green cloth, bottom edges slightly spotted, otherwise nice copy in little chipped and soiled dust jacket.   Second Life Books, Inc.   196 B - 579   2016 $125

Simpson, Louis   *Searching for the Ox.*   New York: Morrow, 1976. First printing, author's presentation to poet William Claire, paper over boards, with cloth spine, top edge slightly spotted, otherwise nice in little chipped and soiled dust jacket.   Second Life Books, Inc.   196 B - 578   2016 $275

Simpson, Margaret   *The Companion to Hard Times.*   London: Helen Information, 1997. First edition, half title, illustrations, original dark green cloth, mint in dust jacket.   Jarndyce Antiquarian Booksellers   CCXVIII - 534   2016   £35

Simrock, Karl   *Die Deutschen Volksbucher, Gesammelt und in Ihrer Ursprunglichen Echtheit Wiederhergestellt.*   Frankfurt: Heinr. Ludw. Bronner, 1845-1867. First edition, 13 volumes, tall 12mo., contemporary green cloth, numerous illustrations and text wood engravings, ex-library with markings.   Oak Knoll Books   310 - 219   2016 $450

Sincera, Rege   *Observations both Historical and Moral Upon the Burning of London, September 1666.*   London: printed by Thomas Ratcliffe and are to be sold by Rohert Pawlet at the Bible in Chancery- lane, 1667. First edition, 4to., untrimmed, head & tailpieces, 4to., modern brown half morocco with brown cloth board, gilt stamped title lettering to spine, blue marbled endpapers, binding near fine, text block with small worm track d3-f2, primarily in lower margin, E4r with small circular prior owner stamp to lower margin, small paper repair to left of same, very good.   Tavistock Books   Getting Around - 25   2016 $2250

Sinclair, Iain   *The Birth Rug.*   Albion Village Press, 1973. First edition, one of 200 copies, printed in navy on light blue paper, 8 pages of photo illustrations, crown 8vo., original sewn blue wrappers printed in silver, very light fading to edges, light rubbing at head, very good, inscribed by author.   Blackwell's Rare Books   B184 - 233   2016   £150

Sinclair, Iain *Lights Out for the Territory.* Goldmark & Granta Books, 1997. First edition, T/26 copies signed by author and artist, with additional sheet of holograph material signed and lettered by author and signed original photo signed and lettered by artist, Marc Atkins in pocket at rear, full page maps and photographic plates, 8vo., original blue cloth with photo inset to upper board, backstrip lettered gilt, matching slipcase trifle dusty on top, near fine.   Blackwell's Rare Books   B184 - 234   2016   £300

Sinclair, Iain *London Orbital. A Walk around the M25.* Goldmark & Granta Books, 2002. First edition, ix/xv hors commerce copies, signed by author with additional holographic material signed and lettered by author in pocket in rear, with an additional chapter to special edition also, 8 plates of photomontage and illustration at head of each section, 8vo., original grey cloth, backstrip lettered in silver, matching slipcase, prospectus laid in at rear, fine. Blackwell's Rare Books   B184 - 235   2016   £350

Sinclair, Iain *Rodinsky's Room.* London: Granta Books, 1999. First edition, octavo, illustrations, cloth with photo mounted on front, signed by author and Rachel Lichtenstein, fine in fine cloth slipcase.   Peter Ellis   112 - 360   2016   £150

Sinclair, Iain *White Chappell Scarlet Tracings.* Uppingham: Goldmark, 1987. First edition, 69/100 copies, signed by author and Rigby Graham (who provides frontispiece), original signed and numbered etching for frontispiece in pocket at rear, 8vo., original grey cloth, backstrip lettered in black, top edge grey, acetate dust jacket, cloth, slipcase, fine.   Blackwell's Rare Books   B184 - 236   2016   £650

Sinclair, John *The History of the Public Revenue of the British Empire.* London: printed for A. Strahan .... and for T. Cadell and W. Davies, 1803. Third edition, 3 volumes, half title in volume I, 8vo., slight paper flaw to top blank corner B2-3 volume i, some offset browning and light foxing to endpapers and pastedowns, handsome set bound in full contemporary polished tree calf, ornate gilt decorated spines, floral bands, wavy lines, oval flower head motifs, dark green morocco labels, slight crack to upper joint volume I, some minor rubbing to head and tail of spines.   Jarndyce Antiquarian Booksellers   CCXVI - 528   2016   £650

Sinclair, May *The Belfry.* New York: Macmillan, 1916. First American edition, faint foxing to half title and titlepage, portion of dust jacket? pasted to verso of flyleaf and slightly offset to half title, single foxspot to border of one page and odd handling mark, crown 8vo., original red cloth with single fillet border blindstamped to upper board, backstrip and upper board lettered in gilt, slight lean to spine, light rubbing to extremities with little bumping to couple of corners, top edge little dusty, fore-edge rough trimmed with few faint foxspots, some very faint foxing to endpapers with bookplate of Henry Festing Jones, good, inscribed by author to Jones. Blackwell's Rare Books   B186 - 283   2016   £115

Sinclair, Upton   1878-1968 *Another Pamela, or Virtue Still Rewarded.* New York: Viking Press, 1950. First edition, red cloth lettered in black, small scratch to upper corner of front cover, extremities rubbed and slightly showing, dust jacket soiled and chipped with faded spine, very good. Argonaut Book Shop   Literature 2015 - 6143   2016 $60

Sinclair, Upton   1878-1968 *Dragon Harvest.* New York: Viking Press, 1945. First edition, red cloth, spine slightly faded, bumped with small faint stain at foot of spine, else fine.   Argonaut Book Shop   Literature 2015 - 5588   2016 $50

Sinclair, Upton   1878-1968 *One Clear Call.* New York: Viking Press, 1948. First edition, red cloth, lettered in silver, dust jacket rubbed and faded at spine with small stain. Argonaut Book Shop   Literature 2015 - 5586   2016 $90

Sinclair, Upton   1878-1968 *The Return of Lanny Budd.* New York: Viking Press, 1953. First edition, red cloth, lettered in silver to spine, lower corners slightly jammed, minor offsetting to front endpapers, dust jacket rubbed with faded spine and blind stamped by San Francisco Public Library (no other library markings found anywhere in book), near fine.   Argonaut Book Shop   Literature 2015 - 6143   2016 $60

Sinclair, Upton   1878-1968 *A World to Win.* New York: Viking Press, 1948. First edition, red cloth lettered in silver, spine slightly dinged along edge near top, minor wear to covers with few faint white spots, very good.   Argonaut Book Shop   Literature 2015 - 6146   2016 $40

Singer, Barry *Black and Blue: the Life and Lyrics of Andy Razaf.* New York: Scribner, 1992. First printing, 8v., author's presentation on half title for Andy Davis, photos, paper over boards with cloth spine, nice in lightly scuffed dust jacket.   Second Life Books, Inc.   196 B - 582   2016 $50

Singer, Charles *A Prelude to Modern Science.* London: 1946. 59 text figures, 6 plates, near fine, original binding and dust jacket, Sir Geoffrey Jefferson's copy.   James Tait Goodrich   X-78 - 539   2016 $495

Singer, Charles *Studies in the History and Method of Science.* Oxford: Clarendon Press, 1917-1921. Colored frontispiece 40 plates, and colored frontispiece, 54 plates, royal 8vo., original cloth, volume 1 has sunned spine. James Tait Goodrich   X-78 - 505   2016 $495

Singer, Charles *Vesalius on the Human Brain.* London: Wellcome, 1952. Original binding, illustrations, very good in dust jacket.   James Tait Goodrich   X-78 - 538   2016 $125

Singer, Isaac Bashevis *Elijah the Slave.* New York: Straus Giroux, 1970. Stated first edition, cloth, fine in fine dust jacket, fabulously illustrated by Antonio Frasconi with striking color woodcuts, this copy signed by artist. Aleph-bet Books, Inc.   111 - 427   2016 $400

Singer, Isaac Bashevis *The Golum.* New York: Farrar, Strauss Giroux, 1982. Limited to 4to numbered cop9es, signed by author and artist, 8vo., cloth, fine in slipcase, faded on edges, full page illustrations by Uri Shulevitz. Aleph-bet Books, Inc.   111 - 428   2016 $400

Singer, Isaac Bashevis *The Pentitent.* New York: Farrar Straus Giroux, 1983. First edition, 8vo., fine in price clipped dust jacket, inscribed by author.   Second Life Books, Inc.   196 B - 583   2016 $75

Singer, Isaac Bashevis *The Topsy-Turvy Emperor of China.* New York: Harper & Row, 1971. First edition, 8vo., pictorial cloth, fine in dust jacket, illustrations by William Pene Du Bois, laid-in photo of Du Bois receiving the Newberry Award for 21 Balloons at the Awards Dinner in 1948, photos is 8 x 10 inches (one corner torn off in margin).   Aleph-bet Books, Inc.   111 - 429   2016 $90

Singer, Isaac Bashevis *Yentl the Veshiva Boy.* New York: Farrar Straus Giroux, 1983. Stated first edition, 8vo., cloth, small soil area on cover, else fine in price clipped dust jacket with scrape in corner, illustrations by Antonio Frasconi with striking color woodcuts, signed by Frasconi.   Aleph-bet Books, Inc.   112 - 463   2016 $200

Singer, Isaac Bashevis *Zlateh the Goat.* New York: Harper & Row, 1966. Limited to 500 copies, signed by Sendak and Singer, 8vo., off white cloth, pictorial paste-on, spine slightly soiled, else fine in original marbelized brown slipcase, 17 wonderful full page illustrations by Maurice Sendak, printed on Andora paper and specially bound. Aleph-bet Books, Inc.   111 - 410   2016 $750

Singer, Samuel Weller *Researches into the History of Playing Cards: with Illustrations of the Origin of Printing and Engraving on Wood.*   London: T. Bensley and Son for Robert Triphook, 1816. Limited to 250 copies, 4to., contemporary quarter leather, engraved frontispiece, 19 plates, 11 engraved and 8 hand-colored woodcuts, black and white illustrations in text, scuffing at edges and along spine, front inside joint cracked, also cracked between frontispiece and title, scattered foxing on plates, 3 leaves bound out of order, facing page 293, rather than facing 284 as in directions for placing plates.   Oak Knoll Books   310 - 8   2016 $2850

Siringo, Charles Angelo   1855-1928 *Riata and Spurs: the Story of a Lifetime Spent in the Saddle as Cowboy and Detective.*   Boston: 1927. First edition, first issue, very good, clean copy with some wear, hinges starting, short tears to top and bottom of spine and browning to endpapers and titlepage.   Dumont Maps and Books   133 - 78   2016 $195

Sis, Peter *The Three Golden Keys.* New York: Doubleday, 1994. Stated first edition, first printing with 1-10 code, 10 1/2 x 12 inches, pictorial boards, fine in dust jacket (creased in lower corner), this copy signed by Sis with nice drawing, illustrations by Sis on every page.   Aleph-bet Books, Inc.   111 - 430   2016 $200

Siskind, Aaron *Aaron Siskind: Photographer.* Rochester: George Eastman House, 1965. First edition, clean and tight, near fine copy in close to near fine dust jacket with some slight wear, signed and inscribed by Siskind for Jack Welpott, fellow worker in the vineyard, rather uncommon thus.   Jeff Hirsch Books   E-List 80 - 28   2016 $500

Sisson, C. H. *An Asiatic Romance.* London: Gaberbocchus Press, 1953. First edition, small octavo, ownership signature, edges slightly spotted, very good in very good, slightly spotted dust jacket with couple of small nicks.   Peter Ellis   112 - 361   2016   £45

Sitwell, Edith   1887-1964 *Jane Barston 1719-1746.* London: Faber and Faber, First edition, one of 250 signed copies on English handmade paper, drawings by R. A. Davies, yellow cloth little soiled, very good.   Second Life Books, Inc.   197 - 294   2016 $150

Sitwell, Edith   1887-1964 *Street Songs.* London: Macmillan, 1942. First edition, 8vo., fine in little soiled and nicked dust jacket, review copy with slip laid in, Sidney Keyes copy.   Second Life Books, Inc.   196 B - 586   2016 $65

Sitwell, Osbert   1892-1969 *Out of the Flame.* London: Grant Richards, 1923. First edition, frontispiece, 8vo., original green cloth with few light spots, backstrip with orange paper label little chipped to border, top edge lightly dust soiled with endpapers faintly browned, good, with holograph copy of 'Superstition', from the library of Baron Emile D'Erlanger, although without any mark of ownership. Blackwell's Rare Books   B186 - 284   2016   £130

Sitwell, Osbert   1892-1969 *The Winstonburg Line.*   The Bomb Shop, 1919. Original wrappers slightly dusty, endpapers very slight foxed, otherwise very good, uncommon.   I. D. Edrich   Winston Spencer Churchill - 2016   £100

Sitwell, Sacheverell *Collected Poems.* London: Duckworth, 1936. First edition, octavo, cover edges just little rubbed, spine slightly creased, prelims little spotted, very good in very good, price clipped dust jacket little rubbed at edges, inscribed by author for Robert Byron.   Peter Ellis   112 - 362   2016   £295

Siwertz, Siegfried *Downstream.* New York: Knopf, 1923. 8vo., author's presentation on half title, black cloth stamped in red, purple and gilt, cover little worn, else very good. Second Life Books, Inc.   196 B - 588   2016 $45

Sjowall, Maj *The Abominable Man.* New York: Pantheon Books, 1972. First American edition, purple cloth lettered in gilt, light rubbing to dust jacket, fine. Argonaut Book Shop Literature 2015 - 8159 2016 $60

Sjowall, Maj *The Fire Engine that Disappeared.* New York: Pantheon, 1970. First American edition, fine in dust jacket. Mordida Books 2015 - 011414 2016 $65

Sjowall, Maj *The Man Who Went Up in Smoke.* New York: Pantheon Books, 1969. First American edition, blue cloth backed boards, top corners slightly bumped, slight fading along extreme edges of covers, spine bit cocked, very good in pictorial dust jacket. Argonaut Book Shop Literature 2015 - 6152 2016 $75

Sjowall, Maj *Murder at the Savoy.* New York: Pantheon Books, 1971. First American edition, blue cloth lettered gilt, minimal rubbing to head of spine, 1 x 3 inch portion torn away and lacking along outer edge of font of dust jacket, , else fine. Argonaut Book Shop Literature 2015 - 6153 2016 $45

Skidmore, Thomas *The Rights of Man to Property Being a Proposition to make it Equal Among the Adults of the Present Generation...* New York: for the author, Alexander Ming Jr., 1829. First edition, Contemporary sheep, signature torn from top of page 3 (preface) costing 2-3 lines of type on verso, light foxing, scattered red pencilled check marks in first part of text, spine scuffed and dry, rear hinge broken, cloth folding box. Joseph J. Felcone, Inc. Books from Five Centuries: a Miscellany - 129 2016 $2800

Skinner & Co. *A Catalogue of the Portland Museum, Lately the Property of the Duchess Dowager of Portland.... which will be sold by auction by Mr. Skinner and Co... 1786.* London: 1786. 4to., engraved frontispiece, neat modern quarter calf, lightly foxed, bit heavier on first and last few leaves, very good. Joseph J. Felcone, Inc. Books from Five Centuries: a Miscellany - 117 2016 $5500

Skinner, Cornelia Otis *Footlights and Spotlights.* Indianapolis: Bobbs Merrill, 1924. First edition, 8vo., illustrations, author's presentation flyleaf, nice in little soiled dust jacket. Second Life Books, Inc. 196 B - 593 2016 $45

Skinner, Cornelia Otis *Madame Sarah.* Boston: Houghton Mifflin, 1967. First edition, illustration, signed Cornelia to Charlie (Brackett), movie director, nice in little worn dust jacket. Second Life Books, Inc. 196 B - 590 2016 $45

Skinner, J. S. *The Dog and the Sportsman Embracing the uses, Breeding, Training, Diseases etc... of Dogs...* Philadelphia: Lea & Blanchard, 1845. First edition, vignette title, 224 pages, plates, original cloth, front hinge opened. M & S Rare Books, Inc. 99 - 290 2016 $425

Sklar, Kathryn Kish *Competing Kingdoms: Women, Mission, Nation and American Protestant Empire 1812-1960.* Durham: Duke University, 2010. First edition, author's signature, red cloth, about as new. Second Life Books, Inc. 196 B - 594 2016 $40

Sklosky, Sidney *Times Square Tintypes.* New York: Ives Washburn, 1930. Second printing, 8vo., caricatures, author's presentation, flap on dust jacket laid in, rest of jacket missing, very good. Second Life Books, Inc. 196 B - 596 2016 $45

Skogman, Carl Johan Alfred *Fregatten 'Eugenies' Resa Omkring Jorden aren 1851-1853...* Stockholm: Adolf Bonnier, n.d., 1854-1855. First edition, 2 volumes in 1, 8vo., lithographic plates, some heightened with varnish, 6 line engravings, 3 folding charts, textual vignettes, contemporary brown half calf, neatly rebacked, new endpapers, light foxing to maps, uncommon. J. & S. L. Bonham Antiquarian Booksellers Voyages 2016 - 7250 2016 £200

Skues, G. E. M. *Silk, Fur and Feather: the Trout-Fly Dresser's Year.* Beckenham: The Fishing Gazette, 1950. First edition in book form, 12mo., original green cloth, gilt lettering to upper cover and spine, rounded covers, all edges green, text illustrations, previous owner's bookplate and inscription, very good. Sotheran's Hunting, Shooting & Fishing - 144 2016 £90

Skurray, Francis *Bidcombe Hill with Other Rural Poems.* London: printed for William Miller, 1808. First edition, 191 x 121mm., contemporary straight grain green morocco, elaborately decorated in gilt and blind, covers with gilt palmette frame enclosing black tooled floral frame, flat spine with panels intricately tooled in gilt and black, gilt rolled turn-ins, marbled endleaves, all edges gilt, with fine pastoral fore-edge painting of Saint Bee's College Cumberland; in later sturdy fleece lined cloth slipcase, 4 engraved plates, spine sunned to light green muted spotting to leather, plates somewhat foxed, other minor defects, still quite pleasing, binding with only insignificant wear, text bright, fresh and clean and margins very ample. Phillip J. Pirages 67 - 162 2016 $1400

Slater, James *Sheridan Lord 1926-1994.* New York: Kelly Winterton Press, 1995. One of 200 copies, signed by author, saddle stitched in wrappers, fine, signed by author. Between the Covers Rare Books 204 - 105 2016 $50

Slater, Michael *Charles Dickens.* New Haven & London:: Yale University Press, 2009. First edition, half title, illustrations, plates, original dark blue cloth, unsigned presentation inscription, mint in dust jacket. Jarndyce Antiquarian Booksellers CCXVIII - 1448 2016 £40

Slater, Michael *Dickens 1970; Centenary Essays....* London: Chapman & Hall in association with The Dickens Fellowship, 1970. First edition, Half title, frontispiece, illustrations, original green cloth, very good in dust jacket. Jarndyce Antiquarian Booksellers   CCXVIII - 1443   2016   £20

Slater, Michael *Dickens on America & the Americans.* London: Harvester Press, 1979. First edition, half title, illustrations, maps on endpapers, original bright blue cloth, very good in slightly worn dust jacket, presentation inscription from author for Thelma Grove.   Jarndyce Antiquarian Booksellers   CCXVIII - 1444   2016   £22

Slater, Michael *Dickens on Women.* London: J. M. Dent & Sons, 1983. First edition, half title, plates, original maroon cloth very good in slightly faded dust jacket.   Jarndyce Antiquarian Booksellers   CCXVIII - 1445   2016   £35

Slavitt, David *The Ecologues of Virgil.* Garden City: Doubleday, 1971. No. 306 of a limited edition of 1139 copies, 8vo., signed and numbered by author, black cloth stamped in silver, nice in box and somewhat scuffed paper labels front and back.   Second Life Books, Inc.   196 B - 601   2016 $75

Sleeman, C. W. *Torpedoes and Torpedo Warfare Containing a Complete and Concise Account of the Rise and Progress of Submarine Warfare...* Portsmouth: Griffin & Co., 1880. First edition, 8vo., modern red half morocco over cloth covered boards, black morocco lettering pieces n spine, original gilt stamped illustration from original binding laid down on front cover, tinted lithographic frontispiece, numerous plates, one plate reinserted with traces of previously used sellotape, initially and at end a little brown spotted, contemporary ownership inscription.   Sotheran's Travel and Exploration - 473   2016   £78

Slidell-MacKenzie, Alexander *A Year in Spain.* London: John Murray, 1831. First edition, 2 volumes, 8vo., recent brown calf, clean, crisp copy.   J. & S. L. Bonham Antiquarian Booksellers   Europe 2016 - 8408   2016   £190

Sloan, Samuel *Sloan's Constructive Architecture: a Guide to the Practical Builder and Mechanic...* Philadelphia: 1866. Large 4to., 66 lithographed plates, neat modern cloth, leather spine label, very nice.   Joseph J. Felcone, Inc.   Books from Five Centuries: a Miscellany - 8   2016 $700

Sloane, Eric *American Yesterday.* New York: Funk, 1986. Small 4to., illustrations by author, author's presentation and sketch, blue cloth stamped in black, edges of cover very slightly scuffed, otherwise nice in scuffed and slightly chipped dust jacket.   Second Life Books, Inc.   196 B - 602   2016 $100

Sloane, Eric *The Seasons of America Past.* New York: Funk, 1958. 4to., drawings and four color plates, maps on endpapers, author's signature and small sketch, rust colored cloth, top edge little spotted, else very good, tight in chipped and slightly soiled dust jacket.   Second Life Books, Inc.   196 B - 603   2016 $125

Sloane, Hans *An Account of a Most Efficacious Medecine for Soreness, Weakness and Several other Distempers of the Eyes.* London: for Dan. Browne, circa, 1750. Second edition, neat modern cloth backed boards, fine.   Joseph J. Felcone, Inc.   Books from Five Centuries: a Miscellany - 97   2016 $475

Slotnikoff, Will *The First Time I Live...* Washington: Manchester Lane Edition, 1966. First edition, 8vo., little worn paper wrappers, review slip tipped to rear endpaper, inscribed by author for poet William Claire, laid in is postcard signed to Claire and 3 page typed letters also to Claire.   Second Life Books, Inc.   196 B - 604   2016 $75

Small Beginning or the Way to Get On. London: James Hogg & sons, 1859. First edition, half title, frontispiece, plates, 4 pages ads, original red cloth, gilt vignette, dulled, cup mark on front board, contemporary signature, Fred Reymer 1862.   Jarndyce Antiquarian Books   CCXV - 48   2016   £35

Small, Eve *The Semiotics of Color. Part II.* Morgantown: Permutation Press, 1987. Limited to 189 numbered copies, small 4to., cloth with inset black cover label.   Oak Knoll Books   27 - 52   2016 $450

Smart, Christopher   1722-1771 *Poems on Several Occasions.* London: printed for the author by W. Strahan, 1752. 4to., errata leaf, frontispiece, one engraved plate, some offsetting from frontispiece, full contemporary tree calf, raised and gilt banded spine, red morocco label, expert repairs to head and tail of spine and to corners, several small abrasions to surface leather on boards, very good.   Jarndyce Antiquarian Booksellers   CCXVI - 529   2016   £780

Smellie, William   1740-1795 *A Set of Anatomical tables with Explanations and an Abridgement of the Practice of Midwifery...* London: n.d., 1925? Facsimile of 1761 second edition, 39 plates, folio, boards, vellum spine, some occasional foxing, very good on thick paper.   Edwin V. Glaser Rare Books   2015 - 10082   2016 $275

Smellie, William   1740-1795 *A Sett of Anatomical Tables with explanations and an Abridgement of the Practice of Midwifery.* W. B. Saunders,circa, 1970. Fine facsimile reprint of 1754 edition, tall folio, handsome half calf and marbled boards, marbled endpapers and placed in cloth slipcase, printed on heavy laid rag paper.   James Tait Goodrich   X-78 - 509   2016 $595

Smet, Pierre Jean De 1801-1873 *Missions De L'Oregon et Voyages Aux Montagnes Rocheuses...1845-46.* Gand (i.e. Ghent): Vander Schelden, 1848. First edition in French, 194 x 117mm., original yellow printed paper wrappers, unopened, modern (slightly soiled and worn) custom made gilt titled folding cloth box, illustrated titlepage, 3 folding maps and 15 plates, wrappers little browned and bit wrinkled at edges, couple of tiny chips to tail of spine, isolated mild foxing, couple of tiny marginal tears, but by and large, very fine, extremely fragile item, obviously never having been read.   Phillip J. Pirages   67 - 111   2016 $1750

Smiles, Samuel *Character.* London: John Murray, 1876. New edition, half title, 14 pages ads, slightly spotted, occasional pencil underlinings, original green cloth, contemporary ownership inscriptions, bookseller's ticket of Burdekin, York, very good.   Jarndyce Antiquarian Books   CCXV - 409   2016   £35

Smiles, Samuel *George Moore, Merchant and Philanthropist.* London: George Routledge, 1878. Second edition, half title, frontispiece, original purple cloth, slight rubbing, bookplate and signature of Peter Carmichael, very good.   Jarndyce Antiquarian Books   CCXV - 949   2016   £58

Smiles, Samuel *Self-Help.* London: John Murray, 1860. 35th thousand, 32 page catalog original maroon cloth blocked in blind, spine lettered gilt, rubbed and worn, inscription from Percival Skelton, July 1861 for father, sound.   Jarndyce Antiquarian Books   CCXV - 410   2016   £120

Smiles, Samuel *Self-Help.* Paris: Henri Plon; Londres: John Murray, 1865. First French edition, half title, original green cloth, slightly marked but very good, bright.   Jarndyce Antiquarian Books   CCXV - 411   2016   £185

Smiles, Samuel *Thrift.* London: John Murray, 1891. 47th thousand, half title, 8 pages ads, original purple cloth, bevelled boards, spine slightly faded, very good.   Jarndyce Antiquarian Books   CCXV - 412   2016   £35

Smiley, Jane *"Not a Pretty Picture" in Novel History.* New York: Simon & Schuster, 2001. First edition, signed by Smiley, upper covers tapped, else fine in fine dust jacket.   Ken Lopez Bookseller   166 - 118   2016 $150

Smiley, Jane *A Thousand Acres.* New York: Knopf, 1991. First edition, fine in fine dust jacket, inscribed by author to Ivan Doig.   Ken Lopez Bookseller   166 - 117   2016 $275

Smith, Adam 1723-1790 *Essays on Philosophical Subjects.* Dublin: printed for Messrs. Wogan, Byrne (and 6 others), 1795. First Dublin edition, 8vo., some foxing, mainly to endpapers and blanks, slight browning, contemporary tree calf, gilt banded spine, red morocco label, joints cracked but firm, corners worn, spine bit rubbed, slightly worn at foot.   Jarndyce Antiquarian Booksellers   CCXVI - 530   2016   £450

Smith, Adam 1723-1790 *An Inquiry into the Nature and Causes of the Wealth of Nations.* London: printed for W. Strahan and T. Cadell, 1776. First edition, large 4to., 2 volumes, contemporary full calf, spines with five raised bands, richly ornamented in gilt and each volume with two contrasting lettering pieces, boards with single gilt fillets, inner dentelles gilt, yellow edges, marbled endpapers, few tables in text, extremities expertly restored by Bernard Middleton, few areas little worn, very few leaves with light spotting, few old and new restorations to paper flaws, page 460 in volume I with loss of one letter due to small paper flaw, overall clean and crisp.   Sotheran's   Piccadilly Notes - Summer 2015 - 10   2016   £120,000

Smith, Adam 1723-1790 *An Inquiry into the Nature and Causes of the Wealth of Nations.* London: printed for A. Strahan and T. Cadell, 1786. Fourth edition, 3 volumes, octavo, contemporary tree calf, rebacked to style, boards tooled gilt, spines with red morocco spine labels and gilt lettering on black morocco onlayed volume numbers, top edge dyed brown, occasional foxing, light dampstain to top margin of volume II, board edges lightly chipping, overall very nice.   Heritage Book Shop   Holiday 2015 - 101   2016 $3000

Smith, Adam 1723-1790 *An Inquiry into the Nature and Causes of the Wealth of Nations.* London: T. Cadell Jun. and W. Davies, 1802. 11th edition, 3 volumes, half titles, tear to fore-edge of pages 171-72, volume I with no loss of text, recent half brown calf, black morocco labels, signature of Joseph Chippendale on titlepage of volumes I and III, half title of volume II.   Jarndyce Antiquarian Booksellers   CCXVII - 259   2016   £1250

Smith, Albert *The Miscellany: a Book for the Field or the Fire Side Amusing Tales and Sketches.* London: David Bogue, 1850. First edition, octavo, later brown half morocco, marbled paper boards, gilt lettering, top edge gilt, 6 pages of publisher's terminal ads, original printed wrappers bound in, scarce, edges and boards rubbed, good copy.   The Brick Row Book Shop   Miscellany 69 - 75   2016 $150

Smith, Albert *Social Zoologies.* London: David Bogue, 1847. First edition, 32mo., 9 parts in 3 volumes, numerous engraved plates, titlepage vignettes and text illustrations, publisher's three quarter black calf, spine gilt extra, red and black labels, corners show some wear, lovely little set.   Argonaut Book Shop   Literature 2015 - 7229   2016 $300

Smith, Albert Richard *The Cricket on the Hearth...a drama in three acts.*   London: John Dicks, 1883?   Disbound, illustrations.   Jarndyce Antiquarian Booksellers   CCXVIII - 382   2016   £20

Smith, Alfred *Twenty Lithographic Views of Ecclesiastical Edifices in the Borough of Stroud...*   Stroud: J. P. Brisley, 1838. First edition, large oblong , 20 lithographs on India pasted onto velin paper, errata slip loosely inserted, prelims bit dusty and with dog eared lower outer corners, otherwise very lightly spotted in places only, original printed wrappers, little worn, lower outer corner of front wrapper torn away front wrapper inscribed by C. S. Fortescue of Shepworth Dec. 1838, dedication leaf signed by artist.   Marlborough Rare Books   List 55 - 63   2016   £950

Smith, Andrew *Possums and Gliders.*   Chipping Norton: Surrey Beatty, 1984. First edition, quarto, slipcase, photos, text illustrations, bookplate, very good in dust jacket.   Andrew Isles Natural History Books   55 - 24045   2016 $200

Smith, Andrew M.   *Roman Palmyra Identity, Community and State Formation.*   Oxford University Press, 2013. First edition, large 8vo., blue boards, bronze lettered, light bumping to end caps and bottom corners, edges lightly dusted, near fine, dust jacket with minor shelfwear, near fine.   Unsworths Antiquarian Booksellers Ltd. E04 - 98   2016   £30

Smith, Benjamin *Vice-Royalty; or Counsels Respecting the Government of the Heart.* London: John Mason, 1863. Second edition, half title, 16 page catalog, original blue cloth, little rubbed and dulled, inner hinges cracking, sound.   Jarndyce Antiquarian Books   CCXV - 413   2016   £40

Smith, Bernard *The Art of the First Fleet and Other Early Australian Drawings.*   New Haven: Yale University Press, 1988. Small folio, illustrations, very good in dust jacket.   Andrew Isles Natural History Books   55 - 13004   2016 $100

Smith, Betty *A Tree Grows in Brooklyn.* New York: Harper & Bros., 1943. First edition, octavo, original dust jacket.   Honey & Wax Booksellers   4 - 58   2016 $4800

Smith, Cecil *The Birds of Guernesey and the Neighbouring Islands Alderney, Sark, Jethou, Herm: Being a Small Contribution to the Channel islands.*   London: R. H. Porter, 1879. Duodecimo, publisher's green cloth, few minor blemishes, otherwise fine, crisp copy.   Andrew Isles Natural History Books   55 - 36214   2016 $450

Smith, Cecil Harcourt *Collection of J. Pierpoint Morgan Bronzes, Antique Greek, Roman, Etc...*   Paris: Libraire Central De Beaux Arts, 1913. One of a likely limitation of 150 copies, folio, original gilt ruled chocolate half morocco over French shell marbled paper covered boards, spine divided into six compartments with raised bands gilt, second and third compartments, gilt titled, remainder decorated with gilt centre tooled floral device set with border comprised of four gilt rules, top edges gilt, remainder uncut, marbled endpapers, half title, title, 66 color heliograve plates printed on thin paper laid to panelled mounts, each with titled guard, 38 color heliogravure illustrations printed on thin paper and laid into text, bright fresh copy. Sotheran's Piccadilly Notes - Summer 2015 - 278   2016   £1950

Smith, Chard Powers *Turn of the Dial.* New York: Scribner's, 1943. First edition, 8vo., author's presentation for poet Barbara Howes, 8vo., nice, dust jacket little chipped and scuffed.   Second Life Books, Inc.   196 B - 606   2016 $50

Smith, Charles *The Antient and present State of the County of Kerry.* Dublin: printed for the author, 1756. 8vo., large folding map, 4 folding plates, lacks plate of Scelig island, 8vo, folding map neatly mounted on to a new guard, several expert repairs on verso, short tear along one fold without loss, slight foxing and little fingermarking to some leading edges, generally good, clean copy, contemporary calf raised bands, red morocco label, joints and head and tail of spine expertly repaired, old vertical crease slightly visible, armorial bookplate of William Perceval Esq., his initials and shelf number to titlepage, gilt crest at foot of spine.   Jarndyce Antiquarian Booksellers   CCXVI - 531   2016   £380

Smith, Clark Ashton *Out of Space and Time.*   Sauk City: Arkham House, 1942. First edition, 1054 copies, octavo, cloth, fine in fine dust jacket, elusive in this condition.   John W. Knott, Jr./L.W. Currey, Inc.   Fall-Winter 2015 - 17365   2016 $5000

Smith, D. Murray *Arctic Expeditions from British and Foreign Shores from the Earliest Times to the Expedition of 1875-1876.* Glasgow: 1877. Small folio, illustrations, 2 folding maps, recent quarter leather, all edges gilt, couple of repairs to larger folding map, else tight and very good.   Dumont Maps and Books   133 - 79   2016 $350

Smith, Dodie *I Capture the Castle.* Folio Society, 1997. Pictorial cloth, illustrations by A. Brouwer, pictorial cloth, fine in slipcase.   Bertram Rota Ltd.   February List 2016 - 53   2016   £20

Smith, E. Boyd *The Country Book.* New York: Frederick Stokes, 1924. First edition, oblong 4to., cloth, pictorial paste-on, school stamp on front and rear endpaper, shows no sign of ever having been circulated, fine in dust jacket, pictorial wrappers, 12 color plates plus numerous black and whites throughout text, great copy, rare.   Aleph-bet Books, Inc.   111 - 431   2016 $500

Smith, Edmund *A Poem on the Death of Mr. John Philips, author of the Splendid Shilling, Blenheim and Cyder.* London: printed for Bernard Lintott, 1710. First edition, folio, some light browning, disbound.   Jarndyce Antiquarian Booksellers   CCXVI - 532   2016   £200

Smith, Edward E. *Skylark of Valeron.* Reading: Fantasy Press, 1949. First edition, octavo, black and white frontispiece and chapter headings by A. J. Donnell, head and tail of spine slightly bumped, pastedowns partially and faintly tanned, very good in like dust jacket chipped and rubbed at edges.   Peter Ellis   112 - 364   2016   £45

Smith, Edward E. *Skylark Three.* Reading: Fantasy Press, 1948. First edition, octavo, head and tail of spine very slightly bumped, near fine in very good, nicked and chipped dust jacket rubbed at the edges.   Peter Ellis   112 - 365   2016   £65

Smith, Edward E. *Spacehounds of IPC - a Tale of Inter-Planetary Corporation.* Reading: Fantasy Press, 1949. Reprint, octavo, signed by author, covers edges little bumped and faded, very good in only frayed, rubbed and torn dust jacket.   Peter Ellis   112 - 366   2016   £35

Smith, Edward E. *Subspace Explorers.* New York: Canaveral Press, 1965. First edition, fewer than 1500 copies printed, octavo, frontispiece by Krenkel, head of spine slightly bumped, near fine in very good dust jacket nicked, torn and creased at top edge.   Peter Ellis   112 - 367   2016   £45

Smith, Egerton *The Melange, a Variety of Original Pieces in Prose and Verse Comprising the Elysium of Animals.* Liverpool: Egerton Smith and Co., 1834. Woodcut illustrations in text, 634 pages, nice copy, various members of the Roddick family recorded in pencil on leading free endpaper.   Jarndyce Antiquarian Booksellers   CCXVII - 260   2016   £180

Smith, Ernest Bramah *Kai Lung Unrolls His Mat.* Garden City: Doubleday Doran, 1928. First American edition, very good, without dust jacket.   Mordida Books   2015 - 001637   2016 $65

Smith, Ernest Bramah *Kai Lung's Golden Hours.* New York: Doran, 1923. First American edition, very good without dust jacket.   Mordida Books   2015 - 011636   2016 $65

Smith, Ernest Bramah *A Little Flutter.* London: Cassell, 1930. Ex-library, very good, uncommon.   I. D. Edrich Crime - 2016   £35

Smith, Ernest Bramah *The Specimen Case.* London: Hodder & Stoughton, 1924. Red cloth titled in black on spine, embossed title on front cover, covers badly faded on fore-edge and spine, none-the-less, very good, tight copy internally.   I. D. Edrich   Crime - 2016   £60

Smith, Ernest Bramah *The Wallet of Kai Lung.* New York: Doran, Reprint edition, very good without dust jacket.   Mordida Books   2015 - 001635   2016 $75

Smith, Ethan *View of the Hebrews: Exhibiting the Destruction of Jerusalem the Certain Restoration of Judah and Israel...* Poultney: Smith & Shute, 1823. First edition, 12mo., contemporary mottled sheep, usual scattered foxing, else very good, tight.   Joseph J. Felcone, Inc.   Books from Five Centuries: a Miscellany - 130   2016 $3000

Smith, Frank *The Life and Work of Sir James Kay-Shuttleworth.* London: John Murray, 1923. First edition, half title, frontispiece, plates, original blue cloth, spine slightly dulled, very good.   Jarndyce Antiquarian Books   CCXV - 805   2016   £30

Smith, George A. *Lovebirds and Related Parrots.* London: Paul Elek, 1979. Parrot Society edition limited to 350 numbered copies, this copy inscribed by author for Australian aviculturist Ross (Hogben), color photos, publisher's cloth and slipcase.   Andrew Isles Natural History Books   55 - 24085   2016 $80

Smith, George A. *The Rise, Progress and Travels of the Church of Jesus Christ of Latter-day Saints...* Salt Lake City: Deseret New Office, 1869. First edition, 8vo., original printed wrappers.   M & S Rare Books, Inc.   99 - 191   2016 $600

Smith, George Charles *Bristol Fair, but no Preaching!* London: Francis Westley, 1824. 6 issues, each of 12 pages, complete and all published, 12mo., little foxed and dust marked here and there, old (19th century) cloth backed marbled boards, some wear to spine, still good.   John Drury Rare Books   2015 - 18372   2016 $350

Smith, Harry B. *The Dickens-Kolle Letters.* Boston: Bibliophile Society, 1910. One of 483 copies, 4to., limitation leaf, frontispiece, uncut in original half vellum, very good in worn slipcase.   Jarndyce Antiquarian Booksellers   CCXVIII - 856   2016   £75

Smith, Harry B. *First Nights and First Editions.* Boston: Little Brown, 1931. 8vo., illustrations, one hinge tender, inscribed by author, very good.   Second Life Books, Inc.   196 B - 608   2016 $45

Smith, Henry *High Pressure Business Life and the Physical and Moral Evils Induced Thereby.* London: published by Henry Smith, M.D., 1876. Half title, 24 page catalog of important medical & social works by Henry Smith, 1876, original brick red cloth. Jarndyce Antiquarian Booksellers CCXVII - 261 2016 £60

Smith, Holland M. *Coral and Brass.* 1949. First edition, near fine, blue cloth, minor wear to edges of binding with near fine dust jacket, frontispiece. Simon Finch 2015 - 002014 2016 $300

Smith, Hugh *Letters to Married Women.* London: printed for G. Kearsley in Ludgate Street, 1767. 8vo., some slight offset browning to edges of titlepage, otherwise fine, clean copy, full contemporary pale calf, gilt ruled borders, raised and gilt banded, unlettered spine, from the Library of Invercauld Castle, Braemar. Jarndyce Antiquarian Booksellers CCXVI - 533 2016 £580

Smith, Ian M. *The Siege of Mafeking.* Johannesburg: The Brenthurst Press, 2001. First edition, one of 850 copies, 4to., 3 volumes, original cloth, illustrated dust jackets (volume 1 in interim boards), highly illustrated in color throughout, very good. Sotheran's Travel and Exploration - 24 2016 £398

Smith, J. L B. *The Sea Fishes of Southern Africa.* South Africa: Central News Agency, 1949. First edition, subscriber's edition limited to 200 numbered copies and signed by author, publisher's half red morocco and gilt, decorated cloth. Andrew Isles Natural History Books 55 - 8085 2016 $600

Smith, J. Lewis *A Treatise on the Diseases of Infancy and Childhood.* Philadelphia: Henry C. Lea, 1869. Original grey publisher's cloth, worn and faded, front joint split. James Tait Goodrich X-78 - 456 2016 $395

Smith, J. Lewis *A Treatise on the Diseases of Infancy and Childhood.* Philadelphia: Henry C. Lea, 1869. First edition, large 8vo. original cloth, spine faded, slight break in cloth at outer top of spine and break at inside lower front cover, owner's April 1879 signature, small contemporary bookseller's bookplate. M & S Rare Books, Inc. 99 - 293 2016 $150

Smith, James *Rejected Addresses or the new Theatrum Poetarum.* London: John Murray, 1833. First edition with these illustrations, 178 x 108mm., animated early 20th century scarlet crushed morocco, richly gilt by Riviere and Son (stamp signed on front turn-in), covers framed by curling vine bearing many berries and leaves, central panel formed and divided into compartments by gilt strapwork, each compartment containing a stylized strapwork and stippled wheel, radiating sections of wheel decorated with leafy fronds, raised bands, spine gilt in similar style, wide gilt turn-ins with plain and dotted label bound in at rear, fleece lined morocco clipped cloth slipcase, engraved frontispiece and 6 engraved illustrations by George Cruikshank, with signed original pencil study for one of the woodcuts and small pen and ink caricature, initialled by Cruikshank with his signature, laid in at front with two autograph letters, signed, tipped in at front, one from James Smith to Lady Blessington and one from Horace Smith to Duby (Edward Dubois - 1774-1850), front joint slightly (and rear joint just faintly) rubbed, spine shade darker than covers, text with faint overall browning because of paper stock, otherwise fine, lovely binding lustrous and altogether pleasing, text very clean and smooth. Phillip J. Pirages 67 - 64 2016 $950

Smith, James Edward *A Defence of the Church and Universities of England...* London: Longman, 1819. 8 page catalog stitched in, uncut, sewn as issued, spine worn with loss, little dusted. Jarndyce Antiquarian Books CCXV - 950 2016 £30

Smith, James Edward *An Introduction to Physiological and Systematical Botany.* London: Longman, Rees, Orme and others, 1827. Sixth edition, octavo, 15 hand colored engraved plates, contemporary brown calf and marbled boards and half calf, gilt spine, some light wear. Andrew Isles Natural History Books 55 - 39000 2016 $350

Smith, Janet L. *A Vintage Murder.* New York: Fawcett, 1994. First edition, advance review copy with review slip and flyler laid in, fine in dust jacket. Mordida Books 2015 - 010632 2016 $55

Smith, Jeremiah Finch *Manchester School Register.* Manchester: Chatham Society, 1866. First edition, 4 volumes, very good, some volumes partly unopened, slight wear at extremities, otherwise very good in original blind-stamped decorative cloth binding. Simon Finch 2015 - 4884 2016 $192

Smith, Jeremiah Finch *Notes and Collections relating to Parish of Aldridge.* Leicester: W. H. Lead, 1884. First edition, half red leather over red cloth, armorial bookplate of Thomas William Fletcher, clean tight text with minor edge spotting, extremities of covers bit rubbed, two autograph letters dated 1884 and 1889, signed by author to Colonel Thomas William Fletcher. Simon Finch 2015 - h014018 2016 $222

Smith, Jessie Willcox *The Jessie Willcox Smith Mother Goose.* New York: Mead Dodd, 1914. first edition, first issue, large oblong 4to., black cloth, pictorial paste-on, cover plate with some soil, faint spotting on first 2 leaves, very good+, illustrations by Smith.   Aleph-bet Books, Inc.   111 - 432   2016 $1350

Smith, John *Gaelic Antiquities Consisting of a History of the Druids, Particularly Those of Caledonia.* Edinburgh: printed for T. Cadell, London and D. Elliot Edinburgh, 1780. First edition, 4to., notes in old hand to prelim blank and some neat marginalia, little staining to margins of pages v-viii, occasional light spots of foxing and ink smudges not affecting text, 19th century brown polished calf over wooden boards, raised bands, both boards with blindstamped celtic knot design and raised central escutcheon, all edges red, marbled endpapers, quite rubbed, joints worn, few scratches, still very good overall, small, apparently hand drawn bookplate in the name of Archibald, two double sided leaves of ms. notes on Druids loosely inserted.   Unsworths Antiquarian Booksellers Ltd.   E05 - 13   2016   £360

Smith, John *Gerochomia Basilike. King Solomons Portraiture of Old Age.* London: for J. Hayes for S. Thomson, 1666. First edition, 8vo., folding letterpress table, some occasional spotting, blank lower corner of H1 torn away, contemporary calf, rebacked, corners repaired and new endpapers, contemporary signature of Edmund Morgan in ink, from the library of James Stevens Cox (1910-1997).   Maggs Bros. Ltd.   1447 - 388   2016   £280

Smith, John *Horological Dialogues in Three Parts: Shewing the Nature, Use and Right Managing of Clocks and Watches.* London: for Jonathan Edwin, 1675. First edition, 8vo., contemporary mottled calf, neatly rebacked in 19th century, lacks prelim blank A1 and binder's blanks, tiny closed tear in top margin of last leaf, else very good. Joseph J. Felcone, Inc.   Books from Five Centuries: a Miscellany - 131   2016 $4500

Smith, John *The Trade & Fishing of Great Britain Displayed' with a Description of the Islands of Orkney and Scotland (sic).* London: By William Godbid and are to be sold by Nathaniel Webb, 1661. First edition, small 4to., bit shorter aong fore-edge, very light worming to inner margin and single worm track to blank fore margin, mid 20th century blue half morocco, from the library of James Stevens Cox (1910-1997) with his pencil annotations.   Maggs Bros. Ltd. 1447 - 389   2016   £1500

Smith, Laurence Dwight *The G-Men in Jeopardy.* New York: Grosset & Dunlap, 1938. First edition, some light staining on front endpapers, otherwise fine in dust jacket with crease and small chip on front panel.   Mordida Books 2015 - 012667   2016 $65

Smith, Laurence Dwight *The G-Men Trap the Spy Ring.* New York: Grosset & Dunlap, 1939. First edition, fine in dust jacket.   Mordida Books   2015 - 012668   2016 $65

Smith, Malcolm *British Reptiles and Amphibia.* Penguin Books, 1949. First edition, 8vo., publisher's paper covere boards, 16 color plates by Paxton Chadwick, very good. Sotheran's   Piccadilly Notes - Summer 2015 - 277   2016 £35

Smith, Martin Cruz *Polar Star.* Franklin Center: Franklin Library, 1989. Limited first edition, signed by author, blue leather, lettered and decoratively stamped in gilt, all edges gilt, very fine, as new, extremely handsome.   Argonaut Book Shop   Literature 2015 - 4019   2016 $60

Smith, Meredith J. *Marsupials of Australia, Volume On: Possums, the Koala and Wombats.* Melbourne: Lansdowne Editions, 1980. Limited to 10 copies signed and numbered by author and artist, Folio, color plates by Rosemary Woodford Ganf, publisher's cloth covered boards with embossed brown calf inset, fine.   Andrew Isles Natural History Books   55 - 1792   2016 $450

Smith, Nora Archibald *Boys and Girls of Bookland.* Philadelphia: David McKay Co., 1923. First edition, 2nd issue, large quarto, eleven full page color plates by Jessie Willcox Smith, publisher's brown paper boards, front cover lettered in black and with color illustration in duplicate of color plate facing page 48 pasted on, spine lettered black, small tape repair to front pastedown, near ink signature to front free endpaper, otherwise near fine, original color pictorial dust jacket little chipped at extremiites.   David Brass Rare Books, Inc.   2015 - 02971   2016 $350

Smith, Patti *Just Kids.* New York: Ecco/Harper Collins, 2010. Uncorrected proof, signed by author, trace rubbing to spine lettering, still fine in wrappers, uncommon proof. Ken Lopez Bookseller   166 - 119   2016 $500

Smith, Patti *M Train.* New York: Alfred A. Knopf, 2015. First edition, as new in new dust jacket with 'signed first edition' sticker, signed by Smith on publisher's tipped-in leaf. Between the Covers Rare Books   208 - 78   2016 $60

Smith, Richard Henry *Twigs for Nests; or Notes on Nursery Nuture.* London: James Nisbet & Co., 1866. First edition, half title, frontispiece, illustrations, 4 pages ads, original green cloth, bevelled boards, blocked in gilt, all edges gilt, fine.   Jarndyce Antiquarian Books   CCXV - 414 2016 £145

Smith, Robert *A Compleat System of Opticks in four books...* Cambridge and London: printed for the author... by Stephen Austen and Robert Dodsley, 1738. First edition, 2 volumes, 4to., 83 folding engraved plates, directions to binder, 2 plates with short tears, 1 plate slightly worn, contemporary mottled calf, rebacked in plain calf, gilt spine titles, rubbed, old rebacking, corner showing wear, all raised bands worn, binder's stamp applied to both front flyleaves, "Stoakley, Cambridge", occasional stains, clean copy, very good.   Jeff Weber Rare Books   183 - 35   2016 $2850

Smith, Robert Angus *To Iceland in a yacht...* Edinburgh: privately printed by Edmonston & Douglas. May, 1873. Sole edition, great rarity, 8vo. original decorated dark green cloth, gilt, gilt vignette to upper cover, 5 lithographic plates, 6 autotype plates from photos, lacking one tissue guard, folding plans, slight wear to extremities, inner hinges strengthened, few pages with minimal markings to margins, else clean and very good, contemporary bookplate of Thomas Hutchinson of Morpeth.   Sotheran's   Travel and Exploration - 442   2016   £898

Smith, Shelley *Death Stalks a Lady.* London: G. G. Swan, 1945. Blue cloth gilt, some spotting of endpapers, otherwise very good, inscribed presentation copy from author with hand written, signed postcard from her, covers faded and spine sunned.   I. D. Edrich   Crime - 2016   £25

Smith, Sherry L. *Sagebrush Soldier - Private William Earl Smith's View of the Sioux War 1876.* Norman: University of Oklahoma Press, 1989. First edition, vintage photos, drawings, very fine, pictorial dust jacket, black cloth, very fine. Argonaut Book Shop   Native American 2015 - 7473   2016 $60

Smith, Stevie *Some are More Human than Others.* London: Gaberbocchus, 1958. First edition, square octavo, 73 line drawings with captions, free endpapers faintly tanned, very good in dust jacket little creased and nicked at edges.   Peter Ellis   112 - 368   2016   £75

Smith, Stewart *Retrievers and How to Break them for Sport and Field Trials.* Horace Cox, 1910. First edition, 12mo., original green cloth, gilt lettering to upper board ad spine, small mark to upper board, near fine.   Sotheran's Hunting, Shooting & Fishing - 97   2016   £50

Smith, Sydney *The Selected Writings.* London: Faber and Faber, 1957. First edition, octavo, small ownership inscription on front free endpaper, spine slightly bruised at head, free endpaper partially tanned and spotted, edges spotted, very good in very good dust jacket, slightly creased at edges.   Peter Ellis   112 - 24   2016   £55

Smith, Walter E. *Charles Dickens in the Original Cloth....* Los Angeles: Heritage Book Shop, 1982-1983. First edition, 2 volumes, 4to., half titles, illustrations, original green cloth, R. G. Taylor booklabels, very good in dust jackets. Jarndyce Antiquarian Booksellers   CCXVIII - 1516   2016 £80

Smith, William *Some Thoughts on Education: with Reasons for Erecting a College in this Province, and Fixing the Same at the City of New York, to which is added a Scheme for Employing Masters or Teachers in the mean Time...* New York: J. Parker, 1752. First edition, Final leaf D4 in very skillfull and almost undetectable facsimile, neat modern paper covered boards, Abraham Keteltas' copy signed and stamped.   Joseph J. Felcone, Inc.   Books from Five Centuries: a Miscellany - 132   2016 $3800

Smith, William Gardner *South Street.* New York: Farrar, Straus and Young, 1954. First edition, spine ends and corners lightly bumped, else near fine in very good dust jacket with short nicks to spine ends and small pen scribble on verso, signed by author on titlepage, scarce in this condition signed.   Between the Covers Rare Books   202 - 101 2016 $700

Smith, William Jay *Big and Little.* Honesdale: Wordsong, 1991. First edition, small quarto, near fine in dust jacket, inscribed and signed by author.   Second Life Books, Inc. 196 B - 616   2016 $75

Smith, William Jay *A Green Place: Modern Poems Compiled by....* New York: Delacorte Press, 1982. First edition, 8vo., nicked and little worn dust jacket, signed by author.   Second Life Books, Inc.   196 B - 622   2016 $45

Smith, William Jay *Ho for a Hat.* Boston: Little Brown, 1989. First paperback edition, 8vo., illustrations in color, signed by author, fine.   Second Life Books, Inc.   196 B - 624   2016 $45

Smith, William Jay *Poems.* New York: Banyan Press, 1947. First edition, one of 500 numbered copies, this copy signed by author, hand set in Weiss and Geramond faces printed on Enfield paper, fine, cloth backed printed boards. Second Life Books, Inc.   196 B - 627   2016 $125

Smith, William Jay *Collected Poems 1939-1989.* New York: Scribner's Sons, 1989. First edition, 8vo., fine in dust jacket, signed by author.   Second Life Books, Inc.   196 B - 618   2016 $50

Smith, William Jay *Poems 1947-1957.* Boston: Little Brown, 1957. First edition, signed, and inscribed by author for William Meredith, 24 Oct. 1959, with 1957 postcard to Meredith announcing a reading by Smith, slight dust spotting to top edge of text, near fine in like dust jacket.   Charles Agvent   William Meredith - 109   2016 $150

Smith, William Jay *The Streaks of the Tulip: Selected Criticism.* New York: Delacorte, 1961. First printing, 8vo., near fine in price clipped dust jacket, signed by author. Second Life Books, Inc.   196 B - 629   2016 $45

Smith, William Jay *The Streaks of the Tulip: Selected Criticism.* New York: Delacourt, 1972. First printing, 8vo., tan cloth with brown spine, author's signature on title, near fine in very slightly soiled dust jacket.   Second Life Books, Inc.   197 - 297   2016 $25

Smith, William Jay *The Traveler's Tree.* New York: Persea Books, 1980. First trade edition, 8vo., near fine in dust jacket, frontispiece and 2 sectional woodcuts, signed by author.   Second Life Books, Inc.   196 B - 630   2016 $45

Smith, William Jay *Up the Hill and Down.* Honesdale: Boyd's Mills Press, Wordsong, 2003. First edition, illustrations by Allan Eitzen, large 8vo., fine in dust jacket, signed by author.   Second Life Books, Inc.   196 B - 631   2016 $45

Smith, Willie Wesley *Out There was silence, too.* New York: Vantage Press, 1968. First edition, octavo, near fine in bright, lightly rubbed and soiled, near fine dust jacket.   Between the Covers Rare Books   202 - 114   2016 $450

Smithes, Marion F. *Children of the Desert...* Kensington (London): Curtis & Davidson, 1910. Very rare first edition, 8vo., original terracotta cloth backed illustrated boards, spine and front cover lettered in black, 8 plates, cover little marked, initially and at end little browned due to offsetting from endpapers, otherwise titlepage.   Sotheran's Travel and Exploration - 371   2016   £248

Smithies, Thomas Bywater *Illustrated Songs and Hymns for the Little Ones.* London: Partridge & Co., 1858. First edition, tall 8vo., color frontispiece, added engraved title and plates, illustrations, few spots, original dark blue cloth with some small discreet repairs, elaborately gilt blocked on front board, all edges gilt.   Jarndyce Antiquarian Booksellers   CCXVII - 262   2016   £150

Smollett, Tobias George   1721-1771 *The Adventures of Roderick Random.* London: printed for J. Osborn, 1750. Third edition, engraved frontispieces after Hayman, 12mo., fine, clean copy, full contemporary sprinkled calf, gilt ruled borders, cornerpiece decoration, raised and gilt banded spines, red and black morocco labels, gilt decoration to each compartment, from the library of Invercauld Castle, Braemar.   Jarndyce Antiquarian Booksellers   CCXVI - 534   2016   £350

Smollett, Tobias George   1721-1771 *The Regicide or James the First of Scotland.* London: printed for J. Osborn and A. Millar, 1749. 8vo., fairly recently rebound in half calf, marbled boards, crimson label.   Jarndyce Antiquarian Booksellers   CCXVI - 470   2016   £250

Smythe, F. S. *Kamet Conquered.* London: Victor Gollancz, 1932. First edition, 8vo., original back cloth, spine lettered gilt, 59 black and white photograph plates and full page maps, one folding, map at end, light wear to extremities, front inner hinge expertly strengthened, frontispiece and titles, little spotted, typewritten letter from author to Geoffrey Bartram to whom the book is inscribed.   Sotheran's   Travel and Exploration - 183   2016   £498

Smythe, Frank S. *Behold the Mountains: Climbing with a Color Camera.* New York: Chanticleer, 1949. First edition, 4to., color and back and white photos by author, light brown cloth with silver lettering on spine, front corners and spine ends very lightly bumped, else fine, in quite worn and tape repaired dust jacket.   Argonaut Book Shop Mountaineering 2015 - 713   2016 $45

Smythies, Bertram Evelyn *The Birds of Borneo.* Edinburgh: Oliver and Boyd, 1960. First edition, octavo, 50 color plates by a. M. Hughes, pholtos, fine in dust jacket, desirable in this condition.   Andrew Isles Natural History Books   55 - 17464   2016 $300

Smythies, Bertram Evelyn *The Birds of Burma.* Edinburgh: Oliver and Boyd, 1953. Second edition, octavo, 31 color plates by A. M. Hughes, folding map, some pale foxing, otherwise good, in chipped dust jacket.   Andrew Isles Natural History Books   55 - 26378   2016 $200

Snicket, Lemony *A Series of Unfortunate Events. Volumes 1-13 Plus Lemony Snicket: The Unauthorized Biography. (plus) The Baby in the Manger.* New York: Harper Trophy, 1999-2006. All first printings, all in original laminated paper boards, pictorial cover designs, paper spines in various colors, all in fine condition, volume 5 has rare dust jacket, 8 are signed and stamped Daniel Handler, last title limited to 65 numbered copies, super set.   Alephbet Books, Inc.   111 - 435   2016 $2850

Snodgrass, Melinda *The Edge of Reason.* New York: Tor Books, 2008. First edition, as new, signed and dated by author shortly after publication, dust jacket.   Gene W. Baade, Books on the West   2015 - 5022009   2016 $61

Snodgrass, W. D. *The Fuhrer Bunker: a Cycle of Poems...* Brockport: BOA editions, 1978. Second impression, 8vo., printed wrappers, fine, inscribed to poet William Claire, by author.   Second Life Books, Inc.   196 B - 635   2016 $75

Snow, David *Raymond Ching: the Bird Paintings.* London: Collins, 1978. Folio, color plates, fine in dust jacket and slipcase.   Andrew Isles Natural History Books   55 - 8961   2016 $450

Snyder, Gary *Life Out in the Rain: New Poems 1947-1985.* San Francisco: North Point Press, 1986. First edition, fine in dust jacket, signed by author.   Second Life Books, Inc.   196 B - 640   2016 $45

Snyder, Gary *The Mountain Spirit.* Hopewell: Pied Oxen printers, 2014. First edition, one of 50 numbered copies signed by poet and printer, from an edition of 60 copies, photo etchings after sumi-ink scroll paintings, original red cedar hand-scroll with black walnut end knobs, bound in Japanese book cloth and handmade washi, publisher's paulownia box by Mihagi-Kougei Co. Ltd. Tokyo, as new, design illustrations, letter press printing and binding all by Daivd Sellars.   James S. Jaffe Rare Books   Occasional List: Winter 2016 - 126   2016 $1500

Snyder, Robert *Anais Nin Observed: from a Film Portrait of a Woman as Artist.* Chicago: Swallow, 1976. First edition, large 8vo., bound in pictorial wrappers, laid in are two ad sheets for the book which has been inscribed by author, very good.   Second Life Books, Inc.   196 B - 641   2016 $50

Soames, Henry *An Inquiry into the Doctrines of the Anglo-Saxon Church in Eight Sermons.* Oxford: Samuel Collingwood, Printer to the University for C. J. G. and F. Rivington, 1830. First edition, 220 x 140mm, very decorative contemporary deep purple straight grain morocco, covers with frame of multiple gilt and blind fillets and featuring a dense gilt roll interlacing at medians, and broad-leaf ornaments, broad raised bands, spine compartments with interlaced lobed ribbons, cornerpieces and central massed tools, turn-ins gilt ruled, moire silk endleaves, all edges gilt with very pleasing fore-edge painting of Canterbury Cathedral, housed in unusually fine, heavily gilt pebble grain morocco clamshell box in convincing imitation of the present binding, armorial bookplate, morocco bookplate of Lucy Smith (Doheny) Battson, lower cover with uneven fading, spine darkened with consequent dulling of gilt, light wear to extremities and joints, otherwise excellent, once extremely pretty binding still appealing with glistening gilt on covers, text very bright, fresh and clean and fore-edge painting perfectly preserved.   Phillip J. Pirages   67 - 163   2016 $2400

Soane, Ely Banister *To Mesopotamia and Kurdistan in Disguise.* London: John Murray, 1926. Revised edition, 8vo., original brown cloth, lettered gilt to upper cover and spine, rarely seen dust jackets, 9 black and white plates from photos, one folding map, wrappers little dusted and with slight loss at head of spine.   Sotheran's   Travel and Exploration - 372   2016   £378

Soane, George *January Eve: a Tale of the Times.* London: E. Churton, 1848. New edition, frontispiece, engraved title, foxed, additional printed title, lacks half title, contemporary half maroon sheep, gilt spine, violet cloth boards, little rubbed, nice.   Jarndyce Antiquarian Booksellers   CCXVIII - 362   2016   £250

Social Etiquette the Art of Cookery and Hints on Carving. London: Houlston & Wright, 1860. Fourth thousand, original decorated blue cloth, little rubbed and dulled, but nice. Jarndyce Antiquarian Books   CCXV - 415   2016   £185

Societe Paritys et Les Tissus Lebotys *Collection Ete 1957.* Paris: Societe Paritys, 1957. Folio, printed in red on stiff stock paper, 16 color fashion drawings, tipped in fabric samples, publisher's color pictorial glazed boards, post binder, 3 brass posts, decorative screw tops, red cloth joints, some general extremity wear to binder with slightly bumped corners, occasional dust soiling, minor foxing, overall very good with cloth samples generally very good+ to near fine, occasional crease ot odd sample or two.   Tavistock Books   Getting Around - 33   2016 $2450

Societe Paritys et Les Tissus Lebotys *Collection ete 1959.* Paris: Societe Paritys/Leboyts, 1959. 16 1/2 x 12 inches, 16 color fashion drawings, 800 pasted and tipped-in fabric samples, post binder with 3 brass posts, publisher's pictorial glazed boards, white cloth joints, light extremity wear to boards, shot split to rear joint, page block lightly foxed, occasional foxing/fraying, overall very good. Tavistock Books   Getting Around - 36   2016 $2450

Societe Paritys et Les Tissus Lebotys *Collection Hiver 1957-1958.* Paris: Societe Paritys/Leboyts, 1957. 16 1/8 12 1/8 inches, 16 color fashion drawings, 740 pasted or tipped in fabric samples, post binder with 3 brass posts, decorative screw tops, publisher's color pictorial glazed boards, blue spine and joints, board edges rubbed and worn, short split to rear outer joint, inner joints tender, paper splitting through cloth, reinforcement beneath intact, page block foxed, occasional foxing/spotting throughout, light off-setting from fabric samples to some pages, fabric sample generally clean and bright, occasional creasing/fraying, overall good+.   Tavistock Books   Getting Around - 34   2016 $245

Societe Paritys et Les Tissus Lebotys *Collection Hiver 1958-59.* Paris: Societe Paritys/Leboyts, 1958. 16 1/8 x 12 1/8 inches, 16 color fashion drawings, 800 pasted and tipped-in fabric samples, post binder with 3 brass posts, publisher's pictorial glazed boards, white cloth joints, light extremity wear to boards, short split to rear joint, page block lightly foxed, occasional foxing/spotting to margins, few white nylon fabric samples discolored by paste beneath, fabric samples otherwise clean and bright, only minor occasional creasing/fraying, overall very good.   Tavistock Books Getting Around - 3t   2016 $2450

Societes De La Froix-Rogue *Troisieme Conference Internationale Des Societes De La Croix-Rogue. Tenue A Geneve Du Ier Au 6 Septembre 1884. Compte Renu.* Geneve: Au Siege Comite International de al Croix Rouge, 1885. First edition, 4to., original blue cloth binding with silver stamped lettering to spine and front board, accompanied by impressed silver and red Red Cross logo, housed in custom chemise and quarter leather slipcase with marbled paper boards, volume shows wear and evidence of damp-staining, rear hinge paper starting at bottom, about very good, chemise and slipcase fine, presentation copy inscribed by Clara Barton for Dr. Joseph Gardner March 15 1889.   Tavistock Books   Bibliolatry - 19   2016 $4250

Society for Growing Australian Plants *Australian Plants.* Sydney: Society for Growing Australian Plants, 1959-1966. Octavo, first 3 volumes, publisher's binders, very good set. Andrew Isles Natural History Books   55 - 38972   2016 $60

Society for Improving the Condition of the Labouring Classes *Industrial Schools at Aberdeen from the Labourers' Friend on Jan. 1849.* London: The Society..., 1849. Unopened, sewn as issued.   Jarndyce Antiquarian Books   CCXV - 953   2016   £120

Society for Promoting Christian Knowledge *Reading Books for Adults. Nos. 1-4.* London: SPCK, 1859. original purple cloth, faded, rubbed and slightly worn, signature of John Boxall, Eashing 1871.   Jarndyce Antiquarian Books CCXV - 954   2016   £35

Society for the Reformation on Principles *The Scholar Armed Against the Errors of Time or a Collection of Tracts on the Principles and Evidences of Christianity....* London: F. C. & J. Rivington, 1812. Third edition, 2 volumes, ads on leading f.e.p. volume I, uncut in original blue boards, brown paper spines slightly chipped paper labels, some rubbing but overall very good in original binding, from the library of Earl John Eldon, with his armorial roundal signature and inscription "The gift of the Earl of Shaftesbury".   Jarndyce Antiquarian Booksellers   CCXVII - 264   2016   £220

Society of Antiquaries of London *A Copy of the Royal Charter and Statutes of the Society of Antiquaries.* London: printed in the Year, 1759. First edition, 2nd issue, 8vo., original marbled wrappers, very good, rare.   John Drury Rare Books   2015 - 19324   2016 $437

Society of Arts *Report of the Committee of the Society of Arts &c. Together with Approved Communications and Evidence Upon the Same....* London: Society of Arts, 1819. First edition, 8vo., modern paper wrappers with paper cover and spine labels, old ink stamp of Mercantile Library of Philadelphia on a number of pages and all the plates, plates faintly waterstained.   Oak Knoll Books   310 - 208   2016 $1250

Society of Dilettanti *Specimens of Antient Sculpture, Aegyptian, Etruscan Greek and Roman.* Reprinted by the Society of Dilettantti T. Payne...and J. White and co., 1809. Payne and Foss, 1835, Large folio, 3 parts in 2 volumes, first volume bound in contemporary full calf, expertly rebacked in late 19th century in burgundy morocco gilt to match later binding of volume II, boards with gilt tooled border composed of a Tudor rose motif containing a second blind tooled border composed of a repeating scroll motif, three single gilt rules, inner rule with gilt foliate spandrels, gilt turn-ins, all edges marbled, marbled endpapers, second volume in late 19th century half burgundy morocco over burgundy pebble grained cloth, all edges gilt, marbled endpapers, bright, fresh set with no library markings other than those described below, centre of upper board of each volume gilt stamped with roundel lettered in gilt "Free Public Library Wigan" and legend "Winnard's Bequest", 75 stipple engraved plates, 3 engraved head and tailpieces, 58 stipple engraved plates, each interleaved with paper guard, 3 similarly engraved head and tailpieces.   Sotheran's Piccadilly Notes - Summer 2015 - 299   2016   £4400

Society of Friends *A Brief Account of the Proceedings of the Committee Appointed in the Year 1795....(with) a Brief Acount Baltimore printed, London reprinted.* Philadelphia: printed: London: reprinted, and sold by Phillips & Fardon, George Yard Lombard Street, 1806. Reprint of first edition, 12mo., disbound.   Jarndyce Antiquarian Booksellers CCXVI - 535   2016   £110

Society of Friends *Some Account of the conduct of the Religious Society of Friends Towards the Indian Tribes in the Settlement of the Colonies of East and West Jersey....* London: Edward Marsh, 1844. Frontispiece map, folding map, original cloth, recased with original spine laid down, slight foxing, maps clean, very good.   Dumont Maps and Books   134 - 47   2016 $350

Society of Friends *A Testimony of the Monthly Meeting of Friends at Pyrmont in Westphalia, Germany.* Philadelphia: printed, London: reprinted by James Phillips & Son, 1798. 18mo., disbound, very good.   Jarndyce Antiquarian Booksellers   CCXVI - 536   2016   £45

Society Small Talk; or What to Say and When to Say It. London: Frederick Warne & Co. circa, 1887. Eighth edition, half title, original mustard cloth, slightly dulled, very good. Jarndyce Antiquarian Books   CCXV - 20   2016   £55

Solis, Antonio De *The History of the Conquest of Mexico by the Spaniards.* London: H. Lintot, 1753. Third edition, 2 volumes, 8vo., frontispiece, 2 folding maps, 6 folding plates, contemporary full polished calf, handsome set.   J. & S. L. Bonham Antiquarian Booksellers   America 2016 - 8256   2016   £400

Sollers, Philippe *Francesca Woodman.* Zurich: Scalo, 1998. First edition, numerous black and white images, tight very near fine in very near fine dust jacket.   Jeff Hirsch Books   E-List 80 - 30   2016 $150

Solomon, Alan *New York: the Art Scene.* New York: Holt, Rinehart and Winston, 1967. First edition, near fine in strong, very good plus dust jacket, price clipped, jacket complete and clean, few minor splits at hinge folds, very attractive, photographs by Ugo Mulas.   Royal Books   51 - 12   2016 $1850

Solomon, Pearl Chester *Dickens and Melville in their Time.* New York: Columbia University Press, 1975. First edition, half title, original maroon cloth, lettered gilt, very good.   Jarndyce Antiquarian Booksellers   CCXVIII - 1452   2016   £35

Soltera, Maria *A Lady's Ride Across Spanish Honduras.* Edinburgh: William Blackwood, 1884. First edition, increasingly rare, 8vo., original green decorative cloth, 6 tinted lithographic plates after drawings by author, spine little rubbed, internally even light browning as usual, inoffensive shelfmark number on title verso, otherwise very good.   Sotheran's Travel and Exploration - 70   2016   £248

Somazzi, Mario *Index of Passages Cited in Bruce Karl Braswell a Commentary on the Fourth Pythian Ode of Pindar.* University press Fribourg, 1992. First edition, 8vo, white paperback, top edge slightly yellowed, top corner lightly bumped, still very good.   Unsworths Antiquarian Booksellers Ltd.   E04 - 99   2016   £45

Some British Ballads. London: Constable and Co., 1919. No,. 348 of 575 large paper copies signed by artist, 292 x 225mm., publisher's paper boards backed with vellum, upper cover and flat spine with titling and vignette in gilt, lower cover with gilt lion and leopard flanked by rose and thistle, top edge gilt, other edges untrimmed, titlepage vignette, black and white illustrations in text and 17 colored plates by Arthur Rackham, as called for, all tipped on and with letterpress guards, binding little soiled, corners rather bumped, light offsetting to free endpaper from binder's glue, otherwise fine, text and plates in especially fresh, clean, bright condition.   Phillip J. Pirages   67 - 297   2016 $950

Some Rules of the Game. Essays on Garden Design.... Carrollton: Press on Scroll Road, n.d. circa, 2004. Limited to 54 numbered copies, 4to., printed from handset Cloister Lightface type in two colors on dampened Twinrocker handmade paper, small green engraving, four page prospectus, green cloth, paper title label on spine, bound by Priscilla Spitler.   Oak Knoll Books   27 - 55   2016 $350

Some Who Do... and One who Doesn't. Exton, Devon: printed by the Whittington Press, Bishops Books, 1998. One of 150 numbered copies printed on Zerkall mouldmade paper, this unnumbered but listed 'out of series', titlepage printed in black and green, royal 8vo., original plain cream sewn card, untrimmed, dust jacket, fine.   Blackwell's Rare Books   B184 - 325   2016   £45

Sondheim, Stephen *Pacific Overtures.* New York: Dodd, Mead and Co., 1977. First edition, photographs and drawing by Al Hirschfield, fine in fine dust jackets, laid in is card signed by actor Mako, who played The Receiver.   Between the Covers Rare Books   208 - 84   2016 $200

The Song of Roland. Cambridge: Riverside Press for Houghton Mifflin & Co., 1906. No. 33 of 220 copies, 445 x 292mm., publisher's quarter vellum over paper boards patterned with rows of alternating fleurs-de-lys and rosettes, flat spine with ink titling, in (somewhat worn) folding chemise, printer's device on titlepage, large arch-topped vignette at beginning of text and roundel vignettes, all colored by hand, printed in red and black with shoulder notes printed in gold. Phillip J. Pirages   67 - 304   2016 $4500

The Song of Rolland. New York: Limited Editions Club, 1938. Limited to 1500 numbered copies, signed by artist, 8vo., vellum backed boards, spine lightly soiled, some of the gilt rubbed else near fine in slipcase (toned on edges and backstrip), half page illustrations and pictorial initials, all hand colored and illuminated by Valenti Angelo, laid in are 2 handwritten letters on Angelo's personal stationery concerning book.   Aleph-bet Books, Inc.   111 - 18   2016 $850

Sonmez, Nedim *Marbled Flowers.* Tubingen: Nedim Sonmez, 2005. Limited to 38 numbered copies signed and numbered, 4to., leather, 12 unique pieces all of which are tipped in and numbered on backing sheet.   Oak Knoll Books   310 - 198   2016 $585

Sonmez, Nedim *Under the Surface: with Ten Original Samples of Marbled Pictures of the Underwater World's Nature.* Izmir: Nedim Sonmez, 2009. Limited edition of 19 signed and numbered copies, containing 10 original tipped-in marbled pictures of sea creatures, oblong folio, leather, gilt lettering on cover and spine, 10 marbled paper samples, each signed by hand.   Oak Knoll Books   310 - 199   2016 $595

Sontag, Susan *Women.* New York: Random House, 1999. First edition, small folio, original printed boards dust jacket, signed by Annie Leibovitz and Sontag, uncommon thus, very fine in dust jacket with some light wear at extremities.   James S. Jaffe Rare Books   Occasional List: Winter 2016 - 114   2016 $850

Sophocles *Oedipus the King: the Greek...* New York: Limited Editions Club, 1955. First edition, one of 1500 copies printed by John. Enschede en zoen, Haarlem, signed by artist, small erasure mark on back cover, spine faded, else fine, original slipcase, wood engravings by Demetrios Galanis. Second Life Books, Inc. 196 B - 644 2016 $85

Sophocles *Oedipus the King: the Greek.* New York: Limited Editions Club, 1955. First edition, limited edition, #339 of 1500 copies signed by artist, Demetrius Galanis, 4to., bound in gilt stamped black cloth, pictorial upper cover stamped in gilt, brown and cream, pictorial endpapers, uncut, wood engravings by Galanis. Second Life Books, Inc. 196 B - 645 2016 $200

Sophocles *(Greek) Tragaediae Septem cum Commentariis etc.* Venice: Aldus Manutius, August, 1502. Editio princeps, 8vo., 196 leaves, 19th century vellum over pasteboard, gilt spine, early title lettered ink on lower edge, Aldus device on verso of final leaf, Greek type, Latin marginalia to Ajax and notes on front blank c. 1800 (slightly cropped), bookplate of Sir Charles James Stuart, 2nd Baronet, Herbert Thompson name inscribed on front flyleaf. Maggs Bros. Ltd. 1474 - 74 2016 £20,000

Sophocles *Tragoediae Septem.* Oxonii: Impensia M. Bliss et R. Bliss, 1809. 2 volumes, 12mo., sporadic very light foxing, contemporary dark green straight grain calf, gilt title to spine, all edges gilt, joints little creased, few tiny chips to edges, lower corners fraying but very good overall, to each front pastedown and armorial bookplate, inscription dated 1959. Unsworths Antiquarian Booksellers Ltd. 30 - 141 2016 £125

Sophocles *The Tragedies.* Cambridge: Cambridge University Press, 1957. fourth impression, Volume I - Volume II, 2 volumes, small 8vo., red cloth, gilt lettered to spine, edges dusted and slightly spotted, volume II red cloth, slightly darker and endcaps just starting to wear, volume I lacks dust jacket, dust jacket to volume I with 2 cm. closed tear to upper jacket, price clipped with price sticker adhered to front flap, bit grubby, still good, ex-libris sticker Barbara McBride, one or two pencil annotations. Unsworths Antiquarian Booksellers Ltd. E04 - 101 2016 £24

Sorrentino, Gilbert *Flawless Play Restored.* Los Angeles: Black Sparrow, 1974. First edition, one of 200 hardcover copies numbered and signed by poet, large 8vo., patterned paper over boards, cloth spine, fine in acrylic dust jacket. Second Life Books, Inc. 196 B - 647 2016 $40

Sorrentino, Gilbert *Selected Poems 1958-1980.* Santa Barbara: Black Sparrow, 1982. First edition, 8vo., one of 200 bound in cloth backed boards, signed by author, fine in original acetate dust jacket, little soiled. Second Life Books, Inc. 196 B - 649 2016 $45

Sorrentino, Gilbert *White Sail.* Santa Barbara: Black Sparrow, 1977. First edition, large 8vo., one of 200 hardcover copies, numbered and signed by poet, paper over boards, cloth spine, fine in slightly scuffed acrylic dust jacket. Second Life Books, Inc. 196 B - 648 2016 $95

Sortore, Abram *Biography and Early Life Sketch of the late Abram Sortore Including His Trip to California and Back. Alexandria Missouri March 25 1909.* Alexandria: n.p., 1909. First edition, 8vo., stapled paper wrappers, very scarce, only few copies known to exist, about fine, nick to edge of one leaf, minor shelfwear. Kaaterskill Books 21 - 91 2016 $500

Sothebys *Catalogue of an Extensive Collection of Children's Books etc. the Property of the Late F. R. Russell, Esq.* London: printed by Kitchen & Barratt, 1945. Frontispiece and plates, original green printed wrappers, very good. Jarndyce Antiquarian Books CCXV - 784 2016 £20

Sothebys *Catalogue of an Extraordinary Series of Leather Abacus, Horn-Books and Lectures of Remarkable Style and Workmanship of the 17th Century...* London: Dryden Press, 1901. Plates, original yellow printed wrappers, some foxing, repaired at spine. Jarndyce Antiquarian Books CCXV - 783 2016 £20

Soul Looks Back in Wonder. New York: Dial Books, 1993. First printing (1-10 code), cloth backed boards, as new in new dust jacket, striking color illustrations on every page, this copy has artist Tom Feelings bold signature laid-in on Dial Stationery. Aleph-bet Books, Inc. 111 - 172 2016 $100

Souljah, Sister *No Disrespect.* New York: Random House, 1994. first edition, 2nd printing, 8vo., author's presentation on flyleaf, paper over boards with cloth spine, nice in little soiled dust jacket. Second Life Books, Inc. 196 B - 651 2016 $40

Soulsby, Lucy H. M. *Stray Thoughts for Teachers.* Oxford & London: James Parker & Co., 1893. 1 pages ads original maroon cloth, unevenly faded, contemporary inscription. Jarndyce Antiquarian Books CCXV - 956 2016 £20

South, Richard *Catalogue of the Collection of Palaerctic Butterflies Formed by the Late John Henry Leech...* London: British Museum (Natural History), 1902. Quarto, uncolored frontispiece, 2 colored plates, publisher's cloth, neat library stamp on titlepages, otherwise fine, crisp copy. Andrew Isles Natural History Books 55 - 35883 2016 $450

Southard, Charles Zibeon *The Evolution of Trout and Trout Fishing in America.* New York: E. P. Dutton and Co., 1928. First edition, no. 84 of 100 deluxe copies signed by author, 4to., original burgundy morocco, spine lettered gilt with gilt centre tools, upper board with gilt block, frontispiece, 2 maps, 9 color plates, little rubbing to extremities, otherwise very good.   Sotheran's   Hunting, Shooting & Fishing - 146   2016   £1450

Southern, Terry *Lollipop (Candy).* Paris: Olympia Press, 1962. First edition thus, revised after 1958 edition suppressed, printed wrappers, very near fine, full page and effusive inscription by author to friend Nelson Lyon, TV producer and writer.   Between the Covers Rare Books   208 - 81   2016 $3500

Southey, Thomas *Chronological History of the West Indies.* London: Longman, Rees, Orme. Brown and Green, 1827. First edition, 8vo., 3 volumes, contemporary calf backed marbled boards, spines each with two gilt stamped lettering pieces and ornamentad in gilt, marbled endpapers and edges, some rubbing to extremities, else very good.   Sotheran's   Travel and Exploration - 71   2016   £1350

Southwick, Remington *The Rhode-Island Almanac for the Year of Our Lord 1801....* Newport: printed and sold by Oliver Farnsworth, 1800. First edition, 16mo. stitched, edgeworn, stitching loose, some soiling one leaf with horizontal tear, faint dampstain along bottom margin of rear leaves, few minor chips, still about very good.   Kaaterskill Books   21 - 115   2016 $250

A Souvenir of Niagara Falls with a Series of Views in Oil colors.... New York: Sage, Sons and Co., 1864. First edition, oblong 4to, 4 splendid full page and color lithographs, fine, original cloth, all edges gilt.   M & S Rare Books, Inc.   99 - 216   2016 $2000

The Sovereigns of England from William the Conquerer to Victoria. London: circa, 1860. Hand colored folding panorama.   Honey & Wax Booksellers   4 - 13   2016 $375

Sowerby, John Edward   1825-1870 *British Wild Flowers Described and Key to the Natural Order...* London: John Van Voorst, 1863. Second edition, octavo, frontispiece, 86 hand colored steel engraved plates, contemporary full gilt morocco, all edges gilt, marbled endpapers, two 19th century ownership inscriptions (one dated 1863), occasional spot, otherwise fine, crisp copy.   Andrew Isles Natural History Books   55 - 38864   2016 $1250

Sowerby, John Edward   1825-1870 *The Ferns of Great Britain. (with) The Fern Allies: a Supplement.* London: Henry G. Bohn, 1859. Octavo 80 hand colored plates, publisher's handsome blindstamped and decorated cloth, all edges gilt, few occasional spots and signature on front endpaper, fine.   Andrew Isles Natural History Books   55 - 15220   2016 $850

Sowers, Pauline *Joan the Maid of Orleans.* San Francisco: Vernon Sowers, 1938. First English translation, one of 525 copies, printed in red and black, 7 initials in blue, 9 initials in red, 22 woodcuts, handset Koch Bibel Gotisch type, blue boards with tan cloth spine, small decoration in gold and blue on front cover, tan spine label printed in red, spine and edges of front cover bit darkened, fine.   Argonaut Book Shop   Biography 2015 - 5791   2016 $150

Spalding, Albert Goodwill *Spalding's Base Ball Guide and Official League Book for 1885. A Complete Hand Book of the National Game of Base Ball.* New York: and Chicago: Pub. by A. G. Splading & Bros., 1885. first printing thus, for this year, illustrated with cuts, original printed pale orange paper wrappers, general wear and soiling to wrappers, some moest paper loss to spine ends, paper yellowing and becoming brittle, withal a solid very good copy.   Tavistock Books   Bibliolatry - 31   2016 $500

Spalding, Frances *Vanessa Bell.* London: Weidenfeld and Nicolson, 1983. First edition, fine in very near fine dust jacket.   Peter Ellis   112 - 36   2016   £35

Spangenberg, Evgeni Pavlovich *Iz Shizini Naturalista.* Moscow: Malodaia Gvardiia, 1953. First edition, 8vo., original cloth backed illustrated boards lettered gilt, spine decorated and lettered in white and gilt, color frontispiece, highly illustated after drawings by Komarov, beautiful copy.   Sotheran's   Travel and Exploration - 282   2016   £198

Spargo, John *The Jew and American Ideals.* New York: Harper, 1921. 8vo., author's presentation to Louis Marshall (one of the founders of the American Jewish Congress), maroon cloth, top edges soiled, cover little scuffed, otherwise very good, tight copy.   Second Life Books, Inc.   196 B - 654   2016 $65

Spargo, John *Karl Marx. His Life and work.* New York: Huebsch, 1910. First edition, 8vo., illustrations, tan cloth, author's presentation, hinges tender, cover little bumped and scuffed, otherwise very good.   Second Life Books, Inc.   196 B - 655   2016 $45

Spater, George *A Marriage of True Minds - an Intimate Portrait of Leonard and Virginia Woolf.* London: Jonathan Cape and the Hogarth Press, 1977. First edition, royal octavo, numerous photos, near fine in like dust jacket.   Peter Ellis   112 - 453   2016   £25

Spears, John R. *The Dangers and Sufferings of Robert Eastburn and His Deliverance from Indian Captivity.* Cleveland: Burrows Bros., 1904. Number 28 of 267 numbered copies, facsimile titlepage, maroon cloth, top edges gilt, very slight rubbing to spine extremities, fine.   Argonaut Book Shop   Native American 2015 - 5953   2016 $90

The Spectator: with Illustratives Notes... London: H. D. Symonds, et al, 1801. Reprint, 8vo., contemporary full marbled calf, spine gilt with black leather spine labels, thousands of pages, minor wear at spine ends, bookplate, well preserved set.   Oak Knoll Books   310 - 54   2016 $550

The Spectator. New York: printed for Limited Editions Club at Curwen Press, 1970. 379/1500 copies, signed by artist, 16 hand colored plates and several other drawings by Lynton Lamb, typographical design to head of some pages printed in brown, imperial 8vo., original patterned cloth, backstrip with maroon leather label lettered gilt, board slipcase with printed label, very good.   Blackwell's Rare Books   B184 - 282   2016   £50

Spedding, Thomas   *Duty and Affection to the King and Reverence and Respect to Magistrates Recommended.* Whitehaven: printed by J. Dunn at the Bible in the market Place, 1771. 4to., contemporary marbled paper wrappers, inscribed "The Gift of A. R. A. at head of titlepage.   Jarndyce Antiquarian Booksellers   CCXVI - 537   2016   £1771

A Speech, Delivered at a Meeting of the Freeholders & Others, of the County of Nottingham, Holden at Mansfield on the 4th of Jan. 1781. Newark: printed by James Tomlinson, n.d.?, 1781. 8vo., half title, preserved in modern wrappers with printed label on upper cover, very good, only edition?, apparently very rare.   John Drury Rare Books   2015 - 26100   2016 $437

Speed, Lancelot   *A Sojourn in the Highlands.* Penrith: David A. H. Grayling, 1996. Limited edition, 116 out of 400 copies, 4to., original red cloth, gilt stamped with antler design to upper cover, in translucent wrapper as issued, near fine, few slight marks of use to wrapper, unusual still having one at all.   Sotheran's   Hunting, Shooting & Fishing - 200   2016   £40

Speed, Samuel   *Prison-Pietie; or Meditations Divine and Moral.* London: by James Cottrel for Samuel Speed, 1677. First edition, 12mo., lacking engraved portrait of Speed, lightly browned throughout, few ink blots and some marginal staining, including a stain in lower corners towards end, marginal flaw in I6 damaging one letter on verso, early 19th century calf tooled in blind, rubbed, corners bumped, early ink underlining and occasional pointing hands or manicules throughout, pencil note Thorpes Cat. 7008 1825, from the library of James Stevens Cox (1910-1997).   Maggs Bros. Ltd.   1447 - 390   2016   £400

Speedy, Tom   *Natural History of Sport in Scotland with Rod and gun.* William Blackwood and sons, 1920. First edition, royal 8vo., original green cloth lettered in gilt on spine with gilt vignette on upper cover, frontispiece and numerous other illustrations by J. G. Millais, previous owner's label to front pastedown and signature, little bumped at extremities very good.   Sotheran's   Hunting, Shooting & Fishing - 201   2016   £150

Spence, Joseph   1699-1768   *Polymetis or an Enquiry Concerning the Agreement Between the Works of the Roman Poets and the Remains of the Antient Artists.* London: printed for R. & J. Dodsley, 1755. Second edition, frontispiece, 41 other engraved plates, some minor spotting, plates offset onto facing pages, folio, contemporary calf, neatly rebacked preserving original gilt spine, gilt now somewhat worn, new green morocco lettering piece to style, boards with elaborate stencilled frame dyed lighter brown, marbled endpapers, some tidy repairs to corners, rubbed, bookplates of Strathallan and Southouse, good.   Blackwell's Rare Books   B186 - 144   2016   £500

Spence, Thomas   *One Pennyworth of Pig's Meat or Lessons for the Winish Multitude.* London: printed for T. Spence, 1793. Part First Number 1-Part Second Number XXIV, frontispiece, titlepage dusted with two small holes possibly paper flaws, not affecting text, frontispiece dusted and browned, chipped at edges, final index, leaf browned, 2 volumes in 1 contemporary half calf expertly rebacked, gilt banded spine red morocco label, boards rather rubbed, corners neatly repaired, from the collection of Michael Foot.   Jarndyce Antiquarian Booksellers   CCXVI - 538   2016   £6800

Spence, William Blundell   *The Lions of Florence and Its Environs or the Stranger Conducted through its Principal Studios, Churches, Palaces and Galleries.* Florence: printed by Felix Le Monnier, 1847. Half title, vignette title, contemporary half black calf, marbled boards, spine gilt, red label, slight rubbing.   Jarndyce Antiquarian Booksellers   CCXVII - 266   2016   £150

Spencer, Baldwin   *Report on the Work of the Horn Expedition to Central Australia, Part Three: Geology and Botany.* London: Dulau and Co., 1896. Quarto, uncolored plates, publisher's printed wrappers, very fragile with missing pieces but all text present, scarce.   Andrew Isles Natural History Books   55 - 18220   2016 $400

Spencer, Baldwin   *Report on the Work of the Horn Expedition to Central Australia, part one: introduction, narrative, summary of results supplement to zoological report, map.* London: Dulau and Co., 1896. Small quarto, folding map, publisher's handsome blue cloth, all edges gilt, few occasional spots and signature on front endpaper, fine.   Andrew Isles Natural History Books   55 - 15220   2016 $850

Spencer, Colin   *The Tyranny of Love.* 1967. First edition, very nice in slightly frayed and soiled dust jacket, bookplate, presentation copy inscribed by author in 1972, signed by him.   Bertram Rota Ltd.   February List 2016 - 54   2016   £45

Spencer, Frank   *Piltdown: a Scientific Forgery.* London: Natural History Museum Publications, 1990. Octavo, text illustrations, signature, near fine in dust jacket.   Andrew Isles Natural History Books   55 - 24527   2016 $80

Spencer, Frank *The Piltdown Papers 1908-1955.* London: Natural History Museum Publications, 1990. Octavo, text illustrations, signature, fine in dust jacket. Andrew Isles Natural History Books 55 - 19719 2016 $80

Spencer, Herbert *Education Intellectual, Moral and Physical.* London: Williams & Norgate, 1861. Fifth thousand, 2 pages initial ads, half title, 16 page catalog, original brown cloth, slightly rubbed at head of spine, library numbers at foot of spine, booklabel of Library of Faculty of Physicians and Surgeons, Glasgow. Jarndyce Antiquarian Books CCXV - 957 2016 £75

Spencer, John *A Discourse Concerning Prodigies; Wherein the Vanity of Presages by them is Reprehended and Their True and Proper Ends Asserted and Vindicated.* London: by John Field for Will. Graves... in Cambridge, 1663. First edition, small 4to., titlepage little dusty and with the lower margin renewed, and lower edge of gathering 'M' folded at little shorter and uncut, late 19th century gilt ruled polished calf by Pratt, spine tooled in gilt and with red and green morocco label, edges gilt, Henry Huth and Alfred Henry Huth copy with leather label, from the library of James Stevens Cox (1910-1997), Sir R. Leicester Harmsworth, 1st Bart (1870-1937). Maggs Bros. Ltd. 1447 - 391 2016 £350

Spencer, O. M. *Indian Captivity: a True Narrative of the Capture of the Rev. O. M. Spencer by the Indians....* New York: Lane & Tippett, 1846. Later printing, 18mo., 4 woodcut plates, 3 woodcut text illustrations, original blindstamped brown cloth, spine worn with some varnish, two inch horizontal tear to one leaf, light damp stain to first ten leaves, very good. Argonaut Book Shop Native American 2015 - 5954 2016 $200

Spencer, Philip *Full Term.* London: Faber and Faber, 1961. First edition, crown 8vo., original red and black boards, backstrip lettered gilt, slight foxing to edges, ownership inscription ot flyleaf, dust jacket designed by Felix Kelly with owner's shelfmark, very good. Blackwell's Rare Books B184 - 212 2016 £30

Spencer, Reuben *To Young Men Going Out into Life.* Manchester: John Heywood, 1891. Original blue cloth, slight marking to spine, presentation inscription with author's compliments for Mr. Hagell, very good. Jarndyce Antiquarian Books CCXV - 416 2016 £58

Spencer, Sydney *Mountaineering.* London: Seeley Service & Co., 1934. First edition, original two-tone cloth, gilt lettered spine, small split and extremely light stain to upper front board, fine and clean, 130 illustrations, including 102 photographic plates, text figures, 9 folding maps. Argonaut Book Shop Mountaineering 2015 - 4459 2016 $90

Spender, Stephen *Cyril Connolly. A Memoir.* Edinburgh: privately printed at Tragara Press, 1978. 59/150 copies, (from an edition of 165 copies), frontispiece, crown 8vo., original quarter black cloth with pale green boards, backstrip with printed label, very good. Blackwell's Rare Books B186 - 346 2016 £40

Spender, Stephen *Engaged in Writing and The Fool and the Princess.* London: Hamish Hamilton, 1958. First edition, 8vo., original boards, fine in dust jacket with slightly faded spine, dedication copy inscribed by author for Hansi Lambert. James S. Jaffe Rare Books Occasional List: Winter 2016 - 130 2016 $1250

Spender, Stephen *Poems of Dedication.* New York: Random House, 1947. First American edition, 8vo., original cloth backed patterned boards, dust jacket, fine in lightly worn dust jacket, presentation inscribed by author to poet Theodore Roethke. James S. Jaffe Rare Books Occasional List: Winter 2016 - 129 2016 $750

Spender, Stephen *The Temple.* London: Faber and Faber Ltd., 1988. First edition, inscribed on titlepage for William Meredith, slight dust spotting to top edge, near fine in fine dust jacket. Charles Agvent William Meredith - 110 2016 $150

Spender, Stephen *W. H. Auden. A Tribute.* New York: Macmillan Pub. Co. Inc., 1975. First American edition, inscribed and signed by editor for William Meredith, fine in near fine dust jacket. Charles Agvent William Meredith - 109 2016 $150

Spene, Joseph *Anecdotes and Observations of Books and Men Collected from the Conversation of Mr. Pope and Other Eminent Persons of His Time.* London: John Russell Smith, 1858. Octavo, publisher's cloth contemporarily rebacked with matching cloth and spine affixed to rear pastedown, corners bumped and modest edgewear, else near fine, Rubaiyat translator Edward Fitzgerald's copy with his pencilled ownership signature, five lines of pencilled notes on rear blank. Between the Covers Rare Books 208 - 80 2016 $2000

Spenser, Edmund 1552-1599 *The Faerie Queen: the Shepheards Calendar: Together with the Other Works of England's Arch-Poet, Edm. Spenser...* London: printed for H L. for Matthew Lownes, 1611. First collected edition, five parts in one folio volumes, folio in sixes, general title within woodcut border, woodcut illustrations and ornamental borders, decorative woodcut head and tailpieces and initials, contemporary polished dark brown calf with central gilt stamped lozenges to front and rear covers, blind stamped letters (TN) to each side of lozenge, expertly rebacked to style, gilt spine lettering, few minor marginal tears, lower corner of D4 torn out (not affecting text), some occasional browning, bookplates of Viscount Birkenhead and Reginald Francis, some notations on front endpaper surrounded by old tape residue, some scuffing to corners, still very nice. Heritage Book Shop   Holiday 2015 - 102   2016 $7500

Spenser, Edmund 1552-1599 *The Faerie Queene.* Chelsea: Ashendene Press, 1923. One of 150 paper copies for sale, of a total of 180 (plus 12 copies printed on vellum), 438 x 311mm., original calf backed thick vellum boards, raised bands, gilt spine titling, untrimmed edges, calf backed clamshell box (quite worn and faded, printer's device in colophon, printed in red, black and blue, just hint of rubbing at spine ends, three corners lightly bumped, vellum with variations in color and grain (tending toward pale orange, with number of cloudy darker areas), otherwise very fine, wear to binding negligible, spine leather extremely bright and pristine internally.   Phillip J. Pirages   67 - 16   2016 $4500

Spenser, Edmund 1552-1599 *The Shepherd's Calendar Containing Twelve Aeglogues, Proportionable to the Twelve Months.* London: 1732. Copper engravings.   Honey & Wax Booksellers   4 - 34   2016 $950

Spenser, Edmund 1552-1599 *The Shepheardes Calendar.* Hammersmith: Kelmscott Press, 1896. One of 255 copies on paper and 6 on vellum, 241 x 171mm., publisher's linen backed blue paper boards, sturdy later cloth slipcase, printer's device in colophon, 12 full page line-block illustrations by A. J. Gaskin, printed in black and red, unsurpassable copy in close to original condition.   Phillip J. Pirages   67 - 224   2016 $7800

Spenser, Edmund 1552-1599 *The Shepheardes Calendar.* London: Cresset Press, 1930. Limited to 350 numbered copies on paper, in an edition of 353 copies, this copy not numbered but has "printer's file copy" written in place of a number, titlepage and 12 headpieces by John Nash, illustrations colored by stencils at Curwen Press, set in 16 pt. Lionotype Granjon Old Face, printed on Barcham Green handmade paper, 4to., half vellum, marbled paper covered boards, gilt title on spine, spine darkened, corners slightly bumped, some shelf wear, nevertheless very good, Robert Elwell's copy with his bookplate, inscribed "With the compliments and high regard of the printer".   Oak Knoll Books   27 - 4   2016 $500

Spenser, Edmund 1552-1599 *The Shepheardes Calendar.* London: Cresset Press, 1930. Limited to 350 numbered copies on paper in an edition of 353 copies, titlepage and 12 headpieces by John Nash illustrations colored by stencils at the Curwen Press, set in 16 pt. Linotype Granjon Old Face, designed by George Jones, printed on Barcham Green handmade paper, 4to., quarter vellum with cream colored raw silk covered boards, title gilt on spine, top edge gilt, slipcase, slight bump to top corner, minor wear to edges, else very good.   Oak Knoll Books 27 - 5 2016 $650

Spenser, Edmund 1552-1599 *The Shepheardes Calendar...* London: Cresset Press, 1930. No. 264 of 350 copies on paper and 3 on vellum, 335 x 205mm., original vellum backed cream colored silk covers, flat spine gilt lettered, top edge gilt, others untrimmed, original ivory printed dust jacket (later enhanced neatly with color), additional title and 12 illustrations (headpieces) by John Nash, colored by stencil process (titlepage and headpiece for January with colors enlived by previous owner), front panel of dust jacket missing 3/8" portion halfway across top and with significant adjacent closed tear, minor soiling, other trivial imperfections, but without restoration and otherwise excellent, volume itself in very fine condition inside and out.   Phillip J. Pirages   67 - 103   2016 $750

Spenser, Edmund 1552-1599 *Spenser's Minor Poems...* Chelsea: Ashendene Press, 1925. One of 200 copies on paper, 175 of them for sale (and 15 copies on vellum, 12 of them for sale), 438 x 305mm., original calf backed thick vellum boards, raised bands, gilt spine titling, edges untrimmed in green slipcase (slightly worn), printer's device in blue in colophon, printed in red black and blue, numerous large and small roman style initials, spine lightly sunned, joints somewhat rubbed and flaked (front joint with thin crack at head, chip to head of rear joint, but binding entirely solid and unsoiled, fine, internally very clean, fresh and bright.   Phillip J. Pirages   67 - 17   2016 $3500

Spenser, Edmund 1552-1599 *The Works of that Famous English Poet Mr. Edmond Spenser.* London: by Henry Hills for Jonathan Edwin, 1679. Folio, engraved frontispiece, some rust spotting in places, otherwise fresh copy, contemporary mottled calf, marbled edges, surface of leather crazed by mottling acid, joints split at top and bottom, front cover wobbly, lower corners chewed, upper headcap and spine label missing, one front flyleaf coming loose, from the library of James Stevens Cox (1910-1997).   Maggs Bros. Ltd.   1447 - 392   2016   £300

Spenser, Edmund 1552-1599 *The Works.* Oxford: Shakespeare Head press, 1930-1932. No. 7 of 375 copies on paper (350 for sale, along with 11 copies on vellum), 292 x 203mm., 8 volumes, publisher's Cockerell marbled paper boards backed with green Hermitage calf, flat spine, vellum tipped corners, five of volumes entirely unopened, with hand colored wood engravings by Hilda Quick in text, headings and initials by Joscelyne Gaskin, cut in wood, spines slightly darkened and little stuffed on couple of volumes, paper boards bit chafed, other trivial imperfections, but bindings all very sturdy and without serious defects, and text in outstanding condition, mostly unopened with signs of use internally. Phillip J. Pirages 67 - 318 2016 $1500

Sperry, Lyman B. *Confidential Talks with Young Women.* Edinburgh and London: Oliphant Anderson & Ferrier, 1894. first English edition, half title, illustrations, 22 page catalog, labels removed from endpapers causing slight tear to leading f.e.p., original green decorated cloth, slightly rubbed, very good. Jarndyce Antiquarian Books CCXV - 417 2016 £45

Sperry, Lyman B. *Confidential Talks with Young Women.* Edinburgh & London: Oliphants, 1897. Ninth thousand, half title, illustrations, 6 pages ads, original olive green cloth, rubbed. Jarndyce Antiquarian Books CCXV - 418 2016 £25

Spewack, Sam *My 3 Angels.* New York: Random House, 1953. First printing, 8vo., illustrations, signed by author, very good in somewhat soiled and slightly torn dust jacket. Second Life Books, Inc. 45 - 662 2016 $50

Speyer, Leonora *Slow Wall: Poems New and Selected.* New York: Knopf, 1939. First edition, 8vo., author's presentation, cover slightly soiled and worn at ends of spine, otherwise very good. Second Life Books, Inc. 196 B - 663 2016 $65

Spicer, Jack *After Lorca.* San Francisco: White Rabbit Press, 1957. First edition, one of 26 lettered copies signed by Spicer with drawing by the poet, out of a total edition of 500 typed on Olivetti Lexikon 80 by Robert Duncan and multilithed by Joe Dunn, cover design by Jess, although not noted, this came from the library of poet Jack Gilbert, covers slightly soiled, otherwise very good, rare, 8vo. original wrappers. James S. Jaffe Rare Books Occasional List: Winter 2016 - 131 2016 $5000

Spielmann, M. H. *The Iconography of Andreas Vesalius...* London: John Bale Sons & Danielson Ltd., 1925. Titlepage printed from original woodblock, 68 plates, 4to., original blue cloth, nice. James Tait Goodrich X-78 - 532 2016 $695

Spielmann, M. H. *Kate Greenaway.* London: A. & C. Black, 1908. Limited to 500 numbered copies signed by John Greenaway (Kate's brother), large thick 4to, white cloth, top edge gilt, fine, original pencil sketch done by Greenaway which is matted and bound in with John Greenaway's signature of authenticity (background of sketch foxed), 50 color plates plus many black and whites. Aleph-bet Books, Inc. 111 - 206 2016 $2250

Spielmann, Percy Edwin *Catalouge of the Library of Miniature Books Collected by....* London: Edward Arnold, 1961. Limited to 500 numbered copies, scarce, 8vo., cloth backed patterned paper covered boards, dust jacket. Oak Knoll Books 310 - 213 2016 $325

Spier, Peter *The Book of Jonah.* New York: Doubleday and Co., 1985. Stated first edition, this copy inscribed by Spier and dated 1935, pictorial cloth, fine in dust jacket (very good+ with small closed tear). Aleph-bet Books, Inc. 111 - 436 2016 $125

Spillane, John D. *The Doctrine of Nerves.* Oxford: Oxford University Press, 1981. 4to., original binding, dust jacket worn, some writing on rear paste board. James Tait Goodrich X-78 - 510 2016 $135

Spingarn, J. E. *Poems.* New York: Harcourt Brace & Co., 1924. First edition, 12mo., original cloth backed boards, printed pictorial label, July 1924 presentation from author. M & S Rare Books, Inc. 99 - 295 2016 $225

Spink, Alfred H. *One Thousand Sport Stories.* Chicago: The Spink Stories Co., 1921. First edition, 3 volumes, red cloth gilt, binding error has left one page corner a bit oversized light soiling to boards, otherwise fine, tight set, scarce complete. Between the Covers Rare Books 208 - 142 2016 $1500

Spinola, George *Rules to Get Children by with Handsome Faces...* London: for R. H., 1642. First edition, small 4to., lightly browned, early 20th century half morocco by Riviere, from the library of James Stevens Cox (1910-1997). Maggs Bros. Ltd. 1447 - 393 2016 £1250

Spock, Benjamin *Spock on Spock.* Franklin Center: Franklin Library, 1989. Limited first edition, signed by Spock and co-author Mary Morgan, dark blue leather, lettered and decoratively stamped in gilt, all edges gilt, very fine, as new, extremely handsome. Argonaut Book Shop Literature 2015 - 4024 2016 $50

Spon, Isaac *The History of the City and State of Geneva; from Its First Foundation to the Present Time.* London: Bernard White, 1687. First edition, folio, 5 plates, contemporary brown full polished calf, joints cracked, corners rubbed, internally clean and crisp. J. & S. L. Bonham Antiquarian Booksellers Europe 2016 - 8716 2016 £650

Spooner, Lysander *National Law or the Science of Justice a Treatise on Natural Law, Natural Justice, Natural Rights, Natural Liberty and Natural Society...* Boston: A. Williams, May, 1882. Second edition, 8vo., old staples, title leaf loose.   M & S Rare Books, Inc.   99 - 297   2016 $300

Spor, Cajus Rudolf Von *Dissertatio Inauguralis Juris Publici et Feudalis de Natura Vasallagii et Sjbjectionis in Territoris S. R. Imperii....* Frankfurt: Philippi Schwartzii, 1739. Title vignette, head and tailpieces, modern marbled wrappers, rare, near fine.   Jeff Weber Rare Books   181 - 35   2016 $75

A Sporting Garland. London: Sands, n.d. circa, 1900. Oblong folio, cloth backed pictorial boards, covers lightly rubbed and tips worn, else fine, pictorial half title for each of the 3 sections and many bold full page illustrations by Cecil Alden, printed on heavy coated paper, stunning book.   Aleph-bet Books, Inc.   111 - 16   2016 $1750

Sprat, Thomas   1635-1713 *The History of the Royal-Society of London for the Improving of natural Knowledge.* London: by T. R. for J. Martyn and J. Allestry, 1667. First edition, small 4to., engraved plate of the arms of the Royal Society, 2 folding plates (slightly shaved) and page 233 with very short tear, but without etched frontispiece by Hollar (often missing), contemporary calf, rebacked, new endleaves, corners repaired, from the library of James Stevens Cox (1910-1997), early 19th century signature of Edw. Williams and John Johnstone, early ink ciphers CR, similar to that of Charles II.   Maggs Bros. Ltd.   1447 - 394   2016   £400

Spratt, G. *Obstetric Tables Comprising Graphic Illustrations with Descriptions and Practical Remarks...* Philadelphia: James A. Bill, 1850. First American edition, small folio, 21 lithographed plates, most hand colored with moveable flaps, contemporary blindstamped leather, sheets and plates loose.   M & S Rare Books, Inc.   99 - 300   2016 $650

Sprigg, William *A Modest Plea, for an Equal Common-Wealth Against Monarchy.* London: for Giles Calvert, 1659. One of two editions, 8vo., blank upper corner of A1-E1 and I8-K4 intermittently dampstained, some occasional light soiling and few light ink drops to gatherings A and B, contemporary sheep, recently rebacked and recornered, new endpapers, from the library of James Stevens Cox (1910-1997), 17th century signatures of Robert Pearce, signature of Sir Frederick Rogers (1716-1777) 4th Baronet of Wisdome in Devon.   Maggs Bros. Ltd.   1447 - 395   2016   £950

Sprigge, Joshua *Anglia Rediviva; Englands Recovery...* London: by R. W. for John Partridge, 1647. First edition, small folio, frontispiece, errata leaf, folding engraved portraits (soiled, backed with later paper), large folding engraved view backed (with later paper and slight damage in folds, few ink blots), folding letterpress table, rather grubby throughout with occasional spots and stains E4v and F1r particularly soiled, contemporary calf, rebacked, 19th century marbled pastedowns, from the library of James Stevens Cox (1910-1997), armorial bookplate of Charles James, 1st Baron Northbourne.   Maggs Bros. Ltd.   1447 - 396   2016   £350

Sprigge, S. Squire *The Methods of Publishing.* London: 1890. Original black buckram, lettered gilt, bookplate sof J. Johnston Abraham and Gavin D. R. Bridson.   Jarndyce Antiquarian Booksellers   CCXVII - 240   2016   £65

Spring, Gardiner *The Doctrine of Election Illustrated and Established in a Sermon Preached on the Evening of the Second Lord's Day in December 1816.* New York: Finch 70 Bowery, 1826. 8vo., removed, quite foxed.   M & S Rare Books, Inc.   99 - 262   2016 $75

Spring, Gardiner *Memoirs of the Rev. Samuel J. Mills, Late Missionary to the South Western Section of the United States and Agent of the American Colonization Society...* New York: New York Evangelical Missionary Society, 1820. First edition, tall octavo, American binding of contemporary mottled sheep with red morocco gilt spine labels and ruled in gilt, early bookplate of Nancy North, Boonville NY, tiny hole on spine, small split at bottom of front joint and little peel along edges of boards, still very good or better.   Between the Covers Rare Books   202 - 100   2016 $400

Spruce, Richard *Notes of a Botanist on the Amazon & Andes.* London: Macmillan, 1908. First edition, 2 volumes, neat bookplate of Harald Hauge, endpapers little foxed, otherwise sound, slight fraying and slight chipping (with no loss) at spine ends and faint signs of shelfwear, decent, about very good set.   Any Amount of Books   2015 - C14253   2016   £650

Spurr, Josiah Edward *Geology of the Aspen Mining District, Colorado with Atlas to accompany Monograph XXXI on the Geology of Aspen Mining District, Colorado.* Washington: GPO, 1898. 2 volumes, 4to. and folio atlas, 43 plates, 10 figures, original maroon gilt stamped cloth, spine ends chipped, rear joint worn, rubbed, inner joints strengthened, good, the atlas, 32 maps in color or tinted, original full green gilt stamped cloth, extremities bit worn, front endleaf crease and torn, very good.   Jeff Weber Rare Books   181 - 8   2016 $1800

Spurzheim, Johann Gaspar   1776-1832 *A View of the Elementary Principles of Education, Founded on the Study of the Nature of Man.* London: Treuttel Wurtz and Richter, 1828. Second edition, half calf, rubbed.   Jarndyce Antiquarian Books   CCXV - 960   2016   £85

Spyri, Johanna *Heidi.* Philadelphia: McKay, 1922. Large 8vo., 10 color illustrations by Jessie Willcox Smith, blue cloth with large pictorial label, covr spotted on spine, little worn at corners and ends of spine, otherwise very good, tight, 10 color illustrations by Jessie Willcox Smith. Second Life Books, Inc. 197 - 190 2016 $50

Spyri, Johanna *Heidi.* Philadelphia: David McKay Co., 1922. First edition illustrated thus, first issue, quarto, color pictorial titlepage, 10 full page color plates and 23 full page plates in text printed in red and black, publisher's blue cloth, front cover with pasted-on illustration, spine lettered in gilt, top edge gilt, color pictorial endpapers, with original color pictorial dust jacket, jacket with quarter inch chips at top of spine, 3/4 inch chip at foot and some additional chipping on edges, near fine, good dust jacket. David Brass Rare Books, Inc. 2015 - 02975 2016 $450

Squier, Ephraim George 1821-1888 *Ancient Monuments of the Mississippi Valley...* New York: Richard O. Jenkins for the Smithsonian Institution in Washington, 1847. First edition forming the entire first volume of The Smithsonian Contributions to Knowledge, large 4to., original cloth, spine lettered gilt, covers blindstamped ruled, 207 fine wood engravings in text, 2 plates of tinted lithographic views (one bound as frontispiece) and 46 lithographic plates, cloth and gilt faded, rear hinge weakened, corners little worn, few prelims with short tears to gutters, page 90 with small paper flaw to gutter, occasionally light spotting, presentation by the Smithsonian to Royal Institution with lithographed letter form printed on blue paper, signatures of Smithsonian secretary Joseph Henry and his assistant secretary tipped onto front flyleaf, lower outer corner of series title with Royal Institution stamp. Sotheran's Travel and Exploration - 72 2016 £698

St. John, Charles William George *Charles St. John's Note Books 1846-1853.* Edinburgh: David Douglas, 1901. First edition, 8vo., original green cloth, gilt shield to upper board, gilt lettering to spine, top edge gilt, frontispiece, 8 plates and text illustrations, previous owner's signature, very good. Sotheran's Hunting, Shooting & Fishing - 206 2016 £50

St. John, Charles William George *Natural History & Sport in Moray.* Edinburgh: David Douglas, 1882. First Illustrated edition, 8vo., sometime rebound in half blue calf over blue cloth, borders decorated in blind with floral motif, gilt spine divided in to six compartments with raised bands, 40 plates, numerous text illustrations, sunning to spine, little rubbing to extremities, otherwise very good. Sotheran's Hunting, Shooting & Fishing - 204 2016 £250

St. John, Charles William George *Short Sketches of the Wild Sports & Natural History of Highlands.* London: John Murray, 1878. Illustrated edition, 8vo., original green cloth, gilt border and vignette of wild cat to upper board, gilt lettering to spine, text illustrations, previous owner's inscription, little foxing to prelims, otherwise very fresh, very good. Sotheran's Hunting, Shooting & Fishing - 203 2016 £150

St. John, Charles William George *A Tour In Sutherlandshire with Extracts from the Field-books of a Sportsman and Naturalist.* London: John Murray, 1849. First edition, 8vo., 2 volumes, original green cloth, gilt vignette of hooded hawk to upper boards, gilt lettering to spine, illustrations, volume I rebacked with original spine laid down, bindings rubbed, previous owner's signature, tape marks to endpapers, internally very good. Sotheran's Hunting, Shooting & Fishing - 205 2016 £100

St. John, Charles William George *Wild Sports & Natural History of the Highlands.* Edinburgh: T. N. Foulis, 1919. First edition thus, 4to., original tan cloth, lettering and design of stag in black to upper board, spine lettered gilt, color plates, black and white illustrations, previous owner's inscription, spine dulled, endpapers browned, internally very clean. Sotheran's Hunting, Shooting & Fishing - 207 2016 £90

St. John, David *Hush.* Boston: Houghton Mifflin, 1976. First edition, signed and inscribed in 1983 for William Meredith, fine in near fine dust jacket with tanned spine. Charles Agvent William Meredith - 111 2016 $60

St. John, John *The Island of St. Marguerite.* London: printed for J. Debrett, 1790. Second edition, half title, 8vo., odd spot, brown boards, brown leather label. Jarndyce Antiquarian Booksellers CCXVI - 471 2016 £40

St. John, Percy B. *The Trapper's Bride: a tale of the Rocky Mountains. With the Rose of Ouisconsin Indian Tribes.* London: 1845. First edition in English, cloth, lacks series title preceding titlepage, else very nice, tight copy. Joseph J. Felcone, Inc. Books from Five Centuries: a Miscellany - 133 2016 $600

St. John, Primus *Looking at a Bus Stop.* Washington: Folger Poetry Series, 1971. First edition, one of 100 copies, printed in letterpress on Rives buff lightweight paper, signed by poet, Press announcemet laid in, fine in dust jacket. Second Life Books, Inc. 196 B - 669 2016 $75

Stace, Machell *An Alphabetical Catalogue of an Extensive Collection of the Writings of Daniel Defoe....* London: printed for Whitmore and Penn, Homer's Head, Charing Cross, 1829. First edition, 8vo., first and last leaves little dust soiled, otherwise clean throughout, stitched as issued, long inscription by William Hazlitt 1811-1893) to Mr. Burn. Marlborough Rare Books List 56 - 16 2016 £225

Stacy, Edmund *The Country Gentleman's Vade Mecum; or His Companion for the Town.* London: for John Harris, 1699. First edition, 8vo., lacking contents leaves (a1-4) which were never bound in, some occasional spotting, small blank piece torn away from corner of D6 and H2, minor rust hole in C3 and H3v lightly stained, contemporary sprinkled sheep, covers panelled in blind, joints split at foot, lower headcap chewed by insects, front pastedown and flyleaf ink spotted, from the library of James Stevens Cox (1910-1997), early signature of Tho(mas) Elton.   Maggs Bros. Ltd. 1447 - 397   2016   £200

Staffe, Blanche Augustine, Baroness *The Lady's Dressing-Room.* London: Cassell & Co., 1893. 22 pages initial ads, half title, final ad leaf, ads on endpapers, original green decorated cloth, very good, attractive copy.   Jarndyce Antiquarian Books   CCXV - 419   2016   £58

Stafford, William *Allegiances.* New York: Harper & Row, 1970. First edition, 8vo., on title, author's presentation to William Claire, paper over boards, top edges little spotted, edges of cover slightly scuffed, otherwise very good, tight in scuffed and very slightly chipped dust jacket.   Second Life Books, Inc.   196 B - 671   2016 $300

Stafford, William *Smoke's Way: Poems from Limited Editions 1968-1981.* Port Townsend: Graywolf Press, 1983. Copy P of 26 lettered copies, very fine in like dust jacket, signed by author.   Jeff Hirsch Books   Holiday List 2015 - 61   2016 $200

Stafford, William *Smoke's Way: Poems from Limited editions 1968-1981.* Port Townsend: Graywolf Press, 1983. First printing, small 8vo., author's signature and copy letter on title, grey paper over boards with blue cloth spine, as new in dust jacket.   Second Life Books, Inc.   196 B - 672   2016 $150

Stafford, William *Someday, Maybe.* New York: Harper Row, 1973. First printing, 8vo., inscribed by author for William Claire, very good, tight clean copy in dust jacket.   Second Life Books, Inc.   196 B - 673   2016 $175

Stafford, William *Traveling through the Dark.* New York: Harper & Row, 1962. First edition, author's presentation to William Claire, paper over boards, fine in dust jacket, 8vo.   Second Life Books, Inc.   196 B - 674   2016 $275

Stagg, Alonzo *A Scientific and Practical Treatise on American Football for Schools and Colleges.* Hartford: Press of the Case, Lockwood & Brainand Company, 1893. First edition, 12mo., diagrams, blue cloth, gilt, , bit of light spotting on front board, else near fine in original unprinted paper dust jacket, with piece cut away on spine in order to reveal the title, else nice, very good or better example, scarce.   Between the Covers Rare Books   204 - 48   2016 $2400

Stahl, E. L. *Holderlin's Symbolism: an Essays.* Oxford: B. H. Blackwell, 1994. First edition, 8vo., original printed wrappers little toned, very good, clean, this is poet Barbara Howes' copy with her bookplate and signature.   Second Life Books, Inc.   196 B - 675   2016 $75

Stahl, P. J. *La Journee De Mademoiselle Lili.* Paris: Bibliotheque D'Education et de la recreation, ads dated, 1864. First edition, Cloth backed pictorial boards, minor soil and rubbing, very good+, tight and clean, printed on one side of paper, every page has lovely engraving by L. Froelich.   Aleph-bet Books, Inc.   112 - 206   2016 $150

Stall, Sylvanus *Purity and Truth.* Philadelphia: the Vir Pub. Co., 1897. First edition, original maroon cloth, slightly rubbed, very good.   Jarndyce Antiquarian Books   CCXV - 420   2016   £48

Stan Rogers Songs from Fogarty's Cove. Canada: OFC publications, 1982. First edition, spiral bound, black and white rproductions of photos, good.   Simon Finch   2015 - 812G3468   2016 $250

Stanbury, Peter *Australia's Animals: Who Discovered Them?* Sydney: Macleay Museum, 1978. Octavo, photos, illustrations, signature, softcover.   Andrew Isles Natural History Books   55 - 14638   2016 $30

Standfast, Richard *Clero-Lacium Condimentum.* Bristol: for Thomas Thomas, 1644. First edition, small 4to., titlepage soiled with prominent crease to inner margin, par 24 and A1v with dark stain along upper margin, corner of B1 dampstained and spotting to lower margins between B2 and C2, final leaf browned on recto, early 20th century cloth backed boards, soiled, from the library of James Stevens Cox (1910-1997).   Maggs Bros. Ltd.   1447 - 398   2016   £300

Standish, Craig Peter *Henry Miller: a book of tributes 1931-1994.* Orland: 1994. First edition, 8vo., presentation card and color portrait of Miller laid in, spine slightly bumped, otherwise nice, one of 100 numbered copies signed by editor.   Second Life Books, Inc.   196 B - 676   2016 $125

Standley, Samuel *An Essay on the Manufacture of Straw Bonnets...* Providence: Barnum Field & Co., 1825. First edition, 18mo., original printed paper covered boards, untrimmed, light overall foxing common to early American paper, light dampstain on front cover, upper hinge split and held by one cord, lovely copy, fragile, original printed boards, inscribed "Please accept this with Lousia E. Northup's repsects Providence Jan. 12 1828".   Joseph J. Felcone, Inc. Books from Five Centuries: a Miscellany - 135   2016 $800

Stanford, Ann *The Descent.* New York: Viking, 1970. First edition, author's presentation to poet William Claire, front edges slightly spotted, otherwise very good, tight copy in scuffed and slightly chipped dust jacket.   Second Life Books, Inc.   196 B - 679   2016 $50

Stanford, Ann *The Weathercock.* New York: Viking, 1966. First edition, author's presentation to poet and editor William Claire, paper over boards with cloth spine, spine somewhat stained, otherwise very good, tight copy in browned, slightly soiled and little chipped dust jacket. Second Life Books, Inc.   196 B - 680   2016 $45

Stanford, Derek *Christopher Fry Album.* London: Nevill, 1952. First edition, large 8vo., signed by Fry, top and bottom of spine little scuffed, otherwise nice, little chipped dust jacket.   Second Life Books, Inc.   196 B - 5691   2016 $50

Stanford, J. K. *And Some in Horses.* London: Faber & Faber, 1965. First edition, 8vo., original brown cloth, dust jacket, ownership inscription, very good.   Sotheran's Hunting, Shooting & Fishing - 227   2016   £25

Stanford, J. K. *A Bewilderment of Birds.* London: Rupert Hart-Davis, 1954. First edition, 8vo., original red cloth, dust jacket little worn, otherwise very good.   Sotheran's Hunting, Shooting & Fishing - 217   2016   £45

Stanford, J. K. *Bledgrave Hall.* London: Faber & Faber, 1950. First edition, 8vo., original green cloth, dust jacket printed in red and black, dust jacket used, otherwise good, internally clean and unfoxed.   Sotheran's Hunting, Shooting & Fishing - 212   2016   £40

Stanford, J. K. *British Friesians - a History of the Breed.* London: Max Parrish, 1956. First edition, 8vo., publisher's green cloth, dust jacket, signed by author, slightly used copy, but sound.   Sotheran's Hunting, Shooting & Fishing - 218   2016   £30

Stanford, J. K. *Death of a Vulpicide.* London: Faber & Faber, 1960. First edition, 8vo., original red cloth, no dust jacket.   Sotheran's Hunting, Shooting & Fishing - 222 2016   £25

Stanford, J. K. *Far Ridges.* London: C. J. & Temple Ltd. c., 1944. First edition, original blue cloth, no dust jacket. Sotheran's Hunting, Shooting & Fishing - 209   2016   £50

Stanford, J. K. *Fox Me.* London: Geoffrey Bles, 1958. First edition, 8vo., original green cloth, titled in silver to spine, illustrated dust jacket, very minor wear to jacket edges, otherwise vivid, very good.   Sotheran's Hunting, Shooting & Fishing - 219   2016   £25

Stanford, J. K. *Full Moon at Sweatenham.* London: Faber & Faber Ltd., 1953. First edition, 8vo., original red cloth, titled in silver to spine, illustrated dust jacket is little worn to spine, otherwise very good.   Sotheran's Hunting, Shooting & Fishing - 216   2016   £40

Stanford, J. K. *Grouse Shooting.* London: Percival Marshall & co., 1963. Small 8vo., green cloth with dust jacket, minor abrasion to upper front dust jacket. Sotheran's Hunting, Shooting & Fishing - 225   2016   £20

Stanford, J. K. *Guns Wanted.* London: Faber & Faber ltd., 1949. First edition, 8vo., original red cloth, used copy. Sotheran's Hunting, Shooting & Fishing - 213   2016   £90

Stanford, J. K. *Jimmy Bundobust.* London: Faber & Faber, 1958. First edition, 8vo., original green cloth, dust jacket, very good, jacket sometime repaired.   Sotheran's Hunting, Shooting & Fishing - 220   2016   £25

Stanford, J. K. *A Keeper's Country.* London: H. F. & G. Witherby Ltd., 1968. First edition, 8vo., original beige cloth, dust jacket, very good.   Sotheran's Hunting, Shooting & Fishing - 230   2016   £30

Stanford, J. K. *Ladies in the sun.* London: Gallery Press, 1962. First edition, 8vo., original blue cloth, dust jacket, slightly used.   Sotheran's Hunting, Shooting & Fishing - 223   2016   £25

Stanford, J. K. *Mixed Bagmen.* London: Herbert Jenkins Ltd., 1947. First edition, original dark green cloth with dust jacket, little damage to upper dust jacket, skillfully repaired. Sotheran's Hunting, Shooting & Fishing - 208   2016   £30

Stanford, J. K. *No Sportsman At All.* London: Faber & Faber, 1952. First edition, 8vo., light green cloth, color printed dust jacket, ink ownership inscription, otherwise very good, not price clipped.   Sotheran's Hunting, Shooting & Fishing - 215   2016   £30

Stanford, J. K. *Partridge Shooting.* London: Percival Marshall & Co., 1963. Small 8vo., green cloth with dust jacket, slightly used.   Sotheran's Hunting, Shooting & Fishing - 226   2016   £20

Stanford, J. K. *Reverie of a Qu' Hai.* London: William Blackwood & Sons, 1951. First edition, 8vo., original red cloth, spine little slanted, otherwise sturdy copy, internally clean, scarce.   Sotheran's Hunting, Shooting & Fishing - 214   2016   £120

Stanford, J. K. *Tail of an Army.* London: Phoenix House, 1966. First edition, 8vo., queen cloth, gilt stamped with pictorial dust jacket, minor foxing to fore edge, otherwise very good.   Sotheran's Hunting, Shooting & Fishing - 228 2016   £90

Stang, Phil *Censored the Goat.* New York: Dodd Mead, 1945. First edition, 4to., pictorial boards, fine in dust jacket, full and partial illustrations by Kurt Wiese. Aleph-bet Books, Inc. 111 - 477 2016 $150

Stanhope, Eugenia *The Deportment of a Married Life laid Down in a Series of Letters...* London: printed for Mr. Hodges Pall Mall, 1798. 8vo., some browning to final leaves, contemporary tree calf, rebacked retaining original spine, inscribed "H. E. Benyon from EB 1800". Jarndyce Antiquarian Books CCXV - 421 2016 £220

Stanislaw, Lem *Solaris.* Warsaw: Wydawnictwo Ministerstwa Obrony Narodowej, 1961. First Polish edition, preceding all others, near fine in wrapper, in near fine example of rare dust jacket with thumbnail size chip at rear panel, else excellent. Royal Books 51 - 2 2016 $4500

Stanley, Arthur Penrhyn *The Life and Correspondence of Thomas Arnold.* London: B. Fellowes, 1845. Fourth edition, 2 volumes, half titles, frontispiece, original dark green-blue cloth blocked in blind, diagonal mark to back board of volume II, otherwise nice. Jarndyce Antiquarian Books CCXV - 312 2016 £75

Stanley, Henry Morton 1841-1904 *How I Found Livingstone.* London: Sampson Low Marston, Searle & Rivington, 1890. New edition, octavo, illustrations, original red gilt and black pictorial cloth, rubber ownership stamp in front pastedown, endpapers starting to split at hinges, spine little faded top inside corner of panel board little bruised, very good. Peter Ellis 112 - 383 2016 £125

Stanley, Henry Morton 1841-1904 *In Darkest Africa or the Quest, Rescue and Retreat of Emin, Governor of Equatoria.* London: William Clowes and Sons, Limited for Sampson Low, Marston, Searle and Rivington ltd., 1890. First edition, 8vo., 2 volumes, original brick red pictorial cloth by Leighton, Son and Hdoge with their ticket on lower pastedown of volume I, upper boards decorated and lettered in black and gilt, spines decorated and lettered in black and gilt, map endpapers, one wood engraved frontispiece and one in photogravure, both retaining tissue guards, 37 wood engraved plates, 3 folding, color printed lithographic maps, one color printed lithographic geological profile, one folding letterpress table, numerous wood engraved illustrations in text, extremities very lightly rubbed, slight foxing throughout (less than usual), maps with minor repaired tears, spines color not sunned at all and consistent with covers, these with sharp corners and edges, unusually good set in original pictorial cloth. Sotheran's Travel and Exploration - 37 2016 £575

Stanley, Henry Morton 1841-1904 *In Darkest Africa or the Quest, Rescue and Retreat of Emin, Governor of Equatoria.* London: Sampson Low Marston, 1907. Reprint, octavo, 150 woodcut illustrations, folding map, original red gilt pictorial cloth, top edge gilt, spine little faded, cover edges slightly rubbed, bookplate removed from front pastedown, prelims little spotted, very good. Peter Ellis 112 - 382 2016 £95

Stanley, Henry Morton 1841-1904 *Through the Dark Continent.* London: Sampson Low, Marston, Searle & Rivington, 1890. New and cheaper edition, octavo, illustrations, folding map at rear, original red gilt and black pictorial cloth, rubber ownership stamp, cloth little bubbled, spine slightly faded, very good. Peter Ellis 112 - 384 2016 £125

Stanley, William Owen *Memoirs on Remains of Ancient Dwellings in Holyhead Island Mostly of Circular Form called Cyttlau'r Gwyddelod...* London/Chester: James Bain/ Marshall & Hughes, 1871. First edition, gold stamped sienna cloth, modest edgewear, signed "Frances Wynne from W. O. Stanley March 26 1881", stunning engraved bookplate of designer Harry Soane for Col. John Charles Wynne Finch, very faint bookstore stamp to front cover, many engravings, fold mout map intact. Simon Finch 2015 - 055187 2016 $225

Stanton, Elizabeth Cady *The History of woman Suffrage Volumes I-III.* New York: Fowler & Wells, 1881. New York: 1882. Rochester: 1887. First edition, volume one has loose hinge in front but it and volume two are in very good condition, volume 3 very worn with some loose prelim matter and well worn binding, volumes one and two have tipped in signature by Susan B. Anthony, all 3 volumes inscribed Lizzie Everett from Flora M. Kimball, National City California April 4 1887. Second Life Books, Inc. 196 B - 684 2016 $2000

Stanton, Elizabeth Cady *History of Woman Suffrage. Volume One only.* New York: Fowler and Wells, 1881. First edition, 8vo., steel engravings, presentation from Matilda Joslyn Gage, dated 1888, maroon cloth, cover quite scuffed and somewhat worn at spine and corners, little foxing, otherwise very good. Second Life Books, Inc. 196 B - 685 2016 $350

Stapf, Ambrosius Joseph *The Spirit and Scope of Education in Promoting Well Being of Society.* Edinburgh: Marsh & Beattie, 1851. First English edition, Uncut in original green cloth, blocked in blind, slight nick to head of spine, otherwise nice. Jarndyce Antiquarian Books CCXV - 963 2016 £45

Stapledon, W. Olaf *Last Men in London.* London: Methuen, 1932. first edition, first issue (ads at rear dated '932', few faint foxspots to prelims and ads, crown 8vo., original blue cloth with blindstamped single fillet border to upper board, backstrip lettered gilt, some light rubbing at extremities, some faint foxing to rough trimmed edges, couple of words noted in pencil at head of rear free endpaper, attractive pictorial second state dust jacket with backstrip panel shade darkened and some very light chpping to corners, very good.   Blackwell's Rare Books   B184 - 237   2016   £800

Stark, Freya *A Winter in Arabia.* London: John Murray, 1940. First edition, 8vo., original green cloth lettered gilt, 1 folding map, numerous illustrations from photos, printed in photogravure, cloth faded along edges and spine, internally apart from occasional very light spotting and offsetting from endpapers, good copy, contemporary bookplate of Antonio Besse inside front cover, two original press photos loosely inserted.   Sotheran's   Travel and Exploration - 378   2016   £185

Stark, Richard *The Handle.* New York: Pocket, 1966. First edition, paperback original, fine, unread copy in wrappers.   Mordida Books   2015 - 007201   2016 $65

Starr, Chester G. *The Roman Imperial Navy 31 B.C. - A.D. 324.* Westport: Greenwood Press, 1975. Reprint, 8vo., cloth, gilt lettering now faded, spine sunned, edges lightly foxed and dusted, minor shelfwear, still very good, no dust jacket.   Unsworths Antiquarian Booksellers Ltd.   E04 - 103   2016   £30

Starrett, Vincent *Late, Later and Possibly Last.* Autolycus Press, One of 500 copies signed by Starrett & Murphy, original black boards, gilt, very good, uncut.   I. D. Edrich   Crime - 2016   £25

Starrett, Vincent *The Private Life of Sherlock Holmes.* London: Nicholson & Watson, 1934. Illustrations, covers sunned, otherwise very good.   I. D. Edrich   Crime - 2016   £25

Statius, Publius Papinius *Statii Syvalrum Libri V: Achilleidos Libri XII...* Venice: Aldus, 1519. Second Aldus edition, small 8vo., bound in early full morocco with gilt rules, marbled endpapers, spine faded, all edges gilt, little rubbed along hinges, but very good, clean copy.   Second Life Books, Inc.   197 - 300   2016 $1500

Staton, Frances M. *A Bibliography of Canadiana, Being Items in the Public Library of Toronto, Canada...* Toronto: Public Library, 1934. 1959. 1985. 1986. First edition, 4 volumes, thick tall 8vo. and 8vo., cloth, leather spine label, cloth, spine of first volume faded.   Oak Knoll Books   310 - 234   2016 $600

Staton, James Taylor *The Visit to'th Greight Paris Eggsibishun of Bobby Shuttle and his Wife Sayroh.* Manchester: Abel Heywood, London: Simpkin, Marshall & Co., Liverpoool: William Gilling, 1867? First edition, with oval woodcut portrait as frontispiece, woodcut head and tail-pieces, few spots, early 20th century light green cloth, original printed yellow wrappers, bound in upper one in incorporating a portrait of Bobby Shuttle, bookplate of Sir William Hesketh Lever and opposite his bookplate as Baron Leverhulme, good.   Blackwell's Rare Books   B184 - 80   2016   £250

Stauffer, R. C. *Charles Darwin's Natural Selection....* London: Cambridge University Press, 1975. Octavo, publisher's blue cloth, staining to first few leaves, pencil annotations.   Andrew Isles Natural History Books   55 - 38688   2016 $80

Stawell, Maud Margaret Key *Fabre's Book of Insects.* London: Hodder & Stoughton, n.d., 1921. Thick 4to., white cloth pictorially stamped in gold, fore edge has few spots, else fine in dust jacket with mounted color plate (dust jacket is frayed with a 2 x 3 inch piece off corner), illustrations by Edward Detmold, with 12 magnificent tipped-in color plates with lettered tissue guards, beautiful copy, scarce in dust jacket.   Aleph-bet Books, Inc.   111 - 120   2016 $600

Stawell, Maud Margaret Key *Fairies I Have Met.* New York: Hodder and Stoughton, 1910. First American edition, octavo, 8 color plates printed on glossy paper by Edmund Dulac, with captions printed in blue, publisher's olive brown cloth, front cover and spine pictorially stamped in black, white and gilt, minimal rubbing to extremities, early ink presentation, dedication leaf browned, otherwise near fine.   David Brass Rare Books, Inc.   2015 - 02920   2016 $550

Steadman, Ralph *Scar Strangled Banger.* London: Harrap, 1987. First British edition, near fine, front free endpaper creased, near fine dust jacket with light creasing to spine ends.   Bella Luna Books   2016 - t7666   2016 $82

Stebbing, E. F. *Jungle By-Ways in India; Laves from the Note-Book of a Sportsman and a Naturalsit.* London: John Lane the Bodley Head, 1911. First edition, 8vo., original pale green cloth, upper cover and spine titled in gilt with triple fillet borders to white, both incorporating various substantial vignettes, also blocked in white, of stags, top edge gilt, collotype frontispiece, 32 photographic or collotype plates on 14 leaves and more than 90 vivid wood engraved illustrations in text, apart from browning to half title and final leaf of ads due to offsetting from pastedowns and few minor spots to rear corner, fine.   Sotheran's   Hunting, Shooting & Fishing - 23   2016   £248

Stebbins, Genevieve *Society Gynmastics ad Voice-Culture.* New York: Edgar S. Werner, 1893. Fourth edition, 4 pages ads, original light brown decorated cloth, slightly rubbed, stamps of Eleanor Miller School of Oratory.   Jarndyce Antiquarian Books   CCXV - 422   2016   £50

Steedman, Amy *Legends and Stories of Italy for Children.* New York and London: Putnam & Jack, 1909. First US edition, 8vo., cloth backed gilt decorative boards, top edge gilt, fine, 12 magnificent tipped in color plates by Katherine Cameron.   Aleph-bet Books, Inc.   111 - 72   2016 $250

Steel, F. A. *English Fairy Tales.* New York: Macmillan, 1918. First American edition, later issue with top edge plain instead of gilt, thick 8vo., red cloth, neat hinge strengthening, edge soil on endpaper and some finger soil on cover, very good+ in beautiful custom half leather box with raised bands, 16 magnificent color plates plus 41 black and whites and pictorial endpapers by Arthur Rackham, this copy with 3 inch charming pen drawing signed and dated by Rackham.   Aleph-bet Books, Inc.   112 - 411   2016 $1975

Steele, Richard   1672-1729   *The Christian Hero.* London: printed for J. and R. Tonson, 1741. Ninth edition, 12mo., final blank sig. E4 present, contemporary sprinkled edges, slight rubbing to hinges some staining, top corners bir bumped, signature of W. Radcliffe, very good, attractive copy.   Jarndyce Antiquarian Booksellers   CCXVI - 540   2016   £95

Steele, Richard   1672-1729   *The Crisis of Property; an Argument Proving that the Annultants for Ninety-Nine Years, as such...*   London: for W. Chetwood, J. Roberts and Charles Little, 1720. First edition, 8vo., titlepage little soiled and outer corners chipped, preserved in modern marbled wrappers, label on upper cover, variant issue without Brotherton's name in imprint and with printer's ornament on page 30.   John Drury Rare Books   2015 - 15795   2016 $350

Steele, Richard   1672-1729   *The Lover and the reader, by the author of the Tatler and Spectator.*   London: printed for J. Tonson..., 1718. Second edition, 12mo., some light browning to endpapers and titlepage, first few leaves foxed, otherwise clean copy, contemporary mottled calf, gilt ruled, borders, spine very rubbed, joints cracked but firm.   Jarndyce Antiquarian Booksellers   CCXVI - 541   2016   £45

Steele, Richard   1672-1729   *The Lying Lover or the Ladies Friendship. (bound with) The Tender Husband or the Accomplish'd Fools.*   London: printed for Bernard Lintott, 1712. Second edition, old waterstain to upper margin, some browning and light foxing, signature of Geo. Yardley 1733 to front endpaper, some pen strokes to inner front board, traces of wax seals removal, full contemporary panelled calf, raised bands, morocco label.   Jarndyce Antiquarian Booksellers   CCXVI - 472   2016   £75

Steele, Richard   1672-1729   *The Romish Ecclesiastical History of Late Years.*   London: printed for J. Roberts, 1714. Engraved frontispiece, 8vo., later 18th century quarter calf, gray paper boards, more recent endpapers.   Jarndyce Antiquarian Booksellers   CCXVI - 542   2016   £60

Steere, Reuben A.   *Sketch of the Life, Personal, Appearance, Character and Manners of Col. R. A. Steere and Wife...*   Danielsonville: F. U. Scofield, 1883. 12mo., printed yellow wrappers, lightly dusted, soft horizontal crease, else very good.   Dramatis Personae   119 - 143   2016 $175

Steig, William   *Bad Island.*   New York: Windmill/Simon & Schuster, 1969. Stated first printing, cloth, fine in dust jacket (taped on verso soiled with chip), later published as Rotten Island, uncommon printing.   Aleph-bet Books, Inc.   112 - 466   2016 $125

Steig, William   *Brave Irene.*   New York: Farrar Straus Giroux, 1986. Stated first edition, 4to., red cloth, as new in dust jacket, color illustrations, this copy signed by author.   Aleph-bet Books, Inc.   111 - 437   2016 $225

Steig, William   *CDC?*   New York: Farrar Straus Giroux, 1984. Stated first edition, 8vo., cloth, fine in dust jacket, illustrations on every page.   Aleph-bet Books, Inc.   111 - 439   2016 $225

Steig, William   *Caleb and Kate.*   New York: Farrar Strauss Giroux, 1977. Stated first edition, 4to., cloth, fine in lightly soiled dust jacket, color illustrations on every page.   Aleph-bet Books, Inc.   111 - 438   2016 $100

Steig, William   *Shrek!*   New York: Farrar, Straus and Giroux, 1990. First edition, fine in glossy pictorial boards.   Between the Covers Rare Books   204 - 22   2016 $125

Stein, Aurel   *Old Routes of Western Iran....*   London: Macmillan, 1940. First edition, 8vo., original maroon cloth lettered gilt on spine, gilt decoration on cover, 31 plates, numerous maps and plans, 1 folding map in pocket at rear, ex-library with usual markings, inner hinge cracked but holding, stamp and label at prelims, but reasonable copy, slightly rubbed at spine ends.   Any Amount of Books   2015 - A85563   2016   £250

Stein, Gertrude   1874-1946   *A Christmas Greeting.*   N.P.: Sans Souci Press, 1969. First published edition, one of 40 numbered copies, signed by publisher William Young, 12mo., 8 page leaflet, printed on three sides, fine.   Bertram Rota Ltd.   Christmas List 2015 - 53   2016   £20

Stein, Gertrude   1874-1946   *Geography and Plays.*   Boston: Four Seas co., 1922. First edition, first state binding, grey paper over boards with stamped blue lettering, rough blue quarter cloth with cream paper label and dark blue lettering, lacking dust jacket, ex-university library with only unobtrusive, one-line name stamp to head of Foreword, no other library markings, light toning, slight discoloration to spine label, small chip to foot of f.f.e.p., binding slightly shaken, text clean, very good.   Tavistock Books   Getting Around - 52   2016 $350

Steinbeck, John Ernst   1902-1968   *Cannery Row.*   New York: Viking Press, 1945. Very rare advance issue, first edition, first issue with "January 1945' on copyright page, publisher's blue wrappers printed on front cover in black, short tear to last leaf, repaired with archival tape, short half inch tear to foot of spine, overall fine, none of the usual chipping to cover edges, housed in folding chemise and dark brown slipcase, superior copy.   Argonaut Book Shop Literature 2015 - 7648   2016 $2500

Steinbeck, John Ernst   1902-1968   *East of Eden.*   New York: Viking Press, 1952. First edition, one of 1500 large paper copies, large 8vo., signed by author, excellent copy of original glassine and rubbed wood grained publisher's box.   Second Life Books, Inc.   196 B - 692   2016 $3750

Steinbeck, John Ernst   1902-1968   *East of Eden.*   New York: Viking Press, 1952. First edition, light green cloth, lettered in navy, red-brown spine label lettered in black, near fine, some light sunning to spine and board edges, former owner's signature to front pastedown, else bright and clean, overall sturdy and pleasing copy.   B & B Rare Books, Ltd. 2016 - JS080   2016 $150

Steinbeck, John Ernst   1902-1968   *The Grapes of Wrath.*   New York: Viking, 1939. First edition, first issue dust jacket with first edition statement at bottom front jacket flap, wrap-around jacket art by Elmer Hader, fine in bright, about fine dust jacket, jacket lightly toned along top flap folds, touch of rubbing to jacket crown, signle tiny closed tear to rear top of rear panel, exceptional copy overall in custom cloth slipcase.   Royal Books   49 - 65   2016 $8250

Steinbeck, John Ernst   1902-1968   *The Grapes of Wrath.*   New York: Viking, 1939. First edition, very nice with light browning to endpapers, good dust jacket, rubbed and worn at folds and nicked to extremities, first issue, with first edition on dust jacket flap.   Second Life Books, Inc.   197 - 310   2016 $4250

Steinbeck, John Ernst   1902-1968   *John Emery as Read at the Services in New York City, Jan 18 1964.*   New York: privately printed, 1964. One of 200 copies, none of which were for sale, 8vo., frontispiece, patterned red paper over boards with black leatherette spine, slightly scuffed at corners, otherwise near fine, rare.   Second Life Books, Inc.   197 - 302   2016 $1200

Steinbeck, John Ernst   1902-1968   *John Steinbeck Replies.*   New York: L. M. Birkhead Friends of Democracy, 1940. First edition, lightly toned, near fine, scarce.   Second Life Books, Inc.   197 - 303   2016 $900

Steinbeck, John Ernst   1902-1968   *Once There was a War.*   New York: Viking, 1958. First edition, 8vo., very good in little nicked and worn dust jacket.   Second Life Books, Inc.   197 - 304   2016 $300

Steinbeck, John Ernst   1902-1968   *The Pastures of Heaven.*   New York: Brewer, Warren and Putnam, 1932. First edition, first issue in second issue dust jacket, inscribed by author for Keith Baker, scarce, especially signed, about near fine in like dust jacket, slight lean, light fading to board edges, light foxing and offsetting to endpapers, jacket has minor chipping to top edge and diagonal crease to rear flap.   Royal Books   48 - 72   2016 $32,500

Steinbeck, John Ernst   1902-1968   *Pastures of Heaven.*   London: Philip Allan, 1933. First UK edition, this author's copy with his and his wife Carol's ownership stamp, very good in scarce dust jacket, fading to spine, few small faint dampstains to boards and short tear to cloth and bottom of front spine, custom clamshell box.   Royal Books   49 - 66   2016 $3500

Steinbeck, John Ernst   1902-1968   *The Red Pony.*   New York: Covici Friede, 1937. First edition, one of 699 numbered copies, this being no. 638 signed by author, near fine with slight browning to boards, matching very good publisher's slipcase, bookplate with faint offsetting to facing page, slipcase lightly rubbed with small chip to top panel, else near fine.   Royal Books   49 - 68   2016 $3250

Steinbeck, John Ernst   1902-1968   *The Red Pony. The Gift II. The Great Mountains III. The Promise.*   New York: Covici Friede, 1937. First edition, limited to 699 copies this is number 341, signed by author, large 8vo., very good, untrimmed, moderately worn original slipcase, printed on handmade La Garde paper and printed by Pynson Printers in September 1937.   Second Life Books, Inc.   197 - 306   2016 $4500

Steinbeck, John Ernst   1902-1968   *The Red Pony.*   New York: Viking, 1945. First edition, 8vo., illustrations by Wesley Dennis, pictorial endpapers, tan cloth with paper illustration on front, stamped in blue and gilt, near fine.   Second Life Books, Inc.   197 - 305   2016 $45

Steinbeck, John Ernst   1902-1968   *Sweet Thursday.*   New York: Viking, 1954. First edition, nice in dust jacket (lacks half inch triangle on rear hinge), first issue dust jacket with author photo on rear panel without reviewer blurbs.   Second Life Books, Inc.   197 - 311   2016 $425

Steinbeck, John Ernst   1902-1968   *Travels with Charley.*   New York: Viking, 1962. First edition, 8vo., very good in little nicked and some toned dust jacket, original first issue dust jacket has $4.95 printed price present on front flap.   Second Life Books, Inc.   197 - 307   2016 $300

Steinbeck, John Ernst   1902-1968   *The Wayward Bus.*   New York: Viking, 1947. First edition, 8vo, very good in little nicked and rubbed dust jacket.   Second Life Books, Inc.   197 - 308   2016 $600

Steiner, Robert *Passion.* Lincoln: Penmaen Press, 1980. One of 1000 copies, 8vo., wood engravings by Berta Golahny, signed by author and artist, brown and tan patterned paper over boards, three quarter tan cloth, very slightly scuffed at bottom of spine, otherwise fine in plastic dust jacket.   Second Life Books, Inc.   196 B - 693   2016 $45

Steinfeldt, Cecilia *Early Texas Furniture and Decorative Arts.* San Antonio: Pub. for the San Antonio Museum Association by Trinity University Press, 1973. First edition, 4to., color and black and white plates, photos, brown linen, gilt titles, color plate on front board, signed by authors, very good+ copy, scattered foxing to edges and endpapers. Kaaterskill Books   21 - 95 2016 $400

Steinman, David B. *I Built a Bridge and Other Poems.* New York: Davidson Press, 1955. First edition, fine+, owner name and address, in fine dust jacket.   Ken Hebenstreit, Bookseller   2016 - 2016 $65

Steinmetz, Andrew *Japan and Her People.* London: Routledge, Warne and Routledge, 1859. First edition, good to very good, original blue pebbled cloth, blindstamped with elaborate gilt design on cover, armorial bookplate of Richard Ponsonby.   Simon Finch   2015 - 000253   2016 $245

Stejneger, Leonard *The Poisonous Snakes of North America.* Washington: Annual Report of the United States National Museum, 1893. Octavo, 19 photos, text illustrations, contemporary quarter, morocco and marbled boards, rubbed.   Andrew Isles Natural History Books   55 - 15386   2016 $250

Stephanchev, Stephen *The Mad Bomber.* Los Angeles: Black Sparrow, 1972. First edition, large 8vo., one of 200 hardcover copies numbered and signed by author, paper over boards with patterned cloth spine, fine in acrylic dust jacket.   Second Life Books, Inc.   196 B - 695   2016 $65

Stephanchev, Stephen *Mining the Darkness.* Los Angeles: Black Sparrow, 1975. One of 200 copies numbered and signed by poet, 8vo., cover slightly faded at edges, otherwise nice and little soiled plastic dust jacket. Second Life Books, Inc.   196 B - 696   2016 $45

Stephens, Ian *Monsoon Morning.* London: Ernest Benn, 1966. First edition, octavo, very good in like dust jacket, price clipped, nicked and rubbed at edges.   Peter Ellis   112 - 179   2016   £35

Stephens, James 1882-1950 *Julia Elizabeth.* New York: Crosby Gaige, 1929. 1/861 copies, Large 8vo., signed by author, cover somewhat browned, owner's bookplate, otherwise nice, tight copy.   Second Life Books, Inc.   196 B - 697   2016 $50

Stephens, James 1882-1950 *Collected Poems.* London: Macmillan, 1926. First edition, limited to 500 large paper copies, signed by author, vellum backed boards, front hinge tender, very good.   Second Life Books, Inc.   196 B - 698   2016 $65

Stephens, John L. *Incidents of Travel in Central America, Chiapas and Yucatan.* London: John Murray, 1841. First UK edition, 2 volumes, numerous illustrations, original brown cloth, spine little faded, internally clean and crisp, extremely good set.   J. & S. L. Bonham Antiquarian Booksellers America 2016 - 9306   2016   £950

Stephenson, Jean Simpson *Of Scandinavia.* N.P.: Jean Simpson Stephenson, n.d., Limited to 22 numbered copies, signed by author/artist, square small 4to., back cloth spine, decorated paper covered boards, cloth clamshell box with orange printed paper labels, illustrations printed on Somerset Satin mouldmade paper, bound by artist.   Oak Knoll Books   27 - 63   2016 $400

Stephenson, Neal *Snow Crash.* New York: Toronto: London: Sydney: Auckland: Bantam Books, 1992. First edition, octavo, cloth backed boards, signed by author, fine in nearly fine dust jacket with hint of tanning along upper front edge.   John W. Knott, Jr./L.W. Currey, Inc.   Fall-Winter 2015 - 18572   2016 $1500

Sterling, George *Songs Lovingly Dedicated to Nellie Holbrook.* San Francisco: Sherman Clay, 1916. First edition, quarto, original printed wrappers, silk ties, , edges and spine little nibbled, very good.   The Brick Row Book Shop Miscellany 69 - 76   2016 $250

Stern, Gerald *Bread without Sugar.* N. P.: Sutton Hoo Press, 1991. Limited to 250 copies, signed by author, artist, Nadya Brown and printer, Chad Oness, one illustration, small 4to., stiff paper wrappers, dust jacket with paper label on front cover, some edges uncut.   Oak Knoll Books   310 - 156   2016 $125

Sterne, Laurence 1713-1768 *The Beauties of Sterne...* London: printed for G. Kearsley, J. Walker and 4 others, 1799. Thirteenth edition, engraved frontispiece and 6 plates, 12mo., frontispiece slightly waterstained, titlepage slightly browned, contemporary calf, gilt floral border, gilt decorated spine with black, gilt label, spine rubbed with slight wear and crack at head, 19th century signature at head of titlepage and on endpaper.   Jarndyce Antiquarian Booksellers   CCXVI - 545   2016   £50

Sterne, Laurence 1713-1768 *Letters of the late Rev. Mr. Laurence Sterne to his Most Intimate Friends.* London: printed for T. Becket the Corner of the Adelphi in the Strand, 1776. New edition, 3 volumes, errata, engraved frontispiece, 12mo., fine set bound in full contemporary calf, raised and gilt banded spines, red morocco title labels, oval black gilt volume labels, recent continental bookplates.   Jarndyce Antiquarian Booksellers   CCXVI - 546   2016   £185

Sterne, Laurence 1713-1768 *La Vie et les Opinions of Tristram Shandy. (with) Suite et fin de la vie et des opinions de Tristram Shandy...* Londres: 1784. 1783., 18mo., 4 volumes, few gatherings lightly discolored, lower blank margins to few leaves in volume 2 slightly torn, uniform in contemporary quarter continental calf, blue marbled boards, vellum tips, spines ruled and decorated to gilt, green and cream morocco labels, slight wear, short splits to hinges repaired, attractive copy.   Jarndyce Antiquarian Booksellers   CCXVI - 547   2016   £280

Sterne, Laurence 1713-1768 *A Sentimental Journey through France and Italy.* London: for T. Becket and P. A. De Hondt, 1768. First edition with text variant 2 in volume 1 and text variant 1 in volume 2, as ususal, 2 volumes, 8vo., engraved coat of arm on Dev, with half titles and list of subscriber names a usual, without rare inserted ad leaf, full sprinkled calf, fully gilt by Riviere, spines bit dry, hinges worn, small chip at crown of volume 2, Hobart Cole bookplate.   Joseph J. Felcone, Inc.   Books from Five Centuries: a Miscellany - 137   2016 $900

Sterne, Laurence 1713-1768 *A Sentimental Journey through France and Italy.* London: George Routledge and Sons, 1885. No. 96 of 550 copies, loosely inserted is an additional half title with an original watercolor signed by Leloir and dated 1884, verso is limitation page for the Edition de Grand Luxe numbered 182 (of 200), plates from this edition loosely inserted together with plates bound in, additional color chromolithographic title, half title, photogravure frontispiece and plates, illustrations, some light foxing, partially uncut in 20th century full crimson crushed morocco by Sotheran, triple borders with floral cornerpieces, raised bands, gilt compartments and elaborate gilt dentelles, slight rubbing to leading hinge and head of spine, top edge gilt, handsome copy.   Jarndyce Antiquarian Booksellers   CCXVII - 267   2016   £680

Sterne, Laurence 1713-1768 *A Sentimental Journey through France and Italy by Mr. Yorick to which are added The Journal to Eliza and a Political Romance.* London: Oxford University Press, 1968. First edition thus, octavo, ownership inscription, edges little spotted, very good in like dust jacket, rubbed at edges and faded at spine.   Peter Ellis   112 - 385   2016   £50

Steven, Edward Millar *Medical Supervision in Schools...* London: Bailliere, Tidnall & Co., 1910. First edition, half title, numerous illustrations, original maroon cloth, library reference at foot of spine, from the library of Bournville Village Trust, very good.   Jarndyce Antiquarian Books   CCXV - 965   2016   £65

Stevens, Benjamin Franklin *Christopher Columbus: His Own Book of Privileges 1502.* London: B. F. Stevens, 1893. Limited to 20 copies, presentation by author to Henry Harrisse, folio, later quarter leather with original paper wrappers bound in, 3 plates, spine slightly rubbed, minor scratching to cover, well preserved.   Oak Knoll Books   310 - 281   2016 $850

Stevens, Edward Thomas *Domestic Economy for Girls.* London: Longmans, 1877. New edition, 3 volumes, initial ad leaf in volumes I and II, half titles, illustrations, volume II lacking leading f.e.p., original brown printed cloth, slightly dulled and rubbed, otherwise nice, attractive set.   Jarndyce Antiquarian Books   CCXV - 423   2016   £85

Stevens, James *Big Jim Turner.* Garden City: Doubleday and Co., 1948. First edition, foxing on endpapers and tiny spots on boards, else near fine in very good dust jacket with some tiny splash marks on spine, inscribed by author for Norman Thomas.   Between the Covers Rare Books   208 - 83   2016 $225

Stevens, James *Paul Bunyan.* New York: Knopf, 1925. First edition, cloth, woodcuts by Allen Lewis, bookseller's label on back pastedown, laid in sheet has author's inscription signed and dated 1944 and 1944 former owner signature, top edge waterstained, mild tide-line on top (2" down) on each leaf of text, still acceptable collectible condition becuase of lovely and scarce dust jacket (couple of short closed tears), very scarce.   Gene W. Baade, Books on the West   2015 - 1003143   2016 $81

Stevens, John *The History of Portugal from the First Ages of the World to the Great Revolution, Under King John IV in the year 1640.* London: W. Rogers, 1698. First edition, 8vo., table, contemporary brown speckled calf, covers scuffed, good, library label of Baron Rolle.   J. & S. L. Bonham Antiquarian Booksellers   Europe 2016 - 8419   2016   £500

Stevens, Robert *Sermons, on Our Duty Towards God, Our Neighbour, and Ourselves: and on Other Subjects.* London: printed for John Booth, 1814. First edition, 225 x 133mm., pleasing contemporary midnight blue straight grain morocco, covers framed by plain gilt rules outlining Greek key and palmette blind rolls, raised bands, compartments with central gilt fleuron radiating densely blind tooled foliage, gilt ruled turn-ins, all edges gilt, with excellent fore-edge painting of Dover Castle; a presentation copy with (slightly foxed) signed autograph letter bound in (with letter offsets) for E. S. Stephenson, unidentified armorial bookplate, bit of wear to corners and joints, very small (ink?) stain to edge of prelim leaves visible at upper left background of fore-edge painting (not affecting primary image), otherwise fine, clean, fresh internally in lustrous binding.   Phillip J. Pirages   67 - 164   2016 $1300

Stevens, Wallace 1879-1955 *The Blue Guitar and the Man with the Blue Guitar.* London and New York: Petersburg Press, 1977. First edition, small squrae 4to., illustrations, original boards, paper onlay on front cover, dust jacket, fox marks on edges of text block, otherwise fine, signed the artist, David Hockney.   James S. Jaffe Rare Books   Occasional List: Winter 2016 - 10   2016 $750

Stevens, Wallace 1879-1955 *Harmonium.* New York: Knopf, 1923. First edition, one of 500 copies bound thus, 8vo., original cloth backed decorated boards with printed label on spine, extreme fore-tips of boards bit bumped and rubbed with bit of surface loss, otherwise fine, bright copy, rare in dust jacket, copies lacking the jacket are rarely seen in such clean condition.   James S. Jaffe Rare Books Occasional List: Winter 2016 - 132   2016 $4500

Stevens, Wallace 1879-1955 *Ideas of Order.* New York: Knopf, 1936. First trade edition, 12mo., little soiled publisher's boards, paper spine label, very good with bookplate of poet Barbara Howes, with Howes' ownership signature, in the yellow binding (#3), one of 1000 copies.   Second Life Books, Inc.   196 B - 701   2016 $250

Stevens, Wallace 1879-1955 *The Man with the Blue Guitar.* London: Petersburg Press, 1977. First edition thus, square 8vo. etchings by David Hockney, 20 sketchings, all in color, boards with decorated title label, fine in very near fine dust jacket.   Peter Ellis   112 - 171   2016   £65

Stevens, Wallace 1879-1955 *The Collected Poems.* New York: Alfred A. Knopf, 1954. First edition, one of 2500 numbered copies, presentation copy inscribed by author Oct. 4 1954 for Jerry Baxter, booklabel on front pastedown, otherwise fine in dust jacket lightly sunned along spine panel with 1 3/4 inch triangular chip along top edge of front panel affecting letters.   James S. Jaffe Rare Books Occasional List: Winter 2016 - 133   2016 $5000

Stevenson, Anne *Black Grate Poems.* Oxford: Inky Parrot Press, 1984. First edition, deluxe issue, one of 15 roman numeraled copies with original manuscript poem and original pen and ink drawing, signed by author and artist, in boardbound issue of 160 copies in total edition of 360, 4to., colored lithographed illustrations, illustrated endpapers, original illustrated paper over boards, publisher's board slipcase, very fine, drawings by Annie Newnham.   James S. Jaffe Rare Books   Occasional List: Winter 2016 - 134   2016 $650

Stevenson, D. E. *The House of the Deer.* New York: Holt, Rinehart and Winston, 1971. First edition, fine in fine dust jacket with minor edge wear.   Ken Hebenstreit, Bookseller   2016 - 2016 $45

Stevenson, John George *The Challenge and other Talks with Boys and Girls.* London: James Clarke & co., 1906. Half title, frontispiece, illustrations, original decorated red cloth, contemporary signature.   Jarndyce Antiquarian Books   CCXV - 424   2016   £25

Stevenson, Lionel *Best Poems of 1964: Borestone Mountain Poetry Awards 1965 Volume XVII.* Palo Alto: Pacific Books, 1965. 8vo., signed by contributor William Jay Smith, tan cloth, cover slightly bumped at ends of spine, otherwise very good, tight copy in scuffed and chipped dust jacket.   Second Life Books, Inc.   197 - 312   2016 $35

Stevenson, M. I., Mrs. *Letters from Samoa 1891-1895.* London: Methuen, 1906. First edition, 8vo., original red cloth with paper label painted in red and black on spine, top edge gilt, frontispiece, tissue guards and 11 plates after photos, spare label tipped in at end, spine little sunned, internally occasionally lightly spotted.   Sotheran's Travel and Exploration - 407   2016   £98

Stevenson, Robert Louis Balfour 1850-1894 *An Apology for Idlers.* Oakland: Ben Kennedy, 1931. Number 81 of 110 numbered copies, illustrations, bound by Lawton Kennedy, small octavo, color titlepage illustration, 5 small text illustrations, cloth backed blue boards printed and illustrated paper label on front cover, light rubbing to spine, boards slightly faded, but fine.   Argonaut Book Shop Private Press 2015 - 6390   2016 $50

Stevenson, Robert Louis Balfour 1850-1894 *Ballads.* London: Chatto & Windus, 1890. First edition, one of 100 large paper copies, signed by R. & R. Clarke, printer, 4to., original cream buckram, uncut on watermarked laid paper, cover soiled and stained, endpapers browned, very good untrimmed copy.   Second Life Books, Inc.   197 - 313   2016 $200

Stevenson, Robert Louis Balfour 1850-1894 *Black Arrow.* New York: Scribner, Oct., 1916. First edition, 4to., black cloth, pictorial paste-on, top edge gilt, near fine, illustrations by N. C. Wyeth, beautiful copy.   Aleph-bet Books, Inc.   111 - 492   2016 $600

Stevenson, Robert Louis Balfour 1850-1894 *The Black Arrow.* New York: Charles Scribner's, 1942. Early edition illustrated thus, Royal 8vo., original polished black cloth with full size onlaid pictorial label to upper board, spine lettered gilt, top edge red, pictorial endpapers protected by original repeat dust jacket, pictorial titlepage and 9 colored plates, slight browning to heel of spine, protected by near fine, unchipped dust jacket with only little dusting.   Sotheran's Piccadilly Notes - Summer 2015 - 280   2016   £128

Stevenson, Robert Louis Balfour 1850-1894 *A Child's Garden of Verses.* London: Longmans, Green and Co., 1885. First edition, first printing, one of 1000 copies printed, 12mo., original dark blue cloth, minor soiling, top edge gilt, fore and bottom edges uncut, usual browning of endpapers and little rubbing of extremities, else excellent in morocco backed cloth slipcase.   Howard S. Mott Inc.   265 - 120   2016 $2000

Stevenson, Robert Louis Balfour 1850-1894 *A Child's Garden of Verses.* London: Longmans, Green and Co., 1885. First edition, first issue of the text and second issue of the binding, few minor spots and stains, 16mo., original bevel edged medium blue cloth, spine gilt lettered, publisher's logo on front cover, top edges gilt, others untrimmed, spine slightly faded and bumped at either end, corners trifle worn, bookplate, cloth chemise and light blue lettered morocco and cloth slipcase, good.   Blackwell's Rare Books   B186 - 145   2016   £1250

Stevenson, Robert Louis Balfour 1850-1894 *A Child's Garden of Verses.* San Francisco: Press at Tuscany Alley, 1978. Limited to 500 numbered copies signed by printer. Limited to 500 numbered copies signed by printer, charming full color illustrations, quarter green cloth, printed boards, fine, illustrations by Joyce Lancaster Wilson.   Jeff Weber Rare Books   181 - 75   2016 $250

Stevenson, Robert Louis Balfour 1850-1894 *David Balfour.* New York: Scribner, 1924. First edition with N. C. Wyeth illustrations, 4to., black cloth, pictorial paste-on, fine in original wrappers with mounted color plate.   Aleph-bet Books, Inc.   112 - 521   2016 $750

Stevenson, Robert Louis Balfour 1850-1894 *The Master of Ballantrae.* London: Cassell & Co., 1889. First published edition, first issue with ads dated July 1889, 8vo., original pictorial cloth, spine slightly faded and worn at either end, minor soiling to covers, bookplate of dedicatee, Sir Percy Florence Shelley.   Blackwell's Rare Books   B184 - 81   2016   £3000

Stevenson, Robert Louis Balfour 1850-1894 *On the Choice of a Profession.* London: Chatto & Windus, 1916. First edition, half title, uncut, original boards, purple cloth spine, contemporary ink monogram, very good.   Jarndyce Antiquarian Books   CCXV - 423   2016   £75

Stevenson, Robert Louis Balfour 1850-1894 *Osbourne. The Wrecker.* London: Cassell, 1892. original blue cloth slightly rubbed, 12 plates, 12 pages ads at rear, slight foxing of endpapers, otherwise very good.   I. D. Edrich   Crime - 2016   £80

Stevenson, Robert Louis Balfour 1850-1894 *Pan's Pipes.* Printed at the Riverside Press, 1910. 93/550 copies, printed on handmade paper, wood engraved title vignette and wood engraved head and tailpiece by Bruce Rogers, 16mo, original scarlet boards, gilt design to front cover, some mild rubbing to spine, very good, signed by Bruce Rogers.   Blackwell's Rare Books   B184 - 309   2016   £150

Stevenson, Robert Louis Balfour 1850-1894 *Poems. Hitherto Unpublished.* Boston: Bibliophile Society, 1921. First edition of these poems, one of 450 copies, frontispiece, 9 facsimiles, three quarter vellum over rust cloth sides, hint of foxing to extremely fore-edge of text block, but fine in very good double slipcase.   Argonaut Book Shop   Literature 2015 - 6820   2016 $125

Stevenson, Robert Louis Balfour 1850-1894 *Songs with Music.* London: T. C. & E. C. Jack Ltd. n.d., circa, 1915. First edition, quarto, color frontispiece, color pictorial titlepage and 12 color headpieces, numerous black and white text illustrations, publisher's quarter cream cloth over paper boards with laid-on color illustration, original gray paper dust jacket with pasted on color illustration (same as on cover), corners very slightly bumped, light offset to endpapers from dust jacket with early ink signature on front free endpaper, minimal chipping to jacket spine extremities, small booksellers label on front pastedown, near fine.   David Brass Rare Books, Inc.   2015 - 02978   2016 $350

Stevenson, Robert Louis Balfour 1850-1894 *Strange Case of Dr. Jekyll and Mr. Hyde.* New York: Charles Scribner's Sons, 1886. First edition, octavo, flyleaves at front and rear, original green cloth, front and spine panels stamped in gold, top edge gilt, initialled and dated March 1886 on front free endpaper by early owner, light wear to cloth at spine ends and corner tips, some rubbing along outer front joint, bright, very good.   John W. Knott, Jr./L.W. Currey, Inc.   Fall-Winter 2015 - 17281   2016 $8500

Stevenson, Robert Louis Balfour 1850-1894 *The Strange Case of Dr. Jekyll & Mr. Hyde.* London: John Lane Bodley Head, 1930. First edition with these illustrations, 8vo., recently rebound in half black morocco, spine lettered and ruled gilt and with gilt centre tools, top edges gilt, illustrated cloth, original front cover and set of pictorial endpapers bound in at end, silhouettes and 8 plates by S. G. Hulme Beaman, very nice.   Sotheran's   Piccadilly Notes - Summer 2015 - 281   2016   £350

Stewart, C. S. *Visit to the South Seas in the U. S. Ship Vincennes....* New York: John P.. Haven, 1831. First edition, very good, rebound in half leather, attractive set, new endpages, 12mo.   Simon Finch   2015 - 31861   2016 $215

Stewart, Frank *Cellar's Market.* London: Collins Crime Club, 1983. First edition, fine in dust jacket.   Mordida Books   2015 - 010856   2016 $65

Stewart, George R. *Bret Harte: Argonaut and Exile.* Boston and New York: Houghton Mifflin Co., 1931. First edition, 10 plates, tan cloth lettered in red, bookplate, fine, scarce.   Argonaut Book Shop   Literature 2015 - 7593   2016 $125

Stewart, George R. *Donner Pass and Those Who Crossed it.* San Francisco: California Historical Society, 1960. First edition, photos, facsimiles, maps, pictorial blue cloth, spine faded, else fine.   Argonaut Book Shop   Literature 2015 - 7354   2016 $40

Stewart, J. I. M. *The Man Who Won the Pools.* London: Victor Gollancz, 1961. First edition, crown 8vo., original red boards backstrip lettered gilt now dulled, very minor bump to bottom corners, edges little toned and spotted, ownership inscription to flyleaf, dust jacket with backstrip panel a shade darkened and owner's shelfmark to front flap, very good.   Blackwell's Rare Books   B184 - 214   2016   £30

Stewart, J. I. M. *Mark Lambert's Supper.* London: Victor Gollancz, 1954. First edition, crown 8vo., original maroon boards, backstrip lettered gilt now dulled, very minor bump to bottom corners, edges lightly dust soiled and faintly spotted, ownership inscription to flyleaf and one or two small foxspots at head of pastedowns, dust jacket with backstrip panel a shade darkened, owner's shelfmark to front flap and short closed tear at head of rear panel, good.   Blackwell's Rare Books   B184 - 213   2016   £30

Stewart, James B. *Blood Sport: the President and His Adversaries.* New York: 1996. First edition, signed by author, black and white photos and reproductions, blue cloth backed boards lettered silver, very fine in pictorial dust jacket.   Argonaut Book Shop   Literature 2015 - 6160   2016 $75

Stewart, Pamela *The Hawley Road Marsh Marigolds.* Iowa City: Meadow Press, 1975. First edition, no. 25 of 70 copies signed by author, large 8vo., tan cloth, woodcut by Leigh McLellan, nice.   Second Life Books, Inc.   196 B - 704   2016 $40

Stewart, T. McCants *Liberia: the Americo-African Republic.* New York: Edward O. Jenkins Sons, 1886. First edition, octavo, illustrations, modern quarter calf and grey paper over boards with black morocco spine label, gilt, very edge of front fly has been archivally strengthened affecting one letter in the inscription, light dampstain in bottom corner of text block, still handsome, very good copy, rare, inscribed by author to wife of journalist T. Thomas Fortune, Mrs. Carrie Fortune.   Between the Covers Rare Books   202 - 99   2016 $5000

Stewart, W. C. *A Caution to Anglers.* Edinburgh: Adam and Charles Black, 1871. First edition, 12mo., original printed wrappers bound into contemporary half blue calf over marbled paper boards, spine panelled and lettered in gilt with emblematic centre tools, little browning to titlepage, otherwise very good, bookplate of writer Dean Sage.   Sotheran's   Piccadilly Notes - Summer 2015 - 282   2016   £298

Stewart, W. C. *The Practical Angler or the Art of Trout Fishing, more particularly Applied to Clear water.* Adam and Charles Black, 1938. Reprint, 8vo original cloth, 6 colored plates and flies in pocket at end, previous owner's bookplate, spine little bumped, very good.   Sotheran's Hunting, Shooting & Fishing - 147   2016   £40

Stickney, Walt Christopher *The Bethesda Preludes.* Washington: Pushkin Press, 1982. First edition, author's presentation on half title to poet William Claire, 8 drawings in color by author, black cloth, nice in scuffed and slightly chipped dust jacket.   Second Life Books, Inc.   196 B - 705   2016 $75

Stigand, C. H. *Hunting the Elephant in Africa.* New York: St. Martin's Press, 1986. First edition, 8vo, original cloth and wrapper, photographic frontispiece, 15 plates, little rubbing to extremities of wrapper, very good.   Sotheran's Hunting, Shooting & Fishing - 24   2016   £70

Stiles, Henry Reed *Bundling, Its Origin, Progress and Decline in America.* Mount Vernon: Peter Pauper Press, 1937. Special edition, #43 of 95 hand colored copies, bound in leather, woodcuts by Herb Roth, red leather lettered in gilt, some rubbing to extremities, front cover slightly bowed, very good.   Argonaut Book Shop   Literature 2015 - 1593   2016 $60

Stillman, J. D. B. *The Horse in Motion.* London: Trubner & Co., 1882. First edition, blindstamped decorated and gilt stamped pictorial cloth, 4to., 107 plates with tissue guards, including 9 drawings, some wear to extremities, some peeling of cloth at two spine corners, rubbing on back cover (long line & spots), some tissue guards with some creases, some slight pulls/short tears at binding on some leaves, three leaves with some burning from laid in news clippings, front hinge separation after prelim blank page has been archivally closed, overall good, very scarce.   Gene W. Baade, Books on the West   2015 - 1506140   2016 $747

Stillwell, Margaret Bingham *Gutenberg and the Catholicon of 1460.* New York: Edmond Byrne Hackett, Brick Row Sheop, 1916. Library edition, large folio, title printed in red and black, original leaves laid into well in back pastedown held by metal stays, original full crimson buckram over bevelled boards by Krumin of Boston (stamp signed), covers decoratively stamped in blind, front cover lettered gilt, fine, chemised in original morocco grain paper over board and slipcase, slipcase shows wear, else fine.   Heritage Book Shop   Holiday 2015 - 72   2016 $7500

Stinson, Alvah *Woman Under the Law.* Boston: Hudson, 1914. First edition, 8vo., author's presentation on blank, blue cloth stamped in gilt, very good.   Second Life Books, Inc.   196 B - 706   2016 $150

Stirling, Edward *The Cricket on the Hearth....as performed at the Theatre Royal, Adelphi.* London: Webster and Co., 1846. original printed wrappers, little dusted, good plus.   Jarndyce Antiquarian Booksellers   CCXVIII - 383   2016   £180

Stockham, Alice Bunker *Karezza: Ethics of Marriage.* New York: Diehl, Landau & Petit, circa, 1903. New edition, original green cloth, very good in dust jacket.   Jarndyce Antiquarian Books   CCXV - 426   2016   £38

Stockton, Frank Richard *The Lady or the Tiger? and Other Stories.* New York: Charles Scribner's Sons, 1884. First edition, former owner's neat bookplate, his inked name top of titlepage and bit of professional touch-up to spine ends, corners and rear cover, else very good in two-tone pictorial cloth.   Buckingham Books   2015 - 37490   2016 $475

Stockton, Frank Richard *The Late Mrs. Null.* New York: Charles Scribner's, 1886. First edition, first issue with 6 pages of ads, octavo, brown decorated cloth, with mis-spelling of 'mattress' as 'mattrass' on page 150, octavo, very good.   Peter Ellis   112 - 386   2016   £50

Stoddard, Anne *Tony Sarg's Alphabet.* New York: Greenberg, n.d. circa, 1920. First edition, 8vo., pictorial boards, some wear to paper spine, tiny chip on endpaper else, very good+, bold clor illustrations by Tony Sarg.   Aleph-bet Books, Inc.   112 - 445   2016 $400

Stoddard, Charles Augustus *Across Russia; from the Baltic to the Danube.* London: Chapman & Hall, 1892. First UK edition, 8vo., 12 illustrations, original black and yellow decorative cloth.   J. & S. L. Bonham Antiquarian Booksellers   Europe 2016 - 8775   2016   £65

Stoddard, Charles Warren *For the Pleasure of His Company: an Affair of the Misty City, Thrice Told.* San Francisco: A. M. Robinson, 1903. First edition, octavo, fine in pictorial cloth in fine dust jacket.   Between the Covers Rare Books   208 - 31   2016 $2500

Stoddart, Thomas Tod *Angling Reminiscenses of the River and Lochs of Scotland.* Hamilton, Adams & Co., 1887. Reprint, 8vo., original blue cloth, gilt lettering and design to spine, spine dulled, partially uncut, some spotting to edges, very good.   Sotheran's   Piccadilly Notes - Summer 2015 - 283   2016   £70

Stoffel, Stephanie Lovett *The Art of Alice in Wonderland.* New York: Wonderland Press, 1998. First edition, quarto, black cloth effect paper over boards with silver stamped title on spine, illustrated endpapers, very good, light rubbing at spine ends and along edges of cover, very good dust jacket with very moderate surface wear.   Ken Sanders Rare Books   E Catalogue # 1 - 15   2016 $35

Stoker, Bram   1847-1912 *Dracula.* New York: Heritage Press, 1965. Wood engravings by Felix Hoffman, red and black cloth, spine faded, else fine in marbled slipcase, slight fading to extremities of fore edge of slipcase, Sandglass pamphlet laid in.   Argonaut Book Shop   Heritage Press 2015 - 7094   2016 $40

Stokes, Vernon *Blobbs at the Fair.* London: Chambers, n.d. circa, 1920. Folio, pictorial boards, slight bit of edge rubbing, else fine in dust jacket, illustrations by Stokes and B. Parker, with 11 fabulous full page chromolithographs and with more than 12 full page black and whites.   Aleph-bet Books, Inc.   111 - 128   2016 $800

Stokes, Vernon *A Town Dog in the Country.* London: Chambers, n.d. circa, 1924. Folio, pictorial boards, narrow 1/16th inch strip of darkening on corner of some pages else fine in dust jacket, 10 fabulous full page chromolithographs and with more full page black and whites, outstanding copy, rarely found so intact with dust jacket.   Aleph-bet Books, Inc.   111 - 129   2016 $800

Stokes, W. Royal *The Jazz Scene: an Informal History from New Orleans to 1990.* New York: Oxford, 1991. First printing, 8vo., author's presentation on flyleaf, photos, paper over boards with cloth spine, very good, tight in dust jacket.   Second Life Books, Inc.   196 B - 708   2016 $150

Stokes, William *Stokes's Rapid Writing for Rapidly Teaching to Within and for Teaching to Write Rapidly.* London: Houlston & Sons, 1874. Ninth edition, 12mo., frontispiece, illustrations, original limp green cloth, leading inner hinge, slight cracking, later signature on title.   Jarndyce Antiquarian Books   CCXV - 966   2016   £38

Stokes, William *A Treatise on the Diagnosis and Treatment of Diseases of the Chest Part 1.* Philadelphia: A. Waldie, 1837. First American edition, new cloth with red leather labels, marbled endpapers.   James Tait Goodrich   X-78 - 511   2016 $495

Stoll, Maximillian *Praelectiones in Diversos Morbows Chronicos Post eius Obitum Edidit et Praefatus est Josephus Eyerel.* Ticini: Balthassaris Comini, 1794. 8vo., cloth, 2 volumes, covers soiled, moderate foxing, good copy.   Edwin V. Glaser Rare Books   2015 - 10225   2016 $175

Stone, Harry *Dickens and the Invisible World: a Fairy Tales, Fantasy and Novel-Making.* London: Macmillan, 1980. First English edition, half title, original red cloth, very good in dust jacket, contemporary newspaper reviews pasted into prelims.   Jarndyce Antiquarian Booksellers   CCXVIII - 1457   2016   £20

Stone, Harry *Dickens' Working Notes for His Novels.* Chicago: University of Chicago Press, 1987. First edition, large 4to., half title, frontispiece and illustrations, original red cloth, very good in slightly worn dust jacket. Jarndyce Antiquarian Booksellers CCXVIII - 1453 2016 £85

Stone, Irving *The Origin: a Biographical Novel of Charles Darwin.* Garden City: Doubleday, 1980. First edition, map, author' signature, brown cloth, edges slightly soiled, otherwise very nice, scuffed and little chipped dust jacket. Second Life Books, Inc. 197 - 314 2016 $85

Stone, Reynolds *Engravings.* London: John Murray, 1977. First trade edition, printed on Basingwerk Parchment paper numerous illustrations with some printed in blue or copper, original blue buckram, backstrip lettered in gilt light rubbing to extremities, top edge blue and trifle dust soiled, dust jacket price clipped with little light dust soiling and few nicks, very good. Blackwell's Rare Books B186 - 341 2016 £50

Stone, Reynolds *The Wood Engravings of Gwen Raverat.* London: Faber and Faber, 1959. First edition, large 4to., original grey flecked cloth with printed label to spine in green and gilt, pictorial dust jacket, hundreds of wood engravings, fine in near fine, price clipped dust jacket with little rubbing at head and tail of spine. Sotheran's Piccadilly Notes - Summer 2015 - 253 2016 £225

Stone, Robert *Outerbridge Reach.* Franklin Center: Franklin Library, 1992. Limited first edition, signed by author, blue leather, lettered and decoratively stamped in gilt, all edges gilt, very fine, as new. Argonaut Book Shop Literature 2015 - 4027 2016 $60

Stone, Thomas *An Essay on Agriculture with a View to Inform Gentlemen of Landed Property....* Lynn: printed by W. Whittingham, 1785. 8vo., large uncut copy in original boards, old stain towards end, affecting final few pages and inner board, some wear to backstrip, original printed label intact, corners bumped. Jarndyce Antiquarian Booksellers CCXVI - 548 2016 £380

Stonehouse, Bernard *The Biology of Marsupials.* London: Macmillan Press, 1977. Octavo, photos, fine in dust jacket. Andrew Isles Natural History Books 55 - 21399 2016 $80

Stonehouse, Bernard *The Biology of Penguins.* London: Macmillan Press, 1975. Octavo, photos, text illustrations, very good in dust jacket, scarce. Andrew Isles Natural History Books 55 - 19885 2016 $150

Stonehouse, John Harrison *Green Leaves, New Chapters in the Life of Charles Dickens.* London: Piccadilly Fountain Press, 1931. First edition, complete in 5 original parts, original pale blue printed wrappers, very good in slightly dulled double slipcase. Jarndyce Antiquarian Booksellers CCXVIII - 1458 2016 £25

Stoner, Winifred Sackville *Facts in Jingles.* Indianapolis: Bobbs Merrill, 1915. 8vo. author's presentation on flyleaf, light blue cloth, printed in gilt, occasional light foxing, cover slightly scuffed at corners and ends of spine, otherwise very good, tight copy. Second Life Books, Inc. 196 B - 710 2016 $45

Stonham, Charles *The Birds of the British Islands.* London: E. Grant Richards, 1906-1911. Large quarto, 5 volumes, 318 uncolored plates by Lillian Medland, publisher's cloth, top edge gilt, few flecks, internally some light spotting. Andrew Isles Natural History Books 55 - 32428 2016 $2000

Stonhouse, J. *Every Man's Assistant and the Sick Man's Friend.* London: C. and J. Rivington, 1825. New edition, original blue sugar boards, newly rebacked, from a note in prelims, this appears to be a third edition, uncut, nice. James Tait Goodrich X-78 - 512 2016 $275

Stookey, Byron *Surgical and Mechanical Treatment of Peripheral Nerves.* Philadelphia: Saunders, 1922. Illustrations plus two colored plates, original cloth, light rubbbing, overll very good, clean tight copy. James Tait Goodrich X-78 - 513 2016 $295

Stookey, Byron *Trigeminal Neuralgia. Its History and Treatment.* Springfield: 1959. original cloth, original dust jacket worn, internally fine, presentation from Joseph Ransohoff for Edgar Houseplan. James Tait Goodrich X-78 - 518 2016 $150

Stopes, Marie *Married Love.* A. C. Fifield, 1918. First edition, 8vo., original brown cloth, previous owner's signature, binding little rubbed, little spotting particularly to last few leaves, very good. Sotheran's Piccadilly Notes - Summer 2015 - 285 2016 £200

Storck, Anton *Annus Medicus quo Sistuntur Observations circa Morbos Acutos et Chronicos. (bound with) Annus Medicus Secundus. (bound with) Nosocomio Civico Pazmariano Physici...* Vienna: Trubner, 1760. 1761. 1760., 8vo., early vellum, binding soiled, internally browned and foxed, completely illegible, good copy only. Edwin V. Glaser Rare Books 2015 - 10380 2016 $100

Storey, Gladys *Dickens and Daughter.* London: Frederick Muller, 1939. First edition, half title, frontispiece, plates, original blue cloth, spine lettered gilt, very good, bright copy. Jarndyce Antiquarian Booksellers CCXVIII - 1460 2016 £35

Stories of Birds. N.P.: 184-? First edition, 18mo., 24 nicely engraved and colored full page plates, original stamped cloth.   M & S Rare Books, Inc.   99 - 61   2016 $350

Storke, Thomas M. *California Editor.* Los Angeles: Westernlore Press, 1958. First edition, frontispiece, 59 illustrations, pictorial endpapers, brown cloth, fine in spine faded dust jacket.   Argonaut Book Shop   Biography 2015 - 3762   2016 $40

Storrs, Ronald *Orientations.* London: Ivor Nicholson & Watson, 1937. First edition, signed presentation inscribed by author to Bertram Thomas, 8vo., original dark blue cloth, blocked gilt, pictorial dust jacket, map endpapers, frontispiece, 13 plates, two text illustrations, foldout map and one map in text, initial blank.   Sotheran's   Travel and Exploration - 380   2016   £498

The Story of a Pupil Teacher. London: SPCK, 1876. Frontispiece, 4 pages ads, original brick red cloth, very good.   Jarndyce Antiquarian Books   CCXV - 969   2016   £40

The Story of the American Firemen. New York: McLoughlin Bros., 1909. Cloth backed pictorial boards, one corner bumped, else fine, scarce, 4 magnificent full page chromolithographs, plus several smaller chromos and many line illustrations, excellent copy, rarely found so clean.   Aleph-bet Books, Inc.   112 - 307   2016 $475

Story of the Three Little Pigs. New York: McLoughlin Bros., 1892. 4to., pictorial wrappers, 2 tiny edge mends, spine slightly rough, else very good+, die cut on top edge in shape of pig's head, 6 fine full page, full color covers, six 4 color lithos and 1 double page 4 color litho.   Aleph-bet Books, Inc.   111 - 275   2016 $325

The Story of the Typewriter 1873-1923. New York: Herkimer, 1923. First edition, octavo, illustrations, original paper boards with cover plate, spine little bruised at head, free endpapers partially and faintly tanned, very good.   Peter Ellis   112 - 413   2016   £50

Stout, Rex *Fer-de-Lance.* New York: Farrar & Rinehart, 1934. First edition, near fine in near fine example of scarce dust jacket, pink topstain very bright, gilt bright and complete, jacket with only a couple of tiny chips, some expert repairs and restoration at upper spine panel and some strengthening along flap folds.   Royal Books   51 - 16   2016 $25,000

Stout, Rex *How Like a God.* New York: Vanguard Press, 1929. 8vo., original purple cloth stamped on front cover "Discussion copy', original purple cloth stamped on front cover, purple cloth slightly faded at spine and edges, else clean, very good to near fine copy, lacking dust jacket, custom chemise and slipcase, laid in is ad leaf from Aug 24 1929 issue of American Mercury.   Sotheran's   Piccadilly Notes - Summer 2015 - 286   2016   £298

Stout, Rex *Over My Dead Body.* New York: Avon, 1945. Paperback edition, Avon no. 62, fine in wrappers with tiny wear at top front corner.   Mordida Books   2015 - 011129   2016 $65

Stout, Rex *The Red Box.* New York: Farrar and Rinehart, 1937. First edition, very good in like dust jacket, spine lean, some wear along joints, else book is bright and clean, jacket complete with touch of fading to red titling on spine, small chips at couple of corners and split along front flap fold running about halfway down, bright presentable copy.   Royal Books   51 - 17   2016 $9500

Stow, Randolph *Tourmaline.* London: Macdonald, 1963. First edition, octavo, covers very faintly stained at edges, very good in like dust jacket, very slightly rubbed.   Peter Ellis   112 - 388   2016   £35

Stowe, Harriet Elizabeth Beecher   1811-1896 *The Key to Uncle Tom's Cabin...* Boston: John P. Jewett & Co., Cleveland: Jewett, Proctor & Worthington, 1853. First edition, tall 8vo., bound in black cloth rubbed at tips, worn at bottom of spine, torn at top with little loss along hinge, lacks part of front blank endpaper.   Second Life Books, Inc.   197 - 315   2016 $400

Strachan, W. J. *Modern Italian Stories.* London: Eyre & Spottiswoode, 1955. First edition, octavo, very good in like dust jacket, slightly chipped, nicked and rubbed dust jacket, bit darkened at spine, presentation from Strachan, inscribed for Nancy and Walter, tipped in is slip on which is typed the review of this book in the Observer newspaper.   Peter Ellis   112 - 389   2016   £80

Strada, Famiano *Prolusiones Academicae.* Oxford: Sheldonian Theatre, 1745. 8vo., engraved publisher's vignette to titlepage, wide margins, little browning on one page, pencilled note to page 216, occasional light foxing, contemporary vellum, marbled edges and endpapers, spine darkened and ink largely rubbed away, boards somewhat marked, corners bumped.   Unsworths Antiquarian Booksellers Ltd.   E01 - Early Printing - 23   2016   £250

The Strand Magazine. 1891-1914. Volumes 1-49, lacking 40, 41, 44, 48, together 45 volumes, 36 being in original publisher's cloth, rest in mixed bindings, very good.   I. D. Edrich   Crime - 2016   £1250

The Strand Magazine. Volume XLII July to December. London: George Newnes Ltd., 1911. First edition, thick 8vo., original pictorial blue cloth, spine stylized titles in black and gold gilt, upper front cover with title and pictorial scene in black, illustrations, all edges gilt, lovely fore-edge painting featuring likeness of Arthur Conan Doyle on one side and portrait of Sherlock Holmes based on illustration on page 609, lightly rubbed at spine ends and corners, else very good, clean, tight, the fore-edge painting in fine condition. Buckingham Books   2015 - 32260   2016 $3750

Strand, Clark *North Star.* N.P.: Red Hydra Press, 1992. Limited to 90 numbered copies signed by author, 15 harrd-bound by artist, this copy thus, 12mo., quarter cloth, gilt paper covered boards, illustrations by Douglas Himes. Oak Knoll Books   310 - 144   2016 $125

Strand, Mark *89 Clouds.* New York: ACA Galleries, 1999. First edition, one of only 20 copies specially bound with original signed monotype by Wendy Mark laid into pocket at back of book, also signed by author and artist, square 8vo., reproductions of monotypes by Wendy Mark, original handmade roma paper over boards with printed paper label on spine by Claudia Cohen, as new.   James S. Jaffe Rare Books   Occasional List: Winter 2016 - 135   2016 $2500

Strand, Robert *Wood Engravings.* n.p., n.d. circa, 2001. First edition, 4to., original printed wrappers, near fine. Blackwell's Rare Books   B186 - 344   2016   £30

A Strange and Wonderful Account of the Great Mischiefs, Sustained by the late Dreadful Thunder, Ligthening and Terrible land Floods... London: J. Wright, I. Clarke, W. Thackery...., 1683. First edition, small 8vo., woodcut, three crude woodcut illustrations on recto final leaf, cropped at foot with lower edge of A1-2 and A7-8 repaired (with loss to imprint and some minor loss of occasional catchwords), titlepage very lightly spotted, staining to fore-margin of A3 (affecting final word on approximately 18 lines), early 19th century half calf and drab boards, front board scuffed, from the library of James Stevens Cox (1910-1997).   Maggs Bros. Ltd.   1447 - 401   2016   £4500

Strange, Edward F. *Alphabets: a Handbook of Lettering with Historical Critical & Practical Descriptions.* London: George Bell & Sons, 1895. First edition, this being one of 75 numbered copies, printed on Japanese vellum, frontispiece and illustrations, 8vo., original stiff paper wrappers, edges uncut, folded paper cover, spine darkened, edges of spine chipped, very light tanning, mainly near edges of text. Oak Knoll Books   310 - 152   2016 $400

Strange, Ian J. *The Falkland Islands.* Newton Abbot: David & Charles, 1972. First edition, 8vo. original cloth, dust jacket, black and white illustrations, near fine. Sotheran's   Piccadilly Notes - Summer 2015 - 287   2016   £40

Strange, Robert *An Inquiry Into the Rise and Establishment of the Royal Academy of Arts.* London: printed for E. and C. Dilly in the Poultry, 1775. First edition, Large copy, stamp of Hampstead Pub. Libraries on titlepage verso and in margins of a number of leaves, waterstaining to upper and lower margins of some leaves, but paper still crisp, plainly bound in full dark brown calf, blind ruled bands to spine, gilt lettering.   Jarndyce Antiquarian Booksellers CCXVI - 549   2016   £185

Stratton, Clarence *Theatron: an Illustrated Record.* New York: Henry Holt, 1928. First edition, 8vo., 150 illustrations, author's presentation on flyleaf, hinge tender, cover worn with some insect damage.   Second Life Books, Inc.   196 B - 713   2016 $45

Strauss, David Friedrich *The Life of Jesus Critically Examined.* London: Chapman Bros., 1846. translated from the fourth German edition, 3 volumes, tall 8vo., half titles, contemporary full brown calf, spines gilt in compartments, maroon and black leather labels, slight rubbing to spine volume III, odd small mark, inner hinges strengthened with brown tape, blindstamps and labels of Birkbeck College Library, good plus.   Jarndyce Antiquarian Booksellers CCXVII - 96   2016   £1250

Streatfeild, Noel *The Circus is Coming.* London: J. M. Dent and Sons ltd., 1938. First edition, 8vo., newly and handsomely bound in half dark blue calf over dark blue polished cloth sides, spine with 5 raised bands ruled and lettered gilt, gilt centres, top edge gilt, original cloth, spine and cover bound in at rear, line drawings by Spurrier, fine. Sotheran's   Piccadilly Notes - Summer 2015 - 289   2016 £198

Street, George Edmund *Brick and Marble in the Middle Ages.* London: John Murray, 1855. First edition, plates, text illustrations, half title, 32 page catalog, Nov. 1856, original dark mustard cloth, boards blocked in blind, spine lettered in gilt.   Jarndyce Antiquarian Booksellers CCXVII - 268   2016   £125

Street, John *Dr. Priestley's Quest.* Geoffrey Bles, 1926. Proof copy, blush bound, as issued, very gentle toning to pages, crown 8vo., original wrappers, backstrip lettered black and slightly sunned with small amount of rubbing at foot, little foxing to front, some pages uncut, very good. Blackwell's Rare Books   B184 - 225   2016   £3000

Streeton, Hesba *Max Kromer. The Story of the Siege of Strasbourg.* London: Religious Tract Society, circa, 1897. Frontispiece, illustrations, original light brown pictorial cloth, prize inscription 1898, very good, bright.   Jarndyce Antiquarian Booksellers   CCXVII - 257   2016   £25

Stribling, T. S. *Clues to the Caribbees.* Garden City: Doubleday, 1929. Very good, name stamps on front endpapers, spine worn and soiled and corner slightly bumped, otherwise very good without dust jacket. Mordida Books 2015 - 009961 2016 $65

Strickland, Hugh *Ornithological Synonyms. Volume One: Accipitres.* London: John Van Voorst, 1855. Octavo, publisher's cloth, some wear, signature and bookplate of H. M. Whittell, scarce. Andrew Isles Natural History Books 55 - 31219 2016 $300

Stringer, Arthur *Night Hawk.* New York: Burt, Reprint edition, fine in very fine, as new dust jacket. Mordida Books 2015 - 012376 2016 $65

Stringer, George Eyre *New Hall Porcelain.* London: Salisbury Square, 1949. First edition, numerous black and white plates, color frontispiece, fine copy in chipped and lightly soiled dust jacket. Argonaut Book Shop Pottery and Porcelain 2015 - 984 2016 $80

Strobridge, William F. *Regulars in the Redwoods.* Spokane: Arthur H. Clark Co., 1994. First edition, one of 1027 copies, 11 maps and views, blue cloth, very fine with pictorial dust jacket. Argonaut Book Shop Native American 2015 - 7139 2016 $75

Strong, James *Joanereidos; or Feminine Valour...* London: reprinted Anno Dom., 1674. Second edition, small 4to., spotted and lightly browned, some tearing in inner margin of title and following two leaves caused by original stitching, many edges uncut, early19th century half calf and marbled boards, headcaps damaged and edges rubbed, from the library of James Stevens Cox (1910-1997), signature of Edward Rowe Mores (1730-1778), the copy of James Boswell the younger (1778-1822), small signature of Thomas Park (1658/9-1834). Maggs Bros. Ltd. 1447 - 402 2016 £1500

Strong, Leonard Alfred George *The Open sky.* London: Victor Gollancz, 1939. First edition, octavo, laid in is Book Society bookplate signed by author, fine in very good, slightly nicked and creased and dust jacket, faded at spine and edges, uncommon in such bright condition. Peter Ellis 112 - 390 2016 £65

Strongman, Phil *John Lennon and the FBI Files.* Sanctuary, 2003. First edition, signed by Alan Parker, 8vo., original paper wrappers, black and white photos, fine. Sotheran's Piccadilly Notes - Summer 2015 - 36 2016 £50

Struther, Jan *The Modern Struwwelpeter.* London: Methuen and Co., 1936. First edition, royal 8vo., original green cloth backed pictorial cream boards, illustrations by E. H. Shepard printed in duotone colors of blue and orange, very acceptable copy with light dusting and rubbing to boards, edges and some of the usual wrinkling of paper to lower cover, internally generally very clean with one or two faint and small marginal splash marks and little cracking, rather scarce. Sotheran's Piccadilly Notes - Summer 2015 - 274 2016 £148

Strutt, Joseph *The Sports and Pastimes of the People of England Including the Rural and Domestic Recreations...* London: printed for Thomas Tegg, 1831. 260 x 165mm., very attractive later 19th century deep forest green crushed morocco, gilt by William Matthews (stamp-signed), covers with gilt French fillet, raised bands, spine gilt in compartments with central hunting themed ornament, stippled scrolling cornerpieces, gilt titling, turn-ins with very elegant gilt scrolling floral decoration, marbled endleaves, all edges gilt, 137 illustrations, full page plate and 136 numbered wood engravings in text, bookplate of George Edward Dimock, isolated very minor foxing, otherwise in very fine condition, unusual clean and fresh internally and accomplished binding lustrous and unworn. Phillip J. Pirages 67 - 56 2016 $1500

Strutt, Joseph *The Sports and Pastimes of the People of England... from the Earliest Period to the Present Time.* London: printed for Thomas Tegg, 1845. New edition, 8vo., many illustrations in text, few spots of light foxing to couple of pages front and rear, generally clean with, claret morocco, heavily gilt spine and borders, green morocco label, all edges gilt, marbled endpapers, spine faded, raised bands, joints and edges worn, few scuffs but still very good. Unsworths Antiquarian Booksellers Ltd. 30 - 144 2016 £150

Stuart-Wortley, A. *The Partridge.* London: Longmans, Green & Co., 1893. First edition, 8vo., original decorative cloth lettered in red with gilt title to spine, illustrations, previous owner's bookplates and signatures, otherwise very good. Sotheran's Hunting, Shooting & Fishing - 99 2016 £50

Stuart-Wortley, A. *The Pheasant.* London: Longmans, Green & Co., 1895. First edition, 8vo., original decorative cloth, lettered in red, gilt title to spine, illustrations, previous owner's bookplate and signature to endpapers, very good. Sotheran's Hunting, Shooting & Fishing - 100 2016 £50

Stuart, Andrew *Letters to the right Honourable Lord Mansfield from Andrew Stuart Esqr.* London: printed in the month of January, 1773. 8vo., excellently rebound in half calf, marbled paper boards, spine ruled in gilt, red morocco label, early bookplate of Chas. Willm. Bigge retained. Jarndyce Antiquarian Booksellers CCXVI - 550 2016 £185

Stuart, Gilbert *A View of Society in Europe....* London: printed for J. Murray, 1783. Second edition, 4to., slight wear to outer corner of A1, light browning to margin of two leaves, bound without half title, half calf, rebacked, spine with gilt twist bands, red gilt morocco label. Jarndyce Antiquarian Booksellers CCXVI - 551 2016 £420

Stuart, Jesse *Danelion on the Acropolis a Journal of Greece.* Archers Editions Press, 1978. Limited numbered edition, no. 18 of 250 copies, signed by author, cloth with gilt stamped spine, photos, fine, as new in snug slipcase, rare. Gene W. Baade, Books on the West 2015 - FTR162 2016 $292

Stuart, Jesse *Foretaste of Glory.* New York: Dutton, 1946. First edition, cloth, presentation copy signed by author, bookplate, very good in chipped dust jacket with several splits archivally repaired. Gene W. Baade, Books on the West 2015 - FTR156 2016 $40

Stuart, Jesse *Head O' W-Hollow.* New York: Dutton, 1936. First edition, pictorial cloth, long presentation inscription signed and dated by Stuart, two former owner's signatures, one on front pastedown and the other above the presentation, covers soiled, spine somewhat darkened, foxing on pastedowns, 2-3 small foxing spots to text, good copy, laid in is ALS from Stuart, rare. Gene W. Baade, Books on the West 2015 - FTR172 2016 $273

Stuart, John *Sir John Kirk.* London: S. W. Partridge & Co., 1907. Second edition, half title, frontispiece, plates, 32 page catalog, text pages slightly browned, few spots, original blue cloth, inner hinges cracking, inscribed by Kirk. Jarndyce Antiquarian Books CCXV - 812 2016 £25

Stuart, John Sobieski *Lays of the Deer Forest.* Diss: Anthony Atha Publishers, 1985. No. 279 of a limited edition of 350 copies, oblong 4to., original green cloth, gilt rules and stag' head to upper board, gilt lettering and decoration to spine, color plates and text illustrations by Ian Oates, fine, inscribed from Lord Lovat to friend Wyndham (Lloyd-Davies). Sotheran's Hunting, Shooting & Fishing - 65 2016 £350

Stuart, Robert *Duncan Ross Detective Sergeant.* Blackie & son, 1935. Covers unevenly faded and little worn, spine tender, front hinge cracking, some edge spotting not affecting text, internally very good. I. D. Edrich Crime - 2016 £30

Stubbes, George *A New Adventure of Telemachus.* London: printed by W. Wilkins, 1731. Titlepage woodcut, large engraved head and tailpieces, decorated initial, 8vo. in 4s, small tear to inner margin of titlepage well clear of text, lower margin close cropped affecting imprint date, disbound, very good, clean copy. Jarndyce Antiquarian Booksellers CCXVI - 552 2016 £90

Studdy, G. E. *Animals in Wonderland Animals.* No publication information, British circa 1940's, Oblong 4to., flexible pictorial card covers, slightest bit of cover fading, else fine, every page with color illustration. Aleph-bet Books, Inc. 112 - 469 2016 $200

Studer, Jacob H. *The Birds of North America.* New York: Natural Science Association of America, 1888. 391 x 298 mm., original turkey half morocco and buckram, upper cover with gilt decorative titling, joints and tips renewed with calf, original backstrip preserved, spine panels with blindstamped fleuron, floral patterned endpapers, all edges gilt, frontispiece, 11 chromolithographs of North American Birds, after crayon drawings by Theodore Jasper, all with tissue guards, some rubbing and scuffing to spine, joints and extremities (noticeable without being severe), small white stain to upper cover, frontispiece rather foxed, isolated minor smudges of thumbing, otherwise very good, text and plates clean and fresh, binding completely sound. Phillip J. Pirages 67 - 321 2016 $750

Studley, Barrett *Practical Flight Training.* London: Macmillan, 1928. First edition, original cloth with dust jacket, fine. Sotheran's Piccadilly Notes - Summer 2015 - 290 2016 £148

Stuhlmann, Gunther *Anais: an International Journal.* LA: 1983-2001. 8vo., printed wrappers, laid in TLS from editor to William Claire, 15 issues in all, volumes 1, 3, 7, 8, 9, 10, 11, 12, 13, 14, 15, 16, 17, 18, 19, very good+. Second Life Books, Inc. 196 B - 715 2016 $275

Sturgeon, Theodore *The Dreaming Jewels.* New York: Greenberg Corwin, 1950. First edition, inscribed by author, slight sunning to board edges and tanning to endpaper, near fine in like dust jacket (lightly rubbed), reader response card laid in. Ken Lopez Bookseller 166 - 123 2016 $250

Sturgeon, Theodore *Maturity.* Minneapolis/St. Paul: Rune Press/Minnesota Science Fiction Society, 1979. Limited edition, of a total edition of 750 copies, this number 337 of 700, signed by author, fine in near fine, very slightly sunned dust jacket. Ken Lopez Bookseller 166 - 124 2016 $75

Sturges, Jock *Radiant Identities.* New York: Aperture, 1994. First edition, quarto, presentation inscription signed by Sturges, half black cloth, gray boards, very fine, pictorial dust jacket, slight wrinkle to laminate on front of jacket (not too bad), no tears or chips. Argonaut Book Shop Photography 2015 - 5560 2016 $250

Sturz, J. J. *A Review, Financial, Statistical & Commercial of the Empire of Brazil and Its Resources.* London: Effingham Wilson, 1837. First edition, 8vo., slightly later dark green pebble grained cloth, spine lettered gilt, yellow endpapers large folding table, others in text, very light marginal wear, title and last leaf little spotted due to offsetting from flyleaves, from Gloucestershire County Library with their stamps and shelfmarks, contemporary engraved armorial bookplate of G. R. Porter.   Sotheran's   Travel and Exploration - 74   2016   £398

Success in Life. A Book for Young men.   London: T. Nelson & Sons, 1881. Frontispiece, original green cloth, blocked in black and gilt, front board slightly dulled and marked, otherwise very nice, prize label.   Jarndyce Antiquarian Books CCXV - 427   2016   £28

Suckling, John   *Fragmenta Aurea. A collection of al the Incomparable Peeces.*   London: for Humphrey Moseley, 1646. First edition, first state, engraved portrait, contemporary calf, gilt fillet and cornerpieces, red morocco spine label, portrait and first two leaves with two very tiny holes at gutter, worm trail in lower margin of first three gatherings, else very nice in lovely contemporary binding, bookplate of C. Pearl Chamberlain and book label of Abel Berland, fine red morocco pull of case, accompanied by ALS of John Suckling (1569-1627) father of the poet to unnamed recipient.   Joseph J. Felcone, Inc.   Books from Five Centuries: a Miscellany - 138   2016 $6000

Sucksmith, Harvey Peter   *The Narrative Art of Charles Dickens...*   Oxford: Clarendon Press, 1970. First edition, half title, frontispiece, original dark blue cloth, very good in dust jacket.   Jarndyce Antiquarian Booksellers   CCXVIII - 1461   2016   £20

Sueter, Murray F.   *The Evolution of the Submarine Boat, Mine and Torpedo from the Sixteenth Century to the Present Time.*   Portsmouth: J. Griffin & Co., 1907. First edition, large 8vo., modern half morocco over marbled boards, spine lettered gilt, boards ruled in gilt, highly illustrated with plates, title and last leaf with light spotting, few plates with minor crinkling, still good.   Sotheran's   Travel and Exploration - 476   2016   £198

Suetonius   *Les Douze Cesars.*   Paris: F. L. Schmied, 1928. No. 165 of 175 copies, signed by artist, 292 x 200mm., dark blue crushed morocco by Gonin (stamp signed), spine lettered in gilt, turn-ins with silver fillet border, royal blue leather doublures and matching moire silk endleaves, original wrappers preserved, housed in later suede backed slipcase, decorative title and section titles printed in gold an 23 color illustrations by Schmied, comprised of 9 vignette tailpieces and 14 full page plates including 12 portraits, cracks with some looseness, along joints (no doubt because of heavy boards), covers with light polish residue, original wrappers heavily foxed, plates and text clean and fresh.   Phillip J. Pirages   67 - 310   2016 $2800

Suffolk & Berkshire, Earl of   *The Encyclopaediae of Sport.*   London: Lawrence and Bullen Ltd., 1897. First edition, large 8vo., 2 volumes, contemporary half red morocco, gilt spines, marbled endpapers, all edges gilt, 40 plates, numerous text illustrations, little rubbing to extremities, very good.   Sotheran's   Hunting, Shooting & Fishing - 231   2016   £500

Sugerman, Danny   *The Doors - The Illustrated History.* New York: William Morrow and Co., 1983. First edition, signed by Ray Manzarek, Danny Sugerman and Robby Krieger, fine in dust jacket.   Buckingham Books   2015 - 11547   2016 $450

Sukenick, Ronald   *Down and In.*   New York: Morrow, 1987. First edition, photos, maps on endpapers, author's presentation on title, paper over boards with cloth spine, corners of covers little bumped, otherwise nice in scuffed and little chipped dust jacket.   Second Life Books, Inc. 196 B - 719   2016 $45

Sukenick, Ronald   *Out: a Novel.*   Chicago: Swallow, 1973. First edition, first printing, 8vo., author's presentation on title, green cloth, nice in little soiled and peeling dust jacket.   Second Life Books, Inc.   196 B - 720   2016 $45

Sullivan, George   *An Address of Members of the House of Representatives of the Congress of the United States, to their Constituents on the Subject of the War with Great Britain.*   Hanover: Printed by Charles Spear, 1812. First edition, 8vo., removed from original binding, very good-, tear along spine tail, with small institutional stamp on top of margin of title, signed by George Sullivan and 33 other Federalist member.   Kaaterskill Books   21 - 112   2016 $100

Sullivan, James   *The History of Land Titles in Massachusetts.*   Boston: I. Thomas and E. T. Andrews for the author, August, 1801. First edition, large 8vo., recent cloth, paper label.   M & S Rare Books, Inc.   99 - 173 2016 $550

Sulpicius   *Letters of Sulpicius, on the Northern Confederacy.*   London: printed by Thomas Baylis for William Cobbett, 1801. First edition, small 8vo., disbound, removed from larger volume, otherwise very good, scattered foxing. Kaaterskill Books   21 - 96   2016 $175

A Summer Month or Recollections of a Visit to the Falls of Niagara and its Lakes.   Philadelphia: H. C. Carey and I. Lea, 1823. First edition, 8vo., original printed boards, stained and soiled, uncut, foxed and waterstained.   M & S Rare Books, Inc.   99 - 211   2016 $325

Sumner, Mary Elizabeth *Nursery Training: a Book for Nurses.* London: Warren & Son, circa, 1892. Third edition, half title, frontispiece, original light brown decorated cloth, very good. Jarndyce Antiquarian Books CCXV - 971 2016 £30

Sumption, Jonathan *The Albigensian Crusade.* London: Faber & Faber, 1978. First edition, 8vo., cloth gilt lettered, edges lightly dusted, very good, dust jacket, minor shelf-wear, near fine, ownership inscription of Michael Hall in pen to front pastedown. Unsworths Antiquarian Booksellers Ltd. E05 - 89 2016 £25

Sunshine for Showery Days. London: S. W. Partridge, circa, 1890? Second edition, folio, frontispiece, illustrations, 2 pages ads, spine cracked in places but still firm, original cream paper printed boards, pictorial blocked in color, green cloth, spine slightly dulled but remarkably well preserved copy, prize label of Bickley & Widmore Sunday School dated 1890. Jarndyce Antiquarian Books CCXV - 800 2016 £75

Sunter, George *Voluntaryism Versus Violence as the Motive Power of Education.* Derby: G Wilkins, 1852. 2nd edition, disbound. Jarndyce Antiquarian Books CCXV - 974 2016 £25

Surrey, Henry Howard, Earl of *Songes and Sonettes.* London: in Fletestrete within Temple Barre at the Signe of the Hand and Tarre, by Richard Tottell, Anno, 1567, reprinted by E. Curll, 1717. Re-issue of Curll's 1717 edition, half title, 8vo. in 4's, disbound, very good. Jarndyce Antiquarian Booksellers CCXVI - 553 2016 £110

Surtees, Robert Smith 1803-1864 *Handley Cross.* London: Bradbury, Agnew & Co. Ltd. circa, 1870. Large 8vo., sometime rebound in half red morocco over marbled paper covered boards, raised bands, gilt lettering and hunting motif to spine, top edge gilt, other edges untrimmed, marbled endpapers, spine sunned, otherwise very good in attractive binding. Sotheran's Hunting, Shooting & Fishing - 48 2016 £198

Surtees, Robert Smith 1803-1864 *Hawbuck Grange; or the Sporting Adventures of Thomas Scott Esq.* London: Bradbury Agnew and Co. Ltd., circa, 1870. Large 8vo., sometime rebound half red morocco, marbled paper covered boards, raised bands, gilt lettering and hunting motifs to spine, top edge gilt, other edges untrimmed, marbled endpapers, spine slightly sunned, past ownership bookplate, owner signature, otherwise very good in attractive binding. Sotheran's Hunting, Shooting & Fishing - 46 2016 £198

Surtees, Robert Smith 1803-1864 *Hillingdon Hall; or the Cockney Squire.* London: George Routledge and Sons, circa, 1870. Large 8vo., sometime rebound in half brown calf over green marbled paper covered boards, all edges gilt, gilt lettering and extensive gilt floral designs to spine, green marbled endpapers, slightly worn or faded in places, but still attractive copy, interior bright and clean, past ownership bookplate. Sotheran's Hunting, Shooting & Fishing - 45 2016 £248

Surtees, Robert Smith 1803-1864 *Hunting with Mr. Jorrocks.* London: Geoffrey Cumberlege, Oxford University Press, 1956. First edition illustrated by Edward Ardizzone, 8vo., newly and handsomely bound in half dark blue calf over dark blue polished cloth boards, spine with 5 raised bands, ruled and lettered gilt with gilt centres, top edges gilt, with a total of 9 colored lithographic plates, fine. Sotheran's Piccadilly Notes - Summer 2015 - 168 2016 £198

Surtees, Robert Smith 1803-1864 *Hunts with Jorrocks.* London: Hodder & Stoughton, 1908. Second edition thus, 4to., original scarlet cloth, gilt lettering and vignette to upper board, gilt lettering to spine, 25 color plate illustrations tipped in to green card, spine dulled, sometime recased, very good. Sotheran's Hunting, Shooting & Fishing - 49 2016 £150

Surtees, Robert Smith 1803-1864 *Jorrocks's Jaunts.* London: George Routledge & sons Ltd. circa, 1870. New edition, large 8vo., half red calf over marbled boards, top edge gilt, gilt panels, lettering and lavish floral decorations to spine, spine sunned and some light wear to corners, good copy, illustrations and text remaining bright, past ownership bookplate, attached to front free endpaper. Sotheran's Hunting, Shooting & Fishing - 44 2016 £248

Surtees, Robert Smith 1803-1864 *Mr. Sponge's Sporting Tour.* London: Bradbury Agnew and Co. Ltd. circa, 1870. Large 4to., sometime bound in half red morocco over marbled paper covered boards, raised bands, gilt lettering and hunting motifs to spine, top edge gilt, other edges untrimmed, marbled endpapers, 4to., spine slightly sunned, past ownership bookplate to front pastedown, endpaper and past owner signature, otherwise very good, in attractive binding, illustrations by John Leech. Sotheran's Hunting, Shooting & Fishing - 47 2016 £198

Surtees, Robert Smith 1803-1864 *Romford's Hounds.* London: Bradbury, Agnew and Co. Ltd. circa, 1870. Large 8vo., sometime bound in half red morocco over marbled paper covered boards, raised bands, gilt lettering and hunting motifs to spine, top edge gilt, other edges untrimmed, marbled endpapers, spine slightly sunned, past ownership bookplate, past owner signature, otherwise very good, attractive binding. Sotheran's Hunting, Shooting & Fishing - 43 2016 £198

Sutherland, Captain *A Tour Up the Straits from Gibraltar to Constaninople; with the leading Events in the Present war Between the Austrians, Russians and the Turks to the Commencement of the year 1789.* London: J. Johnson, 1790. First edition, 8vo., contemporary brown half calf, small crack at base of spine, corners rubbed, library label on front endpaper, but no stamps in text, good.   J. & S. L. Bonham Antiquarian Booksellers   Europe 2016 - 8380   2016   £400

Suzannet, Alain, Comte De *Catalogue of a Further Portion of the Well Known Library, the Property of the Comte De Suzannet, La Petite Chardiere, Lausanne...* Sotheby and Co., 1938. Frontispiece, original green wrappers, slightly spotted & rubbed.   Jarndyce Antiquarian Booksellers   CCXVIII - 1519   2016   £25

Svietlov, Valerian *Anna Pavlova.* Paris: de Brunoff, 1922. No. 30 of 325 copies of French edition, signed by editor, Maurice de Brunoff, 343 x 260mm., pleasing contemporary red (publisher's deluxe?) pebble grain morocco, upper cover with gilt lettering and calligraphic flourish, raised bands, spine panels with gilt sultana centerpiece, gilt titling, mustard yellow endpapers, edges untrimmed, modern marbled paper slipcase, decorative engraved head and tailpieces, 22 plates (with tissue guards), as called for, and more than 50 illustrations in text, two tiny nicks on back cover, one plate with light marginal foxing, otherwise only most trivial imperfections, very fine, especially with clean and fresh leaves and in unworn, lustrous binding.   Phillip J. Pirages   67 - 274   2016 $2250

Svietlov, Valerian *Inedited Works of Bakst.* New York: Brentano's, 1927. No. 66 of 600 copies of the American edition, 337 x 261mm., publisher's ivory paper boards backed with linen upper cover with color vignette by Bakst, scarce original pictorial dust jacket, housed in modern cloth slipcase; woodcut headpieces and decorative initials, and 42 plates, comprised of 20 full page hand colored plates heightened with gold or silver, 9 full page black and white plates, one magenta full page plate and 12 mounted or tipped-on color plates (with tissue guards), all reproducing works by Bakst, dust jacket panels bit toned and lightly foxed, jacket spine with thumb sized portion missing and front joint partly torn, covers and spine of volume itself in fine condition, contents beginning to come loose (though still intact), because of perishing gutta percha, some offsetting from illustrations without tissue guards, text very fresh and vibrantly colored plates clean and pleasing.   Phillip J. Pirages   67 - 20   2016 $3500

Swan, James G. *The Northwest Coast; or Three Years' Residence in Washington Territory.* New York: Harper & Bros., 1857. First edition, publisher's brown buckram, flat spine with gilt tiling, 29 illustrations by author, 18 of these full page, one a folding map, front free endpaper, inscribed by author to Mrs. C. W. Philbrick, with neatly stamped signature of Ellen Philbrick, bookplate of Frederick V. Holman, spine bit sunned, extremities slightly worn, small patches of water(?) stains to boards, other trivial imperfections, really excellent copy, fresh and clean, original fragile binding still solid and generally well preserved.   Phillip J. Pirages   67 - 271   2016 $1100

Swann, Brian *Elizabeth.* Lincoln: Penmaen, 1981. First edition, large 8vo., title illustration by Michael McCurdy, one of 150 copies specially bound, numbered and signed by artist, and author, patterned green and white paper over boards, three quarter linen, fine in acrylic jacket.   Second Life Books, Inc.   196 B - 724   2016 $70

Swanton, John R. *The Indian Tribes of North America.* Washington: GPO, 1952. First edition, one single page map, 4 large folding maps, green cloth, gilt, endpapers renewed, spine slightly faded, overall fine copy.   Argonaut Book Shop   Native American 2015 - 5538   2016 $125

Swarzenski, Hanns *Die Latenischen Illuminierten Handschriften des XIII. Jahrhunderts in Den Landern an Rhein...* Berlin: Deutscher Verein Fur Kunstwissenschaft, 1936. First edition, 2 volumes, folio, half vellum with paper covered boards, 2020 plates, 1096 illustrations, loosely inserted commemorative booklabel indicating this book came from reference library of H. P. Kraus.   Oak Knoll Books   310 - 52   2016 $950

Swedenborg, Emanuel *A Treatise Concerning Heaven and Hell and of the Wonderful Things Therein as Heard and Seen.* Chester: printed by C. W. Leadbeater, 1800. Fourth edition, printed on poor quality greyish paper, slightly browned with occasional light spotting, slight damage to titlepage in 3 places with loss from one character of author's name, 8vo., later half calf, marbled boards (rubbed), neatly rebacked preserving old black lettering piece, red edges, old ownership inscription of Hugh Thomson of Bunbury, Cheshire, sound.   Blackwell's Rare Books   B186 - 146   2016   £250

Swift, Jonathan 1667-1745 *Gulliver's Travels.* London: Cresset Press, 1930. No. 134 of 195 copies on paper and 10 on vellum, 2 volumes, 364 x 256mm., fine recent dark green half morocco gilt by Courtland Benson, lighter green marbled paper sides, raised bands, spines handsomely gilt in compartments in antique style with large elegant floral stamp centerpiece and curling leafy cornerpieces, gilt titling, top edge gilt, others untrimmed; with a total of 27 engravings as called for, title page vignette featuring a bust of Swift (appearing in each volume), 8 head and tailpieces, five full page maps, 12 delicately hand colored engraved plates (including two frontispiece) by Rex Whistler, each within ornate baroque-style frame, front pastedown of volume II with bookplate of Charles J. Rosenbloom, very fine set inside and out.   Phillip J. Pirages   67 - 104   2016 $8500

Swift, Jonathan 1667-1745 *Gulliver's Travels.* London: Cresset Press, 1930. No. VIII of 10 copies on Roman vellum with an extra set of plates on vellum, each of them signed by artist, 343 x 235mm., 2 bound volumes plus portfolio of plates, publisher's special russet morocco by Wood of London, raised bands flanked by simple blind tooling extending onto boards, gilt titling, brass clasps and catches, gilt ruled turn-ins, all edges gilt, vellum endleaves, extra plates housed in silk covered chemise bound into boards covered with matching morocco, whole contained in two extremely fine recent morocco backed felt lined folding boxes with raised bands and gilt titling, giving appearance of three book spines, main volumes with total of 27 engravings (26 images) as called for a little page vignette featuring a bust of Swift (appearing in each volume), 8 head and tailpieces, five full page maps and 12 delicately hand colored copper engraved plates (including two frontispieces) by Rex Whistler each within ornate baroque style frame, with additional suite of all 26 engraved images (the same 12 images that are colored in the main volumes, also colored by hand in this extra suite), each of the 26 extra images signed by Whistler and separately matted, original tissue guards, spines of text and plate volumes rather darkened (though evenly so), morocco boards covering the plate chemise bit soiled and somewhat scratched (scratches well refurbished) but original deluxe bindings showing almost no other wear and retaining much of the original appeal, text and plates with only most trivial of toning of tonal variations to vellum, generally in very fine condition internally.   Phillip J. Pirages 67 - 333   2016 $45,000

Swift, Jonathan 1667-1745 *A Tale of a Tub...* London: printed for Charles Bathurst, 1747. Eleventh edition, engraved frontispiece and 7 engraved plates, 8vo., full contemporary sprinkled calf, gilt panelled spine, red morocco label, joints rebacked but firm, slightly chipped at head of spine.   Jarndyce Antiquarian Booksellers   CCXVI - 534 2016   £85

Swift, Jonathan 1667-1745 *A Tale of a Tub....* London: printed for Joseph Wenman, 1781. 2 volumes in 1, 24mo., some old faint waterstaining, text little dusted, full contemporary calf, gilt banded spine and morocco label, covers rubbed, corners bumped.   Jarndyce Antiquarian Booksellers   CCXVI - 555   2016   £45

Swift, Jonathan 1667-1745 *Travels into Several Remote Nations of the World.* London: printed for Benj. Motte at the Middle Temple Gate in Fleet Street, 1727. Second edition, 4 parts bound in 2 volumes, frontispiece, 5 engraved maps, engraved plate, 8vo., very good, clean copy, waterstaining to margins of endpapers and frontispiece, volume 1, some browning to plates and edges of endpapers and pastedowns, full contemporary sprinkled calf, double gilt ruled borders, raised and gilt banded spines, red morocco labels, expert repairs to joints & spines.   Jarndyce Antiquarian Booksellers   CCXVI - 556   2016   £2500

Swift, Jonathan 1667-1745 *Travels into Several remote Nations of the World.* London: Benjamin Motte, 1727, i.e., 1728. First illustrated edition and first 12mo. edition, engravings executed after Jonathan Swift's own suggestions, 2 volumes, 12mo., contemporary calf gilt, rebacked, 6 engraved maps and plans and four full page pictorial plates, very scarce early edition.   Honey & Wax Booksellers   4 - 48   2016 $6500

Swift, S. C. *The Voyages of Jacques Cartier in Prose and Verse.* Toronto: Thomas Allen, 1934. Quarter centenary edition, blue cloth, dust jacket, half title, 8vo., frontispiece, black and white illustrations, very good.   Schooner Books Ltd.   115 - 207   2016 $40

Swiggett, Howard *The Strong Box.* London: Hodder & Stoughton, 1956. First UK edition, Very slight edge foxing not affecting text but none the less, very good in like dust jacket, uncommon edition.   I. D. Edrich   Crime - 2016   £20

Swinburne, Algernon Charles 1837-1909 *The Ballad of Dead Men's Bay.* London: printed privately, 1889. Half title, uncut, original drab paper wrappers, sewn as issued, fine, in slightly rubbed, half morocco slipcase.   Jarndyce Antiquarian Booksellers   CCXVII - 270   2016   £580

Swinburne, Algernon Charles 1837-1909 *The Bride's Tragedy.* London: privately printed, 1889. Half title, uncut in contemporary full tan calf by Tout, triple ruled gilt borders and floral cornerpieces, gilt dentelles, green morocco label, uplettered gilt, bound with original wrappers, very good.   Jarndyce Antiquarian Booksellers   CCXVII - 271   2016   £580

Swinburne, Algernon Charles 1837-1909 *Grace Darling.* London: printed only for private circulation, 1893. Half title, uncut in 20th century full crimson crushed morocco by Riviere, elaborate gilt dentelles, hinges slightly rubbed with slight wear to head of spine, slight cracking.   Jarndyce Antiquarian Booksellers   CCXVII - 272   2016   £480

Swinburne, Algernon Charles 1837-1909 *The Poems of Algernon Charles Swinburne.* London: Chatto & Windus, 1912. Fifth impression, octavo, 6 volumes, portrait frontispiece in first volume, fine period bindings by Bumpus of full polished calf with raised bands, gilt decoration and rules, red and green morocco title labels, all edges gilt, armorial bookplate in each volume, fine set, attractively bound. Peter Ellis   112 - 391   2016   £875

Swinburne, Algernon Charles 1837-1909 *The Springtide of Life.* London: William Heinemann, 1918. No. 369 of 765 copies signed by Rackham, 286 x 232mm., very attractive red three quarter morocco, gilt stamp signed 'Putnam's', raised bands, spine handsomely gilt in compartments formed by plain and decorative rules, quatrefoil centerpiece surrounded by densely scrolling cornerpieces, sides and endleaves of rose colored linen, top edge gilt, numerous black and white illustrations of cherubic children in text, 9 color plates as called for, tipped onto brown paper and with letterpress guards, morocco with bookplate of W. A. M. Burden, just hint of offsetting from brown mounting paper, otherwise very fine, bright fresh and clean inside and out, with only the most trivial of imperfections.   Phillip J. Pirages   67 - 298   2016 $2250

Swinburne, Algernon Charles 1837-1909 *The Two Knights and Other Poems.* London: printed for private circluation, 1918. Half title, uncut in original pale green printed paper wrappers, sewn as issued, very faint fading to margins, near fine in foldover blue cloth box.   Jarndyce Antiquarian Booksellers   CCXVII - 273   2016   £350

Swinburne, Algernon Charles 1837-1909 *Wearieswa'.* London: printed for private circulation, 1917. Half title, partially unopened in original pale green printed paper wrappers, sewn as issued, very faint fading to margins, near fine in fold over blue cloth box.   Jarndyce Antiquarian Booksellers   CCXVII - 274   2016   £350

Swinburne, Henry *Travels through Spain in the Years 1775 and 1776.* London: P. Elmsley, 1787. Second edition, 2 volumes, 8vo., engraved portrait frontispiece, 10 plates, 2 maps, contemporary brown polished calf, rebacked using original gilt decorated spines.   J. & S. L. Bonham Antiquarian Booksellers   Europe 2016 - 8448   2016   £450

Swinnerton, Frank *Coquette.* London: Methuen & Co., 1921. First edition, fine in very attractive very good dust jacket with some tears at edges and couple of small and unobtrusive chips, housed in older chemise and quarter leather slipcase, inscribed by author to American Publisher Crosby Gaige.   Between the Covers Rare Books   204 - 112   2016 $650

Swire, Herbert *The Voyage of the Challenger a Personal Narrative of the Historic Circumnavigation of the Globe in the Years 1872-1876.* London: Golden Cockerel Press, 1938. One of 300 numbered copie printed in Eric Gill's perpetua on Van Gelder paper, 2 volumes, small folio, colored plates, text illustrations, blue cloth boards, white cloth spines, gilt, fine, publisher's cloth slipcases (lightly rubbed at extremities).   Joseph J. Felcone, Inc.   Books from Five Centuries: a Miscellany - 139   2016 $1000

Sydenham, Thomas *Dissertatio Epistolaris ad Speclatissimum Dochissimung Virum Gulielmum Cole....* London: typis M. D. Impensis Walters Kercilby, 1682. First edition, errata leaf, rebound in quarter calf and marbled boards, bit dusty particularly in margins.   James Tait Goodrich   X-78 - 520   2016 $695

Sykes, Percy *A History of Afghanistan.* London: Macmillan & Co., 1940. First edition, 2 volumes, 8vo.., 11 plates and 4 folding maps, 10 plates and 3 folding maps and 1 further large folding map in pocket at rear volume II, without dust jackets, blue cloth, gilt spine, top edge blue, spines faded, few very light spots and scratches, boards still very good.   Unsworths Antiquarian Booksellers Ltd.   30 - 145   2016   £600

Sylvester, Julie *John Chamberlain: a Catalogue Raisonne of the Scultpure 1954-1985.* New York: Hudson Hill Press, 1986. First edition, 4to., cloth, dust jacket, 313 color plates, 371 black and white illustrations, dust jacket rubbed, ex-private library book with small stamp in ink on titlepage and another on an interior page, card holder on rear pastedown, top dge of text block slightly foxed.   Oak Knoll Books   310 - 235   2016 $400

Sylvester, Martin *A Dangerous Age.* London: Michael Joseph, 1986. First edition, fine in dust jacket.   Mordida Books   2015 - 010614   2016 $65

Sylvester, Martin *A Lethal Vintage.* London: Michael Joseph, 1988. First edition, advance review copy with review slip laid in, fine in dust jacket.   Mordida Books   2015 - 010610   2016 $65

Sylvester, Martin *Rough Red.* London: Michael Joseph, 1989. First edition, fine in dust jacket.   Mordida Books   2015 - 010611   2016 $65

Sylvestre, Henri *The Triumphs of Modern Art.* Philadelphia: Gebbie & Co., n.d. circa, 1890-1900. First edition, 2 volumes, full calf folio, decoratively blindstamped on front covers, gilt title, spine titles, volume numbers and decorative devices in gilt, raised bands, beautifully marbled endpapers with gilt decorated calf over three edges of pastedowns, each volume with 50 magnificent full page photogravures and etchings and each has 100 typogravures.   Gene W. Baade, Books on the West   2015 - TA001   2016 $1950

Symmachus, Quintus Aurelius *Epistolarum Diversos Libri Decem Eustatium Vignon.* Geneva: E. Vignon per Dionysium Probum, 1587. 2 parts in one volume, 8vo., occasional notes and underlining, some notes in old hand to prelim blanks, additional titlepage to second part, little toned towards top edge, few smudges and light stains, contemporary semi limp vellum, number 68 inked to spine, yapp edged, edges lightly sprinkled, slightly yellowed a few marks evidence of lost ties, upper fore-edge a bit creased, endband thongs snapped at gutter but still sound and very good, 20th century bookplate of Daniel Henry Holmes Ingalls (1916-1999). Unsworths Antiquarian Booksellers Ltd. E05 - 14 2016 £475

Symonds, John Addington *In the Key of Blue and Other Prose Essays.* London and New York: Elkin Mathews & John Lane and Macmillan and Co., 1893. First edition one of 50 copies of the large paper copy, original full vellum designed by Charles Ricketts, decorated and lettered gilt, head of spine with minor scuffing, gold little faded from spine, front inner hinge strengthened, few of the entirely uncut margins little browned. Sotheran's Travel and Exploration - 284 2016 £798

Symonds, John Addington *In the Key of Blue and Other Prose Essays.* London: Elkin Mathews & John Lane, 1893. First edition, octavo, one of 50 large paper copies bound in full vellum with elaborate decoration designed by Charles Ricketts, contemporary (1893) art nouveau bookplate of Edmund Bulkley, endpapers bit spotted at edges, very good, lovely with gilt still clear and bright. Peter Ellis 112 - 392 2016 £950

Symons, A. J. A. *A Bibliography of the First Editions of Books by William Butler Yeats.* First Edition Club, 1924. First edition, 106/500 copies printed on Japan paper at the Curwen Press, crown 8vo., original boards, backstrip with printed label, gutters of rear endpaper, trifle dusty with spare label tipped in to rear pastedown, dust jacket lightly toned with short closed tear at head of front panel, original prospectus and order from loosely inserted, very good, inscribed by author to Ambrose Heal. Blackwell's Rare Books B186 - 290 2016 £200

Symons, A. J. A. *H. M. Stanley.* London: Duckworth, 1933. First edition, octavo, covers bit faded at edges, very good in good, chipped, torn and rubbed dust jacket repaired on reverse, presentation copy inscribed by author for Augustus John, July 1933. Peter Ellis 112 - 393 2016 £75

Symons, A. J. A. *The Nonesuch Century: an Appraisal, A Personal Note and a Bibliography of the First Hundred Books Issued by the Press 1923-1934.* London: Nonesuch Press, 1936. No. 663 of 750 copies, 318 x 203mm., original green buckram, flat spine with black morocco label, later sturdy marbled paper slipcase, engraved portrait of Meynell by Eric Gill, 3 pages of printer's devices, six photogravure plates of bindings, 52 pages reproducing illustrative text and titlepages and 45 insets of reprinted leaves mounted on dark gray paper, 25 of those bifolia, front pastedown with bookplate reading "From the Library of the Curwen Press London", spine sunned (as always with this book, one sample bit reased, otherwise very fine. Phillip J. Pirages 67 - 265 2016 $850

Symons, Arthur *The Symbolist Movement in Literature.* London: William Heinemann, 1899. First edition, with the presentation copy blindstamp in titlepage, 8vo., original navy buckram, spine panel lettered gilt, publisher's blindstamp in back cover. James S. Jaffe Rare Books Occasional List: Winter 2016 - 136 2016 $350

Symons, James M. *Meyerhold's Theatre on the Grotesque: The Post Revolutionary Productions 1920-1932.* Coral Gables: University of Miami Press, 1971. 8vo., 16 illustrations, fine in chipped dust jacket. Second Life Books, Inc. 196 B - 727 2016 $45

Symons, Julian *The Belting Inheritance.* New York: Harper & Bros., 1965. First edition, red cloth backed black boards, lettered gilt, minor wear to upper edge of dust jacket, else fine. Argonaut Book Shop Literature 2015 - 6164 2016 $45

Symons, Julian *Bogue's Fortune.* New York: Harper and Bros., 1956. First American edition, black cloth lettered gilt, some foxing to top edge, small sticker and residue to front endpaper, dust jacket heavily rubbed and slightly chipped, very good. Argonaut Book Shop Literature 2015 - 6166 2016 $40

Symons, Julian *The Criminal Comedy of the Contented Couple.* London: Macmillan, 1985. First British edition, black cloth, lettered in gilt on spine, minor soiling to inner flaps of dust jacket, else fine. Argonaut Book Shop Literature 2015 - 6173 2016 $45

Symons, Julian *The Defling Murders.* London: Macmillan, 1982. First edition, grey cloth, lettered in silver on spine, fine in pictorial dust jacket. Argonaut Book Shop Literature 2015 - 8175 2016 $60

Symons, Julian *The End of Solomon Grundy.* London: Collins, 1964. First edition, red and black cloth, lettered gilt on spine, previous owner's inscription of front free endpaper, fine, rubbed dust jacket. Argonaut Book Shop Literature 2015 - 6176 2016 $45

Symons, Julian *The Gigantic Shadow.* London: Collins, 1958. First edition, red cloth, corners and spine ends slightly bumped, minor bump to lower front edge, jacket lightly rubbed with very minor chipping to foot of spine, minor foxing to rear of dust jacket, very good.   Argonaut Book Shop   Literature 2015 - 6168   2016 $100

Symons, Julian *The Name of Annabel Lee.* London: Macmillan, 1983. First British edition, blue cloth, lettered silver on spine, slight foxing along top edge and very faint offsetting to front free endpaper, fine in pictorial dust jacket.   Argonaut Book Shop   Literature 2015 - 6174   2016 $75

Symons, Julian *The Players and the Game.* London: Collins, 1972. First edition, red cloth lettered gilt, small stain to lower rear corner, else fine in lightly rubbed dust jacket.   Argonaut Book Shop   Literature 2015 - 6169   2016 $50

Symons, Julian *The Players and the Game.* New York: Harper & Row, 1972. First American edition, yellow cloth backed boards, minor soiling to dust jacket, else fine.   Argonaut Book Shop   Literature 2015 - 6170   2016 $45

Symson, Patrick *Spiritual songs or Holy Poems.* Edinburgh: by the Heir of Andrew Anderson &c. for William Dickie, 1686? 12mo., small wormhole in lower fore-corner becoming increasingly larger throughout, closed tear to fore margin of A2 and G1, fore-margin of A3 stained, foot of L2, L7, L8 damaged (no loss of text), contemporary sheep, front board detached, covers very worn and scuffed, corners bumped, from the library of James Stevens Cox (1910-1997), armorial bookplate of Patrick Hume, 1st Earl of Marchmont (1641-1724).   Maggs Bros. Ltd.   1447 - 404   2016   £200

Synesius of Cyrene *(Opera).* Paris: Ex officina Andriani Turnebe, 1553. First printing, folio, small rusthole to one leaf affecting one or two characters on each side, some faint dampmarking in places, titlepage dusty and just slightly frayed ar corner, chapters neatly numbered in early hand, folio, early 18th century sprinkled calf, boards bordered with triple gilt fillet, small floral gilt cornerpieces inside, expertly rebacked preserving original spine compartments with central gilt floral tools, new red morocco lettering piece, hinges neatly relined, ownership inscription of Phelipps, good copy.   Blackwell's Rare Books   B184 - 82   2016   £1200

Synge, John Millington   1871-1909 *The Well of the Saints.* London: George Allen & Unwin, 1924. Later printing, inscribed by actor, Laurence Olivier, brown paper covered boards, quarter bound with imitation parchment leather and spine titles in gilt, as issued, brief spotting to boards, backstrip toned, overall very good.   Royal Books   49 - 7   2016 $1850

Syr Percyvelle of Gales. Hammersmith: Kelmscott Press, 1895. One of 350 copies on paper (and 8 on vellum), 210 x 145mm., handsome Gothic style brown blind tooled pigskin by Zaehnsdorf (stamp signed and dated 1895, with firm's exhibition stamp), covers with frame formed by multiple gilt rules, head and tail with gilt titling and date, central panel diapered in ogival compartments containing floral ornaments, raised bands, neatly rebacked, spine with blind tooled panels and gilt titling, blind ruled turn-ins, marbled endpapers, all edges gilt (front hinge carefully repaired), woodcut frontispiece by Edward Burne-Jones, elaborate wide border on frontispiece and first page of text, one page with half border, decorated woodcut initials device in colophon, significant rubbing, couple of small abrasions to upper board, binding lustrous and still generally appealing, fine copy, internally quite clean, fresh and bright.   Phillip J. Pirages   67 - 225   2016 $1500

Syracuse Poems 1970. Syracuse: Syracuse University, 1970. First edition, #102 of 1000, inscribed by editor for William Meredith, near fine, printed wrappers.   Charles Agvent   William Meredith - 19   2016 $60

T

Tacitus, Cornelius *The Annales of Cornelius Tacitus. (with) The End of Nero and Beginning of Galba...* London: by Arnold Hatfield for John Norton, 1612. Second edition of Greneway's translation of the Annales and fourth edition of Savile's translation of the second work, 2 parts in 1, small folio, full page engraving and marginal woodcut, woodcut initials, first and last blanks excised, title and final page little tattered at edges, slight worming from title to pages 107-8 first volume, and few gatherings of second volume, never affecting more than couple of letters, occasional spots of wax and ink not obscuring text, slightly toned toward top edge, contemporary dark brown calf, sturdily rebacked in slightly later shade, corners repaired, some scrapes to lower board, edges worn, still very good. Unsworths Antiquarian Booksellers Ltd. 30 - 147 2016 £600

Tacitus, Cornelius *Taciti Opera Quae Exstant. I. Lipsivis quartum recensuit ...* Lvgdvni Batavorum: Ex Officina Plantiniana Apud Franciscum Raphelengium, 1588. Fourth edition edited by J. Lips, small octavo, 18th century panelled calf, early ink underlinings in text, one earlier marginal note (trimmed in binding) on page 630, boards rubbed, hinges cracked, cords holding, good, sound, from the library of English playwright William Congreve. The Brick Row Book Shop Miscellany 69 - 27 2016 $3500

Tacitus, Cornelius *The Works of Tacitus.* Dublin: printed by A. Rhames for R. Gunne near the Ram in Capel-street, 1728-1732. 4 volumes, 8vo., very good, clean set, full contemporary panelled calf, raised bands, red morocco labels, some old marking to lower edge of one board, probably from damp, no further evidence inside volume or on inner board. Jarndyce Antiquarian Booksellers CCXVI - 556 2016 £850

Taekel, Blair *The Lands of the Tamed Turk.* Boston: L. C. Page, 1910. 8vo., illustrations, folding map, original green decorative cloth, near fine. J. & S. L. Bonham Antiquarian Booksellers Europe 2016 - 8324 2016 £125

Taffrail, Pseud. *Fred Travis, A. B.* London: Hodder and Stoughton, 1939. First edition, near fine, tight in dust jacket (lightly soiled on rear panel). Buckingham Books 2015 - 30072 2016 $450

Taffrail, Pseud. *Operation "M.O".* London: Hodder and Stoughton Ltd., 1938. First edition, near fine, tight copy in dust jacket, moderate foding to unprinted side. Buckingham Books 2015 - 30071 2016 $450

Taffrail, Pseud. *Seventy North (70 Degrees North).* London: Hodder and Stoughton, 1934. First edition, white ink partially missing from spine panel, else near fine, tight copy in lightly rubbed dust jacket with light wear to spine ends and corners. Buckingham Books 2015 - 30065 2016 $450

Tagore, Sourindro Mohun *Hindu Loyalty: a Presentation of the Views and Opinions of the Sanskrit Authorities on the Subject of Loyalty...* Calcutta: printed by I. C. Bose and Co. and Pub. by author, 1883. First edition, 216 x 159mm., publisher's original Calcutta binding of dark green pebbled morocco, richly gilt, front cover with densely gilt frame enclosing gilt rolled panel with central vignette of Shiva (rear cover with an arabesque at center, otherwise identically gilt rolled raised bands, spine compartments heavily gilt with stippling and vegetal forms, gilt hatched turn-ins, all edges gilt, text bordered in red, slight loss of gilt to vignette, hint of dulling to spine, still fine, gilt very bright everywhere else, text remarkably clean and fresh. Phillip J. Pirages 67 - 50 2016 $1250

Taine, John *The Purple Sapphire.* New York: Burt, Reprint edition, very good in fine dust jacket with faint crease on back panel. Mordida Books 2015 - 010041 2016 $65

Tait, Peter Guthrie *On the Value of the Edinburgh Degree of M.A.* Edinburgh: Maclachlan & Stewart, 1866. First edition, initial leaf with coat of arms, uncut in original brown cloth, unevenly faded, otherwise very good. Jarndyce Antiquarian Books CCXV - 978 2016 £35

Taken by Design: Photographs from the Institute of Design 1937-1971. Chicago: University of Chicago Press, 2002. First edition, very near fine copy in photo illustrated flexible boards, signed by Joseph Jachna and additionally inscribed by Joseph Sterling And Alan Cohen. Jeff Hirsch Books E-List 80 - 1 2016 $200

Takhtajan, Armen *Flowering Plants: Origins and Dispersal.* Edinburgh: Oliver and Boyd, 1969. Octavo, photos, text illustrations, fine in dust jacket. Andrew Isles Natural History Books 55 - 37561 2016 $80

Talbot, Eleanor W. *Wondereyes and Whatfor.* London: Cassell Petter Galpin, 1880. 4to., pictorial boards, some edge wear, very good++, printed on one side of paper, each leaf with very fine large chromolithograph, especially lovely. Aleph-bet Books, Inc. 112 - 494 2016 $400

Talbot, Marjorie *Ghosts Incorporated.* New York: Pageant Press, 1957. First edition, about fine in very good or better dust jacket with some rubbing and small nicks at spine ends, nicely inscribed by author, very uncommon. Between the Covers Rare Books 208 - 129 2016 $500

Talbot, William *The Bishop of Oxford His Speech, in the House of Lords on the First Article of the Impeachment of Dr. Henry Sacheverell.* London: printed for Jonah Bowyer, 1710. 8vo., disbound.   Jarndyce Antiquarian Booksellers   CCXVI - 558   2016   £20

A Tale of Two Cities. London & Letchworth: Amex Co., circa, 1950. Abridged version, Printed throughout in red and black, original color printed wrappers, stapled as issued, some splitting to spine, illustrated comic strip forum. Jarndyce Antiquarian Booksellers   CCXVIII - 565   2016   £30

A Tale of Two Cities. London: Strato Publications, circa, 1951? Stapled as issued in original color printed wrappers. Jarndyce Antiquarian Booksellers   CCXVIII - 566   2016   £30

A Tale of Two Cities. New York: Gilbertson Co., 1967. Stapled as issued in original color printed wrappers. Jarndyce Antiquarian Booksellers   CCXVIII - 567   2016   £30

Tallack, William *Malta: Under the Phenicians, Knights and English.* London: A. W. Bennett, 1861. First edition, 8vo., 2 tinted lithographs, 2 illustrations, original brown blind-stamped cloth, slight rubbing to head and tail of spine.   J. & S. L. Bonham Antiquarian Booksellers   Europe 2016 - 9434   2016   £220

Tambours et Trompettes. Paris: December, n.d., 1918. Limited to 500 numbered copies on handmade paper, large folio, loose as issued in pictorial portfolio with ribbon ties, 11 absolutely stunning large pochoir pages, including titlepage, excellent condition.   Aleph-bet Books, Inc.   111 - 24   2016 $1500

Tan, Amy *The Hundred Secret Senses.* New York: Putnam, 1995. First edition, 8vo., fine inscribed by author.   Second Life Books, Inc.   196 B - 730   2016 $75

Tan, Amy *The Joy Luck Club.* New York: Putnam, 1989. Twenty fourth printing, 8vo., fine in price clipped dust jacket, inscribed by author.   Second Life Books, Inc.   196 B - 731   2016 $45

Tan, Amy *The Moon Lady.* New York: Macmillan, 1992. First edition, illustrations by Gretchen Schields, fine in fine dust jacket, signed by author.   Bella Luna Books   2016 - j2240   2016 $82

Tanabe, Y. K. *Biological Rhythms in Birds: Neural and Endocrine Aspects.* Tokyo: Japan Scientific Societies Press, 1980. octavo, black and white photos, text illustrations, graphs, fine in publisher's cloth.   Andrew Isles Natural History Books   55 - 38493   2016 $120

Tannenbaum, Allan *John and Yoko: a New York Love Story.* San Rafael: Insight Editions, 2007. First edition, no. 256 of limited edition of 1250 signed by author, square 4to., original white cloth and wrapper, all edges silver, publisher's white cloth fall-down back box, original mailing carton with photo of John and Yoko pasted to front, color and black and white photos, photographic print signed by Tannenbaum, in portfolio sleeve and facsimile compilation of 3 articles from Dec. 1980 issues of Soho Weekly news about the couple, fine.   Sotheran's   Piccadilly Notes - Summer 2015 - 37   2016   £900

Tannenbaum, Allan *New York in the 70s.* Berlin: Feierabend Verlag OHG, 2003. First edition, 4to., original cloth, dust jacket, black and white and some color illustrations, signed by author, fine.   Sotheran's   Piccadilly Notes - Summer 2015 - 292   2016   £200

Tanner, Henry *The Martyrdom of Lovejoy.* Chicago: Fergus Printing Co., 1880. First edition, 8vo., original cloth with paper spine label, 5 plates, spine label little browned, otherwise very good, presentation inscribed by author for John A. Wheeler.   Sotheran's   Piccadilly Notes - Summer 2015 - 293   2016   £248

Tapie, Michel *Ossorio.* Torino: Edizioni D'Arte Fratelli Pozzo, 1961. First edition, folio, 10 full page tipped in color plates, original wrappers worn along spine near binding staple, very good, clean copy, inscribed by Alfonso Ossorio, for Alfred Cooper.   Second Life Books, Inc.   196 B - 732   2016 $150

Tappan, Henry P. *Public Education: an Address Delivered in the Hall of the House of Representatives.... Jan. 2 1857.* Detroit: H. Barns, 1857. First edition, 12mo., removed.   M & S Rare Books, Inc.   99 - 180   2016 $125

Tapply, William G. *Follow the Sharks.* New York: Scribners, 1985. First edition, very fine in dust jacket, inscribed by author.   Mordida Books   2015 - 011467   2016 $65

Tarachow, Michael *An Exploration of the Granjon Arabesques.* Minneapolis: Pentagram press, 1990. First edition, limited to 312 numbered copies, this one of 40 bound thus and containing a tipped-in specimen of handmade paper printed with two color 'arabesque', presentation from author, tall 8vo., cloth backed paper covered boards, paper spine label.   Oak Knoll Books   310 - 135   2016 $150

Tarantino, Quentin *Reservoir Dogs.* London: Faber and Faber, 1994. First UK edition, wrappers, screenplay with black and white stills, fine.   Peter Ellis   112 - 394   2016   £20

Tarantino, Quentin *True Romance.* London: Faber and Faber, 1995. First UK edition, wrappers, screenlay, fine. Peter Ellis   112 - 393   2016   £20

Tarkington, Booth *Image of Josephine.* New York: Doubleday, 1945. 8vo., fine in dust jacket, this lacks 'first edition' slug on copyright page, inscribed by author for Mrs. Belyea.   Second Life Books, Inc.   196 B - 733   2016 $75

Tarkington, Booth *Kate Fennigate, a Novel.* New York: Doubleday Doran, 1943. Later edition, 8vo., inscribed by author for Kenneth Allen.   Second Life Books, Inc.   196 B - 734   2016 $45

Tarn, Nathaniel *Narrative of This Fall.* Los Angeles: Black Sparrow, 1975. Offprint from Sparrow 32 May 1975, paper wrappers, presentation on front from author for Sonya and Bill Jay Smith, front very slightly creased and spotted, otherwise near fine.   Second Life Books, Inc.   196 B - 736   2016 $45

Taro, Yashima *Crow Boy.* New York: Viking, 1955. First edition, 4to., cloth, fine in very slightly worn dust jacket with few small archival mends on verso, review copy with slip laid in, full color lithographs, beautiful copy.   Aleph-bet Books, Inc.   112 - 526   2016 $400

Tarry, Ellen *My Dog Rinty.* New York: Viking Press, 1966. Eighth printing, illustrated by Alexander and Alexandra Allan from photos, small quarto, slight foxing, very near fine in spine faded very good dust jacket with very small nicks and tears, nicely inscribed by Tarry to Tracy Sugarman.   Between the Covers Rare Books   207 - 26   2016 $450

Tarver, John Charles *Some Observations of a Foster Parent.* Westminster: Archibald Constable & Co., 1897. First edition, half title, 2 pages ads, uncut, original green boards with slight scarring, dark green cloth spine, good. Jarndyce Antiquarian Books   CCXV - 979   2016   £25

Tasso, Torquato   1544-1595 *Dell' Aminta Favola Boschereccia di Torquato Tasso.*   Londra: Presso C. Bennet, 1736. 12mo., full contemporary calf, joints cracked, head and tail of spine worn, later 18th century inscription "the gift of Hernietta Maria Bowdler to Jane Davis".   Jarndyce Antiquarian Booksellers   CCXVI - 559   2016   £75

Tasso, Torquato   1544-1595 *Amintas: a Dramatick Pastoral written Originally in Italian.* London: 1737. First edition of Ayre's translation, 8vo., contemporary calf, front hinge repaired, corners rubbed, leather label, engraved frontispiece and engraved title, very good copy.   Howard S. Mott Inc.   265 - 122   2016 $450

Tasso, Torquato   1544-1595 *The Gerusalemme Liberato of Tasso...* Cambridge: printed by J. Archdeacon printer to the University, 1786. 1792. First edition of volume i, and second edition of volume ii, 8vo., 2 volumes, fine, clean copy bound in full contemporary sprinkled calf, smooth spines, gilt band, red morocco title labels, dark green oval volume labels, lemon yellow edges, signature of Elizabeth Collingridge, Oct. 1842, recent bookplate of Christopher Clark Geest.   Jarndyce Antiquarian Booksellers   CCXVI - 560   2016   £225

Tasso, Torquato   1544-1595 *Godfrey of Bulloigne; or the Recovery of Jerusalem.*   London: by John Macock for George Wells and Abel Swalle, 1687. Second edition, small closed tear to titlepage with evidence of earlier restoration, occasional rust spotting, dampstaining to margin in places, 55mm. piece torn away from fore margin of A7, repaired tear to A8, small piece torn away from corners of H4, 2A1 and with 60mm. closed tear to foot of 2I1 (touching text), contemporary calf, head and tail of spine damaged, corners bumped, label missing, from the library of James Stevens Cox (1910-1997), signature of E. Marshall dated 1769, signature of John Warren dated 1809.   Maggs Bros. Ltd.   1447 - 406   2016   £180

Tasso, Torquato   1544-1595 *Godfrey of Bulloigne or the Recovery of Jerusalem.*   Dublin: printed by and for A. Rhames, 1726. 8vo., some dusting and occasional light marking but generally clean leading hinge weak, head of spine chipped, corners worn, 5 folding engraved plates. Jarndyce Antiquarian Booksellers   CCXVI - 561   2016   £75

Tate, Allen *Christ and the Unicorn.*   West Branch: Cummington Press, 1966. First edition, one of 125 copies, wrappers, slight foxing still fine.   Between the Covers Rare Books   204 - 113   2016 $100

Tate, Allen *The Hovering Fly and other Essays.* Cummington: Cummington Press, 1949. One of 140 copies of the regular unsigned issue on Arches paper, 8vo., woodcuts by Wightman Williams, original quarter calf and boards, fine, very uncommon thus.   James S. Jaffe Rare Books Occasional List: Winter 2016 - 50   2016 $750

Tate, G. H. H.   *The Rodents of Australia and New Guinea.* New York: Bulletin of the American Museum of Natural History, 1951. Softcover, signature.   Andrew Isles Natural History Books   55 - 8256   2016 $60

Tate, G. H. H.   *Studies on the Anatomy and Phylogeny of the Macropodidae (Marsupialia).*   New York: American Museum of Natural History, 1948. quarto, tables, map, signature, softcover.   Andrew Isles Natural History Books   55 - 8354   2016 $50

Tate, James *If it Would All Please Hurry.* Amherst: Shanachie Press, 1980. First edition, one of only 10 lettered copies reserved for author and artist, this being copy 'J' out of a total edition of 35 copies produced, of which 25 roman numeraled copies were for sale, all copies signed by poet and artist, with each of the original prints also numbered and signed in margin by artist, folio, 10 original etchings and engravings by Stephen Riley, on Arches Cover White paper, loose sheets in folding box, presentation copy inscribed by Tate and Riley for Stanley Wiater, portfolio lightly soiled, otherwise very fine, rare.   James S. Jaffe Rare Books   Occasional List: Winter 2016 - 137   2016 $4000

Tate, James *Tracts on the Cases, Prepositions and Syntax of the Greek Language.* Richmond: 1830. Presentation copy inscribed by author, 2 corrections in same hand, 8vo., disbound, scarce.   Blackwell's Rare Books   B186 - 67   2016   £350

Tate, James *Viper Jazz.* Middletown: Wesleyan University Press, 1976. First edition, hardcover issue, fine in very good or better dust jacket with some modest rubbing and some foxing at extremities, very warmly inscribed by Tate to poet David Axelrod, also laid in is warm ALS by Tate to Axelrod.   Between the Covers Rare Books   208 - 85   2016 $275

Tate, Nahum *Poems.* London: by T. M. for Benj. Tooke, 1677. First edition, 8vo., without final blank leaf, small ink stain to blank fore margin of E2, rust spot to F4, some light staining to F6 and H2, 19th century calf, blind panelled, front board detached, from the library of James Stevens Cox (1910-1997), mid 19th century bookplate of John Whiteford Mackenzie, armorial bookplate of Archibald Philip Primrose, 5th Earl of Rosebery.   Maggs Bros. Ltd.   1447 - 407   2016   £150

Tattersall, Ivan *The Avenging Brotherhood.* New York: McBride, 1929. First American edition, endpapers darkened and spotting on page edges, otherwise very good in dust jacket with chipping at spine ends and along edges, slightly darkened spine, several short closed tears.   Mordida Books   2015 - 002148   2016 $55

Taudouze, Gustave *Francois I.* Paris: Boivin, 1909. First edition, folio, pictorial cloth, all edges gilt, corners bumped, slight over soil, very good, each page individually hinged into book, full page color illustrations by Robida.   Aleph-bet Books, Inc.   111 - 183   2016 $600

Taunt, Henry William Edward *A New Map of the River Thames from Oxford to London from Entirely New Surveys.* Oxford: Henry W. Taunt, 1872. First edition, oblong 8vo., double lithograph maps with 79 albumen photos vignette paste-ons, original green pictorial cloth blocked with gold lettering, very good.   Marlborough Rare Books   List 56 - 55   2016   £450

Taurellus, Nicolaus *Emblemata Physico-ethica. (with) Carmina Funebria.* Nuremberg: Paul Kaugmann, 1592. Nuremberg: Gerlach, 1592. First edition, 2 works in one volume, titles within woodcut architectural border, 83 woodcut emblems, two works in one volume, 17th century speckled calf gilt spine with morocco label, red speckled edges, arare, Allan Heywood Bright bookplate and notes.   Maggs Bros. Ltd.   1474 - 75   2016   £7500

Taut, Bruno *Houses and People of Japan.* Tokyo: Sanseido Co. Ltd., 1958. Second edition, large 8vo., royal blue linen, gilt lettered spine, photo illustrated dust jacket, 9 tipped in color plates, including frontispiece, each with loose tissue guard, numerous black and white photos and line drawings, chipping, some loss to upper extremities of front and spine of dust jacket, otherwise bright, fresh.   Sotheran's   Piccadilly Notes - Summer 2015 - 294   2016   £295

Taverner, Eric *Anglers' Fishes and Their Natural History.* London: Seeley Service & Co. Ltd., 1957. First edition, 8vo.,original cloth and dust jacket, 200 illustrations, fine.   Sotheran's   Piccadilly Notes - Summer 2015 - 295   2016   £80

Taverner, Eric *The Making of a Trout Stream.* London: Seeley Service & Co. n.d., 1953. First edition, 8vo., original cloth and wrappers, maps to endpapers, text illustrations, very good.   Sotheran's   Hunting, Shooting & Fishing - 150   2016   £50

Taverner, Eric *Salmon Fishing.* London: Seeley Service & Co., 1931. First edition, 8vo., original brown cloth, gilt crest to upper board, gilt lettering to spine, maps to endpapers, 300 illustrations, very good.   Sotheran's   Hunting, Shooting & Fishing - 149   2016   £80

Taverner, Eric *Trout Fishing from all Angles.* London: Seeley Service & Co., 1929. First edition, 8vo., original brown cloth, gilt crest to upper board, gilt lettering to spine, 250 illustrations, previous owner's signature, very good.   Sotheran's   Hunting, Shooting & Fishing - 148   2016   £80

Taxay, Don *Money of the American Indians and Other Primitive.* New York: Nummus Press, 1970. First edition, photos, facsimile, drawings, rust cloth lettered in silver, very fine with slightly chipped pictorial dust jacket.   Argonaut Book Shop   Native American 2015 - 5715   2016 $50

Taxi Driver Curry - 1. Heathrow 4.30a.m. Terminal 4 to 3, April 2014. Decorah: Solmentes Press, 2015. 11/45 copies from an edition of 50 copies, oblong 8vo., 10 woodcuts, original pictorial cloth, backstrip lettered in white, edges untrimmed, endpapers of handmade paper incorporating grass and rose petals with stamped leaf design, slipcase, fine.   Blackwell's Rare Books   B184 - 316   2016   £300

Taxi Driver Curry - 1 Heathrow 4:30a.m., Terminal 4 to 3, April 2014. Decorah: Solmentes Press, 2015. 26/45 copies from an edition of 50 copies, 10 woodcuts, oblong 8vo., original pictorial cloth, backstrip lettered in white, edges untrimmed, endpapers with stamped repeating eye design in gold and purple, slipcase, fine.   Blackwell's Rare Books   B186 - 339   2016   £300

Taylor, Alrutheus Ambush   *The Negro in Tennessee 1865-1880.*   Washington: Associated Pub. Inc., 1941. First edition, slight offsetting to endpapers from original binder's glue, still fine in attractive, very good or better dust jacket with some sunning to spine, faint dampstain at foot and little splitting on one seam.   Between the Covers Rare Books   202 - 102   2016 $575

Taylor, Andrew   *An Old School Tie.*   London: Gollancz, 1986. First edition, very fine in dust jacket.   Mordida Books   2015 - 005997   2016 $65

Taylor, Ann   *Original Hymns for Sunday Schools.*   Boston: Crocker and Brewster, 1827. First edition?, 16mo., engraved frontispiece, original printed flexible boards (soiled), spine chipped.   M & S Rare Books, Inc.   99 - 135   2016 $175

Taylor, Claire   *Heresy, Crusade and Inquisition in Medieval Quercy.*   York: Medieval Press, 2011. First edition, 8vo., illustrations, laminated pictorial boards, as new.   Unsworths Antiquarian Booksellers Ltd.   E05 - 90   2016   £25

Taylor, Coley   *Yankee Doodle: a Drama of the American Revolution.*   New York: Devin-Adair, 1945. First edition, author's presentation, very good in little worn dust jacket.   Second Life Books, Inc.   196 B - 738   2016 $40

Taylor, Deems   *Of Men and Music.*   New York: Simon and Schuster, 1937. First edition, 8vo., very good in dust jacket (little torn), tipped in card signed by author, also tipped in program from The Colonnades, Essex House, April 14 1938 production of Taylor's "Ramuntcho".   Second Life Books, Inc.   196 B - 739   2016 $150

Taylor, E. G. R.   *The Troublesome Voyage of Captain Edward Fenton 1582-1583.*   Cambridge: Hakluyt, 1959. First edition, 8vo., frontispiece, illustrations, original blue decorative cloth, dust jacket.   J. & S. L. Bonham Antiquarian Booksellers   Voyages 2016 - 8357   2016   £20

Taylor, Edward H.   *The Serpents of Thailand and Adjacent Waters.*   Lawrence: University of Kansas, 1965. Photos, very good, in wrappers.   Andrew Isles Natural History Books   55 - 8278   2016 $120

Taylor, Elizabeth   *The Wedding Group.*   London: Chatto & Windus, 1968. First edition, octavo, covers edges just trilfe bumped, near fine in very good dust jacket, slightly rubbed at edges.   Peter Ellis   112 - 396   2016   £95

Taylor, H. A.   *Handbook of the West African Gold Mines.*   New York: Melbourne: Sydney: Hutchinson's Scientific and Technical Publications, 1946. First edition, 8vo., original blue cloth, lettered in gilt, double page table in red and black, folding lithographic map, loosely inserted, cloth little rubbed and faded, very light toning to paper, good, very rare.   Sotheran's   Travel and Exploration - 39   2016   £228

Taylor, Henry   *Breakings.*   San Luis Obispo: Solo, 1971. One of 400 copies, 8vo., paper wrappers, author's presentation to poet William Claire, cover somewhat bumped at edges, else very good, tight copy.   Second Life Books, Inc.   196 B - 741   2016 $95

Taylor, Henry   *The Horse Show at Midnight: Poems.*   Baton Rouge: Louisiana State University, 1966. First edition, 8vo., author's presentation to poet William Claire, paper over boards, nice, dust jacket scuffed and slightly chipped.   Second Life Books, Inc.   196 B - 742   2016 $50

Taylor, Isaac   *Advice to the Teens; or Practical Help Towards the Formation of One's Own Character.*   London: Rest Fenner, 1818. First edition, frontispiece, some slight spotting, contemporary half calf, library number of head of spine, rubbed and worn, hinges cracking, library label of Carr's Lane Boys' School laid on earlier label, sound copy only.   Jarndyce Antiquarian Books   CCXV - 429   2016   £35

Taylor, Isaac   *Home Education.*   London: Jackson & Walford, 1838. Third thousand, original purple brown cloth, spine slightly faded and rubbed at head, nice, inscription "Presented to Jesse Gouldsmith Esqre by author January 1839", followed by further inscription from Gouldsmith to his daughter 1840.   Jarndyce Antiquarian Books   CCXV - 981   2016   £75

Taylor, Isaac   *Home Education.*   London: Jackson & Walford, 1838. Fourth edition, partially unopened in original dark green cloth, signature of J. H. Ross Farquharson, very good, crisp copy.   Jarndyce Antiquarian Books   CCXV - 430   2016   £50

Taylor, Isaac   *Scenes of British Wealth in Produce, Manufactures and Commerce, for the Amusement and Instruction of Little Tarry at Home Travellers.*   London: H. Harris, St. Paul's Church Yard, 1825. Second edition, 12mo., engraved folding map frontispiece, vignette on titlepage, 84 numbered engraved plates on 28 sheets, original red roan backed boards, rebacked in style.   Marlborough Rare Books   List 55 - 67   2016   £485

Taylor, Isaac *Scenes of Commerce by Land and Sea....* London: John Harris, Corner of St. Paul's Church Yard, 1830. First edition, 12mo. in 6's, 18 engraved plates, including frontispiece each plate containing three scenes, bound in original dark red publisher's round backed marbled boards, good.   Marlborough Rare Books   List 56 - 54   2016   £225

Taylor, Isaac *Self Cultivation Recommended on Hints to a Youth leaving School.* London: Rest Fenner, 1818. Third edition, 12mo., half title, frontispiece, 8 pages ads, contemporary quarter dark blue calf, marbled paper boards, armorial bookplate of North, Thurlsand Castle, very good. Jarndyce Antiquarian Books   CCXV - 431   2016   £60

Taylor, Isaac *Self-Cultivation Recommended.* London: Baldwin Cradock and Joy, 1820. Fourth edition, 12mo., frontispiece slightly waterstained, uncut in original drab boards, paper label, good plus.   Jarndyce Antiquarian Books   CCXV - 432   2016   £65

Taylor, J. E. *The Aquarium: Its Inhabitants, Structure and Management.* Edinburgh: John Grant, 1901. Octavo, text illustrations, publisher's decorated cloth, very good. Andrew Isles Natural History Books   55 - 38994   2016 $100

Taylor, Jane *Practical Hints to Young Females on the Duties of a Wife, a Mother and a Mistress of a Family.* London: Taylor & Hessey, 1822. Eleventh edition, 12mo., frontispiece, 4 pages ads, uncut in original blue boards, brown paper spine, paper label, dulled and rubbed and little worn, sound.   Jarndyce Antiquarian Books   CCXV - 433   2016   £38

Taylor, Jeremy 1613-1667 *A Discourse Concerning Prayer ex Tempore or by Pretence of the Spirit.* N.P.: n.p. in the Yeere, 1646. First edition, small 4to., 15mm. dampstain to foot of titlepage (not touching text), larger dampstain along fore-edge of gatherings B-C and inner margin of E, modern quarter imitation sheep and marbled boards, early ink inscription and few marginal ink crosses, By Bp. Tailour, from the library of James Stevens Cox (1910-1997). Maggs Bros. Ltd.   1447 - 408   2016   £150

Taylor, Jeremy 1613-1667 *The Rule and Exercises of Holy Living... (with) The Rule and Exercises of Holy Dying.* London: printed by J. Heptinstall for Royston and Elizabeth Meredith, 1715. Twenty-second editions, 8vo., 2 volumes bound in uniform full contemporary sprinkled calf, raised bands, red morocco labels, slight waterstain to head of final leaves in Holy Living, small piece of leather worn from rear board of same volume, from the library of Invercauld Castle, Braemar with contemporary note on inner rear board. Jarndyce Antiquarian Booksellers   CCXVI - 562   2016   £200

Taylor, Jeremy 1613-1667 *XXVIII Sermons Preached at Golden Grove; Being for the Summer Half Year...*   London: by R. N. for Richard Royston, 1651. First edition, small folio, some occaisonal spotting, otherwise good, mid 19th century dark green morocco, covers with large early 16th century style acorn panel in blind and with large gilt arms block of the 8th Earl of Scarbrough, gilt spine, marbled endleaves, gilt edges, from the library of James Stevens Cox (1910-1997), occasional underlining and marginal marks in ink including few small florets, bound for John Lumley-Savile, 8th Earl of Scarbrough by descent to his son John Lumley-Savile, 1st Baron Savile of Rufford, Rufford Hall booklabel.   Maggs Bros. Ltd.   1447 - 409   2016   £220

Taylor, John *A Summary of the Roman Law, Taken from Dr. Taylor's Elements of the Civil Law.* London: for T. Payne, 1772. Modern cloth, clean, very good.   Joseph J. Felcone, Inc.   Books from Five Centuries: a Miscellany - 140   2016 $600

Taylor, John 1580-1653 *Cornucopia or Roome for a Ram-head.* London: by John Reynolds, 1642. First edition, small 4to., crude woodcut, each leaf inlaid, first letter of title just shaved, very light staining near inner margin of title, some minor browning throughout, text lightly inked in lower corner of A24 (yet still legible), early 19th century half black morocco and drab boards, spine worn, upper headcap torn away and corners bumped, text coming loose, from the library of James Stevens Cox (1910-1997), old pencil foliation, armorial bookplate of Graham of Gartmore, Perthshire. Maggs Bros. Ltd.   1447 - 410   2016   £1250

Taylor, Marshall W. *The Fastest Bicycle Rider in the World...* Worcester: Wormley Pub. Co., 1928. First edition, octavo, gilt stamped blue cloth, extensively illustrated with photos, bottom corners little bumped, else fine in near fine dust jacket with small nicks and tears.   Between the Covers Rare Books   202 - 194   2016 $4000

Taylor, Marshall W. *The Life, Travels, Labors and Helpers of Mrs. Amanda Smith, the Famous Negro Evangelist.* Cincinnati: printed by Cranston & Stowe for the author, 1887. First edition, frontispiece, original printed pale blue wrappers, light soiling, near fine.   Between the Covers Rare Books   202 - 105   2016 $3500

Taylor, Nora Pitt *Wilhelmina: the Adventures of a Dutch Doll.* New York: International Art n.d. circa, 1910. printed boards, fox spots on several pages, worse at beginning, else very good+, complete with 3 1/2 inch high jointed wooden doll attached to cover with a ribbon, printed on coated paper, 8 wonderful color plates and black and whites on every page by Gladys Hall, rare with doll.   Aleph-bet Books, Inc.   112 - 151   2016 $300

Taylor, Robert Lewis *Two Roads to Guadalupe.* New York: Doubleday & Co., 1964. First edition, map ends, two tone black and tan cloth, very fine with pictorial dust jacket. Argonaut Book Shop   Literature 2015 - 6409   2016 $40

Taylor, Samuel *Sabrina Fair; or a woman of the World a Romantic Comedy.* New York: Random House, 1954. First printing, 8vo., illustrations, very good in little scuffed and soiled, price clipped dust jacket, signed by Lerna Dana, Kim Stanley, Diana Lynn and Margaret Steele, who appeared in the play, illustrations.   Second Life Books, Inc.   196 B - 743   2016 $95

Taylor, Thomas *The History of the Waldenses and Albigenses who Begun the Reformation in the Vallies of Peidmont (sic).* Bolton: printed by J. Higham, 1793. First edition, title within border of printer's ornaments, uniformly slightly browned, 12mo., contemporary sheep, rebacked, gold signature at head of title of Thos. Redwood, Jan. 23 1796.   Blackwell's Rare Books   B184 - 83   2016   £750

Taylor, Thomas Proclus *Dombey and Son or Good Mrs. Brown the Child Stealer.* 1858? Folded as issued, with split to one fold, original buff wrappers, hand colored illustrations, edges little chipped, signed 'F. A. Marshall Aug. 1879', fragile, scarce.   Jarndyce Antiquarian Booksellers   CCXVIII - 462   2016   £85

Teasdale-Buckell, G. T. *The Complete Shot.* London: Methuen & Co., 1924. Fifthe edition, 8vo., original green cloth, gilt lettering to spine, photos, occasional slight foxing, but very nice.   Sotheran's   Hunting, Shooting & Fishing - 102   2016   £98

Teasdale, Sara 1884-1933 *Star Tonight.* New York: Oct., 1930. First edition, 8vo., cloth, owner bookplate, fine in near fine dust jacket with slight soil, color frontispiece plus 16 very beautiful full page black and whites by Dorothy Lathrop, excellent copy.   Aleph-bet Books, Inc.   112 - 285   2016 $225

Tebbel, John *History of Book Publishing in the United States Volume I-Volume 4.* New York: R. R. Bowker, 1972. 1975. 1978. 1981. First edition, large 8vo., 4 volumes, cloth, presentation from author for Mark Carroll, clipped news obits of Alfred Knopf, well preserved.   Oak Knoll Books   310 - 75   2016 $550

Tedder, Arthur William *Air Power in War.* London: issued by the Directorate of Command and Staff Training Air Ministry Sept., 1947. Large 8vo., original printed wrappers with new backstrip, wire stitched as issued, 2 maps, 9 diagrams, 3 folding, one very large, staples bit oxidized, good, rare.   Sotheran's   Travel and Exploration - 488   2016   £198

Tegetmeier, W. B. *Horses, Asses, Zebras, Mules and Mule Breeding.* London: Horace Cox, 1895. Octavo, ads, uncolored frontispiece, 24 uncolored plates, publisher's copy, fine.   Andrew Isles Natural History Books   55 - 34932   2016 $450

Tegetmeier, W. B. *Pheasants: Their Natural History and Practical Management.* London: Horace Cox, 1881. Second edition, 4to., original dark green cloth, upper cover blocked with large centrally placed gilt vignette, inside elaborate interwoven framing device blocked in black (and reprised in blind on lower cover) with further external gilt fillet border, spine titled ot gilt, all edges gilt, yellow endpapers, 13 excellent wood engraved plates, illustrations, previous owner's bookplate, little cockling to lower board, internally very clean, very good.   Sotheran's   Hunting, Shooting & Fishing - 103   2016   £300

Tegg, Thomas *A Present for an Apprentice.* London: William Tegg & Co., 1848. Second edition, illustrations, occasional slight spotting, original red cloth, spine faded, slightly rubbed, presentation label on leading f.e.p. from the Worshipful Company of Shipwrights to Albert Enoch Horton on his being bound apprentice to his father.   Jarndyce Antiquarian Books   CCXV - 434   2016   £40

Tegg, Thomas *The Rise, Progress and Termination of the O. P. War in Poetic Epistles or Hudibrastic Letters...* London: Thomas Tegg, 1810. 12mo., early boards and decorative paper spine, considerable scuffing, edgewear, use markings to covers, some loss and tanning to spine, early paper spine label, rubbed, pages unevenly bound and rough cut, moderately tanned and foxed, early name inscribed on front flyleaf.   Dramatis Personae   119 - 147   2016 $125

Tegg, William *The Cruet Stand or Sauce Piquante to suit all Tastes.* London: William Tegg, 1871. First edition, 32 page catalog, original purple cloth, bevelled boards, blocked in black and gilt, spine faded to brown, back board slightly marked, inscription to Ms. Phelps with editor's kind wishes.   Jarndyce Antiquarian Books   CCXV - 435   2016   £40

Tegner, Esaias *Frithiof's Saga.* Stockholm: Norstedt & Soner, 1953. Limited Edition Club, one of 1500 copies signed by artist, large 8vo., illustrations by Eric Palmquist, paper over boards, cloth spine and corner reinforcement, stamped in black, red and gilt, cover little scuffed, otherwise nice.   Second Life Books, Inc.   196 B - 744   2016 $45

Temple, John *The Irish Rebellion or an History of the Beginnings and First Progress of the General Rebellion...* London: 1724. Sixth edition, reprinted from London edition of 1679, 4to., light browning, frontispiece foxed, titlepage printed in red and black, 4to., light browning, frontispiece foxed, contemporary mottled calf, expert repairs to joints and head and tail of unlettered spine, from the library of Perceval-Maxwell family, contemporary ownership initials WP, 19th century news clipping.   Jarndyce Antiquarian Booksellers   CCXVI - 563   2016   £650

Temple, William *Works...* London: printed for J. Round, J. Tonson, J. Clarke, B. Motte, T. Wotton, S. Birt and T. Osborne, 1731. Second edition, 2 volumes, folio, frontispiece, woodcut head and tailpieces and initials, separate titlepage to each part but continuously paginated, neatly repaired tear (63mm. approx.), frontispiece, light staining to bottom fore-edge, corner of first few gatherings of volume I, contemporary brown calf, sturdily rebacked in calf, corners and edges also repaired, red and green morocco gilt labels and blind tooling in spines, gilt borders and frames, edges sprinkled red.   Unsworths Antiquarian Booksellers Ltd.   E01 - Early Printing - 24   2016   £350

Tempsky, Gustav Ferdinand Von *Mitla: a Narrative of Incidents and Personal Adventures on a Journey in Mexico, Guatemala and Salvador in the Years 1853 to 1855.* London: Longman Brown, 1858. First edition, 8vo., folding map, 5 colored chromolithographs, 9 wood engravings, contemporary full polished calf, Eton Prize binding, handsome copy.   J. & S. L. Bonham Antiquarian Booksellers   America 2016 - 1576   2016   £1100

Ten Little Niggers. London & New York: Frederick Warne, n.d. circa., 1880. Stiff pictorial wrappers, pages mounted on linen, nearly as new, fine chromolithograph to illustration rhyme, rare in such amazing condition.   Aleph-bet Books, Inc.   112 - 60   2016 $1200

Ten Tales. Huntington Beach: Cahill, 1994. Limited to 250 copies, hardcover in slipcase, signed by all 10 authors, fine.   Bella Luna Books   2016 - j1032   2016 $297

Tenison-Woods, J. E. *Fish and Fisheries of New South Wales.* Sydney: Thomas Richards, 1882. Quarto, 45 plates, quarter brown calf, marbled boards, some foxing throughout, otherwise sound.   Andrew Isles Natural History Books   55 - 38483   2016 $350

Tenison, Thomas *The Creed of Mr. Hobbes Examined; in a Feigned Conference Between Him and a Student of Divinity.* London: for Francis Tyson, 1670. First edition, 8vo., with final errata leaf, titlepage lightly soiled and frayed along edges, intermittent light marginal dampstaining, contemporary calf, covers panelled in blind, spine with five raised bands, 35 x 10mm. piece torn from head of spine, foot of spine chipped and cracked with minor loss, joints worn, front cover loose, covers and edges rubbed and worn, from the library of James Stevens Cox (1910-1997).   Maggs Bros. Ltd.   1447 - 411   2016   £550

Tennant, Alan *On the Wing: to the Edge of the Earth with the Peregrine Falcon.* New York: Knopf, 2004. First edition, 8 pages of color photos, fine in dust jacket, inscribed by poet to William Jay Smith.   Second Life Books, Inc.   196 B - 746   2016 $75

Tennant, Eleonora *Spanish Journey - Personal Experiences of the Civil War.* London: Eyre and Spottiswoode, 1926. First edition, octavo, reproductions, endpaper map, spine little bruised at head, sporadic spotting, very good in very good dust jacket darkened at spine, defective at head of spine and torn at fold of upper flap.   Peter Ellis   112 - 375   2016   £95

Tennant, Robert *British Guiana and its Resources.* London: George Philip & Son, 1895. Extremely rare first edition, 8vo., original red cloth, lettered in black, folding map with gold mines printed in yellow, cloth bit marked, otherwise fine, this the publisher's file copy, with label on front cover.   Sotheran's   Travel and Exploration - 75   2016   £248

Teenie Weenie Man's Mother Goose. Chicago: Reilly & Lee, 1921. First edition, 4to., cloth pictorial paste-on, slight soil and rubbing, very good+, over 100 illustrations by William Donahey, including pictorial endpapers and 12 great bright color plates, scarce.   Aleph-bet Books, Inc.   112 - 154   2016 $750

Tennyson, Alfred Tennyson, 1st Baron   1609-1692 *In Memoriam.* London: Edward Moxon, 1850. First edition, half title, without catalog, original vertical grained purple cloth, floral borders blocked in blind, spine lettered in gilt, spine faded, still very good, clean copy.   Jarndyce Antiquarian Booksellers   CCXVII - 275   2016   £550

Tennyson, Alfred Tennyson, 1st Baron   1609-1692 *In Memoriam.* London: Macmillan & co. Ltd., 1899. 155 x 113mm., extremely pretty deep purple morocco very attractively gilt and inlaid, by Ramage, stamp signed, both covers with densely gilt frame of tiny stars and with large gilt outlined hearts as cornerpieces, frame enclosing four inlaid roses of yellow morocco on leafy gilt stems, flowers in a field of alternating rows of tiny open leaves and dots, raised bands, spine gilt in compartments, central heart outlined by frame of stars, gilt titling, broard turn-ins punctuated with 20 gilt rose sprigs flanked by multiple decorative gilt rules, Ivory Moire silk endleaves, all edges gilt, negligible rubbing to front joint and corners, still fine, binding lustrous and interior showing no signs of use.   Phillip J. Pirages   67 - 61   2016 $750

Tennyson, Alfred Tennyson, 1st Baron   1609-1692 *Poems by Two Brothers.* London: printed by J. and J. Jackson, Louth for Simpkin and Marshall, 1827. First edition, 163 x 102mm., lovely late 19th century crimson morocco, elegantly gilt, covers with plain and decorative gilt rules and fleuron cornerpieces, raised bands, spine gilt in double ruled compartments with urn of flowers at center surrounded by small tools, leaf garlands at corners, gilt titling, richly gilt turn-ins, top edge gilt, bookplate of S. A. Thompson Yates, the collection then passed to Allan Heywood Bright, faint discoloration in bottom margin of about 25 leaves, isolated insignificant soiling, otherwise very pretty book in fine condition, text fresh and bright and especially beautiful binding, lustrous and unworn.   Phillip J. Pirages   67 - 325   2016 $3250

Tennyson, Alfred Tennyson, 1st Baron   1609-1692 *Poems.* London: Edward Moxon and Co., 1862. Small 4to., contemporary full brown morocco decorated and stamped in black, all edges gilt, richly gauffered marbled endpapers, illustrations, handsome.   Sotheran's Piccadilly Notes - Summer 2015 - 298   2016   £298

Tennyson, Alfred Tennyson, 1st Baron   1609-1692 *Poems MDCCCXXX. MDCCCXXXIII.* Toronto: privately printed, 1862. Pirated reprint, small square 8vo., original blue printed wrappers, edges uncut and unopened, slight creasing to lower wrapper, otherwise very nice, preserved in custom made cloth covered fall down-back box, spine lettered in gilt.   Sotheran's Piccadilly Notes - Summer 2015 - 297   2016   £225

Tennyson, Alfred Tennyson, 1st Baron   1609-1692 *Poems. MDCCCXXX. MDCCCXXXIII.* Toronto: privately printed, 1862. Piracy by J. Dykes Campbell, blue wrappers, hint of foxing, faint creases on rear wrapper, else very fine, fresh copy.   Joseph J. Felcone, Inc.   Books from Five Centuries: a Miscellany - 141   2016 $450

Tennyson, Alfred Tennyson, 1st Baron   1609-1692 *Seven Poems and Two Translations.* Hammersmith: Doves Press, 1902. One of 325 copies on paper and 25 on vellum, 236 x 165mm., very appealing contemporary brown crushed morocco decorated in Arts and Crafts style by G. C. Creswell (stamp signed), cover with blind tooled strapwork, frame accented with inlaid dots of green and olive morocco, raised bands, vertical titling in blind turn-ins with frame of multiple blind rules and inlaid green and olive dots at corners, binding with total of 296 inlays, all edges gilt, printed in red an black, with (laid in) bookplate of Elizabeth Watson Diamond, featuring etched portrait of T. J. Cobden-Sanderson by Sidney Lawton Smith, spine lightly sunned, extremities little rubbed, four short faint scratches to boards, minor offsetting from turn-ins, mild freckled foxing to edges of half dozen leaves, otherwise excellent copy, text very clean and fresh in quite pleasing amateur binding.   Phillip J. Pirages   67 - 117   2016 $1500

Tennyson, Jesse F. *The Solange Stories.* Macmillan, 1931. First US edition, 8vo., original yellow cloth, titles stamped in black on front cover and spine, very good, elusive dust jacket professionally restored at spine ends and extremities and red color on spine faded.   Buckingham Books   2015 - 37494   2016 $475

Tenon, Jacques Rene *De Cataracta.* Paris: Viduae Defaguette, 1757. 4to., engraved plate, fine in full modern calf, red morocco title label on front cover.   Edwin V. Glaser Rare Books   2015 - 10099   2016 $1000

Tentoonstelling Van Hulpmiddelen Voor Den Boekhandel. Amsterdam: Roeloffzen & Hubner, 1881. First edition, small 4to., publisher's red cloth stamped in gilt and black, minor foxing on prelim pages.   Oak Knoll Books   310 - 187   2016 $450

Terentius Afer, Publius *Comoediae, Andria, Eunuchus....* Paris: Apud Ioannem de Roigny, 1552. First Thierry edition, numerous woodcut illustrations within text, some light spotting, ink splotch to second two leaves, ownership inscriptions to titlepage of Johann Adolph Freitagh, folio, contemporary French mid-brown calf, boards bordered with black strap within gilt fillets, central decorative arabesque panel in gilt and black, flat spine divided by gilt tools, second compartments gilt lettered within gilt shield outline, other compartments with central decoration in black and gilt, spine ends, joints and corners skillfully repaired, some old scratches and marks to leather, dampmark to front endpapers, bookplate removed from front pastedown, smaller modern booklabel in its place, very good.   Blackwell's Rare Books Greek & Latin Classics VII - 83   2016   £3000

Terentius Afer, Publius *Comoediae Sex.* Cambridge: ex officina Ioannis Hayes, 1676. 12mo., titlepage dusty and with small tear in blank area, some light spotting and browning, small intermittent dampmark to lower corner, contemporary panelled calf, rebacked preserving original spine, hinges neatly relined, old leather bit scratched and rubbed, bookplate of Lt. Col. W. H. M. Jackson, sound. Blackwell's Rare Books   B186 - 147   2016   £180

Terentius Afer, Publius *Terence's Comedies.* London: for A. Swall and T. Childe, 1694. First edition, 8vo., small (20mm) piece torn away from fore margin of titlepage, some very light staining, contemporary sprinkled calf, gilt spine, red morocco label, joints cracked, headcaps broken and corners bumped, from the library of James Stevens Cox (1910-1997), signature and initials of Charles Kenneys (1651-1702).   Maggs Bros. Ltd.   1447 - 412   2016   £150

Terentius Afer, Publius *Comoediae.* Cambridge: Apud Cornelium Crownfield, 1726. First Bentley edition, 2 engraved portraits, some soiling in places, 4to., contemporary calf spine gilt, quite rubbed and scratched but now conserved, joints expertly renewed and red morocco lettering piece replaced to style, booklabel of Peter Allen Hansen and ownership inscription of (MP for Durham) R(obert) Shafto, good.   Blackwell's Rare Books   Greek & Latin Classics VII - 84   2016   £400

Terentius Afer, Publius *Comoediae.* Amsterdam: Apud R. & J. Wetstenios & G. Smith, 1727. 3 engraved plates, little light toning but generally quite clean and fresh, 4to., prize binding of marbled calf, circa 1813, boards bordered with gilt roll and with arms of Haarlem blocked in gilt at centre, spine gilt in compartments, printed prize leaf with front endpapers, green silk ties present and wholly intact, label lost from spine, some surface damage to leather of boards, very good.   Blackwell's Rare Books   Greek & Latin Classics VII - 86   2016   £600

Terentius Afer, Publius *Comoedia.* London: Impensis J. et P. Knapton et G. Sandby, 1751. 2 volumes in one, 6 engraved plates, some soiling, last leaf bit stained, 8vo., contemporary vellum, spine lettered in black, somewhat soiled, endpapers renewed preserving old bookplate of William Henry Mason and old flyleaves with pencilled inscription of George William Mason, Trinity College, Cambridge 1840, good.   Blackwell's Rare Books   Greek & Latin Classics VII - 87   2016   £120

Terentius Afer, Publius *The Comedies of Terence.* London: for T. Beckett and P. A. Dehondt and others, 1765. First edition, 4to, full speckled cafl, slightly shelfworn, spine ends abraded, gilt to spine compartments, rubbed, morocco label, upper hinge tender, marbled endpapers, engraved frontispiece and plates, text and plates, clean and bright, speckled edges.   Dramatis Personae   119 - 36   2016 $500

Terentius Afer, Publius *Comoediae ex recensione Danielis Heinsii....* Rome: Impensis Nicolai Roisechii, 1767. Second edition of the Italian translation by Fortiguerra, Folio, titlepage printed in black and red, a number of large engravings within text, folio, untrimmed, contemporary half vellum, paper boards decorated in brown, red and yellow, spines lettered gilt, bookplates of Markham of Becca Lodge in Yorkshire, bindings soiled and worn around edges (particularly corners and spine ends, splash of white paint to backstrip of volume ii, good.   Blackwell's Rare Books   Greek & Latin Classics VII - 88   2016   £600

Terentius Afer, Publius *Comediae.* Birmingham: Typis Johannis Baskerville, 1772. 4to., titlepage toned, little minor spotting, elsewhere, slightly later half red morocco, marbled boards, spine divided by gilt rolls, second compartment gilt lettered direct, rest with central oval or fountain & bird tools, marbled endpapers, spine somewhat faded, slight rubbing to extremities, bookplates of L. W. Greenwood and Lytton Strachey, very good.   Blackwell's Rare Books   Greek & Latin Classics VII - 89   2016   £300

Terentius Afer, Publius *(Comoediae).* Londini: William Pickering, 1822. 48mo., frontispiece, engraved titlepage and addtional titlepage, very lightly toned, head edge and some fore-edges unopened, contemporary crimson silk, small printed paper label to spine, powder blue endpapers, silk covering perished at spine but binding sound, few smudgy marks, edges little worn, very good.   Unsworths Antiquarian Booksellers   30 - 46   2016   £75

The Territory of Wyoming. Its History, Soil, Climate, Resources etc. Laramie City: Daily Sentinel Print Dec., 1874. Blue printed wrappers, long diagonal tear in lower corner of titlepage has been neatly closed with strip of cellophane tape on iethr side, touching one letter of type, spine ends bit chipped, else very good, clean with wrappers in lovely condition.   Joseph J. Felcone, Inc.   Books from Five Centuries: a Miscellany - 155   2016 $4500

Terry, Ellen 1848-1928   *The Story of My Life.* London: Hutchinson, 1908. 1/1000 copies, 1/250 copies signed by author, 8vo., photos, owner's bookplate, cover little yellowed and worn, lacks small piece at top of spine, otherwise very good.   Second Life Books, Inc.   196 B - 749   2016 $250

A Testimonial to Charles J. Paine and Edward Burgess from the City of Boston for Their Successful Defence of the America's Cup. Boston: printed by order of the City Council, 1888. Second edition, limited to 1680 copies, this in seeming scarce special leather binding, 4to., original full black morocco, boards with gilt panels, upper board lettered gilt, lower board with gilt medallion of the city of Boston, spine lettered gilt, gilt panels and centre tools, all edges gilt, rich gilt turn-ins, marbled endpapers, frontispiece, 8 fine black and white photos, diagram, portraits, ink inscription, otherwise near fine.   Sotheran's   Piccadilly Notes - Summer 2015 - 16 2016   £1750

Thacher, James *Observations on Hydrophobia, Produced by the Bite of a Mad Dog...* Plymouth: Joseph Avery, 1812. First edition, hand colored plate, contemporary mottled sheep, foxed (as always) but very attractive copy, binding particularly nice. Joseph J. Felcone, Inc. Books from Five Centuries: a Miscellany - 98 2016 $500

Thackeray, Albert Smith *Comic Almanack: an Ephemeris in Jest Containing Merry Tales, Humorous Poetry Quips and Oddities.* London: Chatto and Windus, 1835-1853. 4 volumes, 12mo., half leather, marbled paper covered boards, marbled endpapers, black and white illustrations, covers rubbed and scuffed at edges and along spine. Oak Knoll Books 310 - 220 2016 $300

Thackeray, William Makepeace 1811-1863 *The Adventures of Philip on His Way through the World...* London: Smith Edler & Co., 1862. First edition, 3 volumes, half title in volume I, original brown coarse morocco grained cloth, boards blocked in blind, spines lettered in gilt, slight bump to fore edge of front board, volume II, superior copy. Jarndyce Antiquarian Booksellers CCXVII - 278 2016 £480

Thackeray, William Makepeace 1811-1863 *The History of Pendennis: His Fortunes and Misfortunes, His Friends and His Greatest Enemy.* Ipswich: Limited Editions Club, 1961. No. 1461 of 1500 copies, 2 volumes, large 8vo., signed by artist, Charles W. Stewart, embossed yellow cloth with spine label in lavender and gilt, volumes as new in box with large wax stain at ne end. Second Life Books, Inc. 197 - 317 2016 $40

Thackeray, William Makepeace 1811-1863 *The Kickleburys on the Rhine.* London: Smith Elder & Co., 1850. First edition, half title, illustrations with 15 hand colored plates, including frontispiece and vignette title, final ad leaf, beautifully bound by Riviere & Son in slightly later full dark green crushed morocco, gilt spine, borders and dentelles, original pale pink printed wrappers bound in at end, fine. Jarndyce Antiquarian Booksellers CCXVII - 279 2016 £400

Thackeray, William Makepeace 1811-1863 *The Kickleburys on the Rhine.* London: Smith, Elder, 1851. Second edition, square 8vo., contemporary half calf over marbled boards, spine lettered and ruled in gilt, marbled edges, title with tinted lithographic vignette, tinted lithographic frontispiece and 13 tinted lithographic plates, all by Thackeray, light wear to extremities, spine little sunned with hinges weakened at head, internally, apart from very light marginal toning a clean and fresh copy, Glasgow bookseller's label inside front cover, contemporary engraved armorial bookplate of C. J. Tennant Dunlop underneath. Sotheran's Travel and Exploration - 286 2016 £125

Thackeray, William Makepeace 1811-1863 *The Memoirs of Barry Lyndon, Edsq. of the Kingdom of Ireland.* London: Bradbury & Evans, 1856. First edition, title and final slightly spotted, excellently rebound in dark blue half straight grained calf, spine gilt, maroon morocco label, very good. Jarndyce Antiquarian Booksellers CCXVII - 280 2016 £750

Thackeray, William Makepeace 1811-1863 *Mrs. Perkin's Ball.* London: Chapman & Hall, 1847. First edition, half title, 22 hand colored plates, frontispiece, vignette title, beautifully bound by Riviere & Son in slightly later full dark green crushed morocco, gilt spine borders & dentelles, all edges gilt, fine, De Luzer's variant without letterpress under the first plate, no list of illustrations and no advertisement. Jarndyce Antiquarian Booksellers CCXVII - 281 2016 £400

Thackeray, William Makepeace 1811-1863 *The Newcomes: memoirs of a most respectable family.* London: Bradbury & Evans, 1855. First edition, volume I later printing (1855) volume II first printing (1855), 2 volumes, wood and steel engravings by Richard Doyle, blue cloth lettered gilt, decorated in blind, pale yellow endpapers, very good, volume I with outer hinge starting at spine head, volume II with cloth very lightly starting to split at front outer hinge, paper hinges very lightly starting inside covers, otherwise sturdy bindings, few small chips to spine ends, minor sunning to spines, few faint and scattered spots to otherwise fresh pages, overall attractive. B & B Rare Books, Ltd. 2016 - WT09 2016 $400

Thackeray, William Makepeace 1811-1863 *Vanity Fair.* Bradbury & Evans, Bouverie Street, 1849. First edition, late impression, half morocco with decorative tooling to spine, marbled boards and fore-edge with matching endpapers, boards and spine scuffed with loss to marbled paper and wear to morocco at extremities, corners slightly bumped, some foxing to interior throughout, former owner's bookplate and ownership inscription. Bertram Rota Ltd. February List 2016 - 55 2016 £100

Tharaud, Jerome *La Fete Arabe.* Paris: Aux Editions Lupina, 1926. No. 177 of 400 copies, 32 color woodcuts by Sureda, spine shows considerable vertical wrinkling from shrinking glue or amateur regluing, otherwise fine in original slipcase, 4to. Beasley Books 2015 - 2016 $800

Thatcher, Margaret *The Path to Power.* London: Harper Collins, 1995. First edition, limited to 500 copies, signed by author, beautiful deluxe edition, numerous photos, thick octavo, original full morocco with gilt spine lettering, all edges gilt, original slipcase, fine. Manhattan Rare Book Company 2016 - 1667 2016 $1450

Thayer, Emma Homan *Wild Flowers of Colorado.* New York: Cassell & Co., 1885. Small folio, 54 pages, illustrations, all edges gilt, pictorial boards and spine faded, hinges and few early pages reinforced top and bottom of spine rubbed, internally clean.   Dumont Maps and Books   134 - 48   2016 $295

Thayer, Lee *The Darkest Spot.* New York: Burt, Reprint edition, very good in fine dust jacket.   Mordida Books 2015 - 10443   2016 $65

Thelwall, John *The Trident of Albion an Epic Effusion...* Liverpool: printed for the author by G. F. Harris, 1805. 8vo., half title and final leaf rather dusty and stained, faint ex-library stamp to titlepage verso expertly bound in recent half calf, gilt banded spine, dark green morocco label, marbled boards.   Jarndyce Antiquarian Booksellers   CCXVI - 564   2016   £1500

Theocritus *The Idyllia, Epigrams and Fragments of Theocritus, Bion and Moschus, with Elegies of Tyrateus.* Bath: printed by R. Cruttwell, 1792. First edition by Polwhele, 2 volumes bound as one, half title, discarded, little minor spotting, ownership inscription of W. Mayer, T.C.D., to titlepage, 8vo., later half maroon roan, marbled boards, spine lettered gilt, corners worn, spine rubbed, shelfmark to front pastedown, good.   Blackwell's Rare Books   Greek & Latin Classics VII - 90   2016   £120

Theocritus *The Second and Seventh Idylls.* London: John Lane, Bodley Head, 1927. First Rivers edition, 8 wood engravings by Elizabeth Rivers, 32mo., original black boards, backstrip and upper board lettered and decorated in white, some splitting along upper joint and some tiny spots of wear to corners, edges rough trimmed and little toned, partial browning to endpapers, good, inscribed by artist to Aunt Mary with love from Elizabeth Rivers.   Blackwell's Rare Books   B186 - 332   2016   £80

Theocritus *Sixe Idillia.* Duckworth, 1922. 173/355 copies (from an edition of 380), printed on handmade paper, signed by artist, 31 wood engravings by Vivien Gribble, one or two tiny foxspots to border of a couple of pages, large 4to., original quarter fawn canvas with design by Gribble to upper board, backstrip lettered in gilt, few spots aorund head and top corners little bumped, edges untrimmed, free endpapers browned, dust jacket with red staining to margin of front and couple of spots of same to upper board and tail edge, good.   Blackwell's Rare Books   B186 - 311   2016   £60

Theocritus *Tade Enestein Ente Garoi se Biblo Eidyllia he Kai Triakonta.* Rome: Zacharias Callierges, 1516. 8vo., early 19th century mid brown polished calf, spine gilt in compartments, red morocco lettering piece, edges red, marbled endpapers, corners slightly worn, joints near invisibly strengthened and front flyleaf re-attached, bookplate of Thomas Gaisford and letter from Earl Spencer to Gaisford, Gaisford's ownership inscription and manuscript table of contents to blank endpapers, good.   Blackwell's Rare Books   B184 - 84   2016   £6500

Theroux, Paul 1941- *Chicago Loop.* London: Hamish Hamilton, 1990. Uncorrected advance proof copy, green and white original wrappers, very good.   I. D. Edrich Crime - 2016   £25

Theroux, Paul 1941- *The Kingdom by the Sea.* London: Hamish Hamilton, 1983. First edition, 8vo., map, original green cloth, dust jacket, near fine.   J. & S. L. Bonham Antiquarian Booksellers   Europe 2016 - 9787   2016   £25

Theroux, Paul 1941- *London Snow: a Christmas Story.* 1979. First edition, one of 450 numbered copies signed by artist, very slight spotting to top and bottom edges of sides, but very nice in original tissue wrapper.   Bertram Rota Ltd.   Christmas List 2015 - 56   2016   £95

Theroux, Paul 1941- *O-Zone.* Franklin Center: Franklin Library, 1986. Limited first edition, signed by author, bound in gray leather, lettered and decoratively stamped in gilt, all edges gilt, very fine, as new.   Argonaut Book Shop Literature 2015 - 4029   2016 $45

Theroux, Paul 1941- *The Shortest Day of the Year: a Christmas Fantasy.* Leamington Spa: Sixth Chamber Press, 1986. First edition, one of 175 numbered copies signed by author (there were a further 26 copies in quarter leather), 4to., 3 color typographical constructions by Sebastian Carter, one repeated and mounted on upper cover, very fine.   Bertram Rota Ltd.   Christmas List 2015 - 57   2016   £110

Thesiger, Wiflred *Visions of a Nomad.* London: Collins, 1987. First edition, quarto, photos, very fine in near fine, price clipped dust jacket.   Peter Ellis   112 - 398   2016   £75

Thewlis, Malford W. *Geriatrics: a Treatise on the Prevention and Treatment of Diseases of Old Age and the Care of the Aged.* St. Louis: 1924. Second edition, 8vo., green cloth, author's presentation on flyleaf, cover little scuffed at edges, otherwise very good.   Second Life Books, Inc.   196 B - 754   2016 $65

Thicknesse, Philip *A Year's Journey through France and part of Spain.* N. Brown, 1778. Second edition, 2 volumes in 1, 8vo., 10 plates, 3 music sheets, 3 pages with marginal tears, contemporary brown speckled calf joint cracked, spine worn and rubbed. J. & S. L. Bonham Antiquarian Booksellers Europe 2016 - 9336 2016 £200

Thielen, Beth *About My Mother.* Pasadena: Beth Thielen, 1996. Revised edition, one of five numbered copies, 4to., black linen covered boards, matching black linen slipcase, paper spine label, unpaginated, accordion fold book with large pages of heavy paper containing drawings in gold ink surrounding a small cut-out book which forms part of the text of the larger book. Oak Knoll Books 27 - 65 2016 $750

Thielen, Beth *Sentences: Words Spoken in Prison to an Artist. (with) Why the Revolving Door....* Pasadena: Beth Thielen, 1990. 1993. First title one of 10 numbered copies, signed by artist in book, as well as on a separate card description, second title Artists' Proof in an edition of 20 numbered copies signed by artist who has also noted that this copy is unique, 7 dramatic pop-up scenes, titlepages handwritten in pencil, small 4to., quarter black linen paper covered boards with monoprints on front and rear covers, specially made black linen slipcase. Oak Knoll Books 27 - 66 2016 $3500

Thimm, Carl Albert *English, French, Turkish and Russian Vocabulary for the Use of the Army, Navy and Travellers.* London: Franz Thimm, 1855. First edition, 12mo., original mauve pebble grained cloth, spine lettered gilt, front cover with blindstamped logo on front cover, wear to spine and one corner, marginal traces of humidity at beginning and end, light browning due to paper stock, one corner with little loss, very rare. Sotheran's Travel and Exploration - 382 2016 £298

Thine, Bawlingly *Something for the Admirers of Baseball.* New York: Glenn Horowitz, 1990. Limited to 150 copies, 8vo., stiff paper wrappers, cord tied, illustration. Oak Knoll Books 310 - 119 2016 $100

The Third Chapter of Accidents and Remarkable Events... Philadelphia: J. Johnson, 1807. 12mo., marbled wrappers, 24 leaves, fine, 12 very fine engravings. Aleph-bet Books, Inc. 112 - 166 2016 $850

This is the House that Jack Built. London: Marcus Ward, n.d. circa, 1890. 6 x 7 inches, die-cut in shape of house, near fine, fine color lithographs on every page by E. Caldwell. Aleph-bet Books, Inc. 112 - 460 2016 $350

This Quarter. Volume 1 number 1. Paris: 1925. 8vo., original paper wrappers (chipped around the edges, lacks, some of the paper on spine, light stain on bottom of cover), frontispiece, very good fragile piece. Second Life Books, Inc. 197 - 318 2016 $450

Thomas A'Kempis 1380-1471 *Opera et Libri vite Fratris Thomas de Kempis Ordinis Canonicorum Regularium Quorum Titulos Vide inPrimo Folio.* Nuremberg: per Caspar Hochfeder, 1494. Second collected edition, sploch of worming to last leaf affecting part of four words, ruled in red throughout with initials and paragraph marks supplied in red and blue and printed capitals picked out in yellow, first leaf bit soiled with some light dustiness and browning elsewhere, one blank corner renewed, folio, early 20th century half vellum, spine lettered in ink, just bit rubbed, bookplate of Bibliotheca Ritmana, very good. Blackwell's Rare Books Marks of Genius - 24 2016 £9000

Thomas Cook & Son *Peking. North China. South Manchuria. Korea.* Yokohama: Box of Curious P. & P. Co. for Thomas Cook & Son in Beijing, 1920. 8vo., original green cloth lettered in black and with printed title label on front cover, 3 folding maps, cloth little marked, maps on brown onion skin paper, as issued, good copy. Sotheran's Travel and Exploration - 103 2016 £198

Thomas, Abel Charles *The Lowell Offering: a Repository of Original Articles.* Lowell: Powers & Bagley, Boston: Saxton & Peirce and Jordan, 1842. First edition, octavo, contemporary blindstamped gray-green cloth, gilt lettering, five woodcut illustrations and vignettes, cloth worn, binding little shaken, very good, fragile. The Brick Row Book Shop Miscellany 69 - 77 2016 $275

Thomas, Alan *Thre Tremayne Case.* London: Ernest Benn, 1929. Black boards, fading, red titling, spine slightly sunned, light edge spotting, otherwise very good, uncommon title. I. D. Edrich Crime - 2016 £50

Thomas, Caitlin *Caitlin - a Warring Absence.* London: Secker & Warburg, 1986. First edition, photos, signed by author, presentation from Thomas's daughter to Judith Karolyi and Zenka Bartek, covers slightly marked, very good in like dust jacket, slightly creased. Peter Ellis 112 - 400 2016 £85

Thomas, Charles Cyrus *A Black Lark Caroling.* Dallas: Kaleidograph Press, 1936. First edition, octavo, about fine in soiled and modestly chipped and stained, good or better dust jacket, uncommon. Between the Covers Rare Books 202 - 106 2016 $350

Thomas, D. M. *Love and Other Deaths: Poems.* 1975. First edition, fine in dust jacket, signed by author. Bertram Rota Ltd. February List 2016 - 57 2016 £30

Thomas, D. M. *Two Voices.* London: Cape Goliard Press, 1968. First edition, royal octavo, number 30 of 50 copies signed by author, clothbound with photographic image mounted on front, fine in original tissue wrapper torn at edges. Peter Ellis 112 - 399 2016 £75

Thomas, David A. *Churchill, the member for Woodford.* 1995. Fine in like dust jacket, inscribed presentation by author as well as Churchill's successor as MP for Woodford Lord (Patrick) Jenkin, fine in like dust jacket.   I. D. Edrich Winston Spencer Churchill - 2016   £65

Thomas, Donna *Hetch Hetchy Flora. A Collection of Wildflowers Painted on May 22 2013.* Santa Cruz: Peter & Donna Thomas, 2013. Number 15 of 35 copies, Thomas designed the book, painted the borders on each of the original watercolors, wrote the text and created original text pages, Peter Thomas created a paper for the project, her original watercolors printed directly onto Peter's paper using a Cannon digital printer, prints were then hand sewn onto accordion folded sheets of 'granite' paper, covers feature a wooden 'plant press' over blue Moroccan grain leather covered boards, pant press is a lattice of strong hardwoods, most of the walnut modeled after those used in early 1900's by botanists like Jepson, 9 watercolor paintings, one watercolor printed map, five ornamental pages of handwritten and rubricated text, book housed in blue cloth clamshell box with decorative title label on front, fine.   The Kelmscott Bookshop   13 - 57   2016 $875

Thomas, Dylan Marlais   1914-1953 *Deaths and Entrances - Poems.* London: J. M. Dent, 1946. First edition, orange cloth, free endpapers slightly spotted, very good in like dust jacket, slightly marked, little rubbed at spine.   Peter Ellis   112 - 401   2016   £350

Thomas, Dylan Marlais   1914-1953 *In Country Sleep and Other Poems.* New York: New Directions, 1952. First trade edition, 8vo., due-tone portrait by Marion Morehouse tipped to titlepage, original boards, dust jacket, fine in dust jacket, presentation copy from author.   James S. Jaffe Rare Books   Occasional List: Winter 2016 - 138   2016 $5000

Thomas, Dylan Marlais   1914-1953 *In Country Sleep and Other Dreams.* New York: New Directions, 1952. First edition, signed by author, octavo, photographic portrait of Thomas tipped in to titlepage, previous owner's signature and date, green paper over boards, dust jacket, jacket spine chipped on top and bottom, two small chips to top of rear panel, very good.   Heritage Book Shop   Holiday 2015 - 103   2016 $1500

Thomas, Edward *Six Poems by Edward Eastaway.* Flansham: Pear Tree Press, 1916. first edition of his rare first book of poems, printed in an edition stated to consist of 100 copies by hand and in color from intaglio plates by Guthrie, 4to., illustrations by James Guthrie, original gray wrappers with printed label, light use at overlap edges of wrappers, two short closed tears in top spine portion, otherwise fine, preserved in custom half morocco folding box.   James S. Jaffe Rare Books   Occasional List: Winter 2016 - 139   2016 $12,500

Thomas, Franklin *The Etiquette of Freemasonry.* London: A. Lewis, 1890. First edition, half title, 6 pages ads, original blue cloth, Foyles bookseller's label, signature of K. G. Prior, very good.   Jarndyce Antiquarian Books CCXV - 436   2016   £75

Thomas, Garfield *The First African Baptist Church of North America.* Savannah: Author, 1925. First edition, errata slip tipped in, drawings, photos, modest soiling to few pages, some pencil notes erased from front fly, light wear to corners, very good or better, scarce.   Between the Covers Rare Books   202 - 107   2016 $350

Thomas, Helen *A Memory of W. H. Hudson.* Wakefield: Fleece Press, 1984. One of 40 copies of an edition of 190, but colophon states 300 copies on Arches were printed, but printer's loosely inserted printed errata slip makes clear tath the issue was by miscalculation printed in an edition of 150, printed on Velin Arches mouldmade paper and signed by Myfawnwy Thomas, full page wood engraving by Michael Renton, errata slip correcting limitation, small 4to., original quarter cream linen, printed label, brown decorated boards, untrimmed, near fine.   Blackwell's Rare Books   B184 - 260   2016   £185

Thomas, J. E. *The Whole New Art of Confectionary also Sugar Boiling, Iceing, Candying....*   Leeds: printed by Henry Spink, 1832. New edition, 8vo., original printed wrappers, spotted and chipped, spine perished, rare.   Howard S. Mott Inc.   265 - 119   2016 $450

Thomas, Joyce Carol *Bitter Sweet.* San Jose: Firesign Press, 1973. First edition, slight spotting on boards, near fine in very good or better dust jacket with little age toning and couple of short tears, scarce.   Between the Covers Rare Books   202 - 108   2016 $150

Thomas, Lately *Between Two Empires. The Life Story of California's First Senator, William Mckendree Gwin.* Boston: Houghton Mifflin, 1969. First edition, grey cloth, small oval bookplate, very fine with dust jacket.   Argonaut Book Shop   Biography 2015 - 3599   2016 $40

Thomas, Peter *Bikupan, the Story of a Trip to visit a Hand Paper Mill in Sweden.* Santa Cruz: Peter & Donna Thomas, 1992. Limited to 119 numbered copies on paper handmade by Peter using white and black rags with blue pigment, small 4to., quarter blue leather over marbled paper covered boards, slipcase, tipped in are 6 samples of paper from Lessebo.   Oak Knoll Books   310 - 159   2016 $350

Thomas, R. S. *Das Helle Feld.* Babel: Schondorf am Ammersee, 1995. First edition thus, octavo, one of 890 copies, wrappers, fine.   Peter Ellis   112 - 402   2016   £45

Thomas, R. S. *The Mountains.* New York: Chilmark Press, 1968. One of 11 special copies in a total edition of 350, signed by author, artist and engraver, with extra set of the 10 engravings, on Japanese Hosho paper tipped in and bound thus, handset in 18 pt. Zapf Palatino on mould made paper from Wookey Hole Mill, prospectus loosely inserted, 4to., quarter dark blue morocco, gilt stamped spine over cloth covered boards, illustrated with wood engraving, top edge gilt, slipcase, very scarce. Oak Knoll Books 27 - 57 2016 $2500

Thomas, R. S. *The Stones of the Field.* Camarthen: Druid Press, 1946. First edition, 8vo., original quarter blue cloth with pale blue boards, gentlest of bumps to corners, ownership inscription to flyleaf, dust jacket with little chipping to corners and backstrip ends, short closd tear at head of rear panel, little pencil erasure at head of front panel, very good. Blackwell's Rare Books B184 - 240 2016 £600

Thomas, Ross *Voodoo, Ltd.* New York: Mysterious Press, 1992. First edition, very fine in pictorial wrappers, inscribed by author, advance reading copy. Mordida Books 2015 - 012384 2016 $65

Thomas, Simon *Hanes y Byd a'r Amseroedd, et Hyfforddiad rhai o'r Cymru.* London: printed by J. Batly, 1721. First London edition, some browning and staining, small 8vo., original sheep, crudely rebacked, new endpapers, sound. Blackwell's Rare Books B186 - 148 2016 £400

Thompson & West *Historical Atlas Map of Santa Clara County.* San Francisco: Thompson & West, 1876. First edition, folio, original cloth rebacked, minor soiling and discoloring of covers, with new endpapers, colored maps, double page map, several black and white scenes, along with plates and other illustrations, wonderful copy, very clean with slightest staining or soiling. M & S Rare Books, Inc. 99 - 38 2016 $5500

Thompson, D'Arcy Wenworth *A Glossary of Greek Birds.* Oxford: Clarendon Press, 1895. Octavo, publisher's cloth, pencil ownership signature of W. Baldwin Spencer, deaccessioned library stamp of royal Australasian Ornithologists' Union and the bookplate of D. L. Serventy. Andrew Isles Natural History Books 55 - 38849 2016 $200

Thompson, Dorothy *Once On Christmas.* New York: Oxford University Press (Oct. 1938, 4th printing, Nov., 1938. Pictorial boards, 2 tips worn, else very good+ in dust jacket that is dusty with some mends on verso, illustrations by Lois Lenski with full and partial page pen and ink drawings, with 3 page handwritten letter written to a children's book collector who had inquired about buying an original from this book. Aleph-bet Books, Inc. 111 - 258 2016 $450

Thompson, George E. *Life in Tripoli with a Peep at Ancient Carthage.* Liverpool: Edward Howell, 1894. First edition, 8vo., original red cloth, decorated in black and lettered gilt, 30 photogravure plates, apart from light slanting and offsetting from endpapers, very good, inscribed by pupil of Castle Cary Collegiate School, Edith Haine, dated 1897. Sotheran's Travel and Exploration - 383 2016 £698

Thompson, H. Epworth *Everybody's Guide to Public Speaking.* London: Saxon & Co., 1896. 16mo., original light brown printed cloth boards, slightly dulled. Jarndyce Antiquarian Books CCXV - 437 2016 £38

Thompson, Hunter S. *Fire in the Nuts.* Woody Creek/ Loose Valley: Blue Grass/High Desert/ Gono International/ Steam Press/Petro III Graphics/Sylph Pub., 2004. Limited edition, of a total of 176 copies, this number 3 of 130 numbered copies, signed in full by author and artist, 13 illustrations by Ralph Steadman, quarterbound in black Ashai cloth with illustrated panels and leather spine label, stamped in gold, fine. Ken Lopez Bookseller 166 - 125 2016 $1250

Thompson, Hunter S. *Generation of Swine - Tales of Shame and Degradation in the '80s.* New York: Summit Books, 1988. First edition, octavo, fine in fine dust jacket, very slightly crinkled at top edge. Peter Ellis 112 - 403 2016 £50

Thompson, Jim *Nothing More than Murder.* New York: Harper and Bros., 1949. First edition, author's copy with his ownership name and notation "Jim Thompson RARE COPY PLEASE RETURN", remnants of Thompson's previous address label on same as well as attempted erasure of his old telephone number, with letter of provenance from Thompson's daughter, Sharon Reed-Thompson, about very good in very good dust jacket. Royal Books 51 - 1 2016 $15,000

Thompson, Kay *Eloise.* New York: Simon and Schuster, 1955. Stated first printing, 4to., white cloth, slight offset on front pastedown, else near fine in very good+ dust jacket with light soil and few small chips, illustrations by Hilary Knight, great copy, increasingly scarce. Aleph-bet Books, Inc. 111 - 445 2016 $2500

Thompson, Kay *Eloise in Paris.* New York: Simon & Schuster, 1957. Board stamped in silver, slight bit of cover soil and wear at bottom of spine, else very good+ in dust jacket with 1 inch piece off front cover, small narrow piece off top of spine, spine has archival repair and small chip to bottom, illustrations by Hilary Knight, this copy inscribed by author. Aleph-bet Books, Inc. 112 - 474 2016 $1250

Thompson, Kay *Eloise in Moscow.* New York: Simon & Schuster, 1959. Stated first printing, boards, fine in dust jacket with 3 very small chips, color illustrations by Hilary Knight, inscribed by artist. Aleph-bet Books, Inc. 112 - 473 2016 $700

Thompson, Ruth Plumly *The Gnome King of Oz.* Chicago: The Reilly & Lee Co., 1927. First edition, first issue with color plate sheets coated on both sides and with emerald green cloth binding, 12 color plates, numerous black and white illustrations by John Neill, light emerald green cloth with pictorial paper pastedown to front cover, all edges stained yellow, bit of minjor spotting to copyright page, very fine.   Argonaut Book Shop   Literature 2015 - 7210   2016 $600

Thompson, Ruth Plumly *Grampa in Oz.* Chicago and New York: Reilly Lee Co., 1928. First edition, first issue with color plates sheet coated only on one side, and with unbroken type of numeral on page 171 and last word in second to last line on page 189, includes the 4 lines of ads at back, printed on rectos only, 12 color plates, numerous black and white illustrations by John R. Neill, brick cloth with pictorial paper pastedown to front cover, lovely copy, fine and clean, very scarce pictorial dust jacket, lightly worn with 1.5 inch section lacking from head of spine.   Argonaut Book Shop   Literature 2015 - 7211   2016 $425

Thompson, Ruth Plumly *Hungry Tiger of Oz.* Chicago: Reilly & Lee, 1926. First edition, first state, H-G XX, 12 color plates by J. R. Neill, 4to., green cloth with pictorial paste on, fine in frayed dust jacket, great copy.   Aleph-bet Books, Inc.   112 - 49   2016 $1750

Thompson, Ruth Plumly *The Perhappsy Chaps.* Chicago: Volland, 1918. First edition, 8vo. pictorial boards, spine ends chipped and corners lightly worn, else very good+ illustrations by author, excellent copy.   Aleph-bet Books, Inc.   111 - 446   2016 $800

Thompson, Ruth Plumly *The Princess of Cozy Town.* Chicago: Volland, 1922. First edition, 8vo., pictorial boards offset on backstrip, else near fine in original pictorial box (very good with flap repair), full page and in text color illustrations, throughout by Janet Laura Scott to accompany 6 original fairy tales, beautiful copy.   Aleph-bet Books, Inc.   111 - 447   2016 $800

Thomsen, Wilhelm *The Relations Between the Ancient Russia and Scandinavia and the Origin of the Russian State.* Oxford: James Parker, 1877. First edition, 8vo., original brown blind stamped cloth, blindstamped on titlepage, very good, unopened copy.   J. & S. L. Bonham Antiquarian Booksellers   Europe 2016 - 8822   2016   £100

Thomson, Donald F. *Birds of Cape York Peninsula: Ecological Notes, Field Observations and Catalogue of Specimens Collected on Three Expeditions to North Queensland.* Melbourne: Government Printer, 1935. Octavo, photos, publisher's printed wrappers, very good.   Andrew Isles Natural History Books   55 - 36369   2016 $60

Thomson, George M. *Wild Life in New Zealand.* Wellington: New Zealand Board of Science and Art, 1921-1926. First edition, octavo, text illustrations, 2 volumes, publisher's cloth, very good.   Andrew Isles Natural History Books   55 - 10283   2016 $100

Thomson, James *The Seasons.* London: Wilkie and Robinson, J. Walker, Cadell and Davies et al, 1811. 191 x 121mm., very pleasing contemporary crimson straight grain morocco, elaborately decorated in gilt and blind, covers with broad gilt fillet perimeter bordering a frame of gilt palmettes and then (closer in) fillets and palmettes in blind, raised bands with gilt dash-roll, spine compartments with symmetrically clustered arabesques, roses, open dots, stars and foliate tools, gilt rolled turn-ins, all edges gilt, 4 engraved allegorical plates designed by T. Unwins, inscribed "L. E./from the library of her brother / H. Duncombe e(x) dono A. Curzon", little foxing to plates, exraordinarily fine, text clean and fresh, lovely binding, very lustrous and virtually unworn.   Phillip J. Pirages   67 - 70   2016 $950

Thomson, John *An Enquiry Concerning the liberty and Licentiousness of the Press and the Uncontrollable Nature of the Human Mind...* New York: Johnson & Stryker for the author, 1801. First and only edition, removed from a bound volume, some foxing and spotting, marginal stains on first few pages and one or two internal pages, good to very good in neat cloth folding box with leather label.   Joseph J. Felcone, Inc.   Books from Five Centuries: a Miscellany - 142   2016 $2800

Thomson, John *Tables of Interest at 3, 4, 4 and 5 per cent.* London: printed for W. Creech & C. Elliot, Edinburgh and T. Longman, G. Robinson & T. Cadell, London, 1783. Third edition, 12mo., contemporary reversed calf, blind decorated rules, red morocco label, excellent copy with engraved bookplate of MacLean of Ardgour.   Jarndyce Antiquarian Booksellers   CCXVI - 565   2016   £110

Thorburn, Archibald *Thorburn's Birds of Prey: a Facsimile of the 1919 Edition.* Lamarsh: Iain Grahame, 1985. Collector's edition limited to 135 numbered copies, Small folio, 12 colored plates, publisher's green half morocco marbled endpapers, slipcase, fine.   Andrew Isles Natural History Books   55 - 8313   2016 $1250

Thorburn, David *The University Endowment Movement: Memorandum Relative Thereto.* Edinburgh: Andrew Elliot, 1866. 1 page ads, original grey printed paper wrappers, sewn as issued, slight vertical crease, very good.   Jarndyce Antiquarian Books   CCXV - 982   2016   £45

Thoreau, Henry David 1817-1882 *Men of Concord.* Boston: Houghton Mifflin, 1936. First edition, 4to., green cloth, small erasure mark on endpaper, else fine in dust jacket (small archival mend at spine, otherwise very good+_, illustrations by N. C. Wyeth, this copy signed and dated by Wyeth on titlepage, great copy.   Aleph-bet Books, Inc.   111 - 493   2016 $2500

Thoreau, Henry David 1817-1882 *The Writings.* Boston and New York: Houghton Mifflin and Co., 1906. One of 600 copies, 229 x 156mm., 20 volumes, fine dark green three quarter morocco, marbled sides and endpapers, spines very handsomely gilt in animated compartments filled, with floral stamps and stars, top edges gilt, other edges rough trimmed, most of the volumes unopened, 104 black and white and 20 colored plates, mostly photogravures, spines faded uniformly and very slightly to a pleasing brown (just hint of fading to perimeter of covers), total of four leaves with expertly repaired tears (one tear of four inches entering text, others smaller and marginal, and no loss in any case, otherwise very fine set, bindings quite bright and virtually unworn and leaves without any significant signs of use, majority of text obviously never having been read.   Phillip J. Pirages   67 - 327   2016 $17,500

Thorley, John *Melisselogia; or The Female Monarchy.* London: printed for the author and sold by N. Thorley and J. Davidson, 1744. First edition, frontispiece, 4 inserted copperplate engravings, one folding, 8vo., handsome modern dark tan half calf, skillfully executed in period style, muted green marbled paper boards, fine, ex-library with 2 stamps, period personal ownership signature and notes dated 1744 to prelim blank, very good+.   Tavistock Books   Bibliolatry - 36   2016 $1250

Thornber, John James *The Fantastic Clan: the Cactus Family.* New York: Macmillan, 1932. First edition, 4 color plates, numerous photographic illustrations, 8vo., drawings, endpaper map, brown pictorial cloth stamped in gilt, spine and upper edge of rear cover with slightest of fading, fine.   Argonaut Book Shop   Natural History 2015 - 7360   2016 $45

Thornbury, Walter *Haunted London.* London: Chatto & Windus, 1880. First edition, extra illustrated with cancel titlepage noting "Special Copy Extended to two volumes by the insertion of a large number of extra illustrations", ALS from Lord Rosebery, 8vo., 2 volumes, sometime bound in full double gilt line panelled full polished calf panelled and lettered gilt on spines, top edges gilt, illustrations by F. W. Fairholt, extra illustrated with 97 plates, joints and heads of spines little worn and rubbed, otherwise very good.   Sotheran's   Piccadilly Notes - Summer 2015 - 304   2016   £750

Thorndike, Russell *Little Dorrit.... told for children.* Oxford: Clarendon Press, 1979. Half title, frontispiece, illustrations, original dark blue cloth, very good without dust jacket.   Jarndyce Antiquarian Booksellers   CCXVIII - 547   2016   £20

Thorne, E. P. *Justice is Mine.* London: Wright & Brown Ltd., 1950. Very good, illustrated dust jacket which has couple of closed tears on rear panel, uncommon.   I. D. Edrich   Crime - 2016   £30

Thornton, J. L. *The Northern Poetical Keepsake.* Newcastle: Fisher (printed by Thomas and James Pigg), 1856. Half title, printed in red and blue, title in green gold & red, contemporary half red morocco, marbled boards.   Jarndyce Antiquarian Booksellers   CCXVII - 282   2016   £250

Thornton, John *Maxims and Directions for Youth on a Variety of Important and Interesting Subjects...*   London: printed for W. Baynes, 1811. 12mo., 4 pages ads, contemporary full tan calf, spine gilt, leading hinge slightly splitting at head, slightly rubbed, contemporary signature of Francis Buckle Jr. and J. Nisbet bookseller's ticket, very nice, scarce.   Jarndyce Antiquarian Books   CCXV - 438   2016   £220

Thornton, Robert John *Illustrations of the School-Virgil in Copper-plates and Wood-cuts...* London: F. C. & J. Rivington, J. Johnson & Newberry &c, 1814. First edition, 62 leaves of plates, 148 woodcut illustrations with binder's page instructions, titlepage slightly dusted and chipped at margins, later 19th century quarter maroon calf, patterned maroon cloth boards, slightly sunned, spine little rubbed.   Jarndyce Antiquarian Books   CCXV - 983   2016   £750

Thornton, Robert John *Thornton's Temple of Flora.* London: Collins, 1951. Limited to 250 numbered copies, signed by three contributors Geoffrey Grigson, Handasyde, Buchanan and William Stearn, large folio, 31 colored and uncolored plates, publisher's half morocco and slipcase, spine slightly sunned.   Andrew Isles Natural History Books   55 - 30581   2016 $500

Thorp, Raymond W. *Spirit Gun of the West. The Story of Doc W. F. Carver.* Glendale: Arthur H. Clark, 1957. First edition, 2nd issue, one of 994 copies bound in blue cloth and issued with dust jacket, photos, very fine with slightly soiled dust jacket, 2000 copies bound in blue cloth and issued with dust jacket, photos, very fine with slightly soiled, dust jacket.   Argonaut Book Shop   Biography 2015 - 5381   2016 $60

Thorpe, Adrian *The Birds of Edward Lear: a Selection of the 12 Finest Bird Plates of the Artist.* London: Ariel Press, 1975. Folio, 12 color plates, very good, in slightly chipped dust jacket.   Andrew Isles Natural History Books   55 - 15375   2016 $250

Thorson, Thomas B. *Investigations of the Ichthyofauna of Nicaraguan lakes.* Lincoln: University of Nebraska Press, 1976. Quarto, photos, signature, very good in chipped dust jacket.   Andrew Isles Natural History Books   55 - 38376   2016 $60

Thouvenel, Pierre *De Corpore Nutritivo et de Nutritione Tentamen Chymico-Medicum.* Pezenas: J. Dent, 1770. Disbound, very good, large engraved coat of arms, 4to.   Edwin V. Glaser Rare Books   2015 - 10083   2016 $125

Thrapp, Dan L. *The Conquest of Apacheria.* Norman: University of Oklahoma, 1975. Reprint, numerous black and white illustrations, fine in very slightly rubbed dust jacket.   Argonaut Book Shop   Native American 2015 - 1971   2016 $75

Three Letters Addressed to a Friend in India by a Proprietor. London: printed for J. Debrett, 1793. First edition, folding table, first few leaves little spotted and with slight dampstain in upper margin, 8vo., disbound, good.   Blackwell's Rare Books   B186 - 54   2016   £400

Three Tiny Pigs. London: Dean & Son, 1861. 4to., pictorial wrappers, small part of spine rubbed, else near fine, printed on one side of the paper, 8 large three quarter page hand colored illustrations, scarce.   Aleph-bet Books, Inc.   111 - 167   2016 $500

Three Tiny Pigs. New York: McLoughlin Bros. n.d. circa, 1864. 4to., pictorial wrappers, some scattered internal soil else very good, printed on one side of the paper, 8 large three quarter page hand colored illustrations with text and story below, scarce.   Aleph-bet Books, Inc.   111 - 276   2016 $600

Through Space to Mars or the Longest Journey on Record. The Great Marvel Series #4. New York: Cupples & Leon Co., 1910, circa, 1935. 12mo., frontispiece, brown cloth stamped in black, red topstain, color pictorial dust jacket, very good+ in very good dust jacket (modest wear/spine panel lightly sunned).   Tavistock Books   Getting Around - 49   2016 $75

Thubron, Colin *Mirror to Damascus.* London: Heinemann, 1967. First edition, 8vo., original burgundy cloth lettered gilt on spine, illustrations, signed presentation from author, faint rubbing at edge, otherwise fine in very good+ complete dust jacket with slight shelfwear (closed tear, slight nick, slight creasing).   Any Amount of Books 2015 - A77296   2016   £150

Thucydides *De Bello Peloponnesiaco Libri VIII.* Geneva: Henri Estienne, 1588. Augmented second edition, folio, Greek and Latin text, Estienne device, ornamental initials and headpieces, 18th century tree calf, expertly rebacked preserving original spine, gilt stamped spine compartments, newer morocco spine label, armorial bookplate, corners bit bumped, aside from some general toning and browning to edges, excellent copy.   Heritage Book Shop   Holiday 2015 - 104   2016 $10,000

Thucydides *De Bello Peloponnesiaco Libri Octo.* Amstelaedami: Apud R. & J. Wetstenios & Gul. Smith, 1731. Folio, engraved frontispiece and 2 folding plates (maps), Greek and Latin parallel texts, titlepages in red and black, engraved vignette, engraved initials and head and tailpieces, occasional toned leaves, generally bright within, contemporary brown calf boards, neatly rebacked, spine gilt with older red morocco label retained, gilt frames and borders, corners reinforced, edges sprinkled red and blue, endpapers renewed, few scrapes and scratches, slight creasing to spine, edges rubbed, but very good, ownership inscription of W. Cokyane Frith.   Unsworths Antiquarian Booksellers Ltd.   30 - 151   2016   £1000

Thucydides *De Bello Poloponneasiaco Libri Octo cum Adnotationibus Integris Henrici Stephani & Joannis Hudsoni.* Amsterdam: Apud R. & Ja. Wetstenios & Gul. Smith, 1731. Folio, engraved frontispiece and two folding plates, some spotting and toning, first few leaves with dampmark to foremargin, slightly later brown calf spine gilt in compartments, joints and corners expertly repaired, new morocco lettering piece, marbled endpapers, old scratches and scrapes to boards, good.   Blackwell's Rare Books   B186 - 151   2016   £750

Thucydides *History of the Peloponnesian War.* Chelsea: Ashendene Press, 1930. One of 260 copies on paper, 240 for sale (and 20 on vellum), 407 x 277, original white pigskin by W. H. Smith & Son (stamp signed), raised bands, gilt titling, edges untrimmed, substantial marbled slipcase (from time of publication?) with pigskin edging to match volume, first initial of each chapter and opening line of each book, designed by Graily Hewitt, printer's device in colophon, printed in red and black, few small scrapes on spine, as almost always, just whisper of soiling to white pigskin, one tiny closed tear at fore edge, extremely fine, essentially unworn binding, much cleaner than we have a right to expect, text virtually pristine.   Phillip J. Pirages   67 - 18   2016 $5500

Thurber, James 1894-1961 *Many Moons.* New York: Harcourt Brace, 1943. I. First edition, 4to., red cloth, fine in price clipped dust jacket frayed at spine ends, short tear on rear panel, overall bright and very good+, this copy inscribed by author illustrations in color by Louis Slobodkin, rare and amazing copy.   Aleph-bet Books, Inc.   111 - 450   2016 $6500

Thurber, James 1894-1961 *Thurber Country.* New York: Simon and Schuster, 1953. First edition, illustrations, cloth backed boards, spine slightly darkened, dust jacket rubbed and chipped, missing portions at ends of spine, else very good.   Argonaut Book Shop   Literature 2015 - 6180   2016 $45

Thurley, Geoffrey *The Dickens Myth: Its Genesis & Structure.* London: Routledge & Kegan Paul, 1976. First edition, half title, original green cloth, spine lettered in white & yellow, very good in dust jacket.   Jarndyce Antiquarian Booksellers   CCXVIII - 1463   2016   £20

Thurley, Norgrove *Death for Dollars.* Stanley Paul, 1951. Very good in slightly aged, chipped, frayed dust jacket. I. D. Edrich Crime - 2016 £30

Thurman, Wallace *The Interne.* New York: Macaulay, 1932. First edition, bit of scuffing at bottom of boards, else near fine in bright, very good dust jacket with some slight spine fading and some modest chipping to spine ends, additionally this copy signed by Thurman as well as co-author, A. L. Furman. Between the Covers Rare Books 207 - 89 2016 $10,000

Thwaite, Ann *The Brilliant Career of Winnie-the-Pooh.* London: Methuen, 1992. First edition, large 8vo., author's presentation on title, copiously illustrated with facsimiles, photos and reproductions, some in color, about as new in very slightly worn dust jacket. Second Life Books, Inc. 196 B - 759 2016 $45

Thwaite, Reuben Gold 1853-1913 *A Short Biography of John Leeth with an Account of His Life Among the Indians.* Cleveland: Burrows Bros. Co., 1904. Number 140 of 267 copies, reprinted from the original edition, maroon cloth, gilt, slight offsetting to endpapers, fine. Argonaut Book Shop Native American 2015 - 5955 2016 $100

Tibbles, Percy Thomas *The Magician's Hanndbook.* London: Marshall & Brookes and Dawbarn & Ward, 1901. First edition, 8vo., original green cloth with illustration, signed presentation from author to Robert Elsley, slight soiling and slight wear to covers, appears to lack front endpaper, slight to prelims, otherwise near very good. Any Amount of Books 2015 - A49177 2016 £170

Tibbs, Delbert L. *Poems Prayers & Logics.* Chicago: ENNAQ, 1984. First edition, softcover, tight near fine in wrappers, uncommon. Jeff Hirsch Books E-List 80 - 29 2016 $50

Tibullus, Albius *The Elegies of Delia of....* Cleveland: Bits Press, 1985. One of 333 copies, large 8vo. not numbered, signed on colophon by translator, with presentation by David Slavitt for Sonja & Bill (Smith). Second Life Books, Inc. 197 - 320 2016 $65

Tibullus, Albius *A Poetical Translation of Elegies of Tibullus.* London: printed for A. Millar, 1759. 2 volumes in one, some foxing to endpapers and first and final pages, otherwise clean copy, late 19th century dark brown cloth, gilt lettered spine, inscribed ex-libris Lud. Du Rieu 1784, ownership inscription of Geoffrey Tillotson. Jarndyce Antiquarian Booksellers CCXVI - 567 2016 £75

Tibullus, Albius *Quae Exstant.* Amsterdam: Ex Officina Weisteniana, 1708. 4to., engraved titlepage, 9 further plates, titlepages in red and black with engraved device, occasional illustrations within text, little staining to edges of margins near front, occasional very light spotting, paper flaw to edge of page 133 not affecting text, contemporary brown speckled calf, recent calf reback with retained red morocco gilt spine label, edges sprinkled red, inner hinges reinforced, few scuffs and marks, corners fraying, still very good, small label with name David Walley and small bookplate with elaborate lettler C and crown motif to front pastedown, based on Scaliger's text with notes and some changes by Van Broekhuyzen. Unsworths Antiquarian Booksellers Ltd. E01 - Early Printing - 27 2016 £300

Ticehrust, Claud B. *The Birds of Mesopotamia.* Bombay: Reprinted from the Journal of the Bombay Natural History Society, 1920-1922. Octavo, photos, 4 parts i single volume binder's cloth, each part inscribed 'author's compliments', few spots throughout, bookplate of Stephen Marchant. Andrew Isles Natural History Books 55 - 12139 2016 $300

Tichenor, G. C. *Letter from the Secretary of the Treasury Transmitting a Further Report Upon the Subject of War Claims of the State of California, Called for by Senate Resolution of Dec. 19 1889.* GPO, 1889. First edition, cloth binder, 190 pages, tables. Buckingham Books 2015 - 27795 2016 $450

Tickell, Richard *Anticipation, Containing the Substance of His M------y's Most Gracious Speech to both H----s of P-l----t on the Opening of the Approaching Session together with a Full and Authentic Account of the Debate...* London: printed for T. Becket...., 1778. First edition, 8vo., some foxing mainly to first two leaves, final leaf badly imposed, obscuring first letters of each line on verso, disbound. Jarndyce Antiquarian Booksellers CCXVI - 568 2016 £35

Tickell, Richard *The Wreath of Fashion or the art of Sentimental Poetry.* London: printed for T. Becket, 1778. Fourth edition, 4to., disbound. Jarndyce Antiquarian Booksellers CCXVI - 569 2016 £60

Ticknor, Caroline *Glimpses of Authors.* Boston: Houghton Mifflin Co., 1922. First edition, 2nd printing, illustrations by Theodore Brown Hapgood, near fine, publisher's decorative maroon cloth designed and signed by Theodore Hapgood, with full gilt floral decorations and rulings to the front board and spine, top edge gilt, near fine, hint of rubbing to extremities, touch of faint toning to spine, otherwise fresh binding, tiny chip to fore edge of list of illustrations, very discreet tape repair to short closed tear to contents page, otherwise extremely fresh interior, overall very attractive copy in beautiful binding. B & B Rare Books, Ltd. 2016 - C51001 2016 $50

Tidsskrift for Kunstindustri. Kjobenhavn: G. E. C. Gad, 1885-1899. 15 volumes bound in 5, 4to., contemporary half parchment, red leather spine labels, all edges stained red, profusely illustrated, parchment spine of fifth volume damaged.   Oak Knoll Books   310 - 188   2016 $1250

Tiedeman, Friedrich   *The Anatomy of the Foetal Brain...* Edinburgh: printed for John Carfrae & Sons and Longman, et al, London, 1826. First edition in English, 8vo., 14 plates, minimal spotting, little more pronounced on plates, especially the first, uncut and partly unopened in original boards, sometime rebacked in cloth, green paper covering of lower cover missing, later presentation inscription, good copy.   Blackwell's Rare Books   B186 - 152   2016   £800

Tijera, Jose De La   *Copia de Carta en que un Amig refiere a otro con Exactind el Hecho...*   Barcelona: Sastres et al, 1801. First edition, folding engraved plate, plate refolded with repair to 2 original folds visible on recto and small area lost to rump of bull inflicting the injury to Hillo's knee, small repairs to last 4 pages with minimal loss to printed border and loss of 2 letters on 1 page, 8vo., modern Spanish half calf, bookplate of S. A. Thompson Yates, good.   Blackwell's Rare Books   B184 - 18   2016   £850

Tillotson, Kathleen   *Novels of the Eighteen-Forties.* Oxford: Clarendon Press, 1956. Reprint, original dark blue cloth, very good in repaired dust jacket.   Jarndyce Antiquarian Booksellers   CCXVIII - 1464   2016   £20

Tim Grin's Jests or the New London Joker...   London: printed for W. Lane, 1788. Third edition, 72 pages, engraved frontispiece, 12mo., expert repair to clean tear without loss B9, disbound.   Jarndyce Antiquarian Booksellers   CCXVI - 322   2016   £350

Timbs, John   *Lady Bountiful's Legacy to her Family and Friends.*   London: Griffith & Farran, 1868. (1867). first and only edition, slight tear to lower corner of title, original green cloth by W. Bone & Son, bevelled boards, attractively blocked in lack and gilt, all edges gilt, bookseller's ticket of B. & J. Meehan, Bath, very good.   Jarndyce Antiquarian Books   CCXV - 439   2016   £125

Timbs, John   *School-Days of Eminent Men.*   London: Kent & Co., 1858. Frontispiece and plates, slight spotting, original purple cloth, spine faded and little rubbed, contemporary signature of Mary Gorset.   Jarndyce Antiquarian Books   CCXV - 70   2016   £20

Timlin, William   *The Ship that Sailed to Mars.*   London: Harrap, n.d., 1923. Large 4to, gilt decorated vellum backed boards, spine darakened along rear joint, some tip and edge wear, clean and very good+, 48 mounted color plates by author that are really magnificent.   Aleph-bet Books, Inc.   111 - 451   2016 $2500

Timothy Trim's Clock Book.   Detroit: Curtis, 1909. Pictorial boards, slight edge rubbing, else near fine, grandfather clock with roman numerals and moveable hands, each page with full color illustration.   Aleph-bet Books, Inc.   112 - 348   2016 $225

Tinkle, Lon   *An American original: the Life of J. Frank Dobie.*   Boston: Little Brown and Co., 1978. First edition, 13 black and white photos, gilt and blindstamped dark brown cloth, very fine with pictorial dust jacket.   Argonaut Book Shop   Biography 2015 - 7280   2016 $45

Tinling, James Forbes Bisset   *Fifteen Hundred Facts and Similes for Sermons and Addresses.*   London: Hodder & Stoughton, 1889. First edition, half title, original olive green cloth, slightly dulled.   Jarndyce Antiquarian Books   CCXV - 440   2016   £30

Tinson, A. R.   *Orders & Medals of the Sultante of Oman.* London: spink, 1995. 4to., original green cloth, decorated and lettered gilt, illustrated dust jackets, illustrations in color, as new, very rare.   Sotheran's   Travel and Exploration - 384   2016   £298

Tip and Top and Tap Look at Ships.   London: Bancroft, 1964. Large square 4to., stiff pictorial ard covers, near fine, 6 double page pop-ups by Kubasta, illustrations in color. Aleph-bet Books, Inc.   111 - 355   2016 $475

Tissot, Samuel Auguste Andre David   *Avis au Peuple sur la Sante.*   Lausanne: Francois Grasset, 1766. Third enlarged edition, 12mo., 2 volumes, later paper boards, very good set.   Edwin V. Glaser Rare Books   2015 - 10109   2016 $150

Tissot, Samuel Auguste Andre David   *Traite des nerfs et de Leurs Maladies.*   Lausanne: Avec Privilege de LL. EE., 1784. early edition, 4 volumes, handsome set, bound in full mottled contemporary calf, gilt tooled spine with raised bands and panelling, all edges gilt, light text browning, otherwise internally very clean and crisp.   James Tait Goodrich   X-78 - 524   2016 $1750

Titelmann, Franz   *De Consideratione Dialectica Libri Sex.* Paris: Jean Louis de Tielt, 1544. Woodcut printer's device on title, crible and woodcut initials, 8o., contemporary deerskin, very rubbed, spine defective, texblock split after first gathering, but withal good copy, preserved in cloth folding box, occasional marginal notes and 3 pages of notes at end. Blackwell's Rare Books   B184 - 85   2016   £600

To My Younger Brother on His Seventeenth Birthday. Chiswick Press, 1916. Uncut, original blue grey printed paper wrappers, sewn as issued, very good.   Jarndyce Antiquarian Books   CCXV - 118   2016   £150

Tobin, Agnes *Letters - Translations - Poems with Some Account of Her Life. (with) Phaedra.* San Francisco: Grabhorn Press for John Howell, 1958. Both copies issued separately and limited to 400 copies, 2 volumes, quarto, frontispiece in color with photographic reproductions in text in first volume, decorations in red in second volume, handset Janson type used in both volumes, blue boards, tan linen spine, titles in black on white spine labels, very fine copies.   Argonaut Book Shop   Literature 2015 - 5865   2016 $125

Tocqueville, Alexis Charles Henri Maurice Clerel De 1805-1859 *De la Democratie en Amerique.* Bruxelles: Louis Hauman et Compe, 1835. First Brussels edition, 2 volumes, 12mo., complete with half titles present, folding, hand colored engraved map laid in, supplied from first edition, rare original printed wrappers, pages uncut, wrappers bit rubbed and chipped, spines split with repairs still holding firm, some occasional light toning, overall very good set, housed in custom full morocco.   Heritage Book Shop Holiday 2015 - 105   2016 $2500

Tocqueville, Alexis Charles Henri Maurice Clerel De 1805-1859 *Democracy in America.* London: Saunders and Otley, 1838. Third edition, half title in volume II, 2 volumes, illustrations, one folding map, 8vo., original brown cloth boards decorated in blind, rebacked to style, very good or better set, boards rubbed rebacked to style, renewed endpapers, some minor restoration to corners, light marginal stain to top edge of last leaves of volume I, contents sharp, map fine.   Kaaterskill Books   21 - 102   2016 $1000

Todd, Edwin M. *The Neuroanatomy of Leonardo da Vinci.* Park Ridge: AANS, 1991. sketches, 4to., cloth, drawing of skull to front board.   James Tait Goodrich   X-78 - 372   2016 $125

Todd, Glenn *Shaped Poetry, a Suite of 30 Typographic Prints Chronicling this Literary Form from 300 BC to the Present.* San Francisco: Arion Press, 1981. First edition, one of 300 copies, folio, suite of 30 lloose typographic prints, each on different handmade paper in black paper wrapper with title letterpress printed on front, with companion volume of two sewn signatures in paper wrapper with letterpress printed title, both volumes in black cloth covered drop-spine case with black styrofoam walls, plus seprate plexiglass display frame.   Kaaterskill Books   21 - 19   2016 $2000

Todd, John *The Daughter at School.* London: T. Nelson & Sons, 1860. Half title, frontispiece, original lilac wavy grained cloth, gilt spine, very good.   Jarndyce Antiquarian Books   CCXV - 984   2016   £40

Todd, Marilyn *Virgin Territory.* London: Macmillan, 1996. First edition, very fine in dust jacket.   Mordida Books 2015 - 002187   2016 $55

Todd, Walter E. *Gathered Treasures.* Washington: Murray Bros. Printing Co., 1912. First edition, 24mo., green cloth gilt, frontispiece, author's name and address stamp on front pastedown, some spotting on turn-ins, else nice, near fine copy of this self published volume.   Between the Covers Rare Books   202 - 109   2016 $750

Toddles Boys. Springfield: McLoughlin, 1927. 4 McLoughlin shape books, pictorial boards, fine in pictorial box with some soil and flap wear, scarce, especially in box. Aleph-bet Books, Inc.   112 - 461   2016 $500

Toffler, Alvin *Future Shock.* New York: Random House, 1970. 2 volumes, a review copy of the first edition and an uncorrected proof copy, first edition has some mild edge foxing and is near fine in very near fine dust jacket with shallow crease to rear panel, folded in fourths and laid in are 3 different 2 legal size pages press releases, the uncorrected proof is tall, fragile padbound proof, text block seems perfectly fine but covers and spine have some staining and insect dagage and covers are likely to detach in time, uncommon advance state.   Ken Lopez Bookseller   166 - 128   2016 $1500

Toland, John *Gods of War.* Franklin Center: Franklin Library, 1985. Limited first edition, signed by author, red leather, lettered and decoratively stamped in gilt, all edges gilt, gilt flaked from small spots on front cover, else fine. Argonaut Book Shop   Literature 2015 - 4030   2016 $45

Toland, John *Infamy: Pearl Harbor and Its Aftermath.* Garden City: Doubleday, 1982. First edition, maps on endpapers, author's signature, paper over boards with cloth spine, owner's name stamp on half title, nice in slightly chipped and soiled dust jacket, very good+.   Second Life Books, Inc.   196 B - 765   2016 $65

The Toliet. London: Frederick Warne and Co., circa, 1875? 32mo., original brown decorated cloth, colour onlay to front board, all edges gilt, very good.   Jarndyce Antiquarian Books   CCXV - 468   2016   £75

Tolkien, John Ronald Reuel 1892-1973 *The Hobbit or Three and Back Again.* London: George Allen & Unwin for the Folio Society, 1976. First edition thus, octavo, plates and endpaper maps, quarter brown leather with cloth sides decorated with gilt labyrinth design but with no mention of the Folio society on titlepage or anywhere else in book, fine in fine slipcase covered in 'leather' paper as called for Hammond and Anderson.   Peter Ellis   112 - 404   2016 £450

Tolkien, John Ronald Reuel 1892-1973 *The Lord of the Rings. The Fellowship of the Ring. The Two Towers. the Return of the King.* London: George Allen & Unwin Ltd., 1966. First British and first hardcover printing of second edition, octavo, 3 volumes, cloth, fine set in fine dust jackets with some minor rubbing at spine ends and price clipped from flap of Fellowship, overall bright, lovely set, quite scarce.   John W. Knott, Jr./L.W. Currey, Inc.   Fall-Winter 2015 - 15987   2016 $1500

Tolkien, John Ronald Reuel 1892-1973 *Songs for the Philologists.* London: privately printed in the Department of English at University College, London, 1936. Wire stitched, without rusting, original blue printed wrappers, inscription on red ink on front wrapper, please return to K. Tillotson, very good.   Jarndyce Antiquarian Booksellers   CCXVII - 284   2016   £12,500

Tollerton, Linda *Wills and Will-Making in Anglo-Saxon England.* York: Medieval Press, 2011. First edition, 8vo., illustrations, laminated pictorial boards, as new.   Unsworths Antiquarian Booksellers Ltd.   E05 - 110   2016   £25

Tolman, Henry & Co. *The Musician's Guide or Henry Tolman & Co.'s Illustrated.* Boston: 1866. Narrow 4to, original printed and pictorial wrappers laid down on cloth.   M & S Rare Books, Inc.   99 - 193   2016 $450

Tolomei, Claudio *Due Orazioni in Lingua Toscana. (bound after) Oratione de la Pace.* Parma: S. Viotto, 1 Jan., 1547. Rome: A Blado, March 1534. Rare first edition, 2 works in one, 4to., volume i with historiated woodcut initials and alphabetic rebus 'quadrangolo' on last leaf, volume ii with titlepage impress of altar of Concordia Augusta taken from a Roman coin, Blado's fine device on final leaf, contemporary vellum backed in 18th century with marbled papper, title lettered along spine, little wear to spine, some burn marks on fore-edge towards end of first work, not affecting text. Maggs Bros. Ltd.   1474 - 76   2016   £3500

Tolstoi, Lev Nikolaevich 1828-1910 *Anna Karenina in 8 parts.* New York: Thomas Y. Crowell, 1886. 8vo., original printed wrappers, few minor tears and small corner lacking front wrappers, but good, tight copy.   M & S Rare Books, Inc.   99 - 306   2016 $750

Tolstoi, Lev Nikolaevich 1828-1910 *The Cossocks.* New York: Grosset & Dunlap, 1928. First photoplay edition, 8vo., original cloth with dust jacket, illustrations, very good. Sotheran's   Piccadilly Notes - Summer 2015 - 305   2016   £128

Tolstoi, Lev Nikolaevich 1828-1910 *The End of the Age.* Christchurch (Hants.): Free Age Press, 1905. First English edition?, 8vo., original green wrappers printed in red, tears in spine little crudely repaired, good.   Blackwell's Rare Books   B186 - 153   2016   £250

Tolstoi, Lev Nikolaevich 1828-1910 *The Complete Works of Count Tolstoy.* Boston: Dana Estes & Co., 1904-1905. Edition deluxe, no. 600 of an edition limited to 1000 copies, 24 volumes, half titles, frontispieces and vignette titles, plates, handsomely bound in later half maroon morocco, spine sgilt in compartments, dark green morocco labels, top edge gilt, other edges untrimmed, fine, attractive. Jarndyce Antiquarian Booksellers   CCXVII - 285   2016   £1200

Tolver Preston, Samuel *Physics of the Ether.* London: E. & F. N. Spon, 1875. First edition, few figures in the text, few spots and little dust staining to first 2 leaves, 8vo., original chocolate brown cloth, lettered gilt on upper cover and on spine, upper joint skilfully repaired, minor wear to corners, bookplate of Glasgow University Library stamped 'withdrawn' inside front cover, below this a barcode, and opposite the remains of a label, good.   Blackwell's Rare Books   B186 - 150   2016   £2000

Tomalin, Claire *The Invisible Woman: the Story of Nelly Ternan and Charles Dickens.* Viking, 1990. First edition, half title, illustrations, original grey cloth, 'Review copy' slip, very good in dust jacket.   Jarndyce Antiquarian Booksellers   CCXVIII - 1465   2016   £40

Tombleson, William *Tombleson's Views of the Rhine.* London: Tombleson, 1852. First edition, 8vo., folding map frontispiece, vignette on titlepage, 67 steel engravings, all edges gilt, contemporary half black morocco, purple pebble boards, joints rubbed, few plates affected by marginal foxing, otherwise very good.   J. & S. L. Bonham Antiquarian Booksellers   Europe 2016 - 4398   2016   £295

Tombleson, William *Tombleson's Views of the Rhine.* London: W. Tombleson & Co., 1852. 2 volumes, contemporary half olive green morocco over olive green moire cloth covered boards, all edges gilt, marbled endpapers, a total of 137 finely engraved plates, each paper guarded, 1 engraved folding map tipped-in to rear of each volume, offsetting to paper guards but overall bright, clean set, Samuel Harris engraved armorial bookplate.   Sotheran's   Piccadilly Notes - Summer 2015 - 306   2016   £495

Tomkis, Thomas *Lingua; or the Combat of the Tongue and the Five Senses for Superiority.* London: for Simon Miller, 1657. Small 8vo., sheet "B" lightly browned, small hole in blank part of title, early 20th century half brown morocco by Artelier Bindery, joints heavily rubbed, rear pastedown torn removing a label, from the library of James Stevens Cox (1910-1997), early inscription.   Maggs Bros. Ltd.   1447 - 414   2016   £300

Tomlinson, Charles *Summer in the Antarctic Regions, a Narrative of Voyages of Discovery Towards the South Pole.* London: Society for Promoting Christian Knowledge, 1848. First edition, small square 8vo., original maroon cloth, spine lettered in gilt, front cover with gilt stamped centrepiece, ornamented in blind, folding steel engraved map, wood engraved illustrations, map bit crinkled and partially laid down, few very light spots only here and there, very good. Sotheran's Travel and Exploration - 443 2016 £298

Tomlinson, Henry Major 1873-1958 *All Our Yesterdays.* New York: Harper & Bros., 1930. First edition, one of 350 copies numbered and signed by author, tan cloth backed blue boards, spine darkened, paper spine label worn, slipcase worn, some of the pages uncut, overall fine. Argonaut Book Shop Literature 2015 - 1621 2016 $150

Tomlinson, Henry Major 1873-1958 *Norman Douglas.* London: Chatto & Windus, 1931. First limited edition, #20 of 260 copies signed by author, 8vo., final two leaves trimmed very close, otherwise fine. Second Life Books, Inc. 196 B - 766 2016 $56

Tomlinson, Henry Major 1873-1958 *The Sea & the Jungle.* London: Duckworth, 1930. First edition, 90/515 copies printed on handmade paper and signed by author, wood engraved frontispiece, 6 wood engraved plates and several wood engraved head and tailpieces by Clare Leighton, 8vo., original apple green buckram, lightly faded backstrip gilt lettered, top edge gilt, others untrimmed, dust jacket little darkened, near fine. Blackwell's Rare Books B184 - 280 2016 £200

Tomlinson, Henry Major 1873-1958 *The Sea and the Jungle.* Barre: Imprint Society, 1971. No. 903 of 1950 copies, 8vo., wood engravings by Garrick Palmer, map, signed by Palmer, green cloth, stamped in gilt with black leather spine, spine slightly scuffed at ends, small hole in pages 165-166, nice in box covered with pictorial paper. Second Life Books, Inc. 197 - 321 2016 $45

Tomlinson, Henry Major 1873-1958 *Thomas Hardy.* New York: Crosby Gaige, 1929. One of 764 numbered copies, signed by author and artist, lithograph by Zhenya Gay, very nice, original orange cloth lettered gilt. Sotheran's Piccadilly Notes - Summer 2015 - 158 2016 £78

Toole, John Kennedy *A Confederacy of Dunces.* Baton Rouge: Louisiana State University, 1980. Very small first printing (reportedly of 2500 copies), one tiny fore edge spot, else fine and tight, boards tend to splay on most copies, very near fine, first issue dust jacket with only trace wear to corners and hint of rubbing near spine crown. Ken Lopez Bookseller 166 - 129 2016 $10,000

Toomer, Jean *Essentials.* Chicago: Private Edition, 1931. First edition, fine, lacking dust jacket, limited to 1000, this copy unnumbered and unsigned.   Between the Covers Rare Books 207 - 90 2016 $650

Toomer, Jean *Essentials. Definitions and Aphorisms.* Chicago: privately printed, 1931. First edition, no. 179 of 1000 copies, numbered and signed by Toomer, 12mo., very good+ with light soiling, spine label bit soiled. Beasley Books 2015 - 2016 $1500

Toose, Alfred *Madame Iago.* London: Thornton Butterworth, 1928. First edition, octavo, half tanned, very good in scarce dust jacket with lovely art deco designs by John Austen, which is slightly chipped and has few short tears.   Peter Ellis 112 - 405 2016 £85

Topolski, Felix *Topolski's Chronicle 1953. Volume I.* London: privately published, 1953. First edition, large folio, plain thick card folder, lettered black and grey with black line drawing on cover, complete with 12 broadsheet style folded pages (a ttoal of 13 sheets with index page), printed black with occasional color on beige, copiously illustrated throughout, folder very slight edgeworn and pages very slightly browned at edges, otherwise very good.   Any Amount of Books 2015 - A85938 2016 £150

Torres-Garcia, J. *La Tradicion del Hombre Abstracto.* Montevideo: Publicationes de la Associacion de Arte Constructivo, 1938. First edition, small 4to., facsimile of author's holograph with illustrations to text by author, some very faint foxing, original brown wrappers printed in black and faintly spotted, little creasing to yapp edges, textblock edges untrimmed, very good, scarce. Blackwell's Rare Books B186 - 287 2016 £900

Torres, Angel *La Historia del Beisbol Cubano 1878-1976.* Los Angeles: Angel Torres, 1976. First edition, large quarto, errata slip or supplement laid in, heavily illustrated from photos, illustrated wrappers little rubbed, very good or better, briefly inscribed by author, very uncommon.   Between the Covers Rare Books 208 - 144 2016 $200

Torriano, Giovanni *Della Lingua Toscana-Romana.* London: for J. Martin and J. Allestrye, 1657. First edition, large 8vo. small hole (printing flaw?) to K1 affecting one or two letters of text, light dampstaining to lower right corner of first few gatherings, recto of last leaf lightly soiled, contemporary reversed calf, heavily worn, joints cracked and exposing sewing, corners chipped, from the library of James Stevens Cox (1910-1997).   Maggs Bros. Ltd. 1447 - 415 2016 £1250

Toure *Soul City.* Boston: Little Brown, 2004. First edition, 8vo. author's signature on title, paper over boards, as new.   Second Life Books, Inc. 197 - 324 2016 $60

Toussaint-Samat, Jean *Ships Aflame!* Philadelphia: J. B. Lippincott, 1935. First American edition, octavo, fine in near fine dust jacket with couple of tiny nicks and tears, handsome copy, very scarce in dust jacket. Between the Covers Rare Books 204 - 81 2016 $400

Toussaint, Francois Vincent *Manners.* London: printed for J. Payne and J. Bouquet, 1749. 8vo., engraved title, slightly creased, otherwise internally crisp and clean, small tear to folding of leading f.e.p., contemporary full speckled calf, raised bands, compartments gilt, red morocco label, very slight wear to leading hinge at tail of spine, exceptional copy. Jarndyce Antiquarian Books CCXV - 441 2016 £450

Towers, Alton *Billy Bunce of the Wanderings of A White Rabbit.* Leeds & London: Alf Cooke, n.d., 1907. 4to., pictorial cloth, slight edge rubbing, else very good-fine, illustrations by Harry Rountree with 20 richly colored color plates and pictorial endpapers, black and whites throughout text by F. Stuart, very rare. Aleph-bet Books, Inc. 111 - 397 2016 $1200

Townsend, John *The Doom of Slavery in the Union....* Charleston: printed by Evans & Cogwell No. 5 Broad and 103 East Bay streets, 1860. First edition, 8vo., sewn as issued, sheets quite browned, ink blots on last couple of leaves affecting text, with small erosion resulting in loss of several letters on last page. M & S Rare Books, Inc. 99 - 292 2016 $275

Toye, Randall *The Agatha Christie Who's Who.* Heron Books, 1980. Fine with original ribbon marker, illustrations in text. I. D. Edrich Crime - 2016 £20

Traherne, Thomas *Christian Ethicks; or Divine Morality.* London: for Jonathan Edwin, 1675. First edition, 8vo., lightly foxed throughout due to poor paper quality, titlepage with some light wrinkles, contemporary calf, spine with four raised bands and red morocco lettered gilt, rebacked with extensive repairs to corners and headcaps, near contemporary signature of Ja(mes) King, 19th century bookplate of Sir John Dashwood King, from the library of James Stevens Cox (1910-1997). Maggs Bros. Ltd. 1447 - 416 2016 £650

Traherne, Thomas *Joys, Passages from the Works.* Llandogo: Old Stile Press, 2003. 92/200 copies from an edition of 226, signed by artist, 9 wood engravings printed in dark blue, 5 woodcuts printed in burnt sienna, linocut borders in sage, text printed in brown, small 4to., original quarter terra cotta cloth with patterned boards, backstrip lettered in silver, beige cloth slipcase with large inset illustration in sage, prospectus laid in at front, fine. Blackwell's Rare Books B186 - 322 2016 £120

Train, Arthur *His children's Children.* New York: Scribner's, 1923. First edition, 8vo., hinges tender, cover somewhat worn, very good, inscribed by author. Second Life Books, Inc. 196 B - 767 2016 $45

Transformation. London: Victor Gollancz, 1943. First edition, first issue, frontispiece and 4 further plates, toning to paper throughout and occasional light foxing, crown 8vo., original wrappers, backstrip little darkened and faint foxing to rear panel, good. Blackwell's Rare Books B184 - 217 2016 £40

Transition No. 21, No, 22, No. 25 and No. 26. The Hague: Servire Press, 1932-1933. 1936. 1937. First editions, 4 separately issued volumes, original pictorial paper wrappers, numerous black and white photos, issue 22 with original (somewhat chipped, but intact), yellow paper band reading 'Revolutionary Romanticism' issue no. 25 with ink inscription "Wallace Liggett April 18 1946" on rear cover, issue no. 26 with ink stamp of Messageries Dawson, Paris on rear cover, few tiny chips to edge of boards, little light soiling, no. 26 with short scratch and pencilled number on front cover, no. 25 with occasional small, faint stains to fore edge, few (inevitable) corner creases, otherwise in fine condition, quite clean, fresh and bright internally in very well preserved paper wrappers. Phillip J. Pirages 67 - 214 2016 $1250

Trant, Carolyn *Art for Life: the Story of Peggy Angus.* Oldham: Incline Press, 2005. Limited to 350 copies, folio, cloth, patterned paper covered boards, portfolio, slipcase, photos, reproductions and prints. Oak Knoll Books 27 - 31 2016 $650

Traubel, Horace *Chants Communal.* New York: Boni, 1914. Second edition, 8vo., author's presentation to J. B. Kelley, paper over boards with cloth spine, partially unopened, from the library of Florence Kelley, spine little scuffed at ends, else very good, tight copy. Second Life Books, Inc. 196 B - 768 2016 $45

Traven, B. *The Rebellion of the Hanged.* London: Knopf, 1952. First edition, fine in near fine dust jacket, price clipped, minor rubbing and fading to spine, exceptionally bright. Bella Luna Books 2016 - j2198 2016 $75

Travers, P. L. *Mary Poppins.* New York: Reynal & Hitchcock, 1934. First American edition, same year as the UK edition, 8vo., illustrations by Mary Shepard, very fine in beautiful dust jacket, laid in is 3 line inscription by author, excellent copy. Aleph-bet Books, Inc. 111 - 452 2016 $3000

Travers, P. L. *Mary Poppins Comes Back.* New York: Reynal & Hitchcock, 1935. First American edition, 8vo., pictorial cloth, fine in dust jacket with 2 edge chips and few small closed tears, overall clean, attractive, very good, illustrations by Mary Shepard. Aleph-bet Books, Inc. 112 - 479 2016 $300

Travers, P. L. *Moscow Excursion.* New York: Reynal and Hitchcock, 1934. First American edition, slight soiling on boards, else fine in very slightly spine toned, about fine, dust jacket, publisher's complimentary copy with slip laid in, stating date of publication as Aug. 8 1934.   Between the Covers Rare Books   204 - 114   2016 $950

Travers, P. L. *Walt Disney's Mary Poppins: a Golden Color and Re-Color Book.*   N.P.:: Walt Disney Productions, 1964. Tall narrow 4to., color pictorial boards, slight cover soil, else fine and unused, scarce in unused condition, 13 panel panorama of black line drawings.   Aleph-bet Books, Inc.   112 - 478   2016 $200

Travers, Rosalind   *Letters from Finland, August 1908- March 1909.*   London: Kegan Paul, 1911. First edition, 8vo., original olive green cloth lettered and ornamented gilt, highly illustrated with plates and one folding map, binding little worn, endpapers with spotting due to offsetting from binder's glue, otherwise good.   Sotheran's   Travel and Exploration - 287   2016   £58

Tree, Viola   *Can I Help You?*   London: Leonard & Virginia Woolf at the Hogarth Press, 1937. First edition, half title, frontispiece and plates, original blue cloth, spine slightly dulled.   Jarndyce Antiquarian Books   CCXV - 442   2016   £20

Trelawny, Edward John   *Adventures of a Younger Son.* London: Oxford University Press, 1974. first edition thus, octavo, fine in very near fine, price clipped dust jacket.   Peter Ellis   112 - 406   2016   £35

Trench, Francis   *Good and Bad Reading in Church, School & Home.*   London: John W. Parker, 1855. First edition, original purple cloth wrappers, tissue laid down on leading f.e.p. over old signature.   Jarndyce Antiquarian Books   CCXV - 986   2016   £20

Trench, Richard Chenevis   *On the Study of Words.* London: Macmillan and Co., 1864. Bound in slightly later half dark blue calf by Rathespeck Trust, their booklabel on leading pastedown, very good.   Jarndyce Antiquarian Books   CCXV - 987   2016   £25

Trench, William Steuart   *Realities of Irish Life.*   London: Longmans, Green and Co., 1869. Fourth edition, half title, frontispiece and plates, one in color, folding map of Ireland, slightly spotted, fine binding by Henry Young and Sons, Liverpool, half dark green crushed morocco, green cloth boards, spine gilt, very good.   Jarndyce Antiquarian Booksellers   CCXVII - 286   2016   £150

Tresselt, Alvin   *White Snow Bright Snow.*   New York: Lothrop Lee Shepard, 1947. First edition, first printing, 4to., pictorial boards, fine in nice dust jacket, few small closed tears, not price clipped, award seal, wonderful color illustrations on every page by Roger Duvoisin-.   Aleph-bet Books, Inc.   111 - 138   2016 $950

Trevanian   *The Eiger Sanction.*   New York: Crown Publishers, 1972. First edition, fine in fine dust jacket with quarter inch tear and wrinkles at top of spine.   Ken Hebenstreit, Bookseller   2016 - 2016 $225

Trevanian   *Shibumi.*   New York: Crown Publishers Inc, 1979. First edition, fine, owner bookplate, fine white dust jacket is slightly toned and has half inch closed tear at bottom of spine.   Ken Hebenstreit, Bookseller   2016 - 2016 $125

Trevelyan, Humphry   *Wood Engravings by Humphry Trevelyan.*   Cambridge: printed by Will Carter, 1964. First edition, 40 engravings with some full page, printed on Basingwerk Parchment paper in black, dark blue sepia and dark green, royal 8vo., original blue boards, backstrip lettered in gilt and tifle faded, Japanese Tairel endpapers, very good,.   Blackwell's Rare Books   B186 - 330   2016   £60

Trevor, William   1928-2016   *Death in Summer.*   Viking, 1998. First edition, fine in dust jacket.   Bertram Rota Ltd. Christmas List 2015 - 58   2016   £40

Trevor, William   1928-2016   *The Love Department.* 1966. First edition, very good only in slightly frayed dust jacket, label partly removed from front pastedown. Bertram Rota Ltd.   February List 2016 - 58   2016   £65

Trevor, William   1928-2016   *Lovers of their Time and Other Stories.*   London: Bodley Head, 1978. First edition, octavo, spine very slightly bumped at head and tail, otherwise fine in fine dust jacket.   Peter Ellis   112 - 407   2016   £85

A Tribute to Jacqueline Kennedy Onassis.   New York: Doubleday, 1995. Book has hint of foxing on half title, but still very near fine, without dust jacket as issued, printed card stating tht "Doubleday would like you to have this special tribute ...", card foxed.   Ken Lopez Bookseller   166 - 62   2016 $450

Tribute to Walter De La Mare on His Seventy-Fifth Birthday. London: Faber & Faber, 1948. First edition, colored lithographic frontispiece, portraits, reproduction of cartoon by Max Beerbohm, 8vo., original blue buckram with De La Mare's monogram in blind to upper board, backstrip lettered gilt partly on pink ground with slight lean to spine, top edge gilt, few faint spots at head of rear pastedown, related newspaper clippings laid in, dust jacket with gentle fading to backstrip panel, some chipping to extremities with flap-folds little rubbed and faded, good, inscribed by author to his secretary Marie Lamigeon.   Blackwell's Rare Books   B186 - 198   2016   £200

Trigen, Cornelli   *Observationum Medico Chirurgicarum Fasciculus.*   Lugduni Batavorum: Apud Petrum Vander Eye..., 1743. Title in black and red, 13 engraved plates, text bit dusty, some staining to parts, tall copy with edges uncut, partially unopened copy, 4to., skillfully rebound in new quarter calf and marbled boards, small library stamps on title and on plates, very uncommon.   James Tait Goodrich   X-78 - 525   2016 $950

Trimmer, Sarah   *Fabulous Histories Designed for the Instruction of Children Respecting their Treatment of Animals.*   London: printed for T. Longman, 1786. Second edition, 12mo., 19th century tree calf, gilt roll tool borders gilt decorated spine, red morocco label, slight rubbing to spine and corners.   Jarndyce Antiquarian Booksellers   CCXVI - 573   2016   £350

Trimmer, Sarah   *A Series of Prints of Scripture History....*   printed and sold by John Marshall, circa, 1790. 24mo., 32 engraved plates, original sheep, gilt ruled borders on sides, spine defective, corners worn, armorial bookplate of Thomas Blayds inside front cover.   Blackwell's Rare Books   B186 - 86   2016   £300

Trimmer, Sarah   *Some Account of the Life and Writings of Mrs. Trimmer...*   London: printed for F. C. and J. Rivington, 1816. Second edition, 2 volumes, half titles, final ad leaf, volume II, contemporary full calf, double ruled gilt borders, raised bands, gilt compartments, neat repairs to hinges, inscription Mary Thornhill the gift of Mrs. Bathurst 1816.   Jarndyce Antiquarian Books CCXV - 968   2016   £225

Triples Changements Merveilleux.   Paris: Guerin - Muller (London: Dean), n.d. circa, 1859. 4to., cloth backed pictorial boards, light soil and rubbing, very good+, 8 moveable pages with hand colored illustrations, each page has two flaps allowing child to make 3 different pictures, extremely rare.   Aleph-bet Books, Inc.   111 - 307   2016 $3750

Trollope, Anthony   1815-1882   *The American Senator.*   London: Chapman and Hall, 1877. First edition in book form, 184 x 127mm., half titles, 3 volumes, fine contemporary dark olive morocco bound for the Earl of Carysfort (with his arms in gilt on center at front covers and with his monogram at foot of spines), backstrips titled in gilt, raised bands flanked by multiple gilt rules, marbled endpapers, all edges gilt, shelf label and engraved Carysfort bookplate, front joint of 2 volumes with hint of wear, one leaf with two tiny tears at top, fine, attractive set, text immaculate and in a lustrous elegant binding.   Phillip J. Pirages   67 - 328   2016 $2250

Trollope, Anthony   1815-1882   *Barchester Towers.*   New York: Limited Editions Club, 1958. First edition thus, 8vo., hand colored title vignette and text illustrations, original quarter leather, gilt back, slipcase, limited to 1500 numbered copies signed by artist, Fritz Kredel, printed on Peter Beilenson in Mount Vernon NY, illustrations hand colored at the studio of Richard Ellis.   Second Life Books, Inc.   196 B - 770   2016 $100

Trollope, Anthony   1815-1882   *British Sports and Pastimes.*   London: Virtue and Co., 1868. First edition, octavo, publisher's pebble grained green cloth with blind-stamped rule on boards and gilt titles and decorations, primrose yellow endpapers with Virtue & Co.'s paper label on rear pastedown, cloth trifle rubbed with few small nicks and stains, inner front hinge, little tender and first gathering little sprung, but a bright very good or better copy, inscribed by Trollope for M. C. Maxwell.   Between the Covers Rare Books   208 - 145   2016 $4500

Trollope, Anthony   1815-1882   *A Letter from Anthony Trollope Describing a Visit to California in 1875.*   San Francisco: Colt Press, 1946. Limited to 500 copies, four wood engravings by Mallette Dean, green cloth backed decorated boards, top edge of covers slightly faded, else fine.   Argonaut Book Shop   Literature 2015 - 2289   2016 $75

Trollope, Anthony   1815-1882   *Phineas Redux. A Novel.*   New York: Harper and Bros., 1874. First American edition, three quarter, three quarter leather binding lettered in gilt to spine, one inch crack along lower rear hinge, corners and head of spine worn, light wear and rubbing to extremities, very good.   Argonaut Book Shop   Literature 2015 - 6196   2016 $50

Trollope, Anthony   1815-1882   *The Small House at Allington.*   New York: Harper & Bros., 1864. First American edition, tall 8vo., little worn and shabby publisher's cloth, very good.   Second Life Books, Inc.   197 - 325   2016 $450

Trollope, Anthony   1815-1882   *Travelling Sketches.* London: Chapman and Hall, 1866. First edition, 8vo., sand-grained red cloth, bevelled boards lettered gilt, slightly marked spine slightly faded, name and address stamed at top of top edge gilt, very good.   Second Life Books, Inc.   197 - 327   2016 $325

Trollope, Anthony   1815-1882   *The Way We Live Now.* New York: Harper & Bros., 1875. First American edition, tall 8vo., little worn and shabby publisher's cloth, very good. Second Life Books, Inc.   197 - 326   2016 $450

Troost, Lewis   *Proceedings of the Public Meeting and Board of Directors of the Mobile and Ohio Rail Road....* Mobile: Office of the Herald & Tribune, 1847. First edition, 8vo., removed, title heavily foxed.   M & S Rare Books, Inc.   99 - 2   2016 $125

Trotter, Lionel J.   *The Life of John Nicholson, Solider and Administrator based on private and hitherto....*   London: John Murray, 1900. First edition, octavo, 2 plates and 3 folding maps, period fine binding by Bumpus, full brown morocco with raised bands, gilt rules and devices to spine, inner dentelles elaborately gilt, top edge gilt, armorial bookplate of Kennet of Dene, contemporary (1900) ownership inscription of a member of the family (Arthur W. Young), near fine, attractive binding.   Peter Ellis   112 - 181   2016   £125

The Troubles of a Good Husband.   Northampton: printed by F. Cordeux, 1818. 12mo., errata leaf page 21 is a cancel, some water staining to lower margins, uncut in original drab boards, brown paper spine, extremities rubbed, loss of paper to spine, contemporary signature of Mary Mayle, good, sound copy.   Jarndyce Antiquarian Books   CCXV - 443   2016   £65

Troubridge, Laura   *The Book of Etiquette.*   London: Associated Bookbuyers' Co., 1926. 2 volumes, half titles, pencil scribbles on endpapers volume II, original blue cloth in slightly torn dust jacket.   Jarndyce Antiquarian Books   CCXV - 444   2016   £45

Troubridge, Laura   *The Book of Etiquette.*   London: World's Work, 1952. Half title, original dark blue cloth.   Jarndyce Antiquarian Books   CCXV - 445   2016   £20

Troy, Hugh   *The Chippendale Dam.*   New York: Oxford University Press, 1941. First edition, cloth, 8vo., fine in dust jacket with narrow chip off rear panel, illustrations by author, this copy has fine inscribed watercolor by author, nice.   Aleph-bet Books, Inc.   111 - 455   2016 $375

A True and Perfect Narrative of the Great and Dreadful Damages Susteyned in Several parts of England... London: for P. Brooksby, 1674. First edition, rare, small 4to., titlepage verso of final leaf lightly soiled, titlepage marginally shorter at foot than other leaves, disbound, cloth folder bowing, tie missing, from the library of James Stevens Cox (1910-1997).   Maggs Bros. Ltd.   1447 - 417   2016   £1800

True, Lye C.   *How and What to Play for Moving Pictures - a Manual and Guide for Pianos.*   San Francisco: Music Supply Co., 1914. First edition, 12mo., 24 pages, stapled printed green wrappers, title library perforation on front wrapper, short tear on rear wrapper else fine.   Between the Covers Rare Books   204 - 45   2016 $250

Truelove, Edward   *In the High Court of Justice, Queen's Bench Division, February 1, 1878. The Queen v. Edward Truelove for publishing the Hon. Robert Dale Owen's Moral Physiology.*   London: Edward Truelove, 1878. First edition, 8vo., half title and final leaf of ads, original brown cloth gilt, long biographical note in pencil verso of half title, very good. John Drury Rare Books   2015 - 19288   2016 $350

Truhlar, Antonin   *Rukovet Humanistickeho Basnictvi Cechach a Na Morave.*   Prague: Ceskoslovenske Akademie Ved, 1966. 8vo., cloth, black and white plates in all volumes, boards and spines lightly soiled.   Oak Knoll Books   310 - 269   2016 $450

Truman, Harry S.   *Mr. Citizen.*   New York: Bernard Geis Associates, 1960. Deluxe author's edition, signed, inscribed and dated in year of publication by Truman to John R. Steelman, near fine quarter morocco leather patterned board binding, gilt lettering spine, mild soil covers, original blue grey slipcase with tipped on label as issued, mild sun, edge wear slipcase, 8vo.   By the Book, L. C.   45 - 6   2016 $2750

Trumbo, Dalton   *Additional Dialogue: Letters of Dalton Trumbo 1942-1962.*   New York: M. Evans, 1970. First edition, boldly signed by author, touch of production bleed from topstain to top page edges on several leaves, else near fine in like dust jacket with none of the fading commonly found on jacket spine, attractive copy.   Royal Books   52 - 49   2016 $950

Trusler, John   *Chronology or the Historian's Vade Mecum.* London: printed for the author and sold by S. Bladon in Paternoster row, F. Ewbery, Ludgate Street (and others), 1773. Sixth edition, frontispiece, 12mo., some dustiness, faint old waterstaining to top outer corner visible on some leaves, little close cropped touching running head in places, final leaf has on seom leaves a little close cropped touching running head in places, final leaf has page number torn away in top corner, contemporary quarter calf, marbled boards, vellum tips, joints cracked, spine worn & chipped. Jarndyce Antiquarian Booksellers   CCXVI - 573   2016   £65

Trusler, John *Principles of Politeness....* London: printed for the author and J. Bell, 1782. Twelfth edition, 3 pages ads, slightly spotted with occasional marginal tears, uncut in original marbled boards, expertly rebacked in tan calf, neat inscription.   Jarndyce Antiquarian Books   CCXV - 446   2016   £260

Trusler, John *Trusler's Domestic Management....* London: John Souter, circa, 1820. New edition, 4 page catalog, contemporary half calf, marbled boards, neatly rebacked, stiff brown card.   Jarndyce Antiquarian Books   CCXV - 447   2016   £125

The Truth about the FEPC Fight. Detroit: National Negro Labor Council, 1952. 8 1/2 x 14 inches, 15 leaves mimeographed on recto only, stapled self wrappers, tear on blank portion of final leaf, old horizontal fold, staple possbily a replacement, else near fine.   Between the Covers Rare Books   202 - 55   2016 $350

Truth, Sojourner *Narrative of SojournerTruth.* Boston: the author, 1874. Third edition, 8vo., joints and spine ends bit rubbed, rear free endpaper adhering to pastedown and showing a tear, otherwise very nice.   Beasley Books   2015 - 2016 $1000

Truths Discovery of a Black Cloud in the north.... n.p., 1646. 4to., bound with numerous blanks in 20th century quarter calf.   Jarndyce Antiquarian Booksellers   CCXVII - 204   2016   £450

Tryon, Thomas *The Way to Health, Long Life and Happiness; or a Discourse of Temperance...* London: printed and are to be sold by most booksellers, 1697. Third edition, titlepage browned and chipped along edges, light marginal staining throughout, light foxing and spotting, 8mm circular hole through centre of P1, mid 20th century green morocco, from the library of James Stevens Cox (1910-1997), 18th century signature of Henry Bradbury, 18th century pencil notes of John Soper.   Maggs Bros. Ltd.   1447 - 418   2016   £200

Tschantre, Gracia *Tin Tan Tales.* London & New York: Nister & Dutton, n.d. circa., 1900. 4to., cloth backed pictorial boards, edges rubbed and some margin soil, else very good+, printed on thick board pages, individualy hinged into book.   Aleph-bet Books, Inc.   112 - 27   2016 $500

Tschantre, Gracia *Tin Tans at Play.* London & New York: Nister & Dutton, n.d. circa, 1910. 4to., cloth backed pictorial boards, minimal shelfwear, near fine, printed rectos only, wonderful chromolithographs on every page, very scarce.   Aleph-bet Books, Inc.   112 - 25   2016 $600

Tsukiyama, Gail *Women of the Silk.* New York: St. Martin's Press, 1991. Presentation inscription signed and dated by author, gray cloth in pictorial dust jacket, very fine.   Argonaut Book Shop   Literature 2015 - 6211   2016 $75

Tuchman, Barbara W. *The March of Folly; from Troy to Vietnam.* New York: Knopf, 1984. First edition, 8vo., author's signature, illustrations, owner's embossed stamp, gray cloth, cover slightly faded at edges, else nice in somewhat scuffed and yellowed dust jacket, very good+.   Second Life Books, Inc.   196 B - 771   2016 $75

Tucker, Abraham *Vocal Sounds by Edward Search, Esq.* Printed by T. Jones and sold by T. Payne, 1773. First edition, small 8vo., 19th century half maroon morocco by E. Riley & Son, very good.   Blackwell's Rare Books   B186 - 155   2016   £900

Tucker, C. M. *Plays for Amatuers and Home Reading.* London: Stead's Publishing House, 1911. Frontispiece, original pale blue printed wrappers, very good.   Jarndyce Antiquarian Booksellers   CCXVIII - 731   2016   £30

Tucker, E. S. *A Cup of Tea.* New York: Worthington, 1892. Oblong 4to., cloth backed pictorial boards, tips worn, light stain on part of rear cover, edge rubbing, very good and internally clean and fine, beautiful Victorian plate book.   Aleph-bet Books, Inc.   112 - 265   2016 $225

Tucker, Sophie *Some of these Days.* N.P.: n.p., 1945. Photos on endpapers, author's presentation, cover little faded and stained, otherwise very good.   Second Life Books, Inc.   196 B - 772   2016 $75

Tudor, Tasha *Alexander the Gander.* New York: Oxford University Press, 1939. First edition, green patterned cloth, slight edge rubbing, else near fine, illustrations by Tudor.   Aleph-bet Books, Inc.   111 - 459   2016 $375

Tudor, Tasha *Becky's Christmas.* New York: Viking, 1961. First edition, 4to., cloth, fine in very good+ dust jacket, lovely color and black and white illustrations.   Aleph-bet Books, Inc.   112 - 485   2016 $400

Tudor, Tasha *The County Fair.* New York: Oxford University Press, 1940. First edition, first printing, 16mo., polka dot patterned cloth, fine in fie dust jacket that is slightly toned, full page color illustrations, pictorial initials and calligraphic text, beautiful copy, rare in this condition.   Aleph-bet Books, Inc.   112 - 482   2016 $1200

Tudor, Tasha *The Doll's Christmas.* New York: Oxford University Press, 1950. First edition, 8vo., red cloth, fine in slightly soiled and frayed dust jacket, full page color illustrations by author.   Aleph-bet Books, Inc.   112 - 484   2016 $450

Tudor, Tasha *Dorcus Porkus.* New York: Oxford University Press, 1942. First edition, first printing, 16mo., yellow polka dotted cloth, fine in dust jacket (soiled, slightly frayed, but still very good), pictorial initials with full page color illustrations, nice, rare. Aleph-bet Books, Inc. 112 - 483   2016 $1400

Tudor, Tasha *Edgar Allan Crow.* New York: Oxford University Press, 1953. First edition, first printing, 8vo., cloth, paste-on, near fine in dust jacket (lightly toned), illustrations in color. Aleph-bet Books, Inc.   112 - 481   2016 $975

Tudor, Tasha *The Great Corgiville Kindapping.* Boston: et al: Little Brown, 1997. Stated first edition, first printing, pictorial boards, fine in fine dust jacket, fantastic full page and smaller color illustrations, this copy signed by Tudor. Aleph-bet Books, Inc.   111 - 457   2016 $150

Tudor, Tasha *Pumpkin Moonshine.* New York: Oxford University Press, 1938. First edition, first printing, 16mo., polka dot patterned boards, edges and joints faded, else near fine in beautiful clean dust jacket with no fraying or tears, with only light browning on edge of inner flaps and small abrasion on backstrip effecting the 'x' in Oxford, beautifully illustrated, this is the dedication copy, inscribed by author for her niece, Sylvie Ann.   Aleph-bet Books, Inc. 111 - 456   2016 $15,850

Tuer, Andrew White   1838-1900 *History of the Horn-Book.* London: Leadenhall Press, 1897. 4to., half title, engraved frontispiece, illustrations, original light brown cloth, bevelled boards, brown leather label, slight rubbing, inner hinge slight cracking, top edge gilt, inscription "To A.M.B. from A.M.L. Nov 20th 1897".   Jarndyce Antiquarian Books   CCXV - 785   2016   £250

Tuer, Andrew White   1838-1900 *History of the Horn Book.* New York: Arno Press, 1979. Reprint edition, frontispiece, illustrations, original red cloth, very good in dust jacket.   Jarndyce Antiquarian Books   CCXV - 786   2016 £30

Tuer, Andrew White   1838-1900 *Pages and Pictures from Forgotten Children's Books.* London: Leadenhall Press, 1898-1899. 8vo., blue cloth, extensive gilt decoration, top edge gilt, offsetting on endpaper, else near fine, 400 illustrations.   Aleph-bet Books, Inc. 112 - 419   2016 $150

Tugay, Emine Foat *Three Centuries: Family Chronicles of Turkey and Egypt.* London: Oxford University Press, 1963. First edition, 8vo., 8 tables at rear, 11 plates, very good in slightly used dust jacket.   Any Amount of Books   2015 - A71205   2016   £150

Tulin, Alexander *Dike Phonou. The Right of Prosecution and Attic Homicide Procedure.* Leipzig: B. G. Teubner, 1996. First edition, 8vo., grey cloth, red lettered, light bumping to corners, small mark to fore-edge, very good, no dust jacket, illegible ownership inscription.   Unsworths Antiquarian Booksellers Ltd.   E05 - 63   2016   £75

Tullis Russell & Co. *Charles Dickens 1812-1870. A biography.* London: Tullis Russell & Co., 1962. First edition, 4to., half title, frontispiece, color plates from originals by Kyd, illustrations, original pale blue cloth, lettered gilt, mint in dust jacket.   Jarndyce Antiquarian Booksellers   CCXVIII - 1468   2016   £20

Turbott, E. G. *Buller's Bird of New Zealand.* Christchurch: Whitcombe & Tombs, 1974. Reprint, folio, tipped-in color plates, fine in dust jacket.   Andrew Isles Natural History Books   55 - 37094   2016 $100

Turgenev, Ivan Sergeevich   1818-1883 *Dym. (in Russian) (Smoke).* Moscow: Tipografia Gracheva, 1868. First bookform edition, some foxing, 8vo., uncut in original printed wrappers, slightly soiled, minor fraying to fore-edges, good.   Blackwell's Rare Books   B184 - 86   2016   £1500

Turing, Alan *A Method of Calculation of the Zeta-Function.* London: C. F. Hodgson & Son Ltd., 1943. First edition, tall octavo, modern three quarter red cloth over linen boards, original wrappers bound in, beautiful fine copy, full margins, rare.   Manhattan Rare Book Company   2016 - 1794   2016 $3900

Turing, Alan *Systems of Logic Based On Ordinals.* London: C. F. Hodgson & Son Ltd., 1939. First edition, tall octavo, modern three quarter red cloth over linen boards, original wrappers bound-in, beautiful fine, full margins and no institutional stamps, rare.   Manhattan Rare Book Company   2016 - 1795   2016 $8000

Turk, Eugene M. *No Big Thing.* New Orleans: Moret Press, 1967. First edition, octavo, staple bound pictorial card wrappers, illustrations, mild cover wear and soiling, very good or better.   Between the Covers Rare Books   202 - 111   2016 $275

Turnbull, David *Travels in the West, Cuba; with Notices of Porto Rico and the Slave Trade.* London: Spottiswoode, 1840. First edition, 8vo., map (little foxed), contemporary brown half calf, spine rubbed, good crisp copy.   J. & S. L. Bonham Antiquarian Booksellers   America 2016 - 8036   2016   £350

Turnebe, Adrien *Adversariorum tomi III.* Basel: Per Thomam Guarinum, 1581. First collected edition, some browning and spotting, old paper repairs to blank upper corners of first 10 leaves, damp marking and blooming to upper corner in second and third sections, expanding in index with little bit of wear to top margin at end, old ownership inscription, cancelled, occasional underlining, folio, 18th century Italian vellum boards, one section of spine dyed yellow and lettered gilt, just slightly marked, 20th century inscription, sound.   Blackwell's Rare Books   Greek & Latin Classics VII - 14   2016   £500

Turner, Alan *The Big Cats and Their Fossil Relatives...* Irvington: Columbia University Press, 1977. Octavo, colour plates, other illustrations, signature, very good in dust jacket. Andrew Isles Natural History Books   55 - 10497   2016 $60

Turner, Edward *The Young Man's Companion or Friendly Advisor.* Halifax: Milner & Sowerby, 1857. 16mo., frontispiece, uncut, original green cloth, slightly rubbed and dulled, gift inscription, embossed library stamp.   Jarndyce Antiquarian Books   CCXV - 448   2016   £45

Turner, Lorenzo Dow *Anti-Slavery sentiment in American Literature Prior to 1865.* Washington: Association for the Study of Negro Life and History Inc., 1929. First edition, lovely, fine, lacking rare dust jacket, inscribed by author to Anna Grace Sawyer, April 9 1936.   Between the Covers Rare Books   202 - 112   2016 $400

Turner, Richard *An Easy Introduction to the Arts and Sciences being a Short but Comprehensive System of Useful and Polite Learning.* London: J. Johnson, 1803. Ninth edition, half title, plates, illustrations, final ad leaf, contemporary speckled calf, lacking label, rubbed, ownership inscription of M. E. Denne, April 11th 1804 ad Arthur Denne Hilton 1866.   Jarndyce Antiquarian Books   CCXV - 991   2016   £45

Turner, Richard *A View of the Heavens; Being a Short but Comprehensive, System of Modern Astronomy....* printed for S. Crowder, 1783. Second edition, folio, 2 full page engraved plates, 1 as frontispiece, 12 engravings in text, 1 with volvelle (complete) and 3 woodcut diagrams in text, some foxing and browning, offsetting of engravings, engraving with volvelle backed with later paper, stitched in original drab paper wrappers, apparently without ever having spine covering, bit stained and worn, sound.   Blackwell's Rare Books   B186 - 156   2016   £1100

Turner, Sharon *The History of the Anglo-Saxons from the earliest Period to the Norman Conquest.* London: Longman, Rees, Orme, Brown, Green & Longman, 1836. Sixth edition, 3 volumes 8vo., folding map to volume 1, map foxed and occasional spots of foxing elsewhere, publisher's half cloth and grey boards, printed paper labels to spines, edges uncut, all volumes neatly rebacked with original spines retained, endpapers replaced, rubbed, edges worn, corners bumped, gift inscription "Agnes M. Scully from her mama Ismera Payne Jan. 25th 1840, library stamp of Abbat S. Martae e. Berholten.   Unsworths Antiquarian Booksellers Ltd.   E05 - 111   2016   £150

Turner, Thomas *The Case of the Bankers and their Creditors Stated and Examined.* London: in the year, 1675. Third edition, 8vo., titlepage lightly soiled, many upper corners slightly creased, small closed tear at foot of F2 (not touching text), blue inkstain in margin of K7r with slight offset on opposite page, contemporary sheep rebacked, new endleaves but old rear flyleaves preserved, rather tightly bound with narrow inner margins, from the library of James Stevens Cox (1910-1997), two early ink inscriptions of Roger Taunton.   Maggs Bros. Ltd.   1447 - 419   2016   £240

Turow, Scott *The Laws of Our Fathers.* New York: Farrar Straus Giroux, 1996. First edition, very fine in dust jacket, signed by author.   Mordida Books   2015 - 002208   2016 $55

Turton, Thomas *Thoughts on the Admission of Persons Without Regard to their Religious Opinions to Certain Degrees in the Universities of England.* Cambridge: printed at the Pitt Press by John Smith &c., 1834. 16 page catalog, sewn as issued, dust jackets, slightly marked, signature of J. B. Hope.   Jarndyce Antiquarian Books   CCXV - 962 2016   £30

Tuska, Jon *The Detective in Hollywood.* Garden City: Doubleday, 1978. First edition, fine in dust jacket. Mordida Books   2015 - 010786   2016 $65

Tusser, Thomas *Five Hundred Points of Good Husbandry.* London: by Thomas Ratcliffe and Mary Daniel for the Company of Stationers, 1672. Small 4to., black letter, heavily browned/spotted in places throughout due to poor paper quality, scorch marks on K1, P1-4, S2 and T2, headlines on the Penultimate leaf just shaved, large lock of ?wool tied in bow loosely inserted between G3-4, late 18th century calf, spine divided by raised bands with red morocco label, upper joint slightly cracked, from the library of James Stevens Cox (1910-1997), engraved initial of Thomas Holt White (1724-1797), and three sucessive Holt White family signatures.   Maggs Bros. Ltd.   1447 - 420   2016   £500

Tusser, Thomas *Five Hundred Pointes of Good Husbandrie.* London: published for the English Dialect Society by Trubner & Co., 1878. 8vo., very lightly yellowed, few small pencil marks to glossary, contemporary half black calf, raised bands, gilt ruled spine with red morocco label, red marbled paper covered boards, edges sprinkled red, spine and edges bit rubbed, few light scratches, but very good, handsome copy, tiny bookbinder's ticket of Broadbere, Pembroke Square, Bargate, Southampton.   Unsworths Antiquarian Booksellers Ltd.   30 - 154   2016   £45

Tutorow, Norman E. *The Governor. The Life and Legacy of Leland Stanford.* Spokane: Arthur H. Clark Co., 2004. First edition, one of 1550 copies, 2 volumes, 175 photos, portraits, maps, reproductions, charts, red cloth, gilt, very set with pictorial dust jackets.   Argonaut Book Shop   Biography 2015 - 7145   2016 $125

Tutorow, Norman E. *The Governor. The Life and Legacy of Leland Stanford.* Spokane: Arthur H. Clark Co., 2004. First edition, one of 1550 copies, presentation inscription signed by author, 2 volumes, 175 photos, portraits, maps, reproductions and charts, red cloth, gilt, very fine, pictorial dust jackets.   Argonaut Book Shop   Biography 2015 - 7140   2016 $175

Tuttle, Richard *Early Auden.* Richard Tuttle, 1991. Artist book printed in an edition of only 80 copies with this being number 17, accordion style book with Tuttle's aquatint illustrations and inset poems by Auden, close to near fine in vellum boards with leather spine, but with some slight bowing, internally fine and bright, possibly missing plain paper wrapping/slipcase, signed by Tuttle, very beautifully realized book.   Jeff Hirsch Books   Holiday List 2015 - 2   2016 $6000

Tweddell, Robert *Account of the Examination of the Elgin-box at the Foreign Office in Downing Street on 7th November 1816 in a letter to James Losh, Esa....* Manchester: printed for the author by C. Wheeler and Son, 7 Pall Mall, King Street, 1817. Sole edition, 4to., uncut in original blue sugar paper wrappers, slight water stained, also affecting initial and following blanks, signature on upper wrapper of WL Charlton.   Jarndyce Antiquarian Booksellers CCXVII - 288   2016   £120

Tweedie, William King *The Early Choice: a Book for Daughters.* London: T. Nelson & Sons, 1858. Additional engraved title, little spotted, contemporary full pebble grained green morocco, decorated gilt, slightly dulled, all edges gilt, attractive copy.   Jarndyce Antiquarian Books CCXV - 449   2016   £75

Tweedie, William King *The Early Choice: a Book for Daughters.* London: T. Nelson & sons, 1873. Frontispiece, additional engraved title, plates, 4 page ads, original green decorated cloth, bevelled boards, spines slightly dulled and rubbed, contemporary inscription "to Maggie Taylor, Dublin 1874.   Jarndyce Antiquarian Books   CCXV - 450   2016 £30

Twelvetrees, R. C. *Seven Little Women.* New York: Frederick Stokes, 1908. Oblong folio, cloth backed pictorial boards, edges and corners worn, covers soiled, tight and clean, scarce.   Aleph-bet Books, Inc.   112 - 487   2016 $475

The 20 Mule-Team Brigade.. New York: Chicago: San Francisco: Pacific Coast Borax, 1904. Oblong 8vo, pictorial books, slight cover soil and one margin mend, else very good++, 11 full page color illustrations, rare.   Aleph-bet Books, Inc.   112 - 336   2016 $1500

Twigden, Blake L. *Pisces Tropicani.* Melbourne: Lansdowne, 1978. Limited to 350 copies numbered and signed by artist, Folio, half morocco and suede.   Andrew Isles Natural History Books   55 - 1787   2016 $300

Two Worlds Monthly. New York: Two Worlds Publishing, July, 1926-. September, 1927, Journal's first 11 issues, 238 x 168mm, original printed paper wrappers, isolated pencilled marginalia, five spines with minor chip at tail, short splits to head of six joints, covers of last issue detached and chipped around edges, covers little soiled, couple of short fore-edge tears, occasional corner creases or short marginal tears, but leaves clean and fresh and fragile volumes otherwise preserved.   Phillip J. Pirages   67 - 215   2016 $3500

Twombly, Cy *Cy Twombly: Photographs 1951-1999.* Munich: Schirmer/Mosel, 2002. 70 color images, very near fine in very near fine dust jacket, boldly signed by artist. Jeff Hirsch Books   Holiday List 2015 - 96   2016 $750

Twysden, Roger *Historiae Anglicanae Scriptores X.* London: Typis Jacobi Flesher sumptibus Cornelii Bee, 1652. Editio princeps, 2 volumes as 1, folio, half title, title in red and black, section, woodcut initials, few tiny wax spots and ink blots not obscuring text, contemporary dark brown calf, blind tooled frame, edges sprinkled brown and red, neatly rebacked, red morocco gilt spine label, few scratches to boards, inner hinges reinforced, 2 armorial bookplates, F. E. Sotheby, Ecton and Derek Baker, third armorial bookplate of Ambrose Isted, fourth armorial bookplate with no name but with motto 'Que Serra Serra".   Unsworths Antiquarian Booksellers Ltd.   E01 - Early Printing - 28   2016   £500

Tyler, John *Message from the President of the United States to the Two Houses of Congress at the Commencement of the Session of the Twenty-Seventh Congress December 7 1841...* Washington: Thomas Allen, Printer, 1841. First edition, 2 black & white maps, one folding, 1 plate and 1 folding chart, 8vo., removed from larger volume else about very good, dampstain to rear leaves at upper spine, mostly marginal, very faint dampstain on fore edge, one leaf chipped at corner affecting about two letters of text.   Kaaterskill Books   21 - 103   2016 $250

Tyler, Michael J. *The Gastric Brooding Frog.* London: Croom Helm, 1983. Octavo, illustrations, signature, fine in dust jacket, scarce.   Andrew Isles Natural History Books   55 - 1879   2016 $120

Tyler, Ron *Audubon's Great National Work.* Austin: W. Thomas Taylor, 1993. First edition, limited to 225 copies, with two original prints, bound in wrappers and laid in at back of box, 4to., illustrations, original green cloth backed paste paper boards, matching green linen folding box, printed spine label, as new.   James S. Jaffe Rare Books Occasional List: Winter 2016 - 27   2016 $1500

Tyndale, William *The Whole Workes of W. Tyndall, John Frith and Doct. Barnes, three Worthy Martyrs and Principall Teachers of this Churche of England...* London: printed by John Daye, 1573. First edition, 3 parts in one folio volume, black letter and Roman letter in double columns, title and two sectional titles with repeated woodcut border, half page woodcut illustrations on A4, woodcut historiated and foliate initials, typographical ornaments, 18th century calf, neatly rebacked to style, covers decoratively bordered in blind, board edges tooled gilt, marbled edges, early paper repair not affecting text, lower blank corner of Xx3 renewed, not affecting text, repaired tear to lower margin of DD1, just touching few letters, but with no loss, paper repair to lower corner of Mmm5 in third part, not affecting text, few minor marginal paper flaws, not affecting text, small dampstain in lower corner of second part and throughout third part, housed in custom quarter brown morocco clamshell, gilt stamped.   Heritage Book Shop   Holiday 2015 - 109   2016 $35,000

Typographica. New Series No. 2. London: Lund Humphries, 1960. 4to., paper wrappers many full color illustrations.   Oak Knoll Books   310 - 193   2016 $100

Typothetae. The Hampshrie Typothetae. Northampton: Hampshire Typothetae, 1977. One of 1500 copies, 8vo., 2 double leaves, paper wrappers, print by Barry Moser laid in, signed by Moser, nice.   Second Life Books, Inc.   196 B - 775   2016 $100

Tyrell, George *Versions and Perversions of Heine & Others.* London: Elkin Mathews, 1909. First edition, boards somewhat marked and browning to endpapers, but nice, presentation copy inscribed by Wilfrid Scawen Blunt for Elizabeth Lawrence Xmas 1909, book dedicated to Wilfrid Blunt.   Simon Finch   2015 - 4159   2016 $252

Tyson, Edward *Carigueya, seu Marsupiale Americanum or the Anatomy of an Opossum, Dissected at Gresham College.* London: for Sam. Smith and Benj. Walford, 1698. First separate edition, small 4to., 2 folding engraved plates, one slightly shaved at foot, corners and edges occasionally bumped, disbound (traces of leather visible on spine), stitched (apparently a fairly early date) into a portion of 17th century printed singing manual, from the library of James Stevens Cox (1910-1997), 18th century ink lot number, Cox's pencil notes inside front cover 'James Yonge's copy.   Maggs Bros. Ltd.   1447 - 421   2016   £1800

Tytler, Sarah, Pseud. *Papers for Thoughtful Girls with Sketches of Some Girls' Lives.* London: Alexander Strahan, 1866. Seventh edition, half title, frontispiece and plates by John Millais, 16 page catalog (Jan. 1866), paper slightly browning, original purple cloth, bevelled boards, blocked and lettered gilt, spine darkened and slightly worn at head and tail, inner hinges cracking, owner's signature, all edges gilt.   Jarndyce Antiquarian Books   CCXV - 451   2016   £40

Tytler, William *An Historical and Critical Enquiry into the Evidence Produced by the Earls of Murray and Morton against Mary Queen of Scots.* Edinburgh: printed by W. Gordon, 1760. 8vo., fine clean copy in full contemporary sprinkled calf, smooth spine, gilt bands, red morocco label, very slight abrasion to upper board, from the library of Invercauld Castle, Braemar.   Jarndyce Antiquarian Booksellers   CCXVI - 576   2016   £380

U

Udall, John *A Demonstration of the Trueth of the Discipline which Christe Hath Prescribed in His Worde for the Government of His Church, in all Times and Places....* East Molesey: R. Waldegrave, 1588. First edition, folding table, titlepage and blank verso of last leaf dust soiled, C4 frayed in fore margin, small 8vo., 17th century calf, panelled in gilt and blind, with central medallion in gilt, rebacked preserving original spine, 18th century ownership inscription of William Groom below errata and also on front free endpaper, that of John Stretton on following flyleaf, good. Blackwell's Rare Books   B184 - 87   2016   £5000

Ueber Die Wirkung und Kreigeschirurgische Bedeutung Der Neuen Handfeuerwaffen Im Auftrage Seiner Exzellentz des Herrn Kriegsministers Bearbeitet von der Medizinal.... Berlin: August Hirschwald, 1894. 79 text illustrations, diagrams and half tones, one hand colored plate, atlas volume with 17 high quality photogravures, two of which are in color, ex-library stamps on titles and spine labels, paper has some toning, plates loosely inserted in atlas volume, contemporary quarter line and marbled boards, spine sunned and binding showing wear.   James Tait Goodrich   X-78 - 399   2016 $2750

Ulanov, Barry *Duke Ellington.* New York: Creative Age Press, 1946. First edition, extremities and lettering rubbed, about very good, lacking dust jacket, inscribed by the subject to Magnifique Marion.   Between the Covers Rare Books   202 - 63   2016 $750

Ullman, James Ramsay *The Age of Mountaineering.* Philadelphia: J. B. Lippincott, 1954. First edition, 24 photos, 6 maps, endpaper maps, addendum tipped in at rear, two tone cloth, very fine with spine faded pictorial dust jacket.   Argonaut Book Shop   Mountaineering 2015 - 7243   2016 $90

Ulloa, Antonio De *A Voyage to South America.* London: Lockyer Davis, 1772. Third edition, 2 volumes, 8vo., early 19th century black half morocco, folding map, plan, 5 plates, some light rubbing to joints and corners, excellent set.   J. & S. L. Bonham Antiquarian Booksellers   America 2016 - 8990   2016   £400

The Undead: The Book Sail 16th Anniversary Catalogue. Orange: McLaughlin Press, 1984. Deluxe first edition, octavo, illustrations, red and black cloth boards with 3D portraits of Elvira mounted on front board with wraparound band, original clear dust jacket and red cloth slipcase, fine with small scrape on portrait with near fine wraparound band with light wear and near fine clear dust jacket with nick, one of 400 deluxe copies signed by Elvira, Ray Bradbury, Robert Bloch, Rowena and with separate first printing of Dandelion Chronicles by Nolan limited to 550 copies and signed in pocket on rear pastedown.   Between the Covers Rare Books   208 - 113   2016 $300

Ungerer, Tomi *I Am Pap Snap and These are My Favorite No Such Stories.* New York: Harper & Row, 1971. Stated first edition, large 4to., cloth, fine in dust jacket, illustrations by author, beautiful copy.   Aleph-bet Books, Inc.   111 - 462   2016 $200

Ungerer, Tomi *Zeralda's Ogre.* New York: Harper & Row, 1967. First edition, Folio, cloth backed pictorial boards, fine in frayed dust jacket, bright color illustrations by author.   Aleph-bet Books, Inc.   111 - 463   2016 $200

Union List of Series (1927) / Union List of Serials Supplement 1925-1931 (1935) / Union List of Serials, Second Edition of Serials Second Supplement 1944-1949 (1953). New York: H. W. Wilson, 1927. First and Second editions and supplements to 1953, 4to. and large 4to. and large 8vo., covers worn, rubbed, scratched, bindings shaken to some degree with splitting at several hinges, ex-library with bookplates.   Oak Knoll Books   310 - 217   2016 $300

United Negro and Allied Veterans of America *UNAVA First National Convention New York City May 30-June 1 1947.* New York: UNAVA, 1947. Large quarto, stapled tan wrappers, illustrations by Jacob Lawrence, tear on rear wrapper and last leaf, slight soiling, very good or better, front wrapper illustration by Lawrence.   Between the Covers Rare Books   207 - 92   2016 $800

United States. Congress. House of Representatives - 1792 *Journal of the House of Representatives of the United States of the First (-Second) Session of the Second Congress.* Philadelphia: Francis Childs and John Saine, 1792-1793. Folio, 2 volumes in 1, bound in modern calf backed marbled boards, very skillfully executed in period style, several gatherings in second volume foxed, else near fine, from the library of James Moll treasurer of NJ.   Joseph J. Felcone, Inc.   Books from Five Centuries: a Miscellany - 143   2016 $2000

United States. Congress. House of Representatives - 1828 *Memorial of Inhabitants of Philadelphia Praying that the Baltimore and Ohio Rail Road Company May Not be Permitted to Import Iron Free of Duty May 12 1828 (with) Documents Accompanying a Memorial of the President and Directors of the Baltimore and Ohio Rail Road Co. May 19 1828. (with) Mr. Buchanan submitted the Following Letter....* Washington: Printed by Gales & Seaton, 1828. First edition, removed, very good with few minor notations. Kaaterskill Books   21 - 107   2016 $150

United States. Congress. Senate - 1794 *In the Senate, May 12th 1794. On Motion, Ordered that the Memorial of Mr. Pinckney, the Answer of Mr. Hammond, and the letter of the Secretary of State on the 1st of May to Mr. Hammond Relative to the British Instruction of the 8th of June Last, be Printed for the Use of the Members of the Senate.* Philadelphia: printed by John Fenno?, 1794. 8vo., printed area bit browned, modern marbled boards, good.   Blackwell's Rare Books   B186 - 154   2016   £450

United States. Congress. Senate - 1880 *In the Senate of the United States Feb. 9 1880. Ordered to be printed Mr. Cameron of Wisconsin, from the Committee on Claims, Submitted the Following Report (to acccompany bill S231). The Committee on Claims, to whom was referred the petition of Benjamin Holladay, Praying Compensation for Spoliations by Indians on his Property While Engaged in Carrying the mail of the United States Under a Contract with the United States.... (with) April 11 1882, Mr. Cameron of Wisconsin from the Committee on Claims, submitted following report (to accompany Bill S 1683)....* Washington: GPO, 1880-1882. 8vo. stapled paper wrappers; stitched paper wrappers, very good copies.   Kaaterskill Books   21 - 68   2016 $350

United States. Continental Congress - 1776 *Journals of Congress. Containing the Proceedings in the Year 1776.* Philadelphia: R. Aitken, 1777. First edition, modern full mottled sheepskin, superbly executed in exact facsimile of original binding, spine with red morocco title label and '1776' tooled in black oval onlay, some internal dampstaining and browning, particularly toward end of text, else very handsome volume, with signature of Samuel McCraw Gunn dated 1822, enclosed in four flap chemise and morocco backed slipcase.   Joseph J. Felcone, Inc.   Books from Five Centuries: a Miscellany - 144   2016 $20,000

United States. Navy - 1866 *Register of the Commissioned, Warrant and Volunteer Officers of the Navy of the United States, Including Officers of the Marine Corps and Others to Jan. 1 1866.* Washington: GPO, 1866. First edition, 8vo., three quarter morocco over marbled paper covered boards, signed by J(essie) E. Dow, clerk in the Navy Dept., heavily annotated, good+, front joint tender, spine ends chipped, edgewear, some scuffing to boards, owner's name on title scattered soil spots and marginalia. Kaaterskill Books   21 - 106   2016 $150

United States. Navy - 1898 *Register of the Commissioned and Warrant Officers of the Navy of the United States and the Marine Corps to Jan. 1 1898 (with) 1899 (with (1900 (with) list and Station July 1, 1898 (with) July 3, 1899 (with) July 1, 1900.* Washington: GPO, 1898-1900. First edition, 8vo., three quarter morocco over marbled boards, front board nearly detached, leather bit dry, binding tight, contents near fine.   Kaaterskill Books   21 - 105   2016 $225

United States. State Department - 1895 *Appendix II: Foreign Relations of the United States 1894: Affairs in Hawaii.* Washington: GPO, 1895. First edition, fat 8vo., bound in red cloth lettered gilt on spine, ex-British Foreign Office library with few library markings, nicked at head of spine, covers very slightly marked, else sound, very good. Any Amount of Books   2015 - A78286   2016   £250

University Press (Cambridge, Massachusetts) *Specimen Book of the University Press John Wilson and Son (Incorporated)....* Cambridge: University Press, 1900. Oblong 4to., cloth, title and logo gilt stamped on front board, title gilt stamped on spine, facsimile titlepage, black and white illustrations, recased with original spine laid down on newer cloth, new endpapers, old library stamp in corner of few pages, very scarce.   Oak Knoll Books   310 - 191   2016 $1350

Unsworth, Barry *The Big Day.* London: Michael Joseph, 1976. First edition, octavo, covers bit bumped at edges very good in like dust jacket with usual fading up spine and edges.   Peter Ellis   112 - 415   2016   £75

Unsworth, Barry *Pascali's Island.* London: Michael Joseph, 1980. First edition, octavo, slight bump to bottom edge of rear cover, otherwise fine in very good dust jacket slightly creased at top edge.   Peter Ellis   112 - 414   2016   £85

Unsworth, Walt *Peaks, Passes and Glaciers.* London: Albert Lane, 1981. First edition, black and white photos, light blue cloth, lettered gilt, slight fading to extreme upper and lower edges of covers, else fine, pictorial dust jacket. Argonaut Book Shop   Mountaineering 2015 - 720   2016 $45

Updike, John 1932-2009 *The Angels.* Pensecola: King and Queen Press, 1968. First edition, 24mo., string tied printed pale blue wrappers, one of 150 hand printed copies, very slight sunning at extremities else fine, issued unsigned, this copy inscribed by author for Herb Yellin, very uncommon.   Between the Covers Rare Books   204 - 118   2016 $1500

Updike, John 1932-2009 *The Beloved.* Northridge: Lord John Press, 1982. First edition, quarter leather and cloth, fine, publisher's file copy, so designated in letterpress type and inscribed by author.   Between the Covers Rare Books   204 - 121   2016 $950

Updike, John   1932-2009   *Brazil.*   Franklin Center: Franklin Library, 1994. Limited first edition, signed by author, brown leather, lettered and decoratively stamped in gilt, all edges gilt, very fine, as new.   Argonaut Book Shop Literature 2015 - 4035   2016 $150

Updike, John   1932-2009   *Buchanan Dying.*   New York: Alfred A. Knopf, 1974. First edition, inscribed and signed for William Meredith, fine in near fine dust jacket with tanned spine.   Charles Agvent   William Meredith - 112   2016 $250

Updike, John   1932-2009   *The Carpentered Hen and Other Tame Creatures.*   New York: Harper and Bros., 1958. First edition, one signature fallen slightly forward as usual, else fine in fine, first issue dust jacket with later (probably publisher's) price sticker over original price, inscribed by author for Herb Yellin.   Between the Covers Rare Books   204 - 116   2016 $2500

Updike, John   1932-2009   *The Complete Henry Bech: Twenty Stories.*   New York: Alfred A. Knopf, 2001. First edition thus, fine in fine dust jacket, inscribed by author for Herb Yellin, notable association, uncomoon edition.   Between the Covers Rare Books   208 - 86   2016 $250

Updike, John   1932-2009   *Couples.*   New York: Alfred A. Knopf, 1968. First edition, publisher's navy blue cloth lettered gilt and metallic silver, original pictorial dust jacket designed by Jeanyee Wong, panels illustrated with details of watercolor drawing by William Blake, fine, hint of light wear to spine ends, slight trace of faint spotting to page edges, otherwise fresh and clean pages, unclipped dust jacket with only hint of light wear to extremities, else fine, overall bright and attractive copy.   B & B Rare Books, Ltd.   2016 - JU015   2016 $75

Updike, John   1932-2009   *Couples: a Short Story.*   Cambridge: Halty Ferguson, 1976. First edition , copy S of 26 lettered copies, decorared wrappers with applied label, fine, signed by printers, William and Raquel Ferguson, dated August 20 1976.   Between the Covers Rare Books   208 - 87   2016 $500

Updike, John   1932-2009   *Hub Fans bid Kid Adieu.*   Northridge: Lord John Press, 1977. First edition, copy number 49 of 300 numbered copies, signed by author, quarter cloth and paper covered boards, fine, housed in custom cloth chemise and slipcase with morocco spine labels gilt, this copy also signed by Ted Williams, laid in is certificate of authenticity issued by Williams' son John Henry Williams.   Between the Covers Rare Books   204 - 120   2016 $1500

Updike, John   1932-2009   *In Memoriam Felix Felis.*   Leamington Spa: Sixth Chamber Press, 1989. First edition, this conforms to the issues of 1/26 lettered copies but unlettered and signed by author and artist, 6 illustrations by R B. Kitaj, quarter cloth and paper covered boards, fine in lightly rubbed near fine illustrated slipcase, inscribed by author for Herb Yellin.   Between the Covers Rare Books   204 - 122   2016 $1500

Updike, John   1932-2009   *Marry Me, a Romance.*   New York: Alfred A. Knopf, 1976. First trade edition, fine in very slightly soiled and crease dust jacket.   Bertram Rota Ltd. February List 2016 - 59   2016   £60

Updike, John   1932-2009   *The Music School.*   New York: Alfred A. Knopf, 1966. First edition, first issue, one corner tiny bit bumped, else fine in slightly spine toned, very near fine dust jacket with two tiny tears, inscribed by author for Herb Yellin.   Between the Covers Rare Books   204 - 117   2016 $850

Updike, John   1932-2009   *On Meeting Authors.*   Newburyport: Wickford Press, 1968. First edition, copy number 12 of 250 numbered copies, stapled wrappers with applied printed label, fine, this copy inscribed by author for Herb Yellin, very uncommon.   Between the Covers Rare Books   204 - 119   2016 $1200

Updike, John   1932-2009   *Problems and Other Stories.*   New York: Alfred A. Knopf, 1979. First edition, publisher's red cloth and gray boards, lettered in silver, black top stain, slight lean to spine, else fine, contemporary with two short closed tears and some creasing to rear panel, light rubbing to extremities, else bright and clean, overall near fine and very attractive.   B & B Rare Books, Ltd.   2016 - JUo27   2016 $45

Updike, John   1932-2009   *Rabbit Angstrom, a Tetralogy: Rabbit, Run, Rabbit Redux, Rabbit Rich, Rabbit at Rest.*   New York: Alfred A. Knopf, 1995. First edition thus, fine in fine dust jacket, inscribed by author for Herb Yellin.   Between the Covers Rare Books   208 - 88   2016 $250

Updike, John   1932-2009   *Rabbit at Rest.*   New York: Alfred A. Knopf, 1990. First edition, indigo cloth, lettered in silver and gilt, lavender top stain, original purple black and gray striped dust jacket, lettered in white, fine, only hint of faint creasing to spine head, beautiful and fresh, fine dust jacket with only few faint scuffs, beautiful copy.   B & B Rare Books, Ltd.   2016 - JU028   2016 $50

Updike, John 1932-2009 *Rabbit, Run.* New York: Alfred A. Knopf, 1960. First edition, teal cloth and slate blue boards, lettered in silver, aqua top stain, original green, blue, yellow and gray striped dust jacket, lettered in white and yellow, near fine, only some faint toning to extremities and minor dimming to top edge, else bright and clean, dust jacket with few small chips to spine head, tiny closed split to front flap, some soiling to spine and panels, faint wear and rubbing to extremities, overall very good and pleasing copy. B & B Rare Books, Ltd. 2016 - JU025 2016 $300

Updike, John 1932-2009 *Rabbit Run; Rabbit, Redux; Rabbit is Rich; Rabbit at Rest.* Norwalk: Easton Press, 1989. First Easton Press edition, 4 volumes, illustrations by Richard Sparks full leather, gilt, fine, no Easton bookplate, each volume inscribed by author for Herb Yellin. Between the Covers Rare Books 204 - 123 2016 $800

Updike, John 1932-2009 *Roger's Version.* London: Andre Deutsch, 1986. First UK edition, octavo, head of spine very slightly bumped, fine in near fine dust jacket slightly creased at edges. Peter Ellis 112 - 416 2016 £25

Updike, John 1932-2009 *The Witches of Eastwick.* Franklin Center: Franklin Library, 1984. Limited first edition, large 8vo. signed by author, green leatherette, all edges gilt, stamped in gilt, as new. Second Life Books, Inc. 196 B - 778 2016 $150

Upfield, Arthur W. *The Body at Madman's Bend.* Garden City: published for the Crime Club by Doubleday, Doran and Co. Inc., 1963. First US edition, octavo, cloth, fine in fine dust jacket, touch or rubbing. John W. Knott, Jr./L.W. Currey, Inc. Fall-Winter 2015 - 17364 2016 $200

Upfield, Arthur W. *Journey to the Hangman.* Garden City: Published for the Crime Club at Doubleday, Doran and Co., 1959. First US edition, octavo, fine in nearly fine dust jacket with some mild rubbing to folds and corners, spine panel has slight color fade. John W. Knott, Jr./L.W. Currey, Inc. Fall-Winter 2015 - 17360 2016 $125

Upfield, Arthur W. *No Footprints in the Bush.* Garden City: Crime Club by Doubleday Doran, 1944. First US edition, octavo, cloth, fine in fine dust jacket with slight wear to upper corner, tips with slight loss to rear tip and touch of edge wear, very nice. John W. Knott, Jr./L.W. Currey, Inc. Fall-Winter 2015 - 17359 2016 $500

Upfield, Arthur W. *Valley of the Smugglers.* Garden City: published for the Crime Club by Doubleday, Doran and Co. Inc., 1960. First US edition, mild rubbing to bottom cloth edge, fine in fine dust jacket with touch of rubbing to upper corner tips and head of spine panel. John W. Knott, Jr./L.W. Currey, Inc. Fall-Winter 2015 - 17361 2016 $150

Upfield, Arthur W. *The White Savage.* Garden City: published for Crime Club by Doubleday Doran and Co., 1961. First US edition, fine in fine dust jacket. John W. Knott, Jr./L.W. Currey, Inc. Fall-Winter 2015 - 17362 2016 $150

Upfield, Arthur W. *The Will of the Tribe.* Garden City: published for the Crime Club by Doubleday Doran and Co., 1962. First US edition, fine in fine dust jacket with tiny closed tear (3mm) to upper left front corner with touch of rubbing to corner with touch of rubbing to corner tips, small rub spot to spine edge and touch of toning to spine panel. John W. Knott, Jr./L.W. Currey, Inc. Fall-Winter 2015 - 17363 2016 $150

Upham, Thomas C. *Elements of Intellectual Philosophy.* Portland: William Hyde, 1827. First edition, 8vo., contemporary two toned back cover, spine much chipped, partial printed label. M & S Rare Books, Inc. 99 - 255 2016 $325

Upham, Thomas C. *A Philosophical and Practical Treatise on the Will.* Portland: William Hyde, 1834. First edition, 8vo., original cloth, leather label, spine shot. M & S Rare Books, Inc. 99 - 254 2016 $500

Upton, William *The School Boy: a Poem.* London: William Darton, 1820. Color engravings, stabbed as issued, red card wrappers, printed label on front torn at lower right corners, spine rubbed and partly splitting, 6 leaves. Jarndyce Antiquarian Books CCXV - 787 2016 £125

Upward, Edward *In the Thirties.* London: Heinemann, 1962. First edition, octavo, fine in fine dust jacket. Peter Ellis 112 - 418 2016 £75

Upward, Edward *The Scenic Railway.* London: Enitharmon Press, 1997. First edition, octavo, number 44 of 50 hardbound copies, signed by author, fine in fine original acetate dust jacket. Peter Ellis 112 - 417 2016 £65

Urbanelli, Lora *The Wood Engravings of Lucien Pissaro & a Bibliography of the Eragny Press.* Cambridge: Silent Books and Ashmolean Museum, Oxford, 1994. First edition, octavo, card wrappers with flaps, well illustrated in color and black and white, bookplate inside front cover, fine. Peter Ellis 112 - 301 2016 £25

Urcullu, Jose De *The California Text-Book.* San Francisco: Marvin & Hitchcock, 1852. First edition, 12mo., publisher's quarter blind tooled red roan over vertically ribbed brown-purple cloth with gilt spine lettering, spine bumped and chipped with small ink smudge, light scattered foxing throughout, some small light waterstaining to upper margin of first half, overall very good, fragile and rare. Heritage Book Shop Holiday 2015 - 110 2016 $2500

Ure, Andrew *The Philosophy of Manufactures....* London: Charles Knight, Ludgate Street, 1835. First edition, 8vo., engraved frontispiece, 1 folding engraving, 1 folding table, engraved illustrations and tables in text, some foxing to title and frontispiece and folding plate common to many copies of this work, contemporary half calf, spine with red label lettered in gilt restored, bookplate of Edward Strutt, first Baron Belper (1801-1880). Marlborough Rare Books List 55 - 70 2016 £150

Uris, Leon *The Haj.* Franklin Center: Franklin Library, 1984. First edition, 8vo., 5 maps, all edges gilt, limited edition signed by author, stamped in gilt, leatherette, nice. Second Life Books, Inc. 196 B - 780 2016 $60

Uris, Leon *Mitla Pass.* New York: Doubleday, 1988. First edition, 8vo., author's signature on blank along with owner's embossed stamp, paper over boards with cloth spine, nice in little scuffed dust jacket, near fine. Second Life Books, Inc. 196 B - 781 2016 $125

Urquhart, D. H. *Commentaries on Classical Learning.* London: T. Cadell and W. Davies, 1803. First edition, titlepage slightly spotted, few thumbmarks, otherwise quite clean and fresh, 8vo., contemporary diced russia, boards bordered with gilt fillet, spine lettered gilt with decorative gilt lozenge shaped tools, extremities the merest touch rubbed, little surface damage to foot of front board, ownership inscription of Eldon, i.e. John Scott, 1st Earl of Eldon (1751-1838) and his armorial bookplate, very good. Blackwell's Rare Books Greek & Latin Classics VII - 15 2016 £150

Urquhart, David *The Lebanon: (Mount Souria) A History and a Diary.* Thomas Cautley Newby, 1860. Very rare first edition, 8vo., 2 volmes in 1, original brick red cloth, gilt, all edges gilt, steel engraved frontispiece to each volume, retaining tissue guard, expertly rebacked, preserving original endpapers, occaisonal spotting or embrowning, contemporary name on title, else very good. Sotheran's Travel and Exploration - 385 2016 £1950

Urquhart, Thomas *But Flashes of Wit. Epigrams from....* Tunbridge Wells: Foundling Press, 1999. 109/300 copies printed on Hahnemuhle paper, 11 wood engravings, printed in black, blue or purple, titlepage printed in black and purple, purple line border, 8vo., original plain plum wrappers, tail edges, rough trimmed, dust jacket, fine. Blackwell's Rare Books B186 - 306 2016 £50

Urrea, Luis Alberto *Nobody's Son.* University of Arizona Press, 1998. First edition, fine, early ARC copy, missing 20 pages and text that was included in the final version, signed by author. Bella Luna Books 2016 - 1096 2016 $75

Urrea, Luis Alberto *Vatos.* Cinco Puntos Press, 2000. First edition, photography by Jose Galvez, fine, paperback original, signed and dated by author, 9.2.00. Bella Luna Books 2016 - t11386 2016 $100

Ursini, Fulvio *Imagines et Elogia Virorum Illustrium.* Venice: Peitro Dechuchino for Antoine Lafrery, 1570. First edition, small folio, 19th century vellum backed marbled boards (rubbed), engraved title within architectural border with figure of fame seated above, signed with monogram of Andrea Marelli, 17 woodcuts and 58 engravings (mostly full page), some light marginal dampstaining, generally fresh copy. Maggs Bros. Ltd. 1474 - 77 2016 £3000

Usherwood, R. D. *Drawing for radio.* London: Bodley Head, 1961. First edition, 8vo., original brown boards lettered in silver, preserved in pictorial dust jacket, profusely illustrated in black and white, bookplate, fine in unclipped dust jacket. Sotheran's Piccadilly Notes - Summer 2015 - 310 2016 £60

Ussher, James *Clio or a Discourse on Taste...* Dublin: printed for John Milliken at No. 10 in Skinner Row, 1770. Second edition, 8vo., signature erased in ink at head of title, contemporary full calf, black morocco label, little rubbed, nice. Jarndyce Antiquarian Books CCXV - 452 2016 £280

Utility or Sketches of Domestic Education. London: Darton Harvey & Darton, 1815. 12mo., frontispiece, 2 pages ads, contemporary speckled calf, red morocco label, slightly rubbed, inscribed for Charles Ferdinand Keele, a gift from his father 27 Sept. 1847. Jarndyce Antiquarian Books CCXV - 994 2016 £65

Utley, Robert M. *The Lance and the Shield. The Life and Times of Sitting Bull.* New York: Henry Holt, 1993. First edition, 51 photographic illustrations, cloth and boards, very fine with pictorial dust jacket. Argonaut Book Shop Native American 2015 - 7652 2016 $45

Uvedale, Thomas *Memoirs of Philip De Comines...* London: John Phillips, 1712. 8vo., 2 volumes, early calf, rubbed and scuffed, joints tender, internally quite nice. Edwin V. Glaser Rare Books 2015 - 10384 2016 $100

V

Vaenius, Ernestus *Physiologicus de Pulchritudine, Juxta ea quae Sponsa in Canticis...* Brussels: F. Foppens, 1662. First and only edition, small octavo, full 18th century mottled calf gilt, engraved title and 28 engravings in text, text in Latin, near fine copy.   Honey & Wax Booksellers   4 - 3   2016 $2800

Val D'Osne *Album No. 2 Fontes D'Art.* Paris: Imprimeriem Typographique de P. Dubreuil 18 Rue Clauzel, 1908. Folio, wood engraved and half tone plates, 'bis' plates, original light green cloth lettered in black and onlaid illustration, unusually clean for a trade Catalogue.   Marlborough Rare Books   List 56 - 57   2016   £550

Valdes, Don Antonio *Derrotero De Las Costas De Espana en el Oceano Atlantico....* Por la Vinda de Ibarra, 1789. First edition, 8vo., contemporary brown full speckled calf, spine rubbed at head and tail, very good, crisp copy.   J. & S. L. Bonham Antiquarian Booksellers   Europe 2016 - 9727   2016   £800

Valdes, Jose Manuel *Disertaciones Medico-Quirurgicus Sobre Varios Puntos Importantes.* Madrid: Sancha, 1815. 12mo., full polished contemporary sheep, binding shows wear but intact, remnants of bookplate.   James Tait Goodrich   X-78 - 527   2016 $850

Valdivia, Pedro De *Prolog e Iconografia Miguel Rojas-Mix Transcripcion y Notas Mario Ferreccio Poedsta.* Madrid: Lumen, 1991. First edition, number 331 of 2000 copies printed, square large 4to., original black boards, illustrated dust jackets, original illustrated slipcase, elaborately illustrated, facsimiles, slipcase with slight bump to one corner, apart from that, fine, from the collection of a descendant of the founder of Chile with his contemporary collector's blindstamp.   Sotheran's   Travel and Exploration - 77   2016   £248

Valentia, George Annesley, Viscount *Voyages and Travels to India, Ceylon, The Red Sea, Abyssinia and Egypt in the Years 1802, 1803, 1804, 1805 and 1806.* London: William Miller, 1809. First edition, 3 volumes, 4to., full marbled calf, spines and borders of boards decorated in gilt in Grecian style, contrasting lettering pieces, marbled endpapers, 3 engraved vignettes, 60 engraved plates, 3 engraved folding plans at end of volume 3, very large folding map, 7 engraved folding maps and plans, rebacked at earlier date, wear to extremities, internally, apart from occasional spotting to plates and minor repairs to large map and light even toning to text, beautiful, wide margined and uniformly bound set, armorial engraved bookplates of William Baldwin, his name on two half titles.   Sotheran's   Travel and Exploration - 198   2016   £2995

Valentia, George Annesley, Viscount *Voyages and Travels to India, Ceylon, The Red Sea, Abyssinia and Egypt in the Years 1802, 1803, 1804, 1805 and 1806.* London: Wm. Miller, 1809. First edition, 3 volumes, quarto, engraved vignettes at head of first chapter of each volume, 66 engraved plates and charts, large folding plan, 2 large folding charts, some occasional browning and spotting volume II, 19th century brown full morocco, joints little rubbed, hinges strengthened.   J. & S. L. Bonham Antiquarian Booksellers   Voyages 2016 - 9376   2016   £1900

Valentine and Orson The Two Sons of the Emperour of Greece. London: by J. W. for E. Tracy, 1694. Small 4to., woodcut frontispiece and ads below, woodcut on titlepage and numerous woodcut illustrations in text, very small piece torn away the upper blank corner of woodcut frontispiece, minor rust hole through P1 (in text) and Dd2 (in margin), small hole worn through foot of 2b2, light worming to fore margin of T2-V3, rust stain to Bb4 (touching text), contemporary sheep, covers ruled in blind, inside joints split, old stain from glass on upper cover, minor staining on rear, faded contemporary inscription of Ann Hill, Albert M Cohn 20th century armorial bookplate, from the library of James Stevens Cox (1910-1997).   Maggs Bros. Ltd.   1447 - 422   2016   £650

Valentine, Mark *In Violet Veils and Other Tales of the Conoisseur.* Horam, East Sussex: Tarraus Press, 1999. First edition, one of 200 numbered copies signed by author, octavo, boards, fine in fine dust jacket.   John W. Knott, Jr./L.W. Currey, Inc.   Fall-Winter 2015 - 17345   2016 $450

Valentine, Mrs. *The Domestic Educator.* London: Frederick Warne & Co., circa, 1882. Half title, illustrations, yellowback, original blue printed paper boards, worn but sound.   Jarndyce Antiquarian Books   CCXV - 453   2016   £65

Valerius Flaccus, Quintus *Argonauticon Libri octo cum Notis Integris.* Leiden: Apud Samuelem Luchtmanus, 1724. 4to., additional engraved titlepage, presentation certificate and folding portrait, titlepage in red and black with engraved device, woodcut initials and ornaments, errata leaf, little toned, some occasional foxing, small loss to fore edge margin of page 19 not affecting text, vellum prize binding, title in red to spine, raised bands, gilt spine borders, frames, Amsterdam coat of arms to each board, edges sprinkled blue and red, bit yellowed, spine slightly darkened, some smudgy marks, ties lost, label removed from front pastedown, overall very good,. Unsworths Antiquarian Booksellers Ltd. E04 - 24 2016 £350

Vallance, Aymer *The Old Colledes of Oxford: their Architectural History Illustrated and Described.* London: Batsford, n.d., 1913. First edition, large 4to., original blue buckram, lettered and decorated gilt on spine and front cover, copiously illustrated in black and white, very good+, excellent. Any Amount of Books 2015 - C13540 2016 £170

Vallee, Rudy *Vagabond Dreams Come True.* New York: Dutton, 1930. First edition, 8vo. photos, very good, inscribed by author for Harry Chaffin, also inscribed to same by Elliott B. MacRae, president of Dutton. Second Life Books, Inc. 196 B - 783 2016 $100

Vallee, Rudy *Vagabond Dreams Come True.* New York: Dutton, 1930. First edition, limited to 299 copies signed by crooner, large paper, 8vo., laid in is camera portrait for frontispiece, boards, cloth spine, small corner bumps, otherwise nice. Second Life Books, Inc. 196 B - 784 2016 $225

Valmore, Marceline Desbordes *Le Livre des Enfants Poesies.* Paris: Garnier Freres, 1924. First edition, large 4to., cloth backed pictorial boards, fine, color illustrations on every page by Andre Helle. Aleph-bet Books, Inc. 111 - 218 2016 $525

Van *Fun with Faces.* Garden City: Garden City Books, 1950. 4to., spiral backed boards, tiny bit of rubbing, else near fine, bright color illustrations by Julian Wehr, 6 comical color plates operated with tabs letting the reader make comical faces. Aleph-bet Books, Inc. 111 - 312 2016 $450

Van Allsburg, Chris *Jumanji.* Boston: Houghton Mifflin, 1981. First edition, first printing with 1-10 code, 4to., cloth, slightest bit of rubbing, else near fine in very good+ dust jacket (slightly darkened in upper corner, slight wear on small part of bottom edge, no award seal, not price clipped), signed by author. Aleph-bet Books, Inc. 112 - 489 2016 $850

Van Allsburg, Chris *Polar Express.* Boston: Houghton Mifflin, 1985. First edition, very good+ in dust jacket with 2 closed edge tears, soiled around edges of front cover and spine, no award seal, magnificent color illustrations. Aleph-bet Books, Inc. 112 - 490 2016 $400

Van Allsburg, Chris *The Sweetest Fig.* Boston: Houghton Mifflin, 1993. First edition, first printing with 1-10 code, cloth backed boards, as new in dust jacket, illustrations in color, signed by author. Aleph-bet Books, Inc. 112 - 491 2016 $125

Van De Wetering, Jan Willem *Robert Van Gulik. His Life His Work.* Miami Beach: Dennis Macmillan Publications, 1967. First edition, limited to 350 copies, each signed and numbered by author, this #14, fine in dust jacket. Buckingham Books 2015 - 26973 2016 $450

Van Der Elsken, Ed *Love on the Left.* London: Andre Deutsch, 1956. First edition, small quarto, fine in nice, near fine dust jacket with little rubbing and couple of very small nicks and tear at extremities, very uncommon. Between the Covers Rare Books 208 - 64 2016 $2500

Van Der Weele, H. W. *Ascalaphiden: Monographisch Bearbeitet.* Brussels: Hayez, Impr. Des Academies, 1908. Large quarto, 2 colored plates, text illustrations, binder's cloth, very good. Andrew Isles Natural History Books 55 - 20344 2016 $400

Van Deusen, John G. *The Black Man in White America.* Washington: Associated Pub., 1944. Revised edition, 8vo., author's signature on title, very good in well worn dust jacket, illustrations by Lois Mailou Jones. Second Life Books, Inc. 196 B - 785 2016 $125

Van Doren, Carl *Swift.* New York: Viking, 1930. First edition, portraits, author's presentation, tan cloth, cover slightly worn at edges and faded, otherwise very good, tight copy. Second Life Books, Inc. 196 B - 786 2016 $40

Van Doren, Mark *Edwin Arlington Robinson.* New York: Literary Guild, 1927. First edition, small 8vo., portrait, cover little soiled, little nicked at top of spine, otherwise very good, this copy inscribed by Robinson "Mark's Copy (given by) Edwin Arlington (Robinson) May 1927". Second Life Books, Inc. 196 B - 790 2016 $150

Van Druten, John *Old Acquaintance.* New York: Random House, 1941. First edition, 8vo., no dust jacket but very good copy, signed by cast of the play, bookplate of critic Hugh Beaumont. Second Life Books, Inc. 196 B - 791 2016 $175

Van Dyke, Henry *The Unknown Quantity.* New York: Scribner's, 1912. First edition, 8vo., illustrations, prayer inscribed by author, bookplate, blue cloth stamped in gilt, orange and blue by Margaret Armstrong, cover little worn at edges, otherwise very good, tight copy. Second Life Books, Inc. 196 B - 792 2016 $65

Van Fossan, Edward *Race to Happiness.* Philadelphia: Dorrance Co., 1971. First edition, foxing on front endpaper, else fine in very slightly spine toned, ele fine, dust jacket, long inscription by author to co-worker, uncommon. Between the Covers Rare Books   208 - 10   2016 $300

Van Gulik, Robert *The Chinese Bell Murders.* London: Michael Joseph, 1958. First edition, fine in price clipped dust jacket, lightly soiled along top edge of rear panel. Buckingham Books   2015 - 14577   2016 $450

Van Gulik, Robert *The Chinese Lake Murders.* London: Michael Joseph, 1960. First edition, fine in price clipped dust jacket, lightly soiled on rear panel and faint evidence of glue residue from removal of small label from front and spine panels. Buckingham Books   2015 - 34201   2016 $450

Van Gulik, Robert *The Chinese Lake Murders.* New York: Harper, 1962. First American edition, fine in dust jacket with chip at base of spine.   Mordida Books   2015 - 007274   2016 $60

Van Gulik, Robert *The Haunted Monastery.* London: Heinemann, 1963. First UK edition, fine in dust jacket, exceptional copy.   Buckingham Books   2015 - 26985   2016 $450

Van Gulik, Robert *The Monkey and the Tiger.* London: Heinemann, 1965. First edition, fine in dust jacket, lightly sunned on spine.   Buckingham Books   2015 - 3424   2016 $450

Van Gulik, Robert *New Year's Eve in Lan-Fang.* Beirut: Imprimerie Catholique, 1958. First edition, limited 200 copies, fine in printed wrappers, very scarce, housed in four point case that is inserted into cloth slipcase with leather labels on spine and titles stamped in gold.   Buckingham Books   2015 - 26901   2016 $3250

Van Loey-Nouri *Specimen De La Fonderie Typograhique Van Loey-Nouri.* Bruxelles: Van Loey-Nouri, n.d. circa, 1930. 4to., original quarter leather over cloth, leather worn along hinges with partially split bottom at front hinge, internally fine.   Oak Knoll Books   310 - 192   2016 $1250

Van Straelen *Resultats Scientifiques du Voyage aux Indes Orientales Neerlandaises.* Brussels: Musee Royal D'Histoire de Belgique, 1933. Quarto, numerous text illustrations and plate, publishers printed wrappers, total of 40 fascicles, few small library stamps and minor blemishes, otherwise sound, clean set.   Andrew Isles Natural History Books   55 - 33118   2016 $400

Van Vechten, Carl   1880-1964 *Nigger Heaven.* New York: Alfred A. Knopf, 1926. First edition, some chipping to cloth at crown, front hinge neatly restored, still sound, very good, lacking rare dust jacket, inscribed by author for Dorothy Peterson, spectacular association copy.   Between the Covers Rare Books   202 - 110   2016 $4000

Van Vechten, Carl   1880-1964 *Spider Boy: a Scenaro for a Moving Picture.* New York: Alfred A. Knopf, 1928. First edition, signed by author, number 174 of 220 copies, original cloth backed blue boards, lettered gilt spine faded, slight rubbing to extremities, glue stain to front endpaper, overall fine.   Argonaut Book Shop   Literature 2015 - 1625   2016 $125

Van Vogt, A. E. *The Mind Cage.* New York: Simon and Schuster, 1957. First edition, octavo, fine in fine dust jacket, very slightly creased at edges.   Peter Ellis   112 - 419   2016   £45

Van Waters, George *Poetical Geography designed to Accompany Outline Maps or School Atlases.* Published at Cincinnati, Philadelphia: Hartford: New York: and Boston, 1849. First edition, uncommon edition, numerous black and white engravings, 8vo., stitched paper wrappers, corners worn on front wrapper and first few leaves, rear wrapper chipped at top edge with minor loss, leaves foxed, horizontal tide line at center, contemporary restitch, adding an additional new plain protective wrapper of which only rear present, still good copy.   Kaaterskill Books   21 - 108   2016 $150

Van Zandt, Townes *For the Sake of the Song.* San Antonio: Wings Press, 1977. First edition, one of 500 copies signed and numbered by Van Zandt and numbered, roughly 100 of were given to Van Zandt as author's copies, near fine in photo illustrated boards with no dust jacket as issued, gift inscribed from Indian Tom.   Royal Books   52 - 8   2016 $2500

Vanbrugh, John *Aesop. A comedy.* London: printed for Richard Wellington, 1702. First few leaves stained at head, recent marble wrappers, 4to.   Jarndyce Antiquarian Booksellers   CCXVI - 473   2016   £120

Vance, John Holbrook *Lyonesse: Suldren's Garden; with Lyonesse: The Green Pearl. with Lyonesse: Madouc.* San Francisco: Columbia: Underwood Miller, 1983. 1985. 1989. First hardcover and first editions, one of 26 lettered sets signed by author, this being set "U", octavo, 3 volumes, quarter leather backed cloth, fine set, cloth slipcase.   John W. Knott, Jr./L.W. Currey, Inc.   Fall-Winter 2015 - 17229   2016 $4500

Vancouver, George *A Voyage of Discovery to the North Pacific Ocean and Round the World.* London: printed for G. G. and J. Robinson and J. Edwards, 1798. First edition, 3 volumes, quarto, plus folio atlas, 18 engraved plates, one of which is a map, with half titles and errata, 10 folding maps and 6 plates of profiles in atlas volume, text volumes bound in contemporary speckled calf, all volumes uniformly rebacked to style, with double blind ruled borders, spines each with blue calf label, red morocco label, stamped and lettered gilt, edges speckled brown, marbled endpapers, boards bit scuffed and bumped, volume I with some minor worming to lower margin, mainly a single hole and not affecting text, remnants of previous owner's old ink inscription on half title of volume 1, now mostly rubbed away, front inner hinge of volume II split but still firm, volume II with minor dampstain to fore edges which shows slightly to bottom margin of few pages and bit darker on final blank, volume Ii has few pages (283-286) with crease through middle affecting text of few lines, plates with some light foxing and pages facing plates, bit toned, otherwise text extremely clean, atlas bound in half modern speckled calf over marbled boards, boards lightly soiled, few folding maps with minor repairs and small tears to creases, with no loss, plate 5 map with 3 inch closed tear at inner margin, also with no loss, overall excellent set, tall, clean and complete. Heritage Book Shop Holiday 2015 - 111 2016 $52,500

Vanderpoel, Halstead *A Catalogue of the VanderPoel Dickens Collection at the University of Texas.* Austin: University of Texas, 1968. Half title, frontispiece, illustrations, original brown cloth, very good in dust jacket. Jarndyce Antiquarian Booksellers CCXVIII - 1523 2016 £25

Vane, C. W. *A Steam Voyage to Constaninople; by the Rhine and the Danube in 1840-1841.* London: Henry Colburn, 1842. First edition, 2 volumes, 8vo., contemporary brown diced calf, expertly rebacked, some occasional light foxing. J. & S. L. Bonham Antiquarian Booksellers Europe 2016 - 9695 2016 £850

Vane, Gillan, Pseud. *A Great Mystery Solved.* London: Sampson Low, Marston & Co., 1914. Half title, 16 page catalog, odd spot, original dark blue cloth lettered in pale blue and gilt, slightly rubbed, small repaired tears at head and tail of spine, Eric Jones-Evans booklabel, good plus. Jarndyce Antiquarian Booksellers CCXVIII - 663 2016 £45

Varavenargues, Luc De Clapeirs, Marquis De *Maximes.* Arthur l. Humphresy, 1903. Handsomely printed edition, 8vo., 3 volumes, half gilt ruled brown morocco, spine panelled and lettered gilt, top edge gilt, very good. Sotheran's Piccadilly Notes - Summer 2015 - 311 2016 £450

Varesi, Gilda *Enter Madame: a Play in three acts.* New York: Putnam, 1921. First edition, 8vo., cloth backed boards, very good, inscribed by author under frontispiece and signed by 10 members of the cast including Norman Trevor, Jane Meredith, Gavin Muir, etc. Second Life Books, Inc. 196 B - i794 2016 $250

Varlo, Charles *A New System of Husbandry Shewing How to Raise Good Crops Without Manure.* Philadelphia: printed for the author, 1785. First American edition, 12mo., 2 volumes, folding plate, lacks folding frontispiece, contemporary calf, runbed, very sound, nice set. M & S Rare Books, Inc. 99 - 314 2016 $650

Varmus, Harold *The Art and Politics of Science.* New York: W. W. Norton, 2009. First edition, 8vo., fine in near fine dust jacket. By the Book, L. C. 45 - 25 2016 $250

Vasarely, Victor *Planetary Folklore.* Greenwich: New York Graphic Society, 1973. First American edition, square 8vo., photos and reproductions in color and black and white, fine in slightly chipped and scuffed dust jacket, signed by artist. Second Life Books, Inc. 196 B - 795 2016 $150

Vasari, Giorgio *Lives of the Most Eminent Painters.* New York: Heritage Press, 1967. 2 volumes, printed boards with burgundy cloth spines, lettered gilt, very fine spot of soiling to edge of spine on volume one and extremely slight rubbing to boards, slight bump to foot of spine of volume two, fine set in slipcases, minor fading and some wear to slipcases, Sandglass pamphlet laid in. Argonaut Book Shop Heritage Press 2015 - 7108 2016 $75

Vaughan, Francis E. *Andrew C. Lawson, Scientist, Teacher, Philosopher.* Glendale: Arthur H. Clark, 1970. First edition, frontispiece, 12 full page illustrations from photographs, facsimile letters, gilt lettered blue cloth, bookplate, else fine. Argonaut Book Shop Biography 2015 - 5383 2016 $60

Vaumoriere, Pierre D'Ortigue *The Art of Pleasing in Conversation.* London: A. Bettesworth & F. Clay, 1722. 12mo., contemporary full calf, spine rubbed and worn and with loss to head and tail, lacking label, signature of John Maxwell, Christ Church College, bookplate of Maxwell of Polloc. Jarndyce Antiquarian Books CCXV - 454 2016 £120

Vaurie, Charles *Tibet and its Birds.* London: H. F. & G. Witherby, 1972. Large octavo, 3 color plates, photos, very good in slightly grubby dust jacket. Andrew Isles Natural History Books 55 - 13713 2016 $150

Vautel, Clement *Resemblances.* Paris: B. Sirvan, n.d. circa, 1925. 4to., cloth backed pictorial boards, light edge rubbing and slight rear over soil, very good+, 9 animals featured, with color lithographs, rare.   Aleph-bet Books, Inc.   111 - 340   2016 $1375

Vaux, Robert *Memoirs of the Life of Anthony Benezet.* York: W. Alexander, 1817. First UK edition, 12mo., frontispiece, original boards with paper backstrip and title label, early name plates (Thomas Marsh and Robert Langdon), some foxing to prelims, cup ring to front cover, backstrip defective, label rubbed, very good, scarce in original state.   Peter Ellis   112 - 363   2016   £750

Vaux, Robert *Memoirs of the Life of Anthony Benezet.* Philadelphia: published by James P. Parke/Merritt, Printer, 1817. First edition, 12mo, lacking front board and frontispiece, rear board detached but present, pages toned but uncut, wear along spine, wear affecting couple of letters of inscription, good plus, inscribed by author for Prince Saunders, housed in half morocco clamshell case, marvelous association copy.   Between the Covers Rare Books   202 - 113   2016 $6500

Veen, Otto Van *Q. Horati Flacci Embelmata.* Antwerp: ex officina Hieronymi Verdussen, 1607. First edition, 4to., oval portrait of Horace on titlepage and 103 full page emblems, 20th century vellum, title lettered ink on spine, 18th century notes on verso of half title, small stamp off ex-libris Alex Martin, fore-margins cropped, closely at times, pages 123 and 129 touching platemark of emblem.   Maggs Bros. Ltd.   1474 - 78   2016   £2600

Velikovsky, Immanuel *Worlds in Collision.* London: Victor Gollancz, 1950. First English edition, 8vo., original dark blue cloth, backstrip lettered in gilt with just touch of softening at foot, some light foxing to edges, ownership inscription to flyleaf with faint partial browning to free endpapers, dust jacket with some light foxing and backstrip panel little sunned, owner's shelfmark at head of front flap, very good.   Blackwell's Rare Books   B184 - 242   2016   £80

Velpeau, A. L. M. *Nouveau Elements de Medeine Operatoire Accompagnes d'un Atlas de 20 Planches in-40 Gravees...*   Paris: J. B. Bailliere, 1832-1839. 191 illustrations in text plus atlas with 20 engraved plates, 8vo., 4 volumes in early three quarter morocco over marbled boards, atlas is folio original printed wrappers, text volumes sound and near fine, some foxing to text but good, partially opened copy.   Edwin V. Glaser Rare Books   2015 - 10230   2016 $750

Venables, Robert *The Experienced Angler or Angling Improv'd.* London: by Benjamin White for B. Tooke and Tho. Sawbridge, 1683. Fifth edition (i.e. fourth edition), small 8vo., engraved frontispiece (backed with old paper and bound right to inner margin with some early blotted ink pen trials at head, ten small engravings in text of various fish, lightly browned, margins spotted throughout, margins trimmed throughout, many sidenotes and few signatures and catchwords shaved, early 20th century plain brown sheep, gilt edges, spine lightly stained, from the library of James Stevens Cox (1910-1997).   Maggs Bros. Ltd.   1447 - 423   2016   £750

Venet, Marc *Photos de Cinema: Autour de la Nouvelle Vague 1958-1968.* Paris: Image France Editions, 2007. First edition, deluxe monograph, fine in illustrated paper covered boards.   Royal Books   49 - 63   2016 $75

Venice Saved from the Sea.   New York: High Tide Press, 1995. Limited to only 15 numbered copies and signed by artist, John Ross, 4to. turquoise cloth boards with wave pattern, lined in blue slubbed silk, matching silk slipcase with recessed paper title label, unpaginated, accordion fold, collagraph images with two three-page foldouts.   Oak Knoll Books   27 - 28   2016 $2000

Venn, Jules *Early Collegiate Life.* Cambridge: W. Heffer & Sons, 1913. Half title, 1 page ads, original dark green pictorial cloth, very good.   Jarndyce Antiquarian Books   CCXV - 379   2016   £25

Venn, Otto Van *Emblemes de l'Amour Divin.* Paris: chez P. Landry, n.d. c., 1670. Engraved titlepage and 59 full page engravings with Latin mottoes and French epigrams, 12mo., exquisitely bound in contemporary red morocco, triple gilt fillet on covers, flat spine gilt in compartments with central fleuron to each panel, double panel for green morocco label lettered in gilt 'EMBLEMES", inscription "Madame de Brebeuf", partly inked over,.   Maggs Bros. Ltd.   1474 - 79   2016   £2500

Vetustissimorum Poetarum Hesiodi, Theocriti, Theognidis, Moschi, Musaei, Bionis....   Paris: Apud Joannem Libert, 1628. Rare edition, ownership inscription of John Nicholas of Queen's College, Oxford dated 1641, general titlepage damaged at gutter from cracked hinge and just starting to loosen, 8vo., contemporary English calf, spine with four raised bands between double blind fillets, boards also bordered with double blind fillet, edges red, bit marked, spine ends worn, some surface loss to leather on front board, joints cracking little but strong, bookplate of Colonel Sir Charles J. J. Hamilton, Baronet.   Blackwell's Rare Books   B186 - 68   2016   £1500

Ventum, Harriet *Selina, a Novel, Founded on Facts.* London: printed for C. Law, 1800. First edition, 3 volumes, titlepage to volume III in very good facsimile on contemporary paper, some browning and finger marking to text in places, offsetting on pastedowns and endpapers, full contemporary sheep, spines rubbed, lacking labels, some cracking across bands, heads chipped but joints sound, early signatures to titlepages of Mary Windale and later 19th century name of T. E. Headlam, Gilmonby Hall (Yorkshire). Jarndyce Antiquarian Booksellers   CCXVI - 577   2016   £750

Verborum Anomalorum in Graeca Lingua Investigatio. In Usum Scholae Regiae Salopiensis. Shrewsbury: Prostant Venales Apud Josh. Eddowes, 1774. 8vo., little minor spotting, original quarter sheep, marbled boards, rather rubbed and worn, joints cracked but cords holding, ownership inscription of Richard Price, August 31st. 1786, with his bookplate, sound, rare, unsophisticated copy.   Blackwell's Rare Books   Greek & Latin Classics VII - 24   2016   £550

Verbruggen, J. F. *The Battle of the Golden Spurs.* Woodbridge: Boydell Press, 2002. First revised edition in English, 8vo., illustrations, light brown cloth, gilt lettered to spine, dust jacket, as new.   Unsworths Antiquarian Booksellers Ltd.   E05 - 91   2016   £25

Verelst, Harry *A View of the Rise, Progress and Present State of the English Government in Bengal...* London: printed for J. Nourse, 1772. First edition, 4to., front endpaper little dusted, some very neat pencil notes in margins, fine, full contemporary pale calf, double gilt fillet border, gilt spine in six compartments, red morocco label, armorial bookplate of William Constable, Esq. of Burton Constable, Yorkshire.   Jarndyce Antiquarian Booksellers   CCXVI - 578   2016   £1100

Vergil, Polydorus *Proverbiorum Libellus.* Venice: per Ioannen de Cereto de Tridino alis Tacuinum, 1503. Rare and early edition, 4to., roughly half the gatherings browned, some light spotting and frequent marginal notes and underlining in early hand (some shaved), recto of final leaf dusty, 4to., modern boards, covered with incunable leaf, lightly soiled and spotted.   Blackwell's Rare Books   B186 - 157   2016   £1500

Vergilius Maro, Publius *The Nyne Fyst Bookes of the Eneidos of Virgil Converted into Englishe...* London: by Rouland Hall for Nicholas Englande, 1562. Woodcut on title, text in black letter, 19th century morocco, ruled in gilt, edges gilt, extremities lightly worn, minor scuffing, first quire washed and neatly extended at top edge, possibly supplied from another copy, few internal repairs, else very good, with excellent full margins, Rubislaw House bookplate of John Morgan, rare early edition.   Joseph J. Felcone, Inc. Books from Five Centuries: a Miscellany - 145   2016 $11,000

Vergilius Maro, Publius *Virgils Aeneis.* Edinburgh: printed by Mr. Andrew Symson and MR. Robert Freebairns and sold at their Shops, 1710. First Ruddman edition, title within double ruled border, occasional foxing or browning (less than usual), some waterstaining at end, mainly marginal diminishing and not extending much beyond index, little, but lesser, staining at beginning, folio, contemporary panelled calf, some wear, cracks at extremities of joints, ownership of Thomas Graham, fourth Laird of Balgowan, modern bookplate of Robert Maxtone Graham.   Blackwell's Rare Books B184 - 35   2016   £650

Vergilius Maro, Publius *Bucolica, Georgica, et Aeneis.* Impensis J. et P. Knapton in Vico Ludgate et Gul. Sandby, 1750. 8vo., contemporary sprinkled calf, boards bordered with decorative gilt roll, rebacked (in different colour) preserving old lettering pieces and endpapers, corners repaired, armorial bookplate, good, 58 engraved plates, paper lightly toned and spotted.   Blackwell's Rare Books Greek & Latin Classics VII - 93   2016   £200

Vergilius Maro, Publius *Bucolica, Georgica, et Aeneis.* Birmingham: typis Johannis Baskerville, 1757. First Baskerville edition, initial blank creased as often, small wormhole to lower blank margin in last quarter of book, stretching into short trail towards end, one leaf in subscriber's list with small dampstain to lower corner, 4to., later mottled calf, spine richly gilt, green morocco lettering piece, marbled endpapers, touch rubbed at extremities, very good. Blackwell's Rare Books   Greek & Latin Classics VII - 94 2016   £1500

Vergilius Maro, Publius *Bucolica, Georgica et Aeneis.* Birmingham: Typis Johannis Baskerville. 1757, but circa, 1770. Concealed second edition, 4to., some light toning and foxing, contemporary red crushed morocco, spine divided by raised bands between double gilt fillets, green morocco lettering pieces in second compartment and at foot, marbled endpapers, edges gilt, board edges and turn-ins gilt, little bit marked and rubbed, spine slightly faded, very good. Blackwell's Rare Books   Greek & Latin Classics VII - 95 2016   £750

Vergilius Maro, Publius *Publii Virgilii Maronis Bucolica et Georgica tabulis Aeneis Olim a Johanne Pine Sculptore Regio...* n.p., 1774. 2 volumes bound as one, 80 plates on 59 sheets (including two frontispieces), titlepages and section titles and 6 engraved dedications, two of them on verso of letterpress pages, one plate folding, frequent further engravings within text, complete with ad leaf at front which is often discarded, some foxing and offsetting from plates, 8vo., contemporary vellum, spine divided by a gilt roll, second compartment dyed yellow and lettered gilt, marbled endpapers, vellum soiled, boards splaying outward somewhat, bookplate of Henry Anthony Littledale and ownership inscription of G. A. Littledale to front endpapers. Blackwell's Rare Books   Greek & Latin Classics VII - 96 2016   £500

Vergilius Maro, Publius *Bucolica et Georgica tabullis Aeneis Olim a Johanne Pine...* n.p., 1774. 2 volumes bound as one, 80 plates on 59 sheets, frequent further engravings within text, ad leaf discarded, 8vo., contemporary tree calf, spine divided by gilt fillet, red morocco lettering piece, other compartments with central sunburst gilt tools, bit rubbed, spine creased, gutters cracking towards middle of textbock but binding perfectly sound, bookplates of Magdalen College, Oxford and Sir Richard Paul Jodrell, with inscription indicating the gift of the volume from the former to the latter dated 1802, good.   Blackwell's Rare Books   B186 - 160   2016   £600

Vergilius Maro, Publius *Les Bucoliques.* Paris: Philippe Gonin, 1951. One of 200 copies, 327 x 248mm., loose as issued in publisher's cream colored wrappers and vellum backed portfolio, black titling on spine, in later patterned paper slipcase with 80 wood engravings by Lucile Passavant, first prelim leaf warmly inscribed to Ed and Mary (Thom?), inscribed by the artist for the Thoms, greeting card illustrated by artist inscribed for Thoms laid in, hint of soil to spine, corners worn to boards, faint freckling to covers, text with isolated trivial foxing, excellent copy, text clean and fresh and binding a good deal more than good enough.   Phillip J. Pirages   67 - 348   2016 $3000

Vergilius Maro, Publius *Les Bucoliques De Virgile.* Paris: Scripta & Picta, 1953. First Villon edition, one of 245 copies (total edition), folio, text pages loosely inserted in publisher's paper folder, chemise and slipcase, 45 original lithographs by Jacques Villon, hors- and in texte, printed on Arches wove paper by F. Mourlot, outer slipcase faded and worn along edges, book very fine, bookplate of Margaret Winkelman, Paul Valery's copy.   Oak Knoll Books   310 - 7   2016 $4500

Vergilius Maro, Publius *Die Eclogen Vergils in Der Ursprache Und Deutsch.* Weimar: Cranach, 1926. No. 42 of 250 copies on handmade, 335 x 247 mm., pure hemp rag (of a total edition of 294), with 8 on vellum and 36 on Kessler Maillol silk rag, recent black crushed morocco, earlier large onlaid crimson crushed morocco label on front cover, raised bands, gilt titling on spine, top edge gilt, housed in later green cloth slipcase, woodcut title vignette, 42 woodcut illustrations, two initials, and press-mark by Aristide Maillol, woodcut lettering and initials by Eric Gill, large paper copy, 3 pages with tiny spot of foxing, but in extremely fine condition, binding unworn, cuts in very fresh impressions and beautiful paper especially fresh, bright and clean.   Phillip J. Pirages   67 - 97   2016 $4500

Vergilius Maro, Publius *Maronis Codex Antiqvissimvs a Rvfio Tvrcio Aproniano V.C. Distinctvs et Emendatvs Qvi Nvnc Florentiae in Bibliotheca Mediceo-Lawrentiana....* Florence: typis Mannianis, 1741. 4to., titlepage printed in red and black, some passages of text also printed in red engraved dedication with architectural border, engraved title vignette, engraved head and tailpieces, engraved initial, some headlines cropped, minor dampstaining at beginning, 4to., 19th or early 20th century italian patterned boards, maroon lettering piece on spine, spine darkened, upper joint split but structure sound, good.   Blackwell's Rare Books   B186 - 159   2016   £500

Vergilius Maro, Publius *(Oper) Cum Veterum Omnium Commentariis et Selectis Recentiorum Notis Nova Editio.* Lugduni Batavorum: ex officina Abraham Commelini, 1646. 4to., engraved titlepage, woodcut initials, slightly narrow margin at head edge, small hole to margin of page 3, repair and tear to page 303, not affecting text, contemporary speckled brown calf prize binding, red morocco label to spine, gilt borders and coat of arms of Hoorn to each board, spine creased and little rubbed, small neat repair headcap, edges bit worn, very good, stub of excised prize certificate just visible after first gathering, Library inkstamp (Amsterdam") to titlepage verso.   Unsworths Antiquarian Booksellers Ltd.   E01 - Early Printing - 29   2016   £650

Vergilius Maro, Publius *The Works of...* London: by Thomas Maxey for Andrew Crook, 1650. Second edition, 8vo., engraved portrait of Ogilby and additional engraved title by William Marshall (both dated 1649), minor rust spots to a number of leaves throughout, with upper corners of last few leaves creased, contemporary sheep covers ruled in blind, later (but old) paper labels on spine, worn, leather along fore-edge of front board chewed away and starting to detach, corners of lower cover chewed, joints split, headcaps missing, corners bumped, 'Charles Moore his Book', early inscription and early signature 'John Ogilvy", from the library of James Stevens Cox (1910-1997).   Maggs Bros. Ltd.   1447 - 424   2016   £180

Vergilius Maro, Publius *The Works of...* London: sold by Tho. Guy, 1684. Ninth edition, 8vo., engraved titlepage by Drapentier and 32 engraved plates, occasional rust spots, small closed tear to blank fore margin of D7 (not affecting text), contemporary sheep (nasty 19th century reback, now worn again with upper joint split, corners and edges chewed, 19th century endpapers), from the library of James Stevens Cox (1910-1997), 19th century armorial bookplate of John Frederick Doveton.   Maggs Bros. Ltd.   1447 - 425   2016   £180

Vergilius Maro, Publius *Opera.* Edinburgh: apud Robertum Freebarnium, 1732. Small stain to blank margin of last quarter, ownership inscription of Allan Livingston (early) and Mary Lloyd Aston (20th century), 24mo., contemporary Scottish red morocco, spine gilt in compartments containing a saltire design, boards with central cross shape made up of arabesques containing dotted lines with thistles at its points, corners with square tools containing fan sprays, endpapers of decorative paper in multiple colours with gilt, edges gilt, joints cracking but strong, leather bit darkened, good.   Blackwell's Rare Books   Greek & Latin Classics VII - 92   2016   £500

Vergilius Maro, Publius *The Works of Virgil.* Birmingham: printed by John Baskerville for the author, 1766. Sole edition, 8vo., later full speckled calf by Bedford, boards with french fillet border, spine richly gilt with contrasting leather labels, joints little rubbed, spine slightly sunned, marginal dampstain to pages 529-536, bookplate of Glenconnor, otherwise very good.   Sotheran's   Piccadilly Notes - Summer 2015 - 315   2016   £500

Vergilius Maro, Publius *Opera Varietate Lectiones et Perpetua Adnotations Illustrata....* Typis T.. Rickaby, Impensis T. Payne, B. & J. White, R. Faulder, & J. Edwards, 1793. Large paper copy, engraved frontispiece and dedication, one bifolium missed by stitching and hence loose, little minor toning and spotting, 4to., contemporary straight grained red morocco by Kalthoeber, with his ticket in volume i, boards bordered with triple gilt fillet, spines divided by raised bands between gilt titles, second and third compartments, gilt lettered direct, edges gilt, marbled endpapers, joints rubbed, spines somewhat scuffed, little darkening to spine and joints, from old polishing attempt?, short tear to head of front joint volume i, armorial bookplate of John Perrett, good.   Blackwell's Rare Books   B184 - 88   2016   £1200

Vergilius Maro, Publius *Opera, Varietate Lectiones et Perpetua Adnotatione Illustrata....* Typis T. Rickaby, Impensis T. Payne, B. & J. White, R. Faulder & J. Edwards, 1793. 8vo., 4 volumes, engraved frontispiece and dedication, some spotting and offsetting, contemporary russia, boards bordered with greek key gilt roll, spines divided by raised bands between gilt fillets, second and fourth compartments gilt lettered direct, first and sixth gilt decoration, third and fifth with same tool in blind behind a smaller central gilt tool, edges patterned with brown dye, touch of rubbing to joints, one raised band, small chip, very good copy.   Blackwell's Rare Books   Greek & Latin Classics VII - 97   2016   £1200

Vergilius Maro, Publius *Opera Omnia.* Oxford and London: Johannes Henricus et Jacobus Parker, 1859. 12mo., few pencil annotations, titlepage slightly separated from flyleaf, toning to occasional leaf but generally clean within, brown calf, gilt spine with red morocco label, all edges red, spine little faded, endcaps rubbed, very good.   Unsworths Antiquarian Booksellers Ltd.   E05 - 64   2016   £20

Verheyen, Philip *Corporis Humani Anatomiae Liber Primus in Quo Tam Veteru Quam Recentiorum Anatomicorum Inventia.* Brussels: Apud Fratres Serstevens, 1710. Second edition, 2 volumes bound in 1, engraved frontispiece, 46 engraved folding plates, small 4to., contemporary full calf, gilt spine with raised bands joints just starting, light browning to text, some fraying to plate edges, otherwise very good, clean tight.   James Tait Goodrich   X-78 - 528   2016 $1795

Verlaine, Paul 1844-1898 *Parallelement.* Argenteuil: R. Colouma and Paris: Cereballaud & Jonnart for the artist and Dec. May 25, 1931. Privately printed number XVI of the 23 copies on Japon ancien reserved for the artist (total print run 198 copies) with Edouard Chimot's aquatint etchings in first state, large 4to., loose and entirely uncut in original printed wrappers, half title, 23 full page etchings with aquatint (some color printed or tinted), spine of wrappers little rubbed and worn, remnants of contemporary half calf folder and slipcase, few leaves with marginal blue ink spots,.   Sotheran's   Piccadilly Notes - Summer 2015 - 313   2016   £3500

Vermeire, Robert *Cocktails: How to Mix Them.* Worcester: The Trinity Press, circa, 1930. Eighth printing, half title, 4 pages ads, original red decorated boards, slightly marked, otherwise very good.   Jarndyce Antiquarian Booksellers   CCXVII - 289   2016   £38

Verne, Jules 1828-1905 *Godfrey Morgan: a Californian Mystery.* London: Sampson Low, Marston, Searle & Rivington, 1883. First British edition, frontispiece, vignette title, illustrations, further 47 plates by Leon Bennett, short tear in upper margin of pages 23/24 without loss, original dark green cloth, pictorially blocked in black, lettered in black and gilt, edges very slightly spotted, still very good, bright.   Jarndyce Antiquarian Booksellers   CCXVII - 290   2016   £500

Verne, Jules 1828-1905 *A Journey to the Centre of the Earth...* New York: Scribner Armstrong & Co. 654 Broadway, n.d., 1874? First printing of Scribner Armstrong's complete edition, 55 full page illustrations and titlepage vignette by Riou original bevel edged blue cloth, 12mo., front and spine panels stamped in black and gold, rear panel stamped in blind, yellow endpapers, tiny early owner's name stamped to titlepage and his small book label affixed to front pastedown, spine ends and corner tips strengthened, inner rear hinge mended, bright, very good, very nice.   John W. Knott, Jr./L.W. Currey, Inc.   Fall-Winter 2015 - 18498   2016 $4500

Verne, Jules 1828-1905 *The Mysterious Island.* Baltimore: Limited Editions Club at the Garamond Pressd, 1959. No. 186 of 1500 copies, numbered and signed by artist, large 8vo., pictorial cloth in pale green and black, top edge gilt green, fine in slightly faded box.   Second Life Books, Inc.   197 - 339   2016 $100

Verne, Jules 1828-1905 *The Myterious Island.* Baltimore: Limited Editions Club at Garamond press, 1959. No. 186 of 1500 copies, numbered and signed on colophon by artist, large 8vo., pictorial cloth, pale green and black, top edge green, fine in slightly faded box, fine.   Second Life Books, Inc.   196 B - 796   2016 $100

Verne, Jules 1828-1905 *Round the World in Eighty Days.* London: George Routledge and Sons, 1879. First edition thus, frontispiece, 8vo., blue cloth blocked in gilt and black, bevelled edge, pale yellow endpapers, very good, spine slightly darkened, personal ownership name to blank side of frontispiece, very scarce translation by Henry Frith.   Tavistock Books   Bibliolatry - 26   2016 $395

Verneuil, Maurice Pillard *Etude de la Plante: Son Application Aux Industries d'Art.* Paris: Librairie Centrale des Beaux Arts, 1903. First edition, 357 x 280, publisher's green cloth lettered and decorated in white, housed in later custom made slipcase, 379 illustrations, mostly printed in color or hand colored in pochoir, many full page, all by author, tip of top corner of upper board missing, half inch tear at tail of front joint, frontispiece and title faintly foxed, handful of leaves elsewhere with just breath of foxing, in most ways unusually fine, cloth virtually spotless and text and plates especially clean and fresh.   Phillip J. Pirages   67 - 289   2016 $1800

Verney, Frances Parthenope *Memoirs of the Verney Family.* London: Longmans Green & Co., 1892. First edition, 4 volumes, photogravure plates, period bindings by Hatchards of three quarter brown morocco with raised bands, gilt rules, cloth sides, marbled endpapers, top edges gilt, armorial bookplate of Kennet of Dene on each board is family's gilt coat of arms, near fine, handsome set.   Peter Ellis   112 - 115   2016   £350

Veron, J. E. N. *Scleractinia of Eastern Australia.* Townsville: Australian Institute of Marine Science, 1976-1984. Quarto, photos, publisher's printed wrappers, very good set.   Andrew Isles Natural History Books   55 - 38498   2016 $150

Vesalius, Andreas *Anatomes Totius aere Insculpta Delineatio.* Paris: Andre Wechel, 1564. First Grevin edition, full page woodcut arms of dedicatee, 47 engraved plates on 40 leaves, folio, modern reversed leather, occasional marginal soiling, scattered ink blots on text leaves, some plates might be washed, folding plate of Adam and Eve was torn and mounted with slight image loss, repaired clean tears across facing D3r and E1v but these not affecting image, bookplate of Crawford W. Adams.   James Tait Goodrich   X-78 - 530   2016 $1500

Vesalius, Andreas *Icones Anatomicae.* Munich: printed by the Breer Press for the Academia Mediinae Nova Eboracensis..., 1934. Elephant folio format, quarter calf backed, linen boards, light rubbing to spine, very faint staining to lower third of front board, front flyleaf and rear joint have been reinforced with white linen, printed on heavy deckled edge hand laid rag paper, all edges trimmed.   James Tait Goodrich   X-78 - 529   2016 $5750

Vesey-Fitzgerald, Brian *It's My Delight.* London: Eyre & Spottiswoode, 1947. First edition, 8vo., original cloth and wrapper, drawings, mark to rear of wrapper, previous owner's signature, very good.   Sotheran's Hunting, Shooting & Fishing - 232   2016   £40

Vesling, Johannes *Syntagma Anatomicvm Locis Plurimis Auctum Emendatum...* Patavii: Typis Pauli Frambotti Bib., 1647. 4to., engraved frontispiece, engraved portrait, 24 engraved plates and 24 leaves of handwritten text figure legends, printed title leaf and text leaves not present, 18th(?) century old plain boards, title and final plate remargined along inner border, some soiling and foxing of pages, final leaf shaved at bottom affecting one line of text.   James Tait Goodrich   X-78 - 540   2016 $3500

Vespa, Giuseppe *Letters in Occasione d'un Nuovo Strumento Inventato per Tagliare la Cornea Lucida nel Fare l'Operatione della...* Florence: Nella Stamperia Moucke, 1769. First edition, 4to., large folding hand tinted plate, bit of staining to rear cover, overall fine copy, early stiff paper wrappers, housed in white cloth, clamshell box.   Edwin V. Glaser Rare Books   2015 - 10102   2016 $750

Vetlina, Vera *Krimskie Puteshestvia.* Moscow: Molodaia Gvardia, 1955. First edition, 8vo., original blue cloth, spine lettered and ornamented in green and gilt, front cover lettered gilt and with mounted colour illustrations, ornamented endpapers, sketch maps, illustrations after drawings in text, plates in color and black and white, folding map in black and yellow at rear, binding little rubbed, internally very clean and fresh.   Sotheran's   Travel and Exploration - 288   2016   £298

Vibius Sequester *De Fluminibus Fontibus Iacubus Nemoribus Paludibus Montibus Gentibus Quorum Poetas Mentio Fit.* Strasbourg: apud Amandum Konig, 1778. 8vo., titlepage bit toned, some faint marginal stains, occasional spots and smudges, contemporary brown calf, neatly rebacked in slightly lighter shade with burgundy morocco spine label, edges sprinkled blue, endpapers renewed, edges worn, corners bumped, but good overall, pencilled code to titlepage.   Unsworths Antiquarian Booksellers Ltd.   30 - 157   2016   £200

Vicaire, Georges *Manuel De l'Amatuer De Livres Du XIXe Siecle 1801-1893.* Teaneck: Somerset House, 1973. Reprint of the 8 original volumes in first edition of 1894, 8 volumes in 1, folio, cloth.   Oak Knoll Books   310 - 270   2016 $450

Vickers-Rich, P. *Vertebrate Palaeontology of Australasia.* Melbourne: Pioner Design Studio, 1991. Octavo, text illustrations, signature dust jacket. Andrew Isles Natural History Books 55 - 11224 2016 $250

Victoria & Albert Museum *Handbook of the Dyce and Forster Collection in the South Kensington Museum.* London: Chapman & Hall, 1884. Later reissue, Half title, plates, illustrations, original dark green cloth, slightly rubbed. Jarndyce Antiquarian Booksellers CCXVIII - 1525 2016 £25

Victoria, Queen of Great Britain *Leaves from the Journal of Our Life in the Highlands from 1848 to 1861.* London: Smith, Elder & Co., 1868. First edition, 8vo., original green cloth, gilt borders and design to upper board, gilt lettering to spine, frontispiece and one other plate, binding little rubbed at extremities, previous owner's signatures, very good. Sotheran's Hunting, Shooting & Fishing - 189 2016 £250

Vidal, Gore *Empire: a Novel.* New York: Random House, 1987. First Random House edition, second printing, 8vo., author's signature, dark blue cloth, owner's embossed stamp on flyleaf and blank nice in little scuffed and faded dust jacket, near fine. Second Life Books, Inc. 196 B - 797 2016 $150

Vidal, Gore *Kalki: a Novel.* New York: Random House, 1978. Stated first trade edition, black cloth backed boards, lettered gilt, some foxing to fore-edge, fine in dust jacket. Argonaut Book Shop Literature 2015 - 6242 2016 $50

Vidal, Gore *Reflections Upon a Sinking Ship.* London: Heinemann, 1969. First UK edition, octavo, signed by author, ownership blindstamp of Lord McAlpine, tail of spine slightly bumped, top edge spotted, very good in like dust jacket, bit creased at top edge. Peter Ellis 112 - 421 2016 £75

Vidal, Gore *Two Sisters: a Memoir in the form of a Novel.* Boston: Little Brown ad Co., 1970. First edition, fine in near fine dust jacket with some light rubbing and couple of very short tears, inscribed by author for Harold Bloom. Between the Covers Rare Books 204 - 125 2016 $550

Vidocq, Eugene *Memoires de Vidocq Chief De La Police De Surete Jusqu'en 1827.* Tenan, Libraire Editeur, 1828-1829. First edition, 8vo., 4 volumes, bound in uniform red leather with maroon and red marbled boards, marbled boards, marbled endpapers, gilt spine lettering and ruled lines, volume 1-3 signed by author, frontispiece volume 4, bookplates, attractive, very good set. Buckingham Books 2015 - 37815 2016 $3000

Viereck, Peter *New and Selected Poems 1932-1967.* Indianapolis: Bobbs Merrill, 1967. 8vo. presentation on half title to poet William Claire, cloth, cover and edges little spotted, otherwise very good, tight copy in little scuffed dust jacket. Second Life Books, Inc. 196 B - 800 2016 $45

Viereck, Peter *The Persimmon Tree...* New York: Scribner's, 1956. First edition, 8vo., author's presentation to William Claire, green cloth, edge sof cover very slightly scuffed, otherwise nice in scuffed and little soiled dust jacket. Second Life Books, Inc. 196 B - 801 2016 $45

Viertel, Peter *Dangerous Friends: at Large with Hemingway and Huston in the Fifties.* New York: Doubleday, 1992. First edition, cloth and boards, illustrations, fine, like new in new dust jacket, rather scarce. Gene W. Baade, Books on the West 2015 - LO1008 2016 $65

Views of Our National Finances as Presented by the leading Newspapers of the Country, Collected and Republished for the Benefit of the Tax Payers and Respectfully Presented to the Governing Class. Washington: Gibson Brothers, 1868. 4to. stitched paper wrappers, good but fragile copy, wrappers soiled, detached and torn in half at fold, leaves with 2 inch tear at fore edge on fold. Kaaterskill Books 21 - 31 2016 $150

Vignelli, Massimo *New York Subway Guide. (with) New York City Graphic Standards Manual.* New York: New York City Transit Authority, 1972. Color printed map and large square folio, publisher's red cloth, 176 color and monochrome plates, three folding. Honey & Wax Booksellers 4 - 1 2016 $750

Vigo, Johannes De *Practica Copiosa in Arte Chirugica (sic).* Venice: heirs of Octavinaus Scotus, 1520. First Venice edition, Folio, 2 parts in one volume, woodcut initials, text dampstained with some worming which is mostly in margins, but not affecting some text, especially gatherings M-N, paper repairs in the last two leaves, part 2 lacking final blank, modern vellum by Omega Bindery, spine lettered in manuscript. James Tait Goodrich X-78 - 542 2016 $5750

Village Harmon or Youth's Assistant to Sacred Musick... Newburyport: E. Little and Co., 1816. Thirteenth edition, oblong 8vo., contemporary paper covered boards (spine and portion of front cover lacking paper). M & S Rare Books, Inc. 99 - 194 2016 $150

Villa-Lobos, H. *Simples Collectianea.* Rio: Casa Mozart, 1920. First edition, folio, printed wrappers, inscribed by composer, very good. Second Life Books, Inc. 196 B - 804 2016 $550

Villa-Lobos, H. *Suite Pour Chant et Violon.* Paris: Max Eschig, 1925. First edition, folio, printed wrappers, inscribed by composer, very good.   Second Life Books, Inc.   196 B - 805   2016 $500

The Village Orphan; a tale for Youth.   printed by C. Whittingham for Longman and Rees, 1797. 25 woodcut vignettes and tailpieces, little bit of browning around edges, sporadic very minor staining, 12mo., uncut, original pink boards, plain paper spine renewed, edges slightly worn, inscription, good.   Blackwell's Rare Books   B186 - 87   2016   £600

Villagra, Gaspar Perez De   *Historia de la Nueva Mexico 1610.*   Albuquerque: University of New Mexico Press, 1992. First revised English translation, quarto, frontispiece, 3 photographic illustrations, map, maroon cloth, gilt, very fine.   Argonaut Book Shop   Literature 2015 - 7246   2016 $75

Villars, Meg   *Dining-Out in Paris.*   Paris: Editions Vendome circa, 1928. First edition, 12mo., vignettes, illustrated paper over boards, owner's name dated 1930 and penciled list of two Paris clubs on rear free endpaper, some penciled marginalia about Paris restaurants, modest chipping at fragile spine ends, else nice, near fine, very scarce.   Between the Covers Rare Books   208 - 19   2016 $450

Villars, Nicolas Pierre Henri   *The Count of Gabalis; or the Extravagant Mysteries of the Cabalists, Exposed in Five Pleasant Discourses on the Secret Sciences.*   London: in the year, 1660. First edition of this translation by Philip Ayres, 12mo., occasional spot or rust mark, fine, contemporary calf, gilt spine, headcap missing, joints rubbed, old paper shelflabel at head of spine, from the library of James Stevens Cox (1910-1997).   Maggs Bros. Ltd.   1447 - 428   2016   £650

Villon, Francois   *Poesies de Villon.*   Paris: 1925. One of 2550 copies, hand painted vellum binding, text in French.   Honey & Wax Booksellers   4 - 25   2016 $175

Villon, Francois   *The Works of Francois Villon.*   London: Eric Partridge at the Scholartis Press, 1930. First edition of this translation, royal octavo, one of 600 copies, ownership signature, very good in like dust jacket, bit nicked and creased at edges and darkened at spine.   Peter Ellis   112 - 428   2016   £65

Vincartius, Joannes   *Sacrarum Heroidum Epistolae.*   Tournai: Adrien Quinque, 1640. Rare first edition, engraved titlepage and 24 oval copperplate emblems by Petrus Rucholle, 12mo., contemporary vellum.   Maggs Bros. Ltd.   1474 - 81   2016   £2250

Vince, Samuel   *A Treatise on Plane and Spherical Trigonometry.*   Cambridge: printed by J. Burges, 1800. 8vo., 2 folding engraved plates, modern boards, good.   Blackwell's Rare Books   B186 - 158   2016   £550

Vincent, George   *Dinners and Dinner Parties.*   London: Chapman & Hall, 1862. First edition, half title, illustrations, original blue cloth decorated gilt, slightly dulled, presentation from author for Mrs. Thellusson, very good.   Jarndyce Antiquarian Books   CCXV - 455   2016 £480

Vincent, Henriette Antoinette   *Studies of Fruit and Flowers Painted from Nature. (bound with) The Elements of Flower and Fruit Painting Illustrated with Engravings.*   London: R. Ackermann, 1814. 356 x 279mm., recent retrospective quarter calf, flat spine divided into panels by gilt Greek key roll, green morocco label, 49 attractive engravings of fruits and flowers, 25 of the plates stipple engraved, printed in colors, finished by hand, occasional mild thumbing, otherwise especially fine, clean and bright internally with rich coloring, unworn binding.   Phillip J. Pirages   67 - 347   2016 $24,000

Vincent, William   *A Defence of Public Education Addressed to the Most Reverend the Lord bishop of Meath.*   London: T. Cadell, 1802. Second edition, paper repair to upper corner of titlepage, disbound.   Jarndyce Antiquarian Books   CCXV - 995   2016   £40

Vincent, William   *A Discourse Addressed to the People of Great Britain May13th 1792.*   Canterbury: printed by Simmons, Kirkby & Jones, 1793. 8vo., disbound.   Jarndyce Antiquarian Booksellers   CCXVI - 579   2016   £65

Viola, Herman   *The Indian Legacy of Charles Bird King.*   Washington: Library of Congress and Doubleday and Co., 1976. First edition, 4to., color and black and white reproductions, early prints, maps, green cloth, very fine with pictorial dust jacket.   Argonaut Book Shop   Native American 2015 - 7247   2016 $45

Virchow, Rudolf   *Die Cellularpathologie in Ihrer Begrilundung auf Physiologie und Pathologische Gewebelchre Vierte...*   Berlin: Hirschwald, 1871. First German edition, 157 illustrations, half contemporary, half leather, worn, ex-library with usual markings, internally clean.   James Tait Goodrich   X-78 - 544   2016 $595

Virues, Cristoval De *El Monserrate...* Madrid: Alonso Martin, 1609. Third edition, large woodcut on titlepage, 2 large woodcut tailpieces, woodcut initial to each Canto, that to first on a slip pasted in, repairs to title and A1 just touching a few letters, some headlines and one catchword cropped, first 2 gatherings slightly browned, small 8vo., 19th century mottled calf for Biblioteca de Slava, with his emblem blocked in gilt on both covers, spine gilt in compartments, black lettering piece, slightly rubbed, some repairs to joints, good, very rare.   Blackwell's Rare Books   B184 - 89   2016   £5000

Vissering, Harry *Zeppelin. the Story of a Great Achievement.* Chicago: printed for the author, 1922. First edition, scarce, square 8vo., original green cloth, gilt design and lettering to upper board, 59 plates, inscribed by author, inscribed with author's compliments, very good, spine slightly stained.   Sotheran's   Piccadilly Notes - Summer 2015 - 316   2016   £350

Vives, Juan Luis *Linguae Latine Exercitatio.* London: Typis Alice Warren cum Societate Stationiarum, 1660. 12mo., title within type ornament border, small rust hole to lower corner of A4 (touching text) and with rust mark to lower margin of A8 and C2, lower fore-corner of A5 missing from paper flaw, no loss of text and upper blank corner of D7 torn away, contemporary sheep, covers ruled in blind, remnants of paper spine label, lower joint damaged by worming at head, single worm hole in upper joint, pastedowns unstuck, ink inscription "John Waddinge his book", from the library of James Stevens Cox (1910-1997).   Maggs Bros. Ltd.   1447 - 429   2016   £420

Vivian, Evelyn Charles *The Way of the Red Cross.* London: Hodder & Stoughton, 1915. First edition, half title, folded facsimile letter from Queen Anne, leading f.e.p. with vertical crease, original blue grey cloth, spine slightly dulled, presentation inscription in secretarial hand no leading f.e.p. "Janet C. Kirkpatrick Yorkhill War Hospital Glasgow. Presentd (sic) by Her majesty Queen Alexandra at Marlborough House May 22nd 1917", very good.   Jarndyce Antiquarian Booksellers   CCXVII - 291   2016   £45

Viviani, Vincenzo *De Maximis et Minimis Geometrica Divinatio in Quintum Coniorcum Apollonii Pergaei adhuc Desideratum.* Florence: G. Cocchini, 1659. First edition, fine copy, title printed in red and black, half title, large folding sheet at end with 2 engraved plates, 2 woodcut plates, diagrams in text, 2 parts in one, folio, contemporary English calf, spine gilt, half title and final page little dusty.   Maggs Bros. Ltd.   1474 - 82   2016   £3500

The Vivisector. London: Jonathan Cape, 1970. First edition, crown 8vo., original terra cotta boards, backstrip lettered gilt, top edge black, dust jacket by Tom Adams, little nicked at head of backstrip panel with couple of nicks to front and rear panels also and gentle rubbing to corners, very good.   Blackwell's Rare Books   B186 - 289   2016   £80

Voge, Hervey *A Climber's Guide to the High Sierra, Routes and Records for California Peaks from Bond Pass to Army Pass and for Rock Climbs...* San Francisco: Sierra Club, 1954. First edition, 12mo., frontispiece and 16 further photos, text drawings and maps, blue cloth stamped in silver, owner's ink presentation, slight darkening to front ends, else fine, lightly edge worn pictorial dust jacket.   Argonaut Book Shop   Mountaineering 2015 - 7248   2016 $50

Voigt, Ellen Bryant *Claiming Kin.* Middletown: Wesleyan University Press, 1976. First edition, inscribed and signed for William Meredith, fine in fine dust jacket.   Charles Agvent   William Meredith - 113   2016 $100

Volbracht, Christian *Mykolibri. Die Bibliothek der Pilzbucher.* Hamburg: MykoLibri, 2006. Limited to 750 numbered and signed copies, this one of the 50 special edition with original plate, 4to., cloth, dust jacket, 8 page booklet in English laid in.   Oak Knoll Books   310 - 271   2016 $335

Volland *Volland Book Catalogue: Books Good for Children.* n.d. circa, 1928. Pictorial wrappers, near fine, illustrations, rare.   Aleph-bet Books, Inc.   111 - 469   2016 $450

Voltaire, Francois Marie Arouet De   1694-1778 *Candidus; or All for the Best.* printed for B. Long and T. Pridden, 1773. Early and scarce edition in English, 12mo., half title stained, staining diminishing over next few leaves, minor staining elsewhere, modern calf backed boards, some lines in pencil in margins, good.   Blackwell's Rare Books   B186 - 161   2016   £600

Voltaire, Francois Marie Arouet De   1694-1778 *Kandide.* Munchen: Kurt Wolff, 1920. First edition, small quarto, 26 pen and ink drawings by Paul Klee, white cloth backed dark blue paper boards, lettered in gilt, cover edges little rubbed, scratch approximately three inches on lower cover, very good.   Peter Ellis   112 - 203   2016   £195

Voltaire, Francois Marie Arouet De   1694-1778 *Elemens de la Philosophie de Neuton.* Amsterdam: Jacques Desbordes, 1738. First edition, title printed in red and black, finely engraved portraits, with frontispiece, 27 engraved vignettes, 6 engraved plates, 58 engravings in text, 22 engraved tailpieces and 1 folding engraved table, fine contemporary paneled sheep with beautiful and crisp blindstamping and gilt borders on front and back covers, spine with gilt decorations in five compartments and gilt titling in sixth, with bookplate of William A. Cole, collector and bibliographer of chemistry, above is contemporary ink signature (crossed out with two diagonal strokes), and on same line 'Bergen 1799", overall fine, bright, clean, very beautiful. Athena Rare Books   List 15 - 1738   2016 $4250

Voltaire, Francois Marie Arouet De 1694-1778 *For the Promotion of Christian Knowledge. the Character of the Christian Mysteries in a Dialogue Betwen a Church of England Missionary Preacher and a Chinese Mandarin....* New York: G. H. Evans?, 1827. First American edition, 8vo., removed, foxed.   M & S Rare Books, Inc.   99 - 93   2016 $275

Voltaire, Francois Marie Arouet De 1694-1778 *The Ignorant Philosopher.* London: printed for S. Bladon in Pater Noster Row, 1767. First English edition, 8vo., half title, some old faint waterstaining to first 10 leaves, slight worming to extreme inner margins at foot of pages 89-109, also at inner margin at head of pages 181 to end, expertly bound in recent quarter sprinkled calf, raised and gilt banded spine, red morocco label, marbled boards, vellum tips.   Jarndyce Antiquarian Booksellers   CCXVI - 580   2016   £285

Voltaire, Francois Marie Arouet De 1694-1778 *Jamforelse Emellan Newtons och Leibnitz's Meningar in Metaphysiken Och Naturalarn.* Stockholm: C. E. Marquard, 1792. 8vo., entirely uncut and unopened in original light blue paper wrappers, fine, rare.   Blackwell's Rare Books   B186 - 162   2016   £800

Voltaire, Francois Marie Arouet De 1694-1778 *Romans...* Paris: de l'Imprimerie et de la Fonderie Stereotypes de Pierre Didot l'aine et de Firmin Didot, 1800. 3 volumes, half titles, 18mo., light damp marking to upper bank margins of few leaves in volume 2, contemporary gilt ruled, tree calf spines, ruled and decorated in gilt, double red morocco labels, lemon edges, silk markers, slight wear, signature of Michelle (?), very attractive.   Jarndyce Antiquarian Booksellers   CCXVI - 581   2016   £85

Voltaire, Francois Marie Arouet De 1694-1778 *Vers de Voltaire au Roi de Prusse.* London: printed for R. and J. Dodsley, 1753. 4to., slight foxing, slight tear without loss along old fold mark on titlepage, recent sugar paper wrappers.   Jarndyce Antiquarian Booksellers   CCXVI - 582   2016   £850

Volter, Maria Louise *Marissa und Die Heinzelmannchen.* Esslington: J. F. Schreiber, n.d., 1982. Pictorial boards, fine, illustrations by Gennadi Spirin, this copy signed by artist.   Aleph-bet Books, Inc.   112 - 465   2016 $125

Voluntary School Association *The School Annual Report of the Committee of the Voluntary School Association.* London: Charles Gilpin, 1850. Corners slightly creased, original blue printed paper wrappers, few marginal tears.   Jarndyce Antiquarian Books   CCXV - 997   2016   £20

Vonnegut, Kurt *Bluebeard.* New York: Delacorte Press, 1987. First edition, inscribed and signed in 1987 by author for William Meredith, fine in fine dust jacket.   Charles Agvent   William Meredith - 114   2016 $850

Vonnegut, Kurt *Gold Bless You, Mr. Rosewater, or Pearls Before Saints.* New York: Holt, Rinehart and Winston, 1965. First edition, signed by author, octavo, original half cloth with color patterned boards, original dust jacket, book near fine, some wear to spine and very minor brown spot in extreme margin of three leaves, dust jacket near fine, only light general wear, exceptionally nice.   Manhattan Rare Book Company   2016 - 1800   2016 $1350

Vonnegut, Kurt *Jailbird.* New York: Delacorte Press, 1979. First edition, black cloth, lettered in silver and gold, original white pictorial dust jacket, near fine or better with few faint spots to page edges, else bright and fresh, dust jacket with hint of faint toning to extremities, very slight dimming to spine, else bright and clean, overall very square and attractive copy.   B & B Rare Books, Ltd.   2016 - KV034   2016 $100

Vonnegut, Kurt *One Great Novelist of the 70's Writes about Another: Kurt Vonnegut, Jr. on Joseph Heller's Something Happened.* New York: Ballantine Books, 1974. First separate edition, fine in stapled wrappers, as issued, uncommon.   Between the Covers Rare Books   204 - 126   2016 $400

Vonnegut, Kurt *Poems Written During the First Five Months of 2005.* N.P.: self published, 2005. Self published velobound photocopies, but this is apparently the originales, signed by author, fine.   Ken Lopez Bookseller   166 - 144   2016 $1500

Vonnegut, Kurt *Slaughterhouse-Five.* New York: Delacorte Press, 1969. First edition, fine in modestly spine toned, else crisp and near fine dust jacket, boldly inscribed by author.   Between the Covers Rare Books   208 - 89   2016 $8500

Vonnegut, Kurt *Slaughterhouse-Five, or The Children's Crusade.* New York: Seymour Lawrence Delacorte Press, 1969. First edition, octavo, original blue cloth, original dust jacket, book near fine with hint of toning at edges, dust jacket bright and clean with what appears to be some white-out on verso, not visible from outside.   Manhattan Rare Book Company   2016 - 1625   2016 $1200

Vonsybel, Heinrich *History of the French Revolution.* London: John Murray, 1867-1869. First edition in English, 235 x 146mm., 4 volumes, very pleasing dark blue half morocco, attractively gilt by Zaehnsdorf for A. C. McClurg & Co. (stamp signed), wide raised bands decorated with five parallel gilt rules, spine compartments with gilt frames composed of stippled rules connected to corner volutes, marbled sides and endpapers, top edge gilt, other edges rough trimmed, hint of chafing to paper sides, occasional minor foxing, never offensive, additional trivial imperfections, otherwise fine set in excellent decorative bindings, leather unusually lustrous and virtually unworn and text very smooth and clean.   Phillip J. Pirages   67 - 166   2016 $850

Voorhis, Robert *Life and Adventures of Robert, the Hermit of Massachusetts, Who Has Lived 14 Years in a Cave....* Providence: printed for H. Trumbell, 1829. First edition, unprinted blue wrappers as issued, leaves untrimmed, woodcut frontispiece, very faint old genealogical society blindstamp, rear wrapper splitting at spine, other light wear, otherwise very good, uncommon.   Between the Covers Rare Books   202 - 98   2016 $500

Vossius, Isaac *De Lucis Natura et Proprietate.* Amsterdam: L. & D. Elzevier, 1662. First edition, woodcut printer's device on title, woodcut illustrations in text, little staining and browning at beginning, 4to., contemporary mottled calf, spine gilt in compartments, bit worn at extremities, flyleaves dampstained, good.   Blackwell's Rare Books   B186 - 163   2016   £4000

Voznesensky, Andrei *Antiworlds: Poetry.* New York: Basic, 1966. Second printing, 8vo., author's presentation on flyleaf to poet Bill Claire, black cloth, nice, somewhat scuffed dust jacket.   Second Life Books, Inc.   196 B - 810   2016 $65

Voznesensky, Andrei *Nostalgia for the Present.* Garden City: Doubleday, 1978. First edition, 8vo., author's presentation to poet William Claire, 4 illustrations, paper over boards with cloth spine, top edges very slightly soiled, otherwise nice in slightly soiled dust jacket.   Second Life Books, Inc.   196 B - 811   2016 $65

Vyse, Charles *The Key to the Tutor's Guide or the Arithmetician's Repository...* London: printed by S. Hamilton, Falcon Court, Fleet Street for G. G. Robinson and J. Robinson..., 1799. 12mo. in sixes, full contemporary unlettered sheep, gilt banded spine, head of spine slightly chipped, leading hinge, slightly cracked, signature of Matthias Millington 1800, very clean copy with clean tear to dust jacket without loss.   Jarndyce Antiquarian Books   CCXV - 998   2016   £65

W

Wa-Sha-Quon-Asin *Tales of an Empty Cabin.* New York: Dodd Mead & Co., 1936. First American edition, back and white photographic illustrations, gray cloth, upper rear corner slightly bumped, minor wear and slight fading, near fine. Argonaut Book Shop   Natural History 2015 - 6145   2016 $60

Wadd, William *Cursory Remarks on Corpulence by a Member of the Royal College of Surgeons.* London: printed for J. Callow, 1810. Later quarter calf and linen boards, spine sunned and endpapers renewed, very good internally. James Tait Goodrich   X-78 - 549   2016 $495

Waddell, Helen *Poetry in the Dark Ages....* Glasgow: Jackson Son, 1948. First edition, octavo, wrappers, presentation from author for Betty Blake, covers little marked and creased, very good.   Peter Ellis   112 - 429   2016   £25

Wadsworth, Edward *Sailing-Ships and Barges of the Western Mediterranean and the Adriatic Seas.* London: Frederick Etchells & Hugh MacDonald, 1926. Limited to 450 numbered copies, 4to., quarter cream colored cloth with orange buckram covered boards, illustration in gilt on cover and spine, copperplate engravings, set in Rudolf Kochs Kursiv printed on Zanders handmade paper, slipcase rubbed and spotted, spine of book faded, minor spotting on endpapers, else very good.   Oak Knoll Books   27 - 67   2016 $700

Wagener, Richard *California in Relief. Thirty Wood Engravings.* San Francisco: Book club of California, 2009. First edition, copy #8 of 300 signed by artist, 30 black and white woodcut images, green cloth spine over taupe paper wrapped boards, wax paper wrapper, slipcase, as new. Tavistock Books   Bibliolatry - 39   2016 $600

Wagner, Henry Raup 1862-1957 *The Plains and the Rockies.* Columbus: Long's College Book Co., 1953. Third edition, number 10 of deluxe edition of 75, illustrations, limitation statement laid in, issued without dust jacket, in slipcase which is rubbed, book near fine.   Dumont Maps and Books   134 - 50   2016 $150

Wagner, Henry Raup 1862-1957 *Sir Francis Drake's Voyage Around the World: Its Aims and Achievements.* San Francisco: John Howell Books, 1926. First edition, although not indicated, one of 1100 copies, quarto, maps, photos and facsimiles, maroon cloth gilt, spine lightly faded, else very fine.   Argonaut Book Shop   Biography 2015 - 7283   2016 $400

Wagner, Henry Raup 1862-1957 *Spanish Explorations in the Strait of Juan De Fuca.* Fine Arts Press, 1933. First edition, #7 of Special illustrated edition of 35 signed copies, from a total first printing of 425, original vellum, 13 maps and plans, large folding plates or maps, Special illustrated edition has 12 extra illustrations, minor professional repair to top of spine and small spot on rear panel else clean, near fine, rare, custom slipcase.   Buckingham Books   2015 - 28354   2016 $3000

Wagner, Richard 1813-1883 *Parsifal.* New York: Crowell, 1912. Full plum colored suede leather binding with gilt design, yap edges, top edge gilt, some splits on edge were suede folds over binding and stain on upper corner of cover (not offensive), very good+, color lithographs in text, 16 tipped in color plates, pictorial borders on text pages, pictorial endpapers and calligraphic text, printed on heavy gray stock, rare binding.   Aleph-bet Books, Inc.   112 - 378   2016 $475

Wagner, Richard 1813-1883 *Siegfried & the Twilight of the Gods.* London: William Heinemann, 1911. Edition deluxe limited to 1150 copies, signed by artist, this number 964, original full vellum, pictorially gilt stamped on front cover, gilt stamped spine, new ties, 10 tipped-in color plates, top edge gilt, otherwise uncut, very good, illustrations by Arthur Rackham.   Heritage Book Shop   Holiday 2015 - 91   2016 $2500

Wagner, Richard 1813-1883 *Siegfried & The Twilight of the Gods.* London & New York: Heinemann & Doubleday, 1911. First American edition, cloth backed gilt pictorial boards, one corner bumped and another rubbed, else very good+, illustrated by Arthur Rackham, 30 magnificent tipped-in colored plates with tissue guards, pictorial titlepage, pictorial endpapers.   Aleph-bet Books, Inc.   112 - 417   2016 $450

Wagoner, David *Dry Sun, Dry Wind.* Bloomington: Indiana University, 1953. First edition, author's presentation on title to William Claire, black cloth, Claire's name on flyleaf, nice in soiled and chipped dust jacket.   Second Life Books, Inc.   196 B - 812   2016 $125

Wagoner, David *A Guide to Dungeness Spit.* Port Townsend: Graywolf Press, 1975. First and only edition, one of 60 copies of a total edition of 225, author's signature, paper wrappers, cover very slightly faded, otherwise nice. Second Life Books, Inc.   196 B - 813   2016 $45

Wagoner, David *Travelling Light.* Port Townsend: Graywolf, 1976. First edition, one of 600 softcover copies out of an edition of 750, pictorial dark brown wrappers, inscribed by author for William Meredith, with TLS to Meredith, with original envelope addressed in Wagoner's hand, fine.   Charles Agvent   William Meredith - 115   2016 $200

Wagstaffe, William *The Character of Richard Style, Esq. with some Remarks by Toby, Abel's Kinsman; or According to Mr. Calamy, A. F. & N.* London: printed for J. Morphew near Stationer's Hall, 1713. 8vo. in fours, half title, engraved frontispiece, fine, clean crisp copy, frontispiece very slightly shaved, full polished calf by Riviere, gilt fillet borders, gilt panelled spine, red gilt morocco labels, all edges gilt. Jarndyce Antiquarian Booksellers CCXVI - 543 2016 £185

Wagstaffe, William *The Character of Richard St---le Esq. with some Remarks by Toby, Abel's Kinsman...* London: printed for J. Morphew near Stationer's Hall, 1713. Second edition, half title, frontispiece, 8vo. in 4's, lower corner of half title torn just affecting lower ruled line, E1-3 affected by old damp at head with some loss to paper, just affecting a single letter of one word, outer leaves dusted, disbound. Jarndyce Antiquarian Booksellers CCXVI - 544 2016 £85

Wain, Louis *A Cat Alphabet.* New York: Dodge, printed in Scotland, n.d., 1914. cloth backed boards, pictorial paste-on edges slightly rubbed and corner wear, else fine, color frontispiece, full color illustrations, rare. Aleph-bet Books, Inc. 112 - 503 2016 $2000

Wain, Louis *Cat's Cradle. A Picture Book for Little Folk.* London: Blackie, n.d., circa, 1908. Small 4to., grey pictorial paper boards, dark grey endpapers, 6 full page color Wain illustrations plus color illustrations, backstrip worn, paper has separated from boards slightly at spine and is slightly chipped, otherwise near very good, rubbed at corners and at lower edges but with very clean text and illustrations. Any Amount of Books 2015 - A72284 2016 £150

Wain, Louis *The Louis Wain Kitten Book.* London: Anthony Treherne and New York H. B. Clafin, 1904. Square 3 inches, pictorial cloth, printed on board pages on one side only, each page of verse faced by marvelous full page color illustrations by Wain. Aleph-bet Books, Inc. 112 - 505 2016 $1250

Wain, Louis *Louis Wain's Annual 1910-1911.* London: George Allen and Soons, 1911. First edition, royal octavo, color frontispiece mounted on gray card, 7 full page mono-color plates and numerous black and white text illustrations, original color printed wrappers with additional color illustration on front wrapper, small chip missing from fore-edge of front wrapper, lower corner of back wrapper torn away, still incredible copy, very rare. David Brass Rare Books, Inc. 2015 - 02988 2016 $450

Wain, Louis *Pa Cats. Ma Cats and their Kittens.* London: Raphael Buck, n.d., 1902. Folio, cloth backed pictorial boards, some cover soil, edges rubbed, ink markings on front and rear paste downs, front hinge strengthened plus 22 full and partial page illustrations in blue, every page illustrated and text printed in blue, very scarce. Aleph-bet Books, Inc. 112 - 504 2016 $1650

Wain, Louis *With Louis Wain to Fairyland.* London: Raphael Tuck, n.d., 1904. Pictorial cloth, old hinge repairs and several margin mends, some cover rubbing, really very good, 12 full page color illustrations plus black and white text illustrations, rare. Aleph-bet Books, Inc. 112 - 506 2016 $1750

Wainewright, Latham *The Literary and Scientific Pursuits Which are Encourage and Enforced in the University of Cambridge briefly described....* London: J. Hatchard, 1813. Half tan calf, green morocco label, spine rubbed, armorial bookplate of Toft Hall. Jarndyce Antiquarian Books CCXV - 580 2016 £85

Wait, Benjamin *Letters from Van Dieman's land.* Buffalo: A. G. Wilgus, 1843. First edition, 12mo., frontispiece and folding map, contemporary calf backed cloth, spine quite worn, folding portion of map lacking, although essentially complete, text foxed. M & S Rare Books, Inc. 99 - 39 2016 $550

Waite, Edgar R. *A Popular Account of Australian Snakes with Complete List of the Species and an Introduction to their Habits and Organisation.* Sydney: Thomas Shine, 1898. Small octavo, 16 chromolithographed plates, publisher's blindstamped cloth, lightly cracked and few flecks, otherwise very good. Andrew Isles Natural History Books 55 - 8444 2016 $950

Waiting at Table: a Practical Guide. London: Frederick Warne, circa, 1894. Half title, 4 pages ads, original blue-grey cloth, fine. Jarndyce Antiquarian Books CCXV - 21 2016 £125

Waiting at Table: a Practical Guide. London: Frederick Warne, circa, 1910. Later reprint of 1894 edition, original olive green decorated cloth, little marked and dulled. Jarndyce Antiquarian Books CCXV - 22 2016 £45

Waiting at Table. London: Universal Publications, 1937. 7 pages ads, illustrations, original orange wrappers, spine slightly creased, very good. Jarndyce Antiquarian Books CCXV - 456 2016 £45

Wake, William *The Genuine Epistles of the Apostolical Fathers S. Barnabas, S. Clement, S. Ignatius, S. Polycarp...* London: Richard Sare, 1693. First edition, 8vo., smart 19th century half tan calf over marbled boards, black spine label lettered gilt, boards little rubbed, later endpapers, ownership stamp, titlepage slightly cropped, not affecting text, small quantity of early annotations in both ink and pencil, overall clean and sound, very good. Any Amount of Books 2015 - C10139 2016 £250

Wake, William *The Missionarie's Arts Discovered; or an Account of their Ways of Insinuation, Their Artifices and Several Methods of Which They Serve Themselves in Making Converts.* London: printed and sold by Randal Taylor, 1688. First edition, 4to., licence/errata leaf (edges bit frayed, not affecting printed surface), recently sympathetically bound in old style quarter calf gilt, good copy. John Drury Rare Books 2015 - 16046 2016 $437

Wakeman, Geoffrey *XIX Century Illustration, Some Methods Used in English Books.* Loughborough: Plough Press, 1970. One of 75 numbered copies, folio, quarter cloth portfolio with paper covered boards, slipcase, (16) cord-tied portfolios, extra-illustrated copy, slipcase rubbed and faded along edges. Oak Knoll Books 310 - 138 2016 $1500

Wakoski, Diane *Inside the Blood Factory.* Garden City: Doubleday and Co., 1968. First edition, inscribed by author for William Meredith, by author, she has added two small drawings handwritten and her printed names, slight fraying to cloth along spine edge at top, near fine in like dust jacket. Charles Agvent   William Meredith - 116   2016 $100

Walcot, John *Bozzy and Piozzi or the British Biographers a Town Eclogue.* London: printed for G. Kearsley at Johnson's Head, 1786. Fifth edition, etched plate, some worming to leading edge, mainly a single tiny hole touching a few letters, close cropped at lower edge affecting a few signatures and footnotes, bound in 19th century cloth, gilt lettered spine, rather faded, additional portrait of Pindar pasted on to inner board, ownership name of James Ford, Bath 1859. Jarndyce Antiquarian Booksellers CCXVI - 583 2016 £50

Walden, Arthur *A List of Birds Known to Inhabit the Island of Celebes.* London: Transactions of the Zoological Society of London, 1872. Quarto, coloured map and 10 hand coloured plates, contemporary brown half morocco and marbled boards, upper corner of drop title restored without affecting text, very good. Andrew Isles Natural History Books 55 - 26603 2016 $850

Walder, Dennis *Dickens and Religion.* London: George Allen & Unwin, 1981. First edition, half title, illustrations, original red cloth, very good in slightly faded dust jacket. Jarndyce Antiquarian Booksellers CCXVIII - 1471 2016 £20

Waldman, Anne *Makeup on Empty Space.* West Branch: Toothpaste Press, 1984. First edition, one of 100 numbered copies, with Ehrhardt Monotype Portrait of author, deluxe edition, printed on Frankfurt White, quarter bound in cloth and Tokutairei Tanabata, a handmade paper, at the Campbell-Logan Bindery, fine in acetate dust jacket. Second Life Books, Inc.   196 B - 817   2016 $125

Waley, Arthur *The Secret History of the Mongols and Other Pieces.* London: George Allen & Unwin, 1963. First edition, octavo, very good in like dust jacket, slightly nicked and dusty dust jacket faded at spine, short tear to bottom edge of front panel.   Peter Ellis 112 - 430 2016 £50

Walford, Edward *The Antiquary Volumes I-X.* London: Elliot Stock, 1880-1884. 10 volumes bound as 5, 4to., numerous illustrations in text, volume IX foxed at front, occasional further light foxing, few unobtrusive pencil notes to margins, later half vellum (flesh side out?) with marbled paper boards and endpapers, tan morocco gilt labels to spines, top edge gilt, others uncut, little rubbed, some loss of color to boards, vellum slightly soiled, some scrapes to spine labels, inner hinges beginning to wear but holding firm, armorial bookplate of Edward Swinfen Harris and his pencilled ownership.   Unsworths Antiquarian Booksellers 30 - 6   2016   £200

Walker, A. Earl *A History of Neurological Surgery.* Baltimore: Williams & Wilkins, 1951. Original cloth. James Tait Goodrich X-78 - 548 2016 $150

Walker, A. Stodart *The Keeper's Book.* Edinburgh: George A. Morton, 1903. First edition, 8vo., original cream decorative cloth, frontispiece, illustrations, previous owner's signature, very good.   Sotheran's   Hunting, Shooting & Fishing - 233 2016 £180

Walker, A. Stodart *The Keeper's Book.* Edinburgh: George A. Morton, 1904. Third impression, 8vo., original cream decorative cloth, frontispiece, illustrations, bookplate with P. Jeffrey Mackie's printed signature, printed signature, binding little rubbed and sunned to spine, internally very good.   Sotheran's   Piccadilly Notes - Summer 2015 - 317 2016   £160

Walker, Alice 1944- *The Third Life of Grange Copeland.* London: Women's Press, 1970. First British edition, very good plus with usual darkening to pages, former owner signature to front free endpaper and small pen stroke to titlepage in close to near fine dust jacket with small tear and some creasing to base of rear pane, signed by author, uncommon thus.   Jeff Hirsch Books   Holiday List 2015 - 62 2016 $85

Walker, Alice 1944- *The Third Life of Grange Copeland.* New York: Harcourt Brace, 1970. First edition, near fine, light wear, no major defects, dust jacket fine, signed by author. Bella Luna Books 2016 - t3874 2016 $264

Walker, Alice 1944- *You Can't Keep a Good Woman Down.* New York: Harcourt Brace, 1981. First edition, fine in near fine dust jacket, light chipping at heel of spine. Bella Luna Books 2016 - ta268 2016 $99

Walker, Donald *Games and Sports...* London: Thomas Hurst, 1837. First edition, half title, frontispiece, additional engraved title, plates, 18 page catalog, some foxing to plates, original maroon cloth by Remnant & Edmonds, gilt vignette, spine slightly faded, small ink mark to back board, booklabel of J. P. Brown-Westhead, Lea Castle, very good, near fine. Jarndyce Antiquarian Books CCXV - 458 2016 £350

Walker, Francis A. *Statistical Atlas of the United States Based on the Results of the Ninth Census 1870....* New York: Julius Bien, 1874. First edition, 60 color lithographed mapsheets and charts, folio, three quarter morocco over cloth boards, gilt titles, marbled endpapers, front joint cracked but sturdy, otherwise very good, spine and extremities worn, few small edge ters to initial leaves, else maps and charts quite bright. Kaaterskill Books 21 - 109 2016 $725

Walker, George *The Three Spaniards.* Dublin: printed by Brett Smith for P. Wogan, J. Rice, G. Folingsby & B. Dornin, 1800. 12mo., contemporary marginal note to page 83 volume I, corner of E12 volume II torn, but with no loss of text, pages rather browned, with some fingermarks and occasional browning with some ink doodles on endpapers, contemporary calf, gilt ruled spines, dark red morocco labels, joints & head and tail of spines expertly repaired, bookplate of Robert Montgomery, Convoy, signature of Tho. Montgomery across titlepages. Jarndyce Antiquarian Booksellers CCXVI - 584 2016 £480

Walker, Jonathan *Trial and Imprisonment... at Pensacola Florida for Aiding Slaves to Escape Their Bondage.* Boston: Anti-Slavery office, 1846. First edition, 12mo., 2 plates, original cloth one signature shaken. M & S Rare Books, Inc. 99 - 232 2016 $375

Walker, Margaret *For My People: (Poems).* New Haven: Yale, 1943. Fourth printing, 8vo., author's presentation, yellow cloth, cover little soiled at edges, otherwise very good, tight in some worn dust jacket. Second Life Books, Inc. 196 B - 818 2016 $650

Walker, Margaret *For My People.* New Haven: Yale, 1969. Seventh printing, 8vo., author's signature, paper wrappers, cover creased and scuffed, otherwise very good. Second Life Books, Inc. 196 B - 819 2016 $65

Walker, Margaret *Prophets for a New Day.* Detroit: Broadside Press, 1970. First edition, 8vo., author's signature on title, paper wrappers, covere slightly scuffed and creased, otherwise very good. Second Life Books, Inc. 197 - 342 2016 $50

Walker, Mary Willis *Zero at the Bone.* New York: St. Martin's Press, 1991. Uncorrected proof, near fine, hint of wear to corners, scarce format, signed by author, printed red wrappers. Bella Luna Books 2016 - 2004 2016 $165

Walker, Meredith *Building for nature: Walter Burley Griffin and Castlecrag.* Castlecrag: Walter Burley Griffin Society, 1994. Horizontal 8vo., black and white photos, presentation by Adrienne Kabos and James Weirick, auction flyer laid in, paper wrappers, about as new. Second Life Books, Inc. 196 B - 821 2016 $75

Walker, Obadiah *Of Education. Especially of Young Gentlemen.* Oxford: in the Theatre, 1673. Second edition, small 8vo., engraved coat-of-arms of Oxford University on title, printer's crease across titlepage engraving, inner margins of title and contents leaves slightly damaged by adhesion, prominent dampstain in top inner margin of most leaves, corners stained in sheets C-D, with small piece torn from corner of M5, early 19th century half calf and paste boards, rubbed and worn with some worming to spine, early ink notes, the copy of the Cooper family of Markree Castle, Co. Sligo, Ireland with blue shield shaped case label, from the library of James Stevens Cox (1910-1997). Maggs Bros. Ltd. 1447 - 430 2016 £150

Walker, Obadiah *Periamma Epidemion; or Vulgar Errours in Practice Censured.* London: for Richard Royston, 1659. First edition, small 8vo., 2 parts, general title ruled in red, severe staining to A1-8, two-line stain (and small hole) to centre of B7, otherwise lightly browned with occasional small stains or rust spots, contemporary mottled calf, rebacked, corners repaired, new endleaves. from the library of James Stevens Cox (1910-1997). Maggs Bros. Ltd. 1447 - 433 2016 £140

Walker, Thomas *Aristology; or the Art of Dining.* London: George Bell & Sons, 1881. Half title, 24 page catalog (Nov. 1880), original red cloth, marked and worn, armorial bookplate of Richard Munkhouse Wilson. Jarndyce Antiquarian Books CCXV - 459 2016 £35

Walker, Thomas Harris *Good Servants, Good Wives and Happy Homes.* London: S. W. Partridge, 1862. First edition, frontispiece, vignette title, plates and illustrations, 32 page catalog, leaves slightly browned, original red cloth, decorated in gilt, dulled and slightly rubbed, signature of Mary Wagstaff June 12th/64, nice. Jarndyce Antiquarian Books CCXV - 460 2016 £75

Walker, William *The Royal Grammar, Commonly Called Lylly's Grammar Explained.* London: for Robert Pawlet and Edward Pawlet, 1674. Second edition, small 8vo., small rust hole through the blank part of the titlepage and upper corner with minor damage due to ink stain, larger hole from paper flaw on B3 (touching top line of text), some occasional minor spots, inkstain along upper edge of I5-K1 and with small piece torn away from bank corner of G4, contemporary calf, spine with four gilt tooled panels, spine label missing, upper joint split at head, endleaves unstuck. from the library of James Stevens Cox (1910-1997), Juvenile ink inscription, Heylar family of Coker Court Somerset, with 19th century armorial bookplate. Maggs Bros. Ltd. 1447 - 432 2016 £200

Walkley, Thomas *A New Catalogue of the Dukes, Marquesses, Earls, Viscounts, Barons of England, Scotland and Ireland...* London: Thomas Walkley, 1652. Second edition, 8vo., dark staining around edges of titlepage and with old inscription above imprint scratched away, remaining leaves browned and dampstained throughout and with some ink staining on final two leaves, later calf, rebacked, new endpapers, from the library of James Stevens Cox (1910-1997). Maggs Bros. Ltd. 1447 - 433 2016 £120

Wall, Berhnardt *The Invitation to Gettysburg.* Lime Rock: 1930. First edition, number 35 of 100 copies signed by author, 2 etchings signed in pencil, limitation leaf signed in pencil, 16mo., original printed wrappers, 8 leaves including 2 signed etchings of Lincoln, uncut. Howard S. Mott Inc. 265 - 80 2016 $375

Wallace, Alfred Russel 1823-1913 *Island Life or the Phenomena and Causes of Insular Faunas and Floras, Including a Revision and Attempted Solution of the Problem of Eccological Climates.* London: Macmillan and co., 1880. First edition, 8vo., 3 maps, further maps and illustrations in text, first bifolium unopened, very slight foxing and browning but good, bound in green publisher's cloth lettered gilt and with gilt Macmillan device to spine, gilt globe stamp to front cover and black Macmillan device to back, simple black linear design to head and foot of spine and covers, brown paper pastedowns and endpapers (rubbed, slightly worn and bumped, front cover touch bent, f.f.e.p. loose), purchase note in pencil dated June 1926, some pencil notes. Unsworths Antiquarian Booksellers Ltd. 30 - 160 2016 £600

Wallace, Alfred Russel 1823-1913 *A Narrative of Travels on the Amazon and Rio Negro with an Account of the Native tribes, and Observations on the Climate, Geology and Natural History of the Amazon Valley.* London: Ward Lock and Co. n.d. c., 1890. Reprint of new Minerva edition, 8vo., sometime bound in full red calf, gilt foliate borders to sides, spine with gilt raised bands and centre tools, green morocco label with gilt lettering, gilt turn-ins, marbled edges and endpapers, frontispiece, 14 wood engraved plates or diagrams, one single page map, little foxing to endpapers and titlepage, else very good, bright copy. Sotheran's Piccadilly Notes - Summer 2015 - 318 2016 £100

Wallace, Alfred Russell 1823-1913 *Tropical Nature and Other Essays.* London: Macmillan & Co., 1878. First edition, 8vo., final leaf with publisher's ads to recto, foxing at beginning and end but good, bound in green publisher's cloth with lettering and publisher's stamp to spine, simple black linear pattern to spine and covers, brown pastedowns and endpapers, blinding slightly rubbed, bumped and discolored and hinges cracked, but good, bookseller's label of Whiteleys, Stationers, Westbourne Grove, inscription dated 1882, pencil purchase note June 1926. Unsworths Antiquarian Booksellers Ltd. 30 - 159 2016 £400

Wallace, Diana *Midsummer Madness.* Hornsey, 1935. One of 24 numbered copies, 5 wood engravings by Barbara Wallace, few faint foxspots, original blue boards, decorated with yellow and brown speckle effect, brown leather backstrip lettered gilt, very slightly rubbed at ends, endpapers faintly foxed, gift inscription, very good. Blackwell's Rare Books B184 - 318 2016 £100

Wallace, Edgar *Four Square Jane.* Readers Library, 1929. Name stamps on front endpaper, dust jacket lightly chipped but practically complete, rarely found in this good condition. I. D. Edrich Crime - 2016 £40

Wallace, Eglantine, Lady *The Ton.* London: printed for T. Hookham, 1788. 8vo., without half title, disbound. Jarndyce Antiquarian Booksellers CCXVI - 474 2016 £40

Wallace, Harold Frank *A Stuart Sketch Book 1542-1746.* London: Eyre & Spottiswoode, 1933. First edition, 4to., recently bound in half red morocco, lettered gilt on spine with gilt centre tools, top edges gilt, color and black and white plates by author and Lionel Edwards, very little spotting to few pages, otherwise near fine. Sotheran's Piccadilly Notes - Summer 2015 - 115 2016 £298

Wallace, Irving *The Seven Minutes.* New York: Simon and Schuster, 1969. First edition, fine in fine dust jacket (minor wear at top of spine). Ken Hebenstreit, Bookseller 2016 - 2016 $40

Wallace, Irving *The Word.* New York: Simon & Schuster, 1969. First edition, fine in fine dust jacket (minor wear at top of spine). Ken Hebenstreit, Bookseller 2016 - 2016 $40

Wallace, John *The Battle of Life.* Manchester: Abel Heywood & sons, 1898. 3 parts, original buff printed wrappers, little dusted, good sound copy. Jarndyce Antiquarian Booksellers CCXVIII - 387 2016 £30

Wallace, Patrick Maxwell Stewart *The Trials of Patrick Maxwell Stewart Wallace and Michael Shaw Stewart Wallace, for Wilfully Destroying the Brig Dryad off Cuba....* London: Williams and Son, 1841. First edition, original blindstamped cloth, rather faded, spine neatly repaired, good, uncut, scarce. John Drury Rare Books 2015 - 21115 2016 $437

Waller, Augustus *Nouvelle Methode Anatomique pour l'Investigation Du Systeme Nerveaux Premiere Partie....* Bonn: Charles Georgi, 1852. 2 plates, large 4to., new marbled wrappers, text with some foxing, otherwise tall uncut copy with wide margins, rare. James Tait Goodrich X-78 - 547 2016 $1495

Waller, Edmund *Mr Waller's Speech in Parliament, at a Conference of Both Houses in the Painted Chamber 6 July 1641.* London: by John Norton for Abel Roper at the black spread Eagle, 1641. First edition, small 4to., title spotted and final page soiled, late 19th century half blue morocco, endleaves, titlepage and final leaf lightly foxed, from the library of James Stevens Cox (1910-1997). Maggs Bros. Ltd. 1447 - 434 2016 £100

Waller, Edmund *Poems &c.* London: by T. W. for Humphrey Mosley, 1645. Second or third unauthorized edition, 8vo., lacking engraved portrait, repair to inner margin of title, touching one rule, single worm hole to upper outer margin extends gradually to three holes, then a trail and disappears, early 19th century russia, covers tooled with single gilt rule and blind roll border, spine tooled in gilt and blind, drab presentation, front joint half split, but holding, lower joint rubbed, nasty dent to second to last panel, from the library of James Stevens Cox (1910-1997). Maggs Bros. Ltd. 1447 - 435 2016 £200

Waller, Edmund *Poems &c.* London: for Henry Herringman, 1668. Later edition, small 8vo., variant with 'London' printed in red in imprint, pastedowns and flyleaves little stained, contemporary sheep, ruled in blind (edges chipped, lower corners bumped, lower headcap torn away), early signature of Margaret Short, pen trials on flyleaves, from the library of James Stevens Cox (1910-1997). Maggs Bros. Ltd. 1447 - 436 2016 £150

Waller, Edmund *Poems, &c. (bound with) The Maid's Tragedy Altered.* London: for H. Herringman and sold by Jacob Tonson, 1694. 1690. Sixth edition of first work, 8vo., small tear to lower blank margin of portrait, light browning, occasional rust spots, blank corner of P1 weak from paper flaw, short closed tear to upper margin, contemporary calf, boards and spine rubbed, bumped and worn, gilt label, faded, joints starting to split, second work with little spotting to E4 and E5, some occasional light modern pencil annotations, from the library of James Stevens Cox (1910-1997). Maggs Bros. Ltd. 1447 - 417 2016 £120

Waller, Edmund *The Poetical Works.... from Mr. Fenton's Quarto Edition.* London: printed for C. Cooke, 1798. Cooke's edition, engraved frontispiece, engraved titlepage, 3 engraved plates, 12mo., some slight waterstaining to few pages, most visible at head of frontispiece and engraved titlepage, full contemporary mottled calf, gilt decorated spine, black morocco label. Jarndyce Antiquarian Booksellers CCXVI - 585 2016 £35

Wallis, Ralph *Room for the Cobbler of Gloucester and His Wife...* London: for the author, 1668. First and only edition, small 4to., lightly foxed, minor tear along upper edge of C3, small piece torn away from blank corner of E1, with some leaves partly uncut, mid 19th century half black morocco and marbled boards, corners little worn, Henry Cunliffe bookplate, from the library of James Stevens Cox (1910-1997). Maggs Bros. Ltd. 1447 - 438 2016 £1100

Walls, William Jacob *Joseph Charles Price: Educator and race Leader, Founder of Livingstone College.* Boston: Christopher Pub. House, 1943. First edition, double frontispiece, photos, inscription, else fine in fine in very good plus pictorial dust jacket with some very shallow chipping at extremities and couple of small dampstains. Between the Covers Rare Books 202 - 119 2016 $300

Walpole, Horace 1719-1797 *The Castle of Otranto, A Gothic Story.* Parma: Printed by Bodoni for J. Edwards, 1791. Sixth edition, one of 300 copies, second state of titlepage, quarto, contemporary red morocco, gilt rules and lettering, two frontispieces, this copy has Hazen's states A & B of frontispiece, bookplate of Charles Walker Andrews, edges little rubbed, some light foxing, very good. The Brick Row Book Shop Miscellany 69 - 8 2016 $950

Walras, Leon *Elements D'Economie Politique Pure ou Theorie de la Richesse Sociale.* Lausanne: F. Rouge, 1889. Second edition, 8vo., original buckram cloth, from the library of economist Lindley Fraser with his signature, mild wear to spine tips, darkening to spine, minimal foxing to endpapers, 8vo., 6 folding plates. By the Book, L. C. 45 - 37 2016 $6000

Walrond, Eric *Tropic Death.* New York: Boni & Liveright, 1926. First edition, 8vo., black cloth slightly cocked, hinge tender, very good, inscribed by author for Philitus Joyce, Sept. 29 1926. Second Life Books, Inc. 196 B - 823 2016 $750

Walsh, James J. *Old-time Makers of Medicine.* New York: Fordham, 1911. Original red cloth, uncut, page tear on page 432, no loss, nice, clean copy. James Tait Goodrich X-78 - 880 2016 $150

Walsh, Robert *The Making of Buffalo Bill. A Study in Heroics.* Indianapolis: Bobbs Merrill, 1928. First edition, frontispiece, 32 illustrations and facsimiles, dark green cloth, gilt, light wear to foot of spine and lower corners, dampstain to gutter of last 10 leaves, very good with worn and soiled pictorial dust jacket. Argonaut Book Shop Biography 2015 - 5918 2016 $125

Walsh, William *A Dialogue Concerning Women being a Defence of the Sex.* London: printed for R. Bensley in Russel street in Covent Garden, 1691. 8vo., paper little browned, stain at end affecting endpapers and last page of text, inner hinges neatly repaired, contemporary calf, expertly rebacked, spine gilt with raised bands, early ownership inscription of John Byrch, oval booklabel of Arnold Muirhead. Jarndyce Antiquarian Booksellers CCXVII - 292 2016 £4200

Walsingham, Lord *Shooting, Moor and Marsh.* London: Longmans, Green & Co., 1889. Third edition, 8vo., original brown decorative cloth, many full page and other illustrations, some foxing, otherwise very good. Sotheran's Hunting, Shooting & Fishing - 104 2016 £130

Walter, L. Edna *Mother Goose's Nursery Tales.* London: A. & C. Black, Autumn, 1923. First edition, Pictorial cloth, fine and bright, 16 fanciful color plates, by Charles Folkard and numerous black and whites plus pictorial endpapers, scarce in such bright condition. Aleph-bet Books, Inc. 112 - 198   2016 $325

Walters, Edward *Printer and Engraver.* Upper Denby: Fleece Press, 2013, but, 2014. One of 240 copies printed on Magnani mouldmade paper, numerous illustrations, device to illustrations and fly-titles printed in red,, 4to., original quarter blue cloth with patterned paper boards, backstrip with printed label, edges untrimmed, fine, with copy of prospectus loosely inserted.   Blackwell's Rare Books   B186 - 303   2016   £195

Walters, John *A Dissertation on the Welsh Language...* Cowbridge: printed for the author by R. and D. Thomas, 1771. First edition, 8vo., half title, name of early owner cut away from upper blank margin of title, well bound in late 19th century dark blue half morocco gilt over marbled boards, top edge gilt, others uncut, very good, scarce. John Drury Rare Books   2015 - 19115   2016 $350

Walters, L. D'O. *The Years at the Spring: an Anthology of Recent Poetry Compiled by....* New York: Brentanos, September, 1920. First edition, 4to., tan pictorial cloth, light foxing in margins, else near fine, illustrations by Harry Clarke.   Aleph-bet Books, Inc.   112 - 110   2016 $400

Walton, Elijah *Vignettes: Alpine and Eastern.. in two Series. Eastern Series.* London: W. M. Thompson, 1873. First edition, folio, original maroon cloth over bevelled boards by Leighton, Son and Hodge, upper board blocked with design in gilt, lower board blocked in blind, spine lettered gilt, lemon yellow endpapers, all edges gilt, mounted chromolithograph plates, each with tissue guard, binding with wear and little faded, front hinge reinforced, occasional light spotting on card mounts, text little browned, else very good.   Sotheran's Travel and Exploration - 388   2016   £1450

Walton, Izaak 1593-1683   *The Complete Angler.* London: printed for F. and C. Rivington, 1792. Fifth edition, engraved frontispiece, 9 plates, 2 engraved leaves of music, woodcuts within text, 8vo., slight browning and occasional foxing to plates, expertly bound in recent full sprinkled calf, raised and gilt bands, gilt device to spine, red morocco label, handsome.   Jarndyce Antiquarian Booksellers   CCXVII - 295   2016   £480

Walton, Izaak 1593-1683   *The Complete Angler...* London: printed for F. and C. Rivington, 1797. Sixth edition, large 12mo., half title, 5 plates, 3 woodcuts, original full speckled calf, neatly rebacked in calf with light brown gilt stamped spine label, 7 ruled bands on spine, corners worn, some rubbing, very good, ownership signature (1806).   Jeff Weber Rare Books   181 - 86 2016 $400

Walton, Izaak 1593-1683   *The Complete Angler.* London: Elliot Stock, 1885? 12mo., bound by R. H. Porter (with his stamp) in full vellum, black and red titling on cover, edges lightly foxed, very good.   Jeff Weber Rare Books   181 - 85   2016 $75

Walton, Izaak 1593-1683   *The Complete Angler...* Boston: Little Brown, 1892. 8vo., lacking volume I, frontispiece, vignettes, dark green gilt stamped cloth, top edge gilt, bit frayed at spine ends, rubbed, top corner hinge splitting, angling themed bookplate of Keith Cushman Russell, good+.   Jeff Weber Rare Books   181 - 88   2016 $45

Walton, Izaak 1593-1683   *The Compleat Angler.* Cambridge: designed by Bruce Rogers for the Riverside Press, 1909. First Bruce Rogers designed edition, limited to 440 copies, 16mo., original brown mottled boards with printed spine label, wood engravings by Lamont Brown after the cuts of fish in the first edition, with spare spine label at rear, very slight pinching to spine at slipcase, finger holes, small blindstamp to front free endpaper, very good in original slipcase.   Sotheran's Piccadilly Notes - Summer 2015 - 320   2016   £248

Walton, Izaak 1593-1683   *The Complete Angler...* London & Edinburgh: T. N. Foulis ltd., 1925. Large 8vo., color frontispiece, 20 full color plates by Thorpe, original quarter green cloth backed cloth, decorative boards, one corner bit worn, angling themed bookplate of Keith Cushman Russell, very good.   Jeff Weber Rare Books   181 - 87   2016 $45

Walton, Izaak 1593-1683   *The Compleat Angler.* London: George Harrap, 1931. 4to. publisher's full green morocco binding stamped in gold and blind top edge gilt, spine very slightly faded, else fine in custom cloth slipcase, pictorial endpapers, 12 color plates, numerous black and whites by Arthur Rackham, rare publisher's binding.   Aleph-bet Books, Inc.   111 - 373   2016 $1250

Walton, Izaak 1593-1683   *The Compleat Angler.* London: George G. Harrap, 1931. First edition illustrated by Rackham, 4to. original polished black cloth gilt, pictorial endpapers, top edge plain, others untrimmed, 12 colored plates with captioned tissues and chapter headings, tailpieces, vignettes, externally fine, handsome copy, slight bubbling to lower joint, internally clean, minor uniform toning and tone tiny closed tear to half title, slight evidence of earlier adhesions to version of couple of plates, later issue binding. Sotheran's Piccadilly Notes - Summer 2015 - 249   2016   £198

Wambaugh, Joseph   *The Onion Field.* New York: Delacorte, 1973. First edition, fine in price clipped dust jacket with crease on inner front flap.   Mordida Books   2015 - 01057   2016 $65

Wandrei, Donald *The Web of Easter Island.* Sauk City: Arkham House, 1948. First edition, octavo, cloth, fine in fine dust jacket, presentation inscription by author to August Derleth.   John W. Knott, Jr./L.W. Currey, Inc.   Fall-Winter 2015 - 17287   2016 $3500

Wanless, Alexander *Threadline Angling.* London: Herbert Jenkins, 1933. First edition, 8vo., original blue cloth with red and black printed dust jacket, little sunned to spine, otherwise good, not price clipped.   Sotheran's Hunting, Shooting & Fishing - 154   2016   £30

Wanless, Alexander *Threadline's Year.* London: Herbert Jenkins, 1952. First edition, small 8vo., original blue cloth with illustrated dust jacket (little worn but not pirce clipped), very good.   Sotheran's Hunting, Shooting & Fishing - 155   2016   £20

Warburton, Sydney *Letters to my Unknown Friends.* London: Longman Brown &c., 1846. First edition, half title, 32 page catalog (Jan. 1847), original pink-brown cloth by Westleys & Clark, slight nick to head of spine, dust jacket signature, very good.   Jarndyce Antiquarian Books   CCXV - 461   2016   £85

Ward, Anne *The Maiden's Prize or Batchelor's Puzzle, being a Miscellany of Theological and Philosophical Queries.* printed and sold in Aldermary Church-Yard, Bow Lane, 1770? 8vo., woodcut on title, woodcut portrait and vignette, lower outer corner of last 2 leaves oil stained, uncut, sewn ingeniously with contemporary pin, good.   Blackwell's Rare Books   B184 - 23   2016   £1250

Ward, Lynd *Madman's Drum.* New York: Jonathan Cape and Harrison Smith, 1930. Very near fine in close to near fine dust jacket with few tiny tears and some very slight wear, overall much nice than usual.   Jeff Hirsch Books   Holiday List 2015 - 63   2016 $500

Ward, Lynd *Vertigo: a Novel in Woodcuts.* New York: Random House, 1937. 8vo., decorative cloth, gilt rubbing, else very good+, more than 200 full page woodcuts.   Aleph-bet Books, Inc.   112 - 509   2016 $400

Ward, Margarete *Born to the Purple: the Karma of Princess Minerva.* Los Angeles: Kellaway-Ide, 1938. First edition, 8vo., purple cloth, gilt stamped, author's presentation on half title, cover somewhat worn, otherwise very good in worn dust jacket.   Second Life Books, Inc.   196 B - 824   2016 $75

Ward, Mary Augusta Arnold 1851-1920 *Fenwick's Career.* New York: Harper, 1906. First American edition, 2 volumes, 8vo., signed by author, illustrations by Albert Sterner, all present but one loose, one hinge tender, otherwise very good.   Second Life Books, Inc.   196 B - 825   2016 $75

Ward, Ned *The Comforts of Matrimony or Lobe's Last Shift.* London: printed for Fielding and Walker, 1780. Lacking frontispiece, title rather dusted, 1 small tear not affecting text, contemporary half calf, sympathetically rebacked, red morocco label.   Jarndyce Antiquarian Books   CCXV - 465   2016   £125

Ward, Seth *Vindiciae Academiarum Containing Some Briefe Animadversions Upon Mr. Websters Book...* Oxford: by Leonard Lichfield for Thomas Robinson, 1654. First edition, small 4to., top margin closely trimmed with page numbers cropped on A2, B3, D2-3, gatherings A-B lightly stained, small hole to D1 affecting text, internally crisp and clean, modern brown half calf and boards, from the library of James Stevens Cox (1910-1997).   Maggs Bros. Ltd.   1447 - 440   2016   £750

Ward, Seth *Vindiciae Academiarum Containing Some Briefe Animadversions Upon Mr. Websters Book....* Oxford: by Leonard Lichfield for Thomas Robinson, 1654. First edition, small 4to., ink stain in upper inner corner of titlepage and marking to C3r and C4, sidenote on A3v shaved, closely shaved at foot touching few catchwords, mid 20th century calf, Rev. Philip Bliss (1787-1857) signature, from the library of James Stevens Cox (1910-1997).   Maggs Bros. Ltd.   1447 - 439   2016   £800

Ward, Thomas *England's Reformation from the Time of King Henry the Eight to the End of Oates's Plot.* Liverpool: printed in the year, 1782. Sixth edition, 8vo., Y7 torn across and repaired neatly without loss of text, fore-edge reinforced on recto, some browning and occasional foxing, blindstamp of Wigan Public Library at foot of titlepage, recent marbled paper wrappers.   Jarndyce Antiquarian Booksellers   CCXVI - 590   2016   £65

Warden, William *Letters Written on Board His Majesty's Ship the Northumberland and Saint Helena...* London: pub. for the author by R. Ackermann, 1816. Fourth edition, half title, engraved frontispiece, 2 plates, 8vo., fine copy, contemporary half russia, gilt banded spine, gilt flower head motifs, from the library of Invercauld Castle, Braemar, bookseller's ticket of A. Brown & Co. Aberdeen.   Jarndyce Antiquarian Booksellers   CCXVI - 591   2016   £280

Wardrop, A. E. *Modern Pig Sticking.* London: Macmillan and Co. Ltd., 1914. 8vo., original dark blue cloth, image of author stamped in gilt on upper cover, spine titled in gilt, 35 plates, very good, some mild and occasional foxing.   Sotheran's   Piccadilly Notes - Summer 2015 - 322   2016   £148

Ward's Miscellany. London: Thomas Ward and Co., Ainsworth & sons, Manchester &c, 1837. Volume I, 52 issues, half black calf, marbled boards, slightly rubbed.   Jarndyce Antiquarian Booksellers   CCXVII - 229   2016   £65

Ware, George W. *German and Austrian Porcelain.* New York: Crown Pub. Inc., 1963. First American edition, color and black and white plates, dust jacket has 1 and half inch tear to front and lightly chipped on spine head, fine. Argonaut Book Shop   Pottery and Porcelain 2015 - 985   2016 $100

Warner, Charles Dudley *My Winter on the Nile Among the Mummies and Moslems...* Hartford: American Pub. Co., 1876. Scarce first edition, 8vo., original decorated cloth, lettered gilt, frontispiece, spine little dulled, tissue guard of frontispiece removed, light spotting to initial blank, otherwise very good.   Sotheran's   Travel and Exploration - 43   2016   £198

Warner, Francis *A Course of Lectures on the Growth and means of Training and Mental Faculty Delivered in the University Press 1890.* Cambridge: at the University Press, 1890. Half title, illustrations, 1 page ads, original brown cloth, slightly rubbed.   Jarndyce Antiquarian Books   CCXV - 999   2016   £35

Warner, Hariette *The Story Song Book with Words and Music.* Chicago: Catherine Cook, 1912. Boards with round pictorial paste-on, fine+, 10 fabulous full page color illustrations by M. T. Ross.   Aleph-bet Books, Inc.   112 - 435   2016 $250

Warner, Rex *Aerodrome - a Love Story.* London: John Lane the Bodley Head, 1941. First edition, octavo, scarce, lettering on spine of dust jacket has offset onto spine, lower corners slightly affected by damp, free endpapers tanned, very good in good, somewhat grubby and nicked dust jacket by Donovan Lloyd, faded at spine and edges, several short enclosed tears at edges.   Peter Ellis   112 - 433   2016   £675

Warner, Richard *Plantae Woodfordienses, a Catalogue of the More Perfect Plants Growing Spontaneously about Woodford in the County of Essex.* London: printed for the author, 1771. First edition, 8vo., engraved monogrammed vignette on title, few gatherings miss-folding, first few leaves with repairs to fore-edge, not affecting text, uncut in modern buckram backed boards, printed paper label on spine, inscribed "From the author".   Marlborough Rare Books   List 56 - 58   2016   £650

Warner, Richard *Rebellion in Bath... (with) The Restoration...* London: G. Wilkie and J. Robinson, 1808-1809. First edition, 4to., vignette on titlepage of first part, few characters identified in pencil, some slight marginal dusting, two voumes bound in one, fairly recent half dark green cloth, marbled boards in 19th century style.   Jarndyce Antiquarian Booksellers   CCXVII - 294   2016   £150

Warner, Tom *The Monster in the Turtles Den.* Cincinnati: Michael Mar Press, 1977. Only edition, 4to., original pictorial full brown morocco, uncut, illustrations in color, produced on handmade paper, inscribed to master papermaker Douglas Morse Howell.   Howard S. Mott Inc. 265 - 75   2016 $1250

Warren, Edwards *Some Account of the Letheom; or, Who is the Discoverer?* Boston: Dutton and Wentworth, 1847. Revised, 8vo, sewn as issued, some foxing and fraying.   M & S Rare Books, Inc.   99 - 7   2016 $850

Warren, John Collins *The Great Tree on Boston Common.* Boston: John Wilson, 1855. First edition, large 8vo., inscribed by author to John Welles, wood engraved frontispiece, tissue guard, double page map.   Second Life Books, Inc.   196 B - 827   2016 $250

Warren, Robert Penn   1905-1989   *Ballad of a Sweet Dream of Peace: a Charade for Easter.* Dallas: Pressworks, 1980. First edition, coy 72 of 350 numbered copies (of a total edition of 376) signed by author and artist, marbled boards with black cloth spine, 3 mounted color illustrations with acetate guards by Bill Komodore, dedicated to William Meredith, his copy though no sign of ownership, fine in fine acetate dust jacket, laid in is the printed musical score by By Alexei Haleff.   Charles Agvent   William Meredith - 117   2016 $200

Warren, Robert Penn   1905-1989   *Brother to Dragons: a Tale in Verse and Voices.* New York: Random, 1983. First printing, author's presentation on flyleaf to William Claire, blue cloth, very good, tight, dust jacket some soiled and chipped, half of presentation on endpaper browned from acidation from something that had been laid in.   Second Life Books, Inc.   196 B - 828   2016 $120

Warren, Robert Penn   1905-1989   *Incarnations: Poems 1966-1968.* New York: Random, 1968. first printing, 8vo., author's presentation to William Claire, small stain to foredge of leaves, very good, tight in some soiled and chipped dust jacket.   Second Life Books, Inc.   196 B - 829   2016 $120

Warren, Robert Penn   1905-1989   *New and Selected Poems 1923-1985.* New York: Random House, 1989. First Random House edition, 8vo., nice in little worn printed wrappers, inscribed by author to poet and editor Barbara Howes.   Second Life Books, Inc.   196 B - 830   2016 $100

Warren, Robert Penn   1905-1989   *Selected Poems: new and Old. 1923-1966.* New York: Random House, 1966. First edition, #235 of 250 large paper copies, printed on special paper and specially bound, signed by author, 8vo., small stain to fore-edge, otherwise fine in dust jacket and publisher's box.   Second Life Books, Inc.   196 B - 831   2016 $225

Warren, Robert Penn 1905-1989 *Two Poems.* Winston Salem: Palaemon Press, 1980. First edition, #72 of 350 numbered copies (of a total edition of 376) signed by author and artist on colophon page, inscribed by publisher Stuart Wright for William Meredith, fine.   Charles Agvent   William Meredith - 118   2016 $150

Warren, Robert Penn 1905-1989 *You, Emperors and Others Poems 1957 1960.* New York: Random House, 1960. First printing, 8vo., author's presentation to William Claire, blue cloth, very good, tight copy, dust jacket some soiled and chipped.   Second Life Books, Inc.   196 B - 832   2016 $120

Warren, Rosanna *Snow Day.* Winston Salem: Palaemon Press, 1981. First edition, one of 550 copies, cloth backed boards, inscribed and signed by author

for William Meredith, laid in prospectus as well as ALS from Warren to Meredith dated 23 dec. 1981, fine.   Charles Agvent   William Meredith - 119   2016 $150

Warren, Stewart *The Wife's Guide and Friend.* London: A. Lambert & Co., 1894. Third edition, small 4to., illustrations, 58 page catalog, original blue cloth, boards marked.   Jarndyce Antiquarian Books   CCXV - 469   2016   £35

Warren, Stewart *The Wife's Guide and Friend...* London: Lambert & Co., 1927. Twenty second edition, illustrations, 68 page catalog, original orange printed cloth, slightly rubbed.   Jarndyce Antiquarian Books   CCXV - 470   2016   £30

Warwick, Frances Evelyn *A Woman and the War.* London: Chapman & Hall, 1916. First edition, 8vo., frontispiece, little foxed red cloth, very good, tight, inscribed by author for Clifford Carver.   Second Life Books, Inc.   196 B - 833   2016 $325

Wascher-James, Sande *Votes for Women.* Whidbey Island: 2015. Artist's book, one in a series of 3, each on various papers and signed by artist, on 12 Varese Floral papers, four of which have gold, , all are Turkish map folded and put on book covers, signed with title hand lettered by artist, page size 11 7/8 x 5 1/4 inches, housed in custom made cornflower blue Irish book cloth over boards lidded box with one of the posters from the suffrage movement on the lid, box measures 12 5/8 x 13 7/8 x 13 7/8 x 12 1/8 inches.   Priscilla Juvelis - Rare Books   66 - 21   2016 $2500

Wase, Christopher *Considerations Concerning Free-Schools, as Settled in England.*   Oxford: at the Theatre and are to be sold there and in London at Mr. Simon Millers, 1678. First edition, 8vo., engraved vignette of the Sheldonian Theatre on title, dampstaining to foot of titlepage and leaves a2-B4, lightly spotted throughout, mid 2th century quarter green morocco and marbled boards, old flyleaves preserved, 19th century ink armorial stamp of Mrs. M. F. Fletcher, from the library of James Stevens Cox (1910-1997).   Maggs Bros. Ltd.   1447 - 441   2016   £700

Wase, Christopher *Senarius sive De Legibus & licentia Veterum Poetarum.* Oxford: e Theatro Sheldoniano, 1687. First edition, 4to., engraved printer's device to titlepage, little light foxing, mostly affecting title, occasional light toning, slight staining to margins towards rear, contemporary vellum, small handwritten label to spine, edges sprinkled red, spine slightly darkened with evidence of small label removed at tail, some smudgy marks, boards little bowed but entirely sound, 'Fletcher' in old hand to rear pastedown.   Unsworths Antiquarian Booksellers Ltd.   E01 - Early Printing - 30   2016   £600

Washington, Booker T. *The Future of the American Negro.* Boston: Small Maynard, 1899. First edition, frontispiece, maroon cloth, very small chip at bottom of front fly, else exceptionally fine and bright.   Between the Covers Rare Books   207 - 93   2016 $500

Washington, Booker T. *My Larger Education: Being Chapters from My Experience.* Garden City: Doubleday Page, 1911. First edition, frontispiece, maroon cloth neat and attractive contemporary ownership signature of Joseph Stannard Baker, offsetting on titlepage and also on blank front a clipping, else exceptionally fine and bright.   Between the Covers Rare Books   207 - 96   2016 $300

Washington, Booker T. *Phelps Hall Bible Training Course...* Tuskegee: Tuskegee Institute Steam Press, 1901. First edition, small octavo, stapled and printed wrappers, staples oxidized, still fine, prospectus for the course.   Between the Covers Rare Books   207 - 94   2016 $950

Washington, Booker T. *Tuskegee and Its People: Their Ideals and Achievements.* New York: D. Appleton and Co., 1905. First edition, frontispiece, illustrations, light rubbing on corners, else bright and fine, in very good example of rare printed dust jacket with some chips and tears particularly where crown meets rear panel and some professional internal reinforcement to folds, jacket rare.   Between the Covers Rare Books   207 - 95   2016 $7500

Washington, Booker T. *Up from Slavery.* New York: Doubleday Page & Co., 1901. First edition, frontispiece, red cloth, gilt, modern gift inscription for Walter Hutchins from Peter Lax, modest wear at spine ends and corners, else tight and bright, near fine.   Between the Covers Rare Books   202 - 117   2016 $300

Washington, George 1732-1799 *Official Letters to the Honourable American Congress, Written during the War Between the United Colonies and Great Britain by his Excellency, George Washington....* London: printed for Cadell Junior and Davies, G. G. and J. Robinson, B. and J. White, W. Otridge and Son, J. Debrett, R. Faulder and T. Egerton, 1795. First edition, second issue without half title and portrait, 8vo., contemporary mottled calf, six compartments, four decorated gilt with flags and crown, red morocco title and black volume number labels, marbled endpapers, very good set, boards rubbed, small circular scuff worn through to rear board of one volume, flyleaves toned opposite endpapers, text quite sharp, armorial bookplate of Otis E. Weld.   Kaaterskill Books   21 - 113   2016 $1200

Washington, M. Bunch *The Art of Romare Bearden: the Prevalance of Ritual.* New York: Harry N. Abrams Inc., 1972. First edition, folio, bit of foxing on fore edge and first and last few leaves, spine tail bumped with half inch tears at joints, else near fine copy in like dust jacket with corresponding tears on spine tail, press release for the book laid in, inscribed by Bearden for Richard Long.   Between the Covers Rare Books   202 - 9   2016 $1500

Wassermann, Caroline *Song Book of the Pacific Coast School for Workers.* Berkeley: Pacific Coast School for Workers, 1939. Third edition, quarto, mimeographed leaves and stapled into mimeographed wrappers illustrated by C. Amys, rear wrapper detached, with stains on both front and back wrappers, small nicks and tears, fair only, very uncommon.   Between the Covers Rare Books   204 - 76   2016 $450

Wassterstein, Wendy *Bachelor Girls.* New York: Knopf, 1990. First trade edition, 8vo., signed by author, fine in dust jacket.   Second Life Books, Inc.   196 B - 834   2016 $45

Wastfield, Robert *A True Testimony of Faithfull Witnesses Recorded.* London: for Giles Calvert, 1657. First edition, small 4to., little dusty, lower right corner of verso of n3 soiled, isolated staining to lower inside of N4, prominent staining to foot of final leaf, fore-edges of first few leaves creased, very fresh, uncut copy, sewn as issued, original buff paper wrappers, spine partly defective, five contemporary ink annotations, from the library of James Stevens Cox (1910-1997).   Maggs Bros. Ltd.   1447 - 442   2016   £500

Watanabe, Sumiharu *Face of Washington Square.* Tokyo: Hashimoto Yuyudo, 1965. Photographs, signed and inscribed by Watanabe in English and Japanese, very nice, uncommon signed, close to near fine in photo-illustrated wrappers with slight bumping to top and bottom corners and some very negligible wear with near fine obi that has small tear to spine in close to near fine printed that cardboard slipcase that has some splitting to top corner.   Jeff Hirsch Books   Holiday List 2015 - 3   2016 $6000

Waterhouse, Benjamin *Cautions to Young Persons Concerning Health in a Public Lecture Delivered at the Close of the Medical Course in Cambridge Nov. 20 1804...* Cambridge: University Press by W. Hilliard, 1805. 32 pages, contemporary marbled paper covers, printed paper label on upper cover, neatly bound in later cloth, light, mostly marginal foxing, some spotting on label, else very good, wide margined copy.   Joseph J. Felcone, Inc.   Books from Five Centuries: a Miscellany - 148   2016 $650

Waterhouse, G. R. *The Naturalist's Library. Volume 24. Mammalia: Marsupialia or Pouched Animals.* Edinburgh: W. H. Lizars, 1855. Second edition, duodecimo, 34 hand colored plates, hand colored half title, publisher's cloth with new endpapers.   Andrew Isles Natural History Books   55 - 3838   2016 $650

Waterman, Catharine H. *Flora's Lexicon...* Philadelphia: Herman Hooker, 1839. First edition, 8vo., three floral colored plates, numerous woodcuts, original cloth, stamped gilt spine, front hinge weak, considerable waterstaining & browning, some pages becoming loose.   M & S Rare Books, Inc.   99 - 62   2016 $300

Waterman, Hugh *A Sermon Preached before the Court of Guardians of the Poor in the City of Bristol at St. Peters Church April 13th 1699.* Bristol: by W. Bonny, 1699. First edition, small 4to., lightly browned and spotted throughout, particularly at end, rust spots in places, lower edges of A1-2 uncut, lower fore-corner of F4 repaired, late 19th early 20th century half maroon morocco and marbled boards, from the library of James Stevens Cox (1910-1997), signature of Alfred J. Waterman, 6 Manor Park, Redland, Bristol dated 1913 and 3 page note on front flyleaves, 1913 clipping from local Bristol newspaper, pencil note "from the Weare collection.   Maggs Bros. Ltd.   1447 - 443   2016   £500

Waters, Ethel *To Me It's Wonderful.* New York: Harper & Row, 1972. First edition, 8vo., photos, nice in slightly chipped, price clipped dust jacket, signed by author.   Second Life Books, Inc.   196 B - 835   2016 $45

Waters, Frank *Brave are My People.* Clear Light Press, 1993. First edition, fine copy in fine dust jacket, signed by Waters and Deloria Vine.   Bella Luna Books   2016 - p2277   2016 $75

Waters, Frank *Flight from Fiesta.* Santa Fe: Rydal Press, 1986. Limited edition, 67/200 copies, signed by author, cloth and paper covered boards, book near fine in lightly worn slipcase, better than it sounds.   Dumont Maps and Books   133 - 82   2016 $75

The Watershed Anthology. La Crosse: University of Wisconsin La Crosse, 1988. 8vo., stiff paper wrapers, sewn, illustrations, foldout broadsides by Gary Young and Jenny Sawle.   Oak Knoll Books   310 - 157   2016 $125

Waterstone, Satella *Short Stories of Musical Melodies.* Chicago: Volland, 1915. 4to., cloth backed boards, stamped in gold, slight edgewear, else very near fine, illustrations by K. Sturges Dodge, full page illustrations, scarce. Aleph-bet Books, Inc. 112 - 502 2016 $300

Waterton, Charles *Wanderings in South America the North-West of the United States and the Antilles in the Years 1812, 1816, 1829 and 1824.* London: A. Applegarth for J. Mawman, 1825. First edition, 4to., contemporary quarter brown morocco, brown paper covered boards, frontispiece, 2 woodcut text illustrations with ALS from Charles Waterton, seal cut out, bookplate of Bertram Savile Ogle, very good. Sotheran's Piccadilly Notes - Summer 2015 - 323 2016 £1550

Waterton, Charles *Wanderings in South America, the North-West of the United States and the Antilles in the Years 1812, 1816, 1820 and 1824.* Macmillan, 1825. First edition, quarto, frontispiece and titlepage foxed, page with ink splash, contemporary brown quarter calf, corners rubbed, joints cracked with small loss at head and tail of spine. J. & S. L. Bonham Antiquarian Booksellers America 2016 - 9903 2016 £250

Waterton, Charles *Wanderings in South America.* London: B. Fellowes, 1828. Second edition, engraved frontispiece, original green linen boards, faded and sunned, front board detached, uncut. James Tait Goodrich X-78 - 551 2016 $650

Waterville, Armand De *Introduction a L'Etude de L'Electronicus des Nerfs Moterus et Sensities chz l'Homme.* Londres: Imprimerie de Ranken et Cie, 1883. 2 plates, original binding. James Tait Goodrich X-78 - 552 2016 $750

Watkins-Pitchford, Denys *The Best of 'BB' an Anthology.* London: Michael Joseph, 1985. First edition, 8vo., original cloth with dust jacket, illustrations by author, near fine. Sotheran's Piccadilly Notes - Summer 2015 - 25 2016 £60

Watkins-Pitchford, Denys *The Bullfinch.* London: Hamish Hamilton, 1957. First edition, 8vo., original bright yellow cloth decorated and lettered in blue, pictorial endpapers, preserved in pictorial dust jacket, illustrations in black and white, externally and internally bright, fresh copy, eually good unclipped dust jacket with slight fading to spine, dusting and soiling to lower panel, wear to spine ends, to a depth of 1mm and little mild rubbing. Sotheran's Piccadilly Notes - Summer 2015 - 24 2016 £498

Watkins-Pitchford, Denys *A Child Alone - The Memoirs of 'B.B.'.* London: Michael Joseph, 1978. First edition, 8vo., original grey cloth, illustrated dust jacket, past ownership bookplate attached to front free endpaper, very good. Sotheran's Hunting, Shooting & Fishing - 242 2016 £90

Watkins-Pitchford, Denys *Letters from Comptom Deverell.* London: Eyre & Spottiswoode, 1950. First edition, royal 8vo., original brown cloth, gilt lettering and wavy lines to upper board and spine, 15 colored plates by the author and with black and white vignette headpiece to each chapter, binding little stained, internally fine. Sotheran's Hunting, Shooting & Fishing - 240 2016 £150

Watkins-Pitchford, Denys *Recollections of a Longshore Gunnet.* Ipswich: Boydell Press, 1976. First edition, slim 8vo., original blue cloth titled in silver to spine, illustrated dust jacket, price clipped dust jacket very slightly faded, otherwise very good, uncommon. Sotheran's Hunting, Shooting & Fishing - 241 2016 £150

Watkins-Pitchford, Denys *The Sportsman's Bedside Book.* London: Eyre & Spottiswoode, 1948. Fourth printing, 8vo., original brown cloth, illustrated dust jacket slightl used, nevertheless a very good copy. Sotheran's Hunting, Shooting & Fishing - 237 2016 £100

Watkins, Daniel Joseph *Freak Power. Hunter S. Thompson's Campaign for Sheriff.* Aspen: Meat Process Press, 2015. First edition, signed by author, fine in fine dust jacket. Ken Lopez Bookseller 166 - 126 2016 $100

Watkins, Henry George *Affectionate Advice to Apprentices and Other Young Men Engaged in Trades or Professions.* London: William Brown & Co., 1869. Eleventh edition, prelims slightly spotted, contemporary full red crushed morocco, elaborate gilt borders, spine gilt, coat of arms of worshipful Company of Goldsmiths, all edges gilt, very good. Jarndyce Antiquarian Books CCXV - 471 2016 £85

Watkins, Vernon *The Ballad of the Outer Dark and Other Poems.* London: Enitharmon Press, 1979. First edition, one of 45 specially bound and numbered copies, octavo, cloth backed patterned boards, top edge gilt, fine. Peter Ellis 112 - 434 2016 £100

Watson, Ian *God's World.* London: Victor Gollancz, 1979. First edition, octavo, presentation copy inscribed to Les, tail of spine very slightly bumped, fine in fine dust jacket. Peter Ellis 112 - 435 2016 £25

Watson, Ina *Silvertail: the Story of a Lyrebird.* Sydney: John Sands Pty. Ltd., 1946. Large octavo, color illustrations, fine in dust jacket. Andrew Isles Natural History Books 55 - 23876 2016 $50

Watson, James D. *The DNA Story.* San Francisco: W. H. Freeman, 1981. First edition, minimal scuffs to covers in near fine dust jacket. By the Book, L. C. 45 - 27 2016 $400

Watson, James D. *Molecular Biology of the Gene.* New York: W. A. Benjamin, 1965. First edition, 8vo., very good++, mild soil to covers, edges, corners bumped, very good dust jacket with closed tears to front panel, 1.5 inch piece missing lower tip, minimal chips, scarce.   By the Book, L. C.   45 - 25   2016 $300

Watson, William *The History of the Reign of Philip the Third King of Spain.* Basil: printed and sold by J. J. Tourneisen, 1792. New edition, 2 volumes, 8vo. slight foxing, several leaves little dusty, upper edge of blank margin of S6 & Y6 volume i not affecting text, 19th century half calf, marbled boards, red morocco labels, repair to spine volume ii, heads of spines rubbed.   Jarndyce Antiquarian Booksellers   CCXVI - 592   2016   £120

Watt, Robert *Rules of Life with Reflections on the manners and Dispositions of Mankind.* Edinburgh: Longman, Hurst &c, 1814. 12mo., name erased from upper corner of title, contemporary full speckled calf, gilt borders and spine, brown morocco labels, hinges slightly rubbed, Fasque booklabel, very good.   Jarndyce Antiquarian Books   CCXV - 472   2016   £75

Watteville, H. De *Waziristan 1919-1920.* London: Constable and Co. Ltd., 1925. First edition, 8vo., original red cloth spine lettered in gilt, 6 plates, 1 folding map and 3 full page sketch maps, spine little sunned, cloth with minor marking, few pages little spotted, one gathering opened crudely.   Sotheran's   Travel and Exploration - 204   2016   £298

Wattleton, Faye *Life on the Line: a Special Limited Edition for Friends of MS Magazine.* New York: Ballantine, 1996. First printing, 8vo., one leaf of corrections laid in, paper over boards, about as new in dust jacket.   Second Life Books, Inc.   196 B - 837   2016 $45

Watts, Alan S. *The Life and Times of Charles Dickens.* London: Studio Editions, 1991. First edition, folio, half title, 250 color and black and white illustrations, original pale blue cloth, very good in dust jacket.   Jarndyce Antiquarian Booksellers   CCXVIII - 1477   2016   £25

Watts, Alan W. *The Wisdom of Insecurity.* New York: Pantheon, 1951. First edition, signed by author, near fine in good, fragile dust jacket that is spine faded and chipped at corners, spine extremities and separated at front fold, gift note tipped to rear free endpaper, Watt's signature is uncommon.   Ken Lopez Bookseller   166 - 147   2016 $750

Watts, George *A Sermon Preached before the Trustees for establishing the Colony of Georgia in America at their Anniversary meeting in... London... March 18, 1735.* London: B. M. Downing, 1736. 4to.. remarkably fine, fresh copy, entirely untrimmed in 19th century quarter roan (broken).   Joseph J. Felcone, Inc.   Books from Five Centuries: a Miscellany - 71   2016 $1800

Watts, Isaac *Divine Songs in Easy Language for the Use of Children.* London: printed for J. Buckland and 5 others, 1775. 12mo., initial license leaf, slight tear without loss to head of B1, pen strokes to opening pages 34-35, otherwise good, clean copy, original hessian cloth boards, front endpaper bears inscription of John Owen, March 30th 1776 and Anne Owen, July 2nd 1796.   Jarndyce Antiquarian Booksellers   CCXVI - 593   2016   £120

Watts, Isaac *Horae Lyricae.* London: printed for J. Buckland, T. Longman, T. Field and E. & C. Dilly, 1770. Twelfth edition, 12mo., portrait frontispiece, engraved by T. Chambers, initial royal license leaf, final page of ads for books by Watts, 2 leaves slightly sprung and creased at fore edge, contemporary gilt ruled and decorated speckled calf, spine ruled gilt, red morocco label, red sprinkled edges, slight wear to joint, very good.   Jarndyce Antiquarian Booksellers   CCXVI - 594   2016   £50

Watts, Isaac *Hymns and Spiritual Songs.* London: printed for W. Strahan and 7 others, 1785. Engraved frontispiece, 12mo., very slight unintrusive worming to gutter margins, full contemporary red morocco, gilt rope twist border, gilt cornerpiece decoration, gilt panelled spine, marbled endpapers, slight rubbing but attractive copy.   Jarndyce Antiquarian Booksellers CCXVI - 595   2016   £150

Watts, Isaac *The Impeachment of the Mind or a Supplement to the Art of Logic...* Norwich: John Stacy, 1822. Half title, contemporary prize binding of full light brown calf, blocked in gilt and blind, black morocco reward label, spine in gilt, maroon morocco labels, slight wear to lower end of following hinge, slightly rubbed and faded, nice, attractive copy, bookseller's ticket of J. Stacy Norwich, contemporary signature of Robert Gummer.   Jarndyce Antiquarian Books   CCXV - 1000   2016   £95

Watts, Isaac *Select Songs for Children.* Newcastle: printed for S. Hodgson and sold by the Booksellers in Town and Country, 1790. Seventh edition, 12mo., a number of leaves rather thumb marked, some browning, final two pages have verses separated by pencil lines, small tear with loss to blank lower corner of titlepage, contemporary calf backed pattered paper boards, spine and corners worn, boards very rubbed, signature of Elizabeth Nelson, Aug. 16th 1794, and of Elizabeth Ingleson Nov. 1821.   Jarndyce Antiquarian Booksellers   CCXVI - 597   2016   £120

Wauchope, Robert *Archaeology of Northern Mesoamerica.* Austin: University of Texas Press, 1971. 2 volumes, illustrations, near fine in like dust jackets.   Dumont Maps and Books   133 - 83   2016 $100

Waugh, Evelyn 1903-1966 *The Holy Places.* Queen Anne Press, 1952. First edition, 488/900 copies (from an edition of 950 copies), printed on mouldmade paper, titlepage printed in red and black, royal 8vo., original red buckram with press device stamped gilt to both boards, backstrip lettered gilt, some rubbing to borders of cloth, edges untrimmed, dust jacket with light toning to borders, few traces of handling and a brief pen mark at foot of rear panel, very good. Blackwell's Rare Books B184 - 243 2016 £225

Waugh, Evelyn 1903-1966 *Ninety-Two Days.* London: Duckworth, 1934. First edition, octavo, 2 pages of ads at rear, 24 photos, folding map, cloth little rubbed at head and tail of spine, corners bumped, some creasing to edges of map, very good, scarce. Peter Ellis 112 - 436 2016 £250

Waugh, Evelyn 1903-1966 *The Ordeal of Gilbert Pinfold.* Boston: Little Brown and Co., 1957. First edition, black cloth backed red boards, lettered silver to spine, minor rubbing to dust jacket, else fine. Argonaut Book Shop Literature 2015 - 6246 2016 $175

Waugh, Evelyn 1903-1966 *Scoop.* London: Chapman and Hall, 1938. First edition, 2nd issue with 'as' on last line of page 88, inscribed by author to H. H. Rawles from author, 8vo., original red and black marbled cloth lettered gilt on spine with second issue dust jacket with some sunning and chipping, closed tears and creases, otherwise very good, bright, signed and inscribed copies scarce. Sotheran's Piccadilly Notes - Summer 2015 - 328 2016 £2995

Waugh, Evelyn 1903-1966 *Scott-Kings Modern Europe.* London: Chapman and Hall, 1947. First edition, color frontispiece by John Piper, titlepage printed in brown, crown 8vo., original blue cloth, backstrip lettered gilt, top edge blue with others faintly foxed, few small foxspots to fore edge, Piper dust jacket with darkened backstrip panel and faint foxing to lighter areas, chipping to corners and ends of backstrip panel with odd nick, good. Blackwell's Rare Books B184 - 244 2016 £30

Waugh, Evelyn 1903-1966 *Unconditional Surrender - the Conclusion of Men at Arms and Officers and Gentlemen.* London: Chapman & Hall, 1961. First edition, octavo, fine in near fine dust jacket without price sticker, found in many copies. Peter Ellis 112 - 437 2016 £75

Waugh, Evelyn 1903-1966 *Vile Bodies.* London: Chapman and Hall, 1930. First edition, octavo, titlepage designed by author, slight rubbing to corners, near fine, no dust jacket, very bright copy. Peter Ellis 112 - 438 2016 £950

Waugh, Frederick J. *The Clan of Munes.* New York: Charles Scribner, Nov., 1916. First edition, Large oblong 4to., light cover soil and rubbing, near fine, full page plates (8 color and 20 black and white) plus decorative initials and illustrations in text. Aleph-bet Books, Inc. 112 - 185 2016 $850

Way, Thomas Robert *Reliques of Old London - later Reliques of Old London - Suburban London...* London: George Bell and Sons, 1896-1899. Limited edition, each one of 250 copies signed by Way, 4 volumes, 4to., 24 lithographs, signed publisher's half 'Art' vellum over decorated boards, spine ornamented and lettered in gilt. Marlborough Rare Books List 55 - 71 2016 £550

Weaver, Robert C. *The Urban Negro Worker in the United States 1925-1936 Volume II.* Washington: US. Government, 1939. First edition, 4to., blue cloth, author's presentation on front, cover somewhat spotted, otherwise very good tight. Second Life Books, Inc. 196 B - 838 2016 $50

Weaver, William D. *Catalogue of the Wheeler Gift of Books, Pamphlets and Periodicals in the Library of the American Institute of Electrical Engineers.* Mansfield Centre: Martino, n.d., Facsimile reprint limited to 150 copies, Thick 8vo., original cloth, 2 volumes in one, fine. Edwin V. Glaser Rare Books 2015 - 7034 2016 $90

Webb, Brian *Think Of It as a Poster.* Upper Denby: Fleece Press, 2010. One of 100 copies (from an edition of 350) printed on Zerkall Rosa paper, the special copies containing 44 stamps after wood engravings or linocuts, 24mo., original quarter salmon pink cloth with patterned paper sides repeating a design by Clare Melinsky, backstrip with printed label, edges rough trimmed, cloth lined wood and metal box, protective foam lined cardboard box, fine. Blackwell's Rare Books B186 - 304 2016 £250

Webb, Jean Francis *No Match for Murder.* New York: Macmillan, 1942. First edition, bottom of page edges stained and residue from book cover along bottom edge of covers and on free endpapers otherwise very good in prce clipped dust jacket with extensive internal tape mends, chip at top of spine and wear at corners. Mordida Books 2015 - 008724 2016 $55

Webb, Sidney *London Education.* London: Longmans, 1904. First edition, half title, 12 pages ads, original blue cloth, slightly dulled. Jarndyce Antiquarian Books CCXV - 1001 2016 £30

Webb, William *Minutes of Remarks on Subjects Picturesque, Moral and Miscellaneous....* London: Baldwin Cradock and Joy, Dublin: William Frederick Wakeman, 1827. First edition, 2 volumes, very pleasing contemporary sea green straight grain morocco, elaborately gilt, covers with gilt floral frame enclosing a central blindstamped arabesque, raised bands, spine compartments densely gilt with floral tools and volutes, turn-ins with decorative gilt densely gilt with floral tools and volutes, turn-ins with decorative gilt roll, light blue watered silk endleaves, all edges gilt, each volume with animated fore-edge painting set in Italian landscape; armorial bookplate of armorial bookplate of John Thornton Down, spines slightly and uniformly sunned, joints with just hint of rubbing, corners little bent, volume I lacking free endleaf at back, trivial imperfections internally, but extremely pretty set in essentially fine condition, bindings entirely solid with especially lustrous covers and text clean and fresh.   Phillip J. Pirages   67 - 165   2016 $2900

Weber, Bruce *Let's get Lost - a Film Journal.* Little Bear Films, 1988. Published as a companion piece to the movie, black and white photos, tight, very near fine with tiny nick to top and bottom of rear panel, otherwise remarkably fresh and clean, housed in custom black cloth clamshell box. Jeff Hirsch Books   Holiday List 2015 - 98   2016 $1250

Weber, Bruce *O Rio De Janeiro.* New York: Alfred A Knopf, 1986. Paperback original, illustrated, includes several gatefold plates, very near fine in photo illustrated wrappers that have minute bit of wear at spine ends and some small spots to front panel and to top of rear panel of spine, very nice.   Jeff Hirsch Books   Holiday List 2015 - 97   2016 $600

Weber, Lenora Mattingly *Happy Birthday, Dear Beany.* New York: Thomas Crowell, 1957. Stated first printing, fine in near fine dust jacket (price clipped, one tiny closed tear), remarkable copy, rarely found in such beautiful condition. Aleph-bet Books, Inc.   111 - 474   2016 $250

Weber, Leopold *Traumgestalten. (The Dream Garden).* Zurich: und Leipzig: Ratapfelverlag, 1922. First edition, 4to, pictorial cloth, light cover soil, very good+, illustrations by Kreidolf with 10 eerie color plates, 3 full page black and whites and endpapers.   Aleph-bet Books, Inc.   111 - 242   2016 $300

Webster, John *Academiarum Examen or the Examination of Academices.* London: for Giles Calvert, 1654. First edition, small 4to., top edge gilt little dusty, ink blot at centre of N3-4, very light dampstaining touching lower blank edge of M4-4, upper edge closely shaved, occasionally touching running titles, early underlining and annotation on M2v, early 20th century calf, ruled in blind, spine lettered gilt, endleaves little foxed, scarce, with century initials "JW or "TW", from the library of James Stevens Cox (1910-1997) with his cipher and pencil annotations.   Maggs Bros. Ltd.   1447 - 444   2016   £2400

Webster, John *A Monumental Columne, Erected to the Liuing Memory of the Euer-Glorious Henry, late Prince of Wales.* London: printed by N. O(kes) for William Welby, 1613. First edition, woodcut ornaments on title, woodcut headpieces, 2 pages printed entirely in black, lacking final 2 leaves (also printed entirely in black, without text), last leaf with a hole with loss of 3 letters from the motto at end of text on recto, slight loss to lower fore-corner of this leaf and extreme corresponding corner of preceeding leaf (no loss of text), A4 (the first black leaf), very slightly defective at top outer corner, title slightly browned, 4to., late 19th century green crushed morocco by Matthews, quadruple gilt fillets on sides with corner ornaments, spine lettered longitudinally in gilt, gilt edges, extra blank leaves bound in at beginning and end, last at front inscribed 'Richard Grant White Esq. with the best wishes of R. H. Stoddard", good.   Blackwell's Rare Books   Marks of Genius - 50   2016   £20,000

Webster, Noah   1758-1843 *An American Dictionary of the English Language.* New York: Published by S. Converse, Printed by Hezekiah Howe, New Haven, 1828. First edition, 289 x 225mm., 2 volumes, contemporary marbled boards expertly and convincingly rebacked and recornered by Courtland Benson using diced Russia of the period, spines divided into panels by double gilt rules, gilt titling, engraved frontispiece of author in volume 1, paper boards bit chafed, two inch abrasion to leather on lower board of volume 1 but artfully and cleverly restored retrospective bindings show no important wear at the same time that they retain their peirod feel, two gatherings (only) with insignificant foxing (frontispiece, title and few leaves here and there with quite minor foxing), other trivial imperfections, altogether pleasing internally, text remarkably fresh and clean, especially fine copy, that looks very attractive on the shelf. Phillip J. Pirages   67 - 351   2016 $22,500

Webster, T. B. L. *Studies in Menander.* Manchester University Press, 1960. Second edition, 8vo., green cloth, gilt lettered to spine, top edge dusted and with very light spotting, endcaps just starting to wear, small bump to rear board bottom edge, very good, light green dust jacket now bit grubby, spine faded with top edge starting to fray, otherwise still good, author's ownership inscription, two slips of author's notes loosely inserted.   Unsworths Antiquarian Booksellers Ltd.   E04 - 122   2016   £25

Webster, William *The Consequences of Trade as to the Wealth and Strength of any Nation of the Woollen Trade in Particular...* London: sold by T. Cooper at the Globe in Pater Noster Row, 1740. Second edition, 8vo., recent sugar paper wrappers, top edge slightly cropped just touching few page numbers.   Jarndyce Antiquarian Booksellers CCXVI - 600   2016   £60

Webster, William *The Draper Confuted or a Candid and Impartial but Full answer to the Consequences of Trade...* London: printed for T. Cooper at the Globe in Pater Noster Row, 1740. 8vo., some light creasing and browning in final leaf, disbound.   Jarndyce Antiquarian Booksellers   CCXVI - 601   2016   £65

Webster, William *Remarks Upon Mr. Webber's scheme and the Draper's Pamphlet.* London: sold by J. Roberts in Warwick Lane, 1741. 12mo., titlepage little dusty, recent sugar paper wrappers. Jarndyce Antiquarian Booksellers CCXVI - 602 2016 £65

A Wedding Gift. London: Darton and Co., circa, 1845. 16mo., contemporary full brown morocco decorated in gilt, slightly rubbed, gift inscription on recto of front, all edges gilt, attractive copy. Jarndyce Antiquarian Books CCXV - 473 2016 £50

Weddington, Sarah *A Question of Choice.* New York: Grosset/Putnam, 1992. First edition, 8vo. fine in dust jacket, signed by author. Second Life Books, Inc. 196 B - 839 2016 $45

Weedon, L. *Child Characters from Dickens re-told by...* London: Ernest Nister, 1905. First edition, half title, frontispiece, plates, illustrations, original grey clcoth, bevelled boards, pictorially blocked in back, red, dark green, yellow and blue, lettering in black and reversed out of gilt, all edges gilt, very good, attractive. Jarndyce Antiquarian Booksellers CCXVIII - 730 2016 £65

Weems, Mason Locke 1759-1825 *God's Revenge Against Murder ; or the Drown'd Wife.* Philadelphia: printed for the author, 1823. Eleventh edition, frontispiece, removed, browned throughout, handsome leather backed slipcase. Joseph J. Felcone, Inc. Books from Five Centuries: a Miscellany - 149 2016 $400

Wehman Bros.' Bartenders' Guide How to Mix Drinks. New York: Wehman Bros., 1912. 24mo., stapled illustrated glazed yellow wrappers, cheaper paper of the pages slightly age toned, but supple and very near fine. Between the Covers Rare Books 204 - 26 2016 $475

Wehr, Julian *Animated Antics in Playland.* Akron: Saalfield, 1946. Oblong 4to., spiral bound pictorial boards fine in dust jacket with small chip at base of spine, else near fine, very uncommon 4 exceptionally nice moveables with multiple parts in action, color illustrations. Aleph-bet Books, Inc. 112 - 328 2016 $300

Weichenhan, Erasmus *Christliche Betrachtungen Ueber die Evangelischen Texte....* Germantown: Michael Billmeyer, 1791. First American edition, square 8vo., title vignette, contemporary calf over boards, original clasps intact, browned, few early margins neatly reinforced, very good. M & S Rare Books, Inc. 99 - 232 2016 $1250

Weier, Debra *Edges.* Madison: Emanon Press, 1979. Limited to 15 numbered copies, signed by Weier and Bill Bridges, small 4to., cloth with blindstamped front cover, illustrations by Bridges, intaglio images printed on rived BFK and Arches, text printed on separate paper paste-ons. Oak Knoll Books 27 - 69 2016 $1500

Weifenbach, Terri *Some Insects.* Portland: Nazraeli Press, 2010. Number 259 from and edition of 500 copies, signed by Weifenbach, very fine in publisher's bag, includes several images along with original tipped in color photo. Jeff Hirsch Books Holiday List 2015 - 99 2016 $75

Weinthal, Leo *Synopsis of Principal Contents.* London: Pioneer Pub. Co. Ltd. and 'The African World', 1923. 4to., original cord bound wrappers, front cover decorated and lettered gilt, numerous specimens of mounted photographic portraits, illustrations from photos, plates, maps, spine of wrappers with less to head and tail, edges little worn, internally fine. Sotheran's Travel and Exploration - 44 2016 £298

Weir, Joanne *Weir Cooking: Recipes from the Wine Country.* Alexandria: Time Life, 1999. First printing, small 4to., signed by author, copiously illustrated with color photos, nice in somewhat scuffed dust jacket. Second Life Books, Inc. 196 B - 843 2016 $45

Weird Tales - Fall 1984. Los Angeles: Bellerophon Network, 1984. Cover art by H. Ro. Kim, quartoer, perfect-bound magazine, tocuh of wear t spine, else fine. Between the Covers Rare Books 208 - 123 2016 $150

Weisgard, Leonard *Cinderella.* New York: Garden City, 1938. First edition, 4to., cloth backed pictorial boards, fine in dust jacket, color lithos. Aleph-bet Books, Inc. 111 - 475 2016 $250

Weiss, Emil Rudolf *The Typography of an Artist: Emil Rudolf Weiss. A Monograph.* Oldham: Incline Press, 2012. Number 118 of 250 copies, large folio, bound in brown paper covered boards with vellum spine and design in red to front cover, housed in brown paper covered slipcase with black cloth edges and title label to spine, fine. The Kelmscott Bookshop 13 - 25 2016 $600

Weissmuller, Johnny *Swimming the American Crawl.* Boston: Houghton Mifflin Co., 1930. First edition, fine in very good or better dust jacket with few tiny nicks and tears, very nice. Between the Covers Rare Books 208 - 146 2016 $600

Welch, Marie *Of a Feather.* N.P.: 1929. First edition?, 4to., untrimmed and uncut, bound in silk backed boards, very good clean in original slipcase, inscribed by artist. Second Life Books, Inc. 196 B - 846 2016 $75

Weldon, Anthony *The Court and Character of King James.* London: by Robert Ibbitson and are to be sold by John Wright, 1650. Small 8vo., engraved portrait, minor stain at top of first few leaves, some light browning and occasional spots, sheet m lightly dusty, small flaw in margin of D4, some leaves uncut at tail, contemporary sheep, coming loose in case, spine heavily worn and d3efective at head, corners bumped, small wormhole to centre of front cover, no pastedowns, from the library of James Stevens Cox (1910-1997), bookplate of James Frampton (1659-1855), earlier signature deleted from front flyleaf. Maggs Bros. Ltd. 1447 - 445 2016 £175

The Well-Bred Boy and Girl... Boston: B. B. Mussey & Co., 1850. Second edition, Presentation plate, additional vignette titlepage, original brown decorated cloth, contemporary gift inscription, very good, bright copy. Jarndyce Antiquarian Books CCXV - 474 2016 £125

Wellby, M. S. *Twixt Sirdar and Menelik.* London: Harper and Brother, 1901. First edition, 8vo., original brown cloth, decorated in black and white, titled in gilt to front and spine, 8 discolorations to spine, little shaky, nonetheless a more attractive copy than most, largely unblemished text. Sotheran's Travel and Exploration - 45 2016 £148

Weller, Thomas H. *Growing pathogens in Tissue Cultures.* Canton: Science History Publications, 2004. First edition, 8vo., near fine in fine dust jacket. By the Book, L. C. 45 - 21 2016 $500

Welles, Orson *Mr. Arkadin.* London: W. H Allen, 1956. First UK edition, inscribed by author, tiny crown stamp to right corner of front endpaper, else about near fine in like dust jacket. Royal Books 52 - 12 2016 $1500

Welles, Orson *Mr. Arkadin.* New York: Thomas Y Crowell, 1956. First edition, inscribed by author, very good plus in very good plus dust jacket. Royal Books 52 - 13 2016 $1250

Wellman, Paul I. *Broncho Apache.* New York: Macmillan Co., 1936. First edition, 8vo., laid into this copy is 1943 TLS from Wellman to news editor, fine in lightly rubbed dust jacket with light wear to spine ends to to extremities, exceptional, lovely copy. Buckingham Books 2015 - 23335 2016 $2750

Wellman, Paul I. *The Callaghan, Yesterday and Today.* Encinal: Callaghan land and Pastoral Co., n.d. 1943 or 1944, First edition, 8vo., pictorial wrappers with extended edges, illustrations, portraits, map, covers lightly rubbed and soiled, light wear to over sized edges, else very good. Buckingham Books 2015 - 37958 2016 $475

Wells, Carolyn *The Furtherest Fury.* New York: Burt, Reprint edition, fine in lightly soiled dust jacket. Mordida Books 2015 - 012412 2016 $65

Wells, Herbert George 1866-1946 *Bealby - a Holiday.* London: Methuen, 1915. First edition, octavo, original gilt decorated red cloth, small hole in cloth near tail of spine, prelims spotted, very good in good, very scarce pictorial dust jacket torn and chipped at head of spine and at folds of flaps and with repairs to reverse. Peter Ellis 112 - 441 2016 £450

Wells, Herbert George 1866-1946 *The First Men in the Moon.* London: George Newnes, 1901. First British edition, first binding, octavo, 12 inserted plates with illustrations by Claude Shepperson, original decorated blue cloth, front and spine panels stamped in gold, black coated endpapers, cloth rubbed along top and bottom edges, spine ends and corners along outer joints, top edge of text block dusty, gift to City of Salford Royal Museum & Library, Peel Park, with gift label affixed to front pastedown and stamp to blank side of frontispiece, verso of titlepage and verso of final blank, some scattered foxing, good, clipped signature of Wells dated 1920. John W. Knott, Jr./L.W. Currey, Inc. Fall-Winter 2015 - 18559 2016 $350

Wells, Herbert George 1866-1946 *The Open Conspiracy, Blueprints for a World Revolution.* London: Victor Gollancz, 1928. First edition, crease to top corner of few leaves, crown 8vo., original black cloth, backstrip lettered in orange and slightly rubbed at tips, tiny amount of wear to corners, top edge dust soiled, faint partial browning to free endpapers, good, notable presentation copy, inscribed by author to friend Eileen Power. Blackwell's Rare Books B186 - 299 2016 £500

Wells, Herbert George 1866-1946 *The Stolen Bacillus.* London: Methuen, 1895. First edition, publisher's list dated Sept. 1895, crown 8vo., original dark blue cloth, backstrip and front cover lettered and decorated in gilt, endpapers lightly browned, bookplate, untrimmed, very good. Blackwell's Rare Books B184 - 245 2016 £1000

Wells, Herbert George 1866-1946 *Tales of Space and Time.* London: and New York: Harper & Bros. 1900, i.e., 1899. First edition, octavo, first leaf blank preceding half title, original decorated tan cloth, front panel stamped in dark brown and gold, spine panel stamped in dark brown, fore and bottom edges untrimmed, cloth bit dusty, endpapers tanned, very good. John W. Knott, Jr./L.W. Currey, Inc. Fall-Winter 2015 - 18561 2016 $450

Wells, Herbert George 1866-1946 *The Time Machine: an Invention.* London: William Heinemann, 1895. First British edition, second cloth binding, no inserted publisher's catalog, signed by author, small octavo, original tan decorated cloth, front and rear panels stamped in purple, spine panel stamped in light blue, binding 18.2cm. vertically, "HEINEMAN" at base of spine set in 12 point type, top edge gilt, fore and bottom edges rough trimmed, neatly signed and dated 1904 in pencil by early owner, tipped onto front pastedown is lengthy letter of provenance, hint of tanning to spine panel some mild spotting to front free endpaper and darkening to rear endpapers, nearly fine, lovely copy, bright, clean, unworn binding.   John W. Knott, Jr./L.W. Currey, Inc.   Fall-Winter 2015 - 17289   2016 $45,000

Wells, Herbert George 1866-1946 *The Time Machine: an Invention.* New York: Henry Holt and Co., 1895. First edition, first printing with author's name incorrectly printed "H. S. WELLS" on recto of title leaf, Small octavo, inserted frontispiece with tissue guard, illustration by W. B. Russell, original decorated tan buckram, front and spine panels stamped in purple, top edge gilt, other edges untrimmed, offsetting to endpapers, previous owner's name in ink to front free endpaper, mild rubbing mainly to edges and spine ends spotting to covers and spine, good copy.   John W. Knott, Jr./L.W. Currey, Inc.   Fall-Winter 2015 - 17382   2016 $8500

Wells, Herbert George 1866-1946 *The Time machine. The War of the Worlds.* New York: Heritage Press, 1964. Gray and mustard cloth lettered gilt, very fine in slipcase, illustrations by Joe Mugnaini, Sandglass pamphlet laid in.   Argonaut Book Shop   Heritage Press 2015 - 7118   2016 $40

Wells, Herbert George 1866-1946 *The War in the Air and Particularly How Mr. Best Smallways Fared While it Lasted....* London: George Bell and Sons, 1908. First edition, first binding with all lettering and decoration on front and spine panel in gold, "George Bell & Sons" at base of spine panel, octavo, 16 inserted plates with illustrations by A. C. Michael, original blue cloth, front and spine panels stamped in gold, page edges foxed, else fine with clean and bright binding.   John W. Knott, Jr./L.W. Currey, Inc.   Fall-Winter 2015 - 18562   2016 $1500

Wells, Herbert George 1866-1946 *The War of the Worlds.* London: William Heinemann, 1898. First edition, second state, 32 page publisher's undated ads at end, instead of 16 pages of dated ads which denotes first issue, original gray cloth lettered in black on front cover and spine, publisher's logo stamped in black on back cover, uncut, binding slightly skewed, spine lightly browned, inner front hinge just barely starting but still quite solid, few pages opened bit rough, overall very good.   Heritage Book Shop   Holiday 2015 - 112   2016 $2250

Wells, Herbert George 1866-1946 *The War of the Worlds.* London: William Heinemann, 1898. First edition, 16 page publisher's catalog dated Autumn mcdddxcvii inserted at rear, octavo, original gray cloth, front and spine panels stamped in black, publisher's monogram stamped in black on rear panel, early copy, owner's signature on front free endpaper, small erasure from front pastedown, few spots to endpapers, very good.   John W. Knott, Jr./L.W. Currey, Inc.   Fall-Winter 2015 - 18563   2016 $2250

Wells, Margaret *Moths.* Wellington: Harry Tombs, n.d., 4to., boards, pictorial paste-on, illustrations by Edna Kuala.   Aleph-bet Books, Inc.   111 - 158   2016 $275

Wells, Nathaniel Armstrong *The Picturesque Antiquities of Spain.* London: Richard Bentley, 1846. First edition, 8vo. 10 plates, illustrations, original brown decorative cloth, inner hinges cracked, good.   J. & S. L. Bonham Antiquarian Booksellers   Europe 2016 - 9487   2016 £150

Welsh, Alexander *The City of Dickens.* Oxford: Clarendon Press, 1971. First edition, half title, plates, original blue cloth, very good in dust jacket.   Jarndyce Antiquarian Booksellers   CCXVIII - 1478   2016   £20

Welsh, Irvine *Ecstasy - Three Tales of Chemical Romance.* London: Jonathan Cape, 1996. First edition, hardbound issue, octavo, head of spine very slightly bumped, fine in very near fine dust jacket.   Peter Ellis   112 - 442   2016   £25

Welsh, Richard *Kiddie-Kar Book.* Philadelphia: Lippincott, 1920. First and probably only edition, oblong 4to., cloth backed boards, pictorial paste-on, fine in dust jacket (slightly frayed), lovely pictorial border and 9 fine color plates plus pictorial endpapers and smaller illustrations, rare.   Aleph-bet Books, Inc.   112 - 468   2016 $875

Welsted, Leonard *The Dissembled Wanton; or My Son and Money.* London: printed for John Watts at the Printing Office in Wild Court, near Lincoln's Inn Fields, 1727. Half title, 8vo., text evenly browned, disbound, lacks final leaf of ads.   Jarndyce Antiquarian Booksellers   CCXVI - 475   2016   £45

Welty, Eudora *A Curtain of Green (Stories).* New York: Doubleday, 1941. First edition, 8vo., some stained on endpaper, inscribed by author for William Claire, one of 2476 copies, scarce.   Second Life Books, Inc.   196 B - 850   2016 $650

Welty, Eudora *One Writer's Beginnings.* Cambridge: Harvard, 1984. First edition, third printing, 8vo., photos, inscribed by author for Barbara Howes, nice in dust jacket.   Second Life Books, Inc.   196 B - 849   2016 $500

Welty, Eudora *The Optimist's Daughter.* New York: Random House, 1972. Limited edition, one of 300 numbered copies, this being no. 99, signed by author, pinhead size splash to page edges, else fine in about fine numbered slipcase without dust jacket as issued, lovely copy, uncommonly found in such bright condition.   Royal Books   49 - 73   2016 $400

Wenckstern, F. Von *Bibliography of the Japanese Empire, Being a Classified List of All Books, essays and Maps in European Languages Relating to Dai Nihon (Great Japan).* Leiden: E. J. Brill, 1895. First editions with all supplements, 2 volumes, thick 8vo., original cloth, each volume enclosed in modern cloth slipcase with cloth chemise, ex-library with markings and library name perforated on titlepage, covers of first volume loose from binding with spine covering torn pages detached in places, paper brittle, scarce edition. Oak Knoll Books   310 - 253   2016 $350

Wentworth, Patricia *Vanishing Point.* Philadelphia: Lippincott, 1953. First edition, fine in dust jacket.   Mordida Books   2015 - 002277   2016 $60

Wentworth, Trelawney *The West India Sketch Book.* London: Whittaker & Co., 1834. First edition, issue with plates, 8vo., 2 volumes, contemporary red half morocco, over marbled boards, 2 engraved maps (one as frontispiece), rose tinted aquatint, frontispiece, 9 engraved plates (one tinted, one printed in red and hand colored, one printed in blue, one hand colored), wood engraved vignettes and musical notations in text, binding with wear and restorations, occasional foxing to plates, text evenly toned.   Sotheran's Piccadilly Notes - Summer 2015 - 329   2016   £1995

Wentz, Roby *The Grabhorne Press, a biography.* San Francisco: Book Club of California, 1981. Limited to 750 copies, initials by Maleltte Dean, 4to., illustrations, quarter white linen backed decorative boards, gilt spine title, plain white dust jacket (as issued), bottom edges of upper cover marred with dual puncture, else very good.   Jeff Weber Rare Books   181 - 63   2016 $45

Wenzel, Jacob Von *A Treatise on the Cataract...* London: D. Dilly, 1791. First edition in English, folding engraved plate, 8vo.., scarce, modern half morocco over marbled boards, very good.   Edwin V. Glaser Rare Books   2015 - 10104   2016 $600

Wescott, Glenway *Images of Truth: Remembrances and Criticism.* New York: Harper & Row, 1962. First edition, author's presentation of Richard Hughes, Aug. 15 1962, excellent copy in slightly soiled dust jacket.   Second Life Books, Inc.   196 B - 851   2016 $188

Wesley, John   1703-1791 *An Extract of the Rec. Mr. John Wesley's Journals.* Philadelphia: printed by Henry Tuckniss and sold by John Dickins, 1795. First American edition, some browning and staining, 12mo, original sheep, rubbed, sound.   Blackwell's Rare Books   B186 - 164   2016   £750

Wesley, John   1703-1791 *Sermons on Several Occasions.* London: printed by W. Bowyer (Volumes II & III by W. Strahan), 1754. 1748. 1750. Volume I second edition, volumes II and III first editions, half title in volume III, 3 volumes, 12mo., slight and even browning but good, clean copy, clean edge tear without loss to M1 volume II, faint traces of old waterstain to lower front edge, full contemporary sprinkled calf, double gilt ruled borders, raised and gilt banded spines, gilt volume numbers, slight chipping to head and tail of volume I, recent bookplate of Christopher Clark Geest.   Jarndyce Antiquarian Booksellers   CCXVI - 603   2016   £1250

Wesley, John   1703-1791 *Thoughts Concerning the Origin of Power.* Bristol: printed by W. Pine in Wine Street, 1772. First edition, 12mo., half inch tear without loss to leading edge, outer pages little dulled, stitched as issued. Jarndyce Antiquarian Booksellers   CCXVI - 604   2016   £280

Wesley, Samuel *The Life of Our Blessed Lord and Saviour Jesus Christ.* London: for Charles Harper and Benj. Motte, 1693. First edition, folio, engraved portrait, engraved architectural title (long tear from lower margin into image repaired), 58 engraved plates, some light browning or spotting in places, few short marginal tears, some corners dog eared, lower blank outer corner on plate at page 21 torn away and piece (60mm. long) torn from outer margin of plate at page 296, minor hole to image of plate at page 333, contemporary sprinkled calf, early paper spine label (joints split, front cover almost detached, piece chewed from foot of spine, two corners chewed, bookplate removed from font pastedown, from the library of James Stevens Cox (1910-1997).   Maggs Bros. Ltd.   1447 - 446   2016   £180

West De Wend Fenton, Michael *The Primrose Path.* privately printed, 1908. First edition one of 50 copies, crown 8vo., small amount of very faint foxing to borders of few pages, original navy blue cloth lettered gilt to backstrip and upper board with design blocked in yellow to the latter, rubbing to extremities, top edge gilt, others untrimmed, faint spotting to free endpapers with few pieces of related ephemera loosely inserted, good, inscribed by author to his mother.   Blackwell's Rare Books   B186 - 214   2016   £400

West Point *Regulations of the U.. S. Military Academy at West Point.* New York: J. J. Harper, 1832. 16m., finely colored map, contemporary calf, stamped in gilt on front cover, three short breaks in folds but fine.   M & S Rare Books, Inc.   99 - 329   2016 $350

West, Dorothy *The Living is Easy.* Old Westbury: Feminist Press, 1982. First Feminist Press edition, 8vo., author's presentation, paper wrappers, cover scuffed, otherwise very good, tight copy.   Second Life Books, Inc.   196 B - 852   2016 $150

West, Jane *Letters Addressed to a Young Man on His First Entrance into Life..* London: printed by A. Strahan for T. N. Longman & O. Rees, 1802. Second edition, 12mo., 3 volumes, full contemporary tre calf, red leather labels, hinges little weak, some rubbing to head and tail of spine, each volume signed "Miss Middle" in contemporary hand.   Jarndyce Antiquarian Books   CCXV - 475   2016   £150

West, Jane *Letters to a Young Lady....* London: Longman, Hurst, Rees and Orme, 1806. Third edition, 3 volumes, 12mo., uncut in contemporary drab boards, paper spines little darkened and chipped at heads and tails with some loss, good, sound copy.   Jarndyce Antiquarian Books   CCXV - 476   2016   £125

West, Jane *Letters to a Young Lady...* London: Longman, Hurst, Rees and Orme, 1806. third edition, contemporary half calf, gilt spine, black morocco labels, slight wear to hinges, chip to lower label of volume I, little rubbed, but nice, attractive copy.   Jarndyce Antiquarian Books   CCXV - 477   2016   £125

West, Nathanael *A Cool Million.* New York: Covici Friede, 1934. First edition, author's sister's copy with her ownership signature 'Laura Weinstein", modest foxing to boards, endpages and page edges, very good in like dust jacket with bit of sunning on and near spine and few very small edge chips, much nicer than usual, in custom clamshell case.   Ken Lopez Bookseller   166 - 146   2016 $7500

West, Nathanael *The Day of the Locust.* New York: Random House, 1939. First edition, octavo, publisher's red cloth, orange paper label on spine, printed in black, top edge gilt in bright publisher's dust jacket, with $2.00 price, jacket with some minor wear along edges and some light rubbing, small circle stain to back panel of jacket and back board of book, outer joints just slightly darkened, still near fine.   Heritage Book Shop   Holiday 2015 - 112   2016 $2250

West, Nathanael *Miss Lonleyhearts.* New York: Liveright, 1933. First edition, first issue, first state, ex-private circulating library copy with small stamps and modest pocket remnant on verso of rear fly, lacking rare dust jacket, front flap of jacket affixed to front fly.   Between the Covers Rare Books   204 - 127   2016 $1500

West, Rebecca 1892-1983 *War Nurse. The True Story of a Woman Who Lived, Loved and Suffered on the Western Front.* New York: Cosmopolitan, 1930. Crown 8vo., black cloth stamped in gilt, red topstain, white dust jacket with color pictorial of nurse to front panel, gilt bright, slight lean, bit of spotting to top edge, withal very good+ in very good dust jacket that shows some edgewear, light soiling and chipping to spine panel ends.   Tavistock Books   Bibliolatry - 21   2016 $375

Westburg, Barry *The Confessional Fictions of Charles Dickens.* Dekalb: Northern Illinois University Press, 1977. Half title, frontispiece, original brown cloth, very good in slightly rubbed dust jacket.   Jarndyce Antiquarian Booksellers   CCXVIII - 1490   2016   £20

Westergaard, Jens Christensen *Synopsis Life History of Jens Christensen Westerngaard.* Portland: Metropolitan Printing Co., 1946. Cloth, very good but without dust jacket, illustrations, inscribed by author.   Dumont Maps and Books   133 - 64   2016 $65

Western Review: a Literary Quarterly. Volume 15 Number 4. Iowa City: Pub. by the State University of Iowa, 1951. Octavo, printed yellow wrappers, fine.   Between the Covers Rare Books   204 - 42   2016 $250

Westlake, Donald *Brothers Keepers.* New York: M. Evans, 1975. First printing, 8vo., author's presentation to poet William Claire, paper over boards with cloth spine, top edges little spotted, otherwise very good, tight in very slightly chipped dust jacket.   Second Life Books, Inc.   196 B - 856   2016 $75

Westlake, Donald *Don't Ask.* New York: Mysterious Press, 1993. First edition, 8vo., author's presentation to William Claire, paper over boards, nice in slightly scuffed dust jacket.   Second Life Books, Inc.   196 B - 857   2016 $75

Westlake, Donald *Drowned Hopes.* New York: Mysterious Press, 1990. First printing, author's presentation to William Claire, paper over boards with cloth spine, corners of cover slightly bumped, edges spotted, otherwise very good, tight in dust jacket.   Second Life Books, Inc.   196 B - 858   2016 $75

Westlake, Donald *Good Behavior.* New York: Mysterious Press, 1985. First printing, author's presentation on title to William Claire, paper over boards with cloth spine, top edges faintly spotted, nice in slightly chipped dust jacket.   Second Life Books, Inc.   196 B - 859   2016 $75

Westlake, Donald *High Adventure.* New York: Mysterious Press, 1985. First edition, 8vo., author's presentation to William Claire, paper over boards with cloth spine, edges lightly spotted, else nice in scuffed dust jacket.   Second Life Books, Inc.   196 B - 862   2016 $75

Westlake, Donald *High Jinx: A Mohonk Mystery.* Miami Beach: Dennis McMillan, 1987. First edition, 8vo., printed wrappers, fine, inscribed by authors to poet William Claire. Second Life Books, Inc.   196 B - 854   2016 $65

Westlake, Donald *Killing Time.* New York: Random House, 1961. First edition, signed by author on titlepage, fine in dust jacket lightly soiled on white rear cover and lightly rubbed at foot of spine, exceptionally fine copy. Buckingham Books   2015 - 35190   2016 $450

Westlake, Donald *Levine.* New York: Mysterious Press, 1984. First edition, 8vo., author's signature on title, black cloth, edges spotted, otherwise very good, tight.   Second Life Books, Inc.   196 B - 860   2016 $65

Westlake, Donald *The Spy in the Ointment.* New York: Random House, 1966. First edition, fine in price clipped dust jacket, remkarable association copy for author's wife, Abby.   Buckingham Books   2015 - 35193   2016 $450

Westlake, Donald *Transylvania Station: a Monhonk Mystery.* Miami Beach: Dennis McMillan, 1987. First edition, 8vo., printed wrappers, fine, inscribed by authors to William Claire.   Second Life Books, Inc.   196 B - 855   2016 $65

Westlake, Donald *Trust me on this.* New York: Mysterious Press, 1988. First printing, author's presentation to William Claire, paper over boards, cloth spine, edges slightly spotted, otherwise nice in dust jacket.   Second Life Books, Inc.   196 B - 861   2016 $75

Westmacott, Mary *A Daughter's Daughter.* London: Heinemann, 1952. First edition, crown 8vo., original red cloth, backstrip lettered gilt, with little rubbing to publisher's name at foot and slight lean to spine, corners little turned in, dust jacket frayed, good, inscribed by author for Mrs. Bush. Blackwell's Rare Books   B184 - 128   2016   £750

Westminster Assembly of Divines *The Shorter Catechism, Composed by the Reverend Assembly of Divines...* London: printed in the year, 1774. 12mo., original dark brown glazed hessian cloth, with name Alfred Cole, Clapton 1810.   Jarndyce Antiquarian Booksellers   CCXVI - 606   2016   £120

Weston, Edward *The Daybooks of...* Millerton: Aperture, 1973. Volume I and II, small 4to., photos, paper wrappers, cover little soiled, small tear top front of spine, donor's presentation on flyleaf, otherwise very good tight copies. Second Life Books, Inc.   197 - 344   2016 $200

Weston, Richard *Directions Left by a Gentleman to His Sonns...* London: by E. T. and R. H. for R. Royston, 1670. First edition, small 4to., titlepage soiled and damaged at head, loss to rule border and crudely repaired on verso of top and bottom edges, A2 soiled and crudely repaired on recto of fore-margin upper edge of B1 and C1 closely shaved (touching headlines), mid 20th century quarter blue morocco and marbled boards, wormhole in lower joint, from the library of James Stevens Cox (1910-1997).   Maggs Bros. Ltd.   1447 - 447   2016   £200

Wetmore, Alexander *The Birds of the Republic of Panama.* Washington: Smithsonian Inst. Press, 2008. First edition, signed and inscribed edition, 5 volumes, 8vo, green cloth, first four in publisher's unclipped dust jackets, first 3 volumes only fair to good condition, bumped tips and light soiling, rubbing and edgewear to covers, staining to page edges and mild waviness and slight staining to interiors from use in final volume 4-5 are in very good condition, only slight bumping and soiling to covers, volume 5 lacks dust jacket, jackets on volume s 1-4 soiled, creased, rubbed and edgeworn, but nicely preserved in clear archival sleeves, overall outstanding complete working set, uncommon signed.   Simon Finch   2015 - 0451-3130   2016 $200

Wetsch, Joseph *Medicina ex Pulsu, Sive Systema Doctrina Sphygnicae.* C. Heydinger, 1771. Small 8vo., woodcut vignette on title and tailpieces, one folding engraved plate, bit browned or foxed in places, stamps of Birmingham General Hospital Library and one later of the Birmingham Medical Institute, small 8vo., modern boards, engraved armorial bookplate of (James) Johnstone and initial E added in manuscript, sound.   Blackwell's Rare Books   B186 - 165   2016   £800

Wey, Francis *Les Anglais Chez eux. Esquisses de Moeurs et de Voyage.* Paris: Giraud, 1854. Very rare first edition, small 8vo., contemporary green half morocco over pebble grained cloth, spine with raised bands, ruled and lettered gilt, light wear to extremities, internally little brown spotted in places only, 1920's Warsaw Library stamp to verso of title, release stamp.   Sotheran's Travel and Exploration - 289   2016   £225

Whalen, Will W. *Strike.* Philadelphia: Dorance and co., 1927. First edition, fine in very nice, near fine dust jacket with very shallow nicks at crown, full page inscription by author to his dentist, very scarce.   Between the Covers Rare Books   208 - 72   2016 $500

Wharton, Edith 1862-1937 *Artemis to Actaeon and Other Verse.* New York: Charles Scribner's Sons, 1909. First edition, small 8vo., original gilt decorated cloth, presentation copy inscribed by author to her personal maid in attendance, Elise Duvlenck, Sept. 1909, faint traces of damp to covers, very good.   Peter Ellis   112 - 443   2016   £2250

Wharton, Edith 1862-1937 *The Descent of Man: and Other Stories.* New York: Charles Scribner's sons, 1914. First edition thus, 8vo., red cloth, spine faded, library stamp on endpaper, very good, tight. Second Life Books, Inc. 197 - 345   2016 $45

Wharton, Edith 1862-1937 *Ethan Frome.* New York: Limited Editions club, 1939. One of 1500 copies signed by artist, small folio, dark blue cloth, upper cover stamped in gilt, fine in rubbed slipcase, water color drawings by Henry Varnum Poor. Second Life Books, Inc. 196 B - 863   2016 $150

Wharton, Edith 1862-1937 *Ethan Frome.* Portland: Ascensius Press, 2002. One of 50 numbered copies, marbled paper covered boards, goatskin fore edges and spine by Daniel Gehnrich, very fine in publisher's cloth clamshell box. Joseph J. Felcone, Inc. Books from Five Centuries: a Miscellany - 150   2016 $900

Wharton, Edith 1862-1937 *Fighting France.* New York: Charles Scribner's Sons, 1915. First edition, 8vo., red cloth stamped in gilt, rear hinge starting, library stamp on bottom of leaves, otherwise very good, clean copy. Second Life Books, Inc. 197 - 346   2016 $100

Wharton, Edith 1862-1937 *The House of Mirth.* New York: Scribner, 1905. First edition with Scribner seal on copyright page, first issue, without ad, 8vo., some numerical figures on endpaper, hinges tender, untrimmed, red cloth, some faded on spine, couple of spots on cover, very good. Second Life Books, Inc. 197 - 347   2016 $300

Wharton, Edith 1862-1937 *Italian Villas and Their Gardens.* New York: Century, 1904. First and only edition, heavily illustrated with photos, drawings and 26 full color plates by Maxfield Parrish, this copy with tipped in ALS written to Mrs. Sage, owner's small tasteful bookplate, this copy extra illustrated, presumably by Mrs. Sage. Ken Lopez Bookseller 166 - 149   2016 $10,000

Wharton, Edith 1862-1937 *Italian Villas and Their Gardens.* New York: Century, 1905. First edition, 2nd issue, 4to., pictorial cloth, little soiled on spine, very good, untrimmed, 52 illustrations, 27 of which are color plates or half tones by Maxfield Parrish, lettered tissue guards, rest being photos and drawings. Second Life Books, Inc. 197 - 348   2016 $950

Wharton, Richard *Fables.* London: printed by T. Bensley... for Payne and Mackinlay, 1804-1805. 8vo., 2 volumes in one, some scattered foxing and light browning, contemporary quarter calf, marbled boards, vellum tips, double gilt bands, red morocco label, slight wear to rear joint and head of spine, armorial bookplate of John Headlam, of Gilmonly Hall Yorkshire. Jarndyce Antiquarian Booksellers CCXVI - 607   2016   £180

Wheat, Carl Irving *Mapping of the Transmississippi West.* San Francisco: Institute of Historical Cartography, 1957-1963. Limited to 1000 copies, 374 facsimile maps, original quarter green gilt stamped cloth, beige linen sides, as issued, very fine. Jeff Weber Rare Books 181 - 9   2016 $2000

Wheat, Carl Irving *Mapping the Transmississippi West.* San Francisco: printed by the Grabhorn Press, volumes II-V printed by Taylor & Taylor and James printing using the designs of Edwin and Robert Grabhorn, 1957-1963. One of 1000 copies, 5 volumes bound in six, 368 x 264mm., publisher's gray linen boards backed with textured buckram, flat spine, in apparently original plain brown dust jacket with ink titling on spines, with 374 maps as called for, five in color, 27 folding, inscribed by author to Irving W. Robbins, Jr., with Robbins' bookplate, prospectus and envelope containing obituaries of Wheat laid in at front of volume), dust jackets bit creased and frayed (though not in tatters), one minor corner crease to map, otherwise volumes themselves extremely fine, clean, fresh and bright inside and out. Phillip J. Pirages   67 - 179   2016 $5400

Wheat, Carl Irving *Mapping the Transmississippi West 1540-1861.* San Francisco: Institute of Historical Cartography, 1959. First edition, limited to 1000 sets, folio, two toned cloth, maps. Oak Knoll Books 310 - 272   2016 $2000

Wheatland, David P. *The Apparatus of Science at Harvard 1765-1800.* Cambridge: Harvard, 1968. First edition, copiously illustrated with several color plates tipped in, warm inscription by author to Paul Buck, red cloth stamped in gilt, nice. Second Life Books, Inc. 196 B - 864   2016 $150

Wheatley, Dennis *Murder Off Miami.* Hutchinson/Crime Club, 1936. First printing, extremely good, fox-free and undamaged, original printed wrappers, ribbon page holder. I. D. Edrich   Crime - 2016   £36

Wheatley, Henry B. *Round About Piccadilly and Pall Mall or a Ramble from the Haymarket to Hyde Part.* London: Smith Elder, 1870. First edition, tall 12mo., tissue guarded frontispiece and 28 illustrations in text, original brown cloth covers, black embossed freeze around edges, gilt embossed cartouche, heavy gilt and black design and lettering on spine, brown endpapers, small bookplate of C. A. W. Finch 1883, neat signature and date 1886, very slight rubbing to edges, inner hinge splitting inside rear cover, some occasional foxing, bright, very attractive copy. Simon Finch   2015 - 1568   2016 $320

Wheeler, Charles *High Relief - The Autobiography of Sir Charles Wheeler, Sculptor.* Fletham: Country Life Books, 1968. First edition, 8vo., photos, presentation from author to Lady Mander, spine little creased, near fine in near fine dust jacket little creased at edges, notes in ink, presumably by Lady Mander. Peter Ellis 112 - 444   2016   £35

Wheeler, Hugh *Candide.* New York: Macmillan/Schirmer Books, 1976. First edition, quarto, deluxe edition, glossy color plates, uncommon, near fine in like dust jacket, inscribed by Stephen Sondheim.   Royal Books   51 - 21   2016 $2000

Wheelock, John Hall *By Daylight and in Dream: new and collected poems 1904-19070.* New York: Scribner's, 1970. First edition, author's signature, paper over boards with cloth spine, poet William Jay Smith's name on flyleaf, very good, tight in slightly scuffed dust jacket.   Second Life Books, Inc.   196 B - 868   2016 $75

Wheelock, John Hall *Poems 1911-1936.* New York: Scribner, 1936. First edition, 8vo., very nice in very lightly worn dust jacket, inscribed by author with 9 line poem to poet Clement Wood.   Second Life Books, Inc.   196 B - 869   2016 $75

Wheelwright, H. W. *Bush Wanderings of a Naturalist or Notes on the Field Spots and Fauna of Australia Felix.* London: Routledge, Warne & Routledge, 1862. Second edition, duodecimo, 16 uncolored plates, publisher's blind-stamped cloth (secondary binding?), contemporary inscription, very good.   Andrew Isles Natural History Books   55 - 37696   2016 $300

When I Grow Up. New York: Century Co., 1909. First edition, first issue with titlepage dated Sept. 1909, 24 full page color illustrations and numerous others in monotone and black and white by W. W. Denslow, original tan cloth, front cover and spine pictorially decorated in orange, white and black, early ink inscription, near fine.   David Brass Rare Books, Inc.   2015 - 02947   2016 $950

Wher, Julian *The Exciting Adventures of Finnie the Fiddler.* New York: Cupples & Leon, 1942. Oblong 4to., spiral backed pictorial boards, near fine, 4 fabulous moveables, text illustrations, very scarce.   Aleph-bet Books, Inc.   112 - 330   2016 $300

Whewell, William   1794-1866 *On the Principles of English University Education.* London: John W. Parker, 1838. Half title, slight spotting to prelims, original purple cloth, largely faded to brown, slight nick to upper leading hinge, libray label on leading pastedown, very good.   Jarndyce Antiquarian Books   CCXV - 1005   2016   £85

Whincop, Thomas *Scanderbeg; or Love and Liberty. A Tragedy.* London: for W. Reeve, 1747. First edition, frontispiece and five engraved plates, plus numerous vignette portraits within text engraved by Nathaniel Parr, modern cloth, neat early repair to corner of pi3, occasional very light soiling, else good to very good.   Joseph J. Felcone, Inc.   Books from Five Centuries: a Miscellany - 151   2016 $650

Whishaw, Constance Mary *Character and Conduct; a Book of Helpful thoughts by Great Writers...* Liverpool: Henry Young & Son, 1905. Third edition, half title, frontispiece, maroon cloth, slightly rubbed.   Jarndyce Antiquarian Books   CCXV - 478   2016   £25

Whistler, Hugh *Popular Handbook of Indian Birds.* Edinburgh: Gurney and Jackson, 1941. Third edition, octavo, color plates, text illustrations, fine, dust jacket, scarce in this condition, bookplate of Roy P. Cooper.   Andrew Isles Natural History Books   55 - 19348   2016 $100

Whistler, James A. M. *The Gentle Art of Making Enemies.* London: William Heinemann, 1890. First English edition ad first authroized edition, one of only 10 special copies, near fine in slightly chipped, publisher's brown gilt decorated wrappers bound into similarly decorated near fine full brown morocco by Zaehnsdorf in 1925, housed in custom quarter morocco slipcase with cloth chemise, inscribed by Whistler to his publishers William Heinemman with his butterfly signature, Chelsea Oct. 1890.   Between the Covers Rare Books   204 - 16   2016 $16,500

Whitaker, John *The Genuine History of the Britons Asserted Against Mr. Macpherson.* London: printed for J. Murray, 1773. Second edition, 8vo., title leaf a cancel, 10 line errata onpage 313, waterstain to top inner blank margins, scattered light foxing, contemporary speckled calf, spine ruled and decorated in gilt, red morocco label, bit rubbed, leading hinge weakening, good plus.   Jarndyce Antiquarian Booksellers   CCXVI - 608   2016   £90

White, Andrew Nathaniel *Trane 'n Me (A Semi-Autobiography): A Treatise on the Music of John Coltrane.* Washington: Andrew's Musical Enterprises, 1981. First edition, quarto, spirial bound printed wrappers, bottom corner with few tiny creases, near fine, inscribed by author, uncommon.   Between the Covers Rare Books   208 - 54   2016 $250

White, Constance *Ice Kids.* Chicago: M. A. Donohue, 1910. 4to., cloth backed pictorial boards, edges worn, some cover soil, overall very good with strong binding and internally fine, rare.   Aleph-bet Books, Inc.   111 - 171   2016 $600

White, Dorothy *The Girl's Week-Day Book.* London: RTS, 1839. Second edition, frontispiece, illustrations, contemporary dark brown calf, spine attractively decorated gilt and red green morocco label, slightly rubbed, prize inscription on inserted sheet following f.e.p., very good.   Jarndyce Antiquarian Books   CCXV - 479   2016   £58

White, Elwyn Brooks *Charlotte's Web.* New York: Harper Bros., 1952. Stated First edition, tan cloth, fine in near fine dust jacket with slight wear to spine ends, illustrations by Garth Williams with more than 40 black and whites plus color wrapper, particulary beautiful copy.   Aleph-bet Books, Inc.   111 - 476   2016 $2250

White, Elwyn Brooks *Stuart Little.* New York: Harper & Bros., 1945. First edition, 8vo., original cloth, pictorial endpapers, dust jacket, very fine, pictures by Garth Williams.   James S. Jaffe Rare Books   Occasional List: Winter 2016 - 143   2016 $2500

White, Ethel Lina *Some Must Watch.* New York: Harper & Bros., 1941. First US edition, light offsetting to front and rear endpapers, else fine in dust jacket with light internal professional restoration to spine ends and corners, scarce, exceptional copy.   Buckingham Books   2015 - 36788   2016 $3000

White, Ethel Lina *Some Must Watch.* New York: Harper and Bros, 1941. First American edition, near fine in very good plus, unrestored example of scarce dust jacket, jacket bright with no loss or fading, some minute rubbing to extremities and faint vertical fold line toward right end of spine panel.   Royal Books   49 - 75   2016 $3750

White, Gerald T. *Baptism in Oil. Stephen F. Peckham in Southern California 1865-66.* San Francisco: Book Club of California, 1984. First edition, limited to 500 copies printed, portraits, plates from photos, cloth backed decorated green boards with gilt lettered spine, very fine.   Argonaut Book Shop   Private Press 2015 - 2526   2016 $60

White, Gilbert   1720-1793 *The Natural History and Antiquities of Selborne in the County of Southampton.* London: J. and J. Arch, 1837. Octavo, text illustrations, early brown half calf and olive cloth, gilt lettering on spine, owner's inscription on half title, fine.   Andrew Isles Natural History Books   55 - 8545   2016 $500

White, Gwen *The Toys Adventures at the Zoo.* London: A. & C. Black, 1929. First edition, 4to., fine in slightly worn dust jacket 8 full page color lithographs, one double page color lithograph, smaller color lithoraphs on each text page.   Aleph-bet Books, Inc.   112 - 372   2016 $325

White, Henry Kirke *The Poetical Works.* London: William Pickering, 1830. 165 x 105mm., contemporary black morocco (unsigned but very possibly by Hayday), covers with border of three blind rules with large complex gilt lyre centerpiece, flat spine with titling and curvilinear panelling in gilt in Romantic style, with gilt decorated turn-ins, all edges gilt, expertly rebacked using original backstrip, blue buckram slipcase; with two fore-edge paintings showing Esher Place, Surrey and British Museum, Russell Street, printer's device on titlepage, frontispiece, front joints and extremities slightly rubbed, minor tear in fore margin of one leaf, scattered minor foxing in text, otherwise attractive, restored binding entirely sound, text clean, bright and fresh.   Phillip J. Pirages   67 - 151   2016 $1500

White, James *A Treatise on Veterinary Medicine. Volume II only.* London: J. Johnson and Co., 1811. Small library number stamp on front cover, other library name on first free endpaper, very good, untrimmed, contemporary blue boards, paper spine label.   Edwin V. Glaser Rare Books   2015 - 10118   2016 $125

White, James *A Treatise on Veterinary Medicine. Volume III (of 3).* London: Longman, Hurst Rees, Orme and Brown, 1812. 8vo., engraved plates, small library rubber stamp on front cover, library name inked on front free endpaper, some light browning and foxing on few pages, very good, unopened and untrimmed, contemporary blue boards with paper spine label.   Edwin V. Glaser Rare Books   2015 - 10119   2016 $125

White, James C. *Pain and the Neurosurgeon.* Springfield: Thomas, 1969. Original binding, nice copy in original dust jacket.   James Tait Goodrich   X-78 - 554   2016 $150

White, John *A Rich Cabinet with Variety of Inventions.* London: William Whitwood at the sign of the Golden Lion in Duck Lane near Smith-field, 1668. Fourth edition, 8vo., 58 woodcuts, diagrams, final ad leaf, small chip in upper left margin of titlepage, occasional browning, contemporary full calf, ruled in blind, appropriately rebacked.   Jarndyce Antiquarian Booksellers   CCXVII - 295   2016   £6500

White, John *A Way to the Tree of Life.* London: Miles Fletcher for R. Royston, 1647. First edition, 8vo., without final blank titlepage browned and slightly shaved at fore-edge, small piece torn away from blank corner of A4, browned throughout with small dark marks on N6-8, final blank page stained by turn-ins and with edges little ragged, contemporary calf, rebacked, corners repaired, new endleaves, small inscription of John Witham, inscription of Philip Pecke, from the library of James Stevens Cox (1910-1997).   Maggs Bros. Ltd.   1447 - 448   2016   £500

White, Joseph *Sermons Preached Before the University of Oxford in the year 1784 at the Lecture founded by the Rev. John Bampton M.A.....* London: 1785. Second edition, 8vo., very good, clean copy, very small marginal rust hole in IL3, contemporary calf, attractive large gilt floral device to each compartment, red morocco label, slight cracks to joints.   Jarndyce Antiquarian Booksellers   CCXVI - 609   2016   £125

White, Lionel *Hijack.* New York: Macfadden, 1969. First edition, paperback original, fine, unread copy in wrappers.   Mordida Books   2015 - 011042   2016 $60

White, Patrick E. *Eurydice Unbound.* Lawrence: Holiseventh Press, 1988. Limited to 30 copies, 5 Artist Proofs not for sale, numbered through 25, signed by White and Talleur, relief prints by John Talleur, oblong 4to., accordion fold in clamshell box, printed on Hosho backed by Kochi, binding and boxing by Louise Reynolds, set by hand in Centaur & Arrighi and printed on a Washington Hoe press by John Talleur with Mark Ritchie, John Coleman and Shawn Henning at Holiseventh Press.   Oak Knoll Books   27 - 29   2016 $1200

White, Randy Wayne *Captiva.* New York: Putnam, 1996. First edition, uncorrected proof, very fine in slick pictorial wrappers.   Mordida Books   2015 - 009561   2016 $65

White, S. A, *The Cruise of the Avocet in Search of Skuas and other Things.* Adelaide: reprinted from the Register, 1917. Sextodecimo, photos, publisher's printed wrappers, fine, scarce.   Andrew Isles Natural History Books   55 - 15036   2016 $550

White, S. A. *Bunya or Mystery Mountains. To Robe via the Coorong. A Camp Out in New South Wales.* Adelaide: reprinted from the Register, 1919. Sextodecimo, photos, publisher's printed wrappers, fine copy, scarce.   Andrew Isles Natural History Books   55 - 15038   2016 $650

White, S. A. *In the Far North-East: A Scientific Expedition.* Adelaide: reprinted from the Register, 1917. Sextodecimo, photos, publisher's printed wrappers, fine, scarce.   Andrew Isles Natural History Books   55 - 12542   2016 $650

White, S. A. *Ooldea on the East-West Railway: o the Flooded Murray River and Other Sketches.* Adelaide: 1919. Sextodecimo, photographic plates, some folding, publisher's printed wrappers, scarc4e.   Andrew Isles Natural History Books   55 - 32459   2016 $350

White, Sarah Parker *A Moral History of Woman.* New York: Doubleday Doran, 1937. First edition, 8vo., inscribed by author for Grace Overton.   Second Life Books, Inc.   196 B - 871   2016 $45

White, T. H. *The Godstone and the Blackymor.* London: Jonathan Cape, 1959. First edition, 8vo., drawings by Edward Ardizzone, pictorial paper boards, head and tail of spine slightly bumped, near fine in slightly nicked dust jacket just faintly rubbed at edges.   Peter Ellis   112 - 446   2016   £45

White, T. H. *The Goshawk.* London: Jonathan Cape, 1951. First edition, 8vo., original cherry red cloth with vignette in blind to upper board, lettered in silver to spine, top edge red, preserved in pictorial red dust jacket, couple of diagrams in text, very fresh copy, both externally and internally, protected by unclipped, dust jacket with slight dusting to spine, otherwise fresh and attactive, scarce.   Sotheran's   Hunting, Shooting & Fishing - 67   2016   £598

White, Theodore *In Search of History: a Personal Adventure.* New York: Harper & Row, 1978. First printing, author's signature on title, maroon cloth, very slight stain on upper edges, otherwise nice, in scuffed and slightly chipped dust jacket, very good+.   Second Life Books, Inc.   196 B - 872   2016 $60

White, Thomas *The Grounds of Obedience and Government.* London: printed by J. Fletcher, 1655. Second edition, engraved folding frontispiece, frontispiece has been repaired and laid down on old paper, title and final leaves heavily soiled, 12mo., contemporary full polished calf later rebacking.   James Tait Goodrich   X-78 - 555   2016 $600

White, William *Mouseknees.* New York: Random House, 1939. 8vo., cloth, very good+ in frayed dust jacket, illustrations by Avery Johnson.   Aleph-bet Books, Inc.   111 - 51   2016 $150

White, William *The Story of the Seven Street and Priory First-Day Schools.* Birmingham: Our Jubilee Year, Headley Bros., 1895. Photographic frontispiece and plates, original mauve decorated cloth, front board marked by damp.   Jarndyce Antiquarian Books   CCXV - 1006   2016   £30

Whitehead, David *The Ideology of the Athenian Metic.* Cambridge Philological Society, 1977. First edition, light yellow paperback, slightly dusted, creases to spine and bottom corner, very good.   Unsworths Antiquarian Booksellers Ltd.   E04 - 124   2016   £45

Whitehead, P. J. P. *Forty drawings of fishes made by the artists who accompanied Captain James Cook on his three voyages to the Pacific 1768-71, 1772-7, 1776-80...* London: Trustees of the British Museum (Natural History), 1968. Folio, dust jacket, 36 color plates.   Andrew Isles Natural History Books   55 - 8549   2016 $300

Whitehead, William *Manners: a Satire.* N.P.: 1739. 16 pages, folio, margins little dusty, later plain blue wrappers.   Jarndyce Antiquarian Booksellers   CCXVI - 610   2016   £60

Whiting, Lilian *The Golden Road.* Boston: Little Brown, 1918. 8vo., author's full page presentation and holograph transcription of a Landor poem, photos, very good in torn dust jacket.   Second Life Books, Inc.   196 B - 873   2016 $45

Whitley, Gilbert P. *Solvol fish Book: the Life and Habits of 80 Australian Fishes.* Sydney: J. Kitchen and Sons, 1942. Colour illustrations, publisher's wrappers, fine.   Andrew Isles Natural History Books   55 - 8559   2016 $30

Whitlock, Dorothy *English Historical Documents. Volume I c. 500-1042.* London: Eyre & Spottiswoode, 1955. First edition, large 8vo., cloth gilt lettered, toning to bottom edge and headcap, crease along length of spine, top edge inked but finger marked, edges dusted, still very good, dust jacket, 10.2 x 3.4cm. tear with loss to bottom edge of lower wrapper, two small tears with loss to headcap, 4.2cm. and 4.6cm. tear without loss to tailpiece, 2.1 cm. tear without loss to top edge of lower wrapper, spine browned and scratched, several small tears without loss to edges, wrappers bit grubby, good, library numbers in spine and cover. Unsworths Antiquarian Booksellers Ltd. 30 - 161 2016 £125

Whitman, Walt 1819-1892 *Drum-Taps.* New York: One of 100 copies, 1865. First edition, second issue with separately printed 'Sequel to Drum Taps', 12mo., brown cloth stamped in blind and gilt, some rubbed on cover and extremities, very good, tight copy, old inscription 'from the author' probably not in author's hand. Second Life Books, Inc. 197 - 350 2016 $5500

Whitman, Walt 1819-1892 *Leaves of Grass.* New York: Grabhorn Press for Random House, 1930. No. 278 of 400 copies, 375 x 256mm., original red Niger backed Philippine mahogany boards, Random House vignette incised on lower corner of front cover, raised bands, blindstamped spine title, with 37 woodcuts by Valenti Angelo, mildest of sunning to spine, slight rubbing to joints and bands, four leaves with light to moderate foxing, otherwise excellent copy with only trivial imperfections, binding with significant wear and very lustrous, text almost entirely fine. Phillip J. Pirages 67 - 180 2016 $1800

Whitman, Walt 1819-1892 *Leaves of Grass.* Mount Vernon: Peter Pauper Press, 1950. Commemorative edition, 4to., printed in Waverley and Lydian types on specially made paper by Hurlbut Paper Co., leather backed boards by Russell Rutter Co., wood engraving printed directly from blocks, 1/1100 copies in publisher's box, some rubbing on box, very fine, uncut. Second Life Books, Inc. 197 - 351 2016 $400

Whitman, Walt 1819-1892 *Specimen Days & Collect.* Philadelphia: David McKay, 1882-1883. First edition, 2nd issue, 192 x 124mm, publisher's citron cloth titled and decorated in gilt, leaves lightly browned, as no doubt in every copy because of paper stock, otherwise exceptionally fine, text clean and fresh, binding immaculate. Phillip J. Pirages 67 - 352 2016 $750

Whitman, Walt 1819-1892 *Specimen Days in America.* London: Walter Scott, 1887. Second English edition, first issue, 12mo. publisher's flexible full red leather, lettered in gilt, all edges gilt, front joint professionally repaired with some residual wear at both joints and edges, rear free endpaper detached and chipped at edges, good only, inscribed by author to a fellow Whitman (Mr. Whitman June 1887 (was it inscribed by poet to himself?). Between the Covers Rare Books 208 - 90 2016 $8500

Whitmarsh, Stuart I. *The Debutante Tradition - Mrs. George Davis Finch, the southern Social Register.* Debutant Register Assoc. Ltd., 1950. First edition, 4to., fine in blue suede leather, gold lettering, all edges gilt, moire endpapers, vinyl dust jacket in gray cloth slipcase, spine is photon faded to gray, otherwise fine. Simon Finch 2015 - 037771 2016 $195

Whitmore, Geoffrey *Theatre in Action.* London: The Studio, 1939. First edition, large 8vo., red cloth, little soiled, very good, this copy inscribed and signed by Frederick Piper, Mihora Campbell, Gabrielle Blunt, Aileen Wyse, Josephine Tarret, James Ottaway and 3 others. Second Life Books, Inc. 196 B - 865 2016 $150

Whitney, Adeline Dutton Train *Mother Goose for Grown Ups.* New York: Rudd & Carlton, 1960. First edition, 8vo., ribbed green cloth stamped in gilt, leaves uniformly browned, small waterstain on fore-edge, fine, presentation inscribed by author for Mrs. Saml. Morrill. Second Life Books, Inc. 196 B - 876 2016 $150

Whitney, Adeline Dutton Train *With Memories.* Boston: Houghton Mifflin, 1894. First edition, 8vo., soiled covers, dust jacket, inscribed by author. Second Life Books, Inc. 196 B - 877 2016 $45

Whitney, John *The Genteel Recreation or the Pleasure of Angling.* Covent Garden: R. H. Burn, printed by J. Johnson, 1820. Second edition, small 8vo., full red morocco boards with double gilt fillet and blind rules, central gilt rococo style cartouche of fish, spine with raised bands bordered in gilt and blind, lettered in gilt, gilt ruled turn-ns, all edges gilt, printed throughout on vellum, very rare privately printed edition of 1700. Sotheran's Hunting, Shooting & Fishing - 156 2016 £4995

Whittemore, Reed *The Feel of the Rock. Poems of Three Decades.* Washington & San Francisco: Dryad Press, 1982. First edition, of a total of 1500 copies, this one of only 30 hardbound and in addition is one of the first 50 copeis signed by poet on colophon page, also inscribed and signed by author for William Meredith, some fading of cloth, very good, likely issued without dust jacket. Charles Agvent William Meredith - 120 2016 $150

Whittier, John Greenleaf 1807-1892 *The Demon Lady and The Struggle for Freedom.* Ashtabula: H. H. Timby, 1919. Number 33 of 65 copies, privately printed and handsomely hand illuminated, with two half page original watercolors. Howard S. Mott Inc. 265 - 147 2016 $300

Whittier, John Greenleaf 1807-1892 *The Tent on the Beach and Other Poems.* Boston: Ticknor Reed and Fields, 1867. First edition, small 8vo., green cloth stamped in gilt, binding B, first printing with perfect "N" on line 2 on page 172, earliest states on pages 31 and 42 and throughout as called for, remnants of bookplate, embossed stamp. Second Life Books, Inc. 197 - 352 2016 $110

Whittlesey, Charles *General Wallace's Division - Battle of Shiloh - was It Tardy?* Cleveland: n.p., 1875. First edition, 8vo., self wrappers, unopened (uncut) and untrimmed copy, edge tears as usual notation of place on wrapper, foxed, few tears at mail fold, about very good.   Kaaterskill Books   21 - 118   2016 $125

Whitty, Edward Michael *Friends of Bohemia or Phases of London Life.* London: Smith Elder & Co., 1857. First edition, 2 volumes, half titles, slightly later half red morocco, gilt spine in compartments, little rubbed, bookplates of Charles W. Butt.   Jarndyce Antiquarian Booksellers   CCXVII - 296   2016   £250

The Whole Art of Legerdemain, or Hocus Focus Laid Open and Explained by those Renowed (sic) Masters, Sena, Sama, Hamed Ben-Alla and all the Other Celebrated and Mysterious Professors of the Art of Natural Magic. New York: C. C. Nafis, 1833. 144 x 85mm., original gray-green printed boards, upper cover with titling and an illustration of a gentleman identified as the author, lower cover with two amusing woodcuts "The Lawyer and his Client", in brown cloth chemise and slightly rubbed matching calf backed slipcase, folding frontispiece, small stains at top and bottom of spine, covers just slightly grubby, endpapers bit browned, text with light, inoffensive foxing, but for what is, an unusually fine copy, fragile binding entirely sound and text remarkably fresh and clean.   Phillip J. Pirages   67 - 246   2016 $7500

The Whole Art of Book-Binding, Containing Valuable Recipes for Sprinklng, Marbling, Colouring &c. Richmond: Peter Cottom, 1824. First American from third English edition, 12mo., contemporary quarter, calf over paper covered boards in later clamshell box, this copy's foldout table in back which lists prices for NY bookbinders is torn with most lacking, but facsimile reprint, with letter from previous bookseller, inserted.   Oak Knoll Books   310 - 2   2016 $8500

Whymper, Edward *Swiss Pictures.* London: Religious Tract Society, 1866. First edition, foolscap folio, original olive green morocco, spines with raised bands and lettered gilt, image blocked in gilt on both covers, inner dentelles gilt, all edges gilt, color lithographic frontispiece, retaining tissue guard, highly illustrated with wood engravings in text (some full page), extremities little worn, endpapers spotted, frontispiece foxed as usual, otherwise clean and fresh, presentation inscription dated 1952, front flyleaf with repaired tear.   Sotheran's   Travel and Exploration - 290   2016   £498

Whymper, Edward *Travels Amongst the Great Andes of the Equator - Supplementary Appendix.* London: R. & R. Clark for John Murray, 1892. -1891. Second edition of Travels, first edition of Appendix, 8vo. in 4s, 2 volumes, original olive green cloth over bevelled boards, upper boards with gilt borders, spines lettered and decorated in gilt, lower boards in blind, mid-brown coated endpapers, uncut, some quires in supplementary volume unopened, wood engraved frontispiece, 43 wood engraved plates and numerous illustrations to text, one wood engraved map, one folding lithographic plan, one folding facsimile map, one large folding lithographic map loose as issued in pocket on lower pastedown volume 1, extremities lightly rubbed and bumped, spines slightly faded, minor damage on front free endpaper of Travels, splitting and old repairs on upper hinge of supplementary volume, offsetting onto verso of loose map, otherwise very good, clean set, engraved bookplate of Thomas Somners Vernon Cocks (1850-1923), boosseller's ticket of Harrison and Sons, London.   Sotheran's   Travel and Exploration - 79   2016   £595

Whyte-Melville, George John *The Gladiators a Tale of Rome and Judaea.* London: Longman, 1863. First edition, 3 volumes, few gatherings little proud in volume III, original embossed red cloth, spine decorated and lettered in gilt, dulled and slightly rubbed, very good.   Jarndyce Antiquarian Booksellers   CCXVII - 297   2016   £350

Whytt, Robert *An Essay on the Virtues of Lime-Water in the Cure of the Stone.* Edinburgh: Hamilton, Balfour & Neil, 1755. Plate, 8vo., full contemporary calf, joints cracking, very clean internally.   James Tait Goodrich   X-78 - 556   2016 $395

Widdemer, Margaret *The Red Castle Woman: a Novel of A Haunting Legend....* Garden City: Doubleday & Co., 1968. First edition, fine-, slight slant, near fine- dust jacket with minor chipping at spine and flap old ends.   Ken Hebenstreit, Bookseller   2016 - 2016 $45

Wideman, John Edgar *The Lynchers.* New York: Harcourt Brace Jovanovich, 1973. Very near fine with letter L on front pastedown most likely from what would have been the beginning of inscription, very near fine dust jacket, signed and inscribed by author for Leon Forrest, very nice association.   Jeff Hirsch Books   Holiday List 2015 - 64   2016 $275

Wieland, Christoph Martin *Dialogues from the German of M. Wieland...* Printed for S. Leacroft, 1775. 2 leaves misbound, in reverse, so as to present their uncut inner margin to the fore-edge, another leaf with folded corner resulting in absence of some letters during printing, occasioal foxing, 8vo., 19th century calf, spine richly gilt, slight wear, good, scarce.   Blackwell's Rare Books   B186 - 166   2016   £850

Wiens, Paul *Min Und Go: Ein Brief Aus China.* Berlin: Der Kinderbuchverlag, 1952. First edition, oblong 4to., cloth backed pictorial boards, light edge wear slight soil, near fine, quite scarce. Aleph-bet Books, Inc. 111 - 365 2016 $1200

Wier, Harrison *The Children's Picture Play Book.* London: James Miller, circa, 1850. First edition, 8vo., richly hand colored engravings, red/brown cloth stamped gilt (some faded), very good. Second Life Books, Inc. 197 - 353 2016 $125

Wiese, Kurt *The Cunning Turtle.* New York: Viking, 1956. First edition, Oblong 4to., pictorial cloth, near fine in dust jacket, (price clipped, light soiled, but very good+), nearly full page 3 color illustrations on almost every page, uncommon. Aleph-bet Books, Inc. 112 - 511 2016 $125

A Wife's Home Duties.... London: Bell & Daldy, 1859. Half title, 4 pages ads, spotting, occasionally heavy, original brown cloth, little dulled, recent bookseller's ticket. Jarndyce Antiquarian Books CCXV - 480 2016 £75

Wiggin, Kate Douglas *A Child's Journey with Dickens.* London: Hodder & Stoughton, 1912. First UK edition, frontispiece, original drab printed boards, brown cloth spine, boards dusted and marked, slightly rubbed. Jarndyce Antiquarian Booksellers CCXVIII - 1482 2016 £25

Wiggin, Kate Douglas *A Child's Journey with Dickens.* Boston and New York: Houghton Mifflin & Co., 1912. First edition, half title, frontispiece, portrait, original drab boards, lettered in dark blue, dark green cloth spine, inscribed by author for Sir Walter Lawrence. Jarndyce Antiquarian Booksellers CCXVIII - 1481 2016 £45

Wiggin, Kate Douglas *Susanna and Sue.* Boston: Houghton Mifflin, 1909. First edition, 8vo. illustrations by Alice Barber Stepehns and N. C. Wyeth, gray cloth stamped in orange and dark green, picture pasted on front, author's presentation, for Henry Marc Fayden, Christmas 1906, covers somewhat scuffed and worn at edges, else very good. Second Life Books, Inc. 196 B - 881 2016 $125

Wiggin, Kate Douglas *Timothy's Quest.* Boston: Houghton Mifflin, 1918. Reprint edition, 8vo., very good in original cloth, inscribed by author. Second Life Books, Inc. 196 B - 882 2016 $85

Wight, Fanny *Nellie's Christmas Eve.* New York: McLoughlin Bros., 1908. 4to., stiff pictorial wrappers, some spine rubbing, else very good, each page mounted on linen, full and partial page chromolithographs. Aleph-bet Books, Inc. 111 - 90 2016 $275

Wigram, W. A. *The Cradle of Mankind Life in Easter Kurdistan.* London: A. & C. Black, 1922. Second edition, 8vo., original blue cloth, spine lettered green, plates after drawings and photos, plans and illustrations in text, folding map, printed in sepia at end, only light wear to extremities, one corner with slight bump, apart from light offsetting from endpapers as usual, contemporary name on front flyleaf, very good. Sotheran's Travel and Exploration - 391 2016 £148

Wilbur, Richard *A Bestiary.* New York: designed and printed by the Spiral Press for Pantheon Books, 1951. Of a total edition of 825 copies, this one of 750 on specially made Curtis Rag paper, numbered and signed by author and artist, Alexander Calder, very nice. Second Life Books, Inc. 196 B - 884 2016 $625

Wilbur, Richard *Ceremony and other Poems.* New York: Harcourt Brace, 1950. First edition, signed by author, 8vo., very good in price clipped dust jacket, issued in an edition of 1500 copies in Oct. 1950. Second Life Books, Inc. 196 B - 886 2016 $200

Wilbur, Richard *The 1996 Frost Medal Lecture.* N.P.: Poetry Society of America, 1997. First edition, one of 100 numbered copies signed by Wilbur and Kunitz who wrote the introduction, 12mo., original blue cloth, printed spine label, fine. James S. Jaffe Rare Books Occasional List: Winter 2016 - 144 2016 $350

Wilcock, Donald E. *Damn Right I've got the blues...* San Francisco: Woodford, 1993. first printing, 8vo., signed by Wilcock and Buddy Guy, Copiousley illustrated with photos, paper wrappers, cover slightly scuffed, otherwise very good, tight copy. Second Life Books, Inc. 196 B - 887 2016 $150

Wilcox, Ella Wheeler *New thought Common Sense and What Life Means to Me.* London: Gay & Hancock, 1925. Seventh edition, half title, leading f.e.p. removed, original pale blue cloth, slightly dulled. Jarndyce Antiquarian Books CCXV - 481 2016 £20

Wild, Robert *Iter Boreale.* London: printed on St. George's Day for George Thomason, 1660. Small 4to., dampstaining to inner margin of titlepage and final leaf, final leaf guarded along inner margin, light staining to foot of A2, minor foxing to A4, B3, C1, corner of C2 repaired, with stain acorss text of B4, rebound in contemporary calf from tract volume, covers panelled in blind, rebacked, corners repaired, new endleaves, old flyleaves preserved, from the library of James Stevens Cox (1910-1997). Maggs Bros. Ltd. 1447 - 449 2016 £180

Wilde, George *A Sermon Preached Upon Sunday the Third of March in St. Maries Oxford, before the General Assembly of the Members of the Honourable House of Commons Assembled.* Oxford: i.e. London: by Leonard Lichfield, 1643. Second edition, small 4to., titlepage, A2 and #4 spotted, lighter spotting and discoloration throughout, early 19th century half morocco and marbled boards, the copy of Rev. Philip Bliss (1787-1857), with signature, from the library of James Stevens Cox (1910-1997). Maggs Bros. Ltd.   1447 - 450   2016   £120

Wilde, Oscar   1854-1900   *After Reading. (and) After Berneval.*   Westminster: Beaumont Press, 1921-1922. First editions, each one of 75 on Japanese vellum of the edition deluxe signed by publisher and artist (of a total of 475 copies), 222 x 152mm., 2 separately issued but companion volumes, original vellum backed decorative paper boards "Reading" with vignette on title in orange and green, two plates in same colors, one facsimile of writing in text, device on final page, stylized illustrations of tree on front and rear endpapers, "Berneval" with woodcuts of Naples and Paris printed in blue on front and rear endpapers, two color title page woodcut, one plate with facsimile of Wilde letter and printer's woodcut device, special deluxe version with 3 additional woodcuts, all woodcuts and cover design by Randolph Schwabe, spine just bit darkened, otherwise fine, unworn copies, obviously little used, as they open stiffly and are immaculate inside and out.   Phillip J. Pirages   67 - 23   2016 $2500

Wilde, Oscar   1854-1900   *The Ballad of Reading Gaol.* London: Leonard Smithers, 1898. Third edition, no. 89 of 99 copies, signed by Wilde, 230 x 145mm., original linen (ivory colored backstrip, plum colored sides), gilt titling on flat spine, gilt vignette after Charles Ricketts on upper cover, top edge, rough trimmed, other edges untrimmed, housed in later fleece lined burgundy silk clamshell box with vellum spine label, spine faintly and uniformly sunned (with three tiny dark flecks), vague mottling to lower cover on ivory linen, little signs of use ot corners and edges, two dots of glue residue (from previously affixed paper description) on blank recto of limitation leaf (with sight show through on verso), light freckled toxing to endpapers, each of these defects minor, all in all a very pleasing copy with unworn joints and very clean text of a book difficult to find in better condition.   Phillip J. Pirages   67 - 354   2016 $15,000

Wilde, Oscar   1854-1900   *The Ballad of Reading Gaol.* Portland: Thomas B. Mosher, 1904. No. 9 of 10 copies on vellum, signed by publisher (of a total edition of 110), 179 x 114mm., publisher's limp vellum, flat spine lettered gilt, green cloth portfolio with silk ribbon ties, faint foxing to covers, perhaps a third of leaves slightly yellow (as often with vellum printings), otherwise very fine, especially fresh and clean inside and out.   Phillip J. Pirages   67 - 344   2016 $6500

Wilde, Oscar   1854-1900   *The Birthday of the Infanta.* New York: Macmillan, Oct., 1929. Limited to 500 copies, numbered and signed by Pamela Bianco, 4to., cloth backed boards, fine in slipcase (just slightly worn at corners), printed on fine paper, beautiful double page color illustrations as well as black and whites by Bianco, laid in is great half page handwritten letter from Bianco to artist Valenti Angelo. Aleph-bet Books, Inc.   111 - 478   2016 $400

Wilde, Oscar   1854-1900   *The Happy Prince.*   New York: Putnam, 1913. First US edition, gilt pictorial purple cloth, top edge gilt, lightly faded in spots of rear cover, light scattered foxing, mainly in beginning pages, very good, illustrations by Charles Robinson.   Aleph-bet Books, Inc.   112 - 426   2016 $850

Wilde, Oscar   1854-1900   *The Harlot's House and Other Poems.*   New York: E. P. Dutton, 1929. Limited to 200 signed copies, this no. 47, signed by artist, John Vassos, near fine, black cloth spine and black and white illustrated paper over boards with gilt lettering spine, top edge gilt, red endpapers, few pages unopened, housed in very good+ matching red and black paper covered slipcase with black lettering on paper paste-down title label, slipcase has mild wear, 8vo.   By the Book, L. C.   45 - 69   2016 $400

Wilde, Oscar   1854-1900   *House of Pomegranates.* London: James Osgood McIlvanie, 1891. First edition, 4to., green cloth spine and decorative cloth boards, slight cover soil, neat hinge repair, else very good++ in attractive custom box, magnificently illustrated by Charles Ricketts with cover, titlepage, endpaper designs and text ornaments, illustrations.   Aleph-bet Books, Inc.   112 - 512   2016 $3500

Wilde, Oscar   1854-1900   *A House of Pomegranates.* London: Methuen, 1915. First edition with these illustrations, 4to., blue pictorial cloth, top edge gilt, slight scattered foxing, else near fine in attractive custom box, illustrations by Jessie King.   Aleph-bet Books, Inc.   112 - 278   2016 $1750

Wilde, Oscar   1854-1900   *An Ideal Husband.*   London: Leonard Smithers & Co., 1899. First edition, one of 1000 copies, lovely, near fine with triviall soiling on boards, spine touch faded and gift inscription.bookplates on front endpapers, long gift inscription from Richard Todd, excellent copy. Heritage Book Shop   Holiday 2015 - 114   2016 $2250

Wilde, Oscar 1854-1900 *The Importance of Being Earnest.* London: Bernard Smithers and Co., 1899. First edition, one of 100 copies, 228 x 157mm., original lavender cloth decorated gilt, edges untrimmed and unopened, leather book label bearing gilt monogram "SSB" on front pastedown, corners little bumped, backstrip rather faded (as virtually always), crumpling and tiny losses to head and tail of spine, light toning throughout interior (as with all copies because of paper stock), apparently lacking final endpaper, still very good, extremely difficult to find in decent shape, binding solid and atypically clean, none of the usual cocking and text with no signs of use, having never been unopened. Phillip J. Pirages   67 - 355   2016 $2500

Wilde, Oscar 1854-1900 *Lady Windermere's Fan - a Play about a Good Woman.* London: Methuen, 1909. Third edition, small octavo, top edge gilt, head and tail of spine little bumped, cover edges slightly rubbed, endpapers faintly spotted, very good.   Peter Ellis   112 - 448   2016   £85

Wilde, Oscar 1854-1900 *The Picture of Dorian Gray.* New York: Limited Editions Club, 1957. First edition thus, one of 1500 signed by artist, large 8vo., leather backed boards little rubbed, near fine in publisher's slipcase (some faded).   Second Life Books, Inc.   196 B - 888   2016 $50

Wilde, Oscar 1854-1900 *Ravenna. Recited in the Theatre, Oxford June 26 1878.* Oxford: Thos. Shrimpton 1878, i.e., 1904. First pirated edition, small octavo, original grey wrappers, pictorial bookplate of A. Squire, smaller printed label from Library of AJA Symons, Brick House, covers just little wrinkled, very good, preserved in custom made green morocco backed patterned board folder.   Peter Ellis   112 - 449   2016   £575

Wilde, Oscar 1854-1900 *Salome.* London: Limited Editions Club, 1938. One of 1500 numbered copies, 4to., maroon cloth with lettering and decorative stamping in gilt, boxed with Salome Drame en Un Acte, with goache drawings on black paper by Andre Derain, paper wrappers, signed by artist, slight foxing on endpapers and title, nice in scuffed box, first volume in black wrappers, signed by Derain.   Second Life Books, Inc.   196 B - 889   the Angel that Troubled the WatersAn $750

Wilde, Oscar 1854-1900 *The Sphinx.* London: printed at the Ballantyne Press for Elkin Mathews & John Lane at the Bodley Head, 1894. One of 25 large paper deluxe copies with extra ornamentation (along with 200 regular copies), 258 x 195mm., original stiff vellum, covers with gilt pictorial designs by Charles Ricketts, flat spine with gilt tooling, ribbon ties, edges untrimmed, marbled drop-back box inside matching purple morocco backed slipcase, with one wood engraved vignette, one woodcut initial and 9 dramatic sepia wood engraved plates by Charles Ricketts, tissue guard between title and first page of text as called for, with publisher's ad laid in, printed in black, red and green, but for significant soiling to vellum, very fine, leaves fresh and bright, gilt glistening.   Phillip J. Pirages   67 - 303   2016 $36,000

Wilde, Oscar 1854-1900 *A Woman of No Importance.* London: John Lane at Sign of the Bodley Head, 1894. First edition, one of 500 copies, book near fine with spine faded, otherwise very nice, after the first four leaves, book entirely unopened at top edge, bookplate of Joseph Groves and short inscription from actor Vincent Price.   Heritage Book Shop   Holiday 2015 - 115   2016 $2000

Wilden, Theodore *To Die Elsewhere.* London: Heinemann, 1976. First edition, inscribed by author to John Le Carre, fine in dust jacket with light restoration to top rear corners.   Buckingham Books   2015 - 38078   2016 $475

Wilder, Laura Ingalls *Little Town on the Prairie.* New York: Harper Bros., 1941. Not first edition, 8vo., pictorial cloth, near fine in dust jacket (with old tape mends and 3 pieces out of backstrip), color dust jacket and frontispiece by Helen Sewell, and in line by Mildred Boyle, this copy signed by author.   Aleph-bet Books, Inc.   111 - 479   2016 $4000

Wilder, Laura Ingalls *Little Town on the Prairie.* New York: Harper, 1941. First edition, 8vo., mild foxing to covers, edges, very good+ in like dust jacket with minimal foxing, chips, short closed tear.   By the Book, L. C.   45 - 7   2016 $2250

Wilder, Laura Ingalls *The Long Winter.* New York: Harper and Bros., 1940. Stated first edition, 8vo., tan pictorial cloth, neat name on free endpaper barely visible else fine, beautiful price clipped dust jacket with just bit of rubbing on spine ends and edges, illustrations by Helen Sewall and Mildred Boyle.   Aleph-bet Books, Inc.   111 - 480   2016 $2500

Wilder, Laura Ingalls *These Happy Golden Years.* New York: Harper & Bros., 1943. Stated first edition, 8vo., pictorial cloth, slight cover soil, near fine in very slightly frayed dust jacket, illustrations by Helen Sewell and Mildred Boyle with color dust jacket, color frontispiece plus full page black and whites, Boyle's copy inscribed by her to hr niece.   Aleph-bet Books, Inc.   112 - 513   2016 $2750

Wilder, Thornton 1896-1976 *The Angel that Troubled the Waters and Other Plays.* New York: Coward McCann, 1928. First edition, large paper copy, one of 775 copies signed by author, large 8vo., printed on Canson Ingres handmade paper, untrimmed, blue cloth in dark blue, near fine,. Second Life Books, Inc. 197 - 354 2016 $175

Wilder, Thornton 1896-1976 *The Angel that Troubled the Waters and Other Plays.* New York: Coward McCann, 1928. First edition, large 8vo., printed on Canson Inges handmade paper, untrimmed, blue cloth in dark blue dust jacket (torn along hinge), price chipped, near fine, large paper copy, one of 775 copies, signed by author. Second Life Books, Inc. 196 B - 891 2016 $175

Wilder, Thornton 1896-1976 *The Bridge of San Luis Rey.* London: Longmans Green, 1927. First UK edition and the correct first, near fine and unread in near fine dust jacket, book has light foxing to prelim pages as a commonly found in this edition, otherwise fine, jacket, especially fresh and bright, light toning to spine and couple of tiny closed tears, housed in custom clamshell box. Royal Books 49 - 72 2016 $975

Wilder, Thornton 1896-1976 *The Bridge of San Luis Rey.* New York: Grosset & Dunalap, circa, 1950. Reprint, fine, dust jacket with some chips at top of front cover and along top of spine, not affecting printing of spine title, inscribed by author for Miss Sara Glass. Second Life Books, Inc. 196B - 896 2016 $188

Wilder, Thornton 1896-1976 *The Bridge of San Luis Rey.* New York: Limited Editions Club, 1962. Limited to 1500 numbered copies signed by artist, 4to., morocco backed buckram, fine in slipcase (soiled on top edge, 2 inches on side panel with some scraping of paper), full page color lithographs by Jean Charlot, laid in is personal Christmas card from Charlot. Aleph-bet Books, Inc. 111 - 88 2016 $175

Wilder, Thornton 1896-1976 *The Bridge of San Luis Rey.* London: Limited Editions Club, 1962. Limited edition, number N-W' of 1500 copies, lithographs by Jean Charlot, fine in publisher's box, tall 8vo., monthly newsletter laid in. Second Life Books, Inc. 197 - 356 2016 $200

Wilder, Thornton 1896-1976 *The Eighth Day.* New York: Harper & Row, 1967. First edition, one of 500 copies printed on special paper, 8vo, specially bound and signed by author, this copy #2 with bookplate of Cass Canfield, publishers' greeting card signed "Evan" and "Cass" laid in and nice inscription on titlepage by author for Cass, fine in publisher's box, inscribed by author to his editor at Harper, Cass Canfield. Second Life Books, Inc. 196 B - 892 2016 $1250

Wilder, Thornton 1896-1976 *Lucrece.* Boston: Houghton Mifflin, 1933. First edition, 8vo., nice in some nicked and soiled, dust jacket, inscribed by author to Stanley. Second Life Books, Inc. 196 B - 893 2016 $225

Wilder, Thornton 1896-1976 *Theophilus North.* New York: Harper & Row, 1973. First edition, 8vo., one of 275 copies printed on special paper, specially bound and signed by author, this copy #216 in publisher's box (little faded), fine. Second Life Books, Inc. 196 B - 894 2016 $188

Wilder, Thornton 1896-1976 *The Skin of Our Teeth. A Play in Three Acts.* New York: Harper, 1942. First edition, 8vo., very good, actor Frederic March's copy with his signature, with presentation card from author, with pencil marks and comments. Second Life Books, Inc. 197 - 355 2016 $600

Wilder, Thornton 1896-1976 *The Woman of Andros.* New York: Boni, 1930. First edition, 8vo., fine, in near fine dust jacket, custom slipcase, inscribed "Greetings of Thornton Wilder". Second Life Books, Inc. 196 B - 895 2016 $175

Wildsmith, Brian *Carousel.* New York: Alfred Knopf, 1988. First edition, first printing (1-10 code), folio, pictorial boards, fine in dust jacket (very good+ with few small closed tears), color illustrations on every page by author, laid in is charming pen drawing of 2 lions, inscribed by him and signed twice. Aleph-bet Books, Inc. 111 - 481 2016 $200

Wiles, Hector V. *The Horn-Book: the First rung on the Ladder of Literacy.* London: printed at the Walthamstow Press, circa, 1952? Ordinary edition, Half title, frontispiece and plates, illustrations, original cream card wrappers, red cloth spine. Jarndyce Antiquarian Books CCXV - 789 2016 £20

Wiles, Hector V. *The Horn-Book: the First rung on the Ladder of Literacy.* London: printed & published by the Walthamstow Press, circa, 1952? No. 83 of 100 copies for private circulation, on thick paper, Half title, frontispiece and plates, illustrations, original white cloth, very good. Jarndyce Antiquarian Books CCXV - 788 2016 £30

Wilkes, Charles *Narrative of the United States Exploring Expedition During the Years 1838-1842.* London: Whittaker, 1845. 8vo., original green blindstamped cloth, spine faded and split on 1 joint and small wear to head and tail. J. & S. L. Bonham Antiquarian Booksellers Voyages 2016 - 5289 2016 £95

Wilkes, John Caesar *The Political Controversy; or Weekly Magazine of Ministerial and Anti-Ministerial Essays...* London: S. Williams, 1762-1763. First edition, 8vo., 5 volumes, soundly rebound in recent black cloth lettered gilt on spines, very good set.   Any Amount of Books   2015 - C16216   2016   £600

Wilkes, Roger *Wallace. The Final Verdict.* London: Bodley Head, 1984. Uncorrected proof copy, very good, original wrappers.   I. D. Edrich   Crime - 2016   £20

Wilkins, H. J. *Edward Colston (1636-1721 A.D.). A Chronological Account of His Life and Work. Together With an Account of the Colston Societies and Memorials in Bristol.* Bristol: J. W. Arrowsmith, 1920. 8vo., foxing mainly to titlepage and preface, text otherwise clean, brown cloth, gilt lettering to spine, little rubbed to endcaps, edges uncut, top edge little dusted and spotted, very good, ownership signature of P(aul) Slack.   Unsworths Antiquarian Booksellers Ltd.   E04 - 15   2016   £25

Wilkins, Thurman *Clarence King. A Biography.* Albuquerque: University of New Mexico Press, 1988. Revised edition, illustrations, very fine.   Argonaut Book Shop   Biography 2015 - 3607   2016 $60

Wilkins, W. H. *The Romance of Isabel Lady Burton: the Story of Her Life.* London: Hutchinson, 1897. Third edition, 2 volumes, 8vo., frontispiece, original brown decorative cloth, fore-edges rubbed and waterstained.   J. & S. L. Bonham Antiquarian Booksellers   Voyages 2016 - 9048   2016   £40

Wilkinson, David Nicholas *Charles Dickens's England.* London: Guerilla Books, 2009. 4to., half title, frontispiece, illustrations in color, original green cloth, mint in dust jacket.   Jarndyce Antiquarian Booksellers   CCXVIII - 1483   2016   £20

Wilkinson, E. S. *Shanghai Birds: a study of Bird Life in Shanghai and the Surrounding Districts.* Shanghai: North China Daily News and Herald, 1929. Small quarto, colored frontispiece and 23 color plates by Gronvold, publisher's handsome decorated cloth with torn dust jacket, scarce in this condition.   Andrew Isles Natural History Books   55 - 16953   2016 $500

Wilkinson, George *Experiments and Observations on the Cortex Salicis Latifoliae....* Newcastle-upon-Tyne: printed for the author by Edw. Walker, 1803. First edition with hand colored engraved frontispiece by Bewick after Assiotti, plate slightly frayed around edges, ink border little corroded, signature on back of plate partly erased, offset onto title, text uniformly slightly browned and few scattered spots, 8vo., modern boards, preserved in cloth folding box with colored copy of the plate inset in upper cover behind glass, sound, very scarce.   Blackwell's Rare Books   B186 - 167   2016   £950

Wilkinson, L. P. *Ovid Recalled.* Bath: Cedric Chivers, 1974. First edition, 8vo., green boards, gilt lettered, green dust jacket laminated, spine slightly faded, price clipped, very good, ownership inscription of C. D. N. Costa in pen, and one postcard loosely inserted.   Unsworths Antiquarian Booksellers Ltd.   E05 - 65   2016   £25

Wilkinson, Margaret *Correct Etiquette for all Occsasions.* Bombay: D. B. Taraporevala Sons & Co., circa, 1935? third Indian edition, half title, original grey paper boards, lilac cloth spine, very good.   Jarndyce Antiquarian Books   CCXV - 482   2016   £45

Willan, Robert *Delineation of Cutaneous Diseases, Exhibiting the Characteristic Appearances of the Principal Genra and Species....* London: H. G. Bohn, 1840. New edition, 4to., 20th century quarter brown calf, marbled boards, spine with raised bands, gilt tools and lettering, top edges gilt, 72 hand colored plates, each with tissue guard and accompanying leaf of text, occasional unobtrusive spots, very good, from the library of the present owner of Willan's house in Sedbergh.   Sotheran's   Piccadilly Notes - Summer 2015 - 332   2016   £3000

Willan, Robert *On Cutaneous Diseases.* London: J. Johnson, 1808. 4to., 20th century quarter brown calf, marbled boards, spine with raised bands, gilt rules, red morocco label with gilt lettering, 33 hand colored plates, loose color photo of Willan's grave, repairs to edges of titlepage, light dampstaining to upper corners of first few leaves and last few plates, foxing to some leaves, otherwise very clean, very good, scarce in handsome binding, inkstamp of Western Medical and Surgical Society to titlepage and corner of one leaf, subsequently this book has spent many years in the library of the previous owner of Willan's house in Sedbergh.   Sotheran's   Piccadilly Notes - Summer 2015 - 331   2016   £4750

Willard, Frances E. *Nineteen Beautiful Years or Sketches of a Girl's life.* Chicago: Woman's Temperance Pub., 1889. Revised edition, 8vo., tan cloth little rubbed and soiled, front flyleaf and hinge loose, good copy, inscribed by author.   Second Life Books, Inc.   196 B - 897   2016 $125

Willeford, Charles *Kiss Your Ass Good-Bye.* Miami Beach: Dennis McMillan, 1987. First edition, limited to 400 copies signed and numbered by author, fine in fine dust jacket with very light creasing to top front cover at spine.   Buckingham Books   2015 - 15577   2016 $450

Willeford, Charles *No Experience necessary.* Chicago: Newstand Library Magenta Book, 1962. First edition, paperback original, fine unread copy in pictorial wrappers, exceptional copy.   Buckingham Books   2015 - 23194   2016 $450

Willeford, Charles *Poontang and Other Poems.* Crescent City: privately printed/New Atheneum Press, 1967. First edition, stapled wrappers, very slight bump to bottom corner, still fine, signed by author, reportedly one of 500 copies, seemingly scarcer variant in gray wrappers. Between the Covers Rare Books   208 - 111   2016 $2500

William L. Clements Library *Author/Title Catalog of Americana 1493-1860 in the William L. Clements Library, University of Michigan, Ann Arbor, Michigan.* Boston: G. K. Hall & Co., 1970. 7 volumes, folio, cloth, staining to top edge of text blocks on volumes 2-7, staining to front edges of text blocks on volumes 3, 4, 5 and 7, interior staining to front pastedown, free endpaper and next two pages of volumes, staining to volume five on front pastedown and free endpaper, slight wrinkling to top edges of text blocks, some rubbing to boards, staining does not affect text.   Oak Knoll Books   310 - 226   2016 $650

William, of Malmsbury *Gesta Regum Angliorum.* London: English Historical Society, 1840. First edition, 2 volumes, 8vo., text in Latin, printed marginalia and footnotes in English, volume I pages 369-384 lacking and replaced with facsimiles, adjacent pages somewhat soiled but text perfectly legible, original brown paper covered boards, skillfully rebacked in well matched brown paper, black morocco gilt labels, edges uncut, some stains and scratches to boards, labels little rubbed, edges dusted, bookplate 'Ex Oblatorum C. Caroli Bibliothecca apud Bayswater', recent bookplate of Eric Poole,, several library ink margins to prelims of both volumes.   Unsworths Antiquarian Booksellers Ltd.   30 - 162   2016   £120

Williams-Ellis, Amabel *Fairy Tales from the British Isles.* London & Glasgow: Blackie, 1960. First edition, color frontispiece and 7 color printed plates, titlepage with vignette printed in red and black, further illustrations by Pauline Baynes throughout text with initial headpiece printed in red and black, one or two faint spots to half title 8vo., original red cloth with few faint spots to this and to fore-edge, color printed endpapers, dust jacket lightly toned in places, laminate lifting little along joint folds, very good, signed by artist. Blackwell's Rare Books   B186 - 181   2016   £700

Williams, Alfred *Folk Songs of the Upper Thames.* London: Duckworth & Co., 1923. First edition, 8vo., little light foxing to first and last few pages, pale green cloth, gilt title to spine and upper board, spine slightly rubbed with some creasing to endcaps, edges lightly foxed, light patches of toning to endpapers, still very good, without dust jacket, small Foyles label to front pastedown.   Unsworths Antiquarian Booksellers Ltd.   30 - 163   2016   £60

Williams, C. J. *Greenacre, or the Edgeware-Road Murder Presenting an Authentic and Circumstantial Account of This Most Sanguinary Outrage of the laws of Humanity...* Derby: published by Thomas Richardson, 1837. 8vo., color folding frontispiece, upper margins stabbed (for string) slightly affecting frontispiece and some headlines, original printed green paper wrappers, minor creasing and short closed tear, else good copy.   John Drury Rare Books   2015 - 25361   2016 $350

Williams, C. K. *Creatures.* Haverford: Green Shade, 2006. First edition, deluxe issue, one of 26 lettered copies printed on Twinrocker handmade paper at the Grenfell Press, specially bound and signed by poet, small 4to., original quarter black morocco and handmade paste paper over boards, publisher's paper slipcase, as new, splendidly bound.   James S. Jaffe Rare Books   Occasional List: Winter 2016 - 145   2016 $850

Williams, Charles *The Bit Bite.* London: Cassell/Crime Connoisseur, 1957. Dust jacket, rubbed, very good.   I. D. Edrich   Crime - 2016   £50

Williams, Charles *Talk of the Town.* New York: Dell, 1958. First edition, very good in wrappers.   Mordida Books   2015 - 010708   2016 $60

Williams, Clara Andrews *The Bettijak Book: Adventures of Jack and Betty.* New York: Frederick Stokes, Sept., 1914. 4to., cloth, pictorial paste-on slats already cut else near fine, cover has large hole which reveals the picture below, color illustrations by George Alfred Williams.   Alephbet Books, Inc.   112 - 514   2016 $350

Williams, Emlyn *Accolade: a Play in Six Scenes.* London: Heinemann, 1951. First edition, 8vo., original cloth, very good in little worn dust jacket, inscribed by author to Michael Weight Jan. 1951.   Second Life Books, Inc.   196 B - 898   2016 $113

Williams, Emlyn *Night Must Fall: a Play in three acts.* London: Victor Gollancz, 1936. First edition, second impression, 8vo., cloth with little soiled dust jacket, inscribed by author for Michael Weight.   Second Life Books, Inc.   196 B - 899   2016 $113

Williams, Gerald *Common Ground.* N.P.: the Bieler Press, 1980. Limited to 150 numbered copies signed by author and artist, 12 illustrations by Schechter, large 8vo., stiff paper wrappers, double endpapers of Fabriano handmade paper.   Oak Knoll Books   310 - 83   2016 $125

Williams, Helen Maria *Julia, a Novel, Interspersed with Some Poetical Pieces.* London: printed for T. Cadell, 1790. 2 volumes, 12mo., little foxing & browning, possibly lacking A1 (blank) in volume II, contemporary half calf, marbled boards, original red morocco labels, black oval volume numbers, slight wear to head of one spine, boards slightly rubbed, contemporary bookplate of Sir Henry Hay Makdougall of Makerstoun, Cuonty Roxburgh, nice, scarce. Jarndyce Antiquarian Booksellers   CCXVI - 612   2016   £5200

Williams, James *The Footman's Guide.* London: Dean and Son, 1856. Sixth edition, appropriate plates and bills of fare, 12mo., 2 folding plates, one slightly dusted and creased at fore edge, contemporary full dark purple grained calf, expertly rebacked, signature of Mr. Coward Rose, bookseller's ticket of Richard & W. F. Larkin.   Jarndyce Antiquarian Books   CCXV - 483   2016   £280

Williams, John *The History of the Gunpowder Treason.* London: for Richard Chiswel, 1678. First edition, small 4to., initial imprimatur leaf, small rust on C34, very minor stain on D2r and with verso of final leaf (D4), very lightly soiled, Amateur binding of early 20th century red boards and white spine, boards, little stained and corners bumped, from the library of James Stevens Cox (1910-1997), bookplate of William Salt Brassington.   Maggs Bros. Ltd.   1447 - 451   2016   £120

Williams, John A. *Love.* Derry: Babcock & Koontz, 1988. No. 43 of 200 copies, not numbered, 8vo., wood engraving on title by Gaylord Schanilec, author's signature, paper wrappers, sewn at fold, applied paper label on front, about as new.   Second Life Books, Inc.   196 B - 900   2016 $65

Williams, John A. *Mothersill and the Foxes.* Garden City: Doubleday, 1975. First edition, signed and dated by author on title, paper over boards, nice in little scuffed and soiled dust jacket.   Second Life Books, Inc.   196 B - 901   2016 $75

Williams, Jonathan *Affilati Attrezzi Per I Giardini Di Catullo.* Milano: Lerici Editori, 1966. First edition, 8vo., paper wrappers, English and Italian on facing pages, inscribed by author for Paul Metcalf.   Second Life Books, Inc.   196 B - 903   2016 $50

Williams, Jonathan *Aposiopeses (Odds & Ends).* Minneapolis: Granary Books, 1988. Limited to 165 numbered copies, this one of the 100 bound in wrappers, signed by author, 4to., stiff paper wrappers, label on spine, top edge gilt, other edges uncut, frontispiece by Kitaj.   Oak Knoll Books   310 - 105   2016 $150

Williams, Jonathan *A Celestial Centennial Reverie for Mr. Charles Ives.* Highlands: Jonathan Williams Feb. 20-27, 1975. Produced on Xerox 4000 in an edition of 100 copies for friends, 4to., self wrappers in plastic binder, inscribed by author for Paul and Nancy Metcalf.   Second Life Books, Inc.   196 B - 905   2016 $150

Williams, Jonathan *Elite/Elate Poems: Selected Poems 1971-1975.* Jargon Society, 1979. First edition, portfolio of photos by Guy Mendes, 4to., little streak on cloth, otherwise fine in dust jacket (little worn), inscribed by author for Paul and Nancy Metcalf.   Second Life Books, Inc.   196 B - 906   2016 $200

Williams, Jonathan *Five from Up T'Dale.* Corn Close: Finial Press in Great Britain, 1974. First edition, square folio, loose sheets in portfolio, prints by A. D. Moore, limited to only 50 numbered copes signed by author and artist, fine. James S. Jaffe Rare Books   Occasional List: Winter 2016 - 63   2016 $450

Williams, Jonathan *Four Stoppages.* Stuttgart: Jonathan Williams/Jargon, 1953. First edition, limited to 200 unnumbered copies, issued as Jargon 5, fragile and scarce, large folio stiff card sheet, folded to make 8 large pages, small stain on last panel, modest age toning, one small corner with archival repair, very good.   Between the Covers Rare Books   208 - 91   2016 $2500

Williams, Jonathan *Glees Swarthy Monotonies Rince Cochon & Chozzerai for Simon.* Roswell: DBA Editions, 1980. First edition, 1/128 copies distributed to friends, not for sale, 4to., very good inscribed by author for Paul Metcalf. Second Life Books, Inc.   196 B - 907   2016 $100

Williams, Jonathan *Homage, Umbrage, Quibble & chicane.* Roswell: DBA Editions, 1981. First edition, one of 120 copies produced for friends, 4to., this #68, inscribed by Paul and Nancy Metcalf.   Second Life Books, Inc.   196 B - 908   2016 $125

Williams, Jonathan *The Lucidites, Sixteen in Visionary Company.* London: Turret Books, 1967. First edition, bound in cloth with illustrations by John Furnival on foil, fine, of a total edition of 280, this one of 250 for sale, inscribed by author for friends, Paul and Nancy Metcalf. Second Life Books, Inc.   196 B - 909   2016 $125

Williams, Jonathan *My Quaker Atheist Friend.* London: Jonathan Williams, 1975. Inscribed by author to poet Paul Metcalf, folded in half and stapled, very good.   Second Life Books, Inc.   196 B - 911   2016 $65

Williams, Jonathan *Shankum Naggum.* Rocky Mount: Friends of the Library NC Wesleyan, 1979. 1/550 copies, tall 8vo., paper wrappers, inscribed by author for poet Paul Metcalf, very good.   Second Life Books, Inc.   196 B - 912   2016 $45

Williams, Jonathan *Sharp Tools for Catullan Gardens.* Bloomington: Fine Arts Dept. University of Indiana, 1968. First edition, one of only 36 copies, printed on Italian paper and signed by author and artist, with each lithograph individually signed by the artist, folio, 24 leaves plus 2 guard sheets in fabricoid portfolio with printed label, 10 lithographs by James McGarrell, fine.   James S. Jaffe Rare Books   Occasional List: Winter 2016 - 147   2016 $5000

Williams, Jonathan *62 Climerikews to Amuse Mr. Ler.* Rosewell/Denver: DBA/JCA Editions, Christmas, 1983. One of 200 numbered and inscribed for friends of author and artist, this is #62 signed for Paul and Nancy (Metcalf) and signed JW, 4to., printed wrappers, nice.   Second Life Books, Inc.   196 B - 902   2016 $150

Williams, Jonathan *Untinears & Antennae for Maurice Ravel.* St. Paul: Truck Books, 1977. First edition, very nice in printed wrappers, inscribed by author for poet Paul Metcalf and wife, Nancy.   Second Life Books, Inc.   196 B - 913   2016 $50

Williams, Joseph J. *Hebrewisms of West Africa.* New York: Lincoln, MacVeagh, The Dial Press, 1930. First edition, 8vo., original black cloth, spine lettered gilt and illustrated in gilt to front cover, original illustrated dust jackets, 2 plates (one a map), five sketch maps, wrappers little dusted with minor fraying to margins, upper outer corner of binding with one bump, front inner hinge with traces of having been stuck together, internally very good and uncut.   Sotheran's Travel and Exploration - 46   2016   £298

Williams, Tennessee 1911-1983 *Camino Real.* Norfolk: New Directions, 1953. First edition, one corner bumped, else fine in near fine dust jacket.   Between the Covers Rare Books   204 - 132   2016 $300

Williams, Tennessee 1911-1983 *Hard Candy a Book of Stories.* New York: New Directions, 1954. First edition, tall octavo, some soiling and small stain along edge of spine, about very good in worn, first issue royal blue slipcase, cutom chemise and quarter morocco clamshell case, dedication copy (for Paul and Jane Bowles), inscribed by author for Paul Bowles.   Between the Covers Rare Books   204 - 135   2016 $35,000

Williams, Tennessee 1911-1983 *The Kingdom of Earth with Hard Candy: a Book of Stories.* New York: New Directions, 1954. No. 15 of 100 copies signed by author, 248 x 152mm., (cancel titlepage tipped-in, as in all copies), publisher's linen backed patterned paper boards, flat spine with author's name in gilt, original blue cardboard slipcase with paper title label on front cover, one small only vague visible discolored spot at head of spine, otherwise mint with leaves that open only reluctantly.   Phillip J. Pirages   67 - 356   2016 $1750

Williams, Tennessee 1911-1983 *One Arm and Other Stories.* New Directions, 1948. Fifth printing, large 8vo., paper wrappers, good, inscribed by author to Ralph Renzi.   Second Life Books, Inc.   197 - 357   2016 $1500

Williams, Tennessee 1911-1983 *A Streetcar named Desire.* New York: New Directions, 1947. First edition, touch of wear at spine ends, else fine in near fine dust jacket with some splitting at front spine fold and spine fold at crown along with some toning, nice.   Between the Covers Rare Books   204 - 131   2016 $2800

Williams, Tennessee 1911-1983 *Suddenly Last Summer.* New York: New Directions, 1958. First edition, fine in fine dust jacket, beautiful copy.   Between the Covers Rare Books   204 - 133   2016 $400

Williams, Tennessee 1911-1983 *Tennessee.* Washington: David Bruce Smith, 2012. First edition, one of 750 numbered copies, elephant sized folio, 3 volumes, hand bound and loosely inserted in custom made clamshell case, specially built heavy cardboard mailer, book design and binding by John Paul Greenawalt.   Oak Knoll Books   310 - 94   2016 $3000

Williams, Tennessee 1911-1983 *Tennessee Williams' Letters to Donald Windham 1940-1965.* Verona: Sandy Campbell, 1976. First edition,, one of only 26 lettered copies printed on blue Fabriano paper and signed by author and Windham, out of a total edition of 526, very fine, 8vo., illustrations, original wrappers, acetate dust jacket, slipcase.   James S. Jaffe Rare Books   Occasional List: Winter 2016 - 149   2016 $1500

Williams, Wellington *The Traveller's and Tourist's Guide through the United States of America, Canada, etc....* Philadelphia: Lippincott Grambo & Co., 1851. First edition, 12mo., publisher's catalog last 20 pages, foldout map, map hand colored in outline, original wallet-style purple leather with gilt title stamping to one side, leather faded to dark tan, old paper repair to top of rear hinge, map with some age-toning along two cnter horizontal fold lines, overall respectable very good+ copy.   Tavistock Books   Bibliolatry - 37   2016 $2500

Williamson, George Charles 1858-1942 *Life and Works of Ozias Humphry.* London: John Lane, Bodley Head, 1918. Limited edition, 1.400 copies, plates, some in color, minor foxing, 4to., original vellum backed boards, top edges gilt, others uncut, good.   Blackwell's Rare Books   B186 - 168   2016   £150

Williamson, Hamilton *Baby Bear.* New York: Doubleday Doran & Co., 1930. Stated first edition, 8vo., pictorial boards, spine bottom chipped, half split at joint, slightly dusty, really very good+ in dust jacket with several pieces off, worn at folds, striking color and black and white lithographs by the Haders, full page watercolor, inscribed by the Haders.   Aleph-bet Books, Inc.   111 - 209   2016 $1000

Williamson, James A. *The Caribbee Islands Under the Proprietary Patents.* Oxford: University Press, 1926. First edition, 2 volumes, quarto, map, 117 plates, portrait frontispiece, vignette on titlepage, contemporary black full calf, gilt, gilt spines and raised bands, all edges gilt, very handsome. J. & S. L. Bonham Antiquarian Booksellers   America 2016 - 9211   2016   £120

Williamson, Kenneth *The Atlantic Islands.* London: Collins, 1948. First edition, 8vo., original cloth, dust jacket, illustrations, sketch map, map endpapers, wrappers chipped to extremities with loss from head and foot of spine, binding sunned, internally clean, very good.   Sotheran's   Piccadilly Notes - Summer 2015 - 333   2016   £60

Williamson, Passmore *Case of Passmore Williamson.* Philadelphia: Uriah Hunt & son, 1856. First edition, octavo, original cloth, bookplate of defucnt library, pocket removed from rear pastedown, call letters on spine, cloth worn down at spine ends, still bright, very good, this copy inscribed by Williamson for H. G. Jones, almost certainly Horatio Gates Jones, historian.   Between the Covers Rare Books   202 - 118   2016 $1850

Williamson, Thomas *Oriental Field Sports.* London: Edward Orme, 1807. First edition, first state, with plate XXXI lettered "Hunting Jackalls", paper watermarks dated 1804, very handsome recent blue straight grain morocco gilt in style of period by Courtland Benson, covers with broad border featuring Greek key roll and starbust corner ornaments, raised bands flanked by multiple plain and decorative rules, spine panels with large central fleuron, marbled endpapers, all edges gilt, engraved pictorial title and 40 dramatic aquatint plates, all attractively colored by hand, frontispiece and two index leaves with flattened creases, titlepage slightly soiled, margin of final page of text bit foxed, faint offsetting from plates onto text, other trivial defects (one short marginal tear, isolated insignificant pinpoint foxing, little smudge here and there), but fine, only quite minor imperfections, with none of the typical and often deadly offsetting from text onto plates, very accomplished replica binding unworn.   Phillip J. Pirages   67 - 357   2016 $19,500

Willis, Ambrose Madison, Mrs. *The Social Rubaiyat of a Bud.* San Francisco: Paul Elder & Co., 1913. First edition, 8vo., original stiff card decorative wrappers, illustrations by Elsie Harrison with color lithographs, heightened with gold of Art Deco images.   Sotheran's   Piccadilly Notes - Summer 2015 - 334   2016   £98

Willis, Fred H. *Theodore Parker in spirit Life. A Narration of Personal Experience.* Boston: Wilson White & Co., 1868. First edition, 8vo., removed, lacks wrappers.   M & S Rare Books, Inc.   99 - 296   2016 $100

Willis, John *Mnemonica or the Art of Memory Drained Out of the Pure Fountains of Art and Nature.* London: printed and are to be sold by Leonard Sowersby, 1661. First complete edition in English, 12mo., woodcut illustration of stage on E4B, browned throughout, stronger in margins, small ink-stain on D6, pages 94-95 somewhat soiled, light marking to fore edges of D8 and M7-8, early 19th century calf, ruled in gilt, spine with five raised bands, covers scuffed, joints just starting to crack, corners bumped, bookplate of Rev. Edward Orlebar Smith, from the library of James Stevens Cox (1910-1997).   Maggs Bros. Ltd.   1447 - 452   2016   £400

Willis, Nathaniel Parker   1806-1867 *Canadian Scenery.* London: Virtue, 1842. First edition, 2 volumes, quarto, map, 117 plates, frontispiece, vignette on titlepage, contemporary black full calf, gilt, gilt spines and raised bands, all edges gilt, very handsome.   J. & S. L. Bonham Antiquarian Booksellers   America 2016 - 9211   2016   £850

Willis, Thomas *The Anatomy of the Brain and Nerves.* Birmingham: Classics of Neurology and Neurosurgery Library, 1983. Engraved frontispiece, full gilt leather, folio, nice, from the library of Edgar Houseplan.   James Tait Goodrich   X-78 - 559   2016 $125

Willis, Thomas *De Anima Brutorum Quae Hominis Vitalis ac Sensitiva est Exercitationes Duae Prior Physiologica Ejusdem Naturam Partes Potentias...* London: Typis E. F. Impensis Ric. Davis, 1672. First octavo edition, Lacking one plate (of 8 folding plates), with an addition two plates torn with some image loss, plate lacking is #8, newly rebound in full contemporary style English panel calf, handsome rebinding, with exception of defects, nice, clean copy. James Tait Goodrich   X-78 - 560   2016 $650

Willis, Thomas *Cerebri Anatome. Cui Accessi Nervorum.* London: Tho. Roycroft for Jo. Martyn & Ja. Allestry, 1664. First Octavo edition, 15 foling engraved plates, 8vo., very nice contemporary vellum with yapped edges, hand lettered spine, contents quite crisp and clean, blank lower edge of title excised and restored, volume placed in folding cloth case, bookplates of the Duke of Braunschweig-Luneburg and Herbert McLean Evans.   James Tait Goodrich   X-78 - 557   2016 $5950

Willis, Thomas *Distribae Duae Medico Philosophicae...* London: Typis Tho. Roycroft, Impensis Jo. martin, Ja. Allestry & Tho. Dicas, 1660. Second edition, 12mo., engraved frontispiece, dampstain to upper inner corner, lower corners of C5-I2 creased, occasional rust spotting throughout, small ink stain to blank lower margin of H6y4, later sheep, ruled in gilt, rubbed, small single wormhole to spine, headcap missing, with two pieces of leather gouged from centre of lower board, single marginal Latin annotation on H34, from the library of James Stevens Cox (1910-1997). Maggs Bros. Ltd.   1447 - 453   2016   £240

Willis, Thomas *Dr. Willis's Practice of Physick.* London: printed for T. Dring, C. Harper and J. Leigh, 1684. Small folio, newly rebound in full English panel calf, raised bands with tooled compartments, text with light browning and foxing, very mild worming in margins and some of the marginal notes have been lightly shaved, done of the plates shaved by later binding, about 1-2mm. James Tait Goodrich X-78 - 558   2016 $6500

Willis, Thomas *Proteus Vinctus.* London: for E. Cotes and are to be sold by Will London bookseller in Newcastle, 1655. First edition, variant issue, 8vo., light dampstaining at beginning and end, some light occasional soiling, overall clean, crisp copy, contemporary sheep rebacked, front cover cracked and stained, rear cover torn away exposing board, corners and edges bumped and chipped, from the library of James Stevens Cox (1910-1997). Maggs Bros. Ltd. 1447 - 454   2016   £350

Willm, Joseph *The Education of the People...* Glasgow: William Lang, 1847. First British edition, errata slip, contemporary half calf by David Bryce, Glasgow, gilt spine, slightly rubbed, morocco label, slightly rubbed and marked, but nice, contemporary signature of G. Walker. Jarndyce Antiquarian Books CCXV - 1008   2016   £48

Willock, Colin *Town Gun.* London: Andre Deutsch, 1973. Reprint, 8vo., original red cloth, illustrated dust jacket (spine sunned, price clipped), internally clean. Sotheran's Hunting, Shooting & Fishing - 105   2016   £30

Wills, Garry *Inventing America: Jefferson's Declaration of Independence.* Garden City: Doubleday & Co., 1978. First edition, fine in fine dust jacket (minor edge wear). Ken Hebenstreit, Bookseller 2016 - 2016 $90

Wills, William Henry *Old Leaves Gathered from Household Words.* London: Chapman & Hall, 1860. First edition, contemporary half red morocco, little rubbed, all edges gilt, large paper, presentation copy from Dickens's sub-editor to Charles Knight. Jarndyce Antiquarian Booksellers CCXVIII - 782   2016   £125

Willson, Dixie *Once Upon a Monday.* Joliet: Volland, 1931. First edition, no additional printings, 8vo., cloth backe pictorial boards, some cover soil else fine in box (cover soil), rare, illustrations by Erick Berry. Aleph-bet Books, Inc. 111 - 466   2016 $450

Willughby, Francis *The Ornithology of Francis Willughby of Middleton in the County of Warwick, Esq...* London: by Andrew Clarke for John Martyn, 1678. First edition in English, folio 78 engraved plates and two engraved plates of snares at page 28, titlepage browned and spotted slightly grubby throughout with marginal browning, occasional spotting, closed tear in outer margin of Kkk3, top corner of Kkk4 (touching rule), small blank piece torn from plate LIX; last 40 plates increasingly stained at outer edge, eventually working into image towards end and final plate damaged in outer margin but roughly repaired with outer half of plate backed with paper at earlyish date, late 18th century marbled boards, rebacked with leather, corners and edges bumped and worn, from the library of James Stevens Cox (1910-1997). Maggs Bros. Ltd. 1447 - 455   2016   £1600

Wilsey, Sean *Oh the glory of It All.* New York: Penguin, 2005. First edition, inscribed by author fine in near fine dust jacket rubbed at edges and folds. Ken Lopez Bookseller 166 - 151   2016 $75

Wilson, Arthur *The History of Great Britain, being the Life and Reign of King James the First...* London: for Richard Lownds, 1653. 4to., contemporary leather, five raised bands on spine, frontispiece, engraved initial letters, frontispiece and title separated, chipped at edges, previous owner's name on title, tanning and some foxing throughout text. Oak Knoll Books 310 - 308   2016 $450

Wilson, Chris *The Myth of Santa Fe, Creating a Modern Regional Tradition.* Albuquerque: 1997. Near fine in like dust jacket, illustrations, signed by author. Dumont Maps and Books 133 - 85   2016 $100

Wilson, Daniel *The Substance of a Conversation with John Bellingham, the Assassin of the Late Right Hon. Spencer Perceval, on Sunday May 17 1812....* London: John Hatchard, 1812. First edition, 8vo., recent marbled boards, lettered on spine, very good, scarce. John Drury Rare Books 2015 - 24459   2016 $437

Wilson, Edward O. *The Diversity of life.* London: Allen Lane, 1992. First edition, octavo, illustrations, signature, very good in dust jacket. Andrew Isles Natural History Books 55 - 38833   2016 $60

Wilson, Ernest Henry *A Naturalist in Western China with Vasculum, Camera and Gun.* London: Methuen, 1913. First edition, octavo, 2 volumes, photos, folding map, publisher's red cloth, minor blemish on lower corner of volume two, fine, crisp set, signed by Wilson 13.12.20, bookplate of Harold Alston. Andrew Isles Natural History Books 55 - 30016   2016 $1500

Wilson, F. Paul *The Keep.* New York: William Morrow and Co., 1981. First edition, fine in fine dust jacket. Between the Covers Rare Books 208 - 128   2016 $100

Wilson, Francis *Francis Wilson's Life of Himself.* Boston: Houghton Mifflin, 1924. First edition, 8vo., numerous illustrations, one of 300 copies signed by Wilson, all edges uncut, cover little soiled, otherwise very good, ex-library with bookplate removed from front endpaper.   Second Life Books, Inc.   196 B - 918   2016 $75

Wilson, George *What is Technology?* Edinburgh: Sutherland & Knox, 1855. Disbound, unsewn, 26 pages.   Jarndyce Antiquarian Books   CCXV - 636   2016   £35

Wilson, Helen Calista *Vagabonding at Fifty. From Siberia to Turkenstan.* New York: Coward McCann, 1929. First edition, issue with gilt binding, as opposed to later and cheaper variant decorated in black, 8vo.,8vo., original red cloth, decorated and lettered in gilt, map endpapers, illustrated wrappers, plates after photos, wrappers little frayed, light even browning, very good in rarely preserved wrappers.   Sotheran's   Travel and Exploration - 207   2016   £148

Wilson, Isaiah W. *A Geography and History of the County of Digby, Nova Scotia.* Belleville: Mika Studio, 1972. Facsimile edition of original 1900 edition, red cloth, 8vo., gilt to spine and front cover, very good, previous owner's stamp inside front cover.   Schooner Books Ltd.   115 - 180   2016 $45

Wilson, James Andrew *James Andrew Wilson Life Travels and Adventures.* Austin: Gammel's Book Store, 1927. First edition, fine in very good+ dust jacket, gilt stamped maroon cloth, drawings, 1962 ink gift inscription, very scarce, fine, dust jacket slightly soiled with couple of small chips.   Gene W. Baade, Books on the West   2015 - O111170   2016 $44

Wilson, James Grant *Appletons' Cyclopaedia of American Biography.* New York: D. Appleton and Co., 1895. Reprint of first edition, 6 volumes complete, thick small 4to., 19th century half calf with marbled paper covered boards, all edges marbled, well preserved set, portraits, illustrations, with 61 steel engraved portraits, covers rubbed, slightly shaken.   Oak Knoll Books   310 - 309   2016 $350

Wilson, Joyce Lancaster *The Work & Play of Adrian Wilson, a Bibliography with Commentary.* Austin: W. Thomas Taylor, 1983. Limited to 325 numbered copies, folio, quarter bound in oasis morocco dyed to match Tuscany red ink used in text, Dutch linen sides stamped with Wilson's type-juggler device, small gouge to back cover, printed on handmade paper, many tipped-in specimens.   Oak Knoll Books   310 - 254   2016 $500

Wilson, Keith *Homestead.* San Francisco: Kayak, 1969. First edition, one of 1000 copies, decorated wrappers, color prints, inscribed and signed by author for William Meredith, laid in is TLS by Wilson to Meredith, near fine.   Charles Agvent   William Meredith - 122   2016 $80

Wilson, Lucy Sarah Atkins *The India Cabinet Opened.* London: printed for Harris and Son..., 1821. First edition, 12mo., hand colored engraved frontispiece, original red morocco backed marbled boards.   Marlborough Rare Books   List 56 - 60   2016   £350

Wilson, Robert, Mrs. *In the Land of the Tui.* London: Sampson Low, 1894. Extremely rare first edition, 8vo., original olive green pictorial cloth, lettered gilt, frontispiece retaining tissue guards and 11 plates, mostly after photos, large folding lithographic plate printed in 3 colors, only light marginal rubbing to binding, apart from very light toning in places, near fine, presentation copy inscribed by author with tipped in ms. note.   Sotheran's   Travel and Exploration - 408   2016   £398

Wilson, S. *Geography simplified: Being a Brief Summary of the Principal Features of the Great Divisions of the earth...* London: Simpkin Marshall & Co., 1849. Third edition, maps, occasional pencil annotations, with further annotations and illustrations on f.e.p.'s, binding cracked in places, contemporary dark green calf, slightly rubbed, original signature of J. Baker.   Jarndyce Antiquarian Books   CCXV - 1009   2016   £25

Wilson, Sadye Tune *Of Coverlets: The Legacies, the Weavers.* Nashville: Tunstede, 1983. First edition, hardback in very good condition, very good dust jacket, 4to., wear to jacket edges.   Simon Finch   2015 - 40814   2016 $275

Wilson, Stephen K. *Australia's Reptiles: a Photographic Reference to the Terrestrial Reptiles of Australia.* Pymble: Cornstalk, 1992. Reprint, quarto, color photos, signature dust jacket.   Andrew Isles Natural History Books   55 - 2423   2016 $80

Wilson, William *Economy of the Kitchen-Garden the Orchard and the Winery with Plain Practical Directions for their Management.* New York: Anderson Davis and Co., 1828. First edition, 12mo., contemporary calf backed boards, much rubbed, lacks endpaper, ink writing on pastedown.   M & S Rare Books, Inc.   99 - 107   2016 $450

Winch, Terence *The Beautiful Indifference.* New York: O Press, 1976. First edition, 4to., stapled wrappers, little soiled, very good, inscription on titlepage, maybe by author.   Second Life Books, Inc.   196 B - 920   2016 $75

Winchester and Nottingham, George James Finch Hatton *Voices through Many Years.* London: Marcus Ward & Co., 1879. First edition, photos of author pasted in as frontispiece in each volume, 3 volumes, 8vo., original vellum over boards with yapp edges, covers blocked in blind with title, smooth spines blocked in blind and lettered gilt, marbled endleaves, uncut, little stained, printed on heavy uncut paper, bound in decorated vellum with yapp edges, volume i inscribed " Cadogan Mansions, Sloan Square. this copy is corrected by author .... July 13 1885". Simon Finch 2015 - 2016 $320

Winchester College *Winchester College 1836-1906. A Register.* Winchester: P. & G. Wells, 1907. Half title, original dark blue cloth, slightly rubbed. Jarndyce Antiquarian Books CCXV - 1011 2016 £30

Winchilsea, Anne Kingsmill Finch, Countess of *The Poems of....* Chicago: Chicago University Press, 1903. First edition, original maroon cloth, gilt lettering, small attractive bookplate of early private owner, old insect damage around lowr edge of covers causing some discoloration in other respects in very good, bright copy. Simon Finch 2015 - 209151 2016 $200

Winchilsea, George James Finch Hatton, Earl of *Flying Childers.* London: 1870. First edition, original green cloth, presentation copy inscribed by author to Earl of Effingham, pictorial half title and one other illustrated leaf, nice, scarce. Simon Finch 2015 - 82172 2016 $240

Winchilsea, Heneage Finch, Earl of *A True and Exact Relation of the Late Prodigious Earthquake & Eruption of Mount Aetna...* London: by T. Newcombe, 1669. First edition, small 4to., lacking folding engraved plate, but with 18th century engraving of Vesuvius erupting in 1630 loosely inserted, dampstained, more heavily at end, upper edge closely trimmed in places, one page number cropped, late 19th century half maroon morocco marbled boards, extremities rubbed, corners bumped, bookplate of John Beresford Clements 2869-1940 of Killadeeon, Co. Kildare, from the library of James Stevens Cox (1910-1997). Maggs Bros. Ltd. 1447 - 456 2016 £120

Windham, Donald *The Dog Star.* New York: Doubleday, 1950. First edition, signed by author on tipped-in-leaf, additionally signed by Tennessee Williams on front jacket flap, light foxing to top page edges, and light toning to jacket spine, near fine in like dust jacket. Royal Books 49 - 71 2016 $300

Windham, William *Speech of the Right Hon. W. Windham, in the House of Commons, June 13 1809 on Lord Erskine's Bill for the More Effectual Prevention of Cruelty Towards Animals.* London: J. Budd, 1810. First separate edition, 8vo., final leaf blank, preserved in modern wrappers with printed title label on upper cover, fine, crisp copy, scarce. John Drury Rare Books 2015 - 24229 2016 $350

Windle, John *Leaf from the Kelmscott Chaucer.* Hammersmith: Kelmscott Press, 1896. Original leaf from Kelmscott Press masterpiece, The Works of Geoffrey Chaucer... accompanied by the bookseller John Windle on its commercial history, leaf is from disbound and dispersed damaged copy and was presented by Windle in paper portfolio in 1994 as a keepsake to members of the Colophon, Roxburghe and Zamorano Clubs, folio sized leaf is from pages 215-216 "The Persouns Tale", there is no illustration but there are 12 small decorated initials, leaf very good except for bit of rubrication (red ink text) bleed through on two shoulder titles and one section heading, little rippling along top edge, very good. The Kelmscott Bookshop 13 - 28 2016 $650

Windsor. 1898. Dec. 1898 issue, lacks wrappers and is missing last 10 pages of the magazine. I. D. Edrich Crime - 2016 £20

Wing, John *The Crowne Conivgall or the Spouse Royall.* Middleburgh: John Hellenius, 1620. First edition, small quarto, titlepage with engraved vignette and engraved initial, without final blank, 19th century half calf, over marbled boards, spine with maroon calf spine label, spine elaborately stamped in gilt, all edges gilt, two small repairs to titlepage, one to top inner corner, other along inner margin, nethier affecting text, few pages with some light chipping along foreedge, previous owner's bookplate, back endpaper with old bookseller slip tipped-in, overall very good. Heritage Book Shop Holiday 2015 - 116 2016 $4000

Wingfield, Lewis Strange *Abigel Rowe.* London: Richard Bentley, 1883. First edition, 3 volumes, contemporary half calf, marbled boards with Beechwood Public library, stamps and blocked in gilt at tails of spines. Jarndyce Antiquarian Booksellers CCXVII - 298 2016 £75

Winkles, Henry *Architectural and Picturesque Illustrations of the Cathedral Churches of England and Wales.* London: Tilt and Bogue, n.d., 1836. 3 volumes, 8vo., all plates as called for, bit foxed, some patchy toning, Ely Cathedral plate facing page 61 little creased, contemporary blind tooled brown calf, two brown morocco gilt labels to each spine, marbled endpapers, edges colorized, scuffed, especially in spines, some scrapes and small surface leaves, joints starting, labels chipped with those for volume III almost entirely lost, sound working set, gift inscription ot Rev. Canon Gardner 3rd July 1907. Unsworths Antiquarian Booksellers Ltd. 30 - 164 2016 £375

Winn, Edith Linwood *The Etudes of Life.* Boston: Carl Fischer, 1908. First edition, little worn suede binding, #6 of limited edition, signed by author, very good. Second Life Books, Inc. 196 B - 922 2016 $55

Winslow, Don *Savages.* New York: Simon and Schuster, 2010. First edition, very fine in dust jacket. Mordida Books 2015 - 012726 2016 $65

Winsor, Justin *Narrative and Critical History of America.* Boston & New York: Houghton Mifflin and Co., 1889. 86-84-84-87-87-88-89. First edition, 279 x 191mm., 8 volumes, simple but pleasing contemporary black half morocco over marbled boards, raised bands accented with gilt rules, gilt titling, marbled endpapers, top edges gilt, more than 1000 in-text illustrations, maps and charts, bookplate of Samuel Nelson Sawyer in each volume, minor wear to raised bands, faint darkening at edges of leaves, otherwise excellent set, attractive bindings very sturdy and fresh, clean leaves with few signs of use. Phillip J. Pirages 67 - 2 2016 $950

Winstanley, William *Historical Rarities and Curious Observations Domestick & Foreign.* London: printed for Rowland Reynolds, 1684. 8vo., frontispiece, some browning and spotting, 8vo., 18th century calf, double gilt fillets on sides, spine gilt ruled in compartments, cracks in joints and spine slightly rubbed, engraved armorial bookplate of Horatio Walpole (first Baron), good. Blackwell's Rare Books B184 - 91 2016 £600

Winstanley, William *Poor Robins Perambulation from Saffron-Walden to London Performed this Month of July 1678 With Allowance July 11 1678.* London: for T. E. and are to be sold by General Assembly of Hawkers, 1678. First edition, only edition, small 4to., light soiling on title and pages 4/5 and a single small wormhole to inner margin throughout (intensifying in gathering C), mid 20th century flexible boards, from the library of James Stevens Cox (1910-1997). Maggs Bros. Ltd. 1447 - 457 2016 £1500

Winter, Milo *Billy Popgun.* Boston: Houghton Mifflin, Oct., 1912. Limited to 350 numbered copies, printed on Japanese paper, illustrations mounted on Japanese paper with a border in gold from a special design by the artist, 4to., vellum backed boards, gilt cover, top edge gilt, spine soiled with light edge rubbing, else near fine, illustrations by author, laid in is publisher's 4 page prospectus and order blank, very scarce. Aleph-bet Books, Inc. 111 - 484 2016 $1200

Winter, William *The Life of David Belasco.* New York: Moffat, Yard, 1918. First edition, 2 volumes, 8vo., portraits, volume 1 inscribed by Belasco July 9 1924, little watermark on fore edge, Belasco has added holograph caption under photo, covers little water stained, volume i has hinge tender and one repaired, very good. Second Life Books, Inc. 196 B - 924 2016 $100

Winter, William *Shakespeare on the Stage: Second Series.* New York: Moffat, Yard, 1915. First edition, 8vo., portraits, author's 12 line presentation, dated April 19 1935, another owner's bookplate on pastedown, very good. Second Life Books, Inc. 196 B - 925 2016 $50

Winter, William *The Wallet of Time.* New York: Moffat Yard and Co., 1913. First edition, limited to 1250 sets, thick 8vo., 2 volumes, frontispiece in each volume, 64 illustrations, most from photos, very good, unopened. Edwin V. Glaser Rare Books 2015 - 10175 2016 $225

Winterbottom, Augustus *The Evolution of Medicine and Surgery as a Science and the evolution of St. George's Hospital as a School.* London: Ballantyne Hanson & co., 1890. Inscription by author, original cream wrappers, lettered gilt, dulled and slightly worn, stamps and label of Westminster Libraries. Jarndyce Antiquarian Books CCXV - 1012 2016 £30

Winterich, John T. *Mademoiselle from Armentieres.* Mount Vernon: Peter Pauper, 1953. Small 8vo., illustrations by Herb Roth, paper over boards, edges of cover somewhat rubbed, otherwise very good, tight in slightly chipped and soiled dust jacket. Second Life Books, Inc. 197 - 158 2016 $45

Winters, Shelley *Shelley; also known as Shirley.* New York: Morrow, 1980. First edition, 8vo., photos, author's presentation on half title very good in dust jacket. Second Life Books, Inc. 196 B - 927 2016 $45

Winterton, Ralph *Poetae Minores Graeci.* Cambridge: Ex Officina Joan Hayes sold by J. Ray, E. Dobson, P. Campbell & J. Milner, Dublin Bibliopolis, 1699. First edition, 12mo., titlepage lightly soiled and spotted with 3 small holes from stitched in inner margin, last page dusty, some occasional spotting and soiling, few headlines shaved by binder, early 18th century calf backed boards, lined with light blue paper (head of spine chipped), blindstamped name on front cover has been scratched out, 18th century armorial bookplate of Wolle family of Forenaughts, Ireland, from the library of James Stevens Cox (1910-1997). Maggs Bros. Ltd. 1447 - 458 2016 £240

Wisden Cricket Monthly. Wisden: Cricket magazines ltd., 1979-1989. 10 volumes, full color photos, bound in brown cloth, very good, some infrequent browning to head of pages. Sotheran's Piccadilly Notes - Summer 2015 - 335 2016 £498

Wise, Daniel *The Young Lady's Counsellor or Outlines and Illustrations of the Sphere, the Duties and the Dangers of Young Women.* New York: Carlton & Porter, circa, 1855. 36th thousand, engraved frontispiece marked, 4 pages ads, slightly spotted, original royal blue cloth, slightly rubbed and marked, contemporary prize inscription. Jarndyce Antiquarian Books CCXV - 484 2016 £35

Wise, Daniel *The Young Lady's Counsellor....* Otley: Yorkshire Joint Stock Pub. & Stationary Co., 1863. 1 page ads, title heavily spotted, some browning and spotting, original brown cloth, sound only, presentation inscription. Jarndyce Antiquarian Books CCXV - 485 2016 £35

Wise, Henry A. *Tales for the Marines.* Boston: Philips Sampson & co., 1835. First edition, 8vo., frontispiece and pictorial title, original cloth, spine rubbed, inscribed by author 16 May 1855 for Miss Clara Elmer. M & S Rare Books, Inc. 99 - 324 2016 $275

Wise, Thomas James 1859-1937 *A Byron Library, a Catalogue of Printed Books, Manuscripts and Autograph Letters by George Gordon Noel, Baron Byron.* London: printed for Private Circulation, 1928. Limited to 200 copies, numerous plates, small 4to., polished cloth, top edge gilt, others uncut, minor fading to spine. Oak Knoll Books 310 - 233 2016 $450

Wise, Thomas James 1859-1937 *Letters of.... to John Henry Wrenn.* New York: Knopf, 1944. First edition, 8vo., several illustrations, black cloth stamped gilt, edges little soiled and spotted, cover slightly scuffed at edges, few spots on title, otherwise very good, tight copy in chipped and somewhat browned dust jacket. Second Life Books, Inc. 197 - 360 2016 $50

Wise, Thomas James 1859-1937 *A Pope Library, a Catalogue of Plays, Poems and Prose writings, Collected by Thomas James Wise.* London: printed for Private Circulation, 1931. First edition, one of 160 copies printed on Antique paper, plates printed on glossy paper, 4to., red polished cloth stamped in gilt, beveled edges, top edge gilt, others uncut, well preserved copy. Oak Knoll Books 310 - 264 2016 $300

Wise, Thomas James 1859-1937 *Two Lake Poets, a Catalogue of Printed Books, Manuscripts and Autograph Letters by William Wordsworth and Samuel Taylor Coleridge.* London: privately printed, 1927. First edition, limited to 130 copies, printed on Antique paper, some foxing of prelim pages, 4to., red cloth, beveled edges, top edge gilt, others uncut, some foxing of prelim pages, scarce. Oak Knoll Books 310 - 273 2016 $300

Wiseman, Richard *Eight Chirurgical Treatises on the Following Heads, viz. I of Tumours. II of Ulcers. III. Of Diseases of the Anus...* London: for B. T. and L. M. and sold by W. Keblewhtie and J. Jones, 1697. Third edition, 18th century paneled calf, very skillfully rebacked retaining original gilt spine, period style label, tin (half inch) repaired tear in lower margin of third leaf, else remarkably fine, fresh copy, contemporary ownership signature of Stewart Sparkes on half title. Joseph J. Felcone, Inc. Books from Five Centuries: a Miscellany - 99 2016 $3200

Wiseman, Samuel *A Short and Serious Narrative of Londons fatal Fire, and Its Diurnal and Nocturnal Progression from Sunday Morning (being) the Second of September Anno Mirabili 1666 until Wednesday Night following A Poem.* London: for Peter Dring, 1667. First edition, small 4to., title within thick black woodcut mourning border, probably washed, early 20th century dark red morocco by Wood, from the library of James Stevens Cox (1910-1997), with bookplate and purchase note. Maggs Bros. Ltd. 1447 - 459 2016 £1500

Wishart, George *Montrose Redivivus or the Portraicture of James late Marquess of Montrose, Earl of Kincardin &c.* London: for Jo. Ridley, 1652. First edition in English, 8vo., engraved portrait, light marginal browning, A3r dust soiled and very lightly dampstained in places, probably washed, late 19th century sprinkled calf by F. Bedford (front cover detached, spine bands, lightly scuffed and chipped), bookplate of Charles George Milnes Gaskell, from the library of James Stevens Cox (1910-1997). Maggs Bros. Ltd. 1447 - 460 2016 £120

Wisniewski, David *Elfwyn's Saga.* New York: Lothrop Lee and Shepard, 1990. first printing (1-10 code), pictorial boards, as new in like dust jacket, stunning color paper cut illustrations. Aleph-bet Books, Inc. 112 - 515 2016 $75

Wisniewski, David *Golem.* Clarion Books/Houghton Mifflin, 1996. First edition, first printing with code 1-10, 4to., glazed pictorial boards, fine in dust jacket with no award seal, color illustrations, signed by Wisniewski. Aleph-bet Books, Inc. 112 - 516 2016 $200

Wister, Owen 1860-1938 *The Virginian: a Horseman of the Plains.* New York: Heritage Press, 1951. Beige cloth decorated and lettered gilt, spine darkened and heavily rubbed, very good in slipcase (faded and lightly worn), illustrations by William Moyers, Sandglass pamphlet laid in. Argonaut Book Shop Heritage Press 2015 - 2061 2016 $40

Wister, Owen 1860-1938 *The Virginian.* Los Angeles: Limited Editions Club, 1951. 1/1500 copies, 4to., illustrations by William Moyers, signed by artist, tan linen, leather label on spine and gold stamped leather picture on front, nice in slipcase. Second Life Books, Inc. 196 B - 932 2016 $125

Wister, Owen 1860-1938 *Watch Your Thrist.* New York: Macmillan, 1923. First edition, 4to., illustrations by George Howe, 1/1000 copies numbered and signed by author, very good in little worn dust jacket. Second Life Books, Inc. 196 B - 929 2016 $200

Witham, Henry *The Internal Structure of Fossil Vegetables Found in the Caroniferous and Oolitic Deposits of Great Britain....* Edinburgh: Adam and Charles Black, 1833. Quarto, 16 engraved plates, contemporary full calf, expertly rebacked, prize binding with contemporary written inscription pasted in. Andrew Isles Natural History Books 55 - 36572 2016 $1200

Wither, George *The Grateful Acknowledgment of a late Trimming Regulator.* London: in the year, 1688. First edition, small 4to., titlepage very slightly soiled and with old manuscript tract number in upper fore-corner, small hole through and some soiling to final leaf (hole touching two lines of text on verso), disbound, from the library of James Stevens Cox (1910-1997). Maggs Bros. Ltd. 1447 - 461 2016 £280

Wither, George *Speculum Speculativum.* London: Ritten June XIII, MDXLX and three imprinted in the same year, 1660. 8vo., titlepage lightly soiled and frayed at edges, small burn mark to blank upper right corner of A4-5 and blank fore margin of A7-8, lightly soiled and stained throughout, small worm track to upper blank margin of final sheet, book block separating from binding, contemporary sheep, lacking endleaves, rubbed, corners bumped, headcaps damaged, from the library of James Stevens Cox (1910-1997). Maggs Bros. Ltd. 1447 - 462 2016 £200

Witherby, H. F. *The Handbook of British Birds.* London: H. F. and G. Witherby, 1946. Reprint, octavo, dust jacket, five volumes, color plates, text illustrations, bookplate of Roy Cooper, fine set in dust jackets. Andrew Isles Natural History Books 55 - 13270 2016 $150

Withering, William *An Account of the Foxglove and Some of Its Medieval Uses.* London: M. Swinney for G. G. J. and J. Robinson, 1785. First edition, half title and hand colored frontispiece present but detached, original paper backed blue sugar boards, front board off, title handwritten on spine, uncut, spine quite worn, paper spine missing from top and bottom compartments, boards spotted and rubbed, folding plate has three short tears not affecting image, some browning and spotting of plate and text, in fine quarter morocco slipcase. James Tait Goodrich X-78 - 563 2016 $18,500

Withers, Philip *Alfred or a Narrative of the Daring and Illegal measures to Suppress a Pamphlet Intituled, Strictures on the Declaration of Horne Tooke, Esq....* London: printed for Fitzherbert, 1789. Fourth edition, 8vo., title and last page bit dusted, small closed tears to signature (B4), ink mark to lower blank margin, signature C1 verso, untrimmed, stitched as issued. Jarndyce Antiquarian Booksellers CCXVI - 613 2016 £60

Withers, William Bramwell *The History of Ballarat from the First Pastoral Settlement to the Present Time.* Ballarat, F. W. Niven and Co., 1887. 8vo., original blue green pictorial blue cloth blocked in dark green and gold, very large folding chromolithographic bird's eye view, large folding color lithographic plan, two facsimiles, 20 lithographic plates (6 tinted), historiated initials, large plate and plan with repaired tears, evenly little browned, as usual, otherwise very clean and fres, presented to Ballarat pioneer James Oddie (1824-1911). Sotheran's Travel and Exploration - 409 2016 £448

Witley, A. F. *Dangereously Blonde.* Pallas Publishing Co., 1938. Proof copy, original wrappers, obviously much read with top and bottom edges of spine little cured and faint name written on front wrapper. I. D. Edrich Crime - 2016 £40

Witt, Ronald *In the Footsteps of the Ancients.* Boston: Brill Academic Pub., 2003. First edition, 8vo., paperback, wrappers little scratched, edges dust marked, very good. Unsworths Antiquarian Booksellers Ltd. E05 - 92 2016 £40

Witte, Gasto Francois De *Genera des Serpents du Congo et du Ruanda-Urundi.* Tervuren: Musee Royal de l'Afrique Centrale, 1962. Octavo, 15 uncolored plates, text illustrations, modern half blue morocco wrappers retained, fine. Andrew Isles Natural History Books 55 - 13775 2016 $200

Witte, Henning *Memoriae Medicorum Nostr Seculi Clarissimorum Renovalate Decas Prima.* Frankfurt am main: Joannes Andreae..., 1676. First edition, frontispiece, early 19th century boards, some foxing to text, front joint showing wear. James Tait Goodrich X-78 - 564 2016 $495

Wittstein, G. C. *The Organic Constitutents of Plants and Vegetable Substances their Chemical Analysis...* Melbourne: M'Carron, Bird and Co., 1878. Octavo, quarter leather and boards, publisher's title wrapper retained, some wear, inscribed by translator, Ferd. von Mueller. Andrew Isles Natural History Books 55 - 38890 2016 $80

Wodehouse, Pelham Grenville 1881-1975 *A Few Quick Ones.* London: Herbert Jenkins, 1959. First edition, red cloth, foot of spine bumped, minor rubbing to head of spine, dust jacket chipped and rubbed, now protected in acetate cover. Argonaut Book Shop Literature 2015 - 6250 2016 $75

Wodehouse, Pelham Grenville 1881-1975 *Ice in the Bedroom.* London: Herbert Jenkins, 1961. First edition, red cloth, light spotting to outer edges of text bock, else fine in fine dust jacket. Argonaut Book Shop Literature 2015 - 6251 2016 $175

Wodehouse, Pelham Grenville   1881-1975   *Mike at Wrykyn.*   New York: Meredith Press, 1953. First American edition, grey cloth, very fine in pictorial dust jacket.   Argonaut Book Shop   Literature 2015 - 6249   2016 $200

Wodehouse, Pelham Grenville   1881-1975   *Plum Pie.* Herbert Jenkins, 1966. First edition, original cloth with dust jacket little sunned and with little wrinkling in original laminate and with some staining to lower panel, otherwise very good, inscribed by author for Ira Gershwin.   Sotheran's Piccadilly Notes - Summer 2015 - 12   2016   £5500

Wodehouse, Pelham Grenville   1881-1975   *The Small Bachelor.*   London: Methuen, 1930. Fourth edition, green cloth, owner's name, cloth at crown worn down to text block front panel of jacket affixed to page facing titlepage and small newspaper image of Wodehouse on page facing half title, sound good only copy signed by author below picture.   Between the Covers Rare Books   208 - 92   2016 $500

Wodehouse, Pelham Grenville   1881-1975   *Summer Moonshine.*   London: Herbert Jenkins, 1938. First English edition, crown 8vo., original bright red linen, backstrip and upper board lettered in black with publisher's device stamped in black to lower board, top edge red now faded, ownership inscription to flyleaf, very good.   Blackwell's Rare Books   B184 - 247   2016   £150

Woiwode, Larry   *Even Tide.*   New York: Farrar, Straus and Giroux, 1977. First edition, inscribed by author for William Meredith, fine in fine dust jacket,.   Charles Agvent   William Meredith - 123   2016 $60

Wolcot, John   1738-1819   *Farewell Odes or the Year 1786.*   London: printed for G. Kearsley, 1789. 4to., half title, fine, clean copy, disbound.   Jarndyce Antiquarian Booksellers   CCXVI - 615   2016   £25

Wolcot, John   1738-1819   *The Louisad, an Heroic Poem Canto I-IV.*   London: printed for T. Evans, 1793. 1793. 1791. 1792, New edition, 4to., 4 parts together, disbound.   Jarndyce Antiquarian Booksellers   CCXVI - 616   2016   £40

Wolcot, John   1738-1819   *Lyric Odes for the Year 1783.* London: printed for G. Kearsley, 1789. 4to., fine, clean, disbound.   Jarndyce Antiquarian Booksellers   CCXVI - 617   2016   £25

Wolcot, John   1738-1819   *Ode Upon Ode; or a Peep at St. James's or New-Year's Day or What you Will.*   London: printed for G. Kearsley, 1787. Sixth edition, etched plate, 4to., very good, clean copy, disbound.   Jarndyce Antiquarian Booksellers   CCXVI - 618   2016   £25

Wolcot, John   1738-1819   *Odes to Mr. Paine author of Rights of Man. (with) The Remonstrance.*   London: printed for J. Evans Paternoster Row, 1791. London: printed for H. D. Symonds, 1792. New editions, 4to., together but disbound, some dusting to titlepage, some slight foxing, but generally good, clean copies.   Jarndyce Antiquarian Booksellers   CCXVI - 619   2016   £45

Wolcot, John   1738-1819   *Tristia; or the Sorrows of Peter.* London: printed by C. Hayden published by J. Walker, 1806. First edition, small 8vo., original boards, some spine chipping, corners little rubbed, printed paper label, half title, title, errata, uncut.   Howard S. Mott Inc.   265 - 148   2016 $450

Wolcot, John   1738-1819   *The Works of Peter Pinder (sic).*   New York: for L. Wayland, 1793. First American edition, Voume I-(III), 8vo., 3 volumes, strip torn from head of titlepage of volume ii without loss of text, but removing a signature (signature present on both other titles), minor dust soiling, contemporary tree calf, rebacked, extremities worn, sound.   Blackwell's Rare Books   B186 - 116   2016 £1200

Wolf, Christa   *Im Stein. (In the Stone).*   Lieberg, Gotha: Edition Balance, 1998. Limited to 130 numbered copies, this one of 100 described as 'Ausgabe B", signed by author and artist, color lithographs and etchings by Helge Lieberg, approximately 23 drypoint etchings by Helge Leiberg, complemented by lithographs, small folio, quarter blue leather with paper covered boards with title and design in blue and red on front board, slipcase, unpaginated.   Oak Knoll Books   27 - 12   2016 $950

Wolf, Friedrich   *The Sailors of Cattaro: a Play in 2 Acts....* New York: Samuel French, 1935. First edition, fine in near fine dust jacket with couple of small chips and few small light stains.   Between the Covers Rare Books   204 - 139 2016 $90

Wolfe, Geoffrey   *The Duke of Deception.*   New York: Random House, 1979. First edition, folded and gathered sheets, mild foxing to fore edge and top edge, near fine, scarce format.   Ken Lopez Bookseller   166 - 152   2016 $200

Wolfe, Humbert   *Homage to Meleager.*   New York: Fountain Press, 1930. First edition, 8vo., uncut in original half leather, rubbed, one of 464 copies signed by author. Second Life Books, Inc.   196 B - 934   2016 $65

Wolfe, Humbert   *News of the Devil.*   London: Ernest Benn Ltd., 1926. First edition limited to 265 copies (250 were for sale), signed by poet, 12mo., black cloth, paper spine label, fine.   Argonaut Book Shop   Literature 2015 - 1629   2016 $150

Wolff, Jens *Sketches and Observations Taken on a Tour through a Part of the South of Europe.* W. Wilson, 1801. First English edition, quarto, contemporary brown half cloth, vignette on title and in text, very light foxing on titlepage, upper cover detached, clean. J. & S. L. Bonham Antiquarian Booksellers Europe 2016 - 9870   2016   £110

Wolff, Joseph *Travels and Adventures of Dr. Wolff.* London: Saunders Otley, 1860. First edition, 8vo., 2 volumes, frontispiece, small vignette on titlepages, contemporary brown half calf, small piece of leather missing at head volume II, good, clean set, scarce. J. & S. L. Bonham Antiquarian Booksellers   Voyages 2016 - 10224   2016   £550

Wollaston, Arthur Naylor *The Sword of Islam.* London: Murray, 1905. First edition, 8vo., original green cloth, ornamented in gilt, 16 plates and folding map, only minor rubbing to extremities and lightly spotted in places internally. Sotheran's Travel and Exploration - 392   2016   £248

Wollaston, Francis *A Country Parson's Address to His Flock, to Caution Them against being Misled by the Wolf in Sheep's Clothing....* London: printed for G. White, 1799. 8vo., disbound, small copy, signature of Benwell(?) on title, Renier on verso.   Jarndyce Antiquarian Booksellers CCXVI - 620   2016   £25

Wollaston, William *The Design of Part of the Book of Ecclesiastes; or the Unreasonableness of Mens Restless Contentions for the Present Enjoyments Represented in an English Poem.* London: for James Knapton, 1691. First edition, 8vo., titlepage slightly grubby and with some minor ink stains, lower blank corner of A2 from a crease and E7 (from a flaw) torn-away, occasional spotting or slight stains, single wormhole through C1-4 (touching text in places), contemporary sprinkled calf, covers panelled in blind, top and bottom spine panels renewed, corners bumped, deleted ink signature, booksellers' pencil notes (some deleted), from the library of James Stevens Cox (1910-1997).   Maggs Bros. Ltd.   1447 - 463   2016   £240

Wollaston, William *The Religion of Nature Delineated.* London: printed by S. Palmer and sold by B. Lintott, W. and J. Innys, J. Oxborn, J. Batley and T. Longman, 1725. Third edition, quarto, contemporary panelled calf, edges little rubbed, some light foxing, very good copy.   The Brick Row Book Shop   Miscellany 69 - 35   2016 $750

Wollstonecraft, Mary 1759-1797 *A Vindication of the Rights of Woman with Strictures on Political and Moral Subjects.* London: printed for J. Johnson, 1792. Second edition, 8vo., very good, large uncut and unpressed copy, expertly bound in recent half mottled calf, rope-twist gilt bands, gilt flower head devices to spine, red morocco label, marbled boards.   Jarndyce Antiquarian Booksellers CCXVI - 621   2016   £1850

A Woman's Thoughts on Public Affairs, Including the Church, Pauperism and the Game Laws.   Norwich: Bacon and Kinnerbrook, 1834. Only edition, 8vo., recent marbled boards lettered on spine, very good, apparently very rare. John Drury Rare Books   2015 - 21070   2016 $350

Woman's World.   Port Sunlight, Cheshire: Lever Bros., 1899. Half title, frontispiece, illustrations, ads on endpapers, original limp pictorial blue cloth, rubbed.   Jarndyce Antiquarian Books   CCXV - 486   2016   £45

The Wonderful and Scientific Museum; or Magazine of Remarkable Characters...   London: R. Kirby, 1803. 1804. 1805. 1813, 4 volumes, frontispieces, plates, illustrations, some offsetting to frontispiece, volume IV, occasional browning and foxing, uniformly bound in contemporary half calf, red morocco labels, slight chip to head of volume I, hinges little rubbed, bookseller's ticket on leading pastedown, overall very nice.   Jarndyce Antiquarian Booksellers   CCXVII - 157   2016   £600

Wonderful England or the Happy Land.   London: Grant Richards, n.d. circa, 1903. Oblong 4to., cloth backed pictorial boards, some edge wear, mild soil, few insignificant margin mends, really very good, boldly colored full page illustrations.   Aleph-bet Books, Inc.   112 - 373   2016 $325

Wood Jones, Frederic *The Mammals of South Australia.* Adelaide: Government Printer, 1923-1925. Octavo, 3 parts, text illustrations, publishers printed wrappers, very good set. Andrew Isles Natural History Books   55 - 8617   2016 $100

Wood, J. G. *Natural History Rambles: Lane and Field.* London: Society for Promoting Christian Knowledge, 1906. small octavo, text engravings, full contemporary tree calf, covers double gilt ruled, spine decoratively tooled and lettered gilt in compartments, gilt board edges and turn-ins marbled edges, marbled endpapers, School prize label dated 1908, near fine.   David Brass Rare Books, Inc. 2015 - 03014   2016 $125

Wood, Casey Albert *The Fundus Oculi of Birds, Especially as viewed through the Microscope: a Study in Comparative Anatomy and Physiology.*   Chicago: Lakeside, 1917. Quarto, 61 color photographic plates, publisher's cloth, library stamps of Royal Australian Ornithologists' Union, a note reading "To Dr.J. A. Leach with compliments of the author" pasted on upper endpaper.   Andrew Isles Natural History Books   55 - 38140   2016 $150

Wood, Charles W. *Glories of Spain.*   London: Macmillan, 1901. First edition, 8vo., illustrations, original green decorative cloth.   J. & S. L. Bonham Antiquarian Booksellers Europe 2016 - 7347   2016   £65

Wood, Edwin O. *Historic Mackinac.* Macmillan Co., 1918. First edition, 2 volumes, original blue cloth, decorations and title in gilt on front cover and spine, top edge gilt, frontispiece, map, corners lightly bumped, overall clean, bright set in near fine.   Buckingham Books   2015 - 35558   2016 $450

Wood, Harvey Freeman   *The Night of the 3D ULT.*   New York: John W. Lovel Co., copyright, 1908. First edition, first issue, octavo, original decorated blue cloth, front and spine panels stamped in silver, all edges stained yellow, significant and very scarce, minute rubs to spine ends and corner tips, bright nearly fine, rare.   John W. Knott, Jr./L.W. Currey, Inc.   Fall-Winter 2015 - 15998   2016 $1250

Wood, Henry   *Change for the American Notes: in Letters from London to New York.*   London: Wiley & Putnam, Stationers, Edinburgh: A. & C. Black; Dublin: W. Curry, 1843. First edition, contemporary full tan calf, gilt spine, borders and dentelles, red leather label, hinges expertly repaired, Cortlandt Field Bishop bookplate, all edges gilt, good plus.   Jarndyce Antiquarian Booksellers   CCXVIII - 329   2016   £180

Wood, Henry   *Change for the American Notes: in Letters from London to New York.*   London: Wiley & Putnam, Stationers; Edinburgh: A. & C. Black, Dublin: W. Curry, 1843. First edition, Original brown cloth, spine dulled and neatly repaired.   Jarndyce Antiquarian Booksellers   CCXVIII - 328   2016   £125

Wood, J. G.   *Strange Dwellings.*   London: Longmans, Green and Co., 1871. First edition thus, octavo, woodcut frontispiece, vignette title page and over 50 wood engravings, bound by Rivingtons (stamp signed on front blank), contemporary full blue calf, covers with double gilt rules, spine with five raised bands, decoratively tooled in gilt in compartments with red morocco label lettered gilt, gilt board edges, all edges marbled, marbled endpaper.   David Brass Rare Books, Inc.   2015 - 03008   2016 $100

Wood, John   *A Description of the Exchange of Bristol, Wherein the Ceremony of laying the First Stone of that Structure....*   Bath: sold by J. Leake, C. Hitch in Paternoster Row, London and B. Hickley in Bristol, 1745. Limited to 300 copies, 8 engraved plates, 6 double page, modern marbled boards with printed label to spine, this copy appears to have been Earl Cowper's copy.   Marlborough Rare Books   List 55 - 73   2016   £1950

Wood, Peggy   *Actors and People.*   New York: Appleton, 1930. First edition, photos, author's presentation on flyleaf, some foxing, else very good.   Second Life Books, Inc.   196 B - 936   2016 $45

Wood, Peggy   *Arts and Flowers.*   New York: William Morrow, 1963. First edition, 8vo., photos, author's presentation on flyleaf, very good in somewhat scuffed and soiled dust jacket.   Second Life Books, Inc.   196 B - 937   2016 $65

Wood, Peggy   *How Young You Look: Memoirs of a Middle Sized actress.*   New York: Farrar & Rinehart, 1941. First edition, illustrations, author's presentation on flyleaf, some pencil marking in text, otherwise very good in worn dust jacket.   Second Life Books, Inc.   196 B - 938   2016 $45

Wood, Robert   *The Ruins of Palmyra, Otherwise Tedmor, in the Desart.*   London: n.p., 1753. First edition, large folio, mid 20th century calf backed marbled boards, spine with raised bands and red morocco lettering piece, 57 numbered plates, engravings of inscriptions in text, binding worn in places, one plate with old repair to one tear, light browning and occasional spotting, wide margined copy.   Sotheran's Travel and Exploration - 393   2016   £2450

Wood, Thomas   *Juvenalis Redivivus or the First Satyr of Juvenal taught to speak plain Englsih.*   London: in the year, 1683. First edition, small 4to., titlepage soiled and with several short fractures from type around weak points in paper and small hole where the full stop after "POEM" has punched though, small tear to fore margin of A1-2 and F24 stained, small piece torn from fore-margin between E4-F2 (nt affecting text), mid 20th century quarter blue morocco and marbled boards, spine slightly faded, illegible early signature, from the library of James Stevens Cox (1910-1997).   Maggs Bros. Ltd.   1447 - 464   2016   £220

Wood, Walter E.   *Venezula: or Two Years on the Spanish Main.*   Middlesborough: Jordison, 1896. First and only edition, 8vo., map, 17 plates, including frontispiece, little foxing or soiling of first few leaves, original brown decorative cloth, trifle rubbed but good, uncommon book.   J. & S. L. Bonham Antiquarian Booksellers   America 2016 - 5921   2016   £190

Woodford, Michael   *A Manual of Falconry.*   Adam & Charles Black, 1961. Reprint, 8vo., original cloth and dust jacket, 8 black and white plates, text illustrations, very good.   Sotheran's Hunting, Shooting & Fishing - 68   2016   £40

Woodhead, Joshua T.   *The Golden Referee, a Guide to Health and the Causes that Prevent it.*   Liverpool: Medicus & Co., 1903. Original pale green printed wrappers, slightly rubbed, torn and spotted, spine slightly chipped, sound only.   Jarndyce Antiquarian Books   CCXV - 489   2016   £35

Woodman, Mary   *Correct Conduct or Etiquette for Everybody.*   London: W. Foulsham & Co., 1922. First edition, half title, original olive green cloth.   Jarndyce Antiquarian Books   CCXV - 490   2016   £25

Woodman, Mary *The House and Home Repairer's Guide.* London: W. Foulsham & Co., 1922. Half title, original green cloth, mark on back board.   Jarndyce Antiquarian Books   CCXV - 491   2016   £20

Woodruff, Elizabeth *Dickey Bird.* Springfield: Milton Bradley, 1928. First edition, large 4to., black imitation leather stamped in yellow, fine in dust jacket (very good, lightly frayed and piece off top of backstrip), illustrations by Tenggren, beautiful copy, rare in dust jacket.   Aleph-bet Books, Inc.   111 - 444   2016 $1500

Woodruff, Elizabeth *Stories from a magic World.* Springfield: McLoughlin, 1938. Large 4to., cloth, pictorial paste-on, slight tip and spine end wear, very good-fine, illustrations by Tengreen with 5 incredible color plates, 13 full page black and whites by Gustaf Tenggren.   Aleph-bet Books, Inc.   112 - 471   2016 $600

Woods, Frederick *A Bibliography of the Works of Sir Winston Spencer Churchill.* 1963. Dust jacket.   I. D. Edrich   Winston Spencer Churchill - 2016   £60

Woods, S. D. *Lights and Shadows of Life on the Pacific Coast.* New York: Funk & Wagnalls Co., 1910. First edition, frontispiece, yellow cloth stamped in black on spine and front cover, lower corners slightly worn, light rubbing to ends of spine, near fine.   Argonaut Book Shop   Biography 2015 - 3815   2016 $60

Woodson, Carter Godwin *The Negro in Our History.* Washington: Associated Pub., 1962. Tenth edition, extensively illustrated, facing pages roughly opened resulting in tiny chips, else near fine in spine faded, very good dust jacket, internal repairs to flap folds.   Between the Covers Rare Books   207 - 104   2016 $375

Woodsworth, J. S. *Hours that Stand Apart.* Ottawa: Mutual Press ltd., 1927? Small 8vo., printed card covers, 8vo., some foxing to cover, otherwise very good.   Schooner Books Ltd.   115 - 210   2016 $55

Woodward, Calvin Milton *Manual Training in Education.* London: Walter Scott, 1890. First edition, half title, final ad leaf, original maroon cloth, rubbed at head of spine, library numbers at foot of spine, booklabel for Library of Faculty of Physicians and Surgeons, Glasgow. Jarndyce Antiquarian Books   CCXV - 1015   2016   £20

Woodward, George Moutard *Eccentric Excursions or Literary & Pictorial Sketches of Countance, Character and Country in Different Parts of England & South Wales.* London: R. S. Kirby, 1817. 4to., hand colored frontispiece, engraved titlepage, 100 numbered hand colored plates, on 99 leaves, page vi/6 mounted on stub, slight tear along plate indent of no. 58, plates largely bright and clean, some occasional slight creasing to text block, slightly later half brown calf, raised bands, black morocco label, little rubbed. Jarndyce Antiquarian Booksellers   CCXVII - 299   2016   £3500

Woodward, Henry *A Letter from Henry Woodward, Comedian, the meanest of all Characters... to Dr. John Hill.* London: printed for M. Cooper, 1752. First edition, 8vo., disbound, 22 pages.   Jarndyce Antiquarian Booksellers CCXVI - 622   2016   £250

Woodward, John *The State of Physick and of Diseases with an Inquiry into the Causes of the late Increase of them but more particularly of the Small-Pox.* London: printed for T. Horne, 1718. First edition, full contemporary calf, gilt panelled spine, head of spine neatly repaired, Author's presentation with note from author to Thomas Hearne.   James Tait Goodrich   X-78 - 565   2016 $1500

Woodward, William *A Memoir of Andrew Jackson Africanus.* N.P.: 1938. One of 150 numbered copies printed at Derrydale Press, plates, half morocco, stamped author's inscription, bookseller's label, bookplate, one inch hole in front flyleaf, else very good.   Joseph J. Felcone, Inc.   Books from Five Centuries: a Miscellany - 153   2016 $750

Woolf, Virginia   1882-1941 *Books and Portraits - some further selections....* London: Hogarth Press, 1977. First edition, octavo, fine in fine dust jacket.   Peter Ellis   112 - 451   2016   £45

Woolf, Virginia   1882-1941 *The Common Reader: Second Series.* London: Pub. by Leonard & Virginia Woolf at Hogarth Press, 1932. First edition, page edges slightly soiled, still about fine in about very good dust jacket with some modest chips and tears, some overall soiling, small Hogarth Press pamphlet advertising Woolf's works laid in, inscribed by author to her typist Margaret Walton, Oct. 13th 1932, inscription has very slightly offset very slightly on front flap.   Between the Covers Rare Books   204 - 137   2016 $25,000

Woolf, Virginia   1882-1941 *Granite and Rainbow.* London: Hogarth Press, 1958. First edition, original blue cloth with dust jacket by Vanessa Bell, jacket little darkened on spine and edges, some discoloration to cover, otherwise very good.   Sotheran's   Piccadilly Notes - Summer 2015 - 337   2016   £198

Woolf, Virginia 1882-1941 *Kew Gardens.* London: Hogarth Press, 1927. Third English edition, limited to 500 numbered copies, 4to., rebacked in matching brown cloth, illustrated paper covered boards, top edge cut, others uncut, illustrations by Vanessa Bell, front board decorated azure blue, lime-green and milk-chocolate brown, titlepage also milk-chocolate brown, text on recto of leaf only, surrounded by black and white illustrations by Bell, printed and engraved by Herbert Reiach, Ltd., spine rebacked, boards soiled and stained, slightly worn at edges, pencil notations, slight tanning.   Oak Knoll Books   310 - 109   2016 $850

Woolf, Virginia 1882-1941 *Moments of Being - Unpublished Autobiographical Writings.* London: Hogarth Press, 1978. New edition, fine in near fine dust jacket little creased at head.   Peter Ellis   112 - 454   2016   £35

Woolf, Virginia 1882-1941 *Orlando: a Biography.* New York: Crosby Gaige, 1928. First edition preceding English trad4e edition, tiny, barely visible scuff on front board, else fine, copy number 688 of 861 numbered copies signed by author, very nice.   Between the Covers Rare Books   208 - 93   2016 $3000

Woolf, Virginia 1882-1941 *Roger Fry: a Biography.* London: Hogarth Press, 1940. First edition, very slight sunning at spine ends, else fine in near fine dust jacket with some modest toing and couple of very short tears.   Between the Covers Rare Books   204 - 138   2016 $1500

Woolf, Virginia 1882-1941 *The Years.* London: published by Leonard and Virginia Woolf at Hogarth Press, 1937. First edition, 191 x 127mm publisher's light green cloth and printed dust jacket, very faint uniform darkening to jacket spine, otherwise especially fine in very fine dust jacket, virtually faultless inside and out.   Phillip J. Pirages   67 - 359   2016 $5500

Woollcombe, William *Remarks on th Frequency and Fatality of Different Diseases, Particularly on the Progressive Increase of Consumption...* London: Longman, Hurst Reees and Orme and Rees and Curtis Plymouth, 1808. First edition, 8vo., half title, tiny hole in A1 resulting in loss of two letters on verso, head margins of many leaves rather browned but particularly so at beginning and end, marginal repairs to final to leaves but printed surface not affected, new endpapers, contemporary marbled boards, now neatly rebacked in sheep, spine lettered gilt.   John Drury Rare Books   2015 - 26207   2016 $437

Woollcott, Alexander *Chateau Theirry: a Friendly Guide for American Pilgrims Between the Marine and the Vesle.* Paris: Lafayette Pub. Co., 1919. First edition, line drawings by Private C. Leroy Baldridge, stapled illustrated wrappers, split along bottom spine, else near fine.   Between the Covers Rare Books   204 - 140   2016 $350

Woolley, Bryan *November 22: a Novel.* New York: Seaview Books, 1981. First edition, fine in fine dust jacket.   Ken Hebenstreit, Bookseller   2016 - 2016 $60

Woolman, John 1720-1772 *The Works of John Woolman.* Philadelphia: Joseph Crukshank, 1774. Contemporary sheep, very skillfully rebacked in period Quaker style, boards scuffed, edges worn, discoloration on pages 146-47 from old laid in newspaper cutting, else very good, inscribed 'Sarah Woolman to Jno. Townsend", later miniscule signature of Charles L. Cresson, superb presentation, John Townsend was author's close friend.   Joseph J. Felcone, Inc.   Books from Five Centuries: a Miscellany - 154   2016 $1200

Woolnoth, William *A Graphical Illustration of the Metropolitan Cathedral Church of Canterbury.* London: T. Cadell & W. Davies and J. Murray, 1816. Large paper copy, royal 4to., 20 plates on India paper, foxing to front and rear blanks and plates, text pages generally clean barring occasional offset toning from plates, neat pencil notes to pages 92-3, early 20th century half burgundy morocco gilt title to spine, blue marbled paper boards, edges sprinkled red, endcaps, joints and corners bit worn, edges slightly chipped but very good overall, bookplate of A. D. Gondinton dated 1901, recent bookplate of Susan Wade, tiny bookbinder's label of R. Hynes, Dover, catalog description pasted in, some pencilled booksellers notes to prelim blanks, note to list of subscribers identifies this as the copy belonging to Mr. Jesse White, Canterbury.   Unsworths Antiquarian Booksellers Ltd.   30 - 165   2016   £350

Woolnough, C. W. *The Whole Art of Marbling as Applied to Paper, Book Edges, etc.* London: George Bell and Sons, 1881. Third edition, 39 plates of marbled paper specimens, some with multiple samples, also with extra section of 9 specimens of marbled paper following tipped-in notice, light wear at spine ends and small hole in back hinge, 8vo., original green cloth.   Oak Knoll Books   310 - 10   2016 $3000

Woolrich, Cornell *Black Alibi.* New York: Simon & Schuster, 1942. First edition, near fine in bright dust jacket with some very light professional restoration to spine ends and corners, handsome, bright copy.   Buckingham Books   2015 - 27079   2016 $3000

Woolrich, Cornell *The Black Angel.* Garden City: published for the Crime Club by Doubleday, Doran and Ind., 1943. First edition, octavo, cloth, some tanning to endpapers, very good in good dust jacket with wear at spine ends and corner tips, some shallow loss at spine ends and thin paper backing on unprinted inner surface.   John W. Knott, Jr./L.W. Currey, Inc.   Fall-Winter 2015 - 17184   2016 $550

Woolrich, Cornell *The Black Curtain.* New York: Simon and Schuster, 1941. First edition, Octavo, original red cloth stamped in white and black, top edge stained red, previous owner's name and address handwritten in ink and in pencil, spine lean, very good with no shelfwear in good pictorial dust jacket with wear and rubbing at edges, shallow loss at spine ends and corner tips, some soiling and abrasion to rear panel, scarce.   John W. Knott, Jr./L.W. Currey, Inc.   Fall-Winter 2015 - 17956   2016 $850

Woolrich, Cornell *The Blue Ribbon.* Philadelphia and New York: J. B. Lippincott Co., 1949. First edition, fine in nearly fine dust jacket with some light rubbing to edges and corner tips.   John W. Knott, Jr./L.W. Currey, Inc.   Fall-Winter 2015 - 17876   2016 $650

Woolrich, Cornell *Phantom Lady.* Philadelphia and New York: J. B. Lippincott Co., 1942. First edition, octavo, cloth, nearly fine in very good or somewhat better dust jacket which rubbed at spine edges and folds, mild shelf wear to spine ends and corner tips, attractive copy.   John W. Knott, Jr./L.W. Currey, Inc.   Fall-Winter 2015 - 17962   2016 $1750

Woolrich, Cornell *Waltz into Darkness.* Philadelphia: J. B. Lippincott, 1947. First edition, fine in bright, near fine dust jacket with light wear to spine ends and corners, few tiny closed tears to top edge of rear cover panel and one to bottom edge.   Buckingham Books   2015 - 38447   2016 $475

Wooster, David *Alpine Plants: Figures and Descriptions of Some of the Most Striking and beautiful of the Alpine Flowers.* London: George Bell and Sons, 1874. Tall octavo, 2 volumes, 108 chromolithographed plates, publisher's blue blindstamped and gilt decorated cloth, some flecking, otherwise bright, crisp set.   Andrew Isles Natural History Books   55 - 38893   2016 $700

Worcester Diocesan Architectural Society *Report of the Proceedings at the Inaugural meeting Held at Worcester on Thursday the 26th of January 1854.* Worcester: Deighton, Eaton & Son and R. Child, 1854. 8vo., original printed wrappers.   Marlborough Rare Books   List 55 - 74   2016   £60

Worcester, Samuel *An Address on Sacred Musick, Delivered before the Middlesex Musical Society and the Handel society of Dartmouth College...* Boston: Manning & Loring, 1811. 8vo., self wrappers sewn, inscribed by author for William Cunningham, very slight foxing in places, edges of leaves little chipped, otherwise very good.   Second Life Books, Inc.   196 B - 941   2016 $75

The Words of the Masters, Reflections on the Fine Art of Type Design. Maple Shade: Pickering Press of John Anderson, 1982. First edition, limited to 75 numbered copies, wood engravings by John De Pol, small 8vo., stiff paper wrappers, cord tinted, presentation from John Anderson.   Oak Knoll Books   310 - 137   2016 $200

Wordsworth, Christopher *Athens & Attica: a Journal of a Residence There.* London: John Murray, 1836. First edition, 8vo., frontispiece, map, 2 lithographic plates, folding table, some foxing to frontispiece and plates, otherwise fine, inscriptions, Marquis of Camden's copy.   J. & S. L. Bonham Antiquarian Booksellers   Europe 2016 - 9215   2016   £400

Wordsworth, William   1770-1850 *Ode on the Intimations of Immorality from Recollections of Early Childhood.* Chipping Campden: Essex House Press, 1903. No. 108 of 150 copies, 194 x 130mm., original stiff vellum with embossed rose on front cover, gilt lettering on spine, hand colored frontispiece by Walter Crane, hand colored printer's device in colophon, illuminated initials by "Miss Power", touch of soiling to head edge of cover, boards tending to splay slightly, pastedowns lifting up at corners, otherwise fine especially clean, fresh and smooth internally.   Phillip J. Pirages   67 - 336   2016 $1250

Wordsworth, William   1770-1850 *The Complete Poetical Works.* Boston and New York: Houghton Mifflin Co., 1910-1911. Large paper edition, one of 500 copies, 279 x 159mm., 10 volumes, lovely dark olive brown three quarter crushed morocco handsomely gilt, marbled sides and endpapers, riased bands, spine compartments densely gilt with floral and foliate tools emanating from a large central rose, top edges gilt, other edges untrimmed, the set entirely unopened, vignette title pages, map of Lake District, 75 photogravure plates (with letterpress tissue guards), one hand colored plate at beginning that duplicates a black and white plate elsewhere in volume, titlepage in red and black, each volume with full page tipped in bookplate of Fannie May Howard, in remarkably fine condition, essentially without any wear, virtually pristine internally and obviously used so little that the volumes open unwillingly.   Phillip J. Pirages   67 - 360   2016 $3250

Wordsworth, William   1770-1850 *The Prelude, or Growth of a Poet's Mind...* London: Edward Moxon, 1850. First edition, octavo, period binding of half burgundy calf with raised gilt decorated bands, marbled boards and endpapers, all edges gilt, 1850 ownership inscription, spine faded and scuffed and rubbed at hinges, corners little rubbed, very good, internally bright.   Peter Ellis   112 - 455   2016   £275

Worecester, Dean Conant *The Phillippines Past and Present...* New York: Macmillan, 1914. Revised edition, 2 volumes, 8vo., original blue cloth, spine lettered gilt, front covers lettered and ornamented in blind, plates after photos by author, very light rubbing to extremities, one flyleaf with repaired corner, otherwise very good and clean, name to front fly-leaf volume one.   Sotheran's   Travel and Exploration - 410   2016   £168

Worlidge, John *Systema Agriculturae the Mystery of Husbandry Discovered.* London: by T. Johnson for Samuel Speed, 1669. First edition, folio, additional engraved titlepage, woodcut illustrations, frontispiece with three wormholes, lower edge of engraved title repaired, small wormhole in middle of first three leaves, small wormhole in blank margin of gatherings A-H, occasional light browning, circular stain to Mm1, contemporary sheep, spine with red morocco and gilt label, covers heavily scuffed, corners bumped, upper headcap torn, lower corner of rear board cracked, H. Raymond Barnett, modern bookplate, from the library of James Stevens Cox (1910-1997).   Maggs Bros. Ltd.   1447 - 465   2016   £350

Worlidge, John *Systema Agriculturae; the Mystery of Husbandry Discovered.* London: for Tho. Dring and are to be sold by R. Cavel, 1681. Third edition, folio, additional engraved titlepage and one plate , short worm trail in lower margin of first few leaves, small piece torn from fore-margin of #2, large rust spot in I1 and with some occasional light staining in places, contemporary calf, rebacked covers worn and rather crazed by damp, some insect damage along lower edges, new endleaves, from the library of James Stevens Cox (1910-1997).   Maggs Bros. Ltd.   1447 - 466   2016   £350

Worm, Piet *Three Little Horses: Blackie, Brownie and Whitey.* New York: Random House, 1958. Probably first edition printed in america, 4to., pictorial boards, slight edge rubbing, else fine, bright color illustrations by Worm, with 9 letters from Worm to a teacher in California who had her class draw pictures about the book that she then sent to Worm.   Aleph-bet Books, Inc.   111 - 488   2016 $600

Worsley, T. C. *Behind the Battle.* London: Robert Hale, 1939. First edition, octavo, very scarce, covers just little darkened and rubbed at edges, free endpapers faintly spotted, very good in like dust jacket, dusty and defective at top edge of upper panel at head and tail of spine.   Peter Ellis   112 - 377   2016   £250

Wotton, Henry *Reliquiae Wottoniane...* London: by T. Roycroft for R. Marriott, F. Tyton, T. Collins and J. Ford, 1672. Third edition, 8vo., four engraved portraits, one portrait and titlepage foxed, minor repairs to corners of a5,-7, early 20th century green morocco, covered and spine bordered with small gilt sequin and dot tool, smooth spine lettered gilt, all edges gilt, spine little faded, small 18th? century signature of G. Smith, from the library of James Stevens Cox (1910-1997) with pencil note of purchase.   Maggs Bros. Ltd.   1447 - 467   2016   £180

Wright, Alan *Bingo and Babs.* London: Blackie, n.d., owner dated 1919, 4to., boards, pictorial paste-on, fw marks on cover, endpaper toned, clean and tight, very good+, 12 lovely color plates and in line, scarce.   Aleph-bet Books, Inc.   112 - 520   2016 $200

Wright, Barton *Kachinas of the Zuni.* Flagstaff: 1985. First edition, illustrations, near fine in like dust jacket, inscribed by author.   Dumont Maps and Books   133 - 85   2016 $85

Wright, Charles *China Trace.* Middletown: Wesleyan University Press, 1977. First edition, signed and inscribed by author for William Meredith, fine in fine dust jacket.   Charles Agvent   William Meredith - 124   2016 $200

Wright, Charles *Country Music. Selected Early Poems.* Middletown: Wesleyan University Press, 1983. First edition, 2nd printing, signed and inscribed by author for William Meredith, spine sunned, near fine.   Charles Agvent William Meredith - 125   2016 $60

Wright, Esther Clark *Samphire Greens. The Story of the Steeves.* Kingsport: Pub. by author, 1961. 8vo., card covers, sketch map at front, cover edges slightly worn with small stain to inside front cover.   Schooner Books Ltd.   115 - 93   2016 $45

Wright, Fred *The Ketchikan & Wrangell Mining Districts Alaska.* Washington: GPO, 1908. First edition, 8vo., 3 maps, illustrations, original grey wrapper, spine chipped with small loss.   J. & S. L. Bonham Antiquarian Booksellers America 2016 - 5416   2016   £30

Wright, Gordon *MacDiarmid - an Illustrated Biography of Christopher Murry Grieve (Hugh MaDiarmind).* Edinburgh: Gordon Wright, 1997. First edition, quarto, copiously illustrated, laminated boards, ends of spine slightly bumped, very good.   Peter Ellis   112 - 240   2016   £25

Wright, Gwendolyn *Moralism and the Model Home.* Chicago: University of Chicago, 1980. First printing, 8vo., photos, drawings, floor plans, author's presentation, blue cloth, edges slightly spotted, otherwise nice in little browned dust jacket.   Second Life Books, Inc.   196 B - 944   2016 $75

Wright, Isa L. *Remarkable Tale of a Whale.* Chicago: Volland, 1920. First edition with no additional printings isted, charming full page and smaller color illustrations, pictorial endpapers by John Held, slim small 8vo., pictorial boards, light edge rubbing, few tiny spots on title, else very good++.   Aleph-bet Books, Inc.   112 - 501   2016 $300

Wright, Richard *Puissance Norie. (Black Power).* Paris: Correa Bucher & Chastel, 1955. First French edition, pages little browned, else fine in wrappers as issued, inscribed by author to photographer and author, Giselle Freund.   Between the Covers Rare Books   202 - 123   2016 $2000

Wright, Thomas *A History of Domestic Manners and Sentiments in England During the Middle Ages.* London: Chapman & Hall, 1862. Fourth edition, half title, illustrations, final ad leaf, original maroon cloth, bevelled boards, blocked in gilt, spine slightly worn at head, later signature.   Jarndyce Antiquarian Books   CCXV - 492   2016   £50

Wright, Willard Huntington   1888-1939 *The Bishop Murder Case.* New York: Charles Scribner's Sons, 1929. First edition, presentation from author to John V. Cravins Jr., author has added inked comment "See page 334", on page 334 he has edited the text in ink in two places, cloth moderately soiled, lightly foxed, old small waterstain visible along bottom margin of first 25 pages, not affecting text, else good in dust jacket with light wear to spine ends and corners.   Buckingham Books   2015 - 33090   2016 $2750

Wrighte, William *Ideas for Rustic Furniture Proper for Garden Seas, Summer Houses, Hermitages, Cottages &c.* London: printed for I. and J. Taylor at the Architectural Library, 1800? First edition, 25 engraved plates, including title, some foxing and staining and offsetting, 8vo., original marbled wrappers, yellow edges.   Blackwell's Rare Books   B184 - 92   2016   £1200

Wrisberg, Henrico Avgvsto *Descriptio Anatomica Embryonis Observationibvs...* Gottingae: svmtibvs Vidvae A. vanderhoeck, 1768. One folding engraved plate, 5 pathological illustrations, quarter calf in contemporary boards, some text foxing and browning.   James Tait Goodrich   X-78 - 567   2016 $750

Wroblewski, David *The Story of Edgar Sawtelle.* New York: Ecco, 2008. First edition, fine in fine dust jacket, signed and dated 6/10/2008.   Bella Luna Books   2016 - p3526   2016 $148

Wroth, Lawrence C. *Benjamin Franklin: Printer at Work.* New York: Privately printed, 1974. Small 8vo., illustrations by John Del Pol with wood engravings in green, yellow paper over boards, stamped in black, cover very slightly soiled, bit faded at spine, very small tear at back of base of spine, leaves very slightly crooked in cover, very good, tight copy.   Second Life Books, Inc.   197 - 361   2016 $45

Wundt, Theodor *Wanderungen in Den Ampezzaner Dolomiten.* Stuttgart: Deutsche Verlags Anstalt, 1895. Second edition, quarto, folding map, illustrations, original green decorative cloth.   J. & S. L. Bonham Antiquarian Booksellers   Europe 2016 - 7137   2016   £380

Wurdemann, Audrey *Bright Ambush.* New York: John Day Co., 1934. First edition, fine in near fine dust jacket with sunning at extremities, modest tear on front panel, inscribed by author for Laura Mae Carlisle oct. 1936.   Between the Covers Rare Books   204 - 142   2016 $600

Wyatt, Matthew Digby *The Art of Illuminating as Practised in Europe from the earliest Times.* London: Day and Son, 1860. First edition, small folio, contemporary full maroon morocco, wide ornamental blind borders, gilt cornerpieces, spine lettered gilt, decorated in gilt and blind, gilt turn-ins, marbled endpapers, all edges gilt, chromolithographed plates, text within decorative borders, mostly printed in red, slight marginal staining to three plates towards the end of the volume, occasional very minor spotting, otherwise very good.   Sotheran's   Piccadilly Notes - Summer 2015 - 338   2016   £450

Wylie, Elinor   1885-1928 *Incidental Numbers.* London: printed by Wm. Clowes & sons, 1912. First edition, one of 65 copies, 16mo., original printed boards (hairline crack in front hinge), Frank Hogan copy, this copy inscribed by author for Christopher Morley, inside front cover is autograph note by Morley, Wylie's first book, elaborate gold stamped Hogan bookplate, nearly fine in slipcase.   Howard S. Mott Inc.   265 - 150   2016 $8000

Wylie, Elinor   1885-1928 *Mr. Hodge & Hazard.* New York: Knopf, 1928. First edition, one of 140 large paper copies printed on Borzoi Rag paper, signed by author, uncut, little worn original cloth, edges of leaves lightly browned, otherwise very good, tight copy.   Second Life Books, Inc.   196 B - 948   2016 $200

Wylie, Elinor   1885-1928 *The Orphan Angel.* New York: Knopf, 1926. First edition, one of 160 large paper copies printed on Borzoi Rag paper, signed by author, faded cloth backed boards, very good, tight copy.   Second Life Books, Inc.   196 B - 949   2016 $200

Wylie, Elinor   1885-1928 *Collected Poems.* New York: Knopf, 1932. First edition, one of 210 copies numbered and signed by editor, William Rose Benet, 8vo., front flyleaf missing, rear hinge tender, cover little worn, otherwise very good.   Second Life Books, Inc.   196 B - 946   2016 $45

Wylie, Elinor   1885-1928 *Trivial Breath (Poems).* New York: Knopf, 1928. First edition, one of 100 large copies signed by author, striped cloth little soiled, excellent uncut copy, printed on Van Gelder handmade paper, designed and made by Pynson printers.   Second Life Books, Inc.   196 B - 951   2016 $125

Wyman & Sons *Authorship & Publication: a Concise Guide for the Authors in Matters Relating to Printing and Publishing...* London: Wyman & sons, 1882. 100 pages, frontispiece, vignette headpieces and illustrations, slightly later olive buckram, maroon leather spine label, very good. Jarndyce Antiquarian Booksellers   CCXVII - 241   2016   £125

Wyndham, John *The Day of the Triffids.* London: Michael Joseph, 1951. First edition, 8vo., original cloth and price clipped dust jacket, jacket little worn at head and tail of spine, some internal tape repair, small Cape Town booksellers stamp inside front cover, good.   Blackwell's Rare Books   B184 - 248   2016   £1500

Wyndham, John *Re-Birth.* New York: Ballantine Books, 1955. First edition, age darkening to text block (quite common with this book), fine in very good or somewhat better dust jacket with short closed tear to upper front panel, mild rubbing to corners and front flap fold and some color fade to lettering of spine panel.   John W. Knott, Jr./L.W. Currey, Inc. Fall-Winter 2015 - 18344   2016 $300

Wyse, Thomas *The Continental Traveller's Oracle or Maxims for Foreign Locomotion.* London: Henry Colburn, 1828. First edition, 2 volumes, small 8vo., original cloth backed drab boards, spine with black paper labels, printed in gold, extremities little darkened and worn, apart from occasional spotting, good, uncut copy in rarely seen binding, housed in purpose made cloth drop-back box, rare edition. Sotheran's   Travel and Exploration - 481   2016   £1250

Wytsman, P. *Genera Insectorum (Homoptera: Family Membracidae.* Brussels: V. Verteneuil and Louis Desmet, 1950. Quarto, 13 uncolored plates, binder's cloth, wrappers retained, few spots.   Andrew Isles Natural History Books   55 - 15505   2016 $300

X Y Z

Xenophon *Cyrupaedia (The Institution and Life of Cyrus).* Newtown: Gregynog Press, 1936. No. 123 of 135 copies (of 150 total, including 15 in different special binding by George Fisher), 311 x 216mm., handsome dark green oasis by Gregynog Bindery (stamp signed), covers with gilt decoration of Persian character, raised bands, gilt ruled spine compartments, top edge gilt, other edges untrimmed, felt lined green moire cloth chemise and excellent matching morocco backed slipcase, 9 floriated wood engraved initials by Loyd Haberly, hand colored in red and green, printed in red and black in Poliphilus type on Batchelor handmade paper, back cover with slightest hint of few shallow scratches, leaves nn-3-4 with slightest hint of few shallow scratches, leaves nn3-4 with light marginal foxing (whisper of foxing on couple of other leaves), otherwise choice, virtually no signs of use. Phillip J. Pirages 67 - 185 2016 $3500

Xenophon *Cyrupaedia: the Institution and Life of Cyrus, The First of that Name, King of Persians.* Newtown: Gregynog Press, 1936. Limited to 150 numbered copies, this one of 135 bound thus by Gregynog Bindery and signed at bottom of back cover on turn-in, 4to., original green oasis decorated with center and cornerpieces onlaid in red and light green, outlined in gilt and blocked in gilt decorations of Persian character, five raised bands gilt paneled spine, top edge gilt, printed under the direction of Lord Haberly who provided floriated wood engraved initials, well preserved inserted in clamshell box with matching green quarter leather. Oak Knoll Books 310 - 108 2016 $2750

Xenophon *Expeditio Cyri. Tomis Quatuor.* London: T. Hutchinson, 1764. 4 volumes, foolscap 8vo. isue with Greek and Latin on subsequent leaves, contemporary mid brown calf, spines gilt, red morocco lettering pieces (one renewed), next compartment down stained darker and gilt lettered direct, little wear to spine ends and slight rubbing to extremities, good. Blackwell's Rare Books Greek & Latin Classics VII - 100 2016 £300

Xenophon *Xenophon's History of the Affairs of Greece.* London: printed for Benjamin White at Horace's Head in Fleet Street, 1770. 4to., index & errata, folding engraved map, clean copy with some very slight foxing, old waterstain to lower margins from page 150 onwards, early 19th century full diced calf, double gilt ruled borders, gilt device in each compartment, translator's name in gilt at foot of spine, head of spine worn, corners bumped, joints racked but firm. Jarndyce Antiquarian Booksellers CCXVI - 623 2016 £180

Xenophon *Kyrou Anbaseos Biblia Hepta.* Oxonii: E. Typographeo Clarendoniano, 1772. 8vo., large printer's device to titlepage, few occasional annotations and inkspots but generally clean within, contemporary light brown calf, gilt spine with orange morocco label, edges sprinkled red, scuffed, spine creased with evidence of tape a tail, joints beginning to split, upper board fraying at top corner, good working copy, Hampshire County Library stamps to titlepage, library card pocket to front pastedown and security sticker to rear pastedown, in old hand, faintly to front pastedown 'an incorrect book'. Unsworths Antiquarian Booksellers Ltd. 30 - 166 2016 £75

Xenophon *Xenophon's Memoirs of Socrates, with a Defence of Socrates, Before His Judges.* Bath: 1762. First edition translated by Sarah Fielding, Honey & Wax Booksellers 4 - 35 2016 $950

Xenos, Stefanos *Depredations; or Overend, Gurney & Co. and the Greek & Oriental Steam Navigation Company.* London: published by the author, 1869. First and only edition?, 8vo., original blindstamped maroon cloth, spine very faded and neatly repaired, good, previous owners' signatures at head of title. John Drury Rare Books 2015 - 26013 2016 $437

Yarrell, William *A History of British Birds.* John Van Voorst, 1837-1843. 1845. 1846. First edition, large paper copy, imperial 8vo., 3 volumes with both supplements bound in to volume 3, bound in full green morocco by P. Bedford, gilt panels with foliate tooling to sides, elaborate gilt spines with gilt raised bands and lettering, gilt turn-ins, marbled endpapers, all edges gilt, engraved illustrations by John Thompson, spine sunned to attractive brown, internally fine, very clean copy in handsome binding, Edward Huth bookplates. Sotheran's Piccadilly Notes - Summer 2015 - 339 2016 £1600

Yashima, Mitsu *Momo's Kitten.* New York: Viking, 1961. No additional printings listed, pictorial cloth, near fine in slightly soiled, very good+ dust jacket repaired on verso, inscribed by artist Taro Yashima, with watercolor drawing. Aleph-bet Books, Inc. 112 - 528 2016 $400

Yashima, Taro *Seashore Story.* New York: Viking, 1967. First edition, cloth, fine in slightly worn dust jacket, beautiful illustrations in color, this copy inscribed by author with color drawing. Aleph-bet Books, Inc. 111 - 496 2016 $275

Yashima, Taro *The Village Tree.* New York: Viking, 1953. First edition, 4to., cloth, fine in very good-fine dust jacket with 2 tiny closed tears, beautifully illustrated, this copy inscribed by author. Aleph-bet Books, Inc. 111 - 497 2016 $350

Yates, Frances A. *The Rosicrucsian Enlightenment.* London & Boston: Routledge & Kegan Paul, 1972. First edition, illustrations, green boards, gilt lettered, endcaps just starting to wear, very good, dust jacket wrapped in plastic film, slightly worn to bottom edge of spine, else near fine, one or two pencil markings to margins of text and pencil annotations of free endpaper. Unsworths Antiquarian Booksellers Ltd. E05 - 113 2016 £50

Yau, John *Notarikon.* New York: Jordan Davies, 1981. Limited to 75 copies signed by author and artist, drawings, some on tissue by Jake Berthot, 8vo., quarter cloth, paper covered boards. Oak Knoll Books 310 - 118 2016 $125

Yeats-Brown, Francis *Golden Horn.* London: Gollancz, 1932. First edition, 8vo., inscribed by author to Faith Baldwin, with TLS with line in holograph signed, cover little worn and torn, else very good. Second Life Books, Inc. 196 B - 953 2016 $75

Yeats, Grant David *A Biographical Sketch of the Life and Writings of Patrick Colquhoun.* London: printed by G. Smeeton, 1818. First edition, 8vo., frontispiece, rather offset on to titlepage, original printed boards but boards rather soiled, presentation copy inscribed in ink at head of title Royal society of Literature from author's son,James 20/3/55, scarce. John Drury Rare Books 2015 - 22810 2016 $323

Yeats, Grant David *A Statement of the Early Symptoms Which Lead to the Disease Water in the Brain...* London: printed for J. Callow, 1815. Half title, publisher's 16 page catalog and ad leaf at end, modern quarter calf and marbled boards. James Tait Goodrich X-78 - 568 2016 $2500

Yeats, Jack B. *In Sand - a play with Green Wave...* Dublin: Dolmen Press, 1964. First edition, octavo, tail of spine, slightly bumped, near fine in near fine, slightly creased dust jacket. Peter Ellis 112 - 460 2016 £35

Yeats, Jack B. *The Late Paintings.* Bristol, London and The Hague: Whitechapel Art Gallery, Hangs Gemeentemuseum, 1991. First edition, quarto, 30 color plates, other black and white reproductions, wrappers, fine in fine dust jacket. Peter Ellis 112 - 459 2016 £35

Yeats, William Butler 1865-1939 *Estrangement: Being some Fifty Thoughts from a Diary Kept... in the Year Nineteen Hundred and Nine.* Dublin: Cuala Press, 1926. First edition, one of 300 copies, 215 x 148mm., publisher's holland backed blue boards, paper label to spine, titlepage with publisher's device in red, with Cuala Press Book List laid in, tail edges of boards with small dent, free endpapers with usual light offsetting from binder's glue, but fine, text clean, fresh and bright and fragile binding unworn and unsoiled. Phillip J. Pirages 67 - 196 2016 $1000

Yeats, William Butler 1865-1939 *"Meditation of the Old Fisherman." in The Irish Monthly October 1886 No. 160 Volume XIV.* Dublin: W. H. Gill & son, 1886. Original blue printed wrappers, slight loss to front wrapper near head of spine, otherwise good. Jarndyce Antiquarian Booksellers CCXVII - 300 2016 £350

Yeats, William Butler 1865-1939 *Michael Robartes and the Dancer.* Churchtown, Dundrum: Cuala Press, 1920. First edition, one of 400 copies, elegantly printed with both red and black type, original half linen over blue paper boards, custom silk box, toning to free endpapers (as usual), small spot of soiling to rear panel, magnificent copy, rare. Manhattan Rare Book Company 2016 - 1822 2016 $2600

Yeats, William Butler 1865-1939 *The Variorum Edition of the Poems of W. B. Yeats.* New York: Macmillan, 1957. Limited edition, one of 825 numbered copies signed by Yeats, fine but for slight sunning to spine, small 4to. Beasley Books 2015 - 2016 $1750

Yeats, William Butler 1865-1939 *Poems of W. B. Yeats.* San Francisco: Arion Press, 1990. First edition, one of 400 numbered copies signed by Diebenkorn, 6 etchings by Richard Diebenkorn, 4to., original quarter red morocco and dark green cloth, publisher's matching cloth and board slipcase, fine. James S. Jaffe Rare Books Occasional List: Winter 2016 - 4 2016 $4000

Yeats, William Butler 1865-1939 *The Shadowy Waters.* London: Hodder and Stoughton, 1900. First edition, small 4to., original dark blue cloth over bevelled boards, design stamped in gilt on front cover, top edge gilt, signed by Yeats in pencil, rear cover lightly stained near top edge, corners bit rubbed, otherwise very good. James S. Jaffe Rare Books Occasional List: Winter 2016 - 150 2016 $3000

Yeats, William Butler 1865-1939 *16.* Dublin: Ester Rising, 2016. 23/150 copies (from an edition of 200 copies), signed by Modern contributors, printed in blue and black, pigment prints by Kathy Prendergast and Michael Canning with former on black paper and with hand applied iridescence, foldout pigment print by Alice Maher and a print from two intaglio plates by Brian O'Doherty, sheet of exclusive commemorative stamps pasted to page following colophon, folio, original grey-blue linen with blue leather vertical band to upper board, stamped in green, red and white to upper board, blue linen slipcase lettered in white, original publisher's mailing box, new. Blackwell's Rare Books B186 - 34 2016 £1375

Yee, Chiang *Yebbin: a Guest from the Wild.* London: Methuen, 1947. First edition, cloth, very good+ in dust jacket (some closed tears and light soil), 4 beautiful color plates and many full and partial page black and whites, this copy signed by Yee. Aleph-bet Books, Inc. 112 - 104 2016 $125

Yenser, Thomas *Who's Who in Colored America....* Brooklyn: Who's Who in Colored America, Thomas Yesner, Editor and Publisher, 1937. Fourth edition, thick quarto, photos, green pebble grained cloth, modest rubbing on boards, nice, very good or better.   Between the Covers Rare Books   207 - 105   2016 $800

Yi-Fang Wu *China Rediscovers Her West. A Symposium.* London: Allen & Unwin, 1942. First UK edition, small 8vo., original red cloth, spine lettered in white, original printed wrappers, map endpapers, vignettes in text, wrappers bit smudged and damaged, otherwise near fine.   Sotheran's Travel and Exploration - 209   2016   £128

Yockney, Alfred *International Art Past and Present.* London: Virtue & Co., n.d., but circa, 1915. 12 parts in 3 volumes, stiff paper wrappers, loosely inserted in later quarter leather slipcases, edges of each part slightly worn, slipcases, lightly dented at corners and rubbed at edges, the sets of 10 plates in each volume complete.   Oak Knoll Books   310 - 53   2016 $350

Yokohama Nursery Co. Ltd. *Maples of Japan.* Yokohama: 1898. Oblong folio, title and introduction, 7 colored pochoir stencil plates with 39 examples of maple, original colored woodcut wrappers, silk ties, old fold with some minor chips to corners.   Marlborough Rare Books   List 55 - 39   2016   £450

Yolen, Jane *Dream Weaver.* Cleveland and New York: Collins, 1979. First edition, 4to., cloth backed boards, as new in as new dust jacket, full page color illustrations by Michael Hague, this copy with warm inscription form author dated 1979 and fantastic pen drawing by Hague and inscribed by Hague.   Aleph-bet Books, Inc.   111 - 498   2016 $350

Yorke, Malcolm *Edward Bawden and His Circle - The Inward Laugh.* London: Collector's Club, 2007. Revised edition, Quarto, color illustrations, fine in fine dust jacket. Peter Ellis   112 - 31   2016   £85

Yorke, Malcolm *Keith Vaughan, His Life and Work.* London: Constable, 1990. First edition, octavo, numerous illustrations in color and black and white, fine in fine dust jacket, just little crinkled at edges.   Peter Ellis   112 - 420   2016   £45

The Yorkshire-Racers. a Poem...   London: printed for the use of all sorts of jockeys....n.d., 1709. First edition, 4to, sewn as issued, cloth slipcase, very good, titlepage bit soiled, last leaf slightly wrinkled, but very good in original condition.   C. R. Johnson Rare Book Collections   Foxon: H-P 2015 - 864   2016 $2298

Yoshimura, Yuji *The Japanese art of Miniature trees and Landscapes: Their Creation, Care and Enjoyment.* Rutland: Tuttle, 1966. Thirteenth printing, small 4to., 25 color plates, 245 halftone plates, 42 explanatory diagrams and 340 plant descriptions, cloth printed in gilt, nice in somewhat soiled corrugated slipcase.   Second Life Books, Inc.   196 B - 957   2016 $50

Yoshishige, Utagawa *Tokaido Gojusan-eki Hachtyama Edyu.* Shinsailbashi: 1848. Probably first or early issue, 8vo., 2 volumes, original illustrated wrappers, one woodcut on pastedown, 56 color woodcuts, wrappers little rubbed, worming, mainly marginal and light surface wear, otherwise good.   Sotheran's   Travel and Exploration - 210   2016   £1250

Yost, Billie Williams *Bread Upon the Sands.* Caldwell: Caxton Printers, 1958. First edition, 16 photo plates, yellow decorated cloth stamped in red, very fine.   Argonaut Book Shop   Native American 2015 - 7554   2016 $75

Youens, William George *Youen's Dance Album and Ball-Room Guide Words and Music.* London: George Routledge & sons, 1873. 16mo., binding slightly cracking in places, original light blue decorated cloth, all edges gilt, very good. Jarndyce Antiquarian Books   CCXV - 493 2016   £85

The Young Ladies' Offering or Gems of Prose and Poetry... Boston: Phillips & Sampson, 1856. Reprint, 8vo., black cloth elaborately stamped in gilt, little worn along hinge and extremities of spine, otherwise bright, with Lydia Sigourney's name as if she were the author, later bookplate, inscribed by Sigourney for Mrs. Jareret.   Second Life Books, Inc.   197 - 291   2016 $150

Young Lady's Book: a Manual of Elegant Recreations, Arts, Sciences and Accomplishments. London: Henry G. Bohn, 1859. Half title, frontispiece, plates ad illustrations, 48 page partially unopened catalog (1864), original olive green cloth, decorated in blind, spine lettered gilt, spine faded to brown, few marks on front board, hinges little weak, ownership signature, overall very nice.   Jarndyce Antiquarian Books CCXV - 494   2016   £150

The Young Man's Own Book. London: Thomas Allman & Son, 1856. Original red cloth, slightly marked, contemporary gift inscription, all edges gilt, very good.   Jarndyce Antiquarian Books   CCXV - 495   2016   £58

The Young Secretary's Guide to an Epistolary Correspondence in Business, Love, Friendship.... Newcastle upon Tyne: printed by Saint for W. Chamley and Whitfield & Co., 1781. 12mo., small repair to corner of A4 affecting few letters made in ms., leaves little dusted with some slight damp marking and browning, contemporary full sheep, neatly rebacked, corners worn, slightly later signature of Richard Lund, sound copy.   Jarndyce Antiquarian Books   CCXV - 496   2016   £120

The Young Travellers; or a Visit to Oxford. By a Lady. London: printed for Williams and Co., 1818. First edition, duodecimo, red quarter morocco and marbled boards, period style, gilt rules and lettering, top edge gilt, others untrimmed, frontispiece and one plate, some slight smudges and foxing, fine.   The Brick Row Book Shop   Miscellany 69 - 22   2016 $600

Young, A. S.   *Sonny Liston: the Champ Nobody Wanted.* Chicago: Johnson Pub. Co., 1963. First edition, near fine in bright, very good plus dust jacket, touch of rubbing to edges of boards and minor wear to edges of jacket, including one tiny chip, brief rubbing and several short closed tears.   Royal Books   48 - 81   2016 $550

Young, Al   *Drowning in the Sea of Love.*   Hopewell: Ecco, 1995. First edition, 8vo. author's presentation for Andy Davis, nice in dust jacket.   Second Life Books, Inc.   196 B - 958   2016 $45

Young, Andrew   *The Thirteenth Key.*   privately printed, 1985. Limited to 100 copies, signed by Alison Young, poet's daughter, very good.   I. D. Edrich   Crime - 2016   £25

Young, Edward   *Night Thoughts on Life, Death & Immortality by....*   London: printed for Chapman & Co., 1793. First collected edition, small quarto, contemporary red morocco richly gilt decorated, marbled endpapers, gilt inner dentelles and lettering, all edges gilt, frontispiece, engraved titlepage and 13 plates, edges slightly worn, light foxing to plates, fien, handsome contemporary binding. The Brick Row Book Shop   Miscellany 69 - 85   2016 $500

Young, Gary   *The Body's Logic.*   Winona: Sutton Hoo Press, 2000. Limited to 126 copies signed by author, square 12mo., cloth, woodcut illustration by author.   Oak Knoll Books   310 - 158   2016 $125

Young, Gary   *In the Durable World.*   Minneapolis: Bieler Press, 1985. Limited to 175 numbered copies, signed by author, 8vo., sewn, stiff paper covers.   Oak Knoll Books 310 - 84   2016 $100

Young, Glen S., Mrs.   *Life and Exploits of S. Glenn Young: World-Famous Law Enforcement Officer.*   Herrin: pub. by Mrs. S. Glenn Young, n.d. circa, 1924. Illustrations, original boards, some wear and spotting, some internal soil, generally good.   Dumont Maps and Books   133 - 87   2016 $50

Young, H. M.   *The Housewife's Manual of Domestic Cookery...*   London: Fletcher, Russell & co., circa, 1900. 27th edition, half title, illustrations, occasional marking and few marginal tears, original red buckram blocked in black, signature of M. L. Gayton, spine slightly faded, leading hinge neatly strengthened, nice.   Jarndyce Antiquarian Books   CCXV - 497   2016   £65

Young, John   *A Criticism on the Elegy Written in a Country Church-Yard.*   Edinburgh: printed for John Ballantyne for Longman, Hurst, Rees and Orme, 1810. Second edition, octavo, original grey boards and printed paper label, untrimmed, leather bookplate of Arthur Gordon Ripley, Denver, bookseller's description pasted to front pastedown, slight foxing, boards little worn, some loss at head of spine, very good.   The Brick Row Book Shop   Miscellany 69 - 51   2016 $625

Young, John   *A Series of Designs for Shop Fronts and Entrances to Buildings, Public and Private.*   London: M. Taylor, 1 Wellington Street, Strand, 1835. 4to., engraved ornamental titlepage, 29 engraved plates, contemporary green ribbed cloth backed drab wrappers, clean. Marlborough Rare Books   List 55 - 75   2016   £1750

Young, Julia   *Black Evan.*   New York: Tennyson Neely, 1901. Large 8vo., frontispiece, author's presentation, black cloth stamped in gilt.   Second Life Books, Inc.   196 B - 960   2016 $45

Young, Karl   *Milestones Set One: 1970-1975.*   Madison: Landlocked Press, 1987. 1/130 copies, inscribed by author for Paul Metcalf, large 8vo., pages not numbered, sewn and bound with vellum strips in two tone paper wrappers, cover little yellowed, otherwise nice.   Second Life Books, Inc. 196 B - 963   2016 $150

Young, Rose   *The Record of the Leslie Woman Suffrage Commission Inc. 1917-1929.*   Leslie Commission, 1929. First edition, small 8vo., little soiled cloth, very good, inscribed by Carrie Chapman Catt for Josephine Fowler Pool.   Second Life Books, Inc.   196A - 263   2016 $600

Young, William   *Portugal in 1828.*   London: Henry Colburn, 1828. First edition, 8vo., contemporary brown half calf, gilt stamp of Signet Library on covers, no stamps in text.   J. & S. L. Bonham Antiquarian Booksellers   Europe 2016 - 8452   2016   £250

Younghusband, Francis   *India and Tibet. A History of the Relations Which Have Subsisted Between the Two Countries...*   London: John Murray, 1910. 8vo., 26 plates and 22 colored maps, foxing and light browning, red publisher's cloth, title stamped gilt to spine, spine darkened, touch of fraying at top of lower joint but good, label of Times Book Club and stamp 27 Jul 1911, inscription of Spencer Ervin, June 1912.   Unsworths Antiquarian Booksellers Ltd.   30 - 167   2016   £150

Younghusband, G. J.   *The Queen's Commission How to Prepare for It, How to Obtain It...*   London: John Murray, 1891. Second edition, original red cloth, white buckram spine, very good.   Jarndyce Antiquarian Books   CCXV - 1018   2016   £40

Zaccaria, Francescantonio *Dissertazioni Varie Italiane a Storia Ecclesiactica...* Roma: Stamperia Salomoni, 1780. 2 volumes, small 8vo., small title woodcut vignettes, head and tailpieces, indexes, corners curling, worming at gutter pages 113-126 of volume i, early ink handwritten notes on rear free endpaper, original marbled printed wrappers, spines worn, some cords loose, bookplates of Ex Oblatorum S. Carolio Bibliotheca Bayswater (Henry Edward Manning 1808-1892) and Pitts Theology Library, along with rubber ink stamps on title and elsewhere, archival folding chemises, very good. Jeff Weber Rare Books 181 - 38 2016 $100

Zagoria, Donald S, *The Sino-Soviet Conflict 1956-1961.* Princeton and London: Princeton University Press and Oxford University, 1962. First edition UK issue with dust jacket price in sterling, octavo, ownership signature of Swedish journalist Britt-Marie Mattson, fine in near fine dust jacket faintly darkened at spine. Peter Ellis 112 - 73 2016 £65

Zahorowski, Hieronim *Secreta Monita Societatis Jesu: the Secret Instructions of the Jesuits.* London: printed for John Walthoe, 1723. 12mo., some light browning and very slight foxing, rebound in half dark calf, raised bands, marbled boards, new endpapers and pastedowns, early name of James Taylor on titlepage. Jarndyce Antiquarian Booksellers CCXVI - 625 2016 £500

Zamyatin, Yevgeny *We.* London: Jonathan Cape, 1970. First English edition, crown 8vo., original grey boards, backstrip lettered gilt, top edge black, dust jacket with very mild toning to backstrip panel and some light scuffing to rear panel, very good, review copy with Cape Review Slip laid in. Blackwell's Rare Books B186 - 291 2016 £300

Zanotti, Giampietro *La Pitture de Pellegrino Tibali e di Nicolo Abbati Existenti nell'Instituto de Bologna.* Venice: n.p., 1756. First edition, folio, contemporary half calf, marbled boards, spine restored, boards rubbed, engraved allegorical frontispiece after G. B. Moretti, engraved vignette incorporating a view of Bologna on title, engraved portraits, 41 plates and 19 head or tailpieces, vignettes or initials, Erno Park Library with their 19th century bookplate, light dampstain in blank lower fore-margin of opening few leaves. Maggs Bros. Ltd. 1474 - 83 2016 £2500

Zapf, Hermann *Manuale Typographicum, 100 Typographical Arrangements with Considerations about Types....* New York: Z Presse Frankfurt, 1968. Limited to 975 numbered and signed copies, 4to., parchment backed cloth, dust jacket, printed in black and red, prospectus loosely inserted, jacket chipped with small tear along edges. Oak Knoll Books 310 - 22 2016 $475

Zapf, Hermann *Typographic Variations Designed by Hermann Zapf on Themes in Contemporary Book Design and Typography in 78 Book and Title Pages.* New York: Museum Books, 1964. Limited to 500 numbered copies for the Aemrican market signed by Zapf, set in 16 languages with types of D. Stempel, 4to., parchment backed boards, vellum tips, dust jacket with faint stain along top of front cover. Oak Knoll Books 310 - 23 2016 $375

Zarate, D'Augustin De *Histoire De La Decouverte et de La conquete Du Perou.* Paris: Compagnie des Libraries, 1742. First edition, 2 volumes, contemporary speckled calf, spine gilt with raised bands, small wear to head of spine, joints rubbed, internally clean and crisp, handsome set. J. & S. L. Bonham Antiquarian Booksellers America 2016 - 8532 2016 £320

Zelazny, Roger *Creatures of Light and Darkness.* London: Faber and Faber, 1970. First UK edition, octavo, edges very slightly spotted, near fine in very good slightly rubbed dust jacket. Peter Ellis 112 - 461 2016 £150

Zelazny, Roger *Lord of Light.* Garden City: Doubleday & Co. Inc., 1967. First edition, octavo, cloth, fine in nearly fine dust jacket with mild rubbing to spine ends and corner tips, some mild rub spots to lower spine panel and to spine fold. John W. Knott, Jr./L.W. Currey, Inc. Fall-Winter 2015 - 17555 2016 $2500

Zemach, Harve *Duffy and the Devil.* New York: Farrar Straus & Giroux, 1973. Stated first edition, 4to., blue cloth, fine in fine dust jacket with little rubbing, no award medal, wonderful color illustrations, laid in is 1974 award Dinner booklet for the Year that Duffy won the award, inscribed by author. Aleph-bet Books, Inc. 111 - 499 2016 $400

Zemach, Harve *A Penny Look.* New York: Farrar Straus Giroux, 1971. Stated first edition, 9 x 8 inches, cloth, fine in near fine dust jacket with light rubbing, this copy has warm inscription with 2 pen drawings, illustrations by Margot Zemach. Aleph-bet Books, Inc. 111 - 500 2016 $225

Zemach, Margot *Jake and Honeybunch Go to Heaven.* New York: Farrar Straus Giroux, 1982. First edition, cloth, fine in slightly frayed dust jacket, striking full page and smaller color illustrations by Margot Zemach, laid in is color illustrated publisher's promotional card for The Princess and Ferggie" with drawings of a bird and a flower inscribed by Zemach and her daughters. Aleph-bet Books, Inc. 112 - 65 2016 $125

Zepeda Y Adrada, Alonso *Epitome de la Fortification Moderns, Assi en lo regular, Como em lo Irregular Relucida a la Regla y al Compas, Por Diversos Modos y los Mas Faciles Para Mover la Tierra...* Brussels: Foppens, 1669. First edition, 4to., English 18th century full polished tree calf, spine elaborately decorated gilt, red morocco lettering pieces, red edges, large engraved coat-of-arms on title, engraved portrait and 34 fold-out engraved plates, front hinge restored at some point internally, apart from small old repair to title and light browning, very good in fine binding made for the Earls of Macclesfield.   Sotheran's Travel and Exploration - 282   2016   £2750

Zeune, Johann August *Belisar, Ueber den Unterriche der Blinden.* Berlin: Johann Friedrich Weiss, 1821. Second edition, 2 parts in 1, with separate registers and pagination, but all called for in Contents, engraved title with vignette, 3 engraved plates, 2 folding, few spots here and there, 8vo., modern marbled boards, good, rare.   Blackwell's Rare Books   B186 - 170   2016   £1200

Zhbankovoi, N. *Spon Vambo. (Vambo the Elephant).* Moscow: G. F. Mirimanvo, n.d. circa, 1925. Oblong 4to, pictorial wrappers, slight soil, very good, 12 fine full page richly colored lithographs by Vasily Vatagin.   Aleph-bet Books, Inc.   111 - 401   2016 $850

Zimmer, John Todd *Catalogue of the Edward E. Ayer Ornithological Library.* Chicago: Field Museum of Natural History, 1926. Octavo, 2 volumes colored frontispiece, publisher's wrappers, both volumes in slipcase, very good set.   Andrew Isles Natural History Books   55 - 13266   2016 $300

Zimmer, Paul *The Republic of Many Voices.* New York: October House, 1969. First edition, inscribed and signed by author Dec. 16 1969 for William Meredith, laid in are 2 TLS's and typed manuscript poem signed and inscribed by author, near fine in like dust jacket with sunned spine.   Charles Agvent   William Meredith - 126   2016 $100

Zimmerman, Hazel L. *Sands of Song.* Metropolitan press, 1926. 1/110 copies signed by author, frontispiece, 8vo., paper over boards with paper label, cover worn at edges and at spine, otherwise very good.   Second Life Books, Inc.   196 B - 973   2016 $45

Zimmermann, Johann Georg *An Essay on National Pride...* London: printed for J. Wilkie and C. Heydinger, 1771. 12mo., frontispiece, light dampstaining at beginning and end, piece torn from blank fore-margin of signature O8, closed tear in O10 the first leaf of index, later gilt decorated half calf, marbled paper boards, spine ruled and decorated gilt, red morocco label, blue sprinkled edges, very lightly rubbed, small bookplate removed from front pastedown, attractive copy.   Jarndyce Antiquarian Booksellers   CCXVI - 627   2016   £110

Zimmermann, Johann Georg *Solitude.* London: printed for the Associated Booksellers, 1798. 7 beautiful engravings by Ridley, frontispiece, additional engraved titlepage, dated Feb. 16th 1797, vignette on printed titlepage, 5 engraved plates, 8vo., some old waterstaining, otherwise good clean copy, 19th century half calf, marbled boards, raised and gilt banded spine, red morocco label.   Jarndyce Antiquarian Booksellers   CCXVI - 626   2016   £50

Zincke, Forster Barham *Some Thoughts about the School of the Future....* London: Longman, Brown, Green & Longmans, 1852. Half title, stain to upper margin of first 3 leaves, original purple cloth, spine faded and little dulled and marked, presentation inscription to the Duke of Bedford.   Jarndyce Antiquarian Books   CCXV - 1019   2016   £180

Zineman, Jakub *50-Lecie "Panstwa Zydowskiego" Teodora Herzia.* Lodz: C. K. Zjednoczenia Sujonistow-Demokratow ICHUD w Polsce Resort Wydawniczy, 1946. Very rare first edition, 8vo., original illustrated wrappers, full page illustration, apart form even light browning, fine.   Sotheran's Travel and Exploration - 293   2016   £248

Zinnes, Harriet *I Wanted to See Something Flying.* New York: Folder Editions, 1976. First edition, author's presentation on flyleaf to William Claire, paper wrappers, cover little scuffed at edges, otherwise very good, tight copy.   Second Life Books, Inc.   196 B - 975   2016 $45

Zola, Emile *Nana.* 1/1500 copies, illustrations by Bernard Lamotte, signed by artist, full maroon cloth, cloth label on spine, spine slightly faded, else nice in rather worn slipcase.   Second Life Books, Inc.   196 B - 976   2016 $75

Zollner, Frank *Leonardo Da Vinci: the Complete Painting and Drawings.* Cologne: London: Los Angeles: Madrid: Paris: Tokyo: Tashen, 2003. First edition, dust jacket, copiously illustrated in color and black and white, fine in fine dust jacket.   Any Amount of Books   2015 - A77754   2016   £150

Zolotow, Charlotte *Mr. Rabbit and the Lovely Present.* New York: Harper & Row, 1962. First edition, oblong 8vo., pictorial boards, fie in dust jacket, illustrations in full color.   Aleph-bet Books, Inc.   112 - 448   2016 $750

Zolotow, Charlotte *Over and Over.* New York: Harper & Bros., 1957. First edition, 4to., cloth backed pictorial boards, near fine in dust jacket, worn at spine ends and some fraying and few closed tears, full page color illustrations by Garth Williams.   Aleph-bet Books, Inc.   111 - 483   2016 $200

The Zooland Postcard Painting Book. London: Valentine & Sons, n.d. circa, 1910. Pictorial card covers, chip off upper corner, spine rubbed, light general wear, paint that originally came with are no longer there but postcards ar all unused, very good+, illustrations by Louis Wain.   Aleph-bet Books, Inc.   112 - 507   2016 $1350

Zuill, William *Bermuda Sampler.*   Richard Clay, 1937. First edition, 8vo., frontispiece, illustrations, original purple cloth, ads on endpapers.   J. & S. L. Bonham Antiquarian Booksellers   America 2016 - 9512   2016   £45

Zukofsky, Louis *After I'S.*   Pittsburgh: Boxwood Mother, 1964. First edition, 12mo., original wrappers, cover little browned, rear stained, good, tight copy, inscribed Dick Moore's copy from Louis Zukofsky 3.16.66.   Second Life Books, Inc.   196 B - 980   2016 $75

Zukofsky, Louis *Prepositions. The Collected Critical Essays of...*   London: Rapp & Carroll,, 1967. First edition, one of a limited edition of 150 signed copies, fine in dust jacket.   Second Life Books, Inc.   196 B - 981   2016 $85

Zussman, Na'ama *Interactions Between Memory and Reality.*   Washington: 2012-2013. Limited to 7 copies, 3 volumes, each volume bound in white laminate covers with title printed in black on cover, fine, 8 x 10 inches, fine.   The Kelmscott Bookshop   13 - 61   2016 $450

Zussman, Na'ama *A Survey of a World.*   Washington: Na'ama Zussman, 2015. Number 7 of 12 copies, bound in brown Cialux book cloth, goatskin leather spine, images created through screen printing process and done on lovely Thai Kozo paper, text composed of Meta Capitals and Constantia, book housed in surveyor's bag made out of grey cashmere with leather string, colophon is a pocket in back of bag, fine.   The Kelmscott Bookshop   13 - 62   2016 $1500

Zwerger, Lisbeth *The Merry Pranks of Till Eulen-Spiegel.* Saxonville: Picture Book Studio, 1990. First English edition thus, 4to., pictorial hardbound, illustrations, fine in dust jacket, scarce.   Gene W. Baade, Books on the West   2015 - 5010030   2016 $40

Zwinger, Ann *John Xantus: the Fort Tejon Letters 1857-1859.*   Tucson: University of Arizona Press, 1986. First edition, frontispiece, text illustrations, cloth backed, cloth covered boards, small oval bookplate fine in pictorial dust jacket.   Argonaut Book Shop   Biography 2015 - 3398   2016 $40

Association Copies

Association – Abdullah, Achmed

Baldwin, Faith *Sign Posts.* Boston: Small, Maynard & Co., 1924. First edition, small octavo, blue decorated cloth stamped in black and gold, trifle rubbed at spine ends, slight foxing on top edge, else very near fine, lacking dust jacket, inscribed by author to Achmed Abdullah.   Between the Covers Rare Books   204 - 11   2016 $450

Association – Abel, B. A.

Graves, Robert 1895-1985 *The Real David Copperfield.* London: Arthur Barker, 1933. First edition, half title, original blue cloth, pencil inscription of John Butt 1938, stamps of B. A. Abel, solicitor, Nottingham, good plus in slightly worn dust jacket.   Jarndyce Antiquarian Booksellers   CCXVIII - 491   2016   £65

Association – Abingdon, Earls

Peck, Francis *Academia Tertia Anglicana; or the Antiquarian Annals of Stanford (sic) in Lincoln, Rutland and Northampton Shires....* London: printed for the author by James Bettenham, 1727. First edition, 14 books in one, bound in early 19th century panelled russia, attractively tooled in blind, rebacked period style by Bernard Middleton, all edges gilt, 33 engraved plates, including large folding engraved frontispiece, 4 small engraved plates within text, numerous attractive wood engraved tailpieces, bright, clean, early 19th century engraved armorial booklabel of Earls of Abingdon, bookplate of John Lea Nevinson (1905-1985).   Sotheran's   Piccadilly Notes - Summer 2015 - 233   2016   £695

Association – Aboussouan, Camille

Martialis, Marcus Valerius *Epigrammata Demptis Obscenis.* Paris: Apud Viduam Simonis Benard, 1693. 12mo., contemporary brown morocco, covers with gilt fleur-de-ls and interlaced crescents at alternate corners, large central gilt arms of town of Bordeau, edges gilt, very pretty copy, bookplates (two) of Camille Aboussouan.   Joseph J. Felcone, Inc.   Books from Five Centuries: a Miscellany - 23   2016 $600

Association – Abraham, J. Johnston

Sprigge, S. Squire *The Methods of Publishing.* London: 1890. Original black buckram, lettered gilt, bookplate sof J. Johnston Abraham and Gavin D. R. Bridson.   Jarndyce Antiquarian Booksellers   CCXVII - 240   2016   £65

Association – Acker, Kathy

Love is Strange: Stories of Postmodern Romance. New York: W. W. Norton & Co., 1993. First edition, illustrated self wrappers, slight waviness on pages, rear bottom corner bumped, else near fine, 'Autographed Copy' sticker, nicely inscribed by contributor, Kathy Acker with drawing, inscription below in unknown hand.   Between the Covers Rare Books   204 - 7   2016 $275

Association – Adams, Charles

Baker, Henry *Employment of the Microscope.* London: printed for R. and J. Dodsley, 1764. Second edition, 2 parts in one volume, 8vo., 17 engraved plates, lightly foxed, titlepage creased, plate facing page 422 torn at fold, modern full calf with original calf mounted on sides, gilt stamped motto "Fide et Virtute" belonging to Cha. Brandling, gilt and blindstamped spine, gilt stamped red leather label, new endleaves, bookplates of Cha. Brandling, Charles Adams, Fred C. Luck and Max Erb, very good+.   Jeff Weber Rare Books   183 - 5   2016 $650

Association – Adams, Crawford

Vesalius, Andreas *Anatomes Totius aere Insculpta Delineatio.* Paris: Andre Wechel, 1564. First Grevin edition, full page woodcut arms of dedicatee, 47 engraved plates on 40 leaves, folio, modern reversed leather, occasional marginal soiling, scattered ink blots on text leaves, some plates might be washed, folding plate of Adam and Eve was torn and mounted with slight image loss, repaired clean tears across facing D3r and Elv but these not affecting image, bookplate of Crawford W. Adams.   James Tait Goodrich   X-78 - 530   2016 $1500

Association – Adams, L. R.

McDougall, William *Character and the Conduct of Life.* London: Methuen, 1928. Third edition, Half title, 8 pages ads, original blue cloth, signature of L. R. Adams 1930.   Jarndyce Antiquarian Books   CCXV - 304   2016   £25

Association – Adamson, George

Huxley, Elspeth *White Man's Country. Lord Delamere and The Making of Kenya.* London: MacMillan, 1935. First edition, 8vo., 2 volumes, original orange cloth, spine lettered in gilt, plate sand four folding maps, light marking to cloth, internally, apart from very few faint discolorations, very good, inscribed by author on both half titles to Joy and George Adamson, dated Dec. 1956, contemporary name boldly on both front covers.   Sotheran's   Travel and Exploration - 14   2016   £498

Association – Adamson, Joy

Huxley, Elspeth *White Man's Country. Lord Delamere and The Making of Kenya.* London: MacMillan, 1935. First edition, 8vo., 2 volumes, original orange cloth, spine lettered in gilt, plate sand four folding maps, light marking to cloth, internally, apart from very few faint discolorations, very good, inscribed by author on both half titles to Joy and George Adamson, dated Dec. 1956, contemporary name boldly on both front covers.   Sotheran's   Travel and Exploration - 14   2016   £498

Association – Addams, Jane

Maurice, C. Edmund *Life of Octavia Hill as told in her Letters.* London: Macmillan, 1913. First edition, 8vo., portraits, untrimmed and partially unopened, very good, clean tight copy, this the copy of author and feminist, Jane Addams (Hull House), from the library of consumer advocate Florence Kelley.   Second Life Books, Inc.   196 B - 157   2016 $250

Association – Addinell, Richard

Dane, Clemence *Come of Age.* New York: Doubleday, Doran, 1934. First edition, 8vo., very good, inscribed by author and Addinell for Edward Wasserman and signed by actress Judith Anderson who starred in the play.   Second Life Books, Inc.   196A - 372   2016 $150

Association – Adler, Stella

Clurman, Harold *Lies Like Truth: Theatre Reviews and Essays.* New York: Macmillan, 1958. First edition, signed by book's dedicatee, actress Stella Adler on dedication page, very good in very good plus dust jacket.   Royal Books   48 - 35   2016 $350

Association – Aikman, Hugh Henry Robertson

Copley, Esther *Cottage Comforts ...* London: Simpkin, Marshall & Co., 1858. Twenty-third edition, original grey-green cloth, hand colored armorial bookplate of Hugh Henry Robertson Aikman, embossed library stamp on leading f.e.p., very good.   Jarndyce Antiquarian Books   CCXV - 133   2016   £45

Association – Ainslie, J. R.

Linton, William *Colossal Vestiages of the Older nations.* London: Longman, Green, Longman & Roberts, 1862. First edition, frontispiece, foldout diagram, untrimmed in original red wavy grained cloth, blocked in blind, front board lettered gilt, some minor repairs to head and tail of spine, bookplates of Charles Dickens, Sara R. Dunn and J. R. Ainslie, with "from the Library of Charles Dickens" label, very good in brown cloth foldover box, inscribed by Marion Bell to Dickens.   Jarndyce Antiquarian Booksellers   CCXVIII - 871   2016   £1650

Association – Alexander, A. S.

Maugham, William Somerset   1874-1965 *The Making of a Saint.* London: T. Fisher Unwin, 1898. First English edition, uncommon second book, original green cloth with gilt title to spine, minor rubbing to boards and minor wear to spine ends, text and endpages slightly browned as is usual with this book, bookplates of three previous owners, A. S. Alexander, Eleanor Jacott and Mark Samuels Lasner, very good.   The Kelmscott Bookshop   12 - 66   2016 $300

Association – Alexander, Katherine

Rice, Elmer *The Left Bank.* New York: Samuel French, 1931. First edition, very good, tight copy, with card list from original play program tipped to front free endpaper and printed photo of leading lady tippped to front pastedown, this copy signed by Katharine Alexander, Horace Braham and Donald Macdonald.   Second Life Books, Inc.   196 B - 475   2016 $125

Association – Alexandra, Queen

Vivian, Evelyn Charles *The Way of the Red Cross.* London: Hodder & Stoughton, 1915. First edition, half title, folded facsimile letter from Queen Anne, leading f.e.p. with vertical crease, original blue grey cloth, spine slightly dulled, presentation inscription in secretarial hand no leading f.e.p. "Janet C. Kirkpatrick Yorkhill War Hospital Glasgow. Presentd (sic) by Her majesty Queen Alexandra at Marlborough House May 22nd 1917", very good.   Jarndyce Antiquarian Booksellers   CCXVII - 291   2016   £45

Association – Alington

Shelley, Percy Bysshe   1792-1822 *Letters... to Leigh Hunt.* London: privately printed, 1894. First edition, one of 6 copies on vellum, with first and last blank leaves, 30 copies were printed on Whatman paper, 8vo., crushed black morocco by Ramage, Herbert S. Leon and Alington bookplates, fine.   Blackwell's Rare Books   Marks of Genius - 48   2016   £6000

Association – Allan, Jewell

Douglas, Lloyd C. *White Banners.* Boston and New York: Houghton Mifflin, 1936. First edition, 8vo., fine, in dust jacket little worn with few small nicks and tears, inscribed by the author for Jewell Allan.   Second Life Books, Inc.   196A - 444   2016 $225

Association – Allen, E.

Dickens, Charles   1812-1870   *Dombey and Son.* London: Bradbury & Evans, 1848. First edition, frontispiece, engraved title and plates by Phiz, 2 errata slips, some foxing to plates, contemporary half dark green calf, spine gilt in compartments, black leather label, little rubbed, contemporary signature of Howard Simcox later details of E. Allen, good, sound copy.   Jarndyce Antiquarian Booksellers   CCXVIII - 442   2016   £220

Association – Allen, Jack

Mallory, Jay   *Sweet aloes: a Play in Three Acts.* London: Cassell, 1935. First edition, orange cloth, very good, tight copy, inscribed by author for producer Hugh Beaumont, also inscribed by actress, Joyce Carey, and signed by 12 members of the cast.   Second Life Books, Inc.   196 B - 126   2016 $225

Association – Allen, Kenneth

Tarkington, Booth   *Kate Fennigate, a Novel.* New York: Doubleday Doran, 1943. Later edition, 8vo., inscribed by author for Kenneth Allen.   Second Life Books, Inc.   196 B - 734   2016 $45

Association – Allen, Mary

Mrabet, Mohamnmed   *Love with a few Hairs.* New York: George Braziller, 1968. Very near fine in near fine, signed and inscribed by Paul Bowles the translator for Mary Allen, 21/5/69, very nice, uncommon.   Jeff Hirsch Books Holiday List 2015 - 55   2016 $300

Association – Allen, R.

Burgh, James   *The Art of Speaking.* London: printed for T. Longman & J. Buckland &c., 1761. 8vo., odd mark and crease, overall nice, clean copy, contemporary full calf, corners repaired, little rubbed, signature of R. Allen, June 21 1799, nice.   Jarndyce Antiquarian Books   CCXV - 89   2016   £380

Association – Allingham, Helen

Allingham, William   *Rhymes for the You Folk.* London: Cassell & Co., n.d., 1867. Large 8vo., original illustrated red paper boards over red cloth, lettered black and white on front board, copiously illustrated, signed presentation from one of the artists, Helen Allingham for Claude and Alan Scott, June 1917, some rubbing and slight chipping along edges and corners with faint foxing to prelims, otherwise sound, clean, attractive, very good.   Any Amount of Books   2015 - C8506   2016   £250

Association – Allsopp, John

Aikin, John   *Letters from a Father to His Son.* London: J. Johnson, 1796. Third edition, 2 volumes, 8vo., uncut in original blue drab boards, cream paper spines, neatly rebacked but with ink volume numbers on spines reversed, contemporary signature of John Allsopp on leading f.e.p. volume 1, very good.   Jarndyce Antiquarian Books   CCXV - 10   2016   £150

Association – Alston, Harold

Wilson, Ernest Henry   *A Naturalist in Western China with Vasculum, Camera and Gun.* London: Methuen, 1913. First edition, octavo, 2 volumes, photos, folding map, publisher's red cloth, minor blemish on lower corner of volume two, fine, crisp set, signed by Wilson 13.12.20, bookplate of Harold Alston.   Andrew Isles Natural History Books   55 - 30016   2016 $1500

Association – Altrocchi, Julie

Hunt, Rockwell   *Mr. California. Autobiography of Rockwell D. Hunt.* San Francisco: Fearon Pub., 1956. First edition, fine with dust jacket, presentation inscription signed by fellow author, Julie Altrocchi, also signed by author.   Argonaut Book Shop   Biography 2015 - 2016 $40

Association – Ames, Winthrop

Kaufman, George   *Beggar on Horseback.* New York: Boni & Liveright, 1924. First edition, 8vo., 2 pages in the middle of text quite darkened from old news clipping that had been laid in, top edges of boards sunned, otherwise very good tight copy in very good, bright dust jacket, inscribed by producer Winthrop Ames to George Barbier who played Mr. Cady, also inscribed by both playwrights, George Kaufman and Marc Connelly, splendid association.   Second Life Books, Inc.   196A - 913   2016 $1500

Association – Anderson, John

The Words of the Masters, Reflections on the Fine Art of Type Design. Maple Shade: Pickering Press of John Anderson, 1982. First edition, limited to 75 numbered copies, wood engravings by John De Pol, small 8vo., stiff paper wrappers, cord tinted, presentation from John Anderson. Oak Knoll Books   310 - 137   2016 $200

Association – Anderson, Judith

Dane, Clemence *Come of Age.* New York: Doubleday, Doran, 1934. First edition, 8vo., very good, inscribed by author and Addinell for Edward Wasserman and signed by actress Judith Anderson who starred in the play.   Second Life Books, Inc.   196A - 372   2016 $150

Jeffers, Robinson   1887-1962 *Medea.* New York: Random House, 1946. Second printing, autographed to Doris Rich by Dedicatee Judith Anderson on dedication page, with short TLS from Anderson to Rich dated Feb. 6 1948, laid in, some notes in pencil that appear to show changes made in production, owner's bookplate, nice in worn dust jacket.   Second Life Books, Inc.   196A - 892   2016 $125

Association – Andrade, E. N. Da C.

Collier, Jane *An Essay on the Art of Ingeniously Tormenting with Proper Rules for the Exercise of that Pleasant Art.* London: printed for A. Millar in the Strand, 1753. 8vo., engraved frontispiece, very nice, clean copy, contemporary full calf, raised bands, compartments in gilt, brown morocco label, rebacked retaining original spine, leading hinge cracked and little worn, spine rubbed and dulled, repair to following inner hinge, armorial bookplate of Sir George Shuckburgh & later label of E. N. Da C. Andrade, good sound copy.   Jarndyce Antiquarian Books   CCXV - 126   2016   £480

Association – Andrews, Charles Walker

The Book of Gems. The Modern Poets and Artists of Great Britain. London: Henry G. Bohn, 1845. 222 x 140mm., very pretty crimson morocco, handsomely gilt by the Doves Bindery (stamp signed and dated 1908), covers with line and dot frames, corners adorned with heart shaped leaves, a poppy seed pod, oak leaves, solid heart and gouge work, raised bands, spine compartments with line and dot frames, central poppy seed pod with leaves above below, turn-ins with gilt rules and oak leaf cluster cornerpieces, all edges gilt with two rows of gauffered dots (upper cover with small repair at fore edge to fill in a gouge), with 43 engraved vignettes, 40 facsimile signatures of poets on four pages following text, wood engraved bookplate of Charles Walker Andrews, hint of wear at upper corners and along top of spine, gilt frame on front cover slightly affected by repair at fore edge, leaves shade less than bright, still excellent copy, lovely binding especially lustrous and pleasing (even with minor flaws).   Phillip J. Pirages   67 - 39   2016 $1900

The Book of Gems. The Poets and Artists of Great Britain. London and Paris: Fisher Son & Co., 1844. 2 volumes, 222 x 140mm., very pretty crimson morocco handsomely gilt by Doves Bindery (stamp signed and dated 1908 on rear turn-in), covers with line and dot frames, corners adorned with heart shaped leaves, a poppy seed pod, oak leaves, solid heart and gouge work, raised bands, spine compartments with line and dot frames, central poppy seed pod with leaves above and below, turn-ins with gilt rules and oak leaf cluster cornerpieces, all edges gilt, with two rows of gauffered dots (expert repairs to tiny portion of top of spine and three small areas of front joint of second volume), with 106 engraved vignettes and four pages of poets' facsimile signatures at end of each volume, front pastedown with wood engraved bookplate of Charles Walker Andrews, front free endpaper with typed copy of a letter from Andrews to the Doves Bindery, about these bindings (which he commissioned) and Cobden-Sanderson's handwritten and signed reply (first apparently a transcript, with later date of a letter sent 29 Jan. 1909, the second dated 9 Feb. 1909), top corners of volume I bit worn, leaves shade less than bright (no doubt as in all copies because of paper stock, still excellent set that looks very attractive on shelf, binding lustrous and appealing despite its defects and text clean, fresh and unread.   Phillip J. Pirages   67 - 38   2016 $3500

Floire et Jeanne *The Tale of King Florus and the Fair Jehane.* Kelmscott Press, 1893. 350 copies printed with an additional 15 copies on vellum, of the 360 copies, 76 copies were purchased in sheets by Tregaskis and sent to book binders, this is probably a trial copy that Rau chose not to send as his exhibition piece but seems more likely that it was a second copy commissioned by a collector who saw the Tretaskis copy in the exhibition or the exhibition catalog, 16mo., choicely bound by E Rau of St. Petersburg in full orange crushed morocco lettered gilt on spine, boards with semi of stylized flowers within a single gilt and dog tooth panel, central initial of 'W" on upper board and "M' on lower, richly gilt inner dentelles over marbled endpapers, double page woodcut border, text printed in black and red in Chaucer type, fine in slipcase, bookplate of Frank Howell and of American collector Charles Walker Andrews, loosely inserted is typed letter from J. and M. L. Tregaskis to Frank Howell.   Sotheran's   Piccadilly Notes - Summer 2015 - 175   2016   £4995

Gray, Thomas   1716-1771 *An Elegy wrote in a Country Churchyard.* London: printed for R. Dodsley and sold by M. Cooper, 1751. Second edition, slight stain on upper margin of titlepage, some light foxing, very good, bookplate of Charles Walker Andrews.   The Brick Row Book Shop Miscellany 69 - 52   2016 $1000

Pater, Walter *Essays from the Guardian.* London: Macmillan and Co., 1901. Second printing, extremely pleasing crimson crushed morocco attractively gilt by Zaehnsdorf (stamp signed), covers with multiple gilt rule frame, central panel with azured cornerpieces and central oval medallion, flat spine in three unequal panels, two with oval medallion tools, one with gilt titling, gilt ruled turn-ins, marbled endpapers, top edge gilt, bookplate of Charles Walker Andrews, spine uniformly sunned to a dark red, light offsetting on free endpapers from turn-in glue, otherwise very fine, binding unworn and especially lustrous, text showing virtually no signs of use.   Phillip J. Pirages 67 - 77   2016 $800

Walpole, Horace   1719-1797 *The Castle of Otranto, A Gothic Story.* Parma: Printed by Bodoni for J. Edwards, 1791. Sixth edition, one of 300 copies, second state of titlepage, quarto, contemporary red morocco, gilt rules and lettering, two frontispieces, this copy has Hazen's states A & B of frontispiece, bookplate of Charles Walker Andrews, edges little rubbed, some light foxing, very good.   The Brick Row Book Shop   Miscellany 69 - 8   2016 $950

Association – Angelo, Valenti

Douglas, Norman   1868-1952 *South Wind.* New York: Dodd Mead and Co., 1928. First American illustrated edition, color illustrated frontispiece, 11 further color plates by Valenti Angelo, royal 8vo., original black buckram stamped in gilt to upper board, backstrip lettered gilt and just little dulled with bruise at head of upper joint, top edge orange, others rough trimmed, illustrated endpapers, slipcase with wear and split along base, otherwise very good, inscribed by the artist for Leon Livingston Sept. 1928.   Blackwell's Rare Books   B186 - 208   2016   £70

Wilde, Oscar   1854-1900 *The Birthday of the Infanta.* New York: Macmillan, Oct., 1929. Limited to 500 copies, numbered and signed by Pamela Bianco, 4to., cloth backed boards, fine in slipcase (just slightly worn at corners), printed on fine paper, beautiful double page color illustrations as well as black and whites by Bianco, laid in is great half page handwritten letter from Bianco to artist Valenti Angelo. Aleph-bet Books, Inc.   111 - 478   2016 $400

Association – Anthony, Susan B.

Stanton, Elizabeth Cady *The History of woman Suffrage Volumes I-III.* New York: Fowler & Wells, 1881. New York: 1882. Rochester: 1887. First edition, volume one has loose hinge in front but it and volume two are in very good condition, volume 3 very worn with some loose prelim matter and well worn binding, volumes one and two have tipped in signature by Susan B. Anthony, all 3 volumes inscribed Lizzie Everett from Flora M. Kimball, National City California April 4 1887.   Second Life Books, Inc.   196 B - 684   2016 $2000

Association – Antles, P. L.

Schott, Gaspar *Magia Optica Das ist Geheime doch Naturmassige Gesicht und Augen-Lehr...* Bamberg: Johann Martin Schonwerters, 1677. First German edition, small 4to., allegorical frontispiece, 25 engraved copper plates, variously browned, foxed or stained, contemporary quarter calf, decorative boards, extremities very worn, ownership signature L. Orssinger and inscription Ex Libris P. Lemigii Antles, Ludovii Kappourr?   Jeff Weber Rare Books   183 - 32 2016 $3000

Association – Antrobus, F.

Dickens, Charles   1812-1870 *Bleak House.* London: Bradbury & Evans, 1852-1853. First edition, xx original parts in xix, original pale blue printed wrappers, generally well preserved with some minor repair work in places, two of three backstrips expertly replaced, following wrapper to part in xix/xx repaired in lower inner margin, earlier parts with signature of F. Antrobus and label of Ingalton, the Eton bookseller, nice, clean set in custom made maroon morocco box.   Jarndyce Antiquarian Booksellers   CCXVIII - 500 2016   £3500

Association – Appel, Doris

Saunders, J. B. *Vesalius. The Illustrations from his works.* New York: 1950. original binding, very good in dust jacket, showing some wear, signed presentation by Doris Appel. James Tait Goodrich   X-78 - 537   2016 $500

Association – Armer, Sidney

Armer, Laura Adams *Waterless Mountain.* New York: Longmans Green, 1935. 4to., cloth, very good in tattered dust jacket, illustrations by Sidney and Laura Armer, this copy inscribed by Laura and laid in is 2 page handwritten letter from Sidney.   Aleph-bet Books, Inc.   112 - 33   2016 $200

Association – Armour, George Allison

Pater, Walter *Appreciations with an Essay on Style.* London: Macmillan, 1890. Third impression, bound for George Allison Armour by Doves Bindery in 1894, very good in full green morocco with gilt title, gilt clover decoration and five raised bands to spine, browning to spine and edges of boards, minor rubbing to hinges, corners and bands, decorative dentelles and full edges gilt, offsetting to endpapers and slight toning to margins of pages, else clean and bright, very good.   The Kelmscott Bookshop   13 - 41   2016 $850

Association – Armytage, George John

Bronte, Patrick   1777-1861 *The Cottage in the Wood; or the Art of Becoming Rich and Happy.* Bradford: T. Inkersley, 1815. Second edition, 18mo., engraved frontispiece after F. James, sculpted by E. Stather, slight offsetting on titlepage, later 19th century full crimson crushed morocco, triple gilt borders, raised bands, gilt compartments and dentelles, green and brown morocco labels, bookplate of George John Armytage, very good.   Jarndyce Antiquarian Booksellers   CCXVII - 48   2016   £2500

Association – Arnold, E. V.

Jameson, Anna Brownell   1794-1860 *Characteristics of Women, Moral, Poetical and Historical.* London: Saunders & Otley, 1832. First edition, 2 volumes, half titles volume I, illustrated with tiny vignette etchings bound in later olive green binder's cloth, maroon leather labels, spines slightly foxed, contemporary signature of Frances Bass on half title, later signature E. V. Anrold, good plus.   Jarndyce Antiquarian Books   CCXV - 272   2016   £150

Association – Arnold, Edward

Amman, Jost *Bibliorum Utriusque Testamenti Icones, Summor Artificio Expressae Historias Sacras and Vivum Exhibentes & Oculis Summa cum Gratia Repraesentantes....* Frankfurt: Christoph Corvinus & Sigmund Feyerabend, 1571. First edition, 8vo., 19th century blue morocco, triple blind fillet on cover, title lettered in gilt on spine, inner edge richly gilt and signed Bauzonnet-Trautz', marbled edges, gilt edges, silk bookmark, woodcut coats of arms of Johann Fichard and Konrad Weis, 200 fine oval woodcuts within ms. frames by Jose Amman, many signed with his initials, IA, bookplates of Edward Arnold, Dorking, E. Yeminez, Lyon and Allan Heywood Bright, London.   Maggs Bros. Ltd.   1474 - 12   2016   £4500

Association – Arnold, Susy

Arnold, Matthew   1822-1888 *Irish Essays and Others.* London: Smith, Elder and Co., 1882. Blue cloth boards, gilt title to spine, ex-library from St. Felix School Southwold with bookplate, tape remnants to spine and boards, top quarter inch of cloth to head of spine has chipped off, small chip to foot of spine, interior remains very clean, some wear to hinges, very good, presentation inscribed by author's sister, Susy.   The Kelmscott Bookshop   12 - 1   2016 $375

Association – Arnold, Thomas

Arnold, Matthew   1822-1888 *Merope: a tragedy.* London: Longman, Brown, Green, Longmans & Roberts, 1858. First edition, presentation copy, inscribed "From the author", with ownership signature of Thomas Arnold, author's brother, dated Dublin 1858, very good in original dark green cloth boards with gilt title to spine and blind stamped decoration to boards, expertly rebacked with original spine laid down, minor rubbing and few spots to boards with minor wear to corners, occasional spots of foxing and light browning to margins of pages, clean overall, type-written description of this book is pasted down to rear free endpaper, very good.   The Kelmscott Bookshop   13 - 2   2016 $450

Association – Arthur, Thomas Glen

Scott, Walter 1771-1832 *The Doom of the Devorgoil, A Melo-Drama. (and) Alichindrane or the Ayrshire Tragedy.* Edinburgh: printed by Ballantyne for Cadell and Co., Edinburgh and Simpkin and Marshall, London, 1830. First separate and complete edition, 229 x 1522m., attractive late 19th century dark green armorial morocco by Maclehose of Glasgow (stamp signed), covers gilt with heraldic pelican crest of Thomas Glen Arthur of Garrick House, Ayr, flat spine with title at head and author at tail and five gilt rnaments in between (comprised of three thistles and two heraldic devices), gold endleaves, top edge gilt, other edges untrimmed (front hinge and joint with careful repairs, front free endpaper and first flyleaf cut near gutter and reattached with cellophane), large paper presentation copy, inscribed by Harry A. Sickles, Christmas 1917 for friend Frank P. Leffingwell, short crack beginning at bottom of front joint, hint of fading and leather dressing residue to covers, otherwise in excellent, binding solid and lustrous, text clean and fresh, margins very commodious.   Phillip J. Pirages   67 - 312   2016 $1000

Association – Artzybasheff, Boris

Colum, Padraic 1881-1972 *Creatures.* New York: Macmillan, 1927. First edition, 8vo., cloth backed decorated boards, near fine in dust jacket with some chips and mends on verso, illustrations by Boris Artzybasheff with striking bold woodcuts, this copy signed by artist.   Alephbet Books, Inc.   111 - 25   2016 $225

Association – Asch, Moses

Hughes, Langston *One-Way ticket.* New York: Alfred A. Knopf, 1949. First edition, inscribed by author for Moses Asch, Aug. 15 1955, near fine in very good dust jacket, jacket bright with some rubbing at folds and small chip at crown, no titling affected.   Royal Books   48 - 28   2016 $1500

Association – Ash, Lee

Handyside, P. D. *Observations on the Arrested Twin Development of Jean Battista Dos Santos, Born at Faro in Portugal in 1846.* Edinburgh (and) London: Maclachlan and Stewart (and) Robert Hardwicke, 1866. First edition, octavo, later decorated wrappers, 2 rather graphic woodcuts, laid in is TNS by book dealer James Tait Goodrich sending the pamphlet to Lee Ash.   Between the Covers Rare Books   204 - 71   2016 $450

Association – Ashbee, C. R.

Longus *Les Amours Pastorales De Daphnis et Chloe.* Chelsea: Ashedene Press, 1933. One of 250 paper copies for sale (of a total of 290) and 20 on vellum, 261 x 185mm., in original peacock green paper boards with vellum spine and tips, circular gold stamping on front cover by Gwendolen Raverat, in original patterned paper slipcase (slightly soiled and rubbed), 29 charming woodcuts by Raverat, four full page; morocco bookplate of C. R. and J. E. Ashbee, marginal notes printed in red, initials and paragraph marks in blue added by hand by Graily Hewitt, half dozen tiny chips missing where paper covering boards meets vellum, spine, otherwise fine, entirely clean, fresh and bright inside and out.   Phillip J. Pirages   67 - 15   2016 $3800

Association – Ashbee, J. E.

Longus *Les Amours Pastorales De Daphnis et Chloe.* Chelsea: Ashedene Press, 1933. One of 250 paper copies for sale (of a total of 290) and 20 on vellum, 261 x 185mm., in original peacock green paper boards with vellum spine and tips, circular gold stamping on front cover by Gwendolen Raverat, in original patterned paper slipcase (slightly soiled and rubbed), 29 charming woodcuts by Raverat, four full page; morocco bookplate of C. R. and J. E. Ashbee, marginal notes printed in red, initials and paragraph marks in blue added by hand by Graily Hewitt, half dozen tiny chips missing where paper covering boards meets vellum, spine, otherwise fine, entirely clean, fresh and bright inside and out.   Phillip J. Pirages   67 - 15   2016 $3800

Association – Ashburner, Walter

Manilius, Marcus *Astronomicon ex Recensione et cum Notis Richardi Bentleii.* London: Typus Henrici Woodfall Sumptibus Pauli et Isaac Vaillant, 1739. 4to., 2 engraved plates, frontispiece folding celestial map, woodcut device to titlepage, engraved headpiece to dedication, occasional neatly pencilled marginal notes, closed tear (85mm. approx) to page 145-6, sporadic light worming to top fore-edge, corner not affecting text, small closed tear to map attachment, some edges little toned, 19th century half vellum, black morocco gilt spine label, marbled paper covered boards, fore and tail edges deckled, vellum darkened, rubbed, edges worn, corners frayed, inkstamp and signature of writer and book collector Walter Ashburner (1864-1936), signature of W. Oates dated 1746.   Unsworths Antiquarian Booksellers Ltd.   E01 - Early Printing - 14   2016   £850

Association – Aston, Joseph

H., M. B. *Home Truths for Home Peace, or "Muddle" Defeated, a Practical Inquiry....* London: Longmans, 1854. Sixth edition, original green cloth by Westley & Co., slightly rubbed, nice, contemporary signature of Joseph R. Aston.   Jarndyce Antiquarian Books   CCXV - 234   2016   £65

Association – Aston, Mary Lloyd

Vergilius Maro, Publius *Opera.* Edinburgh: apud Robertum Freebarnium, 1732. Small stain to blank margin of last quarter, ownership inscription of Allan Livingston (early) and Mary Lloyd Aston (20th century), 24mo., contemporary Scottish red morocco, spine gilt in compartments containing a saltire design, boards with central cross shape made up of arabesques containing dotted lines with thistles at its points, corners with square tools containing fan sprays, endpapers of decorative paper in multiple colours with gilt, edges gilt, joints cracking but strong, leather bit darkened, good.   Blackwell's Rare Books   Greek & Latin Classics VII - 92   2016   £500

Association – Athill, Diana

Blackwood, Caroline *The Fate of Mary Rose.* London: Jonathan, 1981. First edition, octavo, fore-edge very slightly spotted, otherwise fine in very near fine dust jacket, presentation copy from author inscribed for Diana Athill, literary editor.   Peter Ellis   112 - 42   2016   £150

Association – Atkin, Frank

Dickens, Charles   1812-1870 *Oliver Twist or the Parish Boy's Progress.* London: Richard Bentley, 1838. First edition, first issue, 3 volumes, half titles in volumes I and II, frontispieces and plates by George Cruikshank, original purple brown cloth, without imprint at tail of spines, spines faded and with expertly executed minor repairs, bookseller's ticket in volume I - G. Simms, Manchester, later signatures of Frank Atkin, good set.   Jarndyce Antiquarian Booksellers   CCXVIII - 175   2016   £4500

Association – Atkinson, Gertrude

Dickens, Charles   1812-1870 *Master Humphrey's Clock.* London: Chapman and Hall, 1840-1841. First edition, 3 volumes, frontispieces, illustrations, original brown cloth, boards blocked in blind with clock centerpieces, gilt spines, slight wear to hinges, otherwise good, signature of Gertrude E. Atkinson 1850 in volume 1, and initials in volumes II and III, bookplates of G. Maitland Gordon, variant marbled endpapers, cloth slipcase.   Jarndyce Antiquarian Booksellers   CCXVIII - 271   2016   £850

Association – Attwell, Mabel Lucy

Barrie, James Matthew   1860-1937 *Peter Pan and Wendy.* London: Hodder & Stoughton, n.d. circa, 1921. Thick 4to., blue cloth, slight fade spots on covers, else very good+, many black and white text illustrations, 12 beautiful tipped-in color plates by Mabel Lucy Attwell, this copy inscribed by artist with lovely full page watercolor, special copy, exceedingly scarce.   Aleph-bet Books, Inc.   111 - 31   2016 $2750

Association – Aubry, A.

Martin, Gabriel *Catalogus Librorum Bibliothecae Illustrissimi Viri Caroli Henrici Comitis de Hoym...* Parisiis: Gabriele & Claudium Martin, 1738. Small 8vo., 18th century quarter calf, blue paper covered boards, red leather spine label, all edges stained red, individual lots priced in ink in margins, dampstaining to titlepage and few pages that immediately follow, wear to extremities with small chips to head and tail of spine and to one panel between raised bands, small corner of page 99 lacking, bookplate of Paul Lacombe and A. Aubry, loosely inserted is commemorative booklabel which indicates the book came from reference library of H. P. Kraus.   Oak Knoll Books   310 - 64   2016 $1750

Association – Axelrod, David

Tate, James *Viper Jazz.* Middletown: Wesleyan University Press, 1976. First edition, hardcover issue, fine in very good or better dust jacket with some modest rubbing and some foxing at extremities, very warmly inscribed by Tate to poet David Axelrod, also laid in is warm ALS by Tate to Axelrod.   Between the Covers Rare Books   208 - 85   2016 $275

Association – Aynsley, John Murray

Lambe, Robert *An Exact and Circumstantial History of the Battle of Floddon.* Berwick upon Tweed: printed and sold by R. Taylor and E. and C. Dilly in the Poultry and G. Freer, Bell Yard, London, 1774. 8vo., frontispiece, erratum leaf + ads at end, 19th century half calf, marbled boards, grey sprinkled edges, leading hinge weakening, booklabel of John Murray Aynsley.   Jarndyce Antiquarian Booksellers   CCXVI - 354   2016   £75

Association – Backus, Jim

Backus, Henry *What are you doing after the orgy?* Englewood Cliffs: Prentice Hall, 1962. First edition, cartoons, presentation by authors Henry and Jim Backus, nice in little scuffed and soiled dust jacket.   Second Life Books, Inc.   196A - 65   2016 $45

Association – Bagot, M.

Layman, Pseud. *Remarks on the Rev. Dr. Vincent's Defence of Public Education with an Attempt to State Fairly the Question....* London: J. Hatchard, 1802. Second edition, disbound, signature of M. Bagot.   Jarndyce Antiquarian Books   CCXV - 996   2016   £40

Newcome, Peter *The History of the Ancient and Royal Foundation, Called the Abbey of St. Alban in the County of Hertford, from the Founding Thereof in 793 to the dissolution in 1339.* London: printed for the author by J. Nichols, 1795. Reissue, 4to., some slight foxing, generally very clean, bound red labels, some wear to head and tail of spine, gilt little rubbed, minor abrasions to boards, early signature of Mary Bagot.   Jarndyce Antiquarian Booksellers   CCXVI - 426   2016   £225

Association – Baillie, George

Poiret, Pierre *The Divine Oeconomy; or an Universal System of the Works and Purposes of God Towards Men, Demonstrated.* printed for R. Bonwicke, M. Wotton, S. Manship and R. Parker, 1713. 6 volumes bound in 4, each volume with its own titlepage, slight browning, 8vo. contemporary panelled calf, rubbed, 1 headcap defective, sound armorial bookplate, engraved by A. Johnston in each volume of Hon. George Baillie (of Jerviswood).   Blackwell's Rare Books   B186 - 124   2016   £1500

Association – Bain, James

Francesco D'Assisi, Saint   1886-1926 *I Fioretti Del glorioso Poverello Di Cristo S. Francesco Di Assisi. (Little flowers).* Chelsea: Ashendene Press, 1922. One of 200 paper copies for sale of 240 printed (and 12 on vellum), 225 x 156mm., original flexible vellum, green silk ties, gilt lettering on spine, edges untrimmed, printer's device and 53 woodcuts in text, printed in black, blue and red, initials in red or blue designed by Graily Hewitt, laid in at front an inked autograph note on personal note card in its original autograph envelope from C. H. St. John Hornby to London bookseller James S Bain, vellum with naturally occurring variations in color, otherwise very fine, binding unworn and text entirely clean, fresh and smooth.   Phillip J. Pirages   67 - 11   2016 $1250

Hornby, C. H. St. John *A Descriptive Bibliography of Books printed at the Ashendene Press MDCCCXCV-MCMXXXIV.* Chelsea: Ashendene Press, 1935. No. 41 of 390 copies of the original edition, signed by Hornby, 343 x 235mm., publisher's polished cordovan calf, gilt titling on front cover ad spine, edges untrimmed, modern morocco edged slipcase, with 33 plates, several initials hand painted by Graily Hewitt, very good autograph letters from Hornby to London bookseller James Bain, in marbled paper folders laid in, errata and additional errata slips laid in at rear, spine somewhat rubbed and marked with two small dark spots, faint fading to spine and top edge of covers, otherwise binding lustrous and pleasing with virtually no wear to joints, very faint offset to front free endpaper, handful of light and neglibile rust spots, otherwise very fine internally.   Phillip J. Pirages   67 - 14   2016 $2500

Association – Baird, Josie

Blake, Nicholas *The Dreadful Hollow.* New York: Harper & Bros., 1953. First American edition, crown 8vo., original quarter black cloth with terra cotta sides, backstrip lettered in white, top edge little dusty, other edges rough trimmed, dust jacket with small amount of fraying and few spots of internal tape repair, good, inscribed by Cecil Day-Lewis for Josie Baird.   Blackwell's Rare Books   B186 - 196   2016   £60

Association – Baker, Derek

Twysden, Roger *Historiae Anglicanae Scriptores X.* London: Typis Jacobi Flesher sumptibus Cornelii Bee, 1652. Editio princeps, 2 volumes as 1, folio, half title, title in red and black, section, woodcut initials, few tiny wax spots and ink blots not obscuring text, contemporary dark brown calf, blind tooled frame, edges sprinkled brown and red, neatly rebacked, red morocco gilt spine label, few scratches to boards, inner hinges reinforced, 2 armorial bookplates, F. E. Sotheby, Ecton and Derek Baker, third armorial bookplate of Ambrose Isted, fourth armorial bookplate with no name but with motto 'Que Serra Serra".   Unsworths Antiquarian Booksellers Ltd.   E01 - Early Printing - 28   2016   £500

Association – Baker, J.

Wilson, S. *Geography simplified: Being a Brief Summary of the Principal Features of the Great Divisions of the earth...* London: Simpkin Marshall & Co., 1849. Third edition, maps, occasional pencil annotations, with further annotations and illustrations on f.e.p.'s, binding cracked in places, contemporary dark green calf, slightly rubbed, original signature of J. Baker.   Jarndyce Antiquarian Books   CCXV - 1009   2016   £25

Bankes, George Nugent *A Day of My Life.* London: Sampson Low, 1877. First edition, half title, 6 pages ads, original brick red decorated cloth, slight ink mark to front board, little rubbed, bookplate of Oliver Brett & John H. Baker, very good.   Jarndyce Antiquarian Books   CCXV - 673   2016   £35

Association – Baker, Joseph Stannard

Washington, Booker T. *My Larger Education: Being Chapters from My Experience.* Garden City: Doubleday Page, 1911. First edition, frontispiece, maroon cloth neat and attractive contemporary ownership signature of Joseph Stannard Baker, offsetting on titlepage and also on blank front a clipping, else exceptionally fine and bright.   Between the Covers Rare Books   207 - 96   2016 $300

Association – Baker, Keith

Steinbeck, John Ernst 1902-1968 *The Pastures of Heaven.* New York: Brewer, Warren and Putnam, 1932. First edition, first issue in second issue dust jacket, inscribed by author for Keith Baker, scarce, especially signed, about near fine in like dust jacket, slight lean, light fading to board edges, light foxing and offsetting to endpapers, jacket has minor chipping to top edge and diagonal crease to rear flap. Royal Books 48 - 72 2016 $32,500

Association – Baker, Mrs.

Gisborne, Thomas *An Enquiry into the Duties of Men in the Higher and Middle Classes of Society, in Great Britain, Resulting from their Respective Stations, Professions and Employments.* London: printed for B. and J. White, Fleet Street, 1797. Fourth edition, 8vo., full contemporary calf, raised and gilt banded spines, red morocco labels, slight wear to upper rear hinge volume I, spines rubbed, 19th century note on inner front board, Ebbetston Library No. 84 in later hand, gift from Mrs. Baker. Jarndyce Antiquarian Books CCXV - 224 2016 £200

Association – Baldock, Martha

Kilner, Ann *A Course of Lectures for Sunday Evenings Containing Religious Advice to Young Persons.* London: printed and sold by John Marshall 124, 1737-1787. 12mo., ink splash to first titlepage, slight tear to gutter margin first half title, two volumes bound in one, contemporary quarter calf, marbled boards, vellum tips, board edges worn, some slight rubbing to joints, inscribed on front endpaper "Wm. Jones bought miss Baldock's sale 1845", signatures of Martha Baldock 1844 and Eleanor Jones. Jarndyce Antiquarian Booksellers CCXVI - 341 2016 £225

Association – Baldwin, Faith

Yeats-Brown, Francis *Golden Horn.* London: Gollancz, 1932. First edition, 8vo., inscribed by author to Faith Baldwin, with TLS with line in holograph signed, cover little worn and torn, else very good. Second Life Books, Inc. 196 B - 953 2016 $75

Association – Baldwin, Harold

La Fontaine, Jean De 1621-1695 *The Fables of La Fontaine.* New York: Viking, 1954. First edition, one of 400 large copies, large 8vo., fine copy, not signed by inscribed by translator, Marianne Moore for Dr. Harold Baldwin, red cloth, bookplate, neatly removed, fine. Second Life Books, Inc. 196 B - 259 2016 $325

Association – Baldwin, William

Valentia, George Annesley, Viscount *Voyages and Travels to India, Ceylon, The Red Sea, Abyssinia and Egypt in the Years 1802, 1803, 1804, 1805 and 1806.* London: William Miller, 1809. First edition, 3 volumes, 4to., full marbled calf, spines and borders of boards decorated in gilt in Grecian style, contrasting lettering pieces, marbled endpapers, 3 engraved vignettes, 60 engraved plates, 3 engraved folding plans at end of volume 3, very large folding map, 7 engraved folding maps and plans, rebacked at earlier date, wear to extremities, internally, apart from occasional spotting to plates and minor repairs to large map and light even toning to text, beautiful, wide margined and uniformly bound set, armorial engraved bookplates of William Baldwin, his name on two half titles. Sotheran's Travel and Exploration - 198 2016 £2995

Association – Ballett, Richard

Aelfric Grammaticus, Abbot of Eynsham *A Testimonie of Antiquitie.* John Day..., 1566? First edition of the first printed Old English text, fore-margin of titlepage sometime torn away (no loss of text, though slight loss to an early inscription at head of title), some mild dampstaining slightly more pronounced at end corners curling, but attractive and large copy, small 8vo., resewn in original binding of limp vellum, being a fragment of a 12th century manuscript, lacking spine, contemporary ownership inscription of Richard Ballett, twice, once in secretary hand and again in italic, early note on upper cover "Broughton Lib". Blackwell's Rare Books B184 - 2 2016 £12,000

Association – Bandram

Dickens, Charles 1812-1870 *The Poor Traveller; Boots at the Holly-Tree Inn; and Mrs. Gamp.* London: Bradbury & Evans, 1858. First edition, original green printed wrappers, stitching largely missing, spine defective, lacking back wrappers, signed 'Brandram' on front wrapper, with excisions, annotations and amendments in same hand, Bandram 1824-1892 was a barrister. Jarndyce Antiquarian Booksellers CCXVIII - 553 2016 £1500

Association – Bangs, E. Geoffrey

Browne, Lina Fergusson *J. Ross Browne, His Letters, Journals and Writings.* Albuquerque: University of New Mexico Press, 1969. First edition, presentation signed by author to fellow author, E. Geoffrey Bangs, 15 plates, brown cloth, fine with pictorial dust jacket. Argonaut Book Shop Biography 2015 - 3555 2016 $45

Association – Barber, Kate

Blessington, Marguerite Power Farmer Gardiner, Countess of 1789-1849 *The Keepsake for 1844.* London: Longmans, 1844. Engraved frontispiece and title plates, original maroon cloth, attractively blocked in blind and gilt, rebacked, little darkened and rubbed, signature of Kate Barber 1844, armorial bookplates of Algernon Graves, Renier booklabel.   Jarndyce Antiquarian Booksellers   CCXVIII - 430   2016   £120

Association – Barberini

Catholic Church. Liturgy & Ritual *Canon Missae cum Praefationibus & Aliis non Nullius quae in ea Fere Communiter Dicuntur.* Venice: Ciera, 1630. Large title vignette of Last Supper and full page engraving of the Crucifixion, both signed "Johan, Faber / fecit in Venetia", folio, contemporary Italian brown morocco over paste boards, covers richly gilt in fanfare style incorporating at centre three bees and a sunburst tool repeatedly stamped in inner panel and frame, both familiar emblems of the Barberini family (joints and corners rubbed, small burn hole to upper edge of lower cover), very finely gilt tooled 17th century Italian binding for a member of the Barberini dynasty, decorated with their familiar emblems of 3 bees and sunburst, signs of use throughout but exquisite binding.   Maggs Bros. Ltd.   1474 - 19   2016   £3500

Association – Barbier, George

Kaufman, George *Beggar on Horseback.* New York: Boni & Liveright, 1924. First edition, 8vo., 2 pages in the middle of text quite darkened from old news clipping that had been laid in, top edges of boards sunned, otherwise very good tight copy in very good, bright dust jacket, inscribed by producer Winthrop Ames to George Barbier who played Mr. Cady, also inscribed by both playwrights, George Kaufman and Marc Connelly, splendid association.   Second Life Books, Inc.   196A - 913   2016 $1500

Association – Barclay, Charles

Saint Pierre, Jacques Henri Bernardin De 1737-1814 *Paul and Mary an Indian Story.* London: printed for J. Dodsley, Pall Mall, 1789. 2 volumes, bound without half titles, 12mo., tears with slight loss to blank lower margin of few leaves, final blank removal from end of volume II, early 19th century half calf, gilt banded spines, black labels, marbled boards, some rubbing and slight wear to middle of spine volume II, one section little loose, armorial bookplate of Charles Barclay and W. Douro Hoare.   Jarndyce Antiquarian Booksellers   CCXVI - 505   2016   £150

Association – Baring, Maurice

Eliot, George, Pseud. 1819-1880 *Adam Bede.* Edinburgh and London: William Blackwood and Son, 1859. Third edition, 3 volumes, 8vo., few spots and minor stains, text block broken in volume ii and couple of gatherings round, original russet pebble grained cloth, blind stamped panels on sides, spine gilt lettered, corners little worn, hinges strained, Maurice Baring's copy with his bookplate in volumes ii and iii, and his signature.   Blackwell's Rare Books   B184 - 38   2016   £100

Association – Barken, Ben

Levy, Jacques *Cesar Chavez: Autobiography of La Causa.* New York: W. W. Norton, 1975. First edition, inscribed by Chavez for Ben Barken, fine in bright, near fine dust jacket.   Royal Books   48 - 79   2016 $350

Association – Barker, Anthony

Robinson, Thomas *An Essays Towards a National History of Westmorland and Cumberland.* London: printed by J. L. for W. Freeman, 1709. 8vo., lower edge of final ad leaf worn and repaired with no loss of text, some light browning and occasional minor foxing, 19th century ownership name, Anthony Barker at head of titlepage, expertly bound in recent quarter mottled calf, raised and gilt banded spine, red morocco label, marbled boards, vellum tips.   Jarndyce Antiquarian Booksellers   CCXVI - 496   2016   £380

Association – Barker, Roy

Shakespeare, William 1564-1616 *Troilus and Creside.* New York: Limited Editions Club, 1939. 153/950 copies, frontispiece and 5 further full page wood engravings printed in black and brown, folio, original tan buckram with patterned boards, backstrip little darkened and lettered gilt, touch of wear to corners, top edge gilt, others untrimmed and lightly toned, bookplate and ownership inscription of Roy. C. Barker, 4 page descriptive leaflet laid in, very good.   Blackwell's Rare Books   B186 - 316   2016   £60

Association – Barker, Star

Jones, Charlotte Rosalys *The Hypnotic Experiment of Dr. Reeves and other Stories.* London and New York: Bliss, Sands and Foster, Brentano's, 1894. First edition, brown cloth with delicate cream and green design in gilt, edges worn and chipped, interior pages have some browning along margins, some splitting of signatures but text block remains solid, very good, presentation copy from author to Star Barker, further inscribed to Karl Martin.   The Kelmscott Bookshop   12 - 58   2016 $300

Association – Barla, Barbara

Gregory, John *A Father's Legacy to His Daughters.* London: John Sharpe, 1822. Half title, frontispiece and plates, full tan calf, blocked in blind and gilt, raised bands, compartments in gilt, maroon morocco label, little rubbed, contemporary calligraphic ownership signature of Miss Barbara Barla, bookseller's ticket, Maurice Ogle, Glasgow, nice copy.   Jarndyce Antiquarian Books   CCXV - 233   2016   £50

Association – Barnard, John

Quarles, Francis *Divine Poems.* London: by Edward Okes for Benjamin Tooke and Thomas Sawbridge...., 1669. 8vo., engraved frontispiece/title, engraved title and final leaf repaired and strengthened at fore edge, later 20th century calf, from the library of James Stevens Cox (1910-1997), various pen trials, inscription "John Barnard/of Fallm(outh); in/Cornwall" and "To James Edgecom/John Symmons", presumably of Edgcumbe or Edgcombe.   Maggs Bros. Ltd.   1447 - 345   2016   £180

Association – Barnes, Djuna

Ford, Charles Henri *Poems for Painters.* New York: View Editions, 1945. First edition, quarto, wrappers illustrated by Pavel Tchelitchew, this is copy number 24 of 500 copies, signed by author (of a total edition of 1500), near fine in stapled wrappers with some light soiling and modest age toning, inscribed by author for Djuna Barnes.   Between the Covers Rare Books   204 - 49   2016 $950

Association – Barnes, Julian

Daudet, Alphonse *In the Land of Pain.* London: Jonathan Cape, 2002. First Julian Barnes edition, frontispiece, foolscap 8vo., original black boards, backstrip lettered gilt, dust jacket with 'signed copy' sticker to front, fine, signed by Barnes.   Blackwell's Rare Books   B184 - 102   2016   £35

Kriegel, Volker *The Truth About Dogs.* Bloomsbury: 1988. First Julian Barnes edition, Kriegel cartoons, 12mo., original yellow boards, backstrip lettered gilt, dust jacket near fine, signed by Julian Barnes, beneath his crossed through printed name.   Blackwell's Rare Books   B184 - 107   2016   £35

Association – Barnett, H. Raymond

Worlidge, John *Systema Agriculturae the Mystery of Husbandry Discovered.* London: by T. Johnson for Samuel Speed, 1669. First edition, folio, additional engraved titlepage, woodcut illustrations, frontispiece with three wormholes, lower edge of engraved title repaired, small wormhole in middle of first three leaves, small wormhole in blank margin of gatherings A-H, occasional light browning, circular stain to Mm1, contemporary sheep, spine with red morocco and gilt label, covers heavily scuffed, corners bumped, upper headcap torn, lower corner of rear board cracked, H. Raymond Barnett, modern bookplate, from the library of James Stevens Cox (1910-1997).   Maggs Bros. Ltd.   1447 - 465   2016   £350

Association – Barney, Nora Stanton

Blatch, Harriot Stanton *Challenging Years.* New York: Putnams, 1940. First edition, 8vo., very nice in dust jacket, inscribed by author's daughter, Nora Stanton Barney to Winifred A. Tyler.   Second Life Books, Inc.   196A - 157   2016 $150

Association – Barrett, Fred

Leacock, Stephen *The Dry Pickwick and Other Congruities.* London: John Lane, Bodley Head, 1932. First edition, half title, 8 pages ads, original purple cloth lettered in white, spine faded, contemporary pencil signature of Fred Barrett.   Jarndyce Antiquarian Booksellers   CCXVIII - 152   2016   £25

Association – Bartek, Zenka

Thomas, Caitlin *Caitlin - a Warring Absence.* London: Secker & Warburg, 1986. First edition, photos, signed by author, presentation from Thomas's daughter to Judith Karolyi and Zenka Bartek, covers slightly marked, very good in like dust jacket, slightly creased.   Peter Ellis   112 - 400   2016   £85

Association – Barth, John

Lewis, Leon *The Landscape of Contemporary Cinema.* Buffalo: Buffalo Spectrum Press, 1967. First edition, octavo, illustrated perfect bound wrapper, very slight soiling on wrappers, still fine, inscribed by William David Sherman to author John Barth with Barth's ownership signature and ownership stamp, laid in ALS from Sherman to Barth sending the book.   Between the Covers Rare Books   204 - 43   2016 $225

Association – Bartlett, L., Mrs.

Martin, Francois Xavier *The History of Louisiana from the Earliest Period.* New Orleans: printed by Lyman and Beardslee and A. T. Penniman & Co., 1827. First edition, 2 volumes, 248 x 165mm., pleasing later 19th century dark green crushed morocco by Stikeman (signed on front turn-in), covers with triple gilt fillet border and floral sprig corner-pieces, raised bands, spines densely gilt in compartments with center floral sprig in oval medallion, surrounded by swirling gilt tooling accented with small tools, gilt titling, gilt turn-ins, marbled endpapers, top edges gilt, other edges entirely untrimmed, front pastedown with leather bookplate of Marshall Clifford Lefferts and bookplate of Mrs. L. Bartlett, spines sunned to pleasing honey brown (covers bit sunned at edges, with front cover volume II inconspicuously sunned, and showing the darker silhouette of a bookend), few small stains to edges of same board, bindings virtually unworn and otherwise quite pleasing, minor foxing or browning throughout (no doubt affecting all copies because of inferior paper stock), five quires in volume I with one inch dampstain at head, one gathering in volume II noticeably browned, not without condition issues, but with much to please internally, including vast margins, consistent freshness and absence of soiling.   Phillip J. Pirages   67 - 250   2016 $1800

Association – Barton, Clara

Societes De La Froix-Rogue *Troisieme Conference Internationale Des Societes De La Croix-Rogue. Tenue A Geneve Du Ier Au 6 Septembre 1884. Compte Renu.* Geneve: Au Siege Comite International de al Croix Rouge, 1885. First edition, 4to., original blue cloth binding with silver stamped lettering to spine and front board, accompanied by impressed silver and red Red cross logo, housed in custom chemise and quarter leather slipcase with marbled paper boards, volume shows wear and evidence of dampstaining, rear hinge paper starting at bottom, about very good, chemise and slipcase fine, presentation copy inscribed by Clara Barton for Dr. Joseph Gardner March 15 1889.   Tavistock Books   Bibliolatry - 19   2016 $4250

Association – Bartram, Geoffrey

Smythe, F. S. *Kamet Conquered.* London: Victor Gollancz, 1932. First edition, 8vo., original back cloth, spine lettered gilt, 59 black and white photograph plates and full page maps, one foldinj, map at end, light wear to extremities, front inner hinge expertly strengthened, frontispiece and titles, little spotted, typewritten letter from author to Geoffrey Bartram to whom the book is inscribed.   Sotheran's   Travel and Exploration - 183   2016   £498

Association – Barwis

Ruskin, John 1819-1900 *Dame Wiggins of Lee and Her Seven Wonderful Cats.* Sunnyside, Orpington, Kent: George Allen, 1885. Large paper copy from a later edition, inscribed by the artist, Kate Greenaway for F. Locker-Lampson, 1886, illustrations by Greenaway, original brown cloth with gilt title and illustration on front cover, binding rubbed and bumped, with few light stains, interior pages are generally clean, this copy has a plate of Bert M. Barwis Fund of Trenton Public Library stating the book was a personal gift to the library from Miss Barwis, she was the Supervisor of Kindergartens and Primary Schools for the City of Trenton NJ, call number written in white ink on spine and library ownership indicated by stamp to titlepage, despite flaws, still very nice, desirable copy.   The Kelmscott Bookshop   12 - 48   2016 $400

Association – Baskin, Leonard

Browne, Thomas *Of Garlands and Coronary or Garland Plants .... to John Evelyn.* Northampton: Gehenna Press, 1962. wrappers, uncut, fine signed by Leoanrd Baskin. Second Life Books, Inc.   196A - 625   2016 $100

Association – Bass, Frances

Jameson, Anna Brownell 1794-1860 *Characteristics of Women, Moral, Poetical and Historical.* London: Saunders & Otley, 1832. First edition, 2 volumes, half titles volume I, illustrated with tiny vignette etchings bound in later olive green binder's cloth, maroon leather labels, spines slightly foxed, contemporary signature of Frances Bass on half title, later signature E. V. Arnold, good plus.   Jarndyce Antiquarian Books   CCXV - 272   2016   £150

Association – Bassi, Bruno

Plato *The Works of Plato Abridg'd.* London: printed for A. Bell, 1701. First English edition, few leaves browned or spotted, one or two corrections in manuscript, faint dampmark to upper forecorner of first 50 leaves, 8vo., contemporary Cambridge stype panelled calf, red morocco label to spine, slightly rubbed and marked bookplate of Seton of Ekoslund and ownership inscription of Duncan Campbell, more recent chess bookplate of Bruno Bassi, name 'Greeg' in blank area of first page of text, blindstamped. Blackwell's Rare Books   Greek & Latin Classics VII - 73   2016   £2500

Association – Bastard, Edward

Caswall, Edward *A New Art Teaching How to be Plucked Being a Treatise after the Fashion of Aristotle...* Oxford: J. Vincent, 1835. Second edition, 12mo., contemporary full red calf, limp boards, slightly rubbed and dulled, but nice, ownership Edward W. Bastard 1877.   Jarndyce Antiquarian Books   CCXV - 585   2016   £65

Association – Bates, H. E.

Greene, Graham 1904-1991 *The Old School. Essays by Divers Hands.* London: Jonathan Cape, 1934. First edition, faint foxing to prelims and final text pages, occasional faint spot further in, 8vo., original black cloth lettered in blue to upper board with publisher's device in same to lower backstrip lettered in blue, few faint foxspots to gently toned edges, tail edge rough trimmed, few faint spots to endpapers, good, bright copy, scarce edition, with 1 page ALS from H. E. Bates to Greene. Blackwell's Rare Books B186 - 225   2016   £800

Association – Bathurst, Mrs.

Trimmer, Sarah *Some Account of the Life and Writings of Mrs. Trimmer...* London: printed for F. C. and J. Rivington, 1816. Second edition, 2 volumes, half titles, final ad leaf, volume II, contemporary full calf, double ruled gilt borders, raised bands, gilt compartments, neat repairs to hinges, inscription Mary Thornhill the gift of Mrs. Bathurst 1816. Jarndyce Antiquarian Books CCXV - 968   2016   £225

Association – Battson, Lucy Smith Doheny

Soames, Henry *An Inquiry into the Doctrines of the Anglo-Saxon Church in Eight Sermons.* Oxford: Samuel Collingwood, Printer to the University for C. J. G. and F. Rivington, 1830. First edition, 220 x 140mm, very decorative contemporary deep purple straight grain morocco, covers with frame of multiple gilt and blind fillets and featuring a dense gilt roll interlacing at medians, and broad-leaf ornaments, broad raised bands, spine compartments with interlaced lobed ribbons, cornerpieces and central massed tools, turn-ins gilt ruled, moire silk endleaves, all edges gilt with very pleasing fore-edge painting of Canterbury Cathedral, housed in unusually fine, heavily gilt pebble grain morocco clamshell box in convincing imitation of the present binding, armorial bookplate, morocco bookplate of Lucy Smith (Doheny) Battson, lower cover with uneven fading, spine darkened with consequent dulling of gilt, light wear to extremities and joints, otherwise excellent, once extremely pretty binding still appealing with glistening gilt on covers, text very bright, fresh and clean and fore-edge painting perfectly preserved.   Phillip J. Pirages 67 - 163   2016 $2400

Association – Battye, Ivan

Batty, John *The Spirit and Influence of Chivalry.* London: Elliot Stock, 1890. First edition, half title, erratum leaf, slight paper browning, uncut in original olive green cloth, bevelled boards, little rubbed, lower corners slightly worn, 4 page ALS from Batty, 1891 tipped in opposite leading f.e.p., signatures of Richmond Battye 1894 and Ivan(?) Battye 1898.   Jarndyce Antiquarian Books   CCXV - 40   2016   £45

Association – Battye, Richmond

Batty, John *The Spirit and Influence of Chivalry.* London: Elliot Stock, 1890. First edition, half title, erratum leaf, slight paper browning, uncut in original olive green cloth, bevelled boards, little rubbed, lower corners slightly worn, 4 page ALS from Batty, 1891 tipped in opposite leading f.e.p., signatures of Richmond Battye 1894 and Ivan(?) Battye 1898.   Jarndyce Antiquarian Books   CCXV - 40   2016   £45

Association – Bawden, Edward

Malory, Thomas *Sir Thomas Malory's Chronicles of King Arthur.* London: Folio Society, 1982. 3 volumes, 8vo., full red leather with decorative gilt stamping to spines and covers, signed on half title by artist, Edward Bawden, faint rubbing and slight fading at spines, otherwise fine in very good+ slipcase.   Any Amount of Books   2015 - A91761   2016   £170

Association – Baxter, Alexander

Lucianus Samosatensis *Dialogorum Selectorum Libri Duo Graecolatini.* Ingolstadt: Ex officinia typogrpahica Adami Sartorii, 1598. 8vo., final blank discarded, errata leaf present, top margin of last few leaves worn (with loss to running title), titlepage dust soiled and bit frayed at fore-margin, small paper flaw in leaf y4 affecting few characters, occasional marginal annotations in Latin and Greek in early hand, gathering v bound out of order, 8vo, contemporary dark sheep, paper label to spine, rubbed and scratched, some wear to joints, leather since treated to conserve it, various inscriptions in English, Latin and Greek - Andrew Baxter and his son Alexander of Duns Castle, also of Thomas Mein.   Blackwell's Rare Books   Greek & Latin Classics VII - 58   2016   £750

Association – Baxter, Andrew

Lucianus Samosatensis *Dialogorum Selectorum Libri Duo Graecolatini.* Ingolstadt: Ex officinia typogrpahica Adami Sartorii, 1598. 8vo., final blank discarded, errata leaf present, top margin of last few leaves worn (with loss to running title), titlepage dust soiled and bit frayed at fore-margin, small paper flaw in leaf y4 affecting few characters, occasional marginal annotations in Latin and Greek in early hand, gathering v bound out of order, 8vo, contemporary dark sheep, paper label to spine, rubbed and scratched, some wear to joints, leather since treated to conserve it, various inscriptions in English, Latin and Greek - Andrew Baxter and his son Alexander of Duns Castle, also of Thomas Mein.   Blackwell's Rare Books   Greek & Latin Classics VII - 58   2016   £750

Association – Baxter, Jerry

Stevens, Wallace 1879-1955 *The Collected Poems.* New York: Alfred A. Knopf, 1954. First edition, one of 2500 numbered copies, presentation copy inscribed by author Oct. 4 1954 for Jerry Baxter, booklabel on front pastedown, otherwise fine in dust jacket lightly sunned along spine panel with 1 3/4 inch triangular chip along top edge of front panel affecting letters. James S. Jaffe Rare Books Occasional List: Winter 2016 - 133 2016 $5000

Association – Baylis, James

Neale, Charles Montague *An Index to Pickwick.* London: printed for the author by J. Hitchcock, 1897. 4to., addenda slip tipped in uncut in grey printed boards, green cloth spine, little rubbed, leading inner hinge starting, contemporary signature of James H. Baylis. Jarndyce Antiquarian Booksellers CCXVIII - 159 2016 £30

Association – Baynes, Mary

The Gentleman's Library, Containing Rules for Conduct in all Parts of Life. London: printed for E. P. for W. Mears, 1715. First edition, 12mo., frontispiece, contemporary panelled calf, later faded and worn paper label, some expert repairs, ownership inscription of Mary Baynes, good plus. Jarndyce Antiquarian Books CCXV - 218 2016 £520

Association – Baynes, Pauline

Williams-Ellis, Amabel *Fairy Tales from the British Isles.* London & Glasgow: Blackie, 1960. First edition, color frontispiece and 7 color printed plates, titlepage with vignette printed in red and black, further illustrations by Pauline Baynes throughout text with initial headpiece printed in red and black, one or two faint spots to half title 8vo., original red cloth with few faint spots to this and to fore-edge, color printed endpapers, dust jacket lightly toned in places, laminate lifting little along joint folds, very good, signed by artist. Blackwell's Rare Books B186 - 181 2016 £700

Association – Beaglehole, J. C.

Gosse, Philip *The Pirates 'Who's Who' giving Particulars of the Lives and Deaths of the Pirates and Buccaneers.* London: Dulau, 1924. First edition, 8vo., map on endpapers, 6 plates, original red cloth, from the library of J. C. Beaglehole. J. & S. L. Bonham Antiquarian Booksellers America 2016 - 9924 2016 £70

Association – Beard, Joseph

Keach, Benjamin *War with the Devil; or the Young Man's Conflict with the Powers of Darkness.* London: printed for H. P. and sold by Han(nah) Tracy, n.d. circa, 1720. 18th impression, Small 8vo., 19th century divinity calf, red edges, double page woodcut frontispiece (neatly trimmed and mounted), 15 further woodcuts in text, excellent, armorial bookplate of Joseph Beard of Alderley, later book label of L. G. E. Bell. C. R. Johnson Rare Book Collections Foxon: H-P 2015 - 509 2016 $689

Association – Bearden, Romare

Washington, M. Bunch *The Art of Romare Bearden: the Prevalance of Ritual.* New York: Harry N. Abrams Inc., 1972. First edition, folio, bit of foxing on fore edge and first and last few leaves, spine tail bumped with half inch tears at joints, else near fine copy in like dust jacket with corresponding tears on spine tail, press release for the book laid in, inscribed by Bearden for Richard Long. Between the Covers Rare Books 202 - 9 2016 $1500

Association – Beaumont, Hugh

Ervine, St. John *Robert's Wife: aa Comedy in Three Acts.* London: Allen & Unwin, 1938. First edition, 8vo., very good, inscribed by author to actor Hugh Beaumont, this a round robin book signed by 15 members of cast and crew. Second Life Books, Inc. 196A - 539 2016 $450

Mallory, Jay *Sweet aloes: a Play in Three Acts.* London: Cassell, 1935. First edition, orange cloth, very good, tight copy, inscribed by author for producer Hugh Beaumont, also inscribed by actress, Joyce Carey, and signed by 12 members of the cast. Second Life Books, Inc. 196 B - 126 2016 $225

Van Druten, John *Old Acquaintance.* New York: Random House, 1941. First edition, 8vo., no dust jacket but very good copy, signed by cast of the play, bookplate of critic Hugh Beaumont. Second Life Books, Inc. 196 B - 791 2016 $175

Association – Beckford, William

Silius, Italicus *De Secundo Bello Punico.* Amsterdam: G. Jansson, 1620. Engraved titlepage, ruled in red, 16mo., exquisite binding by Mace Ruette, contemporary gilt tooled red morocco, covers framed by outer double fillet, central panel of strait and curved double fillets with small vase of flowers tool at each outer corner in centre of covers a quadrilobe inlay with monogram of H. L. Habert de Montmort and four "S" forms with elaborate pointille sprays of spirals, circles and dots on all four sides, spine with five raised bands, decorated in compartments, inner edges gilt, marbled endpapers, gilt edges, headcaps and joints lightly rubbed, the copy of Habert de Montmort (1600-1679), Colonel Thomas Stanley (1749-1818), William Beckford with his bookseller George Clarke's pencil collation mark, Hamilton Palace Library sale, Thore Virgin inscription dated 1916 with his book label (1886-1957). Maggs Bros. Ltd. 1474 - 72   2016   £2500

Association – Bective

Maitland, James A. *Reminiscences of a Retired Physician.* London: G. Routledge and Co., 1854. First edition, little cut down in contemporary half purple calf, spine gilt, slightly faded, from the Headfort Library, signed Bective 1854. Jarndyce Antiquarian Booksellers   CCXVII - 176   2016   £65

Maxwell, William Hamilton *Rambling Recollections of a Soldier of Fortune.* Dublin: William Curry, Jun. & Co., 1842. Frontispiece and plates by Phiz, frontispiece, slightly foxed, contemporary half brown calf, maroon morocco label, slightly rubbed with slight sign of library label removal from spine, from the Headfort library, 'Bective 1856', nice copy. Jarndyce Antiquarian Booksellers   CCXVII - 183   2016   £150

Association – Bedford, Duke of

Hammer, Meredith *The Auncient Ecclesiastical Histories of the First Six Hundred Yeares After Christ.* London: Richard Field, 1129. Third edition, folio, gap in pagination as called for but lacking first and final blank, separate half title to each section with woodcut device, woodcut decorations, very lightly toned towards edges, few underlinings, occasional specks of wax, green morocco with green cloth boards, previous spine label retained, endpapers and endbands renewed, very good, armorial bookplate of John (Russell), Duke of Bedford. Unsworths Antiquarian Booksellers   30 - 55   2016   £650

Zincke, Forster Barham *Some Thoughts about the School of the Future....* London: Longman, Brown, Green & Longmans, 1852. Half title, stain to upper margin of first 3 leaves, original purple cloth, spine faded and little dulled and marked, presentation inscription to the Duke of Bedford. Jarndyce Antiquarian Books   CCXV - 1019   2016   £180

Association – Beeson, G.

Russell, Bertrand 1872-1970 *On Education, Especially in Early Childhood.* London: George Allen & Unwin, 1927. Third edition, half title, final ad leaf, original blue cloth, blocked in red, slightly rubbed, signature of G. Beeson. Jarndyce Antiquarian Books   CCXV - 929   2016   £20

Association – Beeson, W.

Medicina Flagellata; or the Doctor Scarified. London: printed for J. Bateman and J. Nicks, 1721. First edition, with additional letterpress title with engraved vignette, 8vo., contemporary tree calf, flat spine gilt in compartments, red lettering piece, minor wear, top of upper joint snagged, foot of spine chipped, contemporary signature of W. Beeson, MD, engraved bookplate of Sir Thomas Hesketh and Easton Neston Library shelf label, very good. Blackwell's Rare Books   B186 - 126   2016   £550

Association – Beeton, Mayson

Malton, Thomas *Views of Oxford.* London: White & Co.; Oxford: R. Smith, 1810. First complete edition, appealing 19th century (circa 1860's?), dark green half morocco over lighter green textured cloth by T. Aitken (stamp signed), upper cover with gilt titling, raised bands, spine gilt in compartments with elongated fleuron centerpiece and scrolling cornerpieces, gilt titling, marbled endpapers, all edges gilt (small, very expert repairs to upper outer corners and perhaps at top of joints), mezzotint frontispiece, engraved title, 30 fine plates of interior and exterior views, armorial bookplates of Sir Mayson M. Beeton and Sir Richard Farrant, verso of front free endpaper, ink presentation inscription from author for Sir Charles Locock, Nov. 1860, subscription proposal for work printed by T. Bensley and dated "London, May 30, 1301 (i.e. 1801)", laid in at front, couple of small smudges to boards, portrait faintly foxed and browned, isolated small stains, not affecting images, but fine, plates especially clean and fresh, smooth and pleasing binding with virtually no wear. Phillip J. Pirages   67 - 248   2016 $8500

Association – Bell, Clive

Sassoon, Siegfried Lorraine 1886-1967 *Poems.* London: Duckworth, 1931. First edition, crown 8vo., couple of occasional faint foxspots at head of pages and light handling marks, original black boards, stamped in green to upper board, faint foxing to free endpapers, very good, this copy inscribed by Christabel McLaren May 14th 1931 to Clive Bell. Blackwell's Rare Books   B186 - 280   2016   £100

Association – Bell, Elizabeth

Homerus *The Iliad of Homer. (with) The Odyssey of Homer.* London: printed for J. Whiston &c., 1771. 1771, Iliad in 4 volumes, Odyssey in 5 volumes, together 9 volumes, engraved portraits, 2 plates, 2 folding maps, folding plate uniformly bound in slightly later full sprinkled calf, spines gilt in compartments, maroon and green morocco labels, armorial bookplate in all volumes of Elizabeth Bell, very good, attractive set, fine in 18th century binding. Jarndyce Antiquarian Booksellers   CCXVII - 232   2016   £4250

Association – Bell, James

Settle, Elkanah *The New Athenian Comedy...* London: for Campanella Restio, 1693. First edition, small 4to., browned throughout, author's name written in pencil on titlepage, late 19th century half morocco and marbled boards by Kerr and Richardson (head and foot of spine chipped, front joint lightly chipped), from the library of James Stevens Cox (1910-1997), 20th century signature of James Bell.   Maggs Bros. Ltd.   1447 - 379   2016   £250

Association – Bell, L. G. E.

Keach, Benjamin *War with the Devil; or the Young Man's Conflict with the Powers of Darkness.* London: printed for H. P. and sold by Han(nah) Tracy, n.d. circa, 1720. 18th impression, Small 8vo., 19th century divinity calf, red edges, double page woodcut frontispiece (neatly trimmed and mounted), 15 further woodcuts in text, excellent, armorial bookplate of Joseph Beard of Alderley, later book label of L. G. E. Bell.   C. R. Johnson Rare Book Collections   Foxon: H-P 2015 - 509   2016 $689

Association – Bell, Madison Smartt

Chute, Carolyn *The Beans of Egypt, Maine.* New York: Ticknor and Fields, 1985. Uncorrected proof, with long inscription from author to fellow author Madison Smartt Bell, with Madison Smartt Bell's ownership signature, further inscribed years later by Chute for book collector Rolland Comstock, faint crease to front cover likely from so much inscribing, near fine in wrappers, laid in is folded five page press release from Ticknor, wonderful association.   Ken Lopez Bookseller   166 - 21   2016 $500

Association – Bell, Marion

Linton, William *Colossal Vestiages of the Older nations.* London: Longman, Green, Longman & Roberts, 1862. First edition, frontispiece, foldout diagram, untrimmed in original red wavy grained cloth, blocked in blind, front board lettered gilt, some minor repairs to head and tail of spine, bookplates of Charles Dickens, Sara R. Dunn and J. R. Ainslie, with "from the Library of Charles Dickens" label, very good in brown cloth foldover box, inscribed by Marion Bell to Dickens.   Jarndyce Antiquarian Booksellers   CCXVIII - 871   2016   £1650

Association – Bell, Nathalie

Dahl, Roald *Someone Like You.* New York: Alfred Knopf, 1953. First edition, gift inscription from author for Nathalie Bell Nov. 9th 1953, tiny bump to top and bottom front corners, former owner's neat stamped name and address on front pastedown sheet (completely covered by front jacket flap), else near fine, bright copy in jacket lightly rubbed at head of spine, excellent copy.   Buckingham Books   2015 - 37651   2016 $3750

Association – Bell, Susan

Mott, Abigail *Observations on the Importance of Female Education and Maternal Instruction with Their Beneficial Influence on Society.* New York: printed and sold by Mahlon Day, 1825. First edition, 12mo., old boards, detached, title loose, printed copyright slip pasted to verso of title leaf, printed early bookplate of Susan Bell.   M & S Rare Books, Inc.   99 - 338   2016 $1250

Association – Bellamy, Emma

Bellamy, Edward *Looking Backward 2000-1887.* Boston: Houghton Mifflin, 1926. 8vo., very good in publisher's cloth, stain at hinge of rear endpaper, inscribed by author's wife, Emma for Walter James Henry, also inscribed by Bellamy's daughter, Marian Bellamy Ernshaw, laid in 9 x 6 inch handbill advertising talk given by Marian and Emma Bellamy. Second Life Books, Inc.   196A - 103   2016 $300

Association – Belper, Edward Strutt, 1st Baron

Ure, Andrew *The Philosophy of Manufactures....* London: Charles Knight, Ludgate Street, 1835. First edition, 8vo., engraved frontispiece, 1 folding engraving, 1 folding table, engraved illustrations and tables in text, some foxing to title and frontispiece and folding plate common to many copies of this work, contemporary half calf, spine with red label lettered in gilt restored, bookplate of Edward Strutt, first Baron Belper (1801-1880).   Marlborough Rare Books   List 55 - 70   2016   £150

Association – Belt, Benjamin Lloyd

Burns, Robert *The Poems and Songs of Robert Burns.* London: George Newnes Ltd., 1902. 165 x 102mm., very fine crimson morocco lavishly and intricately gilt in a 'Scottish Wheel' design by Morrell (stamp signed on front turn-ins), covers with large central wheel of 20 compartments, each containing elegant gossamer floral tools between two lines of dots radiating from a central rosette, massed tiny circle tools at head and foot of wheel, above and below these circle tools, triangle formed by small scalloped compartments and multiple tiny flowers, corners with large leaf frond tools and covers generally with many accenting small tools, raised bands, spine compartments, with large quatrefoil containing central daisy radiating floral tools surrounded by gilt dots, elegantly and elaborately gilt turn-ins in swag pattern, ivory watered silk endleaves, all edges gilt, rear joint very expertly renewed, frontispiece, rear free endpaper with ink presentation to Ozite Fleming Cox from Benjamin Lloyd Belt dated May 8 1906, front joint beginning to show a thin crack (but mostly masked with dye), paper stock little dingy (as not doubt in all copies), otherwise very fine, covers and spine unworn and lustrous and text without signs of use.   Phillip J. Pirages   67 - 58   2016 $850

Association – Belyea, Mrs.

Tarkington, Booth *Image of Josephine.*   New York: Doubleday, 1945. 8vo., fine in dust jacket, this lacks 'first edition' slug on copyright page, inscribed by author for Mrs. Belyea.   Second Life Books, Inc.   196 B - 733   2016 $75

Association – Bemens, Clarence

Maidment, James *A Book of Scotish Pasquils 1568-1715.* Edinburgh: William Paterson, 1868. One of 3 copies on vellum (and limited but unspecified number of copies printed on paper), 210 x 130mm., handsome contemporary crimson morocco, attractively gilt by Andrew Grieve (stamp signed on front turn-in), covers gilt with multiple plain and decorative rules enclosing a delicate frame, large and intricate fleuron at center of each cover, spine gilt in double ruled compartments with complex fleuron centerpiece and scrolling floral cornerpieces, turn-ins decorated with plain and decorative gilt rules, patterned burgundy and gold silk endleaves, top edge gilt, slightly worn matching morocco lipped slipcase, woodcut titlepage illustrations, numerous decorative tailpieces and occasional woodcut vignettes in text, front pastedown with armorial bookplate of H. D. Colvill-Scott, armorial bookplate of Clarence S. Bemens, tiny dark spot on spine corners and just hint of rubbing, couple of leaves with slightly rumpled fore edge, still fine, text clean, smooth and bright and binding unusually lustrous, virtually no wear.   Phillip J. Pirages   67 - 346   2016 $4500

Association – Bender, Albert

Bottome, Phyllis *Stella Benson.* San Francisco: Grabhorn Press, 1934. First edition, 250 copies printed, small 8vo., title printed in red and black, marginal titles, initial and colophon in red, handset Garamond type, Oxford gray cloth boards with yellow spine, paper label printed in red on front cover, spine slightly darkened, but very fine, from the collection of Carl I. Wheat, inscribed by Wheat "From the Library of Albert Bender".   Argonaut Book Shop Private Press 2015 - 6276   2016 $60

Association – Benet, Stephen Vincent

Aiken, Conrad   *The Jug of Forslin.*   Boston: Four Seas, 1916. 8vo., bookplate of Thomas Caldecot Chubb, and his name in ink dated Oct. 1919, also signed by Stephen Vincent Benet who signed Christmas 1916, brown stain, top edges darkened, edges of cover and ends of spine little worn, rear cover little spotted, otherwise very good, tight.   Second Life Books, Inc.   197 - 2   2016 $125

Association – Benet, William Rose

Wylie, Elinor   1885-1928   *Collected Poems.* New York: Knopf, 1932. First edition, one of 210 copies numbered and signed by editor, William Rose Benet, 8vo., front flyleaf missing, rear hinge tender, cover little worn, otherwise very good.   Second Life Books, Inc.   196 B - 946   2016 $45

Association – Benjamin, Walter

Deutsche Menschen. Eine Folge Von Briefen.   Luzern: Vita Nova Verlag, 1936. First edition, one of 2000 copies, 8vo., original cloth, presentation copy inscribed by Walter Benjamin for film maker Hans Richter, rare, important association copy, buff linen lightly soiled, otherwise very good, rare inscribed.   James S. Jaffe Rare Books   Occasional List: Winter 2016 - 31   2016 $27,500

Association – Benkovitz, Miriam

Douglas, Norman   1868-1952   *Together.* London: Chapman & Hall, 1923. First edition, 2 plates, foxing ot half title, occasional spots further in, 8vo., original maroon cloth, backstrip lettered gilt and faded, couple of small marks at foot, rubbing to extremities with mottling to leading edge of both boards, successive bookplates of Lytton Strachey and Miriam Benkovitz, with ownership gift inscription by these respective owners, very good, significant association.   Blackwell's Rare Books   B186 - 209   2016   £150

Association – Bennet, Joan

Hirschhorn, Clive *The Films of James Mason.* London: LSP Books, 1975. 4to., heavily illustrated, signatures of Mason and his second wife Clarissa and Joan Bennet, appearing on their pictures, very good in chipped and soiled dust jacket.   Second Life Books, Inc.   196A - 799   2016 $225

Association – Bennet, R. H. A.

Morgan, Sydney Owenson *France.* London: Henry Colburn, 1817. First edition, 4to., 2 volumes in 1, map, contemporary diced calf, spine fully gilt in panels, edges marbled, corners worn, hinges cracked but held by cords and endpapers, light scattered foxing on few gatherings, else fine internally in very nice period binding, R. H. A. Bennet armorial bookplate.   Joseph J. Felcone, Inc.   Books from Five Centuries: a Miscellany - 107   2016 $800

Association – Benyon, H. E.

Stanhope, Eugenia *The Deportment of a Married Life laid Down in a Series of Letters...* London: printed for Mr. Hodges Pall Mall, 1798. 8vo., some browning to final leaves, contemporary tree calf, rebacked retaining original spine, inscribed "H. E. Benyon from EB 1800".   Jarndyce Antiquarian Books   CCXV - 421   2016   £220

Association – Berger, Mildred

Berger, Thomas *Little Big Man.* New York: Dial Press, 1964. First edition, staining on top edge, very good in moderately rubbed, very good or better dust jacket with shallow chip at foot inscribed by author for his parents.   Between the Covers Rare Books   204 - 13   2016 $7500

Berger, Thomas *Reinhart in Love.* New York: Charles Scribner's Sons, 1962. First edition, stains along edges of boards, thus sound, but good only in good but presentable dust jacket with corresponding stain visible only on rear panel, dedication copy inscribed by author to his parents.   Between the Covers Rare Books   204 - 2   2016 $4500

Association – Berger, Thomas Charles

Berger, Thomas *Little Big Man.* New York: Dial Press, 1964. First edition, staining on top edge, very good in moderately rubbed, very good or better dust jacket with shallow chip at foot inscribed by author for his parents.   Between the Covers Rare Books   204 - 13   2016 $7500

Berger, Thomas *Reinhart in Love.* New York: Charles Scribner's Sons, 1962. First edition, stains along edges of boards, thus sound, but good only in good but presentable dust jacket with corresponding stain visible only on rear panel, dedication copy inscribed by author to his parents.   Between the Covers Rare Books   204 - 2   2016 $4500

Association – Berland, Abel

Carter, John   1905-1975 *An Enquiry into the Nature of Certain Nineteenth Century Pamphlets.* London: Constable & Co., 1934. First edition, 8vo., cloth, top edge gilt, dust jacket, this copy inscribed by Carter and Graham Pollard, with bookplate of noted collector Abel Berland, jacket rubbed along spine and hinges along with some fading to spine, rather well preserved.   Oak Knoll Books   310 - 204   2016 $550

Suckling, John *Fragmenta Aurea. A collection of all the Incomparable Peeces.* London: for Humphrey Moseley, 1646. First edition, first state, engraved portrait, contemporary calf, gilt fillet and cornerpieces, red morocco spine label, portrait and first two leaves with two very tiny holes at gutter, worm trail in lower margin of first three gatherings, else very nice in lovely contemporary binding, bookplate of C. Pearl Chamberlain and book label of Abel Berland, fine red morocco pull of case, accompanied by ALS of John Suckling (1569-1627) father of the poet to unnamed recipient.   Joseph J. Felcone, Inc.   Books from Five Centuries: a Miscellany - 138   2016 $6000

Association – Berrigan, Alice

Prince, F. T. *Drypoints of the Hassidim.* London: Menard Press, 1975. First edition, slim book, near fine in stapled wrappers with some faint creasing to top corner of pages, in about very good dust jacket with some slight wear to top, spine and top of rear panel, signed and inscribed by author to Ted and Alice Berrigan, nice association, laid in is article about this book.   Jeff Hirsch Books   E-List 80 - 25   2016 $100

Association – Berrigan, Daniel

O'Brien, Conor Cruise *Maria Cross Imaginative Patterns in a Group of Modern Catholic Writers.* New York: Oxford University Press, 1952. First edition, fine in attractive, near fine dust jacket with tiny tears, inscribed by Daniel and Philip Berrigan, uncommon title.   Between the Covers Rare Books   208 - 58   2016 $500

Association – Berrigan, Philip

O'Brien, Conor Cruise *Maria Cross Imaginative Patterns in a Group of Modern Catholic Writers.* New York: Oxford University Press, 1952. First edition, fine in attractive, near fine dust jacket with tiny tears, inscribed by Daniel and Philip Berrigan, uncommon title.   Between the Covers Rare Books   208 - 58   2016 $500

Association – Berrigan, Ted

Duncan, Robert *The Opening Field, (with) The Opening Field (a second copy).* New York: Grove Press, 1960. First edition, 8vo., original printed wrappers, Ted Berrigan's copies with his ownership signature in pencil of first copy, scattered annotations throughout text of first copy with Berrigan's ownership signature, but they appear to be in another hand, titlepage of this copy detached but present with red stain on top edge, covers soiled and lightly rubbed, presentation copy in fine condition.   James S. Jaffe Rare Books   Occasional List: Winter 2016 - 54   2016 $1500

Guest, Barbara *Poems: the Location of Things, Archaics, the Open Skies.* Garden City: Doubleday, 1962. First edition, 8vo., original boards, dust jacket, fine, jacket slightly dust soiled, presentation copy inscribed by poet to Ted Berrigan, with his ownership signature in pencil.   James S. Jaffe Rare Books   Occasional List: Winter 2016 - 73   2016 $1250

Prince, F. T. *Drypoints of the Hassidim.* London: Menard Press, 1975. First edition, slim book, near fine in stapled wrappers with some faint creasing to top corner of pages, in about very good dust jacket with some slight wear to top, spine and top of rear panel, signed and inscribed by author to Ted and Alice Berrigan, nice association, laid in is article about this book.   Jeff Hirsch Books   E-List 80 - 25   2016 $100

Association – Berry, R. J.

Arbman, Holger *The Vikings.* London: Thames and Hudson, 1962. New edition, 8vo., original cloth and blue wrapper, black and white photos, illustrations and maps, spine of wrapper slightly sunned, very good, signature of R. J. Berry, Emeritus Professor of Genetics of University College London and president of Linnean Society.   Sotheran's   Piccadilly Notes - Summer 2015 - 20   2016   £30

Lionnet, Guy *The Seychelles.* Newton Abbot: David & Charles, 1972. First edition, 8vo., original cloth and wrapper, black and white illustrations, slight dampstain to top edges, very good, signature of R. J. Berry, professor.   Sotheran's   Piccadilly Notes - Summer 2015 - 192   2016   £30

Association – Berry, Wendell

Peters, Jason *Wendell Berry/Life and Work.* Lexington: The University Press of Kentucky, 2007. Second printing with titlepage without paper flaw, 8vo., fine in dust jacket, this is the third (?) issue with titlepage replaced and bound in, this copy signed by Berry.   Second Life Books, Inc.   196 B - 398   2016 $50

Peters, Jason *Wendell Berry/Life and Work.* Lexington: The University of Kentucky, 2007. First edition, first issue with paper flaw at bottom of titlepage, 8vo., fine, issued in an edition of approximately 3000 copies, this copy signed by Berry and 6 contributors Guy Mendes, Ed McClanahn, Morris Grubbs, Norman Wirzba, Katharine Dalton & Jack Shoemaker.   Second Life Books, Inc.   196 B - 397   2016 $150

Reece, Erik *Field Work: Modern Poems from Eastern Forests.* Lexington: The University Press of Kentucky, 2008. First edition, 8vo., fine in dust jacket, signed by contributors Eric Reece, James Baker Hall, Wendell Berry and Richard Taylor.   Second Life Books, Inc.   196 B - 461   2016 $45

Association – Besse, Antonio

Stark, Freya *A Winter in Arabia.* London: John Murray, 1940. First edition, 8vo., original green cloth lettered gilt, 1 folding map, numerous illustrations from photos, printed in photogravure, cloth faded along edges and spine, internally apart from occasional very light spotting and offsetting from endpapers, good copy, contemporary bookplate of Antonio Besse inside front cover, two original press photos loosely inserted.   Sotheran's   Travel and Exploration - 378   2016   £185

Association – Bester, James

Doudney, David Alfred *Try. A Book for Boys.* Bonmahon Industrial Printing School, 1857. First edition, 16mo., frontispiece, laid down within printed border, plates, original green cloth, decorated in gilt, recased, dulled, gift inscription on leading f.e.p. for James Bester.   Jarndyce Antiquarian Books   CCXV - 628   2016   £125

Association – Bianco, Pamela

Wilde, Oscar 1854-1900 *The Birthday of the Infanta.* New York: Macmillan, Oct., 1929. Limited to 500 copies, numbered and signed by Pamela Bianco, 4to., cloth backed boards, fine in slipcase (just slightly worn at corners), printed on fine paper, beautiful double page color illustrations as well as black and whites by Bianco, laid in is great half page handwritten letter from Bianco to artist Valenti Angelo.   Aleph-bet Books, Inc.   111 - 478   2016 $400

Association – Bichlmaier, G. G.

Kolliker, Albert *Handbuch der Gewebelebre des Menschen fur Arzie und Studirende.* Leipzig: Wilhelm Engelmann, 1852. First edition, 8vo., 313 figures, early half maroon sheep, marbled boards, black leather gilt stamped label, extremities worn, spine faded, ownership signature of G. G. Bichlmaier, ink inscription on half title. Jeff Weber Rare Books 183 - 21 2016 $875

Association – Bickley, Tony

Shaw, George Bernard 1856-1950 *Man and Superman.* New York: Dodd, Mead, 1947. First edition, 8vo., very good in little worn dust jacket, some of the photos show little watermark at edge, written on endpaper is note this book is the property of "Maurice Evans Prod. Inc." and is to be returned, this copy signed by Malcolm Keen, Chester Stratton, Victor Sutherland, Carmen Mathews, Jack Manning, Phoebe Mackay and Tony Bickley. Second Life Books, Inc. 196 B - 562 2016 $450

Association – Bigge, Charles William

Stuart, Andrew *Letters to the right Honourable Lord Mansfield from Andrew Stuart Esqr.* London: printed in the month of January, 1773. 8vo., excellently rebound in half calf, marbled paper boards, spine ruled in gilt, red morocco label, early bookplate of Chas. Willm. Bigge retained. Jarndyce Antiquarian Booksellers CCXVI - 550 2016 £185

Association – Birch, Reginald

Burnett, Frances Hodgson *Little Lord Fauntleroy.* New York: Charles Scribner, 1911. First edition with these illustrations, 8vo., blue cloth, pictorial paste-on, top edge gilt, corner of blank endpaper clipped else near fine, this copy inscribed by author to Robert Newell, with lengthy inscription from artist, below is a charming watercolor by artist, super copy, illustrations by Reginald Birch. Aleph-bet Books, Inc. 111 - 65 2016 $1500

Association – Birkenhead, Viscount

Shelley, Percy Bysshe 1792-1822 *Prometheus Unbound. A Lyrical Drama in Four Acts with Other Poems.* London: C. and J. Ollier, 1820. First edition, 2nd issue, with half title, ads at end discarded, 8vo., early 20th century red crushed morocco for William Brown (booksellers), Edinburgh, French fillets on sides, crowned initial B on the upper cover, spine panelled in gilt in compartments, gilt edges, surface of joints partly lifted, F. E. Smith's copy (crowned initial on upper cover), with his bookplate inside front cover as Viscount Birkenhead, bookplate of Fernand Spaak opposite, good. Blackwell's Rare Books Marks of Genius - 49 2016 £2500

Spenser, Edmund 1552-1599 *The Faerie Queen: the Shepheards Calendar: Together with the Other Works of England's Arch-Poet, Edm. Spenser...* London: printed for H L. for Matthew Lownes, 1611. First collected edition, five parts in one folio volumes, folio in sixes, general title within woodcut border, woodcut illustrations and ornamental borders, decorative woodcut head and tailpieces and initials, contemporary polished dark brown calf with central gilt stamped lozenges to front and rear covers, blind stamped letters (TN) to each side of lozenge, expertly rebacked to style, gilt spine lettering, few minor marginal tears, lower corner of D4 torn out (not affecting text), some occasional browning, bookplates of Viscount Birkenhead and Reginald Francis, some notations on front endpaper surrounded by old tape residue, some scuffing to corners, still very nice. Heritage Book Shop Holiday 2015 - 102 2016 $7500

Association – Bishop, Cortlandt

Dickens, Charles 1812-1870 *The Personal History of David Copperfield.* London: 1849-1850. First edition, illustrations by Phiz, xx original parts in xix, plates slightly browned in places, original blue green pictorial wrappers, two or three parts, very slightly chipped at head of tail of spine, back wrapper carefully reattached part xix/xx part xvii wrappers loose, as issued, never glued to text block, overall very well preserved and clean set, virtually no repair work, custom made blue morocco box, armorial bookplate of Cortlandt F. Bishop. Jarndyce Antiquarian Booksellers CCXVIII - 468 2016 £12,500

Horatius Flaccus, Quintus *Carmina Sapphica. (and) Carmina Alcaica.* Chelsea: Ashendene Press, 1903. One of 150 copies on Japanese paper (25 on vellum), 185 x 128mm., 2 volumes, original flexible vellum, gilt titling on spine, housed in custom cloth folding box with separate compartments for each book, initials hand painted by Graily Hewitt, printed in red and black, "Carmina Alcaica" inscribed to Philip Webb by printer and dated 1903 with further ink notation that was given by Webb's executor to Walter Knight Shirley, Earl Ferrers on 22 Feb. 1916 and by him to Charles Winmile Jan 1937, verso of 'Carmina Sapphica" with morocco bookplate of Cortlandt Bishop, pastedowns little waffled, otherwise mint. Phillip J. Pirages 67 - 13 2016 $4000

Wood, Henry *Change for the American Notes: in Letters from London to New York.* London: Wiley & Putnam, Stationers, Edinburgh: A. & C. Black; Dublin: W. Curry, 1843. First edition, contemporary full tan calf, gilt spine, borders and dentelles, red leather label, hinges expertly repaired, Cortlandt Field Bishop bookplate, all edges gilt, good plus. Jarndyce Antiquarian Booksellers CCXVIII - 329 2016 £180

Association – Bishop, Elizabeth

Drayton, Michael *Poems of Michael Drayton.* London: Routledge and Kegam Paul Ltd., 1953. 2 volumes, 12mo., trifle stained near spines, else near fine in near fine dust jackets, each volume with ownership signature of poet Elizabeth Bishop.   Between the Covers Rare Books   204 - 35   2016 $1200

Association – Bisset, William

Mathias, Thomas James *The Pursuits of Literature... (bound with) A Translation of the Passages from Greek, Latin, Italian and French Writers.* London: printed for T. Becket, 1798. Dublin: printed for J. Milliken... 1799. Fifth edition of first work, 8vo., very light marginal damp marking, slightly more intrusive at end, contemporary half vellum, marbled paper boards, little rubbed, little wear to lower joint, green morocco label, blue sprinkled edges, bookplate of William Bisset, Lessondrum, his signature dated 1798 and of Francis White Popham, sound, attractive copy.   Jarndyce Antiquarian Booksellers   CCXVI - 406   2016   £785

Association – Black, Myron

Johnson, Lyndon Baines *State of the Union Message...* 8vo., inscribed by a secreatry, not Johnson, for friend Myron Black, fine copy.   Second Life Books, Inc.   196A - 898   2016 $50

Association – Blackwell, Alice Stone

Cable, George Washington   1844-1925 *Bonaventure, a Prose Pastoral of Acadian Louisiana.* New York: Scribner, 1888. First edition, 8vo., ownership signature of Alice Stone Blackwell's copy with her ownership signature, staining to bottom half of covers which bleeds through to endpapers, tight copy otherwise.   Second Life Books, Inc.   196A - 244   2016 $75

McConnell, Francis John *Borden Parker Bowne, His Life and Philosophy.* New York: Abingdon Press, 1929. First edition, 8vo., very good, Alice Stone Blackwell's copy with her ownership signature.   Second Life Books, Inc.   196A - 155   2016 $75

Association – Blaikie, W. B.

Housman, Laurence   1865-1959 *All-Fellows, Seven Legends Of Lower Redemption with Insets in Verse.* London: Kegan-Paul, Trench, Trubner & Co., 1896. First edition, presentation copy inscribed by author Feb. 18th 1897 to W. B. Blaikie, master printer at T. and A. Constable, lovely engravings, cover design, titlepage and initial letters by Housman, original green cloth with bumping, fading and sunning to spine, interior pages very nice light browning to margins and deckled edges, very good.   The Kelmscott Bookshop   13 - 24   2016 $450

Association – Blair, James

The Academic. Glasgow: Wardlaw and Cunninghame and Richard Baynes, London, 1826. Excellent set of numbers I to IX, with contemporary inscription to Thomas Campbell, Esq. Lord Rector of University of Glasgow with congratulations of admiring constituent James Blair, very scarce,.   John Drury Rare Books   2015 - 6422   2016 $437

Association – Blake, Betty

Waddell, Helen *Poetry in the Dark Ages....* Glasgow: Jackson Son, 1948. First edition, octavo, wrappers, presentation from author for Betty Blake, covers little marked and creased, very good.   Peter Ellis   112 - 429   2016   £25

Association – Bleeck, Alfred

Dickens, Charles   1812-1870 *Memoirs of Joseph Grimaldi.* London: Richard Bentley, 1838. First edition, 2nd issue, 2 volumes, half titles, frontispiece and plates by George Cruikshank, some slightly spotted, 36 page catalog volume II, original pink brown cloth, spine blocked gilt, slightly faded, slight wear and repairs to heads and tails, armorial bookplate of Alfred Bleeck, maroon cloth slipcase.   Jarndyce Antiquarian Booksellers   CCXVIII - 214   2016   £500

Association – Blessington, Lady

Dickens, Charles   1812-1870 *The Chimes.* London: Chapman & Hall, 1844. Proof copy, sent by Dickens to Lady Blessington after 6th December 1844, half title, frontispiece and additional engraved title, illustrations, 19th century full green crushed morocco, hinges skilfully repaired, small mark to front board, bookplates of M. C. Borden and John C. Eckel, all edges gilt. very good, bound after half title is manuscript address leaf in Dickens's hand, cloth slipcase.   Jarndyce Antiquarian Booksellers   CCXVIII - 363   2016   £28,000

Smith, James *Rejected Addresses or the new Theatrum Poetarum.* London: John Murray, 1833. First edition with these illustrations, 178 x 108mm., animated early 20th century scarlet crushed morocco, richly gilt by Riviere and Son (stamp signed on front turn-in), covers framed by curling vine bearing many berries and leaves, central panel formed and divided into compartments by gilt strapwork, each compartment containing a stylized strapwork and stippled wheel, radiating sections of wheel decorated with leafy fronds, raised bands, spine gilt in similar style, wide gilt turn-ins with plain and dotted label bound in at rear, fleece lined morocco clipped cloth slipcase, engraved frontispiece and 6 engraved illustrations by George Cruikshank, with signed original pencil study for one of the woodcuts and small pen and ink caricature, initialled by Cruikshank with his signature, laid in at front with two autograph letters, signed, tipped in at front, one from James Smith to Lady Blessington and one from Horace Smith to Duby (Edward Dubois - 1774-1850), front joint slightly (and rear joint just faintly) rubbed, spine shade darker than covers, text with faint overall browning because of paper stock, otherwise fine, lovely binding lustrous and altogether pleasing, text very clean and smooth.   Phillip J. Pirages   67 - 64   2016 $950

Association – Bliss, Philip

Ward, Seth *Vindiciae Academiarum Containing Some Briefe Animadversions Upon Mr. Websters Book....* Oxford: by Leonard Lichfield for Thomas Robinson, 1654. First edition, small 4to., ink stain in upper inner corner of titlepage and marking to C3r and C4, sidenote on A3v shaved, closely shaved at foot touching few catchwords, mid 20th century calf, Rev. Philip Bliss (1787-1857) signature, from the library of James Stevens Cox (1910-1997).   Maggs Bros. Ltd.   1447 - 439   2016   £800

Wilde, George *A Sermon Preached Upon Sunday the Third of March in St. Maries Oxford, before the General Assembly of the Members of the Honourable House of Commons Assembled.* Oxford: i.e. London: by Leonard Lichfield, 1643. Second edition, small 4to., titlepage, A2 and #4 spotted, lighter spotting and discoloration throughout, early 19th century half morocco and marbled boards, the copy of Rev. Philip Bliss (1787-1857), with signature, from the library of James Stevens Cox (1910-1997).   Maggs Bros. Ltd.   1447 - 450   2016   £120

Association – Blochman, Lawrence

Fischer, Bruno *Crook's Tour.* New York: Dodd Mead, 1953. First edition, fine, inscribed by contributors Lawrence Blochman and Dorothy Gardiner, fine in price clipped dust jacket.   Mordida Books   2015 - 010969   2016 $65

Association – Bloom, Harold

Roth, Philip *Operation Skylock.* New York: Simon & Schuster, 1993. Uncorrected proof, Harold Bloom's copy, with TNS by Roth from two years prior laid in, note folded, else fine, proof has Bloom's notations on front cover and summary page, handling apparent to covers, very good in wrappers, good association.   Ken Lopez Bookseller   166 - 108   2016 $1500

Roth, Philip *The Plot Against America.* Boston: New York: Houghton Mifflin, 2004. Advance reading copy, Literary critic Harold Bloom's copy, with his signature, age toning to pages, near fine in wrappers.   Ken Lopez Bookseller   166 - 109   2016 $350

Vidal, Gore *Two Sisters: a Memoir in the form of a Novel.* Boston: Little Brown ad Co., 1970. First edition, fine in near fine dust jacket with some light rubbing and couple of very short tears, inscribed by author for Harold Bloom.   Between the Covers Rare Books   204 - 125   2016 $550

Association – Blum, Harry

Lewis, Matthew Gregory 1775-1818 *Tales of Wonder.* London: printed by W. Bulmer and Co. for the author, 1801. First edition, 2 volumes, 260 x 159mm., contemporary calf in Etruscan style, possibly by Edwards of Halifax, each cover with gilt floral spray border (unusual for this style of binding) surrounding a terra cotta and deep burnt orange frame with palmettes stamped in black and blind, this frame enclosing panel diced and dotted in blind and with gilt cornerpieces and central medallion featuring an incised monochrome mythological painting, double raised bands flanking gilt pentaglyph and metope roll, gilt ruled spine compartments with open gilt dots and classical ornaments in blind, turn-ins with greek key gilt roll, marbled edges, neatly rebacked using most of original spines, hinges reinforced with matching paper in first volume and matching cloth in second, bookplate of E.L.", bookplate of Harry H. Blum, central images on covers of volume II somewhat indistinct, few leaves with faint spots, otherwise excellent, carefully restored binding, still retaining much of its original impressiveness and text very crisp and clean.   Phillip J. Pirages   67 - 42   2016 $1500

Association – Blumenbach, Joseph Friedrich

Du Verney, Joseph Guichard *Tractatus de Organo Auditus Continens Structuram usum et Morbos Omnium Auris Partium.* Nuremberg: Johann Zieger, 1684. First edition in Latin, 4to., 16 engraved folding plates, 19th century paper wrappers, plate 16 neatly backed, title very lightly soiled, else very good, Joseph Friedrich Blumenbach's copy with his signature, in fine morocco backed clamshell box.   Joseph J. Felcone, Inc.   Books from Five Centuries: a Miscellany - 96   2016 $4800

Association – Blundell, Charles

Knight, Richard Payne *An Analytical Inquiry into the Principles of Taste.* London: printed by Luke Hansard... for T. Payne, 1806. Third edition, 8vo. slight foxing, old closed tear towards foot of titlepage, contemporary half calf, marbled boards, gilt spine, boards slightly rubbed, with Fasque library bookplate of the Gladstone family, inscription "the gift of Cha. Blundell Esq. ... to John Gladstone.. 17 Nov. 1827. Jarndyce Antiquarian Booksellers   CCXVI - 350   2016   £90

Association – Blundell, Robert

Grey, Edward William *The History of and Antiquities of Newbury and Its Environs, Including Twenty-Eight Parishes, Situate in the County of berks...* Speenhamland: Hall and Marsh, 1839. 8vo., 19 plates, folding frontispiece map laid down on tissue and with repaired tear stretching 12mm. from mount, some foxing and spotting elsewhere, half title discarded, later polished green calf, boards with gilt border, spine gilt, green morocco lettering piece, somewhat rubbed, spine sunned, bookplate of Piscatorial Society recording book's gift to Society by Robert Blundell in 1911, good. Blackwell's Rare Books   B184 - 48   2016   £120

Association – Blunt, Wilfrid Scawen

Tyrell, George *Versions and Perversions of Heine & Others.* London: Elkin Mathews, 1909. First edition, boards somewhat marked and browning to endpapers, but nice, presentation copy inscribed by Wilfrid Scawen Blunt for Elizabeth Lawrence Xmas 1909, book dedicated to Wilfrid Blunt.   Simon Finch   2015 - 4159   2016 $252

Association – Boice, Lucy

Rowson, Susanna *Reuben and Rachel or Tales of Old Times.* sold by him and by author (and others), 1798. First edition, 2 volumes in 1, browning and foxing (as usual), staining from turn-ins, textblock strained and few gatherings proud, contemporary ownership inscription of Miss Lucy H. Boice, Worcester, 8vo., original sheep, red lettering piece, worn, spine slightly defective at head and foot, sound. Blackwell's Rare Books   B186 - 136   2016   £1500

Association – Bolland

Cambridge Trifles or Splutterings from an Undergraduate Pen. London: Sampson, Low, Marston, Searle & Rivington, 1881. First edition, dark orange binder's cloth, Bolland collection stamps.   Jarndyce Antiquarian Books   CCXV - 566   2016   £25

Craik, George Lillie *The Pursuit of Knowledge Under Difficulties.* London: Nattali & Bond, circa, 1857. 2 volumes, frontispiece and plates, original green cloth, spines elaborately gilt blocked, little rubbed and dulled, blind-stamps, pressmarks &c. of Bolland Collection LSE Library, good, with signatures of Arthur Bolland Feb. 11th 1857. Jarndyce Antiquarian Books   CCXV - 55   2016   £40

Association – Bonanomus, Hieronimus

Aesopus *Aesopi Phrigis et Aliorum Fabulae Quorum Nomina Sequens Pagella Indicabit.* Venice: Apud Prodoctos, 1686. Rare edition, oval woodcut vignette to titlepage, many more oval woodcuts in text, these showing light coloring in with red crayon or chalk, fables numbered in old hand, one leaf with thin area torn from fore-margin with loss to one letter each in about 10 words, another letter with horizontal closed tear (through two woodcuts with no loss), little other staining and evidence of cheap printing, 12mo. contemporary limp vellum, spine lettered in ink, ruckled, old repair to lower quarter of spine, some wear to edges, label removed, remains of red wax to front flyleaf and rear pastedown, rear flyleaf removed, otherwise inscriptions of Hieronimus Bonanomus (1686) and Canvero Giuseppe (with date 1686, but much later), sound.   Blackwell's Rare Books Greek & Latin Classics VII - 4   2016   £1200

Association – Bonds, W. E.

Radcliffe, Alexander *Ovidius Exulans ur Ovid Travestie.* London: by Peter Lillicrap for Samuel Speed, 1673. First edition, small 8vo., engraved portrait bust, washed and pressed, late 19th century polished calf by F. Bedford, covers with triple gilt fillet, gilt spine, marbled endleaves, gilt edges, joints rubbed. from the library of James Stevens Cox (1910-1997). the copy of W. E. Bonds, of Enderby House, Clapham, London, the copy of George Thorn Drury. Maggs Bros. Ltd.   1447 - 350   2016   £1100

Association – Bone, Stephen

Betjeman, John   1906-1984 *English, Scottish and Welsh landscape 1700-c. 1860.* Frederick Muller, 1944. First edition, crown 8vo., 13 full page illustrations by John Piper, original cloth with Piper lithograph wrapping around, top edge slightly dusty, bookplate of Stephen Bone, flyleaf with little creasing to rear free endpaper, dust jacket repeating cover design little chipped, nicked and rubbed.   Blackwell's Rare Books   B186 - 183   2016   £100

Association – Bonomi, Joseph

Cory, Alexander Turner *The Hieroglyphics of Horapollo Nilous.* London: William Pickering, 1840. 193 x 118mm., very attractive contemporary olive green morocco elaborately gilt by Hering (stamp signed), covers with delicate gilt frame of drawer handle, floral sprig and star tools, raised bands, spine gilt in compartments with similar tooling, densely gilt turn-ins, pale yellow endpapers, all edges gilt, frontispiece, numerous representations of hieroglyphics and 3 plates, pencilled presentation from author to the illustrator of the work, Joseph Bonomi, engraved bookplate of Samuel Ashton Thompson-Yates, just slightest hint of rubbing to joints (well marked with dye), faint graze on rear cover, spine probably sunned (though abundance of gilt making this difficult to determine), significant foxing to prelim leaves, frontispiece and titlepage (moderate foxing to plates II and III and adjacent text leaves), but text otherwise clean and fresh, decorative binding lustrous scarcely worn and altogether pleasing.   Phillip J. Pirages   67 - 49   2016 $1500

Association – Borden, M. C.

Dickens, Charles   1812-1870   *The Chimes.* London: Chapman & Hall, 1844. Proof copy, sent by Dickens to Lady Blessington after 6th December 1844, half title, frontispiece and additional engraved title, illustrations, 19th century full green crushed morocco, hinges skilfully repaired, small mark to front board, bookplates of M. C. Borden and John C. Eckel, all edges gilt. very good, bound after half title is manuscript address leaf in Dickens's hand, cloth slipcase. Jarndyce Antiquarian Booksellers   CCXVIII - 363   2016   £28,000

Association – Borelli, Francois

Borelli, Jules *Ethiopia Meridionale Journal de Mon Voyage aux Pays Anhara, Oromo et Sidama, Septembre 1885 a November 1888.* Paris: Ancienne Maison Quantin, 1890. First edition, 4to., contemporary calf backed marbled boards, spine ruled and lettered gilt, 13 plates, 7 double page maps (one colored), numerous wood engravings, extremities little worn, occasional brown spotting, good, contemporary armorial bookplate of Francois Borelli. Sotheran's   Travel and Exploration - 7   2016   £750

Association – Borsari, Giovanni

Gazzadi, Domenico *Zoologia Morale Exposta in Cento Venti Discrousi in Versi o in Prosa.* Florence: Vincenzo Batelli & Compagni, 1843-1846. First and only edition, folio, 3 volumes, contemporary quarter brown morocco, marbled boards, elaborate gilt tools and lettering to spines, 93 hand colored engraved plates by J. Giarre, binding little rubbed to edges, browning to 3 plates on volume II, closed tear affecting image to bottom margin of plate of St. Bernard's in volume I, occasional marking elsewhere, generally very clean and bright, very good, ownership stamps of Giovanni Borsari, with Borsari's stamp and 2 censor's stamps.   Sotheran's   Piccadilly Notes - Summer 2015 - 6   2016   £20,000

Association – Borthwick, E. Ken

Hesychius of Alexandria *Lexicon Ailiou Diogeneianou Periergopentes Editionem Minorem....* Jenae: sumptibus Hermanni Dufftii (Libraria Maukiana), 1867. Large 8vo., sporadic foxing heavier at front and rear, some neat pencil annotations, later half brown morocco with green cloth covered boards, green gilt spine label, top edge red, rubbed, few scuffs, corners wearing but very good, sound copy, penciled ownership inscription of E. Ken Borthwick to f.f.e.p. Unsworths Antiquarian Booksellers   30 - 72   2016   £90

Association – Boswell, James

Strong, James *Joanereidos; or Feminine Valour...* London: reprinted Anno Dom., 1674. Second edition, small 4to., spotted and lightly browned, some tearing in inner margin of title and following two leaves caused by original stitching, many edges uncut, early19th century half calf and marbled boards, headcaps damaged and edges rubbed, from the library of James Stevens Cox (1910-1997), signature of Edward Rowe Mores (1730-1778), the copy of James Boswell the younger (1778-1822), small signature of Thomas Park (1658/9-1834).   Maggs Bros. Ltd.   1447 - 402   2016   £1500

Association – Bottomley, Gordon

Doolittle, Hilda   1886-1961 *Tribute to the Angels.* London: Oxford University Press, 1945. First edition, crown 8vo., original printed wrappers, small ringstain to front and small trace of surface adhesion at foot of same, otherwise very good, inscribed by author to Gordon Bottomley. Blackwell's Rare Books   B186 - 203   2016   £500

Association – Bouguereau, W. Vincens

Perrault, Charles   1628-1703 *Les Contes De. Ch. Perrault.*   Paris: Librairie des Bibliophiles, 1876. No. 54 of 200 copies, 216 x 197mm., 2 volumes, half titles, lovely contemporary dark green crushed morocco, attractively gilt by Thibaron-Joly (stamp signed), covers with French fillets, raised bands, spine gilt in compartments with central rose sprig and floral cornerpieces, marbled endpapers, all edges gilt, frontispiece and 11 engraved plates, one illustrating each tale, large paper copy, bookplate in each volume of W. Vincens Bouguereau, faint offsetting from engravings, text shade less than bright, couple of vaguest scratches on covers, otherwise very fine, text and plates smooth, fresh and clean, margins far beyond ample and beautifully executed bindings virtually perfect.   Phillip J. Pirages   67 - 69   2016 $1500

Association – Bourne, M. N.

The Murdered Bride or the Victim of Treachery: a Tale of Horror.   London: William Emans, 1837. First edition?, small quarto, engraved frontispiece, additional engraved titlepage and 6 other engraved plates, contemporary half calf over marbled boards, original parts bound together with stabmarks, bound by G. J. Sutton (?) with small binder label on front endpaper, spine heavily tooled gilt in compartments, green morocco spine label, lettered gilt, spine with name M. N. Bourne in gilt at foot, all edges marbled, green endpapers, some toning to plates, bit of foxing throughout, boards bit rubbed, previous owner Bruce Ismery's armorial bookplate, overall very good, extremely rare.   Heritage Book Shop   Holiday 2015 - 3   2016 $3000

Association – Bowdler, Hernietta Maria

Tasso, Torquato   1544-1595 *Dell' Aminta Favola Boschereccia di Torquato Tasso.*   Londra: Presso C. Bennet, 1736. 12mo., full contemporary calf, joints cracked, head and tail of spine worn, later 18th century inscription "the gift of Hernietta Maria Bowdler to Jane Davis".   Jarndyce Antiquarian Booksellers   CCXVI - 559   2016   £75

Association – Bowles, Paul

Mrabet, Mohamnmed   *Love with a few Hairs.*   New York: George Braziller, 1968. Very near fine in near fine, signed and inscribed by Paul Bowles the translator for Mary Allen, 21/5/69, very nice, uncommon.   Jeff Hirsch Books   Holiday List 2015 - 55   2016 $300

Williams, Tennessee   1911-1983   *Hard Candy a Book of Stories.*   New York: New Directions, 1954. First edition, tall octavo, some soiling and small stain along edge of spine, about very good in worn, first issue royal blue slipcase, custom chemise and quarter morocco clamshell case, dedication copy (for Paul and Jane Bowles), inscribed by author for Paul Bowles.   Between the Covers Rare Books   204 - 135   2016 $35,000

Association – Bowles, Thomas

Hume, David   *Essays and treatises on Several Subjects.*   London: printed for A. Millar and A. Kincaid and A. Donaldson, 1764. London: Printed for A. Millar in the Strand, and A. Kincaid, and A. Donaldson at Edinburgh, 1764. New edition, 2 volumes, 8vo., clean, crisp copy throughout, contemporary sprinkled calf, spines with contrasting red and black morocco labels, lettered and numbered in gilt, some light chipping to head and feet of spines, still fine inscribed by Thomas Bowles and dated 13 1767.   Marlborough Rare Books   List 56 - 25   2016   £950

Association – Boxall, John

Society for Promoting Christian Knowledge   *Reading Books for Adults. Nos. 1-4.*   London: SPCK, 1859. original purple cloth, faded, rubbed and slightly worn, signature of John Boxall, Eashing 1871.   Jarndyce Antiquarian Books   CCXV - 954   2016   £35

Association – Boyle, Mildred

Wilder, Laura Ingalls   *These Happy Golden Years.*   New York: Harper & Bros., 1943. Stated first edition, 8vo., pictorial cloth, slight cover soil, near fine in very slightly frayed dust jacket, illustrations by Helen Sewell and Mildred Boyle with color dust jacket, color frontispiece plus full page black and whites, Boyle's copy inscribed by her to her niece.   Aleph-bet Books, Inc.   112 - 513   2016 $2750

Association – Boyle, Peter

Bible. Greek - 1848   *He Palaia Diatheke Kata Tous Ebdomekonta Vetus Testamentum...*   Oxonii: e Typographico Academico, 1848. 3 volumes, small 8vo., text in Greek, little toned, endpapers slightly foxed, generally bright and clean within, contemporary dark brown morcco, gilt titles to spines, all edges gilt, marbled endpapers, rubbed, corners bumped and little worn, very good, ownership inscription of A. Staveley, 47th March 1881 to Roger Garth Hooper, 1925 to Peter A. Boyle, September 1952.   Unsworths Antiquarian Booksellers   30 - 18   2016   £90

Association – Boylen, Michael

Carruth, Hayden *Aura.* West Burke: Janus Press, 1977. First edition, limited to only 50 copies, this copy press lettered especially 'for Michael Boylen' and inscribed by Claire Van Vliet in pencil for Bruce Hubbard, tall folio, printed handmade paper folder, enclosed in publisher's linen folding box with printed paper label on spine, very fine, rare. James S. Jaffe Rare Books   Occasional List: Winter 2016 - 84   2016 $4500

Association – Brace, John

Monck, Mary *Marinda. Poems and Translations Upon Several Occasions.* London: printed by J. Tonson, 1716. First edition, very good, 8vo., contemporary calf, gilt, rebacked, very good, early signatures of John Brace (crossed out) and Elizabeth Lovell, later bookplates of G. W. F. Gregor and Oliver Brett, Viscount Esher.   C. R. Johnson Rare Book Collections   Foxon: H-P 2015 - 617   2016 $2298

Association – Bracket, Charlie

Skinner, Cornelia Otis *Madame Sarah.* Boston: Houghton Mifflin, 1967. First edition, illustration, signed Cornelia to Charlie (Brackett), movie director, nice in little worn dust jacket. Second Life Books, Inc.   196 B - 590   2016 $45

Association – Bradbury, Henry

Tryon, Thomas *The Way to Health, Long Life and Happiness; or a Discourse of Temperance...* London: printed and are to be sold by most booksellers, 1697. Third edition, titlepage browned and chipped along edges, light marginal staining throughout, light foxing and spotting, 8mm circular hole through centre of P1, mid 20th century green morocco, from the library of James Stevens Cox (1910-1997), 18th century signature of Henry Bradbury, 18th century pencil notes of John Soper.   Maggs Bros. Ltd.   1447 - 418   2016   £200

Association – Bradbury, Ray

California Sorcery. Abingdon: Cemetery Dance, 1999. Publisher's copy of the limited edition (26 copies), signed by Ray Bradbury, Richard Matheson, Ellison, Nolan, Tomerlin, Sohl, Fritch and others, stamp of another author, fine in fine dust jacket in publisher's printed gray case.   Ken Lopez Bookseller   166 - 5   2016 $650

Association – Bradfer-Lawrence, Harry Lawrence

Shakespeare, William   1564-1616 *The Works of Shakespeare.* London: Nonesuch Press, New York: Random Huse, 1929-1933. Limited to 1600 sets, this number 359 (of 1050 sets for Great Britain and Ireland and 550 sets for America), 7 volumes, octavo, on Pannekoek mould made paper, publisher's full niger morocco, corners with gilt double fillet border blind and lettered in gilt in compartments, gilt turn-ins, top edge colored pale pink and gilt on rough, others uncut, some very slight variations in colors of spines as usual, some minor offsetting to endpapers, bookplate of previous owner, Harry Lawrence Bradfer-Lawrence, covers and spines with occasional minor discoloration, overall near fine.   Heritage Book Shop   Holiday 2015 - 85   2016 $3000

Association – Brague, M. St.

Dickens, Charles   1812-1870 *The Personal History of David Copperfield.* London: Bradbury & Evans, 1850. First edition, frontispiece and engraved title slightly browned at edges, printed title, plates by Phiz, contemporary half maroon calf, spine gilt to compartments, black leather label, spine faded to tan and slightly rubbed, corner slightly knocked, contemporary signature of M. St. Brague(?) on initial blank, good plus.   Jarndyce Antiquarian Booksellers   CCXVIII - 472   2016   £600

Association – Braham, Horace

Rice, Elmer *The Left Bank.* New York: Samuel French, 1931. First edition, very good, tight copy, with card list from original play program tipped to front free endpaper and printed photo of leading lady tipped to front pastedown, this copy signed by Katharine Alexander, Horace Braham and Donald Macdonald.   Second Life Books, Inc.   196 B - 475   2016 $125

Association – Brainard, William

Rand, Ayn *Atlas Shrugged.* New York: Random House, 1957. First edition, fine and unread in about fine dust jacket, jacket unrestored with uniformly deep colors and brilliant unblemished and unfaded topstain, only touch of rubbing at crown to note and none of the usual toning to spine, wonderful association copy, inscribed by author for William W. Brainard, Jr.   Royal Books   52 - 1   2016 $25,000

Association – Bram, Abraham Cornelis Sebastian

Caille, L'Abbe De La *Lecons Elementaires d'Optique.* Paris: H. L. Guerin & L. F. Delatour, 1756. Second edition, Title vignette, decorative head and tailpieces, 12 folding engraved copperplates, disbound, yet in early marbled wrappers, spine exposed, some signatures loosening, bookplate signed TM of ACS Van Heel, handsome modern blue cloth, drop back box, good, the copy of Abraham Cornelis Sebastian Bram.   Jeff Weber Rare Books   183 - 10   2016 $400

Association – Brampton, Ada

Dickens, Charles   1812-1870   *The Christmas Books.* London: Chapman & Hall, circa, 1880. Charles Dickens Edition, 4 page initial ads, frontispiece and 7 plates, original uniform red cloth, little dulled and slightly rubbed, signature of Ada Brampton, 1928.   Jarndyce Antiquarian Booksellers   CCXVIII - 402   2016   £35

Association – Brand, Dr.

Opie, Amelia   *Illustrations of Lying in all Its Branches.* London: Longman, 1825. First edition, 2 volumes, 12mo., contemporary half calf, black labels, hinges slightly splitting, contemporary signature of Dr. Brand(?).   Jarndyce Antiquarian Books   CCXV - 343   2016   £120

Association – Brandling, Charles

Baker, Henry   *Employment of the Microscope.*   London: printed for R. and J. Dodsley, 1764. Second edition, 2 parts in one volume, 8vo., 17 engraved plates, lightly foxed, titlepage creased, plate facing page 422 torn at fold, modern full calf with original calf mounted on sides, gilt stamped motto "Fide et Virtute" belonging to Cha. Brandling, gilt and blindstamped spine, gilt stamped red leather label, new endleaves, bookplates of Cha. Brandling, Charles Adams, Fred C. Luck and Max Erb, very good+.   Jeff Weber Rare Books   183 - 5   2016 $650

Association – Branfill, Champion

Johnson, Samuel   1709-1784   *A Dictionary of the English Language.*   London: printed by W. Strahan for J. and P. Knapton...., 1755. First edition, 2 volumes, titlepages printed in red and black, smallish (?wax) stain in last leaf of prelims, few leaves little browned, crease in 29F2 (no loss), small circular ink spot 2952v, couple of contemporary notes on sources added in margins, folio, contemporary calf, double gilt fillets on sides, stoutly and skillfully rebacked, repairs to corners, contemporary ownership inscription of Champion Branfill, engraved armorial bookplate of Joseph Cator, very good.   Blackwell's Rare Books   B184 - 52   2016   £17,500

Association – Brassington, William Salt

Williams, John   *The History of the Gunpowder Treason.* London: for Richard Chiswel, 1678. First edition, small 4to., initial imprimatur leaf, small rust on C34, very minor stain on D2r and with verso of final leaf (D4), very lightly soiled, Amateur binding of early 20th century red boards and white spine, boards, little stained and corners bumped, from the library of James Stevens Cox (1910-1997), bookplate of William Salt Brassington.   Maggs Bros. Ltd.   1447 - 451   2016   £120

Association – Braunschweig-Luneburg, Duke of

Willis, Thomas   *Cerebri Anatome. Cui Accessi Nervorum.* London: Tho. Roycroft for Jo. Martyn & Ja. Allestry, 1664. First Octavo edition, 15 folding engraved plates, 8vo., very nice contemporary vellum with yapped edges, hand lettered spine, contents quite crisp and clean, blank lower edge of title excised and restored, volume placed in folding cloth case, bookplates of the Duke of Braunschweig-Luneburg and Herbert McLean Evans.   James Tait Goodrich   X-78 - 557   2016 $5950

Association – Brausen, Erica

Saint Phalle, Niki De   *Aids - You Can't Catch it Holding Hands.*   Munich and Lucerne: Verlag C. J. Bucher, 1986. First edition, color pictorial laminated boards, quarto, facsimile reproduction of author/artist's original illustrated manuscript, presentation copy inscribed by author for Erica Brausen and Toto Koopman, corners bumped at corners, very good.   Peter Ellis   112 - 345   2016   £225

Association – Braxton, Anthony

Lock, Graham   *Forces in Motion: Anthony Braxton and the Meta-Reality of Creative Music.*   London: Quarter, 1988. First edition, 8vo., presentation on flyleaf from Braxton, photos, paper over boards, nice in dust jacket.   Second Life Books, Inc.   196 B - 80   2016 $85

Association – Bray, Charles

Court Etiquette: a Guide to Intercourse with Royal or Titled Persons, to Drawing Rooms, Levees, Courts and Audiences...   London: Charles Mitchell, 1849. First edition, 12mo., frontispiece, 1 page ads, original blue grey cloth, dulled and marked by damp, slightly rubbed, all edges gilt, booklabel of Charles Bray, sound.   Jarndyce Antiquarian Books   CCXV - 138   2016   £85

Association – Brebeuf, Madame De

Venn, Otto Van *Emblemes de l'Amour Divin.* Paris: chez P. Landry, n.d. c., 1670. Engraved titlepage and 59 full page engravings with Latin mottoes and French epigrams, 12mo., exquisitely bound in contemporary red morocco, triple gilt fillet on covers, flat spine gilt in compartments with central fleuron to each panel, double panel for green morocco label lettered in gilt 'EMBLEMES", inscription "Madame de Brebeuf", partly inked over,. Maggs Bros. Ltd. 1474 - 79   2016   £2500

Association – Brennan, Elizabeth

Dickens, Charles   1812-1870 *The Old Curiosity Shop.* London: Chapman & Hall, 1841. First separate edition, frontispiece, illustrations, original maroon cloth blocked in blind, spine lettered gilt, neatly recased, spine and edges faded to brown, corners worn, small booklabel of Elizabeth Brennan, good, sound copy.   Jarndyce Antiquarian Booksellers   CCXVIII - 280   2016   £380

Association – Brett, Lucy

De Salis, Harriet Anne *Tempting Dishes for Small Incomes.* London: Longmans, 1890. First edition, half title, original beige cloth, red cloth spine rather marked, owner inscription of Lucy M. Brett.   Jarndyce Antiquarian Books   CCXV - 152   2016   £45

Association – Brett-Smith, John

Philips, John *Bleinheim, a Poem.* London: printed for Tho. Bennet, 1705. First edition, folio, recent boards, foxed, otherwise very good from the library of John Brett-Smith.   C. R. Johnson Rare Book Collections   Foxon: H-P 2015 - 744   2016 $2298

Association – Brewer, Joe

Hughes, Richard *The Wooden Shepherdess. The Human Predicament volume II.* London: Chatto & Windus, 1973. First edition, fine in dust jacket designed by John Ward, inscribed by author to Joe Brewer, laid in is autograph card from Hughes.   Second Life Books, Inc.   196A - 853   2016 $225

Association – Bridson, Gavin

Alken, Henry *The Art and Practice of Etching; with Directions for Other methods of Light and Entertaining Engraving.* London: S. & J. Fuller, 1849. First edition, square 8vo., original cloth, new spine covering, frontispiece, 8 plates, engraved plates by Alken, bookplate of Gavin Bridson, inside hinges cracked, rebacked with new cloth and with modern paper spine label, ink ownership inscription of titlepage.   Oak Knoll Books   310 - 24   2016 $500

British Museum *List of Serial Publications in the British Museum (Natural History) Library.* London: Trustees of the British Museum (Natural History), 1975. Second edition, 4to., 3 volumes, cloth, dust jacket, ink signature of Gavin Bridson, dust jackets lightly worn with some soiling and spotting.   Oak Knoll Books   310 - 259   2016 $450

Davenport, Cyril *Mezzotints.* London: Methuen and Co., 1904. First edition, one of 50 bound thus, printed on Japanese paper, small 4to., full vellum with top edge gilt, plates, some cover soiling, bookplate and pencil signature of Gavin Bridson.   Oak Knoll Books   310 - 29   2016 $350

Dougall, J. *Cabinent of the Art: Being a New and Universal Drawing Book Forming a Complete System of Drawing...* London: R. Ackermann, n.d., 1821. Second edition, text volume only, without the plate volume, 4to., new cloth spine with paper spine label, original paper covered boards, frontispiece, engraved titlepage, bookplate and pencil signature of Gavin Bridson, wear along edges of covers, inner hinges reinforced with archvial paper repair.   Oak Knoll Books   310 - 33   2016 $650

Sprigge, S. Squire *The Methods of Publishing.* London: 1890. Original black buckram, lettered gilt, bookplate sof J. Johnston Abraham and Gavin D. R. Bridson.   Jarndyce Antiquarian Booksellers   CCXVII - 240   2016   £65

Association – Bright, Allan Heywood

Amman, Jost *Bibliorum Utriusque Testamenti Icones, Summor Artificio Expressae Historias Sacras and Vivum Exhibentes & Oculis Summa cum Gratia Repraesentantes....* Frankfurt: Christoph Corvinus & Sigmund Feyerabend, 1571. First edition, 8vo., 19th century blue morocco, triple blind fillet on cover, title lettered in gilt on spine, inner edge richly gilt and signed Bauzonnet-Trautz', marbled edges, gilt edges, silk bookmark, woodcut coats of arms of Johann Fichard and Konrad Weis, 200 fine oval woodcuts within ms. frames by Jose Amman, many signed with his initials, IA, bookplates of Edward Arnold, Dorking, E. Yeminez, Lyon and Allan Heywood Bright, London.   Maggs Bros. Ltd. 1474 - 12   2016   £4500

Hoogstraten, Franz Van *Het Voorhof der Ziele, Behangen met Leerzaeme Prenten en Zinnebeelden.* Rotterdam: Francois van Hoogstraeten, Boeckverkooper, 1668. First edition, rare, 4to., contemporary mottled calf, gilt spine, red speckled edges, etched engraved title,60 half page etchings by Romeyn de Hooghe, Allan Heywood Bright bookplate.   Maggs Bros. Ltd.   1474 - 42   2016   £4500

Howell, James *Epistolae Ho-Eliana. Familiar Letters Domestic and Forren...* London: printed for Humphrey Moseley, 1645. First edition, small 4to., lacking additional engraved titlepage, woodcut initials and head and tailpieces, few pencil marks and underlinings, some MS. notes in old hand including dates and sometimes locations, occasional wax marks not affecting text, 19th century plum colored faux morocco, gilt label to spine, blindstamped spine and boards, edges sprinkled red, marbled endpapers, rubbed, edges bit worn and some fraying to covers, spine label lifting, armorial bookplate of Frederick William Cosens, MS gift inscription to Allan H. Bright, dated 30th May 1891, from HYS, armorial bookplate of Douglas Kinnaird, tipped to f.f.e.p. a page of handwritten notes on the content of the book with brief chronology of Howell's life in pencil, with note book was purchased from Cosens through Quaritch. Unsworths Antiquarian Booksellers 30 - 82 2016 £300

Taurellus, Nicolaus *Emblemata Physico-ethica. (with) Carmina Funebria.* Nuremberg: Paul Kaugmann, 1592. Nuremberg: Gerlach, 1592. First edition, 2 works in one volume, titles within woodcut architectural border, 83 woodcut emblems, two works in one volume, 17th century speckled calf gilt spine with morocco label, red speckled edges, arare, Allan Heywood Bright bookplate and notes. Maggs Bros. Ltd. 1474 - 75 2016 £7500

Tennyson, Alfred Tennyson, 1st Baron 1609-1692 *Poems by Two Brothers.* London: printed by J. and J. Jackson, Louth for Simpkin and Marshall, 1827. First edition, 163 x 102mm., lovely late 19th century crimson morocco, elegantly gilt, covers with plain amd decorative gilt rules and fleuron cornerpieces, raised bands, spine gilt in double ruled compartments with urn of flowers at center surrounded by small tools, leaf garlands at corners, gilt titling, richly gilt turn-ins, top edge gilt, bookplate of S. A. Thompson Yates, the collection then passed to Allan Heywood Bright, faint discoloration in bottom margin of about 25 leaves, isolated insignificant soiling, otherwise very pretty book in fine condition, text fresh and bright and especially beautiful binding, lustrous and unworn. Phillip J. Pirages 67 - 325 2016 $3250

Association – Bright, James Frank

Livy *Historiarum Libri, Qui Supersunt Omnes et Deperditorum Fragmenta.* Oxonii: Talboys, 1840. 1840. 1841. 1841, 8vo., 4 volumes, little light foxing to front and rear generally clean and bright, v4ellum, gilt red morocco spine labels, marbled endpapers, all edges red, endcaps little creased, some smudges and shelfwear to vellum, generally very good, armorial bookplate of James Frank Bright, stamped "Bound by Wheeler". Unsworths Antiquarian Booksellers 30 - 97 2016 £240

Association – Britain, Radie

Gershwin, Ira *Lyrics on Several Occasions.* New York: Alfred A. Knopf, 1959. First edition, inscribed by Gershwin to noted pianist and composer, Radie Britain, fine in about near fine dust jacket (spine lightly toned and with few nicks and rubs along top edge), lovely copy. Royal Books 48 - 23 2016 $1500

Association – Broadhurst, C. K.

Borden, Mary *Action for Slander.* London: Heinemann, 1936. First edition, octavo, presentation from author to C. K. Broadhurst with compliments of author, edges spotted, some offsetting from dust jacket onto spine, very good in scarce dust jacket which is very good, slightly nicked and bit spotted on rear panel, dust jacket design has playing card motif. Peter Ellis 112 - 306 2016 £150

Association – Broadwood, M. A.

Haslam, John *Sound Mind; or Contributions to the Natural History and Physiology of the Human Intellect.* London: Longman Hurst Rees Orme and Brown, 1819. First edition, few early reader's marks and annotations, light foxing of few early leaves, later 19th century half calf with label, little rubbed but very good, old bookplate of M. A. Broadwood. John Drury Rare Books 2015 - 13669 2016 $437

Association – Bromwell, D. J. G.

Fields, James T., Mrs. *A Shelf of Old Books.* New York: Charles Scribner's Sons, 1895. First edition, 8vo., 54 illustrations and ms. facsimiles, bound in brown gilt stamped cloth, untrimmed, very good, clean, ownership signature on free endpaper "D. J. G. Bromwell/Christmas 1895" with 3 line quote for (S.T.) Coleridge. Second Life Books, Inc. 196A - 369 2016 $2500

Association – Brooke, Thomas

Bible. Greek - 1524 *Novum Testamentum Graece.* Strasbourg: Wolfgang Cephalaeus, 1524. Title within quadripartie woodcut border, printer's device at centre, large device on verso of last leaf with mottoes in Hebrew, Greek and Latin, uniformly little browned and with some slight dampstaining in upper and fore margins, 8vo., contemporary blindstamped pigskin (or deerskin) over bevelled wooden boards, brass clasps and catches, lacking clasps, very rubbed and darkened, spine partly defective, upper cover held by 1 (of 3) cords, 1529 ownership inscription in 2 places of Johannes Hartmann, purchased, the whole extensively annotated by him in Latin and Greek, sometimes in red ink, 19th century bookplate of Thomas Brooke, of Armitage Bridge (Huddersfield), sound, scarce. Blackwell's Rare Books B184 - 13 2016 £5000

Bible. Polyglot - 1512 *Psalterium Daviticum Materna Lingua Expositum.* Paris: A. Verard, circa, 1512. First edition, in French & Latin, small 8vo., 18th cebtury mottled calf, spine gilt in compartments, red morocco label (one label missing, joints and headcaps restored), titlepage with fine metalcut of David and Bathesheba enclosed within ornate metalcut crible border made up of 8 different strips, printed in red and black throughout, little marginal foxing and toning to places but generally good, 17th century? ownership inscription "Collegii Paris Societ. Jesu", bookseller's label, armorial bookplate of Thomas Brooke, FSA, owner of the Pillone library, inscribed of W. Ingham Brooke of Barford Rectory, Warwick 1908 and pencil acquisition note of Lord Kenyon 20 Dec. 1979.   Maggs Bros. Ltd.   1474 - 67   2016   £1500

L'Innocence de la Tresillustre. Tres-chaste, et Debonnaire Princesse, Madame Marie Royne d'Escosse. n.p. Iprime an, 1572. 8vo., signature O omitted in make up, text complete, all pages faintly rubricated, very nice, bound by Bedford in dark blue morocco gilt, dentelles, marbled endpapers, all edges gilt, ownership signature of A. Elphinston(e) on titlepage with dated in lower margin 1600, later armorial bookplate of James Wyllie Guild and Thomas Brooke, FSA, Armitage Bridge, ownership inscription Alexander W. Ruthven Stuart 1923.   Jarndyce Antiquarian Booksellers   CCXVII - 182   2016   £1500

Association – Brooke, W. Ingham

Bible. Polyglot - 1512 *Psalterium Daviticum Materna Lingua Expositum.* Paris: A. Verard, circa, 1512. First edition, in French & Latin, small 8vo., 18th century mottled calf, spine gilt in compartments, red morocco label (one label missing, joints and headcaps restored), titlepage with fine metalcut of David and Bathsheba enclosed within ornate metalcut crible border made up of 8 different strips, printed in red and black throughout, little marginal foxing and toning to places but generally good, 17th century? ownership inscription "Collegii Paris Societ. Jesu", bookseller's label, armorial bookplate of Thomas Brooke, FSA, owner of the Pillone library, inscribed of W. Ingham Brooke of Barford Rectory, Warwick 1908 and pencil acquisition note of Lord Kenyon 20 Dec. 1979.   Maggs Bros. Ltd.   1474 - 67   2016   £1500

Association – Brooks, Cleanth

Richards, L. A. *Coleridge's Minor Poems.* N.P.: n.p., n.d., circa, 1970. First edition, octavo, wrappers, printed label on upper cover, presentation copy inscribed by author to Cleanth Brooks, wrappers faintly faded at edges, very good. Peter Ellis   112 - 330   2016   £45

Association – Brooks, Gwendolyn

Harper, Michael *Photographs: Negatives: History at Apple Tree.* San Francisco: Scarab Press, 1972. First edition, one of 500 numbered copies, signed by author, near fine in slightly foxed and soiled, near fine dust jacket, this copy inscribed to fellow poet Gwendolyn Brooks 26 July 72.   Between the Covers Rare Books   207 - 49   2016 $500

Association – Brooks, Joe

Marston, Edward *On a Sunshine Holyday by the Amateur Angler.* London: Sampson Low and Co., 1897. First edition, 1 of 250 numbered copies on Van Gelder paper initialled by author, 8vo., original vellum backed green cloth boards lettered gilt on spine, frontispiece and 15 India paper proof plates, spine slightly darkened, otherwise very good, bookplate of angling author Joe Brooks.   Sotheran's Piccadilly Notes - Summer 2015 - 198   2016   £198

Association – Brooks, Shirley

Clarke, William *Every night Book or Life after Dark.* London: T. Richardson, Sherwood & Co., 1827. 2 vignette engravings, neatly rebacked in quarter calf, red label, book-label of Shirley Brooks, humorous writer and editor of Punch, with commendatory note which may be in his hand.   Jarndyce Antiquarian Booksellers   CCXVII - 71   2016   £225

Association – Brooks, Van Wyck

Du Bois, W. E. B. *Mansart Builds a School.* New York: Mainstream Publishers, 1959. First edition, bookplate, paper over front hinge cracked but hinge still tight, very good, lacking dust jacket, inscribed by author to fellow author Van Wyck Brooks.   Between the Covers Rare Books   202 - 25   2016 $4500

Association – Brooksby, Josh

Rowe, Elizabeth Singer *Friendship in Death in Letters from the Dead to the Living.* London: C. Cooke, 1797. 12mo., 4 engraved plates, tailpieces, small engraving on title, stained, foxed throughout, original dark calf, heavily worn, cover off, ink signatures on titlepage and title verso (Madam Codman, Josh Brooksby and George Wilson), rubber ink stamped numbers on title verso, blind emboss stamps on first and last few leaves, including title, bookplate of Charles T. Congdon (1821-1891).   Jeff Weber Rare Books   181 - 34   2016 $35

Association – Brossard, J. F.

La Mettrie, Julien Offray De *Traite de la Petite Verole, avec la Maniere de Guerir Cette Maladie Suivant les Principes de Mr. Herman Boerhaave.* Paris: Chez Huart & Briasson, 1740. First edition, contemporary full leather with five raised bands on spine and gilt decorations and gilt title, few light gouges to covers both front and back, but nothing unsightly, lovely contemporary bookplate of J. F. Brossard 1752, otherwise tight, clean, remarkably well preserved. Athena Rare Books   List 15 - 1740   2016 $1500

Association – Broughton, H. H.

Food for the Young. London: W. Darton Jun., 1818. First edition, small 12mo., frontispiece and 2 further plates, leaves little dusted, 20th century quarter red morocco, presentation inscription on leading blank "H.H. Broughton, a present from Mrs. Nightingale 1819", nice.   Jarndyce Antiquarian Books   CCXV - 687   2016   £95

Association – Browlies, Ruth

Elliot, William Hume *The Country and Church of the Cheeryble Brothers.* Selkirk: George Lewis & Son, 1893. First edition, half title, double frontispiece, illustrations, double frontispiece, illustrations, final leaf, original blue cloth, slightly rubbed, inscribed to Ruth Browlies "from the author', top edge gilt.   Jarndyce Antiquarian Booksellers   CCXVIII - 249   2016   £30

Association – Brown, Andrew

Horatius Flaccus, Quintus *The Works of Horace.* Edinburgh: printed for J. Dickson, Exchange, and James Duncan, Glasgow, 1777. 18mo., somewhat spotted and soiled, contemporary sheep, rubbed and worn, lettering pieces lost, joints cracking, spine of volume cracking and one compartment partly defective, front flyleaves excised, remaining endpapers with various scribbles and inscriptions in ink and pencil (including, Andrew Brown of Egypt Park in Paisley dated 1842).   Blackwell's Rare Books   Greek & Latin Classics VII - 45   2016   £200

Association – Brown, Anne

Dickens, Charles 1812-1870 *Sketches by Boz.* Philadelphia: Lee & Blanchard, 1842. New edition, tall 8vo., engraved frontispiece and 19 plates after George Cruikshank (all present), some browning and staining, few carefully repaired tears, original brown cloth, decorated in blind, gilt spine, expertly recased, neat repairs to corners and head and tail of spine, inscribed Ann (sic) Brown from Catherine Dickens NY June 1842, inscription leaf rather browned and has repaired edges, text clear.   Jarndyce Antiquarian Booksellers   CCXVIII - 65   2016   £1500

Association – Brown, Camilla Bryden

Hale, Kathleen *Orlando and the Three Graces.* London: John Murray, 1965. First edition, numerous lithographic illustrations in color and black and white by author, few faint spots to first and last text pages, oblong 8vo., original pictorial boards with few faint spots to edges, dust jacket clipped but still showing price (as issued) with few faint spots, signed by author, bookplate of Camilla Bryden Brown, artist. Blackwell's Rare Books   B186 - 231   2016   £175

Association – Brown, Frederick William

Rossetti, Dante Gabriel 1828-1882 *The Poems of Dante Gabriel Rossetti.* London: Ellis & Elvey, 1904. No. 7 of 30 numbered copies, with plates on Japanese vellum, 25 copies for subscribers and 5 for presentation, lovely set, bound in full vellum, top edge gilt, slight soiling in gilt on fore-edge of volume II, beautifully printed with 18 full page illustrations and frontispieces from Rossetti's paintings and drawings, each protected by tissue guard giving the name of the work, vellum binding in very good condition with just lightest signs of handling, gilt title and author to spine, interior pristine, bookplate of Frederick William Brown affixed to each front pastedown, original blue ribbon placemarks present, housed in modern green cloth slipcase, fine.   The Kelmscott Bookshop   13 - 47   2016 $1300

Association – Brown, Henry Tatnall

Fante, John *Ask the Dust.* New York: Stackpole, 1939. First edition, inscribed by author to collector and bibliographer of Christopher Morley, Henry Tatnall Brown Jr., dated Nov. 14 1939, Brown's bookplate, slight offsetting from bookplate, else fine in near fine dust jacket, spine sunned with very light edge wear, very nice copy.   Ken Lopez Bookseller   166 - 33   2016 $8500

Association – Brown, John

Ellis, Asa *The Country Dyer's Assistant.* Brookfield: pr. by E. Merriam & Co. for the author, 1798. First edition, 16mo., errata & leaf, contemporary calf, gilt stamping on spine, rubbed but very nice, light foxing, signature of John Brown, Esq.   M & S Rare Books, Inc.   99 - 86   2016 $1250

Association – Brown, John Mason

Copeau, Jacques *The House into Which We are Born.* New York: Theatre Arts, 1924. First American edition, 12mo., inscribed by noted US theatre critic John Mason Brown to an American producer, lightly soiled wrappers. Second Life Books, Inc.   196A - 336   2016 $45

McCord, David *Twelve Verses from XII Night.* Boston: St. Botolph Club, 1938. First edition, 8vo., one of 120 copies, this numbered 129! printed paper over boards, paper label, author's presentation to John Mason Brown and his wife, spine little browned and faded, two small spots on front, otherwise nice. Second Life Books, Inc. 196 B - 172 2016 $50

Nathan, George Jean *Art of the Night.* New York: Knopf, 1928. First edition, 8vo., laid in autograph note and postcard by Nathan to critic John Mason Brown, moderate wear. Second Life Books, Inc. 196 B - 301 2016 $50

Nathan, George Jean *The Theatre of the Moment.* New York: Knopf, 1938. First edition, nice, moderately worn dust jacket, inscribed by author to critic John Mason Brown. Second Life Books, Inc. 196 B - 303 2016 $65

Association – Brown, Marcia

Cinderella *Cinderella.* New York: Scribner, 1954. A. First edition, first printing, 4to., cloth, corner slightly worn else fine in very good dust jacket, small chips off spine ends, this copy signed by artist, Marcia Brown. Aleph-bet Books, Inc. 112 - 77 2016 $1500

Dick Whittington and His Cat. New York: Scribner, 1950. First edition, 4to., pictorial cloth, fine in nice dust jacket, rubbed at fold with piece missing from spine ends, wonderful linoleum cuts by Marcia Brown, inscribed by Brown. Aleph-bet Books, Inc. 111 - 56 2016 $750

Association – Brown, Michael

Archibald, Campbell *Lessons for School Life...* Edinburgh: Thomas Constable & Co., 1853. Second edition, contemporary full calf by Charles Thurnam, maroon and green morovco labels, slightly rubbed, inscribed by author for Mrs. Marshall, Apl. 1856, recent ownership label of Dr. Michael Brown. Jarndyce Antiquarian Books CCXV - 928 2016 £45

Association – Brown, N. R.

How to be Happy or Fairy Gifts... London: John Harris, 1828. Frontispiece, plates, 1 page ads, contemporary marbled boards, maroon morocco, spine slightly rubbed, contemporary signature N. R. Brown on leading f.e.p., very good. Jarndyce Antiquarian Books CCXV - 264 2016 £125

Association – Brown-Westhead, J. P.

Walker, Donald *Games and Sports...* London: Thomas Hurst, 1837. First edition, half title, frontispiece, additional engraved title, plates, 18 page catalog, some foxing to plates, original maroon cloth by Remnant & Edmonds, gilt vignette, spine slightly faded, small ink mark to back board, booklabel of J. P. Brown-Westhead, Lea Castle, very good, near fine. Jarndyce Antiquarian Books CCXV - 458 2016 £350

Association – Browne, A. Murray

Newman, John Henry, Cardinal 1801-1890 *Tracts for the Times.* London: printed for J. G. and F. Rivington & J. H. Parker, Oxford, 1834-1841. First editions, complete set, Volume I 1834-4 - Volume V for 1838-40 and Volume VI for 1841, complete set of 90 tracts bound in 6 volumes with titlepages and prelim matter for the first 5 volumes, no volume title to last volume, due no doubt to sudden cessation of the series, contemporary divinity calf, spine little bit scuffed, 1885 inscription A. Murray Browne, later inscription by William Bevil Browne, some pencil underlinings and marginal notes, good. Blackwell's Rare Books B186 - 106 2016 £600

Association – Browne, William Bevil

Newman, John Henry, Cardinal 1801-1890 *Tracts for the Times.* London: printed for J. G. and F. Rivington & J. H. Parker, Oxford, 1834-1841. First editions, complete set, Volume I 1834-4 - Volume V for 1838-40 and Volume VI for 1841, complete set of 90 tracts bound in 6 volumes with titlepages and prelim matter for the first 5 volumes, no volume title to last volume, due no doubt to sudden cessation of the series, contemporary divinity calf, spine little bit scuffed, 1885 inscription A. Murray Browne, later inscription by William Bevil Browne, some pencil underlinings and marginal notes, good. Blackwell's Rare Books B186 - 106 2016 £600

Association – Bruce, J. C.

Kitchiner, William 1775-1827 *The Art of Invigorating and Prolonging Life...* London: Hurst & Robinson & Co., 1822. third edition, 12mo., half title, final ad leaf, uncut in original blue drab boards, neatly rebacked with grey paper spine retaining original label, slight damp mark to back board, signature and booklabel of J. C. Bruce. Jarndyce Antiquarian Books CCXV - 283 2016 £120

Association – Bruce, James

Gibbon, Edward   1737-1794   *The History of the Decline and Fall of the Roman Empire.*   London: Strahan and Cadell, 1788-1790. Early octavo edition, 12 volumes, full contemporary polished calf, frontispiece, 3 folding maps, armorial bookplate of James Bruce, Laird of Kinnaird, near fine set with excellent association.   Honey & Wax Booksellers   4 - 56   2016 $5000

Association – Brunck, Richard Francois Philippe

Estienne, Henri   1528-1598   *Schediasmatum Variorum id est Observationum, Emendationum, Expositioum, Didquisitionum Libri Tres....*   Geneva: Excudebat Henricus Stephanus, 1578-1589. First edition, some light browning, few marginal notes in ink, old ownership inscription to titlepage of Johann Geisel?) Zeigler, 8vo, 2 parts bound together in late 18th century mottled calf spine gilt, red morocco lettering piece, "BRUNCK" lettered direct in gilt at foot, marbled endpapers, front joint splitting but strong, some rubbing to joints and edges, good, this the copy of Richard Francois Philippe Brunck (1729-1803).   Blackwell's Rare Books   B184 - 41   2016   £1200

Association – Bry, Doris

O'Keefe, Georgia   *Some Memories of Drawings.*   New York: Atlantis Edition, 1974. First edition, limited, one of 20 presentation copies, out of a total edition of 120, signed by artist, and book's designer, Leonard Baskin, extraordinary copy, given by O'Keeffe's long time agent Doris Bry to her friend and noted psychiatrist Dr. Lucie Jessner, with letters from Bry to Jessner, 21 charcoal and pencil drawings reproduced on Arches Silkscreen in 300-line offset lithography, each laid into lettered folded leaf of Arches paper.   Manhattan Rare Book Company   2016 - 1626   2016 $10,000

Association – Bryan, Joe

Marshall, Edward   *Four on the shore.*   New York: Dial Books, 1985. First printing (code 1-10), 8vo., pictorial boards, as new in as new dust jacket, wonderful color illustrations by James Marshall to his life partner and dedicatee of the book, Joe Bryan, with charming ink drawing.   Aleph-bet Books, Inc.   111 - 270   2016 $1000

Phillips, Louis   *Haunted House Jokes.*   New York: Viking Kestrel, 1987. First printing, (code -15), 8vo., as new, pictorial boards, illustrations by James Marshall, this copy inscribed to Marshall's life partner, Joe Bryan.   Aleph-bet Books, Inc.   112 - 302   2016 $450

Association – Buchan, David Steuart Erskine, 11th Earl of

Beattie, James   1735-1803   *An Essay on the Nature and Immutability of Truth; in Opposition to Sophistry and Scepticism.*   Edinburgh: Kincaid & J. Bell, 1770. First edition, octavo, inscribed by author for David Steuart Erskine, 11th Earl of Buchan, beautifully preserved contemporary leather with gilt double lines inscribed on front and back panels, spine has five raised bands and title in gilt lettering on red field, second compartment, with Lord Cardrof's bookplate, ink signature, beautiful copy.   Athena Rare Books   List 15 - 1770   2016 $4500

Association – Buchan, John

Churchill, Winston Leonard Spencer   1874-1965   *The World Crisis. 1916-1918 Part II.*   London: Thornton Butterworth, 1927. First edition, 6 folding maps or charts and 2 facsimiles of letters from Haig as well as further maps within text, occasional pencil markings in margin by Buchan with occasional comment or correction, few very faint foxspots to initial and ultimate leaves and one or two light handling marks, 8vo., original dark blue cloth blindstamped to upper board, backstrip lettered gilt, edges lightly toned and free endpapers little browned, very good, John Buchan's copy with his bookplate and his pencilled notes, superb page letter from author to Buchan 22.2.27.   Blackwell's Rare Books   Marks of Genius - 14   2016   £6000

Association – Buchanan, Frank

Duncan, Ronald   *Judas.*   Anthony Blond, 1960. First edition, printed on rose tinted Abbey Mills Glastonbury laid paper, 8 lithographic plates by John Piper, royal 8vo., original blue buckram, upper board blocked in gilt lightest rubbing to extremities, very good, presentation inscribed by author for fellow poet Frank Buchanan.   Blackwell's Rare Books   B184 - 142   2016   £80

Association – Buck, Paul

Wheatland, David P.   *The Apparatus of Science at Harvard 1765-1800.*   Cambridge: Harvard, 1968. First edition, copiously illustrated with several color plates tipped in, warm inscription by author to Paul Buck, red cloth stamped in gilt, nice.   Second Life Books, Inc.   196 B - 864   2016 $150

Association – Buckley, John Camm

Lytton, Edward George Earle Lyton, Bulwer-Lytton, 1st Baron   1803-1873   *Works.*   London: George Routledge and Sons, circa, 1870. Large 8vo., late 19th century green half hard grained morocco, spine with gilt ornaments in compartments, lettered direct, marbled edges, spines faded, bookplate of John Camm Buckley, good.   Blackwell's Rare Books   B186 - 29   2016   £300

Association – Buechner, Frederick

Fischer, Henry *Bred in the Bone. an Anthology.* Princeton: Ampersand Press, 1945. First edition, cloth, #300 of 325 printed, inscribed and signed by one of the contirbutors, Frederick Buechner for William Meredith, Christmas 1974, laid in ALS from Buechner to Meredith, very good, likely issued without dust jacket, with brief ALS by another contributor, Robert Zufall.   Charles Agvent William Meredith - 21   2016 $250

Association – Buel, R. F.

Bible. Greek - 1838 *New Testament Gospels and Acts in Modern Greek.* Athens: Andreou Koronela, 1838. first edition of this version, one of 2000 copies, 8vo., original calf, rubbed, leather bit dry, but very good, internally fine, co-ownership signature of Baptist missionary Rev. R F. Buel, ex-Colgate University with two early bookplates, small accession number and inconspicuous blindstamp on title.   Howard S. Mott Inc.   265 - 9   2016 $650

Association – Buff, Conrad

Buff, Mary *Dancing Cloud the Navajo Boy.* New York: Viking, 1957. First edition thus, 8vo., cloth, fine in slightly worn dust jacket, illustrations by Conrad Buff, this copy inscribed and signed by author and artist.   Aleph-bet Books, Inc.   111 - 61   2016 $200

Buff, Mary *Hah-Nee of the Cliff Dwellers.* Boston: Houghton Mifflin, 1956. 8vo., cloth, fine in very good dust jacket with small piece off backstrip, slight fraying, this copy signed and inscribed by author and artist, full color and black and white lithographs by Conrad Buff.   Aleph-bet Books, Inc.   111 - 63   2016 $150

Buff, Mary *Hurry, Skurry and Flurry.* New York: Viking, 1954. First edition, 8vo., cloth, fine in slightly worn dust jacket, lovely inscribed signed by author and artist, beautiful original cloth by Conrad Buff.   Aleph-bet Books, Inc.   111 - 62   2016 $150

Association – Bulkley, Edmund

Symonds, John Addington *In the Key of Blue and Other Prose Essays.* London: Elkin Mathews & John Lane, 1893. First edition, octavo, one of 50 large paper copies bound in full vellum with elaborate decoration designed by Charles Ricketts, contemporary (1893) art nouveau bookplate of Edmund Bulkley, endpapers bit spotted at edges, very good, lovely with gilt still clear and bright.   Peter Ellis   112 - 392   2016   £950

Association – Bullock, Adrian

Cotman, John Sell *Engravings of Sepulchral Brasses in Norfolk and Suffolk, Tending to Illustrate the Ecclesiastical Military and Civil Costume...* London: Henry G. Bohn, 1839. Second edition, 2 volumes, folio, 171 plates as called for, some folding, hand colored frontispiece, very occasional light foxing, slight faint smudging to titlepages, few folded plates just starting to split a little along their folds, generally in good order, half olive green morocco and gold marbled paper covered boards, matching endpapers, gilt spines, top edge gilt and others uncut, spines little faded, rubbed, few small scrapes, edges worn, inner hinges inconspicuously reinforced with green tape, bookplate of Adrian Bullock to front and back pastedown of each volume.   Unsworths Antiquarian Booksellers   30 - 38   2016   £650

Association – Burden, Carter

Bronk, William *Two Apostrophes.* Concord: William B. Ewert, 1985. One of only 86 copies, this copy marked for presentation, printed folded sheet that holds two broadsides that each contain a single poem "Reduction" and "The Incongruities", each printed in two colors, both in fine condition as is the folder, Bronk has signed and inscribed 'Reduction' to noted collector Carter Burden and simply signed the other broadside, very nice.   Jeff Hirsch Books Holiday List 2015 - 23   2016 $125

Association – Burden, W. A. M.

Swinburne, Algernon Charles 1837-1909 *The Springtide of Life.* London: William heinemann, 1918. No. 369 of 765 copies signed by Rackham, 286 x 232mm., very attractive red three quarter morocco, gilt stamp signed 'Putnam's', raised bands, spine handsomely gilt in compartments formed by plain and decorative rules, quatrefoil centerpiece surrounded by densely scrolling cornerpieces, sides and endleaves of rose colored linen, top edge gilt, numerous black and white illustrations of cherubic children in text, 9 color plates as called for, tipped onto brown paper and with letterpress guards, morocco with bookplate of W. A. M. Burden, just hint of offsetting from brown mounting paper, otherwise very fine, bright fresh and clean inside and out, with only the most trivial of imperfections.   Phillip J. Pirages   67 - 298   2016 $2250

Association – Burgin, G. B.

Phillpotts, Eden 1862-1960 *The End of a Life.* Bristol and London: J. W. Arrowsmith and Simpkin, Marshall, Hamilton, Kent & Co. Ltd., 1891. Presentation copy inscribed to G. B. Burgin, presentation copies from Phillpotts are scarce, very good in original brown cloth with gilt title to spine and black title to front board, front board slightly bowed and spine is somewhat cocked, hinges rubbed, minor soiling to boards, corners bumped, bookplate of Alastair Forbes, text remains bright although there is browning to margins of interior, evidence of a repair to front and rear interior hinges, very good.   The Kelmscott Bookshop   12 - 81   2016 $225

Association – Burn, Mr.

Stace, Machell *An Alphabetical Catalogue of an Extensive Collection of the Writings of Daniel Defoe....* London: printed for Whitmore and Penn, Homer's Head, Charing Cross, 1829. First edition, 8vo., first and last leaves little dust soiled, otherwise clean throughout, stitched as issued, long inscription by William Hazlitt 1811-1893) to Mr. Burn.   Marlborough Rare Books   List 56 - 16   2016   £225

Association – Burne-Jones

Frere, Mary *Old Deccan Days; or Hindoo Fairy Legends; Current in Southern India.* London: John Murray, 1868. First edition, 8vo., 4 colored plates, many further illustrations in text, burgundy publisher's cloth, gilt title to spine, gilt stamped illustrations of Ganesh to upper board, endcaps and joints worn, slight loss to head of upper joint little cracked, still very good, 1920's news clipping on subject of folkloric stories for children passed to prelim blank, ownership inscription of Anna M. Orde, 1868 to titlepage, with "Burne-Jones 1880' ms. to titlepage (not the handwriting of the artist, but according to old bookseller's note, from his library).   Unsworths Antiquarian Booksellers   30 - 59   2016   £40

Association – Burnell, James

Johnson, Samuel 1709-1784 *A Journey to the Western Islands of Scotland.* London: printed for A. Strahan and T. Cadell, 1791. New edition, 8vo., some browning to lower margins of final hundred pages, occasionally rather intrusive, full contemporary sheep, gilt decorated spine, original morocco label, spine slightly chipped at head and tail, joints cracked but firm, armorial bookplate of Revd. James Burnell, with his name on titlepage.   Jarndyce Antiquarian Booksellers   CCXVI - 330   2016   £150

Association – Burton, Virginia Lee

Andersen, Hans Christian 1805-1875 *The Emperor's New Clothes.* Boston: Houghton Mifflin, 1949. Small 4to., cloth, slight bit of cover soil, else fine in dust jacket (very good to fine, very slight wear to spine), illustrations in color, warmly inscribed by artist, Virginia Lee Burton dated 1949, rare thus, beautiful copy.   Aleph-bet Books, Inc.   111 - 68   2016 $850

Association – Butler, A. G.

Roughley, T. C *Fishes of Australia and their Technology.* Sydney: Government printer, 1916. Color plates, publisher's green decorated cloth, inscribed by author to A. G. Butler, very good.   Andrew Isles Natural History Books   55 - 38723   2016 $300

Association – Butler, Jim

Haley, Alex *Roots.* Garden City: Doubleday, 1976. Uncorrected proof, inscribed by author for Jim Butler, about very good in plain beige printed wrappers as issued, wrappers creased at corners and first few dozen leaves creased at bottom right corner from reading, some occasional spotting on pages as well, presentable example, scarce.   Royal Books   52 - 30   2016 $2850

Association – Butler, Lord

Monsarrat, Nicholas *The Cruel Sea.* N.P.: Book Club Associates, 1971. First edition thus, 8vo., full red faux leather lettered gilt on spine and cover, limitation label on front endpaper, this no. 89 inscribed by author for Lord Butler of Saffron Walden, covers very slightly bumped, otherwise very good, sound.   Any Amount of Books   2015 - A84859   2016   £250

Association – Butt, Charles

Whitty, Edward Michael *Friends of Bohemia or Phases of London Life.* London: Smith Elder & Co., 1857. First edition, 2 volumes, half titles, slightly later half red morocco, gilt spine in compartments, little rubbed, bookplates of Charles W. Butt.   Jarndyce Antiquarian Booksellers   CCXVII - 296   2016   £250

Association – Butt, John

Graves, Robert 1895-1985 *The Real David Copperfield.* London: Arthur Barker, 1933. First edition, half title, original blue cloth, pencil inscription of John Butt 1938, stamps of B. A. Abel, solicitor, Nottingham, good plus in slightly worn dust jacket.   Jarndyce Antiquarian Booksellers   CCXVIII - 491   2016   £65

Association – Buxton, A. F.

Butler, Arthur Gray *The Three Friends: a Story of Rugby in the Forties.* London: Henry Frowde, 1900. Original maroon cloth, spine little faded, top edge gilt, signed by A. F. Buxton and Kathleen Tillotson, with ALS from Tillotson to Dorothy M. Ward. Jarndyce Antiquarian Books CCXV - 927 2016 £35

Association – Byass, Kathleen

Patmore, Brigit *The Impassioned Onlooker.* London: Robert Holden, 1926. First edition, one or two faint foxspots to prelims with occasional spot further, few faint handling marks, crown 8vo., original red and black patterned cloth, backstrip gently faded with printed label, small amount of creasing to cloth of upper board, little bleed from red of cloth to top edge and dust jacket interior (single spot showing to front panel), dust jacket with light overall dust soiling and small amount of chipping at corners, good, inscribed by author for Kathleen Byass. Blackwell's Rare Books B186 - 271 2016 £600

Association – Byles, C. E.

Darwin, Charles Robert 1809-1882 *The Origin of Species by Means of Natural Selection...* London: John Murray, 1891. Sixth edition, 8vo., original green cloth gilt, one folding chart, binding little rubbed, slight spotting to prelims, partially uncut, very good, presentation from R. J. Wilson to C. E. Byles the antiquarian writer. Sotheran's Piccadilly Notes - Summer 2015 - 95 2016 £450

Association – Byrch, John

Walsh, William *A Dialogue Concerning Women being a Defence of the Sex.* London: printed for R. Bensley in Russel street in Covent Garden, 1691. 8vo., paper little browned, stain at end affecting endpapers and last page of text, inner hinges neatly repaired, contemporary calf, expertly rebacked, spine gilt with raised bands, early ownership inscription of John Byrch, oval booklabel of Arnold Muirhead. Jarndyce Antiquarian Booksellers CCXVII - 292 2016 £4200

Association – Byron, Robert

Sitwell, Sacheverell *Collected Poems.* London: Duckworth, 1936. First edition, octavo, cover edges just little rubbed, spine slightly creased, prelims little spotted, very good in very good, price clipped dust jacket little rubbed at edges, inscribed by author for Robert Byron. Peter Ellis 112 - 362 2016 £295

Association – Cadman, A. Denys

Iraq Petroleum Company *An Account of the Construction in the Years 1932 to 1934 of the Pipe-Line of the Iraq Petroleum Company Limited ...* London: St. Clements Press, Oct., 1934. First edition, very rare, folio, original petrol blue quarter leather over boards, spine lettered gilt and with two panels blocked in gilt on front cover, folding plan, folding map, numerous superb illustrations in text, wear to extremities of binding, internally fine, contemporary bookplate of A. Denys Cadman, later in the Library of the University of Wyoming with stamp (cancelled), shelfmark label removed. Sotheran's Travel and Exploration - 329 2016 £798

Association – Cahill, John Baptist

Bonaventura, Saint 1221-1274 *Die Legend des Heyligen Vatters Francisci.* Nuremberg: Hieronymus Holtzel for the heirs of Caspar Rosentalet, April, 1512. First German edition, 4to., titlepage with large woodcut, full page woodcuts, smaller woodcuts, 57 woodcuts in all, all in fine contemporary color, predominantly yellows, greens and browns, 4to., 16th century pigskin over wooden boards, panelled and decorated in blind, remains of clasps (rubbed), rare, from the Virtue and Cahill Library (John Vertue formerly Virtue [1826-1900] and John Baptist Cahill [1841-1910]), overprinted bookplate noting war bomb damage to library in 1941, much used copy with some defects, repaired tear to foot of F3 and V1, no loss, I1, M1 &T4 lower outer corner torn away with loss of some text to lower portion of leaves, N1 woodcut with small hole expertly repaired, some old tears repaired, general staining and soiling throughout. Maggs Bros. Ltd. 1474 - 16 2016 £12,500

Association – Calder, Alexander

Aesopus *The Fables of Aesop according to Sir Roger L'Estrange.* Paris: Harrison of Paris, 1931. No. 274 of 595 copies on Auvergne from a total edition of 645, 20 of which were not for sale, 257 x 191mm., publisher's cloth backed boards in original pictorial dust jacket, in original (slightly marked) red cardboard chemise and (neatly repaired) slipcase with paper label, 50 drawings by Alexander Calder, original - very frequently missing or damaged - printed paper knife (for opening pages) laid in, pictorial inscription by the artist, Alexander Calder, one leaf with short fore-edge tear, not affecting text, otherwise very fine, pristine internally. Phillip J. Pirages 67 - 84 2016 $5500

Association – Calhoun, William

More, Henry *Enchiridion Ethicum, Praecipua Moralis Rhilosophiae Rudimenta Complectens Illustrata Utplurimum Veterum Monumentis...* London: J. Downing, 1711. Fourth edition, 8vo. engraved portrait, frontispiece trimmed, contemporary blind tooled calf, rebacked, 4 raised bands, gilt title, new endleaves, signature of Edmund Quincey 1718, donor's note (to Jeremiah Dummer, (Silversmith) dated 1718, signatures of 'William B. Calhoun', foxing, some leaves toned, marginal pen lines, title + first leaf perforated and embossed, very good.   Jeff Weber Rare Books   181 - 23   2016 $295

Association – Calmady, Laura Anne

Rea, John *Flora: seu de Florum Cultura.* London: by T. N. for George Marriott, 1676. Second edition, folio, engraved title, 8 plates, lightly browned, upper margins dusty, worming close to inner margin towards top edge, extends throughout getting worse in middle and then fanning out into a trial in text, hole in Y1 (affecting two lines), closed tear on two of the plate leaves about 3cm. long, contemporary calf, covers panelled in blind, rebacked, lower corners repaired, upper corners worn, new endleaves, old flyleaves preserved, from the library of James Stevens Cox (1910-1997), engraved label inserted between pages 52 and 53 'Laura A(nne) Calmady' of Langdon Court, ms. note on label dated 23 Oct. 1889 and states the book was bought from Wm. Wade at sale of Langdon books by Vincent Pollexfen Calmady.   Maggs Bros. Ltd.   1447 - 361   2016   £500

Association – Calmady, Vincent Pollexfen

Rea, John *Flora: seu de Florum Cultura.* London: by T. N. for George Marriott, 1676. Second edition, folio, engraved title, 8 plates, lightly browned, upper margins dusty, worming close to inner margin towards top edge, extends throughout getting worse in middle and then fanning out into a trial in text, hole in Y1 (affecting two lines), closed tear on two of the plate leaves about 3cm. long, contemporary calf, covers panelled in blind, rebacked, lower corners repaired, upper corners worn, new endleaves, old flyleaves preserved, from the library of James Stevens Cox (1910-1997), engraved label inserted between pages 52 and 53 'Laura A(nne) Calmady' of Langdon Court, ms. note on label dated 23 Oct. 1889 and states the book was bought from Wm. Wade at sale of Langdon books by Vincent Pollexfen Calmady.   Maggs Bros. Ltd.   1447 - 361   2016   £500

Association – Cambsfort

Camerarius, Joachim   1500-1574 *Symbolorum et Emblematum Centuriae Tres....*   Heidelberg: Voegelin, 1605. First collected edition, 4 engraved titlepages, 400 circular engraved illustrations, 4to., 4 parts in one volume, contemporary reversed calf, headcap and corners worn, some tears and marks to covers, contemporary ownership inscription "Cambsfort?", titlepage with old repair to tear (no loss), lightly browned throughout, occasional dampstaining. Maggs Bros. Ltd.   1474 - 18   2016   £4500

Association – Camden, Marquis of

Wordsworth, Christopher *Athens & Attica: a Journal of a Residence There.*   London: John Murray, 1836. First edition, 8vo., frontispiece, map, 2 lithographic plates, folding table, some foxing to frontispiece and plates, otherwise fine, inscriptions, Marquis of Camden's copy.   J. & S. L. Bonham Antiquarian Booksellers   Europe 2016 - 9215   2016   £400

Association – Campbell, Charles Montgomery

Hamilton, Thomas *Men and Manners in America.* Edinburgh: William Blackwood and T. Cadell, London, 1833. First edition, 2 volumes, 8vo., original green patterned cloth, paper labels (little browned), uncut, old repair to front inner hinge of volume 1, rare in original condition, without foxing, rarer still inscribed, presentation copy inscribed by author for Charles Mont(gomer)y Campbell.   Howard S. Mott Inc.   265 - 62   2016 $650

Association – Campbell, Duncan

Plato *The Works of Plato Abridg'd.* London: printed for A. Bell, 1701. First English edition, few leaves browned or spotted, one or two corrections in manuscript, faint dampmark to upper forecorner of first 50 leaves, 8vo., contemporary Cambridge type panelled calf, red morocco label to spine, slightly rubbed and marked bookplate of Seton of Ekoslund and ownership inscription of Duncan Campbell, more recent chess bookplate of Bruno Bassi, name 'Greeg' in blank area of first page of text, blindstamped. Blackwell's Rare Books   Greek & Latin Classics VII - 73   2016   £2500

Association – Campbell, J. Dykes

Campbell, James Dykes *Poems. MDCCCXXX. MDCCCXXXIII.*   Toronto: privately printed, 1862. Pirated edition, uncut in original blue penned paper wrappers, little creased with some very slight wear to head and tail of spine, pencil inscription, given to NIC by Mrs. Dykes Campbell, from JDC's editor, J. Dykes Campbell, library, nice in original wrappers.   Jarndyce Antiquarian Booksellers   CCXVII - 277   2016   £220

Association – Campbell, Martha

Chapone, Hester *Letters on the Improvement of the Mind, Addressed to a Young Lady.* London: printed for J. Walter, Charing Cross and C. Dilly in the Poultry, 1787. New edition, 8vo., , contemporary full speckled calf, rubbed maroon leather label, hinges weakening but sound, slightly chipped at head and tail of spine, armorial bookplate, signature of Martha Campbell & partially removed signature of Harriet Ramsay?, good, sound copy.   Jarndyce Antiquarian Books   CCXV - 105   2016   £50

Association – Canfield, Cass

Falconer, William *The Shipwreck, a Poem.* London: printed for William Miller by W. Bulmer, 1811. 197 x 121mm, very pretty mid 19th century green straight grain morocco, intricately decorated in gilt and blind, by W. Barratt (ticket on front flyleaf), covers with broad, densely gilt frame and central lozenge containing a large and elaborate floral centerpiece, raised bands, spine panels filled with gilt purple watered silk endleaves framed by gilt tolls, all edges gilt, 3 engraved plates and five engraved vignettes, verso of front endleaf with early inscription, "The Bookbinder's Tribute of Gratitude to Benj. Morland" and with bookplate of Cass Canfield, presentation to Canfield from Austen Kark laid in, spine uniformly sunned to olive brown, slight rubbing to corners, bands and joints, muted spotting to silk plates with minor foxing, hint of browning at edges of some leaves, still excellent copy, with none of the condition issues serious and with elaborately decorated covers lustrous and unworn. Phillip J. Pirages   67 - 27   2016 $750

Wilder, Thornton 1896-1976 *The Eighth Day.* New York: Harper & Row, 1967. First edition, one of 500 copies printed on special paper, 8vo, specially bound and signed by author, this copy #2 with bookplate of Cass Canfield, publishers' greeting card signed "Evan" and "Cass" laid in and nice inscription on titlepage by author for Cass, fine in publisher's box, inscribed by author to his editor at Harper, Cass Canfield.   Second Life Books, Inc.   196 B - 892   2016 $1250

Association – Campbell, Thomas

The Academic. Glasgow: Wardlaw and Cunninghame and Richard Baynes, London, 1826. Excellent set of numbers I to IX, with contemporary inscription to Thomas Campbell, Esq. Lord Rector of University of Glasgow with congratulations of admiring constituent James Blair, very scarce,.   John Drury Rare Books   2015 - 6422   2016 $437

Association – Cardew, Gloria

Children's Singing Games. David Nutt, 1894. First edition, Arts & Craft style illustrations to every page with many borders and some full page, every illustration hand colored by Gloria Cardew, small inkspot at foot of one page, 4to., original mottled brown cloth with illustration stamped in black to upper board, little rubbing to corners and light browning to endpapers, very good, inscribed by Cardew.   Blackwell's Rare Books   B184 - 252   2016   £1000

Association – Cardrof, Lord

Beattie, James 1735-1803 *An Essay on the Nature and Immutability of Truth; in Opposition to Sophistry and Scepticism.* Edinburgh: Kincaid & J. Bell, 1770. First edition, octavo, inscribed by author for David Steuart Erskine, 11th Earl of Buchan, beautifully preserved contemporary leather with gilt double lines inscribed on front and back panels, spine has five raised bands and title in gilt lettering on red field, second compartment, with Lord Cardrof's bookplate, ink signature, beautiful copy.   Athena Rare Books   List 15 - 1770   2016 $4500

Association – Cardwell, R.

Cohen, Gustavus *The Formation of Character.* Bloomsbury: Gustavus Cohen, 59 Great Russell Street; Liverpool: 40 Bedford Street North, 1884. original blue cloth, bevelled boards decorated in gilt and black, slightly dulled, illustrations by Fritz Braun, inscription from H. G. Cohen 28th July 1886 to R. Cardwell, very good, bright of family presentation copy.   Jarndyce Antiquarian Books   CCXV - 124   2016   £65

Association – Carey, Chris

Harrison, A. R. W. *The Law of Athens Procedure.* Oxford: Clarendon Press, 1971. First edition, 8vo., cloth, gilt lettered, spine slightly cocked, edges dusted, very good, no dust jacket, crossed out ownership inscription of Birthe Elkrog and gift inscription of Chris (Carey).   Unsworths Antiquarian Booksellers Ltd.   E04 - 57   2016   £30

Lloyd-Jones, H. *Sophocles Second Thought.* Gottingen: Vandenhoeck und Ruprecht, 1997. First edition, 8vo., near fine, paperback, author's gift inscription to Chris Carey. Unsworths Antiquarian Booksellers Ltd.   E04 - 70   2016   £20

Association – Carey, Joyce

Mallory, Jay *Sweet aloes: a Play in Three Acts.* London: Cassell, 1935. First edition, orange cloth, very good, tight copy, inscribed by author for producer Hugh Beaumont, also inscribed by actress, Joyce Carey, and signed by 12 members of the cast.   Second Life Books, Inc.   196 B - 126   2016 $225

Association – Carle, Eric

Fisher, Aileen *Do Bears Have Mothers, Too?* New York: Thomas Y. Crowell, 1973. First edition, beautifully illustrated by Eric Carle, little wear to plastic covering on rear dust jacket, otherwise fine in dust jacket (not price clipped), inscribed by Carle in ink for Catherine Clark, with added drawing of smiling cat, fine.   Second Life Books, Inc.   197 - 47   2016 $1500

Association – Carless, Rosa Fronfins

De Moraes, Vinicius *O Mergulhador.* Rio De Janeiro: Atelier De Arte, 1968. First edition, 4to., illustrated laminated boards, issued without dust jacket, illustrations in black and white with photos, signed presentation from author and his wife to artist Rosa Fronfins Carless, covers very slightly marked but sound clean, pleasing very good+ copy.   Any Amount of Books   2015 - A90864   2016   £550

Association – Carlingford, Lord

Aberdeen, George Hamilton Gordon, Earl of *An Inquiry into the Principles of Beauty in Grecian Architecture...* London: John Murray, 1822. First edition, contemporary or slightly later half tan calf, marbled boards, spine decorated in gilt, dark green morocco label, bookplate of Lord Carlingford, very good.   Jarndyce Antiquarian Booksellers   CCXVII - 1   2016   £85

Andrews, Alexander *The Eighteenth Century or Illustrations of the Manners and Customs of Our Grandfathers.* London: Chapman & Hall, 1856. First edition, half title, original green cloth, spine decorated in gilt, signature of Lord Carlingford, 1878, very good.   Jarndyce Antiquarian Books   CCXV - 14   2016   £60

Gray, Thomas   1716-1771   *The Poetical Works of Thomas Gray....*   York: printed by A. Ward and sold by J. Dodsley and J. Todd, York, 1775. First edition, 4to., contemporary full calf, spine with contrasting red leather label, frontispiece, joints cracking at top head of spine with little chipping, some scrapes to boards and rubbing to spine, little browning to endpapers, otherwise very good, ink note on front free endpaper by Richard Hooper of Upton Vicarage, Berks dated Jul 12 1872, bookplate of Baron Carlingford.   Sotheran's Piccadilly Notes - Summer 2015 - 150   2016   £275

Association – Carlisle, Elsie

Cary, Joyce *The Moonlight.* London: Michael Joseph, 1946. First edition, 8vo., signed presentation from author for Elsie Carlisle, singer, very good+ in chipped, very good- dust jacket.   Any Amount of Books   2015 - A68594   2016   £150

Association – Carlisle, Laura Mae

Wurdemann, Audrey *Bright Ambush.* New York: John Day Co., 1934. First edition, fine in near fine dust jacket with sunning at extremities, modest tear on front panel, inscribed by author for Laura Mae Carlisle oct. 1936.   Between the Covers Rare Books   204 - 142   2016 $600

Association – Carlyon, Horatio

Bacon, Francis   1561-1626   *The Twoo Bookes of Francis Bacon. Of the Proficience and Advancement of Learning, Divine and Humane.*   London: for Henrie Tomes, 1605. First edition, 4to., lacks final blank 3H2 and as always, rare two leaves of errata at end, late 19th century half calf and marbled boards, extremities of boards worn, very skillfully and imperceptibly rebacked, retaining entire original spine, small worm trail at bottom margin of quires 2D-2F, occasional minor marginalia in early hand, else lovely copy, early signature of Row'd Wetherald on title signature of Horatio Carlyon 1861, Sachs bookplate and modern leather book label calf backed clamshell box.   Joseph J. Felcone, Inc. Books from Five Centuries: a Miscellany - 10   2016 $7500

Association – Carmichael, Peter

Smiles, Samuel *George Moore, Merchant and Philanthropist.* London: George Routledge, 1878. Second edition, half title, frontispiece, original purple cloth, slight rubbing, bookplate and signature of Peter Carmichael, very good.   Jarndyce Antiquarian Books   CCXV - 949   2016   £58

Association – Carmichael, Thomas

Bunyan, John, Junior *The Drunkard's Progress...* Edinburgh: Johnstone and Hunter, 1853. 12 full page plates, vignette title and 2 other woodcuts, plate IV, V, VI transposed in binding, contemporary half red calf, cloth boards, front panel lettered with title, ownership inscr. Thos. Carmichael 1854.   Jarndyce Antiquarian Booksellers   CCXVII - 59   2016   £65

Association – Carnegie, Douglas

Pym, Horace N. *Chats in the Book-room.* London: 1896. Number 73 of 150 copies, signed and inscribed to Douglas Carnegie, vellum backed green cloth with gilt title and author to front board and spine, vellum discolored and corners bumped, printed on Arnold's unbleached handmade paper, interior very good except for foxing to frontispiece verso, which are printed on different paper, very good.   The Kelmscott Bookshop   12 - 86   2016 $160

Association – Carnes, A. Burton

Franklin, Benjamin 1706-1790 *Printing Week Library of Benjamin Franklin Keepsakes.* New York: privately printed, 1953-1982. Large 12mo., 30 volumes, complete set, all paper covered boards with some quarter leather and some patterned boards, variously paginated, this set belonged to Ben Lieberman, inscribed to him by designer, A. Burton Carnes. Oak Knoll Books 310 - 31 2016 $350

Association – Caroline, Queen Consort of George IV

Church of England. Book of Common Prayer *The Book of Common Prayer and Administration of the Sacraments.* London: published for John Reeves...sold and G. and W. Nicol and Satcherd and Letterman, 1807. 2 parts in 1 volume, 12mo., contemporary red straight grained morocco, single gilt fillet on sides and an inner border of 2 blind fillets and a blind roll tool, gilt crown of centre of both covers, spine richly tooled gilt and blind lettered in gilt direct, red morocco label inside front cover, gilt edges, trifle worn at extremities, inner hinge neatly repaired, boards trifle warped, good copy, with a letter of provenance on mourning paper from Isabella Speechly of Peterborough stating "The Prayer Book and Hymn Book (latter not present) which belonging to Queen Caroline, were given to the Lady Egmont by Lady Anne Hamilton the Queen's Lady and she have them to my Great Aunt Miss Martha Speechly then living at Darmouth House...". Blackwell's Rare Books Marks of Genius - 11 2016 £6000

Association – Carpentarius, Antonius

Plato *Omnia Opera cum Commentariis Procli in Timaeum & Politica...* Basel: Apud Ioan Valderum, 1534. Editio princeps of the Scholia, 2 volumes bound as 3, some minor spotting and staining, old (probably 17th century) manuscript annotations in ink (in Latin, some shaved) and underlining in red, plus later marginal numbered in pencil, one or two later ink notes in French, marginal dampstaining in volume III, 17th century inscription of 'Ant. Carpetnarius, Doct. med. Paris', folio, late 17th century brown goatskin, spines gilt in compartments with second and third lettered and central tool of a crowned goat's head in others, marbled pastedowns, colouring different in each volume, some wear and old repairs to head and foot of spines, volume i with front flyleaf filled with 8 paragraphs of bibliographic detail in French in later (late 18th century) hand, good. Blackwell's Rare Books Greek & Latin Classics VII - 72 2016 £5000

Association – Carpenter, Anne

Kaufman, George *Beggar on Horseback.* New York: Boni & Liveright, 1924. First edition, 8vo., nice in little chipped dust jacket, section of joike newspaper pasted in on page 167, inscribed by Anne Carpenter (Gladys in the play). Second Life Books, Inc. 196A - 912 2016 $125

Association – Carr, R. L.

Salmon, William *Seplasium. The Compleat English Physician or the Druggist's Shop Opened.* London: for Matthew Gilliflower and George Sawbridge, 1693. First edition, half title and errata/ad leaf and a4 with table on verso that is meant as a slip cancel for the table on X8v bound after X8, small hole through centre of Z8 (damaging two lines), 19th century paper slip tipped in between E32-3 (obscuring small portion of text on first 13 lines), rust spots on Gg1-3, fore corner of Ooo4 folded-in, small rust spot on Ffff4, contemporary calf, front joint and spine repaired, 19th century endleaves, from the library of James Stevens Cox (1910-1997), old signature "R. L. Carr ex donis C. C. Cocks". Maggs Bros. Ltd. 1447 - 373 2016 £650

Association – Carroll, Mark

Tebbel, John *History of Book Publishing in the United States Volume I-Volume 4.* New York: R. R. Bowker, 1972. 1975. 1978. 1981. First edition, large 8vo., 4 volumes, cloth, presentation from author for Mark Carroll, clipped news obits of Alfred Knopf, well preserved. Oak Knoll Books 310 - 75 2016 $550

Association – Carter, Leslie

Ford, James L. *The Story of Du Barry.* New York: Stokes, 1902. Leslie Carter edition, 8vo., illustrations, bound in front is program for the Belasco production, bookplate, signed by Carter, 10 years later Belasco signed and dated page as well, owner's signature on flyleaf, purple cloth stamped in gilt, spine faded, cover little worn, else very good. Second Life Books, Inc. 196A - 571 2016 $75

Association – Cartier, R. E.

De Tournes, Jean De *Insignium Aliquot Virorum Icones.* Lyons: Jean de Tournes, 1559. First and only edition, 8vo., later vellum with red leather label on spine, some soiling, De Tournes' Viper device on title and 145 woodcut portrait medallions, bookplate of R. E. Cartier, Alfred Cartier's nephew and heir, armorial bookplate of Bibliotheca Trautner-Falkiana, i. e. the Augsburg bibliophile Hans Joachim Trautner (1916-2001), little spotted in places. Maggs Bros. Ltd. 1474 - 29 2016 £1800

Association – Carver, Clifford

Warwick, Frances Evelyn *A Woman and the War.* London: Chapman & Hall, 1916. First edition, 8vo., frontispiece, little foxed red cloth, very good, tight, inscribed by author for Clifford Carver. Second Life Books, Inc. 196 B - 833 2016 $325

Association – Carysfort, Earl of

Trollope, Anthony 1815-1882 *The American Senator.* London: Chapman and Hall, 1877. First edition in book form, 184 x 127mm., half titles, 3 volumes, fine contemporary dark olive morocco bound for the Earl of Carysfort (with his arms in gilt on center at front covers and with his monogram at foot of spines), backstrips titled in gilt, raised bands flanked by multiple gilt rules, marbled endpapers, all edges gilt, shelf label and engraved Carysfort bookplate, front joint of 2 volumes with hint of wear, one leaf with two tiny tears at top, fine, attractive set, text immaculate and in a lustrous elegant binding.   Phillip J. Pirages   67 - 328   2016 $2250

Association – Castle Forbes

Aikin, John *Letters from a Father to His Son on Various Topics Relative to Literature and the Conduct of Life.* London: printed for J. Johnson, St. Paul's Churchyard, 1794. Second edition, 8vo., titlepage slightly dusted, otherwise nice clean copy, contemporary or slightly later half scarlet calf, armorial gilt stamp of Forbes family at head of spine, little rubbed, corners slightly bumped, armorial bookplate of Castle Forbes Library.   Jarndyce Antiquarian Books   CCXV - 9 2016   £125

Association – Cator, Joseph

Johnson, Samuel 1709-1784 *A Dictionary of the English Language.* London: printed by W. Strahan for J. and P. Knapton...., 1755. First edition, 2 volumes, titlepages printed in red and black, smallish (?wax) stain in last leaf of prelims, few leaves little browned, crease in 29F2 (no loss), small circular ink spot 2952v, couple of contemporary notes on sources added in margins, folio, contemporary calf, double gilt fillets on sides, stoutly and skillfully rebacked, repairs to corners, contemporary ownership inscription of Champion Branfill, engraved armorial bookplate of Joseph Cator, very good.   Blackwell's Rare Books   B184 - 52   2016   £17,500

Association – Catt, Carrie Chapman

National American Woman Suffrage Association *Victory: How Women Won It.* New York: Wilson, 1940. First edition, 8vo., pages 174, illustrations, blue cloth, spine little faded, otherwise fine, one of 300 Honor Copies inscribed by Carrie Chapman Catt.   Second Life Books, Inc.   196 B - 305   2016 $450

Young, Rose *The Record of the Leslie Woman Suffrage Commission Inc. 1917-1929.* Leslie Commission, 1929. First edition, small 8vo., little soiled cloth, very good, inscribed by Carrie Chapman Catt for Josephine Fowler Pool.   Second Life Books, Inc.   196A - 263   2016 $600

Association – Cawdor, Earl of

Homerus *Ilias kai Odysseia.* Oxonia: ex Ergasteriou Typographikou Akademias, 1800. One of the rare and spectacular copies of the Grenville Homer, only 25 copies printed and used as presentation copies, inscribed by editors, William Wyndham, Lord Grenville and his brother Thomas Grenville, 4to., 5 engraved plates, plates spotted, some light offsetting to text, contemporary red morocco, boards with central gilt stamp, arms of the Earl of Cawdor, spines lettered gilt, red morocco doublures with border of fourteen gilt fillets, edges gilt on rough, spines sunned, touch of rubbing to extremities, doublures offset onto endpapers and outermost leaves of each volume, very good.   Blackwell's Rare Books   Greek & Latin Classics VII - 37   2016   £12,000

Association – Chabrol, Claude

Rohmer, Eric *Hitchcock.* Paris: Editions Universitaires, 1957. First French edition, inscribed by Rohmer and co-author, Claude Chabrol, also laid in is small publisher's prospectus for this title, very good in wrappers.   Royal Books   51 - 37   2016 $3500

Association – Chaffin, Harry

Vallee, Rudy *Vagabond Dreams Come True.* New York: Dutton, 1930. First edition, 8vo. photos, very good, inscribed by author for Harry Chaffin, also inscribed to same by Elliott B. MacRae, president of Dutton.   Second Life Books, Inc.   196 B - 783   2016 $100

Association – Chamberlain, C. Pearl

Suckling, John *Fragmenta Aurea. A collection of al the Incomparable Peeces.* London: for Humphrey Moseley, 1646. First edition, first state, engraved portrait, contemporary calf, gilt fillet and cornerpieces, red morocco spine label, portrait and first two leaves with two very tiny holes at gutter, worm trail in lower margin of first three gatherings, else very nice in lovely contemporary binding, bookplate of C. Pearl Chamberlain and book label of Abel Berland, fine red morocco pull of case, accompanied by ALS of John Suckling (1569-1627) father of the poet to unnamed recipient.   Joseph J. Felcone, Inc.   Books from Five Centuries: a Miscellany - 138   2016 $6000

Association – Chamberlayne, James

Rabelais, Francois *The Works of the Famous Mr. Francis Rabelais, Doctor in Physick...* London: for Richard Bentley and are to be sold by John Starkey, 1664. First edition in English, 2nd issue, small rust spot on E8 and G1, small piece torn away from fore-edge of M8 (not touching text), dark stain near inner margin of D1, minor tear to lower edge of (2) N& (just touching last line of text), lower edge of)2 uncut, contemporary sheep ruled in blind, rebacked, corners repaired, new endleaves, from the library of James Stevens Cox (1910-1997), contemporary ink signature of James Chamberlayne. Maggs Bros. Ltd.   1447 - 348   2016   £950

Association – Chapin, Chester

Adam, Robert Brothwick *The R. B. Adam Library Relating to Dr. Samuel Johnson and His Era.* Buffalo: printed for the author, London and New York: Oxford University Press, 1929. First edition, one of 500 copies, 3 volumes, quarto, original blue buckram, gilt lettering, top edge gilt, others untrimmed, frontispieces and numerous illustrations, from the library of Walpole bibliographer and scholar Allen Tracy Hazen, with his posthumous booklabel, later ink signature of Johnson scholar Chester Chapin, dated Feb. 27 1986, cloth slightly rubbed and worn, very good.   The Brick Row Book Shop   Miscellany 69 - 50   2016 $500

Association – Chapman, Mary

Child, Lydia Maria 1802-1880 *The Frugal Housewife.* London: William Tegg, 1860. Twenty-fourth edition, 16mo., original red cloth, spine gilt, slightly rubbed and dulled, signature of Mary Chapman 1868 on leading f.e.p.   Jarndyce Antiquarian Books   CCXV - 117   2016   £48

Association – Chappell, Warren

Prokofieff, Serge *Peter and the Wolf.* New York: Alfred Knopf, 1940. Stated first edition, Oblong 4to., cloth, pictorial paste-on, fine in faded dust jacket with few mends, inscribed by artist with lovely drawing of Peter laid in note signed by artist on his personal stationery with mailing envelope, super copy, illustrations by Warren Chappell.   Alephbet Books, Inc.   111 - 85   2016 $400

Association – Chargaff, Erwin

Schrader, Franz *Mitosis.* New York: Columbia University Press, 1949. Third printing, 8vo., signed by Erwin Chargaff, fine, hardback.   By the Book, L. C.   45 - 24   2016 $250

Association – Charlotte, Queen

Haller, Ablrecht Von, Baron *Letters from Baron Haller to His Daughter...* London: printed by J. Murray, 1780. Half title, contemporary speckled calf, raised bands, maroon morocco label, neat repairs to hinges, spines slightly rubbed, presentation inscriptions on leading pastedown and initial blank, gift of Queen Charlotte to Mary Hamilton, Queen's House, London Jan. 19th 1781.   Jarndyce Antiquarian Books   CCXV - 241   2016   £1500

Association – Charlton, W. L.

Tweddell, Robert *Account of the Examination of the Elgin-box at the Foreign Office in Downing Street on 7th November 1816 in a letter to James Losh, Esa....* Manchester: printed for the author by C. Wheeler and Son, 7 Pall Mall, King Street, 1817. Sole edition, 4to., uncut in original blue sugar paper wrappers, slight water stained, also affecting initial and following blanks, signature on upper wrapper of WL Charlton.   Jarndyce Antiquarian Booksellers   CCXVII - 288   2016   £120

Association – Chatsworth Library

Homerus *Ilias (and) Odyssea. Batrachomyomachia. Hymni XXXII. Eorundem Multiplex Lectio.* Venice: in officina Lucaeantonii Iuntae, 1537. 8vo., woodcut device with initials "LA on titlepages, some light spotting, titlepage and last page dusty in each volume, second gathering in third section either misbound or misnumbered (but all there), late 18th century red morocco boards, bordered with gilt fillet, spine divided by dotted gilt rules, second and third compartments, gilt lettered direct, rest with small central flower tools, marbled endpapers, edges red, just little rubbed, spines slightly sunned, very good, the Chatsworth copy.   Blackwell's Rare Books   Greek & Latin Classics VII - 33   2016   £5000

Lucretius Carus, Titus *De Rerum Nature Libros Sex, ad Exemplarium Mss. Fidem Recensitos...* Impensis editoris typis A Hamilton, 1796-1797. First Wakefield edition, large paper copy, engraved frontispiece, little spotting and dust soiling here and there, tall 4to., contemporary vellum, boards bordered with gilt roll with central gilt stamp of arms of Duke of Devonshire, spines titled gilt, deep blue endpapers, edges gilt and marbled underneath vellum on each spine split horizontally, just above middle, volume ii in two places (with slight loss of vellum on volumes ii and iii), otherwise just little bit age yellowed and with touch of wear to spine ends, bookplates of Chatsworth Library, red morocco gilt booklabels of Baron Holland, plus modern paper booklabel in volume i, very good.   Blackwell's Rare Books   B186 - 98   2016   £3000

Association – Chavoix, P. H.

Johannes De Aquila *Sermones Quadragesimales (with the Collaboration of Daniel Vincentius).* Venice: Petrus de Quarengiis, Bergomensis for Alexander Calcedonius, 21 October, 1499. Second edition, fine woodcut, opening historiated initial, rubricated in red and black headings and large initials rubricated in red throughout, 8vo., double columns, 19th century French marbled calf, flat spine richly gilt with red morocco label, marbled edges, neat repair to headcap, contemporary inscription, ex libris P H Chavoix typographi. Maggs Bros. Ltd. 1474 - 43 2016 £3000

Association – Chavontier, Charles

Farcot, Henri Eugene Adrien *La Navigation Atmospherique.* Paris: A. Bourdilliat et Cie, 1859. 12mo., folding engraved plate, half title, early 20th century dark green quarter morocco and marbled boards, spine gilt and lettered with balloon motif in gilt in compartments, original printed paper wrappers bound in, attractive association copy with red inkstamps of Charles Chavontier, the Paris airship manufacturers. John Drury Rare Books 2015 - 16246 2016 $437

Association – Chester, Mary

The Female Instructor or Young Woman's Companion... Liverpool: Nuttall, Fisher & Dixon, 1812. Stereotype edition, frontispiece and plates, small worm hole to final 3 leaves, contemporary full mottled calf, black morocco label, expert repair to hinges, contemporary signature of Mary Chester, nice. Jarndyce Antiquarian Books CCXV - 194 2016 £225

Association – Chiaveroti, Carlo

Malpighi, Marcello *Opera Medica et Anatomica Varia...* Venice: Andrea Poletti, 1743. Half title, engraved frontispiece, 20 engraved plates, folio, bound in contemporary vellum boards, boards slightly warped, short crack at top of front joint and bottom of rear joint, some minor foxing on few plates, bookplate of Carlo Chiaveroti on title verso, adhesive discoloration showing through on recto. James Tait Goodrich X-78 - 391 2016 $1250

Association – Chichester, R.

Bird, J. B. *The Laws Respecting Parish Matters, Containing the Several Offices and Duties of Churchwardens...* London: J. and W T. Clarke, 1832. Eighth edition, 8vo., occasional spots of foxing, some early leaves little grubby, small tear to titlepage at lower gutter, contemporary half green morocco, gilt spine, marbled paper covered boards, edges sprinkled brown, upper joint splitting at head with some chips to leather, small loss to tail of spine, rubbed with little surface loss to upper board, endpaper bit stained, worn but sound, ownership inscription of R. Chichester dated June 19th 1835, pencilled bookseller's notes. Unsworths Antiquarian Booksellers 30 - 20 2016 £75

Association – Chilcott, Hugh T.

Dowson, Ernest *Adrian Rome.* London: Methuen & Co., 1899. Original blue cloth with gilt authors and title to spine and front cover, spine and cover also have a lovely filigree gilt design, slight bumping and very small strip of cloth missing along top of spine, interior is bright and clean, 39 page publisher's catalog Feb. 1899, very good, quite scarce, rare presentation copy inscribed by Arthur Moore 2nd May 99 for Hugh T. Chilcott. The Kelmscott Bookshop 12 - 37 2016 $850

Association – Chiles, Sam

Reed, St. Clair Griffin *A History of the Texas Railroads and of Transportation Conditions Under Spain and Mexico and the Republic and the State.* Houston: St. Clair Pub., 1941. First edition, 8vo., blue cloth, gilt titles, presentation copy warmly inscribed by author to Sam Chiles, longtime railroad associate of author, no. 1733 of numbered limited edition signed by author, very good+, faint darkening of spine. Kaaterskill Books 21 - 79 2016 $400

Association – Chimaer, Ludovicus

Horatius Flaccus, Quimtus *Cum Commentariis & Enarrationibus Commentatoris Veteris, et Iacobi Cruquii Messenii...* Antwerp: Ex officina Plantiana Raphelengii, 1611. Final Plantin edition, 4to., paper toned, some spotting, gift inscription dated 1643 (to Ludovicus Chimaer from G. van Alphen) and ownership inscription dated 1669, contemporary vellum, board fore-edges overlapping, spine lettered in ink, soiled and bit nicked, hinges cracking but sound, rear flyleaf removed, armorial bookplate of Rich. Palmer, Esq. Blackwell's Rare Books Greek & Latin Classics VII - 41 2016 £500

Association – Chippendale, Joseph

Smith, Adam 1723-1790 *An Inquiry into the Nature and Causes of the Wealth of Nations.* London: T. Cadell Jun. and W. Davies, 1802. 11th edition, 3 volumes, half titles, tear to fore-edge of pages 171-72, volume I with no loss of text, recent half brown calf, black morocco labels, signature of Joseph Chippendale on titlepage of volumes I and III, half title of volume II.   Jarndyce Antiquarian Booksellers   CCXVII - 259   2016   £1250

Association – Cholmondeley

Pritchett, V. S. *Marching Spain.* London: Ernest Benn, 1928. First edition, octavo, 8 photos, ownership signature of one of the Cholmondeleys, edges bit spotted, cloth bubbled in places, corner bruised, very good in very good, chipped and slightly marked dust jacket bit tanned at spine.   Peter Ellis 112 - 317   2016   £125

Association – Christie, James

Kerr, John *Memories Grave and Gay....* Edinburgh: William Blackwood & Sons, 1902. Half title, frontispiece, plates, 32 page catalog, few leaves roughly opened causing tear to pages 287/288, original green cloth, slightly rubbed and dulled, gift inscription from James Christie, Carlisle 25th March 1902.   Jarndyce Antiquarian Books   CCXV - 809   2016   £20

Association – Chubb, Thomas Caldecot

Aiken, Conrad *The Jug of Forslin.* Boston: Four Seas, 1916. 8vo., bookplate of Thomas Caldecot Chubb, and his name in ink dated Oct. 1919, also signed by Stephen Vincent Benet who signed Christmas 1916, brown stain, top edges darkened, edges of cover and ends of spine little worn, rear cover little spotted, otherwise very good, tight.   Second Life Books, Inc.   197 - 2   2016 $125

Association – Chubova, A. P.

Lee, Harper (title in Cyrillic and English) *Ubit Peresmeshnika/To Kill a Mockingbird.* Moskva: Moldodaia Gvardiia, 1964. First Russian book edition, octavo, text in Russian, octavo, quarter black cloth printed in white and illustrated paper over boards, attractive bookplate in Cyrillic of A. P. Chubova, owner's name in Cyrillic on both sides of first leaf, binding little cocked and spine lettering little rubbed, modest edgewear on edges of paper, overall very good.   Between the Covers Rare Books   204 - 67   2016 $2200

Association – Churchill, Mary

Bible. English - 1903 *The English Bible.* Hammersmith: Doves Press, 1903-1905. One of 500 copies, 331 x 235mm., five volumes, original limp vellum by Doves Bindery (stamp signed), gilt titling on spine, housed within two later oatmeal linen dropback clamshell boxes with black morocco spine labels, elegant initial letters in red by Edward Johnston, including an "I" running the length of the page to open Genesis ("In the beginning"), front flyleaf of volume I inscribed in pencil by Madeleine Whyte for Mary Churchill, with Doves Press invoice for Miss Whyte dated June 27 1905, initaled by "B.H." (i.e. Bessie Hooley, a sewer at the bindery and part-time secretary to Cobden-Sanderson) laid in, vellum with just hint of soiling, but very little of the typical variation in grain, two dozen leaves with minor marginal foxing (never approaching any significance), dozen additional leaves with whisper of foxing, otherwise clean, fresh, bright copy inside and out.   Phillip J. Pirages 67 - 115   2016 $19,500

Association – Cippico, Antonio

Bacon, Francis 1561-1626 *Of Gardens.* London: Eragny Press for Hacon Ricketts, 1902. One of 226 copies, original patterned paper boards, gilt titling on front, wood engraved frontispiece, borders, colophon, printer's device and initials, all by Lucien Pissaro, clipping from promotional material tipped onto front pastedown, front free endpaper with bookplate of Antonio Cippico, front cover with ink inscription "File copy/ not to be/Taken away", paper boards little soiled, usual offsetting to endpapers from binder's glue, half a dozen leaves with faint wrinkling, other minor imperfections but especially interesting copy in very good condition.   Phillip J. Pirages   67 - 129   2016 $1500

Association – Claire, William

Aldridge, Adele *Notepoems.* Riverside: Magic Circle, 1972. Second edition, First printing, 8vo., author's presentation to poet and editor William Claire, 2/17/73, paper wrappers, cover little soiled, otherwise very good, tight.   Second Life Books, Inc.   196A - 22   2016 $50

Becker, Anne *The Transmutation Notebooks: Poems in the Voices of Charles and Emma Darwin.* Washington: Forest Woods Media, 1996. First edition, paper wrappers, author's presentation to poet and editor William Claire, laid in is notecard inviting Claire to a party and flyer announcing poet's readings of her book with note handwritten to invite Claire to same party, fine.   Second Life Books, Inc.   196A - 92   2016 $40

Bogan, Louise *Collected Poems 1923-1953.* New York: Noonday, 1954. First edition, 8vo., author's presentation on flyleaf to poet and editor Bill Claire, erratum slip tipped in, yellow cloth, cover little faded and soiled, otherwise very good, tight copy.   Second Life Books, Inc.   196A - 177   2016 $85

Combs, T. *Briefs.* Franklin: Hillside, 1966. No. 259 of 425 copies, 1 5/16 x 2 inches, yellow cloth with drawing on front and lettering on spine in dark blue, drawings by D. Clark, author's presentation for Bill Claire, cover slightly darkened, else nice, little paper folder.   Second Life Books, Inc.   196 B - 244   2016 $100

Conover, Anne *Caresse Crosby From Black Sun to Roccasinibalda.* Santa Barbara: Capra Press, 1989. First edition, 8vo., fine in dust jacket, inscribed by author to William Claire.   Second Life Books, Inc.   196A - 152   2016 $750

Cowley, Malcolm *Blue Juniata: Collected Poems.* New York: Viking Press, 1968. First edition, 8vo., fine, little worn dust jacket, inscribed by author to poet and editor William Claire.   Second Life Books, Inc.   196A - 344   2016 $85

Dickey, James *Poems 1957-1967.* Middletown: Wesleyan University Press, 1967. First edition, fine in very good dust jacket, inscribed to poet and editor Bill Claire.   Second Life Books, Inc.   196A - 419   2016 $200

Dillard, Annie *Tickets for a Prayer Wheel: Poems.* Columbia: University of Missouri, 1974. First edition, 8vo., author's presentation on half title to poet and editor, William Claire and his wife Helen, orchid cloth over flexible boards, top edges little spotted, otherwise very good tight copy in somewhat toned dust jacket.   Second Life Books, Inc.   196A - 425   2016 $350

Hammond, Mrs. *The Horse Opera; and other poems.* Columbus: Ohio State University, 1966. First edition, author's presentation to poet William Claire, blue cloth, top edges slightly spotted, otherwise nice in very slightly chipped and faded dust jacket.   Second Life Books, Inc.   196A - 712   2016 $45

Hazo, Samuel *Once for the last Bandit.* Pittsburgh: University of Pittsburgh, 1972. 8vo., author's presentation to poet William Claire, orchid cloth, top edges slightly spotted, otherwise nice, in somewhat soiled and chipped dust jacket.   Second Life Books, Inc.   196A - 759   2016 $45

Hazo, Samuel *Sexes: the Marriage Dialogues.* Byblos Press, 1965. First edition, 8vo., author's presentation to William Claire, very good.   Second Life Books, Inc.   196A - 760   2016 $45

Heaney, Seamus 1939- *Poems & a Memoir.* New York: Limited Editions Club, 1982. First edition, tall 8vo., one of 200 copies signed by author, Henry Pearson and Thomas Flanagan, embossed brown morocco by Robert Bulen & son, in brown cardboard slipcase, this copy inscribed by author for Bill Claire, fine.   Second Life Books, Inc.   196A - 761   2016 $1200

Hecht, Roger *Burnt Offerings. Poems by.* Santa Fe: The Lightning Tree, 1979. First printing, small 8vo., author's presentation to poet William Claire, paper wrappers, cover ad edges little foxed, otherwise nice.   Second Life Books, Inc.   196A - 767   2016 $45

Hecht, Roger *27 Poems.* Denver: Alan Swallow, 1966. First edition, 8vo., paper over boards, cover slightly bumped at ends of spine, otherwise nice in slightly scuffed and chipped dust jacket, presentation from author to William Claire.   Second Life Books, Inc.   196A - 766   2016 $50

Heyen, William *The Chestnut Rain.* New York: Ballantine, 1986. First edition, author's presentation on half title to poet and editor, William Claire, paper wrappers, cover slightly soiled and creased, otherwise very good, right copy.   Second Life Books, Inc.   196A - 781   2016 $85

Heyen, William *Noise in the Trees: poems and memoir.* New York: Vanguard, 1974. First edition, author's presentation to poet William Claire, Oct. 20 1989, pale blue cloth stamped in white, edges little spotted, cover slightly faded, otherwise very good, tight copy in price clipped and little scuffed dust jacket.   Second Life Books, Inc.   196A - 782   2016 $95

Hoffman, Daniel *An Armada of Thirty Whales.* New Haven: Yale, 1954. First edition, 8vo., author's presentation opposite title to poet William Claire, paper over boards, first book scarce, edges little spotted, otherwise very good tight in somewhat soiled and little chipped dust jacket with corner of front flap torn off.   Second Life Books, Inc.   196A - 803   2016 $75

Hoffman, Daniel *A Little Geste; and other poems.* New York: Oxford, 1960. 8vo., author's presentation to poet William Claire, signed under crossed-out author's name, green cloth, edges slightly soiled, corners of cover little rubbed, otherwise very good, tight copy in little chipped and soiled dust jacket.   Second Life Books, Inc.   196A - 804   2016 $75

Hoffman, Daniel *Striking the Stones: Poems.* New York: Oxford, 1968. 8vo., author's name crossed out and 'Dan' written below and presentation to William Claire, from author, light yellow cloth, top edges of leaves and edges of cover slightly soiled, very good, tight in little chipped and soiled dust jacket.   Second Life Books, Inc.   196A - 807   2016 $45

Jacobsen, Josephine *The Animal Inside.* Athens: Ohio University, 1966. First edition, yellow cloth, errata slip in between pages, 2 articles about author laid in, edges of cover little soiled, otherwise very good, tight copy in scuffed and chipped dust jacket, author's presentation to poet William Claire.   Second Life Books, Inc.   196A - 884   2016 $45

Jacobsen, Josephine *For the Unlost. Volume four of the Distinguished Poets Series of Contemporary Poetry.* Baltimore: Contemporary Poetry, 1946. First edition, 8vo., frontispiece, author's presentation to poet William Claire, signed again on title, gray cloth, cover slightly yellowed and little scuffed at corners and ends of spine, else nie.   Second Life Books, Inc.   196A - 887   2016 $50

Jacobsen, Josephine *The Sisters.* Columbia: The Bench Press, 1987. First printing, author's presentation on half title to poet William Claire, paper wrappers, about as new.   Second Life Books, Inc.   196A - 886   2016 $45

Kennedy, Ellen Conroy *The Negritude of Poets.* New York: Viking, 1975. 8vo., presentation form editor for William Claire, paper over boards with cloth spine, edges little spotted, otherwise very good, tight copy, little chipped and scuffed dust jacket.   Second Life Books, Inc.   196A - 942   2016 $45

Kunitz, Stanley *A Kind of Order, a Kind of Folly.* Boston: Atlantic Monthly, Little Brown, 1975. First edition, 8vo., author's presentation for William Claire, paper over boards with cloth spine, edges little marked and soiled, edges of cover little scuffed, otherwise very good tight in chipped and lightly soiled dust jacket.   Second Life Books, Inc.   196A - 992   2016 $75

Kunitz, Stanley *Passport to the War.* New York: Holt, 1944. First edition, 8vo. fine in nicked and some worn dust jacket, inscribed by author for William Claire.   Second Life Books, Inc.   196A - 994   2016 $300

Kunitz, Stanley *The Poems of 1928-1978.* Boston: Little Brown, 1979. First edition, 8vo., author's affectionate presentation to Bill Claire, tan cloth, nice, little soiled and stained dust jacket.   Second Life Books, Inc.   196A - 993   2016 $75

Kunitz, Stanley *The Testing-Tree.* Boston: Atlantic Monthly, 1971. First edition, 8vo., fine in little nicked dust jacket, inscribed by author for William Claire.   Second Life Books, Inc.   196A - 995   2016 $225

Kurzweil, Arthur *The Encyclopedia of Jewish Genealogy volume I.* Northvale: Jason Aronson, 1991. First edition, 8vo., presentation to William Claire, black cloth, top edges slightly soiled, otherwise very good, tight copy in browned and little soiled, slightly chipped, dust jacket.   Second Life Books, Inc.   196A - 996   2016 $50

L'Heureux, John *Rubrics for a Revolution.* New York: Macmillan, 1967. First printing, author's presentation to William Claire, black cloth, top edges slightly soiled, otherwise very good, tight in browned and little soiled, slightly chipped dust jacket.   Second Life Books, Inc.   196B - 997   2016 $75

Laughlin, James *Selected Poems.* Norfolk: New Directions, 1959. First edition, 8vo., author's presentation on flyleaf to poet William Claire, paper over boards, little foxing on endpapers, otherwise very good, tight copy in little chipped and somewhat soiled dust jacket.   Second Life Books, Inc.   196 B - 20   2016 $75

Laughlin, James *Quello Che La Maitta Scrive...* Parma: Guanda Editore, 1970. First edition, 12mo., printed wrapper over stiff wrapper, inscribed to poet William Claire, slight tanning to text block, near fine.   Second Life Books, Inc.   196 B - 16   2016 $75

Laughlin, James *The Wild Anemone & Other Poems.* New York: New Directions, 1957. First edition, 12mo., printed wrapper over stiff wrapper, inscribed by author for William Claire, slight tanning to text block, nar fine.   Second Life Books, Inc.   196 B - 19   2016 $75

Leonard, Elmore *Get Shorty.* New York: Delacorte, 1990. First printing, 8vo, paper over boards with cloth spine, author's presentation to Bill Claire, cover slightly darkened at ends of spine, otherwise near fine in slightly yellowed dust jacket.   Second Life Books, Inc.   197 - 208   2016 $200

Logan, John *The Anonymous Lover: new Poems by...* New York: Liveright, 1973. First edition, 8vo., author's presentation on half title to poet and editor William Claire, also signed on title, 3 photos by Aaron Sisking, paper over boards with cloth spine, very slight foxing on first and last two leaves, otherwise nice in dust jacket.   Second Life Books, Inc.   196 B - 85   2016 $75

Logan, John *The Bridge of Change.* Brockport: BOA editions, 1978. One of 200 copies, 8vo., author's presentation on flyleaf to poet and editor William Claire, signed on title, paper wrappers, slight spot on back cover, otherwise nice. Second Life Books, Inc. 196 B - 87 2016 $45

Logan, John *Cycle for Mother Cabrini.* Cloud Marauder Press, 1971. Second printing, 8vo., author's presentation to poet William Claire, woodcuts by James Brunot, paper wrappers, cover slightly faded and very small bump at upper corner, otherwise nice. Second Life Books, Inc. 196 B - 88 2016 $45

Logan, John *Ghosts of the Heart: New Poems...* Chicago: University of Chicago, 1960. First edition, 8vo., signed by author, presentation from author for poet William Claire, red cloth, nice, scuffed and little chipped, dust jacket. Second Life Books, Inc. 196 B - 89 2016 $75

Logan, John *Spring of the Thief: Poems 1960-1962.* New York: Knopf, 1963. First edition, 8vo., author's signature and presentation to William Claire, blue cloth stamped in red and gilt, cover very slightly scuffed at corners and ends of spine, otherwise very good, tight copy in scuffed and chipped dust jacket. Second Life Books, Inc. 196 B - 91 2016 $95

Louichheim, Katie *With or Without Roses.* Garden City: Doubleday, 1966. First edition, 8vo., author's presentation n title to poet William Claire, tan cloth, top edges slightly spotted, few ink marks in contents pages, otherwise very good, tight, scuffed and lightly soiled dust jacket. Second Life Books, Inc. 196 B - 97 2016 $40

Lucas, John *The Poetry of Theodore Roethke.* Oxford Review, 1968. Offprint, 8vo., stapled wrappers, inscribed by author for William Claire, laid in TLS to Claire. Second Life Books, Inc. 196 B - 101 2016 $85

MacLeish, Archibald *New and Collected Poems 1917-1976.* Boston: Houghton Mifflin, 1976. First printing, fine in near fine dust jacket, inscribed for William Claire. Second Life Books, Inc. 196 B - 117 2016 $75

MacLeish, Archibald *Songs for Eve.* Boston: Houghton Mifflin, 1954. First edition, fine in nice and some worn dust jacket, inscribed by author for William Claire. Second Life Books, Inc. 196 B - 119 2016 $45

Marshall, Paule *Praisesong for the Widow.* New York: Putnam, 1983. First edition, 8vo., fine, dust jacket little nicked and worn, inscribed by author to poet William Claire. Second Life Books, Inc. 196 B - 142 2016 $85

McCarthy, Eugene *Other Things and the Aardvark.* Garden City: Doubleday and Co., 1970. Limited to 250 copies, first trade edition, tall 8vo., publisher's boards, inscribed by author for Bill Claire, very good, tight copy. Second Life Books, Inc. 196 B - 165 2016 $75

McHugh, Heather *Dangers: Poems by.* Boston: Houghton Mifflin, 1977. First printing, 8vo., half title, author's presentation to poet William Claire, red cloth stamped in silver, nice, little chipped and soiled dust jacket. Second Life Books, Inc. 196 B - 182 2016 $125

Meredith, William *Hazard the Painter.* N.P.: Ironwood Press, 1972. First edition, 8vo. scarce, inscribed by author for William Claire. Second Life Books, Inc. 196 B - 209 2016 $150

Merrill, James *First Poems.* New York: Knopf, 1951. First edition, one of 999 copies, this #564, 8vo., near fine in dust jacket, inscribed by author for William Claire. Second Life Books, Inc. 196 B - 213 2016 $975

Merrill, James *The Seraglio.* New York: Knopf, 1957. First edition, 8vo., very good tight in scuffed and chipped dust jacket, inscribed by author to Bill Claire. Second Life Books, Inc. 196 B - 214 2016 $175

Nin, Anais *Children of the Albatross.* New York: Dutton, 1947. First edition, 8vo., fine in near fine dust jacket, inscribed by author for Bill Claire. Second Life Books, Inc. 196 B - 315 2016 $400

Nin, Anais *The Diary of Anais Nin. Volume Two 1934-1939.* New York: Swallow Press/Harcourt Brace and world, 1967. First edition, 8vo., photos, very good, tight copy, dust jacket little scuffed and chipped, inscribed by author for Bill Claire. Second Life Books, Inc. 196 B - 317 2016 $400

Nin, Anais *The Diary of.... 1944-1947.* New York: Harcourt Brace Jovanovich, 1971. First edition, 8vo. illustrations, with photos, cover lightly stained, otherwise very good, tight copy in little scuffed and nicked price clipped dust jacket, laid in is advance copy complimentary slip with author's card, also inscribed by author to poet William Claire. Second Life Books, Inc. 196 B - 318 2016 $600

Nin, Anais *The Four Chambered Heart.* New York: Duell, Sloan and Pearce, 1950. First edition, 8vo., grey cloth, pages little toned, very good, inscribed by author for William Claire. Second Life Books, Inc. 196 B - 319 2016 $300

Nin, Anais *Ladders to Fire.* New York: Dutton, 1946. First edition, 8vo., very good in little chipped and worn dust jacket (lacks some of jacket at extremities of spine and on corners), inscribed by author for Bill Claire.   Second Life Books, Inc.   196 B - 321   2016 $450

Pastan, Linda *Aspects of Eve: Poems.* New York: Liveright, 1975. First edition, 8vo., author's presentation on title to poet Bill Claire, brown cloth, nice in slightly scuffed and soiled dust jacket.   Second Life Books, Inc.   196 B - 374   2016 $45

Pastan, Linda *A Perfect Cicle of Sun.* Chicago: Swallow, 1971. First edition, brown cloth, cover very slightly scuffed at corners and ends of spine, but nice in scuffed and little soiled dust jacket, author's presentation to poet William Claire.   Second Life Books, Inc.   196 B - 376   2016 $45

Pauker, John *Yoked by Violence: Poems by...* Denver: Alan Swallow, 1949. Small 8vo., author's presentation to The Cosmos Club and poet William Claire, paper on boards, edges and cover slightly soiled and cover little peeled at lower front edge, otherwise very good, tight copy.   Second Life Books, Inc.   196 B - 384   2016 $75

Poets & Writers, Inc. *...Tenth Birthday Party: Roseland October 22 1980.* New York: Poets & Writers Inc., 1980. Small 4to., paper wrappers, laid in note to poet and editor William Claire, on blue paper with heading Saturday Review, edges very slightly spotted, front corners of cover slightly worn, otherwise very good, tight copy.   Second Life Books, Inc.   196 B - 414   2016 $50

Poulin, A. *Catawba: Omens, Prayers & Songs: Poems by...* Port Townsend: Graywolf Press, 1977. One of 640 copies, small 8vo., illustration by Roy Nydorf, author's signature on title, with presentation to poet William Claire, flyer for book laid in, signed by author, cover slightly spotted, otherwise nice.   Second Life Books, Inc.   196 B - 428   2016 $75

Poulin, A. *A Momentary Order: Poems by...* St. Paul: Graywolf, 1987. First printing, authors's presentation to poet William Claire, signed, paper wrappers, cover slightly scuffed, otherwise nice.   Second Life Books, Inc.   196 B - 430   2016 $50

Poulin, A. *The Widow's Taboo: Poems after the Catawba.* Toyko: Mushinsha, 1977. First edition, small 4to., tipped in illustrations by Nydorf, author's signature and presentation to poet William Claire, brown cloth, nice in chipped, scuffed and little worn dust jacket.   Second Life Books, Inc.   196 B - 431   2016 $225

Powell, Anthony *Talk about Byzantium: Anthony Powell & the BBC.* Charingworth: Evergreen, 2006. First edition, stitched paper wrappers, one of 200 numbered copies, hand set and printed by John Grice in Centaur type on Zekall mouldmade paper, laid in original letter from Powll to William Claire , with ink corrections and additions.   Second Life Books, Inc.   196 B - 432   2016 $1200

Rilke, Rainer Maria   1875-1926 *The Roses & the Windows.* Port Townsend: Greywold press, 1979. First edition, presentation from translator, A. Poulin for William Claire, green cloth stamped in gilt, nice in very slightly yellowed and soiled dust jacket.   Second Life Books, Inc.   196 B - 483   2016 $75

Rogers, W. G. *Wise Men Fish Here...* New York: Harcourt Brace & World, 1965. First edition, yellow cloth, cover lightly stained, otherwise nice in some soiled and chipped dust jacket, inscribed by author for William Claire, with TLS from author to Claire.   Second Life Books, Inc.   196 B - 493   2016 $85

Rukeyser, Muriel *The Green Wave.* New York: Doubleday, 1948. First edition, 8vo., very good in little soiled dust jacket, inscribed by author for Bill Claire.   Second Life Books, Inc.   196 B - 511   2016 $100

Savage, Thomas *Lona Hanson: a bold woman with a Lust for Power.* New York: Signet Books July, 1949. Abridged paperback edition, pictorial wrappers, very good, offered with full page TLS from author to poet and editor Bill Claire.   Second Life Books, Inc.   196 B - 528   2016 $125

Simpson, Louis *Selected Poems.* New York: Harcourt Brace & World, 1965. First edition, 8vo., author's presentation for William Claire, green cloth, bottom edges slightly spotted, otherwise nice copy in little chipped and soiled dust jacket.   Second Life Books, Inc.   196 B - 579   2016 $125

Simpson, Louis *Searching for the Ox.* New York: Morrow, 1976. First printing, author's presentation to poet William Claire, paper over boards, with cloth spine, top edge slightly spotted, otherwise nice in little chipped and soiled dust jacket.   Second Life Books, Inc.   196 B - 578   2016 $275

Slotnikoff, Will *The First Time I Live...* Washington: Manchester Lane Edition, 1966. First edition, 8vo., little worn paper wrappers, review slip tipped to rear endpaper, inscribed by author for poet William Claire, laid in is postcard signed to Claire and 3 page typed letters also to Claire.   Second Life Books, Inc.   196 B - 604   2016 $75

Snodgrass, W. D. *The Fuhrer Bunker: a Cycle of Poems...* Brockport: BOA editions, 1978. Second impression, 8vo., printed wrappers, fine, inscribed to poet William Claire, by author.   Second Life Books, Inc.   196 B - 635   2016 $75

Stafford, William *Allegiances.* New York: Harper & Row, 1970. First edition, 8vo., on title, author's presentation to William Claire, paper over boards, top edges little spotted, edges of cover slightly scuffed, otherwise very good, tight in scuffed and very slightly chipped dust jacket.   Second Life Books, Inc.   196 B - 671   2016 $300

Stafford, William *Someday, Maybe.* New York: Harper Row, 1973. First printing, 8vo., inscribed by author for William Claire, very good, tight clean copy in dust jacket.   Second Life Books, Inc.   196 B - 673   2016 $175

Stafford, William *Traveling through the Dark.* New York: Harper & Row, 1962. First edition, author's presentation to William Claire, paper over boards, fine in dust jacket, 8vo.   Second Life Books, Inc.   196 B - 674   2016 $275

Stanford, Ann *The Descent.* New York: Viking, 1970. First edition, author's presentation to poet William Claire, front edges slightly spotted, otherwise very good, tight copy in scuffed and slightly chipped dust jacket.   Second Life Books, Inc.   196 B - 679   2016 $50

Stickney, Walt Christopher *The Bethesda Preludes.* Washington: Pushkin Press, 1982. First edition, author's presentation on half title to poet William Claire, 8 drawings in color by author, black cloth, nice in scuffed and slightly chipped dust jacket.   Second Life Books, Inc.   196 B - 705   2016 $75

Stuhlmann, Gunther *Anais: an International Journal.* LA: 1983-2001. 8vo., printed wrappers, laid in TLS from editor to William Claire, 15 issues in all, volumes 1, 3, 7, 8, 9, 10, 11, 12, 13, 14, 15, 16, 17, 18, 19, very good+.   Second Life Books, Inc.   196 B - 715   2016 $275

Taylor, Henry *Breakings.* San Luis Obispo: Solo, 1971. One of 400 copies, 8vo., paper wrappers, author's presentation to poet William Claire, cover somewhat bumped at edges, else very good, tight copy.   Second Life Books, Inc.   196 B - 741   2016 $95

Taylor, Henry *The Horse Show at Midnight: Poems.* Baton Rouge: Louisiana State University, 1966. First edition, 8vo., author's presentation to poet William Claire, paper over boards, nice, dust jacket scuffed and slightly chipped.   Second Life Books, Inc.   196 B - 742   2016 $50

Viereck, Peter *New and Selected Poems 1932-1967.* Indianapolis: Bobbs Merrill, 1967. 8vo. presentation on half title to poet William Claire, cloth, cover and edges little spotted, otherwise very good, tight copy in little scuffed dust jacket.   Second Life Books, Inc.   196 B - 800   2016 $45

Viereck, Peter *The Persimmon Tree...* New York: Scribner's, 1956. First edition, 8vo., author's presentation to William Claire, green cloth, edge soft cover very slightly scuffed, otherwise nice in scuffed and little soiled dust jacket.   Second Life Books, Inc.   196 B - 801   2016 $45

Wagoner, David *Dry Sun, Dry Wind.* Bloomington: Indiana University, 1953. First edition, author's presentation on title to William Claire, black cloth, Claire's name on flyleaf, nice in soiled and chipped dust jacket.   Second Life Books, Inc.   196 B - 812   2016 $125

Warren, Robert Penn 1905-1989 *Brother to Dragons: a Tale in Verse and Voices.* New York: Random, 1983. First printing, author's presentation on flyleaf to William Claire, blue cloth, very good, tight, dust jacket some soiled and chipped, half of presentation on endpaper browned from acidation from something that had been laid in.   Second Life Books, Inc.   196 B - 828   2016 $120

Warren, Robert Penn 1905-1989 *Incarnations: Poems 1966-1968.* New York: Random, 1968. first printing, 8vo., author's presentation to William Claire, small stain to foredge of leaves, very good, tight in some soiled and chipped dust jacket.   Second Life Books, Inc.   196 B - 829   2016 $120

Warren, Robert Penn 1905-1989 *You, Emperors and Others Poems 1957 1960.* New York: Random House, 1960. First printing, 8vo., author's presentation to William Claire, blue cloth, very good, tight copy, dust jacket some soiled and chipped.   Second Life Books, Inc.   196 B - 832   2016 $120

Welty, Eudora *A Curtain of Green (Stories).* New York: Doubleday, 1941. First edition, 8vo., some stained on endpaper, inscribed by author for William Claire, one of 2476 copies, scarce.   Second Life Books, Inc.   196 B - 850   2016 $650

Westlake, Donald *Brothers Keepers.* New York: M. Evans, 1975. First printing, 8vo., author's presentation to poet William Claire, paper over boards with cloth spine, top edges little spotted, otherwise very good, tight in very slightly chipped dust jacket.   Second Life Books, Inc.   196 B - 856   2016 $75

Westlake, Donald *Don't Ask.* New York: Mysterious Press, 1993. First edition, 8vo., author's presentation to William Claire, paper over boards, nice in slightly scuffed dust jacket. Second Life Books, Inc. 196 B - 857 2016 $75

Westlake, Donald *Drowned Hopes.* New York: Mysterious Press, 1990. First printing, author's presentation to William Claire, paper over boards with cloth spine, corners of cover slightly bumped, edges spotted, otherwise very good, tight in dust jacket. Second Life Books, Inc. 196 B - 858 2016 $75

Westlake, Donald *Good Behavior.* New York: Mysterious Press, 1985. First printing, author's presentation on title to William Claire, paper over boards with cloth spine, top edges faintly spotted, nice in slightly chipped dust jacket. Second Life Books, Inc. 196 B - 859 2016 $75

Westlake, Donald *High Adventure.* New York: Mysterious Press, 1985. First edition, 8vo., author's presentation to William Claire, paper over boards with cloth spine, edges lightly spotted, else nice in scuffed dust jacket. Second Life Books, Inc. 196 B - 862 2016 $75

Westlake, Donald *High Jinx: A Mohonk Mystery.* Miami Beach: Dennis McMillan, 1987. First edition, 8vo., printed wrappers, fine, inscribed by authors to poet William Claire. Second Life Books, Inc. 196 B - 854 2016 $65

Westlake, Donald *Transylvania Station: a Mohonk Mystery.* Miami Beach: Dennis McMillan, 1987. First edition, 8vo., printed wrappers, fine, inscribed by authors to William Claire. Second Life Books, Inc. 196 B - 855 2016 $65

Westlake, Donald *Trust me on this.* New York: Mysterious Press, 1988. First printing, author's presentation to William Claire, paper over boards, cloth spine, edges slightly spotted, otherwise nice in dust jacket. Second Life Books, Inc. 196 B - 861 2016 $75

Zinnes, Harriet *I Wanted to See Something Flying.* New York: Folder Editions, 1976. First edition, author's presentation on flyleaf to William Claire, paper wrappers, cover little scuffed at edges, otherwise very good, tight copy. Second Life Books, Inc. 196 B - 975 2016 $45

Association – Clanricarde, Earl of

Mozeen, Thomas *Young Scarron.* London: Printed & sold by T. Trye & W. Reeve, 1752. 8vo. half title, contemporary calf, rather rubbed, rebacked, red label, 2 armorial bookplates of Earl of Clanricarde. Jarndyce Antiquarian Booksellers CCXVI - 421 2016 £520

Association – Clark, Barrett

Kelly, George *Behold the Bridegroom.* Boston: Little Brown, 1928. First edition, 8vo., frontispiece, blue cloth with paper label, else near fine in little nicked and soiled dust jacket, rare in dust jacket, inscribed by author for Mr. Barrett Clark, May 1929. Second Life Books, Inc. 196A - 927 2016 $350

Association – Clark, Catherine

Fisher, Aileen *Do Bears Have Mothers, Too?* New York: Thomas Y. Crowell, 1973. First edition, beautifully illustrated by Eric Carle, little wear to plastic covering on rear dust jacket, otherwise fine in dust jacket (not price clipped), inscribed by Carle in ink for Catherine Clark, with added drawing of smiling cat, fine. Second Life Books, Inc. 197 - 47 2016 $1500

Association – Clark, George Oliver

Montgomery, Robert *The Sacred Annual; Being the Messiah, a Poems.* London: John Turrill, 1834. Fourth edition, 191 x 121mm, appealing 19th century black straight grain morocco, covers with gilt filigree and blind rolled frame, raised bands, spine compartments gilt with curling cornerpieces and lancet tools radiating from a central circle, black morocco label, blind rolled turn-ins, marbled endpapers, all edges gilt, extra chromolithographed 'missal' titlepage woodcut tailpiece by John Franklin and 10 color lithographs mounted on heavy stock, 3 of these by John Martin, all lithographs with captioned tissue guards, front pastedown with armorial bookplate, engraved bookplate of George Oliver Clark, with inscription, joints little rubbed (part of front joint with thin crack), spine gilt little muted, corners very slightly worn, binding without any serious condition issues and pleasing, isolated faint spots internally, text and plates generally very clean and fresh. Phillip J. Pirages 67 - 251 2016 $1500

Association – Clark, J.

James, George Payne Rainsford 1799-1860 *The History of Chivalry.* London: Henry Colburn & Richard Bentley, 1830. Second edition, frontispiece, engraved title, original green glazed cloth, dark blue paper label lettered gilt, spine very slightly faded, contemporary signature of J. Clark on engraved title, very good, crisp copy. Jarndyce Antiquarian Books CCXV - 269 2016 £75

James, John Angell *The Young Man from Home.* London: RTS, circa, 1830. Second edition, frontispiece, engraved title, original green glazed cloth, dark blue paper label lettered gilt, spine very slightly faded, contemporary signature of J. Clark on engraved title, very good, crisp copy. Jarndyce Antiquarian Books CCXV - 270 2016 £40

Association – Clark, Tom

Codrescu, Andrei *Selected Poems 1970-1980.* New York: Sun, 1983. First edition, author's presentation, paper wrappers, 8vo., edges, cover and half title little spotted, otherwise very good, laid in is 6 line ALS from author and APC to poet Tom Clark.   Second Life Books, Inc.   196A - 314   2016 $150

Association – Clarke, Barrett

Kelly, George *Daisy Mayme.* Boston: Little Brown, 1927. First edition, blue cloth with little nicked paper label, inscribed by author for Barrett Clarke, laid in is clipped signature of Jessie Busley who played the title role and to whom the plays was dedicated.   Second Life Books, Inc.   196A - 930   2016 $225

Kelly, George *Philip goes Forth.* New York: Samuel French, 1931. First edition, 8vo., fine, inscribed by author to Barrett Clarke from George Kelly.   Second Life Books, Inc.   196A - 935 2016 $188

Kelly, George *The Show-Off.* Boston: Little Brown, 1924. First edition, 8vo., frontispiece, inscribed by author for Barrett H. Clarke, very good.   Second Life Books, Inc.   196A - 938   2016 $350

Kelly, George *The Torch Bearers.* New York: Samuel French, 1924. First Acting edition, 8vo., publisher's wrappers, uncut and unopened, inscribed by author for Barrett Clarke, recipient's bookplate, very good.   Second Life Books, Inc.   196A - 939   2016 $94

Association – Clarke, Cleland

Dickens, Charles   1812-1870 *Works.* London: Chapman & Hall, 1901-1902. Oxford India Paper Dickens, copyright edition with illustrations by Cruikshank, 17 volumes, half titles, illustrations, occasional spotting in prelims, contemporary full dark green crushed and embossed morocco, spine lettered gilt, one or two spines slightly faded, monogram bookplates of Cleland C. Clarke, Southport, top edge gilt, very good.   Jarndyce Antiquarian Booksellers   CCXVIII - 35   2016   £650

Association – Clarke, Julia Maria

Mayhew, Augustus *Acting Charades; or Deeds not Words.* London: D. Bogue, 86 Fleet Street, n.d. c., 1850. First edition, square 16mo., hand colored engraved title and frontispiece, tailpiece by George Cruikshank, original red cloth, upper cover and spine blocked in gilt, lightly dust soiled and rubbed to extremities, inscribed "W. J. Clarke & Julia Maria Clarke from Papa".   Marlborough Rare Books List 55 - 47   2016   £125

Association – Clarke, Maria

Chapone, Hester *Letters on the Improvement of the Mind, Addressed to a Young Lady.* London: printed for Scatherd & Letterman, 1810. 12mo., contemporary full tree calf, black morocco label, spine rubbed, ownership inscription of Maria Clarke, 28th Nov. 1810.   Jarndyce Antiquarian Books CCXV - 106   2016   £50

Association – Clarke, W. J.

Mayhew, Augustus *Acting Charades; or Deeds not Words.* London: D. Bogue, 86 Fleet Street, n.d. c., 1850. First edition, square 16mo., hand colored engraved title and frontispiece, tailpiece by George Cruikshank, original red cloth, upper cover and spine blocked in gilt, lightly dust soiled and rubbed to extremities, inscribed "W. J. Clarke & Julia Maria Clarke from Papa".   Marlborough Rare Books List 55 - 47   2016   £125

Association – Clarke, William Buddell

Burke, Edmund   1729-1797 *An Account of the European Settlements in America.* London: John Joseph Stockdale, 1808. New edition, quarto, two engraved maps, contemporary calf, gilt, with two block morocco spine labels, marbled endpapers and matching edges, minor wear to binding, rubbing to joints, some browning and offsetting to first and lost few leaves, overall near fine, armorial bookplate of William Buddell Clarke, small ticket, clipped quotation mounted ot front pastedown.   Heritage Book Shop   Holiday 2015 - 15   2016 $1500

Association – Claus, Hugo

Appel, Karel *Appel & Alechinsky: Two Brush Paintings their Poems by Hugo Claus.* Paris: Yves Riveire, 1980. First edition, 4to., original publisher's printed wrappers, very good, illustrations in black and white and color, inscribed by Hugo Claus to poet William Jay Smith.   Second Life Books, Inc.   196A - 909   2016 $350

Association – Clayton, George

Brassey, Annie Allnutt, Baroness   1839-1887 *A Voyage in the Sunbeam: Our Home on the Ocean for Eleven Months.* London: Longmans, Green and Co., 1878. First edition, dark grey cloth with gilt title and author to spine and front cover, gilt illustrations to front and back, cloth chipped and faded but still quite attractive, some soiling to prelim pages and tear to front map, otherwise very good, two foldouts and 118 wood engraved illustrations after drawings by Bingham, ownership signature of George Clayton, very good.   The Kelmscott Bookshop   13 - 11   2016 $550

Association – Clearis, Genevieve

Amusemens Francois, ou Contes a Rire: Trattenimenti Italiani... Venice: Dominico Pitteri, 1752. 2 volumes bound as 1, 8vo., French and Italian texts, woodcut device to each title, little annotation (page 195), some pencilled notes to front flyleaves, slightly yellowed, few inkspots and smudges, contemporary dark brown calf rebacked in poor quality leather which is now creased and rather rubbed, all edges red, marbled endpapers, upper joint starting at head and tail, edges rubbed, corners worn, flyleaves dusty, still good copy, ownership inscription of Mademoiselle Genevieve Clea(ris?).   Unsworths Antiquarian Booksellers   30 - 3   2016   £160

Association – Clements, James Beresford

Winchilsea, Heneage Finch, Earl of   *A True and Exact Relation of the Late Prodigious Earthquake & Eruption of Mount Aetna...*   London: by T. Newcombe, 1669. First edition, small 4to., lacking folding engraved plate, but with 18th century engraving of Vesuvius erupting in 1630 loosely inserted, dampstained, more heavily at end, upper edge closely trimmed in places, one page number cropped, late 19th century half maroon morocco marbled boards, extremities rubbed, corners bumped, bookplate of John Beresford Clements 2869-1940 of Killadeeon, Co. Kildare, from the library of James Stevens Cox (1910-1997).   Maggs Bros. Ltd.   1447 - 456   2016   £120

Association – Cleverdon, Douglas

Bythner, Victorinus   *Lyra Prophetica Davidis Regis. Sive Analysis Critico-Practica Psalmorum in quae Omnes & Singulae Voces Hebraeae in Psalterio Contentae...*   Londoni: Jacobi Flesher, 1650. First edition, 4to., text in Hebrew and Latin, titlepage in red and black, separate half title to 'Index Libri Psalmorum', final leaf of errata, tidemark to top fore-edge corner from title to page 81 small worm trail to fore-edge margin of page 333 dwindling away to end of textblock, tiny burnhole to page 3-4 touching couple of letters, contemporary brown sprinkled calf, red morocco gilt label to spine, blind tooled borders and additional vertical line to boards, edges sprinkled blue and red, very early rubricated leaves with accompanying manuscript marginalia used as pastedowns, spine rubbed, lower joint split and upper starting but cords holding firm, some scrapes and stains, corners wearing but sound unsophisticated copy, ownership inscription of Stephen Freeman dated 1787 and bookplate of Douglas Cleverdon.   Unsworths Antiquarian Booksellers   30 - 28   2016   £175

Association – Clifton, Talbot

O'Hamaguchi San   *Fortune Telling by Japanese Swords from Old Japanese Mss.*   London: John Lane, Bodley Head, 1905. First edition, 8vo., very good+, red cloth with gilt lettering and Japanese sword illustration spine, gilt Japanese sun design front cover, top edge gilt, mild spotting to covers, scattered foxing, few pages unopened, rare, signed and inscribed by Talbot Clifton.   By the Book, L. C.   45 - 51   2016 $650

Association – Cloetta, Yvonne

Connell, Mary   *Help is on the Way (Poems).*   Reinhardt, 1896. First edition, line drawings by author, crown 8vo., original light blue card wrappers printed in black, red and white, fine, inscribed by Graham Greene for love of his life Yvonne Cloetta.   Blackwell's Rare Books   B186 - 223   2016   £800

Association – Clonbrook, Robert Dillon, 3rd Baron

Moore, Thomas   *Letters and Journals of Lord Byron with Notices of His Life.*   London: John Murray, 1830. First edition, 273 x 216mm., 2 volumes, especially pleasing contemporary deep blue half roan over marbled boards, spines attractively gilt in compartments with fleuron centerpieces and entwined vines filling corners, gilt titling, marbled endpapers and edges, frontispiece in volume 1, front pastedown with armorial bookplate of Robert Dillon, 3rd Baron Clonbrook (1807-93), hint of rubbing to leather, paper boards, very faintly chafed, one small marginal wax spot, exceptionally fine, clean, smooth and bright internally and in virtually unworn decorated period binding.   Phillip J. Pirages   67 - 83   2016 $950

Association – Clopet, Liliam M. C.

Freeman, Kathleen   *The Work and Life of Solon...*   Cardiff: University of Wales, 1926. First edition, 8vo., pages unopened, very good in scarce dust jacket which is very good, slightly darkened at spine and bit creased at edges, presentation from author inscribed for Lilian M. C. Clopet from Kathleen Freeman July 14th 1926.   Peter Ellis   112 - 136   2016   £125

Association – Close, Chuck

Finch, Christopher   *Chuck Close Work.*   Prestel, 2010. First edition, very good, dust jacket, folio, signed by author and subject, Chuck Close, dust jacket excellent, text clean and free of marks, binding tight and solid boards clean with no wear.   Simon Finch   2015 - 28253   2016 $300

Association – Clutton, Ralph

Dickens, Charles   1812-1870   *The Strange Gentleman.*   London: Chapman & Hall, 1837. First edition, original pale lavender printed wrappers bound into full tan calf, gilt spine, dentelles and borders, green label, bookplate of Ralph Clutton, very good in cloth slipcase.   Jarndyce Antiquarian Booksellers   CCXVIII - 81   2016   £8500

Dickens, Charles   1812-1870   *The Village Coquettes.*   London: Richard Bentley (printed by Samuel Bentley), 1836. First edition, title very slightly browned, tiny marginal repair in final leaf, handsome full calf by F. Bedford, gilt spine, borders & dentelles, dark green leather label, armorial bookplate of Ralph Clutton, very good, rare edition.   Jarndyce Antiquarian Booksellers   CCXVIII - 86   2016   £1500

Association – Coates, Carrol

Alexis, Jacques Stephen   *In the Flicker of an Eyelid.*   Charlottesville: University of Virginia, 2002. First American edition, 8vo., black cloth, review laid in, presentation from Carrol F. Coates, cover very slightly scuffed, otherwise as new.   Second Life Books, Inc.   196A - 24   2016 $45

Association – Cobden-Sanderson

The Book of Gems. The Poets and Artists of Great Britain.   London and Paris: Fisher Son & Co., 1844. 2 volumes, 222 x 140mm., very pretty crimson morocco handsomely gilt by Doves Bindery (stamp signed and dated 1908 on rear turn-in), covers with line and dot frames, corners adorned with heart shaped leaves, a poppy seed pod, oak leaves, solid heart and gouge work, raised bands, spine compartments with line and dot frames, central poppy seed pod with leaves above and below, turn-ins with gilt rules and oak leaf cluster cornerpieces, all edges gilt, with two rows of gauffered dots (expert repairs to tiny portion of top of spine and three small areas of front joint of second volume), with 106 engraved vignettes and four pages of poets' facsimile signatures at end of each volume, front pastedown with wood engraved bookplate of Charles Walker Andrews, front free endpaper with typed copy of a letter from Andrews to the Doves Bindery, about these bindings (which he commissioned) and Cobden-Sanderson's handwritten and signed reply (first apparently a transcript, with later date of a letter sent 29 Jan. 1909, the second dated 9 Feb. 1909), top corners of volume I bit worn, leaves shade less than bright (no doubt as in all copies because of paper stock, still excellent set that looks very attractive on shelf, binding lustrous and appealing despite its defects and text clean, fresh and unread.   Phillip J. Pirages   67 - 38   2016 $3500

Association – Cockayne, E.

Sauvan, Jean Baptiste Balthazar   *Picturesque Tour of the Seine From Paris to the Sea: With Particulars Historical and Descriptive.*   London: R. Ackermann, 1821. First edition, 346 x 273mm., publisher's red buckram, covers with blind-stamped frame upper cover with gilt titling, flat spine stamped with gilt strapwork panels and with gilt titling, all edges gilt, with engraved color vignette on titlepage, unsigned aquatint vignette at foot of last page, engraved color map, 24 fine hand colored aquatint plates, by Augustus Pugin and John Gendall, presentation bookplate "Master E. Cockayne, as the reward of merit by Mr. Bowling Milk Street Academy Sheffield June 23rd 1848, binding little soiled, joints and extremities bit worn, just the slightest off-setting from some plates onto text, one plate with offsetting from text and half a dozen others with just hint of same, other trivial imperfections, still very desirable, binding sturdy and without any major defects, beautiful scenic plates with particularly attractive coloring.   Phillip J. Pirages   67 - 307   2016 $5500

Association – Cockburn, Agnes

Grierson, James   *Delineations of St. Andrews...*   Edinburgh: printed for Peter Hill et al, 1807. First edition, 198 x 114mm., publisher's original blue boards, paper label on spine, edges untrimmed, felt lined morocco backed folding box, 4 engraved plates, inscribed "Edin. 27th April 1807/ Agnes Cockburn/in memory/ of the author", boards little soiled, front joint cracked (rear joint starting at tail), extremities with the expected considerable wear, spine label chipped (with a fourth of the letters gone), but with boards still attached and extremely insubstantial publisher's binding still appealing because of its original materials, titlepage with bit of offsetting from frontispiece, isolated minor foxing in text, other trivial imperfections, but excellent internally, untrimmed leaves bright fresh and clean, with all of their ample margins intact.   Phillip J. Pirages   67 - 175   2016 $6500

Association – Cockerell, C. R.

Pye, John   *Patronage of British Art, an Historical Sketch...*   London: Longman, Brown, Green and Longmans, 1845. First edition, presentation from author, royal 8vo., engraved portrait, one folding table, several facsimile signatures and 17 illustrations in text, original dark green vertically ribbed cloth, spine lettered gilt, inscribed "To C. R. Cockerell Esq. R. A., Professor of Architecture in the Royal Academy &c &c. with John Pye's Compls.", some pencil marginalia in recipient's hand.   Marlborough Rare Books   List 55 - 57   2016   £100

Association – Cockerell, Sydney

Deland, Margaret *The Old Garden.* Boston: Houghton Mifflin, 1894. first US edition, Owner inscription dated 1893, 8vo., pictorial cloth, colors on covers rubbed, else very good, printed on French-fold paper and illustrated in color on every page by Walter Crane, laid in is 3 page handwritten letter to Sydney Cockerell, from Crane, dated August 1892 with mailing envelope.   Aleph-bet Books, Inc.   112 - 123   2016 $750

Morris, William   1834-1896 *A Note by William Morris on his Aims in Founding the Kelmscott Press Together with a Short Description of the Press by S. C. Cockerell...* Hammersmith: Kelmscott Press, 1898. One of 525 copies on paper (and 12 on vellum), 210 x 150mm., original holland backed gray boards, very nice folding box covered with navy blue cloth, spine with morocco label reading "C. H. St.. J. H./ S. C. C./ W.M.", elaborate borders around frontispiece and first page of text, frontispiece drawn by Edward Burne-Jones and cut by William Morris, large decorative woodcut initials, device on last page of text and one full page woodcut of ornaments used in Kelmscott edition of "Love is Enough", printed in red and red black, bookplate of Charles Harry St. John Hornby, presentation from Cockerell to Hornby and his wife as well as tipped-on letter to Hornby, describing, this work, rear pastedown with clipped signature of William Morris pasted down, pristine.   Phillip J. Pirages   67 - 221   2016 $19,500

Association – Cocks, C. C.

Salmon, William *Seplasium. The Compleat English Physician or the Druggist's Shop Opened.* London: for Matthew Gilliflower and George Sawbridge, 1693. First edition, half title and errata/ad leaf and a4 with table on verso that is meant as a slip cancel for the table on X8v bound after X8, small hole through centre of Z8 (damaging two lines), 19th century paper slip tipped in between E32-3 (obscuring small portion of text on first 13 lines), rust spots on Gg1-3, fore corner of Ooo4 folded-in, small rust spot on Ffff4, contemporary calf, front joint and spine repaired, 19th century endleaves, from the library of James Stevens Cox (1910-1997), old signature "R. L. Carr ex donis C. C. Cocks".   Maggs Bros. Ltd.   1447 - 373   2016   £650

Association – Cocks, Thomas Somners Vernon

Whymper, Edward *Travels Amongst the Great Andes of the Equator - Supplementary Appendix.* London: R. & R. Clark for John Murray, 1892. -1891. Second edition of Travels, first edition of Appendix, 8vo. in 4s, 2 volumes, original olive green cloth over bevelled boards, upper boards with gilt borders, spines lettered and decorated in gilt, lower boards in blind, mid-brown coated endpapers, uncut, some quires in supplementary volume unopened, wood engraved frontispiece, 43 wood engraved plates and numerous illustrations to text, one wood engraved map, one folding lithographic plan, one folding facsimile map, one large folding lithographic map loose as issued in pocket on lower pastedown volume 1, extremities lightly rubbed and bumped, spines slightly faded, minor damage on front free endpaper of Travels, splitting and old repairs on upper hinge of supplementary volume, offsetting onto verso of loose map, otherwise very good, clean set, engraved bookplate of Thomas Somners Vernon Cocks (1850-1923), booseller's ticket of Harrison and Sons, London.   Sotheran's Travel and Exploration - 79   2016   £595

Association – Codman, Madam

Rowe, Elizabeth Singer *Friendship in Death in Letters from the Dead to the Living.* London: C. Cooke, 1797. 12mo., 4 engraved plates, tailpieces, small engraving on title, stained, foxed throughout, original dark calf, heavily worn, cover off, ink signatures on titlepage and title verso (Madam Codman, Josh Brooksby and George Wilson), rubber ink stamped numbers on title verso, blind emboss stamps on first and last few leaves, including title, bookplate of Charles T. Congdon (1821-1891).   Jeff Weber Rare Books   181 - 34   2016 $35

Association – Cohen, Alan

Taken by Design: Photographs from the Institute of Design 1937-1971. Chicago: University of Chicago Press, 2002. First edition, very near fine copy in photo illustrated flexible boards, signed by Joseph Jachna and additionally inscribed by Joseph Sterling And Alan Cohen.   Jeff Hirsch Books E-List 80 - 1   2016 $200

Association – Cohen, H. G.

Cohen, Gustavus *The Formation of Character.* Bloomsbury: Gustavus Cohen, 59 Great Russell Street; Liverpool: 40 Bedford Street North, 1884. original blue cloth, bevelled boards decorated in gilt and black, slightly dulled, illustrations by Fritz Braun, inscription from H. G. Cohen 28th July 1886 to R. Cardwell, very good, bright of family presentation copy.   Jarndyce Antiquarian Books CCXV - 124   2016   £65

Association – Cohn, Albert M.

Valentine and Orson The Two Sons of the Emperour of Greece. London: by J. W. for E. Tracy, 1694. Small 4to., woodcut frontispiece and ads below, woodcut on titlepage and numerous woodcut illustrations in text, very small piece torn away the upper blank corner of woodcut frontispiece, minor rust hole through P1 (in text) and Dd2 (in margin), small hole worn through foot of 2b2, light worming to fore margin of T2-V3, rust stain to Bb4 (touching text), contemporary sheep, covers ruled in blind, inside joints split, old stain from glass on upper cover, minor staining on rear, faded contemporary inscription of Ann Hill, Albert M Cohn 20th century armorial bookplate, from the library of James Stevens Cox (1910-1997).   Maggs Bros. Ltd.   1447 - 422   2016   £650

Association – Coigny, Duc De

Richardson, Samuel   1689-1761   *Pamela, ou La Vertu Recompensee.*   Paris: De l'Imprimerie de Plassan, 1821-1822. 2 volumes, 212, 133mm., very attractive quarter calf blindstamped in 'cathedral' style over marbled boards by by Thouvenin (stamp signed in gilt at foot of spine), corners tipped with green vellum, green blindstamped with design of Gothic arched windows, gilt titling, marbled endpapers and edges, half title with ink inscription in French stating that this book was purchased at the sale of the library of Duc de Coigny at Chateau de Franquetot on 24 April (19)12, occasional insignificant smudges or spots of foxing, paper little on inexpensive side, otherwise appealing copy with virtually no signs of use.   Phillip J. Pirages   67 - 302   2016 $900

Association – Cole, Christopher

Babington, Thomas   *A Practical View of Christian Education in Its Early Stages.*   London: J. Hatchard, 1815. Second edition, half title, 2 pages ads, contemporary dark blue morocco, slightly rubbed, bookplate of Christopher Cole, with his signature, very good.   Jarndyce Antiquarian Books   CCXV - 516   2016   £110

Association – Cole, Cordelia

Culpeper, Nicholas   *Pharmacopia Londiensis or the London Dispensatory Further Adorned by the Studies and Collections of the Fellows...*   London: printed by Peter Cole, printer and bookseller...., 1659. (and 1658). One of 3 printing variants of the 6th edition, 8vo., 20th century full calf with raised bands, spine lettered gilt, bound without vertical half title as often, title within two-line typographical border, page 257 with marginal repair, obscuring few words, index with few stains, cut close, never affecting printed surface, little spotted and lightly browned in places, contemporary ink inscription Cordelia Cole, her book, and ink inscription, Benjamin Daves his book.   Sotheran's   Piccadilly Notes - Summer 2015 - 92   2016   £1250

Association – Cole, Hobart

Sterne, Laurence   1713-1768   *A Sentimental Journey through France and Italy.*   London: for T. Becket and P. A. De Hondt, 1768. First edition with text variant 2 in volume 1 and text variant 1 in volume 2, as usual, 2 volumes, 8vo., engraved coat of arm on Dev, with half titles and list of subscriber names a usual, without rare inserted ad leaf, full sprinkled calf, fully gilt by Riviere, spines bit dry, hinges worn, small chip at crown of volume 2, Hobart Cole bookplate.   Joseph J. Felcone, Inc.   Books from Five Centuries: a Miscellany - 137   2016 $900

Association – Cole, William

Voltaire, Francois Marie Arouet De   1694-1778   *Elemens de la Philosophie de Neuton.*   Amsterdam: Jacques Desbordes, 1738. First edition, title printed in red and black, finely engraved portraits, with frontispiece, 27 engraved vignettes, 6 engraved plates, 58 engravings in text, 22 engraved tailpieces and 1 folding engraved table, fine contemporary paneled sheep with beautiful and crisp blindstamping and gilt borders on front and back covers, spine with gilt decorations in five compartments and gilt titling in sixth, with bookplate of William A. Cole, collector and bibliographer of chemistry, above is contemporary ink signature (crossed out with two diagonal strokes), and on same line 'Bergen 1799", overall fine, bright, clean, very beautiful. Athena Rare Books   List 15 - 1738   2016 $4250

Association – Coleman, D. R.

Hart, Joseph C.   *Miriam Coffin; on the Whale Fisherman: a Tale.*   New York: G. & C. & H. Carvill et al, 1834. First edition, 2 volumes in 1, duodecimo, 19th century brown half calf, marbled paper boards, gilt rules and lettering, half titles present, 19th century signature of D. R. Coleman, 517 Ellis St., SF, who apparently had this bound for him, his name gilt stamped at foot of spine, edges bit rubbed, date trimmed by binder on titlepage of volume two, some light foxing, very good.   The Brick Row Book Shop   Miscellany 69 - 46   2016 $500

Association – Coleman, Robert

Golden, John   *Stage-Struck John Golden.*   New York: Samuel French, 1930. First edition, 8vo., photos and drawings, author's presentation on flyleaf, presentation letter from Golden to Robert Coleman at The Mirror in NY laid in, very good in worn dust jacket.   Second Life Books, Inc.   196A - 656   2016 $75

Association – Coleridge, Henry Nelson

Horatius Flaccus, Quintus *Poemata: ex antiquis Codd. & Certis Observationibus...* Londoni: apud Fratres Vaillant et N. Prevost, 1721. First edition, personal copy of Henry Nelson Coleridge, with his ownership signature dated 'Hampstead 1832' to titlepage, full vellum, spine ruled and decorated in blind, handwritten title to spine, all edges stained red, pink marbled endpapers, very good or better, some bowing to boards, minor spotting at spine heads, otherwise sturdy binding, small loss to bottom corner of pages 213;214, few minor and scattered pieces of pencil marginalia, light soiling to pages and page edges, else bright and clean, very good overall, tight copy in early binding.   B & B Rare Books, Ltd.   2016 - STC005   2016 $350

Association – Collamer, J.

Bridge, Horatio *Journal of an African Cruiser.* New York: George P. Putnam & Co., 1853. 12mo., original blind-stamped cloth, superb copy, inscribed in pencil "Hon. J. Collamer(?)... with respects of the author.   M & S Rare Books, Inc.   99 - 102   2016 $1250

Association – Collett, William Michael

Horatius Flaccus, Quintus *Ad Nuperam Richardi Bentleii Editionem Accurate Expressus. Notas Addidit Thomas Bentleius, A. B. Collegii S. Trinitatis apud Cantabrigienses Alumnus.* Cambridge: Typis Academicis Impensis Cornelii Crownfield`, 1713. 8vo., bit of light browning, some marginal annotations, contemporary calf, black morocco, boards panelled in gilt and blind, spine divided by raised bands, flower head tool in gilt to each compartment, marbled endpapers, bound with half a dozen additional binder's blanks at front and rear, the last at front excised, these filled closely with manuscript notes, joints and edges rubbed, small crack to foot of rear joint, bookplate of William Michael Collett, ownership inscription of Woodthorpe Scholefield Collet, struck through, another C. S. Collett, Grammar School, Ipswich to binder's blank, very good.   Blackwell's Rare Books   Greek & Latin Classics VII - 42   2016   £900

Association – Collett, Woodthorpe Scholefield

Horatius Flaccus, Quintus *Ad Nuperam Richardi Bentleii Editionem Accurate Expressus. Notas Addidit Thomas Bentleius, A. B. Collegii S. Trinitatis apud Cantabrigienses Alumnus.* Cambridge: Typis Academicis Impensis Cornelii Crownfield`, 1713. 8vo., bit of light browning, some marginal annotations, contemporary calf, black morocco, boards panelled in gilt and blind, spine divided by raised bands, flower head tool in gilt to each compartment, marbled endpapers, bound with half a dozen additional binder's blanks at front and rear, the last at front excised, these filled closely with manuscript notes, joints and edges rubbed, small crack to foot of rear joint, bookplate of William Michael Collett, ownership inscription of Woodthorpe Scholefield Collet, struck through, another C. S. Collett, Grammar School, Ipswich to binder's blank, very good.   Blackwell's Rare Books   Greek & Latin Classics VII - 42   2016   £900

Association – Collingridge, Elizabeth

Tasso, Torquato   1544-1595 *The Gerusalemme Liberato of Tasso...* Cambridge: printed by J. Archdeacon printer to the University, 1786. 1792. First edition of volume i, and second edition of volume ii, 8vo., 2 volumes, fine, clean copy bound in full contemporary sprinkled calf, smooth spines, gilt band, red morocco title labels, dark green oval volume labels, lemon yellow edges, signature of Elizabeth Collingridge, Oct. 1842, recent bookplate of Christopher Clark Geest.   Jarndyce Antiquarian Booksellers   CCXVI - 560   2016   £225

Association – Collins, Charles

Clarkson, Thomas *The History of the Rise, Progress and Accomplishment of the Abolition of the African Slave-Trade by the British Parliament.* Wilmington: R. Porter, 1816. Second Wilmington edition?, small octavo, 348 pages, vignette, contemporary full calf with morocco spine label gilt, early gift inscription to Stephen Downing from Charles Collins and signatures, small chip on front fly, light wear on boards, very good or better.   Between the Covers Rare Books   202 - 2   2016 $375

Association – Collins, Henry Brown

Collins, Henry Brown *Valentine's Manual of Old New York 1924.* New York: Gracie Mansion, 1923. First edition, 8vo., editor, Henry Brown Collins' presentation on flyleaf, black and white and color illustrations, blue cloth stamped in gilt, top edge gilt, one hinge tender, cover little worn at corners and spine, otherwise very good, inscribed.   Second Life Books, Inc.   196A - 211   2016 $65

Association – Collins, John

Lana, Francesco *Prodromo Ouero Saggio di Alcune Inuentoni Premesso all'Arte Maestra....* Brescia: per li Rizzardi, 1670. First edition, 20 engraved plates with figures numbered I-LXX, folio, contemporary mottled calf over pasteboard, spine wrongly titled, expert repair at edges, possibly belonged to mathematician John Collins (1625-1683), fellow of the Royal Society, first three leaves neatly restored at fore-edges, flyleaves defective at fore-edges, otherwise very clean, crisp copy.   Maggs Bros. Ltd.   1474 - 46   2016   £4500

Association – Collinson, F.

Euclides *Geometricorum Elementorum Libri XV.* Paris: Henri Estienne 7 Jan., 1516-1517. Sixth edition, Roman types, numerous woodcut geometrical diagrams in margins, fine crible initials in a variety of styles and sizes, titlepage soiled and cut down and mounted on old paper, one diagram just cropped at its extreme outer corners, without final blank, folio, 19th century half brown calf by Hatton of Manchester, marbled edges, original order for the binder loosely inserted, the Macclesfield copy with bookplate but no blindstamps and annotated by John Collins, after his death his books were acquired by William Jones and thence to Shirburn Castle, scarce on the market, preserved in cloth folding box, good copy.   Blackwell's Rare Books   Marks of Genius - 16   2016   £12,000

Shaw, George Bernard   1856-1950 *Man and Superman.* London: Constable and Co. ltd., First edition, 8vo., original green cloth, spine gilt lettered, spine faded, inscribed by author for F. Collinson.   Blackwell's Rare Books   B184 - 229   2016   £1500

Association – Collinson, Patrick

Churton, Ralph *The Life of Alexander Nowell, Dean of St. Pauls.* Oxford University Press, for the author, 1809. 8vo., 9 plates, some folding, little noted, sporadic foxing, plates offset, tan diced russia, gilt spine and borders, marbled edges and endpapers, binding sound, skillfully rebacked, edges rubbed, corners worn, hinges repaired with marbled paper, armorial bookplate of J. Paul Rylands, , letter to Prof. Patrick Collinson dated 9.ii.80 loosely inserted.   Unsworths Antiquarian Booksellers   30 - 32   2016 $75

Association – Colquhoun, James

Ireland, John *Hogarth Illustrated. (with) Graphic Illustrations of Hogarth from Pictures, Drawings and Scarce Prints.* J. J. Boydell and R. Faulder, 1791-1794. First edition, 8vo., 3 volumes, uniformly bound in contemporary full diced Russia calf, spines ruled in gilt contrasting black leather labels, 154 engraved plates, spines slightly sunned, some browning and offsetting, otherwise very good, from the library of Sir James Colquhoun of Luss with bookplate. Sotheran's   Piccadilly Notes - Summer 2015 - 170   2016   £1000

Association – Coltor, Mary

Gilman, Charlotte Perkins *The Home, Its Work and Influence.* New York: McClure Phillips, 1903. First edition, 8vo., cloth stamped in gilt fine in dust jacket, some chipping at top of spine above title, very rare in dust jacket, uncommon book, this copy probably inscribed for architect Mary J. Coltor "For Mary J. Coutler (sic)".   Second Life Books, Inc.   197 - 155   2016 $3750

Association – Colum, Padraic

Colum, Mary *Our Friend James Joyce.* New York: Doubleday, 1958. First edition, little faded spine and couple of minor nicks, inscribed by co-author, Padraic Colum.   Second Life Books, Inc.   196A - 322   2016 $150

Association – Colvile, Frederick Leigh

Lewis, Matthew Gregory   1775-1818 *Tales of Wonder.* London: Printed by W. Bulmer & Co, for the author, 1801. First edition, royal octavo, 2 volumes, period binding of full marbled calf with intricate gilt decoration, leather title labels, marbled edges and endpapers, in the middle of each cover is gilt monogram initial "D" surmounted by winged crown, few stains in margins of first volume, upper joint of second volume cracking, very good set, armorial bookplate (Frederick Leigh Colvile) with inscription "from my Uncle Chandos Leigh".   Peter Ellis   112 - 220   2016   £675

Association – Colvill-Scott, H. D.

Maidment, James *A Book of Scotish Pasquils 1568-1715.* Edinburgh: William Paterson, 1868. One of 3 copies on vellum (and limited but unspecified number of copies printed on paper), 210 x 130mm., handsome contemporary crimson morocco, attractively gilt by Andrew Grieve (stamp signed on front turn-in), covers gilt with multiple plain and decorative rules enclosing a delicate frame, large and intricate fleuron at center of each cover, spine gilt in double ruled compartments with complex fleuron centerpiece and scrolling floral cornerpieces, turn-ins decorated with plain and decorative gilt rules, patterned burgundy and gold silk endleaves, top edge gilt, slightly worn matching morocco lipped slipcase, woodcut titlepage illustrations, numerous decorative tailpieces and occasional woodcut vignettes in text, front pastedown with armorial bookplate of H. D. Colvill-Scott, armorial bookplate of Clarence S. Bemens, tiny dark spot on spine corners and just hint of rubbing, couple of leaves with slightly rumpled fore edge, still fine, text clean, smooth and bright and binding unusually lustrous, virtually no wear. Phillip J. Pirages   67 - 346   2016 $4500

Association – Colvin, Frances

Conrad, Joseph   1857-1924   *The Arrow of Gold.*   New York: Doubleday Page, 1919. First edition, octavo, original blue cloth stamped in gilt, from the library of Stanley J. Seeger with his small bookplate, presentation copy from author for Lady (Frances) Colvin, beneath is another presentation inscription to Christopher Wheeler from Sidney Colvin, cover rubbed at spine and edges, cloth bubbled at inside edge of lower cover, good, preserved in green buckram slipcase lettered gilt with inner folding sleeve.   Peter Ellis   112 - 81   2016   £950

Association – Colvin, Sidney

Conrad, Joseph   1857-1924   *The Arrow of Gold.*   New York: Doubleday Page, 1919. First edition, octavo, original blue cloth stamped in gilt, from the library of Stanley J. Seeger with his small bookplate, presentation copy from author for Lady (Frances) Colvin, beneath is another presentation inscription to Christopher Wheeler from Sidney Colvin, cover rubbed at spine and edges, cloth bubbled at inside edge of lower cover, good, preserved in green buckram slipcase lettered gilt with inner folding sleeve.   Peter Ellis   112 - 81   2016   £950

Association – Comstock, Rolland

Chute, Carolyn *The Beans of Egypt, Maine.* New York: Ticknor and Fields, 1985. Uncorrected proof, with long inscription from author to fellow author Madison Smartt Bell, with Madison Smartt Bell's ownership signature, further inscribed years later by Chute for book collector Rolland Comstock, faint crease to front cover likely from so much inscribing, near fine in wrappers, laid in is folded five page press release from Ticknor, wonderful association.   Ken Lopez Bookseller   166 - 21   2016 $500

Association – Con, Robert

Mann, Horace *Report of an Educational tour in Germany and Parts of Great Britain and Ireland...* London: Simpkin, Marshall & Co., 1846. Half title, some pencil markings and annotations, original purple cloth, largely faded to brown, spine rubbed and head and tail following inner hinge cracking, inscribed "Robert Con Esq. with kindest regards from W. B. Hodgson, Liverpool Feb. 1846".   Jarndyce Antiquarian Books   CCXV - 842   2016   £85

Association – Condere, Jules

Lemarchand, Georges *Conseil Municipal de Paris 1911.* Paris: Imprimerie Municipole, 1911. First edition, 4to., contemporary blue half cloth over marbled boards, spine lettered gilt, marbled endpapers, 37 plates, maps and plans, title little browned and with small old repair to corner, signed presentation inscription to poet Jules Condere, with his etched bookplate and signature and address, author's business card tipped in.   Sotheran's   Travel and Exploration - 262   2016   £248

Association – Congdon, Charles Taber

Rowe, Elizabeth Singer *Friendship in Death in Letters from the Dead to the Living.* London: C. Cooke, 1797. 12mo., 4 engraved plates, tailpieces, small engraving on title, stained, foxed throughout, original dark calf, heavily worn, cover off, ink signatures on titlepage and title verso (Madam Codman, Josh Brooksby and George Wilson), rubber ink stamped numbers on title verso, blind emboss stamps on first and last few leaves, including title, bookplate of Charles T. Congdon (1821-1891).   Jeff Weber Rare Books   181 - 34   2016 $35

Association – Congreve, William

Tacitus, Cornelius *Taciti Opera Quae Exstant. I. Lipsivis quartum recensuit ...* Lvgdvni Batavorum: Ex Officina Plantiniana Apud Franciscum Raphelengium, 1588. Fourth edition edited by J. Lips, small octavo, 18th century panelled calf, early ink underlinings in text, one earlier marginal note (trimmed in binding) on page 630, boards rubbed, hinges cracked, cords holding, good, sound, from the library of English playwright William Congreve.   The Brick Row Book Shop   Miscellany 69 - 27   2016 $3500

Association – Connelly, Marc

Farjeon, Eleanor *Mrs. Malone.* London: Oxford University Press, 1962. First edition, 12mo., pictorial boards, fine in slightly worn dust jacket, illustrations by Edward Ardizzone, this copy inscribed by author to Marc Connelly.   Aleph-bet Books, Inc.   111 - 20   2016 $175

Kaufman, George *Beggar on Horseback.* New York: Boni & Liveright, 1924. First edition, 8vo., 2 pages in the middle of text quite darkened from old news clipping that had been laid in, top edges of boards sunned, otherwise very good tight copy in very good, bright dust jacket, inscribed by producer Winthrop Ames to George Barbier who played Mr. Cady, also inscribed by both playwrights, George Kaufman and Marc Connelly, splendid association. Second Life Books, Inc.   196A - 913   2016 $1500

Association – Connolly, Cyril

Sidney, Philip 1554-1586 *Astrophel & Stella.* London: Nonesuch Press, 1931. One of 1210 copies, inscribed by Cyril Connolly to a colleague at the London Sunday times, with Connoly's funeral program laid-in.   Honey & Wax Booksellers   4 - 21   2016 $350

Association – Conover, Chris

Grimm, The Brothers *The Bear and the Kingbird.* New York: Farrar, Strauss, Giroux, 1979. 8vo., cloth, soil along inner edge of rear cover, very good in dust jacket (soil on rear cover), color illustrations by Chris Conover, laid in is charming letter from Conover discussing her book 'Simple Simon' thanking recipient for hr kind words and with a little ink drawing.   Aleph-bet Books, Inc.   111 - 98   2016 $125

Association – Constable, Charles

Kett, Henry *Elements of General Knowledge.* London: Rivington, 1803. Third edition, 2 volumes, contemporary half calf, spines with surface rubbing, otherwise nice and clean, sound copy, bookplates of Charles Constable. Jarndyce Antiquarian Books   CCXV - 810   2016   £120

Association – Constable, William

Verelst, Harry *A View of the Rise, Progress and Present State of the English Government in Bengal...* London: printed for J. Nourse, 1772. First edition, 4to., front endpaper little dusted, some very neat pencil notes in margins, fine, full contemporary pale calf, double gilt fillet border, gilt spine in six compartments, red morocco label, armorial bookplate of William Constable, Esq. of Burton Constable, Yorkshire.   Jarndyce Antiquarian Booksellers   CCXVI - 578   2016   £1100

Association – Conyngham

Gregory, John *A Father's Legacy to his Daughters.* London: for W. Strahan and T. Cadell, 1784. New edition, 8vo., half title, frontispiece, small paper flaw to B2 causing loss of page number, contemporary full tree calf, elaborate gilt spine, dark green morocco label, corners little bumped, some slight rubbing, Conyngham armorial bookplate, signature of 'Denison', handsome copy.   Jarndyce Antiquarian Books   CCXV - 231   2016   £75

Association – Cook, Margaret

Hayes, Dorsha B. *Chicago; Crossroads of an American Enterprise.* New York: Messner, 1944. First edition, very good, tight copy, 8vo., little nicked and chipped dust jacket lacking lower portion of spine, inscribed by author for cousin, Margaret Cook, with her pencil ownership signature. Second Life Books, Inc.   196A - 752   2016 $65

Association – Coombe, Arthur

Horatius Flaccus, Quintus *Opera.* Londini: prostant apud Gul. Sandby typis Jacobi Bettnham 25 Julli, 1749. 2 volumes, 8vo., 35 engraved plates, including frontispiece, titlepage to each volume in red and black with engraved portraits, list of plates on single leaf, without final leaf of binder's instructions, some occasional light foxing, very small number of pencilled marginal notes, tiny paper repair to page 193, contemporary light brown calf, neatly (if not invisibly) rebacked with original gilt spines retained, all edges red, spines worn and crackled, few scuffs and faded patches, but very good set, inscribed for Thomae Coombe, pencilled bookseller's comment, early 20th century bookplate of Arthur Coombe.   Unsworths Antiquarian Booksellers   30 - 81   2016   £250

Association – Coombe, Thomae

Horatius Flaccus, Quintus *Opera.* Londini: prostant apud Gul. Sandby typis Jacobi Bettnham 25 Julli, 1749. 2 volumes, 8vo., 35 engraved plates, including frontispiece, titlepage to each volume in red and black with engraved portraits, list of plates on single leaf, without final leaf of binder's instructions, some occasional light foxing, very small number of pencilled marginal notes, tiny paper repair to page 193, contemporary light brown calf, neatly (if not invisibly) rebacked with original gilt spines retained, all edges red, spines worn and crackled, few scuffs and faded patches, but very good set, inscribed for Thomae Coombe, pencilled bookseller's comment, early 20th century bookplate of Arthur Coombe.   Unsworths Antiquarian Booksellers   30 - 81   2016   £250

Association – Cooney, Barbara

De Gerez, T. *Louhi: Witch of North Farm.* New York: Viking, 1986. First printing (1-5 code), 4to., pictorial boards, as new in dust jacket, magical color illustrations by Barbara Cooney, this copy inscribed by artist. Aleph-bet Books, Inc. 112 - 115 2016 $100

Association – Cooper

Walker, Obadiah *Of Education. Especially of Young Gentlemen.* Oxford: in the Theatre, 1673. Second edition, small 8vo., engraved coat-of-arms of Oxford University on title, printer's crease across titlepage engraving, inner margins of title and contents leaves slightly damaged by adhesion, prominent dampstain in top inner margin of most leaves, corners stained in sheets C-D, with small piece torn from corner of M5, early 19th century half calf and paste boards, rubbed and worn with some worming to spine, early ink notes, the copy of the Cooper family of Markree Castle, Co. Sligo, Ireland with blue shield shaped case label, from the library of James Stevens Cox (1910-1997). Maggs Bros. Ltd. 1447 - 430 2016 £150

Association – Cooper, A. W.

Aldam, W. H. *A Quaint Treatise o 'Flees and the Art Artyfichaill Flee Mkaing" by an old man...* London: John B. Day, 1876. First edition, 2nd issue, scarce, 4to., original green cloth decorated in gilt and black to upper board and spine, all edges gilt, two chromolithographs after James Poole on 6 board leaves, extra illustrated with engraved portrait of Aldam to prelim, little spotting, very good, presentation from author to A. W. Cooper. Sotheran's Hunting, Shooting & Fishing - 106 2016 £2995

Association – Cooper, Alfred

Tapie, Michel *Ossorio.* Torino: Edizioni D'Arte Fratelli Pozzo, 1961. First edition, folio, 10 full page tipped in color plates, original wrappers worn along spine near binding staple, very good, clean copy, inscribed by Alfonso Ossorio, for Alfred Cooper. Second Life Books, Inc. 196 B - 732 2016 $150

Association – Cooper, Bryan

Sebon, Raymond *La Theologie Naturelle...* Rouen: Jean de la Marc, 1641. 8vo., title printed in red and black, woodcut Jesuit device to title, paper flaw at foot of 4L2 separating several letters on recto but without any loss, contemporary limp vellum, later tan label, remains of ties, engraved armorial bookplate of Edward Joshua Cooper of Markree, with label above it marking re-arrangement of castle library by Bryan Cooper, in 1913, good copy. Blackwell's Rare Books B184 - 69 2016 £1750

Association – Cooper, Diana

Greene, Graham 1904-1991 *Getting to Know the General.* London: Bodley Head, 1984. First edition, 8vo., original cloth, near fine, inscribed by author for Lady Diana Cooper. Sotheran's Piccadilly Notes - Summer 2015 - 152 2016 £1250

Association – Cooper, Edward Joshua

Sebon, Raymond *La Theologie Naturelle...* Rouen: Jean de la Marc, 1641. 8vo., title printed in red and black, woodcut Jesuit device to title, paper flaw at foot of 4L2 separating several letters on recto but without any loss, contemporary limp vellum, later tan label, remains of ties, engraved armorial bookplate of Edward Joshua Cooper of Markree, with label above it marking re-arrangement of castle library by Bryan Cooper, in 1913, good copy. Blackwell's Rare Books B184 - 69 2016 £1750

Association – Cooper, George Chester

Gray, Thomas 1716-1771 *The Works of Thomas Gray.* London: Harding, Triphook and Lepard, 1825. 2 volumes, extremely appealing contemporary red straight grain morocco, attractively gilt by Ingalton of Eton (with their ticket), 197 x 114mm., covers with double fillet border enclosing a triple fillet frame with gilt tooled leafy cornerpieces, central panel enclosed by single fillet with roundel corners, raised bands, spine compartments gilt with leafy frames, turn-ins with dense gilt roll, all edges gilt, engraved frontispiece portrait of gray, first prelim leaf to volume I with inked inscription 'George Chester Cooper/Given to him by his friend George Pickering/Eton. March 1830", just vaguest rubbing and abrasions to covers, minor foxing to frontispiece and prelim leaves, pretty set in very fine condition, clean and fresh internally, gleaming bindings with virtually no wear. Phillip J. Pirages 67 - 45 2016 $950

Association – Cooper, Roy

Hingston, R. W. G. *The Meaning of Animal Colour and Adornment.* London: Edward Arnold, 1933. Octavo, text illustrations, bookplate of Roy Cooper, dust jacket. Andrew Isles Natural History Books 55 - 6584 2016 $150

Whistler, Hugh *Popular Handbook of Indian Birds.* Edinburgh: Gurney and Jackson, 1941. Third edition, octavo, color plates, text illustrations, fine, dust jacket, scarce in this condition, bookplate of Roy P. Cooper. Andrew Isles Natural History Books 55 - 19348 2016 $100

Association – Cope, Thomas Pym

Shelley, Mary Wollestonecraft Godwin 1797-1851 *History of a Six Weeks' Tour Through a Part of France, Switzerland, Germany and Holland.*   London: published by T. Hookham Jun., 1817. First edition, little light soiling, 8vo., early 20th century olive morocco by Tout, boards with gilt frame and spine, elaborately gilt top edge gilt, others untrimmed, joints rather rubbed, little wear to headcap, bookplates of H. Bradley Martin and of Robertson Trowbridge (this inscribed to Mark Trowbridge's gift of the volume to Thomas Pym Cope) and of Thomas Jefferson McKee, very good.   Blackwell's Rare Books   Marks of Genius - 43   2016   £3500

Association – Copeland, Aaron

Holland, James R.   *Tanglewood.*   Barre: Barre Pub., 1973. First edition, small 4to., printed wrappers, photos, signed by composer Aaron Copeland, very good+.   Second Life Books, Inc.   196A - 810   2016 $250

Association – Cornell, Katharine

Anderson, Maxwell   *The Wingless Victory.*   Washington: Anderson House, 1936. First edition, 8vo., very good in fine dust jacket, inscribed by prodcer of the play to actress Katharine Cornell.   Second Life Books, Inc.   196A - 36   2016 $113

Association – Cosens, Frederick William

Howell, James   *Epistolae Ho-Eliana. Familiar Letters Domestic and Forren...*   London: printed for Humphrey Moseley, 1645. First edition, small 4to., lacking additional engraved titlepage, woodcut initials and head and tailpieces, few pencil marks and underlinings, some MS. notes in old hand including dates and sometimes locations, occasional wax marks not affecting text, 19th century plum colored faux morocco, gilt label to spine, blindstamped spine and boards, edges sprinkled red, marbled endpapers, rubbed, edges bit worn and some fraying to covers, spine label lifting, armorial bookplate of Frederick William Cosens, MS gift inscription to Allan H. Bright, dated 30th May 1891, from HYS, armorial bookplate of Douglas Kinnaird, tipped to f.f.e.p. a page of handwritten notes on the content of the book with brief chronology of Howell's life in pencil, with note book was purchased from Cosens through Quaritch.   Unsworths Antiquarian Booksellers   30 - 82   2016   £300

Association – Costa, C. D. N.

Brown, Francis   *A Hebrew and English Lexicon of the Old Testament.*   Oxford: Clarendon Press, 1968. First edition, sixth reprint, corrected, 4to., blue boards, gilt lettered to spine, edges spotted, some shelf wear, no dust jacket, still good, ownership inscription of C. D. N. Costa.   Unsworths Antiquarian Booksellers Ltd.   E05 - 21   2016   £25

Gardiner, Alan   *Egyptian Grammar.*   Oxford University Press, 1973. Third edition, large 4to., blue boards, gilt lettered to spine, top edge dated and spotted, little shelfwear, no dust jacket, very good, ownership C. D. N. Costa in pen to front pastedown.   Unsworths Antiquarian Booksellers Ltd.   E05 - 28   2016   £30

Gomme, A. W.   *A Historical Commentary on Thucydides.*   Oxford: Clarendon Press, 1945. 1979. 1978. 1981, 8 books in 5 volumes, 8vo., cloth, gilt lettered bump to top edge of lower wrapper volume III, light toning to upper board volume I, spine of volume IV lightly sunned, edges dusted, all very good, no dust jackets, made up set but with ownership inscription of C. D. N. Costa.   Unsworths Antiquarian Booksellers   30 - 62   2016   £300

Griffin, Jasper   *Homer on Life and death.*   Oxford: Clarendon Press, 1983. First paperback edition, 8vo., spine slightly faded, very minor shelfwear, very good, ownership inscription of C. D. N. Costa and one or two pencil annotations.   Unsworths Antiquarian Booksellers Ltd.   E05 - 30   2016   £30

Hart, John   *Herodotus and Greek history.*   New York: St. Martin's Press, 1982. First edition, 8vo., maps, cloth, gilt lettered top edge, slightly dusted, otherwise near fine, yellow dust jacket, spine bit faded, little shelfwear, very good, ownership inscription of C. D. N. Costa and Croom Helm LTD publisher card with compliments from author.   Unsworths Antiquarian Booksellers Ltd.   E05 - 35   2016   £20

Henbeck, Alfred   *A Commentary on Homer's Odyssey.*   Oxford: Clarendon Press, 1990-1992. 3 volumes, 8vo., figures, paperbacks, spines faded, one light crease along length of spine to volume II and III, little shelfwear, very good set, ownership inscription of C. D. N. Costa with few small and neat annotations to volume II.   Unsworths Antiquarian Booksellers Ltd.   E05 - 36   2016   £90

Innes, Doreen   *Ethics and Rhetoric.*   Oxford: Clarendon Press, 1995. First edition, 8vo., blue boards, gilt lettered to spine, 93cm. scratch to spine, spot of wear to top board, blue dust jacket, spine slightly faded, very good, ownership inscription of C D N. Costa, complimentry copy note loosely inserted.   Unsworths Antiquarian Booksellers Ltd.   E05 - 41   2016   £65

Jones, A. H. M.   *The Later Roman Empire 284-602. A Social, Economic and Administrative Survey.*   Oxford: Basil Blackwell, 1986. Reprint in 2 volumes, 8vo., cloth, gilt lettered, faint mark to upper boards, edges lightly dusted, very good, dust jackets, spine sunned, minor shelfwear, very good, ownership inscription of C. D. N. Costa.   Unsworths Antiquarian Booksellers Ltd.   E05 - 43   2016   £180

Lobel, Edgar *Poetarum Lesbiorum Fragmenta.* Oxford: Clarendon Press, 1997. Reprint of first edition, 8vo. dark blue boards, gilt lettered, one crease along spine, else near fine, lacks dust jacket, ownership inscription of C. D. N. Costa to front pastedown.   Unsworths Antiquarian Booksellers Ltd.   E05 - 48   2016   £28

Long, A. A. *The Hellenistic Philosophers.* Cambridge: Cambridge University Press, 1990. 1989, 8vo., 2 volumes, paperback .5cm closed tear to spine of volume II, .3cm. closed tear to spine of volume I, bump to top corner of volume II, edges slightly dusted, price stickers to lower wrappers, very good, ownership inscription of C. D. N. Costa.   Unsworths Antiquarian Booksellers Ltd.   E05 - 49   2016   £40

MacDonell, Arthur Anthony *A Practical Sanskrit Dictionary.* London: Oxford University Press, 1976. First edition, 7th photographic reprint, 4to., cloth, gilt lettered, light toning to upper board, 12 small brown marks to endpapers, edges lightly dusted, very good, no dust jacket, ownership inscription of C. D. N. Costa.   Unsworths Antiquarian Booksellers Ltd.   E05 - 51   2016   £25

Page, D. I. *Poetae Melici Graeci Alcamanais steishori Ibyci Anacreontis Simonidis Corinnae Poetarum Minorum Reliquias Carmina Popularia Et Convivialia.* Oxford: Clarendon Press, 1967. First reprint, 8vo., red boards, gilt lettered, spine faded, endcaps slightly worn, little shelfwear, very good, ownership inscription of C. D. N. Costa to front pastedown and with few pencil annotations.   Unsworths Antiquarian Booksellers Ltd.   E05 - 54   2016   £50

Russell, D. A. *Antonine Literature.* Oxford: Clarendon Press, 1990. First edition, 8vo., blue boards, gilt lettered to spine, green dust jacket, near fine, ownership inscription of C. D. N. Costa, Oxford University Press complimentary advice note loosely inserted.   Unsworths Antiquarian Booksellers Ltd.   E05 - 59   2016   £35

Wilkinson, L. P. *Ovid Recalled.* Bath: Cedric Chivers, 1974. First edition, 8vo., green boards, gilt lettered, green dust jacket laminated, spine slightly faded, price clipped, very good, ownership inscription of C. D. N. Costa in pen, and one postcard loosely inserted.   Unsworths Antiquarian Booksellers Ltd.   E05 - 65   2016   £25

Association – Couchman, John

Allot, Robert *Wit Theater of the Little World.* printed by J(ames) R(oberts) for N(icholas) L(ing), 1599. First edition, few catchwords trimmed, first 2 and last 4 leaves soiled, small hole in blank area of title, repair to lower margin of title, rust hole in X5 with loss of a few leaves, small 8vo., 19th century dark burgundy morocco, double gilt fillets on sides, double gilt rules on either side of 3 raised bands on spine and at head and foot, lettered and dated in gilt direct, signature of John Couchman dated 1699.   Blackwell's Rare Books   B184 - 4   2016   £5000

Association – Coushaine, Anna

Anthony, Susan B. *The History of Woman Suffrage.* Rochester: Susan B. Anthony, 1902. First edition, Volume IV only, 8vo., frontispiece, publisher's maroon cloth, front hinge loose, lacks the last 3 leaves of index, good copy housed in cloth clamshell box, inscribed by Anthony for Miss Anna B. Coushaine.   Second Life Books, Inc.   196 B - 685a   2016 $2500

Association – Cowper, Earl

Wood, John *A Description of the Exchange of Bristol, Wherein the Ceremony of laying the First Stone of that Structure....* Bath: sold by J. Leake, C. Hitch in Paternoster Row, London and B. Hickley in Bristol, 1745. Limited to 300 copies, 8 engraved plates, 6 double page, modern marbled boards with printed label to spine, this copy appears to have been Earl Cowper's copy.   Marlborough Rare Books   List 55 - 73   2016   £1950

Association – Cox, Claude

Doughty, Henry Montagu *Chronicles of Theberton. A Suffolk Village.* Cambridge: University of Cambridge; London: Macmillan, 1910. First edition, original green cloth, spine ruled and lettered gilt, spine sunned, light bumping to corners, little spotting to endpapers, frontispiece, plates, 3 maps, printed in green and black, occasional light spotting, good, early ownership inscription of Jack Simmons and pictorial bookplate of Claude and Joan Cox, very rare.   Sotheran's   Piccadilly Notes - Summer 2015 - 111   2016   £148

Association – Cox, E. M.

Brooke, Fulke Greville, 1st Baron *Certaine Learned and Elegant Workes of the Right Honorable Fulke Lord Brooke.* E. P(urslowe) for Henry Seyle, 1633. First edition, tall copy of ordinary paper issue, folio, full morocco gilt by Riviere, all edges gilt, initial and terminal blanks, repaired rust hole in d2 with loss of few letters, slight soiling to first leaves, otherwise very good, large copy, contemporary inscription D. Johannis Mallet, later bookplate of E. M. Cox.   Sotheran's Piccadilly Notes - Summer 2015 - 155   2016   £2750

Association – Cox, James Stevens

Quarles, Francis *Divine Fancies Digested into Epigrams, Meditations and Observations.* London: T(homas) D(awks) for John Williams, 1675. Seventh edition, 8vo., small dampstain to upper margin and very light foxing to titlepage, large rust spot to centre of B2 and C1, dampstain in corner of D2-N2, early 19th century half russia and marbled boards, reback, boards soiled and corners worn, from the library of James Stevens Cox (1910-1997). Maggs Bros. Ltd. 1447 - 344 2016 £120

Quarles, Francis *Divine Poems.* London: by Edward Okes for Benjamin Tooke and Thomas Sawbridge...., 1669. 8vo., engraved frontispiece/title, engraved title and final leaf repaired and strengthened at fore edge, later 20th century calf, from the library of James Stevens Cox (1910-1997), various pen trials, inscription "John Barnard/of Fallm(outh); in/Cornwall" and "To James Edgecom/John Symmons", presumably of Edgcumbe or Edgcombe. Maggs Bros. Ltd. 1447 - 345 2016 £180

Quarles, John *Divine Meditations Upon Several Subjects.* London: by Thomas Johnson for Peter Parker, 1671. Third edition, 8vo., engraved portrait, title roughly torn along inner margin and mounted on stub (with slight loss to imprint), browned and foxed throughout (more so in margins), corners of B8 and C1 bumped and with some light worming, scorchmark (45 x 25mm.) to centre of L2 (and with loss to upper margin) also affecting L3, contemporary sheep rebacked, corners repaired, new endleaves, from the library of James Stevens Cox (1910-1997). Maggs Bros. Ltd. 1447 - 346 2016 £180

Quevedo, Francisco De *Forture in Her Wits; or the Hour of all Men.* London: for R. Sare, F. Saunders and Tho. Bennet, 1697. First edition in English, 8vo., minor worming to inner margin of A1-A3 touching printed border of top edge gilt and two letters of text on A3, small stain to lower inner margin of D5-D6, small ink stain to blank lower margin of f1, early ownership inscription cropped from head of titlepage, 19th century calf, corners bumped and chipped, joints rubbed, from the library of James Stevens Cox (1910-1997), inscribed "W(illiam) M. Marrow, his booke 1720", inscription of Alicia Anne Shring 1835. Maggs Bros. Ltd. 1447 - 347 2016 £350

Rabelais, Francois *The Works of the Famous Mr. Francis Rabelais, Doctor in Physick...* London: for Richard Bentley and are to be sold by John Starkey, 1664. First edition in English, 2nd issue, small rust spot on E8 and G1, small piece torn away from fore-edge of M8 (not touching text), dark stain near inner margin of D1, minor tear to lower edge of (2) N& (just touching last line of text), lower edge of)2 uncut, contemporary sheep ruled in blind, rebacked, corners repaired, new endleaves, from the library of James Stevens Cox (1910-1997), contemporary ink signature of James Chamberlayne. Maggs Bros. Ltd. 1447 - 348 2016 £950

Radcliffe, Alexander *Ovidius Exulans ur Ovid Travestie.* London: by Peter Lillicrap for Samuel Speed, 1673. First edition, small 8vo., engraved portrait bust, washed and pressed, late 19th century polished calf by F. Bedford, covers with triple gilt fillet, gilt spine, marbled endleaves, gilt edges, joints rubbed. from the library of James Stevens Cox (1910-1997). the copy of W. E. Bonds, of Enderby House, Clapham, London, the copy of George Thorn Drury. Maggs Bros. Ltd. 1447 - 350 2016 £1100

Raleigh, Walter *Judicious and Select Essayes and Observations.* London: by T. Warren for Humphrey Moseley, 1650. First edition, small 8vo., engraved portrait, but without 4 leaves of Moseley's ads, blank verso of engraved portrait and blank verso of last leaf stained by turn-ins and with edges slightly chipped, small repair to foot of titlepage, just touching decorated border, minor closed tear in lower inner margin of A1-2, dampstaining to inner margins of G4-(2)C8 (touching text in places), small hole through (3)A-3 (touching two lines of text), some occasional rust spotting, mid 20th century calf, from the library of James Stevens Cox (1910-1997), early inscription of John Spelman, signature Robertus (?) Culsett, armorial bookplate of William Miller Ord (1834-1902). Maggs Bros. Ltd. 1447 - 351 2016 £350

Randolph, Thomas *Poems with the Muses Looking-Glass and Amyntas.* Oxford: for F. Bowman and are to be sold by John Crosley, 1668. Fifth (i.e. sixth) edition, small 8vo., with half title, leaves A1-P8 lightly browned, small piece torn away from blank corner of C4 and with small closed tear to lower margin of L4, some small spots, minor hole through P7 (touching text) and with sheet S closely trimmed, but with no loss of text, early 20th century calf, gilt spine by Birdsall & Son of Northampton, joints rubbed and slightly cracked at head and tail, some insect damage at foot of spine, from the library of James Stevens Cox (1910-1997), armorial bookplate, Ambrose Isted (1717-81) of Ecton Hall, Northamptonshire. Maggs Bros. Ltd. 1447 - 354 2016 £180

Randolph, Thomas *Poems with the Muses Looking-Glasse, and the Amyntas.* London: in the year, 1643. Third edition, titlepage lightly soiled, some light soiling and staining, full modern calf, from the library of James Stevens Cox (1910-1997), with his pencil annotations to front pastedown, signature of Thomas Stringer, 1678, (K?) Stringer signature dated 1693,. Maggs Bros. Ltd. 1447 - 352 2016 £250

Randolph, Thomas *Poems.* London: for F. Bowman, and are to be sold by William Roybould, 1652. Fourth edition, small 8vo., engraved titlepage, small stain at head of engraved titlepage, paper flaw in lower corner of (2)(N), upper corners of (2)C1-7 dampstained, rust spot to head of I1, type ornament border of title closely shaved and border of subtitle to 'Aristippus' slightly shaved, early 19th century calf, covers ruled in blind, front joint cracked, lower joint and headcaps rubbed, small hole in spine, from the library of James Stevens Cox (1910-1997), contemporary signature of Dorothy Howland with crude ink drawing. Maggs Bros. Ltd. 1447 - 353 2016 £150

Ravenscroft, Edward *The London Cuckolds.* London: for Jos. Hindmarsh, 1688. Second edition, small 4to., small dampstain to blank fore-margin throughout, closely cropped along lower edge with occasional cropping of signatures, 20th century half morocco and marbled boards, from the library of James Stevens Cox (1910-1997) with note of Maggs Bros. sale to him and his notes on front pastedown. Maggs Bros. Ltd. 1447 - 355 2016 £150

Rawlet, John *Poetick Miscellanies of Mr. John Rawlet, B.D.....* London: for Samuel Tidmarsh, 1687. First edition, 8vo., portrait trimmed down and mounted at later date, without first blank leaf, long crease with very small closed tear (5mm) to titlepage, two ink spots recto of K4 (one just touching text), small rust spot, modern half red morocco and cloth boards, from the library of James Stevens Cox (1910-1997). Maggs Bros. Ltd. 1447 - 356 2016 £320

Ray, John *A Collection of English Proverbs Digested into a Convenient Method for the Speedy Finding Any One Upon Occasion; with Short Annotations.* Cambridge: by John Hayes for W. Morden, 1678. Second edition, 8vo., light intermittent soiling and dampstaining throughout, blank margin of B5 soiled, 19th century calf, ruled in blind, rebacked, new endpapers, from the library of James Stevens Cox (1910-1997), 18th century ownership inscription James Nicol, Traquair Manse. Maggs Bros. Ltd. 1447 - 358 2016 £300

Ray, John *Catalogus Plantarum Circa Cantabrigiam Nascentium....* Cambridge: Excudebat Joann. Fieldd., Impensis Gulielmi Nealand, 1660. First edition, 8vo., Keynes' corrected titlepage 'B', lightly browned throughout and with some spotting to D1-4 and L4, contemporary limp vellum, painted green (paint rubbing away) particularly on spine, from the library of James Stevens Cox (1910-1997). Maggs Bros. Ltd. 1447 - 157 2016 £575

Ray, John *Synopsis Methodica Animalium Quadruperdum et Serpentini Generis.* London: Impensis S. Smith & B. Walford, 1693. First edition, 8vo., engraved portrait, sheets B-M browned due to poor paper quality, all others clean, printer's crease across lower corner of page 67 but no loss of text, contemporary sprinkled calf, front cover detached, label missing, from the library of James Stevens Cox (1910-1997), contemporary inscription 'AAA 50', inscription 'E Libris Eduardi Nelthorpe Admi/1720', and "E Libris G. D. Kent CCC Oxon". Maggs Bros. Ltd. 1447 - 359 2016 £220

Ray, John *The Wisdom of God Manifested in the Works of the Creation, in Two Parts.* London: for Samuel Smith, 1692. Second edition, 8vo., contemporary calf, covers panelled gilt with vase and flower tool in each corner, gilt spine with red morocco label (corners worn, top corner of lower cover chewed, area of surface insect damage at foot of the lower cover), from the library of James Stevens Cox (1910-1997), inscribed "The Gift of Mrs. Ray to John Morley July 31 1707", and signatures 'Jane Dorothy Harvey 1849' and 'C. H. Rikerman(?) 1885'. Maggs Bros. Ltd. 1447 - 360 2016 £500

Rea, John *Flora: seu de Florum Cultura.* London: by T. N. for George Marriott, 1676. Second edition, folio, engraved title, 8 plates, lightly browned, upper margins dusty, worming close to inner margin towards top edge, extends throughout getting worse in middle and then fanning out into a trial in text, hole in Y1 (affecting two lines), closed tear on two of the plate leaves about 3cm. long, contemporary calf, covers panelled in blind, rebacked, lower corners repaired, upper corners worn, new endleaves, old flyleaves preserved, from the library of James Stevens Cox (1910-1997), engraved label inserted between pages 52 and 53 'Laura A(nne) Calmady' of Langdon Court, ms. note on label dated 23 Oct. 1889 and states the book was bought from Wm. Wade at sale of Langdon books by Vincent Pollexfen Calmady. Maggs Bros. Ltd. 1447 - 361 2016 £500

Record, Robert *Records Arithmetick or the Ground of Arts.* London: by J. Flesher for John Harrison..., 1652. 8vo., numerous engraved tables and mathematical illustrations, large dampstains to corners in places, very small hole through 2N4 (just touching text), text-block starting to split in places, contemporary sheep spine rubbed and creased, corners slightly rubbed, from the library of James Stevens Cox (1910-1997). Maggs Bros. Ltd. 1447 - 362 2016 £650

Record, Robert *Records Arithmetick; or the Ground of Arts...* London: by James Flesher and are to be sold by Joseph Cranford, 1662. 8vo., rust holes through E8, F8, 2A2, 2A5 and 2H4, ink blots on F2v and F34, S1-T1 lightly browned and with occasional light damp staining along the fore-margins, contemporary calf, surface cracking on spine, area of surface insect damage on lower corner, joints, corners and edges rubbed, from the library of James Stevens Cox (1910-1997). Maggs Bros. Ltd. 1447 - 363 2016 £600

A Relation of Several Hundreds of Children and others that Prophesie and Preach in Their Sleep &c. London: for Richard Baldwin, 1689. First edition, small 4to., some light soiling to first few leaves, mid 20th century half blue morocco and marbled boards by William Matthews for Maggs, from the library of James Stevens Cox (1910-1997). Maggs Bros. Ltd. 1447 - 364 2016 £180

Ridpath, George *The Stage Condem'd and the Encouragement Given to the Immoralities and Profaneness of the Theatre....* London: for John Salusbury, 1698. First edition, foxed and browned throughout, heavily in places and dampstained at end, contemporary panelled calf, rebacked, leather crackled by damp, corners repaired, new endleaves, from the library of James Stevens Cox (1910-1997), 'E- libris Ge(o)r(ge) Luke pr. 0£ 2s-6d". Maggs Bros. Ltd. 1447 - 365 2016 £220

Robinson, John *An Account of Sueden; Together with an Extract of the History of the Kingdom.* London: Tim Goodwin, 1694. First edition, 8vo., initial leaf with half title on recto and ad on verso, A1-4 browned, E8-8 and O1-2 browned and spotted, small semi-circular chip from fore-edge of front flyleaf, contemporary sprinkled calf, spine with gilt thistle crest in fourth panel and gilt shelf mark in final one (covers detached, edges and corners worn, headcaps torn away and with small white splash of paint on upper board), from the library of James Stevens Cox (1910-1997) the copy of Rev. Kene Percival (1709?-74?) with his gilt thistle crest, S. or J. Foley signature. Maggs Bros. Ltd. 1447 - 366 2016 £100

Rochester, John Wilmot, 2nd Earl of 1647-1680 *Poems (&c) on Several Occasions.* London: for Jacob Tonson, 1696. Reprint of 1691 edition, 8vo., slightly dusty in places, very small worm trail in lower inner margin of final few leaves, contemporary plain mottled calf, covers ruled in blind, joints rubbed, stain on rear endleaves, from the library of James Stevens Cox (1910-1997). Maggs Bros. Ltd. 1447 - 367 2016 £750

Rogers, Thomas *A Posie for Lovers; or the Terrestrial Venus Unmaskt.* London: for Thomas Speed, 1694. First edition, small 4to., titlepage and verso of final leaf lightly soiled and with a number of uncut edges, early 20th century half calf and marbled boards, from the library of James Stevens Cox (1910-1997) with his cipher pencilled on front pastedown and notes attributing the work to Rogers. Maggs Bros. Ltd. 1447 - 368 2016 £1250

Rusden, Moses *A Further Discovery of Bees.* London: for the author and by Henry Million, 1679. First edition, engraved frontispiece and 3 folding plates (out inch of first plate is missing where it would have been folded-in, with loss to image), some heavy browning and spotting, stronger in margins, short (25mm) closed tear to fore margin of C5 (just touching text), frontispiece and first plate heavily browned, contemporary sheep, rebacked, large areas of insect damage to covers, corners worn, old reback wearing again with an area of insect damage at foot, from the library of James Stevens Cox (1910-1997). Maggs Bros. Ltd. 1447 - 369 2016 £300

Rutherford, Samuel *Joshua Redivivus or Mr. Rutherford's Letters, Divided in two parts.* Rotterdam: in the Year, 1664. First edition, 8vo., some occasional light dampstaining, larger ink blots, very small hole through V1 (touching text on verso), late 19th century 'Presbyterian blue' morocco by Riviere & Son, panelled and lettered gilt, gilt gauffered edges, contemporary flyleaves and 'Dutch-gilt' pastedowns preserved from original binding, from the library of James Stevens Cox (1910-1997), 17th century calligraphic inscription 'Mrs. Anna Montgomerie Her Booke", long list of numbers and letters written in ink on front flyleaf, mid 19th century bookplate of John Whiteoord Mackenize. Maggs Bros. Ltd. 1447 - 370 2016 £500

Rymer, Thomas *The Tragedies of the Last Age Consider'd and examin'd by the Practice of the Ancients and by the Common sense of All the Ages.* London: for Richard Tonson, 1678. First edition, 8vo., A1-4 lightly foxed, short tear at foot of title, small stains to corner of C5-6, rust spot to E8, F4, leaves K4-8 heavily foxed, 45 x 25mm. piece cut from flyleaf, probably to removed earlier signature, early 19th century half calf and marbled boards, rubbed, corners bumped, from the library of James Stevens Cox (1910-1997). Maggs Bros. Ltd. 1447 - 371 2016 £180

Salmon, William *Seplasium. The Compleat English Physician or the Druggist's Shop Opened.* London: for Matthew Gilliflower and George Sawbridge, 1693. First edition, half title and errata/ad leaf and a4 with table on verso that is meant as a slip cancel for the table on X8v bound after X8, small hole through centre of Z8 (damaging two lines), 19th century paper slip tipped in between E32-3 (obscuring small portion of text on first 13 lines), rust spots on Gg1-3, fore corner of Ooo4 folded-in, small rust spot on Ffff4, contemporary calf, front joint and spine repaired, 19th century endleaves, from the library of James Stevens Cox (1910-1997), old signature "R. L. Carr ex donis C. C. Cocks". Maggs Bros. Ltd. 1447 - 373 2016 £650

Saltmarsh, John *Perfume Against the Sulpherous Stinke of the Snuffe of the Light for Smoak, called Novello-Mastix.* London: by Elizabeth Purslow, April 19, 1646. First edition, small 4to., small defect from paper fault in lower fore-corner of title (touching type-ornament border), disbound, uncut, from the library of James Stevens Cox (1910-1997). Maggs Bros. Ltd. 1447 - 373 2016 £200

Sarbiewski, Maciej Kazimierz 1595-1640 *Mathiae Casimiri Sarbievii Lycircorum Libri IV.* Cambridge: Richard Green, 1684. 12mo., fore-margin of A1-4 (and second fly-leaf) dampstained and slightly ragged, contemporary calf, ruled in blind with small tool in each corner, front joint rubbed, from the library of James Stevens Cox (1910-1997), the copy of John Loveday (1711-1689) with signature. Maggs Bros. Ltd.   1447 - 374   2016   £120

Selden, John 1584-1654 *Table-Talk: Being the Discourses of John Selden Esq. or His Sence of Various Matters of Weight and High Consequence Relating Especially to Religion and State.* London: for E. Smith, 1689. First edition, small 4to., browned throughout, dampstain to fore-margin,of (A)4 and D1, very small hole through inner margin of C3, foxing to edges of H3-4, lower corner of last leaf torn-away (just touching two letters), some lower edges uncut, mid 20th century half calf and marbled boards, from the library of James Stevens Cox (1910-1997). Maggs Bros. Ltd.   1447 - 376   2016   £400

Selden, John 1584-1654 *The Priviledges of the Baronage of England, when they Sit in Parliament.* London: by T. Badger for Matthew Wallbanck, 1642. First edition, small 8vo., without first blank leaf, dampstained and browned throughout, shaved at head, with some loss to page numbers, late 19th century vellum (label missing), from the library of James Stevens Cox (1910-1997), bookplate of Charles Edward Doble (d. 1914).   Maggs Bros. Ltd.   1447 - 375   2016   £170

Selden, John 1584-1654 *Theanthropos; or God Made Man.* London: by J. G. for Nathaniel Brooks, 1661. First edition, 8vo., engraved portrait, contemporary calf, covers ruled in blind, gilt spine with red morocco label, inside joints broken, spine defective at head and tail, covers rubbed, pastedowns unstuck, flyleaves include waste from 12mo. edition of Cicero, from the library of James Stevens Cox (1910-1997), bookplate and signature of John, first and last Baron Rolle of Stevenstone (1750-1842), Exeter.   Maggs Bros. Ltd.   1447 - 377   2016   £160

Settle, Elkanah *The New Athenian Comedy...* London: for Campanella Restio, 1693. First edition, small 4to., browned throughout, author's name written in pencil on titlepage, late 19th century half morocco and marbled boards by Kerr and Richardson (head and foot of spine chipped, front joint lightly chipped), from the library of James Stevens Cox (1910-1997), 20th century signature of James Bell.   Maggs Bros. Ltd.   1447 - 379   2016   £250

Shannon, Francis, Viscount *Discourses Useful for the Vain Modish Ladies and their Gallants.... (bound after) Essays and Discourses, Moral and Divine, Upon Several Subjects.* London: for J. Taylor, 1696. Second edition, the two parts usually bound in reverse, lacking combined general titlepage, old ink stain along lower edge of D5 and centre of B1, contemporary mottled calf, corners bumped and spine split, from the library of James Stevens Cox (1910-1997). Maggs Bros. Ltd.   1447 - 380   2016   £750

Sharrock, Robert *The History of the Propagation & Improvement of Vegetables by the Concurrence of Art and Nature...* Oxford: A. Lichfield for Tho. Robinson, 1660. First edition, small 8vo., with two additional illustrated leaves and ad at end, very inky thumb prints on titlepage, very occasional minor rust spotting, endleaves stained by turn-ins, early 20th century calf, from the library of James Stevens Cox (1910-1997), with bookplate.   Maggs Bros. Ltd.   1447 - 381   2016   £700

Shelton, Thomas *Tachygraphy.* London: by Thomas Milbourn for Dorman Newman, 1693. Small 8vo., adddi-tional engraved architectural title, 9 pages of engraved examples, engraved title frayed at head and repaired (touching frame) and shaved at foot affecting second line of imprint, small pin-hole through centre of first 15 leaves, letterpress title dampstained in upper inner margin, little soiled throughout and with margins closely trimmed in places, mid 20th century half calf and marbled boards, Edmund Herbert's early signature, from the library of James Stevens Cox (1910-1997).   Maggs Bros. Ltd.   1447 - 382   2016   £350

Shiers, William *A Familiar Discourse or Dialogue Concerning the Mine-Adventure.* London: in the year, 1700. First edition, 8vo., light dampstaining to fore-margins, tables spotted, first one torn affecting five lines of text, book block split, pastedowns detached, contemporary sheep, panelled in blind, spine split with dust jacket paper label, shelfmark, spine worn and torn at foot, sewing broken, coming loose in case, endleaves unstuck, from the library of James Stevens Cox (1910-1997).   Maggs Bros. Ltd.   1447 - 383   2016   £700

Shirley, James 1596-1666 *Via ad Latinam Linguam Companta.* London: by R. W. for John Stephenson, 1649. First edition, 8vo., lacking engraved title by Thomas Cross, some light soiling to titlepage and A2, two small inkstains to A24 and A3v, edges slightly bumped throughout and with some gatherings beginning to come loose, contemporary blind ruled sheep (corner of upper board chewed, bumped and rubbed), from the library of James Stevens Cox (1910-1997), 18th century name of Joseph Spry.   Maggs Bros. Ltd.   1447 - 384   2016   £200

Shotterel, Robert *Archerie Reviv'd or the Bow-Man's Excellence.* London: by Thomas Roycroft, 1676. First edition, 8vo., first blank leaf, light marginal browning, a number of margins have also been closely trimmed, contemporary sheep, covers ruled blind (slightly rubbed, front cover with 90mm scuff and with some minor staining on rare board, from the library of James Stevens Cox (1910-1997). Maggs Bros. Ltd.   1447 - 385   2016   £750

Simons, Mathew *A Direction for the English Traveller.* London: are to be sold by Thomas Jenner at the South Entrance of the Exchange, 1643. Fourth edition, small 4to., engraved leaves, paginated in manuscript by near contemporary hand, few pen trials to titlepage, occasional spotting and soiling, contemporary blind ruled sheep (front cover with early repair, covers with scrapes, piece torn from rear cover, edges chipped, joints cracked), with 8 page manuscript of Dance Steps by choreographer, Kenelm Tomlinson, with Tomlinson signature, from the library of James Stevens Cox (1910-1997).   Maggs Bros. Ltd.   1447 - 387   2016   £6000

Smith, John *Gerochomia Basilike. King Solomons Portraiture of Old Age.* London: for J. Hayes for S. Thomson, 1666. First edition, 8vo., folding letterpress table, some occasional spotting, blank lower corner of H1 torn away, contemporary calf, rebacked, corners repaired and new endpapers, contemporary signature of Edmund Morgan in ink, from the library of James Stevens Cox (1910-1997).   Maggs Bros. Ltd.   1447 - 388   2016   £280

Smith, John *The Trade & Fishing of Great Britain Displayed' wtih a Description of the Islands of Orkney and Shotland (sic).* London: By William Godbid and are to be sold by Nathaniel Webb, 1661. First edition, small 4to., bit shorter along fore-edge, very light worming to inner margin and single worm track to blank fore margin, mid 20th century blue half morocco, from the library of James Stevens Cox (1910-1997) with his pencil annotations.   Maggs Bros. Ltd.   1447 - 389   2016   £1500

Speed, Samuel *Prison-Pietie; or Meditations Divine and Moral.* London: by James Cottrel for Samuel Speed, 1677. First edition, 12mo., lacking engraved portrait of Speed, lightly browned throughout, few ink blots and some marginal staining, including a stain in lower corners towards end, marginal flaw in I6 damaging one letter on verso, early 19th century calf tooled in blind, rubbed, corners bumped, early ink underlining and occasional pointing hands or manicules throughout, pencil note Thorpes Cat. 7008 1825, from the library of James Stevens Cox (1910-1997).   Maggs Bros. Ltd.   1447 - 390   2016   £400

Spencer, John *A Discourse Concerning Prodigies; Wherein the Vanity of Presages by them is Reprehended and Their True and Proper Ends Asserted and Vindicated.* London: by John Field for Will. Graves... in Cambridge, 1663. First edition, small 4to., titlepage little dusty and with the lower margin renewed, and lower edge of gathering 'M' folded at little shorter and uncut, late 19th century gilt ruled polished calf by Pratt, spine tooled in gilt and with red and green morocco label, edges gilt, Henry Huth and Alfred Henry Huth copy with leather label, from the library of James Stevens Cox (1910-1997), Sir R. Leicester Harmsworth, 1st Bart (1870-1937).   Maggs Bros. Ltd. 1447 - 391   2016   £350

Spenser, Edmund   1552-1599   *The Works of that Famous English Poet Mr. Edmond Spenser.* London: by Henry Hills for Jonathan Edwin, 1679. Folio, engraved frontispiece, some rust spotting in places, otherwise fresh copy, contemporary mottled calf, marbled edges, surface of leather crazed by mottling acid, joints split at top and bottom, front cover wobbly, lower corners chewed, upper headcap and spine label missing, one front flyleaf coming loose, from the library of James Stevens Cox (1910-1997).   Maggs Bros. Ltd.   1447 - 392   2016   £300

Spinola, George *Rules to Get Children by with Handsome Faces...* London: for R. H., 1642. First edition, small 4to., lightly browned, early 20th century half morocco by Riviere, from the library of James Stevens Cox (1910-1997). Maggs Bros. Ltd.   1447 - 393   2016   £1250

Sprat, Thomas   1635-1713   *The History of the Royal-Society of London for the Improving of natural Knowledge.* London: by T. R. for J. Martyn and J. Allestry, 1667. First edition, small 4to., engraved plate of the arms of the Royal Society, 2 folding plates (slightly shaved) and page 233 with very short tear, but without etched frontispiece by Hollar (often missing), contemporary calf, rebacked, new endleaves, corners repaired, from the library of James Stevens Cox (1910-1997), early 19th century signature of Edw. Williams and John Johnstone, early ink ciphers CR, similar to that of Charles II.   Maggs Bros. Ltd.   1447 - 394 2016   £400

Sprigg, William *A Modest Plea, for an Equal Common-Wealth Against Monarchy.* London: for Giles Calvert, 1659. One of two editions, 8vo., blank upper corner of A1-E1 and I8-K4 intermittently dampstained, some occasional light soiling and few light ink drops to gatherings A and B, contemporary sheep, recently rebacked and recornered, new endpapers, from the library of James Stevens Cox (1910-1997), 17th century signatures of Robert Pearce, signature of Sir Frederick Rogers (1716-1777) 4th Baronet of Wisdome in Devon.   Maggs Bros. Ltd.   1447 - 395 2016   £950

Sprigge, Joshua *Anglia Rediviva; Englands Recovery...* London: by R. W. for John Partridge, 1647. First edition, small folio, frontispiece, errata leaf, folding engraved portraits (soiled, backed with later paper), large folding engraved view backed (with later paper and slight damge in folds, few ink blots), folding letterpress table, rather grubby throughout with occasional spots and stains E4v and F1r particularly soiled, contemporary calf, rebacked, 19th century marbled pastedowns, from the library of James Stevens Cox (1910-1997), armorial bookplate of Charles James, 1st Baron Northbourne.   Maggs Bros. Ltd.   1447 - 396   2016   £350

Stacy, Edmund *The Country Gentleman's Vade Mecum; or His Companion for the Town.*   London: for John Harris, 1699. First edition, 8vo., lacking contents leaves (a1-4) which were never bound in, some occasional spotting, small blank piece torn away from corner of D6 and H2, minor rust hole in C3 and H3v lightly stained, contemporary sprinkled sheep, covers panelled in blind, joints split at foot, lower headcap chewed by insects, front pastedown and flyleaf ink spotted, from the library of James Stevens Cox (1910-1997), early signature of Tho(mas) Elton.   Maggs Bros. Ltd.   1447 - 397   2016   £200

Standfast, Richard *Clero-Lacium Condimentum.*   Bristol: for Thomas Thomas, 1644. First edition, small 4to., titlepage soiled with prominent crease to inner margin, par 24 and A1v with dark stain along upper margin, corner of B1 dampstained and spotting to lower margins between B2 and C2, final leaf browned on recto, early 20th century cloth backed boards, soiled, from the library of James Stevens Cox (1910-1997).   Maggs Bros. Ltd.   1447 - 398   2016   £300

A Strange and Wonderful Account of the Great Mischiefs, Sustained by the late Dreadful Thunder, Liggtening and Terrible Land Floods...   London: J. Wright, I. Clarke, W. Thackery...., 1683. First edition, small 8vo., woodcut, three crude woodcut illustrations on recto final leaf, cropped at foot with lower edge of A1-2 and A7-8 repaired (with loss to imprint and some minor loss of occasional catchwords), titlepage very lightly spotted, staining to fore-margin of A3 (affecting final word on approximately 18 lines), early 19th century half calf and drab boards, front board scuffed, from the library of James Stevens Cox (1910-1997).   Maggs Bros. Ltd.   1447 - 401   2016   £4500

Strong, James *Joanereidos; or Feminine Valour...*   London: reprinted Anno Dom., 1674. Second edition, small 4to., spotted and lightly browned, some tearing in inner margin of title and following two leaves caused by original stitching, many edges uncut, early 19th century half calf and marbled boards, headcaps damaged and edges rubbed, from the library of James Stevens Cox (1910-1997), signature of Edward Rowe Mores (1730-1778), the copy of James Boswell the younger (1778-1822), small signature of Thomas Park (1658/9-1834).   Maggs Bros. Ltd.   1447 - 402   2016   £1500

Symson, Patrick *Spiritual songs or Holy Poems.*   Edinburgh: by the Heir of Andrew Anderson &c. for William Dickie, 1686? 12mo., small wormhole in lower fore-corner becoming increasingly larger throughout, closed tear to fore margin of A2 and G1, fore-margin of A3 stained, foot of L2, L7, L8 damaged (no loss of text), contemporary sheep, front board detached, covers very worn and scuffed, corners bumped, from the library of James Stevens Cox (1910-1997), armorial bookplate of Patrick Hume, 1st Earl of Marchmont (1641-1724).   Maggs Bros. Ltd.   1447 - 404   2016   £200

Tasso, Torquato 1544-1595 *Godfrey of Bulloigne; or the Recovery of Jerusalem.*   London: by John Macock for George Wells and Abel Swalle, 1687. Second edition, small closed tear to titlepage with evidence of earlier restoration, occasional rust spotting, dampstaining to margin in places, 55mm. piece torn away from fore margin of A7, repaired tear to A8, small piece torn away from corners of H4, 2A1 and with 60mm. closed tear to foot of 2I1 (touching text), contemporary calf, head and tail of spine damaged, corners bumped, label missing, from the library of James Stevens Cox (1910-1997), signature of E. Marshall dated 1769, signature of John Warren dated 1809.   Maggs Bros. Ltd.   1447 - 406   2016   £180

Tate, Nahum *Poems.*   London: by T. M. for Benj. Tooke, 1677. First edition, 8vo., without final blank leaf, small ink stain to blank fore margin of E2, rust spot to F4, some light staining to F6 and H2, 19th century calf, blind panelled, front board detached, from the library of James Stevens Cox (1910-1997), mid 19th century bookplate of John Whitefoord Mackenzie, armorial bookplate of Archibald Philip Primrose, 5th Earl of Rosebery.   Maggs Bros. Ltd.   1447 - 407   2016   £150

Taylor, Jeremy 1613-1667 *A Discourse Concerning Prayer ex Tempore or by Pretence of the Spirit.*   N.P.: n.p. in the Yeere, 1646. First edition, small 4to., 15mm. dampstain to foot of titlepage (not touching text), larger dampstain along fore-edge of gatherings B-C and inner margin of E, modern quarter imitation sheep and marbled boards, early ink inscription and few marginal ink crosses, By Bp. Tailour, from the library of James Stevens Cox (1910-1997).   Maggs Bros. Ltd.   1447 - 408   2016   £150

Taylor, Jeremy 1613-1667 *XXVIII Sermons Preached at Golden Grove; Being for the Summer Half Year...*   London: by R. N. for Richard Royston, 1651. First edition, small folio, some occaisonal spotting, otherwise good, mid 19th century dark green morocco, covers with large early 16th century style acorn panel in blind and with large gilt arms block of the 8th Earl of Scarbrough, gilt spine, marbled endleaves, gilt edges, from the library of James Stevens Cox (1910-1997), occasional underlining and marginal marks in ink including few small florets, bound for John Lumley-Savile, 8th Earl of Scarbrough by descent to his son John Lumley-Savile, 1st Baron Savile of Rufford, Rufford Hall booklabel.   Maggs Bros. Ltd.   1447 - 409   2016   £220

Taylor, John 1580-1653 *Cornucopia or Roome for a Ram-head.*   London: by John Reynolds, 1642. First edition, small 4to., crude woodcut, each leaf inlaid, first letter of title just shaved, very light staining near inner margin of title, some minor browning throughout, text lightly inked in lower corner of A24 (yet still legible), early 19th century half black morocco and drab boards, spine worn, upper headcap torn away and corners bumped, text coming loose, from the library of James Stevens Cox (1910-1997), old pencil foliation, armorial bookplate of Graham of Gartmore, Perthshire.   Maggs Bros. Ltd.   1447 - 410   2016   £1250

Tenison, Thomas *The Creed of Mr. Hobbes Examined; in a Feigned Conference Between Him and a Student of Divinity.*   London: for Francis Tyson, 1670. First edition, 8vo., with final errata leaf, titlepage lightly soiled and frayed along edges, intermittent light marginal dampstaining, contemporary calf, covers panelled in blind, spine with five raised bands, 35 x 10mm. piece torn from head of spine, foot of spine chipped and cracked with minor loss, joints worn, front cover loose, covers and edges rubbed and worn, from the library of James Stevens Cox (1910-1997).   Maggs Bros. Ltd.   1447 - 411   2016   £550

Terentius Afer, Publius *Terence's Comedies.*   London: for A. Swall and T. Childe, 1694. First edition, 8vo., small (20mm) piece torn away from fore margin of titlepage, some very light staining, contemporary sprinkled calf, gilt spine, red morocco label, joints cracked, headcaps broken and corners bumped, from the library of James Stevens Cox (1910-1997), signature and initials of Charles Kenneys (1651-1702).   Maggs Bros. Ltd.   1447 - 412   2016   £150

The Session of the Poets, Holden at the Foot of Parnassus-Hill July the 9th 1696.   London: for Elizabeth Whitlock, 1696. First edition, 8vo., uncut, engraved frontispiece, little dusty, some creasing to edges, small piece torn away from lower corner of D1, unsophisticated copy, sewn as issued in original pale blue paper wrappers, wrappers creased, short tear at head and tille stained, (original stitching partly loose), from the library of James Stevens Cox (1910-1997).   Maggs Bros. Ltd.   1447 - 378   2016   £1500

Tomkis, Thomas *Lingua; or the Combat of the Tongue and the Five Senses for Superiority.*   London: for Simon Miller, 1657. Small 8vo., sheet "B" lightly browned, small hole in blank part of title, early 20th century half brown morocco by Artelier Bindery, joints heavily rubbed, rear pastedown torn removing a label, from the library of James Stevens Cox (1910-1997), early inscription.   Maggs Bros. Ltd.   1447 - 414   2016   £300

Torriano, Giovanni *Della Lingua Toscana-Romana.*   London: for J. Martin and J. Allestrye, 1657. First edition, large 8vo. small hole (printing flaw?) to K1 affecting one or two letters of text, light dampstaining to lower right corner of first few gatherings, recto of last leaf lightly soiled, contemporary reversed calf, heavily worn, joints cracked and epxosing sewing, corners chipped, from the library of James Stevens Cox (1910-1997).   Maggs Bros. Ltd.   1447 - 415   2016   £1250

Traherne, Thomas *Christian Ethicks; or Divine Moraltiy.*   London: for Jonathan Edwin, 1675. First edition, 8vo., lightly foxed throughout due to poor paper quality, titlepage with some light wrinkles, contemporary calf, spine with four raised bands and red morocco lettered gilt, rebacked with extensive repairs to corners and headcaps, near contemporary signature of Ja(mes) King, 19th century bookplate of Sir John Dashwood King, from the library of James Stevens Cox (1910-1997).   Maggs Bros. Ltd.   1447 - 416   2016   £650

A True and Perfect Narrative of the Great and Dreadful Damages Susteyned in Several parts of England...   London: for P. Brooksby, 1674. First edition, rare, small 4to., titlepage verso of final leaf lightly soiled, titlepage marginally shorter at foot than other leaves, disbound, cloth folder bowing, tie missing, from the library of James Stevens Cox (1910-1997).   Maggs Bros. Ltd.   1447 - 417   2016   £1800

Tryon, Thomas *The Way to Health, Long Life and Happiness; or a Discourse of Temperance...*   London: printed and are to be sold by most booksellers, 1697. Third edition, titlepage browned and chipped along edges, light marginal staining throughout, light foxing and spotting, 8mm circular hole through centre of P1, mid 20th century green morocco, from the library of James Stevens Cox (1910-1997), 18th century signature of Henry Bradbury, 18th century pencil notes of John Soper.   Maggs Bros. Ltd.   1447 - 418   2016   £200

Turner, Thomas *The Case of the Bankers and their Creditors Stated and Examined.* London: in the year, 1675. Third edition, 8vo., titlepage lightly soiled, many upper corners slightly creased, small closed tear at foot of F2 (not touching text), blue inkstain in margin of K7r with slight offset on opposite page, contemporary sheep rebacked, new endleaves but old rear flyleaves preserved, rather tightly bound with narrow inner margins, from the library of James Stevens Cox (1910-1997), two early ink inscriptions of Roger Taunton.   Maggs Bros. Ltd.   1447 - 419   2016   £240

Tusser, Thomas *Five Hundred Points of Good Husbandry.* London: by Thomas Ratcliffe and Mary Daniel for the Company of Stationers, 1672. Small 4to., black letter, heavily browned/spotted in places throughout due to poor paper quality, scorch marks on K1, P1-4, S2 and T2, headlines on the Penultimate leaf just shaved, large lock of ?wool tied in bow loosely inserted between G3-4, late 18th century calf, spine divided by raised bands with red morocco label, upper joint slightly cracked, from the library of James Stevens Cox (1910-1997), engraved initial of Thomas Holt White (1724-1797), and three successive Holt White family signatures.   Maggs Bros. Ltd.   1447 - 420   2016   £500

Tyson, Edward *Carigueya, seu Marsupiale Americanum or the Anatomy of an Opossum, Dissected at Gresham College.* London: for Sam. Smith and Benj. Walford, 1698. First separate edition, small 4to., 2 folding engraved plates, one slightly shaved at foot, corners and edges occasionally bumped, disbound (traces of leather visible on spine), stitched (apparently a fairly early date) into a portion of 17th century printed singing manual, from the library of James Stevens Cox (1910-1997), 18th century ink lot number, Cox's pencil notes inside front cover 'James Yonge's copy.   Maggs Bros. Ltd.   1447 - 421   2016   £1800

Valentine and Orson The Two Sons of the Emperour of Greece. London: by J. W. for E. Tracy, 1694. Small 4to., woodcut frontispiece and ads below, woodcut on titlepage and numerous woodcut illustrations in text, very small piece torn away the upper blank corner of woodcut frontispiece, minor rust hole through P1 (in text) and Dd2 (in margin), small hole worn through foot of 2b2, light worming to fore margin of T2-V3, rust stain to Bb4 (touching text), contemporary sheep, covers ruled in blind, inside joints split, old stain from glass on upper cover, minor staining on rear, faded contemporary inscription of Ann Hill, Albert M Cohn 20th century armorial bookplate, from the library of James Stevens Cox (1910-1997).   Maggs Bros. Ltd.   1447 - 422 2016   £650

Venables, Robert *The Experienced Angler or Angling Improv'd.* London: by Benjamin White for B. Tooke and Tho. Sawbridge, 1683. Fifth edition (i.e. fourth edition), small 8vo., engraved frontispiece (backed with old paper and bound right to inner margin with some early blotted ink pen trials at head, ten small engravings in text of various fish, lightly browned, margins spotted throughout, margins trimmed throughout, many sidenotes and few signatures and catchwords shaved, early 20th century plain brown sheep, gilt edges, spine lightly stained, from the library of James Stevens Cox (1910-1997).   Maggs Bros. Ltd.   1447 - 423   2016   £750

Vergilius Maro, Publius *The Works of...* London: by Thomas Maxey for Andrew Crook, 1650. Second edition, 8vo., engraved portrait of Ogilby and additional engraved title by William Marshall (both dated 1649), minor rust spots to a number of leaves throughout, with upper corners of last few leaves creased, contemporary sheep covers ruled in blind, later (but old) paper labels on spine, worn, leather along fore-edge of front board chewed away and starting to detach, corners of lower cover chewed, joints split, headcaps missing, corners bumped, 'Charles Moore his Book', early inscription and early signature 'John Ogilvy", from the library of James Stevens Cox (1910-1997).   Maggs Bros. Ltd.   1447 - 424   2016   £180

Vergilius Maro, Publius *The Works of...* London: sold by Tho. Guy, 1684. Ninth edition, 8vo., engraved titlepage by Drapentier and 32 engraved plates, occasional rust spots, small closed tear to blank fore margin of D7 (not affecting text), contemporary sheep (nasty 19th century reback, now worn again with upper joint split, corners and edges chewed, 19th century endpapers), from the library of James Stevens Cox (1910-1997), 19th century armorial bookplate of John Frederick Doveton.   Maggs Bros. Ltd.   1447 - 425 2016   £180

Villars, Nicolas Pierre Henri *The Count of Gabalis; or the Extravagant Mysteries of the Cabalists, Exposed in Five Pleasant Discourses on the Secret Sciences.* London: in the year, 1660. First edition of this translation by Philip Ayres, 12mo., occasional spot or rust mark, fine, contemporary calf, gilt spine, headcap missing, joints rubbed, old paper shelflabel at head of spine, from the library of James Stevens Cox (1910-1997).   Maggs Bros. Ltd.   1447 - 428 2016   £650

Vives, Juan Luis *Linguae Latine Exercitatio.* London: Typis Alice Warren cum Societate Stationiarum, 1660. 12mo., title within type ornament border, small rust hole to lower corner of A4 (touching text) and with rust mark to lower margin of A8 and C2, lower fore-corner of A5 missing from paper flaw, no loss of text and upper blank corner of D7 torn away, contemporary sheep, covers ruled in blind, remnants of paper spine label, lower joint damaged by worming at head, single worm hole in upper joint, pastedowns unstuck, ink inscription "John Waddinge his book", from the library of James Stevens Cox (1910-1997). Maggs Bros. Ltd. 1447 - 429 2016 £420

Walker, Obadiah *Of Education. Especially of Young Gentlemen.* Oxford: in the Theatre, 1673. Second edition, small 8vo., engraved coat-of-arms of Oxford University on title, printer's crease across titlepage engraving, inner margins of title and contents leaves slightly damaged by adhesion, prominent dampstain in top inner margin of most leaves, corners stained in sheets C-D, with small piece torn from corner of M5, early 19th century half calf and paste boards, rubbed and worn with some worming to spine, early ink notes, the copy of the Cooper family of Markree Castle, Co. Sligo, Ireland with blue shield shaped case label, from the library of James Stevens Cox (1910-1997). Maggs Bros. Ltd. 1447 - 430 2016 £150

Walker, Obadiah *Periamma Epidemion; or Vulgar Errours in Practice Censured.* London: for Richard Royston, 1659. First edition, small 8vo., 2 parts, general title ruled in red, severe staining to A1-8, two-line stain (and small hole) to centre of B7, otherwise lightly browned with occasional small stains or rust spots, contemporary mottled calf, rebacked, corners repaired, new endleaves. from the library of James Stevens Cox (1910-1997). Maggs Bros. Ltd. 1447 - 433 2016 £140

Walker, William *The Royal Grammar, Commonly Called Lylly's Grammar Explained.* London: for Robert Pawlet and Edward Pawlet, 1674. Second edition, small 8vo., small rust hole through the blank part of the titlepage and upper corner with minor damage due to ink stain, larger hole from paper flaw on B3 (touching top line of text), some occasional minor spots, inkstain along upper edge of I5-K1 and with small piece torn away from bank corner of G4, contemporary calf, spine with four gilt tooled panels, spine label missing, upper joint split at head, endleaves unstuck. from the library of James Stevens Cox (1910-1997), Juvenile ink inscription, Heylar family of Coker Court Somerset, with 19th century armorial bookplate. Maggs Bros. Ltd. 1447 - 432 2016 £200

Walkley, Thomas *A New Catalogue of the Dukes, Marquesses, Earls, Viscounts, Barons of England, Scotland and Ireland...* London: Thomas Walkley, 1652. Second edition, 8vo., dark staining around edges of titlepage and with old inscription above imprint scratched away, remaining leaves browned and dampstained throughout and with some ink staining on final two leaves, later calf, rebacked, new endpapers, from the library of James Stevens Cox (1910-1997). Maggs Bros. Ltd. 1447 - 433 2016 £120

Waller, Edmund *Mr Waller's Speech in Parliament, at a Conference of Both Houses in the Painted Chamber 6 July 1641.* London: by John Norton for Abel Roper at the black spread Eagle, 1641. First edition, small 4to., title spotted and final page soiled, late 19th century half blue morocco, endleaves, titlepage and final leaf lightly foxed, from the library of James Stevens Cox (1910-1997). Maggs Bros. Ltd. 1447 - 434 2016 £100

Waller, Edmund *Poems &c.* London: by T. W. for Humphrey Mosley, 1645. Second or third unauthorized edition, 8vo., lacking engraved portrait, repair to inner margin of title, touching one rule, single worm hole to upper outer margin extends gradually to three holes, then a trail and disappears, early 19th century russia, covers tooled with single gilt rule and blind roll border, spine tooled in gilt and blind, drab presentation, front joint half split, but holding, lower joint rubbed, nasty dent to second to last panel, from the library of James Stevens Cox (1910-1997). Maggs Bros. Ltd. 1447 - 435 2016 £200

Waller, Edmund *Poems &c.* London: for Henry Herringman, 1668. Later edition, small 8vo., variant with 'London' printed in red in imprint, pastedowns and flyleaves little stained, contemporary sheep, ruled in blind (edges chipped, lower corners bumped, lower headcap torn away), early signature of Margaret Short, pen trials on flyleaves, from the library of James Stevens Cox (1910-1997). Maggs Bros. Ltd. 1447 - 436 2016 £150

Waller, Edmund *Poems, &c. (bound with) The Maid's Tragedy Altered.* London: for H. Herringman and sold by Jacob Tonson, 1694. 1690. Sixth edition of first work, 8vo., small tear to lower blank margin of portrait, light browning, occasional rust spots, blank corner of P1 weak from paper flaw, short closed tear to upper margin, contemporary calf, boards and spine rubbed, bumped and worn, gilt label, faded, joints starting to split, second work with little spotting to E4 and E5, some occasional light modern pencil annotations, from the library of James Stevens Cox (1910-1997). Maggs Bros. Ltd. 1447 - 417 2016 £120

Wallis, Ralph *Room for the Cobler of Goucester and His Wife...* London: for the author, 1668. First and only edition, small 4to., lightly foxed, minor tear along upper edge of C3, small piece torn away from blank corner of E1, with some leaves partly uncut, mid 19th century half black morocco and marbled boards, corners little worn, Henry Cunliffe bookplate, from the library of James Stevens Cox (1910-1997).   Maggs Bros. Ltd.   1447 - 438   2016   £1100

Ward, Seth *Vindiciae Academiarum Containing Some Briefe Animadversions Upon Mr. Websters Book....* Oxford: by Leonard Lichfield for Thomas Robinson, 1654. First edition, small 4to., ink stain in upper inner corner of titlepage and marking to C3r and C4, sidenote on A3v shaved, closely shaved at foot touching few catchwords, mid 20th century calf, Rev. Philip Bliss (1787-1857) signature, from the library of James Stevens Cox (1910-1997).   Maggs Bros. Ltd.   1447 - 439   2016   £800

Ward, Seth *Vindiciae Academiarum Containing Some Briefe Animadversions Upon Mr. Websters Book...* Oxford: by Leonard Lichfield for Thomas Robinson, 1654. First edition, small 4to., top margin closely trimmed with page numbers cropped on A2, B3, D2-3, gatherings A-B lightly stained, small hole to D1 affecting text, internally crisp and clean, modern brown half calf and boards, from the library of James Stevens Cox (1910-1997).   Maggs Bros. Ltd.   1447 - 440   2016   £750

Wase, Christopher *Considerations Concerning Free-Schools, as Settled in England.* Oxford: at the Theatre and are to be sold there and in London at Mr. Simon Millers, 1678. First edition, 8vo., engraved vignette of the Sheldonian Theatre on title, dampstaining to foot of titlepage and leaves a2-B4, lightly spotted throughout, mid 2th century quarter green morocco and marbled boards, old flyleaves preserved, 19th century ink armorial stamp of Mrs. M. F. Fletcher, from the library of James Stevens Cox (1910-1997).   Maggs Bros. Ltd.   1447 - 441   2016   £700

Wastfield, Robert *A True Testimony of faithfull Witnesses Recorded.* London: for Giles Calvert, 1657. First edition, small 4to., little dusty, lower right corner of verso of n3 soiled, isolated staining to lower inside of N4, prominent staining to foot of final leaf, fore-edges of first few leaves creased, very fresh, uncut copy, sewn as issued, original buff paper wrappers, spine partly defective, five contemporary ink annotations, from the library of James Stevens Cox (1910-1997).   Maggs Bros. Ltd.   1447 - 442   2016   £500

Waterman, Hugh *A Sermon Preached before the Court of Guardians of the Poor in the City of Bristol at St. Peters Church April 13th 1699.* Bristol: by W. Bonny, 1699. First edition, small 4to., lightly browned and spotted throughout, particularly at end, rust spots in places, lower edges of A1-2 uncut, lower fore-corner of F4 repaired, late 19th early 20th century half maroon morocco and marbled boards, from the library of James Stevens Cox (1910-1997), signature of Alfred J. Waterman, 6 Manor Park, Redland, Bristol dated 1913 and 3 page note on front flyleaves, 1913 clipping from local Bristol newspaper, pencil note "from the Weare collection.   Maggs Bros. Ltd.   1447 - 443   2016   £500

Webster, John *Academiarum Examen or the Examination of Academices.* London: for Giles Calvert, 1654. First edition, small 4to., top edge gilt little dusty, ink blot at centre of N3-4, very light dampstaining touching lower blank edge of M4-4, upper edge closely shaved, occasionally touching running titles, early underlining and annotation on M2v, early 20th century calf, ruled in blind, spine lettered gilt, endleaves little foxed, scarce, with century initials "JW or "TW", from the library of James Stevens Cox (1910-1997) with his cipher and pencil annotations.   Maggs Bros. Ltd.   1447 - 444   2016   £2400

Webster, John *Academiarum Examen or the Examination of Academices.* London: for Giles Calvert, 1654. First edition, small 4to., top edge gilt little dusty, ink blot at centre of N3-4, very light dampstaining touching lower blank edge of M4-4, upper edge closely shaved, occasionally touching running titles, early underlining and annotation on M2v, early 20th century calf, ruled in blind, spine lettered gilt, endleaves little foxed, scarce, with century initials "JW or "TW", from the library of James Stevens Cox (1910-1997) with his cipher and pencil annotations.   Maggs Bros. Ltd.   1447 - 444   2016   £2400

Weldon, Anthony *The Court and Character of King James.* London: by Robert Ibbitson and are to be sold by John Wright, 1650. Small 8vo., engraved portrait, minor stain at top of first few leaves, some light browning and occasional spots, sheet m lightly dusty, small flaw in margin of D4, some leaves uncut at tail, contemporary sheep, coming loose in case, spine heavily worn and d3efective at head, corners bumped, small wormhole to centre of front cover, no pastedowns, from the library of James Stevens Cox (1910-1997), bookplate of James Frampton (1659-1855), earlier signature deleted from front flyleaf.   Maggs Bros. Ltd.   1447 - 445   2016   £175

Wesley, Samuel *The Life of Our Blessed Lord and Saviour Jesus Christ.* London: for Charles Harper and Benj. Motte, 1693. First edition, folio, engraved portrait, engraved architectural title (long tear from lower margin into image repaired), 58 engraved plates, some light browning or spotting in places, few short marginal tears, some corners dog eared, lower blank outer corner on plate at page 21 torn away and piece (60mm. long) torn from outer margin of plate at page 296, minor hole to image of plate at page 333, contemporary sprinkled calf, early paper spine label (joints split, front cover almost detached, piece chewed from foot of spine, two corners chewed, bookplate removed from font pastedown, from the library of James Stevens Cox (1910-1997). Maggs Bros. Ltd. 1447 - 446 2016 £180

Weston, Richard *Directions Left by a Gentleman to His Sonns...* London: by E. T. and R. H. for R. Royston, 1670. First edition, small 4to., titlepage soiled and damaged at head, loss to rule border and crudely repaired on verso of top and bottom edges, A2 soiled and crudely repaired on recto of fore-margin upper edge of B1 and C1 closely shaved (touching headlines), mid 20th century quarter blue morocco and marbled boards, wormhole in lower joint, from the library of James Stevens Cox (1910-1997). Maggs Bros. Ltd. 1447 - 447 2016 £200

White, John *A Way to the Tree of Life.* London: Miles Fletcher for R. Royston, 1647. First edition, 8vo., without final blank titlepage browned and slightly shaved at fore-edge, small piece torn away from blank corner of A4, browned throughout with small dark marks on N6-8, final blank page stained by turn-ins and with edges little ragged, contemporary calf, rebacked, corners repaired, new endleaves, small inscription of John Witham, inscription of Philip Pecke, from the library of James Stevens Cox (1910-1997). Maggs Bros. Ltd. 1447 - 448 2016 £500

Wild, Robert *Iter Boreale.* London: printed on St. George's Day for George Thomason, 1660. Small 4to., dampstaining to inner margin of titlepage and final leaf, final leaf guarded along inner margin, light staining to foot of A2, minor foxing to A4, B3, C1, corner of C2 repaired, with stain across text of B4, rebound in contemporary calf from tract volume, covers panelled in blind, rebacked, corners repaired, new endleaves, old flyleaves preserved, from the library of James Stevens Cox (1910-1997). Maggs Bros. Ltd. 1447 - 449 2016 £180

Wilde, George *A Sermon Preached Upon Sunday the Third of March in St. Maries Oxford, before the General Assembly of the Members of the Honourable House of Commons Assembled.* Oxford: i.e. London: by Leonard Lichfield, 1643. Second edition, small 4to., titlepage, A2 and #4 spotted, lighter spotting and discoloration throughout, early 19th century half morocco and marbled boards, the copy of Rev. Philip Bliss (1787-1857), with signature, from the library of James Stevens Cox (1910-1997). Maggs Bros. Ltd. 1447 - 450 2016 £120

Williams, John *The History of the Gunpowder Treason.* London: for Richard Chiswel, 1678. First edition, small 4to., initial imprimatur leaf, small rust on C34, very minor stain on D2r and with verso of final leaf (D4), very lightly soiled, Amateur binding of early 20th century red boards and white spine, boards, little stained and corners bumped, from the library of James Stevens Cox (1910-1997), bookplate of William Salt Brassington. Maggs Bros. Ltd. 1447 - 451 2016 £120

Willis, John *Mnemonica or the Art of Memory Drained Out of the Pure Fountains of Art and Nature.* London: printed and are to be sold by Leonard Sowersby, 1661. First complete edition in English, 12mo., woodcut illustration of stage on E4B, browned throughout, stronger in margins, small ink-stain on D6, pages 94-95 somewhat soiled, light marking to fore edges of D8 and M7-8, early 19th century calf, ruled in gilt, spine with five raised bands, covers scuffed, joints just starting to crack, corners bumped, bookplate of Rev. Edward Orlebar Smith, from the library of James Stevens Cox (1910-1997). Maggs Bros. Ltd. 1447 - 452 2016 £400

Willis, Thomas *Distribae Duae Medico Philosophicae...* London: Typis Tho. Roycroft, Impensis Jo. martin, Ja. Allestry & Tho. Dicas, 1660. Second edition, 12mo., engraved frontispiece, dampstain to upper inner corner, lower corners of C5-I2 creased, occasional rust spotting throughout, small ink stain to blank lower margin of H6y4, later sheep, ruled in gilt, rubbed, small single wormhole to spine, headcap missing, with two pieces of leather gouged from centre of lower board, single marginal Latin annotation on H34, from the library of James Stevens Cox (1910-1997). Maggs Bros. Ltd. 1447 - 453 2016 £240

Willis, Thomas *Proteus Vinctus.* London: for E. Cotes and are to be sold by Will London bookseller in Newcastle, 1655. First edition, variant issue, 8vo., light dampstaining at beginning and end, some light occasional soiling, overall clean, crisp copy, contemporary sheep rebacked, front cover cracked and stained, rear cover torn away exposing board, corners and edges bumped and chipped, from the library of James Stevens Cox (1910-1997). Maggs Bros. Ltd. 1447 - 454 2016 £350

Willughby, Francis *The Ornithology of Francis Willughby of Middleton in the County of Warwick, Esq...* London: by Andrew Clarke for John Martyn, 1678. First edition in English, folio 78 engraved plates and two engraved plates of snares at page 28, titlepage browned and spotted slightly grubby throughout with marginal browning, occasional spotting, closed tear in outer margin of Kkk3, top corner of Kkk4 (touching rule), small blank piece torn from plate LIX; last 40 plates increasingly stained at outer edge, eventually working into image towards end and final plate damaged in outer margin but roughly repaired with outer half of plate backed with paper at earlyish date, late 18th century marbled boards, rebacked with leather, corners and edges bumped and worn, from the library of James Stevens Cox (1910-1997). Maggs Bros. Ltd. 1447 - 455 2016 £1600

Winchilsea, Heneage Finch, Earl of *A True and Exact Relation of the Late Prodigious Earthquake & Eruption of Mount Aetna...*   London: by T. Newcombe, 1669. First edition, small 4to., lacking folding engraved plate, but with 18th century engraving of Vesuvius erupting in 1630 loosely inserted, dampstained, more heavily at end, upper edge closely trimmed in places, one page number cropped, late 19th century half maroon morocco marbled boards, extremities rubbed, corners bumped, bookplate of John Beresford Clements 2869-1940 of Killadeeon, Co. Kildare, from the library of James Stevens Cox (1910-1997).   Maggs Bros. Ltd.   1447 - 456   2016   £120

Winstanley, William *Poor Robins Perambulation from Saffron-Walden to London Performed this Month of July 1678 With Allowance July 11 1678.*   London: for T. E. and are to be sold by General Assembly of Hawkers, 1678. First edition, only edition, small 4to., light soiling on title and pages 4/5 and a single small wormhole to inner margin throughout (intensifying in gathering C), mid 20th century flexible boards, from the library of James Stevens Cox (1910-1997).   Maggs Bros. Ltd.   1447 - 457   2016   £1500

Winterton, Ralph *Poetae Minores Graeci.*   Cambridge: Ex Officina Joan Hayes sold by J. Ray, E. Dobson, P. Campbell & J. Milner, Dublin Bibliopolis, 1699. First edition, 12mo., titlepage lightly soiled and spotted with 3 small holes from stitched in inner margin, last page dusty, some occasional spotting and soiling, few headlines shaved by binder, early 18th century calf backed boards, lined with light blue paper (head of spine chipped), blindstamped name on front cover has been scratched out, 18th century armorial bookplate of Wolle family of Forenaughts, Ireland, from the library of James Stevens Cox (1910-1997).   Maggs Bros. Ltd.   1447 - 458   2016   £240

Wiseman, Samuel *A Short and Serious Narrative of Londons fatal Fire, and Its Diurnal and Nocturnal Progression from Sunday Morning (being) the Second of September Anno Mirabili 1666 until Wednesday Night following A Poem.*   London: for Peter Dring, 1667. First edition, small 4to., title within thick black woodcut mourning border, probably washed, early 20th century dark red morocco by Wood, from the library of James Stevens Cox (1910-1997), with bookplate and purchase note.   Maggs Bros. Ltd.   1447 - 459   2016   £1500

Wishart, George *Montrose Redivivus or the Portraicture of James late Marquess of Montrose, Earl of Kincardin &c.* London: for Jo. Ridley, 1652. First edition in English, 8vo., engraved portrait, light marginal browning, A3r dust soiled and very lightly dampstained in places, probably washed, late 19th century sprinkled calf by F. Bedford (front cover detached, spine bands, lightly scuffed and chipped), bookplate of Charles George Milnes Gaskell, from the library of James Stevens Cox (1910-1997).   Maggs Bros. Ltd.   1447 - 460   2016   £120

Wither, George *Speculum Speculativum.*   London: Ritten June XIII, MDXLX and thre imprinted in the same year, 1660. 8vo., titlepage lightly soiled and frayed at edges, small burn mark to blank upper right corner of A4-5 and blank fore margin of A7-8, lightly soiled and stained throughout, small worm track to upper blank margin of final sheet, book block separating from binding, contemporary sheep, lacking endleaves, rubbed, corners bumped, headcaps damaged, from the library of James Stevens Cox (1910-1997).   Maggs Bros. Ltd.   1447 - 462   2016   £200

Wither, George *The Grateful Acknowledgment of a late Trimming Regulator.*   London: in the year, 1688. First edition, small 4to., titlepage very slightly soiled and with old manuscript tract number in upper fore-corner, small hole through and some soiling to final leaf (hole touching two lines of text on verso), disbound, from the library of James Stevens Cox (1910-1997).   Maggs Bros. Ltd.   1447 - 461   2016   £280

Wollaston, William *The Design of Part of the Book of Ecclesiastes; or the Unreasonableness of Mens Restless Contentions for the Present Enjoyments Represented in an English Poem.*   London: for James Knapton, 1691. First edition, 8vo., titlepage slightly grubby and with some minor ink stains, lower blank corner of A2 from a crease and E7 (from a flaw) torn-away, occasional spotting or slight stains, single wormhole through C1-4 (touching text in places), contemporary sprinkled calf, covers panelled in blind, top and bottom spine panels renewed, corners bumped, deleted ink signature, booksellers' pencil notes (some deleted), from the library of James Stevens Cox (1910-1997).   Maggs Bros. Ltd.   1447 - 463   2016   £240

Wood, Thomas *Juvenalis Redivivus or the First Satyr of Juvenal taught to speak plain Englsih.*   London: in the year, 1683. First edition, small 4to., titlepage soiled and with several short fractures from type around weak points in paper and small hole where the full stop after "POEM" has punched though, small tear to fore margin of A1-2 and F24 stained, small piece torn from fore-margin between E4-F2 (nt affecting text), mid 20th century quarter blue morocco and marbled boards, spine slightly faded, illegible early signature, from the library of James Stevens Cox (1910-1997).   Maggs Bros. Ltd.   1447 - 464   2016   £220

Worlidge, John *Systema Agriculturae the Mystery of Husbandry Discovered.*   London: by T. Johnson for Samuel Speed, 1669. First edition, folio, additional engraved titlepage, woodcut illustrations, frontispiece with three wormholes, lower edge of engraved title repaired, small wormhole in middle of first three leaves, small wormhole in blank margin of gatherings A-H, occasional light browning, circular stain to Mm1, contemporary sheep, spine with red morocco and gilt label, covers heavily scuffed, corners bumped, upper headcap torn, lower corner of rear board cracked, H. Raymond Barnett, modern bookplate, from the library of James Stevens Cox (1910-1997).   Maggs Bros. Ltd.   1447 - 465   2016   £350

Worlidge, John *Systema Agriulturae; the Mystery of Husbandry Discovered.* London: for Tho. Dring and are to be sold by R. Cavel, 1681. Third edition, folio, additional engraved titlepage and one plate, short worm trail in lower margin of first few leaves, small piece torn from fore-margin of #2, large rust spot in I1 and with some occasional light staining in places, contemporary calf, rebacked covers worn and rather crazed by damp, some insect damage along lower edges, new endleaves, from the library of James Stevens Cox (1910-1997).   Maggs Bros. Ltd.   1447 - 466   2016   £350

Wotton, Henry *Reliquiae Wottoniane...* London: by T. Roycroft for R. Marriott, F. Tyton, T. Collins and J. Ford, 1672. Third edition, 8vo., four engraved portraits, one portrait and titlepage foxed, minor repairs to corners of a 5,-7, early 20th century green morocco, coverd and spine bordered with small gilt sequin and dot tool, smooth spine lettered gilt, all edges gilt, spine little faded, small 18th? century signature of G. Smith, from the library of James Stevens Cox (1910-1997) with pencil note of purchase.   Maggs Bros. Ltd.   1447 - 467   2016   £180

Association – Cox, Joan

Doughty, Henry Montagu *Chronicles of Theberton. A Suffolk Village.* Cambridge: University of Cambridge; London: Macmillan, 1910. First edition, original green cloth, spine ruled and lettered gilt, spine sunned, light bumping to corners, little spotting to endpapers, frontispiece, plates, 3 maps, printed in green and black, occasional light spotting, good, early ownership inscription of Jack Simmons and pictorial bookplate of Claude and Joan Cox, very rare.   Sotheran's   Piccadilly Notes - Summer 2015 - 111   2016   £148

Association – Cox, Ozite Fleming

Burns, Robert *The Poems and Songs of Robert Burns.* London: George Newnes Ltd., 1902. 165 x 102mm., very fine crimson morocco lavishly and intricately gilt in a 'Scottish Wheel' design by Morrell (stamp signed on front turn-ins), covers with large central wheel of 20 compartments, each containing elegant gossamer floral tools between two lines of dots radiating from a central rosette, massed tiny circle tools at head and foot of wheel, above and below these circle tools, triangle formed by small scalloped compartments and multiple tiny flowers, corners with large leaf frond tools and covers generally with many accenting small tools, raised bands, spine compartments, with large quatrefoil containing central daisy radiating floral tools surrounded by gilt dots, elegantly and elaborately gilt turn-ins in swag pattern, ivory watered silk endleaves, all edges gilt, rear joint very expertly renewed, frontispiece, rear free endpaper with ink presentation to Ozite Fleming Cox from Benjamin Lloyd Belt dated May 8 1906, front joint beginning to show a thin crack (but mostly masked with dye), paper stock little dingy (as not doubt in all copies), otherwise very fine, covers and spine unworn and lustrous and text without signs of use.   Phillip J. Pirages   67 - 58   2016 $850

Association – Coxe, John Redman

Morgagni, Giovanni Battista   1682-1771 *The Seats and Causes of Disease Investigated by Anatomy in the Books Containing a Great Variety of Dissections with Remarks.* London: for A. Millar and others, 1769. First edition in English, thick 4to., 3 volumes, recent quarter morocco and linen boards, raised bands, gilt spine lettering, lacking half title in volume one, neat repairs on verso of titlepages, light text browning, early ownership markings on title, signature of John Redman Coxe.   James Tait Goodrich   X-78 - 405   2016 $3750

Association – Coylestone, F.

Ashe, Thomas *Songs of a Year.* London: Chiswick Press privately printed, 1888. First edition, paperback edition, scarce, presentation from author to F Coylestone, Feb. 1888, original paper wrappers, covers stained, creased on right corner and chipped along edges, hinges tender but text block in tight and clean, very good.   The Kelmscott Bookshop   13 - 3   2016 $220

Ashe, Thomas *Songs of a Year.* London: Chiswick press, privately printed, 1888. First edition, scrace, original paper wrappers, covers stained, creased on right corner and chipped along edges, hinges tender but text block is tight and clean, very good, presentation copy from author for F. Coylestone Feb. 1888.   The Kelmscott Bookshop   12 - 3   2016 $220

Association – Cradock-Hartopp, John William, 4th Baronet

Gould, John 1804-1881 *The Birds of Great Britain.* published by the author, 1862-1873. First edition, imperial folio, 25 parts in 5 volumes, bound by George Gregory of Bath in half green morocco, spines with gilt raised bands, lettering and elaborate tooling in custom made (c. 1990) walnut display case 38 x 36 x 25 inches, with lockable drawers, one for each volume, together with lockable hinged glass compartment that can be positioned like a lectern; with 367 hand colored lithographs, one text gathering bound in upside down in volume IV, slightly rubbed at extremities, occasional spots, otherwise extremely clean, very good, subscriber's copy with bookplate of Sir John William Cradock-Hartopp, 4th Baronet (1829-1888). Sotheran's Piccadilly Notes - Summer 2015 - 7   2016   £90,000

Association – Cram, Donald

McPhee, John *Annals of the Former World.* New York: FSG, 1998. First edition, signed by author, with signature of 1987 Nobel Prize winning chemist, Donald J. Cram, bit of shelfwear to lower edges of cloth, slight spine lean, very near fine in fine dust jacket.   Ken Lopez Bookseller 166 - 83   2016 $1000

Association – Cramb, John, Mrs.

Davidson, John *Smith: a Tragedy.* Glasgow: Frederick W. Wilson and Brother, 1888. First edition, 300 copies printed, scarce presentation copy inscribed by author to Mrs. John A Cramb, original parchment wrappers, which are browned and lightly soiled, otherwise very good, interior pages clean and bright, very light rippling caused by tight signature, enclosed in red cloth folder, which is inserted into red cloth slipcase with quarter leather spine, gilt title, author, date and 'presentation copy' to spine, very good in wrappers.   The Kelmscott Bookshop   12 - 32   2016 $675

Association – Crane, Walter

Deland, Margaret *The Old Garden.* Boston: Houghton Mifflin, 1894. first US edition, Owner inscription dated 1893, 8vo., pictorial cloth, colors on covers rubbed, else very good, printed on French-fold paper and illustrated in color on every page by Walter Crane, laid in is 3 page handwritten letter to Sydney Cockerell, from Crane, dated August 1892 with mailing envelope.   Aleph-bet Books, Inc.   112 - 123   2016 $750

Association – Craven, Thomas

Carmer, Carl *Listen to a Lonesome Drum.* New York: Farrar, 1936. First edition, 8vo., cover slightly soiled, very good, presentation by author to art critic and author Thomas Craven.   Second Life Books, Inc.   196A - 255   2016 $65

Association – Cravins, John

Wright, Willard Huntington 1888-1939 *The Bishop Murder Case.* New York: Charles Scribner's Sons, 1929. First edition, presentation from author to John V. Cravins Jr., author has added inked comment "See page 334", on page 334 he has edited the text in ink in two places, cloth moderately soiled, lightly foxed, old small waterstain visible along bottom margin of first 25 pages, not affecting text, else good in dust jacket with light wear to spine ends and corners.   Buckingham Books   2015 - 33090   2016 $2750

Association – Creighton, Mandell

Shaw, George T. *History of the Athenaeum.* Liverpool: printed for the Committee of the Athenaeum by Rockcliff Bros. Ltd. 44 Castle Street, 1898. Small folio, contemporary full chocolate brown crushed morocco by Fazakerley of Liverpool, gilt stamped monogram to centre of the upper board, spine divided into six compartments with raised bands, lettered and dated in second and third compartments, gilt ruled edges, gilt dentelles, top edge gilt, marbled endpapers, gilt lettered brown morocco, presentation label to front pastedown, black and white photo frontispiece and 6 plates, 3 plans, bright, crisp, copy, presentation to Mandell Creighton, Bp. of London, bookplate of Sir Albert Richardson (1880-1964).   Sotheran's   Piccadilly Notes - Summer 2015 - 273   2016   £295

Association – Cressey, E. H.

Blackwell, Elizabeth *The Laws of Life with Special Reference to the Physical Education of Girls.* New York: George P. Putnam, 1852. First edition, slate gray cloth, edges stained red, spine bit faded, few very tiny spots, else remarkably fresh, tight copy as close to fine as one could hope for, contemporary signature of E. H. Cressey, lovely near fine copy, very scarce.   Joseph J. Felcone, Inc. Books from Five Centuries: a Miscellany - 24   2016 $12,000

Association – Cresswell, J.

Fuller, Thomas 1608-1661 *A Pisgah Sight of Palestine and the Confines Thereof...* London: printed by J. E. for John Williams, 1650. First edition, 28 plates + frontispiece and additional titlepage, neat repair to upper corner of pages 279-280, plates mouned on later stubs, exceptionally clean, folio, mid 19th century full dark green crushed morocco, gilt and blind ruled borders, raised bands, ruled in gilt with compartments ruled in blind and gilt, little dulled, bookplate of J. Cresswell on leading pastedown and later bookplate of Helene Jung, inscribed in remembrance of her great kindness to Wm. Howson and his family Dec. 1858, handsome copy. Jarndyce Antiquarian Booksellers   CCXVII - 103   2016   £3500

Association – Crewe, Robert Crewe-Milnes, Marquess of

Buchanan, George *The Very learned Scotsman, Mr. George Buchanan's Fratres Fraterrimi.* Edinburgh: printed by the heirs and successors of Andrew Anderson, 1708. First edition, small 8vo., 19th century calf, gilt crest on upper cover by J. Leighton, fine, very scarce, early inscription of Robert Mylne, later bookplate of Robert Crewe-Milnes, Marquess of Crewe. C. R. Johnson Rare Book Collections Foxon: H-P 2015 - 622 2016 $2298

Association – Crompton, Millicent

Mundy, Francis Noel Clarke *Needwood Forest. (bound with) The Fall of Needwood.* Lichfield: printed by John Jackson; Derby: printed at the Office of J. Drewry, 1766. or c. 1790, & 1808. First editions, 4to., frontispiece, some foxing to 3 leaves of second work, contemporary ink note to one passage, pencil quotation from the Letters of Anna Seward in first work, 2 volumes in one, bound in early 19th century half red morocco, marbled boards, some rubbing to boards, corners worn, ownership name of Henry Smedley 1812 and Millicent Crompton, tipped in as a slip of blue sugar paper for Miss Mary French's friend. Jarndyce Antiquarian Booksellers CCXVI - 422 2016 £180

Association – Crosby, Harry

Crosby, Caresse *Poems for Harry Crosby.* Paris: Black Sun Press, 1931. First edition, 8vo., half white morocco (little soiled), 6 1/4 x 1/8 vertical stain on front cover, red diagonal backstrip (faintly faded at bottom), paper label (little soiled, abrasion at bottom taking first two numerals of the date), fore and bottom edges uncut, copy H of 44 lettered copies, on Hollande Van Gelder paper, of an edition of 544, two leaves little roughly opened 15 top, from the collection of Harry Crosby. Howard S. Mott Inc. 265 - 39 2016 $375

Association – Cross, John Neville

Dickens, Charles 1812-1870 *Sketches by Boz.* London: Chapman and Hall, 1839. Half title, frontispiece, engraved title, plates, uncut in slightly later dark green crushed morocco by Riviere & Son, gilt spine, borders and dentelles, armorial bookplate of John Neville Cross, top edge gilt, very good, handsome copy. Jarndyce Antiquarian Booksellers CCXVIII - 60 2016 £850

Association – Crossley, John

Satchell, William *The Angler's Notebook and Naturalist's Record.* London: William Satchell, Elliot Stock, 1880. 1888, Square 8vo., 12 illustrations, occasional marginalia, original dark green blind and gilt stamped cloth, extremities worn, spine ends chipped especially on second series volume, bookplate of John H. Crossley, good. Jeff Weber Rare Books 181 - 84 2016 $100

Association – Crouse, Lindsey

Clurman, Harold *Ibsen.* New York: Macmillan, 1977. First edition, inscribed by author to director David Mamet and his then wife, Lindsey Crouse Dec. 31. 1977, near fine in like dust jacket. Royal Books 48 - 36 2016 $650

Association – Crown, Dennis

Corbett, James J. *The Roar of the Crowd: The True Tale of the Rise and Fall of a Champion.* New York: G. P. Putnam's sons, 1925. First edition, front hinge neatly restored, else fine in very good or better dust jacket with modest chips at spine ends, short split at front flap fold, inscribed by author for boxing champion Dennis Crown. Between the Covers Rare Books 208 - 133 2016 $2500

Association – Cruikshank, George

Dickens, Charles 1812-1870 *Sketches by Boz.* London: John Macrone, 1836-1837. First edition, 2 volumes, 12mo., frontispiece in volume 1 and plates by George Cruikshank, small tear to margin pages 277 and 278 neatly repaired with archival tape, volumes little affected by damp, handsomely rebound in full dark green morocco, gilt dentelles and edges, top edge gilt, cloth slipcase, inscribed "Mrs. George Cruikshank with publisher's best respects" and signed by George Cruikshank. Jarndyce Antiquarian Booksellers CCXVIII - 53 2016 £5500

Association – Cruikshank, Norah

D'Arlingcourt, Charles Victor Prevot, Le Vicomte *Ipsiboe.* London: J. Robins & Co., 1823. First English edition, 2 volumes, half titles, later half calf, red and green labels, signature of George Cruikshank at head of titlepage, volume I and dated by him 1823, later c. 1850 bookplates of George S. Davis, very good, attractive copy. Jarndyce Antiquarian Booksellers CCXVII - 234 2016 £180

Pitter, Ruth *The Art of Reading in Ignorance.* London: Constable, n.d. circa, 1971. First edition, wrappers, presentation from author, inscribed to Norah Cruikshank from Ruth Pitter 19 Mar 71, staples rusted, covers slightly marked and creased, small smudge on upper cover slightly affecting presentation inscription, very good. Peter Ellis 112 - 302 2016 £75

Association – Culsett, Robert

Raleigh, Walter *Judicious and Select Essayes and Observations.* London: by T. Warren for Humphrey Moseley, 1650. First edition, small 8vo., engraved portrait, but without 4 leaves of Moseley's ads, blank verso of engraved portrait and blank verso of last leaf stained by turn-ins and with edges slightly chipped, small repair to foot of titlepage, just touching decorated border, minor closed tear in lower inner margin of A1-2, dampstaining to inner margins of G4-(2)C8 (touching text in places), small hole through (3)A-3 (touching two lines of text), some occasional rust spotting, mid 20th century calf, from the library of James Stevens Cox (1910-1997), early inscription of John Spelman, signature Robertus (?) Culsett, armorial bookplate of William Miller Ord (1834-1902).   Maggs Bros. Ltd.   1447 - 351   2016   £350

Association – Cunliffe, Henry

Cicero, Marcus Tullius *Cato Major and His Discourse of Old Age.* Philadelphia: Printed and sold by B. Franklin, 1744. First edition, 4to., printed on imported Genoese 'trois-O' paper, titlepage in red and black, contemporary sprinkled calf, gilt fillet roll around covers, blind sawtooth roll on edges, pages edges sprinkled red, very skillfully and almost imperceptibly rehinged, retaining entire original spine, just the slightest bit of foxing at edges of margins on few pages, else probably the nicest copy we have ever handled, bookplate of 19th century book collector Henry Cunliffe, in neat gold tooled calf backed slipcase.   Joseph J. Felcone, Inc. Books from Five Centuries: a Miscellany - 64   2016 $20,000

Wallis, Ralph *Room for the Cobler of Goucester and His Wife...* London: for the author, 1668. First and only edition, small 4to., lightly foxed, minor tear along upper edge of C3, small piece torn away from blank corner of E1, with some leaves partly uncut, mid 19th century half black morocco and marbled boards, corners little worn, Henry Cunliffe bookplate, from the library of James Stevens Cox (1910-1997).   Maggs Bros. Ltd.   1447 - 438   2016   £1100

Association – Currer, Frances Mary Richardson

Baxter, William *Glossarium Antiquitatum Britannicarum, Sive Syllabus...* London: impensis T. Woodward, C. Davis, J. Hazard, W. Bickerton & R. Chandler, 1773. Second edition, 8vo., frontispiece, woodcut head and last pieces and initials, few old repairs to titlepage, contemporary brown calf, red morocco gilt title label, relaid to spine, double fillet gilt border to boards, edges red, rebacked in slightly lighter shade, chips to label, edges worn, endpapers replaced, but no recently, second bookplate just visible beneath first, armorial bookplate of Frances Mary Richardson Currer.   Unsworths Antiquarian Booksellers Ltd.   E01 - Early Printing - 1   2016   £140

Association – Currie, Elizabeth

Binney, Thomas *Is It Possible to Make the Best of Both Worlds?* London: James Nisbet & Co., 1865. Fifteenth edition, pencil signature of Elizabeth Currie on title and preface and pencil note on following f.e.p., fine.   Jarndyce Antiquarian Books   CCXV - 47   2016   £35

Association – Currie, Philip

De La Ramee, Marie Louise   1839-1908 *Two Offenders.* London: Chatto & Windus, 1893. First edition, inscribed by author for Sir Philip and Lady Currie, bound in cream cloth with gilt ruling and design to front cover, boards smudged and show other signs of handling, small red spot on front board that may be ink, spine browned and slightly chipped, interior has light foxing to some pages and slight loosening of few signatures, although text block tight, all edges gilt, very good.   The Kelmscott Bookshop   12 - 78   2016 $525

Association – Curzon, A.

Thomson, James *The Seasons.* London: Wilkie and Robinson, J. Walker, Cadell and Davies et al, 1811. 191 x 121mm., very pleasing contemporary crimson straight grain morocco, elaborately decorated in gilt and blind, covers with broad gilt fillet perimeter bordering a frame of gilt palmettes and then (closer in) fillets and palmettes in blind, raised bands with gilt dash-roll, spine compartments with symmetrically clustered arabesques, roses, open dots, stars and foliate tools, gilt rolled turn-ins, all edges gilt, 4 engraved allegorical plates designed by T. Unwins, inscribed "L. E./from the library of her brother / H. Duncombe e(x) dono A. Curzon", little foxing to plates, extraordinarily fine, text clean and fresh, lovely binding, very lustrous and virtually unworn. Phillip J. Pirages   67 - 70   2016 $950

Association – D'Erlanger, Emile, Baron

Sitwell, Osbert   1892-1969 *Out of the Flame.* London: Grant Richards, 1923. First edition, frontispiece, 8vo., original green cloth with few light spots, backstrip with orange paper label little chipped to border, top edge lightly dust soiled with endpapers faintly browned, good, with holograph copy of 'Superstition', from the library of Baron Emile D'Erlanger, although without any mark of ownership. Blackwell's Rare Books   B186 - 284   2016   £130

Association – Dailey, Irene

Gilroy, Frank *About Those Roses or How not to Do a Play and Succeed.* New York: Random House, 1965. First edition, 8vo., signed by Irene Dailey who played Nettie Cleary in the 1964 production, very good in little worn dust jacket. Second Life Books, Inc.   196A - 642 2016 $65

Association – Dall, Caroline

Hale, Edward Everett *Seven Spanish Cities and the Way to Them.* Boston: Roberts, 1883. First edition, 8vo., blue cloth stamped in gilt (worn at top of spine), front flyleaf separate, ownership signature of Caroline H(ealey) Dall, contemporary book review tipped to front pastedown, very good.   Second Life Books, Inc.   196A - 702   2016 $150

Association – Dallas, Thomas

Dallas, George *A Vindication of the Justice and Policy of the late Wars Carried on in Hindostan and the Deckan by Marquis Wellesley....* London: for John Stockdale, 1806. First edition, contemporary acid mottled calf, gilt, extremities worn, else very good, Sir Thomas Dallas's copy with his contemporary signature and armorial bookplate.   Joseph J. Felcone, Inc.   Books from Five Centuries: a Miscellany - 79   2016 $400

Association – Dalone, Mr.

Lister, Martin *Conchyliorum Bivalvium Utriusque Aquae Exercitatio Anatomica Tertia...* London: Sumptibus authoris impressa, 1696. 4to., 10 engraved plates, complete with terminal blank Z4 in first work, contemporary sprinkled calf, very skillfully rebacked in period style, small early shelfmark in red ink on endpaper and on title, minor paper flaw in S2 just grazing catchword, very faint foxing in fore-edge, very lovely copy with text and plates clean and fresh, armorial bookplate of A. Gifford, DD of the Museum, presentation copy inscribed by author for Mr. Dalone.   Joseph J. Felcone, Inc.   Books from Five Centuries: a Miscellany - 91   2016 $10,000

Association – Dana, Lerna

Taylor, Samuel *Sabrina Fair; or a woman of the World a Romantic Comedy.* New York: Random House, 1954. First printing, 8vo., illustrations, very good in little scuffed and soiled, price clipped dust jacket, signed by Lerna Dana, Kim Stanley, Diana Lynn and Margaret Steele, who appeared in the play, illustrations.   Second Life Books, Inc. 196 B - 743   2016 $95

Association – Daniel, George

Phillips, Edward *Theatrum Poetarum Anglicanorum,...* London: Canterbury, 1800. First printing of this enlarged, updated edition, 203 x 121mm., appealing recent brown quarter morocco over linen boards, raised bands, red morocco label, front flyleaf with ownership inscription of 'G.D./Canonbury' (George Daniel of Canonbury Square, Islington, titlepage with small discreet embossed stamp of 'Mark Pattison, Lincoln College, Oxon", in exceptionally fine condition inside and out.   Phillip J. Pirages   67 - 243   2016 $750

Association – Danson, John Raymond

Grazzini, Antonis Francesco, called Il Lasca   1503-1584 *The Story of Doctor Manente.* Florence: Orioli, 1929. First edition, 49.200 copies signed by author, printed on Binda handmade paper (of an edition of 1200), frontispiece, 2 further plates, original vellum, oval ornament stamped in red to upper board, little browning and few small foxspots to lower board, backstrip lettered in red and darkened Lawrence phoenix bookplate and Stephen Gooden, bookplate for John Raymond Danson, untrimmed, protective glassine jacket, good.   Blackwell's Rare Books   B184 - 176   2016   £350

Association – Dao, Bei

Hamod, Sam *Dying with the Wrong Name.* Princeton: Contemporary Poetry Press, 2013. New edition, inscribed by author for poet Bei Dao, near fine in near fine dust jacket, laid in typescript copy of Hamod's poem "Sabra/Shatilla: In Sorrow".   Ken Lopez Bookseller   166 - 42   2016 $150

Association – Darwood, John William

Innes, Emily *Chersonese with the gilding Off.* London: Richard Bentley, 1885. First edition, 2 volumes, frontispiece illustrations, original green pictorial cloth lettered gilt, from the library of John William Darwood with his bookplate in each volume, founder of the tram system in Burma as well as the Strand Hotel in Rangoon, with errata slip, covers little marked and little bruised at edges, edges of free endpaper to volume I, just little chipped, very good, scarce.   Peter Ellis   112 - 246   2016   £550

Association – Daubeney, Robert

Parker, John Henry *The Architectural Antiquities of the City of Wells.* London: James Parker and Co., 1866. First edition, vignette title, 29 numbered plates, plate XVII foxed, sewing of plates slightly weak, original purple cloth, slightly faded and marked, inscribed "From the author" verso of leading f.e.p., armorial bookplate of Robert Daubeney. Jarndyce Antiquarian Booksellers   CCXVII - 212   2016 £40

Association – Davenport, George

Fenelon, Francois Salignac De La Mothe, Abp.   1651-1715 *The Adventures of Telemachus.* London: printed by W. Wilson for R. Edwards, 1792. 2nd edition, 4to., rubbed full calf, front hinge loose in volume one, contemporary bookplate (Samuel Fothergill Lettsom), later ownership signature of Dr. George Davenport, engraved portrait in volume one, engraved titlepages in both volumes, 24 engraved plates (foxed).   Second Life Books, Inc.   197 - 234   2016 $225

Association – Daves, Benjamin

Culpeper, Nicholas *Pharmacopia Londiensis or the London Dispensatory Further Adorned by the Studies and Collections of the Fellows...* London: printed by Peter Cole, printer and bookseller...., 1659. (and 1658). One of 3 printing variants of the 6th edition, 8vo., 20th century full calf with raised bands, spine lettered gilt, bound without vertical half title as often, title within two-line typographical border, page 257 with marginal repair, obscuring few words, index with few stains, cut close, never affecting printed surface, little spotted and lightly browned in places, contemporary ink inscription Cordelia Cole, her book, and ink inscription, Benjamin Daves his book.   Sotheran's   Piccadilly Notes - Summer 2015 - 92   2016   £1250

Association – David, Florence Nightingale

Quetelet, Lambert Adolphe Jacques *Letters Addressed to H. R. H the Grand Duke of Saxe Coburg and Gotha on the Theory of Probabilities as Applied to the Moral and Political Sciences.* London: Charles & Edwin Layton, 1849. First edition in English, 8vo., tables, original blind-stamped brown cloth by Lewis (binder's ticket at rear), rebacked, new spine label, fine, inscribed by translator Olinthus Gregory Downes to J. J. Sylvester, Esq., bookplate of Percy Alexander MacMahon, bookplate of Francis Galton Laboratory, initials of Florence Nightingale David, 1845. Jeff Weber Rare Books   183 - 29   2016 $1000

Association – Davidson, Alan

Kirwan, Andrew Valentine *Host and Guest.* London: Bell & Daldy, 1864. First edition, half title, uncut in original blue cloth by Bone & Son, little rubbed and dulled, recent booklabel of Alan Davidson, good plus.   Jarndyce Antiquarian Books   CCXV - 282   2016   £120

Association – Davie, Donald

MacDonald, Ross *Black Money.* New York: Knopf, 1966. First edition, inscribed by author to poet Donald Davie and wife, Doreen, fine in dust jacket with one tiny rub at head of spine.   Buckingham Books   2015 - 20957   2016 $2750

Association – Davie, Doreen

MacDonald, Ross *Black Money.* New York: Knopf, 1966. First edition, inscribed by author to poet Donald Davie and wife, Doreen, fine in dust jacket with one tiny rub at head of spine.   Buckingham Books   2015 - 20957   2016 $2750

Association – Davis, Andy

Coleman, Janet *Mingus/Mingus: Two Memoirs.* Berkeley: Creative Arts, 1989. First edition, photos, green cloth, nice in slightly scuffed dust jacket, Al Young's presentation for Andy Davis.   Second Life Books, Inc.   196A - 317   2016 $45

Singer, Barry *Black and Blue: the Life and Lyrics of Andy Razaf.* New York: Scribner, 1992. First printing, 8v., author's presentation on half title for Andy Davis, photos, paper over boards with cloth spine, nice in lightly scuffed dust jacket.   Second Life Books, Inc.   196 B - 582   2016 $50

Young, Al *Drowning in the Sea of Love.* Hopewell: Ecco, 1995. First edition, 8vo. author's presentation for Andy Davis, nice in dust jacket.   Second Life Books, Inc.   196 B - 958   2016 $45

Association – Davis, George

D'Arlingcourt, Charles Victor Prevot, Le Vicomte *Ipsiboe.* London: J. Robins & Co., 1823. First English edition, 2 volumes, half titles, later half calf, red and green labels, signature of George Cruikshank at head of titlepage, volume I and dated by him 1823, later c. 1850 bookplates of George S. Davis, very good, attractive copy.   Jarndyce Antiquarian Booksellers   CCXVII - 234   2016   £180

Association – Davis, Jane

Tasso, Torquato   1544-1595 *Dell' Aminta Favola Boschereccia di Torquato Tasso.* Londra: Presso C. Bennet, 1736. 12mo., full contemporary calf, joints cracked, head and tail of spine worn, later 18th century inscription "the gift of Hernietta Maria Bowdler to Jane Davis".   Jarndyce Antiquarian Booksellers   CCXVI - 559   2016   £75

Association – Davis, Reuben Robert

Dickens, Charles   1812-1870 *The Lamplighter.* London: privately printed, 1879. First edition, no. 129 of 250 copies, half title, original blue-gray wrappers bound into contemporary royal blue pebble grained cloth, triple ruled borders in blind, spine and front board lettered gilt, hinges very slightly rubbed, armorial bookplate of Reuben Robert Davis, very good, attractive copy.   Jarndyce Antiquarian Booksellers   CCXVIII - 701   2016   £250

Association – Davis, Susannah

Dickens, Charles 1812-1870 *The Battle of Life. A Love Story.* London: Bradbury & Evans, 1846. First edition, 2nd state of engraved title, woodcuts, small 8vo., original red cloth with gilt stamped lettering and cover design, all edges gilt, bright gilt, square and tight, period personal ownership of Susannah Davis dated 21st Dec. 1846, withal pleasing, near fine.   Tavistock Books   Bibliolatry - 6   2016 $1750

Association – Dawson, Douglas

Clausewitz, Carl Von *On War.* London: N. Trubner & Co., 1871. First edition in English, 3 small quarto volumes in one, mounted photographic frontispiece portrait of author, original full blue cloth, boards ruled in black, spine stamped in gilt, orange paper spine label, lettered in gilt, brown coated endpapers, spine bit darkened, boards bit rubbed, head and tail of spine with some minor shelfwear, front inner hinge starting but firm, previous owner Douglas Dawson's large bookplate, overall very good.   Heritage Book Shop   Holiday 2015 - 21   2016 $4000

Association – Dawson, Thomas

Kitchiner, William 1775-1827 *The House Keeper's Oracle.* London: Whittaker, Treacher & Co., 1829. Frontispiece, illustrations, title trimmed close at foot with loss of date, slightly later full maroon calf, raised gilt bands, green morocco label, spine faded to brown, little rubbed at hinges and head and tail of spine, armorial bookplate of Thomas Dawson, nice.   Jarndyce Antiquarian Books   CCXV - 284   2016   £180

Association – Day-Lewis, Cecil

Blake, Nicholas *The Dreadful Hollow.* New York: Harper & Bros., 1953. First American edition, crown 8vo., original quarter black cloth with terra cotta sides, backstrip lettered in white, top edge little dusty, other edges rough trimmed, dust jacket with small amount of fraying and few spots of internal tape repair, good, inscribed by Cecil Day-Lewis for Josie Baird.   Blackwell's Rare Books   B186 - 196   2016   £60

Association – De Contant-Delessert, A.

Conty, Henry Alexis De *Suisse Francaise Oberland Bernois. Guide Pratique et Illustre...* Paris: Faure, circa, 1867. First (?) edition, 12mo., original blue blindstamped flexible cloth, ornamented and lettered gilt, printed on blue paper, wood engravings, folding lithographic map printed in black, red and blue, folding lithographic railway map, 8 page booklet with wood engraved vignette on title inside rear pocket, bold of binding bit faded, only light rubbing, evenly little browned due to paper stock, railway map, little brown spotted, name of Swiss photographer A de Contant-Delessert, inscribed inside front cover.   Sotheran's   Travel and Exploration - 228 2016   £325

Association – De Cronin Hastings, Hubert

Richards, J. M. *The Castles on the Ground.* Architectural Press, 1946. First edition, frontispiece and 7 other lithographic plates in brown from drawings by John Piper, crown 8vo., original dark brown cloth, backstrip lettered gilt, faint endpaper foxing, very good, inscribed by Hubert De Cronin Hastings, for Dick & Bride.   Blackwell's Rare Books   B184 - 304   2016   £60

Association – De Guinzbourg, Victor

Pedant, Gilles *Recueil de Diverses Sentences, Prouerbes & Dictions Remarquables.* Paris: Pierre Ramier, 1628. 8vo., marbled wrappers, upper cover nearly detached, little browned and minor staining, bookplate of Colonel Victor De Guinzbourg, sound.   Blackwell's Rare Books   B186 - 114   2016   £850

Association – De Jonge, T.

Fichte, Johann Gottlieb *Grundlage des Naturrechts nach Principien der Wissenschaftslehre.* Jena und Leipzig: Christian Ernst Gabler, 1796. First edition, contemporary quarter calf with marbled boards, spine with gilt lettering, ornamental devices and four raised bands, from the library of T. De Jonge with his armorial bookplate, minor foxing to text, absolutely beautiful matched set.   Athena Rare Books   List 15 - 1796   2016 $1200

Association – De La Rue, Emile

Dickens, Charles 1812-1870 *A Child's History of England.* London: Bradbury & Evans, 1853-1854. Volume I 1853, volumes II and III first edition, 3 volumes, half titles, frontispiece by F. W. Topham, 1 page ads in all volumes, old tape repairs to inner hinges volume I, original violet pink cloth blocked in blind, front boards decorated n gilt, heads and tails of spine slightly rubbed with some slight loss, boards little dulled and marked, dedication leaf volume i inscribed by author frontispiece Feb. 5th 1854 for Emile de la Rue, signed by De la Rue, later bookplate of H. Lettenorier, fold over box.   Jarndyce Antiquarian Booksellers   CCXVIII - 495   2016   £16,500

Association – De Mille, Cecil B.

Raleigh, Walter *The Historie of the World in Five Books.* London: printed for B. White I. Place & G. Dawes, 1666. Early edition, small folio, 8 double page engraved maps, modern full brown calf, decoratively blindstamped on spine with five raised bands, few contemporary notations throughout, Cecil B. De Mille's copy with his bookplate.   Heritage Book Shop   Holiday 2015 - 96   2016 $2000

Association – De Texada, Rosita

Moore, George 1852-1933 *Martin Luther. A Tragedy in Five Acts.* London: Remington & Co., 1879. First edition, original blindstamped black cloth with gilt title and authors to front cover and title to spine, corners lightly bumped and small piece missing from top on spine, interior pages very nice, ownership signature of Henry Knight, bookplate of Rosita de Texada, very good, housed in green silk folding case.   The Kelmscott Bookshop   13 - 41   2016 $2550

Association – Dean, Peter

Hill, Richard *An Address to Persons of Fashion. Relating to Balls...* Shrewsbury: printed by J. Eddowes, 1771. Sixth edition, half title, 12mo., good clean copy, manuscript footnote on page 34, blue marginal line marking a paragraph on pages 154-155, recent full tan calf, raised bands, red morocco label, fresh contemporary endpapers and pastedowns, early signature of Peter Dean on titlepage.   Jarndyce Antiquarian Books   CCXV - 252   2016   £200

Association – Dearden, James

Common Sense or Every Body's Magazine. London: JGF & J. Rivington & Whittaker & Co., 1842. Volume I (of two published), 8 numbers, May-December, original purple brown cloth, slightly faded, early signature of James Dearden, Renier booklabel, very good.   Jarndyce Antiquarian Booksellers   CCXVII - 221   2016   £45

Association – Deats, Hiram

Moorehead, Warren K. *The Bird-Stone Ceremonial.* Saranac Lake: 1899. One of 600 copies privately printed, large 4to., illustrations, plate, wrappers, very fine, fresh, from the library of antiquarian Hiram E. Deats.   Joseph J. Felcone, Inc.   Books from Five Centuries: a Miscellany - 105   2016 $450

Association – Debary, P.

Lancaster, Joseph *Improvements in Education.* London: printed & sold by J. Lancaster, Free School, Borough Rd., 1806. Fourth edition, full contemporary tree calf, gilt spine, black morocco label, little rubbed and worn at corners, inscribed by author for P. Debary in the Egham Coach Apt. 25 1807.   Jarndyce Antiquarian Books   CCXV - 819   2016   £380

Association – Debenham, Ernest Ridley

Brown, Robert *A Treatise on Agriculture and Rural Affairs; Being th Substance of the Article Agriculture....* Edinburgh: Oliphant and Balfour and Brown andCrombie and Longman, &c. London, 1811. First separate edition, 2 volumes, 8vo., 6 engraved plates (these little offset), half titles, contemporary uniform mottled calf, spines with gilt lines and labels lettered gilt, very good, sometime in the library of Sir Ernest Ridley Debenham, with his bookplate in each volume.   John Drury Rare Books   2015 - 25653   2016 $437

Association – Deland, Lorin

Martin, Edward Sandford *The Unrest of Women.* New York: Appleton, 1913. First edition, 8vo., ex-library with bookplate, cloth, very good, author Martha Deland's copy with her ownership signature and note that it was presented from publisher, note from the Library of Lorin Deland and library bookplate.   Second Life Books, Inc.   196 B - 144   2016 $75

Association – Deland, Margaret

Martin, Edward Sandford *The Unrest of Women.* New York: Appleton, 1913. First edition, 8vo., ex-library with bookplate, cloth, very good, author Martha Deland's copy with her ownership signature and note that it was presented from publisher, note from the Library of Lorin Deland and library bookplate.   Second Life Books, Inc.   196 B - 144   2016 $75

Association – Delano, Frederic

Fisher, Irving 1867-1947 *Stable Money. A History of the Movement.* New York: Adelphi Co., 1934. First edition, limited, no. 634, 8vo., signed and inscribed by Fisher, Frederic Delano and James Rand, original blue cloth with mild wear cover edges, marginal dampstain, very good+.   By the Book, L. C.   45 - 28   2016 $3000

Association – Delcavo, Tony

Gore, Al *Earth in Balance.* Boston: Houghton Mifflin, 1992. First edition, fine in fine dust jacket, inscribed by author for Tony Delcavo.   Bella Luna Books   2016 - ta87   2016 $396

Association – Delillo, Don

Auster, Paul *Leviathan.* New York: Viking, 1992. Fine in fine dust jacket, signed by author and additionally signed by dedicatee Don Delillo, very uncommon thus.   Jeff Hirsch Books   Holiday List 2015 - 19   2016 $175

Association – Demetsosie, Hoke

Clark, Ann Nolan *The Little Herded in Summer.* United States Office of Indian Affair, 1942. Oblong 4to., pictorial cloth, slight soil near fine, illustrations, inscribed by artist, Hoke Demetsosie.   Aleph-bet Books, Inc.   111 - 226   2016 $475

Association – Deming, Edwin

Deming, Therese *Red Folk and Wild Folk with Indian Folk Lore Stories.* New York: Frederick Stokes, Sept., 1902. 4to., yellow cloth, pictorial paste-on, slight soil, else fine, this copy inscribed and signed by author and artist (Edwin Deming), 12 color plates plus many half tones in text, printed on coated paper, rare inscribed.   Aleph-bet Books, Inc. 111 - 117   2016 $400

Association – Denbigh, Maria

Sigourney, Lydia Huntley *Letters to Young Ladies.* London: Thomas Ward & Co., 1834. First English edition, 16mo., frontispiece, original brown patterned cloth, contemporary signature of Maria Denbigh on leading free endpaper, very good.   Jarndyce Antiquarian Books   CCXV - 408   2016   £75

Association – Denby, Edwin

Berrigan, Ted *"C" a Journal of Poetry.* New York: Lornez Gude et al May, 1963. -May 1966., I: 1-10; II-11 and 13 (of 13), 12 issues, tall legal format, mimeographed and stapled in printed wrappers and in pictorial wrappers with cover design by Joe Brainard, and one issue with silk screen cover design by Andy Warhol, some numbers inscribed by Berrigan and signed by Joe Brainard, presentation inscriptions to Tony Towle from Warhol, Berrigan, Edwin Denby, Gerard Malanga and John Wieners.   James S. Jaffe Rare Books   Occasional List: Winter 2016 - 24   2016 $22,500

Association – Denne, M. E.

Turner, Richard *An Easy Introduction to the Arts and Sciences being a Short but Comprehensive System of Useful and Polite Learning.* London: J. Johnson, 1803. Ninth edition, half title, plates, illustrations, final ad leaf, contemporary speckled calf, lacking label, rubbed, ownership inscription of M. E. Denne, April 11th 1804 ad Arthur Denne Hilton 1866.   Jarndyce Antiquarian Books   CCXV - 991   2016   £45

Association – Denny, Tom

Asimov, Isaac *I. Robot.* New York: Gnome Press, 1950. First edition, octavo, illustrations, cloth, inscribed by author Oct. 14 '82 for Tom Denny, nearly fine in very good dust jacket with moderate rubbing to front panel, light edge wear and light wear to spine ends, closd tear upper front spine fold, spine panel color faded.   John W. Knott, Jr./L.W. Currey, Inc.   Fall-Winter 2015 - 17581   2016 $2500

Association – Dent, Edward Joseph

Burton, Richard Francis   1821-1890 *Wanderings in West Africa from Liverpool to Fernando Po.* London: Tinsley Brothers, 18 Catherine St. Strand, 1863. First edition, 8vo., 2 volumes, original blindstamped maroon cloth lettered gilt to spine, one folding map frontispiece to volume I, wood engraved frontispiece to volume II, very minor rubbing to extremities, nice and clean, engraved armorial bookplates of Edward Joseph Dent and Norman Douglas Simpson.   Sotheran's   Travel and Exploration - 10   2016   £4000

Association – DePol, John

Krapf, Norbert *Heartwood.* Roslyn Harbor: Stone House Press, 1983. Limited to 150 numbered copies signed by author, presentation from artist, John DePol, wood engravings by DePol, 8vo., cloth backed decorated paper boards.   Oak Knoll Books   310 - 150   2016 $135

Association – Derby, Stanley, Earl of

Morell, Thomas *Thesaurus Graecae Poeseros; sive Lexicon Graeco-Prosodiacum Versus et Synonyma....* Etonae: Ex Typographia et Impensis Josephi Pote, Bibliopolae, 1762. First edition, large 4to., frontispiece, but lacking half title (with bookseller's catalog to verso), titlepage in red and black with engraved vignette, light sporadic foxing, some leaves little yellowed, slightly later half dark brown calf with marbled paper covered boards, neatly rebacked with spine retained, raised band, gilt title to spine, corners reinforced, edges sprinkled reddish brown, rubbed, some loss of surface pattern to marbled pages, edges worn, endpapers little dusty with short closed tear to f.f.e.p., but sound and very good overall, bookplate of Stanley family, Earls of Derby.   Unsworths Antiquarian Booksellers   30 - 110   2016   £225

Association – Derleth, August

Bloch, Robert *Pleasant Dreams-Nightmares.* Sauk City: Arkham House, 1960. First edition, presentation from author to August Derleth, fine in fine dust jacket, fine association copy, octavo, cloth.   John W. Knott, Jr./L.W. Currey, Inc.   Fall-Winter 2015 - 17254   2016 $2500

Campbell, Ramsey *The Inhabitant of the Lake and Less Welcome Tenants.* Sauk City: Arkham House, 1964. First edition, 2009 copies printed, presentation copy with signed inscription by Campbell to August Derleth, fine in fine dust jacket. John W. Knott, Jr./L.W. Currey, Inc. Fall-Winter 2015 - 17256   2016 $3500

Metcalfe, John *The Feasting Dead.* Sauk City: Arkham House, 1954. First edition, octavo, cloth, presentation from author to his publisher August Derleth, fine in fine dust jacket, rare signed or inscribed. John W. Knott, Jr./L.W. Currey, Inc. Fall-Winter 2015 - 17275   2016 $3000

Wandrei, Donald *The Web of Easter Island.* Sauk City: Arkham House, 1948. First edition, octavo, cloth, fine in fine dust jacket, presentation inscription by author to August Derleth. John W. Knott, Jr./L.W. Currey, Inc. Fall-Winter 2015 - 17287   2016 $3500

Association – Devisme, G.

Herodotus *Historia.* Glasgow: In aedibus Academicis, excuderbant Robertus et Andreas Foulis, 1761. First Foulis edition, first issue on less fine paper but with all blanks present and correct, 8vo., contemporary calf, spines gilt, red and green morocco lettering pieces (about half of them renewed with consummate skill), joints and extremities worn, some leather cracking but all boards firm held, front endpapers volume I renewed, bookplate of G. Devisme in all volumes except first, good copy. Blackwell's Rare Books Greek & Latin Classics VII - 30   2016   £1500

Association – Dewey

Marston, William Moulton *F. F. Proctor.* New York: Richard Smith, 1943. First edition, photos and program reproductions, inscribed by Mrs Proctor to Governor Dewey of NY, nice, little scuffed and chipped dust jacket. Second Life Books, Inc.   196 B - 143   2016 $75

Association – Di Maggio, Joe

Rust, Art *The Art Rust Jr. Baseball Quiz Book.* New York: Facts On File Publications, 1985. First edition, fine in fine dust jacket, inscribed to Joe DiMaggio 7/13/85, with letter of provenance signed by DiMaggio's two granddaughters. Between the Covers Rare Books   202 - 11   2016 $600

Association – Diamond, Elizabeth Watson

Tennyson, Alfred Tennyson, 1st Baron   1609-1692 *Seven Poems and Two Translations.* Hammersmith: Doves Press, 1902. One of 325 copies on paper and 25 on vellum, 236 x 165mm., very appealing contemporary brown crushed morocco decorated in Arts and Crafts style by G. C. Creswell (stamp signed), cover with blind tooled strapwork, frame accented with inlaid dots of green and olive morocco, raised bands, vertical titling in blind turn-ins with frame of multiple blind rules and inlaid green and olive dots at corners, binding with total of 296 inlays, all edges gilt, printed in red an black, with (laid in) bookplate of Elizabeth Watson Diamond, featuring etched portrait of T. J. Cobden-Sanderson by Sidney Lawton Smith, spine lightly sunned, extremities little rubbed, four short faint scratches to boards, minor offsetting from turn-ins, mild freckled foxing to edges of half dozen leaves, otherwise excellent copy, text very clean and fresh in quite pleasing amateur binding. Phillip J. Pirages   67 - 117   2016 $1500

Association – Dickens, Catherine

Dickens, Charles   1812-1870 *Sketches by Boz.* Philadelphia: Lee & Blanchard, 1842. New edition, tall 8vo., engraved frontispiece and 19 plates after George Cruikshank (all present), some browning and staining, few carefully repaired tears, original brown cloth, decorated in blind, gilt spine, expertly recased, neat repairs to corners and head and tail of spine, inscribed Ann (sic) Brown from Catherine Dickens NY June 1842, inscription leaf rather browned and has repaired edges, text clear. Jarndyce Antiquarian Booksellers   CCXVIII - 65   2016   £1500

Association – Dickens, Charles

Dousseau, Jean Jacques *Oeuvres Completees.* Paris: Chez A. Belin, imprimeur libaraire, 1817. Contemporary full tree calf, spine gilt in compartments, gilt borders and dentelles, maroon and green leather labels, carefully rebacked, slightly rubbed, bookplate of Charles Dickens as well as 'from the Library of Charles Dickens' label, further bookplate of Cordell William Firebrace. Jarndyce Antiquarian Booksellers   CCXVIII - 872   2016   £950

Egan, Pierce   1772-1849 *Tom & Jerry. Life in London....* London: John Camden Hotten, 1869. Half title, color frontispiece and 35 color plates, text little browned, original blue sand grained cloth, pictorially blocked and lettered gilt, spine little darkened and carefully repaired at head, inner hinge slight splitting, armorial bookplate of Charles Dickens and "From the Library of Charles Dickens" label June 1870. Jarndyce Antiquarian Booksellers   CCXVIII - 870   2016   £1100

Lytton, Edward George Earle Lyton, Bulwer-Lytton, 1st Baron 1803-1873 *Works.* London: G. Routledge and Co., Chapman and Hall, 1851-1860. New edition, 19 titles in 20 volumes, frontispieces, occasional spotting and dusting, one or two gatherings slightly proud, uniformly bound in contemporary half maroon calf blocked in blind, spines decorated in gilt, dark green leather labels, armorial bookplates of Charles Dickens, with "From the Library of Charles Dickens" label in all volumes.   Jarndyce Antiquarian Booksellers   CCXVIII - 869   2016   £4500

Linton, William   *Colossal Vestiages of the Older nations.* London: Longman, Green, Longman & Roberts, 1862. First edition, frontispiece, foldout diagram, untrimmed in original red wavy grained cloth, blocked in blind, front board lettered gilt, some minor repairs to head and tail of spine, bookplates of Charles Dickens, Sara R. Dunn and J. R. Ainslie, with "from the Library of Charles Dickens" label, very good in brown cloth foldover box, inscribed by Marion Bell to Dickens.   Jarndyce Antiquarian Booksellers   CCXVIII - 871   2016   £1650

Association – Dickens, Charles, Mrs.

Pope, Alexander   1688-1744   *The Poetical Works of Alexander Pope.* London: printed for private circulation by Bradbury & Evans,, 1848. Contemporary full dark green morocco, spine with blindstamped compartments, blind and gilt borders, gilt dentelles, slightly rubbed, small mark on front board, all edges gilt, attractive, well preserved, presentation from editor, William Macready to Mrs. Charles Dickens, then in turn, given by her to writer Edward Dutton Cook.   Jarndyce Antiquarian Booksellers   CCXVIII - 878   2016   £350

Association – Dickens, Joe

Dickens, Charles   1812-1870   *The Life and Adventures of Nicholas Nickleby.* London: Chapman & Hall, 1891. Half title, 39 plates by Phiz, contemporary half dark blue morocco, blue cloth sides, spine with raised bands, devices gilt later family inscription "From Joe Dickens".   Jarndyce Antiquarian Booksellers   CCXVIII - 236   2016   £110

Association – Dickens, Mamie

Dickens, Charles   1812-1870   *The Life and Adventures of Martin Chuzzlewit.* London: Chapman & Hall, 1872. Household edition, 4to., frontispiece, vignette title, illustrations by J. Barnard, original green cloth blocked and lettered in black and gilt, very good, presentation from author's daughter, Mamie for Penton Reading Room.   Jarndyce Antiquarian Booksellers   CCXVIII - 421   2016   £120

Association – Dickerson, George

Griffiths, Julia   *Autographs for Freedom.*   Auburn/Rochester: Alden, Beardsley & Co./Wanzer Beardsley & Co., 1854. Second edition, publisher's brown figured cloth, gilt (no priority), slight contemporary name stamp of George H. Dickerson, slight spotting on boards and light wear at extremities, else near fine.   Between the Covers Rare Books   207 - 3   2016 $600

Association – Dickinson, William

Lucretius Carus, Titus   *De Rerum Natura Libri Sex.* Berlin: Impensis Georgii, 1850. 8vo., 2 volumes bound as one, little foxing at beginning and end, contemporary vellum, boards ruled in blue, spine gilt, red and green morocco lettering pieces, green morocco date piece at foot (albeit with wrong date, 1840), marbled edges and endpapers, boards just slightly bowed, touch of rubbing to extremities, bookplate and ownership inscription of William Dickinson (Trinity college 1851), very good.   Blackwell's Rare Books   Greek & Latin Classics VII - 63   2016   £1000

Association – Didler, James Franklin

Burke, Edmund   1729-1797   *A Philosophical Enquiry Into the Origin of Our ideas of the Sublime and Beautiful.* London: for R. and J. Dodsley, 1757. First edition, contemporary mottled calf, marbled endpapers, neatly early repair to spine ends, half title with short tear and red stamped name of early owner, occasional minor spotting, withal very good, from the library of Franklin James Didler with his signature, chemise and morocco backed slipcase.   Joseph J. Felcone, Inc.   Books from Five Centuries: a Miscellany - 32   2016 $2000

Association – Digby, Robert

Jenyns, Soane   *Thoughts on the Causes and Consequences of the Present High Price of Provisions.* London: printed for J. Dodsley, 1767. Second edition, 8vo., half title, final blank signature, entirely untrimmed, stitched as issue, signature of Robt. Digby, very good.   Jarndyce Antiquarian Booksellers   CCXVI - 319   2016   £85

Association – Diggle, Alfred

Hand-Book of Etiquette: Being a Complete Guide to the Usages of Polite Society. London: Cassell, Petter & Galpin, Half title, 24 page catalog, original red brown limp cloth boards, little faded, slight lifting of cloth on front board, pencil inscription of Alfred Diggle, nice copy.   Jarndyce Antiquarian Books   CCXV - 242   2016   £75

Association – Dikty, Ted

Bester, Alfred *The Demolished Man.* Chicago: Shasta Publishers, 1953. First edition, octavo, cloth backed boards, very fine association, signed inscribed by author to his editor Ted Dikty, fine in virtually as new fine dust jacket. John W. Knott, Jr./L.W. Currey, Inc. Fall-Winter 2015 - 18564   2016 $3000

Association – Dill, Charles

Ireland, William Henry   1777-1835 *Memoirs of Jeanne D'Arc Surnamed La Pucelle D'Orleans with the History of Her Times.* London: Robert Triphook, 1824. 2 volumes bound in 4, 241 x 152mm., pleasing 19th century dark blue three quarter morocco flat spines decorated in gilt and inlaid with four tan fleurs-de-lys, marbled sides and endpapers, top edge gilt, with 27 plates, including five called for (one a double page, another folding color scene) and extra-illustrated with 22 plates, four of them in color, large paper copy, front flyleaf with signature of Charles G. Dill dated 31 May 1909; joints and extremities with hint of rubbing (but well masked with dye), small chip out of spine top, backstrips lightly and uniformly sunned, but the pretty bindings solid and with no serious condition issues, flyleaves and final leaf in each volume somewhat browned, (one opening with small portion of pages similarly browned from a laid-in acidic object), variable offsetting from the plates (perhaps a dozen rather noticeably offset), intermittent spotted foxing (isolated leaves more heavily foxed), not without problems internally, but with text still fresh, without many signs of use and printed within vast margins.   Phillip J. Pirages   67 - 204   2016 $850

Association – Dimock, George Edward

Strutt, Joseph *The Sports and Pastimes of the People of England Including the Rural and Domestic Recreations...* London: printed for Thomas Tegg, 1831. 260 x 165mm., very attractive later 19th century deep forest green crushed morocco, gilt by William Matthews (stamp-signed), covers with gilt French fillet, raised bands, spine gilt in compartments with central hunting themed ornament, stippled scrolling cornerpieces, gilt titling, turn-ins with very elegant gilt scrolling floral decoration, marbled endleaves, all edges gilt, 137 illustrations, full page plate and 136 numbered wood engravings in text, bookplate of George Edward Dimock, isolated very minor foxing, otherwise in very fine condition, unusual clean and fresh internally and accomplished binding lustrous and unworn.   Phillip J. Pirages   67 - 56   2016 $1500

Association – Dixon, Jean

Kelly, George *The Deep Mrs. Sykes.* New York: Samuel French, 1946. First edition, photos of two sets, fine, inscribed by author for Jean Dixon, she starred in this play. Second Life Books, Inc.   196A - 933   2016 $350

Association – Doble, Charles Edward

Selden, John   1584-1654 *The Priviledges of the Baronage of England, when they Sit in Parliament.* London: by T. Badger for Matthew Wallbanck, 1642. First edition, small 8vo., without first blank leaf, dampstained and browned throughout, shaved at head, with some loss to page numbers, late 19th century vellum (label missing), from the library of James Stevens Cox (1910-1997), bookplate of Charles Edward Doble (d. 1914).   Maggs Bros. Ltd.   1447 - 375   2016   £170

Association – Dodgson, Frances Anne

Maxims, Morals and Golden Rules. London: J. Madden & Co., 1839. Original limp green cloth, creased and rubbed, all edges gilt, contemporary gift inscription on leading pastedown from Frances Anne Dodgson for father, additional later presentation leaf tipped in.   Jarndyce Antiquarian Books CCXV - 313   2016   £60

Association – Dodgson, Mary

Dodgson, Charles Lutwidge   1832-1898 *Phantasmagoria and Other Poems.* London: macmillan, 1869. 8vo., blue cloth with gilt decorations, all edges gilt, two signatures sprung, light fraying to spine ends, spine and covers darkened a bit, very good in custom cloth clamshell box, this copy inscribed by author to his sister, Mary Dodgson.   Aleph-bet Books, Inc.   111 - 75   2016 $7500

Association – Doheny, Estelle

Shelley, Percy Bysshe   1792-1822 *The Cenci. A Tragedy, in Five Acts.* Italy (Livorgno): printed for C. and J. Ollier, 1819. First edition, only 250 copies printed, without initial blank, 8vo., brown crushed morocco gilt by Zaehnsdorf with their exhibition stamp, wide multiple roll tooled borders on sides, gilt in gilt on cover (within a frame) and spine, gilt edges and iner dentelles, Estelle Doheny's copy with her morocco gilt book label inside front cover, fine. Blackwell's Rare Books   Marks of Genius - 45   2016 £4000

Association – Doig, Ivan

Smiley, Jane *A Thousand Acres.* New York: Knopf, 1991. First edition, fine in fine dust jacket, inscribed by author to Ivan Doig.   Ken Lopez Bookseller   166 - 117 2016 $275

Association – Dollar, Robert

Noyes, Charles *Redwood and Lumbering in California Forests.* San Francisco: E. Cherry, 1884. First edition, 4to., 24 mounted original albumen photos, with 15 captioned in purple ink, original brown cloth, green patterned paper endpapers, housed in custom chemise and quarter leather slipcase, binding show wear with some cloth loss (two horizontal strips 1 inch wide) to rear board, with board showing, first gathering coming loose, last quarter of text block has tide-line in upper and right margins (not affecting text), prior owner inscriptions to first blank page, including presentation inscription to contributor, Robert Dollar 1844-1932 (unknown inscriber), occasional marginal note, some photos with age fading to edges though not adversely affecting overall image, good+ to very good.   Tavistock Books   Bibliolatry - 38   2016 $7500

Association – Donaldson, Edward Andrew

Allbut, Robert *London and Country Rambles with Charles Dickens.* London: Shepherd & St. John, 1888? Frontispiece and plates, original red cloth, spine and front board lettered in gilt, front board with gilt border, spine slightly dulled small mark on fron board, armorial bookplate of Edward Andrew Donaldson & his signature on titlepage, all edges gilt, very good plus.   Jarndyce Antiquarian Booksellers   CCXVIII - 1056   2016   £40

Association – Dorr, Thomas Wilson

Saint Pierre, Jacques Henri Bernardin De   1737-1814 *Beauties of the Studies of nature Selected form the Works of.* New York: Davis for Caritat, 1799. First American edition, 8vo., contemporary calf, front cover nearly detached, signature of RI reformer T(homas) W(ilson) Dorr.   M & S Rare Books, Inc.   99 - 78   2016 $750

Association – Douglas, Fannie H.

Church, Roberta *The Robert R. Churches of Memphis: a Father and Son Who Achieved in Spite of Race.* Ann Arbor: Edwards Brothers, 1974. First edition, photos, page edges slightly rumpled, still near fine, bit worn but very good dust jacket with some light chipping and faint staining, inscribed by Annette and Roberta Church to Fannie H. Douglas (wife of James H. Douglas).   Between the Covers Rare Books   207 - 27   2016 $250

Association – Doveton, John Frederick

Vergilius Maro, Publius *The Works of...*   London: sold by Tho. Guy, 1684. Ninth edition, 8vo., engraved titlepage by Drapentier and 32 engraved plates, occasional rust spots, small closed tear to blank fore margin of D7 (not affecting text), contemporary sheep (nasty 19th century reback, now worn again with upper joint split, corners and edges chewed, 19th century endpapers), from the library of James Stevens Cox (1910-1997), 19th century armorial bookplate of John Frederick Doveton.   Maggs Bros. Ltd.   1447 - 425   2016   £180

Association – Dow, Jessie

United States. Navy - 1866 *Register of the Commissioned, Warrant and Volunteer Officers of the Navy of the United States, Including Officers of the Marine Corps and Others to Jan. 1 1866.* Washington: GPO, 1866. First edition, 8vo., three quarter morocco over marbled paper covered boards, signed by J(essie) E. Dow, clerk in the Navy Dept., heavily annotated, good+, front joint tender, spine ends chipped, edgewear, some scuffing to boards, owner's name on title scattered soil spots and marginalia.   Kaaterskill Books   21 - 106   2016 $150

Association – Down, John Thornton

Webb, William *Minutes of Remarks on Subjects Picturesque, Moral and Miscellaneous....* London: Baldwin Cradock and Joy, Dublin: William Frederick Wakeman, 1827. First edition, 2 volumes, very pleasing contemporary sea green straight grain morocco, elaborately gilt, covers with gilt floral frame enclosing a central blindstamped arabesque, raised bands, spine compartments densely gilt with floral tools and volutes, turn-ins with decorative gilt densely gilt with floral tools and volutes, turn-ins with decorative gilt roll, light blue watered silk endleaves, all edges gilt, each volume with animated fore-edge painting set in Italian landscape; armorial bookplate of armorial bookplate of John Thornton Down, spines slightly and uniformly sunned, joints with just hint of rubbing, corners little bent, volume I lacking free endleaf at back, trivial imperfections internally, but extremely pretty set in essentially fine condition, bindings entirely solid with especially lustrous covers and text clean and fresh.   Phillip J. Pirages   67 - 165   2016 $2900

Association – Downes, Olinthus Gregory

Quetelet, Lambert Adolphe Jacques *Letters Addressed to H. R. H the Grand Duke of Saxe Coburg and Gotha on the Theory of Probabilities as Applied to the Moral and Political Sciences.* London: Charles & Edwin Layton, 1849. First edition in English, 8vo., tables, original blindstamped brown cloth by Lewis (binder's ticket at rear), rebacked, new spine label, fine, inscribed by translator Olinthus Gregory Downes to J. J. Sylvester, Esq., bookplate of Percy Alexander MacMahon, bookplate of Francis Galton Laboratory, initials of Florence Nightingale David, 1845.   Jeff Weber Rare Books   183 - 29   2016 $1000

Association – Downing, Stephen

Clarkson, Thomas *The History of the Rise, Progress and Accomplishment of the Abolition of the African Slave-Trade by the British Parliament.* Wilmington: R. Porter, 1816. Second Wilmington edition?, small octavo, 348 pages, vignette, contemporary full calf with morocco spine label gilt, early gift inscription to Stephen Downing from Charles Collins and signatures, small chip on front fly, light wear on boards, very good or better. Between the Covers Rare Books 202 - 2 2016 $375

Association – Drummond, John

La Fontaine, Jean De 1621-1695 *Fables Choisies ...* Paris: chez Desaint & Saillant et Durond..., 1755. First edition, large paper copy, 4 volumes, handsomely bound in contemporary French mottled calf, red and green morocco spine labels with rich gilt detailing, marbled endpapers and all edges marbled, discrete repairs to spine ends without rebacking, internal contents are generally in excellent condition although with occasional spot of foxing and with few warm pinholes running through the blank margins, front inner hinge of volume IV cracked but holding and slight age toning to text leaves in volume, engraved frontispiece, extra engraved portrait (found only in some copies) and 275 other engraved plates, bookplate of John Drummond in all volumes volume and second bookplate with name illegible. Heritage Book Shop Holiday 2015 - 69 2016 $35,000

Association – Drury, Collins

Phillips, Charles Henry *The History of the Colored Methodist Episcopal Church in America....* Jackson: Pub. House C. M. E. Church, 1925. Third edition of Book one, first edition of book two, publisher's cloth gilt, frontispiece, photos, couple of small tears on spine, else nice, near fine, inscribed by author to another Bishop in the Church, Collins Drury Feb. 15 1926. Between the Covers Rare Books 207 - 81 2016 $950

Association – Drury, Emmie

Dodgson, Charles Lutwidge 1832-1898 *Rhyme? and Reason?* London: Macmillan, 1983. First edition, 8vo., white vellum stamped in gold with picture of ghost on cover, all edges gilt, minor insect damage to hinges, else clean, tight and very good+ in custom clamshell box, in rear vellum for presentation, this copy warmly inscribed by author for dear friend Emmie Drury (Wyper), illustrations in color and black and white. Aleph-bet Books, Inc. 111 - 74 2016 $7500

Association – Drury, George Thorn

Radcliffe, Alexander *Ovidius Exulans ur Ovid Travestie.* London: by Peter Lillicrap for Samuel Speed, 1673. First edition, small 8vo., engraved portrait bust, washed and pressed, late 19th century polished calf by F. Bedford, covers with triple gilt fillet, gilt spine, marbled endleaves, gilt edges, joints rubbed. from the library of James Stevens Cox (1910-1997). the copy of W. E. Bonds, of Enderby House, Clapham, London, the copy of George Thorn Drury. Maggs Bros. Ltd. 1447 - 350 2016 £1100

Association – Du Priest, Oscar

Connor, Nellie Victoria *Essence of Good Perfume.* Burbank: Ivan Deach Jr., 1940. First edition, one of 100 numbered copies signed by author, frontispiece, cloth soiled, endpapers bit smudged, very good without dust jacket, probably as issued, this copy inscribed twice to Hon. Oscar and Mrs. Du Priest. Between the Covers Rare Books 207 - 31 2016 $485

Association – Du Rieu, L.

Tibullus, Albius *A Poetical Translation of Elegies of Tibullus.* London: printed for A. Millar, 1759. 2 volumes in one, some foxing to endpapers and first and final pages, otherwise clean copy, late 19th century dark brown cloth, gilt lettered spine, inscribed ex-libris Lud. Du Rieu 1784, ownership inscription of Geoffrey Tillotson. Jarndyce Antiquarian Booksellers CCXVI - 567 2016 £75

Association – Duart, Arbuthnot Charles Guthrie

Dickens, Charles 1812-1870 *Great Expectations.* London: Chapman and Hall, 1861. First edition, first impression of volume one, volume II and III second edition, second impression, 3 volumes, odd spot in prelims, contemporary half dark green calf, spines gilt in compartments, brown morocco spine labels, marbled boards, edges and endpapers, armorial bookplate of Arbuthnot Charles Guthrie Duart, very good, attractive set. Jarndyce Antiquarian Booksellers CCXVIII - 585 2016 £6500

Association – Dubois, Edward

Smith, James *Rejected Addresses or the new Theatrum Poetarum.* London: John Murray, 1833. First edition with these illustrations, 178 x 108mm., animated early 20th century scarlet crushed morocco, richly gilt by Riviere and Son (stamp signed on front turn-in), covers framed by curling vine bearing many berries and leaves, central panel formed and divided into compartments by gilt strapwork, each compartment containing a stylized strapwork and stippled wheel, radiating sections of wheel decorated with leafy fronds, raised bands, spine gilt in similar style, wide gilt turn-ins with plain and dotted label bound in at rear, fleece lined morocco clipped cloth slipcase, engraved frontispiece and 6 engraved illustrations by George Cruikshank, with signed original pencil study for one of the woodcuts and small pen and ink caricature, initialled by Cruikshank with his signature, laid in at front with two autograph letters, signed, tipped in at front, one from James Smith to Lady Blessington and one from Horace Smith to Duby (Edward Dubois - 1774-1850), front joint slightly (and rear joint just faintly) rubbed, spine shade darker than covers, text with faint overall browning because of paper stock, otherwise fine, lovely binding lustrous and altogether pleasing, text very clean and smooth.   Phillip J. Pirages   67 - 64   2016 $950

Association – Dubourg, Mrs.

Dodgson, Charles Lutwidge   1832-1898 *Sylvie and Bruno.* London: Macmillan, 1889. First edition, 8vo., red cloth stamped in gold, all edges gilt, front gutter and right edge have small holes, rear corner soft, some gilt dulled, prelim pages faded, overall really very good in custom chemise and leather slipcase, this copy inscribed by author for Mrs. Dubourg, wonderfully illustrated by Harry Furniss.   Aleph-bet Books, Inc.   111 - 80   2016 $3250

Dodgson, Charles Lutwidge   1832-1898 *Sylvie and Bruno Concluded.* London: Macmillan, 1893. First edition, 8vo., red cloth stamped in gold, all edges gilt, offsetting on half title and tissue guard foxed, else near fine and bright, inscribed by author for Mrs. Dubourg, wonderfully illustrated by Harry Furniss with full and partial page drawings.   Aleph-bet Books, Inc.   111 - 79   2016 $3750

Association – Duce, C,

Bolton, Robert *Instructions for a Right Comfoorting Afflicted Consequences...*   imprinted by Felix Kyngston for Thomas Weaver, 1631. First edition, woodcut printer's device on title, very slight dampstaining in upper margins, initial blank discarded, small 4to., contemporary mottled calf, blind tooled corner ornaments, author's name in gilt on spine, top compartment of spine defective early initials "PC" opposite signature B, inscription on titlepage "Christo Duce, R.C.", 17th century of T. Browne, 20th century acquisition note by Reginald Chas. Tudor Hutchins, very good.   Blackwell's Rare Books   B186 - 22   2016   £1750

Association – Dummer, Jeremiah

More, Henry *Enchiridion Ethicum, Praecipua Moralis Rhilosophiae Rudimenta Complectens Illustrata Utplurimum Veterum Monumentis...* London: J. Downing, 1711. Fourth edition, 8vo. engraved portrait, frontispiece trimmed, contemporary blind tooled calf, rebacked, 4 raised bands, gilt title, new endleaves, signature of Edmund Quincey 1718, donor's note (to Jeremiah Dummer, (Silversmith) dated 1718, signatures of 'William B. Calhoun', foxing, some leaves toned, marginal pen lines, title + first leaf perforated and embossed, very good.   Jeff Weber Rare Books   181 - 23   2016 $295

Association – Duncombe, Charlotte

Pinchard, Elizabeth Sibthorpe *The Blind Child.* London: printed for E. Newbery, 1798. Fifth edition, 12mo., some foxing to frontispiece, titlepage dusted and little browned, full contemporary tree calf, double gilt banded spine, red morocco label, joints cracked but firm, some slight wear, inscription "given to the Miss Fludyers by Lady Charlotte Duncombe, June 1801".   Jarndyce Antiquarian Books   CCXV - 370   2016   £75

Association – Duncombe, H.

Thomson, James *The Seasons.* London: Wilkie and Robinson, J. Walker, Cadell and Davies et al, 1811. 191 x 121mm., very pleasing contemporary crimson straight grain morocco, elaborately decorated in gilt and blind, covers with broad gilt fillet perimeter bordering a frame of gilt palmettes and then (closer in) fillets and palmettes in blind, raised bands with gilt dash-roll, spine compartments with symmetrically clustered arabesques, roses, open dots, stars and foliate tools, gilt rolled turn-ins, all edges gilt, 4 engraved allegorical plates designed by T. Unwins, inscribed "L. E./from the library of her brother / H. Duncombe e(x) dono A. Curzon", little foxing to plates, extraordinarily fine, text clean and fresh, lovely binding, very lustrous and virtually unworn.   Phillip J. Pirages   67 - 70   2016 $950

Association – Dunlop, C. J. Tennant

Thackeray, William Makepeace   1811-1863 *The Kickleburys on the Rhine.* London: Smith, Elder, 1851. Second edition, square 8vo., contemporary half calf over marbled boards, spine lettered and ruled in gilt, marbled edges, title with tinted lithographic vignette, tinted lithographic frontispiece and 13 tinted lithographic plates, all by Thackeray, light wear to extremities, spine little sunned with hinges weakened at head, internally, apart from very light marginal toning a clean and fresh copy, Glasgow bookseller's label inside front cover, contemporary engraved armorial bookplate of C. J. Tennant Dunlop underneath.   Sotheran's   Travel and Exploration - 286   2016   £125

Association – Dunn, Sara

Linton, William *Colossal Vestiages of the Older nations.* London: Longman, Green, Longman & Roberts, 1862. First edition, frontispiece, foldout diagram, untrimmed in original red wavy grained cloth, blocked in blind, front board lettered gilt, some minor repairs to head and tail of spine, bookplates of Charles Dickens, Sara R. Dunn and J. R. Ainslie, with "from the Library of Charles Dickens" label, very good in brown cloth foldover box, inscribed by Marion Bell to Dickens.   Jarndyce Antiquarian Booksellers   CCXVIII - 871   2016   £1650

Association – Durand, Emile

Gancel, Joseph *Gancel's Ready Reference Book of Menu Terms.* New York: Joseph Joseph Gancel, 1910. First edition, 8vo., original cloth lettered gilt on upper board, very good, ownership inscription of Emile Durand, head chef for Miami Biltmore Kitchen.   Sotheran's   Piccadilly Notes - Summer 2015 - 141   2016   £298

Association – Durante, Jimmy

Fowler, Gene *Schnozzola: the Story of Jimmy Durante.* New York: Viking, 1951. First edition, 8vo., presentation from Durante, illustrations, very good in somewhat scuffed and chipped dust jacket.   Second Life Books, Inc.   196A - 574   2016 $85

Association – Duru, Leon

Perreaux, Louis Guillaume *Lois De L'Univers: Principe de la Creation.* Paris: Edouard Baltenweck Editeur 7 rue Horore Chevalier, 1877. First edition, 2 volumes, 8vo., titles printed in red and black, colored frontispiece in first volume, paper discolored in places, original printed wrappers, joints to wrappers to volume on repaired, some minor chipping to edge of upper wrapper in volume two, inscribed by author to Leon Duru, rare.   Marlborough Rare Books   List 56 - 43   2016   £550

Association – Dutour, Etienne-Francois

Persius *Satyrae sex.* Paris: Apud Sebastianum Cramoisy, Architypographum Regium & Gabrielem Cramoisy, 1644. Scarce small format printing, some spotting and light browning, contemporary vellum, slightly soiled letterpress booklabel of Etienne-Francois Dutour (1711-1784), very good.   Blackwell's Rare Books   Greek & Latin Classics VII - 67   2016   £500

Association – Dutton Cook, Edward

Pope, Alexander 1688-1744 *The Poetical Works of Alexander Pope.* London: printed for private circulation by Bradbury & Evans,, 1848. Contemporary full dark green morocco, spine with blindstamped compartments, blind and gilt borders, gilt dentelles, slightly rubbed, small mark on front board, all edges gilt, attractive, well preserved, presentation from editor, William Macready to Mrs. Charles Dickens, then in turn, given by her to writer Edward Dutton Cook.   Jarndyce Antiquarian Booksellers   CCXVIII - 878   2016   £350

Association – Duvlenck, Elise

Wharton, Edith 1862-1937 *Artemis to Actaeon and Other Verse.* New York: Charles Scribner's Sons, 1909. First edition, small 8vo., original gilt decorated cloth, presentation copy inscribed by author to her personal maid in attendance, Elise Duvlenck, Sept. 1909, faint traces of damp to covers, very good.   Peter Ellis   112 - 443   2016   £2250

Association – Dyer-Bennet, Richard

Homerus *The Odyssey.* Garden City: Anchor Press/Doubledday, 1961. Reprint, illustrations by Hans Erni, inscribed and signed by translator Robert Fitzgerald for William Meredith in 1979, also inscribed in Greek and signed by folk singer Richard Dyer-Bennet, laid in is ticket and program to a Library of Congress event presenting Dyer-Bennet premier, fine in close ot fine dust jacket.   Charles Agvent   William Meredith - 55   2016 $100

Association – Dyer, Mr.

Lawrence, Alfred Henry *Reminiscences of Cambridge Life.* London: for private circulation only, 1889. Half title, original light blue cloth, bevelled boards, all edges gilt, later presentation inscription from author's wife to Mr. Dyer, very good.   Jarndyce Antiquarian Books   CCXV - 574   2016   £65

Association – Eamonson, B.

Keith, Thomas *The Complete Practical Arithmetician.* London: printed for J. Scatcherd etc., 1798. Second edition, 12mo., page of ads for books, occasional ink blot or other sign of use, lower corners bit creased, contemporary sheep spine gilt ruled, unlettered, bit worn, corners bumped, signature of B. Eamonson 1832.   Jarndyce Antiquarian Books   CCXV - 806   2016   £120

Association – Easton, Sarah

Gessner, Salomon *The Death of Abel.* Newport: printed by Peter Edes, 1787. Rare American printing, browned, text on titlepage underlined with pinpricks, early ownership inscription of Sarah J. Easton, 12mo., contemporary sheep, spine ruled in gilt, rubbed, some wear to front joint and tail of spine, sound. Blackwell's Rare Books B186 - 62 2016 £400

Association – Eckel, John C.

Dickens, Charles 1812-1870 *The Chimes.* London: Chapman & Hall, 1844. Proof copy, sent by Dickens to Lady Blessington after 6th December 1844, half title, frontispiece and additional engraved title, illustrations, 19th century full green crushed morocco, hinges skilfully repaired, small mark to front board, bookplates of M. C. Borden and John C. Eckel, all edges gilt. very good, bound after half title is manuscript address leaf in Dickens's hand, cloth slipcase. Jarndyce Antiquarian Booksellers CCXVIII - 363 2016 £28,000

Association – Edel, Leon

Horgan, Paul *Lamy of Santa Fe: His Life and Times.* New York: Farrar, Straus & Giroux, 1973. First edition, large paper limited edition of 490 copies signed by author, this number 12, tall 8vo., 20 black and whites plates, and 12 beautifully colored plates, cloth backed paper boards, top edge gilt, couple of light age spots on titlepage, else fine in publisher's box, presentation copy from author for Leon Edel, with his ownership signature. Second Life Books, Inc. 196A - 821 2016 $275

Association – Edgecombe, James

Quarles, Francis *Divine Poems.* London: by Edward Okes for Benjamin Tooke and Thomas Sawbridge...., 1669. 8vo., engraved frontispiece/title, engraved title and final leaf repaired and strengthened at fore edge, later 20th century calf, from the library of James Stevens Cox (1910-1997), various pen trials, inscription "John Barnard/of Fallm(outh); in/Cornwall" and "To James Edgecom/John Symmons", presumably of Edgcumbe or Edgcombe. Maggs Bros. Ltd. 1447 - 345 2016 £180

Association – Edridge, Catherine Elizabeth

Bible. Latin - 1666 *Novum Testamentum Domini Nostri Iesu Christi.* Cambridge: John Field, 1666. Pretty copy of a pocket New Testament, engraved title within architectural frame with Royal arms at top, few headlines just shaved, minor browning and occasional small stain, small circular indistinct stamp of the Corporation of Southampton thrice on verso of last leaf, 24mo., contemporary Cambridge black morocco richly gilt, gilt edges, trifle rubbed at extremities, early ownership inscription Cath. Eliz. Edridge, very good. Blackwell's Rare Books B186 - 16 2016 £600

Association – Edson, Katherine Philips

Neuhaus, Eugen *The Art of the Exposition.* San Francisco: Paul Elder, 1915. First edition, 8vo., illustrations, untrimmed, dust jacket with pieces missing to fore-edge, part of lower corner of front board nicked and about 1 inch of paper missing, good copy, this the copy of consumer advocate Florence Kelley, presentation to Kelley from Katherine Philips Edson May 29th 1915, nice association. Second Life Books, Inc. 196 B - 310 2016 $95

Association – Edwards, George Wharton

Seitz, Don C. *The Buccaneers rough Verse.* New York: Harper & Bros., 1912. First edition, decorations by Howard Pyle, octavo, with frontispiece and two text illustrations, publisher's black cloth, front cover with additional Pyle color plate pasted on, lettered gilt, inscribed by author to American impressionist George Wharton Edwards, near fine. David Brass Rare Books, Inc. 2015 - 02981 2016 $350

Association – Edwards, H. Holland

Le Sage, Alain Rene 1668-1747 *The Adventures of Gil Blas of Santillane.* London: printed for Richard Phillips, 1807. 203 x 121mm., 4 volumes, extremely pleasing contemporary deep blue straight grain morocco, handsomely gilt by Samuel Welcher (with his ticket on verso of front endpaper), covers bordered gilt with triple rules and framed with palmette roll, inside is a rule with small ring and floral tools at corners, raised bands, spines ornately gilt in lobed compartments, featuring stippled ground, quatrefoil centerpiece with delicate foliate, sprays at sides and fleurons at ends, turn-ins gilt with single rule and fleuron and ring tools at corners, all edges gilt, with 160 engravings comprised of 100 copperplates by Warner, Tomlinson and others, and extra illustrated with 60 plates by Conrad Martin Metz, armorial bookplate of H. Holland Edwards, Pennant Erithlyn, North Wales; front joints just little flaked, backstrips slightly sunned, covers with minor variation in color, several plates little foxed, generally only in margins and more frequently on added plates), one leaf with light ink stain in lower margin, light dampstain in margin at head of one plate, isolated very minor marginal soiling, very pleasing set, decorative bindings very well preserved and internally clean, fresh and bright. Phillip J. Pirages 67 - 72 2016 $1750

Association – Edwards, J. O.

Homerus *The Iliads of Homer Prince of Poets (with) Homer's Odysses. (with) The Crowne of all Homers Worckes Batrachomyonmachia or the Battaile of Frogs and Mise...* London: printed (by Richard Field) for Nathaniel Butter, 1611-1615. Worckes - London: printed by Iohn Bill, 1624. First Complete edition in English of first two works, first edition in English of third, titlepage engraved (some expert repair work around outer edges), inner edge just disappearing into gutter, initial blank discarded, final blank present, additional leaves of sonnets bound in prelims, some dust soiling and marks; titlepage engraved (some expert repair work around edges), initial and final blanks discarded, Y2 slightly shorter and probably supplied, little marginal worming in second half expertly repaired, occasionally touching letter, no significant loss; top edge gilt (earliest state with "Worckes" instead of "Workes"), initial blank discarded, folio, 3 volumes, washed and pressed in 19th century red morocco by Riviere, boards with central lozenge shape made of wreaths and flowers and containing a circular frame, blocked in gilt, spines elaborately gilt, bookplate of Thomas Gaisford, leather booklabel of 'Terry' and small booklabel of J. O. Edwards, modern bookplate, very good. Blackwell's Rare Books   Marks of Genius - 22   2016   £40,000

Association – Edwards, Jeffery

Miller, Hugh *My Schools and Schoolmasters or the Story of My Education.* Edinburgh: Thomas Constable and Co., 1858. contemporary speckled calf, gilt spine, lacking label, little rubbed, contemporary gift inscription on leading pastedown "Jeffery Edwards from his friend & school fellow, Henry Lee Warner....". Jarndyce Antiquarian Books   CCXV - 838   2016   £38

Association – Effingham, Earl of

Winchilsea, George James Finch Hatton, Earl of *Flying Childers.* London: 1870. First edition, original green cloth, presentation copy inscribed by author to Earl of Effingham, pictorial half title and one other illustrated leaf, nice, scarce. Simon Finch   2015 - 82172   2016 $240

Association – Egmont, Lady

Church of England. Book of Common Prayer *The Book of Common Prayer and Administration of the Sacraments.* London: published for John Reeves...sold and G. and W. Nicol and Satcherd and Letterman, 1807. 2 parts in 1 volume, 12mo., contemporary red straight grained morocco, single gilt fillet on sides and an inner border of 2 blind fillets and a blind roll tool, gilt crown of centre of both covers, spine richly tooled gilt and blind lettered in gilt direct, red morocco label inside front cover, gilt edges, trifle worn at extremities, inner hinge neatly repaired, boards trifle warped, good copy, with a letter of provenance on mourning paper from Isabella Speechly of Peterborough stating "The Prayer Book and Hymn Book (latter not present) which belonging to Queen Caroline, were given to the Lady Egmont by Lady Anne Hamilton the Queen's Lady and she have them to my Great Aunt Miss Martha Speechly then living at Dartmouth House...".   Blackwell's Rare Books   Marks of Genius - 11   2016   £6000

Association – Ehmann, Neville Howell

Hedin, Sven *The Flight of the 'Big Horse'.* New York: Darton and Co., 1936. First US edition, publisher's blue cloth, pictorial dust jacket, red lettering to spine and upper cloth cover, map endpapers (browned as usual, over 10 full page illustrations from photos, rubbing and creasing to extremities of dust jacket with closed tear to back, very good, bookplate of Neville Howell Ehmann.   Sotheran's Piccadilly Notes - Summer 2015 - 162   2016   £298

Hedin, Sven *The Flight of the "Big Horse" the Trail of War in Central Asia.* New York: Dutton, 1936. First US edition, 8vo., publisher's blue cloth, pictorial dust jacket, red lettering to spine and upper cloth cover, map endpapers (browned as usual) over 100 full page photo illustrations, rubbing and creasing to extremities of dust jacket ad closed tear to back, very good, bookplate Neville Howell Ehmann.   Sotheran's Travel and Exploration - 132   2016   £298

Association – Eldon, John Scott, 1st Earl of

Cranmer, Thomas *A Defence of the True and Catholick Doctrine of the Sacrament of the Body and Blood of Our Saviour Jesus Christ....* London: C. and J. Rivington &c., 1825. First edition, uncut in original blue-grey boards, paper label, some slight rubbing with slight cracking to lower corner of front board, from the library of Earl John Eldon with his armorial roundle and signature Eldon, very good in original binding.   Jarndyce Antiquarian Booksellers   CCXVII - 78   2016   £180

Dundonald, Archibald Cochrane, 9th Earl of *A Treatise Shewing the Intimate Connection that Subsists between Agriculture and Chemistry.* printed for the author and sold by R. Edwards, March, 1795. First edition, printed on blueish paper, inscribed "From the author" and below signature J(ohn) Scott, first Lord Eldon, with his bookplate, 4to., uncut in original drab boards, little soiling and wear, spine defective a little at head and foot, very good. Blackwell's Rare Books   B186 - 44   2016   £300

Society for the Reformation on Principles *The Scholar Armed Against the Errors of Time or a Collection of Tracts on the Principles and Evidences of Christianity....* London: F. C. & J. Rivington, 1812. Third edition, 2 volumes, ads on leading f.e.p. volume I, uncut in original blue boards, brown paper spines slightly chipped paper labels, some rubbing but overall very good in original binding, from the library of Earl John Eldon, with his armorial roundal signature and inscription "The gift of the Earl of Shaftesbury". Jarndyce Antiquarian Booksellers   CCXVII - 264   2016   £220

Urquhart, D. H. *Commentaries on Classical Learning.* London: T. Cadell and W. Davies, 1803. First edition, titlepage slightly spotted, few thumbmarks, otherwise quite clean and fresh, 8vo., contemporary diced russia, boards bordered with gilt fillet, spine lettered gilt with decorative gilt lozenge shaped tools, extremities the merest touch rubbed, little surface damage to foot of front board, ownership inscription of Eldon, i.e. John Scott, 1st Earl of Eldon (1751-1838) and his armorial bookplate, very good. Blackwell's Rare Books   Greek & Latin Classics VII - 15   2016   £150

Association – Eldridge, Florence

Hemingway, Ernest Millar   1899-1961 *The Sun Also Rises.* New York: Charles Scribner's Sons, 1926. First edition, 2nd issue, 8vo., bound in black publisher's cloth with paper label (chipped on spine, affecting couple of letters), good clean, Florence Eldridge's copy with her bookplate. Second Life Books, Inc.   197 - 178   2016 $350

Association – Elkrog, Birthe

Harrison, A. R. W. *The Law of Athens Procedure.* Oxford: Clarendon Press, 1971. First edition, 8vo., cloth, gilt lettered, spine slightly cocked, edges dusted, very good, no dust jacket, crossed out ownership inscription of Birthe Elkrog and gift inscription of Chris (Carey). Unsworths Antiquarian Booksellers Ltd.   E04 - 57   2016   £30

Association – Ellington, Duke

Ulanov, Barry *Duke Ellington.* New York: Creative Age Press, 1946. First edition, extremities and lettering rubbed, about very good, lacking dust jacket, inscribed by the subject to Magnifique Marion. Between the Covers Rare Books   202 - 63   2016 $750

Association – Elliott, Denholm

Fry, Christopher *A Sleep of Prisoners, a Play.* London: Oxford University Press, 1951. First edition, presentation from actor Denham Elliott one month after opening in London and signed by author and producer and other members of the cast, fine in dust jacket. Second Life Books, Inc.   196A - 589   2016 $150

Association – Elliott, J. E.

Drew, Joseph *The Mystery of Creation: a Lay Sermon.* Wymouth: printed by Sherren and Son, 1879. Half title, text within double rule borders, original black cloth bevelled boards, block in gilt, slightly rubbed and dulled, ownership inscription of J. E. Elliott 1879 and Lawrence Lyall 1903, scarce. Jarndyce Antiquarian Booksellers   CCXVII - 91   2016   £45

Association – Elliott, John

Cozzens, Fred S. *The Sayings of Dr. Bushwhacker and Other Learned Men.* New York: Simpson, 1867. First edition, 8vo, little worn purple cloth, leaves browned, very good, inscribed by author to John Elliott, bookplate removed, very good. Second Life Books, Inc.   196A - 346   2016 $150

Association – Ellis, J. P. William

Justice, James *The British Gardener's Director...* Edinburgh: printed for A. Kincaid and J. Bell and R. Fleming, 1764. 8vo., some very slight marginal worming, well clear of text, only affecting few leaves, contemporary sheep neatly rebacked, with plain raised bands, original red morocco label, contemporary signature of J. P. Wm. Ellis. Jarndyce Antiquarian Booksellers   CCXVI - 338   2016   £320

Association – Ellis, William

Ellis, William *Philo-Socrates. Part V.* London: Smith, Elder & Co., 1863. Original light brown printed paper wrappers, hinges slightly splitting with some repair to head of leading hinge, inscription Caroline Lindley from her friend William Ellis. Jarndyce Antiquarian Books CCXV - 640   2016   £85

Association – Ellison, Fanny Mae

Ellison, Ralph *Invisible Man.* New York: The Modern Library, 1952. Modern Library edition, slight wear to boards, near fine in about very good dust jacket with some small chips and repaired along front flap fold with archival tape, inscribed by author to his wife Fanny Mae. Between the Covers Rare Books   202 - 32   2016 $4500

Association – Ellison, Ralph

California Sorcery. Abingdon: Cemetery Dance, 1999. Publisher's copy of the limited edition (26 copies), signed by Ray Bradbury, Richard Matheson, Ellison, Nolan, Tomerlin, Sohl, Fritch and others, stamp of another author, fine in fine dust jacket in publisher's printed gray case.   Ken Lopez Bookseller   166 - 5   2016 $650

Sackheim, Eric   *The Blues Line: a Collection of Blues Lyrics.*   New York: Grossman Pub., 1969. First edition, quarto, fine in age toned, very good dust jacket, author Ralph Ellison's copy with his ownership signature.   Between the Covers Rare Books   207 - 41   2016 $800

Association – Ellison, T. H.

Burton, William   *A Commentary on Antoninus His Itinerary or Journies of the Romanae Empire, so far As It Concernth Britain.*   London: printed by Tho. Roycroft for Henry Twyford ad T. Twyford, 1658. Small folio, 2 plates, portrait frontispiece by Hollar, double page map, lacking single leaf 'preface to the reader', titlepage in red and black, woodcut initials, illustrations in text, errata to final leaf verso, small burn hole to pages 33-4 just touching few letters, page 141-2 creased during binding, very occasional spotting and few slight smudges, front and rear blanks darkened at edges, contemporary calf, gilt ruled panels with various mottled effects, all edges gilt, rebacked with dark brown morocco, original spine label retained, spine rubbed, few chips and bookplate of T. H. Ellison, underneath Pemberton plate a piece of paper crossed through in ink, possibly patching a removed third bookplate, Latin annotation in old hand to prelim blank.   Unsworths Antiquarian Booksellers Ltd.   E01 - Early Printing - 3   2016   £750

Association – Elmer, Clara

Wise, Henry A.   *Tales for the Marines.*   Boston: Philips Sampson & co., 1835. First edition, 8vo., frontispiece and pictorial title, original cloth, spine rubbed, inscribed by author 16 May 1855 for Miss Clara Elmer.   M & S Rare Books, Inc.   99 - 324   2016 $275

Association – Elphinstone, A.

L'Innocence de la Tresillustre. Tres-chaste, et Debonnaire Princesse, Madame Marie Royne d'Escosse.   n.p. Iprime an, 1572. 8vo., signature O omitted in make up, text complete, all pages faintly rubricated, very nice, bound by Bedford in dark blue morocco gilt, dentelles, marbled endpapers, all edges gilt, ownership signature of A. Elphinston(e) on titlepage with dated in lower margin 1600, later armorial bookplate of James Wyllie Guild and Thomas Brooke, FSA, Armitage Bridge, ownership inscription Alexander W. Ruthven Stuart 1923.   Jarndyce Antiquarian Booksellers CCXVII - 182   2016   £1500

Association – Elsley, Robert

Tibbles, Percy Thomas   *The Magician's Hanndbook.* London: Marshall & Brookes and Dawbarn & Ward, 1901. First edition, 8vo., original green cloth with illustration, signed presentation from author to Robert Elsley, slight soiling and slight wear to covers, appears to lack front endpaper, slight to prelims, otherwise near very good.   Any Amount of Books   2015 - A49177   2016   £170

Association – Elton, Thomas

Stacy, Edmund   *The Country Gentleman's Vade Mecum; or His Companion for the Town.*   London: for John Harris, 1699. First edition, 8vo., lacking contents leaves (a1-4) which were never bound in, some occasional spotting, small blank piece torn away from corner of D6 and H2, minor rust hole in C3 and H3v lightly stained, contemporary sprinkled sheep, covers panelled in blind, joints split at foot, lower headcap chewed by insects, front pastedown and flyleaf ink spotted, from the library of James Stevens Cox (1910-1997), early signature of Tho(mas) Elton.   Maggs Bros. Ltd. 1447 - 397   2016   £200

Association – Elwell, Henry

Simms, Rupert   *Bibliotheca Staffordiensis.*   Lichfield: A. C. Lomax, 1894. Limited to 200 numbered copies, large 4to., original cloth, uncut pages with top edge gilt, bookplate of Donald and Mary Hyde, ink inscription by Henry Elwell, also signed by Elwell, hinges, head and tail of spine worn, corners rubbed, both covers scuffed.   Oak Knoll Books   310 - 267   2016 $350

Association – Elwell, Robert

Spenser, Edmund   1552-1599   *The Shepheardes Calendar.*   London: Cresset Press, 1930. Limited to 350 numbered copies on paper, in an edition of 353 copies, this copy not numbered but has "printer's file copy" written in place of a number, titlepage and 12 headpieces by John Nash, illustrations colored by stencils at Curwen Press, set in 16 pt. Linotype Granjon Old Face, printed on Barcham Green handmade paper, 4to., half vellum, marbled paper covered boards, gilt title on spine, spine darkened, corners slightly bumped, some shelf wear, nevertheless very good, Robert Elwell's copy with his bookplate, inscribed "With the compliments and high regard of the printer".   Oak Knoll Books   27 - 4   2016 $500

Association – Embleton, H. C.

Dickens, Charles 1812-1870 *American Notes for General Circulation.* London: Chapman and Hall, 1842. First edition, first issue, 2 volumes, half titles, ad leaf preceding half title volume I, glazed yellow endpapers, original purple cloth blocked in blind, spines lettered in gilt, some minimal dampstaining to prelims, armorial bookplate of H. C. Embleton volume II, later William Wapler bookplate in both volumes, very good in slipcase.   Jarndyce Antiquarian Booksellers   CCXVIII - 316   2016   £1600

Association – England, Pat

Heyeck, Robin *Marbling at the Heyeck Press.* Woodside: Heyeck, 1986. Limited to 150 numbered copies, signed by author, 4to., quarter morocco with marbled paper covered sides, slipcase, printed on dampened handmade paper and having a total of 28 samples, loosely inserted is a bill for this copy made out to collector, Pat England with note by Robin Heyeck written on it, also present is Christmas card from Heyeck to England.   Oak Knoll Books   27 - 37   2016 $850

Association – Ensor, Paul

Bustani, Emile *March Arabesque.* London: Robert Hale, 1961. First edition, octavo, presentation from author for friend Paul Ensor, very good in rubbed and creased dust jacket with several short tears.   Peter Ellis   112 - 15   2016   £95

Association – Erb, Max

Baker, Henry *Employment of the Microscope.* London: printed for R. and J. Dodsley, 1764. Second edition, 2 parts in one volume, 8vo., 17 engraved plates, lightly foxed, titlepage creased, plate facing page 422 torn at fold, modern full calf with original calf mounted on sides, gilt stamped motto "Fide et Virtute" belonging to Cha. Brandling, gilt and blindstamped spine, gilt stamped red leather label, new endleaves, bookplates of Cha. Brandling, Charles Adams, Fred C. Luck and Max Erb, very good+.   Jeff Weber Rare Books   183 - 5   2016 $650

Association – Erno Park Library

Zanotti, Giampietro *La Pitture de Pellegrino Tibali e di Nicolo Abbati Existenti nell'Instituto de Bologna.* Venice: n.p., 1756. First edition, folio, contemporary half calf, marbled boards, spine restored, boards rubbed, engraved allegorical frontispiece after G. B. Moretti, engraved vignette incorporating a view of Bologna on title, engraved portraits, 41 plates and 19 head or tailpieces, vignettes or initials, Erno Park Library with their 19th century bookplate, light dampstain in blank lower fore-margin of opening few leaves.   Maggs Bros. Ltd.   1474 - 83   2016   £2500

Association – Ernshaw, Marian Bellamy

Bellamy, Edward *Looking Backward 2000-1887.* Boston: Houghton Mifflin, 1926. 8vo., very good in publisher's cloth, stain at hinge of rear endpaper, inscribed by author's wife, Emma for Walter James Henry, also inscribed by Bellamy's daughter, Marian Bellamy Ernshaw, liad in 9 x 6 inch handbill advertising talk given by Marian and Emma Bellamy.   Second Life Books, Inc.   196A - 103   2016 $300

Association – Ervin, Spencer

Dasent, George Webbe *Popular Tales from the Nourse.* Edinburgh: Edmonston and Douglas, 1859. First edition with this collection, 8vo., light browning, bound in brown rough grained publisher's cloth, panelled in blind, title, author and imprint in gilt in spine, binding slightly rubbed, cloth at tail pushed in but good, yellow-brown waxed pastedowns and endpapers, purchase notes of S(pencer) E(rvin) to half title, contents slightly loosening, slight loosening also at hinges.   Unsworths Antiquarian Booksellers Ltd.   E05 - 72   2016   £150

Leclercq, Jules *Un Sejour Dans l'Ile de Java. Le Pays, Les Habitants, Le Systeme Colonial.* Paris: Librarie Plon, 1898. 8vo., plates, slightly toned, green cloth, gilt title to spine, edges sprinkled brown, spine little darkened, very good, pencilled ownership inscription of Spencer Ervin.   Unsworths Antiquarian Booksellers   30 - 94   2016   £30

Younghusband, Francis *India and Tibet. A History of the Relations Which Have Subsisted Between the Two Countries...* London: John Murray, 1910. 8vo., 26 plates and 22 colored maps, foxing and light browning, red publisher's cloth, title stamped gilt to spine, spine darkened, touch of fraying at top of lower joint but good, label of Times Book Club and stamp 27 Jul 1911, inscription of Spencer Ervin, June 1912.   Unsworths Antiquarian Booksellers Ltd.   30 - 167   2016   £150

Association – Esher, Lord

Barrie, James Matthew 1860-1937 *Jane Annie or the Good Conduct Prize.* London: Chappell & Co., 1893. Paperback, original printed wrappers, very nice, uncommon, particularly in this condition, variant issue, housed in slipcase, bookplates of Lord Esher and Clark Hunter, very good.   The Kelmscott Bookshop   12 - 5   2016 $700

Association – Esher, Oliver Brett, Viscount

Bankes, George Nugent *A Day of My Life.* London: Sampson Low, 1877. First edition, half title, 6 pages ads, original brick red decorated cloth, slight ink mark to front board, little rubbed, bookplate of Oliver Brett & John H. Baker, very good.   Jarndyce Antiquarian Books   CCXV - 673   2016   £35

Monck, Mary *Marinda. Poems and Translations Upon Several Occasions.* London: printed by J. Tonson, 1716. First edition, very good, 8vo., contemporary calf, gilt, rebacked, very good, early signatures of John Brace (crossed out) and Elizabeth Lovell, later bookplates of G. W. F. Gregor and Oliver Brett, Viscount Esher.   C. R. Johnson Rare Book Collections   Foxon: H-P 2015 - 617   2016 $2298

Shelley, Percy Bysshe 1792-1822 *Rosalind and Helen, a Modern Eclogue, with Other Poems.* London: printed for C. and J. Ollier, 1819. First edition, with final ad leaves, first few leaves slightly spotted, 8vo., polished calf by F. Bedford, spine gilt red lettering piece, gilt edges, minimal wear to extremities, the Hibbert-Esher copy with bookplates and acquisition notes by Oliver Brett, good.   Blackwell's Rare Books   Marks of Genius - 47   2016   £2500

Association – Essex, Duke of

Freeman, G. J. *Sketches in Wales or a Diary of Three Walking Excursions in that Principality.* London: Longman, Rees Orme, Brown and Green, 1826. First edition, 8vo., full claret leather with attractive gilt tooling, corners and edges lightly bumped and worn, spine has title and lots of gilt tooling, edges lightly bumped internally, marbled endpapers, Duke of Essex bookplate, bookplate of Charles Arthur Wynne Finch, 15 black and white plates.   Simon Finch   2015 - 004316   2016 $296

Association – Estill, Anthony David

Heath, Henry *Domestic Bliss. (with) Domestic Miseries.* London: D. Bogue, 1848. Oblong folio, 6 numbered plates, all with numerous caricature sketches, all slightly dusted, small tear to upper margin of no. 3., marginal tears to number 6, repaired with archival tape, Miseries with plates number 7, 8 and 9, creased, dusted and with numerous marginal tears repaired, archvial tape, recent black cloth, fold over case, booklabel of Anthony David Estill.   Jarndyce Antiquarian Books   CCXV - 247   2016   £350

Pinnock, William *Roman History made easy...* London: W. Sell, 1831. Color map frontispiece, plate and illustrations, slight spotting, slight paper damage to inner margin of front and title, original printed paper boards, paper label slightly rubbed, contemporary ownership signatures of Charles Little, bookplate of Anthony David Estill, nice.   Jarndyce Antiquarian Books   CCXV - 904   2016   £68

Secker, William *The Wedding Ring.* Wakefield: William Nicholson & sons, cicra, 1870. Original yellow wrappers, decorated title onlay with embossed gilt floral border, illustrated and lettered in blue, exceptional copy, custom made foldover case, label of Anthony David Estill.   Jarndyce Antiquarian Books   CCXV - 400   2016   £120

Association – Evans, Edith

Craig, Edward Gordon 1872-1966 *Henry Irving.* London: J. M. Dent & Sons, 1930. First edition, this being one of 75 specially bound copies, containing 2 extra illustrations and signed by author, Dame Edith Evans's copy with posthumous bookplate, original quarter leather, spine lettered gilt, top edge gilt, coloured frontispiece, 23 portraits and other illustrations, very good.   Sotheran's Piccadilly Notes - Summer 2015 - 171   2016   £498

Association – Evans, F.

Carlisle, Isabella Howard, Countess of *Thoughts in the Form of maxims Addressed to Young Ladies.* London: printed for T. Cornwell, 1790. Second edition, 8vo., half title, contemporary tree calf, neat repairs to extremities expertly rebacked, maroon morocco label, contemporary inscription "E. D. Parr from F. Evans".   Jarndyce Antiquarian Books   CCXV - 98   2016   £30

Association – Evans, Herbert McLean

Willis, Thomas *Cerebri Anatome. Cui Accessi Nervorum.* London: Tho. Roycroft for Jo. Martyn & Ja. Allestry, 1664. First Octavo edition, 15 folding engraved plates, 8vo., very nice contemporary vellum with yapped edges, hand lettered spine, contents quite crisp and clean, blank lower edge of title excised and restored, volume placed in folding cloth case, bookplates of the Duke of Braunschweig-Luneburg and Herbert McLean Evans.   James Tait Goodrich   X-78 - 557   2016 $5950

Association – Everett, Lizzie

Stanton, Elizabeth Cady *The History of woman Suffrage Volumes I-III.* New York: Fowler & Wells, 1881. New York: 1882. Rochester: 1887. First edition, volume one has loose hinge in front but it and volume two are in very good condition, volume 3 very worn with some loose prelim matter and well worn binding, volumes one and two have tipped in signature by Susan B. Anthony, all 3 volumes inscribed Lizzie Everett from Flora M. Kimball, National City California April 4 1887.   Second Life Books, Inc.   196 B - 684   2016 $2000

Association – Everson, William

Jeffers, Robinson 1887-1962 *Granite & Cypress: Rubbins from the Rock.* University of California at Santa Cruz: Lime Kiln Press, 1975. Limited to 100 numbered copies, exceptionally rare, Oblong folio, printed on English Hayle handmade paper, titlepage woodcut by William Prochnow, bound by Schuberth Bookbindery in German linen, open laced deerskin over Monterey Cypress spine, Japanese Uwa endpapers, custom slipcase made of Monterey Cypress inlaid with square 'window' of granite from Jeffers; stoneyard (drawn by the poet from the sea), built to stand erect on felt lined cypress stand case, with hairline crack, else fine, signed by printer, William Everson, presentation signed by Everson and three proof sheets laid in.   Jeff Weber Rare Books   181 - 67   2016 $15,000

Association – Evetts, Deborah

Bertin, Charles *Christopher Columbus.* Roslyn: John Carter Brown Library, 1992. Limited to 200 numbered copies signed by artist, binder and printer, this being one of 20 of the deluxe edition, 8vo., quarter leather, cloth, inserted in clamshell case with separate portfolio containing 6 woodcuts on individual plates, from the library of Deborah Evetts, binder and contains pen and ink drawing of design used on front cover, sample stamped in green leather of this design.   Oak Knoll Books   310 - 148   2016 $850

Association – Evill, Wilfird

Olivier, J. *Fencing Familiarized; or a New Treatise on the Art of Sword Play.* London: John Bell, 1771-1772. First edition, 8vo., contemporary polished calf, sometime rebacked with contrasting leather spine label, engraved folding frontispiece and 8 plates, some rubbing and wear to boards, small wormhole to top corner of first 15 pages, offsetting from plates, little occasional browning, bookplate of Wilfrid Evill, otherwise very good.   Sotheran's   Piccadilly Notes - Summer 2015 - 220   2016   £398

Association – Eyre, Francis

Horatius Flaccus, Quintus *Opera.* Londini: Iohannes Pine, 1733. 1737. First issue with "Post Est" rather than correct "Potest" engraved around Caesar medal volume 2 page 108), 2 volumes, 8vo., multiple lists of subscribers to each volume, but without letterpress printed list of antiquities sometimes found, entirely engraved by John Pine, with frontispieces, title vignettes, 8 full page illustrations, culs-de-lampe and 4 line opening initial to each poem, volume I has small intermittent stain to lower margin near gutter, handful of upper corners creased, occasional light foxing, contemporary dark brown calf, gilt spines with red and green title labels, green possibly replaced or sympathetically retooled, all edges red, spines rubbed with tail of volume II quite worn, joints neatly repaired, few scuffs, endpapers little toned, very good, armorial bookplate of Francis Eyre (c. 1732-104) of Warkworth, serviceable copy.   Unsworths Antiquarian Booksellers   30 - 80   2016   £850

Association – Faber, Geoffrey

Lewis, Clive Staples 1898-1963 *Out of the Silent Planet.* London: Bodley Head, 1938. First edition, occasional light foxing to borders with couple of pages more heavily spotted, crown 8vo., original burgundy cloth, backstrip lettered gilt with slight lean to spine, very slight bowing to boards, edges little rubbed, top edge dust soiled with color faded, few spots to other edges, pencilled numerals (some dates) to rear pastedown, bookseller label at foot, ownership inscription of Geoffrey Faber.   Blackwell's Rare Books   B186 - 257   2016   £1750

Association – Fabre, Michael

Himes, Chester *La Croisade de Lee Lordon. (Lonely Crusade).* Paris: Correa, 1952. First French edition, pages with little browning, else fine in lightly worn, near fine dust jacket, inscribed by Himes to Michael Fabre, a Sorbonne professor.   Between the Covers Rare Books   202 - 41   2016 $2000

Association – Fabvi, Renie

Fordyce, James *Sermons to Young Women in Two Volumes.* London: printed for A. Millar & T. Cadell, J. Dodsley & J. Payne, 1767. Fourth edition, 8vo., slight marking to titlepage in volume two, contemporary full lightly speckled calf, raised bands, compartments with double gilt vertical rules, red morocco labels, small chip to front board of volume I with old repair, signature of Renie Fabvi, very good, handsome copy.   Jarndyce Antiquarian Books   CCXV - 204   2016   £380

Association – Fahey, Herbert

Lewis, Oscar *The Lost Years. A biographical fantasy.* New York: Alfred A. Knopf, 1951. First edition, presentation inscription signed by author to bookbinder and designer, Herbert Fahey, illustrations by Mallette Dean, brown and white decorated boards, fine with pictorial dust jacket (slight chip), laid in is photos of author.   Argonaut Book Shop   Literature 2015 - 7190   2016 $60

Association – Fairbanks, Douglas

Dialogue. Journal des Livres et des Idees No. 3. Lausanne: September, 1967. Folio, original self wrappers, printed on all sides, light overall toning, quarter folded with horizontal points starting, from the library of actor Douglas Fairbanks Jr. with his loose bookplate in separate envelope, very good, warmly inscribed to Ezra Pound by Piero Sanavio.   Blackwell's Rare Books   B186 - 274   2016   £650

Association – Farquharson

Bellegarde, Jean Baptiste Morvan De *Reflexions Upon Ridicule or What It Is That Makes a Man Ridiculous and the Means to Avoid It. (with) Reflexions Upon the Politeness of Manners, with Maxims of Civil Society...* London: printed for Tho. Newborough, 1707. 8vo., bound in two volumes, contemporary panelled calf, slightly later gilt volume numbers, boards slightly marked with head of spine, volume I slightly rubbed, armorial bookplate of Farquharson of Invercald, very good, first volume with slight paper damage to initial blank. Jarndyce Antiquarian Books CCXV - 46 2016 £450

Association – Farquharson, J. H. Ross

Pike, John Gregory *Parental Care for the Salvation of Children Explained and Enforced with Advice on their Religious Education.* London: RTS, 1839. Original brown cloth, signature of J. H. Ross Farquharson, very good. Jarndyce Antiquarian Books CCXV - 901 2016 £35

Taylor, Isaac *Home Education.* London: Jackson & Walford, 1838. Fourth edition, partially unopened in original dark green cloth, signature of J. H. Ross Farquharson, very good, crisp copy. Jarndyce Antiquarian Books CCXV - 430 2016 £50

Association – Farrant, Richard

Malton, Thomas *Views of Oxford.* London: White & Co.; Oxford: R. Smith, 1810. First complete edition, appealing 19th century (circa 1860's?), dark green half morocco over lighter green textured cloth by T. Aitken (stamp signed), upper cover with gilt titling, raised bands, spine gilt in compartments with elongated fleuron centerpiece and scrolling cornerpieces, gilt titling, marbled endpapers, all edges gilt (small, very expert repairs to upper outer corners and perhaps at top of joints), mezzotint frontispiece, engraved title, 30 fine plates of interior and exterior views, armorial bookplates of Sir Mayson M. Beeton and Sir Richard Farrant, verso of front free endpaper, ink presentation inscription from author for Sir Charles Locock, Nov. 1860, subscription proposal for work printed by T. Bensley and dated "London, May 30, 1301 (i.e. 1801)", laid in at front, couple of small smudges to boards, portrait faintly foxed and browned, isolated small stains, not affecting images, but fine, plates especially clean and fresh, smooth and pleasing binding with virtually no wear. Phillip J. Pirages 67 - 248 2016 $8500

Association – Fasque

Watt, Robert *Rules of Life with Reflections on the manners and Dispositions of Mankind.* Edinburgh: Longman, Hurst &c, 1814. 12mo., name erased from upper corner of title, contemporary full speckled calf, gilt borders and spine, brown morocco labels, hinges slightly rubbed, Fasque booklabel, very good. Jarndyce Antiquarian Books CCXV - 472 2016 £75

Association – Faulkner, Maud

Faulkner, William Harrison 1896-1962 *Doctor Martino and Other Stories.* New York: Smith and Haas, 1934. First edition, fine with slightest of seemingly inevitable fading to spine, without dust jacket as issued, copy number 1 of 360 numbered copies, signed by author, with letter from antiquarian bookseller detailing provenance directly from Dean Faulkner Wells who inherited it from her grandmother, Maud. Between the Covers Rare Books 204 - 40 2016 $12,000

Association – Fay, Joseph

Moss, Arthur B. *The Workman's Foe.* London: Watts & Co., 1898? Presentation copy inscribed by author for Joseph Fay 25 June 98, brown cloth with titles and author in gilt to cover and original wrappers bound in, waterstaining on pastedowns and free endpapers, partially affecting inscription, some pages loose and paper has browned, cloth binding slightly rubbed and worn, very good given fragility of the items. The Kelmscott Bookshop 12 - 75 2016 $750

Association – Fay, W.

Dickens, Charles 1812-1870 *Charles Dickens as editor. Being Letters Written by hi to William Henry Wills.* London: Smith, Elder & Co., 1912. First edition, half title, frontispiece, plates, original red cloth lettered in blind and gilt, spine faded, bookplate of W. Fay, good plus. Jarndyce Antiquarian Booksellers CCXVIII - 866 2016 £35

Association – Fayden, Henry Marc

Wiggin, Kate Douglas *Susanna and Sue.* Boston: Houghton Mifflin, 1909. First edition, 8vo. illustrations by Alice Barber Stephens and N. C. Wyeth, gray cloth stamped in orange and dark green, picture pasted on front, author's presentation, for Henry Marc Fayden, Christmas 1906, covers somewhat scuffed and worn at edges, else very good. Second Life Books, Inc. 196 B - 881 2016 $125

Association – Featherstone-Witty, Evy

Cleary, Jon *Fall of an Eagle.* New York: Morrow, 1964. First edition, 8vo., dedication copy, signed by author, with 3 good signed typed letters loosely inserted, with 2 bookplates of recipients, Gordon and Evy Featherstone-Witty, slight tape marks to front endpaper.   Any Amount of Books 2015 - A72358   2016   £150

Association – Featherstone-Witty, Gordon

Cleary, Jon *Fall of an Eagle.* New York: Morrow, 1964. First edition, 8vo., dedication copy, signed by author, with 3 good signed typed letters loosely inserted, with 2 bookplates of recipients, Gordon and Evy Featherstone-Witty, slight tape marks to front endpaper.   Any Amount of Books 2015 - A72358   2016   £150

Association – Feelings, Tom

Soul Looks Back in Wonder. New York: Dial Books, 1993. First printing (1-10 code), cloth backed boards, as new in new dust jacket, striking color illustrations on every page, this copy has artist Tom Feelings bold signature laid-in on Dial Stationery.   Aleph-bet Books, Inc.   111 - 172   2016 $100

Association – Fernandez, Isidoro

Bonaventura, Saint   1221-1274   *Tractado en la Contempacion de la Vida de Nuestro Senor Iesu Christo Agora Nueuamente Corregdio y Emendado yy con Licentia Impresso.* Valladolid: M. Borras...., 1588. Rare illustrated Spanish edition, small 8vo., blue morocco gilt a la Francaise by Brugalla, title lettered on spine, covers with device of Isidoro Fernandez, gilt turn-ins, all edges gilt, titlepage with woodcut of the Trinity, 21 woodcuts in text, booklabels of Isidoro Fernandez, book collector of Barcelona.   Maggs Bros. Ltd.   1474 - 15   2016   £1800

Guzman, Francisco De   *Triumphos Morales...* Seville: Alonso Escribano, 1575. 8vo., red morocco gilt a la Francaise by Brugalla dated 1937, with gilt emblematic stamp on covers, printer's device on title, 14 full page woodcuts, title with marginal repairs, repaired tear to K3 and N3 with some smaller repairs to other leaves, whole lightly washed, washed out inscriptions on titlepage of the library of Compania de Jesus, Barcelona, green morocco booklabel of Isidoro Fernandez (1876-1963).   Maggs Bros. Ltd.   1474 - 39   2016   £4000

Association – Ferrers, Walter Knight Shirley, Earl of

Horatius Flaccus, Quintus   *Carmina Sapphica. (and) Carmina Alcaica.* Chelsea: Ashendene Press, 1903. One of 150 copies on Japanese paper (25 on vellum), 185 x 128mm., 2 volumes, original flexible vellum, gilt titling on spine, housed in custom cloth folding box with separate compartments for each book, initials hand painted by Graily Hewiett, printed in red and black, "Carmina Alcaica" inscribed to Philip Webb by printer and dated 1903 with further ink notation that was given by Webb's executor to Walter Knight Shirley, Earl Ferrers on 22 Feb. 1916 and by him to Charles Winmile Jan 1937, verso of 'Carmina Sapphica" with morocco bookplate of Cortlandt Bishop, pastedowns little waffled, otherwise mint.   Phillip J. Pirages   67 - 13   2016 $4000

Association – Festing, R. A. G.

Mascall, Leonard   *A Book of Fishing with Hooke and Line...* London: S. Watchell, 1884. One of 200 copies, 222 x 178mm., original brown quarter morocco over cloth boards, flat spine with titling in gilt, marbled endpapers, top edge gilt, 12 illustrations, from woodcuts, front pastedown with bookplate of R. A. G. Festing, extremities slightly rubbed, spine with minor marks, endpapers bit foxed, otherwise excellent copy, binding completely sound and without any major flaw and text clean and pleasing.   Phillip J. Pirages   67 - 3   2016 $750

Association – Ffeilden, Joseph

Nichols, John   *Genuine Works of William Hogarth...* London: Longman, Hurst, Rees, & Orme, 1808. 1810, 2 volumes, 4to., frontispiece portraits, plates, some light foxing overall, nice, clean copy, contemporary full calf, elaborate blind and gilt borders, raised gilt bands, spines in blind and gilt, some rubbing to hinges, armorial bookplate of Joseph Ffeilden, Esq., Lancaster, bookseller's ticket of Row & Waller, London, fine and handsome.   Jarndyce Antiquarian Booksellers   CCXVII - 127   2016   £450

Association – Field, Alexander

Lyndon, Barre   *The Amazing Dr. Clitterhouse.* London: Hamish Hamilton, 1936. First edition, 8vo. fine in little soiled and worn dust jacket, photos, signed by 12 members of the first NY production, including Alexander Field, Edward Fulang, Muriel Hutchinson, Stephen Fox and others.   Second Life Books, Inc.   196 B - 108   2016 $225

Association – Finch, Aurberon

Papers Relative to the Discussion with Spain in 1802, 1803 and 1804. London: A. Strahan, 1805. First edition, contemporary mottled calf, spine gilt ruled and with black label, spine rubbed, upper joints cracked but holding, bookplate of Aurberon Finch with his stamp, scarce.   Simon Finch 2015 - 22284   2016 $102

Association – Finch, C. A. W.

Wheatley, Henry B. *Round About Piccadilly and Pall Mall or a Ramble from the Haymarket to Hyde Part.* London: Smith Elder, 1870. First edition, tall 12mo., tissue guarded frontispiece and 28 illustrations in text, original brown cloth covers, black embossed freeze around edges, gilt embossed cartouche, heavy gilt and black design and lettering on spine, brown endpapers, small bookplate of C. A. W. Finch 1883, neat signature and date 1886, very slight rubbing to edges, inner hinge splitting inside rear cover, some occasional foxing, bright, very attractive copy.   Simon Finch   2015 - 1568   2016 $320

Association – Finch, Helen Bess

Roberts, Kenneth *Sun Hunting.* Indianapolis: Bobbs Merrill, 1922. First edition, first state, very good+ in dark green cloth covered boards, faded gilt text on spine and bold gilt text stamped on front board, 12mo., without dust jacket, signed warmly inscribed by author to Helen Bess Finch, black and white photos.   Simon Finch   2015 - TB01648   2016 $200

Association – Finch, John Charles Wynne

Stanley, William Owen *Memoirs on Remains of Ancient Dwellings in Holyhead Island Mostly of Circular Form called Cyttlau'r Gwyddelod...* London/Chester: James Bain/Marshall & Hughes, 1871. First edition, gold stamped sienna cloth, modest edgewear, signed "Frances Wynne from W. O. Stanley March 26 1881", stunning engraved bookplate of designer Harry Soane for Col. John Charles Wynne Finch, very faint bookstore stamp to front cover, many engravings, fold out map intact.   Simon Finch   2015 - 055187   2016 $225

Association – Finch, Robert

East Indian Railway Company *Rules and Regulations of the East Indian Railway Company. Together with the act for Regulating Railways in British India.* Calcutta: East Indian Railway Company's Press, 1867. First edition thus, original green cloth backed marbled wrappers, worn with cloth tape spine worn at top and bottom, illustrations from drawings, previous owner's handstamp on inside front cover and rear blank, rare in any condition, owner name Robert Finch with his signature.   Simon Finch   2015 - 103632   2016 $220

Association – Firebrace, Cordell William

Dousseau, Jean Jacques *Oeuvres Completees.* Paris: Chez A. Belin, imprimeur libaraire, 1817. Contemporary full tree calf, spine gilt in compartments, gilt borders and dentelles, maroon and green leather labels, carefully rebacked, slightly rubbed, bookplate of Charles Dickens as well as 'from the Library of Charles Dickens' label, further bookplate of Cordell William Firebrace.   Jarndyce Antiquarian Booksellers   CCXVIII - 872   2016   £950

Association – Firusky, Maurice

Hillyer, Robert *The Death of Captain nemo.* New York: Knopf, 1949. First edition, 8vo., laid in ALS from author to bookseller Maurice Firusky, May 1949 on Poetry Socetiy of America Stationary, nice in little faded dust jacket.   Second Life Books, Inc.   196A - 794   2016 $45

Association – Fischer, Margaret Jane

Geilgud, John *Stage Directions.* New York: Random House, 1963. Second printing, 8vo., frontispiece in color and 11 illustrations, Drama League award to Margaret Jane Fischer and inscription to her from author, fine.   Second Life Books, Inc.   196A - 631   2016 $45

Association – Fisher, Edward

Hooper, Franklin William *Plan of an Institution Devoted to Liberal Education.* New York: S. W. Green's Sons, 1881. Folding plate, later grey paper wrappers, rebacked, inscribed "Henry Norman with compliments of Edward T. Fisher".   Jarndyce Antiquarian Books   CCXV - 743   2016   £85

Association – Fisher, W. C.

Barrie, James Matthew   1860-1937 *Auld Licht Idylls.* London: Hodder and Stoughton, 1888. First edition, 8vo., original bevel edged navy buckram, backstrip lettered gilt with very slight lean to spine, gentlest of rubbing to extremities, top edge gilt, others untrimmed, brown endpapers, very good, inscribed by author for W. C. Fisher.   Blackwell's Rare Books   B186 - 178   2016   £450

Barrie, James Matthew   1860-1937 *When a Man's Single.* London: Hodder & Stoughton, 1888. First edition, 8vo., original bevel edged navy bukram, backstrip lettered gilt, trifling spot of wear at one corner and odd light graze, top edge gilt, others untrimmed, green endpapers, very good, inscribed by author for W. C. Fisher.   Blackwell's Rare Books   B186 - 179   2016   £450

Association – Fitzgerald, Francis

Spene, Joseph *Anecdotes and Observations of Books and Men Collected from the Conversation of Mr. Pope and Other Eminent Persons of His Time.* London: John Russell Smith, 1858. Octavo, publisher's cloth contemporarily rebacked with matching cloth and spine affixed to rear pastedown, corners bumped and modest edgewear, else near fine, Rubaiyat translator Edward Fitzgerald's copy with his pencilled ownership signature, five lines of pencilled notes on rear blank.   Between the Covers Rare Books   208 - 80   2016 $2000

Association – Fitzgerald, Thomas

Pinnock, William *Pinnock's Juvenile reader...* London: G. & W. B. Whittaker, 1822. Eleventh edition, 12mo., frontispiece, illustrations, contemporary mottled tree sheep, red morocco label, slight wear to foot of spine, corners slightly bumped, armorial bookplate of Thomas Fitzgerald & bookseller's ticket of King & Co., Cork. Jarndyce Antiquarian Books   CCXV - 903   2016   £40

Association – Fleming, Tris

Baldwin, Louisa *The Story of a Marriage.* London: J. M. Dent and Co., 1895. Publisher's dark blue cloth with gilt title and author to spine, bumped, rubbed, light stains and slightly cocked, interior pages very good with typical offsetting to free endpapers, 6 illustrations by J. A. Symington, very good despite binding flaws, very good, inscribed by author to Tris Fleming Nov. 1900.   The Kelmscott Bookshop   13 - 4   2016 $150

Association – Fletcher, M. F., Mrs.

Wase, Christopher *Considerations Concerning Free-Schools, as Settled in England.* Oxford: at the Theatre and are to be sold there and in London at Mr. Simon Millers, 1678. First edition, 8vo., engraved vignette of the Sheldonian Theatre on title, dampstaining to foot of titlepage and leaves a2-B4, lightly spotted throughout, mid 2th century quarter green morocco and marbled boards, old flyleaves preserved, 19th century ink armorial stamp of Mrs. M. F. Fletcher, from the library of James Stevens Cox (1910-1997).   Maggs Bros. Ltd.   1447 - 441   2016   £700

Association – Fletcher, Thomas William

Smith, Jeremiah Finch *Notes and Collections relating to Parish of Aldridge.* Leicester: W. H. Lead, 1884. First edition, half red leather over red cloth, armorial bookplate of Thomas William Fletcher, clean tight text with minor edge spotting, extremities of covers bit rubbed, two autograph letters dated 1884 and 1889, signed by author to Colonel Thomas William Fletcher.   Simon Finch   2015 - h014018   2016 $222

Association – Flexner, Anne Crawford

Mason, Alfred Edward Woodley   1865-1948 *Miranda of the Balcony.* London: Macmaillan and Co. Limited, 1899. First edition, inscribed on titlepage by Anne Crawford Flexner who secured the dramatic rights for Mason's Novel, original blue cloth with bright gilt title stamped to cover and spine, along with lovely embossed floral design, top edge gilt, light wear to edges and spine ends, foxing to endpapers but rest of interior is extremely clean and bright, tightly bound, very good.   The Kelmscott Bookshop   12 - 65   2016 $150

Association – Flick, Reuben Jay

Dickens, Charles   1812-1870 *Sketches by Boz. First Series. (with) Second Series.* London: John Macrone, 1836-1837. First edition, frontispiece and plates by George Cruikshank, 2 volumes, uncut in original dark green embossed cloth, heads of spines decorated and lettered in gilt, spines little darkened, carefully recased with some expertly executed minor repairs, second series with half title, frontispiece, engraved title plates, by Cruikshank, 19 page catalog (Dec. 1836), uncut in original pink pebble grained cloth, panelled spine pigmented black at head and tail to give impression of labels, carefully recased with small neat repairs to hinges and head and tail of spine, all volumes with armorial bookplate of Reuben Jay Flick, generally well preserved in custom made dark blue crushed morocco and cloth double slipcase by Heritage Bindery.   Jarndyce Antiquarian Booksellers   CCXVIII - 54   2016   £2800

Association – Flinn, Janet

Olsen, Penny *Feather and Brush: Three Centuries of Australian Bird Art.* Melbourne: CSIRO Pub., 2001. Quarto, color illustrations, signature of Janet Flinn (an artist represented in the book), very good in dust jacket.   Andrew Isles Natural History Books   55 - 14253   2016 $120

Association – Fludyers

Pinchard, Elizabeth Sibthorpe *The Blind Child.* London: printed for E. Newbery, 1798. Fifth edition, 12mo., some foxing to frontispiece, titlepage dusted and little browned, full contemporary tree calf, double gilt banded spine, red morocco label, joints cracked but firm, some slight wear, inscription "given to the Miss Fludyers by Lady Charlotte Duncombe, June 1801".   Jarndyce Antiquarian Books   CCXV - 370   2016   £75

Association – Foley, Jack

Arguelles, Ivan *New Poetry from California: Dead Requiem.* Berkeley: Pantograph Press, 1998. 4to., Presentation from Jack Foley for William Jay Smith, paper wrappers, as new.   Second Life Books, Inc.   196A - 48   2016 $45

Association – Fonda, Henry

Houghton, Norris *But Not Forgotten.* New York: William Sloane Associates, 1951. First edition, near fine in near very good dust jacket with couple of chips and long closed tear, signed by three members of the troupe, Henry Fonda, Joshua Logan and Mildred Narwick.   Between the Covers Rare Books   204 - 58   2016 $500

Association – Fontanne, Lynn

Coward, Noel 1899-1973 *Quadrille: a Romantic Comedy in Three Acts.* London: Heinemann, 1952. First edition, signed by 17 members of the English cast and by producer Jack Wilson and by Lynn Fontanne and Alfred Lunt on dedication page (play is dedicated to them), inscribed by Coward to Dorothy Sands (Octavia in the NY production), two more signed cards by Lunt and Fontanne tipped in and 3 notes by Lunt to Sands laid in, with tipped in signed photo of sands, nice in somewhat signed dust jacket.   Second Life Books, Inc.   196A - 342   2016 $500

Association – Foot, A. H.

Hill, John   *The Conduct of a Married Life.*   London: printed for R. Baldwin, 1753. 12mo., tear to lower corner of H*5 with no loss of text, contemporary full brown calf, double ruled gilt borders, raised bands, compartments, double ruled in gilt, some expert repairs to hinges, slightly rubbed, later pencil signature of A. H. Foot, nice.   Jarndyce Antiquarian Books   CCXV - 251   2016   £950

Association – Foot, Michael

Paine, Thomas 1737-1809   *Rights of Man.*   London: part I printed for J. S. Jordan, Part II printed for H. D. Symonds, 1792. 12mo., cheap coarse paper, old but not intrusive waterstaining, occasional dusting, bound in contemporary calf backed marbled boards, vellum fore-edges, boards rubbed and neatly rebacked, Michael Foot's copy with his signature and note on front endpaper.   Jarndyce Antiquarian Booksellers   CCXVI - 439   2016   £2500

Paine, Thomas 1737-1809   *The Whole Proceedings on the Trial of an Information Exhibited ex officio by the king's Attorney Against Thomas Paine for a Libel Upon the Revolution and the Bill of Rights....*   London: sold by Martha Gurney No. 128, Holborn Hill, 1793. 8vo., contemporary half calf, expertly rebacked, gilt banded spine, red morocco label, marbled boards, corners neatly repaired, bookplate of Michael Foot with pencil notes to front endpaper, pencil underlinings with the ownership signature of Thomas Holcroft 1745-1809.   Jarndyce Antiquarian Booksellers CCXVI - 441   2016   £1800

Spence, Thomas   *One Pennyworth of Pig's Meat or Lessons for the Winish Multitude.*   London: printed for T. Spence, 1793. Part First Number 1-Part Second Number XXIV, frontispiece, titlepage dusted with two small holes possibly paper flaws, not affecting text, frontispiece dusted and browned, chipped at edges, final index, leaf browned, 2 volumes in 1 contemporary half calf expertly rebacked, gilt banded spine red morocco label, boards rather rubbed, corners neatly repaired, from the collection of Michael Foot. Jarndyce Antiquarian Booksellers   CCXVI - 538   2016   £6800

Association – Foote, G. W.

Meredith, George 1828-1909   *A Reading of Earth.* Macmillan and Co., 1888. First edition, apparently a presentation copy with inserted sheet printed "From the author" and with bookplate of recipient G. W. Foote, original dark blue cloth with light bumping to corners, interior page very good with light aging to margins and occasional pencil mark next to passage, inserted sheet has a browned crease along top edge, very good.   The Kelmscott Bookshop   12 - 69   2016 $175

Association – Forbes, Alastair

Phillpotts, Eden 1862-1960   *The End of a Life.*   Bristol and London: J. W. Arrowsmith and Simpkin, Marshall, Hamilton, Kent & Co. Ltd., 1891. Presentation copy inscribed to G. B. Burgin, presentation copies from Phillpotts are scarce, very good in original brown cloth with gilt title to spine and black title to front board, front board slightly bowed and spine is somewhat cocked, hinges rubbed, minor soiling to boards, corners bumped, bookplate of Alastair Forbes, text remains bright although there is browning to margins of interior, evidence of a repair to front and rear interior hinges, very good.   The Kelmscott Bookshop   12 - 81   2016 $225

Association – Forbes, Bryan

Bates, Herbert Ernest 1905-1974   *The Hessian Prisoner.* William Jackson Books ltd., 1930. First edition, limited to 550 copies signed by author, 8vo., original red buckram lettered gilt on spine and upper board, frontispiece by John Austen, spine slightly sunned, otherwise near fine, this copy inscribed by author for film director Bryan Forbes, with bookplate.   Sotheran's   Piccadilly Notes - Summer 2015 - 31   2016   £148

Bates, Herbert Ernest 1905-1974   *The Seekers.*   John and Edward Bumpus, 1926. First edition, signed by author on half title, additionally inscribed by author to writer and actor, Bryan Forbes, with Forbes' bookplate, 8vo., original paper covered boards with glassine wrapper, little chipping and loss to glassine, otherwise very good.   Sotheran's Piccadilly Notes - Summer 2015 - 30   2016   £98

Association – Ford, Gordon Lester

Murray, John   *Jerubbaal or Tyranny's Grove Destroyed and the Altar of Liberty Finished.*   Newbury-port: John Mycalf, 1784. First edition, 12mo., three quarter morocco over marbled boards, few spots and stains but very good, from the Gordon Lester Ford Collection of NY Public Library with their duplicate sold stamp, lacks final four leaves. Edwin V. Glaser Rare Books   2015 - 10379   2016 $240

Association – Ford, James

Pascal, Blaise *Thoughts on Religion and Other Subjects.* Edinburgh: printed by R. Fleming for W. Gray, 1751. 12mo., old ink splash to leading edge of book block, intruding on to page but disappearing by page 28, ownership name of James Ford 1828, some underlining to text, marginal pen strokes, expertly bound in recent quarter sprinkled calf, marbled boards, vellum tips, raised and gilt banded spine, red morocco label. Jarndyce Antiquarian Booksellers CCXVI - 442 2016 £280

Walcot, John *Bozzy and Piozzi or the British Biographers a Town Eclogue.* London: printed for G. Kearsley at Johnson's Head, 1786. Fifth edition, etched plate, some worming to leading edge, mainly a single tiny hole touching a few letters, close cropped at lower edge affecting a few signatures and footnotes, bound in 19th century cloth, gilt lettered spine, rather faded, additional portrait of Pindar pasted on to inner board, ownership name of James Ford, Bath 1859. Jarndyce Antiquarian Booksellers CCXVI - 583 2016 £50

Association – Foreman, John

Shepard, Leslie *The History of the Horn Book.* London: 1977. Original printed wrappers, bound into marbled boards, brown cloth spine, handmade paper endpapers, compliments slip bearing note from John Foreman to Leslie Shepard. Jarndyce Antiquarian Books CCXV - 781 2016 £20

Association – Forman, H. Buxton

Haggard, Henry Rider 1856-1925 *The Wizard.* Bristol: J. W. Arrowsmith, 1896. first edition in cloth, publisher's brown cloth blocked in black on front cover, blind on rear cover and gilt on spine, charcoal endpapers, spine ends lightly worn, corners rubbed, front inner hinge very slightly cracked, but very good, from the library of H. Buxton Forman, with his bookplate and initialled note in pencil on front endpaper. Joseph J. Felcone, Inc. Books from Five Centuries: a Miscellany - 76 2016 $650

Association – Forrest, Leon

Wideman, John Edgar *The Lynchers.* New York: Harcourt Brace Jovanovich, 1973. Very near fine with letter L on front pastedown most likely from what would have been the beginning of inscription, very near fine dust jacket, signed and inscribed by author for Leon Forrest, very nice association. Jeff Hirsch Books Holiday List 2015 - 64 2016 $275

Association – Forrester, William

Dunbar, George *Key to the Greek Exercises.* Edinburgh: Stirling & Kenney, 1830. Few ink annotations on final page, disbound, contemporary signature of William Forrester, Edinburgh. Jarndyce Antiquarian Books CCXV - 630 2016 £28

Association – Forster, Edward Morgan

Browning, Robert 1812-1889 *The Ring and The Book.* London: Smith, Elder, 1868-1869. First edition, 4 volumes, 8vo., occasional light scattered foxing to free endleaves, original black stamped green cloth, gilt stamped spines by Harrison, quarter gilt stamped calf over blue cloth slipcase, volume 3 rear hinge cracked with light front pastedown soiling, volumes 1 and 2 hinges cracked, Robert Browning's signature tipped in volume I, opposite titlepage, ownership signatures of W. J. (...?) Settle (Sherborne Dorset, Feb. 21, 1869) and F. Rowlandson, ownership signatures of E. M. Forster in volume 2 to free front endleaf and titlepage, attractive, very good, with cut-out signature tipped in of Robert Browning. Jeff Weber Rare Books 181 - 42 2016 $4000

Goldsmith, Oliver 1730-1774 *The Works of Oliver Goldsmith.* London: John Murray, 1854. 4 volumes, additional engraved titlepage in each volume, frontispiece volume 1, contemporary red pebble grain morocco prize binding from Trinity College, Cambridge, boards with college arms blocked in gilt, spines lettered gilt direct with arms at head and foot, prize label to front pastedown with ownership labels to endpapers, edges gilt, merest touch of rubbing, few minor marks, very good, award as prize at Trinity College Cambridge, to Henry Thornton Forster, label of L. M. Forster (Laura Mary Forster), Edward Morgan Llewellyn Forster's label, then to Novelist E. M. Forster. Blackwell's Rare Books B184 - 45 2016 £600

Association – Forster, Henry Thornton

Goldsmith, Oliver 1730-1774 *The Works of Oliver Goldsmith.* London: John Murray, 1854. 4 volumes, additional engraved titlepage in each volume, frontispiece volume 1, contemporary red pebble grain morocco prize binding from Trinity College, Cambridge, boards with college arms blocked in gilt, spines lettered gilt direct with arms at head and foot, prize label to front pastedown with ownership labels to endpapers, edges gilt, merest touch of rubbing, few minor marks, very good, award as prize at Trinity College Cambridge, to Henry Thornton Forster, label of L. M. Forster (Laura Mary Forster), Edward Morgan Llewellyn Forster's label, then to Novelist E. M. Forster. Blackwell's Rare Books B184 - 45 2016 £600

Association – Forster, Laura Mary

Goldsmith, Oliver 1730-1774 *The Works of Oliver Goldsmith.* London: John Murray, 1854. 4 volumes, additional engraved titlepage in each volume, frontispiece volume 1, contemporary red pebble grain morocco prize binding from Trinity College, Cambridge, boards with college arms blocked in gilt, spines lettered gilt direct with arms at head and foot, prize label to front pastedown with ownership labels to endpapers, edges gilt, merest touch of rubbing, few minor marks, very good, award as prize at Trinity College Cambridge, to Henry Thornton Forster, label of L. M. Forster (Laura Mary Forster), Edward Morgan Llewellyn Forster's label, then to Novelist E. M. Forster. Blackwell's Rare Books   B184 - 45   2016   £600

Association – Forster, Sybil

Galsworthy, John 1867-1933 *The Man of Property.* London: Heinemann, 1906. First edition, some foxing at either end (as often) and on edges, 3 leaves little proud at top edge (for no apparent reason), 8vo., original cloth, title in gilt on upper cover, spine gilt lettered, little shaken and worn, contemporary signature of Sybil A. Forster dated 1806, modern bookplate.   Blackwell's Rare Books   B184 - 156   2016   £200

Association – Fortescue, C. S.

Smith, Alfred *Twenty Lithographic Views of Ecclesiastical Edifices in the Borough of Stroud...* Stroud: J. P. Brisley, 1838. First edition, large oblong , 20 lithographs on India pasted onto velin paper, errata slip loosely inserted, prelims bit dusty and with dog eared lower outer corners, otherwise very lightly spotted in places only, orginal printed wrappers, little worn, lower outer corner of front wrapper torn away front wrapper inscribed by C. S. Fortescue of Shepworth Dec. 1838, dedication leaf signed by artist.   Marlborough Rare Books   List 55 - 63   2016   £950

Association – Fortune, Brian

Mortimer, J. *The Whole Art of Husbandry...* London: printed by J. H. for J. Mortlock and J. Robinson, 1708. Second edition, 8vo., some woodcut illustrations in text, little toned towards edges, occasional spots and stains, one or two small annotations, recently rebound in half brown cloth with marbled paper covered boards, red cloth and gilt label to spine, endpapers renewed, very good, sound copy, recent bookplate of Brian Fortune.   Unsworths Antiquarian Booksellers Ltd.   30 - 112   2016   £250

Association – Fortune, Carrie

Stewart, T. McCants *Liberia: the Americo-African Republic.* New York: Edward O. Jenkins Sons, 1886. First edition, octavo, illustrations, modern quarter calf and grey paper over boards with black morocco spine label, gilt, very edge of front fly has been archivally strengthened affecting one letter in the inscription, light dampstain in bottom corner of text block, still handsome, very good copy, rare, inscribed by author to wife of journalist T. Thomas Fortune, Mrs. Carrie Fortune.   Between the Covers Rare Books   202 - 99   2016 $5000

Association – Fothergill

Cooper, James Fenimore 1789-1851 *The Last of the Mohicans; a Narrative of 1757.* London: John Miller, 1826. First English edition, 3 volumes, 12mo., slight spotting to prelims, bound without half titles in slightly later 19th century half tan calf, spine with double ruled gilt bands, compartments blocked in blind, volume numbers in gilt, dark green moroco labels, slightly rubbed, Fothergill armorial bookplate, very good.   Jarndyce Antiquarian Booksellers   CCXVII - 77   2016   £2200

Association – Foulis

Newton, Isaac 1642-1727 *Philosophiae Naturalis Principia Mathematica.* London: William and John Innys, 1726. Third edition, title printed in red and black, engraved frontispiece, 1 engraving and numerous diagrams in text, complete with half title and final ad leaf, some foxing at beginning and end, few scattered minor stains, repairs to margins of front flyleaves, late 19th century half red hard grained morocco, spine gilt in compartments and lettered direct, red edges, rebacked preserving previous spine, early inscription at head of title, little cropped at top and faded, seems to say 'gifted to Mr. William Scott of Babecan advocate by me ( ) Foulis', 19th century signature stamp of Dugald Macdonald at centre of titlepage, bookplate of Quebecois George G. Leroux, very good.   Blackwell's Rare Books   Marks of Genius - 32   2016   £11,000

Association – Fowle, Fulwar William

Gregory, Saint, the Great *Opera.* Paris: Francois Regnault, 1521. Early reissue of 1518 editio princeps, titlepage printed in red and black, scattering of small wormholes in title and first section (index), reducing to 3 by the start of text and wholly extinguished by f. 50, 3 further small holes in last 30ff., sometimes touching a character but rarely affecting legibility, frequent short marginal early ink notes, bit of dust soiling and marginal damp marking at end, folio, early 19th century English sprinkled calf, backstrip with four raised bands, remains of old label in second compartment, boards bordered in blind, front joint and backstrip ends expertly renewed, bit rubbed and scratched, ownership inscription with Latin motto dated 1578 at head of title with initials T. G. (further initial lost), 17th century inscription by Roger Kay, early 19th century bookplate of Fulwar William Fowle, good.   Blackwell's Rare Books   Marks of Genius - 20   2016   £950

Association – Fowler, Harry Alfred

The Order of Chivalry. Kelmscott Press, 1892-1893. One of 225 copies of an edition of 235 copies, printed in black and red in Chaucer type on Flower paper of two sizes, woodcut frontispiece designed by Burne-Jones, first woodcut initial, recently hand colored with green and red, small 4to. and 8vo., original limp vellum, backstrip lettered gilt, green silk ties, just lightly soiled, bookplate of Harry Alfred Fowler, very good.   Blackwell's Rare Books   B184 - 279   2016   £3000

Association – Fowles, John

Mogridge, George *Sergeant Bell and His Raree-show.* London: Thomas Tegg, First edition, frontispiece illustrations, contemporary half red sheep, marbled boards, little rubbed and worn, bookplate of novelist John Fowles, news clipping relating to Seregeat Bell publishing history tipped in, good plus, internally clean, scarce.   Jarndyce Antiquarian Booksellers   CCXVIII - 268   2016   £200

Association – Fox, Stephen

Lyndon, Barre *The Amazing Dr. Clitterhouse.* London: Hamish Hamilton, 1936. First edition, 8vo. fine in little soiled and worn dust jacket, photos, signed by 12 members of the first NY production, including Alexander Field, Edward Fulang, Muriel Hutchinson, Stephen Fox and others.   Second Life Books, Inc.   196 B - 108   2016 $225

Association – Foxcroft, Thomas Hammond

Moore, John *Edward. Various Views of Human Nature...* London: printed for A. Strahan and T. Cadell Jun. and W. Davies, 1796. 2 volumes, 8vo., very good, clean, contemporary marbled boards, vellum tips, ex-expertly rebacked, calf spines, double gilt bands, red morocco title labels, small circular green morocco volume numbers, armorial crest & booklabel of Thomas Hammond Foxcroft and his signature at head of each titlepage.   Jarndyce Antiquarian Booksellers   CCXVI - 415   2016   £160

Association – Frampton, James

Weldon, Anthony *The Court and Character of King James.* London: by Robert Ibbitson and are to be sold by John Wright, 1650. Small 8vo., engraved portrait, minor stain at top of first few leaves, some light browning and occasional spots, sheet m lightly dusty, small flaw in margin of D4, some leaves uncut at tail, contemporary sheep, coming loose in case, spine heavily worn and d3efective at head, corners bumped, small wormhole to centre of front cover, no pastedowns, from the library of James Stevens Cox (1910-1997), bookplate of James Frampton (1659-1855), earlier signature deleted from front flyleaf.   Maggs Bros. Ltd.   1447 - 445   2016   £175

Association – Francis, C.

Demeunier, Jean Nicolas *L'Esprit des Usages et des Coutumes des Differens Peuples, on Observations Tirees des Voyagers & des Historens.* Londres: Paris: Chez Pissot, 1776. First edition, 3 volumes, 8vo., half titles, title woodcut vignettes, head and tailpieces, original full mottled calf, decorative gilt stamped spine, raised bands, marbled endpapers and edges, joints cracked but holding head and tail worn, head portion missing on volume 3, later shelf sticker on spine foot, ownership signature of C. Francis 1836 and rubber ink and blind embossed stamps on first and last few pages, good, rare.   Jeff Weber Rare Books   181 - 14   2016 $450

Association – Francis, Reginald

Spenser, Edmund 1552-1599 *The Faerie Queen: the Shepheards Calendar: Together with the Other Works of England's Arch-Poet, Edm. Spenser...* London: printed for H L. for Matthew Lownes, 1611. First collected edition, five parts in one folio volumes, folio in sixes, general title within woodcut border, woodcut illustrations and ornamental borders, decorative woodcut head and tailpieces and initials, contemporary polished dark brown calf with central gilt stamped lozenges to front and rear covers, blind stamped letters (TN) to each side of lozenge, expertly rebacked to style, gilt spine lettering, few minor marginal tears, lower corner of D4 torn out (not affecting text), some occasional browning, bookplates of Viscount Birkenhead and Reginald Francis, some notations on front endpaper surrounded by old tape residue, some scuffing to corners, still very nice.   Heritage Book Shop   Holiday 2015 - 102   2016 $7500

Association – Francotte, Henri Joseph

Bible. Latin - 1549 *Testamenn Novi Editio Vulgata.* Lyon: Sebastien Gryphe, 1549. One of several illustrated editions produced by Gryphius, 16mo., 19th century half brown morocco, marbled boards, printer's woodcut device on titlepage and 108 woodcuts, three of them signed "IF", few ornamental borders and initials, bookplate of Henri Joseph Francotte, titlepage lightly soiled, otherwise fresh. Maggs Bros. Ltd.   1474 - 11   2016   £1250

Association – Franklin, Mary Mac

Handy, W. C. *Saint Louis Blues.* New York: Handy Brothers Music Co. Inc., 1940. Quarto, bi-folium with loose leaf laid in as issued, some rubbing with faint creases, very good, small affixed typed label "When Mary Mac's review of W. C. Handy's autobiography appeared in the Memphis Commerical Appeal in June 1941, Handy in appreciation sent her this autographed presentation copy, inscribed to same by author for Mary Mac Franklin, note laid in by recipient reiterating information on typed label.   Between the Covers Rare Books   202 - 62   2016 $550

Association – Frasconi, Antonio

Farber, Norma   *How the Left-Behind Beasts Built Ararat.* New York: Walker and Co.,   1978. First printing, (correct number code), 4to., cloth, fine in dust jacket, color woodcuts by Antonio Frasconi, mounted on half title, is decorative typed card with book title, signed by artist.   Aleph-bet Books, Inc.   112 - 199   2016 $125

Association – Fraser, Lindley

Walras, Leon   *Elements D'Economie Politique Pure ou Theorie de la Richesse Sociale.*   Lausanne: F. Rouge, 1889. Second edition, 8vo., original buckram cloth, from the library of economist Lindley Fraser with his signature, mild wear to spine tips, darkening to spine, minimal foxing to endpapers, 8vo., 6 folding plates.   By the Book, L. C.   45 - 37   2016 $6000

Association – Fraser, Lovat

The Mariner's Concert, Being a New Collection of the Most Favorite Sea Songs...   printed by J. Evans, 1797. Large woodcut vignette on title, poorly printed on cheap paper with bit of consequent browning, 4to., early 20th century navy blue buckram, lettered on upper cover, slight worn, pencil note inside front cover, form the library of Lovat Fraser, good, rare.   Blackwell's Rare Books   B186 - 141   2016   £250

Association – Fraser, Victoria

Hughes, Ted   1930-1998   *Chiasmadon.*   Baltimore: Charles Seluzicki, 1977. First edition, one of 5 or 6 copies specially bound for participants of the edition, out of a total of 175 copies, square 8vo., original quarter black leather and decorated paper boards by Susan Johanknecht, this ad personam copy, designated for "Victoria Fraser" in Van Vliet's hand, very fine copy.   James S. Jaffe Rare Books Occasional List: Winter 2016 - 82   2016 $4500

Association – Freedman, Lillian

Cowley, Malcolm   *Think Back On us.*   Carbondale: Southern Illinois University, 1967. 8vo., author's presentation on half title to Lillian Freedman, green cloth, top edges of leaves little soiled, edges of cover little worn in spots, otherwise very good, tight in chipped dust jacket.   Second Life Books, Inc.   196A - 345   2016 $75

Association – Freeman, Emily

Hawthorne, Nathaniel   1804-1864   *The Scarlet Letter.* Boston: Ticknor, Reed and Fields,   1850. First edition, 12mo., later full crimson morocco (original cloth and endpapers bound in), inscribed ads dated March 1, 1850, pasted opposite title, which is printed in black and red-orange, is fine example of Hawthorne's holograph signature, signed as surveyor of the port of Salem, Mass., 19h century ownership signature 'Emily G. Freeman, nearly fine with bookplate of Carolyn Wells, author.   Howard S. Mott Inc.   265 - 65   2016 $2000

Association – Freeman, Robert

Clark, Walter   *Histories of the Several regiments and Battalions from North Carolina in the Great War 1861-1865.* Raleigh: E. M. Uzzell, printer and binder,   1901. First edition, thick 8vo., gray cloth stamped in blue, red, white and lettered gilt, presentation from author to Adjutant Robert M. Freeman, covers rubbed with wear at spine ends, inside hinges cracked with some signatures sprung.   Oak Knoll Books   310 - 280   2016 $650

Association – Freeman, Stephen

Bythner, Victorinus *Lyra Prophetica Davidis Regis. Sive Analysis Critico-Practica Psalmorum in quae Omnes & Singulae Voces Hebraeae in Psalterio Contentae...* Londoni: Jacobi Flesher, 1650. First edition, 4to., text in Hebrew and Latin, titlepage in red and black, separate half title to 'Index Libri Psalmorum', final leaf of errata, tidemark to top fore-edge corner from title to page 81 small worm trail to fore-edge margin of page 333 dwindling away to end of textblock, tiny burnhole to page 3-4 touching couple of letters, contemporary brown sprinkled calf, red morocco gilt label to spine, blind tooled borders and additional vertical line to boards, edges sprinkled blue and red, very early rubricated leaves with accompanying manuscript marginalia used as pastedowns, spine rubbed, lower joint split and upper starting but cords holding firm, some scrapes and stains, corners wearing but sound unsophisticated copy, ownership inscription of Stephen Freeman dated 1787 and bookplate of Douglas Cleverdon.   Unsworths Antiquarian Booksellers   30 - 28   2016   £175

Association – Freeman, Thomas Edwards

Homerus *The Iliad. (with) The Odyssey.* London: printed by W. Bowyer for Bernard Lintott, 1715-1726. First editions translated by Alexander Pope, 11 volumes bound as 6, large paper copies, titlepages of Odyssey printed in red and black, with all plates except Troy plate (often missing), double page map hand colored in outline, some spotting in volume iii of the Iliad, less in v, worming in lower margins of iv of Odyssey extending slightly into v, no loss of text, one or two other minor faults, sporadic minor dust staining in upper margins, staining to 2 leaves in postscript to Odyssey, folio, uniform contemporary mottled calf, spines richly gilt in compartments, tan lettering pieces, some joints cracked, some wear, engraved bookplate of Thomas Edwards Freeman in most volumes (removed from others), good.   Blackwell's Rare Books   Marks of Genius - 38   2016   £6000

Association – Freer, Allan

Hume, Abraham *The Learned Societies and printing Clubs of the United Kingdom...* London: G. Willis, 1853. Half title, original brown cloth, little rubbed, inner hinges cracking, monogram bookplate of Allan Freer, Fordel, good plus.   Jarndyce Antiquarian Booksellers   CCXVII - 131   2016   £85

Association – Freitagh, Johann Adolph

Terentius Afer, Publius *Comoediae, Andria, Eunuchus....* Paris: Apud Ioannem de Roigny, 1552. First Thierry edition, numerous woodcut illustrations within text, some light spotting, ink splotch to second two leaves, ownership inscriptions to titlepage of Johann Adolph Freitagh, folio, contemporary French mid-brown calf, boards bordered with black strap within gilt fillets, central decorative arabesque panel in gilt and black, flat spine divided by gilt tools, second compartments gilt lettered within gilt shield outline, other compartments with central decoration in black and gilt, spine ends, joints and corners skillfully repaired, some old scratches and marks to leather, dampmark to front endpapers, bookplate removed from front pastedown, smaller modern booklabel in its place, very good.   Blackwell's Rare Books   Greek & Latin Classics VII - 83   2016   £3000

Association – Frere, Alexander Stuart

Douglas, Norman 1868-1952 *Birds and Beasts of the Greek Anthology.* Florence: privately printed at the Tipografia Giuntina, 1927. First edition, 444/500 copies, signed by author, frontispiece, 2 smaller plates tipped-in, 8vo., original blue boards, backstrip with printed label, lettered in black, little rubbing to very tip of backstrip, top edge dust soiled, others untrimmed and uncut, dust jacket with few short closed tears, darkened backstrip panel with some liquid staining predominantly to front, adhesive trace at front flap, very good, inscribed by author for Alexander Stuart Frere.   Blackwell's Rare Books   B186 - 204   2016   £360

Association – Freund, Giselle

Wright, Richard *Puissance Norie. (Black Power).* Paris: Correa Bucher & Chastel, 1955. First French edition, pages little browned, else fine in wrappers as issued, inscribed by author to photographer and author, Giselle Freund.   Between the Covers Rare Books   202 - 123   2016 $2000

Association – Frey, Eberhard

Schott, Gaspar *Schola Steganographica in Classes Octo Distributa...* Nuremberg: Jobus Hertz for Johann Andrea..., 1665. First edition, small 4to., extra engraved titlepage, half title, titlepage printed in red and black, engraved arms of Ferdinand Maximilan, 1625-1669, 3 tables, text engravings, woodcut initials, head and tailpieces, contemporary vellum, title in old hand on spine, edges speckled red, minor toning and foxing, vellum browned as usual, one tie remains, bookplate of Hedwig & Eberhard Frey dated 1920, one plate with repaired tears at blank table, otherwise fine.   Jeff Weber Rare Books   183 - 33   2016 $3250

Association – Frey, Hedwig

Schott, Gaspar *Schola Steganographica in Classes Octo Distributa...* Nuremberg: Jobus Hertz for Johann Andrea..., 1665. First edition, small 4to., extra engraved titlepage, half title, titlepage printed in red and black, engraved arms of Ferdinand Maximilan, 1625-1669, 3 tables, text engravings, woodcut initials, head and tailpieces, contemporary vellum, title in old hand on spine, edges speckled red, minor toning and foxing, vellum browned as usual, one tie remains, bookplate of Hedwig & Eberhard Frey dated 1920, one plate with repaired tears at blank table, otherwise fine. Jeff Weber Rare Books 183 - 33 2016 $3250

Association – Friedman, Carol

Giddins, Gary *A Moment's Notice: Portraits of American Jazz Musicians.* New York: Schrimer, 1983. First printing, 4to., presentation by Carol Friedman to Martin Scorsese, paper over boards, nice in slightly browned dust jacket. Second Life Books, Inc. 196A - 629 2016 $95

Association – Fritch

California Sorcery. Abingdon: Cemetery Dance, 1999. Publisher's copy of the limited edition (26 copies), signed by Ray Bradbury, Richard Matheson, Ellison, Nolan, Tomerlin, Sohl, Fritch and others, stamp of another author, fine in fine dust jacket in publisher's printed gray case. Ken Lopez Bookseller 166 - 5 2016 $650

Association – Frith, W. Cokayne

Herodotus *Historiarum Libri IX.* Amstelodami: sumptibus Petri Schovtenii, 1763. Folio, engraved additional titlepage and 1 folding plate, Greek and Latin text, titlepage in red and black with engraved vignette, half title, engraved initials and head and tailpieces, internally bright and clean, contemporary brown calf boards, neatly rebacked in slightly lighter shade, spine heavily gilt, older red morocco spine label, edges sprinkled red, marbled endpapers little rubbed, few light scratches, rear flyleaf repaired with tape, very good, ownership inscription of W. Cokayne Frith, bookbinders label E. A. Weeks & Son, London. Unsworths Antiquarian Booksellers 30 - 71 2016 £1000

Thucydides *De Bello Peloponnesiaco Libri Octo.* Amstelaedami: Apud R. & J. Wetstenios & Gul. Smith, 1731. Folio, engraved frontispiece and 2 folding plates (maps), Greek and Latin parallel texts, titlepages in red and black, engraved vignette, engraved initials and head and tailpieces, occasional toned leaves, generally bright within, contemporary brown calf boards, neatly rebacked, spine gilt with older red morocco label retained, gilt frames and borders, corners reinforced, edges sprinkled red and blue, endpapers renewed, few scrapes and scratches, slight creasing to spine, edges rubbed, but very good, ownership inscription of W. Cokyane Frith. Unsworths Antiquarian Booksellers Ltd. 30 - 151 2016 £1000

Association – Frohman, Daniel

Phillpotts, Eden 1862-1960 *Folly and Fresh Air.* London: Trischler and Comany, 1891. First edition, inscribed by author to Daniel Frohman 18 June 1892, very good in green cloth boards with dark red title and author to spine and dark red author, title and design to front cover, some chipping and bumping and bit of light soiling to boards, floral decorated endpages, endpages and text pages lightly browned from age. The Kelmscott Bookshop 12 - 82 2016 $150

Association – Fromanteel, Abraham

Locke, John 1632-1704 *An Essay Concerning Humane Understanding in Four Books.* London: for Awnsham and John Churchil (sic), 1700. Fourth edition, engraved portrait, some browning and spotting, purchase inscription 'Fromanteel pr. 13s' to titlepage, gift inscription 'The gift of Abraham Fromanteel of London, to Daniel Fromanteel Sen. of Norwich after his decease to be & remaine in hs family, London November 27 1709', folio, contemporary Cambridge style panelled calf, rebacked, hinges relined, boards pitted, edges worn, sound. Blackwell's Rare Books Marks of Genius - 25 2016 £950

Association – Fromanteel, Daniel

Locke, John 1632-1704 *An Essay Concerning Humane Understanding in Four Books.* London: for Awnsham and John Churchil (sic), 1700. Fourth edition, engraved portrait, some browning and spotting, purchase inscription 'Fromanteel pr. 13s' to titlepage, gift inscription 'The gift of Abraham Fromanteel of London, to Daniel Fromanteel Sen. of Norwich after his decease to be & remaine in hs family, London November 27 1709', folio, contemporary Cambridge style panelled calf, rebacked, hinges relined, boards pitted, edges worn, sound. Blackwell's Rare Books Marks of Genius - 25 2016 £950

Association – Frost, Elias Harry

Holbein, Hans *Les Images de la Mort, aux Quelles Saint Adioustees Douze Figures.* Lyon: Jean Freelon, 1547. Third edition in French, seventh edition overall, small octavo, modern full black morocco, printer's device on titlepage, woodcut initials throughout text, 53 woodcuts after designs by Holbein, bookplate and owner signatures of 19th century collector Elias Harry Frost, text in French, near fine. Honey & Wax Booksellers 4 - 47 2016 $17,500

Association – Fry, Joseph

Monro, George *Extracts. Doctrinal, Practical and Devotional.* London: William Darton and Son, 1836. 19th century blind stamped binding, inscribed by editor, Joseph Fry for Raymond & Louisa Polly, , octavo, full contemporary decoratively blindstamped blue morocco, spine lettered gilt, all edges gilt, near fine.   David Brass Rare Books, Inc.   2015 - 03012   2016 $150

Association – Fry, Roger

Cervantes Saavedra, Miguel De   1547-1616 *Don Quixote De La Mancha.* London: Nonesuch Press, 1930. First press edition, limited to 1475 copies, 2 volumes, octavo, publisher's full morocco, 21 color plates, presentation from artist, E. McKnight Kauffer to Roger Fry, near fine.   Honey & Wax Booksellers   4 - 2   2016   £2200

Association – Fulang, Edward

Lyndon, Barre *The Amazing Dr. Clitterhouse.* London: Hamish Hamilton, 1936. First edition, 8vo. fine in little soiled and worn dust jacket, photos, signed by 12 members of the first NY production, including Alexander Field, Edward Fulang, Muriel Hutchinson, Stephen Fox and others.   Second Life Books, Inc.   196 B - 108   2016 $225

Association – Fuller, John

The Bazar Book of the Household Marriage Establishment, Children, Servants, Home Life, Housekeeping, Company. New York: Harper & Bros., 1875. Original green cloth, bevelled boards, front board marked and little scuffed, Guille-Alles library stamps, its label removed from front board, sound, booklabel of John Fuller.   Jarndyce Antiquarian Books   CCXV - 41   2016   £30

Association – Furman, A. L.

Thurman, Wallace *The Interne.* New York: Macaulay, 1932. First edition, bit of scuffing at bottom of boards, else near fine in bright, very good dust jacket with some slight spine fading and some modest chipping to spine ends, additionally this copy signed by Thurman as well as co-author, A. L. Furman.   Between the Covers Rare Books   207 - 89   2016 $10,000

Association – Furstenberg, Hans

The Historie of Frier Rush: How He Came to a House of Religion to Seeke Service... London: Harding and Wright for Robert Triphook, 1810. One of 4 copies on vellum, contemporary red velvet by H. Faulkner (ticket on verso front flyleaf), covers with wide Greek key border rolled in blind, flat spine with small remnant of leather backstrip (that has been laid on to hide a binder's titling error), red moire silk endleaves, turn-ins and pastedowns with rolls in blind, all edges gilt, housed in very good later leather edged slipcase, woodcut vignette on title, verso to front flyleaf with bookplate of Edward Vernon Utterson and morocco bookplate of Hans Furstenberg, bookplate of John Kershaw, contemporary inked note listing original owner of each of the four vellum copies of the present book, later pencilled note on same "Ths copy was after-wards in the possession of Mr. George Smith and it was (sold in his (s)ale for £9.15.0", spine mostly covered with (glue?) residue left by now basically missing leather backstrip, corners rubbed to board, portions of the joints torn, velvet nap somewhat diminished, a bit of natural rumpling to the vellum, very few inoffensive spots to margins, entirely solid (apart from spine remnants) an agreeable copy of this curious book.   Phillip J. Pirages   67 - 341   2016 $4500

Association – Gage, Matilda Joslyn

Stanton, Elizabeth Cady *History of Woman Suffrage. Volume One only.* New York: Fowler and Wells, 1881. First edition, 8vo., steel engravings, presentation from Matilda Joslyn Gage, dated 1888, maroon cloth, cover quite scuffed and somewhat worn at spine and corners, little foxing, otherwise very good.   Second Life Books, Inc.   196 B - 685   2016 $350

Association – Gahagan, Henry

Herodotus *Historiarum Libri IX...* Lugduni Batavorum: apud Samuelem Luchtmann, 1715. Engraved frontispiece titlepage dated 1716, first edition, folio, without separate titlepage to appendix (after page 554), found in some copies, half title, additional engraved title, titlepage in red and black, foldout engraved illustration after page 135, two small illustrations in text (pages 912 and 997), woodcut initials, engraved tailpieces, Greek and Latin parallel text, occasional small annotations, some light ink spotting to half title, little toned in gutters and towards end of text, small ink blot to top edge sporadically visible at upper margins but never approaching text, contemporary vellum, raised bands, gilt morocco spine label, blind tooled boards, edges sprinkled red and blue, bit grubby, prelim blanks tattered with some loss, old discolored repair to top corner but very good, ownership inscriptions of Henry Gahagan, student at Christ Church Oxford and Rev. Reginald (Lake?) Nov. 30 1880.   Unsworths Antiquarian Booksellers Ltd.   E04 - 21   2016   £650

Association – Gaige, Crosby

Cavendish, George *The Life of Thomas Wolsey, Cardinall Archbishop of York.* London: sold by Reeves & Turner (Hammersmith), 1893. One of 250 paper copies of an edition of 256, octavo, woodcut border to page 1 and numerous initials, full limp vellum with green silk ties, yapp edges, spine lettered gilt, edges uncut, previous owner Crosby Gaige bookplate, vellum slightly warped, and little discoloration, overall very good.   Heritage Book Shop   Holiday 2015 - 63   2016 $2500

Swinnerton, Frank *Coquette.* London: Methuen & Co., 1921. First edition, fine in very attractive very good dust jacket with some tears at edges and couple of small and unobtrusive chips, housed in older chemise and quarter leather slipcase, inscribed by author to American Publisher Crosby Gaige.   Between the Covers Rare Books   204 - 112   2016 $650

Association – Gaisford, Thomas

Homerus *The Iliads of Homer Prince of Poets (with) Homer's Odysses. (with) The Crowne of all Homers Worckes Batrachomyonmachia or the Battaile of Frogs and Mise...* London: printed (by Richard Field) for Nathaniel Butter, 1611-1615. Worckes - London: printed by Iohn Bill, 1624. First Complete edition in English of first two works, first edition in English of third, titlepage engraved (some expert repair work around outer edges), inner edge just disappearing into gutter, initial blank discarded, final blank present, additional leaves of sonnets bound in prelims, some dust soiling and marks; titlepage engraved (some expert repair work around edges), initial and final blanks discarded, Y2 slightly shorter and probably supplied, little marginal worming in second half expertly repaired, occasionally touching letter, no significant loss; top edge gilt (earliest state with "Worckes" instead of "Workes"), initial blank discarded, folio, 3 volumes, washed and pressed in 19th century red morocco by Riviere, boards with central lozenge shape made of wreaths and flowers and containing a circular frame, blocked in gilt, spines elaborately gilt, bookplate of Thomas Gaisford, leather booklabel of 'Terry' and small booklabel of J. O. Edwards, modern bookplate, very good.   Blackwell's Rare Books   Marks of Genius - 22   2016   £40,000

Theocritus *Tade Enestein Ente Garoi se Biblo Eidyllia he Kai Triakonta.* Rome: Zacharias Callierges, 1516. 8vo., early 19th century mid brown polished calf, spine gilt in compartments, red morocco lettering piece, edges red, marbled endpapers, corners slightly worn, joints near invisibly strengthened and front flyleaf re-attached, bookplate of Thomas Gaisford and letter from Earl Spencer to Gaisford, Gaisford's ownership inscription and manuscript table of contents to blank endpapers, good.   Blackwell's Rare Books   B184 - 84   2016   £6500

Association – Gallien, Andre

Paroissien: Elzevir, Rite Romain. Paris: Gruel et Englemann, 1889. 165 x 83mm., striking contemporary burgundy morocco, elaborately gilt by Gruel (stamp signed at tail of spine), upper cover with large and richly detailed oval bas-relief plaquette of the last supper framed above and below by a large panel of interlacing open strapwork comprised of abstracted gilt floral and foliate curls and other decorative elements, lower cover similarly decorated, with its central medallion containing a gilt cipher in intertwined majuscules, raised bands, spine gilt in double ruled compartments with central arabesque, gilt filigree turn-ins, claret moire silk endleaves, all edges gilt, original brass clasps with strapwork decoration, with 26 illustrations, composed of 22 large black and white woodcut headpieces and four chromolithographed plates with gold highlights, along with numerous uncolored woodcut initials, front free endleaf gilt stamp '24 Mai 1891', first Communion card of Andre Gallien dated 9 May 1895, laid in, very fine, morocco lustrous and leaves entirely crisp and clean.   Phillip J. Pirages   67 - 47   2016 $1100

Association – Galsworthy, Ada

Galsworthy, John 1867-1933 *Glimpses and Reflections.* London: Heinemann, 1937. First edition, 8vo. inscribed by Ada Galsworthy for Molly Kerr, with Mrs. Galsworthy's compliments card laid in, light foxing on front and back pages and on edges, else very good.   Second Life Books, Inc.   196A - 606   2016 $45

Association – Galsworthy, E.

Clemens, Samuel Langhorne 1835-1910 *A Tramp Abroad.* London: Chatto & Windus, 1880. Third edition, 2 volumes, half titles, 32 page catalog (April 1880), original olive green cloth, front boards pictorially blocked and lettered in black, spines blocked in black and lettered in gilt, publisher's monogram at centre of following boards, very slightly rubbed, signed "Kate Restall, May 29th/80", additional inscription "To Mr. E. Galsworthy, 2 Gladstone Terrance, Grosvenor Road".   Jarndyce Antiquarian Booksellers   CCXVII - 287   2016   £120

Association – Garden Ltd.

Bunyan, John 1628-1688 *Pilgrim's Progress.* London: printed by Bernard Newdigate at the Shakespeare Head Press for the Cresset Press, 1928. Number 6 of 10 special copies printed on vellum (and 195 on paper), 2 volumes, plus portfolio of plates, fine publisher's russet morocco by Sangorski & Sutcliffe (stamp signed on front turn-in), covers lettered gilt, metal clasps, raised bands, wide turn-ins with multiple ruled border, all edges gilt, volumes housed along with extra suite of engravings, in a (slightly worn but still very good), fleece lined matching cloth box and slipcase, 2 large vignettes and 10 powerful expressionistic engraved plates on vellum, vignettes and 6 of the plates by Blair Hughes-Stanton, the other four by Gertrude Hermes with matted duplicates of all plates (all of the engravings signed), extras done on thin paper and contained in their own portfolio, bookplate of the Garden Collection assembled by Haven O'More, a couple of faint scratches to boards, spines shade darker than covers, small handful of leaves with usual faint discoloration that is inevitable with vellum, otherwise superb set, text clean and fresh, smooth, bright vellum leaves, bindings unworn.   Phillip J. Pirages   67 - 332   2016 $35,000

Association – Gardiner, Dorothy

Fischer, Bruno *Crook's Tour.* New York: Dodd Mead, 1953. First edition, fine, inscribed by contributors Lawrence Blochman and Dorothy Gardiner, fine in price clipped dust jacket.   Mordida Books   2015 - 010969   2016 $65

Association – Gardner, Carl

Dodson, Owen *Powerful Long Ladder.* New York: Farrar Straus, 1946. Second printing, fine in lightly rubbed, very good plus dust jacket, inscribed for Carl Gardner, by author Dec. 11 1958.   Between the Covers Rare Books   207 - 36   2016 $275

Association – Gardner, Erle Stanley

Dixon, Jeane *My Life and Prophecies: Her Own Story.* New York: William Morrow & Co., 1969. First edition, fine in just about fine dust jacket with slight wrinkling on lamination at the bottom of the front panel, inscribed by Dixon to writer Mr. (and Mrs. Erle Stanley Gardner.   Between the Covers Rare Books   208 - 57   2016 $225

Association – Gardner, Joseph

Societes De La Froix-Rogue *Troisieme Conference Internationale Des Societes De La Croix-Rogue. Tenue A Geneve Du Ier Au 6 Septembre 1884. Compte Renu.* Geneve: Au Siege Comite International de al Croix Rouge, 1885. First edition, 4to., original blue cloth binding with silver stamped lettering to spine and front board, accompanied by impressed silver and red Red cross logo, housed in custom chemise and quarter leather slipcase with marbled paper boards, volume shows wear and evidence of damp-staining, rear hinge paper starting at bottom, about very good, chemise and slipcase fine, presentation copy inscribed by Clara Barton for Dr. Joseph Gardner March 15 1889.   Tavistock Books   Bibliolatry - 19   2016 $4250

Association – Garley, Granville

Davenport, Richard Alfred *Lives of Individuals Who Raised Themselves from Poverty to Eminence or Fortune.* London: Thomas Tegg, 1841. First edition, half title, final ad leaf, tipped in label removed from leading pastedown, original printed cloth boards, slightly rubbed and marked, typed booklabel of Granville Garley.   Jarndyce Antiquarian Books   CCXV - 59   2016   £38

Association – Garrick, Carrington

Caesar, Gaius Julius *Quae Extant Omnia.* Venice: Societatis Albritianae, 1737. Engraved frontispiece, folding map, 5 plates (two folding) plus engravings in text area, few leaves with marginal dampmarks, some foxing and finger soiling (heavier in one or two places), one leaf with chip from blank margin, bit of spotting, 4to., contemporary vellum borads, brown morocco lettering piece to spine, soiled and bit scratched vellum covering worn in places (particularly patch at front joint and another at fore-edge of rear board), bookplates of Carrington and David Garrick to front pastedown, good.   Blackwell's Rare Books   B186 - 34   2016   £950

Association – Garrick, David

Caesar, Gaius Julius *Quae Extant Omnia.* Venice: Societatis Albritianae, 1737. Engraved frontispiece, folding map, 5 plates (two folding) plus engravings in text area, few leaves with marginal dampmarks, some foxing and finger soiling (heavier in one or two places), one leaf with chip from blank margin, bit of spotting, 4to., contemporary vellum borads, brown morocco lettering piece to spine, soiled and bit scratched vellum covering worn in places (particularly patch at front joint and another at fore-edge of rear board), bookplates of Carrington and David Garrick to front pastedown, good.   Blackwell's Rare Books   B186 - 34   2016   £950

Association – Garver, Tom

Coleman, Allan D. *Confirmation.* Brooklyn: ADCO Enterprises, 1975. Number 86 from an edition of 250, 12 black and white images of Jazz great Charlie Parker grave stone signed by Coleman, also includes signed note from Coleman to curator and author Tom Garver, terrific copy with nice association, fine in wrappers.   Jeff Hirsch Books   Holiday List 2015 - 7   2016 $75

Association – Gascoyne, David

Auden, Wystan Hugh   1907-1973 *The Enchafed Flood or the Romantic Iconography of the Sea.* London: Faber and Faber, 1951. First English edition, crown 8vo., original blue cloth, backstrip lettered gilt now dulled, dustiness to boards and textblock, edges of browning to free endpapers, dust jacket browned, frayed and lightly spotted, good, David Gascoyne's copy with his notes, signed by author.   Blackwell's Rare Books   B184 - 97   2016   £400

Association – Gaskell, Charles George Milnes

Wishart, George *Montrose Redivivus or the Portraicture of James late Marquess of Montrose, Earl of Kincardin &c.* London: for Jo. Ridley, 1652. First edition in English, 8vo., engraved portrait, light marginal browning, A3r dust soiled and very lightly dampstained in places, probably washed, late 19th century sprinkled calf by F. Bedford (front cover detached, spine bands, lightly scuffed and chipped), bookplate of Charles George Milnes Gaskell, from the library of James Stevens Cox (1910-1997).   Maggs Bros. Ltd.   1447 - 460   2016   £120

Association – Gault, Bill

MacDonald, Ross *The Far Side of the Dollar.* New York: Alfred A. Knopf, 1965. First edition, 8vo., fine in fine dust jacket, inscribed Jan. 15 1965 for Bill Gault, by author, exceptional copy, housed in cloth slipcase with red leather labels on spine, titles and date stamped in gold.   Buckingham Books   2015 - 25474   2016 $2750

Association – Gaunt, David

Quintilianus, Marcus Fabius *De Institutione Oratoria Libri Duodecim ad Codicum Veterum Fidem...* Lipsiae: Sumtibus Siegfried Lebrecht Crusi (Volumes I_IV) Sumptiubs Frid. Christ. Guil. Vogelii (Volumes V-VI), 1798-1834. 6 volumes, 8vo., occasional spots of foxing, generally bright, small closed tear to vol. IV titlepage, mid 20th century half light tan calf, red morocco spine labels, red marbled paper boards, edges lightly sprinkled brown, contrasting marbled endpapers, some patchy color variation to spines, possibly from leather dressing, little rubbed but very good set, with "David M. Gaunt (rebound Jan. 1968)".   Unsworths Antiquarian Booksellers Ltd.   E05 - 10   2016   £675

Association – Gayton, J. L.

Young, H. M. *The Housewife's Manual of Domestic Cookery...* London: Fletcher, Russell & co., circa, 1900. 27th edition, half title, illustrations, occasional marking and few marginal tears, original red buckram blocked in black, signature of M. L. Gayton, spine slightly faded, leading hinge neatly strengthened, nice.   Jarndyce Antiquarian Books   CCXV - 497   2016   £65

Association – Geers, A. W

Estienne, Charles   1504-1564 *Dictionarium Historicum, Geographicum, Poeticom....* Genevae: apud Samuelem de Tournes, 1693. Reissue of the new edition, quarto, titlepage printed in red and black, contemporary binding of full tree calf with gilt decoration, marbled endpapers, from the library of Dutch theologian Johannes Henricus Scholten (1811-1885) tipped in before titlepage is leaf printed with announcement of the Latin School at Delft with Schotlen's name inserted by hand, signed by Rector A. W. Geers and four other teachers, some light foxing here and there.   Peter Ellis   112 - 117   2016   £475

Association – Geest, Christopher Clark

Browning, Elizabeth Barrett   1806-1861 *Poems.* London: Edward Moxon, 1844. First edition, 2 volumes, ad leaf at end of volume I, original green vertical fine ribbed cloth, blocked in blind, spines lettered gilt, booklabels of Miss S. Sheppard with her signatures on verso of titlepages and dated May 1848, modern labels of Christopher Clark Geest, slight marking to leading free endpaper from old insertion, otherwise lovely crisp copy, green cloth fold over box.   Jarndyce Antiquarian Booksellers   CCXVII - 53   2016   £1250

Hale, Virginia Sidney *A Book of Etiquette, good form on all occasions.* New York: Dell Pub. Co., 1923. Original illustrated cream wrappers, stapled as issued, illustrations, bookplate of Christopher Clark Geest.   Jarndyce Antiquarian Books   CCXV - 238   2016   £45

Hawthorne, Nathaniel   1804-1864 *Our Old Home: a Series of English Sketches.* Boston: Ticknor and Fields, 1863. First edition, 2nd state with page (399) blank, brown cloth decorated in blind, lettered gilt, brown coated endpapers, about near fine with some light wear to extremities, tiny holes to hinges at spine tail, boards lightly rubbed, otherwise bright and sturdy binding, Christopher Geest's bookplate, former owner's pencil inscription, faint tide marks to bottom corners of last few leaves, otherwise very bright and fresh, overall very clean and sturdy copy.   B & B Rare Books, Ltd.   2016 - NH024   2016 $100

Tasso, Torquato 1544-1595 *The Gerusalemme Liberato of Tasso...* Cambridge: printed by J. Archdeacon printer to the University, 1786. 1792. First edition of volume i, and second edition of volume ii, 8vo., 2 volumes, fine, clean copy bound in full contemporary sprinkled calf, smooth spines, gilt band, red morocco title labels, dark green oval volume labels, lemon yellow edges, signature of Elizabeth Collingridge, Oct. 1842, recent bookplate of Christopher Clark Geest.   Jarndyce Antiquarian Booksellers   CCXVI - 560   2016   £225

Wesley, John 1703-1791 *Sermons on Several Occasions.* London: printed by W. Bowyer (Volumes II & III by W. Strahan), 1754. 1748. 1750. Volume I second edition, volumes II and III first editions, half title in volume III, 3 volumes, 12mo., slight and even browning but good, clean copy, clean edge tear without loss to M1 volume II, faint traces of old waterstain to lower front edge, full contemporary sprinkled calf, double gilt ruled borders, raised and gilt banded spines, gilt volume numbers, slight chipping to head and tail of volume I, recent bookplate of Christopher Clark Geest.   Jarndyce Antiquarian Booksellers   CCXVI - 603   2016   £1250

Association – Geismar, Maxwell

Kent, Rockwell *Rockewll Kent's Greenland Journal.* New York: Ivan Obolensky Inc., 1962. First edition, inscribed by Kent for friend Maxwell Geismar, drawings by Kent, 8vo., green cloth, silver stamped lettering to spine, map endpapers, dust jacket, very good+ in similar jacket which has slightly sun tanned spine panel.   Tavistock Books   Getting Around - 31   2016 $750

Association – Gell

Godwin, William 1756-1836 *Things as They Are, or the Adventures of Caleb Williams.* London: printed for B. Crosby, 1794. First edition, 12mo., some spotting, early signature (largely illegible, but from the Gell family), and watercolour coat of arms on half titles, critical quotation from Monthly Review to verso volume i titlepage (partly cropped), early quarter blue roan, marbled boards, spines divided by gilt fillets and lettered direct to gilt, marbled endpapers, little bit rubbed, modern bookplate, very good.   Blackwell's Rare Books   Marks of Genius - 19   2016   £5000

Association – Gensmer, Margaret Wadsworth

Beard, Mary R. *On Understanding Women.* New York: Longmans, Green, 1931. First edition, 8vo., very good, laid in is TLS about book from author to Mrs. Margaret Wadsworth Gensmer who is thanked by Beard in prefatory note for having 'volunteered to spend in the Congressional Library at Washington DC such leisure as they could command, helping with researches".   Second Life Books, Inc.   196A - 76   2016 $275

Association – Gershwin, Ira

Hughes, Langston *The Weary Blues.* New York: Alfred A. Knopf, 1926. First edition, one of 1500 copies, small 8vo., original blue cloth backed decorated boards, inscribed by author to Ira Gershwin, covers lightly rubbed, lacking rare dust jacket, otherwise very good.   James S. Jaffe Rare Books   Occasional List: Winter 2016 - 81   2016 $35,000

Wodehouse, Pelham Grenville 1881-1975 *Plum Pie.* Herbert Jenkins, 1966. First edition, original cloth with dust jacket little sunned and with little wrinkling in original laminate and with some staining to lower panel, otherwise very good, inscribed by author for Ira Gershwin.   Sotheran's Piccadilly Notes - Summer 2015 - 12   2016   £5500

Association – Gerwing, Howard

Matrix 1-26 (with index to volumes 1-21). Whittington Press, 1980-2006. Together 27 volumes, 4to, original harlequin wrappers, profusely illustrated, near fine run, with ALS from John Randle to Howard Gerwing.   Sotheran's Piccadilly Notes - Summer 2015 - 307   2016   £3750

Association – Gibbings, Robert

Brook, George Leslie *The Language of Dickens.* London: Andre Deutsch, 1970. First edition, original blue cloth, half title, very good in slightly torn dust jacket, Robert Gibbing's signed copy.   Jarndyce Antiquarian Booksellers   CCXVIII - 1084   2016   £25

Association – Gibbs, Cecil Armstrong

De La Mare, Walter 1873-1956 *Crossings.* London: W. Collins, 1923. First edition, 8vo., with music by Cecil Armstrong Gibbs, cloth backed pictorial boards, worn leather label, signed by De La Mare with presentation by Gibbs (?) seemingly signed "Cecil".   Second Life Books, Inc.   197 - 63   2016 $125

Association – Gibson, Walter

Grant, Maxwell *The Eyes of the Shadow.* New York: Street & Smith, 1931. First edition, inscribed by author for Walter B. Gibson, front hinge cracking, else very good, attractive copy, fragile cheaply made book in pictorial papers over boards, issued without.   Buckingham Books   2015 - 6358   2016 $450

Association – Gibson, William

Nepos, Cornelius *Quae extant ex Editione Io. And. Bosil.* Amsterdam: Typis Petri Mortier, 1704. Pleasant copy of this pocket edition, ownership inscription of William Gibson dated 1746, 16mo., contemporary sprinkled calf, spine with four raised bands, red morocco lettering piece, other compartments decorated in gilt, little rubbed and much worn at extremities, slightly scratched, good.   Blackwell's Rare Books   B186 - 105   2016   £125

Association – Gifford, A.

Lister, Martin *Conchyliorum Bivalvium Utriusque Aquae Exercitatio Anatomica Tertia...* London: Sumptibus authoris impressa, 1696. 4to., 10 engraved plates, complete with terminal blank Z4 in first work, contemporary sprinkled calf, very skillfully rebacked in period style, small early shelfmark in red ink on endpaper and on title, minor paper flaw in S2 just grazing catchword, very faint foxing in fore-edge, very lovely copy with text and plates clean and fresh, armorial bookplate of A. Gifford, DD of the Museum, presentation copy inscribed by author for Mr. Dalone.   Joseph J. Felcone, Inc.   Books from Five Centuries: a Miscellany - 91   2016 $10,000

Association – Gilbert, Jack

Ginsberg, Allen *Howl and Other Poems.* San Francisco: City Lights Pocket Bookshop, 1956. First edition, one of 1000 copies printed letterpress, 12mo., original printed wrappers, printed cover label lightly soiled, otherwise fine, presentation from author to poet Jack Gilbert.   James S. Jaffe Rare Books   Occasional List: Winter 2016 - 64   2016 $15,000

Spicer, Jack *After Lorca.* San Francisco: White Rabbit Press, 1957. First edition, one of 26 lettered copies signed by Spicer with drawing by the poet, out of a total edition of 500 typed on Olivetti Lexikon 80 by Robert Duncan and multilithed by Joe Dunn, cover design by Jess, although not noted, this came from the library of poet Jack Gilbert, covers slightly soiled, otherwise very good, rare, 8vo. original wrappers.   James S. Jaffe Rare Books   Occasional List: Winter 2016 - 131   2016 $5000

Association – Gili, Jonathan

Cervantes Saavedra, Miguel De   1547-1616 *El Ingenioso Hidalgo Don Quixote de la Mancha.* Madrid: J. Ibarra, 1780. 4 volumes, 4to., additional engraved titles, map, plates and vignettes, contemporary Spanish binding of green marbled calf, covers further 'marbled' with inlaid octagonal panel of brown morocco set in gilt tooled border, spines gilt in compartments, red morocco labels, marbled endpapers, gilt edges, slight worn damage to boot of spine of volume I, head of spine of volume 4 slightly chipped, fine, armorial bookplate of Sarah Sophia Child (Villiers), Countess of Jersey (1785-1867) with old pressmarks of Osterley Park Library, bookplate of Jonathan and Phillida Gili (by Reynolds Stone), it is said about 1500 copies printed, borders of few plates foxed.   Maggs Bros. Ltd.   1474 - 23   2016   £12,500

Sallustius Crispus, C. *La Conjuracion e Catilina y la Guerra de Jugurta.* Madrid: J. Ibarra, 1772. Folio, contemporary Spanish binding of red morocco, covers decorated with gilt Greek key border having gilt suns at corners, enclosing an inner roll border of foliate design, falt spine gilt at either end with central neo-classical motif built of various tools, green morocco label, green silk doublures and marker, edges gilt, slight chip at headband, small worm holes at head and foot of spine, excellent copy, engraved titlepage by Montfort, portrait, 3 engraved plates (including a map) and numerous engravings by Montfort and Carmona after Maella, 3 engraved plates by Fabregat and Ballester and two plates of scripts, one of Phoenician coins, without half title found in most copies, bookplate of Jonathan and Phillida Gili, by Reynolds Stone.   Maggs Bros. Ltd.   1474 - 71   2016 $8500

Association – Gili, Phillida

Cervantes Saavedra, Miguel De   1547-1616 *El Ingenioso Hidalgo Don Quixote de la Mancha.* Madrid: J. Ibarra, 1780. 4 volumes, 4to., additional engraved titles, map, plates and vignettes, contemporary Spanish binding of green marbled calf, covers further 'marbled' with inlaid octagonal panel of brown morocco set in gilt tooled border, spines gilt in compartments, red morocco labels, marbled endpapers, gilt edges, slight worn damage to boot of spine of volume I, head of spine of volume 4 slightly chipped, fine, armorial bookplate of Sarah Sophia Child (Villiers), Countess of Jersey (1785-1867) with old pressmarks of Osterley Park Library, bookplate of Jonathan and Phillida Gili (by Reynolds Stone), it is said about 1500 copies printed, borders of few plates foxed.   Maggs Bros. Ltd.   1474 - 23   2016   £12,500

Sallustius Crispus, C. *La Conjuracion e Catilina y la Guerra de Jugurta.* Madrid: J. Ibarra, 1772. Folio, contemporary Spanish binding of red morocco, covers decorated with gilt Greek key border having gilt suns at corners, enclosing an inner roll border of foliate design, falt spine gilt at either end with central neo-classical motif built of various tools, green morocco label, green silk doublures and marker, edges gilt, slight chip at headband, small worm holes at head and foot of spine, excellent copy, engraved titlepage by Montfort, portrait, 3 engraved plates (including a map) and numerous engravings by Montfort and Carmona after Maella, 3 engraved plates by Fabregat and Ballester and two plates of scripts, one of Phoenician coins, without half title found in most copies, bookplate of Jonathan and Phillida Gili, by Reynolds Stone.   Maggs Bros. Ltd.   1474 - 71   2016 $8500

Association – Gill, Eric

Betjeman, John   1906-1984 *Ghastly Good Taste; or a Depressing Story of the rise and Fall of English Architecture.* London: 1933. First edition, the copy of Eric Gill.   Honey & Wax Booksellers   4 - 15   2016 $500

Pepler, Hillary Douglas Clark *The Devil's Devices..* S. Dominic's Press, 1915. First edition, 11 wood engravings by Eric Gill, foolscap 8vo., original quarter black cloth, scarlet boards, Gill engraving and lettering on front cover, all printed in black, cover rubbed, more so to rear cover, untrimmed, good, Eric Gill's bookplate.   Blackwell's Rare Books   B184 - 311   2016   £300

Association – Gill, Herbert

Bruce, William *Marriage.* London: Jemaes Spiers, 1871. Half title, printed in gold, original white cloth, bevelled boards, elaborately decorated and lettered gilt, little dulled with slight marking to lower board, gift inscription to Mr. & Mrs. Herbert Gill from Mr. and Mrs. Wilkins, March 15 (18)89.   Jarndyce Antiquarian Books   CCXV - 83   2016   £85

Association – Ginsberg, Allen

Barney, Rosset *Evergreen Review: Volume I Number 4 1957.* New York: Grove Press, 1957. First edition, general light rubbing, near fine, inscribed by Allen Ginsberg by his contribution.   Between the Covers Rare Books   208 - 32   2016 $325

Nahm, Milton C. *Selections from Early Greek Philosophy.* New York: F. S. Crofts, 1945. Second edition, fifth edition, small 8vo., original cream cloth lettered brown on spine and cover, Allen Ginsberg's copy with his name written 3 times on front endpaper.   Any Amount of Books   2015 - A71815   2016   £550

Association – Giuseppe, Canavero

Aesopus *Aesopi Phrigis et Aliorum Fabulae Quorum Nomina Sequens Pagella Indicabit.* Venice: Apud Prodoctos, 1686. Rare edition, oval woodcut vignette to titlepage, many more oval woodcuts in text, these showing light coloring in with red crayon or chalk, fables numbered in old hand, one leaf with thin area torn from fore-margin with loss to one letter each in about 10 words, another letter with horizontal closed tear (through two woodcuts with no loss), little other staining and evidence of cheap printing, 12mo. contemporary limp vellum, spine lettered in ink, ruckled, old repair to lower quarter of spine, some wear to edges, label removed, remains of red wax to front flyleaf and rear pastedown, rear flyleaf removed, otherwise inscriptions of Hieronimus Bonanomus (1686) and Canvero Giuseppe (with date 1686, but much later), sound.   Blackwell's Rare Books   Greek & Latin Classics VII - 4   2016   £1200

Association – Gladstone

Scruton, James *The Practical Counting House...* Glasgow: printed for James Duncan, 1777. 8vo., titlepage dusted and foxed, some worming ot upper margin at start of book, disappearing to single hole by page 26 ending at page 103, some pen marks against entries, other ink splashes to few pages and edge of book block, pen calculations on inner front board, without free endpapers, Fasque library bookplate of Gladstone family, full contemporary calf, raised and gilt banded spine, red morocco label, covers rubbed, some old ink marks to boards.   Jarndyce Antiquarian Booksellers   CCXVI - 512   2016   £420

Association – Gladstone, John

Heywood, B. A. *Addresses Delivered at the Meetings of the Proprietors of the Liverpool Royal Institution on the 27th February 1822 and 13 February 1824.* Liverpool: printed by Harris and Co., 1824. First edition, 4to., frontispiece woodcut on India paper laid down on blank, vignette of the seal and one plate, on India paper of the Minerva Ergane, excellently rebound in half calf, marbled boards, maroon morocco label, from the library of John Gladstone, Fasque House, very good.   Jarndyce Antiquarian Booksellers   CCXVII - 125   2016   £280

Knight, Richard Payne *An Analytical Inquiry into the Principles of Taste.* London: printed by Luke Hansard... for T. Payne, 1806. Third edition, 8vo. slight foxing, old closed tear towards foot of titlepage, contemporary half calf, marbled boards, gilt spine, boards slightly rubbed, with Fasque library bookplate of the Gladstone family, inscription "the gift of Cha. Blundell Esq. ... to John Gladstone.. 17 Nov. 1827.   Jarndyce Antiquarian Booksellers   CCXVI - 350   2016   £90

Association – Gladstone, Thomas

Adam, Francis *On Ornithology as a Branch of Liberal Education.* Aberdeen: John Smith, 1859. Few ink corrections, first ad final leaves slightly dusted and marked, vertical fold, sewn as issued, inscribed by author for Sir Thomas Gladstone.   Jarndyce Antiquarian Books   CCXV - 500   2016   £40

Association – Gladwin, Julie

Coles, Manning *Pray Silence.* London: Hodder & Stoughton Limited, 1940. First edition, inscribed by author for Julie J. Gladwin, signed by Adelaide Manning, spine slightly browned and light offsetting to front and rear endpapers, else very good in dust jacket with light restoration to spine ends, rare in jacket, rarer still inscribed by author.   Buckingham Books   2015 - 2016 $4875

Association – Glass, Sara

Wilder, Thornton 1896-1976 *The Bridge of San Luis Rey.* New York: Grosset & Dunalap, circa, 1950. Reprint, fine, dust jacket with some chips at top of front cover and along top of spine, not affecting printing of spine title, inscribed by author for Miss Sara Glass.   Second Life Books, Inc.   196B - 896   2016 $188

Association – Gleason, Joseph

Marsh, Richard Ogelsby *White Indians of Darien.* New York: Putnam's Sons, 1934. First edition, 8vo., original red buckram, lettered in black, map endpapers, frontispiece and plates after photos, very good and fresh, library card pocket removed from rear flyleaf, provenance of Monsigneur Joseph M. Gleason's pictorial engraved bookplate.   Sotheran's   Travel and Exploration - 64   2016   £198

Association – Glenconnor

Vergilius Maro, Publius *The Works of Virgil.* Birmingham: printed by John Baskerville for the author, 1766. Sole edition, 8vo., later full speckled calf by Bedford, boards with french fillet border, spine richly gilt with contrasting leather labels, joints little rubbed, spine slightly sunned, marginal dampstain to pages 529-536, bookplate of Glenconnor, otherwise very good.   Sotheran's   Piccadilly Notes - Summer 2015 - 315   2016   £500

Association – Glynn, William Anthony

More, Hannah 1745-1833 *An Estimate of the Religion of the Fashionable World.* London: T. Cadell, 1793. Fifth edition, 8vo., very slight worm damage in lower margins of prelims bound without half title but with ad leaf, contemporary tree calf, spine gilt in compartments, red label, slight rubbing, armorial bookplate of William Anthony Glynn, nice copy.   Jarndyce Antiquarian Booksellers   CCXVI - 419   2016   £65

Association – Godman, Frederick Ducane

Salt, Henry *A Voyage to Abyssinia and Travels into the Interior of that Country...* London: W. Bulmer & Co. for F. C. and J. Rivington, 1814. First edition, large paper copy in good Regency binding, large 4to., contemporary full tan calf, spine gilt in compartments and lettered in one, highly decorated in gilt, all edges gilt, 28 engraved plates, 2 engraved head and tailpieces, 6 engraved maps, 5 folding and one hand coloured in outline, illustrations in text, roman, greek and arabic types, retaining half title, only minor rubbing to extremities, expertly rebacked, some variable light spotting and browning, armorial bookplate of Frederick Ducane Godman inside front cover.   Sotheran's   Travel and Exploration - 31   2016   £2995

Association – Godson, Rufus

Mann, Tom *From Single Tax to Syndicalism.* London: Guy Bowman, 1913. 8vo., few slight smudges to title, otherwise very bright outside, half black morocco, dark grey cloth boards, gilt title to spine, edges sprinkled red, spine rubbed and worn but holding firm, corners rubbed, owner hinges reinforced with cloth tape, very good, ownership inscription of Rufus Godson.   Unsworths Antiquarian Booksellers   30 - 105   2016   £50

Association – Goldman, Robert

Bianchi, Daniel B. *Some Recollections of the Merrymount Press.* Berkeley: George I. Harding & Roger Levenson, 1978. First edition, 12mo., black cloth lettered and decorated in gilt on front cover and spine, bookplate tipped to inner cover, else fine, tipped in bookplates of book collector, Robert Goldman.   Argonaut Book Shop   Private Press 2015 - 6274   2016 $45

Association – Goldstone, Adrian

Cole, G. D. H. *Birthday Gifts & Other Stories.* London: Polybooks, 1946. First edition, Goldstone bookplate, near fine in dust jacket.   Mordida Books   2015 - 011725   2016 $65

Association – Gollancz

Meyrink, Gustav *The Golem.* London: Gollancz, 1928. First English edition, half title, original black cloth in pictorial dust jacket by Edward McKnight Kauffer, spine of dust jacket slightly dulled, Gollanz family copy.   Jarndyce Antiquarian Booksellers   CCXVII - 187   2016   £580

Association – Gondinton, A. D.

Woolnoth, William *A Graphical Illustration of the Metropolitan Cathedral Church of Canterbury.* London: T. Cadell & W. Davies and J. Murray, 1816. Large paper copy, royal 4to., 20 plates on India paper, foxing to front and rear blanks and plates, text pages generally clean barring occasional offset toning from plates, neat pencil notes to pages 92-3, early 20th century half burgundy morocco gilt title to spine, blue marbled paper boards, edges sprinkled red, endcaps, joints and corners bit worn, edges slightly chipped but very good overall, bookplate of A. D. Gondinton dated 1901, recent bookplate of Susan Wade, tiny bookbinder's label of R. Hynes, Dover, catalog description pasted in, some pencilled booksellers notes to prelim blanks, note to list of subscribers identifies this as the copy belonging to Mr. Jesse White, Canterbury.   Unsworths Antiquarian Booksellers Ltd.   30 - 165   2016   £350

Association – Gooch, Alfred Sherlock

Birkbeck, George *George Birkbeck, the Pioneer of Popular Education.* London and Derby: Bemrose and Sons, 1884. First edition, half title, frontispiece, original brown cloth, bevelled boards, marked, signature of Alfred Sherlock Gooch, April 3, 84, very good.   Jarndyce Antiquarian Books   CCXV - 534   2016   £125

Purnell, Thomas *Dust and Diamonds.* London: Ward & Downey, 1888. First edition, half title, unopened, 16 page Ward & Downey catalog Nov. 1888, original turquoise cloth, gilt, very good, armorial bookplate of Sir Alfred Sherlock Gooch.   Jarndyce Antiquarian Booksellers   CCXVII - 242   2016   £45

Association – Gooden, Stephen

Grazzini, Antonis Francesco, called Il Lasca   1503-1584 *The Story of Doctor Manente.* Florence: Orioli, 1929. First edition, 49.200 copies signed by author, printed on Binda handmade paper (of an edition of 1200), frontispiece, 2 further plates, original vellum, oval ornament stamped in red to upper board, little browning and few small foxspots to lower board, backstrip lettered in red and darkened Lawrence phoenix bookplate and Stephen Gooden, bookplate for John Raymond Danson, untrimmed, protective glassine jacket, good.   Blackwell's Rare Books   B184 - 176   2016   £350

Association – Goodman, Bill

Hercules, Frank *Where the Hummingbird Flies.* New York: Harcourt Brace, 1961. First edition, author's presentation on flyleaf for Bill Goodman, Feb. 10 1970, rust cloth, cover little soiled, but very good tight copy in scuffed and slightly chpped dust jacket, scarce first book.   Second Life Books, Inc.   196A - 777   2016 $150

Association – Goodman, Thomas

Powell, W. J. *The Zulu Rebellion of 1906.* Johannesburg: Transvaal Leader, 1906. First edition, oblong 4to., original green illustrated cloth, illustrated mainly with photographs, binding minimally spotted and rubbed, good, clean copy, neat contemporary ownership inscription Thomas Goodman from Tom, very rare.   Sotheran's   Piccadilly Notes - Summer 2015 - 246   2016   £995

Association – Goodrich, James Tait

Handyside, P. D. *Observations on the Arrested Twin Development of Jean Battista Dos Santos, Born at Faro in Portugal in 1846.* Edinburgh (and) London: Maclachlan and Stewart (and) Robert Hardwicke, 1866. First edition, octavo, later decorated wrappers, 2 rather graphic woodcuts, laid in is TNS by book dealer James Tait Goodrich sending the pamphlet to Lee Ash.   Between the Covers Rare Books   204 - 71   2016 $450

Association – Gordon, G. Maitland

Dickens, Charles   1812-1870 *Master Humphrey's Clock.* London: Chapman and Hall, 1840-1841. First edition, 3 volumes, frontispieces, illustrations, original brown cloth, boards blocked in blind with clock centerpieces, gilt spines, slight wear to hinges, otherwise good, signature of Gertrude E. Atkinson 1850 in volume 1, and initials in volumes II and III, bookplates of G. Maitland Gordon, variant marbled endpapers, cloth slipcase.   Jarndyce Antiquarian Booksellers   CCXVIII - 271   2016   £850

Association – Gordon, James

Cox, Irwin Edward Bainbridge *The Country House....* London: Horace Cox, 1883. Third edition, illustrations, slight paper flaw to upper margin of titlepage, original green cloth, front board slightly marked, ex-libris James Gordon, good.   Jarndyce Antiquarian Books   CCXV - 139   2016   £65

Association – Gordon, Ruth

Belloc Lowndes, Marie *Lizzie Border: a Study in Conjecture.* New York: Longmans, Green, 1939. First edition, inscribed by author to actor/writer Ruth Gordon, with bookplate signed by Gordon and husband Garson Kanin, included is TLS by author to Gordon, very good plus in very good dust jacket, jacket spine lightly faded, chipping to edges and light creasing, letter with horizontal fold, near fine overall.   Royal Books   52 - 9   2016 $2500

Kanin, Garson *Hollywood.* New York: Viking Press, 1974. First edition, 8vo., inscribed by author to wife Ruth Gordon, with notations by Gordon, a working copy. Second Life Books, Inc.   196A - 906   2016 $75

Association – Gorset, Mary

Timbs, John *School-Days of Eminent Men.* London: Kent & Co., 1858. Frontispiece and plates, slight spotting, original purple cloth, spine faded and little rubbed, contemporary signature of Mary Gorset.   Jarndyce Antiquarian Books   CCXV - 70   2016   £20

Association – Gosling, E. T.

Cicero, Marcus Tullius *Three Books Touching the Nature of the Gods.* London: printed for Joseph Hindmarsh, 1683. 12mo., publisher'ds ads to first leaf, edges neatly repaired, little toned, occasional spotting, leaves a7 and 19 grubby at fore edge with few small holes not affecting text, paper flaw to fore-edge margin leaf c2 resulting in small area of loss but not affecting text, contemporary dark brown calf neatly rebacked, raised bands, morocco gilt spine label, blind tooling to boards, edges sprinkled red, rubbed, corners repaired, front endpapers renewed, lower hinge neatly repaired, overall very good, indecipherable ownership inscription and another of Ed. Th. Gosling, Stockwell (?) 1884.   Unsworths Antiquarian Booksellers   30 - 33   2016   £275

Association – Gough, Miss

Moore, George 1852-1933 *Mike Fletcher: a Novel.* London: Ward and Downey, 1889. First edition, probable second state with leaf of press notices for Moore's novels, with tipped in two-page letter from Moore to his secretary, Miss Gough on administrative matters, blue cloth boards with gilt title to spine, orange patterned decoration to spine and front board, minor wear to edges and corners, bookplate of John Stuart Groves, clean interior and tight binding, housed in turquoise half morocco slipcase, very good plus. The Kelmscott Bookshop   12 - 71   2016 $225

Association – Gouldsmith, Jesse

Taylor, Isaac *Home Education.* London: Jackson & Walford, 1838. Third thousand, original purple brown cloth, spine slightly faded and rubbed at head, nice, inscription "Presented to Jesse Gouldsmith Esqre by author January 1839", followed by further inscription from Gouldsmith to his daughter 1840.   Jarndyce Antiquarian Books   CCXV - 981   2016   £75

Association – Goulliard, Pierre

Lewandowski, Ranier *Die Filme von Volker Schlondorff.* Hildesham: Olma Presse, 1981. First edition, trade softcover original, inscribed by Volker Schlondorff for Pierre Goulliard, near fine, profusely illustrated with photos, stiff perfect bound wrappers, fine, 8.5 x 9.5 inches.   Royal Books   49 - 24   2016 $1250

Association – Goux-Stern

Du Breul, Jacques *Le Theatre des Antiquitez de Paris.* Paris: Claude de La Tour, 1612. First edition, 4to., late 17th century full calf, spine with raised bands, ornamented and lettered in gilt, edges sprinkled in red, woodcut coat of arms on title, 111 engravings in text, few almost full page, wear to corners, head and tail of spines and hinges, lower cover with few small wormholes, even light toning, handful of leaves with inoffensive ink spots, single wormhole from page 1193 to end, good and clean, Portugese bookseller's label and bookplate of Paris collector Goux-Stern.   Sotheran's Travel and Exploration - 237   2016   £1350

Association – Govi, Gilbert

Cherubin D'Orleans, Francois Lasseri *La Vision Parfaite; ou la Concourt des Dens Asssxis de la Vision et un Seul Poin le O'ject.* Paris: Chez Sebastien Mabre Cramoisy Imprimeur du Roy, 1677. First edition in French, 4 parts in one, folio, large engraved allegorical frontispiece, title vignette, 16 engraved plates, contemporary full calf, gilt spine titles, extremities worn, joints repaired, titlepage with signature of Gilbert Govi, 1854, bookseller's description tipped in, possibly that of Henry Sotheran, rare.   Jeff Weber Rare Books   183 - 12   2016 $8000

Association – Grable, Betty

Parsons, Louella *The Gay Illiterate.* Garden City: Doubleday Doran, 1944. First edition, fine in price clipped, very good dust jacket with slight loss at crown, inscribed by Parson for Betty Grable and husband Harry James. Between the Covers Rare Books   204 - 51   2016 $650

Association – Graham

Taylor, John 1580-1653 *Cornucopia or Roome for a Ram-head.* London: by John Reynolds, 1642. First edition, small 4to., crude woodcut, each leaf inlaid, first letter of title just shaved, very light staining near inner margin of title, some minor browning throughout, text lightly inked in lower corner of A24 (yet still legible), early 19th century half black morocco and drab boards, spine worn, upper headcap torn away and corners bumped, text coming loose, from the library of James Stevens Cox (1910-1997), old pencil foliation, armorial bookplate of Graham of Gartmore, Perthshire.   Maggs Bros. Ltd.   1447 - 410   2016   £1250

Association – Graham, Robert Maxtone

Vergilius Maro, Publius *Virgils Aeneis.* Edinburgh: printed by Mr. Andrew Symson and MR. Robert Freebairns and sold at their Shops, 1710. First Ruddman edition, title within double ruled border, occasional foxing or browning (less than usual), some waterstaining at end, mainly marginal diminishing and not extending much beyond index, little, but lesser, staining at beginning, folio, contemporary panelled calf, some wear, cracks at extremities of joints, ownership of Thomas Graham, fourth Laird of Balgowan, modern bookplate of Robert Maxtone Graham.   Blackwell's Rare Books   B184 - 35   2016   £650

Association – Graham, Thomas

Vergilius Maro, Publius *Virgils Aeneis.* Edinburgh: printed by Mr. Andrew Symson and MR. Robert Freebairns and sold at their Shops, 1710. First Ruddman edition, title within double ruled border, occasional foxing or browning (less than usual), some waterstaining at end, mainly marginal diminishing and not extending much beyond index, little, but lesser, staining at beginning, folio, contemporary panelled calf, some wear, cracks at extremities of joints, ownership of Thomas Graham, fourth Laird of Balgowan, modern bookplate of Robert Maxtone Graham.   Blackwell's Rare Books   B184 - 35   2016   £650

Association – Grams, Alfred

Joyce, Patrick Weston *A Hand-Book of School Management and Methods of teaching.* Dublin: M. H. Gill & Son, 1879. Sixth edition, illustrations, original purple cloth, unevenly faded, presentation from author for Alfred P. Grams.   Jarndyce Antiquarian Books   CCXV - 799   2016   £48

Association – Grant, A.

Chapone, Hester *The Works of.* Edinburgh: James Ballantyne & Co., 1807. Some occasional marking and creasing, contemporary full calf, gilt spine, black morocco label, slightly rubbed, inscribed 'From A. Grant to Jane Grant... May 14th 1809'.   Jarndyce Antiquarian Books   CCXV - 107   2016   £60

Association – Grant, Jane

Chapone, Hester *The Works of.* Edinburgh: James Ballantyne & Co., 1807. Some occasional marking and creasing, contemporary full calf, gilt spine, black morocco label, slightly rubbed, inscribed 'From A. Grant to Jane Grant... May 14th 1809'.   Jarndyce Antiquarian Books   CCXV - 107   2016   £60

Association – Gration-Maxfield, Brent

Bunny, Edmund *Of Divorce for Adutlerie and Marrying Againe...* Oxford: Joseph Barnes, 1610. Folindg table, frontispiece, inoffensive staining from **1 to A4 including folding table, foremargin of last 2 leaves trimmed, with minor loss, 20th century full panelled calf, raised bands, spine lettered gilt, some slight rubbing to hinges and extremities, pencil notes on initial inserted blank of the collector Brent Gration-Maxfield.   Jarndyce Antiquarian Booksellers   CCXVII - 58   2016   £3200

Association – Graux, Lucien

Erasmus, Desiderius 1466-1536 *Moriae Encomium Erasmi Roterodami Declamatio....* Paris: Jehan Lalyseau, 1514. 4to., 19th century morocco backed marbled boards, Lalyseau's fine device on titlepage, one large and one small crible initial, extremely rare early Paris edition, 19th century monogramed stamp on flyleaf, Docteur Lucien Graux (1878-1944) with his red label.   Maggs Bros. Ltd.   1474 - 31   2016   £12,500

Association – Graves, Algernon

Blessington, Marguerite Power Farmer Gardiner, Countess of 1789-1849 *The Keepsake for 1844.* London: Longmans, 1844. Engraved frontispiece and title plates, original maroon cloth, attractively blocked in blind and gilt, rebacked, little darkened and rubbed, signature of Kate Barber 1844, armorial bookplates of Algernon Graves, Renier booklabel.   Jarndyce Antiquarian Booksellers   CCXVIII - 430   2016   £120

Association – Graves, R. P.

Clough, Arthur Hugh *Poems.* Cambridge: Macmillan, 1862. First collected edition, 8vo., original green honeycomb cloth, gilt, minor wear to extremities, good, inscribed by author for Revd. R. P. Graves.   Blackwell's Rare Books   B186 - 43   2016   £375

Association – Gray, Cynthia

Quarles, Benjamin *Black History's Diversified Clientele: a Lecture at Howard University.* Washington: Dept. of History, Howard University, 1971. First edition, blue cloth boards, gilt, fine, issued without dust jacket. inscribed by historian Rayford Logan to Cynthia Gray in year of publication, very scarce. Between the Covers Rare Books 202 - 81 2016 $650

Association – Gray, Denis

Bradley, Rose M. *The English Housewife in the Seventeenth & Eighteenth Centuries.* London: Edward Arnold, 1912. Half title, frontispiece, 7 plates, 8 page catalog, slight spotting, original decorated red cloth, spine and back board faded, otherwise very good, bright, presentation copy stamp on titlepage, bookplate of Denis Gray, inserted is ALS recording book as a gift from Frances Lane, Bristol. Jarndyce Antiquarian Books CCXV - 78 2016 £45

Association – Gray, Donald

Kapham, Mortimer *Dickens Children Stories.* Chicago & New York: Donohue, 1929. 4to., illustrations by Ella Dolbear, color frontispiece and plates, original olive green cloth, lettered gilt, front board with rubbed color onlay, bookplate of Donald S. Gray, this copy inscribed by author. Jarndyce Antiquarian Booksellers CCXVIII - 744 2016 £30

Association – Gray, Mary

Dickens, Charles 1812-1870 *A Christmas Carol.* London: Chapman & Hall, 1843. Second edition, half title and title in blue, hand colored frontispiece and 3 color plates, text woodcuts, final ad leaf, pale yellow endpapers, original salmon pink vertical fine ribbed cloth, boards blocked with borders in blind, front board and spine decorated and lettered gilt, tiny ink spot on following board, very slight wear to corners and head and tail of spine, signature of Mary Gray 1843, all edges gilt, good plus. Jarndyce Antiquarian Booksellers CCXVIII - 331 2016 £1500

Association – Greaves, John

Fridlender, Y. V. *Charles Dickens: Bibliografia...* Moskva: Pub. House of All-Union Palace of Books, 1962. First edition, frontispiece, original paper covered stiff boards, cloth spine, little rubbed, good plus, presentation from co-author I. Katarskii, to Sir John Greaves. Jarndyce Antiquarian Booksellers CCXVIII - 1499 2016 £25

Association – Green, Joseph

Sewall, Joseph *A Sermon Preached at the Thursday-Lecture in Boston, September 16, 1761 Before the Great and General Court... on the Joyful news of the Reduction ...* Boston: by John Draper and by Edes and Gil, 1762. Stitched and untrimmed, stitching breaking, else very good, contemporary signature of Jos. Green, chemise and cloth slipcase. Joseph J. Felcone, Inc. Books from Five Centuries: a Miscellany - 53 2016 $550

Association – Greenaway, Kate

Ruskin, John 1819-1900 *Dame Wiggins of Lee and Her Seven Wonderful Cats.* Sunnyside, Orpington, Kent: George Allen, 1885. Large paper copy from a later edition, inscribed by the artist, Kate Greenaway for F. Locker-Lampson, 1886, illustrations by Greenaway, original brown cloth with gilt title and illustration on front cover, binding rubbed and bumped, with few light stains, interior pages are generally clean, this copy has a plate of Bert M. Barwis Fund of Trenton Public Library stating the book was a personal gift to the library from Miss Barwis, she was the Supervisor of Kindergartens and Primary Schools for the City of Trenton NJ, call number written in white ink on spine and library ownership indicated by stamp to titlepage, despite flaws, still very nice, desirable copy. The Kelmscott Bookshop 12 - 48 2016 $400

Association – Greene, Graham

Connell, Mary *Help is on the Way (Poems).* Reinhardt, 1896. First edition, line drawings by author, crown 8vo., original light blue card wrappers printed in black, red and white, fine, inscribed by Graham Greene for love of his life Yvonne Cloetta. Blackwell's Rare Books B186 - 223 2016 £800

Association – Greene, Joseph

Lindley, John 1799-1865 *Pomologia Britannica; or Figures and Descriptions of the Most Important Varieties of Fruit Cultivated in Great Britain.* London: Henry G. Bohn, 1841. First edition, 3 volumes, 245 x 150mm, contemporary green half morocco with marbled boards, spine gilt with fruit motifs, raised bands, red and brown morocco labels, gilt edges, 152 beautiful hand colored plates, bookplate of Joseph Greene and that of Sir Thomas Neame, edges and joints, bit rubbed, covers little scuffed, couple of minor marginal stains and occasional foxing, mostly on paper guards and very rarely affecting leaves with text, otherwise all plates fine, with particularly bright colors. Phillip J. Pirages 67 - 242 2016 $15,000

Association – Greene, Nancy

Penzer, Norman *The Most Noble and Famous Travels of Marco Polo, Together with the Travels of Nicolo de Conti.* London: Argonaut Press, 1937. First edition thus, quarto, one of 1050 numbered copies, color frontispiece, titlepage vignette by William Monk, several maps, one of which is folding, original binding of quarter vellum backed with yellow buckram sides, armorial shield on upper cover, printed on Japon vellum, presentation copy from editor Norman Penzer May 28th 1934 for Nancy and Wilfred Greene, armorial bookplate of recipient, bookplate, edges bit spotted, very good.   Peter Ellis   112 - 247   2016   £175

Association – Greene, Wilfred

Penzer, Norman *The Most Noble and Famous Travels of Marco Polo, Together with the Travels of Nicolo de Conti.* London: Argonaut Press, 1937. First edition thus, quarto, one of 1050 numbered copies, color frontispiece, titlepage vignette by William Monk, several maps, one of which is folding, original binding of quarter vellum backed with yellow buckram sides, armorial shield on upper cover, printed on Japon vellum, presentation copy from editor Norman Penzer May 28th 1934 for Nancy and Wilfred Greene, armorial bookplate of recipient, bookplate, edges bit spotted, very good.   Peter Ellis   112 - 247   2016   £175

Association – Greenshields, J. Blackwood

Cervantes Saavedra, Miguel De   1547-1616 *The Life and Exploits of the Ingenious Gentleman Don Quixote de la Mancha.* London: printed for J. and R. Tonson, 1749. Second edition, 2 volumes, engraved frontispiece, 23 engraved plates, 8vo., some light browning, blank upper corners volume I G5-6 torn away, contemporary calf, gilt ruled borders, expertly rebacked in matching style, raised and gilt banded spines, red morocco labels, armorial bookplate of John Hallifax, Esq., Kenilworth on inner front boards, 19th century bookplate of J. Blackwood Greenshields on front endpapers.   Jarndyce Antiquarian Booksellers   CCXVII - 66   2016   £1500

Association – Greenwood, C. J.

Rickwood, Edgell *Invocations to Angels and The Happy New Year.* Wishart, 1928. First edition, foolscap 8vo., original quarter black cloth with patterned paper boards, just little rubbed to edges, edges rough trimmed, dust jacket, very good, inscribed by author to C. J. Greenwood.   Blackwell's Rare Books   B186 - 277   2016   £275

Association – Greenwood, L. W.

Terentius Afer, Publius *Comediae.* Birmingham: Typis Johannis Baskerville, 1772. 4to., titlepage toned, little minor spotting, elsewhere, slightly later half red morocco, marbled boards, spine divided by gilt rolls, second compartment gilt lettered direct, rest with central oval or fountain & bird tools, marbled endpapers, spine somewhat faded, slight rubbing to extremities, bookplates of L. W. Greenwood and Lytton Strachey, very good.   Blackwell's Rare Books   Greek & Latin Classics VII - 89   2016   £300

Association – Gregor, G. W. F.

Monck, Mary *Marinda. Poems and Translations Upon Several Occasions.* London: printed by J. Tonson, 1716. First edition, very good, 8vo., contemporary calf, gilt, rebacked, very good, early signatures of John Brace (crossed out) and Elizabeth Lovell, later bookplates of G. W. F. Gregor and Oliver Brett, Viscount Esher.   C. R. Johnson Rare Book Collections   Foxon: H-P 2015 - 617   2016 $2298

Association – Gregory, John

Marriott, Joseph *Prosaic Effusions or Essays on Various Subjects and Miscellaneous observations.* Whitchurch: printed and sold by R. B. Jones, circa, 1829? Index, errata leaf, uncut in original blue boards, drab paper spine & label, hinges weakening, early ownership stamp of John Gregory with his signatue.   Jarndyce Antiquarian Booksellers   CCXVII - 181   2016   £120

Association – Greive, Mary

Fry, Caroline *The Assistant of Education; Religious and Literary.* London: published for the author by T. Baker, 1823-1824. 2 volumes, 12mo., plates, some light spotting, contemporary half brown calf, little dulled with some slight wear to leading hinge of volume I, inscription on leading blank for Aubrey Lum from sister Mary Greive 2nd July 1869, nice.   Jarndyce Antiquarian Books   CCXV - 695   2016   £75

Association – Grenville, Baron

Juvenalis, Decimus Junius *Satyrae.* Cambridge: Prostant Venales Londini apud Gul. Sandby, 1763. 8vo., 15 engraved plates (including frontispiece), light spotting, contemporary mid-brown calf, boards bordered with gilt roll, gilt in compartments, lettering piece in second compartment (rather chipped), boards with later Chancellor's Prize stamp in blind (i.e. arms of Baron Grenville, as chancellor of Oxford), marbled endpapers, extremities rubbed, head of spine chipped, front joint cracking but strong, armorial bookplate of Revd Charles Lyttelton, good.   Blackwell's Rare Books   Greek & Latin Classics VII - 54   2016   £250

Association – Grenville, Thomas

Homerus *Ilias kai Odysseia.* Oxonia: ex Ergasteriou Typographikou Akademias, 1800. One of the rare and spectacular copies of the Grenville Homer, only 25 copies printed and used as presentation copies, inscribed by editors, William Wyndham, Lord Grenville and his brother Thomas Grenville, 4to., 5 engraved plates, plates spotted, some light offsetting to text, contemporary red morocco, boards with central gilt stamp, arms of the Earl of Cawdor, spines lettered gilt, red morocco doublures with border of fourteen gilt fillets, edges gilt on rough, spines sunned, touch of rubbing to extremities, doublures offset onto endpapers and outermost leaves of each volume, very good. Blackwell's Rare Books   Greek & Latin Classics VII - 37   2016   £12,000

Association – Grenville, William Wyndham

Homerus *Ilias kai Odysseia.* Oxonia: ex Ergasteriou Typographikou Akademias, 1800. One of the rare and spectacular copies of the Grenville Homer, only 25 copies printed and used as presentation copies, inscribed by editors, William Wyndham, Lord Grenville and his brother Thomas Grenville, 4to., 5 engraved plates, plates spotted, some light offsetting to text, contemporary red morocco, boards with central gilt stamp, arms of the Earl of Cawdor, spines lettered gilt, red morocco doublures with border of fourteen gilt fillets, edges gilt on rough, spines unned, touch of rubbing to extremities, doublures offset onto endpapers and outermost leaves of each volume, very good. Blackwell's Rare Books   Greek & Latin Classics VII - 37   2016   £12,000

Association – Grey, Baron

Laconics or New Maxims of State and Conversation. printed for Thomas Hodges..., 1701. 8vo., nice, clean copy, contemporary panelled calf, red morocco label, rebacked retaining original spine, armorial bookplate of William Lord North of Carthlage and Baron Grey of Rolleston 1703. Jarndyce Antiquarian Books   CCXV - 205   2016   £250

Association – Grey, Elizabeth

Corbet, John *Self Employment in Secret.* Hull: printed by J. Ferraby, 1795. New edition, 12mo., contemporary full dark blue calf, gilt bands, compartments gilt, two original brass clasps, slightly rubbed, contemporary signature of Elizabeth Grey, all edges gilt, very good, attractive. Jarndyce Antiquarian Books   CCXV - 134   2016   £225

Association – Gribbel, John

Bible. English - 1929 *The Apocrypha.* London: Cresset Press, 1929. No. XXX of 30 large paper copies on handmade paper and 450 copies on mould made paper, with additional suite of plates, each signed by artist, 350 x 227mm., publisher's black stiff vellum by Wood (stamp signed), flat spine with gilt titling, yapp edges, top edge gilt, other edges untrimmed, housed with (slightly scuffed) portfolio of plates in later black slipcase, 14 woodcuts, each by different artist, with additional suite of the plates printed on Japanese paper and signed by artist responsible for each, (original?) tissue guards in volume, with two of the original wood blocks for the engravings by Eric Jones and Wladislaw Skoczylas, remains of bookplate, prospectus laid in, spine lightly and uniformly faded, slivers of the binding's black dye faintly worn away along portions of joints and edges (and dye very carefully renewed in few small places, otherwise extremely fine, binding essentially unworn and not splayed, text immaculate, from the collection of John Gribbel (1858-1936) and was lot 217 in the 30 Oct. 1940 sale of his collection at Parke-Bernet.   Phillip J. Pirages   67 - 100   2016 $6500

Association – Griffin, Lepel H.

Burnet, Gilbert, Bp. of Salisbury 1643-1715 *Bishop Burnet's History of His Own Time.* Oxford: Clarendon Press, 1823. First edition, 8vo., 6 volumes, full brown with gilt decorated spine and five raised bands, top hinge slightly tender on first volume, occasional slight marks to leather, slight rubbing but handsome set with frontispiece portrait, armorial bookplate of Lepel H. Griffin, Glenthorne.   Any Amount of Books   2015 - A82541   2016   £250

Association – Griffiths, Joseph

Robeson, Paul *Here I Stand.* London: Dennis Dobson, 1958. first UK edition, octavo, spine just little faded, free endpapers partially tanned, front free endpaper little creased, very good in like dust jacket, little nicked and rubbed at edges, presentation inscribed by author to Joseph Griffiths.   Peter Ellis   112 - 333   2016   £350

Association – Grist, William

Kitton, Frederic George *Dickensiana: a Bibliography of the Literature Relating to Charles Dickens and His Writings.* London: George Redway, 1886. First edition, only 500 copies printed, half title, title, frontispiece, 24 page catalog (1886), untrimmed in original fine grained green cloth by Westleys, spine lettered gilt, leading inner hinge cracking, booklabel of William Grist, good plus.   Jarndyce Antiquarian Booksellers   CCXVIII - 1329   2016   £75

Association – Grobosky, Louis

Milne, Alan Alexander 1882-1956 *The House at Pooh Corner.* London: Methuen & Co., 1928. First edition, one of 350 numbered copies printed on handmade paper, signed by author and artist, presentation copy inscribed by author to Louis Grobosky on titlepage, with his small bookplate, small quarto, text illustrations, original quarter blue cloth over cream colored boards, printed paper label on front cover, rare bottom right corner bumped with professional repair, some foxing to covers, dust jacket with repairs to verso folds, very good, housed in custom blue cloth chemise and quarter blue morocco slipcase, gilt stamped.   Heritage Book Shop   Holiday 2015 - 81   2016 $6500

Association – Groom, Amy

Fenning, Daniel *The Young Man's Book of Knowledge.* London: printed for S. Crowder, 1793. Fifth edition, frontispiece and plates, but lacking final music plate, 12mo., contemporary full calf, neat repair to hinges, 19th century inscription on recto of front of Amy Groom.   Jarndyce Antiquarian Books   CCXV - 196   2016   £120

Association – Groom, William

Udall, John *A Demonstration of the Trueth of the Discipline which Christe Hath Prescribed in His Worde for the Gouernment of His Church, in all Times and Places....* East Molesey: R. Waldegrave, 1588. First edition, folding table, titlepage and blank verso of last leaf dust soiled, C4 frayed in fore margin, small 8vo., 17th century calf, panelled in gilt and blind, with central medallion in gilt, rebacked preserving original spine, 18th century ownership inscription of William Groom below errata and also on front free endpaper, that of John Stretton on following flyleaf, good.   Blackwell's Rare Books   B184 - 87   2016   £5000

Association – Grossman, Edith

Garcia Marquez, Gabriel *Love in the time of Cholera.* New York: Alfred A. Knopf, 1988. First American edition, inscribed by translator, Edith Grossman, black cloth lettered gilt, with postcard from publisher's laid in, dust jacket, beautiful copy.   B & B Rare Books, Ltd.   2016 - GGM044   2016 $200

Association – Grove, Thelma

Ackroyd, Peter *Dickens' London an Imaginative Vision...* London: Guild Publishing, 1987. First edition, half title, illustrations, original white cloth, booklabel, very good in price clipped dust jacket, photos, signed presentation inscription from author for Thelma Grove.   Jarndyce Antiquarian Booksellers   CCXVIII - 1051   2016   £20

Allen, Michael *Charles Dickens' Childhood.* London: Macmillan, 1988. First edition, half title, plates, maps, original brown cloth, Thelma Grove booklabel, very good in slightly faded dust jacket, signed by author.   Jarndyce Antiquarian Booksellers   CCXVIII - 1059   2016   £25

Morgenstaler, Goldie *Dickens and Heredity...* London: Macmillan Press, 2000. Inscribed by author to Thelma Grove and with some loosely inserted correspondence, half title, original black cloth, very good in dust jacket.   Jarndyce Antiquarian Booksellers   CCXVIII - 1386   2016   £30

Philip, Neil *Charles Dickens: a December Vision.* London: Collins, 1986. First edition, 8vo., half title, vignette title, illustrations in black and white, original green cloth, booklabel of Thelma Grove, very good in price clipped dust jacket.   Jarndyce Antiquarian Booksellers   CCXVIII - 1412   2016   £20

Slater, Michael *Dickens on America & the Americans.* London: Harvester Press, 1979. First edition, half title, illustrations, maps on endpapers, original bright blue cloth, very good in slightly worn dust jacket, presentation inscription from author for Thelma Grove.   Jarndyce Antiquarian Booksellers   CCXVIII - 1444   2016   £22

Association – Grove, Thomas

Metz, Nancy Ayrcock *The Companion to Martin Chuzzlewit.* London: Helm Information, 2001. First edition, half title, illustrations, maps, original dark green cloth, booklabel of Thomas Grove, mint in dust jacket.   Jarndyce Antiquarian Booksellers   CCXVIII - 429   2016   £35

Association – Groves, John Stuart

Moore, George 1852-1933 *Mike Fletcher: a Novel.* London: Ward and Downey, 1889. First edition, probable second state with leaf of press notices for Moore's novels, with tipped in two-page letter from Moore to his secretary, Miss Gough on administrative matters, blue cloth boards with gilt title to spine, orange patterned decoration to spine and front board, minor wear to edges and corners, bookplate of John Stuart Groves, clean interior and tight binding, housed in turquoise half morocco slipcase, very good plus.   The Kelmscott Bookshop   12 - 71   2016 $225

Association – Groves, Joseph

Wilde, Oscar 1854-1900 *A Woman of No Importance.* London: John Lane at Sign of the Bodley Head, 1894. First edition, one of 500 copies, book near fine with spine faded, otherwise very nice, after the first four leaves, book entirely unopened at top edge, bookplate of Joseph Groves and short inscription from actor Vincent Price.   Heritage Book Shop   Holiday 2015 - 115   2016 $2000

Association – Guild, James Wyllie

L'Innocence de la Tresillustre. Tres-chaste, et Debonnaire Princesse, Madame Marie Royne d'Escosse. n.p. Iprime an, 1572. 8vo., signature O omitted in make up, text complete, all pages faintly rubricated, very nice, bound by Bedford in dark blue morocco gilt, dentelles, marbled endpapers, all edges gilt, ownership signature of A. Elphinston(e) on titlepage with dated in lower margin 1600, later armorial bookplate of James Wyllie Guild and Thomas Brooke, FSA, Armitage Bridge, ownership inscription Alexander W. Ruthven Stuart 1923.   Jarndyce Antiquarian Booksellers   CCXVII - 182   2016   £1500

Association – Guildford, Earl of

Lucanus, Marcus Annaeus *Pharsalia.* Twiceknham: Strawberry Hill, 1760. 4to., engraved vignette on titlepage and dedication, prelims in first state, some light spotting, contemporary calf, rebacked and recornered in slightly different shade, preserving original lettering piece, spine gilt in compartments, marbled endpapers preserved, old leather scratched, bookplate of Earl of Guildford to front pastedown, good.   Blackwell's Rare Books   Greek & Latin Classics VII - 57   2016   £500

Association – Guillebaud, Henry Lea

Dickens, Charles   1812-1870   *A Tale of Two Cities.* London: Chapman & Hall, 1859. First edition, 2nd issue, frontispiece, engraved title, plates by Phiz, uncut, original red cloth, blocked in blind, spine lettered gilt, expertly recased with small repairs to head and tail of spine, odd spot, bookplate of Henry Lea Guillebaud, good plus, scarce in original cloth.   Jarndyce Antiquarian Booksellers   CCXVIII - 561   2016   £1500

Association – Guitet

Caventou, Joseph Bienaime   *Nouvelle Nomenclature Chimique d'Apres la Classification Adoptee par M. Thenard...*   Paris: Chez Crochard and Chez Gabon, 1816. First edition, 8vo., half title, vignette, large folding table, index, 1 leaf of errata, quarter calf, paste paper over boards, parchment corners, red leather spine label, ornately gilt spine, rubbed, ownership rubberstamp of Guitet, Pharmacien, very good.   Jeff Weber Rare Books   183 - 11   2016 $750

Association – Gummer, Robert

Watts, Isaac   *The Impeachment of the Mind or a Supplement to the Art of Logic...*   Norwich: John Stacy, 1822. Half title, contemporary prize binding of full light brown calf, blocked in gilt and blind, black morocco reward label, spine in gilt, maroon morocco labels, slight wear to lower end of following hinge, slightly rubbed and faded, nice, attractive copy, bookseller's ticket of J. Stacy Norwich, contemporary signature of Robert Gummer.   Jarndyce Antiquarian Books   CCXV - 1000   2016   £95

Association – Gunkle, William

Burke, B. W.   *A Compendium of the Anatomy, Physiology and Pathology of the Horse.*   Philadelphia: James Humphreys, 1806. First American edition, 2 plates, 12mo., contemporary mottled sheep, plates moderately foxed, upper spine cap partly chipped, small chip from spine label, else very attractive in handsome period binding, ownership signature of Wm. Gunkle, 1818.   Joseph J. Felcone, Inc.   Books from Five Centuries: a Miscellany - 31   2016 $1000

Association – Gunn, Samuel McCraw

United States. Continental Congress - 1776   *Journals of Congress. Containing the Proceedings in the Year 1776.* Philadelphia: R. Aitken, 1777. First edition, modern full mottled sheepskin, superbly executed in exact facsimile of original binding, spine with red morocco title label and '1776' tooled in black oval onlay, some internal dampstaining and browning, particularly toward end of text, else very handsome volume, with signature of Samuel McCraw Gunn dated 1822, enclosed in four flap chemise and morocco backed slipcase.   Joseph J. Felcone, Inc.   Books from Five Centuries: a Miscellany - 144   2016 $20,000

Association – Guthrie, Robin

Eckert, Robert P.   *Edward Thomas. A Biography and a Bibliography.*   London: J. M. Dent, 1937. First edition, frontispiece, 9 further plates, few foxspots to prelims and index, 8vo., original green cloth, backstrip lettered gilt against brown ground with tiny amount of wear to tips of lower joint, little spotting around head of cloth and at foot of upper board, some surface wear to tips of lower joint, little spotting around head of cloth and at foot of upper board, some surface grazing and corners a touch bumped, top edge green, few spots to endpapers and two ownership inscriptions, dust jacket frayed with light soiling and some loss at backstrip ends, good, this the copy of Robin Guthrie, artist-son of James Guthrie of Pear Tree press with his ownership inscription dated 1942.   Blackwell's Rare Books   B186 - 286   2016   £135

Association – Guthrie, Stuart

Guthrie, James *The Elf.* Pear Tree Press, printed at the Old Bourne Press, 1903. One of 250 numbered copies, this unnumbered, Autumn number, titlepage with elaborate woodcut border printed in terra cotta, frontispiece and 6 further full page wood engravings, with one printed in terra cotta and one with tissue guard, 3 pages with decorative borders in terracotta small 4to., original quarter beige cloth, blue board with floral design printed in terra cotta, printed label to upper board, small amount of wear to corners and some light dust soiling, edges untrimmed, endpapers with repeated wood engraved illustrations, good, inscribed by James Guthrie for Stuart Guthrie. Blackwell's Rare Books B186 - 325   2016   £450

Association – Guy, Buddy

Wilcock, Donald E. *Damn Right I've got the blues...* San Francisco: Woodford, 1993. first printing, 8vo., signed by Wilcock and Buddy Guy, Copiously illustrated with photos, paper wrappers, cover slightly scuffed, otherwise very good, tight copy. Second Life Books, Inc. 196 B - 887   2016 $150

Association – Gwilt, Joseph

Poleni, Giovanni *Memorie Istoriche Della gran Cupola Del Tempio Vaticano...* Padova: Nella Stamperia dei Seminario, 1748. Folio, five books in one volume, contemporary quarter calf over patterned paper covered boards, brown morocco and gilt lettering piece to spine, all edges speckled red, folding etched plates, binding rather rubbed at extremities, corners bumped some loss of paper covering boards, internally bright, crisp copy, ink signature of John Lewis Wolfe, engraved armorial bookplate of Joseph Gwilt (1784-1863), engraved bookplate of Sir Albert Richardson (1880-1964). Sotheran's Piccadilly Notes - Summer 2015 - 239   2016   £3955

Association – Habert de Montmort, H. L..

Silius, Italicus *De Secundo Bello Punico.* Amsterdam: G. Jansson, 1620. Engraved titlepage, ruled in red, 16mo., exquisite binding by Mace Ruette, contemporary gilt tooled red morocco, covers framed by outer double fillet, central panel of strait and curved double fillets with small vase of flowers tool at each outer corner in centre of covers a quadrilobe inlay with monogram of H. L. Habert de Montmort and four "S" forms with elaborate pontille sprays of spirals, circles and dots on all four sides, spine with five raised bands, decorated in compartments, inner edges gilt, marbled endpapers, gilt edges, headcaps and joints lightly rubbed, the copy of Habert de Montmort (1600-1679), Colonel Thomas Stanley (1749-1818), William Beckford with his bookseller George Clarke's pencil collation mark, Hamilton Palace Library sale, Thore Virgin inscription dated 1916 with his book label (1886-1957). Maggs Bros. Ltd. 1474 - 72   2016   £2500

Association – Habgood, R.

Heyrick, Thomas *Miscellany Poems.* Cambridge: by John Hayes for the author, 1691. First edition, very scarce, woodcut alma mater device on title, late 19th century half morocco (hinges lightly scuffed), some foxing and light browning, chiefly on first and last few pages and largely confined to margins, small piece torn from upper corner of titlepage, short marginal tear on K1, signature of Rd. Habgood 1774. Joseph J. Felcone, Inc.   Books from Five Centuries: a Miscellany - 78   2016 $3000

Association – Haddington, Earl of

Penn, Granville *Remarks Preparatory to the Issue of the Reserved Negotiation for Peace.* London: printed by James Bateson for T. Beckett, Pall Mall, 1797. 8vo., presentation inscription to Earl of Haddington from his father the author, very good, clean copy, disbound. Jarndyce Antiquarian Booksellers   CCXVI - 444   2016   £75

Association – Hader, Berta

Williamson, Hamilton *Baby Bear.* New York: Doubleday Doran & Co., 1930. Stated first edition, 8vo., pictorial boards, spine bottom chipped, half split at joint, slightly dusty, really very good+ in dust jacket with several pieces off, worn at folds, striking color and black and white lithographs by the Haders, full page watercolor, inscribed by the Haders. Aleph-bet Books, Inc. 111 - 209   2016 $1000

Association – Hader, Elmer

Hader, Berta *Jamaica Johnny.* New York: Macmillan, Oct., 1935. First edition, 8 3/4 inch square, green pictorial cloth, fine in very good+ dust jacket with few chips and small closed tears, wonderful full page color lithographs and smaller black and white lithos, this copy has fabulous full page watercolor signed by Berta and Elmer Hader. Aleph-bet Books, Inc.   111 - 210   2016 $1500

Williamson, Hamilton *Baby Bear.* New York: Doubleday Doran & Co., 1930. Stated first edition, 8vo., pictorial boards, spine bottom chipped, half split at joint, slightly dusty, really very good+ in dust jacket with several pieces off, worn at folds, striking color and black and white lithographs by the Haders, full page watercolor, inscribed by the Haders. Aleph-bet Books, Inc. 111 - 209   2016 $1000

Association – Hagell, Mr.

Spencer, Reuben *To Young Men Going Out into Life.* Manchester: John Heywood, 1891. Original blue cloth, slight marking to spine, presentation inscription with author's compliments for Mr. Hagell, very good. Jarndyce Antiquarian Books   CCXV - 416   2016   £58

Association – Hague, Michael

Yolen, Jane *Dream Weaver.* Cleveland and New York: Collins, 1979. First edition, 4to., cloth backed boards, as new in as new dust jacket, full page color illustrations by Michael Hague, this copy with warm inscription form author dated 1979 and fantastic pen drawing by Hague and inscribed by Hague.   Aleph-bet Books, Inc.   111 - 498   2016 $350

Association – Haine, Edith

Thompson, George E. *Life in Tripoli with a Peep at Ancient Carthage.* Liverpool: Edward Howell, 1894. First edition, 8vo., original red cloth, decorated in black and lettered gilt, 30 photogravure plates, apart from light slanting and offsetting from endpapers, very good, inscribed by pupil of Castle Cary Collegiate School, Edith Haine, dated 1897.   Sotheran's   Travel and Exploration - 383   2016   £698

Association – Haines, Joseph

Arabian Nights *Sinbad Le Marin et D'Autres Contes Des Mille et Une Nuits. (Sinbad the Sailor and Other Tales from the Thousand and One Nights).* Paris: H. Piazza, 1919. First edition in French, 305 x 241mm., no. 520 of 1500 copies, especially attractive rich green morocco by Root & son (signed), covers framed in gilt with triple rules, inner rule entwined at corners with ivy leaf terminations, raised bands, spine gilt in compartments formed by double rule and featuring ivy leaf cornerpieces around an inner central panel, wide ruled turn-ins, with foliate cornerpieces, marbled endpapers, top edge gilt, other edges rough trimmed, original wrappers preserved, decorative initials and titlepage, decorative borders throughout and 27 color plates by Edmund Dulac (each laid down within decorative frame, with captioned tissue guard), printed in pale orange and black throughout, pastedown with bookplate of Joseph H. Haines, upper corners slightly bumped, verso of free endpapers, little discolored (from glue?), otherwise very fine.   Phillip J. Pirages   67 - 122   2016 $1950

Association – Hall, Daisy Patterson

Homerus *The Works.* Oxford: Shakespeare Head Press, 1930-1931. No. 302 of 450 copies on paper (and 10 on vellum), five volumes, 292 x 203mm., original burnt-orange half morocco over cream colored buckram, edges untrimmed, later paper covered slipcase, 52 wood engravings by John Farleigh, comprised of two frontispieces, woodcut framed titlepages to volumes I and V, and 48 full page cuts, ink ownership inscription of Daisy Patterson Hall, overall fading and significant chafing to spines, minor dressing residue to leather, faint dampstain covering about a third of back cover of volume V (few tiny stray stains on spine and of same volume), bindings showing little wear, other sides of other volumes, often found foxed, virtually spotless and very pleasing, internally beautiful copy, as fresh and clean as one could hope for.   Phillip J. Pirages   67 - 315   2016 $1250

Association – Hall, Edward

Haile, Berard, Father *Prayer Stick Cutting in a Five Night Navaho Cermonial of the male branch of Shootingway.* Chicago: University of Chicago Press, 1947. 9 folding plates, illustrations, original printed wrappers, dampstain to some pages of fore edge and waviness to those surrounding, previous owner name stamp to front cover and f.f.e.p. of Edward Hall.   Dumont Maps and Books   134 - 36   2016 $125

Association – Hall, James Baker

Reece, Erik *Field Work: Modern Poems from Eastern Forests.* Lexington: The University Press of Kentucky, 2008. First edition, 8vo., fine in dust jacket, signed by contributors Eric Reece, James Baker Hall, Wendell Berry and Richard Taylor.   Second Life Books, Inc.   196 B - 461   2016 $45

Association – Hall, Michael

Sumption, Jonathan *The Albigensian Crusade.* London: Faber & Faber, 1978. First edition, 8vo., cloth gilt lettered, edges lightly dusted, very good, dust jacket, minor shelfwear, near fine, ownership inscription of Michael Hall in pen to front pastedown.   Unsworths Antiquarian Booksellers Ltd.   E05 - 89   2016   £25

Association – Hallifax, John

Cervantes Saavedra, Miguel De   1547-1616 *The Life and Exploits of the Ingenious Gentleman Don Quixote de la Mancha.* London: printed for J. and R. Tonson, 1749. Second edition, 2 volumes, engraved frontispiece, 23 engraved plates, 8vo., some light browning, blank upper corners volume I G5-6 torn away, contemporary calf, gilt ruled borders, expertly rebacked in matching style, raised and gilt banded spines, red morocco labels, armorial bookplate of John Hallifax, Esq., Kenilworth on inner front boards, 19th century bookplate of J. Blackwood Greenshields on front endpapers.   Jarndyce Antiquarian Booksellers   CCXVII - 66   2016   £1500

Association – Halward, L. V.

Hedin, Sven *Trans-Himalaya. Discoveries and adventures in Tibet.* London: R. & R. Clark, Limited for Macmillan and Co. Limited, 1910-1913. First English edition, 8vo., 3 volumes, original red cloth, upper boards blocked with gilt vignette, spines lettered gilt, top edges gilt, frontispieces, retaining tissue guards, hundreds of plates, extremities little worn and bumped, light offsetting onto free endpapers, some occasional light spotting, short, skillfully repaired tears on 2 folding maps, nonetheless very good, clean set in original cloth, all volumes with neat ownership inscription of L. V. Halward dated Cambridge Feb. 1921.   Sotheran's   Piccadilly Notes - Summer 2015 - 161   2016   £498

Association – Hambleden, William Henry Smith, 3rd Viscount

Boccaccio, Giovanni   1313-1375   *Il Decameron.* Chelsea: Ashedene Press, 1920. One of 80 paper copies for sale (of 105 printed), along with 6 on vellum, 419 x 292 mm., original linen backed blue paper boards, printed paper label on spine, fine printed initials in red and blue designed by Graily Hewitt, text printed in black, red and blue, bookplate of William Henry Smith, 3rd Viscount Hambleden (1903-48), cover with a number of superficial marks and handful of small abrasions (two more prominent), faint fading along two edges of each board, surprisingly solid, only trivial wear to corners and internally pristine.   Phillip J. Pirages   67 - 9   2016 $5000

Association – Hamilton, Anne

Church of England. Book of Common Prayer   *The Book of Common Prayer and Administration of the Sacraments.* London: published for John Reeves...sold and G. and W. Nicol and Satcherd and Letterman, 1807. 2 parts in 1 volume, 12mo., contemporary red straight grained morocco, single gilt fillet on sides and an inner border of 2 blind fillets and a blind roll tool, gilt crown of centre of both covers, spine richly tooled gilt and blind lettered in gilt direct, red morocco label inside front cover, gilt edges, trifle worn at extremities, inner hinge neatly repaired, boards trifle warped, good copy, with a letter of provenance on mourning paper from Isabella Speechly of Peterborough stating "The Prayer Book and Hymn Book (latter not present) which belonging to Queen Caroline, were given to the Lady Egmont by Lady Anne Hamilton the Queen's Lady and she have them to my Great Aunt Miss Martha Speechly then living at Dartmouth House...".   Blackwell's Rare Books   Marks of Genius - 11   2016   £6000

Association – Hamilton, Charles J. J.

Vetustissimorum Poetarum Hesiodi, Theocriti, Theognidis, Moschi, Musaei, Bionis.... Paris: Apud Joannem Libert, 1628. Rare edition, ownership inscription of John Nicholas of Queen's College, Oxford dated 1641, general titlepage damaged at gutter from cracked hinge and just starting to loosen, 8vo., contemporary English calf, spine with four raised bands between double blind fillets, boards also bordered with double blind fillet, edges red, bit marked, spine ends worn, some surface loss to leather on front board, joints cracking little but strong, bookplate of Colonel Sir Charles J. J. Hamilton, Baronet.   Blackwell's Rare Books   B186 - 68   2016   £1500

Association – Hamilton, J. A.

Churchill, Winston Leonard Spencer   1874-1965   *Marlborough: His Life and Times.* London: George G. Harrap & Co., 1939. First edition thus, 4 volumes, large 8vo., original purple cloth, lettered gilt on spine, illustrations, foldout maps, neat name "J. A Hamilton". otherwise very good+ in like dust jackets (very slight edgewear), slight fading to spines of books and jackets.   Any Amount of Books   2015 - C5426   2016   £650

Association – Hamilton, Mary

Haller, Ablrecht Von, Baron   *Letters from Baron Haller to His Daughter...*   London: printed by J. Murray, 1780. Half title, contemporary speckled calf, raised bands, maroon morocco label, neat repairs to hinges, spines slightly rubbed, presentation inscriptions on leading pastedown and initial blank, gift of Queen Charlotte to Mary Hamilton, Queen's House, London Jan. 19th 1781.   Jarndyce Antiquarian Books   CCXV - 241   2016   £1500

Association – Hansen, Peter Allen

Terentius Afer, Publius   *Comoediae.*   Cambridge: Apud Cornelium Crownfield, 1726. First Bentley edition, 2 engraved portraits, some soiling in places, 4to., contemporary calf spine gilt, quite rubbed and scratched but now conserved, joints expertly renewed and red morocco lettering piece replaced to style, booklabel of Peter Allen Hansen and ownership inscription of (MP for Durham) R(obert) Shafto, good.   Blackwell's Rare Books   Greek & Latin Classics VII - 84   2016   £400

Association – Hapgood, Theodore Brown

Ticknor, Caroline   *Glimpses of Authors.*   Boston: Houghton Mifflin Co., 1922. First edition, 2nd printing, illustrations by Theodore Brown Hapgood, near fine, publisher's decorative maroon cloth designed and signed by Theodore Hapgood, with full gilt floral decorations and rulings to the front board and spine, top edge gilt, near fine, hint of rubbing to extremities, touch of faint toning to spine, otherwise fresh binding, tiny chip to fore edge of list of illustrations, very discreet tape repair to short closed tear to contents page, otherwise extremely fresh interior, overall very attractive copy in beautiful binding.   B & B Rare Books, Ltd.   2016 - C51001   2016 $50

Association – Harbin, W.

Johnson, John *The Clergyman's Vade-Mecum or an Account of the Ancient and Present Church of England... (with) Part II.* London: printed for Robert Knaplock and Ballard, 1731. 1723. Sixth edition and third edition of part II, 12mo., contemporary gilt ruled calf, lettered only with volume number, just little wear to extremities, but very good with 18th century signature of W. Harbin; part II with few leaves creased, but very good, crisp copy also with Harbin's signature and in matching binding.   John Drury Rare Books   2015 - 228827   2016 $350

Association – Harding, H. W.

Herrick, Robert   **1591-1674**   *The Hesperides & Noble Numbers.* London: Lawrence & Bullen, 1898. Revised edition, small octavo, 2 volumes, superb period bindings by Riviere of full dark pink morocco with raised bands, ornate gilt spine with inner dentelles, gilt rules, top edge gilt, bookplate of poet H. W. Harding, spines little darkened and joints just faintly rubbed, very good.   Peter Ellis   112 - 167   2016   £650

Association – Hardman, Gerald

Mahony, Francis Sylvester   *Facts & Figures from Italy.* London: Richard Bentley, 1847. First edition, 4 page ad, original pale yellow vertical fine ribbed cloth blocked with gilt lettering and blind decoration, papal marks in black on front and in blind on back board, spine slightly sunned, marks on front board, small tear in leading f.e.p., Ecclesiastical bookplate of Gerald J. Hardman.   Jarndyce Antiquarian Booksellers   CCXVIII - 435   2016   £300

Association – Hardy, Thomas

Couvreur, Jesse Catherine Huybers   *In Her Earliest Youth.* London: Kegan Paul, Trench, Trubner & Co., 1891. 8vo., original gilt stamped red cloth, spine slightly faded, author Thomas Hardy's copy signed copy, with his Max Gate bookplate.   Howard S. Mott Inc.   265 - 38   2016 $950

Gibson, Wilfrid   *Krindlesyke.* London: Macmillan, 1922. First edition, 8vo., original tan boards, printed paper spine label, extreme fore-tips lightly bumped, offset on free endpapers, delimited by jacket flaps, otherwise fine in dust jacket, stained on front panel, presentation copy inscribed by author for Thomas Hardy, with Hardy's Max Gate booklabel.   James S. Jaffe Rare Books   Occasional List: Winter 2016 - 75   2016 $750

Association – Harley, Edward

Prior, Matthew   **1664-1721**   *Poems on Several Occasionas.* London: for Jacob Tonson and John Barber, 1718. First collected edition, large paper copy, gift from Edward Harley for Mary Popham, royal folio, engraved frontispiece, titlepage vignette, headpieces and initial letters, engraved portrait of Prior dated 1719 neatly mounted to front flyleaf, contemporary calf, boards with two-line gold fillet enclosing blind decorative roll, board edges with gold decorative roll, spine very skillfully rebacked retaining original label, recornered, marbled endpapers, just lightest occasional foxing, else very good, lovely copy.   Joseph J. Felcone, Inc.   Books from Five Centuries: a Miscellany - 120   2016 $1400

Association – Harmsworth, R. Leicester

Spencer, John   *A Discourse Concerning Prodigies; Wherein the Vanity of Presages by them is Reprehended and Their True and Proper Ends Asserted and Vindicated.* London: by John Field for Will. Graves... in Cambridge, 1663. First edition, small 4to., titlepage little dusty and with the lower margin renewed, and lower edge of gathering 'M' folded at little shorter and uncut, late 19th century gilt ruled polished calf by Pratt, spine tooled in gilt and with red and green morocco label, edges gilt, Henry Huth and Alfred Henry Huth copy with leather label, from the library of James Stevens Cox (1910-1997), Sir R. Leicester Harmsworth, 1st Bart (1870-1937).   Maggs Bros. Ltd.   1447 - 391   2016   £350

Association – Harpham, H. T.

Friswell, James Hain   *The Better Self...* London: Henry S. King & Co., 1875. Half title, 48 page catalog, original decorated brown cloth, bevelled boards, ownership stamp of H. T. Harpham.   Jarndyce Antiquarian Books   CCXV - 211   2016   £35

Association – Harrell, E.

Dickens, Charles   **1812-1870**   *The Chimes.* London: Chapman & Hall, 1845. Twelfth edition, half title, frontispiece, additional engraved title, illustrations, original red cloth gilt, carefully recased, inscribed by author for Thomas Powell, September fourth 1845, later ownership inscription of Ellen Maria Streater, and E. Harrell, all edges gilt, morocco backed box.   Jarndyce Antiquarian Booksellers   CCXVIII - 364   2016   £25,000

Association – Harrington, Lady

Dodgson, Charles Lutwidge 1832-1898 *Sylvie and Bruno.* London: Macmillan, 1889. First edition, 8vo., bound by Riviere in full blue calf with extensive tooling on spine, all edges gilt, gilt turn-ins and with original covers bound in at back, inscribed by author for Lady Harrington, wonderfully illustrated by Harry Furniss with full and partial page drawings.   Aleph-bet Books, Inc.   111 - 78   2016 $3500

Association – Harris, Edward Swinfen

Walford, Edward *The Antiquary Volumes I-X.* London: Elliot Stock, 1880-1884. 10 volumes bound as 5, 4to., numerous illustrations in text, volume IX foxed at front, occasional further light foxing, few unobtrusive pencil notes to margins, later half vellum (flesh side out?) with marbled paper boards and endpapers, tan morocco gilt labels to spines, top edge gilt, others uncut, little rubbed, some loss of color to boards, vellum slightly soiled, some scrapes to spine labels, inner hinges beginning to wear but holding firm, armorial bookplate of Edward Swinfen Harris and his pencilled ownership.   Unsworths Antiquarian Booksellers   30 - 6   2016   £200

Association – Harris, John

Overton, Thomas Collins *Original Designs of Temples and Other Ornamental Buildings for Parks and Gardens, in the Greek, Roman and Gothic Taste.* London: printed for the author and sold by Henry Webley, 1766. First edition, royal 8vo., contemporary full speckled calf, gilt spine, red morocco and gilt label, little worn at head and foot of spine, 50 engraved plates printed on thick paper, early bookplate of John Ward, recent bookplate of John Harris, particularly fine copy.   Sotheran's   Piccadilly Notes - Summer 2015 - 227   2016   £2400

Association – Harris, Samuel

Tombleson, William *Tombleson's Views of the Rhine.* London: W. Tombleson & Co., 1852. 2 volumes, contemporary half olive green morocco over olive green moire cloth covered boards, all edges gilt, marbled endpapers, a total of 137 finely engraved plates, each paper guarded, 1 engraved folding map tipped-in to rear of each volume, offsetting to paper guards but overall bright, clean set, Samuel Harris engraved armorial bookplate.   Sotheran's   Piccadilly Notes - Summer 2015 - 306   2016   £495

Association – Harrison, Rex

Behrman, S. N. *No Time for comedy: a Play in Three Acts.* London: Hamish Hamilton, 1939. First edition, 8vo., original worn printed wrappers, (also issued in cloth), round-robin copy, signed by members of the London production, Diane Wyngard, Rex Harrison, Lilian Palmer, Elizabeth Welch and 3 others.   Second Life Books, Inc.   196A - 97   2016 $250

Association – Harrisse, Henry

Stevens, Benjamin Franklin *Christopher Columbus: His Own Book of Privileges 1502.* London: B. F. Stevens, 1893. Limited to 20 copies, presentation by author to Henry Harrisse, folio, later quarter leather with original paper wrappers bound in, 3 plates, spine slightly rubbed, minor scratching to cover, well preserved.   Oak Knoll Books   310 - 281   2016 $850

Association – Hart, J. N.

De La Mare, Walter 1873-1956 *Songs of Childhood.* London: Longmans, Green, 1902. First edition, 12mo., blue cloth stamped in gold, parchment spine, top edge gilt, other edges uncut, fine in custom cloth case, gravure frontispiece by Richard Doyle, this copy inscribed by De La Mare and also has 1 page hand written letter from De La Mare laid in, book inscribed by author for friend, J. N. Hart Jan. 1942, and has written 12 lines of verse from his poem 'Gone', plus laid in handwritten letter on 2 sides of an 8vo.. sheet of paper from author to Hart, special copy, rare.   Aleph-bet Books, Inc.   111 - 115   2016 $1850

Association – Hart, Thomas

Pritchard, Andrew *The Microscopic Cabinet of Select animated Objects....* London: Whittaker, Treacher and Arnot, 1832. First edition, 8vo., numerous figures, 13 plates, modern quarter calf, original marbled boards, black spine label, original calf corners, new endleaves, bookplate of Fred C. Luck, early pencil ownership signature of Thomas B. Hart(?) 1834, very good.   Jeff Weber Rare Books   183 - 28   2016 $875

Association – Harte, Bret

Adeler, Max *Elbow Room, a Novel without a plot.* London: Ward Lock, 1883. Authorized edition, First UK edition, 8vo., stamped cloth, very good, Bret Harte's copy with bookplate and ex-libris, some external wear, very good.   Second Life Books, Inc.   196A - 730   2016 $150

Association – Harteis, Richard

Merwin, W. S. *Asian Figures.* New York: Atheneum, 1975. First edition, pictorial wrappers, inscribed by poet for Richard Harteis via Bill Meredith and Bill Merwin, laid in is brief ANS from Meredith to Harteis, his partner of many years, fine. Charles Agvent William Meredith - 83 2016 $150

Association – Hartmann, Johannes

Bible. Greek - 1524 *Novum Testamentum Graece.* Strasbourg: Wolfgang Cephalaeus, 1524. Title within quadripartie woodcut border, printer's device at centre, large device on verso of last leaf with mottoes in Hebrew, Greek and Latin, uniformly little browned and with some slight dampstaining in upper and fore margins, 8vo., contemporary blindstamped pigskin (or deerskin) over bevelled wooden boards, brass clasps and catches, lacking clasps, very rubbed and darkened, spine partly defective, upper cover held by 1 (of 3) cords, 1529 ownership inscription in 2 places of Johannes Hartmann, purchased, the whole extensively annotated by him in Latin and Greek, sometimes in red ink, 19th century bookplate of Thomas Brooke, of Armitage Bridge (Huddersfield), sound, scarce. Blackwell's Rare Books B184 - 13 2016 £5000

Association – Harvey, Jane Dorothy

Ray, John *The Wisdom of God Manifested in the Works of the Creation, in Two Parts.* London: for Samuel Smith, 1692. Second edition, 8vo., contemporary calf, covers panelled gilt with vase and flower tool in each corner, gilt spine with red morocco label (corners worn, top corner of lower cover chewed, area of surface insect damage at foot of the lower cover), from the library of James Stevens Cox (1910-1997), inscribed "The Gift of Mrs. Ray to John Morley July 31 1707", and signatures 'Jane Dorothy Harvey 1849' and 'C. H. Rikerman(?) 1885'. Maggs Bros. Ltd. 1447 - 360 2016 £500

Association – Harwood, A. E.

Dickens, Charles 1812-1870 *The Personal History of David Copperfield.* London: Bradbury & Evans, 1850. First edition, early issue, without half title, engraved frontispiece, title and plates by Phiz, waterstain to lower outer corner of plates, some foxing, original olive green fine diaper cloth, blocked in blind, spine lettered gilt, spine little faded, neat repairs to inner hinges, ownership inscription of A. E. Harwood, superior copy. Jarndyce Antiquarian Booksellers CCXVIII - 469 2016 £2500

Association – Hase, R. H.

Cosson, Anthony De *Mareotis, Being a Short Account of the History and Ancient Monments of the North-Western Desert of Egypt and of Leke Mareotis.* London: Country Life, 1935. First edition, 8vo., original black cloth with illustrated dust jacket, frontispiece in sepia photogravure, photogravure plate, 3 folding plans and folding map (this re-inserted and with repaired tears, see below), cloth lightly rubbed, endpapers with foxing (offsetting to half title), inscribed by R. H. Hase dated Alexandria Dec. 1935. Sotheran's Travel and Exploration - 312 2016 £98

Association – Hassall, Joan

Burnett, David *The Heart's Undesign.* Edinburgh: The Tragra Press, 1977. One of 200 copies, titlepage vignette and tailpiece by Joan Hassall, foolscap 8vo., original printed green wrappers, edges rough trimmed, very good, inscribed for Hassall by Burnett. Blackwell's Rare Books B184 - 274 2016 £60

Burnett, David *The True Vine.* Hedgehog Press, 1975. One of 100 copies, frontispiece and tailpiece by Joan Hassall, errata slip tipped in at rear, foolscap 8vo., original sewn orange wrappers, little darkened along spine, good, inscribed by author for Joan Hassall. Blackwell's Rare Books B184 - 275 2016 £45

Association – Hasse, Doc

Blochman, Lawrence G. *Clues for Dr. Coffee. A Second Casebook.* Philadelphia: J. B. Lippincott Co., 1964. First edition, signed on titlepage by author, presentation by author for Doc Hasse, exceptional copy. Buckingham Books 2015 - 29111 2016 $450

Association – Hatfeild, Randall

Du Refuge, Eustache *Arcana Aulica; or Walsingham's manual of Prudential Maxims for the States-man and Courtier.* printed for Matthew Gillyflower at the Spread-Eagle in Westminster-Hall, 1694. 12mo., engraved frontispiece, 12mo., little browning, mainly marginal or to original endpapers and pastedowns, recent full antique calf, blind ruled borders, raised bands, retaining original endpapers with bookplate of Randall Hatfeild on leading pastedown. Jarndyce Antiquarian Books CCXV - 165 2016 £280

Association – Hauge, Harald

Spruce, Richard *Notes of a Botanist on the Amazon & Andes.* London: Macmillan, 1908. First edition, 2 volumes, neat bookplate of Harald Hauge, endpapers little foxed, otherwise sound, slight fraying and slight chipping (with no loss) at spine ends and faint signs of shelfwear, decent, about very good set. Any Amount of Books 2015 - C14253 2016 £650

Association – Hauptmann, Gerhart

Bolsche, Wilhelm *Charles Darwin. Ein Lebensbild.* Leipzig: Voigtlander, 1898. First edition, presentation copy inscribed by author to his brother, Gerhart Hauptmann dated 1898, small 8vo., contemporary red cloth, portrait frontispiece, light wear to binding, few pages with very light spotting, old Polish library stamp on verso of list of contents and release note in pencil on title.   Sotheran's   Piccadilly Notes - Summer 2015 - 51   2016   £248

Association – Haverland

Austen, Jane   1775-1817 *Sense and Sensibility.* London: Richard Bentley, 1833. First Bentley edition, frontispiece, engraved title, slight spotting to prelims, contemporary full tan calf, double ruled gilt borders, spine gilt with bands, dark brown morocco label, slightly rubbed, Haverland armorial bookplate, very nice.   Jarndyce Antiquarian Booksellers   CCXVII - 19   2016   £450

Association – Hawkes, Dougall

Le Blanc, Charles *Manuel De l'Amateur D'Estampes Contenant Le Dictionnaire des Graveurs de Toutes Les Nations.* Paris: Emile Bouillon, 1854-1890. 8vo., contemporary quarter leather, marbled paper covered boards, original paper wrappers bound in, 4 volumes, illustrations, laid in letter from Mr. James Hillhouse of New Haven to Mr. Dougall Hawkes of NY describes research done on this copy, ex-library, bookplate and markings, spines of first 3 volumes loose, front hinges of first two volumes cracked, scuffing and rubbing at edges of all volumes.   Oak Knoll Books   310 - 43   2016 $450

Association – Hawkins, Arthur

Cain, James M. *The Postman Always Rings Twice.* New York: Alfred A. Knopf, 1934. First edition, boards slightly soiled and near fine, with supplied proof dust jacket which came directly from estate of artist Arthur Hawkins Jr., jacket folded with crease at spine, Knopf's small Borzoi logo has been cut away , date '1933' on front flap, although book wasn't released until 1934, however this is exceptionally bright and otherwise fine and about 1/4 inch taller than the finished version.   Between the Covers Rare Books   208 - 99   2016 $10,000

Association – Hawkins, Robert

Landowska, Wanda *Landowska on Music.* New York: Stein & Day, 1964. First edition, 8vo., frontispiece, photos, nice in scuffed slipcase, this copy neatly signed in ink by editors, Denise Restout and Robert Hawkins.   Second Life Books, Inc.   196 B - 8   2016 $100

Association – Hayes, Helen

Leatherman, Leroy *Martha Graham.* New York: Knopf, 1966. First edition, 4to., photos by Martha Swope, signed by Leatherman and Swope, inscribed by Swope to Helen Hayes, nice copy.   Second Life Books, Inc.   196 B - 37   2016 $250

Association – Haynes, E. S. P.

Davies, William Henry   1871-1940 *The Soul's Destroyer and Other Poems.* Alston Rivers, 1970. Second (first trade) edition, foxing throughout, small wormhole at foot of first few leaves, crown 8vo., original grey-green wrappers printed in blue to front, spine little ragged and upper cover detached and held internally by thin strips of brown tape, sound, inscribed by author to E. S. P. Haynes, close friend.   Blackwell's Rare Books   B186 - 195   2016   £700

Association – Hayward, Eric

Bradley-Birt, F. B. *The Romance of an Eastern Capital.* London: Smith, Elder & Co., 1906. First edition, 8vo., original cloth lettered gilt, front cover with gilt stamped vignette of a sailing ship, plates after photos, spine sunned, light offsetting from endpapers very good, presentation copy inscribed by author to Eric Hayward (pictorial bookplate).   Sotheran's   Travel and Exploration - 91   2016   £198

Association – Hayward, John

Barnes, Djuna *Nightwood.* London: Faber & Faber, 1936. First edition, 8vo., original purple cloth, dust jacket, few small chips at lower fore-corner of jacket, tiny bit of edgewear elsewhere, otherwise fine, rare, inscribed presentation from author to John Hayward, laid into this copy is brief autographed card signed by Barnes to Hayward, exceptional association.   James S. Jaffe Rare Books Occasional List: Winter 2016 - 29   2016 $9500

Association – Hazen, Allen Tracy

Adam, Robert Brothwick *The R. B. Adam Library Relating to Dr. Samuel Johnson and His Era.* Buffalo: printed for the author, London and New York: Oxford University Press, 1929. First edition, one of 500 copies, 3 volumes, quarto, original blue buckram, gilt lettering, top edge gilt, others untrimmed, frontispieces and numerous illustrations, from the library of Walpole bibliographer and scholar Allen Tracy Hazen, with his posthumous booklabel, later ink signature of Johnson scholar Chester Chapin, dated Feb. 27 1986, cloth slightly rubbed and worn, very good.   The Brick Row Book Shop   Miscellany 69 - 50   2016 $500

Association – Hazlerigg, Arthur

Shakespeare, William 1564-1616 *The Works of William Shakespeare.* London: Macmillan & Co., 1899. Eversley edition, 10 volumes, half titles, some slight foxing, occasional pencil marking, armorial bookplate of Arthur & Dorothy Hazlerigg, contemporary half olive green morocco, spines with gilt floral motif, some very slight rubbing to extremities, attractive set.   Jarndyce Antiquarian Booksellers   CCXVII - 256   2016   £1850

Association – Hazlerigg, Dorothy

Shakespeare, William 1564-1616 *The Works of William Shakespeare.* London: Macmillan & Co., 1899. Eversley edition, 10 volumes, half titles, some slight foxing, occasional pencil marking, armorial bookplate of Arthur & Dorothy Hazlerigg, contemporary half olive green morocco, spines with gilt floral motif, some very slight rubbing to extremities, attractive set.   Jarndyce Antiquarian Booksellers   CCXVII - 256   2016   £1850

Association – Hazlitt, William

Stace, Machell *An Alphabetical Catalogue of an Extensive Collection of the Writings of Daniel Defoe....* London: printed for Whitmore and Penn, Homer's Head, Charing Cross, 1829. First edition, 8vo., first and last leaves little dust soiled, otherwise clean throughout, stitched as issued, long inscription by William Hazlitt 1811-1893) to Mr. Burn. Marlborough Rare Books List 56 - 16   2016   £225

Association – Head, Henry, Mrs.

Henley, William Ernest 1849-1903 *For England's Sake: Verses and Songs in Time of War.* London: David Nutt, 1900. First edition, signed presentation from author for Mrs. Henry Head, wife of Sir Henry Head, brownish purple wrappers with faded gold lettering on stiff archival boards, sunning to spine and edges of boards, interior yellowed but text clear and crisp, housed in brown cloth covered box, scarce in presentation from, very good-.   The Kelmscott Bookshop 12 - 50   2016 $175

Association – Headfort, Marquess of

Maitland, James A. *Reminiscences of a Retired Physician.* London: G. Routledge and Co., 1854. First edition, little cut down in contemporary half purple calf, spine gilt, slightly faded, from the Headfort Library, signed Bective 1854.   Jarndyce Antiquarian Booksellers   CCXVII - 176   2016   £65

Maxwell, William Hamilton *Rambling Recollections of a Soldier of Fortune.* Dublin: William Curry, Jun. & Co., 1842. Frontispiece and plates by Phiz, frontispiece, slightly foxed, contemporary half brown calf, maroon morocco label, slightly rubbed with slight sign of library label removal from spine, from the Headfort library, 'Bective 1856', nice copy. Jarndyce Antiquarian Booksellers   CCXVII - 183   2016   £150

Plato *Platonis Dialogui V.* Oxonii: E Typogrpaheo Clarendoniano, 1752. 8vo., titlepage vignette, few pencil underlinings, full contemporary sprinkled caf raised & gilt banded spine, small gilt device in compartment, red morocco label, armorial bookplate of Marquess of Headfort. Jarndyce Antiquarian Booksellers   CCXVI - 455   2016   £85

Shaftesbury, Anthony Ashley Cooper, 3rd Earl of 1671-1713 *Characteristicks of Men, Manners, Opinions, Times &c.* London: printed in the year, 1733. 3 volumes, 12mo., collective titlepage in volume I, separate titles with imprint for each volume, some light browning to paper, several leaves of index, untrimmed in top corner and folded back into binding, contemporary mottled calf, spines rubbed, only faint traces of black morocco labels, armorial bookplate of Marquess of Headfort, nice, unsophisticated copy. Jarndyce Antiquarian Books   CCXV - 400   2016   £225

Sheridan, Thomas *British Education or the Source of the Disorders of Great Britain.* London: printed for R. and J. Dodsley, 1756. Half title, 8vo., early 19th century calf, expertly rebacked, raised bands, gilt motifs, original red morocco, armorial bookplate of Marquess of Headfort. Jarndyce Antiquarian Books   CCXV - 845   2016   £480

Association – Headlam, Arthur

Prior, Matthew 1664-1721 *A New Collection of Poems on Several Occasions.* London: printed for Tho. Osborne, 1725. 12mo., some browning, mainly affecting endpapers, and pastedowns, engraved frontispiece, 3 engraved plates, full contemporary panelled calf, raised bands, joints cracked but firm, spine and corners rather rubbed, 19th century bookplate of Arthur Headlam.   Jarndyce Antiquarian Booksellers   CCXVI - 482   2016   £65

Association – Headlam, John

Johnson, Samuel 1709-1784 *The Lives of the Most Eminent English Poets...* London: printed for J. Buckland, C. Bathurst and T. Davies, 1793. New edition, frontispiece, 12mo., some browning to endpapers and pastedowns, some marginal browning to next few leaves, each volume, one leaf torn right across in volume III, without loss, full contemporary sprinkled calf, gilt banded spines, rather dry & rubbed, red morocco labels intact, two joints cracked but firm, wear to one headcap and to foot of one spine, contemporary bookplate of John Headlam, and his signature dated 1796. Jarndyce Antiquarian Booksellers CCXVI - 331 2016 £200

Wharton, Richard *Fables.* London: printed by T. Bensley... for Payne and Mackinlay, 1804-1805. 8vo., 2 volumes in one, some scattered foxing and light browning, contemporary quarter calf, marbled boards, vellum tips, double gilt bands, red morocco label, slight wear to rear joint and head of spine, armorial bookplate of John Headlam, of Gilmonly Hall Yorkshire. Jarndyce Antiquarian Booksellers CCXVI - 607 2016 £180

Association – Headlam, T. E.

Ventum, Harriet *Selina, a Novel, Founded on Facts.* London: printed for C. Law, 1800. First edition, 3 volumes, titlepage to volume III in very good facsimile on contemporary paper, some browning and finger marking to text in places, offsetting on pastedowns and endpapers, full contemporary sheep, spines rubbed, lacking labels, some cracking across bands, heads chipped but joints sound, early signatures to titlepages of Mary Windale and later 19th century name of T. E. Headlam, Gilmonby Hall (Yorkshire). Jarndyce Antiquarian Booksellers CCXVI - 577 2016 £750

Association – Heal, Ambrose

Symons, A. J. A. *A Bibliography of the First Editions of Books by William Butler Yeats.* First Edition Club, 1924. First edition, 106/500 copies printed on Japan paper at the Curwen Press, crown 8vo., original boards, backstrip with printed label, gutters of rear endpaper, trifle dusty with spare label tipped in to rear pastedown, dust jacket lightly toned with short closed tear at head of front panel, original prospectus and order from loosely inserted, very good, inscribed by author to Ambrose Heal. Blackwell's Rare Books B186 - 290 2016 £200

Association – Heaphy, Thomas

Dodgson, Charles Lutwidge 1832-1898 *Phantasmagoria and other Poems.* London: Macmillan, 1869. 8vo., blue cloth with gilt decorations, all edges gilt, except for light fraying to spine ends, near fine in custom cloth clamshell box, this copy inscribed by author to artist, Thomas Heaphy the Younger. Aleph-bet Books, Inc. 111 - 76 2016 $5000

Association – Hearne, Thomas

Woodward, John *The State of Physick and of Diseases with an Inquiry into the Causes of the late Increase of them but more particularly of the Small-Pox.* London: printed for T. Horne, 1718. First edition, full contemporary calf, gilt panelled spine, head of spine neatly repaired, Author's presentation with note from author to Thomas Hearne. James Tait Goodrich X-78 - 565 2016 $1500

Association – Hedderwick, James

The Salt Water Gazette for MDCCCXXXV. Glasgow: James Hedderwick & son, 1835. Issues 1 to 14 (all published), later maroon morocco grained cloth, probably 1857 from pencil date, spine lettered gilt, publisher's own copy. Jarndyce Antiquarian Booksellers CCXVII - 228 2016 £180

Association – Heelis, Mrs.

Potter, Beatrix 1866-1943 *The Tale of Jemima Puddle-Duck.* London: Frederick Warne and Co. Ltd., 1943. Early edition, 12mo., original green paper covered boards with onlaid pictorial label to upper cover, pictorial endpapers, color illustrations after watercolours by author, very good and clean, externally lightly rubbed with couple of tiny closed nicks to joints at head of spine, now neatly repaired and almost unnoticeable, internally a touch shaken and sometime expertly tightened, some sporadic light thumbing, pale marking and occasional minor cracking, scarce signed, presentation copy inscribed "For Isabel/from Mrs. Heelis/Beatrix Potter/Feb. 16th 1943". Sotheran's Piccadilly Notes - Summer 2015 - 244 2016 £1400

Association – Heinemann, William

Whistler, James A. M. *The Gentle Art of Making Enemies.* London: William Heinemann, 1890. First English edition ad first authorized edition, one of only 10 special copies, near fine in slightly chipped, publisher's brown gilt decorated wrappers bound into similarly decorated near fine full brown morocco by Zaehnsdorf in 1925, housed in custom quarter morocco slipcase with cloth chemise, inscribed by Whistler to his publishers William Heinemman with his butterfly signature, Chelsea Oct. 1890. Between the Covers Rare Books 204 - 16 2016 $16,500

Association – Hemsworth, Sarah Jane

The New Female Instructor; or Young Woman's Guide... London: Thomas Kelly, 1822. Frontispiece, additional engraved title, plates, frontispiece strengthened using original endpaper, plates slightly browned and with some damp marking, paper repair to contents leaf, handsomely rebound in half tan calf, black morocco label, signature of Sarah Jane Hemsworth, April 1829.   Jarndyce Antiquarian Books CCXV - 338   2016   £180

Association – Henderson, David

Lucas, W. F. *Bottom Fishing: a Novella and Other Stories.* Knoxville: Carpetbag Press, 1974. First edition, 8vo., 8vo., author's presentation on inside of cover for David Henderson, some very light spots at bottom of some leaves, cover soiled, otherwise very good, tight copy.   Second Life Books, Inc.   196 B - 102   2016 $150

Association – Henderson, George William Mercer

Murray, Thomas Boyles *Pitcairn: the Island, the People and the Pastor...*   London: Society for Promoting Christian Knowledge, 1854. Fourth edition, 8vo., original brown grained cloth, spine lettered gilt, vignette blocked in gilt onto upper cover ornamented in blind, 13 engraved plates, very light marking to binding, very good, contemporary bookplate of George William Mercer Henderson.   Sotheran's Travel and Exploration - 405   2016   £225

Association – Hendrick, Charles

Roberti, Antonius *Clavis Homerica. Sive Lexicon Vocabulorum Omnium Quae Continentur in Homeri Iliade et Potissima Parte Odysseaeae.*   London: Impensis J. Walthoe, J. Knapton, R. Knaplock, J. & B. Sprint (etc), 1727. Ad leaf discarded, ownership inscriptions of Charles and Edward Hendrick to titlepage, along with ink blot causing small hole in blank area, short wormtrack in blank gutter of last 5 leaves, just some minor soiling otherwise, 8vo., contemporary Cambridge style panelled calf, bit rubbed, touch of wear to extremities, some old scratches, good, pleasant copy, scarce printing.   Blackwell's Rare Books Greek & Latin Classics VII - 23   2016   £200

Association – Hendrick, Edward

Roberti, Antonius *Clavis Homerica. Sive Lexicon Vocabulorum Omnium Quae Continentur in Homeri Iliade et Potissima Parte Odysseaeae.*   London: Impensis J. Walthoe, J. Knapton, R. Knaplock, J. & B. Sprint (etc), 1727. Ad leaf discarded, ownership inscriptions of Charles and Edward Hendrick to titlepage, along with ink blot causing small hole in blank area, short wormtrack in blank gutter of last 5 leaves, just some minor soiling otherwise, 8vo., contemporary Cambridge style panelled calf, bit rubbed, touch of wear to extremities, some old scratches, good, pleasant copy, scarce printing.   Blackwell's Rare Books Greek & Latin Classics VII - 23   2016   £200

Association – Henry, Walter James

Bellamy, Edward *Looking Backward 2000-1887.* Boston: Houghton Mifflin, 1926. 8vo., very good in publisher's cloth, stain at hinge of rear endpaper, inscribed by author's wife, Emma for Walter James Henry, also inscribed by Bellamy's daughter, Marian Bellamy Ernshaw, laid in 9 x 6 inch handbill advertising talk given by Marian and Emma Bellamy.   Second Life Books, Inc.   196A - 103   2016 $300

Association – Herbert, Edmund

Shelton, Thomas *Tachygraphy.*   London: by Thomas Milbourn for Dorman Newman, 1693. Small 8vo., additional engraved architectural title, 9 pages of engraved examples, engraved title frayed at head and repaired (touching frame) and shaved at foot affecting second line of imprint, small pin-hole through centre of first 15 leaves, letterpress title dampstained in upper inner margin, little soiled throughout and with margins closely trimmed in places, mid 20th century half calf and marbled boards, Edmund Herbert's early signature, from the library of James Stevens Cox (1910-1997).   Maggs Bros. Ltd.   1447 - 382   2016   £350

Association – Heron-Allen, Edward

Dickens, Charles 1812-1870 *The Loving Ballad of Lord Bateman.*   London: Tilt & Bogue, 1842? Half title, plates by George Cruikshank, original green cloth blocked gilt, slightly dulled, leading inner hinge slightly cracked and repaired, bookplate of Edward Heron-Allen, good plus.   Jarndyce Antiquarian Booksellers   CCXVIII - 258   2016   £150

Association – Herz

Cockburn, John *A Journey Over Land from the Gulf of Honduras to the Great South-Sea.*   London: for C. Rivington, 1735. First edition, folding map, contemporary sprinkled calf, very skillfully rebacked with entire original spine and label retained, lovely copy, text clean and fresh and entirely unfoxed, Wolfgang Herz copy with his small booklabel.   Joseph J. Felcone, Inc.   Books from Five Centuries: a Miscellany - 44   2016 $3500

Jourtel, Henri *A Journal of the Last Voyage Perform'd by Monsr. de la Sale to the Gulph of Mexico to find out the Mouth of the Mississippi River...* London: for A. Bell, B. Lintot and J. Baker, 1714. First edition in English, engraved folding map, short closed tear, contemporary calf, extremities rubbed, top of spine bit worn, else lovely untouched copy, text clean and fresh and entirely unfoxed, Peter A Porter bookplate and Wolfgang Herz label. Joseph J. Felcone, Inc. Books from Five Centuries: a Miscellany - 85 2016 $15,000

Ludolf, Hiob *A New History of Ethiopia.* London: for Samuel Smith, 1682. First edition in English, folio, 8 engraved plates, engraved plate of Ethiopic alphabet and folding genealogical table, contemporary or early 18th century calf, front hinge cracked but held by cords, corners worn, some light browning, but very good with signatures of Edmund and Rufus Marsden, latter dated 1762, Herz booklabel. Joseph J. Felcone, Inc. Books from Five Centuries: a Miscellany - 92 2016 $2200

Association – Hesketh, Thomas

Juvenalis, Decimus Junius *The Satires of Juvenal.* Cambridge: printed for J. Nicholson, 1777. Some light soiling and toning, frequent underlining and marginal notes in early hand, 8vo., later mottled calf, rebacked preserving original endpapers, spine gilt somewhat crudely, armorial bookplate of Thomas Hesketh and shelfmark and label of Easton Neston library, good. Blackwell's Rare Books Greek & Latin Classics VII - 51 2016 £400

Medicina Flagellata; or the Doctor Scarified. London: printed for J. Bateman and J. Nicks, 1721. First edition, with additional letterpress title with engraved vignette, 8vo., contemporary tree calf, flat spine gilt in compartments, red lettering piece, minor wear, top of upper joint snagged, foot of spine chipped, contemporary signature of W. Beeson, MD, engraved bookplate of Sir Thomas Hesketh and Easton Neston Library shelf label, very good. Blackwell's Rare Books B186 - 126 2016 £550

Association – Heyen, Kristen

Heyen, William *The Ash.* Potsdam: Tamarack Editions, 1978. First edition, of a total edition of 326, this #48 of 126 to contain a special drawing, hand colored by Kristen Heyen, 12 year old daughter of author, and signed by author and artist, inscribed and signed by same for William Meredith, original envelope addressed in Heyen's hand to Meredith, fine. Charles Agvent William Meredith - 36 2016 $100

Association – Heyen, William

Manassas Review. William Heyen Issue. Manassas: Northern Virginia Community College, 1978. First edition, printed wrappers, this copy signed and inscribed by William Heyen for William Meredith, laid in is full ALS from Heyen to Meredith in original envelope addressed in Heyen's hand to Meredith, fine. Charles Agvent William Meredith - 46 2016 $100

Association – Heylar

Walker, William *The Royal Grammar, Commonly Called Lylly's Grammar Explained.* London: for Robert Pawlet and Edward Pawlet, 1674. Second edition, small 8vo., small rust hole through the blank part of the titlepage and upper corner with minor damage due to ink stain, larger hole from paper flaw on B3 (touching top line of text), some occasional minor spots, inkstain along upper edge of I5-K1 and with small piece torn away from bank corner of G4, contemporary calf, spine with four gilt tooled panels, spine label missing, upper joint split at head, endleaves unstuck. from the library of James Stevens Cox (1910-1997), Juvenile ink inscription, Heylar family of Coker Court Somerset, with 19th century armorial bookplate. Maggs Bros. Ltd. 1447 - 432 2016 £200

Association – Hibbert

Shelley, Percy Bysshe 1792-1822 *Rosalind and Helen, a Modern Eclogue, with Other Poems.* London: printed for C. and J. Ollier, 1819. First edition, with final ad leaves, first few leaves slightly spotted, 8vo., polished calf by F. Bedford, spine gilt red lettering piece, gilt edges, minimal wear to extremities, the Hibbert-Esher copy with bookplates and acquisition notes by Oliver Brett, good. Blackwell's Rare Books Marks of Genius - 47 2016 £2500

Association – Hicks, Isaac

Convention of Delegates from the Abolition Societies *Minutes of the Proceedings of the... Convention of Delegates from the Abolition Societies...* Philadelphia: Printed by Zacharian Poulson Junr., 1794-1801. First, second, third, fourth, fifth and seventh conventions, 6 sewn pamphlets in plain paper wrappers, 3 are untrimmed in original plain paper wrappers, the other three trimmed in early plain paper wrappers, contemporary signature of Samuel Rodman, contemporary signature of Isaac Hicks, front wrapper of fourth pamphlet detached, very good set. Between the Covers Rare Books 202 - 4 2016 $10,000

Association – Hicks, Madame

Moliere, Jean Baptiste Pouquelin De 1622-1673 *Le Tartuffe. (and) Don Juan.* Nice and Paris: l'Imprimerie Nationale de Monaco, 1954. No. IX of XXV copies reserved for the collaborators and friends of the artist (in addition to 700 regular copies), 241 x 191mm., contemporary green crushed morocco by Jean Santin (stamp-signed), smooth spine with gilt titling, gilt ruled turn-ins, pale green watered silk endleaves, all edges gilt, titlepage vignettes, frontispiece at beginning of each work and numerous illustrations in text by Jean Gradassi, all hand colored by atelier of Edmond Vairel using pochoir technique, with extra suite of 45 illustrations, bound in after text and with original version of an illustration from Don Juan inscribed by the artist to Madame Hicks and identified by him on verso, bound in at front, pages ruled in red, two half titles printed in red, joints little rubbed, spine uniformly sunned, just hint of soiling to covers, otherwise very fine, binding lustrous and text immaculate. Phillip J. Pirages 67 - 285 2016 $850

Association – Hiethold, Hugh

Cleghorn, Thomas *The Hydro-Aeronaut or Navigators Life Buoy...* London: J. M. Richardson, 1810. First edition, 12mo., half title, frontispiece, engraved title, errata leaf, contemporary sprinkled calf, gilt spine, red morocco lael, some worm damage to head of spine and following hinge, extremities little rubbed, signature of Hugh Hiethold 1946, overall good plus. Jarndyce Antiquarian Booksellers CCXVII - 72 2016 £220

Association – Highfield, Dr.

Quammen, David *To Walk the Line.* New York: Knopf, 1970. First edition, fine, dust jacket fine with letter to Dr. Highfield, handwritten, signed and dated by author 1/31/71, inscribed by author. Bella Luna Books 2016 - ta276 2016 $132

Association – Hill, Ann

Valentine and Orson The Two Sons of the Emperour of Greece. London: by J. W. for E. Tracy, 1694. Small 4to., woodcut frontispiece and ads below, woodcut on titlepage and numerous woodcut illustrations in text, very small piece torn away the upper blank corner of woodcut frontispiece, minor rust hole through P1 (in text) and Dd2 (in margin), small hole worn through foot of 2b2, light worming to fore margin of T2-V3, rust stain to Bb4 (touching text), contemporary sheep, covers ruled in blind, inside joints split, old stain from glass on upper cover, minor staining on rear, faded contemporary inscription of Ann Hill, Albert M Cohn 20th century armorial bookplate, from the library of James Stevens Cox (1910-1997). Maggs Bros. Ltd. 1447 - 422 2016 £650

Association – Hill, John Woern

Galton, Francis 1822-1911 *The Art of Travel or Shifts and Contrivances Available in Wild Coutnries.* London: John Murray, 1860. Third edition, woodcut, illustrations, original scarlet cloth by Edmonds and Remnants, spine faded, slightly dulled, leading inner hinge slightly cracked, ex-libris John Woern Hill. Jarndyce Antiquarian Booksellers CCXVII - 106 2016 £150

Association – Hill, M. J. M.

Froissart, Jean De *Chronicles of England, France, Spain and the Adjoining Counties....* London and New York: George Routledge and Sons, 1868. 2 volumes, many illustrations in text, fore-edge margins somewhat discolored towards rear of volume 1, contemporary light brown calf, blind tooled with gilt embossed 'Oxford Local Examinations, London' centerpieces, red morocco gilt labels and blind tooling to spines, rebacked well but in different shade, boards scuffed, edges worn, corners neatly repaired, bookplates of M. J. M. Hill from London Committee of Oxford Local Examinations. Unsworths Antiquarian Booksellers 30 - 60 2016 £140

Association – Hill, Maurice

Grimble, Augustus *More Leaves from My Game Book.* London: printed for R. Clay and Sons Ltd., 1917. First edition, limited to 250 copies, 8vo., original half vellum over marbled boards with red leather label on spine, 45 illustrations, vellum bit rubbed and discolored but good, inscribed by author to Maurice Hill Aug. 1917. Sotheran's Hunting, Shooting & Fishing - 176 2016 £300

Association – Hill, Roy

Hernton, Calvin C. *Coming Together: Black Power, White Hatred and Sexual Hang-Ups.* New York: Random House, 1971. First edition, bottom corner of few pages creased, tiny burn mark on fore-edge else near fine in lightly soiled about fine dust jacket, effusively inscribed by author for Roy Hill, poet/author. Between the Covers Rare Books 207 - 52 2016 $125

Association – Hill, W. S.

Redding, Cyrus *Every man His Own Butler.* London: Whitaker & Co., 1839. First edition, engraved title, original ribbed purple cloth, gilt illustrated, largely faded to brown, spine slightly rubbed at head and tail, signs of label removal, later signature of W. S. Hill, good plus copy. Jarndyce Antiquarian Books CCXV - 381 2016 £480

Association – Hillary, Edmund

Hunt, John *The Ascent of Everest.* London: Hodder & Stoughton, 1953. First edition, signed by Sir Edmund Hillary, 48 black and white photos, 8 color photos, numerous maps, drawings, etc., blue cloth, fine, lightly chipped and faded pictorial dust jacket.   Argonaut Book Shop   Mountaineering 2015 - 7162   2016 $500

Association – Hillhouse, James

Le Blanc, Charles *Manuel De l'Amateur D'Estampes Contenant Le Dictionnaire des Graveurs de Toutes Les Nations.* Paris: Emile Bouillon, 1854-1890. 8vo., contemporary quarter leather, marbled paper covered boards, original paper wrappers bound in, 4 volumes, illustrations, laid in letter from Mr. James Hillhouse of New Haven to Mr. Dougall Hawkes of NY describes research done on this copy, ex-library, bookplate and markings, spines of first 3 volumes loose, front hinges of first two volumes cracked, scuffing and rubbing at edges of all volumes.   Oak Knoll Books   310 - 43   2016 $450

Association – Hillier, Bevis

Haworth-Booth, Mark *E. McKnight Kauffer: a Designer and His Public.* Gordon Fraser, 1979. 4to., original boards, dust jacket, illustrations in color and black and white, very good, inscribed to art design critic, Bevis Hillier from author.   Sotheran's   Piccadilly Notes - Summer 2015 - 197   2016   £198

Association – Hilton, Arthur Denne

Turner, Richard *An Easy Introduction to the Arts and Sciences being a Short but Comprehensive System of Useful and Polite Learning.* London: J. Johnson, 1803. Ninth edition, half title, plates, illustrations, final ad leaf, contemporary speckled calf, lacking label, rubbed, ownership inscription of M. E. Denne, April 11th 1804 ad Arthur Denne Hilton 1866.   Jarndyce Antiquarian Books   CCXV - 991   2016   £45

Association – Hind, C. Lewis

Moore, George   1852-1933 *Confessions of a Young Man.* London: Swan Sonnenschein, Lowrey & Co., 1888. First edition, author's presentation copy to his brother Maurice Moore, tipped in at back is autograph letter from Moore to editor C. Lewis Hind, dated June 18 1900, original cloth with pictorial illustration of a young woman on cover, spine somewhat darkened as usual, corners of book and spine bumped, still nice, hinges tender, otherwise very good, tipped in is an ad for Moore's Parnell and His Island, housed in grey cloth chemise and quarter leather slipcase, very good.   The Kelmscott Bookshop   13 - 42   2016 $3000

Association – Hind, J. G.

Beazley, J. D. *The Development of Attic Black Figure.* Berkeley & Los Angeles: University of California Press, 1964. First edition reprinted, large 8vo., grey cloth, gilt lettered to spine, now fading, little shelfwear, very good, no dust jacket, ownership inscription of J. G. Hind.   Unsworths Antiquarian Booksellers Ltd.   E05 - 17   2016   £20

Brauer, George C. *The Age of the Soldier Emperors. Imperial Rome A.D. 244-284.* New Jersey: Noyes Press, 1985. First edition, 8vo., cloth, gilt lettered to spine, endcaps just starting to wear, top edge slightly dusted and spotted, very good, dust jacket, three large tears, one with loss, some smaller closed tears, fraying, faded to spine, good only, ownership inscription J. G. Hind, School of History, Univ. of Leeds with one or two ink annotations.   Unsworths Antiquarian Booksellers Ltd.   E04 - 35   2016   £30

MacMullen, Ramsey *Soldier and Civilian in the later Roman Empire.* Cambridge: Harvard University Press, 1967. First reprinting, small 8vo. 4 plates, cloth, gilt lettered spine slightly cocked, edges dusted, very good, dust jacket with 1.7 cm. closed tear to lower jacket, few small tears to headcap with bit of loss, .8cm. closed tear to top edge of upper jacket, spine lightly sunned, two small pencil marks to upper jacket, minor shelfwear, top corner of front flyleaf clipped, very good, ownership inscription J. G. Hind.   Unsworths Antiquarian Booksellers Ltd.   E05 - 52   2016   £30

Meiggs, Russell *The Athenian Empire.* Oxford: Clarendon Press, 1979. First paperback edition, 8vo., figures and maps, edges faded and worn, creased, bit grubby, still good, correspondence from author to J. G. Hind loosely inserted.   Unsworths Antiquarian Booksellers Ltd.   E04 - 75   2016   £20

Seager, Robin *Amnianus Marcellinus. Seven Studies in His Language and Thought.* Columbia University of Missouri Press, 1986. First edition, 8vo., cloth, blue lettered, some very small marks to spine, edges dusted, jacket has closed tears to top edge of upper jacket, minor shelfwear, very good, from the library of Prof. J. G. Hind, with his ms translation of sections of annotations loosely inserted.   Unsworths Antiquarian Booksellers Ltd.   E05 - 61   2016   £35

Association – Hinde, Robert

Camden, William *Rerum Anglicarum et Hibernicarum Annales, Regnante Elisabetha.* Lugd. Batavorum: Elzevir, 1639. 8vo, engraved portrait, titlepage in red and black, woodcut printer's device, copious notes in old hand to endpapers and prelim blanks, further marginalia in Latin and English with occasional manicules, few pages with pencil ticks to margins, sporadic light foxing, one or two marginal paper flaws, small hole in centre of page 359, affecting only few letters, contemporary vellum, gilt to spine evidence of lost label replaced with ink title, yapp edges, spine slightly darkened, little soiled with some smudges and stains, small (burn?) hole to spine, some bands broken and inner hinge split but binding sound, small loss to top corner of f.f.e.p., armorial bookplate of Robert Hinde, bookplate of Frances Massey O'Brien and an anonymous catalogue description affixed to front pastedown, ownership inscriptions of Sunderland Nov. 23rd 1805, Eton, L. M. Robinson 1923, and Frances Massey O'Brien, July 1967, FMO's pencil note. Unsworths Antiquarian Booksellers Ltd. E01 - Early Printing - 4   2016   £300

Association – Hinkson, Katharine Tynan

Rhymers' Club *The Second Book of the Rhymers' Club.* London: Elkin Mathews & John Lane, 1894. One of 650 copies, presentation from publisher John Lane, inscribed in pencil to Irish poet and novelist Katharine Tynan Hinkson, extremely uncommon thus, original brown cloth with gilt title to spine, light browning to margins of interior pages, bookplates of writer J. G. E. Hopkins, culinary writer Helmut Lothar Ripperger and collector Mark Samuels Lasner, very good.   The Kelmscott Bookshop   13 - 59   2016 $950

Association – Hinsdale, Isabelle

Horgan, Paul *Humble Powers.* London: Macmillan, 1954. First British edition thus, cloth, laid into corner photo mounts on f.f.e.p is black and white photo of Horgan with his aunt, and godchild, gilt inscription written by his aunt, Marie Rhor to Isabelle Hinsdale, fine in slightly edge worn dust jacket with two small chips and couple of short tears, very scarce.   Gene W. Baade, Books on the West   2015 - FTR091   2016 $131

Association – Hirschfeld, Al

Atkinson, Brooks *The Lively Years 1920-1973.* New York: Association Press, 1973. 8vo., cartoons by Hirschfeld, inscribed by Hirschfeld, top edge of spine damaged, otherwise very good in little worn dust jacket. Second Life Books, Inc.   196A - 54   2016 $125

Association – Hoare, Henry Merrik

Reresby, John *The Memoirs of the Hon. Sir John Reresby, Bart....* London: printed for Samuel Harding, 1734. First edition in 8vo, 2 titlepages with slightly different content, first in red and black, each with woodcut device, lightly toned, sporadic foxing, few smudgy marks particularly to first titlepage, pages 225-6 torn with loss to upper corner affecting about a quarter of the text, infilled with plain paper, contemporary light brown calf, gilt label to spine, edges lightly sprinkled blue, scuffed, joints neatly repaired, some speckled marks to upper board, bookplate little offset to f.f.e.p., very good, armorial bookplate of Henry Merrik Hoare.   Unsworths Antiquarian Booksellers Ltd.   30 - 129   2016   £125

Association – Hoare, W. Douro

Saint Pierre, Jacques Henri Bernardin De 1737-1814 *Paul and Mary an Indian Story.* London: printed for J. Dodsley, Pall Mall, 1789. 2 volumes, bound without half titles, 12mo., tears with slight loss to blank lower margin of few leaves, final blank removal from end of volume II, early 19th century half calf, gilt banded spines, black labels, marbled boards, some rubbing and slight wear to middle of spine volume II, one section little loose, armorial bookplate of Charles Barclay and W. Douro Hoare.   Jarndyce Antiquarian Booksellers   CCXVI - 505   2016   £150

Association – Hobhouse, Arthur

Gesner, Johann Mathias *Scriptores Rei Rusticae Veretes Latini.* Leipzig: sumtibus Caspari Fritsch, 1773. 1774. Second edition, 2 volumes, frontispiece to volume I and 6 further folding plates, engraved vignette to each titlepage, some spotting and browning due to paper quality as usual with fritsch but less than sometimes seen, final plate little oversized and therefore crumpled at edges, contemporary speckled tan calf red and green morocco gilt spine labels, edges sprinkled red, volume I head cap little chipped, few small stains and patchy fading, overall very good, armorial bookplate of Right Hon. Henry Hobhouse (1854-1937) and Stephen Hobhouse (1881-1961) and Arthur Hobhouse (1886-1965).   Unsworths Antiquarian Booksellers Ltd. E05 - 12   2016   £350

Association – Hobhouse, Henry

Epictetus *Epicteti Enchiridion Latinis Versibus Adumbratum.* Oxford: E. Theatro Sheldoniano, 1715. First edition, frontispiece, two leaves with fore-edges dusty, few minor marks elsewhere, 8vo., contemporary sprinkled calf, spine divided by double gilt fillets, black morocco lettering piece, other compartments with gilt wheel tool, edges sprinkled red, slightest bit rubbed at extremities, armorial bookplate of Henry Hobhouse, very good, very pleasant. Blackwell's Rare Books   B184 - 40   2016   £300

Gesner, Johann Mathias *Scriptores Rei Rusticae Veretes Latini.* Leipzig: sumtibus Caspari Fritsch, 1773. 1774. Second edition, 2 volumes, frontispiece to volume I and 6 further folding plates, engraved vignette to each titlepage, some spotting and browning due to paper quality as usual with fritsch but less than sometimes seen, final plate little oversized and therefore crumpled at edges, contemporary speckled tan calf red and green morocco gilt spine labels, edges sprinkled red, volume I head cap little chipped, few small stains and patchy fading, overall very good, armorial bookplate of Right Hon. Henry Hobhouse (1854-1937) and Stephen Hobhouse (1881-1961) and Arthur Hobhouse (1886-1965). Unsworths Antiquarian Booksellers Ltd. E05 - 12 2016 £350

Scriptores Rei Rusticae Veretes Latini. Lipsiae: sumptibus Caspari Fritsch, 1773-1774. Second edition, 2 volumes, 4to., frontispiece to volume 1, 6 further folding plates, engraved vignette to each titlepage, some spotting and browning due to paper quality as usual with Fritsch (but less than sometimes seen), final plate little oversized and therefore crumpled at edges, contemporary speckled tan calf, red and green morocco gilt spine labels, edges sprinkled red, volume 1 head-cap little chipped, few small stains and patchy fading but overall very good set, armorial bookplate of Right Hon, Henry Hobhouse (1854-1937). Unsworths Antiquarian Booksellers Ltd. 30 - 136 2016 £350

Association – Hobhouse, Stephen

Gesner, Johann Mathias *Scriptores Rei Rusticae Veretes Latini.* Leipzig: sumtibus Caspari Fritsch, 1773. 1774. Second edition, 2 volumes, frontispiece to volume I and 6 further folding plates, engraved vignette to each titlepage, some spotting and browning due to paper quality as usual with fritsch but less than sometimes seen, final plate little oversized and therefore crumpled at edges, contemporary speckled tan calf red and green morocco gilt spine labels, edges sprinkled red, volume I head cap little chipped, few small stains and patchy fading, overall very good, armorial bookplate of Right Hon. Henry Hobhouse (1854-1937) and Stephen Hobhouse (1881-1961) and Arthur Hobhouse (1886-1965). Unsworths Antiquarian Booksellers Ltd. E05 - 12 2016 £350

Association – Hockney, David

Stevens, Wallace 1879-1955 *The Blue Guitar and the Man with the Blue Guitar.* London and New York: Petersburg Press, 1977. First edition, small square 4to., illustrations, original boards, paper onlay on front cover, dust jacket, fox marks on edges of text block, otherwise fine, signed the artist, David Hockney. James S. Jaffe Rare Books Occasional List: Winter 2016 - 10 2016 $750

Association – Hodgkinson, Vera

Dickens, Charles 1812-1870 *Dickens to His Oldest Friend.* London: Putnam, 1932. One of 500 copies, half title, slight foxing to prelims, uncut in original dark green buckram, spine darkened, bookplate of Vera Hodgkinson. Jarndyce Antiquarian Booksellers CCXVIII - 848 2016 £30

Dickens, Charles 1812-1870 *Dickens to His Oldest Friend. The Letters of a Lifetime from Charles Dickens to Thomas Beard.* London: Putnam, 1932. One of 500 copies, Half title, slight foxing to prelims, uncut, original dark green buckram, spine darkened, bookplates of Vera Hodgkinson. Jarndyce Antiquarian Booksellers CCXVIII - 848 2016 £30

Association – Hodgson, W. B.

Mann, Horace *Report of an Educational tour in Germany and Parts of Great Britain and Ireland...* London: Simpkin, Marshall & Co., 1846. Half title, some pencil markings and annotations, original purple cloth, largely faded to brown, spine rubbed and head and tail following inner hinge cracking, inscribed "Robert Con Esq. with kindest regards from W. B. Hodgson, Liverpool Feb. 1846". Jarndyce Antiquarian Books CCXV - 842 2016 £85

Association – Hogan, Frank

Wylie, Elinor 1885-1928 *Incidental Numbers.* London: printed by Wm. Clowes & sons, 1912. First edition, one of 65 copies, 16mo., original printed boards (hairline crack in front hinge), Frank Hogan copy, this copy inscribed by author for Christopher Morley, inside front cover is autograph note by Morley, Wylie's first book, elaborate gold stamped Hogan bookplate, nearly fine in slipcase. Howard S. Mott Inc. 265 - 150 2016 $8000

Association – Hogben, Ross

Smith, George A. *Lovebirds and Related Parrots.* London: Paul Elek, 1979. Parrot Society edition limited to 350 numbered copies, this copy inscribed by author for Australian aviculturist Ross (Hogben), color photos, publisher's cloth and slipcase. Andrew Isles Natural History Books 55 - 24085 2016 $80

Association – Holcroft, Thomas

Paine, Thomas 1737-1809 *The Whole Proceedings on the Trial of an Information Exhibited ex officio by the king's Attorney Against Thomas Paine for a Libel Upon the Revolution and the Bill of Rights....* London: sold by Martha Gurney No. 128, Holborn Hill, 1793. 8vo., contemporary half calf, expertly rebacked, gilt banded spine, red morocco label, marbled boards, corners neatly repaired, bookplate of Michael Foot with pencil notes to front endpaper, pencil underlinings with the ownership signature of Thomas Holcroft 1745-1809. Jarndyce Antiquarian Booksellers CCXVI - 441 2016 £1800

Association – Holden, Irene

Pickering, Harold G. *Dog-Days on Trout Waters.* New York: Derrydale Press, 1933. One of 199 numbered copies signed by author, this additionally inscribed by Pickering to good friend Irene Holden, illustrations by Donald Gardner, paper covered boards, cloth spine, printed paper labels, bookplate, very light soiling and fading of boards, two facing leaves darkened from laid-in news cutting, else very good, not quite fine. Joseph J. Felcone, Inc. Books from Five Centuries: a Miscellany - 116 2016 $800

Association – Holland, Baron

Lucretius Carus, Titus *De Rerum Nature Libros Sex, ad Exemplarium Mss. Fidem Recensitos...* Impensis editoris typis A Hamilton, 1796-1797. First Wakefield edition, large paper copy, engraved frontispiece, little spotting and dust soiling here and there, tall 4to., contemporary vellum, boards bordered with gilt roll with central gilt stamp of arms of Duke of Devonshire, spines titled gilt, deep blue endpapers, edges gilt and marbled underneath vellum on each spine split horizontally, just above middle, volume ii in two places (with slight loss of vellum on volumes ii and iii), otherwise just little bit age yellowed and with touch of wear to spine ends, bookplates of Chatsworth Library, red morocco gilt booklabels of Baron Holland, plus modern paper booklabel in volume i, very good. Blackwell's Rare Books B186 - 98 2016 £3000

Association – Holley, Nan

Bacchylides *The Poems of Bacchylides.* London: by order of the trustees of The British museum, 1897. First edition, 8vo, cloth, gilt lettered, spine slightly cocked, spine sunned, toning to upper board, corners and endcaps bumped and starting to fray, edges dusted and uncut, spit to rear endpapers, good, library number cellotaped to spine, ex-libris bookplate of Nan Holley, ownership inscription of N. M. Halley. Unsworths Antiquarian Booksellers Ltd. E05 - 16 2016 £30

Association – Hollis, Roger

Bingham, John *A Case for Libel.* London: Victor Gollancz, 1963. First edition, crown 8vo., original red boards, backstip lettered gilt with lean to spine, top edge trifle dusty, dust jacket bright but rather frayed, good, inscribed by author to then Director of MIT, Roger Hollis. Blackwell's Rare Books B184 - 116 2016 £150

Bingham, John *Murder Plan Six.* London: Victor Gollancz, 1958. First edition, crown 8vo., original red boards, backstrip lettered gilt with lean to spine, top edge trifle dusty, dust jacket bright, backstrip panel shade darkened, light dust soiling to rear panel, some light chipping to corners and backstrip ends and short closed tear at foot of upper joint fold, good, inscribed by author to then Director of MI5, Roger Hollis. Blackwell's Rare Books B184 - 117 2016 £200

Bingham, John *Night's Black Agent.* London: Victor Gollancz, 1961. First edition, touch of creasing to bottom corners of two leaves, crown 8vo., original red boards, backstrip lettered in black with lean to spine, top edge trifle dusty, dust jacket bright with light chipping to corners and backstrip ends, small amount of speckling at head of lower joint fold and one or two light marks, good, inscribed by author to then Director of MI5, Roger Hollis. Blackwell's Rare Books B184 - 118 2016 £200

Association – Hollrik, Dr.

Holyoake, George Jacob *The Jubilee History of the Leeds Industrial Co-Operative Society from 1847 to 1897.* Leeds: Central Cooperative Offices, 1897. First edition, 8vo., publiser's cloth somewhat worn, spine lacking cloth at extremities, corporate library bookplate, inscribed for friend Dr. Hollrik (sp?), good copy, large foldout map of the city of Leeds with stores run by Industrial Society noted, photos. Second Life Books, Inc. 196A - 812 2016 $65

Association – Holman, Frederick

Swan, James G. *The Northwest Coast; or Three Years' Residence in Washington Territory.* New York: Harper & Bros., 1857. First edition, publisher's brown buckram, flat spine with gilt tiling, 29 illustrations by author, 18 of these full page, one a folding map, front free endpaper, inscribed by author to Mrs. C. W. Philbrick, with neatly stamped signature of Ellen Philbrick, bookplate of Frederick V. Holman, spine bit sunned, extremities slightly worn, small patches of water(?) stains to boards, other trivial imperfections, really excellent copy, fresh and clean, original fragile binding still solid and generally well preserved. Phillip J. Pirages 67 - 271 2016 $1100

Association – Holmes, Daniel Henry

Silvestre, Armand *Roses D'Octobre.* Paris: G. Charpentier et Cie, 1890. No. 9 of 10 copies on Holland paper, 187 x 12mm., charming contemporary dark green morocco gilt and inlaid by Salvador David (stamp-signed on front turn-in), covers framed by gilt branches, entwined with inlaid pink morocco roses, raised bands, spine compartments with central inlaid pink now surrounded by gilt foliage, densely gilt turn-ins, all edges gilt, original wrappers bound in, bookplate of Daniel Henry Holmes Jr., tiny fox spot every 40 pages, text with overall faint darkening (perhaps as in all copies because of paper stock), spine probably just a shade darker than the covers, still obviously fine, completely clean and smooth internally, and in unworn, lustrous binding. Phillip J. Pirages   67 - 35   2016 $750

Association – Holmes, Emma Maria

Creasy, Edward Shepherd *The Fifteen Decisive Battles of the world from Marathon to Waterloo.* London: Richard Bentley, 1851. Second edition, 2 volumes, , inscribed in both volumes to Emma Maria Holmes from ESP April 13th '52 with pencil notes indicating that the volumes were later given to Emma's brother, William George Holmes and suggesting that the original recipient may have been Stanley Poole, very good.   Jarndyce Antiquarian Booksellers   CCXVII - 70   2016   £150

Association – Holmes, William George

Creasy, Edward Shepherd *The Fifteen Decisive Battles of the world from Marathon to Waterloo.* London: Richard Bentley, 1851. Second edition, 2 volumes, , inscribed in both volumes to Emma Maria Holmes from ESP April 13th '52 with pencil notes indicating that the volumes were later given to Emma's brother, William George Holmes and suggesting that the original recipient may have been Stanley Poole, very good.   Jarndyce Antiquarian Booksellers   CCXVII - 70   2016   £150

Association – Holstein-Hoisteinborg

Marchand, Prosper *Dictionnaire Historiques ou Memoires Critiques et Litterires, Concernant La Vie et les Ouvrages de Divers Personnage Distingues, Particulierement Dans La Republique des Lettres.* La Haye: Pierre de Hondt, 1758-1759. 2 volumes bound as one, three quarter brown leather with decorated brown paper boards, six raised bands to spine with brown leather title label in second compartment, chipping and small tears to leather as well as to paper covers, interior pages show light aging, otherwise lean and bright, offsetting on free endpapers from leather borders, previous owner bookplate and small stamp "Holstein-Hoisteinborg", very good.   The Kelmscott Bookshop   13 - 36   2016 $750

Association – Holt White, Thomas

Tusser, Thomas *Five Hundred Points of Good Husbandry.* London: by Thomas Ratcliffe and Mary Daniel for the Company of Stationers, 1672. Small 4to., black letter, heavily browned/spotted in places throughout due to poor paper quality, scorch marks on K1, P1-4, S2 and T2, headlines on the Penultimate leaf just shaved, large lock of ?wool tied in bow loosely inserted between G3-4, late 18th century calf, spine divided by raised bands with red morocco label, upper joint slightly cracked, from the library of James Stevens Cox (1910-1997), engraved initial of Thomas Holt White (1724-1797), and three successive Holt White family signatures.   Maggs Bros. Ltd.   1447 - 420   2016   £500

Association – Holt, Lester

Hughes, Langston *The Weary Blues.* New York: Knopf, 1944. Ninth printing, 8vo, yellow cloth, dust jacket lacks some paper at extremities of spine and small hole which affects two letters of author's name, very good, inscribed by author for Mrs. Lester Holt Nov. 14 1945.   Second Life Books, Inc.   196A - 851   2016 $450

Association – Holte, Clarence

Quarles, Benjamin *Allies for Freedom: Blacks and John Brown.* New York: Oxford University Press, 1974. First edition, fine in attractive, near fine dust jacket with very slight fading to spine lettering and very small nick on rear panel, inscribed by author for Clarence Holte, ad exec.   Between the Covers Rare Books   202 - 82   2016 $350

Association – Hooper, Richard

Gray, Thomas   1716-1771 *The Poetical Works of Thomas Gray....* York: printed by A. Ward and sold by J. Dodsley and J. Todd, York, 1775. First edition, 4to., contemporary full calf, spine with contrasting red leather label, frontispiece, joints cracking at top head of spine with little chipping, some scrapes to boards and rubbing to spine, little browning to endpapers, otherwise very good, ink note on front free endpaper by Richard Hooper of Upton Vicarage, Berks dated Jul 12 1872, bookplate of Baron Carlingford.   Sotheran's Piccadilly Notes - Summer 2015 - 150   2016   £275

Association – Hooper, Roger Garth

Bible. Greek - 1848 *He Palaia Diatheke Kata Tous Ebdomekonta Vetus Testamentum...* Oxonii: e Typographico Academico, 1848. 3 volumes, small 8vo., text in Greek, little toned, endpapers slightly foxed, generally bright and clean within, contemporary dark brown morocco, gilt titles to spines, all edges gilt, marbled endpapers, rubbed, corners bumped and little worn, very good, ownership inscription of A. Staveley, 47th March 1881 to Roger Garth Hooper, 1925 to Peter A. Boyle, September 1952.   Unsworths Antiquarian Booksellers   30 - 18   2016   £90

Association – Hooten, Peter

Merrill, James *Peter.* Dublin: Old Deerfield: The Deerfield Press/The Gallery Press, 1982. First edition, one of 300 numbered copies by poet on colophon page, this copy inscribed by author and Peter Hooten for William Meredith, fine in fine dust jacket.   Charles Agvent   William Meredith - 81   2016 $350

Association – Hope, A. J. Beresford

Catholic Church. Liturgy & Ritual *Missale ad Consuetudinem Ecclesie Romanae...* Paris: in alma Parisiorum Academia Impensis Thielmanni Kerver 23 March, 1506. 8vo., Kerver's fine device on titlepage, full page woodcut of Crucifixion, large crible initial of Crucifixion, crible initials, music on four-line staves, printed in red and black, decorative line fillers in red and black, 8vo., 19th century purple brown morocco richly gilt in 16th century style by J. Wright, binder, gauffered edges, headcaps rubbed, bookseller's note stating this was from the library of A. J. Beresford Hope (1820-1887), bookplate and inscription of Herbert Watney (1843-1932).   Maggs Bros. Ltd.   1474 - 53   2016   £4500

Association – Hope, J. B.

Turton, Thomas *Thoughts on the Admission of Persons Without Regard to their Religious Opinions to Certain Degrees in the Universities of England.* Cambridge: printed at the Pitt Press by John Smith &c., 1834. 16 page catalog, sewn as issued, dust jackets, slightly marked, signature of J. B. Hope.   Jarndyce Antiquarian Books   CCXV - 962   2016   £30

Association – Hopkins, Francis

Montmort, Pierre Remond De *Essay d'Analyse sur les Jeux de Hazard.* Paris: Chez Jacque Quillau, 1708. First edition, 4to, engraved title vignette, 3 vignettes depicting gambling scenes, decorative initials and tailpieces, 3 folding tables, occasional browning, pages 127-8 with closed tear, small marginal burn hole pages 101-102, original full vellum with maroon calf spine label, ink inscription of author, armorial bookplate of Sir Francis Hopkins, 1st Baronet 1756-1814, very good.   Jeff Weber Rare Books   183 - 24   2016 $7000

Association – Hopkins, J. G. E.

Rhymers' Club *The Second Book of the Rhymers' Club.* London: Elkin Mathews & John Lane, 1894. One of 650 copies, presentation from publisher John Lane, inscribed in pencil to Irish poet and novelist Katharine Tynan Hinkson, extremely uncommon thus, original brown cloth with gilt title to spine, light browning to margins of interior pages, bookplates of writer J. G. E. Hopkins, culinary writer Helmut Lothar Ripperger and collector Mark Samuels Lasner, very good.   The Kelmscott Bookshop   13 - 59   2016 $950

Association – Horbury, William

Bible. Greek - 1835 *Vetus Testamentum Graece.* Lipsiae: sumptibus et typis Caroli Tauchnitii, 1835. Editio stereotypa, 8vo., sporadic light foxing, contemporary vellum, gilt spine with two dark green morocco labels, marbled endpapers, all edges red, vellum little darkened, some smudgy marks but still very good, ownership inscriptions, first of J. Thorp, Jan. 1860 and second of William Horbury dated iv, xlii, Thorps's signature again in pencil to titlepage.   Unsworths Antiquarian Booksellers   30 - 17   2016   £60

Association – Hornby, Charles Harry St. John

Francesco D'Assisi, Saint   1886-1926 *I Fioretti Del glorioso Poverello Di Cristo S. Francesco Di Assisi. (Little flowers).* Chelsea: Ashendene Press, 1922. One of 200 paper copies for sale of 240 printed (and 12 on vellum), 225 x 156mm., original flexible vellum, green silk ties, gilt lettering on spine, edges untrimmed, printer's device and 53 woodcuts in text, printed in black, blue and red, initials in red or blue designed by Graily Hewitt, laid in at front an inked autograph note on personal note card in its original autograph envelope from C. H. St. John Hornby to London bookseller James S Bain, vellum with naturally occurring variations in color, otherwise very fine, binding unworn and text entirely clean, fresh and smooth.   Phillip J. Pirages   67 - 11   2016 $1250

Morris, William   1834-1896 *A Note by William Morris on his Aims in Founding the Kelmscott Press Together with a Short Description of the Press by S. C. Cockerell...* Hammersmith: Kelmscott Press, 1898. One of 525 copies on paper (and 12 on vellum), 210 x 150mm., original holland backed gray boards, very nice folding box covered with navy blue cloth, spine with morocco label reading "C. H. St.. J. H./ S. C. C./ W.M.", elaborate borders around frontispiece and first page of text, frontispiece drawn by Edward Burne-Jones and cut by William Morris, large decorative woodcut initials, device on last page of text and one full page woodcut of ornaments used in Kelmscott edition of "Love is Enough", printed in red and red black, bookplate of Charles Harry St. John Hornby, presentation from Cockerell to Hornby and his wife as well as tipped-on letter to Hornby, describing, this work, rear pastedown with clipped signature of William Morris pasted down, pristine.   Phillip J. Pirages   67 - 221   2016 $19,500

Association – Horton, Albert Enoch

Tegg, Thomas *A Present for an Apprentice.* London: William Tegg & Co., 1848. Second edition, illustrations, occasional slight spotting, original red cloth, spine faded, slightly rubbed, presentation label on leading f.e.p. from the Worshipful Company of Shipwrights to Albert Enoch Horton on his being bound apprentice to his father.   Jarndyce Antiquarian Books   CCXV - 434   2016   £40

Association – Horton, William

Mirabeau, Honore Gabrielle Riquetti, Comte De 1749-1791 *Considerations on the Order of Cincinnatus. To Which are Added Several Original Papers...* Philadelphia: printed by T. Seddon, 1786. New edition, first American edition, 8vo. 19th century three quarter morocco over marbled boards, very good copy, untrimmed, chips to spine ends, scuffed tips, owner's bookplate son front free endpapers and first blank, tight binding, the copy of Frank Maier and William S. S. Horton, M.De. with armorial bookplate. Kaaterskill Books 21 - 55 2016 $750

Association – Hosmer, Herbert

Krauss, Ruth *A Hole is to Dig.* New York: Harper and Row, 1952. Later printing, 12mo., pictorial cloth, fine in dust jacket, illustrations by Maurice Sendak, this copy inscribed by artist for Herbert Hosmer. Aleph-bet Books, Inc. 111 - 413 2016 $850

Association – Hottelet

Hearn, Gordon *A Handbook for Traveller's in India and Pakistan, Burma and Ceylon, Including the Portuguese and French Possessions and the Indian States...* London: Murray, 1952. 8vo., original orange cloth, lettered in gilt, rarely seen dust jacket, printed in red, large folding map in rear pocket, numerous folding maps and plans, small repaired tear to wrappers, bought from Calcutta booksellers by C. R. Hottelet of NY. Sotheran's Travel and Exploration - 130 2016 £128

Association – Houghton, Henry

Blagdon, Francis William *A New Dictionary of Classical Quotations.* London: printed for Robert Stodart, 1819. First edition, light age toning, 12mo., untrimmed in original boards, paper label to spine, joints rubbed, some slight wear, early ink inscription of Henry Houghton and later monogram stamp of STC, good. Blackwell's Rare Books B186 - 20 2016 £120

Association – Houghton, William

Lily, William *A Short Introduction of Grammar, Generally to be Used.* printed by Bonham Norton, 1630. 4to., titlepage dusty, dampmark to fore-corners, some other spots and stains, repairs to blank, corners of titlepage and also to just some corners tips of next two and last six leaves, contemporary ownership inscription of William Houghton to titlepage and third leaf, 4to., sometime stitched into limp wrappers reusing a parchment manuscript of the sixteenth century, parchment somewhat unevenly trimmed around edges and externally dust soiled, sound. Blackwell's Rare Books Greek & Latin Classics VII - 55 2016 £1500

Association – Houseplan, Edgar

Pool, J. Lawrence *Acoustic Nerve Tumors. Early Diagnosis and Treatment.* Springfield: Thomas, 1970. Original binding, near fine in dust jacket, presentation from author to Ed Houseplan. James Tait Goodrich X-78 - 471 2016 $175

Pool, J. Lawrence *Adventures and Ventures of a New York Neurosurgeon.* published by the author, 1988. Blue printed wrappers, illustrations, nice, presentation note to Edgar Houseplan from author. James Tait Goodrich X-78 - 473 2016 $95

Pool, J. Lawrence *Aneurysma and Arteriovenous Snomnalies of the Brain Diagnois and Treatment.* New York: Hoeber, 1965. 271 illustrations, 4 in full color, near fine, original binding, dust jacket, presentation form author March 16 1965 to Ed Houseplan. James Tait Goodrich X-78 - 469 2016 $150

Pool, J. Lawrence *The Early Diagnosis and Treatment of Acoustic Nerve Tumors.* Springfield: Thomas, 1957. Original binding, near fine in dust jacket, presentation copy to Ed Houseplan from author Oct. 29 1957. James Tait Goodrich X-78 - 470 2016 $125

Pool, J. Lawrence *The Neurological Institute of New York 1909-1974.* Pocket Knife Press, 1975. Original printed wrappers, spine soiled, illustrations, presentation by author for Edgar Houseplan. James Tait Goodrich X-78 - 475 2016 $125

Riley, Henry Alsop *An Atlas of the Basal Ganglia, Brain Stem and Spinal Cord.* New York: Hafner Pub., 1960. Oblong 4to., original binding, very nice, excellent illustrations, signature of E. H. Houseplan. James Tait Goodrich X-78 - 491 2016 $395

Stookey, Byron *Trigeminal Neuralgia. Its History and Treatment.* Springfield: 1959. original cloth, original dust jacket worn, internally fine, presentation from Joseph Ransohoff for Edgar Houseplan. James Tait Goodrich X-78 - 518 2016 $150

Willis, Thomas *The Anatomy of the Brain and Nerves.* Birmingham: Classics of Neurology and Neurosurgery Library, 1983. Engraved frontispiece, full gilt leather, folio, nice, from the library of Edgar Houseplan. James Tait Goodrich X-78 - 559 2016 $125

Association – Housman, A. E.

Manilius, Marcus *Astronomicon. Liber Quintus.* London: Richards Press, 1930. One of 400 copies, 8vo. original tape backed printed boards, printed paper spine label, with ALS by A. E. Housman to G. N. Wiggins, tipped to front free endpaper, spine panel lightly sunned, dust soiling to top edge of textblock, few fox marks and fold from mailing letter is fine.   James S. Jaffe Rare Books   Occasional List: Winter 2016 - 80   2016 $1000

Association – Howard, Fannie May

Wordsworth, William 1770-1850 *The Complete Poetical Works.* Boston and New York: Houghton Mifflin Co., 1910-1911. Large paper edition, one of 500 copies, 279 x 159mm., 10 volumes, lovely dark olive brown three quarter crushed morocco handsomely gilt, marbled sides and endpapers, raised bands, spine compartments densely gilt with floral and foliate tools emanating from a large central rose, top edges gilt, other edges untrimmed, the set entirely unopened, vignette title pages, map of Lake District, 75 photogravure plates (with letterpress tissue guards), one hand colored plate at beginning that duplicates a black and white plate elsewhere in volume, titlepage in red and black, each volume with full page tipped in bookplate of Fannie May Howard, in remarkably fine condition, essentially without any wear, virtually pristine internally and obviously used so little that the volumes open unwillingly.   Phillip J. Pirages 67 - 360   2016 $3250

Association – Howard, R.

Hawtrey, Stephen Thomas *Reminiscences of a French Eton.* London: printed by Mary S. Rickerby, 1847. Original green cloth wrappers, red edges, presentation inscription "R. Howard Esq. from the writer".   Jarndyce Antiquarian Books CCXV - 723   2016   £35

Association – Howell, Douglas Morse

Warner, Tom *The Monster in the Turtles Den.* Cincinnati: Michael Mar Press, 1977. Only edition, 4to., original pictorial full brown morocco, uncut, illustrations in color, produced on handmade paper, inscribed to master papermaker Douglas Morse Howell.   Howard S. Mott Inc. 265 - 75   2016 $1250

Association – Howell, Frank

Floire et Jeanne *The Tale of King Florus and the Fair Jehane.* Kelmscott Press, 1893. 350 copies printed with an additional 15 copies on vellum, of the 360 copies, 76 copies were purchased in sheets by Tregaskis and sent to book binders, this is probably a trial copy that Rau chose not to send as his exhibition piece but seems more likely that it was a second copy commissioned by a collector who saw the Tretaskis copy in the exhibition or the exhibition catalog, 16mo., choicely bound by E Rau of St. Petersburg in full orange crushed morocco lettered gilt on spine, boards with semi of stylized flowers within a single gilt and dog tooth panel, central initial of 'W' on upper board and "M' on lower, richly gilt inner dentelles over marbled endpapers, double page woodcut border, text printed in black and red in Chaucer type, fine in slipcase, bookplate of Frank Howell and of American collector Charles Walker Andrews, loosely inserted is typed letter from J. and M. L. Tregaskis to Frank Howell.   Sotheran's Piccadilly Notes - Summer 2015 - 175   2016   £4995

Association – Howes, Barbara

Acton, Harold *Four Cautionary Tales.* New York: Wyn, 1948. First American edition, 8vo., little faded yellow cloth, inscribed by author to poet and editor Barbara Howes with her bookplate, included is original photo by Cecil Beaton with his name stamp on verso.   Second Life Books, Inc. 196A - 6   2016 $350

Barzun, Jacques *Romanticism and the Modern Ego.* Boston: Little Brown, 1943. First edition, 8vo., very good, tight, clean copy, inscribed by author to poet/editor Barbara Howes with her bookplate.   Second Life Books, Inc. 196A - 82   2016 $150

Bly Aleixandre, Vicente *Twenty Poems.* Madison: Seventies Press, 1977. First edition, 8vo., bounf in plain paper wrappers with printed dust jacket, inscribed by author to poet Barbara Howes, nice copy.   Second Life Books, Inc. 196A - 166   2016 $65

Clark, Eleanor *Baldur's Gate.* New York: Pantheon, 1970. First edition, 8vo., inscribed by author to noted American poet Barbara Howes, very nice in dust jacket with Howes' notes on rear endpaper.   Second Life Books, Inc. 196A - 293   2016 $75

Clark, Eleanor *Dr. Heart: a Novella & other Stories.* New York: Pantheon, 1976. First edition, 8vo., inscribed by author to poet Barbara Howes.   Second Life Books, Inc. 196A - 294   2016 $65

Collis, John Stewart *The Worm Forgives the Plow.* New York: George Braziller, 1975. First American edition, 8vo., illustrations by Oscar Ratti, very good in price clipped dust jacket, inscribed by poet Barbara Howes for her first husband and his wife. Second Life Books, Inc. 196A - 320 2016 $75

Cozzens, James Gould *S. S. San Pedro and Castaway.* New York: Modern Library Paperback by Random House, 1957? 8vo. paperback, spine loose, good, this was poet and editor Barbara Howe's copy and laid in are 10 (6 x 4 inch) sheets of paper on which Howes has commented on Cozzens as a writer and on these short stories. Second Life Books, Inc. 196A - 75 2016 $350

Dinesen, Isak 1885-1962 *Karen Blixens Kunst (Tegninger og Malerier). the Art of Karen Blixen (Drawings & Paintings).* Denmark: Karen Blixen Museet, 2001. First edition, 4to., illustrations in black and white and color, printed boards, near fine, this the copy of William Jay Smith who wrote 16 lines of holograph about his personal memories of his wife, poet Barbara Howes meeting Blixen in Denmark. Second Life Books, Inc. 196A - 161 2016 $125

Holland, Rupert Sargent *Pirates of the Delaware.* Philadelphia: Lippincott, 1925. First edition, author's presentation to poet Barbara Howes, cream cloth, pictorial stamping in dark blue, edges slightly spotted, cover somewhat scuffed and soiled, spine little worn at ends, else very good, tight copy. Second Life Books, Inc. 196A - 811 2016 $65

Jacobsen, Josephine *On the Island.* Princeton: Ontario Review Press, 1989. First printing, 8vo., signed on titlepage by author, presentation from author to editor Barbara Howes, gray-green cloth, nice in slightly chipped dust jacket. Second Life Books, Inc. 196A - 885 2016 $65

Jung, Carl G. *Eranos 1941.* Zurich: 1941. Mimeographed, 182 pages bound in stiff boards, signed by poet Barbara Howes, very good. Second Life Books, Inc. 196A - 904 2016 $50

Lewis, Sinclair 1885-1951 *Ann Vickers.* London: Cape, 1933. Second impression, 8vo., publisher's cloth some soiled, very good, inscribed by author for Elizabeth Farmer Feb. 23 1933, bookplate of author Barbara Howes. Second Life Books, Inc. 196 B - 65 2016 $600

Merrill, James *The Changing Light at Sandover.* New York: Atheneum, 1982. First edition, 8vo, photographs inside covers, paper wrappers, author's presentation to Barbara Howes, errata slip laid in, first five leaves loose, else very good. Second Life Books, Inc. 196 B - 212 2016 $300

O'Faolain, Sean *A Summer In Italy.* New York: Devin-Adair, 1950. First edition, 8vo., signed by author, bookplate of Barbara Howes. Second Life Books, Inc. 196 B - 332 2016 $40

Porter, Katherine Anne 1890-1980 *A Christmas Story.* New York: Delacorte, 1967. First edition, 12mo., very good, tight, clean copy in little toned dust jacket, inscribed by author for friend, poet Barbara Howes, 12mo., very good, clean, tight copy in little toned dust jacket. Second Life Books, Inc. 196 B - 425 2016 $700

Reid, Alastair *To Lighten My House.* New York: Morgan & Morgan, 1953. One of 850 copies, 8vo., author's presentation on half title to author and editor, Barbara Howes, with her bookplate, gray cloth, stamped in red, edges little soiled, cover slightly faded, otherwise nice in very slightly chipped and soiled dust jacket. Second Life Books, Inc. 196 B - 469 2016 $100

Smith, Chard Powers *Turn of the Dial.* New York: Scribner's, 1943. First edition, 8vo., author's presentation for poet Barbara Howes, 8vo., nice, dust jacket little chipped and scuffed. Second Life Books, Inc. 196 B - 606 2016 $50

Stahl, E. L. *Holderlin's Symbolism: an Essays.* Oxford: B. H. Blackwell, 1994. First edition, 8vo., original printed wrappers little toned, very good, clean, this is poet Barbara Howes' copy with her bookplate and signature. Second Life Books, Inc. 196 B - 675 2016 $75

Stevens, Wallace 1879-1955 *Ideas of Order.* New York: Knopf, 1936. First trade edition, 12mo., little soiled publisher's boards, paper spine label, very good with bookplate of poet Barbara Howes, with Howes' ownership signature, in the yellow binding (#3), one of 1000 copies. Second Life Books, Inc. 196 B - 701 2016 $250

Warren, Robert Penn 1905-1989 *New and Selected Poems 1923-1985.* New York: Random House, 1989. First Random House edition, 8vo., nice in little worn printed wrappers, inscribed by author to poet and editor Barbara Howes. Second Life Books, Inc. 196 B - 830 2016 $100

Welty, Eudora *One Writer's Beginnings.* Cambridge: Harvard, 1984. First edition, third printing, 8vo., photos, inscribed by author for Barbara Howes, nice in dust jacket. Second Life Books, Inc. 196 B - 849 2016 $500

Association – Howland, Dorothy

Randolph, Thomas *Poems.* London: for F. Bowman, and are to be sold by William Roybould, 1652. Fourth edition, small 8vo., engraved titlepage, small stain at head of engraved titlepage, paper flaw in lower corner of (2)(N), upper corners of (2)C1-7 dampstained, rust spot to head of I1, type ornament border of title closely shaved and border of subtitle to 'Aristippus' slightly shaved, early 19th century calf, covers ruled in blind, front joint cracked, lower joint and headcaps rubbed, small hole in spine, from the library of James Stevens Cox (1910-1997), contemporary signature of Dorothy Howland with crude ink drawing.   Maggs Bros. Ltd.   1447 - 353   2016   £150

Association – Hoyland, Clement Hoyland

Dickens, Charles   1812-1870 *Bleak House.* London: Bradbury & Evans, 1853. First edition, primary binding variant, with date in Roman numerals at tail of spine, half title, frontispiece and engraved title, plates, occasional very slight offsetting, generally very clean and fresh, original olive green fine diaper cloth, blocked in blind, spine lettered gilt, very slightly faded, armorial bookplate of Clement Edward Hoyland with signature in pencil, very good.   Jarndyce Antiquarian Booksellers   CCXVIII - 501   2016   £2500

Association – Hubbard, Bruce

Carruth, Hayden *Aura.* West Burke: Janus Press, 1977. First edition, limited to only 50 copies, this copy press lettered especially 'for Michael Boylen' and inscribed by Claire Van Vliet in pencil for Bruce Hubbard, tall folio, printed handmade paper folder, enclosed in publisher's linen folding box with printed paper label on spine, very fine, rare.   James S. Jaffe Rare Books   Occasional List: Winter 2016 - 84   2016 $4500

Association – Hubbard, Elbert

Dickens, Charles   1812-1870 *A Christmas Carol in Prose.* East Aurora: Roycroft Shop, 1902. First edition thus, printed on Japanese vellum, frontispiece, titlepage decorations, head bands and tailpieces by Samuel Warner, 8vo., three quarter blue morocco binding with marbled paper boards and endpapers, spine gilt decorated, top edge gilt, light wear, handsome, very good+ copy, signed by Elbert Hubbard.   Tavistock Books   Bibliolatry - 2   2016 $1500

Association – Hubbell, H. P.

Dickens, Charles   1812-1870 *Bleak House.* Philadelphia: Getz & Buck, 1853. Appears to be first American edition, Frontispiece, plates, uncut in original pale green printed wrappers, slightly worn in upper and lower margins, contemporary signature of H. P. Hubbell (?) NY.   Jarndyce Antiquarian Booksellers   CCXVIII - 515   2016   £450

Association – Hughes, Arthur

Rossetti, Dante Gabriel   1828-1882 *Poems.* London: F. S. Ellis, 1870. 8vo., presentation inscription from author for friend, Arthur Hughes; dark green cloth boards with gilt title to spine, attractive gilt decoration to spine and boards, minor wear to edges and slight discoloration to boards, clean, bright interior with decorative endpieces, housed in black cloth covered clamshell box, gilt label to spine, very good.   The Kelmscott Bookshop   12 - 93   2016 $6400

Association – Hughes, Dorothy

Reed, Eliot *The Maras Affair.* Garden City: Doubleday Crime Club, 1953. First edition, advance review copy with review slip laid in, signed by Dorothy Hughes, very good in dust jacket with chipped spine ends, slightly faded spine and wear at corners.   Mordida Books   2015 - 012572   2016 $65

Association – Hughes, Richard

Wescott, Glenway *Images of Truth: Remembrances and Criticism.* New York: Harper & Row, 1962. First edition, author's presentation of Richard Hughes, Aug. 15 1962, excellent copy in slightly soiled dust jacket.   Second Life Books, Inc.   196 B - 851   2016 $188

Association – Hughes, William

Eklekta. In Usum Scholae Regiae Westmonasteriensis. Sumptibus Gulielmi Ginger, ad Insignia Collegii Westmonasteriennsis..., 1781. Sole edition, second leaf of ads, bound following titlepage instead of at end, little minor spotting, 8vo. original linen, bit marked and rubbed, ownership inscription of William Hughes, alumnus of Felsted School to front flyleaf, his name repeated with date 1784 at rear, very good, rare.   Blackwell's Rare Books   Greek & Latin Classics VII - 25   2016   £600

Association – Hunt, Fanny

Radcliffe, Ann Ward   1764-1823 *The Romance of the Forest.* London: printed for T. Hookham and J. Carpenter, 1792. Third edition, 3 volumes, 12mo., old stain to gutter margin pages 200-206 volume I, otherwise very clean, early ownership name of Fanny (?) Hunt, Christian names erased causing hole to volume 1 titlepage, key pattern bands, gilt stars, red and black morocco labels, hinges and spines little rubbed, very good.   Jarndyce Antiquarian Booksellers   CCXVI - 485   2016   £280

Association – Hunter, Clark

Barrie, James Matthew 1860-1937 *Jane Annie or the Good Conduct Prize.* London: Chappell & Co., 1893. Paperback, original printed wrappers, very nice, uncommon, particularly in this condition, variant issue, housed in slipcase, bookplates of Lord Esher and Clark Hunter, very good.   The Kelmscott Bookshop   12 - 5   2016 $700

Association – Hunter, J. T.

Hunter, George *Reminiscences of an Old Timer.* Battle Creek: Review and Herald, 1889. Fourth edition, 8vo., illustrations, warmly inscribed "Compliments of the author..... to J. T. Hunter, as in other words Hunter to Hunter.... July 8th 90", also signed with his Indian name, red cloth stamped in gilt, little worn, hinge tender, very good.   Second Life Books, Inc.   196A - 864   2016 $350

Association – Hunter, Richard

Huet, Pierre Daniel *De Imbecillitate Mentis Humanae Libri Tres.* Amsterdam: Apud H. Du. Sauzet, 1738. 12mo., title in red and black, engraved frontispiece, portrait, spine strengthened with clear tape, good copy in contemporary grey blue boards, presentation slip "With the compliments of Dr. Richard A. Hunter" laid in, with Stonor armorial bookplate.   Edwin V. Glaser Rare Books   2015 - 19212   2016 $300

Association – Hupkirk, Peter

Austin, Ethel Mildred King Britten *Unending Journey.* London: Thornton Butterworth, 1939. First edition, original brick red cloth, spine lettered gilt, illustrated dust jackets (price clipped), map, spine little sunned, wrappers with few minor chips, very good, from the collection of travel writer Peter Hupkirk, ownership inscription of Wilfred G. Wright dated April 1939.   Sotheran's   Piccadilly Notes - Summer 2015 - 23   2016   £278

Association – Hurck, Henrico Petro Van

Lucanus, Marcus Annaeus *Pharaslia, cum Commentario Petri Burmanni.* Leidae: apud Conradum Wishoff, Danielem Goetval et Georg. Jacob Wishoff fil, Conrad, 1740. 4to., presentation certificate bound in, titlepage in red and black with large engraved vignette, some woodcut initials, 3 page errata to rear, occasional light foxing, some leaves little grubby towards top and fore-edges, contemporary prize vellum, gilt spine and boards with Utrecht coat-of-arms centerpiece to both boards, edges sprinkled red and blue, spine darkened, quite soiled, joint beginning to crack but holding firm, endpapers bit dusty, very good, presentation certificate dated 1776 bound in before titlepage, inscribed to Henrico Petro van Hurck and signed by various academics, small leaf of calculations in old hand loosely inserted.   Unsworths Antiquarian Booksellers   30 - 98   2016   £300

Association – Hurst, Joseph Stancliffe

Hamilton, Elizabeth *A Series of Popular Essays Illustrative of Principles Essentially Connected with the Improvement of the Understanding, the Imagination and the Heart.* Edinburgh: printed for Manners and Miller, 1813. First edition, 2 volumes, 5 pages ads volume II, contemporary full tan calf, gilt spines, , red morocco labels, some slight rubbing, bookplates of William Jacomb and Joseph Stancliffe Hurst, handsome.   Jarndyce Antiquarian Books   CCXV - 715   2016   £320

Association – Hurwitz, Donald

Ben-Gurion, David *Israel. A Personal History.* New York: Tel Aviv: Funk & Wagnalls/Sabra Books, 1971. First edition, small 4to., fine, original slipcase with mild soil edge wear, slipcase indicates the volume was presented to participants in the United Jewish Appeal 1972 study Conference, presentation for Mr. and Mrs. Donald Hurwitz.   By the Book, L. C.   45 - 2   2016 $1600

Association – Hustler, John

Pascal, Blaise *Les Provinciales; or The Mysterie of Jersuitisme.* London: printed by J.. G. for R. Royston, 1657. First edition in English, 12mo., prelim blank, postscript leaf, two final leaves of errata and ads, added engraved titlepage by Robert Vaughan, 18th century panelled calf, neatly rebacked, retaining old morocco lettering label, spine lettered gilt with decorative gilt board edges, 18th century armorial bookplate of John Hustler of Acklam mounted on verso of engraved titlepage, early ink notations at bottom of engraved titlepage, leaves Q thru Q12 have been affected by printer's ink, mostly just little snugging, verso of Q10 is the only page where two lines of text have been affected, apart from few flaws, fine copy, very rare.   Heritage Book Shop   Holiday 2015 - 86   2016 $2000

Association – Hutchins, Reginald C. Tudor

Bolton, Robert *Instructions for a Right Comforting Afflicted Consequences...* imprinted by Felix Kyngston for Thomas Weaver, 1631. First edition, woodcut printer's device on title, very slight dampstaining in upper margins, initial blank discarded, small 4to., contemporary mottled calf, blind tooled corner ornaments, author's name in gilt on spine, top compartment of spine defective early initials "PC" opposite signature B, inscription on titlepage "Christo Duce, R.C.", 17th century of T. Browne, 20th century acquisition note by Reginald Chas. Tudor Hutchins, very good.   Blackwell's Rare Books   B186 - 22   2016   £1750

Association – Hutchins, Walter

Washington, Booker T. *Up from Slavery.* New York: Doubleday Page & Co., 1901. First edition, frontispiece, red cloth, gilt, modern gift inscription for Walter Hutchins from Peter Lax, modest wear at spine ends and corners, else tight and bright, near fine.   Between the Covers Rare Books   202 - 117   2016 $300

Association – Hutchinson, Muriel

Lyndon, Barre *The Amazing Dr. Clitterhouse.* London: Hamish Hamilton, 1936. First edition, 8vo. fine in little soiled and worn dust jacket, photos, signed by 12 members of the first NY production, including Alexander Field, Edward Fulang, Muriel Hutchinson, Stephen Fox and others.   Second Life Books, Inc.   196 B - 108   2016 $225

Association – Hutchinson, Ruth

Milhouse, Katherine *With Bells On.* New York: Charles Scribner, 1955. A. First edition, 4to., aqua pictorial cloth, fine in dust jacket with piece out of corner, many full page color illustrations by author, this copy inscribed by Milhous to author Ruth Hutchinson with color pencil drawing, also signed by her, laid in are two handwritten letters from Milhouse to Hutchinson.   Aleph-bet Books, Inc.   111 - 281   2016 $450

Association – Hutchinson, Thomas

Homerus *The Odyssey of Homer.* London: printed for John Bell, 1774. 2 volumes, some light spotting, later ownership inscription of Thomas Hutchinson of St. John's College to titlepages (possibly the vicar of Kimbolton and nephew of William Wordsworth), 8vo., contemporary sprinkled sheep, rubbed and worn, red and green morocco lettering pieces to volume i (lost from volume ii), joints cracking, sound, rare.   Blackwell's Rare Books   Greek & Latin Classics VII - 35   2016   £400

Horne, Herbert Percy *Diversi Colores.* London: published by author at the Chiswick Press, 1891. First edition, probably one of 250 copies, duodecimo, original gray-green boards and printed paper label, decorated titlepage and colophon designed by author, form the library of school teacher Thomas Hutchinson with his initials and shelf number on front pastedown and note on front free endpaper, scarce little book, label little darkened, edges slightly rubbed, fine copy.   The Brick Row Book Shop   Miscellany 69 - 47   2016 $225

Smith, Robert Angus *To Iceland in a yacht...* Edinburgh: privately printed by Edmonston & Douglas. May, 1873. Sole edition, great rarity, 8vo. original decorated dark green cloth, gilt, gilt vignette to upper cover, 5 lithographic plates, 6 autotype plates from photos, lacking one tissue guard, folding plans, slight wear to extremities, inner hinges strengthened, few pages with minimal markings to margins, else clean and very good, contemporary bookplate of Thomas Hutchinson of Morpeth.   Sotheran's   Travel and Exploration - 442   2016   £898

Association – Huth, Alfred Henry

Spencer, John *A Discourse Concerning Prodigies; Wherein the Vanity of Presages by them is Reprehended and Their True and Proper Ends Asserted and Vindicated.* London: by John Field for Will. Graves... in Cambridge, 1663. First edition, small 4to., titlepage little dusty and with the lower margin renewed, and lower edge of gathering 'M' folded at little shorter and uncut, late 19th century gilt ruled polished calf by Pratt, spine tooled in gilt and with red and green morocco label, edges gilt, Henry Huth and Alfred Henry Huth copy with leather label, from the library of James Stevens Cox (1910-1997), Sir R. Leicester Harmsworth, 1st Bart (1870-1937).   Maggs Bros. Ltd.   1447 - 391   2016   £350

Association – Huth, Edward

Yarrell, William *A History of British Birds.* John Van Voorst, 1837-1843. 1845. 1846. First edition, large paper copy, imperial 8vo., 3 volumes with both supplements bound in to volume 3, bound in full green morocco by P. Bedford, gilt panels with foliate tooling to sides, elaborate gilt spines with gilt raised bands and lettering, gilt turn-ins, marbled endpapers, all edges gilt, engraved illustrations by John Thompson, spine sunned to attractive brown, internally fine, very clean copy in handsome binding, Edward Huth bookplates.   Sotheran's   Piccadilly Notes - Summer 2015 - 339   2016   £1600

Association – Huth, Henry

Spencer, John *A Discourse Concerning Prodigies; Wherein the Vanity of Presages by them is Reprehended and Their True and Proper Ends Asserted and Vindicated.* London: by John Field for Will. Graves... in Cambridge, 1663. First edition, small 4to., titlepage little dusty and with the lower margin renewed, and lower edge of gathering 'M' folded at little shorter and uncut, late 19th century gilt ruled polished calf by Pratt, spine tooled in gilt and with red and green morocco label, edges gilt, Henry Huth and Alfred Henry Huth copy with leather label, from the library of James Stevens Cox (1910-1997), Sir R. Leicester Harmsworth, 1st Bart (1870-1937).   Maggs Bros. Ltd.   1447 - 391   2016   £350

Association – Hyde, Donald

Simms, Rupert *Bibliotheca Staffordiensis.* Lichfield: A. C. Lomax, 1894. Limited to 200 numbered copies, large 4to., original cloth, uncut pages with top edge gilt, bookplate of Donald and Mary Hyde, ink inscription by Henry Elwell, also signed by Elwell, hinges, head and tail of spine worn, corners rubbed, both covers scuffed.   Oak Knoll Books   310 - 267   2016 $350

Association – Hyde, Mary

Simms, Rupert *Bibliotheca Staffordiensis.* Lichfield: A. C. Lomax, 1894. Limited to 200 numbered copies, large 4to., original cloth, uncut pages with top edge gilt, bookplate of Donald and Mary Hyde, ink inscription by Henry Elwell, also signed by Elwell, hinges, head and tail of spine worn, corners rubbed, both covers scuffed.   Oak Knoll Books   310 - 267   2016 $350

Association – Hyde, Salem

MacKail, John William *William Morris, an Address Delivered the XIth November MDCCCC at Kelmscott House, Hammersmith, before Hammersmith Socialist Society.* London: Doves Press, 1901. One of 300 copies (of an edition of 315), printed in black and red on handmade paper, 8vo., original limp cream vellum by Doves Bindery, backstrip gilt lettered, untrimmed, slight wear to head of boards, bookplate of Charles Walker Andrews, very good, Andrews pencil note records that the book came from Salem Hyde's Library (Hyde being his father in law).   Blackwell's Rare Books   Marks of Genius - 30   2016   £500

Association – Ignatow, David

Ray, David *Gathering Firewood. New Poems and Selected.* Middletown: Wesleyan University Press, 1974. First edition, decorated wrappers, inscribed and signed in 1974 for William Meredith, ALS with postcard by Ray to Meredith as well as large promotional card for the book from David Ingatow, near fine.   Charles Agvent   William Meredith - 104   2016 $60

Association – Impey, Catherine

Harper, Frances E. W. *Iola Leroy, or Shadows Uplifted.* Philadelphia: Garrigues Brothers, 1892. First edition, brown cloth, gilt, frontispiece, fine with just slightest of bumping at corners and hinges repaired, gilt bright and unrubbed, small stamp of Anti-Slavery and Aborigines Protection Society, inscribed by author for Catherine Impey.   Between the Covers Rare Books   207 - 50   2016 $35,000

Association – Indian Tom

Van Zandt, Townes *For the Sake of the Song.* San Antonio: Wings Press, 1977. First edition, one of 500 copies signed and numbered by Van Zandt and numbered, roughly 100 of which were given to Van Zandt as author's copies, near fine in photo illustrated boards with no dust jacket as issued, gift inscribed from Indian Tom.   Royal Books   52 - 8   2016 $2500

Association – Ingalls, Daniel Henry Holmes

Symmachus, Quintus Aurelius *Epistolarum Diversos Libri Decem Eustatium Vignon.* Geneva: E. Vignon per Dionysium Probum, 1587. 2 parts in one volume, 8vo., occasional notes and underlining, some notes in old hand to prelim blanks, additional titlepage to second part, little toned towards top edge, few smudges and light stains, contemporary semi limp vellum, number 68 inked to spine, yapp edged, edges lightly sprinkled, slightly yellowed a few marks evidence of lost ties, upper fore-edge a bit creased, endband thongs snapped at gutter but still sound and very good, 20th century bookplate of Daniel Henry Holmes Ingalls (1916-1999).   Unsworths Antiquarian Booksellers Ltd.   E05 - 14   2016   £475

Association – Ingleson, Elizabeth

Watts, Isaac *Select Songs for Children.* Newcastle: printed for S. Hodgson and sold by the Booksellers in Town and Country, 1790. Seventh edition, 12mo., a number of leaves rather thumb marked, some browning, final two pages have verses separated by pencil lines, small tear with loss to blank lower corner of titlepage, contemporary calf backed pattered paper boards, spine and corners worn, boards very rubbed, signature of Elizabeth Nelson, Aug. 16th 1794, and of Elizabeth Ingleson Nov. 1821.   Jarndyce Antiquarian Booksellers   CCXVI - 597   2016   £120

Association – Invercauld Castle

King, William *The Original Works of William King, LL.D.* London: printed for the Editor and sold by N. Conant, successor to Mr. Whiston in Fleet street, 1776. 8vo., 3 volumes, half titles, engraved vignette portrait to each titlepage, one full page woodcut, one very slight marginal tear to T1 volume II, some offset browning on endpapers, fine, clean set bound in full contemporary sprinkled calf, smooth spines, gilt bands, red morocco title labels, dark green oval volume labels set within gilt wreaths, from the library of Invercauld Castle, Braemar.   Jarndyce Antiquarian Booksellers   CCXVI - 345   2016   £680

La Fontaine, Jean De 1621-1695 *Fables Choisies Mises en Vers...* Paris: Le Breton, 1769. Nouvelle edition, 2 parts in 1, half titles, titlepages printed in red and black, engraved frontispiece, 12mo., fine, clean copy, full contemporary calf, raised and gilt banded spine, red morocco label, paper flaw to blank lower corner L1, from the library of Invercauld Castle, Braemar.   Jarndyce Antiquarian Booksellers   CCXVI - 353   2016   £250

Langhorne, John *The Effusions of Friendship and Fancy.* London: printed for T. Becket and P. A De Hondt, 1766. Second edition, 12mo., 2 volumes, fine, clean copy, full contemporary calf, raised and gilt banded spine, red and black morocco labels, from the Library of Invercauld Castle, Braemar.   Jarndyce Antiquarian Booksellers   CCXVI - 355   2016   £350

Lennox, Charlotte 1720-1804 *The Female Quioxte, or the Adventures of Arabella.* London: printed for A. Millar...., 1752. First edition, 12mo., small marginal tear without loss to C2 volume I, long vertical tear to left hand edge N2 in same volume, possibly original paper flaw, several gatherings little proud in binding, full contemporary sprinkled calf, raised & gilt banded spines, red morocco labels, gilt volume numbers, small gilt device for each compartment, from the library of Invercauld Castle, Braemar.   Jarndyce Antiquarian Booksellers   CCXVI - 361   2016   £850

Lucas, Richard *An Enquiry into the Happiness.* London: printed by J. Buckland (and 8 others), 1764. Tenth edition, 8vo, near fine in full contemporary sprinkled calf, raised and gilt banded spines, red morocco labels, from the library of Invercauld Casatle, Braemar.   Jarndyce Antiquarian Booksellers   CCXVI - 373   2016   £450

Marmontel, Jean Francois 1723-1799 *The Incas or the Destruction of the Empire of Peru.* London: printed for J. Nourse (and 3 others), 1777. First English edition, 12mo., half titles, fine, clean copy, full contemporary sprinkled calf, raised and gilt banded spines, red morocco labels, gilt volume numbers, from the library of Invercauld Castle, Braemar.   Jarndyce Antiquarian Booksellers   CCXVI - 402   2016   £580

Marmontel, Jean Francois 1723-1799 *Les Incas; ou la Destruction d l'Empire de Peru.* Paris: chez Lacombe, 1777. First edition in French, 2 volumes, half titles, engraved frontispiece, 10 engraved plates, 12mo., very clean, slight waterstain to blank upper margin of one plate, small tear without loss to leading edge of first titlepage, full contemporary English sprinkled calf, raised and gilt banded spines, red morocco labels, gilt volume numbers, from the Library of Invercauld Castle, Braemar, very good.   Jarndyce Antiquarian Booksellers   CCXVI - 401   2016   £480

Royal Dublin Society *Essays and Observations on the Following Subjects Viz. O Trade - Husbandry of flax - raising Banks Against Tides and Floods - Hops....* Dublin: printed: London: Reprinted and sold by Charles Corbett, 1740. 4 engraved folding plates, 8vo., fine, clean copy, full contemporary calf, raised and gilt banded spine, repeat gilt flower head device, red morocco label, from the Library Of Invercauld Castle, Braemar.   Jarndyce Antiquarian Booksellers   CCXVI - 498   2016   £1500

Santa Croce, Antonio *Secretaria di Apollo or Letters from Apollo....* London: printed for R. Smith at the Angel and Bible...., 1704. 8vo., engraved frontispiece, very crisp, clean, fine full contemporary panelled calf, simple raised spine bands, from the library of Invercauld Castle Braemar, armorial bookplate.   Jarndyce Antiquarian Booksellers   CCXVI - 508   2016   £480

Smith, Hugh *Letters to Married Women.* London: printed for G. Kearsley in Ludgate Street, 1767. 8vo., some slight offset browning to edges of titlepage, otherwise fine, clean copy, full contemporary pale calf, gilt ruled borders, raised and gilt banded, unlettered spine, from the Library of Invercauld Castle, Braemar.   Jarndyce Antiquarian Booksellers   CCXVI - 533   2016   £580

Smollett, Tobias George 1721-1771 *The Adventures of Roderick Random.* London: printed for J. Osborn, 1750. Third edition, engraved frontispieces after Hayman, 12mo., fine, clean copy, full contemporary sprinkled calf, gilt ruled borders, cornerpiece decoration, raised and gilt banded spines, red and black morocco labels, gilt decoration to each compartment, from the library of Invercauld Castle, Braemar.   Jarndyce Antiquarian Booksellers   CCXVI - 534   2016 £350

Taylor, Jeremy 1613-1667 *The Rule and Exercises of Holy Living... (with) The Rule and Exercises of Holy Dying.* London: printed by J. Heptinstall for Royston and Elizabeth Meredith, 1715. Twenty-second editions, 8vo., 2 volumes bound in uniform full contemporary sprinkled calf, raised bands, red morocco labels, slight waterstain to head of final leaves in Holy Living, small piece of leather worn from rear board of same volume, from the library of Invercauld Castle, Braemar with contemporary note on inner rear board.   Jarndyce Antiquarian Booksellers   CCXVI - 562   2016   £200

Tytler, William *An Historical and Critical Enquiry into the Evidence Produced by the Earls of Murray and Morton against Mary Queen of Scots.* Edinburgh: printed by W. Gordon, 1760. 8vo., fine clean copy in full contemporary sprinkled calf, smooth spine, gilt bands, red morocco label, very slight abrasion to upper board, from the library of Invercauld Castle, Braemar.   Jarndyce Antiquarian Booksellers   CCXVI - 576   2016   £380

Warden, William *Letters Written on Board His Majesty's Ship the Northumberland and Saint Helena...* London: pub. for the author by R. Ackermann, 1816. Fourth edition, half title, engraved frontispiece, 2 plates, 8vo., fine copy, contemporary half russia, gilt banded spine, gilt flower head motifs, from the library of Invercauld Castle, Braemar, bookseller's ticket of A. Brown & Co. Aberdeen. Jarndyce Antiquarian Booksellers CCXVI - 591 2016 £280

Association – Irving, Edward

Carlyle, Thomas 1795-1881 *Sartor Resartus.* London: privately printed, James Fraser, 1834. First separate edition, one of only 58 copies, titlepage re-laid, dusted and with few small tears, one affecting final 'v' in imprint date, bound without wrappers in slightly later brown calf by M. Patterson, Glasgow, rubbed, presentation for Edward Irving, from author. Jarndyce Antiquarian Booksellers CCXVII - 64 2016 £5800

Association – Isherwood, Christopher

Petronius *The Satyricon of T. Petronius Arbiter.* London: Simpkin Marshall, Hamilton, Kent and Co., circa, 1926. 8vo., original blue cloth, lettered gilt on spine, gilt very dulled, ornaments of Martin Travers, slight rubbing to extremities, otherwise very good, without dust jacket, Christopher Isherwood's copy with ownership signature dated Oxford Dec. 1926. Sotheran's Piccadilly Notes - Summer 2015 - 235 2016 £750

Association – Ismery, Bruce

The Murdered Bride or the Victim of Treachery: a Tale of Horror. London: William Emans, 1837. First edition?, small quarto, engraved frontispiece, additional engraved titlepage and 6 other engraved plates, contemporary half calf over marbled boards, original parts bound together with stabmarks, bound by G. J. Sutton (?) with small binder label on front endpaper, spine heavily tooled gilt in compartments, green morocco spine label, lettered gilt, spine with name M. N. Bourne in gilt at foot, all edges marbled, green endpapers, some toning to plates, bit of foxing throughout, boards bit rubbed, previous owner Bruce Ismery's armorial bookplate, overall very good, extremely rare. Heritage Book Shop Holiday 2015 - 3 2016 $3000

Association – Isted, Ambrose

Randolph, Thomas *Poems with the Muses Looking-Glass and Amyntas.* Oxford: for F. Bowman and are to be sold by John Crosley, 1668. Fifth (i.e. sixth) edition, small 8vo., with half title, leaves A1-P8 lightly browned, small piece torn away from blank corner of C4 and with small closed tear to lower margin of L4, some small spots, minor hole through P7 (touching text) and with sheet S closely trimmed, but with no loss of text, early 20th century calf, gilt spine by Birdsall & Son of Northampton, joints rubbed and slightly cracked at head and tail, some insect damage at foot of spine, from the library of James Stevens Cox (1910-1997), armorial bookplate, Ambrose Isted (1717-81) of Ecton Hall, Northamptonshire. Maggs Bros. Ltd. 1447 - 354 2016 £180

Twysden, Roger *Historiae Anglicanae Scriptores X.* London: Typis Jacobi Flesher sumptibus Cornelii Bee, 1652. Editio princeps, 2 volumes as 1, folio, half title, title in red and black, section, woodcut initials, few tiny wax spots and ink blots not obscuring text, contemporary dark brown calf, blind tooled frame, edges sprinkled brown and red, neatly rebacked, red morocco gilt spine label, few scratches to boards, inner hinges reinforced, 2 armorial bookplates, F. E. Sotheby, Ecton and Derek Baker, third armorial bookplate of Ambrose Isted, fourth armorial bookplate with no name but with motto 'Que Serra Serra". Unsworths Antiquarian Booksellers Ltd. E01 - Early Printing - 28 2016 £500

Association – Izou, Elizabeth

Morris, William 1834-1896 *The Earthly Paradise.* London: Ellis and Green, 1872. Popular edition in 10 parts, 10 volumes, frontispiece volume I, original flexible blue green cloth, slight lifting in places, otherwise good plus, ownership inscribed in all volumes of Elizabeth Izou. Jarndyce Antiquarian Booksellers CCXVII - 190 2016 £125

Association – Jachna, Joseph

Taken by Design: Photographs from the Institute of Design 1937-1971. Chicago: University of Chicago Press, 2002. First edition, very near fine copy in photo illustrated flexible boards, signed by Joseph Jachna and additionally inscribed by Joseph Sterling And Alan Cohen. Jeff Hirsch Books E-List 80 - 1 2016 $200

Association – Jack, Aquinto

Laughlin, James *New Directions in Poetry and Prose.* Norfolk: New Directions, 1936. First edition, 8vo., printed boards, somewhat soiled, signed by author to Aquinto Jack, one of 513 copies. Second Life Books, Inc. 196 B - 14 2016 $300

Association – Jack, Ian

Arnold, Matthew 1822-1888 *Higher Schools and Universities in Germany.* London: Macmillan & Co., 1874. Second edition, half title, 83 page catalog (Oct. 1873), original brown cloth, slightly rubbed and dulled, library label at foot of spine, booklabel of Ian Jack. Jarndyce Antiquarian Books   CCXV - 508   2016   £35

Association – Jackson, Ebenezer

Adams, John Quincy 1767-1848 *Oration on the Life and Character of Gilbert Motier De Lafayette...* Washington: 1835. First edition, thick paper copy, inscribed by author on inserted slip in front of titlepage, as usual, signed for Ebenezer Jackson, octavo, contemporary full straight grain navy blue morocco, handsomely rebacked to style, spine stamped and lettered gilt, boards ruled in gilt, blue drab endpapers, original plain wrappers bound in, pages bit toned, inner hinges repaired, previous owners ink signature and address label, some owner's blind embossed notary stamp on signature sheet and page 49, very good.   Heritage Book Shop   Holiday 2015 - 1   2016 $5000

Association – Jackson, Harry

Patrick, John *The Teahouse of the August Moon.* New York: Putnam, 1952. Second impression, 8vo., Harry Jackson's copy (Sgt. Gregovich in the play), signed by David Wayne and 15 members of the cast, presentation from Jackson, light edge bumps, tear on blank, otherwise very good in little chipped and stained dust jacket.   Second Life Books, Inc.   196 B - 380   2016 $200

Association – Jackson, R. D.

McCarthy, Justin *A History of Our Own Times.* London: Chatto & Windus, 1880-1905. First editions, 7 volumes, large 8vo., contemporary half blue morocco, spine gilt ruled in compartments and lettered direct by Bicker and Son, last 3 volumes signed, small piece missing form foot of spine, some shelfwear, armorial bookplate inside front cover of R. D. Jackson, sound.   Blackwell's Rare Books   B186 - 99   2016   £250

Association – Jackson, W. H. M.

Terentius Afer, Publius *Comoediae Sex.* Cambridge: ex officina Ioannis Hayes, 1676. 12mo., titlepage dusty and with small tear in blank area, some light spotting and browning, small intermittent dampmark to lower corner, contemporary panelled calf, rebacked preserving original spine, hinges neatly relined, old leather bit scratched and rubbed, bookplate of Lt. Col. W. H. M. Jackson, sound.   Blackwell's Rare Books   B186 - 147   2016   £180

Association – Jackson, William

Midgley, Samuel *Halifax and Its Gibbet Law Placed in a True Light.* Halifax: printed by P. Darby for John Bentley, 1761. First edition thus, small 8vo., frontispiece and 1 additional folding plate, little toned, occasional underlining, light foxing, frontispiece edges delicate with few small repairs, later tan marbled calf, apparently by Riviere, spine gilt, raised bands, all edges gilt, endpapers renewed, joints creased, upper just starting, free endpapers toned at edges, very good, handsome copy, elaborate ownership inscription of William Jackson, Halifax 1679.   Unsworths Antiquarian Booksellers Ltd.   E05 - 8   2016   £175

Association – Jacomb, William

Hamilton, Elizabeth *A Series of Popular Essays Illustrative of Principles Essentially Connected with the Improvement of the Understanding, the Imagination and the Heart.* Edinburgh: printed for Manners and Miller, 1813. First edition, 2 volumes, 5 pages ads volume II, contemporary full tan calf, gilt spines, , red morocco labels, some slight rubbing, bookplates of William Jacomb and Joseph Stancliffe Hurst, handsome.   Jarndyce Antiquarian Books   CCXV - 715   2016   £320

Association – Jacott, Eleanor

Maugham, William Somerset 1874-1965 *The Making of a Saint.* London: T. Fisher Unwin, 1898. First English edition, uncommon second book, original green cloth with gilt title to spine, minor rubbing to boards and minor wear to spine ends, text and endpages slightly browned as is usual with this book, bookplates of three previous owners, A. S. Alexander, Eleanor Jacott and Mark Samuels Lasner, very good.   The Kelmscott Bookshop   12 - 66   2016 $300

Association – James, Alice

James, William *The Letters of...* Boston: Atlantic Monthly, 1920. Limited edition, #1 of 600 sets, 2 volumes, 8vo., photos and facsimiles, gray paper over boards, embossed medallion on front and blue cloth spine, paper label, top edge gilt, little foxing here and there, covers little worn at edges and corners, otherwise very good, tight set, Alice James' copy of the set with her name on blank, perhaps written by publisher.   Second Life Books, Inc.   196A - 891   2016 $350

Association – James, Harry

Parsons, Louella *The Gay Illiterate.* Garden City: Doubleday Doran, 1944. First edition, fine in price clipped, very good dust jacket with slight loss at crown, inscribed by Parson for Betty Grable and husband Harry James.   Between the Covers Rare Books   204 - 51   2016 $650

Association – James, Revd.

Caraccioli, Louis Antoine *Advice from a Lady of Quality to Her Children in the Last Stage of a Lingering Illness.* Gloucester: printed by R Raikes and sold by J. F. & C. Rivington, 1766. Fourth edition, 8vo., full contemporary green crushed morocco, boards elaborately blocked in gilt, raised bands, compartments in gilt, spine slightly faded and rubbed, 2 small nicks to front board, presentation inscription "Penelope Phipps given by Revd. James Esqr. August 18th 1805, with additional inscription beneath dated 1851, all edges gilt, very good, handsome copy. Jarndyce Antiquarian Books CCXV - 97 2016 £420

Association – Jamieson, Jessica Duncan

Hopper, Nora *Under Quickens Boughs.* London: John Lane, Bodley Head, 1896. First edition, highly decorated green cloth with red and black floral designs on front and back boards, title and author in gilt to spine, very good with light bumping to corners, interior very good, untrimmed fore-edges, inscription and poem in th hand of Jessica Duncan Jamieson, as well as tipped in rebuttal poet title to JDJ with slip of paper reading "William Parker" securing it, another poem written in pencil. The Kelmscott Bookshop 12 - 55 2016 $175

Association – Janvrin, Francis

Grimaldi, Stacey *A suit of Armour for Youth.* published by the proprietor, 1824. First edition, engraved frontispiece, 11 engraved plates each with flap, 1 of the flaps re-attached, some offsetting, 12mo., contemporary calf, gilt roll tooled borders on sides, spine gilt, rebacked (little crudely), corners worn, contemporary ownership inscription of Jane Janvrin and inscription by her presenting volume to her brother, Francis, sound. Blackwell's Rare Books B186 - 70 2016 £450

Association – Janvrin, Jane

Grimaldi, Stacey *A suit of Armour for Youth.* published by the proprietor, 1824. First edition, engraved frontispiece, 11 engraved plates each with flap, 1 of the flaps re-attached, some offsetting, 12mo., contemporary calf, gilt roll tooled borders on sides, spine gilt, rebacked (little crudely), corners worn, contemporary ownership inscription of Jane Janvrin and inscription by her presenting volume to her brother, Francis, sound. Blackwell's Rare Books B186 - 70 2016 £450

Association – Jarcho, Saul

Osler, William 1849-1919 *Bibliotheca Osleriana.* Montreal: 1969. Thick 4to., original red cloth, light wear, from the collection of Saul Jarcho, M.D. with his signature, photocopied addenda and corrigenda laid in. James Tait Goodrich X-78 - 439 2016 $125

Packard, Francis R. *History of Medicine in the United States.* New York: 1931. Second edition, 2 volumes, light cloth wear, else very good, from the library of Saul Jarcho, MD with his signature on each of front flyleaves. James Tait Goodrich X-78 - 449 2016 $250

Association – Jareret, Mrs.

The Young Ladies' Offering or Gems of Prose and Poetry... Boston: Phillips & Sampson, 1856. Reprint, 8vo., black cloth elaborately stamped in gilt, little worn along hinge and extremities of spine, otherwise bright, with Lydia Sigourney's name as if she were the author, later bookplate, inscribed by Sigourney for Mrs. Jareret. Second Life Books, Inc. 197 - 291 2016 $150

Association – Jean-Aubry, Gerard

Conrad, Joseph 1857-1924 *Laughing Anne and One Day More - two plays.* London: Castle, 1924. First combined edition, octavo, from the library of Gerard Jean-Aubry, author's close friend and first biographer, from the library of Stanley Seeger with his small bookplate, tipped on blank facing page 19 (a summary description of personages in the play), an original sketch in blue crayon of the stage layout, and positioning of the characters written in black ink by Conrad, at lower corner is note in green ink in Jean-Abury's hand "Plan de la scene - fait par Joseph Conrad", with much rougher sketch for final scene, free endpapers tanned, otherwise fine in very good, nicked and creased dust jacket with enclosed tear at head of upper hinge, preserved in green buckram slipcase lettered gilt and with inner folding sleeve. Peter Ellis 112 - 82 2016 £1250

Association – Jebb, Julian

Fraser, Antonia *Cool Repentance.* London: Weidenfeld & Nicholson, 1982. very good copy in like dust jacket, loosely inserted invitation card from author presentation from author for Julian (Jebb). I. D. Edrich Crime - 2016 £30

Association – Jefferey, F. J.

Monaldini, Giuseppe Antonio *Instituzione Antiquaria Numismatica o sia Introduzione allo Studio delle Antiche Medaglie in due Libri Proposa.* Rome: A Spese di Venanzio Monaldini nella Stamperia Giovanni Zempel, 1772. First edition, title printed in red and black with engraved vignette, 3 folding engraved plates, half title, apparently lacking initial blank, 8vo., contemporary sheep backed russet boards, all but 1 of the sheep tips lacking, stamp (19th century) on half title of English numismatics dealer, F. J. Jefferey, good, scarce. Blackwell's Rare Books B184 - 66 2016 £350

Association – Jefferson, Geoffrey

Singer, Charles *A Prelude to Modern Science.* London: 1946. 59 text figures, 6 plates, near fine, original binding and dust jacket, Sir Geoffrey Jefferson's copy.   James Tait Goodrich   X-78 - 539   2016 $495

Association – Jeniken, Sebastianus

Bible. Latin - 1578 *Biblia Sacra Veteris et Novi Testament.* Basle: Thomas Guarinus, 1578. First titlepage within a broad ornamental woodcut border showing Aaron and Moses, incorporating printer's device, larger version of device on titles to other two parts, 190 woodcut illustrations by Tobias Stimmer, 3 double page maps and full page map, 3 parts in one volume, 8vo., contemporary blind tooled pigskin over wooden boards, panelled and outer ornamental roll, inner roll with historiated figure of the virgus Fides, Spes, Fortunado etc. dated 1563, with central panels of the Crucifixion on upper cover with legend below, and of the Resurrection on lower cover with legend below, dated 1583 on upper cover, 7 cornerpieces remain, clasps of catches intact though one replaced, some wear, initials on upper cover erased, superbly illustrated bible, inscribed by Sebastianus Jeniken 1613 with his notes on division of Bible facing the titlepage 18th and 19th century inscriptions on flyleaf, scattering of wormholes towards end, mostly marginal, title lightly soiled, few spots and ink stains, but generally handsome copy in original binding.   Maggs Bros. Ltd.   1474 - 13   2016   £3500

Association – Jenkin, Patrick

Thomas, David A. *Churchill, the member for Woodford.* 1995. Fine in like dust jacket, inscribed presentation by author as well as Churchill's successor as MP for Woodford Lord (Patrick) Jenkin, fine in like dust jacket.   I. D. Edrich   Winston Spencer Churchill - 2016   £65

Association – Jenkyn, James

Montaigne, Michel De 1533-1592 *Essays of Michael Seigneur de Montaigne in Three Books.* London: printed for T. Basset, 1693. Early edition, 3 volumes, small 8vo., engraved frontispiece portrait of author, some early ink underlining, lacks rear free endpaper (volume I), original full mottled calf (mismatched set), raised bands, gilt spines, red leather title labels, inner joints reinforced with Kozo, worn, ownership signatures of J. Merton (?), Arthur Rogers - June 1933, Reverend James Jenkyn (d. 1825 of Herfordshire?) and Myles Standish Slocum, Pasadena.   Jeff Weber Rare Books   181 - 22   2016 $275

Association – Jennett, Sean

Conrad, Joseph 1857-1924 *The Nature of a Crime.* London: Duckworth, 1924. First edition, small octavo, 2 bookplates on front pastedown, one of which is that of travel writer Sean Jennett, typographer at Faber and Faber and that of Conrad collector, Stanley J. Seeger, spine slightly faded at head and just little bumped at tail, very good, preserved in custom made green buckram slipcase, lettered gilt on spine, inner folding sleeve.   Peter Ellis   112 - 78   2016   £95

Association – Jersey, Sarah Sophia Child Villiers, Countess of

Cervantes Saavedra, Miguel De 1547-1616 *El Ingenioso Hidalgo Don Quixote de la Mancha.* Madrid: J. Ibarra, 1780. 4 volumes, 4to., additional engraved titles, map, plates and vignettes, contemporary Spanish binding of green marbled calf, covers further 'marbled' with inlaid octagonal panel of brown morocco set in gilt tooled border, spines gilt in compartments, red morocco labels, marbled endpapers, gilt edges, slight worn damage to boot of spine of volume I, head of spine of volume 4 slightly chipped, fine, armorial bookplate of Sarah Sophia Child (Villiers), Countess of Jersey (1785-1867) with old pressmarks of Osterley Park Library, bookplate of Jonathan and Phillida Gili (by Reynolds Stone), it is said about 1500 copies printed, borders of few plates foxed.   Maggs Bros. Ltd.   1474 - 23   2016   £12,500

Association – Jespersen, Beryl Schreiber

Schreiber, Hazel Snell *Coastland Curfew and Other Poems.* San Francisco: Privately published, 1957. One of 250 copies, Memorial edition, presentation from Beryl Schreiber Jespersen to Ina Coolibrth Circle SF, titlepage printed in red and black, tan cloth backed blue/gray boards, gilt, fine.   Argonaut Book Shop   Private Press 2015 - 6377   2016 $60

Association – Jessner, Lucie

O'Keefe, Georgia *Some Memories of Drawings.* New York: Atlantis Edition, 1974. First edition, limited, one of 20 presentation copies, out of a total edition of 120, signed by artist, and book's designer, Leonard Baskin, extraordinary copy, given by O'Keeffe's long time agent Doris Bry to her friend and noted psychiatrist Dr. Lucie Jessner, with letters from Bry to Jessner, 21 charcoal and pencil drawings reproduced on Arches Silkscreen in 300-line offset lithography, each laid into lettered folded leaf of Arches paper.   Manhattan Rare Book Company   2016 - 1626   2016 $10,000

Association – Jessop, Thomas

Hodgkin, John *Calligraphia Graeca et Poecilographia Graeca.* n.p., 1794-1807. Engraved titlepage, dedication and 17 other engraved plates, plates toned and somewhat spotted, letterpress more heavily spotted, ownership inscription of Thomas Jessop to titlepage, folio, contemporary quarter red roan, marbled boards, spine lettered vertically in gilt, front binder's blank with hand lettered 'half title' reading 'Poikilographia Ellenika' in Greek alphabet, followed by reference to discussion of the work in the Classical Journal, rubbed, some light wear to extremities, ownership stamp of Grace Richardson to endpaper, good.   Blackwell's Rare Books   Greek & Latin Classics VII - 27   2016   £800

Association – Jewett, Sarah Orne

Greenaway, Kate   1846-1901 *Under the Window.* London: George Routledge & Sons, New York: 416 Broome St., n.d., 1878. First edition, green glazed pictorial boards, blue spine, blue endpapers, yellow edges, light edgewear an hinge rubbing, half title quite foxed, else very good+, this copy signed by Sarah Orne Jewett, her copy.   Aleph-bet Books, Inc.   112 - 224   2016 $600

Association – JOB

Bouchot, Henri *L'Epopee Du Costume Militiaire Francais.* Paris: Societe Feancaise D'Editions D'Art/L. Henry May, 1898. First edition, thick 4to., original handsome full embossed leather with gold and red designs, all edges gilt, fine, illustrations by JOB, laid in is 3 page handwritten letter from JOB regarding the publication of one of his books.   Aleph-bet Books, Inc.   112 - 269   2016 $2750

Mongorgueil, G. *Murat.* Paris: Hachette, 1903. gilt pictorial cloth, endpaper slightly frayed, slight cover rubbing, else fine, 40 magnificent full page color illustrations by JOB, this copy inscribed by him.   Aleph-bet Books, Inc.   112 - 270   2016 $2250

Association – Jodrell, Richard Paul

Vergilius Maro, Publius *Bucolica et Georgica tabullis Aeneis Olim a Johanne Pine...* n.p., 1774. 2 volumes bound as one, 80 plates on 59 sheets, frequent further engravings within text, ad leaf discarded, 8vo., contemporary tree calf, spine divided by gilt fillet, red morocco lettering piece, other compartments with central sunburst gilt tools, bit rubbed, spine creased, gutters cracking towards middle of textbock but binding perfectly sound, bookplates of Magdalen College, Oxford and Sir Richard Paul Jodrell, with inscription indicating the gift of the volume from the former to the latter dated 1802, good.   Blackwell's Rare Books   B186 - 160   2016   £600

Association – John, Augustus

Symons, A. J. A. *H. M. Stanley.* London: Duckworth, 1933. First edition, octavo, covers bit faded at edges, very good in good, chipped, torn and rubbed dust jacket repaired on reverse, presentation copy inscribed by author for Augustus John, July 1933.   Peter Ellis   112 - 393   2016   £75

Association – Johnson, Adelaide

Brown, Olympia *Acquaintances, Old and New, Among Reformers.* Milwaukee: by the author, 1911. First edition, grey cloth, photos, fine, inscribed by author to sculptor Adelaide Johnson, Xmas 1913.   Second Life Books, Inc.   196A - 216   2016 $950

Association – Johnson, Dan

Baker, Houston A. *Modernism and the Harlem Renaissance.* Chicago: University of Chicago, 1987. First printing, 8vo., several illustrations, review laid in, author's presentation to Dan Johnson, maroon cloth, edges spotted cover little scuffed at corners and end of spine, otherwise nice in dust jacket.   Second Life Books, Inc.   196A - 70   2016 $75

Gates, Henry Louis *The Signifying Monkey.* New York: Oxford, 1988. Second printing, author's presentation for Dan Johnson, paper over boards, cloth spine, edges of cover slightly rubbed, otherwise nice in dust jacket.   Second Life Books, Inc.   196A - 623   2016 $75

Association – Johnson, Gerard

Dickens, Charles   1812-1870 *The Personal History of David Copperfield.* London: Bradbury & Evans, 1850. First edition, frontispiece and engraved title, printed title, plates by Phiz, some browning to plates, lacks leading f.e.p., contemporary full dark blue black morocco, ruled in gilt, little rubbed, repairs to head of leading hinge, contemporary signature of Gerard Johnson, all edges gilt.   Jarndyce Antiquarian Booksellers   CCXVIII - 473   2016   £320

Association – Johnstone, John

Sprat, Thomas   1635-1713 *The History of the Royal-Society of London for the Improving of natural Knowledge.* London: by T. R. for J. Martyn and J. Allestry, 1667. First edition, small 4to., engraved plate of the arms of the Royal Society, 2 folding plates (slightly shaved) and page 233 with very short tear, but without etched frontispiece by Hollar (often missing), contemporary calf, rebacked, new endleaves, corners repaired, from the library of James Stevens Cox (1910-1997), early 19th century signature of Edw. Williams and John Johnstone, early ink ciphers CR, similar to that of Charles II.   Maggs Bros. Ltd.   1447 - 394   2016   £400

Association – Jones, Barbara

Senn, Charles Herman *The Art of the Table...* London: Ward, Lock & Co., 1923. Third edition, half title, photo frontispiece and illustrations, original grey decorated cloth, ex-libris Barbara Jones, very good.   Jarndyce Antiquarian Books   CCXV - 402   2016   £40

Association – Jones, Charlotte Harriet

Cats, Jacob *Moral Emblems with Aphorisms, Adages and Proverbs of all Ages and Nations.* London: Longman, Green, Longman and Roberts, 1860. First edition with these illustrations, 276 x 197mm., fine contemporary green straight grain morocco, handsomely gilt, covers framed by multiple rues and wide, ornate dentelle, whole enclosing detailed Greek urn centerpiece, raised bands, spine densely gilt in compartment featuring many small botanical and floral tools, gilt turn-ins, all edges gilt, frontispiece, 60 large tondo emblems and 60 tailpieces, ink presentation 'Wilhemina Colquhoun Jones/1863/ with Charlotte Harriet Jones/ love and best wishes', spine darkened to olive brown (as almost always with green morocco), just faintest hint of wear to joints, occasional minor foxing or stains, extremely attractive, very decorative contemporary binding bright and scarcely worn, text very fresh and showing no signs of use.   Phillip J. Pirages   67 - 236   2016 $750

Association – Jones, Eleanor

Kilner, Ann *A Course of Lectures for Sunday Evenings Containing Religious Advice to Young Persons.* London: printed and sold by John Marshall 124, 1737-1787. 12mo., ink splash to first titlepage, slight tear to gutter margin first half title, two volumes bound in one, contemporary quarter calf, marbled boards, vellum tips, board edges worn, some slight rubbing to joints, inscribed on front endpaper "Wm. Jones bought miss Baldock's sale 1845", signatures of Martha Baldock 1844 and Eleanor Jones.   Jarndyce Antiquarian Booksellers   CCXVI - 341   2016   £225

Association – Jones, Gloria

Giles, James R. *James Jones.* Boston: Twayne, 1981. One of the dedication copies, inscribed by Giles to Jones's widow, Gloria and their children, boards foxed, very good, without dust jacket, presumably as issued.   Ken Lopez Bookseller   166 - 59   2016 $250

Association – Jones, H. G.

Williamson, Passmore *Case of Passmore Williamson.* Philadelphia: Uriah Hunt & son, 1856. First edition, octavo, original cloth, bookplate of defunct library, pocket removed from rear pastedown, call letters on spine, cloth worn down at spine ends, still bright, very good, this copy inscribed by Williamson for H. G. Jones, almost certainly Horatio Gates Jones, historian.   Between the Covers Rare Books   202 - 118   2016 $1850

Association – Jones, Henry Festing

Sinclair, May *The Belfry.* New York: Macmillan, 1916. First American edition, faint foxing to half title and titlepage, portion of dust jacket? pasted to verso of flyleaf and slightly offset to half title, single foxspot to border of one page and odd handling mark, crown 8vo., original red cloth with single fillet border blindstamped to upper board, backstrip and upper board lettered in gilt, slight lean to spine, light rubbing to extremities with little bumping to couple of corners, top edge little dusty, fore-edge rough trimmed with few faint foxspots, some very faint foxing to endpapers with bookplate of Henry Festing Jones, good, inscribed by author to Jones.   Blackwell's Rare Books   B186 - 283   2016   £115

Association – Jones, James

Chase-Riboud, Barbara *From Memphis & Peking.* New York: Random House, 1974. First edition, bit of foxing to endpapers, else near fine in dust jacket, inscribed by author to author James Jones and his wife.   Between the Covers Rare Books   207 - 23   2016 $350

Association – Jones, Jehoshaphat

Camden, William *Institutio Graecae Grammatices Compendiaria.* London: Exeuderunt S. Buckley, et T. Longman, 1790. Relatively late edition, 8vo., original linen, covered at an early date with a dust jacket of rough paper, its flaps folded over pastedowns and stitched together rather crudely with green thread, outer surface of paper now worn, inscription 'Jehoshaphat Jones's Book, Bought at Mr. North's Brecon, May 4th 1802", this inscription repeated in various forms on endpapers.   Blackwell's Rare Books Greek & Latin Classics VII - 26   2016   £300

Association – Jones, Wilhemina Colquhoun

Cats, Jacob *Moral Emblems with Aphorisms, Adages and Proverbs of all Ages and Nations.* London: Longman, Green, Longman and Roberts, 1860. First edition with these illustrations, 276 x 197mm., fine contemporary green straight grain morocco, handsomely gilt, covers framed by multiple rues and wide, ornate dentelle, whole enclosing detailed Greek urn centerpiece, raised bands, spine densely gilt in compartment featuring many small botanical and floral tools, gilt turn-ins, all edges gilt, frontispiece, 60 large tondo emblems and 60 tailpieces, ink presentation 'Wilhemina Colquhoun Jones/1863/ with Charlotte Harriet Jones/ love and best wishes', spine darkened to olive brown (as almost always with green morocco), just faintest hint of wear to joints, occasional minor foxing or stains, extremely attractive, very decorative contemporary binding bright and scarcely worn, text very fresh and showing no signs of use.   Phillip J. Pirages   67 - 236   2016 $750

Association – Jones, William

Kilner, Ann *A Course of Lectures for Sunday Evenings Containing Religious Advice to Young Persons.* London: printed and sold by John Marshall 124, 1737-1787. 12mo., ink splash to first titlepage, slight tear to gutter margin first half title, two volumes bound in one, contemporary quarter calf, marbled boards, vellum tips, board edges worn, some slight rubbing to joints, inscribed on front endpaper "Wm. Jones bought miss Baldock's sale 1845", signatures of Martha Baldock 1844 and Eleanor Jones. Jarndyce Antiquarian Booksellers CCXVI - 341 2016 £225

Euclides *Geometricorum Elementorum Libri XV.* Paris: Henri Estienne 7 Jan., 1516-1517. Sixth edition, Roman types, numerous woodcut geometrical diagrams in margins, fine crible initials in a variety of styles and sizes, titlepage soiled and cut down and mounted on old paper, one diagram just cropped at its extreme outer corners, without final blank, folio, 19th century half brown calf by Hatton of Manchester, marbled edges, original order for the binder loosely inserted, the Macclesfield copy with bookplate but no blindstamps and annotated by John Collins, after his death his books were acquired by William Jones and thence to Shirburn Castle, scarce on the market, preserved in cloth folding box, good copy. Blackwell's Rare Books Marks of Genius - 16 2016 £12,000

Association – Jordan-Smith, Paul

Penn, William *Some Fruits of Solitude.... (with, as issued) More Fruits....* Newport: printed by James Franklin, 1749. First American edition, 12mo., 2 parts in 1 volume, occasional browning and spotting, few leaves little defective in fore margin, original sheep, cracks in joints, upper one repaired, corners worn, slip-in case ownership inscription of Mary Monry 1876, later bookplate of Paul Jordan-Smith. Blackwell's Rare Books B186 - 115 2016 £2250

Association – Josey, Clint

Casement, Dan Dillon *The Abbreviated Autobiography of a Joyous Pagan.* privately printed, 1944. First edition, original red wrappers, frontispiece, plates, portraits, inscribed by author for family friend, from the library of Clint and Dot Josey with their inked signature and their penciled notation at top of last page, also pencilled notation of collector Larry Myers on last page below Josey notation, laid in is newspaper article dated June 10 1952 advising of Casement's recognition of the Kiwanis Club, a copy of the guest editorial and newspaper clipping advising of Casement's death March 7, 1953, also laid in 1952 Christmas card that pictures Casement, rare, lightly rubbed along spine and covers, else very good, housed in original four-point cloth case with titles stamped in silver on spine. Buckingham Books 2015 - 32934 2016 $4500

Garrard, Lewis H. *Wah-to-Yah and the Taos Trail...* H. W. Derby & Co., 1850. First edition, first state, from the library of Clint and Dorothy Josey with their bookplate, original black blindstamped cloth with original spine replaced, original title in gilt on spine, professionally rebacked with title portion of original spine remaining, front and rear endpapers replaced and some pages lightly foxed, else near fine, tight copy, housed in slipcase. Buckingham Books 2015 - 28736 2016 $3000

Association – Josey, Dorothy

Casement, Dan Dillon *The Abbreviated Autobiography of a Joyous Pagan.* privately printed, 1944. First edition, original red wrappers, frontispiece, plates, portraits, inscribed by author for family friend, from the library of Clint and Dot Josey with their inked signature and their penciled notation at top of last page, also pencilled notation of collector Larry Myers on last page below Josey notation, laid in is newspaper article dated June 10 1952 advising of Casement's recognition of the Kiwanis Club, a copy of the guest editorial and newspaper clipping advising of Casement's death March 7, 1953, also laid in 1952 Christmas card that pictures Casement, rare, lightly rubbed along spine and covers, else very good, housed in original four-point cloth case with titles stamped in silver on spine. Buckingham Books 2015 - 32934 2016 $4500

Garrard, Lewis H. *Wah-to-Yah and the Taos Trail...* H. W. Derby & Co., 1850. First edition, first state, from the library of Clint and Dorothy Josey with their bookplate, original black blindstamped cloth with original spine replaced, original title in gilt on spine, professionally rebacked with title portion of original spine remaining, front and rear endpapers replaced and some pages lightly foxed, else near fine, tight copy, housed in slipcase. Buckingham Books 2015 - 28736 2016 $3000

Association – Joyce, Philitus

Walrond, Eric *Tropic Death.* New York: Boni & Liveright, 1926. First edition, 8vo., black cloth slightly cocked, hinge tender, very good, inscribed by author for Philitus Joyce, Sept. 29 1926. Second Life Books, Inc. 196 B - 823 2016 $750

Association – Juneman, Helen Fay

Adventures of Jack Ninepins. New York: Harper Bros., 1944. Stated first edition, 6 1/4 x 8 1/2 inches, cloth, fine in frayed dust jacket, I in color by Averill, this copy from the library of Bertha Mahony Miller with her bookplate, laid in are 6 handwritten letters from Averill to Helen Fay (Juneman) Book Store owner and lecturer on children's books. Aleph-bet Books, Inc. 111 - 28 2016 $1200

Association – Jung, Helen

Fuller, Thomas 1608-1661 *A Pisgah Sight of Palestine and the Confines Thereof...* London: printed by J. E. for John Williams, 1650. First edition, 28 plates + frontispiece and additional titlepage, neat repair to upper corner of pages 279-280, plates mounted on later stubs, exceptionally clean, folio, mid 19th century full dark green crushed morocco, gilt and blind ruled borders, raised bands, ruled in gilt with compartments ruled in blind and gilt, little dulled, bookplate of J. Cresswell on leading pastedown and later bookplate of Helene Jung, inscribed in remembrance of her great kindness to Wm. Howson and his family Dec. 1858, handsome copy. Jarndyce Antiquarian Booksellers CCXVII - 103 2016 £3500

Association – Kabos, Adrienne

Walker, Meredith *Building for nature: Walter Burley Griffin and Castlecrag.* Castlecrag: Walter Burley Griffin Society, 1994. Horizontal 8vo., black and white photos, presentation by Adrienne Kabos and James Weirick, auction flyer laid in, paper wrappers, about as new. Second Life Books, Inc. 196 B - 821 2016 $75

Association – Kaline, Al

Ewald, Dan *Six. A Salute to Al Kaline.* Detroit: Detroit Tigers and Olympia Entertainment, 2010. First edition, fine, signed by Kaline, oversized paperback original. Bella Luna Books 2016 - t9510a 2016 $132

Association – Kamp, Fritz

Meredith, George 1828-1909 *One of Our Conqueors.* London: Chapman and Hall, 1891. 3 volumes, original royal blue coarse morocco grained cloth, front board blocked in black back board with publisher's monogram in blind, spine gilt lettered and ruled, fine, pale yellow endpapers, signature of Fritz Kamp. Jarndyce Antiquarian Booksellers CCXVII - 175 2016 £220

Association – Kanin, Garson

Belloc Lowndes, Marie *Lizzie Border: a Study in Conjecture.* New York: Longmans, Green, 1939. First edition, inscribed by author to actor/writer Ruth Gordon, with bookplate signed by Gordon and husband Garson Kanin, included is TLS by author to Gordon, very good plus in very good dust jacket, jacket spine lightly faded, chipping to edges and light creasing, letter with horizontal fold, near fine overall. Royal Books 52 - 9 2016 $2500

Association – Kaplan, Sherman

McGuane, Thomas *Panama.* New York: Straus & Giroux, 1978. First edition, signed and inscribed by author for Sherman Kaplan, green cloth and green paper boards, lettered in blind and silver, top edge green, original white dust jacket lettered in red and black, near fine with some light off-setting to boards, else bright and clean, dust jacket with some faint toning to extremities, few faint spots of light soiling, very tight copy. B & B Rare Books, Ltd. 2016 - TMG002 2016 $50

Association – Kappourr, Ludovii

Schott, Gaspar *Magia Optica Das ist Geheime doch Naturmassige Gesicht und Augen-Lehr...* Bamberg: Johann Martin Schonwerters, 1677. First German edition, small 4to., allegorical frontispiece, 25 engraved copper plates, variously browned, foxed or stained, contemporary quarter calf, decorative boards, extremities very worn, ownership signature L. Orssinger and inscription Ex Libris P. Lemigii Antles, Ludovii Kappourr? Jeff Weber Rare Books 183 - 32 2016 $3000

Association – Karfiol, Edward

Hawthorne, Nathaniel 1804-1864 *The Marble Faun or the Romance of Monte Beni.* Boston and New York: printed at the Riverside Press for Houghton Mifflin and Co., 1890. 2 volumes, quite pretty contemporary sky blue crushed morocco lavishly gilt, covers with multiple plain and decorative rules enclosing a central panel seme with gilt daisies, raised bands, spine compartments densely gilt with central daisy enclosed by small tools and filigree cornerpieces, marbled endpapers, all edges gilt, 51 photogravure plates, including portrait of Hawthorne, front pastedowns and verso of front free endpapers, bookplate of Edward Karfiol, spines just slightly different shade of blue, especially fine set, bindings lustrous and unworn, immaculate internally. Phillip J. Pirages 67 - 48 2016 $950

Association – Kark, Austen

Falconer, William *The Shipwreck, a Poem.* London: printed for William Miller by W. Bulmer, 1811. 197 x 121mm, very pretty mid 19th century green straight grain morocco, intricately decorated in gilt and blind, by W. Barratt (ticket on front flyleaf), covers with broad, densely gilt frame paned central lozenge containing a large and elaborate floral centerpiece, raised bands, spine panels filled with gilt purple watered silk endleaves framed by gilt tolls, all edges gilt, 3 engraved plates and five engraved vignettes, verso of front endleaf with early inscription, "The Bookbinder's Tribute of Gratitude to Benj. Morland" and with bookplate of Cass Canfield, presentation to Canfield from Austen Kark laid in, spine uniformly sunned to olive brown, slight rubbing to corners, bands and joints, muted spotting to silk plates with minor foxing, hint of browning at edges of some leaves, still excellent copy, with none of the condition issues serious and with elaborately decorated covers lustrous and unworn. Phillip J. Pirages   67 - 27   2016 $750

Association – Karolyi, Judith

Thomas, Caitlin *Caitlin - a Warring Absence.* London: Secker & Warburg, 1986. First edition, photos, signed by author, presentation from Thomas's daughter to Judith Karolyi and Zenka Bartek, covers slightly marked, very good in like dust jacket, slightly creased.   Peter Ellis   112 - 400   2016   £85

Association – Katarskii, I.

Fridlender, Y. V. *Charles Dickens: Bibliografia...* Moskva: Pub. House of All-Union Palace of Books, 1962. First edition, frontispiece, original paper covered stiff boards, cloth spine, little rubbed, good plus, presentation from co-author I. Katarskii, to Sir John Greaves.   Jarndyce Antiquarian Booksellers   CCXVIII - 1499   2016   £25

Association – Kauffer, E. McKnight

Cervantes Saavedra, Miguel De   1547-1616 *Don Quixote De La Mancha.* London: Nonesuch Press, 1930. First press edition, limited to 1475 copies, 2 volumes, octavo, publisher's full morocco, 21 color plates, presentation from artist, E. McKnight Kauffer to Roger Fry, near fine. Honey & Wax Booksellers   4 - 2   2016   £2200

Association – Kay, Celia

O'Dell, Scott *Island of the Blue Dolphins.* Boston: Houghton Mifflin, 1960. First edition, first printing, 8vo., cloth, fine in dust jacket (not price clipped, no award seal, irregular piece off top of spine, ink name on flap, few closed tears), still very good-, this copy inscribed by O'Dell and laid in is TLS by artist, Eveline Ness in 1976 on her personal letterhead, Ness illustrated the color dust jacket, also laid in 4 page playbill for the movie made in 1964, signed by Celia Kay who starred in the movie.   Aleph-bet Books, Inc.   112 - 350   2016 $875

Association – Kay, Roger

Gregory, Saint, the Great *Opera.* Paris: Francois Regnault, 1521. Early reissue of 1518 editio princeps, titlepage printed in red and black, scattering of small wormholes in title and first section (index), reducing to 3 by the start of text and wholly extinguished by f. 50, 3 further small holes in last 30ff., sometimes touching a character but rarely affecting legibility, frequent short marginal early ink notes, bit of dust soiling and marginal damp marking at end, folio, early 19th century English sprinkled calf, backstrip with four raised bands, remains of old label in second compartment, boards bordered in blind, front joint and backstrip ends expertly renewed, bit rubbed and scratched, ownership inscription with Latin motto dated 1578 at head of title with initials T. G. (further initial lost), 17th century inscription by Roger Kay, early 19th century bookplate of Fulwar William Fowle, good.   Blackwell's Rare Books   Marks of Genius - 20   2016   £950

Association – Kazin, Alfred

Halley, Anne *Between the Wars and Other Poems.* Northampton: Gehenna Press, 1965. First edition, green cloth stamped in gilt, little faded and worn dust jacket, #11 of 500 copies, this copy inscribed by author for writer/critic Alfred Kazin, fine.   Second Life Books, Inc.   196A - 710   2016 $125

Sedgwick, William Ellery *Herman Melville: the Tragedy of Mind.* Cambridge: Harvard, 1944. First edition, green cloth, cover very slightly scuffed at corners and ends of spine, ownership signature of Alfred Kazin, 1944, some pencil marking throughout, otherwise very good, tight, price clipped, chipped and browned dust jacket.   Second Life Books, Inc.   196 B - 203   2016 $100

Association – Keele, Charles Ferdinand

Utility or Sketches of Domestic Education. London: Darton Harvey & Darton, 1815. 12mo., frontispiece, 2 pages ads, contemporary speckled calf, red morocco label, slightly rubbed, inscribed for Charles Ferdinand Keele, a gift from his father 27 Sept. 1847.   Jarndyce Antiquarian Books   CCXV - 994   2016   £65

Association – Keen, Malcolm

Shaw, George Bernard 1856-1950 *Man and Superman.* New York: Dodd, Mead, 1947. First edition, 8vo., very good in little worn dust jacket, some of the photos show little watermark at edge, written on endpaper is note this book is the property of "Maurice Evans Prod. Inc." and is to be returned, this copy signed by Malcolm Keen, Chester Stratton, Victor Sutherland, Carmen Mathews, Jack Manning, Phoebe Mackay and Tony Bickley.   Second Life Books, Inc.   196 B - 562   2016 $450

Association – Keeshan, Robert

Blatty, William Peter *The Exorcist.* New York: Harper and Row, 1971. First edition, touch of foxing to top page edges, else lovely, easily near fine in like dust jacket, this the copy of Robert Keeshan (Captain Kangaroo).   Royal Books   52 - 14   2016 $1375

Association – Keightley, Thomas

Rossetti, Dante Gabriel 1828-1882 *The Early Italian Poets from Ciullo d'Alcamo t Dante Alighieri....*   London: Smith, Elder & Co., 1861. First edition, one of 600 copies, presentation copy inscribed by author to Thomas Keightley, original brown cloth, gilt title to spine and cover design by author, professionally recased, common repair for this title due to text block being too heavy for binding, light rubbing to edges and boards, short, expertly repaired closed tear to book cloth along rear board and spine, interior clean and bright, housed in handsome green half morocco slipcase with few scuff marks to spine, very good.   The Kelmscott Bookshop   12 - 92 2016 $3200

Association – Kelley, Florence

Bragdon, Claude *Four Dimensional Vistas.* New York: Knopf, 1916. First edition, purple cloth stamped in gilt, author's presentation on flyleaf to Florence Kelley, cover somewhat faded and spotted, slightly worn at corners and ends of spine, interior shows light moisture staining bottom of leaves, otherwise very good.   Second Life Books, Inc.   196A - 186   2016 $45

Elder, William *A Memoir of Henry C. Carey; Read before the Historical Society of Pennsylvania.* Philadelphia: Henry Carey Baird Co., 1880. First edition, 8vo., brown cloth stamped in black, blind and gilt, small scrape on front cover, otherwise very good, presentation "Hon. William D. Kelley/ with the compliments/ Wm. E. Ringwalt/April 2nd/84", from the library of consumer advocate Florence Kelley, this was presented to her father, Judge and Congressman.   Second Life Books, Inc.   196A - 497   2016 $65

Kelley, William D. *Speeches, Addresses and Letters on Industrial and Financial Question...* Philadelphia: Henry Carey Baird, 1872. First edition, 8vo., bound in green cloth, some external wear, cloth torn along lower hinge, hinges starting, good copy, presentation from author's daughter, Florence Kelley to her son Nicholas.   Second Life Books, Inc.   196A - 923   2016 $300

Loti, Pierre *La Mort De Notre Chere France en Orient.* Paris: Calmann-Levy, 1920. Third edition, chipped wrappers, cover separate, this was the copy of consumer advocate, Florence Kelley with her signature and 12 lines of her holograph, fragile pulpy paper.   Second Life Books, Inc.   196 B - 94   2016 $50

Maurice, C. Edmund *Life of Octavia Hill as told in her Letters.* London: Macmillan, 1913. First edition, 8vo., portraits, untrimmed and partially unopened, very good, clean tight copy, this the copy of author and feminist, Jane Addams (Hull House), from the library of consumer advocate Florence Kelley.   Second Life Books, Inc.   196 B - 157   2016 $250

Neuhaus, Eugen *The Art of the Exposition.* San Francisco: Paul Elder, 1915. First edition, 8vo., illustrations, untrimmed, dust jacket with pieces missing to fore-edge, part of lower corner of front board nicked and about 1 inch of paper missing, good copy, this the copy of consumer advocate Florence Kelley, presentation to Kelley from Katherine Philips Edson May 29th 1915, nice association.   Second Life Books, Inc.   196 B - 310   2016 $95

Pickens, William *Bursting Bonds...* Boston: Jordan & More Press, 1923. Second edition, 8vo., boards with paper label, lacking some of the paper on spine, some staining to cover, nice and clean inside, inscribed by author to consumer advocate Florence Kelley from her library.   Second Life Books, Inc.   196 B - 406   2016 $325

Traubel, Horace *Chants Communal.* New York: Boni, 1914. Second edition, 8vo., author's presentation to J. B. Kelley, paper over boards with cloth spine, partially unopened, from the library of Florence Kelley, spine little scuffed at ends, else very good, tight copy.   Second Life Books, Inc.   196 B - 768   2016 $45

Association – Kelley, J. B.

Traubel, Horace *Chants Communal.* New York: Boni, 1914. Second edition, 8vo., author's presentation to J. B. Kelley, paper over boards with cloth spine, partially unopened, from the library of Florence Kelley, spine little scuffed at ends, else very good, tight copy.   Second Life Books, Inc.   196 B - 768   2016 $45

Association – Kelley, Nicholas

Kelley, William D. *Speeches, Addresses and Letters on Industrial and Financial Question...* Philadelphia: Henry Carey Baird, 1872. First edition, 8vo., bound in green cloth, some external wear, cloth torn along lower hinge, hinges starting, good copy, presentation from author's daughter, Florence Kelley to her son Nicholas.   Second Life Books, Inc.   196A - 923   2016 $300

Association – Kelley, William

Elder, William *A Memoir of Henry C. Carey; Read before the Historical Society of Pennsylvania.* Philadelphia: Henry Carey Baird Co., 1880. First edition, 8vo., brown cloth stamped in black, blind and gilt, small scrape on front cover, otherwise very good, presentation "Hon. William D. Kelley/ with the compliments/ Wm. E. Ringwalt/April 2nd/84", from the library of consumer advocate Florence Kelley, this was presented to her father, Judge and Congressman.   Second Life Books, Inc.   196A - 497   2016 $65

Association – Kelly, John F.

Nutt, Alfred *Popular Studies in Mythology, Romance and Folklore.* London: David Nutt, 1899-1902. Volumes 1-12 bound as 1, 8vo., original green wrappers bound in, little toned, some occasional foxing, some wrappers faded, bound together in red buckram, gilt title to spine, edges little rubbed, top edge dusty but robustly bound and very good, nos. 11 and 12 signed " John F. Kelly".   Unsworths Antiquarian Booksellers Ltd.   30 - 114   2016   £300

Association – Kennard, Thomas

Johnson, Samuel   1709-1784 *The Idler.* London: printed for J. Hodges and 6 others, 1790. Sixth edition, 8vo., some browning, waterstain to upper corner of first three leaves of volume II, full contemporary tree calf, gilt borders, smooth spines, gilt decoration, black morocco labels, some rubbing to hinges and spines, early ownership name of Thos. Kennard.   Jarndyce Antiquarian Booksellers   CCXVI - 329   2016   £125

Johnson, Samuel   1709-1784 *The Rambler.* London: printed for J. Hodges and 6 others, 1791. 4 volumes, 8vo., some foxing, faint waterstaining, one opening with old ink splash, top corner volume I B6 torn with slight loss to page number, full contemporary tree calf, gilt borders, smooth spines, gilt decoration, black morocco labels, some rubbing to hinges and spines, early ownership name of Thos. Kennard.   Jarndyce Antiquarian Booksellers   CCXVI - 332   2016   £200

Association – Kennedy, Ethel

Abel, Elie *The Missile Crisis.* Philadelphia and New York: J. B. Lippincott, 1966. First edition, well used, very good, without dust jacket, inscribed by author to Robert Kennedy and wife Ethel, with Kennedy's extensive notes.   Between the Covers Rare Books   204 - 62   2016 $10,000

Association – Kennedy, Evory Hamilton

Dante Alighieri   1265-1321 *La Divina Commedia.* Oxford: M. A. Nella Stameria dell' Universita, 1900. First edition thus, octavo, period binding by W. Matthews of full brown morocco raised bands, gilt rules, all edges gilt, ownership signature of "E(vory) H(amilton) Kennedy - Betchworth 1937, he was Vicar of Betchworth, bound in at front are five pages of his notes, armorial bookplate of Edward Hilton Young, 1st Baron Kennet of Denne, corners slightly bumped, very good.   Peter Ellis   112 - 90   2016   £150

Association – Kennedy, Helen Weber

Bashford, Herbert *A Man Unafraid. The Story of John Charles Fremont.* San Francisco: Hart Wagner, 1927. First edition, tinted frontispiece, 19 plates, 2 tipped-in color illustrations, green cloth, gilt, minor dampstain at foot of spine, light offsetting to front endpaper, near fine, photos, prints, portraits, two color illustrations after paintings, signature on inner cover of Helen Weber Kennedy, direct descendant of Captain Weber.   Argonaut Book Shop   Biography 2015 - 5429   2016 $90

Association – Kennedy, Robert

Abel, Elie *The Missile Crisis.* Philadelphia and New York: J. B. Lippincott, 1966. First edition, well used, very good, without dust jacket, inscribed by author to Robert Kennedy and wife Ethel, with Kennedy's extensive notes.   Between the Covers Rare Books   204 - 62   2016 $10,000

Association – Kennet, Edward Hilton Young, 1st Baron

Crabbe, George *The Life of George Crabbe, by his son.* London: Oxford University Press, Humphrey Milford, 1932. First edition with this introduction, small 8vo., bound by Morrell in full leather, raised bands, gilt decorated spine, gilt rules, marbled endpapers and edges, stamped in gilt with crown and letter K on upper cover, armorial bookplate of Edward Hilton Young, 1st Baron Kennet of the Dene; presentation copy inscribed by author for Kennet, fine.   Peter Ellis   112 - 130   2016   £450

Dante Alighieri 1265-1321 *La Divina Commedia.* Oxford: M. A. Nella Stameria dell' Universita, 1900. First edition thus, octavo, period binding by W. Matthews of full brown morocco raised bands, gilt rules, all edges gilt, ownership signature of "E(vory) H(amilton) Kennedy - Betchworth 1937, he was Vicar of Betchworth, bound in at front are five pages of his notes, armorial bookplate of Edward Hilton Young, 1st Baron Kennet of Denne, corners slightly bumped, very good.   Peter Ellis   112 - 90   2016   £150

Froude, James Anthony 1818-1894 *Letters and Memorials of Jane Welsh Carlyle.* London: Longmans, Green and Co., 1883. First edition, octavo, 3 volumes, period binding of half dark green morocco with raised bands, gilt decoration to spine, marbled boards, edges and endpapers, armorial bookplate of Kennet of the Dene in each volume, covers slightly rubbed at edges, very good.   Peter Ellis   112 - 62   2016   £225

Pascal, Blaise *Les Provinciales ou Lettres Ecrites par Louis de Montalte...*   Paris: Charpentier, 1875. New edition, octavo, period binding of full blue straight grain calf, raised bands, gilt decorated spine, gilt rules and inner and outer dentelles, marbled endpapers, all edges gilt, armorial bookplate of Edward Hilton Young, 1st Baron Kennet of the Dene, gift inscription "Arthur William Young with best wishes from Margaret Lucia Young 27th June 1882", slight scuffing to hinges, very good.   Peter Ellis   112 - 287   2016   £150

Trotter, Lionel J. *The Life of John Nicholson, Solider and Administrator based on private and hitherto....* London: John Murray, 1900. First edition, octavo, 2 plates and 3 folding maps, period fine binding by Bumpus, full brown morocco with raised bands, gilt rules and devices to spine, inner dentelles elaborately gilt, top edge gilt, armorial bookplate of Kennet of Dene, contemporary (1900) ownership inscription of a member of the family (Arthur W. Young), near fine, attractive binding.   Peter Ellis   112 - 181   2016   £125

Verney, Frances Parthenope *Memoirs of the Verney Family.* London: Longmans Green & Co., 1892. First edition, 4 volumes, photogravure plates, period bindings by Hatchards of three quarter brown morocco with raised bands, gilt rules, cloth sides, marbled endpapers, top edges gilt, armorial bookplate of Kennet of Dene on each board is family's gilt coat of arms, near fine, handsome set.   Peter Ellis   112 - 115   2016   £350

Association – Kenneys, Charles

Terentius Afer, Publius *Terence's Comedies.* London: for A. Swall and T. Childe, 1694. First edition, 8vo., small (20mm) piece torn away from fore margin of titlepage, some very light staining, contemporary sprinkled calf, gilt spine, red morocco label, joints cracked, headcaps broken and corners bumped, from the library of James Stevens Cox (1910-1997), signature and initials of Charles Kenneys (1651-1702).   Maggs Bros. Ltd.   1447 - 412   2016   £150

Association – Kensington, Lady

Rattigan, Nancy *The Confessions of a Siamese Cat Prince.* Lahore: printed at the Civil and Military Press, 1914. 4to., original illustrated cream printed paper boards, light blue cloth spine, inscription "To Lady Kensington with love from Nancy 12 March 1914".   Jarndyce Antiquarian Booksellers   CCXVII - 246   2016   £180

Association – Kent, George Davies

Ray, John *Synopsis Methodica Animalium Quadruperdum et Serpentini Generis.* London: Impensis S. Smith & B. Walford, 1693. First edition, 8vo., engraved portrait, sheets B-M browned due to poor paper quality, all others clean, printer's crease across lower corner of page 67 but no loss of text, contemporary sprinkled calf, front cover detached, label missing, from the library of James Stevens Cox (1910-1997), contemporary inscription 'AAA 50', inscription 'E Libris Eduardi Nelthorpe Admi/1720', and "E Libris G. D. Kent CCC Oxon".   Maggs Bros. Ltd.   1447 - 359   2016   £220

Association – Kenyon, F. G.

Martialis, Marcus Valerius *Epigrammaton Libri XIII.* Lyon: Apud Seb. Gryphium, 1546. Pocket edition, few minor spots, ownership inscription erased from titlepage, 16mo., 19th century mottled calf, spine gilt in compartment, boards bordered with triple gilt fillet, marbled endpapers, label lost from spine, extremities worn, label removed from front pastedown, ownership inscription of F. G. Kenyon, good.   Blackwell's Rare Books   Greek & Latin Classics VII - 65   2016   £250

Association – Kenyon, Lord

Bible. Polyglot - 1512 *Psalterium Daviticum Materna Lingua Expositum.* Paris: A. Verard, circa, 1512. First edition, in French & Latin, small 8vo., 18th cebtury mottled calf, spine gilt in compartments, red morocco label (one label missing, joints and headcaps restored), titlepage with fine metalcut of David and Bathesheba enclosed within ornate metalcut crible border made up of 8 different strips, printed in red and black throughout, little marginal foxing and toning to places but generally good, 17th century? ownership inscription "Collegii Paris Societ. Jesu", bookseller's label, armorial bookplate of Thomas Brooke, FSA, owner of the Pillone library, inscribed of W. Ingham Brooke of Barford Rectory, Warwick 1908 and pencil acquisition note of Lord Kenyon 20 Dec. 1979.   Maggs Bros. Ltd.   1474 - 67   2016   £1500

Association – Kenyon-Lees, Lorna

Pitter, Ruth *Persephone in Hades.* Auch, Gers, France: privately printed by A. Sauriac, 1931. First edition, one of 100 numbered copies, this being no. 1, octavo, wrappers, printed on Pur Fil Lafuma, covers marked and darkened at edges, short closed tear at top edge of lower cover, very good, rare, presentation from author for Lorna Kenyon-Lees, Jan. 1933.   Peter Ellis   112 - 303   2016   £275

Association – Kermode, Frank

Doctorow, E. L. *Welcome to Hard Times.* New York: Simon & Schuster, 1960. First edition, signed by author, 8vo., toned, particularly towards edges, quarter cream buckram with orange paper covered boards, black title to spine and upper board, spine little yellowed, edges very slightly faded, faint mark at lower edge of upper board, still very good, dust jacket little crease and worn at head and tail of spine and joints, bit toned, some shelf wear but good, author's inscription to literary critic Frank Kermode dated 1972.   Unsworths Antiquarian Booksellers   30 - 48   2016   £600

Association – Kerr, Molly

Galsworthy, John   1867-1933 *Glimpses and Reflections.* London: Heinemann, 1937. First edition, 8vo. inscribed by Ada Galsworthy for Molly Kerr, with Mrs. Galsworthy's compliments card laid in, light foxing on front and back pages and on edges, else very good.   Second Life Books, Inc.   196A - 606   2016 $45

Association – Kerr, Rose

Boyle, Eleanor Vere *Sylvana's Letters to an Unknown Friend.* London: Macmillan and Co., 1900. First edition, 2nd impression, presentation copy inscribed by author for Rose Kerr (1882-1944), with her bookplate, original purple cloth, slightly rubbed, endpapers brown, not in very good condition, black and white illustrations, very good.   The Kelmscott Bookshop   12 - 40   2016 $150

Association – Kershaw, J. A.

Salvin, Osbert *Catalogue of the Picariae in the Collection of the British Museum.* London: British Museum (Natural History), 1892. Octavo, 14 chromolithograph plates, publisher's cloth, 2 small library stamps of Royal Society of Victoria, ownership signature of J. A. Kershaw (ornithologist of Horn Expedition), fine.   Andrew Isles Natural History Books   55 - 15576   2016 $750

Sclater, Philip Lutley *Catalogue of the Passeriformes or Perching Birds, in the Collection of the British Museum.* London: British Museum Natural History, 1888. Octavo, 18 chromolithograph plates by Smit, publisher's cloth, two small library stamps of Royal Society of Victoria, ownership signature of J. A. Kershaw (ornithologist of Horn Expedition), fine.   Andrew Isles Natural History Books   55 - 37794   2016 $500

Association – Kershaw, John

The Historie of Frier Rush: How He Came to a House of Religion to Seeke Service... London: Harding and Wright for Robert Triphook, 1810. One of 4 copies on vellum, contemporary red velvet by H. Faulkner (ticket on verso front flyleaf), covers with wide Greek key border rolled in blind, flat spine with small remnant of leather backstrip (that has been laid on to hide a binder's titling error), red moire silk endleaves, turn-ins and pastedowns with rolls in blind, all edges gilt, housed in very good later leather edged slipcase, woodcut vignette on title, verso to front flyleaf with bookplate of Edward Vernon Utterson and morocco bookplate of Hans Furstenberg, bookplate of John Kershaw, contemporary inked note listing original owner of each of the four vellum copies of the present book, later pencilled note on same "This copy was after-wards in the possession of Mr. George Smith and it was (sold in his (s)ale for £9.15.0", spine mostly covered with (glue?) residue left by now basically missing leather backstrip, corners rubbed to board, portions of the joints torn, velvet nap somewhat diminished, a bit of natural rumpling to the vellum, very few inoffensive spots to margins, entirely solid (apart from spine remnants) an agreeable copy of this curious book.   Phillip J. Pirages   67 - 341   2016 $4500

Association – Kessler, Charles

Adams, Harry *Beyond the Barrier with Byrd. An Authentic Story of the Byrd Antarctic Exploring Expedition.* Chicago and New York: M. A. Donohue & Co., 1932. First edition, first issue binding, 8vo., original green cloth gilt, upper board lettered gilt and blocked to blind with ship, spine lettered in gilt and blocked to blind with penguin, remnant of pictorial dust jacket with picture of Byrd on upper panel, photographic frontispiece and 15 photographic plates, full page facsimile of letter by Byrd, cloth in fine condition, text evenly little browned as usual, signed presentation from Lt. Comdr. Tom Mulroy to Charles L. Kessler.   Sotheran's   Travel and Exploration - 412   2016   £298

Association – Keteltas, Abraham

Smith, William *Some Thoughts on Education: with Reasons for Erecting a College in this Province, and Fixing the Same at the City of New York, to which is added a Scheme for Employing Masters or Teachers in the mean Time...* New York: J. Parker, 1752. First edition, Final leaf D4 in very skillfull and almost undetectable facsimile, neat modern paper covered boards, Abraham Keteltas' copy signed and stamped.   Joseph J. Felcone, Inc.   Books from Five Centuries: a Miscellany - 132   2016 $3800

Association – Kettaneh, Francis

Andrews, William Loring *Bibliopegy in the United States and Kindred Subjects.* New York: printed by the Gillis Press for Dodd, Mead and Co., 1902. First edition, deluxe issue, one of 36 copies printed on Imperial Japan vellum, out of an edition of 177, 8vo., frontispiece and color and black and white illustrations, engraved chapter titles and vignettes, original gilt stamped vegetable parchment over boards, silk ribbon marker, dust jacket, neat two inch hairline split in joint near spine of front cover, leather booklabel of Francis Kettaneh on verso of front free endpaper, otherwise fine in dust jacket, sunned at spine panel.   James S. Jaffe Rare Books   Occasional List: Winter 2016 - 32   2016 $875

Association – Kettilby, Samuel

Hedericus, Benjamin *Lexicon Manuale Graecum, Omnibus sui Generis Lexicis quae quidem Exstant...* London: Excudit S. Palmer, Impensis J. & J. Knapton et al, 1727. 4to., titlepage in red and black, final leaf with publisher's catalog, occasional light spots and smudges, generally clean, closed tear to leaf M4, trimmed little close but never touching text, contemporary tan calf boards, neatly rebacked, raised bands, gilt to spine, older label retained, edges patterned, endpapers renewed, some scratches and stains, area of lower board neatly patched with calf, corners fraying, still very good and sound, armorial bookplates of Rev. Samuel Kettilby, and Edward Oates, and Robert Washington Oates, commentary of Oates to first flyleaf verso, pencilled inscription "From Henry (Cooper?) to Mrs. Edward Oates 17 Nov. 1849".   Unsworths Antiquarian Booksellers   30 - 68   2016   £175

Association – Ketton-Cremer, R. W.

Everitt, Alan *Suffolk and the Great Rebellion 1640-1660.* Suffolk Records Society, 1961. First edition, large 8vo., cloth, gilt lettered, few faint marks to lower board, spine slightly browned, very small dark mark to upper board, corners bumped and slightly frayed, edges lightly dusted, still very good, ownership inscription of R. W. Ketton Cremer in pen and bequeathed to him by the Library of the University of East Anglia as noted on the Library's bookplate, various library marks, elsewhere.   Unsworths Antiquarian Booksellers Ltd.   E05 - 102   2016   £45

Association – Keyes, Sidney

Sitwell, Edith   1887-1964 *Street Songs.* London: Macmillan, 1942. First edition, 8vo., fine in little soiled and nicked dust jacket, review copy with slip laid in, Sidney Keyes copy.   Second Life Books, Inc.   196 B - 586   2016 $65

Association – Kiefer, J. G.

Kipling, Rudyard   1865-1936 *Plain Tales from the Hills.* London: Macmillan and Co., 1928. Pocket edition on India paper, half title, frontispiece, slight worming at end, original flexible maroon cloth, front board and spine gilt, spine slightly darkened with minimal repairs, signed presentation from author to J. G. Kiefer.   Jarndyce Antiquarian Booksellers   CCXVII - 152   2016   £225

Association – Kimball, Flora

Stanton, Elizabeth Cady *The History of woman Suffrage Volumes I-III.* New York: Fowler & Wells, 1881. New York: 1882. Rochester: 1887. First edition, volume one has loose hinge in front but it and volume two are in very good condition, volume 3 very worn with some loose prelim matter and well worn binding, volumes one and two have tipped in signature by Susan B. Anthony, all 3 volumes inscribed Lizzie Everett from Flora M. Kimball, National City California April 4 1887. Second Life Books, Inc. 196 B - 684 2016 $2000

Association – Kimber, W. J. T.

Duncan, John *The Education of the Ordinary Child.* London: Thomas Nelson & Sons, 1942. First edition, Half title, original red cloth, booklabel and stamp of National Bureau for Co-operation in Child Care Library, presented to the library by Dr. W. J. T. Kimber. Jarndyce Antiquarian Books CCXV - 631 2016 £20

Association – King, James

Traherne, Thomas *Christian Ethicks; or Divine Moraltiy.* London: for Jonathan Edwin, 1675. First edition, 8vo., lightly foxed throughout due to poor paper quality, titlepage with some light wrinkles, contemporary calf, spine with four raised bands and red morocco lettered gilt, rebacked with extensive repairs to corners and headcaps, near contemporary signature of Ja(mes) King, 19th century bookplate of Sir John Dashwood King, from the library of James Stevens Cox (1910-1997). Maggs Bros. Ltd. 1447 - 416 2016 £650

Association – King, John Dashwood

Traherne, Thomas *Christian Ethicks; or Divine Moraltiy.* London: for Jonathan Edwin, 1675. First edition, 8vo., lightly foxed throughout due to poor paper quality, titlepage with some light wrinkles, contemporary calf, spine with four raised bands and red morocco lettered gilt, rebacked with extensive repairs to corners and headcaps, near contemporary signature of Ja(mes) King, 19th century bookplate of Sir John Dashwood King, from the library of James Stevens Cox (1910-1997). Maggs Bros. Ltd. 1447 - 416 2016 £650

Association – King, Martha

Broonzy, William *Big Bill Blues.* London: Cassell, 1955. First edition, 8vo., dust jacket, photos and drawings, donor's presentation on flyleaf, author's presentation under his frontispiece photo to Mrs. Martha King, top edges slightly soiled, otherwise very good, tight copy, little chipped and somewhat soiled dust jacket, scarce signature. Second Life Books, Inc. 196A - 204 2016 $1500

Association – Kinnaird, Douglas

Howell, James *Epistolae Ho-Eliana. Familiar Letters Domestic and Forren...* London: printed for Humphrey Moseley, 1645. First edition, small 4to., lacking additional engraved titlepage, woodcut initials and head and tailpieces, few pencil marks and underlinings, some MS. notes in old hand including dates and sometimes locations, occasional wax marks not affecting text, 19th century plum colored faux morocco, gilt label to spine, blindstamped spine and boards, edges sprinkled red, marbled endpapers, rubbed, edges bit worn and some fraying to covers, spine label lifting, armorial bookplate of Frederick William Cosens, MS gift inscription to Allan H. Bright, dated 30th May 1891, from HYS, armorial bookplate of Douglas Kinnaird, tipped to f.f.e.p. a page of handwritten notes on the content of the book with brief chronology of Howell's life in pencil, with note book was purchased from Cosens through Quaritch. Unsworths Antiquarian Booksellers 30 - 82 2016 £300

Association – Kirk, John

Stuart, John *Sir John Kirk.* London: S. W. Partridge & Co., 1907. Second edition, half title, frontispiece, plates, 32 page catalog, text pages slightly browned, few spots, original blue cloth, inner hinges cracking, inscribed by Kirk. Jarndyce Antiquarian Books CCXV - 812 2016 £25

Association – Kirkpatrick, Janet

Vivian, Evelyn Charles *The Way of the Red Cross.* London: Hodder & Stoughton, 1915. First edition, half title, folded facsimile letter from Queen Anne, leading f.e.p. with vertical crease, original blue grey cloth, spine slightly dulled, presentation inscription in secretarial hand no leading f.e.p. "Janet C. Kirkpatrick Yorkhill War Hospital Glasgow. Presented (sic) by Her majesty Queen Alexandra at Marlborough House May 22nd 1917", very good. Jarndyce Antiquarian Booksellers CCXVII - 291 2016 £45

Association – Kisby, Allston

Duncan, George P. *The Gentleman's Book of Manners or Etiquette.* Wakefield: William Nicholson & Cos., circa, 1880? 16mo., half title, color frontispiece, 18 page catalog, original blue glazed cloth, blocked in black, slightly rubbed, booklabel of Allston A. Kisby on leading pastedown. Jarndyce Antiquarian Books CCXV - 168 2016 £45

Association – Klopfer, Donald

Blumenthal, Joseph *Typographic Years.* New York: printed for members of the Grolier Club, 1982. First edition, one of 300 copies, numbered and signed by author, fine in original slipcase, thi copy inscribed on endpaper to Random House founder Donald Klopfer. Second Life Books, Inc. 196A - 164 2016 $150

Association – Klupfel, Engelbert

Petau, Denis ...*Opus de Theologicis Dogmatibus Nunc primum Septem Voluminibus Comprehensum, in Mediorem Ordinem Redactum...* Venice: Remondiana, 1757. Best edition, 6 books in 7 and bound in 2 volumes, folio, title in red and black, half title, each book with its separate title, titlepage portrait engraving of Denis and additional woodcut initials and head and tailpieces all volumes, first volume free endpapers slightly torn, contemporary full vellum, gilt stamped spines, first volume stained, second volume lower corners gently bumped, bookplates of Ex Oblatororum S. Caroli Bibliotheca Bayswater (Henry Edward Manning 1808-1892), Pitts Theology Library bookplates, C. J. Stewart bookseller label, titlepage ownership signatures and inscriptions of Engelbert Klupfel, 1769 and Steph. Wirelo(?), rare, fine. Jeff Weber Rare Books 181 - 26 2016 $750

Association – Knight, Charles

Wills, William Henry *Old Leaves Gathered from Household Words.* London: Chapman & Hall, 1860. First edition, contemporary half red morocco, little rubbed, all edges gilt, large paper, presentation copy from Dickens's sub-editor to Charles Knight. Jarndyce Antiquarian Booksellers CCXVIII - 782 2016 £125

Association – Knight, Henry

Moore, George 1852-1933 *Martin Luther. A Tragedy in Five Acts.* London: Remington & Co., 1879. First edition, original blindstamped black cloth with gilt title and authors to front cover and title to spine, corners lightly bumped and small piece missing from top on spine, interior pages very nice, ownership signature of Henry Knight, bookplate of Rosita de Texada, very good, housed in green silk folding case. The Kelmscott Bookshop 13 - 41 2016 $2550

Association – Knight, Hillary

Thompson, Kay *Eloise in Moscow.* New York: Simon & Schuster, 1959. Stated first printing, boards, fine in dust jacket with 3 very small chips, color illustrations by Hilary Knight, inscribed by artist. Aleph-bet Books, Inc. 112 - 473 2016 $700

Association – Knollys, Eardley

Carpenter, Alejo *The War of Time.* London: Victor Gollancz, 1970. First UK edition, head of spine and one corner slightly bumped, very good in like dust jacket (slightly dusty), presentation copy by translator, Frances Partridge to Bloomsbury artist Eardley Knollys. Peter Ellis 112 - 63 2016 £200

Association – Knott, John

Priestley, Joseph 1733-1804 *The History and Present State of Discoveries Relating to Vision, Light and Colours.* London: printed for J. Johnson, 1772. First edition, 4to., folding frontispiece, errata, 24 folding plates, the copy of John Knott, MD Nov. 21 1904, red inked signature on title and frequent marginal notes, bookplate of Trinity College, Dublin, lending Library, duplicate sold. Jeff Weber Rare Books 183 - 27 2016 $1600

Association – Kobler, John

Joyce, James 1882-1941 *Haveth Childers Everywhere.* Paris: Henry Babou and Jack Kahane; New York: Fountain Press, 1930. No. 24 of 100 copies on iridescent handmade Japan, signed by author (plus an additional 500 on paper and 75 writer's copies), 283 x 191mm., original white paper covers with printed titling on front and spine, leaves untrimmed and unopened in original glassine protected wrapper, the whole in original (slightly rubbed) three panel stiff card folder covered with gilt paper, without original slipcase, title printed in green and black, initials and headlines printed in green, inside front cover of folder and bookplate of John Kobler, corners just slightly bumped, one small faint brown spot to tissue cover, outstanding copy, very fragile and always torn glassine entirely intact, text with no signs of use, most of it never having seen the light of day. Phillip J. Pirages 67 - 209 2016 $15,000

Joyce, James 1882-1941 *A Portrait of the Artist as a Young Man.* New York: B. W. Huebsch, 1916. First edition, 194 x 127mm., publisher's blue cloth, blindstamped title on front cover, flat spine with gilt tilting, bookplates of John Kobler and of "Porcaro", very slight chafing to joints and extremities, spine ends just little curled, otherwise fine, binding especially clean, spine gilt very bright, text virtually pristine. Phillip J. Pirages 67 - 211 2016 $7000

Association – Koopman, Toto

Saint Phalle, Niki De *Aids - You Can't Catch it Holding Hands.* Munich and Lucerne: Verlag C. J. Bucher, 1986. First edition, color pictorial laminated boards, quarto, facsimile reproduction of author/artist's original illustrated manuscript, presentation copy inscribed by author for Erica Brausen and Toto Koopman, corners bumped at corners, very good. Peter Ellis 112 - 345 2016 £225

Association – Koteliansky, S. S.

Dostoevsky, Fyodor Mikhailovich 1821-1881 *New Dostoevsky Letters.* London: Mandrake Press, n.d. circa, 1930. First edition, frontispiece, little ink offsetting to first page, foolscap 8vo., original quarter black cloth with gilt snakeskin patterned sides, backstrip with printed label, top edge little dusty, dust jacket with darkened backstrip panel, one or two small spots and some light handling marks, very good, inscribed by translator, S. S. Koteliansky. Blackwell's Rare Books B186 - 249 2016 £150

Association – Kraus, H. P.

Brun, Carl *Schweizerisches Kunstler-Lexikon, Herausgegeben Mit Unterstutzung des Bundes Und Kunstrefundlicher Privater vom Schweizerischen Kunstverein.* Frauenfeld: Von Huber & Co., 1905-1917. Thick 8vo., half cloth over pastepaper covered boards loosely inserted commemorative booklabel, which indicates this came from reference library of H. P. Kraus. Oak Knoll Books 310 - 26 2016 $750

Cerretti, Luigi *Modonese Notizie Biografiche e Letterrarie Con Prose e Versi Mancanti Nell' Edizioni Dell'autore.* Reggio: Torreggiani, 1833-1837. First edition, 5 volumes, large 8vo., contemporary quarter green gilt leather spine, marbled paper covered boards, all edges speckled blue, slight rubbing on boards, slight damage to top edge of spine on volume five, in all very well preserved set, loosely inserted commemorative book label which indicated this set came from reference library of H. P. Kraus. Oak Knoll Books 310 - 235 2016 $850

Chevalier, Ulysse *Repertoire des Sources Historiques du Moyen Age, Topo-Bibliographie.* Montbeliard: Societe Anonyme d'Imprimerie Montbeliardaise, 1894-1900. First edition, printed in an edition of 2000 copies, 2 volumes, small 4to., modern cloth, leather spine labels, marginal staining, loosely inserted commemorative booklabel which indicated this set came from reference library of H. P. Kraus. Oak Knoll Books 310 - 237 2016 $350

Martin, Gabriel *Catalogus Librorum Bibliothecae Illustrissimi Viri Caroli Henrici Comitis de Hoym...* Parisiis: Gabriele & Claudium Martin, 1738. Small 8vo., 18th century quarter calf, blue paper covered boards, red leather spine label, all edges stained red, individual lots priced in ink in margins, dampstaining to titlepage and few pages that immediately follow, wear to extremities with small chips to head and tail of spine and to one panel between raised bands, small corner of page 99 lacking, bookplate of Paul Lacombe and A. Aubry, loosely inserted is commemorative booklabel which indicates the book came from reference library of H. P. Kraus. Oak Knoll Books 310 - 64 2016 $1750

Palermo, Francesco *I Manoscritti Palatini Di Firenze.* Firenze: Biblioteca Palatina, 1853-1869. First edition, 4to. modern cloth, leather spine labels, uncut, 4 pages of plates and facsimiles, light foxing throughout, bookplate indicates this book came from the reference library of H. P. Kraus. Oak Knoll Books 310 - 216 2016 $450

Schonbrunner, J. *Handzeichnungen Alter Meister aus Der Albertina Und Anderen Sammlungen.* Wien: Gerlach & Schenk, 1896-1908. First edition, folio, 12 volumes, half calf portfolio, cloth backed boards, gilt stamping and illustration on upper boards with tipped in illustration, hundreds of plates, commemorative booklabel which indicates this set came from the H. P. Kraus reference library. Oak Knoll Books 310 - 303 2016 $2000

Swarzenski, Hanns *Die Latenischen Illuminierten Handschriften des XIII. Jahrhunderts in Den Landern an Rhein...* Berlin: Deutscher Verein Fur Kunstwissenschaft, 1936. First edition, 2 volumes, folio, half vellum with paper covered boards, 2020 plates, 1096 illustrations, loosely inserted commemorative booklabel indicating this book came from reference library of H. P. Kraus. Oak Knoll Books 310 - 52 2016 $950

Association – Krauss, Max

Epicurus *Brief an Menoikeus.* N.P.: Fischbachpresse, 2007. Limited to 144 numbered copies signed by binder, Max Krauss, 12 copies, each with different states of binding, bound by Krauss and Wolfgang Kreuzer, woodcut illustrations by Kraus, paper covered boards, sewn, leather spine label, top edge cut, other edges uncut, slipcase, presentation laid in with signatures of Krauss and Kreuzer. Oak Knoll Books 310 - 100 2016 $350

Association – Krawitz, Herman

Chagall, Marc *Illustrations for the Bible.* New York: Harcourt Brace and Co., 1956. First American edition, inscribed by artist with stunning original page color drawing of Moses for Lenette and George Nayor, 1966, and from the collection of Herman Krawitz, former assistant manager of the Metropolitan Opera House, complete with 16 lithographs in color, 12 in black and white plus lithograph cover, also illustrated with reproductions in heliograuvre of the 106 etchings made by Chagall for the illustrations of the bible, folio, original pictorial boards, original dust jacket, book with tape residue to endpapers, otherwise book and lithographs fine, extremely scarce dust jacket (almost never seen) with chipping, edgewear and damage to spine. Manhattan Rare Book Company 2016 - 1646 2016 $40,000

Association – Kreuzer, Wolfgang

Epicurus *Brief an Menoikeus.* N.P.: Fischbachpresse, 2007. Limited to 144 numbered copies signed by binder, Max Krauss, 12 copies, each with different states of binding, bound by Krauss and Wolfgang Kreuzer, woodcut illustrations by Kraus, paper covered boards, sewn, leather spine label, top edge cut, other edges uncut, slipcase, presentation laid in with signatures of Krauss and Kreuzer.   Oak Knoll Books   310 - 100   2016 $350

Association – Krieger, Robby

Sugerman, Danny *The Doors - The Illustrated History.* New York: William Morrow and Co., 1983. First edition, signed by Ray Manzarek, Danny Sugerman and Robby Krieger, fine in dust jacket.   Buckingham Books   2015 - 11547   2016 $450

Association – Kyriss, Ernst

Rothschild, James De, Le Baron *Catalogue Des Livres Composant La Bibliotheque De Feli M. Le Baron James De Rothschild.* Paris: Damascene Morgand, 1884-1920. First edition, no. 400 of 400 copies, 260 x 171mm., 5 volumes, pleasing red three quarter morocco, raised bands, gilt titling, top edges gilt, other edges untrimmed, frontispiece, numerous illustrations in text and 52 plates, 14 of these folding, 8 plates in color highlighted with gold, front free endpaper with tiny 'EK' ink stamp of Ernst Kyriss, extremities just slightly rubbed, isolated, mild offsetting from in-text illustrations, but fine, clean, fresh and bright inside and out.   Phillip J. Pirages   67 - 305   2016 $2250

Association – Kyrle, William Money

Boswell, Thomas Alexander *The Journal of an Exile.* London: Saunders and Otley, British and Foreign Public Library, 1825. First edition, 2 volumes, some minor foxing, contemporary, probably Scottish binding with thistle motifs on spines, half calf, maroon morocco labels, little rubbed, nice, bookplates of William Money Kyrle.   Jarndyce Antiquarian Booksellers   CCXVII - 37   2016   £320

Association – La Bedoyere, Comte H. De

Bonet, Honore *L'Apparition De Jehan de Meun ou Le Songe Du Prieur De Salon.* Paris: Imprime par Crapelet pour la Societe des Bibliophiles Franai, 1845. No. 7 of 17 copies on vellu, plus 100 copies issued on paper, 235 x 181mm., recent fine white pigskin, decorated in blind in medieval style by Courtland Benson, housed in titled custom made morocco backed folding cloth box, 10 engraved plates replicating illustrations from early manuscript copies of the week, pastedown with morocco bookplate of Comte H. De La Bedoyere and engraved bookplate of Marcellus Schlimovich, front free endpaper with embossed library stamp of Dr. Detlef Mauss, half title with ink library stamp of Sociedad Hebraica Argentina, fine, especially clean and bright internally with only most trivial imperfections and in striking new retrospective binding.   Phillip J. Pirages   67 - 343   2016 $2750

Association – La Farge, Consuelo

Maxwell, William *The Chateau.* New York: Knopf, 1961. First edition, inscribed by author to author Oliver La Farge and wife Consuelo, fine in very near fine dust jacket with slight loss of crimson to spine extremities.   Ken Lopez Bookseller   166 - 78   2016 $575

Association – La Farge, Oliver

Maxwell, William *The Chateau.* New York: Knopf, 1961. First edition, inscribed by author to author Oliver La Farge and wife Consuelo, fine in very near fine dust jacket with slight loss of crimson to spine extremities.   Ken Lopez Bookseller   166 - 78   2016 $575

Association – La Rocher, A.

Dickens, Charles   1812-1870 *Great Expectations.* Philadelphia: T. B. Peterson & Bros., 1861. Half title, frontispiece, engraved and printed title, 34 illustrations, original uniform brown cloth, boards blocked and lettered in blind, spines blocked and lettered gilt, tail of spine little chipped, slight split to head of leading hinge, contemporary signature of A. La Rocher, good plus.   Jarndyce Antiquarian Booksellers   CCXVIII - 590   2016   £450

Association – La Roux, Susan

Ryder, John *The Case for Legibility.* London: Bodley Head, 1979. First edition, foolscap 8vo., original blue cloth, backstrip lettered in gilt with very slight lean to spine, dust jacket with very gentle fading to backstrip panel, very good, inscribed by author for Susan La Roux.   Blackwell's Rare Books   B186 - 278   2016   £50

Association – Laber, Fritz

Mizauldo, Antonio *Centuriae IX Memorabilium Utilium Ac Juncdorum in Aphorismos...* Frankfurt: Nicolas Hoffman, 1613. Small folio, 3 parts in 1 volume, some misnumbering of pages, printer's device on each of the three titles, light paper toning, occasional stains, contemporary limp vellum, manuscript spine title, lacks ties, rear joint partly torn, bookplate signed by Fritz Laber of Dr. Carl Wurth, early ownership signatures of Ernnet Casparus Maismis, very good. Jeff Weber Rare Books   181 - 21   2016 $600

Association – Labourer, H.

Herskovits, Melville J. *The Anthropometry of the American Negro.* New York: Columbia University Press, 1930. First edition, boards little bowed, else fine, without dust jacket, possibly as issued, inscribed by author for Prof. H. Labourer with compliments and kind regards of the author, scarce.   Between the Covers Rare Books   202 - 39   2016 $650

Association – Lacombe, Paul

Martin, Gabriel *Catalogus Librorum Bibliothecae Illustrissimi Viri Caroli Henrici Comitis de Hoym...* Parisiis: Gabriele & Claudium Martin, 1738. Small 8vo., 18th century quarter calf, blue paper covered boards, red leather spine label, all edges stained red, individual lots priced in ink in margins, dampstaining to titlepage and few pages that immediately follow, wear to extremities with small chips to head and tail of spine and to one panel between raised bands, small corner of page 99 lacking, bookplate of Paul Lacombe and A. Aubry, loosely inserted is commemorative booklabel which indicates the book came from reference library of H. P. Kraus.   Oak Knoll Books   310 - 64   2016 $1750

Association – Laird, David

Poston, Charles D. *Apache-Land.* San Francisco: A. L. Bancroft & Co., 1878. Frontispiece, 12 litho views, remains of label on spine, front hinge starting, previous owner's bookplate of David Laird, bookseller and bibliographer, else good.   Dumont Maps and Books   133 - 74   2016 $125

Association – Lake, Reginald

Herodotus *Historiarum Libri IX...* Lugduni Batavorum: apud Samuelem Luchtmann, 1715. Engraved frontispiece titlepage dated 1716, first edition, folio, without separate titlepage to appendix (after page 554), found in some copies, half title, additional engraved title, titlepage in red and black, foldout engraved illustration after page 135, two small illustrations in text (pages 912 and 997), woodcut initials, engraved tailpieces, Greek and Latin parallel text, occasional small annotations, some light ink spotting to half title, little toned in gutters and towards end of text, small ink blot to top edge sporadically visible at upper margins but never approaching text, contemporary vellum, raised bands, gilt morocco spine label, blind tooled boards, edges sprinkled red and blue, bit grubby, prelim blanks tattered with some loss, old discolored repair to top corner but very good, ownership inscriptions of Henry Gahagan, student at Christ Church Oxford and Rev. Reginald (Lake?) Nov. 30 1880. Unsworths Antiquarian Booksellers Ltd.   E04 - 21   2016   £650

Association – Lamb, Edith

Morris, William   1834-1896 *The Earthly Paradise.* London: Reeves and Turner, 1890. Unusual presentation copy inscribed by author for Miss Edith Lamb July 15 1891, she was the family's nurse, bound in three quarter vellum with black leather title, author and date spine labels and gilt decorated compartments, boards marbled blue, gilt and cream paper, as are the end pages bumping and some chipping to top of boards and spine and along edge of rear board, vellum has light smudging, paper boards have faded, interior very good, housed in modern white cloth clamshell box, very good.   The Kelmscott Bookshop   12 - 73   2016 $2200

Association – Lambert, Hansi

Spender, Stephen *Engaged in Writing and The Fool and the Princess.* London: Hamish Hamilton, 1958. First edition, 8vo., original boards, fine in dust jacket with slightly faded spine, dedication copy inscribed by author for Hansi Lambert.   James S. Jaffe Rare Books   Occasional List: Winter 2016 - 130   2016 $1250

Association – Lamigeon, Marie

Tribute to Walter De La Mare on His Seventy-Fifth Birthday. London: Faber & Faber, 1948. First edition, colored lithographic frontispiece, portraits, reproduction of cartoon by Max Beerbohm, 8vo., original blue buckram with De La Mare's monogram in blind to upper board, backstrip lettered gilt partly on pink ground with slight lean to spine, top edge gilt, few faint spots at head of rear pastedown, related newspaper clippings laid in, dust jacket with gentle fading to backstrip panel, some chipping to extremities with flap-folds little rubbed and faded, good, inscribed by author to his secretary Marie Lamigeon.   Blackwell's Rare Books   B186 - 198   2016   £200

Association – Lancaster, Robert

Langley, Batty *The City and Country Builders and Workman's Treasury of Designs of the Art of Drawing and Working the Ornamental Parts of Architecture Illustrated.* London: printed for J. Ilive for Thomas Langley, 1740. First edition, bookplate, signature and stamp of Robert Lancaster, one of the listed subscribers, 4to., contemporary full calf rebacked with original red leather spine label laid down, spine in 6 compartments, 187 engraved plates, mild wear to cover edges, mild scattered foxing, soiling, bit of worming lower margin of first third of volume, no text or plates affected later owner name f.f.e.p., scarce. By the Book, L. C. 45 - 4   2016 $2750

Association – Lane, Francis

Bradley, Rose M. *The English Housewife in the Seventeenth & Eighteenth Centuries.* London: Edward Arnold, 1912. Half title, frontispiece, 7 plates, 8 page catalog, slight spotting, original decorated red cloth, spine and back board faded, otherwise very good, bright, presentation copy stamp on titlepage, bookplate of Denis Gray, inserted is ALS recording book as a gift from Frances Lane, Bristol. Jarndyce Antiquarian Books   CCXV - 78   2016   £45

Association – Lane, John

Rhymers' Club *The Second Book of the Rhymers' Club.* London: Elkin Mathews & John Lane, 1894. One of 650 copies, presentation from publisher John Lane, inscribed in pencil to Irish poet and novelist Katharine Tynan Hinkson, extremely uncommon thus, original brown cloth with gilt title to spine, light browning to margins of interior pages, bookplates of writer J. G. E. Hopkins, culinary writer Helmut Lothar Ripperger and collector Mark Samuels Lasner, very good. The Kelmscott Bookshop   13 - 59   2016 $950

Association – Langdon, Robert

Vaux, Robert *Memoirs of the Life of Anthony Benezet.* York: W. Alexander, 1817. First UK edition, 12mo., frontispiece, original boards with paper backstrip and title label, early name plates (Thomas Marsh and Robert Langdon), some foxing to prelims, cup ring to front cover, backstrip defective, label rubbed, very good, scarce in original state. Peter Ellis   112 - 363   2016   £750

Association – Langner, Lawrence

Guiterman, Arthur *The School for Husbands.* New York: Samuel French, 1933. 8vo., illustrations, signed by Guiterman and Lawrence Langner, very good in little worn dust jacket. Second Life Books, Inc.   196A - 691   2016 $50

Association – Lankes, J. J.

Frost, Robert Lee 1874-1963 *New Hampshire: a Poem with Notes and Graces Notes.* New York: Holt, 1924. Second printing, 8vo., woodcuts J. J. Lankes who has signed in pencil on blank, dated 1924, paper over boards with cloth spine, edge darkened, cover corners and ends of spine little worn, otherwise very good, tight copy. Second Life Books, Inc.   197 - 131   2016 $125

Association – Lasner, Mark Samuels

Clough, Arthur Hugh *Bothie of Toper-Na-Fuoisich. A Long Vacation Pastoral.* Oxford: Francis Macpherson, 1848. First edition, very good in original blue cloth, flexible boards with gilt title to front cover, minor wear to edges of covers, few small chip to edges of several pages, binding split in few places, however all of the pages remain bound in, bookplate of collector Mark Samuels Lasner, very good. The Kelmscott Bookshop   12 - 25   2016 $400

De Lyrienne, Richard *The Quest of the Gilt-edged Girl.* London: John Lane, Bodley Head, 1897. First edition, rare, near fine in orange paper wrappers with brown title to spine and front panel, short closed tear to front endpage, otherwise fine, housed in portfolio within grey cloth slipcase with black and gilt leather title label in spine and bookplate of Mark Samuels Lasner on inside board of portfolio, near fine in slipcase. The Kelmscott Bookshop   12 - 34   2016 $250

Maugham, William Somerset 1874-1965 *The Making of a Saint.* London: T. Fisher Unwin, 1898. First English edition, uncommon second book, original green cloth with gilt title to spine, minor rubbing to boards and minor wear to spine ends, text and endpages slightly browned as is usual with this book, bookplates of three previous owners, A. S. Alexander, Eleanor Jacott and Mark Samuels Lasner, very good. The Kelmscott Bookshop   12 - 66   2016 $300

Orczy, Emmuska *The Emperor's Candlesticks.* London: C. Arthur Pearson Limited, 1899. First edition, original tan cloth boards with brown title to spine and front board, minor wear to edges and spine ends, light rubbing to boards, few spots of foxing to interior, else very clean, bookplate of collector Mark Samuels Lasner, tipped in, very good. The Kelmscott Bookshop   12 - 77   2016 $550

Platt, William *Men, Women and Chance.* London: T. Fisher Unwin, 1898. First edition, rare, very nice in original grey cloth with gilt cover design, bookplate of Mark Samuels Lasner. The Kelmscott Bookshop   12 - 84   2016 $200

Rhymers' Club *The Second Book of the Rhymers' Club.* London: Elkin Mathews & John Lane, 1894. One of 650 copies, presentation from publisher John Lane, inscribed in pencil to Irish poet and novelist Katharine Tynan Hinkson, extremely uncommon thus, original brown cloth with gilt title to spine, light browning to margins of interior pages, bookplates of writer J. G. E. Hopkins, culinary writer Helmut Lothar Ripperger and collector Mark Samuels Lasner, very good.   The Kelmscott Bookshop   13 - 59   2016 $950

Association – Latham, Henry

Melanchthon, Philipp 1497-1560 *Epigrammata Selectiota Formulis Precum, Historiis Paraphrasi Dictorum Divinorum...* Frankfurt: Johanne & Sigismund Feyerabend, 1583. First edition edited by Peter Jensen, 4to., printer's device on titlepage and larger version on recto of penultimate leaf, woodcut dedicatory arms, map, 95 oval woodcuts within fine mannerist borders, many signed I.A. (Jost Amman), late 18th century calf, sides with gilt ruled and blind roll tooled border, gilt edges, spine with later gilt lettering, marbled endpapers, neat repairs to head and foot of spine, joints rubbed, blank corner of titlepage cut away and neatly replaced, few spots and stains but generally fresh, inscription dated 1818 of Rev. Henry White of Lichfield, dated 1818, armorial bookplate of Henry Latham.   Maggs Bros. Ltd.   1474 - 52   2016   £2800

Association – Lathes, Stanley

Nicols, Arthur *Chapters from the Physical History of the Earth.* London: C. Kegan Paul & Co., 1880. First edition, half title, 32 page catalog 10/79, tipped in 'Opinions of the Press' leaf, original dark brown cloth, little marked, author's own copy with his notes, corrections amendments together with insertions, 4 page ALS from F. W. Ridler of Museum of Practical Geology, brief note from Kegan Paul, brief ALS from H. G. Seeley, ALS postcard from Sir Stanley Lathes.   Jarndyce Antiquarian Booksellers   CCXVII - 205   2016   £380

Association – Lathrop, Dorothy

Artzybasheff, Boris *As I See.* New York: Dodd Mead, 1954. First edition, 4to., tan cloth, very good+ in chipped dust jacket with some mends on verso, drawings and paintings, include with this is Christmas Greeting poster from artist, 13 1/2 x 12 inches, with intricate and bizarre illustrations, also laid in is greeting card inscribed by artist for Dorothy Lathrop, with illustration on cover.   Aleph-bet Books, Inc.   111 - 26   2016 $800

Association – Latimore, Sarah

Ford, Julia Ellsworth *Imagina.* New York: Duffield, 1914. First edition, 4to., cloth, slight fading on rear cover else, fine, this copy inscribed by Ford to Sarah Latimore, Rackham bibliographer.   Aleph-bet Books, Inc.   111 - 371   2016 $950

Politi, Leo *Juanita.* New York: Charles Scribner's Son, 1948. A. First edition, cloth, fine dust jacket, inscribed and dated 1948 to Sarah Latimore, with very fine finished watercolor.   Aleph-bet Books, Inc.   112 - 381   2016 $850

Quiller-Couch, Arthur Thomas 1863-1944 *The Twelve Dancing Princesses and Other Fairy Tales Retold by Sir Arthur Quiller-Couch.* New York: George H. Doran, n.d. circa, 1915. 8vo., blue gilt pictorial cloth, fine in dust jacket, dust jacket very good to fine with some minor wear, this copy inscribed by artist, Kay Nielsen to Sarah Briggs Latimore, 16 magnificent tipped-in color plates, black and whites in text, pictorial endpapers, cover and dust jacket design, beautiful copy.   Aleph-bet Books, Inc.   111 - 324   2016 $2000

Association – Lawless, James

Dickens, Charles 1812-1870 *The Posthumous Papers of the Pickwick Club.* London: Chapman & Hall, 1837. First edition, Weller title, frontispiece and engraved title spotted, plates with some marginal spotting and staining, contemporary half calf, black leather label, carefully rebacked, spine and corners rubbed, endpapers at some point, contemporary signature of James Lawless, Exeter, good, sound copy.   Jarndyce Antiquarian Booksellers   CCXVIII - 97   2016   £180

Association – Lawrence, Elizabeth

Tyrell, George *Versions and Perversions of Heine & Others.* London: Elkin Mathews, 1909. First edition, boards somewhat marked and browning to endpapers, but nice, presentation copy inscribed by Wilfrid Scawen Blunt for Elizabeth Lawrence Xmas 1909, book dedicated to Wilfrid Blunt.   Simon Finch   2015 - 4159   2016 $252

Association – Lawrence, Walter

Wiggin, Kate Douglas *A Child's Journey with Dickens.* Boston and New York: Houghton Mifflin & Co., 1912. First edition, half title, frontispiece, portrait, original drab boards, lettered in dark blue, dark green cloth spine, inscribed by author for Sir Walter Lawrence.   Jarndyce Antiquarian Booksellers   CCXVIII - 1481   2016   £45

Association – Lawson, Frank

Rogers, William *Reminiscences of William Rogers.* London: Kegan Paul, Trench & Co., 1888. First edition, half title, frontispiece, 43 page catalog (11.87), 4 pages ads, original maroon cloth, bevelled boards, little rubbed, presentation inscription on title for Frank Lawson.   Jarndyce Antiquarian Books   CCXV - 923   2016   £40

Association – Lawson, James

Goldsmith, Oliver 1730-1774 *Dr. Goldsmith's History of Greece....* Gainsborough: H. Mozley, 1814. New edition, 12mo., frontispiece, contemporary full speckled sheep, spine slightly rubbed at head and tail back board slightly marked, inscription "James Lawson Feb. 24 1818", good plus. Jarndyce Antiquarian Books   CCXV - 701   2016   £35

Association – Lawson, John

Hamilton, Elizabeth *Letters on the Elementary Principles of Education.* London: G. & J. Robinson, 1801. Volume I second edition, volume II first edition, half title in volume II, 1 page ads in both volumes, uncut in contemporary light blue paper boards, red morocco labels, some slight rubbing, overall, nice, bookplate of John Lawson.   Jarndyce Antiquarian Books   CCXV - 714   2016   £240

Pemble, William *A Briefe Introduction to Geography Containing a Description of the Grounds, and Generall part Thereof...* Oxford: Iohn Lichfield for Edward Forest, 1630. First edition, small 4to., 1 folding table, printer's device on titlepage, 2 woodcut headpieces, very faint waterstain on a few pages, modern full vellum, gilt stamped spine title, book-label of John Lawson, fine, rare.   Jeff Weber Rare Books   181 - 25   2016 $2500

Association – Lax, Peter

Washington, Booker T. *Up from Slavery.* New York: Doubleday Page & Co., 1901. First edition, frontispiece, red cloth, gilt, modern gift inscription for Walter Hutchins from Peter Lax, modest wear at spine ends and corners, else tight and bright, near fine.   Between the Covers Rare Books   202 - 117   2016 $300

Association – Layton, William Edward

Page, Augustine *Memoranda Concerning the Boys' Hospital at Ampton, in Suffolk, Founded by James Calthorpe, Esq. A.D. 1702.* Ipswich: printed by J. Page St. Clement's Fore Street, for private circulation, 1838. First edition, 4to., several early ms. annotations in ink, original boards with printed short title on upper cover, boards generally bit grubby, neatly rebacked with cloth, armorial bookplate of William Edward Layton, very rare.   John Drury Rare Books   2015 - 21915   2016 $350

Association – Le Blanc, Lee

Silsby, Wilson *Etching Methods and Materials.* New York: Dodd Mead & Co., 1943. First edition, 8vo., cloth, presentation copy to artist Lee Le Blanc, signed by author and by Le Blanc, small spot on fore edge of front cover, else near fine.   Gene W. Baade, Books on the West   2015 - 5001115   2016 $109

Association – Le Carre, John

Wilden, Theodore *To Die Elsewhere.* London: Heinemann, 1976. First edition, inscribed by author to John Le Carre, fine in dust jacket with light restoration to top rear corners.   Buckingham Books   2015 - 38078   2016 $475

Association – Le Gallienne, Eva

Middleton, George *Hiss! Boom!! Blah!!!* New York: Samuel French, 1933. 8vo., author's presentation to Eva Le Gallienne with her bookplate, lacks dust jacket.   Second Life Books, Inc.   196 B - 224   2016 $45

Association – Le Gresley, Robert

Hawthorne, Nathaniel 1804-1864 *The Scarlet Letter.* Boston: Ticknor, Reed and Fields, 1850. First edition, first issue with ads dated march 1 1850 with misprint on page 21 line 20 'reduplicate' for 'repudiate', 181 x 111mm., fine modern dark brown crushed morocco by Bayntun (stamp-signed on front turn-in), covers with single gilt fillet border, raised bands, spine gilt in single ruled compartments containing antique style letter 'A', gilt titling and turn-ins, marbled endpapers, all edges gilt, original blindstamped brown cloth covers bound in at rear, bookplate of Robert Le Gresley, leaves shade less than bright (as in the typical copy), occasional corner creases, isolated spots of mild foxing, otherwise fine, text clean and fresh, pristine binding.   Phillip J. Pirages   67 - 192   2016 $3900

Association – Leach, J. A.

Wood, Casey Albert *The Fundus Oculi of Birds, Especially as viewed through the Microscope: a Study in Comparative Anatomy and Physiology.* Chicago: Lakeside, 1917. Quarto, 61 color photographic plates, publisher's cloth, library stamps of Royal Australian Ornithologists' Union, a note reading "To Dr.J. A. Leach with compliments of the author" pasted on upper endpaper.   Andrew Isles Natural History Books   55 - 38140   2016 $150

Association – Leat, Noel

Allfree, P. S. *Hawks of the Hadhramaut.* London: Robert Hale Ltd., 1967. First edition, 8vo., original cloth, dust jacket, sketch map, illustrations from photos, light rubbing to edges of jacket, initially few minor spots, else fine, ownership inscription Noel E. Leat.   Sotheran's   Travel and Exploration - 296   2016   £98

Association – Lee, Harper

Clanahan, James F. *The History of Pickens County, Alabama 1540-1920.* Carrollton: Clanahan Publications, 1964. First edition, fine in modestly soiled very good or better dust jacket with couple of stains and small shallow chip at crown, inscribed by Harper Lee.   Between the Covers Rare Books   204 - 66   2016 $3500

Association – Lee, Jonathan

Bonnycastle, John *An Introduction to Mensuration and Practical Geometry.* London: J. Johnson, 1802. Seventh edition, half title, engraved frontispiece, contemporary mottled calf, rubbed and little worn, inscription 'Jonathan Lee's book Dec. 15th 1806", sound.   Jarndyce Antiquarian Books CCXV - 542   2016   £60

Association – Lefferts, Marshall Clifford

Martin, Francois Xavier *The History of Louisiana from the Earliest Period.* New Orleans: printed by Lyman and Beardslee and A. T. Penniman & Co., 1827. First edition, 2 volumes, 248 x 165mm., pleasing later 19th century dark green crushed morocco by Stikeman (signed on front turn-in), covers with triple gilt fillet border and floral sprig corner-pieces, raised bands, spines densely gilt in compartments with center floral sprig in oval medallion, surrounded by swirling gilt tooling accented with small tools, gilt titling, gilt turn-ins, marbled endpapers, top edges gilt, other edges entirely untrimmed, front pastedown with leather bookplate of Marshall Clifford Lefferts and bookplate of Mrs. L. Bartlett, spines sunned to pleasing honey brown (covers bit sunned at edges, with front cover volume II inconspicuously sunned, and showing the darker silhouette of a bookend), few small stains to edges of same board, bindings virtually unworn and otherwise quite pleasing, minor foxing or browning throughout (no doubt affecting all copies because of inferior paper stock), five quires in volume I with one inch dampstain at head, one gathering in volume II noticeably browned, not without condition issues, but with much to please internally, including vast margins, consistent freshness and absence of soiling.   Phillip J. Pirages   67 - 250   2016 $1800

Association – Leffingwell, Frank

Scott, Walter   1771-1832 *The Doom of the Devorgoil, A Melo-Drama. (and) Alichindrane or the Ayrshire Tragedy.* Edinburgh: printed by Ballantyne for Cadell and Co., Edinburgh and Simpkin and Marshall, London, 1830. First separate and complete edition, 229 x 1522m., attractive late 19th century dark green armorial morocco by Maclehose of Glasgow (stamp signed), covers gilt with heraldic pelican crest of Thomas Glen Arthur of Garrick House, Ayr, flat spine with title at head and author at tail and five gilt ornaments in between (comprised of three thistles and two heraldic devices), gold endleaves, top edge gilt, other edges untrimmed (front hinge and joint with careful repairs, front free endpaper and first flyleaf cut near gutter and reattached with cellophane), large paper presentation copy, inscribed by Harry A. Sickles, Christmas 1917 for friend Frank P. Leffingwell, short crack beginning at bottom of front joint, hint of fading and leather dressing residue to covers, otherwise in excellent, binding solid and lustrous, text clean and fresh, margins very commodious.   Phillip J. Pirages   67 - 312   2016 $1000

Association – Lehmann, Helen

Lowell, Amy *Six French Poets.* New York: Macmillan, 1916. First edition, 2nd printing, 8vo., blue cloth stamped in gilt, very good, tight copy, inscribed by author for Helen Lehmann.   Second Life Books, Inc.   196 B - 99   2016 $200

Lowell, Amy *Some Imagist Poets 1916.* Boston & New York: Houghton Mifflin, 1916. First edition, 8vo., printed wrappers, front hinge torn, spine paper worn, inscribed by Lowell for Helen Lehmann.   Second Life Books, Inc.   196 B - 98   2016 $250

Association – Lehmann, John

Mortimer, Raymond *Channel Packet.* London: Hogarth Press, 1942. First edition, octavo, fine in very good dust jacket, slightly nicked and creased at edges, presentation copy inscribed by author for John (Lehmann), managing director of Hogarth Press.   Peter Ellis   112 - 264   2016   £150

Association – Leibowitz, Herbert

George, Emery *A Gift of Nerve.* Ann Arbor: Kylix Press, 1978. 8vo., very good+ in dust jacket, laid in is one page ALS from Herbert Leibowitz, publisher of Parnassus to poet Paul Metcalf requesting a review, also laid in 3 page holograph MS. review of the book by metcalf.   Second Life Books, Inc.   196A - 627   2016 $250

Association – Leigh, Chandos

Horatius Flaccus, Quintus *Opera, cum Scholiis Veteribus Castigavit et Notis Illustravit Gulielmus Baxteruus...* Edinburgh: Ex Prelo Academico... apud Mundell Doig et Stevenson, 1806. 4to., contemporary red straight grained morocco, boards bordered in gilt and blind enclosing a further frame combining a rectangle and lozenge shape, spine lettered gilt and also decorated in gilt and blind, marbled endpapers, edges gilt and minimally guaffered, bit rubbed at joints and extremities, few small marks, bookplates and ownership inscription of Chandos Leigh, very good. Blackwell's Rare Books   Greek & Latin Classics VII - 48   2016   £550

Lewis, Matthew Gregory 1775-1818 *Tales of Wonder.* London: Printed by W. Bulmer & Co, for the author, 1801. First edition, royal octavo, 2 volumes, period binding of full marbled calf with intricate gilt decoration, leather title labels, marbled edges and endpapers, in the middle of each cover is gilt monogram initial "D" surmounted by winged crown, few stains in margins of first volume, upper joint of second volume cracking, very good set, armorial bookplate (Frederick Leigh Colvile) with inscription "from my Uncle Chandos Leigh".   Peter Ellis   112 - 220   2016   £675

Association – Leinster, Duke of

Pemberton, Henry *A View of Newton's Philosophy.* S. Palmer, 1728. First edition, 4to., recent half mottled brown calf, marbled boards, spine with raised bands and red morocco label with gilt lettering, 12 unnumbered folding plates, engraved titlepage vignette, initials, headpieces and tailpieces by John Pine after J. Grison, very bright and clean, very good, engraved bookplate and library labels of Duke of Leinster.   Sotheran's   Piccadilly Notes - Summer 2015 - 216   2016   £1500

Association – Lentner, Edith

Atkinson, Ethel Tindal *A Garden of Shadows.* London: Macmillan, 1907. First edition, octavo, 8 full page black and white art nouveau illustrations by Byam Shaw, pages unopened, presentation copy inscribed by author for Edith Lentner, May 1941, free endpapers lightly tanned, edges and prelims spotted, very good in very good slightly rubbed, nicked and creased dust jacket slightly darkened at spine and chipped at tail of spine.   Peter Ellis   112 - 357   2016   £50

Association – Leo, Richard

Halfer, Josef *Die Fortschritte der Marmorierkunst. ein Praktisches Handbuch fur Buchbinder und Buntpapierfabrikanten.* Stuttgart: Wilhelm Leo, 1891. Second edition, 8vo., later half red calf, marbled paper covered boards, five raised bands, top edge gilt, signed binding by Zaehnsdorf, with 5 leaves of single mounted marbled paper specimens + 5 leaves each with 6 mounted marbled paper specimens, from the reference library of Zaehnsdorf and Company with commemorative booklabel loosely inserted, with bookplate of Zaehnsdorf Co., tipped in is two page ALS by Richard Leo to Mr. Zaehnsdorf, rubbed along hinges and soiled along edges.   Oak Knoll Books   310 - 9   2016 $3500

Association – Leon, Herbert

Shelley, Percy Bysshe 1792-1822 *Letters... to Leigh Hunt.* London: privately printed, 1894. First edition, one of 6 copies on vellum, with first and last blank leaves, 30 copies were printed on Whatman paper, 8vo., crushed black morocco by Ramage, Herbert S. Leon and Alington bookplates, fine.   Blackwell's Rare Books   Marks of Genius - 48   2016   £6000

Association – Leroux, George

Newton, Isaac 1642-1727 *Philosophiae Naturalis Principia Mathematica.* London: William and John Innys, 1726. Third edition, title printed in red and black, engraved frontispiece, 1 engraving and numerous diagrams in text, complete with half title and final ad leaf, some foxing at beginning and end, few scattered minor stains, repairs to margins of front flyleaves, late 19th century half red hard grained morocco, spine gilt in compartments and lettered direct, red edges, rebacked preserving previous spine, early inscription at head of title, little cropped at top and faded, seems to say 'gifted to Mr. William Scott of Babecan advocate by me ( ) Foulis', 19th century signature stamp of Dugald Macdonald at centre of titlepage, bookplate of Quebecois George G. Leroux, very good.   Blackwell's Rare Books   Marks of Genius - 32   2016   £11,000

Association – Lettenorier, H.

Dickens, Charles 1812-1870 *A Child's History of England.* London: Bradbury & Evans, 1853-1854. Volume I 1853, volumes II and III first edition, 3 volumes, half titles, frontispiece by F. W. Topham, 1 page ads in all volumes, old tape repairs to inner hinges volume I, original violet pink cloth blocked in blind, front boards decorated n gilt, heads and tails of spine slightly rubbed with some slight loss, boards little dulled and marked, dedication leaf volume i inscribed by author frontispiece Feb. 5th 1854 for Emile de la Rue, signed by De la Rue, later bookplate of H. Lettenorier, fold over box.   Jarndyce Antiquarian Booksellers   CCXVIII - 495   2016   £16,500

Association – Lettsom, Samuel Fothergill

Fenelon, Francois Salignac De La Mothe, Abp. 1651-1715 *The Adventures of Telemachus.* London: printed by W. Wilson for R. Edwards, 1792. 2nd edition, 4to., rubbed full calf, front hinge loose in volume one, contemporary bookplate (Samuel Fothergill Lettsom), later ownership signature of Dr. George Davenport, engraved portrait in volume one, engraved titlepages in both volumes, 24 engraved plates (foxed).   Second Life Books, Inc.   197 - 234   2016 $225

Association – Lever, William Hesketh

Staton, James Taylor   *The Visit to'th Greight Paris Eggsibishun of Bobby Shuttle and his Wife Sayroh.* Manchester: Abel Heywood, London: Simpkin, Marshall & Co., Liverpoool: William Gilling, 1867? First edition, with oval woodcut portrait as frontispiece, woodcut head and tailpieces, few spots, early 20th century light green cloth, original printed yellow wrappers, bound in upper one in incorporating a portrait of Bobby Shuttle, bookplate of Sir William Hesketh Lever and opposite his bookplate as Baron Leverhulme, good.   Blackwell's Rare Books   B184 - 80   2016   £250

Association – Leverhulme, Baron

Staton, James Taylor   *The Visit to'th Greight Paris Eggsibishun of Bobby Shuttle and his Wife Sayroh.* Manchester: Abel Heywood, London: Simpkin, Marshall & Co., Liverpool: William Gilling, 1867? First edition, with oval woodcut portrait as frontispiece, woodcut head and tailpieces, few spots, early 20th century light green cloth, original printed yellow wrappers, bound in upper one in incorporating a portrait of Bobby Shuttle, bookplate of Sir William Hesketh Lever and opposite his bookplate as Baron Leverhulme, good.   Blackwell's Rare Books   B184 - 80   2016   £250

Association – Levertov, Denise

Garcia Lorca, Federico   *Romance de la Guardia Civil Espanol.*   Philadelphia: Janus Press, 1962. First printing of this edition, slim quarto, printed in Monotype Bembo on Okawara paper, one of 45 numbered copies, this being no. 35, signed by artist, Jerome Kaplan, light fading overall and small chip to front wrappers, else near fine, this Denise Levertov's copy.   Royal Books   48 - 69   2016 $650

Association – Lewes, M. E.

Eliot, George, Pseud. 1819-1880 *The Writings of George Eliot.*   Boston: Houghton Mifflin, 1908. Illustrated large paper edition, 25 volumes, contemporary full blue morocco gilt, photogravures in color ALS by author to M. E. Lewes typed into volume I, fine set.   Honey & Wax Booksellers   4 - 6   2016 $7500

Association – Lewis, Sinclair

Henry, John M.   *Nine Above the Law: Our Supreme Court.* Pittsburgh: R. T. Lewis Co., 1936. First edition, small quarto, red brown cloth gilt, some rubbing to extremities, very good or better, inscribed by author, to Sinclair Lewis, also with bookplate of Lewis's wife, activist/author Dorothy Thompson.   Between the Covers Rare Books   208 - 37   2016 $300

Association – Lewis, Winslow

Moll, Herman   *The British Empire in America, Containing the History of the Discovery, Settlement, Progress and Present State of all the British Colonies...*   London: printed for John Nicholson at the King's Arms in Little Britain, Benjamin Took at Middle Temple Gate, Fleetstreet and Richard Parker and Ralph Smith...., 1708. First edition, 8 engraved folding maps, small 8vo. contemporary paneled calf, rebacked in morocco, raised bands, red morocco lettering piece, gilt, very good set, boards rubbed with one small split small stickers on each front cover and front pastedown, browning to corners, volume I has damp marking to upper part of title and first few leaves of introduction, volume II has worming to corners of free front endpapers and first blank, faint damp marking along top edge, tear to one map through blank area, few minor nicks to edges of two other maps, stickers from Dr. Winslow Lewis (1799-1875) of Boston.   Kaaterskill Books   21 - 67   2016 $5000

Association – Leyland, Frederick

Rossetti, Dante Gabriel 1828-1882 *Ballads and Sonnets.*   London: Ellis and White, 1881. First edition, exceptional association copy, inscribed by author for Frederick Leyland (1832-1892), original green cloth with gilt flower and lattice design by Rossetti on covers and spine, spotting to prelim leaves and at end of book, including inscription page, but this does not obscure inscription, closed half inch margin to page 327, very good plus, housed in modern green cloth clamshell box.   The Kelmscott Bookshop   12 - 91   2016 $4500

Association – Leylet, Francois

Hyde, Philip   *The Last Redwoods.*   San Francisco: Sierra Club, 1963. First edition, presentation inscription, signed by Francois Leylet, 78 black and white photos and 8 color photos, large folding map, grayish brown cloth, very fine with pictorial dust jacket.   Argonaut Book Shop Photography 2015 - 7165   2016 $150

Association – Liagre, Alfred De

Giradoux, Jean   *The Madwoman of Chaillot.*   New York: Random, 1947. First printing, 2 photos, presentation on flyleaf by Alfred de Liagre, Jr., director of the 1948 production of Belasco Theatre on Dec. 27 1948.   Second Life Books, Inc.   196A - 646   2016 $50

Association – Lichtenstein, Rachel

Sinclair, Iain *Rodinsky's Room.* London: Granta Books, 1999. First edition, octavo, illustrations, cloth with photo mounted on front, signed by author and Rachel Lichtenstein, fine in fine cloth slipcase. Peter Ellis 112 - 360 2016 £150

Association – Lieberman, Ben

Franklin, Benjamin 1706-1790 *Printing Week Library of Benjamin Franklin Keepsakes.* New York: privately printed, 1953-1982. Large 12mo., 30 volumes, complete set, all paper covered boards with some quarter leather and some patterned boards, variously paginated, this set belonged to Ben Lieberman, inscribed to him by designer, A. Burton Carnes. Oak Knoll Books 310 - 31 2016 $350

Association – Liggett, Wallace

Transition No. 21, No, 22, No. 25 and No. 26. The Hague: Servire Press, 1932-1933. 1936. 1937. First editions, 4 separately issued volumes, original pictorial paper wrappers, numerous black and white photos, issue 22 with original (somewhat chipped, but intact), yellow paper band reading 'Revolutionary Romanticism' issue no. 25 with ink inscription "Wallace Liggett April 18 1946" on rear cover, issue no. 26 with ink stamp of Messageries Dawson, Paris on rear cover, few tiny chips to edge of boards, little light soiling, no. 26 with short scratch and pencilled number on front cover, no. 25 with occasional small, faint stains to fore edge, few (inevitable) corner creases, otherwise in fine condition, quite clean, fresh and bright internally in very well preserved paper wrappers. Phillip J. Pirages 67 - 214 2016 $1250

Association – Lilford, Lord

Phaedrus *Phaedri Fabulae et P. Syrimimi Sententiae.* Hagae Contitum: apud Petrum Gosse, 1723. 8vo., titlepage printed in red and black, engraved vignette frontispiece, full contemporary sheep, raised bands, gilt decorated spine red morocco label, joints cracked but firm, head of spine chipped, engraved bookplate and label of Lord Lilford's Library at Lilford Hall, Northamptonshire. Jarndyce Antiquarian Booksellers CCXVI - 447 2016 £125

Association – Lilienthal, Joseph

De La Mare, Walter 1873-1956 *The Veil: and other Poems.* London: Constable, 1921. First edition, #88 of 250 numbered copies, signed, large paper copies, 8vo., untrimmed, bound in cloth backed boards, spine soiled, worn leather label, small bookplate on front endpaper noting that this book was the property of poet laureate John Masefield, also bookplate of Joseph Lilienthal, nice and clean. Second Life Books, Inc. 197 - 64 2016 $135

Association – Lima, Frank

Ceravolo, Joseph *Fits of Dawn.* New York: C Press, 1965. First edition, 4to., original illustrated wrappers, stapled as issued, wrappers lightly to moderately soiled, otherwise fine, scarce, presentation from author for Frank Lima and his wife. James S. Jaffe Rare Books Occasional List: Winter 2016 - 36 2016 $2250

Association – Lindley, Caroline

Ellis, William *Philo-Socrates. Part V.* London: Smith, Elder & Co., 1863. Original light brown printed paper wrappers, hinges slightly splitting with some repair to head of leading hinge, inscription Caroline Lindley from her friend William Ellis. Jarndyce Antiquarian Books CCXV - 640 2016 £85

Association – Lines, Kate

Lines, Samuel *A Few Incidents in the Life of Samuel Lines, Sen.* Birmingham: printed by Josiah Allen, Jun., 1862. First edition, 8vo., inscribed " To my granddaughter, Kate Lines May 31st 1862, original embossed cloth, printed paper label, clean copy. Marlborough Rare Books List 55 - 43 2016 £185

Association – Lingard, D., Mrs.

Craik, George Lillie *The Pursuit of Knowledge Under Difficulties.* London: M. A. Nattali, 1846. 2 volumes, frontispiece and plates, partially unopened in original green cloth, spines faded with small chip to head of spine, volume i, otherwise very good, contemporary signature of Mrs. D. Lingard. Jarndyce Antiquarian Books CCXV - 34 2016 £40

Association – Lish, Gordon

Nabokov, Vladimir 1899-1977 *Look at the Harlequins!* New York: McGraw Hill, 1974. First edition, fine in fine dust jacket, inscribed by author for Gordon Lish, with author's corrections, housed in cloth chemise and quarter morocco and cloth slipcase. Between the Covers Rare Books 204 - 84 2016 $9500

Association – Lister, Pamela

Merrifield, Mary Philadelphia *The Art of Fresco painting as Practised by the Old Italian and Spanish Masters with a Preliminary Inquiry into the nature of the Colours Used in Fresco Painting...* for the author by Charles Gilpin and Arthur Wallace, Brighton, 1846. First edition, half title, index, largely unopened, fine, bright in original green cloth blocked in blind, lettered gilt, Reynolds Stone booklabel of Pamela and Raymond Lister. Jarndyce Antiquarian Booksellers CCXVII - 186 2016 £125

Association – Lister, Raymond

Merrifield, Mary Philadelphia *The Art of Fresco painting as Practised by the Old Italian and Spanish Masters with a Preliminary Inquiry into the nature of the Colours Used in Fresco Painting...* for the author by Charles Gilpin and Arthur Wallace, Brighton, 1846. First edition, half title, index, largely unopened, fine, bright in original green cloth blocked in blind, lettered gilt, Reynolds Stone booklabel of Pamela and Raymond Lister. Jarndyce Antiquarian Booksellers CCXVII - 186 2016 £125

Association – Littell, Guy

Bible. English - 1932 *The Revelation of Saint John the Divine.* Montgomeryshire: Gregynog Press, 1932. No. 51 of 250 copies, 347 x 205mm., publisher's deep red Hermitage calf over bevelled boards, top edge sprinkled, housed in (somewhat worn) later quarter leather slipcase; 41 striking wood engraved illustrations by Blair Hughes-Stanton, 13 of them full page, text printed in red and black, first three words on titlepage wood engraved, front pastedown with morocco bookplate of Neva and Guy Littell, spine mildly faded, few minor shallow grazes to leather, otherwise very fine with binding lustrous and showing little use and text and plates especially fresh and clean. Phillip J. Pirages 67 - 181 2016 $3000

Association – Littell, Neva

Bible. English - 1932 *The Revelation of Saint John the Divine.* Montgomeryshire: Gregynog Press, 1932. No. 51 of 250 copies, 347 x 205mm., publisher's deep red Hermitage calf over bevelled boards, top edge sprinkled, housed in (somewhat worn) later quarter leather slipcase; 41 striking wood engraved illustrations by Blair Hughes-Stanton, 13 of them full page, text printed in red and black, first three words on titlepage wood engraved, front pastedown with morocco bookplate of Neva and Guy Littell, spine mildly faded, few minor shallow grazes to leather, otherwise very fine with binding lustrous and showing little use and text and plates especially fresh and clean. Phillip J. Pirages 67 - 181 2016 $3000

Association – Little, Charles

Pinnock, William *Roman History made easy...* London: W. Sell, 1831. Color map frontispiece, plate and illustrations, slight spotting, slight paper damage to inner margin of front and title, original printed paper boards, paper label slightly rubbed, contemporary ownership signatures of Charles Little, bookplate of Anthony David Estill, nice. Jarndyce Antiquarian Books CCXV - 904 2016 £68

Association – Littledale, G. A.

Vergilius Maro, Publius *Publii Virgilii Maronis Bucolica et Georgica tabulis Aeneis Olim a Johanne Pine Sculptore Regio...* n.p., 1774. 2 volumes bound as one, 80 plates on 59 sheets (including two frontispieces), titlepages and section titles and 6 engraved dedications, two of them on verso of letterpress pages, one plate folding, frequent further engravings within text, complete with ad leaf at front which is often discarded, some foxing and offsetting from plates, 8vo., contemporary vellum, spine divided by a gilt roll, second compartment dyed yellow and lettered gilt, marbled endpapers, vellum soiled, boards splaying outward somewhat, bookplate of Henry Anthony Littledale and ownership inscription of G. A. Littledale to front endpapers. Blackwell's Rare Books Greek & Latin Classics VII - 96 2016 £500

Association – Littledale, Henry Anthony

Vergilius Maro, Publius *Publii Virgilii Maronis Bucolica et Georgica tabulis Aeneis Olim a Johanne Pine Sculptore Regio...* n.p., 1774. 2 volumes bound as one, 80 plates on 59 sheets (including two frontispieces), titlepages and section titles and 6 engraved dedications, two of them on verso of letterpress pages, one plate folding, frequent further engravings within text, complete with ad leaf at front which is often discarded, some foxing and offsetting from plates, 8vo., contemporary vellum, spine divided by a gilt roll, second compartment dyed yellow and lettered gilt, marbled endpapers, vellum soiled, boards splaying outward somewhat, bookplate of Henry Anthony Littledale and ownership inscription of G. A. Littledale to front endpapers. Blackwell's Rare Books Greek & Latin Classics VII - 96 2016 £500

Association – Livingston, Allan

Vergilius Maro, Publius *Opera.* Edinburgh: apud Robertum Freebarnium, 1732. Small stain to blank margin of last quarter, ownership inscription of Allan Livingston (early) and Mary Lloyd Aston (20th century), 24mo., contemporary Scottish red morocco, spine gilt in compartments containing a saltire design, boards with central cross shape made up of arabesques containing dotted lines with thistles at its points, corners with square tools containing fan sprays, endpapers of decorative paper in multiple colours with gilt, edges gilt, joints cracking but strong, leather bit darkened, good. Blackwell's Rare Books Greek & Latin Classics VII - 92 2016 £500

Association – Livingston, Leon

Douglas, Norman 1868-1952 *South Wind.* New York: Dodd Mead and Co., 1928. First American illustrated edition, color illustrated frontispiece, 11 further color plates by Valenti Angelo, royal 8vo., original black buckram stamped in gilt to upper board, backstrip lettered gilt and just little dulled with bruise at head of upper joint, top edge orange, others rough trimmed, illustrated endpapers, slipcase with wear and split along base, otherwise very good, inscribed by the artist for Leon Livingston Sept. 1928.   Blackwell's Rare Books   B186 - 208   2016   £70

Association – Lloyd, Bertram

Campbell, Roy 1901-1957 *The Flaming Terrapin.* London: Jonathan Cape, 1924. First edition, frontispiece, crown 8vo. original first state binding of quarter green cloth with patterned boards, backstrip with printed label, light toning to boards, little rubbing to extremities, top edge lightly dust soiled, others untrimmed, free endpapers lightly browned, small bookseller sticker, good, inscribed by Ezra Pound for Bertram Lloyd.   Blackwell's Rare Books   B186 - 273   2016 £300

Association – Lloyd, Wyndham Edward Buckley

Lewis, Wyndham 1882-1957 *The Apes of God.* Arthur Press, 1930. First edition, 341/750 copies signed by author, recurrent light foxing to borders, royal 8vo., original tan cloth with little spotting overall, backstrip lettered in green spotting to edges, armorial bookplate of Wyndham Edward Buckley Lloyd, foxing to free endpapers, dust jacket darkened and lightly dust soiled overall, rubbed at folds with edges little frayed, light chipping to corners and tips of backstrip panel with small hole at foot of Latter, good. Blackwell's Rare Books   B186 - 259   2016   £425

Association – Lloyd-Davies, Wyndham

Stuart, John Sobieski *Lays of the Deer Forest.* Diss: Anthony Atha Publishers, 1985. No. 279 of a limited edition of 350 copies, oblong 4to., original green cloth, gilt rules and stag' head to upper board, gilt lettering and decoration to spine, color plates and text illustrations by Ian Oates, fine, inscribed from Lord Lovat to friend Wyndham (Lloyd-Davies).   Sotheran's   Hunting, Shooting & Fishing - 65   2016   £350

Association – Lo, Margaret

Mennie, Donald *The Grandeur of the Gorges.* Shanghai: A. S. Watson & Co. (The Shanghai Pharmacy Ltd.), Kelly & Walsh Limited, 1926. First edition, no. 889 of 1000 copies, 4to, original silk, image of Yangtze Gorge in colours to upper cover, 50 mounted plates from photos, including 12 colored, nice, bright copy, inscribed by Margaret Lo for Mrs. W. J. Souchow?   Sotheran's   Travel and Exploration - 155   2016   £1950

Association – Locker-Lampson, Frederick

Ruskin, John 1819-1900 *Dame Wiggins of Lee and Her Seven Wonderful Cats.* Sunnyside, Orpington, Kent: George Allen, 1885. Large paper copy from a later edition, inscribed by the artist, Kate Greenaway for F. Locker-Lampson, 1886, illustrations by Greenaway, original brown cloth with gilt title and illustration on front cover, binding rubbed and bumped, with few light stains, interior pages are generally clean, this copy has a plate of Bert M. Barwis Fund of Trenton Public Library stating the book was a personal gift to the library from Miss Barwis, she was the Supervisor of Kindergartens and Primary Schools for the City of Trenton NJ, call number written in white ink on spine and library ownership indicated by stamp to titlepage, despite flaws, still very nice, desirable copy.   The Kelmscott Bookshop   12 - 48   2016 $400

Association – Locock, Charles

Malton, Thomas *Views of Oxford.* London: White & Co.; Oxford: R. Smith, 1810. First complete edition, appealing 19th century (circa 1860's?), dark green half morocco over lighter green textured cloth by T. Aitken (stamp signed), upper cover with gilt titling, raised bands, spine gilt in compartments with elongated fleuron centerpiece and scrolling cornerpieces, gilt titling, marbled endpapers, all edges gilt (small, very expert repairs to upper outer corners and perhaps at top of joints), mezzotint frontispiece, engraved title, 30 fine plates of interior and exterior views, armorial bookplates of Sir Mayson M. Beeton and Sir Richard Farrant, verso of front free endpaper, ink presentation inscription from author for Sir Charles Locock, Nov. 1860, subscription proposal for work printed by T. Bensley and dated "London, May 30, 1301 (i.e. 1801)", laid in at front, couple of small smudges to boards, portrait faintly foxed and browned, isolated small stains, not affecting images, but fine, plates especially clean and fresh, smooth and pleasing binding with virtually no wear.   Phillip J. Pirages   67 - 248   2016 $8500

Association – Logan, Joshua

Osborn, Paul *On Borrowed Time.* New York: Knopf, 1938. First edition, very good, tight copy in little worn dust jacket, laid in is program from Chicago production of the play from 1938 that includes some of the NY cast, signed by director, Joshua Logan as well as all of the cast.   Second Life Books, Inc.   196 B - 353   2016 $350

Houghton, Norris *But Not Forgotten.* New York: William Sloane Associates, 1951. First edition, near fine in near very good dust jacket with couple of chips and long closed tear, signed by three members of the troupe, Henry Fonda, Joshua Logan and Mildred Narwick.   Between the Covers Rare Books   204 - 58   2016 $500

Association – Logan, Rayford

Quarles, Benjamin *Black History's Diversified Clientele: a Lecture at Howard University.* Washington: Dept. of History, Howard University, 1971. First edition, blue cloth boards, gilt, fine, issued without dust jacket. inscribed by historian Rayford Logan to Cynthia Gray in year of publication, very scarce. Between the Covers Rare Books 202 - 81 2016 $650

Association – Lomax, Caleb

Lockman, John *A New Roman History, by Question and Answer.* London: T. Astley, 1737. First edition, titlepage fore-edge little creased, last two leaves containing publisher's ads, 12mo., contemporary sheep, joints cracked and strengthened with glue internally, extremities worn, label lost, early inscriptions of Caleb Lomax to flyleaves, sound. Blackwell's Rare Books Greek & Latin Classics VII - 77 2016 £150

Association – Lombard, Barthelemy

Courtivron, Gaspard Le Compasseur Cresquy-Montfort De *Traite d'Optique Ou l'on Done la Theorie de la Lumiere dans le Systeme Newtonien...* Paris: Chez Durand & Pissot, 1752. First edition, small 4to., errors in pagination, collated complete, 7 engraved folding plates, original full mottled calf, raised bands, gilt spine, compartments, brown leather, title label, minor worming to joints and back cover, signature of Barthelemy Lombard, rare. Jeff Weber Rare Books 183 - 14 2016 $3750

Association – Lombroso, Cesare

Levi, Primo *Se Questo e un Uomo. (If This a man).* Torino: Einaudi, 1963. Fourth edition, 8vo., original cloth, dust jacket, signed by author, cocked, ink owner's name, otherwise very good in somewhat worn jacket, reinforced with cellotape in few places, from the library of Dr. Cesare Lombroso, of Harvard med. School, rare signed. James S. Jaffe Rare Books Occasional List: Winter 2016 - 92 2016 $2500

Association – Long, Richard

Bearden, Romare *Romare Bearden: Rituals of the Obeah.* New York: Cordier & Ekstrom, 1984. First edition, oblong octavo, illustrations in color, stapled wrappers, fine exhibition catalog, inscribed by artist to Richard Long, with original mailing envelope hand addressed by Bearden. Between the Covers Rare Books 207 - 12 2016 $1500

Washington, M. Bunch *The Art of Romare Bearden: the Prevalance of Ritual.* New York: Harry N. Abrams Inc., 1972. First edition, folio, bit of foxing on fore edge and first and last few leaves, spine tail bumped with half inch tears at joints, else near fine copy in like dust jacket with corresponding tears on spine tail, press release for the book laid in, inscribed by Bearden for Richard Long. Between the Covers Rare Books 202 - 9 2016 $1500

Association – Lorant, Stefan

Ayoux, Jean Jacques *Melville.* New York: Grove Press, London: Evergreen Books, 1960. First edition, small 8vo., illustrations, very nice, inscribed by historian Stefan Lorant to Melville's granddaughter, Eleanor Melville Metcalf. Second Life Books, Inc. 196 B - 200 2016 $50

Association – Lord, Mary

Farley, Harriet *The Lowell Offering. Series 4 no. 8 June 1844.* Lowell: Misses Curtis & Farley, 1844. First edition, little nicked at top of cover, near fine, scarce, former owner's signature "Mary J. Lord". Second Life Books, Inc. 197 - 107 2016 $150

Association – Lossing, Benson John

Murphy, Henry C. *Anthology of New Netherland or Translations from the Early Dutch Poets of New York with Memoirs of their Lives.* New York: Bradford Club, 1865. Number 86 of an edition of 125 copies, 4to., later flexible leatherette, frontispiece, accompanied by two manuscript letters, first from John B. Moreau making the presentation to Benson Lossing on behalf of Bradford Club and second from Lossing to Moreau, very good copy. Edwin V. Glaser Rare Books 2015 - 10275 2016 $450

Association – Lourie, Richard

Hughes, Langston *Troubled Island: an Opera in Three Acts by William Grant Still, Libretto by Langston Hughes.* New York: Leeds Music Corp., 1949. First edition, 8vo. little soiled light blue printed wrappers, near fine, inscribed by Hughes for Richard M. Lourie. Second Life Books, Inc. 196A - 849 2016 $600

Association – Lovat, Lord

Stuart, John Sobieski *Lays of the Deer Forest.* Diss: Anthony Atha Publishers, 1985. No. 279 of a limited edition of 350 copies, oblong 4to., original green cloth, gilt rules and stag' head to upper board, gilt lettering and decoration to spine, color plates and text illustrations by Ian Oates, fine, inscribed from Lord Lovat to friend Wyndham (Lloyd-Davies). Sotheran's Hunting, Shooting & Fishing - 65 2016 £350

Association – Loveday, John

Sarbiewski, Maciej Kazimierz 1595-1640 *Mathiae Casimiri Sarbievii Lycircorum Libri IV.* Cambridge: Richard Green, 1684. 12mo., fore-margin of A1-4 (and second fly-leaf) dampstained and slightly ragged, contemporary calf, ruled in blind with small tool in each corner, front joint rubbed, from the library of James Stevens Cox (1910-1997), the copy of John Loveday (1711-1689) with signature. Maggs Bros. Ltd. 1447 - 374 2016 £120

Association – Lovell, Elizabeth

Monck, Mary *Marinda. Poems and Translations Upon Several Occasions.* London: printed by J. Tonson, 1716. First edition, very good, 8vo., contemporary calf, gilt, rebacked, very good, early signatures of John Brace (crossed out) and Elizabeth Lovell, later bookplates of G. W. F. Gregor and Oliver Brett, Viscount Esher. C. R. Johnson Rare Book Collections Foxon: H-P 2015 - 617 2016 $2298

Association – Luck, Fred

Baker, Henry *Employment of the Microscope.* London: printed for R. and J. Dodsley, 1764. Second edition, 2 parts in one volume, 8vo., 17 engraved plates, lightly foxed, titlepage creased, plate facing page 422 torn at fold, modern full calf with original calf mounted on sides, gilt stamped motto "Fide et Virtute" belonging to Cha. Brandling, gilt and blindstamped spine, gilt stamped red leather label, new endleaves, bookplates of Cha. Brandling, Charles Adams, Fred C. Luck and Max Erb, very good+. Jeff Weber Rare Books 183 - 5 2016 $650

Pritchard, Andrew *The Microscopic Cabinet of Select animated Objects....* London: Whittaker, Treacher and Arnot, 1832. First edition, 8vo., numerous figures, 13 plates, modern quarter calf, original marbled boards, black spine label, original calf corners, new endleaves, bookplate of Fred C. Luck, early pencil ownership signature of Thomas B. Hart(?) 1834, very good. Jeff Weber Rare Books 183 - 28 2016 $875

Association – Luke, George

Ridpath, George *The Stage Condem'd and the Encouragement Given to the Immoralities and Profaneness of the Theatre....* London: for John Salusbury, 1698. First edition, foxed and browned throughout, heavily in places and dampstained at end, contemporary panelled calf, rebacked, leather crackled by damp, corners repaired, new endleaves, from the library of James Stevens Cox (1910-1997), 'E- libris Ge(o)r(ge) Luke pr. 0£ 2s-6d". Maggs Bros. Ltd. 1447 - 365 2016 £220

Association – Lum, Aubrey

Fry, Caroline *The Assistant of Education; Religious and Literary.* London: published for the author by T. Baker, 1823-1824. 2 volumes, 12mo., plates, some light spotting, contemporary half brown calf, little dulled with some slight wear to leading hinge of volume I, inscription on leading blank for Aubrey Lum from sister Mary Greive 2nd July 1869, nice. Jarndyce Antiquarian Books CCXV - 695 2016 £75

Association – Lund, Richard

The Young Secretary's Guide to an Epistolary Correspondence in Business, Love, Friendship.... Newcastle upon Tyne: printed by Saint for W. Chamley and Whitfield & Co., 1781. 12mo., small repair to corner of A4 affecting few letters made in ms., leaves little dusted with some slight damp marking and browning, contemporary full sheep, neatly rebacked, corners worn, slightly later signature of Richard Lund, sound copy. Jarndyce Antiquarian Books CCXV - 496 2016 £120

Association – Lunt, Alfred

Coward, Noel 1899-1973 *Quadrille: a Romantic Comedy in Three Acts.* London: Heinemann, 1952. First edition, signed by 17 members of the English cast and by producer Jack Wilson and by Lynn Fontanne and Alfred Lunt on dedication page (play is dedicated to them), inscribed by Coward to Dorothy Sands (Octavia in the NY production), two more signed cards by Lunt and Fontanne tipped in and 3 notes by Lunt to Sands laid in, with tipped in signed photo of sands, nice in somewhat signed dust jacket. Second Life Books, Inc. 196A - 342 2016 $500

Association – Lyall, Lawrence

Drew, Joseph *The Mystery of Creation: a Lay Sermon.* Wymouth: printed by Sherren and Son, 1879. Half title, text within double rule borders, original black cloth bevelled boards, block in gilt, slightly rubbed and dulled, ownership inscription of J. E. Elliott 1879 and Lawrence Lyall 1903, scarce. Jarndyce Antiquarian Booksellers CCXVII - 91 2016 £45

Association – Lynch, Brendan

Kavanagh, Patrick *Lapped Furrows - Correspondence 1933-1967 Between Patrick and Peter Kavanagh with other Documents.* New York: Peter Kavanagh Hand Press, 1969. First edition, octavo, presentation copy inscribed by editor for Brendan Lynch, octavo, covers slightly marked, near fine. Peter Ellis 112 - 201 2016 £85

Association – Lynes, Honore d'Albert, Duc De

Gerhard, Friedrich Wilhelm Eduard *Etruskische und Kampanische Vasenbilder des Koniglichen Museums zu Berlin.* Berlin: Verlag von G. Reimer, 1843. First edition, imperial folio, contemporary calf over marbled blue paper boards, 30 color and five monochrome plates, library label of the Duc de Lynes, text in German, from the library of Honore d'Albert, 8th Duc de Luynes, noted archaeologist and collector of antiquities. Honey & Wax Booksellers 4 - 5 2016 $9000

Association – Lynn, Diana

Taylor, Samuel *Sabrina Fair; or a woman of the World a Romantic Comedy.* New York: Random House, 1954. First printing, 8vo., illustrations, very good in little scuffed and soiled, price clipped dust jacket, signed by Lerna Dana, Kim Stanley, Diana Lynn and Margaret Steele, who appeared in the play, illustrations. Second Life Books, Inc. 196 B - 743 2016 $95

Association – Lynne, J. W.

Dexter, Walter *The London of Dickens.* London: Cecil Palmer, 1930. Third & pocket edition, half title, original brown embossed cloth, booklabel on leading pastedown obscuring excised booklabel, very good, signed by author for J. W. Lynne. Jarndyce Antiquarian Booksellers CCXVIII - 1158 2016 £20

Association – Lyon, Nelson

Southern, Terry *Lollipop (Candy).* Paris: Olympia Press, 1962. First edition thus, revised after 1958 edition suppressed, printed wrappers, very near fine, full page and effusive inscription by author to friend Nelson Lyon, TV producer and writer. Between the Covers Rare Books 208 - 81 2016 $3500

Association – Lyon, William

Gale, Zona *The Secret Way.* New York: Macmillan, 1921. First edition, 8vo., bound in cloth backed printed boards, fine, inscribed by author to Dr. William Lyon. Second Life Books, Inc. 196A - 596 2016 $200

Association – Lyster, A. C.

Our Paper. Jan. to Dec., 1856. (1855).with No. 10 being for Oct. -Dec., editor's own copy, with his monogram stamp on leading free endpaper and titlepage and signed by him on leading blank, A. C. Lyster Grennan Lodge, Lessners, Heath, Kent St., contemporary red binder's cloth, little worn, recased, all edges gilt. Jarndyce Antiquarian Booksellers CCXVII - 227 2016 £1250

Association – Lyttelton, Charles

Juvenalis, Decimus Junius *Satyrae.* Cambridge: Prostant Venales Londini apud Gul. Sandby, 1763. 8vo., 15 engraved plates (including frontispiece), light spotting, contemporary mid-brown calf, boards bordered with gilt roll, gilt in compartments, lettering piece in second compartment (rather chipped), boards with later Chancellor's Prize stamp in blind (i.e. arms of Baron Grenville, as chancellor of Oxford), marbled endpapers, extremities rubbed, head of spine chipped, front joint cracking but strong, armorial bookplate of Revd Charles Lyttelton, good. Blackwell's Rare Books Greek & Latin Classics VII - 54 2016 £250

Association – Macauley, Ian

Clarke, Arthur C. *Islands in the Sky.* Philadelphia: John C. Winston, 1952. First edition, small ownership of Ian Macauley, some wear to crown, very good in supplied dust jacket with small chip on front board, couple of tiny tears and some general wear at extremities along with original tattered, poor dust jacket, dedication copy inscribed by author to his protege and friend Ian Macauley. Between the Covers Rare Books 208 - 117 2016 $25,000

Association – Macclesfield, Earl of

Bude, Guillaume *De Asse et Partibus Etus, Libri Quinque....* Cologne: Johannes Soter, 1528. First American edition, 2 parts in 1 volume, woodcut printer's device on title, title to second part within woodcut border, woodcut initials, more elaborate woodcut device on verso of last leaf, some text in Greek, small hole in titlepage with loss of 1 letter from headline on verso, 2 leaves with small repairs to fore-margin, few gatherings slightly browned, minor dampstaining, small 8vo., contemporary vellum over flexible boards, lettered in ink on spine, minor soiling, some contemporary annotation, the Macclesfield copy with bookplate and blindstamp, very good, scarce. Blackwell's Rare Books B186 - 28 2016 £1200

Callimachus *Hymni, Epigrammata et Fragmenta.* Paris: Excudebat Sebastianus Mabre-Cramoisy, 1675. First Dacier edition, gently washed and pressed at time of rebinding, browned titlepage then also expertly mounted on an old binder's blank, two sets of Macclesfield blindstamps to first three leaves, 4to., 19th century green pebbled morocco by Hatton of Manchester, spine faded, front joint rubbed, Macclesfield arms in gilt to front board, all edges gilt, marbled endpapers, bookplate, good. Blackwell's Rare Books B186 - 35 2016 £500

Caron, Francois *A True Description of the Mighty Kingdoms of Japan and Siam.* printed for Robert Boutler, 1671. Second edition in English, large folding engraved map (tears at either end on one fold, no loss and two emanating from inner margin), little discoloration around edges, particularly from turn-ins, some dust soiling among prelims, small 8vo., contemporary speckled calf, fleurons in blind at corners, rebacked, slightly worn at extremities, calf backed folding box, the Macclesfield copy. Blackwell's Rare Books B184 - 19 2016 £6500

Cebes *Tabula.* Impensis Authoris, 1720. First and last pages slightly dusty, little faint toning, embossment of Earls of Macclesfield to titlepage, one name in preface corrected in early ink, 8vo., slightly later sprinkled calf, boards bordered with decorative blind roll within double gilt fillet, spine divided by raised bands, red morocco lettering piece, other compartments with gilt acorn tools in quarters within gilt dentelles borders, small paper shelfmark labels at head and foot, Macclesfield bookplate of South Library Shirburn Castle, joints little rubbed, very good. Blackwell's Rare Books B186 - 38 2016 £600

Euclides *Geometricorum Elementorum Libri XV.* Paris: Henri Estienne 7 Jan., 1516-1517. Sixth edition, Roman types, numerous woodcut geometrical diagrams in margins, fine crible initials in a variety of styles and sizes, titlepage soiled and cut down and mounted on old paper, one diagram just cropped at its extreme outer corners, without final blank, folio, 19th century half brown calf by Hatton of Manchester, marbled edges, original order for the binder loosely inserted, the Macclesfield copy with bookplate but no blindstamps and annotated by John Collins, after his death his books were acquired by William Jones and thence to Shirburn Castle, scarce on the market, preserved in cloth folding box, good copy. Blackwell's Rare Books Marks of Genius - 16 2016 £12,000

The Hampstead Congress; or the Happy Pair. London: printed and sold by M. Cooper, A. Dodd and G. Woodfall (sic), 1745. First edition, 4to., recent half calf and marbled boards, very good, from the Macclesfield library. C. R. Johnson Rare Book Collections Foxon: H-P 2015 - 442 2016 $2681

Philo, Judaeus *In Libros Mosis: De Mundi Opificio, Historicos, de Legibus Eiusdem Libri Singulares.* Paris: e officina Adriani Turnebi typographi Regii, 1552. Editio princeps, lightly toned, titlepage little dusty, 3 small wormholes, briefly stretching to a short trail in blank margin at beginning, blindstamp of Earls of Macclesfield to initial leaves, folio, 18th century panelled calf, rubbed and scuffed, some wear to joints, bookplate of Shirburn Castle, good. Blackwell's Rare Books Greek & Latin Classics VII - 69 2016 £2750

Pitati, Pietro *Compendivm.... Super Annua Solaris Atque Lunaris anni Quantitate...* Verona: Paolo Ravagnano, 1560. First edition, woodcut printer's device on title, woodcut initials, Register and colophon on recto and heraldic woodcut on verso of last leaf, lacking final (blank) leaf, few headlines shaved, little waterstaining at beginning towards top, 4to., 18th century ?Italian mottled calf, spine gilt in compartments, unlettered green lettering piece, yellow marbled edges, Macclesfield copy with bookplate and blindstamps. Blackwell's Rare Books B186 - 119 2016 £1500

Rowlands, Henry *Mona Antiqua Restaurata.* Dublin: printed by Aaron Rhames for Robert Owen, 1723. First edition, 4to., 10 plates, titlepage in red and black, woodcut initials, some lineages illustrated in text, lightly toned, occasional light foxing, small blind embossed coat of arms to titlepage and following three pages, contemporary brown mottled calf, gilt spine with brown label, raised bands, all edges red, marbled endpapers, rubbed, endcaps worn with some loss, joints split but cards holding, very good, armorial bookplate of Earls of Macclesfield. Unsworths Antiquarian Booksellers Ltd. E05 - 11 2016 £360

Zepeda Y Adrada, Alonso *Epitome de la Fortification Moderns, Assi en lo regular, Como em lo Irregular Relucida a la Regla y al Compas, Por Diversos Modos y los Mas Faciles Para Mover la Tierra...* Brussels: Foppens, 1669. First edition, 4to., English 18th century full polished tree calf, spine elaborately decorated gilt, red morocco lettering pieces, red edges, large engraved coat-of-arms on title, engraved portrait and 34 fold-out engraved plates, front hinge restored at some point internally, apart from small old repair to title and light browning, very good in fine binding made for the Earls of Macclesfield. Sotheran's Travel and Exploration - 282 2016 £2750

Association – MacDonald, Donald

Rice, Elmer *The Left Bank.* New York: Samuel French, 1931. First edition, very good, tight copy, with card list from original play program tipped to front free endpaper and printed photo of leading lady tipped to front pastedown, this copy signed by Katharine Alexander, Horace Braham and Donald Macdonald. Second Life Books, Inc. 196 B - 475 2016 $125

Association – MacDonald, Dugald

Newton, Isaac 1642-1727 *Philosophiae Naturalis Principia Mathematica.* London: William and John Innys, 1726. Third edition, title printed in red and black, engraved frontispiece, 1 engraving and numerous diagrams in text, complete with half title and final ad leaf, some foxing at beginning and end, few scattered minor stains, repairs to margins of front flyleaves, late 19th century half red hard grained morocco, spine gilt in compartments and lettered direct, red edges, rebacked preserving previous spine, early inscription at head of title, little cropped at top and faded, seems to say 'gifted to Mr. William Scott of Babecan advocate by me ( ) Foulis', 19th century signature stamp of Dugald Macdonald at centre of titlepage, bookplate of Quebecois George G. Leroux, very good. Blackwell's Rare Books   Marks of Genius - 32   2016   £11,000

Association – MacDonald, George

Dickens, Charles 1812-1870 *Letters of Charles Dickens to Wilkie Collins 1851-1876.* London: James R. Osgood, McIlvaine & Co., 1892. Half title, original dark blue cloth, dulled, inner hinges cracking, inscribed by A. P. Watt for friend George Macdonald. Jarndyce Antiquarian Booksellers   CCXVIII - 850   2016   £280

Association – MacDonald, Grenville Matheson

Graves, Alfred Perceval *Songs of Killarney.* London: Bradbury Agnew & Co., 1873. First edition, half title, vignette signed AC, slightly dusted, original green cloth, front board and spine decorated in black, lettered gilt, back board in blind, half title inscribed "With the author's Respects", Grenville Matheson MacDonald's bookplate, later ownership inscription of R. G. F. Sandbach, nice. Jarndyce Antiquarian Booksellers   CCXVII - 112   2016   £150

Association – Macfie, Robert

Munro, Thomas *The Life of Major General Sir Thomas Munro, Bart....* London: Henry Colburn and Richard Bentley, 1830. First edition, 3 volumes, frontispiece, folding map volume I, contemporary half red morocco, marbled boards, ownership inscription in all volumes of Robert Macfie, Ardis. 1865, very good, attractive copy. Jarndyce Antiquarian Booksellers   CCXVII - 194   2016   £380

Association – MacKay, Phoebe

Shaw, George Bernard 1856-1950 *Man and Superman.* New York: Dodd, Mead, 1947. First edition, 8vo., very good in little worn dust jacket, some of the photos show little watermark at edge, written on endpaper is note this book is the property of "Maurice Evans Prod. Inc." and is to be returned, this copy signed by Malcolm Keen, Chester Stratton, Victor Sutherland, Carmen Mathews, Jack Manning, Phoebe Mackay and Tony Bickley. Second Life Books, Inc. 196 B - 562   2016 $450

Association – MacKenzie, John Whiteoord

Rutherford, Samuel *Joshua Redivivus or Mr. Rutherford's Letters, Divided in two parts.* Rotterdam: in the Year, 1664. First edition, 8vo., some occasional light dampstaining, larger ink blots, very small hole through V1 (touching text on verso), late 19th century 'Presbyterian blue' morocco by Riviere & Son, panelled and lettered gilt, gilt gauffered edges, contemporary flyleaves and 'Dutch-gilt' pastedowns preserved from original binding, from the library of James Stevens Cox (1910-1997), 17th century calligraphic inscription 'Mrs. Anna Montgomerie Her Booke", long list of numbers and letters written in ink on front flyleaf, mid 19th century bookplate of John Whiteoord Mackenize. Maggs Bros. Ltd.   1447 - 370   2016   £500

Tate, Nahum *Poems.* London: by T. M. for Benj. Tooke, 1677. First edition, 8vo., without final blank leaf, small ink stain to blank fore margin of E2, rust spot to F4, some light staining to F6 and H2, 19th century calf, blind panelled, front board detached, from the library of James Stevens Cox (1910-1997), mid 19th century bookplate of John Whiteoord Mackenzie, armorial bookplate of Archibald Philip Primrose, 5th Earl of Rosebery. Maggs Bros. Ltd.   1447 - 407   2016   £150

Association – MacKenzie, Kenneth

Ardene, Jean Paul De Rome D' *Traite des Renoncules, qui Contient Outre ce Qui Regarde des Fleurs Beaucoup d'Observations, Physiques & de Remarques Utiles Soit Pour l'Agriculture, Soit Pour le Jardinge.* Avignon: Louis Chambeau, 1763. Third edition, small 8vo., contemporary green boards, rebacked in matching morocco with part of original gilt spine preserved, monogram AS in gilt on upper cover, bookplate of NY Horticultural Society, Bequest of Kenneth Mackenzie, inside front cover. Blackwell's Rare Books   B186 - 9   2016   £600

Association – Mackie, P. Jeffrey

Walker, A. Stodart *The Keeper's Book.* Edinburgh: George A. Morton, 1904. Third impression, 8vo., original cream decorative cloth, frontispiece, illustrations, bookplate with P. Jeffrey Mackie's printed signature, printed signature, binding little rubbed and sunned to spine, internally very good. Sotheran's Piccadilly Notes - Summer 2015 - 317   2016   £160

Association – MacLean

Gener, S. *Translations of M. Gener, Being a Selection of letters on Life and Manners.* Edinburgh: printed for Peter Hill, 1808. First English edition, half title, contemporary full tree calf, red label, slightly rubbed, booklabel of Maclean of Ardgour, very good. Jarndyce Antiquarian Books   CCXV - 217   2016   £65

Hamilton, Elizabeth *A Series of Popular Essays, Illustrative of Principles Essentially Connected with the Improvement of the Understanding, the Imagination and the Heart.*   Edinburgh: printed for Manners and Miller and Longman &c. London, 1813. 2 volumes, 8vo, half titles, contemporary calf, flat spines gilt and labelled, but numbering pieces wanting, very good contemporary armorial bookplate in each of Maclean of Ardgour.   John Drury Rare Books   2015 - 25845   2016 $437

Thomson, John *Tables of Interest at 3, 4, 4 and 5 per cent.*   London: printed for W. Creech & C. Elliot, Edinburgh and T. Longman, G. Robinson & T. Cadell, London, 1783. Third edition, 12mo., contemporary reversed calf, blind decorated rules, red morocco label, excellent copy with engraved bookplate of MacLean of Ardgour.   Jarndyce Antiquarian Booksellers   CCXVI - 565   2016   £110

Association – Maclehose

MacEwen, William *Pyogenic Infective Diseases of the Brain and Spinal Cord.*   Glasgow: Maclehose, 1893. 60 illustrations, original green cloth, light wear, internally fresh, clean and uncut, penned "With Mess. Maclehose Compliments, and "William Thorburn Reviewer for Medical Chronicle", this appears to have been sent by publisher for review.   James Tait Goodrich   X-78 - 384   2016 $1295

Association – MacLeish, Archibald

Colby Library Quarterly. Edwin Arlington Robinson Centennial Issue #1. Waterville: Colby College, March, 1969. First edition, pictorial wrappers, inscribed and signed by Archibald Macleish for William Meredith, with two ink corrections in his essay and original envelope addressed in MacLeish's hand, fine.   Charles Agvent   William Meredith - 66   2016 $80

Association – MacLeod, Robert Bruce Aeneas

Sheridan, Richard Brinsley Butler   1751-1816   *The Works of the late Right Honourable Richard Brinsley Sheridan.* London: J. Murray, James Ridgway and Thomas Wilkie, 1821. First collected edition, 2 volumes, 236 x 154mm., contemporary dun colored publisher's boards, flat spines with paper labels, edges untrimmed, modern blue buckram, chemises inside matching morocco backed slipcases with gilt titling on spines, engraved armorial bookplate of R. B. AE Macleod of Cadboll, Invergordon Castle, 1877, paper boards little soiled, extremities with vague wear, occasional was drippings (noticeable, without being disfiguring, at bottom of perhaps 20 openings), otherwise excellent, leaves fresh and bright with generous signs and insubstantial boards entirely solid and showing, very few signs of use.   Phillip J. Pirages   67 - 320   2016 $1000

Association – MacMahon, Percy Alexander

Quetelet, Lambert Adolphe Jacques *Letters Addressed to H. R. H the Grand Duke of Saxe Coburg and Gotha on the Theory of Probabilities as Applied to the Moral and Political Sciences.*   London: Charles & Edwin Layton, 1849. First edition in English, 8vo., tables, original blind-stamped brown cloth by Lewis (binder's ticket at rear), rebacked, new spine label, fine, inscribed by translator Olinthus Gregory Downes to J. J. Sylvester, Esq., bookplate of Percy Alexander MacMahon, bookplate of Francis Galton Laboratory, initials of Florence Nightingale David, 1845.   Jeff Weber Rare Books   183 - 29   2016 $1000

Association – MacNeice, Louis

Clark, Leonard *The Mirror and Other Poems.*   London: Allan Wingate, 1948. First edition, crown 8vo., original grey-green cloth, backstrip lettered gilt, bottom corners trifle bumped, dust jacket little sunned to borders and backstrip panel with minor chipping to corners and backstrip panel ends, very good, inscribed to fellow poet Louis MacNeice.   Blackwell's Rare Books   B184 - 130   2016   £45

Association – MacRae, Elliott B.

Vallee, Rudy *Vagabond Dreams Come True.*   New York: Dutton, 1930. First edition, 8vo. photos, very good, inscribed by author for Harry Chaffin, also inscribed to same by Elliott B. MacRae, president of Dutton.   Second Life Books, Inc.   196 B - 783   2016 $100

Association – Macready, William

Pope, Alexander   1688-1744 *The Poetical Works of Alexander Pope.*   London: printed for private circulation by Bradbury & Evans,, 1848. Contemporary full dark green morocco, spine with blindstamped compartments, blind and gilt borders, gilt dentelles, slightly rubbed, small mark on front board, all edges gilt, attractive, well preserved, presentation from editor, William Macready to Mrs. Charles Dickens, then in turn, given by her to writer Edward Dutton Cook.   Jarndyce Antiquarian Booksellers   CCXVIII - 878   2016   £350

Association – Maier, Frank

Mirabeau, Honore Gabrielle Riquetti, Comte De   1749-1791   *Considerations on the Order of Cincinnatus. To Which are Added Several Original Papers...*   Philadelphia: printed by T. Seddon, 1786. New edition, first American edition, 8vo. 19th century three quarter morocco over marbled boards, very good copy, untrimmed, chips to spine ends, scuffed tips, owner's bookplate son front free endpapers and first blank, tight binding, the copy of Frank Maier and William S. S. Horton, M.De. with armorial bookplate.   Kaaterskill Books   21 - 55   2016 $750

Association – Maierus, M. J. Jacobus

Caesar, Gaius Julius *Commentaria Caesaris Prius a Locundo Impressioni datae...* Florence: ex officina Philippi de Giunta, 1514. First Giunti edition of Caesar, 5 full page woodcuts and 2 double page woodcut maps included in pagination, manuscript marginal numbers added to first few pages, some light spotting, one or two small marginal tears, ownership inscription of M. Joh. Jacobus Maierus to titlepage, later ms. Latin quotation recto of final leaf (blank apart from device on verso), 8vo., 17th century walnut brown calf, boards bordered with blind decorative roll inside triple gilt fillet, endpapers renewed early 20th century, recently rebacked in expertly sympathetic fashion, fore-edge lettered in ink (with date '1541'), very good. Blackwell's Rare Books Greek & Latin Classics VII - 9 2016 £2500

Association – Maismis, Ernnet Casparus

Mizauldo, Antonio *Centuriae IX Memorabilium Utilium Ac Juncdorum in Aphorismos...* Frankfurt: Nicolas Hoffman, 1613. Small folio, 3 parts in 1 volume, some misnumbering of pages, printer's device on each of the three titles, light paper toning, occaisonal stains, contemporary limp vellum, manuscript spine title, lacks ties, rear joint partly torn, bookplate signed by Fritz Laber of Dr. Carl Wurth, early ownership signatures of Ernnet Casparus Maismis, very good. Jeff Weber Rare Books 181 - 21 2016 $600

Association – Makdougall, Henry Hay

Williams, Helen Maria *Julia, a Novel, Interspersed with Some Poetical Pieces.* London: printed for T. Cadell, 1790. 2 volumes, 12mo., little foxing & browning, possibly lacking A1 (blank) in volume II, contemporary half calf, marbled boards, original red morocco labels, black oval volume numbers, slight wear to head of one spine, boards slightly rubbed, contemporary bookplate of Sir Henry Hay Makdougall of Makerstoun, Cuonty Roxburgh, nice, scarce. Jarndyce Antiquarian Booksellers CCXVI - 612 2016 £5200

Association – Mako

Sondheim, Stephen *Pacific Overtures.* New York: Dodd, Mead and Co., 1977. First edition, photographs and drawing by Al Hirschfield, fine in fine dust jackets, laid in is card signed by actor Mako, who played The Receiver. Between the Covers Rare Books 208 - 84 2016 $200

Association – Malamud, Ann

Broughton, T. Alan *The Man on the Moon.* New York: Barlemir House, 1979. First edition, 8vo., paper covered boards, fine, inscribed by author for Ann and Bernard Malamud. Second Life Books, Inc. 196A - 205 2016 $45

Association – Malamud, Bernard

Broughton, T. Alan *The Man on the Moon.* New York: Barlemir House, 1979. First edition, 8vo., paper covered boards, fine, inscribed by author for Ann and Bernard Malamud. Second Life Books, Inc. 196A - 205 2016 $45

Howard, Richard *Quantities. Poems.* Middletown: Wesleyan University Press, 1962. First edition, issue in wrappers, signed and inscribed by author for William Meredith, additionally signed by Bernard Malamud , to Meredith, with TLS from Malamud apologizing for signing the book, some dust spotting to top edge, near fine. Charles Agvent William Meredith - 57 2016 $500

Association – Malan de Merindol

Harvey, William 1578-1657 *De Motu Cordis et Sanguinis in Animalibus Anatomica Exercitatio....* Padua: Cadorinum, 1689. 12mo., old vellum, base of spine with old nicely done repair, author's name in ink on spine, few old ink ownership marks on blindstamped, leather slipcase with mild edge wear, bookplate of Malan de Merindol, very good+. By the Book, L. C. 45 - 17 2016 $3000

Association – Malanga, Gerard

Berrigan, Ted *"C" a Journal of Poetry.* New York: Lornez Gude et al May, 1963. -May 1966., I: 1-10; II-11 and 13 (of 13), 12 issues, tall legal format, mimeographed and stapled in printed wrappers and in pictorial wrappers with cover design by Joe Brainard, and one issue with silk screen cover design by Andy Warhol, some numbers inscribed by Berrigan and signed by Joe Brainard, presentation inscriptions to Tony Towle from Warhol, Berrigan, Edwin Denby, Gerard Malanga and John Wieners. James S. Jaffe Rare Books Occasional List: Winter 2016 - 24 2016 $22,500

Himma 3 December 1977. Indianapolis: Ron Bernard, 1977. Oblong octavo, stapled gray decorated wrappers, little rust on staples, else fine, signed by Gerard Malanga, contributor. Between the Covers Rare Books 204 - 70 2016 $150

Association – Malina, Judith

MacLow, Jackson *Barnesbook: Four Poems Derived from Sentences by Djuna Barnes.* Los Angeles: Sun & Moon Press, 1996. First edition, small octavo, illustrated wrappers, fine inscribed by author to Judith Malina. Between the Covers Rare Books 204 - 69 2016 $450

Association – Mallet, Johannis

Brooke, Fulke Greville, 1st Baron *Certaine Learned and Elegant Workes of the Right Honorable Fulke Lord Brooke.* E. P(urslowe) for Henry Seyle, 1633. First edition, tall copy of ordinary paper issue, folio, full morocco gilt by Riviere, all edges gilt, initial and terminal blanks, repaired rust hole in d2 with loss of few letters, slight soiling to first leaves, otherwise very good, large copy, contemporary inscription D. Johannis Mallet, later bookplate of E. M. Cox.   Sotheran's Piccadilly Notes - Summer 2015 - 155   2016   £2750

Association – Mallinson, C. L.

Baines, Thomas   1806-1881 *Lancashire and Cheshire Past and Present.* London: William Mackenzie, c., 1867. 4 volumes, 4to., 25 plates and engraved titlepages to first part of each volume, some foxing, especially near front and rear, publisher's crimson morocco, heavy gilt spines, boards and dentelles, armorial centre pieces to boards, all edges gilt, spines darkened, joints rubbed, some slight scrapes and dents to boards with very occasional small areas of surface loss, ownership inscription of C. L. Mallinson.   Unsworths Antiquarian Booksellers Ltd.   E04 - 4   2016   £400

Association – Malo, D. Gregorio Lopez

Plutarchus *Vitae Illustrium Virorum.*   Rome: Ulrich Han, 1470. First edition, volume I, large folio, mid to late 19th century dark brown morocco over bevelled boards by William Townsend and Son, Sheffield with other blindstamp inside front covers panelled with simple blind fillets and ornamental rolls, spine decorated in same way, red morocco label, illuminated opening page with white vine stem border, on three sides extending into fore-margin, border incorporates 9 line initial "I" in gold and wreath on each border, one in lower margin left blank for a coat-of-arms, remaining two with rosettes, also four birds found in lower border, all in burnished gold, blue, green, purple, 54 further initials in gold, mostly 9 to 11 lines, against intricate white vine backgrounds infilled with blue green and purple, which extend into margins, 4 line initial in gold infilled with green and purple against blue background, some rubrication, early ms. headings and foliation, heavy inkstain affecting ff. vIv and v2r and initial, some dampstaining, mostly marginal but heavier towards end affecting c. 9 initials, foxed and spotted in places, near contemporary marginal annotations plentiful for first 35ff and intermittent thereafter, acquisition note of Dom Munor de Suessa, Dean of Iabelda-Logrono 1632, 18th century inscription of D. Gregorio Lopez Malo, 2 pages of 19th century bibliographical notes cut down and mounted at end.   Maggs Bros. Ltd.   1474 - 64   2016   £45,000

Association – Malsey, William

Boethius, Anicius Manlius Severinus   *De Consolatione Philosophiae, Libri Quinque.*   Antwerp: ex officina Plantiniana, 1607. 8vo., printer's device to titlepage and final leaf, woodcut initials, very light toning towards edges, ink blot to page 279-80 not affecting text to recto, obscuring a few letters to verso, contemporary vellum, raised bands, title inked to spine, blind tooled borders, vellum darkened with some marks, corners worn and small areas of loss, narrow strip of vellum lost to top edge of lower board, some bookseller's pencil notes, notes in old hand to rear pastedown, very good, armorial bookplate of William Malsey of St. John's College, Cambridge.   Unsworths Antiquarian Booksellers Ltd.   E05 - 3   2016   £575

Association – Mamet, David

Clurman, Harold   *Ibsen.* New York: Macmillan, 1977. First edition, inscribed by author to director David Mamet and his then wife, Lindsey Crouse Dec. 31. 1977, near fine in like dust jacket.   Royal Books   48 - 36   2016 $650

Association – Mandell, Jo

Sampson, Anthony   *Mandela. the Authorised Biography.* London: Harper Collins, 1999. First edition, signed and inscribed by Jo. Mandell, who co-directed the 1996 official film biography of Nelson Mandela, for Gritta Weil (1924-2009).   Sotheran's   Travel and Exploration - 33   2016   £78

Association – Mander, Lady

Wheeler, Charles   *High Relief - The Autobiography of Sir Charles Wheeler, Sculptor.*   Fletham: Country Life Books, 1968. First edition, 8vo., photos, presentation from author to Lady Mander, spine little creased, near fine in near fine dust jacket little creased at edges, notes in ink, presumably by Lady Mander.   Peter Ellis   112 - 444   2016   £35

Association – Manger, H.

Clare, Martin   *Youth's Introduction to Trade and Business.* London: by Benjamin Webb, G. Keith, J. Fuller & 11 others, 1769. Tenth edition, 8vo., slightly dusted, hansomely rebound in half brown calf, red morocco label, signature of H. Manger, 1853 on leading blank.   Jarndyce Antiquarian Books   CCXV - 120   2016   £280

Association – Mangnall, Richmal

Grant, Anne MacVicar 1755-18838 *Essays on the Superstitions on the Highlanders of Scotland.* London: and Edinburgh: Longman, Hurst, Rees, Orme, etc., 1811. First edition, octavo, 2 volumes, period binding of full calf with gilt decorated spines, gilt rules, black leather title labels, lettered gilt, bookplate of English schoolmistress Richmal Mangnall (1769-1820) ad armorial bookplate of each volume, covers little rubbed and bruised at corners and just little defective at extreme head of volume 1, prelims spotted, very good. Peter Ellis   112 - 350   2016   £195

Association – Manning, Adelaide,

Coles, Manning *Pray Silence.* London: Hodder & Stoughton Limited, 1940. First edition, inscribed by author for Julie J. Gladwin, signed by Adelaide Manning, spine slightly browned and light offsetting to front and rear endpapers, else very good in dust jacket with light restoration to spine ends, rare in jacket, rarer still inscribed by author. Buckingham Books   2015 - 2016 $4875

Association – Manning, Henry Edward

Zaccaria, Francescantonio *Dissertazioni Varie Italiane a Storia Ecclesiactica...* Roma: Stamperia Salomoni, 1780. 2 volumes, small 8vo., small title woodcut vignettes, head and tailpieces, indexes, corners curling, worming at gutter pages 113-126 of volume i, early ink handwritten notes on rear free endpaper, original marbled printed wrappers, spines worn, some cords loose, bookplates of Ex Oblatorum S. Carolio Bibliotheca Bayswater (Henry Edward Manning 1808-1892) and Pitts Theology Library, along with rubber ink stamps on title and elsewhere, archival folding chemises, very good.   Jeff Weber Rare Books   181 - 38   2016 $100

Petau, Denis *...Opus de Theologicis Dogmatibus Nunc primum Septem Voluminibus Comprehensum, in Mediorem Ordinem Redactum...* Venice: Remondiana, 1757. Best edition, 6 books in 7 and bound in 2 volumes, folio, title in red and black, half title, each book with its separate title, titlepage portrait engraving of Denis and additional woodcut initials and head and tailpieces all volumes, first volume free endpapers slightly torn, contemporary full vellum, gilt stamped spines, first volume stained, second volume lower corners gently bumped, bookplates of Ex Oblatororum S. Caroli Bibliotheca Bayswater (Henry Edward Manning 1808-1892), Pitts Theology Library bookplates, C. J. Stewart bookseller label, titlepage ownership signatures and inscriptions of Engelbert Klupfel, 1769 and Steph. Wirelo(?), rare, fine.   Jeff Weber Rare Books   181 - 26   2016 $750

Association – Manning, Jack

Shaw, George Bernard 1856-1950 *Man and Superman.* New York: Dodd, Mead, 1947. First edition, 8vo., very good in little worn dust jacket, some of the photos show little watermark at edge, written on endpaper is note this book is the property of "Maurice Evans Prod. Inc." and is to be returned, this copy signed by Malcolm Keen, Chester Stratton, Victor Sutherland, Carmen Mathews, Jack Manning, Phoebe Mackay and Tony Bickley.   Second Life Books, Inc.   196 B - 562   2016 $450

Association – Manny, Louise

Fraser, James A. *A History of Caton's Island.* Chatham: Miramichi Historical Society, Feb. 15, 1968. First printing, limited to 500 copies, this #2, felt covers, small 8vo., 1 map and 11 black and white photo illustrations, very good, author's presentation inscription to Dr Louise Manny. Schooner Books Ltd.   115 - 32   2016 $55

Association – Mantle, Burns

Atkinson, Brooks *Broadway Scrapbook.* New York: Theatre Arts, 1947. First edition, 8vo., cartoons by Al Hirschfeld, author's presentation to Burns Mantle, with Mantle's bookplate, cover little yellowed and worn, else very good, tight copy.   Second Life Books, Inc.   196A - 55   2016 $75

Association – Manzarek, Ray

Sugerman, Danny *The Doors - The Illustrated History.* New York: William Morrow and Co., 1983. First edition, signed by Ray Manzarek, Danny Sugerman and Robby Krieger, fine in dust jacket.   Buckingham Books   2015 - 11547   2016 $450

Association – Marceau, Robert

Cottle, Joseph *Early Recollections: Chiefly Relating to the late Samuel Taylor Coleridge.* London: Longman, Rees & Co., 1837. First edition, 200 x 127mm, 2 volumes, fine polished calf, elegantly gilt by R. W. Smith (stamp signed on front flyleaf), covers bordered with double gilt rules, spines with raised bands and compartments featuring pleasing dense gilt scrollwork, red and deep blue morocco labels, intricately gilt turn-ins, marbled endpapers, top edge gilt, 6 engraved plates, large modern bookplate of Robert Marceau, engravings rather foxed, little darkening and very minor intermittent foxing in text, otherwise excellent internally in beautiful, virtually unworn binding.   Phillip J. Pirages   67 - 93   2016 $750

Association – March, Frederic

Wilder, Thornton 1896-1976 *The Skin of Our Teeth. A Play in Three Acts.* New York: Harper, 1942. First edition, 8vo., very good, actor Frederic March's copy with his signature, with presentation card from author, with pencil marks and comments. Second Life Books, Inc. 197 - 355 2016 $600

Association – Marchant, Philip

Fitzgerald, Francis Scott Key 1896-1940 *Taps at Reveille.* New York: Charles Scribner's Sons, 1935. First edition, first state, Rockwell Kent designed bookplate of Philip Marchant, else superlative, very fine with spine lettering bright, lacking dust jacket. Between the Covers Rare Books 208 - 28 2016 $2000

Association – Marchant, Stephen

Chapin, James P. *The Birds of the Belgian Congo.* New York: American Museum of Natural History, 1932-1954. Only 300 copies printed, Octavo, 4 volumes, 3 color plates, photos and other illustrations, binder's red cloth, all edges speckled, bookplate and signatures of Stephen Marchant (previous editor of The Emu), very good, scarce. Andrew Isles Natural History Books 55 - 12104 2016 $1200

Ticehrust, Claud B. *The Birds of Mesopotamia.* Bombay: Reprinted from the Journal of the Bombay Natural History Society, 1920-1922. Octavo, photos, 4 parts i single volume binder's cloth, each part inscribed 'author's compliments', few spots throughout, bookplate of Stephen Marchant. Andrew Isles Natural History Books 55 - 12139 2016 $300

Association – Marchmont, Patrick Hume, 1st Earl of

Symson, Patrick *Spiritual songs or Holy Poems.* Edinburgh: by the Heir of Andrew Anderson &c. for William Dickie, 1686? 12mo., small wormhole in lower fore-corner becoming increasingly larger throughout, closed tear to fore margin of A2 and G1, fore-margin of A3 stained, foot of L2, L7, L8 damaged (no loss of text), contemporary sheep, front board detached, covers very worn and scuffed, corners bumped, from the library of James Stevens Cox (1910-1997), armorial bookplate of Patrick Hume, 1st Earl of Marchmont (1641-1724). Maggs Bros. Ltd. 1447 - 404 2016 £200

Association – Markham

Terentius Afer, Publius *Comoediae ex recensione Danielis Heinsii....* Rome: Impensis Nicolai Roisechii, 1767. Second edition of the Italian translation by Fortiguerra, Folio, titlepage printed in black and red, a number of large engravings within text, folio, untrimmed, contemporary half vellum, paper boards decorated in brown, red and yellow, spines lettered gilt, bookplates of Markham of Becca Lodge in Yorkshire, bindings soiled and worn around edges (particularly corners and spine ends, splash of white paint to backstrip of volume ii, good. Blackwell's Rare Books Greek & Latin Classics VII - 88 2016 £600

Association – Marrow, William

Quevedo, Francisco De *Forture in Her Wits; or the Hour of all Men.* London: for R. Sare, F. Saunders and Tho. Bennet, 1697. First edition in English, 8vo., minor worming to inner margin of A1-A3 touching printed border of top edge gilt and two letters of text on A3, small stain to lower inner margin of D5-D6, small ink stain to blank lower margin of f1, early ownership inscription cropped from head of titlepage, 19th century calf, corners bumped and chipped, joints rubbed, from the library of James Stevens Cox (1910-1997), inscribed "W(illiam) M. Marrow, his booke 1720", inscription of Alicia Anne Shring 1835. Maggs Bros. Ltd. 1447 - 347 2016 £350

Association – Marsden, Edmund

Ludolf, Hiob *A New History of Ethiopia.* London: for Samuel Smith, 1682. First edition in English, folio, 8 engraved plates, engraved plate of Ethiopic alphabet and folding genealogical table, contemporary or early 18th century calf, front hinge cracked but held by cords, corners worn, some light browning, but very good with signatures of Edmund and Rufus Marsden, latter dated 1762, Herz booklabel. Joseph J. Felcone, Inc. Books from Five Centuries: a Miscellany - 92 2016 $2200

Association – Marsden, Rufus

Ludolf, Hiob *A New History of Ethiopia.* London: for Samuel Smith, 1682. First edition in English, folio, 8 engraved plates, engraved plate of Ethiopic alphabet and folding genealogical table, contemporary or early 18th century calf, front hinge cracked but held by cords, corners worn, some light browning, but very good with signatures of Edmund and Rufus Marsden, latter dated 1762, Herz booklabel. Joseph J. Felcone, Inc. Books from Five Centuries: a Miscellany - 92 2016 $2200

Association – Marsh, Mary

Fisher, Anne *The Pleasing Instructor or Entertaining Moralist....* Newcastle upon Tyne: S. Hodgson, circa, 1800. Title vignette, plates, slightly foxed, contemporary mottled calf, spine rubbed and darkened, hinges cracked, ownership inscription of Mary Marsh 1819, sound. Jarndyce Antiquarian Books   CCXV - 686   2016   £48

Association – Marsh, Thomas

Vaux, Robert *Memoirs of the Life of Anthony Benezet.* York: W. Alexander, 1817. First UK edition, 12mo., frontispiece, original boards with paper backstrip and title label, early name plates (Thomas Marsh and Robert Langdon), some foxing to prelims, cup ring to front cover, backstrip defective, label rubbed, very good, scarce in original state. Peter Ellis   112 - 363   2016   £750

Association – Marshall, E.

Tasso, Torquato   1544-1595 *Godfrey of Bulloigne; or the Recovery of Jerusalem.* London: by John Macock for George Wells and Abel Swalle, 1687. Second edition, small closed tear to titlepage with evidence of earlier restoration, occasional rust spotting, dampstaining to margin in places, 55mm. piece torn away from fore margin of A7, repaired tear to A8, small piece torn away from corners of H4, 2A1 and with 60mm. closed tear to foot of 2I1 (touching text), contemporary calf, head and tail of spine damaged, corners bumped, label missing, from the library of James Stevens Cox (1910-1997), signature of E. Marshall dated 1769, signature of John Warren dated 1809.   Maggs Bros. Ltd.   1447 - 406   2016   £180

Association – Marshall, F. A.

Taylor, Thomas Proclus *Dombey and Son or Good Mrs. Brown the Child Stealer.* 1858? Folded as issued, with split to one fold, original buff wrappers, hand colored illustrations, edges little chipped, signed 'F. A. Marshall Aug. 1879', fragile, scarce.   Jarndyce Antiquarian Booksellers   CCXVIII - 462   2016   £85

Association – Marshall, John Nairn

Austen, Jane   1775-1817 *Austen's Novels in five volumes with a Memoir.* London: Richard Bentley, 1885-1886. 6 volumes, half title, frontispiece, contemporary half red morocco, spine extra gilt, leading inner hinge of Pride and Prejudice slightly weak but sound, very nice, attractive set, bookplates of John Nairn Marshall.   Jarndyce Antiquarian Booksellers   CCXVII - 18   2016   £1200

Association – Marshall, Louis

Spargo, John *The Jew and American Ideals.* New York: Harper, 1921. 8vo., author's presentation to Louis Marshall (one of the founders of the American Jewish Congress), maroon cloth, top edges soiled, cover little scuffed, otherwise very good, tight copy.   Second Life Books, Inc.   196 B - 654   2016 $65

Association – Marshall, Mrs.

Archibald, Campbell *Lessons for School Life...* Edinburgh: Thomas Constable & Co., 1853. Second edition, contemporary full calf by Charles Thurnam, maroon and green morocco labels, slightly rubbed, inscribed by author for Mrs. Marshall, Apl. 1856, recent ownership label of Dr. Michael Brown.   Jarndyce Antiquarian Books   CCXV - 928   2016   £45

Association – Martin, Alex

Veen, Otto Van *Q. Horati Flacci Embelmata.* Antwerp: ex officina Hieronymi Verdussen, 1607. First edition, 4to., oval portrait of Horace on titlepage and 103 full page emblems, 20th century vellum, title lettered ink on spine, 18th century notes on verso of half title, small stamp off ex-libris Alex Martin, fore-margins cropped, closely at times, pages 123 and 129 touching platemark of emblem.   Maggs Bros. Ltd.   1474 - 78   2016   £2600

Association – Martin, Franca Mercati

Kinman, Diane *Franca's Story Survival in World War II Italy.* Mercer Island: Wimer Pub. Co., 2005. First edition, signed by author and Franca Mercati Martin, illustrations by Martin, endpaper maps, as new.   Gene W. Baade, Books on the West   2015 - 5021022   2016 $121

Association – Martin, H. Bradley

Meredith, George   1828-1909 *Farina: a Legend of Cologne.* London: Smith, Elder and Co., 1857. First edition, rare, inscribed by author for friend, F. Maxse, original apple green cloth, professionally recased, binding rubbed and easily soiled, interior pages clean and bright, July 1857 publisher's catalog, bookplate of noted collector, H. Bradley Martin, green cloth clamshell box with paper title and author label to spine, exceptional association copy in extremely scarce original cloth, very good.   The Kelmscott Bookshop   12 - 68   2016 $4900

Shelley, Mary Wollestonecraft Godwin 1797-1851
History of a Six Weeks' Tour Through a Part of France, Switzerland, Germany and Holland. London: published by T. Hookham Jun., 1817. First edition, little light soiling, 8vo., early 20th century olive morocco by Tout, boards with gilt frame and spine, elaborately gilt top edge gilt, others untrimmed, joints rather rubbed, little wear to headcap, bookplates of H. Bradley Martin and of Robertson Trowbridge (this inscribed to Mark Trowbridge's gift of the volume to Thomas Pym Cope) and of Thomas Jefferson McKee, very good.   Blackwell's Rare Books   Marks of Genius - 43   2016   £3500

Association – Martin, Karl

Jones, Charlotte Rosalys   *The Hypnotic Experiment of Dr. Reeves and other Stories.*   London and New York: Bliss, Sands and Foster, Brentano's, 1894. First edition, brown cloth with delicate cream and green design in gilt, edges worn and chipped, interior pages have some browning along margins, some splitting of signatures but text block remains solid, very good, presentation copy from author to Star Barker, further inscribed to Karl Martin.   The Kelmscott Bookshop   12 - 58   2016 $300

Association – Martin, W.

De Quincey, Thomas 1785-1859   *Revolt of the Tatars; or Flight of the Kalmuck Khan and His People from the Russian Territories to the Frontiers of China.*   London: Dropmore Press, 1948. first edition thus, quarto, illustrations, including endpapers by Stuart Boyle, printed on handpress on handmade paper, half brown leather with gilt decoration, cloth sides, top edge gilt, presentation copy inscribed "W. Martin from the Dropmore Press Christmas 1948 - Edward Shanks".   Peter Ellis   112 - 106   2016   £85

Association – Martineau, James

Cockburn, William   *Strictures on Clerical Education in the University of Cambridge.*   London: J. Hatchard &c., 1809. Some largely inoffensive dampstaining to upper margins, disbound, ownership signature of James Martineau, 36 pages.   Jarndyce Antiquarian Books   CCXV - 570   2016   £40

Association – Martineau, M. E.

Dickens, Charles 1812-1870   *Pictures from Italy.*   London: published for author by Bradbury & Evans, 1846. First edition, vignette title, contemporary full dark green calf, spine gilt in compartments, double ruled borders in gilt, maroon and brown morocco labels, spine slightly rubbed at head and tail contemporary signature of M. E. Martineau, good plus, attractive.   Jarndyce Antiquarian Booksellers   CCXVIII - 434   2016   £250

Association – Masefield, John

De La Mare, Walter 1873-1956   *The Veil: and other Poems.*   London: Constable, 1921. First edition, #88 of 250 numbered copies, signed, large paper copies, 8vo., untrimmed, bound in cloth backed boards, spine soiled, worn leather label, small bookplate on front endpaper noting that this book was the property of poet laureate John Masefield, also bookplate of Joseph Lilienthal, nice and clean.   Second Life Books, Inc.   197 - 64   2016 $135

Association – Mashiter, F.

Plinius Caecilius Secundus, Gaius   *The Letters of Pliny the Counsul; with Occasional Remarks.*   London: printed for J. Dodsley, 1748. Third edition, 2 volumes, 8vo., titlepages printed in red and black with small numismatic engravings, half title in each volume, occasional light foxing, particularly to front and rear, few smudgy marks, contemporary dark brown speckled calf, neatly rebacked, gilt borders, edges sprinkled red, spines darkened and bit creased, few small chips and scrapes, very good, ownership inscription of F. Mashiter to each front pastedown, together with several library codes, pictorial bookplate, ownership inscription of Thomas Short to each titlepage122.   Unsworths Antiquarian Booksellers Ltd.   30 - 122   2016   £160

Association – Mason, Clarissa

Hirschhorn, Clive   *The Films of James Mason.*   London: LSP Books, 1975. 4to., heavily illustrated, signatures of Mason and his second wife Clarissa and Joan Bennet, appearing on their pictures, very good in chipped and soiled dust jacket.   Second Life Books, Inc.   196A - 799   2016 $225

Association – Mason, George William

Terentius Afer, Publius   *Comoedia.*   London: Impensis J. et P. Knapton et G. Sandby, 1751. 2 volumes in one, 6 engraved plates, some soiling, last leaf bit stained, 8vo., contemporary vellum, spine lettered in black, somewhat soiled, endpapers renewed preserving old bookplate of William Henry Mason and old flyleaves with pencilled inscription of George William Mason, Trinity College, Cambridge 1840, good.   Blackwell's Rare Books   Greek & Latin Classics VII - 87   2016   £120

Association – Mason, James

Hirschhorn, Clive   *The Films of James Mason.*   London: LSP Books, 1975. 4to., heavily illustrated, signatures of Mason and his second wife Clarissa and Joan Bennet, appearing on their pictures, very good in chipped and soiled dust jacket.   Second Life Books, Inc.   196A - 799   2016 $225

Association – Matheson, Richard

California Sorcery. Abingdon: Cemetery Dance, 1999. Publisher's copy of the limited edition (26 copies), signed by Ray Bradbury, Richard Matheson, Ellison, Nolan, Tomerlin, Sohl, Fritch and others, stamp of another author, fine in fine dust jacket in publisher's printed gray case. Ken Lopez Bookseller 166 - 5 2016 $650

Association – Mathews, Carmen

Shaw, George Bernard 1856-1950 *Man and Superman.* New York: Dodd, Mead, 1947. First edition, 8vo., very good in little worn dust jacket, some of the photos show little watermark at edge, written on endpaper is note this book is the property of "Maurice Evans Prod. Inc." and is to be returned, this copy signed by Malcolm Keen, Chester Stratton, Victor Sutherland, Carmen Mathews, Jack Manning, Phoebe Mackay and Tony Bickley. Second Life Books, Inc. 196 B - 562 2016 $450

Association – Matthay, Tobias

Ortmann, Otto *The Physiological Mechanics of Piano Technique.* London: Kegan Paul, Trench, Trubner & Co. Ltd. and Curwen & Sons, 1929. First edition, diagrams in text, photographic plates, original cloth, blindstamped borders on sides, spine gilt lettered, spine and portion of boards faded, lower outer corner of upper board completely faded or perhaps affected by Damp, Tobias Matthay's copy annotated in pencil, extensively dog-eared, good. Blackwell's Rare Books B184 - 72 2016 £750

Association – Matthiessen, Peter

Cardenas, Jeffrey *Marquesa.* Stone Harbor: Meadow Run Press, 1995. First printing, one of 1500 copies, fine in fine slipcase with promotional postcard laid in, letter from publisher dated Jan 23 1995, transmitting to book to author Peter Matthiesson on behalf of author. Ken Lopez Bookseller 166 - 16 2016 $350

Chaskey, Scott *December Songs.* Porthenrys: self published, 1988. Copy #58 of 100, inscribed by author to Peter Matthiessen with TLS laid in, near fine in self wrappers. Ken Lopez Bookseller 166 - 30 2016 $200

Costello, Ruth *Poems for Evan Connell.* Self published: undated, circa 1980's, Near fine, laid in is printout of 1983 Costello poem "For Lama Anagarika Govinda", unmarked, but from the library of Peter Matthiessen. Ken Lopez Bookseller 166 - 24 2016 $150

Costello, Ruth *Poems for Herb Gold.* undated, circa 1980's, self published, Velobound in gold stamped plastic covers, unmarked, from the library of Peter Matthiessen, highly uncommon. Ken Lopez Bookseller 166 - 23 2016 $150

Dodge, Jim *A Book of Ku.* N.P.: Tangram, 2013. One of 200 copies, saddle stitched self wrappers, small spot to rear cover, else fine, laid in to this copy is letter from publishers Jerry Reddan to Peter (Matthiessen), uncommon. Ken Lopez Bookseller 166 - 30 2016 $250

Association – Mattson, Britt Marie

Zagoria, Donald S, *The Sino-Soviet Conflict 1956-1961.* Princeton and London: Princeton University Press and Oxford University, 1962. First edition UK issue with dust jacket price in sterling, octavo, ownership signature of Swedish journalist Britt-Marie Mattson, fine in near fine dust jacket faintly darkened at spine. Peter Ellis 112 - 73 2016 £65

Association – Mauss, Detlef

Bonet, Honore *L'Apparition De Jehan de Meun ou Le Songe Du Prieur De Salon.* Paris: Imprime par Crapelet pour la Societe des Bibliophiles Franai, 1845. No. 7 of 17 copies on vellu, plus 100 copies issued on paper, 235 x 181mm., recent fine white pigskin, decorated in blind in medieval style by Courtland Benson, housed in titled custom made morocco backed folding cloth box, 10 engraved plates replicating illustrations from early manuscript copies of the week, pastedown with morocco bookplate of Comte H. De La Bedoyere and engraved bookplate of Marcellus Schlimovich, front free endpaper with embossed library stamp of Dr. Detlef Mauss, half title with ink library stamp of Sociedad Hebraica Argentina, fine, especially clean and bright internally with only most trivial imperfections and in striking new retrospective binding. Phillip J. Pirages 67 - 343 2016 $2750

Association – Maxse, F.

Meredith, George 1828-1909 *Farina: a Legend of Cologne.* London: Smith, Elder and Co., 1857. First edition, rare, inscribed by author for friend, F. Maxse, original apple green cloth, professionally recased, binding rubbed and easily soiled, interior pages clean and bright, July 1857 publisher's catalog, bookplate of noted collector, H. Bradley Martin, green cloth clamshell box with paper title and author label to spine, exceptional association copy in extremely scarce original cloth, very good. The Kelmscott Bookshop 12 - 68 2016 $4900

Association – Maxwell, Henry

Dickens, Charles 1812-1870 *Oliver Twist.* London: Richard Bentley, 1839. Second edition, 3 volumes, frontispieces and plates, volume i unopened, slight spotting to plates, uncut in original purple brown vertical grained cloth, imprints at tails of spines, carefully recased, armorial bookplates and signatures of Henry Maxwell, small bookseller's ticket, good plus.   Jarndyce Antiquarian Booksellers   CCXVIII - 178   2016   £580

Association – Maxwell, John

Vaumoriere, Pierre D'Ortigue *The Art of Pleasing in Conversation.* London: A. Bettesworth & F. Clay, 1722. 12mo., contemporary full calf, spine rubbed and worn and with loss to head and tail, lacking label, signature of John Maxwell, Christ Church College, bookplate of Maxwell of Polloc.   Jarndyce Antiquarian Books   CCXV - 454   2016   £120

Association – Maxwell, M. C.

Trollope, Anthony 1815-1882 *British Sports and Pastimes.* London: Virtue and Co., 1868. First edition, octavo, publisher's pebble grained green cloth with blind-stamped rule on boards and gilt titles and decorations, primrose yellow endpapers with Virtue & Co.'s paper label on rear pastedown, cloth trifle rubbed with few small nicks and stains, inner front hinge, little tender and first gathering little sprung, but a bright very good or better copy, inscribed by Trollope for M. C. Maxwell.   Between the Covers Rare Books   208 - 145   2016 $4500

Association – Maxwell, Robert

Seneca, Lucius Annaeus *Tragoediae: Post Omnes Omnium Editiones Recensione Editae Denuo & Notis....* Excudebat Rogerus Daniel, 1659. 12mo., first leaf blank, one leaf with paper flaw to fore-edge affecting few characters of side note, small wormhole in gutter of a few gatherings sometimes touching a line number, few minor marks, bookplate of Robert Maxwell of Finnebrogue to titlepage verso, 12mo., original blind ruled sheep, worn paper label to spine, rear joint damaged near head revealing structure of binding, but binding still entirely sound, slightly marked and rubbed, good.   Blackwell's Rare Books   Greek & Latin Classics VII - 82   2016   £200

Association – Maxwell, William

Humphries, Sydney *A Calendar of Verse.* London: privately printed, 1912. One of 20 copies, 225 x 155mm., printed recto only, excellent full vellum over boards by Riviere & Son (stamp-signed), compiler's gilt coat of arms on each cover and foot of spine, flat spine with gilt titling, densely gilt turn-ins, ivory moire silk endleaves, top edge gilt, other edges untrimmed, fleece lined blue cloth slipcase, frontispiece with monographs of Humphries and his wife, surrounded by putti and other symbols of love, engraved coat of arms on title, ink inscription from author to William Maxwell, master printer at R. & R Clark, where the volume was printed, extremely pleasing, binding unworn, entirely clean, fresh and bright, inside and out.   Phillip J. Pirages   67 - 244   2016 $1250

Association – May, Dick

Jackson, Charles *The Lost Weekend.* New York: Farrar & Rinehart, 1944. First edition, Fine bright copy in dust jacket with some minor professional restoration to spine ends, sharp copy, author's warm contemporary presentation inscription to Dick May Jan. 27 '44.   Buckingham Books   2015 - 26213   2016 $3750

Association – Mayer, Elizabeth

Moore, Marianne 1887-1972 *The Arctic Ox.* London: Faber and Faber, 1964. First edition, one of 1500 copies, presentation copy inscribed by author for Elizabeth Mayer, 8vo., original cloth, dust jacket, light offsetting from binding adhesive on rear free endpaper, else very fine in jacket.   James S. Jaffe Rare Books   Occasional List: Winter 2016 - 99   2016 $850

Association – Mayer, W.

Theocritus *The Idyllia, Epigrams and Fragments of Theocritus, Bion and Moschus, with Elegies of Tyrateus.* Bath: printed by R. Cruttwell, 1792. First edition by Polwhele, 2 volumes bound as one, half title, discarded, little minor spotting, ownership inscription of W. Mayer, T.C.D., to titlepage, 8vo., later half maroon roan, marbled boards, spine lettered gilt, corners worn, spine rubbed, shelfmark to front pastedown, good.   Blackwell's Rare Books   Greek & Latin Classics VII - 90   2016   £120

Association – Mayle, Mary

The Troubles of a Good Husband. Northampton: printed by F. Cordeux, 1818. 12mo., errata leaf page 21 is a cancel, some water staining to lower margins, uncut in original drab boards, brown paper spine, extremities rubbed, loss of paper to spine, contemporary signature of Mary Mayle, good, sound copy.   Jarndyce Antiquarian Books   CCXV - 443   2016   £65

Association – Mays, Willie

Einstein, Charles *Willie's Time: a memoir.* New York: Lippincott, 1979. First edition, cloth and boards, pictorial endpapers, signed by Willie Mays, very, very scarce signed, very good+ in dust jacket.　Gene W. Baade, Books on the West　2015 - SHEL689　2016　$135

Association – McAlpine, Lord

Vidal, Gore *Reflections Upon a Sinking Ship.* London: Heinemann, 1969. First UK edition, octavo, signed by author, ownership blindstamp of Lord McAlpine, tail of spine slightly bumped, top edge spotted, very good in like dust jacket, bit creased at top edge.　Peter Ellis　112 - 421　2016　£75

Association – McBride, Barbara

Plato *Plato's Phaedo.* London: Routledge & Kegan Paul, 1955. First edition, 8vo., cloth, gilt lettered, spine slightly cocked, edges dusted, top edges slightly foxed, light toning to free endpapers, very good, white dust jacket bit grubby, minor shelfwear, very good, ex-libris of Barbara McBride. Unsworths Antiquarian Booksellers Ltd.　E04 - 85　2016　£25

Sophocles *The Tragedies.* Cambridge: Cambridge University Press, 1957. fourth impression, Volume I - Volume II, 2 volumes, small 8vo., red cloth, gilt lettered to spine, edges dusted and slightly spotted, volume II red cloth, slightly darker and endcaps just starting to wear, volume I lacks dust jacket, dust jacket to volume I with 2 cm. closed tear to upper jacket, price clipped with price sticker adhered to front flap, bit grubby, still good, ex-libris sticker Barbara McBride, one or two pencil annotations. Unsworths Antiquarian Booksellers Ltd.　E04 - 101　2016 £24

Association – McCann, Frazier

Rabier, Benjamin *Le Buffon de Benjamin Rabier.* Paris: Librairie Garnier Freres, n.d., 1913. First edition, 4to., contemporary quarter red morocco, gilt lettering and decoration to spine, marbled boards, marbled endpapers, top edges gilt, 33 full color plates, color text illustrations, little rubbing to edges of binding, little chipping to fore-edge of first couple of leaves, otherwise very good, prize bookplate and ex-libris bookplate of Frazier McCann.　Sotheran's　Piccadilly Notes - Summer 2015 - 248　2016　£800

Association – McCants, Andrew

Braithwaite, William Stanley *Anthology of Magazine Verse for 1920.* Boston: Small Maynard, 1920. First edition, corners little bumped, else about fine lacking scarce dust jacket, inscribed by author as well as by dedicatee, Boston bookseller Andrew McCants.　Between the Covers Rare Books　207 - 11　2016　$300

Association – McClanahan, Ed

Kesey, Ken *Kesey's Jail Journal.* New York: Viking, 2003. First edition, large 8vo., fine in dust jacket, signed by Ed McClanahan (introducer).　Second Life Books, Inc. 196A - 949　2016　$45

Association – McClintic, Guthrie

Howard, Sidney *Yellow Jack, a History...* New York: Harcourt Brace, 1933. First edition, 8vo., full brown morocco by Brentanos, spine gilt in compartments, this copy presented by author to play's director Guthrie McClintic, with initials 'G McC' on front board.　Second Life Books, Inc. 196A - 833　2016　$375

Association – McCormick, Edith Rockefeller

Herodotus *Herodoti Libri Novem. Quibus Musarum Sunt Nomina.* Venice: Aldus Manutius, 1502. First edition, folio, printed in Green type with Aldine anchor on title and last page, full 18th century French crimson levant morocco stamped in gilt, triple gilt fillets on sides and gilt inside borders, marbled endpapers, all edges gilt, previous cataloger noted the binding was probably done by Derome, part of lower right of titlepage restored, barely affecting few letters of dedication letter, contemporary manuscript marginalia on some leaves, fine, large copy, wide margins, bookplate of Edith Rockefeller McCormick.　Second Life Books, Inc. 197 - 180　2016　$47,500

Association – McCutcheon, John T.

Davis, Richard Harding *The Deserter.* New York: Scribners, 1917. First edition, 8vo., uncut and partially unopened, fine in very slightly worn original dust jacket, upper corner of first 3 leaves of prelim matter clipped off, inscribed by (introducer) John T. McCutcheon, tipped to endpaper is ALS 12.5/17 from author's brother responding to a request for an autograph, tipped to flyleaf if ALS from author to his brother.　Second Life Books, Inc.　196A - 388　2016 $150

Association – McDonell, John M.

Dyson, Walter *Howard University: The Capstone of Negro Education. A History 1867-1940.* Washington: Graduate School Howard University, 1941. First edition, 553 pages, illustrations, fine, lacking dust jacket, inscribed by author for Mr. John M. McDonell, scarce.   Between the Covers Rare Books   202 - 45   2016 $700

Association – McElderry, Margaret

Anglund, Joan Walsh *Cowboy and His Friend.* New York: Harcourt Brace World, 1961. Stated first edition, 8vo., cloth, fine in dust jacket, illustrations by Anglund, laid in is marvelous drawing of little girl and her cat, inscribed by Anglund and signed by Margaret McElderry.   Aleph-bet Books, Inc.   111 - 19   2016 $400

Association – McKean, Thomas

Cunningham, Peter *The Story of Nell Gwyn and the Sayings of Charles II.* London: Bradbury & Evans, 1852. First edition in book form, 2 volumes, very pretty brown crushed morocco elaborately gilt by Zaehnsdorf, (stamp signed), covers with frame comprising plain and decorative gilt rules, an inlaid maroon morocco strap, ornate gilt cornerpieces of many small floral tools on a stippled background, raised bands, spines densely gilt in compartments with floral branches radiating form a central circle, background stippled and with small circlets, delicate floral frame on turn-ins, leather hinges, olive and gold silk jacquard endleaves, top edges gilt, extra illustrated with 179 engraved plates, (plates listed alphabetically on printed leaves following the Table of Contents obviously prepared either for this copy alone or else for very limited number of copies, engraved armorial bookplate of Thomas McKean, small nick to one board, otherwise just hint of use to attractive lustrous and scarcely worn bindings, majority of inserted plates foxed (two dozen of them noticebly so), variable offsetting from engraved material, otherwise excellent internally.   Phillip J. Pirages   67 - 74   2016 $950

Association – McKee, Louis

Metz, Leon *Robert E. McKee: Master Builder of Structures Beyond the Ordinary.* El Paso: Robert E. & Evelyn McKee Foundation, 1997. First edition, 4to., attractive pictorial silver stamped cloth, illustrations, signed by Metz and Louis McKee, fine in fine slipcase, very scarce.   Gene W. Baade, Books on the West   2015 - 1111113   2016 $356

Association – McKee, Thomas Jefferson

Shelley, Mary Wollestonecraft Godwin   1797-1851 *History of a Six Weeks' Tour Through a Part of France, Switzerland, Germany and Holland.* London: published by T. Hookham Jun., 1817. First edition, little light soiling, 8vo., early 20th century olive morocco by Tout, boards with gilt frame and spine, elaborately gilt top edge gilt, others untrimmed, joints rather rubbed, little wear to headcap, bookplates of H. Bradley Martin and of Robertson Trowbridge (this inscribed to Mark Trowbridge's gift of the volume to Thomas Pym Cope) and of Thomas Jefferson McKee, very good.   Blackwell's Rare Books   Marks of Genius - 43   2016   £3500

Association – McLaren, Christabel

Sassoon, Siegfried Lorraine   1886-1967 *Poems.* London: Duckworth, 1931. First edition, crown 8vo., couple of occasional faint foxspots at head of pages and light handling marks, original black boards, stamped in green to upper board, faint foxing to free endpapers, very good, this copy inscribed by Christabel McLaren May 14th 1931 to Clive Bell.   Blackwell's Rare Books   B186 - 280   2016   £100

Association – McLellan, Leigh

McPherson, Sandra *Sensing.* San Francisco: Meadow Press, 1980. No. 67 of 100 copies, signed by author and Leigh McLellan, woodcut and printing by McLellan, patterned paper over boards with cloth spine, nice in little yellowed and chipped plain paper dust jacket.   Second Life Books, Inc.   196 B - 190   2016 $65

Association – McLuhan, Marshall

MacDonald, Ross *The Wycherly Woman.* New York: Knopf, 1961. First edition, presentation inscription dated 1961, month of publication to the Marshall McLuhans, fine in dust jacket lightly soiled on rear panel and with some very minor restoration to spine ends and corners.   Buckingham Books   2015 - 31440   2016 $3750

Association – McMurtry, Larry

Shakespeare, William   1564-1616 *Complete Works.* London: Oxford University Press, 1969. 8vo., publisher's cloth, very good, tight copy, bookseller, author, Larry McMurtry's copy, with his 1969 ownership signature, card with 7 lines of holograph and slip with 6 lines of holograph laid in.   Second Life Books, Inc.   196 B - 555   2016 $50

Association – McNaghton, Alex

Segar, Simon *Honores Anglicani or Titles of Honour the Temporal Nobility of the English Nation.* London: printed for John Baker at the Black Boy in Pater Noster Row, 1712. 8vo., some foxing and browning, contemporary panelled calf, raised bands, red morocco label, faint gilt crest at foot, expert repairs to joints and head and tail of spine, armorial bookplate of William Perceval, signature on titlepage and shelf number at head and early name Alex. McNaghton. Jarndyce Antiquarian Booksellers CCXVI - 513 2016 £380

Association – McNamee, Greg

Abbey, Edward *Resist Much, Obey Little - Some Notes on Edward Abbey.* Salt Lake City: Dream Garden Press, 1985. First edition, fine, this copy signed by Greg Mcnamee. Bella Luna Books 2016 - 3680 2016 $76

Association – McPhee, David

Davidson, Rodney *A Book Collector's Notes on Items Relating to the Discovery of Australia the First Settlement and the Early Coastal Exploration of the Continent.* North Melbourne: Cassell Australia, 1970. Limited to 250 numbered and signed copies, octavo, photos, publisher's cloth and slipcase, bookplate of David McPhee. Andrew Isles Natural History Books 55 - 37026 2016 $150

Association – Mechlin, Jacob

Mair, John *An Introduction to Latin Syntax...* Philadelphia: printed for Campbell Conrad & Co. by J. Bioren, 1799. First American edition, lightly toned and spotted, ownership inscription of Daniel Turny to titlepage and Jacob Mechlin to second leaf, contemporary marbled sheep, rubbed, worn at extremities, red morocco lettering piece partly worn away, sound. Blackwell's Rare Books B186 - 102 2016 £200

Association – Medlicott

Puffendorf, Samuel, Freiherr Von 1632-1694 *The Compleat History of Sweden....* London: printed for J. Brudenell, 1701. 8vo., some browning to several gatherings, otherwise very good, clean, full contemporary calf, lighter mottled board panels, blindstamped tulip cornerpieces, ornate gilt panelled spine, red morocco label, armorial bookplate with Medlicott family motto. Jarndyce Antiquarian Booksellers CCXVI - 483 2016 £350

Association – Meeenger, W.

Marshall, Francis James Charles *Physical Education in Boys' Schools.* London: University of London Press, 1933. First edition, half title, frontispiece, plates and illustrations, original light blue cloth, spine faded, slightly dulled, booklabel of W. Meenger, St. Luke's College, Exeter. Jarndyce Antiquarian Books CCXV - 856 2016 £20

Association – Mein, Thomas

Lucianus Samosatensis *Dialogorum Selectorum Libri Duo Graecolatini.* Ingolstadt: Ex officinia typogrpahica Adami Sartorii, 1598. 8vo., final blank discarded, errata leaf present, top margin of last few leaves worn (with loss to running title), titlepage dust soiled and bit frayed at fore-margin, small paper flaw in leaf y4 affecting few characters, occasional marginal annotations in Latin and Greek in early hand, gathering v bound out of order, 8vo, contemporary dark sheep, paper label to spine, rubbed and scratched, some wear to joints, leather since treated to conserve it, various inscriptions in English, Latin and Greek - Andrew Baxter and his son Alexander of Duns Castle, also of Thomas Mein. Blackwell's Rare Books Greek & Latin Classics VII - 58 2016 £750

Association – Melchet Court

Newton, Isaac 1642-1727 *Mathematical Principles of Natural Philosophy Book the First (all published).* London: printed by A. Strahan for T. Cadell, Jun. and W. Davies, 1802. 22 folding engraved plates, some dampstaining mainly throughout, usually pale but little more pronounced in places, the last leaf a cancel, 4to., 19th century half calf and marbled boards, flat spine gilt tooled on either side of raised bands, skillfully rebacked and recornered, new labels, stamp of Melchet Court, Romsey with initial A circled by a crown in centre, few mathematical notes in margins, good. Blackwell's Rare Books Marks of Genius - 33 2016 £2500

Association – Mellinger, William

Hazard, Caroline *Threads from the Distaff of History and Contemplation.* Providence: Roger Williams Press, 1934. First edition, 8vo., frontispiece, paper over boards, cloth back, paper labels, author's presentation to William Mellinger, president of Wellesley College on flyleaf, another owner's name on flyleaf, cover little scuffed and worn at edges, else very good, tight copy. Second Life Books, Inc. 196A - 756 2016 $45

Association – Mellor, G.

Edleston, Richard *Marriage its Uses, Duties and Blessings.* Leeds: J. Heaton, 1849. Occasional ink annotation, original brown cloth, slightly rubbed maroon morocco label, slight damp mark to front board, ownership stamps of G. Mellor. Jarndyce Antiquarian Books   CCXV - 173   2016   £45

Association – Mendham

Bedford, William Riland *The Midland Forester. By a Woodman of Arden.* Birmingham: printed and published by R. Wrightson Athenaeum 8 New Street, 1829. First edition, 12mo., contemporary ownership signature (Mendham) in upper margin of title, bound recently in cloth with printed title label on upper cover, very good, apparently of great rarity. John Drury Rare Books   2015 - 26076   2016 $437

Association – Merchant, Vivien

Pinter, Harold *The Birthday Party.* London: Encore Pub., 1959. First edition, trifle rubbed, still fine in wrappers, uncommon true first edition of author's first play, inscribed by him to his first wife, Vivien Merchant Dec. 59, very uncommon, housed in custom full cloth clamshell box. Between the Covers Rare Books   204 - 83   2016 $40,000

Association – Meredith, Jane

Varesi, Gilda *Enter Madame: a Play in three acts.* New York: Putnam, 1921. First edition, 8vo., cloth backed boards, very good, inscribed by author under frontispiece and signed by 10 members of the cast including Norman Trevor, Jane Meredith, Gavin Muir, etc.   Second Life Books, Inc.   196 B - i794   2016 $250

Association – Meredith, William

Abse, Dannie *A Strong Dose of Myself.* London: Hutchinson, 1983. First edition, presentation from author for William Meredith, slight dust spotting to top edge, fine in fine dust jacket.   Charles Agvent   William Meredith - 4   2016 $100

Abse, Dannie *Dannie Abse. The Pocket Poets.* London: Vista, 1963. First edition, fine, inscribed by author for William Meredith.   Charles Agvent   William Meredith - 1   2016 $80

Abse, Dannie *Doctors and Patients.* Oxford: Oxford University Press, 1984. First edition, inscribed for William Meredith, signed twice on titlepage, fine in fine dust jacket.   Charles Agvent   William Meredith - 8   2016 $80

Abse, Dannie *Funland. A Poem in Nine Parts.* Swansea: Portland University Library, 1971. First edition, inscribed and signed by poet for William Meredith, near fine.   Charles Agvent   William Meredith - 2   2016 $80

Abse, Dannie *Modern European Verse. The Pocket Poets.* London: Vista Books, 1964. First edition, inscribed for William Meredith, by Abse, small skim mark on rear, otherwise fine.   Charles Agvent   William Meredith - 9   2016 $80

Abse, Dannie *Poems Golders Green.* London: Hutchinson, 1962. First edition, inscribed for William Meredith, near fine in like dust jacket with some wear to spine.   Charles Agvent   William Meredith - 3   2016 $150

Abse, Dannie *Tenants of the House. Poems 1951-1956.* New York: Criterion Books, 1959. First American edition, poet William Meredith's copy with his signature, below inscription from author, laid in is promotional photo of author, fine in near fine dust jacket.   Charles Agvent   William Meredith - 6   2016 $200

Abse, Dannie *Three Question Plays.* Lowestoft: Scorpion Press, 1967. First edition, inscribed by author for William Meredith, pictorial wrappers, some soiling to covers, very good.   Charles Agvent   William Meredith - 7   2016 $60

Appleman, Philip *Kites on a Windy Day.* Nottingham: The Byron Press, 1967. First edition, inscribed and signed for William Meredith, laid in are two TLS's, along with copies of Appleman's resume and reviews, near fine.   Charles Agvent   William Meredith - 10   2016 $60

Auden, Wystan Hugh 1907-1973 *Poesies Choiseies.* Paris: Gallimard, 1976. First edition, printed wrappers, William Meredith's copy signed by poet, near fine.   Charles Agvent   William Meredith - 76   2016 $60

Balaban, John *Walking Down into Cebolla Canyon.* Greensboro: Unicorn, 1980. First edition, wrappers, reproduction of photo by William Clift on cover, broadside poem folded in ours, one of 500 copies, inscribed for William Meredith by Balaban, with original envelope addressed in Balaban's hand, fine.   Charles Agvent   William Meredith - 12   2016 $80

Barker, George *Collected Poems 1903-1955.* London: Faber and Faber, 1957. First edition, inscribed by author for William Meredith, fine in near fine dust jacket.   Charles Agvent   William Meredith - 13   2016 $150

Barker, George *Sacred and Secular Elegies.* Norfolk: New Directions, 1943. First edition, inscribed and signed for William Meredith, fine in near fine dust jacket. Charles Agvent   William Meredith - 14   2016 $200

Bidart, Frank *Golden State.* New York: George Braziller, 1973. First edition, one of 500 copies, this copy inscribed by author for William Meredith, fine in fine dust jacket. Charles Agvent   William Meredith - 16   2016 $500

Bidart, Frank *The Book of the Body.* New York: Farrar, Straus & Giroux, 1977. First edition, this copy inscribed for William Meredith, by author on April 3, 1977, laid in is shipping label from envelope Bidart used to send the book, filled out in Bidart's hand, bit of dust spotting to top edge of bulked text, about fine in close to fine dust jacket. Charles Agvent   William Meredith - 15   2016 $200

Booth, Philip *Margins. A Sequence of New and Selected Poems.* New York: Viking Press, 1970. First edition, advance reading copy with letter from editor laid in, inscribed and signed by author April 16th 1971 for William Meredith, mild sunning to top edge, near fine in lightly soiled, near fine dust jacket. Charles Agvent   William Meredith - 18   2016 $100

Booth, Philip *The Islanders.* New York: Viking Press, 1961. First edition, inscribed and signed by author March 26th 1962 for William Meredith, slight dust spotting to top edge, fine in price clipped, near fine dust jacket. Charles Agvent   William Meredith - 17   2016 $150

Booth, Philip *Weathers and Edges.* New York: Viking Press, 1966. First edition, signed with publisher's compliments card laid in, inscribed and signed for William Meredith, slight dust spotting to top edge, fine in lightly soiled, near fine dust jacket. Charles Agvent   William Meredith - 20   2016 $100

Ciardi, John *Other Skies.* Boston: Little Brown and co., 1947. First edition, inscribed by poet for William Meredith, June 9 1980, fine in close to fine dust jacket with tanned spine. Charles Agvent   William Meredith - 22   2016 $250

Colby Library Quarterly. Edwin Arlington Robinson Centennial Issue #1. Waterville: Colby College, March, 1969. First edition, pictorial wrappers, inscribed and signed by Archibald Macleish for William Meredith, with two ink corrections in his essay and original envelope addressed in MacLeish's hand, fine. Charles Agvent   William Meredith - 66   2016 $80

Cole, Henri *The Look of Things.* New York: Alfred A. Knopf, 1995. First edition, inscribed and signed by poet March 7 1995, for William Meredith, faint dampstain to top of rear panel of both book and dust jacket, not terribly noticeable, near fine in like dust jacket. Charles Agvent   William Meredith - 23   2016 $150

Cooper, Jane *The Weather of Six Mornings. Poems.* New York: London: Macmillan, 1969. First edition, inscribed and signed by author for William Meredith, fine in near fine dust jacket with tanned spine. Charles Agvent   William Meredith - 24   2016 $100

Cummings, Edward Estlin   1894-1962 *Collected Poems.* New York: Harcourt Brace and co., 1946. Reprint, later printing, William Meredith's copy, signed by poet Princeton 1947, near fine in very good dust jacket. Charles Agvent   William Meredith - 77   2016 $60

Davison, Peter *Dark Houses.* Cambridge: Halty Ferguson, 1971. First edition, one of 300 handprinted copies, dark blue decorated wrappers, fine, inscribed by author June 1972 for William Meredith, 3 corrections in text by author. Charles Agvent   William Meredith - 25   2016 $100

Davison, Peter *Walking the Boundaries. Poems 1957-1974.* New York: Atheneum, 1974. First American edition, inscribed and signed by author June 4 1980, for William Meredith, with author's business card laid in, fine in fine dust jacket. Charles Agvent   William Meredith - 26   2016 $80

Doolittle, Hilda   1886-1961 *Trilogy; The Walls Do Not Fall; Tribute to the Angels; and the Flowering of the Rod.* New York: New Directions, 1973. First edition, William Meredith's copy, signed by poet, review copy with slip from publisher laid in, near fine in near fine dust jacket. Charles Agvent   William Meredith - 78   2016 $50

Eliot, Thomas Stearns   1888-1965 *Collected Poems 1909-1935.* New York: Harcourt Brace and co., 1936. First edition, early printing, William Meredith's copy, signed by poet Princeton 1940, extensively annotated by Meredith in pencil with few pages of notes by Meredith laid in, covers faded and stained, good only, lacking dust jacket. Charles Agvent   William Meredith - 79   2016 $500

Empson, William *The Gathering Storm.* London: Faber and Faber Ltd., 1940. First edition, James Merrill's copy with his signature dated 1974, signed by William Meredith, faint stain to bottom of front cover, very good in good only dust jacket, split into two pieces. Charles Agvent   William Meredith - 82   2016 $150

Feldman, Irving *The Pripet Marshes and Other Poems.* New York: Viking, 1965. First edition, signed and inscribed by author in 1971 for William Meredith, laid in is ALS from author to Meredith, some dust spotting to top of bulked text, near fine in very good dust jacket with some darkening to spine and top edges with short tear at rear.   Charles Agvent   William Meredith - 28   2016 $100

Feldman, Irving *Work and Days.* London: Andre Deutsch, 1961. First British edition, inscribed by author in 1971 for William Meredith, some dust spotting to top of bulked text, near fine in like dust jacket with some staining to spine.   Charles Agvent   William Meredith - 29   2016 $80

Fischer, Henry *Bred in the Bone. an Anthology.* Princeton: Ampersand Press, 1945. First edition, cloth, #300 of 325 printed, inscribed and signed by one of the contributors, Frederick Buechner for William Meredith, Christmas 1974, laid in ALS from Buechner to Meredith, very good, likely issued without dust jacket, with brief ALS by another contributor, Robert Zufall.   Charles Agvent   William Meredith - 21   2016 $250

Francis, Robert *The Face Against Glass.* Amherst: by the author, 1950. First edition, inscribed by author May 2 1960 for William Meredith, near fine, printed wrappers. Charles Agvent   William Meredith - 30   2016 $60

Ginsberg, Allen *Kaddish.* San Francisco: City Lights, 1961. First edition, printed wrappers, inscribed and signed by the poet for William Meredith, with several drawings by Ginsberg, light wear, near fine.   Charles Agvent   William Meredith - 32   2016 $1000

Gluck, Louise *The House on Marshland.* New York: Ecco Press, 1975. First edition, review copy with material from publisher laid in, although there is no indication of such, this book came from the library of William Meredith, fine in close to fine dust jacket.   Charles Agvent   William Meredith - 33   2016 $200

Hecht, Anthony *Jiggery-Pokery: a Compendium of Double Dactyls.* New York: Atheneum, 1967. First edition, inscribed and signed by author for William Meredith, illustrations by Milton Glaser, fine in near fine dust jacket. Charles Agvent   William Meredith - 34   2016 $150

Hecht, Anthony *The Hard Hours. Poems.* New York: Atheneum, 1967. First edition, issue in wrappers, inscribed and signed for William Meredith, near fine.   Charles Agvent William Meredith - 35   2016 $100

Heyen, William *Depth of Field. Poems.* Baton Rouge: Louisiana State University Press, 1970. First edition, inscribed and signed by author for William Meredith, slight wrinkling to top of text and dampstaining to top of dust jacket, still near fine in very good dust jacket.   Charles Agvent William Meredith - 37   2016 $80

Heyen, William *Erika. Poems of the Holocaust.* St. Louis: Time Being Books, 1991. New edition, lengthily inscribed and signed by author for William Meredith, slight dust spotting to top edge, fine in fine dust jacket.   Charles Agvent William Meredith - 38   2016 $100

Heyen, William *Fires.* Athens: Croissant & Co., 1977. First edition, printed red wrappers, #87 of 300 copies, this copy inscribed and signed by author for William Meredith in 1977, fine, original envelope addressed in Heyen's hand to Meredith.   Charles Agvent   William Meredith - 39   2016 $100

Heyen, William *Long Island Light. Poems and a Memoir.* New York: Vanguard Press, 1979. First edition, inscribed and signed in 1979 by author for William Meredith, slight dust spotting to top edge of text, fine in near fine dust jacket. Charles Agvent   William Meredith - 40   2016 $100

Heyen, William *My Holocaust Songs.* Concord: William B. Ewert, 1980. First edition, #146 of 180 signed by author and artist, Michael McCurdy, signed and inscribed by author for William Meredith, slight dust spotting to top edge of text, mild sunning to spine, near fine, issued without dust jacket. Charles Agvent   William Meredith - 41   2016 $100

Heyen, William *Noise in the Trees. Poems and a Memoir.* New York: Vanguard Press, 1974. First edition, copy 28 of 50 signed copies from a total edition of 2500, additionally inscribed and signed by author for William Meredith, slight dust spotting to top edge of text, fine in fine dust jacket. Charles Agvent   William Meredith - 42   2016 $150

Heyen, William *The Ash.* Potsdam: Tamarack Editions, 1978. First edition, of a total edition of 326, this #48 of 126 to contain a special drawing, hand colored by Kristen Heyen, 12 year old daughter of author, and signed by author and artist, inscribed and signed by same for William Meredith, original envelope addressed in Heyen's hand to Meredith, fine.   Charles Agvent   William Meredith - 36 2016 $100

Heyen, William *The Swastika Poems 1957-1974.* New York: Vanguard Press, 1977. First edition, signed and inscribed by author for William Meredith, fine in close to fine dust jacket with short tear at rear.   Charles Agvent William Meredith - 43   2016 $100

Heyen, William *XVII Machines.* Pittsburg: and Derry: Sisyphus Editions, 1976. First edition, printed wrappers, #20 of 503, inscribed and signed in 1977 by author for William Meredith, laid in is 4 page ALS from author to Meredith, in original envelope addressed in Heyen's hand, fine.   Charles Agvent   William Meredith - 44   2016 $150

Hoffman, Daniel *A Little Geste and Other Poems.* New York: Oxford University Press, 1958. First edition, inscribed and signed by author April 75 for William Meredith, fine in near fine dust jacket with tanned spine.   Charles Agvent   William Meredith - 49   2016 $50

Hoffman, Daniel *An Armada of thirty Whales.* New Haven: Yale University Press, 1954. First edition, inscribed by author for William Meredith, with small original color photo of Meredith with little girl annotated on rear by Hoffman, with ALS from Hoffman to Meredith on postcard, fine in lightly soiled, near fine dust jacket with tanned spine.   Charles Agvent   William Meredith - 47   2016 $350

Hoffman, Daniel *The City of Satisfaction.* New York: Oxford University Press, 1963. First edition, fine in near fine dust jacket with sunned spine, inscribed by author for William Meredith.   Charles Agvent   William Meredith - 48   2016 $50

Hollander, John *A Crackling of Thorns.* New Haven: Yale University Press, 1958. First edition, inscribed and signed by poet for William Meredith, May 1958, near fine in very good dust jacket.   Charles Agvent   William Meredith - 50   2016 $200

Hollander, John *Movie-going and Other Poems.* New York: Atheneum, 1962. First edition, wrapper issue, inscribed and signed by author for William Meredith, near fine.   Charles Agvent William Meredith - 51   2016 $80

Hollander, John *Reflections on Espionage. The Question of Cupcake.* New York: Atheneum, 1976. First edition, inscribed and signed by author for William Meredith, fine in near fine dust jacket.   Charles Agvent   William Meredith - 53   2016 $80

Hollander, John *Tales Told of the Fathers. Poems.* New York: Atheneum, 1975. First edition, inscribed by author for William Meredith, fine in near fine dust jacket.   Charles Agvent William Meredith - 54   2016 $100

Homerus *The Odyssey.* Garden City: Anchor Press/ Doubleday, 1961. Reprint, illustrations by Hans Erni, inscribed and signed by translator Robert Fitzgerald for William Meredith in 1979, also inscribed in Greek and signed by folk singer Richard Dyer-Bennet, laid in is ticket and program to a Library of Congress event presenting Dyer-Bennet premier, fine in close ot fine dust jacket.   Charles Agvent   William Meredith - 55   2016 $100

Howard, Richard *Fellow Feelings. Poems.* New York: Atheneum, 1976. First edition, issue in wrappers, inscribed and signed by author for William Meredith, foxing to top and side edges, very good.   Charles Agvent   William Meredith - 56   2016 $80

Howard, Richard *Quantities. Poems.* Middletown: Wesleyan University Press, 1962. First edition, issue in wrappers, signed and inscribed by author for William Meredith, additionally signed by Bernard Malamud , to Meredith, with TLS from Malamud apologizing for signing the book, some dust spotting to top edge, near fine.   Charles Agvent   William Meredith - 57   2016 $500

Howard, Richard *Two-Part Inventions. Poems.* New York: Atheneum, 1974. First edition, issue in wrappers, inscribed and signed by author for William Meredith, some dust spotting to top edge, near fine.   Charles Agvent   William Meredith - 58   2016 $150

Howard, Richard *Untitled Subjects. Poems.* New York: Atheneum, 1969. First edition, paperback original, inscribed and signed by author for William Meredith, some dust spotting to top edge, near fine.   Charles Agvent   William Meredith - 59   2016 $200

Irving, John 1942- *The 158-Pound Marriage.* New York: Random House, 1974. First edition, inscribed and signed by author for William Meredith, fine in near fine dust jacket.   Charles Agvent   William Meredith - 60   2016 $300

Jacobsen, Josephine *The Shade-Seller New and Selected Poems.* Garden City: Doubleday and Co., 1974. First edition, hardbound issue, inscribed and signed by author for William Meredith, offsetting from clippings slightly affecting inscription, near fine in soiled, very good dust jacket.   Charles Agvent   William Meredith - 61   2016 $60

Kumin, Maxine *Looking for Luck. Poems.* New York: W. W. Norton & co., 1992. First edition, inscribed and signed on titlepage by author for William Meredith, laid in is 1994 flyer announcing Kumin reading and addressed to Meredith, fine in fine dust jacket.   Charles Agvent William Meredith - 63   2016 $80

Kumin, Maxine *Nurture. Poems.* New York: Viking, 1989. First edition, signed on titlepage for William Meredith, fine in fine dust jacket.   Charles Agvent   William Meredith - 64   2016 $60

Kumin, Maxine *The Long Approach. Poems.* New York: Viking, 1985. First edition, inscribed and signed by author for William Meredith, near fine in fine dust jacket.   Charles Agvent   William Meredith - 62   2016 $50

Kumin, Maxine *Women, Animals and Vegetables. Essays and Stories.* New York: W. W. Norton and Co., 1994. First edition, inscribed and signed for William Meredith, laid in is photographic Christmas card signed by Kumin, fine in fine dust jacket.   Charles Agvent   William Meredith - 65   2016 $100

Manassas Review. William Heyen Issue. Manassas: Northern Virginia Community College, 1978. First edition, printed wrappers, this copy signed and inscribed by William Heyen for William Meredith, laid in is full ALS from Heyen to Meredith in original envelope adressed in Heyen's hand to Meredith, fine.   Charles Agvent   William Meredith - 46   2016 $100

Matthews, William *Sticks and Stones.* Milwaukee: Pentagram Press, 1975. First edition, one of 600 copies, pictorial wrappers, inscribed by author for William Meredith, quarter size light stain on front cover, near fine.   Charles Agvent   William Meredith - 69   2016 $100

Merrill, James *Peter.* Dublin: Old Deerfield: The Deerfield Press/The Gallery Press, 1982. First edition, one of 300 numbered copies by poet on colophon page, this copy inscribed by author and Peter Hooten for William Meredith, fine in fine dust jacket.   Charles Agvent   William Meredith - 81   2016 $350

Merwin, W. S. *Asian Figures.* New York: Atheneum, 1975. First edition, pictorial wrappers, inscribed by poet for Richard Harteis via Bill Meredith and Bill Merwin, laid in is brief ANS from Meredith to Harteis, his partner of many years, fine.   Charles Agvent   William Meredith - 83   2016 $150

Milosz, Czeslaw *Bells In Winter.* New York: Ecco Press, 1978. First edition, review copy with photo of author and broadside with poem 'Encounters' laid in, inscribed by author for William Meredith, fine in fine dust jacket.   Charles Agvent   William Meredith - 84   2016 $500

Moss, Howard *A Swim off the Rocks. Light Verse.* New York: Atheneum, 1978. First edition, pictorial wrappers, inscribed by poet on front endpaper for William Meredith, fine.   Charles Agvent   William Meredith - 86   2016 $50

Moss, Howard *A Swimmer in the Air: Poems.* New York: Charles Scribner's Sons, 1957. First edition, inscribed by the poet for William Meredith, fine in near fine dust jacket.   Charles Agvent   William Meredith - 87   2016 $150

Moss, Howard *Buried City.* New York: Atheneum, 1975. First edition, inscribed and signed by poet for William Meredith, near fine in fine dust jacket.   Charles Agvent   William Meredith - 85   2016 $130

Murray, Joan *Poems.* New Haven: Yale University Press, 1947. First edition, although there is not indication, this book came from William Meredith's library, slight dust spotting to top edge of text, near fine in near fine dust jacket.   Charles Agvent   William Meredith - 88   2016 $100

Nemerov, Howard *Gnomes & Occasions. Poems.* Chicago and London: The University of Chicago Press, 1973. First edition, inscribed and signed by author for William Meredith, near fine.   Charles Agvent   William Meredith - 90   2016 $100

Nemerov, Howard *The Collected Poems of....* Chicago and London: University of Chicago Press, 1977. First edition, inscribed and signed by author for William Meredith, fine in near fine dust jacket.   Charles Agvent   William Meredith - 89   2016 $250

Nemerov, Howard *The Oak in the Acorn; on Remembrance of Things and on Teaching Proust...* Baton Rouge & London: Louisiana State University Press, 1987. First edition, inscribed and signed by author for William Meredith, near fine in like dust jacket.   Charles Agvent   William Meredith - 91   2016 $100

Nemerov, Howard *The Western Approaches. Poems 1973-75.* Chicago: and London: University of Chicago Press, 1975. First edition, inscribed and signed on half title by author for William Meredith, slight dust spotting to top edge, fine in fine dust jacket.   Charles Agvent   William Meredith - 93   2016 $150

Nemerov, Howard *War Stories. Poems About Long Ago and Now.* Chicago & London: University of Chicago Press, 1987. First edition, inscribed and signed by author for William Meredith, near fine in like dust jacket with glass ring on front cover.   Charles Agvent   William Meredith - 92   2016 $100

Ostriker, Alicia *Once More Out of Darkness and Other Poems.* Berkeley: Berkeley Poet's Workshop & Press, 1974. First edition, pictorial wrappers, inscribed by poet for William Meredith, fine.   Charles Agvent   William Meredith - 94   2016 $50

Pastan, Linda *Aspects of Eve. Poems.* New York: Liveright, 1975. First edition, hardcover issue, inscribed and signed for William Meredith, faint spotting to cloth, very good in like dust jacket. Charles Agvent William Meredith - 96 2016 $100

Pastan, Linda *Aspects of Eve. Poems.* New York: Liveright, 1975. First edition, wrapper issue, inscribed and signed for William Meredith, near fine. Charles Agvent William Meredith - 95 2016 $50

Pastan, Linda *The Five Stages of Grief. Poems.* New York: W. W. Norton & co., 1978. First edition, inscribed and signed on titlepage for William Meredith, also signed in full by Pastan, near fine in near fine dust jacket. Charles Agvent William Meredith - 97 2016 $80

Pastan, Linda *Waiting for My Life. Poems.* New York: W. W. Norton & Co., 1981. First edition, inscribed and signed by author for William Meredith, near fine in like dust jacket. Charles Agvent William Meredith - 98 2016 $80

Pinsky, Robert *An Explanation of America.* Princeton: Princeton University Press, 1979. First edition, inscribed and signed by author for William Meredith, fine in near fine dust jacket with sunned spine. Charles Agvent William Meredith - 100 2016 $250

Pinsky, Robert *Sadness and Happiness. Poems.* Princeton: Princeton University Press, 1975. First edition, inscribed and signed by author for William Meredith, fine in fine dust jacket. Charles Agvent William Meredith - 101 2016 $150

Plath, Sylvia 1932-1963 *Ariel.* New York: Harper & Row, 1966. First edition, William Meredith's copy signed by poet with several annotations in pencil, near fine in very good dust jacket. Charles Agvent William Meredith - 80 2016 $300

Pollitt, Katha *Antarctic Traveller. Poems.* New York: Alfred A. Knopf, 1982. First edition, uncorrected proof, printed white wrappers, with TLS for William Meredith, forwarding the galleys 'with warm regards from your old student', near fine. Charles Agvent William Meredith - 103 2016 $150

Pollitt, Katha *Antarctic Traveller: Poems.* New York: Alfred A. Knopf, 1982. First edition, inscribed and signed by author for William Meredith, Dec. 7 1984, fine in fine dust jacket. Charles Agvent William Meredith - 102 2016 $150

Ray, David *Gathering Firewood. New Poems and Selected.* Middletown: Wesleyan University Press, 1974. First edition, decorated wrappers, inscribed and signed in 1974 for William Meredith, ALS with postcard by Ray to Meredith as well as large promotional card for the book from David Ingatow, near fine. Charles Agvent William Meredith - 104 2016 $60

Rich, Adrienne *Diving into the Wreck.* New York: W. W. Norton, 1973. First edition, as usual, price at bottom corner of front flap clipped, with price present at top, review copy with material from publisher laid in, although no indication of such, this book from William Meredith's library, fine in near fine dust jacket with small tear at rear. Charles Agvent William Meredith - 105 2016 $150

Simic, Charles *Dismantling the Silence Poems.* New York: George Braziller, 1971. First edition, printed wrappers, inscribed and signed by author for William Meredith, 4-2-75, with personal letter from publisher and handwritten description of book in uknown hand, near fine. Charles Agvent William Meredith - 106 2016 $200

Simic, Charles *Return to a Place Lit by a Glass of Milk. Poems.* New York: George Braziller, 1974. First edition, printed wrappers, inscribed and signed for William Meredith, by author, 4-19-77, near fine. Charles Agvent William Meredith - 107 2016 $150

Smith, William Jay *Poems 1947-1957.* Boston: Little Brown, 1957. First edition, signed, and inscribed by author for William Meredith, 24 Oct. 1959, with 1957 postcard to Meredith announcing a reading by Smith, slight dust spotting to top edge of text, near fine in like dust jacket. Charles Agvent William Meredith - 109 2016 $150

Spender, Stephen *The Temple.* London: Faber and Faber Ltd., 1988. First edition, inscribed on titlepage for William Meredith, slight dust spotting to top edge, near fine in fine dust jacket. Charles Agvent William Meredith - 110 2016 $150

Spender, Stephen *W. H. Auden. A Tribute.* New York: Macmillan Pub. Co. Inc., 1975. First American edition, inscribed and signed by editor for William Meredith, fine in near fine dust jacket. Charles Agvent William Meredith - 109 2016 $150

St. John, David *Hush.* Boston: Houghton Mifflin, 1976. First edition, signed and inscribed in 1983 for William Meredith, fine in near fine dust jacket with tanned spine. Charles Agvent William Meredith - 111 2016 $60

Syracuse Poems 1970. Syracuse: Syracuse University, 1970. First edition, #102 of 1000, inscribed by editor for William Meredith, near fine, printed wrappers.   Charles Agvent   William Meredith - 19   2016 $60

Updike, John 1932-2009   *Buchanan Dying.* New York: Alfred A. Knopf, 1974. First edition, inscribed and signed for William Meredith, fine in near fine dust jacket with tanned spine.   Charles Agvent   William Meredith - 112   2016 $250

Voigt, Ellen Bryant   *Claiming Kin.* Middletown: Wesleyan University Press, 1976. First edition, inscribed and signed for William Meredith, fine in fine dust jacket.   Charles Agvent   William Meredith - 113   2016 $100

Vonnegut, Kurt   *Bluebeard.* New York: Delacorte Press, 1987. First edition, inscribed and signed in 1987 by author for William Meredith, fine in fine dust jacket.   Charles Agvent   William Meredith - 114   2016 $850

Wagoner, David   *Travelling Light.* Port Townsend: Graywolf, 1976. First edition, one of 600 softcover copies out of an edition of 750, pictorial dark brown wrappers, inscribed by author for William Meredith, with TLS to Meredith, with original envelope addressed in Wagoner's hand, fine.   Charles Agvent   William Meredith - 115   2016 $200

Wakoski, Diane   *Inside the Blood Factory.* Garden City: Doubleday and Co., 1968. First edition, inscribed by author for William Meredith, by author, she has added two small drawings handwritten and her printed names, slight fraying to cloth along spine edge at top, near fine in like dust jacket.   Charles Agvent   William Meredith - 116   2016 $100

Warren, Robert Penn   1905-1989   *Ballad of a Sweet Dream of Peace: a Charade for Easter.* Dallas: Pressworks, 1980. First edition, coy 72 of 350 numbered copies (of a total edition of 376) signed by author and artist, marbled boards with black cloth spine, 3 mounted color illustrations with acetate guards by Bill Komodore, dedicated to William Meredith, his copy though no sign of ownership, fine in fine acetate dust jacket, laid in is the printed musical score by By Alexei Haleff.   Charles Agvent   William Meredith - 117   2016 $200

Warren, Robert Penn   1905-1989   *Two Poems.* Winston Salem: Palaemon Press, 1980. First edition, #72 of 350 numbered copies (of a total edition of 376) signed by author and artist on colophon page, inscribed by publisher Stuart Wright for William Meredith, fine.   Charles Agvent   William Meredith - 118   2016 $150

Warren, Rosanna   *Snow Day.* Winston Salem: Palaemon Press, 1981. First edition, one of 550 copies, cloth backed boards, inscribed and signed by author for William Meredith, laid in prospectus as well as ALS from Warren to Meredith dated 23 dec. 1981, fine.   Charles Agvent   William Meredith - 119   2016 $150

Whittemore, Reed   *The Feel of the Rock. Poems of Three Decades.* Washington & San Francisco: Dryad Press, 1982. First edition, of a total of 1500 copies, this one of only 30 hardbound and in addition is one of the first 50 copies signed by poet on colophon page, also inscribed and signed by author for William Meredith, some fading of cloth, very good, likely issued without dust jacket.   Charles Agvent   William Meredith - 120   2016 $150

Wilson, Keith   *Homestead.* San Francisco: Kayak, 1969. First edition, one of 1000 copies, decorated wrappers, color prints, inscribed and signed by author for William Meredith, laid in is TLS by Wilson to Meredith, near fine.   Charles Agvent   William Meredith - 122   2016 $80

Woiwode, Larry   *Even Tide.* New York: Farrar, Straus and Giroux, 1977. First edition, inscribed by author for William Meredith, fine in fine dust jacket,.   Charles Agvent   William Meredith - 123   2016 $60

Wright, Charles   *China Trace.* Middletown: Wesleyan University Press, 1977. First edition, signed and inscribed by author for William Meredith, fine in fine dust jacket.   Charles Agvent   William Meredith - 124   2016 $200

Wright, Charles   *Country Music. Selected Early Poems.* Middletown: Wesleyan University Press, 1983. First edition, 2nd printing, signed and inscribed by author for William Meredith, spine sunned, near fine.   Charles Agvent   William Meredith - 125   2016 $60

Zimmer, Paul   *The Republic of Many Voices.* New York: October House, 1969. First edition, inscribed and signed by author Dec. 16 1969 for William Meredith, laid in are 2 TLS's and typed manuscript poem signed and inscribed by author, near fine in like dust jacket with sunned spine.   Charles Agvent   William Meredith - 126   2016 $100

Association – Mergenthaler, Frank

Adams, George *Mathematical Instrument Maker, the Elder, A Treatise Describing the Construction and Explaining the Use of New Celestial and terrestrial Globes.* London: printed for and sold by the author at Tycho Brahe's Head, 1769. Second edition, 8vo., 14 engraved plates, frontispiece, fore-edge trimmed, left margin frontispiece trimmed, occasional spotting, titlepage defaced bit (eliminating the 'X' from the date, creating at date that didn't exist), offsetting on half title from ads, modern period style calf, gilt stamped, raised bands, elegant red spine label, edges sprinkled red, ownership ink signature of Frank Mergenthaler August 28 1928. Jeff Weber Rare Books 183 - 1 2016 $1250

Association – Merrill, James

Empson, William *The Gathering Storm.* London: Faber and Faber Ltd., 1940. First edition, James Merrill's copy with his signature dated 1974, signed by William Meredith, faint stain to bottom of front cover, very good in good only dust jacket, split into two pieces. Charles Agvent William Meredith - 82 2016 $150

Association – Merritt, H. S.

Hawes, Robert *The History of Framingham in the County of Suffolk, Including Brief Notices of the Masters and Fellows of Pembroke-Hall in Cambridge, from the Foundation of the College to the Present Time.* Woodbridge: printed by and for R. Loder, 1798. 4to., frontispiece, 10 further engraved plates, final ad leaf list of subscribers, inside cockled towards the front, plates somewhat foxed, contemporary half tan calf, gilt spine, marbled boards, edges sprinkled red, very much rubbed with some surface, loss to spine, label lost, upper just beginning to split at head, edges worn, ownership inscription of H. S. Merritt (?). Unsworths Antiquarian Booksellers Ltd. E01 - Early Printing - 9 2016 £250

Association – Merton, J.

Montaigne, Michel De 1533-1592 *Essays of Michael Seigneur de Montaigne in Three Books.* London: printed for T. Basset, 1693. Early edition, 3 volumes, small 8vo., engraved frontispiece portrait of author, some early ink underlining, lacks rear free endpaper (volume I), original full mottled calf (mismatched set), raised bands, gilt spines, red leather title labels, inner joints reinforced with Kozo, worn, ownership signatures of J. Merton (?), Arthur Rogers - June 1933, Reverend James Jenkyn (d. 1825 of Herfordshire?) and Myles Standish Slocum, Pasadena. Jeff Weber Rare Books 181 - 22 2016 $275

Association – Metcaf, Paul

Enslin, Theodore *Music for Several Occasions.* Milwaukee: Membrane Press, 1985. First edition, 8vo., printed wrappers, fine, inscribed to poet Paul Metcalf. Second Life Books, Inc. 196A - 524 2016 $50

Association – Metcalf, David

Putnam, Wallace *Moby Dick Seen Again.* New York: Blue Moon Press, 1975. First edition, issued in an edition of 365 copies+, 4to., some toning to top of some leaves, 35 loose folders, 11.25 x 9.25 inches, each enclosed in wraparound folder with author an title on cover, printed on Crane Artificial parchment rag paper by Yorktown Printing Corp., 15 of these also included original drawing, imperfect copy issued without box, signed and inscribed by the artist to David Metcalf, also signed on colophon noting this is a "HC" copy, this was actually given to Paul Metcalf, Melville's great grandson. Second Life Books, Inc. 196 B - 202 2016 $2000

Association – Metcalf, Eleanor Melville

Ayoux, Jean Jacques *Melville.* New York: Grove Press, London: Evergreen Books, 1960. First edition, small 8vo., illustrations, very nice, inscribed by historian Stefan Lorant to Melville's granddaughter, Eleanor Melville Metcalf. Second Life Books, Inc. 196 B - 200 2016 $50

Melville, Herman 1819-1891 *Melville's Agatha Letter to Hawthorne.* Portland: Southworth Press, 1929. First separate printing, green paper wrapper, spine little discolored, very good, signed by Melville's granddaughter Elenaor M(elville) Metcalf, rare. Second Life Books, Inc. 196 B - 199 2016 $750

Association – Metcalf, Nancy

Williams, Jonathan *A Celestial Centennial Reverie for Mr. Charles Ives.* Highlands: Jonathan Williams Feb. 20-27, 1975. Produced on Xerox 4000 in an edition of 100 copies for friends, 4to., self wrappers in plastic binder, inscribed by author for Paul and Nancy Metcalf. Second Life Books, Inc. 196 B - 905 2016 $150

Williams, Jonathan *Elite/Elate Poems: Selected Poems 1971-1975.* Jargon Society, 1979. First edition, portfolio of photos by Guy Mendes, 4to., little streak on cloth, otherwise fine in dust jacket (little worn), inscribed by author for Paul and Nancy Metcalf. Second Life Books, Inc. 196 B - 906 2016 $200

Williams, Jonathan *Homage, Umbrage, Quibble & chicane.* Roswell: DBA Editions, 1981. First edition, one of 120 copies produced for friends, 4to., this #68, inscribed by Paul and Nancy Metcalf.   Second Life Books, Inc.   196 B - 908   2016 $125

Williams, Jonathan *The Lucidites, Sixteen in Visionary Company.* London: Turret Books, 1967. First edition, bound in cloth with illustrations by John Furnival on foil, fine, of a total edition of 280, this one of 250 for sale, inscribed by author for friends, Paul and Nancy Metcalf. Second Life Books, Inc.   196 B - 909   2016 $125

Williams, Jonathan *Untinears & Antennae for Maurice Ravel.* St. Paul: Truck Books, 1977. First edition, very nice in printed wrappers, inscribed by author for poet Paul Metcalf and wife, Nancy.   Second Life Books, Inc.   196 B - 913   2016 $50

Association – Metcalf, Paul

Adams, Alexander *Geronimo: a Biography.* New York: Putnams, 1971. First edition, 8vo., photos, inscribed by author to poet Paul Metcalf and his wife.   Second Life Books, Inc.   196A - 8   2016 $45

Atkinson, Ron *Looking for My Name.* Lenox: Bookstore Press, 1974. First edition, 8vo. paper wrappers, inscribed by author to poet, Paul Metcalf and his wife, two typewritten poems laid in, very good.   Second Life Books, Inc.   196A - 57   2016 $45

Boer, Charles *Varmint Q.* Chicago: Swallow Press, 1972. 8vo., woodcuts by David Hayes, includes signed letter from author to poet Paul Metcalf laid in, very good in somewhat stained and chipped dust jacket.   Second Life Books, Inc.   196A - 175   2016 $50

David, Gary *Eye of the Heart.* Barred Owl Publications, 1981. 8vo., inscribed by author to Paul Metcalf, paper wrappers, very good.   Second Life Books, Inc.   196A - 381   2016 $35

David, Gary *Vineland Distillations.* Rapid City: D'Vine Press, 1980. Paper wrappers, inscribed by author to poet Paul Metcalf and his wife, very good.   Second Life Books, Inc.   196A - 380   2016 $45

Dawson, Fielding *On Duberman's Black Mountain & B. H. Friedman's biography of Jackson Pollock.* Toronto: Coach House Press, 1973. First edition, 12mo., self wrappers, very good, inscribed by author to friend Paul Metcalf.   Second Life Books, Inc.   196A - 392   2016 $75

Dawson, Fielding *On Shortstop as the figure of Kinesis.* Durham: Duke University, 1975. First edition, 1/300 copies, horizontal small 8vo., brown paper wrappers, inscribed by author to Paul Metcalf, very good.   Second Life Books, Inc.   196A - 393   2016 $75

Enslin, Theodore *Ascensions.* Santa Barbara: Black Sparrow, May, 1977. Printed self wrappers, very good inscribed by author to friend, poet Paul Metcalf.   Second Life Books, Inc.   196A - 508   2016 $45

Enslin, Theodore *Case Book.* Elmwood: Poets & Poets Press, 1987. First edition, 8vo., printed wrappers, fine, inscribed by author to poet Paul Metcalf.   Second Life Books, Inc.   196A - 509   2016 $50

Enslin, Theodore *Circles.* Lewiston: Great Raven Press, 1977. First edition, 8vo., one of 325 copies, printed wrappers, fine, inscribed by author to Paul Metcalf.   Second Life Books, Inc.   196A - 519   2016 $50

Enslin, Theodore *Concentrations.* Dennis: Salt Works press, 1977. First edition, 1/400 copies, printed wrappers, fine, inscribed by author to poet Paul Metcalf.   Second Life Books, Inc.   196A - 512   2016 $50

Enslin, Theodore *The Country of Our Consciousness.* Berkeley: Sand Dollar Books # 5, 1971. First edition, 8vo., printed wrappers, very good, inscribed by author to poet Paul Metcalf. Second Life Books, Inc.   196A - 513   2016 $65

Enslin, Theodore *Etudes.* New Rochelle: Elizabeth Press, 1972. First edition, 8vo., printed paper wrappers, designed by Martino Mardersteig and printed from Garmond type on rag paper by Stamperia Valdonega, Verona, one of 400 copies, inscribed by author for Paul Metcalf and his wife.   Second Life Books, Inc.   196A - 514   2016 $50

Enslin, Theodore *The Fifth Direction.* Markesan: Pentagram Press, 1980. First edition, one of 424 copies in printed wrappers, fine, inscribed by author to poet Paul Metcalf.   Second Life Books, Inc.   196A - 515   2016 $50

Enslin, Theodore *The Flare of Beginning is In November.* Brooklyn: Jordan Davis, 1980. First edition, 12mo., printed wrappers, limited to 150 copies, signed, this copy inscribed by author to Paul Metcalf, very nice.   Second Life Books, Inc.   196A - 516   2016 $75

Enslin, Theodore *Fragments--- Epigrammata.* Vineyard Haven: Salt-works Press, 1982. First edition, 8vo., of a total edition of 400, handset in Italian oldstyle types on Ticonderoga text paper, this one of 100 bound in cloth, numbered and signed by author, this copy inscribed by author for friend Paul Metcalf, fine. Second Life Books, Inc. 196A - 506 2016 $75

Enslin, Theodore *From Near the Great Pine.* Peoria: Spoon River Poetry Press, 1988. First edition, 8vo., printed wrappers, fine, inscribed by author to poet Paul Metcalf. Second Life Books, Inc. 196A - 517 2016 $50

Enslin, Theodore *The Further Regions.* Milwaukee: Pentagram, 1977. First edition, printed wrappers, fine, of an edition of 376 copies, this one of 300 unsigned, inscribed by author to poet Paul Metcalf. Second Life Books, Inc. 196A - 518 2016 $50

Enslin, Theodore *In the Keeper's House.* Dennis: Salt-works Press, 1973. First edition, printed wrappers, very nice, inscribed by author to poet Paul Metcalf. Second Life Books, Inc. 196A - 519 2016 $50

Enslin, Theodore *The July Book.* Berkeley: San Dollar, 1976. First edition, 8vo. inscribed by author to poet Paul Metcalf, nice. Second Life Books, Inc. 196A - 520 2016 $50

Enslin, Theodore *Landler.* New Rochelle: The Elizabeth Press, 1975. First edition, 8vo., printed paper wrappers, one of 250 copies, printed from Baskerville type on Magnani rag paper by Stamperia Valdonega, Verno, nice, inscribed by author to poet Paul Metcalf. Second Life Books, Inc. 196A - 521 2016 $50

Enslin, Theodore *May Fault.* Fort Kent: Great Raven Press, 1979. First edition, stiff printed wrappers, nice, inscribed by author for poet Paul Metcalf. Second Life Books, Inc. 196A - 522 2016 $50

Enslin, Theodore *The Mornings.* Berkeley: Shama Drum, 1974. First edition, small 8vo., printed wrappers, fine, one of 500 issued, this copy inscribed by author for poet Paul Metcalf. Second Life Books, Inc. 196A - 523 2016 $50

Enslin, Theodore *Papers.* New Rochelle: Elizabeth Press, 1976. First edition, 8vo., printed paper wrappers, one of 250 copies, nice, inscribed by author to poet Paul Metcalf, printed from Imprint type on Magnani rag paper by Stamperia Voldonega, Verona. Second Life Books, Inc. 196A - 525 2016 $50

Enslin, Theodore *Passacaglia (Poems).* Bayonne: Beehive Press, 1982. First edition, spiral bound wrappers, nice, inscribed by author to poet Paul Metcalf. Second Life Books, Inc. 196A - 526 2016 $50

Enslin, Theodore *Ranger CXXII & CXXVIII.* New York: Station Hill, 1977. First edition, limited to 500 copies, 8vo., paste paper wrappers, fine, inscribed by author to poet Paul Metcalf. Second Life Books, Inc. 196A - 527 2016 $50

Enslin, Theodore *Sitio January 1969 November 1970.* Hanover: Granite Publications, 1973. First edition, 8vo., printed wrappers, fine, inscribed by author to poet Paul Metcalf. Second Life Books, Inc. 196A - 528 2016 $50

Enslin, Theodore *Views.* New Rochelle: Elizabeth Press, 1972. First edition, 8vo., printed paper wrappers, designed by Mardersteig and printed from Garamond type on Magnani rag paper, one of 400 copies, nice, inscribed to poet Paul Metcalf. Second Life Books, Inc. 196A - 529 2016 $50

Enslin, Theodore *With Light Reflected, Poems 1970-1972.* Fremont: Sumac Press, 1973. First edition, 1/1000 copies in printed wrappers, warmly inscribed by author to poet Paul Metcalf and his wife Nancy. Second Life Books, Inc. 196A - 530 2016 $50

Ferrini, Vincent *Hermit of the Clouds, the Autobiography of...* Gloucester: Ten Pound Island Book Co., 1988. First edition, printed wrappers, perfect bound with some loose pages, inscribed by author for Paul Metcalf and his wife Nancy. Second Life Books, Inc. 196A - 559 2016 $45

Ferrini, Vincent *Know Fish.* Storrs: University of Conn. Library, 1979. First edition, 8vo. printed wrappers, nice, inscribed by author to Paul Metcalf who wrote preface, laid in is 2 page ALS to same from author. Second Life Books, Inc. 196A - 554 2016 $150

Ferrini, Vincent *Know Fish: Book III, the navigators.* Storrs: University of Conn. Library, 1984. First edition, printed wrappers, nice, inscribed by Paul Metcalf. Second Life Books, Inc. 196A - 551 2016 $50

Ferrini, Vincent *Know Fish: Book IV & V. The Community of Self.* Storrs: University of Conn. Library, 1986. First edition, 8vo., printed wrappers, nice, inscribed by authr to Paul Metcalf. Second Life Books, Inc. 196A - 552 2016 $50

Ferrini, Vincent *Know Fish: Book VI & VII This Other Ocean.* Storrs: University of Conn. Library, 1991. First edition, 8vo., printed wrappers, nice, inscribed by author to Paul Metcalf and his wife Nancy.   Second Life Books, Inc. 196A - 553   2016 $50

Ferrini, Vincent *A Tale of Psyche.* Bedford: Igneus Press, 1991. First edition, 8vo., printed wrappers, fine, inscribed by author to Paul Metcalf and wife Nancy. Second Life Books, Inc.   196A - 555   2016 $50

Ferrini, Vincent *Undersea Bread.* Storrs: University of California Lib., 1989. First edition, 8vo., printed wrappers, very nice, inscribed by author to poet Paul Metcalf and his wife Nancy.   Second Life Books, Inc.   196A - 556   2016 $50

Ferrini, Vincent *War in Heaven.* Storrs: University of CT. Library, 1987. First edition, 8vo., inscribed by author to poet Paul Metcalf, very nice, tight copy.   Second Life Books, Inc.   196A - 557   2016 $50

Finley, Mike *Home Trees.* St. Peter Publishing House, 1978. First edition, printed wrappers, very good, laid in is 9 line holograph review by poet Paul Metcalf.   Second Life Books, Inc.   196A - 562   2016 $75

George, Emery *A Gift of Nerve.* Ann Arbor: Kylix Press, 1978. 8vo., very good+ in dust jacket, laid in is one page ALS from Herbert Leibowitz, publisher of Parnassus to poet Paul Metcalf requesting a review, also laid in 3 page holograph MS. review of the book by metcalf.   Second Life Books, Inc.   196A - 627   2016 $250

Gillman, Richard *Lunch at Carcassonne.* Manchester: The X Press, 1976. First edition, of a total of 500 copies, this one of 450 signed by author, 8vo., printed wrappers, laid in 3 page typed review, with holograph corrections by writer Paul Metcalf.   Second Life Books, Inc.   196A - 639   2016 $125

Glaze, Andrew *The Trash Dragon of Shensi.* Providence: Copper Beech Press, 1978. First edition, printed wrappers, very good, laid in is 1 page typed ms. review of this book by poet Paul Metcalf.   Second Life Books, Inc.   196A - 651   2016 $100

Hannigan, Paul *The Carnation.* Boston: Barn Dream Press, 1972. First edition, of an edition of 1100 copies, this one of 100 in printed wrappers, 8vo., inscribed by author to poet Paul Metcalf, in addition there is one page TLS from author to Metcalf laid in.   Second Life Books, Inc.   196A - 718   2016 $45

Hausman, Gerald *Circle Meadow.* Lenox: Bookstore Press, 1972. Paper wrappers, inscribed by author to poet, Paul Metcalf, very good.   Second Life Books, Inc.   196A - 739   2016 $355

Hausman, Gerald *New Marlboro Stage.* Lenox: Bookstore Press, 1971. 8vo., paper wrappers, inscribed by author to poet Paul Metcalf, very good.   Second Life Books, Inc.   196A - 741   2016 $45

Hellman, Lillian *The Autumn Garden.* Boston: Little Brown, 1951. First edition, 8vo., very good in dust jacket mended on verso, presentation from author to Paul (Metcalf) and wife.   Second Life Books, Inc.   196A - 771   2016 $450

Hueter, Diane *Kansas: Just Before Sleep...* Lawrence: Cottonwood Review, 1978. First edition, printed wrappers, very good, this copy belonged to Paul Metcalf and several of the poems have pencil marks next to them in his holograph, in addition, laid in is 2 page typed review of the book with line in his holography.   Second Life Books, Inc.   196A - 844   2016 $85

Humphrey, James *An Homage the End of some More Land.* Woods Hole: the Job Shop, 1972. First edition, 1/500 copies, 8vo. paper wrappers, inscribed by author to poet Paul Metcalf, very good.   Second Life Books, Inc. 196A - 858   2016 $40

Joris, Pierre *Turbulence.* Rhinebeck: St. Lazaire, 1991. First edition, 8vo., paper wrappers, inscribed by author for poet Paul Metcalf.   Second Life Books, Inc.   196A - 902   2016 $45

Ostriker, Alicia *Songs.* New York: Rinehart and Winston, 1969. First edition, 8vo., inscribed by author for Paul Metcalf, and his wife, very good in dust jacket little yellowed. Second Life Books, Inc.   196 B - 357   2016 $50

Putnam, Wallace *Moby Dick Seen Again.* New York: Blue Moon Press, 1975. First edition, issued in an edition of 365 copies+, 4to., some toning to top of some leaves, 35 loose folders, 11.25 x 9.25 inches, each enclosed in wraparound folder with author an title on cover, printed on Crane Artificial parchment rag paper by Yorktown Printing Corp., 15 of these also included original drawing, imperfect copy issued without box, signed and inscribed by the artist to David Metcalf, also signed on colophon noting this is a "HC" copy, this was actually given to Paul Metcalf, Melville's great grandson.   Second Life Books, Inc.   196 B - 202   2016 $2000

Quasha, George *Giving the Lily back her Hands.* Barrytown: Station Hill Press, 1979. First edition, tall 8vo., paper wrappers, inscribed by author for Paul Metcalf, very good. Second Life Books, Inc. 196 B - 448 2016 $45

Williams, Jonathan *Affilati Attrezzi Per I Giardini Di Catullo.* Milano: Lerici Editori, 1966. First edition, 8vo., paper wrappers, English and Italian on facing pages, inscribed by author for Paul Metcalf. Second Life Books, Inc. 196 B - 903 2016 $50

Williams, Jonathan *Glees Swarthy Monotonies Rince Cochon & Chozzerai for Simon.* Roswell: DBA Editions, 1980. First edition, 1/128 copies distributed to friends, not for sale, 4to., very good inscribed by author for Paul Metcalf. Second Life Books, Inc. 196 B - 907 2016 $100

Williams, Jonathan *My Quaker Atheist Friend.* London: Jonathan Williams, 1975. Inscribed by author to poet Paul Metcalf, folded in half and stapled, very good. Second Life Books, Inc. 196 B - 911 2016 $65

Williams, Jonathan *Shankum Naggum.* Rocky Mount: Friends of the Library NC Wesleyan, 1979. 1/550 copies, tall 8vo., paper wrappers, inscribed by author for poet Paul Metcalf, very good. Second Life Books, Inc. 196 B - 912 2016 $45

Williams, Jonathan *A Celestial Centennial Reverie for Mr. Charles Ives.* Highlands: Jonathan Williams Feb. 20-27, 1975. Produced on Xerox 4000 in an edition of 100 copies for friends, 4to., self wrappers in plastic binder, inscribed by author for Paul and Nancy Metcalf. Second Life Books, Inc. 196 B - 905 2016 $150

Williams, Jonathan *Elite/Elate Poems: Selected Poems 1971-1975.* Jargon Society, 1979. First edition, portfolio of photos by Guy Mendes, 4to., little streak on cloth, otherwise fine in dust jacket (little worn), inscribed by author for Paul and Nancy Metcalf. Second Life Books, Inc. 196 B - 906 2016 $200

Williams, Jonathan *Homage, Umbrage, Quibble & chicane.* Roswell: DBA Editions, 1981. First edition, one of 120 copies produced for friends, 4to., this #68, inscribed by Paul and Nancy Metcalf. Second Life Books, Inc. 196 B - 908 2016 $125

Williams, Jonathan *The Lucidites, Sixteen in Visionary Company.* London: Turret Books, 1967. First edition, bound in cloth with illustrations by John Furnival on foil, fine, of a total edition of 280, this one of 250 for sale, inscribed by author for friends, Paul and Nancy Metcalf. Second Life Books, Inc. 196 B - 909 2016 $125

Williams, Jonathan *Untinears & Antennae for Maurice Ravel.* St. Paul: Truck Books, 1977. First edition, very nice in printed wrappers, inscribed by author for poet Paul Metcalf and wife, Nancy. Second Life Books, Inc. 196 B - 913 2016 $50

Young, Karl *Milestones Set One: 1970-1975.* Madison: Landlocked Press, 1987. 1/130 copies, inscribed by author for Paul Metcalf, large 8vo., pages not numbered, sewn and bound with vellum strips in two tone paper wrappers, cover little yellowed, otherwise nice. Second Life Books, Inc. 196 B - 963 2016 $150

Association – Michelson, Charles

Bierce, Ambrose 1842-1914 *Tales of Soldiers and Civilians.* San Francisco: E. L. G. Steele, 1891. First edition, octavo, original gray cloth, front and spine panels stamped in gold, presentation copy inscribed by author to fellow journalist Charles Michelson, cloth rubbed at spine ends, bit of darkening to spine panel, minor bubbling to cloth on rear cover, just bit of fading at upper edge of front cover, else fine, very nice, custom cloth slipcase. John W. Knott, Jr./L.W. Currey, Inc. Fall-Winter 2015 - 17253 2016 $8500

Association – Middleton, Hastings Nathaniel

Browne, Moses *Angling Sports in Nine Piscatory Eclogues.* London: printed for Edward and Charles Dilly, 1773. Small 8vo., frontispiece, apparently inscribed by author to Mr. Betteroth?, original calf, rebacked with handsome new spine and red morocco gilt stamped spine label, bookplate of Hastings Nathaniel Middleton, some minor ink annotations to title, very good. Jeff Weber Rare Books 181 - 79 2016 $175

Association – Miller, Adelaide

Faulkner, William Harrison 1896-1962 *The Town.* New York: Random House, 1957. First edition in second issue dust jacket, without the '5/57' on front flap, signed by author for Miss Adeliade (sic) and Chuck Miller, very near fine with tiny tear at crown in near fine dust jacket with mild foxing to flap folds and on verso very attractive copy, notoriously uncommon signature. Ken Lopez Bookseller 166 - 34 2016 $12,500

Association – Miller, Bertha Mahony

Adventures of Jack Ninepins. New York: Harper Bros., 1944. Stated first edition, 6 1/4 x 8 1/2 inches, cloth, fine in frayed dust jacket, I in color by Averill, this copy from the library of Bertha Mahony Miller with her bookplate, laid in are 6 handwritten letters from Averill to Helen Fay (Juneman) Book Store owner and lecturer on children's books. Aleph-bet Books, Inc. 111 - 28 2016 $1200

Association – Miller, Chuck

Faulkner, William Harrison 1896-1962 *The Town.* New York: Random House, 1957. First edition in second issue dust jacket, without the '5/57' on front flap, signed by author for Miss Adeliade (sic) and Chuck Miller, very near fine with tiny tear at crown in near fine dust jacket with mild foxing to flap folds and on verso very attractive copy, notoriously uncommon signature.   Ken Lopez Bookseller   166 - 34   2016 $12,500

Association – Miller, W.

Kitton, Frederic George *Dickens Illustrations, Facsimiles of Original Drawings, Sketches and Studies for Illustrations in the Works of Charles Dickens...* London: George Redway, 1900. Folio, half title, list of plates (unopened), 28 plates, loosely inserted into original green cloth foldover case, bookplate of W. Miller, the Dickensian, very good.   Jarndyce Antiquarian Booksellers   CCXVIII - 955   2016   £100

Association – Millington, Matthias

Vyse, Charles *The Key to the Tutor's Guide or the Arithmetician's Repository...* London: printed by S. Hamilton, Falcon Court, Fleet Street for G. G. Robinson and J. Robinson..., 1799. 12mo. in sixes, full contemporary unlettered sheep, gilt banded spine, head of spine slightly chipped, leading hinge, slightly cracked, signature of Matthias Millington 1800, very clean copy with clean tear to dust jacket without loss.   Jarndyce Antiquarian Books   CCXV - 998   2016   £65

Association – Mills, John

Kipling, Rudyard 1865-1936 *The Years Between.* London: Methuen, 1919. First edition, half title, 32 page Methuen catalog at end coded IK/2/19, uncut in original maroon cloth, spine lettered gilt, top edge gilt, original dust jacket, tear to back wrapper repaired without loss, bookplate of John H. Mills, Derby, small ownership stamp of F. Alan Underwood.   Jarndyce Antiquarian Booksellers   CCXVII - 156   2016   £150

Association – Mills, Samuel

Dickens, Charles 1812-1870 *Immorteles from Charles Dickesn.* London: John Moxon, 1856. Half title, few spots, original royal blue cloth by Bone & son, lettered gilt, little worn at corners, bookplate of Samuel J. Mills, good, sound copy.   Jarndyce Antiquarian Booksellers   CCXVIII - 725   2016   £65

Association – Milne, David

Brown, Thomas, the Elder, Pseud. *Brighton or the Steyne.* London: printed for the author, sold by Sherwood, Neely and Jones, 1818. First edition, 3 volumes bound in 1 volume, 12mo., half title volume I with ad on verso, contemporary blue green moire cloth, little rubbed, bookplate of David Milne, Advocate with his trimmed signatures to titles volumes ii and iii, Renier booklabel, nice.   Jarndyce Antiquarian Booksellers   CCXVII - 51   2016   £750

Association – Milne, Douglas Stuart William

Nicoll, William Robertson *The Problem of 'Edwin Drood' a study in the methods of Dickens.* London: Hodder & Stoughton, 1912. First edition, half title, frontispiece, original full vellum, spine and front board lettered gilt, slightly spotted, very good, signed presentation from author to Captain Douglas Stuart William Milne on his marriage in 1916.   Jarndyce Antiquarian Booksellers   CCXVIII - 682   2016   £45

Association – Milner, Alfred, Viscount

Delandes, Andre Francois *The Art of Being Easy at all Times and in all Places.* London: printed for C. Rivington at the Bible and Crown, 1724. Second edition, 12mo., leading pastedown not laid down, contemporary half sheep, worn but sound, signature of Ch. Milner & label of Alfred Viscount Milner.   Jarndyce Antiquarian Books   CCXV - 157   2016   £650

Association – Milner, C.

Delandes, Andre Francois *The Art of Being Easy at all Times and in all Places.* London: printed for C. Rivington at the Bible and Crown, 1724. Second edition, 12mo., leading pastedown not laid down, contemporary half sheep, worn but sound, signature of Ch. Milner & label of Alfred Viscount Milner.   Jarndyce Antiquarian Books   CCXV - 157   2016   £650

Association – Minto, Countess of

Holmes, Oliver Wendell 1809-1894 *John Lothrop Motley: a Memoir.* Boston: Houghton, Osgood and Co., 1879. First US edition, large 8vo., original orange cloth lettered gilt on spine and on front cover, signed presentation from author to Countess of Minto, slight mottled and very slight rubbing, else clean, very good+.   Any Amount of Books   2015 - C12763   2016   £170

Association – Mitchell, Joseph

Jackson, Shirley *Hangsaman.* New York: Farrar Straus and Young, 1951. First edition, extremities of boards little worn, else fine in price clipped, very good dust jacket with some foxing on rear panel, inscribed by author for Joseph Mitchell and his wife, very nice copy.   Between the Covers Rare Books   208 - 41   2016 $4800

Association – Mitchell, Richard

Mee, Margaret Ursula *Flowers of the Brazilian Forests Collected and Painted by Margaret Mee.* London: L. van Leer & Co. for the Tryon Gallery in association with George Rainbird, 1968. First and only edition, limited to 500 copies, this no. 27 of 100 deluxe copies signed by Mee and with original gouache by Mee, folio, original full natural vellum by Zaehnsdorf gilt facsimile of author's signature blocked on upper board, vignette of a teja-assu lizard after Mee blocked in gilt on lower board, spine lettered in gilt, endpapers with printed vignettes of teja assu after Mee, top edges gilt, original green cloth slipcase with gilt lettering piece on upper panel, original shipping carton address to Richard Mitchell, Aldham, Essex with limitation numbers, printed in green and black, loose original prospectus, fine.   Sotheran's Piccadilly Notes - Summer 2015 - 9   2016   £7000

Association – Moholy-Nagy, Lucia

Moholy-Nagy, Laszlo *Bauhaus Buchet 14: Von matrial zu Architektur.* Munchen: Albert Langen Verlag, 1929. First edition, small quarto, extensively illustrated with photos, yellow cloth decorated in red, some rubbing on spine lettering and age toning on boards, very good in very good original card slipcase rubber stamped with title and publisher, inscribed by author to his wife Lucia.   Between the Covers Rare Books   208 - 65   2016 $8000

Association – Moll, James

United States. Congress. House of Representatives - 1792 *Journal of the House of Representatives of the United States of the First (-Second) Session of the Second Congress.* Philadelphia: Francis Childs and John Saine, 1792-1793. Folio, 2 volumes in 1, bound in modern calf backed marbled boards, very skillfully executed in period style, several gatherings in second volume foxed, else near fine, from the library of James Moll treasurer of NJ.   Joseph J. Felcone, Inc.   Books from Five Centuries: a Miscellany - 143   2016 $2000

Association – Monry, Mary

Penn, William *Some Fruits of Solitude.... (with, as issued) More Fruits....* Newport: printed by James Franklin, 1749. First American edition, 12mo., 2 parts in 1 volume, occasional browning and spotting, few leaves little defective in fore margin, original sheep, cracks in joints, upper one repaired, corners worn, slip-in case ownership inscription of Mary Monry 1876, later bookplate of Paul Jordan-Smith.   Blackwell's Rare Books   B186 - 115   2016   £2250

Association – Montgomerie, Anna

Rutherford, Samuel *Joshua Redivivus or Mr. Rutherford's Letters, Divided in two parts.* Rotterdam: in the Year, 1664. First edition, 8vo., some occasional light dampstaining, larger ink blots, very small hole through V1 (touching text on verso), late 19th century 'Presbyterian blue' morocco by Riviere & Son, panelled and lettered gilt, gilt gauffered edges, contemporary flyleaves and 'Dutch-gilt' pastedowns preserved from original binding, from the library of James Stevens Cox (1910-1997), 17th century calligraphic inscription 'Mrs. Anna Montgomerie Her Booke", long list of numbers and letters written in ink on front flyleaf, mid 19th century bookplate of John Whitefoord Mackenize.   Maggs Bros. Ltd.   1447 - 370   2016   £500

Association – Montgomery, James

MacPherson, James *The Poems of Ossian.* London: printed for Cadell and Davies, 1807. New edition, 2 volumes, 8vo., half title, some light browning, full contemporary tree calf, gilt decorated spines, dark green morocco label, spines and joints little rubbed, armorial bookplate of Sir Jas. Montgomery Bart. of Stanhope.   Jarndyce Antiquarian Booksellers   CCXVI - 377   2016   £150

Association – Montgomery, Robert

Walker, George *The Three Spaniards.* Dublin: printed by Brett Smith for P. Wogan, J. Rice, G. Folingsby & B. Dornin, 1800. 12mo., contemporary marginal note to page 83 volume I, corner of E12 volume II torn, but with no loss of text, pages rather browned, with some fingermarks and occasional browning with some ink doodles on endpapers, contemporary calf, gilt ruled spines, dark red morocco labels, joints & head and tail of spines expertly repaired, bookplate of Robert Montgomery, Convoy, signature of Tho. Montgomery across titlepages.   Jarndyce Antiquarian Booksellers CCXVI - 584   2016   £480

Association – Montgomery, Thomas

Walker, George *The Three Spaniards.* Dublin: printed by Brett Smith for P. Wogan, J. Rice, G. Folingsby & B. Dornin, 1800. 12mo., contemporary marginal note to page 83 volume I, corner of E12 volume II torn, but with no loss of text, pages rather browned, with some fingermarks and occasional browning with some ink doodles on endpapers, contemporary calf, gilt ruled spines, dark red morocco labels, joints & head and tail of spines expertly repaired, bookplate of Robert Montgomery, Convoy, signature of Tho. Montgomery across titlepages.   Jarndyce Antiquarian Booksellers   CCXVI - 584   2016   £480

Association – Moody, John Sadlier

Mayer, John *The Sportsman's Directory or Park and Gamekeeper's Companion.* London: printed for Baldwin and Cradock et al, 1828. Fifth edition, 191 x 121mm., appealing mid 19th century black straight grain half morocco over marbled paper boards, raised bands, gilt spine titling, marbled endpapers, top edge gilt, woodcut tailpiece, sewn illustrations in text and one engraved plate, titlepage with ink ownerhship signature of John Sadlier Moody, upper corners slightly bumped, top edge gilt obviously browned from facing frontispiece, light offsetting and isolated trivial foxing in text, excellent copy, binding without significant wear and leaves almost entirely quite fresh and clean.   Phillip J. Pirages   67 - 4   2016 $750

Association – Moore, Arthur

Dowson, Ernest *Adrian Rome.* London: Methuen & Co., 1899. Original blue cloth with gilt authors and title to spine and front cover, spine and cover also have a lovely filigree gilt design, slight bumping and very small strip of cloth missing along top of spine, interior is bright and clean, 39 page publisher's catalog Feb. 1899, very good, quite scarce, rare presentation copy inscribed by Arthur Moore 2nd May 99 for Hugh T. Chilcott.   The Kelmscott Bookshop   12 - 37   2016 $850

Association – Moore, Charles

Vergilius Maro, Publius *The Works of...* London: by Thomas Maxey for Andrew Crook, 1650. Second edition, 8vo., engraved portrait of Ogilby and additional engraved title by William Marshall (both dated 1649), minor rust spots to a number of leaves throughout, with upper corners of last few leaves creased, contemporary sheep covers ruled in blind, later (but old) paper labels on spine, worn, leather along fore-edge of front board chewed away and starting to detach, corners of lower cover chewed, joints split, headcaps missing, corners bumped, 'Charles Moore his Book', early inscription and early signature 'John Ogilvy', from the library of James Stevens Cox (1910-1997).   Maggs Bros. Ltd.   1447 - 424   2016   £180

Association – Moore, Dick

Zukofsky, Louis *After I'S.* Pittsburgh: Boxwood Mother, 1964. First edition, 12mo., original wrappers, cover little browned, rear stained, good, tight copy, inscribed Dick Moore's copy from Louis Zukofsky 3.16.66.   Second Life Books, Inc.   196 B - 980   2016 $75

Association – Moore, Marianne

La Fontaine, Jean De 1621-1695 *The Fables of La Fontaine.* New York: Viking, 1954. First edition, one of 400 large copies, large 8vo., fine copy, not signed by inscribed by translator, Marianne Moore for Dr. Harold Baldwin, red cloth, bookplate, neatly removed, fine.   Second Life Books, Inc.   196 B - 259   2016 $325

Association – Moore, Maurice

Moore, George 1852-1933 *Confessions of a Young Man.* London: Swan Sonnenschein, Lowrey & Co., 1888. First edition, author's presentation copy to his brother Maurice Moore, tipped in at back is autograph letter from Moore to editor C. Lewis Hind, dated June 18 1900, original cloth with pictorial illustration of a young woman on cover, spine somewhat darkened as usual, corners of book and spine bumped, still nice, hinges tender, otherwise very good, tipped in is an ad for Moore's Parnell and His Island, housed in grey cloth chemise and quarter leather slipcase, very good.   The Kelmscott Bookshop   13 - 42   2016 $3000

Association – Moore, Philip

A Just, Genuine and Impartial History of the Memorable Sea-Fight in the Mediterranean Between the Combined Fleets of France and Spain... printed of the author and sold by R. Walker, 1745. First edition, folding engraved plate as frontispiece and folding engraved plate with 2 maps, uniformly slightly browned, minor soiling, frontispiece foxed and with short tear (no loss), old flyleaf at front, defective in lower outer corner, bearing ownership inscription of Philip Moore, dated 2nd 1745, 8vo., modern leatherette, sound.   Blackwell's Rare Books   B184 - 71   2016   £850

Association – Moreau, John

Murphy, Henry C. *Anthology of New Netherland or Translations from the Early Dutch Poets of New York with Memoirs of their Lives.* New York: Bradford Club, 1865. Number 86 of an edition of 125 copies, 4to., later flexible leatherette, frontispiece, accompanied by two manuscript letters, first from John B. Moreau making the presentation to Benson Lossing on behalf of Bradford Club and second from Lossing to Moreau, very good copy.   Edwin V. Glaser Rare Books   2015 - 10275   2016 $450

Association – Mores, Edward Rowe

Strong, James *Joanereidos; or Feminine Valour...* London: reprinted Anno Dom., 1674. Second edition, small 4to., spotted and lightly browned, some tearing in inner margin of title and following two leaves caused by original stitching, many edges uncut, early19th century half calf and marbled boards, headcaps damaged and edges rubbed, from the library of James Stevens Cox (1910-1997), signature of Edward Rowe Mores (1730-1778), the copy of James Boswell the younger (1778-1822), small signature of Thomas Park (1658/9-1834).   Maggs Bros. Ltd.   1447 - 402   2016   £1500

Association – Morgan, Edmund

Smith, John *Gerochomia Basilike. King Solomons Portraiture of Old Age.* London: for J. Hayes for S. Thomson, 1666. First edition, 8vo., folding letterpress table, some occasional spotting, blank lower corner of H1 torn away, contemporary calf, rebacked, corners repaired and new endpapers, contemporary signature of Edmund Morgan in ink, from the library of James Stevens Cox (1910-1997).   Maggs Bros. Ltd.   1447 - 388   2016   £280

Association – Morgan, John

Perkins, William *The Workes of the Famous and Worthy Minister of Christ...(The First Volume) The Foundation of Christian Religion, Gathered into Six Princples. (with) A Golden Chaine or the Description of Theologie...* London: Iohn Legatt, printer to the Universitie of Cambridge, 1616. Second collected edition, Volume 1 (of 3), folio, 6 tables, lacking first four leaves (general title, address to the reader and table of contents) and folding table, margins dust soiled and dampstained, few leaves frayed to blank margin, modern half dark brown calf with marbled boards, spine in 7 compartments with raised bands, red morocco compartment, little cocked when upright, but binding sound, 19th century ownership inscription of John Morgan of Warrington to title.   Unsworths Antiquarian Booksellers Ltd.   30 - 118   2016   £600

Vergilius Maro, Publius *The Nyne Fyst Bookes of the Eneidos of Virgil Converted into Englishe...* London: by Rouland Hall for Nicholas Englande, 1562. Woodcut on title, text in black letter, 19th century morocco, ruled in gilt, edges gilt, extremities lightly worn, minor scuffing, first quire washed and neatly extended at top edge, possibly supplied from another copy, few internal repairs, else very good, with excellent full margins, Rubislaw House bookplate of John Morgan, rare early edition.   Joseph J. Felcone, Inc.   Books from Five Centuries: a Miscellany - 145   2016 $11,000

Association – Morgenstern, Charles

Graves, Robert   1895-1985 *The Isles of Unwisdom.* London: Cassell, 1950. First English edition, double page map, foolscap 8vo., original black cloth, backstrip gilt lettered, light edge spotting, dust jacket with backstrip panel trifle sunned and with internal sellotape repair at head, very good, inscribed by author for Charles (Morgenstern).   Blackwell's Rare Books   B186 - 222   2016   £450

Association – Morley, Christopher

Wylie, Elinor   1885-1928 *Incidental Numbers.* London: printed by Wm. Clowes & sons, 1912. First edition, one of 65 copies, 16mo., original printed boards (hairline crack in front hinge), Frank Hogan copy, this copy inscribed by author for Christopher Morley, inside front cover is autograph note by Morley, Wylie's first book, elaborate gold stamped Hogan bookplate, nearly fine in slipcase.   Howard S. Mott Inc.   265 - 150   2016 $8000

Association – Morley, John

Ray, John *The Wisdom of God Manifested in the Works of the Creation, in Two Parts.* London: for Samuel Smith, 1692. Second edition, 8vo., contemporary calf, covers panelled gilt with vase and flower tool in each corner, gilt spine with red morocco label (corners worn, top corner of lower cover chewed, area of surface insect damage at foot of the lower cover), from the library of James Stevens Cox (1910-1997), inscribed "The Gift of Mrs. Ray to John Morley July 31 1707", and signatures 'Jane Dorothy Harvey 1849' and 'C. H. Rikerman(?) 1885'.   Maggs Bros. Ltd.   1447 - 360   2016   £500

Association – Morrell, I.

Freemasons. Grand Lodge of Pennsylvania *Ahiman Rezon Abridged and Digested as a Help to All that Are or Would be Free and Accepted Masons.* Philadelphia: Hall and Sellers, 1783. First American edition, engraved frontispiece, contemporary sheep, skillfully rebacked in period style, some overall soiling and dampstaining, free endpaper and frontispiece browned at edges and neatly guarded, small early ownership stamp of I. Morrell on first two leaves, good.   Joseph J. Felcone, Inc.   Books from Five Centuries: a Miscellany - 66   2016 $1800

Association – Morrill, Sam, Mrs.

Whitney, Adeline Dutton Train *Mother Goose for Grown Ups.* New York: Rudd & Carlton, 1960. First edition, 8vo., ribbed green cloth stamped in gilt, leaves uniformly browned, small waterstain on fore-edge, fine, presentation inscribed by author for Mrs. Saml. Morrill.   Second Life Books, Inc.   196 B - 876   2016 $150

Association – Morris, Margery

Dickens, Charles 1812-1870 *Sketches of Young Couples and Young Gentlemen.* London: Chapman & Hall, circa, 1870? Frontispiece and plates by Phiz, original pebble grained maroon cloth, blocked in black, lettered gilt, slightly rubbed, bookplate of Peter & Margery Morris. Jarndyce Antiquarian Booksellers CCXVIII - 165 2016 £85

Association – Morris, Peter

Dickens, Charles 1812-1870 *Sketches of Young Couples and Young Gentlemen.* London: Chapman & Hall, circa, 1870? Frontispiece and plates by Phiz, original pebble grained maroon cloth, blocked in black, lettered gilt, slightly rubbed, bookplate of Peter & Margery Morris. Jarndyce Antiquarian Booksellers CCXVIII - 165 2016 £85

Association – Morris, William

Bible. Latin - 1512 *Epistola ad Rhomanos. Epistola Prima ad Cori(n)thios etc.* Paris: Henricus Stephanus Dec. 15, 1512. First edition of Lefevre's revision of the Vuglate text of St. Paul's Epistles, woodcut title border, colored red by contemporary hand, 42 fine large crible initials, all but one coloured in red by contemporary hand and numerous smaller initials, rubricated throughout, some passages pasted over or deleted in ink, few manuscript notes, clean tear just into text on K4 with edges marked from sellotape, Blackwell catalog description and illustration pasted to verso of last leaf (small repaired tear) and rear pastedown, folio, contemporary blindstamped calf over wooden boards by the Carthusians at Wedderen, near Dulmen, backstrip with five raised bands and exposed endbands, titled ink on red stained ground, shelfmark on white bound, boards with outer panels with series of blindstamped medallions and inner panels with "IHS", "MA" and "IOHS" circular stamps within diaper pattern, front board more closely filled than the rear, vellum endpapers, two fore-edge clasps sometime renewed, some expert repair to joints, ownership inscription to front flyleaf (one of the Carthusian house at Dulmen, the other dated 1959), bookplate of William Morris and old bookseller's description to front pastedown, very good copy. Blackwell's Rare Books   Marks of Genius - 31   2016 £20,000

Association – Morton, Louisa

Pilkington, Mrs. *Marmontel's Tales, selected and abridged for the instruction and amusement of Youth by....* London: Vernor and Hood, 1799. First edition, engraved frontispiece and 26 woodcuts, little spotted, 12mo., original sheep, joints cracked but cords firm, corners worn, contemporary signature of Louisa Morton, 2 brief lines of inscription scored out, good.   Blackwell's Rare Books   B186 - 85   2016   £350

Association – Mosch, Erwin

Ovidius Naso, Publius *Liber Heroidum Epistolarum. Liber Sapphus Libellus in Ibin...* Lyon: JeanThomas & Stephane Gueynard, Nov., 1513. 4to., 19th century blind tooled calf, title lettered gilt on spine, title within fine four piece white-on-black border made up of putti and classical ornaments, woodcut, title in red and black, large opening woodcut and 21 woodcuts in text, some pages with ornamental borders, numerous initials verso of final leaf with circular diagram of winds and regions of the globe, beautifully produced, early 20th century signature and bookplate of Erwin Mosch. Maggs Bros. Ltd.   1474 - 56   2016   £2800

Association – Mosel, Tad

Connelly, Marc *The Green Pastures.* New York: Farrar & Rinehart, 1930. First edition, 4to., #206 of 550 copies signed by author and artist, Robert Edmond Jones, laid in is TLS from author to author Tad Mosel thanking him for his birthday greeting, beautiful pochoir frontispiece, color of boards little retouched, fine in publisher's box.   Second Life Books, Inc.   196A - 325   2016 $350

Horgan, Paul *A Certain Climate: Essays in History, Arts and Letters.* Middletown: Wesleyan University, 1988. First edition, with short note from author to Tad Mosel laid in, as well as clipping of Horgan's obit, fine in dust jacket. Second Life Books, Inc.   196A - 819   2016 $45

Association – Mosher, Thomas B.

Dickson, Robert *Annals of Scottish Printing from the Introduction of the Art in 1507 to the Beginning of the Seventeenth Century.* Cambridge: Macmillan & Bowes, 1890. Limited to 600 numbered copies signed by John Philip Edmond, this one of the 1000 large paper copies bound thus, illustrations, 4to., original creme colored paper spine with light green paper covers, illustrations, bookplate of Thomas B. Mosher, slight soiling on covers, internally very near fine, unopened.   Oak Knoll Books   310 - 181 2016 $850

Association – Moss, Stanley

Laughlin, James *New Directions in Poetry and Prose. Number 11.* Norfolk: New Directions, 1949. First edition, 8vo., tan cloth and nicked and somewhat worn dust jacket, inscribed by poet Stanley Moss for Ella, with ink drawing, he has also made ink corrections in text of his poems. Second Life Books, Inc.   196 B - 15   2016 $85

Association – Muir, Gavin

Varesi, Gilda *Enter Madame: a Play in three acts.* New York: Putnam, 1921. First edition, 8vo., cloth backed boards, very good, inscribed by author under frontispiece and signed by 10 members of the cast including Norman Trevor, Jane Meredith, Gavin Muir, etc. Second Life Books, Inc. 196 B - i794 2016 $250

Association – Muir, Margaret

Birrell, Augustine *Obiter Dicta.* London: Elliott Stock, 1884. First edition, inscribed by author for friend Margaret Muir, interesting hand written sentence on first page of last chapter titled 'Falstaff', very good in original green cloth with gilt title and small rectangle gilt design to front cover, spine faded, some bumping to spine and corners, interior pages clean with slight pulling away of rear hinge, nice, relatively scarce, very good. The Kelmscott Bookshop 12 - 13 2016 $225

Association – Muirhead, Arnold

Walsh, William *A Dialogue Concerning Women being a Defence of the Sex.* London: printed for R. Bensley in Russel street in Covent Garden, 1691. 8vo., paper little browned, stain at end affecting endpapers and last page of text, inner hinges neatly repaired, contemporary calf, expertly rebacked, spine gilt with raised bands, early ownership inscription of John Byrch, oval booklabel of Arnold Muirhead. Jarndyce Antiquarian Booksellers CCXVII - 292 2016 £4200

Association – Mulgrave, Earl of

Darwin, Charles Robert 1809-1882 *On the Origin of Species by means of natural Selection...* London: W. Clowes and Sons for John Murray, 1859. First edition, 8vo. in 12's, original green cloth by Edmonds & Remnants, London retaining their ticket on lower pastedown, boards blocked in blind, rules enclosing foliate designs and central panel, spine gilt, mid brown endpapers, green cloth solander box with printed paper label to spine, 32 publisher's catalog dated June 1859, Freeman variant 3, folding lithographic plate by William West after Darwin, slight rubbing and bumping to extremities with very small ink spot to front board, hinges skillfully restored, little chipped to edges of endpapers and few leaves, nonetheless very bright, fresh copy in original cloth, bookplate of Pownoll William Phipps (b. 1835) using arms and motto of Earls of Mulgrave, whom he was a cousin. Sotheran's Piccadilly Notes - Summer 2015 - 5 2016 £95,000

Association – Mullins, John Lane

Grosse, E. M. *Series of Seventeen Colour Lithographed Plates from the 1913 Expedition to the Coral Reefs of the Torres Straits of Department of Marine Biology of the Carnegie Inst. of Washington.* Sydney: Government Printer, 1914. Quarto, 17 plates (numbered to 19), typescript insert inscribed to J. Lane Mullins by F. Walsh. Andrew Isles Natural History Books 55 - 38216 2016 $650

Scott, A. W. *Mammalia, Recent and Extinct: an Elementary Treatise for the Use of the Public Schools of New South Wales.* Sydney: Government printer, 1873. Octavo, quarter calf on marbled boards, some foxing, bookplate of John Lane Mullins, inscription from author, scarce. Andrew Isles Natural History Books 55 - 7985 2016 $300

Association – Mulroy, Thomas

Adams, Harry *Beyond the Barrier with Byrd. An Authentic Story of the Byrd Antarctic Exploring Expedition.* Chicago and New York: M. A. Donohue & Co., 1932. First edition, first issue binding, 8vo., original green cloth gilt, upper board lettered gilt and blocked to blind with ship, spine lettered in gilt and blocked to blind with penguin, remnant of pictorial dust jacket with picture of Byrd on upper panel, photographic frontispiece and 15 photographic plates, full page facsimile of letter by Byrd, cloth in fine condition, text evenly little browned as usual, signed presentation from Lt. Comdr. Tom Mulroy to Charles L. Kessler. Sotheran's Travel and Exploration - 412 2016 £298

Association – Munby, A. N. L.

Prior, Matthew 1664-1721 *Poems on Several Occasions.* London: printed for Jacob Tonson and John Barber, 1718. Large folio, fine, engraved frontispiece, contemporary black morocco, covers panelled gilt, spine and inner dentelles gilt, dark red morocco label, all edges gilt, joints and corners bit rubbed, sumptuous edition, this one of a relatively small number of copies printed on superfine copy, with watermark of a fleur-de-lys surmounting a shield as opposed to ordinary copies for subscribers with a Strasburg band watermark and copies of the trade issue with London arms watermark, numerous engraved headpieces and tailpieces, some dampmarks in blank upper margins, otherwise fine in handsome morocco binding of the period, bold armorial bookplate of Philip Southcote and booklabel of bibliography A. N. L. Munby. C. R. Johnson Rare Book Collections Foxon: H-P 2015 - 798 2016 $2298

Association – Munn, W. A.

Dawson, Samuel *Brest on the Quebec Labrador.* Toronto: Copp-Clark Co., 1905. 8vo. rebound in green cloth, original printed wrappers, pamphlet folded at one time with resulting creases, W. A. Munn's copy with some notations in pencil on outer margins.   Schooner Books Ltd.   115 - 99   2016 $45

Association – Munro, Harold

Davies, William Henry   1871-1940 *Shorter Lyrics of the Twentieth Century 1900-1922.* Poetry Bookshop, 1922. First edition, this being one of 200 numbered copies on large paper, inscirbed by poet Harold Munro, 8vo., recently finely bound in full dark green morocco, gilt fillet border to sides spine lettered gilt and ruled gilt and with gilt centre tools, marbled endpapers, top edges gilt, fine.   Sotheran's Piccadilly Notes - Summer 2015 - 96   2016   £298

Association – Murphy, Bernardine

Aristophanes *Le Comedie de'l Facetis, Simo Aristofane...* Venice: Appresso Vicenzo Vaugris, 1545. First edition in Italian, some light foxing and few tiny dampmarks to early leaves 18th century vellum boards, spine lettered gilt within yellow dyed compartment, marbled endpapers, little bit soiled, bookplate of Bernardine Murphy, very good.   Blackwell's Rare Books   B186 - 19   2016   £900

Association – Murray, H.

Homerus *The Odyssey of Homer.* London: printed for C. and J. Rivington (and 16 other firms), 1823. 12mo., additional engraved titlepage and frontispiece, untrimmed in original printed boards, front board replicating the titlepage and rear board, rubbed, some wear to extremities, ownership inscription of H. Murray dated 1844 on front pastedown, good, scarce in original boards.   Blackwell's Rare Books   Greek & Latin Classics VII - 39   2016   £150

Association – Murray, John

Fermor, Patrick Leigh *A Time of Gifts. On Foot to Constantinople: from the Hook of Holland to the Middle Danube.* London: Murray, 1978. First edition, 2nd issue, 8vo., original blue cloth, upper board with gilt crane design, spine lettered gilt, dust jacket with design after Craxton not price clipped, frontispiece, double page map printed on light brown paper, dust jacket slightly faded on spine (as often), past ownership bookplate attached to front free endpaper, gift inscription dated 1979 by John Murray, probably publisher, dust jacket very slightly rubbed at edges, nonetheless very fresh and bright.   Sotheran's   Travel and Exploration - 247   2016   £75

Paston, George *At John Murray's Records of a Literary Circle 1843-1892.* London: John Murray, 1932. First edition, 8vo., frontispiece, plates, original black cloth, presentation from John Murray to Mr. Williams.   J. & S. L. Bonham Antiquarian Booksellers   Voyages 2016 - 8794   2016   £65

Paston, George *At John Murray's - Records of a Literary Circle 1843-1892.* London: John Murray, 1932. First edition, plates, head and tail of spine slightly bumped, near fine in very good, slightly torn and repaired price clipped dust jacket faded at spine and edges, presentation copy inscribed for Henry Schollick, by John G. Murray, below that his Son John R. Murray has added his signature.   Peter Ellis   112 - 318   2016   £75

Association – Myers, Christopher

Myers, Walter *Harlem.* New York: Scholastic Press, 1997. First edition, folio, pictorial boards, new in dust jacket, illustrations by Christopher Myers with color collages, this copy signed by author and artist, with signed poster laid in.   Aleph-bet Books, Inc.   111 - 48   2016 $125

Association – Myers, Larry

Casement, Dan Dillon *The Abbreviated Autobiography of a Joyous Pagan.* privately printed, 1944. First edition, original red wrappers, frontispiece, plates, portraits, inscribed by author for family friend, from the library of Clint and Dot Josey with their inked signature and their penciled notation at top of last page, also pencilled notation of collector Larry Myers on last page below Josey notation, laid in is newspaper article dated June 10 1952 advising of Casement's recognition of the Kiwanis Club, a copy of the guest editorial and newspaper clipping advising of Casement's death March 7, 1953, also laid in 1952 Christmas card that pictures Casement, rare, lightly rubbed along spine and covers, else very good, housed in original four-point cloth case with titles stamped in silver on spine.   Buckingham Books   2015 - 32934   2016 $4500

Association – Mylne, Robert

Buchanan, George *The Very learned Scotsman, Mr. George Buchanan's Fratres Fraterrimi.* Edinburgh: printed by the heirs and successors of Andrew Anderson, 1708. First edition, small 8vo., 19th century calf, gilt crest on upper cover by J. Leighton, fine, very scarce, early inscription of Robert Mylne, later bookplate of Robert Crewe-Milnes, Marquess of Crewe.   C. R. Johnson Rare Book Collections   Foxon: H-P 2015 - 622   2016 $2298

Association – Nall-Cain, Charles Alexander

Dowling, Francis *Fistiana; or the Oracle of the Ring.* London: William Clement, Jun., 1841. First edition, half title, frontispiece and 4 plates, frontispiece slightly foxed, slight adhesive tear to leading endpapers, early 20th century full speckled calf, raised bands, compartments ruled gilt, red morocco label, bound in at front is slightly trimmed down original illustrated cloth binding, armorial bookplate of Sir Charles Alexander Nall-Cain, Baronet, all edges gilt, very good.   Jarndyce Antiquarian Booksellers   CCXVII - 87   2016   £680

Association – Narwick, Mildred

Houghton, Norris *But Not Forgotten.* New York: William Sloane Associates, 1951. First edition, near fine in near very good dust jacket with couple of chips and long closed tear, signed by three members of the troupe, Henry Fonda, Joshua Logan and Mildred Narwick.   Between the Covers Rare Books   204 - 58   2016 $500

Association – Nayor, George

Chagall, Marc *Illustrations for the Bible.* New York: Harcourt Brace and Co., 1956. First American edition, inscribed by artist with stunning original page color drawing of Moses for Lenette and George Nayor, 1966, and from the collection of Herman Krawitz, former assistant manager of the Metropolitan Opera House, complete with 16 lithographs in color, 12 in black and white plus lithograph cover, also illustrated with reproductions in heliograuvre of the 106 etchings made by Chagall for the illustrations of the bible, folio, original pictorial boards, original dust jacket, book with tape residue to endpapers, otherwise book and lithographs fine, extremely scarce dust jacket (almost never seen) with chipping, edgewear and damage to spine.   Manhattan Rare Book Company   2016 - 1646   2016 $40,000

Association – Nayor, Lenette

Chagall, Marc *Illustrations for the Bible.* New York: Harcourt Brace and Co., 1956. First American edition, inscribed by artist with stunning original page color drawing of Moses for Lenette and George Nayor, 1966, and from the collection of Herman Krawitz, former assistant manager of the Metropolitan Opera House, complete with 16 lithographs in color, 12 in black and white plus lithograph cover, also illustrated with reproductions in heliograuvre of the 106 etchings made by Chagall for the illustrations of the bible, folio, original pictorial boards, original dust jacket, book with tape residue to endpapers, otherwise book and lithographs fine, extremely scarce dust jacket (almost never seen) with chipping, edgewear and damage to spine.   Manhattan Rare Book Company   2016 - 1646   2016 $40,000

Association – Neame, Thomas

Lindley, John   1799-1865 *Pomologia Britannica; or Figures and Descriptions of the Most Important Varieties of Fruit Cultivated in Great Britain.* London: Henry G. Bohn, 1841. First edition, 3 volumes, 245 x 150mm, contemporary green half morocco with marbled boards, spine gilt with fruit motifs, raised bands, red and brown morocco labels, gilt edges, 152 beautiful hand colored plates, bookplate of Joseph Greene and that of Sir Thomas Neame, edges and joints, bit rubbed, covers little scuffed, couple of minor marginal stains and occasional foxing, mostly on paper guards and very rarely affecting leaves with text, otherwise all plates fine, with particularly bright colors.   Phillip J. Pirages   67 - 242   2016 $15,000

Association – Neild, Alfred

Dickens, Charles   1812-1870 *Hard Times for These Times.* London: Bradbury & Evans, 1854. First edition, original olive green horizontal ribbed moire cloth, blocked in blind on boards and spine, spine lettered in gilt, spine little faded and with some expertly executed minor repairs to head and tail of spine, simple bookplate of Alfred Neild, good plus.   Jarndyce Antiquarian Booksellers   CCXVIII - 525   2016   £750

Association – Nelson, Elizabeth

Watts, Isaac *Select Songs for Children.* Newcastle: printed for S. Hodgson and sold by the Booksellers in Town and Country, 1790. Seventh edition, 12mo., a number of leaves rather thumb marked, some browning, final two pages have verses separated by pencil lines, small tear with loss to blank lower corner of titlepage, contemporary calf backed pattered paper boards, spine and corners worn, boards very rubbed, signature of Elizabeth Nelson, Aug. 16th 1794, and of Elizabeth Ingleson Nov. 1821.   Jarndyce Antiquarian Booksellers   CCXVI - 597   2016   £120

Association – Nelson, Paul

MacDonald, Ross *The Instant Enemy.* New York: Alfred A. Knopf, 1968. First edition, octavo, blue cloth backstrip over yellow paper boards, dust jacket with mild toning to jacket, recipient's name in inscription, presentation inscribed by author for Paul Nelson.   Heritage Book Shop   Holiday 2015 - 76   2016 $1250

Association – Nelthorpe, Eduardi

Ray, John *Synopsis Methodica Animalium Quadruperdum et Serpentini Generis.* London: Impensis S. Smith & B. Walford, 1693. First edition, 8vo., engraved portrait, sheets B-M browned due to poor paper quality, all others clean, printer's crease across lower corner of page 67 but no loss of text, contemporary sprinkled calf, front cover detached, label missing, from the library of James Stevens Cox (1910-1997), contemporary inscription 'AAA 50', inscription 'E Libris Eduardi Nelthorpe Admi/1720', and "E Libris G. D. Kent CCC Oxon".   Maggs Bros. Ltd.   1447 - 359   2016   £220

Association – Nesbit, Paris

Nesbit, Edith *A Pomander of Verse.* London: John Lane at the Bodley Head, 1895. First edition, 1 of 750 copies, inscribed by author's cousin, Paris Nesbit, tan boards with gilt cover design by Laurence Housman, who also did the charming illustration for titlepage, very good with bumping to board corners and chipping to spine edges, interior clean with slight aging to margins of untrimmed pages, very good-.   The Kelmscott Bookshop   12 - 76   2016 $250

Association – Ness, Eveline

O'Dell, Scott *Island of the Blue Dolphins.* Boston: Houghton Mifflin, 1960. First edition, first printing, 8vo., cloth, fine in dust jacket (not price clipped, no award seal, irregular piece off top of spine, ink name on flap, few closed tears), still very good-, this copy inscribed by O'Dell and laid in is TLS by artist, Eveline Ness in 1976 on her personal letterhead, Ness illustrated the color dust jacket, also laid in 4 page playbill for the movie made in 1964, signed by Celia Kay who starred in the movie.   Aleph-bet Books, Inc.   112 - 350   2016 $875

Association – Netter, Frank

Salter, Robert B. *Textbook of Disorders and Injuries of the Musculoskeletal System.* Baltimore: 1970. Light wear, else good, from the library of Frank H. Netter, with note to that effect on front fly, original binding.   James Tait Goodrich   X-78 - 498   2016 $75

Association – Neuburg, Victor

Craik, George Lillie *The Pursuit of Knowledge Under Difficulties.* London: John Murray, 1858. New edition, 2 volumes in 1, frontispiece, plates and illustrations, original purple cloth, gilt vignette of Craik on frontispiece, faint circular mark on front board, spine faded, all edges gilt, contemporary and recent inscriptions on leading f.e.p, Victor Neuburg's copy.   Jarndyce Antiquarian Books   CCXV - 56   2016   £35

Jones, Mary Gladys *The Charity School Movement.* London: Frank Cass & Co., 1964. New impression, half title, plates, original turqoise cloth, very good in slightly torn dust jacket with repair to tail of spine, Victor Neuburg's copy.   Jarndyce Antiquarian Books   CCXV - 798   2016   £20

Association – Neville-Cross, John

Dickens, Charles   1812-1870 *The Uncommercial Traveller.* London: Chapman & Hall, 1861. First edition, half title, 32 page catalog (Dec. 1860), contemporary full dark green crushed morocco by Riviere, gilt spine, borders and dentelles, part of original purple cloth board bound in at end, armorial bookplate of John Neville-Cross, top edge gilt, very good handsome copy.   Jarndyce Antiquarian Booksellers   CCXVIII - 597   2016   £600

Association – Nevinson, John Lea

Peck, Francis *Academia Tertia Anglicana; or the Antiquarian Annals of Stanford (sic) in Lincoln, Rutland and Northampton Shires....* London: printed for the author by James Bettenham, 1727. First edition, 14 books in one, bound in early 19th century panelled russia, attractively tooled in blind, rebacked period style by Bernard Middleton, all edges gilt, 33 engraved plates, including large folding engraved frontispiece, 4 small engraved plates within text, numerous attractive wood engraved tailpieces, bright, clean, early 19th century engraved armorial booklabel of Earls of Abingdon, bookplate of John Lea Nevinson (1905-1985).   Sotheran's   Piccadilly Notes - Summer 2015 - 233   2016   £695

Association – Newbold, H. LeRoy

Lugar, Robert *Villa Architecture: a Collection of Views with Plans, of Buildings Executed in England, Scotland &c.* London: J. Taylor, 1828. First edition, folio, 42 plates, of 2hich 26 are handcolored aquatints, 16 floral plans, modern half red morocco, margins of first two leaves bit soiled, few tiny chips, two leaves of preface moderately foxed, occasional spot of foxing, but plates clean and bright and fine, signature of H. LeRoy Newbold, NY 1836.   Joseph J. Felcone, Inc.   Books from Five Centuries: a Miscellany - 7   2016 $4500

Association – Newell, Robert

Burnett, Frances Hodgson *Little Lord Fauntleroy.* New York: Charles Scribner, 1911. First edition with these illustrations, 8vo., blue cloth, pictorial paste-on, top edge gilt, corner of blank endpaper clipped else near fine, this copy inscribed by author to Robert Newell, with lengthy inscription from artist, below is a charming watercolor by artist, super copy, illustrations by Reginald Birch.   Aleph-bet Books, Inc.   111 - 65   2016 $1500

Association – Newman, Murray

Dibdin, Thomas Frognall 1776-1847 *The Library Companion or the Young Man's Guide and the Old Man's Comfort in the Choice of a Library.* printed for Harding, Triphook and Legard, 1824. First edition, 8vo., 2 volumes, contemporary full polished calf with gilt and blind panels to boards, both volumes rebacked preserving original spines, little rubbing and scratching to boards, otherwise very good, from the library of Murray A. W. Newman with his bookplate and ownership signature.   Sotheran's   Piccadilly Notes - Summer 2015 - 104   2016   £250

Association – Nicholas, John

Vetustissimorum Poetarum Hesiodi, Theocriti, Theognidis, Moschi, Musaei, Bionis.... Paris: Apud Joannem Libert, 1628. Rare edition, ownership inscription of John Nicholas of Queen's College, Oxford dated 1641, general titlepage damaged at gutter from cracked hinge and just starting to loosen, 8vo., contemporary English calf, spine with four raised bands between double blind fillets, boards also bordered with double blind fillet, edges red, bit marked, spine ends worn, some surface loss to leather on front board, joints cracking little but strong, bookplate of Colonel Sir Charles J. J. Hamilton, Baronet.   Blackwell's Rare Books   B186 - 68   2016   £1500

Association – Nicholls, R.

Reider, William D. *The New Tablet of memory...* London: John Clements, 1841. Slightly browned, contemporary half calf, lacking label, little rubbed, later ownership signature of R. Nicholls.   Jarndyce Antiquarian Books   CCXV - 917   2016   £48

Association – Nicol, James

Ray, John *A Collection of English Proverbs Digested into a Convenient Method for the Speedy Finding Any One Upon Occasion; with Short Annotations.* Cambridge: by John Hayes for W. Morden, 1678. Second edition, 8vo., light intermittent soiling and dampstaining throughout, blank margin of B5 soiled, 19th century calf, ruled in blind, rebacked, new endpapers, from the library of James Stevens Cox (1910-1997), 18th century ownership inscription James Nicol, Traquair Manse.   Maggs Bros. Ltd.   1447 - 358   2016   £300

Association – Nielsen, Kay

Quiller-Couch, Arthur Thomas 1863-1944 *The Twelve Dancing Princesses and Other Fairy Tales Retold by Sir Arthur Quiller-Couch.* New York: George H. Doran, n.d. circa, 1915. 8vo., blue gilt pictorial cloth, fine in dust jacket, dust jacket very good to fine with some minor wear, this copy inscribed by artist, Kay Nielsen to Sarah Briggs Latimore, 16 magnificent tipped-in color plates, black and whites in text, pictorial endpapers, cover and dust jacket design, beautiful copy.   Aleph-bet Books, Inc.   111 - 324   2016 $2000

Association – Niesart, Johann Heinrich Joseph

Albertus Magnus, St. *De Laudibus Beate Virginis Mariae.* Cologne: Ulrich Zel not after, 1473. First edition, folio, 165 leaves (of 166, lacking final blank), Gothic type, 2-4 line initial spaces, alternating spaces filled in red, red paragraph marks, underlining and capital strokes, single pinhole visible in lower margins, early 19th century ochre paper boards, spine label in red lettered in gilt red edges, spine darkened, little soiled and marked, preserved in a box, pinhole visible in lower margin, inner margin of first leaf lightly soiled, otherwise extremely fresh, from Bibliotheae J(ohann Heinrich Joseph) Niesart 1766-1841, pastor in Velen 1816, with his manuscript inscription and his bibliographical notes on loose inserted leaf.   Maggs Bros. Ltd.   1474 - 3   2016   £14,000

Association – Nightingale, Mrs.

Food for the Young. London: W. Darton Jun., 1818. First edition, small 12mo., frontispiece and 2 further plates, leaves little dusted, 20th century quarter red morocco, presentation inscription on leading blank "H.H. Broughton, a present from Mrs. Nightingale 1819", nice.   Jarndyce Antiquarian Books   CCXV - 687   2016   £95

Association – Nolan

California Sorcery. Abingdon: Cemetery Dance, 1999. Publisher's copy of the limited edition (26 copies), signed by Ray Bradbury, Richard Matheson, Ellison, Nolan, Tomerlin, Sohl, Fritch and others, stamp of another author, fine in fine dust jacket in publisher's printed gray case.   Ken Lopez Bookseller   166 - 5   2016 $650

Association – Norman, Frederick Henry

Mill, John Stuart 1806-1873 *Principles of Political Economy with some of Their Applications to Social Philosophy.* John W. Parker, 1849. Second edition, 8vo., 2 volumes, contemporary half calf over marbled boards, spines with new morocco labels with gilt lettering, neat repairs to joints and extremities, spines little darkened, very clean internally, very good, bookplate of Frederick Henry Norman.   Sotheran's   Piccadilly Notes - Summer 2015 - 205   2016   £700

Association – Norman, Haskell

Buonanni, Filippo 1638-1725 *Observations circa Viventia, quae in Rebus non Viventibus Repriuntur. Cum Micrographia Curiosa....* Rome: Typs Dominci Antonii Herculis, 1691. First edition, small 4to., 3 parts in one volume, title woodcut vignette, engraved title, 69 engraved copperplate plates, title with mended hole, ownership mark excised on outer margin, with slight affect to 1 letter, frequent browning, lacks famous frontispiece, original full vellum, gilt spine title, added ink manuscript, bookplate of Haskell F. Norman, early ink ownership mark on title 1778. Jeff Weber Rare Books   183 - 7   2016 $3750

Association – Norman, Henry

Clark, John Spencer *Drawing in Public Education, the Features of the Study which Should be Taught in Primary, Grammar and High School.* Boston: L. Prang & Co., 1880. Plates, some color, original printed wrappers, slight wear to back wrapper, small repairs to spine, the copy of journalist politician Henry Norman.   Jarndyce Antiquarian Books   CCXV - 594   2016   £48

Hooper, Franklin William *Plan of an Institution Devoted to Liberal Education.* New York: S. W. Green's Sons, 1881. Folding plate, later grey paper wrappers, rebacked, inscribed "Henry Norman with compliments of Edward T. Fisher".   Jarndyce Antiquarian Books   CCXV - 743   2016   £85

Association – Norman, Patience

Haywood, William D. *Bill Haywood's Book.* New York: International Pub., 1929. First edition, owner's signature, Patience W. Norman, else fine in attractive, very good or better dust jacket with couple of modest chips and tears, nice, clean copy.   Between the Covers Rare Books   204 - 64   2016 $350

Association – North, Nancy

Spring, Gardiner *Memoirs of the Rev. Samuel J. Mills, Late Missionary to the South Western Section of the United States and Agent of the American Colonization Society...* New York: New York Evangelical Missionary Society, 1820. First edition, tall octavo, American binding of contemporary mottled sheep with red morocco gilt spine labels and ruled in gilt, early bookplate of Nancy North, Boonville NY, tiny hole on spine, small split at bottom of front joint and little peel along edges of boards, still very good or better. Between the Covers Rare Books   202 - 100   2016 $400

Association – North, William

Laconics or New Maxims of State and Conversation. printed for Thomas Hodges..., 1701. 8vo., nice, clean copy, contemporary panelled calf, red morocco label, rebacked retaining original spine, armorial bookplate of William Lord North of Carthage and Baron Grey of Rolleston 1703. Jarndyce Antiquarian Books   CCXV - 205   2016   £250

Association – Northbourne, Charles James, 1st Baron

Sprigge, Joshua *Anglia Rediviva; Englands Recovery...* London: by R. W. for John Partridge, 1647. First edition, small folio, frontispiece, errata leaf, folding engraved portraits (soiled, backed with later paper), large folding engraved view backed (with later paper and slight damge in folds, few ink blots), folding letterpress table, rather grubby throughout with occasional spots and stains E4v and F1r particularly soiled, contemporary calf, rebacked, 19th century marbled pastedowns, from the library of James Stevens Cox (1910-1997), armorial bookplate of Charles James, 1st Baron Northbourne.   Maggs Bros. Ltd.   1447 - 396   2016   £350

Association – Northbourne, Edith

Bunyan, John 1628-1688 *Pilgrim's Progress from this World to that Which is to Come.* London: printed for the Society by J. Haddon, 1847. First edition, 8vo., finely bound by Ramage in full brown morocco boards panelled gilt and black with oak leaf and acorn corner tools and central gilt block, spine panelled and lettered gilt, all edges gilt, uppper joint little rubbed, little spotting to endpapers, leather booklabel of Edith Northbourne, otherwise very good. Sotheran's   Piccadilly Notes - Summer 2015 - 59   2016   £498

Association – Northumberland, Duke of

Richmond, William *A Series of Maritime and Mercantile Tables Illustrative of the Shipping as Connected with the Trade and Commerce of Great Britain..* Newcastle upon Tyne: printed by Hernaman and Perring, 1833. First and only edition, Large folio, handsome presentation binding of black morocco, embossed in blind, sides gilt panelled and gilt lettered on upper cover, all edges gilt, spines and extremities rather worn and covers just little warped, contents in fine state of preservation, notable presentation copy inscribed and signed in ink by author to Duke of Northumberland with Duke's armorial bookplate, scarce. John Drury Rare Books   2015 - 26048   2016 $437

Association – Northup, Louisa

Standley, Samuel *An Essay on the Manufacture of Straw Bonnets...* Providence: Barnum Field & Co., 1825. First edition, 18mo., original printed paper covered boards, untrimmed, light overall foxing common to early American paper, light dampstain on front cover, upper hinge split and held by one cord, lovely copy, fragile, original printed boards, inscribed "Please accept this with Louisa E. Northup's respects Providence Jan. 12 1828".   Joseph J. Felcone, Inc. Books from Five Centuries: a Miscellany - 135   2016 $800

Association – Novak, Alvin

Blake, William   1757-1827 *Poems from William Blake's Songs of Innocence.*   London: Bodley Head, 1967. Limited to only 275 copies for presentation by publisher,, this copy inscribed by artist to pianist Alvin Novak, with drawing, Dec. '67, pictorial wrappers, fine, illustrations by Maurice Sendak with pictorial cover and 8 color illustrations.   Aleph-bet Books, Inc.   111 - 406   2016 $7500

Association – O'Brien, Frances Massey

Camden, William *Rerum Anglicarum et Hibernicarum Annales, Regnante Elisabetha.*   Lugd. Batavorum: Elzevir, 1639. 8vo, engraved portrait, titlepage in red and black, woodcut printer's device, copious notes in old hand to endpapers and prelim blanks, further marginalia in Latin and English with occasional manicules, few pages with pencil ticks to margins, sporadic light foxing, one or two marginal paper flaws, small hole in centre of page 359, affecting only few letters, contemporary vellum, gilt to spine evidence of lost label replaced with ink title, yapp edges, spine slightly darkened, little soiled with some smudges and stains, small (burn?) hole to spine, some bands broken and inner hinge split but binding sound, small loss of top corner of f.f.e.p., armorial bookplate of Robert Hinde, bookplate of Frances Massey O'Brien and an anonymous catalogue description affixed to front pastedown, ownership inscriptions of Sunderland Nov. 23rd 1805, Eton, L. M. Robinson 1923, and Frances Massey O'Brien, July 1967, FMO's pencil note.   Unsworths Antiquarian Booksellers Ltd.   E01 - Early Printing - 4   2016   £300

Association – O'Byrne, James

Bentley's Miscellany. Volumes I-VI.   London: Richard Bentley, 1837-1839. Frontsipiece, plates, contemporary half tan calf, marbled boards, lacking spine strips but sound, armorial bookplate of James O'Byrne, decent working copy.   Jarndyce Antiquarian Booksellers   CCXVIII - 765   2016   £350

Association – O'More, Haven

Doves Press *Catalogue Raisonne of Books printed & Published at the Doves Press No. 1 The Terrace Hammersmith.*   Hammersmith: Doves Press, 1908. One of 300 copies, 234 x 167mm., russet morocco by the Doves Bindery (stamp signed and dated 1908), covers with simple frame of gilt rules accented with circlets where the lines intersect, neatly rejointed, raised bands, gilt titling, all edges gilt, later felt lined green cloth drop-back box; printed in red and black, engraved bookplate of Henry Fairfield Osborn with leather book label of Haven O'More, front free endpaper inscribed to Professor Osborne (sic) by Cobden-Sanderson, signed 'C S" and dated 12 November 1908 accompanied by the booklet "The Closing of the Doves Press: a keepsake from the opening of a 1969 exhibition at Stanford University devoted to Cobden-Sanderson, the Doves Press and the Doves Bindery; spine and significant portion of front cover rather darkened, joints and extremities bit rubbed, half a dozen water spots to boards, restored binding entirely solid and very clean and fresh internally.   Phillip J. Pirages   67 - 116   2016 $1250

Association – O'Reilly, E. J.

Arnold, Thomas Kerchever *A First Verse Book.*   London: printed for J. G. F. & J. Rivington, 1841. Final ad leaf, some pencil marks in text, original brown ribbed cloth, paper label, little bumped and marked, ownership inscription of E. J. O'Reilly, 1879.   Jarndyce Antiquarian Books   CCXV - 513   2016   £40

Association – Oakes, E. Ann

Saint Pierre, Jacques Henri Bernardin De   1737-1814 *Studies of Nature.*   London: printed by J. W. Myers for W. West, 1798. 8vo., without half title, contemporary half mottled calf, gilt spine, green label, very good, signature of E. Ann Oakes.   Jarndyce Antiquarian Booksellers   CCXVI - 507   2016   £180

Association – Oakley, Thornton

Masson, Elsie *Folk Tales of Brittany.*   Philadelphia: Macrae Smith, 1929. First edition, 4to., cloth backed pictorial boards, corner rubbed, else fine in dust jacket (very good, with few mends on verso and half inch piece off top of backstrip), pictorial endpapers, 15 full page illustrations plus many partial page illustrations and striking color wrapper by Thornton Oakley, with Oakley inscription and sketch.   Aleph-bet Books, Inc.   111 - 326   2016 $450

Association – Oakley, Violet

Eddy, Mary Baker Glover *Christ My Refuge: One of Seven Hymns by...* Boston: Pub. by the Trustees under the Will of Mary Baker Eddy, 1939. White cloth, gilt pictorial cover, very good-fine, printed on one side of the page, calligraphic text done in 4 colors with pictorial and illuminated initials, pictorial headpiece and tailpece, title, and cover illustrations plus full page color illustrations by Violet Oakley, beautiful book.   Aleph-bet Books, Inc.   111 - 327   2016 $75

Association – Oates, Edward

Hedericus, Benjamin *Lexicon Manuale Graecum, Omnibus sui Generis Lexicis quae quidem Exstant...* London: Excudit S. Palmer, Impensis J. & J. Knapton et al, 1727. 4to., titlepage in red and black, final leaf with publisher's catalog, occasional light spots and smudges, generally clean, closed tear to leaf M4, trimmed little close but never touching text, contemporary tan calf boards, neatly rebacked, raised bands, gilt to spine, older label retained, edges patterned, endpapers renewed, some scratches and stains, area of lower board neatly patched with calf, corners fraying, still very good and sound, armorial bookplates of Rev. Samuel Kettilby, and Edward Oates, and Robert Washington Oates, commentary of Oates to first flyleaf verso, pencilled inscription "From Henry (Cooper?) to Mrs. Edward Oates 17 Nov. 1849".   Unsworths Antiquarian Booksellers   30 - 68   2016   £175

Association – Oates, Robert Washington

Doran, John *Knights and Their Days.* London: Richard Bentley, 1856. First edition, half title, frontispiece, lacking following f.e.p., original orange decorated cloth, spine faded, leading inner hinge crudely repaired, bookplate of Robert Washington Oates.   Jarndyce Antiquarian Books   CCXV - 162   2016   £25

Hedericus, Benjamin *Lexicon Manuale Graecum, Omnibus sui Generis Lexicis quae quidem Exstant...* London: Excudit S. Palmer, Impensis J. & J. Knapton et al, 1727. 4to., titlepage in red and black, final leaf with publisher's catalog, occasional light spots and smudges, generally clean, closed tear to leaf M4, trimmed little close but never touching text, contemporary tan calf boards, neatly rebacked, raised bands, gilt to spine, older label retained, edges patterned, endpapers renewed, some scratches and stains, area of lower board neatly patched with calf, corners fraying, still very good and sound, armorial bookplates of Rev. Samuel Kettilby, and Edward Oates, and Robert Washington Oates, commentary of Oates to first flyleaf verso, pencilled inscription "From Henry (Cooper?) to Mrs. Edward Oates 17 Nov. 1849".   Unsworths Antiquarian Booksellers   30 - 68   2016   £175

Association – Oates, W.

Manilius, Marcus *Astronomicon ex Recensione et cum Notis Richardi Bentleii.* London: Typus Henrici Woodfall Sumptibus Pauli et Isaac Vaillant, 1739. 4to., 2 engraved plates, frontispiece folding celestial map, woodcut device to titlepage, engraved headpiece to dedication, occasional neatly pencilled marginal notes, closed tear (85mm. approx) to page 145-6, sporadic light worming to top fore-edge, corner not affecting text, small closed tear to map attachment, some edges little toned, 19th century half vellum, black morocco gilt spine label, marbled paper covered boards, fore and tail edges deckled, vellum darkened, rubbed, edges worn, corners frayed, inkstamp and signature of writer and book collector Walter Ashburner (1864-1936), signature of W. Oates dated 1746.   Unsworths Antiquarian Booksellers Ltd.   E01 - Early Printing - 14   2016   £850

Association – Oddie, James

Withers, William Bramwell *The History of Ballarat from the First Pastoral Settlement to the Present Time.* Ballarat, F. W. Niven and Co., 1887. 8vo., original blue green pictorial blue cloth blocked in dark green and gold, very large folding chromolithographic bird's eye view, large folding color lithographic plan, two facsimiles, 20 lithographic plates (6 tinted), historiated initials, large plate and plan with repaired tears, evenly little browned, as usual, otherwise very clean and fres, presented to Ballarat pioneer James Oddie (1824-1911).   Sotheran's   Travel and Exploration - 409   2016   £448

Association – Odell, George

Housman, Laurence   1865-1959 *Prunella or Love in a Dutch Garden.* London: Sigwick & Jackson, 1911. Third edition, new impression, square 8vo., untrimmed frontispiece by Housman, printed boards, bookplate removed from front pastedown, closed tear to front blank, very good, signed and dated by actor George Odell who played the Tenor, in addition this copy signed by about 25 members of the NY cast,.   Second Life Books, Inc.   196A - 830   2016 $225

Association – Ofili, Chris

Choon, Angela *Chris Ofili: Devil's Pie.* New York and Gottingen: Steidl and David Zwimer, 2008. First edition, 4to., original purple cloth lettered silver on spine and cover, signed presentation from Ofili, about fine.   Any Amount of Books   2015 - A75550   2016   £150

Association – Ogilvy, John

Vergilius Maro, Publius *The Works of...* London: by Thomas Maxey for Andrew Crook, 1650. Second edition, 8vo., engraved portrait of Ogilby and additional engraved title by William Marshall (both dated 1649), minor rust spots to a number of leaves throughout, with upper corners of last few leaves creased, contemporary sheep covers ruled in blind, later (but old) paper labels on spine, worn, leather along fore-edge of front board chewed away and starting to detach, corners of lower cover chewed, joints split, headcaps missing, corners bumped, 'Charles Moore his Book', early inscription and early signature 'John Ogilvy', from the library of James Stevens Cox (1910-1997). Maggs Bros. Ltd. 1447 - 424 2016 £180

Association – Ogle, Bertram Savile

Waterton, Charles *Wanderings in South America the North-West of the United States and the Antilles in the Years 1812, 1816, 1829 and 1824.* London: A. Applegath for J. Mawman, 1825. First edition, 4to., contemporary quarter brown morocco, brown paper covered boards, frontispiece, 2 woodcut text illustrations with ALS from Charles Waterton, seal cut out, bookplate of Bertram Savile Ogle, very good. Sotheran's   Piccadilly Notes - Summer 2015 - 323   2016   £1550

Association – Olds, William P.

Ford, Worthington Chauncey *George Washington.* New York: Goupil & Co. and Charles Scribner's Sons, 1900. One of 200 copies of Edition de Luxe, 267 x 203mm., 2 volumes, attractive green crushed morocco covers with two-line gilt frame, raised bands, gilt framed compartments and gilt titling, red morocco doublures surrounded by inch wide green morocco turn-ins with four gilt fillets, watered silk endleaves, top edges gilt, other edges untrimmed, 88 full page plates, as wll as 32 tailpieces, chapter initials in black and red, bookplate of William P. Olds laid in at front of each volume, large paper copy, hint of wear to joints and extremities, spines mildly faded to olive green (spine of second volume with just slightly irregular fading), still fine copy of this deluxe edition, morocco bindings solid and pleasing, text and plates virtually pristine. Phillip J. Pirages 67 - 349 2016 $950

Association – Oliver, David

Mortensen, Greg *Three Cups of Tea.* New York: Viking, 2006. 10th printing, illustrations, signed by Mortenson and David Oliver, scarce thus, fine in dust jacket. Gene W. Baade, Books on the West 2015 - SHEL787 2016 $75

Association – Olivier, Laurence

Synge, John Millington 1871-1909 *The Well of the Saints.* London: George Allen & Unwin, 1924. Later printing, inscribed by actor, Laurence Olivier, brown paper covered boards, quarter bound with imitation parchment leather and spine titles in gilt, as issued, brief spotting to boards, backstrip toned, overall very good.   Royal Books 49 - 7 2016 $1850

Association – Ord, William Miller

Raleigh, Walter *Judicious and Select Essayes and Observations.*   London: by T. Warren for Humphrey Moseley, 1650. First edition, small 8vo., engraved portrait, but without 4 leaves of Moseley's ads, blank verso of engraved portrait and blank verso of last leaf stained by turn-ins and with edges slightly chipped, small repair to foot of titlepage, just touching decorated border, minor closed tear in lower inner margin of A1-2, dampstaining to inner margins of G4-(2)C8 (touching text in places), small hole through (3)A-3 (touching two lines of text), some occasional rust spotting, mid 20th century calf, from the library of James Stevens Cox (1910-1997), early inscription of John Spelman, signature Robertus (?) Culsett, armorial bookplate of William Miller Ord (1834-1902).   Maggs Bros. Ltd. 1447 - 351 2016   £350

Association – Orde, Anna

Frere, Mary *Old Deccan Days; or Hindoo Fairy Legends; Current in Soutehrn India.* London: John Murray, 1868. First edition, 8vo., 4 colored plates, many further illustrations in text, burgundy publisher's cloth, gilt title to spine, gilt stamped illustrations of Ganesh to upper board, endcaps and joints worn, slight loss to head of upper joint little cracked, still very good, 1920's news clipping on subject of folkloric stories for children passed to prelim blank, ownership inscription of Anna M. Orde, 1868 to titlepage, with "Burne-Jones 1880' ms. to titlepage (not the handwriting of the artist, but according to old bookseller's note, from his library).   Unsworths Antiquarian Booksellers 30 - 59 2016   £40

Association – Orssinger, L.

Schott, Gaspar *Magia Optica Das ist Geheime doch Naturmassige Gesicht und Augen-Lehr...* Bamberg: Johann Martin Schonwerters, 1677. First German edition, small 4to., allegorical frontispiece, 25 engraved copper plates, variously browned, foxed or stained, contemporary quarter calf, decorative boards, extremities very worn, ownership signature L. Orssinger and inscription Ex Libris P. Lemigii Antles, Ludovii Kappourr?   Jeff Weber Rare Books   183 - 32 2016 $3000

Association – Osborn, Edward Oliver

Littleton, Adam *Latin Dictionary.* London: printed for J. Walthoe, J. J. and P. Knapton, et al, 1735. Sixth edition, 4to., frontispiece and 2 maps, lacking front and rear free endpapers, little yellowed, some light ink spots and smudges, contemporary brown calf boards rebacked in vellum, slotted to accommodate raised bands, ownership inscriptions to frontispiece and titlepage of Edward Oliver Osborn, also to titlepage, inscription of William Osborn dated 1739. Unsworths Antiquarian Booksellers 30 - 96 2016 £150

Association – Osborn, Henry Fairfield

Doves Press *Catalogue Raisonne of Books printed & Published at the Doves Press No. 1 The Terrace Hammersmith.* Hammersmith: Doves Press, 1908. One of 300 copies, 234 x 167mm., russet morocco by the Doves Bindery (stamp signed and dated 1908), covers with simple frame of gilt rules accented with circlets where the lines intersect, neatly rejointed, raised bands, gilt titling, all edges gilt, later felt lined green cloth drop-back box; printed in red and black, engraved bookplate of Henry Fairfield Osborn with leather book label of Haven O'More, front free endpaper inscribed to Professor Osborne (sic) by Cobden-Sanderson, signed 'C S" and dated 12 November 1908 accompanied by the booklet "The Closing of the Doves Press: a keepsake from the opening of a 1969 exhibition at Stanford University devoted to Cobden-Sanderson, the Doves Press and the Doves Bindery; spine and significant portion of front cover rather darkened, joints and extremities bit rubbed, half a dozen water spots to boards, restored binding entirely solid and very clean and fresh internally. Phillip J. Pirages 67 - 116 2016 $1250

Association – Osborn, William

Littleton, Adam *Latin Dictionary.* London: printed for J. Walthoe, J. J. and P. Knapton, et al, 1735. Sixth edition, 4to., frontispiece and 2 maps, lacking front and rear free endpapers, little yellowed, some light ink spots and smudges, contemporary brown calf boards rebacked in vellum, slotted to accommodate raised bands, ownership inscriptions to frontispiece and titlepage of Edward Oliver Osborn, also to titlepage, inscription of William Osborn dated 1739. Unsworths Antiquarian Booksellers 30 - 96 2016 £150

Association – Osborne, Lewis

American Type Founders Co. Kelly Press Division *Style B Kelly Automatic Press Book of Instructions.* Elizabeth: Kelly Press Division, American Type Founders Co., April, 1927. Oblong quarto, original printed red wrappers, 20 illustrations, laid into this copy is typed postcard from printer Lewis Osborne of Ashland, Oregon dated Jan. 9 1973 to printer Adrian Wilson, well used, worn and stained, as one would expect, with scotch tape reinforcement, etc, but complete, and rare. The Brick Row Book Shop Miscellany 69 - 66 2016 $225

Association – Osler, William

Guillemeau, Jacques *Child-Birth or the Happy Delivery of Women Wherein is Set Down the Government of Woman in the Time of their Breeding Childe...* London: Anne Griffin for Joyce Norton and Richard Whitaker, 1635. Small 4to., new English sytle panel calf with raised bands, text foxed and some marginal dampstaining, title soiled and institutional stamp, lower portion of X4 torn with text loss, original French edition, bookplate, noting this was a gift of William Osler. James Tait Goodrich X-78 - 398 2016 $2500

Association – Ossorio, Alfonso

Tapie, Michel *Ossorio.* Torino: Edizioni D'Arte Fratelli Pozzo, 1961. First edition, folio, 10 full page tipped in color plates, original wrappers worn along spine near binding staple, very good, clean copy, inscribed by Alfonso Ossorio, for Alfred Cooper. Second Life Books, Inc. 196 B - 732 2016 $150

Association – Ouseley, Gore

Delille, Jacques *L'Homme des Champs ou les Georgiques Francoises.... (bound with) Dithyrame sur l'Immoralite de l'Ame, Suivi du Passage du St. Gothard....* Basel: Chez Jacques Decker, 1800. Paris: Chez Giguet et Michaud, 1802. First editions, first work,4 plates, dampstaining throughout at tail of gutter margin, some browning, second work with frontispiece, bound together, 12mo., contemporary dark blue straight grain morocco, smooth backstrip divided by double gilt rules, second compartment gilt letter direct, single gilt rule on sides, gilt ball roll on board edges and turn-ins, marbled endpapers, touch of rubbing to joints, very good, bookplate of Sir Gore Ouseley, Baronet. Blackwell's Rare Books B186 - 51 2016 £150

Association – Overton, Grace

White, Sarah Parker *A Moral History of Woman.* New York: Doubleday Doran, 1937. First edition, 8vo., inscribed by author for Grace Overton. Second Life Books, Inc. 196 B - 871 2016 $45

Association – Owen, Anne

Watts, Isaac *Divine Songs in Easy Language for the Use of Children.* London: printed for J. Buckland and 5 others, 1775. 12mo., initial license leaf, slight tear without loss to head of B1, pen strokes to opening pages 34-35, otherwise good, clean copy, original hessian cloth boards, front endpaper bears inscription of John Owen, March 30th 1776 and Anne Owen, July 2nd 1796. Jarndyce Antiquarian Booksellers CCXVI - 593 2016 £120

Association – Owen, John

Watts, Isaac *Divine Songs in Easy Language for the Use of Children.* London: printed for J. Buckland and 5 others, 1775. 12mo., initial license leaf, slight tear without loss to head of B1, pen strokes to opening pages 34-35, otherwise good, clean copy, original hessian cloth boards, front endpaper bears inscription of John Owen, March 30th 1776 and Anne Owen, July 2nd 1796. Jarndyce Antiquarian Booksellers CCXVI - 593 2016 £120

Association – Page, William Hussey

Holmes, Oliver Wendell 1809-1894 *Boylston Prize Dissertations for the Years 1836 and 1837.* Boston: Charles C. Little and James Brown, 1838. First edition, octavo, folding map frontispiece with state borders outlined by hand in colors, brown ribbon embossed cloth (oak-leaf and acorn pattern), gilt spine title, couple of short closed tears at spinal extremities and few scattered spots of light foxing in text, lovely near fine, this copy inscribed by author to William Hussey Page, Boston physician. Between the Covers Rare Books 208 - 39 2016 $4950

Association – Palmer, Lilian

Behrman, S. N. *No Time for comedy: a Play in Three Acts.* London: Hamish Hamilton, 1939. First edition, 8vo., original worn printed wrappers, (also issued in cloth), round-robin copy, signed by members of the London production, Diane Wyngard, Rex Harrison, Lilian Palmer, Elizabeth Welch and 3 others. Second Life Books, Inc. 196A - 97 2016 $250

Association – Palmer, Richard

Horatius Flaccus, Quimtus *Cum Commentariis & Enarrationibus Commentatoris Veteris, et Iacobi Cruquii Messenii...* Antwerp: Ex officina Plantiana Raphelengii, 1611. Final Plantin edition, 4to., paper toned, some spotting, gift inscription dated 1643 (to Ludovicus Chimaer from G. van Alphen) and ownership inscription dated 1669, contemporary vellum, board fore-edges overlapping, spine lettered in ink, soiled and bit nicked, hinges cracking but sound, rear flyleaf removed, armorial bookplate of Rich. Palmer, Esq. Blackwell's Rare Books Greek & Latin Classics VII - 41 2016 £500

Association – Pankova, Libuse

Eliot, Thomas Stearns 1888-1965 *Tam Domov Mas. (East Coker).* East Coker: PEN Clubs, 1941. First Czech edition, one of 750 copies, foolscap 8vo., tipped in frontispiece by John Piper, one or two instances of Pencil annotation to margins, original stapled printed wrappers tifle dust soiled, laid slip laid in, very good, inscribed by translator, Libuse Pankova. Blackwell's Rare Books B186 - 212 2016 £300

Association – Panton, Jan

Inchbald, Elizabeth *A Simple Story.* London: printed for G. G. J. and J. Robinson, 1791. Second edition, half titles discarded, ownership inscription of Jan Panton, touch of light soiling and browning, one leaf in volume I with small paper flaw to blank margin, one gathering in volume iii rough at bottom edge (missed by binder's knife), 8vo., late 19th century half calf, sometime rebacked to style, dark brown morocco lettering pieces, marbled boards, edges and endpapers, slightly rubbed, corners bit worn, hinges neatly relined, good. Blackwell's Rare Books B186 - 80 2016 £500

Association – Paoly, Charles

Frederick, J. George *Long Island Seafood Cook Book.* New York: Business Course, 1939. First edition, octavo, fine in just about fine dust jacket, inscribed by Frederick for Charles Paoly, Sea Isle Hotel, Miami Beach, beautiful copy. Between the Covers Rare Books 204 - 33 2016 $800

Association – Pardonneau

Prudentius Clemens, Aurelius *Opera.* Amsterdam: Apud Danielem Elzevirium, 1667. 12mo., title in red and black with printer's device and hand ruled lines, separate half title to Heinsius notes, occasional engraved initials and head and tailpieces, little toned but generally clean, contemporary vellum, title inked to spine in old hand, yapp edges, edges sprinkled blue, some smudgy marks, endcaps creased, turn-ins lifting slightly causing cracks to edges of endpapers, but all holding firm, Pardonneau of Tours to front pastedown, armorial bookplate of Samuel Alfred Steinthal. Unsworths Antiquarian Booksellers Ltd. E01 - Early Printing - 19 2016 £175

Association – Pargeter, Edmund Ellis

Peters, Ellis *The Lily Hand: and Other Stories.* London: Heinemann, 1965. First edition, octavo, boards, signed inscriptions, first from author to brother Edmund Ellis Pargeter, second to Sue (could be Sue Feder), fine in nearly fine dust jacket with touch of dustiness and very mild stress wrinkle to lower front panel. John W. Knott, Jr./L.W. Currey, Inc. Fall-Winter 2015 - 16212 2016 $325

Association – Paris, Gaston

Jusserand, J. J. *La Vie Nomade et Les Routes D'Angleterre au XIVe Siecle.* Paris: Hachette, 1884. 8vo., quarter black roan with marbled boards, spine in seven compartments with raised bands, gilt, rubbed, corners bit bumped and worn, marble endpapers, prelims darkened a little but text block clean, edges uncut, general dustiness but still good, author's inscription to Gaston Paris, philanthropist, stamp of St. Ignatius College Amsterdam. Unsworths Antiquarian Booksellers 30 - 90 2016 £60

Association – Park, Thomas

Strong, James *Joanereidos; or Feminine Valour...* London: reprinted Anno Dom., 1674. Second edition, small 4to., spotted and lightly browned, some tearing in inner margin of title and following two leaves caused by original stitching, many edges uncut, early19th century half calf and marbled boards, headcaps damaged and edges rubbed, from the library of James Stevens Cox (1910-1997), signature of Edward Rowe Mores (1730-1778), the copy of James Boswell the younger (1778-1822), small signature of Thomas Park (1658/9-1834).   Maggs Bros. Ltd.   1447 - 402   2016   £1500

Association – Parke, Florence

Frost, Robert Lee   1874-1963   *A Masque of Reason.* New York: Holt, 1945. First edition, #724 of 800 large paper copies, signed by author, inscribed by author to Florence Parke, 8vo., fine in some worn slip-case, untrimmed.   Second Life Books, Inc.   197 - 136   2016 $650

Association – Parker, Gilbert

Jones, Henry Arthur   *Patriotism and Popular Education...* London: Chapman & Hall, 1919. Presentation inscription, from author for Gilbert Parker.   Jarndyce Antiquarian Books   CCXV - 795   2016   £65

Association – Parker, R.

Bewick, Thomas   1753-1828   *History of British Birds.* Newcastle: Edward Walker for T. Bewick, 1804, but, 1814-1816. 1804.Fifth edition of volume I (Land Birds), variant B with vignette of ploughman and milkmaid added to page 296; first edition
volume II Water Birds, first state of woodcuts, 241 x 149mm., very pleasing contemporary diced calf, covers with triple fillet rules and blindstamped palmette roll border, raised bands, spine compartments with elaborate assemblage of gilt fleurons, gilt titling, gilt rolled turn-ins, marbled endleaves; with 218 fine woodcut figures of birds as well as 227 charming vignettes by Thomas Bewick, large paper copy, verso of front free endpapers with small ink ownership stamp of R. Parker; one joint just slightly rubbed, couple of short black (ink?) marks to one board, one leaf with neat repairs to two short tears at inner margin, one gathering (only) rather foxed, isolated trivial foxing elsewhere, otherwise especially fine, fresh copy internally and in very well preserved original binding.   Phillip J. Pirages   67 - 25   2016 $1600

Association – Parlade, Jaime

Bacon, Francis   1909-1992   *Francis Bacon.* Paris: Galeries Nationales du Grand Palais, 1971. First edition, small quarto, numerous color reproductions, presentation from Bacon for Spanish interior designer Jaime Parlade, one of two of the folding plates creased at fore-edge, very good.   Peter Ellis   112 - 26   2016   £1500

Association – Parr, E. D.

Carlisle, Isabella Howard, Countess of   *Thoughts in the Form of maxims Addressed to Young Ladies.*   London: printed for T. Cornwell, 1790. Second edition, 8vo., half title, contemporary tree calf, neat repairs to extremities expertly rebacked, maroon morocco label, contemporary inscription "E. D. Parr from F. Evans".   Jarndyce Antiquarian Books   CCXV - 98   2016   £30

Association – Parsons, Fanny

Arbis, Robert   *The Lord's Woods. The Passing of an American Woodland.*   New York: Norton, 1971. First edition, inscribed by author for Fanny Parsons, small owner label apparently over another name on front flyleaf, near fine in very good, modestly rubbed and spine faded dust jacket internally tape strengthened at spine base.   Ken Lopez Bookseller   166 - 6   2016 $200

Association – Partridge, Frances

Carpenter, Alejo   *The War of Time.*   London: Victor Gollancz, 1970. First UK edition, head of spine and one corner slightly bumped, very good in like dust jacket (slightly dusty), presentation copy by translator, Frances Partridge to Bloomsbury artist Eardley Knollys.   Peter Ellis   112 - 63   2016   £200

Association – Passavant, Lucile

Vergilius Maro, Publius   *Les Bucoliques.*   Paris: Philippe Gonin, 1951. One of 200 copies, 327 x 248mm., loose as issued in publisher's cream colored wrappers and vellum backed portfolio, black titling on spine, in later patterned paper slipcase with 80 wood engravings by Lucile Passavant, first prelim leaf warmly inscribed to Ed and Mary (Thom?), inscribed by the artist for the Thoms, greeting card illustrated by artist inscribed for Thoms laid in, hint of soil to spine, corners worn to boards, faint freckling to covers, text with isolated trivial foxing, excellent copy, text clean and fresh and binding a good deal more than good enough.   Phillip J. Pirages   67 - 348   2016 $3000

Association – Passmore, Elsie

Dickens, Charles 1812-1870 *Hard Times for These Times.* London: Bradbury & Evans (Chapman & Hall), 1870. First edition, remainder issue using original sheets, remainder binding, original green pebble grained cloth, carefully recased, slight rubbing, good plus, half title obscured by Elsie and Stanley Passmore booklabel, repairs to inner hinges. Jarndyce Antiquarian Booksellers CCXVIII - 528 2016 £350

Association – Passmore, Stanley

Dickens, Charles 1812-1870 *Hard Times for These Times.* London: Bradbury & Evans (Chapman & Hall), 1870. First edition, remainder issue using original sheets, remainder binding, original green pebble grained cloth, carefully recased, slight rubbing, good plus, half title obscured by Elsie and Stanley Passmore booklabel, repairs to inner hinges. Jarndyce Antiquarian Booksellers CCXVIII - 528 2016 £350

Association – Patmore, Coventry

Davison, Henry *Dove Sono.* London: Kegan Paul Trench, Trubner & Co., 1894. Half title, original olive green cloth, gilt, slightly rubbed, inscribed by Coventry Patmore for Francis Patmore. Jarndyce Antiquarian Booksellers CCXVII - 82 2016 £125

Association – Patmore, Francis

Davison, Henry *Dove Sono.* London: Kegan Paul Trench, Trubner & Co., 1894. Half title, original olive green cloth, gilt, slightly rubbed, inscribed by Coventry Patmore for Francis Patmore. Jarndyce Antiquarian Booksellers CCXVII - 82 2016 £125

Association – Pattison, Mark

Phillips, Edward *Theatrum Poetarum Anglicanorum,...* London: Canterbury, 1800. First printing of this enlarged, updated edition, 203 x 121mm., appealing recent brown quarter morocco over linen boards, raised bands, red morocco label, front flyleaf with ownership inscription of 'G.D./Canonbury' (George Daniel of Canonbury Square, Islington, titlepage with small discreet embossed stamp of 'Mark Pattison, Lincoln College, Oxon", in exceptionally fine condition inside and out. Phillip J. Pirages 67 - 243 2016 $750

Association – Payne, Ismera

Turner, Sharon *The History of the Anglo-Saxons from the earliest Period to the Norman Conquest.* London: Longman, Rees, Orme, Brown, Green & Longman, 1836. Sixth edition, 3 volumes 8vo., folding map to volume 1, map foxed and occasional spots of foxing elsewhere, publisher's half cloth and grey boards, printed paper labels to spines, edges uncut, all volumes neatly rebacked with original spines retained, endpapers replaced, rubbed, edges worn, corners bumped, gift inscription "Agnes M. Scully from her mama Ismera Payne Jan. 25th 1840, library stamp of Abbat S. Martae e. Berholten. Unsworths Antiquarian Booksellers Ltd. E05 - 111 2016 £150

Association – Peacock, Henry

The Self-Instructor or Young Man's Companion... London: Henry Fisher, c., 1823. Additional engraved title and 8 plates, plates slightly browned and with small damp marking, contemporary half calf, red morocco label, rubbed, overall nice, signature of Henry S. Peacock, Maddlockstones. Jarndyce Antiquarian Books CCXV - 401 2016 £220

Association – Peale, Norman Vincent

Hoover, Herbert *The Problems of Lasting Peace.* Garden City: Doubleday Doran and Co., 1942. 2nd printing (as per jacket), about fine in very good, internally tape repaired dust jacket with several small nicks and tears, inscribed by author for Norman Vincent Peale. Between the Covers Rare Books 204 - 57 2016 $950

Association – Pearce, Robert

Sprigg, William *A Modest Plea, for an Equal Common-Wealth Against Monarchy.* London: for Giles Calvert, 1659. One of two editions, 8vo., blank upper corner of A1-E1 and I8-K4 intermittently dampstained, some occasional light soiling and few light ink drops to gatherings A and B, contemporary sheep, recently rebacked and recornered, new endpapers, from the library of James Stevens Cox (1910-1997), 17th century signatures of Robert Pearce, signature of Sir Frederick Rogers (1716-1777) 4th Baronet of Wisdome in Devon. Maggs Bros. Ltd. 1447 - 395 2016 £950

Association – Pearson, E. Kendall

On the Origin of Sam Weller and the Real Cause of the Success of the Posthumous Papers of the Pickwick Club by a Lover of Charles Dickens's Works. Together with a Facsimile Reprint of the Beauties of Pickwick. London: J. W. Jarvis, 1883. Frontispiece, title in red and black, original blue printed wrappers, small tear in outer margin of front cover not affecting text, ownership signature of E. Kendall Pearson. Jarndyce Antiquarian Booksellers CCXVIII - 134 2016 £20

Association – Pearson, Karl

Poisson, Simeon Denis *Recherches sur la Probabilite des Jugements en Matiere Criminelle et en Matiere Civile Precedes des Regeles Generales de Calcul des Probabilites.* Paris: Bachelier, 1837. First edition, half title, light foxing within, original quarter dark green gilt stamped calf, marbled boards, extremities worn, very good, signature of Karl Pearson (1857-1936). Jeff Weber Rare Books 183 - 25   2016 $4000

Association – Pearson, S., Mrs.

Jones, Robert *Artificial Fireworks, Improved to the Modern Practice, from the Minutest to the Highest Branches.* Chelmsford: printed and sold by Meggy and Chalk, 1801. 210 x 137mm., very pleasing recent retrospective smooth calf, raised bands, red morocco label, edges entirely untrimmed, with 20 copper engraved plates (printed on both sides of leaves) showing various pyrotechnical apparatuses, inscription in 19th century hand for Mrs. S. Pearson, Steeton; minor foxing and soiling there, but generally text in excellent condition, unexpectedly clean and fresh, unworn sympathetic binding. Phillip J. Pirages 67 - 290   2016 $950

Association – Pease, John William

Dibdin, Thomas Frognall   1776-1847 *An Introduction to the Knowledge of Rare and Valuable Editions of the Greek and Latin Classics.* London: printed for Harding & Lepard, 1827. Fourth edition, 2 volumes, 292 x 1977, handsome early 20th century brown straight grain morocco, covers with gilt double fillet border, fleuron cornerpieces, raised bands, spines richly gilt with panels dominated by bold and complex quatrefoil incorporating spade-like tools and with palmette cornerpieces, turn-ins with two gilt fillets, marbled endpapers, all edges gilt, with facsimile of Greek and Latin text from the Complutensian Polyglot and volume I with specimen leaf laid down, as called for, large paper copy, engraved armorial bookplate of John William Pease, rear pastedown with vellum armorial bookplate of Lord Wardington, touch of rubbing to tail edge of boards, one leaf with thin band of soiling along four inches of the fore edge, light glue stain at lower corner of specimen leaf, endpapers with faint fox spots (isolated minor foxing elsewhere), other trivial imperfections but generally, very fine, text clean and fresh with vast margins and decorative bindings with no significant wear. Phillip J. Pirages 67 - 112   2016 $4500

Association – Pecke, Philip

White, John *A Way to the Tree of Life.* London: Miles Fletcher for R. Royston, 1647. First edition, 8vo., without final blank titlepage browned and slightly shaved at fore-edge, small piece torn away from blank corner of A4, browned throughout with small dark marks on N6-8, final blank page stained by turn-ins and with edges little ragged, contemporary calf, rebacked, corners repaired, new endleaves, small inscription of John Witham, inscription of Philip Pecke, from the library of James Stevens Cox (1910-1997). Maggs Bros. Ltd. 1447 - 448   2016   £500

Association – Peckhove, Elizabeth

Beddow, Mrs. *Use Them; or Gathered Fragments: Missionary Hints and Anecdotes for the Young.* London: Hamilton Adams & Co., 1842. Second edition, 12mo., original brown cloth, contemporary inscription of Elizabeth Peckhove, very good. Jarndyce Antiquarian Books CCXV - 531   2016   £50

Association – Peel, Robert

Ireland, William Henry   1777-1835 *Memoirs of Jeanne D'Arc surnamed La Pucelle D'Orleans with the History of Her Times.* London: printed for Robert Triphood, 1824. 2 volumes, 8vo., 2 plates, sporadic foxing, some toning to plates and offsetting to facing pages, half green morocco marbled paper covered boards, raised bands, gilt title to spine, top edge gilt, other edges uncut, marbled endpapers, spines faded and little scratched, joints and endcaps rubbed, little scuffed, still very good, armorial bookplate of Sir Robert Peel, later bookplate of John Porter, small inkstamp "Mentmore". Unsworths Antiquarian Booksellers 30 - 87   2016   £180

Association – Pelser, Joanni Petro

Claudianus, Claudius *Opera quae Exstant Omnia ad Membranarum Veterum Fidem Castigata.* Amstelodami: ex officina Schouteniana, 1760. First edition thus 4to., additional presentation certificate bound in, titlepage in red and black, woodcut device, woodcut had and tailpieces and initials, titlepage little dusty, occasional light spots of foxing, slightly toned towards top edge, generally clean within, contemporary Dutch prize vellum, raised bands, blind tooling and black morocco label to spine, gilt panels and centerpieces to both boards with coat of arms of Amsterdam, edges lightly sprinkled blue, two small holes to vellum at spine, label chipped, ties lost, somewhat grubby but very good, sound, overall, printed prize certificate dated 1796 made out by hand to Joanni Petro Pelser and signed by College of Amsterdam rector H. Hana. Unsworths Antiquarian Booksellers 30 - 36   2016   £350

Association – Perceval, William

Dissertations and Miscellaneous Pieces Relating to the History and Antiquities, the Arts, Sciences and Literature of Asia. Dublin: printed for Messrs. P. Byrne, Grafton Street and W. Jones, Dame Street, 1793. 8vo., contemporary tree calf, gilt banded spine, red morocco label, joints and head and tail of spine expertly repaired, armorial bookplate of William Perceval, Esq., faint gilt crest and number at foot of spine.   Jarndyce Antiquarian Booksellers   CCXVI - 334   2016   £285

Moule, Thomas   *Great Britain Illustrated.*   London: Charles Tilt, 1830. First edition in book form, striking, contemporary embossed 'Relievo' burgundy morocco by Remnant & Edmonds (their stamp), covers densely patterned with three very complex foliate frames around a central medallion featuring the muses Erato, Calliope and Euterpe, flat spine with gilt titling at head and an elaborate embossed pattern below, turn-ins with floral gilt roll all edges gilt, extra engraved titlepage with vignette and 118 engraved views on 59 plates by William Westall, as called for, original tissue guards, front pastedown with armorial bookplate of William Perceval, majority of plates with minor foxing and offsetting (two or three engravings foxed, bit more, engraved title and facing page rather noticeably affected), spine slightly and uniformly sunned, joints with vaguest hint of rubbing but text especially fresh clean and bright and stricking binding virtually unworn, very lustrous covers that retain all of the original sharpness of their intricate blind decoration.   Phillip J. Pirages   67 - 62   2016 $1000

Segar, Simon   *Honores Anglicani or Titles of Honour the Temporal Nobility of the English Nation.*   London: printed for John Baker at the Black Boy in Pater Noster Row, 1712. 8vo., some foxing and browning, contemporary panelled calf, raised bands, red morocco label, faint gilt crest at foot, expert repairs to joints and head and tail of spine, armorial bookplate of William Perceval, signature on titlepage and shelf number at head and early name Alex. McNaghton.   Jarndyce Antiquarian Booksellers   CCXVI - 513   2016   £380

Smith, Charles   *The Antient and present State of the County of Kerry.*   Dublin: printed for the author, 1756. 8vo., large folding map, 4 folding plates, lacks plate of Skelig island, 8vo, folding map neatly mounted on to a new guard, several expert repairs on verso, short tear along one fold without loss, slight foxing and little fingermarking to some leading edges, general good, clean copy, contemporary calf raised bands, red morocco label, joints and head and tail of spine expertly repaired, old vertical crease slightly visible, armorial bookplate of William Perceval Esq., his initials and shelf number to titlepage, gilt crest at foot of spine.   Jarndyce Antiquarian Booksellers   CCXVI - 531   2016   £380

Association – Perceval-Maxwell

Roberts, George   *The Four Years Voyages of Capt. George Roberts....*   London: printed for A. Bettesworth, 1726. 8vo., folding frontispiece map, 4 engraved plates, paper rather browned but in good sound condition, full contemporary panelled calf, raised bands, expert repairs to joints and head and tail of spine, from the library of Perceval-Maxwell with shelf number at head of titlepage, faint gilt crest and number at foot of spine.   Jarndyce Antiquarian Booksellers   CCXVI - 495   2016   £480

Temple, John   *The Irish Rebellion or an History of the Beginnings and First Progress of the General Rebellion...*   London: 1724. Sixth edition, reprinted from London edition of 1679, 4to., light browning, frontispiece foxed, titlepage printed in red and black, 4to., light browning, frontispiece foxed, contemporary mottled calf, expert repairs to joints and head and tail of unlettered spine, from the library of Perceval-Maxwell family, contemporary ownership initials WP, 19th century news clipping.   Jarndyce Antiquarian Booksellers   CCXVI - 563   2016   £650

Association – Percival, Kene

Robinson, John   *An Account of Sueden; Together with an Extract of the History of the Kingdom.*   London: Tim Goodwin, 1694. First edition, 8vo., initial leaf with half title on recto and ad on verso, A1-4 browned, E8-8 and O1-2 browned and spotted, small semi-circular chip from fore-edge of front flyleaf, contemporary sprinkled calf, spine with gilt thistle crest in fourth panel and gilt shelf mark in final one (covers detached, edges and corners worn, headcaps torn away and with small white splash of paint on upper board), from the library of James Stevens Cox (1910-1997) the copy of Rev. Kene Percival (1709?-74?) with his gilt thistle crest, S. or J. Foley signature.   Maggs Bros. Ltd.   1447 - 366   2016   £100

Association – Perelman, S. J.

Lewis, Norman   *Darkness Visible - a Novel.*   London: Jonathan Cape, 1960. First edition, octavo, little bumped and faded at edges, very good, in very good dust jacket, marked, nicked and rubbed at edges, presentation copy inscribed by author for S. J. Perelman and his wife.   Peter Ellis   112 - 224   2016   £650

Lewis, Norman   *Samara.*   London: Jonathan Cape, 1949. First edition, octavo, very scarce, presentation copy inscribed by author to American humourist S. J. Perelman, very good in very good price clipped dust jacket, tanned and little defective at head and tail of spine and little torn, nicked and creased at edges.   Peter Ellis   112 - 221   2016   £1250

Lewis, Norman *A Single Pilgrim - a Novel.* London: Jonathan Cape, 1953. First edition, octavo, presentation copy inscribed by author for S. J. Perelman, covers bruised at head of spine and at top edge of upper board, very good in very good nicked, rubbed and creased dust jacket with closed tear at fold of upper flap.   Peter Ellis   112 - 222   2016   £650

Lewis, Norman *The Tenth Year of the Ship.* London: Collins, 1962. First edition, octavo, head of spine and upper corners little bruised, very good in very good dust jacket, nicked and rubbed, little defective at tail of spine, presentation copy inscribed by author for S. J. Perelman and his wife.   Peter Ellis   112 - 225   2016   £650

Association – Perowne, Stewart

Grahame, Kenneth 1859-1932 *The Wind in the Willows.* London: Methuen and Co., 1908. First edition, gilt lettering and designs fresh and bright, little wear at edges and covers, few very light stains, some professional color restoration, prelims and endleaves somewhat darkened and foxed as usual and edges of some leaves also foxed, nice, increasingly scarce, ownership inscription erased from flyleaf, but from the library of Dame Freya Stark and husband Stewart Perowne, bearing their Asolo bookplate.   Bertram Rota Ltd.   Christmas List 2015 - 13   2016   £4000

Association – Perrett, John

Vergilius Maro, Publius *Opera Varietate Lectiones et Perpetua Adnotations Illustra....* Typis T.. Rickaby, Impensis T. Payne, B. & J. White, R. Faulder, & J. Edwards, 1793. Large paper copy, engraved frontispiece and dedication, one bifolium missed by stitching and hence loose, little minor toning and spotting, 4to., contemporary straight grained red morocco by Kalthoeber, with his ticket in volume i, boards bordered with triple gilt fillet, spines divided by raised bands between gilt titles, second and third compartments, gilt lettered direct, edges gilt, marbled endpapers, joints rubbed, spines somewhat scuffed, little darkening to spine and joints, from old polishing attempt?, short tear to head of front joint volume i, armorial bookplate of John Perrett, good.   Blackwell's Rare Books   B184 - 88   2016   £1200

Association – Peterson, Dorothy

Van Vechten, Carl 1880-1964 *Nigger Heaven.* New York: Alfred A. Knopf, 1926. First edition, some chipping to cloth at crown, front hinge neatly restored, still sound, very good, lacking rare dust jacket, inscribed by author for Dorothy Peterson, spectacular association copy.   Between the Covers Rare Books   202 - 110   2016 $4000

Association – Phelipps

Homerus *The Iliad of Homer.* London: printed by W. Bowyer for Bernard Lintott, 1715-1720. First edition translated by Alexander Pope, folio, plates and maps, period full paneled calf, bindings with spine labels to volumes 1, 5 and 6 only, personal owner gilt stamped name ("I. Phelipps Y", label to volume 6 chipped, some wear to spines and joints tender though bindings overall sound and quite appealing, minor worming to margins of volumes 1, 3, 5 and 6, some gatherings little browned as often found, short tear to volume II f.f.e.p., period personal ownership signature to front free endpapers, withal very good set.   Tavistock Books   Bibliolatry - 16   2016 $7500

Synesius of Cyrene *(Opera).* Paris: Ex officina Andriani Turnebe, 1553. First printing, folio, small rusthole to one leaf affecting one or two characters on each side, some faint dampmarking in places, titlepage dusty and just slightly frayed ar corner, chapters neatly numbered in early hand, folio, early 18th century sprinkled calf, boards bordered with triple gilt fillet, small floral gilt cornerpieces inside, expertly rebacked preserving original spine compartments with central gilt floral tools, new red morocco lettering piece, hinges neatly relined, ownership inscription of Phelipps, good copy.   Blackwell's Rare Books   B184 - 82   2016   £1200

Association – Phelps, Ms.

Tegg, William *The Cruet Stand or Sauce Piquante to suit all Tastes.* London: William Tegg, 1871. First edition, 32 page catalog, original purple cloth, bevelled boards, blocked in black and gilt, spine faded to brown, back board slightly marked, inscription to Ms. Phelps with editor's kind wishes.   Jarndyce Antiquarian Books   CCXV - 435   2016   £40

Association – Phelps, Professor

Savidge, Eugene Coleman *The American In Paris.* Philadelphia: Lippincott, 1896. Second edition, 12mo., brown cloth stamped in silver, inscribed by author to Professor Phelps with author's compliments, very good, tight copy.   Second Life Books, Inc.   196 B - 530   2016 $85

Association – Philbrick, C. W.

Swan, James G. *The Northwest Coast; or Three Years' Residence in Washington Territory.* New York: Harper & Bros., 1857. First edition, publisher's brown buckram, flat spine with gilt tiling, 29 illustrations by author, 18 of these full page, one a folding map, front free endpaper, inscribed by author to Mrs. C. W. Philbrick, with neatly stamped signature of Ellen Philbrick, bookplate of Frederick V. Holman, spine bit sunned, extremities slightly worn, small patches of water(?) stains to boards, other trivial imperfections, really excellent copy, fresh and clean, original fragile binding still solid and generally well preserved.   Phillip J. Pirages   67 - 271   2016 $1100

Association – Philbrick, Ellen

Swan, James G. *The Northwest Coast; or Three Years' Residence in Washington Territory.* New York: Harper & Bros., 1857. First edition, publisher's brown buckram, flat spine with gilt tiling, 29 illustrations by author, 18 of these full page, one a folding map, front free endpaper, inscribed by author to Mrs. C. W. Philbrick, with neatly stamped signature of Ellen Philbrick, bookplate of Frederick V. Holman, spine bit sunned, extremities slightly worn, small patches of water(?) stains to boards, other trivial imperfections, really excellent copy, fresh and clean, original fragile binding still solid and generally well preserved. Phillip J. Pirages 67 - 271 2016 $1100

Association – Philles, E. P.

Dickens, Charles 1812-1870 *The Haunted Man and the Ghost's Bargain.* New York: Harper & Bros., 1849. First American edition, slightly spotted, sewn as issued in original brown printed wrappers, old stab holes in inner margin, contemporary signature of E. P. Philles, very good. Jarndyce Antiquarian Booksellers CCXVIII - 392 2016 £350

Association – Phillipps, Robert Biddulph

Plot, Robert *The Natural History of Oxford-shire.* Oxford: printed by Leon Litchfield for Charles Brome... and John Nicholson, 1705. Second edition, folio, 17 plates including folded map, occasional spotting but generally bright and clean, map very slightly toned with small tear near attachment, contemporary tan calf boards, neatly rebacked in marginally lighter shade, raised bands, green morocco gilt title label, all edges red upper hinge reinforced, little ms. to f.f.e.p., rear endpapers renewed, few small scrapes and marks but very good, armorial bookplates of Powell Snell and Robert Biddulh Phillipps, bookseller's ticket of Myers and Co. Unsworths Antiquarian Booksellers Ltd. E05 - 9 2016 £1500

Association – Phillips, Ernest

Murray, L. *The Young Man's Best Companion and Book of General Knowledge...* London: Thomas Kelly, 1822. Additional engraved title, plates, some occasional pencil markings, heavy in places, lacing following f.e.p., contemporary black calf, borders in gilt and blind, gilt bands and compartments, red morocco label, boards little marked, signature of Ernest Phillips 1892, good plus. Jarndyce Antiquarian Books CCXV - 331 2016 £110

Association – Phillips, John Charles

Ireland, Alleyne *The Far Eastern Tropics, Studies in the administration of tropical Dependencies.* Boston and New York: Houghton Mifflin and Co., 1905. First edition, 8vo., original green ribbed cloth lettered in gilt, very light toning, near fine, signed presentation inscribed by author to John C. Phillips. Sotheran's Travel and Exploration - 138 2016 £398

Association – Phillips, William G.

Reynolds, Joshua *The Works Containing His Discourses, Idlers, A Journey to Flanders and Holland....* London: printed for T. Cadell Jun. and W. Davies, 1797. 2 volumes in one, 4to., frontispiece causing light offset to title, some lower and outer margins untrimmed, volume 1 title and one or two gatherings in volume 2 lightly foxed, closed tears in lower blank portion of last leaf, contemporary gilt ruled diced calf, spine ruled and decorated in gilt, brown morocco label, marbled endpapers and edges, silk marker, trifle rubbed, engraved bookplate of Revd. Willm. G. Phillips, Elling. Hants, very handsome, clean copy with wide margins. Jarndyce Antiquarian Booksellers CCXVI - 490 2016 £380

Association – Phipps, Penelope

Caraccioli, Louis Antoine *Advice from a Lady of Quality to Her Children in the Last Stage of a Lingering Illness.* Gloucester: printed by R Raikes and sold by J. F. & C. Rivington, 1766. Fourth edition, 8vo., full contemporary green crushed morocco, boards elaborately blocked in gilt, raised bands, compartments in gilt, spine slightly faded and rubbed, 2 small nicks to front board, presentation inscription "Penelope Phipps given by Revd. James Esqr. August 18th 1805, with additional inscription beneath dated 1851, all edges gilt, very good, handsome copy. Jarndyce Antiquarian Books CCXV - 97 2016 £420

Association – Phipps, Pownoll William

Darwin, Charles Robert 1809-1882 *On the Origin of Species by means of natural Selection...* London: W. Clowes and Sons for John Murray, 1859. First edition, 8vo. in 12's, original green cloth by Edmonds & Remnants, London retaining their ticket on lower pastedown, boards blocked in blind, rules enclosing foliate designs and central panel, spine gilt, mid brown endpapers, green cloth solander box with printed paper label to spine, 32 publisher's catalog dated June 1859, Freeman variant 3, folding lithographic plate by William West after Darwin, slight rubbing and bumping to extremities with very small ink spot to front board, hinges skillfully restored, little chipped to edges of endpapers and few leaves, nonetheless very bright, fresh copy in original cloth, bookplate of Pownoll William Phipps (b. 1835) using arms and motto of Earls of Mulgrave, whom he was a cousin. Sotheran's Piccadilly Notes - Summer 2015 - 5 2016 £95,000

Association – Pickering, George

Gray, Thomas 1716-1771 *The Works of Thomas Gray.* London: Harding, Triphook and Lepard, 1825. 2 volumes, extremely appealing contemporary red straight grain morocco, attractively gilt by Ingalton of Eton (with their ticket), 197 x 114mm., covers with double fillet border enclosing a triple fillet frame with gilt tooled leafy cornerpieces, central panel enclosed by single fillet with roundel corners, raised bands, spine compartments gilt with leafy frames, turn-ins with dense gilt roll, all edges gilt, engraved frontispiece portrait of gray, first prelim leaf to volume I with inked inscription 'George Chester Cooper/Given to him by his friend George Pickering/Eton. March 1830", just vaguest rubbing and abrasions to covers, minor foxing to frontispiece and prelim leaves, pretty set in very fine condition, clean and fresh internally, gleaming bindings with virtually no wear.   Phillip J. Pirages   67 - 45   2016 $950

Association – Pilgate, Hadie

Philp, Robert Kemp *The Practical Housewife, a Complete Encyclopaedia of Domestic Economy and Family Medical guide.* London: Houlston & Wright, 1860. New edition, half title, frontispiece, illustrations, original dark green cloth, blocked in blind and gilt, expertly recased, ownership signature of Hadie Pilgate, inscription, nice.   Jarndyce Antiquarian Books   CCXV - 366   2016   £85

Association – Plunkett, R. E.

Mignan, Robert *Travels in Chaldaea, Including a Journey from Bussourah to Bagdad, Hillah and Babylon, performed on foot in 1827...* London: Henry Colburn, 1829. First edition, 8vo., contemporary original blue cloth, yellow endpapers, aquatint frontispiece and five aquatint plates printed in sepia, retaining tissue guards, two engraved folding maps, wood engraved illustrations in text, light rubbing to cloth, here and there little spotted, very good in rarely seen publisher's binding, contemporary ownership inscription of R. E. Plunkett.   Sotheran's   Travel and Exploration - 346   2016   £798

Association – Plymell, Charles

Burroughs, William S. *Naked Lunch.* Paris: Olympia Press, 1965. Reprint, printed green wrappers, modest edgewear, slight tear at base of spine, very good or better, without dust jacket, inscribed by author to poet and publisher Charles Plymell, with program for the memorial Service held for Burroughs in Lawrence, Kansas in 1997, fine, with small business card sized poem, signed by Plymell.   Between the Covers Rare Books   208 - 14   2016 $5000

Association – Politi, Leo

Clark, Ann Nolan *Magic Money.* New York: Viking, 1950. First edition, 8vo., red cloth, fine in very good dust jacket frayed at head of spine and bit worn at fold, wonderful color illustrations by Leo Politi, laid in is note from Politi and two color photos of him.   Aleph-bet Books, Inc.   112 - 386   2016 $175

Association – Pollard, Graham

Carter, John 1905-1975 *An Enquiry into the Nature of Certain Nineteenth Century Pamphlets.* London: Constable & Co., 1934. First edition, 8vo., cloth, top edge gilt, dust jacket, this copy inscribed by Carter and Graham Pollard, with bookplate of noted collector Abel Berland, jacket rubbed along spine and hinges along with some fading to spine, rather well preserved.   Oak Knoll Books   310 - 204   2016 $550

Association – Polly, Louisa

Monro, George *Extracts. Doctrinal, Practical and Devotional.* London: William Darton and Son, 1836. 19th century blind stamped binding, inscribed by editor, Joseph Fry for Raymond & Louisa Polly, , octavo, full contemporary decoratively blindstamped blue morocco, spine lettered gilt, all edges gilt, near fine.   David Brass Rare Books, Inc.   2015 - 03012   2016 $150

Association – Polly, Raymond

Monro, George *Extracts. Doctrinal, Practical and Devotional.* London: William Darton and Son, 1836. 19th century blind stamped binding, inscribed by editor, Joseph Fry for Raymond & Louisa Polly, octavo, full contemporary decoratively blindstamped blue morocco, spine lettered gilt, all edges gilt, near fine.   David Brass Rare Books, Inc.   2015 - 03012   2016 $150

Association – Ponsonby, Richard

Steinmetz, Andrew *Japan and Her People.* London: Routledge, Warne and Routledge, 1859. First edition, good to very good, original blue pebbled cloth, blindstamped with elaborate gilt design on cover, armorial bookplate of Richard Ponsonby.   Simon Finch   2015 - 000253   2016 $245

Association – Pool, Josephine Fowler

Young, Rose *The Record of the Leslie Woman Suffrage Commission Inc. 1917-1929.* Leslie Commission, 1929. First edition, small 8vo., little soiled cloth, very good, inscribed by Carrie Chapman Catt for Josephine Fowler Pool.   Second Life Books, Inc.   196A - 263   2016 $600

Association – Poole, Eric

William, of Malmsbury *Gesta Regum Angliorum.* London: English Historical Society, 1840. First edition, 2 volumes, 8vo., text in Latin, printed marginalia and footnotes in English, volume I pages 369-384 lacking and replaced with facsimiles, adjacent pages somewhat soiled but text perfectly legible, original brown paper covered boards, skillfully rebacked in well matched brown paper, black morocco gilt labels, edges uncut, some stains and scratches to boards, labels little rubbed, edges dusted, bookplate 'Ex Oblatorum C. Caroli Bibliothecca apud Bayswater', recent bookplate of Eric Poole,, several library ink margins to prelims of both volumes.   Unsworths Antiquarian Booksellers Ltd.   30 - 162   2016   £120

Association – Poole, Gray

Shawn, Ted *One Thousand and One Night Stands.* New York: Doubleday, 1960. First edition, signed by Shawn and inscribed by his collaborator Gray Poole, very good.   Second Life Books, Inc.   196 B - 563   2016 $75

Association – Poor, Henry William

Dante Alighieri   1265-1321 *The New Life of Dante Alghieri.* Cambridge: printed at the Riverside Press, 1892. No. 1 of 250 copies, 202 x 140mm., handsome brown crushed morocco, gilt by Club Bindery (stamp signed), covers with gilt french fillet border, central panel with double gilt rule frame and oblique fleuron cornerpieces, raised bands, spine gilt in compartments with floral cornerpieces and central floral ornament enclosed by a lozenge of small tools, gilt titling, densely gilt turn-ins, top edge gilt, other edges untrimmed, versos of front free endpaper, bookplate of Henry William Poor, "Bound to be the Best: The Club Bindery", just vague hint of rubbing to joints, free endpapers with usual offset shadow from binder's glue, couple of trivial spots internally, but fine, text clean, fresh and bright and in lustrous, scarcely worn binding.   Phillip J. Pirages   67 - 34   2016 $3250

Association – Popham, Francis White

Mathias, Thomas James *The Pursuits of Literature... (bound with) A Translation of the Passages from Greek, Latin, Italian and French Writers.* London: printed for T. Becket, 1798. Dublin: printed for J. Milliken... 1799. Fifth edition of first work, 8vo., very light marginal damp marking, slightly more intrusive at end, contemporary half vellum, marbled paper boards, little rubbed, little wear to lower joint, green morocco label, blue sprinkled edges, bookplate of William Bisset, Lessondrum, his signature dated 1798 and of Francis White Popham, sound, attractive copy.   Jarndyce Antiquarian Booksellers   CCXVI - 406   2016   £785

Association – Popham, Mary

Prior, Matthew   1664-1721 *Poems on Several Occasions.* London: for Jacob Tonson and John Barber, 1718. First collected edition, large paper copy, gift from Edward Harley for Mary Popham, royal folio, engraved frontispiece, titlepage vignette, headpieces and initial letters, engraved portrait of Prior dated 1719 neatly mounted to front flyleaf, contemporary calf, boards with two-line gold fillet enclosing blind decorative roll, board edges with gold decorative roll, spine very skillfully rebacked retaining original label, recornered, marbled endpapers, just lightest occasional foxing, else very good, lovely copy.   Joseph J. Felcone, Inc.   Books from Five Centuries: a Miscellany - 120   2016 $1400

Association – Porter, G. R.

Sturz, J. J. *A Review, Financial, Statistical & Commercial of the Empire of Brazil and Its Resources.* London: Effingham Wilson, 1837. First edition, 8vo., slightly later dark green pebble grained cloth, spine lettered gilt, yellow endpapers large folding table, others in text, very light marginal wear, title and last leaf little spotted due to offsetting from flyleaves, from Gloucestershire County Library with their stamps and shelfmarks, contemporary engraved armorial bookplate of G. R. Porter.   Sotheran's   Travel and Exploration - 74   2016   £398

Association – Porter, John

Ireland, William Henry   1777-1835 *Memoirs of Jeanne D'Arc surnamed La Pucelle D'Orleans with the History of Her Times.* London: printed for Robert Triphood, 1824. 2 volumes, 8vo., 2 plates, sporadic foxing, some toning to plates and offsetting to facing pages, half green morocco marbled paper covered boards, raised bands, gilt title to spine, top edge gilt, other edges uncut, marbled endpapers, spines faded and little scratched, joints and endcaps rubbed, little scuffed, still very good, armorial bookplate of Sir Robert Peel, later bookplate of John Porter, small inkstamp "Mentmore".   Unsworths Antiquarian Booksellers   30 - 87   2016   £180

Association – Porter, Katherine Anne

Moore, Marianne   1887-1972 *Collected Poems.* New York: Macmillan Co., 1951. First edition, American issue, 8vo., original reddish orange cloth, dust jacket, errata sheet tipped to page 9, one of 1500 copies printed (out of total printing of 5000 copies), presentation inscribed by author for Katherine Anne Porter, Dec. 3 1951, covers bit splayed, small photo of Moore affixed to front pastedown, otherwise very good in jacket (spine tanned with few small chips and split along spine gold).   James S. Jaffe Rare Books   Occasional List: Winter 2016 - 97   2016 $2250

Association – Porter, Peter

Jourtel, Henri *A Journal of the Last Voyage Perform'd by Monsr. de la Sale to the Gulph of Mexico to find out the Mouth of the Mississippi River...* London: for A. Bell, B. Lintot and J. Baker, 1714. First edition in English, engraved folding map, short closed tear, contemporary calf, extremities rubbed, top of spine bit worn, else lovely untouched copy, text clean and fresh and entirely unfoxed, Peter A Porter bookplate and Wolfgang Herz label. Joseph J. Felcone, Inc. Books from Five Centuries: a Miscellany - 85 2016 $15,000

Association – Portland, Duke of

Fosbroke, Thomas Dudley *Foreign Topography; or an Encyclopedick Account Alphabetically Arraigned....* London: J. B. Nichols, 1828. First edition, quarto, 11 plates, illustrations, contemporary full calf, spine little rubbed, there were 22 additional plates issued but not always bound in, bookplate of Duke of Portland. J. & S. L. Bonham Antiquarian Booksellers Voyages 2016 - 7712 2016 £120

Guibelet, Jourdain *Examen de l'Examen des Esprits.* Paris: M. Soly, 1631. First edition, 8vo., contemporary vellum, engraved printer's device on title, very scarce, bit of soiling to binding, else very good, large armorial bookplate of Duke of Portland. Edwin V. Glaser Rare Books 2015 - 10407 2016 $1200

Association – Poulin, A.

Our Exagmination Round His Factification for Incaminatiom of Work in Progress. Paris: Shakespeare and Co., 1929. First printing, one of 96 special copies in the limited edition (and 200 copies in the trade edition), 191 x 140mm., original printed paper wrappers designed by Sylvia Beach, front flyleaf with ink ownership inscription of "Arthur W. Poulin/ November 1944/San Francisco", one inch tears top of front and bottom of rear joint, spine little scuffed, covers with faint soiling, two small chips to fore edge of front cover, otherwise fragile wrappers in excellent condition, except for slight browning at edges because of paper stock, fine internally. Phillip J. Pirages 67 - 217 2016 $4000

Rike, Rainer, Maria 1875-1926 *The Astonishment of Origins.* Port Townsend: Graywolf Press, 1982. First printing, 12mo., blue cloth, stamped in gilt, signed by translator, A. Poulin, nice in dust jacket. Second Life Books, Inc. 196 B - 481 2016 $95

Rilke, Rainer Maria 1875-1926 *The Roses & the Windows.* Port Townsend: Greywold press, 1979. First edition, presentation from translator, A. Poulin for William Claire, green cloth stamped in gilt, nice in very slightly yellowed and soiled dust jacket. Second Life Books, Inc. 196 B - 483 2016 $75

Rilke, Rainer Maria 1875-1926 *The Roses and the Windows.* Port Townsend: Graywolf Press, 1979. One of 48 copies numbered and inscribed by translator, A. Poulin and W, D. Snodgrass, 12mo., green cloth stamped gilt, about as new in dust jacket. Second Life Books, Inc. 196 B - 482 2016 $250

Association – Pound, Ezra

Campbell, Roy 1901-1957 *The Flaming Terrapin.* London: Jonathan Cape, 1924. First edition, frontispiece, crown 8vo. original first state binding of quarter green cloth with patterned boards, backstrip with printed label, light toning to boards, little rubbing to extremities, top edge lightly dust soiled, others untrimmed, free endpapers lightly browned, small bookseller sticker, good, inscribed by Ezra Pound for Bertram Lloyd. Blackwell's Rare Books B186 - 273 2016 £300

Dialogue. Journal des Livres et des Idees No. 3. Lausanne: September, 1967. Folio, original self wrappers, printed on all sides, light overall toning, Quarter folded with horizontal points starting, from the library of actor Douglas Fairbanks Jr. with his loose bookplate in separate envelope, very good, warmly inscribed to Ezra Pound by Piero Sanavio. Blackwell's Rare Books B186 - 274 2016 £650

Eliot, Thomas Stearns 1888-1965 *Ezra Pound: His Metric and Poetry.* New York: Knopf, 1917. first edition of author's second book, one of 1000 copies, 12mo., frontispiece by Henri Gaudier Brzeska, original rose boards, top edge of boards near head of spine bumped, spine faded, otherwise very good, one of Ezra Pound's retained copies, with his contemporary blindstamped address and his holograph annotations to bibliography at back of book, top edge of boards near head of spine bumped, spine faded, otherwise very good. James S. Jaffe Rare Books Occasional List: Winter 2016 - 56 2016 $4500

Association – Powell, Thomas

Dickens, Charles 1812-1870 *The Chimes.* London: Chapman & Hall, 1845. Twelfth edition, half title, frontispiece, additional engraved title, illustrations, original red cloth gilt, carefully recased, inscribed by author for Thomas Powell, September fourth 1845, later ownership inscription of Ellen Maria Streater, and E. Harrell, all edges gilt, morocco backed box. Jarndyce Antiquarian Booksellers CCXVIII - 364 2016 £25,000

Association – Power, Eileen

Wells, Herbert George 1866-1946 *The Open Conspiracy, Blueprints for a World Revolution.* London: Victor Gollancz, 1928. First edition, crease to top corner of few leaves, crown 8vo., original black cloth, backstrip lettered in orange and slightly rubbed at tips, tiny amount of wear to corners, top edge dust soiled, faint partial browning to free endpapers, good, notable presentation copy, inscribed by author to friend Eileen Power.   Blackwell's Rare Books   B186 - 299   2016   £500

Association – Pratten, W. S.

Clarke, Mary Victoria Cowden *The Complete Concordance to Shakespeare.* London: Charles Knight & Co., 1845. First edition in book form, 4to., subscriber's copy, signed by author, clean and bright within, few spots of foxing to prelims, half tan calf, gilt spine with slightly cracked dark brown morocco label, marbled paper boards, endpapers and edges, rubbed spine bit scuffed, lower hinge repaired, very good, faded ownership inscription of 'W. S. Pratten, Compton Lodge".   Unsworths Antiquarian Booksellers Ltd.   30 - 138   2016   £150

Association – Prentice, Alta Rockefeller

McFarland, J. Horace *Modern Roses II.* New York: Macmillan, 1940. Second edition, 8vo., color and black and white photos, red cloth, author's signature on back of frontispiece photo, fine, from the library of Alta Rockefeller Prentice.   Second Life Books, Inc.   196 B - 176   2016 $45

Association – Preston, Guliolmi

Crucius, Jacobus *Epistolarun Libri IV. Cum Duplici Indice.* Delphis: ex officina Johannes Andreae Koleting, 1633. First edition, 8vo., woodcut initials, f.f.e.p. and following blank both with top fore-edge corner excised, titlepage bit grubby, some light foxing to blanks front and rear, contemporary vellum, title inked to spine, yapp edges, vellum darkened, quite heavily marked especially to spine but entirely sound, inscribed "Antonius (surname obscured) Col. Reg. Oxon ex dondo Guliolmi Preston 1743".   Unsworths Antiquarian Booksellers Ltd.   E01 - Early Printing - 6   2016   £200

Association – Price, Margaret Davies

Bewick, Thomas 1753-1828 *Memorial Edition of the Works.* Newcastle upon tyne: printed by R. Ward and Sons for Bernard Quaritch... London, 1885-1887. Limited to 750 numbered copies signed by publisher, 3 volumes, original half brown morocco, spine with raised bands, lettered gilt and with animal and bird tools in top and bottom panels, marbled endpaper, top edges gilt, many wood engravings by Thomas Bewick, very good, TLS dated August 17th 1889 from W J May, VP of Atchison, Topeka and Santa Fe Railroad to Mr. Price urging him to buy this set of books, each volume with bookplate of Margaret Davies Price.   Sotheran's   Piccadilly Notes - Summer 2015 - 47   2016   £1400

Association – Price, Reynolds

Hijuelos, Oscar *Mr. Ives' Christmas.* New York: Harper Collins, 1995. First edition, fine in fine dust jacket, inscribed by author for Reynolds Price.   Between the Covers Rare Books   208 - 38   2016 $275

Association – Price, Richard

Verborum Anomalorum in Graeca Lingua Investigatio. In Usum Scholae Regiae Salopiensis. Shrewsbury: Prostant Venales Apud Josh. Eddowes, 1774. 8vo., little minor spotting, original quarter sheep, marbled boards, rather rubbed and worn, joints cracked but cords holding, ownership inscription of Richard Price, August 31st. 1786, with his bookplate, sound, rare, unsophisticated copy.   Blackwell's Rare Books   Greek & Latin Classics VII - 24   2016   £550

Association – Price, Vincent

Wilde, Oscar 1854-1900 *A Woman of No Importance.* London: John Lane at Sign of the Bodley Head, 1894. First edition, one of 500 copies, book near fine with spine faded, otherwise very nice, after the first four leaves, book entirely unopened at top edge, bookplate of Joseph Groves and short inscription from actor Vincent Price.   Heritage Book Shop   Holiday 2015 - 115   2016 $2000

Association – Priestley, J. C.

Dickens, Charles 1812-1870 *The Life and Adventures of Martin Chuzzlewit.* London: Chapman & Hall, 1844. first edition, first state with '1000' on engraved title, errata pages has 13 lines and thus, according to Hatton and Cleaver is the earlier issue, half title, frontispiece, engraved title, plates by Phiz, plates fairly evenly browned, plate opposite page 415 with small marginal repair, contemporary half black morocco, carefully recased, bookplates of W. H. Wills and Sir W. O. Priestley and handwritten statement inserted in prelims concerning ownership by W. H. Wills, signed J. C. Priestley, cloth slipcase.   Jarndyce Antiquarian Booksellers CCXVIII - 412   2016   £1800

Association – Priestley, W. O.

Dickens, Charles 1812-1870 *The Life and Adventures of Martin Chuzzlewit.* London: Chapman & Hall, 1844. first edition, first state with '1000' on engraved title, errata pages has 13 lines and thus, according to Hatton and Cleaver is the earlier issue, half title, frontispiece, engraved title, plates by Phiz, plates fairly evenly browned, plate opposite page 415 with small marginal repair, contemporary half black morocco
o, carefully recased, bookplates of W. H. Wills and Sir W. O. Priestley and handwritten statement inserted in prelims concerning ownership by W. H. Wills, signed J. C. Priestley, cloth slipcase. Jarndyce Antiquarian Booksellers CCXVIII - 412 2016 £1800

Association – Prindle, William

Coolidge, Calvin *Have Faith in Massachusetts.* Boston and New York: Houghton Mifflin, 1919. Second edition, 8vo., inscribed by the President to William F. Prindle, Aug. 1920, very good, tight copy. Second Life Books, Inc. 196A - 330 2016 $750

Association – Prior, K. G.

Thomas, Franklin *The Etiquette of Freemasonry.* London: A. Lewis, 1890. First edition, half title, 6 pages ads, original blue cloth, Foyles bookseller's label, signature of K. G. Prior, very good. Jarndyce Antiquarian Books CCXV - 436 2016 £75

Association – Pritchett, V. S.

Norwich, John Julius *A Christmas Cracker: being a Commonplace Selection.* N.P.: 1993. wrappers, slight damp marks throughout, otherwise very nice, inscribed by compiler for Victor and Dorothy, from the library of V. S. Pritchett. Bertram Rota Ltd. Christmas List 2015 - 30 2016 £20

Association – Proctor, Mrs.

Marston, William Moulton *F. F. Proctor.* New York: Richard Smith, 1943. First edition, photos and program reproductions, inscribed by Mrs Proctor to Governor Dewey of NY, nice, little scuffed and chipped dust jacket. Second Life Books, Inc. 196 B - 143 2016 $75

Association – Pumpelly, Raphael

Fischer, Heinrich *Knitische Mikroskopisch-mineralogische Studien.* Freiburg: Carl Troemer, 1869. 1871. 1873. First edition, 3 works in 1, small 8vo., 2 colored plates, some brittleness to paper, quite browned, early half brown morocco, lighter brown pebbled cloth, gilt stamped spine with original yellow printed wrappers, bound in, rubbed, printed wrapper chipped, others fine, ownership signatures of R. Pumpelly, very good, rare. Jeff Weber Rare Books 183 - 18 2016 $300

Association – Pym, Horatio Noble

Dodsley, Robert 1703-1764 *A Select Collection of Old English Plays.* London: Reeves and Turner, 1874. Fourth edition, one of a handful of large paper copies on fine laid paper, one of a handful of large paper copies on fine laid paper, 229 x 152mm., 15 volumes, elegant contemporary polished calf by Mansell (stamp-signed each volume), gilt in compartments, circular brown morocco volume label in garland and wheel pattern, each spine with additional red light brown and black morocco labels, gilt inner dentelles, marbled endpapers, top edges gilt, others untrimmed, 10 woodcut illustrations on one leaf in volume I, front pastedowns with armorial bookplate of Horatio Noble Pym, rear cover of final volume somewhat marked and soiled, spines uniformly just bit darker than boards with occasional minor abrasions, blanks and text leaves lightly foxed at beginning and end of few volumes, otherwise handsome set in fine, clean condition, virtually immaculate internally. Phillip J. Pirages 67 - 52 2016 $2000

Association – Pynchon, Thomas Ruggles

Munro, H. H. *The Novels and Plays of Saki.* New York: Viking Press, 1933. Stated "Second Omnibus" volume, rebound in blue half morocco gilt, paper covered boards, probably soon after publication, spine expertly preserved, otherwise nice, near fine, with two identical examples of the armorial bookplate of Thomas Ruggles Pynchon, presumably that of author Thomas Pynchon's father. Between the Covers Rare Books 204 - 99 2016 $950

Association – Queen, Ellery

Golding, Louis *Pale Blue Nightgown.* Corvinus Press, 1936. first edition, one of 60 copies printed on Potal Whitechurch paper, numbered and signed by author, this copy 17, 8vo., limited to 100 signed by author, quarter blue leather and gray cloth with all four corners bound in blue leather and titles stamped in gold gilt on spine, affixed to front flyleaf is statement of provenance advising that this copy came from the library of Ellery Queen, former owner's armorial bookplate, front pastedown sheet, blue spine panel lightly sunned, else near fine. Buckingham Books 2015 - 38201 2016 $3500

Association – Quincey, Edmund

More, Henry *Enchiridion Ethicum, Praecipua Moralis Rhiosophiae Rudimenta Complectens Illustrata Utplurimum Veterum Monumentis...* London: J. Downing, 1711. Fourth edition, 8vo. engraved portrait, frontispiece trimmed, contemporary blind tooled calf, rebacked, 4 raised bands, gilt title, new endleaves, signature of Edmund Quincey 1718, donor's note (to Jeremiah Dummer, (Silversmith) dated 1718, signatures of 'William B. Calhoun', foxing, some leaves toned, marginal pen lines, title + first leaf perforated and embossed, very good.   Jeff Weber Rare Books   181 - 23   2016 $295

Association – Quinn, John

Jonson, Ben   1572-1637 *Volpone; or the Foxe.* New York: John Lane, 1898. No, 43 of 100 copies on Japanese Imperial vellum, each containing an extra suite of plates (of a total edition of 1100 for England and America), 295 x 225mm., publisher's original vellum over bevelled boards, upper cover elaborately gilt in design by Beardsley, smooth spine lettered gilt, top edge gilt, others untrimmed, housed in later cloth slipcase, 13 illustrations by Aubrey Beardsley, woodcut bookplate of John Quinn, splaying to boards, otherwise especially fine, very clean and smooth and fresh inside and out.   Phillip J. Pirages   67 - 22   2016 $2900

Association – Quittner, Walter

Adler, Egon *Die Entdeckung Karlsbads Eine Satire.* privately printed, 1922. No. 36 of 50 copies, this with plates hand colored, 4to., pages 63, copiously illustrate in color throughout, name of recipient tipped in at colophon (Walter Quittner) with short handwritten sentiment initialled E.A., original marbled boards over beige cloth lettered gilt at spine, very slight fraying at spine ends, otherwise clean, very good.   Any Amount of Books   2015 - A84565   2016   £550

Association – Rabassa, Gregory

Garcia Marquez, Gabriel *The Autumn of the Patriarch.* New York: Harper and Row, 1976. First American edition, fifth printing, signed by translator Gregory Rabassa, blue cloth lettered gilt, pale blue top stain, original pictorial dust jacket lettered in white and orange, about fine, jacket with hint of rubbing to extremities, faint creasing to spine head, else bright and clean, beautiful copy.   B & B Rare Books, Ltd.   2016 - GGM043   2016 $60

Garcia Marquez, Gabriel *Innocent Erendira and Other Stories.* New York: Harper and Row, 1978. First American edition, signed by translator, Gregory Rabassa, publisher's dark blue cloth, spine lettered gilt, top edge orange, original colorful pictorial dust jacket, about fine with only hint of rubbing to spine ends, else fine, unclipped dust jacket with touch of faint rubbing to extremities, else bright and fresh, very clean and square copy.   B & B Rare Books, Ltd.   2016 - GGM042   2016 $150

Association – Rabinowitz, Harry

Bugge, Thomas *De Forste Grunde til den Sphaeriske og Theoretiske Astronomie...* Kjobenhavn: S. Poulsens, 1796. Mottled leather spine and tips with tan paste paper covered boards and leather title label to spine, gilt spine label, chipping to top edge of title label which effects few letters in author's name, minor wear to corners and edges of boards, bumping to corners, rubbing to boards and hinges, few chips to paper covering boards, bookplate of Harry Rabinowitz, notes in pen to endpages, soiling to corners of few pages, occasional small spots of foxing, 12 plates, very good.   The Kelmscott Bookshop   13 - 12   2016 $175

Association – Rackham, Arthur

Barham, Richard Harris   1788-1845 *Ingoldsby Legends.* London: Dent, 1907. Limited to 560 signed by Rackham, (500 for sale), large thick 4to., full gilt pictorial vellum, inconspicuous mend on 2 text pages, else fine with new ties, 24 beautiful tipped-in color plates mounted on dark paper, 12 full page tinted illustrations and 66 black and white drawings, plus pictorial endpapers, this copy with fine half page watercolor drawing signed by artist, Arthur Rackham.   Aleph-bet Books, Inc.   111 - 372   2016 $13,500

Goldsmith, Oliver   1730-1774 *Vicar of Wakefield.* London: Harrap, 1929. First edition, 4to., gilt cloth, top edge gilt, endpaper foxed, light wear, very good+, illustrated by Arthur Rackham, this copy has large half page pen drawing signed and dated Nov. 1929 by artist.   Aleph-bet Books, Inc.   112 - 407   2016 $2200

Association – Radcliffe, W.

Steele, Richard   1672-1729 *The Christian Hero.* London: printed for J. and R. Tonson, 1741. Ninth edition, 12mo., final blank sig. E4 present, contemporary sprinkled edges, slight rubbing to hinges some staining, top corners bit bumped, signature of W. Radcliffe, very good, attractive copy.   Jarndyce Antiquarian Booksellers   CCXVI - 540   2016   £95

Association – Rae, Kenneth

Blunden, Edmund *Choice or Chance, New Poems.* London: Cobden Sanderson, 1934. First edition, one of 45 numbered copies, this unnumbered, being one of 10 for presentation, signed by author, 8vo., original pink buckram, gilt lettered backstrip faded, free endpapers, lightly browned, top edge gilt, others untrimmed, with Rex Whistler designed bookplate of Kenneth Rae.   Blackwell's Rare Books   B186 - 184   2016   £160

Blunden, Edmund *Halfway House. A Miscellany of New Poems.* London: Cobden Sanderson, 1932. First edition, one of 70 numbered copies, this unnumbered, being one of 10 for presentation signed by author, 8vo., original orange buckram faintly spotted, gilt lettered backstrip little faded, free endpapers lightly browned, top edge gilt, others untrimmed, good, with Kenneth Rae bookplate designed by Rex Whistler.   Blackwell's Rare Books   B186 - 185   2016   £160

Blunden, Edmund *Retreat.* Cobden-Sanderson, 1928. First edition, one of 112 nubered copies, this unnumbered, being one of 12 for presentation, printed on handmade paper and signed by author title printed in black and red, crown 8vo., original tan buckram, darkened backstrip gilt lettered, free endpapers lightly browned, untrimmed, very good, inscribed by author to Kenneth Rae, with Rae's signature.   Blackwell's Rare Books   B186 - 186   2016   £250

Association – Rae, Mrs.

Blunt, Wilfrid Scawen   1840-1922   *The Love Sonnets of Proteus.* London: Kegan Paul, Trench & Co., 1885. Fifth edition, original green cloth lettered and decorated in gilt, cloth just little worn and slight spotting to endpapers, otherwise very nice, presentation inscribed by author for Mrs. Rae.   Bertram Rota Ltd.   February List 2016 - 7   2016   £250

Association – Ralli, Stephen

Clarke, Edward H. *Sex In Education or a Fair Chance for Girls.* Boston & New York: Houghton Mifflin & Co., 1886. 13 page catalog, original green cloth, armorial bookplate of Stephen Ralli, very good.   Jarndyce Antiquarian Books   CCXV - 596   2016   £35

Association – Rampling, Charlotte

Charlotte Rampling with Compliments. London: Quartet Books, 1973. First edition, signed by Rampling, near fine in fine dust jacket, photographic plates.   Royal Books   48 - 22   2016 $950

Association – Ramsay, Harriet

Chapone, Hester *Letters on the Improvement of the Mind, Addressed to a Young Lady.* London: printed for J. Walter, Charing Cross and C. Dilly in the Poultry, 1787. New edition, 8vo., , contemporary full speckled calf, rubbed maroon leather label, hinges weakening but sound, slightly chipped at head and tail of spine, armorial bookplate, signature of Martha Campbell & partially removed signature of Harriet Ramsay?, good, sound copy.   Jarndyce Antiquarian Books   CCXV - 105   2016   £50

Association – Ramsey, Zephyr

Branson, Helen Kitchin *Let there Be Life: the Contemporary Account of Edna L. Griffin M.D.* Pasadena: pub. by M. S. Sewn, 1947. First edition, tall octavo, 135 pages, frontispiece, green cloth title stamped on front board in pale yellow, net owner's name Zephyr M. Ramsey, bit of rubbing at spine ends, else very near fine, no dust jacket, almost certainly as issued.   Between the Covers Rare Books   202 - 14   2016 $650

Association – Rand, James

Fisher, Irving   1867-1947   *Stable Money. A History of the Movement.* New York: Adelphi Co., 1934. First edition, limited, no. 634, 8vo., signed and inscribed by Fisher, Frederic Delano and James Rand, original blue cloth with mild wear cover edges, marginal dampstain, very good+.   By the Book, L. C.   45 - 28   2016 $3000

Association – Randall, Elizabeth

Kettilby, Mary *A Collection of Above Three Hundred Receipts in Cookery, Physick and Surgery; for the Use of all Good Wives, Tender Mothers and Careful Nurses.* London: for Richard Wilkin, 1714. First edition, contemporary paneled calf, neatly rebacked, light overall toning, minor marginal foxing and dampstaining, upper margin of A3 clipped and neatly restored, just grazing running head on verso, 3 leaves of early owners' recipes bound in at end, early ownership signature of Tho. tipping, dated at several locations in Herfordshire 1714-1739, later signature of Elizabeth Randall 1771, modern cookery bookplate, very nice in portfolio and leather backed slipcase.   Joseph J. Felcone, Inc.   Books from Five Centuries: a Miscellany - 49   2016 $2800

Association – Randall, M.

Hulme, F. Edward *Bards and Blossoms or the Poetry, History and Associations of Flowers.* London: Marcus Ward & Co., 1877. First edition, half title, colour frontispiece and 7 further color plates, original green cloth beveled boards, elaborately decorated in gilt, black and pink, all edges gilt, attractive gift inscription "L. A. Richardson from her loving friend M. Randall, June 15 1878", fine, attractive copy.   Jarndyce Antiquarian Booksellers   CCXVII - 130   2016   £180

Association – Randeria

Schmidt, Adolf *Bucheinbande Aus Dem XIV-XIX Jahrhundert in Der Landesbibliothek zu Darmstadt.* Leipzig: Karl W. Hiersemann, 1921. Thick folio, cloth, leather spine label, 41 pages followed by 100 full page plates, magnificent folio, some spotting of covers, with Randeria bookplate.   Oak Knoll Books   310 - 19   2016 $550

Association – Randle, John

Matrix 1. Number One Autumn 1981. Manor Farm: Whittington Press, 1981. First edition, limited to 30 numbered copies, 4to., stiff paper wrappers, very scarce, fading to spine and spine edges of back cover/top of front cover, inserted is ALS form John Randle, slight shelfwear, some sunning to spine.   Oak Knoll Books   310 - 172   2016 $1000

Matrix 1-26 (with index to volumes 1-21). Whittington Press, 1980-2006. Together 27 volumes, 4to, original harlequin wrappers, profusely illustrated, near fine run, with ALS from John Randle to Howard Gerwing.   Sotheran's Piccadilly Notes - Summer 2015 - 307   2016   £3750

Association – Randolph, Harold

Irving, Washington   1783-1859 *Chronicle of the Conquest of Granada. (and) The Alhambra.* New York and London: Printed at the Knickerbocker Press for G. P. Putnam's Sons, 1893-1894. 229 x 165mm., 4 volumes, representing two separately published works, each in two volumes, publisher's ivory buckram, ornately embellished with Moorish inspired design by Alice Cordelia Morse, covers with elaborate decoration in colors and gilt, flat spines with gilt titling, decoration and patterned endpapers, top edge gilt, in original blue cloth dust jacket, gilt titling on spine, 61 photogravures of the Alhambra and Granada, each with lettered tissue guard, engraved bookplate of Ella C. Smith (Alhambra) and Harold Randolph (Granada), mild browning to leaves opposite illustrations from acidic tissue guards, otherwise extraordinarily fine set, clean and fresh in very pretty publisher's bindings beautifully protected by original fine dust jackets.   Phillip J. Pirages   67 - 202   2016 $950

Association – Raney, William

Kelley, William Melvin *A Different Drummer.* Garden City: Doubleday, 1962. First edition, 8vo., author's presentation for William Raney, paper over boards, cloth spine, very good, tight copy in little scuffed and soiled dust jacket.   Second Life Books, Inc.   196A - 924   2016 $225

Association – Rankin, Mary

Kipling, Rudyard   1865-1936 *Just So Stories for Little children.* New York: Doubleday Page and Co., 1909. Pocket edition, 12th impression, half title, original limp maroon cloth, front board and spine gilt, spine slightly darkened with some repairs, signed presentation by author for Mary Rankin Xmas 09.   Jarndyce Antiquarian Booksellers CCXVII - 150   2016   £380

Association – Ransohoff, Joseph

Stookey, Byron *Trigeminal Neuralgia. Its History and Treatment.* Springfield: 1959. original cloth, original dust jacket worn, internally fine, presentation from Joseph Ransohoff for Edgar Houseplan.   James Tait Goodrich X-78 - 518   2016 $150

Association – Ransom, Will

The Dictes and Sayings of The Philosophers. Detroit: Cranbrook press, 1901. No. 21 of 244 copies, 282 x 215mm., original half vellum, brown paper sides, calf label on spine, edges untrimmed and unopened, fleece lined slipcase with brown morocco lip, first opening with 3 1/2 x 4 3/4" woodcut vignette on either page, from drawings, vignettes surrounded by elaborate strapwork border, 3 other pages with similar borders, as well as woodcut initials, headpieces and tailpieces, in elaborate style, rear pastedown with library label of Will Ransom, corners slightly bumped, hint of soiling to covers and spine, otherwise very fine, immaculate internally.   Phillip J. Pirages   67 - 98   2016 $1250

Association – Rapoport, Kenneth

Juvenalis, Decimus Junius *Satyrae with commentary of Domitius Calderinus.* Venice: Bartholomaeus de Zanis 3 Oct., 1487. Folio, spaces left for capitals illuminated with four large white vine initials of 4 to 8 lines in size, initials in gold with swirling white stems surrounding them against backgrounds of red, green and blue, two small 3 line initials and gold against a red and green background, some rubrication in blue and red, two smaller initials in gold against red and green background, lacking final blank, Romam letter, 61 lines of commentary surrounding text, 19th century half brown morocco, rubbed and scuffed, tear to upper margins of ff. b1 and b2, neatly repaired, one or two wormholes at beginning and end, little browned or stained in places, Kenneth Rapoport copy.   Maggs Bros. Ltd.   1474 - 44 2016   £7500

Association – Rawles, H. H.

Waugh, Evelyn 1903-1966 *Scoop.* London: Chapman and Hall, 1938. First ediion, 2nd issue with 'as' on last line of page 88, inscribed by author to H. H. Rawles from author, 8vo., original red and black marbled cloth lettered gilt on spine with second issue dust jacket with some sunning and chipping, closed tears and creases, otherwise very good, bright, signed and inscribed copies scarce.   Sotheran's Piccadilly Notes - Summer 2015 - 328   2016   £2995

Association – Ray, Mrs.

Ray, John *The Wisdom of God Manifested in the Works of the Creation, in Two Parts.* London: for Samuel Smith, 1692. Second edition, 8vo., contemporary calf, covers panelled gilt with vase and flower tool in each corner, gilt spine with red morocco label (corners worn, top corner of lower cover chewed, area of surface insect damage at foot of the lower cover), from the library of James Stevens Cox (1910-1997), inscribed "The Gift of Mrs. Ray to John Morley July 31 1707", and signatures 'Jane Dorothy Harvey 1849' and 'C. H. Rikerman(?) 1885'.   Maggs Bros. Ltd.   1447 - 360   2016   £500

Association – Raymond, Isabella

The Romish Mass-Book Faithfully Translated into English with Notes and Observations Thereupon... London: printed by George Larkin for Thomas Malthus, 1683. 12mo., engraved frontispiece, publisher's catalog, frontispiece almost detached, little yellowed, with few small spots, worming to lower margin page 12 onwards, final leaf slightly adhered to r.f.e.p. causing some tearing near gutter, contemporary brown sheep, edges sprinkled reddish brown, spine worn and narrow 4cm. piece missing at tail and adjacent stain to lower board, some other small stains and speckling, pastedowns lifting with lower part of front pastedown excised, number 17 inked in old hand in inner front board where exposed to lifted pastedown and to fore edge, ownership inscription of Isabella Raymond dated 1756.   Unsworths Antiquarian Booksellers   30 - 5   2016   £450

Association – Raymond, J.

N., J. *Select Lessons in Prose and Verse, from Various Authors...* Bristol: printed by S. Farley, 1774. 8vo., 4 lines crossed out in contemporary ink, 19th century marbled boards, handsomely rebacked in brown calf, red morocco label, signature of J. Raymond 1778.   Jarndyce Antiquarian Books   CCXV - 334   2016   £220

Association – Rayner, A. B.

Hodson, W. *Hodson's Self Instructing Copy Book.* London: W. Hodson, circa, 1860. Engraved head lines partially completed in ink and pencil, 7 leaves without ms., original orange illustrated printed paper wrappers, wrappers sewn as issued, inscription "Charles Rayner, Schoolmistress, Miss A. B. Rayner, Wallinton, Herts".   Jarndyce Antiquarian Books   CCXV - 739   2016   £30

Association – Rayner, Charles

Hodson, W. *Hodson's Self Instructing Copy Book.* London: W. Hodson, circa, 1860. Engraved head lines partially completed in ink and pencil, 7 leaves without ms., original orange illustrated printed paper wrappers, wrappers sewn as issued, inscription "Charles Rayner, Schoolmistress, Miss A. B. Rayner, Wallinton, Herts".   Jarndyce Antiquarian Books   CCXV - 739   2016   £30

Association – Raynes, F.

Churchill, Seton *Forbidden Fruit for Young Men.* London: James Nisbet & Co., circa, 1895. Sixth edition, half title, 6 pages ads, slight spotting, original blue cloth, slightly dulled, signature of F. Raynes 1895.   Jarndyce Antiquarian Books   CCXV - 119   2016   £40

Association – Read, Frank

Cornwallis, Harris, William *Portraits of the Game and Wild Animals of Southern Africa.* Mazoe: Frank Read Press, 1977. Card portfolio, 66.5 x 49cm., containing 4 prints, each 59 x 43cm., on handmade, painted with Read Press blindstamp, signed by Frank Read and date stamped 9th Dec. 1977, fine.   Sotheran's   Piccadilly Notes - Summer 2015 - 86   2016   £450

Association – Reddan, Jerry

Dodge, Jim *A Book of Ku.* N.P.: Tangram, 2013. One of 200 copies, saddle stitched self wrappers, small spot to rear cover, else fine, laid in to this copy is letter from publishers Jerry Reddan to Peter (Matthiessen), uncommon.   Ken Lopez Bookseller   166 - 30   2016 $250

Association – Redwood, Thomas

Taylor, Thomas *The History of the Waldenses and Albigenses who Begun the Reformation in the Vallies of Peidmont (sic).* Bolton: printed by J. Higham, 1793. First edition, title within border of printer's ornaments, uniformly slightly browned, 12mo., contemporary sheep, rebacked, gold signature at head of title of Thos. Redwood, Jan. 23 1796.   Blackwell's Rare Books   B184 - 83   2016   £750

Association – Reece, Clifford

Morris, John *Traveller from Tokyo.* London: Cresset Press, 1943. First edition, octavo, very good in slightly chipped dust jacket tanned at spine, presentation from author inscribed for Clifford & Sibyl Lawton Reece, 2 Oct. 1943. Peter Ellis 112 - 193 2016 £35

Association – Reece, Eric

Reece, Erik *Field Work: Modern Poems from Eastern Forests.* Lexington: The University Press of Kentucky, 2008. First edition, 8vo., fine in dust jacket, signed by contributors Eric Reece, James Baker Hall, Wendell Berry and Richard Taylor. Second Life Books, Inc. 196 B - 461 2016 $45

Association – Reece, Sibyl Lawton

Morris, John *Traveller from Tokyo.* London: Cresset Press, 1943. First edition, octavo, very good in slightly chipped dust jacket tanned at spine, presentation from author inscribed for Clifford & Sibyl Lawton Reece, 2 Oct. 1943. Peter Ellis 112 - 193 2016 £35

Association – Reed, Joe

Ellison, Ralph *Invisible Man.* New York: Vintage, 1972. first paperback edition?, small 8vo., author's presentation to Joe Reed and family, paper wrappers, ink markings on front edges, cover creased and scuffed, very good, tight copy. Second Life Books, Inc. 196A - 499 2016 $700

Association – Reed, Warmington

Parfit, Joseph T. *Among the Druzes of Lebanon and Bashan.* London: Hunter & Longhurst, 1917. First edition, octavo, photos, original green cloth, scarce, presentation copy inscribed by author for Mr. and Mrs. Warmington Reed, covers little marked and rubbed at edges, free endpapers tanned, very good. Peter Ellis 112 - 107 2016 £250

Association – Reede, W.

Correlli, Marie *Free Opinions Freely expressed on Certain Phases of Modern Social Life and Conduct.* London: Archibald Constable, 1905. First edition, half title, final ad leaf, 16 page catalog, original dark blue cloth, blocked and lettered in gilt, spine slightly faded, modern bookplate of Ronald George Taylor, inscribed by author on leading f.e.p. "Mr. W. Reede 34 Marstell Place - Leicester". Jarndyce Antiquarian Books CCXV - 135 2016 £58

Association – Refregier, Anton

Lowenfels, Walter *Song of Peace.* New York: Roving Eye Prress, 1959. One of 125 copies in hardcover, Blockprints by Anton Refregier, folio, cloth and illustrated paper over boards, cloth quite foxed, thus about very good, laid in broadside on card with block print by Refregier and with blurb by Linus Pauling (foxed and with crease), volume signed by Lowenfels and Refregier, also inscribed for James Roman by Lowenfels', laid in letter dated 9/4/65 on Lowenfels' stationary. Between the Covers Rare Books 204 - 68 2016 $150

Association – Reis, David

Acker, Kathy *Algeria: a Series of Invocations Because Nothing Else Works.* London: Aloes Books, 1984. First edition, octavo, stapled illustrated wrappers, slight sunning on spine, else about fine, signed by Acker, laid in is ANS from Acker to David Reis, uncommon signed. Between the Covers Rare Books 204 - 6 2016 $1000

Association – Reitlinger, Gerald

Powell, Anthony *Agents and Patients.* London: Duckworth, 1936. First edition, faint foxing to prelims and final few leaves, little to edges, foolscap 8vo., original pink cloth cocked, faded backstrip gilt lettered with chafing to its head and tail, good, with friendly 2 page ALS from Powell loosely tucked into book, addressed to Gerald Reitlinger. Blackwell's Rare Books B186 - 275 2016 £800

Association – Renier, Anne

Blessington, Marguerite Power Farmer Gardiner, Countess of 1789-1849 *The Keepsake for 1844.* London: Longmans, 1844. Engraved frontispiece and title plates, original maroon cloth, attractively blocked in blind and gilt, rebacked, little darkened and rubbed, signature of Kate Barber 1844, armorial bookplates of Algernon Graves, Renier booklabel. Jarndyce Antiquarian Booksellers CCXVIII - 430 2016 £120

Brown, Thomas, the Elder, Pseud. *Brighton or the Steyne.* London: printed for the author, sold by Sherwood, Neely and Jones, 1818. First edition, 3 volumes bound in 1 volume, 12mo., half title volume I with ad on verso, contemporary blue green moire cloth, little rubbed, bookplate of David Milne, Advocate with his trimmed signatures to titles volumes ii and iii, Renier booklabel, nice. Jarndyce Antiquarian Booksellers CCXVII - 51 2016 £750

Common Sense or Every Body's Magazine. London: JGF & J. Rivington & Whittaker & Co., 1842. Volume I (of two published), 8 numbers, May-December, original purple brown cloth, slightly faded, early signature of James Dearden, Renier booklabel, very good.   Jarndyce Antiquarian Booksellers   CCXVII - 221   2016   £45

Crowe, Catherine   *The Seeress of Prevost Being Revelations Concerning the Inner Life of Man....*   London: J. C. Moore, 1845. First English edition, half title, 2 pages ads, original blue cloth blocked in blind, spine lettered gilt, spine slightly faded, very good, Renier booklabel.   Jarndyce Antiquarian Booksellers   CCXVII - 80   2016   £125

Dickens, Charles   1812-1870   *Sketches by Boz.* London: Chapman & Hall, 1877. Half title, vignette title, ads on endpapers slightly spotted, 'Yellowback', original pale green printed boards, spine darkened and little worn at head and tail, hinges rubbed, corners slightly knocked, Renier booklabel.   Jarndyce Antiquarian Booksellers   CCXVIII - 71   2016   £120

The Double Perplexity or the Mysterious Marriages. London: printed by J. Roach, at the Britannia Printing Office, 1796. 12mo., some foxing and staining, one section detached in stitching, disbound, from the Renier collection. Jarndyce Antiquarian Booksellers   CCXVI - 456   2016   £120

The Halfpenny Magazine.   London: R. Seton at the Tatler Office, Covent Garden, 1832. Nos. 1-13, 16-17, May-August 1832, contemporary marbled boards, later paper spine, hand lettered, booklabels of R. G. Scotland and Reniers.   Jarndyce Antiquarian Booksellers   CCXVII - 222   2016   £65

The Harbinger.   London: William Freeman, 1862. 12 issues, Jan.-Dec., lacking leading f.e.p., original wavy grained green cloth, gilt, Renier booklabel.   Jarndyce Antiquarian Booksellers   CCXVII - 223   2016   £35

The Iris. London: printed for E. Livermore, published by J. Gifford, 1825. Volume I, nos. I-XXVI, contemporary boards, rather worn, roughly rebacked, 4to., Renier booklabel. Jarndyce Antiquarian Booksellers   CCXVII - 226   2016   £85

Kitton, Frederic George   *"Phiz".* London: George Redway, 1882. First edition, half title, frontispiece, plates, 2 page 'note', original brown wrappers, slightly chipped with minor loss to edges and spine, bookplate of Anne & Fernand Renier.   Jarndyce Antiquarian Booksellers   CCXVIII - 1089   2016   £35

O'Bryen, Denis   *Utrum Horum? The government or the Country?*   London: printed for J. Debrett, 1796. 8vo., half title, final blank Q2, disbound, slightly dusted, signature of Anne Renier.   Jarndyce Antiquarian Booksellers   CCXVI - 435   2016   £40

Russell, George   *Sunday School and Other Anecdotes.* London: printed by Pewtress, Low & Pewtress, 1819. Errata slip, contemporary tree calf, gilt spine and borders, leading hinge slightly splitting, Renier booklabel, nice. Jarndyce Antiquarian Books   CCXV - 931   2016   £25

Saint Pierre, Jacques Henri Bernardin De   1737-1814 *Paul and Virginia.*   London: printed for Vernor & Hood, 1799. Fourth edition, frontispiece, engraved title and printed title, 6 plates and numerous woodcuts, 8vo., frontispiece and engraved title browned, some staining to text, contemporary full dark green morocco, gilt spine, borders and dentelles, slight rubbing to spine, good plus, Renier bookplate. Jarndyce Antiquarian Booksellers   CCXVI - 506   2016 £85

Association – Renier, Fernand

Blessington, Marguerite Power Farmer Gardiner, Countess of   1789-1849   *The Keepsake for 1844.* London: Longmans, 1844. Engraved frontispiece and title plates, original maroon cloth, attractively blocked in blind and gilt, rebacked, little darkened and rubbed, signature of Kate Barber 1844, armorial bookplates of Algernon Graves, Renier booklabel.   Jarndyce Antiquarian Booksellers CCXVIII - 430   2016   £120

Brown, Thomas, the Elder, Pseud.   *Brighton or the Steyne.*   London: printed for the author, sold by Sherwood, Neely and Jones, 1818. First edition, 3 volumes bound in 1 volume, 12mo., half title volume I with ad on verso, contemporary blue green moire cloth, little rubbed, bookplate of David Milne, Advocate with his trimmed signatures to titles volumes ii and iii, Renier booklabel, nice.   Jarndyce Antiquarian Booksellers   CCXVII - 51   2016   £750

Common Sense or Every Body's Magazine. London: JGF & J. Rivington & Whittaker & Co., 1842. Volume I (of two published), 8 numbers, May-December, original purple brown cloth, slightly faded, early signature of James Dearden, Renier booklabel, very good.   Jarndyce Antiquarian Booksellers   CCXVII - 221   2016   £45

Crowe, Catherine   *The Seeress of Prevost Being Revelations Concerning the Inner Life of Man....*   London: J. C. Moore, 1845. First English edition, half title, 2 pages ads, original blue cloth blocked in blind, spine lettered gilt, spine slightly faded, very good, Renier booklabel.   Jarndyce Antiquarian Booksellers   CCXVII - 80   2016   £125

Dickens, Charles 1812-1870 *Sketches by Boz.* London: Chapman & Hall, 1877. Half title, vignette title, ads on endpapers slightly spotted, 'Yellowback', original pale green printed boards, spine darkened and little worn at head and tail, hinges rubbed, corners slightly knocked, Renier booklabel.   Jarndyce Antiquarian Booksellers   CCXVIII - 71   2016   £120

The Double Perplexity or the Mysterious Marriages. London: printed by J. Roach, at the Britannia Printing Office, 1796. 12mo., some foxing and staining, one section detached in stitching, disbound, from the Renier collection. Jarndyce Antiquarian Booksellers   CCXVI - 456   2016 £120

The Halfpenny Magazine.   London: R. Seton at the Tatler Office, Covent Garden, 1832. Nos. 1-13, 16-17, May-August 1832, contemporary marbled boards, later paper spine, hand lettered, booklabels of R. G. Scotland and Reniers.   Jarndyce Antiquarian Booksellers   CCXVII - 222   2016   £65

The Harbinger.   London: William Freeman, 1862. 12 issues, Jan.-Dec., lacking leading f.e.p., original wavy grained green cloth, gilt, Renier booklabel.   Jarndyce Antiquarian Booksellers   CCXVII - 223   2016   £35

The Iris. London: printed for E. Livermore, published by J. Gifford, 1825. Volume I, nos. I-XXVI, contemporary boards, rather worn, roughly rebacked, 4to., Renier booklabel. Jarndyce Antiquarian Booksellers   CCXVII - 226   2016 £85

Kitton, Frederic George   *"Phiz".* London: George Redway, 1882. First edition, half title, frontispiece, plates, 2 page 'note', original brown wrappers, slightly chipped with minor loss to edges and spine, bookplate of Anne & Fernand Renier.   Jarndyce Antiquarian Booksellers CCXVIII - 1089   2016   £35

Russell, George *Sunday School and Other Anecdotes.* London: printed by Pewtress, Low & Pewtress, 1819. Errata slip, contemporary tree calf, gilt spine and borders, leading hinge slightly splitting, Renier booklabel, nice. Jarndyce Antiquarian Books   CCXV - 931   2016   £25

Saint Pierre, Jacques Henri Bernardin De   1737-1814 *Paul and Virginia.* London: printed for Vernor & Hood, 1799. Fourth edition, frontispiece, engraved title and printed title, 6 plates and numerous woodcuts, 8vo., frontispiece and engraved title browned, some staining to text, contemporary full dark green morocco, gilt spine, borders and dentelles, slight rubbing to spine, good plus, Renier bookplate. Jarndyce Antiquarian Booksellers   CCXVI - 506   2016 £85

Association – Renzi, Ralph

Williams, Tennessee   1911-1983 *One Arm and Other Stories.* New Directions, 1948. Fifth printing, large 8vo., paper wrappers, good, inscribed by author to Ralph Renzi. Second Life Books, Inc.   197 - 357   2016 $1500

Association – Restall, Kate

Clemens, Samuel Langhorne   1835-1910 *A Tramp Abroad.* London: Chatto & Windus, 1880. Third edition, 2 volumes, half titles, 32 page catalog (April 1880), original olive green cloth, front boards pictorially blocked and lettered in black, spines blocked in black and lettered in gilt, publisher's monogram at centre of following boards, very slightly rubbed, signed "Kate Restall, May 29th/80", additional inscription "To Mr. E. Galsworthy, 2 Gladstone Terrance, Grosvenor Road".   Jarndyce Antiquarian Booksellers CCXVII - 287   2016   £120

Association – Restout, Denise

Landowska, Wanda *Landowska on Music.* New York: Stein & Day, 1964. First edition, 8vo., frontispiece, photos, nice in scuffed slipcase, this copy neatly signed in ink by editors, Denise Restout and Robert Hawkins.   Second Life Books, Inc.   196 B - 8   2016 $100

Association – Revoil, B. H.

Ainsworth, William Harrison   1807-1896 *Le Gentilhomme Des Grandes-Routes.* Paris: Imprimerie de Dubisson et cie, n.d., First French edition, 4to., original plain wrappers, very good copy, presentation copy from translator, B. H. Revoil to Ainsworth.   Second Life Books, Inc.   196A - 18   2016 $750

Association – Reymer, Fred

Small Beginning or the Way to Get On. London: James Hogg & sons, 1859. First edition, half title, frontispiece, plates, 4 pages ads, original red cloth, gilt vignette, dulled, cup mark on front board, contemporary signature, Fred Reymer 1862.   Jarndyce Antiquarian Books   CCXV - 48 2016   £35

Association – Reynolds, John Taylor

Combe, William 1742-1823 *The Three Tours of Dr. Syntax. In Search of the Picturesque... In Search of Consolation... In Search of a Wife.* London: R. Ackermann's Repository of Arts, 1812. 1820. 1821. First editions in book form, 3 volumes, volume III with eight pages of ads and original wrappers and ads from the three monthly parts bound in at rear, very handsome gilt decorated early 20th century dark blue rushed morocco by Riviere & Son (stamp-signed on front turn-in), covers with French fillet border, spines lavishly and elegantly gilt in compartments with flower filled cornucopia centerpiece surrounded by small tools and volute cornerpieces, inner gilt dentelles, top edges gilt, other edges untrimmed, one woodcut illustration, one engraved tailpiece and 80 partfully hand colored aquatint plates by Thomas Rowlandson, engraved armorial bookplate of John Taylor Reynolds, spines uniformly more black than blue, four of the covers with just hint of soiling, most plates with variable offsetting (usually faint but noticeable in half dozen cases), other trivial imperfections, but extremely desirable set, nevertheless with strong impressions and good coloring of first edition plates, with good coloring of first edition plates, very spacious margins, lovely bindings that are lustrous and virtually unworn.   Phillip J. Pirages   67 - 306   2016 $3500

Association – Rhinelander, Mary

Irving, Washington 1783-1859 *The Life and Voyages of Christopher Columbus.* New York: N. and J. White, 1834. Plates, contemporary straight grain morocco, title with gilt box on front cover, marbled endpapers and edges, foxing, hinges cracking very slightly but quite secure, presentation inscribed by author for Mary Rhinelander, uncommon.   Joseph J. Felcone, Inc.   Books from Five Centuries: a Miscellany - 81   2016 $2600

Association – Rhods, Brianne

Bemelmans, Ludwig *Madeline: Story and Pictures by....* London: Derek Veraschoyle, 1952. First US edition, first impression with publisher's address matching on copyright page, inscribed by author with drawing to Brianne Rhods, 1952, illustrated paper boards, matching dust jacket with price still intact, tips lightly rubbed, jacket with light wear along extremities, custom beige cloth slipcase, overall very good, very scarce with original signed drawing.   Heritage Book Shop   Holiday 2015 - 8   2016 $5000

Association – Rich, Doris

Jeffers, Robinson 1887-1962 *Medea.* New York: Random House, 1946. Second printing, autographed to Doris Rich by Dedicatee Judith Anderson on dedication page, with short TLS from Anderson to Rich dated Feb. 6 1948, laid in, some notes in pencil that appear to show changes made in production, owner's bookplate, nice in worn dust jacket.   Second Life Books, Inc.   196A - 892   2016 $125

Association – Richards, Grant

Clodd, Edward *Grant Allen. A Memoir.* London: Grant Richards, 1900. First edition, presentation from author to book's publisher, Grant Richards, original dark brown cloth boards, gilt title to spine, minor sunning to spine, small chip to foot of spine and few spots to boards, offsetting to endpapers, else clean, very good.   The Kelmscott Bookshop   13 - 13   2016 $650

Association – Richardson, Albert

Poleni, Giovanni *Memorie Istoriche Della gran Cupola Del Tempio Vaticano...* Padova: Nella Stamperia dei Seminario, 1748. Folio, five books in one volume, contemporary quarter calf over patterned paper covered boards, brown morocco and gilt lettering piece to spine, all edges speckled red, folding etched plates, binding rather rubbed at extremities, corners bumped some loss of paper covering boards, internally bright, crisp copy, ink signature of John Lewis Wolfe, engraved armorial bookplate of Joseph Gwilt (1784-1863), engraved bookplate of Sir Albert Richardson (1880-1964). Sotheran's   Piccadilly Notes - Summer 2015 - 239   2016   £3955

Shaw, George T. *History of the Athenaeum.* Liverpool: printed for the Committee of the Athenaeum by Rockcliff Bros. Ltd. 44 Castle Street, 1898. Small folio, contemporary full chocolate brown crushed morocco by Fazakerley of Liverpool, gilt stamped monogram to centre of the upper board, spine divided into six compartments with raised bands, lettered and dated in second and third compartments, gilt ruled edges, gilt dentelles, top edge gilt, marbled endpapers, gilt lettered brown morocco, presentation label to front pastedown, black and white photo frontispiece and 6 plates, 3 plans, bright, crisp, copy, presentation to Mandell Creighton, Bp. of London, bookplate of Sir Albert Richardson (1880-1964).   Sotheran's   Piccadilly Notes - Summer 2015 - 273   2016   £295

Association – Richardson, Grace

Hodgkin, John *Calligraphia Graeca et Poecilographia Graeca.* n.p., 1794-1807. Engraved titlepage, dedication and 17 other engraved plates, plates toned and somewhat spotted, letterpress more heavily spotted, ownership inscription of Thomas Jessop to titlepage, folio, contemporary quarter red roan, marbled boards, spine lettered vertically in gilt, front binder's blank with hand lettered 'half title' reading 'Poikilographia Ellenika' in Greek alphabet, followed by reference to discussion of the work in the Classical Journal, rubbed, some light wear to extremities, ownership stamp of Grace Richardson to endpaper, good.   Blackwell's Rare Books   Greek & Latin Classics VII - 27   2016   £800

Association – Richardson, L. A.

Hulme, F. Edward *Bards and Blossoms or the Poetry, History and Associations of Flowers.* London: Marcus Ward & Co., 1877. First edition, half title, colour frontispiece and 7 further color plates, original green cloth beveled boards, elaborately decorated in gilt, black and pink, all edges gilt, attractive gift inscription "L. A. Richardson from her loving friend M. Randall, June 15 1878", fine, attractive copy. Jarndyce Antiquarian Booksellers   CCXVII - 130   2016   £180

Association – Richardson, L. F.

Ritter, H. *Historia Philosophiae.* Gothae: sumtibus Frider Andr. Perthes, 1878. Sixth edition, 8vo., pencil underlinings and annotations, little toned, light foxing to prelims, half tan morocco, darker brown cloth, gilt and blind tooling to spine, marbled endpapers, edges sprinkled red, rubbed, joints slightly worn, very good, ownership inscription of L. F. Richardson.   Unsworths Antiquarian Booksellers Ltd.   30 - 131   2016   £30

Association – Richie, A. Muriel

Dickens, Charles   1812-1870 *Hard Times for These Times.* London: Bradbury & Evans, 1854. First edition, half title, some light unobtrusive staining pages 11-14, slightly later half red morocco, spine gilt in compartments, marbled boards and edges, booklabel of A. Muriel Ritchie, very good.   Jarndyce Antiquarian Booksellers   CCXVIII - 527   2016   £520

Association – Richter, Hans

Deutsche Menschen. Eine Folge Von Briefen. Luzern: Vita Nova Verlag, 1936. First edition, one of 2000 copies, 8vo., original cloth, presentation copy inscribed by Walter Benjamin for filmmaker Hans Richter, rare, important association copy, buff linen lightly soiled, otherwise very good, rare inscribed.   James S. Jaffe Rare Books   Occasional List: Winter 2016 - 31   2016 $27,500

Association – Riddell, Chris

Hardinge, Francis *The Lie Tree.* London: Macmillan Children's Books, 2016. Special edition, double signed by author and artist, Chris Riddell, beautifully illustrated, book and jacket fine, jacket fitted with new removable clear cover.   Gemini Books   2016 - 31899   2016 $40

Association – Ridler, F. W.

Nicols, Arthur *Chapters from the Physical History of the Earth.* London: C. Kegan Paul & Co., 1880. First edition, half title, 32 page catalog 10/79, tipped in 'Opinions of the Press' leaf, original dark brown cloth, little marked, author's own copy with his notes, corrections amendments together with insertions, 4 page ALS from F. W. Ridler of Museum of Practical Geology, brief note from Kegan Paul, brief ALS from H. G. Seeley, ALS postcard from Sir Stanley Lathes.   Jarndyce Antiquarian Booksellers   CCXVII - 205   2016   £380

Association – Ridley, Harrison

Hill, Leslie Pinckney *Toussaint L'Ouverture: a Dramatic History.* Boston: Christopher Pub. House, 1928. First edition, owner's stamp of Harrison A. Ridley Jr., repeated on prelim leaves, numbers on bottom page (as was Ridley's custom), else near fine, handsome, very near fine dust jacket (scarce).   Between the Covers Rare Books   207 - 53   2016 $750

Association – Riek, Edgar

Moore, Raymond C. *Treatise on Invertebrate Palaeontology part R: Arthropoda volume four (Crustacea).* Lawrence: University of Kansas, 1969. Octavo, 2 volumes, text illustrations, very good in cloth binding, signed by author for Edgar Riek.   Andrew Isles Natural History Books   55 - 20337   2016 $250

Association – Rigg, H. C.

Scott, Walter   1771-1832 *Border Antiquities of England and Scotland...* London: printed for Longman, Hurst, Rees, Orme and Brown, J. Murray...., 1814. 1817. First edition, large paper copy, 2 volumes, folio, 94 engraved plates, including 2 engraved titlepages, Morpeth Castle plate loose, volume I engraved title almost loose, pages civ-cv little discolored apparently by insertion of a leaf between them, occasional light foxing with volume I engraved titlepage bit more affected, contemporary half deep red straight grain morocco, green marbled paper covered boards, edges uncut, endcaps, joints and board edges worn, boards much rubbed, edges little toned but still good copy overall, front pastedown of each volume is ownership inscription of H. C. Rigg, Crossrigg Hall and recent bookplate of Susan Wade.   Unsworths Antiquarian Booksellers Ltd.   30 - 135   2016   £200

Association – Rikerman, C. H.

Ray, John *The Wisdom of God Manifested in the Works of the Creation, in Two Parts.* London: for Samuel Smith, 1692. Second edition, 8vo., contemporary calf, covers panelled gilt with vase and flower tool in each corner, gilt spine with red morocco label (corners worn, top corner of lower cover chewed, area of surface insect damage at foot of the lower cover), from the library of James Stevens Cox (1910-1997), inscribed "The Gift of Mrs. Ray to John Morley July 31 1707", and signatures 'Jane Dorothy Harvey 1849' and 'C. H. Rikerman(?) 1885'.   Maggs Bros. Ltd.   1447 - 360   2016   £500

Association – Ringwalt, William

Elder, William *A Memoir of Henry C. Carey; Read before the Historical Society of Pennsylvania.* Philadelphia: Henry Carey Baird Co., 1880. First edition, 8vo., brown cloth stamped in black, blind and gilt, small scrape on front cover, otherwise very good, presentation "Hon. William D. Kelley/ with the compliments/ Wm. E. Ringwalt/April 2nd/84", from the library of consumer advocate Florence Kelley, this was presented to her father, Judge and Congressman.   Second Life Books, Inc.   196A - 497   2016 $65

Association – Rintoul, C. R.

Murphy, Arthur *Ranger's Progress; Consisting of a Variety of Poetical Essays....* London: printed for the author and sold by T. Kinnersly in St. paul's Church Yard and to be had of all othr Booksellers in Town and Country, 1760. 8vo., full contemporary calf, gilt ruled border, spine gilt in six compartments with repeat floral device, upper inch of joints little cracked, head and tail chipped, signature of C. R. Rintoul 1888 on f.e.p., very good, clean copy.   Jarndyce Antiquarian Booksellers   CCXVI - 423   2016   £280

Association – Ripley, Arthur Gordon

Young, John *A Criticism on the Elegy Written in a Country Church-Yard.* Edinburgh: printed for John Ballantyne for Longman, Hurst, Rees and Orme, 1810. Second edition, octavo, original grey boards and printed paper label, untrimmed, leather bookplate of Arthur Gordon Ripley, Denver, bookseller's description pasted to front pastedown, slight foxing, boards little worn, some loss at head of spine, very good.   The Brick Row Book Shop   Miscellany 69 - 51   2016 $625

Association – Ripperger, Helmut Lothar

Rhymers' Club *The Second Book of the Rhymers' Club.* London: Elkin Mathews & John Lane, 1894. One of 650 copies, presentation from publisher John Lane, inscribed in pencil to Irish poet and novelist Katharine Tynan Hinkson, extremely uncommon thus, original brown cloth with gilt title to spine, light browning to margins of interior pages, bookplates of writer J. G. E. Hopkins, culinary writer Helmut Lothar Ripperger and collector Mark Samuels Lasner, very good.   The Kelmscott Bookshop   13 - 59   2016 $950

Association – Ripstein, Sylvia

Garcia Marquez, Gabriel *La Incredible y Triste Historia de la Candida Erendira y de su Abuela Desalmada. (Innocent Erendira).* Mexico: Editorial Hermes, 1972. First Mexican edition, pictorial paper wrappers, illustrations to panels, lettered gilt, presentation inscribed by author to Sylvia Ripstein, his granddaughter, near fine with some light wear to spine ends, faint toning to extremities, minor offsetting from a small piece of removed tape to front free endpaper, otherwise fresh interior, overall bright and attractive copy.   B & B Rare Books, Ltd.   2016 - GGM046   2016 $2000

Association – Risenfield, William

Chaucer, Geoffrey 1340-1400 *The Canterbury Tales.* Waltham St. Lawrence: Golden Cockerel Press, 1929-1931. No. 343 of 485 copies on paper (and 15 on vellum), 4 volumes, 318 x 197mm., original morocco backed patterned paper boards by Sangorski & Sutcliffe, raised bands, gilt titling, top edges gilt, others untrimmed, in cloth slipcase, red and blue initials and very pleasing wood engraved borders (frequently inhabited) by Eric Gill on every page except in last part of volume IV, verso of front free endpapers with bookplate of William Risenfield, joints somewhat rubbed and bit darkened (from dye), portions of upper joint volume I cracked (no other cracking), corners rather mashed, leather little marked, but all volumes solid, covers unsoiled, spines uncharacteristically close in color, very fresh, clean and bright internally.   Phillip J. Pirages   67 - 172   2016 $8500

Association – Ritchie, Neil

Acton, Harold *Modern Chinese Poetry.* London: Duckworth, 1936. First edition, 8vo., original blue cloth little scuffed overall stamped in gilt to front, backstrip lettered in gilt, little wear at tips, slight lean to spine, top edge gilt, erased ownership inscription, flyleaf and others toned and fore edge untrimmed, good, inscribed by author for (his bibliographer) Neil Ritchie.   Blackwell's Rare Books   B186 - 172   2016   £125

Association – Rivero de la Calle, Manuel

Neruda, Pablo *Cancion de Gesta (Song of Protest).* N.P.: Imprenta Nacional de Cuba, 1960. True first edition, inscribed by author to Manuel Rivero de la Calle, 1960, mild foxing to pages, multiple dampstains to boards, tiny pencil annotations on cover, good copy.   Ken Lopez Bookseller   166 - 91   2016 $2500

Association – Rivers, Elizabeth

Theocritus *The Second and Seventh Idylls.* London: John Lane, Bodley Head, 1927. First Rivers edition, 8 wood engravings by Elizabeth Rivers, 32mo., original black boards, backstrip and upper board lettered and decorated in white, some splitting along upper joint and some tiny spots of wear to corners, edges rough trimmed and little toned, partial browning to endpapers, good, inscribed by artist to Aunt Mary with love from Elizabeth Rivers.   Blackwell's Rare Books   B186 - 332   2016   £80

Association – Rixey, P. H.

Derleth, August *Someone in the Dark.* Sauk City: Arkham House, 1941. First edition, first printing, 1115 copies, octavo cloth, presentation from author to M. P. Shiel, inscribed again by author for Major P. H. Rixey, some tanning to front endpapers, rear endpaper has tape residue to edges and rear paste down has the bookplate of P. H. Rixey affixed to it, top page edges dusty, upper front right corner little bumped, about very good in very good dust jacket which has small tear with wrinkle and small piece missing at upper right front panel affecting the edge of the "E" in title lettering SOMEONE, some light rubs to corner tips and spine ends, some tanning to edges of rear panel.   John W. Knott, Jr./L.W. Currey, Inc.   Fall-Winter 2015 - 16236   2016 $2500

Association – Roadstrum, V. N.

Finch, James A. *Federal Anti-Trust Decisions. Cases Decided in the United States Courts Arising Under, Involving or Growing Out of the Enforcement of the Anti-Trust Act of July 2 1890....* Washington: GPO, 1912. First edition, 4 volumes, inscribed by John Qullin Tilson (1866-1958), Conn. Congressman, with stamp of V. N. Roadstrum, attorney for J.P. Morgan Estate, very good or better, edges lightly soiled, otherwise very tight and clean, handsome set, original maroon buckram.   Simon Finch   2015 - 27510   2016 $300

Association – Robbins, Irving W.

Wheat, Carl Irving *Mapping the Transmississippi West.* San Francisco: printed by the Grabhorn Press, volumes II-V printed by Taylor & Taylor and James printing using the designs of Edwin and Robert Grabhorn, 1957-1963. One of 1000 copies, 5 volumes bound in six, 368 x 264mm., publisher's gray linen boards backed with textured buckram, flat spine, in apparently original plain brown dust jacket with ink titling on spines, with 374 maps as called for, five in color, 27 folding, inscribed by author to Irving W. Robbins, Jr., with Robbins' bookplate, prospectus and envelope containing obituaries of Wheat laid in at front of volume), dust jackets bit creased and frayed (though not in tatters), one minor corner crease to map, otherwise volumes themselves extremely fine, clean, fresh and bright inside and out.   Phillip J. Pirages   67 - 179   2016 $5400

Association – Robeson, Paul

Dunbar, Paul Laurence *Lyrics of Lowly Life.* London: Chapman & Hall, 1897. First English edition, octavo, publisher's green cloth, frontispiece, ownership signature of Paul Robeson.   Honey & Wax Booksellers   4 - 55   2016 $2500

Association – Robinson, Alfred

Priestley, Joseph 1733-1804 *Lectures on History and General Policy...* London: Thomas Tegg, 1826. 2 folding plates, later functional purple cloth, spine faded, later signature of Alfred H. Robinson.   Jarndyce Antiquarian Books   CCXV - 908   2016   £60

Association – Robinson, Commander

Jane, Fred T. *The Lordship The Passen and We.* London: A. D. Innes, 1897. First edition, 8vo., original blue cloth lettered gilt on spine and cover, pages uncut, signed presentation from author to Commander Robinson.   Any Amount of Books   2015 - A99784   2016   £250

Association – Robinson, Edwin Arlington

Van Doren, Mark *Edwin Arlington Robinson.* New York: Literary Guild, 1927. First edition, small 8vo., portrait, cover little soiled, little nicked at top of spine, otherwise very good, this copy inscribed by Robinson "Mark's Copy (given by) Edwin Arlington (Robinson) May 1927".   Second Life Books, Inc.   196 B - 790   2016 $150

Association – Robinson, Eli K., Mrs.

Jernegan, Marcus Wilson *Progress of Nations. The Story of the World And Its Peoples from the Dawn of History to the Present Day.* Chicago: Dept. of Rehabilitation, Disabled American Veterans of the World War, 1930-1931. Unknown Soldier edition, 10 volumes, 229 x 156mm., this copy #604 especially prepared for Mrs. Eli K. Robinson, remarkably fine publisher's deluxe black pebble grain morocco, ornately gilt, front covers with decorative gilt rule border enclosing elaborate floral rococo-style frame, frame around a central medallion featuring a knight's plumed helmet, raised bands, gilt titling, gilt turn-ins with compartments elegantly decorated with volutes and small floral tools, gilt titling, gilt turn-ins with curling floral rolls, sky blue pictorial endpapers, all edges gilt, with more than 2000 illustrations, including more than 200 maps and charts, 53 images in color, perhaps trivial imperfection somewhere, but essentially in as new condition, amazingly well preserved set, virtually as it was delivered to its original owner.   Phillip J. Pirages   67 - 195   2016 $1800

Association – Robinson, Frederick

Emancipation of the Negro Slaves in the West India Colonies Considered with Reference to its Impolicy and Injustice, in Answer to Mr. Wilberforce's Appeal. London: Whitmore & Fen, 1824. Half title, slight crease to first 2 leaves, unopened, sewn as issued, backed with later brown paper, slightly worn at head and tail, inscribed "Rt. Hon. Fredk. Robinson MP".   Jarndyce Antiquarian Booksellers   CCXVII - 257   2016   £350

Association – Robinson, G. H.

Sallustius Crispus, C. *Opera Quae Suerpsunt Omnia.* Andreapoli: in aedibus academicis excudebat Jacobus Morison, 1796. 12mo., half title, lightly dust soiled in places, largely untrimmed in early 20th century green pebbled cloth, spine lettered gilt, backstrip sunned, headcap lightly worn, ownership inscription of G. H. Robinson, good.   Blackwell's Rare Books   B186 - 138   2016   £200

Association – Robinson, James

Dickens, Charles   1812-1870 *Christmas Stories from "Household Worlds" and "All the Year Round".* London: Chapman & Hall, 1879. Household edition, 4to., frontispiece, vignette title, plates and illustrations by Dalziel, odd spot, contemporary half calf, spine with raised gilt bands and black leather labels, spine little rubbed, Jas. Robinson with small booklabel, good plus.   Jarndyce Antiquarian Booksellers   CCXVIII - 774   2016   £35

Association – Robinson, L. M.

Camden, William *Rerum Anglicarum et Hibernicarum Annales, Regnante Elisabetha.* Lugd. Batavorum: Elzevir, 1639. 8vo, engraved portrait, titlepage in red and black, woodcut printer's device, copious notes in old hand to endpapers and prelim blanks, further marginalia in Latin and English with occasional manicules, few pages with pencil ticks to margins, sporadic light foxing, one or two marginal paper flaws, small hole in centre of page 359, affecting only few letters, contemporary vellum, gilt to spine evidence of lost label replaced with ink title, yapp edges, spine slightly darkened, little soiled with some smudges and stains, small (burn?) hole to spine, some bands broken and inner hinge split but binding sound, small loss to top corner of f.f.e.p., armorial bookplate of Robert Hinde, bookplate of Frances Massey O'Brien and an anonymous catalogue description affixed to front pastedown, ownership inscriptions of Sunderland Nov. 23rd 1805, Eton, L. M. Robinson 1923, and Frances Massey O'Brien, July 1967, FMO's pencil note.   Unsworths Antiquarian Booksellers Ltd.   E01 - Early Printing - 4   2016   £300

Association – Robson, Harriet

Patmore, Coventry *Poems. I. Amelia. II. Angel in the House. III. Victories of Love. IV. The Unknown Eros.* London: George Bell & sons, 1879. Half titles, 4 volumes, contemporary quarter green morocco, green sand grained cloth sides, spines lettered gilt, slight rubbing, very good, discreet presentation inscription from author for H. R. (likely Harriet Robson who became Patmore's third wife).   Jarndyce Antiquarian Booksellers   CCXVII - 214   2016   £320

Association – Rodman, Samuel

Convention of Delegates from the Abolition Societies *Minutes of the Proceedings of the... Convention of Delegates from the Abolition Societies...* Philadelphia: Printed by Zacharian Poulson Junr., 1794-1801. First, second, third, fourth, fifth and seventh conventions, 6 sewn pamphlets in plain paper wrappers, 3 are untrimmed in original plain paper wrappers, the other three trimmed in early plain paper wrappers, contemporary signature of Samuel Rodman, contemporary signature of Isaac Hicks, front wrapper of fourth pamphlet detached, very good set.   Between the Covers Rare Books   202 - 4   2016 $10,000

Association – Roethke, Theodore

Spender, Stephen *Poems of Dedication.* New York: Random House, 1947. First American edition, 8vo., original cloth backed patterned boards, dust jacket, fine in lightly worn dust jacket, presentation inscribed by author to poet Theodore Roethke.   James S. Jaffe Rare Books   Occasional List: Winter 2016 - 129   2016 $750

Association – Roger, Susan

National Training School for Cookery *High Class Cookery Recipes as Taught in School.* London: W. H. Allen & Co., 1885. 10 pages ads, 44 page catalog (July 1883), 4 pages ads, ink recipe for Xmas cake on verso of title, endpapers brittle, leading f.e.p. loose, original contemporary signature of Susan Roger.   Jarndyce Antiquarian Books CCXV - 335   2016   £45

Association – Rogers, Arthur

Montaigne, Michel De   1533-1592 *Essays of Michael Seigneur de Montaigne in Three Books.* London: printed for T. Basset, 1693. Early edition, 3 volumes, small 8vo., engraved frontispiece portrait of author, some early ink underlining, lacks rear free endpaper (volume I), original full mottled calf (mismatched set), raised bands, gilt spines, red leather title labels, inner joints reinforced with Kozo, worn, ownership signatures of J. Merton (?), Arthur Rogers - June 1933, Reverend James Jenkyn (d. 1825 of Herfordshire?) and Myles Standish Slocum, Pasadena.   Jeff Weber Rare Books   181 - 22   2016 $275

Association – Rogers, Frederick

Sprigg, William *A Modest Plea, for an Equal Common-Wealth Against Monarchy.* London: for Giles Calvert, 1659. One of two editions, 8vo., blank upper corner of A1-E1 and I8-K4 intermittently dampstained, some occasional light soiling and few light ink drops to gatherings A and B, contemporary sheep, recently rebacked and recornered, new endpapers, from the library of James Stevens Cox (1910-1997), 17th century signatures of Robert Pearce, signature of Sir Frederick Rogers (1716-1777) 4th Baronet of Wisdome in Devon.   Maggs Bros. Ltd.   1447 - 395   2016   £950

Association – Rogers, Samuel

Gruner, Ludwig *The Decorations of the Garden Pavilion in the Grounds of Buckingham Palace.* London: Published by John Murray, 1846. First edition, large folio, 15 engraved plates, some light spotting, original red cloth, upper board lettered and tooled in gilt, rebacked, armorial bookplate of Samuel Rogers.   Marlborough Rare Books   List 55 - 31   2016   £950

Association – Rogert, William Benezet

Gould, Nat *The Magic of Sport; Mainly Autobiographical.* London: John Long, 1909. First edition, bookplate and owner's inked name of William Benezet Rogert, spine ends bit chipped, else near fine in modestly chipped and internally repaired, about very good, very scarce.   Between the Covers Rare Books   208 - 134   2016 $225

Association – Rohr, Marie

Horgan, Paul *Humble Powers.* London: Macmillan, 1954. First British edition thus, cloth, laid into corner photo mounts on f.f.e.p is black and white photo of Horgan with his aunt, and godchild, gilt inscription written by his aunt, Marie Rhor to Isabelle Hinsdale, fine in slightly edge worn dust jacket with two small chips and couple of short tears, very scarce.   Gene W. Baade, Books on the West   2015 - FTR091   2016 $131

Association – Rolle, Baron

Stevens, John *The History of Portugal from the First Ages of the World to the Great Revolution, Under King John IV in the year 1640.* London: W. Rogers, 1698. First edition, 8vo., table, contemporary brown speckled calf, covers scuffed, good, library label of Baron Rolle.   J. & S. L. Bonham Antiquarian Booksellers   Europe 2016 - 8419   2016   £500

Selden, John   1584-1654 *Theanthropos; or God Made Man.* London: by J. G. for Nathaniel Brooks, 1661. First edition, 8vo., engraved portrait, contemporary calf, covers ruled in blind, gilt spine with red morocco label, inside joints broken, spine defective at head and tail, covers rubbed, pastedowns unstuck, flyleaves include waste from 12mo. edition of Cicero, from the library of James Stevens Cox (1910-1997), bookplate and signature of John, first and last Baron Rolle of Stevenstone (1750-1842), Exeter.   Maggs Bros. Ltd.   1447 - 377   2016   £160

Association – Rolls, John Etherington Welch

Barry, William Whittaker *A Walking Tour in Normandy.* London: Richard Bentley, 1868. First edition, original blue cloth by Edmonds & Remnants, slightly dulled, bookplate of John Etherington Welch Rolls, esq., The Hendre Co. Monmoth, very good.   Jarndyce Antiquarian Booksellers CCXVII - 26   2016   £75

Association – Roman, James

Lowenfels, Walter *Song of Peace.* New York: Roving Eye Press, 1959. One of 125 copies in hardcover, Blockprints by Anton Refregier, folio, cloth and illustrated paper over boards, cloth quite foxed, thus about very good, laid in broadside on card with block print by Refregier and with blurb by Linus Pauling (foxed and with crease), volume signed by Lowenfels and Refregier, also inscribed for James Roman by Lowenfels', laid in letter dated 9/4/65 on Lowenfels' stationary.   Between the Covers Rare Books   204 - 68   2016 $150

Association – Romie, Richard

Bearden, Romare *Six Black Masters of American Art.* Garden City: Doubleday & Co./Zenith Books, 1972. Second edition?, hardcover issue, simultaneous issue, octavo, pictorial cloth, fine in near fine dust jacket with short tear and little rubbing, inscribed by Bearden for Richard Romie, very scarce signed.   Between the Covers Rare Books   202 - 7   2016 $1000

Association – Rose, Coward

Williams, James *The Footman's Guide.* London: Dean and Son, 1856. Sixth edition, appropriate plates and bills of fare, 12mo., 2 folding plates, one slightly dusted and creased at fore edge, contemporary full dark purple grained calf, expertly rebacked, signature of Mr. Coward Rose, bookseller's ticket of Richard & W. F. Larkin.   Jarndyce Antiquarian Books   CCXV - 483   2016   £280

Association – Rose, Kenneth

Day, J. Wentworth *King George V as a Sportsman: an Informal Study of the first Country Gentleman.* London: Cassell & Co., 1935. 8vo. in 12's, original green cloth, spine titled gilt, 52 photographic plates and illustrations, spine sunned, otherwise very good, from the library of Kenneth Rose (1924-12014), with his signature.   Sotheran's   Piccadilly Notes - Summer 2015 - 97   2016   £50

Hart-Davis, Rupert *The Lyttelton Hart-Davis Letters. Correspondence of George Lyttelton and Rupert Hart-Davis.* London: John Murray, 1978-1984. First edition, 8vo., 6 volumes in original cloth with dust jackets, near fine set, this set from the library of historian Kenneth Rose, without ownership markings, occasional marginal lines in his hand.   Sotheran's   Piccadilly Notes - Summer 2015 - 159   2016   £198

Association – Rosebery, Archibald Philip Primrose, 5th Earl of

Tate, Nahum *Poems.* London: by T. M. for Benj. Tooke, 1677. First edition, 8vo., without final blank leaf, small ink stain to blank fore margin of E2, rust spot to F4, some light staining to F6 and H2, 19th century calf, blind panelled, front board detached, from the library of James Stevens Cox (1910-1997), mid 19th century bookplate of John Whitefoord Mackenzie, armorial bookplate of Archibald Philip Primrose, 5th Earl of Rosebery.   Maggs Bros. Ltd.   1447 - 407   2016   £150

Association – Rosebery, Lord

Thornbury, Walter *Haunted London.* London: Chatto & Windus, 1880. First edition, extra illustrated with cancel titlepage noting "Special Copy Extended to two volumes by the insertion of a large number of extra illustrations", ALS from Lord Rosebery, 8vo., 2 volumes, sometime bound in full double gilt line panelled full polished calf panelled and lettered gilt on spines, top edges gilt, illustrations by F. W. Fairholt, extra illustrated with 97 plates, joints and heads of spines little worn and rubbed, otherwise very good.   Sotheran's   Piccadilly Notes - Summer 2015 - 304   2016   £750

Association – Rosenbloom, Charles

Swift, Jonathan 1667-1745 *Gulliver's Travels.* London: Cresset Press, 1930. No. 134 of 195 copies on paper and 10 on vellum, 2 volumes, 364 x 256mm., fine recent dark green half morocco gilt by Courtland Benson, lighter green marbled paper sides, raised bands, spines handsomely gilt in compartments in antique style with large elegant floral stamp centerpiece and curling leafy cornerpieces, gilt titling, top edge gilt, others untrimmed; with a total of 27 engravings as called for, title page vignette featuring a bust of Swift (appearing in each volume), 8 head and tailpieces, five full page maps, 12 delicately hand colored engraved plates (including two frontispiece) by Rex Whistler, each within ornate baroque-style frame, front pastedown of volume II with bookplate of Charles J. Rosenbloom, very fine set inside and out.   Phillip J. Pirages   67 - 104   2016 $8500

Association – Rosenthal, Tom

Orwell, George 1903-1950 *The Complete Works of George Orwell.* London: Secker & Warburg, 1998. First complete edition, from the library of publisher, Tom Rosenthal with his bookplate, 8vo., 20 volumes in original cloth with dust jackets, little light sunning to spines of few wrappers, otherwise near fine set.   Sotheran's   Piccadilly Notes - Summer 2015 - 224   2016   £2750

Association – Rotomagoeus, Ludovicus Martellus

Horatius Flaccus, Quintus *Ex Antiquissimus Undecim Lib. M. S. et Schedis Aliquot Emendatus.* Antwerp: Christophori Plantini, 1578. Small 4to., printer's device to titlepage, some small illustrations in text, woodcut initials, occasional tiny annotations and underlinings in old hand, few small paper flaws, two marginal and one affecting couple of words to page 441-2, little light toning towards edges, odd spots of ink, modern green morocco, red label to spine, edges red, marbled endpapers, spine faded to yellowish tan, little shelfwear, very good, signature of Ludovicus Martellus Rotomagoeus, illegible library ink stamp, few ms. codes to prelim blanks.   Unsworths Antiquarian Booksellers Ltd.   E01 - Early Printing - 11   2016   £475

ssociation – Rouse, H.

Payne Gallwey, Ralph *The Fowler Ireland.* London: John Van Voorst, Paternoster Row, 1882. First edition, inscribed by author for H. Rouse, large 8vo, recently rebound in half blue morocco over blue cloth, spine decorated in gilt and stamped with hunting motifs, marbled endpapers, top edge gilt, very good, internally clean.   Sotheran's   Hunting, Shooting & Fishing - 91   2016   £200

Association – Rowell, Galen

Muir, John **1838-1914** *The Yosemite.* San Francisco: Sierra Club, 1989. First edition, signed by photographer, Galen Rowell, 4to., 101 full color plates, many full page, black cloth, gilt, very fine in original pictorial dust jacket. Argonaut Book Shop   Natural History 2015 - 7460   2016 $175

Association – Rowlandson, F.

Browning, Robert **1812-1889** *The Ring and The Book.* London: Smith, Elder, 1868-1869. First edition, 4 volumes, 8vo., occasional light scattered foxing to free endleaves, original black stamped green cloth, gilt stamped spines by Harrison, quarter gilt stamped calf over blue cloth slipcase, volume 3 rear hinge cracked with light front pastedown soiling, volumes 1 and 2 hinges cracked, Robert Browning's signature tipped in volume I, opposite titlepage, ownership signatures of W. J. (...?) Settle (Sherborne Dorset, Feb. 21, 1869) and F. Rowlandson, ownership signatures of E. M. Forster in volume 2 to free front endleaf and titlepage, attractive, very good, with cut-out signature tipped in of Robert Browning.   Jeff Weber Rare Books   181 - 42   2016 $4000

Association – Rudd, Donald

Goodchild, George *McLean Prevails.* London & Melbourne: Ward, Lock & Co., 1935. First edition, 8vo., original olive green cloth, lettered black on spine and front cover, from the Donald Rudd collection, very slight browning to endpapers with small Father Christmas sticker, otherwise near fine in price clipped, very good+ dust jacket, very slight shelfwear, excellent condition.   Any Amount of Books   2015 - C11014   2016   £170

Association – Rule, Daniel

Kurt, Weill *An American Opera.* New York: Chappell & Co., 1948. First edition, large quarto, printed wrappers, top corner very slightly bumped, trifle age toned on wrappers, publisher's price sticker on titlepage, near fine, ownership signature of Daniel Rule, director of NYC Opera.   Between the Covers Rare Books   204 - 77   2016 $900

Association – Rumbold

Austen, Jane **1775-1817** *Northanger Abbey and Persuasion.* London: John Murray, 1818. First edition, 4 volumes, bound without half titles and blanks, sporadic foxing, small hole in C12 in volume i, affecting 2 letters on verso, volume iv, waterstained, 12mo., contemporary half calf, 2 of the spines partially scorched, lacking lettering pieces, 1 spine slightly defective at head, cracks in 4 joints, engraved bookplate in volume i (Rumbold family), pencil ownership inscription on flyleaf (almost loose) of volume iv of C. E. Rumbold, Walton.   Blackwell's Rare Books   Marks of Genius - 6   2016   £6000

Austen, Jane **1775-1817** *Sense and Sensibility.* London: printed for the author by C. Roworth and published by T. Egerton, 1813. Second edition, 3 volumes, bound without half titles and terminal blanks, sporadic foxing as usual, slight defect to inner margin of 1 leaf in volume i, 4 leaves almost loose in volume ii (never caught by edge sewing), minor worming in lower margin volume iii, 12mo., contemporary half calf, flat spines gilt in compartments, lacking lettering pieces, minor wear, engraved armorial bookplate inside front covers volumes i and ii (Rumbold family), good copy.   Blackwell's Rare Books   Marks of Genius - 3   2016   £8000

Association – Ruskin, John

Leslie, George Dunlop *Letters to Marco.* London: Macmillan, 1893. Presentation to John Ruskin from G. D. Leslie, Dec. 20, 1993, very good in original dark green cloth boards, gilt title to spine and gilt floral decoration to front cover, minor wear to edges of boards and corners, interior clean overall, occasional spots of foxing, short closed tear to bottom edge of titlepage, minor repairs to both interior hinges, very good.   The Kelmscott Bookshop   13 - 31   2016 $450

Association – Russell, Keith Cushman

Walton, Izaak **1593-1683** *The Complete Angler...* Boston: Little Brown, 1892. 8vo., lacking volume I, frontispiece, vignettes, dark green gilt stamped cloth, top edge gilt, bit frayed at spine ends, rubbed, top corner hinge splitting, angling themed bookplate of Keith Cushman Russell, good+.   Jeff Weber Rare Books   181 - 88   2016 $45

Walton, Izaak **1593-1683** *The Complete Angler...* London & Edinburgh: T. N. Foulis ltd., 1925. Large 8vo., color frontispiece, 20 full color plates by Thorpe, original quarter green cloth backed cloth, decorative boards, one corner bit worn, angling themed bookplate of Keith Cushman Russell, very good.   Jeff Weber Rare Books   181 - 87   2016 $45

Association – Ryan, Nigel

Cooper, Diana *Autobiography Consisting of the Rainbow comes & Goes, Light of Common Fay. Trumpets from the Steel.* London: Rupert Hart Davis, 1958-1960. First edition, 8vo., 3 volumes, original cloth with dust jackets, photographs, cloth on Rainbow somewhat worn and with repaired and rather tatty dust jacket, dust jackets on other two volumes little chipped, creased and stained, all volumes inscribed by author for friend Nigel Ryan.   Sotheran's Piccadilly Notes - Summer 2015 - 84   2016   £248

Association – Ryder, John

Bernard Shaw & Max Beerbohm at Covent Garden. London: Bodley Head, 1981. First edition, one of 225 copies, press device to titlepage, foolscap 8vo., original sewn card wrappers, dust jacket with Beerbohm caricature, very gentle fading to borders, very good, inscribed by book's designer, John Ryder.   Blackwell's Rare Books   B186 - 282   2016   £30

Association – Ryland, William

Monro, Alexander   *Three Treatises on the Brain, the Eye and the Ear.* Edinburgh: Bell & Bradfute, G. G. & J. Robinson and J. Johnson, Edinburgh, 1797. First edition, 24 engraved plates, some folding, one partially hand colored, first two leaves moderately browned with occasional light toning throughout, margins of title expertly mended, some offsetting from a number of plates, signature of William Ryland, Edinburgh dated 1819, very attractive, untrimmed copy.   Edwin V. Glaser Rare Books   2015 - 10131   2016 $2500

Association – Rylands, J. Paul

Churton, Ralph   *The Life of Alexander Nowell, Dean of St. Pauls.* Oxford University Press, for the author, 1809. 8vo., 9 plates, some folding, little noted, sporadic foxing, plates offset, tan diced russia, gilt spine and borders, marbled edges and endpapers, binding sound, skillfully rebacked, edges rubbed, corners worn, hinges repaired with marbled paper, armorial bookplate of J. Paul Rylands, , letter to Prof. Patrick Collinson dated 9.ii.80 loosely inserted.   Unsworths Antiquarian Booksellers   30 - 32   2016 $75

Association – Sachs

Bacon, Francis   1561-1626   *The Twoo Bookes of Francis Bacon. Of the Proficience and Advancement of Learning, Divine and Humane.* London: for Henrie Tomes, 1605. First edition, 4to., lacks final blank 3H2 and as always, rare two leaves of errata at end, late 19th century half calf and marbled boards, extremities of boards worn, very skillfully and imperceptibly rebacked, retaining entire original spine, small worm trail at bottom margin of quires 2D-2F, occasional minor marginalia in early hand, else lovely copy, early signature of Row'd Wetherald on title signature of Horatio Carlyon 1861, Sachs bookplate and modern leather book label calf backed clamshell box.   Joseph J. Felcone, Inc. Books from Five Centuries: a Miscellany - 10   2016 $7500

Association – Sackville-West, Victoria

Lyric Love. London: and New York: Macmillan and Co., 1892. 159 x 105mm., lovely contemporary blue-gray crushed morocco elegantly and elaborately gilt by Bumpus (stamp signed), covers with delicate filigree frame and large densely intricate central medallion composed of hundreds of small tools, fan shaped cornerpieces of similar design, raised bands, spine gilt in compartments with central medallion and scrolling cornerpieces, pastedowns framed by turquoise morocco with gilt filigree borders, fleuron cornerpieces and alternating dot and crescent tools along the four sides, ivory silk endleaves, all edges gilt, titlepage vignette, front pastedown with engraved bookplate of Victoria Sackville-West, spine sunned to pleasant slightly darker blue green, joints with just a hint of water, light offsetting to free endleaves from turn-ins as usual, isolated corner creases, other trivial imperfections, but most attractive little book, especially smooth and clean internally and in flamboyant binding showing almost no wear.   Phillip J. Pirages   67 - 33   2016 $1500

Association – Sage, Dean

Stewart, W. C.   *A Caution to Anglers.* Edinburgh: Adam and Charles Black, 1871. First edition, 12mo., original printed wrappers bound into contemporary half blue calf over marbled paper boards, spine panelled and lettered in gilt with emblematic centre tools, little browning to titlepage, otheriwse very good, bookplate of writer Dean Sage. Sotheran's   Piccadilly Notes - Summer 2015 - 282   2016 £298

Association – Sage, Mrs.

Wharton, Edith   1862-1937   *Italian Villas and Their Gardens.* New York: Century, 1904. First and only edition, heavily illustrated with photos, drawings and 26 full color plates by Maxfield Parrish, this copy with tipped in ALS written to Mrs. Sage, owner's small tasteful bookplate, this copy extra illustrated, presumably by Mrs. Sage.   Ken Lopez Bookseller   166 - 149   2016 $10,000

Association – Salazar, A.

Lafragua, Jose Maria *Reglamento de la Direccion De Colonizacion.* Mexico: Reglamento de la Direccion, 1846. First edition, 16mo., contemporary calf, bookplate of A. Salazar, very good, boards lightly scuffed, some faded ink spots on titlepage, small bookplate on front pastedown. Kaaterskill Books 21 - 13 2016 $1000

Association – Sales D'Olivier, Gabriel Theodore Francois, De

Abailard, Pierre 1079-1142 *Lettre d'Heloise & Abailard. (with, as issued) Reponse d'Abailard a La Lettre d'Heloise.* Tours: Louis Vauquer, 1695. Extremely rare edition, woodcut ornament on title, little browned in places, 12mo., contemporary mottled calf, spine gilt, upper joint cracked, corners slightly worn, bookplate of Gabriel-Theodore-Francois de Sales d'Olivier, sound. Blackwell's Rare Books B186 - 1 2016 £800

Association – Salomon, I. L.

Luzi, Mario *In the Dark Body of Metamorphosis & Other Poems.* New York: Norton, 1972. First edition, blue cloth, nice in little scuffed and soiled dust jacket, presentation by translator to I. L. Salomon. Second Life Books, Inc. 197 - 219 2016 $45

Association – Salt, Thomas

Fortescue, Hugh, 3rd Earl of *Public Schools for the Middle Classes.* London: Longman Green, 1864. First edition, half title, original brown cloth, bookplate of Thomas Salt, very good. Jarndyce Antiquarian Books CCXV - 688 2016 £60

Association – Saltmarshe, Philip

Finch-Hatton, Harold *Advance Australia! An Account of Eight Years Work....* London: W. H. Allen Co., 1885. First edition, 8vo., black and white frontispiece, 13 other black and white plates plus folding black and white map, original blue cloth, gilt spine lettering, gilt vignette to front, rubbed, some marks to boards, frontispiece detached, spotted and with frayed edge, some spots to prelims, plates and text tight and clean, armorial bookplate of Philip Saltmarshe, good++. Simon Finch 2015 - 8854586565 2016 $320

Association – Salvadori

Sharpe, R. Bowdler *Catalogue of the Passeriformes, or Perching Birds, in the Collection of the British Museum. Fringilliformes: part three.* London: British Museum, 1888. Octavo, 16 chromolithograph plates by Hart and Keulemans, publisher's cloth, double page manuscript letter from Salvadori to Sharpe tipped-in. Andrew Isles Natural History Books 55 - 9260 2016 $500

Association – Sanavio, Piero

Dialogue. Journal des Livres et des Idees No. 3. Lausanne: September, 1967. Folio, original self wrappers, printed on all sides, light overall toning, quarter folded with horizontal points starting, from the library of actor Douglas Fairbanks Jr. with his loose bookplate in separate envelope, very good, warmly inscribed to Ezra Pound by Piero Sanavio. Blackwell's Rare Books B186 - 274 2016 £650

Association – Sanborn, Frank B.

Parker, Theodore *Lessons from the World of Matter and The World of Man.* Boston: Published by Charles W. Slack, 1865. First edition, green cloth, gilt, few tears at bottom of spine, short crack to paper over front hinge, modest wear to boards, very good, inscribed by editor to author and Thomas biographer, Frank B. Sanborn. Between the Covers Rare Books 202 - 71 2016 $600

Association – Sandbach, R. G. F.

Graves, Alfred Perceval *Songs of Killarney.* London: Bradbury Agnew & Co., 1873. First edition, half title, vignette signed AC, slightly dusted, original green cloth, front board and spine decorated in black, lettered gilt, back board in blind, half title inscribed "With the author's Respects", Grenville Matheson MacDonald's bookplate, later ownership inscription of R. G. F. Sandbach, nice. Jarndyce Antiquarian Booksellers CCXVII - 112 2016 £150

Association – Sands, Dorothy

Coward, Noel 1899-1973 *Quadrille: a Romantic Comedy in Three Acts.* London: Heinemann, 1952. First edition, signed by 17 members of the English cast and by producer Jack Wilson and by Lynn Fontanne and Alfred Lunt on dedication page (play is dedicated to them), inscribed by Coward to Dorothy Sands (Octavia in the NY production), two more signed cards by Lunt and Fontanne tipped in and 3 notes by Lunt to Sands laid in, with tipped in signed photo of sands, nice in somewhat signed dust jacket. Second Life Books, Inc. 196A - 342 2016 $500

Association – Sassoon, Philip

Sieveking, Lance *The Woman She Was.* London: Cassell, 1934. First edition, 2 plates, presentation from author, inscribed for Sir Philip Sassoon, edges spotted, spine dull, good in good, chipped and torn dust jacket defective at head and tail of spine. Peter Ellis 112 - 358 2016 £95

Association – Saunders, Prince

Vaux, Robert *Memoirs of the Life of Anthony Benezet.* Philadelphia: published by James P. Parke/Merritt, Printer, 1817. First edition, 12mo, lacking front board and frontispiece, rear board detached but present, pages toned but uncut, wear along spine, wear affecting couple of letters of inscription, good plus, inscribed by author for Prince Saunders, housed in half morocco clamshell case, marvelous association copy.   Between the Covers Rare Books   202 - 113   2016 $6500

Association – Saunders, William

Dickens, Charles 1812-1870 *Memoirs of Joseph Grimaldi.* London: Richard Bentley, 1838. First edition, 2nd issue, 2 volumes, half titles, frontispiece, plates by George Cruikshank, 36 page catalog volume II, later full scarlet morocco for Hatchards. gilt spines and double ruled borders, original pink cloth, spine strips bound in at end of each volume, armorial bookplate of William H. R. Saunders, top edge gilt, very good.   Jarndyce Antiquarian Booksellers   CCXVIII - 216   2016   £420

Association – Savage, David

Roth, Philip *Portnoy's Complaint.* New York: Random House, 1969. First edition, inscribed by author in month of publication to photographer Naomi Savage and her husband the artist, David Savage, bit of offsetting to endpapers and between pages 200-201, small spot to topstain near fine in very near fine, corner clipped but not price clipped dust jacket with slightest wear to spine extremities.   Ken Lopez Bookseller   166 - 107   2016 $2500

Association – Savage, Naomi

Roth, Philip *Portnoy's Complaint.* New York: Random House, 1969. First edition, inscribed by author in month of publication to photographer Naomi Savage and her husband the artist, David Savage, bit of offsetting to endpapers and between pages 200-201, small spot to topstain near fine in very near fine, corner clipped but not price clipped dust jacket with slightest wear to spine extremities.   Ken Lopez Bookseller   166 - 107   2016 $2500

Association – Savage, S. M.

Powlett, Edmund *The General Contents of the British Museum; with Remarks Serving as a Directory...*   London: printed for R. and J. Dodsley, 1762. Second edition, half title, 12mo., some light browning, but very good, clean copy, full contemporary sprinkled calf, gilt ruled borders, raised and gilt banded spine, red morocco label, expert repairs to joints and corners, armorial bookplate of Strahallan contemporary signature on front endpaper of S. M. Savage dated 1762 with a number of ms. corrections and observations.   Jarndyce Antiquarian Booksellers   CCXVI - 480   2016   £1250

Association – Saville, John Lumley Savile, 1st Baron

Taylor, Jeremy   1613-1667 *XXVIII Sermons Preached at Golden Grove; Being for the Summer Half Year...*   London: by R. N. for Richard Royston, 1651. First edition, small folio, some occasional spotting, otherwise good, mid 19th century dark green morocco, covers with large early 16th century style acorn panel in blind and with large gilt arms block of the 8th Earl of Scarbrough, gilt spine, marbled endleaves, gilt edges, from the library of James Stevens Cox (1910-1997), occasional underlining and marginal marks in ink including few small florets, bound for John Lumley-Savile, 8th Earl of Scarbrough by descent to his son John Lumley-Savile, 1st Baron Savile of Rufford, Rufford Hall booklabel.   Maggs Bros. Ltd.   1447 - 409   2016   £220

Association – Sawyer, Anna Grace

Turner, Lorenzo Dow   *Anti-Slavery sentiment in American Literature Prior to 1865.*   Washington: Association for the Study of Negro Life and History Inc., 1929. First edition, lovely, fine, lacking rare dust jacket, inscribed by author to Anna Grace Sawyer, April 9 1936.   Between the Covers Rare Books   202 - 112   2016 $400

Association – Sawyer, Samuel Nelson

Winsor, Justin *Narrative and Critical History of America.* Boston & New York: Houghton Mifflin and Co., 1889. 86-84-84-87-87-88-89. First edition, 279 x 191mm., 8 volumes, simple but pleasing contemporary black half morocco over marbled boards, raised bands accented with gilt rules, gilt titling, marbled endpapers, top edges gilt, more than 1000 in-text illustrations, maps and charts, bookplate of Samuel Nelson Sawyer in each volume, minor wear to raised bands, faint darkening at edges of leaves, otherwise excellent set, attractive bindings very sturdy and fresh, clean leaves with few signs of use.   Phillip J. Pirages   67 - 2   2016 $950

Association – Scarbrough, John Lumley Savile, 8th Earl of

Taylor, Jeremy   1613-1667 *XXVIII Sermons Preached at Golden Grove; Being for the Summer Half Year...*   London: by R. N. for Richard Royston, 1651. First edition, small folio, some occasional spotting, otherwise good, mid 19th century dark green morocco, covers with large early 16th century style acorn panel in blind and with large gilt arms block of the 8th Earl of Scarbrough, gilt spine, marbled endleaves, gilt edges, from the library of James Stevens Cox (1910-1997), occasional underlining and marginal marks in ink including few small florets, bound for John Lumley-Savile, 8th Earl of Scarbrough by descent to his son John Lumley-Savile, 1st Baron Savile of Rufford, Rufford Hall booklabel.   Maggs Bros. Ltd.   1447 - 409   2016   £220

Association – Schiller

Denslow, W. W. *Denslow's Mother Goose.* New York: McClure Phillips Co., 1901. First edition, 2nd issue, 4to., cloth backed pictorial boards, edges and covers rubbed, else clean, tight and very good+ in original pictorial dust jacket chipped at corner folds, (missing 1 1/2 inch piece off spine with some other chipping, overall very good), this is the Schiller auction copy, this copy with large signature of Denslow plus Seahorse drawing,. Aleph-bet Books, Inc. 112 - 140   2016 $8000

Association – Schimmel, Stuart B.

Browning, Robert   1812-1889 *Ferishtah's Fancies.* London: Smith, Elder & Co., 1884. First edition, forged presentation "To FG Watts from Robert Browning Dec. 1884" (not in Browning's hand), in very good original dark brown cloth boards with gilt title to spine and black decoration to front board, rubbing to hinges, edges and corners with short open tear to book cloth along front hinge, foxing to first and last few pages with few light pencil bracket marks to text and occasional folded corners, blue endpages, from the collection of Stuart B. Schimmel.   The Kelmscott Bookshop 12 - 20   2016 $450

Association – Schlesinger, Carl

Digby, Joan *John Depol, from Dark to Light, Wood Engravings for the Stone House Press.* New York: Stone House Press, 1988. Limited to 200 signed and numbered copies, this one of 155 for sale, this copy signed by Digbys, DePol and Gelfand, 60 wood engravings executed by De Pol, 8vo., quarter cloth with patterned paper over boards, this copy inscribed by DePol for Carl Schlesinger.   Oak Knoll Books   310 - 149   2016 $425

Association – Schlimovich, Marcellus

Bonet, Honore *L'Apparition De Jehan de Meun ou Le Songe Du Prieur De Salon.* Paris: Imprime par Crapelet pour la Societe des Bibliophiles Franai, 1845. No. 7 of 17 copies on vellu, plus 100 copies issued on paper, 235 x 181mm., recent fine white pigskin, decorated in blind in medieval style by Courtland Benson, housed in titled custom made morocco backed folding cloth box, 10 engraved plates replicating illustrations from early manuscript copies of the week, pastedown with morocco bookplate of Comte H. De La Bedoyere and engraved bookplate of Marcellus Schlimovich, front free endpaper with embossed library stamp of Dr. Detlef Mauss, half title with ink library stamp of Sociedad Hebraica Argentina, fine, especially clean and bright internally with only most trivial imperfections and in striking new retrospective binding.   Phillip J. Pirages   67 - 343   2016 $2750

Association – Schlondorff, Volker

Lewandowski, Ranier *Die Filme von Volker Schlondorff.* Hildesham: Olma Presse, 1981. First edition, trade softcover original, inscribed by Volker Schlondorff for Pierre Goulliard, near fine, profusely illustrated with photos, stiff perfect bound wrappers, fine, 8.5 x 9.5 inches.   Royal Books   49 - 24   2016 $1250

Association – Schmid, H.

Duemmler, Ernest *Poetae Latini Aevi Carolini.* Berlin: Weidmann, 1964. Reprinted from edition of 1881-1896, 4 volumes in 7, including supplement, 8vo., black and white plates to rear of each volume except III, green cloth, gilt, top edge green, slightly faded and dusty, couple of spots to rear endpapers in two volumes, still very good, bookplate of Dr. H. Schmid, Munchen 40.   Unsworths Antiquarian Booksellers   30 - 49   2016   £210

Association – Schmied, Francois Louis

Mardrus, J. C. *Histoire Charmante De L'Adolescente Sucre D'Amour.* Paris: F. L. Schmied, 1927. First edition, no. 50 of 170 copies signed by artist, 318 x 241mm., unbound as issued in original printed paper wrappers, 14 full page color wood engravings, including frontispiece, signed in pencil by artist, Francois Louis Schmied, and 635 color panel borders, line fillers and tailpieces in Art Deco style, all by Schmied, recto of limitations page with facsimile inscription by author to Schmied, short ink mark to margin of titlepage, just faintest isolated smudge or freckled foxing, otherwise very fine, clean, fresh, fragile wrapper unsoiled and remarkably well preserved.   Phillip J. Pirages   67 - 309 2016 $6500

Association – Schollick, Henry

Paston, George *At John Murray's - Records of a Literary Circle 1843-1892.* London: John Murray, 1932. First edition, plates, head and tail of spine slightly bumped, near fine in very good, slightly torn and repaired price clipped dust jacket faded at spine and edges, presentation copy inscribed for Henry Schollick, by John G. Murray, below that his Son John R. Murray has added his signature.   Peter Ellis   112 - 318   2016   £75

Association – Scholten, Johannes Henricus

Estienne, Charles 1504-1564 *Dictionarium Historicum, Geographicum, Poeticom....* Genevae: apud Samuelem de Tournes, 1693. Reissue of the new edition, quarto, titlepage printed in red and black, contemporary binding of full tree calf with gilt decoration, marbled endpapers, from the library of Dutch theologian Johannes Henricus Scholten (1811-1885) tipped in before titlepage is leaf printed with announcement of the Latin School at Delft with Schotlen's name inserted by hand, signed by Rector A. W. Geers and four other teachers, some light foxing here and there.   Peter Ellis   112 - 117   2016   £475

Association – Schomburgk, R.

Mueller, Ferdinand Von *Western Australia.* Perth: Government Printer, 1882. Quarto, two (folding) colored maps, one tinted and 20 uncolored lithographic plates, publisher's cloth with label, hinges cracked, crudely repaired, bookplate of R. Schomburgk, director of Adelaide Botanic Gardens.   Andrew Isles Natural History Books   55 - 37716   2016 $450

Association – Scorsese, Martin

Giddins, Gary *A Moment's Notice: Portraits of American Jazz Musicians.* New York: Schrimer, 1983. First printing, 4to., presentation by Carol Friedman to Martin Scorsese, paper over boards, nice in slightly browned dust jacket.   Second Life Books, Inc.   196A - 629   2016 $95

Association – Scotland, R. G.

The Halfpenny Magazine. London: R. Seton at the Tatler Office, Covent Garden, 1832. Nos. 1-13, 16-17, May-August 1832, contemporary marbled boards, later paper spine, hand lettered, booklabels of R. G. Scotland and Reniers.   Jarndyce Antiquarian Booksellers   CCXVII - 222   2016   £65

Association – Scott, A.

Kingdom, William *The Secretary Assistant...* London: Whittaker & Co., 1838. Seventh edition, original purple cloth, largely faded to brown, booklabel of A. Scott over earlier removed label, very good.   Jarndyce Antiquarian Books   CCXV - 280   2016   £60

Association – Scott, Alan

Allingham, William *Rhymes for the You Folk.* London: Cassell & Co., n.d., 1867. Large 8vo., original illustrated red paper boards over red cloth, lettered black and white on front board, copiously illustrated, signed presentation from one of the artists, Helen Allingham for Claude and Alan Scott, June 1917, some rubbing and slight chipping along edges and corners with faint foxing to prelims, otherwise sound, clean, attractive, very good.   Any Amount of Books   2015 - C8506   2016   £250

Association – Scott, Claude

Allingham, William *Rhymes for the You Folk.* London: Cassell & Co., n.d., 1867. Large 8vo., original illustrated red paper boards over red cloth, lettered black and white on front board, copiously illustrated, signed presentation from one of the artists, Helen Allingham for Claude and Alan Scott, June 1917, some rubbing and slight chipping along edges and corners with faint foxing to prelims, otherwise sound, clean, attractive, very good.   Any Amount of Books   2015 - C8506   2016   £250

Association – Scott, Thomas

Catlin, George 1796-1872 *O'Kee-Pa: a Religious Ceremony: and Other Customs of the Mandans.* London: Trubner and Co., 1867. First edition, with rare 'Folium Servatum' bound in at rear', presentation copy inscribed by Nicholas Trubner to Thomas Scott, 13 chromolithographed plates, publisher's purple cloth, gilt, all edges gilt, binding lightly soiled and faded, extremities lightly worn, spine ends more so, occasional minor foxing, very good, fragile book difficult to find in fine condition.   Joseph J. Felcone, Inc.   Books from Five Centuries: a Miscellany - 36   2016 $20,000

Association – Scott, William

Newton, Isaac 1642-1727 *Philosophiae Naturalis Principia Mathematica.* London: William and John Innys, 1726. Third edition, title printed in red and black, engraved frontispiece, 1 engraving and numerous diagrams in text, complete with half title and final ad leaf, some foxing at beginning and end, few scattered minor stains, repairs to margins of front flyleaves, late 19th century half red hard grained morocco, spine gilt in compartments and lettered direct, red edges, rebacked preserving previous spine, early inscription at head of title, little cropped at top and faded, seems to say 'gifted to Mr. William Scott of Babecan advocate by me ( ) Foulis', 19th century signature stamp of Dugald Macdonald at centre of titlepage, bookplate of Quebecois George G. Leroux, very good.   Blackwell's Rare Books   Marks of Genius - 32   2016   £11,000

Association – Scrivener, Alan

Coles, Elisha *The Compleat English Schoolmaster 1674.* Scholar Press, 1969. Facsimile of 1674 edition, original red cloth, very good, Alan Scrivener's copy.   Jarndyce Antiquarian Books CCXV - 601   2016   £25

Association – Scully, Agnes

Turner, Sharon *The History of the Anglo-Saxons from the earliest Period to the Norman Conquest.* London: Longman, Rees, Orme, Brown, Green & Longman, 1836. Sixth edition, 3 volumes 8vo., folding map to volume 1, map foxed and occasional spots of foxing elsewhere, publisher's half cloth and grey boards, printed paper labels to spines, edges uncut, all volumes neatly rebacked with original spines retained, endpapers replaced, rubbed, edges worn, corners bumped, gift inscription "Agnes M. Scully from her mama Ismera Payne Jan. 25th 1840, library stamp of Abbat S. Martae e. Berholten.   Unsworths Antiquarian Booksellers Ltd.   E05 - 111   2016   £150

Association – Searle, Ronald

Leiris, Michel *Verve - The French Review of Art Volume VIII No. 29/30.* Paris: Teriade, 1954. First English edition distributed in Great Britain by A. Swemmer, folio, double number devoted to Picasso, 180 drawings, 16 color lithographs, 164 heliogravures, color pictorial boards by Picasso, ownership signature of Ronald Searle, covers bit rubbed at edges, tail of spine slightly chipped, very good.   Peter Ellis   112 - 296   2016   £1500

Association – Sears, Charles

Coras, Jean De *The Qualifications and the Duties of a Good and Complete Judge...* Montreal: 1934. First edition, with his signature dated Autumn 1934, original cloth, spine somewhat rubbed and discolored, else very good, Charles B. Sears's copy.   Simon Finch   2015 - 23032   2016 $250

Association – Secunderabad, Elsie Stockley

Kenney-Herbert, Arthur Russell *Culinary Jottings. A Treatise in Thirty Chapters on Reformed Cookery for Anglo-Indian Exiles...* Madras: Higginbotham & Co., 1891. Half title, some offset browning from f.e.p.'s, original brown cloth, slightly rubbed, signature of Elsie Stockley Secunderabad, Oct. 1898, nice.   Jarndyce Antiquarian Books   CCXV - 274   2016   £120

Association – Seeger, Stanley

Conrad, Joseph 1857-1924   *Laughing Anne and One Day More - two plays.* London: Castle, 1924. First combined edition, octavo, from the library of Gerard Jean-Aubry, author's close friend and first biographer, from the library of Stanley Seeger with his small bookplate, tipped on blank facing page 19 (a summary description of personages in the play), an original sketch in blue crayon of the stage layout, and positioning of the characters written in black ink by Conrad, at lower corner is note in green ink in Jean-Abury's hand "Plan de la scene - fait par Joseph Conrad", with much rougher sketch for final scene, free endpapers tanned, otherwise fine in very good, nicked and creased dust jacket with enclosed tear at head of upper hinge, preserved in green buckram slipcase lettered gilt and with inner folding sleeve.   Peter Ellis   112 - 82   2016   £1250

Conrad, Joseph 1857-1924   *The Children of the Sea - A Tale of the Forecastle.* New York: Dodd, Mead, n.d. circa, 1908. Early edition, small octavo, original dark blue pictorial cloth, depicting a sailing ship in silhouette against a background of clouds and waves, from the library of Stanley Seeger with his bookplate, contemporary (1908) ownership inscription, covers slightly scuffed, very good.   Peter Ellis   112 - 85   2016   £95

Conrad, Joseph 1857-1924   *The Complete Short Stories of Joseph Conrad.* London: Hutchinson, 1933. First edition, 2nd issue, octavo, original black cloth lettered in yellow, slight crease at outer edge of front free endpaper, near fine in very good pictorial dust jacket little nicked and creased at edges, 3'6 reduced price sticker on spine, from the library of Stanley J. Seeger.   Peter Ellis   112 - 84   2016   £125

Conrad, Joseph 1857-1924   *The First and Last of Conrad - Almayer's Folly, an Outcast of the Islands, the Arrow of Gold & the Rover.* London: Ernest Benn, 1929. First edition, octavo, very good in like dust jacket, slightly marked and littled nicked and creased at edges, from the library of Stanley Seeger with his small bookplate.   Peter Ellis   112 - 83   2016   £125

Conrad, Joseph 1857-1924   *The Shadow-Line - a Confession.* London: J. M. Dent, 1917. Second impression, published same month as the first, 2200 copies printed, 8vo., original green decorated cloth, from library of Stanley J. Seeger with his bookplate, presentation from author for The British Farmers' Red Cross Fund No. 1917, cloth little scuffed in two patches on upper board, very good in good only dust jacket, extensively torn at lower hinge and defective at head and tail of spine, preserved in green buckram slipcase lettered gilt with folding inner sleeve.   Peter Ellis   112 - 80   2016   £550

Conrad, Joseph   1857-1924   *Tales of Hearsay.*   London: T. Fisher Unwin, 1925. First edition, octavo, fomer the library of Conrad collector, Stanley J. Seeger with his small bookplate, prelims and edges little spotted, free endpapers partially and lightly tanned, very good in like pictorial dust jacket with several short closed tears, one of them at head of spine which is also creased, preserved custom made green buckram slipcase, lettered in gilt on spine, inner folding sleeve.   Peter Ellis   112 - 79   2016   £250

Conrad, Joseph   1857-1924   *The Nature of a Crime.* London: Duckworth, 1924. First edition, small octavo, 2 bookplates on front pastedown, on of which is that of travel writer Sean Jennett, typographer at Faber and Faber and that of Conrad collector, Stanley J. Seeger, spine slightly faded at head and just little bumped at tail, very good, preserved in custom made green buckram slipcase, lettered gilt on spine, inner folding sleeve.   Peter Ellis   112 - 78   2016   £95

Conrad, Joseph   1857-1924   *The Arrow of Gold.*   New York: Doubleday Page, 1919. First edition, octavo, original blue cloth stamped in gilt, from the library of Stanley J. Seeger with his small bookplate, presentation copy from author for Lady (Frances) Colvin, beneath is another presentation inscription to Christopher Wheeler from Sidney Colvin, cover rubbed at spine and edges, cloth bubbled at inside edge of lower cover, good, preserved in green buckram slipcase lettered gilt with inner folding sleeve.   Peter Ellis   112 - 81   2016   £950

Association – Seeley, H. G.

Nicols, Arthur   *Chapters from the Physical History of the Earth.*   London: C. Kegan Paul & Co., 1880. First edition, half title, 32 page catalog 10/79, tipped in 'Opinions of the Press' leaf, original dark brown cloth, little marked, author's own copy with his notes, corrections amendments together with insertions, 4 page ALS from F. W. Ridler of Museum of Practical Geology, brief note from Kegan Paul, brief ALS from H. G. Seeley, ALS postcard from Sir Stanley Lathes.   Jarndyce Antiquarian Booksellers   CCXVII - 205   2016   £380

Association – Seide, Michael

Malamud, Bernard   1914-1986   *Pictures of Fidelman.* New York: FSG, 1969. First edition, inscribed by author for Michael Seide and wife Katharine Shattuck, fine in near fine dust jacket.   Ken Lopez Bookseller   166 - 73   2016 $350

Malamud, Bernard   1914-1986   *The Fixer.*   New York: FSG, 1966. First edition, inscribed by author for Katharina Shattuck and Michael Seide, fine in near fine dust jacket with mild foxing to spine lettering and bit of wear to crown, excellent association copy.   Ken Lopez Bookseller   166 - 72   2016 $750

Malamud, Bernard   1914-1986   *The Tenants.*   New York: FSG, 1971. First edition, inscribed by author for Catharine and Mike, (Katharine Shattuck and Michael Seide), fine in near fine dust jacket, fading to spine lettering and wear to crown.   Ken Lopez Bookseller   166 - 74   2016 $250

Association – Selden

Sand, George, Pseud. of Mme. Dudevant   1804-1876 *Andre.*   Paris: Felix Bonnaire Editeur, 1837. Second edition, octavo, 19th century dark red straight grained half morocco, marbled boards, gilt rules and lettering, 2 armorial Selden bookplates, some spotting to front endpapers, edges slightly rubbed, minor foxing, very good in handsome binding.   The Brick Row Book Shop   Miscellany 69 - 36   2016 $300

Sand, George, Pseud. of Mme. Dudevant   1804-1876 *Lelia.*   Paris: Henri Dupuy, Imprimeur Editeur, L. Tenre, Libraire, 1833. First edition, 2 volumes, octavo, 19th century dark red straight grained half morocco, marbled paper boards, gilt rules and lettering, two armorial Selden bookplates, spotting to front endpapers, moderate foxing, very good in handsome binding.   The Brick Row Book Shop   Miscellany 69 - 37   2016 $600

Sand, George, Pseud. of Mme. Dudevant   1804-1876 *Mauprat.*   Paris: Felix Bonnaire, Editer, 1837. First Paris edition in book form and first authorized edition, 2 volumes, octavo, 19th century dark red straight grained half morocco, marbled paper boards, gilt rules and lettering, frontispiece, light spotting to front endpapers, some light foxing, very good in handsome binding, two armorial Selden bookplates. The Brick Row Book Shop   Miscellany 69 - 38   2016   £750

Association – Self

Dickens, Charles   1812-1870   *Edwin Drood. Complete (Part Second) by te Spirit-Pen of Charles Dickens, through a Medium).*   Brattleboro: T. P. James, 1873. Original brown cloth, bevelled boards, lettered gilt, little rubbed, Suzannet, Starling & Self booklabels, good plus.   Jarndyce Antiquarian Booksellers   CCXVIII - 647   2016   £120

Association – Sendak, Maurice

Blake, William   1757-1827   *Poems from William Blake's Songs of Innocence.*   London: Bodley Head, 1967. Limited to only 275 copies for presentation by publisher,, this copy inscribed by artist to pianist Alvin Novak, with drawing, Dec. '67, pictorial wrappers, fine, illustrations by Maurice Sendak with pictorial cover and 8 color illustrations.   Aleph-bet Books, Inc.   111 - 406   2016 $7500

Krauss, Ruth *A Hole is to Dig.* New York: Harper and Row, 1952. Later printing, 12mo., pictorial cloth, fine in dust jacket, illustrations by Maurice Sendak, this copy inscribed by artist for Herbert Hosmer. Aleph-bet Books, Inc. 111 - 413 2016 $850

Association – Senhouse, Roger

Buonarroti, Michel Angelo 1475-1564 *The Sonnets of Michael Angelo Buonarroti and Tommaso Campanella Now for the First time Translated into Rhymed English...* London: Smith Elder & Co., 1878. First complete translation, 8vo., original smooth blue/purple cloth, lettered gilt on spine, borders of lines and stars in black on boards, slightly cocked, spine little darkened, little spotting to prelims, otherwise very good, from the library of Bloomsbury Group publisher and translator, Roger Senhouse. Sotheran's Piccadilly Notes - Summer 2015 - 203 2016 £198

Musil, Robert *The Man Without Qualities. Volume III. Into the Millennium.* London: Secker & Warburg, 1959, but, 1960. Uncorrected proof copy, correction to publication date on titlepage and extensive notes in pencil and red ink by Roger Senhouse, crown 8vo., original printed wrappers, little fading to backstrip and borders and slight lean to spine, pencilled note of date going to press to front, short split at head of upper joint, good. Blackwell's Rare Books B186 - 267 2016 £1000

Association – Serventy, D. L.

Thompson, D'Arcy Wenworth *A Glossary of Greek Birds.* Oxford: Clarendon Press, 1895. Octavo, publisher's cloth, pencil ownership signature of W. Baldwin Spencer, deaccessioned library stamp of royal Australasian Ornithologists' Union and the bookplate of D. L. Serventy. Andrew Isles Natural History Books 55 - 38849 2016 $200

Association – Seton

Plato *The Works of Plato Abridg'd.* London: printed for A. Bell, 1701. First English edition, few leaves browned or spotted, one or two corrections in manuscript, faint dampmark to upper forecorner of first 50 leaves, 8vo., contemporary Cambridge type panelled calf, red morocco label to spine, slightly rubbed and marked bookplate of Seton of Ekoslund and ownership inscription of Duncan Campbell, more recent chess bookplate of Bruno Bassi, name 'Greeg' in blank area of first page of text, blindstamped. Blackwell's Rare Books Greek & Latin Classics VII - 73 2016 £2500

Association – Settle, W. J.

Browning, Robert 1812-1889 *The Ring and The Book.* London: Smith, Elder, 1868-1869. First edition, 4 volumes, 8vo., occasional light scattered foxing to free endleaves, original black stamped green cloth, gilt stamped spines by Harrison, quarter gilt stamped calf over blue cloth slipcase, volume 3 rear hinge cracked with light front pastedown soiling, volumes 1 and 2 hinges cracked, Robert Browning's signature tipped in volume I, opposite titlepage, ownership signatures of W. J. (...?) Settle (Sherborne Dorset, Feb. 21, 1869) and F. Rowlandson, ownership signatures of E. M. Forster in volume 2 to free front endleaf and titlepage, attractive, very good, with cut-out signature tipped in of Robert Browning. Jeff Weber Rare Books 181 - 42 2016 $4000

Association – Sewell, Michael Gerveys

Gill, Eric 1882-1940 *War Memorial.* Ditchling: St. Dominics Press, 1923. First edition, small 8vo., original heavy grey wrappers, with front cover and titlepage illustration from wood engraving by David Jones and single wood engraving by Gill, wrappers slightly browned otherwise, very good, bookplate of Michael Gerveys Sewell. Sotheran's Piccadilly Notes - Summer 2015 - 145 2016 £495

Association – Shaftesbury, Earl of

Society for the Reformation on Principles *The Scholar Armed Against the Errors of Time or a Collection of Tracts on the Principles and Evidences of Christianity....* London: F. C. & J. Rivington, 1812. Third edition, 2 volumes, ads on leading f.e.p. volume I, uncut in original blue boards, brown paper spines slightly chipped paper labels, some rubbing but overall very good in original binding, from the library of Earl John Eldon, with his armorial roundal signature and inscription "The gift of the Earl of Shaftesbury". Jarndyce Antiquarian Booksellers CCXVII - 264 2016 £220

Association – Shafto, Robert

Terentius Afer, Publius *Comoediae.* Cambridge: Apud Cornelium Crownfield, 1726. First Bentley edition, 2 engraved portraits, some soiling in places, 4to., contemporary calf spine gilt, quite rubbed and scratched but now conserved, joints expertly renewed and red morocco lettering piece replaced to style, booklabel of Peter Allen Hansen and ownership inscription of (MP for Durham) R(obert) Shafto, good. Blackwell's Rare Books Greek & Latin Classics VII - 84 2016 £400

Association – Shanilec, Gaylord

Hampl, Patricia *Resort: a Poem by...* St. Paul: Bookslinger Editions, 1982. One of 50 copies numbered and signed by author, 8vo., frontispiece and ornamental rose by Gaylord Shanilec, author's presentation and signature on half title, also signed by artist, paper wrappers, cover very slightly scuffed at top of spine, faintly dog eared, otherwise nice, inscribed by author for Scott Walker, signed by artist in pencil "Hi Scott Gaylord".   Second Life Books, Inc. 196A - 715   2016 $250

Association – Shapes, Katharine

De Garis, Frederic *We Japanese: Being Descriptions of Many of the Customs, Manners, Ceremonies, Festivals....* Miyanoshita: Fujiya Hotel, 1936. Third printing, 8vo., copiously illustrated, paper wrappers, covered with brocade, sewn in Japanese style, with paper label, in cloth covered folding case, fastened with cords and bone pins, cover of book slightly soiled on front, case little worn at corners and slightly unglued at interior spine, otherwise very good, tight copy, presentation from H. S. K. Yamaguchi for Katharine A. Shapes.   Second Life Books, Inc. 196A - 397   2016 $150

Association – Sharp, G. A.

Boyd, John Edward *Reply to Mr. Swinyard's Reports on the prince Edward Island Railway...* Charlottetown: printed by order of the Government of Prince Edward Island, 1875. 8vo., printed wrappers with stitch bound, covers lightly soiled, spine split and pieces missing along spine, very small pieces missing from bottom right corner and small hole through top corner margin through pamphlet but not into text, presentation from G. A. Sharp.   Schooner Books Ltd.   115 - 182   2016 $200

Newton, Isaac 1642-1727 *Correspondence Respecting the Prince Edward Island Raily and Report of....* Charlottetown: 1873. 8vo., printed wrappers stitch bound, browned along edges and with some foxing, very small pieces misising from spine and small hole through top corner margin through pamphlet but not into text, presentation from G. A. Sharp.   Schooner Books Ltd.   115 - 183   2016 $175

Association – Shattuck, Katharine

Malamud, Bernard 1914-1986 *Pictures of Fidelman.* New York: FSG, 1969. First edition, inscribed by author for Michael Seide and wife Katharine Shattuck, fine in near fine dust jacket. Ken Lopez Bookseller   166 - 73   2016 $350

Malamud, Bernard 1914-1986 *The Fixer.* New York: FSG, 1966. First edition, inscribed by author for Katharine Shattuck and Michael Seide, fine in near fine dust jacket with mild foxing to spine lettering and bit of wear to crown, excellent association copy.   Ken Lopez Bookseller   166 - 72   2016 $750

Malamud, Bernard 1914-1986 *The Tenants.* New York: FSG, 1971. First edition, inscribed by author for Catharine and Mike, (Katharine Shattuck and Michael Seide), fine in near fine dust jacket, fading to spine lettering and wear to crown.   Ken Lopez Bookseller   166 - 74   2016 $250

Association – Shaw, Charlotte

Le Corbeau, Adrien *The Forest Giant.* London: Jonathan Cape, 1924. First English edition, frontispiece and decorative border to titlepage with decorations at head of each text page, little very faint foxing to prelims and pencil note identifying Lawrence to titlepage, foolscap 8vo., original quarter yellow cloth with green boards, backstrip with printed label, a touch of wear to one corner, edges rough trimmed, dust jacket with darkened backstrip panel frayed at either end with some loss at foot, little chipping to corners, darkened overall, good, presentation copy inscribed by Charlotte F. Shaw to J. G. Wilson of Bumpus.   Blackwell's Rare Books B186 - 252   2016   £400

Association – Shaw, George Bernard

Cowley, Abraham 1618-1667 *Poems: viz I. Miscellanies. II. Mistress; or Love Verses. III. Pindarique Odes. and IV. Davides, or a Sacred Poem of the Troubles of David.* London: For Humphrey Moseley, 1656. First collected edition, contemporary paneled calf, edges gilt, very skillfully rebacked to style, later endpapers, occasional minor spots and repaired marginal tears, 3L2 soiled and with paper defect costing several letters, lovely copy, early signature of Edmund Henry Marshal on title "Ex Libris George Bernard Shaw".   Joseph J. Felcone, Inc.   Books from Five Centuries: a Miscellany - 52   2016 $2500

Association – Shaw, William Starmer

Defoe, Daniel *The Original Power of the Collective Body of the People of England, Examined and Asserted...* London: printed and sold by R. Baldwin, n.d. circa, 1770. Third edition, 8vo., uncut, evidence of original stab-stitching to gutters, edges little dusty, pencil annotations of page 5 and few pencil marks to titlepage, 19th century half brown calf, textured cloth covered boards, gilt title to spine, spine scuffed with little loss to endcaps, rubbed, corners worn, titlepage separating slightly, some bibliographical pencil notes, binding little shabby but very good internally, label showing book from collection of William Starmer Shaw. Unsworths Antiquarian Booksellers   30 - 42   2016 $95

Association – Shawn, Ted

Dreier, Katherine S. *Shawn: the Dancer.* New York: Barnes, 1933. First edition, 4to., silver coated cloth, numerous full page photos, inscribed by Shawn to critic Walter Terry, cover slightly soiled, but very good, tight, clean copy. Second Life Books, Inc. 196A - 452 2016 $200

Association – Shelley, Percy Florence

Stevenson, Robert Louis Balfour 1850-1894 *The Master of Ballantrae.* London: Cassell & Co., 1889. First published edition, first issue with ads dated July 1889, 8vo., original pictorial cloth, spine slightly faded and worn at either end, minor soiling to covers, bookplate of dedicatee, Sir Percy Florence Shelley. Blackwell's Rare Books B184 - 81 2016 £3000

Association – Shellick, George

The Gardener: A Synopsis of the Principles and Practice of His Art and Calling. London: Houlston & sons, circa, 1870. original brick brown cloth blocked in gilt and black, slightly rubbed few small marks on back board, bookseller's ticket of George H. Shellick, Plymouth on leading pastedown, good plus. Jarndyce Antiquarian Books CCXV - 260 2016 £110

Association – Shepard, Leslie

Knott, Robert R. *The new Aid to memory...* London: printed for the author, circa, 1840. New edition, half title, color plates, original red cloth, slightly dulled and marked, all edges gilt, very good, Leslie Shepard's copy. Jarndyce Antiquarian Books CCXV - 815 2016 £75

Association – Sheppard, S.

Browning, Elizabeth Barrett 1806-1861 *Poems.* London: Edward Moxon, 1844. First edition, 2 volumes, ad leaf at end of volume I, original green vertical fine ribbed cloth, blocked in blind, spines lettered gilt, booklabels of Miss S. Sheppard with her signatures on verso of titlepages and dated May 1848, modern labels of Christopher Clark Geest, slight marking to leading free endpaper from old insertion, otherwise lovely crisp copy, green cloth fold over box. Jarndyce Antiquarian Booksellers CCXVII - 53 2016 £1250

Association – Sherman, William David

Lewis, Leon *The Landscape of Contemporary Cinema.* Buffalo: Buffalo Spectrum Press, 1967. First edition, octavo, illustrated perfect bound wrapper, very slight soiling on wrappers, still fine, inscribed by William David Sherman to author John Barth with Barth's ownership signature and ownership stamp, laid in ALS from Sherman to Barth sending the book. Between the Covers Rare Books 204 - 43 2016 $225

Association – Sherwin, Henry

The Innocent Epicure; or the Art of Angling. London: printed by H. Meere for R. Gosling, 1713. Second edition, small 8vo., contemporary calf, gilt, neatly rebacked, spine gilt, red morocco label, presentation copy, inscribed 'Ex dono authoris', fine, bookplates of Edwin Snow and Henry Sherwin. C. R. Johnson Rare Book Collections Foxon: H-P 2015 - 487 2016 $3831

Association – Shiel, M. P.

Derleth, August *Someone in the Dark.* Sauk City: Arkham House, 1941. First edition, first printing, 1115 copies, octavo cloth, presentation from author to M. P. Shiel, inscribed again by author for Major P. H. Rixey, some tanning to front endpapers, rear endpaper has tape residue to edges and rear paste down has the bookplate of P. H. Rixey affixed to it, top page edges dusty, upper front right corner little bumped, about very good in very good dust jacket which has small tear with wrinkle and small piece missing at upper right front panel affecting the edge of the "E" in title lettering SOMEONE, some light rubs to corner tips and spine ends, some tanning to edges of rear panel. John W. Knott, Jr./L.W. Currey, Inc. Fall-Winter 2015 - 16236 2016 $2500

Association – Shirley, Walter

Shaftesbury, Anthony Ashley Cooper, 3rd Earl of 1671-1713 *Characteristicks of Men, Manners, Opinions, Times.* N.P.: n.p., 1708-1711. 3 volumes, , lovely contemporary boards with spines beautifully and unobtrusively rebacked to style, top front spine edge of volume three just beginning to crack (about 2") but very firm, small bookplate to inside front cover of volume I (Walter T. Shirley II), contemporary ink signature, overall very pretty, rare first issue. Athena Rare Books List 15 - 1711 2016 $4500

Association – Short, Margaret

Waller, Edmund *Poems &c.* London: for Henry Herringman, 1668. Later edition, small 8vo., variant with 'London' printed in red in imprint, pastedowns and flyleaves little stained, contemporary sheep, ruled in blind (edges chipped, lower corners bumped, lower headcap torn away), early signature of Margaret Short, pen trials on flyleaves, from the library of James Stevens Cox (1910-1997). Maggs Bros. Ltd.   1447 - 436   2016   £150

Association – Short, Thomas

Plinius Caecilius Secundus, Gaius *The Letters of Pliny the Counsul; with Occasional Remarks.* London: printed for J. Dodsley, 1748. Third edition, 2 volumes, 8vo., titlepages printed in red and black with small numismatic engravings, half title in each volume, occasional light foxing, particularly to front and rear, few smudgy marks, contemporary dark brown speckled calf, neatly rebacked, gilt borders, edges sprinkled red, spines darkened and bit creased, few small chips and scrapes, very good, ownership inscription of F. Mashiter to each front pastedown, together with several library codes, pictorial bookplate, ownership inscription of Thomas Short to each titlepage122.   Unsworths Antiquarian Booksellers Ltd.   30 - 122   2016   £160

Association – Shorter, Clement K.

Dickens, Charles   1812-1870   *Letters to Mark Lemon.* London: printed for Private Circulation, 1927. Printed for Thomas J. Wise, limited to 30 copies, half title, original purple printed wrappers, bound into contemporary half dark blue calf, Clement K. Shorter's booklabel and stamped "C" on initial blank, very good.   Jarndyce Antiquarian Booksellers   CCXVIII - 860   2016   £250

Association – Shorthouse, J. Henry

Arnold, Matthew   1822-1888   *Culture and Anarchy: an Essay in Political and Social Criticism.* London: Smith, Elder & Co., 1869. First edition, half title, pencil notes, original brown cloth, bevelled boards, little rubbed, armorial booklabel "Presented by Bishop Wordsworth's family", ownership signature of J. Henry Shorthouse.   Jarndyce Antiquarian Booksellers   CCXVII - 15   2016   £420

Association – Shring, Alicia Anne

Quevedo, Francisco De *Forture in Her Wits; or the Hour of all Men.* London: for R. Sare, F. Saunders and Tho. Bennet, 1697. First edition in English, 8vo., minor worming to inner margin of A1-A3 touching printed border of top edge gilt and two letters of text on A3, small stain to lower inner margin of D5-D6, small ink stain to blank lower margin of f1, early ownership inscription cropped from head of titlepage, 19th century calf, corners bumped and chipped, joints rubbed, from the library of James Stevens Cox (1910-1997), inscribed "W(illiam) M. Marrow, his booke 1720", inscription of Alicia Anne Shring 1835.   Maggs Bros. Ltd.   1447 - 347   2016   £350

Association – Shuckburgh, George

Collier, Jane   *An Essay on the Art of Ingeniously Tormenting with Proper Rules for the Exercise of that Pleasant Art.*   London: printed for A. Millar in the Strand, 1753. 8vo., engraved frontispiece, very nice, clean copy, contemporary full calf, raised bands, compartments in gilt, brown morocco label, rebacked retaining original spine, leading hinge cracked and little worn, spine rubbed and dulled, repair to following inner hinge, armorial bookplate of Sir George Shuckburgh & later label of E. N. Da C. Andrade, good sound copy.   Jarndyce Antiquarian Books   CCXV - 126   2016   £480

Association – Sickles, Harry

Scott, Walter   1771-1832   *The Doom of the Devorgoil, A Melo-Drama. (and) Alichindrane or the Ayrshire Tragedy.* Edinburgh: printed by Ballantyne for Cadell and Co., Edinburgh and Simpkin and Marshall, London, 1830. First separate and complete edition, 229 x 1522m., attractive late 19th century dark green armorial morocco by Maclehose of Glasgow (stamp signed), covers gilt with heraldic pelican crest of Thomas Glen Arthur of Garrick House, Ayr, flat spine with title at head and author at tail and five gilt ornaments in between (comprised of three thistles and two heraldic devices), gold endleaves, top edge gilt, other edges untrimmed (front hinge and joint with careful repairs, front free endpaper and first flyleaf cut near gutter and reattached with cellophane), large paper presentation copy, inscribed by Harry A. Sickles, Christmas 1917 for friend Frank P. Leffingwell, short crack beginning at bottom of front joint, hint of fading and leather dressing residue to covers, otherwise in excellent, binding solid and lustrous, text clean and fresh, margins very commodious.   Phillip J. Pirages   67 - 312   2016 $1000

Association – Sigourney, Lydia

The Young Ladies' Offering or Gems of Prose and Poetry... Boston: Phillips & Sampson, 1856. Reprint, 8vo., black cloth elaborately stamped in gilt, little worn along hinge and extremities of spine, otherwise bright, with Lydia Sigourney's name as if she were the author, later bookplate, inscribed by Sigourney for Mrs. Jareret.   Second Life Books, Inc.   197 - 291   2016 $150

Association – Simcox, Howard

Dickens, Charles   1812-1870   *Dombey and Son.* London: Bradbury & Evans, 1848. First edition, frontispiece, engraved title and plates by Phiz, 2 errata slips, some foxing to plates, contemporary half dark green calf, spine gilt in compartments, black leather label, little rubbed, contemporary signature of Howard Simcox later details of E. Allen, good, sound copy.   Jarndyce Antiquarian Booksellers   CCXVIII - 442   2016   £220

Association – Simmons, Jack

Doughty, Henry Montagu   *Chronicles of Theberton. A Suffolk Village.*   Cambridge: University of Cambridge; London: Macmillan, 1910. First edition, original green cloth, spine ruled and lettered gilt, spine sunned, light bumping to corners, little spotting to endpapers, frontispiece, plates, 3 maps, printed in green and black, occasional light spotting, good, early ownership inscription of Jack Simmons and pictorial bookplate of Claude and Joan Cox, very rare. Sotheran's   Piccadilly Notes - Summer 2015 - 111   2016   £148

Association – Simmons, Roscoe Conkling

Johnson, Georgia Douglas   *Bronze.*   Boston: B. J. Brimmer Co., 1922. First edition, printed paper over boards, boards slightly splayed and corners little worn, else near fine, fragile volume, without dust jacket, rear panel and rear flap are laid in, warmly inscribed by author to Roscoe Conkling Simmons.   Between the Covers Rare Books   202 - 50   2016 $4500

Association – Simpson, Norman Douglas

Burton, Richard Francis   1821-1890   *Wanderings in West Africa from Liverpool to Fernando Po.*   London: Tinsley Brothers, 18 Catherine St. Strand, 1863. First edition, 8vo., 2 volumes, original blindstamped maroon cloth lettered gilt to spine, one folding map frontispiece to volume I, wood engraved frontispiece to volume II, very minor rubbing to extremities, nice and clean, engraved armorial bookplates of Edward Joseph Dent and Norman Douglas Simpson.   Sotheran's   Travel and Exploration - 10   2016   £4000

Association – Singleton, E. A.

Marston, Philip Bourke   *Song-Tide and Other Poems.* London: Ellis and Green, 1871. First edition, inscribed presentation from author for aunt E. A. Singleton, exceptionally uncommon inscription, very good in original green cloth with gilt title to spine and front board, bump to head of spine ad to lower front cover, slight wear to boards, browning to endpages and few small spots of foxing to interior, very good. The Kelmscott Bookshop   12 - 64   2016 $300

Association – Skelton, Percival

Smiles, Samuel   *Self-Help.*   London: John Murray, 1860. 35th thousand, 32 page catalog original maroon cloth blocked in blind, spine lettered gilt, rubbed and worn, inscription from Percival Skelton, July 1861 for father, sound.   Jarndyce Antiquarian Books   CCXV - 410   2016   £120

Association – Skene

Pindarus   *Olympia, Nemea, Pythia, Isthmia.*   Oxford: E. Theatro Sheldoniano, 1697. First English edition of the Greek text, edited by Richard West and Robert Welsted, engraved frontispiece and large titlepage vignette by M. Burghers, final section printed on poorer paper and rather browned, some spotting and toning elsewhere, folio, 18th century speckled calf, spine gilt in compartments, marbled endpapers, rather rubbed, joints cracking at ends, bookplate of Skene Library and early 20th century Blackwell's bookseller label to front pastedown, good.   Blackwell's Rare Books   Greek & Latin Classics VII - 71   2016   £700

Association – Skrimshire, Fenwick

Clare, John   *The Village Minstrel and Other Poems.* London: Taylor & Hessey, Fleet Street and E. Drury, Stamford, 1821. First edition, 2 volumes bound in 1, 12mo., modern dark green calf over marbled paper boards, frontispiece in volume 1, ownership signatures of Fenwick Skrimshire, near fine copy.   Honey & Wax Booksellers   4 - 57   2016 $5500

Association – Slack, Paul

Wilkins, H. J.   *Edward Colston (1636-1721 A.D.). A Chronological Account of His Life and Work. Together With an Account of the Colston Societies and Memorials in Bristol.*   Bristol: J. W. Arrowsmith, 1920. 8vo., foxing mainly to titlepage and preface, text otherwise clean, brown cloth, gilt lettering to spine, little rubbed to endcaps, edges uncut, top edge little dusted and spotted, very good, ownership signature of P(aul) Slack.   Unsworths Antiquarian Booksellers Ltd.   E04 - 15   2016   £25

Association – Slavitt, David

Tibullus, Albius *The Elegies of Delia of....* Cleveland: Bits Press, 1985. One of 333 copies, large 8vo. not numbered, signed on colophon by translator, with presentation by David Slavitt for Sonja & Bill (Smith). Second Life Books, Inc. 197 - 320 2016 $65

Association – Slocum, Milton

Shakespeare, William 1564-1616 *The Works of William Shakespeare.* New York: Random House, 1929-1933. Limited to 1600 sets, 7 volumes, 8vo., original full gilt stamped Niger morocco, top edge gilt, clean and unfaded, near fine, originally issued in individual slipcases, not present here, this is the Milton S. Slocum San Marino, CA copy with original invoice from 1955. Jeff Weber Rare Books 181 - 71 2016 $2000

Association – Slocum, Myles Standish

Montaigne, Michel De 1533-1592 *Essays of Michael Seigneur de Montaigne in Three Books.* London: printed for T. Basset, 1693. Early edition, 3 volumes, small 8vo., engraved frontispiece portrait of author, some early ink underlining, lacks rear free endpaper (volume I), original full mottled calf (mismatched set), raised bands, gilt spines, red leather title labels, inner joints reinforced with Kozo, worn, ownership signatures of J. Merton (?), Arthur Rogers - June 1933, Reverend James Jenkyn (d. 1825 of Herfordshire?) and Myles Standish Slocum, Pasadena. Jeff Weber Rare Books 181 - 22 2016 $275

Association – Smedley, Henry

Mundy, Francis Noel Clarke *Needwood Forest. (bound with) The Fall of Needwood.* Lichfield: printed by John Jackson; Derby: printed at the Office of J. Drewry, 1766. or c. 1790, & 1808. First editions, 4to., frontispiece, some foxing to 3 leaves of second work, contemporary ink note to one passage, pencil quotation from the Letters of Anna Seward in first work, 2 volumes in one, bound in early 19th century half red morocco, marbled boards, some rubbing to boards, corners worn, ownership name of Henry Smedley 1812 and Millicent Crompton, tipped in as a slip of blue sugar paper for Miss Mary French's friend. Jarndyce Antiquarian Booksellers CCXVI - 422 2016 £180

Association – Smith, Addie Viola

McCormick, Elsie *Audacious Angles of China.* Shanghai: Chinese American Pub. Co., 1922. First book edition, printed marbled card stock covers, printed cloth tape spine (added later?), average wear, tightly bound, pulling on beginning & terminal leaves, very good, signature of former owner Addie Viola Smith (1893-1975). Tavistock Books Getting Around - 41 2016 $250

Association – Smith, Benjamin

Bruce, James *An Interesting Narrative of the Travels of James Bruce Esq. into Abyssinia to Discover the Source of the Nile.* New York: for Berry and Rogers, 1790. First American edition, 12mo, engraved folding map, contemporary sheep, neatly rebacked with original label laid down, 19th century signature of Benj. H. Smith, usual moderate foxing common to American books of this period, else very good. Joseph J. Felcone, Inc. Books from Five Centuries: a Miscellany - 30 2016 $550

Association – Smith, Bill

Shapiro, Harvey *Lauds.* New York: Sun, 1975. First edition, 8vo., author's presentation for Bill Smith, paper wrappers, cover slightly soiled, otherwise nice. Second Life Books, Inc. 197 - 288 2016 $45

Association – Smith, Edward Orlebar

Willis, John *Mnemonica or the Art of Memory Drained Out of the Pure Fountains of Art and Nature.* London: printed and are to be sold by Leonard Sowersby, 1661. First complete edition in English, 12mo., woodcut illustration of stage on E4B, browned throughout, stronger in margins, small ink-stain on D6, pages 94-95 somewhat soiled, light marking to fore edges of D8 and M7-8, early 19th century calf, ruled in gilt, spine with five raised bands, covers scuffed, joints just starting to crack, corners bumped, bookplate of Rev. Edward Orlebar Smith, from the library of James Stevens Cox (1910-1997). Maggs Bros. Ltd. 1447 - 452 2016 £400

Association – Smith, Ella

Irving, Washington 1783-1859 *Chronicle of the Conquest of Granada. (and) The Alhambra.* New York and London: Printed at the Knickerbocker Press for G. P. Putnam's Sons, 1893-1894. 229 x 165mm., 4 volumes, representing two separately published works, each in two volumes, publisher's ivory buckram, ornately embellished with Moorish inspired design by Alice Cordelia Morse, covers with elaborate decoration in colors and gilt, flat spines with gilt titling, decoration and patterned endpapers, top edge gilt, in original blue cloth dust jacket, gilt titling on spine, 61 photogravures of the Alhambra and Granada, each with lettered tissue guard, engraved bookplate of Ella C. Smith (Alhambra) and Harold Randolph (Granada), mild browning to leaves opposite illustrations from acidic tissue guards, otherwise extraordinarily fine set, clean and fresh in very pretty publisher's bindings beautifully protected by original fine dust jackets. Phillip J. Pirages 67 - 202 2016 $950

Association – Smith, F. E.

Shelley, Percy Bysshe 1792-1822 *Prometheus Unbound. A Lyrical Drama in Four Acts with Other Poems.* London: C. and J. Ollier, 1820. First edition, 2nd issue, with half title, ads at end discarded, 8vo., early 20th century red crushed morocco for William Brown (booksellers), Edinburgh, French fillets on sides, crowned initial B on the upper cover, spine panelled in gilt in compartments, gilt edges, surface of joints partly lifted, F. E. Smith's copy (crowned initial on upper cover), with his bookplate inside front cover as Viscount Birkenhead, bookplate of Fernand Spaak opposite, good.   Blackwell's Rare Books   Marks of Genius - 49   2016   £2500

Association – Smith, G.

Wotton, Henry *Reliquiae Wottoniane...*   London: by T. Roycroft for R. Marriott, F. Tyton, T. Collins and J. Ford, 1672. Third edition, 8vo., four engraved portraits, one portrait and titlepage foxed, minor repairs to corners of a5,-7, early 20th century green morocco, covered and spine bordered with small gilt sequin and dot tool, smooth spine lettered gilt, all edges gilt, spine little faded, small 18th? century signature of G. Smith, from the library of James Stevens Cox (1910-1997) with pencil note of purchase.   Maggs Bros. Ltd.   1447 - 467   2016   £180

Association – Smith, G. N. G.

Parvan, Vasile *Dacia. An Outline of the early Civilizations of the Carpatho-Danubian Countries.*   Cambridge University Press, 1928. First edition, 8vo., plates and maps, green cloth, gilt lettered spine, some separation at gutter between pages 64/65, little wear to endcaps and corners, but binding sound, still good copy, ownership inscription of G. N. G. Smith.   Unsworths Antiquarian Booksellers Ltd.   E05 - 55   2016   £20

Association – Smith, George

The Historie of Frier Rush: How He Came to a House of Religion to Seeke Service...   London: Harding and Wright for Robert Triphook, 1810. One of 4 copies on vellum, contemporary red velvet by H. Faulkner (ticket on verso front flyleaf), covers with wide Greek key border rolled in blind, flat spine with small remnant of leather backstrip (that has been laid on to hide a binder's titling error), red moire silk endleaves, turn-ins and pastedowns with rolls in blind, all edges gilt, housed in very good later leather edged slipcase, woodcut vignette on title, verso to front flyleaf with bookplate of Edward Vernon Utterson and morocco bookplate of Hans Furstenberg, bookplate of John Kershaw, contemporary inked note listing original owner of each of the four vellum copies of the present book, later pencilled note on same "Ths copy was after-wards in the possession of Mr. George Smith and it was (sold in his (s)ale for £9.15.0", spine mostly covered with (glue?) residue left by now basically missing leather backstrip, corners rubbed to board, portions of the joints torn, velvet nap somewhat diminished, a bit of natural rumpling to the vellum, very few inoffensive spots to margins, entirely solid (apart from spine remnants) an agreeable copy of this curious book.   Phillip J. Pirages   67 - 341   2016 $4500

Association – Smith, Horace

Smith, James   *Rejected Addresses or the new Theatrum Poetarum.*   London: John Murray, 1833. First edition with these illustrations, 178 x 108mm., animated early 20th century scarlet crushed morocco, richly gilt by Riviere and Son (stamp signed on front turn-in), covers framed by curling vine bearing many berries and leaves, central panel formed and divided into compartments by gilt strapwork, each compartment containing a stylized strapwork and stippled wheel, radiating sections of wheel decorated with leafy fronds, raised bands, spine gilt in similar style, wide gilt turn-ins with plain and dotted label bound in at rear, fleece lined morocco clipped cloth slipcase, engraved frontispiece and 6 engraved illustrations by George Cruikshank, with signed original pencil study for one of the woodcuts and small pen and ink caricature, initialled by Cruikshank with his signature, laid in at front with two autograph letters, signed, tipped in at front, one from James Smith to Lady Blessington and one from Horace Smith to Duby (Edward Dubois - 1774-1850), front joint slightly (and rear joint just faintly) rubbed, spine shade darker than covers, text with faint overall browning because of paper stock, otherwise fine, lovely binding lustrous and altogether pleasing, text very clean and smooth.   Phillip J. Pirages   67 - 64   2016 $950

Association – Smith, Lucius

Paine, Martyn *Letters on the Cholera Asphyxia as It Has Appeared in the City of New York.* New York: Collins & Harvey, 1832. First edition, thin 8vo., spine label and covers chipped and slightly soiled, library label on front pastedown, some marginal staining on few pages, some scattered foxing, inscription to Rev. Lucius Smith, very good, untrimmed, cloth backed paper boards with paper spine label. Edwin V. Glaser Rare Books 2015 - 10282 2016 $150

Association – Smith, Sonja

Day, Douglas *Journey of the Wolf.* New York: Atheneum, 1977. First edition, 8vo., paper over boards with cloth spine, review laid in, map on endpapers, nice in little scuffed and slightly chipped dust jacket, author's presentation for Wm. (Jay Smith) & Sonja. Second Life Books, Inc. 197 - 62 2016 $95

Tarn, Nathaniel *Narrative of This Fall.* Los Angeles: Black Sparrow, 1975. Offprint from Sparrow 32 May 1975, paper wrappers, presentation on front from author for Sonya and Bill Jay Smith, front very slightly creased and spotted, otherwise near fine. Second Life Books, Inc. 196 B - 736 2016 $45

Tibullus, Albius *The Elegies of Delia of....* Cleveland: Bits Press, 1985. One of 333 copies, large 8vo. not numbered, signed on colophon by translator, with presentation by David Slavitt for Sonja & Bill (Smith). Second Life Books, Inc. 197 - 320 2016 $65

Association – Smith, Thomas

MacGowan, John *Death, a Vision or the Solemn departure of Saints and Sinners...* London: printed for G. G. J. & J. Robinson, 1789. Fifth edition, half title, 12mo., some slight foxing, full contemporary calf, gilt banded spine, red morocco label, joints slightly cracked but very firm, some insect damage to lower corner of upper board, early name of Thos. Smith on front endpaper, later inscription to half title "Hephzibah Smith the gift of her affectionate mother Feb. 3rd 1828". Jarndyce Antiquarian Booksellers CCXVI - 375 2016 £125

Association – Smith, Tom

Crane, Hart **1899-1932** *The Bridge.* New York: Horace Liveright, 1930. First American edition, photo by Walker Evans, fine in very good, spine faded dust jacket with couple of internally repaired short tear, in custom cloth chemise and quarter morocco slipcase, inscribed by Crane for Tom Smith. Between the Covers Rare Books 204 - 30 2016 $50,000

Association – Smith, William Jay

Appel, Karel *Appel & Alechinsky: Two Brush Paintings their Poems by Hugo Claus.* Paris: Yves Riveire, 1980. First edition, 4to., original publisher's printed wrappers, very good, illustrations in black and white and color, inscribed by Hugo Claus to poet William Jay Smith. Second Life Books, Inc. 196A - 909 2016 $350

Arguelles, Ivan *New Poetry from California: Dead Requiem.* Berkeley: Pantograp Press, 1998. 4to., Presentation from Jack Foley for William Jay Smith, paper wrappers, as new. Second Life Books, Inc. 196A - 48 2016 $45

Beekman, E. M. *Lame Duck a Novel.* Boston: Houghton Mifflin, 1971. First edition, 8vo., fine in slightly worn dust jacket, inscribed by author to poet William Jay Smith, signed again on titlepage. Second Life Books, Inc. 196A - 95 2016 $45

Benchley, Nathaniel *Catch a Falling Spy.* New York: McGraw Hill, 1963. Third printing, 8vo., very good in wrinkled and worn dust jacket, inscribed by author, probably to poet William Jay Smith. Second Life Books, Inc. 196A - 105 2016 $125

Blegvad, Lenore *Kitty and Mr. Kipling: neighbors in Vermont.* New York: McElderry, 2005. First printing, 8vo., illustrations by Erik Blegvad, inscribed by author to poet William Jay Smith, signed by artist as well, paper over boards. Second Life Books, Inc. 196A - 158 2016 $45

Chukovsky, Kornei *The Telephone.* New York: Delacorte Press, 1977. First edition, 8vo., unpaged, illustrations by Blair Lent, fine in little worn dust jacket signed by translator, William Jay Smith. Second Life Books, Inc. 196A - 284 2016 $75

Day, Douglas *Journey of the Wolf.* New York: Atheneum, 1977. First edition, 8vo., paper over boards with cloth spine, review laid in, map on endpapers, nice in little scuffed and slightly chipped dust jacket, author's presentation for Wm. (Jay Smith) & Sonja. Second Life Books, Inc. 197 - 62 2016 $95

Dinesen, Isak **1885-1962** *Karen Blixens Kunst (Tegninger og Malerier). the Art of Karen Blixen (Drawings & Paintings).* Denmark: Karen Blixen Museet, 2001. First edition, 4to., illustrations in black and white and color, printed boards, near fine, this the copy of William Jay Smith who wrote 16 lines of holograph about his personal memories of his wife, poet Barbara Howes meeting Blixen in Denmark. Second Life Books, Inc. 196A - 161 2016 $125

Dorset, Gerald *Cloud 4 Shadows.* London: Poets and Painters' Press, 1969. First edition, 8vo., publisher's printed wrappers (little bent and soiled), very good, inscribed by author to poet william Jay Smith. Second Life Books, Inc. 196A - 441   2016 $50

Enright, D. J. *Selected Poems 1990: Oxford Poets.* New York: Oxford University Press, 1990. First edition, 8vo., printed wrappers, near fine, inscribed by author for William Jay Smith and Sonja. Second Life Books, Inc. 196A - 505   2016 $50

Goyen, William *Selected Letters from a Writer's Life.* Austin: University of Texas Press, 1995. First edition, 8vo., fine in dust jacket, inscribed by editor to poet William Jay Smith. Second Life Books, Inc. 196A - 670   2016 $65

Hall, Wade *The Smiling Phoenix.* Gainesville: University of Florida Press, 1968. Second printing, large 8vo., very good in torn in dust jacket, inscribed by author to pot William Jay Smith. Second Life Books, Inc. 196A - 709   2016 $45

Howes, Barbara *The Blue Garden.* Middletown: Wesleyan Univ. Press, 1972. First edition, very good in little stained and worn price clipped dust jacket, inscribed by author to first husband William Jay Smith and his wife. Second Life Books, Inc. 196A - 839   2016 $200

Howes, Barbara *From the Green Antilles...* New York: Macmillan, 1966. First edition, 8vo., very good, tight copy, dust jacket little wrinkled and soiled, inscribed by author to her first husband William Jay Smith. Second Life Books, Inc. 196A - 835   2016 $150

Howes, Barbara *Light and Dark: Poems.* Middletown: Wesleyan, 1959. First edition, 8vo., very good in dust jacket, little soiled, inscribed by author to husband William Jay Smith. Second Life Books, Inc. 196A - 836   2016 $200

Howes, Barbara *A Private Signal, Poems New and Selected.* Middletown: Wesleyan Univ., 1977. First edition, 8vo., fine in little soiled and stained dust jacket, inscribed by author for her ex-husband William Jay Smith and his wife. Second Life Books, Inc. 196A - 842   2016 $200

Kennedy, X. J. *French Leave.* Florence: Robert L. Barth, 1983. Number F of 200 signed and numbered copies, 8vo, presentation for William Jay Smith, paper wrappers, nice, near fine. Second Life Books, Inc. 196A - 945   2016 $45

Laforgue, Jules *Moral Tales.* New Directions, 1985. First edition, 8vo., fine in dust jacket, signed by William Jay Smith. Second Life Books, Inc. 196 B - 1   2016 $145

Least Heat Moon, William *Blue Highways.* Boston: Little Brown, 1982. First edition, 18th printing, 8vo., nice in little chipped and worn, price clipped dust jacket, signed by author for friend Bill Smith. Second Life Books, Inc. 196 B - 36   2016 $75

MacDonald, George 1824-1905 *The Golden Key.* New York: Farrar Straus and Giroux, 1967. First printing, 8vo., illustrations by Maurice Sendak, blue cloth with decorative stamping in silver, William Jay Smith's copy with his signature, little scuffed at top edge of spine, otherwise nice in slightly soiled dust jacket. Second Life Books, Inc. 197 - 220   2016 $135

Paley, Grace *Just as I Thought.* New York: Farrar Straus, Giroux, 1998. First edition, 8vo., fine in little soiled dust jacket, inscribed by author for poet William Jay Smith. Second Life Books, Inc. 196 B - 365   2016 $75

Shepard, Odell *Connecticut Past and Present.* New York: Knopf, 1939. First edition, 8vo., bound in blue cloth with colored map on endpapers, little chipped dust jacket, inscribed by author for William Jay Smith. Second Life Books, Inc. 196 B - 565   2016 $75

Stevenson, Lionel *Best Poems of 1964: Borestone Mountain Poetry Awards 1965 Volume XVII.* Palo Alto: Pacific Books, 1965. 8vo., signed by contributor William Jay Smith, tan cloth, cover slightly bumped at ends of spine, otherwise very good, tight copy in scuffed and chipped dust jacket. Second Life Books, Inc. 197 - 312   2016 $35

Tarn, Nathaniel *Narrative of This Fall.* Los Angeles: Black Sparrow, 1975. Offprint from Sparrow 32 May 1975, paper wrappers, presentation on front from author for Sonya and Bill Jay Smith, front very slightly creased and spotted, otherwise near fine. Second Life Books, Inc. 196 B - 736   2016 $45

Tennant, Alan *On the Wing: to the Edge of the Earth with the Peregrine Falcon.* New York: Knopf, 2004. First edition, 8 pages of color photos, fine in dust jacket, inscribed by poet to William Jay Smith. Second Life Books, Inc. 196 B - 746   2016 $75

Tibullus, Albius *The Elegies of Delia of....* Cleveland: Bits Press, 1985. One of 333 copies, large 8vo. not numbered, signed on colophon by translator, with presentation by David Slavitt for Sonja & Bill (Smith). Second Life Books, Inc. 197 - 320   2016 $65

Wheelock, John Hall *By Daylight and in Dream: new and collected poems 1904-19070.* New York: Scribner's, 1970. First edition, author's signature, paper over boards with cloth spine, poet William Jay Smith's name on flyleaf, very good, tight in slightly scuffed dust jacket. Second Life Books, Inc. 196 B - 868 2016 $75

Association – Smyth, Diana

Hoare, Louisa *Hints for the Improvement of Early education and Nursery Discipline.* London: J. Hatchard & Son, 1841. Fourteenth edition, original blue grey cloth, spine faded and slightly rubbed, 2 small ink marks, inscription Diana Smyth 23 Wilton Place, May 1844, nice. Jarndyce Antiquarian Books CCXV - 235 2016 £45

Association – Smyth, Herbert Weir

Aeschylus *Tragodiae VII.* Antwerp: Ex Officina Christophori Plaintini, 1850. First Carter edition, dampmark stretching from upper margin and sometimes fore-edge, some spotting, bound little tightly but unlike many copies not trimmed close at other margins, 16mo., late 19th century vellum boards, spine with three raised bands, red morocco lettering piece, soiled, bookplate and release stamp of Harvard College Library Herbert Weir Smyth gift, good. Blackwell's Rare Books B186 - 3 2016 £950

Association – Smyth, James

Pitt, Christopher *Poems and Translations.* London: printed for Bernard Lintot and Arthur Bettesworth, 1727. First edition, folio, contemporary panelled calf, red morocco label, very good on large paper, early signature of James Smyth. C. R. Johnson Rare Book Collections Foxon: H-P 2015 - 752 2016 $613

Association – Smythe, Clifford

Atherton, Gertrude *The White Morning: a Novel of the Power of German women in Wartime.* New York: Stokes, 1918. First edition, 8vo., inscribed by author to Clifford Smythe, previous owner's name on endpaper, good, tight copy. Second Life Books, Inc. 196A - 53 2016 $65

Association – Snell, Powell

Plot, Robert *The Natural History of Oxford-shire.* Oxford: printed by Leon Litchfield for Charles Brome... and John Nicholson, 1705. Second edition, folio, 17 plates including folded map, occasional spotting but generally bright and clean, map very slightly toned with small tear near attachment, contemporary tan calf boards, neatly rebacked in marginally lighter shade, raised bands, green morocco gilt title label, all edges red upper hinge reinforced, little ms. to f.f.e.p., rear endpapers renewed, few small scrapes and marks but very good, armorial bookplates of Powell Snell and Robert Biddulh Phillipps, bookseller's ticket of Myers and Co. Unsworths Antiquarian Booksellers Ltd. E05 - 9 2016 £1500

Association – Snodgrass, W. D.

Rilke, Rainer Maria 1875-1926 *The Roses and the Windows.* Port Townsend: Graywolf Press, 1979. One of 48 copies numbered and inscribed by translator, A. Poulin and W. D. Snodgrass, 12mo., green cloth stamped gilt, about as new in dust jacket. Second Life Books, Inc. 196 B - 482 2016 $250

Association – Snow, Edwin

The Innocent Epicure; or the Art of Angling. London: printed by H. Meere for R. Gosling, 1713. Second edition, small 8vo., contemporary calf, gilt, neatly rebacked, spine gilt, red morocco label, presentation copy, inscribed 'Ex dono authoris', fine, bookplates of Edwin Snow and Henry Sherwin. C. R. Johnson Rare Book Collections Foxon: H-P 2015 - 487 2016 $3831

Association – Snyder, Gary

Antoninus, Brother 1912-1994 *Tendril in the Mesh.* Aromas: Cayucos Books, 1973. First edition, one of an unspecified number of lettered copies (this copy N) in a total edition of 250 signed by author, printed by Clifford Burke on Wookey Hole Mill paper, 4to., original quarter leather and paste paper over boards, presentation copy inscribed by author to Gary Snyder, spine ends and fore-tips very lightly rubbed, faint offset from binding adhesive along gutters of endsheets, otherwise fine, publisher's prospectus laid in. James S. Jaffe Rare Books Occasional List: Winter 2016 - 59 2016 $1250

Brand, Stewart *The Media Lab.* New York: Penguin, 1988. First edition thus, softcover, inscribed by author to Gary Snyder in 1990, with Synder's ownership signature, nice association copy. Ken Lopez Bookseller 166 - 9 2016 $200

Association – Soames, Arthur

Lyons, Daniel *Magna Britannia; Being a Concise Topographical Account of the Several Counties of Great Britain.* London: printed for T. Cadell and W. Davies, 1806-1822. Large paper copy, 346 x 260mm., 6 volumes bound in 10, pleasing contemporary red hard-grain half morocco over marbled boards by J. Mackenzie & son (stamp signed), raised bands, spines attractively gilt in compartments with very large and complex central fleuron surrounded by small tools and volute cornerpieces, gilt titling, marbled endpapers, all edges gilt, with 398 plates of maps, plans, views and architecture, 264 as called for and extra illustrated with 134, the total including 72 double page, 7 folding and 13 in color, engraved armorial bookplate of Arthur Soames, signed and dated in the plate by C. Hebard, paper boards somewhat chafed, extremities (especially bottom edge of boards), rather rubbed, spines slightly (but uniformly) darkened, few of the leather corners abraded, small portions of morocco dulled from preservatives, but bindings completely solid with no cracking to joints and still impressive on shelf, handsomely decorated spines unmarked, majority of plates with variable foxing (usually minimal, but perhaps two dozen noticeably foxed), a number of engravings with small, faint dampstains at very edge of top margin, text itself very fine, looking remarkably clean, fresh, smooth within its vast margins.   Phillip J. Pirages   67 - 245   2016 $5900

Association – Sobol, Louis

Kingsley, Sidney *Men in White.* New York: Covici Friede, 1933. First edition, First edition, 8vo., printed cloth in crinkled and worn dust jacket, advance review with slip tipped to front endpaper, inscribed by author to columnist Louis Sobol.   Second Life Books, Inc.   196A - 961   2016 $500

Association – Sohl

California Sorcery. Abingdon: Cemetery Dance, 1999. Publisher's copy of the limited edition (26 copies), signed by Ray Bradbury, Richard Matheson, Ellison, Nolan, Tomerlin, Sohl, Fritch and others, stamp of another author, fine in fine dust jacket in publisher's printed gray case.   Ken Lopez Bookseller   166 - 5   2016 $650

Association – Sondheim, Norman

Milton, John   1608-1674 *Samson Agonistes.* Florence: Stamperia del Santuccio, 1931. No. 51 of 95 copies, 340 x 229mm., in peculiar amateur binding of blue crushed morocco, upper cover with short black and orange lines onlaid at upper left and lower right corners, centerpiece of onlaid black coffin like ornament entwined by orange snake flat spine with onlaid orange sword with gilt titling, ivory moire silk endleaves, matching velvet lined orange linen, folding box with orange morocco back and lip, onlaid sword on back, printed in black and bistre, bookplate of Norman J. Sondheim, leather little spotted, soiled and with slight variation of color, isolated very trivial flecks of foxing, otherwise fine, text brilliantly white and clean, binding unworn.   Phillip J. Pirages   67 - 187   2016 $5500

Association – Sondheim, Stephen

Wheeler, Hugh *Candide.* New York: Macmillan/Schirmer Books, 1976. First edition, quarto, deluxe edition, glossy color plates, uncommon, near fine in like dust jacket, inscribed by Stephen Sondheim.   Royal Books   51 - 21   2016 $2000

Association – Soper, John

Tryon, Thomas *The Way to Health, Long Life and Happiness; or a Discourse of Temperance...* London: printed and are to be sold by most booksellers, 1697. Third edition, titlepage browned and chipped along edges, light marginal staining throughout, light foxing and spotting, 8mm circular hole through centre of P1, mid 20th century green morocco, from the library of James Stevens Cox (1910-1997), 18th century signature of Henry Bradbury, 18th century pencil notes of John Soper.   Maggs Bros. Ltd.   1447 - 418   2016   £200

Association – Sotheby F. E.

Twysden, Roger *Historiae Anglicanae Scriptores X.* London: Typis Jacobi Flesher sumptibus Cornelii Bee, 1652. Editio princeps, 2 volumes as 1, folio, half title, title in red and black, section, woodcut initials, few tiny wax spots and ink blots not obscuring text, contemporary dark brown calf, blind tooled frame, edges sprinkled brown and red, neatly rebacked, red morocco gilt spine label, few scratches to boards, inner hinges reinforced, 2 armorial bookplates, F. E. Sotheby, Ecton and Derek Baker, third armorial bookplate of Ambrose Isted, fourth armorial bookplate with no name but with motto 'Que Serra Serra".   Unsworths Antiquarian Booksellers Ltd.   E01 - Early Printing - 28   2016   £500

Association – Sotheby, Charles William Hamilton

Manilius, Marcus *Astronomicon Interpretatione et Notis ac Figuris Illustravit Michael fayus...* Parisiis: Apud Fredericum Leonard, 1679. 4to., engraved additional titlepage, woodcut had and tailpieces, initials and device to titlepage, several illustrations and tables in text, toning to some gatherings occasional very light smudges, contemporary brown speckled calf, rebacked neaty but in slightly lighter ton, riased bands, recent black and gilt spine label, edges sprinkled red and brown, rubbed, few scrapes, corners fraying but very good, bookplate of Charles William Hamilton Sotheby (a1820-1887). Unsworths Antiquarian Booksellers 30 - 104 2016 £450

Association – Souchow, W. J., Mrs.

Mennie, Donald *The Grandeur of the Gorges.* Shanghai: A. S. Watson & Co. (The Shanghai Pharmacy Ltd.), Kelly & Walsh Limited, 1926. First edition, no. 889 of 1000 copies, 4to, original silk, image of Yangtze Gorge in colours to upper cover, 50 mounted plates from photos, including 12 colored, nice, bright copy, inscribed by Margaret Lo for Mrs. W. J. Souchow? Sotheran's Travel and Exploration - 155 2016 £1950

Association – Southcote, Philip

Prior, Matthew 1664-1721 *Poems on Several Occasions.* London: printed for Jacob Tonson and John Barber, 1718. Large folio, fine, engraved frontispiece, contemporary black morocco, covers panelled gilt, spine and inner dentelles gilt, dark red morocco label, all edges gilt, joints and corners bit rubbed, sumptuous edition, this one of a relatively small number of copies printed on superfine copy, with watermark of a fleur-de-lys surmounting a shield as opposed to ordinary copies for subscribers with a Strasburg band watermark and copies of the trade issue with London arms watermark, numerous engraved headpieces and tailpieces, some dampmarks in blank upper margins, otherwise fine in handsome morocco binding of the period, bold armorial bookplate of Philip Southcote and booklabel of bibliography A. N. L. Munby. C. R. Johnson Rare Book Collections Foxon: H-P 2015 - 798 2016 $2298

Association – Southouse

Spence, Joseph 1699-1768 *Polymetis or an Enquiry Concerning the Agreement Between the Works of the Roman Poets and the Remains of the Antient Artists.* London: printed for R. & J. Dodsley, 1755. Second edition, frontispiece, 41 other engraved plates, some minor spotting, plates offset onto facing pages, folio, contemporary calf, neatly rebacked preserving original gilt spine, gilt now somewhat worn, new green morocco lettering piece to style, boards with elaborate stencilled frame dyed lighter brown, marbled endpapers, some tidy repairs to corners, rubbed, bookplates of Strathallan and Southouse, good. Blackwell's Rare Books B186 - 144 2016 £500

Association – Sowell, Tobitha

Brown, Elder John *Hymns for the use of the United Baptists of Illinois and the West.* Alton: Courier Steam Printing House, 1857. Second edition, 18mo., contemporary gilt stamped calf, last leaf with loss of few letters, stamped "Tobitha Sowell" on inside front cover and ink note indicating that Sowell bought this hymn book with her across the plains in 1863. M & S Rare Books, Inc. 99 - 110 2016 $750

Association – Spaak, Fernand

Shelley, Percy Bysshe 1792-1822 *Prometheus Unbound. A Lyrical Drama in Four Acts with Other Poems.* London: C. and J. Ollier, 1820. First edition, 2nd issue, with half title, ads at end discarded, 8vo., early 20th century red crushed morocco for William Brown (booksellers), Edinburgh, French fillets on sides, crowned initial B on the upper cover, spine panelled in gilt in compartments, gilt edges, surface of joints partly lifted, F. E. Smith's copy (crowned initial on upper cover), with his bookplate inside front cover as Viscount Birkenhead, bookplate of Fernand Spaak opposite, good. Blackwell's Rare Books Marks of Genius - 49 2016 £2500

Association – Sparkes, Stewart

Wiseman, Richard *Eight Chirurgical Treatises on the Following Heads, viz. I of Tumours. II of Ulcers. III. Of Diseases of the Anus...* London: for B. T. and L. M. and sold by W. Keblewhtie and J. Jones, 1697. Third edition, 18th century paneled calf, very skillfully rebacked retaining original gilt spine, period style label, tin (half inch) repaired tear in lower margin of third leaf, else remarkably fine, fresh copy, contemporary ownership signature of Stewart Sparkes on half title. Joseph J. Felcone, Inc. Books from Five Centuries: a Miscellany - 99 2016 $3200

Association – Speechly, Martha

Church of England. Book of Common Prayer *The Book of Common Prayer and Administration of the Sacraments.* London: published for John Reeves...sold and G. and W. Nicol and Satcherd and Letterman, 1807. 2 parts in 1 volume, 12mo., contemporary red straight grained morocco, single gilt fillet on sides and an inner border of 2 blind fillets and a blind roll tool, gilt crown of centre of both covers, spine richly tooled gilt and blind lettered in gilt direct, red morocco label inside front cover, gilt edges, trifle worn at extremities, inner hinge neatly repaired, boards trifle warped, good copy, with a letter of provenance on mourning paper from Isabella Speechly of Peterborough stating "The Prayer Book and Hymn Book (latter not present) which belonging to Queen Caroline, were given to the Lady Egmont by Lady Anne Hamilton the Queen's Lady and she have them to my Great Aunt Miss Martha Speechly then living at Darmouth House...". Blackwell's Rare Books Marks of Genius - 11 2016 £6000

Association – Spelier, Sophia

Female Excellence or Hints to Daughters. London: RTS, circa, 1852. Half title, slight creasing in prelims, uncut in original brown cloth by E. Littler, little dulled with slight rubbing to head and tail of spine, leading f.e.p., signed 'Sophia Spelier, Jan. 31 1852', good plus. Jarndyce Antiquarian Books CCXV - 330 2016 £35

Association – Spelman, John

Raleigh, Walter *Judicious and Select Essayes and Observations.* London: by T. Warren for Humphrey Moseley, 1650. First edition, small 8vo., engraved portrait, but without 4 leaves of Moseley's ads, blank verso of engraved portrait and blank verso of last leaf stained by turn-ins and with edges slightly chipped, small repair to foot of titlepage, just touching decorated border, minor closed tear in lower inner margin of A1-2, dampstaining to inner margins of G4-(2)C8 (touching text in places), small hole through (3)A-3 (touching two lines of text), some occasional rust spotting, mid 20th century calf, from the library of James Stevens Cox (1910-1997), early inscription of John Spelman, signature Robertus (?) Culsett, armorial bookplate of William Miller Ord (1834-1902). Maggs Bros. Ltd. 1447 - 351 2016 £350

Association – Spencer, Earl

Theocritus *Tade Enestein Ente Garoi se Biblo Eidyllia he Kai Triakonta.* Rome: Zacharias Callierges, 1516. 8vo., early 19th century mid brown polished calf, spine gilt in compartments, red morocco lettering piece, edges red, marbled endpapers, corners slightly worn, joints near invisibly strengthened and front flyleaf re-attached, bookplate of Thomas Gaisford and letter from Earl Spencer to Gaisford, Gaisford's ownership inscription and manuscript table of contents to blank endpapers, good. Blackwell's Rare Books B184 - 84 2016 £6500

Association – Spencer, W. Baldwin

Thompson, D'Arcy Wenworth *A Glossary of Greek Birds.* Oxford: Clarendon Press, 1895. Octavo, publisher's cloth, pencil ownership signature of W. Baldwin Spencer, deaccessioned library stamp of royal Australasian Ornithologists' Union and the bookplate of D. L. Serventy. Andrew Isles Natural History Books 55 - 38849 2016 $200

Association – Spender, Stephen

Raine, Kathleen *The Collected Poems of Kathleen Raine.* London: Hamish Hamilton, 1956. First edition, fine in fine dust jacket, from the library of Stephen Spender with his bookplate. Peter Ellis 112 - 320 2016 £65

Association – Spingarn, Arthur

Cartwright, William *Comedies, Tragi-Comedies with other Poems.* London: for Humphrey Moseley, 1651. First edition, 8vo., engraved portrait, 5 section titles with duplicate leaves U1-3 as usual, blank I4 present, b2 foxed and untrimmed to preserved shoulder notes, modern calf, very skillfully executed in 17th century style, title and dedication leaf and few running heads slightly cropped by binder's knife, and one note to binder cropped, very nice, Arthur Spingarn copy, rebound with his bookplate and collation notes laid in. Joseph J. Felcone, Inc. Books from Five Centuries: a Miscellany - 35 2016 $2400

Association – Spirin, Gennadli

Volter, Maria Louise *Marissa und Die Heinzelmannchen.* Esslington: J. F. Schreiber, n.d., 1982. Pictorial boards, fine, illustrations by Gennadi Spirin, this copy signed by artist. Aleph-bet Books, Inc. 112 - 465 2016 $125

Association – Spitz, Joel

Alken, Henry *Illustrations for Landscape Scenery.* London: published by S. & J. Fuller, at the Temple of Fancy, 34 Rathbone Place..., 1821. First edition, scarce edition, oblong small folio, 26 hand colored engraved plates, numbered 1-24 and 2 unnumbered, uncut in original grey boards, upper cover with printed label, rebacked in modern red cloth slipcase, upper cover lettered gilt, bookplate of Joel Spitz. Marlborough Rare Books List 55 - 1 2016 £1500

Association – Sprowson, Josephine

Dickens, Charles 1812-1870 *The Life and Adventures of Nicholas Nickleby.* London: Chapman & Hall, 1848. First cheap edition, frontispiece little spotted, original green cloth slightly bubbled, blocked in blind, gilt spine slightly faded and little worn at head and tail, small nick in following hinge, contemporary signature of Josephine Sprowson on leading pastedown, bookseller's blindstamp H. Whitmore, Manchester, good plus. Jarndyce Antiquarian Booksellers CCXVIII - 229 2016 £75

Association – Spry, Joseph

Shirley, James 1596-1666 *Via ad Latinam Linguam Companta.* London: by R. W. for John Stephenson, 1649. First edition, 8vo., lacking engraved title by Thomas Cross, some light soiling to titlepage and A2, two small inkstains to A24 and A3v, edges slightly bumped throughout and with some gatherings beginning to come loose, contemporary blind ruled sheep (corner of upper board chewed, bumped and rubbed), from the library of James Stevens Cox (1910-1997), 18th century name of Joseph Spry. Maggs Bros. Ltd. 1447 - 384 2016 £200

Association – Squire, A.

Wilde, Oscar   1854-1900   *Ravenna. Recited in the Theatre, Oxford June 26 1878.*   Oxford: Thos. Shrimpton 1878, i.e., 1904. First pirated edition, small octavo, original grey wrappers, pictorial bookplate of A. Squire, smaller printed label from Library of AJA Symons, Brick House, covers just little wrinkled, very good, preserved in custom made green morocco backed patterned board folder.   Peter Ellis 112 - 449   2016   £575

Association – St. Aubyn, John

Fenelon, Francois Salignac De La Mothe, Abp.   1651-1715   *On the Education of Daughters.* London: W. Darton, 1812. 12mo., frontispiece, slight offsetting, odd spot, handsomely bound in slightly later full light blue grey calf raised bands, gilt compartments, maroon morocco label, little rubbed and marked, attractive copy, gift inscription Juliana St. Aubyn, the gift of Sir. John St. Aubyn.   Jarndyce Antiquarian Books   CCXV - 681   2016   £85

Association – St. Aubyn, Juliana

Fenelon, Francois Salignac De La Mothe, Abp.   1651-1715   *On the Education of Daughters.* London: W. Darton, 1812. 12mo., frontispiece, slight offsetting, odd spot, handsomely bound in slightly later full light blue grey calf raised bands, gilt compartments, maroon morocco label, little rubbed and marked, attractive copy, gift inscription Juliana St. Aubyn, the gift of Sir. John St. Aubyn.   Jarndyce Antiquarian Books   CCXV - 681   2016   £85

Association – St. John, Ambrose

Newman, John Henry, Cardinal   1801-1890   *Sermons Bearing on Subjects of the Day.*   London: J. G. F. and J. Rivington, 1843. First edition, half title, original blue green cloth, slightly browned and chipped paper label, small nick to lower margin of spine with slight loss, spine rubbed at head and tail, inner hinges little weak, presentation inscription "Ambrose St. John with affectionate regards of JHN DEC. 8 1843".   Jarndyce Antiquarian Booksellers   CCXVII - 199   2016   £1250

Association – St. Quintin, Willliam

Darrell, William   *The Gentleman Instructed, in the conduct of a Virtuous and Happy life.*   London: printed by W. B. for E. Smith and sold by Rich. Wilkin, 1720. Seventh edition, 8vo., occasional slight foxing, contemporary panelled calf, brown morocco label, leading hinge with slight cracking, otherwise very good, armorial bookplate of William St. Quintin. Jarndyce Antiquarian Books   CCXV - 144   2016   £480

Association – Stacey, Frederick

Nesfield, William Eden   *Specimens of Mediaeval Architecture, Chiefly Selected from Examples of the 12th and 13th Centuries in France and Italy.*   London: Day and Son at gate Street Near Lincoln Inn Fields, Jan. A.D., 1862. First edition, folio, wood engraved title by Dalziel after author, including figures by Albert Moore, 100 lithographic plates, including one in chromolithography by A. Newman, original purple roan backed brick colored cloth blocked in black, upper cover reproducing title leaf with inlaid panel of red calf blocked in gold spine decorated and lettered gilt and black, all edges gilt, binder ticket of Leighton Son and Hodge, contemporary bookplate of Frederick Stacey. Marlborough Rare Books   List 55 - 50   2016   £250

Association – Stanfield, H. H.

Dickens, Charles   1812-1870   *Pictures from Italy.* London: published for the author by Bradbury & Evans, 1846. first edition, 2nd issue, half title, vignette title, initial and final ad leaves, original blue fine diaper cloth blocked in blind, spine lettered gilt, spine slightly dulled, contemporary signature of H. H. Stanfield, very good in blue cloth slipcase. Jarndyce Antiquarian Booksellers   CCXVIII - 433   2016 £350

Association – Stanley, Arthur Penrhyn

Dodgson, Charles Lutwidge   1832-1898   *Phantasmagoria and other Poems.*   London: Macmillan, 1869. First edition, first issue with page 94 printed correctly, 8vo., beautifully bound by Riviere in full blue calf with extensive gilt toning on spine, gilt rules on covers, gilt turn-ins, all edges gilt and with original covers bound in, fine copy, inscribed by author to Arthur Penrhyn Stanley, beautiful copy.   Aleph-bet Books, Inc.   111 - 77   2016 $6500

Association – Stanley, Kim

Taylor, Samuel   *Sabrina Fair; or a woman of the World a Romantic Comedy.*   New York: Random House, 1954. First printing, 8vo., illustrations, very good in little scuffed and soiled, price clipped dust jacket, signed by Lerna Dana, Kim Stanley, Diana Lynn and Margaret Steele, who appeared in the play, illustrations.   Second Life Books, Inc. 196 B - 743   2016 $95

Association – Stanley, Thomas

Silius, Italicus *De Secundo Bello Punico.* Amsterdam: G. Jansson, 1620. Engraved titlepage, ruled in red, 16mo., exquisite binding by Mace Ruette, contemporary gilt tooled red morocco, covers framed by outer double fillet, central panel of strait and curved double fillets with small vase of flowers tool at each outer corner in centre of covers a quadrilobe inlay with monogram of H. L. Habert de Montmort and four "S" forms with elaborate pointille sprays of spirals, circles and dots on all four sides, spine with five raised bands, decorated in compartments, inner edges gilt, marbled endpapers, gilt edges, headcaps and joints lightly rubbed, the copy of Habert de Montmort (1600-1679), Colonel Thomas Stanley (1749-1818), William Beckford with his bookseller George Clarke's pencil collation mark, Hamilton Palace Library sale, Thore Virgin inscription dated 1916 with his book label (1886-1957). Maggs Bros. Ltd. 1474 - 72   2016   £2500

Association – Stanley, W. O.

Stanley, William Owen *Memoirs on Remains of Ancient Dwellings in Holyhead Island Mostly of Circular Form called Cyttlau'r Gwyddelod...* London/Chester: James Bain/Marshall & Hughes, 1871. First edition, gold stamped sienna cloth, modest edgewear, signed "Frances Wynne from W. O. Stanley March 26 1881", stunning engraved bookplate of designer Harry Soane for Col. John Charles Wynne Finch, very faint bookstore stamp to front cover, many engravings, fold mout map intact. Simon Finch   2015 - 055187   2016 $225

Association – Staples, Leslie

Dickens, Charles 1812-1870 *Barnaby Rudge.* London: Chapman & Hall, 1841. First separate edition, complete in one volume, illustrations by Cattermole and Phiz, original olive green cloth, borders blocked in blind, spine with blind compartments and lettered gilt, spine very slightly faded, booklabel of Leslie C. Staples, very good, bright copy. Jarndyce Antiquarian Booksellers   CCXVIII - 297   2016   £1500

Association – Stark, Freya

Grahame, Kenneth 1859-1932 *The Wind in the Willows.* London: Methuen and Co., 1908. First edition, gilt lettering and designs fresh and bright, little wear at edges and covers, few very light stains, some professional color restoration, prelims and endleaves somewhat darkened and foxed as usual and edges of some leaves also foxed, nice, increasingly scarce, ownership inscription erased from flyleaf, but from the library of Dame Freya Stark and husband Stewart Perowne, bearing their Asolo bookplate. Bertram Rota Ltd.   Christmas List 2015 - 13   2016   £4000

Association – Starkey, Elizabeth

Rowe, James *Five Years to Freedom.* Boston: Little Brown, 1971. First edition, signed by author, additionally this copy inscribed and annotated by Elizabeth Starkey, a nurse at the 24th Evac. Hospital in Long Binh where Rowe was taken, inscribed by Starkey with long paragraph telling her story, near fine in very good dust jacket with internal tape mending. Ken Lopez Bookseller   166 - 138   2016 $450

Association – Starling

Dickens, Charles 1812-1870 *Edwin Drood. Complete (Part Second) by te Spirit-Pen of Charles Dickens, through a Medium).* Brattleboro: T. P. James, 1873. Original brown cloth, bevelled boards, lettered gilt, little rubbed, Suzannet, Starling & Self booklabels, good plus. Jarndyce Antiquarian Booksellers   CCXVIII - 647   2016   £120

Saunders, Montagu *The Mystery in the Drood Family.* Cambridge: University Press, 1914. Half title, original light green cloth, paper label, spine little faded, Starling booklabel, very good. Jarndyce Antiquarian Booksellers   CCXVIII - 686   2016   £25

Association – Starrett, Vincent

Dazey, Charles T. *In Old Kentucky.* Detroit: Dramatists Play service, 1937. First edition, 1/350 copies in special binding, numbered and signed by author, 8vo., bookplate of Vincent Starrett with his ownership signature, very good in somewhat chipped and soiled dust jacket. Second Life Books, Inc.   196A - 396   2016 $65

Association – Staryley

The Housemaid. London: Houlston & Stoneman, circa, 1860. Leaves little dusted, original limp green cloth boards, dulled and slightly affected by damp, signature "Staryley' on title. Jarndyce Antiquarian Books   CCXV - 261   2016   £125

Association – Staveley, A.

Bible. Greek - 1848 *He Palaia Diatheke Kata Tous Ebdomekonta Vetus Testamentum...* Oxonii: e Typographico Academico, 1848. 3 volumes, small 8vo., text in Greek, little toned, endpapers slightly foxed, generally bright and clean within, contemporary dark brown morcco, gilt titles to spines, all edges gilt, marbled endpapers, rubbed, corners bumped and little worn, very good, ownership inscription of A. Staveley, 47th March 1881 to Roger Garth Hooper, 1925 to Peter A. Boyle, September 1952. Unsworths Antiquarian Booksellers   30 - 18   2016   £90

Association – Stedman, Thomas

The Ladies Charity School House Roll of Highgate or a Subscription of Many Noble, Well Disposed Ladies for the Ease of Carrying it On. London: 1670. First edition, octavo, contemporary red morocco with elaborate gilt decorated patterns of floral ornaments, handles, knobs and shells on covers and five compartments on spine, with repeating pattern of smaller handles and knobs around spider like figures, 4 engraved plates, edges rubbed, two silk ties lacking (two present), lacking front free endpaper, very good, ink signature of Thomas Stedman, Oct. 1763. The Brick Row Book Shop Miscellany 69 - 12 2016 $2750

Association – Steed, Elizabeth

Guthrie, A. B. *The Big Sky.* New York: Sloane, 1947. First edition, signed by author and inscribed in Lexington Kentucky for Elizabeth and Virgil (Steed), moderate dampstaining to cloth with loss to spine lettering, very good in very good spine sunned dust jacket with small, internally tape reinforced edge chips. Ken Lopez Bookseller 166 - 40 2016 $575

Association – Steed, Virgil

Guthrie, A. B. *The Big Sky.* New York: Sloane, 1947. First edition, signed by author and inscribed in Lexington Kentucky for Elizabeth and Virgil (Steed), moderate dampstaining to cloth with loss to spine lettering, very good in very good spine sunned dust jacket with small, internally tape reinforced edge chips. Ken Lopez Bookseller 166 - 40 2016 $575

Association – Steel, Miss

Margam Abbey an Historical romance of the Fourteenth Century. London: John Green, 1837. Marginal tear to pages 117-119 without loss to text, full dark green grained calf, attractively blocked in gilt, rubbed, chip to head and tail of spine, inscription to Miss Steel, March 18th 1849, all edges gilt. Jarndyce Antiquarian Booksellers CCXVII - 7 2016 £250

Association – Steele, Margaret

Taylor, Samuel *Sabrina Fair; or a woman of the World a Romantic Comedy.* New York: Random House, 1954. First printing, 8vo., illustrations, very good in little scuffed and soiled, price clipped dust jacket, signed by Lerna Dana, Kim Stanley, Diana Lynn and Margaret Steele, who appeared in the play, illustrations. Second Life Books, Inc. 196 B - 743 2016 $95

Association – Steelman, John

Truman, Harry S. *Mr. Citizen.* New York: Bernard Geis Associates, 1960. Deluxe author's edition, signed, inscribed and dated in year of publication by Truman to John R. Steelman, near fine quarter morocco leather patterned board binding, gilt lettering spine, mild soil covers, original blue grey slipcase with tipped on label as issued, mild sun, edge wear slipcase, 8vo. By the Book, L. C. 45 - 6 2016 $2750

Association – Stegner, Marion

Decker, William *To Be a Man.* Boston: Little Brown, 1967. First edition, inscribed by author to Wallace Stegner's son, the writer Peter Stegner and his wife Marion, nice association, fine in very good dust jacket with few small stains to spine and rear panel which also sports very supportive blurb by Wallace Stegner. Ken Lopez Bookseller 166 - 22 2016 $375

Association – Stegner, Peter

Decker, William *To Be a Man.* Boston: Little Brown, 1967. First edition, inscribed by author to Wallace Stegner's son, the writer Peter Stegner and his wife Marion, nice association, fine in very good dust jacket with few small stains to spine and rear panel which also sports very supportive blurb by Wallace Stegner. Ken Lopez Bookseller 166 - 22 2016 $375

Association – Steinbeck, Carol

Steinbeck, John Ernst 1902-1968 *Pastures of Heaven.* London: Philip Allan, 1933. First UK edition, this author's copy with his and his wife Carol's ownership stamp, very good in scarce dust jacket, fading to spine, few small faint dampstains to boards and short tear to cloth and bottom of front spine, custom clamshell box. Royal Books 49 - 66 2016 $3500

Association – Steinthal, Samuel Alfred

Prudentius Clemens, Aurelius *Opera.* Amsterdam: Apud Danielem Elzevirium, 1667. 12mo., title in red and black with printer's device and hand ruled lines, separate half title to Heinsius notes, occasional engraved initials and head and tailpieces, little toned but generally clean, contemporary vellum, title inked to spine in old hand, yapp edges, edges sprinkled blue, some smudgy marks, endcaps creased, turn-ins lifting slightly causing cracks to edges of endpapers, but all holding firm, Pardonneau of Tours to front pastedown, armorial bookplate of Samuel Alfred Steinthal. Unsworths Antiquarian Booksellers Ltd. E01 - Early Printing - 19 2016 £175

Association – Stephens, S.

Laishley, Richard *Education and Educators.* London: Waterlow & Sons, March, 1884. inscribed by author for Prof. S. Stephens, original red cloth, spine faded. Jarndyce Antiquarian Books CCXV - 817 2016 £20

Association – Stephenson, E. S.

Stevens, Robert *Sermons, on Our Duty Towards God, Our Neighbour, and Ourselves: and on Other Subjects.* London: printed for John Booth, 1814. First edition, 225 x 133mm., pleasing contemporary midnight blue straight grain morocco, covers framed by plain gilt rules outlining Greek key and palmette blind rolls, raised bands, compartments with central gilt fleuron radiating densely blind tooled foliage, gilt ruled turn-ins, all edges gilt, with excellent fore-edge painting of Dover Castle; a presentation copy with (slightly foxed) signed autograph letter bound in (with letter offsets) for E. S. Stephenson, unidentified armorial bookplate, bit of wear to corners and joints, very small (ink?) stain to edge of prelim leaves visible at upper left background of fore-edge painting (not affecting primary image), otherwise fine, clean, fresh internally in lustrous binding. Phillip J. Pirages 67 - 164 2016 $1300

Association – Sterling, Joseph

Taken by Design: Photographs from the Institute of Design 1937-1971. Chicago: University of Chicago Press, 2002. First edition, very near fine copy in photo illustrated flexible boards, signed by Joseph Jachna and additionally inscribed by Joseph Sterling And Alan Cohen. Jeff Hirsch Books E-List 80 - 1 2016 $200

Association – Stevenson, Adlai

Rey, H. A. *The Stars: a New Way to See Them.* Boston: Houghton Mifflin, 1952. First edition, 4to., pictorial cloth, small bit of edge fading, else fine in dust jacket (some soil, fraying and few closed tears), inscribed by author for Adlai Stevenson. Aleph-bet Books, Inc. 112 - 422 2016 $1750

Simpson, C. L. *The Memoirs of C. L. Simpson: the Symbol of Liberia.* London: Diplomatic Press and Pub. Co., 1961. First edition, octavo, blue cloth gilt, trifle rubbed, paper edges slightly toned, still about fine, inscribed by Simpson to Adlai Stevenson. Between the Covers Rare Books 202 - 95 2016 $450

Association – Stewart, C. J.

Petau, Denis *...Opus de Theologicis Dogmatibus Nunc primum Septem Voluminibus Comprehensum, in Mediorem Ordinem Redactum...* Venice: Remondiana, 1757. Best edition, 6 books in 7 and bound in 2 volumes, folio, title in red and black, half title, each book with its separate title, titlepage portrait engraving of Denis and additional woodcut initials and head and tailpieces all volumes, first volume free endpapers slightly torn, contemporary full vellum, gilt stamped spines, first volume stained, second volume lower corners gently bumped, bookplates of Ex Oblatororum S. Caroli Bibliotheca Bayswater (Henry Edward Manning 1808-1892), Pitts Theology Library bookplates, C. J. Stewart bookseller label, titlepage ownership signatures and inscriptions of Engelbert Klupfel, 1769 and Steph. Wirelo(?), rare, fine. Jeff Weber Rare Books 181 - 26 2016 $750

Association – Stewart, Hinton

Dickens, Charles 1812-1870 *Great Expectations.* London: Chapman & Hall, 1861. First edition, third impression, third impression and first impression respectively, 3 volumes, half title and color frontispiece volume I, color plates 32 page catalog volume III May 1861, slightly later full scarlet crushed morocco by Riviere & Son, spines gilt in compartments, triple ruled borders and gilt dentelles, original purple cloth bound in at end of each volume, armorial bookplates of Hinton A Stewart, top edge gilt, very good, attractive, handsome copy, extra illustrated by Pailthorpe with 21 full color etchings. Jarndyce Antiquarian Booksellers CCXVIII - 588 2016 £6500

Association – Stewart, Jimmy

Reed, Rex *Travolta to Keaton.* New York: Morrow, 1979. First edition, 8vo., portraits, signed by Jimmy Stewart, very good in dust jacket. Second Life Books, Inc. 196 B - 463 2016 $65

Association – Stewart, Rosalie

Kelly, George *Craig's Wife, a Drama.* Boston: Little Brown, 1926. First edition, 8vo., very nice tight copy, inscribed by author for Josephine Williams (played part of Mrs. Harold in NY production), also signed by rest of the cast and inscribed by producer Rosalie Stewart. Second Life Books, Inc. 196A - 929 2016 $1500

Association – Stickney, Dorothy

Kelly, George *Philip Goes Forth.* New York: Samuel French, 1931. First edition, 8vo., fine in dust jacket missing some pieces at edges and corners, inscribed by author to Dorothy Stickney with her name stamp, also signed by the complete cast. Second Life Books, Inc. 196A - 936 2016 $650

Association – Stimson, Frederic

Lowell, Percival *Noto an Unexplored corner of Japan.* Boston: Houghton Mifflin/Riverside Press, 1891. First edition, small 8vo., presentation slip from author tipped-in, very good++, black cloth covered boards with gilt lettered spine, red ink stamped design front cover, titlepage, minimal scuffs spine, soil to rear endpaper, bookplate of Frederic J. Stimson.   By the Book, L. C.   45 - 50   2016 $650

Association – Stoddard, R. H.

Webster, John *A Monumental Colummne, Erected to the Liuing Memory of the Euer-Glorious Henry, late Prince of Wales.* London: printed by N. O(kes) for William Welby, 1613. First edition, woodcut ornaments on title, woodcut headpieces, 2 pages printed entirely in black, lacking final 2 leaves (also printed entirely in black, without text), last leaf with a hole with loss of 3 letters from the motto at end of text on recto, slight loss to lower fore-corner of this leaf and extreme corresponding corner of preceding leaf (no loss of text), A4 (the first black leaf), very slightly defective at top outer corner, title slightly browned, 4to., late 19th century green crushed morocco by Matthews, quadruple gilt fillets on sides with corner ornaments, spine lettered longitudinally in gilt, gilt edges, extra blank leaves bound in at beginning and end, last at front inscribed 'Richard Grant White Esq. with the best wishes of R. H. Stoddard", good.   Blackwell's Rare Books   Marks of Genius - 50   2016   £20,000

Association – Stone, Richard

Bray, F. Sewell *Accounting Research.* London: Cambridge University Press, 1948. First edition, wrappers, 8vo., each issue about 70 pages, 36 issues, from the library of economist Sir Richard Stone.   Any Amount of Books   2015 - A72995   2016   £600

Association – Stonor

Huet, Pierre Daniel *De Imbecillitate Mentis Humanae Libri Tres.* Amsterdam: Apud H. Du. Sauzet, 1738. 12mo., title in red and black, engraved frontispiece, portrait, spine strengthened with clear tape, good copy in contemporary grey blue boards, presentation slip "With the compliments of Dr. Richard A. Hunter" laid in, with Stonor armorial bookplate.   Edwin V. Glaser Rare Books   2015 - 19212   2016 $300

Association – Stoughton, John Clarke

Cruise, William *An Essay on the Nature and Operation of Fines and Recoveries...* London: printed by His Majesty's Law Printers for E. Brooke, 1786. Second edition, 2 volumes, 8vo., contemporary calf, some minor abrasions to bindings and wear to joints, still sound, attractive, original labels, each volume with early 19th century armorial bookplate of John Clarke Stoughton of Wymondham in Norfolk.   John Drury Rare Books   2015 - 22907   2016 $350

Association – Strachey, Lytton

Terentius Afer, Publius *Comediae.* Birmingham: Typis Johannis Baskerville, 1772. 4to., titlepage toned, little minor spotting, elsewhere, slightly later half red morocco, marbled boards, spine divided by gilt rolls, second compartment gilt lettered direct, rest with central oval or fountain & bird tools, marbled endpapers, spine somewhat faded, slight rubbing to extremities, bookplates of L. W. Greenwood and Lytton Strachey, very good.   Blackwell's Rare Books   Greek & Latin Classics VII - 89   2016   £300

Douglas, Norman 1868-1952 *Together.* London: Chapman & Hall, 1923. First edition, 2 plates, foxing to half title, occasional spots further in, 8vo., original maroon cloth, backstrip lettered gilt and faded, couple of small marks at foot, rubbing to extremities with mottling to leading edge of both boards, successive bookplates of Lytton Strachey and Miriam Benkovitz, with ownership gift inscription by these respective owners, very good, significant association.   Blackwell's Rare Books   B186 - 209   2016   £150

Association – Strand, Mark

Brodsky, Joseph *Verses on the Winter Campaign.* London: Anvil Press Poetry, 1981. First edition, one of 250 copies signed by author and translator, Alan Myers, out of a total edition of 500 copies, 12mo., original unprinted wrappers, dust jacket, presentation copy inscribed by author to friend, the poet Mark Strand, with Brodsky's corrections in verse, fine.   James S. Jaffe Rare Books   Occasional List: Winter 2016 - 34   2016 $1250

Association – Strathallan

Hill, David Octavius *Sketches of Scenery in Perthshire.* Perth: Published by Thos. Hill and sold by W. Blackwood, Edinburgh & Matin & Ackermann, London and printed by J. Roberston, Edinburgh, 1821-1823. First edition, 6 parts, oblong folio, 30 lithographed plates, parts 1-3 printed by J. Robertson, Edinburgh, parts 4-6 printed by Hulmandel, stitched as issued in original buff wrappers, preserved in modern green cloth, folder, upper with gilt morocco label, the copy of James Drummond, later 8th Viscount Strathallan, fine.   Marlborough Rare Books   List 55 - 35   2016   £5500

Powlett, Edmund *The General Contents of the British Museum; with Remarks Serving as a Directory...* London: printed for R. and J. Dodsley, 1762. Second edition, half title, 12mo., some light browning, but very good, clean copy, full contemporary sprinkled calf, gilt ruled borders, raised and gilt banded spine, red morocco label, expert repairs to joints and corners, armorial bookplate of Strahallan contemporary signature on front endpaper of S. M. Savage dated 1762 with a number of ms. corrections and observations.   Jarndyce Antiquarian Booksellers   CCXVI - 480   2016   £1250

Spence, Joseph   1699-1768 *Polymetis or an Enquiry Concerning the Agreement Between the Works of the Roman Poets and the Remains of the Antient Artists.* London: printed for R. & J. Dodsley, 1755. Second edition, frontispiece, 41 other engraved plates, some minor spotting, plates offset onto facing pages, folio, contemporary calf, neatly rebacked preserving original gilt spine, gilt now somewhat worn, new green morocco lettering piece to style, boards with elaborate stencilled frame dyed lighter brown, marbled endpapers, some tidy repairs to corners, rubbed, bookplates of Strathallan and Southouse, good. Blackwell's Rare Books   B186 - 144   2016   £500

Association – Stratton, Chester

Shaw, George Bernard   1856-1950 *Man and Superman.* New York: Dodd, Mead, 1947. First edition, 8vo., very good in little worn dust jacket, some of the photos show little watermark at edge, written on endpaper is note this book is the property of "Maurice Evans Prod. Inc." and is to be returned, this copy signed by Malcolm Keen, Chester Stratton, Victor Sutherland, Carmen Mathews, Jack Manning, Phoebe Mackay and Tony Bickley.   Second Life Books, Inc.   196 B - 562   2016 $450

Association – Streater, Maria Ellen

Dickens, Charles   1812-1870 *The Chimes.* London: Chapman & Hall, 1845. Twelfth edition, half title, frontispiece, additional engraved title, illustrations, original red cloth gilt, carefully recased, inscribed by author for Thomas Powell, September fourth 1845, later ownership inscription of Ellen Maria Streater, and E. Harrell, all edges gilt, morocco backed box.   Jarndyce Antiquarian Booksellers   CCXVIII - 364   2016   £25,000

Association – Streatfield, Henry

Ancourt, Abbe D' *The Lady's Preceptor.* London: printed for J. Watts and sold by B. Dod, 1743. Second edition, 8vo., title in red and black, contemporary full calf, double ruled gilt borders, hinges cracked but remaining firm, little rubbed with slight loss to foot of spine, contemporary ownership signature of Henry Streatfield on title with Streatfield family armorial bookplate.   Jarndyce Antiquarian Books   CCXV - 12   2016   £750

Association – Stretton, John

Udall, John *A Demonstration of the Trueth of the Discipline which Christe Hath Prescribed in His Worde for the Gouernment of His Church, in all Times and Places....* East Molesey: R. Waldegrave, 1588. First edition, folding table, titlepage and blank verso of last leaf dust soiled, C4 frayed in fore margin, small 8vo., 17th century calf, panelled in gilt and blind, with central medallion in gilt, rebacked preserving original spine, 18th century ownership inscription of William Groom below errata and also on front free endpaper, that of John Stretton on following flyleaf, good. Blackwell's Rare Books   B184 - 87   2016   £5000

Association – Strickland, Henry Eustachius

Chamberlayne, John *Magnae Britanniae Notitia or the Present State of Great Britain.*   printed for Timothy Goodwin...., 1718. 2 parts in 1, second with separate titlepage, engraved frontispiece, one gathering in first part and 5 in second browned, 8vo., contemporary panelled sheep, red lettering piece on spine, date gilt at foot, little worn, cracks in joint headcap defective, agricultural armorial bookplate of Henry Eustachius Strickland, sound.   Blackwell's Rare Books   B186 - 39   2016   £400

Association – Strickland, William

Roscoe, William *Considerations on the Causes, Objects and Consequences of the Present War and on the Expediency or the Danger of Peace with France.* London: printed by J. McCreery for Cadell & Davies, 1808. First edition, title little browned, uncut sewn as issued, small library duplicate stamp on final page, contemporary signature of William Strickland on titlepage, very good.   Jarndyce Antiquarian Booksellers   CCXVII - 250   2016   £95

Association – Stringer, Thomas

Randolph, Thomas *Poems with the Muses Looking-Glasse, and the Amyntas.* London: in the year, 1643. Third edition, titlepage lightly soiled, some light soiling and staining, full modern calf, from the library of James Stevens Cox (1910-1997), with his pencil annotations to front pastedown, signature of Thomas Stringer, 1678, (K?) Stringer signature dated 1693,.   Maggs Bros. Ltd.   1447 - 352   2016   £250

Association – Stuart, Alexander W. Ruthven

L'Innocence de la Tresillustre. Tres-chaste, et Debonnaire Princesse, Madame Marie Royne d'Escosse. n.p. Iprime an, 1572. 8vo., signature O omitted in make up, text complete, all pages faintly rubricated, very nice, bound by Bedford in dark blue morocco gilt, dentelles, marbled endpapers, all edges gilt, ownership signature of A. Elphinston(e) on titlepage with dated in lower margin 1600, later armorial bookplate of James Wyllie Guild and Thomas Brooke, FSA, Armitage Bridge, ownership inscription Alexander W. Ruthven Stuart 1923.   Jarndyce Antiquarian Booksellers   CCXVII - 182   2016   £1500

Association – Stuart, Charles James

Sophocles   (Greek) *Tragaediae Septem cum Commentariis etc.*   Venice: Aldus Manutius, August, 1502. Editio princeps, 8vo., 196 leaves, 19th century vellum over pasteboard, gilt spine, early title lettered ink on lower edge, Aldus device on verso of final leaf, Greek type, Latin marginalia to Ajax and notes on front blank c. 1800 (slightly cropped), bookplate of Sir Charles James Stuart, 2nd Baronet, Herbert Thompson name inscribed on front flyleaf.   Maggs Bros. Ltd.   1474 - 74   2016   £20,000

Association – Sturdy, Katherine Nora

Osborne, Dorothy   *Letters from Dorothy Osborne to Sir William Temple 1652-54.*   London and Manchester: Sherratt and Hughes, 1903. 184 x 127mm, quite pretty russet crushed morocco by Roger De Coverly & Sons (signed on rear turn-in), covers with double gilt rule border, raised bands, spines richly gilt in compartments with quatrefoil centerpiece surrounded by daisies, shamrocks and rose leaves, gilt titling, turn-ins ruled in gilt with trefoil cornerpieces, all edges gilt, portraits of Osborne and Temple and a plate depicting Osborne's family home, Chicksands Priory, front free endpaper with engraved bookplate of Katherine Nora Sturdy, usual offsetting to free endpapers from turn-in glue, mild foxing to blanks at beginning and end, as well as to leaves opposite two of the plates, but fine, clean, fresh internally and in a bright, unworn binding.   Phillip J. Pirages   67 - 36   2016 $950

Association – Sturgis, Maria

Meredith, George   1828-1909   *Diana of the Crossways.*   New York: Scribner's, 1910. one hinge slightly tender, otherwise very good, 8vo., frontispiece, presentation by author's daughter, Marie Sturgis.   Second Life Books, Inc.   196 B - 206   2016 $75

Association – Sugarman, Tracy

Tarry, Ellen   *My Dog Rinty.*   New York: Viking Press, 1966. Eighth printing, illustrated by Alexander and Alexandra Allan from photos, small quarto, slight foxing, very near fine in spine faded very good dust jacket with very small nicks and tears, nicely inscribed by Tarry to Tracy Sugarman.   Between the Covers Rare Books   207 - 26   2016 $450

Association – Summers, A. Montague

Pope, Alexander   1688-1744   *Selecta Poemata Italorum qui Latine Scripserunt.*   London: impensis J. & P. Knapton, 1740. 2 volumes, 8vo., touch of foxing to titlepages, contemporary sprinkled calf, spines in six compartments with raised bands, numbered in gilt, rest with gilt decoration, much rubbed, joints and corners neatly repaired, spines bit darkened with endcaps worn down and labels lost, but sound, ownership inscriptions of Geoffrey Woledge, Birmingham 1937 and A. Montague Summers (1899).   Unsworths Antiquarian Booksellers Ltd.   E01 - Early Printing - 18   2016   £300

Association – Surtees, Robert

Paris, Matthew   1200-1259   *Flores Historiarum per Matthaeum Westmonasteriensem Collecti, Praecipue de rebus Britannicis ab Exordio Mundi Usque ad Annum Domini 1307.*   ex officina Thomae Marshii, 1570. Folio, titlepage trimmed close to woodcut border, final blank leaf discarded, index bound at front of text, one leaf with original paper flaw affecting few characters, first leaf of index with bottom margin folded over to preserve early manuscript note, verso of title also filled with text in early manuscript (trimmed at bottom), few short notes or marks later on, last dozen leaves showing a faint but substantial dampmark, some soiling/minor staining elsewhere, touch of worming to blank fore-edge margin, two leaves remargined, gathering Ttt in earlier (?) state without (and not calling for) additional unsigned singleton leaf, folio, 18th century mottled calf, spine with five raised bands, red morocco lettering pieces in second and third compartment, rubbed, front joint cracking (but strong) with little peeling to leather, light wear to endcaps, marbled endpapers, bookplates of Robert Surtees and his Mainsforth Library, sound.   Blackwell's Rare Books   B186 - 111   2016   £1100

Association – Sussex, Augustus Frederick, Duke of

Dionysius of Halicarnassus *Antiquitates Romanae.* Treviso: per Bernardinum Celerium du Luer, 24th Feb., 1480. Editio princeps, initial blank discarded. first leaf and last leaf little soiled, some light spotting and finger soiling elsewhere, one tiny wormhole in last few leaves, occasional marginal notes and manicules in early hand, sometimes shaved, old inscription, later vellum, early 19th century black lettering piece to spine, slightly soiled, touch of wear to spine ends, small old patch at head of front joint peeling, armorial bookplate of Augustus Frederick, Duke of Sussex, very good.   Blackwell's Rare Books   B184 - 34   2016   £7500

Association – Sutherland, Donald

Nathanason, E. M. *The Dirty Dozen.* Arthur Barker, 1966. First UK edition, 8vo, original cloth, dust jacket little rubbed with some internal residual tape marks, small stain to top edge of front endpaper, otherwise very good, signed by actor Donald Sutherland who played Vernon Pinkley in the Aldrich film.   Sotheran's   Piccadilly Notes - Summer 2015 - 214   2016   £98

Association – Sutherland, Peter

MacKenzie, William Leslie *The Medical Inspection of School Children...* Edinburgh & Glasgow: William Hodge & Co., 1904. First edition, Half title, folding plate, original maroon cloth, slightly rubbed, ownership inscription "Peter L. Sutherland Feb. 1908".   Jarndyce Antiquarian Books   CCXV - 836   2016   £38

Association – Sutherland, Victor

Shaw, George Bernard   1856-1950 *Man and Superman.* New York: Dodd, Mead, 1947. First edition, 8vo., very good in little worn dust jacket, some of the photos show little watermark at edge, written on endpaper is note this book is the property of "Maurice Evans Prod. Inc." and is to be returned, this copy signed by Malcolm Keen, Chester Stratton, Victor Sutherland, Carmen Mathews, Jack Manning, Phoebe Mackay and Tony Bickley.   Second Life Books, Inc.   196 B - 562   2016 $450

Association – Suzannet, Alain De

Dickens, Charles   1812-1870 *Edwin Drood. Complete (Part Second) by te Spirit-Pen of Charles Dickens, through a Medium).* Brattleboro: T. P. James, 1873. Original brown cloth, bevelled boards, lettered gilt, little rubbed, Suzannet, Starling & Self booklabels, good plus.   Jarndyce Antiquarian Booksellers   CCXVIII - 647   2016   £120

Dickens, Charles   1812-1870 *The Life and Adventures of Nicholas Nickleby.* London: Chapman & Hall, 1838-1839. First edition, illustrations by Phiz, original pale blue printed wrappers, one or two expertly executed minor repairs, very good in custom made slipcase and dark blue morocco box, gilt, exceptionally well preserved set, excellent library from the collection of Comte Alain de Suzannet, with his armorial bookplate.   Jarndyce Antiquarian Booksellers   CCXVIII - 221   2016   £5000

Association – Swinburne

Kendall, Edward Augustus *The Crested Wren.* London: printed for E. Newbery at the Cornr of St. Paul's Church Yard, 1799. 12mo., half title and final ad leaf, engraved frontispiece, titlepage vignette, lacking ads pages 155-156, B3 torn with slight loss to blank top corner, original dark green vellum spine, marbled boards, chipped paper spine label, corners little worn, A Swinburne family copy with signature.   Jarndyce Antiquarian Booksellers   CCXVI - 340   2016   £85

Association – Swinnerton, C. E.

Dickens, Charles   1812-1870 *Oliver Twist. (with) Great Expectations.* London: Chapman and Hall, 1871. 1876. Household edition, 4to., 2 volumes in 1, first work, frontispiece with small tear in outer margin, without loss, illustrations by J. Mahony, second work illustrations by F. A. Fraser, contemporary half dark green morocco, blue patterned cloth sides, spines little faded and slightly rubbed at head and tail, contemporary signature of C. E. Swinnerton.   Jarndyce Antiquarian Booksellers   CCXVIII - 189   2016   £120

Dickens, Charles   1812-1870 *Sketches by Boz. (with) Hard Times.* London: Chapman & Hall, 1876-1877. Household edition, vignette titles, illustrations by F. Barnard, 2 volumes in 1, contemporary half dark green morocco, blue patterned cloth sides, spine little faded and slightly rubbed and head and tail, contemporary signature of C. E. Swinnerton, good plus.   Jarndyce Antiquarian Booksellers   CCXVIII - 70   2016   £50

Association – Swope, Martha

Leatherman, Leroy *Martha Graham.* New York: Knopf, 1966. First edition, 4to., photos by Martha Swope, signed by Leatherman and Swope, inscribed by Swope to Helen Hayes, nice copy.   Second Life Books, Inc.   196 B - 37   2016 $250

Association – Sylvester, J. J.

Quetelet, Lambert Adolphe Jacques *Letters Addressed to H. R. H the Grand Duke of Saxe Coburg and Gotha on the Theory of Probabilities as Applied to the Moral and Political Sciences.* London: Charles & Edwin Layton, 1849. First edition in English, 8vo., tables, original blind-stamped brown cloth by Lewis (binder's ticket at rear), rebacked, new spine label, fine, inscribed by translator Olinthus Gregory Downes to J. J. Sylvester, Esq., bookplate of Percy Alexander MacMahon, bookplate of Francis Galton Laboratory, initials of Florence Nightingale David, 1845. Jeff Weber Rare Books 183 - 29 2016 $1000

Association – Symmons, John

Quarles, Francis *Divine Poems.* London: by Edward Okes for Benjamin Tooke and Thomas Sawbridge...., 1669. 8vo., engraved frontispiece/title, engraved title and final leaf repaired and strengthened at fore edge, later 20th century calf, from the library of James Stevens Cox (1910-1997), various pen trials, inscription "John Barnard/of Fallm(outh); in/Cornwall" and "To James Edgecom/John Symmons", presumably of Edgcumbe or Edgcombe. Maggs Bros. Ltd. 1447 - 345 2016 £180

Association – Symons, A. J. A.

Wilde, Oscar 1854-1900 *Ravenna. Recited in the Theatre, Oxford June 26 1878.* Oxford: Thos. Shrimpton 1878, i.e., 1904. First pirated edition, small octavo, original grey wrappers, pictorial bookplate of A. Squire, smaller printed label from Library of AJA Symons, Brick House, covers just little wrinkled, very good, preserved in custom made green morocco backed patterned board folder. Peter Ellis 112 - 449 2016 £575

Association – Tabori, Paul

Isherwood, Christopher *Lions and Shadows an Education the Twenties.* London: Hogarth Press, 1938. First edition, photographic frontispiece, foolscap 8vo, original blue cloth, first issue with backstrip blocked in black, partial browning to free endpapers, dust jacket with design by Robert Medley reproduced on front panel, backstrip panl darkened and trifle frayed at head and tail, few small ink spots to rear panel, good, bookplate of Paul Tabori. Blackwell's Rare Books B186 - 241 2016 £200

Association – Tailour

Taylor, Jeremy 1613-1667 *A Discourse Concerning Prayer ex Tempore or by Pretence of the Spirit.* N.P.: n.p. in the Yeere, 1646. First edition, small 4to., 15mm. dampstain to foot of titlepage (not touching text), larger dampstain along fore-edge of gatherings B-C and inner margin of E, modern quarter imitation sheep and marbled boards, early ink inscription and few marginal ink crosses, By Bp. Tailour, from the library of James Stevens Cox (1910-1997). Maggs Bros. Ltd. 1447 - 408 2016 £150

Association – Talbot, D'Arcy

Constable, John *The Conversation of Gentlmen Considered...* London: printed by J. Hoyles and sold by the booksellers of London and Westminster, 1738. 12mo., engraved frontispiece, late 18th century quarter calf, red morocco label, corners bumped & worn, some slight rubbing, otherwise nice, inscription "John H. Talbot M.P. from his brother D'Arcy Talbot June 28th 1834", armorial bookplate of John H. Talbot. Jarndyce Antiquarian Books CCXV - 128 2016 £285

Association – Talbot, John

Constable, John *The Conversation of Gentlemen Considered...* London: printed by J. Hoyles and sold by the booksellers of London and Westminster, 1738. 12mo., engraved frontispiece, late 18th century quarter calf, red morocco label, corners bumped & worn, some slight rubbing, otherwise nice, inscription "John H. Talbot M.P. from his brother D'Arcy Talbot June 28th 1834", armorial bookplate of John H. Talbot. Jarndyce Antiquarian Books CCXV - 128 2016 £285

Association – Talhurst, Beatrix

Dodgson, Charles Lutwidge 1832-1898 *The Hunting of the Snark. (and) An Easter Greeting to every Child Who Loves Alice.* London: Macmillan, 1876. First edition, one of 100 copies bound specially for Dodgson (100 in red and gold, 20 in blue and gold, 20 in white and gold), 8vo., bright red cloth with extensive gilt pictorial covers, 6 gilt rules on cover edges, all edges gilt, except for small pinhole in front gutter, near fine and bright, 9 incredibly detailed and fanciful full page illustrations by Henry Holliday, this copy inscribed by author for Beatrix Talhurst. Aleph-bet Books, Inc. 112 - 97 2016 $9500

Association – Tarr, Katherine

Mosley, Walter *Life Out of Context.* New York: Nation Books, 2006. First Printing, 8vo., author's presentation to Katherine Tarr, paper wrappers, near fine. Second Life Books, Inc. 196 B - 281 2016 $75

Association – Tathwell, Sophia

Scott, Walter 1771-1832 *Ivanhoe.* Edinburgh: Archibald Constable and Co., 1820. First edition, first issue, complete with half titles and publisher's ads, 3 volumes, octavo, original boards rebacked, some wear to boards, text extremely clean, faint signature and date (1820) of Sophia Tathwell, tiny faint library stamp on ad leaf of volume 1 and second half titles of volumes 2 and 3.   Manhattan Rare Book Company   2016 - 1756   2016 $5500

Association – Taunton, Roger

Turner, Thomas *The Case of the Bankers and their Creditors Stated and Examined.*   London: in the year, 1675. Third edition, 8vo., titlepage lightly soiled, many upper corners slightly creased, small closed tear at foot of F2 (not touching text), blue inkstain in margin of K7r with slight offset on opposite page, contemporary sheep rebacked, new endleaves but old rear flyleaves preserved, rather tightly bound with narrow inner margins, from the library of James Stevens Cox (1910-1997), two early ink inscriptions of Roger Taunton.   Maggs Bros. Ltd.   1447 - 419   2016   £240

Association – Taylor, Eleanor Ross

Lowell, Robert 1917-1977 *Notebook 1967-1968.*   New York: Farrar Straus Giroux, 1969. First edition, fine in about fine dust jacket with small crease on rear flap, from the library of author Peter Taylor and his wife, Eleanor Ross Taylor, inscribed by Lowell to same.   Between the Covers Rare Books   208 - 2   2016 $2750

Association – Taylor, Maggie

Tweedie, William King   *The Early Choice: a Book for Daughters.*   London: T. Nelson & sons, 1873. Frontispiece, additional engraved title, plates, 4 page ads, original green decorated cloth, bevelled boards, spines slightly dulled and rubbed, contemporary inscription "to Maggie Taylor, Dublin 1874.   Jarndyce Antiquarian Books   CCXV - 450   2016   £30

Association – Taylor, Peter

Lowell, Robert 1917-1977 *Notebook 1967-1968.*   New York: Farrar Straus Giroux, 1969. First edition, fine in about fine dust jacket with small crease on rear flap, from the library of author Peter Taylor and his wife, Eleanor Ross Taylor, inscribed by Lowell to same.   Between the Covers Rare Books   208 - 2   2016 $2750

Association – Taylor, Richard

Reece, Erik   *Field Work: Modern Poems from Eastern Forests.*   Lexington: The University Press of Kentucky, 2008. First edition, 8vo., fine in dust jacket, signed by contributors Eric Reece, James Baker Hall, Wendell Berry and Richard Taylor.   Second Life Books, Inc.   196 B - 461   2016 $45

Association – Taylor, Ronald George

Correlli, Marie   *Free Opinions Freely expressed on Certain Phases of Modern Social Life and Conduct.*   London: Archibald Constable, 1905. First edition, half title, final ad leaf, 16 page catalog, original dark blue cloth, blocked and lettered in gilt, spine slightly faded, modern bookplate of Ronald George Taylor, inscribed by author on leading f.e.p. "Mr. W. Reede 34 Marstell Place - Leicester".   Jarndyce Antiquarian Books   CCXV - 135   2016   £58

Dickens, Charles   1812-1870   *Dombey and Sons.* London: Bradbury & Evans, 1848. First edition, bound in 2 volumes, half title, frontispiece and vignette title volume I, plates by Phiz, 8 line errata leaf volume II, later half morocco by Dubois D'Enghlen, spines gilt in compartments, black leather labels, spines uniformly faded, booklabels of Ronald George Taylor, very good, handsome.   Jarndyce Antiquarian Booksellers   CCXVIII - 440   2016   £380

Dickens, Charles   1812-1870   *Master Humphrey's Clock.* London: Chapman & Hall, 1840-1841. First edition, frontispiece and illustrations by George Cattermole & Phiz, marbled endpapers, original purple brown vertically ribbed cloth, decorated in blind in gilt, spines slightly chipped at heads and tails, poor copy, booklabels of Ronald George Taylor. Jarndyce Antiquarian Booksellers   CCXVIII - 272   2016   £200

Smith, Walter E.   *Charles Dickens in the Original Cloth....* Los Angeles: Heritage Book Shop, 1982-1983. First edition, 2 volumes, 4to., half titles, illustrations, original green cloth, R. G. Taylor booklabels, very good in dust jackets. Jarndyce Antiquarian Booksellers   CCXVIII - 1516   2016   £80

Association – Taylor, Thomas, Mrs.

King, Martin Luther   *Where Do We Go From Here: Chaos or Community?*   New York: Harper & Row, 1967. First edition, fine in fine dust jacket, inscribed by author to Mrs. Thomas Taylor.   Between the Covers Rare Books   207 - 61   2016 $12,500

Association – Temple, Nigel

Horatius Flaccus, Quintus *(Opera).* Londini: Gulielmus Pickering, 1828. second titlepage dated 1824 and frontispiece dated 1828. Second edition from Pickering's Diamond Classics series, 48mo., 2 plates, engraved frontispiece and titlepage, plates very slightly toned but generally bright and clean within, contemporary tan calf, gilt title to spine, all edges gilt, little rubbed, few light scuffs to spine, very good gift inscription, plus name Nigel Temple pencilled in. Unsworths Antiquarian Booksellers   30 - 45   2016   £100

Repton, Humphry   1752-1818 *An Enquiry into the Changes of Taste in Landscape Gardening to Which are Added Some Observations on Its Theory and Practice....* London: J. Taylor, 1806. First edition, 8vo., original blue paper covered boards, original titled paper label to spine, half title, some wear to spine, internally very good, Dr. Nigel Temple copy with his booklabel.   Sotheran's Piccadilly Notes - Summer 2015 - 255   2016   £2500

Association – Terry, Reg

Fisher, Leona W. *Lemon, Dickens and Mr. Nightingale's Diary; a Victorian Farce.* Victoria: University of Virginia, 1988. Plates, original card wrappers, marked, presentation to Kathleen Tillotson by Reg. Terry in 1989 and heavily annotated.   Jarndyce Antiquarian Booksellers   CCXVIII - 1225   2016   £35

Association – Terry, Walter

Dreier, Katherine S. *Shawn: the Dancer.* New York: Barnes, 1933. First edition, 4to., silver coated cloth, numerous full page photos, inscribed by Shawn to critic Walter Terry, cover slightly soiled, but very good, tight, clean copy.   Second Life Books, Inc.   196A - 452   2016 $200

Association – Thellusson, Mrs.

Vincent, George *Dinners and Dinner Parties.* London: Chapman & Hall, 1862. First edition, half title, illustrations, original blue cloth decorated gilt, slightly dulled, presentation from author for Mrs. Thellusson, very good.   Jarndyce Antiquarian Books   CCXV - 455   2016 £480

Association – Theuart, Jean Francois

Plautus, Titus Maccius *Plautus Integer cum Interpretatione Joannisba Pristae.* Milan: Ulrich Scinzenzelet, 18 Jan., 1500. Folio, 60 lines of commentary plush headline, Roman and Greek letter, some printing in red (on Aa2), last leaf with register, 17th century Parisian binding of citron morocco, gilt panel on covers, spine elaborately gilt, marbled edges, few marginal wormholes in first 3 leaves, covers of binding with some abrasions (no loss of leather), some annotations slightly cropped by binder, finely bound copy, the copy of Jean Francois Theuart of Paris, 1674, to whom awarded as a prize, inscription "ex libris JF Theuart".   Maggs Bros. Ltd.   1474 - 61   2016   £9000

Association – Theyre-Smith, S.

Dickens, Charles   1812-1870 *The Uncommercial Traveller.* London: Chapman & Hall, 1861. Third edition, half title, original mauve wavy grained cloth, blocked in blind, spines faded, very good, signature of dramatist S. Theyre-Smith.   Jarndyce Antiquarian Booksellers   CCXVIII - 599   2016   £250

Association – Thom, Ed

Vergilius Maro, Publius *Les Bucoliques.* Paris: Philippe Gonin, 1951. One of 200 copies, 327 x 248mm., loose as issued in publisher's cream colored wrappers and vellum backed portfolio, black titling on spine, in later patterned paper slipcase with 80 wood engravings by Lucile Passavant, first prelim leaf warmly inscribed to Ed and Mary (Thom?), inscribed by the artist for the Thoms, greeting card illustrated by artist inscribed for Thoms laid in, hint of soil to spine, corners worn to boards, faint freckling to covers, text with isolated trivial foxing, excellent copy, text clean and fresh and binding a good deal more than good enough.   Phillip J. Pirages   67 - 348   2016 $3000

Association – Thom, Mary

Vergilius Maro, Publius *Les Bucoliques.* Paris: Philippe Gonin, 1951. One of 200 copies, 327 x 248mm., loose as issued in publisher's cream colored wrappers and vellum backed portfolio, black titling on spine, in later patterned paper slipcase with 80 wood engravings by Lucile Passavant, first prelim leaf warmly inscribed to Ed and Mary (Thom?), inscribed by the artist for the Thoms, greeting card illustrated by artist inscribed for Thoms laid in, hint of soil to spine, corners worn to boards, faint freckling to covers, text with isolated trivial foxing, excellent copy, text clean and fresh and binding a good deal more than good enough.   Phillip J. Pirages   67 - 348   2016 $3000

Association – Thomas, Bertram

Storrs, Ronald *Orientations.* London: Ivor Nicholson & Watson, 1937. First edition, signed presentation inscribed by author to Bertram Thomas, 8vo., original dark blue cloth, blocked gilt, pictorial dust jacket, map endpapers, frontispiece, 13 plates, two text illustrations, foldout map and one map in text, initial blank.   Sotheran's   Travel and Exploration - 380   2016   £498

Association – Thomas, Isaiah

Massachusetts Historical Society *Collections of the Massachusetts Historical Society Volume II of the Second Series.* Boston: printed by John Eliot, 1814. First edition, signed with gift inscription to the American Antiquarian Society by Isaiah Thomas, 8vo., original blue gray paper covered boards with paper label on spine, spine and label well worn, ends and joints chipped, institutional stamp on title, gift inscription on free front endpaper, leaves untrimmed, about good.   Kaaterskill Books   21 - 50   2016 $500

Association – Thomas, Leo G. Watlyn

Russell, John Fuller *The Ancient Knight or Chapters on Chivalry.* London: W. J. Cleaver, 1849. Frontispiece, 14 page catalog, original scarlet cloth by Bone & Son, largely faded to brown, little rubbed, spine chipped at head, contemporary signature of Leo. G. Watlyn Thomas.   Jarndyce Antiquarian Books   CCXV - 392   2016   £40

Association – Thomas, Norman

Stevens, James *Big Jim Turner.* Garden City: Doubleday and Co., 1948. First edition, foxing on endpapers and tiny spots on boards, else near fine in very good dust jacket with some tiny splash marks on spine, inscribed by author for Norman Thomas.   Between the Covers Rare Books   208 - 83   2016 $225

Association – Thompson, Cecil

Ovidius Naso, Publius *Opera.* Leiden: ex officina Elzeviriana, 1629. First edition thus, 3 volumes, 16mo., engraved titlepage to volume I, 'Kalendarium' in red and black, occasional foxing mostly to endpapers, 35mm. closed tear to page 393, volume III, volume I has top fore-edge corner of r.f.e.p. excised, contemporary vellum, titles inked to spines, yapp edges, edges speckled blue, little yellowed, some smudgy marks, top edges darkened, still very good, armorial bookplate of Cecil Thompson to each front pastedown.   Unsworths Antiquarian Booksellers Ltd.   E01 - Early Printing - 15   2016   £500

Association – Thompson, Dorothy

Henry, John M. *Nine Above the Law: Our Supreme Court.* Pittsburgh: R. T. Lewis Co., 1936. First edition, small quarto, red brown cloth gilt, some rubbing to extremities, very good or better, inscribed by author, to Sinclair Lewis, also with bookplate of Lewis's wife, activist/author Dorothy Thompson.   Between the Covers Rare Books   208 - 37   2016 $300

Association – Thompson, Henry Yates

Coryate, Thomas *Coryats Crudities, Hastily gobbled up in five Moneths....* London: printed by VV(illiam) S(tansby for the author), 1611. First edition, 4to., full Regency diced tan calf by Charles Hering (engraved label, firm active in London 1794-1844), spine with raised bands, ornamented and lettered gilt, ornamented in blind as well, boards with filigree gilt stamped fleurons in corners, dotted gilt ruling, gothic ornamentation in blind, edges and inner dentelles ornamented in gilt, marbled endpapers, red edges, engraved title, engraved full page portrait and one heraldic engraving, 4 engraved plates, woodcut ornaments in text, rebacked retaining original spine, gathering 2N with tiny traces of worming in upper margins, very light even browning or minimal spotting, folding plate of Strasbourg clock little cropped as usual, title little cropped at upper margin, very good, elaborate binding, bookplate of Henry Yates Thompson (1838-1928).   Sotheran's   Travel and Exploration - 230   2016   £17,000

Association – Thompson, Herbert

Sophocles *(Greek) Tragaediae Septem cum Commentariis etc.* Venice: Aldus Manutius, August, 1502. Editio princeps, 8vo., 196 leaves, 19th century vellum over pasteboard, gilt spine, early title lettered ink on lower edge, Aldus device on verso of final leaf, Greek type, Latin marginalia to Ajax and notes on front blank c. 1800 (slightly cropped), bookplate of Sir Charles James Stuart, 2nd Baronet, Herbert Thompson name inscribed on front flyleaf.   Maggs Bros. Ltd.   1474 - 74   2016   £20,000

Association – Thompson, Kate

Hurston, Zora Neale *Jonah's Gourd Vine.* Philadelphia: Lippincott, 1934. Scarce first edition, octavo, original dust jacket, presentation inscription from author to Kate Thompson.   Honey & Wax Booksellers   4 - 54   2016 $5200

Association – Thompson-Yates, Samuel Ashton

Cory, Alexander Turner *The Hieroglyphics of Horapollo Nilous.* London: William Pickering, 1840. 193 x 118mm., very attractive contemporary olive green morocco elaborately gilt by Hering (stamp signed), covers with delicate gilt frame of drawer handle, floral sprig and star tools, raised bands, spine gilt in compartments with similar tooling, densely gilt turn-ins, pale yellow endpapers, all edges gilt, frontispiece, numerous representations of hieroglyphics and 3 plates, pencilled presentation from author to the illustrator of the work, Joseph Bonomi, engraved bookplate of Samuel Ashton Thompson-Yates, just slightest hint of rubbing to joints (well marked with dye), faint graze on rear cover, spine probably sunned (though abundance of gilt making this difficult to determine), significant foxing to prelim leaves, frontispiece and titlepage (moderate foxing to plates II and III and adjacent text leaves), but text otherwise clean and fresh, decorative binding lustrous scarcely worn and altogether pleasing. Phillip J. Pirages 67 - 49 2016 $1500

Tennyson, Alfred Tennyson, 1st Baron 1609-1692 *Poems by Two Brothers.* London: printed by J. and J. Jackson, Louth for Simpkin and Marshall, 1827. First edition, 163 x 102mm., lovely late 19th century crimson morocco, elegantly gilt, covers with plain and decorative gilt rules and fleuron cornerpieces, raised bands, spine gilt in double ruled compartments with urn of flowers at center surrounded by small tools, leaf garlands at corners, gilt titling, richly gilt turn-ins, top edge gilt, bookplate of S. A. Thompson Yates, the collection then passed to Allan Heywood Bright, faint discoloration in bottom margin of about 25 leaves, isolated insignificant soiling, otherwise very pretty book in fine condition, text fresh and bright and especially beautiful binding, lustrous and unworn. Phillip J. Pirages 67 - 325 2016 $3250

Alciati, Andrea *Emblemata Latinogallica. Les Emblems Ltin-Francois... la Version Francoise non Encorveu cy Devant.* Paris: Jean Richet, 1584. First edition thus, woodcut device on titlepage and last leaf, portrait on verso of title and 211 woodcut emblems, 12mo., contemporary vellum, remains of later ties, titlepage with contemporary inscription of Bibliotheque Deprins, bookplate of Samuel Ashton Thompson Yates. Maggs Bros. Ltd. 1474 - 5 2016 £3000

Aneau, Barthelemy *Imagination Poetique Tradicte en Vers Francois des Latins & Grece....* Lyons: Mace Bonhomme, after 8 September, 1552. Extremely rare first edition, titlepage with Bonhomme's Perseus device and 105 cuts attributed to Pierre Eskrich (from metal plates), small 8vo., limp ivory vellum by Leighton, upper cover with gilt lettered title and date within elaborate frame, flat gilt spine, bookplate of S. A. Thompson Yates 1894. Maggs Bros. Ltd. 1474 - 6 2016 £12,000

Bible. Italian - 1588 *Figure del Nuovo testamento, Illustrate da Versi Vulgari Italiani.* Lyon: Guillaume Rouille, 1588. Fine illustrated Italian verse adaptation of the New Testament, Rouille's eagle and serpent device on titlepage, and 160 woodcuts, mostly by Pierre Eskrich, fine typographic ornament on verso of otherwise blank final leaf, 8vo., grained brown morocco by Duru dated 1859, title lettered in gilt on spine, inner edges richly gilt, Samuel Ashton Thompson Yates emblematic bookplate dated 1894. Maggs Bros. Ltd. 1474 - 14 2016 £1500

Hoffer, Johann *Icones Catecheseos, et Virtutum ac Uitiorum Illusrtatae Numeris...* Wittenberg: Johannes Crato, 1558. Small 8vo., fine device on titlepage and larger version on recto of final leaf, 77 half page woodcuts by Jakob Lucius?, late 19th century brown morocco by Riviere & Son, covers panelled in blind, spine lettered gilt, gilt edges, bookplate of Samuel Ashton Thompson-Yates, 1894. Maggs Bros. Ltd. 1474 - 41 2016 £2500

Pictorius, Georg *Apotheseos tam Exterarum Gentium Quam Romanorum Deorum Libri Tres.* Basle: Nicolaus Brylinger, 1558. First illustrated edition, printer's device on titlepage, 25 woodcuts, woodcut initials, small 8vo., late 19th century half brown morocco by Roger De Coverly, spine lettered gilt, gilt edges, bookplate of Samuel Ashton Thompson Yates dated 1894. Maggs Bros. Ltd. 1474 - 59 2016 £2500

Tijera, Jose De La *Copia de Carta en que un Amig refiere a otro con Exactind el Hecho...* Barcelona: Sastres et al, 1801. First edition, folding engraved plate, plate refolded with repair to 2 original folds visible on recto and small area lost to rump of bull inflicting the injury to Hillo's knee, small repairs to last 4 pages with minimal loss to printed border and loss of 2 letters on 1 page, 8vo., modern Spanish half calf, bookplate of S. A. Thompson Yates, good. Blackwell's Rare Books B184 - 18 2016 £850

Association – Thomson, Edward

Pardon, George Frederick *The Faces in the Fire; a Story for the Seasons.* London: Willoughby & Co., 1849? First edition, frontispiece, engraved title and 2 plates, woodcut vignettes, slight staining to pages 128/9, handsome crimson straight grained morocco, gilt spine, borders and dentelles, bookplate of Edward Thomson, all edges gilt, very good. Jarndyce Antiquarian Booksellers CCXVIII - 408 2016 £150

Association – Thomson, Hugh

Swedenborg, Emanuel *A Treatise Concerning Heaven and Hell and of the Wonderful Things Therein as Heard and Seen.* Chester: printed by C. W. Leadbeater, 1800. Fourth edition, printed on poor quality greyish paper, slightly browned with occasional light spotting, slight damage to titlepage in 3 places with loss from one character of author's name, 8vo., later half calf, marbled boards (rubbed), neatly rebacked preserving old black lettering piece, red edges, old ownership inscription of Hugh Thomson of Bunbury, Cheshire, sound.   Blackwell's Rare Books   B186 - 146   2016   £250

Shakespeare, William   1564-1616   *As You Like It.* London: Hodder & Stoughton, n.d., 1909. Limited to 500 numbered copies signed by Thomson, this copy 0000 for presentation, presentation inscription from artist to J. E. Hodder Williams, director at Hodder & Stoughton, this is accompanied by lovely watercolor on half title, printed on fine paper, illustrated with 40 beautiful tipped in color plates by Hugh Thomson, with lettered tissue guards, large thick 4to., full vellum, gilt pictorial cover, original silk ties, few minor marks on cover and endpaper, boxed as usual, else fine.   Aleph-bet Books, Inc.   112 - 475   2016 $5000

Association – Thorburn, William

MacEwen, William   *Pyogenic Infective Diseases of the Brain and Spinal Cord.* Glasgow: Maclehose, 1893. 60 illustrations, original green cloth, light wear, internally fresh, clean and uncut, penned "With Mess. Maclehose Compliments, and "William Thorburn Reviewer for Medical Chronicle", this appears to have been sent by publisher for review.   James Tait Goodrich   X-78 - 384   2016 $1295

Association – Thornhill, Mary

Trimmer, Sarah   *Some Account of the Life and Writings of Mrs. Trimmer...* London: printed for F. C. and J. Rivington, 1816. Second edition, 2 volumes, half titles, final ad leaf, volume II, contemporary full calf, double ruled gilt borders, raised bands, gilt compartments, neat repairs to hinges, inscription Mary Thornhill the gift of Mrs. Bathurst 1816. Jarndyce Antiquarian Books CCXV - 968   2016   £225

Association – Thorp, J.

Bible. Greek - 1835   *Vetus Testamentum Graece.* Lipsiae: sumptibus et typis Caroli Tauchnitii, 1835. Editio stereotypa, 8vo., sporadic light foxing, contemporary vellum, gilt spine with two dark green morocco labels, marbled endpapers, all edges red, vellum little darkened, some smudgy marks but still very good, ownership inscriptions, first of J. Thorp, Jan. 1860 and second of William Horbury dated iv, xlii, Thorps's signature again in pencil to titlepage. Unsworths Antiquarian Booksellers   30 - 17   2016   £60

Association – Thorp, Thomas

Horatius Flaccus, Quintus   *(Opera).* Gulielmus Pickering, 1826. Large paper copy, engraved titlepage (slightly browned), bound without engraved frontispiece dated 1828 and the letterpress titlepage dated 1824, 8vo., original rose cloth, printed paper label to spine, sunned and little bit marked, spine ends chipped, cloth cracked at front joint, pencilled purchase note of Thomas Thorp, dated 13th oct. 1928, earlier bookplate of William Ellis Wall, good. Blackwell's Rare Books   B186 - 78   2016   £120

Association – Throckmorton, Lilian

Shaw, George Bernard   1856-1950   *Saint Joan.* London: Constable, 1924. First edition, inscribed by author for Lilian Throckmorton, with original silverprint of Shaw and recipient posing in a garden, with Throckmorton's bookplate, fine. Second Life Books, Inc.   196 B - 561   2016 $750

Association – Thurlow, Violet

Blunt, Wilfrid Scawen   1840-1922   *Esther, Love Lyrics and Natalia's Resurrection.* London: Kegan, Paul, Trench, Trubner & Co. ltd., 1892. First edition, original green cloth lettered and decorated in gilt, cloth little rubbed at edges and endpapers, somewhat browned, otherwise nice, presentation copy inscribed by author for Violet Thurlow.   Bertram Rota Ltd.   February List 2016 - 8   2016   £175

Association – Thurlsand Castle

Taylor, Isaac   *Self Cultivation Recommended on Hints to a Youth leaving School.* London: Rest Fenner, 1818. Third edition, 12mo., half title, frontispiece, 8 pages ads, contemporary quarter dark blue calf, marbled paper boards, armorial bookplate of North, Thurlsand Castle, very good. Jarndyce Antiquarian Books   CCXV - 431   2016   £60

Association – Thwaite, Anthony

Larkin, Philip   1922-1985   *The Less Deceived: Poems.* Hessle: Marvell Press, 1955. First edition, This is an early copy (one of 120) of the first impression with flat spine and the misprint on page 38 (which is here corrected in pencil), little foxing, very nice in dust jacket which has touch of wear at head and foot of spine panel, signed by author in pencil on front free endpaper with few pencil markings and annotations by Anthony Thwaite, loosely inserted are 3 carbon typescript poems by Larkin.   Bertram Rota Ltd.   Christmas List 2015 - 20   2016   £2000

McEwan, Ian   *First Love Last Rites.* London: Jonathan Cape, 1975. First edition, endpapers little spotted, very nice in dust jacket with has just little trivial wear at head of spine panel, Anthony Thwaite's ownership signature and inscription from author Nov. 1990.   Bertram Rota Ltd. February List 2016 - 37   2016   £1000

Association – Tillotson, Geoffrey

Dickens, Charles 1812-1870 *The Christmas Books.* London: Chapman & Hall, circa, 1868. Half title, frontispiece and 7 plates, plain dark turquoise endpapers, original brown cloth lettered in black and gilt, spine slightly marked, otherwise very good, from the library of Kathleen & Geoffrey Tillotson, numerous notes loosely inserted in unusual variant binding.   Jarndyce Antiquarian Booksellers   CCXVIII - 400   2016   £30

Tibullus, Albius *A Poetical Translation of Elegies of Tibullus.* London: printed for A. Millar, 1759. 2 volumes in one, some foxing to endpapers and first and final pages, otherwise clean copy, late 19th century dark brown cloth, gilt lettered spine, inscribed ex-libris Lud. Du Rieu 1784, ownership inscription of Geoffrey Tillotson.   Jarndyce Antiquarian Booksellers   CCXVI - 567   2016   £75

Association – Tillotson, Kathleen

Bentley's Miscellany Volumes I-IX. London: Richard Bentley, 1837-1841. Frontispieces, plates, contemporary half calf, spines gilt in compartment, black leather labels, marbled boards, hinges and corners little rubbed, signature of Kathleen Tillotson.   Jarndyce Antiquarian Booksellers   CCXVIII - 764   2016   £850

Bentley's Miscellany. Volumes I-IX. London: Richard Bentley, 1837-1841. Volumes I-IX, frontispiece and plates, contemporary half calf, spines gilt in compartments, , black leather labels, marbled boards, hinges and corners little rubbed, signature of Kathleen Tillotson.   Jarndyce Antiquarian Booksellers   CCXVIII - 764   2016   £850

Butler, Arthur Gray *The Three Friends: a Story of Rugby in the Forties.* London: Henry Frowde, 1900. Original maroon cloth, spine little faded, top edge gilt, signed by A. F. Buxton and Kathleen Tillotson, with ALS from Tillotson to Dorothy M. Ward.   Jarndyce Antiquarian Books   CCXV - 927   2016   £35

Caswall, Edward *Sketches of Young Ladies...* London: Chapman & Hall, 1837. Fifth edition, frontispiece and plates by Phiz, original green printed boards, spine strip missing, little dulled and rubbed, good, sound copy, Kathleen Tillotson's copy.   Jarndyce Antiquarian Booksellers   CCXVIII - 172   2016   £85

Dickens, Charles 1812-1870 *American Notes for General Circulation.* London: Chapman & Hall, 1842. First edition, first issue, 2 volumes, half titles, ad leaf preceding half title volume I, original purple cloth, blocked in blind, spines lettered gilt, expertly recased, spines faded to brown, Kathleen Tillotson's copy.   Jarndyce Antiquarian Booksellers   CCXVIII - 317   2016   £850

Dickens, Charles 1812-1870 *The Christmas Books.* London: Chapman & Hall, circa, 1868. Half title, frontispiece and 7 plates, plain dark turquoise endpapers, original brown cloth lettered in black and gilt, spine slightly marked, otherwise very good, from the library of Kathleen & Geoffrey Tillotson, numerous notes loosely inserted in unusual variant binding.   Jarndyce Antiquarian Booksellers   CCXVIII - 400   2016   £30

Dickens, Charles 1812-1870 *The Letters of Charles Dickens. Volumes I-VI.* Oxford: Clarendon Press, 1965-1988. Pilgrim edition, volumes I-VI, original pink cloth (volume 1) and red cloth, dulled and marked, volume I with spine strip torn away, volumes III and IV slightly loose, Kathleen Tillotson's copies.   Jarndyce Antiquarian Booksellers   CCXVIII - 840   2016   £380

Fisher, Leona W. *Lemon, Dickens and Mr. Nightingale's Diary; a Victorian Farce.* Victoria: University of Virginia, 1988. Plates, original card wrappers, marked, presentation to Kathleen Tillotson by Reg. Terry in 1989 and heavily annotated.   Jarndyce Antiquarian Booksellers   CCXVIII - 1225   2016   £35

Harbage, Alfred B. *A Kind of Power, the Shakespeare Dickens Analogy.* Philadelphia: American Philosophical Society, 1975. First edition, Half title, original blue cloth, lettered gilt, very good in dust, presentation to Kathleen Tillotson.   Jarndyce Antiquarian Booksellers   CCXVIII - 1278   2016   £20

Kaplan, Fred *Dickens and Mesmerism: the Hidden Springs of Fiction.* Princeton: Princeton University Press, First edition, half title, plates, original brown cloth, very good in dust jacket, Kathleen Tillotson's copy with notes relating to this work.   Jarndyce Antiquarian Booksellers   CCXVIII - 1325   2016   £45

Lohrli, Anne *Household Words: a Weekly Journal 1850-1859.* Toronto: University of Toronto Press, 1973. Half title, original maroon cloth, slightly marked, Kathllen Tillotson's copy, with occasional pencil annotations in text.   Jarndyce Antiquarian Booksellers   CCXVIII - 780   2016   £50

Sanders, Andrew *The Companion of a Tale of Two Cities.* London: Unwin Hyman, 1988. First edition, half title, illustrations, original green cloth, very good in slightly dusted dust jacket, Kathleen Tillotson's copy with some of her notes loosely inserted.   Jarndyce Antiquarian Booksellers   CCXVIII - 571   2016   £30

Tolkien, John Ronald Reuel 1892-1973 *Songs for the Philologists.* London: privately printed in the Department of English at University College, London, 1936. Wire stitched, without rusting, original blue printed wrappers, inscription on red ink on front wrapper, please return to K. Tillotson, very good.   Jarndyce Antiquarian Booksellers   CCXVII - 284   2016   £12,500

Association – Tilson, John Quillin

Finch, James A. *Federal Anti-Trust Decisions. Cases Decided in the United States Courts Arising Under, Involving or Growing Out of the Enforcement of the Anti-Trust Act of July 2 1890....* Washington: GPO, 1912. First edition, 4 volumes, inscribed by John Qullin Tilson (1866-1958), Conn. Congressman, with stamp of V. N. Roadstrum, attorney for J.P. Morgan Estate, very good or better, edges lightly soiled, otherwise very tight and clean, handsome set, original maroon buckram.   Simon Finch   2015 - 27510   2016 $300

Association – Tindal, C. J.

Horatius Flaccus, Quintus *Opera cum Scholiis Veteribus Castigavit....* Glasgow: in Aedibus Academicis Excudebat Jacobus Mundell, 1796. 8vo., some light foxing, Jesuit library stamp of Milltown Park to titlepage, ownership inscription of C. J. Tindal, Trinity College, 1838 to initial blank, 8vo., contemporary straight grained red morocco, boards bordered with single gilt fillet, spine divided by single gilt fillet, gilt crest in top compartment, title lettered direct in second and pale and date at foot, spine bit darkened, few tiny marks here and there, marbled endpapers, all edges gilt, with thin roll of gauffering near front and back hinge, cracking little at titlepage and headband partly loose, label removed from front pastedown, good.   Blackwell's Rare Books   Greek & Latin Classics VII - 47   2016   £500

Association – Tipping, Mrs.

Eckley, Sophia May *Minor Chords.* London: Bell and Daldy, 1869. Presentation inscribed by author for Mrs Tipping, original green cloth with black ruling and design to covers and gilt author and title to spine, some bumping and chipping, otherwise very good, spotting to endpaper and occasional spotting in text, very good.   The Kelmscott Bookshop   12 - 41   2016 $150

Association – Tobias, Henry

Adams, Joey *The Borscht Belt.* New York: Bobbs Merrill, 1966. First printing, 8vo., illustrations, presentation by Henry Tobias, nice in dust jacket little yellowed and chipped.   Second Life Books, Inc.   196A - 9   2016 $50

Association – Todd, Mike

Roos, William *January Thaw.* Chicago: Dramatic Pub., 1946. 8vo., 2 photo, one stage diagram, author's presentation on half title to producer Mike Todd, cover slightly worn at corners and spine, else very good.   Second Life Books, Inc.   196 B - 495   2016 $45

Association – Todd, Richard

Wilde, Oscar 1854-1900 *An Ideal Husband.* London: Leonard Smithers & Co., 1899. First edition, one of 1000 copies, lovely, near fine with trivial soiling on boards, spine touch faded and gift inscription bookplates on front endpapers, long gift inscription from Richard Todd, excellent copy.   Heritage Book Shop   Holiday 2015 - 114   2016 $2250

Association – Todd, William

Carter, John 1905-1975 *Working Papers for a Second Edition of an enquiry into the nature of Certain Nineteenth Century Pamphlets.* Oxford: privately printed, 1967. 1969. 1970. First editions of all parts, limited to 140, 200 and 400 copies respectively, volumes, 2, 3 and 4 (of 4), small 8vo., stiff paper wrappers, this set once belonged to Wise bibliographer William Todd, corner of cover loosely inserted photocopy of a review of this title written by Todd and has pencil notes, loosely inserted photocopy of this title, Todd pencil notes throughout.   Oak Knoll Books   310 - 221   2016 $495

Association – Tomerlin

California Sorcery. Abingdon: Cemetery Dance, 1999. Publisher's copy of the limited edition (26 copies), signed by Ray Bradbury, Richard Matheson, Ellison, Nolan, Tomerlin, Sohl, Fritch and others, stamp of another author, fine in fine dust jacket in publisher's printed gray case.   Ken Lopez Bookseller   166 - 5   2016 $650

Association – Tomlinson, H. M.

Coleridge, Samuel Taylor 1772-1834 *Letters, Conversations and Recollections.* London: Edward Moxon, 1836. First edition, 2 volumes, contemporary black half calf, spines gilt, lacking half titles, binding badly rubbed at extremities and text somewhat browned at margins throughout, very good, each volume with H. M. Tomlinson's ownership signature.   Bertram Rota Ltd.   February List 2016 - 11   2016   £100

Association – Tomlinson, Kenelm

Simons, Mathew *A Direction for the English Traveller.* London: are to be sold by Thomas Jenner at the South Entrance of the Exchange, 1643. Fourth edition, small 4to., engraved leaves, paginated in manuscript by near contemporary hand, few pen trials to titlepage, occasional spotting and soiling, contemporary blind ruled sheep (front cover with early repair, covers with scrapes, piece torn from rear cover, edges chipped, joints cracked), with 8 page manuscript of Dance Steps by choreographer, Kenelm Tomlinson, with Tomlinson signature, from the library of James Stevens Cox (1910-1997).   Maggs Bros. Ltd.   1447 - 387   2016   £6000

Association – Toomer, Jean

Brunini, John Gilland *Whereon to Stand.* New York: Harper and Bros., 1946. Later printing, light sunning at crown, else fine in spine faded, very good plus with wrinkled on front panel, inscribed by author to author Jean Toomer.   Between the Covers Rare Books   207 - 91   2016 $400

Association – Towneley

Marchionni, Domenico *Discorsi Morali Intorno alla Venuta del Messia Alla Verginita di Maria anche dopo il Parto....* Ferrara: per Alonso, e Gio. Battista Maresti, 1664. Small emblematic device on titlepage, title in red and black, woodcut device on page 219, woodcut initials, small 4to., contemporary Italian red morocco gilt over paste board, cover's elaborately decorated with four outer narrow decorative rolls enclosing central panel of large circular fan ornament with four corner fan sections, flat spine richly decorated, gilt edges, some rubbing to extremities, lacks silk ties, Towneley Library near Burnley, Lancashire copy, 19th century pencil note inside cover, sold in Towneley Hall library auction.   Maggs Bros. Ltd.   1474 - 51   2016   £2800

Association – Townsend, J. Barton

The Death Fetch, or the Student of Gottingen Founded on a Popular Opinion, Prevalent Even at the Present Time.... London: printed for T. Hughes, 35 Ludgate Street, n.d., 1826. First edition, 12mo. inserted folded frontispiece with color frontispiece, original three quarter brown levant morocco, tooled and titled in gold by Morrell of London, armorial bookplate of J. Barton Townsend, later bookplate of William Hartmann Woodin.   John W. Knott, Jr./L.W. Currey, Inc.   Fall-Winter 2015 - 17501   2016 $2500

Association – Townsend, John

Woolman, John   1720-1772 *The Works of John Woolman.* Philadelphia: Joseph Crukshank, 1774. Contemporary sheep, very skillfully rebacked in period Quaker style, boards scuffed, edges worn, discoloration on pages 146-47 from old laid in newspaper cutting, else very good, inscribed 'Sarah Woolman to Jno. Townsend", later miniscule signature of Charles L. Cresson, superb presentation, John Townsend was author's close friend.   Joseph J. Felcone, Inc.   Books from Five Centuries: a Miscellany - 154   2016 $1200

Association – Trafton, A. G.

Bronte, The Sisters *Poems by Currer, Ellis and Acton Bell.* Philadelphia: Lea and Blanchard, 1848. First American edition, original brown paper covered boards, printed paper spine label, outer brown paper worn from along hinges and at tips of spine revealing lighter paper underneath, scattered foxing, else very nice, very tight in fragile original boards, 1848 ownership signature of A. G. Trafton.   Joseph J. Felcone, Inc.   Books from Five Centuries: a Miscellany - 29   2016 $2800

Association – Trautner, Hans Joachim

De Tournes, Jean De *Insignium Aliquot Virorum Icones.* Lyons: Jean de Tournes, 1559. First and only edition, 8vo., later vellum with red leather label on spine, some soiling, De Tournes' Viper device on title and 145 woodcut portrait medallions, bookplate of R. E. Cartier, Alfred Cartier's nephew and heir, armorial bookplate of Bibliotheca Trautner-Falkiana, i. e. the Augsburg bibliophile Hans Joachim Trautner (1916-2001), little spotted in places.   Maggs Bros. Ltd.   1474 - 29   2016   £1800

Association – Trevor, Norman

Varesi, Gilda *Enter Madame: a Play in three acts.* New York: Putnam, 1921. First edition, 8vo., cloth backed boards, very good, inscribed by author under frontispiece and signed by 10 members of the cast including Norman Trevor, Jane Meredith, Gavin Muir, etc.   Second Life Books, Inc.   196 B - i794   2016 $250

Association – Trilling, Lionel

Joyce, James   1882-1941 *Stephen Hero.* New Directions, 1944. First American edition, the copy of Lionel Trilling.   Honey & Wax Booksellers   4 - 39   2016 $600

Association – Trimmington, W.

Jones, Joseph *Historical Sketch of the Art and Literary Institutions of Wolverhampton...* London: Alexander & Shepherd, 1897. Half title, frontispiece, plates, original blue cloth, slightly rubbed and dulled, signature of W. Trimmington, nice.   Jarndyce Antiquarian Books   CCXV - 799   2016   £40

Association – Trissel, Jim

Kroll, Ernest *Marianne Moore at the Dial Commissions - an article on the Movies.* Colorado Springs: Press at Colorado College, n.d., Limited to 100 numbered copies, 8vo., quarter faux leather, marbled paper covered boards, paper spine label, printed accordian style, with two page ALS from the printer, Jim Trissel, to editor, Kroll.   Oak Knoll Books   310 - 141   2016 $400

Association – Trowbridge, Robertson

Shelley, Mary Wollestonecraft Godwin   1797-1851 *History of a Six Weeks' Tour Through a Part of France, Switzerland, Germany and Holland.* London: published by T. Hookham Jun., 1817. First edition, little light soiling, 8vo., early 20th century olive morocco by Tout, boards with gilt frame and spine, elaborately gilt top edge gilt, others untrimmed, joints rather rubbed, little wear to headcap, bookplates of H. Bradley Martin and of Robertson Trowbridge (this inscribed to Mark Trowbridge's gift of the volume to Thomas Pym Cope) and of Thomas Jefferson McKee, very good.   Blackwell's Rare Books   Marks of Genius - 43   2016   £3500

Association – Trubner, Nicholas

Catlin, George   1796-1872 *O'Kee-Pa: a Religious Ceremony: and Other Customs of the Mandans.* London: Trubner and Co., 1867. First edition, with rare 'Folium Servatum' bound in at rear', presentation copy inscribed by Nicholas Trubner to Thomas Scott, 13 chromolithographed plates, publisher's purple cloth, gilt, all edges gilt, binding lightly soiled and faded, extremities lightly worn, spine ends more so, occasional minor foxing, very good, fragile book difficult to find in fine condition.   Joseph J. Felcone, Inc. Books from Five Centuries: a Miscellany - 36   2016 $20,000

Association – Truscott, G. F.

Philp, Robert Kemp *Enquire within Upon Everything.* London: Houlston & Stoneman, 1856. First edition, 2 lines ms. notes on page 352, original blue green cloth, blocked in blind and gilt, spine faded and slightly rubbed at head and tail, contemporary inscription of G. F. Truscott, booksellers embossed stamp, nice.   Jarndyce Antiquarian Books CCXV - 361   2016 £250

Association – Tucker, G. W.

Dresser, Christopher *Principles of Decorative Design.* London: Cassell, Petter, Galpin and Co., circa, 1887. Fourth edition, half title, color frontispiece and plate, illustrations, 8 page catalog (July 1887), original brown cloth, decorated in black and gilt, some slight wear to head and tail of spine, otherwise very good, signature of G. W. Tucker.   Jarndyce Antiquarian Booksellers   CCXVII - 90   2016   £280

Association – Tucker, J. Jones

Pritchard, Andrew *History of Infusoria Living and Fossil...* London: Whittaker, 1841. First edition, subscriber's copy with ownership signature on title, of J. Jones Tucker, R. N., Dublin, tipped in notice of author, errata, 1 figure, 12 plates, heavy staining between pages 126-178, original brown embossed cloth, rebacked preserving original spine, very good but for internal staining.   Jeff Weber Rare Books   183 - 26   2016 $175

Association – Tully, William

Berkeley, George *Alciphron or the Minute Philosopher in Seven Dialogues.* New Haven: Increase Cooke & Co., 1803. First American edition from fourth London edition, 213 x 130mm, without leaf of ads at end, original American binding of sheepskin, flat spine divided into panels by gilt rules, original red morocco label, front free endpaper and titlepage with ink ownership inscription of "William Tully.... Yale College 1805", front joint cracked with just slight give to board, leather at corner worn through, covers with handful of short scratches and bit of minor soiling, faint offsetting throughout text, excellent example of early America sheep binding, completely unsophisticated, text fresh and clean, generally very much finer state of preservation than is typical.   Phillip J. Pirages   67 - 24   2016 $1500

Association – Turny, Daniel

Mair, John *An Introduction to Latin Syntax...* Philadelphia: printed for Campbell Conrad & Co. by J. Bioren, 1799. First American edition, lightly toned and spotted, ownership inscription of Daniel Turny to titlepage and Jacob Mechlin to second leaf, contemporary marbled sheep, rubbed, worn at extremities, red morocco lettering piece partly worn away, sound.   Blackwell's Rare Books   B186 - 102   2016   £200

Association – Turton, William

Brookes, Richard *An Introduction to Physic and Surgery.* printed for J. Newbery, 1754. 8vo., contemporary speckled calf, double gilt fillets on sides, dark red lettering piece, joints cracked, headcaps defective, corners slightly worn, engraved armorial bookplate of William Turton (overlaying earlier one), sound, small burn hole in Kk2 affecting few words, occasional browning spotting or staining, still good.   Blackwell's Rare Books   B186 - 27   2016   £500

Association – Tyler, E. W.

Peck, Bradford *The World a Department Store.* Lewiston: Bradford Peck, 1900. First edition, 8vo., lacks half of folding frontispiece, inscribed with compliments of author for E. W. Tyler.   Second Life Books, Inc.   196 B - 782   2016 $175

Association – Tyler, Winifred

Blatch, Harriot Stanton *Challenging Years.* New York: Putnams, 1940. First edition, 8vo., very nice in dust jacket, inscribed by author's daughter, Nora Stanton Barney to Winifred A. Tyler.   Second Life Books, Inc.   196A - 157   2016 $150

Association – Tyrrell, T. N.

Dickens, Charles 1812-1870 *Some Letters of Charles Dickens.* Pittsburgh: privately printed, 1907. No. 9 of 200 copies, Untrimmed in original green wrappers, spine slightly faded, very good, signed presentation to T. N. Tyrrell.   Jarndyce Antiquarian Booksellers   CCXVIII - 865   2016   £20

Association – Tyrwhitt, Thomas

Kirchner, Athanasius 1602-1680 *Ars Magna Lucis et Umbrae: in decem Libros Digesta.* Rome: Sumptibus Hermanni Scheus, 1645. 2 volumes bound in one, engraved frontispiece and 38 plates, 2 double sided tables, engraved frontispiece has been expertly backed, fore edge of pages 513/4 slightly shaved affecting headline, lower margin of pages 563/4 also slightly shaved just affecting catchword, full modern brown morocco, covers panelled in blind, spine with four raised bands ruled in blind and lettered in gilt, all edges sprinkled red, excellent and very fresh copy, rebound about 20 years ago, little tightly but this only affects ease of opening large double page folding plate, ownership inscription of Thomas Tyrwhitt at top of frontispiece.   David Brass Rare Books, Inc.   2015 - 02989   2016 $14,500

Association – Underwood, F. Alan

Kipling, Rudyard 1865-1936 *The Years Between.* London: Methuen, 1919. First edition, half title, 32 page Methuen catalog at end coded IK/2/19, uncut in original maroon cloth, spine lettered gilt, top edge gilt, original dust jacket, tear to back wrapper repaired without loss, bookplate of John H. Mills, Derby, small ownership stamp of F. Alan Underwood.   Jarndyce Antiquarian Booksellers   CCXVII - 156   2016   £150

Association – Utterson, Edward Vernon

The Historie of Frier Rush: How He Came to a House of Religion to Seeke Service...   London: Harding and Wright for Robert Triphook, 1810. One of 4 copies on vellum, contemporary red velvet by H. Faulkner (ticket on verso front flyleaf), covers with wide Greek key border rolled in blind, flat spine with small remnant of leather backstrip (that has been laid on to hide a binder's titling error), red moire silk endleaves, turn-ins and pastedowns with rolls in blind, all edges gilt, housed in very good later leather edged slipcase, woodcut vignette on title, verso to front flyleaf with bookplate of Edward Vernon Utterson and morocco bookplate of Hans Furstenberg, bookplate of John Kershaw, contemporary inked note listing original owner of each of the four vellum copies of the present book, later pencilled note on same "Ths copy was after-wards in the possession of Mr. George Smith and it was (sold in his (s)ale for £9.15.0", spine mostly covered with (glue?) residue left by now basically missing leather backstrip, corners rubbed to board, portions of the joints torn, velvet nap somewhat diminished, a bit of natural rumpling to the vellum, very few inoffensive spots to margins, entirely solid (apart from spine remnants) an agreeable copy of this curious book.   Phillip J. Pirages   67 - 341   2016 $4500

Association – Valery, Paul

Vergilius Maro, Publius *Les Bucoliques De Virgile.* Paris: Scripta & Picta, 1953. First Villon edition, one of 245 copies (total edition), folio, text pages loosely inserted in publisher's paper folder, chemise and slipcase, 45 original lithographs by Jacques Villon, hors- and in texte, printed on Arches wove paper by F. Mourlot, outer slipcase faded and worn along edges, book very fine, bookplate of Margaret Winkelman, Paul Valery's copy.   Oak Knoll Books   310 - 7   2016 $4500

Association – Van Alphen, G.

Horatius Flaccus, Quimtus *Cum Commentariis & Enarrationibus Commentatoris Veteris, et Iacobi Cruquii Messenii...* Antwerp: Ex officina Plantiana Raphelengii, 1611. Final Plantin edition, 4to., paper toned, some spotting, gift inscription dated 1643 (to Ludovicus Chimaer from G. van Alphen) and ownership inscription dated 1669, contemporary vellum, board fore-edges overlapping, spine lettered in ink, soiled and bit nicked, hinges cracking but sound, rear flyleaf removed, armorial bookplate of Rich. Palmer, Esq.   Blackwell's Rare Books   Greek & Latin Classics VII - 41   2016   £500

Association – Van Heel, A. C. S.

Caille, L'Abbe De La *Lecons Elementaires d'Optique.* Paris: H. L. Guerin & L. F. Delatour, 1756. Second edition, Title vignette, decorative head and tailpieces, 12 folding engraved copperplates, disbound, yet in early marbled wrappers, spine exposed, some signatures loosening, bookplate signed TM of ACS Van Heel, handsome modern blue cloth, drop back box, good, the copy of Abraham Cornelis Sebastian Bram.   Jeff Weber Rare Books   183 - 10   2016 $400

Association – Van Heyden De Lancey, Cornelius

Beatson, Alexander *Tracts Relative to the Island of St. Helena....* London: W. Bulmer and Co. for G. and W. Nicol and J. Booth, 1816. First and only edition, 4to. original boards with printed label on spine, aquatint frontispiece, 5 aquatint plates by Daniell after Davis and one engraved plan of the island by Girtin, most plates by tissue guard, some spotting to plates, as usual and occasionally to text, else very good in very good original binding slightly worn, 20th century bookplate of Cornelius Van Heyden De Lancey inside front cover.   Sotheran's   Travel and Exploration - 5   2016   £1795

Association – Van Vliet, Claire

Nyholm, Janet *From a Housewife's Diary...* West Burke: Janus Press, 1978. First edition, no. 213 of 250 copies with Claire Van Vilet's presentation on colophon, large 8vo., illustrations hand colored with pencils, two flyers for Janus Press laid in, almost as new, bound in full cloth (red and white disthtowel) with paper spine label, printed on Mohawk Superfine by Van Vliet, illustrated with eraser stamps by Jerome Kaplan which were "colored 31 times eventually 37, by Victoria Fraser & anyone else she could con".   Second Life Books, Inc.   196 B - 330   2016 $175

Association – Vanderlip, Frank

Bentham, Jeremy   1748-1832 *The Book of Fallacies from Unfinished Papers of Jeremy Bentham.* John and H. L. Hunt, 1824. First edition, contemporary black morocco, gilt foliate borders to sides, gilt lettering and tools to spine, all edges gilt, bookplate of Frank Vanderlip, American banker, another previous owner's signature on titlepage.   Sotheran's   Piccadilly Notes - Summer 2015 - 44   2016   £550

Association – Vandermin, Doctor

Hardy, Florence *The Early Life of Thomas Hady 1840-1891. (and) The Later Years of Thomas Hardy 1892-1928.* London: Macmillan, 1928-1933. First editions, 2 volumes, frontispiece portraits, plates, 8vo., original mid green cloth, lettering on backstrips and hardy medallion on front covers, all gilt blocked, faint endpaper foxing, small newspaper clipping pasted to rear free endpaper, top edge gilt, dust jackets chipped with short tears, very good, Doctor Vandermin's copy, with presentation to same from Florence Hardy.   Blackwell's Rare Books   B186 - 233   2016   £550

Association – Verplanck, Guilian Crommelin

Sandys, William *Christmastide: In History, Festivities and Carols.* London: John Russell Smith, 1852. First edition, 8vo., original blindstamped blue cloth, minor corner wear, spine elaborately gilt, 8 lithographed plates, including frontispiece, 17 in text vignettes, with 1856 ownership signature of G(ulian) C(rommelin) Verplanck (1786-1870), excellent copy.   Howard S. Mott Inc.   265 - 34a   2016 $350

Association – Vershbow, Arthur

Capaccio, Giulio Cesare *Delle Imprese Trattato in tre Libri Diviso.* Naples: Horatio Salviani for Giovanni Giacomo Carlino and Antonio Pace, 1592. First edition, 3 parts in one volume, 4to., clasped hands printer's device on each titlepage, 303 mostly oval woodcut emblems, cuts on book, 3 have decorative corner pieces filling out the block some groups of shields and circular cuts, woodcut initials, head and tailpieces, contemporary vellum over thin pasteboard, title lettered in ink at head of spine, remains of vellum ties and paper shelflabel at foot of spine, label of Arthur and Charlotte Vershbow.   Maggs Bros. Ltd.   1474 - 20   2016   £3500

Association – Vershbow, Charlotte

Capaccio, Giulio Cesare *Delle Imprese Trattato in tre Libri Diviso.* Naples: Horatio Salviani for Giovanni Giacomo Carlino and Antonio Pace, 1592. First edition, 3 parts in one volume, 4to., clasped hands printer's device on each titlepage, 303 mostly oval woodcut emblems, cuts on book, 3 have decorative corner pieces filling out the block some groups of shields and circular cuts, woodcut initials, head and tailpieces, contemporary vellum over thin pasteboard, title lettered in ink at head of spine, remains of vellum ties and paper shelflabel at foot of spine, label of Arthur and Charlotte Vershbow. Maggs Bros. Ltd. 1474 - 20 2016 £3500

Association – Vertue, John

Bonaventura, Saint 1221-1274 *Die Legend des Heyligen Vatters Francisci.* Nuremberg: Hieronymus Holtzel for the heirs of Caspar Rosentalet, April, 1512. First German edition, 4to., titlepage with large woodcut, full page woodcuts, smaller woodcuts, 57 woodcuts in all, all in fine contemporary color, predominantly yellows, greens and browns, 4to., 16th century pigskin over wooden boards, panelled and decorated in blind, remains of clasps (rubbed), rare, from the Virtue and Cahill Library (John Vertue formerly Virtue [1826-1900] and John Baptist Cahill [1841-1910]), overprinted bookplate noting war bomb damage to library in 1941, much used copy with some defects, repaired tear to foot of F3 and V1, no loss, I1, M1 &T4 lower outer corner torn away with loss of some text to lower portion of leaves, N1 woodcut with small hole expertly repaired, some old tears repaired, general staining and soiling throughout. Maggs Bros. Ltd. 1474 - 16 2016 £12,500

Association – Vickery, Patti

Nixon, Richard Milhous *Six Crises.* New York: Doubleday, 1962. First edition, large 8vo., very good, tight in little worn but unclipped dust jacket, inscribed by author for Patti Vickery. Second Life Books, Inc. 196 B - 322 2016 $600

Association – Vickery, Willis

Mason, Stuart *Bibliography of Oscar Wilde.* London: T. Werner Laurie, 1914. First edition, edition deluxe, number 29 of 100 copies numbered and signed, frontispieces, bookplate of Willis Vickery, near fine in beige cloth boards with gilt titles to spines and front boards, few spots of foxing to top edges of boards, good - but rare - brown dust jackets with black titles to spines and front panels, heavy chipping rubbing, browning and wear to jackets, they are protected from further wear with archival plastic cover,. The Kelmscott Bookshop 13 - 37 2016 $975

Association – Villiers, Charles

Babbage, Charles 1792-1871 *Observations on the Temple of Serapis at Pozzuoli Near Naples.* privately printed, 1847. First edition, 8vo., 2 lithographed plates, 6 figures, original blind and gilt stamped red cloth with gilt motif of temple on upper cover, gilt spine title, spine ends worn, some soiling, small paper label on upper cover, neat bookplate of Stirling Public Library (The Thomson Collection, Glasgow), very good, inscribed by author for Hon. Charles Villiers, M.P. Jeff Weber Rare Books 183 - 4 2016 $3750

Association – Vincent, Howard

Mason, Ronald *The Spirit above the Dust: a Study of Herman Melville.* New York: Paul Appel, 1972. Second edition, 8vo., inscribed by author and Howard Vincent (provided introduction), fine, without dust jacket. Second Life Books, Inc. 196 B - 201 2016 $45

Association – Virgin, Thore

Silius, Italicus *De Secundo Bello Punico.* Amsterdam: G. Jansson, 1620. Engraved titlepage, ruled in red, 16mo., exquisite binding by Mace Ruette, contemporary gilt tooled red morocco, covers framed by outer double fillet, central panel of strait and curved double fillets with small vase of flowers tool at each outer corner in centre of covers a quadrilobe inlay with monogram of H. L. Habert de Montmort and four "S" forms with elaborate pointille sprays of spirals, circles and dots on all four sides, spine with five raised bands, decorated in compartments, inner edges gilt, marbled endpapers, gilt edges, headcaps and joints lightly rubbed, the copy of Habert de Montmort (1600-1679), Colonel Thomas Stanley (1749-1818), William Beckford with his bookseller George Clarke's pencil collation mark, Hamilton Palace Library sale, Thore Virgin inscription dated 1916 with his book label (1886-1957). Maggs Bros. Ltd. 1474 - 72 2016 £2500

Association – Visme, G. De

Herodotus *Historia.* Glasgow: in aedibus Academicis excudebant Robertus et Andreas Foulis, 1761. First Foulis edition, issue on less fine paper but with all blanks present and correct, 8vo., contemporary calf, spines gilt, red and green morocco lettering pieces (about half of them renewed with consummate skill), joints and extremities worn, some leather cracking but all boards firmly held, front endpapers volume 1 renewed, bookplate of G. de Visme in all volumes, except the first, good. Blackwell's Rare Books B186 - 71 2016 £1500

Association – Vitale, Lydia Modi

Nash, Graham *The Graham Nash Collection.* Los Angeles: Nash Press, 1978. First edition, one of 100 numbered copies specially bound and signed by Nash, oblong 4to., illustrations, leather backed cloth over boards, marbled front pastedown, original illustrated front wrapper, bound in publisher's matching slipcase, very fine, scarce, presentation from author to Lydia Modi Vitale, laid is is carbon copy signed of single page TL from Nash to an administrator at the University, also laid in is 1 page TLS to Vitale from visitor to the exhibition.   James S. Jaffe Rare Books Occasional List: Winter 2016 - 115   2016 $1000

Association – Vivian, Arthur Pendarves

Ferguson, Samuel *The Cromlech on Howth. A Poem...* London: Day & Son, 1861. First edition, very rare, folio, original Celtic green cloth, spine lettered and ornamented gilt, front cover ornamented in gilt, rear cover in blind, all edges gilt, title printed in red and black, additional chromolithographic titlepage, black and white illustrations, 15 chromolithographic plates, ornamental borders, 7 superb mounted chromolithographic landscape plates retaining tissue guards, two minor spots to lower cover, apart from foxing to initial blank, title and to lesser degree to text and plates as usual, very good, Day & Son's contemporary bindery label, slightly later armorial bookplate of Arthur Pendarves Vivian. Sotheran's   Travel and Exploration - 244   2016   £998

Association – Volkmann, Daniel

Ferry, Hypolite *Description de la Nouvelle Californie Geographique, Politique et Moralecontenant l'Histoire de la Decouverte de Cette Contree...* Paris: 1850. Second edition, octavo, large frontispiece folding map, 3 engraved maps, 4 engraved plates, with half title, contemporary quarter red morocco over pebble boards, spine stamped and lettered gilt, edges speckled blue, board edges rubbed, outer hinges cracked but holding, spine with crack across upper top portion, mostly light foxing throughout, two leaves with minor closed tears with no loss of text, large folding map with some minor closed tears and foxing, previous owner Daniel Volkmann Jr. bookplate, other small bookplate as well, overall nice, housed in custom cloth clamshell. Heritage Book Shop   Holiday 2015 - 39   2016 $2500

Association – Von Mueller, F.

Wittstein, G. C. *The Organic Constitutents of Plants and Vegetable Substances their Chemical Analysis...* Melbourne: M'Carron, Bird and Co., 1878. Octavo, quarter leather and boards, publisher's title wrapper retained, some wear, inscribed by translator, Ferd. von Mueller.   Andrew Isles Natural History Books   55 - 38890   2016 $80

Association – Waddinge, John

Vives, Juan Luis *Linguae Latine Exercitatio.* London: Typis Alice Warren cum Societate Stationiarum, 1660. 12mo., title within type ornament border, small rust hole to lower corner of A4 (touching text) and with rust mark to lower margin of A8 and C2, lower fore-corner of A5 missing from paper flaw, no loss of text and upper blank corner of D7 torn away, contemporary sheep, covers ruled in blind, remnants of paper spine label, lower joint damaged by worming at head, single worm hole in upper joint, pastedowns unstuck, ink inscription "John Waddinge his book", from the library of James Stevens Cox (1910-1997). Maggs Bros. Ltd.   1447 - 429   2016   £420

Association – Wade, S. M.

Poole, George Ayliffe *An Historical and Descriptive Guide to York Cathedral and its Antiquities with a History and Description of the Munster Organ.* York: published by R. Sunter, 1850. 4to., 41 lithographic plates of which 3 are double page and 3 are colored, bit toned, particularly to titlepage, sporadic foxing, later quarter tan calf, brown morocco label with gilt title to spine, marbled paper covered boards, edges uncut, spine faded, little shelf wear, endpapers slightly grubby but overall very good, sound, ownership inscription of S. M. Wade.   Unsworths Antiquarian Booksellers Ltd.   E04 - 14   2016   £175

Association – Wade, Susan

Bonney, T. G. *Cathedrals, Abbeys and Churches of England and Wales.* London: Cassell & Co., 1891. 2 volumes, 4to., 18 plates as called for, numerous further illustrations in text, some plates little foxed, few neatly pencilled annotations, slightly later cloth, half bound in two shades of green, red morocco gilt title labels to spines, edge sprinkled red, few scratches, joints little rubbed but still very good, recent bookplate of Susan Wade, news clipping pasted to f.f.e.p. and volume I and few other relevant clippings, loosely inserted.   Unsworths Antiquarian Booksellers Ltd.   E04 - 5   2016   £100

Britton, John *Cathedral Antiquities. Historical and Descriptive Accounts (...) of the Following English Cathedrals.* London: M. A. Nattali, 1836. 5 volumes, 4to., each volume contains two or three parts, collates complete, all plates as called for, each volume with a series title, volume title and section title, some woodcuts in text, occasional spot or smudge but overall very clean and bright within, later 19th century half green morocco, gilt spine, marbled boards and endpapers, all edges gilt, boards little rubbed, some scuffed to joints, still very good, handsome set, recent bookplate of Susan Wade to each front pastedown.   Unsworths Antiquarian Booksellers   30 - 25   2016   £750

Scott, Walter 1771-1832 *Border Antiquities of England and Scotland...* London: printed for Longman, Hurst, Rees, Orme and Brown, J. Murray...., 1814. 1817. First edition, large paper copy, 2 volumes, folio, 94 engraved plates, including 2 engraved titlepages, Morpeth Castle plate loose, volume I engraved title almost loose, pages civ-cv little discolored apparently by insertion of a leaf between them, occasional light foxing with volume I engraved titlepage bit more affected, contemporary half deep red straight grain morocco, green marbled paper covered boards, edges uncut, endcaps, joints and board edges worn, boards much rubbed, edges little toned but still good copy overall, front pastedown of each volume is ownership inscription of H. C. Rigg, Crossrigg Hall and recent bookplate of Susan Wade. Unsworths Antiquarian Booksellers Ltd. 30 - 135 2016 £200

Woolnoth, William *A Graphical Illustration of the Metropolitan Cathedral Church of Canterbury.* London: T. Cadell & W. Davies and J. Murray, 1816. Large paper copy, royal 4to., 20 plates on India paper, foxing to front and rear blanks and plates, text pages generally clean barring occasional offset toning from plates, neat pencil notes to pages 92-3, early 20th century half burgundy morocco gilt title to spine, blue marbled paper boards, edges sprinkled red, endcaps, joints and corners bit worn, edges slightly chipped but very good overall, bookplate of A. D. Gondinton dated 1901, recent bookplate of Susan Wade, tiny bookbinder's label of R. Hynes, Dover, catalog description pasted in, some pencilled booksellers notes to prelim blanks, note to list of subscribers identifies this as the copy belonging to Mr. Jesse White, Canterbury. Unsworths Antiquarian Booksellers Ltd. 30 - 165 2016 £350

Association – Wade, William

Rea, John *Flora: seu de Florum Cultura.* London: by T. N. for George Marriott, 1676. Second edition, folio, engraved title, 8 plates, lightly browned, upper margins dusty, worming close to inner margin towards top edge, extends throughout getting worse in middle and then fanning out into a trial in text, hole in Y1 (affecting two lines), closed tear on two of the plate leaves about 3cm. long, contemporary calf, covers panelled in blind, rebacked, lower corners repaired, upper corners worn, new endleaves, old flyleaves preserved, from the library of James Stevens Cox (1910-1997), engraved label inserted between pages 52 and 53 'Laura A(nne) Calmady' of Langdon Court, ms. note on label dated 23 Oct. 1889 and states the book was bought from Wm. Wade at sale of Langdon books by Vincent Pollexfen Calmady. Maggs Bros. Ltd. 1447 - 361 2016 £500

Association – Wagstaff, Mary

Walker, Thomas Harris *Good Servants, Good Wives and Happy Homes.* London: S. W. Partridge, 1862. First edition, frontispiece, vignette title, plates and illustrations, 32 page catalog, leaves slightly browned, original red cloth, decorated in gilt, dulled and slightly rubbed, signature of Mary Wagstaff June 12th/64, nice. Jarndyce Antiquarian Books CCXV - 460 2016 £75

Association – Wagstaff, William

Arnold, Thomas *Miscellaneous Works.* London: B. Fellowes, 1845. Half title, unopened in original dark green blue cloth, blocked in blind, spine lettered gilt, booklabel with signature of William Wagstaff, attractive copy, near fine. Jarndyce Antiquarian Books CCXV - 311 2016 £60

Association – Wainwright, Alexander

Parish, Morris L. *Charles Kingsley and Thomas Hughes. First editions (with a Few Exceptions) the library of Dormy House, Pine Valley, New Jersey.* London: 1936. One of 150 numbered copies, 4to., plate, facsimiles, addenda/errata, cloth, pristine, lovely dust jacket with just few tiny chips at spine ends, the personal copy of Alexander Wainwright (curator of Parrish collection of Victorian novelists at Princeton), lovely copy. Joseph J. Felcone, Inc. Books from Five Centuries: a Miscellany - 114 2016 $600

Association – Waldman, Max

Mostel, Zero *Zero by Mostel.* New York: Horizon, 1965. First edition, 4to., presentation by Max Waldman, many photos of Mostel in pantomime and section on his role as Tevye in Fiddler, drawings by Mosel and interview, very good in chipped and soiled dust jacket. Second Life Books, Inc. 196 B - 284 2016 $60

Association – Walford, Cornelius

Roberts, George *The History of Lyme Regis, Dorset...* Sherborne: Printed for the author by Langdon and Harker, and for Baldwin, Cradock and Joy and S. Bagster, London, 1823. First edition, 8vo., 2 hand colored folding lithograph plates by C. Hullmandel after Thomas Mann Baynes, later black morocco backed boards, armorial bookplate of Cornelius Walford. Marlborough Rare Books List 55 - 60 2016 £375

Association – Walker, G.

Willm, Joseph *The Education of the People...* Glasgow: William Lang, 1847. First British edition, errata slip, contemporary half calf by David Bryce, Glasgow, gilt spine, slightly rubbed, morocco label, slightly rubbed and marked, but nice, contemporary signature of G. Walker. Jarndyce Antiquarian Books CCXV - 1008 2016 £48

Association – Walker, Scott

Carver, Raymond *Fires: Essays Poems Stories.* New York: Vintage, 1984. First Vintage edition, 12mo., author's presentation to publisher, Scott Walker, paper wrappers, cover little soiled, else very good, tight, inscribed by author. Second Life Books, Inc. 196A - 257 2016 $250

Dubie, Norman *Popham of the New Song: and Other Poems.... Volume one Number Two of "Twelve Poems" a poetry quarterly.* Port Townsend: Graywolf Press, 1975. First edition, large 8vo., paper wrappers, author's presentation and number on colophon, cover very slightly creased at lower corner, otherwise fine, this is number 27 (sic) of 26 numbered copies inscribed from author to publisher Scott Walker. Second Life Books, Inc. 196A - 457 2016 $400

Haines, John *New Poems: 1980-88.* Brownsville: Story Line Press, 1990. First edition, 8vo., author's presentation to publisher of Graywolf Press, Scott (Walker), paper wrappers, cover scuffed, but very tight. Second Life Books, Inc. 196A - 699 2016 $150

Haines, John *Where the Twilight Never Ends. Poems.* Boise: Limberlost Press, 1994. One of 400 copies, 12mo., author's presentation to Scott Walker, publisher of Graywolf Press, paper wrappers, nice. Second Life Books, Inc. 196A - 701 2016 $125

Hampl, Patricia *Resort: a Poem by...* St. Paul: Bookslinger Editions, 1982. One of 50 copies numbered and signed by author, 8vo., frontispiece and ornamental rose by Gaylord Shanilec, author's presentation and signature on half title, also signed by artist, paper wrappers, cover very slightly scuffed at top of spine, faintly dog eared, otherwise nice, inscribed by author for Scott Walker, signed by artist in pencil "Hi Scott Gaylord". Second Life Books, Inc. 196A - 715 2016 $250

Lawhead, Terry *Nothing Lives Long.* Port Townsend: Graywolf Press, No. 1 of 50 copies, numbered and signed by author, 8vo., paper wrappers, sewn at spine, inscribed to publisher and dedicatee, Scott (Walker), cover slightly faded, otherwise nice. Second Life Books, Inc. 196 B - 25 2016 $50

Association – Wall, William Ellis

Horatius Flaccus, Quintus *(Opera).* Gulielmus Pickering, 1826. Large paper copy, engraved titlepage (slightly browned), bound without engraved frontispiece dated 1828 and the letterpress titlepage dated 1824, 8vo., original rose cloth, printed paper label to spine, sunned and little bit marked, spine ends chipped, cloth cracked at front joint, pencilled purchase note of Thomas Thorp, dated 13th oct. 1928, earlier bookplate of William Ellis Wall, good. Blackwell's Rare Books B186 - 78 2016 £120

Association – Wallace, Walter Thomas

The Library of Fiction, or Family Story-Teller... London: Chapman & Hall, 1836-1837. First edition, first issue, 2 volumes, half title volume 1 only, plates by Robert Seymour, Buss, etc, original dark blue diaper cloth, boards blocked in blind, spines lettered gilt within triple border frame, small repairs to spines & hinges, bookplates of Walter Thomas Wallace. Jarndyce Antiquarian Booksellers CCXVIII - 51 2016 £1600

Association – Waller, Pickford

Davidson, John *The Last Ballad & Other Poems.* London: John Lane, 1899. First edition in rare variant binding, copies usually found in black cloth, this copy bound in red cloth with gilt title, author and Art Nuveau influenced flowers and birds to front cover, very good with some light scraping to cloth along bottom of front cover, interior pages are clean and tight, bookplate of artist Pickford Waller, very good. The Kelmscott Bookshop 12 - 30 2016 $100

Maeterlinck, Maurice *The Treasure of the Humble.* London: George Allen, 1897. octavo, Pickford Waller's copy with his bookplate, designed by him, book specially bound by him in full cream parchment on which he has painted red tulips, together with leaves, three on upper cover and one on lower, book's title and author's name written in his hand on both upper cover and spine, laid in is what appears to be part of a dust jacket, prelims spotted, covers in excellent state, bright and clean. Peter Ellis 112 - 431 2016 £150

Association – Walley, David

Tibullus, Albius *Quae Exstant.* Amsterdam: Ex Officina Weisteniana, 1708. 4to., engraved titlepage, 9 further plates, titlepages in red and black with engraved device, occasional illustrations within text, little staining to edges of margins near front, occasional very light spotting, paper flaw to edge of page 133 not affecting text, contemporary brown speckled calf, recent calf reback with retained red morocco gilt spine label, edges sprinkled red, inner hinges reinforced, few scuffs and marks, corners fraying, still very good, small label with name David Walley and small bookplate with elaborate lettler C and crown motif to front pastedown, based on Scaliger's text with notes and some changes by Van Broekhuyzen.   Unsworths Antiquarian Booksellers Ltd.   E01 - Early Printing - 27   2016   £300

Association – Wallis, B.

Ellis, Havelock *The New Spirit.* London: George Bell and Sons, 1890. First edition, very good in original red cloth boards with gilt title to spine, few spots of soiling to boards, minor wear to edges, light browning to spine and few spots of foxing to interior, still nice, signature of previous owner B. Wallis, very good.   The Kelmscott Bookshop   12 - 43   2016 $375

Association – Walpole, Horatio

Winstanley, William *Historical Rarities and Curious Observations Domestick & Foreign.* London: printed for Rowland Reynolds, 1684. 8vo., frontispiece, some browning and spotting, 8vo., 18th century calf, double gilt fillets on sides, spine gilt ruled in compartments, cracks in joints and spine slightly rubbed, engraved armorial bookplate of Horatio Walpole (first Baron), good.   Blackwell's Rare Books   B184 - 91   2016   £600

Association – Walsh, F.

Grosse, E. M. *Series of Seventeen Colour Lithographed Plates from the 1913 Expedition to the Coral Reefs of the Torres Straits of Department of Marine Biology of the Carnegie Inst. of Washington.* Sydney: Government Printer, 1914. Quarto, 17 plates (numbered to 19), typescript insert inscribed to J. Lane Mullins by F. Walsh.   Andrew Isles Natural History Books 55 - 38216   2016 $650

Association – Walton, Margaret

Woolf, Virginia 1882-1941 *The Common Reader: Second Series.* London: Pub. by Leonard & Virginia Woolf at Hogarth Press, 1932. First edition, page edges slightly soiled, still about fine in about very good dust jacket with some modest chips and tears, some overall soiling, small Hogarth Press pamphlet advertising Woolf's works laid in, inscribed by author to her typist Margaret Walton, Oct. 13th 1932, inscription has very slightly offset very slightly on front flap.   Between the Covers Rare Books   204 - 137   2016 $25,000

Association – Wapler, William

Dickens, Charles 1812-1870 *American Notes for General Circulation.* London: Chapman and Hall, 1842. First edition, first issue, 2 volumes, half titles, ad leaf preceding half title volume I, glazed yellow endpapers, original purple cloth blocked in blind, spines lettered in gilt, some minimal dampstaining to prelims, armorial bookplate of H. C. Embleton volume II, later William Wapler bookplate in both volumes, very good in slipcase.   Jarndyce Antiquarian Booksellers   CCXVIII - 316   2016   £1600

Association – Ward, Dorothy

Butler, Arthur Gray *The Three Friends: a Story of Rugby in the Forties.* London: Henry Frowde, 1900. Original maroon cloth, spine little faded, top edge gilt, signed by A. F. Buxton and Kathleen Tillotson, with ALS from Tillotson to Dorothy M. Ward.   Jarndyce Antiquarian Books   CCXV - 927   2016   £35

Association – Ward, G. A.

Paine, Thomas 1737-1809 *The Rights of Man; Being an Answer to Mr. Burke's Attack on the French revolution...* Boston: printed by I. Thomas and E. T. Andrews, 1791. First Boston edition, self wrappers, stitched as issued, untrimmed, some light foxing, wear and scattered stains, overall very good in original state, contemporary ink notation "Essex Hist. Soc./fr. G. A. Ward".   The Brick Row Book Shop   Miscellany 69 - 61   2016 $1250

Association – Ward, Harry

McNeer, May *The Golden Flash.* New York: Viking, 1947. First edition, signed by author and artist, presented to owner by Harry Ward (Lynd Ward's father), cloth, slight soil, near fine in dust jacket with edge chipping and archvial mends on verso, color lithos by Lynd Ward.   Aleph-bet Books, Inc.   112 - 510   2016 $200

Association – Ward, John

Overton, Thomas Collins *Original Designs of Temples and Other Ornamental Buildings for Parks and Gardens, in the Greek, Roman and Gothic Taste.* London: printed for the author and sold by Henry Webley, 1766. First edition, royal 8vo., contemporary full speckled calf, gilt spine, red morocco and gilt label, little worn at head and foot of spine, 50 engraved plates printed on thick paper, early bookplate of John Ward, recent bookplate of John Harris, particularly fine copy.   Sotheran's   Piccadilly Notes - Summer 2015 - 227   2016   £2400

Association – Ward, Lynd

McNeer, May *The Golden Flash.* New York: Viking, 1947. First edition, signed by author and artist, presented to owner by Harry Ward (Lynd Ward's father), cloth, slight soil, near fine in dust jacket with edge chipping and archival mends on verso, color lithos by Lynd Ward.   Aleph-bet Books, Inc.   112 - 510   2016 $200

Association – Wardington, Lord

Dibdin, Thomas Frognall 1776-1847 *An Introduction to the Knowledge of Rare and Valuable Editions of the Greek and Latin Classics.* London: printed for Harding & Lepard, 1827. Fourth edition, 2 volumes, 292 x 1977, handsome early 20th century brown straight grain morocco, covers with gilt double fillet border, fleuron cornerpieces, raised bands, spines richly gilt with panels dominated by bold and complex quatrefoil incorporating spade-like tools and with palmette cornerpieces, turn-ins with two gilt fillets, marbled endpapers, all edges gilt, with facsimile of Greek and Latin text from the Complutensian Polyglot and volume I with specimen leaf laid down, as called for, large paper copy, engraved armorial bookplate of John William Pease, rear pastedown with vellum armorial bookplate of Lord Wardington, touch of rubbing to tail edge of boards, one leaf with thin band of soiling along four inches of the fore edge, light glue stain at lower corner of specimen leaf, endpapers with faint fox spots (isolated minor foxing elsewhere), other trivial imperfections but generally, very fine, text clean and fresh with vast margins and decorative bindings with no significant wear.   Phillip J. Pirages   67 - 112   2016 $4500

Association – Warhol, Andy

Berrigan, Ted *"C" a Journal of Poetry.* New York: Lornez Gude et al May, 1963. -May 1966., I: 1-10; II-11 and 13 (of 13), 12 issues, tall legal format, mimeographed and stapled in printed wrappers and in pictorial wrappers with cover design by Joe Brainard, and one issue with silk screen cover design by Andy Warhol, some numbers inscribed by Berrigan and signed by Joe Brainard, presentation inscriptions to Tony Towle from Warhol, Berrigan, Edwin Denby, Gerard Malanga and John Wieners.   James S. Jaffe Rare Books   Occasional List: Winter 2016 - 24   2016 $22,500

Association – Warner, Henry Lee

Miller, Hugh *My Schools and Schoolmasters or the Story of My Education.* Edinburgh: Thomas Constable and Co., 1858. contemporary speckled calf, gilt spine, lacking label, little rubbed, contemporary gift inscription on leading pastedown "Jeffery Edwards from his friend & school fellow, Henry Lee Warner....".   Jarndyce Antiquarian Books CCXV - 838   2016   £38

Association – Warre, John Ashley

Beattie, James 1735-1803 *The Ministrel; or the Progress of Genius with Some Other Poems.* London: printed for J. Mawman, 1801. 170 x 102mm., contemporary red straight grain morocco, covers with gilt ruled border, flat spine divided into panels by single gilt rule, gilt titling, turn-ins with decorative bead roll, marbled endpapers, all edges gilt, with pleasing fore-edge painting of the harbor and seaside town of Whitby, in excellent brown morocco pull-off case by Sangorski & Sutcliffe for J. W. Robinson Co., 4 engravings, front pastedown with engraved bookplate of John Ashley Warre, spine slightly and uniformly sunned to a darker red, occasional spotting or staining, still quite decent copy, binding solid and lustrous, text smooth and fresh, painting very well preserved.   Phillip J. Pirages   67 - 147   2016 $800

Association – Warren, John

Tasso, Torquato 1544-1595 *Godfrey of Bulloigne; or the Recovery of Jerusalem.* London: by John Macock for George Wells and Abel Swalle, 1687. Second edition, small closed tear to titlepage with evidence of earlier restoration, occasional rust spotting, dampstaining to margin in places, 55mm. piece torn away from fore margin of A7, repaired tear to A8, small piece torn away from corners of H4, 2A1 and with 60mm. closed tear to foot of 2I1 (touching text), contemporary calf, head and tail of spine damaged, corners bumped, label missing, from the library of James Stevens Cox (1910-1997), signature of E. Marshall dated 1769, signature of John Warren dated 1809.   Maggs Bros. Ltd.   1447 - 406   2016   £180

Association – Warwick, Elwin

Lytton, Edward Robert Bulwer-Lytton, 1st Earl of 1831-1891 *After Paradise or Legends of Exile with Other Poems.* London: David Stott, 1887. First edition, original blue cloth with gilt title to spine, minor wear to edges, interior is very clean with some light foxing to last few pages, tight binding, nice copy apart from presence of a circulating library label, bookplate stating the book was presented to the Norfolk and Norwich Library by the Rev. Elwin in 1907, scarce, very good, presentation copy inscribed W. E. by author (Rev. Warwick Elwin, close friend).   The Kelmscott Bookshop   12 - 61   2016 $175

Association – Wasserman, Edward

Dane, Clemence *Come of Age.* New York: Doubleday, Doran, 1934. First edition, 8vo., very good, inscribed by author and Addinell for Edward Wasserman and signed by actress Judith Anderson who starred in the play.   Second Life Books, Inc.   196A - 372   2016 $150

Association – Waterman, Alfred

Waterman, Hugh *A Sermon Preached before the Court of Guardians of the Poor in the City of Bristol at St. Peters Church April 13th 1699.* Bristol: by W. Bonny, 1699. First edition, small 4to., lightly browned and spotted throughout, particularly at end, rust spots in places, lower edges of A1-2 uncut, lower fore-corner of F4 repaired, late 19th early 20th century half maroon morocco and marbled boards, from the library of James Stevens Cox (1910-1997), signature of Alfred J. Waterman, 6 Manor Park, Redland, Bristol dated 1913 and 3 page note on front flyleaves, 1913 clipping from local Bristol newspaper, pencil note "from the Weare collection.   Maggs Bros. Ltd.   1447 - 443   2016   £500

Association – Waterton, Charles

Waterton, Charles *Wanderings in South America the North-West of the United States and the Antilles in the Years 1812, 1816, 1829 and 1824.* London: A. Applegath for J. Mawman, 1825. First edition, 4to., contemporary quarter brown morocco, brown paper covered boards, frontispiece, 2 woodcut text illustrations with ALS from Charles Waterton, seal cut out, bookplate of Bertram Savile Ogle, very good.   Sotheran's   Piccadilly Notes - Summer 2015 - 323   2016   £1550

Association – Watney, Herbert

Catholic Church. Liturgy & Ritual *Missale ad Consuetudinem Ecclesie Romanae...* Paris: in alma Parisiorum Academia Impensis Thielmanni Kerver 23 March, 1506. 8vo., Kerver's fine device on titlepage, full page woodcut of Crucifixion, large crible initial of Crucifixion, crible initials, music on four-line staves, printed in red and black, decorative line fillers in red and black, 8vo., 19th century purple brown morocco richly gilt in 16th century style by J. Wright, binder, gauffered edges, headcaps rubbed, bookseller's note stating this was from the library of A. J. Beresford Hope (1820-1887), bookplate and inscription of Herbert Watney (1843-1932).   Maggs Bros. Ltd.   1474 - 53   2016   £4500

Association – Watney, Vernon

Erasmus, Desiderius   1466-1536 *L'Eloge de la Folie Nouvellement traduit du Latin d'Esrame par M. De la Veaux.* Basle: imprime avec des caracteres de G. Haas chez J. J. Thurneysen, le Jeune, 1780. Triple portrait frontispiece, additional engraved titlepage, further portrait engraved by Samuel Granicher, illustrations, few leaves browned or foxed, 8vo., 19th century crushed red morocco by Cape, lettered gilt on spine (giving the place as Berlin), gilt edges, minimal wear to corners, overall morocco book label of Vernon Watney inside front cover and his signature on verso of front free endpaper, very good.   Blackwell's Rare Books   Marks of Genius - 15   2016   £300

Association – Watson, Charles

Norie, John William *A Complete Epitome of Practical Navigation...* London: printed for the author and sold by Charles Wilson, 1856. Sixteenth (Stereotyped) edition, 222 x 137mm., very plain contemporary sprinkled sheep, flat spine divided into panels by single gilt rules, dun-colored endpapers, 9 engraved plates, 19th century ink signature of Charles Watson, tiny cracks just beginning at top and bottom of joints, minor smudge upper cover, lower board with small trailing wormhole, minor offsetting from plates, still especially fine, entirely bright, fresh and clean inside and out.   Phillip J. Pirages   67 - 266   2016 $750

Association – Watson, John

Arabian Nights *The Thousand and One Nights, Commonly called in England The Arabian Nights' Entertainments.* London: Charles Knight and Co., 1839-1841. First edition in book form, 3 volumes, 254 x 165mm, pleasing late 19th century crimson half morocco, raised bands, gilt ruled compartments with central ornament of gilt rosette within a star, marbled pastedowns, top edge gilt, more than 300 wood engravings from designs by William Harvey, bookplate of John Watson, volume i with translator's "Advertisement" giving spelling and pronunciation of various bookplate, occasional rust spots, few isolated margin smudges, but really excellent copy with few signs of wear inside or out.   Phillip J. Pirages   67 - 5   2016 $1000

Association – Watson, Richard

Priestley, Joseph   1733-1804 *Miscellaneous Observations relating to Education.* Bath: printed for R. Cruttwell for J. Johnson, 1778. 8vo., occasional slight damp marking, some long and shorthand contemporary annotations, attractively rebound in quarter calf, raised bands, red morocco label, vellum tips, ownership signature of Rich'd Watson, later inscription "Presented to me by Dr. Williams' Library London...".   Jarndyce Antiquarian Books   CCXV - 909   2016   £580

Association – Watt, A. P.

Dickens, Charles 1812-1870 *Letters of Charles Dickens to Wilkie Collins 1851-1876.* London: James R. Osgood, McIlvaine & Co., 1892. Half title, original dark blue cloth, dulled, inner hinges cracking, inscribed by A. P. Watt for friend George Macdonald.   Jarndyce Antiquarian Booksellers   CCXVIII - 850   2016   £280

Association – Watt, Colleen

Ginsberg, Allen *Howl.* New York: Harper & Row, 1986. First edition thus, limited edition, quarto, slightly bowed boards with some spotting, else about near fine in about fine dust jacket, signed by author, with elaborate illustration to writer Colleen Watt.   Between the Covers Rare Books 208 - 33   2016 $500

Association – Watts, Margaret

The Female Aegis; or the Duties of Women from childhood to Old Age and in Most Situations of Life Exemplified. London: printed by Sampson Low for J. Gigner, 1798. First edition, frontispiece, 12mo., contemporary mottled calf, black morocco label, hinges cracking, spine worn at head and tail, calligraphic signature of Margaret Watts, 1805, bookseller's ticket, sound copy.   Jarndyce Antiquarian Books   CCXV - 193   2016   £220

Association – Wayne, David

Patrick, John *The Teahouse of the August Moon.* New York: Putnam, 1952. Second impression, 8vo., Harry Jackson's copy (Sgt. Gregovich in the play), signed by David Wayne and 15 members of the cast, presentation from Jackson, light edge bumps, tear on blank, otherwise very good in little chipped and stained dust jacket.   Second Life Books, Inc.   196 B - 380   2016 $200

Association – Weare

Waterman, Hugh *A Sermon Preached before the Court of Guardians of the Poor in the City of Bristol at St. Peters Church April 13th 1699.* Bristol: by W. Bonny, 1699. First edition, small 4to., lightly browned and spotted throughout, particularly at end, rust spots in places, lower edges of A1-2 uncut, lower fore-corner of F4 repaired, late 19th early 20th century half maroon morocco and marbled boards, from the library of James Stevens Cox (1910-1997), signature of Alfred J. Waterman, 6 Manor Park, Redland, Bristol dated 1913 and 3 page note on front flyleaves, 1913 clipping from local Bristol newspaper, pencil note "from the Weare collection.   Maggs Bros. Ltd.   1447 - 443   2016   £500

Association – Weatherall, Thelma

Langton, Robert *The Childhood and Youth of Charles Dickens.* London: Hutchinson & Co., 1891. First Published edition, half title, frontispiece, illustrations, original pale green cloth, lettered gilt, little dulled, front board slightly creased, signature of Thelma Weatherall April 1891, top edge gilt.   Jarndyce Antiquarian Booksellers   CCXVIII - 1347   2016   £20

Association – Weaver, William

Calvino, Italo *Le Cosmicomiche.* Torino: Einaudi, 1965. First edition, 8vo., original pale green cloth, fine in dust jacket with few short tears, presentation copy inscribed by author to William Weaver, the English translator of Cosmicomics, with a number of discreet pencil annotations by Weaver.   James S. Jaffe Rare Books   Occasional List: Winter 2016 - 37   2016 $4500

Association – Webb, John

Fisher, George *The Instructor or Young Man's Best Companion.* London: printed for J. Clarke, 1742. Sixth edition, frontispiece, plates, illustrations, 12mo., pages little browned, handsomely rebound in half calf, vellum tips, red morocco label, inscription "John Webb his book Jan. 24 1837".   Jarndyce Antiquarian Books   CCXV - 202   2016   £75

Association – Webb, Philip

Horatius Flaccus, Quintus *Carmina Sapphica. (and) Carmina Alcaica.* Chelsea: Ashendene Press, 1903. One of 150 copies on Japanese paper (25 on vellum), 185 x 128mm., 2 volumes, original flexible vellum, gilt titling on spine, housed in custom cloth folding box with separate compartments for each book, initials hand painted by Graily Hewiett, printed in red and black, "Carmina Alcaica" inscribed to Philip Webb by printer and dated 1903 with further ink notation that was given by Webb's executor to Walter Knight Shirley, Earl Ferrers on 22 Feb. 1916 and by him to Charles Winmile Jan 1937, verso of 'Carmina Sapphica" with morocco bookplate of Cortlandt Bishop, pastedowns little waffled, otherwise mint.   Phillip J. Pirages 67 - 13   2016 $4000

Association – Webbe, Egerton

Boxhorn, Marcus Zuertius *Poetae Satyrici Minores de Corrupto Republicae Statu Marcus Zuerius Boxhornius...* Lugduni Batavorum: ex officina Isaaci Commelini, 1633. First edition, 12mo., titlepage in red and black, splatter marks seemingly ink, to few pages but not interfering with text, paper little browned, marginal paper flaw to very edge of page 101, contemporary vellum title inked to spine, edges sprinkled blue, spine darkened, few grey scuff marks but very good, inscription of Egerton Webbe dated 1837 (1810?-1840).   Unsworths Antiquarian Booksellers Ltd.   E01 - Early Printing - 2   2016   £400

Association – Webber, Anne

Fry, Caroline *The Listener.* London: James Nisbet, 1832. Third edition, 2 volumes, half titles, original pink moire cloth, spines lettered gilt, imprint at tails, price 12s, spine faded, slight damp marking, signature of Anne Webber 1833, nice.   Jarndyce Antiquarian Books   CCXV - 696   2016   £48

Association – Webber, John Henry

The Footman: His Duties and How to Perform Them. London: Houlston & sons, circa, 1870. Original brick brown cloth, blocked in gilt and black, ownership inscription and stamp of John Henry Webber on verso of leading f.e.p., very good.   Jarndyce Antiquarian Books   CCXV - 259   2016   £150

Association – Webster, Edgar

Flanagan, Thomas Jefferson *The Road to Mount McKeithan and Other Verse.* Atlanta: Independent (sic) Publishers Corporation, 1927. First edition, frontispiece, one printed illustration, paper covered boards, modest erosion to boards, else nice, very good or better, inscribed by author to Professor and Mrs. Edgar H. Webster and dated in year of publication.   Between the Covers Rare Books   202 - 33   2016 $750

Association – Wedderburn, James

Dickens, Charles 1812-1870 *Oliver Twist.* London: Richard Bentley, 1838. First edition, 2nd issue, 3 volumes, half titles volumes I and II, frontispieces and plates by George Cruikshank, original purple-brown cloth, spines lettered gilt, Bentley imprint at tail, spines little faded, armorial bookplates of James Wedderburn, very nice.   Jarndyce Antiquarian Booksellers CCXVIII - 176   2016   £2800

Association – Weight, Michael

Williams, Emlyn *Accolade: a Play in Six Scenes.* London: Heinemann, 1951. First edition, 8vo., original cloth, very good in little worn dust jacket, inscribed by author to Michael Weight Jan. 1951.   Second Life Books, Inc.   196 B - 898   2016 $113

Williams, Emlyn *Night Must Fall: a Play in three acts.* London: Victor Gollancz, 1936. First edition, second impression, 8vo., cloth with little soiled dust jacket, inscribed by author for Michael Weight.   Second Life Books, Inc.   196 B - 899   2016 $113

Association – Weil, Gritta

Sampson, Anthony *Mandela. the Authorised Biography.* London: Harper Collins, 1999. First edition, signed and inscribed by Jo. Mandell, who co-directed the 1996 official film biography of Nelson Mandela, for Gritta Weil (1924-2009).   Sotheran's   Travel and Exploration - 33   2016   £78

Association – Weinstein, Laura

West, Nathanael *A Cool Million.* New York: Covici Friede, 1934. First edition, author's sister's copy with her ownership signature 'Laura Weinstein", modest foxing to boards, endpages and page edges, very good in like dust jacket with bit of sunning on and near spine and few very small edge chips, much nicer than usual, in custom clamshell case.   Ken Lopez Bookseller   166 - 146   2016 $7500

Association – Weir, J. L.

Jamieson, John *Catalogue of the Extensive Library, Bronzes, Roman Antiquities, Prints &c &c.* Edinburgh: Colston, Printer, East Rose Street Lane, 1839. 8vo., modern red cloth, spine lettered gilt, book label of J. L.. Weir, inserted on title by the famous Glasgow bookseller, John Smith, rare.   Marlborough Rare Books   List 56 - 27   2016   £325

Association – Weirick, James

Walker, Meredith *Building for nature: Walter Burley Griffin and Castlecrag.* Castlecrag: Walter Burley Griffin Society, 1994. Horizontal 8vo., black and white photos, presentation by Adrienne Kabos and James Weirick, auction flyer laid in, paper wrappers, about as new.   Second Life Books, Inc.   196 B - 821   2016 $75

Association – Welch, Elizabeth

Behrman, S. N. *No Time for comedy: a Play in Three Acts.* London: Hamish Hamilton, 1939. First edition, 8vo., original worn printed wrappers, (also issued in cloth), round-robin copy, signed by members of the London production, Diane Wyngard, Rex Harrison, Lilian Palmer, Elizabeth Welch and 3 others.   Second Life Books, Inc.   196A - 97   2016 $250

Association – Weld, Otis E.

Washington, George   1732-1799   *Official Letters to the Honourable American Congress, Written during the War Between the United Colonies and Great Britain by his Excellency, George Washington....*   London: printed for Cadell Junior and Davies, G. G. and J. Robinson, B. and J. White, W. Otridge and Son, J. Debrett, R. Faulder and T. Egerton, 1795. First edition, second issue without half title and portrait, 8vo., contemporary mottled calf, six compartments, four decorated gilt with flags and crown, red morocco title and black volume number labels, marbled endpapers, very good set, boards rubbed, small circular scuff worn through to rear board of one volume, flyleaves toned opposite endpapers, text quite sharp, armorial bookplate of Otis E. Weld.   Kaaterskill Books   21 - 113   2016 $1200

Association – Welfare, Sarah

A Manual of the Etiquette of Love, Courtship and Marriage. London: Allman & Son, 1859. 16mo., frontispiece, original red decorated cloth, rubbed, dulled and slightly marked, all edges gilt, contemporary signature of Sarah Welfare.   Jarndyce Antiquarian Books   CCXV - 308   2016   £45

Association – Weller, George

Markland, George   *Pteryplegia; or the Art of Shooting-Flying.*   London: printed for Stephen Austen, 1727. Second edition, 8v., disbound, titlepage slightly spotted, very good, contemporary signature of George Weller.   C. R. Johnson Rare Book Collections   Foxon: H-P 2015 - 574   2016 $613

Association – Welles, John

Warren, John Collins   *The Great Tree on Boston Common.*   Boston: John Wilson, 1855. First edition, large 8vo., inscribed by author to John Welles, wood engraved frontispiece, tissue guard, double page map.   Second Life Books, Inc.   196 B - 827   2016 $250

Association – Wells, Carolyn

Hawthorne, Nathaniel   1804-1864   *The Scarlet Letter.* Boston: Ticknor, Reed and Fields, 1850. First edition, 12mo., later full crimson morocco (original cloth and endpapers bound in), inscribed ads dated March 1, 1850, pasted opposite title, which is printed in black and red-orange, is fine example of Hawthorne's holograph signature, signed as surveyor of the port of Salem, Mass., 19h century ownership signature 'Emily G. Freeman, nearly fine with bookplate of Carolyn Wells, author.   Howard S. Mott Inc.   265 - 65   2016 $2000

Association – Wells, Dean Faulkner

Faulkner, William Harrison   1896-1962   *Doctor Martino and Other Stories.*   New York: Smith and Haas, 1934. First edition, fine with slightest of seemingly inevitable fading to spine, without dust jacket as issued, copy number 1 of 360 numbered copies, signed by author, with letter from antiquarian bookseller detailing provenance directly from Dean Faulkner Wells who inherited it from her grandmother, Maud.   Between the Covers Rare Books   204 - 40   2016 $12,000

Association – Wells, Joel Cheney

Lamb, Charles   1775-1834   *The Works of Charles and Mary Lamb and the Life of Charles Lamb.*   London: Methuen & Co., 1903-1905. 9 volumes, 222 x 146mm., especially attractive contemporary red morocco, elaborately gilt (stamp signed 'Charles E. Lauriat'), covers framed by two plain gilt rules, raised bands, spines lavishly gilt in compartments with large central fleuron surrounded by a lozenge of small tools and intricate scrolling cornerpieces, densely gilt turn-ins, top edges gilt, extravagantly extra illustrated with 653 plates, five of these folding, two double page, and two colored, engraved bookplate of Joel Cheney Wells, just vaguest hint of rubbing to extremities, isolated small marginal stains, still handsomely bound in fine condition, fresh and clean internally and in lustrous bindings with few signs of wear.   Phillip J. Pirages   67 - 132   2016 $4500

Romer, Isabella Frances *Filia Dolorosa. Memoirs of Marie Therese Charlotte, Duchess of Angouleme, The Last Dauphnies.* London: Richard Bentley, 1852. First edition, 225 x 140mm., 2 volumes, attractive later sky blue crushed morocco by Bayntun of Bath for his bookseller Charles E. Lauriat co. of Boston (stamp signed on front turn-in), covers with frame of black and gilt rules cinched to the center of each side by a decorative quatrefoil, raised bands, spine compartments framed by black and gilt rules, gilt titling, turn-ins ruled in gilt and black with decorative cornerpieces, marbled endpapers, all edges gilt, hand colored frontispiece portrait, extra illustrated with portraits and views, 20 of the portraits hand colored, bookplate of Joel Cheney Wells, designed by Elisha Brown Bird, spines uniformly faded further toward gray than blue, isolated trivial defects internally, otherwise very pleasing copy, entirely clean and fresh as in bindings with spine lustrous covers and virtually no signs of use. Phillip J. Pirages 67 - 39 2016 $750

Association – Welpott, Jack

Siskind, Aaron *Aaron Siskind: Photographer.* Rochester: George Eastman House, 1965. First edition, clean and tight, near fine copy in close to near fine dust jacket with some slight wear, signed and inscribed by Siskind for Jack Welpott, fellow worker in the vineyard, rather uncommon thus. Jeff Hirsch Books E-List 80 - 28 2016 $500

Association – Wender, Deborah

Schwartz, Lynne Sharon *The Accounting.* Great Barrington: Penmaen Press, 1983. First edition, title illustration by Michael McCurdy, with original print of same wood engraving, signed by artist, laid in, one of 50 copies numbered and signed by author and artist and casebound by Deborah Wender, fine in little chipped and soiled tissue dust jacket. Second Life Books, Inc. 196 B - 546 2016 $150

Association – Wescott, Glenway

Moore, Marianne 1887-1972 *Le Mariage.* New York: Ibex Press, 1965. First edition, one of 26 lettered copies from a total edition of 50 copies, 12mo., original unprinted wrappers, illustrated dust jacket by Laurence Scott, publisher's printed envelope, presentation inscribed by author for Glenway Wescott, binding adhesive lightly offset to spine portion of jacket, otherwise fine in lightly toned and dust soiled publisher's envelope, scarce. James S. Jaffe Rare Books Occasional List: Winter 2016 - 100 2016 $1250

Association – West De Wend Fenton, Mrs.

West De Wend Fenton, Michael *The Primrose Path.* privately printed, 1908. First edition one of 50 copies, crown 8vo., small amount of very faint foxing to borders of few pages, original navy blue cloth lettered gilt to backstrip and upper board with design blocked in yellow to the latter, rubbing to extremities, top edge gilt, others untrimmed, faint spotting to free endpapers with few pieces of related ephemera loosely inserted, good, inscribed by author to his mother. Blackwell's Rare Books B186 - 214 2016 £400

Association – West, Harriet

MacKenzie, Henry *Julia De Roubigne a Tale.* London: printed for W. Strahan, 1777. One of two imprints of the first edition of 17777, this one without addition of W. Creech, Edinburgh, half titles and final ad leaf volume II, 12mo., slight browning and offsetting from turn-ins of first few and final leaves, 2 volumes in one, contemporary mottled calf, boards slightly pitted, corners worn, expertly rebacked with raised and gilt banded spine, red morocco label, near contemporary ownership signature of Harriet West. Jarndyce Antiquarian Booksellers CCXVI - 376 2016 £280

Association – Westlake, Abby

Westlake, Donald *The Spy in the Ointment.* New York: Random House, 1966. First edition, fine in price clipped dust jacket, remarkable association copy for author's wife, Abby. Buckingham Books 2015 - 35193 2016 $450

Association – Westwood, Thomas

Folkard, Henry Coleman *The Wild Fowler: a Treatise on Ancient and Modern Wild-Fowling, Historical and Practical.* Piper, Stephenson and Spence, 1859. First edition, sometime rebound in half green morocco, gilt lettering to spine, marbled boards, marbled endpapers, frontispiece and 12 steel engraved plates, 5 woodcuts in text, spine sunned, very good, bookplate of Thomas Westwood, poet and angling bibliographer. Sotheran's Hunting, Shooting & Fishing - 81 2016 £300

Association – Wetherald, R.

Bacon, Francis 1561-1626 *The Twoo Bookes of Francis Bacon. Of the Proficience and Advancement of Learning, Divine and Humane.* London: for Henrie Tomes, 1605. First edition, 4to., lacks final blank 3H2 and as always, rare two leaves of errata at end, late 19th century half calf and marbled boards, extremities of boards worn, very skillfully and imperceptibly rebacked, retaining entire original spine, small worm trail at bottom margin of quires 2D-2F, occasional minor marginalia in early hand, else lovely copy, early signature of Row'd Wetherald on title signature of Horatio Carlyon 1861, Sachs bookplate and modern leather book label calf backed clamshell box. Joseph J. Felcone, Inc. Books from Five Centuries: a Miscellany - 10 2016 $7500

Association – Wettenhall, Norman

Greenewalt, Crawford H. *Hummingbirds.* Garden City: American Museum of Natural History, 1960. Quarto, 68 tipped-in color photos by author, text illustrations, fine, slightly chipped dust jacket, bookplate of Norman Wettenhall. Andrew Isles Natural History Books 55 - 13280 2016 $400

Association – Wheat, Carl Irving

Bottome, Phyllis *Stella Benson.* San Francisco: Grabhorn Press, 1934. First edition, 250 copies printed, small 8vo., title printed in red and black, marginal titles, initial and colophon in red, handset Garamond type, Oxford gray cloth boards with yellow spine, paper label printed in red on front cover, spine slightly darkened, but very fine, from the collection of Carl I. Wheat, inscribed by Wheat "From the Library of Albert Bender". Argonaut Book Shop Private Press 2015 - 6276 2016 $60

Association – Wheatley, Charles

Hincliff, Thomas Woodbine *Over the Sea and Far Away.* London: Longman, Green, 1876. First edition, 8vo., 14 illustrations, recent brown half calf, rare, Charles Wheatley's copy. J. & S. L. Bonham Antiquarian Booksellers Voyages 2016 - 9874 2016 £220

Association – Wheatley, Dennis

Bennett, Arnold 1867-1931 *The Old Wives' Tale.* London: Chapman & Hall, 1908. First edition, presentation copy, blindstamp to title and following leaf, few spots at beginning, 8vo., original dark rose cloth lettered white on upper cover, spine faded and white lettering gone, Dennis Wheatley's copy with his bookplate, modern bookplate opposite, sound. Blackwell's Rare Books B184 - 108 2016 £375

Association – Wheatley, Doris

Hughes, Ted 1930-1998 *Winter Pollen.* New York: Picador, 1995. First American edition, 8vo., original quarter black cloth with blue boards, backstrip lettered in silver, dust jacket with just small amount of creasing to extremities, various clippings about author laid in, inscribed by author for mentor, Doris Wheatley. Blackwell's Rare Books B186 - 240 2016 £1500

Association – Wheeler, Christopher

Conrad, Joseph 1857-1924 *The Arrow of Gold.* New York: Doubleday Page, 1919. First edition, octavo, original blue cloth stamped in gilt, from the library of Stanley J. Seeger with his small bookplate, presentation copy from author for Lady (Frances) Colvin, beneath is another presentation inscription to Christopher Wheeler from Sidney Colvin, cover rubbed at spine and edges, cloth bubbled at inside edge of lower cover, good, preserved in green buckram slipcase lettered gilt with inner folding sleeve. Peter Ellis 112 - 81 2016 £950

Association – Wheeler, John A.

Tanner, Henry *The Martyrdomn of Lovejoy.* Chicago: Fergus Printing Co., 1880. First edition, 8vo., original cloth with paper spine label, 5 plates, spine label little browned, otherwise very good, presentation inscribed by author for John A. Wheeler. Sotheran's Piccadilly Notes - Summer 2015 - 293 2016 £248

Association – Wheeler, Joseph Mazzini

Levesque, Pierre Charles *Collection des Moralistes Anciens Dedies au Roi.* Paris: Didot and Burre, 1782-1783. First French edition, 12mo., 2 volumes in one, calf backed pebble grained cloth of about 1835, spine ruled and lettered gilt, marbled endpapers, head and tail of spine little worn, internally clean and fresh, ink name of Joseph Mazzini Wheeler, translator and editor. Sotheran's Travel and Exploration - 149 2016 £348

Association – White, Henry

Melanchthon, Philipp 1497-1560 *Epigrammata Selectiota Formulis Precum, Historiis Paraphrasi Dictorum Divinorum...* Frankfurt: Johanne & Sigismund Feyerabend, 1583. First edition edited by Peter Jensen, 4to., printer's device on titlepage and larger version on recto of penultimate leaf, woodcut dedicatory arms, map, 95 oval woodcuts within fine mannerist borders, many signed I.A. (Jost Amman), late 18th century calf, sides with gilt ruled and blind roll tooled border, gilt edges, spine with later gilt lettering, marbled endpapers, neat repairs to head and foot of spine, joints rubbed, blank corner of titlepage cut away and neatly replaced, few spots and stains but generally fresh, inscription dated 1818 of Rev. Henry White of Lichfield, dated 1818, armorial bookplate of Henry Latham. Maggs Bros. Ltd. 1474 - 52 2016 £2800

Association – White, James

Penfield, Wilder *The Excitable Cortex in Conscious Man.* Liverpool: 1958. Original binding,m with tipped in reprint of review of this book by Stanley Cobb, note on front fly "James C. White set by W. P. 5-15-58" in White's hand. James Tait Goodrich X-78 - 461 2016 $125

Association – White, Jesse

Woolnoth, William *A Graphical Illustration of the Metropolitan Cathedral Church of Canterbury.* London: T. Cadell & W. Davies and J. Murray, 1816. Large paper copy, royal 4to., 20 plates on India paper, foxing to front and rear blanks and plates, text pages generally clean barring occasional offset toning from plates, neat pencil notes to pages 92-3, early 20th century half burgundy morocco gilt title to spine, blue marbled paper boards, edges sprinkled red, endcaps, joints and corners bit worn, edges slightly chipped but very good overall, bookplate of A. D. Gondinton dated 1901, recent bookplate of Susan Wade, tiny bookbinder's label of R. Hynes, Dover, catalog description pasted in, some pencilled booksellers notes to prelim blanks, note to list of subscribers identifies this as the copy belonging to Mr. Jesse White, Canterbury. Unsworths Antiquarian Booksellers Ltd. 30 - 165 2016 £350

Association – White, Paul Dudley

Cushing, Harvey Williams 1869-1939 *A Bio-Bibliography of Andreas Vesalius.* New York: Schuman, 1943. Limited to 800 copies, quarter green morocco and linen boards, armorial crest on front board, numerous illustrations, very clean, nice copy, minimal wear, from the library of Paul Dudley White, signed by "Paul Dudley White Christmas 1944 from other". James Tait Goodrich X-78 - 533 2016 $850

Association – White, Richard Grant

Webster, John *A Monumental Colummne, Erected to the Liuing Memory of the Euer-Glorious Henry, late Prince of Wales.* London: printed by N. O(kes) for William Welby, 1613. First edition, woodcut ornaments on title, woodcut headpieces, 2 pages printed entirely in black, lacking final 2 leaves (also printed entirely in black, without text), last leaf with a hole with loss of 3 letters from the motto at end of text on recto, slight loss to lower fore-corner of this leaf and extreme corresponding corner of preceding leaf (no loss of text), A4 (the first black leaf), very slightly defective at top outer corner, title slightly browned, 4to., late 19th century green crushed morocco by Matthews, quadruple gilt fillets on sides with corner ornaments, spine lettered longitudinally in gilt, gilt edges, extra blank leaves bound in at beginning and end, last at front inscribed 'Richard Grant White Esq. with the best wishes of R. H. Stoddard", good. Blackwell's Rare Books Marks of Genius - 50 2016 £20,000

Association – White, Robert

The Habits of Good Society: a Handbook of Etiquette for Ladies and Gentleman. London: James Hogg & sons, 1859. First edition, original brown cloth, recased, rubbed and dulled, signature of Robert White, sound copy only. Jarndyce Antiquarian Books CCXV - 236 2016 £50

Association – Whiteley, W.

Kingsford, Anna Bonus *Health, Beauty and the Toilet.* London: Frederick Warne & Co., 1886. First edition, endpapers with marginal tear to leading f.e.p., original light brown cloth, bookseller's ticket of W. Whiteley, very good. Jarndyce Antiquarian Books CCXV - 281 2016 £150

Association – Whiting, Frances

Gallico, Paul *Confessions of a Story Writer.* New York: Alfred A. Knopf, 1946. First edition, 8vo., original red cloth, spine lettered in gilt, upper board centrally blindstamped, lower board blindstamped with publisher's device in bottom right hand corner in original dust jacket with pink paper wraparound band, top edges orange, extremities very slightly rubbed, very light tearing to head and foot of spine, small triangular tear ad some fading to band, nonetheless very fresh, rare with band, author's inscription to his editor Frances Whiting. Sotheran's Piccadilly Notes - Summer 2015 - 140 2016 £298

Association – Whitmore, William

Euclides *Elements Book 1-6 Latin and Greek.* London: Excudebat Gulielmus Iones, 1620. First edition to be printed in England, woodcut ornament on title, woodcut initials and tailpieces, Greek and Latin in parallel columns, 2 sidenotes shaved, little mild dampstaining at beginning, few leaves slightly browned, folio, contemporary calf, blind ruled borders on sides, pair of double rules near spine, hatching in top and bottom compartments, dark blue edges, rather rubbed, corners (especially top front) worn, crack at foot of upper joint and top of lower one, contemporary signature of Will. Whitmore, good. Blackwell's Rare Books Marks of Genius - 18 2016 £2750

Association – Whittaker, Lawson

Dickens, Charles 1812-1870 *The Christmas Books.* London: Chapman & Hall, 1863. Frontispiece, plates, contemporary full green calf, spine gilt in compartments, maroon lather label, slightly marked, contemporary hand written ownership label of Lawson Whittaker, attractive copy. Jarndyce Antiquarian Booksellers CCXVIII - 398 2016 £85

Association – Whittell, H. M.

Strickland, Hugh *Ornithological Synonyms. Volume One: Accipitres.* London: John Van Voorst, 1855. Octavo, publisher's cloth, some wear, signature and bookplate of H. M. Whittell, scarce. Andrew Isles Natural History Books 55 - 31219 2016 $300

Association – Whyte, Madeleine

Bible. English - 1903 *The English Bible.* Hammersmith: Doves Press, 1903-1905. One of 500 copies, 331 x 235mm., five volumes, original limp vellum by Doves Bindery (stamp signed), gilt titling on spine, housed within two later oatmeal linen dropback clamshell boxes with black morocco spine labels, elegant initial letters in red by Edward Johnston, including an "I" running the length of the page to open Genesis ("In the beginning"), front flyleaf of volume I inscribed in pencil by Madeleine Whyte for Mary Churchill, with Doves Press invoice for Miss Whyte dated June 27 1905, initialled by "B.H." (i.e. Bessie Hooley, a sewer at the bindery and part-time secretary to Cobden-Sanderson) laid in, vellum with just hint of soiling, but very little of the typical variation in grain, two dozen leaves with minor marginal foxing (never approaching any significance), dozen additional leaves with whisper of foxing, otherwise clean, fresh, bright copy inside and out. Phillip J. Pirages 67 - 115 2016 $19,500

Association – Wiater, Stanley

Dark Forces. New York: Viking, 1980. Light inkstain throughout first several pages of the introduction, not affecting any text, near fine in near fine dust jacket with light wear to corners, signed or inscribed by 15 writers including, Stephen King, Bloch, Richard Matheson, Joe Haldeman, Gahan Wilson, Campbell, Wolfe, Dennis Etchison, Karl Edward Wagner, Manly Wade Wellman, Edward Bryant, Charles L. Grant and editor, Kirby McCauley, with ownership signature of Stanley Wiater and with his Gahan Wilson bookplate. Ken Lopez Bookseller 166 - 3 2016 $3000

Tate, James *If it Would All Please Hurry.* Amherst: Shanachie Press, 1980. First edition, one of only 10 lettered copies reserved for author and artist, this being copy 'J' out of a total edition of 35 copies produced, of which 25 roman numeraled copies were for sale, all copies signed by poet and artist, with each of the original prints also numbered and signed in margin by artist, folio, 10 original etchings and engravings by Stephen Riley, on Arches Cover White paper, loose sheets in folding box, presentation copy inscribed by Tate and Riley for Stanley Wiater, portfolio lightly soiled, otherwise very fine, rare. James S. Jaffe Rare Books Occasional List: Winter 2016 - 137 2016 $4000

Association – Wieners, John

Berrigan, Ted *"C" a Journal of Poetry.* New York: Lornez Gude et al May, 1963. -May 1966., I: 1-10; II-11 and 13 (of 13), 12 issues, tall legal format, mimeographed and stapled in printed wrappers and in pictorial wrappers with cover design by Joe Brainard, and one issue with silk screen cover design by Andy Warhol, some numbers inscribed by Berrigan and signed by Joe Brainard, presentation inscriptions to Tony Towle from Warhol, Berrigan, Edwin Denby, Gerard Malanga and John Wieners. James S. Jaffe Rare Books Occasional List: Winter 2016 - 24 2016 $22,500

Association – Wiggins, G. N.

Manilius, Marcus *Astronomicon. Liber Quintus.* London: Richards Press, 1930. One of 400 copies, 8vo. original tape backed printed boards, printed paper spine label, with ALS by A. E. Housman to G. N. Wiggins, tipped to front free endpaper, spine panel lightly sunned, dust soiling to top edge of textblock, few fox marks and fold from mailing letter is fine. James S. Jaffe Rare Books Occasional List: Winter 2016 - 80 2016 $1000

Association – Wightman, Julia Parker

Pierre Legrain, Relieur. Repertoire Descriptif et Bibliographique de Mille Deux Trente-Six reliures. Paris: Libraire Auguste Blaizot, 1965. Limited to 600 numbered copies, 4to., signatures loosely inserted in white stiff paper wrapper, brown cloth slipcase, 205 pages in full color, 243 reproductions in collotype, leather bookplate of Julia Parker Wightman, only minor fading of spine.   Oak Knoll Books   310 - 17   2016 $800

Association – Wilkins

Bruce, William   *Marriage.*   London: Jemaes Spiers, 1871. Half title, printed in gold, original white cloth, bevelled boards, elaborately decorated and lettered gilt, little dulled with slight marking to lower board, gift inscription to Mr. & Mrs. Herbert Gill from Mr. and Mrs. Wilkins, March 15 (18)89.   Jarndyce Antiquarian Books   CCXV - 83   2016   £85

Association – Wilkins, William Gylde

Cary, Thomas G.   *Letter to a Lady in France on the Supposed Failure of a National Blank, the Supposed Delinquency of the National Government...*   Boston: Benjamin H. Greene, 1844. Second edition, sewn as issued in original pale blue printed wrappers, slight wear to head and tail of spine, bookplate of William Gylde Wilkins, very good.   Jarndyce Antiquarian Booksellers   CCXVIII - 327   2016   £150

Association – Wilkinson, Gillian A.

Cary, M.   *The Ancient Explorers.*   London: Methuen & Co., 1929. First edition, 8vo., maps, cloth, gilt lettered, spine browned, small mark to lower board, bumping and wear to corners and end caps, edges dusted, light toning to free endpapers, shelfwear, very good, no dust jacket, small white sticker to spine, gilt plate to Bedford College, ownership inscription of Gillian A. Wilkinson.   Unsworths Antiquarian Booksellers Ltd.   E05 - 24   2016   £40

Association – Williams, Edward

Sprat, Thomas   1635-1713   *The History of the Royal-Society of London for the Improving of natural Knowledge.*   London: by T. R. for J. Martyn and J. Allestry, 1667. First edition, small 4to., engraved plate of the arms of the Royal Society, 2 folding plates (slightly shaved) and page 233 with very short tear, but without etched frontispiece by Hollar (often missing), contemporary calf, rebacked, new endleaves, corners repaired, from the library of James Stevens Cox (1910-1997), early 19th century signature of Edw. Williams and John Johnstone, early ink ciphers CR, similar to that of Charles II.   Maggs Bros. Ltd.   1447 - 394   2016   £400

Association – Williams, Garth

Selden, George   *The Cricket in Times Square.*   New York: Farrar Straus and Cudahy, 1960. Stated first printing, 8vo., pink cloth, fine in very good+ dust jacket (price clipped, no award seal), illustrations by Garth Williams, signed by Selden with TLS by Williams laid in.   Aleph-bet Books, Inc.   111 - 482   2016 $750

Association – Williams, J. E. Hodder

Shakespeare, William   1564-1616   *As You Like It.*   London: Hodder & Stoughton, n.d., 1909. Limited to 500 numbered copies signed by Thomson, this copy 0000 for presentation, presentation inscription from artist to J. E. Hodder Williams, director at Hodder & Stoughton, this is accompanied by lovely watercolor on half title, printed on fine paper, illustrated with 40 beautiful tipped in color plates by Hugh Thomson, with lettered tissue guards, large thick 4to., full vellum, gilt pictorial cover, original silk ties, few minor marks on cover and endpaper, boxed as usual, else fine.   Aleph-bet Books, Inc.   112 - 475   2016 $5000

Association – Williams, John

Dickens, Charles   1812-1870   *Master Humphrey's Clock.*   London: Chapman & Hall, 1840-1841. First edition, 3 volumes, frontispieces and illustrations by George Cattermole and Phiz, few spots, contemporary half green morocco, green cloth boards, gilt spines, slight rubbing, bookplates of John Williams, very good, attractive copy.   Jarndyce Antiquarian Booksellers   CCXVIII - 274   2016   £350

Association – Williams, Josephine

Kelly, George   *Craig's Wife, a Drama.*   Boston: Little Brown, 1926. First edition, 8vo., very nice tight copy, inscribed by author for Josephine Williams (played part of Mrs. Harold in NY production), also signed by rest of the cast and inscribed by producer Rosalie Stewart.   Second Life Books, Inc.   196A - 929   2016 $1500

Association – Williams, Miller

O'Connor, Flannery   1925-1964   *Wise Blood.*   New York: Harcourt Brace & Co., 1952. First edition, modest stain on top edge that is just touching top of boards and split at bottom front joint, spine worn down to text block, sound, good copy in presentable supplied, about very good dust jacket, ownership name of Miller Williams stamp on top of page edges, inscribed to same by author.   Between the Covers Rare Books   204 - 1   2016 $12,000

Association – Williams, Mr.

Paston, George *At John Murray's Records of a Literary Circle 1843-1892.* London: John Murray, 1932. First edition, 8vo., frontispiece, plates, original black cloth, presentation from John Murray to Mr. Williams. J. & S. L. Bonham Antiquarian Booksellers Voyages 2016 - 8794 2016 £65

Association – Williams, Ted

Updike, John 1932-2009 *Hub Fans bid Kid Adieu.* Northridge: Lord John Press, 1977. First edition, copy number 49 of 300 numbered copies, signed by author, quarter cloth and paper covered boards, fine, housed in custom cloth chemise and slipcase with morocco spine labels gilt, this copy also signed by Ted Williams, laid in is certificate of authenticity issued by Williams' son John Henry Williams. Between the Covers Rare Books 204 - 120 2016 $1500

Association – Williams, Tennessee

Windham, Donald *The Dog Star.* New York: Doubleday, 1950. First edition, signed by author on tipped-in-leaf, additionally signed by Tennessee Williams on front jacket flap, light foxing to top page edges, and light toning to jacket spine, near fine in like dust jacket. Royal Books 49 - 71 2016 $300

Association – Wills, W. H.

Dickens, Charles 1812-1870 *The Life and Adventures of Martin Chuzzlewit.* London: Chapman & Hall, 1844. first edition, first state with '1000' on engraved title, errata pages has 13 lines and thus, according to Hatton and Cleaver is the earlier issue, half title, frontispiece, engraved title, plates by Phiz, plates fairly evenly browned, plate opposite page 415 with small marginal repair, contemporary half black morocco, carefully recased, bookplates of W. H. Wills and Sir W. O. Priestley and handwritten statement inserted in prelims concerning ownership by W. H. Wills, signed J. C. Priestley, cloth slipcase. Jarndyce Antiquarian Booksellers CCXVIII - 412 2016 £1800

Association – Wilson, Adrian

American Type Founders Co. Kelly Press Division *Style B Kelly Automatic Press Book of Instructions.* Elizabeth: Kelly Press Division, American Type Founders Co., April, 1927. Oblong quarto, original printed red wrappers, 20 illustrations, laid into this copy is typed postcard from printer Lewis Osborne of Ashland, Oregon dated Jan. 9 1973 to printer Adrian Wilson, well used, worn and stained, as one would expect, with scotch tape reinforcement, etc, but complete, and rare. The Brick Row Book Shop Miscellany 69 - 66 2016 $225

Association – Wilson, Andrew

Deslandes, Andre Francois *The Art of Being Easy at all Times and in all Places.* London: printed for C. Rivington at the Bible and Crown, 1724. First edition, 12mo., without half title and final blank but with initial blank leaf, some old waterstaining to edges of first few leaves and neat endpapers and lower margins of main text contemporary unlettered calf, slight wear to head of spine, note on endpaper "Andrew Wilson - Owner 1730". Jarndyce Antiquarian Books CCXV - 156 2016 £1100

Association – Wilson, Danny

Lyttelton, Edward *Mothers and Sons or Problems in the Home Training of Boys.* London: Macmillan and Co., 1893. Half title, 4 pages ads, original blue cloth, contemporary signature of Danny Wilson, very good. Jarndyce Antiquarian Books CCXV - 302 2016 £25

Association – Wilson, Edward

Martialis, Marcus Valerius *Epigrammaton Libri.* Londini: Excudebat Felix Kingstonius impensis Gulielmi Welby, 1615. Small 8vo., woodcut headpieces and motif to titlepage, light toning, small piece missing from bottom corner of editor's dedication and small stain to margin of following page but neither affecting text, very good overall, recent light brown morocco, blind tooled raised bands to spine with black morocco gilt label, gilt date to tail of spine, all edges red, endpapers replaced, tan buckram slipcase, binding and case fine, ownership inscription of Edward Wilson in old hand to initial blank and titlepage, second similar ownership inscription also to title with first name William but illegible surname, some numbers in old hand to rear blank tiny binder's stamp 'Delrue'. Unsworths Antiquarian Booksellers 30 - 108 2016 £500

Association – Wilson, Erasmus

Denny, Henry *Monographia Pselaphidarum et Scydmaenidarum Britanniae...* Norwich: S. Wilkin, 1825. 8vo. in 4's, 14 hand colored plates, small paper flaw to p. 3, uncut in original olive green cloth, paper label, signature of Erasmus Wilson, March 1922, very nice. Jarndyce Antiquarian Booksellers CCXVII - 85 2016 £450

Raffray, Achille *Coleoptera: Family Pselaphidae.* Brussels: L. Desmet-Verteneuil, 1908. Quarto, 9 lithographed plates, contemporary half green morocco, rubbed, the copy of Erasmus Wilson. Andrew Isles Natural History Books 55 - 38319 2016 $350

Association – Wilson, George

Rowe, Elizabeth Singer *Friendship in Death in Letters from the Dead to the Living.* London: C. Cooke, 1797. 12mo., 4 engraved plates, tailpieces, small engraving on title, stained, foxed throughout, original dark calf, heavily worn, cover off, ink signatures on titlepage and title verso (Madam Codman, Josh Brooksby and George Wilson), rubber ink stamped numbers on title verso, blind emboss stamps on first and last few leaves, including title, bookplate of Charles T. Congdon (1821-1891). Jeff Weber Rare Books   181 - 34   2016 $35

Association – Wilson, J. G.

Le Corbeau, Adrien *The Forest Giant.* London: Jonathan Cape, 1924. First English edition, frontispiece and decorative border to titlepage with decorations at head of each text page, little very faint foxing to prelims and pencil note identifying Lawrence to titlepage, foolscap 8vo., original quarter yellow cloth with green boards, backstrip with printed label, a touch of wear to one corner, edges rough trimmed, dust jacket with darkened backstrip panel frayed at either end with some loss at foot, little chipping to corners, darkened overall, good, presentation copy inscribed by Charlotte F. Shaw to J. G. Wilson of Bumpus.   Blackwell's Rare Books   B186 - 252   2016   £400

Association – Wilson, J. M.

Party-Giving on Every Scale or the Cost of Entertainments with the Fashionable Modes of Arrangement. London: Frederick Warne & Co., 1882. Second edition, half title, original mustard decorated cloth, slightly rubbed and marked, signature of J. M. Wilson.   Jarndyce Antiquarian Books   CCXV - 19   2016   £75

Association – Wilson, James Lee

Craig, Edward Gordon 1872-1966 *Nothing or the Bookplate.* London: Chatto & Windus, 1924. First edition, limited edition, no. 33 of 280 copies, crown 8vo., original russet buckram lettered gilt on spine and cover, loosely inserted 2 original bookplates by E. G. Craig, this with further bookplate signed by Craig, bookplates hand colored, from the library of James Lee Wilson with his small neat bookplate by Leo Wyatt, loosely inserted compliments slip from London, otherwise very good+.   Any Amount of Books   2015 - C4661   2016   £250

Association – Wilson, Joseph

Brookes, Thomas *Apples of Gold for Young men and women...* London: Book Society for Promoting Christian Knowledge, 1831. New edition, contemporary half purple calf, little rubbed, spine faded, armorial bookplate of Joseph Wilson.   Jarndyce Antiquarian Books   CCXV - 81   2016   £20

Association – Wilson, Langford

Melfi, Leonard *Encounters: Six One-Act Plays.* New York: Random House, 1967. First printing, 8vo., author's 10 line presentation to playwright Langford Wilson, with recipient's name stamp, nice, scarce.   Second Life Books, Inc.   196 B - 196   2016 $100

Association – Wilson, Mary

Adams, Samuel *The Complete Servant.* London: Knight & Lacey, 1825. First edition, illustrations, later endpapers, contemporary half plain sheep, little rubbed, contemporary signature of Mary Wilson.   Jarndyce Antiquarian Books   CCXV - 6   2016   £125

Association – Wilson, R. J.

Darwin, Charles Robert 1809-1882 *The Origin of Species by Means of Natural Selection...* London: John Murray, 1891. Sixth edition, 8vo., original green cloth gilt, one folding chart, binding little rubbed, slight spotting to prelims, partially uncut, very good, presentation from R. J. Wilson to C. E. Byles the antiquarian writer.   Sotheran's Piccadilly Notes - Summer 2015 - 95   2016   £450

Association – Wilson, Richard Munkhouse

Walker, Thomas *Aristology; or the Art of Dining.* London: George Bell & Sons, 1881. Half title, 24 page catalog (Nov. 1880), original red cloth, marked and worn, armorial bookplate of Richard Munkhouse Wilson.   Jarndyce Antiquarian Books   CCXV - 459   2016   £35

Association – Wilson, Susan

Fenwick, Eliza *Visits to the Juvenile Library or Knowledge Proved to be the Source of Happiness.* London: printed by Bernard & Sultzer for Tabart & Co...., 1805. First edition, frontispiece, plates, 36 page catalog, 20th century quarter calf with earlier marbled boards, lower board slightly creased, contemporary signature of Susan Wilson.   Jarndyce Antiquarian Books   CCXV - 682   2016   £120

Association – Windale, Mary

Ventum, Harriet *Selina, a Novel, Founded on Facts.* London: printed for C. Law, 1800. First edition, 3 volumes, titlepage to volume III in very good facsimile on contemporary paper, some browning and finger marking to text in places, offsetting on pastedowns and endpapers, full contemporary sheep, spines rubbed, lacking labels, some cracking across bands, heads chipped but joints sound, early signatures to titlepages of Mary Windale and later 19th century name of T. E. Headlam, Gilmonby Hall (Yorkshire). Jarndyce Antiquarian Booksellers   CCXVI - 577   2016   £750

Association – Winiarczyk, Andrew

Kelly, Edward F. *Steady-On! The Combat History of Co C 25th Tank BN.* Munich: Buch un Kunstdruckerei Hanns Lindner, 1945. First edition, quarto, photos, maps, stapled wrappers, small tears at spine ends, slightly age toned, very good or better, signed by the commanding officer Lt. Col. Andrew Winiarczyk, very uncommon.   Between the Covers Rare Books   204 - 145   2016 $250

Association – Winkelman, Margaret

Vergilius Maro, Publius *Les Bucoliques De Virgile.* Paris: Scripta & Picta, 1953. First Villon edition, one of 245 copies (total edition), folio, text pages loosely inserted in publisher's paper folder, chemise and slipcase, 45 original lithographs by Jacques Villon, hors- and in texte, printed on Arches wove paper by F. Mourlot, outer slipcase faded and worn along edges, book very fine, bookplate of Margaret Winkelman, Paul Valery's copy.   Oak Knoll Books   310 - 7   2016 $4500

Association – Winmile, Charles

Horatius Flaccus, Quintus *Carmina Sapphica. (and) Carmina Alcaica.* Chelsea: Ashendene Press, 1903. One of 150 copies on Japanese paper (25 on vellum), 185 x 128mm., 2 volumes, original flexible vellum, gilt titling on spine, housed in custom cloth folding box with separate compartments for each book, initials hand painted by Graily Hewiett, printed in red and black, "Carmina Alcaica" inscribed to Philip Webb by printer and dated 1903 with further ink notation that was given by Webb's executor to Walter Knight Shirley, Earl Ferrers on 22 Feb. 1916 and by him to Charles Winmile Jan 1937, verso of 'Carmina Sapphica" with morocco bookplate of Cortlandt Bishop, pastedowns little waffled, otherwise mint.   Phillip J. Pirages   67 - 13   2016 $4000

Association – Winter, William

Hatton, Joseph *Cigarette Papers: for After-Dinner Smoking.* Philadelphia: Lippincott, 1892. 8vo., drawings, letter from author to dramatist William Winter laid in, gray cloth stamped in black, red, gilt and white, cover somewhat worn, hinge tender, otherwise very good.   Second Life Books, Inc.   196A - 736   2016 $65

Association – Winters, Roland

Krasna, Norman *Who Was that lady I Saw You With?* New York: Random House, 1958. First edition, 8vo., very good in little soiled and worn dust jacket, cast member Roland Winters' copy, signed by 30 members of the cast.   Second Life Books, Inc.   196A - 984   2016 $325

Association – Wirelo, S.

Petau, Denis *...Opus de Theologicis Dogmatibus Nunc primum Septem Voluminibus Comprehensum, in Mediorem Ordinem Redactum...* Venice: Remondiana, 1757. Best edition, 6 books in 7 and bound in 2 volumes, folio, title in red and black, half title, each book with its separate title, titlepage portrait engraving of Denis and additional woodcut initials and head and tailpieces all volumes, first volume free endpapers slightly torn, contemporary full vellum, gilt stamped spines, first volume stained, second volume lower corners gently bumped, bookplates of Ex Oblatororum S. Caroli Bibliotheca Bayswater (Henry Edward Manning 1808-1892), Pitts Theology Library bookplates, C. J. Stewart bookseller label, titlepage ownership signatures and inscriptions of Engelbert Klupfel, 1769 and Steph. Wirelo(?), rare, fine.   Jeff Weber Rare Books   181 - 26   2016 $750

Association – Witham, John

White, John *A Way to the Tree of Life.* London: Miles Fletcher for R. Royston, 1647. First edition, 8vo., without final blank titlepage browned and slightly shaved at fore-edge, small piece torn away from blank corner of A4, browned throughout with small dark marks on N6-8, final blank page stained by turn-ins and with edges little ragged, contemporary calf, rebacked, corners repaired, new endleaves, small inscription of John Witham, inscription of Philip Pecke, from the library of James Stevens Cox (1910-1997).   Maggs Bros. Ltd.   1447 - 448   2016   £500

Association – Woledge, Geoffrey

Pope, Alexander 1688-1744 *Selecta Poemata Italorum qui Latine Scripserunt.* London: impensis J. & P. Knapton, 1740. 2 volumes, 8vo., touch of foxing to titlepages, contemporary sprinkled calf, spines in six compartments with raised bands, numbered in gilt, rest with gilt decoration, much rubbed, joints and corners neatly repaired, spines bit darkened with endcaps worn down and labels lost, but sound, ownership inscriptions of Geoffrey Woledge, Birmingham 1937 and A. Montague Summers (1899).   Unsworths Antiquarian Booksellers Ltd.   E01 - Early Printing - 18   2016   £300

Association – Wolfe, John Lewis

Poleni, Giovanni *Memorie Istoriche Della gran Cupola Del Tempio Vaticano...* Padova: Nella Stamperia dei Seminario, 1748. Folio, five books in one volume, contemporary quarter calf over patterned paper covered boards, brown morocco and gilt lettering piece to spine, all edges speckled red, folding etched plates, binding rather rubbed at extremities, corners bumped some loss of paper covering boards, internally bright, crisp copy, ink signature of John Lewis Wolfe, engraved armorial bookplate of Joseph Gwilt (1784-1863), engraved bookplate of Sir Albert Richardson (1880-1964).   Sotheran's   Piccadilly Notes - Summer 2015 - 239   2016   £3955

Association – Wollascott, William

Pitt, Robert *The Antidote; or the preservative of Health and Life and the Restorative of Physick to its Sincerity and Perfection.* London: printed for John Nutt near Stationers Hall, 1704. One of two issues of the first edition, this issue with second line of imprint beginning "Stationers", 8vo. half title, very good, clean copy, full contemporary panelled calf, raised bands, slight wear to head of spine, very slight crack to upper section of front joint, small faint ink splash to leading edge of book block, bookplate of William Wollascott.   Jarndyce Antiquarian Booksellers   CCXVI - 454   2016   £350

Association – Wolle

Winterton, Ralph *Poetae Minores Graeci.* Cambridge: Ex Officina Joan Hayes sold by J. Ray, E. Dobson, P. Campbell & J. Milner, Dublin Bibliopolis, 1699. First edition, 12mo., titlepage lightly soiled and spotted with 3 small holes from stitched in inner margin, last page dusty, some occasional spotting and soiling, few headlines shaved by binder, early 18th century calf backed boards, lined with light blue paper (head of spine chipped), blindstamped name on front cover has been scratched out, 18th century armorial bookplate of Wolle family of Forenaughts, Ireland, from the library of James Stevens Cox (1910-1997).   Maggs Bros. Ltd.   1447 - 458   2016   £240

Association – Wood, Clement

Wheelock, John Hall *Poems 1911-1936.* New York: Scribner, 1936. First edition, 8vo., very nice in very lightly worn dust jacket, inscribed by author with 9 line poem to poet Clement Wood.   Second Life Books, Inc.   196 B - 869   2016 $75

Association – Wood, John

Dickens, Charles 1812-1870 *Sketches by Boz.* London: Chapman & Hall, 1839. First collected edition in original cloth, frontispiece, two engraved titles, one with Chapman and Hall imprint and one without, plates, slight foxing, excellently executed repairs to inner hinges, uncut in original vertical grained cloth, blocked in blind, spine lettered gilt, spine little faded, armorial bookplate of John Wood, green cloth foldover box, slightly spotted, very good, bright.   Jarndyce Antiquarian Booksellers   CCXVIII - 59   2016   £2250

Association – Woodin, William Hartmann

The Death Fetch, or the Student of Gottingen Founded on a Popular Opinion, Prevalent Even at the Present Time.... London: printed for T. Hughes, 35 Ludgate Street, n.d., 1826. First edition, 12mo. insesrted folded frontispiece with color frontispiece, original three quarter brown levant morocco, tooled and titled in gold by Morrell of London, armorial bookplate of J. Barton Townsend, later bookplate of William Hartmann Woodin.   John W. Knott, Jr./L.W. Currey, Inc.   Fall-Winter 2015 - 17501   2016 $2500

Association – Woods, Grosvenor

Franquet De Frangueville, Sophia Matilda Palmer, Countess *Mrs. Penicott's Lodger and Other Stories.* London: Macmillan & Co., 1887. Half title, original pale blue cloth, blocked and lettered in red, spine lettered gilt, spine faded, otherwise very good, signed by author "Connaught House" and bookplate of Grosvenor Woods.   Jarndyce Antiquarian Booksellers   CCXVII - 211   2016   £75

Association – Woolman, Sarah

Woolman, John   1720-1772 *The Works of John Woolman.* Philadelphia: Joseph Cruikshank, 1774. Contemporary sheep, very skillfully rebacked in period Quaker style, boards scuffed, edges worn, discoloration on pages 146-47 from old laid in newspaper cutting, else very good, inscribed 'Sarah Woolman to Jno. Townsend", later miniscule signature of Charles L. Cresson, superb presentation, John Townsend was author's close friend.   Joseph J. Felcone, Inc.   Books from Five Centuries: a Miscellany - 154   2016 $1200

Association – Wordsworth

Arnold, Matthew   1822-1888 *Culture and Anarchy: an Essay in Political and Social Criticism.* London: Smith, Elder & Co., 1869. First edition, half title, pencil notes, original brown cloth, bevelled boards, little rubbed, armorial booklabel "Presented by Bishop Wordsworth's family", ownership signature of J. Henry Shorthouse.   Jarndyce Antiquarian Booksellers   CCXVII - 15   2016   £420

Association – Wordsworth, Charles

Lucretius Carus, Titus *Der Rerum Natura Libri Sex.* Birmingham: Typis Johannis Baskerville, 1772. 12mo. light age toning, few marginal pencil marks, contemporary calf, spine divided by gilt fillets, red morocco lettering piece, other compartments with central gilt fillets, rubbed, front joint cracking but strong, bookplate of Charles Wordsworth (1806-1902) covering earlier bookplate, good.   Blackwell's Rare Books   Greek & Latin Classics VII - 60   2016   £150

Association – Worms, Maurice

Seneca, Lucius Annaeus *Singulares Sententiae Centum Aliquot Versibus ex Codd Pall & Frising Auctae & Correctae, Studio & Opera Jani Gruteri...* Lugduni Batavorum: apud Johannem du Vivie, 1708. 8vo., additional engraved titlepage, titlepage in red and plate with engraved vignette, woodcut head and tailpieces, sporadic light foxing, evidence in gutter preceding engraved title of presentation certificate removal, contemporary vellum prize binding, gilt spine with red morocco label, gilt crest of The Hague to each board, edges sprinkled red, spine label little chipped, some greyish marks, boards slightly bowed, top edge dusty, bookplate of Maurice B. Worms, modern ink inscription "A.S.B. from A.J.C. Easter mcmlx". Unsworths Antiquarian Booksellers Ltd. 30 - 137 2016 £200

Association – Wray, Bert

Duncan, George P. *The Gentleman's Book of Manners or Etiquette.* London: William Nicholson & Sons, circa, 1890. Half title, frontispiece, final ad leaf, original red cloth, bevelled boards, slight worming to following inner hinge, signature of Bert Wray, Nov. 1904, onc leading f.e.p. Jarndyce Antiquarian Books CCXV - 169 2016 £30

Association – Wright, Michael

Larkin, Philip 1922-1985 *Miscellaneous Pieces 1955-1982.* London: Faber and Faber, 1983. First edition, first impression, paperback original, 8vo., original photographic wrappers, soft crease in top corner of front wrapper, otherwise very fine, presentation by author for Michael Wright of Faber and Faber. James S. Jaffe Rare Books Occasional List: Winter 2016 - 90 2016 $3500

Association – Wright, Stuart

Goyen, William *Wonderful Plant.* Winston-Salem: Palaemon Press ltd., 1980. Limited numbered edition of 160, 100 numbered 1-100 for public sale, 60 numbered i-lx for distribution, marbled boards made by Daniel Guyot of Seattle, this copy No. 1 signed by author, presentation from author to publisher Stuart Wright, note from author to publisher laid in along with copy of news clipping. Oak Knoll Books 310 - 130 2016 $300

Warren, Robert Penn 1905-1989 *Two Poems.* Winston Salem: Palaemon Press, 1980. First edition, #72 of 350 numbered copies (of a total edition of 376) signed by author and artist on colophon page, inscribed by publisher Stuart Wright for William Meredith, fine. Charles Agvent William Meredith - 118 2016 $150

Association – Wright, Wilfred

Austin, Ethel Mildred King Britten *Unending Journey.* London: Thornton Butterworth, 1939. First edition, original brick red cloth, spine lettered gilt, illustrated dust jackets (price clipped), map, spine little sunned, wrappers with few minor chips, very good, from the collection of travel writer Peter Hupkirk, ownership inscription of Wilfred G. Wright dated April 1939. Sotheran's Piccadilly Notes - Summer 2015 - 23 2016 £278

Association – Wurth, Carl

Mizauldo, Antonio *Centuriae IX Memorabilium Utilium Ac Juncdorum in Aphorismos...* Frankfurt: Nicolas Hoffman, 1613. Small folio, 3 parts in 1 volume, some misnumbering of pages, printer's device on each of the three titles, light paper toning, occaisonal stains, contemporary limp vellum, manuscript spine title, lacks ties, rear joint partly torn, bookplate signed by Fritz Laber of Dr. Carl Wurth, early ownership signatures of Ernnet Casparus Maismis, very good. Jeff Weber Rare Books 181 - 21 2016 $600

Association – Wyatt-Paine

Hone, William *The Every-Day Book and Table Book or Everlasting Calendar of Popular Amusements, Sports, Pastimes....* London: William Tegg and Co., 1847. 1848., Volumes I-III + Year Book, 8vo., frontispiece to each volume, publisher's catalog rear of first volume, volume III final leaf loosening, small paper repair to Year Book not affecting text, little toned, occasional marginal smudges, recent red cloth, black morocco gilt spine labels, endcaps creased little rubbed, some light scratches, edges uncut and dusted, bookplate of Wyatt-Paine. Unsworths Antiquarian Booksellers 30 - 75 2016 £140

Association – Wyatt, Leo

Craig, Edward Gordon 1872-1966 *Nothing or the Bookplate.* London: Chatto & Windus, 1924. First edition, limited edition, no. 33 of 280 copies, crown 8vo., original russet buckram lettered gilt on spine and cover, loosely inserted 2 original bookplates by E. G. Craig, this with further bookplate signed by Craig, bookplates hand colored, from the library of James Lee Wilson with his small neat bookplate by Leo Wyatt, loosely inserted compliments slip from London, otherwise very good+. Any Amount of Books 2015 - C4661 2016 £250

Association – Wyatt, Stephen

Kneale, Nigel *The Year of the Sex Olympics and Other TV Plays.* London: Ferret Fantasy, 1976. First edition, original ochre cloth lettered gilt on spine, ownership signature of S(tephen) Wyatt, author of Doctor Who books, about fine in very good, slightly tanned dust jacket, complete with no nicks or tears, excellent condition. Any Amount of Books 2015 - A6882 2016 £150

Association – Wyeth, N. C.

Thoreau, Henry David   1817-1882 *Men of Concord.* Boston: Houghton Mifflin, 1936. First edition, 4to., green cloth, small erasure mark on endpaper, else fine in dust jacket (small archival mend at spine, otherwise very good+_, illustrations by N. C. Wyeth, this copy signed and dated by Wyeth on titlepage, great copy.   Aleph-bet Books, Inc.   111 - 493   2016 $2500

Association – Wylde, C. A.

Becke, Louis *Ridan the Devil and Other Stories.* London: T. Fisher Unwin, 1899. First edition, presentation copy inscribed by author for C. A. Wylde, May 10 1899, quite scarce thus, very good in original black cloth boards with gilt title to spine, light rubbing to boards, tips of corners exposed, minor wear to spine ends and hinges, light rubbing to boards, tips of corners exposed, minor wear to spine ends and hinges, slight cock to spine, light foxing to endpages and few creased corners, else interior clean, very good.   The Kelmscott Bookshop   12 - 9   2016 $250

Association – Wyndham, Francis

Blackwood, Caroline *The Stepdaughter.* London: Duckworth, 1976. First edition, quarto, near fine in like dust jacket slightly creased at bottom edge, presentation copy from author inscribed for fellow writer Francis Wyndham.   Peter Ellis   112 - 41   2016   £150

Association – Wyngard, Diane

Behrman, S. N. *No Time for comedy: a Play in Three Acts.* London: Hamish Hamilton, 1939. First edition, 8vo., original worn printed wrappers, (also issued in cloth), round-robin copy, signed by members of the London production, Diane Wyngard, Rex Harrison, Lilian Palmer, Elizabeth Welch and 3 others.   Second Life Books, Inc.   196A - 97   2016 $250

Association – Wynne-Finch, Charles Arthur

Freeman, G. J. *Sketches in Wales or a Diary of Three Walking Excursions in that Principality.* London: Longman, Rees Orme, Brown and Green, 1826. First edition, 8vo., full claret leather with attractive gilt tooling, corners and edges lightly bumped and worn, spine has title and lots of gilt tooling, edges lightly bumped internally, marbled endpapers, Duke of Essex bookplate, bookplate of Charles Arthur Wynne Finch, 15 black and white plates.   Simon Finch   2015 - 004316   2016 $296

Association – Wynne, Frances

Stanley, William Owen *Memoirs on Remains of Ancient Dwellings in Holyhead Island Mostly of Circular Form called Cyttlau'r Gwyddelod...* London/Chester: James Bain/Marshall & Hughes, 1871. First edition, gold stamped sienna cloth, modest edgewear, signed "Frances Wynne from W. O. Stanley March 26 1881", stunning engraved bookplate of designer Harry Soane for Col. John Charles Wynne Finch, very faint bookstore stamp to front cover, many engravings, fold out map intact.   Simon Finch   2015 - 055187   2016 $225

Association – Wynne, Mary

Ovidius Naso, Publius *Metamorphoses in Fifteen Books.* Dublin: printed by S. Powell for G. Risk, G. Ewing and W. Smith, 1727. 12mo., engraved frontispiece, 16 plates, few plates little frayed at edges, one with part of fore-and lower-edge lost outside of platemark, some soiling and staining, early ownership inscription of Owen and Mary Wynne to titlepage, contemporary dark calf label lost from spine, rear flyleaf excised, two corners and head of spine, some old scratches and little rubbing, sound.   Blackwell's Rare Books   Greek & Latin Classics VII - 66   2016   £200

Association – Wynne, Maurice

Callieres, Francois De *The Knowledge of the World and the Attainments Useful in the Conduct of Life.* London: printed for the translator and sold by R. Baldwin &c., 1770? half title, 12mo., prelims misbound, corners creased, tear to H4 affecting 4 words, lacking following f.e.p., uncut in contemporary quarter calf, marbled boards, leading hinge little worn, elaborate signature of Maurice Wynne on leading f.e.p., very unsophisticated copy.   Jarndyce Antiquarian Books   CCXV - 95   2016   £520

Association – Wynne, Owen

Ovidius Naso, Publius *Metamorphoses in Fifteen Books.* Dublin: printed by S. Powell for G. Risk, G. Ewing and W. Smith, 1727. 12mo., engraved frontispiece, 16 plates, few plates little frayed at edges, one with part of fore-and lower-edge lost outside of platemark, some soiling and staining, early ownership inscription of Owen and Mary Wynne to titlepage, contemporary dark calf label lost from spine, rear flyleaf excised, two corners and head of spine, some old scratches and little rubbing, sound.   Blackwell's Rare Books   Greek & Latin Classics VII - 66   2016   £200

Association – Yamaguchi, H. S. K.

De Garis, Frederic *We Japanese: Being Descriptions of Many of the Customs, Manners, Ceremonies, Festivals....* Miyanoshita: Fujiya Hotel, 1936. Third printing, 8vo., copiously illustrated, paper wrappers, covered with brocade, sewn in Japanese style, with paper label, in cloth covered folding case, fastened with cords and bone pins, cover of book slightly soiled on front, case little worn at corners and slightly unglued at interior spine, otherwise very good, tight copy, presentation from H. S. K. Yamaguchi for Katharine A. Shapes.   Second Life Books, Inc. 196A - 397   2016 $150

Association – Yaw, Margot Couzens

Dickens, Charles   1812-1870 *Life of Our Lord.* New York: Simon & Schuster, 1934. First American edition, half title, title printed in red and black, deluxe copy in full cream embossed parchment, spine lettered gilt, contemporary gift inscription, booklabel of Margot Couzens Yaw, very good. Jarndyce Antiquarian Booksellers   CCXVIII - 715   2016   £70

Association – Yeats, James

Yeats, Grant David *A Biographical Sketch of the Life and Writings of Patrick Colquhoun.* London: printed by G. Smeeton, 1818. First edition, 8vo., frontispiece, rather offset on to titlepage, original printed boards but boards rather soiled, presentation copy inscribed in ink at head of title Royal society of Literature from author's son, James 20/3/55, scarce.   John Drury Rare Books   2015 - 22810   2016 $323

Association – Yellin, Herb

Oates, Joyce Carol   1938- *All the Good People I've Left Behind.* Santa Barbara: Black Sparrow Press, 1979. First edition, some sunning at edge of boards, very good or better in fine, original unprinted glassine dust jacket, one of 1000 hardbound copies, dedication copy inscribed by author Herb Yellin.   Between the Covers Rare Books   204 - 90   2016 $1500

Oates, Joyce Carol   1938- *New Heaven, New Earth: The Visionary Experience in Literature.* New York: Vanguard Press, 1974. First edition, fine in fine dust jacket, inscribed by author to Herb Yellin, fairly uncommon.   Between the Covers Rare Books   208 - 60   2016 $250

Oates, Joyce Carol   1938- *With Shuddering Fall.* New York: Vanguard Press, 1964. First edition, near fine in spine sunned, very good dust jacket with ink spot on front panel, warmly inscribed by Oates to Herb Yellin.   Between the Covers Rare Books   208 - 59   2016 $400

Updike, John   1932-2009 *The Angels.* Pensecola: King and Queen Press, 1968. First edition, 24mo., string tied printed pale blue wrappers, one of 150 hand printed copies, very slight sunning at extremities else fine, issued unsigned, this copy inscribed by author for Herb Yellin, very uncommon.   Between the Covers Rare Books   204 - 118   2016 $1500

Updike, John   1932-2009 *The Carpentered Hen and Other Tame Creatures.* New York: Harper and Bros., 1958. First edition, one signature fallen slightly forward as usual, else fine in fine, first issue dust jacket with later (probably publisher's) price sticker over original price, inscribed by author for Herb Yellin.   Between the Covers Rare Books   204 - 116   2016 $2500

Updike, John   1932-2009 *The Complete Henry Bech: Twenty Stories.* New York: Alfred A. Knopf, 2001. First edition thus, fine in fine dust jacket, inscribed by author for Herb Yellin, notable association, uncommon edition.   Between the Covers Rare Books   208 - 86   2016 $250

Updike, John   1932-2009 *In Memoriam Felix Felis.* Leamington Spa: Sixth Chamber Press, 1989. First edition, this conforms to the issues of 1/26 lettered copies but unlettered and signed by author and artist, 6 illustrations by R B. Kitaj, quarter cloth and paper covered boards, fine in lightly rubbed near fine illustrated slipcase, inscribed by author for Herb Yellin.   Between the Covers Rare Books   204 - 122   2016 $1500

Updike, John   1932-2009 *The Music School.* New York: Alfred A. Knopf, 1966. First edition, first issue, one corner tiny bit bumped, ele fine in slightly spine toned, very near fine dust jacket with two tiny tears, inscribed by author for Herb Yellin.   Between the Covers Rare Books   204 - 117   2016 $850

Updike, John   1932-2009 *On Meeting Authors.* Newburyport: Wickford Press, 1968. First edition, copy number 12 of 250 numbered copies, stapled wrappers with applied printed label, fine, this copy inscribed by author for Herb Yellin, very uncommon.   Between the Covers Rare Books   204 - 119   2016 $1200

Updike, John   1932-2009 *Rabbit Angstrom, a Tetralogy: Rabbit, Run, Rabbit Redux, Rabbit Rich, Rabbit at Rest.* New York: Alfred A. Knopf, 1995. First edition thus, fine in fine dust jacket, inscribed by author for Herb Yellin.   Between the Covers Rare Books   208 - 88   2016 $250

Updike, John 1932-2009 *Rabbit Run; Rabbit, Redux; Rabbit is Rich; Rabbit at Rest.* Norwalk: Easton Press, 1989. First Easton Press edition, 4 volumes, illustrations by Richard Sparks full leather, gilt, fine, no Easton bookplate, each volume inscribed by author for Herb Yellin. Between the Covers Rare Books 204 - 123 2016 $800

Association – Yeminez, E.

Amman, Jost *Bibliorum Utriusque Testamenti Icones, Summor Artificio Expressae Historias Sacras and Vivum Exhibentes & Oculis Summa cum Gratia Repraesentantes....* Frankfurt: Christoph Corvinus & Sigmund Feyerabend, 1571. First edition, 8vo., 19th century blue morocco, triple blind fillet on cover, title lettered in gilt on spine, inner edge richly gilt and signed Bauzonnet-Trautz', marbled edges, gilt edges, silk bookmark, woodcut coats of arms of Johann Fichard and Konrad Weis, 200 fine oval woodcuts within ms. frames by Jose Amman, many signed with his initials, IA, bookplates of Edward Arnold, Dorking, E. Yeminez, Lyon and Allan Heywood Bright, London. Maggs Bros. Ltd. 1474 - 12 2016 £4500

Association – Yonge, James

Tyson, Edward *Carigueya, seu Marsupiale Americanum or the Anatomy of an Opossum, Dissected at Gresham College.* London: for Sam. Smith and Benj. Walford, 1698. First separate edition, small 4to., 2 folding engraved plates, one slightly shaved at foot, corners and edges occasionally bumped, disbound (traces of leather visible on spine), stitched (apparently a fairly early date) into a portion of 17th century printed singing manual, from the library of James Stevens Cox (1910-1997), 18th century ink lot number, Cox's pencil notes inside front cover 'James Yonge's copy. Maggs Bros. Ltd. 1447 - 421 2016 £1800

Association – Yorke, James

Hesiod *Opera et Dies. Theogonia. Scutum Herculis.* Venice: in aedibus Batholomaei Zanetti, 1537. First edition with Scholia, first text leaf printed in red and black, several woodcuts within text, including one full page, margins of early leaves dusty and with one or two small tidy repairs, occasional dampstaining to lower margin, particularly at end, gathering (omicron) bound out of order and inside gathering, occasional old underlining and notes in red crayon, 4to., 17th century English calf, boards ruled in gilt and blind with central decorative gilt lozenge, rebacked preserving old backstrip, little marked and chipped, gift bookplate of James Yorke, bishop of Ely, good. Blackwell's Rare Books Greek & Latin Classics VII - 31 2016 £300

Hesiod *Opera et Dies.* Venice: in aedibis Bartholomaei Zanetti, 1537. First edition with Scholia, first text leaf printed in red and black, several woodcuts within text, margins of early leaves dusty and with one or two small tidy repairs, occasional dampstaining to lower margin (particularly at end), gathering (omicron) bound out of order and inside gathering (xi), occasional old underlining and notes in red crayon, 4to., 17th century English calf, boards ruled in gilt and blind with central decorative gilt lozenge, rebacked preserving old backstrip, little marked and chipped, gift bookplate of James Yorke, Bishop of Ely, good. Blackwell's Rare Books B186 - 73 2016 £3000

Association – Young, Al

Coleman, Janet *Mingus/Mingus: Two Memoirs.* Berkeley: Creative Arts, 1989. First edition, photos, green cloth, nice in slightly scuffed dust jacket, Al Young's presentation for Andy Davis. Second Life Books, Inc. 196A - 317 2016 $45

Association – Young, Alison

Young, Andrew *The Thirteenth Key.* privately printed, 1985. Limited to 100 copies, signed by Alison Young, poet's daughter, very good. I. D. Edrich Crime - 2016 £25

Association – Young, Arthur William

Pascal, Blaise *Les Provinciales ou Lettres Ecrites par Louis de Montalte...* Paris: Charpentier, 1875. New edition, octavo, period binding of full blue straight grain calf, raised bands, gilt decorated spine, gilt rules and inner and outer dentelles, marbled endpapers, all edges gilt, armorial bookplate of Edward Hilton Young, 1st Baron Kennet of the Dene, gift inscription "Arthur William Young with best wishes from Margaret Lucia Young 27th June 1882", slight scuffing to hinges, very good. Peter Ellis 112 - 287 2016 £150

Trotter, Lionel J. *The Life of John Nicholson, Solider and Adminstrator based on private and hitherto....* London: John Murray, 1900. First edition, octavo, 2 plates and 3 folding maps, period fine binding by Bumpus, full brown morocco with raised bands, gilt rules and devices to spine, inner dentelles elaborately gilt, top edge gilt, armorial bookplate of Kennet of Dene, contemporary (1900) ownership inscription of a member of the family (Arthur W. Young), near fine, attractive binding. Peter Ellis 112 - 181 2016 £125

Association – Young, Margaret Lucia

Pascal, Blaise *Les Provinciales ou Lettres Ecrites par Louis de Montalte...* Paris: Charpentier, 1875. New edition, octavo, period binding of full blue straight grain calf, raised bands, gilt decorated spine, gilt rules and inner and outer dentelles, marbled endpapers, all edges gilt, armorial bookplate of Edward Hilton Young, 1st Baron Kennet of the Dene, gift inscription "Arthur William Young with best wishes from Margaret Lucia Young 27th June 1882", slight scuffing to hinges, very good.   Peter Ellis   112 - 287   2016   £150

Association – Zaehnsdorf

Berjeau, J. P. *Book-Worm (First two volumes) the The Bookworm, a Literary and Bibliographical Review.* London: Worm, 1867-1871. volumes 2-5 (of 5 total), tall 8vo., contemporary half blue calf with marbled paper covered boards, top edge gilt, signed bindings by Zaehnsdorf, from the Zaehnsdorf reference library with bookplate, rubbed along hinges,.   Oak Knoll Books   310 - 57   2016 $600

Bonnardot, A. *Die Kusnt, Kupferstiche zu Restauriren und Flecken aus Papier zu Entfernen.* Quedlinburg: G. Basse, 1859. First German edition, small 8vo., contemporary quarter brown calf, red cloth, top edge gilt, covers rubbed with wear at head of spine, from the reference library of Zaehnsdorf Co. with commemorative booklabel loosely inserted with their bookplate.   Oak Knoll Books   310 - 12   2016 $1500

Halfer, Josef *Die Fortschritte der Marmorierkunst. ein Praktisches Handbuch fur Buchbinder und Buntpapierfabrikanten.* Stuttgart: Wilhelm Leo, 1891. Second edition, 8vo., later half red calf, marbled paper covered boards, five raised bands, top edge gilt, signed binding by Zaehnsdorf, with 5 leaves of single mounted marbled paper specimens + 5 leaves each with 6 mounted marbled paper specimens, from the reference library of Zaehnsdorf and Company with commemorative booklabel loosely inserted, with bookplate of Zaehnsdorf Co., tipped in is two page ALS by Richard Leo to Mr. Zaehnsdorf, rubbed along hinges and soiled along edges.   Oak Knoll Books   310 - 9   2016 $3500

Association – Zeigler, Johann Geisel

Estienne, Henri   1528-1598 *Schediasmatum Variorum id est Observationum, Emendationum, Expositioum, Didquisitionum Libri Tres....* Geneva: Excudebat Henricus Stephanus, 1578-1589. First edition, some light browning, few marginal notes in ink, old ownership inscription to titlepage of Johann Geisel?) Zeigler, 8vo, 2 parts bound together in late 18th century mottled calf spine gilt, red morocco lettering piece, "BRUNCK" lettered direct in gilt at foot, marbled endpapers, front joint splitting but strong, some rubbing to joints and edges, good, this the copy of Richard Francois Philippe Brunck (1729-1803).   Blackwell's Rare Books   B184 - 41   2016   £1200

Association – Zelinksky, Paul

Grimm, The Brothers *Rapunzel.* New York: Dutton, 1997. Stated first edition, first printing with 1-10 code, pictorial boards, as new in as new dust jacket, illustrations by artist, Paul Zelinsky, this copy inscribed by artist.   Aleph-bet Books, Inc.   112 - 529   2016 $225

Association – Zemach, Margot

Grimm, The Brothers *The Fisherman and His Wife.* New York: Farrar, Straus Giroux, 1908. Stated first edition, cloth, fine in dust jacket creased on corner, else very good+, full and partial page color illustrations by Margot Zemach, laid in are 2 handwritten letters from artist.   Aleph-bet Books, Inc.   112 - 530   2016 $150

Association – Zufall, Robert

Fischer, Henry *Bred in the Bone. an Anthology.* Princeton: Ampersand Press, 1945. First edition, cloth, #300 of 325 printed, inscribed and signed by one of the contributors, Frederick Buechner for William Meredith, Christmas 1974, laid in ALS from Buechner to Meredith, very good, likely issued without dust jacket, with brief ALS by another contributor, Robert Zufall.   Charles Agvent   William Meredith - 21   2016 $250

Association – Zukofsky, Louis

Duncan, Robert *From the Maginogion.* Princeton: Quarterly Review of Literature, 1959. First edition, offprint from Quarterly Review of Lit. Volume XII, 8vo., printed wrappers, one of a small number of special copies used as Christmas greeting by Duncan with original drawing, signed "FD 63" on inside front wrapper, Louis Zukofsky's copy with his ownership signature dated 1963 at top of front wrapper, fine.   James S. Jaffe Rare Books   Occasional List: Winter 2016 - 53   2016 $1250

Fine Bindings

Binding – 16th Century

Bible. Latin - 1504 *Biblia Latina cum Postilla Hugo nis de Sancto charo.* Basle: Johann Froben for Johann Amerbach & Johann Petri and Anton Koberger in Nuremberg, 1504. Large folio, contemporary South German blind tooled deerskin? over wooden boards, upper panelled in blind and infilled with various large tools, leafy stems thistles and central compartment with acorns and eagle stamps, lower cover with diagonal fillets forming large lozenge, compartments infilled with same large tools plus further ornamental and leafy tool, spine with three raised bands infilled with repeated large leafy tool (some worming and minor areas of wear, lacks clasps and catches), superb example of monastic
 binding from the turn of the 16th century, ownership inscription in the hand of Bridgettines at Altomunster, Barvaria dated 1537, with title and shelfmark, pencil note recording in duplicate of Royal Library at Munich.   Maggs Bros. Ltd.   1474 - 10   2016   £3500

Binding – 17th Century

Catholic Church. Liturgy & Ritual *Canon Missae cum Praefationibus & Aliis non Nullius quae in ea Fere Communiter Dicuntur.* Venice: Ciera, 1630. Large title vignette of Last Supper and full page engraving of the Crucifixion, both signed "Johan, Faber / fecit in Venetia", folio, contemporary Italian brown morocco over paste boards, covers richly gilt in fanfare style incorporating at centre three bees and a sunburst tool repeatedly stamped in inner panel and frame, both familiar emblems of the Barberini family (joints and corners rubbed, small burn hole to upper edge of lower cover), very finely gilt tooled 17th century Italian binding for a member of the Barberini dynasty, decorated with their familiar emblems of 3 bees and sunburst, signs of use throughout but exquisite binding.   Maggs Bros. Ltd.   1474 - 19   2016   £3500

The Ladies Charity School House Roll of Highgate or a Subscription of Many Noble, Well Disposed Ladies for the Ease of Carrying it On. London: 1670. First edition, octavo, contemporary red morocco with elaborate gilt decorated patterns of floral ornaments, handles, knobs and shells on covers and five compartments on spine, with repeating pattern of smaller handles and knobs around spider like figures, 4 engraved plates, edges rubbed, two silk ties lacking (two present), lacking front free endpaper, very good, ink signature of Thomas Stedman, Oct. 1763.   The Brick Row Book Shop   Miscellany 69 - 12   2016 $2750

Binding – 18th Century

Epictetus *Enchiridion.* Parma: in aedibus Palatinis, typis Bodonianis, 1793. 2 pages with light offsetting from ribbon bookmark, 8vo., contemporary Italian sheep, strikingly marbled in shades of brown and green, boards bordered with triple gilt fillet, gilt flower cornerpieces, spine divided by raised bands, red morocco lettering pieces in second and third compartments, rest with central and corner gilt tools, marbled endpapers, edges gilt, merest touch of rubbing to extremities, modern booklabel, near fine, striking binding.   Blackwell's Rare Books   B186 - 58 2016   £1200

Homerus *The Iliad of Homer. (with) The Odyssey of Homer.* London: printed for J. Whiston &c., 1771. 1771, Iliad in 4 volumes, Odyssey in 5 volumes, together 9 volumes, engraved portraits, 2 plates, 2 folding maps, folding plate uniformly bound in slightly later full sprinkled calf, spines gilt in compartments, maroon and green morocco labels, armorial bookplate in all volumes of Elizabeth Bell, very good, attractive set, fine in 18th century binding.   Jarndyce Antiquarian Booksellers   CCXVII - 232   2016   £4250

Sallustius Crispus, C. *La Conjuracion e Catilina y la Guerra de Jugurta.* Madrid: J. Ibarra, 1772. Folio, contemporary Spanish binding of red morocco, covers decorated with gilt Greek key border having gilt suns at corners, enclosing an inner roll border of foliate design, falt spine gilt at either end with central neo-classical motif built of various tools, green morocco label, green silk doublures and marker, edges gilt, slight chip at headband, small worm holes at head and foot of spine, excellent copy, engraved titlepage by Montfort, portrait, 3 engraved plates (including a map) and numerous engravings by Montfort and Carmona after Maella, 3 engraved plates by Fabregat and Ballester and two plates of scripts, one of Phoenician coins, without half title found in most copies, bookplate of Jonathan and Phillida Gili, by Reynolds Stone.   Maggs Bros. Ltd.   1474 - 71   2016 $8500

Vergilius Maro, Publius *Opera.* Edinburgh: apud Robertum Freebarnium, 1732. Small stain to blank margin of last quarter, ownership inscription of Allan Livingston (early) and Mary Lloyd Aston (20th century), 24mo., contemporary Scottish red morocco, spine gilt in compartments containing a saltire design, boards with central cross shape made up of arabesques containing dotted lines with thistles at its points, corners with square tools containing fan sprays, endpapers of decorative paper in multiple colours with gilt, edges gilt, joints cracking but strong, leather bit darkened, good.   Blackwell's Rare Books   Greek & Latin Classics VII - 92   2016   £500

Binding – 19th Century

Byron, George Gordon Noel, 6th Baron   1788-1824   *The Works of Lord Byron in Verse and Prose.*   New York: Alexander V. Blake, 1838. Thick 4to., illustrations and facsimiles, fine full contemporary gilt stamped red morocco, some darkening of covers, but very good, browning of text. M & S Rare Books, Inc.   99 - 27   2016 $375

Campbell, Thomas   *The Pleasures of Hope.*   Glasgow: At the University Press, printed by J. Mundell, 1800. Fourth edition, 168 x 98mm., very attractive contemporaneous Etruscan style calf featuring blind gilt and acid treated decorations, very possibly by Edwards of Halifax, covers with gilt Greek key border, palmette frame and central panel containing a lyre from which thickening radiations emanate, smooth spine, divided into panels by multiple gilt rules, each panel with blindstamped lyre centerpiece enclosed by gilt flourishes, gilt dots on turn-ins, marbled endpapers, all edges gilt, 4 engraved plates of scenes from the poem, rear joint with thin half inch crack at bottom, extremities slightly rubbed, offsetting from engravings, leaves a shade less than bright, flyleaves faintly spotted, other trivial imperfections, still attractive copy, text with no serious condition issues, very pretty unsophisticated binding, remarkably well preserved. Phillip J. Pirages   67 - 41   2016 $1100

Ewald, Herman Frederik   *The Story of Waldemar Krone's Youth.*   Edinburgh: Edmonston and Douglas, 1867. First edition in English, 2 volumes, 184 x 121mm., attractive Arts and Crafts style dark green morocco elaborately gilt, each cover with 40 gilt lotus flowers (in five vertical rows of eight), flowers all flanked by gilt dot in each of the four corners, raised bands, spine panels with similar floral decoration, gilt titling ad turn-ins, all edges gilt, green spines inevitably sunned to an olive brown, joints and corners little rubbed, very isolated minor foxing, otherwise fine, clean and fresh internally, appealing binding lustrous and without significant wear.   Phillip J. Pirages   67 - 43   2016 $750

Gautier, Theophile   *Jean and Jeanette.*   Paris: Society des Beau Arts, 1890's, One of 550 numbered copies of the large paper 'Salon edition', royal 8vo., original half dark green morocco, spine decorated gilt with curving leafy stems with red floral onlays, small gilt butterflies, marbled paper sides and endpapers, top edges gilt, others untrimmed, engraved frontispiece, tinted vignette on titlepage, numerous tinted plates ad vignettes, all by Lalauze, tissue guards present, spine faded to brown, very nice.   Sotheran's Piccadilly Notes - Summer 2015 - 142   2016   £98

Gautier, Theophile   *Jean and Jeanette.*   Paris: Societe des Beaux Arts, circa, 1895. One of 20 copies of the edition de Deux Mondes (this copy numbered with a star), 270 x 200mm., sumptuous azure crushed morocco, lavishly gilt and inlaid in Art Nouveau style, covers with large central fleur-de-lys in gilt and lilac morocco within an elaborate frame by lily bouquets and garlands inlaid in lilac, orange and white, raised bands, spine gilt in compartments, smaller ones at head and tail with inlaid maroon fleur-de-lys, large central compartment with spray of lilies in orange and white and two compartments with gilt titling, very wide turn-ins with elaborate gilt floral and foliate decoration enclosing burnt orange morocco doublures, front doublure featuring an oval inset of white kidskin (or perhaps vellum) with hand colored engraving of female nude, ivory watered silk endleaves, blue marbled flyleaves, top edge gilt, other edges untrimmed and unopened with 76 charming engraved vignettes (representing 25 images, one in four states, the others in three states, black and white in text, black and white printed on mounted India paper and hand colored on special textured stock, latter two states with tiny additional accompanying figure in black and white or colored, all by Adolphe Lalauze, tissue guards, large paper copy, small vague scar on front cover (well masked with dye), spine faintly and evenly sunned, otherwise lovely book in fine condition, clean, fresh and bright inside and out.   Phillip J. Pirages   67 - 66   2016 $1250

Hawthorne, Nathaniel   1804-1864   *The Marble Faun or the Romance of Monte Beni.*   Boston and New York: printed at the Riverside Press for Houghton Mifflin and Co., 1890. 2 volumes, quite pretty contemporary sky blue crushed morocco lavishly gilt, covers with multiple plain and decorative rules enclosing a central panel seme with gilt daisies, raised bands, spine compartments densely gilt with central daisy enclosed by small tools and filigree cornerpieces, marbled endpapers, all edges gilt, 51 photogravure plates, including portrait of Hawthorne, front pastedowns and verso of front free endpapers, bookplate of Edward Karfiol, spines just slightly different shade of blue, especially fine set, bindings lustrous and unworn, immaculate internally.   Phillip J. Pirages   67 - 48   2016 $950

Lewis, Matthew Gregory 1775-1818 *Tales of Wonder.* London: printed by W. Bulmer and Co. for the author, 1801. First edition, 2 volumes, 260 x 159mm., contemporary calf in Etruscan style, possibly by Edwards of Halifax, each cover with gilt floral spray border (unusual for this style of binding) surrounding a terra cotta and deep burnt orange frame with palmettes stamped in black and blind, this frame enclosing panel diced and dotted in blind and with gilt cornerpieces and central medallion featuring an incised monochrome mythological painting, double raised bands flanking gilt pentaglyph and metope roll, gilt ruled spine compartments with open gilt dots and classical ornaments in blind, turn-ins with greek key gilt roll, marbled edges, neatly rebacked using most of original spines, hinges reinforced with matching paper in first volume and matching cloth in second, bookplate of E.L.", bookplate of Harry H. Blum, central images on covers of volume II somewhat indistinct, few leaves with faint spots, otherwise excellent, carefully restored binding, still retaining much of its original impressiveness and text very crisp and clean.   Phillip J. Pirages 67 - 42 2016 $1500

Lytton, Edward George Earle Lyton, Bulwer-Lytton, 1st Baron 1803-1873 *The Works of Edward Lytton Bulwer...* Philadelphia: E. L. Carey and A. Hart, 1836. Small 4to., 2 volumes, fine contemporary gilt stamped red morocco, some wear but very good, rare set.   M & S Rare Books, Inc. 99 - 26 2016 $450

Tagore, Sourindro Mohun *Hindu Loyalty: a Presentation of the Views and Opinions of the Sanskrit Authorities on the Subject of Loyalty...* Calcutta: printed by I. C. Bose and Co. and Pub. by author, 1883. First edition, 216 x 159mm., publisher's original Calcutta binding of dark green pebbled morocco, richly gilt, front cover with densely gilt frame enclosing gilt rolled panel with central vignette of Shiva (rear cover with an arabesque at center, otherwise identically gilt rolled raised bands, spine compartments heavily gilt with stippling and vegetal forms, gilt hatched turn-ins, all edges gilt, text bordered in red, slight loss of gilt to vignette, hint of dulling to spine, still fine, gilt very bright everywhere else, text remarkably clean and fresh.   Phillip J. Pirages 67 - 50 2016 $1250

Thomson, James *The Seasons.* London: Wilkie and Robinson, J. Walker, Cadell and Davies et al, 1811. 191 x 121mm., very pleasing contemporary crimson straight grain morocco, elaborately decorated in gilt and blind, covers with broad gilt fillet perimeter bordering a frame of gilt palmettes and then (closer in) fillets and palmettes in blind, raised bands with gilt dash-roll, spine compartments with symmetrically clustered arabesques, roses, open dots, stars and foliate tools, gilt rolled turn-ins, all edges gilt, 4 engraved allegorical plates designed by T. Unwins, inscribed "L. E./from the library of her brother / H. Duncombe e(x) dono A. Curzon", little foxing to plates, extraordinarily fine, text clean and fresh, lovely binding, very lustrous and virtually unworn.   Phillip J. Pirages 67 - 70 2016 $950

Webb, William *Minutes of Remarks on Subjects Picturesque, Moral and Miscellaneous....* London: Baldwin Cradock and Joy, Dublin: William Frederick Wakeman, 1827. First edition, 2 volumes, very pleasing contemporary sea green straight grain morocco, elaborately gilt, covers with gilt floral frame enclosing a central blindstamped arabesque, raised bands, spine compartments densely gilt with floral tools and volutes, turn-ins with decorative gilt densely gilt with floral tools and volutes, turn-ins with decorative gilt roll, light blue watered silk endleaves, all edges gilt, each volume with animated fore-edge painting set in Italian landscape; armorial bookplate of armorial bookplate of John Thornton Down, spines slightly and uniformly sunned, joints with just hint of rubbing, corners little bent, volume I lacking free endleaf at back, trivial imperfections internally, but extremely pretty set in essentially fine condition, bindings entirely solid with especially lustrous covers and text clean and fresh.   Phillip J. Pirages 67 - 165 2016 $2900

White, Henry Kirke *The Poetical Works.* London: William Pickering, 1830. 165 x 105mm., contemporary black morocco (unsigned but very possibly by Hayday), covers with border of three blind rules with large complex gilt lyre centerpiece, flat spine with titling and curvilinear panelling in gilt in Romantic style, with gilt decorated turn-ins, all edges gilt, expertly rebacked using original backstrip, blue buckram slipcase; with two fore-edge paintings showing Esher Place, Surrey and British Museum, Russell Street, printer's device on titlepage, frontispiece, front joints and extremities slightly rubbed, minor tear in fore margin of one leaf, scattered minor foxing in text, otherwise attractive, restored binding entirely sound, text clean, bright and fresh.   Phillip J. Pirages 67 - 151 2016 $1500

Binding – 20th Century

Dibdin, Thomas Frognall 1776-1847 *An Introduction to the Knowledge of Rare and Valuable Editions of the Greek and Latin Classics.* London: printed for Harding & Lepard, 1827. Fourth edition, 2 volumes, 292 x 1977, handsome early 20th century brown straight grain morocco, covers with gilt double fillet border, fleuron cornerpieces, raised bands, spines richly gilt with panels dominated by bold and complex quatrefoil incorporating spade-like tools and with palmette cornerpieces, turn-ins with two gilt fillets, marbled endpapers, all edges gilt, with facsimile of Greek and Latin text from the Complutensian Polyglot and volume I with specimen leaf laid down, as called for, large paper copy, engraved armorial bookplate of John William Pease, rear pastedown with vellum armorial bookplate of Lord Wardington, touch of rubbing to tail edge of boards, one leaf with thin band of soiling along four inches of the fore edge, light glue stain at lower corner of specimen leaf, endpapers with faint fox spots (isolated minor foxing elsewhere), other trivial imperfections but generally, very fine, text clean and fresh with vast margins and decorative bindings with no significant wear.   Phillip J. Pirages 67 - 112 2016 $4500

Dobson, Austin 1840-1921 *Old-World Idyls. (with) At the Sign of the Lyre.* London: Kegan Paul, Trench & Co., 1885. 1886, 159 x 102mm., 2 volumes, very attractive dark green crushed morocco gilt, (stamp-signed "S. E. H. February 23 1907" - binder not identified), covers bordered by double gilt rules with tulip cornerpieces, raised bands, spines gilt in compartments tooled with gilt curls and tulips, gilt titling, turn-ins with plain and decorative gilt rules and volute cornerpieces, brown silk endleaves, top edges gilt, other edges untrimmed in (slightly rubbed) suede lined and morocco lipped marbled paper slipcase, "Lyre" with engraved frontispiece and endpiece, few spots of faint foxing to two plates, faint browning at edges because of paper stock, otherwise very fine set, clean and smooth internally and in lustrous, unworn bindings. Phillip J. Pirages 67 - 37 2016 $750

The Drama, Its History, Literature and Influence on Civilization. London: Athenian Society, 1903-1904. Athenian Edition, one of 250 sets, 22 volumes, extremely attractive very deep blue or black half morocco, marbled sides and endpapers, raised bands, top and bottom spine panel with gilt theatrical ornament (lyre or crossed swords), the second and fourth panels with gilt titling and elongated center panel with prominent variable onlays employing one of more flowers in various colors, top edge gilt, other edges rough trimmed, 120 plates, including two frontispieces in each of the first 20 volumes, one in black and white, the other in color) as well as 20 titlepages with illustrated frames (the first in color, the rest in sepia), and 20 borders, one at beginning of each prologue (19 sepia one black and white) and 13 sepia tailpieces, each coming at end of prologue, letterpress tissue guards, one leaf in final volume with paper flaw and two inch closed tear at top, just reaching text, no loss in either case, two other leaves with very minor closed marginal tear, trivial browning at edges of some of the text, otherwise attractively bound set in remarkably fine condition, bindings extremely bright and virtually unworn, text with almost no signs of use. Phillip J. Pirages 67 - 40 2016 $3900

Lowell, James Russell 1819-1891 *The Complete Writings.* Cambridge: Riverside Press, 1904. Edition de luxe, one of 1000 copies, 222 x 146mm., 16 volumes, last 3 volumes containing 'Letters' edited by Charles Eliot Norton, very handsome dark green morocco extravagantly gilt, covers with wavy gilt border and charming floral ornaments at corners, central panel with square notched corners formed by 6 parallel gilt lines, raised bands, spine compartments attractively gilt with scrolling flowers and foliage enclosing floral fleuron centerpiece, wide turn-ins with elaborate gilt decoration featuring many large and small roses and leaves on stylized lattice work, turn-ins enclosing scarlet colored polished morocco doublures, crimson watered silk free endleaves, top edge gilt, other edges rough trimmed, mostly unopened (6 of the volumes entirely unopened and all but one of the others largely so), 80 mounted photogravure illustrations on India paper (including frontispieces, one double plate and one plate with four portraits), original tissue guards, joints of volume I with hint of wear (half dozen other joints with very slight rubbing), spines evenly sunned to attractive olive brown (though a handful of spines bit lighter than others), one small cover scuff, two leaves roughly opened (with no serious consequences), other isolated trivial imperfections, near fine set in quite attractive binding, leather lustrous and mostly unopened, text essentially undisturbed. Phillip J. Pirages 67 - 51 2016 $2500

Martial De Salviac, P. *Un People Antique Au Pays De Menelik Les Galla.* Paris: H. Oudin, 1991. Second edition, 4to., slightly later crushed orange red morocco with raised bands, top edge gilt, dust jacket in half orange-red morocco over marbled paper boards, inside lined with black calf, spine lettered gilt, marbled paper covered slipcase with morocco edges, original printed wrappers bound in (these little spotted and with wear to spine), black and white illustrations after drawings and photos, near fine, incredibly luxurious binding, very rare. Sotheran's Travel and Exploration - 20 2016 £298

Binding – Adjarian, Max

Shakespeare, William 1564-1616 *The Sonnets of William Shakespeare.* Los Angeles: Zeitlin & Ver Brugge April, 1974. Limited to 120 numbered copies, this number 74, small 8vo., 2 illustrations, original binding by Max Adjarian in quarter levant morocco, decorative paper, raised bands, gilt spine, fine. Jeff Weber Rare Books 181 - 72 2016 $5500

Binding – Aitken, T.

Malton, Thomas *Views of Oxford.* London: White & Co.; Oxford: R. Smith, 1810. First complete edition, appealing 19th century (circa 1860's?), dark green half morocco over lighter green textured cloth by T. Aitken (stamp signed), upper cover with gilt titling, raised bands, spine gilt in compartments with elongated fleuron centerpiece and scrolling cornerpieces, gilt titling, marbled endpapers, all edges gilt (small, very expert repairs to upper outer corners and perhaps at top of joints), mezzotint frontispiece, engraved title, 30 fine plates of interior and exterior views, armorial bookplates of Sir Mayson M. Beeton and Sir Richard Farrant, verso of front free endpaper, ink presentation inscription from author for Sir Charles Locock, Nov. 1860, subscription proposal for work printed by T. Bensley and dated "London, May 30, 1301 (i.e. 1801)", laid in at front, couple of small smudges to boards, portrait faintly foxed and browned, isolated small stains, not affecting images, but fine, plates especially clean and fresh, smooth and pleasing binding with virtually no wear.   Phillip J. Pirages   67 - 248   2016 $8500

Binding – Aked, J.

Bazaar and National Exposition of Manufactures *Presented by the Council of the League to the Ladies Who Assisted at the Bazaar and National Exposition of Manufacturers Held in Covent Garden Theatre, London May 1845.* London: designed & printed by Petty & Ernest & Co., 1845. First edition, 4to., ornamental lithograph title, original decorated cloth the upper cover blocked in pattern of gilt and colors, slightly worn at extremities, stamp J. Aked, Bookbinder, Palgrave, London.   Marlborough Rare Books List 56 - 6   2016   £385

Binding – Ammering, Ernst

Bible. Latin - 1977 *The Gutenberg Bible.* Munich: Idion Verlag, 1977-1978. One of a small number of copies in special deluxe binding (of a total of 955 copies printed, 895 of them for sale), 2 volumes, with additional volume of commentary (in German), very ornate blindstamped calf over thick wooden boards by Ernst Ammering, covers panelled with central diapered field, multiple blind rules forming several compartments on covers and spines containing nearly 500 individual stamps (mostly ornamental, but charming stamp of a lute player on either side of central panel on each cover), large brass corner and center bosses, double raised bands, spine panels with decoration in blind similar to the covers, leather thongs with brass clasps and catches, initials, chapter numbers and headlines printed in red and blue, approximately 100 illuminated initials, some with marginal extension, the openings of each of the books of the Bible with large illuminated initials (many of these containing miniatures in several colors and gold and with elaborate fanciful marginal borders, incorporating flowers, foliage, animals, etc., the whole reproduced in collotype in as many as 10 colors and gold.   Phillip J. Pirages   67 - 142   2016 $11,000

Binding – Arias & Sons

Ciruelo, Pedro *Reprovacion de la Supersticiones y Hechizerias.* Salamanca: Pedro de Castro, 1548. Rare early edition, 8vo., title printed in red and black within woodcut architectural border, woodcut initials, antique style brown blind tooled calf by Arias and Sons, stamped on upper cover, gilt letters on spine, titlepage with neat repairs to edges, small burnhole to folio lxviii affecting one or two letters, lightly spotted and browned in places.   Maggs Bros. Ltd.   1474 - 26   2016   £4500

Binding – Art Nouveau

Gautier, Theophile *King Candaules.* Paris: Societe des Beaux Arts circa, 1895. On of 20 lettered copies of the edition De Dux Mondes (this copy lettered out of sequence and stamped with red star), sumptuous azure crushed morocco, lavishly gilt and inlaid in Art Nouveau style, covers with large central fleur-de-lys in gilt and lilac morocco within an elaborate frame of lily bouquets and garlands inlaid in lilac, orange and white, raised bands, spine gilt in compartments, smaller ones at head and tail with inlaid lilac fleur-de-lys, large central compartment with spray of lilies in orange and white, two compartments with gilt titling, very wide turn-ins with elaborate gilt floral and foliate decoration enclosing burnt orange morocco doublures, front doublure featuring an oval inset of white kidskin with hand colored engraving of female nude, ivory watered silk endleaves, blue marbled flyleaves, top edge gilt, others untrimmed, partially unopened, with 61 illustrations by Paul Avril, comprised of 20 in three states, plain India proof and colored and one in single state, all with tissue guards, spine faintly sunned, otherwise fine as fresh and bright as one could hope for.   Phillip J. Pirages 67 - 67   2016 $2200

Binding – Artelier Bindery

Tomkis, Thomas *Lingua; or the Combat of the Tongue and the Five Senses for Superiority.* London: for Simon Miller, 1657. Small 8vo., sheet "B" lightly browned, small hole in blank aprt of title, early 20th century half brown morocco by Artelier Bindery, joints heavily rubbed, rear pastedown torn removing a label, from the library of James Stevens Cox (1910-1997), early inscription.   Maggs Bros. Ltd.   1447 - 414   2016   £300

Binding – Ascoli, Jan

D'Arbeloff, Natalie *Love.* London: NdA Press, 1992. Limited to 16 numbered copies, plus 2 Artists Proofs, text and illustrations by d'Arbeloff, 34 color etchings with aquatint, printed intaglio and relief on Zerkall, oblong 16mo., concertina binding by Jan Ascoli with cover papers by artist, red slipcase with title in black on spine, 16 leaves.   Oak Knoll Books   27 - 43   2016 $700

Binding – Bain

MacLean, Fitzroy *Back to Bokhara.* London: Jonathan Cape, 1959. First edition, 8vo., original blue cloth by A. W. Bain & Co., spine lettered gilt, top edge blue, photographic endpapers, dust jacket retaining price, double page map printed in ochre and black, 8 monochomre plates, bearing photographic illustrations recto and verso dust jacket minimally rubbed, price clipped, otherwise very good, author's presentation 1959.   Sotheran's   Travel and Exploration - 150   2016   £178

Shakespeare, William   1564-1616   *The Works.* New York: Nonesuch Press, 1929-1933. One of 1600 copies, 242 x 155mm., 7 volumes, original russet niger morocco by A. W. Bain, covers with gilt double fillet frame, raised bands, gilt titling on spines, a total of five (oil?) spots (one the size of a quarter, the others smaller), spines sunned as always (but atypically uniform in color), free endpapers with offset shadow from binder's glue, otherwise very fine, bindings with virtually no wear and interiors essentially undisturbed.   Phillip J. Pirages   67 - 264   2016 $3600

Binding – Bannen, Franny

Danticat, Edwidge   *The Coriolis Effect.*   Stockholm: Midnight Paper Sales, 2002. Limited to 170 numbered copies, hand set in monotype Walbaum and signed by him and author, Large 12mo., printed by Gaylord Schanilec on Zerkall paper, cover paper marbled by Carol Scott, bound by Franny Bannen and Lucy Graber, color illustrations.   Oak Knoll Books   310 - 123   2016 $125

Binding – Barratt, W.

Falconer, William   *The Shipwreck, a Poem.*   London: printed for William Miller by W. Bulmer, 1811. 197 x 121mm, very pretty mid 19th century green straight grain morocco, intricately decorated in gilt and blind, by W. Barratt (ticket on front flyleaf), covers with broad, densely gilt frame and central lozenge containing a large and elaborate floral centerpiece, raised bands, spine panels filled with gilt purple watered silk endleaves framed by gilt tolls, all edges gilt, 3 engraved plates and five engraved vignettes, verso of front endleaf with early inscription, "The Bookbinder's Tribute of Gratitude to Benj. Morland" and with bookplate of Cass Canfield, presentation to Canfield from Austen Kark laid in, spine uniformly sunned to olive brown, slight rubbing to corners, bands and joints, muted spotting to silk plates with minor foxing, hint of browning at edges of some leaves, still excellent copy, with none of the condition issues serious and with elaborately decorated covers lustrous and unworn.   Phillip J. Pirages   67 - 27   2016 $750

Binding – Bauzonnet-Trautz

Amman, Jost   *Bibliorum Utriusque Testamenti Icones, Summor Artificio Expressae Historias Sacras and Vivum Exhibentes & Oculis Summa cum Gratia Repraesentantes....*   Frankfurt: Christoph Corvinus & Sigmund Feyerabend, 1571. First edition, 8vo., 19th century blue morocco, triple blind fillet on cover, title lettered in gilt on spine, inner edge richly gilt and signed Bauzonnet-Trautz', marbled edges, gilt edges, silk bookmark, woodcut coats of arms of Johann Fichard and Konrad Weis, 200 fine oval woodcuts within ms. frames by Jose Amman, many signed with his initials, IA, bookplates of Edward Arnold, Dorking, E. Yeminez, Lyon and Allan Heywood Bright, London.   Maggs Bros. Ltd. 1474 - 12   2016   £4500

Binding – Bayntun

Ackermann, Rudolph   1764-1834   *The History of the Abbey Church of St. Peter's Westminster, Its Antiquities and Monuments.*   London: for R. Ackermann, 1812. First edition, large 4to., 2 volumes, plan, portrait, 81 hand colored aquatint plates, beautifully found in full straight grain red morocco, spines, covers and turn-ins richly gilt by Bayntun, cloth slipcases, very slight offsetting onto text from some plates as usual, just hint of foxing on two or three plates, else remarkably bright and flawless set, upper hinges just beginning to crack slightly, otherwise binding fine and fresh, fine, very desirable copy.   Joseph J. Felcone, Inc.   Books from Five Centuries: a Miscellany - 1   2016 $3200

Arabian Nights   *The Thousand and One Nights, Commonly Called the Arabian Nights' Entertainments.*   London: Chatto & Windus, 1841. 3 volumes, 8vo. handsomely bound set, probably by Bayntun of Bath, late 1940's red half morocco over red cloth boards, spine with raised bands, ornamented and lettered gilt, top edge gilt, marbled endpapers, wood engraved illustrations, light spotting only at beginning and end.   Sotheran's   Travel and Exploration - 335   2016   £1250

Butler, Samuel   1612-1680   *Hudibras, a poem....*   London: printed for Akermann, 1822. 2 volumes, octavo, 12 hand colored engraved plates by J. Clark, full crushed red morocco by Bayntun, covers elaborately tooled and stamped in gilt and black, front boards featuring pictorial inlaid centerpieces made up of several different pieces of dyed morocco, tooled in black, spines tooled, lettered and stamped in gilt in compartments, board edges and turn-ins decoratively gilt, all edges gilt marbled doublures and free endpapers, binding's calligraphic inscription in black and sepia on recto of front free endpapers, occasional light offsetting or spotting, else near fine, clean and bright, fore-edge painting revealed by fanning the outer edge of each text block, after drawing by Hogarth.   Heritage Book Shop Holiday 2015 - 40   2016 $6000

Carlyle, Thomas 1795-1881 *Oliver Cromwell's Letters and Speeches with Elucidations.* London: Chapman and Hall, 1845. First edition, stout 8vo., 2 volumes bound by Bayntun in half single gilt ruled morocco, spines lettered and panelled in gilt, top edges gilt, frontispiece portrait in volume I extra illustrated with insertion of c. 160 engraved portraits upper joint of volume one little tender with small repaired split in bottom, little occasional light spotting, generally very good set. Sotheran's Piccadilly Notes - Summer 2015 - 68 2016 £998

Casanova De Seingalt, Girolamo 1725-1798 *The Memoirs.* London: Casanova Society, 1922. One of 1000 copies, 12 volumes bound in 6, 254 x 203mm., attractive later burgundy half morocco over red linen boards by Bayntun (stamp signed), raised bands flanked by gilt rules, spine panels with gilt chandelier-like centerpiece, each spine with two olive brown morocco labels, top edges gilt, 12 frontispieces, large foldout map, foldout facsimile, engraving, two portraits of Casanova, portrait of Manon Baletti, engravings, corners bit worn, joints of early volumes little rubbed (two joints cracked and boards consequently with little wobble), one volume with small loss of leather at bottom of spine, still quite attractive set, bindings entirely sound and without any serious wear, wide margined text, virtually unused condition. Phillip J. Pirages 67 - 87 2016 $750

Craik, Dinah Maria Mulock 1826-1887 *John Halifax Gentleman.* London: Hurst and Blackett, 1856. First edition, 191 x 114mm., 3 volumes with 3 pages of ads at end of first volume and 2 pages at end of third, extremely pleasing medium green straight grain morocco, attractively gilt by Bayntun (stamp-signed on front flyleaf), gilt double fillet border on covers, raised bands, gilt spine compartments with filigree lozenge centerpiece and cornerpiece volutes, blue and red morocco labels, heavily gilt turn-ins, marbled endpapers, all edges gilt, joints of first volume bit flaked, tiny cracks just beginning, two leaves with neatly repaired tear (one in lower fore margin, the other into text, but without loss), text faintly browned at edges because of inexpensive paper, still quite appealing set, decorative bindings bright and almost entirely unworn, text very clean and smooth. Phillip J. Pirages 67 - 96 2016 $750

Crebillon, Claude Prosper Jolyt De *The Happy Orphans an Authentic History of Persons in High Life.* printed for H. Woodgate and S. Brooks, 1759. First edition of this translation, 2 volumes, occasional minor browning or spotting, few paper repairs (no loss), 12mo., recent half calf by Bayntun, spines gilt, contrasting lettering pieces, good, rare. Blackwell's Rare Books B184 - 31 2016 £2500

Doyle, Arthur Conan 1859-1930 *The Memoirs of Sherlock Holmes.* London: George Newnes, 1894. First edition, quarto, early blue crushed morocco by Bayntun, gilt dentelles, marbled endpapers, all edges gilt, original cloth front cover and spine bound in superficial split to end of joints (all holding), tied uniform fading to spine, beautiful copy. Manhattan Rare Book Company 2016 - 1648 2016 $3000

Hawthorne, Nathaniel 1804-1864 *The Scarlet Letter.* Boston: Ticknor, Reed and Fields, 1850. First edition, first issue with ads dated march 1 1850 with misprint on page 21 line 20 'reduplicate' for 'repudiate', 181 x 111mm., fine modern dark brown crushed morocco by Bayntun (stamp-signed on front turn-in), covers with single gilt fillet border, raised bands, spine gilt in single ruled compartments containing antique style letter 'A", gilt titling and turn-ins, marbled endpapers, all edges gilt, original blindstamped brown cloth covers bound in at rear, bookplate of Robert Le Gresley, leaves shade less than bright (as in the typical copy), occasional corner creases, isolated spots of mild foxing, otherwise fine, text clean and fresh, pristine binding.   Phillip J. Pirages 67 - 192 2016 $3900

Jameson, Anna Brownell 1794-1860 *Memoirs of Early Italian Painters.* London: John Murray, 1891. New edition, octavo, 58 engraved portraits, bound by Bayntun (stamp-signed on front turn-in) circa 1925, full purple morocco over beveled boards, covers ruled gilt, spine with fine raised bands, paneled and lettered gilt, decorative gilt board edges, decorative gilt turn-ins, all edges gilt, marbled endpapers, spine slightly faded, otherwise near fine. David Brass Rare Books, Inc. 2015 - 03011 2016 $175

Langdale, Charles *Memoirs of Mrs. Fitzherbert; with an Account of Her Marriage with H. E. H. the Prince of Wales, Afterwards King George IV.* London: R. Bentley, 1856. First edition, 225 x 140mm., pleasing early 20th century turquoise crushed morocco by Bayntun of Bath for C. E. Lauriat of Boston (stamp-signed on front turn-in), covers with two interlaced rectangular frames of gilt and black, foliate cornerpieces, raised bands, spine compartments with concentric black and gilt frames, gilt titling, turn-ins with gilt French fillet frame and arabesque cornerpieces, marbled endpapers, all edges gilt, housed in felt lined blue buckram slipcase, 38 engraved plates, 10 in color comprised of hand colored frontispiece portrait (as issued) and 37 extra illustrations, all with tissue guards, spine sunned to olive brown, otherwise fine, leather lustrous and virtually by unworn, text with almost no signs of use, tissue guards preventing offsetting the frequently affects extra illustrated copies.   Phillip J. Pirages 67 - 28 2016 $1000

Le Sage, Alain Rene   1668-1747   *The Adventures of Gil Blas of Santillane.*   London: J. C. Nimmo and Bain, 1881. 191 x 121mm., 3 volumes, reddish brown crushed morocco gilt by Bayntun (stamp signed on front turn-in), covers with gilt French fillet border and cricket cornerpieces, raised bands, spine compartments similarly decorated, gilt ruled turn-ins, marbled endpapers, all edges gilt, 12 original etchings as called for and extra illustrated with 95 hand colored plates, one board detached, other joints rather worn, couple with older cracks repaired by glue, spines bit scuffed, other general wear couple of tiny fore-edge tears to one plate, otherwise text and inserted plates especially fine.   Phillip J. Pirages   67 - 237   2016 $850

Liechtenstein, Princess Marie   *Holland House.*   London: Macmillan and Co., 1874. First edition, 2 volumes, handsome early 20th century blue gray crushed morocco by Bayntun, signed on front turn-ins, covers with double gilt fillet border, large central frame of gilt and black, elegant interlacing quatrefoil centerpiece (also in gilt and black), raised bands decorated with gilt dots, spines gilt in compartments repeating cover design elements, turn-ins with gilt French fillet, marbled endpapers, all edges gilt, original cloth binding at back of each volume, titlepage portrait miniatures, numerous woodcut illustrations in text, three portraits and 8 autograph facsimiles as called for, extra illustrated with 140 plates, 20 of these colored, mostly portraits, but with 24 views, three of these double page, isolated faint offsetting and other trivial imperfections, especially fine and pretty set, clean, fresh and bright internally, in lustrous virtually unworn binding.   Phillip J. Pirages   67 - 30   2016 $1750

Pepys, Samuel   1633-1703   *Memoirs of Samuel Pepys: Comprising his Diary from 1659 to 1669 and a Selection from His Private Correspondence.*   London: Henry Colburn, 1825. First decoded edition, 295 x 229mm., 2 volumes, fine honey brown morocco by Bayntun (stamp signed), covers with intricate strapwork frame in gilt and black, raised bands, spines with similar strapwork compartments, gilt turn-ins with complex fleuron cornerpieces, marbled endpapers, leather hinges, all edges gilt, 21 called-for illustrations, including folding map, 7 portraits and an interior view (13 illustrations hand colored) and extra illustrated with 158 plates, 31 of these in color, 20 of them folding, three or four trivial (neatly refurbished) nicks in leather, paper used for mounting extra illustrated material acidic and consequently browned (and with facing pages slightly darkened as well), index in first volume faintly spotted, couple of short marginal tears to folding plates, other insignificant imperfections, but extremely attractive set, text clean and fresh, animated decorative bindings lustrous and scarcely worn.   Phillip J. Pirages   67 - 31   2016 $3900

Porter, William Sydney   1862-1910   *The Best of O. Henry.*   London: Hodder and Stoughton, 1956. Reprint of the first collected edition, 8vo., recently rebound in half red morocco by Bayntun, spine lettered gilt, gilt centre tools, marbled endpapers, top edge gilt, near fine.   Sotheran's Piccadilly Notes - Summer 2015 - 163   2016   £148

Romer, Isabella Frances   *Filia Dolorosa. Memoirs of Marie Therese Charlotte, Duchess of Angouleme, The Last Dauphnies.*   London: Richard Bentley, 1852. First edition, 225 x 140mm., 2 volumes, attractive later sky blue crushed morocco by Bayntun of Bath for his bookseller Charles E. Lauriat co. of Boston (stamp signed on front turn-in), covers with frame of black and gilt rules cinched to the center of each side by a decorative quatrefoil, raised bands, spine compartments framed by black and gilt rules, gilt titling, turn-ins ruled in gilt and black with decorative cornerpieces, marbled endpapers, all edges gilt, hand colored frontispiece portrait, extra illustrated with portraits and views, 20 of the portraits hand colored, bookplate of Joel Cheney Wells, designed by Elisha Brown Bird, spines uniformly faded further toward gray than blue, isolated trivial defects internally, otherwise very pleasing copy, entirely clean and fresh as in bindings with spine lustrous covers and virtually no signs of use.   Phillip J. Pirages   67 - 39   2016 $750

Binding – Bayntun-Riviere

Austen, Jane   1775-1817   *The Novels.*   London: Dent, 1894-1897. 10 volumes bound in 5, 8vo., mid 20th century half green calf by Bayntun-Riviere, spines gilt, twin red lettering pieces, top edges gilt, bookplate removed, good, attractive set.   Blackwell's Rare Books   B184 - 7   2016   £2000

Defoe, Daniel   *The Adventures of Robinson Crusoe.* Bickers and Bush, 1862. First edition illustrated thus, 8vo., sometime bound by Bayntun-Riviere in full double gilt line panelled black straight grain morocco, spine lettered and panelled gilt with gilt centre tools, marbled endpapers, all edges gilt, 8 plates and 38 woodcuts, handsome volume. Sotheran's Piccadilly Notes - Summer 2015 - 102   2016   £498

Dickens, Charles   1812-1870   *A Child's History of England.*   London: Bradbury & Evans, 1852. 1853. 1854. First edition, 3 volumes, half titles, frontispieces by F. W. Topham, final ad leaves, sumptuously bound in full tan calf by Bayntun Riviere, gilt spines, double ruled borders and dentelles, maroon & tan morocco labels, original maroon cloth bound in at end of each volume, all edges gilt, fine. Jarndyce Antiquarian Booksellers   CCXVIII - 497   2016   £1500

Dickens, Charles   1812-1870   *Great Expectations.* London: Chapman & Hall, 1866. Library edition, 8vo., 8 illustrations by Marcus Stone, engraved by Dalziel, finely bound by Bayntun-Riviere in full red crushed morocco with decorated spine, gilt bust of Dickens to front board, gilt facsimile signature to rear board, gilt dentelles, all edges gilt, marbled endpapers, fine, brilliant copy.   Tavistock Books Bibliolatry - 11   2016 $1250

Dickens, Charles   1812-1870   *A Tale of Two Cities.* London: Chapman and Hall, 1859. First edition, first issue, frontispiece, engraved title and plates by Phiz, 32 page catalog (Nov. 1859), catalog with expertly executed minor repairs, handsomely bound in full scarlet crushed morocco by Bayntun-Riviere, gilt spine, single ruled borders and dentelles, all edges gilt, very good, attractive.   Jarndyce Antiquarian Booksellers   CCXVIII - 559   2016   £3800

Rosenthal, Leonard   *Au Royaume De La Perle. (The Kingdom of the Pearl).*   Paris: H. Piazza, 1920. First printing with these illustrations, no. 430 of 1500 copies, 289 x 230mm., fine later black crushed morocco gilt by Bayntun-Riviere (stamp signed), covers with dotted roll border incorporating gilt cornerpieces, upper cover with lobed centerpiece panel enclosing gilt crown set with 26 tiny seed pearls, raised bands, gilt ruled and decorated compartments, wide turn-ins with gilt rolls and cornerpieces, marbled endpapers, top edge gilt, housed in somewhat worn and faded but still sturdy felt-lined drop-back clamshell cloth box; decorated title, initials, head and tailpieces, borders, 10 color plates by Edmund Dulac, mounted within decorative frames, captioned tissue guards, four initials carefully hand colored by previous owner, imitation page with convincing signature of Dulac, which appears to be a forgery, beautifully bound in pristine condition.   Phillip J. Pirages   67 - 120   2016 $1900

Binding – Bedford

Dickens, Charles   1812-1870   *The Village Coquettes.* London: Richard Bentley (printed by Samuel Bentley), 1836. First edition, title very slightly browned, tiny marginal repair in final leaf, handsome full calf by F. Bedford, gilt spine, borders & dentelles, dark green leather label, armorial bookplate of Ralph Clutton, very good, rare edition. Jarndyce Antiquarian Booksellers   CCXVIII - 86   2016   £1500

L'Innocence de la Tresillustre. Tres-chaste, et Debonnaire Princesse, Madame Marie Royne d'Escosse.   n.p. Iprime an, 1572. 8vo., signature O omitted in make up, text complete, all pages faintly rubricated, very nice, bound by Bedford in dark blue morocco gilt, dentelles, marbled endpapers, all edges gilt, ownership signature of A. Elphinston(e) on titlepage with dated in lower margin 1600, later armorial bookplate of James Wyllie Guild and Thomas Brooke, FSA, Armitage Bridge, ownership inscription Alexander W. Ruthven Stuart 1923.   Jarndyce Antiquarian Booksellers   CCXVII - 182   2016   £1500

Mitford, Mary Russell   1787-1855   *Our Village, Illustrated.* London: Sampson Low, 1879. First edition thus, full straight grained dark green morocco by F. Bedford, gilt rules and spine decoration, all edges gilt, very good, attractive copy, 4to.   Jarndyce Antiquarian Booksellers   CCXVII - 188   2016   £280

Radcliffe, Alexander   *Ovidius Exulans ur Ovid Travestie.* London: by Peter Lillicrap for Samuel Speed, 1673. First edition, small 8vo., engraved portrait bust, washed and pressed, late 19th century polished calf by F. Bedford, covers with triple gilt fillet, gilt spine, marbled endleaves, gilt edges, joints rubbed. from the library of James Stevens Cox (1910-1997). the copy of W. E. Bonds, of Enderby House, Clapham, London, the copy of George Thorn Drury. Maggs Bros. Ltd.   1447 - 350   2016   £1100

Shelley, Percy Bysshe   1792-1822   *Rosalind and Helen, a Modern Eclogue, with Other Poems.*   London: printed for C. and J. Ollier, 1819. First edition, with final ad leaves, first few leaves slightly spotted, 8vo., polished calf by F. Bedford, spine gilt red lettering piece, gilt edges, minimal wear to extremities, the Hibbert-Esher copy with bookplates and acquisition notes by Oliver Brett, good.   Blackwell's Rare Books   Marks of Genius - 47   2016   £2500

Vergilius Maro, Publius   *The Works of Virgil.* Birmingham: printed by John Baskerville for the author, 1766. Sole edition, 8vo., later full speckled calf by Bedford, boards with french fillet border, spine richly gilt with contrasting leather labels, joints little rubbed, spine slightly sunned, marginal dampstain to pages 529-536, bookplate of Glenconnor, otherwise very good.   Sotheran's   Piccadilly Notes - Summer 2015 - 315   2016   £500

Wishart, George   *Montrose Redivivus or the Portraicture of James late Marquess of Montrose, Earl of Kincardin &c.* London: for Jo. Ridley, 1652. First edition in English, 8vo., engraved portrait, light marginal browning, A3r dust soiled and very lightly dampstained in places, probably washed, late 19th century sprinkled calf by F. Bedford (front cover detached, spine bands, lightly scuffed and chipped), bookplate of Charles George Milnes Gaskell, from the library of James Stevens Cox (1910-1997).   Maggs Bros. Ltd.   1447 - 460   2016   £120

Yarrell, William   *A History of British Birds.*   John Van Voorst, 1837-1843. 1845. 1846. First edition, large paper copy, imperial 8vo., 3 volumes with both supplements bound in to volume 3, bound in full green morocco by P. Bedford, gilt panels with foliate tooling to sides, elaborate gilt spines with gilt raised bands and lettering, gilt turn-ins, marbled endpapers, all edges gilt, engraved illustrations by John Thompson, spine sunned to attractive brown, internally fine, very clean copy in handsome binding, Edward Huth bookplates.   Sotheran's   Piccadilly Notes - Summer 2015 - 339   2016   £1600

Binding – Benson, Courtland

Bonet, Honore *L'Apparition De Jehan de Meun ou Le Songe Du Prieur De Salon.* Paris: Imprime par Crapelet pour la Societe des Bibliophiles Franai, 1845. No. 7 of 17 copies on vellum, plus 100 copies issued on paper, 235 x 181mm., recent fine white pigskin, decorated in blind in medieval style by Courtland Benson, housed in titled custom made morocco backed folding cloth box, 10 engraved plates replicating illustrations from early manuscript copies of the week, pastedown with morocco bookplate of Comte H. De La Bedoyere and engraved bookplate of Marcellus Schlimovich, front free endpaper with embossed library stamp of Dr. Detlef Mauss, half title with ink library stamp of Sociedad Hebraica Argentina, fine, especially clean and bright internally with only most trivial imperfections and in striking new retrospective binding.   Phillip J. Pirages   67 - 343   2016 $2750

Swift, Jonathan 1667-1745 *Gulliver's Travels.* London: Cresset Press, 1930. No. 134 of 195 copies on paper and 10 on vellum, 2 volumes, 364 x 256mm., fine recent dark green half morocco gilt by Courtland Benson, lighter green marbled paper sides, raised bands, spines handsomely gilt in compartments in antique style with large elegant floral stamp centerpiece and curling leafy cornerpieces, gilt titling, top edge gilt, others untrimmed; with a total of 27 engravings as called for, title page vignette featuring a bust of Swift (appearing in each volume), 8 head and tailpieces, five full page maps, 12 delicately hand colored engraved plates (including two frontispiece) by Rex Whistler, each within ornate baroque-style frame, front pastedown of volume II with bookplate of Charles J. Rosenbloom, very fine set inside and out.   Phillip J. Pirages   67 - 104   2016 $8500

Binding – Bickers

Bronte, The Sisters *The Novels of the Sisters Bronte.* London: Downey and Co. Ltd., 1898. Thornton edition, 12 volumes, contemporary three quarter red morocco leather backed red cloth boards with gilt titles and decoration to spines, binding signed by Bickers and Son, leather on spines browned, though gilt remains bright on all volumes, minor wear/chipping to spine ends of few volumes, minor wear to corners, minor rubbing to hinges and minor scuffing to boards of some volumes, few cracks to spine leather of several volumes, later owner's name neatly handwritten along top of each bookplate, third owner name written in very small neat lettering on top of free front endpaper in few volumes, interiors printed on laid paper and remain very clean, titlepages with tissue guards appear at beginning of most volumes, all volumes tightly bound, very good.   The Kelmscott Bookshop   12 - 17   2016 $1400

Bunyan, John 1628-1688 *The Pilgrim's Progress from this World to that Which is to Come.* London: Essex House Press, 1899. Number 627 of 750 copies, lovely book bound and signed by Bickers and Son in brown crushed pigskin with five bands and blind embossed title on spine, top edges gilt and marbled endpapers, front hinge repaired, printed in black and red type on fine handmade paper, frontispiece illustrations by Reginald Savage protected by tissue guard, very good plus.   The Kelmscott Bookshop   12 - 44   2016 $395

Burton, Richard Francis 1821-1890 *The Lake Regions of Central America: a Picture of Exploration.* London: Longmans, Green, Longman and Roberts, 1860. First edition, 8vo., 5 volumes, Victorian full red calf by Bickers & Son, spine with raised bands, ornamented in gilt and with contrasting lettering pieces, boards with gilt ruled double fillets, all edges marbled, marbled endpapers, 12 printed plates, combining wood engraving with lithography, 22 wood engraved illustrations, 1 folding colored map, 2 corners with slight bumps, apart from minor spotting initially and at end of volume, very fresh and clean set.   Sotheran's   Travel and Exploration - 9   2016   £3995

Kingsley, Charles 1819-1875 *The Water-Babies; a Fairy Tale for a Land-Baby.* London: Macmillan and Co., 1889. New edition, King Edward VI School, Berkhamsted, Prize Binding with prize label, maroon full calf, sides ruled in gilt with armorial crest gilt on upper cover, spine in compartments with raised bands, elaborately gilt and green leather label, lettered gilt by Bickers & Son, extremities with very slight wear, very nice.   Bertram Rota Ltd.   Christmas List 2015 - 17   2016   £150

McCarthy, Justin *A History of Our Own Times.* London: Chatto & Windus, 1880-1905. First editions, 7 volumes, large 8vo., contemporary half blue morocco, spine gilt ruled in compartments and lettered direct by Bicker and Son, last 3 volumes signed, small piece missing form foot of spine, some shelfwear, armorial bookplate inside front cover of R. D. Jackson, sound.   Blackwell's Rare Books   B186 - 99   2016   £250

Binding – Birdsall

Defoe, Daniel *The Novels and Miscellaneous Works.* Oxford: Thomas Tegg, 1840. 20 volumes, half titles, contemporary half blue calf by Birdsall, top edge gilt, nice. Jarndyce Antiquarian Booksellers   CCXVII - 84   2016   £2850

Dodgson, Charles Lutwidge 1832-1898 *Alice's adventures in Wonderland. and Through the Looking-Glass.* London: Macmillan and Co., 1927. 2 volumes, 203 x 130mm, quite appealing dark blue half morocco over blue linen boards by Birdsall (stamp signed on verso of front free endpaper), spines with three raised bands delineating one short and one long compartment, both framed by gilt rules, smaller upper compartment with gilt titling, elongated compartment below featuring ornate gilt hand mirror, marbled endpapers, top edge gilt, other edges untrimmed, with 29 illustrations by John Tenniel as called for, hint of rubbing to extremities, two boards with smattering of tiny faint orange dots, 'Alice' with one inch stain to tail edge of frontispiece titlepage, isolated tears from rough opening, otherwise fine set, very fresh and clean internally, in lustrous virtually unworn bindings.   Phillip J. Pirages   67 - 114   2016 $750

Eliot, George, Pseud. 1819-1880 *Middlemarch.* Edinburgh: William Blackwood, 1871-1872. First edition, 4 volumes, half titles, 8 books bound as 4 in slightly later full dark blue morocco by Birdsall, gilt spines, borders and dentelles, top edge gilt, very good, attractive copy, bound in at end are original pale green wrappers to the 8 separately issued books.   Jarndyce Antiquarian Booksellers   CCXVII - 95   2016   £3500

Randolph, Thomas *Poems with the Muses Looking-Glass and Amyntas.* Oxford: for F. Bowman and are to be sold by John Crosley, 1668. Fifth (i.e. sixth) edition, small 8vo., with half title, leaves A1-P8 lightly browned, small piece torn away from blank corner of C4 and with small closed tear to lower margin of L4, some small spots, minor hole through P7 (touching text) and with sheet S closely trimmed, but with no loss of text, early 20th century calf, gilt spine by Birdsall & Son of Northampton, joints rubbed and slightly cracked at head and tail, some insect damage at foot of spine, from the library of James Stevens Cox (1910-1997), armorial bookplate, Ambrose Isted (1717-81) of Ecton Hall, Northamptonshire.   Maggs Bros. Ltd.   1447 - 354   2016   £180

Binding – Blinn, Carol

Saroyan, William *An Act or Two of Foolish Kindness...* Lincoln: Penmaen press, 1977. First edition, 8vo., 178 of 300 copies signed by author and artist, engravings by Helen Siegl, printed on Curtis Rag paper, paste paper bindings by Carol Blinn, fine.   Second Life Books, Inc.   196 B - 522   2016 $75

Binding – Blunson & Co.

Dickens, Charles 1812-1870 *Works.* London: Chapman & Hall, 1881. Edition deluxe, 30 volumes, half titles, frontispieces, illustrations, with India proofs after original plates, some occasional light foxing, contemporary half maroon morocco by Blunson & Co., spines lettered gilt, top edge gilt, very good.   Jarndyce Antiquarian Booksellers   CCXVIII - 30   2016   £3800

Binding – Bone

Dickens, Charles 1812-1870 *Immorteles from Charles Dickesn.* London: John Moxon, 1856. Half title, few spots, original royal blue cloth by Bone & son, lettered gilt, little worn at corners, bookplate of Samuel J. Mills, good, sound copy.   Jarndyce Antiquarian Booksellers   CCXVIII - 725   2016   £65

Hotten, John Camden *Charles Dickens the story of his life by the author.* London: John Camden Hotten, 1870. First edition, vignette title, plates, 20 page catalog, original green cloth by W. Bone & Son, slight rubbing.   Jarndyce Antiquarian Booksellers   CCXVIII - 1306   2016   £35

Kirwan, Andrew Valentine *Host and Guest.* London: Bell & Daldy, 1864. First edition, half title, uncut in original blue cloth by Bone & Son, little rubbed and dulled, recent booklabel of Alan Davidson, good plus.   Jarndyce Antiquarian Books   CCXV - 282   2016   £120

Lankester, Edwin *Half Hours with the Microscope.* London: Robert Hardwicke, 1860. New edition, illustrated by Tuffen West, half title, frontispiece, plates, 2 pages ads, original pink brown cloth by W. Bone & Son, spine slightly faded, very good.   Jarndyce Antiquarian Booksellers   CCXVII - 160   2016   £50

Menken, Adah Isaacs *Infelicia.* London: Paris: New York: privately printed, 1868. Half title, frontispiece, portrait, illustrations, original green cloth, bevelled boards by W. Bone, bit rubbed, all edges gilt.   Jarndyce Antiquarian Booksellers   CCXVIII - 863   2016   £100

Rock, William Frederick *The Anniversary: a Christmas Story.* London: David Bogue, 1856. First edition, half title, frontispiece, engraved title and 6 further plates by Thomas Onwhyn, original red wavy-grained cloth by Bone & Son, blocked in blind, lettered and decorated gilt, small split in following inner hinge, all edges gilt, very good, bright. Jarndyce Antiquarian Booksellers   CCXVIII - 409   2016   £120

Russell, John Fuller *The Ancient Knight or Chapters on Chivalry.* London: W. J. Cleaver, 1849. Frontispiece, 14 page catalog, original scarlet cloth by Bone & Son, largely faded to brown, little rubbed, spine chipped at head, contemporary signature of Leo. G. Watlyn Thomas.   Jarndyce Antiquarian Books   CCXV - 392   2016   £40

Timbs, John *Lady Bountiful's Legacy to her Family and Friends.* London: Griffith & Farran, 1868. (1867). first and only edition, slight tear to lower corner of title, original green cloth by W. Bone & Son, bevelled boards, attractively blocked in lack and gilt, all edges gilt, bookseller's ticket of B. & J. Meehan, Bath, very good.   Jarndyce Antiquarian Books   CCXV - 439   2016   £125

Binding – BookLab

Brecht, Bertolt *The Seven Deadly Sins of the Lower Middle Class.* New York: Vincent FitzGerald, 1992. No. 3 in an edition of 50 copies signed by artist and translator and Kurt Weill, etchings and lithographs by Max Beard, printed on rives paper, water colored, folio, bound by Zahra Partovi in association with BookLab in 19th century Hub style binding with black leather and Dacron polyester zebra striped fabric in purple and black, black cloth clamshell box with purple leather cover label, titled gilt.   Oak Knoll Books   27 - 15   2016 $7500

Binding – Bretault, Joseph

Epictetus *The Discourses in English.* London: Arthur L. Humphreys, 1897. Reprinted from the translation of George Long, first printing of this edition, 229 x 1844m., pleasing contemporary olive green crushed morocco, gilt by Joseph Bretault (stamp signed), covers with triple gilt fillet border, upper cover of both volumes with elaborate heraldic centerpiece bannered beneath a Scottish lion rampant at top and "And Choille" bannered below a crowned lion's head at bottom (centerpiece also featuring a bee to the right, leeks at center, flowered thistle to the left, and at center an opened book with "ET" on left page and "AM" on right, smooth spines with elongated panels formed by concentric fillets, top edges gilt, others untrimmed, large paper copy, titles printed in red and black, woodcut initials, spines uniformly sunned to warm brown, boards with slight fading as well, otherwise fine, leather lustrous and with only trivial signs of use, text immaculate.   Phillip J. Pirages   67 - 128   2016 $1200

Binding – Broadbere

Tusser, Thomas *Five Hundred Pointes of Good Husbandrie.* London: published for the English Dialect Society by Trubner & Co., 1878. 8vo., very lightly yellowed, few small pencil marks to glossary, contemporary half black calf, raised bands, gilt ruled spine with red morocco label, red marbled paper covered boards, edges sprinkled red, spine and edges bit rubbed, few light scratches, but very good, handsome copy, tiny bookbinder's ticket of Broadbere, Pembroke Square, Bargate, Southampton.   Unsworths Antiquarian Booksellers Ltd.   30 - 154   2016   £45

Binding – Brockman, James

Shakespeare, William 1564-1616 *Comedies, Histories and Tragedies.* London: printed for H. Herringman, E. Brewster and R. Bentley, 1685. Magnificent engraved portrait by Martin Doreshout above the verses To the Reader on verso of first leaf, title with fleur-de-lis-device, double column text within typographical rules, woodcut initials, frontispiece skillfully repaired at inner margin, tear (repaired) in top inner corner just passing through engraved surface for about 1 cm. (hatched area), titlepage with tears repaired, 2 small lacunae filled in, some of the repaired tears passing through letters but without loss, paperflaw in *BBB1 with loss of 7 letters on recto and several more on verso (failure to print), waterstaining in inner margins at beginning, diminishing until absent in gathering E, intermittant waterstaining to lower margins, last leaf mounted and defective at head and foot without loss of text, minor worming strictly in fore-margin in third pagination, few ink splashes here and there and odd small rust hole, tears in lower margin of 'Bbb6 with loss to blank margin not affecting text, another Kkk4 entering the text but without loss, modern panelled calf over boards by James Brockman, spine richly gilt contrasting lettering pieces, black velvet lined maroon buckram folding box with black lettering piece, good.   Blackwell's Rare Books Marks of Genius - 42   2016   £85,000

Binding – Brugalla

Bonaventura, Saint 1221-1274 *Tractado en la Contempacion de la Vida de Nuestro Senor Iesu Christo Agora Nueuamente Corregdio y Emendado yy con Licentia Impresso.* Valladolid: M. Borras...., 1588. Rare illustrated Spanish edition, small 8vo., blue morocco gilt a la Francaise by Brugalla, title lettered on spine, covers with device of Isidoro Fernandez, gilt turn-ins, all edges gilt, titlepage with woodcut of the Trinity, 21 woodcuts in text, booklabels of Isidoro Fernandez, book collector of Barcelona.   Maggs Bros. Ltd.   1474 - 15   2016   £1800

Binding – Bryce, David

Willm, Joseph *The Education of the People...* Glasgow: William Lang, 1847. First British edition, errata slip, contemporary half calf by David Bryce, Glasgow, gilt spine, slightly rubbed, morocco label, slightly rubbed and marked, but nice, contemporary signature of G. Walker. Jarndyce Antiquarian Books CCXV - 1008 2016 £48

Binding – Buchbinderei Burkhardt

Melling, Antoine Ignace *Voyage Pittoresque de Constatinople des Rives du Bosophore.* Bern: Ertug & Kocabiyuk, 2002. No. 46 of 50 specially bound copies, (of a total edition of 350), 670 x 508mm., publisher's scarlet morocco by Buchbinderei Burkhardt AG, covers with gilt rolled border, cornerpieces tooled in gilt, upper cover with gilt calligraphic Arabic centerpiece, lower cover with gilt central heraldic device, marbled endleaves, all edges gilt, frontispiece, 48 double page plates and 3 double page maps, virtually as new. Phillip J. Pirages 67 - 143 2016 $12,500

Binding – Bumpus

Bible. English - 1909 *The Song of Songs Which is Solomon's.* London: Printed at the Ricardi Press for Philip Lee Warner, Publisher to the Medici Society, 1909. No. 61 of 500 copies, 260 x 194mm., pleasing olive brown crushed morocco by Bumpus (stamp signed), cover framed with three sets of triple fillets, raised bands, spine compartments similarly framed, gilt titling and turn-ins, all edges gilt, vignette on titlepage and colophon, both in blue and 10 color plates by William Russell Flint, mounted on stiff paper, each of the plates accompanied by tissue guard and an additional captioned paper guard, spine faded to soft hazel brown (as usual with green) boards with just hint of same fading, very sight rubbing to small portion of joints, usual offsetting from turn-ins to endleaves, one tissue guard with one inch strip torn at head edge, still very appealing, attractive binding lustrous and with no significant wear and interior clean and fresh. Phillip J. Pirages 67 - 301 2016 $2250

Furnivall, Frederick James *The Babee's Book: Medieval Managers for the Young...* London: Chatto & Windus, 1923. Engraved title frontispiece and plates, contemporary full brown calf by Bumpus of Oxford, all edges gilt, very good. Jarndyce Antiquarian Books CCXV - 213 2016 £38

Hamilton, Anthony 1646-1720 *Memoirs of the Count De Grammont.* London: John Lane The Bodley Head, 1928. Numbered, limited edition of 1000 copies, 8vo., bound for Bumpus in contemporary half brown morocco over marbled boards, lettered gilt on spine, top edges gilt, wood engravings by Wilfred Jones, little light spotting to few leaves, otherwise very good. Sotheran's Piccadilly Notes - Summer 2015 - 156 2016 £98

Lyric Love. London: and New York: Macmillan and Co., 1892. 159 x 105mm., lovely contemporary blue-gray crushed morocco elegantly and elaborately gilt by Bumpus (stamp signed), covers with delicate filigree frame and large densely intricate central medallion composed of hundreds of small tools, fan shaped cornerpieces of similar design, raised bands, spine gilt in compartments with central medallion and scrolling cornerpieces, pastedowns framed by turquoise morocco with gilt filigree borders, fleuron cornerpieces and alternating dot and crescent tools along the four sides, ivory silk endleaves, all edges gilt, titlepage vignette, front pastedown with engraved bookplate of Victoria Sackville-West, spine sunned to pleasant slightly darker blue green, joints with just a hint of water, light offsetting to free endleaves from turn-ins as usual, isolated corner creases, other trivial imperfections, but most attractive little book, especially smooth and clean internally and in flamboyant binding showing almost no wear. Phillip J. Pirages 67 - 33 2016 $1500

Swinburne, Algernon Charles 1837-1909 *The Poems of Algernon Charles Swinburne.* London: Chatto & Windus, 1912. Fifth impression, octavo, 6 volumes, portrait frontispiece in first volume, fine period bindings by Bumpus of full polished calf with raised bands, gilt decoration and rules, red and green morocco title labels, all edges gilt, armorial bookplate in each volume, fine set, attractively bound. Peter Ellis 112 - 391 2016 £875

Trotter, Lionel J. *The Life of John Nicholson, Solider and Administrator based on private and hitherto....* London: John Murray, 1900. First edition, octavo, 2 plates and 3 folding maps, period fine binding by Bumpus, full brown morocco with raised bands, gilt rules and devices to spine, inner dentelles elaborately gilt, top edge gilt, armorial bookplate of Kennet of Dene, contemporary (1900) ownership inscription of a member of the family (Arthur W. Young), near fine, attractive binding. Peter Ellis 112 - 181 2016 £125

Binding – Burn

Andrews, Alexander *The Eighteenth Century or Illustrations of the Manners and customs of Our Grandfathers.* London: Chapman & Hall, 1856. First edition, half title, pencil notes on following pastedown, original brown cloth by Burn & Co., spine slightly rubbed at head. Jarndyce Antiquarian Books CCXV - 13 2016 £50

Eliot, George, Pseud. 1819-1880 *Felix Holt the Radical.* Edinburgh and London: William Blackwood & Sons, 1866. New edition, 2 volumes, original cottage red sand grained cloth, bevelled boards, front boards and spines decorated and lettered in gilt, back boards with borders in blind by Burn, with ticket at end of volume 1, slight marking, half titles,. Jarndyce Antiquarian Booksellers CCXVII - 94 2016 £320

MacDonald, George 1824-1905 *At the Back of the North Wind.* London: Strahan & Co., 1871. (1870). First edition, half title, 76 illustrations after Arthur Hughes, 13 page catalog, original green cloth blocked in black, gilt and blind by Burn and Co. with their ticket, slight marking to endpapers, some mottling and rubbing of cloth, all edges gilt, still very good, scarce edition. Jarndyce Antiquarian Booksellers CCXVII - 171   2016   £2500

MacDonald, George 1824-1905 *Works of Fancy and Imagination.* London: Strahan and Co., 1871. First edition, 16mo., 10 volumes, half titles, original green cloth, beveled boards, elaborately blocked in gilt by Burn, all edges gilt, very good apart from rubbing to gilt on spine volume VI, scarce first edition.   Jarndyce Antiquarian Booksellers CCXVII - 173   2016   £1200

Martin, William *Noble Boys: Thei Deeds of Love and Duty.* London: Strahan and Co., 1870. First edition, half title, frontispiece, plates and illustrations, 32 page catalog (Nov. 1870), original brick red cloth by Burn & Co., little dulled, some slight repair to following hinge, prize label and school report laid on to leading free endpapers, good plus.   Jarndyce Antiquarian Books   CCXV - 67   2016   £38

Binding – Campbell-Logan Bindery

Cassay, Neal *O Fatal Practicality!* Louisville: Contre Coup Press, 2014. First edition, limited to 19 copies printed and bound at Campbell-Logan Bindery, Louisville, quarto, tipped-in photo frontispiece and additional tipped in photos of Cassady and Kerouac, quarter gray silk and decorated paper over boards with printed paper spine label, fine.   Between the Covers Rare Books   204 - 24   2016 $450

Waldman, Anne *Makeup on Empty Space.* West Branch: Toothpaste Press, 1984. First edition, one of 100 numbered copies, with Ehrhardt Monotype Portrait of author, deluxe edition, printed on Frankfurt White, quarter bound in cloth and Tokutairei Tanabata, a handmade paper, at the Campbell-Logan Bindery, fine in acetate dust jacket.   Second Life Books, Inc.   196 B - 817   2016 $125

Binding – Cape

Erasmus, Desiderius 1466-1536 *L'Eloge de la Folie Nouvellement traduit du Latin d'Esrame par M. De la Veaux.* Basle: imprime avec des caracteres de G. Haas chez J. J. Thurneysen, le Jeune, 1780. Triple portrait frontispiece, additional engraved titlepage, further portrait engraved by Samuel Granicher, illustrations, few leaves browned or foxed, 8vo., 19th century crushed red morocco by Cape, lettered gilt on spine (giving the place as Berlin), gilt edges, minimal wear to corners, overall morocco book label of Vernon Watney inside front cover and his signature on verso of front free endpaper, very good.   Blackwell's Rare Books Marks of Genius - 15   2016   £300

Binding – Cape Masson-Debonnelle

Holbein, Hans *Le Triomphe De La Mort.* Paris: Simon Racon et Comp. 1780 (but mid 19th century), 146 x 114mm., very pleasing 19th century maroon crushed morocco, Jansenist, by Cape Masson-Debonnelle (stamp signed), covers with central gilt skull with crossbone cornerpieces, raised bands, spine panels alternating gilt skull and crossbones, gilt titling densely gilt turn-ins, marbled endpapers, al edges gilt, fine black quarter morocco folding box, with 47 copper engravings by Christian Von Mechel, 46 of these after original designs of Holbein, one (double page plate) added by Mechel, quarter inch at top of front joint, bit rubbed, occasional faint offsetting from plates, otherwise very fine, especially clean, fresh and bright internally with rich impressions of the plates in lustrous, essentially unworn.   Phillip J. Pirages   67 - 109   2016 $4500

Binding – Carss & Coy

Scott, Walter 1771-1832 *Rob Roy.* Edinburgh: printed by James Ballantyne and Co. for Archibald Constable and Co., 1818. First edition, 3 volumes, with half titles, finely bound in tan polished calf and brown marbled boards by Carss and Coy of Glasgow, five raised bands to spine, contrasting maroon title labels to spine, lettered and ruled in gilt, spine compartments decorated in blind, all edges speckled, green ribbon bookmarks, near fine, volume with some discreet repairs to leaves 33-41 and first two leaves washed, some minor wear to boards and extremities, light toning to spines, few faint spots to calf, volume III with minor spot to top edge, few scattered spots to otherwise fresh pages, overall very clean and handsome.   B & B Rare Books, Ltd. 2016 - SWS078   2016 $750

Binding – Charriere, Gerard

Beard, Mark *The Utah Reader.* New York: Vincent FitzGerald, 1986. Limited to 40 numbered copies signed by artist, oblong 4to., blue green silk over boards, hand lettered title stamped in orange by Gerard Charriere, inserted in specially constructed black cloth clamshell box with paper spine label, 42 hand colored linocuts, 32 Japanese papers used in collage prints executed by Zahra Partovi, extensively hand colored by artist, offset lithography text printed on Arches paper by John Hutucheson.   Oak Knoll Books   27 - 16   2016 $5000

Kondoleon, Harry *The Cote D'Azur Triangle.* New York: Vincent FitzGerald & Co., 1985. Signed limited edition, one of 125 copies only on rives BFK, all signed by author and artist, hand set in Janson, lithographs and etchings, bound by Gerard Charriere, 12 x 14 cloth of vibrant yellow, title stamped in blue within red triangle on front cover, housed in black clamshell box by Charriere.   Oak Knoll Books   310 - 101   2016 $4000

Binding – Club Bindery

Dante Alighieri   1265-1321   *The New Life of Dante Alghieri.*   Cambridge: printed at the Riverside Press, 1892. No. 1 of 250 copies, 202 x 140mm., handsome brown crushed morocco, gilt by Club Bindery (stamp signed), covers with gilt french fillet border, central panel with double gilt rule frame and oblique fleuron cornerpieces, raised bands, spine gilt in compartments with floral cornerpieces and central floral ornament enclosed by a lozenge of small tools, gilt titling, densely gilt turn-ins, top edge gilt, other edges untrimmed, versos of front free endpaper, bookplate of Henry William Poor, "Bound to be the Best: The Club Bindery", just vague hint of rubbing to joints, free endpapers with usual offset shadow from binder's glue, couple of trivial spots internally, but fine, text clean, fresh and bright and in lustrous, scarcely worn binding.   Phillip J. Pirages   67 - 34   2016 $3250

Binding – Cohen, Claudia

Hiebert, Helen   *Interluceo.*   Red Cliff: Helen Hiebert Studio, 2015. Artist's book, one of 25 copies, each signed by Hiebert and dated on titlepage, all on her own handmade papers, 75% cotton, 25% abaca blend paper to showcase watermarks, pigmented abaca pulp to create rainbow spectrum of translucent papers, 9 3/16 x 9 3/16 inches, bound by Claudia Cohen, handsewn exposed spine, grey paper wrapper printed with title and geometric shapes in darker grey on front panel, housed in custom made plum silk over boards box with title printed blind on grey paper laid onto spine, 7 handcut paper illustrations,.   Priscilla Juvelis - Rare Books   66 - 5   2016 $1750

Strand, Mark   *89 Clouds.*   New York: ACA Galleries, 1999. First edition, one of only 20 copies specially bound with original signed monotype by Wendy Mark laid into pocket at back of book, also signed by author and artist, square 8vo., reproductions of monotypes by Wendy Mark, original handmade roma paper over boards with printed paper label on spine by Claudia Cohen, as new.   James S. Jaffe Rare Books   Occasional List: Winter 2016 - 135   2016 $2500

Binding – Collet, Paul

Graves, Ida   *Epithalamion.*   Higham, Colchester: Gemini Press, 1934 but released by Basilisk Press in, 1980. No. 252 of 280 copies on paper (of a total of 330), our copy signed by artist, 349 x 207mm., 23 dramatic full page wood engravings by Blair Hughes-Stanton, publisher's light brown morocco designed by Hughes-Stanton and executed by Paul Collet and David Sellars, flat spine with vertical gilt titling, mint condition.   Phillip J. Pirages   67 - 197   2016 $1000

Binding – Conant, Judi

Rand, Harry   *The Clouds.*   Washington: Dove Press, 1996. Limited to 35 numbered copies, this one of 25 regular signed copies, 4to., gray cloth with darker gray morocco, spine printed in palladium, publisher's slipcase, 10 original lithographs by Elaine Kurtz, 8 full page lithographs hand pulled by Judith Slodkin in collaboration with the artist at Solo Impressions, NY, with two double-page images of approximately 14 x 20 inches, many images required multiple plates and the artist's hand applique of color and mica, design and typography of book by Jerry Kelly, text printed letterpress by Stinehour Press, Lunenberg, VT, type face is Robert Slimbach's Minion Paper for both text and images is Heavyweight Rives BFK 250 gsm., each print has Japanese paper overlay imprinted with short segment from the text, sewn and hand bound by Judi Conant, 4to., gray cloth with darker gray morocco spine printed in palladium, publisher's slipcase.   Oak Knoll Books   27 - 9   2016 $1250

Binding – Craig & Lea

Bible. English - 1791   *The Holy Bible Containing the Old and New Testaments...*   Trenton: Isaac Collins, 1791. First Bible printed in NJ, 4to., contemporary blind paneled sheep by Craig and Lea, with their decorative printed binder's label on front pastedown, binding worn at extremities as usual, front hinge cracking but held strongly by cords, internally the first several leaves have some erosion at extreme edges (about quarter inch) and there is the usual scattered foxing inherent in early American paper, very good, tight copy.   Joseph J. Felcone, Inc.   Books from Five Centuries: a Miscellany - 20   2016 $3000

Binding – Creswell, G. C.

Tennyson, Alfred Tennyson, 1st Baron   1609-1692   *Seven Poems and Two Translations.*   Hammersmith: Doves Press, 1902. One of 325 copies on paper and 25 on vellum, 236 x 165mm., very appealing contemporary brown crushed morocco decorated in Arts and Crafts style by G. C. Creswell (stamp signed), cover with blind tooled strapwork, frame accented with inlaid dots of green and olive morocco, raised bands, vertical titling in blind turn-ins with frame of multiple blind rules and inlaid green and olive dots at corners, binding with total of 296 inlays, all edges gilt, printed in red an black, with (laid in) bookplate of Elizabeth Watson Diamond, featuring etched portrait of T. J. Cobden-Sanderson by Sidney Lawton Smith, spine lightly sunned, extremities little rubbed, four short faint scratches to boards, minor offsetting from turn-ins, mild freckled foxing to edges of half dozen leaves, otherwise excellent copy, text very clean and fresh in quite pleasing amateur binding.   Phillip J. Pirages   67 - 117   2016 $1500

Binding – Curtis, S.

Johnson, John *Original Letters Written by the Late Mr. John Johnson of Liverpool.* Norwich: printed and sold by Crouse, Stevenson and Matchett, sold also by W. Robinson, Liverpool, 1798-1800. First edition, 2 volumes, some foxing to both volumes, some worming in volume I, confined to upper and lower margins, 8vo., contemporary brown straight grained morocco by S. Curtis with his ticket, triple blind ruled borders on sides, black lettering pieces in 2nd and 4th of 5 compartments on spine, raised bands, gilt tooled, hinges rubbed, small knock at foot of spine of volume I, some contemporary annotations to first letter, sound. Blackwell's Rare Books   B186 - 82   2016   £300

Binding – D'Ambroisio, Joseph

D'Ambrosio, Joseph *Trapeze.* Chicago: Joseph J. D'Ambrosio, 1976. First edition, no. 2 of 50 copies signed by artist and printer, Elmore Mundell, 257 x 206mm., 48 leaves, creative original tan vinyl cloth over wood by D'Ambrosio, unusual spine hinging vertically in middle with portion to the right becoming a seriographed shadow box, and with strings running through holes in various locations (spine, wide lip at bottom of front boards and at 11 places on surface of front cover), all contributing to image of circus tent, with taunt ropes holding it up, paper title label on spine portion of shadow box, Japanese mulberry paper endpapers, sturdy card sleeve covered in Japanese mulberry paper, with 20 original color serigraphs signed and numbered by artist, duplicate photocopies of two lettes from artist to original purchaser laid in at front, little creasing to left part of spine, otherwise virtually mint. Phillip J. Pirages   67 - 108   2016 $950

Binding – David, Salvador

Silvestre, Armand *Roses D'Octobre.* Paris: G. Charpentier et Cie, 1890. No. 9 of 10 copies on Holland paper, 187 x 12mm., charming contemporary dark green morocco gilt and inlaid by Salvador David (stamp-signed on front turn-in), covers framed by gilt branches, entwined with inlaid pink morocco roses, raised bands, spine compartments with central inlaid pink now surrounded by gilt foliage, densely gilt turn-ins, all edges gilt, original wrappers bound in, bookplate of Daniel Henry Holmes Jr., tiny fox spot every 40 pages, text with overall faint darkening (perhaps as in all copies because of paper stock), spine probably just a shade darker than the covers, still obviously fine, completely clean and smooth internally, and in unworn, lustrous binding. Phillip J. Pirages   67 - 35   2016 $750

Binding – De Coverly, Roger

Osborne, Dorothy *Letters from Dorothy Osborne to Sir William Temple 1652-54.* London and Manchester: Sherratt and Hughes, 1903. 184 x 127mm, quite pretty russet crushed morocco by Roger De Coverly & Sons (signed on rear turn-in), covers with double gilt rule border, raised bands, spines richly gilt in compartments with quatrefoil centerpiece surrounded by daisies, shamrocks and rose leaves, gilt titling, turn-ins ruled in gilt with trefoil cornerpieces, all edges gilt, portraits of Osborne and Temple and a plate depicting Osborne's family home, Chicksands Priory, front free endpaper with engraved bookplate of Katherine Nora Sturdy, usual offsetting to free endpapers from turn-in glue, mild foxing to blanks at beginning and end, as well as to leaves opposite two of the plates, but fine, clean, fresh internally and in a bright, unworn binding. Phillip J. Pirages   67 - 36   2016 $950

Pictorius, Georg *Apotheseos tam Exterarum Gentium Quam Romanorum Deorum Libri Tres.* Basle: Nicolaus Brylinger, 1558. First illustrated edition, printer's device on titlepage, 25 woodcuts, woodcut initials, small 8vo., late 19th century half brown morocco by Roger De Coverly, spine lettered gilt, gilt edges, bookplate of Samuel Ashton Thompson Yates dated 1894. Maggs Bros. Ltd.   1474 - 59   2016   £2500

Binding – Delrue

Martialis, Marcus Valerius *Epigrammaton Libri.* Londini: Excudebat Felix Kingstonius impensis Gulielmi Welby, 1615. Small 8vo., woodcut headpieces and motif to titlepage, light toning, small piece missing from bottom corner of editor's dedication and small stain to margin of following page but neither affecting text, very good overall, recent light brown morocco, blind tooled raised bands to spine with black morocco gilt label, gilt date to tail of spine, all edges red, endpapers replaced, tan buckram slipcase, binding and case fine, ownership inscription of Edward Wilson in old hand to initial blank and titlepage, second similar ownership inscription also to title with first name William but illegible surname, some numbers in old hand to rear blank tiny binder's stamp 'Delrue'. Unsworths Antiquarian Booksellers   30 - 108   2016   £500

Binding – Derome

Herodotus *Herodoti Libri Novem. Quibus Musarum Sunt Nomina.* Venice: Aldus Manutius, 1502. First edition, folio, printed in Green type with Aldine anchor on title and last page, full 18th century French crimson levant morocco stamped in gilt, triple gilt fillets on sides and gilt inside borders, marbled endpapers, all edges gilt, previous cataloger noted the binding was probably done by Derome, part of lower right of titlepage restored, barely affecting few letters of dedication letter, contemporary manuscript marginalia on some leaves, fine, large copy, wide margins, bookplate of Edith Rockefeller McCormick. Second Life Books, Inc.   197 - 180   2016 $47,500

Binding – Doves Bindery

Bible. English - 1903 *The English Bible.* Hammersmith: Doves Press, 1903-1905. One of 500 copies, 331 x 235mm., five volumes, original limp vellum by Doves Bindery (stamp signed), gilt titling on spine, housed within two later oatmeal linen dropback clamshell boxes with black morocco spine labels, elegant initial letters in red by Edward Johnston, including an "I" running the length of the page to open Genesis ("In the beginning"), front flyleaf of volume I inscribed in pencil by Madeleine Whyte for Mary Churchill, with Doves Press invoice for Miss Whyte dated June 27 1905, initialed by "B.H." (i.e. Bessie Hooley, a sewer at the bindery and part-time secretary to Cobden-Sanderson) laid in, vellum with just hint of soiling, but very little of the typical variation in grain, two dozen leaves with minor marginal foxing (never approaching any significance), dozen additional leaves with whisper of foxing, otherwise clean, fresh, bright copy inside and out.   Phillip J. Pirages   67 - 115   2016 $19,500

The Book of Gems. The Poets and Artists of Great Britain. London and Paris: Fisher Son & Co., 1844. 2 volumes, 222 x 140mm., very pretty crimson morocco handsomely gilt by Doves Bindery (stamp signed and dated 1908 on rear turn-in), covers with line and dot frames, corners adorned with heart shaped leaves, a poppy seed pod, oak leaves, solid heart and gouge work, raised bands, spine compartments with line and dot frames, central poppy seed pod with leaves above and below, turn-ins with gilt rules and oak leaf cluster cornerpieces, all edges gilt, with two rows of gauffered dots (expert repairs to tiny portion of top of spine and three small areas of front joint of second volume), with 106 engraved vignettes and four pages of poets' facsimile signatures at end of each volume, front pastedown with wood engraved bookplate of Charles Walker Andrews, front free endpaper with typed copy of a letter from Andrews to the Doves Bindery, about these bindings (which he commissioned) and Cobden-Sanderson's handwritten and signed reply (first apparently a transcript, with later date of a letter sent 29 Jan. 1909, the second dated 9 Feb. 1909), top corners of volume I bit worn, leaves shade less than bright (no doubt as in all copies because of paper stock, still excellent set that looks very attractive on shelf, binding lustrous and appealing despite its defects and text clean, fresh and unread.   Phillip J. Pirages   67 - 38   2016 $3500

The Book of Gems. The Modern Poets and Artists of Great Britain. London: Henry G. Bohn, 1845. 222 x 140mm., very pretty crimson morocco, handsomely gilt by the Doves Bindery (stamp signed and dated 1908), covers with line and dot frames, corners adorned with heart shaped leaves, a poppy seed pod, oak leaves, solid heart and gouge work, raised bands, spine compartments with line and dot frames, central poppy seed pod with leaves above below, turn-ins with gilt rules and oak leaf cluster cornerpieces, all edges gilt with two rows of gauffered dots (upper cover with small repair at fore edge to fill in a gouge), with 43 engraved vignettes, 40 facsimile signatures of poets on four pages following text, wood engraved bookplate of Charles Walker Andrews, hint of wear at upper corners and along top of spine, gilt frame on front cover slightly affected by repair at fore edge, leaves shade less than bright, still excellent copy, lovely binding especially lustrous and pleasing (even with minor flaws).   Phillip J. Pirages   67 - 39   2016 $1900

Cobden-Sanderson, Thomas James   1840-1922
London: a Paper Read at a Meeting of the Art Workers Guild... March 6 1891. Hammersmith: Doves Press, 1906. One of 5 copies on vellum (and 300 on paper), 235 x 165mm., dark brown crushed morocco by Doves Bindery (stamp signed and dated 1921), gilt ruled covers, raised bands, spine compartments and turn-ins ruled gilt, all edges gilt, neatly rebacked using most of original backstrip, boards with slight humpbacked browning (as nearly always with vellum printed books), hint of rubbing to edges and corners, minor loss of gilt from spine, otherwise near fine.   Phillip J. Pirages   67 - 334   2016 $4500

Doves Press *Catalogue Raisonne of Books printed & Published at the Doves Press No. 1 The Terrace Hammersmith.* Hammersmith: Doves Press, 1908. One of 300 copies, 234 x 167mm., russet morocco by the Doves Bindery (stamp signed and dated 1908), covers with simple frame of gilt rules accented with circlets where the lines intersect, neatly rejointed, raised bands, gilt titling, all edges gilt, later felt lined green cloth drop-back box; printed in red and black, engraved bookplate of Henry Fairfield Osborn with leather book label of Haven O'More, front free endpaper inscribed to Professor Osborne (sic) by Cobden-Sanderson, signed 'C S" and dated 12 November 1908 accompanied by the booklet "The Closing of the Doves Press: a keepsake from the opening of a 1969 exhibition at Stanford University devoted to Cobden-Sanderson, the Doves Press and the Doves Bindery; spine and significant portion of front cover rather darkened, joints and extremities bit rubbed, half a dozen water spots to boards, restored binding entirely solid and very clean and fresh internally.   Phillip J. Pirages   67 - 116   2016 $1250

MacKail, John William *William Morris, an Address Delivered the XIth November MDCCCC at Kelmscott House, Hammersmith, before Hammersmith Socialist Society.* London: Doves Press, 1901. One of 300 copies (of an edition of 315), printed in black and red on handmade paper, 8vo., original limp cream vellum by Doves Bindery, backstrip gilt lettered, untrimmed, slight wear to head of boards, bookplate of Charles Walker Andrews, very good, Andrews pencil note records that the book came from Salem Hyde's Library (Hyde being his father in law). Blackwell's Rare Books Marks of Genius - 30   2016   £500

Pater, Walter *Appreciations with an Essay on Style.* London: Macmillan, 1890. Third impression, bound for George Allison Armour by Doves Bindery in 1894, very good in full green morocco with gilt title, gilt clover decoration and five raised bands to spine, browning to spine and edges of boards, minor rubbing to hinges, corners and bands, decorative dentelles and full edges gilt, offsetting to endpapers and slight toning to margins of pages, else clean and bright, very good.   The Kelmscott Bookshop   13 - 41   2016 $850

Binding – Duru

Bible. Italian - 1588 *Figure del Nuovo testamento, Illustrate da Versi Vulgari Italiani.* Lyon: Guillaume Rouille, 1588. Fine illustrated Italian verse adaptation of the New Testament, Rouille's eagle and serpent device on titlepage, and 160 woodcuts, mostly by Pierre Eskrich, fine typographic ornament on verso of otherwise blank final leaf, 8vo., grained brown morocco by Duru dated 1859, title lettered in gilt on spine, inner edges richly gilt, Samuel Ashton Thompson Yates emblematic bookplate dated 1894. Maggs Bros. Ltd.   1474 - 14   2016   £1500

Binding – Durvand

La Belle Ali Bois Dormant et Quelques Autres Contes de Jadis. Paris: Piazza & Cie, 1910. First edition in French, 303 x 230mm, no. 258 of 400 copies on Japon signed by Durvand (stamp signed), covers with triple gilt fillet border enclosing an elaborate gilt frame with cupids at corners and fancy gilt title lettering at center, flat spine with gilt decoration and lettering, gilt ruled turn-ins, marbled endleaves, top edge gilt, original wrappers bound in; with head and tailpieces, border designs for text and chapter pages, four decorative initials, two small medallions, 30 color plates by Edmund Dulac, mounted within decorative frames captioned in French, each with tissue guard, thin two inch crack at bottom of front joint, trivial marks and soiling to covers, faint residue from leather dressing, spine evenly sunned, otherwise excellent copy with bright gilt and text plates and tissue guards in pristine condition.   Phillip J. Pirages   67 - 119   2016 $1600

Binding – Dusel, Philip

Ritson, Joseph *Gammer Garton's Garland; or the Nursery Parnassus.* London: printed for R. Tiphood, 1810. First complete edition, octavo, modern dark purple morocco by Philip Dusel, gilt decorations and lettering, paper with scattered light browning, fine with wide margins.   The Brick Row Book Shop   Miscellany 69 - 24   2016 $2750

Binding – Edmond, J.

Dickens, Charles   1812-1870 *Bleak House.* London: Bradbury & Evans, circa, 1863? First edition, half title, frontispiece, engraved title, plates by Phiz, odd spot, contemporary half black calf by J. Edmond, Aberdeen, spine with raised gilt bands, devices in blind, morocco leather label, slightly rubbed, good plus, attractive.   Jarndyce Antiquarian Booksellers   CCXVIII - 503 2016   £450

Binding – Edmonds & Remnants

Barry, William Whittaker *A Walking Tour in Normandy.* London: Richard Bentley, 1868. First edition, original blue cloth by Edmonds & Remnants, slightly dulled, bookplate of John Etherington Welch Rolls, esq., The Hendre Co. Monmoth, very good.   Jarndyce Antiquarian Booksellers   CCXVII - 26   2016   £75

Darwin, Charles Robert   1809-1882 *On the Origin of Species by means of natural Selection...* London: W. Clowes and Sons for John Murray, 1859. First edition, 8vo. in 12's, original green cloth by Edmonds & Remnants, London retaining their ticket on lower pastedown, boards blocked in blind, rules enclosing foliate designs and central panel, spine gilt, mid brown endpapers, green cloth solander box with printed paper label to spine, 32 publisher's catalog dated June 1859, Freeman variant 3, folding lithographic plate by William West after Darwin, slight rubbing and bumping to extremities with very small ink spot to front board, hinges skilfully restored, little chipped to edges of endpapers and few leaves, nonetheless very bright, fresh copy in original cloth, bookplate of Pownoll William Phipps (b. 1835) using arms and motto of Earls of Mulgrave, whom he was a cousin.   Sotheran's   Piccadilly Notes - Summer 2015 - 5   2016   £95,000

Galton, Francis   1822-1911 *The Art of Travel or Shifts and Contrivances Available in Wild Coutnries.* London: John Murray, 1860. Third edition, woodcut, illustrations, original scarlet cloth by Edmonds and Remnants, spine faded, slightly dulled, leading inner hinge slightly cracked, ex-libris John Woern Hill.   Jarndyce Antiquarian Booksellers   CCXVII - 106   2016   £150

Binding – Embroidered

Massime Cristiane. Proposte a Meditarsi in Ciascun Giorno Del Mese. Milano: Per Federico Agnelli, 1774. 10th printing, page text with double rule border, head - tailpieces, decorative initial capital letters, 12mo., white cloth with green, black, yellow, pink and blue flower embroidery, all edges gilt, average wear and soiling to binding, period personal owner signature to front pastedown, respectable copy, rare.   Tavistock Books   Bibliolatry - 24   2016 $950

Binding – Enghlen, Dubois

Dickens, Charles   1812-1870   *Dombey and Sons.* London: Bradbury & Evans, 1848. First edition, bound in 2 volumes, half title, frontispiece and vignette title volume I, plates by Phiz, 8 line errata leaf volume II, later half morocco by Dubois D'Enghlen, spines gilt in compartments, black leather labels, spines uniformly faded, booklabels of Ronald George Taylor, very good, handsome.   Jarndyce Antiquarian Booksellers   CCXVIII - 440   2016   £380

Binding – Fairbairn

Mongez, Antoine   *Tableaux, Statues, Bas Reliefs E5 Camera De La Galerie De Florence et du PalaisPitti...* Paris: Lacombe, 1789-1814. 4 volumes bound in 2, frontispiece, 187 engraved illustrations on 200 sheets of India paper laid down on thick paper, with accompanying leaves of descriptive text, foxing as usual, some offsetting, tear to inner margin of dedication leaf, folio, contemporary green hard grained morocco by Fairbairn, multiple gilt and blind fillets on sides, outermost being wide and gilt, spines similarly decorated gilt, gilt edges, corners bumped and joints little rubbed.   Blackwell's Rare Books   B184 - 68   2016   £2000

Binding – Faulkner, H.

The Historie of Frier Rush: How He Came to a House of Religion to Seeke Service...   London: Harding and Wright for Robert Triphook, 1810. One of 4 copies on vellum, contemporary red velvet by H. Faulkner (ticket on verso front flyleaf), covers with wide Greek key border rolled in blind, flat spine with small remnant of leather backstrip (that has been laid on to hide a binder's titling error), red moire silk endleaves, turn-ins and pastedowns with rolls in blind, all edges gilt, housed in very good later leather edged slipcase, woodcut vignette on title, verso to front flyleaf with bookplate of Edward Vernon Utterson and morocco bookplate of Hans Furstenberg, bookplate of John Kershaw, contemporary inked note listing original owner of each of the four vellum copies of the present book, later pencilled note on same "Ths copy was after-wards in the possession of Mr. George Smith and it was (sold in his (s)ale for £9.15.0", spine mostly covered with (glue?) residue left by now basically missing leather backstrip, corners rubbed to board, portions of the joints torn, velvet nap somewhat diminished, a bit of natural rumpling to the vellum, very few inoffensive spots to margins, entirely solid (apart from spine remnants) an agreeable copy of this curious book.   Phillip J. Pirages   67 - 341   2016 $4500

Binding – Fazakerley

Robinson, Jacob   *North Country Sports and Pastimes. Wrestling and Wrestlers...*   London: Bemrose & Sons, Carlisle: The Wordsworth Press, 1893. First edition, scarce, 8vo., contemporary half red morocco by Fazakerley, lettered to gilt on spine, original printed wrappers bound in, little occasional browning, otherwise very good.   Sotheran's Hunting, Shooting & Fishing - 192   2016   £498

Shaw, George T.   *History of the Athenaeum.*   Liverpool: printed for the Committee of the Athenaeum by Rockcliff Bros. Ltd. 44 Castle Street, 1898. Small folio, contemporary full chocolate brown crushed morocco by Fazakerley of Liverpool, gilt stamped monogram to centre of the upper board, spine divided into six compartments with raised bands, lettered and dated in second and third compartments, gilt ruled edges, gilt dentelles, top edge gilt, marbled endpapers, gilt lettered brown morocco, presentation label to front pastedown, black and white photo frontispiece and 6 plates, 3 plans, bright, crisp, copy, presentation to Mandell Creighton, Bp. of London, bookplate of Sir Albert Richardson (1880-1964).   Sotheran's   Piccadilly Notes - Summer 2015 - 273   2016   £295

Binding – Forester, W.

The Gentleman's Library, Containing Rules for Conduct in all Parts of Life. London: published and sold by booksellers, 1813. New edition, 12mo., frontispiece, prelims browned and waterstained, some spotting and slight browning, contemporary full turquoise calf by W. Forester, dulled, spine chipped at head and tail, lacking label, contemporary signature on titlepage.   Jarndyce Antiquarian Books   CCXV - 219   2016   £45

Binding – Frost

Burton, Richard Francis   1821-1890   *The Book of the Thousand Nights and a Night. (and) Supplemental Nights.* Benares: printed by the Kamashastra Society for private subscribers only, 1885-1888. first printing of this edition, 16 volumes, 254 x 159mm., very pleasing rose colored half morocco over buckram boards by Brian Frost & Co. (signed each volume), raised bands, spine panels with gilt floral centerpiece or titling, marbled endpapers, top edge gilt titlepage printed in red and black, first and last few leaves of each volume generally with light foxing to these leaves bit more foxed, text shade less than bright because of paper stock chosen, still very fine, especially lustrous binding without fault with no signs of use internally.   Phillip J. Pirages   67 - 6   2016 $9500

Binding – Gehnrich, Daniel

Wharton, Edith   1862-1937   *Ethan Frome.*   Portland: Ascensius Press, 2002. One of 50 numbered copies, marbled paper covered boards, goatskin fore edges and spine by Daniel Gehnrich, very fine in publisher's cloth clamshell box.   Joseph J. Felcone, Inc.   Books from Five Centuries: a Miscellany - 150   2016 $900

Binding – Gerlach, Gerhard

Hunter, Dard   *Papermaking by Hand in India.*   New York: Pynson Printers, 1939. Limited to 370 numbered copies, signed by Hunter and by Elmer Adler, small folio, hand blocked India print cloth covered boards, black calf back by Gerhard Gerlach, deckled fore and bottom edges, slipcase, 42 leaves of illustrations, 27 actual specimens of handmade paper, slipcase rubbed on spine, few tiny scuff marks on leather spine, much better preserved binding than usually found.   Oak Knoll Books   310 - 194   2016 $1000

Binding – Giannini, Giulio

Oliphant, Laurence   1829-1888   *Altiora Peto.*   Leipzig: Bernhard Tauchnitz, 1883. First Tauchnitz edition, small octavo, 2 volumes, bound by Giulio Giannini of Florence, in full parchment with elaborate gilt stencilling and handpainting tempura in green and red, in manner that has been dubbed 'Florentine style", book's title on spine in black mediaeval script with red uncials, gilt floral endpapers, all edges gilt, binding is roughly contemporaneous with book's publication date, early gift inscription, very good.   Peter Ellis   112 - 281   2016   £125

Binding – Gonin

Suetonius   *Les Douze Cesars.*   Paris: F. L. Schmied, 1928. No. 165 of 175 copies, signed by artist, 292 x 200mm., dark blue crushed morocco by Gonin (stamp signed), spine lettered in gilt, turn-ins with silver fillet border, royal blue leather doublures and matching moire silk endleaves, original wrappers preserved, housed in later suede backed slipcase, decorative title and section titles printed in gold an 23 color illustrations by Schmied, comprised of 9 vignette tailpieces and 14 full page plates including 12 portraits, cracks with some looseness, along joints (no doubt because of heavy boards), covers with light polish residue, original wrappers heavily foxed, plates and text clean and fresh.   Phillip J. Pirages   67 - 310   2016 $2800

Binding – Graber, Lucy

Danticat, Edwidge   *The Coriolis Effect.*   Stockholm: Midnight Paper Sales, 2002. Limited to 170 numbered copies, hand set in monotype Walbaum and signed by him and author, Large 12mo., printed by Gaylord Schanilec on Zerkall paper, cover paper marbled by Carol Scott, bound by Franny Bannen and Lucy Graber, color illustrations.   Oak Knoll Books   310 - 123   2016 $125

Binding – Gray, John

Ballantine, James   *Poems.*   Edinburgh: Thomas Constable & Co., 1856. First edition, original pink morocco grained cloth by John Gray of Edinburgh, front board with central ornament in gilt, spine lettered gilt, bit rubbed, front broad with 2 small stains and slight crease.   Jarndyce Antiquarian Booksellers   CCXVIII - 885   2016   £50

Binding – Greenawalt, John Paul

Williams, Tennessee   1911-1983   *Tennessee.* Washington: David Bruce Smith, 2012. First edition, one of 750 numbered copies, elephant sized folio, 3 volumes, hand bound and loosely inserted in custom made clamshell case, specially built heavy cardboard mailer, book design and binding by John Paul Greenawalt.   Oak Knoll Books   310 - 94   2016 $3000

Binding – Gregory, George

Gould, John 1804-1881 *The Birds of Great Britain.* published by the author, 1862-1873. First edition, imperial folio, 25 parts in 5 volumes, bound by George Gregory of Bath in half green morocco, spines with gilt raised bands, lettering and elaborate tooling in custom made (c. 1990) walnut display case 38 x 36 x 25 inches, with lockable drawers, one for each volume, together with lockable hinged glass compartment that can be positioned like a lectern; with 367 hand colored lithographs, one text gathering bound in upside down in volume IV, slightly rubbed at extremities, occasional spots, otherwise extremely clean, very good, subscriber's copy with bookplate of Sir John William Cradock-Hartopp, 4th Baronet (1829-1888).   Sotheran's Piccadilly Notes - Summer 2015 - 7   2016   £90,000

Binding – Gregynog Bindery

Bible. Welsh - 1929 *Psalmali Dafydd Yn Ol William Morgan 1588. (The Psalms of David).*   Newtown: Gregynog Press, 1929. No. 199 of 200 copies of a total edition of 225, 298 x 220mm., original Niger backed patterned paper boards (stamped 'Gregynog Press Bindery" on rear pastedown), buckram corners, raised bands, gilt spine titling, top edge gilt, decorative wood engraved openings and initials by Horace Walter Bray, initials in red or blue, wood engraved title (with device) in red and black, part of text printed in blue, head of spine faintly darkened, trivial soiling to front board, mild spots of foxing and one small marginal stain to four leaves, otherwise very fine, binding unworn and text lean, fresh and bright.   Phillip J. Pirages   67 - 182   2016 $1000

Xenophon *Cyrupaedia (The Institution and Life of Cyrus).* Newtown: Gregynog Press, 1936. No. 123 of 135 copies (of 150 total, including 15 in different special binding by George Fisher), 311 x 216mm., handsome dark green oasis by Gregynog Bindery (stamp signed), covers with gilt decoration of Persian character, raised bands, gilt ruled spine compartments, top edge gilt, other edges untrimmed, felt lined green moire cloth chemise and excellent matching morocco backed slipcase, 9 floriated wood engraved initials by Loyd Haberly, hand colored in red and green, printed in red and black in Poliphilus type on Batchelor handmade paper, back cover with slightest hint of few shallow scratches, leaves nn-3-4 with slightest hint of few shallow scratches, leaves nn3-4 with light marginal foxing (whisper of foxing on couple of other leaves), otherwise choice, virtually no signs of use.   Phillip J. Pirages   67 - 185   2016 $3500

Xenophon *Cyrupaedia: the Institution and Life of Cyrus, The First of that Name, King of Persians.*   Newtown: Gregynog Press, 1936. Limited to 150 numbered copies, this one of 135 bound thus by Gregynog Bindery and signed at bottom of back cover on turn-in, 4to., original green oasis decorated with center and cornerpieces onlaid in red and light green, outlined in gilt and blocked in gilt decorations of Persian character, five raised bands gilt paneled spine, top edge gilt, printed under the direction of Lord Haberly who provided floriated wood engraved initials, well preserved inserted in clamshell box with matching green quarter leather.   Oak Knoll Books   310 - 108   2016 $2750

Binding – Grieve

The Library of Fiction, or Family Story-Teller... London: Chapman and Hall, 1836-1837. First edition, first issue, 2 volumes, half titles, plates by Robert Seymour, Buss &c., uncut in later 19th century full crushed red morocco by Grieve of Edinburgh, gilt spines, borders & dentelles, elaborate gilt cornerpieces, original spine strips laid in, slight rubbing, overall very good, handsome, top edge gilt.   Jarndyce Antiquarian Booksellers   CCXVIII - 52   2016   £1250

Maidment, James *A Book of Scotish Pasquils 1568-1715.* Edinburgh: William Paterson, 1868. One of 3 copies on vellum (and limited but unspecified number of copies printed on paper), 210 x 130mm., handsome contemporary crimson morocco, attractively gilt by Andrew Grieve (stamp signed on front turn-in), covers gilt with multiple plain and decorative rules enclosing a delicate frame, large and intricate fleuron at center of each cover, spine gilt in double ruled compartments with complex fleuron centerpiece and scrolling floral cornerpieces, turn-ins decorated with plain and decorative gilt rules, patterned burgundy and gold silk endleaves, top edge gilt, slightly worn matching morocco lipped slipcase, woodcut titlepage illustrations, numerous decorative tailpieces and occasional woodcut vignettes in text, front pastedown with armorial bookplate of H. D. Colvill-Scott, armorial bookplate of Clarence S. Bemens, tiny dark spot on spine corners and just hint of rubbing, couple of leaves with slightly rumpled fore edge, still fine, text clean, smooth and bright and binding unusually lustrous, virtually no wear.   Phillip J. Pirages   67 - 346   2016 $4500

Binding – Gruel

Paroissien: Elzevir, Rite Romain. Paris: Gruel et Englemann, 1889. 165 x 83mm., striking contemporary burgundy morocco, elaborately gilt by Gruel (stamp signed at tail of spine), upper cover with large and richly detailed oval bas-relief plaquette of the last supper framed above and below by a large panel of interlacing open strapwork comprised of abstracted gilt floral and foliate curls and other decorative elements, lower cover similarly decorated, with its central medallion containing a gilt cipher in intertwined majuscules, raised bands, spine gilt in double ruled compartments with central arabesque, gilt filigree turn-ins, claret moire silk endleaves, all edges gilt, original brass clasps with strapwork decoration, with 26 illustrations, composed of 22 large black and white woodcut headpieces and four chromolithographed plates with gold highlights, along with numerous uncolored woodcut initials, front free endleaf gilt stamp '24 Mai 1891', first Communion card of Andre Gallien dated 9 May 1895, laid in, very fine, morocco lustrous and leaves entirely crisp and clean.   Phillip J. Pirages   67 - 47   2016 $1100

Rabelais, Francois *Pantagruel.* Paris: Albert Skira, 1943. No. 85 of 275 copies on velin d'arches, signed by artist, 350 x 285mm., magnificent contemporary chocolate brown crushed morocco, elaborately inlaid and gilt by Leon Gruel (stamp signed on front turn-in), covers with exuberant Groliersque design of intricate dark red morocco strapwork accented with swirling azured gilt foliage and small tools, raised bands, spine in compartments framed by red morocco inlays, gilt fleuron centerpieces, gilt titling, chocolate brown morocco doublures framed with multiple gilt rules and azured foliate cornerpieces, rose colored watered silk endleaves, all edges gilt, original printed wrappers bound in, housed in original suede-lined chestnut morocco backed chemise and matching morocco trimmed slipcase, with 180 hand colored wood engravings by Andre Derain, 22 of them full page, 94 in text, 34 initials, 27 tailpieces, title engraving to front wrapper, frontispiece and title vignette, printed in Garamond typeface by Georges Gerard, wood engravings printed by Roger Lacouriere, flawless copy.   Phillip J. Pirages   67 - 46   2016 $33,000

Binding – Guild of Women Binders

Caldecott, Randolph *R. Caldecott's Picture Books.* London: Frederick Warne & Co., circa, 1900. Later edition, 2 quarto volumes, one in portrait format, one in landscape, contemporary full russet crushed morocco, Art Nouveau botanical designs tooled in blind and gilt, both volumes signed by Guild of Women Binders, color plates and sepia illustrations throughout text, stunning set.   Honey & Wax Booksellers   4 - 49   2016 $4500

Binding – Hammer, Trisha

Clemens, Samuel Langhorne   1835-1910   *The Innocents Abroad.* Chicago: Sherwin Beach Press, 1998. Number 57 of 200 copies, numbered and illustrated by the bookmakers, 2 volumes, non-adhesive binding with exposed spine sewing consists of 7 black double raised cords attached to hard covers wrapped in red cloth, each volume has cut-out to front cover with small black and white illustrations= along with author, title and volume number, the volumes in turn housed in black and white linen covered hard case wrapper and black leather straps over brass studs and leather suitcase-type label, intended to suggest a portmanteau, printed in Montype Bell on Johannot paper, designed by Bob McCamant and printed by Martha Chiplis, binding designed and executed by Trisha Hammer, fine.   The Kelmscott Bookshop   13 - 56   2016 $1200

Sandlin, Lee *Saving His Life.* Chicago: Sherwin Peach Press, 2008. Number 18 of 50 copies, signed by author and bookmakers, numerous family photos by Nina Sandlin, designed by Martha Chiplis, set in Monoytype Ehrhardt by Winifred and Michael Bixler, printed by Chiplis on handmade Twinrocker Taupe paper, photo etchings from family photos printed on Hosho, inset into book in debossed panels, map, Trisha Hammer has designed and executed a hidden crossed-structure binding in Nigerian goatskin with endpapers of Japanese silk housed in silk drawstring bag, fine. The Kelmscott Bookshop   13 - 54   2016 $1915

Shen, Juliet *Searching for Morris Fuller Benton: Discovering the Designer through his Typefaces.* Chicago: Sherwin Beach Press, 2011. No. 65 of 75 copies, signed by author, designed by Robert McCamant, set in Cloister Oldstyle cast by Dale Guild Type Foundry from ATF matrices and typeset by Art Larson and Rose Wisotzky at Horton Tank Graphics, printed on Mohawk Superfine, letterpress by Micahl Russeum of Kat Ran Press, offset illustrations and captions by Capitol Offset, Trisha Hammer designed and executed the black cloth binding with red stitching to open spine, fine.   The Kelmscott Bookshop   13 - 55   2016 $450

Binding – Harcourt Bindery

Shelley, Mary Wollestonecraft Godwin   1797-1851 *Frankenstein or the Modern Prometheus.* Northampton: Pennyroyal Press, 1983. No 175 of 305 copies, 2 volumes (including portfolio of prints), original tan quarter morocco over maroon with boards by Sam Ellenport at the Harcourt Bindery, raised bands, maroon leather label with calligraphic titling, matching publishers' folding cloth box just slightly marked, with the extra suite of plates by Barry Moser signed by him, very faint foxing to fore and tail edges of book block, half dozen pages with hardly perceptible very small spots of foxing, otherwise spotless and unworn.   Phillip J. Pirages   67 - 279   2016 $3000

Binding – Hatchards

Dickens, Charles 1812-1870 *Memoirs of Joseph Grimaldi.* London: Richard Bentley, 1838. First edition, 2nd issue, 2 volumes, half titles, frontispiece, plates by George Cruikshank, 36 page catalog volume II, later full scarlet morocco for Hatchards. gilt spines and double ruled borders, original pink cloth, spine strips bound in at end of each volume, armorial bookplate of William H. R. Saunders, top edge gilt, very good.   Jarndyce Antiquarian Booksellers CCXVIII - 216   2016   £420

Verney, Frances Parthenope *Memoirs of the Verney Family.* London: Longmans Green & Co., 1892. First edition, 4 volumes, photogravure plates, period bindings by Hatchards of three quarter brown morocco with raised bands, gilt rules, cloth sides, marbled endpapers, top edges gilt, armorial bookplate of Kennet of Dene on each board is family's gilt coat of arms, near fine, handsome set.   Peter Ellis   112 - 115   2016   £350

Binding – Hatton

Callimachus *Hymni, Epigrammata et Fragmenta.* Paris: Excudebat Sebastianus Mabre-Cramoisy, 1675. First Dacier edition, gently washed and pressed at time of rebinding, browned titlepage then also expertly mounted on an old binder's blank, two sets of Macclesfield blindstamps to first three leaves, 4to., 19th century green pebbled morocco by Hatton of Manchester, spine faded, front joint rubbed, Macclesfield arms in gilt to front board, all edges gilt, marbled endpapers, bookplate, good.   Blackwell's Rare Books B186 - 35   2016   £500

Euclides *Geometricorum Elementorum Libri XV.* Paris: Henri Estienne 7 Jan., 1516-1517. Sixth edition, Roman types, numerous woodcut geometrical diagrams in margins, fine crible initials in a variety of styles and sizes, titlepage soiled and cut down and mounted on old paper, one diagram just cropped at its extreme outer corners, without final blank, folio, 19th century half brown calf by Hatton of Manchester, marbled edges, original order for the binder loosely inserted, the Macclesfield copy with bookplate but no blindstamps and annotated by John Collins, after his death his books were acquired by William Jones and thence to Shirburn Castle, scarce on the market, preserved in cloth folding box, good copy.   Blackwell's Rare Books   Marks of Genius - 16   2016   £12,000

Binding – Hayday

Jones, Owen 1809-1874 *The Sermon on the Mount.* London: Longman & Co., 1844. 36 pages, text illuminated by Owen Jones & chromolithographed in color, some spotting and (mainly) marginal marking, original dark purple by Hayday, blocked in blind with onlaid paper labels to both boards, all edges gilt, contemporary gift inscription, very rare.   Jarndyce Antiquarian Booksellers   CCXVII - 142   2016   £280

Binding – Hayes, W.

Ingram, James *Memorials of Oxford.* Oxford: John Henry Parker; H. Slatter and W. Graham, 1837. First edition, Volume I-(III), 3 general views as frontispieces, folding plan in volume iii, and 94 plates, all steel engraved, some foxing as usual, wood engraved titlepage vignettes and numerous text illustrations, 8vo., contemporary green morocco by W. Hayes of Oxford, extremities very slightly rubbed, spine with raised bands, gilt lettered direct in second and third compartments, remainder panelled with wheel decoration, sides gilt panelled with wide gilt borders, single fillet on board edges, gilt roll on turn-ins, gilt edges, very good. Blackwell's Rare Books   B186 - 109   2016   £70

Binding – Henderson & Bisset

Coleridge, Samuel Taylor 1772-1834 *The Rime of the Ancient Mariner.* Edinburgh: R. & R. Clark Ltd., 1945. Limited to 700 copies, frontispiece and color illustrations, five total, by Duncan Grant, marginal notes printed in red, plates made and printed by Raynard Press on Arnold handmade paper, binding executed by Henderson and Bisset, Edinburgh and the medallion and lettering on binding designed by Percy Metcalfe, 8vo., full blue leather, front board stamped with gilt design, top edge gilt, other edges uncut, spine faded, faint stain along bottom of back cover. Oak Knoll Books   310 - 36   2016 $300

Binding – Hering

Cory, Alexander Turner *The Hieroglyphics of Horapollo Nilous.* London: William Pickering, 1840. 193 x 118mm., very attractive contemporary olive green morocco elaborately gilt by Hering (stamp signed), covers with delicate gilt frame of drawer handle, floral sprig and star tools, raised bands, spine gilt in compartments with similar tooling, densely gilt turn-ins, pale yellow endpapers, all edges gilt, frontispiece, numerous representations of hieroglyphics and 3 plates, pencilled presentation from author to the illustrator of the work, Joseph Bonomi, engraved bookplate of Samuel Ashton Thompson-Yates, just slightest hint of rubbing to joints (well marked with dye), faint graze on rear cover, spine probably sunned (though abundance of gilt making this difficult to determine), significant foxing to prelim leaves, frontispiece and titlepage (moderate foxing to plates II and III and adjacent text leaves), but text otherwise clean and fresh, decorative binding lustrous scarcely worn and altogether pleasing.   Phillip J. Pirages   67 - 49   2016 $1500

Coryate, Thomas *Coryats Crudities, Hastily gobled up in five Moneths....* London: printed by VV(illiam) S(tansby for the author), 1611. First edition, 4to., full Regency diced tan calf by Charles Hering (engraved label, firm active in London 1794-1844), spine with raised bands, ornamented and lettered gilt, ornamented in blind as well, boards with filigree gilt stamped fleurons in corners, dotted gilt ruling, gothic ornamentation in blind, edges and inner dentelles ornamented in gilt, marbled endpapers, red edges, engraved title, engraved full page portrait and one heraldic engraving, 4 engraved plates, woodcut ornaments in text, rebacked retaining original spine, gathering 2N with tiny traces of worming in upper margins, very light even browning or minimal spotting, folding plate of Strasbourg clock little cropped as usual, title little cropped at upper margin, very good, elaborate binding, bookplate of Henry Yates Thompson (1838-1928). Sotheran's Travel and Exploration - 230 2016 £17,000

Gerning, Johann Isaac Von, Baron *A Picturesque Tour along the Rhine.* London: R. Ackermann, 1820. First edition in English, first issue, one of 50 large paper copies, 422 x 324mm., excellent contemporary red half morocco over marbled boards by Charles Hering (stamp signed), newly rebacked and recornered to style by Courtland Benson, wide raised bands and panels, attractively gilt in scrolling designs, gilt titling, all edges gilt, 24 hand colored plates of the Rhine (plus one folding map), armorial bookplate "RGV" with evidence of bookplate removal, offsetting onto tissue guards (indicating they have done their job), one tissue guard missing (but not offsetting onto text in this case), isolated trivial thumbing, foxing or rust spots, but fine and especially desirable copy, beautifully restored binding unworn, text and plates with only most minor imperfections and margins of special copy remarkably broad. Phillip J. Pirages 67 - 167 2016 $10,000

Binding – Hertzberg, Ernst, & Sons

Hawthorne, Nathaniel 1804-1864 *The Complete Works.* Cambridge: Printed at the Riverside Press, 1883. No. 68 of 250 copies of the Riverside edition, 248 x 159mm. restrained but attractive early 20th century brown crushed morocco by Ernst Hertzberg & Sons (stamp-signed), covers with frame formed by pairs of plain gilt rules and single gilt dot at each corner, raised bands, spine compartments gilt in same design as covers, gilt titling, turn-ins densely gilt in palmette pattern, marbled endpaper, top edges gilt, other edges rough trimmed, all volumes with frontispieces and titlepages with etched vignette, large paper copy on laid paper, titlepages in red and black, spines faintly and evenly sunned, just hint of wear to tops of three spines, beautiful set, lustrous bindings almost entirely unworn and text unusually clean, fresh and bright. Phillip J. Pirages 67 - 193 2016 $2000

Binding – Hollingsworth, Marsha

Anderson, Jon *Cypresses: Poems.* Port Townsend: Graywolf Press, 1981. First edition, one of 325 copies, printed in Bembo type on Frankfurt Creme paper, one of 100 copies, hand bound by Marsha Hollingsworth, this copy # 12 signed by poet. Second Life Books, Inc. 196A - 31 2016 $75

Carlile, Henry *Running Lights: Poems by...* Port Townsend: Dragon Gate, 1981. First edition, 1/30 special copies, gray cloth with black spine, hand bound by Marsha Hollingsworth, illustration by Carl Morris applied on front, signed by Carlile and Morris. Second Life Books, Inc. 196A - 253 2016 $75

Binding – Hoyt-Koch, Shelley

Poage, Michael *Handbook of Ornament.* San Francisco: Black Stone Press, 1979. Limited to 500 copies, this one of 26 numbered copies, signed by author, hand bound by Shelley Hoyt-Koch, 8vo., quarter cloth, paper covered boards, label on spine. Oak Knoll Books 310 - 86 2016 $125

Binding – Hynes, R.

Woolnoth, William *A Graphical Illustration of the Metropolitan Cathedral Church of Canterbury.* London: T. Cadell & W. Davies and J. Murray, 1816. Large paper copy, royal 4to., 20 plates on India paper, foxing to front and rear blanks and plates, text pages generally clean barring occasional offset toning from plates, neat pencil notes to pages 92-3, early 20th century half burgundy morocco gilt title to spine, blue marbled paper boards, edges sprinkled red, endcaps, joints and corners bit worn, edges slightly chipped but very good overall, bookplate of A. D. Gondinton dated 1901, recent bookplate of Susan Wade, tiny bookbinder's label of R. Hynes, Dover, catalog description pasted in, some pencilled booksellers notes to prelim blanks, note to list of subscribers identifies this as the copy belonging to Mr. Jesse White, Canterbury. Unsworths Antiquarian Booksellers Ltd. 30 - 165 2016 £350

Binding – Ingalton

Gray, Thomas 1716-1771 *The Works of Thomas Gray.* London: Harding, Triphook and Lepard, 1825. 2 volumes, extremely appealing contemporary red straight grain morocco, attractively gilt by Ingalton of Eton (with their ticket), 197 x 114mm., covers with double fillet border enclosing a triple fillet frame with gilt tooled leafy cornerpieces, central panel enclosed by single fillet with roundel corners, raised bands, spine compartments gilt with leafy frames, turn-ins with dense gilt roll, all edges gilt, engraved frontispiece portrait of gray, first prelim leaf to volume I with inked inscription 'George Chester Cooper/Given to him by his friend George Pickering/Eton. March 1830", just vaguest rubbing and abrasions to covers, minor foxing to frontispiece and prelim leaves, pretty set in very fine condition, clean and fresh internally, gleaming bindings with virtually no wear.   Phillip J. Pirages   67 - 45   2016 $950

Binding – Isacke

Dickens, Charles 1812-1870 *American Notes for General Circulation.* London: Chapman and Hall, 1842. First edition, first issue, 2 volumes in 1, half title, volume I only with small tear in outer margin, contemporary half brown calf by Isacke of Edgeware Rd., spine gilt in compartments, red and green leather labels, slightly chipped at head of spine , little rubbed, good plus.   Jarndyce Antiquarian Booksellers   CCXVIII - 318   2016   £250

Binding – Johanknecht, Susan

Hughes, Ted 1930-1998 *Chiasmadon.* Baltimore: Charles Seluzicki, 1977. First edition, one of 5 or 6 copies specially bound for participants of the edition, out of a total of 175 copies, square 8vo., original quarter black leather and decorated paper boards by Susan Johanknecht, this ad personam copy, designated for "Victoria Fraser" in Van Vliet's hand, very fine copy.   James S. Jaffe Rare Books Occasional List: Winter 2016 - 82   2016 $4500

Binding – Joubert

Horatius Flaccus, Quintus *(Opera).* Londini: Gulielmus Pickering, 1824. Large paper copy, 32mo., portrait frontispiece, 1 engraved plate, very light occasional foxing but still nice and bright inside, contemporary red morocco by Joubert, gilt title to spine, gilt dentelles, bright blue morocco doublures, top edge gilt, joints and corners little worn, small split starting at head of lower board, slight discoloration to free endpapers from leather joints, illegible inscription ot f.f.e.p, verso bookseller's pencilled notes to rear.   Unsworths Antiquarian Booksellers   30 - 44   2016   £250

Binding – Joyce, Carol

Paz, Octavio *Three Poems. Tres Poems.* New York: Limited Editions Club, 1987. Limited to 750 signed copies, this #543, elephant folio, original lithographs by Robert Motherwell with tissue guards, bound in linen with red paper label front cover, black lettering spine, types used are Bauer Bodoni Bold and Bauer Bodoni Bold Italic, cast by Fundicion Tipografica Neufville, text handset at Stamperia Valdonega, with label rear paste-down staining the book was hand-sewn and bound by Carol Joyce, text printed on mould made paper from Cartiere Enrico Magnani, lithographs printed at Trestle Editions on various handmade Japanese papers, in fine original clamshell box with black lettering on spine.   By the Book, L. C.   45 - 62   2016 $2700

Binding – Kalthoeber

Vergilius Maro, Publius *Opera Varietate Lectiones et Perpetua Adnotations Illustrata....* Typis T.. Rickaby, Impensis T. Payne, B. & J. White, R. Faulder, & J. Edwards, 1793. Large paper copy, engraved frontispiece and dedication, one bifolium missed by stitching and hence loose, little minor toning and spotting, 4to., contemporary straight grained red morocco by Kalthoeber, with his ticket in volume i, boards bordered with triple gilt fillet, spines divided by raised bands between gilt titles, second and third compartments, gilt lettered direct, edges gilt, marbled endpapers, joints rubbed, spines somewhat scuffed, little darkening to spine and joints, from old polishing attempt?, short tear to head of front joint volume i, armorial bookplate of John Perrett, good.   Blackwell's Rare Books   B184 - 88   2016   £1200

Binding – Kennedy, Lawton

Stevenson, Robert Louis Balfour 1850-1894 *An Apology for Idlers.* Oakland: Ben Kennedy, 1931. Number 81 of 110 numbered copies, illustrations, bound by Lawton Kennedy, small octavo, color titlepage illustration, 5 small text illustrations, cloth backed blue boards prin ted and illustrated paper label on front cover, light rubbing to spine, boards slightly faded, but fine.   Argonaut Book Shop Private Press 2015 - 6390   2016 $50

Binding – Kerr & Richardson

Settle, Elkanah *The New Athenian Comedy...* London: for Campanella Restio, 1693. First edition, small 4to., browned throughout, author's name written in pencil on titlepage, late 19th century half morocco and marbled boards by Kerr and Richardson (head and foot of spine chipped, front joint lightly chipped), from the library of James Stevens Cox (1910-1997), 20th century signature of James Bell.   Maggs Bros. Ltd.   1447 - 379   2016   £250

Binding – Krauss, Max

Epicurus *Brief an Menoikeus.* N.P.: Fischbachpresse, 2007. Limited to 144 numbered copies signed by binder, Max Krauss, 12 copies, each with different states of binding, bound by Krauss and Wolfgang Kreuzer, woodcut illustrations by Kraus, paper covered boards, sewn, leather spine label, top edge cut, other edges uncut, slipcase, presentation laid in with signatures of Krauss and Kreuzer. Oak Knoll Books   310 - 100   2016 $350

Binding – Kreuzer, Wolfgang

Epicurus *Brief an Menoikeus.* N.P.: Fischbachpresse, 2007. Limited to 144 numbered copies signed by binder, Max Krauss, 12 copies, each with different states of binding, bound by Krauss and Wolfgang Kreuzer, woodcut illustrations by Kraus, paper covered boards, sewn, leather spine label, top edge cut, other edges uncut, slipcase, presentation laid in with signatures of Krauss and Kreuzer. Oak Knoll Books   310 - 100   2016 $350

Binding – Krumin

Stillwell, Margaret Bingham *Gutenberg and the Catholicon of 1460.* New York: Edmond Byrne Hackett, Brick Row Sheop, 1916. Library edition, large folio, title printed in red and black, original leaves laid into well in back pastedown held by metal stays, original full crimson buckram over bevelled boards by Krumin of Boston (stamp signed), covers decoratively stamped in blind, front cover lettered gilt, fine, chemised in original morocco grain paper over board and slipcase, slipcase shows wear, else fine. Heritage Book Shop   Holiday 2015 - 72   2016 $7500

Binding – Larkins

Glascock, William Nugent *Land Sharks and Sea Gulls.* London: Richard Bentley, 1838. First edition, 3 volumes, frontispiece and plates, small marginal tear to plate facing page 58 volume III, handsomely rebound by J. Larkins in half red morocco, raised bands, decorated and lettered gilt, top edge gilt, very good. Jarndyce Antiquarian Booksellers   CCXVII - 110   2016   £450

Kipling, Rudyard   1865-1936 *The Jungle Book & The Second Jungle Book.* London: Macmillan, 1894. 1895. First editions, 2 volumes, half titles, frontispiece in volume I, illustrations, slight spotting to prelims in volume II, some offsetting from dentelles on f.e.p.'s, finely bound in full dark blue crushed morocco by J. Larkins, double ruled gilt borders with floral corner pieces, raised gilt ruled bands, compartments in gilt, elaborate gilt dentelles, very light rubbing to extremities, fine and handsome set. Jarndyce Antiquarian Booksellers   CCXVII - 149   2016   £1500

Binding – Lauriat

Lamb, Charles   1775-1834 *The Works of Charles and Mary Lamb and the Life of Charles Lamb.* London: Methuen & Co., 1903-1905. 9 volumes, 222 x 146mm., especially attractive contemporary red morocco, elaborately gilt (stamp signed 'Charles E. Lauriat'), covers framed by two plain gilt rules, raised bands, spines lavishly gilt in compartments with large central fleuron surrounded by a lozenge of small tools and intricate scrolling cornerpieces, densely gilt turn-ins, top edges gilt, extravagantly extra illustrated with 653 plates, five of these folding, two double page, and two colored, engraved bookplate of Joel Cheney Wells, just vaguest hint of rubbing to extremities, isolated small marginal stains, still handsomely bound in fine condition, fresh and clean internally and in lustrous bindings with few signs of wear. Phillip J. Pirages   67 - 132   2016 $4500

Binding – Leighton

Aneau, Barthelemy *Imagination Poetique Tradicte en Vers Francois des Latins & Grece....* Lyons: Mace Bonhomme, after 8 September, 1552. Extremely rare first edition, titlepage with Bonhomme's Perseus device and 105 cuts attributed to Pierre Eskrich (from metal plates), small 8vo., limp ivory vellum by Leighton, upper cover with gilt lettered title and date within elaborate frame, flat gilt spine, bookplate of S. A. Thompson Yates 1894. Maggs Bros. Ltd.   1474 - 6   2016   £12,000

Binding – Leighton, Henry

Marlowe, Christopher   1564-1593 *Hero and Leander.* London: printed at the Ballantyne Press, 1894. One of 220 copies, 200 for sale, publisher's full vellum by Henry Leighton (stamp signed with his cipher at lower right corner of covers), tooled in gilt, abstract geometric design by Charles Ricketts, covers with compartmentalized central panel, large gilt leaves at corners interlocking "Cs" and date in Roman numerals, spine with gilt title at head and "VI" device at tail, fine modern navy folding cloth box; with elaborate woodcut initials, full white vine border on opening page and 7 wood engravings by Ricketts and Shannon, bookplate of "Beach", significant splaying to covers, one leaf with old repair to corner (torn by rough opening?), three openings and rear flyleaves rather foxed, text a shade less than bright, other minor problems internally, still pleasant copy because of clean, unworn binding. Phillip J. Pirages   67 - 329   2016 $2200

Binding – Leighton, Son & Hodge

Nesfield, William Eden *Specimens of Mediaeval Architecture, Chiefly Selected from Examples of the 12th and 13th Centuries in France and Italy.*   London: Day and Son at gate Street Near Lincoln Inn Fields, Jan. A.D., 1862. First edition, folio, wood engraved title by Dalziel after author, including figures by Albert Moore, 100 lithographic plates, including one in chromolithography by A. Newman, original purple roan backed brick colored cloth blocked in black, upper cover reproducing title leaf with inlaid panel of red calf blocked in gold spine decorated and lettered gilt and black, all edges gilt, binder ticket of Leighton Son and Hodge, contemporary bookplate of Frederick Stacey. Marlborough Rare Books   List 55 - 50   2016   £250

Pyle, Howard *Otto of the Silver Hand.* London: Sampson Low, Marston & Co., 1893. Ad leaf preceding half title, frontispiece, plates, original turquoise cloth by Leighton Son & Hodge, pictorially blocked and lettered in black, silver and gilt, slightly dulled, contemporary ownership inscription, top edge gilt, good plus.   Jarndyce Antiquarian Booksellers   CCXVII - 243   2016   £85

Stanley, Henry Morton   1841-1904 *In Darkest Africa or the Quest, Rescue and Retreat of Emin, Governor of Equatoria.*   London: William Clowes and Sons, Limited for Sampson Low, Marston, Searle and Rivington ltd., 1890. First edition, 8vo., 2 volumes, original brick red pictorial cloth by Leighton, Son and Hodge with their ticket on lower pastedown of volume I, upper boards decorated and lettered in black and gilt, spines decorated and lettered in black and gilt, map endpapers, one wood engraved frontispiece and one in photogravure, both retaining tissue guards, 37 wood engraved plates, 3 folding, color printed lithographic maps, one color printed lithographic geological profile, one folding letterpress table, numerous wood engraved illustrations in text, extremities very lightly rubbed, slight foxing throughout (less than usual), maps with minor repaired tears, spines color not sunned at all and consistent with covers, these with sharp corners and edges, unusually good set in original pictorial cloth.   Sotheran's   Travel and Exploration - 37   2016   £575

Walton, Elijah *Vignettes: Alpine and Eastern.. in two Series. Eastern Series.* London: W. M. Thompson, 1873. First edition, folio, original maroon cloth over bevelled boards by Leighton, Son and Hodge, upper board blocked with design in gilt, lower board blocked in blind, spine lettered gilt, lemon yellow endpapers, all edges gilt, mounted chromolithograph plates, each with tissue guard, binding with wear and little faded, front hinge reinforced, occasional light spotting on card mounts, text little browned, else very good.   Sotheran's   Travel and Exploration - 388   2016   £1450

Binding – Lintott, Mark

Dickinson, Emily   1830-1886 *A Thought Went Up in My Mind To-day.* Octon: Verdigris Press, 2014. Artist's book, one of 10 copies from a total issue of 14, all on Hahnemulhe paper, each copy signed and numbered by artist, Judith Rothchild, page size 4 x 3 1/8 inches, 10 pages, bound by printer, Mark Lintott, in Venetian marbled ochre and lime papers over boards, leporello-style title debossed in blind on front cover, also title printed in black on Venetian marbled paper affixed to brown linen spine of book, slipcase housed housed in matching ochre colored paper over boards slipcase.   Priscilla Juvelis - Rare Books   66 - 17   2016 $700

Lawrence, David Herbert   1885-1930 *Snake.* Octon: Verdigris Press, 2014. Artist's book, one of 4 deluxe copies, from a total edition of 50, deluxe with original copperplate drawing, page size 5 1/4 x 12 inches, bound by Mark Lintott, leporello style in brown boards with title printed in blind on front panel, drawing housed in same brown paper over boards, housed in gold faux snakeskin portfolio laid into clamshell box, copperplate inset into front panel of clamshell box, slipcase and clamshell box of same gold faux snakeskin, manmade material, painted and sanded by artist to resemble belly of a snake, title printed in brown on front panel, title, author, artist and press printed in brown on spine, four mezzotints by Judith Rothchild.   Priscilla Juvelis - Rare Books   66 - 18   2016 $2200

Binding – Lloyd, F. R. S.

Aesopus *Aesop's Fables.* printed for John Stockdale, 1793. First edition, 8vo., 2 volumes, later full red crushed morocco by F. R. S. Lloyd, boards with gilt panels, spines richly decorated and lettered gilt with green morocco onlay raised bands, 112 engraved plates, including vignette titles, little rubbing to joints, some light offsetting from plates, very good.   Sotheran's   Piccadilly Notes - Summer 2015 - 14   2016   £1500

Binding – Lloyd, Trevor

Eden, Frederic Morton *The State of the Poor.* London: J. David for B. & J. White, G. G. & J. Robinson, T. Payne, R. Faulder, T. Gerton, J. Debrett and D. Bremmer, 1797. First edition, 3 volumes, quarto, bound without final leaf of volume III (directions to binder), which was usually omitted when book was bound, superby rebound to style by Trevor Lloyd in full tree calf, covers ruled gilt with a metope-and-septaglyph roll, spines richly gilt with red morocco lettering pieces, volumes numbered on red oval onlays over black morocco labels, inner dentelles ruled in gilt with Greek-key roll, marbled endpapers, an excellent copy,.   Heritage Book Shop   Holiday 2015 - 36   2016 $10,000

Binding – Loeber, Nancy

Maret, Russell *Linear A to Linear Z: Twenty-Six Linoleum Cuts by Russell Maret.* New York: Russell Maret, 2015. Limited to 90 copies, this one of 70 copies bound in paper wrappers by Nancy Loeber.   Oak Knoll Books   310 - 121   2016 $675

Binding – Luis Pettingell Bindery

Cohen, Henry-Jacques *Sous Le Signe Du Rossignol. (Under the Sight of the Nightingale).* Paris: Sur les Presses de Pierre Frazier, Oct. 15, 1923. First edition, no. 121 of 1500 copies, 306 x 235mm., later coral colored quarter morocco over marbled boards by the Luis Pettingell Bindery of Berkeley, California (ticket), raised bands, gilt ruled compartments with central fleuron, 19 color plates by Kay Nielsen, each mounted within a decorative frame with captioned and decorated tissue guard, spine rather sunned, with gilt bit dulled, light purple stain to edge of front free endpaper, otherwise very fine, no signs of use.   Phillip J. Pirages   67 - 262   2016 $1250

Binding – Mackenzie, J.

Lyons, Daniel *Magna Britannia; Being a Concise Topographical Account of the Several Counties of Great Britain.* London: printed for T. Cadell and W. Davies, 1806-1822. Large paper copy, 346 x 260mm., 6 volumes bound in 10, pleasing contemporary red hard-grain half morocco over marbled boards by J. Mackenzie & son (stamp signed), raised bands, spines attractively gilt in compartments with very large and complex central fleuron surrounded by small tools and volute cornerpieces, gilt titling, marbled endpapers, all edges gilt, with 398 plates of maps, plans, views and architecture, 264 as called for and extra illustrated with 134, the total including 72 double page, 7 folding and 13 in color, engraved armorial bookplate of Arthur Soames, signed and dated in the plate by C. Hebard, paper boards somewhat chafed, extremities (especially bottom edge of boards), rather rubbed, spines slightly (but uniformly) darkened, few of the leather corners abraded, small portions of morocco dulled from preservatives, but bindings completely solid with no cracking to joints and still impressive on shelf, handsomely decorated spines unmarked, majority of plates with variable foxing (usually minimal, but perhaps two dozen noticeably foxed), a number of engravings with small, faint dampstains at very edge of top margin, text itself very fine, looking remarkably clean, fresh, smooth within its vast margins.   Phillip J. Pirages   67 - 245   2016 $5900

Binding – MacKenzie, John Whitefoord

Nisbet, Alexander *An Essay on the Ancient and Modern Use of Armories; Shewing their Origin, Definition and Division of them into their Several Species.* Edinburgh: printed by William Adam Junior, for Mr. James Mackeuen, 1718. First edition, fine in beautiful binding, 4to., mid 19th century full red morocco 18th century style, bound by John Whitefoord MacKenzie, elaborately gilt, gilt spine (slightly faded) in 7 compartments, raised bands, black leather label, gilt edges, inner gilt dentelles, marbled endpaper, engraved plates, all edges gilt.   Howard S. Mott Inc.   265 - 101   2016 $600

Binding – Maclehose

Scott, Walter   1771-1832 *The Doom of the Devorgoil, A Melo-Drama. (and) Alichindrane or the Ayrshire Tragedy.* Edinburgh: printed by Ballantyne for Cadell and Co., Edinburgh and Simpkin and Marshall, London, 1830. First separate and complete edition, 229 x 1522m., attractive late 19th century dark green armorial morocco by Maclehose of Glasgow (stamp signed), covers gilt with heraldic pelican crest of Thomas Glen Arthur of Garrick House, Ayr, flat spine with title at head and author at tail and five gilt rnaments in between (comprised of three thistles and two heraldic devices), gold endleaves, top edge gilt, other edges untrimmed (front hinge and joint with careful repairs, front free endpaper and first flyleaf cut near gutter and reattached with cellophane), large paper presentation copy, inscribed by Harry A. Sickles, Christmas 1917 for friend Frank P. Leffingwell, short crack beginning at bottom of front joint, hint of fading and leather dressing residue to covers, otherwise in excellent, binding solid and lustrous, text clean and fresh, margins very commodious.   Phillip J. Pirages   67 - 312   2016 $1000

Binding – Mansell

Dodsley, Robert   1703-1764 *A Select Collection of Old English Plays.* London: Reeves and Turner, 1874. Fourth edition, one of a handful of large paper copies on fine laid paper, one of a handful of large paper copies on fine laid paper, 229 x 152mm., 15 volumes, elegant contemporary polished calf by Mansell (stamp-signed each volume), gilt in compartments, circular brown morocco volume label in garland and wheel pattern, each spine with additional red light brown and black morocco labels, gilt inner dentelles, marbled endpapers, top edges gilt, others untrimmed, 10 woodcut illustrations on one leaf in volume I, front pastedowns with armorial bookplate of Horatio Noble Pym, rear cover of final volume somewhat marked and soiled, spines uniformly just bit darker than boards with occasional minor abrasions, blanks and text leaves lightly foxed at beginning and end of few volumes, otherwise handsome set in fine, clean condition, virtually immaculate internally.   Phillip J. Pirages   67 - 52   2016 $2000

Binding – Marius Michel

Hamilton, Anthony 1646-1720 *Memoirs of Count Grammont.* London and Edinburgh: printed by Ballantyne, Hanson and Co., 1889. Number 101 of 780 copies, 292 x 191mm., extended to 2 volumes and extra illustrated with portraits, views etc. by John Runkle, very fine contemporary scarlet morocco elaborately gilt by Marius Michel (stamp signed on front doublures), covers featuring concentric French fillet panels with intricate cornerpieces between them, raised bands, gilt ruled spine of compartments with elegant foliate curls and complex central lozenge composed of several fleurons, forest green morocco doublures with large central panel formed by lobed French fillets, gilt tooled inner and outer cornerpieces and sidepieces, gilt decorated turn-ins, marbled endpapers, 33 etchings, along with 167 engraved extra illustrations for a total of 200 images, large paper copy, color of spines just shade different from cover, isolated vague spotting of no consequence in the text, inserted plates occasionally with minor foxing, especially attractive set in fine condition, text clean and fresh, margins vast and bindings lustrous and unworn.   Phillip J. Pirages 67 - 53   2016 $1250

Muller, Eugene *La Mionette.* Paris: Librairie L. Conquet, 1885. No. 12 of 150 large paper copies (and 850 regular copies), 197 x 133mm., lovely dark green crushed morocco, gilt and inlaid by Marius Michel (stamp signed on front turn-in), covers with double gilt rule frame enclosing central floral wreath bearing red and white morocco roses, leafy rose branch at corners with red or white blossom, tiny gilt bees whimsically buzzing around flowers (one on upper cover, three on lower), raised bands, spine gilt in compartments with central rose sprig bearing a red or white bloom, foliate cornerpieces, densely gilt turn-ins, marbled endpapers, all edges gilt, original pink wrappers bound in (front cover with small portrait), housed in marbled paper slipcase, with a total of 84 illustrations by Oreste Cortazzo (two large and 26 smaller vignettes, each in three states, eau fort pure, before letters and complete, the third state of the smaller vignettes always printed in the text, rest on pages that are otherwise blank), with an additional state of the wrapper portrait printed on China paper, quite minor offsetting from engravings (though always onto blank page, never onto text), otherwise virtually perfect, lovely binding and unworn, text and cuts in very fine condition.   Phillip J. Pirages 67 - 54   2016 $850

Binding – Matthews

Dibdin, Thomas Frognall 1776-1847 *A Bibliographical Antiquarian and Picturesque Tour in the Northern Counties of England and Scotland.* London: printed for the author by C. Richards, 1838. First edition, 2 volumes, 251 x 156mm., list of subscribers in volume 1, handsome early 20th century red morocco gilt by Matthews (stamp-signed on front turn-in), covers with gilt French fillet border enclosing a simple lobed panel, raised bands, spines very attractively gilt in compartments with spiral cornerpieces and centerpiece featuring either a fleur-de-lys, a manuscript scroll and quill or Dibdin's cipher, gilt inner dentelles, marbled endpapers, all edges gilt, numerous engravings in text, and 44 engraved plates as called for, tiniest bit of rubbing to joints and corners, minor foxing (mostly marginal) to all but a handful of plates, otherwise, especially pleasing set in fine condition, text clean and bright and decorative bindings very lustrous with almost no signs of use.   Phillip J. Pirages 67 - 55   2016 $2250

Strutt, Joseph *The Sports and Pastimes of the People of England Including the Rural and Domestic Recreations...* London: printed for Thomas Tegg, 1831. 260 x 165mm., very attractive later 19th century deep forest green crushed morocco, gilt by William Matthews (stamp-signed), covers with gilt French fillet, raised bands, spine gilt in compartments with central hunting themed ornament, stippled scrolling cornerpieces, gilt titling, turn-ins with very elegant gilt scrolling floral decoration, marbled endleaves, all edges gilt, 137 illustrations, full page plate and 136 numbered wood engravings in text, bookplate of George Edward Dimock, isolated very minor foxing, otherwise in very fine condition, unusual clean and fresh internally and accomplished binding lustrous and unworn.   Phillip J. Pirages 67 - 56   2016 $1500

Webster, John *A Monumental Columnne, Erected to the Liuing Memory of the Euer-Glorious Henry, late Prince of Wales.* London: printed by N. O(kes) for William Welby, 1613. First edition, woodcut ornaments on title, woodcut headpieces, 2 pages printed entirely in black, lacking final 2 leaves (also printed entirely in black, without text), last leaf with a hole with loss of 3 letters from the motto at end of text on recto, slight loss to lower fore-corner of this leaf and extreme corresponding corner of preceding leaf (no loss of text), A4 (the first black leaf), very slightly defective at top outer corner, title slightly browned, 4to., late 19th century green crushed morocco by Matthews, quadruple gilt fillets on sides with corner ornaments, spine lettered longitudinally in gilt, gilt edges, extra blank leaves bound in at beginning and end, last at front inscribed 'Richard Grant White Esq. with the best wishes of R. H. Stoddard", good.   Blackwell's Rare Books Marks of Genius - 50 2016   £20,000

Binding – Matthews, William

A Relation of Several Hundreds of Children and others that Prophesie and Preach in Their Sleep &c. London: for Richard Baldwin, 1689. First edition, small 4to., some light soiling to first few leaves, mid 20th century half blue morocco and marbled boards by William Matthews for Maggs, from the library of James Stevens Cox (1910-1997). Maggs Bros. Ltd. 1447 - 364 2016 £180

Binding – Maziarcyk, Clare

Nash, Paul *Dear Mercia - Paul Nash Letters to Mercia Oakley 1909-18.* Wakefield: Fleece Press, 1991. First edition, 4to., illustrations include facsimiles of drawings in the letters, as well as color plate in rear pocket, quarter cloth with interesting patterned paste paper boards by Clare Maziarcyk in NY, one of 300 printed on Zerkall paper, fine in fine slipcase. Peter Ellis 112 - 273 2016 £85

Binding – McLeish

Dobson, Austin 1840-1921 *Eighteenth Century Vignettes. (and) Eighteenth Century Vignettes. Second Series.* London: Chatto & Windus, 1892. 1894. First editions, 2 separately issued (though obviously companion) volumes, 184 x 127mm, very pleasing black morocco tastefully gilt by C. & C. McLeish (stamp signed on rear turn-ins), covers with gilt rule border and cornerpieces of gilt lilies against a mist of gilt dots, raised bands, each spine compartment with similar design but featuring three inlaid gray morocco lilies at center and trefoil floral ornaments at compartment extremes, all against a stippled ground, turn-ins with gilt fillets and gilt foliate tools at corners, all edges gilt, folding engraved frontispiece to volume 1, large paper copy of each volume, virtually pristine set, nearly as clean and fresh as the day it left the bindery. Phillip J. Pirages 67 - 57 2016 $1250

Binding – Middleton, Bernard

Junius, Franciscus *Etymologicum Anglicanum.* Oxonii: e Theatro Sheldoniano, 1743. Folio, frontispiece, corrigenda and list of subscribers, bound out of order at front, occasional light foxing towards edges, leaf 352 folded and therefore partially uncut, recent blind tooled brown morocco with green morocco spine label by Bernard Middleton, few slight scuffs, endpapers little toned, very good. Unsworths Antiquarian Booksellers 30 - 89 2016 £500

Binding – Miles, Tony

Defoe, Daniel *The Life & Strange Surprising Adventures of Robinson Crusoe of York.* London: Basilisk Press, 1979. No. 6 of 25 specially bound copies with 10 original prints (of a total edition of 515), 328 x 245mm., publisher's original dark blue morocco by Tony Miles of London, upper board with gilt vignette reproducing Craig's woodcut portrait of Crusoe, raised bands, gilt spine titling, gilt dragon ornament to tail panel, decorative blind roll to turn-ins, marbled endpapers, top edge gilt, without publisher's box, with more than 80 small wood engravings in text by Edward Gordon Craig, with 10 original prints, 6 of them signed, with initials and dated, these bound in the rear in windowed French fold leaves, original prospectus laid in, designed by Bernard Roberts and printed at John Roberts Press on Van Gelder mouldmade paper, mint. Phillip J. Pirages 67 - 95 2016 $5000

Binding – Moore, Suzanne

Moore, Suzanne *A Musings.* Vashon Island: 2015. Artist's Book, one of 26 copies, all on Rives BFK paper and Revere papers, lettered A to Z, signed and dated by artist, page size 9 x 15 inches, bound by artist, painted maized colored Magnani paper with letter "A" tooled in silver and gold gilt on front panel, rather abstract as if assemblage of bamboo, paper portfolio to house book, titlepage extends across two pages and features a large script A followed by smaller printed MUSINGS, separated by gold gilt dot, designed, hand lettered and painted and collaged, printed monotype debossed and handcut by artist with handset type composition and letterpress printing by Jessica Spring at Springtide Press, each page an original composition capable of standing on its own. Priscilla Juvelis - Rare Books 66 - 9 2016 $1100

Binding – Morley

Flaubert, Gustave 1821-1880 *Oeuvres Completes.* Paris: Louis Conard, 1910-1954. Mostly late printings, 28 volumes, 8vo, uniformly bound in orange cloth gilt by Morley, spines slightly darkened and edges of some covers little damp marked, associated slight bubbling to pastedown endpapers, otherwise nice. Bertram Rota Ltd. February List 2016 - 17 2016 £500

Plutarchus *The Lives of the Noble Grecians and Romanes Compared Together by that Grave Learned Philosopher....*   Stratford-on-Avon: Shakespeare Head Press, 1928. No. 6 of 100 sets, on handmade paper and in deluxe binding, signed by artist (along with 500 regular copies), 241 x 159 mm., publisher's black half morocco over burnt orange linen by Morley of Oxford (stamp signed), raised bands decorated with thick and thin gilt rules, top edges gilt, tondo portrait of author on titlepage, portrait of Elizabeth I a head of dedication page and portrait of appropriate subject at beginning of each biography, laid-in carbon copy of description from Philip C. Duschnes ((perhaps 1960-70s) describing this set as in perfect condition, one cover with tiny blemish and vague dent to tail edge, but beautifully well preserved, entirely clean, fresh and bright internally, virtually unworn binding.   Phillip J. Pirages   67 - 317   2016 $4500

Binding – Morrell

Affecting History of the Dreadful Distresses of Frederic Manheim's Family...with an Account of the Destruction of the Settlements at Wyoming.   Philadelphia: by Henry Sweitzer for Mathew Carey, 1800. 48 pages, woodcut frontispiece, modern half crushed brown levant, spine attractively gilt by Morrell, fine, fresh, handsomely bound.   Joseph J. Felcone, Inc.   Books from Five Centuries: a Miscellany - 80   2016 $4000

The Death Fetch, or the Student of Gottingen Founded on a Popular Opinion, Prevalent Even at the Present Time.... London: printed for T. Hughes, 35 Ludgate Street, n.d., 1826. First edition, 12mo. inserted folded frontispiece with color frontispiece, original three quarter brown levant morocco, tooled and titled in gold by Morrell of London, armorial bookplate of J. Barton Townsend, later bookplate of William Hartmann Woodin.   John W. Knott, Jr./L.W. Currey, Inc.   Fall-Winter 2015 - 17501   2016 $2500

Burns, Robert *The Poems and Songs of Robert Burns.* London: George Newnes Ltd., 1902. 165 x 102mm., very fine crimson morocco lavishly and intricately gilt in a 'Scottish Wheel' design by Morrell (stamp signed on front turn-ins), covers with large central wheel of 20 compartments, each containing elegant gossamer floral tools between two lines of dots radiating from a central rosette, massed tiny circle tools at head and foot of wheel, above and below these circle tools, triangle formed by small scalloped compartments and multiple tiny flowers, corners with large leaf frond tools and covers generally with many accenting small tools, raised bands, spine compartments, with large quatrefoil containing central daisy radiating floral tools surrounded by gilt dots, elegantly and elaborately gilt turn-ins in swag pattern, ivory watered silk endleaves, all edges gilt, rear joint very expertly renewed, frontispiece, rear free endpaper with ink presentation to Ozite Fleming Cox from Benjamin Lloyd Belt dated May 8 1906, front joint beginning to show a thin crack (but mostly masked with dye), paper stock little dingy (as not doubt in all copies), otherwise very fine, covers and spine unworn and lustrous and text without signs of use.   Phillip J. Pirages   67 - 58   2016 $850

Crabbe, George *The Life of George Crabbe, by his son.* London: Oxford University Press, Humphrey Milford, 1932. First edition with this introduction, small 8vo., bound by Morrell in full leather, raised bands, gilt decorated spine, gilt rules, marbled endpapers and edges, stamped in gilt with crown and letter K on upper cover, armorial bookplate of Edward Hilton Young, 1st Baron Kennet of the Dene; presentation copy inscribed by author for Kennet, fine.   Peter Ellis   112 - 130   2016   £450

Goldsmith, Oliver 1730-1774 *The Vicar of Wakefield, a Tale.* London: R. Ackermann, 1823. Second edition, reissue of the plates form first edition of 1817, hand colored aquatint plates by Thomas Rowlandson, full tan polished calf, richly gilt, spine gilt in compartments with red and green labels by Morrell, occasional very minor spots of foxing or offsetting, else fine and fresh, in chemise and red polished calf slipcase.   Joseph J. Felcone, Inc.   Books from Five Centuries: a Miscellany - 74   2016 $750

Binding – Mullins, Vincent

Adams, Ansel *Taos Pueblo.* New York: Graphic Society Books, 1977. Facsimile edition of rare original printing, number 822 of 950 copies signed by Adams, photos, bound by Vincent Mullins in half tan Niger leather with orange linen covered boards, title stamped in blind on front cover, marbled ends, very fine, new copy, matching slipcase.   Argonaut Book Shop   Photography 2015 - 7440   2016 $3000

Binding – Newbold and Collins

Reader's Digest Complete Book of Australian Birds. Sydney: Reader's Digest, 1983. Second edition, quarto, color photos, maps, handsome modern grey morocco (Newbold and Collins, Sydney), with raised bands and two colored title inlays, decorative gilt rule, marbled endpapers, fine.   Andrew Isles Natural History Books   55 - 26559   2016 $400

Binding – Okamoto Bindery

Michener, James A.   *The Modern Japanese Print.* Rutland & Tokyo: Charles E. Tuttle, 1962. First edition, one of 510 numbered copies, this being number 214, signed by author and 10 contributing artists, large folio, original full page prints, each signed by artist, text handset in Perpetua type, printed on handmade kyokushi or Japanese vellum, bound in Okamoto Bindery in original tri-tone linen, stamped in gilt on front boards and spine, uncut, housed in original slipcase of unvarnished spruce or Japanese cedar, japanese title burned onto wood on front panel of slipcase, spine sunned, slipcase and book with some scuffs, altogether very good copy of exquisite book with 10 original signed prints.   Heritage Book Shop   Holiday 2015 - 80   2016 $3500

Binding – Omega Bindery

Vigo, Johannes De   *Practica Copiosa in Arte Chirugica (sic).* Venice: heirs of Octavinaus Scotus, 1520. First Venice edition, Folio, 2 parts in one volume, woodcut initials, text dampstained with some worming which is mostly in margins, but not affecting some text, especially gatherings M-N, paper repairs in the last two leaves, part 2 lacking final blank, modern vellum by Omega Bindery, spine lettered in manuscript.   James Tait Goodrich   X-78 - 542   2016 $5750

Binding – Padeloup

Foglietta, Uberto   *Ex Universa Historia Rerum Europae...* Naples: Giuseppe Cocchi, 1571. First edition, 4to., mid 18th century maroon moroco by Padeloup of Paris (engraved binder's label at lower margin of title), spine ornamented and lettered in gilt, triple fillets around boards in gilt, inner dentelles, gilt, gilt lined edges of boards, all edges gilt, marbled endpapers, woodcut printer's device on title, light wear to hinges and extremities, variable browning (as frequently the case), two prelim leaves remargined in 18th century, f. 94 with small hole, not touching any letter, 16th century inked out Italian ownership inscription.   Sotheran's Travel and Exploration - 253   2016   £1250

Binding – Parrot, Gray

Clemens, Samuel Langhorne   1835-1910   *Adventures of Huckleberry Finn.* Northampton: Pennyroyal Press, 1985. No. 138 of 350 copies, Portfolio, two volumes, including portfolio of prints, publisher's dark green crushed morocco by Gray Parrot, covers bordered by four gilt fillets, upper cover with gilt medallion containing interlinek dates '1885' and '1985', flat spine with gilt titling, housed with beige portfolio in matching linen slipcase, 49 woodcuts by Barry Moser, as called for in volume, with additional suite of plates in portfolio, calligraphy by Rutledge, spine sunned to light green, otherwise near fine.   Phillip J. Pirages   67 - 276   2016 $2400

Miller, Arthur   *Death of a Salesman...*   New York: Limited Editions Club, 1984. First edition, 1/500 copies, signed by author and artist, five etchings by Leonard Baskin, bound in full brown morocco by Gray Parrot, fine in little worn original slipcase, 4to.   Second Life Books, Inc.   196 B - 235   2016 $750

Moser, Barry   *Fifty Wood Engravings.*   Northampton: Pennyroyal Press, 1978. No. 24 of 100 copies signed by artist, 575 x 445mm., unbound as issued in linen chemise and portfolio backed with mahogany morocco by E. Gray Parrot, 50 wood engravings on 38 plates, mint.   Phillip J. Pirages   67 - 278   2016 $2400

Neruda, Pablo   *Skystones.*   Easthampton: Emanon Press, 1981. Limited to 60 numbered copies signed by Ben Belitt, Debra Weier and Bill Bridges, bound by Gray Parrot in Fabriano over boards printed to a design by Debra Weier and brown leather trim, beige cloth clamshell box with author's name in gilt on spine, box lined with paper to match binding, handset in Virgin Bodoni Book by artists and Bill Bridgers, printed on Arches buff and Rives BFK tan, with one page of Japanese paper, five two-plate color etchings printed on Rives BFK and Arches.   Oak Knoll Books   27 - 14   2016 $1500

Binding – Partovi, Zahra

Brecht, Bertolt   *The Seven Deadly Sins of the Lower Middle Class.*   New York: Vincent FitzGerald, 1992. No. 3 in an edition of 50 copies signed by artist and translator and Kurt Weill, etchings and lithographs by Max Beard, printed on rives paper, water colored, folio, bound by Zahra Partovi in association with BookLab in 19th century Hub style binding with black leather and Dacron polyester zebra striped fabric in purple and black, black cloth clamshell box with purple leather cover label, titled gilt.   Oak Knoll Books   27 - 15   2016 $7500

Binding – Patterson, M.

Carlyle, Thomas 1795-1881 *Sartor Resartus.* London: privately printed, James Fraser, 1834. First separate edition, one of only 58 copies, titlepage re-laid, dusted and with few small tears, one affecting final 'v' in imprint date, bound without wrappers in slightly later brown calf by M. Patterson, Glasgow, rubbed, presentation for Edward Irving, from author.   Jarndyce Antiquarian Booksellers   CCXVII - 64   2016   £5800

Binding – Pictorial

Goldsmith, Oliver 1730-1774 *The Vicar of Wakefield.* London: Bombay. Sydney: George G. Harrap & Co., 1929. First trade edition, appealing publisher's special gray persian morocco upper cover with multi color pictorial inlays reproducing illustration "an Epitaph for my Wife", flat spine with gilt titling, pictorial endpapers, top edge gilt, other edges untrimmed, 35 illustrations by Arthur Rackham, front free endpaper with neatly inked contemporary gift inscription, slight uniform sunning to spine, boards with hint of splaying, title with very faint mottled foxing, other trivial imperfections, still very pleasing copy, binding unworn and lustrous, volume clean and fresh inside and out.   Phillip J. Pirages   67 - 59   2016 $1000

Binding – Porter, R. H.

Walton, Izaak 1593-1683 *The Complete Angler.* London: Elliot Stock, 1885? 12mo., bound by R. H. Porter (with his stamp) in full vellum, black and red titling on cover, edges lightly foxed, very good.   Jeff Weber Rare Books   181 - 85   2016 $75

Binding – Pratt

Spencer, John *A Discourse Concerning Prodigies; Wherein the Vanity of Presages by them is Reprehended and Their True and Proper Ends Asserted and Vindicated.* London: by John Field for Will. Graves... in Cambridge, 1663. First edition, small 4to., titlepage little dusty and with the lower margin renewed, and lower edge of gathering 'M' folded at little shorter and uncut, late 19th century gilt ruled polished calf by Pratt, spine tooled in gilt and with red and green morocco label, edges gilt, Henry Huth and Alfred Henry Huth copy with leather label, from the library of James Stevens Cox (1910-1997), Sir R. Leicester Harmsworth, 1st Bart (1870-1937).   Maggs Bros. Ltd.   1447 - 391   2016   £350

Binding – Prize

Claudianus, Claudius *Opera quae Exstant Omnia ad Membranarum Veterum Fidem Castigata.* Amstelodami: ex officina Schouteniana, 1760. First edition thus 4to., additional presentation certificate bound in, titlepage in red and black, woodcut device, woodcut had and tailpieces and initials, titlepage little dusty, occasional light spots of foxing, slightly toned towards top edge, generally clean within, contemporary Dutch prize vellum, raised bands, blind tooling and black morocco label to spine, gilt panels and centerpieces to both boards with coat of arms of Amsterdam, edges lightly sprinkled blue, two small holes to vellum at spine, label chipped, ties lost, somewhat grubby but very good, sound, overall, printed prize certificate dated 1796 made out by hand to Joanni Petro Pelser and signed by College of Amsterdam rector H. Hana.   Unsworths Antiquarian Booksellers   30 - 36   2016   £350

Goldsmith, Oliver 1730-1774 *The Works of Oliver Goldsmith.* London: John Murray, 1854. 4 volumes, addtitional engraved titlepage in each volume, frontispiece volume 1, contemporary red pebble grain morocco prize binding from Trinity College, Cambridge, boards with college arms blocked in gilt, spines lettered gilt direct with arms at head and foot, prize label to front pastedown with ownership labels to endpapers, edges gilt, merest touch of rubbing, few minor marks, very good, award as prize at Trinity College Cambridge, to Henry Thornton Forster, label of L. M. Forster (Laura Mary Forster), Edward Morgan Llewellyn Forster's label, then to Novelist E. M. Forster.   Blackwell's Rare Books   B184 - 45   2016   £600

Seneca, Lucius Annaeus *Singulares Sententiae Centum Aliquot Versibus ex Codd Pall & Frising Auctae & Correctae, Studio & Opera Jani Gruteri...* Lugduni Batavorum: apud Johannem du Vivie, 1708. 8vo., additional engraved titlepage, titlepage in red and plate with engraved vignette, woodcut head and tailpieces, sporadic light foxing, evidence in gutter preceding engraved title of presentation certificate removal, contemporary vellum prize binding, gilt spine with red morocco label, gilt crest of The Hague to each board, edges sprinkled red, spine label little chipped, some greyish marks, boards slightly bowed, top edge dusty, bookplate of Maurice B. Worms, modern ink inscription "A.S.B. from A.J.C. Easter mcmlx".   Unsworths Antiquarian Booksellers Ltd.   30 - 137   2016   £200

Binding – Putnams

Goldsmith, Oliver 1730-1774 *The Vicar of Wakefield.* Philadelphia: David McKay Co., 1929. No. 95 of 200 copies for American and 575 for England, signed by artist, 10 1/2 x 8 1/8 inches, very attractive red three quarter morocco gilt, stamp signed 'Putnams' along front turn-in), raised bands, spine handsomly gilt in compartment formed by plain and decorative rules, quatrefoil centerpiece surround by densely scrolling cornerpieces, sides and endleaves of rose colored linen, top edge gilt, other edges untrimmed and mostly unopened, 12 color plates by Rackham, including frontispiece, as well as five full page and several smaller illustrations in text by Arthur Rackham, front board with insignficant small round spot to cloth, but fine, unusually bright and clean inside and out with almost no signs of use. Phillip J. Pirages   67 - 292   2016 $2500

Grimm, The Brothers *The Fairy Tales of the Brothers Grimm.* London: Constable & Co. Ltd, 1909. No. 732 of 750 copies signed by artist, 292 x 235mm., very attractive red three quarter morocco gilt stamp signed 'Putnams' along front turn-in, raised bands, spine handsomely gilt in compartments formed by plain and decorative rules, quatrefoil centerpiece surrounded by densely scrolling cornerpieces, sides and endleaves of rose colored linen, top edge gilt (front joint and headcap very expertly repaired by Courtland Benson), titlepage with pictorial frame, numerous black and white illustrations in text, 10 full page black and white illustrations and 40 color plates by Arthur Rackham, as called for mounted on cream stock and protected by lettered tissue guards, front cover with faint minor soiling, just hint of wear to corners, small corner tear to one plate, two tissue guards with minor creasing or chipped edges, otherwise fine, handsome binding, text and plates clean, fresh and bright. Phillip J. Pirages   67 - 293   2016 $3750

Binding – Ramage

Bunyan, John 1628-1688 *Pilgrim's Progress from this World to that Which is to Come.* London: printed for the Society by J. Haddon, 1847. First edition, 8vo., finely bound by Ramage in full brown morocco boards panelled gilt and black with oak leaf and acorn corner tools and central gilt block, spine panelled and lettered gilt, all edges gilt, upper joint little rubbed, little spotting to endpapers, leather booklabel of Edith Northbourne, otherwise very good. Sotheran's   Piccadilly Notes - Summer 2015 - 59   2016 £498

Keats, John 1795-1821 *Poetical Works.* London: Macmillan & co., 1927. 146 x 92mm., lovely turquoise crushed morocco intricately gilt by Ramage of London (stamp signed on front turn-in), covers with multiple gilt rolls bordering a rich an densely gilt plaitwork frame enclosing an open panel with petite, gilt tooled cornerpieces, raised bands, spine compartments reiterating the frame's design, turn-ins decorated with decorative rolls and small tools, ivory moire silk endleaves, all edges gilt, titlepage with engraved vignette, first prelim blank with neat inked inscription, faintest hint of scratch on one cover, spine probably darker than boards (though hard to tell, with so much gilt in the way), but very fine, text clean and fresh, elaborately decorated binding, lustrous and virtually unworn.   Phillip J. Pirages   67 - 60   2016 $850

Omar Khayyam *Rubaiyat.* London: Macmillan and Co., 1905. Small octavo, magnificently bound by Ramage, elaborate contemporary binding of dark green morocco inlaid in Padeloup-style mosaic pattern, covers bordered with decorative and plain gilt rules, rest of boards entirely covered with inlaid diapering featuring rows of pale yellow lozenges tooled gilt with gilt fleurons, these flanked on all four sides with inlaid navy circles, green morocco tooled with curving gilt lines attracted to the dots, spine compartments with similar inlaid pale yellow lozenges tooled gilt and title in gilt, pastedowns framed by dark green morocco inlaid with pale yellow circles at corners and with gilt floral tooling, cream colored watered silk endleaves, faint evidence of owner stamp on verso of front free endpaper tiny chip to top of spine, outstanding binding, extremely well preserved. Manhattan Rare Book Company   2016 - 1707   2016 $2400

Shelley, Percy Bysshe 1792-1822 *Letters... to Leigh Hunt.* London: privately printed, 1894. First edition, one of 6 copies on vellum, with first and last blank leaves, 30 copies were printed on Whatman paper, 8vo., crushed black morocco by Ramage, Herbert S. Leon and Alington bookplates, fine.   Blackwell's Rare Books   Marks of Genius - 48   2016   £6000

Tennyson, Alfred Tennyson, 1st Baron 1609-1692 *In Memoriam.* London: Macmillan & co. Ltd., 1899. 155 x 113mm., extremely pretty deep purple morocco very attractively gilt and inlaid, by Ramage, stamp signed, both covers with densely gilt frame of tiny stars and with large gilt outlined hearts as cornerpieces, frame enclosing four inlaid roses of yellow morocco on leafy gilt stems, flowers in a field of alternating rows of tiny open leaves and dots, raised bands, spine gilt in compartments, central heart outlined by frame of stars, gilt titling, board turn-ins punctuated with 20 gilt rose sprigs flanked by multiple decorative gilt rules, Ivory Moire silk endleaves, all edges gilt, negligible rubbing to front joint and corners, still fine, binding lustrous and interior showing no signs of use.   Phillip J. Pirages   67 - 61   2016 $750

Binding – Ramsey, Eleanore

Franklin, Colin *The Mystique of Vellum.* Boston: printed at the Stinehour Press for Anne and David Bromer, 1984. One of 13 copies printed on vellum and 225 on paper, 305 x 229mm., four blank vellum leaves at front and three at back, errata slip in original envelope, laid in, hand bound by Eleanore Ramsey and Janice Schopfer in full burgundy morocco, covers with handsome central panel stamped in blind and titled in gilt, gray silk doublures, gray suede and papers, publisher's fine matching suede endpapers, publisher's fine matching suede lined morocco drop back box, front cover repeating book's design, fine large woodcut on title, delicate woodcut headpiece on contents page, both cuts showing Medieval scribe at work, six highly burnished raised gold initials painted by Thomas Ingmire, printed in russet gray and black, box with small areas of minor discoloration, otherwise mint.   Phillip J. Pirages   67 - 338   2016 $7500

Binding – Rau, E.

Floire et Jeanne *The Tale of King Florus and the Fair Jehane.* Kelmscott Press, 1893. 350 copies printed with an additional 15 copies on vellum, of the 360 copies, 76 copies were purchased in sheets by Tregaskis and sent to book binders, this is probably a trial copy that Rau chose not to send as his exhibition piece but seems more likely that it was a second copy commissioned by a collector who saw the Tretaskis copy in the exhibition or the exhibition catalog, 16mo., choicely bound by E Rau of St. Petersburg in full orange crushed morocco lettered gilt on spine, boards with semi of stylized flowers within a single gilt and dog tooth panel, central initial of 'W" on upper board and "M' on lower, richly gilt inner dentelles over marbled endpapers, double page woodcut border, text printed in black and red in Chaucer type, fine in slipcase, bookplate of Frank Howell and of American collector Charles Walker Andrews, loosely inserted is typed letter from J. and M. L. Tregaskis to Frank Howell.   Sotheran's   Piccadilly Notes - Summer 2015 - 175   2016   £4995

Binding – Remnant & Edmonds

Heavisides, Edward Marsh *The Poetical and Prose Remains.* London: Longmans, Stockton Jennett & Co, 1850. First edition, original purple cloth by Remnant & Edmonds, decorative borders in blind, spine blocked and lettered gilt, spine slightly faded, very good.   Jarndyce Antiquarian Booksellers   CCXVIII - 1296   2016   £60

Moule, Thomas *Great Britain Illustrated.* London: Charles Tilt, 1830. First edition in book form, striking, contemporary embossed 'Relievo' burgundy morocco by Remnant & Edmonds (their stamp), covers densely patterned with three very complex foliate frames around a central medallion featuring the muses Erato, Calliope and Euterpe, flat spine with gilt titling at head and an elaborate embossed pattern below, turn-ins with floral gilt roll all edges gilt, extra engraved titlepage with vignette and 118 engraved views on 59 plates by William Westall, as called for, original tissue guards, front pastedown with armorial bookplate of William Perceval, majority of plates with minor foxing and offsetting (two or three engravings foxed, bit more, engraved title and facing page rather noticeably affected), spine slightly and uniformly sunned, joints with vaguest hint of rubbing but text especially fresh clean and bright and striking binding virtually unworn, very lustrous covers that retain all of the original sharpness of their intricate blind decoration.   Phillip J. Pirages   67 - 62   2016 $1000

Walker, Donald *Games and Sports...* London: Thomas Hurst, 1837. First edition, half title, frontispiece, additional engraved title, plates, 18 page catalog, some foxing to plates, original maroon cloth by Remnant & Edmonds, gilt vignette, spine slightly faded, small ink mark to back board, booklabel of J. P. Brown-Westhead, Lea Castle, very good, near fine.   Jarndyce Antiquarian Books   CCXV - 458   2016   £350

Binding – Reynolds, Louise

White, Patrick E. *Eurydice Unbound.* Lawrence: Holiseventh Press, 1988. Limited to 30 copies, 5 Artist Proofs not for sale, numbered through 25, signed by White and Talleur, relief prints by John Talleur, oblong 4to., accordion fold in clamshell box, printed on Hosho backed by Kochi, binding and boxing by Louise Reynolds, set by hand in Centaur & Arrighi and printed on a Washington Hoe press by John Talleur with Mark Ritchie, John Coleman and Shawn Henning at Holiseventh Press.   Oak Knoll Books   27 - 29   2016 $1200

Binding – Riley, E.

Tucker, Abraham *Vocal Sounds by Edward Search, Esq.* Printed by T. Jones and sold by T. Payne, 1773. First edition, small 8vo., 19th century half maroon morocco by E. Riley & Son, very good.   Blackwell's Rare Books   B186 - 155   2016   £900

Binding – Riviere

Apperly, Charles James *The Chace. The Turf. The Road.* London: John Murray, 1870. New edition, octavo, hand colored frontispiece, extra engraved title in two states, plain and colored, 13 hand colored engraved plates by Alken, some in aquatint, 9 text illustrations black and white by unknown hand, bound c. 1900 by Riviere and Son in full crimson crushed morocco with French fillets, gilt rolled raised bands, decorated and ornamented compartments, gilt rolled board edges, elaborately gilt dentelles, top edge gilt, expertly and rear invisibly rebacked, fine copy.   David Brass Rare Books, Inc.   2015 - 02798   2016 $550

Brooke, Fulke Greville, 1st Baron *Certaine Learned and Elegant Workes of the Right Honorable Fulke Lord Brooke.* E. P(urslowe) for Henry Seyle, 1633. First edition, tall copy of ordinary paper issue, folio, full morocco gilt by Riviere, all edges gilt, initial and terminal blanks, repaired rust hole in d2 with loss of few letters, slight soiling to first leaves, otherwise very good, large copy, contemporary inscription D. Johannis Mallet, later bookplate of E. M. Cox.   Sotheran's Piccadilly Notes - Summer 2015 - 155   2016   £2750

Byron, George Gordon Noel, 6th Baron   1788-1824 *Childe Harold's Pilgrimage.* London: John Murray, 1841. Large 8vo., full red morocco by Riviere, boards with elaborate gilt borders, spine lettered and panelled gilt with gilt centre tools, richly gilt turn ins over patterned endpapers, top edge gilt, frontispiece, engraved title, folding map and 59 engravings in text, handsome volume.   Sotheran's Piccadilly Notes - Summer 2015 - 65   2016   £998

Chesterton, Gilbert Keith   1874-1936 *A Short History of England.* London: Chatto and Windus, 1917. Author's original corrected typescript, signed with extensive holograph corrections and additions, 4to., bound in red crushed and polished levant, lettered and bordered in gilt, elaborately gilt dentelles and marbled endpapers by Riviere & son, cloth slipcase, light wear along joint of front cover, light soiling to typescript consistent with use, otherwise fine.   James S. Jaffe Rare Books   Occasional List: Winter 2016 - 41   2016 $25,000

Collins, Wilkie   1824-1889 *After Dark.* London: Smith, Elder and Co., 1856. First book edition, 8vo., Riviere & Son full brown calf bindings with elaborate gilt decorated spine, gilt edge tooling, gilt dentelles and marbled paper endpapers, top edge gilt, later maroon leather title labels to spine, original green cloth, covers bound in at rear, minor rubbing to binding extremities, very good+ set.   Tavistock Books   Bibliolatry - 25   2016 $2750

Combe, William   1742-1823 *The Three Tours of Dr. Syntax. In Search of the Picturesque... In Search of Consolation... In Search of a Wife.* London: R. Ackermann's Repository of Arts, 1812. 1820. 1821. First editions in book form, 3 volumes, volume III with eight pages of ads and original wrappers and ads from the three monthly parts bound in at rear, very handsome gilt decorated early 20th century dark blue rushed morocco by Riviere & Son (stamp-signed on front turn-in), covers with French fillet border, spines lavishly and elegantly gilt in compartments with flower filled cornucopia centerpiece surrounded by small tools and volute cornerpieces, inner gilt dentelles, top edges gilt, other edges untrimmed, one woodcut illustration, one engraved tailpiece and 80 partfully hand colored aquatint plates by Thomas Rowlandson, engraved armorial bookplate of John Taylor Reynolds, spines uniformly more black than blue, four of the covers with just hint of soiling, most plates with variable offsetting (usually faint but noticeable in half dozen cases), other trivial imperfections, but extremely desirable set, nevertheless with strong impressions and good coloring of first edition plates, with good coloring of first edition plates, very spacious margins, lovely bindings that are lustrous and virtually unworn.   Phillip J. Pirages 67 - 306   2016 $3500

Congreve, William   1670-1729 *The Works of Mr. William Congreve.* Birmingham: printed by John Baskerville for J. and R. Tonson, 1764. First Baskerville edition, 8vo., 3 volumes, handsomely bound by Riviere in full dark green morocco, boards with gilt line and greek key borders, spines richly gilt with contrasting leather labels, all edges gilt, engraved portrait after Kneller, 5 plates engraved by Grignion after Hayman, little occasional light browning, otherwise very nice, much cleaner than usual and in attractive binding.   Sotheran's   Piccadilly Notes - Summer 2015 - 83   2016   £1000

Dickens, Charles   1812-1870 *Great Expectations.* London: Chapman & Hall, 1861. First edition, third impression, third impression and first impression respectively, 3 volumes, half title and color frontispiece volume I, color plates 32 page catalog volume III May 1861, slightly later full scarlet crushed morocco by Riviere & Son, spines gilt in compartments, triple ruled borders and gilt dentelles, original purple cloth bound in at end of each volume, armorial bookplates of Hinton A Stewart, top edge gilt, very good, attractive, handsome copy, extra illustrated by Pailthorpe with 21 full color etchings.   Jarndyce Antiquarian Booksellers CCXVIII - 588   2016   £6500

Dickens, Charles   1812-1870 *The Pic Nic Papers.* London: Henry Colburn, 1841. First edition, 2nd issue with corrected 'young publisher in preface, 8vo., 3 volumes, sometime bound by Riviere & son in full dark green morocco, boards with French fillet panel, spines lettered and decorated in gilt, original boards bound in at rear, frontispiece and plates by George Cruikshank, Phiz, &c., little rubbing to joints, gilt on spines little dulled, otherwise very good set preserved in marbled paper covered slipcase.   Sotheran's Piccadilly Notes - Summer 2015 - 106   2016   £1250

Dickens, Charles 1812-1870 *Sketches by Boz.* London: Chapman and Hall, 1839. Half title, frontispiece, engraved title, plates, uncut in slightly later dark green crushed morocco by Riviere & Son, gilt spine, borders and dentelles, armorial bookplate of John Neville Cross, top edge gilt, very good, handsome copy. Jarndyce Antiquarian Booksellers CCXVIII - 60   2016   £850

Dickens, Charles 1812-1870 *Sunday Under Three Heads.* London: Chapman & Hall, 1836. First edition, frontispiece, plates by Phiz, original buff pictorial wrappers, at some point neatly respined, good plus in custom made tan calf slipcase by Riviere & Son, imitating a bound volume. Jarndyce Antiquarian Booksellers   CCXVIII - 78   2016   £1800

Dickens, Charles 1812-1870 *The Uncommercial Traveller.* London: Chapman & Hall, 1861. First edition, half title, 32 page catalog (Dec. 1860), contemporary full dark green crushed morocco by Riviere, gilt spine, borders and dentelles, part of original purple cloth board bound in at end, armorial bookplate of John Neville-Cross, top edge gilt, very good handsome copy.   Jarndyce Antiquarian Booksellers   CCXVIII - 597   2016   £600

Dickens, Charles 1812-1870 *The Uncommercial Traveller.* London: Chapman & Hall, 1861. First edition, 32 page catalog dated Dec. 1860, 8vo., 19th century deep maroon full morocco by Riviere, with elaborate gilt decorated spine, top edge gilt, gilt dentelles, minor extremity wear with lower tips showing slight abrasion, bookplate (Barnton), pencil note to prelim blank, "This copy sold in the McKenzie sale", withal handsome, very good+ copy.   Tavistock Books Getting Around - 29   2016 $1500

Dodgson, Charles Lutwidge   1832-1898 *Phantasmagoria and other Poems.* London: Macmillan, 1869. First edition, first issue with page 94 printed correctly, 8vo., beautifully bound by Riviere in full blue calf with extensive gilt toning on spine, gilt rules on covers, gilt turn-ins, all edges gilt and with original covers bound in, fine copy, inscribed by author to Arthur Penrhyn Stanley, beautiful copy.   Aleph-bet Books, Inc.   111 - 77   2016 $6500

Egan, Pierce 1772-1849 *Real Life in London or the Rambles and Adventures of Bob Tallyho, Esq. and His Cousin the Hon. Tom Dashall through the Metropolis.* London: printed for Jones and Co., 1821-1822. First edition, first issue with "Oxford Arms Passage" in imprint, complete with two plates not included in list of plates, 8vo., 2 volumes, full red morocco by Riviere and Son, french fillet border to sides, richly gilt panelled spines, gilt turn-ins, all edges gilt, 34 hand colored aquatint plates, including frontispieces and engraved titles, designed and engraved by Alken, Dighton, Brooke and Rowlandson, etc., little spotting to endpapers and edges, some occasional browning, bookplates, otherwise excellent set.   Sotheran's Piccadilly Notes - Summer 2015 - 116   2016   £1000

Frith, William Powell *John Leech His Life and Work.* London: Richard Bentley and son, 1891. First edition, 2 volumes, 222 x 146mm, very handsome scarlet straight grain morocco gilt by Riviere & son (stamp signed on front turn-in), covers with French fillets, raised bands, spine compartments gilt with sporting center ornament and volute cornerpieces, gilt titling, richly gilt turn-ins, all edges gilt, 176 illustrations, comprised of the 97 called for plus 79 extra inserted engraved plates, 49 of these hand colored and 13 double page, except for few inserted plates, light foxing or minor stains, virtually perfect copy, attractive bindings lustrous and unworn, volumes entirely fresh clean inside and out.   Phillip J. Pirages   67 - 234   2016 $1250

Hallam, Isaac *The Cocker, a Poem.* Stanford: Francis Howgrave, 1742. First edition, 4to., frontispiece, full brown morocco gilt, all edges gilt, by Riviere & Son, fine, very rare. C. R. Johnson Rare Book Collections   Foxon: H-P 2015 - 4397h-p   2016 $5363

Herrick, Robert 1591-1674 *The Hesperides & Noble Numbers.* London: Lawrence & Bullen, 1898. Revised edition, small octavo, 2 volumes, superb period bindings by Riviere of full dark pink morocco with raised bands, ornate gilt spine with inner dentelles, gilt rules, top edge gilt, bookplate of poet H. W. Harding, spines little darkened and joints just faintly rubbed, very good.   Peter Ellis   112 - 167   2016   £650

Hoffer, Johann *Icones Catecheseos, et Virtutum ac Uitiorum Illusrtatae Numeris...* Wittenberg: Johannes Crato, 1558. Small 8vo., fine device on titlepage and larger version on recto of final leaf, 77 half page woodcuts by Jakob Lucius?, late 19th century brown morocco by Riviere & Son, covers panelled in blind, spine lettered gilt, gilt edges, bookplate of Samuel Ashton Thompson-Yates, 1894.   Maggs Bros. Ltd.   1474 - 41   2016   £2500

FINE BINDINGS

Homerus *The Iliads of Homer Prince of Poets (with) Homer's Odysses. (with) The Crowne of all Homers Worckes Batrachomyonmachia or the Battaile of Frogs and Mise...* London: printed (by Richard Field) for Nathaniel Butter, 1611-1615. Worckes - London: printed by Iohn Bill, 1624. First Complete edition in English of first two works, first edition in English of third, titlepage engraved (some expert repair work around outer edges), inner edge just disappearing into gutter, initial blank discarded, final blank present, additional leaves of sonnets bound in prelims, some dust soiling and marks; titlepage engraved (some expert repair work around edges), initial and final blanks discarded, Y2 slightly shorter and probably supplied, little marginal worming in second half expertly repaired, occasionally touching letter, no significant loss; top edge gilt (earliest state with "Worckes" instead of "Workes"), initial blank discarded, folio, 3 volumes, washed and pressed in 19th century red morocco by Riviere, boards with central lozenge shape made of wreaths and flowers and containing a circular frame, blocked in gilt, spines elaborately gilt, bookplate of Thomas Gaisford, leather booklabel of 'Terry' and small booklabel of J. O. Edwards, modern bookplate, very good. Blackwell's Rare Books   Marks of Genius - 22   2016   £40,000

Humphries, Sydney *A Calendar of Verse.* London: privately printed, 1912. One of 20 copies, 225 x 155mm., printed recto only, excellent full vellum over boards by Riviere & Son (stamp-signed), compiler's gilt coat of arms on each cover and foot of spine, flat spine with gilt titling, densely gilt turn-ins, ivory moire silk endleaves, top edge gilt, other edges untrimmed, fleece lined blue cloth slipcase, frontispiece with monographs of Humphires and his wife, surrounded by putti and other symbols of love, engraved coat of arms on title, ink inscription from author to William Maxwell, master printer at R. & R Clark, where the volume was printed, extremely pleasing, binding unworn, entirely clean, fresh and bright, inside and out.   Phillip J. Pirages   67 - 244   2016 $1250

Jonson, Ben 1572-1637 *The Workes.* London: Will Stansby, 1616. London: Richard Meighen, 1640, 3 volumes in 2, engraved title by W. Hole in volume I, 2 divisional titles within woodcut border, engraved portrait by Vaughan inserted from second edition, engraved title neatly repaired at inner margin of A4 of "The Magnetic Lady" restored at margins, very small hole in penultimate leaf of the second volume, occasional light browning, folio, red crushed morocco by Riviere, French fillets on sides, spines richly gilt, gilt edges, upper hinges slightly rubbed, very good. Blackwell's Rare Books   Marks of Genius - 23   2016   £15,000

Midgley, Samuel *Halifax and Its Gibbet Law Placed in a True Light.* Halifax: printed by P. Darby for John Bentley, 1761. First edition thus, small 8vo., frontispiece and 1 additional folding plate, little toned, occasional underlining, light foxing, frontispiece edges delicate with few small repairs, later tan marbled calf, apparently by Riviere, spine gilt, raised bands, all edges gilt, endpapers renewed, joints creased, upper just starting, free endpapers toned at edges, very good, handsome copy, elaborate ownership inscription of William Jackson, Halifax 1679.   Unsworths Antiquarian Booksellers Ltd.   E05 - 8   2016   £175

Rutherford, Samuel *Joshua Redivivus or Mr. Rutherford's Letters, Divided in two parts.* Rotterdam: in the Year, 1664. First edition, 8vo., some occasional light dampstaining, larger ink blots, very small hole through V1 (touching text on verso), late 19th century 'Presbyterian blue' morocco by Riviere & Son, panelled and lettered gilt, gilt gauffered edges, contemporary flyleaves and 'Dutch-gilt' pastedowns preserved from original binding, from the library of James Stevens Cox (1910-1997), 17th century calligraphic inscription 'Mrs. Anna Montgomerie Her Booke", long list of numbers and letters written in ink on front flyleaf, mid 19th century bookplate of John Whitefoord Mackenize.   Maggs Bros. Ltd.   1447 - 370   2016   £500

Selden, John 1584-1654 *Table Talk.* London: J. M. Dent, 1906. 16mo., full blue calf by Riviere & Son circa 1920, covers double ruled gilt, spine decoratively tooled in compartments, two tan morocco labels lettered gilt, gilt board edges and turn-ins, marbled endpapers, all edges gilt, fine.   David Brass Rare Books, Inc.   2015 - 03010   2016 $150

Smith, James *Rejected Addresses or the new Theatrum Poetarum.* London: John Murray, 1833. First edition with these illustrations, 178 x 108mm., animated early 20th century scarlet crushed morocco, richly gilt by Riviere and Son (stamp signed on front turn-in), covers framed by curling vine bearing many berries and leaves, central panel formed and divided into compartments by gilt strapwork, each compartment containing a stylized strapwork and stippled wheel, radiating sections of wheel decorated with leafy fronds, raised bands, spine gilt in similar style, wide gilt turn-ins with plain and dotted label bound in at rear, fleece lined morocco clipped cloth slipcase, engraved frontispiece and 6 engraved illustrations by George Cruikshank, with signed original pencil study for one of the woodcuts and small pen and ink caricature, initialled by Cruikshank with his signature, laid in at front with two autograph letters, signed, tipped in at front, one from James Smith to Lady Blessington and one from Horace Smith to Duby (Edward Dubois - 1774-1850), front joint slightly (and rear joint just faintly) rubbed, spine shade darker than covers, text with faint overall browning because of paper stock, otherwise fine, lovely binding lustrous and altogether pleasing, text very clean and smooth.   Phillip J. Pirages   67 - 64   2016 $950

Spinola, George *Rules to Get Children by with Handsome Faces...* London: for R. H., 1642. First edition, small 4to., lightly browned, early 20th century half morocco by Riviere, from the library of James Stevens Cox (1910-1997). Maggs Bros. Ltd.   1447 - 393   2016   £1250

Sterne, Laurence   1713-1768 *A Sentimental Journey through France and Italy.* London: for T. Becket and P. A. De Hondt, 1768. First edition with text variant 2 in volume 1 and text variant 1 in volume 2, as usual, 2 volumes, 8vo., engraved coat of arm on Dev, with half titles and list of subscriber names a usual, without rare inserted ad leaf, full sprinkled calf, fully gilt by Riviere, spines bit dry, hinges worn, small chip at crown of volume 2, Hobart Cole bookplate.   Joseph J. Felcone, Inc.   Books from Five Centuries: a Miscellany - 137   2016 $900

Swinburne, Algernon Charles   1837-1909 *Grace Darling.* London: printed only for private circulation, 1893. Half title, uncut in 20th century full crimson crushed morocco by Riviere, elaborate gilt dentelles, hinges slightly rubbed with slight wear to head of spine, leding inner hinge, slight cracking.   Jarndyce Antiquarian Booksellers   CCXVII - 272   2016   £480

Thackeray, William Makepeace   1811-1863 *Mrs. Perkin's Ball.* London: Chapman & Hall, 1847. First edition, half title, 22 hand colored plates, frontispiece, vignette title, beautifully bound by Riviere & Son in slightly later full dark green crushed morocco, gilt spine borders & dentelles, all edges gilt, fine, De Luzer's variant without letterpress under the first plate, no list of illustrations and no advertisement.   Jarndyce Antiquarian Booksellers   CCXVII - 281   2016   £400

Wagstaffe, William *The Character of Richard Style, Esq. with some Remarks by Toby, Abel's Kinsman; or According to Mr. Calamy, A. F. & N.* London: printed for J. Morphew near Stationer's Hall, 1713. 8vo. in fours, half title, engraved frontispiece, fine, clean crisp copy, frontispiece very slightly shaved, full polished calf by Riviere, gilt fillet borders, gilt panelled spine, red gilt morocco labels, all edges gilt.   Jarndyce Antiquarian Booksellers   CCXVI - 543   2016   £185

Binding – Rivingtons

Wood, J. G. *Strange Dwellings.* London: Longmans, Green and Co., 1871. First edition thus, octavo, woodcut frontispiece, vignette title page and over 50 wood engravings, bound by Rivingtons (stamp signed on front blank), contemporary full blue calf, covers with double gilt rules, spine with five raised bands, decoratively tooled in gilt in compartments with red morocco label lettered gilt, gilt board edges, all edges marbled, marbled endpaper.   David Brass Rare Books, Inc.   2015 - 03008   2016 $100

Binding – Roach, W.

The Dial: a Magazine of Literature, Philosophy and Religion. Volume 1 no. 1 - July 1840 through volume I no. 4 April 1841. Boston: Weeks, Jordan, London, Wiley and Putnam, 1841. First edition, 8vo., lacks original wrappers, bound in later three quarter maroon morocco by W. Roach of NY, top edge gilt, some foxing and staining, very good, 4 issues, very scarce.   Second Life Books, Inc.   197 - 255   2016 $2200

The Dial: a Magazine of Literature, Philosophy and Religion. Volume II no. 1-July 1841 through Volume II no. 4 - April 1842. Boston: Elizabeth Palmer Peabody and London: John Green, 1842. First edition, 8vo., lacks original wrappers, bound in later three quarter maroon morocco by W. Roach of New York with Index, top edge gilt, nice, clean copy, fine, 4 issues, very scarce.   Second Life Books, Inc.   197 - 254   2016 $2200

Binding – Root

Arabian Nights *Sinbad Le Marin et D'Autres Contes Des Mille et Une Nuits. (Sinbad the Sailor and Oter Tales from the Thousand and One Nights).* Paris: H. Piazza, 1919. First edition in French, 305 x 241mm., no. 520 of 1500 copies, especially attractive rich green morocco by Root & son (signed), covers framed in gilt with triple rules, inner rule entwined at corners with ivy leaf terminations, raised bands, spine gilt in compartments formed by double rule and featuring ivy leaf cornerpieces around an inner central panel, wide ruled turn-ins, with foliate cornerpieces, marbled endpapers, top edge gilt, other edges rough trimmed, original wrappers preserved, decorative initials and titlepage, decorative borders throughout and 27 color plates by Edmund Dulac (each laid down within decorative frame, with captioned tissue guard), printed in pale orange and black throughout, pastedown with bookplate of Joseph H. Haines, upper corners slightly bumped, verso of free endpapers, little discolored (from glue?), otherwise very fine.   Phillip J. Pirages   67 - 122   2016 $1950

Dickens, Charles   1812-1870 *The Posthumous Papers of the Pickwick Club.* London: Chapman and Hall, 1837. First edition, Veller title, 2 volumes, additional plates published by E. Grattan in 1817, with original illustrations, in varying states, bound by Root & Son in blue morocco with Dickens's signature in gilt on covers, gilt floral dentelles, edges ruled in gilt spines evenly faded, top edge gilt, in slipcase, extra illustrated with 45 additional plates.   Jarndyce Antiquarian Booksellers   CCXVIII - 92   2016   £2500

Morford, Henry *John Jasper's Secret....* London: publishing Offices no. 142 Strand, 1872. First UK edition, frontispiece and plates, contemporary half purple morocco by Root & Son, spine with floral devices in gilt, leading hinge little worn with small split at head, marbled boards, slightly rubbed, original blue part wrapper bound in at end, along with original ads, front wrapper to part IV dampstained, otherwise very good. Jarndyce Antiquarian Booksellers CCXVIII - 660 2016 £280

Rogers, Samuel *Italy, a Poem (and) Poems.* London: printed for T. Cadell, 1830. First illustrated editions, 202 x 135mm., 2 separately published works, bound in two volumes, (but often found as companion volumes), very pretty sky blue morocco gilt, by Root & son (stamp-signed on front turn-ins), covers with gilt frame bedecked with a profusion of flowers, raised bands, spines gilt in compartments with large floral spray centerpiece, gilt titling, turn-ins decorated with gilt rules and floral garland, marbled endpapers, all edges gilt, 2 volumes with a total of four plates, 20 illustrations in text, more than 100 fine steel engraved headpieces and tailpieces after designs, mostly by J. M. W. Turner and Thomas Sothard, spines slightly and uniformly sunned, trivial defects internally, extremely pretty set in very fine condition, immaculate text with virtually no signs of use and glittering rulings, unworn. Phillip J. Pirages 67 - 65 2016 $950

Binding – Ruette, Mace

Silius, Italicus *De Secundo Bello Punico.* Amsterdam: G. Jansson, 1620. Engraved titlepage, ruled in red, 16mo., exquisite binding by Mace Ruette, contemporary gilt tooled red morocco, covers framed by outer double fillet, central panel of strait and curved double fillets with small vase of flowers tool at each outer corner in centre of covers a quadrilobe inlay with monogram of H. L. Habert de Montmort and four "S" forms with elaborate pointille sprays of spirals, circles and dots on all four sides, spine with five raised bands, decorated in compartments, inner edges gilt, marbled endpapers, gilt edges, headcaps and joints lightly rubbed, the copy of Habert de Montmort (1600-1679), Colonel Thomas Stanley (1749-1818), William Beckford with his bookseller George Clarke's pencil collation mark, Hamilton Palace Library sale, Thore Virgin inscription dated 1916 with his book label (1886-1957). Maggs Bros. Ltd. 1474 - 72 2016 £2500

Binding – Russell-Rutter Co.

Dumas, Alexander *Marguerite De Valois....* New York: Limited Editions Club, 1969. Limited edition of 1500 copies, large 8vo., presentation slip from directors of LEC laid in, drawings by Edy Legrand hand printed and then hand colored, paper specially made by Curtis Paper Co. and binding done by Russell-Rutter Co., this is number "J.W." signed by artist, fine in publisher's slipcase. Second Life Books, Inc. 196A - 477 2016 $45

Schreiner, Olive 1855-1920 *The Story of an African Farm.* Westerham: Limited Editions Club, 1961. first edition thus, one of 1500 numbered copies, signed by artist, large 8vo., bound by Russell-Rutter Co. in full bark cloth from Uganda, title stamped in gold, illustrations are drawings and original color lithographs by Paul Horgan. Second Life Books, Inc. 196 B - 539 2016 $75

Whitman, Walt 1819-1892 *Leaves of Grass.* Mount Vernon: Peter Pauper Press, 1950. Commemorative edition, 4to., printed in Waverley and Lydian types on specially made paper by Hurlbut Paper Co., leather backed boards by Russell Rutter Co., wood engraving printed directly from blocks, 1/1100 copies in publisher's box, some rubbing on box, very fine, uncut. Second Life Books, Inc. 197 - 351 2016 $400

Binding – Sangorski & Sutcliffe

Aesopus *Aesop's Fables.* London: George G. Harrap & Co., 1936. No. 5 of 8 copies on vellum, signed by the artist (and 525 on paper), 283 x 213mm., very fine publisher's special russet crushed morocco designed by artist and executed by Sangorski & Sutcliffe (stamp signed on front turn-in), covers gilt with strapwork frame featuring grape clusters in corners and prancing fox in center, raised bands flanked by gilt rules, spine panels with central gilt grape cluster, gilt titling, gilt ruled turn-ins, marbled endpapers, all edges gilt on rough, excellent brown textured cloth box with matching slipcase, 201 charming historiated initials, hand colored in part by a former owner and 12 fine engraved illustrations by Stephen Gooden, including engraved titlepage, couple of these partially hand colored, leather with minor naturally occurring variations in color, one plate with very faint dampstain, handful of tiny marginal smudges of stray coloring, otherwise extremely pleasing copy, vellum particularly smooth and bright and special binding lustrous and unworn. Phillip J. Pirages 67 - 339 2016 $29,000

Bible. English - 1931 *The Four Gospels.* Waltham St. Lawrence: Golden Cockerel press, 1931. No. 392 of 500 copies (first 32 on vellum), 343 x 242mm., publisher's half pigskin and wheat colored buckram sides by Sangorski & Sutcliffe, raised bands, gilt rules and titling on spine, top edge gilt, other edges untrimmed, original (lightly soiled and worn) plain card slipcase, 4 large woodcuts on section titles and scores of striking large and small woodcut illustrations, decorative elements and initials by Eric Gill, printed on Batchelor handmade paper; extraordinarily fine, perhaps unsurpassable copy, pristine internally, binding virtually so. Phillip J. Pirages 67 - 170 2016 $19,500

Bunyan, John 1628-1688 *Pilgrim's Progress.* London: printed by Bernard Newdigate at the Shakespeare Head Press for the Cresset Press, 1928. Number 6 of 10 special copies printed on vellum (and 195 on paper), 2 volumes, plus portfolio of plates, fine publisher's russet morocco by Sangorski & Sutcliffe (stamp signed on front turn-in), covers lettered gilt, metal clasps, raised bands, wide turn-ins with multiple ruled border, all edges gilt, volumes housed along with extra suite of engravings, in a (slightly worn but still very good), fleece lined matching cloth box and slipcase, 2 large vignettes and 10 powerful expressionistic engraved plates on vellum, vignettes and 6 of the plates by Blair Hughes-Stanton, the other four by Gertrude Hermes with matted duplicates of all plates (all of the engravings signed), extras done on thin paper and contained in their own portfolio, bookplate of the Garden Collection assembled by Haven O'More, a couple of faint scratches to boards, spines shade darker than covers, small handful of leaves with usual faint discoloration that is inevitable with vellum, otherwise superb set, text clean and fresh, smooth, bright vellum leaves, bindings unworn.   Phillip J. Pirages   67 - 332   2016 $35,000

Bunyan, John 1628-1688 *The Pilgrim's Progress.* London: printed by Bernard Newdigate at the Shakespeare Head Press for the Cresset Press, 1928. No. 102 of 195 copies on paper (and 10 on vellum), 2 volumes, 368 x 264mm, publisher's black stained vellum by Sangorski & Sutcliffe (stamp signed), raised bands, gilt titling on upper cover and spine, 2 large vignettes ad 10 engraved plates, by Blair Hughes-Stanton, and Gertrude Hermes, hint of rubbing to extremities, one leaf with closed marginal tear but fine set, quite clean, fresh and bright inside and out. Phillip J. Pirages   67 - 101   2016 $1600

Chaucer, Geoffrey 1340-1400 *The Canterbury Tales.* Waltham St. Lawrence: Golden Cockerel Press, 1929-1931. No. 343 of 485 copies on paper (and 15 on vellum), 4 volumes, 318 x 197mm., original morocco backed patterned paper boards by Sangorski & Sutcliffe, raised bands, gilt titling, top edges gilt, others untrimmed, in cloth slipcase, red and blue initials and very pleasing wood engraved borders (frequently inhabited) by Eric Gill on every page except in last part of volume IV, verso of front free endpapers with bookplate of William Risenfield, joints somewhat rubbed and bit darkened (from dye), portions of upper joint volume I cracked (no other cracking), corners rather mashed, leather little marked, but all volumes solid, covers unsoiled, spines uncharacteristically close in color, very fresh, clean and bright internally.   Phillip J. Pirages   67 - 172   2016 $8500

Chaucer, Geoffrey 1340-1400 *Troilus and Criseyde.* Waltham St. Lawrence: Godlen cockerel Press, 1927. No. 22 of 225 numbered copies on paper (and six on vellum), 318 x 203mm., original patterned paper sides by Sangorski & Sutcliffe (stamp signed on front pastedown), new replica spine of russet morocco with raised bands and gilt titling by Court land Benson, top edge gilt, others untrimmed (sides with dots in paper pattern enhanced by previous owner in pleasing, scarcely noticeable manner), in later suede backed marbled paper slipcase, pictorial woodcut borders to fore margins of every text page and five full page wood engravings, all by Eric Gill, section titlepages with red or blue lettering, occasional text initials in red or blue, light to moderate rubbing along edges, otherwise very fine, expertly renewed binding entirely pleasing, text fresh, bright and immaculate from first leaf to last.   Phillip J. Pirages   67 - 173   2016 $7500

Coutts, J. *The Complete Book of Gardening.* London: Ward Lock & Co., 1931. Second edition, 8vo., bound by Sangorski & Sutcliffe in half green morocco, spine with gilt raised bands, gilt lettering and gilt foliate centre tools with red morocco inlays, boards and endpapers in matching floral design, top edges gilt, binder's stamp to verso of f.f.e.p., 16 color plates, numerous black and white plates, text illustrations, very good in extremely handsome binding. Sotheran's   Piccadilly Notes - Summer 2015 - 88   2016   £150

Hayden, Arthur *Old English Porcelain. The Lady Ludlow Collection.* London: John Murray, 1932. First edition, limited to 100 numbered copies signed by author, 91 hand printed photogravures, 41 tipped-on color plates, printed throughout in light blue and black, handset type, beautifully bound by Sangorski & Sutcliffe in three quarter turquoise blue levant morocco, light blue cloth boards gilt emblem on front cover and spine, gilt lettered spine, raised bands, top edges gilt, very fine, very rare.   Argonaut Book Shop   Pottery and Porcelain 2015 - 4994   2016 $2750

Ireland, Alexander *The Book-Lover's Enchiridion.* London: Simpkin Marshall and Co., 1883. Third edition, octavo, finely bound by Sangorski & Sutcliffe circa 1930 in full red calf covers with double gilt rules, front cover lettered gilt, spine with five raised bands, decoratively tooled in gilt in compartments, two blue morocco labels lettered gilt, gilt board edges and decorative turn-ins, top edge gilt, marbled endpapers, fine binding example.   David Brass Rare Books, Inc.   2015 - 03007   2016 $225

Jones, David *The Chester Play of the Deluge.* London: printed by Will Carter at the Rampant Lions Press for Clover Hill Editions, 1977. Copy "E" of 7 copies printed on vellu, 343 x 264mm., 2 volumes, including portfolio, original special russet crushed morocco by Sangorski & Sutcliffe (stamp-signed), raised bands, gilt titling, turn-ins ruled in gilt and black, marbled endpapers, portfolio in marbled paper clamshell box backed with matching morocco, both in lightly rubbed felt lined slipcase, 10 wood engravings by David Jones and three additional suites of plates, one on vellum, another on handmade paper and third on Japon, engravings printed from original wood blocks on an Albion handpress by Ian Mortimer at I. M. Imprimit, errata slip laid in at colophon, pristine.   Phillip J. Pirages   67 - 342   2016 $15,000

Joyce, James 1882-1941 *Ulysses.* London: John Lane, the Bodley Head, 1936. One of 100 copies signed by author, there were also 100 unsigned copies, first edition printed in England, original vellum, gilt titling on spine, large stylized gilt bow on each cover, top edge gilt, other edges untrimmed and mostly unopened, original (slightly worn but very solid) black and white patterned paper slipcase with paper label housed in fine silk lined grey morocco clamshell box by Sangorski & Sutcliffe, title printed in blue and black, prospectus laid in at front, perhaps hint of smudging to vellum (or perhaps just natural variation in color), but in any case, virtually mint, binding entirely unworn and especially bright and mostly unopened text pristine.   Phillip J. Pirages   67 - 213   2016 $36,000

Kipling, Rudyard 1865-1936 *The Jungle Book. (with) The Second Jungle Book.* London: Macmillan and Co., 1894-1895. First editions, small octavo, frontispiece, text illustrations, second work small octavo with text illustrations, original bright blue cloth pictorially gilt stamped on front covers and spines, all edges gilt, tips rubbed, mostly at top and bottom of spines, corner of tissue guard torn in volume 1, beautifully housed together in custom quarter snakeskin slipcase by Sangorski & Sutcliffe, gilt stamped morocco label on spine, very handsome set.   Heritage Book Shop   Holiday 2015 - 66   2016 $4250

Maeterlinck, Maurice *The Inner Beauty.* London: Humphreys, 1912. Reprint, small octavo, top edge gilt, full red morocco stamped in gilt by Sangorski & Sutcliffe, inner dentelles, little rubbed along hinge, nice, clean copy.   Second Life Books, Inc.   197 - 222   2016 $75

Mitchell, Margaret 1900-1949 *Gone with the Wind.* New York: Macmillan Co., 1936. First edition, first issue with published May 1936 on copyright page and no note of further printing, 222 x 152mm., signed by author, very pleasing gray crushed morocco by Sangorski & Sutcliffe (stamp-signed), covers with single gilt rule border, raised bands decorated with stippled rule and flanked by gilt rules, panels with intricate gilt fleuron centerpiece and gilt titling, gilt ruled turn-ins, marbled endpapers, top edge gilt, upper right corner of back cover slightly soiled (with a series of short, thin, faint parallel lines about two to three inches in length descending from top edge), spine slightly and evenly sunned to pleasant light brownish gray, trivial internal imperfections, otherwise very fine.   Phillip J. Pirages   67 - 256   2016 $5000

Quiller-Couch, Arthur Thomas 1863-1944 *In Powder and Crinoline.* London: Hodder and Stoughton, 1913. 318 x 229mm., fine green morocco by Sangorski & Sutcliffe (stamp-signed), covers with single gilt fillet border upper cover with gilt titling, raised bands, gilt ruled compartments, turn-ins with single gilt fillet, marbled endleaves, top edges gilt, 26 color plates by Kay Nielsen, tipped-in on gray stock with decorative frames, each with captioned and decorated tissue guards, two leaves with short closed tear to fore margin, slight browning to edges of leaves additional trivial defects, but quite fine, clean internally in unworn binding.   Phillip J. Pirages   67 - 263   2016 $2900

Reade, Charles 1814-1884 *Peg Woffington.* London: George Allen, 1899. First Thomson illustrated edition, 8vo., rebound in full dark blue morocco by Sangorski & Sutcliffe, spine lettered and ruled in gilt with emblematic gilt centre tools, single gilt fillet border to sides, gilt border to turn-ins, marbled endpapers, all edges gilt, illustrations by Hugh Thomson, very nice.   Sotheran's   Piccadilly Notes - Summer 2015 - 303   2016   £198

Binding – Santin, Jean

Moliere, Jean Baptiste Pouquelin De 1622-1673 *Le Tartuffe. (and) Don Juan.* Nice and Paris: l'Imprimerie Nationale de Monaco, 1954. No. IX of XXV copies reserved for the collaborators and friends of the artist (in addition to 700 regular copies), 241 x 191mm., contemporary green crushed morocco by Jean Santin (stamp-signed), smooth spine with gilt titling, gilt ruled turn-ins, pale green watered silk endleaves, all edges gilt, titlepage vignettes, frontispiece at beginning of each work and numerous illustrations in text by Jean Gradassi, all hand colored by atelier of Edmond Vairel using pochoir technique, with extra suite of 45 illustrations, bound in after text and with original version of an illustration from Don Juan inscribed by the artist to Madame Hicks and identified by him on verso, bound in at front, pages ruled in red, two half titles printed in red, joints little rubbed, spine uniformly sunned, just hint of soiling to covers, otherwise very fine, binding lustrous and text immaculate.   Phillip J. Pirages   67 - 285   2016 $850

Binding – Schopfer, Janice

Franklin, Colin *The Mystique of Vellum.* Boston: printed at the Stinehour Press for Anne and David Bromer, 1984. One of 13 copies printed on vellum and 225 on paper, 305 x 229mm., four blank vellum leaves at front and three at back, errata slip in original envelope, laid in, hand bound by Eleanore Ramsey and Janice Schopfer in full burgundy morocco, covers with handsome central panel stamped in blind and titled in gilt, gray silk doublures, gray suede and papers, publisher's fine matching suede endpapers, publisher's fine matching suede lined morocco drop back box, front cover repeating book's design, fine large woodcut on title, delicate woodcut headpiece on contents page, both cuts showing Medieval scribe at work, six highly burnished raised gold initials painted by Thomas Ingmire, printed in russet gray and black, box with small areas of mino discoloration, otherwise mint.   Phillip J. Pirages   67 - 338   2016 $7500

Binding – Schuberth Bookbindery

Jeffers, Robinson   1887-1962 *Granite & Cypress: Rubbins from the Rock.* University of California at Santa Cruz: Lime Kiln Press, 1975. Limited to 100 numbered copies, exceptionally rare, Oblong folio, printed on English Hayle handmade paper, titlepage woodcut by William Prochnow, bound by Schuberth Bookbindery in German linen, open laced deerskin over Monterey Cypress spine, Japanese Uwa endpapers, custom slipcase made of Monterey Cypress inlaid with square 'window' of granite from Jeffers; stoneyard (drawn by the poet from the sea), built to stand erect on felt lined cypress stand case, with hairline crack, else fine, signed by printer, William Everson, presentation signed by Everson and three proof sheets laid in.   Jeff Weber Rare Books   181 - 67   2016 $15,000

Binding – Scopes, W. J.

McKeon, Hugh *An Inquiry into the Rights of the Poor, of the Parish of Lavenham, in Suffolk with Historical Notes and Observations.* London: Baldwin and Cradock and sold by Loder Woodbridge &c., 1829. First edition, 8vo., later 19th century half morocco over marbled boards, spine lettered gilt with raised bands, top edge gilt, others uncut by W. J. Scopes of Ipswich, with his ticket, very good.   John Drury Rare Books   2015 - 19691   2016 $323

Binding – Sellars, David

Snyder, Gary *The Mountain Spirit.* Hopewell: Pied Oxen printers, 2014. First edition, one of 50 numbered copies signed by poet and printer, from an edition of 60 copies, photo etchings after sumi-ink scroll paintings, original red cedar hand-scroll with black walnut end knobs, bound in Japanese book cloth and handmade washi, publisher's paulownia box by Mihagi-Kougei Co. Ltd. Tokyo, as new, design illustrations, letter press printing and binding all by Daivd Sellars.   James S. Jaffe Rare Books   Occasional List: Winter 2016 - 126   2016 $1500

Graves, Ida *Epithalamion.* Higham, Colchester: Gemini Press, 1934 but released by Basilisk Press in, 1980. No. 252 of 280 copies on paper (of a total of 330), our copy signed by artist, 349 x 207mm., 23 dramatic full page wood engravings by Blair Hughes-Stanton, publisher's light brown morocco designed by Hughes-Stanton and executed by Paul Collet and David Sellars, flat spine with vertical gilt titling, mint condition.   Phillip J. Pirages   67 - 197   2016 $1000

Binding – Smith, R. W.

Cottle, Joseph *Early Recollections: Chiefly Relating to the late Samuel Taylor Coleridge.* London: Longman, Rees & Co., 1837. First edition, 200 x 127mm, 2 volumes, fine polished calf, elegantly gilt by R. W. Smith (stamp signed on front flyleaf), covers bordered with double gilt rules, spines with raised bands and compartments featuring pleasing dense gilt scrollwork, red and deep blue morocco labels, intricately gilt turn-ins, marbled endpapers, top edge gilt, 6 engraved plates, large modern bookplate of Robert Marceau, engravings rather foxed, little darkening and very minor intermittent foxing in text, otherwise excellent internally in beautiful, virtually unworn binding.   Phillip J. Pirages   67 - 93   2016 $750

Binding – Smith, W. H.

Cervantes Saavedra, Miguel De   1547-1616 *The First (and Second) Part of The History of the Valorous and Wittie Knight-Errant Don Quixote of the Mancha.* Chelsea: Ashendene Press, 1927-1928. One of 225 copies on paper (and 20 on vellum), 432 x 305mm., 2 volumes, fine original dark green morocco by W. H. Smith & Son (stamp signed inside rear covers), raised bands, gilt titling on spine, lovely woodcut initials and borders designed by Louise Powell, cut on wood by W. M. Quick and George H. Ford, superb copy, entirely fresh, clean and bright internally, and in unworn glittering bindings.   Phillip J. Pirages   67 - 10   2016 $15,000

Thucydides *History of the Peloponnesian War.* Chelsea: Ashendene Press, 1930. One of 260 copies on paper, 240 for sale (and 20 on vellum), 407 x 277, original white pigskin by W. H. Smith & Son (stamp signed), raised bands, gilt titling, edges untrimmed, substantial marbled slipcase (from time of publication?) with pigskin edging to match volume, first initial of each chapter and opening line of each book, designed by Graily Hewitt, printer's device in colophon, printed in red and black, few small scrapes on spine, as almost always, just whisper of soiling to white pigskin, one tiny closed tear at fore edge, extremely fine, essentially unworn binding, much cleaner than we have a right to expect, text virtually pristine.   Phillip J. Pirages   67 - 18   2016 $5500

Binding – Sotheran

Hood, Thomas *Poems by Thomas Hood.* London: E. Moxon, 1871. First edition thus, 22 exquisite engravings by Birket Foster, quarto, fine period binding by H. Sotheran of full straight grain morocco with raised bands, gilt decoration and rules, all edges gilt, bit of foxing here and there, otherwise fine. Peter Ellis 112 - 132 2016 £500

Sterne, Laurence 1713-1768 *A Sentimental Journey through France and Italy.* London: George Routledge and Sons, 1885. No. 96 of 550 copies, loosely inserted is an additional half title with an original watercolor signed by Leloir and dated 1884, verso is limitation page for the Edition de Grand Luxe numbered 182 (of 200), plates from this edition loosely inserted together with plates bound in, additional color chromolithographic title, half title, photogravure frontispiece and plates, illustrations, some light foxing, partially uncut in 20th century full crimson crushed morocco by Sotheran, triple borders with floral cornerpieces, raised bands, gilt compartments and elaborate gilt dentelles, slight rubbing to leading hinge and head of spine, top edge gilt, handsome copy. Jarndyce Antiquarian Booksellers CCXVII - 267 2016 £680

Binding – Souze

Brassey, Annie Allnutt, Baroness 1839-1887 *Aux Indes et en Australie dans le Yacht le 'Sunbeam'.* Tours: Alfred Mame et fils, 1893. Splendid first French edition, small folio, original red pictorial cloth, all edges gilt by A. Souze, numerous wood engraved illustrations (several full page), binding minimally spotted and rubbed, internally, apart from sporadic light spotting, very clean and fresh. Sotheran's Travel and Exploration - 395 2016 £498

Binding – Spitler, Priscilla

Some Rules of the Game. Essays on Garden Design.... Carrollton: Press on Scroll Road, n.d. circa, 2004. Limited to 54 numbered copies, 4to., printed from handset Cloister Lightface type in two colors on dampened Twinrocker handmade paper, small green engraving, four page prospectus, green cloth, paper title label on spine, bound by Priscilla Spitler. Oak Knoll Books 27 - 55 2016 $350

Binding – Stephenson, Jean Simpson

Stephenson, Jean Simpson *Of Scandinavia.* N.P.: Jean Simpson Stephenson, n.d., Limited to 22 numbered copies, signed by author/artist, square small 4to., back cloth spine, decorated paper covered boards, cloth clamshell box with orange printed paper labels, illustrations printed on Somerset Satin mouldmade paper, bound by artist. Oak Knoll Books 27 - 63 2016 $400

Binding – Stikeman

Binyon, Laurence 1869-1943 *Dream come True.* London: Eragny Press, 1905. One of 175 copies for sale (with 10 copies on vellum), 182 x 110mm., pleasing purple morocco by Stikeman & Co. NY, covers with double fillet border and inner frame with elegant flueronated cornerpieces, raised bands, spine attractively gilt in compartments, elaborate gilt turn-ins, first two text leaves with woodcut frames and engravings by Binyon in green and red, woodcut initials and publisher's device in colophon, front pastedown with bookplate engraved by Silvain Guillot, joints little worn, otherwise fine, internally with virtually no signs of use. Phillip J. Pirages 67 - 130 2016 $600

Martin, Francois Xavier *The History of Louisiana from the Earliest Period.* New Orleans: printed by Lyman and Beardslee and A. T. Penniman & Co., 1827. First edition, 2 volumes, 248 x 165mm., pleasing later 19th century dark green crushed morocco by Stikeman (signed on front turn-in), covers with triple gilt fillet border and floral sprig cornerpieces, raised bands, spines densely gilt in compartments with center floral sprig in oval medallion, surrounded by swirling gilt tooling accented with small tools, gilt titling, gilt turn-ins, marbled endpapers, top edges gilt, other edges entirely untrimmed, front pastedown with leather bookplate of Marshall Clifford Lefferts and bookplate of Mrs. L. Bartlett, spines sunned to pleasing honey brown (covers bit sunned at edges, with front cover volume II inconspicuously sunned, and showing the darker silhouette of a bookend), few small stains to edges of same board, bindings virtually unworn and otherwise quite pleasing, minor foxing or browning throughout (no doubt affecting all copies because of inferior paper stock), five quires in volume I with one inch dampstain at head, one gathering in volume II noticeably browned, not without condition issues, but with much to please internally, including vast margins, consistent freshness and absence of soiling. Phillip J. Pirages 67 - 250 2016 $1800

Richardson, Ethel M. *The Lion and the Rose.* New York: E. P. Dutton & Co., 1923. First edition, fine, 1920's Grolieresque binding by Stikeman & Co., 18 full page illustrations on art paper, 2 volumes, octavo, 16 photogravure plates, handsomely bound by Stikeman (stamp signed on rear turn-ins), in full contemporary red crushed levant morocco, covers elaborately stamped in gilt marked endpapers, fine set. David Brass Rare Books, Inc. 2015 - 03049 2016 $1950

Binding – Stoakley

Smith, Robert *A compleat System of Opticks in four books...* Cambridge and London: printed for the author... by Stephen Austen and Robert Dodsley, 1738. First edition, 2 volumes, 4to., 83 folding engraved plates, directions to binder, 2 plates with short tears, 1 plate slightly worn, contemporary mottled calf, rebacked in plain calf, gilt spine titles, rubbed, old rebacking, corner showing wear, all raised bands worn, binder's stamp applied to both front flyleaves, "Stoakley, Cambridge", occasional stains, clean copy, very good.   Jeff Weber Rare Books   183 - 35   2016 $2850

Binding – Sutton, G. J.

The Murdered Bride or the Victim of Treachery: a Tale of Horror. London: William Emans, 1837. First edition?, small quarto, engraved frontispiece, additional engraved titlepage and 6 other engraved plates, contemporary half calf over marbled boards, original parts bound together with stabmarks, bound by G. J. Sutton (?) with small binder label on front endpaper, spine heavily tooled gilt in compartments, green morocco spine label, lettered gilt, spine with name M. N. Bourne in gilt at foot, all edges marbled, green endpapers, some toning to plates, bit of foxing throughout, boards bit rubbed, previous owner Bruce Ismery's armorial bookplate, overall very good, extremely rare.   Heritage Book Shop   Holiday 2015 - 3   2016 $3000

Binding – Taffin

Goncourt, Edmond *L'Amour Au Dix-Huiteme Siecle.* Paris: E. Dentu, 1875. First separate edition, 194 x 143mm., elegant fin-de-Siecle brown crushed morocco by A. Taffin of Paris (stamp-signed), covers with ornate gilt frame of flowers, leaves and small tools enclosing two inlaid salmon pink morocco bands separated by a gilt chain roll, raised bands, spine gilt in compartments with floral frame, gilt titling, turn-ins lavishly gilt, green silk endleaves, top edge gilt, other edges untrimmed, original wrappers bound in, text within full woodcut inhabited frames, engraved frontispiece, headpiece and tailpiece and extra illustrated with 19 engravings in black and white or bistro, spine mildly but uniformly sunned towards a chocolate brown, other trivial imperfections, very fine, extremely pretty decorative binding lustrous and virtually unworn and text clean and fresh.   Phillip J. Pirages   67 - 68   2016 $1000

Binding – Thibaron-Joly

Perrault, Charles 1628-1703 *Les Contes De. Ch. Perrault.* Paris: Librairie des Bibliophiles, 1876. No. 54 of 200 copies, 216 x 197mm., 2 volumes, half titles, lovely contemporary dark green crushed morocco, attractively gilt by Thibaron-Joly (stamp signed), covers with French fillets, raised bands, spine gilt in compartments with central rose sprig and floral cornerpieces, marbled endpapers, all edges gilt, frontispiece and 11 engraved plates, one illustrating each tale, large paper copy, bookplate in each volume of W. Vincens Bouguereau, faint offsetting from engravings, text shade less than bright, couple of vaguest scratches on covers, otherwise very fine, text and plates smooth, fresh and clean, margins far beyond ample and beautifully executed bindings virtually perfect.   Phillip J. Pirages   67 - 69   2016 $1500

Binding – Thouvenin

Herodian *Historiarum Libri Octo Graece.* Halle: in libraria Orphanotrophei, 1792. First Wolf edition, poor quality paper browned and bit spotted, 8vo., untrimmed in contemporary quarter red straight grained morocco by Thouvenin, signed at foot of spine, red paste paper boards, spine divided by five raised bands, second and fourth compartments gilt lettered, rest with central gilt stamps of harp-shapes formed with scallop and beasts' heads tools, marbled endpapers, 2 additional binder's blanks (one paper, one vellum), board edges little worn, leather slightly darkened and rubbed, very good.   Blackwell's Rare Books   Greek & Latin Classics VII - 29   2016   £200

Richardson, Samuel 1689-1761 *Pamela, ou La Vertu Recompensee.* Paris: De l'Imprimerie de Plassan, 1821-1822. 2 volumes, 212, 133mm., very attractive quarter calf blindstamped in 'cathedral' style over marbled boards by by Thouvenin (stamp signed in gilt at foot of spine), corners tipped with green vellum, green blindstamped with design of Gothic arched windows, gilt titling, marbled endpapers and edges, half title with ink inscription in French stating that this book was purchased at the sale of the library of Duc de Coigny at Chateau de Franquetot on 24 April (19)12, occasional insignificant smudges or spots of foxing, paper little on inexpensive side, otherwise appealing copy with virtually no signs of use.   Phillip J. Pirages   67 - 302   2016 $900

Binding – Thurnam, Charles

Archibald, Campbell *Lessons for School Life...* Edinburgh: Thomas Constable & Co., 1853. Second edition, contemporary full calf by Charles Thurnam, maroon and green morovco labels, slightly rubbed, inscribed by author for Mrs. Marshall, Apl. 1856, recent ownership label of Dr. Michael Brown.   Jarndyce Antiquarian Books   CCXV - 928   2016   £45

Binding – Tomlinson, James

An Alphabetical List of the Poll for the Election of Two Representatives to Serve in Parliament for the Borough of Newark-upon-Tyne, Taken before the Worshipful Wm. Martin, Esq. Mayor on the 9th day of September 1780.... Newark: printed for James Tomlinson, 1780. Only edition, 12mo., contemporary (original?) elaborately gilt stamped red morocco by James Tomlinson, covers with decorative and ruled borders, "Newark Election 1780" within center gilt ruled rectangular box, spine elaborately tooled in 6 compartments, gilt edges, marbled endpapers, all edges gilt, binding has few trifling imperfections, but lovely copy.   Howard S. Mott Inc.   265 - 98   2016 $1250

Binding – Tout

Reade, Charles   1814-1884   *The Cloister and the Hearth.* London: Trubner and Co., 1861. First edition, 4 volumes, octavo, black half morocco by Tout, marbled paper sides, matching endpapers, gilt rules and lettering, top edge gilt, some foxing to blanks on volume one (apparently caused by manuscript leaf), fine, enclosed in blue cloth slipcase.   The Brick Row Book Shop   Miscellany 69 - 69   2016 $2500

Shelley, Mary Wollestonecraft Godwin   1797-1851 *History of a Six Weeks' Tour Through a Part of France, Switzerland, Germany and Holland.*   London: published by T. Hookham Jun., 1817. First edition, little light soiling, 8vo., early 20th century olive morocco by Tout, boards with gilt frame and spine, elaborately gilt top edge gilt, others untrimmed, joints rather rubbed, little wear to headcap, bookplates of H. Bradley Martin and of Robertson Trowbridge (this inscribed to Mark Trowbridge's gift of the volume to Thomas Pym Cope) and of Thomas Jefferson McKee, very good.   Blackwell's Rare Books   Marks of Genius - 43   2016   £3500

Swinburne, Algernon Charles   1837-1909   *The Bride's Tragedy.*   London: privately printed, 1889.   Half title, uncut in contemporary full tan calf by Tout, triple ruled gilt borders and floral cornerpieces, gilt dentelles, green morocco label, uplettered gilt, bound with original wrappers, very good. Jarndyce Antiquarian Booksellers   CCXVII - 271   2016 £580

Binding – Townsend, William & Son

Plutarchus   *Vitae Illustrium Virorum.*   Rome: Ulrich Han, 1470.   First edition, volume I, large folio, mid to late 19th century dark brown morocco over bevelled boards by William Townsend and Son, Sheffield with other blindstamp inside front covers panelled with simple blind fillets and ornamental rolls, spine decorated in same way, red morocco label, illuminated opening page with white vine stem border, on three sides extending into fore-margin, border incorporates 9 line initial "I" in gold and wreath on each border, one in lower margin left blank for a coat-of-arms, remaining two with rosettes, also four birds found in lower border, all in burnished gold, blue, green, purple, 54 further initials in gold, mostly 9 to 11 lines, against intricate white vine backgrounds infilled with blue green and purple, which extend into margins, 4 line initial in gold infilled with green and purple against blue background, some rubrication, early ms. headings and foliaton, heavy inkstain affecting ff. vlv and v2r and initial, some dampstaining, mostly marginal but heavier towards end affecting c. 9 initials, foxed and spotted in places, near contemporary marginal annotations plentiful for first 35ff and intermittent thereafter, acquisition note of Dom Munor de Suessa, Dean of labelda-Logrono 1632, 18th century inscription of D. Gregorio Lopez Malo, 2 pages of 19th century bibliographical notes cut down and mounted at end. Maggs Bros. Ltd.   1474 - 64   2016   £45,000

Binding – Trissel, James

Collison, Beth   *Seven Characters.*   Colorado Springs: Press at Colorado College, 1980. Limited to 75 numbered copies, bound by James Trissel, oblong 4to., stiff paper wrappers.   Oak Knoll Books   310 - 139   2016 $300

Binding – Turner, Winifred

Shakespeare, William   1564-1616   *The Sonnets.* Birmingham: Birmingham Guild of Handicraft Press, 1895. One of 500 copies, and 50 large paper copies, 222 x 178mm, pleasing rich brown morocco in the Arts and Crafts style by Winifred Turner (signed and dated by her in 1930), covers divided into geometric compartments by blind and gilt rules, at center a lozenge filled with entwined gilt roses, raised bands, spine compartments ruled in gilt and blind, linen pastedowns framed by gilt beading, top edge gilt, with woodcut white vine initials, some with extensions, 12 half borders and two three quarter borders, all by Ernest G. Treglown, engraved on wood by Charles Carr Tomkinson, spine lightly sunned, little soiling to lower cover, neither trivial nor serious, titlepage bit foxed, other insignificant imperfections internally, but excellent copy, text clean and lustrous binding essentially unworn.   Phillip J. Pirages   67 - 73 2016 $900

Binding – Walbys

Howard, H. Eliot *An Introduction to the Study of Bird Behaviour.* Cambridge: Cambridge University Press, 1929. Quarto, 10 uncolored plates, contemporary red half calf by Walbys of Oxford, apart from few minor spots, handsome copy.   Andrew Isles Natural History Books   55 - 28239   2016 $300

Binding – Welcher, Samuel

Le Sage, Alain Rene   1668-1747 *The Adventures of Gil Blas of Santillane.* London: printed for Richard Phillips, 1807. 203 x 121mm., 4 volumes, extremely pleasing contemporary deep blue straight grain morocco, handsomely gilt by Samuel Welcher (with his ticket on verso of front endpaper), covers bordered gilt with triple rules and framed with palmette roll, inside is a rule with small ring and floral tools at corners, raised bands, spines ornately gilt in lobed compartments, featuring stippled ground, quatrefoil centerpiece with delicate foliate, sprays at sides and fleurons at ends, turn-ins gilt with single rule and fleuron and ring tools at corners, all edges gilt, with 160 engravings comprised of 100 copperplates by Warner, Tomlinson and others, and extra illustrated with 60 plates by Conrad Martin Metz, armorial bookplate of H. Holland Edwards, Pennant Erithlyn, North Wales; front joints just little flaked, backstrips slightly sunned, covers with minor variation in color, several plates little foxed, generally only in margins and more frequently on added plates), one leaf with light ink stain in lower margin, light dampstain in margin at head of one plate, isolated very minor marginal soiling, very pleasing set, decorative bindings very well preserved and internally clean, fresh and bright.   Phillip J. Pirages   67 - 72   2016 $1750

Binding – Westleys

Andersen, Hans Christian   1805-1875 *A Poet's Day Dreams.* London: Richard Bentley, 1853. Half title, 4 pages ads, original brown grained cloth by Westleys, gilt spine darkened and slightly rubbed at head, some splits in following hinge.   Jarndyce Antiquarian Booksellers   CCXVIII - 884   2016   £85

Freeman, Gage Earle *Five Christmas Poems.* London: Longman and Roberts, 1860. First edition, half title, 24 page catalog, September 1859, original green cloth by Westleys, boards blocked in blind, front board blocked and lettered gilt, inscribed "From the author", very good, crisp copy.   Jarndyce Antiquarian Booksellers   CCXVII - 100   2016   £125

Guthrie, Thomas *Seed-time a Harvest of Ragged Schools...* Edinburgh: Adam and Charles Black, 1860. Half title, frontispiece, 9 pages ads, some slight dusting, original maroon cloth by Westleys & Co., slightly rubbed, publisher's ad slip tipped in, bookseller's ticket, very good.   Jarndyce Antiquarian Books   CCXV - 710   2016   £150

H., M. B. *Home Truths for Home Peace, or "Muddle" Defeated, a Practical Inquiry....* London: Longmans, 1854. Sixth edition, original green cloth by Westley & Co., slightly rubbed, nice, contemporary signature of Joseph R. Aston.   Jarndyce Antiquarian Books   CCXV - 234   2016   £65

Heywood, James *The Ancient Laws of the Century, for King's College, Cambridge and for the Public School of Eton College.* London: Longman, 1850. First edition, frontispiece and plate, original dull green cloth by Westleys, small labels and stamps of the British Library of Political Science, otherwise very good.   Jarndyce Antiquarian Books   CCXV - 573   2016   £45

Johnson, Charles Plumptre *Hints to Collectors of Original Editions of the Works of Charles Dickens.* London: George Redway, 1885. First edition, half title, 4 page catalog, uncut, full parchment by Westleys, lettered gilt, bevelled boards, spotted and marked, large format.   Jarndyce Antiquarian Booksellers   CCXVIII - 1506   2016   £30

Kay-Shuttleworth, James *Four Periods of Public education as reviewed in 1832-1839-1846-1862.* London: Longman, 1862. First edition, half title, library stamps, crossed out in ink, slight signs of label removed from leading pastedown, original brown cloth by Westley & Co., slightly rubbed.   Jarndyce Antiquarian Books   CCXV - 803   2016   £110

Kitton, Frederic George *Dickensiana: a Bibliography of the Literature Relating to Charles Dickens and His Writings.* London: George Redway, 1886. First edition, only 500 copies printed, half title, title, frontispiece, 24 page catalog (1886), untrimmed in original fine grained green cloth by Westleys, spine lettered gilt, leading inner hinge cracking, booklabel of William Grist, good plus.   Jarndyce Antiquarian Booksellers   CCXVIII - 1329   2016   £75

Paris, Louis Philippe Albert D'Orleans, Comte De   1838-1894 *Damas et le Liban. Extraits du Journal d'un Voyage en Syrie au Printemps de 1860.* London: W. Jeffs... Foreign Bookseller to the Royal Family, 1861. First edition, 8vo., original maroon cloth by Westleys in London, spine (rebacked) lettered and dated gilt, covers ornamented in blind, covers with few minor spots, half title, little dusted, name of anonymous author supplied in pencil and with underlining in crayon.   Sotheran's   Travel and Exploration - 358   2016   £448

Binding – Westleys & Clark

Warburton, Sydney *Letters to my Unknown Friends.* London: Longman Brown &c., 1846. First edition, half title, 32 page catalog (Jan. 1847), original pink-brown cloth by Westleys & Clark, slight nick to head of spine, dust jacket signature, very good.   Jarndyce Antiquarian Books   CCXV - 461   2016   £85

Binding – Wheeler, William

Maundeville, John *The Voiage and Travaile of Sir John Maundevile, Kt.* New York: printed by the Grabhorn Press, San Francisco for Random House, 1928. No. 104 of 150 copies, 368 x 242mm., publisher's Philippine mahogany boards backed with brown Niger morocco by William Wheeler, raised bands, spine with tilting in blind "TKD" embossed in blank on portion of spine leather extending onto front board, paragraph marks in red or blue, 32 woodcut in text, 34 large hand illuminated initials in red, blue and gold by Valenti Angelo, one page with faint paint residue in margin, but very fine, binding extremely bright and virtually unworn, text showing no signs of use.   Phillip J. Pirages 67 - 178   2016 $2500

Binding – Wieck, Cathy

Coleridge, Samuel Taylor   1772-1834 *The Devil's Thoughts and Apologia Pro Vita Sua.* New York: Kelly Winterton Press, 1989. Limited to 60 numbered copies, 4to., quarter cloth, marbled paper covered boards, top edge gilt, others uncut, hand bound by George and Cathy Wieck. Oak Knoll Books   310 - 120   2016 $225

Binding – Wieck, George

Coleridge, Samuel Taylor   1772-1834 *The Devil's Thoughts and Apologia Pro Vita Sua.* New York: Kelly Winterton Press, 1989. Limited to 60 numbered copies, 4to., quarter cloth, marbled paper covered boards, top edge gilt, others uncut, hand bound by George and Cathy Wieck. Oak Knoll Books   310 - 120   2016 $225

Binding – Wood

Bible. English - 1929 *The Apocrypha.* London: Cresset Press, 1929. No. XXX of 30 large paper copies on handmade paper and 450 copies on mould made paper, with additional suite of plates, each signed by artist, 350 x 227mm., publisher's black stiff vellum by Wood (stamp signed), flat spine with gilt titling, yapp edges, top edge gilt, other edges untrimmed, housed with (slightly scuffed) portfolio of plates in later black slipcase, 14 woodcuts, each by different artist, with additional suite of the plates printed on Japanese paper and signed by artist responsible for each, (original?) tissue guards in volume, with two of the original wood blocks for the engravings by Eric Jones and Wladislaw Skoczylas, remains of bookplate, prospectus laid in, spine lightly and uniformly faded, slivers of the binding's black dye faintly worn away along portions of joints and edges (and dye very carefully renewed in few small places, otherwise extremely fine, binding essentially unworn and not splayed, text immaculate, from the collection of John Gribbel (1858-1936) and was lot 217 in the 30 Oct. 1940 sale of his collection at Parke-Bernet.   Phillip J. Pirages   67 - 100   2016 $6500

Hassell, John *Picturesque Rides and Walks with Excursions by Water Thirty Miles round the British Metropolis.* London: printed for J. Hassell, 1817-1818. First edition, 162 x 102mm, quite attractive late 19th century jade green crushed morocco in Arts and Crafts designs by Wood of London, stamp signed, covers with gilt rule border and stippled cornerpieces incorporating drawer handles and three graceful tulips, raised bands, spines gilt in compartments with wide frame formed by drawer handles, heart ornaments and much stippling, turn-ins decorated with charming gilt tulips, marbled endpapers, top edges gilt, other edges rough trimmed, 120 hand colored aquatint engravings, front joint of one volume with just hint of rubbing at head, faint minor spotting to covers, spines just slightly sunned to richer green, trivial imperfections internally, but particularly fine and pretty set, text and plates very clean and fresh, ornate bindings lustrous and no significant wear. Phillip J. Pirages   67 - 191   2016 $2400

Swift, Jonathan   1667-1745 *Gulliver's Travels.* London: Cresset Press, 1930. No. VIII of 10 copies on Roman vellum with an extra set of plates on vellum, each of them signed by artist, 343 x 235mm., 2 bound volumes plus portfolio of plates, publisher's special russet morocco by Wood of London, raised bands flanked by simple blind tooling extending onto boards, gilt titling, brass clasps and catches, gilt ruled turn-ins, all edges gilt, vellum endleaves, extra plates housed in silk covered chemise bound into boards covered with matching morocco, whole contained in two extremely fine recent morocco backed felt lined folding boxes with raised bands and gilt titling, giving appearance of three book spines, main volumes with total of 27 engravings (26 images) as called for a little page vignette featuring a bust of Swift (appearing in each volume), 8 head and tailpieces, five full page maps and 12 delicately hand colored copper engraved plates (including two frontispieces) by Rex Whistler each within ornate baroque style frame, with additional suite of all 26 engraved images (the same 12 images that are colored in the main volumes, also colored by hand in this extra suite), each of the 26 extra images signed by Whistler and separately matted, original tissue guards, spines of text and plate volumes rather darkened (though evenly so), morocco boards covering the plate chemise bit soiled and somewhat scratched (scratches well refurbished) but original deluxe bindings showing almost no other wear and retaining much of the original appeal, text and plates with only most trivial of toning of tonal variations to vellum, generally in very fine condition internally.   Phillip J. Pirages 67 - 333   2016 $45,000

Wiseman, Samuel *A Short and Serious Narrative of Londons fatal Fire, and Its Diurnal and Nocturnal Progression from Sunday Morning (being) the Second of September Anno Mirabili 1666 until Wednesday Night following A Poem.* London: for Peter Dring, 1667. First edition, small 4to., title within thick black woodcut mourning border, probably washed, early 20th century dark red morocco by Wood, from the library of James Stevens Cox (1910-1997), with bookplate and purchase note.   Maggs Bros. Ltd.   1447 - 459   2016   £1500

Binding – Worrall, Edmund

Dibdin, Thomas Frognall 1776-1847 *Bibliotheca Spenceriana or a Descriptive Catalogue of the Books Printed in the Fifteenth Century...in the Library of George John Earl Spencer (with) Supplement to the Bibliotheca Spenceriana. (with) Aedes Althorpianae; or an Account of the Mansion, Books and Pictures at Althorp (with A Descriptive Catalogue of the Books printed in the Fifteenth Century, Lately forming Part of the Library of the Duke of Dassano Serra and now the Property of George John Earl Spencer.* London: for the author by Shakespeare Press, 1814-1815. 1822-1823, 7 volumes, 4to., profusely illustrated with engraved plates, hundreds of facsimiles of early woodcuts and type, some printed in color, modern full tan morocco, richly gilt, covers with central arms and corner-pieces within two-line fillet, board edges and turn-ins gilt, spines fully gilt in compartments by Edmund Worrall of Birmingham, with his ticket in each volume, engraved plates mostly toned and offset to facing pages, some minor text offsetting, few random gatherings (maybe 12-15 leaves in all), very heavily foxed, else very good set in very fine, fresh bindings.   Joseph J. Felcone, Inc.   Books from Five Centuries: a Miscellany - 55   2016 $2800

Binding – Wright, J.

Catholic Church. Liturgy & Ritual *Missale ad Consuetudinem Ecclesie Romanae...* Paris: in alma Parisiorum Academia Impensis Thielmanni Kerver 23 March, 1506. 8vo., Kerver's fine device on titlepage, full page woodcut of Crucifixion, large crible initial of Crucifixion, crible initials, music on four-line staves, printed in red and black, decorative line fillers in red and black, 8vo., 19th century purple brown morocco richly gilt in 16th century style by J. Wright, binder, gauffered edges, headcaps rubbed, bookseller's note stating this was from the library of A. J. Beresford Hope (1820-1887), bookplate and inscription of Herbert Watney (1843-1932).   Maggs Bros. Ltd.   1474 - 53   2016   £4500

Binding – Young, Henry & Sons

Trench, William Steuart *Realities of Irish Life.* London: Longmans, Green and Co., 1869. Fourth edition, half title, frontispiece and plates, one in color, folding map of Ireland, slightly spotted, fine binding by Henry Young and Sons, Liverpool, half dark green crushed morocco, green cloth boards, spine gilt, very good.   Jarndyce Antiquarian Booksellers   CCXVII - 286   2016   £150

Binding – Zaehnsdorf

Beethoven, Ludwig Van *Ludwig Van Beethoven's Werke.* Leipzig: Breitkopf und Hartel, n.d. circa, 1850's, 4to., contemporary red calf with marbled paper covered boards, all edges gilt, from the reference library of Zaehnsdorf Co. with commemorative booklabel loosely inserted, with their bookplate, wear along hinges.   Oak Knoll Books   310 - 276   2016 $300

Berjeau, J. P. *Book-Worm (First two volumes) the The Bookworm, a Literary and Bibliographical Review.* London: Worm, 1867-1871. volumes 2-5 (of 5 total), tall 8vo., contemporary half blue calf with marbled paper covered boards, top edge gilt, signed bindings by Zaehnsdorf, from the Zaehnsdorf reference library with bookplate, rubbed along hinges,.   Oak Knoll Books   310 - 57   2016 $600

Browning, Elizabeth Barrett 1806-1861 *Sonnets from the Portuguese.* London: Vale Press, 1897. One of 300 copies on paper (and 8 on vellum), 152 x 121mm., pleasing blue-gray crushed morocco by Zaehnsdorf (stamp signed with firm's oval exhibition stamp), covers with delicate gilt frame of swirling tendrils bearing azured leaves, flat spine with gilt tendrils and titling, turn-ins with multiple plain and decorative rules, crimson watered silk endleaves, top edge gilt, 2 large woodcut white vine initials by Charles Ricketts, printed in red, spine evenly sunned, small dark stain, half inch in diameter, at middle of fore-edge of book block (just barely extending onto margin of most pages), otherwise fine, binding unworn and text fresh and clean.   Phillip J. Pirages   67 - 79   2016 $750

Butler, Samuel 1612-1680 *Hudibras. the First Part with The Second Part. The Third and Last Part.* London: by J. G. for Richard Marriot, 1663. London: by T. R. for John Martyn and James Allestry, 1664. London: for Simon Miller, 1678, First authorized editions of volumes 1 and 2, first edition of volume 3, 3 volumes, washed and rebound in uniform simple full brown levant, edges gilt by Zaehnsdorf for A. C. McClurg, some residual soiling, volume 2 with closed tear in title and front hinge cracking slightly and cropped at bit closely cutting into running heads and shoulder notes.   Joseph J. Felcone, Inc.   Books from Five Centuries: a Miscellany - 34   2016 $2200

Cunningham, Peter *The Story of Nell Gwyn and the Sayings of Charles II.* London: Bradbury & Evans, 1852. First edition in book form, 2 volumes, very pretty brown crushed morocco elaborately gilt by Zaehnsdorf, (stamp signed), covers with frame comprising plain and decorative gilt rules, an inlaid maroon morocco strap, ornate gilt corner-pieces of many small floral tools on a stippled background, raised bands, spines densely gilt in compartments with floral branches radiating form a central circle, background stippled and with small circlets, delicate floral frame on turn-ins, leather hinges, olive and gold silk jacquard endleaves, top edges gilt, extra illustrated with 179 engraved plates, (plates listed alphabetically on printed leaves following the Table of Contents obviously prepared either for this copy alone or else for very limited number of copies, engraved armorial bookplate of Thomas McKean, small nick to one board, otherwise just hint of use to attractive lustrous and scarcely worn bindings, majority of inserted plates foxed (two dozen of them noticeably so), variable offsetting from engraved material, otherwise excellent internally.   Phillip J. Pirages   67 - 74   2016 $950

Dickens, Charles 1812-1870 *The Life and Adventures of Nicholas Nickleby.* London: Chapman and Hall, 1839. First edition, half title, steel engraved frontispiece in first state, 39 etched plates, first four in first state with imprint, errors on page 123 and page 160, faint toning and one or two spots, short tears to few plates repaired, generally very clean with plates unusually free from foxing, 8vo., late 19th or early 20th century polished blue calf by Zaehnsdorf, French fillets on sides with floral tools at corners, spine richly gilt in compartments, twin burgundy lettering pieces, top edge gilt, others uncut, very good.   Blackwell's Rare Books B184 - 33   2016   £1200

Dickens, Charles 1812-1870 *The Life and Adventures of Nicholas Nickleby.* London: Chapman & Hall, 1857. Early edition, frontispiece, 39 plates by Phiz, contemporary full tan calf by Zaehnsdorf, gilt spine, borders and dentelles, brown morocco labels, all edges gilt, very good.   Jarndyce Antiquarian Booksellers   CCXVIII - 230   2016   £150

Halfer, Josef *Die Fortschritte der Marmorierkunst. ein Praktisches Handbuch fur Buchbinder und Buntpapierfabrikanten.* Stuttgart: Wilhelm Leo, 1891. Second edition, 8vo., later half red calf, marbled paper covered boards, five raised bands, top edge gilt, signed binding by Zaehnsdorf, with 5 leaves of single mounted marbled paper specimens + 5 leaves each with 6 mounted marbled paper specimens, from the reference library of Zaehnsdorf and Company with commemorative booklabel loosely inserted, with bookplate of Zaehnsdorf Co., tipped in is two page ALS by Richard Leo to Mr. Zaehnsdorf, rubbed along hinges and soiled along edges.   Oak Knoll Books   310 - 9   2016 $3500

Hardy, Thomas 1840-1928 *Under the Greenwood Tree.* London: Tinsley Bros., 1872. First edition, 2 volumes, 192 x 130mm., one of presumably 500 copies (according to Purdy), fine maroon crushed morocco by Zaehnsdorf (stamp signed), covers with triple gilt fillet border, raised bands, spines gilt in compartments with vase and garland centerpiece, gilt titling, turn-ins with gilt floral vine roll, marbled endpapers, top edges gilt, beautiful copy, bindings entirely unworn and unusually bright, text with no signs of use, handsomely bound.   Phillip J. Pirages   67 - 190   2016 $5000

Henley, William Ernest 1849-1903 *A Book of Verses.* London: Published by David Nutt, 1897. 171 x 18mm., fine scarlet crushed morocco elaborately gilt by Zaehnsdorf (blindstamped exhibition mark to lower pastedown), covers with gilt ruled border enclosing panel of double fillets capturing a field with rows of repeated gilt flowers (28 on each cover), flowers on stems with azured leaves and delicate gilt dotted element below each, gilt ruled raised bands and gilt spine compartments repeating these floral and foliate tools, red silk endleaves, all edges gilt, engraved vignette to title, spine uniformly sunned to darker red, very slight rubbing to joints, well masked with dye, otherwise fine, lovely binding especially bright and text showing no signs of use.   Phillip J. Pirages   67 - 75   2016 $850

Hunt, P. Francis *Orchidaceae.* Bourton: Bourton Press, 1973. Limited to 600 numbered copies, signed, Folio, 40 colored plates by Mary Grierson, publisher's full vellum by Zaehnsdorf, all edges gilt, cloth slipcase, fine.   Andrew Isles Natural History Books   55 - 3535   2016 $750

Irving, Washington 1783-1859 *The Adventures of Captain Bonneville.* New York: and London: printed by Knickerbocker Press for G. P. Putnam's, 1895. No. 3 of 100 copies of the Colorado edition, 253 x 180mm., 2 volumes, handsome scarlet crushed morocco by Zaehnsdorf (stamp signed), covers with gilt triple fillet border, raised bands, spines gilt in double-ruled compartments with anthemion centerpiece in gilt and inlaid black morocco, gilt titling, richly gilt turn-ins, marbled endpapers, all edges centerpiece in gilt and inlaid black morocco, gilt titling, richly gilt turn-ins, marbled endpapers, all edges gilt, folding map, 28 plates printed on Japan as called for, all with captioned tissue guards, text framed in gold, small faintly darkened area at top of front cover of volume II, otherwise especially beautiful set in extraordinarily fine, bindings remarkably lustrous and entirely unworn, text and plates pristine.   Phillip J. Pirages   67 - 201   2016 $1250

Jones, Paul *Flora Magnifica: Selected and Painted by the Artist.* London: Tryon Gallery, 1976. Limited to 506 numbered and signed copies, Folio, 15 plates with tissue guards, publisher's half vellum, and maroon cloth boards by Zaehnsdorf, slipcase.   Andrew Isles Natural History Books   55 - 31426   2016 $650

Keats, John 1795-1821 *Life, Letters and Literary Remains. (and) The Poetical Works.* London: Edward Moxon & Co., 1848. First edition of the first work, all volumes with half title, 3 volumes, 171 x 108mm., very pretty early 20th century slate blue crushed morocco by Zaehnsdorf (stamp signed, oval exhibition stamp), covers with delicate gilt rule frame, inlaid red morocco tulips at corners, raised bands, spines gilt in compartments with inlaid red tulip, gilt titling, turn-ins with leafy gilt border, marbled endpapers, top edges gilt, frontispiece in each volume with tissue guard; spines lightly and uniformly sunned, free endpapers with offset shadow from binder's glue, frontispiece from 'Remains' detached and little soiled, still pretty set in excellent condition, text clean and fresh, decorative bindings unworn.   Phillip J. Pirages   67 - 76   2016 $1000

Mee, Margaret Ursula *Flowers of the Brazilian Forests Collected and Painted by Margaret Mee.* London: L. van Leer & Co. for the Tryon Gallery in association with George Rainbird, 1968. First and only edition, limited to 500 copies, this no. 27 of 100 deluxe copies signed by Mee and with original gouache by Mee, folio, original full natural vellum by Zaehnsdorf gilt facsimile of author's signature blocked on upper board, vignette of a teja-assu lizard after Mee blocked in gilt on lower board, spine lettered in gilt, endpapers with printed vignettes of teja assu after Mee, top edges gilt, original green cloth slipcase with gilt lettering piece on upper panel, original shipping carton address to Richard Mitchell, Aldham, Essex with limitation numbers, printed in green and black, loose original prospectus, fine.   Sotheran's Piccadilly Notes - Summer 2015 - 9   2016   £7000

Pater, Walter *Essays from the Guardian.* London: Macmillan and Co., 1901. Second printing, extremely pleasing crimson crushed morocco attractively gilt by Zaehnsdorf (stamp signed), covers with multiple gilt rule frame, central panel with azured cornerpieces and central oval medallion, flat spine in three unequal panels, two with oval medallion tools, one with gilt titling, gilt ruled turn-ins, marbled endpapers, top edge gilt, bookplate of Charles Walker Andrews, spine uniformly sunned to a dark red, light offsetting on free endpapers from turn-in glue, otherwise very fine, binding unworn and especially lustrous, text showing virtually no signs of use.   Phillip J. Pirages   67 - 77   2016 $800

Rackham, Arthur *Arthur Rackham's Book of Pictures.* London: William Heinemann, 1913. No. 511 of 1030 copies signed by artist, 294 x 230mm., appealing burgundy morocco by Zaehnsdorf for E. Joseph (stamp-signed), upper cover with gilt titling and pelican insignia, raised bands, densely gilt turn-ins, marbled endpapers, top edge gilt, other edges untrimmed, few vignettes in text, 44 color plates mounted on brown paper, all with lettered tissue guards, faint crease to frontispiece plate, tiny notch at bottom edge of frontispiece mount, otherwise extremely fine, binding unusually lustrous and virtually unworn, plates clean and fresh, bright copy.   Phillip J. Pirages   67 - 291   2016 $1900

Shakespeare, William 1564-1616 *The Sonnets.* London: published by George Bell and Sons, 1899. 164 x 130mm, very pretty burgundy crushed morocco gilt, by Zaehnsdorf (stamp signed and with firm's oval stamp in blind, covers with thin fillet borders enclosing a central panel featuring rose medallions in each corner and at center a lobed and leafy lozenge contain Shakespeare's initials within flames, raised bands, spine compartments with either lozenge, rose or "W S" monogram at center, gilt titling , turn-ins with foliate tooling, red linen endleaves, top edge gilt, other edges untrimmed and unopened, woodcut initials and elaborate Kelmscott-style white-vine woodcut borders around first opening, hint of rubbing to upper joint, spine just shade darker than covers, pages faintly browned at edges, otherwise fine, binding lustrous, text obviously never read.   Phillip J. Pirages   67 - 78   2016 $950

Shakespeare, William 1564-1616 *The Works.* London: Macmillan and Co., 1902-1905. Cambridge edition, 9 volumes, 235 x 159mm, very appealing in brown half morocco over green linen by Zaehnsdorf (stamp signed on verso of front free endpaper), raised bands, spines gilt in double ruled compartments with dotted inner frame and floral cornerpieces as well as large central ornament formed by two crossed swords, crown and garland, marbled endpapers, top edge gilt, other edges rough trimmed, spines uniformly sunned ot very pleasing honey brown, first volume with shallow chipping at top of spine with one band little abraded, otherwise only trivial defects, bindings in other ways showing only very minor signs of use, text quite clean and fresh.   Phillip J. Pirages   67 - 319   2016 $1900

Shelley, Percy Bysshe 1792-1822 *The Cenci. A Tragedy, in Five Acts.* Italy (Livorgno): printed for C. and J. Ollier, 1819. First edition, only 250 copies printed, without initial blank, 8vo., brown crushed morocco gilt by Zaehnsdorf with their exhibition stamp, wide multiple roll tooled borders on sides, gilt in gilt on cover (within a frame) and spine, gilt edges and iner dentelles, Estelle Doheny's copy with her morocco gilt book label inside front cover, fine.   Blackwell's Rare Books   Marks of Genius - 45   2016   £4000

Syr Percyvelle of Gales. Hammersmith: Kelmscott Press, 1895. One of 350 copies on paper (and 8 on vellum), 210 x 145mm., handsome Gothic style brown blind tooled pigskin by Zaehnsdorf (stamp signed and dated 1895, with firm's exhibition stamp), covers with frame formed by multiple gilt rules, head and tail with gilt titling and date, central panel diapered in ogival compartments containing floral ornaments, raised bands, neatly rebacked, spine with blind tooled panels and gilt titling, blind ruled turn-ins, marbled endpapers, all edges gilt (front hinge carefully repaired), woodcut frontispiece by Edward Burne-Jones, elaborate wide border on frontispiece and first page of text, one page with half border, decorated woodcut initials device in colophon, significant rubbing, couple of small abrasions to upper board, binding lustrous and still generally appealing, fine copy, internally quite clean, fresh and bright.   Phillip J. Pirages   67 - 225   2016 $1500

Vonsybel, Heinrich *History of the French Revolution.* London: John Murray, 1867-1869. First edition in English, 235 x 146mm., 4 volumes, very pleasing dark blue half morocco, attractively gilt by Zaehnsdorf for A. C. McClurg & Co. (stamp signed), wide raised bands decorated with five parallel gilt rules, spine compartments with gilt frames composed of stippled rules connected to corner volutes, marbled sides and endpapers, top edge gilt, other edges rough trimmed, hint of chafing to paper sides, occasional minor foxing, never offensive, additional trivial imperfections, otherwise fine set in excellent decorative bindings, leather unusually lustrous and virtually unworn and text very smooth and clean.   Phillip J. Pirages   67 - 166   2016 $850

Whistler, James A. M. *The Gentle Art of Making Enemies.* London: William Heinemann, 1890. First English edition ad first authroized edition, one of only 10 special copies, near fine in slightly chipped, publisher's brown gilt decorated wrappers bound into similarly decorated near fine full brown morocco by Zaehnsdorf in 1925, housed in custom quarter morocco slipcase with cloth chemise, inscribed by Whistler to his publishers William Heinemman with his butterfly signature, Chelsea Oct. 1890.   Between the Covers Rare Books   204 - 16   2016 $16,500

Binding – Zanardi

Nasti, Mauro *Schmied.* Vicenza: Guido Tamoni, 1991. No. LVI of LVI Delux copies (and 1000 regular copies), publisher's deluxe vellum binding by I. Zanardi, volume housed in dark brown gilt titled folding cloth box, profusely illustrated with examples of Schmied's work, this copy with bifolium on Lamb's vellum (from 1930-33 edition of L'Odyssee), featuring an illustration after Schmied colored au pochoir by Jean Saude, bioflium laid in inside vellum folder, box with few small marks, otherwise mint.   Phillip J. Pirages   67 - 311   2016 $1500

Binding – Zweig, Christian

Kleist, Heirnich Von *On Puppet Shows.* Hamburg: Otto Rohse Press, 1991. Limited to 75 numbered copies signed by Rohse, folio, leather, cloth slipcase, engravings by Rohse, binding by Christian Zweig.   Oak Knoll Books   310 - 127   2016 $1500

Melville, Herman 1819-1891 *Cock-a-Doodle-Doo! or The Crowing of the Noble Cock.* N.P.: Otto Rohse Press, 1986. Limited to 150 numbered copies, signed by Otto Rohse, wood engravings by Rohse, 4to., paper covered boards, illustrated front cover, top edge cut, other edges uncut, slipcase, binding by Christian Zweig.   Oak Knoll Books   310 - 128   2016 $300

Fore-edge Paintings

Fore-edge – 1801

Beattie, James 1735-1803 *The Minstrel; or the Progress of Genius with Some Other Poems.* London: printed for J. Mawman, 1801. 170 x 102mm., contemporary red straight grain morocco, covers with gilt ruled border, flat spine divided into panels by single gilt rule, gilt titling, turn-ins with decorative bead roll, marbled endpapers, all edges gilt, with pleasing fore-edge painting of the harbor and seaside town of Whitby, in excellent brown morocco pull-off case by Sangorksi & Sutcliffe for J. W. Robinson Co., 4 engravings, front pastedown with engraved bookplate of John Ashley Warre, spine slightly and uniformly sunned to a darker red, occasional spotting or staining, still quite decent copy, binding solid and lustrous, text smooth and fresh, painting very well preserved. Phillip J. Pirages 67 – 147 2016 $800

Fore-edge – 1805

Scott, Walter 1771-1832 *The Lay of the Last Minstrel, a Poem.* London and Edinburgh: printed for Longman, Hurst Rees and Orme and for A. Constable by James Ballantyne, 1805. Second edition, 213 x 133mm., contemporary red straight grain morocco, covers bordered by gilt rule and cresting blind roll, flat spine divided into panels by single gilt rules, gilt titling, turn-ins with gilt bead roll, marbled endpapers, all edges gilt, with fore-edge painting of Dumbarton Castle and the River Clyde, in paper slipcase, joints significantly rubbed (but this well masked with dye), small notch out at top of front joint, slight wear with bit of loss at corners and spine ends, minor spotting and darkening to boards, other trivial defects externally but binding, still firm and entirely satisfactory, scattered foxing at edges, leaves less than bright because of paper stock, but text still fresh and dramatic fore-edge painting well preserved. Phillip J. Pirages 67 – 160 2016 $1400

Fore-edge – 1808

Skurray, Francis *Bidcombe Hill with Other Rural Poems.* London: printed for William Miller, 1808. First edition, 191 x 121mm., contemporary straight grain green morocco, elaborately decorated in gilt and blind, covers with gilt palmette frame enclosing black tooled floral frame, flat spine with panels intricately tooled in gilt and black, gilt rolled turn-ins, marbled endleaves, all edges gilt, with fine pastoral fore-edge painting of Saint Bee's College Cumberland; in later sturdy fleece lined cloth slipcase, 4 engraved plates, spine sunned to light green muted spotting to leather, plates somewhat foxed, other minor defects, still quite pleasing, binding with only insignificant wear, text bright, fresh and clean and margins very ample. Phillip J. Pirages 67 – 162 2016 $1400

Fore-edge – 1810

Mason, James *Cornelia and Alcestis: Two Operas.* London: printed for T. Payne, 1810. First edition, 194 x 124mm., harmless contemporary purple straight grain morocco, covers with gilt fillet border, raised bands flanked by plain gilt rules, gilt titling, all edges gilt, excellent later fore-edge painting of the Acropolis, joints somewhat rubbed and flaked, boards little stained and rather faded, rear board with two small abraded patches, otherwise excellent copy, clean, fresh internally, solid, inoffensive binding with vividly colored painting in fine condition. Phillip J. Pirages 67 – 156 2016 $1100

Fore-edge – 1814

Gray, Thomas 1716-1771 *The Poems of Thomas Gray.* London: printed for White, Cochrane & Co., 1814. Octavo, portrait frontispiece and one engraved plate, full contemporary red straight grain morocco, covers elaborately decorated in gilt, spine with raised bands decoratively lettered and tooled in gilt, gilt board edges, gilt turn-ins, all edges gilt, marbled endpapers, 2 neat ink inscriptions on blank leaves, fine, with a 'two-way-double" fore-edge painting by Martin Frost (signed with initials on right-hand side of oval of the Tomb scene) of a bucolic rural scene and a view of Gray's tomb at Stoke Poges, tipped in at back of book is Martin Frost's printed certificate "hidden under the gilt edge of the book you can find a FORE-EDGE PAINTING by Martin Frost", fine example by Frost. David Brass Rare Books, Inc. 2015 – 02892 2016 $1850

Fore-edge – 1814

Stevens, Robert *Sermons, on Our Duty Towards God, Our Neighbour, and Ourselves: and on Other Subjects.* London: printed for John Booth, 1814. First edition, 225 x 133mm., pleasing contemporary midnight blue straight grain morocco, covers framed by plain gilt rules outlining Greek key and palmette blind rolls, raised bands, compartments with central gilt fleuron radiating densely blind tooled foliage, gilt ruled turn-ins, all edges gilt, with excellent fore-edge painting of Dover Castle; a presentation copy with (slightly foxed) signed autograph letter bound in (with letter offsets) for E. S. Stephenson, unidentified armorial bookplate, bit of wear to corners and joints, very small (ink?) stain to edge of prelim leaves visible at upper left background of fore-edge painting (not affecting primary image), otherwise fine, clean, fresh internally in lustrous binding. Phillip J. Pirages 67 – 164 2016 $1300

Fore-edge – 1822

Butler, Samuel 1612-1680 *Hudibras, a poem....* London: printed for Akermann, 1822. 2 volumes, octavo, 12 hand colored engraved plates by J. Clark, full crushed red morocco by Bayntun, covers elaborately tooled and stamped in gilt and black, front boards featuring pictorial inlaid centerpieces made up of several different pieces of dyed morocco, tooled in black, spines tooled, lettered and stamped in gilt in compartments, board edges and turn-ins decoratively gilt, all edges gilt marbled doublures and free endpapers, binding's calligraphic inscription in black and sepia on recto of front free endpapers, occasional light offsetting or spotting, else near fine, clean and bright, fore-edge painting revealed by fanning the outer edge of each text block, after drawing by Hogarth. Heritage Book Shop Holiday 2015 – 40 2016 $6000

Fore-edge – 1823

Church of England. Book of Common Prayer *The Book of Common Prayer...together with the Psalter or Psalms of David...* Oxford: Printed at the Clarendon Press by Samuel Collingwood & Co., 1823. 254 x 152mm., contemporary burgundy straight grain morocco, blindstamped in cathedral style, covers with central panel of an altar with rose window and gothic ownership lettering in gilt ('Eatington Chapel 1826'), panel within a floral frame of gothic motif, wide raised bands, spine panels each blindstamped with two gothic windows, gilt titling, gilt rolled turn-ins, marbled endpapers, all edges gilt; with large fore-edge painting showing Lincoln from the River Witham, spine with hint of sunning, joints and corners slightly worn (front joint perhaps getting ready to crack), final two leaves with faint dampstain at upper right (small, insignificant dampstain at top of some other leaves), very presentable copy, binding solid and not at all unattractive, text unusually bright and quite fresh and painting entirely as it should be. Phillip J. Pirages 67 – 148 2016 $950

Fore-edge – 1827

Gilpin, Joshua *Twenty-One Discourses Delivered in the Parish Church of Wrockwardine in the County of Salop.* London: John Hatchard and Son, 1827. Apparently first edition, 219 x 133mm., appealing contemporary red straight grain morocco, covers with gilt rule border and small sunburst cornerpieces, raised bands flanked by plain and decorative gilt rules, turn-ins with decorative gilt roll, marbled endpapers, all edges gilt, front joint very expertly renewed, with very accomplished fore-edge painting of West Gate, Canterbury; flyleaf facing titlepage with faint but readable offset of the (backward) text of a previously tipped in presentation letter from author; corners bit bruised, spine little dried, leather slightly marked and soiled, expertly repaired binding sound and attractive with lustrous covers, two inch horizontal tear to front endpaper, titlepage bit soiled, text remarkably clean, bright and fresh. Phillip J. Pirages 67 – 155 2016 $1250

Fore-edge – 1827

Webb, William *Minutes of Remarks on Subjects Picturesque, Moral and Miscellaneous....* London: Baldwin Cradock and Joy, Dublin: William Frederick Wakeman, 1827. First edition, 2 volumes, very pleasing contemporary sea green straight grain morocco, elaborately gilt, covers with gilt floral frame enclosing a central blindstamped arabesque, raised bands, spine compartments densely gilt with floral tools and volutes, turn-ins with decorative gilt roll, light blue watered silk endleaves, all edges gilt, each volume with animated fore-edge painting set in Italian landscape; armorial bookplate of armorial bookplate of John Thornton Down, spines slightly and uniformly sunned, joints with just hint of rubbing, corners little bent, volume I lacking free endleaf at back, trivial imperfections internally, but extremely pretty set in essentially fine condition, bindings entirely solid with especially lustrous covers and text clean and fresh. Phillip J. Pirages 67 – 165 2016 $2900

ISBN-13: 978-1-4103-1795-7
ISBN-10: 1-4103-1795-1